SECOND EDITION

Drug Abuse Handbook

SECOND EDITION

Drug Abuse Handbook

Editor-in-Chief
Steven B. Karch, MD, FFFLM

Consultant Pathologist and Toxicologist
Berkeley, California

CRC Press
Taylor & Francis Group
Boca Raton   London   New York

CRC Press is an imprint of the
Taylor & Francis Group, an informa business

CRC Press
Taylor & Francis Group
6000 Broken Sound Parkway NW, Suite 300
Boca Raton, FL 33487-2742

© 2007 by Taylor & Francis Group, LLC
CRC Press is an imprint of Taylor & Francis Group, an Informa business

No claim to original U.S. Government works
Printed in the United States of America on acid-free paper
10 9 8 7 6 5 4 3 2 1

International Standard Book Number-10: 0-8493-1690-1 (Hardcover)
International Standard Book Number-13: 978-0-8493-1690-6 (Hardcover)

Library of Congress Cataloging-in-Publication Data

Drug abuse handbook / [editor-in-chief] Steven B. Karch.-- 2nd ed.
        p. ; cm.
    Includes bibliographical references and index.
    ISBN-13: 978-0-8493-1690-6 (alk. paper)
    ISBN-10: 0-8493-1690-1 (alk. paper)
    1. Drugs of abuse--Handbooks, manuals, etc. 2. Drug abuse--Handbooks, manuals, etc. 3. Forensic toxicology--Handbooks, manuals, etc.
    [DNLM: 1. Street Drugs--pharmacology--Handbooks. 2. Forensic Medicine--Handbooks. 3. Substance
Abuse Detection--Handbooks. 4. Substance-Related Disorders--Handbooks. QV 39 D794 2006]
    I. Karch, Steven B.

RM316.D76 2006
615'.19--dc22   2006008334

Visit the Taylor & Francis Web site at
http://www.taylorandfrancis.com

and the CRC Press Web site at
http://www.crcpress.com

Preface

By the time this weighty volume is published, more than 10 years will have passed since I first approached Taylor & Francis (formerly CRC Press) about this project. I was surprised and delighted when they agreed to undertake this second edition. In the preface to the first edition I told readers that "a tremendous amount" had been learned about the problem of drug abuse, and I observed that most of the learning had been done not by pathologists, or even toxicologists, but rather by molecular biologists and neurochemists. That observation remains true today, even after all of the opiate receptors have been cloned, at a time when it impossible to look at drug–receptor interactions in ways that were inconceivable only a decade ago.

In the preface to the first edition I also complained about the slow progress being made in more traditional, less "exotic" fields. The advent of the phenomenally popular *CSI* television show helped raise public awareness of crime scene investigation. Industry is certainly aware of the amazing progress and has not been slow to capitalize upon it, even to the extent of funding some badly need research. The same kind of progress in understanding the effects of drug abuse has not occurred in the field of pathology, or any other medical specialties, for that matter. To the best of my knowledge, during the last decade, The National Institute of Drug Abuse (NIDA) has not funded even a single pathologist interested in studying the effects of abused drugs on the heart, or pancreas, or any other organ in the body; no pathologist sits on any of the NIH review boards. Some might say this is the very opposite of progress. There is very little difference between the way doctors treat cases of drug toxicity nowadays and the way they did so 30 years ago. The last really great advance in this field was the introduction of naloxone. "Compassionate," or not, the medical management of sick drug users is no more a priority of our current administration than of the previous one.

Like it or not, the scientific study of drug abuse–related disease constitutes an important part of forensic science. When are drugs the cause of death and when do they cause impairment? It turns out that the metabolism of different drugs varies greatly from individual to individual. Some of these differences remain apparent even after death, but many, if not most, are not visible to the naked eye. Not many medical examiners have the training, let alone the equipment, to test for invisible disease.

Does a very high fluoxetene level in a dead child signify a lethal overdose, or attempted murder, or is it a fluke of nature? The questions are more than academic, because the answers may determine whether criminal charges will be filed against the parents. Accordingly, this second edition of the handbook contains new chapters on both toxicogenetics and on the genetics of sudden cardiac death. Anyone who felt that they had mastered the art of DNA had best rethink their conclusions. Far from being a developed discipline, DNA testing is still only in its infancy. Should there be a third edition of this book, it will no doubt focus largely on DNA-related science; a great deal more than matching up single nucleotide polymorphisms is involved.

Readers will also note the addition of a section on legal notions of causation. Doctors have known for years that the search for scientific truth is best carried on outside of the courtroom. What most doctors do not know is that in the minds of jury members, their opinions carry no more, and no less, weight than the opinion of any laboratory technician. Worse, both doctor and technician are likely to have only a vague idea of what constitutes proof, and what constitutes junk science.

But, in fact, there is an easy way to tell: just use the scientific method. Most of this book is concerned with forensic science, the clinical management of toxic patients, and the management of addicted patients. At some point there must a convergence of these fields, and at some point all of these different disciplines become an evidence-based field. Case reports describing possible episodes of drug toxicity in solitary patients 30 years ago are insufficient to establish causation, not in the courtroom and not in the laboratory. Isolated post-mortem blood drug levels, no matter how "significant," are insufficient to establish the cause of death. A great deal more work and knowledge are required before that can be done. No matter how great the scientific advances of the next decade, there will be no real and lasting impact on everyday practice, at least not until what we do is, in fact, evidence based.

As should be apparent from the size of this volume, many individuals expended considerable energy to produce this book. It is probably a good thing that this book took so long to prepare because most of the truly exciting discoveries have occurred only in the last few years.

My thanks to all of the contributors, and my best wishes to the next editor. I do hope he or she will have more positive and exciting things to report.

Steven B. Karch, M.D., FFFLM

The Editor

Steven B. Karch, M.D., FFFLM, received his undergraduate degree from Brown University. He attended graduate school in anatomy and cell biology at Stanford University. He received his medical degree from Tulane University School of Medicine. Dr. Karch did postgraduate training in neuropathology at the Royal London Hospital and in cardiac pathology at Stanford University. For many years he was a consultant cardiac pathologist to San Francisco's Chief Medical Examiner.

In the U.K., Dr. Karch served as a consultant to the Crown and helped prepare the cases against serial murder Dr. Harold Shipman, who was subsequently convicted of murdering 248 of his patients. He has testified on drug abuse–related matters in courts around the world. He has a special interest in cases of alleged euthanasia, and in episodes where mothers are accused of murdering their children by the transference of drugs, either *in utero* or by breast feeding.

Dr. Karch is the author of nearly 100 papers and book chapters, most of which are concerned with the effects of drug abuse on the heart. He has published seven books. He is currently completing the fourth edition of *Pathology of Drug Abuse*, a widely used textbook. He is also working on a popular history of Napoleon and his doctors.

Dr. Karch is forensic science editor for Humana Press, and he serves on the editorial boards of the *Journal of Cardiovascular Toxicology*, the *Journal of Clinical Forensic Medicine* (London), *Forensic Science, Medicine and Pathology*, and *Clarke's Analysis of Drugs and Poisons*.

Dr. Karch was elected a fellow of the Faculty of Legal and Forensic Medicine, Royal College of Physicians (London) in 2006. He is also a fellow of the American Academy of Forensic Sciences, the Society of Forensic Toxicologists (SOFT), the National Association of Medical Examiners (NAME), the Royal Society of Medicine in London, and the Forensic Science Society of the U.K. He is a member of The International Association of Forensic Toxicologists (TIAFT).

Contributors

Wilmo Andollo, B.S.
Quality Assurance Officer
Dade County Medical Examiner Toxicology
  Laboratory
Miami, Florida

Lidia Avois-Mateus, Ph.D.
Swiss Laboratory for Doping Analyses
University Institute of Legal Medicine
Lausanne, Switzerland

Sanjay J. Ayirookuzhi, M.D.
Department of Cardiology and Internal
  Medicine
University of California
Davis, California

Joanna Banbery, M.B.B.S.
The Leeds Addiction Unit
Leeds, U.K.

Michael H. Baumann, Ph.D.
Clinical Psychopharmacology Section
Intramural Research Program
National Institute on Drug Abuse
National Institutes of Health
Department of Health and Human Services
Baltimore, Maryland

Norbert Baume, Ph.D.
Swiss Laboratory for Doping Analyses
University Institute of Legal Medicine
Lausanne, Switzerland

Michael R. Baylor, Ph.D.
Health Sciences Unit
Science and Engineering Group
RTI International
Research Triangle Park, North Carolina

Michael D. Bell, M.D.
District Medical Examiner
Palm Beach Medical Examiner Office
West Palm Beach, Florida

Neil L. Benowitz, M.D.
Division of Clinical Pharmacology and
  Experimental Therapeutics
University of California
San Francisco, California

John W. Boja, Ph.D.
U.S. Consumer Product Safety Commission
Directorate for Health Sciences
Bethesda, Maryland

Marc D. Bollman, M.D.
University Institute of Legal Medicine
Lausanne, Switzerland

Joseph P. Bono, M.A.
Supervisory Chemist
Drug Enforcement Administration
Special Testing and Research Laboratory
McLean, Virginia

Darlene H. Brunzell, Ph.D.
Department of Psychiatry
Yale University School of Medicine
New Haven, Connecticut

Allen P. Burke, M.D.
Professor of Pathology and Medical Director
Kernan Hospital Pathology Laboratory
University of Maryland Medical Center
Baltimore, Maryland

Donna M. Bush, Ph.D., DABFT
Drug Testing Team Leader
Division of Workplace Programs
Center for Substance Abuse Prevention
Substance Abuse and Mental Health Services
  Administration
Rockville, Maryland

Jonica Calkins, M.D.
Department of Cardiology and Internal
  Medicine
University of California
Davis, California

Yale H. Caplan, Ph.D., DABFT
National Scientific Services
Baltimore, Maryland

Vincent Cirimele, Ph.D.
ChemTox Laboratory
Illkirch, France

Edward J. Cone, Ph.D.
ConeChem Research
Severna Park, Maryland

Kelly P. Cosgrove, Ph.D.
Department of Psychiatry
Yale University School of Medicine
New Haven, Connecticut
and
VA Connecticut Healthcare System
West Haven, Connecticut

Dennis J. Crouch, M.B.A.
Director
Sports Medicine Research and Testing
  Laboratory
and
Co-Director
Center for Human Toxicology
University of Utah
Salt Lake City, Utah
and
Consulting Toxicologist
The Walsh Group, P.A.
Bethesda, Maryland

Susan D. Crumpton, M.S.
Health Sciences Unit
Science and Engineering Group
RTI International
Research Triangle Park, North Carolina

Henrik Druid M.D., Ph.D.
Associate Professor
Department of Forensic Medicine
Karolinska Institute
Stockholm, Sweden

Kenneth C. Edgell, M.S.
Past Director (2001–2004)
Office of Drug and Alcohol Policy and
  Compliance
U.S. Department of Transportation
Washington, D.C.

David H. Epstein, Ph.D.
Clinical Pharmacology and Therapeutics
  Branch
National Institute on Drug Abuse
National Institutes of Health
Department of Health and Human Services
Baltimore, Maryland

Francis M. Esposito, Ph.D.
Health Science Unit
Science and Engineering Group
RTI International
Research Triangle Park, North Carolina

Irina Esterlis, Ph.D.
Department of Psychiatry
Yale University School of Medicine
New Haven, Connecticut
and
VA Connecticut Healthcare System
West Haven, Connecticut

Andrew Farb, M.D.
U.S. Food and Drug Administration
Rockville, Maryland

Christian Giroud, Ph.D.
Swiss Laboratory for Doping Analyses
University Institute of Legal Medicine
Lausanne, Switzerland

Kathryn A. Glatter, M.D.
Department of Cardiology and Internal
  Medicine
University of California
Davis, California

Bruce A. Goldberger, Ph.D.
University of Florida College of Medicine
Gainesville, Florida

Colin N. Haile, Ph.D.
Department of Psychiatry
Yale University School of Medicine
New Haven, Connecticut
and
VA Connecticut Healthcare System
West Haven, Connecticut

W. Lee Hearn, Ph.D.
Director
Dade County Medical Examiner Toxicology
  Laboratory
Miami, Florida

Stephen J. Heishman, Ph.D.
Clinical Pharmacology and Therapeutics
  Branch
National Institute on Drug Abuse
National Institutes of Health
Department of Health and Human Services
Baltimore, Maryland

Anders Helander, Ph.D.
Department of Clinical Neuroscience
Karolinska Institute and Karolinska University
  Hospital
Stockholm, Sweden

Bradford R. Hepler, Ph.D.
Toxicology Laboratory
Wayne County Medical Examiner's Office
Detroit, Michigan

Joe G. Hollingsworth, J.D.
Spriggs & Hollingsworth
Washington, D.C.

Jonathan Howland, Ph.D.
Social and Behavioral Sciences Department
Boston University School of Public Health
Boston, Massachusetts

Marilyn A. Huestis, Ph.D.
Chemistry and Drug Metabolism Section
Intramural Research Program
National Institute on Drug Abuse
National Institutes of Health
Department of Health and Human Services
Baltimore, Maryland

Daniel S. Isenschmid, Ph.D.
Toxicology Laboratory
Wayne County Medical Examiner's Office
Detroit, Michigan

Amanda J. Jenkins, Ph.D.
The Office of the Cuyahoga County Coroner
Cleveland, Ohio

Alan Wayne Jones, D.Sc.
Department of Forensic Toxicology
University Hospital
Linköping, Sweden

Graham R. Jones, Ph.D., DABFT
Office of the Chief Medical Examiner
Edmonton, Alberta, Canada

Leo Kadehjian, Ph.D.
Biomedical Consulting
Palo Alto, California

Steven B. Karch, M.D., FFFLM
Consultant Pathologist/Toxicologist
Berkeley, California

Thomas H. Kelly, Ph.D.
Department of Behavioral Science
University of Kentucky College of Medicine
Lexington, Kentucky

Pascal Kintz, Pharm.D., Ph.D.
ChemTox Laboratory
Illkirch, France

Frank D. Kolodgie, Ph.D.
Armed Forces Institute of Pathology
Washington, D.C.

Suchitra Krishnan-Sarin, Ph.D.
Department of Psychiatry
Yale University School of Medicine
New Haven, Connecticut
and
VA Connecticut Healthcare System
West Haven, Connecticut

Eric G. Lasker, J.D.
Spriggs & Hollingsworth
Washington, D.C.

Nick Lintzeris, M.B.B.S., Ph.D.
National Addiction Centre
South London and Maudsley NHS Trust
London, U.K.

Barry K. Logan, Ph.D.
Director
Washington State Toxicology Laboratory
Department of Laboratory Medicine
University of Washington
Seattle, Washington

Patrice Mangin, Ph.D.
University Institute of Legal Medicine
Lausanne, Switzerland

Christopher S. Martin, Ph.D.
Western Psychiatric Institute and Clinic
Department of Psychiatry
University of Pittsburgh School of Medicine
Pittsburgh, Pennsylvania

Deborah C. Mash, Ph.D.
Departments of Neurology and Molecular and
  Cellular Pharmacology
University of Miami
Miller School of Medicine
Miami, Florida

William M. Meil, Ph.D.
Department of Psychology
Indiana University of Pennsylvania
Indiana, Pennsylvania

John M. Mitchell, Ph.D.
Health Science Unit
Science and Engineering Group
RTI International
Research Triangle Park, North Carolina

Florabel G. Mullick, M.D.
Armed Forces Institute of Pathology
Washington, D.C.

Rudy Murillo, B.A.
Clinical Pharmacology and Therapeutics
  Branch
National Institute on Drug Abuse
National Institutes of Health
Department of Health and Human Services
Baltimore, Maryland

Carol S. Myers, Ph.D.
Clinical Pharmacology and Therapeutics
  Branch
National Institute on Drug Abuse
National Institute of Health
Department of Health and Human Services
Baltimore, Maryland

Jagat Narula, M.D., Ph.D.
University of California, Irvine
School of Medicine and Medical Center
Irvine, California

Kent R. Olson, M.D.
Division of Clinical Pharmacology and
  Experimental Therapeutics
University of California
San Francisco, California

Wallace B. Pickworth, Ph.D.
Battelle Centers for Public Health Research and
  Evaluation
Baltimore, Maryland

Anya Pierce, M.Sc., M.B.A.
Toxicology Department
Beaumont Hospital
Dublin, Ireland, U.K.

Derrick J. Pounder, M.D.
Department of Forensic Medicine
University of Dundee
Scotland, U.K.

Kenzie L. Preston, Ph.D.
Clinical Pharmacology and Therapeutics
  Branch
National Institute on Drug Abuse
National Institutes of Health
Department of Health and Human Services
Baltimore, Maryland

Duncan Raistrick, M.B.B.S.
The Leeds Addiction Unit
Leeds, U.K.

Neil Robinson, Ph.D.
Swiss Laboratory for Doping Analyses
University Institute of Legal Medicine
Lausanne, Switzerland

Brett A. Roth, M.D.
University of Texas Southwestern Medical
  Center
Dallas, Texas

Richard B. Rothman, M.D., Ph.D.
Clinical Psychopharmacology Section
Intramural Research Program
National Institute on Drug Abuse
National Institutes of Health
Department of Health and Human Services
Baltimore, Maryland

Angela Sampson-Cone, Ph.D.
ConeChem Research
Severna Park, Maryland

Christophe Saudan, Ph.D.
Swiss Laboratory for Doping Analyses
University Institute of Legal Medicine
Lausanne, Switzerland

Martial Saugy, Ph.D.
Swiss Laboratory for Doping Analyses
University Institute of Legal Medicine
Lausanne, Switzerland

John P. Schmittner, M.D.
Clinical Pharmacology and Therapeutics
  Branch
National Institute on Drug Abuse
National Institutes of Health
Department of Health and Human Services
Baltimore, Maryland

Theodore F. Shults, J.D., M.S.
Chairman
American Association of Medical Review
  Officers
Research Triangle Park, North Carolina

Julie K. Staley, Ph.D.
Department of Psychiatry
Yale University School of Medicine
New Haven, Connecticut
and
VA Connecticut Healthcare System
West Haven, Connecticut

Craig A. Sutheimer, Ph.D.
Health Sciences Unit
Science and Engineering Group
RTI International
Research Triangle Park, North Carolina

Richard C. Taylor, M.A.
Clinical Pharmacology and Therapeutics
  Branch
National Institute on Drug Abuse
National Institutes of Health
Department of Health and Human Services
Baltimore, Maryland

**Joseph A. Thomasino, M.D., M.S.,
  FACPM**
JAT MRO, Inc.
Jacksonville, Florida

Jane S. C. Tsai, Ph.D.
Roche Diagnostics
Indianapolis, Indiana

Alain Verstraete, M.D., Ph.D.
Ghent University Hospital
Laboratory of Clinical Biology–Toxicology
Ghent, Belgium

Marion Villain, M.S.
ChemTox Laboratory
Illkirch, France

Renu Virmani, M.D., F.A.C.C.
Medical Director
CVPath
International Registry of Pathology
Gaithersburg, Maryland

H. Chip Walls, B.S.
Department of Pathology
Forensic Toxicology Laboratory
University of Miami
Miami, Florida

J. Michael Walsh, Ph.D.
The Walsh Group, P.A.
Bethesda, Maryland

Sharon L. Walsh, Ph.D.
Department of Behavioral Science
Center on Drug and Alcohol Research
University of Kentucky College of Medicine
Lexington, Kentucky

Charles V. Wetli, M.D.
Chief Medical Examiner
Office of the Suffolk County Medical Examiner
Hauppage, New York

Robert M. White, Sr., Ph.D.
Technical Director
DSI Laboratories
Fort Myers, Florida

Kim Wolff, Ph.D.
King's College London
Institute of Psychiatry
National Addiction Centre
London, U.K.

Steven H.Y. Wong, Ph.D.
Professor of Pathology
and
Director
Clinical Chemistry/Toxicology
TDM, Pharmacogenomics, Proteomics
Medical College of Wisconsin
and
Scientific Director
Toxicology Department
Milwaukee County Medical Examiner's Office
Milwaukee, Wisconsin

J. Robert Zettl, B.S., M.P.A., DABFE
Forensic Consultants, Inc.
Centennial, Colorado

Shoshanna Zevin, M.D.
Department of Internal Medicine
Shaare Zedek Medical Center
Jerusalem, Israel

Contents

CHAPTER 1

Criminalistics: Introduction to Controlled Substances

Joseph P. Bono, M.A.
Supervisory Chemist, Drug Enforcement Administration, Special Testing and Research Laboratory, McLean, Virginia

CONTENTS

INTRODUCTION

This chapter is concerned with the identification and analysis of physical evidence derived from drugs and drug users. The chapter begins with an introduction to the most popular synthetic routes preferred by clandestine drug makers. Sections are devoted to brief regulatory historics and overviews of the most common drugs (heroin, cocaine, and marijuana) as well as some of the lesser known licit and illicit drug agents. An overview is provided of what information is required to make a defensible forensic identification. This includes an introduction to drug logos, tablet markings and capsule imprints, and blotter acid. The remaining sections provide introductions to the various field and laboratory screening and confirmatory testing procedures. Techniques of comparative analysis are explained, and methods for comparing cocaine and heroin courtroom exhibits are presented. The trade names of commonly encountered chemicals are listed. The chapter concludes with tabular listings of controlled substances by schedule number.

1.1 DEFINITION AND SCHEDULING OF CONTROLLED SUBSTANCES

A "controlled substance" is a drug or substance of which the use, sale, or distribution is regulated by the federal government or a state government entity. These controlled substances are listed specifically or by classification on the federal level in the Controlled Substances Act (CSA) or in Part 1308 of the Code of Federal Regulations. The purpose of the CSA is to minimize the quantity of usable substances available to those who are likely to abuse them. At the same time, the CSA provides for the legitimate medical, scientific, and industrial needs of these substances in the U.S.

1.2 SCHEDULING OF CONTROLLED SUBSTANCES

Eight factors are considered when determining whether or not to schedule a drug as a controlled substance:

1. Actual or relative potential for abuse
2. Scientific evidence of pharmacological effect
3. State of current scientific knowledge
4. History of current pattern of abuse
5. Scope, duration, and significance of abuse
6. Risk to the public health
7. Psychic or physiological dependence liability
8. Immediate precursor

The definition of potential for abuse is based on individuals taking a drug of their own volition in sufficient amounts to cause a health hazard to themselves or to others in the community. Data are then collected to evaluate three factors: (1) actual abuse of the drug; (2) the clandestine manufacture of the drug; (3) trafficking and diversion of the drug or its precursors from legitimate channels into clandestine operations. Preclinical abuse liability studies are then conducted on animals to evaluate physiological responses to the drug. At this point, clinical abuse liability studies can be conducted with human subjects, which evaluate preference studies and epidemiology.

Accumulating scientific evidence of a drug's pharmacological effects involves examining the scientific data concerning whether the drug elicits a stimulant, depressant, narcotic, or hallucinogenic response. A determination can then be made regarding how closely the pharmacology of the drug resembles that of other drugs that are already controlled.

Evidence is also accumulated about the scientific data on the physical and chemical properties of the drug. This can include determining which salts and isomers are possible and which are available. There is also a concern for the ease of detection and identification using analytical chemistry. Because many controlled substances have the potential for clandestine synthesis, there is a requirement for evaluating precursors, possible synthetic routes, and theoretical yields in these syntheses. At this phase of the evaluation, medical uses are also evaluated.

The next three factors — (1) history and patterns of abuse; (2) scope, duration, and significance of abuse; and (3) risks to public health — all involve sociological and medical considerations. The results of these studies focus on data collection and population studies. Psychic and physiological dependence liability studies must be satisfied for a substance to be placed on Schedules II through V. This specific finding is not necessary to place a drug on Schedule I. A practical problem here is that it is not always easy to prove a development of dependence.

The last factor is one that can involve the forensic analyst. Under the law, an "immediate precursor" is defined as a substance that is an immediate chemical intermediary used or likely to be used in the manufacture of a specific controlled substance. Defining synthetic pathways in the clandestine production of illicit controlled substances requires knowledge possessed by the experienced analyst.

A controlled substance will be classified and named in one of five schedules. Schedule I includes drugs or other substances that have a high potential for abuse, no currently accepted use in the treatment of medical conditions, and little, if any, accepted safety criteria under the supervision of a medical professional. Use of these substances will almost always lead to abuse and dependence. Some of the more commonly encountered Schedule I controlled substances are heroin, marijuana, lysergic acid diethylamide (LSD), 3,4-methylenedioxy-amphetamine (MDA), and psilocybin mushrooms.

Progressing from Schedule II to Schedule V, abuse potential decreases. Schedule II controlled substances also include drugs or other substances that have a high potential for abuse, but also have some currently accepted, but severely restricted, medical uses. Abuse of Schedule II substances may lead to dependence, which can be both physical and psychological. Because Schedule II controlled substances do have some recognized medical uses, they are usually available to health professionals in the form of legitimate pharmaceutical preparations. Cocaine hydrochloride is still used as a topical anesthetic in some surgical procedures. Methamphetamine, up until a few years ago, was used in the form of Desoxyn to treat hyperactivity in children. Raw opium is included in Schedule II. Amobarbital and secobarbital, which are used as central nervous system depressants, are included, as is phencyclidine (PCP), which was used as a tranquilizer in veterinary pharmaceutical practices. In humans, PCP acts as a hallucinogen. Although many of the substances seized under Schedule II were not prepared by legitimate pharmaceutical entities, cocaine hydrochloride and methamphetamine are two examples of Schedule II drugs that, when confiscated as white to off-white powder or granules in plastic or glassine packets, have almost always been prepared on the illicit market for distribution. As one progresses from Schedules III through V, most legitimate pharmaceutical preparations are encountered.

1.3 CONTROLLED SUBSTANCE ANALOGUE ENFORCEMENT ACT OF 1986

In recent years, the phenomenon of controlled substance analogues and homologues has presented a most serious challenge to the control of drug trafficking and successful prosecution of clandestine laboratory operators. These homologues and analogues are synthesized drugs that are chemically and pharmacologically similar to substances that are listed in the Controlled Substances Act, but which themselves are not specifically controlled by name. (The term "designer drug" is sometimes used to describe these substances.) The concept of synthesizing controlled substance analogues in an attempt to circumvent existing drug law was first noticed in the late 1960s. At about this time there were seizures of clandestine laboratories engaged in the production of analogues of controlled phenethylamines. In the 1970s variants of methaqualone and phencyclidine were being seized in clandestine laboratories. By the 1980s, Congress decided that the time had come to deal with this problem with a federal law enforcement initiative. The Controlled Substance Analogue Enforcement Act of 1986 amends the Comprehensive Drug Abuse Prevention and Control Act of 1970 by including the following section:

Section 203. A controlled substance analogue shall to the extent intended for human consumption, be treated, for the purposes of this title and title III as a controlled substance in schedule I.

The 99th Congress went on to define the meaning of the term "controlled substance analogue" as a substance:

(i) the chemical structure of which is substantially similar to the chemical structure of a controlled substance in schedule I or II;

(ii) which has a stimulant, depressant, or hallucinogenic effect on the central nervous system that is substantially similar to or greater than the stimulant, depressant, or hallucinogenic effect on the central nervous system of a controlled substance in schedule I or II; or

(iii) with respect to a particular person, which person represents or intends to have a stimulant, depressant, or hallucinogenic effect on the central nervous system of a controlled substance in schedule I or II.

The Act goes on to exclude:

(i) a controlled substance

(ii) any substance for which there is an approved new drug application

(iii) with respect to a particular person any substance, if an exemption is in effect for investigational use, for that person, under section 505 … to the extent conduct with respect to such substance is pursuant to such exemption; or

(iv) any substance to the extent not intended for human consumption before such an exemption takes effect with respect to that substance.

Treatment of exhibits falling under the purview of the federal court system is described in Public Law 91-513 or Part 1308 of the Code of Federal Regulations. Questions relating to controlled substance analogues and homologues can usually be answered by reference to the Controlled Substances Analogue and Enforcement Act of 1986.

1.4 CONTROLLED SUBSTANCES

1.4.1 Heroin

Whenever one thinks about drugs of abuse and addiction, heroin is one of the most recognized drugs. Heroin is a synthetic drug, produced from the morphine contained in the sap of the opium poppy. The abuse of this particular controlled substance has been known for many years. The correct chemical nomenclature for heroin is O^3,O^6-diacetylmorphine. Heroin is synthesized from morphine in a relatively simple process. The first synthesis of diacetylmorphine reported in the literature was in 1875 by two English chemists, G.H. Beckett and C.P. Alder Wright.[1] In 1898 in Elberfeld, Germany, the Farbenfabriken vorm. Friedrich Bayer & Co. produced the drug commercially. An employee of the company, H. Dresser, named the morphine product "heroin."[2] There is no definitive documentation as to where the name "heroin" originated. However, it probably had its origin in the "heroic remedies" class of drugs of the day.

Heroin was used in place of codeine and morphine for patients suffering from lung diseases such as tuberculosis. Additionally, the Bayer Company advertised heroin as a cure for morphine addiction. The analgesic properties of the drug were very effective. However, the addictive properties were quite devastating. In 1924, Congress amended the Narcotic Drug Import and Export Act to prohibit the importation of opium for the manufacture of heroin. However, stockpiles were still available and could be legally prescribed by physicians. The 1925 International Opium Convention imposed drug controls that began to limit the supply of heroin from Europe. Shortly thereafter, the clandestine manufacture of heroin was reported in China. The supplies of opium in the Far East provided a ready source of morphine — the starting material for the synthesis. The medical use of heroin in the U.S. was not banned until July 19, 1956 with the passage of Public Law 728, which required all inventories to be surrendered to the federal government by November 19, 1956.

In the past 50 or so years, the source countries for opium used in clandestine heroin production have increased dramatically. Political and economic instability in many areas of the world accounts for much of the increased production of heroin. The opium that is used to produce the heroin that enters the U.S. today has four principal sources. Geographically all of these regions are characterized by a temperate climate with appropriate rainfall and proper soil conditions. However, there are differences in the quality of opium, the morphine content, and the number of harvests from each of these areas. Labor costs are minimal and the profit margins are extremely high for those in the upper echelons of heroin distribution networks.

1.4.1.1 Heroin Sources by Region

Southeast Asia — The "Golden Triangle" areas of Burma, China, and Laos are the three major source countries in this part of the world for the production of illicit opium. Of these three countries, 60 to 80% of the total world supply of heroin comes from Burma. Heroin destined for the U.S. transits a number of countries including Thailand, Hong Kong, Japan, Korea, the Philippines, Singapore, and Taiwan. Southeast Asian heroin is usually shipped to the U.S. in significant quantities by bulk cargo carriers. The techniques for hiding the heroin in the cargo are quite ingenious. The shipment of Southeast Asian (SEA) heroin in relatively small quantities is also commonplace. Criminal organizations in Nigeria have been deeply involved in the small-quantity smuggling of SEA heroin into the U.S. The "body carry" technique and ingestion are two of the better known methods of concealment by the Nigerians. SEA heroin is high quality and recognized by its white crystalline appearance. Although the cutting agents are numerous, caffeine and acetaminophen appear quite frequently.

Southwest Asia — Turkey, Iraq, Iran, Afghanistan, Pakistan, India, Lebanon, and the newly independent states of the former Soviet Union (NIS) are recognized as source countries in this part of the world. Trafficking of Southwest Asian heroin has been on the decline in the U.S. since the end of 1994. Southwest Asian heroin usage is more predominant in Europe than in the U.S. The Southwest Asian heroin that does arrive in the U.S. is normally transshipped through Europe, Africa, and the NIS. The political and economic conditions of the NIS and topography of the land make these countries ideal as transit countries for heroin smuggling. The rugged mountainous terrain and the absence of significant enforcement efforts enable traffickers to proceed unabated. Most Southwest Asian heroin trafficking groups in the originating countries, the transiting countries, and the U.S. are highly cohesive ethnic groups. These groups rely less on the bulk shipment and more on smaller quantity commercial cargo smuggling techniques. Southwest Asian heroin is characterized by its off-white to tan powdery appearance as compared to the white SEA heroin. The purity of Southwest Asian heroin is only slightly lower than that of SEA heroin. The cutting agents are many: phenobarbital, caffeine, acetaminophen, and calcium carbonate appear quite frequently.

Central America — Mexico and Guatemala are the primary source countries for heroin in Central America. Mexico's long border with the U.S. provides easy access for smuggling and distribution networks. Smuggling is usually small scale and often involves illegal immigrants and migrant workers crossing into the U.S. Heroin distribution in the U.S. is primarily the work of Mexican immigrants from the States of Durango, Michoacan, Nuevo Leon, and Sinaloa. Concealment in motor vehicles, public transportation, external body carries, and commercial package express are common. This heroin usually ranges from a dark brown powder to a black tar. The most commonly encountered adulterants are amorphous (formless and indeterminate) materials and sugars. The dark color of Mexican heroin is attributed to processing by-products. The purity of Mexican heroin varies greatly from seizure to seizure.

South America — Heroin production in this part of the world is a relatively new phenomenon. Cultivation of opium has been documented along the Andean mountain range within Colombia in the areas of Cauca, Huila, Tolima, and Santaner. There have been a number of morphine base and heroin processing facilities seized in Colombia in the past few years. Smuggling of South American heroin into the U.S. increased dramatically in 1994 and 1995. The primary method of smuggling has been by Colombian couriers aboard commercial airliners using false-sided briefcases and luggage, hollowed out shoes, or by ingestion. Miami and New York are the primary ports of entry into the U.S. One advantage that the traffickers from South America have is the importation networks that are already in place for the distribution of cocaine into the U.S. Transshipment of this heroin through other South American countries and the Caribbean is also a common practice. South American heroin has many of the same physical characteristics of Southwest Asian heroin. However, the purity of South American heroin is higher, with fewer adulterants than Southwest Asian heroin. Cocaine in small quantities is oftentimes encountered in South American heroin exhibits. In such cases, it is not always clear whether the cocaine is present as a contaminant introduced due to common packaging locations of cocaine and heroin, or whether it has been added as an adulterant.

1.4.1.2 *Isolation of Morphine and Heroin Production*

There are some very specific methods for producing heroin. However, all involve the same four steps: (1) The opium poppy (*Papaver somniferum* L.) is cultivated; (2) the poppy head is scored and the opium latex is collected; (3) the morphine is isolated from the latex; and (4) the morphine is treated with an acetylating agent. Isolation of the morphine in Step 3 is accomplished using a rendition of one of the following five methods:

1. **Thiboumery and Mohr Process (TMP)** — This is the best known of the reported methods for isolating morphine followed by the acetylation to heroin. Dried opium latex is dissolved in three times its weight of hot water. The solution is filtered hot, which removes undissolved botanical substances. These undissolved botanicals are washed with hot water and filtered. This is done to ensure a maximized yield of morphine in the final product. The filtrate is reduced to half its volume by boiling off the water. The laboratory operator then adds to the filtrate a boiling solution of calcium hydroxide, which forms the water-soluble calcium morphinate. The precipitates, which include the insoluble alkaloids from the opium, and the insoluble materials from this step are filtered. These insolubles are then washed three more times with water and filtered. The resulting filtrate, which contains calcium morphinate still in solution, is then evaporated to a weight of approximately twice the weight of the original weight of the opium and then filtered. This results in a concentrated calcium morphinate solution, which is heated to a boil. Ammonium chloride is then added to reduce the pH below 9.85. When this solution cools, morphine base precipitates and is collected by filtration. The morphine base is dissolved in a minimum volume of warm hydrochloric acid. When this solution cools the morphine hydrochloride precipitates. The precipitated morphine hydrochloride is then isolated by filtration.

2. **Robertson and Gregory Process (RGP)** — This method is similar to TMP. The laboratory operator washes the opium with five to ten times its weight of cold water. The solution is then evaporated to a syrup, which is then re-extracted with cold water and filtered. The filtrate is evaporated until the specific gravity of the solution is 1.075. The solution is boiled and calcium chloride is added. Cold water is added to the calcium morphinate solution, which is then filtered. The solution is concentrated and the calcium morphinate then precipitates out of solution as the liquid evaporates. The calcium morphinate is then redissolved in water and filtered. To the filtrate is added ammonia, which allows the morphine base to precipitate. This morphine base can then be further treated to produce the pharmaceutical quality morphine.

The TMP and RGP are used by commercial suppliers for the initial isolation of morphine from opium. In clandestine laboratories, the same methodologies and rudimentary steps are followed. However, since the operators are using "bucket chemistry," there are modifications to hasten and shortcut the processes.

Three other methods can then be utilized to convert the relatively crude morphine base through purification processes to high-quality morphine base or morphine hydrochloride crystals. Modifications of these purifications are used by clandestine laboratory operators.

3. **Barbier Purification** — The morphine base is dissolved in 80°C water. Tartaric acid is added until the solution becomes acidic to methyl orange. As the solution cools, morphine bitartrate precipitates, is filtered, washed with cold water, and dried. The morphine bitartrate is then dissolved in hot water and ammonia is added to pH 6. This results in a solution of morphine monotartrate. The laboratory operator then adds activated carbon black, sodium bisulfite, sodium acetate, and ammonium oxalate. This process results in a decolorization of the morphine. When this decolorization process is complete, ammonia is added to the solution, which results in white crystals of morphine base. These purified morphine base crystals are then filtered and dried. This high-quality morphine base is converted to morphine hydrochloride by adding 30% ethanolic HCl to a warm solution of morphine in ethanol. The morphine hydrochloride crystallizes from solution as the solution cools.

4. **Schwyzer Purification** — The acetone-insoluble morphine base (from either the TMB or RGP) is washed in with acetone. The morphine base is then re-crystallized from hot ethyl alcohol.

5. **Heumann Purification** — The laboratory operator washes the morphine base (from either the TMB or RGP) with trichloroethylene, followed by a cold 40% ethanol wash. This is subsequently followed by an aqueous acetone wash.

The quality of the clandestine product is usually evaluated by the color and texture of the morphine from one of these processes. If the clandestine laboratory is producing morphine as its end product, with the intention of selling the morphine for conversion by a second laboratory, the morphine will usually be very pure. However, if the operator continues with the acetylation of the morphine to heroin, the "intermediate" morphine will frequently be relatively impure.

Heroin can be produced synthetically, but requires a ten-step process and extensive expertise in synthetic organic chemistry. The total synthesis of morphine has been reported by Gates and Tschudi in 1952 and by Elad and Ginsburg in 1954.[3,4] A more recent synthesis was reported by Rice in 1980.[5] All these methods require considerable forensic expertise and result in low yield. There are also methods reported in the literature for converting codeine to morphine using an *O*-demethylation. The morphine can then be acetylated to heroin. One of these procedures is referred to as "homebake" and was described in the literature by Rapoport et al.[6] This particular procedure has been reported only in New Zealand and Australia.

Acetylation of Morphine to Diacetylmorphine (Heroin) — This process involves placing dried morphine into a reaction vessel and adding excess acetic anhydride (Figure 1.4.1). Sometimes a co-solvent is also used. The mixture is heated to boiling and stirred for varying periods of time ranging from 30 min up to 3 or 4 h. The vessel and contents are cooled and diluted in cold water. A sodium carbonate solution is then added until precipitation of the heroin base is complete and

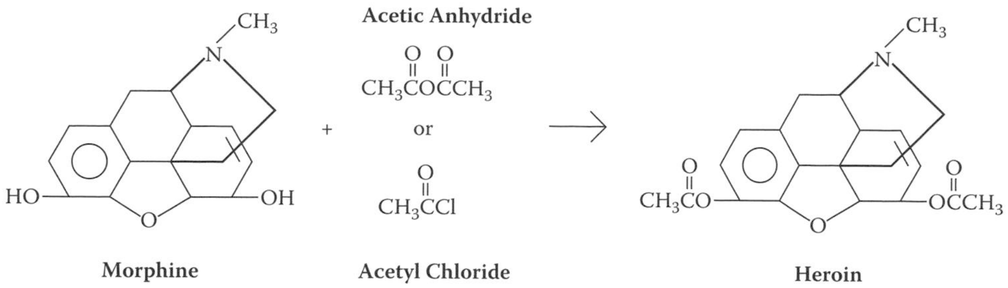

Figure 1.4.1 Clandestine laboratory synthesis of heroin.

settles to the bottom of the reaction vessel. The heroin base is then either filtered and dried or undergoes further processing to enhance the purity or to convert the base to heroin hydrochloride.

Processing By-Products and Degradation Products in Heroin — Pharmaceutical-grade heroin has a purity of greater than 99.5%. Impurities include morphine, the O-3- and O-6-monoacetylmorphines, and other alkaloidal impurities and processing by-products. The impurities found in clandestinely produced heroin include, but are certainly not limited to: the monoacetylmorphines, morphine, codeine, acetylcodeine, papaverine, noscapine, thebaine, meconine, thebaol, acetylthebaol, norlaudanosine, reticuline, and codamine. These impurities (from both quantitative and qualitative perspectives) are retained as the result of anomalies in processing methodologies.

REFERENCES

1. Anon., Heroin, *J. Chem. Soc. London,* 28, 315–318, 1875.
2. Anon., Heroin, *Arch. Ges. Physiol.,* 72, 487, 1898.
3. Gates, M. and Tschudi, G., The synthesis of morphine, *J. Am. Chem. Soc.,* 74, 1109–1110, 1952.
4. Elad, E. and Ginsburg, D., The synthesis of morphine, *J. Am. Chem. Soc.,* 76, 312–313, 1954.
5. Rice, K.C., Synthetic opium alkaloids and derivatives. A short total synthesis of (±)-dihydrothebainone, (±)-dihydrocodinone, and (±)-nordihydrocodinone as an approach to the practical synthesis of morphine, codeine, and congeners, *J. Org. Chem.,* 45, 3135–3137, 1980.
6. Rapoport, H. and Bonner, R.M., delta-7-Desoxymorphine, *J. Am. Chem. Soc.,* 73, 5485, 1951.

1.4.2 Cocaine

The social implications of cocaine abuse in the U.S. has been the subject of extensive media coverage from the 1980s to the present day. As a result, the general public has acquired some of the terminology associated with the cocaine usage. "Smoking crack" and "snorting coke" are terms that have become well understood in the American culture from elementary school through adulthood. However, there are facts associated with this drug that are not well understood by the general public. There are documented historical aspects associated with coca and cocaine abuse that go back 500 years. Recognizing some of these historical aspects enables the public to place today's problem in perspective. Cocaine addiction has been with society for well over 100 years.

There are four areas of interest this section will address: (1) Where does cocaine come from? (2) How is cocaine isolated from the coca plant? (3) What does one take into the body from cocaine purchased on the street? (4) How does the chemist analyzing the drug identify and distinguish between the different forms of cocaine?

Cocaine is a Schedule II controlled substance. The wording in Title 21, Part 1308.12(b)(4) of the Code of Federal Regulations states:

Coca leaves (9040) and any salt, compound, derivative or preparation of coca leaves (including cocaine (9041) and ecgonine (9180) and their salts, isomers, derivatives and salts of isomers and derivatives), and any salt, compound, derivative, or preparation thereof which is chemically equivalent or identical with any of these substances, except that the substances shall not include decocanized coca leaves, or extractions of coca leaves, do not contain cocaine or ecgonine.

It is significant that the term "coca leaves" is the focal point of that part of the regulation controlling cocaine. The significance of this fact will become more apparent as this discussion progresses.

1.4.2.1 Sources of Cocaine

Cocaine is just one of the alkaloidal substances present in the coca leaf. Other molecules, some of them psychoactive (norcocaine being the most prominent), are shown in Figure 1.4.2. Cocaine is extracted from the leaves of the coca plant. The primary of source of cocaine imported into the U.S. is South America, but the coca plant also grows in the Far East in Ceylon, Java, and India. The plant is cultivated in South America on the eastern slopes of the Andes in Peru and Bolivia. There are four varieties of coca plants — *Erythroxylon coca* var. *coca* (ECVC), *E. coca* var. *ipadu*, *E. novogranatense* var. *novogranatense*, and *E. novogranatense* var. *truxillense*.[1–3] ECVC is the variety that has been used for the manufacture of illicit cocaine. While cultivated in many countries of South America, Peru and Bolivia are the world's leading producers of the coca plant. Cocaine is present in the coca leaves from these countries at dry weight concentrations of from 0.1 to 1%. The average concentration of cocaine in the leaf is 0.7%. The coca shrub has a life expectancy of 50 years and can be harvested three or four times a year.

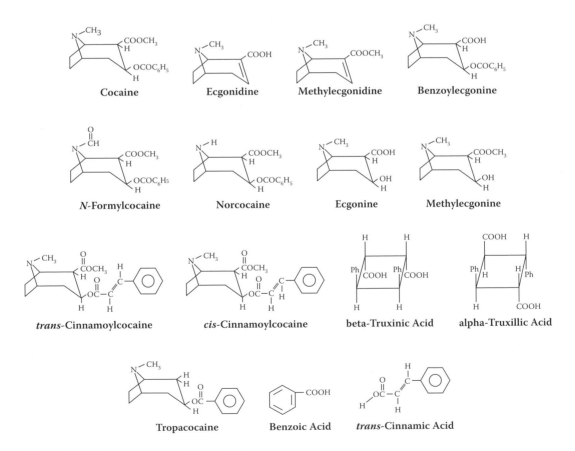

Figure 1.4.2 Substances present in coca leaf.

The method of isolating cocaine from the coca leaf does not require a high degree of technical expertise or experience. It requires no formal education or expensive scientific equipment or chemicals. In most instances the methodology is passed from one generation to the next.

1.4.2.2 Historical Considerations

Prior to the 1880s, the physiological properties of cocaine and the coca leaf were not readily distinguishable in the literature. During that year, H.H. Rusby and W.G. Mortimer made the distinction between the physiological properties of "isolated" cocaine and the coca leaf. Mortimer wrote:

> [T]he properties of cocaine, remarkable as they are, lie in an altogether different direction from those of coca.[1]

In 1884, two significant papers appeared in the literature. Sigmund Freud published the first of his five papers on the medicinal properties of cocaine.[2] A few months later, Karl Koller discovered the use of cocaine as local anesthetic.[3] In 1886, Sir Arthur Conan Doyle, an eye specialist who had studied at Vienna General Hospital, where Freud and Koller made their discoveries, made reference to Sherlock Holmes's use of cocaine in *The Sign of Four*.[4] That same year in Atlanta, Georgia, John Pemberton introduced to this country, caught up in the frenzy of alcohol prohibition, a beverage consisting of coca leaf extracts, African kola nuts, and a sweet carbonated syrup. The product was named "Coca-Cola."[5] Pemberton received his inspiration from Angelo Mariani, a Corsican pharmacist working in Paris, who had been selling a coca leaf-Bordeaux wine tincture since the early 1860s. Mariani's product was the most popular tonic of its time, and was used by celebrities, poets, popes, and presidents.[6] Patterns of coca consumption changed dramatically in the 20th century. In the 19th century, cocaine was available only in the form of a botanical product or a botanical product in solution. When chemical houses, such as Merck, began to produce significant quantities of refined cocaine, episodes of toxicity became much more frequent, the views of the medical profession changed, and physicians lost much of their enthusiasm for the drug.

Until 1923, the primary source of cocaine was from the coca leaf. In that year, Richard Willstatter was able to synthesize a mixture of D-cocaine, L-cocaine, D-pseudococaine, and L-pseudococaine. This multistep synthesis requires a high degree of technical expertise in organic chemistry and results in low yields.[7] These financial and technical factors make the extraction of cocaine from the coca leaf the method by which most, if not all, of the cocaine is isolated for distribution on both the licit and illicit markets.

1.4.2.3 Isolation and Purification

The extraction and isolation of cocaine from the coca leaf is not difficult. There is more than one way to do it. South American producers improvise depending on the availability of chemicals. All of the known production techniques involve three primary steps: (1) extraction of crude coca paste from the coca leaf; (2) purification of coca paste to cocaine base; and (3) conversion of cocaine base to cocaine hydrochloride. The paste and base laboratories in South America are deeply entrenched and widespread with thousands of operations, whereas the conversion laboratories are more sophisticated and centralized. They border on semi-industrial pilot-plant type laboratories involving a knowledge of chemistry and engineering.

The primary isolation method used until recently is a Solvent Extraction Technique. The essential methodology involves macerating a quantity of coca leaves with lime water, and then adding kerosene with stirring. After a while the kerosene is separated from the aqueous layer. A dilute sulfuric acid solution is added to the kerosene with stirring. This time the kerosene is separated from the aqueous layer and set aside. It is common to save the kerosene for another extraction of the leaves. The aqueous layer is retained and neutralized with limestone or some other alkaline substance. The material that precipitates after the addition of limestone is crude coca paste containing anywhere from 30 to 80% cocaine, with the remainder of the cocaine matrix composed primarily of other alkaloids, hydrolysis products, and basic inorganic salts used in the processing. This solid material is isolated by filtration for purification of the cocaine.

The coca paste is then dissolved in dilute sulfuric acid, and dilute potassium permanganate solution is added to oxidize the impurities. This solution is then filtered, and ammonium hydroxide is added to the filtrate to precipitate cocaine base. This "cocaine" is not ready for shipment to the U.S. The cocaine will first be converted to hydrochloride for easier packaging, handling, and shipment.

A second method of isolating cocaine from the leaf, which is more predominant today, is the Acid Extraction Technique. In this method, the cocaine leaves are placed directly in the maceration pit with enough sulfuric acid to cover the leaves. The pit is a hole dug into the ground and lined with heavy-duty plastic. The leaves are macerated by workers who stomp in the sulfuric acid/coca leaf pit. This stomping leaches the cocaine base from the leaf and forms an aqueous solution of cocaine sulfate. This stomping can continue for a matter of hours to ensure maximum recovery of the cocaine.

After stomping is complete, the coca solution is poured through a coarse filter to remove the insolubles including the plant material. More sulfuric acid is added to the leaves and a second or even third extraction of the remaining cocaine will take place. Maximized recovery of cocaine is important to the laboratory operators. After the extractions and filterings are completed, an excess basic lime or carbonate solution is added to the acidic solution with stirring and neutralizing the excess acid and cocaine sulfate. A very crude coca paste forms. The addition of the base is monitored until the solution is basic to an ethanolic solution of phenolphthalein. The coca paste is then back-extracted with a small volume of kerosene. The solution sets until a separation of the layers occurs. The kerosene is then back-extracted this time with a dilute solution of sulfuric acid. Then, an inorganic base is added to precipitate the coca paste. This coca paste is essentially the same as that generated by the solvent extraction method. The advantage to this Acid Extraction Technique is that a minimal volume of organic solvent is required. And while it is more labor intensive, the cost of labor in Bolivia, the major producing country of coca paste, is very low when compared to the financial return.

The resultant cocaine base, produced by either technique, is dissolved in acetone, ether, or a mixture of both. A dilute solution of hydrochloric acid in acetone is then prepared. The two solutions are mixed and a precipitate of cocaine hydrochloride forms almost immediately and is allowed to settle to the bottom of the reaction vessel (usually an inexpensive bucket). The slurry will then be poured through clean bed sheets filtering the cocaine hydrochloride from the solvent. The sheets are then wrung dry to eliminate excess acetone, and the high-quality cocaine hydrochloride is dried in microwave ovens, under heat lamps, or in the sunlight. It is then a simple matter to package the cocaine hydrochloride for shipment. One of the more common packaging forms encountered in laboratories analyzing seizures of illicit cocaine is the "one kilo brick." This is a brick-shaped package of cocaine wrapped in tape or plastic, sometimes labeled with a logo, with the contents weighing near 1 kg. Once the cocaine hydrochloride arrives in the U.S., drug wholesalers may add mannitol or inositol as diluents, or procaine, benzocaine, lidocaine, or tetracaine as adulterants. This cocaine can then be sold on the underground market in the U.S. either in bulk or by repackaging into smaller containers.

1.4.2.4 Conversion to "Crack"

"Crack" is the term used on the street and even in some courtrooms to describe the form of cocaine base that has been converted from the cocaine hydrochloride and can be smoked in a pipe.

This procedure of conversion from the acid to the base is usually carried out in the U.S. Cocaine base usually appears in the form of a rock-like material, and is sometimes sold in plastic packets, glass vials, or other suitable packaging. Cocaine hydrochloride is normally ingested by inhalation through a tube or straw, or by injection. Cocaine base is ingested by smoking in an improvised glass pipe. Ingestion in this manner results in the cocaine entering the bloodstream through the lungs and rushes to the brain very quickly.

Cocaine hydrochloride is converted to cocaine base in one of two ways. The first method involves dissolving the cocaine hydrochloride in water and adding sodium bicarbonate or household ammonia. The water is then boiled for a short period until all of the precipitated cocaine base melts to an oil, and ice is added to the reaction vessel. This vessel will usually be a metal cooking pan or a deep glass bowl. As the water cools, chunks of cocaine base oil will solidify at the bottom of the cooking vessel. After all the cocaine base has formed, the water can be cooled and then poured off leaving the solid cocaine base, which is easily removed from the collection vessel. The cocaine base can be cut with a knife or broken into "rocks," which can then be dried either under a heat lamp or in a microwave oven. It is not unusual when analyzing cocaine base produced from this method to identify sodium bicarbonate mixed with the rock-like material. This cocaine base sometimes has a high moisture content due to incomplete drying.

A second method of producing cocaine base from cocaine hydrochloride involves dissolving the salt (usually cocaine hydrochloride) in water. Sodium bicarbonate or household ammonia is added to the water and mixed well. Diethyl ether is then added to the solution and stirred. The mixture then separates into two layers with the ether layer on top of the aqueous layer. The ether is decanted leaving the water behind. The ether is then allowed to evaporate and high-quality cocaine base remains. If any of the adulterants mentioned previously (excluding sugars, which are diluents) are mixed with the cocaine hydrochloride prior to conversion, then they will also be converted to the base and will be a part of the rock-like material that results from this process. The term "free base" is used to describe this form of cocaine. Cocaine base in this form is also smoked in a glass pipe. However, residual (and sometimes substantial) amounts of ether remaining in these samples from the extraction process make ignition in a glass pipe very dangerous.

1.4.2.5 Other Coca Alkaloids

In the process of examining cocaine samples in the laboratory, it is not uncommon to identify other alkaloids and manufacturing by-products with the cocaine. These other alkaloids are carried over from the coca leaf in the extraction of the cocaine. Many manufacturing by-products result from the hydrolysis of the parent alkaloids (benzoylecgonine from cocaine, or truxillic acid from truxilline). As a forensic chemist, it is important to recognize the sources of these alkaloids as one progresses through an analytical scheme.

The major alkaloidal "impurities" present in the coca leaf that are carried over in the cocaine extraction are the *cis-* and *trans*-cinnamoylcocaines and the truxillines. There are 11 isomeric truxillic and truxinic acids resulting from the hydrolysis of truxilline. Another naturally occurring minor alkaloid from the coca leaf is tropacocaine. The concentration of tropacocaine will rarely, if ever, exceed 1% of the cocaine concentration and is well below the concentrations of the *cis-* and *trans*-cinnamoylcocaines and the truxillines. Two other alkaloids from the coca leaf which have been identified are cuscohygrine and hygrine. These two products are not found in cocaine, just in the leaf.

The second class of substances found in the analysis of cocaine samples is the result of degradation or hydrolysis. Ecgonine, benzoylecgonine, and methylecgonine found in cocaine samples will be the result of the hydrolysis of cocaine. It is important to recognize that some of these manufacturing by-products, such as ecgonine, can be detected by gas chromatography only if they are derivatized prior to injection. Methyl ecgonidine is a by-product of the hydrolysis of cocaine and is oftentimes identified in the laboratory by gas chromatography/mass spectrometry (GC/MS).

This artifact can also result from the thermal degradation of cocaine or the truxillines in the injection port of the GC. Benzoic acid is the other product identified when this decomposition occurs.

There are at least two substances that result directly from the permanganate oxidation of cocaine. N-Formyl cocaine results from oxidation of the N-methyl group of cocaine to an N-formyl group. Norcocaine is a hydrolysis product resulting from a Schiff's base intermediate during the permanganate oxidation. There is also evidence that norcocaine can result from the N-demethylation of cocaine, a consequence of the peroxides in diethyl ether.

1.4.2.6 Cocaine Adulterants

The primary adulterants identified in cocaine samples are procaine and benzocaine. Lidocaine is also found with less regularity. These adulterants are found in both the cocaine base and cocaine hydrochloride submissions. The primary diluents are mannitol and inositol. Many other sugars have been found, but not nearly to the same extent. Cocaine hydrochloride concentrations will usually range from 20 to 99%. The moisture content of cocaine hydrochloride is usually minimal. Cocaine base concentrations will usually range from 30 to 99%. There will usually be some moisture in cocaine base ("crack") submissions from the water/sodium bicarbonate or water/ammonia methods. The concentration of cocaine base ("free base") from the ether/sodium bicarbonate or ether/ammonia methods will usually be higher and free of water.

The methods for identifying cocaine in the laboratory include but are not limited to: infrared spectrophotometry (IR), nuclear magnetic resonance spectroscopy (NMR), mass spectrometry (MS), and gas chromatography (GC). IR and NMR will enable the analyst to distinguish between cocaine hydrochloride and cocaine base. However, it is not possible to identify the form in which the cocaine is present utilizing this instrumentation.

1.4.2.7 Conclusion

The user of either cocaine base or cocaine hydrochloride not only ingests the cocaine, but also other alkaloids from the coca plant, processing by-products, organic and inorganic reagents used in processing, diluents, and adulterants. There is no realistic way in which a cocaine user can ensure the quality of the cocaine purchases on the street, and "innocent" recreational drug use may provide more danger than the user would knowingly risk.

REFERENCES

1. Rusby, H.H., Bliss, A.R., and Ballard, C.W., *The Properties and Uses of Drugs,* Blakiston's Son & Co., Philadelphia, 1930, 125, 386, 407.
2. Byck, R., Ed., *Cocaine Papers by Sigmund Freud,* Stonehill, New York, 1975.
3. Pendergrast, M., *For God, Country, and Coca-Cola; The Definitive History of the Great American Soft Drink and the Company That Makes It,* Basic Books, New York, 2000.
4. Musto, D., A study in cocaine: Sherlock Holmes and Sigmund Freud, *J. Am. Med. Assoc.,* 204: 125, 1968.
5. Brecher, E. and the Editors of Consumer Reports, *Licit and Illicit Drugs,* Little, Brown, Boston, 1972, 33–36, 270.
6. Mariani, A., Ed., *Album Mariani, Les Figures Contemporaines. Contemporary Celebrities from the Album Mariani, etc.,* various publishers for Mariani & Co., 13 Vols., 1891–1913.
7. Willstatter, R., Wolfes, O., and Mader, H., Synthese des Naturlichen Cocains, *Justus Liebigs's Ann. Chim.,* 434, 111–139, 1923.
8. Casale, J.F. and Klein, R.F.X., Illicit cocaine production, *Forensic Sci. Rev,* 5, 96–107, 1993.

1.4.3 Marijuana

1.4.3.1 History and Terminology

Marijuana is a Schedule I controlled substance. In botanical terms, "marijuana" is defined as *Cannabis sativa* L. Legally, marijuana is defined as all parts of the plant *C. sativa* L. (and any of its varieties) whether growing or not, the seeds thereof, the resin extracted from any part of the plant, and every compound, manufacture, salt, derivative, mixture, or preparation of such plant; its seeds and resins. Such terms do not include the mature stalk of the plants, fibers produced from such plants, oils or cakes made from the pressed seeds of such plants, any other compound, manufacture, salt derivative, mixture or preparation of such mature stalks (except the resin extracted therefrom), fiber, oil or cake, pressed seed, or the sterilized seed which is incapable of germination.[1] Pharmaceutical preparations that contained the resinous extracts of cannabis were available on the commercial market from the 1900s to 1937. These products were prescribed for their analgesic and sedative effects. In 1937 the U.S. Food and Drug Administration declared these products to be of little medical utility, and they were removed from the market. Cannabis, in the forms of the plant material, hashish, and hashish oil, is the most abused illicit drug in the world.

Cannabis is cultivated in many areas of the world. Commercial *C. sativa* L. is referred to as "hemp." The plant is cultivated for cloth and rope from its fiber. A valuable drying oil used in art and a substitute for linseed oil is available from the seeds. Bird seed mixtures are also found to contain sterilized marijuana seeds. In the early days of the U.S., hemp was grown in the New England colonies. Its cultivation spread south into Pennsylvania and Virginia. From there it spread south and west most notably into Kentucky and Missouri. Its abundance in the early days of the country is still evident by the fact that it still grows wild in many fields and along many roadways. The plant is now indigenous to many areas, and adapts easily to most soil and moderate climatic conditions.

Marijuana is classified as a hallucinogenic substance. The primary active constituents in the plant are cannabinol, cannabidiol, and the tetrahydrocannabinols, illustrated in Figure 1.4.3. The tetrahydrocannabinols (THCs) are the active components responsible for the hallucinogenic properties of marijuana. The THC of most interest is the Δ^9 tetrahydrocannabinol. The other THCs of interest in marijuana are the Δ^1 *cis-* and *trans-*tetrahydrocannabinols, the Δ^6 *cis-* and *trans-*tetrahydrocannabinols, and the Δ^3 and Δ^4 tetrahydrocannabinols. The concentrations vary dramatically from geographic area to geographic area, from field to field, and from sample to sample. This concentration range varies from less than 1% to as high as 30%. In recent hash oil exhibits, the highest official reported concentration of Δ^9-THC is 43%.[2] Five other terms associated with marijuana are as follows:

Hashish: Resinous material removed from cannabis. Hashish is usually found in the form of a brown to black cake of resinous material. The material is ingested by smoking in pipes or by consuming in food.

Hashish oil: Extract of the marijuana plant which has been heated to remove the extracting solvents. The material exists as a colorless to brown or black oil or tar-like substance.

Sinsemilla: The flowering tops of the unfertilized female cannabis plant. (There are no seeds on such a plant.) Sinsemilla is usually considered a "gourmet" marijuana because of its appearance and relatively high concentrations of the THCs.

Thai sticks: Marijuana leaves tied around stems or narrow-diameter bamboo splints. Thai sticks are considered a high-quality product by the drug culture. The THC concentrations of the marijuana leaves on Thai sticks are higher than domestic marijuana. Unlike hashish and sinsemilla, seeds and small pieces of stalks and stems are found in Thai sticks.

Brick or **Kilo:** Marijuana compressed into a brick-shaped package with leaves, stems, stalk, and seeds. The pressed marijuana is usually tightly wrapped in paper and tape. This is the form of marijuana encountered in most large-scale seizures. These large-scale seizure packages weigh approximately

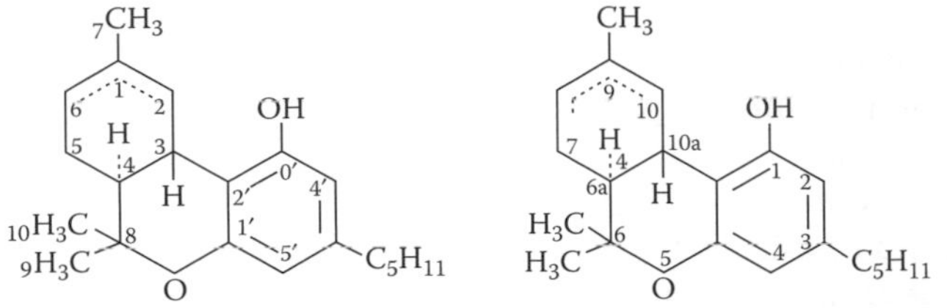

Δ^{1}-THC = Δ^{9}-THC

Δ^{6}-THC = $\Delta^{1(6)}$-THC = Δ^{8}-THC

Tetrahydrocannabinol

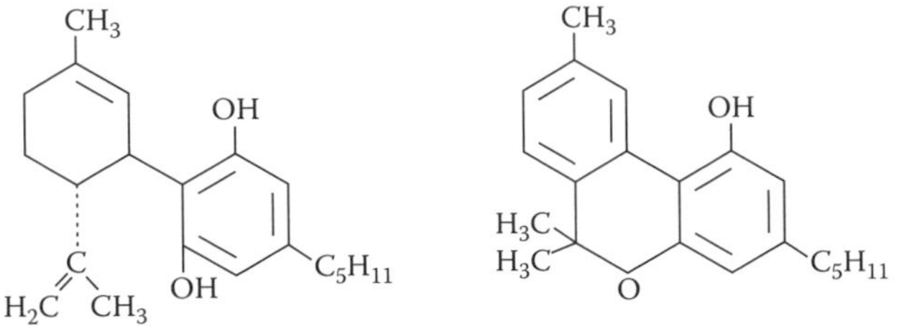

Cannabidiol **Cannabinol**

Figure 1.4.3 The primary active constituents in marijuana.

1000 g (1 kg). This is the packaging form of choice for clandestine operators because of the ease of handling, packaging, shipping, and distribution.

1.4.3.2 Laboratory Analysis

The specificity of a marijuana analysis is still a widely discussed topic among those in the forensic and legal communities. In the course of the past 25 years, the consensus of opinion concerning the analysis of marijuana has remained fairly consistent. In those situations where plant material is encountered, the marijuana is first examined using a stereomicroscope. The presence of the bear claw cystolithic hairs and other histological features are noted using a compound microscope. The plant material is then examined chemically using Duquenois–Levine reagent in a modified Duquenois–Levine testing sequence. These two tests are considered to be conclusive within the realm of existing scientific certainty in establishing the presence of marijauana.[3–5]

The modified Duquenois–Levine test is conducted using Duquenois reagent, concentrated hydrochloric acid, and chloroform. The Duquenois reagent is prepared by dissolving 2 g of vanillin and 0.3 ml of acetaldehyde in 100 ml of ethanol. Small amounts (25 to 60 mg is usually sufficient) of suspected marijuana leaf is placed in a test tube and approximately 2 ml of Duquenois reagent is added. After 1 min, approximately 1 ml of concentrated hydrochloric acid is added. Small bubbles rise from the leaves in the liquid. These are carbon dioxide bubbles produced by the reaction of the hydrochloric acid with the calcium carbonate at the base of the cystolithic hair of the marijuana. A blue to blue-purple color forms very quickly in the solution. Approximately 1 ml of chloroform is then added to the Duquenois reagent/hydrochloric acid mixture. Because chloroform is not miscible with water, and because it is heavier than water, two liquid layers are visible in the tube — the Duquenois reagent/hydrochloric acid layer is on top, and the chloroform layer is on the bottom. After mixing with a vortex stirrer and on settling, the two layers are again clearly distinguishable. However, the chloroform layer has changed from clear to the blue to blue-purple color of the Duquenois reagent/hydrochloric acid mixture.

One variation in this testing process involves pouring off the Duquenois reagent sitting in the tube with the leaves before adding the hydrochloric acid. The remainder of the test is conducted using only the liquid. Another variation involves conducting the test in a porcelain spot plate. This works, although some analysts find the color change a bit more difficult to detect. A third variation involves extracting the cannabis resin with ether or some other solvent, separating the solvent from the leaves, allowing the solvent to evaporate, and conducting the modified Duquenois–Levine test on the extract.

Marquis reagent is prepared by mixing 1 ml of formaldehyde solution with 9 ml of sulfuric acid. The test is done by placing a small amount of sample (1 to 5 mg) into the depression of a spot plate, adding one or two drops of reagent, and observing the color produced. This color will usually be indicative of the class of compounds, and the first color is usually the most important. A weak response may fade, and samples containing sugar will char on standing because of the sulfuric acid. Marquis reagent produces the following results:

1. Purple with opiates (heroin, codeine).
2. Orange turning to brown with amphetamine and methamphetamine.
3. Black with a dark purple halo with 3,4-methylenedioxyamphetamine (MDA) and 3,4-methylene-dioxymethamphetamine (MDMA).
4. Pink with aspirin.
5. Yellow with diphenhydramine.

A thin-layer chromatographic (TLC) analysis, which detects a systematic pattern of colored bands, can then be employed as an additional test.[6,7] Though it is not required, some analysts will run a GC/MS analysis to identify the cannabinoids in the sample.

The solvent insoluble residue of hashish should be examined with the compound microscope. Cystolythic hairs, resin glands, and surface debris should be present. However, if most of the residue is composed of green leaf fragments, the material is pulverized marijuana or imitation hashish.

1.4.4   Peyote

Peyote is a cactus plant that grows in rocky soil in the wild. Historical records document use of the plant by Indians in northern Mexico from as far back as pre-Christian times, when it was used by the Chichimaec tribe in religious rites. The plant grows as small cylinder-like "buttons." The buttons were used to relieve fatigue and hunger, and to treat victims of disease. The peyote buttons were used in group settings to achieve a trance state in tribal dances.[8]

It was used by native Americans in ritualistic ceremonies. In the U.S., peyote was cited in 1891 by James Mooney of the Bureau of American Ethnology.[9] Mooney talked about the use of peyote by the Kiowa Indians, the Comanche Indians, and the Mescalero Apache Indians, all in the southern part of the country. In 1918, he came to the aid of the Indians by incorporating the "Native American Church" in Oklahoma to ensure their rights in the use of peyote in religious ceremonies. Although several bills have been introduced over the years, the U.S. Congress has never passed a law prohibiting the Indians' religious use of peyote. Both mescaline and peyote are listed as Schedule I controlled substances in the Comprehensive Drug Abuse Prevention and Control Act of 1970.

The principal alkaloid of peyote responsible for its hallucinogenic response is mescaline, a derivative of β-phenethylamine. Chemically, mescaline is 3,4,5-trimethoxyphenethylamine. As illustrated in Figure 1.4.4, its structure is similar to the amphetamine group in general. Mescaline was first isolated from the peyote plant in 1894 by the German chemist A. Heffter.[10] The first complete synthesis of mescaline was in 1919 by E. Späth.[11] The extent of abuse of illicit mescaline has not been accurately determined. The use of peyote buttons became popular in the 1950s and

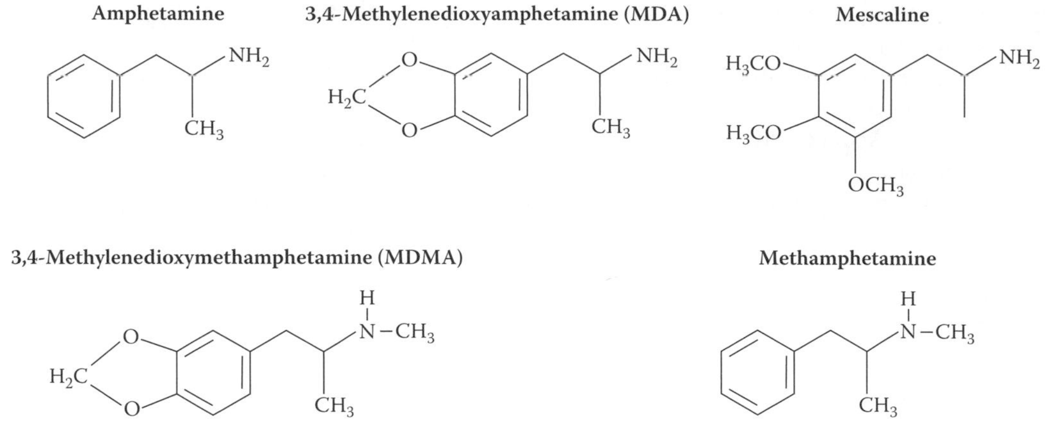

Amphetamine   3,4-Methylenedioxyamphetamine (MDA)   Mescaline

Figure 1.4.4 Chemical structure of mescaline.

3,4-Methylenedioxymethamphetamine (MDMA)   Methamphetamine

again in the period from 1967 to 1970. These two periods showed a dramatic increase in experimentation with hallucinogens in general.

1.4.5 Psilocybin Mushrooms

The naturally occurring indoles responsible for the hallucinogen properties in some species of mushrooms are psilocybin (Figure 1.4.5) and psilocin.[12] The use of hallucinogenic mushrooms dates to the 16th century, occurring during the coronation of Montezuma in 1502.[8] In 1953, R.G. Wassen and V.P. Wasson were credited with the rediscovery of the ritual of the Indian cultures of Mexico and Central America.[13] They were able to obtain samples of these mushrooms. The identification of the mushrooms as the species *Psilocybe* is credited to the French mycologist, Roger Heim.[14]

Albert Hofmann (the discoverer of lysergic acid diethylamine) and his colleagues at Sandoz Laboratories in Switzerland are credited with the isolation and identification of psilocybin (phosphorylated 4-hydroxydimethyltryptamine) and psilocin (4-hydroxydimethyltryptamine).[15] Psilocybin was the major component in the mushrooms, and psilocin was found to be a minor component. However, psilocybin is very unstable and is readily metabolized to psilocin in the body. This phenomenon of phosphate cleavage from the psilocybin to form the psilocin occurs quite easily in the forensic science laboratory. This can be a concern in ensuring the specificity of identification.

The availability of the mushroom has existed worldwide wherever proper climactic conditions exist — that means plentiful rainfall. In the U.S., psilocybin mushrooms are reported to be plentiful in Florida, Hawaii,[16] the Pacific Northwest, and Northern California.[17] Mushrooms analyzed in the forensic science laboratory confirm the fact that the mushrooms spoil easily. The time factor between harvesting the mushrooms and the analysis proves to be the greatest detriment to successfully identifying the psilocybin or psilocin. Storage prior to shipment is best accomplished by drying the mushrooms. Entrepreneurs reportedly resort to storage of mushrooms in honey to preserve the psychedelic properties.[18]

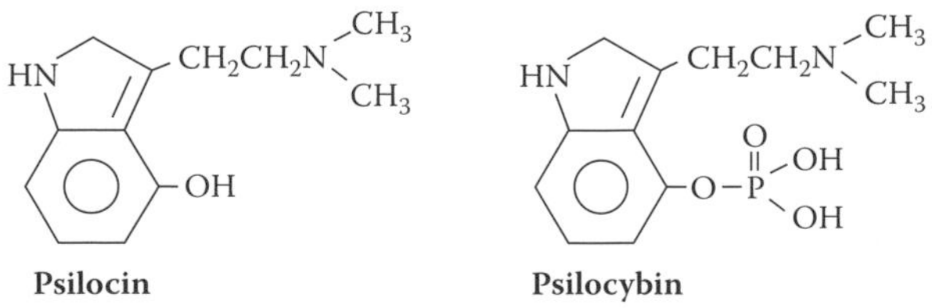

Psilocin   Psilocybin

Figure 1.4.5 Chemical structure of psilocin and psilocybin.

Progressing through the analytical scheme of separating and isolating the psilocybin and psilocin from the mushroom matrix, cleavage of the phosphate occurs quite easily. Prior to beginning the analysis, drying the mushrooms in a desiccator with phosphorus pentoxide ensures a dry starting material. In many instances, the clean-up procedure involves an extraction process carried out through a series of chloroform washes from a basic extract and resolution of the components by TLC. The spots or, more probably, streaks are then scraped from the plate, separated by a back-extraction, and then analyzed by IR. Direct analysis by GC is very difficult because both psilocybin and psilocin are highly polar and not suitable for direct GC analysis. Derivatization followed by GC/MS is an option except in those instances where the mushrooms have been preserved in sugar.[19] With the development and availability of high-performance liquid chromatography (HPLC), the identification and quantitation of psilocybin and psilocyn in mushrooms are becoming more feasible for many forensic science laboratories.[20]

REFERENCES

1. Section 102 (15), Public Law 91-513.
2. ElSohly, M.A. and Ross, S.A., Quarterly Report Potency Monitoring Project, Report 53, January 1, 1995 to March 31, 1995.
3. Nakamura, G.R., Forensic aspects of cystolithic hairs of cannabis and other plants, *J. Assoc. Off. Anal. Chem.*, 52, 5–16, 1969.
4. Thornton, J.I. and Nakamura, G.R., The identification of marijuana, *J. Forensic Sci. Soc.*, 24, 461–519, 1979.
5. Hughes, R.B. and Warner, V.J., A study of false positives in the chemical identification of marijuana, *J. Forensic Sci.*, 23, 304–310, 1978.
6. Hauber, D.J., Marijuana analysis with recording of botanical features present with and without the environmental pollutants of the Duquenois-Levine test, *J. Forensic Sci.*, 37, 1656–1661, 1992.
7. Hughes, R.B. and Kessler, R.R., Increased safety and specificity in the thin-layer chromatographic identification of marijuana, *J. Forensic Sci.*, 24, 842–846, 1979.
8. Report Series, National Clearinghouse for Drug Abuse Information, Mescaline, Series 15, No. 1, May 1973.
9. Mooney, J., The mescal plant and ceremony, *Ther. Gaz.*, 12, 7–11, 1896.
10. Heffter, A., Ein Beitrag zur pharmakologishen Kenntniss der Cacteen, *Arch. Exp Pathol. Pharmakol.*, 34, 65–86, 1894.
11. Spath, E., Über die Anhalonium-Alkaloide, Anhalin und Mescalin, *Monatsh. Chem. Verw. TL*, 40, 1929, 1919.
12. Hofman, A., Heim, R., Brack, A., and Kobel, H., Psilocybin, ein psychotroper Wirkstoff aus dem mexikanishen Rauschpitz *Psilocybe mexicana* Heim, *Experiencia*, 14, 107–109, 1958.
13. Wasson, V.P. and Wasson, R.G., *Mushrooms, Russia, and History.* Pantheon Books, New York, 1957.
14. Heim, R., Genest, K., Hughes, D.W., and Belec, G., Botanical and chemical characterisation of a forensic mushroom specimen of the genus psilocybe, *Forensic Sci. Soc. J.*, 6, 192–201, 1966.
15. Hofmann, A., Chemical aspects of psilocybin, the psychotropic principle from the Mexican fungus, *Psilocybe mexicana* Heim, in Bradley, P.B., Deniker, P., and Radouco-Thomas, C., Eds. *Neuropsychopharmacology,* Elsevier, Amsterdam, 1959, 446–448.
16. Pollock, S.H., A novel experience with Panaeolus: a case study from Hawaii, *J. Psychedelic Drugs,* 6, 85–90, 1974.
17. Weil, H., Mushroom hunting in Oregon, *J. Psychedelic Drugs*, 7, 89–102, 1975.
18. Pollock, S.H., Psilocybin mycetismus with special reference to *Panaeolus, J. Psychedelic Drugs*, 8(1), 50.
19. Repke, D.B., Leslie, D.T., Mandell, D.M., and Kish, N.G., GLC-mass spectral analysis of psilocin and psilocybin, *J. Psychedelic Drugs*, 66, 743–744, 1977.
20. Thomas, B.M., Analysis of psilocybin and psilocin in mushroom extracts by reversed-phase high performance liquid chromatography, *J. Forensic Sci.*, 25, 779–785, 1980.

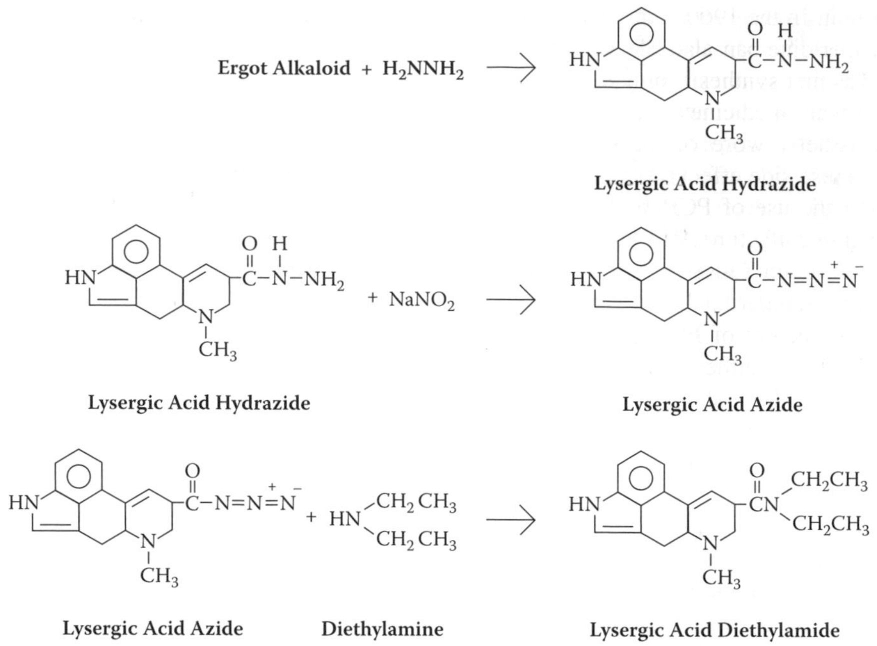

Ergot Alkaloid + H_2NNH_2 ⟶

Lysergic Acid Hydrazide

Lysergic Acid Hydrazide + $NaNO_2$ ⟶

Lysergic Acid Azide

Lysergic Acid Azide + Diethylamine ⟶

Lysergic Acid Diethylamide

Figure 1.4.6 Synthetic route utilized for the clandestine manufacture of LSD.

1.4.6 Lysergic Acid Diethylamide

LSD is a hallucinogenic substance produced from lysergic acid, a substance derived from the ergot fungus (*Clavica purpurea*), which grows on rye. It can also be derived from lysergic acid amide, which is found in morning glory seeds.[1] LSD is also referred to as LSD-25 because it was the 25th in a series of compounds produced by Dr. Albert Hofmann in Basel, Switzerland. Hoffman was interested in the chemistry of ergot compounds, especially their effect on circulation. He was trying to produce compounds that might improve circulation without exhibiting the other toxic effects associated with ergot poisoning. One of the products he produced was Methergine™, which is still in use today. When LSD-25 was first tested on animals, in 1938, the results were disappointing. Then, 5 years later, in 1943, Hoffman decided to reevaluate LSD-25. The hallucinogenic experience that ensued when he accidentally ingested some of the compound led to the start of experimentation with "psychedelic" drugs.

LSD is the most potent hallucinogenic substance known to humans. Dosages of LSD are measured in micrograms (one microgram equals one one-millionth of a gram). By comparison, dosage units of cocaine and heroin are measured in milligrams (one milligram equals one one-thousandth of a gram). LSD is available in the form of very small tablets ("microdots"), thin squares of gelatin ("window panes"), or impregnated on blotter paper ("blotter acid"). The most popular of these forms in the 1990s was blotter paper perforated into 1/4-in. squares. This paper is usually brightly colored with psychedelic designs or line drawings. There have been recent reports of LSD impregnated on sugar cubes.[2] Such LSD-laced sugar cubes were commonplace in the 1970s. The precursor to LSD, lysergic acid, is a Schedule III controlled substance. LSD is classified as a Schedule I controlled substance. The synthetic route utilized for the clandestine manufacture of LSD is shown in Figure 1.4.6.

1.4.7 Phencyclidine

The chemical nomenclature of phencyclidine (PCP) is phenylcyclohexylpiperidine. The term "PCP" is used most often used when referring to this drug. The acronym PCP has two origins that are consistent. In the 1960s phencyclidine was trafficked as a peace pill ("**P**ea**C**e**P**ill"). **P**henyl**C**y-clohexyl**P**iperidine can also account for the PCP acronym.

PCP was first synthesized in 1926.[3] It was developed as a human anesthetic in 1957, and found use in veterinary medicine as a powerful tranquilizer. In 1965 human use was discontinued because, as the anesthetic wore off, confusional states and frightening hallucinations were common. Strangely, these side effects were viewed as desirable by those inclined to experiment with drugs. Today even the use of PCP as a primate anesthetic has been all but discontinued. In 1978, the commercial manufacture of PCP ceased and the drug was transferred from Schedule III to Schedule II of the Controlled Substances Act. Small amounts of PCP are manufactured for research purposes and as a drug standard.

The manufacture of PCP in clandestine laboratories is simple and inexpensive. Figure 1.4.7 shows three of the synthetic routes utilized for its illegal production. The first clandestinely produced PCP appeared in 1967 shortly after Parke Davis withdrew phencyclidine as a pharmaceutical.[4] The clandestine laboratory production of PCP requires neither formal knowledge of chemistry nor a large inventory of laboratory equipment. The precursor chemicals produce phencyclidine when combined correctly using what is termed "bucket chemistry." The opportunities for a contaminated product from a clandestine PCP are greatly enhanced because of the recognized simplicity of the chemical reactions in the production processes. The final product is often contaminated with starting materials, reaction intermediates, and by-products.[5] Clandestine laboratory operators have been known to modify the manufacturing processes to obtain chemically related analogues capable of producing similar physiological responses. The most commonly encountered analogues are *N*-ethyl-1-phenylcyclohexylamine (PCE), 1-(1-phenylcyclohexyl)-pyrrolidine (PCPy), and 1-[1-(2-thienyl-cyclohexyl)]-piperidine (TCP).

In the 1960s, PCP was distributed as a white to off-white powder or crystalline material and ingested orally. In recent years, PCP has been encountered as the base and dissolved in diethyl ether. The liquid is then placed into small bottles that normally would hold commercial vanilla extract. This ether solution is then sprayed on leaves such as parsley and smoked. PCP is commonly encountered on long thin dark cigarettes ("Sherms") that have been dipped in the PCP/ether solution.

1.4.8 Fentanyl

Fentanyl [the technical nomenclature is *N*-(1-phenethyl-4-piperidyl)propionanilide] is a synthetic narcotic analgesic approximately 50 to 100 times as potent as morphine.[6] The drug had its origin in Belgium as a synthetic product of Janssen Pharmaceutica.[7] In the 1960s in Europe and in the 1970s in the U.S., it was introduced for use as an anesthesia and for the relief of post-operative pain. Almost 70% of all surgical procedures in the U.S. use fentanyl for one of these purposes.[8]

Fentanyl has been called "synthetic heroin." This is a misnomer. Victims of fentanyl overdoses were often heroin abusers with "tracks" and the typical paraphernalia. The fentanyls as a class of drugs are highly potent synthetic narcotic analgesics with all the properties of opiates and opioids.[4] However, the fentanyl molecule does not resemble heroin. Fentanyl is strictly a synthetic product while the morphine used in heroin production is derived from the opium poppy.

Beginning in the late 1970s with -methylfentanyl,[9] nine homologues and one analogue (excluding enantiomers) of fentanyl appeared on the illicit marketplace.[10] The degrees of potency vary among the fentanyl homologues and analogues. The potencies of the fentanyl derivatives are much higher than those of the parent compound. But the high potencies cited above explain why even dilute exhibits result in the deaths of users who believe they are dealing with heroin. Another name used by addicts when referring to fentanyl and its derivatives is "China White." This term was first used to described substances seized and later identified as alpha-methylfentanyl in 1981.[11]

There are many fentanyl homologues and analogues. Because of the size and complexity of fentanyl derivatives, the interpretation of IR, MS, and NMR spectral data proves very valuable in elucidating specific structural information required for the identification of the material.[10]

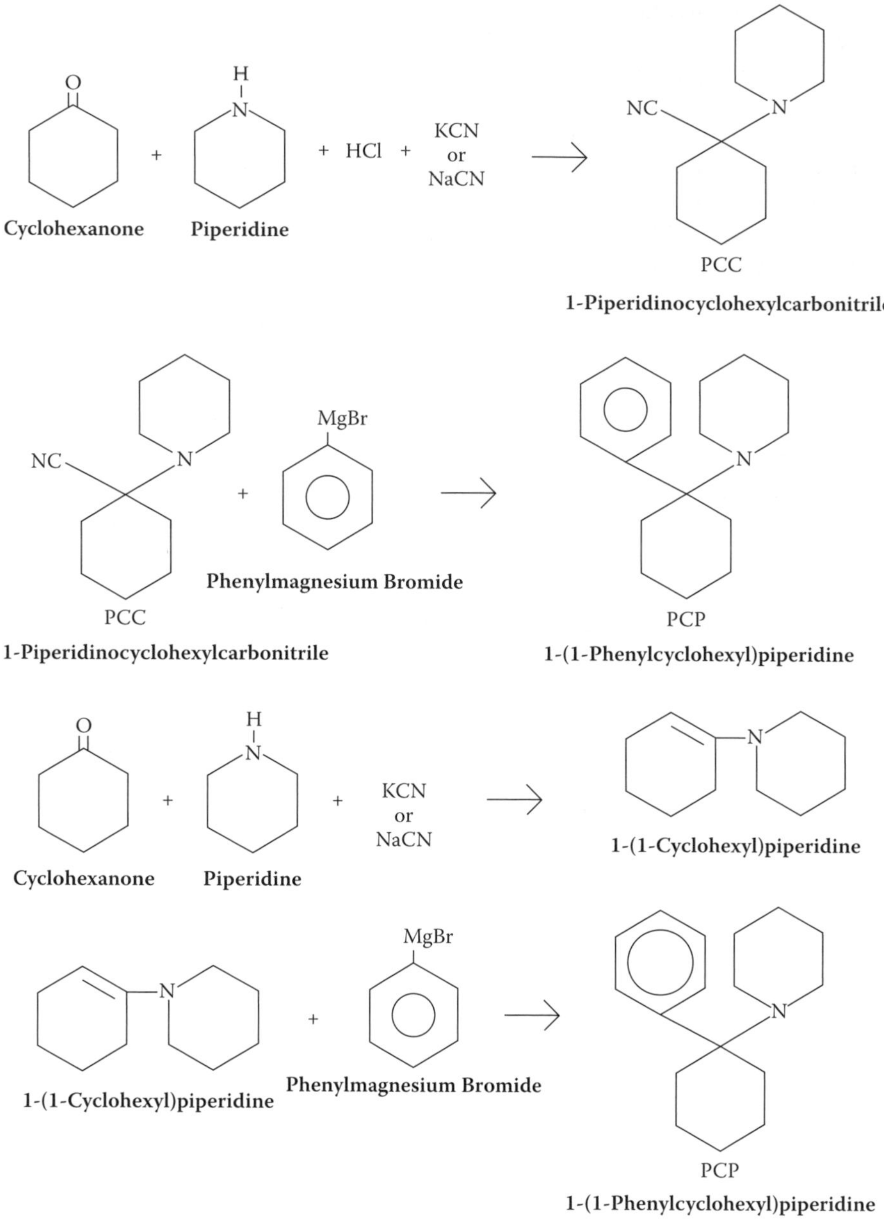

Figure 1.4.7 Synthetic routes utilized for illegal production of PCP.   *Continued.*

Several synthetic routes are possible. As shown in Figure 1.4.8a and b, one of the methods requires that fentanyl precursor, *N*-(1-phenetyl)-4-piperidinlyl) analyine, be produced first. Alternatively, fentanyl can be produced by reacting phenethylamine and methylacrylate to produce the phenethylamine diester (see Figure 1.4.9).

1.4.9 Phenethylamines

The class of compounds with the largest number of individual compounds on the illicit drug market is the phenethylamines. This class of compounds consists of a series of compounds having

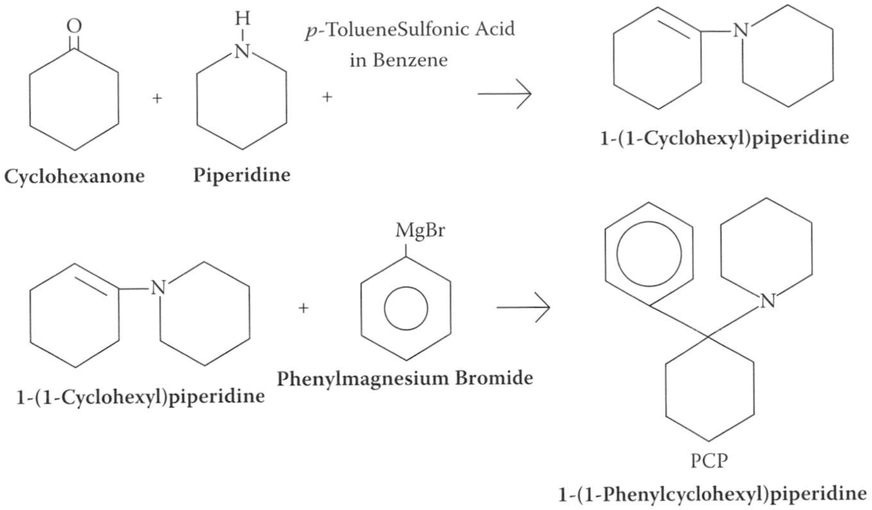

Figure 1.4.7 Continued.

a phenethylamine skeleton. Phenethylamines are easily modified chemically by adding or changing substituents at various positions on the molecule. Phenethylamines fall into one of two categories in terms of physiological effects — these compounds are either stimulants or hallucinogens. Phenethylamines are suitable for clandestine laboratory production. The parent compound in the phenethylamine series is amphetamine, a central nervous system (CNS) stimulant. With this molecule, the modifications begin by adding a methyl group to the nitrogen on the side chain. The resulting structure is the most popular clandestinely produced controlled substance in the U.S. — methamphetamine (Figure 1.4.10).

Like amphetamine, methamphetamine is also a CNS stimulant. It is easily produced in clandestine laboratories using two basic synthetic routes. The traditional route used by "meth cooks" began with phenyl-2-propanone; however, when bulk sales were limited by law, most clandestine chemists began using ephedrine as a precursor (Figure 1.4.11), although, as illustrated in Figure 1.4.11, some now synthesize their own supply of phenyl-2-propanone, and still other routes are possible (Figure 1.4.12). New legislation has now limited bulk purchases of ephedrine in the U.S., though not in neighboring countries. And the chemical structure is such that further molecular synthetic modifications are easily accomplished, resulting in a number of homologues and analogues. Few of the synthetic modifications of phenethylamines by clandestine laboratory "chemists" are novel. Most have been documented either in the scientific literature or in underground scientific literature. And the Internet now provides answers to anyone tenacious enough to search for a simple method to synthesize any analogue or homologue of a phenethylamine.

The parent compound of a second set of phenethylamine homologues and analogues (Figure 1.4.13) is 3,4-methylenedioxyamphetamine (MDA). This compound was first reported in the literature in 1910.[12] In the mid-1980s, the N-methyl analogue of MDA came into vogue and was known then and is still referred to as "Ecstasy." The synthesis of 3,4-methylenedioxymethamphetamine (MDMA) follows the same synthetic protocols as the less complicated phenethylamines. The clandestine laboratory operator or research chemist selectively adds one N-methyl group, an N,N-dimethyl group, an N-ethyl group, an N-propyl, an N-isopropyl group, and so on. In 1985 the N-hydroxy MDA derivative was reported.[13] This was significant because here the modification involved the addition of a hydroxyl group as opposed to an alkyl substitution on the nitrogen. Clandestine laboratory synthesis of MDA and MDMA are shown in Figure 1.4.13 and Figure 1.4.14.

The identification of the phenethylamines in the laboratory requires great care because of the chemical and molecular similarities of the exhibits. IR combined with MS and NMR spectrometry

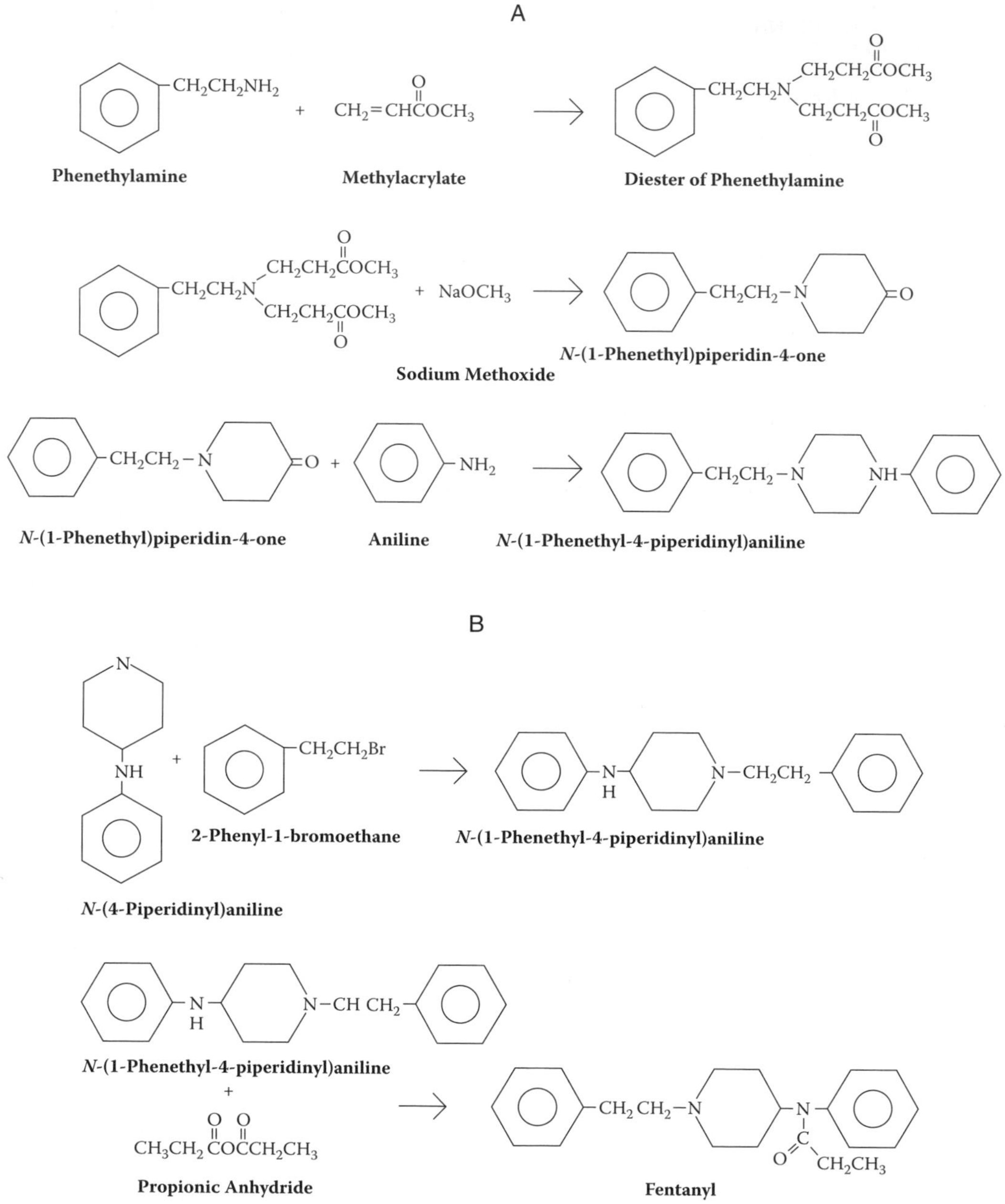

A

B

Figure 1.4.8 (A) Clandestine laboratory synthesis of fentanyl precursor. (B) Clandestine laboratory synthesis of fentanyl.

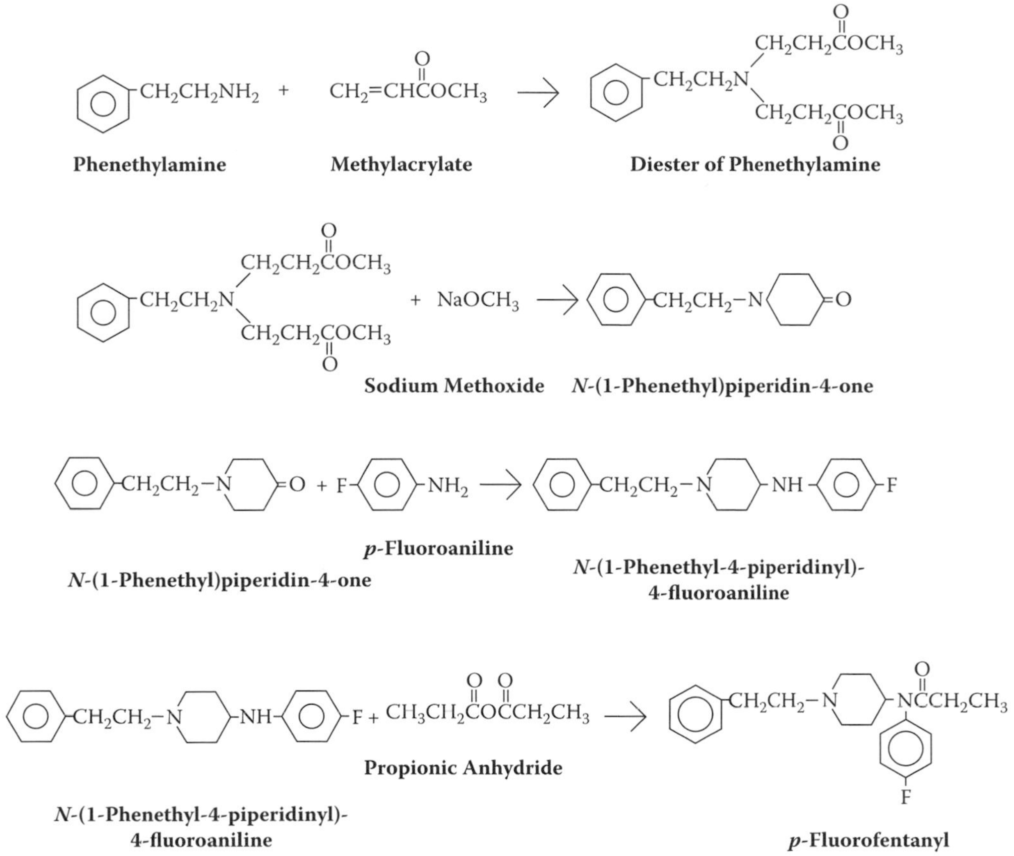

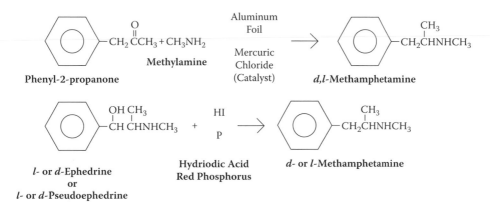

Figure 1.4.9 Clandestine laboratory synthesis of *p*-fluorofentanyl.

Figure 1.4.10 Clandestine laboratory synthesis of methamphetamine.

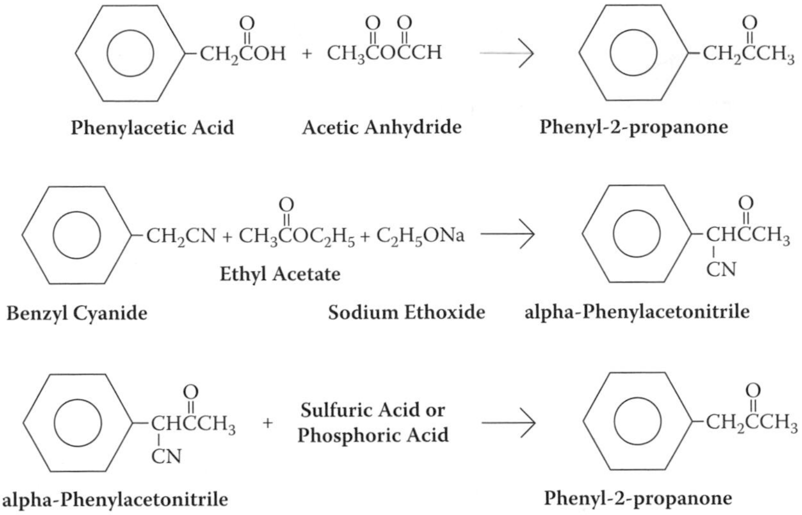

Figure 1.4.11 Clandestine laboratory synthesis of phenyl-2-propanone (p-2-p).

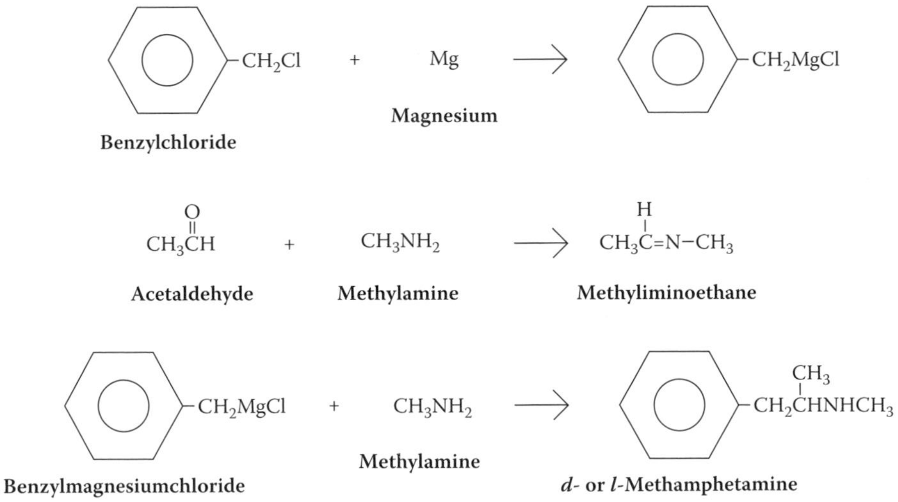

Figure 1.4.12 Clandestine laboratory synthesis of methamphetamine.

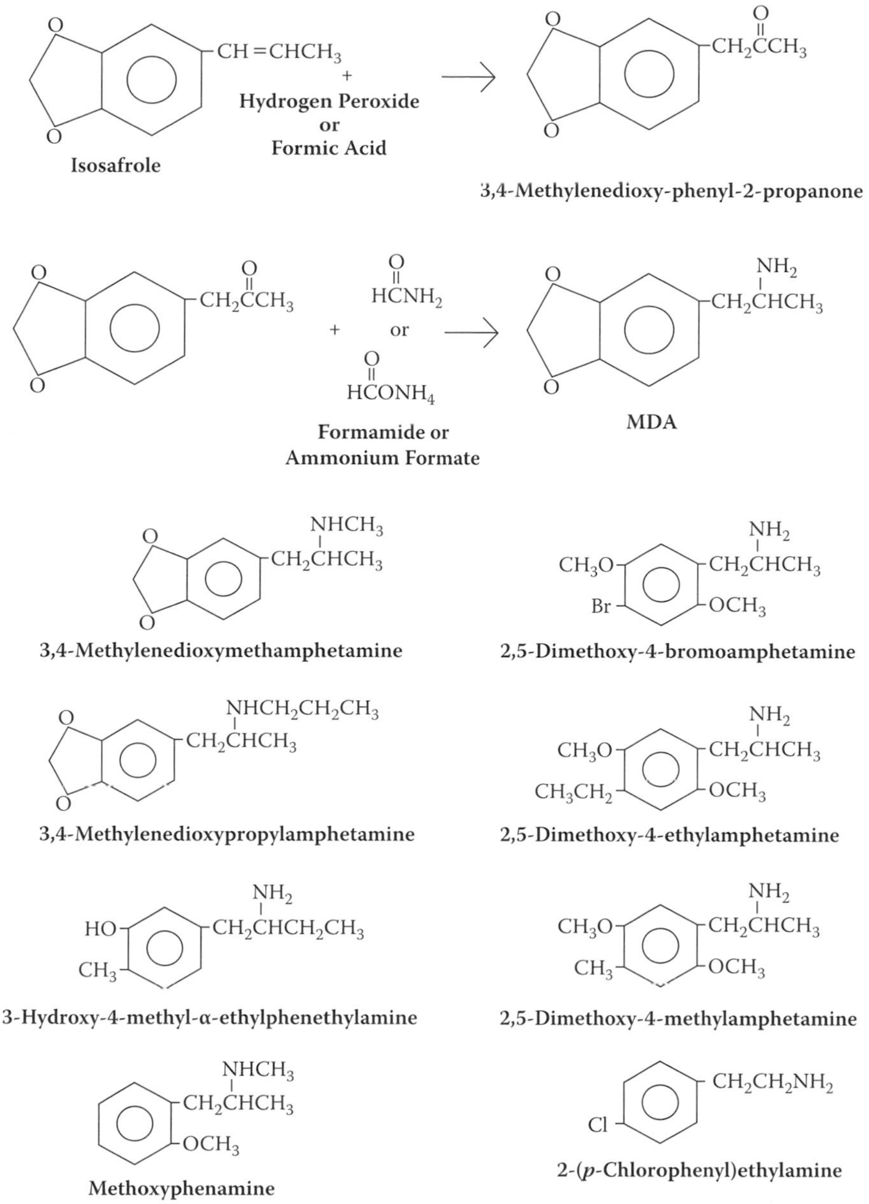

Figure 1.4.13 Clandestine laboratory synthesis of MDA.

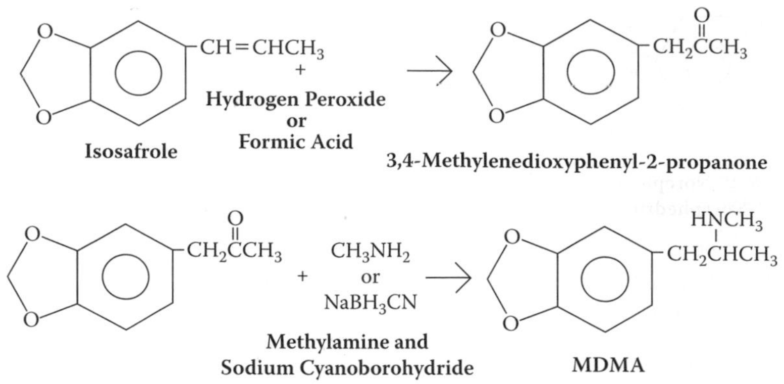

Figure 1.4.14 Clandestine laboratory synthesis of MDMA.

provide the most specificity in the identifications of phenethylamines in the forensic science laboratory.[13,14] From a legal perspective, the laboratory identification of the phenethylamine is part 1 in the forensic process. If prosecution is an option and the phenethylamine in question is not specified as a controlled substance under Public Law 91-513[15] or Part 1308 of the Code of Federal Regulations, another legal option is available.

In 1986, the U.S. Congress realized that the legal system was at a standstill in attempting to prosecute clandestine laboratory operators involved in molecular modification of phenethylamines and other homologues and analogues of controlled substances. The attempted closing of this loophole was the passage of the Controlled Substances Analogue and Enforcement Act of 1986.[16]

1.4.10 Methcathinone

Methcathinone (CAT) is a structural analogue of methamphetamine and cathinone (Figure 1.4.15 and Figure 1.4.16). It is potent and it, along with the parent compound, is easily manufactured. They are sold in the U.S. under the name CAT. Methcathinone is distributed as a white to off-white chunky powdered material and is sold in the hydrochloride salt form. Outside of the U.S., methcathinone is known as ephedrone and is a significant drug of abuse in Russia and some of the Baltic States.[17]

Methcathinone was permanently placed in Schedule I of the Controlled Substances Act in October 1993. Prior to its scheduling, two federal cases were effectively prosecuted in Ann Arbor and Marquette, Michigan, utilizing the analogue provision of the Controlled Substances Analogue and Enforcement Act of 1986.

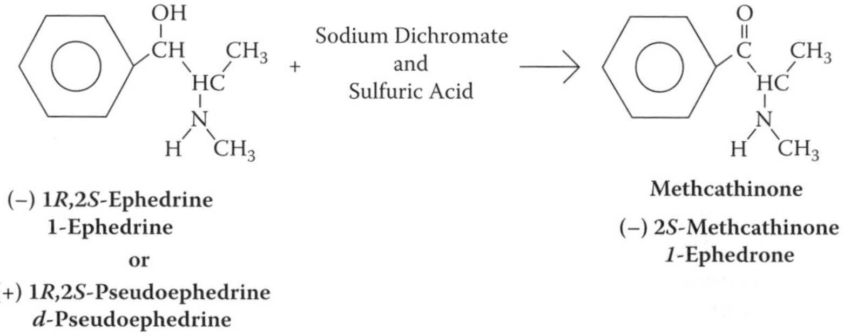

Figure 1.4.15 Clandestine laboratory synthesis of methcathinone.

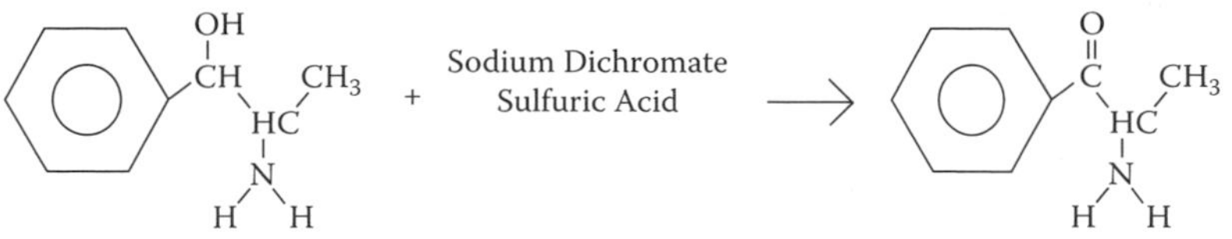

(−) 1*R*,2*S*-Norephedrine
l-Norephedrine

or

(+) 1*R*,2*S*-Norpseudoephedrine
d-Norpseudoephedrine

Cathinone

(−) 2*S*-Cathinone
l-Cathinone

Figure 1.4.16   Clandestine laboratory synthesis of cathinone.

1.4.11   *Catha edulis* (Khat)

Khat consists of the young leaves and tender shoots of the *Catha edulis* plant that is chewed for its stimulant properties.[18] *Catha edulis*, a species of the plant family Celastraceae, grows in eastern Africa and southern Arabia. Its effects are similar to the effects of amphetamine. The active ingredients in Khat are cathinone [(−)-a-aminopropiophenone], a Schedule I controlled substance that is quite unstable, and cathine [(+)-norpseudoephedrine], a Schedule IV controlled substance. Identification of cathinone in the laboratory presents problems because of time and storage requirements to minimize degradation.[19] Some of the decomposition or transformation products of *C. edulis* are norpseudoephedrine, norephedrine, 3,6-dimethyl-2,5-diphenylpyrazine, and 1-phenyl-1,2-propanedione.[20]

REFERENCES

1. Drugs of Abuse, U.S. Department of Justice, Drug Enforcement Administration, 1989, p. 49.
2. Kilmer, S.D., The isolation and identification of lysergic acid diethylamide (LSD) from sugar cubes and a liquid substrate, *J. Forensic Sci.,* 39, 860–862, 1994.
3. Feldman, H.W., Agar, M.H., and Beschner, G.M., Eds., *Angel Dust, An Ethnographic Study of PCP Users*, Lexington Books, Lexington, MA, 1979, 8.
4. Henderson, G.L., Designer drugs: past history and future prospects, *J. Forensic Sci.,* 33, 569–575, 1988.
5. Angelos, S.A., Raney, J.K., Skoronski, G.T., and Wagenhofer, R.J., The identification of unreacted precursors, impurities, and by-products in clandestinely produced phencyclidine preparations, *J. Forensic Sci.,* 35, 1297–1302, 1990.
6. Smialek, J.E., Levine, B., Chin, L., Wu, S.C., and Jenkins, A.J., A fentanyl epidemic in Maryland 1992, *J. Forensic Sci.,* 3, 159–164, 1994.
7. Janssen, P.A.J., U.S. patent 316400, 1965.
8. Henderson, G.L., The fentanyls, *Am. Assoc. Clin. Chem. in-Serv. Train Continuing Ed.,* 12(2), 5–17, 1990.
9. Riley, R.N. and Bagley, J.R., *J. Med. Chem.,* 22, 1167–1171.
10. Cooper, D., Jacob, M., and Allen, A., Identification of fentanyl derivatives, *J. Forensic Sci.,* 31, 511–528, 1986.
11. Kram, T.C., Cooper, D.A., and Allen, A., Behind the identification of China White, *Anal. Chem.,* 53, 1379–1386, 1981.
12. Mannich, C. and Jacobsohn, W., Hydroxyphenylalkylamines and dihydroxyphenylalkylamines, *Berichte*, 43, 189–197, 1910.
13. Dal Cason, T.A., The characterization of some 3,4-methylenedioxyphenyl- isopropylamine (MDA) analogues, *J. Forensic Sci.,* 34, 928–961, 1989.
14. Bost, R.O., 3,4-Methylenedioxymethamphetamine (MDMA) and other amphetamine derivatives, *J. Forensic Sci.,* 33, 576–587, 1988.
15. Comprehensive drug abuse prevention and control act of 1970, Public Law 91-513, 91st Congress, 27 Oct. 1970.

16. Controlled substance analogue and enforcement act of 1986, Public Law 99-570, Title I, Subtitle E, 99th Congress, 27 Oct. 1986.

17. Zhingel, K.Y., Dovensky, W., Crossman, A., and Allen, A., Ephedrone: 2-methylamino-1-phenylpropan-1-one (jell), *J. Forensic Sci.,* 36, 915–920, 1991.

18. *Cath edulis* (khat): some introductory remarks, *Bull. Narcotics,* 32, 1–3, 1980.

19. Lee, M.M., The identification of cathinone in khat (*Catha edulis*): a time study, *J. Forensic Sci.,* 40, 116–121, 1995.

20. Szendrei, K., The chemistry of khat, *Bull. Narcotics,* 32, 5–34, 1980.

1.4.12 Anabolic Steroids

1.4.12.1 *Regulatory History*

In recent years anabolic steroid abuse has become a significant problem in the U.S. There are two physiological responses associated with anabolic steroids: **androgenic activity** induces the development of male secondary sex characteristics; **anabolic activity** promotes the growth of various tissues including muscle and blood cells. The male sex hormone testosterone is the prototype anabolic steroid. Individuals abuse these drugs in an attempt to improve athletic performance or body appearance. The more common agents are shown in Figure 1.4.17.

Black market availability of anabolic steroids has provided athletes and bodybuilders with a readily available supply of these drugs. Both human and veterinary steroid preparations are found in the steroid black market. Anabolic steroid preparations are formulated as tablets, capsules, and oil- and water-based injectable preparations. There is also a thriving black market for preparations that are either counterfeits of legitimate steroid preparations or are simply bogus.

Control of Steroids

In 1990, the U.S. Congress passed the Anabolic Steroid Control Act. This act placed anabolic steroids, along with their salts, esters, and isomers, as a class of drugs, into Schedule III of the Federal Controlled Substances Act (CSA). This law provided 27 names of steroids that were specifically defined under the CSA as anabolic steroids. This list, which is provided in the *Federal Code of Regulations,* is reproduced below.

1. Boldenone	15. Methenolone
2. Chlorotestosterone	16. Methyltestosterone
3. Clostebol	17. Mibolerone
4. Dehydrochlormethyltestosterone	18. Nandrolone
5. Dihydrotestosterone	19. Norethandrolone
6. Drostanolone	20. Oxandrolone
7. Ethylestrenol	21. Oxymesterone
8. Fluoxymesterone	22. Oxymetholone
9. Formebolone	23. Stanolone
10. Mesterolone	24. Stanozolol
11. Methandienone	25. Testolactone
12. Methandranone	26. Testosterone
13. Methandriol	27. Trenbolone
14. Methandrostenolone	

Unfortunately, the list contains three sets of duplicate names (chlorotestosterone and Clostebol; dihydrotestosterone and stanolone; and methandrostenolone and methandienone) as well as one name (methandranone) for a drug that did not exist. So, the actual number of different steroids specifically defined under the law as anabolic steroids is 23, not 27. Realizing that the list of 23

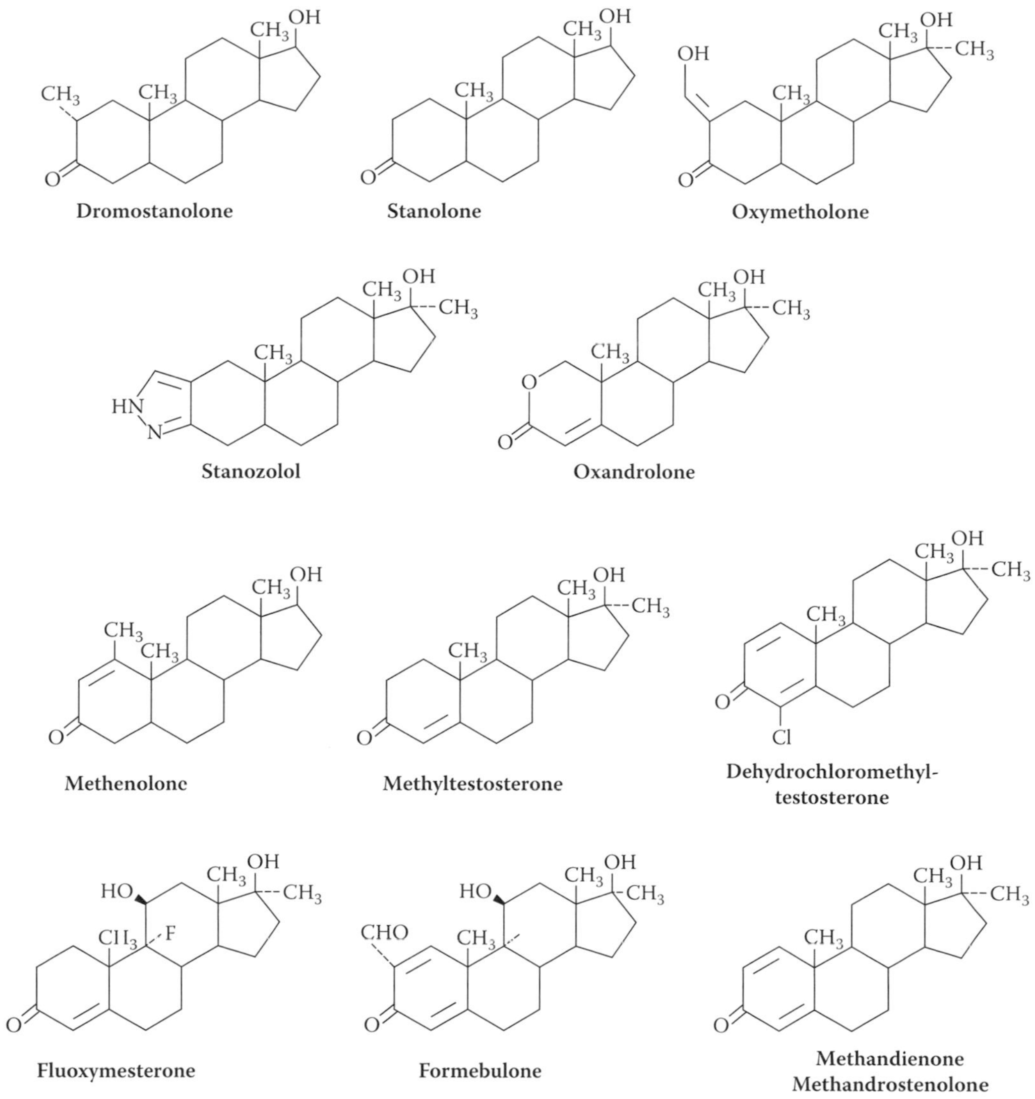

Figure 1.4.17 Common agents.

substances would not be all inclusive, Congress went on to define within the law the term "anabolic steroid" to mean "any drug or hormonal substance, chemically or pharmacologically related to testosterone (other than estrogens, progestins, and corticosteroids) and that promote muscle growth."

The scheduling of anabolic steroids has necessitated forensic laboratories to analyze exhibits containing steroids. In those cases involving the detection of 1 or more of the 23 steroids specifically defined as anabolic steroids under the law, questions of legality are not likely to arise. However, when a steroid is identified that is not specifically defined under the law, it becomes necessary to further examine the substance to determine if it qualifies as an anabolic steroid under the definition of such a substance under the CSA. The forensic chemist must positively identify the steroid and convey to the pharmacologist the entire structure of the steroid. It then becomes the responsibility of the pharmacologist to determine the pharmacological activity, including effects on muscle growth, of the identified steroid.

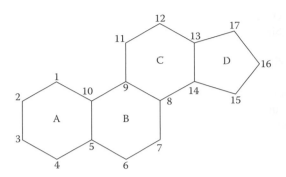

Figure 1.4.18 Cyclopentanoperhydrophenanthrene.

1.4.12.2 Structure–Activity Relationship

The pharmacology of the identified steroid may be evaluated in at least two ways. The first, and most important way, is to examine the scientific, medical, and patent literature for data on the pharmacological effects of the steroid. Over the years, numerous steroids have been examined in animal and/or human studies for anabolic/androgenic activity. It is possible that the identified steroid will be among that group of steroids. The second method is to evaluate possible pharmacological activity using **structure–activity relationships**. Such analysis is based on the assumption of a relationship between the structure of the steroid and its pharmacological effects. Small alterations of chemical structure may enhance, diminish, eliminate, or have no effect on the pharmacological activity of the steroid. The structure–activity relationships of androgens and anabolic steroids have been reviewed extensively.[1,2]

Extensive studies of the structure–activity relationships of anabolic/androgenic steroids have demonstrated that the following structural attributes are necessary for maximal androgenic and anabolic effects: rings A and B must be in the *trans* configuration;[3] hydroxy function at C-17 must be in the β conformational state;[5,6] and high electron density must be present in the area of C_2 and C_33.[7] The presence of a keto or hydroxl group at position 3 in the A-ring usually enhances androgenic and anabolic activity, but it is not absolutely necessary for these effects.[7] A few examples of structural alterations that enhance anabolic activity include removal of the C-19 methyl group;[8] methyl groups at the 2a and 7a positions;[9,10] a fluorine at the 9a position; or a chlorine at the 4a position.[10,11] To make it easier to visualize where these modifications are made in the ring structure, a numbered steroid skeletal ring structure, namely, the cyclopentanoperhydrophenanthrene ring, is shown in Figure 1.4.18.

It is essential to understand that structure–activity analysis can predict only whether or not a steroid is likely to produce androgenic/anabolic effects. It then becomes necessary to examine the steroid in the laboratory to determine whether the prediction is, in fact, true. It is also important to note that numerous studies performed over the years and designed to separate androgenic activity from anabolic activity have failed to obtain such a separation of pharmacological effect. That is, steroids found to possess androgenic activity also have anabolic activity, and vice versa. An examination of the scientific and medical literature reveals that there are, indeed, additional steroids that are not specifically listed in the law but that do, based on available data, probably produce androgenic/anabolic effects. A listing of some of these steroids is provided below.

Androisoaxazole	Mestanolone
Bolandiol	Methyltrienolone
Bolasterone	Norbolethone
Bolenol	Norclostebol
Flurazebol	Oxabolone Cypionate

Mebolazine   Quinbolone
Mesabolone   Stenbolone

1.4.12.3 *Forensic Analysis*

For the forensic chemist, when a steroid is tentatively identified, an additional problem arises, namely, obtaining an analytical standard. Many products found in the illicit U.S. market are commercially available only outside of the U.S. Locating and making contact with a foreign distributor is one problem. Requesting and then receiving a legitimate standard is another problem. The expense incurred in obtaining these standards can be quite high. Once the standard has been received, authentication then enters the analytical process. If a primary standard is unavailable, an optimized analytical process presents a real problem. Fortunately, most steroids received by forensic science laboratories are labeled directly or have labeled packaging. So a manufacturer can be identified, and there is a starting point for the chemist in confirming the material as a particular steroid.

There are no known color tests, crystal tests, or TLC methods that are specific to anabolic steroids. Screening can be accomplished by GLC or HPLC. GLC sometimes presents a problem because of thermal decomposition in the injection port, thereby resulting in several peaks. The steroid will not always be the largest peak. On-column injection will usually solve this problem. However, oil-base steroids rapidly foul or degrade GC columns. Samples in oils can be extracted with methanol/water 9:1 prior to injection onto a GC. Retention times for some anabolic steroids are quite long and nearly triple or quadruple that of heroin. Recognizing that several anabolic steroids are readily oxidized in polar, protic solvents vs. halogenated hydrocarbons, screening and analysis must be accomplished as soon as possible after isolation and dilution.

GC/MS does provide definitive spectra; however, different MS systems may provide differences in the spectra for the same steroid. These differences can be traced to the quality of the MS source and the injection liner, thermal decomposition products, and induced hydration reactions related to high source temperatures set by the MS. $C^{13}NMR$ is the most rigorous identification technique. The limitation here is the need for pure samples and high sample concentrations. Identification by infrared alone can result in problems due to polymorphism. This can be minimized by ensuring that the sample and standard are recrystallized from the same solvent.

Ideally, all anabolic steroids should be identified using two analytical methodologies that yield the same conclusions. The collection of a library of analytical data on different anabolic steroids is essential for the subsequent identification of steroids sent to the laboratory. An ability to interpret MS data will be important in making an identification insofar as determining a molecular formula. Interpreting NMR data will be important in determining how substitutents are attached to the parent steroid ring structure.

It should be noted that selected steroids, such as testosterone, nandrolone, methenolone, boldenone, methandriol, and trenbolone, will often be encountered by the laboratory, not as the parent drug, but instead as an ester. The type of ester will be dependent on the particular steroid. For example, nandrolone is primarily found as a decanoate, laurate, or phenpropionate ester. Testosterone, although it is found as a parent drug, is actually most commonly encountered as the propionate, enanthate, cypionate, decanoate, isocaproate, or undecanoate esters. Less commonly encountered testosterone esters include the acetate, valerate, and undecylenate esters. Methenolone is almost always found in either the acetate or enanthate esterified form.

Upon reaching the forensic science laboratory, steroid preparations will be handled differently depending on the way each preparation is formulated. Tablets can be handled by finely grinding and extracting with chloroform or methanol. Aqueous suspensions can be handled by dilution/solution with methanol for HPLC screening or by extraction with chloroform for GC screening. Oils require a more specialized extraction.

What steroids have been the most predominant in the U.S. in the past few years? Although the last decade has seen the introduction of many new "designer steroids," the list of most abused steroids has changed very little in the past 10 years. From January 1990 to October 1994, the following steroids or their esters were identified by DEA laboratories. This list provides an objective evaluation of what this chemist has encountered in the not-too-distant past. The data on these particular steroids should form the basis of a reference collection for comparison with future submissions.

Steroids or Esters of a Steroid	Numbers of	
	Cases	Exhibits
Testosterone	260	882
Nandrolone	140	244
Methenolone	99	189
Methandrostenolone	76	158
Oxymetholone	67	103
Stanozolol	61	115
Fluoxymesterone	54	7
Methyltestosterone	48	75
Boldenone	24	28
Mesterolone	21	22
Oxandrolone	16	21
Trenbolone	13	20
Methandriol	10	8
Drostanolone	6	7
Mibolerone	4	7
Stanolone	2	2
Testolactone	1	1

Acknowledgment

The author wishes to acknowledge the assistance of Dr. James Tolliver, Pharmacologist, of the DEA Office of Diversion Control, for collaborating in the preparation of this work.

REFERENCES

1. Counsell, R.E. and Klimstra, P.D., Androgens and anabolic agents, in *Medicinal Chemistry,* 3rd ed., Burger, A., Ed., Wiley-Interscience, New York, 1970, 923.
2. Vida, J.A., *Androgens and Anabolic Agents: Chemistry and Pharmacology,* Academic Press, New York, 1969.
3. Huggins, C., Jensen, E.V., and Cleveland, A.S., Chemical structure of steroids in relation to promotion of growth of the vagina and uterus of the hypophysectomized rat, *J. Exp. Med.,* 100, 225–246, 1954.
4. Gabbard, R.B. and Segaloff, A., Facile preparation of 17 beta-hydroxy-5 beta-androstan-3-one and its 17 alpha-methyl derivative, *J. Organic Chem.,* 27, 655, 1962.
5. Kochakian, C.D., *Recent Progress in Hormonal Research,* 1, 177, 1948.
6. Kochakian, C.D., *Am. J. Physiol.,* 160, 53, 1950.
7. Bowers, A., Cross, A.D., Edwards, J.A., Carpio, H., Calzada, M.C., and Denot, E., *J. Med. Chem.,* 6, 156, 1963.
8. Hershberger, L.G., Shipley, E.G., and Meyer, R.K., *Proc. Soc. Exp. Biol. Med.,* 83, 175, 1953.
9. Counsell, R.E., Klimstra, P.D., and Colton, F.B., Anabolic agents, derivatives of 5 alpha-androst-1-ene, *J. Organic Chem.,* 27, 248, 1962.
10. Sala, G. and Baldratti, G., *Proc. Soc. Exp. Biol. Med.,* 95, 22, 1957.
11. Backle, R.M., *Br. Med. J.,* 1, 1378, 1959.

1.5 LEGITIMATE PHARMACEUTICAL PREPARATIONS

The Controlled Substances Act (CSA) of 1970 created a closed system for the production and distribution of legitimately manufactured controlled substances. The CSA includes contingencies to regulate the domestic commerce, importation, and exportation of these pharmaceutical preparations. Even with all of the controls that are in place, legitimate pharmaceuticals intended to help those in need are diverted onto the illegitimate market. Most of the diversion of these pharmaceuticals occurs at the retail rather than the wholesale level.

The analysis of pharmaceutical preparations in the forensic science laboratory is one of the most straightforward types of analysis. These samples are usually recognizable by their labels, which usually include the manufacturer's logo and name. There are some samples that even have the name of the product inscribed on the tablet or capsule. In those instances where the manufacturer's logo is not recognized, the *Physician's Desk Reference* (PDR) is a readily available source of information, which includes photographs and descriptions of the product along with information of the formulation. Another source of this information is the *Logo Index for Tablets and Capsules.*[1] This particular text lists data including inscriptions on most known products including generics. After the tablet or capsule has been tentatively identified in a reference text, it is the responsibility of the forensic chemist to conduct a series of analyses to verify the presence of a controlled substance. This verification process will usually consist of many of the same analytical processes utilized in the analysis and evaluation of any controlled substance.

1.5.1 Benzodiazepines

The benzodiazepines form one of the largest classes of abused pharmaceuticals. These products are sedative/hypnotics, tranquilizers, and anti-anxiety drugs; they produce a calming effect and are often prescribed as tranquilizers. The drugs in this class are numerous and are included under Schedule IV control because, while they do have a potential for abuse, there are recognized medical benefits that are both physiological and psychological. The most frequently diverted and abused benzodiazepines are alprazolam (Xanax) and diazepam (Valium). Other frequently abused benzodiazepines are lorazepam (Activan), triazolam (Halcion), chlordiazepoxide (Librium), flurazepam (Dalmane), and temazepam (Restoril). Another phenomenon that has been noted for several years is the abuse of legitimate pharmaceuticals in conjunction with illicit controlled substances. Clonazepam (Klonipin) is just such a product. It is an anxiety reducer that is used in combination with methadone and heroin.

There has been a recent influx of flunitrazepam (Rohypnol) into the Gulf Coast and other areas of the U.S. This product is a benzodiazepine manufactured principally in Colombia, Mexico, and Switzerland. It is also manufactured in lesser amounts in Argentina, Brazil, Peru, Uruguay, and Venezuela. It is neither manufactured nor marketed legally in the U.S. This is a powerful drug reported to be seven to ten times more potent than diazepam.

1.5.2 Other Central Nervous System Depressants

The oldest of the synthetic sleep-inducing drugs dates back to 1862. Chloral hydrate is marketed as a soft gelatinous capsule under the name Noctec, and controlled under Schedule V. Its popularity declined after the introduction of barbiturates. Barbiturates are the drugs prescribed most frequently to induce sedation. Roughly 15 derivatives of barbituric acid are currently in use to calm nervous conditions. In larger doses they are used to induce sleep.

The actions of barbiturates fall into four categories. Some of the ultrashort acting barbiturates are hexobarbital (Sombulex), methohexital (Brevital), thiamylal (Surital), and thiopental (Pentothal). Short-acting and intermediate-acting barbiturates include pentobarbital (Nembutal), seco-

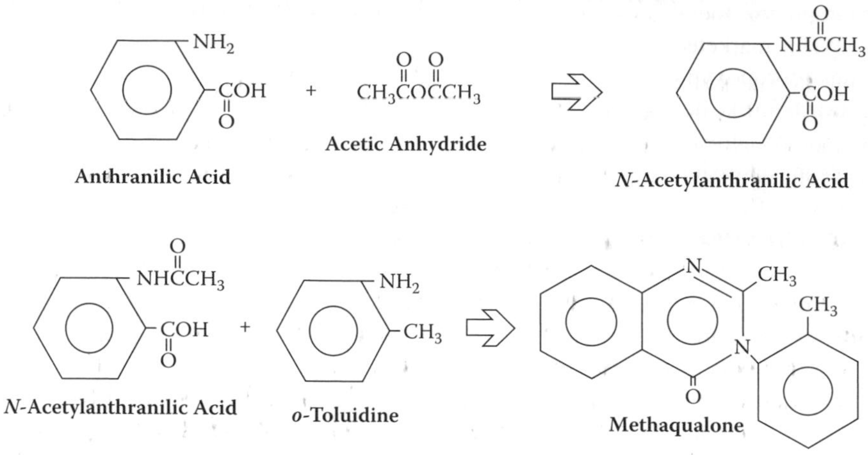

Figure 1.5.1 Clandestine laboratory synthesis of methaqualone.

barbital (Seconal), and amobarbital (Amytal). These three drugs have been among the most abused barbituric acid derivatives. Also included in these categories but not as abused are butabarbital (Butisol), talbutal (Lotusate), and aprobarbital (Alurate). The last category is the long-acting barbiturates. These drugs are used medicinally as sedatives, hypnotics, and anticonvulsants. The group includes phenobarbital (Luminal), mephobarbital or methylphenobarbital (Mebaral), and metharbital (Gemonil).

Three other CNS depressants that have been marketed as legitimate pharmaceutical preparations and have a history of abuse include glutethimide (Doriden), methaqualone (Quaalude, Parest, Mequin, Optimil, Somnafac, Sopor, and Mandrax), and meprobamate (Miltown, Equanil, and SK-Bamate). The route for the clandestine synthesis of methaqualone is shown in Figure 1.5.1.

1.5.3 Narcotic Analgesics

When one thinks of opium-like compounds, morphine and heroin immediately come to mind. However, there is another subset of this class of compounds that includes pharmaceutical preparations used to relieve pain, which are purchased legitimately or illegitimately from a pharmacy with a prescription. Frequently used pharmaceutical opiates include oxycodone (Percodan), hydromorphone (Dilaudid), hydrocodone (Tussionex and Vicodin), pentazocine (Talwin), and codeine combinations such as Tylenol with Codeine and Empirin with Codeine. All of these compounds are addictive.

Along with Tylenol with Codeine and Empirin with Codeine, which are Schedule III controlled substances, codeine is also available in combination with another controlled substance (butalbital) and sold under the trade name of Fiorinal with Codeine. It is available with acetaminophen in Phenaphen. Codeine is available in liquid preparations under the manufacturers' names Cosanyl, Robitussin A-C, Cheracol, Cerose, and Pediacof. Because of the amounts of codeine in these preparations, they are controlled under Schedule V. There are also pharmaceutical codeine tablets, which contain no drug other than codeine and are controlled under Schedule II.

While the compounds listed above are considered opiates, there is another class of compounds also classified as narcotic, but with synthetic origins. Meperidine (Demerol) is one of the most widely used analgesics for the relief of pain. Methadone (Amidone and Dolophine) is another of these synthetic narcotics. It was synthesized during World War II by German scientists because of a morphine shortage. Although it is chemically unlike morphine or heroin, it produces many of the same effects and is often used to treat narcotic addictions.

Dextropropoxyphene is one of those drugs that falls into one of two controlled substance schedules. When marketed in dosage form under the trade names Darvon, Darvocet, Dolene, or Propacet, dextropropoxyphene is a Schedule IV controlled substance. However, when marketed in bulk non-dosage forms, dextropropoxyphene is a Schedule II controlled substance. The significance here is that the penalties for possession of a Schedule II controlled substance are usually much greater than for possession of a Schedule IV controlled substance.

1.5.4 Central Nervous System Stimulants

Amphetamine (Benzedrine and Biphetamine), dextroamphetamine (Dexedrine), and methamphetamine (Desoxyn) are three of the best-known CNS stimulants and were prescribed for many years to treat narcolepsy. At one time, these drugs were sold over the counter without a prescription. For many years these drugs were sold as appetite suppressants. Their availability in the form of prescription drugs has all but been eliminated except under the close scrutiny of a physician. However, the clandestine laboratory production of methamphetamine in the form of a powder or granular material has been one of the major problems facing law enforcement personnel in the past 20 or so years in the U.S.

Phenmetrazine (Preludin) and methylphenidate (Ritalin) are two other CNS stimulants that have patterns of abuse similar to the amphetamine and methamphetamine products. In recent years, a number of pharmaceutical products have appeared on the market as appetite suppressants and as replacements for the amphetamines. These anorectic drugs include benzphetamine (Didrex), chlorphentermine (Pre-Sate), clortermine (Voranil), diethylpropion (Tenuate and Tepanil), fenfluramine (Pondimin), mazindol (Sanorex and Mazanor), phendimetrazine (Plegine, Bacarate, Melifat, Statobex, and Tanorex), and phentermine (Ionamin, Fastin, and Adipex-P).

1.5.5 Identifying Generic Products

There are a number of generic products on the market that are legitimate pharmaceutical preparations. These products will usually contain the active ingredient of the brand name product, but at the same time have a different formulation in the way of diluents and binders. These products are cataloged in various publications. When these products are encountered in the forensic science laboratory, the analyst will usually make a preliminary identification using one of the many publications listing the tablet or capsule's description and the code number that appears in the face of the product. This "preliminary" identification affords a starting point in the analytical process. The analyst will then proceed using the standard chemical techniques and instrumental methods to make an independent identification.

REFERENCE

1. Franzosa, E.S. and Harper W.W., The Logo Index for Tablets and Capsules, 3rd ed., U.S. Government Printing Office, Washington, D.C., 1995, 392–2401.

1.6 UNIQUE IDENTIFYING FACTORS

1.6.1 Packaging Logos

There are unique factors associated with controlled substance examinations that involve packaging. Heroin and cocaine are usually imported into the U.S. clandestinely packaged. Sometimes this packaging takes the form of legitimate household or commercial products that have been hollowed out or have natural crevices into which drugs can be stored for shipment. These kinds of packages will usually be transported via commercial carriers to distributors who will reclaim the drugs and repackage them for street distribution. Sometimes drugs are shipped via human beings who store packages in body cavities, or swallow small packages in order to clear customs checks at points of entry. In these cases, it is not unusual for the packaging to break while in the body of the person transporting the drug. This usually results in severe injury or death.

Another common way of transporting controlled substances is to package the controlled substance in brick-size, 1-kg packages for shipment to the U.S. This is often the case with shipments of heroin, cocaine, and marijuana, and the packages are usually wrapped in paper or tape. Sometimes a logo, serving as a type of trademark for the illicit distributor, will be affixed. Logos can take the form of any number of designs. They are applied using a stamping or printing device. Some commonly encountered designs include, but are not limited to, animals, symbols from Greek mythology, replications of brand name product logos, replications of the names of political figures, cartoon characters, and numbers.

When a number of these logos are encountered, examinations can be conducted to determined whether two logos have a common source. If the examiner determines that two logos are the same, and were produced using the same printing or stamping device, then the two packages must have originated from the same source. This kind of information is especially useful in tracking distribution networks.

Glassine envelopes measuring approximately 1×2 in. are commonly used to distribute heroin "on the street" directly to the primary user. More often than not, these glassine envelopes have rubber-stamped images affixed. These rubber stamped images take many forms. Cartoon characters or words with social implications are common. The examiner can determine whether these rubber-stamped images have a commonality of source and use this information to track distribution patterns of heroin within a geographical area.

1.6.2 Tablet Markings and Capsule Imprints

Counterfeit tablets and capsules, which closely resemble tablets and capsules of legitimate pharmaceutical companies, are readily available on the clandestine market. They generally contain controlled substances that have been formulated in such a way as to mimic legitimate pharmaceutical preparations.[1] They are designed to be sold either on the clandestine or the legitimate market. These counterfeits sometimes are expertly prepared and closely resemble the pharmaceutical products that they are designed to represent. At other times, they are poorly made, inadequate representations of the products they are purported to represent.

The examiner in these types of cases will evaluate the suspected tablets or capsules by examining both the class and individual characteristics of the products. Legitimate products are usually prepared with few significant flaws on tablet or capsule surfaces. The lettering or numbering will be symmetrical in every way. The tablet surfaces will have minimal chips or gouges and will usually be symmetrical. The homogeneity of the tablet will be of the highest quality. Counterfeits will usually have tabletting flaws. These flaws can take the forms of imperfect lettering or numbering, rough surfaces, or inconsistencies in the tablet formulation. This can result in different hardening characteristics of the tablet. Legitimate capsules will be highly symmetrical. The lettering or numbering will usually line up on both halves of the capsule.[2,3]

In recent years, methamphetamine and amphetamine tablets and capsules, crafted to mimic Dexedrine and Benzedrine, have been encountered with some frequency. These two products were distributed and used quite extensively on the legitimate market up until the 1970s. And while they are still available commercially with a prescription, they have been controlled under Schedule II since 1972 and their legal distribution and usage in the medical community has become fairly limited. Counterfeit barbiturate, methaqualone, and benzodiazepine tablets, sometimes from documented clandestine source laboratories from 20 years ago, have been encountered in recent seizures. Counterfeit Quaalude, Mandrax, and Valium tablets are examples of legitimate trademark products that have been the favorites of clandestine laboratory operators. The "look-alike" market was especially lucrative in the 1970s and 1980s and became a $50,000,000 a year industry.[4,5]

A unique problem, encountered with regularity up until 1975, involved the refilling of capsules. Legitimate capsules were diverted from legitimate manufacturing sources. The capsules were then emptied of their contents and refilled with some innocuous material, such as starch or baking soda, and sold. The original filling, usually containing a controlled substance, was then diverted for sale on the illicit market. These capsules can usually be identified by imperfections in their surface characteristics. There may be small indentations on the gelatinous surface of the capsule and fingerprints indicating excessive handling. The seal holding both halves of the capsule together will not be tight. And there will usually be traces of powder around the seal of the capsule. Refilling capsules by hand or by improvised mechanical devices is not easy and usually results in these visible powder residues. A more common problem today is the refilling of over-the-counter capsules with heroin for distribution at the retail level.

A similar problem that is encountered with some frequency in the forensic science laboratory is the pre-packaged syringe from a hospital, which is labeled and supposed to contain an analgesic such as meperidine. Patients complain they are receiving no relief from the injection they have been given. The syringes are then sent to the laboratory for analysis. Not infrequently, they are found to contain water, substituted for the active drug by an addicted doctor or nurse.

1.6.3   Blotter Paper LSD

LSD has been available for years in the forms of small tablets (microdots), small gelatinous squares, clear plastic-like squares (window panes), powders or crystals, liquid, or in capsules. The most commonly encountered form of LSD available today is impregnated blotter paper. This LSD medium is prepared by dissolving the clandestinely produced LSD powder in an alcohol solution, and then spraying or soaking the paper with the solution. The alcohol solution used most frequently is EverClear, a commercial ethyl alcohol product available in liquor stores. This LSD-impregnated paper is referred to as "blotter acid." It is usually distributed on sheets of paper perforated into 1/4 × 1/4 in. squares. These sheets of paper range in size to hold from 1 square up to 1000 squares. These sheets of blotter paper can be plain white or single colored with no design imprints. More often than not, there will be a brightly colored design on the paper. The design can be simple such as a black and white circle, or it can be extremely intricate. One such design was brightly colored and with a detailed depiction of the crucifixion of Jesus Christ. The design can cover each and every individual square of a 1000-perforated square sheet of paper, or one design can cover the entire sheet of blotter paper where each 1/4 × 1/4 in. perforation square makes up 1/1000 of the total design.

By examining the intricate designs on LSD blotter paper from different seizures, it is possible to determine whether there is a common source. Depending on the printing process and the quality of the image, the examiner may be able to characterize an exhibit as having originated from the image transfer process and a specific printing device. This ability to determine source commonality is most valuable in determining the origins of LSD exhibits seized from different parts of the world.

The processes described above are most valuable in linking seizures to a particular source. Investigators who are skillful and fortunate enough to seize printing or tabletting devices even without the actual controlled substances can have their efforts rewarded by terminating a controlled substance production operation. A qualified scientific examiner has the opportunity to use these devices as standards and to search reference collections of tablets, capsules, LSD blotter paper designs, or heroin or cocaine packaging logos to determine possible associations to past seizures. When this happens, the opportunity to eliminate another source of illicit drug distribution becomes a possibility.

REFERENCES

1. Franzosa, E.S., Solid dosage forms: 1975–1983, *J. Forensic Sci.*, 30, 1194–1205, 1985.
2. Eisenberg, W.V. and Tillson, A.H., Identification of counterfeit drugs, particularly barbiturates and amphetamines by microscopic, chemical, and instrumental techniques, *J. Forensic Sci.*, 11, 529–551, 1966.
3. Tillson, A.H. and Johnson, D.W., Identification of drug and capsule evidence as to source, *J. Forensic Sci.*, 19, 873–883, 1974.
4. Crockett, J. and Franzosa, E., Illicit solid dosage forms: drug trafficking in the United States, paper presented at the 6th Interpol Forensic Sciences Symposium in 1980.
5. Crockett, J. and Sapienza, F., Illicit solid dosage forms: drug trafficking in the United States, paper presented at the 10th Interpol Forensic Sciences Symposium in 1983.

1.7 ANALYZING DRUGS IN THE FORENSIC SCIENCE LABORATORY

1.7.1 Screening Tests

No other topic related to the identification of controlled substances causes as much controversy as testing specificity. Forensic science laboratories conduct two different categories of tests. Tests in the first category are called "screening tests." They include a series of tests used to make a preliminary determination of whether a particular drug or class of drugs is present. It must be emphasized that screening tests are not used to positively identify any drug. At best, screening tests can only be used to determine the possibility that members of a particular class of drug may be present. Some say that screening tests can result in "false positives," meaning either that the test indicates the possible presence of a controlled substance when none is present or that the test indicates the possible presence of one controlled substance when a different controlled substance is present. That should not be a problem, so long as it is understood that screening tests have very little if any specificity, and that a false positive test will only lead to more testing, not a false conclusion. The identification of any drug by a chemical analysis is a systematic process involving a progression from less specific methods to more specific methods. The most specific methods involve instrumental analyses. Properly trained scientists should know when a false positive is possible, and how to take steps to narrow the focus of the testing. The more tests used, the fewer the chances for error.

False negative screening tests also occur. Very weak or diluted samples containing controlled substances may yield a negative screening test. An example of this situation would be a 1% heroin sample cut with a brown powder. Testing this sample with Marquis reagent, which contains sulfuric acid and formaldehyde, may result in a charring of the brown powder and subsequent masking of the bleeding purple color characteristic of an opium alkaloid. Weak or old reagents may also yield false negatives. Examiner fallibility or inexperience in discerning colors may also result in false negatives. The possibility of a false negative leads many examiners to conduct a series of screening tests or, when warranted, to progress directly to more narrowly focused screening tests.

Specificity is the key to the forensic identification of controlled substances. There is no one method that will work as a specific test for any and all exhibits at any and all times. The choice of which specific method one utilizes must be determined by the type of controlled substance, the concentration of the controlled substance in the sample, the nature of the diluents and adulterants, the available instrumentation, and the experience of the examiner. There is an ongoing debate whether one can achieve this scientific certainty by combining a series of nonspecific tests. This is discussed later in this section.

1.7.1.1 Physical Characteristics

Occasionally an experienced forensic analyst can just look at an exhibit in a drug case and determine the probable nature of the substance. However, "probable natures" are not enough for an identification, and most examiners will usually conduct more than one test before reporting the presence of a controlled substance. The morphology of botanical substances such as marijuana and the peyote cactus are familiar enough to many laboratory analysts. Marijuana is one of those controlled substances that is examined with such frequency in the laboratory that a preliminary identification is probable based on the morphology of the botanical substance, gross physical appearance, texture, and odor. However, even after a microscopic examination of the cystolithic hairs using a microscope, the modified Duquenois–Levine test is usually run to corroborate the identification. The peyote cactus with its button-like appearance is also unique. In a like manner, the identification of the opium poppy requires a confirmation of the morphine; and the identification of the psilocybin mushroom requires an identification of the psilocybin or the psilocin.

The physical characteristics of these four agronomic substances might enable an expert witness with a background in plant taxonomy and botany to make an identification based solely on these characteristics. The forensic analyst relies on the physical characteristics and corroborating chemical examinations to identify these materials as controlled substances.

1.7.1.2 Color Tests

The color test is usually the first chemical examination examiners conduct after a package suspected of containing controlled substances is opened and weighed. Small amounts of the unknown material are placed in depressions in a porcelain spot plate or a disposable plastic or glass spot plate. Chemical reagents are then added to the depressions and the results noted: color changes, the way in which the color changes take place (flashing or bleeding), the rate at which the color changes take place, and the intensity of the final colors. The most common color reagents are the Marquis reagent for opium alkaloids, amphetamines, and phenethylamines such as MDA or MDMA; cobalt thyocyanate reagent for cocaine and phencyclidine (PCP); Dille-Koppanyi reagent for barbiturates; Duquenois reagent for marijuana; and Ehrlich's reagent for LSD. A more complete listing of these tests is available in the literature.[1] Many of these tests are multistep and multicomponent.

These color tests are designed as a starting place for the examiner in deciding how to proceed as the pyramid of focus narrows in forming a conclusion. Adulterants and diluents can also cause color changes and are sometimes said to be responsible for "false positives." The resulting color changes are not really false. They simply reflect the presence of a substance that is not the primary focus of the analytical scheme. Problems of "false negatives" and "false positives" are usually recognized very early in the analytical scheme, and they are resolved logically and rationally.

1.7.1.3 Thin-Layer Chromatography

Thin-layer chromatography (TLC) is a separation technique. The method utilizes a glass plate that is usually coated evenly with a thin layer of adsorbant. The most commonly used adsorbant is silica gel. A small amount of the sample is put into solution with a chemical solvent. A capillary pipette is then used to place a small amount of the liquid onto the TLC plate approximately 2 cm from the bottom of the plate. A second capillary pipette containing a small amount of a known controlled substance in solution is used to place a second spot on the plate usually next to, but not overlapping, the first spot.

The plate is then placed into a tank containing a solvent system, which rises about 1 cm from the bottom of the tank. Through capillary action, the solvent will migrate up the plate, and the components of the unknown will usually separate as the solvent migrates. The separated components can usually be visualized using long-wave or shortwave ultraviolet light, a chemical spray, or some combination of both. The distance each sample migrates is then divided by the distance the solvent in the tank migrates up the plate (know as the Rf value). The result is then compared to published values that have been established for pure samples of the abused drugs. If one of the components of the unknown migrates the same distance up the plate as the known, the examiner has another piece of corroborating information. If the unknown does not contain a component that migrates the same distance as the known, there are many explanations. Perhaps the known and unknown are not the same. Perhaps there is a component in the unknown solution that is binding the chemical of interest to the silica gel. The explanations for matches are numerous. The explanations for non-matches are just as numerous.

The literature is replete with values for drug/solvent migration ratios. However, these values can be affected by many factors, including the storage conditions of the TLC plates and solvent temperature. It is not uncommon for the Rf values in the laboratory to differ from those in the literature. The importance of a TLC analysis lies in its ability to separate components in a mixture. A match is another piece of corroborating information. A non-match can usually be explained.

Using TLC to identify marijuana, hashish, or hash oil is a much more complicated process than using it to identify other controlled substances.[2] The TLC analysis of cannabis exhibits results in a series of bands on the thin-layer plate. Depending on the solvent system, the number of bands can range from at least three to at least six bands.[3] Each band will have a specific color and lie at a specified place on the plate corresponding to the known cannabinoids in a standard marijuana, hashish, or THC sample.[4] The key point here is that this type of identification involves a specific chromatographic pattern as opposed to one spot where a known is compared directly with an unknown. Even with the increased specificity of a TLC analysis in the examination of cannabis or a cannabis derivative, a modified Duquenois–Levine test is suggested.

1.7.2 Confirmatory Chemical Tests

1.7.2.1 Microcrystal Identifications

Microcrystal tests are conducted using a polarized light microscope and chemical reagents. These microscopic examinations are not screening tests. The analyst will usually place a small amount of the sample on a microscope slide, add a chemical reagent, and note the formation of a specific crystal formation. These crystals are formed from specified reagents. There should be very little subjectivity in evaluating a microcrystal test.[5] Either the crystal forms or it does not form. If the appropriate crystal forms in the presence of the reagent, the drug is present. If the crystal does not form and the drug is present, the problem is usually one in which the drug concentration is too dilute, or the reagent has outlived its shelf life.

One disadvantage of microcrystal tests is the absence of a hard copy of what the analyst sees. Unless a photograph is taken of the crystal formation, the examiner cannot present for review documentation of what he saw under the microscope. Microcrystal tests are an excellent way of evaluating the relative concentration of a drug in a sample to determine the kind of extraction technique for separation and further confirmation.

1.7.2.2 Gas Chromatography

Gas chromatography (GC) has been a standard operating procedure in forensic science laboratories for the past three decades. In this technique, a gaseous mobile phase is passed through a column containing a liquid-coated, stationary, solid, support phase. The most common form of GC uses a capillary column of a very fine diameter for separating the component of a mixture. The sample is usually put into solution using an organic solvent such as methanol. The liquid is then introduced into the injection port of the gas chromatograph using a fine needle syringe capable of delivering microliter quantities of the solution. The amount injected depends on the concentration of the sample: 1 µl (one-one hundredth of a milliliter) of 1 mg of solute per 1 ml of solvent is a typical injection amount. The sample is vaporized in the heated injection port, and with the aid of a carrier gas travels through the long capillary column where the different components are separated. There are many different kinds of capillary columns with different internal coatings, lengths (which can vary from one foot up to tens of meters), and diameters (measured in micrometers). This separation is determined by the polarity and molecular size of each component. Each component exits the column onto a detector. A flame ionization detector (FID) is the most common detector used in most laboratories. Other types of less frequently encountered detectors include the nitrogen phosphorus detector and the electron capture detector.

As each component elutes from the column through the FID, a signal is generated, which results in a "peak" on a recording device. The recorder is used to document the resulting data. This recorder is usually a part of a data station that not only generates a representation of the chromatogram on a monitor, but also controls instrument parameters and ensures the consistency of the analysis. The peaks of interest are evaluated by their retention times (RTs) and by the areas under the peaks. The retention time data can be used either as confirmation of the probable identity of the substance generating the peak, or the data can be evaluated as screening information to determine the possible presence of a controlled substance. These RT data are compared to the retention time of a known standard injected onto the same column in the same instrument at the same temperature and rate flow conditions. The RTs of the known and the unknown should be almost the same within a very narrow window. The area under the peak can be used to quantitatively determine the relative concentration of the substance.

There are some disadvantages of GC. Retention times are not absolute and usually fall within a narrow window. Other compounds may fall within this same RT window. One way to overcome this problem is to analyze the same sample using a second capillary column with a different internal coating and to note its retention time as compared to the known standard. The values should be the same within a narrow RT window. A second disadvantage of GC is that some samples degrade in the injection liner at high temperatures and must be evaluated by using a derivatizing agent. This derivatizing agent is added to the drug and forms a molecular complex. The molecule complex remains intact as it passes from the injection port, through the column, and onto the detector.

GC by itself is a very powerful tool for the forensic analyst. Its most useful application today remains one in which it is interfaced with a mass spectrometer (mass selective detector), which serves as a detector and separate instrumental identification method unto itself. Gas chromatography/mass spectrometry (GS/MS) is discussed later in this section.

1.7.2.3 *High-Performance Liquid Chromatography*

This chromatographic technique is also a separation technique, but with a bit more selectivity than GC. In high-performance liquid chromatography (HPLC), the mobile phase is a liquid and the stationary phase is a solid support or a liquid-coated solid support. In GC, a carrier gas is used to carry the sample through the chromatography column. In HPLC, a high-pressure pump is used to carry the solvent containing the compound of interest through the column. Separation results from selective interactions between the stationary phase and the liquid mobile phase.[6] Unlike GC, the mobile phase plays a major role in the separation. HPLC can be used for the direct analysis of a wide spectrum of compounds and is not dependent on solute volatility or polarity. The operator need not worry about chemical changes in the molecule that can occur in GC due to thermal degradation.

HPLC chromatograms are evaluated based on retention time and area under the peak of interest. Retention time is not an absolute value, but a time within a narrowly defined window. The five basic parts of the liquid chromatograph include the solvent reservoir, the pump, the sample injection system, the column, and the detector. A recorder is used to document the resulting data. This recorder is usually a part of a data station that controls instrument parameters and ensures the consistency of the analysis. The most common detectors are the ultraviolet/visible detector (UV/VIS), the florescence detector, the electrochemical detector, the refractive index detector, and the mass spectrometer. The UV/VIS detector is the most widely used device, and it is dependent on the ability of the solute to absorb UV or visible light. The variable wavelength detector allows the analyst to select any wavelength in the UV or visible range. The diode array or rapid scan detector is also used, which allows a rapid scan of the entire UV spectrum to identify the components eluting from the column.

Because the components elute from the UV detector in solution, they do not undergo degradation or destruction. This one very useful characteristic of HPLC affords the analyst the option of collecting fractions of the eluent for further analysis. This is not possible in GC because the eluent is destroyed by the FID.

1.7.2.4 Capillary Electrophoresis

Capillary electrophoresis (CE) is a technique that separates components on the basis of charge-to-mass ratios under the influence of an electrical field. It uses high voltage for fast separations and high efficiencies. Osmotic flow is the main driving force in CE, especially at higher pH values, and results primarily from the interaction of positive ions in solution with the silanol groups on the capillary in the presence of an applied field. Narrow bore capillary columns of uncoated fused silica are used for heat dissipation during the separation process. The detector is normally a UV detector.

Micellar electrokinetic capillary chromatography (MECC) is a form of CE that allows for the separation of cations, neutral solutes, and anions.

CE has several advantages over HPLC and GC. The method can be used with ionic and neutral solutes, which present problems in GC. There is a higher efficiency, resolving power, and speed of analysis compared to HPLC. From a cost perspective, CE requires much less solvent than HPLC, and the CE capillary column is much less expensive than the HPLC or GC capillary columns. Two disadvantages of CE are the limited sensitivity for UV detection (30 to 100 times less than that of HPLC); and fraction collection is troublesome because of mechanical problems and small sample size. This technique uses a micelle as a run buffer additive to give separations that are both electrophoretic and chromatographic.

One of the advantages of MECC is the ability to separate racemic mixtures of compounds into the D- and L-isomers. This is an ability that is extremely valuable when identifying compounds where one isomer is controlled (dextropropoxyphene) and the other isomer is not controlled (levopropoxyphene). This is usually accomplished by adding cyclodextrins to the run buffer.

1.7.2.5 Infrared Spectrophotometry

Infrared (IR) spectrophotometry is one of the most specific instrumental methods for the identification of a controlled substance. A pure drug as a thin film on a KBr salt plate, or as crystals mounted in a KBr matrix, is placed into the sample compartment of the IR spectrophotometer. A source of electromagnetic radiation in the form of light from a Nernst glower passes light through the sample. The instrument, through a mechanical means, splits the beam into a reference beam and an incident beam. The reference beam passes unobstructed through a monochromer to a photometer; the incident beam passes through the mounted sample through the same monochrometer to the photometer. The reference beam passes 100% unobstructed to the photometer. The incident beam passing through the sample has some of its energy absorbed by the sample. This energy is absorbed at different wavelengths across the infrared spectrum from 4000 cm^{-1} down to 250 cm^{-1}. The amount of relative absorption and where on this spectrum the absorption takes place are dependent on the molecular structure and, more specifically, the functional groups of the drug. Different functional groups and molecular interactions brought on by symmetrical and asymmetrical molecular stretching vibrations and in-plane and out-of-plane bending vibrations result in a number of peaks and valleys on the IR chart. The resultant spectrum is usually formed on an x/y coordinate axis. The wavelength (μ) or wave number (cm^{-1}) where the absorption occurs is depicted on the *x*-axis, and a measure of the amount of light absorbed by the sample, but usually referenced by transmittance units from 0 to 100%, is depicted on the *y*-axis.

The IR spectrum of a suspected drug results in a specific pattern that can be used to positively determine the identity of the substance. For most controlled substances, the resulting spectrum consists of 20 to 70 peaks. These peaks form a pattern that is unique to the chemical structure of the drug. This pattern can then be compared with a reference IR spectrum of a primary drug standard. If the analyst determines that the two spectra match within the limits of scientific certainty, an identification is possible. It is rarely, if ever, possible to overlay the reference spectra with the spectra of the unknown and have a "perfect match." The analyst is looking for a match in the patterns. Any shifts in peak intensity or wave number must be evaluated in conjunction with the pattern. Small shifts of 1 or 2 cm^{-1} and minor intensity variations of individual peaks are expected. However, major variations must be evaluated on a case by case basis. Some authors refer to IR as a "fingerprint" identification method. This implies an ability to overlay two spectra and obtain a perfect match in every way. This degree of perfection is rarely, if ever, possible.

Another factor that must be considered is that when two spectra are being compared peak-by-peak as opposed to pattern-by-pattern, they ideally should be from the same instrument and collected at about the same time. Comparing a literature reference spectrum with an unknown for a pattern match is acceptable. Comparing the same literature reference spectrum wave number by wave number, absolute transmittance value by absolute transmittance value will probably result in minor differences.

IR does have limitations. To obtain an acceptable spectrum, the sample must be very clean and dry. For forensic exhibits, this usually means that most samples must go through extraction processes to remove impurities. In the past, sample size was a problem. However, because of advances in Fourier transform IR technology and the interfacing of an IR spectrophotometer with a microscope, evaluating microgram quantities of a sample results in excellent spectra that are conclusive for the identification of a controlled substance. IR has very definite limitations in its ability to quantitate controlled substances, and differentiating some isomers of controlled substances can pose problems.

1.7.2.6 Gas Chromatography/Mass Spectrometry

GC/MS is by far the most popular method of identifying controlled substances in the forensic science laboratory. In this method, a gas chromatograph is interfaced with a mass selective detector (MSD). The sample undergoing an examination is placed into solution with a solvent such as methanol. A very small injection volume of 1 or 2 μl is injected into the GC injection port. It then travels through the column where the different components of the sample are separated. The separated components can then be directed into the ionization chamber of MSD where they are bombarded by an electron beam. In electron impact gas chromatography/mass spectrometry (EI MS), high-energy electrons impact the separated component molecules. The resulting spectrum of each component is typically complex with a large number of mass fragments. These fragments are represented as peaks of varying intensity that provide the basis for comparison with a primary reference standard. The components are then ionized and positively charged. This ionization also results in a fission or fragmentation process. The molecular fragments traverse into a magnetic field where they are separated according to their masses. In this magnetic field, larger mass fragments are less affected by the magnetic field, and smaller fragments are more affected and undergo a deflection. Upon exiting the magnetic field, these fragments impact a detector losing the charge generated by the beam of electrons impacting the sample. The result of this fragmentation process is a pattern unique for the substance that is being analyzed.

The resulting mass spectrum consists of an *x*/*y* coordinate axis. The numerical value on the *x*-axis represents the mass number determined by the number of neutrons and protons in the nucleus. It is usually the molecular weight of a specific fragment. The largest magnitude peak on the *x*-axis will often be the **molecular ion** and will represent the molecular weight of the unfragmented compound. There will usually be a very small peak to the right of the molecular ion which represents the molecular weight plus 1. The y-axis represents the relative abundance of each peak comprising the mass spectrum. The tallest peak on the y-axis is the **base peak** and represents that part of the molecule that is the most stable and undergoes the least amount of fragmentation. The base peak is assigned a relative abundance value of 100. The other peaks in the resulting spectrum are assigned relative values along the y-axis.

The numerical values on the x- and y-axis are calculated and assigned by the data station, which is interfaced with the mass spectrometer. The accuracy of these numbers is predicated on the fact that the instrument has been properly tuned. This tuning process can be compared to checking the channel tuning on a television set. This might be accomplished by opening a television guide to determine what programs are scheduled at a particular hour. The television is then turned on and the program for each channel checked. If the programs cited in the television magazine appear on corresponding channels at the proper times, the television has been proved to be properly tuned. The tuning of a mass analyzer presents an analogous situation.

The tuning process of a mass analyzer involves a procedure in which a chemical of a known molecular weight and fragmentation pattern is analyzed and the resulting data evaluated. This process includes verifying instrument parameters and the resulting spectrum. If the response of the tuning process falls within specified limits, the mass spectrometer is deemed operationally reliable, and the resulting data can be considered reliable. One such chemical used to tune mass spectrometers is perflurotributylamine (PFTBA).

Fragmentation patterns of controlled substances are typically unique. Once a fragmentation pattern has been obtained, the forensic analyst should be able to explain the major peaks of the spectrum and relate them to the molecular structure. If properly evaluated, mass spectral data can usually be used to form a conclusion as to the identity of a controlled substance.

GC/MS has many advantages in the analysis of controlled substances. The sample being analyzed need not be pure. Multicomponent samples are separated and each soluble organic component can be individually identified. The analyst must be aware of isomeric compounds that have very similar chemical structures and similar fragmentation patterns. These kinds of situations can usually be handled by noting the GC retention time data to discriminate between similar compounds. Possible coelution of compounds from the capillary GC column and thermal degradation as noted in the gas chromatography section of this chapter should also be recognized. GC/MS does not allow the forensic analyst to directly identify the salt form of the drug. This task can be accomplished by considering the solubility properties of the drug being analyzed. In using this knowledge and performing extractions prior to injection onto the GC column, the salt form can be determined indirectly.

When all methods of instrumental analysis of controlled substances are considered, GC/MS is recognized in most instances as one of the efficient analytical techniques. If the analyst is cognizant of maintaining instrument reliability standards and the guidelines of mass spectral interpretation, GC/MS affords one of the highest degrees of specificity in the identification of controlled substances.

1.7.2.7 Nuclear Magnetic Resonance Spectroscopy

Nuclear magnetic resonance (NMR) spectroscopy is one of the most powerful instrumental techniques available to the forensic chemist. In those laboratories fortunate enough to have NMR technology, extensive capabilities exist. Data interpretation of NMR spectra requires a high degree of expertise. This instrumental technique allows the analyst to detect paramagnetic atoms. (^{1}H, ^{2}H, ^{13}C, ^{15}N, ^{17}O, ^{31}P, ^{11}B, and ^{19}F are examples.) Most forensic applications of NMR focus on ^{1}H and ^{13}C. The resonant frequency of hydrogen (^{1}H) in the current high-field magnets ranges from 200 to 750 mHz. This instrument generates a high magnetic field more than capable of damaging encrypted data on the back of a credit card. The NMR is a very expensive instrument requiring a high degree of specialized expertise to maintain and interpret the resulting data. The NMR is the one instrument that affords the analyst the ability to determine both the molecular structure and the three-dimensional orientation of some individual atoms of the molecule. This means that structural isomers can be determined directly. However, the extent of this kind of information is usually required only by research scientists in those instances where no other information is available from other instrumental methods, or where no primary analytical standard is available to confirm the presence of a controlled substance.

The major component of the NMR spectrometer is a high-field super-conducting magnet. The sample is dissolved in a deuterated solvent and then transferred to a long cylindrical glass tube usually measuring 5 mm in diameter. The tube is placed into the NMR probe located near the center of the magnetic field. In proton NMR, the magnetic field causes the hydrogen atoms on the molecule to orient in a particular direction. To obtain high-resolution spectra, the field produced by the magnet must be homogeneous over the entire area of the sample in the probe. The resonance frequencies for all protons in a molecule may be different. These frequencies are dependent on the molecular environment of the nucleus. This correlation between resonance frequencies and molecular environment enables the analyst to make judgments regarding the structure of the drug being analyzed.

The NMR spectrum is traced on a two-dimensional x/y coordinate axis. By evaluating an NMR proton spectrum, an analyst can determine an important factor that facilitates the identification of the compound — the area under each peak indicates the number of nuclei that are undergoing a transition and the number of protons that are present.

There are other types of examinations that are possible with high-field NMR. A carbon-13 (^{13}C) evaluation enables an analyst to determine the number of carbons and their relative positioning in the molecule. ^{13}C is an isotope of the more abundant ^{12}C. About 1% of naturally occurring carbon is ^{13}C. There are two additional NMR "2D experiments" that are very valuable to the forensic analyst. Correlation spectroscopy (COSY) measures proton to proton (^{1}H to ^{1}H) interactions; and nuclear overhauser effect spectroscopy (NOESY) measures the interaction of protons that are close to one another, but not necessarily on adjoining atoms. Carbon-13, COSY, and NOESY spectra are all much more difficult to interpret and require specialized knowledge.

In the forensic analysis of controlled substances, most molecules comprise carbon and hydrogen. Proton NMR provides a unique spectral pattern that can be used to identify a controlled substance. This pattern also enables the analyst to distinguish between the basic and a salt form of the drug. NMR cannot distinguish halogenated salt forms. For instance, it cannot distinguish between heroin hydrochloride and heroin hydrobromide. But it can distinguish between a heroin salt and heroin base.

REFERENCES

1. Johns, S.H., Wist, A.A., and Najam, A.R., Spot tests: a color chart reference for forensic chemists, *J. Forensic Sci.*, 24, 631–649, 1979.
2. Hughes, R.B. and Kessler, R.R., Increased safety and specificity in the thin-layer chromatographic identification of marijuana, *J. Forensic Sci.*, 24, 842–846, 1979.
3. Baggi, T.R., 3-Methylbenzthiazolinone-2-hydrazone (MBTH) as a new visualization reagent in the detection of cannabinoids on thin-layer chromatography, *J. Forensic Sci.*, 25, 691–694, 1980.
4. Parker, K.D., Wright, J.A., Halpern, A.F., and Hine, C.H., Preliminary report on the separation and quantitative determination of cannabis constituents present in plant material and when added to urine by thin-layer and gas chromatography, *Bull. Narc.*, 20, 9–14, 1968.
5. Fulton, C.C., *Modern Microcrystal Tests for Drugs*, John Wiley & Sons, New York, 1969.
6. Lurie, I.S. and Witmer, J.D., *High Performance Liquid Chromatography*, Marcel Decker, New York, 1983.

1.7.3 Controlled Substances Examinations

Every examination made by a forensic chemist has a potential legal ramification or consequence. Forensic chemists must be prepared to depart from the familiar natural science setting of the laboratory and to enter the confrontational setting of the courtroom and be able to communicate with a prosecuting attorney, a defense attorney, a judge, 12 jurors, and on occasion, the press. The forensic chemist must be able to explain the significance of complicated analytical procedures to individuals with little or no scientific training. If the forensic analyst is to have any credibility on the witness stand, he must be able to describe what he has done in terminology understood by those individuals with whom he is communicating.

1.7.3.1 *Identifying and Quantitating Controlled Substances*

Whenever a controlled substance is identified, the possibility exists that an individual could be imprisoned or suffer some other legal consequence as a result. There is, therefore, an absolute, uncompromised requirement for certainty in the identification of controlled substances. Prior to 1960, the results of microscopic crystal tests, color screening tests, and TLC were considered definitive. From the 1960s through the mid-1970s, UV spectrophotometry and GC gained acceptance. It is interesting to look back 30 years and contemplate the absolute faith placed in a retention time on a gas chromatogram, or upon the UV absorption maxima in acidic or basic solutions. In some instances these numerical values were measured with a ruler!

From 1975 through 1985 there were major advances in IR and MS. During those years "specificity," as we understand the term today, was, for the first time, actually attainable in most cases. As the technology continually evolved, with increased Fourier transform peak resolution in IR and NMR, and multicomponent separations improved with capillary column GS, specificity also increased.

In the mid-1980s the advent of "designer drugs" (properly referred to as "controlled substance analogues") resurrected the problem of specificity. In attempts at circumventing existing controlled substance laws, clandestine laboratory chemists began to alter chemical structures of controlled drugs by increasingly sophisticated syntheses. By replacing a methyl group with an ethyl group, or by using a five-membered ring instead of a six-membered ring in a synthesis, these clandestine laboratory chemists developed what at the time were non-controlled analogues. The Controlled Substance Analogue and Enforcement Act of 1986 was passed by Congress, largely as a response to this problem. This particular piece of legislation also reinforced the responsibility of the chemist to accurately discriminate between controlled substances and endless lists of possible analogues.

A direct consequence of the new law's passage was the development of analytical procedures in Fourier transform infrared spectrophotometry (FTIR), Fourier transform nuclear magnetic resonance spectroscopy (FTNMR), gas chromatography/Fourier transform infrared spectroscopy (GC/FTIR), and CE. These instrumental methods have made their way into the forensic science laboratory and now provide the increased specificity required by the courts.

Controlled substances sold on the street are usually mixed with adulterants and diluents in a crude and mostly unspecified manner. In some laboratories, analysts are required to identify and quantitate both the controlled substance and the adulterant drugs and diluent materials. Color tests, TLC, and microcrystal tests of the pre-1960s vintage are still used for screening. These testing procedures were valid then and are still valid today, but today additional instrumental techniques are utilized to make the absolute identification and quantitation.

After the analysis has been completed, it must be documented. The final report must be clear, concise, and accurate, with all conclusions substantiated by analytical data. The data may be in the form of notations on paper in the analyst's writing, or on chromatograms, spectra, or other instrumental printouts. Dates must be checked, and the documented description of the exhibit(s) must be consistent with the actual exhibit. Each time a report is signed, the analyst places his or her reputation and credibility before the scrutiny of the court and his or her peers. Discovering a "mistake" after the report has been submitted to the courts is not good.

Cocaine can exist as either the hydrochloride (HCl) salt or as the base. Pursuant to federal law, there are sentencing guidelines based on the identification of cocaine as either the base or as the salt form (usually HCl). Cocaine can be adulterated with benzocaine, procaine, lidocaine, or any combination of these non-controlled drugs, and further diluted with mannitol, lactose, or other processing sugars. A variety of instrumental techniques can be used to distinguish cocaine HCl from cocaine base. FTIR spectrophotometry is commonly available and used in many laboratories. The IR spectra of cocaine HCl and cocaine base are quite different and easily distinguished. The IR spectrum of a cocaine HCl sample mixed with an adulterant presents a problem. The same sample analyzed by GC/FTIR presents the chemist with a total response chromatogram showing all peaks in a mixture. The resulting IR spectrum and mass spectrum are identifiable. However, in this technique, cocaine HCl and cocaine base cannot be distinguished. At this point, NMR can provide a solution to distinguishing the two forms of cocaine and identifying the adulterants.

The solubility properties of controlled substances can be used to separate different forms of controlled substances. For instance, cocaine base is soluble in diethyl ether; cocaine HCl is insoluble. Therefore, if an analyst is analyzing a material that is believed to be cocaine in a questionable form, the analyst can try placing the material into solution with diethyl ether, separate the ether from the insolubles, evaporate the diethyl ether, and analyze the resulting powder by GC/MS. The resulting cocaine spectrum would indicate the presence of cocaine base because cocaine HCl would not have gone into solution.

Methamphetamine is produced in clandestine laboratories from the reaction of ephedrine with hydriodic acid and red phosphorus, or from the reaction of phenyl-2-propanone (P-2-P) with methylamine. Methamphetamine samples submitted to the forensic science laboratory usually contain precursors from the synthesis, by-products for side reactions, and adulterants such as nicotinamide that have been added by the clandestine laboratory operator. As is true of the mass spectrum of some other phenethylamines, the mass spectrum of methamphetamine may not provide enough specificity for positive identification. The most accurate way to identify many phenethylamines is with IR. However, NMR is at least as specific as FTIR, and it also allows for an identification in the presence of diluents. Unfortunately, NMR is not available in many laboratories. Nicotinamide is one of the more commonly encountered adulterants with methamphetamine and can easily be distinguished from isonicotinamide by NMR spectroscopy.

The IR spectrum of methamphetamine hydrochloride in a potassium chloride salt matrix is very specific, and GC/FTIR is excellent at separating the components of a methamphetamine sample. However, this method requires great care in selecting the optimized temperature and flow parameters, and column selection.

GC/MS is the method most often used for identifying heroin. The mass spectrum of heroin is very specific. Heroin is relatively simple to separate, and identification of the degradation products and the by-products of the heroin synthesis, from morphine and acetic anhydride, is relatively straightforward. Because morphine is derived from opium, many of the by-products from the opium processing are carried over to the final heroin product. Acetylcodeine and acetylmorphine are clearly identified from the corresponding mass spectra. The GC/FTIR also provides excellent spectra for making identifications of heroin, its by-products, degradation products, and precursors. The chloroform insoluble diluents from heroin samples can also be identified in a potassium bromide matrix by FTIR. These materials will usually consist of sugars such as mannitol and inositol. When the heroin has been isolated from diluents and adulterants, FTIR and NMR can be utilized to confirm the salt form of the heroin.

Phencyclidine, more properly identified as phenylcyclohexylpiperidine (PCP), is usually submitted to the laboratory as an exhibit of PCP base in diethyl ether, a powder, or sprayed or coated on marijuana. The analysis of PCP is relatively direct by GC/MS. The resulting mass spectrum is specific. The GC/FTIR spectrum of PCP is not as specific when one compares this spectrum with that of PCP analogues and precursors such as phenylcyclohexyl carbonitrile (PCC) and phenylcyohexyl pyrrolidine (PCPy). FTIR spectrophotometry of the solid in a potassium bromide matrix is very specific. A word of caution is in order for anyone handling PCP. PCP is a substance that is believed to be easily absorbed through the skin of the analyst. Minimum handling is recommended.

1.7.3.2   Identifying Adulterants and Diluents

The terms *adulterants* and *diluents* are sometimes used in the context of illicitly distributed controlled substances. Adulterants are chemicals added to illicit drugs that, in and of themselves, can affect some sort of a physiological response. This response can range from very mild to quite severe. Diluents are chemicals added to controlled substances that are used more as fillers than to elicit a physiological response. They can be added to affect the color and composition for the sake of satisfying the user. Adulterants and diluents are usually added to the controlled substance mixture by those involved in illicit distribution. There is a third class of materials that is found in controlled substance mixtures. This class includes by-products. These by-products can be processing by-products, or they can exist as naturally occurring by-products found in botanical substances such as the coca leaf or the opium poppy.

Most "street" exhibits of heroin and cocaine contain adulterants and diluents. Samples taken from large-scale, brick-size, kilogram seizures will be relatively pure. Except for some by-products from the opium poppy and the coca leaf, there will be little in the way of foreign materials. Adulterants are encountered, in increasing proportions, as the heroin and cocaine progress down the distribution chain from the main supplier to the dealers to the users.

Adulterants commonly encountered in heroin include quinine, procaine, acetaminophen, caffeine, diphenhydramine, aspirin, phenobarbital, and lidocaine. Adulterants commonly encountered in cocaine include procaine, benzocaine, and lidocaine. Diluents found in heroin include different kinds of starches. It is not uncommon to find in heroin substances, such as calcium carbonate, that had been added during the morphine extraction processes. Diluents found in both cocaine and heroin include lactose, mannitol, sucrose, and dextrose.

The identification of adulterants and diluents may or may not be a requirement as a part of the identification scheme in the forensic science laboratory. In most instances, the requirements of the judicial system will be limited to the identification of the controlled substance. This will usually be accomplished by separating the sample into its component parts, and then identifying all or some of these components. In the case of a heroin exhibit, cut with quinine and mannitol, a capillary GC/MS examination might result in a chromatogram and corresponding spectra with an acetylcodeine peak, an acetylmorphine peak, a morphine peak, a quinine peak, and a heroin peak. The first two peaks are most probably processing by-products; the morphine is from the opium poppy; the heroin is the main peak of interest, and the quinine has probably been added as an adulterant. There is no need to separate the components by extractions to make the identifications. However, if the analyst is desirous of conducting an IR examination or a NMR examination to identify the heroin, an extraction of the heroin from a 3 N hydrochloric acid medium using chloroform is an option. Depending on whether the heroin exists as a salt (heroin hydrochloride) or as heroin base, a set of serial extractions can be conducted to isolate the heroin from the quinine and the other substances. The identification of cocaine in a mixture follows the same procedures. Depending on the type of analysis, the cocaine may or may not need to be chemically separated from the adulterants for an identification.

The simplest way to identify diluents in controlled substance mixtures is by microscopic identification. Common diluents along with the sugars/carbohydrates/starches described above include sodium chloride, calcium carbonate, and various types of amorphous materials. Because of their optical properties, these materials lend themselves well to a microscopic identification. Chemical separations are fairly easy because these materials are usually insoluble in solvents such as diethyl ether or hexane, and slightly soluble in solvents such as methanol. Most organic materials are soluble in methanol or some other polar solvent. The sugars/carbohydrates/starches can be further identified using IR following the separation if only one sugar is present. If not, HPLC can be used to identify the sugars.

Even if the identification of all adulterants, diluents, and by-products is not required in the final report generated by the analyst, such information can prove useful in evaluating trends and possible distribution patterns.

1.7.3.3 Quantitating Controlled Substances

A number of different methods can be used to quantitate controlled substances. Capillary column GC or HPLC are probably the two most utilized instrumental methods to accomplish this task. The choice of which instrumental method to use depends on the chemical properties of the substance in question. GC works well with those compounds that are not highly polar, are relatively stable at high temperatures, and are soluble in organic solvents such as methanol or chloroform. Even if these conditions exist, GC can still be used if a derivatizing agent is used.

If GC is used, the most common analytical method for quantitation involves the use of an internal standard, providing a consistent concentration of a known chemical in solution. To avoid the obvious problem of choosing an internal standard, which might be present in the sample as an adulterant or diluent, the internal standard can be a straight-chain hydrocarbon (tetracosane, eicosane, or dodecane) that is added in equal amounts to both the sample being analyzed and the calibration samples. The internal standard method is especially advantageous because the expected flame ionization detector response for the internal standard to the drug can be checked for each and every injection. The critical factor for each injection is the ratio of the detector response of the internal standard to the calibration solution of known concentration. This is especially critical if the sample size of the injection is off target by a minuscule amount. The absolute integration values for the known peak and the internal standard peaks may vary. However, the ratio will not be affected. If the detector is responding properly to the internal standard in solution, it is also responding properly for the substance being quantitated.

Controlled substances can also be quantitated using what is referred to as the external standard method. In this method, calibration standards of known concentrations are prepared. Injections are then made into the GC injection port, and a calibration table is established. The accuracy of this method is quite good, provided that the injection amounts used in establishing the calibration table are exactly the same from injection to injection. Even small variations of less than 10% volume, when dealing with a 1-μl injection, can lead to less than optimized results. This problem can be overcome by making multiple injections and checking the consistency of the detector response and the injection volume. The ability to be consistent can be developed by an analyst with a good eye. The ability to read the sample size on the microsyringe is, for some, as much an art as a scientific technique. Automatic injectors are now available on many gas chromatographs, which approach consistency from one injection to the next. However, this method will work only when there is a verifiable linear response of the detector within a specified concentration range.

In both the internal and external standard methods, there must be a linear response of the detector to the solutions of different concentrations. This is determined by injecting solutions of known concentrations and establishing a calibration table. With most instrument data stations, this is relatively simple. The instrument will then calculate the response ratio of internal standard to drug for the solution of unknown concentration and compare this to the response ratios of internal standard to drug for the solutions of known concentrations in the calibration table. This ratio can then be used to calculate the concentration of the drug that is being analyzed.

HPLC can be useful for quantitating controlled substances in solution. This instrumental method also measures the response of different compounds at different ultraviolet/visible absorption bands. These responses are then compared to calibration table values. Internal standards can be used in the same way they are used in GC quantitations. The limitations and comparisons of HPLC and GC are discussed elsewhere.

Ultraviolet/visible spectrophotometry (UV/VIS) is a technique that has been in use for many years. UV/VIS uses one of the basic tenets of physics — Beer's law. Absorption of monochromatic light is proportional to the concentration of a sample in solution. The concentration of an exhibit in solution can be determined by comparison with calibration tables. This type of analysis is dependent on the solubility properties of the substance being quantitated in acid, basic, and organic solutions. The UV/VIS method is accurate and reliable only when the compound of interest is pure with no interfering substances. GC and HPLC are used more often because of the added reliability check provided by the internal standard methodology.

NMR spectrometry can also be used for the quantitation of controlled substances. The quantitative analytical techniques in NMR are more complicated than those discussed above and require a specialized instrumental expertise.

All of the methods discussed are reliable and accurate when properly and conscientiously conducted. There is one very important difference that applies to any quantitative method when compared to an identification method. With proper methods, an analyst can make an identification of a controlled substance with scientific certainty. The quantitation of a controlled substance will usually result in values falling within a narrowly defined "window" of n m one-tenth to one or two absolute percent. The reported value will usually be an average value.

1.7.3.4 Reference Standards

The first step in ensuring the accuracy of the identification of any controlled substance should be a collection of authenticated reference standards. Reference standards for the forensic science examinations should be 98+% pure. They can be purchased from a reputable manufacturer or distributor, synthesized by an organic chemist within the laboratory, or purified from a bulk secondary standard by using an appropriate methodology. "Reference Standards" that have been authenticated are available from the United States Pharmacopoeia (USP) and National Formulary (NF). Samples obtained from any other source should be authenticated using the appropriate methodology. This authentication process will involve a two-step process of first positively identifying the proposed reference standard and then determining the purity of this standard.

At a minimum, the identification of a reference standard should be conducted using IR and MS. The resulting spectra are then compared with reference spectra in the literature. The chemist should be able to evaluate data from both of these instruments and be able to explain the major peaks using, respectively, a functional group analysis or a molecular fragmentation analysis. If no literature spectra are available, a more sophisticated structural analysis such as NMR spectroscopy will be necessary to verify the chemical structure. Additional methods that can be used to supplement, but not replace, IR, MS, and NMR include optical crystallography, X-ray crystallography, and a melting point analysis.

The next step in the process is to quantitate the reference standard against a "primary standard." A primary standard is a sample that has been subjected to the authentication process and meets the criteria of a positive identification and 98+% purity. The quantitation methods of choice are GC or HPLC. With either method, the concentrations of the injections of both the primary standard and the authentication sample must be within the linear range of the detector. The method should utilize an internal standard. The results of all injections should have a relative standard deviation of less than 3%.[1]

If a primary standard is not available, a purity determination can be accomplished by a peak area percent determination using capillary GC with a flame ionization detector and HPLC using a photo-array ultraviolet detector. A third instrumental method using a differential scanning calorimeter (DSC) should also be considered. In a peak area percent analysis, the area percent of the standard compound is determined vs. any impurities that are present in the batch. A blank injection of the solvent is done prior to the standard injection to detect peaks common to both the solvent and the authentication standard. The GC solution is checked for insolubles. If these insolubles are present, they can be isolated and identified by IR. Of course, if there are insolubles, the sample is no longer considered an authentication standard until it is purified and the foreign material is removed.

HPLC can also be used in a peak area percent analysis. For basic drugs, the analyst would use a gradient mobile phase using methanol and an acidic aqueous phosphate buffer. For neutral and acidic drugs, he would use a gradient with methanol and an acidic aqueous phosphate buffer containing sodium dodecyl sulfate. For anabolic steroids, he would use a methanol/water gradient mobile phase. As is the case with GC, with HPLC a blank injection of the solvent always precedes the injection of the authentication standard. Three wavelengths, 210 nm, 228 nm, and 240 nm, are monitored for most drugs. For anabolic steroids, the analyst should monitor 210 nm, 240 nm, and 280 nm. If the resulting UV spectra of all pertinent peaks are similar, the integration of the peaks with the most sensitive wavelengths are used for the calculation of purity.

DSC is a method of adding heat to a preweighed sample and monitoring temperature and heat flow as the sample goes through its melting point.[2] If decomposition does not occur during the melt, the peak shown on the thermogram can be used to determine melting point and the molar concentration of any melt soluble impurities present. With these data, the analyst can determine the purity of the authentication standard. One drawback of DSC is that structurally dissimilar impurities such as sugars in a supposed heroin "standard" are not always detected by this method. This is because the impurity does not go into solution in the melting main component. With almost all authentication standards, most impurities will be structurally similar to the drug of interest. The dissimilar compounds should have been removed prior to the DSC analysis or detected by GC or HPLC.

REFERENCES

1. *CRC Handbook of Tables for Probability and Statistics*, 2nd ed., CRC Press, Boca Raton, FL, 1968, 5.
2. McNaughton, J.L. and Mortimer, C.T., Differential scanning calorimetry, *IRS; Phys. Chem. Ser. 2*, 10, 1975.

1.8 COMPARATIVE ANALYSIS

1.8.1 Determining Commonality of Source

Two different kinds of controlled substance analyses are routinely conducted in the forensic science laboratory. The first is the "identification." The goal is self-evident — to identify a controlled substance by name. The second, less common, type of analysis is the "comparative analysis." Its purpose is to determine a commonality of source. A comparative analysis will include a comprehensive examination of the sample's chemical and physical characteristics, with the goal of demonstrating, with a high degree of certainty, a common origin for two or more samples.[1]

Sometime it is possible to determine when two items of evidence have a common origin just by physically fitting them together. This applies to exhibits such as a screwdriver and a broken blade, two large paint chips that have broken apart, or a piece of paper torn in two or more pieces. In the forensic examination of illicit drugs, it is possible to state with a high degree of certainty that two exhibits of a white powder share a common source. The wording in stating such a conclusion is critical. Words must be carefully selected to convey the conclusion clearly and concisely, without overstepping the scientific certainty that exists. The following quote, about two samples of cocaine, is from the transcript of drug trial held in 1991. It illustrates the appropriate language to be used on such occasions.

After a review of all analytical data, it can be stated with a high level of scientific certainty and beyond a reasonable doubt that a close chemical relationship exists between [the two samples] strongly suggesting that they were derived from the same manufacturing process … and that they were probably derived from the same batch.[2]

Before undertaking a detailed examination of two samples, a broad overview is desirable. The color and granularity of the exhibits should be examined, and then the components of the sample identified and quantitated. If all of the data from one exhibit compare favorably with all of the data from the second exhibit, the analyst can proceed to a second set of procedures to evaluate the processing by-products and trace materials in the exhibits. It is important to realize that to successfully evaluate two exhibits to determine commonality of source, each exhibit must be analyzed in the same way using the same methodology, instruments, and chemicals and solvents from the same containers.

Controlled substances such as cocaine and heroin are the simplest to compare because they are derived from botanical substances (the coca leaf and the opium poppy, respectively).[3,4] Many naturally occurring by-products from the plants are carried through the processing stages of the drugs, and these can be used to confirm the existence of a common source.

1.8.2 Comparing Heroin Exhibits

Capillary column gas chromatography (ccGC) and HPLC are the two methods most often utilized in comparing two or more heroin exhibits to determine whether they came from the same source. HPLC can be utilized in the first part of the analytical scheme because the components being evaluated usually are present in substantial amounts. The major components, including heroin, acetylmorphine, acetylcodeine, morphine, codeine, noscapine, papaverine, thebaine, and most diluents can be identified and quantitated. A high degree of resolving power is not required at this point in the analytical scheme. If the HPLC analysis demonstrates that the samples being compared are similar, the analyst proceeds to the second part of the analytical scheme.

In the second part of this scheme to evaluate the trace components of the exhibits, ccGC is usually the method of choice, both because of its resolving power and because of its ability to detect minute quantities of the component of interest. The second step of the isolation process involves multiple extractions and derivatizations to isolate the acidic and neutral compounds for analysis and evaluation. This process isolates the precursors, solvents, and respective contaminants, by-products, intermediates, and degradation products. It is desirable to remove the heroin from the sample during the extraction processes in order to keep most of the trace components at the same level of chromatographic attenuation. Once the heroin has been identified and quantitated, only then are the other elements analyzed. If after these two processes the analyst sees no chromatographic differences in the samples being evaluated, a conclusion can be formulated. The number of components from this second part of the process can number from 100 to 300. If all of these components are present in both exhibits at similar relative levels, a conclusion regarding commonality of source is warranted.

1.8.3 Comparing Cocaine Exhibits

The process is different for cocaine comparisons. For one thing, the cocaine need not be removed from the sample. Four different ccGC examinations can be conducted that evaluate and compare the by-products and impurities down to trace levels by:

1. Flame ionization gas chromatography (GC-FID) to evaluate cocaine hydrolysis products, manufacturing impurities, and naturally occurring alkaloids[5]

2. GC-FID to determine trimethoxy-substituted alkaloids as well as other minor naturally occurring tropanes[6]

3. Electron capture gas chromatography (GC-ECD) to determine the hydroxycocaines and N-nor related compounds[4]

4. GC-ECD to determine the ten intact truxillines[7]

These four gas chromatographic methods provide an in-depth evaluation of trace level components and allow the precise comparison of two different cocaine exhibits. The number of components evaluated ranges in the hundreds. These data provide the analyst with an abundance of analytical points to form a conclusion regarding commonality of source.

Extraction of the impurities and by-products can be accomplished using a derivatizing reagent.[8,9] Heptafluorobutyric anhydride (HFBA) is often used for this purpose. The GC-FID and GC-ECD analyses that follow will result in organic profiles of the many compounds from the cocaine and heroin samples being analyzed. A further MS analysis may serve to identify the chemical composition of many of the components of each exhibit. Many of the resulting peaks represent compounds formed during the manufacturing process; others will be oxidation or hydrolysis products of known compounds; and other peaks will have a degree of uncertainty regarding their exact chemical structure. However, what will be known is that these peaks are present in both exhibits being compared using the ccGC methods and represent cocaine and heroin manufacturing impurities or by-products.

REFERENCES

1. Perillo, B.A., Klein, R.F.X., and Franzosa, E.S., Recent advances by the U.S. drug enforcement administration in drug signature and comparative analysis, *Forensic Sci. Int.,* 69, 1–6, 1994.

2. Moore, J.M., Meyers, R.P., and Jiminez, M.D., The anatomy of a cocaine comparison case: a prosecutorial and chemistry perspective, *J. Forensic Sci.,* 38, 1305–1325, 1993.

3. Moore, J.M. and Cooper, D.A., The application of capillary gas chromatography-electron capture detection in the comparative analyses of illicit cocaine samples, *J. Forensic Sci.,* 38, 1286–1304, 1993.

4. Moore, J.M. and Casale, J.F., In-depth chromatographic analyses of illicit cocaine and its precursor, coca leaves, *J. Chromatogr.,* 674, 165–205, 1994.

5. Casale, J.F. and Waggoner, R.W., A chromatographic impurity signature profile analysis for cocaine using capillary gas chromatography, *J. Forensic Sci.,* 36, 1321–1330, 1991.

6. Casale, J.F. and Moore, J.M., 3´,4´,5´-Trimethoxy-substituted analogues of cocaine, *cis-/trans*-cinnamoylcocaine and tropacocaine: Characterization and quantitation of new alkaloids in coca leaf, coca paste and refined illicit cocaine, *J. Forensic Sci.,* 39, 462–472, 1994.

7. Moore, J.M., Cooper, D.A., Lurie, I.S., Kram, T.C., Carr, S., Harper, C., and Yeh, J., Capillary gas chromatographic-electron capture detection of coca leaf related impurities of illicit cocaine: 2,4-diphenylcyclobutane-1,3-dicarboxylic acids, 1,4-diphenylcyclobutane-2,3-dicarboxylic acids and their alkaloidal precursors, the truxillines, *J. Chromatogr.,* 410, 297–318, 1987.

8. Moore, J.M., Allen, A.C., and Cooper, D.A., Determination of manufacturing impurities in heroin by capillary gas chromatography with electron capture detection after derivatization with heptafluorobutyric acid, *Anal. Chem.,* 56, 642–646, 1984.

9. Moore, J.M., The application of chemical derivatization in forensic drug chemistry for gas and high performance liquid chromatographic methods of analysis, *Forensic Sci. Rev.,* 2, 79–124, 1990.

1.9 CLANDESTINE LABORATORIES

There are two kinds of clandestine laboratories. The first is the **operational** clandestine laboratory. This laboratory, usually operating in secrecy, is engaged in the production of controlled substances, precursors to controlled substances, or controlled substance homologues or analogues. The second is the **non-operational** clandestine laboratory. This usually is a storage facility that is under investigation because of information obtained from precursor and essential chemical monitoring.[1]

For the forensic scientist involved in the seizure of a clandestine laboratory, the task of evaluating the possibilities and probabilities begins prior to arrival at the laboratory site. The individual tasked with securing the laboratory for the purpose of collecting evidence must, for his own protection, be trained and certified competent in dealing with the safety and technical considerations of clandestine laboratory seizures. Forensic chemists may be asked to provide assistance in preparing search warrants based on available information, as when investigators know that certain chemicals and pieces of analytical equipment such as gas cylinders, and glassware such as large triple neck round bottom flasks have been purchased. This sort of information is critical in determining what kind of synthesis is taking place. The forensic scientist will also provide technical advice regarding the importance of specific safety considerations and offer suggestions on handling situations such as on-going reactions.

After the clandestine laboratory site has been secured by the appropriate law enforcement authorities, the forensic scientist may enter the site to evaluate the environment and decide on the most appropriate actions. The investigator's most important function is to minimize any health risk to enforcement personnel. This may involve ventilating the environment by opening doors, windows, and using a fan; securing open containers, turning off gases and water; and removing obstacles on the floor, which may prove hazardous to anyone entering the site. The investigator may also decide on whether chemical reactions in progress should be stopped or allowed to proceed. After all of these and other decisions are made and the site is secure, the forensic analyst will begin to sample, package, and mark evidence containers. This process will usually proceed slowly and methodically to ensure accuracy and completeness.

Once the clandestine laboratory has been seized and the evidence collected, the forensic analyst will proceed to the laboratory to complete the administrative processes of ensuring accountability and security. When the time approaches for the analytical procedures to commence, the person tasked with this process will attempt to identify as many of the samples as deemed necessary for the required judicial action. This may mean identifying any and all exhibits that were seized, or it may mean that only those exhibits required to form a conclusion regarding an identification of the final product are necessary. The extent of the analysis can be more of a legal question than a scientific question. The forensic scientist should be able to provide the basics of the reaction mechanisms. This information will be based on the chemicals at the site and those identified in the reaction mixtures. He should also be able to provide a theoretical yield of the final product based on the amounts of the chemical precursors.

After the work in the laboratory has been completed, the forensic scientist has the responsibility of assisting the legal authorities in understanding what was happening in the clandestine laboratory — what was being synthesized, how was it being synthesized, and what environmental ramifications existed due to the disposing of waste solvents and other chemicals found in the soil or plumbing. The forensic analyst must recognize his responsibilities as an expert witness and provide factual information in as much detail as necessary. However, this task carries with it the responsibility of avoiding unsubstantiated speculation.

Evaluating a clandestine laboratory, from the time of notification until the time of testimony in the courtroom, requires an open-minded and analytical approach. As information is gathered and data collection proceeds, the analyst may be involved in an ever-evolving decision-making process. This will probably require him to change his strategies as more information becomes available. Conclusions should be reserved until all the necessary exhibits have been collected and analyzed, the clandestine laboratory operator has been debriefed, the analytical data have been evaluated, and, if necessary, consultations with colleagues have been completed. In the courtroom, the forensic analyst will preserve his status as a credible expert witness by basing his testimony on factual data and possibilities that are within the realm of scientific probability.

1.9.1 Safety Concerns

A hazard evaluation is an absolute requirement prior to entering a clandestine laboratory. This should involve an evaluation of the physical and environmental hazards that may be present. This evaluation is usually the result of questioning other law enforcement personnel familiar with the laboratory, or the laboratory operator. Great care should be exercised in evaluating and acting on information from the laboratory operator. The forensic analyst should determine the minimum level of safety equipment required for entry into the laboratory. If there is knowledge regarding the type of drug being synthesized in the clandestine laboratory and the processing methodology, the forensic scientist will have some idea about the types of chemicals that may be encountered. If records are available regarding the purchasing activity of the clandestine laboratory operator, the quantities of the chemicals facing the investigators will be available.

All this information should be documented and used to decide the safest and most prudent manner in which to enter the clandestine laboratory. Other concerns that must be considered are the weather conditions, and entry and egress options. Extremes in either heat or cold can affect the way the safety and sampling equipment will function. These conditions will also affect how long the forensic chemist can be expected to work in the appropriate clothing. Egress options from a clandestine laboratory must be determined before entry. In the event of a fire or explosion, those individuals processing the clandestine laboratory must know how to exit the dangerous environment. As a part of the planning scenario for processing the clandestine laboratory, the appropriate authority should make the nearest medical facility aware of the fact that if an investigator is injured, medical attention will be sought. The medical facility may have some requirement for treating a chemical injury. This should be determined beforehand and a protocol to meet these requirements should be established.

The most important responsibility of the forensic analyst involved in a clandestine laboratory investigation and seizure is safety. Safety must be considered from a number of perspectives. The forensic scientist must be concerned with the safety and well-being of anyone entering the suspected clandestine laboratory. His training and experience will have prepared him to recognize many of the obvious dangers of the chemical hazards and physical hazards at the site. This awareness is not stagnant. There will usually be a condition that requires an immediate adjustment and reevaluation. He must be constantly aware of the possible hazards when the combination of two minimally unsafe conditions result in fatalities. This results from a failure to recognize that while each condition is dangerous in its own right, combining the dangers is a recipe for disaster if certain precautions are not followed.

For instance, if the odor of ether is detected in an enclosed dark room, a possible first step might be to turn on the lights. However, any short circuit in the light switch resulting in a spark could cause the ether vapors in combination with the oxygen in the air to explode. The correct action would be to obtain outside lighting equipment to determine the source of the ether vapors, rectify the conditions resulting in the ether vapors, ventilate the room, check the light switch and wiring, and then turn on the lights. This situation is one in which a chemical hazard and a physical hazard could combine and result in serious injury or death.

Before entering the clandestine laboratory, the forensic analyst must take precautions to ensure eye, lung, and skin protection. This will usually mean proper clothing including head gear, boots, outerwear, and gloves; safety glasses and/or a face shield; and the appropriate air purification and breathing apparatus. Consideration should also be given to use of air-monitoring devices, which can detect concentrations of combustible gases or vapors in the atmosphere, oxygen deficiencies, and gas concentrations to lower explosive limits. There are also devices available in the form of glass tubes filled with specific detection granules, which allow for the reasonable determination of airborne chemical hazards in the atmosphere. When these devices are used properly, the forensic scientist entering the clandestine laboratory maximizes his chances for protecting the safety of the seizure team, including himself.

Even after the atmosphere has been sampled and ventilation has progressed, once inside the clandestine laboratory, the forensic chemist should be aware of the many possibilities posing a threat. The potential chemical dangers include an explosion potential, flammable and combustible chemicals, corrosive chemicals, oxidizers, poisons, compressed gases, irritants, and booby traps. Physical hazards include but are certainly not limited to broken glass, bare electrical wiring, slippery floors, and loud noises. These chemical and physical hazards can be accentuated by a reduction in dexterity because of safety equipment and clothing, a narrow field of vision due to a breathing apparatus, diminished communications, physical and mental stress, heat or cold stress, a confined work space environment, and a prolonged period of time spent processing the clandestine laboratory.

After the laboratory processing has been completed, the forensic scientist should be a part of the team that reduces the level of environmental contamination to a controllable level. This will usually involve prior planning for the proper disposal of hazardous chemicals and protective clothing by a waste disposal authority. There should be a standard operating procedure for the decontamination of anyone who entered the clandestine laboratory. This should include provisions for an emergency shower and an eyewash station, first aid kits, and decontamination procedures for injured workers.

One of the most important factors anyone processing a clandestine laboratory must remember is the following: no matter how much protective clothing is available, no matter how much pre-planning is done, no matter how careful a person might be in collecting chemicals and assessing danger, if that person fails to recognize his or her limitations in knowledge or physical ability, a disaster is waiting to happen. The greatest danger facing anyone who processes a clandestine laboratory is a false sense of security.

1.9.2 Commonly Encountered Chemicals in the Clandestine Laboratory

The following tabulation of data is intended as an overview of those chemicals most frequently encountered as precursors in clandestine laboratory settings. A **precursor** is a chemical that becomes a part of the controlled substance either as the basis of the molecular skeleton or as a substituent of the molecular skeleton. This list is not all-inclusive. Modifications to typical synthetic routes on the parts of ingenious organic chemists are typical and cannot always be predicted.

Precursor	Controlled Substance
Acetic anhydride	Heroin
	Methaqualone
	Phenyl-2-Propanone (P2P)
Acetonitrile	Amphetamine
N-Acetylanthranilic acid	Methaqualone
	Mecloqualone
Acetylacetone	Methaqualone
4-Allyl-1,2-methylenedioxybenzene	3,4-Methylenedioxyamphetamine (MDA)
Ammonium formate	Amphetamine
	MDA
Amphetamine	alpha-Methyl fentanyl
Aniline	alpha-Methyl fentanyl
Anthranilic acid	Methaqualone
Benzaldehyde	Amphetamine
	P-2-P
Benzene	Amphetamine
	P-2-P
Benzyl cyanide	Methamphetamine
Bromobenzene	N-Ethyl-1-phenylcyclohexylamine (PCE)
	Phencyclidine (PCP)
	1-Phenylcyclohexylpyrrolidine (PCPy)
	P-2-P

Precursor	Controlled Substance
1-Bromo-2,5-dimethoxybenzene	4-Bromo-2,5-dimethoxyamphetamine (DOB)
Bromohydroquinone	DOB
5-Bromoisatin	Lysergic acid
ortho-Bromophenol	4-Bromo-2,5-dimethoxyphenethylamine (Nexus)
Bromosafrole	3,4-Methylenedioxyethylamphetamine (MDEA)
	3,4-Methylenedioxymethamphetamine (MDMA)
2-Bromothiophene	1-[1-(2-Thienyl)cyclohexyl]piperidine (TCP)
Chloroacetic acid	P-2-P
Chloroacetone	P-2-P
1-Chloro2,5-dimethoxybenzene	Nexus
2-Chloro-N,N-dimethylpropylamine	Methadone
2-Chloroethylbenzene	Fentanyl
alpha-Chloroethylmethyl ether	P-2-P
Chlorohydroquinone	DOB
Chlorosafrole	MDEA
	MDMA
ortho-Cresol	4-Methyl-2,5-dimethoxyamphetamine (STP)
Diethylamine	Diethyltryptamine
	Lysergic acid diethylamide (LSD)
Ephedrine	Methamphetamine
	Methcathinone
Ergonovine	LSD
Ergotamine	LSD
Ethylamine	Ethylamphetamine
	3,4-Methylenedioxyethylamphetamine (MDEA)
N-Ethylephedrine	N-Ethyl-N-methylamphetamine
N-Ethylpseudoephedrine	N-Ethyl-N-methylamphetamine
ortho-Ethylphenol	4-Ethyl-2,5-dimethoxyamphetamine
Formamide	Amphetamine
	MDA
Hydroxycodeinone	Oxycotin
Isosafrole	4-Methylenedioxyamphetamine (MDA)
	3,4-Methylenedioxymethamphetamine (MDMA)
	MDEA
Lysergic acid	LSD
Methylamine	Methamphetamine
	MDMA
3,4-Methylenedioxyphenyl-2-propanon	MDA
	MDMA
	MDEA
N-Methyephedrine	N,N-Dimethylamphetamine
N-Methylpseudoephedrine	N,N-Dimethylamphetamine
Nitroethane	P-2-P
	Amphetamine
	MDA
1,2-Methylenedioxy-4-propenylbenzene	MDEA
N-Methylephedrine	P-2-P
N-Methylformamide	Methamphetamine
N-Methylformanilide	STP
2-Methyl-4-[3H]-quinazolinone	Methaqualone
Methyl-3,4,5-trimethoxybenzoate	Mescaline
Norpseudoephedrine	4-Methylaminorex
Phenethylamine	Fentanyl
	para-Fluoro fentanyl
	2-Methyl fentanyl
N-(1-Phenethyl)-Piperidin-4-one	Fentanyl
	para-Fluoro fentanyl
N-(1-Phenethyl-4-piperidinyl)-aniline	Fentanyl
Phenylacetic acid	P-2-P

Precursor	Controlled Substance
Phenylacetonitrile	P-2-P
Phenylacetyl chloride	P-2-P
D-Phenylalanine	Amphetamine
	Methamphetamine
2-Phenyl-1-bromoethane	Fentanyl
1-Phenyl-2-bromopropane	alpha-Methyl fentanyl
Phenylmagnesium bromid	PCP
	PCPy
	P-2-P
Phenylpropanolamine	Amphetamine
	4-Methylaminorex
Phenyl-2-propanone (P-2-P)	Amphetamine
	Methamphetamine
Piperidin	Phencyclidine (PCP)
N-(4-Piperidinyl)aniline	Fentanyl
	alpha-Methyl fentanyl
Piperonal	MDA
	MDMA
	MDEA
Piperonylacetone	N-Hydroxy MDA
Propionic Anhydride1	Fentanyl analogues
Propiophenone	Methamphetamine
Pyrrolidine	PCPy
Pseudoephedrine	Methamphetamine
Safrole	MDA
	MDMA
	3,4-Methylenedioxy P-2-P
3,4,5-Trimethoxybenzaldehyde	Mescaline
	3,4,5-Trimethoxyamphetamine

REFERENCE

1. Frank, R.S., The clandestine laboratory situation in the United States, *J. Forensic Sci.*, 28, 18–31, 1993.

1.9.3   Tables of Controlled Substances

1.9.3.1   *Generalized List by Category of Physiological Effects and Medical Uses of Controlled Substances*

Controlled Substances — Categorized Listing of the Most Commonly Encountered Controlled Substances

Drug	CSA Schedules	Trade or Other Names	Medical Uses
		Narcotics	
Heroin	I	Diacetylmorphine, Horse, Smack	None in U.S., analgesic, antitussive
Morphine	II	Duramorph, MS-Contin, Roxanol, Oramorph SR	Analgesic
Codeine	II, III, IV	Tylenol w/Codeine, Empirin w/Codeine, Robitussin A-C, Fiorinal w/Codeine, APAP w/Codeine	Analgesic, antitussive
Hydrocodone	II, III	Tussionex, Vicodin, Dycodan, Lorcet	Analgesic, antitussive

Controlled Substances — Categorized Listing of the Most Commonly Encountered Controlled Substances *(Continued)*

Drug	CSA Schedules	Trade or Other Names	Medical Uses
Hydromorphone	II	Dilaudid	Analgesic
Oxycodone	II	Percodan, Percocet, Tylox, Roxicet, Roxidone	Analgesic
Methadone and LAAM	I, II	Dolophine, Levo-alpha-acetylmethadol, Levomethadyl acetate	Analgesic, treatment of dependence
Fentanyl and analogues	I, II	Innovar, Sublimaze, Alfenta, Sufenta, Duragesic	Analgesic, adjunct to anesthesia, anesthetic
Other narcotics	II, III, IV, V	Percocan, Percocet, Tylox, Opium, Darvon, Talwin,[a] Buprenorphine, Meperidine (Pethidine)	Analgesic, antidiarrheal
Depressants			
Chloral hydrate	IV	Noctec, Somnos, Felsules	Hypnotic
Barbiturates	II, III, IV	Amytal, Fiorinal, Membutal, Seconal, Tuinal, Penobarbital, Pentobarbital	Sedative hypnotic, veterinary euthanasia agent
Benzodiazepines	IV	Ativan, Dalmane, Diazepam, Librium, Xanax, Serax, Valium, Tranxene, Verstran, Versed, Halcion, Paxipam, Restoril	Antianxiety, sedative, anticonvulsant, hypnotic
Glutethimide	II	Doriden	Sedative, hypnotic
Other depressants	I, II, III, IV	Equanil, Miltown, Noludar, Placidyl, Valmid, Methaqualone	Antianxiety, sedative, hypnotic
Stimulants			
Cocaine[b]	II	Coke, Flake, Snow, Crack	Local anesthetic
Amphetamine/methamphetamine	II	Biphetamine, Desoxyn, Dexedrine, Obetrol, Ice	Attention-deficit disorder, narcolepsy, weight control
Methylphenidate	II	Ritalin	Attention-deficit disorder
Other stimulants	I, II, III, IV	Adipex, Didrex, Ionamin, Melfiat, Plegine, Captagon, Sanorex, Tenuate, Tepanil, Prelu-2, Preludin	Weight control
Cannabis			
Marijuana	I	Pot, Acapulco Gold, Grass, Reefer, Sinsemilla, Thai Sticks	None
Tetrahydro-cannabinol	I, II	THC, Marinol	Antinauseant
Hashish and hashish oil	I	Hash, Hash Oil	None
Hallucinogens			
LSD	I	Acid, Blotter Acid, Microdots	None
Mescaline and peyote	I	Mescal, Buttons, Cactus	None
Phenethylamines	I	2,5-DMA, STP, MDA, MDMA, Ecstasy, DOM, DOB	None
Phencyclidine and analogues	I, II	PCP, PCE, PCPy, TCP, Hog, Loveboat, Angel Dust	None
Other hallucinogens	I	Bufotenine, Ibogaine, DMT, DET, Psilocybin, Psilocin	None

Controlled Substances — Categorized Listing of the Most Commonly Encountered Controlled Substances *(Continued)*

Drug	CSA Schedules	Trade or Other Names	Medical Uses
Anabolic Steroids			
Testosterone	III	Depo-testosterone, Delatestryl (Cypionate, Enanthate)	Hypogonadism
Nandrolone	III	Nandrolone, Durabolin, Deca-Durabolin, Deca	Anemia, breast cancer
Oxymetholone	III	Anadrol-50	Anemia

[a] Not designated a narcotic under the CSA.
[b] Designated a narcotic under the CSA.

1.9.3.2 Listing of Controlled Substances by Schedule Number

Listed below are those substances specifically controlled under the Controlled Substances Act as of June 26, 2006. This list does not include all controlled steroids or controlled substance analogues. These are classes of compounds that are controlled based on chemical and pharmacological criteria that were discussed earlier in this chapter.

Schedule I Controlled Substances

Controlled Substance	Synonym(s)
1-(1-Phenylcyclohexyl)pyrrolidine	PCPy, PHP, rolicyclidine
1-[1-(2-Thienyl)cyclohexyl]piperidine	TCP, tenocyclidine
1-[1-(2-Thienyl)cyclohexyl]pyrrolidine	TCPy
1-Methyl-4-phenyl-4-propionoxypiperdine	MPPP, synthetic heroin
1-(2-Phenylethyl)-4-phenyl-4-acetoxypiperidine	PEPAP, synthetic heroin
2,5-Dimethoxyamphetamine	DMA, 2,5-DMA
2,5-Dimethoxy-4-ethylamphetamine	DOET
2,5-Dimethoxy-4-(n)-propylthiophenethylamine	2C-T-7
3,4,5-Trimethoxyamphetamine	TMA
3,4-Methylenedioxyamphetamine	MDA, Love Drug
3,4-Methylenedioxymethamphetamine	MDMA, Ecstasy, XTC
3,4-Methylenedioxy-N-ethylamphetamine	N-ethyl MDA, MDE, MDEA
3-Methylfentanyl	China White, fentanyl
3-Methylthiofentanyl	China White, fentanyl
4-Bromo-2,5-dimethoxyamphetamine	DOB, 4-bromo-DMA
4-Bromo-2,5-dimethoxyphenethylamine	Nexus, 2-CB, has been sold as Ecstasy, i.e., MDMA
4-Methoxyamphetamine	PMA
4-Methyl-2,5-dimethoxyamphetamine	DOM, STP
4-Methylaminorex (cis isomer)	U4Euh, McN-422
5-Methoxy-3,4-methylenedioxyamphetamine	MMDA
5-Methoxy-N,N-diisopropyltryptamine	5-MeO-DIPT
Acetorphine	
Acetyldihydrocodeine	Acetylcodone
Acetylmethadol	Methadyl acetate
Acetyl-alpha-methylfentanyl	
Allylprodine	
Alphacetylmethadol except levo-alphacetylmethadol	
alpha-Ethyltryptamine	ET, Trip
Alphameprodine	
Alphamethadol	
alpha-Methylfentanyl	China White, fentanyl
alpha-Methylthiofentanyl	China White, fentanyl
alpha-Methyltryptamine	AMT

Schedule I Controlled Substances *(Continued)*

Controlled Substance	Synonym(s)
Aminorex	Has been sold as methamphetamine
Benzethidine	
Benzylmorphine	
Betacetylmethadol	
Betameprodine	
Betamethadol	
Betaprodine	
beta-Hydroxyfentanyl	China White, fentanyl
beta-Hydroxy-3-methylfentanyl	China White, fentanyl
Bufotenine	Mappine, N,N-dimethylserotonin
Cathinone	Constituent of "Khat" plant
Clonitazene	
Codeine methylbromide	
Codeine-N-oxide	
Cyprenorphine	
Desomorphine	
Dextromoramide	Palfium, Jetrium, Narcolo
Diampromide	
Diethylthiambutene	
Diethyltryptamine	DET
Difenoxin	Lyspafen
Dihydromorphine	
Dimenoxadol	
Dimepheptanol	
Dimethylthiambutene	
Dimethyltryptamine	DMT
Dioxaphetyl butyrate	
Dipipanono	Dipipan, phenylpiperone HCL, Diconal, Wellconal
Drotebanol	Metebanyl, oxymethebanol
Ethylmethylthiambutene	
Etonitazene	
Etorphine (except HCL)	
Etoxeridine	
Fenethylline	Captagon, amfetyline, ethyltheophylline amphetamine
Furethidine	
Gamma hydroxybutyric acid	GHB, gamma hydroxybutyrate, sodium oxybate
Heroin	Diacetylmorphine, diamorphine
Hydromorphinol	
Hydroxpethidine	
Ibogaine	Constituent of "Tabernanthe iboga" plant
Ketobemidone	Cliradon
Levomoramide	
Levophenacylmorphan	
Lysergic acid diethylamide	LSD, lysergide
Marihuana	Cannabis, marijuana
Mecloqualone	Nubarene
Mescaline	Constituent of "Peyote" cacti
Methaqualone	Quaalude, Parest, Somnafac, Opitimil, Mandrax
Methcathinone	N-Methylcathinone, "cat"
Methyldesorphine	
Methyldihydromorphine	
Morpheridine	
Morphine methylbromide	
Morphine methylsulfonate	
Morphine-N-oxide	
Myrophine	
N-Benzylpiperazine	BZP, 1-benzylpiperazine
N-Ethyl-1-phenylcyclohexylamine	PCE

Schedule I Controlled Substances *(Continued)*

Controlled Substance	Synonym(s)
N-Ethylamphetamine	NEA
N-Ethyl-3-piperidyl benzilate	JB 323
N-Hydroxy-3,4-methylenedioxyamphetamine	N-hydroxy MDA
N-Methyl-3-piperidyl benzilate	JB 336
N,N-Dimethylamphetamine	
Nicocodeine	
Nicomorphine	Vilan
Noracymethadol	
Norlevorphanol	
Normethadone	Phenyldimazone
Normorphine	
Norpipanone	
Parahexyl	Synhexyl
para-Fluorofentanyl	China White, fentanyl
Peyote	Cactus that contains mescaline
Phenadoxone	
Phenampromide	
Phenomorphan	
Phenoperidine	Operidine, Lealgin
Pholcodine	Copholco, Adaphol, Codisol, Lantuss, Pholcolin
Piritramide	Piridolan
Proheptazine	
Properidine	
Propiram	Algeril
Psilocybin	Constituent of "Magic Mushrooms"
Psilocyn	Psilocin, constituent of "Magic Mushrooms"
Racemoramide	
Tetrahydrocannabinols	THC, Delta-8 THC, Delta-9 THC, and others
Thebacon	Acetylhydrocodone, Acedicon, Thebacetyl
Thiofentanyl	China White, fentanyl
Tilidine	Tilidate, Valoron, Kitadol, Lak, Tilsa
Trimeperidine	Promedolum

Schedule II Controlled Substances

Controlled Substance	Synonym(s)
1-Phenyleyelohexylamine	Precursor of PCP
1-Piperidinoeyelohexanecarbonitrile	PCC, precursor of PCP
Alfentanil	Alfenta
Alphaprodine	Nisentil
Amobarbital	Amytal, Tuinal
Amphetamine	Dexedrine, Adderall, Obetrol
Anilerdine	Leritine
Benzoylecgonine	Cocaine metabolite
Bezitramide	Burgodin
Carfentanil	Wildnil
Coca leaves	
Cocaine	Methyl benzoylecgonine, Crack
Codeine	Morphine methyl ester, methyl morphine
Dextropropoxyphene, bulk (non-dosage forms)	Propoxyphene
Dihydrocodeine	Didrate, Parzone
Dihydroetorphine	DHE
Diphenoxylate	
Diprenorphine	M50-50
Ecgonine	Cocaine precursor, in coca leaves
Ethylmorphine	Dionin
Etorphine HCL	M 99

Schedule II Controlled Substances *(Continued)*

Controlled Substance	Synonym(s)
Fentanyl	Duragesic, Oralet, Actiq, Sublimaze, Innovar
Glutethimide	Doriden, Dorimide
Hydrocodone	Dihydrocodeinone
Hydromorphone	Dilaudid, dihydromorphinone
Isomethadone	Isoamidone
Levo-alphacetylmethadol	LAAM, long-acting methadone, levomathadyl acetate
Levomethorphan	
Levorphanol	Levo-Dromoran
Meperidine	Demerol, Mepergan, pethidine
Meperidine intermediate-A	Meperidine precursor
Meperidine intermediate-B	Meperidine precursor
Meperidine intermediate-C	Meperidine precursor
Metazocine	
Methadone	Dolophine, Methadose, Amidone
Methadone intermediate	Methadone precursor
Methamphetamine	Desoxyn, D-desoxyephedrine, ICE, Crank, Speed
Methylphenidate	Concerta, Ritalin, Methylin
Metopon	
Moramide-intermediate	
Morphine	MS Contin, Roxanol, Oramorph, Duramorph, RMS, MSIR
Nabilone	Cesamet
Opium, granulated	Granulated opium
Opium, powdered	Powdered opium
Opium, raw	Raw opium, gum opium
Opium extracts	
Opium fluid extract	
Oplum poppy	Papaver somniferum
Opium tincture	Laudanum
Oxycodone	OxyContin, Percocet, Endocet, Roxicodone, Roxicet
Oxymorphone	Numorphan
Pentabarbital	Nembutal
Phenazocine	Narphen, Prinadol
Phencyclidine	PCP, Sernylan
Phenmetrazine	Preludin
Phenylacetone	P2P, phenyl-2-propanone, benzyl methyl ketone
Piminodine	
Poppy straw	Opium poppy capsules, poppy heads
Poppy straw concentrate	Concentrate of poppy straw, CPS
Racemethorphan	
Racemorphan	Dromoran
Remifentanil	Ultiva
Secobarbital	Seconel, Tuinal
Sufentanil	Sufenta
Thebaine	Precursor of many narcotics

Schedule III Controlled Substances

Controlled Substance	Synonym(s)
1-Androstenediol	
1-Androstenedione	
3α,17β-Dihydroxy-5α-androstane	
3β,17β-Dihydroxy-5α-androstane	
4-Androstenediol	4-AD
4-Androstenedione	
4-Dihydrotestosterone	Anabolex, Andractim, Pesomax, Stanolone
4-Hydrotestosterone	

Schedule III Controlled Substances *(Continued)*

Controlled Substance	Synonym(s)
4-Hydroxy-19-nortestosterone	
5-Androstenediol	
5-Androstenedione	
13β-Ethyl-7β-hydroxygon-4-en-3-one	
17α-Methyl-3β,17β-dihydroxy-5α-androstane	
17α-Methyl-3α,17β-dihydroxy-5α-androstane	
17α-Methyl-3α,17β-dihydroxyandrost-4-ene	
17α-Methyl-4-hydroxynandrolone	
17α-Methyl-Δ¹-dihydrotestosterone	17α-Methyl-1-testosterone
19-Nor-4-androstenediol	
19-Nor-5-androstenediol	
19-Nor-4-androstenedione	
19-Nor-5-androstenedione	
Amobarbital suppository dosage form	
Amobarbital and noncontrolled active ingredients	Amobarbital/ephedrine capsules
Anabolic steroids	"Body Building" drugs
Androstanedione	
Aprobarbital	Alurate
Barbituric acid derivative	Barbiturates not specifically listed
Benzphetamine	Didrex, Inapetyl
Boldenone	Equipoise, Parenebol, Vebonol, dehydrotestosterone
Bolasterone	
Buprenorphine	Buprenex, Temgesic, Subutex, Suboxone
Buprenorphine	Buprenex, Temgesic
Butabarbital (sec butabarbital)	Butisol, Butibel
Butalbital	Fiorinal, Butalbital with aspirin
Butobarbital (butethal)	Soneryl (UK)
Calusterone	Methosarb
Chlorhexadol	Mechloral, Mecoral, Medodorm, Chloralodol
Chlorotestosterone (same as clostebol)	If 4-chlorotestosterone then clostebol
Chlorphentermine	Pre-Sate, Lucofen, Apsedon, Desopimon
Clortermine	Voranil
Clostebol	alpha-Trofodermin, Clostene, 4-chlorotestosterone
Codeine combination product 90 mg/du	Emprin, Fiorinal, Tylenol, ASA or APAP w/codeine
Codeine and isoquinoline alkaloid 90 mg/du	Codeine with papaverine or noscapine
Dehydrochlormethyltestotsterone	Oral-Turinabol
Dihydrocodeine combination product 90 mg/du	Synalgos-DC, Compal
Delta1-dihydrotestosterone	1-Testosterone
Dronabinol in sesame oil in soft gelatin capsule	Marinol, synthetic THC in sesame oil/soft gelatin
Dihydrotestosterone (same as stanolone)	See stanolone
Drostanolone	Drolban, Masterid, Permastril
Ethylestrenol	Maxibolin, Orabolin, Durabolin-O, Duraboral
Ethylmorphine combination product 15 mg/du	
Formebolone	Esiclene, Hubernol
Furazabol	Frazalon, Miotolon, Qu Zhi Shu
Gamma Hydroxybutyric Acid preparations	Zyrem
Fluoxymesterone	Anadroid-F, Halotestin, Ora-Testryl
Hydrocodone combination product <15 mg/du	Lorcet, Lortab, Vicodin, Vicoprofen, Tussionex, Norco
Hydrocodone and isoquinoline alkaloid <15 mg/du	Dihydrocodeinone + papaverine or noscapine
Ketamine	Ketaset, Ketalar, Special K, K
Lysergic acid	LSD precursor
Lysergic acid amide	LSD precursor
Mesterolone	Androviron, Proviron, Testiwop
Mestanolone	Assimil, Ermalone, Methylbol, Tanterone
Methandienone	Dianabol, Metabolina, Nerobol, Perbolin
Methandriol	Sinesex, Stenediol, Troformone

Schedule III Controlled Substances *(Continued)*

Controlled Substance	Synonym(s)
Methenolone	Primobolan, Primobolan Depot, Primobolan S
Methyldienolone	
Methyltestosterone	Android, Oreton, Testred, Virilon
Methyltrienolone	Metribolone
Methyprylon	Noludar
Mibolerone	Cheque, Matenon
Morphine combination product/ 50 mg/100 ml or g	
Nalorphine	Nalline
Nandrolone	Deca-Durabolin, Durabolin, Durabolin-50
Norbolethone	Genabol
Norclostebol	Anabol-4-19, Lentabol
Norethandrolone	Nilavar, Pronabol, Solevar
Opium combination product 25 mg/du	Paregoric, other combination products
Oxandrolone	Anavar, Lonavar, Provitar, Vasorome
Oxymesterone	Anamidol, Balnimax, Oranabol, Oranabol 10
Oxymetholone	Anadrol-50, Adroyd, Anapolon, Anasteron, Pardroyd
Pentobarbital suppository dosage form	WANS
Pentobarbital and noncontrolled active ingredients	FP-3
Phendimetrazine	Plegine, Prelu-2, Bontril, Melfiat, Statobex
Secobarbital suppository dosage form	Various
Secobarbital and noncontrolled active ingredients	Various
Stanozolol	Winstrol, Winstrol-V
Stenbolone	
Stimulant compounds previously excepted	Mediatric
Sulfondiethylmethane	
Sulfonethylmethane	
Sulfonmethane	
Talbutal	Lotusate
Tetrahydrogestrinone	THG
Testolactone	Teolit, Teslac
Testosterone	Android-T, Adrolan, Depotest, Dalatestryl
Thiamylal	Surital
Thiopental	Pentothal
Tiletamine and zolazepam combination product	Telazol
Trenbolone	Finaplix-S, Finajet, Parabolan
Vinbarbital	Delvinal, Vinbarbitone

Schedule IV Controlled Substances

Controlled Substance	Synonyms
Alprazolam	Xanax
Barbital	Veronal, Plexonal, barbitone
Bromazepam	Lexotan, Lexatin, Lexotanil
Camazepam	Albego, Limpidon, Paxor
Cathine	Constituent of "Khat" plant, (+)-norpseudoephedrine
Chloral betaine	Beta Chlor
Chloral hydrate	Noctac
Chlordiazepoxide	Librium, Libritabs, Lombitrol, SK-Lygen
Clobazam	Urbadan, Urbanyl
Clonazepam	Klonopin, Clonopin
Clorazepate	Tranxene
Clotiazepam	Trecalmo, Rize, Clozan, Veratran
Cloxazolam	Akton, Lubalix, Olcadil, Sepazon
Delorazepam	
Dexfenfluramine	Redux
Dextropropoxyphene dosage forms	Darvon, propoxyphene, Darvocet, Propacet

Controlled Substance	Synonyms
Diazepam	Valium, Diastat
Dichloralphenazone	Midrin, dichloralantipyrine
Diethylpropion	Tenuate, Tepanil
Difenoxin 1 mg/25 µg AtSO4/du	Motofen
Estazolam	ProSom, Domnamid, Eurodin, Nuctalon
Ethchlorvynol	Placidyl
Ethinamate	Valmid, Valamin
Ethyl loflazepate	
Fencamfamin	Reactivan
Fenfluramine	Pondimin, Ponderal
Fenproporex	Gacilin, Solvolip
Fludiazepam	
Flunitrazepam	Rohypnol, Narcozep, Darkene, Roipnol
Flurazepam	Dalmane
Halazepam	Paxipam
Haloxazolam	
Ketazolam	Anxon, Loftran, Solatran, Contamex
Loprazolam	
Lorazepam	Ativan
Lormetazepam	Noctamid
Mazindol	Sanorex, Mazanor
Mebutamate	Capla
Medazepam	Nobrium
Mefenorex	Anorexic, Amexate, Doracil, Pondinil
Meprobamate	Miltown, Equanil, Deprol, Equagesic, Meprospan
Methohexital	Brevital
Methylphenobarbital (mephobarbital)	Mebaral, mephobarbital
Midazolam	Versed
Modafinil	Provigil
Nimetazepam	Erimin
Nitrazepam	Mogadon
Nordiazepam	Nordazepam, Demadar, Madar
Oxazepam	Serax, Serenid-D
Oxazolam	Serenal, Convertal
Paraldehyde	Paral
Pemoline	Cylert
Pentazocine	Talwin, Talwin NX, Talacen, Talwin Compound
Petrichloral	Pentaerythritol chloral, Periclor
Phenobarbital	Luminal, Donnatal, Bellergal-S
Phentermine	Ionamin, Fastin, Adipex-P, Obe-Nix, Zantryl
Pinazepam	Domar
Pipradrol	Detaril, Stimolag Fortis
Prazepam	Centrax
Quazepam	Doral
Sibutramine	Meridia
SPA	1-Dimethylamino-1,2-diphenylethane, Lefetamine
Temazepam	Restoril
Tetrazepam	Myolastan, Musaril
Triazolam	Halcion
Zaleplon	Sonata
Zopiclone	Lunesta
Zolpidem	Ambien, Ivadal, Stilnoct, Stilnox

Schedule V Controlled Substances

Controlled Substance	Synonyms
Codeine preparations — 200 mg/100 ml or 100 g	Cosanyl, Robitussin A-C, Cheracol, Cerose, Pediacof
Difenoxin preparations — 0.5 mg/25 µg AtSO4/du	Motofen
Dihydrocodeine preparations — 10 mg/200 ml or 100 g	Cophene-S, various others
Diphenoxylate preparations — 2.5 mg/25 µg AtSO4	Lomotil, Logen
Ethylmorphine preparations — 100 mg/100 ml or 100 g	
Opium preparations — 100 mg/100 ml or 100 g	Parepectolin, Kapectolin PG, Kaolin, Pectin P.G.
Pregabalin	Lyrica
Pyrovalerone	Centroton, Thymergix

The author gratefully acknowledges the assistance of Dr. Judy Lawrence, Pharmacologist, DEA Office of Diversion Control, for providing information utilized in compiling this listing of controlled substances.

CHAPTER **2**

Pathology of Drug Abuse

Edited by Charles V. Wetli, M.D.
Chief Medical Examiner, Office of the Suffolk County Medical Examiner, Hauppauge, New York

CONTENTS

INTRODUCTION

In a very broad sense, the pathology of drug abuse is determined by the particular drug abused, and the way it is used and administered, not to mention its toxic effects and the behavioral modifications it produces. A comprehensive overview of drug abuse pathology would, therefore, include physical injuries from drunk driving and hallucinogenic drugs, a variety of communicable diseases such as viral hepatitis and AIDS acquired from needle sharing, and indirect complications of addiction, such as homicide, prostitution, child abuse and neglect. However, this section is devoted to the pathological changes resulting from the pharmacologic effects of various drugs that are abused, and from the ways that these drugs are administered. In short, we review the changes one would likely encounter at the autopsy table.

A large volume of literature on drug abuse and the pathologic changes it produces has been amassed over the past three or four decades. Much of this material has recently been collected into several excellent comprehensive treatises.[1,2] Instead of repeating these accomplishments, this chapter focuses on issues of pathology not adequately covered in other references, and concentrates on emerging concepts and newly discovered phenomena. Accordingly, emphasis is placed on death scene investigation, evaluation of the drug abuse victim (living or deceased), and cardiovascular pathology. In many instances, the authors have relied on their own academic and investigative experiences to provide a practical approach to evaluating these victims of drug abuse.

Much of what is known about the pathology of drug abuse has been derived from thorough and carefully performed autopsies. It should therefore be expected that much of this section deals with the autopsy and will be of particular interest to pathologists. However, far from this being an academic exercise, it is hoped that the reader will discern applications to clinical situations. This, in fact, has been accomplished over the years as clinicians have come to better appreciate the pathophysiology of diseases resulting from drug abuse. What is lacking currently, however, is the proper toxicologic evaluation of the drug abuse victim at the time of admission to a hospital. Except for ethanol, reliance is too often made on a urine drug screen. Blood specimens for toxicologic testing, if obtained at all, are too often quantitatively insufficient or qualitatively inadequate due to lack of proper preservation. Should death occur, for whatever reason, days or weeks later, it is often impossible to adequately evaluate the victim toxicologically. In such cases hair testing may prove to be of some value. In many instances (e.g., delayed deaths from cocaine-induced psychosis) this lack of concrete data leads to deleterious speculation about who may be responsible for the death (e.g., police action or inaction) and this void in knowledge may form the nidus of lawsuits. Conversely, adequate analysis undertaken at the beginning may readily eliminate much needless speculation, and absolve or implicate culpability on the part of others.

Although such evaluations are ideal, the goal is not likely to be met in the immediate future with an environment of cost containment and a medical focus that best describes a patient as a problem of "here and now." This leaves little consideration for events or questions that may arise in the future regarding adequacy of patient care, or subsequent questions posed by future investigators, including medical examiners, police, and attorneys.[3]

REFERENCES

1. Karch, S.B., *The Pathology of Drug Abuse,* 3rd ed., CRC Press, Boca Raton, FL, 2001.
2. Lowinson, J.H., Ruiz, P., and Millman, R.B. (Eds.) and Lancrod, J.G. (Assoc. Ed.), *Substance Abuse — A Comprehensive Textbook,* Williams & Wilkins, Baltimore, 1992.
3. Wetli, C.V., Forensic issues, in *The Textbook of Penetrating Trauma,* Ivatury, R.R. and Cayten, C.G., Eds., Williams & Wilkins, Media, PA, 1996, chap. 85, pp. 1084–1097.

2.1 THE SCENE OF DEATH AND THE AUTOPSY

Charles V. Wetli, M.D.
Chief Medical Examiner, Office of the Suffolk County Medical Examiner, Hauppauge, New York

Paramount to any investigation, evaluation, or inquiry is the knowledge of terminal events, and pre-terminal characteristics of the victim. In most hospital deaths, the medical record readily provides this. In the world of forensic pathology, such history is often lacking, and reliance must be placed on an open mind with a conscious realization that drug abuse may have had a significant contribution to a person's death regardless of initial impressions: Infectious diseases such as hepatitis or endocarditis may be the result of intravenous drug abuse; cocaine may trigger convulsions or precipitate hypertensive crises and myocardial ischemia; central nervous system (CNS) depressants may lead to positional asphyxia, etc. And there must also be awareness that people with natural disease may, intentionally or not, abuse drugs, which may exacerbate their underlying disease process and significantly contribute to their death. Drugs create pathological states, with or without death, by their immediate pharmacologic effects, the way in which the drug is taken, by the cumulative effects of chronic abuse, and by interaction with pre-existing pathologic conditions.[1,2] Therefore, what once could have been discussed as a complication of hypertension (e.g., spontaneous aortic dissection) must now be evaluated as a possible effect of acute and chronic cocaine abuse.[3,4]

As noted in the prologue, every death scene must be approached with a conscious effort to evaluate the role of drugs and alcohol regardless of the apparent cause or manner of death. The scene investigator must therefore be ever cognizant of two possibilities: (1) Because a person has

Figure 2.1.1 Packets of drugs.

a disease it does not necessarily mean it is the cause of death, and (2) the scene of a drug overdose is frequently cleaned before investigators are even called. Consequently, it is important to evaluate all medication containers at the death scene, noting the identity of the drug and its purpose, the instructions for usage, and the number remaining. Such a preliminary inventory (followed later by a more complete inventory and drug confirmation) often leads to a suspicion of drug overdose. However, since others may well have previously tampered with the scene, a search should be made for containers that may be concealed: wastebaskets, beneath the bed, in a purse, etc. All medication and medication containers should be confiscated for a more complete inventory and possible toxicologic evaluation.[2] Likewise, all drug paraphernalia must be removed from the premises. Recognizing such paraphernalia requires that the investigator be aware of what illicit drugs prevail in a particular community and how they are used. Thus, a small spoon attached to the cap of a small vial, a gold-plated razor with a mirror, and a soda can with holes punched in the sides are all paraphernalia of cocaine abuse. Packets of drugs (often with a crude logo; Figure 2.1.1) and used syringes are particularly important because these items may be the only way to determine the type of drug being abused, its purity, and its excipients. This is especially true for "designer drugs," which may be many thousand times more potent than heroin and therefore difficult to detect on routine toxicologic analysis of biological specimens.

Besides actual drug containers and paraphernalia, observations should be made that might reflect orientation toward a drug subculture: certain tattoos, evidence of gang affiliation (clothes, hair style, etc.), magazines, posters of drug-oriented music groups, etc. Periodicals and books of right-to-die organizations such as the Hemlock Society and its members should suggest the possibility of suicide or assisted suicide. This literature provides specific instructions about using drugs and plastic bags to commit suicide, and gives suggestions about avoiding (or cooperating) with a medical examiner investigation.[5,6]

Following scrutiny of the environment, attention should turn to the victim. Of particular importance is to ascertain the exact position of the body when it was found[2] to establish the possibility of postural or positional asphyxia.[7] This is a situation where a person collapses in a position such that the airway (nose, mouth) is partially or completely obstructed. Because of the anesthetic effect of the drugs (with or without alcohol), the victim does not move to create an unobstructed airway, and death results from mechanical asphyxia. If the airway obstruction is partial, it may take some hours for death to actually occur from respiratory acidosis and carbon dioxide retention. During this time, the drugs and alcohol continue to be metabolized and eliminated in urine, sweat, or breath. Toxicologic analysis will then reveal a low level of drugs and, if the likelihood of positional asphyxia cannot be established, the cause of death may be a conundrum. At the scene of death it is important to interview the person who first discovered the body and ask specific questions to ascertain whether the airway could have been obstructed.

Examination of the victim at the scene should include a careful inspection of the hands and mouth for drug residue or pills, palpation for hyperthermia (or, better, a direct measurement with a plastic indicator strip or rectal thermometer), which could suggest death from a stimulant drug; tattoos, which could suggest a drug culture; and fine parallel scars of the wrists or neck suggestive of a prior suicide attempt. A nearby plastic bag, particularly in the death of an elderly person with a chronic disease, suggests a death from the combination of asphyxia and drug overdose to terminate prolonged suffering (a method advocated by right-to-die organizations).

A fairly common mistake of some scene investigators is failure to turn the body over (which may reveal previously hidden drugs or drug paraphernalia) and failure to adequately examine the clothing. Pockets must be turned out or cut open, and underwear searched since they may contain packets or residue of drugs. Two death scenes have sufficient characteristics to suggest specific syndromes of cocaine abuse: cocaine-induced excited delirium, and the cocaine body packer.

2.1.1 Excited Delirium

Excited delirium is a medical emergency with a psychiatric presentation.[8] The etiology may be infectious or pharmacologic and today it is most often seen with the abuse of cocaine or amphetamines. A similar syndrome of acute exhaustive mania may be seen with psychiatric patients or schizophrenics who have been treated with neuroleptic medication and who have recently stopped taking their medication. Today, the term agitated or excited delirium is used for the same syndrome regardless of etiology (i.e., infectious, toxic, pharmacologic, or psychiatric. Clinical and neuropharmacologic studies have linked the neuroleptic malignant syndrome and drug-induced excited delirium to disturbances of dopamine release and transport in the striatum of the CNS.[9] The syndrome is characterized by bizarre and violent behavior, hyperthermia, and tremendous, unexpected, strength. It usually takes several people to restrain the victim who is otherwise likely to injure himself or herself or others. Shortly after being restrained, the victim suddenly collapses and dies, often in police custody. If cardiopulmonary resuscitation (CPR) is successful, there is still a potential for death in a few days from myoglobinuric nephrosis secondary to massive rhabdomyolysis.[10,11] The violence is often associated with extensive property damage, inappropriate disrobing, and varying injuries incurred from smashing glass or the struggle with law enforcement personnel. The injuries may, of themselves, be lethal and hence require careful evaluation and documentation. With cocaine-induced excited delirium, blood and brain concentrations of cocaine are typically quite low whereas concentrations of benzoylecgonine are relatively high.[12,13] The "typical" scenario is most often that of a male who has been in a violent struggle, who may be naked and with usually minor injuries sustained in a struggle with police. The most common injuries are those involving the ankles or wrists from fighting against handcuffs or hobble restraints. Scalp and neck injuries may also be seen, and require careful evaluation to exclude a traumatic death. Body temperatures of 104°F or more are common, and there is usually evidence of extensive property damage, especially smashed glass.

The exact mechanism of death in excited delirium has yet to be elucidated.[14,15] The sudden loss of vital signs with asystole or bradycardic pulse-less electrical activity strongly suggests a cardiac mechanism of death, which is also frequently accompanied by an underlying abnormality of the heart (e.g., hypertensive type cardiomegaly) and profound lactic acidosis with a pH of 7.0 or less. Since death often occurs shortly after a violent struggle with the police, there are often allegations that law enforcement tactics generally regarded as a sublethal use of force actually caused or contributed to the death. Most often such allegations allege death resulted from so-called restraint or positional asphyxia, the use of pepper spray or mace, the use of electric stun guns, or the misapplication of a law enforcement neck hold.[16]

2.1.2 Body Packers

Body packers are individuals who swallow packets of drugs in one country and transport them to another, and subsequently retrieve the packets by the use of laxatives.[17] Occasionally, larger packets may be inserted in the vagina or rectum. The most popular drug smuggled by this method into the United States in the past two decades has been cocaine. More recently, a number of heroin body packers have been reported.[18] The amount smuggled may total nearly a kilogram of the drug. Death may occur from a pharmacologic overdose if a drug packet breaks or leaks, or if water should cross a semipermeable membrane (e.g., a condom used as a drug packet) and allow the drug to dialyze into the gastrointestinal lumen to be absorbed rapidly into the blood. Intestinal obstruction is another potentially fatal complication. Cocaine body packers may collapse or have fatal grand mal seizures aboard an airplane or in the airport, or may be found dead in a hotel room. Evidence in the hotel room death scene usually consists of passports, foreign currency, or airplane tickets indicating recent arrival from a drug-supplying country (e.g., Colombia), hyperthermia (high body temperature, wet towels, or other evidence suggesting attempts at cooling), seizure activity (usually bite marks of the lower lip or tongue), presence of laxatives or enemas and, sometimes, drug packets hidden in a closet or suitcase. Heroin body packers do not have evidence of hyper-thermia or of seizure activity, but often have a massive amount of white frothy pulmonary edema fluid about the nose and mouth. Also, the bodies of heroin body packers are more likely to be dumped alongside a roadway, and accomplices may have attempted to remove the packets via a crude post-mortem laparotomy.[15]

Drug packets have been fashioned from balloons, condoms, and other materials. Most com-monly, however, the drug is compressed into a cylinder about 1/2 in. in diameter and 1 in. long, wrapped in plastic and heat-sealed, and wrapped again in several layers of latex (e.g., fingers of latex gloves). The ends are tied and sometimes the packet is dipped in wax. The drug packets are visible radiographically, and they may be accentuated by a halo of radiolucency as gas seeps between the layers of wrapping material.[19]

2.1.3 The Autopsy

External examination in cases of oral drug abuse (i.e., pills or liquid medications) is generally not rewarding unless actual medication or medication residue is observed in the mouth or on the hands. However, as noted earlier, multiple parallel scars on the wrists or neck suggest prior suicide attempts and a subsequent suicidal drug overdose. Bite marks (contusions and lacerations) of the tongue and lower lip should be specifically sought since these frequently accompany terminal convulsions, which may be the result of cocaine or tricyclic antidepressant toxicity.

The prevalence of cocaine requires careful inspection of the nasal septum (preferably with a nasal speculum) to detect inflammation, necrosis, or perforation (Figure 2.1.2) from the chronic nasal insufflation (snorting) of cocaine hydrochloride. Also, it should be noted that crystals of cocaine might occasionally be observed in the nasal hairs or attached to the bristles of a mustache.

Stigmata of intravenous drug abuse are, naturally, the identification of fresh, recent, and old injection sites (Figure 2.1.3). Sometimes these may not be evident if the user makes a conscious attempt to conceal such marks by using very small gauge needles, rotating injection sites, and by injecting in areas normally concealed even by warm weather clothing. This is especially likely to occur among those in the health professions or in occupations where inspections are frequent (e.g., police, military personnel). These abusers may inject into the ankle or foot, beneath a watchband, in the auxiliary region, or even directly through the abdominal wall and into the peritoneal cavity. If the suspicion is high, "blind" incisions into these areas as well as more likely areas (e.g., antecubital fossae) may reveal extravasated blood in the subcutaneous tissue and around a vein, which is typical for a fresh or recent injection (Figure 2.1.4). Mostly, however, fresh and recent injection sites appear as small subcutaneous ecchymoses surrounding a cutaneous puncture. With

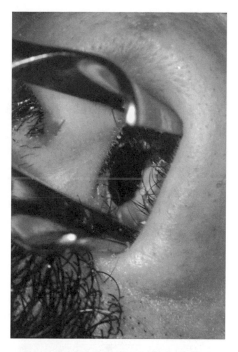

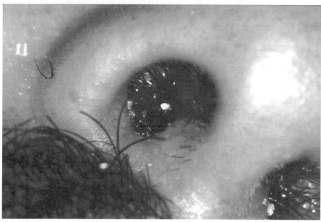

Figure 2.1.2 Inspection of the nasal septum.

cocaine, the needle puncture may be surrounded by a clear halo, which in turn is surrounded by an extensive ecchymoses; recent injection sites appear as poorly demarcated ecchymoses. Intravenous cocaine users may have little or no perivenous scarring even after years of intravenous injections.[4]

Repeated intravenous injections of narcotics generally leave characteristic hyperpigmented or hypopigmented zones of perivenous scarring commonly referred to as "tracks." These arise because narcotic addicts frequently mix heroin with oral medication containing starch or talc fillers.[1] These act like myriad microscopic splinters to elicit inflammatory (particularly granulomatous) reactions, which eventually form scar tissue. This process, plus venous thrombosis, may eventually occlude the vein. Externally, these tracks appear as irregular subcutaneous "ropes" that follow the veins of the hands and forearms.

Round atrophic scars clustered predominantly on the arms and legs are frequently seen in intravenous drug abusers,[4] particularly cocaine abusers. These may represent healed abscesses or healed ischemic ulcers due to the vasoconstrictive effect of cocaine (which is also directly toxic to

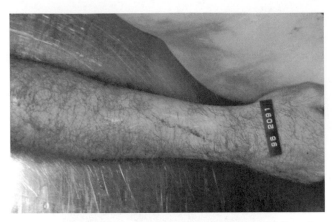

Figure 2.1.3 Stigmata of intravenous drug abuse are the identification of injection sites.

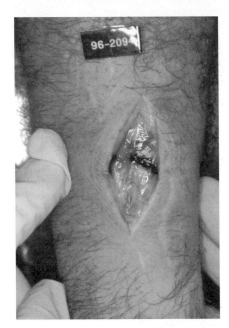

Figure 2.1.4 "Blind" incision reveals extravasated blood in the subcutaneous tissue and around a vein. This is typical for a fresh or recent injection.

capillary endothelium). More rarely encountered are dramatic instances of necrotizing fasciitis (Figure 2.1.5), which may involve an entire extremity and be accompanied by a severe lymphedema, multiple surrounding ovoid scars, and cellulitis. In extreme cases, auto-amputation of the extremity may occur. The etiology of the fasciitis and the lymphedema is unknown.

Internally, some drugs (e.g., alcohol, ethchlorvynol) may impart a characteristic odor, and some medications contain dyes that may impart a red, green, or blue discoloration to the gastrointestinal tract. *In situ* changes typical of intravenous narcotic abuse include hepatosplenomegaly, enlargement of lymph nodes about the celiac axis and/or porta hepatis, and fecal impaction (from the pharmacologic property of opiates that inhibits intestinal motility).

Toxicologic analysis requires specimens be obtained for drug screening, confirmation, and quantitation as well as tissue distribution and evaluation of drug metabolites. Thus, samples for alcohol determination should be obtained from peripheral blood (e.g., femoral vein), vitreous fluid, and central blood (e.g., aorta or pulmonary trunk); brain alcohol determinations are often useful as well. Urine is ideal for qualitative drug screening. Drugs such as tricyclic antidepressants and

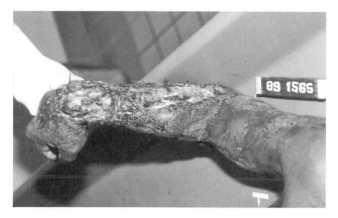

Figure 2.1.5 Necrotizing fasciitis.

propoxyphene are best evaluated by analyzing liver for concentrations of the parent drug and its major metabolites. This is also important for drugs that give spuriously elevated levels in post-mortem blood because of leaching from tissue (tricyclic antidepressants and digitalis are particularly well known to leach from tissues and cause spurious increases in post-mortem blood samples). Other drugs, such as cocaine, not only readily hydrolyze in the post-mortem state but may leach from tissues as well, rendering interpretation of post-mortem drug concentrations in blood even more difficult. For cocaine, brain is the best substance for toxicologic analysis. For routine toxicologic evaluation, samples from the following sites are recommended: peripheral (femoral) blood, blood from aorta and pulmonary trunk, vitreous fluid, bile, liver, brain, and gastric content. In addition, one sample of blood should be centrifuged for post-mortem serum (preserved by freezing) and one preserved with sodium fluoride and refrigerated for long-term storage. Injection sites, the contents of the entire small intestine, hair, and other samples should be obtained as the case dictates.

In recent years, the concept of "post-mortem re-distribution of drugs" has emerged. This is based on the realization that many drugs may have slight or moderate elevations in the post-mortem state, and that the interpretation of post-mortem drug levels does not always correlate with ante-mortem levels. Consequently, popular references now include the post-mortem re-distribution ratio to allow for a more accurate interpretation of post-mortem drug levels.[18]

Finally, as a cautionary note, it should be realized that the gastric mucosa is an excretory organ. As such, water-soluble drugs will pass from the blood into gastric juices and therefore be detected in analysis of gastric contents, usually in very low or trace quantities. Therefore, trace amounts of drugs in the gastric content do not imply oral ingestion of the drug. Likewise, very low levels of alcohol in the gastric content do not imply recent ingestion. In evaluating drugs in gastric content, be sure to calculate the absolute amount of the drug present since most laboratories will report out the concentration of the drug, not the total amount present. Thus, 1 mg/L of drug in 50-mL total gastric content calculates to a total drug content of 0.05 mg.

REFERENCES

1. Wetli, C.V., in *Illicit Drug Abuse in Pathology of Environmental and Occupational Disease,* Craighead, J.D., Ed., Mosby-Year Book, St. Louis, chap. 15, 259–268, 1995.
2. Wetli, C.V., Investigation of drug-related deaths — An overview, *Am. J. Forensic Med. Pathol.,* 5:111–120, 1984.
3. Mittleman, R.E. and Wetli, C.V., Cocaine and apparent "natural death," *J. Forensic Sci.,* 32, 11–19, 1987.
4. Mittleman, R.E. and Wetli, C.V., The pathology of cocaine abuse, *Adv. Pathol. Lab. Med.,* 4, 37–73, 1991.

5. Humphry, D., *Final Exit*, The Hemlock Society, Eugene, OR, 1991.
6. Haddix, T.L., Harruff, R.C., Reay, D.T., and Haglund, W.D., Asphyxial suicides, *Am. J. Forensic Pathol.*, 17, 308–311, 1996.
7. Bell, M.D., Rao, V.J., Wetli, C.V., and Rodriguez, R.N., Positional asphyxiation in adults — a series of 30 cases from the Dade and Broward County Florida Medical Examiner Offices from 1982 to 1990, *Am. J. Forensic Med. Pathol.*, 13(2), 101–107, 1992.
8. Wetli, C.V. and Fishbain, D.A., Cocaine-induced psychosis and sudden death in recreational cocaine users, *J. Forensic Sci.*, 30, 873–880, 1985.
9. Wetli, C.V., Mash, D., and Karch, S.B., Cocaine-associated agitated delirium and the neuroleptic malignant syndrome, *Am. J. Emerg. Med.*, 14, 425–428, 1996.
10. Mittleman, R.E., Rhabdomyolysis associated with cocaine and ethanol abuse, *Am. Soc. Clin. Pathol.*, 37, 95–104, 1995.
11. Roth, D., Alarcon, F.J., Fernandez, J.A. et al., Acute rhabdomyolysis associated with cocaine intoxication, *N. Engl. J. Med.*, 319, 673–677, 1988.
12. Raval, M.P. and Wetli, C.V., Sudden death from cocaine induced excited delirium: an analysis of 45 cases (abstract), *Am. J. Clin. Pathol.*, 104(3), 329, 1995.
13. Ruttenber, A.J., Lawler-Hernandez, J., Yin, M., et al., Fatal excited delirium following cocaine use: epidemiologic findings provide new evidence for mechanism of cocaine toxicity, *J. Forensic Sci.*, 42, 25–31, 1997.
14. Wetli, C.V., Excited delirium, in *Encyclopedia of Forensic and Legal Medicine*, Vol. 2, Payne-James, J. et al., Eds., Elsevier, Glasgow, 2005, 276–281.
15. Wetli, C.V., in *Excited Delirium in Death in Police Custody*, Ross, D. and Chan, T., Eds., Humana, Totowa, NJ, 2005.
16. Wetli, C.V., Death in custody, United States of America, in *Encyclopedia of Forensic and Legal Medicine*, Vol. 2, Payne-James, J. et al., Eds., Elsevier, Glasgow, 2005, 65–73.
17. Wetli, C.V. and Mittleman, R.E., The body packer syndrome — toxicity following ingestion of illicit drugs packaged for transportation, *J. Forensic Sci.*, 26, 492–500, 1981.
18. Wetli, C.V., Rao, A., and Rao, V.J., Fatal heroin body packing, *Am. J. Forensic Med. Pathol.*, 18(3), 312–318, 1997.
19. Beerman, R., Nunez, D., and Wetli, C.V., Radiographic evaluation of the cocaine smuggler, *Gastrointest. Radiol.*, 11, 3512–3540, 1986.

2.2 HEART DISEASE

2.2.1 Techniques for Examination of the Heart*

Renu Virmani, M.D., F.A.C.C.,[1] Allen P. Burke, M.D.,[2] and Andrew Farb, M.D.[3]
[1] Medical Director, CVPath, International Registry of Pathology, Gaithersburg, Maryland
[2] Kernan Hospital Pathology Laboratory, University of Maryland Medical Center, Baltimore, Maryland
[3] U.S. Food and Drug Administration, Rockville, Maryland

The forensic pathologist must examine the heart carefully and methodically in order to obtain maximal information to establish the cause of death. In establishing the manner of death, exclusion of non-cardiac causes is as important as establishing an arrhythmogenic cardiac substrate, because many natural deaths are due to chronic heart diseases that lower the threshold for ventricular

---

* Reproduced in part and modified from Virmani, R., Ursell, P.C., and Fenoglio, J.J., Jr., Examination of the heart, *Human Pathology*, 18, 432, 1987, and Virmani, R., Ursell, P.C., and Fenoglio, J.J., Jr., Examination of the heart, in *Cardiovascular Pathology*, Virmani, R., Atkinson, J.B., and Fenoglio, J.J., Jr., Eds., W.B. Saunders, Philadelphia, 1991, pp. 1–20.

The opinions or assertions contained herein are the private views of the authors and are not to be construed as official or as reflecting the views of the Department of the Army or Navy or the Department of Defense.

fibrillation, without an acute finding. However, it is becoming more important to pinpoint the cause of natural deaths, for genetic counseling of surviving relatives, for instances of civil litigation, and in occasional deaths where the distinction between natural and accidental death may be difficult.

There is no one "correct" method of examining the heart. In cases of sudden unexpected death in adults, an approach should be utilized that evaluates a large portion of the ventricular myocardium, the site of the vast majority of lethal tachyarrhythmias, and that thoroughly inspects the coronary arteries, the most common site of the cause of ischemic ventricular lesions. In addition, preservation of basic anatomy, in case of further review when the heart can be retained, should be a goal in potentially difficult cases. Last, preservation of frozen tissue or blood in unexplained arrhythmic deaths in young people should be considered.

The preferred method of examination of the heart combines opening of each of the four chambers according to the direction of the flow of blood with bread loafing the myocardium.[1,2] After inspecting the heart *in situ* for pericardial disease, pericardial fluid, saddle emboli, intraventricular air, and relationships to surrounding structures, the heart is removed. The epicardial surfaces and origins of the great arteries are inspected. The coronary arteries are sectioned serially, and the valves inspected from above. The heart is bread-loafed from the apex to the papillary muscles, without cutting the atrioventricular valves, allowing measurements of ventricular free walls, assessment of ventricular dilatation, and characterization of scars and necrosis, facilitating diagnosis of ischemic heart disease and cardiomyopathies. Then, the base of the heart is opened by direction of flow of blood. Briefly, the right atrium is opened from the inferior vena cava to the tip of the atrial appendage; the right ventricle is opened along its lateral border through the tricuspid valve and annulus to the apex of the right ventricle with extension to the pulmonary outflow tract close to the ventricular septum. The left atrium is opened by cutting across the roof of the atrium between the left and right pulmonary veins, and the left ventricle is opened laterally between the anterior and posterior papillary muscles to the apex and then cut along the anterior wall adjacent to the ventricular septum through the aortic outflow tract.

2.2.1.1 Removal of the Heart

The examination of the adult heart begins after the anterior chest plate has been removed. A longitudinal cut through the anterior aspect of the pericardial sac is made. The amount of pericardial fluid is measured, and its character is noted. The surface of the visceral as well as parietal pericardium is also examined for exudates, adhesions, tumor nodules, or other lesions. A short longitudinal incision 2 cm above the pulmonary valve will enable a check for thromboemboli in the main pulmonary trunk *in situ*. The heart is removed by cutting the inferior vena cava just above the diaphragm and lifting the heart by the apex, reflecting it anteriorly and cephalad to facilitate exposure of the pulmonary veins at their pericardial reflection. After it is confirmed that the pulmonary veins enter normally into the left atrium, the pulmonary veins are cut. The aorta and the pulmonary trunk, the last remaining connections, are cut transversely 2 cm above the semilunar valves. Following removal of the heart from the pericardial cavity and before weighing the specimen, post-mortem blood clots should be removed manually and gently by flushing the heart with water from the left and right atria.

2.2.1.2 Examination of Coronary Arteries

For research in coronary atherosclerosis, the ideal method of examining the coronary arterial tree requires injecting the coronary arteries with a barium-gelatin mixture and studying the vessels in radiographs.[3,4] Alternatively, in cases of suspected coronary artery disease, the heart may be perfusion fixed with 10% buffered formaldehyde retrograde from the ascending aorta at 100 mm Hg pressure (Figure 2.2.1) for at least 1 h. In the absence of perfusion fixation, which is impractical for routine forensic evaluation, careful dissection of fresh or immersion-fixed coronary arteries is

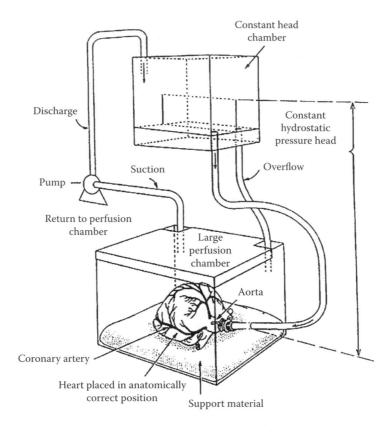

Figure 2.2.1 Diagram showing the method used for perfusion fixation of the heart. The constant head chamber
is placed 135 cm above the perfusion chamber, and is connected via polyethylene tubing to the
ascending aorta through the Lucite plug. The excess formaldehyde is suctioned back into the
constant head chamber via a pump. Both chambers are covered in order to reduce formalin vapors.
(Courtesy J. Frederick Cornhill, D. Phil.)

acceptable, provided that it is understood that precise assessment of percent stenosis is not possible,
and that all segments are sectioned adequately in decalcified arteries if necessary.

For perfusion fixation, a specially constructed Lucite plug or a rubber stopper with central
tubing is inserted into the aorta, taking care that the Lucite/rubber plug does not touch the aortic
valve. The Lucite plug is attached to tubing that is connected to the perfusion chamber.[5] The latter
is placed 135 cm above the specimen, and this provides gravity perfusion pressure that is equivalent
to 100 mm Hg. As a result, the coronary arteries are fixed in a distended state that approximates
the dimensions observed in living patients. Myocardial fixation is also affected, but cardiac chambers are not fixed in a distended state.

This method is fairly simple, does not require sophisticated equipment to achieve good fixation,
and allows for immediate dissection after perfusion for approximately 30 min. If perfusion fixation
is impractical, the heart should be fixed for 24 h in 10% formaldehyde (10 parts of formaldehyde
to 1 part of specimen) before cutting. Radiography of the heart is recommended to determine the
extent of coronary and valvular calcification but is not essential; if coronary arteries are heavily
calcified, they need to be decalcified prior to cutting at 3- to 4-mm intervals.

The vessels that must be examined in all hearts include the four major epicardial coronary
arteries: the left main, the left anterior descending, the left circumflex, and the right coronary
arteries. However, it is not unusual to see severe luminal narrowing in smaller branches of the main
coronary arteries; left diagonals, left obtuse marginal, ramus (intermediate) branch, and the posterior
descending coronary arteries (Figure 2.2.2).

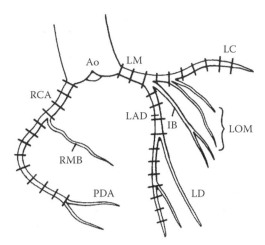

Figure 2.2.2 Diagram of the right and left epicardial coronary arteries as they arise from the aorta. The four major arteries that must be described in detail are right (RCA), left main (LM), left anterior descending coronary (LAD), and the left circumflex (LC) coronary arteries. Not uncommonly severe coronary (>75% cross-sectional area luminal narrowing) artery disease may affect the smaller branches (IB = intermediate or also called ramus branch, LD = left diagonal, LOM= left obtuse marginal, PDA = posterior descending artery, and RMB = right marginal branch).

Following fixation and/or decalcification, the coronary arteries are cut transversely at 3- to 4-mm intervals with a sharp scalpel blade by a gentle sawing motion (not by firm pressure) to confirm sites of narrowing and to evaluate the pathologic process (e.g., atherosclerotic plaques, thrombi, dissections) directly. If the coronary arteries are heavily calcified, it is desirable to remove the coronary arteries intact. Following dissection of the vessel from the epicardial surface, each coronary artery is carefully trimmed of excess fat and the intact arterial tree is placed in a container of formic acid for slow decalcification over 12 to 18 h.

Decalcification of isolated segments of vessel may be sufficient for cases in which the coronary arteries are only focally calcified. The areas of maximal narrowing are noted by specifying the degrees of reduction of the cross-sectional area of the lumen (e.g., 0 to 25%, 26 to 50%, 51 to 75%, 76 to 90%, 91 to 99%, and 100%). Most cardiologists agree that, in the absence of other cardiac disease, significant or severe coronary artery narrowing is that exceeding a 75% cross-sectional luminal narrowing. Particular attention should be paid to the left main coronary artery because disease in this vessel is very important clinically but frequently overlooked at autopsy.[6]

Cross sections from areas of maximal narrowing from each of the four major epicardial coronary arteries or their branches are selected for histological examination. Sections of all coronary arteries containing thrombi are taken to aid in determining the type of underlying plaque morphology, i.e., plaque rupture, or plaque erosion (ulceration). The site of maximal narrowing must be specified, i.e., proximal, middle, or distal coronary involvement. This is of great medicolegal importance in cases where the patient may have been inadequately examined in the physician's office or emergency room or in the hospital following chest pain. It is the location of the severe narrowing that determines if the patient is operable or not; presence of distal disease signifies non-operability.

2.2.1.3 Examination of Coronary Interventions

Coronary interventions consist primarily of open bypass surgery and percutaneous coronary interventions (PCI). The technique for evaluation of bypass grafts is tailored to the circumstances of death. In cases of perioperative death, or when there is question of graft patency, careful dissection is necessary. In cases where it is not possible to perfusion-fix the heart, the heart may be immersion fixed in 10% buffered formalin overnight. Prior to cutting the arteries and the grafts, it is

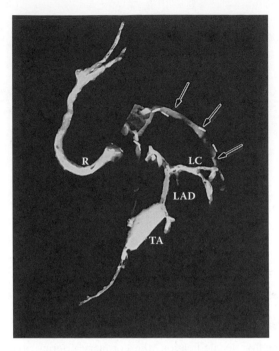

Figure 2.2.3 Radiograph of epicardial coronary arteries and saphenous vein bypass graft (arrows) to left circumflex (LC) removed at autopsy. Note focal calcification of the native arteries and absence of calcification of the vein graft. A portion of the left anterior coronary artery is surrounded by myocardium (bridged or tunneled coronary artery). Arteries are decalcified prior to sectioning and embedding in paraffin. (From Virmani, R., Ursell, P.C., and Fenoglio, J.J., Examination of the heart, in Virmani, R., Atkinson, J.B., and Fenoglio, J.J., Eds., *Cardiovascular Pathology*, W.B. Saunders, Philadelphia, 1991, pp. 1–20. With permission.)

useful to radiograph and decalcify them when necessary (Figure 2.2.3). The important features to document are the numbers of the grafts, patency of aortic anastomoses, sites of distal anastomoses, and patency of run-off arteries. It is helpful to remember that grafts that were never patent or closed soon after surgery have a cord-like appearance, without open lumen; that all types of anastomoses are possible, including Y-grafts, touch-down (end-to-end) anastomoses, and interpositions of radial arteries; and that characteristics of native artery at the distal anastomoses (presence of plaque, size of vessel) influence long-term patency.

After inspecting the aortic origin of vein grafts, the grafts themselves are inspected for lumen patency, fibrous intimal thickening, atherosclerotic plaques with or without calcification, and aneurysms. Twists, as well as excessive tautness between aorta and distal anastomosis, are noted.[7] Anastomotic sites are sectioned in different ways depending on whether the connection is end to end or end to side (Figure 2.2.4). When reporting the findings in the heart, it is important to mention each graft separately; including the location of the aortic orifice, whether it is involved by atherosclerotic ulcerated lesion or not, and if present mention if atheroemboli could have embolized and may be the source of the infarct noted in the heart. Describe the course of the graft and the native coronary vessel to which it is distally anastomosed. Give the size of the native vessel, i.e., less than or greater than 1 mm diameter; vessels less than 1 mm in diameter usually do not carry enough blood to meet the demands of the myocardium. Also, determine if there is severe distal disease present in the grafted vessel.

If the cause of death is related to surgery, the full extent of the saphenous vein grafts is best visualized by barium–gelatin mixture followed by radiography. It is best to inject all the vein grafts simultaneously and to obtain radiographs before injection of the coronary arteries. This enables more detailed study of the native coronary arteries distal to the graft as well as at the coronary

Coronary artery bypass grafts

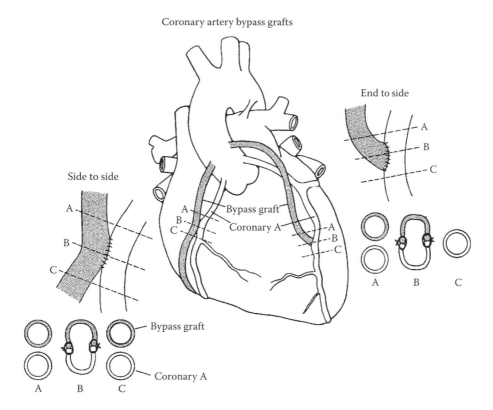

Figure 2.2.4 Diagram illustrating coronary artery bypass grafts that have end-to-side and side-to-side anasto-moses in two separate grafts (shaded area) to left anterior descending and right coronary arteries, respectively. The figure illustrates the method used for sectioning of anastomotic site with end-to-side and side-to-side anastomoses to demonstrate if any of the three mechanisms for obstruction in the anastomotic site are present (i.e., compression or loss of arterial lumen, which may occur if the majority of the arterial wall has been used for anastomosis; thrombosis at the site of anastomosis; and dissection of the native coronary–artery at the site of anastomosis) and if the coronary artery has severe narrowing at the site of anastomosis due to severe atherosclerotic change. (Modified from Bulkley, B.H. and Hutchins, G.M., Pathology of coronary artery bypass graft surgery, *Arch. Pathol.*, 102:273, 1978. From Virmani, R., Ursell, P.C., and Fenoglio, J.J., Examination of the heart, in Virmani, R., Atkinson, J.B., and Fenoglio, J.J., Eds., *Cardiovascular Pathology*, W.B. Saunders, Philadelphia, 1991, pp. 1–20. With permission.)

graft anastomosis. Measurements of lumen diameters may be made from the radiographs. In those cases in which the internal mammary artery is anastomosed to the coronary system, the internal mammary artery is injected from where it has been severed during removal of the heart. The native coronary arteries are injected, fixed, and radiographed to evaluate the extent of disease in the remainder of the coronary arterial tree. If, as mentioned previously, it is not feasible to inject the heart with a barium–gelatin mixture, then the heart may be perfusion fixed with formaldehyde from the aortic stump taking care that the graft orifices are below the Lucite plug and the internal mammary artery should be ligated near the site of severance from the chest wall.

The grafts and native arteries may then be removed from the heart, radiographed, and cut at 3- to 4-mm intervals to determine the extent of luminal narrowing, the presence or absence of thrombi, and/or the extent of atherosclerosis in vein grafts and coronary arteries.[8–11]

The forensic pathologist is encountering intracoronary stents at an ever-increasing pace. As is the case with bypass grafts, the degree of evaluation depends on the circumstances of death. Incidentally found stents are commonly encountered in patients with a history of ischemic heart disease by post-mortem radiography. If a death occurs soon after PCI, the heart should be radiographed, site(s) of stenting established, and the stented segments fixed in formalin. The only method for determining in-stent thrombosis involves plastic embedding and sectioning or stent removal without damaging the lumen contents. Either of these procedures requires consultation with a laboratory specializing in such techniques. Immediate fixation of the stented segments and mailing them in adequate formalin to the consultant will provide for documentation of adequacy of stent placement, characterization of underlying plaque, therapeutic misadventures, and in-stent thrombosis.

2.2.1.4 Examination of the Myocardium in Ischemic Heart Disease

In the presence or absence of acute or healed myocardial infarction, the myocardium is best examined by slicing the ventricles in a manner similar to a loaf of bread. To evaluate the specimen, a series of short-axis cuts are made through the ventricles from apex to base (Figure 2.2.5A). This method is best accomplished using a long, sharp knife on the intact fixed specimen following examination of the coronary arteries. With the anterior aspect of the heart downward (against the cutting board), the cuts are made parallel to the posterior atrioventricular sulcus at 1- to 1.5-cm intervals from the apex of the heart to a point approximately 2 cm caudal to the sulcus or up to the mid-portion of the papillary muscles of the left ventricle.

The result is a series of cross sections through the ventricles, including papillary muscles with the atrioventricular valve apparatus left intact in the remainder of the specimen. The location and extent of the infarct is noted. Locations may be stated using terms relating to the standard anatomic terms of reference (e.g., anteroseptal, posterolateral). The extent of infarction may be described in terms of circumference of the ventricle involved[12–14] and longitudinal portion of the ventricle involved (e.g., basal third, middle third, apical third; Figure 2.2.5A and B).

The distribution within the wall is also described (e.g., transmural or subendocardial; transmural when the infarct extends from the endocardium to the epicardium, and subendocardial when <50% of the left ventricular wall is infarcted). The gross pathologic appearance of the myocardium serves as a relatively good index as to the age of the infarct but must be confirmed by histologic examination. Even if infarction cannot be identified grossly, it is important to section the myocardium in the distribution of the severely diseased coronary arteries more extensively.

2.2.1.5 Examination of the Heart in Cardiomyopathy

The short-axis sectioning (bread-loafing) method described above serves well for the examination of the cardiomyopathic heart. Cardiac hypertrophy and dilation may be demonstrated quite effectively by this method. If the left ventricular cavity measures >4 cm, excluding the papillary muscles, it is considered that the patient was in congestive heart failure prior to death even if there is no history to corroborate the autopsy findings. Left ventricular hypertrophy is said to be present if the left ventricular wall measures >1.5 cm. On the other hand, if the left ventricular wall measures <1.5 cm but the heart weight is increased and the left ventricular cavity is enlarged, then there will be microscopic appreciation of myocyte hypertrophy.

Histological examination of the myocardium is critical to determining the cause of the cardiomyopathy. Thus, in addition to sections of tissue with obvious gross pathology, samples of the walls of all four cardiac chambers, the septum, and papillary muscles should be taken. In the past, the right ventricle has been relatively ignored, but because of the greater awareness of right ventricular infarction and right ventricular dysplasia/cardiomyopathy, it should be a routine to examine the right ventricle carefully. For establishing the diagnosis of right ventricular cardiomyopathy, the most helpful single observation to make is one of fibrosis or scarring in the right ventricular wall with intermingling of fat; these lesions are most often seen in the inflow region of the right ventricle on the posterior wall or in the anterior wall of the right ventricular outflow tract. These lesions can be commonly appreciated grossly if a careful examination of the heart is carried out.

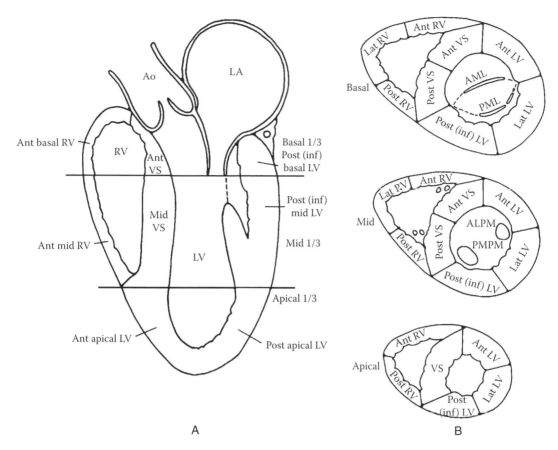

A   B

Figure 2.2.5 The location and extent of myocardial infarction must be indicated by the size, that is, how much of the base to apex is infarcted: basal one third, and/or middle one third, and/or apical one third or more than one third from base to apex. The diagram in (A) shows a long-axis view of the heart with regional nomenclature. (B) The location of the myocardial infarction in the left ventricle must also indicate the wall in which the infarction occurred: anterior, posterior, lateral, septal, or any combination of these. This diagram illustrates a short-axis view through the basal, middle, and apical portions of the right and left ventricles. (Ao = aorta; Ant = anterior; ALPM = anterolateral papillary muscle; AML = anterior mitral leaflet; Inf = inferior; LA = left atrium; LV = left ventricle; Mid = middle; PML = posterior mitral leaflet; PMPM = posteromedial papillary muscle; Post = posterior; RV = right ventricle; VS = ventricular septum) (Modified from Edwards, W.D., Tajik, A.J., and Seward, J.B., Standardized nomenclature and anatomic basis for regional tomographic analysis of the heart, *Mayo Clin. Proc.*, 56:479, 1981. From Virmani, R., Ursell, P.C., and Fenoglio, J.J., Examination of the heart, in Virmani, R., Atkinson, J.B., and Fenoglio, J.J., Eds., *Cardiovascular Pathology*, W.B. Saunders, Philadelphia, 1991, pp. 1–20. With permission.

The heart also may be cut in four-chamber view by cutting the heart from the apex to base, along the acute margin of the right ventricle and the obtuse margin of the left ventricle and continuing the plane of section through the atria (Figure 2.2.6). This four-chamber view is best for evaluating the atrial and ventricular chamber size. In cases of hypertrophic cardiomyopathy, the heart should be cut in the long axis view of the left ventricular outflow tract. The plane of dissection of the aortic valve leaflet is through the right coronary and the posterior non-coronary leaflets, the anterior and the posterior mitral leaflets, the posterior and the anterior left atrial wall, ventricular septum, posterolateral wall of the left ventrical and the anterior right ventricular wall (Figure 2.2.7). Sections to determine the presence of fibromuscular disarray are taken in the transverse plane, usually from the septal location with the largest dimension.

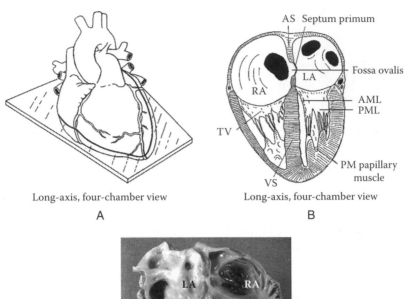

Long-axis, four-chamber view

A

Long-axis, four-chamber view

B

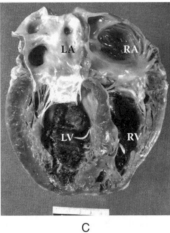

C

Figure 2.2.6 (A) Diagram of the heart demonstrating the ultrasonic tomographic plane used for obtaining the long-axis view of the heart. This four-chamber view is best used for evaluating the atrial and ventricular dimensions, intracavitary masses, ventricular and atrial septal defects, atrioventricular valve abnormalities, ventricular aneurysms, and the drainage of pulmonary veins. (B) Diagram demonstrating the four-chamber view of the heart. This method involves sectioning the heart from apex to base, along the acute margin of the right ventricle and the obtuse margin of the left ventricle and continuing the plane of sectioning through the atria. The bisected specimen that is photographed should match the ante-mortem cardiac image. (C) Tomographic analysis of a heart from a 17-year-old boy who developed progressive heart failure over the course of 8 months, showing four-chamber view with biventricular hypertrophy, four-chamber dilatation, and apical right and left ventricular thrombus. (RA = right atrium; LA = left atrium; VS = ventricular septum; TV = tricuspid valve; AML = anterior mitral leaflet; PML = posterior mitral leaflet) (Modified from Tajik, A.L., Seward, I., Hager, D.J., Muir, D.D., and Lie, J.T., Two-dimensional real-time ultrasonic imaging of the heart and great vessels: Technique, image orientation, structure identification and validation, *Mayo Clin. Proc.*, 53:271, 1978. From Virmani, R., Ursell, P.C., and Fenoglio, J.J., Examination of the heart, in Virmani, R., Atkinson, J.B., and Fenoglio, J.J., Eds., *Cardiovascular Pathology*, W.B. Saunders, Philadelphia, 1991, pp. 1–20. With permission.)

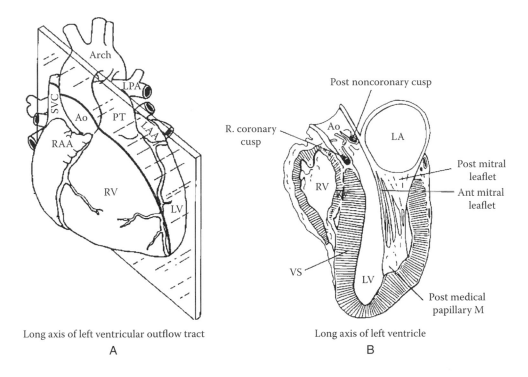

Long axis of left ventricular outflow tract

A

Long axis of left ventricle

B

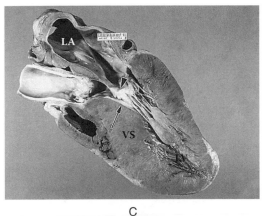

C

Figure 2.2.7 (A) Diagram of the heart demonstrating the ultrasonic plane of the long-axis view of the left ventricular outflow tract. The normal anatomic relationship of septal-aortic and mitral-aortic continuity is best shown by this plane of dissection. This method is used for aortic root pathology, including valvular, supravalvular, and intravalvular obstructions, left ventricular chamber size, posterior wall abnormalities, ventricular septal defects, mitral valve disease, and left atrial size. (B) Anatomic landmarks seen with a long-axis view of the left ventricle. The plane of dissection of aortic valve leaflets is through the right coronary and posterior non-coronary leaflets. (C) Left ventricular long-axis section in hypertrophic cardiomyopathy, showing asymmetric septal hypertrophy with a discrete left ventricular outflow tract plaque (arrow) and a thickened anterior mitral leaflet (arrow head). (Ao = aorta; LA = left atrium; LPA = left pulmonary artery; LV = left ventricle; RAA = right atrial appendage; RV = right ventricle; SVC = superior vena cava; VS = ventricular septum) (Modified from Tajik, A.J., Seward, J.B., Hager, D.J., Muir, D.D., and Lie, J.T., Two-dimensional real-time ultrasonic imaging of the heart and great vessels: Technique, image orientation, structure identification and validation, *Mayo Clin. Proc.*, 53.271, 1978. From Virmani, R., Ursell, P.C., and Fenoglio, J.J., Examination of the heart, in Virmani, R., Atkinson, J.B., and Fenoglio, J.J., Eds., *Cardiovascular Pathology*, W.B. Saunders, Philadelphia, 1991, pp. 1–20. With permission.)

2.2.1.6 Examination of the Heart Valves

In the case of valvular heart disease, the valves are best studied intact. The atrial and ventricular aspect of the atrioventricular valves and the ventricular and arterial aspects of the semilunar valves are examined (Figure 2.2.8). Thus, the tricuspid valve is exposed by a lateral incision through the right atrium from the superior vena cava to 2 cm above the valve annulus. Similarly, the mitral valve may be studied following opening of the left atrium via an incision extending from one of the left pulmonary veins to one of the right pulmonary veins and another incision continuing through the atrium laterally to a point 2 cm above the annulus. If a valve abnormality requires closer inspection, the atria, including the interatrial septum, may be removed 1 to 2 cm above the atrioventricular valves (Figure 2.2.8A). The ventricular aspects of the atrioventricular valves may be viewed following removal of the serial slices of ventricle as described previously.

The semilunar valves are best studied after removal of the aorta (Figure 2.2.8C) and the main pulmonary artery at a point just above the coronary ostia or valve annulus. In selected cases, the valvular pathology may be best visualized using a four-chamber cut[15–17] in the plane including both

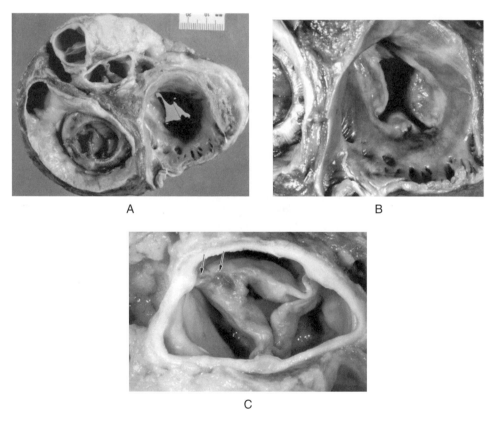

A

B

C

Figure 2.2.8 (A) The appearance of the atrioventricular valves after removal of both the atria. The mitral valve has been replaced with a bioprosthetic porcine valve, which shows a tear in the muscular leaflet close to the ring. (B) The right atrium has been removed close to the tricuspid valve. Note the valve margins are thickened and the commissure between the posterior and the septal leaflet is fused secondary to chronic rheumatic valvulitis. (C) The aortic valve is examined on removal of the aorta close to sinotubular junction. There is diffuse thickening of the valve, which is more marked at the free margins with one of the three commissures fused (arrow). These changes are consistent with chronic rheumatic valvulitis. (AV = aortic valve; MV = mitral valve; PV = pulmonary valve; TV = tricuspid valve). (From Virmani, R., Ursell, P.C., and Fenoglio, J.J., Examination of the heart, in Virmani, R., Atkinson, J.B., and Fenoglio, J.J., Eds., *Cardiovascular Pathology*, W.B. Saunders, Philadelphia, 1991, pp. 1–20. With permission.)

the acute and obtuse margins of the heart (Figure 2.2.6). The aortic valve may be demonstrated by a left ventricular long-axis cut passing from the apex through the outflow tract, ventricular septum, anterior mitral valve leaflet, and aortic valve (Figure 2.2.7). Measurement of the circumference of annuli, especially in valvular stenosis, is on the whole not very useful. In ectasia of the aorta, it is indeed a must to measure the aortic annulus as the valve will be normal in appearance but the annulus will be dilated. Examination of the heart valves should document the type and severity of the valvular disease and its effect on the cardiac chambers and this includes microscopic evaluation.

In cases in which histology of a valve may be helpful, the leaflets are sectioned together with a portion of the adjacent chambers and/or vessel walls. For example, the posterior leaflet of the mitral valve is sectioned including a portion of the left atrium and left ventricular free wall, while the anterior leaflet includes ventricular septum and non-coronary cusp of the aortic valve. In cases of rheumatic heart disease, sections of the atrial appendages are submitted for histological examination because the incidence of Aschoff's nodules is highest in these structures.

2.2.1.7 Prosthetic Heart Valves

The objectives for examinations of valve implants include determination of (1) the type of implant (bioprosthesis or mechanical valve) and its size and position regarding annulus and chamber; (2) adequacy of movement of the valve apparatus; (3) presence of thrombi, vegetations, and paravalvular abscesses or leaks; and (4) evidence of valve degeneration.[15] In particular, paravalvular abscesses may not be visible without careful inspection of the native annulus following removal of the implant. Demonstration of any pathology may be enhanced using short-axis cuts through the atrioventricular junction.

2.2.1.8 Examination of the Aorta

Because atherosclerosis is the most common lesion affecting the aorta, the aorta should be opened longitudinally along its posterior or dorsal aspect from the ascending aorta through the bifurcation and into both common iliac arteries. The extent of disease and the types of lesions may then be described. While this method enables inspection of the complete intimal surface, it may not be optimal for certain types of pathology, such as aortic aneurysms, which may best be demonstrated by cross-sectional slices 1 to 1.5 cm apart in the perfusion-fixed, distended specimen (Figure 2.2.9). Aortic dissections may be examined by a longitudinal cut (long-axis cut) with the aorta cut into anterior and posterior halves (Figure 2.2.10) or by transverse cut at 1- to 1.5-cm intervals after the aorta has been allowed to fix for 24 h in a distended state or free floating in anatomic position in formaldehyde.

2.2.1.9 Examination of the Heart in Apparent Cardiac Death without Morphologic Abnormality

In a significant proportion of apparent arrhythmic deaths, in which toxicologic and scene investigation do not result in a non-natural cause, the gross and histological examination of the heart is normal. In the past, it was assumed that histological examination of the specialized conduction system held the key to finding a possible abnormality to explain death. In the last decades, however, it has become clearer that a large proportion of sudden deaths with normal hearts are due to genetic defects in the cardiac ion channels. It must always be kept in mind that the origin of arrhythmias is generally in the working myocardium. Nevertheless, examination of the conduction system is still worthwhile, in that it allows evaluation of areas at the base of the heart, including small vessels, which may be prone to arterial dysplasia, or small vessel disease, which has been implicated in sudden death.

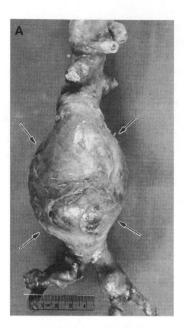
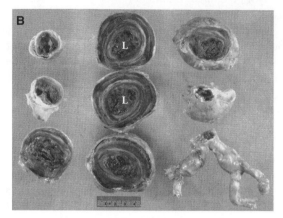

Figure 2.2.9 (A) External view of the abdominal aorta with an infrarenal aneurysm (arrows). Note the size, which is best expressed as the largest diameter. In this case, it is 7 cm. (B) Same aneurysm cut transversely at 1.0 to 1.5 cm apart. Note the extent of luminal (L) narrowing secondary to an organizing thrombus. (From Virmani, R., Ursell, P.C., and Fenoglio, J.J., Examination of the heart, in Virmani, R., Atkinson, J.B., and Fenoglio, J.J., Eds., *Cardiovascular Pathology*, W.B. Saunders, Philadelphia, 1991, pp. 1–20. With permission.)

With practice and careful attention to anatomic landmarks, the conduction system is relatively easily sampled histologically.[18,19] In most humans, the sinus node is a spindle-shaped structure located in the sulcus terminalis on the lateral aspect of the superior vena cava and the right atrium (Figure 2.2.11). In some patients, it is a horseshoe-shaped structure wrapped across the superior aspect of this cavoatrial junction. Histologically, the sinus node consists of relatively small diameter, haphazardly oriented atrial muscle cells admixed with connective tissue, collagen, and elastic fibers (Figure 2.2.12). Often, the artery to the sinus node can be identified in or around the nodal tissue. Because the sinus node is not visible grossly, the entire block of tissue from the suspected area should be taken and serially sectioned, either in the plane perpendicular to the sulcus terminalis (parallel to the long axis of the superior vena cava) or in the plane containing the sulcus (perpendicular to the vessel). In small infants, serial sectioning of the entire cavoatrial junction is preferred.

There are no anatomically distinct muscle tracts for conduction through the atria. The impulse is collected in the atrioventricular node, which is located within the triangle of Koch in the floor of the right atrium. In the heart dissected in the traditional manner along the lines of blood flow, this region is delineated by the following landmarks: the tricuspid valve annulus inferiorly, the coronary sinus posteriorly, and the continuation of the valve guarding the coronary sinus (tendon of Todaro) superiorly (Figure 2.2.11). The atrioventricular node lies within Koch's triangle (Figure 2.2.11), and the apex of the triangle anteriorly denotes the point at which the common bundle of His penetrates the fibrous annulus to reach the left ventricle. After penetrating the fibrous annulus at the crest of the ventricular septum, the bundle of His divides into left and right bundle branches.

Thus, the tissue excised for study of the conduction system must include this area completely. From the opened right atrioventricular aspect (with the aortic outflow tract adjacent to the cutting surface) the block to be excised reaches from the anterior margin of the coronary sinus to the

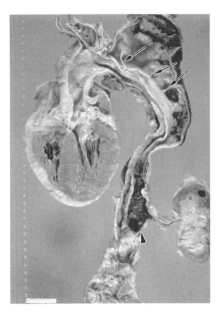

Figure 2.2.10   The heart has been cut in the long-axis plane, exposing the right and left ventricles and the aortic root and valve. In this plane, the anterior wall of the aorta has been removed. Note the dissecting aneurysm that starts just distal to the subclavian artery and extends along the greater curvature of the aorta to just below the left renal artery (arrowhead). Within the false lumen there are fibrous strands (arrows) connecting the outer media and adventitia to the inner media and intima. Note also the organizing thrombus within a fusiform aneurysm distal to the subclavian and within the abdominal aorta of the false lumen. (From Virmani, R., Ursell, P.C., and Fenoglio, J.J., Examination of the heart, in Virmani, R., Atkinson, J.B., and Fenoglio, J.J., Eds., *Cardiovascular Pathology*, W.B. Saunders, Philadelphia, 1991, pp. 1–20. With permission.)

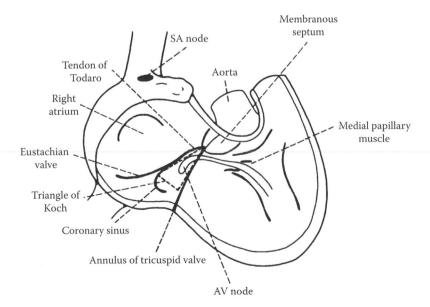

Figure 2.2.11   Diagram of location of the atrioventricular (AV) and sinoatrial (SA) nodes along with the landmarks that help in locating their positions during sectioning of the heart. (Modified from Davies, M.J., Anderson, R.H., and Becker, A.E., *The Conduction System of the Heart*, Butterworth & Co, London, 1983. From Virmani, R., Ursell, P.C., and Fenoglio, J.J., Examination of the heart, in Virmani, R., Atkinson, J.B., and Fenoglio, J.J., Eds., *Cardiovascular Pathology*, W.B. Saunders, Philadelphia, 1991, pp. 1–20. With permission.)

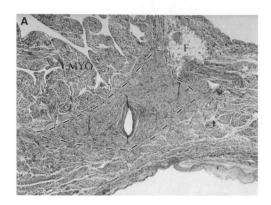 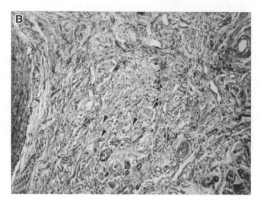

Figure 2.2.12 (A) The sinus node (outlined) lies in the subepicardium. The superficial layer is surrounded by epicardial fat (F), and the deeper layers anastomose with the surrounding atrial myocardium (MYO). (Movat stain, × 25.) (From Virmani, R., Ursell, P.C., and Fenoglio, J.J., Examination of the heart, in Virmani, R., Atkinson, J.B., and Fenoglio, J.J., Eds., *Cardiovascular Pathology*, W.B. Saunders, Philadelphia, 1991, pp. 1–20. With permission.) (B) High-power view of the SA node showing fibrous tissue, elastin fibers, and small SA node haphazardly arranged fibers.

medial papillary muscle of the right ventricle, including 1 cm of atrium and ventricle on both sides of the valve. Alternatively, from the left ventricle outflow tract, the block can be cut perpendicular to the aortic valve from the margin of attachment of the anterior leaflet of the mitral valve to the left edge of the membranous septum.

The block should include the non-coronary cusp of the aortic valve and the crest of the ventricular septum (Figure 2.2.13). In either case, the block of tissue removed should be divided in the plane perpendicular to the annulus, from posterior to anterior; the block to be sectioned should be marked with India ink so its orientation can be maintained throughout the embedding process. The atrioventricular node, bundle, and bundle branches are histologically easily identifiable. The atrioventricular node consists of a network of muscle fibers that are smaller than the atrial and ventricular fibers. The cytoplasm is pale in comparison with the ventricular myocardium, but striations and intercalated disk are present. The nuclei are oval in longitudinal sections. The conduction tissue is markedly cellular due to the presence of a large number of endothelial cells and there is a greater amount of elastic tissue than in the surrounding myocardium. As the node extends to penetrate the fibrous body and become bundle of His, the fibers are less plexiform and more longitudinally oriented (Figure 2.2.14).

Genetic analysis of mutations that may be the cause of sudden cardiac death in morphologically normal hearts is a complex undertaking. The numerous syndromes associated with sudden death without structural heart disease were originally described by clinical features (e.g., long QT syndrome, Brugada syndrome, polymorphous ventricular tachycardia). As the genetic bases for these lesions have been discovered, terminology has slowly shifted to the genes or proteins involved, including sodium and potassium channels (LQT genes/Brugada syndrome), calcium channel–related genes (ryanodine receptor/RyR2), ankyrin-B, etc. From a diagnostic standpoint, some of these mutations are more likely to cause sudden death during exertion, some more specifically with drowning, and others at rest. From this starting point, the hundreds of possible mutations may potentially be screened, in the dozens of exons in each target gene. Archiving frozen tissue is critical in maintaining the possibility of a genetic diagnosis, as enhanced techniques allowing for simultaneous screening of multiple genes becomes possible. At the time of this writing, the genetic diagnosis of sudden death due to cardiac ion channel disease, in the absence of a family history, is difficult and time-consuming, and nearly impossible with archived paraffin-embedded tissue, which greatly limits the size of DNA segments that can be sequenced.

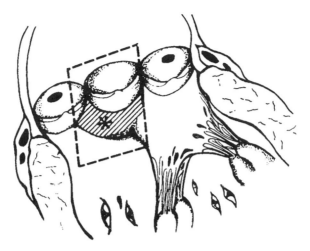

Figure 2.2.13 Diagram of landmarks for excising the major conduction from the left outflow tract. The membranous septum is marked by an asterisk. (From Virmani, R., Ursell, P.C., and Fenoglio, J.J., Examination of the heart, in Virmani, R., Atkinson, J.B., and Fenoglio, J.J., Eds., *Cardiovascular Pathology*, W.B. Saunders, Philadelphia, 1991, pp. 1–20. With permission.)

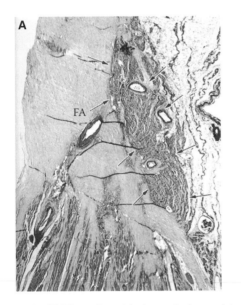

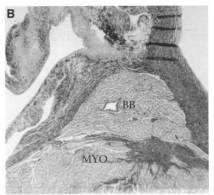

Figure 2.2.14 (A) The atrioventricular node (arrows) is shown nested against the fibrous annulus (FA). (From Virmani, R., Ursell, P.C., and Fenoglio, J.J., Examination of the heart, in Virmani, R., Atkinson, J.B., and Fenoglio, J.J., Eds., *Cardiovascular Pathology*, W.B. Saunders, Philadelphia, 1991, pp. 1–20. With permission.) (B) The bundle of His branching portion. Note the location underneath the fibrous body (FB) and above the septal myocardium (MYO). (Movat stain, × 25.)

2.2.1.10 Evaluating Cardiac Hypertrophy

One of the most important decisions while examining the heart is to determine if the heart is normal or abnormal. The heart may not show any anatomic structural abnormality except that it is hypertrophied. Because cardiac hypertrophy may be a cause of death if severe, and physiologic in cases of chronic conditioning, the criteria for increased heart weight are important. We usually utilize the tables published from the Mayo Clinic giving the 95% confidence intervals for the height and weight of male and female individuals from birth to 99 years.[20,21] We recommend that at least four sections of the left ventricle be examined from the four walls of the heart and one section of the posterior wall of the right ventricle; sections should be taken from the mid-ventricular slice. In elderly individuals we also like to take one section each from both the atria, as amyloidosis and drug reactions may be limited to the atria.

2.2.1.11 Conclusions

This brief description of the examination of the heart is no substitute for the practice of examination and cutting open the heart oneself. In practice, not all methods may be applicable in each laboratory, for each individual, or in all situations. The description is geared more to the forensic pathologist and the examination of the adult heart with intent of making the method easy yet thorough; a careful examination of the heart is worth the time and effort.

REFERENCES

1. Layman, T.E. and Edwards, J.E., A method for dissection of the heart and major pulmonary vessels, *Arch. Pathol.*, 82, 314, 1966.
2. Ludwig, J. and Titus, J.L., Heart and vascular system, in Ludwig, J., Ed., *Current Method of Autopsy Practice,* W.B. Saunders, Philadelphia, 1979.
3. Hales, M.R. and Carrington, C.B., A pigment gelatin mass for vascular injection, *Yale J. Biol. Med.,* 43, 257, 1971.
4. Hutchins, G.M., Buckley, B.H., Ridolfi, R.L. et al., Correlation of coronary arteriograms and left ventriculograms with postmortem studies, *Circulation,* 56, 32, 1977.
5. Glagov, S., Eckner, F.A.O., and Ler, M., Controlled pressure fixation approaches for hearts, *Arch. Patrol.,* 76, 640, 1963.
6. Isner, J.M., Kishel, J., Kent, K.M. et al., Accuracy of angiographic determination of the left main coronary arterial narrowing: angiographic-histologic correlative analysis in 28 patients, *Circulation,* 63, 1056, 1981.
7. Roberts, W.C., Lachman, A.S., and Virmani, R., Twisting of an aortic-coronary bypass conduit: a complication of coronary surgery, *J. Thorac. Cardiovasc. Surg.,* 75, 722, 1978.
8. Atkinson, J.B., Forman, M.B., Perry, J.M., and Virmani, R., Correlation of saphenous vein bypass graft angiography with histologic changes at autopsy, *Am. J. Cardiol.,* 55, 952, 1985.
9. Atkinson, J.B., Forman, M.B., Vaughn, W.K. et al., Morphologic changes in long-term saphenous bypass grafts, *Chest,* 88, 341, 1985.
10. Buckley, B.H. and Hutchins, C.M., Accelerated "atherosclerosis": A morphologic study of 97 saphenous vein coronary artery bypass grafts, *Circulation,* 55, 163, 1977.
11. Buckley, B.H. and Hutchins, G.M., Pathology of coronary artery bypass graft surgery, *Arch. Pathol.,* 102, 273, 1978.
12. Virmani, R. and Roberts, W.C., Quantification of coronary arterial narrowing and of left ventricular myocardial scarring in healed myocardial infarction with chronic, eventually fatal, congestive heart failure, *Am. J. Med.,* 68, 831, 1980.
13. Hackel, B.D. and Ratliff, N.J., Jr., A technique to estimate the quantity of infarcted myocardium post mortem, *Am. J. Pathol.,* 61, 242, 1974.
14. Lichtig, C., Glagov, S., Feldman, S., and Wissler, R.W., Myocardial ischemia coronary artery atherosclerosis: A comprehensive approach to postmortem studies, *Med. Clin. North Am.,* 57, 79, 1973.
15. Roberts, W.C., Technique of opening the heart at autopsy, in *The Heart,* 5th ed., Hurst, J.W., Logue, R.B., Schlant, R.C., and Wenger, N.K., Eds., McGraw-Hill, New York, 1982.
16. Edwards, W.D., Anatomic basis for tomographic analysis of the heart at autopsy, in *Cardiology Clinics: Cardiac Morphology,* Vol. 2, No. 4, Weller, B.F., Ed., W.B. Saunders, Philadelphia, 1984.
17. Tajik, A.J., Seward, J.B., Hagler, D.J. et al., Two dimensional real time ultrasonic imaging of the heart and great vessels: Techniques, image orientation, structure identification and validation, *Mayo Clin. Proc.,* 53, 271, 1978.
18. Davies, M.J., Anderson, R.H., and Becker, A.E., *The Conduction System of the Heart,* Butterworth, London, 1983.

19. Anderson, R.H., Ho, S.Y., Smith, A. et al., Studies of the cardiac conduction tissue in the pediatric age group, *Diagn. Histopathol.*, 4, 3 1981.

20. Scholz, D.G., Kitzman, D.W., Hagen, P.T., Ilstrup, D.M., and Edwards, W.D., Age-related changes in normal human hearts during the first 10 decades of life. Part I (Growth): a quantitative anatomic study of 200 specimens from subjects from birth to 19 years old, *Mayo Clin. Proc.*, 63, 126, 1988.

21. Kitzman, D.W., Scholz, D.G., Hagen, P.T., Ilstrup, D.M., and Edwards, W.D., Age-related changes in normal human hearts during the first 10 decades of life. Part II (Maturity): a quantitative anatomic study of 765 specimens from subjects 20–99 years old, *Mayo Clin. Proc.*, 63, 137, 1988.

22. Virmani, R., Ursell, P.C., and Fenoglio, J.J., Examination of the heart, in *Cardiovascular Pathology*, Virmani, R., Atkinson, J.B., and Fenoglio, J.J., Eds., W.B. Saunders, Philadelphia, 1991, 1–20.

2.2.2 Vascular Effects of Substance Abuse*

Frank D. Kolodgie, Ph.D.,[1] **Allen P. Burke, M.D.,**[2] **Jagat Narula, M.D., Ph.D.,**[3]
Florabel G. Mullick, M.D.,[1] **and Renu Virmani, M.D., F.A.C.C.**[4]

[1] Armed Forces Institute of Pathology, Washington, D.C.

[2] Kernan Hospital Pathology Laboratory, University of Maryland Medical Center, Baltimore, Maryland

[3] University of California, Irvine School of Medicine and Medical Center, Irvine, California

[4] CVPath, International Registry of Pathology, Gaithersburg, Maryland

Statistics provided by the Drug Abuse Warning Network (DAWN) over the past two decades have documented an increasing prevalence in substance abuse as manifested by emergency room and Medical Examiner data (i.e., drug mentions). For example, the Office of the Chief Medical Examiner (OCME) has reported a marked increase in the number of drug abuse deaths in Maryland from 1986 to 1993, with drug deaths increasing sharply from 119 cases in 1986 to 356 in 1993, a 199% increase over seven years.[1] Narcotic drugs, specifically heroin, have played a major role in the rising number of drug abuse deaths.[1] Not surprisingly, cardiovascular complications have accompanied this increase. However, characterizing the effects of drugs of abuse on the vasculature is difficult because not all abused drugs result in anatomic changes. Direct human studies are scarcely available, and the studies that exist are performed under limited, controlled conditions which do not replicate the usage picture or conditions of the drug abuser. The drugs may have multiple effects depending on the dose, route of administration, impurities, underlying risk factors for cardiovascular disease, and concomitant use of other drugs such as ethanol and caffeine. In this section, the underlying pathogenic mechanisms associated with substance abuse leading to vascular complications (Table 2.2.1) is discussed.

Vasoconstriction at the epicardial or microvascular level may result in ischemia of almost any organ, but the vessel often fails to show any morphologic change. Drugs may also lead to formation of intravascular thrombi resulting in organ infarcts. A common complication of drug abuse may be cutaneous or cerebral manifestations of vasculitis. In some instances, acute hemodynamic worsening of hypertension may also lead to dissection of the aorta and rupture of arterial aneurysms resulting in intracranial hemorrhage.

There are several morphologic manifestations of drug-induced vascular disease. Vasoconstriction in itself is rarely identifiable by histologic methods, although contraction band necrosis of smooth muscle cells has rarely been reported in cases of clinically documented vasoconstriction. Chronic vasoconstriction may result in medial hypertrophy. Luminal thrombosis may be secondary to endothelial damage, underlying atherosclerosis, or effects of drugs on the clotting cascade. Atherosclerosis, which is a complex process involving lipid metabolism, endothelial dysfunction, immune activation, and thrombosis may be accelerated in persons exposed to drugs (Figure 2.2.15).

---

* The opinions or assertions contained herein are the private views of the authors and are not to be construed as official or as reflecting the views of the Department of the Army or Navy or the Department of Defense.

Table 2.2.1　Pathologic Vascular Manifestations of Substance Abuse

Drugs	Vasospasm	Thrombosis	Hypersensitivity Vasculitis	Necrotozing (Toxic) Arteritis	Fibrointimal Proliferation	Accelerated Atherosclerosis	Veno-Occlusive Disease
Recreational							
Cocaine	X	X	X	X	X	X	—
Heroin	—	—	X	—	—	—	X
Amphetamine and methamphetamine	X	X	—	X	X	—	—
Nicotine	X	X	X	—	—	X	—
Glue sniffing/solvents	X	—	—	—	—	—	—
Prescription							
Tricyclic antidepressants and phenothiazines	X	—	—	—	—	—	—
Ergot alkaloids	X	X	—	—	X	—	—
Ephedrine/pseudoephedrine	X	—	X	X	—	—	—
Non-Prescription							
Phenylpropanolamine and anorexiants	X	—	—	X	—	—	—
L-Tryptophan	X	—	—	X	X	—	—

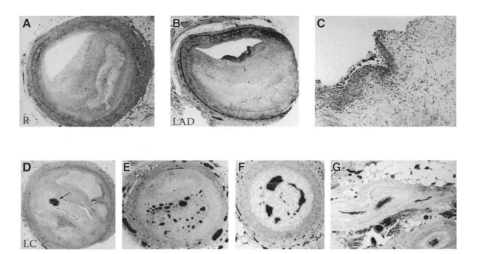

Figure 2.2.15 Cocaine-induced coronary atherosclerosis. The right (A) and the left anterior descending (LAD, B) coronary arteries are severely narrowed by atheroscletrotic plaque. The LAD (B) shows a superficial luminal thrombus (plaque erosion) consisting of fibrin and few inflammatory cells. The left circumflex (D,E,F) shows organized thrombus totally occluding the lumen. In (D), the recannalized channel is occluded by a thrombus (arrow). (G) Epicardial small branches of coronary arteries show severe intimal proliferation probably secondary to an organizing thrombus. The patient, a 30-year-old male, was a known cocaine abuser.

Fibrointimal proliferation (increased numbers of intimal smooth muscle cells either via migration from the media or intimal proliferation) may be secondary to toxic endothelial damage. Inflammatory vascular diseases (vasculitis) have been described as a drug-related effect. The two major types of drug-induced vasculitis occur either via antigen-antibody complex deposition, usually in arterioles and venules (small vessel or hypersensitivity vasculitis, Figure 2.2.16), or via direct toxic damage (toxic vasculitis, Figure 2.2.17), generally involving muscular arteries. Both types of vasculitis are characterized by fibrinoid necrosis of vascular walls, especially toxic vasculitis with occlusion by luminal thrombosis and/or fibrointimal proliferation and vessel rupture.

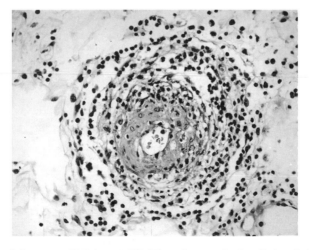

Figure 2.2.16 Small cell (hypersensitivity) vasculitis. There is a predominantly lymphoid infiltrate surrounding an arteriole, with focal neutrophilic karyorrhexis within the arterial wall. The patient had a cutaneous rash (palpable purpura) following exposure to diazepam, to which she was sensitized.

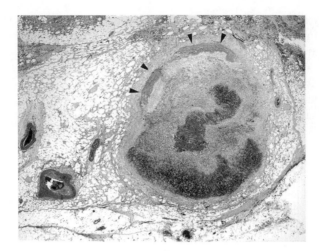

Figure 2.2.17   Toxic arteritis (polyarteritis). There is segmental destruction of the media with aneurysm formation. Residual intact media is present (arrowheads). The patient was a 24-year-old amphetamine
addict who expired from mesenteric arteritis and peritoneal hemorrhage.

2.2.2.1   Cocaine

Of all the known drugs of abuse associated with vascular toxicity, cocaine abuse is the most
common. The recent increase in cocaine abuse has predominantly occurred due to the availability
of cocaine base, known on the streets as crack, which produces an instant euphoria when smoked.
The mechanisms of cocaine-induced vascular toxicity are complex. Acute administration of cocaine
(whether in the base or hydrochloride form) causes an increase in heart rate and blood pressure.
Myocardial oxygen consumption increases from systemic catecholamine release and increased alpha-
adrenergic effects due to a blockade of norepinephrine reuptake.[2-4] Cocaine also acts as a local
anesthetic by inhibiting sodium influx into cells, and this is most likely responsible for the vasodilatory action of the drug. The anesthetic effects of cocaine are expected at higher doses while the
sympathomimetic actions are more likely to be prevalent at lower concentrations. Cocaine is detected
in the circulation immediately after its consumption with a plasma half-life of approximately 1 h.
However, the half-life for euphoria is less than 1 h which may lead to the repetitive use of cocaine.

The blood cocaine levels required to produce the euphoric effects is approximately 10^{-7} to 10^{-5}
mol/L; median plasma levels following intravenous cocaine use in cocaine related deaths is reported
to be approximately 6×10^{-7} mol/L to 3×10^{-4} mol/L.[5-7] "Binge users" of cocaine are known to
use high doses for extended periods, oftentimes up to 200 h.[8] Plasma concentrations during a
"binge" have not been documented although it is thought that the effects of cocaine on the
cardiovascular system are especially significant during bingeing. Following absorption, cocaine is
cleared from the circulation, primarily hydrolyzed to benzoylecgonine and metabolized to ecgonine
methyl ester (by plasma cholinesterases). At least in cerebral vessels, cocaine metabolites appear
to be biologically active and may partially contribute to cocaine's toxic effects.[9] Furthermore,
because of individual variability in plasma cholinesterase activity, cocaine abusers with low enzyme
levels may be predisposed to the cardiotoxic effects of the drug. In humans, cocaine is rapidly
metabolized, and less than 1% is excreted in urine; the major fraction of an administered dose of
cocaine is recovered in urine predominantly as ecgonine methyl ester and benzoylecgonine.[10,11]

Vasospasticity and Microvascular Resistance

Coronary spasm has been repeatedly proposed as a mechanism of the unexplained sudden cardiac
death in young cocaine abusers.[12] Clinical studies with intranasal cocaine administration in patients

undergoing coronary arteriography for the evaluation of chest pain have demonstrated a moderate reduction in luminal caliber and microvascular resistance.[13] Although cocaine-induced vasospasm has not been demonstrated clinically, ergonovine-induced coronary spasm has been reported to occur at the site of severe coronary lesions in young cocaine abusers.[14] Animal experiments have confirmed that cocaine results in only a minimal diffuse diminution in coronary artery caliber.[15] Such non-critical reduction in luminal diameter is presumably clinically insignificant. It therefore seems likely that acceleration of atherosclerotic lesions must form a substrate for the hypersensitive vasoconstrictive response of a vessel to cocaine consumption. In support of this, cocaine-induced vasoconstriction has been shown to be enhanced at sites of significant fixed stenosis.[16]

Alternatively, coronary vasospasm in cocaine abusers may be associated with an increase in adventitial mast cells. A significantly higher prevalence of adventitial mast cells in victims of cocaine-associated sudden cardiac death have been reported when compared to individuals without a history of substance abuse.[17] Similarly, increased adventitial mast cells have been demonstrated at autopsy in patients who had clinically documented vasospastic angina in the absence of severe atherosclerotic coronary disease.[18] Mast cells are a rich source of histamine, which is often used as a provocative test to induce spasm in patients with suspected variant angina.[19,20] Furthermore, other mast cell products such as prostaglandin D2 and leukotrienes C4 and D4 are also modulators of vascular smooth muscle tone; prostaglandin D2-induced vasoconstriction is 5- to 10-fold more potent than norepinephrine.[21]

Thrombosis

Multiple studies have reported angiographic evidence of coronary thrombosis in young cocaine abusers, predominantly associated with minor atherosclerotic irregularities of coronary arteries. On the other hand, the autopsy data from the young patients with cocaine abuse-associated acute coronary thrombosis leading to sudden cardiac death have demonstrated that approximately 40% of patients suffer from severe atherosclerotic lesions of one or more major coronary arteries.[22,23] The average age of the cocaine abusers in these reports was approximately 30 years. However, the decreased prevalence of angiographically determined atherosclerotic disease in cocaine abusers may result from angiographic underestimation of the atherosclerotic lesions due to the relatively diffuse nature of the disease.[24-26] The thrombi isolated from these autopsy examinations have been demonstrated to be rich in platelets[17,22,23] and are characteristically not associated with rupture of the underlying plaques (Figure 2.2.18).

The mechanism of cocaine-induced thrombosis is not clear. Reports of the direct effects of cocaine on platelet function *in vitro* have been inconclusive and contradictory: cocaine either stimulates or inhibits aggregation.[27-31] However, it is thought that cocaine-induced platelet activation may occur *in vivo* due to indirect effects of the drug. Evidence in support of this hypothesis comes from studies in which platelet activation assessed *ex vivo* by P-selectin expression was increased in long-term habitual cocaine abusers and in dogs treated with cocaine.[32,33] Alternatively, coronary spasm may also explain the increased prevalence of thrombosis associated with cocaine abuse.

Accelerated Atherosclerosis

Recent post-mortem studies in patients have emphasized that accelerated atherosclerosis may be an important etiologic factor in cocaine-induced acute coronary syndromes.[17,22-24] Kolodgie et al.[35] conducted a retrospective analysis of aortic sudanophilic lesions in asymptomatic young (median age, 25 years) cocaine abusers. After controlling for known risk factors of atherosclerosis, cocaine abuse was the only significant predictor of the extent of sudanophilia, suggesting that cocaine abuse was an independent risk factor for lipid infiltration in the vessel wall.[35] Accelerated atherosclerosis attributed to cocaine has been demonstrated experimentally in hypercholesterolemia-induced atherosclerosis in rabbits.[36] Also, cocaine abusers with coronary thrombosis have an

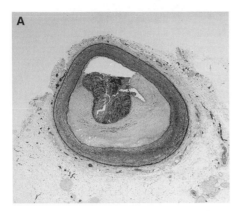
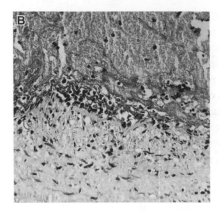

Figure 2.2.18 Cocaine-induced coronary thrombosis. (A) There is moderate (50%) luminal narrowing by atherosclerotic plaque composed of fibrointimal thickening consisting of smooth muscle cells in a proteoglycan-collagen matrix. (B) A higher magnification demonstrating a platelet thrombus overlying a plaque rich in smooth muscle cells and proteoglycans (plaque erosion).

increase in inflammatory cell infiltrate in severely narrowed atherosclerotic coronary arteries (Figure 2.2.15). Various mechanisms such as cocaine-related increase in plasma lipids, direct and indirect increase in endothelial permeability, higher prevalence of mast cells and other inflammatory cells in plaques may contribute to the lesions as discussed below.

Endothelial Dysfunction

As described above, atherosclerotic lesions occur prematurely and are likely to be more severe in cocaine abusers. Furthermore, these lesions develop regardless of the presence of conventional risk factors. Cocaine-induced endothelial cell dysfunction may be one of the predisposing factors, but whether this involves a direct and/or indirect action of the drug is unknown. Cocaine has been shown to disrupt the balance of endothelial prostacyclin and thromboxane production, which may be related to the increased tendency toward thrombosis and vasospasm observed in some cocaine abusers.[37,38] *In vitro* cell culture studies have demonstrated that cocaine increases the permeability function of endothelial cell monolayers as a possible mechanism of accelerated atherosclerosis.[36] Cocaine-treated endothelial cell monolayers demonstrated an increased permeability to horseradish peroxidase without affecting cell viability. Furthermore, cocaine-induced release of intracellular calcium stores may result in dysregulation of cytoskeletal integrity.[39] It has also been suggested that cocaine may suppress endothelial cell growth,[39] cause focal loss of endothelial cell integrity, or produce areas of extensive endothelial cell sloughing.[40,41]

As discussed earlier, the sympathomimetic effects of cocaine are associated with a transient but marked increase in blood pressure and some degree of vasoconstriction. These transient hemodynamic aberrations may cause endothelial injury. Indeed, cholesterol-fed rabbits typically develop atherosclerotic lesions in the thoracic aorta at sites of increased endothelial cell turnover.

Cocaine-related endothelial dysfunction may be associated with impairment of endothelium-dependent vasorelaxation. Forearm blood flow during acetylcholine infusion in long-term cocaine abusers was significantly lower when compared with subjects without a prior history of drug abuse.[42] Whether attenuation of endothelial-dependent vasodilatory mechanisms by cocaine results from lethal injury to the endothelium, insensitivity of smooth muscle cells to nitric oxide, or inhibition of enzymatic pathways responsible for nitric oxide synthesis remains to be determined.

Hemodynamic Alterations

Hypertension related vascular complications have been commonly reported with sympathomimetic drugs such as cocaine. Sympathomimetic actions secondary to acute or chronic cocaine abuse are well documented and may result from peripheral inhibition of neuronal reuptake of monoamines and increased epinephrine release from the adrenal medulla as well as central activation of the sympathetic nervous system. The transient increase in blood pressure, at least after acute cocaine abuse, has been associated with aortic dissection (Figure 2.2.19), rupture of aortic aneurysms, and hemorrhagic strokes in patients with preexisting hypertension.[43-45] Recently, intracranial hemorrhage has also been shown to be associated with cocaine abuse.[46-49] Of the 17 non-traumatic cases of intracranial hemorrhage analyzed at autopsy, 10 were associated with cocaine: 7 cases had intracerebral hemorrhage while 3 had ruptured berry aneurysms.[49] No pathologic evidence of vasculopathy was present in these patients.

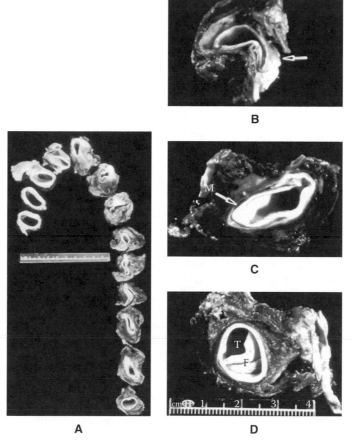

Figure 2.2.19 Cocaine-induced aortic dissection. (A) Multiple cross-sections through the aorta from the ascending aorta to the descending thoracic segment demonstrate dissection beginning at the aortic arch. (B) A cross-section through the descending thoracic aorta demonstrates the rupture site (arrow) of the false lumen. This rupture resulted in hemothorax and the death of the patient, who was a 24-year-old habitual cocaine abuser. (C) The dissection plane within the media (M) is clearly evident in this cross-section that demonstrates the intimal tear. (D) The true (T) and false (F) lumens can be distinguished readily in this cross-section demonstrating the medial flap.

Vasculitis

Cocaine-vasculitis has rarely been observed. Occasional cases of hypersensitivity vasculitis, similar to development of an Arthus reaction in experimental animals,[50-56] have been observed. Vasculitis characteristically results in fibrinoid necrosis of arteriolar and venular walls associated with disintegrating polymorphonuclear cells and histochemical localization of immunoglobulins and complement.[57,58] The lesions may eventually evolve into loose granulomas consisting of pallisading lymphocytes admixed with eosinophils and macrophages and, seldom, giant cells.[57,58] The most common site of vascular involvement in humans is skin; kidneys are involved in one half and liver in a third.[58]

Cocaine is also reported to induce systemic necrotizing arteritis of predominantly medium and small-sized cerebral arterial vessels frequently at branch points.[54,59] Affected areas characteristically have marked necrotic lesions with neutrophilic infiltration and various stages of healing. No giant cells or granulomas are seen, and the vascular adventitia is not involved. The mechanism of drug-induced necrotizing vasculitis has not been established and could be either immunological or directly toxic.

Synergy with Other Drugs

It is estimated that half the individuals consume alcohol during cocaine bingeing, and this promotes hepatic transformation of cocaine to cocaethylene.[60-67] Cocaethylene has a substantially longer half-life and therefore its persistent systemic presence may increase the likelihood of cocaine cardiotoxicity. Cocaethylene has more potent sodium channel blocking activity compared to cocaine and its proar-rhythmic effects may also be related to sudden death in the setting of ischemic myocardium.[69]

Another common drug that may be abused with cocaine is morphine. Morphine is a known secretogogue of mast cells that have been shown to be present in strikingly higher numbers in cocaine-associated atherosclerotic lesions. Mast cells are believed to play an important role in cocaine-related vasospastic manifestations.[70]

Similarly, synergistic interactions have been demonstrated for cocaine and cigarette smoking. Both agents are known to increase the metabolic demands on the heart but may also reduce oxygen supply. Moliteno et al.[71] have reported the influence of intranasal cocaine and cigarette smoking, alone and together, on myocardial oxygen demand and coronary artery dimensions in 42 subjects with and without atherosclerosis. Although none of the patients developed chest pain or ischemic electrocardiographic changes after cocaine use or cigarette smoking, oxygen demand increased by approximately 10% after either cigarette smoking or cocaine use, and by 50% after their simultaneous consumption. While the diameter of the normal coronary artery decreased by 6 to 7% with the use of either or both substances, reduction in the luminal diameter of the diseased artery segments for cigarette smoking, cocaine use, and both substances was 5%, 10%, and 20%, respectively.

2.2.2.2 *Methamphetamine*

The vascular effects of amphetamines have considerable similarity with sympathomimetic amines (ephedrine, phenylpropanolamine) and cocaine, which is alike structurally. Methamphetamine is abused orally, intravenously, or smoked in a crystal form ("ice"). Methamphetamine is metabolized to amphetamine, independent of the route of administration. Acute toxicity to amphetamine may manifest as rhabdomyolysis, disseminated intravascular coagulation, pulmonary edema, vascular spasm, and acute myocardial infarction. The ring substituted amphetamines 3,4-methylenedioxymethyl-amphetamine (MDMA, "ecstasy") and 3,4-methylenedioxyethylamphetamine (MDEA, "eve") have emerged as popular recreational drugs of abuse over the last decade.[72] Pharmacological studies indicate that these substances produce a mixture of central stimulant and psychedelic effects, many of which appear to be mediated by brain monoamines, particularly serotonin and dopamine.[73]

Chronic use of amphetamines may result in systemic and coronary artery vasospasm that results in an increased cardiac workload, impaired myocardial blood supply, and congestive failure, similar to end-stage hypertension. Sudden cardiac death may also occur. A few reports describe acute myocardial infarction associated with amphetamine abuse.[74] Potential explanations include coronary vasospasm, excessive catecholamine discharge resulting in ischemic myocardial necrosis, and catecholamine-mediated platelet aggregation with subsequent thrombus formation. The syndrome closely resembles acute myocardial infarction by cocaine abuse. As with cocaine toxicity, a deleterious effect of associated treatment with beta-blockers in the setting of myocardial infarction has also been observed.[71,75] Acute renal failure due to accelerated hypertension following the ingestion of 3,4-methylenedioxymethamphetamine ("ecstasy") has been reported.[76]

A necrotizing vasculitis resembling polyarteritis nodosa (Figure 2.2.17) has been reported in young abusers of methamphetamine, which may affect cerebral or visceral arteries. Histologically, there is fibrinoid necrosis of the media and intima of muscular arteries, with a neutrophilic eosinophilic, lymphocytic, and histiocytic infiltrate. Lesions at various stages may be seen with fresh thrombi in early lesions, florid intimal proliferation with marked luminal narrowing in subacute lesions, and destruction of the elastic lamina with replacement by collagen and luminal obliteration in later lesions. The cerebral effects of amphetamines are similar to those of other sympathomimetic amines (ephedrine and phenylpropranolamine).

Heroin

Heroin (diacetylmorphine) is a synthetic morphine derivative which, after administration, is hydrolytically deacetylated to 6-acetyl-morphine and excreted in the urine. Heroin has been associated with cerebral arteritis[77] and visceral polyarteritis.[78] Heroin may also have a direct toxic effect on the terminal hepatic veins,[79] the acute lesion being described as an inflammatory infiltrate of neutrophils and mononuclear cells in sinusoidal lumina and terminal veins, which progresses to fibrosis of the central veins. Heroin is also associated with glomerular injury which may result in malignant hypertension. This heroin-associated nephropathy seen in African-American intravenous drug addicts has given way in the 1990s to HIV-associated nephropathy as a result of shared needles.[80]

Nicotine

Nicotine is well known to simulate the release of catecholamines, resulting in vasoconstriction and other vascular effects of catecholamine release.[81,82] In addition, there may be direct toxicity of nicotine to vascular endothelial cells *in vitro*,[83] and an inhibition of apoptosis, which may contribute to an increase in smooth muscle cells within atherosclerotic plaques, possibly by monoclonal proliferation.[84] Nicotine has been found to be chemotactic for human neutrophils but not monocytes,[85] and in contrast to most other chemoattractants for neutrophils, does affect degranulation or superoxide production. Thus, nicotine may promote inflammation which may indirectly contribute to some of the associated vasculopathies. Nicotine transdermal patches used to help nicotine addiction have been associated with a leucocytoclastic vasculitis.[86,87]

Solvents ("Glue Sniffing")

Inhalation abuse of volatile solvents, previously known generically as "glue sniffing," is typically pursued by adolescents.[88] Glue sniffing has been associated with myocardial infarction, presumably secondary to coronary spasm as no fixed coronary lesions were identified by angiography.[89] The mechanism of sudden death in solvent sniffers is believed to be related to enhanced cardiac sensitivity to endogenous catecholamines.[90]

Vasculopathies Associated with Legitimate Medications

The sympathomimetic effects of tricyclic antidepressants are well documented, and overdose with these tricyclic amines is a major source of morbidity and mortality.[91] The most common cardiovascular effect of tricyclic amines is orthostatic hypotension, which is particularly serious in the elderly because it may lead to falls resulting in serious physical injuries. Severe orthostatic hypotension is more likely to develop in depressed patients with left ventricular impairment and/or in patients taking other drugs such as diuretics or vasodilators.[92] With chronic therapeutic administration, tricyclic antidepressants and phenothiazines have been associated with myocardial ischemia and infarction in the absence of fixed coronary lesions.[93]

Ergot Alkaloids — The ergot alkaloids are characterized by a nucleus of lysergic acid with the addition of side chains which divide the group into amino acids and amine alkaloids. Ergotamine, an example of an amino acid alkaloid, and methysergide, an example of an amine alkaloid, are both currently used in the prophylaxis and treatment of migraine headaches. The scleroticum of the fungus *Claviceps purpurea* is especially rich in ergot alkaloid, and was responsible for outbreaks of epidemic ergotism (St. Anthony's fire) following the mass ingestion of improperly stored rye in wet seasons. Ergot alkaloids have been used in large doses as an abortafacient.[94]

The toxic effects of ergot alkaloids include acute poisoning resulting in vasospasm and gangrene (usually as a complication of the induction of abortion), and acute idiosyncratic vasospasm secondary to a small dose of the drug. In this country, by far the most common form of ergot alkaloid toxicity is secondary to chronic ingestion of ergotamine, although outbreaks of St. Anthony's fire are still occasionally documented in developing countries.[94,95] Of recent incidence, bromocriptine mesylate, when used for the suppression of lactation in the puerperium, has been reported to cause generalized or focal vasospasm affecting the cardiac and/or cerebral blood vessels.[95]

The most common clinical manifestations of ergot alkaloid vasospasm are upper and lower extremity ischemia, which may result in claudication and ischemic ulcers of gangrene.[96] Other vasospastic sequelae of methylsergide or ergotamine toxicity include transient ischemic attacks, stroke (Figure 2.2.20), cardiac angina, and intestinal angina. Angiographic studies reveal narrowed

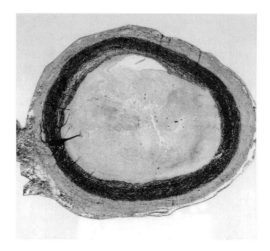

Figure 2.2.20   Ergotomine-induced fibrointimal proliferation. The carotid artery demonstrates marked narrowing by minimally cellular fibrointimal proliferation. The patient was a 45-year-old woman with chronic ergotamine toxicity who expired from a cerebrovascular accident. Elastic van Gieson stain.

vessels, which may show gradual smooth narrowing or irregular outlines with focal stenosis.[96,97] Laboratory studies are generally normal. A history will reveal chronic ingestion of ergotamine or methysergide, usually for migraine headaches, often by self-medication or doses exceeding the therapeutic recommendations. Symptoms often remit following cessation or lowering of medication dosage.

Pathologically, there are few vascular changes in acute cases of ergot poisoning, although contraction bands and medial necrosis may be noted within arterial walls. Chronic forms of ergotamine toxicity may have normal histologic findings[98] or changes consistent with chronic vasoconstriction, including medial hypertrophy, intimal proliferation, intimal hyalinization, and luminal thrombosis.

The mechanism(s) of ergot alkaloid toxicity are not yet completely clear. Physiologic doses result in vasoconstriction of painfully dilated cranial arteries, generally by the interaction of ergot with alpha-adrenergic receptors (alpha-adrenergic blockade) and serotonin antagonism.[99] Toxic vasoconstriciton may occur secondarily to a direct effect of ergot on the arterial media, exacerbated by a direct toxic effect on the capillary endothelium. High levels of platelet-derived growth factor have been detected in an individual with chronic ergotism, suggesting that growth factors are released as a result of chronic endothelial damage.[98]

Ephedrine and Pseudoephedrine

Ephedrine and pseudoephedrine are sympathomimetic amines that may cause hypertension and tachyarrhythmias due to beta-adrenergic stimulation. Toxic effects may result from overdose, drug interactions (e.g., serotonin reuptake inhibitors), or diseases that increase sensitivity to sympathomimetic agents.[100] Reported adverse events range in severity from tremor and headache to death and include reports of stroke, myocardial infarction, chest pain, seizures, insomnia, nausea and vomiting, fatigue, and dizziness.[101,102] Ephedrine is the preferred vasoconstrictor for the treatment of hypotension after epidural and spinal anesthesia in obstetrics because it preserves uterine perfusion better than pure alpha-adrenergic agonists. Although during pregnancy the vasoconstrictor response to ephedrine is diminished, its stimulatory effect on nitric oxide synthase may release nitric oxide.[103]

The incidence of patients developing cerebral hemorrhage, presumably by the development of toxic vasculitis, is rare.[104] Reported cases of cerebral hemorrhage secondary to ephedrine are fewer than those complicating the use of phenylpropanolamine and amphetamines.[104-107] Clinical management of ephedrine overdose is mostly supportive and requires establishing respiration, initiating emesis, administering activated charcoal and a cathartic, and monitoring the patient's blood pressure, ECG, fluid intake, and urinary output.[108]

Phenylpropanolamine

Phenylpropanolamine is a synthetic sympathomimetic amine that is found in cold medications and diet pills. Although the vascular effects of phenylpropanolamine were previously considered minor, relative to ephedrine and amphetamine, increasing reports of toxicity in patients taking larger doses of this drug, especially in diet pills, have led to a reappraisal of the potential toxicity of the drug.

Cerebral hemorrhage has been reported in phenylpropanolamine toxicity after a dose of 50 mg or more.[106] In some commonly used anorexiants, including methamphetamine and phenylpropanolamine, an association with stroke has been reported.[108,109] Angiography in individuals with phenylpropanolamine toxicity has demonstrated vascular beading that has been ascribed to both vasospasm and to vasculitis.[106,110] In occasional instances in which histologic examination was performed, a necrotizing vasculitis has been identified.[105,106] It is unknown what proportions of phenylpropanolamine-, amphetamine-, and ephedrine-induced cerebral hemorrhages are due to vasculitis, and what proportions are due to vasospam related to catecholamine release.[106]

L-Tryptophan

The eosinophilia-myalgia syndrome associated with the ingestion of L-tryptophan was first recognized in late 1989.[111] Similar pathologic manifestations of eosinophilic myalgia syndrome share many features with the toxic oil syndrome caused by ingestion of adulterated rapeseed oil in Spain.[112] Although available over the counter in the U.S., L-tryptophan is dispensed only by prescription in Germany. Epidemiologic studies strongly suggest that the offending toxin is a contaminant used in the preparation of tryptophan, and not tryptophan itself.[113] Putative offending agents from suspected lots of L-tryptophan include 1,1'-ethylidenebis(tryptophan) and 3-pheny-lamino-1,2-propanediol, an aniline derivative. Most symptomatic patients are those that chronically ingest large doses of tryptophan (500 mg to several grams a day), although a dose-related toxic effect was not observed in an epidemiological study of German patients.[111] Vascular effects include pulmonary hypertension resulting from obstruction of pulmonary vessels.[112] Intermittent coronary spasm resulting in episodes of myocardial damage has also been reported.[115] Fibrointimal proliferation of small coronary arteries has also been described in patients with eosinophilia myalgia syndrome associated with L-tryptophan.[116]

Because L-tryptophan is metabolized to a number of compounds, including kynurenine, quinolate, serotonin, 5-hydroxyindoacetic acid, and homovanillic acid, a potential vasospastic role of one or more of these compounds has been investigated. A recent study did not find a link between any of these compounds and coronary vasospasm, but implicated increased levels of eosinophil granule major basic protein.[115]

REFERENCES

1. Li L, Smialek JE. Observations on drug abuse deaths in the state of Maryland. *J Forensic Sci* 1996;41:106–9.
2. Muscholl E. Effect of cocaine and related drugs on the uptake of noradrenaline by heart and spleen. *Br J Pharmacol* 1961;62:352.
3. Fuder H, Bath F, Wiebelt H, Muscholl E. Autoinhibition of noradrenaline release from the rat heart as a function of the biophase concentration. Effects of exogenous alpha-adrenoceptor agonists, cocaine, and perfusion rate. *Naunyn Schmiedebergs Arch Pharmacol* 1984;325:25–33.
4. Perper JA, Van Thiel DH. Cardiovascular complications of cocaine abuse. *Recent Dev Alcohol* 1992;10:343–61.
5. Van Dyke C, Barash PG, Jatlow P, Byck R. Cocaine: plasma concentrations after intranasal application in man. *Science* 1976;191:859–61.
6. Poklis A, Maginn D, Barr JL. Tissue disposition of cocaine in man: a report of five fatal poisonings. *Forensic Sci Int* 1987;33:83–8.
7. Poklis A, Mackell MA, Graham M. Disposition of cocaine in fatal poisoning in man. *J Anal Toxicol* 1985;9:227–9.
8. Gawin FH. Cocaine addiction: psychology and neurophysiology [published erratum appears in Science 1991 Aug 2;253(5019):494]. *Science* 1991;251:1580–6.
9. Madden JA, Powers RH. Effect of cocaine and cocaine metabolites on cerebral arteries *in vitro*. *Life Sci* 1990;47:1109–14.
10. Ambre J. The urinary excretion of cocaine and metabolites in humans: a kinetic analysis of published data. *J Anal Toxicol* 1985;9:241–5.
11. Jeffcoat AR, Perez-Reyes M, Hill JM, Sadler BM, Cook CE. Cocaine disposition in humans after intravenous injection, nasal insufflation (snorting), or smoking. *Drug Metab Dispos* 1989;17:153–9.
12. Minor RL, Jr., Scott BD, Brown DD, Winniford MD. Cocaine-induced myocardial infarction in patients with normal coronary arteries [see comments]. *Ann Intern Med* 1991;115:797–806.

13. Lange RA, Cigarroa RG, Yancy CW, Jr., Willard JE, Popma JJ, Sills MN, McBride W, Kim AS, Hillis LD. Cocaine-induced coronary-artery vasoconstriction [see comments]. *N Engl J Med* 1989;321:1557–62.

14. Smith HW, Liberman HA, Brody SL, Battey LL, Donohue BC, Morris DC. Acute myocardial infarction temporally related to cocaine use. Clinical, angiographic, and pathophysiologic observations. *Ann Intern Med* 1987;107:13–8.

15. Hale SL, Alker KJ, Rezkalla S, Figures G, Kloner RA. Adverse effects of cocaine on cardiovascular dynamics, myocardial blood flow, and coronary artery diameter in an experimental model. *Am Heart J* 1989;118:927–33.

16. Flores ED, Lange RA, Cigarroa RG, Hillis LD. Effect of cocaine on coronary artery dimensions in atherosclerotic coronary artery disease: enhanced vasoconstriction at sites of significant stenoses. *J Am Coll Cardiol* 1990;16:74–9.

17. Kolodgie FD, Virmani R, Cornhill JF, Herderick EE, Smialek J. Increase in atherosclerosis and adventitial mast cells in cocaine abusers: an alternative mechanism of cocaine-associated coronary vasospasm and thrombosis. *J Am Coll Cardiol* 1991;17:1553–60.

18. Forman MB, Oates JA, Robertson D, Robertson RM, Roberts LJ, Virmani R. Increased adventitial mast cells in a patient with coronary spasm. *N Engl J Med* 1985;313:1138–41.

19. Kaski JC, Crea F, Meran D, Rodriguez L, Araujo L, Chierchia S, Davies G, Maseri A. Local coronary supersensitivity to diverse vasoconstrictive stimuli in patients with variant angina. *Circulation* 1986;74:1255–65.

20. Ginsburg R, Bristow MR, Kantrowitz N, Baim DS, Harrison DC. Histamine provocation of clinical coronary artery spasm: implications concerning pathogenesis of variant angina pectoris. *Am Heart J* 1981;102:819–22.

21. Burke JA, Levi R, Guo ZG, Corey EJ. Leukotrienes C4, D4 and E4: effects on human and guinea-pig cardiac preparations *in vitro*. *J Pharmacol Exp Ther* 1982;221:235–41.

22. Mittleman RE, Wetli CV. Cocaine and sudden "natural" death. *J Forensic Sci* 1987;32:11–9.

23. Dressler FA, Malekzadeh S, Roberts WC. Quantitative analysis of amounts of coronary arterial narrowing in cocaine addicts. *Am J Cardiol* 1990;65:303–8.

24. Sheikh KH, Harrison JK, Harding MB, Himmelstein SI, Kisslo KB, Davidson CJ, Bashore TM. Detection of angiographically silent coronary atherosclerosis by intracoronary ultrasonography. *Am Heart J* 1991;121:1803–7.

25. Tobis JM, Mallery J, Mahon D, Lehmann K, Zalesky P, Griffith J, Gessert J, Moriuchi M, McRae M, Dwyer ML, et al. Intravascular ultrasound imaging of human coronary arteries *in vivo*. Analysis of tissue characterizations with comparison to *in vitro* histological specimens. *Circulation* 1991;83:913–26.

26. McPherson DD, Hiratzka LF, Lamberth WC, Brandt B, Hunt M, Kieso RA, Marcus ML, Kerber RE. Delineation of the extent of coronary atherosclerosis by high-frequency epicardial echocardiography. *N Engl J Med* 1987;316:304–9.

27. Heesch CM, Negus BH, Steiner M, Snyder RW, II, McIntire DD, Grayburn PA, Ashcraft J, Hernandez JA, Eichhorn EJ. Effects of *in vivo* cocaine administration on human platelet aggregation. *Am J Cardiol* 1996;78:237–9.

28. Kugelmass AD, Oda A, Monahan K, Cabral C, Ware JA. Activation of human platelets by cocaine. *Circulation* 1993;88:876–83.

29. Jennings LK, White MM, Sauer CM, Mauer AM, Robertson JT. Cocaine-induced platelet defects. *Stroke* 1993;24:1352–9.

30. Rezkalla SH, Mazza JJ, Kloner RA, Tillema V, Chang SH. Effects of cocaine on human platelets in healthy subjects. *Am J Cardiol* 1993;72:243–6.

31. Togna G, Tempesta E, Togna AR, Dolci N, Cebo B, Caprino L. Platelet responsiveness and biosynthesis of thromboxane and prostacyclin in response to *in vitro* cocaine treatment. *Haemostasis* 1985;15:100–7.

32. Kugelmass AD, Shannon RP, Yeo EL, Ware JA. Intravenous cocaine induces platelet activation in the conscious dog. *Circulation* 1995;91:1336–40.

33. Rinder HM, Ault KA, Jatlow PI, Kosten TR, Smith BR. Platelet alpha-granule release in cocaine users. *Circulation* 1994;90:1162–7.

34. Fogo A, Superdock KR, Atkinson JB. Severe arteriosclerosis in the kidney of a cocaine addict. *Am J Kidney Dis* 1992;20:513–5.

35. Kolodgie FD, Virmani R, Cornhill JF, Herderick EE, Malcom GT, Mergner WJ. Cocaine: an independent risk factor for aortic sudanophilia. A preliminary report. *Atherosclerosis* 1992;97:53–62.
36. Kolodgie FD, Wilson PS, Cornhill JF, Herderick EE, Mergner WJ, Virmani R. Increased prevalence of aortic fatty streaks in cholesterol-fed rabbits administered intravenous cocaine: the role of vascular endothelium. *Toxicol Pathol* 1993;21:425–35.
37. Eichhorn EJ, Demian SE, Alvarez LG, Willard JE, Molina S, Bartula LL, Prince MD, Inman LR, Grayburn PA, Myers SI. Cocaine-induced alterations in prostaglandin production in rabbit aorta. *J Am Coll Cardiol* 1992;19:696–703.
38. Cejtin HE, Parsons MT, Wilson L, Jr. Cocaine use and its effect on umbilical artery prostacyclin production. *Prostaglandins* 1990;40:249–57.
39. Welder AA, Grammas P, Fugate RD, Rohrer P, Melchert RB. A primary culture system of rat heart-derived endothelial cells for evaluating cocaine-induced vascular injury. *Toxicol Methods* 1993;3:109–18.
40. Gilloteaux J, Dalbec JP. Transplacental cardiotoxicity of cocaine: atrial damage following treatment in early pregnancy. *Scanning Microsc* 1991;5:519–29; discussion 29–31.
41. Jones LF, Tackett RL. Chronic cocaine treatment enhances the responsiveness of the left anterior descending coronary artery and the femoral artery to vasoactive substances. *J Pharmacol Exp Ther* 1990;255:1366–70.
42. Havranek EP, Nademanee K, Grayburn PA, Eichhorn EJ. Endothelium-dependent vasorelaxation is impaired in cocaine arteriopathy. *J Am Coll Cardiol* 1996;28:1168–74.
43. Gadaleta D, Hall MH, Nelson RL. Cocaine-induced acute aortic dissection. *Chest* 1989;96:1203–5.
44. Cohle SD, Lie JT. Dissection of the aorta and coronary arteries associated with acute cocaine intoxication. *Arch Pathol Lab Med* 1992;116:1239–41.
45. McDermott JC, Schuster MR, Crummy AB, Acher CW. Crack and aortic dissection. *Wis Med J* 1993;92:453–5.
46. Aggarwal SK, Williams V, Levine SR, Cassin BJ, Garcia JH. Cocaine-associated intracranial hemorrhage: absence of vasculitis in 14 cases. *Neurology* 1996;46:1741–3.
47. Nalls G, Disher A, Daryabagi J, Zant Z, Eisenman J. Subcortical cerebral hemorrhages associated with cocaine abuse: CT and MR findings. *J Comput Assist Tomogr* 1989;13:1–5.
48. Green RM, Kelly KM, Gabrielsen T, Levine SR, Vanderzant C. Multiple intracerebral hemorrhages after smoking "crack" cocaine. *Stroke* 1990;21:957–62.
49. Nolte KB, Brass LM, Fletterick CF. Intracranial hemorrhage associated with cocaine abuse: a prospective autopsy study. *Neurology* 1996;46:1291–6.
50. Merkel PA, Koroshetz WJ, Irizarry MC, Cudkowicz ME. Cocaine-associated cerebral vasculitis. *Semin Arthritis Rheum* 1995;25:172–83.
51. Gradon JD, Wityk R. Diagnosis of probable cocaine-induced cerebral vasculitis by magnetic resonance angiography. *South Med J* 1995;88:1264–6.
52. Giang DW. Central nervous system vasculitis secondary to infections, toxins, and neoplasms. *Semin Neurol* 1994;14:313–9.
53. Morrow PL, McQuillen JB. Cerebral vasculitis associated with cocaine abuse. *J Forensic Sci* 1993;38:732–8.
54. Fredericks RK, Lefkowitz DS, Challa VR, Troost BT. Cerebral vasculitis associated with cocaine abuse. *Stroke* 1991;22:1437–9.
55. Kaye BR, Fainstat M. Cerebral vasculitis associated with cocaine abuse. *JAMA* 1987;258:2104–6.
56. Cerebral vasculitis associated with cocaine abuse or subarachnoid hemorrhage? [letter]. *JAMA* 1988;259:1648–9.
57. Krendel DA, Ditter SM, Frankel MR, Ross WK. Biopsy-proven cerebral vasculitis associated with cocaine abuse. *Neurology* 1990;40:1092–4.
58. Enriquez R, Palacios FO, Gonzalez CM, Amoros FA, Cabezuelo JB, Hernandez F. Skin vasculitis, hypokalemia and acute renal failure in rhabdomyolysis associated with cocaine [letter]. *Nephron* 1991;59:336–7.
59. Daras M, Tuchman AJ, Koppel BS, Samkoff LM, Weitzner I, Marc J. Neurovascular complications of cocaine. *Acta Neurol Scand* 1994;90:124–9.
60. Barinaga M. Miami vice metabolite [news]. *Science* 1990;250:758.

61. Hearn WL, Flynn DD, Hime GW, Rose S, Cofino JC, Mantero-Atienza E, Wetli CV, Mash DC. Cocaethylene: a unique cocaine metabolite displays high affinity for the dopamine transporter. *J Neurochem* 1991;56:698–701.

62. Jatlow P, Hearn WL, Elsworth JD, Roth RH, Bradberry CW, Taylor JR. Cocaethylene inhibits uptake of dopamine and can reach high plasma concentrations following combined cocaine and ethanol use. *NIDA Res Monogr* 1991;105:572–3.

63. Hearn WL, Rose S, Wagner J, Ciarleglio A, Mash DC. Cocaethylene is more potent than cocaine in mediating lethality. *Pharmacol Biochem Behav* 1991;39:531–3.

64. Perez-Reyes M, Jeffcoat AR. Ethanol/cocaine interaction: cocaine and cocaethylene plasma concentrations and their relationship to subjective and cardiovascular effects. *Life Sci* 1992;51:553–63.

65. Perez-Reyes M. Subjective and cardiovascular effects of cocaethylene in humans. *Psychopharmacology (Berl)* 1993;113:144–7.

66. Covert RF, Schreiber MD, Tebbett IR, Torgerson LJ. Hemodynamic and cerebral blood flow effects of cocaine, cocaethylene and benzoylecgonine in conscious and anesthetized fetal lambs. *J Pharmacol Exp Ther* 1994;270:118–26.

67. Wilson LD, Henning RJ, Suttheimer C, Lavins E, Balraj E, Earl S. Cocaethylene causes dose-dependent reductions in cardiac function in anesthetized dogs. *J Cardiovasc Pharmacol* 1995;26:965–73.

68. Randall T. Cocaine, alcohol mix in body to form even longer lasting, more lethal drug [news]. *JAMA* 1992;267:1043–4.

69. Xu YQ, Crumb WJ, Jr., Clarkson CW. Cocaethylene, a metabolite of cocaine and ethanol, is a potent blocker of cardiac sodium channels. *J Pharmacol Exp Ther* 1994;271:319–25.

70. Klein LM, Lavker RM, Matis WL, Murphy GF. Degranulation of human mast cells induces an endothelial antigen central to leukocyte adhesion. *Proc Natl Acad Sci USA* 1989;86:8972–6.

71. Moliterno DJ, Willard JE, Lange RA, Negus BH, Boehrer JD, Glamann DB, Landau C, Rossen JD, Winniford MD, Hillis LD. Coronary-artery vasoconstriction induced by cocaine, cigarette smoking, or both. *N Engl J Med* 1994;330:454–9.

72. Milroy CM, Clark JC, Forrest AR. Pathology of deaths associated with "ecstasy" and "eve" misuse. *J Clin Pathol* 1996;49:149–53.

73. Steele TD, McCann UD, Ricaurte GA. 3,4-Methylenedioxymethamphetamine (MDMA, "Ecstasy"): pharmacology and toxicology in animals and humans. *Addiction* 1994;89:539–51.

74. Bashour TT. Acute myocardial infarction resulting from amphetamine abuse: a spasm-thrombus interplay? *Am Heart J* 1994;128:1237–9.

75. Ragland AS, Ismail Y, Arsura EL. Myocardial infarction after amphetamine use. *Am Heart J* 1993;125:247–9.

76. Woodrow G, Harnden P, Turney JH. Acute renal failure due to accelerated hypertension following ingestion of 3,4-methylenedioxymethamphetamine ('ecstasy'). *Nephrol Dial Transplant* 1995;10:399–400.

77. King J, Richards M, Tress B. Cerebral arteritis associated with heroin abuse. *Med J Aust* 1978;2:444–5.

78. Citron BP, Halpern M, McCarron M, Lundberg GD, McCormick R, Pincus IJ, Tatter D, Haverback BJ. Necrotizing angiitis associated with drug abuse. *N Engl J Med* 1970;283:1003–11.

79. de Araujo MS, Gerard F, Chossegros P, Porto LC, Barlet P, Grimaud JA. Vascular hepatotoxicity related to heroin addiction. *Virchows Arch A Pathol Anat Histopathol* 1990;417:497–503.

80. Bakir AA, Dunea G. Drugs of abuse and renal disease. *Curr Opin Nephrol Hypertens* 1996;5:122–6.

81. Murphy DA, O'Blenes S, Nassar BA, Armour JA. Effects of acutely raising intracranial pressure on cardiac sympathetic efferent neuron function. *Cardiovasc Res* 1995;30:716–24.

82. Grassi G, Seravalle G, Calhoun DA, Bolla GB, Giannattasio C, Marabini M, Del Bo A, Mancia G. Mechanisms responsible for sympathetic activation by cigarette smoking in humans. *Circulation* 1994;90:248–53.

83. Pitillo R, Cigarette smoking and endothelial injury: A review. *Tobacco Smoking and Atherosclerosis.* 1989, New York: Plenum Press.

84. Wright SC, Zhong J, Zheng H, Larrick JW. Nicotine inhibition of apoptosis suggests a role in tumor promotion. *FASEB J* 1993;7:1045–51.

85. Totti Nd, McCusker KT, Campbell EJ, Griffin GL, Senior RM. Nicotine is chemotactic for neutrophils and enhances neutrophil responsiveness to chemotactic peptides. *Science* 1984;223:169–71.

86. Lagrue G, Verra F, Lebargy F. Nicotine patches and vascular risks [letter; comment]. *Lancet* 1993;342:564.

87. Van der Klauw MM, Van Hillo B, Van den Berg WH, Bolsius EP, Sutorius FF, Stricker BH. Vasculitis attributed to the nicotine patch (Nicotinell). *Br J Dermatol* 1996;134:361–4.

88. Steffee CH, Davis GJ, Nicol KK. A whiff of death: fatal volatile solvent inhalation abuse. *South Med J* 1996;89:879–84.

89. Cunningham SR, Dalzell GW, McGirr P, Khan MM. Myocardial infarction and primary ventricular fibrillation after glue sniffing. *Br Med J (Clin Res Ed)* 1987;294:739–40.

90. McLeod AA, Marjot R, Monaghan MJ, Hugh-Jones P, Jackson G, Timmis AD, Smyth P, Monaghan M, Walker L, Daly K, McLeod AA, Jewitt DE. Chronic cardiac toxicity after inhalation of 1,1,1-trichloroethane Milrinone in heart failure. Acute effects on left ventricular systolic function and myocardial metabolism. *Br Med J (Clin Res Ed)* 1987;294:727–9.

91. Warrington SJ, Padgham C, Lader M. The cardiovascular effects of antidepressants. *Psychol Med Monogr Suppl* 1989;16:i–iii, 1–40.

92. Glassman AH, Preud'homme XA. Review of the cardiovascular effects of heterocyclic antidepressants. *J Clin Psychiatry* 1993;54 Suppl:16–22.

93. Chamsi-Pasha H, Barnes PC. Myocardial infarction: a complication of amitriptyline overdose. *Postgrad Med J* 1988;64:968–70.

94. Magee R. Saint Anthony's fire revisited. Vascular problems associated with migraine medication. *Med J Aust* 1991;154:145–9.

95. Weaver R, Phillips M, Vacek JL. St. Anthony's fire: a medieval disease in modern times: case history. *Angiology* 1989;40:929–32.

96. Iffy L, McArdle JJ, Ganesh V, Hopp L. Bromocriptine related atypical vascular accidents postpartum identified through medicolegal reviews. *Med Law* 1996;15:127–34.

97. McKiernan TL, Bock K, Leya F, Grassman E, Lewis B, Johnson SA, Scanlon PJ. Ergot induced peripheral vascular insufficiency, non-interventional treatment. *Cathet Cardiovasc Diagn* 1994;31:211–4.

98. Raroque HG, Jr., Tesfa G, Purdy P. Postpartum cerebral angiopathy. Is there a role for sympathomimetic drugs? *Stroke* 1993;24:2108–10.

99. Pietrogrande F, Caenazzo A, Dazzi F, Polato G, Girolami A. A role for platelet-derived growth factor in drug-induced chronic ergotism? A case report. *Angiology* 1995;46:633–6.

100. Oliver JW, Abney LK, Strickland JR, Linnabary RD. Vasoconstriction in bovine vasculature induced by the tall fescue alkaloid lysergamide. *J Anim Sci* 1993;71:2708–13.

101. Skop BP, Finkelstein JA, Mareth TR, Magoon MR, Brown TM. The serotonin syndrome associated with paroxetine, an over-the-counter cold remedy, and vascular disease [see comments]. *Am J Emerg Med* 1994;12:642–4.

102. Wiener I, Tilkian AG, Palazzolo M. Coronary artery spasm and myocardial infarction in a patient with normal coronary arteries: temporal relationship to pseudoephedrine ingestion. *Cathet Cardiovasc Diagn* 1990;20:51–3.

103. Adverse events associated with ephedrine-containing products — Texas, December 1993–September 1995. *MMWR Morb Mortal Wkly Rep* 1996;45:689–93.

104. Li P, Tong C, Eisenach JC. Pregnancy and ephedrine increase the release of nitric oxide in ovine uterine arteries. *Anesth Analg* 1996;82:288–93.

105. Wooten MR, Khangure MS, Murphy MJ. Intracerebral hemorrhage and vasculitis related to ephedrine abuse. *Ann Neurol* 1983;13:337–40.

106. Glick R, Hoying J, Cerullo L, Perlman S. Phenylpropanolamine: an over-the-counter drug causing central nervous system vasculitis and intracerebral hemorrhage. Case report and review. *Neurosurgery* 1987;20:969–74.

107. Forman HP, Levin S, Stewart B, Patel M, Feinstein S. Cerebral vasculitis and hemorrhage in an adolescent taking diet pills containing phenylpropanolamine: case report and review of literature. *Pediatrics* 1989;83:737–41.

108. Nadeau SE. Intracerebral hemorrhage and vasculitis related to ephedrine abuse [letter]. *Ann Neurol* 1984;15:114–5.

109. Sawyer DR, Conner CS, Rumack BH. Managing acute toxicity from nonprescription stimulants. *Clin Pharm* 1982;1:529–33.

110. Kokkinos J, Levine SR. Possible association of ischemic stroke with phentermine. *Stroke* 1993;24:310–3.

111. Fallis RJ, Fisher M. Cerebral vasculitis and hemorrhage associated with phenylpropanolamine. *Neurology* 1985;35:405–7.

112. Mayeno AN, Gleich GJ. The eosinophilia-myalgia syndrome: lessons from Germany [editorial; comment]. *Mayo Clin Proc* 1994;69:702–4.

113. Tabuenca JM. Toxic-allergic syndrome caused by ingestion of rapeseed oil denatured with aniline. *Lancet* 1981;2:567–8.

114. Carr L, Ruther E, Berg PA, Lehnert H. Eosinophilia-myalgia syndrome in Germany: an epidemiologic review [see comments]. *Mayo Clin Proc* 1994;69:620–5.

115. Campagna AC, Blanc PD, Criswell LA, Clarke D, Sack KE, Gold WM, Golden JA. Pulmonary manifestations of the eosinophilia-myalgia syndrome associated with tryptophan ingestion. *Chest* 1992;101:1274–81.

116. Hertzman PA, Maddoux GL, Sternberg EM, Heyes MP, Mefford IN, Kephart GM, Gleich GJ. Repeated coronary artery spasm in a young woman with the eosinophilia-myalgia syndrome. *JAMA* 1992;267:2932–4.

117. Hayashi T, James TN. Immunohistochemical analysis of lymphocytes in postmortem study of the heart from fatal cases of the eosinophilia myalgia syndrome and of the toxic oil syndrome. *Am Heart J* 1994;127:1298–308.

2.3 MYOCARDIAL ALTERATIONS IN DRUG ABUSERS

Steven B. Karch, M.D., FFFLM
Consultant Pathologist and Toxicologist, Berkeley, California

Specific diseases of the myocardium of drug abusers are rarely reported, and the true incidence of myocardial disease in this group remains unknown. The absence of myocardial disease among drug abusers is probably more apparent than real. Many pathologists still do not recognize modest degrees of hypertrophy as representing disease. Another confounder preventing accurate estimation of myocardial disease in drug abusers is that observed frequency of any particular myocardial lesion depends upon the population being studied, and the drugs that they use. Patterns of drug abuse have changed a great deal over the last decade. It is likely that the type of lesions encountered has changed as well.

Prior to the advent of the cocaine and HIV pandemics, when heroin was the main drug of abuse, the incidence of myocardial disease among drug users was apparently the same as in controls. In Siegel and Helpern's classic paper on the "Diagnosis of Death from Intravenous Narcotism," heart disease was never even mentioned,[1] nor were any significant cardiac abnormalities recorded in Wetli's study of 100 consecutively autopsied drug abusers.[2] When Louria analyzed the discharge diagnosis of addicts admitted to Bellevue Hospital's general medical service, 40 years ago, he found that the incidence of endocarditis was less than 10%; no other types of heart disease were mentioned.[3]

The advent of HIV, coupled with the rise in cocaine and methamphetamine abuse, has drastically changed the landscape. So has the unarguable fact that we now live (or soon will live) in the age of the molecular autopsy; hearts that look normal at autopsy, and which even appear normal under the microscope may, in fact, be diseased (channelopathies and other heritable disorders). At the same time, it has also become very clear that the extracellular matrix, the tissue surrounding myocytes, is not just inert scaffolding but, rather, an active, hormone-secreting tissue, exerting potent effects on myocardial structure (the process of myocardial remodeling).

2.3.1　Epidemiology

Whether or not damage occurs to the myocardium depends both on the drug and the way it is administered. In areas where the injection of pills meant for oral use is common practice, granulomatous lung disease and pulmonary hypertension will be encountered.[4–6] Both abnormalities are induced by the expients found in the pills, rather than the drug itself. Even though granulomatous disease involving the pulmonary vasculature and interstitium is relatively common among injection drug users, the clinical consequences of these lesions are difficult to estimate, and the finding may often be overlooked.[7] The practice of injecting crushed pills is much more common in some places than others, so the presence of granulomas, while diagnostically useful, cannot always be assumed. Most adult drug abusers practice polypharmacy; attempts at correlating specific drugs with certain types of lesions is a difficult, if not impossible exercise.

Earlier studies of heart disease in drug users must be interpreted with very great caution, particularly those studies where the diagnosis was not confirmed by toxicological testing. One study of 168 drug-related deaths found a 100% incidence of heart disease,[8] but since toxicological findings were not known for all the patients, and since the limits of detection for drugs were far higher in the early 1980s than today, and since all of the patients were referred because they were suspected of having heart disease in the first place, not a great deal can be concluded about the real incidence of the problem.

Sudden unexpected death in young adults, aged 18 to 35 years, accounts for an important subset of drug-related deaths. A study of cases occurring over a 10-year period in Galway, Ireland, found that a large proportion, over one third, of sudden deaths in young adults were secondary to epilepsy, and/or chemical/drug poisoning. In total, these deaths amounted to 9% of the deaths occurring in the study population.[9] In Australia, where the lifetime use of cocaine is rising, only 3% of the population over age 14 was using cocaine in 1991, but that number had increased to 4.5% in 1998, and cocaine accounted for 10% of all illicit drug-related deaths in that country. Most of these deaths appear to have been the result of acute myocardial infarction.[10] Reliable statistics for the incidence of cocaine-related and/or heroin-related heart disease in the United States are not available.

2.3.2　Mechanism of Myocardial Hypertrophy

Even in the absence of solid epidemiological data, certain generalizations are possible. The hearts of chronic stimulant abusers, whether of cocaine or methamphetamine, or even MDMA, are enlarged, and often manifest changes consistent with the known effects of prolonged catecholamine excess. Myocardial hypertrophy in cocaine abusers has been confirmed by comparisons of cocaine abusers' electrocardiograms to those of age-sex-matched controls, to those of asymptomatic cocaine users in rehabilitation, and to cocaine users seeking treatment for chest pain.[11–13] Myocardial hypertrophy has been reported in separate, controlled, autopsy studies of cocaine, methamphetamine, MDMA, and ephedrine users.[14–17] The increases are generally quite modest, averaging 10 to 11% over that predicted by standard nomograms.[18]

Molecular biologists have shown that stimulant-type drugs cause increases in the myocardial expression and activation of cAMP response binding protein, otherwise known as CREB. CREB is one of the transcriptional factors that regulate gene expression, mainly through the action of a large group of different kinases. These include protein kinase A, calcium calmodulin kinase II, and mitogen-activated protein kinase. All three can induce CREB phosphorylation at serine position 133.[19] The result is increased myosin production and myocardial hypertrophy,[20] primarily because more calmodulin is produced. Calmodulin is a small, acidic protein. It binds to Ca^{2+}-binding proteins and, in conjunction with calcium and other molecules, it acts as a second messenger, controlling diverse biochemical processes in many different cell types, not just myocytes. Calmodulin kinase II activity is required for normal atrioventricular nodal conduction,[21] and camodulin itself protects against structural heart disease.[22] It appears that cocaine users develop myocardial hypertrophy because cocaine directly activates calmodulin kinase II.[23] Whether the same process occurs in methamphetamine, ephedrine, or MDMA abusers is not yet known.

The hearts of heroin abusers generally do not show evidence of myocardial hypertrophy unless, of course, the abusers are simultaneously abusing stimulants, an increasingly common practice. It appears that heroin does not lead to CREB phosphorylation, at least not in the myocardium, although there is evidence for CREB activation in the brain.[24] Heroin abusers may not be uniquely subject to myocardial hypertrophy, but HIV-related disease is common among heroin users, as are a multitude of other "lifestyle" disorders such as hepatitis (types A, B, and C)[25,26] and tuberculosis.[27] If one of these associated disorders leads to restriction of the pulmonary bed, and pulmonary hypertension, at least some degree of right ventricular hypertrophy is to be anticipated.

2.3.3 Consequences of Myocardial Hypertrophy

Left ventricular hypertrophy is the normal cardiac adaptation to a prolonged increase in arterial blood pressure or, at least, to the activation of the genes responding to a pressure increase. One of the earliest results of the pioneering Framingham Study was the clear demonstration that patients with electrocardiographic evidence of left ventricular hypertrophy are at increased risk both for sudden cardiac death and for acute myocardial infarction.[28] Hypertensive patients with left ventricular hypertrophy have substantially more premature ventricular beats than normotensives,[29] and even more than hypertensives who still have normal size hearts. Recent studies have shown that calmodulin-dependent mechanisms are responsible for both the increase in ectopy and for the occurrence of sudden death in cocaine users (and non-drug-using hypertensives), even in the absence of clinically apparent myocyte hypertrophy. Enlarged hearts are prone to QT dispersion (defined as the different between the longest and shortest QT interval measured in each of the 12 leads of the cardiogram). Dispersion equates to electrical inhomogeneity; the greater the degree of dispersion, the higher the probability a reentrant type arrhythmia will occur.[30,31]

The problem for death investigators is that changes in heart weight, amounting to less than 10% of predicted weight, are likely to go unrecognized at autopsy. The result is that a possible cause of death may be missed. Even if wall thickness is fastidiously measured, which is not always the case, a 10% increase is likely go undetected. Small changes go unnoticed mainly because several different systems are used for determining normality. Some pathologists still believe that arbitrary cutoffs can be used: 380 or 400 g for men and 350 g for women. Others determine normality by using a formula; heart weights less than 0.4% of the body weight (0.45% for women) are considered normal.[32] The most accurate approach is to use a nomogram based on a large series of autopsies. Several have been published, including the Mayo Clinic nomogram relating heart weight both to height and to weight.[18] Any value more than 2 standard deviations above the predicted mean is considered abnormal (see Appendix III for copies of the nomogram). Unfortunately, the range is so wide that some hearts may wrongly be classified as normal.

2.3.4 Other Stimulant-Related Disorders

Reports of cardiomyopathy in cases where neither biopsy nor arteriogram was performed[33–37] are difficult to interpret, and the diagnosis of cardiomyopathy in such cases should be considered unconfirmed; the underlying disease is as likely to be ischemic as to be drug mediated. The few reported cases of ephedrine-related cardiomyopathy fall into this category, although when cases have occurred, it has only been in abusers consuming massive amounts of ephedrine for prolonged periods.[38–40] However, dilated cardiomyopathy, in the proven absence of ischemia, has been documented in methamphetamine abusers,[41] and it seems likely that the reported number of new cases will increase.

When direct examination of the hearts of stimulant users has been performed, most of the observed changes appear to be related to catecholamine.[42,43] Chronic catecholamine toxicity is a well-recognized entity in humans and animals. In fact, norepinephrine "myocarditis" was first described nearly 50 years ago,[44,45] and its histological features are indistinguishable from those seen in patients with pheochromocytoma. Contraction band necrosis is the earliest recognizable lesion in both humans and animals.[46]

Several distinct features can be used to distinguish catecholamine-induced necrosis from ischemic necrosis. The most obvious is the distribution of the lesions. In ischemic injury, all cells supplied by a given vessel are affected, leading to a homogeneous zone of necrosis. In catecholamine injury, individual necrotic myocytes are to be found interspersed between normal cells, and the pattern of injury cannot be related to the pattern of blood supply.[47] Ischemic and catecholamine necrosis can also be distinguished by the arrangement of the myofilaments. In ischemia the myofilaments remain in register. In cases of catecholamine toxicity, the arrangement of the filaments is disrupted. In addition, a mononuclear, predominantly lymphocytic, infiltrate may be seen after 12 h (as opposed to the neutrophilic infiltrate seen during the initial phases of ischemic infarction). Necrotic myocytes are eventually reabsorbed and replaced by non-conducting fibrous tissues. After repeated bouts of necrosis, the myocardium becomes increasingly fibrotic, leading to systolic dysfunction and, more importantly, abnormal impulse propagation.[47]

Biopsy findings in a group of cocaine users with recent onset of chest pain and congestive heart failure demonstrated changes very similar to those described above, with microfocal interstitial fibrosis evident in all cases.[43] Lymphocytic infiltrates were seen in only two of the cases, and there were no eosinophils present. Contraction band necrosis (CBN) is a prominent artifact of endomyocardial biopsies, so the presence of these lesions in biopsied drug users is impossible to assess, even though CBN may well be associated with cocaine use. In fact the first reports of CBN in cocaine users were published in the European literature in the 1920s. They were promptly forgotten for another 50 years, until they were rediscovered in a report that appeared in the *New England Journal of Medicine* in 1986.[48]

A biopsy of one of the patients in the *New England Journal of Medicine* report did show eosinophilic myocarditis, but such cases are extremely rare and still reportable. In fact, there has only been one additional reported instance of cocaine-associated eosinophilic myocarditis in the last decade.[49] Even if a known cocaine user were found to have an eosinophilic infiltrate in his or her heart, it would more likely be the result of allergy to expients mixed with the drug, than from the cocaine itself. The variety of expients used to dilute cocaine and heroin is not tracked by any official agency (although it very likely is by some government agencies), and it clearly varies by location and drug origin. An Italian report, now more than a decade old, found that lidocaine and caffeine were the two agents most frequently used to adulterate cocaine. More recently, an assortment of medications has been detected in cocaine specimens, including multiple samples containing diltiazem.

Amphetamines seem to be associated with the same changes in the heart that are associated with cocaine abuse.[50,51] The Japanese literature contains one report describing a long-term methamphetamine abuser who collapsed while being arrested. His heart was hypertrophied, but there was no evidence of myocardial disarray. Endocardial thickening, with increased numbers of elastic fibers, was apparent in all the ventricles and in the atria. There was also narrowing of the lumen of the AV nodal artery secondary to interstitial fibrosis and scar formation. The authors believed that compression of the nodal artery by scarring accounted for the individual's sudden death.[52]

2.3.5 Myocardial Disease in Opiate Abusers

Distinctions between the hearts of opiate and stimulant abusers have become increasingly blurred. In the uncommon situation where an individual is a pure opiate abuser, morphologic changes are uncommon. Autopsy studies of heroin abusers done during the 1960s and early 1970s did not even mention the occurrence of heart disease.[1,53] Clinical studies from that period are equally unrevealing. Among addicts admitted to Bellevue Hospital's general medicine service, the incidence of endocarditis was under 10% and no other cardiac disorders were even mentioned.[3] Whether or not opiates visibly damage the myocardium, undetectable interactions may be occurring at the molecular level. Randomized clinical trials published in 2005 showed convincingly that the mortality of patients with myocardial infarction increases when they are treated with morphine.[54] Why that should be is impossible to say.

Myocardial fibrosis is not uncommon in opiate abusers, but it probably just signifies concomitant stimulant abuse. Larger areas of fibrosis may represent zones of healed infarction, even if they were not diagnosed during life. Although a handful of case reports have appeared in the literature,[55,56] there is no evidence that coronary artery disease is more common among heroin abusers than in the general population. Nonetheless, intravenous drug injectors, no matter what the drug, are prone to pulmonary hypertension as a consequence of granuloma formation in the pulmonary bed.[57] Rarely a talc granuloma may be seen in the myocardium.[58]

Infectious disease now accounts for most of the changes seen in the hearts of drug abusers (see Chapter 2.4 for a discussion of endocarditis in drug abusers). HIV may involve the heart. The most common manifestations of HIV are dilated cardiomyopathy, myocarditis, pulmonary hypertension, pericardial effusion, endocarditis, and HIV-associated malignant neoplasm. Although highly active antiretroviral therapy (HAART) does prolong many patients' lives, it has no effect on the cardiac sequelae of HIV, which will continue to evolve without specific treatment.[59]

There are also reports of myocardial infarction in young patients infected with HIV receiving protease inhibitors, raising concerns about premature arteriosclerosis and coronary artery disease in this patient group. It appears that metabolic alterations produced by antiretroviral therapy worsen the cardiovascular risk profile of patients infected with HIV.[60] When coronary artery disease occurs in an HIV-infected drug abuser, it is impossible to say whether it is a consequence of disease or addiction. Unfortunately, drug users continue to use drugs even after they are infected with HIV. As with coronary artery disease, in many cases it will also be impossible to tell whether sudden death in a drug user is related to the drug or to the virus. Some cardiotropic viruses can cause myocardial infarction and even myocarditis, but are detectable only by advanced DNA polymerase technology, a methodology beyond the reach of most medical examiners' offices.[61]

REFERENCES

1. Siegel, H., M. Helpern, and T. Ehrenreich, The diagnosis of death from intravenous narcotism. With emphasis on the pathologic aspects, *J. Forensic Sci.*, 11(1), 1–16.
2. Wetli, C.V., J.H. Davis, and B.D. Blackbourne, Narcotic addiction in Dade County, Florida. An analysis of 100 consecutive autopsies, *Arch. Pathol.*, 93(4), 330–343, 1972.
3. Louria, D.B., T. Hensle, and J. Rose, The major medical complications of heroin addiction, *Ann. Intern. Med.*, 67(1), 1–22. 1967.
4. Bainborough, A.R. and K.W. Jericho, Cor pulmonale secondary to talc granulomata in the lungs of a drug addict, *Can. Med. Assoc. J.*, 103(12), 1297–1298, 1970.
5. Arnett, E.N., W.E. Battle, J.V. Russo, and W.C. Roberts, Intravenous injection of talc-containing drugs intended for oral use. A cause of pulmonary granulomatosis and pulmonary hypertension, *Am. J. Med.*, 1976. 60(5), 711–718, 1976.
6. Conen, D., D. Schilter, L. Bubendorf, M.H. Brutsche, et al., Interstitial lung disease in an intravenous drug user, *Respiration*, 70(1), 101–103, 2003.
7. Wolff, A.J. and A.E. O'Donnell, Pulmonary effects of illicit drug use. *Clin. Chest Med.*, 25(1), 203–216, 2004.
8. Dressler, F.A. and W.C. Roberts, Modes of death and types of cardiac diseases in opiate addicts: analysis of 168 necropsy cases, *Am. J. Cardiol.*, 64(14), 909–920, 1989.
9. Bennani, F.K. and C.E. Connolly, Sudden unexpected death in young adults including four cases of SADS: a 10-year review from the west of Ireland (1985–1994). *Med. Sci. Law*, 37(3), 242–247, 1997.
10. Vasica, G. and C.C. Tennant, Cocaine use and cardiovascular complications, *Med. J. Aust.*, 177(5), 260–262, 2002.

11. Brickner, M.E., J.E. Willard, E.J. Eichhorn, J. Black, et al., Left ventricular hypertrophy associated with chronic cocaine abuse, *Circulation*, 84(3), 1130–5, 1991.

12. Om, A., S. Ellahham, G.W. Vetrovec, C. Guard, et al., Left ventricular hypertrophy in normotensive cocaine users, *Am. Heart. J.*, 125(5 Pt. 1), 1441–1443, 1993.

13. Chakko, S., S. Sepulveda, K.M. Kessler, M.C. Sotomayor, et al., Frequency and type of electrocardiographic abnormalities in cocaine abusers (electrocardiogram in cocaine abuse), *Am. J. Cardiol.*, 74(7), 710–713, 1994.

14. Karch, S.B., G.S. Green, and S. Young, Myocardial hypertrophy and coronary artery disease in male cocaine users, *J. Forensic Sci.*, 40(4), 591–595, 1995.

15. Karch, S.B., B.G. Stephens, and C.H. Ho, Methamphetamine-related deaths in San Francisco: demographic, pathologic, and toxicologic profiles, *J. Forensic Sci.*, 44(2), 359–368, 1999.

16. Blechman, K., S.B. Karch, and B. Stephens, Demographic, pathologic, and toxicological profiles of 127 decedents testing positive for ephedrine alkaloids, *Forensic Sci. Int.*, 139(2–3), 271, 2004.

17. Patel, M.M., M.G. Belson, A.B. Longwater, K.R. Olson, and M. Miller, Methylenedioxymethamphetamine (ecstasy)-related myocardial hyperthermia, *J. Emerg. Med.*, 29(4), 451–454, 2005.

18. Kitzman, D.W., D.G. Scholz, P.T. Hagen, D.M. Ilstrup, et al., Age-related changes in normal human hearts during the first 10 decades of life. Part II (Maturity): A quantitative anatomic study of 765 specimens from subjects 20 to 99 years old, *Mayo Clin. Proc.*, 63(2), 137–146, 1988.

19. Bilecki, W. and R. Przewlocki, Effect of opioids on Ca^{2+}/cAMP responsive element binding protein, *Acta Neurobiol. Exp.* (Warsaw), 60(4), 557–567, 2000.

20. Sun, L.S. and A. Quamina, Extracellular receptor kinase and cAMP response element binding protein activation in the neonatal rat heart after perinatal cocaine exposure, *Pediatr. Res.*, 56(6), 947–952, 2004.

21. Khoo, M.S., P.J. Kannankeril, J. Li, R. Zhang, et al., Calmodulin kinase II activity is required for normal atrioventricular nodal conduction, *Heart Rhythm*, 2(6), 634–640, 2005.

22. Zhang, R., M.S. Khoo, Y. Wu, Y. Yang, et al., Calmodulin kinase II inhibition protects against structural heart disease, *Nat. Med.*, 11(4), 409–417, 2005.

23. Henning, R., D. Ivancsits, J. Haley, et al., Cocaine activates calmodulin kinase II and causes cardiac ventricular hypertrophy and arrhythmias, *Circulation*, III, iii–603, 2004.

24. Laviolette, S.R., R.A. Gallegos, S.J. Henriksen, and D. van der Kooy, Opiate state controls bi-directional reward signaling via GABAA receptors in the ventral tegmental area, *Nat. Neurosci.*, 7(2), 160–169, 2004.

25. Schaefer, M., A. Heinz, and M. Backmund, Treatment of chronic hepatitis C in patients with drug dependence: time to change the rules? *Addiction*, 99(9), 1167–1175, 2004.

26. Piccolo, P., L. Borg, A. Lin, D. Melia, et al., Hepatitis C virus and human immunodeficiency virus-1 co-infection in former heroin addicts in methadone maintenance treatment, *J. Addict Dis.*, 21(4), 55–66, 2002.

27. Muga, R., H. Guardiola, and C. Rey-Joly, Evaluation of drug addicts with associated pathology. Clinical and therapeutic aspects of the integral attention, *Med. Clin.* (Barcelona), 122(16), 624–635, 2004.

28. Gordon, T. and W.B. Kannel, Premature mortality from coronary heart disease. The Framingham study. *J. Am Med. Assoc.*, 215(10), 1617–1625, 1971.

29. Messerli, F.H., H.O. Ventura, D.J. Elizardi, F.G. Dunn, et al., Hypertension and sudden death. Increased ventricular ectopic activity in left ventricular hypertrophy, *Am. J. Med.*, 77(1), 18–22, 1984.

30. Hnatkova, K., M. Malik, J. Kautzner, Y. Gang, et al., Adjustment of QT dispersion assessed from 12 lead electrocardiograms for different numbers of analysed electrocardiographic leads: comparison of stability of different methods, *Br. Heart J.*, 72(4), 390–396, 1994.

31. Anderson, K.P., Sympathetic nervous system activity and ventricular tachyarrhythmias: recent advances, *Ann. Noninvasive Electrocardiol.*, 8(1), 75–89, 2003.

32. Ludwig, J., *Current Methods of Autopsy Practice*, 2nd ed., W.B. Saunders, Philadelphia, 1979.

33. Wiener, R.S., J.T. Lockhart, and R.G. Schwartz, Dilated cardiomyopathy and cocaine abuse. Report of two cases, *Am. J. Med.*, 81(4), 699–701, 1986.

34. Chokshi, S.K., R. Moore, N.G. Pandian, and J.M. Isner, Reversible cardiomyopathy associated with cocaine intoxication, *Ann. Intern. Med.*, 111(12), 1039–1040, 1989.

35. Duell, P.B., Chronic cocaine abuse and dilated cardiomyopathy, *Am. J. Med.*, 83(3), 601, 1987.

36. Hogya, P.T. and A.B. Wolfson, Chronic cocaine abuse associated with dilated cardiomyopathy, *Am. J. Emerg. Med.*, 8(3), 203–204, 1990.

37. Mendelson, M.A. and J. Chandler, Postpartum cardiomyopathy associated with maternal cocaine abuse, *Am. J. Cardiol.*, 70(11), 1092–1094, 1992.
38. Naik, S.D. and R.S. Freudenberger, Ephedra-associated cardiomyopathy, *Ann. Pharmacother.*, 38(3), 400–403, 2004.
39. To, L.B., J.F. Sangster, D. Rampling, and I. Cammens, Ephedrine-induced cardiomyopathy, *Med. J. Aust.*, 2(1), 35–36, 1980.
40. Schafers, M., D. Dutka, C.G. Rhodes, A.A. Lammertsma, et al., Myocardial presynaptic and postsynaptic autonomic dysfunction in hypertrophic cardiomyopathy, *Circ. Res.*, 82(1), 57–62, 1998.
41. Wijetunga, M., T. Seto, J. Lindsay, and I. Schatz, Crystal methamphetamine-associated cardiomyopathy: tip of the iceberg? *J. Toxicol. Clin. Toxicol.*, 41(7), 981–986, 2003.
42. Karch, S.B. and M.E. Billingham, The pathology and etiology of cocaine-induced heart disease, *Arch. Pathol. Lab. Med.*, 112(3), 225–230, 1988.
43. Peng, S.K., W.J. French, and P.C. Pelikan, Direct cocaine cardiotoxicity demonstrated by endomyocardial biopsy, *Arch. Pathol. Lab. Med.*, 113(8), 842–845, 1989.
44. Szakacs, J.E., R.M. Dimmette, and E.C. Cowart, Jr., Pathologic implication of the catechol amines, epinephrine and norepinephrine, *U.S. Armed Forces Med. J.*, 10, 908–925, 1959.
45. Szakacs, J.E. and A. Cannon, L-Norepinephrine myocarditis, *Am. J. Clin. Pathol.*, 30(5), 425–434, 1958.
46. Rosenbaum, J.S., M.E. Billingham, R. Ginsburg, G. Tsujimoto, et al., Cardiomyopathy in a rat model of pheochromocytoma. Morphological and functional alterations, *Am. J. Cardiovasc. Pathol.*, 1(3), 389–399, 1988.
47. Karch, S.B. and M.E. Billingham, Myocardial contraction bands revisited, *Hum. Pathol.*, 17(1), 9–13, 1986.
48. Isner, J.M., N.A. Estes III, P.D. Thompson, M.R. Costanzo-Nordin, et al., Acute cardiac events temporally related to cocaine abuse, *N. Engl. J. Med.*, 315(23), 1438–1443, 1986.
49. Talebzadeh, V.C., J.C. Chevrolet, P. Chatelain, C. Helfer, et al., Eosinophilic myocarditis and pulmonary hypertension in a drug-addict. Anatomo-clinical study and brief review of the literature, *Ann. Pathol.*, 10(1), 40–46, 1990.
50. Smith, H.J., A.H. Roche, M.F. Jausch, and P.B. Herdson, Cardiomyopathy associated with amphetamine administration, *Am. Heart J.*, 91(6), 792–797, 1976.
51. Rajs, J. and B. Falconer, Cardiac lesions in intravenous drug addicts, *Forensic Sci. Int.*, 13(3), 193–209, 1979.
52. Nishida, N., N. Ikeda, K. Kudo, and R. Esaki, Sudden unexpected death of a methamphetamine abuser with cardiopulmonary abnormalities: a case report, *Med. Sci. Law*, 43(3), 267–271, 2003.
53. Kringsholm, B. and P. Christoffersen, Lung and heart pathology in fatal drug addiction. A consecutive autopsy study, *Forensic Sci. Int.*, 34(1–2), 39–51, 1987.
54. Meine, T.J., M.T. Roe, A.Y. Chen, M.R. Patel, et al., Association of intravenous morphine use and outcomes in acute coronary syndromes: results from the CRUSADE Quality Improvement Initiative, *Am. Heart J.*, 149(6), 1043–1049, 2005.
55. Yu, S.L., C.P. Liu, Y.K. Lo, and S.L. Lin, Acute myocardial infarction after heroin injections, *Jpn. Heart J.*, 45(6), 1021–1028, 2004.
56. Sztajzel, J., H. Karpuz, and W. Rutishauser, Heroin abuse and myocardial infarction, *Int. J. Cardiol.*, 47(2), 180–182, 1994.
57. Robertson, C.H., Jr., R.C. Reynolds, and J.E. Wilson III, Pulmonary hypertension and foreign body granulomas in intravenous drug abusers. Documentation by cardiac catheterization and lung biopsy, *Am. J. Med.*, 61(5), 657–664, 1976.
58. Riddick, L., Disseminated granulomatosis through a patent foramen ovale in an intravenous drug user with pulmonary hypertension, *Am. J. Forensic Med. Pathol.*, 8(4), 326–333, 1987.
59. Barbaro, G. and E.C. Klatt, HIV infection and the cardiovascular system, *AIDS Rev.*, 4(2), 93–103, 2002.
60. Neumann, T., M. Miller, S. Esser, G. Gerken, et al., Atherosclerosis in HIV-positive patients, *Z. Kardiol.*, 91(11), 879–888, 2002.
61. Kuhl, U., M. Pauschinger, T. Bock, K. Klingel, et al., Parvovirus B19 infection mimicking acute myocardial infarction, *Circulation*, 108(8), 945–950, 2003.

2.4 VALVULAR HEART DISEASE

Michael D. Bell, M.D.
District Medical Examiner, Palm Beach Medical Examiner Office, West Palm Beach, Florida

2.4.1 Infective Endocarditis

Although intravenous (IV) drug abuse is a recognized risk factor for infectious endocarditis, this complication is not a frequent complication among IV drug users. The incidence of infective endocarditis in IV drug abusers is estimated at 1.5 to 2.0 cases per 1000 IV drug abusers admitted to the hospital[1] or 1 to 20 cases per 10,000 IV drug users per year. IV drug abusers with infective endocarditis are more likely to be young men (average age = 29 years, M:F = 3:1) compared with non-addicts with endocarditis (average age = 50, M:F = 2:1).[2] The frequency of underlying heart disease in IV drug abusers with endocarditis is 26% compared with 60% of non-addicts with endocarditis. In a cohort of 85 IV drug abusers, echocardiography failed to detect any valvular vegetation consistent with endocarditis.[3] Eight IV drug abusers had thickened or redundant leaflets (with or without prolapse) of the mitral, aortic, or tricuspid valve. Focally thickened leaflets of the mitral and tricuspid valves have been reported in other series of asymptomatic IV drug abusers who were examined by echocardiography.[4] These subtle morphologic abnormalities may be the stratum upon which endocarditis builds. Most researchers agree that endothelial injury or damage initiates fibrin, platelet, and bacterial depositions that produce endocarditis.

In Dressler and Robert's series of 80 autopsied IV drug abusers with infective endocarditis, the tricuspid valve was involved in half of the victims compared with 15% of victims dying of acute endocarditis who did not use IV drugs.[5] Why IV drug users are more likely to develop right-sided endocarditis than non-IV drug users is not known. Postulated factors include physical damage by injected particulate debris, especially if pills are crushed and then injected. Drug-induced pulmonary hypertension in IV drug abusers may cause increased right ventricular pressure and more turbulence flow, resulting in tricuspid valve injury. However, IV drug abusers can, and often do, have left-sided valve involvement. The aortic and mitral valves are involved in 25% and 20% respectively of IV drug abusers with infective endocarditis. Most cases of acute endocarditis in IV drug abusers are caused by *Staphylococcus aureus* as compared with other streptococcal species commonly responsible for endocarditis in those not injecting IV drugs.[6] Outbreaks of methacillin-resistant *S. aureus* endocarditis in IV drug users have been reported in Detroit, Boston, and Zurich. Polymicrobial infection is seen in 8 to 9% of cases of infective endocarditis that involve IV drug abusers, while *Streptococcus viridans* causes right-sided endocarditis in 11% of IV drug abusers. Fungal, usually non-albicans *Candida* species endocarditis is usually superimposed on valves previously damaged by an earlier episode of bacterial endocarditis and usually has a more indolent clinical course. Other unusual pathogens causing endocarditis in IV drug abusers are summarized in Table 2.4.1.

Grossly, infective endocarditis is characterized by friable, white or tan vegetations found on the valve leaflets along the closure lines. Vegetations may be single or, more often, multiple. In one clinical series the mean vegetation size in IV drug abusers with acute right-sided bacterial endocarditis was 1.5 0.7 cm.[6] The size, color, and appearance of the vegetations can vary, however. Streptococcal vegetations grow more slowly than staphylococcal vegetations, but may become larger. Fungal vegetations are usually larger than bacterial vegetations. Vegetations occur more often on the atrial side of the atrioventricular valves and on the ventricular side of the aortic or pulmonic valves. Suppurative bacteria such as *Staphylococcus* may cause valve perforation, resulting in acute valvular insufficiency. Infection may extend into the adjacent myocardium producing necrotic fistulas, aneurysms, or ring abscess (usually of the aortic valve). Further extension results

Table 2.4.1   Uncommon Pathogens in Endocarditis of Intravenous Drug Abusers[11]

Group B *Streptococcus* (*Streptococcus agalactiae*)[12]
Coagulase-negative *Staphylococcus*
Gram-negative bacteria (*Pseudomonas, Serratia, Kingella*, etc.)
Corynebacterium spp., *Neisseria sicca, Rothia denticariosua*
Haemophilus spp.
Erysipelothrix
Anaerobic bacteria (*Bacteroides, Veillonella, Eikenella,*
  Fusobacterium spp., *Clostridium* spp., etc.)
Fungi (*Candida* spp.)

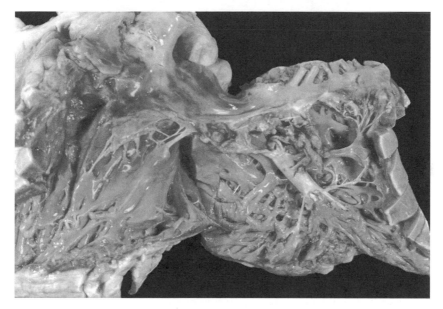

Figure 2.4.1   Large necrotizing vegetations on the tricuspid valve of this 31-year-old addict who commonly injected drug subcutaneously ("skin popping"). Blood cultures were positive for *Streptococcus hominus.*

in pericarditis, found in 4 to 27% of cases of left-sided infective endocarditis.[7] Involvement of the chordae tendinae may lead to rupture and valvular insufficiency. Tricuspid and pulmonic vegetations may embolize to the lungs, resulting in the formation of suppurative abscesses (Figure 2.4.1 and Figure 2.4.2). Perforation, indentation, or aneurysm of the valve cusp or chordae tendinae is presumptive evidence of healed endocarditis.

Microscopically, acute bacterial endocarditis is characterized by masses of fibrin, platelets, and polymorphonuclear leukocytes with bacterial colonies on the valve surface. Bacteria are less frequent after antibiotic treatment, and may not be demonstrable by Gram stain, even if present.[8] Later, the microscopic appearance is characterized by organization with capillary proliferation, a mixed cellular infiltrate, and the formation of granulation tissue. If the individual survives, the lesions eventually heal by fibrosis and re-endothelialization. Calcification may be present in the healed lesions.

The clinical diagnosis of acute infectious endocarditis includes the acute onset of fever, chills, and heart murmur. Right-sided valve murmurs (as in IV drug abusers) may be less audible than left-sided valve murmurs because the reduced chamber pressures of the right heart produce less turbulence and less noise. Signs of early tricuspid insufficiency may be minimal with only an atrial or ventricular gallop and no murmur. Later, a systolic regurgitant murmur, louder with inspiration, appears. Large "v" waves in the neck veins and a pulsating liver are signs of severe tricuspid

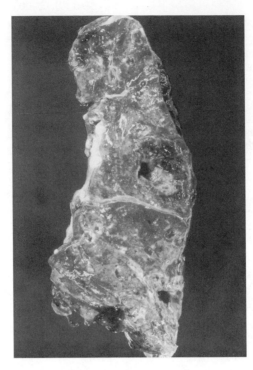

Figure 2.4.2 The lung from the victim in Figure 2.4.1 has multiple suppurative abscesses and extensive dark red consolidation.

regurgitation.[9] Confirmation of the diagnosis includes isolation of the causative organism from two or more blood cultures and identification of valvular vegetation by echocardiography. The criteria for the clinical diagnosis of infective endocarditis have recently been revised. Bacteremia is characteristic of endocarditis, and most IV drug abusers with endocarditis have positive blood cultures even after a few days of antibiotic treatment. True culture-negative endocarditis is rare in IV drug abusers, and negative blood cultures suggest another cause for their illness.

The occurrence of chest pain with dyspnea, along with characteristic abnormalities of the chest radiograph (multiple segmental infiltrates with lower lobe predilection), suggests septic pulmonary emboli from a right-sided valvular vegetation. Systemic embolization can occur in right-sided endocarditis from septic pulmonary vein thrombi, left-sided valvular involvement, or paradoxical embolization through a patent foramen ovale. Table 2.4.2 compares the clinical features of right-sided and left-sided endocarditis.[10] Mortality in IV drug abusers with acute right-sided endocarditis varies from 4 to 14%.[6]

Table 2.4.2 Comparison of Right-Sided and Left-Sided Endocarditis

Right-Sided	Left-Sided
IV drug abusers most common	Congenital heart disease most common
Staphylococcus aureus most common	*Streptococcus viridans* most common
Occasional polymicrobial involvement	Polymicrobial involvement rare
Presents with pleuropneumonic symptoms	Symptoms from distal systemic embolization more common
10% of all infective endocarditis	90% of all infective endocarditis
Heart failure is unusual	Heart failure is common
Good prognosis with frequent cure after medical therapy	Poor prognosis with poor success rate using medical therapy
Surgery usually does not require immediate valve replacement	Surgery usually requires immediate valve replacement

The source of the infecting organisms is usually from the addict's own body (skin or mouth flora), or soft tissue infection at the injection site, not contaminants in the drugs or the drug paraphernalia.[13] Cultures of heroin samples and drug paraphernalia have failed to demonstrate the presence of common pathogens.

2.4.2 Fenfluramine-Associated Regurgitant Valve Disease

Fenfluramine is a sympathomimetic amine chemically similar to amphetamine, but with less stimulant activity. Fenfluramine was a popular anorectic agent in the 1990s, prescribed alone or in combination with another sympathomimetic amine, phentermine. Prescriptions for these appetite suppressants exceeded 18 million in 1996. Fenfluramine's anorectic effect is thought to result from its ability to promote serotonin release and decrease brain re-uptake.

Connolly et al.[14] described 24 women with regurgitant valve disease that had its onset after they took fenfluramine-phentermine ("fen-phen") for 1 to 28 months. One fifth of these women required valve surgery and one third developed pulmonary hypertension. Macroscopic features in the removed valves from these women included irregular nodular leaflet thickening, thickened and tethered glistening white leaflets, leaflets with "stuck on" or "onlay" plaques, and chordal fusion. Valve vegetations, commissural fusion, and annular dilatation were not seen. Microscopically, fibromyxoid plaques and nodules were seen to lie on top of the affected leaflet or encase the chordae tendinae. Myofibroblasts proliferated in the extracellular matrix. The onlay plaques are usually found to be superficial to the elastic fiber layer in the mitral valve. Ultimately these pathologic changes result in a thickened immobile regurgitant valve. Other pathologists have confirmed these findings.[15,16] Later case control and meta-analysis studies,[17,18] however, did not demonstrate as much clinically significant mitral valve disease as the original Connolly study, but by then, fenfluramine was already removed from the U.S. market.

REFERENCES

1. Weinstein, L. and Brusch, J.L., Endocarditis in intravenous drug abusers, in *Infective Endocarditis*, Weinstein, L. and Brusch, J.L., Eds., Oxford University Press, New York, 1996, 194–209.
2. Reisberg, B.E., Infective endocarditis in the narcotic addict, *Prog. Cardiovasc. Dis.*, 22, 193–204, 1979.
3. Willoughby, S.B., Vlahov, D., and Herskowitz, A., Frequency of left ventricular dysfunction and other echocardiographic abnormalities in human immunodeficiency virus seronegative intravenous drug abusers, *Am. J. Cardiol.*, 71, 446–447, 1993.
4. Pons-Llado, G., Carreras, F., Borras, X. et al., Findings on Doppler echocardiography in asymptomatic intravenous heroin users, *Am. J. Cardiol.*, 69, 238–241, 1992.
5. Dressler, F. and Roberts, W., Infective endocarditis in opiate addicts: analysis of 80 cases studied at autopsy, *Am. J. Cardiol.*, 63, 1240–1257, 1989.
6. Hecht, S.R. and Berger, M., Right-sided endocarditis in intravenous drug users: prognostic features in 102 episodes, *Ann. Int. Med.*, 117, 560–566, 1992.
7. Buchbinder, N.A. and Roberts, W.C., Left-sided valvular active infective endocarditis: a study of forty-five patients. *Am. J. Med.*, 53, 20–35, 1972.
8. McFarland, M.M., Pathology of infective endocarditis, in *Infective Endocarditis*, 2nd ed., Kaye, D., Ed., Raven Press, New York, 1992, 57–83.
9. Cannon, N.J. and Cobbs, C.G., Infective endocarditis in drug addicts, in *Infective Endocarditis*, Kaye, D., Ed., University Park Press, Baltimore, 1976, 111–127.
10. Chan, P., Ogilby, J.D., and Segal, B., Tricuspid valve endocarditis, *Am. Heart J.*, 117, 1140–1146, 1989.
11. Sande, M.A., Lee, B.L., Mills, J., Chambers, H.F., III, Endocarditis in intravenous drug users, in *Infective Endocarditis*, 2nd ed., Kaye, D., Ed., Raven Press, New York, 1992, 345–359.
12. Watanakunakorn, C. and Habte-Gabr, E., Group B streptococcal endocarditis of tricuspid valve, *Chest*, 100, 569–571, 1991.

13. Wetli, C.V., in *Illicit Drug Abuse in Pathology of Environmental and Occupational Disease,* Craighead, J.D., Ed., Mosby-Year Book, St. Louis, 1995, 259–268.

14. Connolly, H.M., Crary, J.L., McGoon, M.D., Hensrud, D.D., Edwards, B.S., Edwards, W.D., and Schaff, H.V., Valvular heart disease associated with fenfluramine-phentermine, *N. Engl. J. Med.,* 337, 581–588, 1997.

15. Volmar, K.E. and Hutchins, G.M., Aortic and mitral fenfluramine-phentermine valvulopathy in 64 patients treated with anorectic agents, *Arch. Pathol. Lab. Med.,* 125, 1555–1561, 2001.

16. Steffee, C.H., Singh, H.K., and Chitwood, W.R., Histologic changes in three explanted native cardiac valves following use of fenfluramines, *Cardiovasc. Pathol.,* 8, 245–253, 1999.

17. Gardin, J.M., Schumacher, D., Constantine, G. et al., Valvular abnormalities and cardiovascular status following exposure to dexfenfluramine or phentermine/fenfluramine, *J. Am. Med. Assoc.,* 283, 1738–1740, 2000.

18. Sachdev, M., Miller, W.C., Ryan, T., and Jollis, J.G., Effect of fenfluramine-derivative diet pills on cardiac valves: a meta-analysis of observational studies, *Am. Heart J.,* 144, 1065–1073, 2002.

2.5 LUNG DISEASE

Michael D. Bell, M.D.

District Medical Examiner, Palm Beach Medical Examiner Office, West Palm Beach, Florida

2.5.1 Pulmonary Effects and Pathology of Smoked Illicit Drugs

Heroin is usually smoked by heating a mixture of heroin and caffeine on foil, then inhaling the resultant vapor through a straw. Cocaine freebase or "crack" cocaine is also heated and the vapors inhaled, as is crystallized methamphetamine. Finally, dried *Cannabis sativa* is smoked as a cigarette, or in a pipe. Ascribing a specific pulmonary dysfunction or pathology to a specific drug is difficult, because drug users consistently smoke more than one drug. In one study of 100 heroin users, 88% smoked heroin, 79% inhaled cocaine, 71% smoked marijuana, and 98% smoked cigarettes[1] and had been, on average, for 26 years. These confounding factors must be considered before assigning causation of a specific pathology to a specific drug. Several review articles summarizing the pulmonary changes in drug users have been published.

Bailey et al.[2] performed an autopsy study of cocaine abusers' lungs and found the most common changes were pulmonary congestion (88%), edema (77%), and acute/chronic alveolar hemorrhage (71%). Similar findings were reported by Murray et al.[3,4] who found hemosiderin-laden macrophages in 35% (7 of 20) of the victims of cocaine intoxication and concluded that occult alveolar hemorrhage occurs more frequently in cocaine users than is clinically recognized. Murray also noted pulmonary artery medial hypertrophy in 20% (4 of 20) of cocaine abusers who had no histological evidence of foreign material embolization. The cause of the alveolar hemorrhage was thought to be ischemic damage to the capillary endothelium secondary to constriction of the pulmonary vascular bed after cocaine inhalation, or possibly a result of some direct toxic effect of cocaine on the capillary endothelium. Neither hypothesis is proved.

Hemosiderin-laden macrophages may be seen in bronchoalveolar lavage fluid or in bronchoscopy biopsy specimens. One cocaine abuser who presented with diffuse alveolar hemorrhage had no vasculitis, and electron microscopy did not demonstrate any disruption in the alveolar or capillary basement membranes.[4] Pulmonary hemorrhage has not only been associated with alkaloidal "crack" cocaine smoking, but also with intravenous and nasal routes of administration.[5] Pulmonary congestion in fatal cocaine intoxication is usually ascribed to the slow cessation of cardiac function associated with brain stem hypoxia during terminal seizures, or else to direct cocaine toxicity.

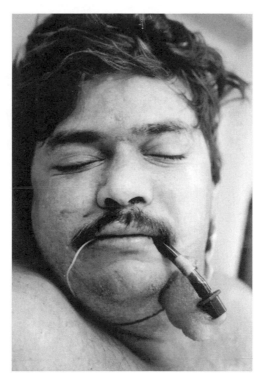

Figure 2.5.1 Abundant blood-tinged foam escapes from the end of the endotrachial tube in this drug abuser with pulmonary edema.

Fatal and nonfatal pulmonary edema (Figure 2.5.1) has been reported in cocaine smokers who have no obvious cardiac or central nervous system disease.[5–8] In some of these individuals the pulmonary edema resolved without specific treatment, and chest radiographs have shown normal cardiac silhouettes. The homodynamic status of patients with cocaine-associated pulmonary edema has never been studied. One patient underwent bronchoalveolar lavage and the lavage fluid was found to have an elevated protein level (four times normal), suggesting that the edema was due to altered alveolar capillary permeability.[7] Bronchial biopsy usually has shown no histological abnormalities[7] or only "mild interstitial inflammatory changes."[8]

Pneumonitis, as defined by widening of the alveolar septae in the presence of a polymorphous infiltrate (lymphocytes, neutrophils, macrophages, eosinophils) or fibrosis, was seen in one fourth of the victims studied by Bailey et al.,[2] while Patel et al.[9] have described a patient with broncholitis obliterans and organizing pneumonia (BOOP) associated with regular use of free-base cocaine during the weeks prior to the onset of his clinical symptoms (nonproductive cough, fever, dyspnea). An open lung biopsy revealed patchy bronchocentric interstitial and intra-alveolar chronic inflammation, with lymphocytes, macrophages, and few polymorphonuclear leukocytes and eosinophils; granulation tissue and collagen occupied bronchioles and adjacent alveolar ducts, but the blood vessels were normal. A hypersensitivity reaction to cocaine, or a cocaine adulterant, was the presumed cause. A similar mechanism also presumably explains the occurrence of "crack lung," a clinical syndrome characterized by chest pain, hemoptysis, and diffuse alveolar infiltrates, a constellation of symptoms and signs see only with smoking "crack" cocaine (Figure 2.5.2). Finally, 11% of the cocaine fatalities have polarizable birefringent material, usually talc, within the lungs. Most of these victims were, not unexpectedly, intravenous drug abusers.[10,11] Other diluents, such as starch and cellulose fibers, may be recognized by their typical pattern of birefringence.

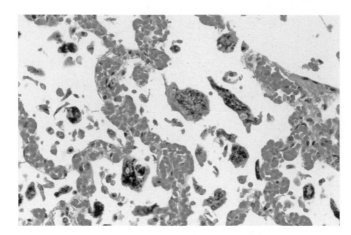

Figure 2.5.2 Intra-alveolar macrophages contain coarse black pigment in a crack cocaine abuser.

Sometimes users of cocaine freebase, or "crack" cocaine, forcefully blow smoke into another user's mouth in order to augment the drug's effect (more absorption). Smokers also prolong the Valsalva maneuver in order to avoid expiring the precious cocaine smoke. The resulting increased intra-alveolar pressure ruptures the alveolar walls, allowing air to dissect along the perivascular tissues, into the mediastinum and surrounding cavities. This basic mechanism has been responsible for all types of barotrauma including pneumothorax, pneumo-mediastinum,[12–14] pneumo-pericardium,[15] pneumoperitoneum,[16] and subcutaneous emphysema. In the few cases to be reported,[17] where the duration of cocaine use prior to clinical symptoms was accurately known, patients freebased cocaine for 8 to 12 h and snorted cocaine for 1 h. Thus, it seems unlikely to occur on the first puff, but the possibility cannot be dismissed either. The clinical course of cocaine-associated barotrauma is generally nonfatal. This barotrauma is a nonspecific finding; it has been described in marijuana smokers,[18] and presumably occurs in smokers of methamphetamine as well.

Individuals with asthma who smoke heroin and cocaine are subject to acute severe exacerbation of their asthma.[19–22] There is nothing to distinguish nondrug-related asthma from asthma occurring secondary to drug usage, although bronchial mucus plugs and pulmonary hyperinflation were observed at autopsy in 64.7% of those with asthma who also had a history of drug or alcohol abuse.[23] Sudden death in this population may be the result of status asthmaticus, although it could also be the result of cocaine's arrhythmic effects, direct or indirect in the setting of an acute asthmatic attack. Insufflation of cocaine hydrochloride has also been associated with near-fatal status asthmaticus.[24] Blackened sputum and pulmonary cytologic specimens with excessive carbonaceous material are highly suggestive of crack cocaine use.[25] As crack is smoked, a dark, tarry residue forms on the inside of the pipe's bowl and barrel. Many smokers consider this residue to be concentrated cocaine and they scrape it free, reheat it, and vigorously inhale it. As a result, coarse, intracellular black particles, and intra-alveolar macrophages filled with black pigment, may be seen in crack cocaine abusers at autopsy (Figure 2.5.2).

The long-term pulmonary effects and pathology of smoking cocaine are unknown. Pulmonary function studies are confounded by the fact that cocaine smokers also smoke tobacco and marijuana in addition to cocaine. Cocaine smokers have a reduced diffusing capacity of carbon monoxide, but no spirometric abnormalities have been demonstrated.[26] Marijuana and tobacco smoking both produce similar changes in the bronchial mucosa; the histopathological changes include basal and goblet cell hyperplasia, squamous cell metaplasia, basement membrane thickening, inflammation, and increased nuclear variation and N/C ratio. Cocaine smoking does not produce these changes to the degree seen in the former groups.

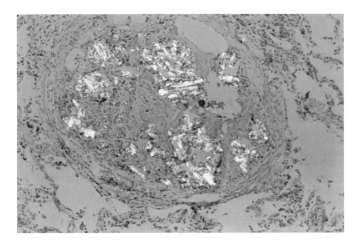

Figure 2.5.3 Abundant birefringent material lies within this pulmonary artery thrombus from an intravenous drug abuser (Hematoxylin and eosin, polarized light, original magnification 80×).

2.5.2 Complications of Intravenous Drug Abuse: Granulomatous Pneumonitis/Arteriopathy

Intravenous drug abusers may crush oral medications and suspend them in water for intravenous injection. Methadone[27] and propoxyphene[28] are examples of oral drugs abused in this fashion. Pill filler material contains insoluble particles. Once these insoluble particles reach the lung, they cause thrombosis, granulomatous inflammation, and fibrosis. The granulomas have numerous multinucleated giant cells and contain birefringent foreign material (Figure 2.5.3; Table 2.5.1). When abundant, the granulomas and foreign material impart a granular texture to the lung. In addition to their morphology, the foreign particles can be identified by selected-area electron diffraction and energy dispersive x-ray analysis. The functional consequence of these lesions is often pulmonary hypertension with its accompanying complications, including cor pulmonale and sudden death. In nonfatal cases, patients may present with dyspnea, mild hypoxemia, and diffuse micronodules apparent on their chest radiographs. Gallium scanning can be used to demonstrate reduced diffusion across the parenchyma capacity; serum angiotensin-converting enzyme concentration in the lung is also elevated. The granulomatous and fibrotic reaction may be in the interstitium, presumably because the particles migrate through the arterial walls[29] and vascular remodeling occurs. Thromboembolic vascular remodeling produces recanalized arteries and intimal fibrosis. Plexiform and angiomatoid vascular lesions may also be seen. Large fibrotic pulmonary masses have been described with huge particle counts and occasional giant cells. The fibrotic masses are usually bilateral, asymmetric, and confined to the middle and upper lung fields. These are similar to the progressive massive fibrosis seen in complicated pneumoconiosis.[30–32]

Pulmonary hypertension due to pulmonary artery thromboses has been reported to result from the repeated intravenous injection of "blue velvet," a mixture of paregoric and tripelennamine (Pyribenzamine) tablets,[33,34] although this practice no longer seems very popular. Methylphenidate (Ritalin) tablets contain talc (magnesium silicate) and cornstarch, which can cause pulmonary hypertension and sudden death, often within 6 to 7 months of abusing the drugs. It is a practice in some areas to use Ritalin tablets as stimulants to counteract the sedative effects of methadone maintenance in addicts.

While cornstarch can cause foreign body granulomas to form, the reaction is generally milder and less frequent than the granulomatous inflammation caused by talc,[35] which is irritating to tissues and may cause thrombosis with occlusion of pulmonary arterioles and capillaries, and a granulomatous inflammation with parenchyma fibrosis.[29] The end result is a restrictive lung disease with

Table 2.5.1 Common Foreign Material Found in the Lungs of IV Drug Abusers

Foreign Material	Drugs	Appearance	Notes
Talc	Methylphenidale (Ritalin) Methadone Tripelennamine HCl (Pyribenzamine) Propoxyphene (Darvon) Meperidine (Demerol) Benzedrine Dilaudid	Birefringent refractile crystalline needles 5–23 μm long or plates, colorless or pale yellow on H & E	Most common type of foreign material
Cornstarch	Barbiturates Paragoric Tripelennamine HCl (Pyribenzamine) Pentazocine (Talwin)	Birefringent refractile 8–12 μm round particles of varying size, colorless on H & E, form "Maltese cross" with polarized light, PAS+, diastase resistant	Often seen with talc particles
Microcrystalline cellulose	Pentazocine (Talwin) Methaqualone (Quaalude) Percodan Acetaminophen/aspirin with codeine Phenobarbital	Large (10–250 μm), irregular birefringent crystals, pale gray on H & E, PAS+ diastase resistant, Congo red+, methenamine silver+	
Cotton fibers	Heroin and other IV drugs	Refractile, birefringent small filaments, ring-shape or curvilinear on cross-section, very pale blue on H & E	
Crospovidone	Hydromorphone, propoxyphene	100 μm basophilic globular or coral-shaped mass; does not polarize; seen with H & E, mucicarmine, Congo Red, and Movat stains	

impaired oxygen transfer across the alveolar-capillary membrane and pulmonary hypertension. The pulmonary arteries may have multiple intravascular and perivascular foreign body granulomas filled with birefringent talc. The pulmonary arteries may also have medial hypertrophy, fibrointimal hyperplasia, and angiomatoid lesions (Figure 2.5.4).[36,37]

Pulmonary emphysema has been described in a subgroup of intravenous drug abusers who inject methylphenidate (Ritalin-SA). These patients present, complaining of dyspnea, at an average

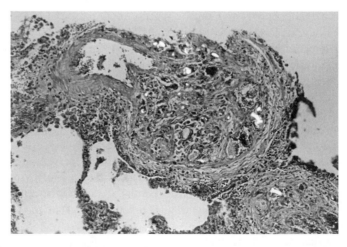

Figure 2.5.4 Angiomatoid lesion with birefringent talc in an intravenous drug abuser (Hematoxylin and eosin, polarized light, original magnification 80×).

Figure 2.5.5 This sectioned lung has multiple abscess cavities. The victim was a 31-year-old cocaine "skin popper."

age of 36 years. All have moderate to severe airflow obstruction with hyperinflation on chest radiography. The bullae are often seen in the lower lobes and the disease may mimic the emphysema seen in alpha-1-antitrypsin deficiency. Morphologically, there is panacinar emphysema with no interstitial fibrosis and variable degrees of pulmonary talc granulomatosis.[38]

2.5.3 Aspiration Pneumonia

Alcoholism is a common predisposing condition for aspiration pneumonia. Aspiration of orogastric material (bacteria, acid, food. including milk, and charcoal-lavage material) can also occur in victims rendered unconscious by drugs directly (narcotics) or indirectly by drug-induced seizures (cocaine). The posterior segments of the upper lobes or superior segments of the left lower lobe are involved when the victim is recumbent during aspiration. The basal lung segments are affected when the victim is upright and the anterior segment of the middle lobe is involved when the victim is prone or inclined forward. Gastric acid can produce bronchiolitis, hemorrhagic edema, and diffuse alveolar damage if the agonal period is prolonged is delayed. Microscopically, gastric acid aspiration produces a distinctive bronchocentric pallor of the pulmonary tissues. Fluid contaminated with *Streptococcus pneumoniae* or *Klebsiella pneumoniae* characteristically produces subpleural pneumonia with hemorrhagic edema.[39] Aspiration pneumonia often is found to consist of a mixture of both aerobic and anaerobic bacteria. Striated muscle and vegetable fibers can be seen within the bronchioles and alveoli microscopically. Necrotizing bacteria may produce lung abscesses. Septic thromboemboli from tricuspid valve endocarditis can also produce multiple lung abscesses and pneumonia in the intravenous drug abuser (Figure 2.5.5 and Figure 2.5.6).

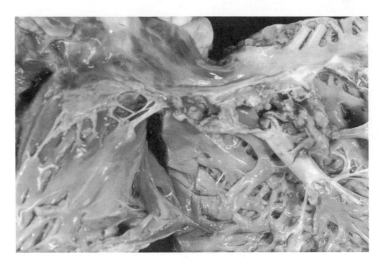

Figure 2.5.6 The victim in Figure 2.5.5 had acute bacterial endocarditis of the tricuspid valve with septic thromboemboli.

REFERENCES

1. Buster, M.C.A., Rook, L., van Brussel, G.H., et al., Chasing the dragon, related to the impaired lung function among heroin users, *Drug Alcohol Depend.*, 68, 221–228, 2002.
2. Bailey, M.E., Fraire, A.E., Greenberg, S.D., Barnard, J., and Cagle, P.T., Pulmonary histopathology in cocaine abusers, *Hum. Pathol.*, 25, 203–207, 1994.
3. Murray, R.J., Smialek, J.E., Golle, M., and Albin, R.J., Pulmonary artery medial hypertrophy in cocaine users without foreign particle microembolization, *Chest*, 96, 1050–1053, 1989.
4. Murray, R.J., Albin, R.J., Mergner, W., and Criner, G.J., Diffuse alveolar hemorrhage temporally related to cocaine smoking, *Chest*, 93, 427–429, 1988.
5. Allred, R.J. and Ewer, S., Fatal pulmonary edema following intravenous "freebase" cocaine use, *Ann. Emerg. Med.* 10, 441–442, 1981.
6. Efferen, L., Palat, D., and Meisner, J., Nonfatal pulmonary edema following cocaine smoking, *NY State J. Med.*, 89, 415–416, 1989.
7. Cucco, R.A., Yoo, O.H., Cregler, L., and Chang, J.C., Nonfatal pulmonary edema after "freebase" cocaine smoking, *Am. Rev. Respir. Dis.*, 136, 179–181, 1987.
8. Hoffman, C.K. and Goodman, P.C., Pulmonary edema in cocaine smokers, *Radiology*, 172, 463–465, 1989.
9. Patel, R.C., Dutta, D., and Schonfeld, S.A., Freebase cocaine use associated with bronchiolitis obliterans organizing pneumonia, *Ann. Intern. Med.*, 107, 186–187, 1987.
10. Forrester, J.M., Steele, A.W., Waldron, J.A., and Parsons, P.E., Crack lung: an acute pulmonary syndrome with a spectrum of clinical and histopathologic findings, *Am. Rev. Respir. Dis.*, 142, 462–467, 1990.
11. Kissner, D.G., Lawrence, W.D., Selis, J.E., and Flint, A., Crack lung: pulmonary disease caused by cocaine abuse, *Am. Rev. Respir. Dis.*, 136, 1250–1252, 1987.
12. Shesser, R., Davis, C., and Edelstein, S., Pneumomediastinum and pneumothorax after inhaling alkaloidal cocaine, *Ann. Emerg. Med.*, 10, 213–215, 1981.
13. Aroesty, D.J., Stanley, R.B., and Crockett, D.M., Pneumomediastinum and cervical emphysema from the inhalation of "freebase" cocaine: report of three cases, *Otolaryngol. Head Neck Surg.*, 94, 372–374, 1986.
14. Bush, M.N., Rubenstein, R., Hoffman, I., and Bruno, M.S., Spontaneous pneumomediastinum as a consequence of cocaine use, *NY State J. Med.*, 84, 618–619, 1984.
15. Adrouny, A. and Magnusson, P., Pneumopericardium from cocaine inhalation [letter], *N. Engl. J. Med.*, 313, 48–49, 1985.

16. Andreone, P., L'Heureux, P., and Strate, R.G., An unusual case of massive nonsurgical pneumoperi-toneum: case report, *J. Trauma*, 29, 1286–1288, 1989.

17. Shesser, R., Davis, C., and Edelstein, S., Pneumomediastinum and pneumothorax after inhaling alkaloidal cocaine, *Ann. Emerg. Med.*, 10, 213–215, 1981.

18. Birrer, R.B. and Calderon, J., Pneumothorax, pneumomediastinum, and pneumopericardium following Valsalva maneuver during marijuana smoking, *NY State J. Med.*, 84, 619–620, 1984.

19. Rubin, R.B. and Neugarten, J., Cocaine-associated asthma, *Am. J. Med.*, 88, 438–439, 1990.

20. Rebhun, J., Association of asthma and freebase smoking, *Ann. Allergy*, 60, 339–342, 1988.

21. Rao, A.N., Polos, P.G., and Walther, F.A., Crack abuse and asthma: a fatal combination, *NY State J. Med.*, 511–512, 1990.

22. Hughes, S. and Calvery, P.M.A., Heroin inhalation and asthma, *Br. Med. J.*, 297, 1511–1512, 1988.

23. Levenson, T., Greenberger, P.A., Donoghue, E.R., and Lifschultz, B.D., Asthma deaths confounded by substance abuse: an assessment of fatal asthma, *Chest*, 110, 604–610, 1996.

24. Averbach, M., Casey, K.K., and Frank, E., Near fatal status asthmaticus induced by nasal insufflation of cocaine, *South. Med. J.*, 89, 340–341, 1996.

25. Greenebaum, E., Copeland, A., and Grewal, R., Blackened bronchoalveolar lavage fluid in crack smokers: a preliminary study, *Am. J. Clin. Pathol.*, 100, 481–487, 1993.

26. Itkonen, J., Schnoll, S., and Glassroth, J., Pulmonary dysfunction in "freebase" cocaine users, *Arch. Intern. Med.*, 144, 2195–2197, 1984.

27. Lamb, D. and Roberts, G., Starch and talc emboli in drug addicts' lungs, *J. Clin. Pathol.*, 25, 876–881, 1972.

28. Butz, W.C., Pulmonary arteriole foreign body granulomata associated with angiomatoids resulting from the intravenous injection of oral medications, e.g. Propoxyphene hydrochloride (Darvon), *J. Forensic Sci.*, 14, 317–326, 1969.

29. Puro, H.E., Wolf, P.J., Skirgaudas, J., and Vazquez, J., Experimental production of human "Blue Velvet" and "Red Devil" lesions, *J. Am. Med. Assoc.*, 197, 1100–1102, 1966.

30. Crouch, E. and Churg, A., Progressive massive fibrosis of the lung secondary to intravenous injection of talc. A pathologic and mineralogic analysis, *Am. J. Clin. Pathol.*, 80, 520–526, 1983.

31. Pare, J.A.P., Fraser, R.G., Hogg, J.C., Howlett, J.G., and Murphy, S.B., Pulmonary "mainline" gran-ulomatosis: talcosis of intravenous methadone abuse, *Medicine*, 58, 229–239, 1979.

32. Sieniewicz, D.J. and Nidecker, A.C., Conglomerate pulmonary disease: a form of talcosis in intrave-nous methadone abusers, *Am. J. Roent.*, 135, 697–702, 1980.

33. Wendt, V.E., Puro, II.E., Shapiro, J., Mathews, W., and Wolf, P.L., Angiothrombotic pulmonary hypertension in addicts, *J. Am. Med. Assoc.*, 188, 755–757, 1964.

34. Szwed, J.J., Pulmonary angiothrombosis caused by "blue velvet" addiction, *Ann. Intern. Med.*, 73, 771–774, 1970.

35. Hahn, H.H., Schweid, A.I., and Beaty, H.N., Complications of injecting dissolved methylphenidate tablets, *Arch. Int. Med.*, 123, 656–659, 1969.

36. Lewman, L.V., Fatal pulmonary hypertension from intravenous injection of methylphenidate (Ritalin) tablets, *Hum. Pathol.*, 3, 67–70, 1972.

37. Hopkins, G.B. and Taylor, D.G., Pulmonary talc granulomatosis, *Am. Rev. Resp. Dis.*, 101, 101–104, 1970.

38. Sherman, C.B., Hudson, L.D., and Pierson, D.J., Severe precocious emphysema in intravenous meth-ylphenidate (Ritalin) abusers, *Chest*, 92, 1085–1087, 1987.

39. Wright, J.L., Consequences of aspiration and bronchial obstruction, in Thurlbeck, W.M. and Churg, A.M., *Pathology of the Lung*, 2nd ed., Thieme Medical, New York, 1995, chap. 31.

2.6 DISORDERS OF THE CENTRAL NERVOUS SYSTEM

Michael D. Bell, M.D.
District Medical Examiner, Palm Beach Medical Examiner Office, West Palm Beach, Florida

2.6.1 Alcohol Related

Marchiafava-Bignami[1–3] disease is a demyelinating disorder affecting the corpus callosum. It was first described in malnourished Italian men who drank cheap red wine. It has since been described in other countries and as occurring with other alcoholic beverages. Grossly, there is a discolored or partially cystic demyelinated region in the genu and body of the corpus callosum with sparing of the thin fibers along the dorsal[4] and ventral surfaces of the corpus callosum. The optic chiasm and anterior commissures may also be involved. The lesion is bilateral and symmetric with sparing of the gray matter. Microscopically, there is demyelination sparing of the axon cylinders. The number of oligodendrocytes is reduced. Lipid-laden macrophages are often abundant.

Central pontine myelinolysis (CPM) is a demyelinating disorder of the central basis pons that was first described in malnourished alcoholics by Adams.[4] Patients with CPM experience a sudden change in mental status, flaccid quadriparesis with hyperreflexia, pseudobulbar palsy, and an extensor plantar response unless coma obscures these signs. CPM is associated with the rapid correction or overcorrection of hyponatremia[5] and the symptoms appear a few days (average 6 days) after overcorrection with intravenous sodium leads to a rise of at least 20 mmol/L. Grossly, victims will be found to have a discolored, finely granular demyelinated zone in the central basis pontis, with sparing of the tegmentum, ventral pons, and corticospinal tracts (Figure 2.6.1).[6] Extrapontine myelinolysis has become more recognized.[7] The demyelinated area varies from a few millimeters to the entire basis pontis and may be triangular, diamond, or butterfly shaped. Microscopically, there is demyelination with relative preservation of axon cylinders and neurons. Axonal spheroids are commonly observed. Acute lesions contain lipid-laden macrophages, but no other inflammatory cells. Oligodendrocytes are reduced or absent and reactive astrocytes are present.

Cerebellar degeneration of alcoholics is clinically manifested by truncal instability, lower extremity ataxia, and wide-based gait, symptoms appearing gradually over months or years.[3] The pathogenesis is still unknown and may be due to the direct toxic effect of alcohol or to thiamine deficiency, or from rapid correction or overcorrection of hyponatremia similar to central pontine

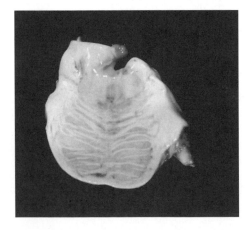

Figure 2.6.1 Discolored granular zone of myelinolysis in the central pons of this 28-year-old alcoholic who was treating aggressively for hyponatremia.

myelinolysis. Grossly, the folia of the rostral vermis and anterosuperior cerebellar hemispheres are atrophic and shrunken with widened interfolial sulci. A sagittal section through the vermis rather than the usual coronal sectioning best demonstrates this. Microscopically, the folial crests are more severely affected than the depths of the interfolial sulci, which help to distinguish the changes from those seen in anoxic-ischemic injury. There is Purkinje cell loss, patchy granular cell loss, molecular layer atrophy, and gliosis with Bregmann glial proliferation.

Acute alcohol intoxication can cause death due to central cardiopulmonary paralysis.[3] While blood ethanol concentrations over 450 to 500 mg/dl are usually considered lethal, there is considerable variability due to tolerance. Children are considered more susceptible to the lethal effects than are adults. Cerebral edema may be present or the neuropathologic examination may be normal. Delirium tremens or withdrawal seizures are not associated with any specific neuro-pathologic abnormalities.[8]

Chronic alcohol use may be associated with cerebral atrophy, although this is a disputed effect of alcoholism.[3] The cerebral atrophy thought to be a result of chronic alcoholism involves the upper dorsolateral frontal lobes, but may extend inferiorly to the inferior frontal gyri and posteriorly to the superior parietal lobule.[1] There is mild ventricular enlargement. Microscopic changes are not specific. This type of cerebral atrophy may be associated with a dementia that is potentially reversible at its early stages.[9]

Fetal alcohol syndrome is a constellation of birth defects found in children of alcohol-abusing mothers. It is the most common cause of birth defects associated with mental retardation. Other clinical manifestations include irritability, seizures, hypotonia, and cerebellar dysfunction. The neuropathology findings are nonspecific and include microcephaly, compensatory hydrocephalus, neuroglial heterotopia of the ventricles or leptomeninges, and atrophy or hypoplasia of the cere-bellum or centrum semiovale.[3,10]

The autopsy manifestations of Warnicke's encephalopathy (gaze paralysis, ataxia, nystagmus, and mental confusion) and Korsakoff psychosis (retrograde amnesia, impaired short-term memory) seen in alcoholics[11] include petechiae and pink discoloration of the mammillary bodies (Figure 2.6.2).[3] The morphologic features (seen in 1.7 to 2.7% of consecutive autopsies) include petechiae and pink discoloration of the mammillary bodies (Figure 2.6.2), hypothalamus, periventricular region of the thalamus, periaqueductal gray matter, and beneath the floor of the fourth ventricle.[1] The lesions are bilateral and symmetric when present. These gross features are seen in only 50% of acute cases;[12] therefore, microscopic examination is essential. The lesions vary with the stage and severity of the deficiency. Acute lesions consist of dilated, congested capillaries with perivas-cular ball and ring hemorrhages and ischemic neuronal changes (Figure 2.6.3). Chronic lesions have vascular endothelial cell swelling and proliferation and gliosis. Affected blood vessels may have irregular or bead-like swellings.

2.6.2 Drug Related: Excited Delirium

Excited delirium is a drug-induced delirium or psychosis accompanied by agitation, and hyper-thermia, and often ending with respiratory arrest and sudden death. Cocaine is the drug most often implicated in this syndrome,[13] but amphetamines have also been implicated in some cases. The syndrome is not due to any contaminants ingested along with the drug.

Chronic cocaine users have increased synaptic dopamine uptake in the ventral striatum. Victims of fatal cocaine-associated excited delirium, however, do not show this increase. Cocaine abusers also have increased serotonin transporter upregulation in dopaminergic areas of the brain. Serotonin is thought to modulate dopamine transmission. Some researchers believe that victims of fatal cocaine-associated excited delirium have a distinctive receptor phenotype differing from that of chronic cocaine users without excited delirium. The pathogenesis of cocaine-induced excited delirium is unknown. One hypothesis is that cocaine initially elevates brain dopamine levels causing the delirium. This cocaine-induced brain dopamine elevation has been demonstrated in animals.[14]

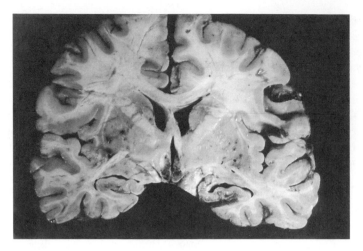

Figure 2.6.2 Coronal section of cerebrum demonstrates the mammillary body hemorrhage in Wernicke–Korsakoff syndrome.

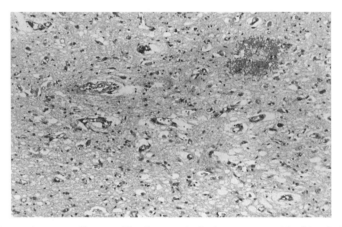

Figure 2.6.3 Ball hemorrhage, capillary proliferation, and gliosis are present in this alcoholic with Wernicke encephalopathy (Hematoxylin and eosin, original magnification 20×).

Chronic cocaine use reduces brain dopamine metabolism[15] potentiating the effect of cocaine on brain dopamine levels. As the cocaine concentration falls, brain dopamine falls triggering the syndrome, which is similar to the neuroleptic malignant syndrome (NMS) in Parkinson's disease or in patients withdrawn from levodopa, a dopaminergic drug. Some authors consider cocaine-induced psychosis as a variant of NMS in which patients also have hyperthermia, autonomic instability, and delirium (Table 2.6.1). NMS is characterized by diffuse muscular rigidity, but this is not seen in cocaine-induced excited delirium. One author has suggested that akinesia of the respiratory muscles may be the fatal mechanism of sudden death in these victims.[16]

There are no specific gross or microscopic findings in victims dying of cocaine-induced agitated delirium. A post-mortem core body temperature, if taken soon after death, will be elevated. A thorough post-mortem examination is essential to rule out other causes of sudden death. Cocaine and its metabolites must be present in toxicology specimens. Victims dying of agitated delirium have post-mortem blood cocaine concentrations (average = 0.6 mg/L with range of 0.14 to 0.92 mg/L) that are ten times lower than those concentrations in victims of cocaine overdose.[17]

Agitated delirium may occur following cocaine ingestion by all routes of administration (snorting, smoking, injection), but never after just chewing coca leaves. The majority of victims are men. Soon after cocaine ingestion, the person becomes paranoid, delirious, and aggressive. The victim

Table 2.6.1 Comparison between Neuroleptic
            Malignant Syndrome and Cocaine-Induced
            Agitated Delirium

Symptom	NMS	Cocaine Delirium
Hyperthermia	++	++
Delirium	++	++
Agitation	+	++
Akinesia/rigidity	++	−

Note: ++ = present in almost all cases; + = present in many
cases; − = may occur late during syndrome.[16]

is often seen running, yelling, breaking glass and overturning furniture, disrobing, and hiding.
Witnesses report that the person has unexpected strength. The victim often becomes calm and quiet
before having a cardiopulmonary arrest, often during police custody or medical transport. This
disorder is frequently accompanied by sudden death. Restraint procedures that could compromise
respiration should be avoided. The restrained person should be closely observed, especially after
the agitation subsides.[18]

2.6.3   Drug-Induced Cerebrovascular Disease

Drug-induced cerebrovascular disease or stroke is any nontraumatic intracerebral hemorrhage
(including subarachnoid hemorrhage) or cerebral infarction that results directly or indirectly from
drug ingestion. An accurate clinical history and/or positive toxicologic testing are needed to
corroborate the recent drug ingestion. In all, 47% of patients less than 35 years old who present
with an acute stroke have drug use as a predisposing condition.[19] Clinically, a patient with cerebrovascular disease presents with sudden loss of function, neurologic deficit, and involvement of
the corresponding vascular supply that occurs within minutes or rarely hours after drug ingestion.
If the blood vessel is occluded through pharmacological vasoconstriction or vasospasm, ischemia
and infarction occurs. If the vessel is damaged, hemorrhage results.

Cocaine is frequently associated with intracerebral hemorrhage.[20–24] Other stimulant drugs
including amphetamine,[19,25] phenylpropanolamine,[26] phencyclidine,[26] pseudoephedrine,[26] and methylphenidate,[19,26] have all been associated with intracranial hemorrhage.

Cocaine blocks the uptake of catecholamines at adrenergic nerve endings, potentiating sympathetic responses, leading to a dose-dependent elevation of arterial pressure and heart rate in humans[27]
and dogs.[28] Amphetamine and methamphetamine can also produce transient hypertension and
tachycardia. Researchers postulated that intracerebral hemorrhage occurs because of sudden marked
elevation in systemic blood pressure in susceptible persons with preexisting vascular malformations.
This would include such disorders as arterio-venous malformations, berry aneurysms,[29] or Charcot–
Bouchard microaneurysms in hypertensive individuals.

In half of patients with cocaine-associated intracerebral or subarachnoid hemorrhage, no demonstrable structural lesion is identified.[30–32] Another postulated mechanism of intraparenchymal hemorrhage in cocaine users is acute increased cerebral blood flow into an area of ischemia produced
by prior cocaine-induced vasoconstriction.[33] Interestingly, intrauterine exposure to cocaine does
not influence the prevalence or severity of intraventricular hemorrhage in the preterm infant.[34]

Cocaine can cause cerebral infarction by arterial thrombosis, arterial embolism, arterial spasm,
and circulatory compromise with secondary cerebral hypoperfusion. In the latter case, cocaine can
cause acute myocardial infarction or ventricular arrhythmia resulting in hypotension and secondary
cerebral hypoperfusion. The middle cerebral artery is most commonly affected with resulting sudden
paraplegia.[35] The anterior cerebral, posterior cerebral, and basilar/vertebral arteries can also be
affected resulting in a variety of clinical signs and symptoms (Figure 2.6.4 and Figure 2.6.5). Most
victims develop symptoms suddenly, within 3 h of cocaine ingestion. Other victims wake up with

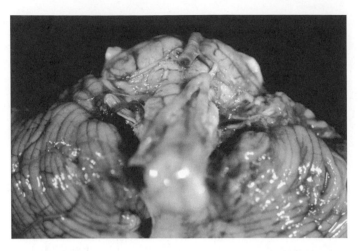

Figure 2.6.4 There is an occlusive thrombus in the basilar artery of this 28-year-old cocaine addict.

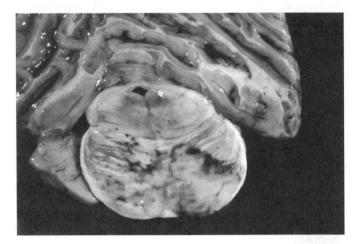

Figure 2.6.5 There is an irregular zone of infarction in the basis pontis of the victim in Figure 2.6.4. He was found comatose at home.

the neurologic deficit after heavy drug use the previous evening. Cannabis has recently been implicated in causing multiple nonfatal ischemic strokes in a 36-year-old man with no other risk factors. The mechanism for cannabis-induced stroke is unknown. No matter how convincing the case report, causation is established only by randomized clinical trials or, as in this case, with a nested case control study. Such studies are lacking.

The most common sites of cocaine-induced intracerebral hemorrhage are the cerebral hemispheres (57%) followed by the putamen (18%), and subarachnoid and intraventricular sites (Figure 2.6.6 and Figure 2.6.7). Cocaine-induced subarachnoid hemorrhage is usually due to rupture of a preexisting arterio-venous malformation or berry aneurysm of the cerebral arteries[35] (Figure 2.6.8). In a recent retrospective study from San Diego, 21% of victims dying from ruptured berry aneurysms had cocaine or methamphetamine (or both) in their post-mortem blood.[36] This was higher than the 5% incidence of cocaine or methamphetamine intoxication in all adult autopsies from the same jurisdiction.

If no vascular malformation is found to explain the subarachnoid hemorrhage in a drug addict, one must consider a traumatic cause for the subarachnoid hemorrhage (such as extracranial vertebral artery laceration[37]) before blithely ascribing it to cocaine or another stimulant. Intraparenchymal hemorrhage due to cocaine use can occur in sites typical of patients with hypertension-related

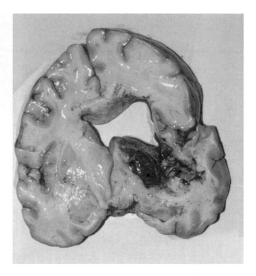

Figure 2.6.6 This 35-year-old woman developed an acute intracerebral hematoma after cocaine use.

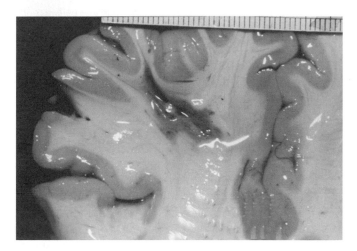

Figure 2.6.7 This brown slit-like cavity in the frontal white matter is all that remains of a previous cocaine-induced intracerebral hemorrhage.

intracerebral hemorrhage. The blood vessels, when examined, are usually normal both on gross and microscopic exam.[38] Charcot–Bouchard microaneurysms, or lipohyalinosis, are typically seen in hypertensive cerebral hemorrhage[39] and are not seen in drug-induced intracerebral hemorrhage. Patients are usually in their third to fifth decades of life with both men and women affected equally. Intracerebral hemorrhage occurs after snorting, smoking, or injecting cocaine. The time between drug use and symptom onset is usually within 3 h, but can range from immediate to 12 h. Most patients present with acute headache or in coma. Confusion is a less frequent presenting symptom. There is 36% mortality in patients who present to the emergency room with acute stroke strongly linked to recent drug use.[19]

2.6.4   Drug-Associated Cerebral Vasculitis

Cerebral vasculitis has been associated with cocaine, ephedrine, and amphetamine use. The association between cerebral vasculitis and cocaine use is tenuous and supported by a only few (eight) case reports, some of which have only angiographic evidence ("beading" or segmental

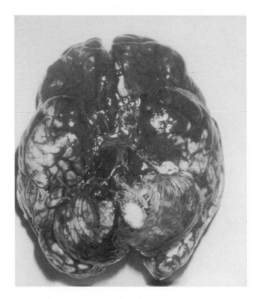

Figure 2.6.8 Subarachnoid hemorrhage in cocaine abusers is often due to a berry aneurysm that ruptures from the sudden blood pressure elevation caused by cocaine.

arterial narrowing) of vasculitis with no histological confirmation (Table 2.6.2).[40,41] Since "beading" is considered by many to be a sign of vasospasm, the causation argument becomes circular. The remaining case reports do show histological evidence of vasculitis, but no angiographic narrowing or other abnormalities.[42–45] Half of the victims presented with encephalopathy and coma without intracranial hemorrhage or infarction. The other half presented with intracerebral hemorrhage or cerebral infarction. Transient ischemic attacks (TIA) with multimodal segmental arterial stenosis on angiography have been reported in chronic cocaine users.[46] All these patients were young (mean age = 28 years with age range = 22 to 36) with multiple routes of drug administration used (nasal insufflation, smoking, intravenous injection). Histological examination demonstrated acute and chronic small vessel inflammation. Four cases had lymphocytic infiltration in the cerebral blood vessels. Two cases had polymorphonuclear leukocyte infiltration in the small arteries and venules of the brain. No giant cells or granulomas were seen in any case. The pathogenesis of cocaine-associated cerebral vasculitis remains unknown. Methamphetamine and structurally related drugs have reportedly caused necrotizing cerebral vasculitis.

2.6.5 Drug-Induced Seizure Disorder

Drug-induced seizures are, by definition, seizures that occur after the ingestion of a drug, that are not caused by other pathologic processes (intracranial hemorrhage or blunt head trauma). An accurate clinical history or positive toxicology testing should corroborate actual ingestion of the drug.

Cocaine has been reported to lower the threshold for seizures and commonly does cause seizures.[47] In one series of patients with seizure activity as the primary admitting diagnosis, cocaine was the most common drug of abuse detected.[48] At least in this series, cocaine-induced seizure was found to be more likely brief and self-limiting, compared to seizures caused by the other drugs of abuse (amphetamine, methamphetamine, phencyclidine, and sedative-hypnotic withdrawal). Seizures may also initiate a terminal cardiac arrhythmia, a theory that has gained more acceptance, but the suggestion has yet to be proved.[49,50]

Fatal seizures associated with cocaine use have been reported.[51] There are no specific gross or microscopic neuropathologic findings in fatal cocaine-induced seizure victims. Tongue contusions are nonspecific findings in patients who die of terminal seizures (Figure 2.6.9).

Table 2.6.2 Reported Cases of Cocaine-Associated Vasculitis

Report	Age/Sex	Route	Clinical syndrome	Angiogram	Time interval	Pathology	Outcome
Kaye, 1987	22 M	Nasal	Cerebral infarct	Beading, occlusion, narrowing	Unknown	None	Improvement with steroids
Klonoff, 1989	29 F	Smoke	ICH	Beading, narrowing	Unknown	None	Stabilized after hematoma removed
Krendel, 1990	36 M	Smoke	Weakness, dysarthria, confusion	Occlusion, narrowing	3.5 weeks	Acute vasculitis, small cortical vessels, cortical infarct with multinucleated giant cells	Improvement with steroids
Krendell, 1990	31 F	Smoke, IV	Coma, cerebral edema	Normal	42 days	Lymphocytic infiltration, small vessels and larger vessel normal, no granulomas, multiple cystic, necrotic, and gliotic areas in white matter with multinucleated giant cells	Death
Fredericks, 1991	32 M	Nasal, IV	Confusion, ataxia	Normal	13 days	Lymphocytic infiltration, small vessels and endothelial swelling	Improvement with steroids
Morrow, 1993	25 F	Nasal	Seizure, coma	Not done	5 days	Lymphocytic infiltration in small vessels of cortex and brainstem, small infarcts, cerebral edema with diffuse encephalomalacia	Death
Merkel, 1995	32 M	Nasal	ICH	Normal	2 days	Non-necrotizing leukocytoclastic vasculitis, neutrophils and mononuclear cells in venules	Improvement without steroids
Merkel, 1995	20 M	Nasal	ICH	Narrowing	<6 months	Neutrophil infiltration and fibrinoid degeneration in small arterioles and veins	Partial recovery

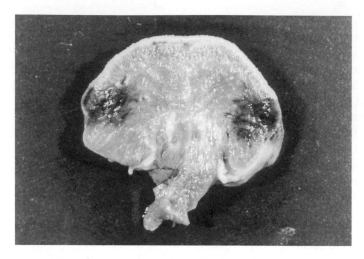

Figure 2.6.9 This cross section of tongue demonstrates the contusions that may be seen in drug-induced
seizures.

Cocaine-induced seizure is a common neurologic complication (2.3 to 8.4%) of cocaine users
who present with seizures to the emergency room[52] that affects both men and women.[53] The average
age is 27 years with a range of 17 to 42 years. Seizures occur after snorting, smoking, or injecting
cocaine. The seizures are usually generalized, tonic–clonic, isolated, and self-limiting. They usually
last less than 5 min and can occur with first-time and chronic cocaine users. The interval between
cocaine ingestion and seizure onset varies from minutes to 12 h. In one emergency room study, 11
of 137 patients (8%) with cocaine intoxication presented with seizures as their chief problem and
none died.[52]

2.6.6   Drug-Induced Movement Disorders

Parkinson's syndrome has been reported in addicts who receive the synthetic meperidine analog
contaminated with MPTP (1-methyl-4-phenyl-1,2,3,6-tetrahydropyridine). MPTP is produced during the careless synthesis of MPPP (1-methyl-4-phenyl-4-propionoxypiperidene) in clandestine
laboratories. Neurotoxic symptoms include resting tremor, rigidity, bradykinesia, and other signs
and symptoms of parkinsonism. Neuropathologic examination has demonstrated substantia nigra
degeneration confined to the zona compacta. There is astrocytosis, focal gliosis, and deposition of
extraneuronal melanin pigment.[54] It has been reported that MPPP contaminated with MPTP causes
a Parkinson's syndrome within days of inject.[55] MPTP-induced Parkinson's syndrome can also
result from snorting the drug.[56] The severe rigidity observed in MPTP-induced parkinonism has
been implicated in the asphyxiation death of one victim who was unable to move his head from a
suffocating posture.[57] Post-mortem neuropathological examination of this individual also revealed
severe neuronal loss in his substantia nigra. Cocaine use also has been associated with movement
disorders. This may be related to the fact that concentrations of alpha-synmuclein, a pre-synaptic
protein found in Lewy bodies in Parkinson's disease, are increased in the midbrain dopamine
neurons of chronic cocaine abusers.

2.6.7   Drug-Induced Anoxic Ischemic Encephalopathy

Abused drugs commonly produce anoxic-ischemic encephalopathy.[58–60] This can occur from
insufficient oxygen reaching the blood from the lungs, insufficient oxygen carriage, or inadequate
cerebral blood perfusion. This is a common mechanism in drug abusers who have a delayed death
after drug intoxication. In the older literature on fatal heroin overdose, cerebral edema with

increased brain weight was observed in nearly 90%. This finding conflicts with the author's own experience, where most cases of fatal heroin intoxication manifested neither cerebral edema nor increased brain weight.

The morphology of anoxic-ischemic encephalopathy is variable in its affect on different parts of the brain. In the gray matter, the watershed zones are commonly affected with laminar necrosis involving lamina zones III, V, VI. The h1 segment (Sommer's sector) and end plate in the hippocampus, are commonly involved. Other vulnerable sites include the Purkinje cells of the cerebellum, the caudate, and the putamen. The brain is often swollen and soft with a pale or dusky gray matter. Laminar necrosis may be apparent if sufficient time has elapsed between the time of anoxia and death. Microscopic changes are not recognizable until 6 to 8 h after the anoxic-ischemic insult. The affected neurons become shrunken with eosinophilic cytoplasm and nuclear pyknosis, and gradually disappear. There is also nonspecific capillary proliferation, with endothelial swelling, spongiform change, and gliosis in the affected neuropil. Hypoxic injury to the cerebral white matter with glossy softening and loss of myelin (hypoxic leukoencephlaopathy) is less commonly seen in drug overdoses where death is delayed.

2.6.8 Drug-Associated Central Nervous System Infections

Primary fungal cerebritis due to *Rhizopus* has been reported in cocaine,[61] heroin,[62–66] and amphetamine[67] users with no other systemic foci identified at autopsy. Victims are usually men in their third or fourth decades of life. They present with hemiplegia, facial weakness, and headache. The brain lesions are usually multiple with frequent bilateral involvement of the basal ganglia. The phycomycoses are angiotrophic fungi that commonly occlude and invade the cerebral blood vessels causing hemorrhagic infarcts. Fungal cerebritis or meningitis has been reported in intravenous drug abusers (Figure 2.6.10 and Figure 2.6.11) with human immunodeficiency virus (HIV) infection. In addition to fungal cerebritis, HIV-infected intravenous drug abusers can develop a large variety of central nervous infections and neoplasms (Table 2.6.3), thereby fulfilling the criterion for acquired immunodeficiency syndrome (AIDS). Intravenous drug abusers with valvular endocarditis may develop central nervous system complications from emboli, both septic and bland infarction, which may affect a single or multiple vessels. The resultant lesions may be ischemic or suppurative, resulting in septic or aseptic meningitis, brain abscess, or encephalopathy.[68] This is more likely to occur with left-sided valvular endocarditis than right-sided endocarditis alone. *Staphylococcus aureus* is a more common etiologic microorganism in intravenous drug abusers than non-intravenous drug abusers and it is more likely to produce neurologic complications. Intravenous drug abusers

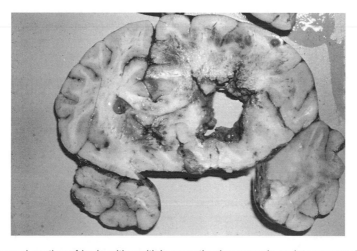

Figure 2.6.10 Coronal section of brain with multiple necrotic abscesses in an intravenous drug abuser.

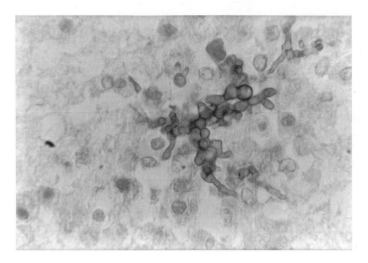

Figure 2.6.11 Within the necrotic cerebral cavities on the patient in this figure are branching, septated fungi (Gomori methanamine silver, original magnification 80×).

Table 2.6.3 Central Nervous System Infections in Intravenous Drug Abusers with AIDS

HIV encephalitis
Progressive multifocal leukoencephalopathy
Cytomegalovirus ventriculitis and *cerebritis*
Toxoplasma cerebritis
Cryptococcal meningitis and *cerebritis*
Histoplasma cerebritis
Nocardia cerebritis
Mycobacterium infections (including tuberculosis, avian-intracellulare)
Fungal meningitis and cerebritis (*Candida, Aspergillus, Rhizopus*)
Cysticercosis
Entameba histolytica
Acanthameba castellani

can develop significant and life-threatening neurologic sequelae from toxins produced by *Clostridium tetani and botulinum* wound infections. Tetanus is commonly associated with subcutaneous injection or "skin popping." Mexican "Black tar" heroin use was a risk factor in cases of botulism occurring in intravenous drug abusers during the mid-1990s. Nasal insufflation of drugs can also cause frontal sinusitis and overlying frontal lobe abscess.[69] Clostridia outbreaks reported from the United Kingdom involved mainly Iranian heroin.[70]

2.6.9 Heroin Smokers Encephalopathy

Spongiform encephalopathy of obscure origin occurs in users of smoked drugs, but most cases have been in heroin abusers. An epidemic outbreak of spongiform leukoencephalopathy occurred in the Netherlands in 1982. It involved nearly 50 patients, many of whom died, none of whom fully recovered.[71] The only factor common to all the individuals was that they all smoked heroin. All of the reported cases have had thorough toxicological investigation, but no agents have been identified. Sporadic cases have occurred over the last quarter century, mainly in Europe. A few of the victims have been cocaine users and several have been drug injectors. More recent magnetic resonance imaging (MRI) studies have shown diffuse white matter changes in all cases. Histologically there is widespread confluent vacuolar degeneration of the deep white matter, with evidence of severe, extensive, axonal injury.[72] Various etiologies have been proposed including some uncharacterized defect in mitochondrial function or a direct toxic effect upon lipid-rich myelin. It may be that the disease has a latent period after the putative toxin is absorbed, but before symptoms appear. If so, that would explain the consistently negative toxicology testing results.

REFERENCES

1. Courville, C.B., *Effects of Alcohol on the Nervous System of Man*, San Lucas Press, Los Angeles, 1966.
2. Bohrod, M.G., Primary degeneration of the corpus callosum (Marchiafava's disease), *Arch. Neurol. Psychiatry*, 47, 465–473, 1942.
3. Schocet, S.S., Jr., Exogenous toxic-metabolic diseases including vitamin deficiency, in Davis, R.L. and Robertson, D.M., Eds., *Textbook of Neuropathology*, Williams & Wilkins, Baltimore, 1985, 372–402.
4. Adams, R.D., Victor, M., and Mancall, E.L., Central pontine myelinolysis: a hitherto undescribed disease occurring in alcoholics and malnourished patients, *Arch. Neurol. Psychiatry*, 81, 154–172, 1959.
5. Norenberg, M.D., Leslie, K.O., and Robertson, A.S.. Association between rise in serum sodium and central pontine myelinolysis, *Ann. Neurol.*, 11, 128–135, 1982.
6. Norenberg, M.D. and Gregorios, J.B., Central nervous system manifestations of systemic disease, in Davis, R.L. and Robertson, D.M., Eds., *Textbook of Neuropathology*, Williams & Wilkins, Baltimore, 1985, 422–423.
7. Laureno, R. and Karp, B.I., Myelinolysis after correction of hyponatremia, *Ann. Intern. Med.*, 126, 57–62, 1997.
8. Powers, J.M. and Haroupian, D.S., Central nervous system, in Damjanov, I. and Linder, J., Eds., *Anderson's Pathology*, 10th ed., Mosby-Year Book, St. Louis, 1996, 2791.
9. Tomlinson, B.E., Aging and the dementias, in Adams, J.H. and Duchen, L.W., Eds., *Greenfield's Neuropathology*, 5th ed., Oxford University Press, New York, 1992.
10. Claren, S.K., Recognition of fetal alcohol syndrome, *J. Am. Med. Assoc.*, 245, 2436–2439, 1981.
11. Cravioto, H., Korein, J., and Silberman, J., Wernicke's encephalopathy: a clinical and pathological study of 28 autopsied cases, *Arch. Neurol.*, 4, 510–519,1961.
12. Harper, C., Wernicke's encephalopathy: a more common disease than realized. A neuropathological study of 51 cases, *J. Neurol. Neurosurg. Psychiatry*, 42, 226–231, 1979.
13. Campbell, B.G., Cocaine abuse with hyperthermia, seizures and fatal complications, *Med. J. Aust.*, 149, 387–389, 1988.
14. Pettit, H.O., Pan, H., Parsons, L.H.. Justice, J.B., Jr., Extracellular concentrations of cocaine and dopamine are enhanced during chronic cocaine administration, *J. Neurochem.*, 55, 798–804, 1990.
15. Karoum, F., Suddath, R.L., and Wyatt, R.J., Chronic cocaine and rat brain catecholamines: long term reduction in hypothalamic and frontal cortex dopamine metabolism, *Eur. J. Pharm.*, 186, 1–8, 1990.
16. Kosten, T.R. and Kleber, H.D., Rapid death during cocaine abuse: a variant of the neuroleptic malignant syndrome? *Am. J. Drug Alcohol Abuse*, 14, 335–346, 1988.
17. Wetli, C.V. and Fishbain, D.A., Cocaine-induced psychosis and sudden death in recreational cocaine users, *J. Forensic Sci.*, 30, 873–880, 1985.
18. Davis, G.D., Cocaine-induced excited delirium. *Forensic Pathology Check Sample*, No. FP 96-9, American Society of Clinical Pathologists, Chicago, 1996.
19. Kaku, D.A. and Lowenstein, D.H., Emergence of recreational drug abuse as a major risk factor for stroke in young adults, *Ann. Intern. Med.*, 113, 821–827, 1990.
20. Levine, S.R., Brust, J.C.M., Futrell, N., Ho, K.L., Blake, D., Millikan, C.H. et al., Cerebrovascular complications of the use of the "crack" form of alkaloidal cocaine, *N. Engl. J. Med.*, 323, 699–704, 1990.
21. Mody, C.K., Miller, B.L., McIntyre, H.B., Cobb, S.K., and Goldberg, M.A., Neurologic complications of cocaine abuse, *Neurology*, 38, 1189 1193, 1988.
22. Mangiardi, J.R., Daras, M., Geller, M.E., Weitzner, I., and Tuchman, A.J., Cocaine-related intracranial hemorrhage. Report of nine cases and review, *Acta Neurol. Scand.*, 77, 177–180, 1988.
23. Aggarwal, S.K., Cocaine-associated intracranial hemorrhage: absence of vasculitis in 14 cases, *Neurology*, 46, 1741–1743, 1996.

24. Buttner, A., Mall, G., Penning, R. et al., The neuropathology of cocaine abuse, *Leg. Med.*, 5, S240–S242, 2003.
25. Harrington, H., Heller, H.A., Dawson, D., Caplan, L., and Rumbaugh, C., Intracerebral hemorrhage and oral amphetamine, *Arch. Neurol.*, 40, 503–507, 1983.
26. Sloan, M.A., Kittner, S.J., Rigamonti, D., and Price, T.R., Occurrence of stroke associated with use/abuse of drugs, *Neurology*, 41, 1358–1364, 1991.
27. Fischman, M.W., Schuster, C.R., Resnekov, L., Shick, J.F.E., Krasnegar, N.A., Fennell, W., and Freedman, D.X., Cardiovascular and subjective effects of intravenous cocaine administration in humans, *Arch. Gen. Psych.*, 33, 983–989, 1976.
28. Wilkerson, R.D., Cardiovascular effects of cocaine in conscious dogs: Importance of fully functional autonomic and central nervous systems, *J. Pharmacol. Exp. Ther.*, 246, 466–471, 1988.
29. Davis, G.D. and Swalwell, C.I., The incidence of acute cocaine or methamphetamine intoxication in deaths due to ruptured cerebral (berry) aneurysms, *J. Forensic Sci.*, 41, 626–628, 1996.
30. Nolte, K.B., Brass, L.M., and Fletterick, C.F., Intracranial hemorrhage associated with cocaine abuse: a prospective autopsy study, *Neurology*, 46, 1291–1296, 1996.
31. Levine, S.R., Brust, J.C.M., Futrell, N., Brass, L.M., Blake, D., Fayad, P., Schultz, L.R., Millikan, C.H., Ho, K.-L., and Welch, K.M.A., A comparative study of the cerebrovascular complications of cocaine: alkaloidal versus hydrochloride: a review, *Neurology*, 41, 1173–1177, 1991.
32. Fessler, R.D., Esshaki, C.M., Stankewitz, R.C., Johnson, R.R., and Diaz, F.G., The neurovascular complications of cocaine, *Surg. Neurol.*, 47, 339–345, 1997.
33. Caplan, L., Intracerebral hemorrhage revisited, *Neurology*, 38, 624–627, 1988.
34. McLenan, D.A., Ajayi, O.A., Rydman, R.J., and Pildes, R.S., Evaluation of the relationship between cocaine and intraventricular hemorrhage, *J. Nat. Med. Assoc.*, 86, 281–287, 1994.
35. Daras, M., Tuchman, A.J., Koppel, B.S., Samkoff, L.M., Weitzner, I., and Marc, J., Neurovascular complications of cocaine, *Acta Neurol. Scand.*, 90, 124–129, 1994.
36. Davis, G.G. and Swalwell, C.I., The incidence of acute cocaine or methamphetamine intoxication in deaths due to ruptured cerebral (berry) aneurysms, *J. Forensic Sci.*, 41, 626–628, 1996.
37. Contostavlos, D.L., Massive subarachnoid hemorrhage due to laceration of the vertebral artery associated with fracture of the transverse process of the atlas, *J. Forensic Sci.*, 16, 40–56, 1971.
38. Nolte, K.B. and Gelman, B.B., Intracerebral hemorrhage associated with cocaine abuse, *Arch. Pathol. Lab. Med.*, 113, 812–813, 1989.
39. Fisher, C.M., Pathological observations in hypertensive cerebral hemorrhage, *J. Neuropathol. Exp. Neurol.*, 30, 536–550, 1971.
40. Kaye, B.R. and Fainstat, M., Cerebral vasculitis associated with cocaine abuse, *J. Am. Med. Assoc.*, 258, 2104–2106, 1987.
41. Klonoff, D.C., Andrews, B.T., and Obana, W.G., Stroke associated with cocaine use, *Arch. Neurol.*, 46, 989–993, 1989.
42. Krendel, D.A., Ditter, S.M., Frankel, M.R., and Ross, W.K., Biopsy-proven cerebral vasculitis associated with cocaine abuse, *Neurology*, 40, 1092–1094, 1990.
43. Morrow, P.L. and McQuillen, J.B., Cerebral vasculitis associated with cocaine abuse, *J. Forensic Sci.*, 38, 732–738, 1993.
44. Fredericks, R.K., Lefkowitz, D.S., Challa, V.R. et al., Cerebral vasculitis associated with cocaine abuse, *Stroke*, 22, 1437–1439, 1991.
45. Merkel, P.A., Koroshetz, W.J., Irizarry, M.C., and Cudkowicz, M.E., Cocaine-associated cerebral vasculitis, *Sem. Arthritis Rheum.*, 25, 172–183, 1995.
46. Moore, P.M. and Peterson, P.L., Nonhemorrhagic cerebrovascular complications of cocaine abuse, *Neurology*, 39, 302, 1989 (Suppl. 1; abstr.).
47. Pascual-Leone, A., Dhuna, A., Altafullah, I., and Anderson, D.C., Cocaine-induced seizures, *Neurology*, 40, 404–407, 1990.
48. Olson, K.R., Kearney, T.E., Dyer, J.E., Benowitz, N.L., and Blanc, P.D., Seizures associated with poisoning and drug overdose, *Am. J. Emerg. Med.*, 12, 392–395, 1994.
49. Rugg-Gunn, F.J., Simister, R.J., Squirrell, M., Holdright, D.R., and Duncan, J.S., Cardiac arrhythmias in focal epilepsy: a prospective long-term study, *Lancet*, 364, 2212–2219, 2004.

50. P-Codrea Tigaran, S., Dalager-Pedersen, S., Baandrup, U., Dam, M., and Vesterby-Charles, A., Sudden unexpected death in epilepsy: is death by seizures a cardiac disease? *Am. J. Forensic Med. Pathol.,* 26(2), 99–105, 2005.

51. Lathers, C.M., Tyau, L.S.Y., Spino, M.M., and Agarwal, I., Cocaine induced seizures, arrhythmias and sudden death, *J. Clin. Pharmacol.,* 28, 584–593, 1988.

52. Derlet, R.W. and Albertson, T.E., Emergency department presentation of cocaine intoxication, *Ann. Emerg. Med.,* 18, 182–186, 1989.

53. Lowenstein, D.H., Massa, S.M., Rowbotham, M.C., Collins, S.D., McKinney, H.E., and Simon, R.P., Acute neurologic and psychiatric complications associated with cocaine abuse, *Am. J. Med.,* 83, 841–846, 1987.

54. Davis, G., Williams, A., Markey, S. et al., Chronic parkinsonism secondary to intravenous injection of meperedine analogs, *Psych. Res.,* 1, 249–254, 1979.

55. Langston, J., Ballard, P., Tetrud, J., and Irwin, I., Chronic parkinsonism in humans due to a product of meperidine-analog synthesis, *Science,* 219, 979–980, 1983.

56. Wright, J.M., Wall, R.A., Perry, T.L., and Paty, D.W., Chronic parkinsonism secondary to intranasal administration of a product of meperidine-analog synthesis [letter], *N. Engl. J. Med.,* 310, 325, 1984.

57. Kaplan, J. and Karluk, D., Suffocation due to drug-induced parkinsonism [abstr.], paper presented at National Association of Medical Examiner Meeting, Traverse City, MI, Sept. 1996.

58. Brierley, J., The neuropathology of brain hypoxia, in *Scientific Foundations of Neurology,* M. Critchley, Ed., F.A. Davis, Philadelphia, 1972.

59. Adams, J., Brierley, J., Connor, R., and Treip, C.S., The effects of systemic hypotension upon the human brain: clinical and neuropathological observations in 11 cases, *Brain,* 89, 235–268, 1966.

60. Norenberg, M.D. and Gregorios, J.B., Central nervous system manifestations of systemic disease, in Davis, R.L. and Robertson, D.M., Eds., *Textbook of Neuropathology,* Williams & Wilkins, Baltimore, MD, 1985, 403–414.

61. Wetli, C.V., Weiss, S.D., Cleary, T.J., and Gyori, E.L., Fungal cerebritis from intravenous drug abuse, *J. Forensic Sci.,* 29, 260–268, 1984.

62. Hameroff, S., Eckholdt, J., and Linderburg, R., Cerebral phycomycosis in a heroin addict, *Neurology,* 20, 261–265, 1970.

63. Kasantikul, V., Shuangshoti, S., and Taecholarn, C., Primary phycomycosis of the brain in heroin addicts, *Surg. Neurol.,* 28, 468–472, 1987.

64. Masucci, E.F., Fabara, J.A., Saini, N., and Kurtzke, J.F., Cerebral mucomycosis (phycomycosis) in a heroin addict, *Arch. Neurol.,* 39, 304–306, 1982.

65. Adelman, L. and Aronson, S., The neuropathologic complications of narcotics addiction, *Bull. N.Y. Acad. Med.,* 45, 225–234, 1969.

66. Pierce, P.F., Jr., Solomon, S.L., Kaufman, L., Garagusi, V.F., Parker, R.H., and Ajello, L., Zygomycetes brain abscesses in narcotic addicts with serological diagnosis, *J. Am. Med. Assoc.,* 248, 2881–2882, 1982.

67. Micozzi, M.S. and Wetli, C.V., Intravenous amphetamine abuse, primary mucomycosis, and acquired immunodeficiency, *J. Forensic Sci.,* 30, 504–510, 1985.

68. Ziment, I., Nervous system complications in bacterial endocarditis, *Am. J. Med.,* 47, 593–607, 1969.

69. Rao, A.N., Brain abscess: a complication of cocaine inhalation, *N.Y. State J. Med.,* 10, 548–550, 1988.

70. Severe illness and death among injecting drug users in Scotland: a case-control study, *Epidemiol. Infect.,* 133(2), 193–204, 2005.

71. Wolters, E.C., van Wijngaarden, G.K., Stam, F.C. et al., Leucoencephalopathy after inhaling "heroin" pyrolysate, *Lancet,* 4;2(8310), 1233–1237, 1982.

CHAPTER 3

Pharmacokinetics: Drug Absorption, Distribution, and Elimination

Amanda J. Jenkins, Ph.D.
The Office of the Cuyahoga County Coroner, Cleveland, Ohio

CONTENTS

INTRODUCTION

Pharmacokinetics is defined as the study of the quantitative relationship between administered doses of a drug and the observed plasma/blood or tissue concentrations.[1] The pharmacokinetic model is a mathematical description of this relationship. Models provide estimates of certain parameters, such as elimination half-life, which provide information about basic drug properties. The models may be used to predict concentration vs. time profiles for different dosing patterns.

The field of pharmacokinetics is concerned with drug absorption, distribution, biotransformation, and excretion or elimination. These processes, in addition to the dose, determine the concentration of drug at the effector or active site and, therefore, the intensity and duration of drug effect. The practice of pharmacokinetics has been used in clinical medicine for many years in order to optimize the efficacy of medications administered to treat disease. Through a consideration of pharmacokinetics, physicians are able to determine the drug of choice, dose, route, and frequency of administration and duration of therapy, in order to achieve a specific therapeutic objective. In the same manner, study of the pharmacokinetics of abused drugs aids investigators in addiction medicine, forensic toxicology, and clinical pharmacology in understanding why particular drugs are abused, factors that affect their potential for abuse, how their use can be detected and monitored over time, and also provide a rational, scientific basis for treatment therapies.

3.1 BASIC CONCEPTS AND MODELS

3.1.1 Transfer across Biological Membranes

The processes of absorption, distribution, biotransformation, and elimination of a particular substance involve the transfer or movement of a drug across biological membranes. Therefore, it is important to understand those properties of cell membranes and the intrinsic properties of drugs that affect movement. Although drugs may gain entry into the body by passage through a single layer of cells, such as the intestinal epithelium, or through multiple layers of cells, such as the skin, the blood cell membrane is a common barrier to all drug entry and therefore is the most appropriate membrane for general discussion of cellular membrane structure. The cellular blood membrane consists of a phospholipid bilayer of 7- to 9-nm thickness with hydrocarbon chains oriented inward and polar head groups oriented outward. Interspersed between the lipid bilayer are proteins, which may span the entire width of the membrane permitting the formation of aqueous pores.[2] These proteins act as receptors in chemical and electrical signaling pathways and also as specific targets for drug actions.[3] The lipids in the cell membrane may move laterally, conferring fluidity at physiological temperatures and relative impermeability to highly polar molecules. The fluidity of plasma membranes is largely determined by the relative abundance of unsaturated fatty acids. Between cell membranes are pores that may permit bulk flow of substances. This is considered to be the main mechanism by which drugs cross the capillary endothelial membranes, except in the central nervous system (CNS), which possesses tight junctions that limit intercellular diffusion.[3]

Physicochemical properties of a drug also affect its movement across cell membranes. These include its molecular size and shape, solubility, degree of ionization, and relative lipid solubility of its ionized and non-ionized forms. Another factor to consider is the extent of protein binding to plasma and tissue components. Although such binding is reversible and usually rapid, only the free unbound form is considered capable of passing through biological membranes.

Drugs cross cell membranes through passive and active or specialized processes. Passive movement across biological membranes is the dominant process in the absorption and distribution of drugs. In passive transfer, hydrophobic molecules cross the cell membrane by simple diffusion along a concentration gradient. In this process there is no expenditure of cellular energy. The magnitude of drug transfer in this manner is dependent on the magnitude of the concentration gradient across the membrane and the lipid:water partition coefficient. Once steady state has been reached, the concentration of free (unbound) drug will be the same on both sides of the membrane. The exception to this situation is if the drug is capable of ionization under physiological conditions. In this case, concentrations on either side of the cell membrane will be influenced by pH differences across the membrane. Small hydrophilic molecules are thought to cross cell membranes through the aqueous pores.[4] Generally, only unionized forms of a drug cross biological membranes due to their relatively high lipid solubility. The movement of ionized forms is dependent on the pKa of the drug and the pH gradient. The partitioning of weak acids and bases across pH gradients may be predicted by the Henderson–Hasselbalch equation. For example, an orally ingested weakly acidic drug may be largely unionized in the acidic environs of the stomach but ionized to some degree at the neutral pH of the plasma. The pH gradient and difference in the proportions of ionized/non-ionized forms of the drug promote the diffusion of the weak acid through the lipid barrier of the stomach into the plasma.

Water moves across cell membranes either by the simple diffusion described above or as the result of osmotic differences across membranes. In the latter case, when water moves in bulk through aqueous pores in cellular membranes due to osmotic forces, any molecule that is small enough to pass through the pores will also be transferred. This movement of solutes is called filtration. Cell membranes throughout the body possess pores of different sizes; for example, the pores in the kidney glomerulus are typically 70 nm, but the channels in most cells are <4 nm.[2]

The movement of some compounds across membranes cannot be explained by simple diffusion or filtration. These are usually high-molecular-weight or very lipid soluble substances. Therefore, specialized processes have been postulated to account for the movement. Active processes typically involve the expenditure of cellular energy to move molecules across biological membranes. Characteristics of active transport include selectivity, competitive inhibition, saturability, and movement across an electrochemical or concentration gradient. The drug complexes with a macromolecular carrier on one side of the membrane, traverses the membrane, and is released on the other side. The carrier then returns to the original surface. Active transport processes are important in the elimination of xenobiotics. They are involved in the movement of drugs in hepatocytes, renal tubular cells, and neuronal membranes. For example, the liver has four known active transport systems, two for organic acids, one for organic bases, and one for neutral organic compounds.[2] A different specialized transport process is termed "facilitated diffusion." This transport is similar to the carrier-mediated transport described above except that no active processes are involved. The drug is not moved against an electrochemical or concentration gradient and there is no expenditure of energy. A biochemical example of such transport is the movement of glucose from the gastrointestinal tract through the intestinal epithelium.

3.1.1.1 Absorption

In order for a drug to exert its pharmacological effect, it must first gain entry into the body, be absorbed into the bloodstream, and transported or distributed to its site of action. This is true except in the case of drugs that exert their effect locally or at the absorption site. The absorption site, or port of entry, is determined by the route of drug administration.

Routes of administration are either enteral or parenteral. The former term denotes all routes pertaining to the alimentary canal. Therefore, sublingual, oral, and rectal are enteral routes of administration. All other routes, such as intravenous, intramuscular, subcutaneous, dermal, vaginal, and intraperitoneal, are parenteral routes.

Absorption describes the rate and extent to which a drug leaves its site of administration and enters the general circulation. Factors that, therefore, affect absorption include the physicochemical properties of the drug that determine transfer across cell membranes as described earlier; formulation or physical state of the drug; site of absorption; concentration of drug; circulation at absorption site; and area of absorbing surface.

Gastrointestinal

Absorption of drug may occur at any point along the tract including the mouth, stomach, intestine, and rectum. Because the majority of drugs are absorbed by passive diffusion, the non-ionized, lipid soluble form of the drug is favored for rapid action. Therefore, according to the Henderson–Hasselbalch equation, the absorption of weak acids should be favored in the stomach and the absorption of weak bases in the alkaline environment of the small intestine. However, other factors such as relative surface area will influence absorption. The stomach is lined by a relatively thick mucus-covered membrane to facilitate its primary function of digestion. In comparison, the epithelium of the small intestine is thin, with villi and microvilli providing a large surface area to facilitate its primary function of absorption of nutrients. Therefore, any factor that increases gastric emptying will tend to increase the rate of drug absorption, regardless of the ionization state of the drug.

The gastrointestinal (GI) tract possesses carrier-mediated transport systems for the transfer of nutrients and electrolytes across the gastric wall. These systems may also carry drugs and other xenobiotics into the organism. For example, lead is absorbed by the calcium transporter.[5] Absorption also depends on the physical characteristics of a drug. For example, a highly lipid soluble drug will not dissolve in the stomach. In addition, solid dosage forms will have little contact with gastric mucosa and the drug will not be absorbed until the solid is dissolved. Further, the particle size affects absorption, since dissolution rate is proportional to particle size.[6] Compounds that increase intestinal permeability or increase the residence time in the intestine by altering intestinal motility will thereby increase absorption of other drugs through that segment of the alimentary canal.

Once a drug has been absorbed through the GI tract, the amount of the compound that reaches the systemic circulation depends on several factors. The drug may be biotransformed by the GI cells or removed by the liver through which it must pass. This loss of drug before gaining access to the systemic circulation is known as the first pass effect.

Although oral ingestion is the most common route of GI absorption, drugs may be administered sublingually. Despite the small surface area for absorption, certain drugs which are non-ionic and highly lipid soluble are effectively absorbed by this route. The drugs nitroglycerin and buprenorphine are administered by this route. The blood supply in the mouth drains into the superior vena cava and, because of this anatomic characteristic, drugs are protected from first pass metabolism by the liver.

Although an uncommon route by which abused drugs are self-administered, rectal administration is used in medical practice when vomiting or other circumstances preclude oral administration. Approximately 50% of the drug that is absorbed will bypass the liver.[3] The disadvantage of this route for drug absorption is that the process is often incomplete and irregular and some drugs irritate the mucosal lining of the rectum.

Pulmonary

Gases, volatile liquids, and aerosols may be absorbed through the lungs. Access to the circulation by this route is rapid because of the large surface area of the lungs and extensive capillary network in close association with the alveoli. In the case of absorption of gases and volatilizable liquids, the ionization state and lipid solubility of the substance are less important than in GI absorption. This is because diffusion through cell membranes is not the rate-limiting step in the absorption process. The reasons include low volatility of ionized molecules, the extensive capillary network in close association with the alveoli resulting in a short distance for diffusion, and the rapid removal of absorbed substances by the blood. Some substances may not reach the lungs because they are deposited and absorbed in the mucosal lining of the nose.

Drugs may be atomized or volatilized and inhaled as droplets or particulates in air; a common example is the smoking of drugs. The advantages of this route include rapid transport into the blood, avoidance of first pass hepatic metabolism, and avoidance of the medical problems associated with other routes of illicit drug administration. Disadvantages include local irritant effect on the tissues of the nasopharynx and absorption of particulate matter in the nasopharynx and bronchial tree. For a drug to be effectively absorbed it should reach the alveoli. However, absorption of particulate matter is governed by particulate size and water solubility. Particles with diameters >5 μm are usually deposited in the nasopharyngeal region;[2] particles in the 2- to 5-μm range are deposited in the tracheobronchiolar region and particles 1 μm and smaller reach the alveolar sacs.

Dermal

The skin is impermeable to most chemicals. For a drug to be absorbed it must pass first through the epidermal layers or specialized tissue such as hair follicles or sweat and sebaceous glands. Absorption through the outer layer of skin, the stratum corneum, is the rate-limiting step in the dermal absorption of drugs. This outer layer consists of densely packed keratinized cells and is commonly referred to as the "dead" layer of skin because the cells comprising this layer are without nuclei. Drug substances may be absorbed by simple diffusion through this layer. The lower layers of the epidermis, and the dermis, consist of porous nonselective cells that pose little barrier to absorption by passive diffusion. Once a chemical reaches this level, it is then rapidly absorbed into the systemic circulation because of the extensive network of venous and lymphatic capillaries located in the dermis. Drug absorption through the skin depends on the characteristics of the drug and on the condition of the skin. Since the stratum corneum is the main barrier to absorption, damage to this area by sloughing of cells due to abrasion or burning enhances absorption, as does any mechanism that increases cutaneous blood flow. Hydration of the stratum corneum also increases its permeability and therefore enhances absorption of chemicals.

Parenteral Injection

Drugs are often absorbed through the GI tract, lungs, and skin but many illicit drugs have historically been self-administered by injection. These routes typically include intravenous, intramuscular, and subcutaneous administration. The intravenous route of administration introduces the drug directly into the venous bloodstream, thereby eliminating the process of absorption altogether. Substances that are locally irritating may be administered intravenously since the blood vessel walls are relatively insensitive. This route permits the rapid introduction of the drug to the systemic circulation and allows high concentrations to be quickly achieved. Intravenous administration may result in unfavorable physiological responses because, once introduced, the drug cannot be removed.

This route of administration is dependent on maintaining patent veins and can result in extensive scar tissue formation due to chronic drug administration. Insoluble particulate matter deposited in the blood vessels is another medical problem associated with the intravenous route.

Intramuscular and subcutaneous administration involves absorption from the injection site into the circulation by passive diffusion. The rate of absorption is limited by the size of the capillary bed at the injection site and by the solubility of the drug in the interstitial fluid.[3] If blood flow is increased at the administration site, absorption will be increased. Conversely, if blood pressure is decreased for any reason (such as cardiogenic shock) absorption will be prolonged.

3.1.1.2 Distribution

After entering circulation, drugs are distributed throughout the body. The extent of distribution is dependent on the physicochemical properties of the drug and physiological factors. Drugs cross cell membranes throughout the body by passive diffusion or specialized transport processes. Small water-soluble molecules and ions cross cell membranes through aqueous pores whereas lipid soluble substances diffuse through the membrane lipid bilayer. The rate of distribution of a drug is dependent on blood flow and the rate of diffusion across cell membranes of various tissues and organs. The affinity of a substance for certain tissues also affects the rate of distribution.

Because only unbound drug (the free fraction) is in equilibrium throughout the body, disposition is affected by binding to or dissolving in cellular constituents. While circulating in blood, drugs may be reversibly bound to several plasma proteins. For example, basic compounds often bind to α1-acid glycoprotein; acidic compounds bind to albumin. The extent of plasma protein binding varies among drugs: nicotine is 5% bound whereas the barbiturate, secobarbital, is 50% bound, and the benzodiazepine, diazepam, is 96% bound.[7] The fraction of drug that is bound is governed by the drug concentration, the drug's affinity for binding sites, and the number of binding sites available for binding. At low drug concentrations, the fraction bound is a function of the number of binding sites and the dissociation constant, a measure of binding affinity. When drug concentrations exceed the dissociation constant, concentration also governs the amount of protein binding. Therefore, published protein binding fractions for drugs only apply over a certain concentration range, usually the therapeutic concentration. Plasma protein binding limits the amount of drug entering tissues. Because plasma protein binding of drugs is relatively non-selective, drugs and endogenous substances compete for binding sites, and drug displacement from binding sites by another substance can contribute to toxicity by increasing the free fraction.

Binding to Tissue Constituents

In addition to binding to plasma proteins, drugs may bind to tissue constituents. The liver and kidney have a large capacity to act as storage depots for drugs. The mechanisms responsible for transfer of many drugs from the blood appear to be active transport processes.[2] Ligandin, a cytoplasmic liver protein, has a high affinity for many organic acids while metallothionein binds metals in the kidney and liver.

Lipid-soluble drugs are stored in neutral fat by dissolution. Since the fat content of an obese individual may be 50% body weight, it follows that large amounts of drug can be stored in this tissue. Once stored in fat, the concentration of drug is lowered throughout the body, in the blood and also in target organs. Any activity, such as dieting or starvation, which serves to mobilize fat, could potentially increase blood concentrations and hence contribute to an increase in the risk of drug toxicity.

Drugs may also be stored in bone. Drugs diffuse from the extracellular fluid through the hydration shell of the hydroxyapatite crystals of the bone mineral. Lead, fluoride, and other compounds may be deposited and stored in bone. Deposition may not necessarily be detrimental. For example, lead is not toxic to bone tissue. However, chronic fluoride deposition results in the condition known as skeletal fluorosis. Generally, storage of compounds in bone is a reversible process. Toxicants may be released from the bone by ion exchange at the crystal surface or by dissolution of the bone during osteoclastic activity. If osteolytic activity is increased, the hydroxyapatite lattice is mobilized, resulting in an increase in blood concentrations of any stored xenobiotics.

Blood-Brain-Barrier

The blood-brain-barrier is often viewed as an impenetrable barrier to xenobiotics. However, this is not true and a more realistic representation is as a site that is less permeable to ionized substances and high-molecular-weight compounds than other membranes. Many toxicants do not enter the brain because the capillary endothelial cells are joined by tight junctions with few pores between cells; the capillaries of the CNS are surrounded by glial processes; and the interstitial fluid of the CNS has a low protein concentration. The first two anatomical processes limit the entry of small- to medium-sized water-soluble molecules, whereas the entry of lipid-soluble compounds is limited by the low protein content, which restricts paracellular transport. It is interesting to note that the permeability of the brain to toxicants varies from area to area. For example, the cortex, area postrema, and pineal body are more permeable than other regions.[2] This may be due to differences in blood supply or the nature of the barrier itself. Entrance of drugs into the brain is governed by the same factors that determine transfer across membranes in other parts of the body. Only the unbound fraction is available for transfer, and lipid solubility and the degree of ionization dictate the rate of entry of drugs into the brain. It should be noted that the blood-brain-barrier is not fully developed at birth. In animal studies, morphine has been found to be three to ten times more toxic to newborns than adults.[8]

Pregnancy

During pregnancy, drugs may also be distributed from the mother to the fetus by simple diffusion across the placenta. The placenta comprises several cell layers between the maternal and fetal circulations. The number of layers varies between species and state of gestation. The same factors govern placental drug transfer as movement by passive diffusion across other membranes. The placenta plays an additional role in preventing transfer of xenobiotics to the fetus by possessing biotransformation capabilities.

3.1.2   Biotransformation

Lipophilicity, a desirable drug characteristic for absorption and distribution across biological membranes, is a hindrance to elimination. To prevent accumulation of xenobiotics, the body chemically alters lipophilic compounds to more water soluble products. The sum of all the processes that convert lipophilic substances to more hydrophilic metabolites is termed biotransformation. These biochemical processes are usually enzymatic and are commonly divided into Phase I and Phase II reactions.[9] Phase I reactions generally expose or introduce a polar group to the parent drug, thereby increasing its water solubility. These reactions are oxidative or hydrolytic in nature and include N- and O-dealkylation, aliphatic and aromatic hydroxylation, N- and S-oxidation, and deamination. These reactions usually result in loss of pharmacological activity, although there are numerous examples of enhanced activity. Indeed, formation of a Phase I product is desirable in the case of administration of prodrugs.

Phase II reactions are conjugation reactions and involve covalent bonding of functional groups with endogenous compounds. Highly water soluble conjugates are formed by combination of the drug or metabolite with glucuronic acid, sulfate, glutathione, amino acids, or acetate. Again, these products are generally pharmacologically inactive or less active than the parent compound. An exception is the metabolite morphine-6-glucuronide. In this case, glucuronidation at the 6-position increases the affinity of morphine for binding at the mu receptor and results in equivalent or enhanced pharmacological activity.[10]

The enzymes that catalyze the biotransformation of drugs are found mainly in the liver. This is not surprising considering the primary function of the liver is to handle compounds absorbed from the GI tract. In addition, the liver receives all the blood perfusing the splanchnic area. Therefore, this organ has developed a high capacity to remove substances from blood, and store, transform, and/or release substances into the general circulation. In its primary role of biotransformation, the liver acts as a homogeneous unit, with all parenchymal cells or hepatocytes exhibiting enzymatic activity. In tissues involved in extrahepatic biotransformation processes, typically only one or two cell types are used. Many organs have demonstrated activity toward foreign compounds but the major extrahepatic tissues are those involved in the absorption or excretion of chemicals. These include the kidney, lung, intestine, skin, and testes. The main cells containing biotransformation enzymes in these organs are the proximal tubular cells, clara cells, mucosa lining cells, epithelial cells, and seminiferous tubules, respectively.

3.1.2.1 Phase I Enzymes

Phase I enzymes are located primarily in the endoplasmic reticulum of cells. These enzymes are membrane bound within a lipoprotein matrix and are referred to as microsomal enzymes. This is in reference to the subcellular fraction isolated by differential centrifugation of a liver homogenate. The two most important enzyme systems involved in Phase I biotransformation reactions are the cytochrome P450 system and the mixed function amine oxidase.

With the advances in recombinant DNA technology, eight major mammalian gene families of hepatic and extrahepatic cytochrome P450 have been identified.[2] A comprehensive discussion of the cytochrome P450 system is beyond the scope of this chapter and the reader is referred to a number of reviews.[11–13] Briefly, this system comprises two coupled enzymes: NADPH-cytochrome P450 reductase and a heme containing enzyme, cytochrome P450. Numerous oxidative pathways for xenobiotics exist, both in humans and other animals. Much drug oxidation is performed by a group of enzymes known as CYPs (from *CY*tochrome *P*450, the 450 being derived from the cytochrome's maximal absorbance of light at 450 nm). The cytochrome P450s or CYPs are categorized according to amino acid sequence homology. CYPs that have less than 40% homology are placed in a different family (e.g., 1, 2, 3, and so on). CYPs that are 40 to 55% identical are assigned to different subfamilies (e.g., 1A, 1B, 1C, and so on). P450 enzymes that are more than 55% identical are classified as members of the same subfamily (e.g., 2B1, 2B2, 2B3). The P450 enzymes are expressed in numerous tissues, but are especially prevalent in the liver. For more information on this topic, see Chapter 5, which deals specifically with the subject of toxicogenetics. This complex is associated with another cytochrome, cytochrome b_5 with a reductase enzyme. In reactions catalyzed by cytochrome P450, the substrate combines with the oxidized form of cytochrome P450 (Fe^{3+}) to form a complex. This complex accepts an electron from NADPH, which reduces the iron in the cytochrome P450 heme moiety to Fe^{2+}. This reduced substrate–cytochrome P450 complex then combines with molecular oxygen, which in turn accepts another electron from NADPH. In some cases, the second electron is provided by NADH via cytochrome b_5. Both electrons are transferred to molecular oxygen, resulting in a highly reactive and unstable species. One atom of the unstable oxygen molecule is transferred to the substrate and the other is reduced to water. The substrate then dissociates as a result, regenerating the oxidized form of cytochrome P450.

3.1.2.2 Phase II Enzymes

Many of the Phase II enzymes are located in the cytosol or supernatant fraction after differential centrifugation of a liver homogenate. These reactions are biosynthetic and therefore require energy.

This is accomplished by transforming the substrate or cofactors to high-energy intermediates. One of the major Phase II reactions is glucuronidation. The resultant glucuronides are eliminated in the bile or urine. The enzyme uridine diphosphate (UDP) glucuronosyltransferase is located in the endoplasmic reticulum. This enzyme catalyzes the reaction between UDP–glucuronic acid and the functional group of the substrate. The location of this enzyme means that it has direct access to the products of Phase I enzymatic reactions. Another important conjugation reaction in humans is sulfation of hydroxyl groups. The sulfotransferases are a group of soluble enzymes, classified as aryl, hydroxysteroid, estrone, and bile salt sulfotransferases. Their primary function is the transfer of inorganic sulfate to the hydroxyl moiety of phenol or aliphatic alcohols.

Another important family of enzymes is the glutathione-S-transferases, which are located in both the cytoplasm and endoplasmic reticulum of cells. The activity of the cytosolic transferase is 5 to 40 times greater than the endoplasmic enzyme. These transferase enzymes catalyze the reaction between the sulfhydryl group of the tripeptide glutathione with substances containing electrophilic carbon atoms. The glutathione conjugates are cleaved to cysteine derivatives, primarily in the kidney. These derivatives are then acetylated resulting in mercapturic acid conjugates, which are excreted in the urine.

Many factors affect the rate at which a drug is biotransformed. One of the important factors is obviously the concentration of the drug at the site of action of biotransforming enzymes. Physicochemical properties of the drug, such as lipophilicity, are important, in addition to dose and route of administration. Certain physiological, pharmacological, and environmental factors may also affect the rate of biotransformation of a compound. Numerous variables affect biotransformation including sex, age, genetic polymorphisms, time of day or circadian rhythms, nutritional status, enzyme induction or inhibition, hepatic injury, and disease states.

3.1.3 Elimination

Drugs are excreted or eliminated from the body as parent compounds or metabolites. The organs involved in excretion, with the exception of the lungs, eliminate water-soluble compounds more readily than lipophilic substances. The lungs are important for the elimination of anesthetic gases and vapors. The processes of biotransformation generally produce more polar compounds for excretion. The most important excretory organ is the kidney. Substances in the feces are mainly unabsorbed drugs administered orally or compounds excreted into the bile and not reabsorbed. Drugs may also be excreted in breast milk[14] and, even though the amounts are small, they represent an important pathway because the recipient of any drugs by this route is the nursing infant.

For a comprehensive discussion of renal excretion of drugs, the reader is referred to Weiner and Mudge.[15] Excretion of drugs and their metabolites involves three processes, namely, glomerular filtration, passive tubular reabsorption, and active tubular secretion. The amount of a drug that enters the tubular lumen of the kidney is dependent on the glomerular filtration rate and the fraction of drug that is plasma protein bound. In the proximal renal tubular organic anions and cations are added to the filtrate by active transport processes. Glucuronide drug metabolites are secreted in this way by the carrier-mediated system for naturally occurring organic acids. In the proximal and distal tubules of the kidney, the non-ionized forms of weak acids and bases are passively reabsorbed. The necessary concentration gradient is created by the reabsorption of water with sodium. The passive reabsorption of ionized forms is pH dependent because the tubular cells are less permeable to these moieties. Therefore, in the treatment of drug poisoning, the excretion of some drugs can be increased by alkalinization or acidification of the urine.

Under normal physiological conditions, excretion of drugs in the sweat, saliva, and by the lacrimal glands is quantitatively insignificant. Elimination by these routes is dependent on pH and diffusion of the unionized lipid-soluble form of the drug through the epithelial cells of the glands. Drugs excreted in saliva enter the mouth and may be reabsorbed and swallowed. Drugs have also been detected in hair and skin, and although quantitatively unimportant, these routes may be useful in drug detection and therefore have forensic significance.

3.1.4 Pharmacokinetic Parameters

Pharmacokinetics assumes that a relationship exists between the concentration of drug in an accessible site, such as the blood, and the pharmacological or toxic response. The concentration of drug in the systemic circulation is related to the concentration of drug at the site of action. Pharmacokinetics attempts to quantify the relationship between dose and drug disposition and provide the framework, through modeling, to interpret measured concentrations in biological fluids.[3] Several pharmacokinetic parameters are utilized to explain various pharmacokinetic processes. It is often changes in these parameters, through disease, genetic abnormalities, or drug interactions, that necessitate modifications of dosage regimens for therapeutic agents. The most important parameters are clearance, the ability of the body to eliminate drug, volume of distribution, a measure of the apparent volume of the body available to occupy the drug, bioavailability, the proportion of drug absorbed into the systemic circulation, and half-life, a measure of the rate of drug elimination from the blood. These concepts are discussed below.

3.1.4.1 Clearance

Clearance is defined as the proportionality factor that relates the rate of drug elimination to the blood or plasma drug concentration:[16]

$$Clearance = Rate\ of\ elimination/Concentration$$

In the above equation, the concentration term refers to drug concentration at steady state. The units of clearance are volume per unit time and, therefore, this parameter measures the volume of biological fluid, such as blood, that would have to have drug removed to account for drug elimination. Therefore, clearance is not a measure of the amount of drug removed.

The concept of clearance is useful in pharmacokinetics because clearance is usually constant over a wide range of concentrations, provided that elimination processes are not saturated. Saturation of biotransformation and excretory processes may occur in overdose and toxicokinetic effects should be considered. If a constant fraction of drug is eliminated per unit time, the elimination follows first-order kinetics. However, if a constant amount of drug is eliminated per unit time, the elimination is described by zero-order kinetics. Some drugs, for example, ethanol, exhibit zero-order kinetics at "normal" or non-intoxicating concentrations. However, for any drug that exhibits first-order kinetics at therapeutic or nontoxic concentrations, once the mechanisms for elimination become saturated, the kinetics become zero order and clearance becomes variable.[3]

Clearance may also be viewed as the loss of drug from an organ of elimination such as the liver or kidney. This approach enables evaluation of the effects of a variety of physiological factors such as changes in blood flow, plasma protein binding, and enzyme activity. Therefore, total systemic clearance is determined by adding the clearance (CL) values for each elimination organ or tissue:

$$CL_{systemic} = CL_{renal} + CL_{hepatic} + CL_{lung} + CL_{other}$$

Clearance from an individual organ is a product of blood flow and the extraction ratio. The extraction ratio is derived from the concentration of drug in the blood entering the organ and the concentration of drug in the blood leaving the organ. If the extraction ratio is 0, no drug is removed. If it is 1, then all the drug entering the organ is removed from the blood. Therefore, the clearance of an organ may be determined from the following equation:

$$CL_{organ} = Q(C_A - C_V/C_A) = Q \times E$$

where

Q = blood flow
C_A = arterial drug concentration
C_V = venous drug concentration
E = extraction ratio

3.1.4.2 Volume of Distribution

The plasma drug concentration reached after distribution is complete is a result of the dose and the extent of uptake by tissues. The extent of distribution can be described by relating the amount of drug in the body to the concentration. This parameter is known as the volume of distribution. This volume does not indicate a defined physiological dimension but the volume of fluid required to contain all the drug in the body at the same concentration as in the plasma or blood. Therefore, it is often called the apparent volume of distribution (V) and is determined at steady state when distribution equilibrium has been reached between drug in plasma and tissues.

$$V = \text{Amount in body/Plasma drug concentration}$$

The volume of distribution depends on the pKa of the drug, the degree of plasma protein and tissue binding, and the lipophilicity of the drug. As would be expected, drugs that distribute widely throughout the body have large volumes of distribution (for example, the V_d of fluphenazine, which is a widely distributed drug, is 11; the V_d for ketoconozole is only 0.7, indicating that very little drug leaves the circulation). In the equation above, the body is considered one homogeneous unit and therefore exhibits a one-compartment model. In this model, drug administration occurs in the central compartment, and distribution is instantaneous throughout the body. For most drugs, the simple one-compartment model does not describe the time course of drug in the body adequately and drug distribution and elimination is more completely described in multiple exponential terms using multicompartmental models. In these models, the volume of distribution, V_{area}, is calculated as the ratio of clearance to the rate of decline of the concentration during the elimination phase:

$$V_{area} = CL/k$$

where k = rate constant.

3.1.4.3 Bioavailability

The bioavailability of a drug refers to the fraction of the dose that reaches the systemic circulation. This parameter is dependent on the rate and extent of absorption at the site of drug administration. Obviously, it follows that drugs administered intravenously do not undergo absorption, but immediately gain access to the systemic circulation and are considered 100% bioavailable. In the case of oral administration, if the hepatic extraction ratio is known, it is possible to predict the maximum bioavailability of drug by this route assuming first-order processes, according to the following equation:[3]

$$F_{max} = 1 - E = 1 - (CL_{hepatic}/Q_{hepatic})$$

The bioavailability of a drug by various routes may also be determined by comparing the area under the curve (AUC) obtained from the plasma concentration vs. time curve after intravenous and other routes of administration:[9]

$$\text{Bioavailability} = \text{AUC}_{\text{oral}}/\text{AUC}_{\text{IV}}$$

3.1.4.4 Half-Life

The half-life is the time it takes for the plasma drug concentration to decrease by 50%. Half-life is usually determined from the log-terminal phase of the elimination curve. However, it is important to remember that this parameter is a derived term and is dependent on the clearance and volume of distribution of the drug. Therefore, as CL and V change with disease, drug interactions, and age, so a change in the half-life should be expected. The half-life is typically calculated from the following equation:

$$t_{1/2} = 0.693/k$$

where $t_{1/2}$ = half life and k = elimination rate constant.

Because $k = \text{CL}/V$, the interrelationship between these parameters is clearly evident.

3.1.5 Dosage Regimens

Pharmacokinetic principles, in addition to clinical factors such as the state of the patient, are utilized in determining dosage regimens. Factors that relate to the safety and efficacy of the drug such as activity–toxicity relationships (therapeutic window and side effects), and pharmaceutical factors, such as dosage form and route of administration, must be considered.[16]

The goal of a therapeutic regimen is to achieve therapeutic concentrations of a drug continuously or intermittently. The latter is useful if tolerance to the drug develops, or if the therapeutic effects of the drug persist and increase in intensity even with rapid drug disappearance. Adjustments to the dosage regimen are made to maintain therapeutically effective drug concentrations and minimize undesirable effects. Optimization of drug therapy is typically determined empirically, that is, changing the dose based on response of the individual. However, there is often better correlation between blood or plasma concentration or amount of drug in the body than the dose administered. Therefore, pharmacokinetic data are useful in the design of dosage regimens. In theory, data following a single dose may be used to estimate plasma concentrations following any dosing design.

For drugs whose effects are difficult to measure, or whose therapeutic index is low, a target-level or steady-state plasma concentration is desirable. A dose is computed to achieve this level, drug concentrations are measured, and the dose is adjusted accordingly. To apply this strategy, the therapeutic range should be determined. For many drugs the lower limit of this range appears to be the concentration that produces 50% maximal response. The upper limit is determined by drug toxicity and is commonly determined by the concentration at which 5 to 10% of patients experience a toxic effect.[3] The target concentration is then chosen at the middle of the therapeutic range.

3.1.5.1 Loading Doses

The loading dose is one or a series of doses that are administered at the beginning of therapy. The objective is to reach the target concentration rapidly. The loading dose can be estimated using the following formula:

$$\text{Loading Dose} = \text{Target } C_p \times V_{ss}/F$$

where C_p = concentration in plasma, V_{ss} = volume of distribution at steady state, and F = fractional bioavailability of the dose.

A loading dose is desirable if the time to achieve steady state is long compared to the need for the condition being treated. One disadvantage of a loading dose is the acute exposure to high concentrations of the drug, which may result in toxic effects in sensitive individuals.

3.1.5.2 Dosing Rate

In the majority of clinical situations, drugs are administered as a series of repeated doses or as a continuous infusion in order to maintain a steady-state concentration. Therefore, a maintenance dose must be calculated such that the rate of input is equal to the rate of drug loss. This may be determined using the following formula:

$$\text{Dosing Rate} = \text{Target} \times \text{CL}/F$$

where CL = clearance and F = fractional bioavailability of the dose.

It is obvious from the above that in order to design an appropriate dosage regimen, several pharmacokinetic factors, including CL, F, V_{ss}, and half-life, must be known in addition to an understanding of the principles of absorption and distribution of the drug in question. The clinician must also be aware of variations in these factors in a particular patient. One should note that even "normal" individuals exhibit variations in these parameters. For example, one standard deviation on clearance values may be 50%. These unpredicted variations in pharmacokinetic parameters may result in a wide range of drug concentrations. This is unacceptable in most cases especially for those drugs with a low therapeutic index. Therefore, C_p should be measured and estimates of CL, F, and V_{ss} calculated directly.

3.1.6 Therapeutic Drug Monitoring

Blood or plasma drug concentrations at steady state are typically measured to refine estimates of CL/F for the individual. Updated estimates are then used to adjust maintenance doses to reach the desired target concentration. Drug concentrations can be misleading if the relevant pharmacokinetics (and toxicokinetics; see Section 3.4) are not considered. In addition, individual variability in drug response, due to multiple drug use, disease, genetic differences, and tolerance, must be considered. Pharmacokinetic characteristics of drugs may differ with development and age. Therefore, drug effects may vary considerably between infants, children, and adults. For example, water constitutes 80% of the weight of a newborn whereas in adults it constitutes approximately 60%. These differences affect distribution of drugs throughout the body.

3.1.6.1 Plasma

Measurement of drug concentrations in plasma is the cornerstone of therapeutic drug monitoring (TDM), but it is not without pitfalls. In many instances, clinical response does not correlate with plasma drug concentrations. Other considerations may be as follows.

Time Delays

It often takes time for a response to reflect a given plasma concentration due to the individual kinetics of the drug. Until this equilibrium is reached, correlation between response and concentration is difficult and may lead to misinterpretation of the clinical picture. Delay may be due to lack of equilibration between plasma and target organ as the drug distributes throughout the body. In addition, delay may be because the response measured is an indirect measure of drug effect, e.g., a change in blood pressure is an indirect measure of either change in peripheral resistance or cardiac output or both.

Active Metabolites

Poor correlation may be found between response and plasma concentration of parent drug if active metabolites are present and not measured. Formation of active metabolites may be a function of the route of drug administration because oral ingestion generally produces an initial surge of metabolites due to the first-pass effect of the liver compared with drugs administered intravenously.

Exposure Duration

Some drugs exhibit unusual concentration/response relationships, which minimizes the utility of TDM. In these cases, clinical response correlates more with duration of dosing than the actual dose or resultant plasma concentrations.

Tolerance

The effectiveness of a drug may diminish with continual use. Tolerance denotes a decreased pharmacological responsiveness to a drug. This is demonstrated by several drugs of abuse including ethanol and heroin. The degree of tolerance varies but is never complete. For example, tolerance to the effects of morphine quickly develops, but the user is not totally unresponsive to the pharmacological effects. To compensate for the development of tolerance, the dose is increased. Tolerance may develop slowly, such as in the case of tolerance to the CNS effects of ethanol, or can occur acutely (tachyphylaxis) as in the case of nicotine. In these cases, a correlation may be found between plasma drug concentration and the intensity of response at a given moment, but the relationship is not consistent and varies with time.[16]

3.1.6.2 Saliva

In recent years, saliva has been utilized for TDM. The advantage is that collection is noninvasive and painless and so it has been used as a specimen of choice in pediatric TDM. Due to the low protein content of saliva, it is considered to represent the unbound or free fraction of drug in plasma. Since this is the fraction considered available for transfer across membranes and therefore responsible for pharmacological activity, its usefulness is easy to understand. Saliva collection methods are known to influence drug concentrations, but if these are compensated for and a standardized procedure utilized, correlation between plasma and saliva drug concentrations may be demonstrated for several drugs (e.g., phenytoin). Inconsistent results have been found for some drugs such as phenobarbital, so additional studies are needed to clearly define the limitations of testing saliva for TDM.

3.2 PHARMACOKINETIC MODELING

3.2.1 Compartmental Modeling

The pharmacokinetic profile of a drug is described by the processes of absorption, distribution, metabolism, and excretion. The disposition of a drug in the body may be further delineated by mathematical modeling. These models are based on the concept that the body may be viewed as a series of compartments in which the drug is distributed. If the compartmental concept is considered literally, then each tissue and organ becomes an individual compartment. However, in pharmaco-kinetic modeling, several organs or tissues exhibit similar characteristics in drug deposition and are often considered the same compartment. The pharmacokinetic profiles of many drugs may be explained using one- or two-compartment models, but more complex models exist and, with the advances in computer software, the ability to describe drug disposition has increased. The use of models does not mean that the drug distributes into distinct physiological compartments, but that these mathematical models adequately describe the fate of the drug in the human body.

3.2.1.1 One-Compartment Models

In the one-compartment model the entire body is considered as one unit (Figure 3.2.1A). The drug is administered into the compartment and distributed throughout the compartment (the body) instantaneously.[17] Similarly, the drug is eliminated directly from the one compartment at a rate measured by k_{el}, the elimination rate constant. The time course of the drug, as measured in the readily accessible blood or plasma, is typically graphed as a log concentration vs. time profile. Figure 3.2.1B shows the log plasma concentration vs. time plot for a drug that distributes according to a one-compartment model. The dotted line demonstrates the time course after intravenous administration and the solid line demonstrates the time course after oral administration. Since intravenous administration does not have an absorption phase, the time course of drug in the plasma is linear. For oral administration, the drug concentration on the blood is slower to reach a peak due to absorptive processes of the GI tract.

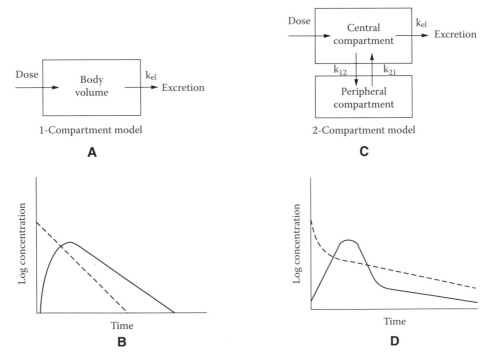

Figure 3.2.1 (A) Schematic representation of a one-compartment model. (B) Log plasma concentration vs. time curve after intravenous (---) and oral (-) administration. (C) Schematic representation of a two-compartment model. (D) Log plasma concentration vs. time curve after intravenous (---) and oral (-) administration. (Adapted from Hagan, R.L., Basic Pharmacokinetics. In-Service Training and Continuing Education AACC/TDM, American Association for Clinical Chemistry, Inc., Washington, D.C., 17(9), 231–247, 1996.)

3.2.1.2 Two-Compartment Models

Figure 3.2.1C illustrates the concept of the two-compartment model. In this model, the drug is administered into the central compartment and then there is a time lag due to slower distribution into other tissues and organs. These other organs are represented by the peripheral compartment(s). More complex models may be developed if distribution to other organs occurs at different rates that can be mathematically differentiated. In the two-compartment model, equilibrium is reached between the central and peripheral compartments and this marks the end of the distribution phase. The beginning of the distribution phase may be observed graphically by an initial rapid decline after peaking in the drug concentration in the central compartment (represented by the plasma/blood) as shown in Figure 3.2.1D. Rate constants may be estimated for drug movement between the central and peripheral compartments, but drug elimination from the body is assumed to occur from the central compartment.[17] As mentioned previously, more complex models may be developed including models in which the number of compartments into which the drug distributes is not assumed in the initial modeling.

3.2.1.3 Elimination Kinetics

The concept of zero- or first-order kinetics may be utilized to describe any rate process in pharmacokinetics. Therefore, if we are discussing drug absorption, a drug exhibits zero-order kinetics if a constant amount of drug is absorbed regardless of dose.[9] Conversely, a drug exhibits first-order absorption kinetics if the amount absorbed is dependent on dose, i.e., is a fraction of the dose. Similarly, when considering drug excretion, ethanol exhibits zero-order elimination kinetics because a constant amount of drug is excreted per unit time regardless of the drug concentration (unless processes become saturated). Most drugs exhibit first-order elimination kinetics in which a constant fraction of drug is eliminated per unit time.

Zero-order elimination kinetics are described by the following equation:[17]

$$C = C_0 - kt$$

where C = drug concentration at time t, C_0 = the concentration at time zero or the initial concentration, and k = the elimination rate constant.

A plot of this equation is linear with a slope, $-k$, and a y-intercept, C_0. The elimination half-life may be calculated from this equation for a drug that exhibits zero-order elimination. When $t = t_{1/2}$, then $C = 1/2 \ C_0$, the initial or peak concentration. This results in the following equation:

$$t_{1/2} = 1/2 \ C_0/k$$

This equation has a concentration term, C_0, indicating that the half-life is variable and dependent on drug concentration. Changes in pharmacokinetic parameters that occur as a function of dose or drug concentration are referred to as nonlinear pharmacokinetic processes. Nonlinearity is usually due to saturation of protein binding, hepatic metabolism, or active renal transport of the drug.[3]

First-order elimination kinetics are described by the equation:[17]

$$C = C_0 e^{-kt}$$

Taking the natural logarithm of this equation and plotting it semilogarithmically results in a linear graph with a slope of $-k$, and a y-intercept of ln C_0. Again, to determine the half-life, $1/2 \ C_0$ is substituted into the equation to give:

$$1/2 \ C_0 = C_0 e^{-kt1/2}$$

Taking natural logs and solving for $t_{1/2}$:

$$t_{1/2} = 0.693/k$$

It is important to note that the elimination half-life is a derived term, and any process that changes k will change the half-life of the drug. Factors that may affect pharmacokinetic parameters are discussed elsewhere, but in this example may include disease states, changes in urinary pH, changes in plasma protein binding, and coadministration of other drugs.

3.2.2 Physiological Models

An alternative method of building a pharmacokinetic profile of a drug in the body is to utilize anatomic and physiological information. Such a model does not make assumptions about body compartments or first-order processes for drug absorption and elimination.[16] The first step in such modeling is to decide whether drug distribution into a particular tissue is perfusion rate or membrane transport limited.[2] These decisions are based on the physicochemical characteristics of the drug and physiological conditions in addition to reference to any experimental data. In order to write a mass balance equation, blood flow, Q, and the volume, V, of the organ or tissue of interest is needed and may be obtained from the literature. The other parameters, venous drug concentration, C_v, and the partition coefficient, R, are determined experimentally.[2] A simple mass balance equation may be written as:[2]

$$V_t \times dC_t/dt = Q_t \times [C_v - C_t/R_t]$$

where t = tissue.

Mass balance equations may be constructed for each organ or tissue considered and algebraic equations added to account for growth, changes in tissue weight ratios, and other physiological parameters. The advantage of this modeling over the more traditional compartmental method is provision of a time course of drug distribution to any organ or tissue, and this model allows estimation of the effects of changing physiological parameters on tissue concentrations. Disadvantages include the need for complex mathematical equations and the lack of data on the physiological parameters necessary to construct the differential equations.[2]

3.3 PHARMACOKINETIC–PHARMACODYNAMIC CORRELATIONS

Pharmacodynamics (PD) may be defined as the quantitative relationship between the measured plasma or tissue concentration of the active moiety and the magnitude of the observed pharmacological effect(s).[1] The study of pharmacokinetics (PK) has been defined previously. A PK/PD model is a mathematical description of the relationship. Knowledge of the model and model parameter estimates permits prediction of concentration vs. time and effect vs. time profiles for different dosing regimens.[1] Different drugs are characterized by different PK and PD models and by differences in model parameters such as volume of distribution and receptor affinity. Understanding the PK/PD model permits comparison of the pharmacological properties for different drugs. For a specific compound, there may be significant variation in model parameters between individuals. PK/PD modeling allows assessment of the contribution of the variability in model parameters to the overall variability in drug response.[1]

To fully understand the significance of PK/PD modeling, it is important to note that the observed effect vs. time profile for a particular individual is determined by several factors. These include (1) drug input dose, rate, and route of administration; (2) intrinsic PK drug properties; and (3) intrinsic PD drug properties. Modeling allows estimation of PK/PD parameters. Further, PK/PD modeling provides dose–response curves for the onset, magnitude, and duration of effects that can be utilized to optimize dose and dosing regimens. Models have been described for reversible and irreversible drug effects and for a range of drug classes including analgesics, benzodiazepines, and anticonvulsants. For a more detailed explanation of PK/PD modeling and correlations and description of computer applications, the reader is referred elsewhere.[1]

3.4 TOXICOKINETICS

Toxicokinetics is the study of drug disposition in overdose. The biochemical processes that constitute the science of pharmacokinetics may be altered when drugs are administered in high concentrations. GI absorption may be altered in overdose due to delayed gastric emptying, changes in intestinal motility, and therapy with activated charcoal.[2] Drugs such as morphine, ethanol, and barbiturates delay gastric emptying and as a consequence slow drug movement into the small intestine. In addition, morphine decreases intestinal motility, resulting in increased transit time through the intestine and increased absorption. Little is known about changes in drug distribution throughout the body after overdose. Several mechanisms may be at work in overdose to cause changes in drug disposition. For example, the bioavailability of a drug with a high first pass metabolism may be increased when the hepatic metabolizing enzymes become saturated. In a similar manner, the concentration of free drug in the plasma may be increased when protein binding becomes saturated. This may result in significant toxicity for those drugs that are highly plasma protein bound. Also, changes in peripheral blood flow due to the cardiac effects of some drugs may result in prolonged drug distribution and higher blood drug concentrations.

Drug metabolism may be altered in overdose when those enzymes responsible for metabolism become saturated. In this event, clearance is decreased, half-life is prolonged, and therefore high drug concentrations exist for a longer time. If multiple drugs are co-ingested, competitive inhibition of metabolism may occur. In addition, if hepatic blood flow is decreased, due to impaired liver function or cardiovascular drug effects, biotransformation of xenobiotics may be decreased.

Renal excretion may or may not be altered in drug overdose. Alteration of renal drug clearance may be utilized therapeutically to enhance drug elimination. Urinary pH is adjusted to increase the clearance of acidic and basic drugs. For example, administration of sodium bicarbonate will raise the urine pH above 7.5, concentrating the ionized form in the renal tubule and, therefore, enhancing elimination of salicylate. Conversely, acidification of the urine may be utilized to enhance renal excretion of basic drugs. However, with some drugs, such as phencyclidine, there is controversy about the role of urinary acidification in enhanced excretion and whether this procedure improves clinical outcome. Acidification is contraindicated with myoglobinuria and may also increase the risk of metabolic complications.[18]

3.5 FACTORS AFFECTING PHARMACOKINETIC PARAMETERS

Toxicokinetics is utilized to describe the changes in pharmacokinetic processes as a result of drug overdose. Other factors may contribute to changes in pharmacokinetic parameters when nontoxic doses are therapeutically or illicitly administered. Besides species differences in the variability in drug response, which are not discussed here, other factors that contribute to changes in parameters include drug formulation and route of administration, gender differences, age, weight or body composition, disease, genetic abnormalities, and drug interactions.

3.5.1 Genetic Factors

When a distinguishable difference between individuals is under genetic control, it is known as genetic polymorphism. Some drug responses have been found to be genetically determined. For example, the activity of the liver enzyme N-acetyltransferase differs between individuals such that the population may be divided into slow and fast acetylators. Approximately 60% of the U.S. population are slow acetylators and may show toxicity unless doses of drugs requiring acetylation for metabolism are reduced. Other inherited variations in pharmacokinetics include deficiency of one or more hepatic cytochrome-P450 isozymes or plasma cholinesterase.[2]

3.5.2 Sex Differences

Examples of sex differences in drug pharmacokinetics have also been identified. These differences may be due to variations in body composition, hepatic metabolism, renal elimination, protein binding, or absorption. Differences in weight may influence muscle mass, organ blood flow, body water spaces, and hence affect the pharmacokinetic parameters of many drugs. In addition, women tend to have a higher percentage of body fat than men, which will affect the volume of distribution of lipophilic drugs. The clinical significance of differences in body composition is unclear but there are some important examples: women have a lower volume of distribution (V) of ethanol[19] and a higher V for diazepam than men.

A number of studies have examined the effect of gender on hepatic metabolism and drug elimination. Greenblatt et al.[20] found that young women have a significantly higher CL for diazepam than young men. In contrast, clearances of oxazepam[21] and chlordiazepoxide[22] are higher in men than in women and no sex difference has been observed in the metabolism of nitrazepam or lorazepam.[19] Differences can be explained by differences in metabolic pathways because oxazepam is metabolized primarily through conjugation, nitrazepam is metabolized by reduction of the nitro group, and most of the other benzodiazepines are metabolized by various cytochrome P450 isozymes. It has been found that the isozyme cytochrome 3A4, responsible for the metabolism of many drugs, is approximately 1.4 times more active in women than men. The isozymes P2D6 and P2C19 display genetic polymorphism that is not influenced by gender. The isozyme P1A2 may be influenced by sex although the data are inconclusive. The work of Relling et al.[23] suggests that the activity of this isozyme is lower in women than men. As mentioned above, gender differences have been demonstrated in the elimination of drugs that are metabolized solely by conjugation. The male:female clearance ratio for oxazepam is approximately 1.5:1.

When considering renal elimination, the glomerular filtration rate (GFR) is on average higher in men than women,[19] but this may be a weight rather than a gender effect as GFR is directly proportional to weight. The effects of gender on tubular secretion and reabsorption have not been well characterized. The influence of gender on plasma protein binding appears to be minimal. Albumin levels are not altered by gender in contrast to the protein α1-acid glycoprotein, which is reduced by estrogen.[24] Other plasma constituents whose levels are influenced by gender include cortico-steroid binding globulin and various lipoproteins.[25] Gender differences in the binding of diazepam and chlordiazepoxide have been demonstrated.

Some studies have suggested that gender influences gastric emptying rate and intestinal transit time.[26] Women empty solids from the stomach more slowly than men and the activity of a stomach enzyme, alcohol dehydrogenase, may be much lower in women. The GI tract also contains large concentrations of the isozyme cytochrome P3A4, so gender differences in the activity of this enzyme could affect the bioavailability of certain drugs. Gender differences observed after intramuscular drug administration may be due to differences in blood flow or incorrect injection into fat in women.

Drug absorption in the lung may differ according to gender. Knight et al.[27] found significantly less deposition of an aerosolized drug in women than men, which the authors attributed to differences in breathing characteristics.

It should be noted that female-specific issues may have significant effects on drug distribution and metabolism. For example, pregnancy may increase the elimination of certain drugs, reducing their efficacy. In addition, oral contraceptive use can affect the metabolism of drugs. The effects of menopause, menstruation, and hormone replacement on the pharmacokinetics of drugs are largely unknown.

3.5.3   Age

Changes in the rate but not the extent of drug absorption are usually observed with age.[16] Factors that affect drug absorption, such as gastric pH and emptying, intestinal motility, and blood flow, change with age. Gastric acid secretion does not approach adult levels until the age of 3 and gastric emptying and peristalsis is slow during the first few months of life. Because skeletal muscle mass is limited, muscle contractions, which aid blood flow, are minimal, and therefore will limit the distribution of intramuscularly administered drug. Higher gastric pH, delayed gastric emptying, and decreased intestinal motility and blood flow are observed in elderly individuals.

3.5.4   Drug and Disease Interactions

The pharmacokinetics of several drugs have been shown to be influenced by concurrent disease processes.[16] The clearance of many drugs decreases in those individuals with chronic hepatic disease such as cirrhosis. In contrast, in acute reversible liver conditions, such as acute viral hepatitis, the clearance of some drugs is decreased or the half-life increased and, for others, no change is detected. The volumes of distribution of some drugs are unaltered in hepatic disease while an increase is observed for other drugs, especially those bound to albumin in individuals with cirrhosis. This phenomenon is due to the decreased synthesis of albumin and other proteins. The influence of liver disease on drug absorption is unclear. It is probable, however, that the oral bioavailability of drugs highly extracted from the liver is increased in cirrhosis. The reasons are decreased first pass hepatic metabolism and the development of portal bypass in which blood enters the superior vena cava directly via esophageal varices.

Renal diseases such as uremia may result in decreased renal clearance of certain drugs.[16] Gastrointestinal diseases, such as Crohn's disease, result in increased plasma protein binding of several drugs due to increased levels of binding proteins. Further, respiratory diseases such as cystic fibrosis increase the renal clearance of some drugs.

Patients commonly receive two or more drugs concurrently and most individuals who abuse drugs are polydrug users. Multiple drug use may result in drug interactions. This occurs when the pharmacokinetics or pharmacodynamics of one drug is altered by another. This concept is important to consider because interaction may result in decreased therapeutic efficacy or an increased risk of toxicity. The degree of drug interaction depends on the relative concentrations and therefore dose and time.[16] Changes in absorption rate, competition for binding sites on plasma proteins, oral bioavailability, volume of distribution, and hepatic and renal clearance have been demonstrated for therapeutic drugs. Few studies have systematically documented pharmacokinetic interactions between illicit drugs.

REFERENCES

1. Derendorf, H. and Hochhaus, G., Eds., *Handbook of Pharmacokinetic/Pharmacodynamic Correlation,* CRC Press, Boca Raton, FL, 1995.

2. Amdur, M.O., Doull, J., and Klaassen, C.D., Eds., *Casarett and Doull's Toxicology: The Basic Science of Poisons,* Pergamon Press, Elmsford, New York, 1991.
3. Hardman, J.G. and Limbird, L.E., Eds., *Goodman & Gilman's The Pharmacological Basis of Therapeutics,* McGraw-Hill, New York, 1996.
4. Benz, R., Janko, K., and Langer, P., Pore formation by the matrix protein (porin) to *Escherichia coli* in planar bilayer membranes, *Ann. N.Y. Acad. Sci.,* 358, 13–24, 1980.
5. Sobel, A.E., Gawron, O., and Kramer, B., Influence of vitamin D in experimental lead poisoning, *Proc. Soc. Exp. Biol. Med.,* 38, 433–435, 1938.
6. Bates, T.R. and Gibaldi, M., Gastrointestinal absorption of drugs. In Swarbuck, J., Ed.: *Current Concepts in the Pharmaceutical Sciences: Biopharmaceutics,* Lea & Febiger, Philadelphia, 1970.
7. Baselt, R.C. and Cravey, R.H., *Disposition of Toxic Drugs and Chemicals in Man,* Chemical Toxicology Institute, Foster City, CA, 1995.
8. Kupferberg, H.J. and Way, E.L., Pharmacologic basis for the increased sensitivity of the newborn rat to morphine, *J. Pharmacol. Exp. Ther.,* 141, 105–112,1963.
9. Pratt, W.B. and Taylor, P., Eds., *Principles of Drug Action: The Basis of Pharmacology,* Churchill Livingstone, New York, 1990.
10. Mulder, G.J., Ed., *Sulfation of Drugs and Related Compounds,* CRC Press, Boca Raton, FL, 1981.
11. Schenkman, J.B. and Kupfer, D., Eds., *Hepatic Cytochrome P-450 Monooxygenase System,* Pergamon Press, Oxford, 1982.
12. Gonzalez, F.J., The molecular biology of cytochrome P450s, *Pharmacol. Rev.,* 40, 243, 1988.
13. Conney, A.H., Induction of microsomal cytochrome P-450 enzymes, *Life Sci.,* 39, 2493, 1986.
14. Stowe, C.M. and Plaa, G.L., Extrarenal excretion of drugs and chemicals, *Annu. Rev. Pharmacol.,* 8, 337–356, 1968.
15. Weiner, I.M. and Mudge, G.H., Renal tubular mechanisms for excretion of organic acids and bases, *Am. J. Med.,* 36, 743–762, 1964.
16. Rowland, M. and Tozer, T.N., *Clinical Pharmacokinetics Concepts and Applications,* Lea & Febiger, Philadelphia, 1989.
17. Hagan, R.L., Basic pharmacokinetics: in-service training and continuing education AACC/TDM, American Association for Clinical Chemistry, Inc., Washington, D.C., 17(9), 231–247, 1996.
18. Ellenhorn, M.J., and Barceloux, D.G., *Medical Toxicology, Diagnosis and Treatment of Human Poisoning,* Elsevier, New York, 1988.
19. Harris, R.Z., Benet, L.Z., and Schwartz, J.B., Gender effects in pharmacokinetics and pharmacodynamics, *Drugs,* 50(2), 222–239, 1995.
20. Greenblatt, D.J., Allen, M.D., and Harmatz, J.S., Diazepam disposition determinants, *Clin. Pharmacol. Ther.,* 27, 301–312, 1980.
21. Greenblatt, D.J., Divoll, M., and Harmatz, J.S., Oxazepam kinetics: effects of age and sex, *J. Pharmacol. Exp. Ther.,* 215, 86–91, 1980.
22. Greenblatt, D.J., Divoll, M., and Abernathy, D.R., Age and gender effects on chlordiazepoxide kinetics: relation to antipyrine disposition, *Pharmacology,* 38, 327–334, 1989.
23. Relling, M.V., Lin, J.S., and Ayers, G.D., Racial and gender differences in *N*-acetyltransferase, xanthine oxidase, and CYP1A2 activities, *Clin. Pharmacol. Ther.,* 52, 643–658, 1992.
24. Routledge, P.A., Stargel, W.W., and Kitchell, B.B., Sex-related differences in the plasma protein binding of lignocaine and diazepam, *Br. J. Clin. Pharmacol.,* 11, 245–250, 1981.
25. Wilson, K., Sex-related differences in drug disposition in man, *Clin. Pharmacokinet.,* 9, 189–202, 1984.
26. Yonkers, K.A., Kando, J.C., and Cole, J.O., Gender differences in pharmacokinetics and pharmacodynamics of psychotropic medication, *Am. J. Psychiatry,* 149, 587–595, 1992.
27. Knight, V., Yu, C.P., and Gilbert, B.E., Estimating the dosage of ribavirin aerosol according to age and other variables, *J. Infect. Dis.,* 158, 443–447, 1988.

3.6 PHARMACOKINETICS OF SPECIFIC DRUGS

3.6.1 Amphetamine

The term *amphetamine* refers to the group of stimulants that includes amphetamine, methamphetamine, methylenedioxyamphetamine, and methylenedioxymethamphetamine. These low-molecular-weight basic drugs are sympathomimetic phenethylamine derivatives possessing central and peripheral stimulant activity. Amphetamines suppress appetite and produce CNS and cardiovascular stimulation. These effects are mediated by increasing synaptic concentrations of norepinephrine and dopamine either by stimulating neurotransmitter release or inhibiting uptake, or both. Clinical uses of amphetamine and methamphetamine include chronic administration for the treatment of narcolepsy in adults and attention-deficit/hyperactivity disorder in children.[1]

These drugs are abused for their stimulant effect. The effects are usually longer lasting than those of cocaine and may prevent fatigue. The latter factor has led to their study in athletes and in military field situations. It is postulated that the disturbances in perception and psychotic behavior, which may occur at high doses, may be due to dopamine release from dopaminergic neurons and also serotonin release from tryptaminergic neurons located in the mesolimbic area of the brain.

Amphetamine and methamphetamine occur as structural isomers and stereoisomers. Structural isomers are compounds with the same empirical formula but a different atomic arrangement, e.g., methamphetamine and phentermine. Stereoisomers differ in the three-dimensional arrangement of the atoms attached to at least one asymmetric carbon and are nonsuperimposable mirror images. Therefore, amphetamine and methamphetamine occur as both D- and L- isomeric forms. The two isomers together form a racemic mixture. The D-amphetamine form has significant stimulant activity, and possesses approximately three to four times the central activity of the L-form. It is also important to note that the D- and L-enantiomers may have not only different pharmacological activity but also varying pharmacokinetic characteristics.

When indicated for therapeutic use, 5 to 60 mg or 5 to 20 mg of amphetamine or methamphetamine, respectively, are administered orally. An oral dose of amphetamine typically results in a peak plasma concentration of 110 ng/ml.[2] When abused, amphetamines may be self-administered by the oral, intravenous, or smoked route. The last route of administration is common for methamphetamine. With heavy use, addicts may ingest up to 2000 mg per day.

3.6.1.1 Absorption

Limited data are available on the GI absorption of amphetamine in humans. Beckett et al.[3] reported serum concentrations of amphetamine in two healthy volunteers after a 15-mg oral dose of the D-isomer. Peak serum concentrations of 48 and 40 ng/ml were achieved at 1.25 h when the volunteers' urine was acidified. Slightly higher serum concentrations were observed (52 and 47 ng/ml) if the urine pH conditions were not controlled. Rowland[4] observed a peak blood concentration of 35 ng/ml, 2 h after a 10-mg oral dose of D-amphetamine to a healthy 66 kg adult. The half-life for the D-isomer was 11 to 13 h compared with a 39% longer half-life for the L-isomer. If the urine was acidified, excretion was enhanced and the half-lives of both isomers were reduced to approximately 7 h.[5] Amphetamine demonstrates a linear one-compartment open model over the dose range 20 to 200 mg.

3.6.1.2 Distribution

The plasma protein binding of amphetamine in humans is approximately 16 to 20% and is similar in drug-dependent and naive subjects.[6] Research by Rowland[4] and Franksson and Anggard[6] indicated that there was a difference in the volume of distribution between non-users (3.5 to 4.6 L/kg) and drug-dependent individuals (6.1 L/kg). It has been suggested that the larger V_d observed in drug-dependent subjects may be due to a higher tissue affinity for amphetamine in these individuals. Evidence to support this suggestion is found in studies with amphetamine-dependent animals in which higher tissue concentrations of amphetamine were found.[7]

3.6.1.3 Metabolism and Excretion

Amphetamine is metabolized by deamination, oxidation, and hydroxylation. Figure 3.6.1 illustrates the metabolic scheme for amphetamine. Deamination produces an inactive metabolite, phenylacetone, which is further oxidized to benzoic acid and then excreted in urine as hippuric acid and glucuronide conjugates. In addition, amphetamine is also converted to norephedrine by oxidation and then this metabolite and the parent compound are p-hydroxylated. Several metabolites, including norephedrine, its hydroxy metabolite, and hydroxyamphetamine, are pharmacologically active. The excretion of amphetamine depends on urinary pH. In healthy men who were administered 5 mg of isotopically labeled D,L-amphetamine, approximately 90% of the dose was excreted in the urine within 3 to 4 days.[8] Approximately 70% of the dose was excreted in the 24-h urine with 30% as unchanged drug. This was increased to 74% under acidic conditions and reduced to 1% in alkaline urine. Under normal conditions, <1% is excreted as phenylacetone, 16 to 28% as hippuric acid, 4% as benzoylglucuronide, 2% as norephedrine, <0.5% as p-hydroxynorephedrine, and 2 to 4% as p-hydroxyamphetamine.[9] L-Amphetamine is not as extensively metabolized as the D-isomer. When volunteers were orally administered 5 to 15 mg of D- or L-amphetamine, the mean excretion of unchanged D-amphetamine was 33% of the dose and that of the L-isomer was 49% of the dose.[2]

The metabolism of amphetamine has been studied in those presenting with amphetamine psychosis. In the presence of acidified urine, the renal elimination of amphetamine increased significantly. The intensity of the psychosis was found to correlate with the amount of basic polar metabolites excreted in the urine, such as norephedrine and p-hydroxyamphetamine, and not with the plasma amphetamine concentration. This suggests that these metabolites may play an important role in the development of paranoid psychosis in chronic amphetamine users.[6]

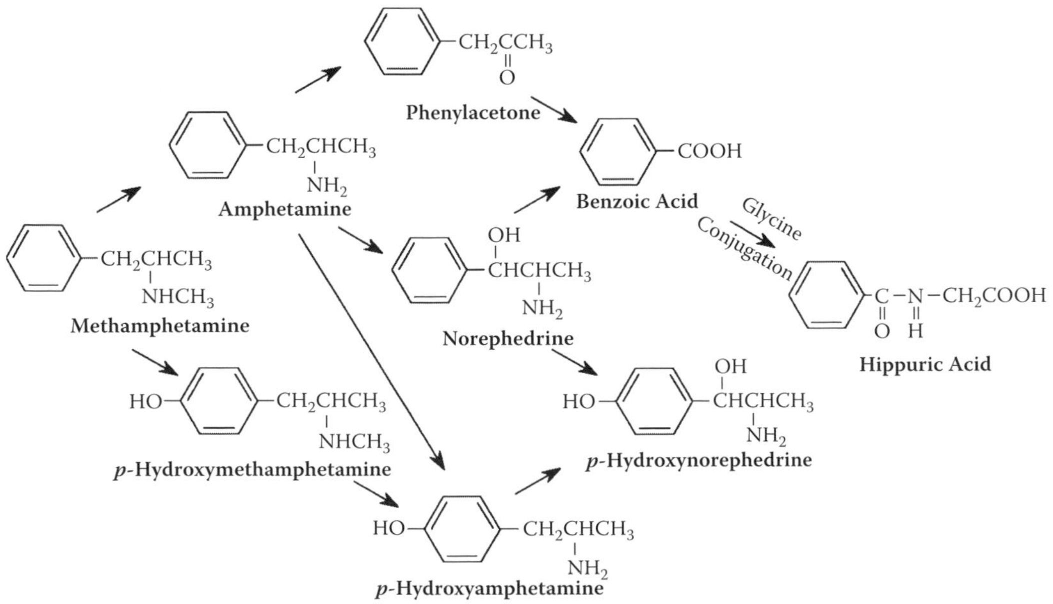

Figure 3.6.1 Metabolic pathway of amphetamine and methamphetamine.

3.6.2   Methamphetamine

D-Methamphetamine, the *N*-methyl derivative of amphetamine, was first synthesized in 1919. Methamphetamine is available in the D- and L-forms. The D-form has reportedly greater central stimulant activity than the L-isomer, which has greater peripheral sympathomimetic activity. The D-form is the commonly abused form while the L-isomer is typically found in nonprescription inhalers as a decongestant.

Although initially available as an injectable solution for the treatment of obesity, D-methamphetamine hydrochloride is currently available as conventional and prolonged release tablets. Illicit methamphetamine is synthesized from the precursors phenylacetone and *N*-methylformamide (DL mixture) or alternatively from ephedrine or pseudoephedrine by red phosphorus/acid reduction.

3.6.2.1   Absorption

Doses of 5 to 10 mg methamphetamine typically result in blood concentrations between 20 to 60 ng/ml. In one study,[10] six healthy adults were orally administered a single dose of 0.125 mg/kg methamphetamine. Peak plasma concentrations were achieved at 3.6 h with a mean concentration of 20 ng/ml. In a second study, Lebish et al.[11] observed a peak blood concentration of 30 ng/ml, 1 h after a single oral dose of 10 mg methamphetamine to one subject. In a study by Schepers et al.[12] eight subjects were administered four oral doses of 10 mg methamphetamine hydrochloride as sustained release tablets within 7 days. At 3 weeks later five subjects received four oral 20-mg doses. After the first dose, methamphetamine was detected in plasma between 0.25 and 2 h, the c_{max} was 14.5 to 33.8 ng/ml (10 mg dose) and 26.2 to 44.3 ng/ml (20 mg) and occurred within 2 to 12 h. Methamphetamine was first detected in oral fluid in this study 0.08 to 2 h post dose, with a c_{max} of 24.7 to 312.2 and 75.3 to 321.7 ng/ml after the 10 and 20 mg doses, respectively. Peak methamphetamine concentrations in oral fluid occurred at 2 to 12 h and the median oral fluid-plasma concentration ratio was 2.0 for 24 h. In general, the detection window for drug in oral fluid exceeded that in plasma.

3.6.2.2   Metabolism and Excretion

In humans, both the D- and L-forms undergo hydroxylation and *N*-demethylation to their respective *p*-hydroxymethamphetamine and amphetamine metabolites. Amphetamine is the major active metabolite of methamphetamine. Under normal conditions, up to 43% of a D-methamphetamine dose is excreted unchanged in the urine in the first 24 hours and 4 to 7% will be present as amphetamine. In acidic urine, up to 76% is present as parent drug[10] compared with 2% under alkaline conditions. Approximately 15% of the dose was present as *p*-hydroxymethamphetamine and the remaining minor metabolites were similar to those found after amphetamine administration. Urine concentrations of methamphetamine are typically 0.5 to 4 mg/L after an oral dose of 10 mg. However, methamphetamine and amphetamine urine concentrations vary widely among abusers. Lebish et al.[11] reported urine methamphetamine concentrations of 24 to 333 mg/L and amphetamine concentrations of 1 to 90 mg/L in the urine of methamphetamine abusers.

L-Methamphetamine is biotransformed in a similar manner to the D-isomer but at a slower rate. Following a 13.7 mg oral dose, the 24 h urine contained an average of 34% of the dose as L-methamphetamine and 1.7% of the dose as L-amphetamine.[3] Oyler et al.[13] described the appearance of methamphetamine and amphetamine in urine after volunteers (*n* = 8) ingested 4 × 10 mg doses of methamphetamine hydrochloride daily for 7 days followed by 4 × 20 mg daily several weeks later. Parent and metabolite were generally detected in the first or second void post dose in a concentration range of 82 to 1827 and 12 to 180 ng/ml, respectively. Peak methamphetamine urine concentrations (1871 to 6004 ng/ml) occurred within 1.5 to 60 h after a single dose.

D-Methamphetamine is commonly self-administered by the smoked route. Both the free-base and hydrochloride salt of methamphetamine are volatile and >90% of parent drug can be recovered intact when heated to temperatures of 300°C. When cigarettes containing tobacco mixed with methamphetamine were pyrolyzed, amphetamine, phenylacetone, dimethylamphetamine, and N-cyanomethyl methamphetamine were the major resulting products.[14] Cook[15] conducted a study in which six volunteers were administered 30 mg D-methamphetamine from a pipe that was heated to approximately 300°C. Blood samples and physiological and subjective measures were collected after drug administration. Plasma methamphetamine concentrations rose rapidly after the start of smoking. However, concentrations plateaued (40 to 44 ng/ml) after 1 h with a slight increase in concentration over the next 1 h. Thereafter, concentrations in plasma declined slowly, reaching the same concentration at 8 h on the downward side of the curve as reached at 30 min on the upward side. The authors used a noncompartmental model to determine an average elimination half-life of 11.7 h with a range of 8 to 17 h. These authors also administered methamphetamine (0.250 mg/kg) orally and the resulting plasma data were fit to a one-compartment model with first-order elimination and a lag time. A maximum plasma concentration of 35 to 38 ng/ml was achieved at 3.1 h with a terminal elimination half-life of 10 h. Although the plasma concentration time curves for smoked and oral methamphetamine appeared similar, the subjective effects were markedly different, with a greater "high" being reported after smoked methamphetamine. This indicates that it may be the rate of change of plasma drug concentrations that is a significant factor in determining subjective effects. Other investigators[16] have reported the bioavailability of methamphetamine after intranasal and smoked drug to be 79 and 67% (of estimated delivered dose), respectively. Maximum blood concentrations of parent drug occurred at 2.7 and 2.5 h after intranasal and smoked doses ($n = 8$).

3.6.3   3,4-Methylenedioxyamphetamine

3,4-Methylenedioxyamphetamine (MDA) is a potent psychotropic amphetamine derivative first synthesized in 1910 (Figure 3.6.2). It has no accepted medical use but is self-administered orally or intravenously in doses of 50 to 250 mg for illicit use.[10] Blood concentrations following normal use have not been reported and, to date, there are no reported clinical studies delineating the pharmacokinetic or pharmacodynamic characteristics of this drug. Blood concentrations in humans have been reported following overdose. The average blood concentration in 12 fatal cases was 9.3 mg/L (range 1.8 to 26).[10] The metabolism of MDA in humans has not been studied, but in other animals MDA is metabolized by O-dealkylation, deamination, and conjugation.[17] Polymorphically expressed CYP2D6 is the major isozyme catalyzing the metabolic steps in the metabolism of MDA and MDMA.[18]

3.6.4   3,4-Methylenedioxymethamphetamine

3,4-Methylenedioxymethamphetamine (MDMA) is a ring-substituted derivative of metham-phetamine (Figure 3.6.2) that has widespread use as a recreational drug. Self-administration is typically by the oral route in doses of 100 to 150 mg. Helmlin et al.[19] reported a mean peak plasma

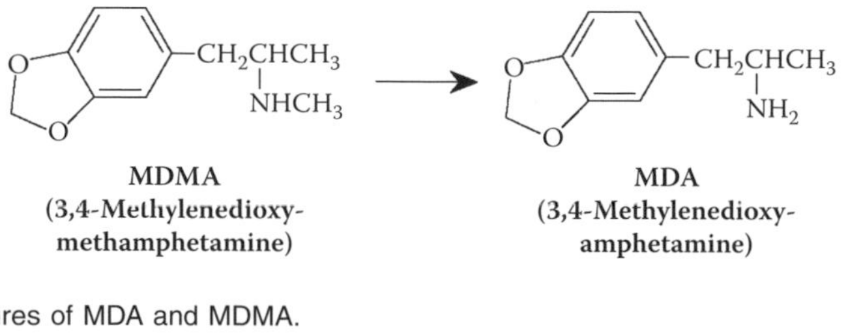

MDMA
(3,4-Methylenedioxy-
methamphetamine)

MDA
(3,4-Methylenedioxy-
amphetamine)

Figure 3.6.2 Structures of MDA and MDMA.

MDMA concentration of 300 ng/ml at 2.3 h after an oral dose of 1.5 mg/kg to adult subjects; de la Torre et al. studied eight healthy volunteers and reported a peak MDMA concentration of 180 ng/m occurring 1.8 h after a 75-mg oral dose, with an MDA peak of 78 ng/ml 5 h after administration. MDMA presents nonlinear pharmacokinetics. In a randomized double blind cross-over placebo-controlled study with nine healthy male subjects, Farre et al.[20] reported increased plasma MDMA concentrations after a second dose of 100 mg, 24 h after the initial dose, were greater than expected by accumulation. The authors suspected the reason to be due to metabolic inhibition. Parameters such as blood pressure, heart rate, and subjective effects were higher after the second dose than after the first.

MDMA is metabolized to MDA with 65% of the dose excreted as parent drug within 3 days. Both MDMA and MDA are hydroxylated to mono- and di-hydroxy derivatives and subsequently conjugated before elimination. The plasma half-life has been reported to be 7.6 h.[10]

If MDMA is co-administered with ethanol, as 100 mg plus 0.8g/kg ethanol, plasma concentrations of the former demonstrate a 13% increase compared with MDMA administered alone.[21] Plasma concentrations of ethanol decreased 9 to 15% after MDMA administration ($n = 9$).

MDMA has also been reported in alternative biological specimens. After a single oral dose of 75 mg in human volunteers, MDMA concentrations in oral fluid exceeded those in plasma with a mean peak concentration of 1215 ng/ml ($n = 12$) and a range of 50 to 6982 ng/ml compared with an average peak plasma concentration of 178 ng/ml (range 21 to 295 ng/ml).[22] In sweat the average concentration was 25 ng/wipe when measured 4 to 5 h after ingestion of a similar dose.[23] When MDMA and MDA concentrations measured in ante-mortem samples have been compared, consistent and significant increases in the postmortem concentrations have been observed.[24]

REFERENCES

1. *Physicians Desk Reference 2005.* Medical Economics Data, a division of Medical Economics Company, Inc., p. 1315, Montvale, NJ.
2. Baylor, M.R. and Crouch, D.J., Sympathomimetic amines: pharmacology, toxicology, and analysis. in-service training and continuing education AACC/TDM, American Association for Clinical Chemistry, Inc., Washington, D.C., 14(5), 101–111, 1993.
3. Beckett, A.H. and Rowland, M., Urinary excretion kinetics of amphetamine in man, *J. Pharm. Pharmacol.,* 17, 628–639, 1965.
4. Rowland, M., Amphetamine blood and urine levels in man, *J. Pharm. Sci.,* 58, 508–509, 1969.
5. Matin, S.B., Wan, S.H., and Knight, J.B., Quantitative determination of enantiomeric compounds, *Biomed. Mass Spectrosc.,* 4, 118–121, 1977.
6. Franksson, G. and Anggard, E., The plasma protein binding of amphetamine, catecholamines and related compounds, *Acta Pharmacol. Toxicol.,* 28, 209–214, 1970.
7. Ellison, T., Siegel., M, Silverman, A.G., and Okun, R., Comparative metabolism of D,L H3-amphetamine hydrochloride in tolerant and non tolerant cats, *Proc. Western Pharmacol. Soc.,* 11, 75–77, 1968.
8. Dring, L.G., Smith, R.L., and Williams, R.T., The metabolic fate of amphetamine in man and other species, *Biochem. J.,* 116, 425–435, 1970.
9. Sever, P.S., Caldwell, J., Dring, L.G., and Williams, R.T., The metabolism of amphetamine in dependent subjects, *Eur. J. Clin. Pharm.,* 6, 177–180, 1973.
10. Baselt, R.C. and Cravey, R.H., *Disposition of Toxic Drugs and Chemicals in Man,* 4th ed., Chemical Toxicology Institute, Foster City, CA, 1995.
11. LeBish, P., Finkle, B.S., and Brackett, J.W., Jr., Determination of amphetamine, methamphetamine, and related amines in blood and urine by gas chromatography by hydrogen-flame ionization detector, *Clin. Chem.,* 16, 195–200, 1970.
12. Schepers, R.J.F., Oyler, J.M., Joseph, R.E., Cone, E.J., Moolchan, E.T., and Huestis, M.A., Methamphetamine and amphetamine pharmacokinetics in oral fluid and plasma after controlled oral methamphetamine administration to human volunteers, *Clin. Chem.,* 49(1), 121–132, 2003.

13. Oyler, J.M., Cone, E.J., Joseph, R.E., Moolchan, E.T., and Huestis, M.A., Duration of detectable methamphetamine and amphetamine excretion in urine after controlled oral administration of methamphetamine to humans, *Clin. Chem.*, 48(10), 1703–1714, 2002.
14. Sekine, H. and Nakahara, Y., Abuse of smoking methamphetamine mixed with tobacco: I. Inhalation efficiency and pyrolysis products of methamphetamine, *J. Forensic Sci.*, 32(5), 1271–1280, 1987.
15. Cook, C.E., Pyrolytic characteristics, pharmacokinetics, and bioavailability of smoked heroin, cocaine, phencyclidine and methamphetamine, NIDA Research Monograph 99, 6–23. DHHS Pub. No. 1990.
16. Harris, D.S., Boxenbaum, H., Everhart, E.T., Sequeira, G., Mendelson, J.E., and Jones, R.T., The bioavailability of intranasal and smoked methamphetamine, *Clin. Pharmacol. Ther.*, 74(5), 475–486, 2003.
17. Midha, K.K., McGilveray, I.J., Bhatnager, S.P., and Cooper, J.K., GLC identification and determination of 3,4-methylenedioxyamphetamine *in vivo* in dog and monkey, *Drug Met. Disp.*, 6, 623–630, 1978.
18. Maurer, H.H., Kraemer, T., Springer, D., and Staack, R.F., Chemistry, pharmacology, toxicology, and hepatic metabolism of designer drugs of the amphetamine (ecstasy), piperazine, and pyrrolidinophenone types: a synopsis, *Ther. Drug Monit.*, 26(2), 127–131, 2004.
19. Helmlin, H.J., Bracher, K., Salamone, S.J., and Brenneisen, R., Analysis of 3,4-methylenedioxymethamphetamine (MDMA) and its metabolites in human plasma and urine, Society of Forensic Toxicologists, Inc., Phoenix, AZ, October 1993 [Abstract].
20. Farre, M., de la Torre, R., Mathuna, B.O., Roset, P.N., Peiro, A.M., Torrens, M., Ortuno, J., Pujadas, M., and Cami, J., Repeated doses administration of MDMA in humans: pharmacological effects and pharmacokinetics, *Psychopharmacology* (Berlin), 173(3–4), 364–375, 2004.
21. Hernandez-Lopez, C., Farre, M., Roset, P.N., Menoyo, E., Pizarro, N., Ortuno, J., Torrens, M., Cami, J., and de la Torre, R., 3,4-Methylenedioxymethamphetamine (ecstasy) and alcohol interactions in humans: psychomotor performance, subjective effects, and pharmacokinetics, *J. Pharmacol. Exp. Ther.*, 300(1), 236–244, 2002.
22. Samyn, N., De Boeck, G., Wood, M., Lamers, C.T., De Waard, D., Brookhuis, K.A., Verstraete, A.G., and Riedel, W.J., Plasma, oral fluid and sweat wipe ecstasy concentrations in controlled and real life conditions, *Forensic Sci. Int.*, 128(1–2), 90–97, 2002.
23. de la Torre, R., Farre, M., Ortuno, J., Mas, M., Brenneisen, R., Roset, P.N., Segura, J., and Cami, J., Non-linear pharmacokinetics of MDMA ("ecstasy") in humans, *Br. J. Clin. Pharmacol.*, 49(2), 104–109, 2000.
24. Elliott, S.P., MDMA and MDA concentrations in antemortem and postmortem specimens in fatalities following hospital admission, *J. Anal. Toxicol.*, 29(5), 296–300, 2005.

3.6.5 Barbiturates

Barbituric acid, 2,4,6-trioxohexahydropyrimidine, was first synthesized in 1864.[1] In 1903 it was marketed for use as an antianxiety and sedative hypnotic medication. Barbituric acid is without CNS depressant activity but by substituting an aryl or alkyl group on C-5, anxiolytic and sedative properties may be conferred. Substitution of sulfur on C-2 produces the thiobarbituates, which have characteristically greater lipophilicity. Generally, structural changes that increase lipophilicity result in decreased duration of action, decreased latency to onset of action, increased biotransformation, and increased hypnotic potency.[2] Although the use of barbiturates as sedative-hypnotic agents has largely been replaced by the benzodiazepines, the barbiturates maintain an important role as anticonvulsant and anesthetic drugs.

3.6.5.1 Pharmacology

As a class of drugs, barbiturates exert hypnotic, sedative, anxiolytic, anticonvulsant, and anesthetic properties. The clinical use of these drugs is based on their shared properties and also unique properties of individual drugs within this class.[1] As CNS depressants, barbiturates exert effects on excitatory and inhibitory synaptic neurotransmission. Barbiturates are known to decrease excitatory amino acid release and post-synaptic response in experimental animals by blocking the excitatory glutamate response. This may be due to a direct effect on the glutamate sensitive channel, or an indirect effect on calcium channels.[1] The ultra short acting barbiturates used for anesthesia, such as thiopental, depress excitatory neuronal transmission to a greater extent than the anticonvulsant barbiturates.[3]

Barbiturates also exert an effect on gamma-amino butyric acid (GABA) neurotransmission. Barbiturates, such as pentobarbital, enhance the binding of GABA to $GABA_A$ receptors. This effect occurs both in the CNS and the spinal cord. The enhanced action of GABA depresses both normal physiological processes, such as post-synaptic potential evocation, and pathophysiological processes such as seizures.[1] Barbiturates also enlarge GABA-induced chloride currents by extending the time for chloride channel opening.[3] It is important to note that some barbiturates such as 5-(1,3-dimethylbutyl)-5-ethyl barbituric acid (DMBB) promote convulsions by directly depolarizing the neuronal membrane and increasing transmitter release.

3.6.5.2 Absorption

When utilized as sedative hypnotics, barbiturates are administered orally. They are rapidly and completely absorbed by this route with nearly 100% bioavailability and an onset of action ranging from 10 to 60 min.[3] Sodium salts are more rapidly absorbed than free acids. Intramuscular injections of sodium salts should be made deep into the muscle to prevent pain and tissue damage. Some barbiturates are also administered rectally; barbiturates utilized for the induction and maintenance of anesthesia (thiopental) or for treating status epilepticus (phenobarbital) are administered intravenously.

Pentobarbital is a short-acting barbiturate available for oral, intramuscular, rectal, and intravenous administration. After a single oral dose of 100 mg, peak serum concentrations of 1.2 to 3.1 mg/L were achieved at 0.5 to 2.0 h.[4] These concentrations diminished slowly to an average of 0.3 mg/L at 48 h. When administered intravenously, in a 5-min continuous infusion of 50 mg, plasma concentrations averaged 1.18 mg/L ($n = 5$) at 0.08 h, declining to 0.54 mg/L after 1 h and reaching 0.27 mg/L after 24 h.[5] Repeated intravenous doses of pentobarbital, typically 100 to 200 mg every 30 to 60 min, are administered to reduce intracranial pressure and decrease cerebral oxygen demand in patients with severe head trauma or anoxic brain damage.[6] Doses are adjusted to maintain plasma concentrations between 25 to 40 mg/L.

Amobarbital is a barbituric acid derivative of intermediate duration of action. It is administered orally in doses of 15 to 200 mg as a sedative hypnotic and in ampoules of 65 to 500 mg for intravenous and intramuscular injection for the seizure control.[6] Following a single oral dose of 120 mg, peak serum concentrations averaged 1.8 mg/L after 2 h.[7] After an oral dose of 600 mg distributed over a 3-h period, the peak blood concentration was achieved after 30 min, averaging 8.7 mg/L, with a decline to 4.1 mg/L by 18 h.[6]

Phenobarbital is utilized as a daytime sedative and anticonvulsant. It also induces several cytochrome P450 isozymes. Compared to other barbiturates, phenobarbital has a low oil/water partition coefficient, which results in slow distribution into the brain. It is available for oral, intravenous, or intramuscular administration. Doses for epileptic patients range from 60 to 200 mg per day. After a single oral dose of 30 mg, peak serum concentrations averaged 0.7 mg/L ($n = 3$). Repeated doses over a period of 7 days resulted in an average peak concentration of 8.1 mg/L.[6] Chronic administration of 200 mg per day as anticonvulsant medication resulted in an average blood concentration of 29 mg/L (range = 16 to 48 mg/L).[9]

3.6.5.3 Distribution

Barbiturates are generally widely distributed throughout the body. The highly lipophilic barbiturates, especially those used to induce anesthesia, undergo redistribution when administered intravenously. Barbiturates enter less vascular tissues over time, such as muscle and adipose tissue, and this redistribution decreases concentrations in the blood and brain. With drugs such as thiopental, this redistribution results in patients waking up within 5 to 15 minutes after injection of an anesthetic dose.

Pentobarbital is 65% plasma protein bound with a volume of distribution of 0.5 to 1.0 L/kg.[6] After intravenous administration, estimates of the plasma half-life have averaged between 20 to 30 h. Amobarbital is similar to pentobarbital in the degree of plasma protein binding (59%) with a slightly larger volume of distribution (0.9 to 1.4 L/kg). The plasma half-life, however, is dose dependent, with a range of 15 to 40 h.[6] Phenobarbital is approximately 50% plasma protein bound with a volume of distribution of 0.5 to 0.6 L/kg. The plasma half-life averages 4 days with a range of 2 to 6 days.

3.6.5.4 Metabolism and Elimination

Generally, barbiturates are metabolized by oxidation and conjugation in the liver prior to renal excretion. The oxidation of substituents at the C-5 position is the most important factor in terminating pharmacological activity.[2] Oxidation of barbiturates results in the formation of alcohols, phenols, ketones, or carboxylic acids with subsequent conjugation with glucuronic acid. Other metabolic transformations include N-hydroxylation, desulfuration of thiobarbiturates to oxybarbiturates, opening of the barbituric acid ring, and N-dealkylation of N-alkylbarbiturates to active metabolites, e.g., mephobarbital to phenobarbital.[2]

Pentobarbital is biotransformed by oxidation of the penultimate carbon of the methyl butyl side-chain to produce a mixture of alcohols, and by N-hydroxylation. The alcoholic metabolites of pentobarbital are pharmacologically inactive. Approximately 86% of a radioactive dose is excreted in the urine in 6 days, about 1% as unchanged drug and up to 73% as the L- and D-diastereoisomers of 3′-hydroxypentobarbital in a 5.4:1 ratio, and up to 15% as N-hydroxypentobarbital.[8] None of these metabolites is eliminated as a conjugate.

Amobarbital is extensively metabolized to polar metabolites in a process that is saturable and best described by zero-order kinetics at therapeutic doses.[10] Two major metabolites are produced by hydroxylation and N-glycosylation. 3′-Hydroxyamobarbital possesses pharmacological activity. Approximately 92% of a single dose is excreted in the urine with 5% excreted in the feces over a 6-day period. Approximately 2% is excreted unchanged in the urine, 30 to 40% is excreted as free 3′-hydroxyamobarbital, 29% as N-glycosylamobarbital, and 5% as the minor metabolite, 3′-carboxyamobarbital.

Phenobarbital is primarily metabolized via N-glycosylation and by oxidation to form p-hydroxyphenobarbital followed by conjugation with glucuronic acid (Figure 3.6.3). A dihydrohydroxy

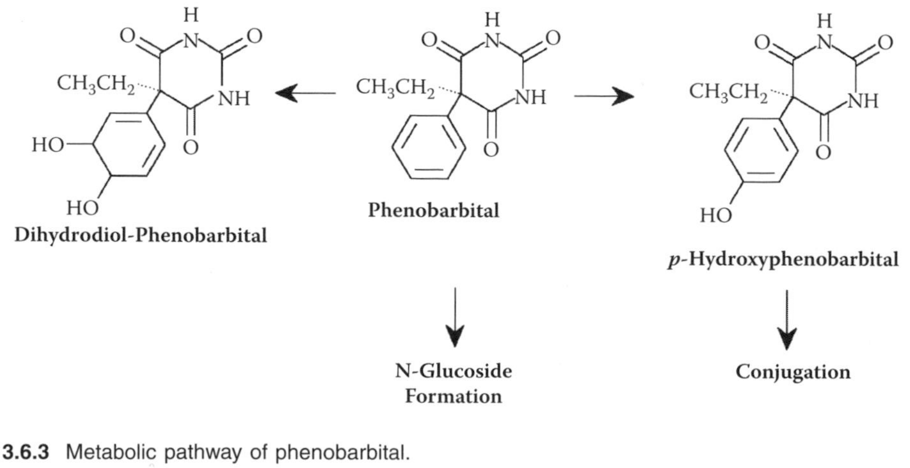

Figure 3.6.3 Metabolic pathway of phenobarbital.

metabolite has been identified in minor amounts, thought to arise from an epoxide intermediate.[11] Approximately 80% of a single labeled dose is excreted in the urine within 16 days. Unchanged drug accounts for 25 to 33% of the dose, *N*-glucosyl-phenobarbital for 24 to 30%, and free or conjugated *p*-hydroxyphenobarbital for 18 to 19%.[12] When administered chronically, approximately 25% of the dose is excreted unchanged in the 24-h urine with 8% free and 9% conjugated *p*-hydroxyphenobarbital.

REFERENCES

1. Smith, M.C. and Riskin, B.J., The clinical use of barbiturates in neurological disorders, *Drugs,* 42(3), 365–378, 1991.
2. Hardman, J.G. and Limbird, L.E., Eds., *Goodman & Gilman's The Pharmacological Basis of Therapeutics,* McGraw-Hill, New York, 1996.
3. MacDonald, R.L. and Barker, J.L., Anticonvulsant and anesthetic barbiturates: different postsynaptic action in cultured mammalian neurons, *Neurology,* 29, 432–477, 1979.
4. Sun, S. and Chun, A.H.C., Determination of pentobarbital in serum by electron capture GLC, *J. Pharm. Sci.,* 66, 477–480, 1977.
5. Smith, R.B., Dittert, L.W., Griffen, W.O., Jr., and Doluisio, J.T., Pharmacokinetics of pentobarbital after intravenous and oral administration, *J. Pharm. Biopharm.,* 1, 5–16, 1973.
6. Baselt, R.C. and Cravey, R.H., *Disposition of Toxic Drugs and Chemicals in Man,* Chemical Toxicology Institute, Foster City, CA, 1995.
7. Tang, B.K., Inaba, T., Endrenyi, L., and Kalow, W., Amobarbital-a probe of hepatic drug oxidation on man, *Clin. Pharmacol. Ther.,* 20, 439–444, 1976.
8. Tang, B.K., Inaba, T., and Kalow, W., *N*-Hydroxylation of pentobarbital in man, *Drug Met. Disp.,* 5, 71–74, 1977.
9. Plaa, G.L. and Hine, C.H., Hydantoin and barbiturate blood levels observed in epileptics, *Arch. Int. Pharm. Ther.,* 128, 375–383, 1960.
10. Garrett, E.R., Bres, J., Schnelle, K., and Rolf, L.L., Jr., Pharmacokinetics of saturably metabolized amobarbital, *J. Pharm. Biopharm.,* 2, 43–103, 1974.
11. Harvey, D.L., Glazener, L., and Stratton, L., Detection of a 5-(3,4-dihydroxy-1,5-cyclohexadien 1 yl) metabolite of phenobarbital and mephobarbital in rat, guinea pig and human, *Res. Comm. Chem. Pathol. Pharm.,* 3, 557–565, 1972.
12. Tang, B.K., Kalow, W., and Grey, A.A., Metabolic fate of phenobarbital in man, *Drug Met. Disp.,* 7, 315–318, 1979.

3.6.6 Benzodiazepines

The benzodiazepines are among the most commonly encountered prescribed drugs in forensic analysis. It has been estimated that between 10 and 20% of the adult population in the Western world has ingested these drugs within any year.[1] They are prescribed for the treatment of anxiety or panic disorder, and as a sleeping aid, anticonvulsant, or muscle relaxant. Abuse of this family of drugs is observed primarily in two forms: persistent therapeutic use, i.e., use longer than generally recommended; and illicit use, in which the drug is self-administered without physician approval or supervision. The former type of abuse is common and typically involves use at low doses compared to the rarely encountered illicit use that may involve high doses and clear indications of acute intoxication and impairment.[2]

3.6.6.1 Pharmacology

Benzodiazepines exert central depressant effects on spinal reflexes, in part mediated by the brainstem reticular system.[3] For example, chlordiazepoxide depresses the duration of electrical after-discharge in the limbic system. Most benzodiazepines elevate the seizure threshold and therefore may be used as anticonvulsant medications. Diazepam, clonazepam, and clorazepate may be prescribed for this therapeutic purpose.

Benzodiazepines potentiate the inhibitory effects of GABA and neurophysiological studies have identified specific benzodiazepine binding sites in the cerebellum, cerebral cortex, and limbic system.[4] These sites are located in a complex protein macromolecule that includes $GABA_A$ receptors and a chloride channel. Binding of benzodiazepines is modulated by both GABA and chloride. Several benzodiazepine antagonists, such as flumazenil, and inverse agonists (compounds with opposite physiological effects to benzodiazepines), such as ethyl-β-carboline-3-carboxylate, competitively inhibit the binding of benzodiazepines.

Benzodiazepines are used as hynoptics because they have the ability to increase total sleep time. They demonstrate minimal cardiovascular effects, but do have the ability to increase heart rate and decrease cardiac output. Most CNS depressants, including the benzodiazepines, exhibit the ability to relax skeletal muscles. Clozapine, a dibenzodiazepine, is used in the treatment of schizophrenia. It has both sedative and antipsychotic actions, and is the only FDA-approved medication indicated for treatment-resistant schizophrenia, and for reducing the risk of suicidal behavior in patients with schizophrenia. This drug can have potentially life-threatening side effects, but appears to have no abuse potential and will not be considered further.

3.6.6.2 Absorption

The benzodiazepines comprise a large family of lipophilic acids (diazepam pKa = 3.4) with high octanol/water coefficients. They demonstrate a wide range of absorption rates when orally administered. Diazepam is absorbed rapidly, with peak concentrations occurring in 1 h in adults and as rapidly as 15 to 30 min in children. Following a single oral dose of 10 mg, peak blood diazepam concentrations averaged 148 ng/ml at 1 h, declining to 37 ng/ml by 24 h.[5] Bioavailability is dependent on drug formulation and route of administration, with approximately 100% bioavailability of diazepam when administered orally as tablets or in suspension, decreasing to 50 to 60% when administered intramuscularly or as suppositories. The rapid rate of absorption may be explained in part by the lipophilicity of diazepam. In contrast, less lipophilic benzodiazepines, such as lorazepam, exhibit slower rates of absorption, with an average time to peak blood concentration of 2 h. Prazepam and clorazepate act as prodrugs and are decarboxylated in the stomach to nordiazepam. Consequently, absorption is slowed and a delay occurs to the onset of action of these drugs.

3.6.6.3 Distribution

The benzodiazepines exhibit a two-compartment pharmacokinetic model.[6] Central compartment distribution is rapid and a slower distribution occurs into less perfused tissues, such as adipose. One-compartment pharmacokinetic models have been described for some benzodiazepines, such as lorazepam.[5] It is obvious that the more lipophilic benzodiazepines distribute more rapidly than less lipophilic drugs. Therefore, after a single dose, diazepam, a highly lipophilic drug, will have a shorter duration of action than lorazepam because it will be rapidly redistributed throughout the body. This may not be easily understood when considering the half-life because diazepam has a longer half-life (approximately 30 h) than lorazepam (12 to 15 h). Therefore, a long elimination half-life does not necessarily imply long duration of action after a single dose.

The majority of benzodiazepines are highly bound to plasma proteins (85 to 95%) with apparent volumes of distribution ranging from 1 to 3 L/kg[3] due to rapid removal from plasma to brain, lungs, and adipose tissue.

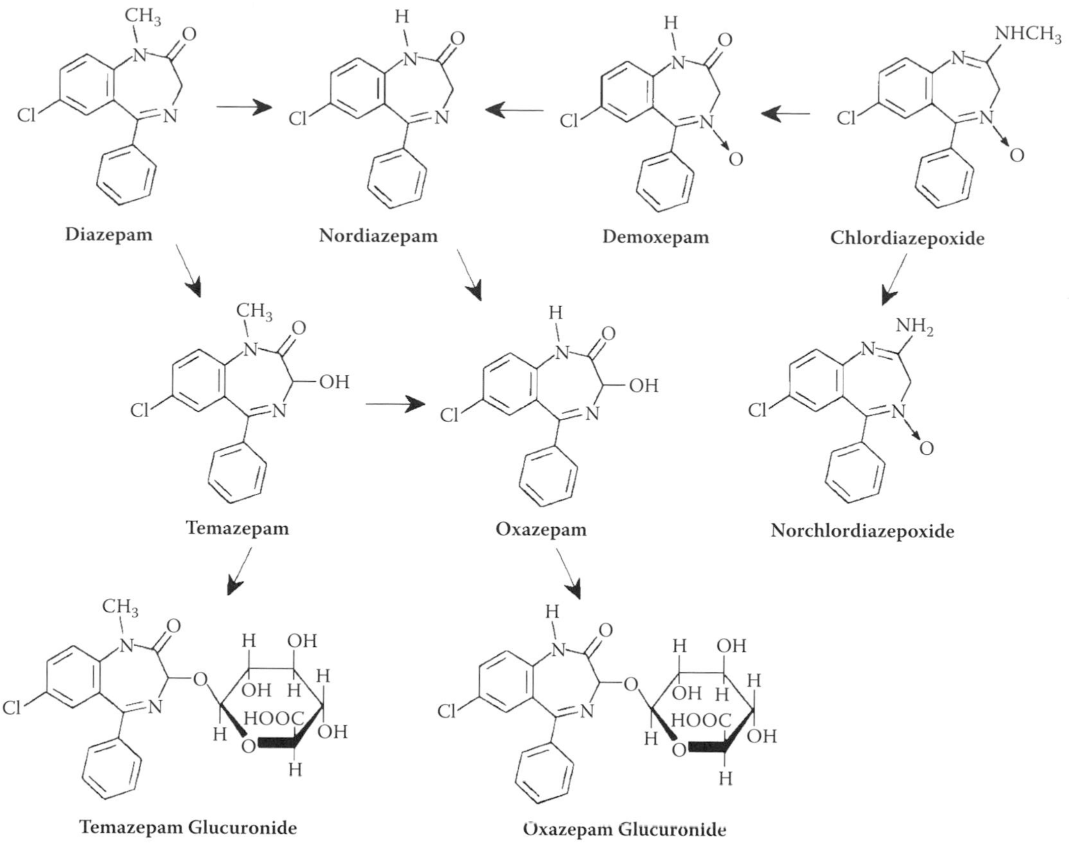

Figure 3.6.4 Metabolic pathway of the benzodiazepines.

3.6.6.4 *Metabolism and Elimination*

The benzodiazepines are extensively metabolized producing multiple metabolites, many of which share common pathways (Figure 3.6.4). Metabolic processes include hydroxylation, demethylation, and glucuronidation.

Diazepam undergoes *N*-demethylation to an active metabolite, nordiazepam. Both of these compounds are then hydroxylated to temazepam and oxazepam, respectively. These metabolites are also active, but are usually rapidly excreted and do not accumulate in plasma. Only small amounts of diazepam and nordiazepam are detected in urine, with 33% of a dose excreted as oxazepam glucuronide and another 20% excreted as various conjugates.[5] Oxazepam, the 3-hydroxy metabolite of nordiazepam, is rapidly conjugated with glucuronic acid to form an inactive metabolite. This conjugate accounts for 61% of an oral dose in the 48-h urine. Trace amounts of free drug are detected in the urine and other hydroxylation products account for less than 5% of a dose.[7] Lorazepam is also rapidly conjugated, forming the inactive product, lorazepam glucuronide. This conjugate is not rapidly excreted but may achieve plasma concentrations exceeding the parent drug, with an elimination half-life of approximately 16 h.[5] Approximately 75% of a dose is eliminated in the urine as the conjugate over 5 days. Minor metabolites, such as ring hydroxylation products and quinazoline derivatives, constitute another 14% of the dose. Trace amounts of free drug are found in urine.

Chlordiazepoxide is metabolized to four active metabolites. The drug is *N*-demethylated to norchlordiazepoxide, then deaminated to form demoxepam. These metabolites demonstrate pharmacological activity similar to the parent drug. Demoxepam is reduced to form nordiazepam, which accumulates in plasma with multiple dosing. Nordiazepam is then hydroxylated to produce oxazepam. Less than 1% of the dose is excreted unchanged in the urine with approximately 6% excreted as demoxepam and the rest as glucuronide conjugates.[8] Temazepam undergoes N-demethylation to form the active metabolite oxazepam. Both parent and metabolite are subsequently conjugated. An average of 82% of a dose is excreted in urine and 12% in the feces.[5]

Alprazolam, a triazolobenzodiazepine, is also extensively metabolized by oxidation and conjugation. Metabolites include a-hydroxyalprazolam, 4-hydroxyalprazolam, and a,4-dihydroxyalprazolam. The first two metabolites possess approximately 66 and 19% of the pharmacological activity of the parent, respectively. 3-Hydroxy-5-methyltriazolyl, an analogue of chlorobenzophenone, is also formed. Approximately 94% of a dose is excreted within 72 h with 80% excreted in the urine.[9] Flunitrazepam, the N-methyl-2´-fluoro analogue of nitrazepam, undergoes biotransformation via N-demethylation, 3-hydroxylation, and glucuronidation. In addition, the nitro group is reduced to an amine and is subsequently acetylated. Approximately 84% of a labeled dose is excreted in the urine over 1 week, and 11% is excreted in the feces.[5] Less than 0.5% is excreted unchanged. Norflunitrazepam and 7-aminoflunitrazepam may be detected in plasma for 1 day after a single dose of 2 mg. Triazolam is extensively metabolized by hydroxylation and subsequent conjugation. The major metabolite, 1-hydroxymethyltriazolam, possesses pharmacological activity. Only trace amounts of unchanged drug are excreted in the urine, with approximately 80% of a dose appearing in the urine in 72 h, mainly as glucuronide conjugates.

Since benzodiazepines are metabolized by the cytochrome P450 family of isozymes,[1] potential inhibitors of these may produce significant increases in blood concentrations of benzodiazepines. An example of this inhibition is the drug midazolam, administered as a pre-surgical anesthetic. Lam et al.[11] reported a mean increase in the area under the curve of midazolam by ketoconazole (772%) and nefazodone (444%) in a group of 40 healthy human subjects administered 200 mg ketoconazole per day and 400 mg nefazodone per day. The authors concluded that caution should be exercised when use of midazolam is warranted with potent CYP3A4 inhibitors.[11]

REFERENCES

1. Balter, M.B., Manheimer, D.I., Mellinger, G.D., and Uhlenhuth, E.H., A cross-national comparison of anti-anxiety/sedative drug use, *Curr. Med. Res. Opin.,* 8(Suppl. 4), 5–20, 1984.
2. Busto, U., Bendayan, R., and Sellers, E.M., Clinical pharmacokinetics of non-opiate abused drugs, *Clin. Pharmacokinet.,* 16, 1–26, 1989.
3. Hardman, J.G. and Limbird, L.E., Eds., *Goodman & Gilman's The Pharmacological Basis of Therapeutics,* McGraw-Hill, New York, 1996.
4. Potokar, J. and Nutt, D.J., Anxiolytic potential of benzodiazepines receptor partial agonists, *CNS Drugs,* 1, 305–315, 1994.
5. Baselt, R.C. and Cravey, R.H., *Disposition of Toxic Drugs and Chemicals in Man,* Chemical Toxicology Institute, Foster City, CA, 1995.
6. Bailey, L., Ward., M., and Musa, M.N., Clinical pharmacokinetics of benzodiazepines, *J. Clin. Pharmacol.,* 34, 804–811, 1994.
7. Knowles, J.A. and Ruelius, H.W., Absorption and excretion of 7-chloro-1,3-dihydro-3-hydroxy-5-phenyl-2H-1,4-benzodiazepin-2-one (oxazepam) in humans, *Arz. Forsch.,* 22, 687–692, 1972.
8. Schwartz, M.A., Pathways of metabolism of benzodiazepines. In *The Benzodiazepines*, Garattini, S., Mussini, E., and Randall, L.O., Eds., Raven Press, New York, 1973, 53–74.
9. Dawson, G.W., Jue, S.G., and Brogden, R.N., Alprazolam. A review of its pharmacodynamic properties and efficacy in the treatment of anxiety and depression, *Drugs,* 27, 132–147, 1984.
10. Moody, D.E., Drug interactions with benzodiazepines. In *Handbook of Drug Interactions: A Clinical and Forensic Guide,* Mozayani, A. and Raymon, L.P., Eds., Humana Press, Totowa, NJ, 2004.

11. Lam, Y.W., Alfaro, C.L., Ereshefsky, L., and Miller, M., Pharmacokinetic and pharmacodynamic interactions of oral midazolam with ketoconazole, fluoxetine, fluvoxamine, and nefazodone, *J. Clin. Pharmacol.*, 43(11), 1274–1282, 2003.

3.6.7 Cocaine

Cocaine is a naturally occurring alkaloid obtained from the plant *Erythroxylon coca* L. This plant grows in the Andes region of South America, ideally at elevations between 1500 and 5000 ft.[1] A second closely related species has been identified, *Erythroxylon novogranatense* H., and each species has one variety known as *E. coca* var. *ipadu* Plowman and *E. coca novogranatense* var. *truxillense*, respectively. Cocaine may also be chemically synthesized with cold aqueous succinaldehyde and cold aqueous methylamine, methylamine hydrochloride, and the potassium salt of acetone-dicarboxylic acid monomethyl ester.[2]

Cocaine is used medically by otorhinolaryngologists and plastic surgeons as an epinephrine cocaine mixture. Solutions for topical application are typically less than 4% cocaine hydrochloride. In the U.S. cocaine is a scheduled drug under the federal Controlled Substances Act of 1970. Refined cocaine, in the form of the base or hydrochloride salt, is self-administered by many routes, including snorting, smoking, genital application, and by injection.

3.6.7.1 Pharmacology

Cocaine inhibits the presynaptic reuptake of the neurotransmitters norepinehrine, serotonin, and dopamine at synaptic junctions. This results in increased concentrations in the synaptic cleft. Since norepinephrine acts within the sympathetic nervous system, increased sympathetic stimulation is produced. Physiological effects of this stimulation include tachycardia, vasoconstriction, mydriasis, and hyperthermia.[3] CNS stimulation results in increased alertness, diminished appetite, and increased energy. The euphoria or psychological stimulation produced by cocaine is thought to be related to the inhibition of serotonin and dopamine reuptake. Cocaine also acts as a local anesthetic due to its ability to block sodium channels in neuronal cells.[3]

3.6.7.2 Absorption

Cocaine is rapidly absorbed from mucous membranes and the pulmonary vasculature. However, the rate at which cocaine appears in the blood is dependent on the route of administration. Coca leaves have been chewed by native South Americans for more than 3000 years. Recent studies of the oral route of administration found that chewing powdered coca leaves containing between 17 and 48 mg of cocaine produced peak plasma concentrations of 11 to 149 ng/ml ($n = 6$) at 0.4 to 2 h after administration.[4] In another study, healthy male volunteers were administered cocaine hydrochloride (2 mg/kg) in gelatin capsules. Peak plasma concentrations of 104 to 424 ng/ml were achieved at 50 to 90 min. One of the most common routes of self-administration of cocaine in North America is the intranasal route. Wilkinson et al.[5] found that peak plasma concentrations of cocaine were reached 35 to 90 min after "snorting" but another study using equivalent doses found that peak plasma concentrations were achieved between 120 and 160 min.[6] Intravenous administration of 32-mg cocaine hydrochloride resulted in an average peak plasma concentration of 308 ng/ml at 5 min.[6] Cocaine may also be self-administered by the smoked route in the form of cocaine base, commonly called "crack" or by a process known as "free-basing" in which powdered cocaine hydrochloride is converted into its base form. In a study of six subjects who each smoked 50 mg of cocaine, the average peak plasma cocaine concentration of 203 ng/ml was achieved at 5 min.[7] The bioavailability of cocaine after smoking depends on several factors including the temperature of volatilization and drug loss in main- and sidestream smoke.

Perez-Reyes et al.[8] estimated that only 32% of a dose of cocaine base placed in a pipe is actually inhaled by the smoker. Cone[9] compared the pharmacokinetics and pharmacodynamics of cocaine by the intravenous, intranasal, and smoked routes of administration in the same subjects. Venous plasma cocaine concentrations peaked within 5 min by the intravenous and smoked routes. Estimated peak cocaine concentrations ranged from 98 to 349 ng/ml and 154 to 345 ng/ml after intravenous administration of 25-mg cocaine hydrochloride and 42-mg cocaine base by the smoked route, respectively. After dosing by the intranasal route (32 mg cocaine hydrochloride) estimated peak plasma cocaine concentrations ranged from 40 to 88 ng/ml after 0.39 to 0.85 h.[9] In this study, the average bioavailability of cocaine was 70.1% by the smoked route, and 93.7% by the intranasal route. Jenkins et al.[10] described the correlation between pharmacological effects and plasma cocaine concentrations in seven volunteers after they had smoked 10 to 40 mg cocaine. The mean plasma cocaine concentration 2 min after smoking 40 mg cocaine was 153 ± 107.5 ng/ml. Peak concentrations ranged from 160.8 ± 99.1 ng/ml. Increases in pupil diameter, systolic and diastolic blood pressure, heart rate, and subjective measures of drug effect occurred early after drug administration, with maximum effects observed at 2 min (first measure) for blood pressure and subjective measures, or after a brief delay (at 5 to 10 min post dose) for others, notably heart rate and pupil diameter.

3.6.7.3 Distribution

After an intravenous dose of radiolabeled cocaine to rats, the highest concentrations were found in the brain, spleen, kidney, and lung after 15 min, with the lowest concentrations in the blood, heart, and muscle.[11] Plasma protein binding in humans is approximately 91% at low concentrations.[11] Cocaine binds to the plasma protein, albumin, and also to $\alpha 1$-acid glycoprotein. The steady-state volume of distribution is large (1.6 to 2.7 L/kg), reflecting extensive extravascular distribution.[12] In 1991 Ambre et al.[13] studied the pharmacokinetics of benzoylecgonine in nine human volunteers. The metabolite is much more polar than the parent and liphophobic, explaining why the measured mean V_d was only 0.71.

A two-compartment open linear model has been described for the pharmacokinetic profile of cocaine after intravenous administration.[14] The distribution phase after cocaine administration is rapid and the elimination half-life estimated as 31 to 82 min.[14] Cone[9] fitted data to a two-compartment model with bolus input and first-order elimination for the intravenous and smoked routes. For the intranasal route, data were fitted to a two-compartment model with first-order absorption and first-order elimination. The average elimination half-life ($t_1/2\beta$) was 244 min after intravenous administration, 272 min after smoked administration, and 299 min after intranasal administration.

The disposition of cocaine in nontraditional testing matrices has been described. For example, Lester et al.[15] measured cocaine and benzoylecgonine (BE) concentrations in skin, interstitial fluid (IF), sebum, and stratum corneum in five volunteers after the intravenous 1-h infusion of 1 mg/kg cocaine d_5. Peak cocaine concentrations in the skin were achieved at 1.5 h and were undetectable after 6 h. No BE was measured in the skin. Peak cocaine concentrations were achieved at 5 h after administration in the IF and were nondetectable by 24 h. BE was found in the IF. In the sebum peak cocaine concentrations occurred between 3 to 24 h but in the stratum corneum cocaine was detected in only one subject.

3.6.7.4 Metabolism

In humans, the principal route of metabolism of cocaine is by hydrolysis of the ester linkages. Pseudocholinesterase and liver esterases produce the inactive metabolite, ecgonine methyl ester (EME) (Figure 3.6.5). The second major metabolite, BE, is formed spontaneously at physiological pH. In addition, there is evidence that BE may be formed enzymatically from cocaine by liver carboxylesterases. N-Demethylation of BE produces benzoylnorecgonine. Further metabolism of EME and BE produces ecgonine. Further hydrolysis of cocaine and BE produce minor metabolites,

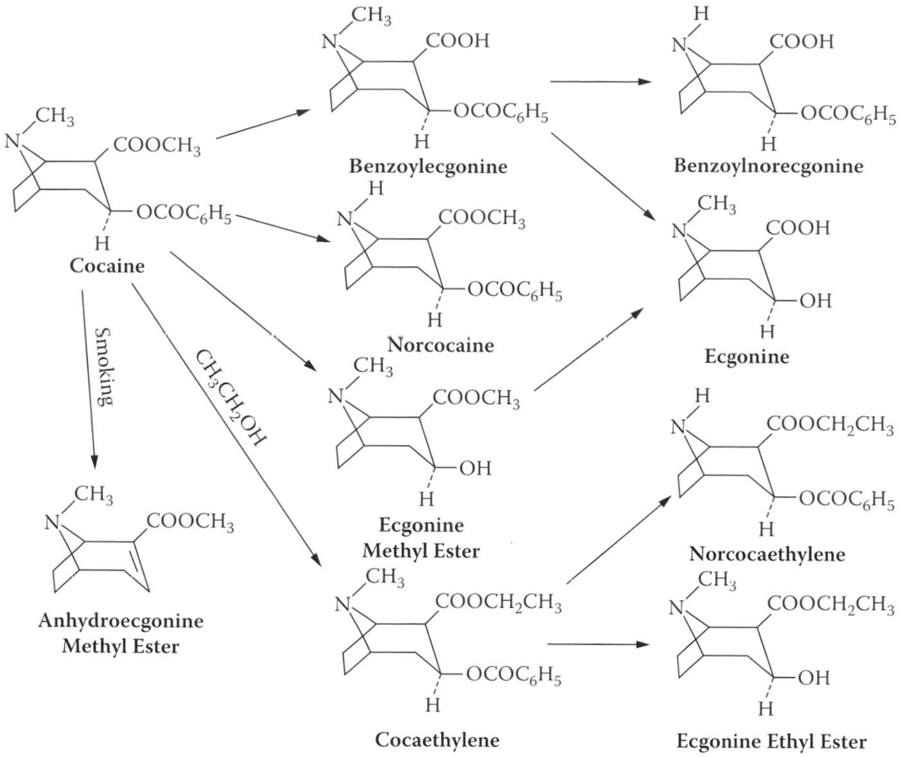

Figure 3.6.5 Metabolic pathway of cocaine.

meta- and para-hydroxy-cocaine and -BE. The proportion of each metabolite produced and the activity of the individual metabolites have yet to be completely determined.

Cocaine may be *N*-demethylated by the cytochrome P450 system to produce an active metabolite, norcocaine. Further breakdown produces *N*-hydroxynorcocaine and norcocaine nitroxide. Further metabolism produces a highly reactive free radical that is thought to be responsible for the hepatotoxicity observed in cocaine users.[1]

When cocaine is coadministered with ethanol, cocaethylene (CE) is formed in the liver by transesterification by liver methylesterase. CE may also be formed by fatty acid ethyl synthase.[16] This lipophilic compound crosses the blood–brain barrier and is known to contribute to the psychological effects produced by cocaine.[1] Harris et al.[17] administered deuterium-labeled cocaine (0.3 to 1.2 mg/kg) intravenously 1 h after an oral dose of ethanol (1 g/kg) to ten volunteers. When coadministered with ethanol, $17 \pm 6\%$ (mean ± S.D.) of the cocaine was converted to cocaethylene. Ethanol ingestion prior to cocaine administration decreased urine BE levels by 48%. When cocaine is smoked, a pyrolysis product, anhydroecgonine methyl ester (AEME), is formed. Therefore, the presence of this compound indicates exposure to smoked cocaine. The pharmacological and toxicological properties of this compound have not been studied.

3.6.7.5 Elimination

Approximately 85 to 90% of a cocaine dose is recovered in the 24-h urine.[18] Unchanged drug accounts for 1 to 9% of the dose depending on urine pH, BE, 35 to 54%, and EME, 32 to 49%. In one study, excretion data were obtained from subjects administered a bolus intravenous injection of cocaine followed by an intravenous infusion, supplying total doses of 253, 444, and 700 mg cocaine.[19] Elimination half-lives averaged 0.8, 4.5, and 3.1 h, for cocaine, BE, and EME, respectively. After intranasal application of 1.5 mg/kg, urine cocaine concentrations averaged 6.7 mg/L during the first hour, and BE concentrations peaked between 4 to 8 hours at 35 mg/L.[11] Oral ingestion of 25 mg cocaine by a single individual resulted in a peak urine BE concentration of 7.9 mg/L in the 6- to 12-h collection period, with a decline to 0.4 mg/L by 48 h.[20] Oral consumption of coca tea of Peruvian origin containing approximately 4 mg of cocaine resulted in a peak urine BE concentration of 3.9 mg/L after 10 h in one individual.[21] The cumulative urinary excretion of BE after approximately 48 h was 3.1 mg. Consumption of coca tea of Bolivian origin by the same individual, containing a similar amount of cocaine, resulted in a peak urine BE level of 4.9 mg/L at 3.5 h.[21] The cumulative BE excreted in urine was 2.6 mg. The minor metabolites, including the p- and m-hydroxy metabolites, and also the pyrolysis product, AEME, have been detected in urine after cocaine administration.[22,23]

REFERENCES

1. Karch, S., *The Pathology of Drug Abuse,* CRC Press, Boca Raton, FL, 1993.
2. Saferstein, R., *Forensic Science Handbook,* Vol. II, Prentice Hall, Englewood Cliffs, NJ, 1988.
3. Warner, E.A., Cocaine abuse, *Ann. Int. Med.,* 119(3), 226–235, 1993.
4. Holmstedt, B., Lindgren, J., Rivier, L., and Plowman, T., Cocaine in blood of coca chewers, *J. Ethnopharm.,* 1, 69–78, 1979.
5. Wilkinson, P., Van Dyke, C., Jatlow, P., Barash, P., and Byck, R., Intranasal and oral cocaine kinetics, *Clin. Pharmacol. Ther.,* 27, 386–394, 1980.
6. Javaid, J.I., Musa, M.N., Fischman, M., Schuster, C.R., and Davis, J.M., Kinetics of cocaine in humans after intravenous and intranasal administration, *Biopharm. Drug Disp.,* 4, 9–18, 1983.
7. Jeffcoat, A.R., Perez-Reyes, M., and Hill, J.M., Cocaine disposition in humans after intravenous injection, nasal insufflation (snorting), or smoking, *Drug Met. Disp.,* 17, 153–159, 1989.
8. Perez-Reyes, M., DiGuiseppi, S., Ondrusek, G., Jeffcoat, A.R., and Cook, C.E., Free base cocaine smoking, *Clin. Pharmacol. Ther.,* 32, 459–465, 1982.
9. Cone, E.J., Pharmacokinetics and pharmacodynamics of cocaine, *J. Anal. Toxicol.,* 19, 459–478, 1995.
10. Jenkins, A.J., Keenan, R.M., Henningfield, J.E., and Cone, E.J., Correlation between pharmacological effects and plasma cocaine concentrations after smoked administration, *J. Anal. Toxicol.,* 26, 382–392, 2002.
11. Busto, U., Bendayan, R., and Sellers, E.M., Clinical pharmacokinetics of non-opiate abused drugs, *Clin. Pharmacokinet.,* 16, 1–26, 1989.
12. Baselt, R.C. and Cravey, R.H., *Disposition of Toxic Drugs and Chemicals in Man,* 4th ed., Chemical Toxicology Institute, Foster City, CA, 1995.
13. Ambre, J.J., Connelly, T.J., and Ruo, T.I., A kinetic model of benzoylecgonine disposition after cocaine administration in humans, *J. Anal. Toxicol.,* 15(1), 17–20, 1991.
14. Chow, M.J., Ambre, J.J., Ruo, T.I., Atkinson, A.J., and Bowsher, D.J., Kinetics of cocaine distribution, elimination and chronotropic effects, *Clin. Pharmacol. Ther.,* 38:318–324, 1985.
15. Lester, L., Uemura, N., Ademola, J., Harkey, M.R., Nath, R.P., Kim, S.J., Jerschow, E., Henderson, G.L., Mendelson, J., and Jones, R.T., Disposition of cocaine in skin, interstitial fluid, sebum, and stratum corneum, *J. Anal. Toxicol.,* 26, 547–553, 2002.
16. Isenschmid, D.S., Cocaine. In *Principles of Forensic Toxicology,* 2nd ed., B.S. Levine, Ed., AACC Press, Washington, D.C., 2003.
17. Harris, D.S., Everhart, E.T., Mendelson, J., and Jones, R.T., The pharmacology of cocaethylene in humans following cocaine and ethanol administration, *Drug Alcohol Depend.,* 72(2), 169–182, 2003.
18. Jatlow, P., Cocaine: analysis, pharmacokinetics and disposition, *Yale J. Biol. Med.,* 61, 105–113, 1988.
19. Ambre, J., Ruo, T.I., Nelson, J., and Belknap, S., Urinary excretion of cocaine, benzoylecgonine, and ecgonine methyl ester in humans, *J. Anal. Toxicol.,* 12:301–306, 1988.
20. Baselt, R. and Chang, R., Urinary excretion of cocaine and benzoylecgonine following oral ingestion in a single subject, *J. Anal. Toxicol.,* 11, 81–82, 1987.
21. Jenkins, A.J., Llosa, T., Montoya, I., and Cone, E.J., Identification and quantitation of alkaloids in coca tea, *Forensic Sci. Int.,* 77, 179–189, 1996.

22. Jacob, P., III, Lewis, E.R., Elias-Baker, B.A., and Jones, R., A pyrolysis product, anhydroecgonine methyl ester (methylecgonidine) is in the urine of cocaine smokers, *J. Anal. Toxicol.*, 14, 353–357, 1990.
23. Zhang, J.Y. and Foltz, R.L., Cocaine metabolism in man: identification of four previously unreported cocaine metabolites in human urine, *J. Anal. Toxicol.*, 14, 201–205, 1990.

3.6.8　Lysergic Acid Diethylamide

Lysergic acid diethylamide (LSD) is an indolealkylamine discovered by Albert Hoffman of Sandoz Laboratories in 1943.[1] It may be synthesized from lysergic acid and diethylamine. Lysergic acid, a naturally occurring ergot alkaloid, is present in grain parasitized by the fungus *Claviceps purpurea*. A closely related alkaloid, lysergic acid amide, is present in morning glory seeds and the Hawaiian baby wood rose.[1] In the 1950s, LSD was used as an aid in the treatment of alcoholism, opioid addiction, psychoneurosis, and sexual disorders, but currently it is classified under Schedule I of the federal Controlled Substances Act with no accepted medical use in the U.S. It is available illicitly as a powder, tablet, or gelatin capsule, or impregnated in sugar cubes, gelatin squares, blotter paper, or postage stamps.

3.6.8.1　Pharmacology

LSD is a potent centrally acting drug. The D-isomer is pharmacologically active while the L-isomer is apparently inactive.[1] Neuropharmacological studies have shown that LSD exerts a selective inhibitory effect on the brain's raphe system by causing a cessation of the spontaneous firing of serotonin-containing neurons of the dorsal and median raphe nuclei. In this way, LSD acts as an indirect serotonin antagonist. However, inhibition of raphe firing is not sufficient to explain the psychotomimetic effects of LSD because the compound lisuride is a more potent inhibitor of the raphe system yet does not demonstrate hallucinogenic potential in humans. Therefore, other post-synaptic mechanisms such as action on glutamate or serotonin receptors may be involved.[2] Also, there is evidence that LSD indirectly exerts effects on the cytoskeleton by reducing the amount of serotonin released by the raphe system.[3] LSD produces sympathomimetic, parasympathomimetic, and neuromuscular effects, which include mydriasis, lacrimation, tachycardia, and tremor.

3.6.8.2　Absorption

LSD may be self-administered orally, nasally, or by parenteral ingestion; however, the oral route is the most common. Doses of 50 to 300 µg are ingested, with a minimum effective dose of 20 to 25 µg. Absorption is rapid and complete regardless of the route of administration. However, food in the stomach slows absorption when ingested. Effects are observed within 5 to 10 min, with psychosis evident after 15 to 20 min. Peak effects have been reported 30 to 90 min after dosing; effects decline after 4 to 6 h.[5] The duration of effects may be 8 to 12 h.

Pharmacokinetic studies in humans are limited with much of the data dating from the 1960s. Following intravenous administration of 2 µg/kg, a peak plasma LSD concentration of 5 ng/ml was observed after 1 h.[1] At 8 h, the plasma concentration had declined to 1 ng/ml.[1] In much more recent studies a method using liquid chromatography with electrospray ionization and tandem mass spectrometric detection has been developed and validated for LSD and iso-LSD. Using this technique the lower limit for quantitative determination was 0.02 µg/L for LSD and iso-LSD. Peak plasma levels were slightly higher than earlier reports (case 1 plasma LSD = 0.31 µg/L, iso-LSD = 0.27 µg/L and in a second case LSD = 0.24 µg/L, iso-LSD = 0.6 µg/L in urine).

3.6.8.3　Distribution

Plasma protein binding of LSD is >80%. As the drug penetrates the CNS, it is concentrated in the visual brain areas, and the limbic and reticular activating systems, correlating with perceived

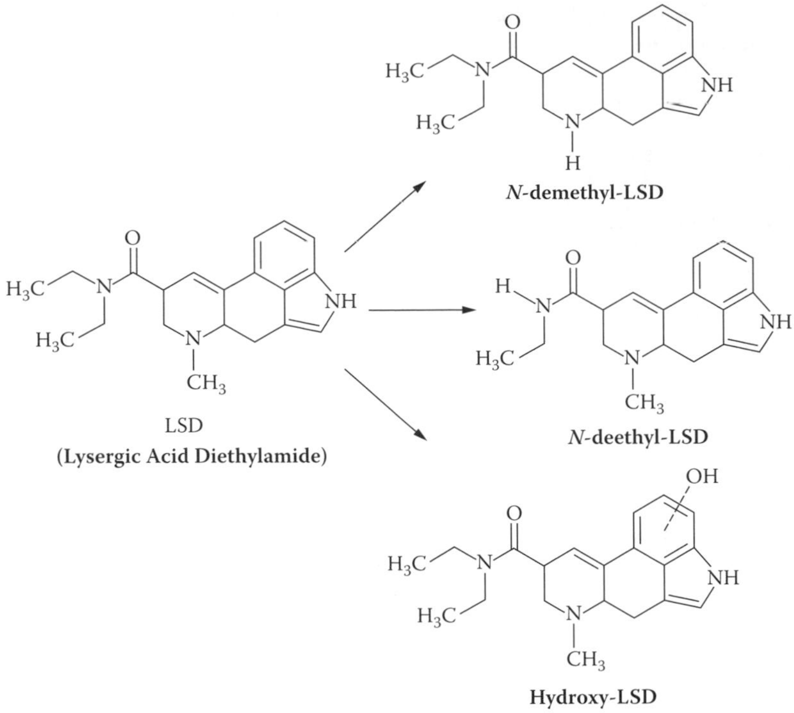

Figure 3.6.6 Metabolic pathway of LSD.

effects. LSD is also found in the liver, spleen, and lungs.[4] The volume of distribution is reported to be low at 0.28 L/kg.[1] Wagner et al.[6] described a two-compartment open model for LSD with an elimination half-life of 3 h.

3.6.8.4 *Metabolism and Excretion*

LSD metabolism was investigated using MS-MS. Metabolites were determined using MS-MS. The main metabolite was 2-oxo-3-hydroxy-LSD (O-H-LSD) present in urine at the concentrations of 2.5 and 6.6 µg/L, respectively, for case 1 and 2, but it was not detected at all in plasma. Nor-LSD was also found in urine at 0.15 and 0.01 µg/L levels. Nor-iso-LSD, lysergic acid ethylamide (LAE), trioxylated-LSD, lysergic acid ethyl-2-hydroxyethylamide (LEO), and 13- and 14-hydroxy-LSD and their glucuronide conjugates were detected in urine using specific MS-MS transitions.[5]

The metabolism and elimination of LSD in humans has received limited study. Animal studies demonstrated extensive biotransformation via *N*-demethylation, *N*-deethylation, and hydroxylation to inactive metabolites (Figure 3.6.6).[7] In humans, demethylation and aromatic hydroxylation occur to produce *N*-desmethyl-LSD and 13- and 14-hydroxy-LSD. Hydroxylated metabolites undergo glucu-ronidation to form water-soluble conjugates. Excretion into the bile accounts for approximately 80% of a dose.[4] Concentrations of unchanged drug ranged from 1 to 55 ng/ml in the 24-h urine after ingestion of 200 to 400 µg LSD in humans.[8] LSD or its metabolites were detectable for 34 to 120 h following a 300-µg oral dose in seven human subjects.[9] The clearance of LSD in humans is unknown.

REFERENCES

1. Baselt, R.C. and Cravey, R.H., *Disposition of Toxic Drugs and Chemicals in Man,* 4th ed., Chemical Toxicology Institute, Foster City, CA, 1995.

2. Goldberger, B.A., Lysergic acid diethylamide. In-service training and continuing education AACC/TDM, American Association for Clinical Chemistry, Inc., Washington, D.C. 14(6), 99–100, 1993.
3. Van Woerkom, A.E., The major hallucinogens and the central cytoskeleton: an association beyond coincidence? Towards sub-cellular mechanisms in schizophrenia, *Med. Hypoth.*, 31, 7–15, 1990.
4. Canezin, J., Cailleux, A., Turcant, A., Le Bouil, A., Harry, P., and Allain, P., Determination of LSD and its metabolites in human biological fluids by high-performance liquid chromatography with electrospray tandem mass spectrometry, *J. Chromatogr. B Biomed. Sci. Appl.*, 765(1), 15–27, 2001.
5. Leikin, J.B., Karantz, A.J., Zell-Kanter, M., Barkin, R.L., and Hryhorczuk, D.O., Clinical features and management of intoxication due to hallucinogenic drugs, *Med. Toxicol. Adverse Drug Exp.*, 4(5), 324–350, 1989.
6. Wagner, J.G., Aghajanian, G.K., and Bing, O.H.L., Correlation of performance test scores with "tissue concentration" of lysergic acid diethylamide in human subjects, *Clin. Pharmacol. Ther.*, 9, 635–638, 1968.
7. Axelrod, J., Brady, R.O., Witkop, B., and Evarts, E.V., Metabolism of lysergic acid diethylamide, *Nature*, 178, 143–144, 1956.
8. Taunton-Rigby, A., Sher, S.E., and Kelley, P.R., Lysergic acid diethylamide: radioimmunoassay, *Science*, 181, 165–166, 1973.
9. Peel, H.W. and Boynton, A.L., Analysis of LSD in urine using radioimmunoassay — excretion and storage effects, *Can. Soc. For. Sci. J.*, 13, 23–28, 1980.

3.6.9 Marijuana

The term "marijuana" refers to all parts of the plant *Cannabis sativa* L., whether growing or not: the seeds; resin extracted from any part of such plant; and every compound, salt, derivative or mixture; but does not include the mature stalks, fiber produced from the stalks, or oil or cake prepared from the seeds.[1] *Cannabis sativa* L. is an annual plant that grows in all parts of the world to a height of 16 to 18 ft. Commercially, it is cultivated for hemp production, with the bulk of the plant consisting of stalks with very little foliage, except at the apex. In contrast, the wild plant and those cultivated illegally possess numerous branches as the psychoactive ingredient is concentrated in the leaves and flowering tops. There may be significant differences in the gross appearance of marijuana plants due to climatic and soil conditions, the closeness of other plants during growth, and the origin of the seed. Marijuana is the crude drug derived from the plant *Cannabis sativa* L., a plant that is currently accepted as belonging to a family (Cannabaceae) that has only one genus (*Cannabis*) with only one species (*sativa*) that is highly variable.[2]

In 1980 the total number of natural compounds identified in *C. sativa* L. was 423[3] By 1995 the number had risen to 483, and recently 6 new compounds, 4 new cannabinoids and 2 new flavonoids, have been described.[4]

The major psychoactive constituent of marijuana is delta-9-tetrahydrocannabinol, commonly referred to as THC. Different parts of the plant contain varying concentrations of THC, with leaves containing <1% to 10% THC by weight, and hashish, a resin prepared from the flowering tops, containing approximately 15% THC. THC may be synthesized using citral and olivetol in boron trifluoride and methylene chloride.[5] Although no reports have appeared within the published peer-reviewed literature, persistent reports from the enforcement community suggest that intensive cross-breeding has led to production of plants that have a THC content well over 20%. These "super" plants appear to be grown mainly along the Canadian–American border, primarily by Asian gangs.

3.6.9.1 Pharmacology

Marijuana is typically self-administered orally or by smoking in doses of 5 to 20 mg.[6] It may produce a variety of pharmacological effects including sedation, euphoria, hallucinations, and temporal distortion. In addition, THC possesses activity at benzodiazepine, opioid, and cannabinoid receptors and also exerts effects on prostaglandin synthesis, DNA, RNA, and protein metabolism.[7,8] Early workers thought that THC effects were nonspecific, but in the late 1980s a specific cannabinoid receptor was identified in the brains of rats. It is now apparent that there are two types of cannabinoid receptor — CB1 and CB2 — and these receptors are the primary targets of endogenous cannabinoids (endocannabinoids). THC binds to both cannabinoid receptors. The CB1 receptor is mostly found in the brain, while the CB2 receptor is found in immune tissues such as the spleen, thymus, and tonsils[8] but not in the brain. Specific antagonists exist for each of the CB1 and CB2 receptors.

Cannabinoid-coupled G protein–coupled receptors are involved in the control of many processes, including metabolic regulation, craving, pain, anxiety, bone growth, and immune function. The exogenous cannabinoids found in marijuana plants can also exert effects via G(i/o) proteins, negatively modulating cyclic AMP levels, and activating the inward rectifying K(+) channels.[9] Manipulation at either receptor site may have important clinical consequences and therapies involving cannabinoid receptors are under development. Manipulation at either receptor site may have important clinical consequences and therapies based on cannabinoid–receptor interactions are under development. Cannabinoids mediate a decrease in blood pressure and can suppress cardiac contractility in hypertension. Conversely, if the CB1-mediated cardiodepressor and vasodilator effects of anandamide are enhanced (by blocking its hydrolysis), blood pressure tends to normalize.[10] Many clinical developments taking advantage of these properties are likely to occur. By the time of publication of this book, rimonabant (Acompliat™), a C1 blocking agent, will have been approved for weight loss by the FDA.[11]

3.6.9.2 Absorption

Marijuana is commonly self-administered by the smoked route by rolling dried marijuana leaves in tobacco paper and smoking as a cigarette. Smoking results in rapid drug delivery from the lungs to the brain. However, loss of drug occurs during the smoking process due to pyrolysis and sidestream smoke. In an *in vitro* study in which loss due to sidestream smoke was minimized, Davis et al.[12] reported a 30% loss of THC due to pyrolysis. Sidestream THC losses of 40 to 50% have been reported. Once THC reaches the lungs, it is rapidly absorbed. Peak plasma THC concentrations of 100 to 200 ng/ml occur after 3 to 8 min and THC is present in blood after the first puff from a marijuana cigarette. Mean ± SD THC concentrations of 7.0 ± 8.1 ng/ml and 18.1 ± 12.0 ng/ml were observed after the first inhalation of low- or high-dose marijuana cigarettes (1.75%, 3.55%), respectively.[13] Peak concentrations occurred at 9 min after the first puff. Lemberger et al.[14] demonstrated that physiological and subjective measures of drug effect occurred simultaneously with the rise in blood THC concentrations.

After oral administration, THC is 90 to 95% absorbed. However, the oral route results in lower peak plasma concentrations at a later time. Perez-Reyes et al. reported a mean peak plasma THC concentration of 6 ng/ml after ingestion of 20 mg.[15] Wall and Perez-Reyes noted that peak plasma THC concentrations occurred 30 min after intravenous administration of 4 to 5 mg, with a mean concentration ($n = 7$) of 62 ng/ml.[16] Reported values for the bioavailability of THC after smoking have ranged from 18 to 50%.[14] This wide range reflects the large inter- and intrasubject variability that occurs in smoking dynamics.[18] Altering the number, duration, and spacing of puffs, the length of time the inhalation is held, and the inhalation volume or depth of puff[19] may vary the amount of drug delivered. Measures to minimize the loss of side- and mainstream smoke as well as optimizing the temperature for drug volatilization will, in turn, increase the amount of drug available for delivery to the lungs. One facet of smoking that cannot be controlled by the smoker is drug deposition on non- or poorly absorbing surfaces within the body. Deposition outside of the lungs is usually a function of drug particle or vapor size. Drug may be deposited in the nasopharyngeal region or the upper bronchial tree. This reduces the amount of drug reaching the lung alveoli where rapid absorption into the blood and subsequent transport to the brain occurs.

Ohlsson et al. compared the bioavailability of THC after intravenous, smoked, and oral administration. Eleven healthy subjects were administered 5 mg intravenously, 19 mg smoked, and 20 mg orally. Plasma concentrations rose rapidly after intravenous administration, reaching 161 to 316 ng/ml at 3 min and declining rapidly thereafter. Peak plasma concentrations also occurred at 3 min after smoking, with lower concentrations of THC ranging from 33 to 118 ng/ml. The plasma concentration time curve after smoking was similar to that obtained after intravenous administration but at lower concentrations. In contrast, low THC concentrations were found after oral administration, with much higher intersubject variability. The authors determined the bioavailability of THC to be 8 to 24% after smoking compared with 4 to 12% after oral ingestion.[20]

3.6.9.3 Distribution

THC is 97 to 99% plasma protein bound with little present in red blood cells. Due to its lipophilicity, THC distributes rapidly into tissues. Highly perfused organs, such as the brain, accumulate THC rapidly after administration, whereas THC distributes more slowly into poorly perfused tissues such as fat.[21] Harvey et al. reported finding maximum THC concentrations in the brains of mice 30 min after a single intravenous dose. The distribution of THC into various tissues and organs such as brain, liver, heart, kidney, salivary glands, breast milk, fat, and lung is reflected in the large volume of distribution (4 to 14 L/kg).[20,22] Hunt and Jones proposed a four-compartment model to describe four tissue composites into which THC distributes after intravenous injection.[23] They observed average half-lives of 1 min, 4 min, 1 h, and 19 h to describe these compartments. They concluded that a "pseudoequilibrium" is achieved between plasma and tissues 6 h after an intravenous dose. Thereafter, THC is slowly eliminated as THC diffuses from tissue to the blood. The terminal elimination half-life is approximately 1 day but has been reported to be 3 to 13 days in frequent users.[24,25]

3.6.9.4 Metabolism and Excretion

Metabolism is the major route of elimination of THC from the body as little is excreted unchanged. In humans, over 20 metabolites have been identified in urine and feces.[26] Metabolism in humans involves allylic oxidation, epoxidation, aliphatic oxidation, decarboxylation, and conjugation. The two monohydroxy metabolites (Figure 3.6.7) 11-hydroxy (OH)-THC and 8-beta-hydroxy THC are active, with the former exhibiting similar activity and disposition to THC, while the latter is less potent. Plasma concentrations of 11-OH-THC are typically <10% of the THC concentration after marijuana smoking. Two additional hydroxy compounds have been identified, namely, 8-alpha-hydroxy-THC and 8,11-dihydroxy-THC, and are believed to be devoid of THC-like activity. Oxidation of 11-OH-THC produces the inactive metabolite, 11-nor-9-carboxy-THC, or THC-COOH. This metabolite may be conjugated with glucuronic acid and is excreted in substantial amounts in the urine.

The average plasma clearance is 600 to 980 ml/min with a blood clearance of 1.0 to 1.6 L/min, which is close to hepatic blood flow. This indicates that the rate of metabolism of THC is dependent on hepatic blood flow. Approximately 70% of a dose of THC is excreted in the urine (30%) and feces (40%) within 72 h.[26] Because a significant amount of the metabolites are excreted in the feces, enterohepatic recirculation of THC metabolites may occur. This would also contribute to the slow elimination and hence long plasma half-life of THC. Unchanged THC is present in low amounts in the urine and 11-OH-THC accounts for only 2% of a dose.

The remainder of the urinary metabolites consist of conjugates of THC-COOH and unidentified acidic products. Following a single smoked 10-mg dose of THC, urinary THC-COOH concentrations peaked within 16 h of smoking, at levels of 6 to 129 ng/ml ($n = 10$).[27] Huestis and Cone[25] reported a mean (± SEM) urinary excretion half-life for THC-COOH of 31.5 ± 1 h and 28.6 ± 1.5 h for six healthy volunteers after administration of a single marijuana cigarette containing 1.75

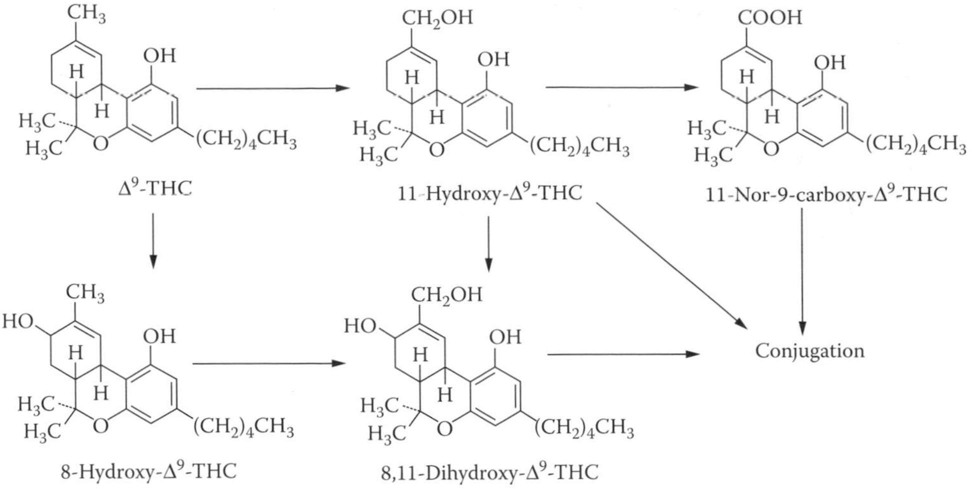

Figure 3.6.7 Metabolic pathway of delta-9-THC.

or 3.55% THC, respectively. Passive exposure to marijuana smoke may also produce detectable urinary metabolite concentrations. Cone et al. exposed five volunteers to the smoke of 16 marijuana cigarettes (2.8% THC content) for 1 h each day for 6 consecutive days.[24] After the first session, THC-COOH concentrations in urine ranged from 0 to 39 ng/ml. A maximum THC-COOH concentration of 87 ng/ml was detected in one subject on day 4 of the study.

THC may be ingested orally by consuming food products containing the seeds or oil of the hemp plant. Ingestion of 0.6 mg/day (equivalent to 125 ml hemp oil containing 5 µg/g of THC or 300 g hulled seeds at 2 µg/g) for 10 days resulted in urine THC-COOH concentrations of <6 ng/ml.[28] The maximum urinary concentration of THC-COOH in another study after ingestion of hemp oil containing 0.39 to 0.47 mg THC/day for 5 days was 5.4 to 38.2 ng/ml (n = 7).[20] After oral administration of a higher dose (7.5 and 14.8 mg THC/day) peak concentrations of THC-COOH ranged from 19.0 to 436 ng/ml. Controlled studies have shown that at the federally mandated cannabinoid cutoffs, it is possible but unlikely for a urine specimen to test positive after ingestion of manufacturer-recommended doses of low-THC hemp oils.[29] On the other hand, patients taking Marinol®, the synthetic form of THC approved by the FDA for the control of nausea and vomiting in cancer patients, will almost certainly test positive. Dronabinol or synthetic THC is present in Marinol® capsules and ElSohly et al. found that within 24 h of administering a single 15-mg dose of dronabinol to four subjects, peak urine THC-COOH concentrations were between 189 and 362 ng/ml.[30]

REFERENCES

1. Farnsworth, N.R., Pharmacognosy and chemistry of "*Cannabis sativa*," *J. Am. Pharm. Assoc.*, 9(8), 410–414, 1969.
2. ElSohly, M.A. and Slade, D., Chemical constituents of marijuana: The complex mixture of natural cannabinoids, *Life Sci.*, 78(5), 539–548, 2005.
3. Turner, C.E., ElSohly, M.A., and Boeren, E.G., Constituents of *Cannabis sativa* L. XVII. A review of the natural constituents, *J. Nat. Prod.*, 43(2), 169–234, 1980.
4. Ross, S.A. et al., Flavonoid glycosides and cannabinoids from the pollen of *Cannabis sativa* L., *Phytochem. Anal.*, 16(1), 45–48, 2005.
5. Lander N. et al., Total synthesis of cannabidiol and delta1-tetrahydrocannabinol metabolites, *J. Chem Soc.* (Perkin 1), 1, 8–16, 1976.
6. Kiplinger, G.F. and Manno, J.E., Dose-response relationships to cannabis in human subjects, *Pharmacol. Rev.*, 23(4), 339–347, 1971.

7. Cabral, G.A. and Staab, A., Effects on the immune system, *Handb. Exp. Pharmacol.*, 168, 385–423, 2005.

8. Vaughan, C.W. and Christie, M.J., An analgesic role for cannabinoids, *Med. J. Aust.*, 173(5), 270–272, 2000.

9. Petrzilka, T. and Demuth, L.M., Synthesis of (–)-11 hydroxy-delta8-6a,10a-transtetrahydrocannabinol, *Helv. Chim. Acta*, 57(1), 121–150, 1974.

10. Begg, M. et al., Evidence for novel cannabinoid receptors, *Pharmacol. Ther.*, 106(2), 133–145, 2005.

11. Heusser, K. et al., Influence of sibutramine treatment on sympathetic vasomotor tone in obese subjects, *Clin. Pharmacol. Ther.*, 79(5), 500–508, 2006.

12. Perez-Reyes, M. et al., Passive inhalation of marihuana smoke and urinary excretion of cannabinoids, *Clin. Pharmacol. Ther.*, 34(1), 36–41, 1983.

13. Huestis, M.A. et al., Characterization of the absorption phase of marijuana smoking, *J. Clin. Pharmacol. Ther.*, 52(1), 31–41, 1992.

14. Lemberger, L. et al., Marihuana: Studies on the disposition and metabolism of delta-9-tetrahydrocannabinol in man, *Science*, 170(964), 1320–1322, 1970.

15. Perez-Reyes, M., Owens, S.M., and Di Guiseppi, S., The clinical pharmacology and dynamics of marihuana cigarette smoking, *J. Clin. Pharmacol.*, 21(8–9 Suppl.), 201S–207S, 1981.

16. Wall, M.E., Brine, D.R., and Perez-Reyes, M., Metabolism and disposition of naltrexone in man after oral and intravenous administration, *Drug Metab. Dispos.*, 9(4), 369–375, 1981.

17. Robinson, K., Beyond resinable doubt? *J. Clin. Forensic Med.*, 12(3), 164–166, 2005.

18. McGilveray, I.J., Pharmacokinetics of cannabinoids, *Pain Res. Manag.*, 10(A), 15A–22A, 2005.

19. Grotenhermen, F., Pharmacokinetics and pharmacodynamics of cannabinoids, *Clin. Pharmacokinet.*, 42(4), 327–360, 2003.

20. Ohlsson, A. et al., Plasma delta-9 tetrahydrocannabinol concentrations and clinical effects after oral and intravenous administration and smoking, *Clin. Pharmacol. Ther.*, 28(3), 409–416, 1980.

21. Babor, T.F. et al., Marijuana, affect and tolerance: A study of subchronic self-administration in women, *NIDA Res. Monogr.*, 49, 199–204, 1984.

22. Johansson, E. et al., Single-dose kinetics of deuterium-labelled cannabinol in man after intravenous administration and smoking, *Biomed. Environ. Mass Spectrom.*, 14(9), 495–499, 1987.

23. Hunt, C.A. and Jones, R.T., Tolerance and disposition of tetrahydrocannabinol in man, *J. Pharmacol. Exp. Ther.*, 215(1), 35–44, 1980.

24. Huestis, M.A., Mitchell, J.M., and Cone, E.J., Detection times of marijuana metabolites in urine by immunoassay and GC-MS, *J. Anal. Toxicol.*, 19(6), 443–449, 1995.

25. Huestis, M.A., Mitchell, J.M., and Cone, E.J., Urinary excretion profiles of 11-nor-9-carboxy-delta 9-tetrahydrocannabinol in humans after single smoked doses of marijuana, *J. Anal. Toxicol.*, 20(6), 441–452, 1996.

26. Widman, M. et al., Metabolism of delta1-tetrahydrocannabinol by the isolated perfused dog lung: Comparison with in vitro liver metabolism, *J. Pharm. Pharmacol.*, 27(11), 842–848, 1975.

27. Manolis, A., McBurney, L.J., and Bobbie, B.A., The detection of delta 9-tetrahydrocannabinol in the breath of human subjects, *Clin. Biochem.*, 16(4), 229–233, 1983.

28. Leson, G. et al., Evaluating the impact of hemp food consumption on workplace drug tests, *J. Anal. Toxicol.*, 25(8), 691–698, 2001.

29. Gustafson, R.A. et al., Urinary cannabinoid detection times after controlled oral administration of delta9-tetrahydrocannabinol to humans, *Clin. Chem.*, 49(7), 1114–1124, 2003.

30. ElSohly, M.A. et al., Delta9-tetrahydrocannabivarin as a marker for the ingestion of marijuana versus Marinol®: Results of a clinical study, *J. Anal. Toxicol.*, 25(7), 565–571, 2001.

3.6.10 Opioids

Members of the group of natural, semi-synthetic, or synthetic alkaloid compounds prepared from opium are referred to as "opioids." This group includes natural compounds usually denoted "opiates," such as morphine and codeine, and the synthetic and semisynthetic compounds such as oxycodone, buprenorphine, fentanyl, methadone, and tramadol. The pharmacological effects and pharmacokinetic parameters of these drugs share many common characteristics and are illustrated with the prototypic drug in this class, morphine.

Morphine is obtained from the latex of the opium poppy, *Papaver somniferum*. Morphine, codeine, and other opiates are extracted from a milky exudate that forms within 12 h when unripe seed capsules are incised. When dried, the material is called raw opium. The principal alkaloid in raw opium is morphine, constituting 8 to 19% of opium by dry weight. The actual percentage is highly dependent on growing conditions and location.[1] Morphine is the analgesic of choice for the treatment of both chronic pain syndromes and acute myocardial infarction. Whether it will remain so for long is not clear. The results of recently published observational studies strongly suggest that in patients with acute coronary syndrome, the use of morphine, either alone, or in combination with nitroglycerin, is associated with an increased mortality rate.[2]

Morphine remains the prototypic mu-opioid analgesic. And, even though other opioids share similar structures, there is overwhelming proof that morphine is different from other similar appearing agents. In the past, these differences had been explained by different pharmacokinetics, but now it appears that heroin and morphine act via different receptor mechanisms. As a result, the concept of multiple mu receptors has emerged. Multiple splice variants of the cloned mu-opioid receptor (abbreviated as M) R-1) have been identified. Nonetheless, a relatively large volume of pharmacokinetic data exists describing morphine clinical applications, which is reviewed here.[3] It is becoming increasingly obvious that knowledge of the molecular mechanisms involved in causing drug dependence and in providing pain relief is mandatory if there are to be clinical advances.

3.6.10.1 *Morphine*

Pharmacology

Morphine and other related opioids produce their pharmacological effects by binding to opiate receptors located throughout the body. Three types of opiate receptor μ (mu), κ (kappa), and δ (delta) are recognized; they are approximately 70% homologous. Differences between receptors occur mainly at the N and C terminal ends. The mu receptor is thought to be the most important, because it is where morphine (and like drugs) exerts its effect. When a mu receptor binds with an agonist, such as morphine, or heroin, or oxycodone, a G protein attached to the third intracellular loop of the receptor is activated (opiate receptors have seven loops, also called transmembrane domains).[4] The genes that determine the various receptor subtypes are located on different chromosomes. There are two mu, three kappa, and two delta subtypes. It is assumed that these receptors arise from post-translational modifications (i.e., they arise at a late stage in protein synthesis), because their genes have not been identified. A purported fourth opiates receptor, referred to as the sigma receptor, is now recognized as a completely unrelated entity.[5]

Mu receptors are almost always located proximally, on the presynaptic side of the synapse. The periaqueductal gray is the region containing the most mu receptors, but they are also found in the superficial dorsal horn of the spinal cord, the external plexiform layer of the olfactory bulb, the nucleus accumbens (an area deeply implicated in the process of addiction), in some parts of the cerebral cortex, and in some of the nuclei of the amygdala. Mu receptors avidly bind enkephalins and beta-endorphin, but they have a low affinity for dynorphins (primarily a kappa receptor agonist).[6]

The obvious clinical effects of morphine are papillary constriction due to its excitatory action on the parasympathetic nerves that supply the pupil. Respiratory depression also occurs because mu agonists exert a direct effect on brain stem respiratory centers, reducing their responsiveness to carbon dioxide. In addition, mu-stimulation depresses respiratory centers located in the pons. Small doses of morphine merely depress the respiratory rate, while large doses cause respiratory arrest, the accepted mechanism of death in cases of narcotic drug overdose. Nausea and vomiting are also associated with the use of mu receptor activation because opioids directly stimulate the chemoreceptor vomiting trigger zone in the medulla. Morphine provides effective and convenient pain relief, largely because there is no upper limit to the amount that can be given, provided enough time is allowed for tolerance to the respiratory effects to develop. Morphine, or compounds that bind the mu receptor are also used to treat diarrhea, and the cough associated with malignancy and tuberculosis.[7] Heroin, which is converted to morphine within the body, was originally marketed by Bayer as a cough suppressant.[8]

Activation of kappa receptors also produces analgesia, but it simultaneously induces nausea and dysphoria. Kappa receptors are located mainly on pain neurons located in the spinal cord and, to a lesser extent in the brain. They bind to an endogenously occurring ligand called dynorphin. The exact function of dynorphin is unknown, but evidence suggests that it is produced to counter the pleasurable effects of produced by cocaine and is, to some degree, neuroprotective.[9] Some believe dynorphin may play an important role in determining an individual's risk for addiction. Blocking the actions of dynorphin helps to alleviate depression.[10]

Delta receptor activation also produces analgesia, but it can also cause seizures as well. Delta receptors normally bind to a class of endogenous ligand known as enkephalins, but unlike mu receptors, information about delta receptors is limited. Enkephalins are peptides that are produced by the pituitary gland. Several different enkephalins have been identified. β-Enkephalin resembles opiates because when it binds to a delta receptor, it relieves pain.[11]

Absorption

Morphine can be given orally, or by subcutaneous, intramuscular injection, or intravenous injection.[7] Increasingly, as the purity of street heroin has risen, heroin is also being inhaled ("chasing the dragon").[12] Heroin is also administered epidurally, either as an individual dose or continuous infusion.[13] Parenteral morphine is well absorbed, and in individuals with normal blood pressure, resultant plasma levels after subcutaneous, intramuscular, and intravenous injection are very similar.[14] The oral bioavailability of morphine is quite low due to extensive first pass hepatic metabolism. A 10-mg bolus given to healthy volunteers undergoing elective surgery produced peak blood of 200 to 400 ng/ml 5 min after injection.[15] After either intramuscular or subcutaneous injection, morphine plasma levels peak in 10 to 20 min. In healthy volunteers a dose of 10 mg/70 kg given intravenously produces a free morphine concentration of 80 ng/ml at 5 min, compared to a peak of 74 ng/ml at 15 min after the same dose was given as an intravenous bolus.[14] Oral administration is a mainstay in the management of patients with cancer. In stable patients receiving sufficient oral morphine to produce acceptable analgesia, the mean trough serum morphine concentration is on the order of 18 ng/ml with roughly equal concentrations of the active metabolite M6G.[16]

Distribution

The volume of distribution of morphine ranges from 2 to 5 L/kg in humans,[17] although values as high as 7 L/kg have been reported.[18] The wide variation could be explained by the health of the volunteers being studied. In patients with incompletely compensated heart failure, and increased body water from any cause, higher values would be expected. Conversely, in patients with renal failure, where intravascular volume may be decreased, smaller values would be expected. Plasma protein binding of morphine in healthy humans ranges from 12 to 35% and appears to be independent of concentration over approximately a 1000-fold range, although a slight decrease (24 to 20% bound) was observed when the concentration was increased from therapeutic by 60-fold.[19] Morphine is bound mainly to albumin with approximately 5% bound to γ-globulin and 5% to α-1-acid glycoprotein. In healthy humans, the blood/plasma concentration ratio for morphine averages 1.02.[17] This ratio was found to be consistent in the concentration range of 35 to 140 nM. The plasma half-life averaged 1.8 and 2.9 h in female and male surgical patients, respectively.[20]

Morphine is relatively hydrophilic and therefore distributes slowly into tissues, where it may be detected in fat, even after death.[21] Morphine crosses the blood–brain barrier, but not so freely as heroin and codeine, which possess an aromatic hydroxyl group at the C3 position. Morphine's passage across the blood–brain barrier is mediated by P-glycoprotein (P-gp) concentrated in brain capillary endothelium. Drugs that interfere with P-gp, such as doxyrubrin, can alter brain morphine uptake and disposition. Lopermide, which is widely used to treat diarrheal disease, avidly binds the mu receptor but, because it does not bind to P-gp, it never enters the brain and never causes any of the psychological changes produced by morphine.[22]

Metabolism and Excretion

The major pathway for morphine metabolism is conjugation with glucuronic acid (Figure 3.6.8). The free phenolic hydroxyl group undergoes glucuronidation to produce morphine-3-glucuronide (M3G), a highly water soluble metabolite. Metabolism occurs primarily in the liver with 90% of a dose excreted in the urine and 10% in the feces. There is extensive enterohepatic circulation of both conjugated and unconjugated morphine. Approximately 87% of a dose of morphine is excreted in the 72-h urine, 75% as M3G, 10% as free morphine, and the remainder as morphine-6-glucuronide, morphine-3-sulfate, normorphine, and conjugates. The clearance of morphine was found to vary between 1.2 to 1.9 L/min/70 kg in several studies of humans.[19]

M3G is the predominant metabolite in young children. The total body morphine clearance is 80% of an adult at 6 months of age.[23] When the brains of experimental animals are directly injected with M3G, neuroexcitatory and anti-analgesic responses result, although this does not happen after system administration. Nonetheless, small amounts of M3G do cross the blood–brain barrier, and this may account for some reports of neuroexcitatory responses to morphine in humans. Attempts at correlating M3G plasma concentrations or M3G:morphine or M3G:M6G concentration ratios

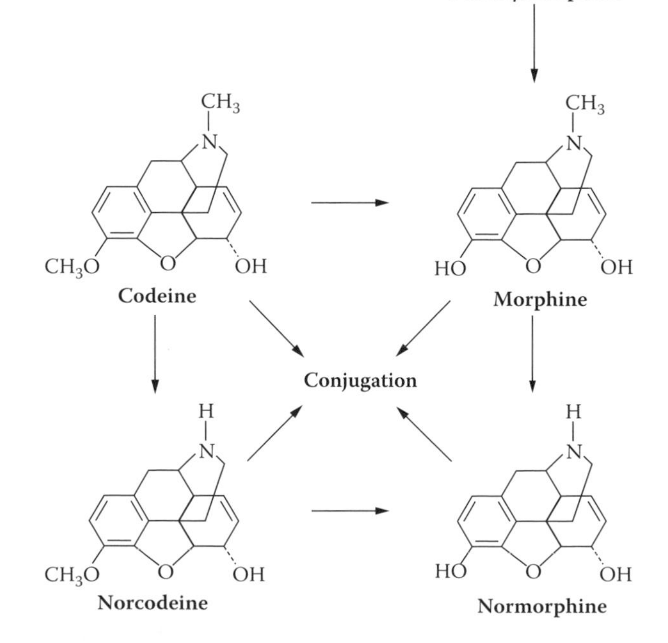

Figure 3.6.8 Metabolic pathway of heroin and morphine.

with the clinical activity of M3G have sometimes been successful, and sometimes not. To date, there are only two published studies describing the effects of injecting M3G directly into humans; both studies yielded equivocal results.[24]

M6G, on the other hand, is pharmacologically active and exerts important clinical opioid effects, especially when it is allowed to accumulate in the plasma of patients who have renal failure. However, after short-term morphine administration, the contribution of M6G to both analgesia and the occurrence of side effects is probably negligible.[25] M6G may have peripheral analgesic effects.[26] In a placebo-controlled, double blind, crossover study in ten healthy volunteers, M6G was given intravenously as a bolus followed by an infusion sufficient to maintain plasma concentrations of 500 ng/ml for 2 h. Analgesia was produced, but miotic effects were not, suggesting that the pain relief was a consequence of some peripheral effect exerted by M6G.

A small amount of morphine, on the order of 5%, is N-demethylated by hepatic CYP3A4, and to a lesser extent CYP2C8, to form normorphine.[27] This metabolite itself has pharmacological activity, but it is less potent than morphine and is present in lower concentrations.

3.6.10.2 Heroin

C.R. Wright first synthesized heroin, or 3,6-diacetylmorphine, from morphine in 1874. The Bayer Company of Germany advertised heroin as an antitussive in 1898. Under U.S. law (but not the laws of many other countries) heroin has no accepted medical use; it is classified as a Schedule I drug under the Controlled Substances Act of 1970.

Heroin is typically self-administered by intramuscular or intravenous injection and also by nasal insufflation ("snorting") or smoking. Peak heroin concentrations in blood are achieved within 1 to 5 min after intravenous and smoked administration[20] and within 5 min after intranasal and intramuscular administration.[28] In a study in which the method of smoked heroin delivery was optimized to reduce losses due to pyrolysis and sidestream smoke, Jenkins et al.[20] reported similar pharmacokinetic profiles for the smoked and intravenous routes. Mean elimination half-lives for two subjects across three doses of heroin were 3.3 and 3.6 min, after smoked and intravenous administration, respectively. The mean residence time of heroin was less than 10 min after all doses by both routes. Cone et al.[28] reported that the pharmacokinetic profile of intranasal heroin was equivalent to that for the intramuscular route. Mean elimination half-lives (hours plus or minus SD) were determined to be 0.09 ± 0.05, 0.07 ± 0.02, and 0.13 ± 0.07, following intranasal administration of 6 and 12 mg, and intramuscular administration of 6 mg of heroin, respectively. The relative potency of intranasal heroin was estimated to be approximately one half that of intramuscular administration.

Heroin may also be administered orally. In drug users this is an uncommon route since hydrolysis in the GI tract and loss due to first pass metabolism results in slow and inefficient delivery to the brain. Following low dose administration of 10 mg heroin hydrochloride, no heroin or 6-acetylmorphine was detected in blood.[29] Peak morphine concentrations ranging from 2 to 15 ng/ml (mean = 8 ng/ml, $n = 6$) were achieved 7.5 min to 4 h after drug administration. In another study, 400 mg of heroin was orally administered, followed 359 min later by a second dose of 400 mg.[30] In this study as well, heroin and 6-acetylmorphine were not detected in blood. Morphine and its conjugates were detected. Peak morphine concentrations were measured 1 to 2 h after the initial dose and were 0.73 and 1.34 mg/L in the two subjects. Girardin et al.[31] administered heroin by three different routes to eight heroin addicts. The intramuscular route demonstrated linear pharmacokinetics for heroin and the metabolites 6-acetylmorphine (6-AM) and morphine. The oral route resulted in low blood concentrations of heroin and 6-AM but linear kinetics for morphine and its glucuronides.

It is known from *in vitro* studies that heroin is rapidly deacetylated to an active metabolite, 6-AM, which is then hydrolyzed to morphine (Figure 3.6.8). Spontaneous hydrolysis to 6-AM may occur under various conditions. Heroin is susceptible to base-catalyzed hydrolysis but will also hydrolyze in the presence of protic compounds such as ethanol, methanol, and aqueous media.

The addition of two acetyl-ester groups to the morphine molecule produces a more lipophilic compound. Experimental evidence suggests that heroin and morphine may exert their effects via different receptor mechanisms.[32,33]

Following intravenous infusion of 70 mg of heroin to human volunteers, 45% of the dose was recovered in urine after 40 h. More than 38% was recovered as conjugated morphine, approximately 4% as free morphine, 1% as 6-acetylmorphine, and 0.1% as heroin.[14] Urinary elimination half-lives of 0.6, 4.4, and 7.9 h were reported for 6-AM, morphine, and conjugated morphine, respectively, after administration of 6 mg of heroin by the intramuscular route.[34]

3.6.10.3 Methadone

Methadone is a synthetic opioid, clinically available in the U.S. since 1947.[8] It exists in the dextro- and levo-rotatory forms with the levo-isoform possessing approximately 8 to 50 times more pharmacological activity.[27,34] Methadone acts on the CNS and cardiovascular system producing respiratory and circulatory depression. Methadone also produces miosis and increases the tone of smooth muscle in the lower gastrointestinal tract while decreasing the amplitude of contractions. It is used clinically for the treatment of severe pain and in maintenance programs for morphine and heroin addicts.[34]

Methadone is typically administered orally, with peak blood concentrations occurring after 4 h. Inturrisi and Verebely[35] reported a peak plasma concentration of 75 ng/ml at 4 h after a single 15-mg oral dose. Concentrations declined slowly, with a half-life of 15 h, reaching 30 ng/ml by 24 h. A single 10-mg intravenous dose of methadone resulted in initial plasma concentrations of 500 ng/ml declining to 50 ng/ml after 1 to 2 h.[29] Peak plasma concentrations (mean = 830 ng/ml) after 4 h were also observed with chronic oral administration of 100 to 200 mg/day.[28] Concentrations of methadone reach a maximum in brain tissue approximately 1 to 2 h after an oral dose.[27] Methadone is highly plasma protein bound (87%) with 70% bound to albumin.[28] Methadone distributes rapidly to tissues, especially the lungs, liver, kidneys, and spleen. The volume of distribution is 4 to 5 L/kg.[34]

Methadone is metabolized in the liver by N-demethylation to produce unstable metabolites, which undergo cyclization to form the metabolites, 2-ethylidene-1,5-dimethyl-3,3-diphenylpyrrolidine (EDDP) and 2-ethyl-5-methyl-3,3-diphenylpyrroline (EMDP) (Figure 3.6.9). These metabolites and the parent drug undergo para-hydroxylation with subsequent conjugation with glucuronic acid. All three are excreted in the bile and are the major excretory products measured in the urine after methadone administration. Minor metabolites, methadol, and normethadol exhibit pharmacological activity similar to methadone but are produced in low concentrations. Metabolism to EDDP is achieved by multiple cytochrome P450 isoforms, namely, CYP2B6, 2C19, and 3A4.[30] Michaelis–Menten data demonstrated that the highest V_{max} and lowest K_m occurred with CYP2B6. CYP2B6 and 2C19 showed stereoselective metabolism, with the former preferentially metabolizing S-methadone and the latter the R-enantiomer.[30] Shiran et al.[36] reported that methadone appears to inhibit CYP2D6 activity.

Large individual variations in the urine excretion of methadone are observed depending on urine volume and pH, the dose and rate of metabolism. Acidification of the urine may increase the urinary output of methadone from 5 to 22%.[37] Typically, following a 5-mg oral dose, methadone and EDDP account for 5% of the dose in the 24-h urine. In those individuals on maintenance therapy, methadone may account for 5 to 50% of the dose in the 24-h urine and EDDP may account for 3 to 25% of the dose. (S)-and (R)-methadone and EDDP have been reported in saliva[38] and methadone and (S)- and (R)-methadone in human breast milk.[39,40]

3.6.10.4 Oxycodone

Oxycodone is a semisynthetic opioid derived from thebaine and used for oral pain relief. It is commonly formulated as an immediate-release medication with acetaminophen or aspirin. A con-

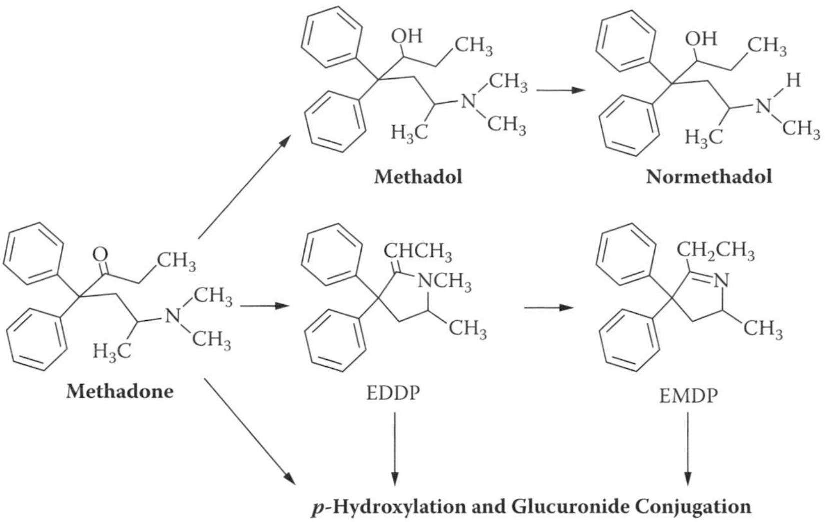

Figure 3.6.9 Metabolic pathway of methadone.

trolled-release oxycodone formulation is used for the treatment of moderate to severe pain; it provides controlled drug delivery over 12 h. The oral bioavailability of this formulation is 60 to 87%.[35] The results of clinical studies of patients with postoperative and cancer pain show that oxycodone has a potency 1.5 times that of morphine.

The absorption half-life of the immediate-release oral formulation is 0.4 h in healthy adults. In contrast the controlled-release form exhibits a biphasic absorption pattern with two apparent half-lives of 0.6 and 6.9 h.[41] Peak plasma concentrations are achieved in approximately 1.6 h with the immediate release compared with 2 to 3 h with the controlled-release formulation. After a 10-mg oral dose of the immediate release formulation, peak plasma concentrations ranged from 13 to 46 ng/ml (mean = 30 ng/ml, n = 12).[36] After the administration of 20 mg of the prolonged-release formulation the peak plasma concentration averaged 23 ng/ml in a group of 28 adults.[41] The plasma half-life has been reported to be 4 to 6 h with a volume of distribution of 1.8 to 3.7 L/kg.[42]

Oxycodone is metabolized in the liver by the cytochrome P450 isozymes and the elimination half-life is prolonged in individuals with liver disease, such as cirrhosis. Metabolism by O- and N-demethylation produces the metabolites oxymorphone and noroxycodone. The O-demethylated metabolite, oxymorphone, is a very powerful μ receptor agonist, providing ten times the relief of morphine in patients with cancer,[43] and at one time it was believed that most of oxycodone's ability to relieve pain was due to oxymorphone formation. However, recent studies have shown that so little oxymorphone is formed that it cannot account for the relief afforded by the parent compound.[44–46] Both the O- and N-demethylated forms are then conjugated with glucuronic acid. CYP2D6 metabolizes oxycodone and is encoded by a polymorphic gene with three mutations (*3, *4, and *5) with a combined 95% allelic frequency and approximately 10% prevalence.[47] Less than 65% of a single dose is excreted in the urine over a period of 24 h with 13 to 19% comprising free oxycodone.

3.6.10.5 Hydrocodone

Hydrocodone is a semisynthetic opioid derived from codeine.[8] It is utilized as an analgesic and antitussive available for oral administration, often in combination with acetaminophen or ibuprofen. As a rule, potent analgesics containing a methoxyl group at position 3 (e.g., hydrocodone, K_i = 19.8 nM) bind the mu receptor relatively weakly, but their O-demethylated metabolites, such as hydromorphone, K_i = 0.6 nM), bind more strangely. As with oxycodone, the possibility exists that some of their ability to relieve pain may actually derive from their active metabolites.[48]

Hydrocodone has multiple actions, mainly involving the CNS and smooth muscle. Peak serum concentrations after single therapeutic doses are typically less than 30 ng/ml and occur within 1.5 h after drug administration.[25] The plasma half-life has been reported to range from 3.4 to 8.8 h with a volume of distribution of 3.3 to 4.7 L/kg.[25] In humans, hydrocodone is metabolized by O-demethylation (by the action of CYP2D6) and N-demethylation (by the action of CYP3A4) and also reduction of the 6-keto groups. This produces multiple metabolites including hydromorphone, norhydrocodone, hydrocodol, and hydromorphol. The last two metabolites exist as stereoisomers (6-alpha-hydrocodol is also known as dihydrocodeine). Hydromorphone and hydromorphol are then conjugated to form glucuronides. The unconjugated metabolites are believed to exhibit pharmacological activity and, therefore, may contribute to the actions of the drug. Hydrocodone is principally excreted by the kidneys. Approximately 26% of the drug from a single dose is eliminated in the 72-h urine, with less than 15% as unchanged drug.

3.6.10.6 Fentanyl

Fentanyl is a fast-acting potent synthetic opioid introduced in the U.S. in the early 1960s for use as an anesthetic supplement. It interacts with the opioid mu receptors located in the brain, spinal cord, and smooth muscle. Fentanyl is highly lipophilic and, therefore, crosses the blood–brain barrier rapidly. Therapeutic use involves the CNS, producing pharmacological actions as pain relief and sedation. In addition to its use as an anesthetic agent, fentanyl is prescribed clinically to treat chronic pain. It is available in an oral transmucosal solid formulation and also as a transdermal delivery system (patches). In opioid nontolerant individuals effective analgesia occurs at blood concentrations of 1 to 2 ng/ml.[25] Surgical anesthesia occurs at concentrations of 10 to 20 ng/ml.

The transmucosal formulation of fentanyl is designed to be dissolved slowly in the mouth, permitting absorption through the buccal mucosa, and a more prolonged absorption, after swallowing, in the GI tract. Bioavailability is dependent on the fraction of the dose absorbed by both routes. Typically 25% of the dose is rapidly absorbed through the buccal mucosa and approximately 33% of the remaining dose, which is swallowed, becomes systemically available. The time to reach peak blood concentrations after this form of drug delivery is generally 20 to 40 minutes after drug administration.

The transdermal system provides continuous systemic delivery of fentanyl for 72 h. The amount of drug released from the system per hour is proportional to the surface area. Following application of the patch to the skin, a depot of fentanyl concentrates in the upper skin layers. This is then available to the systemic circulation. There is an initial rise in blood fentanyl concentration after application followed by a leveling off that occurs 12 to 24 h later. Peak blood concentrations occur between 24 and 72 h after application. The skin does not appear to metabolize fentanyl when delivered transdermally.

Fentanyl is highly lipophilic. It is rapidly distributed to tissues such as the brain, heart, kidneys, and lungs, followed by slower movement into muscle and fat.

Fentanyl is approximately 80% bound to plasma proteins, principally α-1-acid glycoprotein. The volume of distribution reportedly ranges from 3 to 8 L/kg. The plasma half-life is 3 to 12 h.[49] Fentanyl is metabolized in the liver and intestinal mucosa by cytochrome P450 3A4 isozyme by N-dealkylation to form the pharmacologically inactive metabolite norfentanyl.[35] Hydroxylated inactive metabolites include hydroxyfentanyl and hydroxynorfentanyl. Fentanyl is primarily excreted in the urine with up to 85% of a single dose eliminated in 3 to 4 days. Norfentanyl is the principal compound detected in urine comprising 26 to 55% of a single dose.[50]

3.6.10.7 Buprenorphine

Buprenorphine is derived from thebaine. It is a partial mu agonist with kappa antagonist activity. Buprenorphine has 25 to 50 times the potency of morphine. It is used to produce a longer-lasting analgesia than morphine. Effects of buprenorphine last longer because it is released more slowly from mu receptors than morphine. It is available as an injectable for intramuscular (IM) or intravenous administration in a 1 ml solution containing 0.3 mg buprenorphine (as buprenorphine HCl) for the relief of moderate to severe pain. It is also available to treat opioid dependence in the formulation of a tablet,[51] alone or in combination with naloxone, in 2 or 8 mg doses to be administered sublingually (SL).[25] The recommended sublingual daily dose is 12 to 16 mg/day.

Pharmacological effects occur within 15 min of IM administration, peaking at approximately 1 h and persisting for up to 6 h. After SL administration, peak pharmacological effects typically occur after 100 min. After an intravenous dose of 0.3 mg, plasma concentrations are typically less than 1 ng/ml. Sublingual maintenance therapy of 8 mg/day resulted in plasma buprenorphine concentrations of 1 to 8 ng/ml.[52]

The bioavailability of the buprenorphine/naloxone tablet appears to be greater than the buprenorphine-alone formulation, with the former similar to the drug in liquid form. Buprenorphine is approximately 96% plasma protein bound, primarily to α- and β-globulin. The plasma half-life is 2 to 4 h with a volume of distribution of 2.5 L/kg. The drug undergoes N-dealkylation by CYP3A4 isozyme to norbuprenorphine, a pharmacologically active metabolite. This metabolite and parent are subject to glucuronidation. Buprenorphine is eliminated primarily in the feces as free drug with low concentrations occurring in the urine.

3.6.10.8 Tramadol

Tramadol has about one tenth the pain-relieving ability of morphine.[53] There are two enantiomers, and both contribute to pain relief, but via different mechanisms. (+)-Tramadol and the metabolite (+)-O-desmethyl-tramadol, which is referred to as M1, are agonists of the mu opioid receptor. (+)-Tramadol inhibits serotonin reuptake and (−)-tramadol inhibits norepinephrine reuptake.[25] This latter action enhances the inhibitory effects on pain transmission in the spinal cord. Because the actions of the two enantiomers are complementary, they are usually supplied as a racemic mixture. However, because it is a serotonin-reuptake blocker, interaction with other medications can lead to the occurrence of serotonin syndrome.[54]

Tramadol is available as drops, capsules, and sustained-release formulations for oral use, suppositories for rectal use, and solution for intramuscular, intravenous, and subcutaneous injection. After oral administration, tramadol is rapidly and almost completely absorbed. Sustained-release tablets release the active ingredient over a period of 12 h, reach peak concentrations after 4.9 h and have a bioavailability of 87 to 95% compared with capsules. One 100-mg dose given to healthy volunteers resulted in plasma levels of 375 ng/ml at 1.5 h.[55] Tramadol is 20% bound to plasma protein and it is rapidly distributed in the body; it is mainly metabolized by O- and N-demethylation forming glucuronides and sulfates that are excreted by the kidney.

The mean elimination half-life is about 6 h. The O-demethylation of tramadol to M1, the main analgesic effective metabolite, is catalyzed by cytochrome P450 (CYP) 2D6, whereas N-demethylation to M2 is catalyzed by CYP2B6 and CYP3A4. The wide variability in the pharmacokinetic properties of tramadol can partly be ascribed to CYP polymorphism. O- and N-demethylation of tramadol as well as renal elimination are stereoselective.[56]

Pharmacokinetic–pharmacodynamic characterization of tramadol is difficult because of differences between tramadol concentrations in plasma and at the site of action, and because of pharmacodynamic interactions between the two enantiomers of tramadol and its active metabolites.[53]

3.6.10.9 Hydromorphone

Sold as Dilaudid™ in the U.S., hydromorphone is a semisynthetic, differing from morphine only by presence of a 6-keto group, and the hydrogenation of the double bond at the 7–8 position of the molecule.[57] Like morphine, it acts primarily at the mu opioid receptors, and to a lesser degree at delta receptors.

As a hydrogenated ketone of morphine, it shares common pharmacologic properties with other opioid analgesics.[25] These include the expected changes in the CNS, including increased cerebrospinal fluid pressure, increased biliary pressure, and increased parasympathetic activity. It can also produce transient hyperglycemia. It is generally viewed as a second tier analgesic and is not that widely prescribed.

Hydromorphone is well absorbed from the small intestine and is extensively metabolized in the liver, mainly to 3-glucuronide which, like morphine, is devoid of analgesic effect, but can cause significant neuroexcitation. It undergoes extensive first pass metabolism (62%), accounting for its relatively low bioavailability. A single 8-mg dose of hydromorphone yields blood concentrations of approximately 2 ng/ml, while a 12-mg time-release formulation gives plasma concentrations half as high.[58,59]

Depending on the country where the drug is manufactured, a number of different time-release preparations are available. Palladone™, a controlled-release preparation consisting of hydromorphone HCl pellets, was withdrawn from the U.S. market in 2005. When taken with alcohol the pellets rapidly released their contents leading to dangerously elevated peak plasma concentrations.[60] Interaction with ethanol and "dose dumping" is not the only concern. Any CNS depressant may enhance the depressant effects of hydromorphone.

REFERENCES

1. Anon., The opium alkaloids, *Bull. Narcotics*, 19, 13–14, 1963.
2. Meine, T.J., M.T. Roe, A.Y. Chen, M.R. Patel, et al., Association of intravenous morphine use and outcomes in acute coronary syndromes: results from the CRUSADE Quality Improvement Initiative, *Am. Heart J.*, 149(6), 1043–1049, 2005.
3. Hoskin, P.J. and G.W. Hanks, Morphine: pharmacokinetics and clinical practice, *Br. J. Cancer,* 62(5), 705–707, 1990.
4. Hann, V. and P. Chazot, G-proteins, *Curr. Anaesth. Crit. Care*, 15(1), 79–81, 2004.
5. Bodnar, R.J. and G.E. Klein, Endogenous opiates and behavior: 2003, *Peptides,* 25(12), 2205–2256, 2004.
6. Evans, C.J., Secrets of the opium poppy revealed, *Neuropharmacology,* 47(Suppl. 1), 293–299, 2004.
7. Skaer, T.L., Practice guidelines for transdermal opioids in malignant pain, *Drugs*, 64(23), 2629–38, 2004.
8. Karch, S.B., *Karch's Pathology of Drug Abuse,* 3rd ed., CRC Press, Boca Raton, FL, 2002.
9. Hauser, K.F., J.V. Aldrich, K.J. Anderson, G. Bakalkin, et al., Pathobiology of dynorphins in trauma and disease, *Front. Biosci.*, 10, 216–235, 2005.
10. Morley, J.E., Anorexia of aging: physiologic and pathologic, *Am. J. Clin. Nutr.*, 66(4), 760–773, 1997.
11. Bodnar, R.J. and G.E. Klein, Endogenous opiates and behavior: 2004, *Peptides*, 2005.
12. Klous, M.G., A.D. Huitema, E.J. Rook, M.J. Hillebrand, et al., Pharmacokinetic comparison of two methods of heroin smoking: "chasing the dragon" versus the use of a heating device, *Eur. Neuropsychopharmacol.*, 15(3), 263–269, 2005.
13. Robertson, S.A. and P.M. Taylor, Pain management in cats — past, present and future. Part 2. Treatment of pain — clinical pharmacology, *J. Feline Med. Surg.,* 6(5), 321–333, 2003.
14. Stuart-Harris, R., S.P. Joel, P. McDonald, D. Currow, et al., The pharmacokinetics of morphine and morphine glucuronide metabolites after subcutaneous bolus injection and subcutaneous infusion of morphine, *Br. J. Clin. Pharmacol.*, 49(3), 207–214, 2000.
15. Berkowitz, B.A., S.H. Ngai, J.C. Yang, J. Hempstead, et al., The disposition of morphine in surgical patients, *Clin. Pharmacol. Ther.*, 17(6), 629–635, 1975.
16. Klepstad, P., S. Kaasa, and P.C. Borchgrevink, Start of oral morphine to cancer patients: effective serum morphine concentrations and contribution from morphine-6-glucuronide to the analgesia produced by morphine, *Eur. J. Clin. Pharmacol.*, 55(10), 713–719, 2000.

17. Milne, R.W., R.L. Nation, and A.A. Somogyi, The disposition of morphine and its 3- and 6-glucuronide metabolites in humans and animals, and the importance of the metabolites to the pharmacological effects of morphine, *Drug Metab. Rev.*, 28(3), 345–472, 1996.

18. Lotsch, J., A. Stockmann, G. Kobal, K. Brune, et al., Pharmacokinetics of morphine and its glucuronides after intravenous infusion of morphine and morphine-6-glucuronide in healthy volunteers, *Clin. Pharmacol. Ther.*, 60(3), 316–325, 1996.

19. Mazoit, J.X., P. Sandouk, P. Zetlaoui, and J.M. Scherrmann, Pharmacokinetics of unchanged morphine in normal and cirrhotic subjects, *Anesth. Analg.*, 66(4), 293–298, 1987.

20. Jenkins, A.J., R.M. Keenan, J.E. Henningfield, and E.J. Cone, Pharmacokinetics and pharmacodynamics of smoked heroin, *J. Anal. Toxicol.*, 18(6), 317–330, 1994.

21. Levisky, J.A., D.L. Bowerman, W.W. Jenkins, D.G. Johnson, et al., Drugs in postmortem adipose tissues: evidence of antemortem deposition, *Forensic Sci. Int.*, 121(3), 157–160, 2001.

22. Daugherty, L.M., Loperamide hydrochloride, *Am. Pharm.*, NS30(12), 45–48, 1990.

23. Bouwmeester, N.J., B.J. Anderson, D. Tibboel, and N.H. Holford, Developmental pharmacokinetics of morphine and its metabolites in neonates, infants and young children, *Br. J. Anaesth.*, 92(2), 208–217, 2004.

24. Skarke, C., G. Geisslinger, and J. Lotsch, Is morphine-3-glucuronide of therapeutic relevance? *Pain*, 116(3), 177–180, 2005.

25. Lotsch, J., Opioid metabolites, *J. Pain Symptom Manage.*, 29(5 Suppl.), S10–24, 2005.

26. Tegeder, I., S. Meier, M. Burian, H. Schmidt, et al., Peripheral opioid analgesia in experimental human pain models, *Brain*, 126(Pt. 5), 1092–1102, 2003.

27. Projean, D., P.E. Morin, T.M. Tu, and J. Ducharme, Identification of CYP3A4 and CYP2C8 as the major cytochrome P450s responsible for morphine *N*-demethylation in human liver microsomes, *Xenobiotica*, 33(8), 841–854, 2003.

28. Cone, E.J., B.A. Holicky, T.M. Grant, W.D. Darwin, et al., Pharmacokinetics and pharmacodynamics of intranasal "snorted" heroin, *J. Anal. Toxicol.*, 17(6), 327–337, 1993.

29. Jenkins, A.J., B.A. Holicky, T.M. Grant, W.D. Darwin, et al., Blood concentrations and pharmacological effects after oral heroin administration, paper presented at Society of Forensic Toxicologists/The International Association of Forensic Toxicologists, Joint Conference (October 1994), abstr. 127, 1994.

30. Gyr, E., R. Brenneisen, D. Bourquin, T. Lehmann, et al., Pharmacodynamics and pharmacokinetics of intravenously, orally and rectally administered diacetylmorphine in opioid dependents, a two-patient pilot study within a heroin-assisted treatment program, *Int. J. Clin. Pharmacol. Ther.*, 38(10), 486–491, 2000.

31. Girardin, F., K.M. Rentsch, M.A. Schwab, M. Maggiorini, et al., Pharmacokinetics of high doses of intramuscular and oral heroin in narcotic addicts, *Clin. Pharmacol. Ther.*, 74(4), 341–352, 2003.

32. Rady, J.J., A.E. Takemori, P.S. Portoghese, and J.M. Fujimoto, Supraspinal delta receptor subtype activity of heroin and 6-monoacetylmorphine in Swiss Webster mice, *Life Sci.*, 55(8), 603–609, 1994.

33. Gilbert, A.K., S. Hosztafi, L. Mahurter, and G.W. Pasternak, Pharmacological characterization of dihydromorphine, 6-acetyldihydromorphine and dihydroheroin analgesia and their differentiation from morphine, *Eur. J. Pharmacol.*, 492(2–3), 123–130, 2004.

34. Cone, E.J., P. Welch, J.M. Mitchell, and B.P. Paul, Forensic drug testing for opiates: I, *J. Anal. Toxicol.*, 15, 1–7, 1991.

35. Inturrisi, C.E. and K. Verebely, Disposition of methadone in man after a single oral dose, *Clin. Pharmacol. Ther.*, 13(6), 923–930, 1972.

36. Shiran, M.R., J. Chowdry, A. Rostami-Hodjegan, S.W. Ellis, et al., A discordance between cytochrome P450 2D6 genotype and phenotype in patients undergoing methadone maintenance treatment, *Br. J. Clin. Pharmacol.*, 56(2), 220–224, 2003.

37. Chamberlain, N., Patterns of drug use in dependent opioid users in methadone treatment, *N.Z. Med. J.*, 110(1047), 258–259, 1997.

38. Rosas, M.E., K.L. Preston, D.H. Epstein, E.T. Moolchan, et al., Quantitative determination of the enantiomers of methadone and its metabolite (EDDP) in human saliva by enantioselective liquid chromatography with mass spectrometric detection, *J. Chromatogr. B Anal. Technol. Biomed. Life Sci.*, 796(2), 355–370, 2003.

39. Begg, E.J., T.J. Malpas, L.P. Hackett, and K.F. Ilett, Distribution of R- and S-methadone into human milk during multiple, medium to high oral dosing, *Br. J. Clin. Pharmacol.*, 52(6), 681–685, 2001.

40. McCarthy, J.J. and B.L. Posey, Methadone levels in human milk, *J. Hum. Lact.*, 16(2), 115–120, 2000.

41. Kalso, E., Oxycodone, *J. Pain Symptom Manage.*, 29(5 Suppl.), S47–56, 2005.

42. Davis, M.P., J. Varga, D. Dickerson, D. Walsh, et al., Normal-release and controlled-release oxycodone: pharmacokinetics, pharmacodynamics, and controversy, *Support. Care Cancer*, 11(2), 84–92, 2003.

43. Beaver, W.T., S.L. Wallenstein, R.W. Houde, and A. Rogers, Comparisons of the analgesic effects of oral and intramuscular oxymorphone and of intramuscular oxymorphone and morphine in patients with cancer, *J. Clin. Pharmacol.*, 17(4), 186–198, 1977.

44. Kaiko, R.F., Pharmacokinetics and pharmacodynamics of controlled-release opioids, *Acta Anaesthesiol. Scand.*, 41(1 Pt. 2), 166–174, 1997.

45. Heiskanen, T., K.T. Olkkola, and E. Kalso, Effects of blocking CYP2D6 on the pharmacokinetics and pharmacodynamics of oxycodone, *Clin. Pharmacol. Ther.*, 64(6), 603–611, 1998.

46. Poyhia, R., T. Seppala, K.T. Olkkola, and E. Kalso, The pharmacokinetics and metabolism of oxycodone after intramuscular and oral administration to healthy subjects, *Br. J. Clin. Pharmacol.*, 33(6), 617–621, 1992.

47. Wong, S.H., M.A. Wagner, J.M. Jentzen, C. Schur, et al., Pharmacogenomics as an aspect of molecular autopsy for forensic pathology/toxicology: does genotyping CYP 2D6 serve as an adjunct for certifying methadone toxicity? *J. Forensic Sci.*, 48(6), 1406–1415, 2003.

48. Chen, Z.R., R.J. Irvine, A.A. Somogyi, and F. Bochner, Mu receptor binding of some commonly used opioids and their metabolites, *Life Sci.*, 48(22), 2165–2171, 1991.

49. Poklis, A., Fentanyl: a review for clinical and analytical toxicologists, *J. Toxicol. Clin. Toxicol.*, 33(5), 439–447, 1995.

50. Poklis, A. and R. Backer, Urine concentrations of fentanyl and norfentanyl during application of Duragesic transdermal patches, *J. Anal. Toxicol.*, 28(6), 422–425, 2004.

51. Stock, C. and J.H. Shum, Bupreorphine: a new pharmacotherapy for opioid addictions treatment, *J. Pain Palliat. Care Pharmacother.*, 18(3), 35–54, 2004.

52. Perez de los Cobos, J., S. Martin, A. Etcheberrigaray, J. Trujols, et al., A controlled trial of daily versus thrice-weekly buprenorphine administration for the treatment of opioid dependence, *Drug Alcohol Depend.*, 59(3), 223–233, 2000.

53. Grond, S. and A. Sablotzki, Clinical pharmacology of tramadol, *Clin. Pharmacokinet.*, 43(13), 879–923, 2004.

54. Jones, D. and D.A. Story, Serotonin syndrome and the anaesthetist, *Anaesth. Intensive Care*, 33(2), 181–187, 2005.

55. Gambaro, V., C. Benvenuti, L. De Ferrari, L. Dell'Acqua, et al., Validation of a GC/MS method for the determination of tramadol in human plasma after intravenous bolus, *Farmaco*, 58(9), 947–950, 2003.

56. Pedersen, R.S., P. Damkier, and K. Brosen, Tramadol as a new probe for cytochrome P450 2D6 phenotyping: a population study, *Clin. Pharmacol. Ther.*, 77(6), 458–467, 2005.

57. Babul, N., A.C. Darke, and N. Hagen, Hydromorphone metabolite accumulation in renal failure, *J. Pain Symptom Manage.*, 10(3), 184–186, 1995.

58. Vashi, V., S. Harris, A. El-Tahtawy, D. Wu, et al., Clinical pharmacology and pharmacokinetics of once-daily hydromorphone hydrochloride extended-release capsules, *J. Clin. Pharmacol.*, 45(5), 547–554, 2005.

59. Murray, A. and N. Hagen, Hydromorphone, *J. Pain Symptom Manage.*, 29(5, Suppl. 1), 57–66, 2005.

60. Murray, S. and E. Wooltorton, Alcohol-associated rapid release of a long-acting opioid, *CMAJ*, 173(7), 756, 2005.

3.6.11 Phencyclidine

Phencyclidine, PCP, or 1-(1-phenylcyclohexyl) piperidine, is an arylcyclohexamine with structural similarities to ketamine. It is a lipophilic weak base with a pKa of 8.5. Phencyclidine was originally synthesized and marketed under the trade name Sernyl®, by Parke-Davis for use as an intravenously administered anesthetic agent in humans. Distribution began in 1963 but was discontinued in 1965 due to a high incidence (10 to 20%) of post-operative delirium and psychoses. However, its use continued as a veterinary tranquilizer for large animals until 1978, when all manufacture was prohibited and PCP was placed in Schedule II of the federal Controlled Substances Act (1970).

Illicit use of PCP as a hallucinogenic agent was first reported in San Francisco in 1967.[1] It was first abused in oral form but then gained popularity in the smoked form as this mode of drug delivery allowed better control over dose. Because illicit synthesis is relatively easy and inexpensive, abuse became widespread in the 1970s and early 1980s. Today, use of PCP tends to be highly regionalized and located in certain areas of the U.S., notably the Washington D.C./Baltimore corridor, New York City, and Los Angeles.[2]

3.6.11.1 Pharmacology

Phencyclidine binds with high affinity to sites located in the cortex and limbic structures of the brain. Binding results in blockade of N-methyl-D-aspartic acid (NMDA)-type glutamate receptors. The actions of glutamate and aspartate at the NMDA receptor allow movement of cations across the cell membrane. PCP exerts its action by binding to the glutamate receptor, thus preventing the flux of cations.[3] PCP is also known to exert effects on catecholamines, serotonin, gamma-hydroxy butyric acid, and acetylcholine neurotransmitter release, but its role is incompletely defined. Due to its action on several systems, the physiological and behavioral effects of PCP are varied and depend on not only the dose, but also the route of administration and user's previous experience.

3.6.11.2 Absorption

Phencyclidine is typically self-administered by the oral, intravenous, or smoked routes. After oral administration to healthy human volunteers, the bioavailability was found to vary between 50 to 90%.[4] In this study, peak plasma concentrations were achieved after 1.5 h and appeared to correlate with the time to reach maximum pharmacological effects. However, because there have been no comprehensive clinical controlled studies of phencyclidine, a correlation between PCP blood concentrations and pharmacological effects has not been definitively documented. Maximum serum PCP concentrations ranged between 2.7 and 2.9 ng/ml after 1 mg PCP administered orally.[4]

PCP is commonly self-administered by the smoked route. Liquid PCP is soaked in parsley flakes and rolled as a cigarette; powdered PCP is sprinkled over a marijuana joint, or the end of a tobacco cigarette is dipped in liquid PCP and then smoked. Cook et al.[5] studied the pharmacokinetic properties of PCP deposited on parsley cigarettes. Upon smoking, PCP is partially volatilized to 1-phenylcyclohexene (PC). These investigators found that 69 ± 5% of the PCP available in the cigarette was inhaled, 39% as PCP and 30% as PC.[5] The pharmacological and toxicological properties of PC have not been established. Peak plasma concentrations of PCP were reached within 5 to 20 min. In 80% of the subjects, a second peak was observed in plasma PCP concentrations, occurring 1 to 3 h after the end of smoking. This may have been due to trapping of PCP in the mouth, where it could be released and absorbed by the GI tract or, alternatively, it could be due to absorption by the lung and bronchial tissue with slower release into the systemic circulation.[6] Long-term users of PCP report feeling the effects of the drug within 2 to 5 min of smoking, with a peak effect after 15 to 30 min and residual effects for 4 to 6 h.[7]

3.6.11.3 Distribution

Plasma protein binding of PCP in healthy individuals remains relatively constant between 60 to 70% over the concentration range of 0.007 to 5000 ng/ml.[5] PCP binding to serum albumin accounts for only 24% of the binding,[6] which suggests binding to another protein may occur to a significant extent. When studied *in vitro*, α_1-acid glycoprotein was also found to bind phencyclidine.[6] The volume of distribution has been shown to be large, between 5.3 and 7.5 L/kg,[8] providing evidence of extensive distribution to extravascular tissues.

Wall et al.[9] administered 1.3 µg/kg of 3H-PCP intravenously to human volunteers and collected blood samples for 72 h. Data from this study suggested a two-compartment pharmacokinetic model with a plasma half-life for PCP of 7 to 16 h. Domino et al.[10] further analyzed the data from Wall et al. and developed a more complex three-compartment PK model. The reported half-lives for each compartment were 5.5 min, 4.6 h, and 22 h. The specific tissues and organs represented by the multicompartment model were not identified. Half-lives of greater than 3 days have been reported in cases of PCP overdose.[11]

3.6.11.4 Metabolism and Excretion

PCP is metabolized by the liver through oxidative hydroxylation. Unchanged PCP, two mono-hydroxylated, and one dihydroxylated metabolite have been identified in urine after oral and intravenous administration.[12] The monohydroxlyated metabolites have been identified as 4-phenyl-4-(1-piperidinyl)-cyclohexanol (PPC) and 1-(1-phenylcyclohexyl)-4-hydroxypiperidine (PCHP). These metabolites are pharmacologically inactive in humans and PPC is present in both cis- and trans-isomeric forms. The cis/trans ratio was found to be 1:1.4 in human urine.[5] The dihydroxylated metabolite was identified as 4-(4-hydroxypiperidino)-4-phenylcyclohexanol (HPPC). These metab-olites are present in urine as glucuronide conjugates in addition to their unconjugated forms.[8]

Approximately 30 to 50% of a labeled intravenous dose is excreted over a 72-h period in urine as unchanged drug (19.4%) and 80.6% as polar metabolites, mainly 4-phenyl-4-(1-piperidinyl) cyclohexanol.[5] Only 2% of a dose is excreted in feces.[10] After 10 days, an average of 77% of an intravenous dose is found in the feces and urine.[9] Green et al.[12] reported urine PCP concentrations between 40 to 3400 ng/ml in ambulatory users.

Urine pH is an important determinant of renal elimination of PCP. In a study in which urine pH was uncontrolled (6.0 to 7.5), the average total clearance of PCP was 22.8 ± 4.8 L/h after intravenous administration.[4] In the same study, renal clearance was 1.98 ± 0.48 L/h. When the urine was made alkaline, the renal clearance of PCP was found to decrease to 0.3 ± 0.18 L/h. If the urine was acidified (pH 6.1) in the same subjects, renal clearance increased to 2.4 ± 0.78 L/h.[13] Aronow et al.[14] determined that if the urine pH was decreased to <5.0, renal clearance increased significantly to 8.04 ± 1.56 L/h. There is disagreement about the utility of urine acidification in the treatment of PCP overdose, even though excretion may be increased by as much as 100-fold.[15] It should be noted that acidification may increase the risk of metabolic complications.[16]

REFERENCES

1. Nicholl, A.M., The non therapeutic use of psychoactive drugs, N. Engl. J. Med., 308, 925–933, 1983.
2. Epidemiologic trends in drug abuse, data from the Drug Abuse Early Warning Network, Vol. 11, Department of Health and Human Services, National Institute on Drug Abuse, Rockville, MD, June 1994.
3. Stone, J.A., Phencyclidine. In-Service Training and Continuing Education AACC/TDM, American Association for Clinical Chemistry, Inc., Washington, D.C., 17(8), 199–202, 1996.
4. Cook, C.E., Brine, D.R., Jeffcoat, A.R., Hill, J.M., and Wall, M.E., Phencyclidine disposition after intravenous and oral doses, Clin. Pharmacol. Ther., 31, 625–634, 1982.
5. Cook, C.E., Brine, D.R., Quin, G.D., Perez-Reyes, M., and DiGuiseppi, S.R., Phencyclidine and phenylcyclohexene disposition after smoking phencyclidine, Clin. Pharmacol. Ther., 31, 635–641, 1982.
6. Busto, U., Bendayan, R., and Sellers, E.M., Clinical pharmacokinetics of non-opiate abused drugs, Clin. Pharmacokinet., 16, 1–26, 1989.
7. Perry, D.C., PCP revisited, Clin. Toxicol., 9, 339–348, 1976.
8. Baselt, R.C. and Cravey, R.H., Disposition of Toxic Drugs and Chemicals in Man, 4th ed., Chemical Toxicology Institute, Foster City, CA, 1995.

9. Wall, M.E., Brine, D.R., Jeffcoat, R.A., and Cook, C.E., Phencyclidine metabolism and disposition in man following a 100 µg intravenous dose, *Res. Commun. Substance Abuse,* 2, 161–172, 1981.

10. Domino, S.E., Domino, L.E., and Domino, E.F., Comparison of two and three compartment models of phencyclidine in man, *Subst. Alcohol Actions Misuse,* 2, 205–211, 1982.

11. Done, A.K., Aronow, R., and Miceli, J.N., The pharmacokinetics of phencyclidine in overdosage and its treatment, National Institute on Drug Abuse, Rockville, MD, Res. Monograph 21, 210–217, 1978.

12. Green, D.E., Chao, F.C., Loeffler, K.O., and Lemon, R., Phencyclidine blood levels by probability based matching GC/MS, *Proc. West. Pharm. Soc.,* 19, 355–361, 1976.

13. Perez-Reyes, M., DiGuiseppi, S., Brine, D.R., Smith, H., and Cook, C.E., Urine pH and phencyclidine excretion, *Clin. Pharmacol. Ther.,* 32, 635–641, 1982.

14. Aronow, R., Miceli, J.N., and Done, A.K., Clinical observations during phencyclidine intoxication and treatment based on ion-trapping, National Institute on Drug Abuse, Rockville, MD, Res. Monograph Ser. 21, 218–228, 1978.

15. Milhorn, H.T., Diagnosis and management of phencyclidine intoxication, *Am. Fam. Physician,* 43, 1293–1301, 1991.

16. Ellenhorn, M.J. and Barceloux, D.G., *Medical Toxicology, Diagnosis and Treatment of Human Poisoning,* Elsevier, New York, 1988, 764–777.

3.6.12 Ketamine

Ketamine, a weakly basic compound structurally and pharmacologically similar to phencyclidine, is utilized in the U.S. to induce anesthesia.[1] It is available in solution for intravenous or intramuscular injection. Since the drug is pharmacologically similar to PCP it has the potential of producing hallucinogenic effects and, therefore, in recent years has become a drug of abuse.

After intravenous administration of 175 mg/70 kg to five individuals, the average peak serum concentration was 1.0 mg/L achieved at 12 min.[2] The concentration declined by 50% within 30 min. The plasma half-life is reported to be 3 to 4 h with a volume of distribution of 3 to 5 L/kg.[1] Continuous infusion of 41 µg/kg/min after a 2 mg/kg bolus produced an average ($n = 31$) steady-state plasma concentration of 2.2 mg/L.[3]

Two metabolites are formed that achieve serum concentrations similar to ketamine and may also exhibit the depressant effects of the parent compound. Norketamine is produced by *N*-demethylation.[4] Norketamine is then dehydrogenated to form dehydronorketamine. Parent drug and metabolites are then subject to hydroxylation and conjugation. Approximately 2% of a single dose of ketamine is excreted in the 72-h urine as unchanged drug. In a recent study urine ketamine concentrations ranged from 6 to 7744 ng/ml (mean = 1083 ng/ml) in 33 subjects following illegal consumption.[5]

REFERENCES

1. Baselt, R.C. and Cravey, R.H., *Disposition of Toxic Drugs and Chemicals in Man,* 4th ed., Chemical Toxicology Institute, Foster City, CA, 1995.

2. Wieber, J., Gugler, R., Hengstmann, J.H., and Dengler, H.J., Pharmacokinetics of ketamine in man, *Anaesthesia,* 24, 260–263, 1975.

3. Idvall, J., Ahlgren, I., Aronsen, K.F., and Stenberg, P., Ketamine infusions: pharmacokinetics and clinical effects, *Br. J. Anaesth.,* 51, 1167–1173, 1979.

4. Jenkins, A.J., Hallucinogens. In *Principles of Forensic Toxicology,* 2nd ed., B.S. Levine, Ed., AACC Press, Washington, D.C., 2003.

5. Moore, K.A., Sklerov, J., Levine, B., and Jacobs, A.J., Urine concentrations of ketamine and norketamine following illegal consumption, *J. Anal. Toxicol.,* 25, 583–588, 2001.

CHAPTER 4

Pharmacodynamics

Edited by Stephen J. Heishman, Ph.D.
Clinical Pharmacology and Therapeutics Branch, National Institute on Drug Abuse, National Institutes of
Health, Department of Health and Human Services, Baltimore, Maryland

CONTENTS

INTRODUCTION

Pharmacodynamics is the study of the physiological and behavioral mechanisms by which a drug exerts its effects in living organisms. An effect is initiated by the drug binding to receptor sites in a cell's membrane, setting in motion a series of molecular and cellular reactions culminating in some physiological (e.g., opioid-induced analgesia) or behavioral (e.g., alcohol-induced impairment) effect. Drugs typically have multiple effects. For example, a benzodiazepine will produce its primary anxiolytic effect, but may also cause side effects of sedation and impaired performance.

Central to an understanding of drug abuse and its treatment is a complete knowledge of the pharmacodynamics of psychoactive drugs. The question of the behavioral effects of abused drugs has been the focus of research by behavioral pharmacologists for many decades. In this section, we focus on the performance effects of drugs of abuse and the abuse of several marketed drugs. Because of the widespread use of psychoactive drugs throughout society, employers have become increasingly concerned about drugs in the workplace and the potential for impaired job performance and onsite drug-related accidents. There are now computerized tests that employers can use to aid in the detection of impaired employees. Some drugs of abuse also produce characteristic effects on the visual system, and for this reason, devices that detect eye movement and function are also being tested for their ability to predict drug ingestion and potential impairment in the workplace.

4.1 EFFECTS OF ABUSED DRUGS ON HUMAN PERFORMANCE: LABORATORY ASSESSMENT

Stephen J. Heishman, Ph.D. and Carol S. Myers, Ph.D.
Clinical Pharmacology and Therapeutics Branch, National Institute on Drug Abuse, National Institutes of Health, Department of Health and Human Services, Baltimore, Maryland

4.1.1 Introduction

The experimental investigation of the effects of psychoactive drugs on human performance has enjoyed a long history. Some of the earliest university laboratories in departments of psychology and physiology were dedicated to the study of caffeine, nicotine, and other drugs.[1,2] Advances in technology and methodology have resulted in a comprehensive body of research, and for most drugs of abuse, we have a general idea of their effects on performance. For example, it is well known that psychomotor stimulants, such as D-amphetamine, increase one's ability to sustain attention over prolonged periods of time when performing monotonous tasks.[3,4] However, numerous inconsistencies exist in the literature concerning the effects of certain drugs on various aspects of human performance, and few studies take into account nonpharmacological variables that, in addition to the drug dose, ultimately determine behavioral effects of psychoactive drugs.[5,6]

The purpose of this chapter is to provide an overview of the effects of abused drugs on human performance as assessed in the laboratory. This is not an exhaustive review of the literature. Rather, we take as our starting point several general overviews[7-9] and drug-specific reviews[3,4,6,10-18] and update these findings with recent studies. The classes of drugs included in this review are (1) psychomotor stimulants, including D-amphetamine, cocaine, and 3,4-methylenedioxymethamphetamine (MDMA, ecstasy); (2) nicotine and tobacco; (3) sedative-hypnotics, focusing on benzodiazepines as the prototypical sedative-hypnotic in use today (effects of ethanol are discussed elsewhere in this volume); (4) opioid analgesics and anesthetics; and (5) marijuana. Within each drug category, results will be organized into sensory, motor, attentional, and cognitive abilities. Such a classification scheme allows a focus on behavior compared with, for example, a classification based on specific performance tests.

4.1.2 Psychomotor Stimulants

4.1.2.1 Cocaine and D-Amphetamine

The psychomotor stimulants, cocaine and D-amphetamine, are considered together because they share a similar psychopharmacological profile.[19,20] Low to moderate doses of both drugs given acutely to nontolerant, nonanxious subjects produce increases in positive mood (euphoria), energy, and alertness. Experienced cocaine users were unable to distinguish between intravenous (IV) cocaine and D-amphetamine,[21] and cross-tolerance between cocaine and D-amphetamine with respect to their anorectic effect has been demonstrated.[22] Additionally, the toxic psychosis observed after days or weeks of continued use of both psychostimulants is very similar. The fully developed toxic syndrome, characterized by vivid auditory and visual hallucinations, paranoid delusions, and disordered thinking, is often indistinguishable from paranoid schizophrenia.[20] Derlet et al.[23] reported that the most prominent presenting symptoms seen in 127 cases of amphetamine toxicity were agitation, suicidal ideation, hallucinations, delusions, confusion, and chest pain. Once drug use ceases, symptoms usually resolve within 1 week.

Research studies on human performance have typically involved the administration of cocaine and D-amphetamine in single doses that do not produce toxic psychosis. In the studies reviewed, D-amphetamine was administered orally (PO). Given that the performance effects of D-amphetamine have been studied for more than 60 years and its widespread use during World War II,[24] it is not surprising that much is known about the effects of D-amphetamine on vigilance and attention. However, the effect of psychostimulants on higher-order cognitive processes has not been widely studied.

Sensory Abilities

A frequently used measure of central nervous system (CNS) functioning is critical flicker frequency (CFF) threshold. The task requires subjects to view a light stimulus and to note the point (frequency) at which the steady light begins to flicker (or vice versa), as the experimenter changes the frequency of the light. An increase in CFF threshold indicates increased cortical and behavioral arousal, whereas a decrease suggests lowered CNS arousal.[25] D-Amphetamine reliably increases CFF threshold.[8,25] In the only study, to our knowledge, intranasal cocaine (100 mg) had no effect on CFF threshold.[26]

Motor Abilities

Finger tapping is considered to be a measure of relatively pure motor activity. One study found that D-amphetamine (10 mg) produced a 5% increase in tapping rate,[27] whereas three other studies reported no effect.[28-30] The circular lights test is a measure of gross motor coordination in which subjects extinguish lights by pressing buttons that are arranged in a 72-cm-diameter circle on a wall-mounted panel. The test is typically performed for 1 min. D-Amphetamine (25 mg) increased response rate on the circular lights test in one study,[31] but another study reported no effect of 20 mg D-amphetamine.[32] The effect of cocaine on finger tapping and circular lights performance has not been examined.

Attentional Abilities

Attention is a broad psychological category encompassing behaviors such as searching, scanning, and detecting visual and auditory stimuli for brief or long periods of time.[33,34] In nearly all performance tests assessing attention, responding is measured in some temporal form, such as reaction or response time, time off target, or response rate. If appropriate, response accuracy is also reported. Because of differential drug effects, it can be helpful to distinguish among focused, selective, divided, and sustained attention.[6]

Focused attention involves attending to one task for a brief period of time, usually about 5 min or less. In this regard, D-amphetamine[7] and cocaine[26] have been shown to improve performance in auditory and visual reaction time tests, although other studies have reported no effect of D-amphetamine. A brief, frequently used test of psychomotor skills and attention is the digit symbol substitution test (DSST), which originated as a paper and pencil subtest of the Wechsler Adult Intelligence Scale and now exists in a computerized version.[35] The DSST requires subjects to draw the symbol or type the pattern associated with each numeral 1 to 9. The number of attempted and correct symbols or patterns during the 90-s test is recorded. In general, D-amphetamine[7,36] and cocaine[37–39] enhanced performance on the DSST, although Foltin et al.[40] reported that cocaine decreased number of attempted trials, and others have reported no effect of smoked cocaine[41] or D-amphetamine.[42,43]

A few recent studies have looked at behavioral inhibition using reaction time tasks that require the participant to make quick responses to "go" signals and inhibit responding to "stop" signals. An impairment in the ability to inhibit responses is used as a measure of impulsivity. Cocaine administered orally to cocaine users dose-dependently impaired the ability to inhibit responses.[44] However, in another study in which cocaine was smoked, there was no effect on reaction time.[41] In contrast, D-amphetamine administered orally to healthy volunteers improved inhibition, but only in those people who had slow baseline stop responses.[45]

Examining selective attention, two studies reported that D-amphetamine improved accuracy,[46,47] and either increased[46] or decreased[47] reaction time. The effect of D-amphetamine and cocaine on divided attention has not been widely investigated; two studies reported small increases in accuracy on a divided attention test after administration of D-amphetamine.[48,49] Several studies have shown that D-amphetamine reliably enhanced performance in tests of visual and auditory vigilance.[7,50] The time of effect in these studies was 1 to 4 h after drug administration, suggesting that D-amphetamine improved performance by preventing the vigilance decrement that typically occurs in tests of sustained attention.

Cognitive Abilities

Psychostimulants have produced inconsistent effects on tests of cognition. Several studies have investigated the effect of cocaine on a test of repeated acquisition and performance of response sequences. In the acquisition component, subjects attempt to learn by trial and error a predetermined sequence of 10 numbers within 20 trials. Subjects learn a new sequence each time they perform the test. In the performance component, the response sequence remains constant throughout the experiment, and thus subjects repeat an already learned sequence. Two studies have reported no effect of either intranasal (IN) or IV cocaine on the test.[37,40] However, Higgins et al.[51] reported that cocaine (96 mg, IN) decreased response rate during the acquisition phase and increased response accuracy during the performance component. In a similar serial acquisition procedure, cocaine has been shown to have no effect.[52,53]

Cocaine[26] and D-amphetamine[7] had no effect on simple arithmetic skills. With respect to memory, most studies have also indicated no effect of D-amphetamine on immediate recall of lists of numbers.[7] However, Soetens et al.[54] reported that D-amphetamine (10 mg) administered PO before learning and intramuscularly (IM) after learning enhanced recall of a word list for up to 3 days. D-Amphetamine also enhanced performance on a working memory task, but only in subjects with a low baseline working memory capacity. In contrast, amphetamine diminished performance in high-baseline subjects.[55]

Summary

The performance effects of D-amphetamine have been studied to a greater extent than those of cocaine; however, because of their similar pharmacology, both drugs generally produce comparable effects. Psychostimulants in low to moderate doses typically produce behavioral and cortical arousal, and thus D-amphetamine reliably increases CFF threshold and has been shown in some studies to increase finger tapping rate and gross motor coordination. A relatively large body of literature indicates that D-amphetamine and cocaine enhance attentional abilities, including brief tests requiring focused attention and vigilance tasks requiring sustained attention. The majority of studies have shown that cocaine and D-amphetamine have no effect on learning, memory, and other cognitive processes, such as solving arithmetic problems.

4.1.2.2   3,4-Methylenedioxymethamphetamine (MDMA; Ecstasy)

Since the late 1980s, MDMA (ecstasy) has become an increasingly popular recreational drug among teenagers and young adults. MDMA has structural similarities to hallucinogens and psychomotor stimulants and acts to release presynaptic monoamines, primarily serotonin. Cardiovascular effects are similar to other stimulants and include increases in heart rate and blood pressure due to peripheral norepinephrine release. Users report a sense of well-being, heightened responsiveness to emotions, and feelings of intimacy toward other people. These effects are sometimes accompanied by mild hallucinations and perceptual disturbances, thought to be due to the drug's interaction with postsynaptic 5-HT2 receptors.[56] There have been reports of MDMA-generated psychotic syndrome, anxiety-related disorders, and other psychiatric symptoms.

MDMA is most often taken orally in a typical dose range per tablet of 50 to 100 mg.[57,58] Neurotoxicity of MDMA to serotonergic systems has been demonstrated in animal studies; therefore for ethical reasons most research has been accomplished using light to heavy MDMA users. Methodological confounds associated with this include the sometimes extensive previous or concurrent use of other drugs, the existence of premorbid psychiatric syndromes often is not explored or reported, and variability in the components of street drugs sold as "ecstasy."

Sensorimotor Abilities

Prepulse inhibition (PPI) of acoustic startle is the reduction of a startle response to a stimulus when that stimulus is preceded by a weaker stimulus. PPI has been used as an operational measure to study sensorimotor gating in a variety of populations. In a double-blind, placebo-controlled study, MDMA (1.7 mg) was administered orally to healthy, non-MDMA-using volunteers to determine the effect on PPI. MDMA produced a slight but significant increase in startle reactivity.[59] Using a trail-making test to assess psychomotor speed, there were no differences in performance between current and former MDMA users, polydrug users, and drug naïve participants.[60] Similarly, users of MDMA were asked to perform a simple reaction time task after administration of 75 and 125 mg of MDMA and neither dose affected task performance.[61]

Attentional Abilities

There are several reports of decrements in attentional processes among MDMA users. Focused attention, as assessed by the DSST, was significantly worse among MDMA users who were administered 125 mg MDMA.[61] In another study employing a similar task, MDMA users who were abstinent for 3 weeks prior to testing were significantly less accurate than non-MDMA users at baseline.[62] On a divided attention task requiring attention to simultaneously presented visual and auditory cues, participants who were regular users of both cannabis and MDMA performed more poorly than cannabis users only and than participants who used neither drug. These MDMA/cannabis users also performed more poorly than either comparison group on a selective attention task requiring visual memory, target selection, and response inhibition.[63] Adolescent MDMA users performed significantly worse as compared to drug naïve adolescents on both selective and divided attention tasks.[64] However, another group reported no impairment in divided attention in either current or former MDMA users.[60]

Reports of sustained attention performance are mixed. In studies that used the Continuous Performance Task (CPT), no differences were observed between MDMA users and drug naïve controls.[64,65] Using a visual search scan, regular (>10 times) and novice (≤10 times) users of MDMA were compared to MDMA naïve participants. Subjects were tested off-drug, when the user groups were actively self-administering MDMA, and at three times (up to 7 days) after the last drug use. Visual scanning was impaired only when the user groups were on MDMA.[66] This was confirmed in a second study in which these groups were tested only while they were drug-free, and there were no differences in sustained attention performance between the three groups.[67] In contrast is a report of MDMA users who were abstinent for 3 weeks prior to testing, yet still had performance decrements on a sustained attention task that required arithmetic calculations.[62]

Cognitive Abilities

Many studies that have assessed cognitive processes have demonstrated impairment in both active and abstinent users of MDMA, particularly on memory performance. Memory decrements have been reported long after users had ceased taking the drug. For example, immediate[67] and delayed recall was significantly worse in novice[66] and regular MDMA users,[66–68] compared to MDMA-naïve participants, whether they were on or off drug.[66,67] Memory scores remained poor in the regular MDMA users up to 7 days after drug use.[66] Other studies have confirmed that memory difficulties can persist after drug use has ended. MDMA users who were abstinent 1 week,[69] 3 weeks,[62] 2 months,[70] 6 months,[68,71] and at least 1 year[70] showed impaired performances on short-term memory,[62,69–71] delayed recall,[68,70] working memory,[62,71] and logical reasoning[62] compared to MDMA-naïve control groups. However, another study found no decrements in working memory in MDMA users,[60] and Parrott[18] mentioned several unpublished reports in which unimpaired learning or memory task performance was observed in users.

One problem, as noted earlier, is that cognitive deficits reported in these studies might be confounded by concurrent use of other drugs. For example, one investigator[72] reported that it was impossible to recruit MDMA users who did not also use cannabis. Exploring the relationship of these two drugs, one group reported that cannabis-only users and drug-naïve participants performed significantly better on tests of working memory, immediate recall, selective and divided attention, and logical thinking compared to users of MDMA + cannabis.[63] In that group, the use of cannabis was related to more pronounced cognitive deficits. In contrast, other investigators have reported that both drug-using groups each performed significantly worse than non-users on several measures of memory and other cognitive processes,[72,73] suggesting that coincident cannabis use might account for the cognitive impairment in MDMA users. However, in one of those studies[72] the MDMA + cannabis group did perform worse on two delayed recall tasks and others also have reported similar findings on various cognitive tasks.[17,18,57,58]

Summary

Simple cognitive processes such as reaction time seem to be normal among MDMA users, with the exception of one report of altered sensorimotor gating. More complex cognitive processes, such as attentional processes, appear to be more susceptible to disruption by MDMA. Although the literature is mixed, the use of MDMA has been reported to disrupt focused, divided, selective, and sustained attention. There is a growing body of evidence that even light recreational use of MDMA can have long-lasting effects on memory, including verbal and visual recall and working memory. The degree of memory impairment is associated with the extent and intensity of drug use and might be enhanced by concurrent cannabis use, and memory deficits can be long lasting.

4.1.3   Nicotine and Tobacco

The vast majority of people who use nicotine (either cigarettes or smokeless tobacco products) use the drug on a daily basis and are considered to be addicted to or dependent on nicotine. In contrast, a minority of people who use the other psychoactive drugs considered in this chapter for nonmedical purposes develop a drug dependence. Daily smokers accumulate plasma levels of nicotine that increase during the day, decline overnight, but never reach zero. This poses a unique problem when conducting behavioral studies with smokers. When improvements in performance are observed after nicotine is given to smokers who have been tobacco-deprived overnight (a common design strategy), it is impossible to determine whether such improvements represent a true enhancement of performance or the alleviation of withdrawal-induced performance deficits. The latter explanation would simply represent a reversal to the person's normal smoking behavioral baseline, not a true enhancement above baseline performance. Unlike other drugs of abuse that are typically tested in nondependent, nontolerant subjects, this issue must always be considered when interpreting the effects of nicotine on smokers' performance.

Two papers have thoroughly reviewed the literature on the effects of nicotine and cigarette smoking on human performance.[6,15] In general, both reviews concluded that nicotine does not universally enhance performance and cognition and that any nicotine-induced performance improvements are small in magnitude. Heishman et al.[6] suggested that the limited performance-enhancing effects of nicotine are not likely to be an important factor in the initiation of cigarette smoking by adolescents (the modal age for starting tobacco use is between 11 and 15; beginning after high school is rare[74]). However, once an individual is dependent on nicotine, data suggest that nicotine deprivation maintains smoking, at least in part, because nicotine can reverse withdrawal-induced performance decrements.[6]

Because the majority of studies in this area are methodologically deficient, only studies that used placebo-control conditions and single- or double-blind drug administration procedures are included in this section. Additionally, because of the problem of interpreting nicotine-induced changes in smokers' performance as discussed above, a distinction will be made between studies that administered nicotine to subjects under conditions of nicotine deprivation and no deprivation. Studies involving no nicotine deprivation include nondeprived smokers and nonsmokers.

4.1.3.1   Sensory Abilities

Sherwood et al.[75] administered nicotine polacrilex gum (0 and 2 mg) three times at 1-h intervals to smokers who were overnight deprived and measured CFF after each administration. CFF threshold was increased over predose baseline after the first 2-mg dose, but no further increase after the second and third doses was observed. Thus, the initial dose appeared to reverse a deprivation-induced deficit, and subsequent doses maintained normal functioning. Baseline CFF was not measured before subjects were tobacco abstinent. No effect of nicotine on CFF was reported following administration of nicotine polacrilex or subcutaneous (SC) nicotine injections to 24-h abstinent smokers, nonabstinent smokers, and nonsmokers.[76–79] The lack of effect of nicotine in the absence of nicotine deprivation is consistent with the data of Sherwood et al.,[75] further suggesting that nicotine reverses withdrawal-induced deficits, but does not produce true enhancement of CFF threshold.

4.1.3.2 Motor Abilities

Perkins et al.[80] administered placebo and nicotine nasal spray (15 µg/kg) to smokers who were tobacco deprived for at least 12 h. Nicotine reliably increased finger tapping rate in all subjects, and produced a nonsignificant trend toward improved hand steadiness. In a subsequent study, Perkins et al.[81] reported that nicotine (5, 10, and 20 µg/kg) increased finger tapping rate, but impaired hand steadiness and hand tremor in nonsmokers and overnight tobacco abstinent smokers. Finger tapping rate was also increased by nicotine in nonsmokers who were administered nicotine nasal solution or spray[80,82] or SC nicotine injections.[77] In contrast, Foulds et al.[79] found that nicotine injections (0.3 and 0.6 mg, SC) had no effect on finger tapping rate in nonsmokers, and only 0.3 mg nicotine produced a slight tapping rate increase in 24-h abstinent smokers. Heishman and Henningfield[83] administered nicotine polacrilex gum (0, 2, 4, 8 mg) to nonsmokers each day for 8 days and found that the 8-mg dose impaired gross motor performance on the circular lights test.

4.1.3.3 Attentional Abilities

Numerous studies investigating focused attention have used reaction time tests. Nicotine polacrilex gum (2 mg) produced faster motor reaction time, but did not affect recognition reaction time in overnight deprived smokers,[75] nonabstinent smokers,[76] and a group of nonabstinent smokers and nonsmokers.[78] Le Houezec et al.[84] found that SC nicotine (0.8 mg) increased the number of fast reaction times, but did not affect task accuracy. Griesar et al.[85] reported faster reaction time following administration of transdermal nicotine patch compared to placebo patch in nonsmokers. However, Hindmarch et al.[76] reported no effect of 2-mg polacrilex on reaction time in nonsmokers.

Selective attention can be defined as the ability to attend to a target stimulus while simultaneously ignoring irrelevant or distracting stimuli. In 12-h tobacco-deprived smokers, nicotine polacrilex (2 and 4 mg) reversed deprivation-induced impairments in letter searching to pre-deprivation baseline[86] and had no effect on Stroop and letter cancellation tests.[87] The Stroop test compares the time required for subjects to name the ink color of color words that are incongruent (e.g., the word red printed in blue ink) vs. the ink color of neutral stimuli, such as non-color words or colored squares. Typically, the incongruent task takes more time than the neutral stimulus task because the tendency to read the color word interferes with naming its ink color; the difference in time between the two tasks is considered a measure of selective attention or distractibility.[88] In two studies comparing abstinent smokers and nonsmokers on the Stroop test, nicotine nasal spray (5, 10, and 20 µg/kg) improved response time, but impaired accuracy with regard to the Stroop conflict,[81] whereas nicotine injections (0.3 and 0.6 mg, SC) had no effect.[79] Using the Stroop test with nonsmokers, Wesnes and Revell[89] found no effect of 1.5-mg nicotine tablets, whereas Provost and Woodward[90] reported faster response time after 2-mg nicotine polacrilex. In two studies with nonsmokers, nicotine polacrilex (2 and 4 mg) had no effect on letter searching response time or accuracy,[91] whereas 8-mg polacrilex impaired letter searching accuracy.[83]

Using a divided attention test that required subjects to perform simultaneously a central tracking task and respond to peripheral visual stimuli, Sherwood et al.[75] found that 2-mg polacrilex decreased tracking errors, but had no effect on reaction time to the peripheral lights in overnight deprived smokers. There were fewer tracking errors after the third nicotine dose compared to the first dose, and placebo responding was unchanged, suggesting a true enhancement of performance. In the same divided attention test, nicotine decreased errors on the tracking task in nonabstinent smokers[76,78] but had no effect in nonsmokers.[76]

The rapid visual information processing (RVIP) test has been used in numerous studies investigating the effects of smoking and nicotine on sustained attention. This test requires subjects to press a button when they detect three consecutive even or odd digits in a series of single digits presented on a video monitor at 600-ms intervals. In tobacco-deprived smokers, RVIP accuracy was improved after subjects smoked cigarettes,[92] were administered nicotine polacrilex,[87,93] or received SC injections of nicotine.[79] However, there was no effect on RVIP performance in smokers who were abstinent for 2 h and given polacrilex (4 mg)[94] and in nondeprived smokers allowed to smoke one cigarette.[95] Wesnes et al.[96] reported that the decline in signal detection during an 80-min vigilance test was less after active nicotine tablets compared with placebo in 12-h deprived smokers. Testing nonsmokers, three studies reported that nicotine had no effect on the RVIP test compared to placebo conditions,[77,97,98] whereas Foulds et al.[79] reported faster reaction time after nicotine injections (0.3 and 0.6 mg, SC). Levin et al.[99] found that transdermal nicotine decreased errors of omission on a continuous performance test in nonsmokers. Nonsmokers were also administered nicotine tablets in the Wesnes et al.[96] study, and no difference between abstinent smokers and nonsmokers was observed, suggesting that nicotine functioned to reverse deprivation-induced deficits in the 12-h abstinent smokers.

4.1.3.4 Cognitive Abilities

Testing a verbal rote learning paradigm in overnight-deprived smokers, Andersson and Post[100] reported that after the first cigarette, anticipatory responding was improved in the placebo compared to the nicotine condition, but after the second cigarette, there was no difference between conditions. Another study reported that, after learning a word-pair list, smoking a cigarette reduced errors when subjects were tested 1 week later.[101]

The effects of nicotine and smoking on memory have been widely investigated. In two studies conducted with 10-h abstinent smokers,[102,103] most subjects recalled a greater number of words after nicotine tablets or cigarettes; however, some subjects' recall improved after placebo tablets or denicotinized cigarettes, and some showed no difference between conditions. More recent studies with 12- to 24-h abstinent smokers found that nicotine nasal spray[81] and SC nicotine injections[79] improved recognition memory. In a study with minimally tobacco deprived (1 h) smokers, three experiments found no effect of smoking after word list presentation on delayed intentional word recall.[104] In contrast, three experiments found improved free recall when subjects either smoked[104,105] or received 2-mg polacrilex gum[106] before list presentation. Krebs et al.[107] reported that subjects' recall of prose passages was better after smoking a 0.7-mg nicotine cigarette compared to 0.1- or 1.5-mg nicotine cigarettes, suggesting that optimal arousal was produced by the medium, compared with the high, nicotine-containing cigarette. Reaction time on the Sternberg memory test, which measures scanning and retrieval from short-term memory, was faster after smoking[75,108] and administration of nicotine polacrilex[109] compared to placebo conditions; however, Foulds et al.[79] reported no effect of SC nicotine on the Sternberg memory test in 24-h abstinent smokers and nonsmokers.

In contrast to these positive effects of nicotine on memory, three studies[86,93,110] reported no effect of nicotine on tests of immediate and delayed recall in nicotine-deprived smokers, and Houston et al.[111] reported that immediate and delayed recall was impaired after smoking a nicotine cigarette compared to a nicotine-free cigarette. In studies of nondeprived smokers or nonsmokers, two reported that nicotine improved some aspects of memory in patients with Alzheimer's disease,[77,112] two found enhanced reaction time on the Sternberg memory test,[78,109] four reported no effect of nicotine on tests of immediate and delayed recall,[76,77,91,113] and two found that nicotine polacrilex impaired immediate and/or delayed recall accuracy.[83,114] Foulds et al.[79] reported that SC nicotine enhanced response time but decreased accuracy in a digit recall test in nonsmokers.

Several studies have examined the effect of nicotine on other cognitive abilities. Snyder and Henningfield[86] reported that polacrilex (2 and 4 mg) enhanced response time but had no effect on accuracy in an arithmetic test and had no effect on either speed or accuracy in a test of logical reasoning in 12-h abstinent smokers. However, Foulds et al.[79] reported that nicotine injections (0.3 and 0.6 mg, SC) improved response time on the logical reasoning test in 24-h deprived smokers. Five studies conducted with nonsmokers reported no effect of nicotine on several cognitive tests, including the ability to generate correct answers to word and number problems[114] and logical reasoning and mental arithmetic.[79,83,91,113]

4.1.3.5 Summary

As discussed previously, results of studies conducted with nicotine-deprived smokers are difficult to interpret. Without pre-deprivation baseline data, which few studies report, it is difficult to conclude whether nicotine reversed deprivation-induced deficits or enhanced performance beyond that observed in the nondeprived state. In general, however, nicotine and smoking at least reversed deprivation-induced deficits in certain abilities in abstinent smokers, but such beneficial effects have not been observed consistently across a range of performance measures. For example, about half of the studies that measured sustained attention and memory reported a positive effect of nicotine; however, the effects were limited to some subjects or one aspect of test performance.

The strongest conclusions concerning the effects of nicotine and smoking on human performance can be drawn from studies conducted with nondeprived smokers and nonsmokers. These studies indicated that nicotine enhanced finger tapping rate and motor responding in tests of focused and divided attention. Additionally, nicotine produced faster motor responses in the Sternberg memory test, enhanced recognition memory, and reversed the vigilance decrement in a sustained attention test. However, no studies reported true enhancement of sensory abilities, selective attention, learning, and other cognitive abilities.

4.1.4 Sedative-Hypnotics: Benzodiazepines

Since their advent in the 1960s, benzodiazepines have been prescribed widely as anxiolytic and sedative-hypnotic medications, essentially replacing barbiturates because of their greater safety margin. Compared with barbiturates, an acute benzodiazepine overdose is much less likely to produce fatal respiratory depression.[20] There are currently more than a dozen benzodiazepines available for medical use; all produce sedation with varying potency. Benzodiazepines with longer duration of action, such as diazepam and lorazepam, are typically prescribed for the treatment of anxiety disorders, whereas those with shorter duration of action, such as triazolam, are used as hypnotics for insomnia. A concern with benzodiazepines being used at night to induce sleep has been the potential for sedation and impaired performance the next day. A review of 52 studies[115] indicated that all benzodiazepine hypnotics, at high enough doses, produced next-day performance impairment. The degree of impairment was dose related, suggesting that the lowest effective hypnotic dose should be prescribed.

As with all drugs that produce changes in mood, benzodiazepines have the potential to be abused,[116,117] and methodologies have been developed to test the abuse liability of benzodiazepines and related drugs in the laboratory.[118] The pattern of benzodiazepine abuse varies from occasional episodes of intoxication to daily, compulsive use of large doses. Tolerance and physical dependence develop with continued use, such that individuals taking therapeutic doses of benzodiazepines for several months typically experience withdrawal symptoms even if the dose is gradually tapered.[20] The benzodiazepine withdrawal syndrome includes insomnia, restlessness, dizziness, nausea, headache, inability to concentrate, and fatigue. Although unpleasant, benzodiazepine withdrawal is not life-threatening, unlike withdrawal from barbiturates.

The effects of benzodiazepines have been studied extensively with respect to human performance and cognition. Because of their sedative effects, not surprisingly, benzodiazepines generally impair all aspects of performance.[7,119] However, some decrements, such as the well-studied anterograde amnesia, have been shown to be independent of general sedation.[12] Benzodiazepines will be considered as the prototypic sedative-hypnotic drug, recognizing that other CNS depressant drugs, such as barbiturates and ethanol, produce somewhat distinct performance impairment profiles. In the studies reviewed, benzodiazepines were administered PO.

4.1.4.1 Sensory Abilities

Consistent with their depressant and sedative effects, benzodiazepines administered acutely typically decrease CFF threshold.[119,120] Specifically, significant decreases have been reported for 1 mg alprazolam, 10 mg diazepam, and 15 mg quazepam;[121] 4 to 11 mg midazolam;[122] 7.5 to 50 mg oxazepam;[123] 1 and 2 mg lorazepam;[124] and 0.5 mg triazolam and 1 mg flunitrazepam.[120] As is evident, this effect on CFF threshold was observed at therapeutic doses of each drug, and when multiple doses were tested, the effect was dose-related. However, there are reports of acute, therapeutic doses of diazepam (5 mg)[125] and lorazepam (1 and 2 mg)[125,126] having no effect on CFF threshold. One study investigating numerous benzodiazepines[120] reported next-day impairment after acute doses of triazolam (0.5 mg) and lormetazepam (1 to 2 mg). No studies were found that examined the effect of chronic benzodiazepine administration on CFF threshold.

Blom et al.[121] recorded horizontal saccadic eye movements as subjects viewed the successive illumination of red light stimuli. They reported that alprazolam, diazepam, and quazepam reduced peak saccadic velocity; alprazolam produced the greatest degree of impairment. Maximal reductions occurred 1 to 4 h after dosing, and effects had not returned to placebo levels at 8 h. Rettig et al.[127] reported that 1 mg lormetazepam and 15 mg midazolam given the night before increased imbalance of the ocular muscles as measured by the Maddox Wing test. This muscular imbalance produces strabismus, which is the inability of both eyes to converge directly on a visual stimulus. Such ocular impairment could be the basis of a wide range of benzodiazepine-induced performance deficits.

4.1.4.2 Motor Abilities

Numerous studies have reported that various benzodiazepines decrease finger tapping rate.[119,122,124,128] Kunsman et al.[119] noted that finger tapping rate was generally less sensitive to the effects of benzodiazepines than more complex tasks, such as reaction time and tracking. However, the studies reporting decreases in tapping rate used doses that were in the therapeutic range; thus simple motor skills can be impaired at clinically relevant doses.

A large number of studies have shown that benzodiazepines impair gross motor coordination, as measured by the ability to balance on one leg and the circular lights test. Alprazolam (0.5 to 2 mg),[129] lorazepam (1 and 4 mg),[130,131] and triazolam (0.25 to 0.75)[132–135] impaired balance or circular lights performance in a dose-related manner. In a population of sedative abusers, acute administration of 40 or 80 mg diazepam and 1 or 2 mg triazolam impaired circular lights performance, and diazepam, but not triazolam, impaired performance the next day.[136] Stoops and Rush[137] reported that tolerance to impaired performance on the circular lights task developed over several sessions of triazolam (0.375 mg) administration. Bond et al.[128] reported that 1 mg alprazolam increased body sway as measured in an automated ataxiameter.

In contrast to these reports of benzodiazepine-induced motor impairment, Kumar et al.[138] found that chronic administration of 1 mg lorazepam and 0.5 mg alprazolam for 5 days had no effect on fine motor coordination as assessed using a standard pegboard test. Additionally, Tobler et al.[139] reported that performance on a typing test was not impaired the day after an acute dose of 7.5 mg midazolam.

4.1.4.3 Attentional Abilities

The effects of benzodiazepines on reaction time tests and the DSST have been investigated in many studies, the majority of which reported impairment of attentional abilities necessary to perform such tests successfully. Because these tests typically are of short duration (less than 5 min), focused attention is primarily required, although other abilities are also involved. Numerous studies have reported that simple or choice reaction time to visual stimuli was increased (slowed) by acute, therapeutic doses of various benzodiazepines, including adinazolam,[140] alprazolam,[129] diazepam and flunitrazepam,[141] lorazepam,[130,142] oxazepam,[123] temazepam,[119] and triazolam.[132] Linnoila et al.[143,144] reported that diazepam, alprazolam, and adinazolam impaired reaction time and accuracy in a word recognition test. Flurazepam (30 mg, but not 15 mg) produced next-day impairment of simple and choice visual reaction time, whereas 15 mg midazolam had no residual effect.[145] In contrast, diazepam (5 mg) and lorazepam (1 mg) had no effect on an auditory reaction time test.[125] It is possible that, compared with visual tests, auditory reaction time tests are less sensitive to the impairing effects of benzodiazepines. To investigate this, Pompeia et al.[146] compared the effects of equipotent doses of lorazepam and flunitrazepam on visual and auditory event-related potentials. Both benzodiazepines produced performance decrements on auditory delayed recall; however, flunitrazepam increased P3 latencies in both visual and auditory modalities whereas lorazepam increased visual latencies only.

Like reaction time tests, nearly all studies have reported that acute administration of benzodiazepines impair performance on the DSST. Lorazepam (1 to 9 mg),[125,130,142,147–149] triazolam (0.25 to 0.75 mg),[132,134,135,148,150–153] alprazolam (0.5 to 4 mg),[129,147] temazepam (15 to 60 mg),[119,150] diazepam (5 to 10 mg),[147,154] clonazepam,[155] and estazolam (1 to 4 mg)[152] have been shown to impair response speed and/or accuracy on the DSST in a dose-related manner. However, Kelly et al.[156] reported that diazepam (5 or 10 mg) had no effect on DSST performance. It is unlikely that low doses of diazepam accounted for the lack of effect, as suggested by Kelly et al.,[156] because numerous studies have reported DSST impairment after 10 mg diazepam.[7] In a test similar to the DSST, symbol copying, Saano et al.[125] reported no effect of diazepam (5 mg) and lorazepam (1 mg). Acute triazolam (0.375 mg) administration decreased the number of trials completed on the DSST task, but tolerance to this decrement developed with each of three subsequent doses.[137]

Another test requiring focused attention is digit or letter cancellation, in which subjects mark through a certain numeral in a page of random numbers or a certain letter in a page of text or random letters. The typical duration of cancellation tests is 1 to 2 min. Two studies reported that diazepam (10 or 15 mg)[157] and lorazepam (1 and 2 mg)[124] impaired digit cancellation performance. Interestingly, Brown et al.[157] found that impaired focused attention was not correlated with the ability to encode associative information. These studies confirm numerous previous studies that reported benzodiazepine-induced decrements in cancellation tests.[7]

Brief tests of tracking abilities can also be considered tests of focused attention. In such tests, subjects attempt to maintain a moving target within a certain area of the video monitor or a cursor within a moving target. Tracking performance is uniformly impaired by benzodiazepines at doses similar to those reported above for reaction time and DSST impairment.[119,143,144] One study investigating the effects of multiple doses of three benzodiazepines reported that lorazepam produced the greatest degree of tracking impairment, followed by alprazolam and then diazepam.[147] Because the manipulandum used to control the moving target in some studies was a steering wheel, tracking tests have occasionally been considered laboratory tests of driving ability. In studies of on-road driving, Volkerts et al.[158] reported that driving was impaired the morning after dosing with oxazepam (50 mg) and slightly impaired after lormetazepam (1 mg). Brookhuis et al.[159] found that next-day driving was significantly impaired after flurazepam (30 mg) and less impaired after lormetazepam (2 mg). Diazepam (15 mg) impaired performance on a clinical test for drunkenness, which comprised 13 tests assessing motor, vestibular, mental, and behavioral functioning.[160]

Compared with focused attention, fewer studies have examined the effects of benzodiazepines on selective attention. Two studies have shown that performance on the Stroop test was impaired by lorazepam.[119,131] Acute administration of triazolam and lorazepam produced dose-dependent decrements in response rate and accuracy in a simultaneous matching-to-sample task, which required subjects to determine which of two comparison visual stimuli was identical to the sample stimulus.[148,161] The drug effects differed as a function of task difficulty, such that the benzodiazepine-induced impairment was reduced when discriminability of the non-matching stimulus was increased.

Benzodiazepines have been shown to impair divided attention.[119] Two groups of investigators reported that oxazepam (7.5 to 50 mg)[123] and alprazolam (0.5 mg)[162] impaired performance on a test that required subjects to divide their attention between a central tracking task and responding to stimuli in the peripheral visual field. Using a similar test of divided attention, Moskowitz et al.[145] found that 30 mg flurazepam and 15 mg midazolam impaired performance the day after drug administration.

Consistent with the other types of attention, benzodiazepines impair performance in tests of sustained attention or vigilance.[14,143,145] There is no evidence that benzodiazepines exacerbate the vigilance decrement normally observed during prolonged, tedious tests. The impairment caused by benzodiazepines in tests of sustained attention is not secondary to sedation, but rather a direct effect on perceptual sensitivity, resulting in decreased hits and increased response time in detecting stimulus targets.

4.1.4.4 Cognitive Abilities

The most widely studied aspect of cognition with respect to benzodiazepines is memory.[12,163] One of the most reliable effects of benzodiazepines is to impair recall of information presented after drug administration (anterograde amnesia). In contrast, information presented before administration of benzodiazepines is not affected. The memory decrement produced by benzodiazepines is a function of task difficulty, such that little or no impairment is observed for immediate recall of a few items, whereas more complex or delayed memory tests reveal profound impairment.[12] The benzodiazepine antagonist flumazenil has been used to block the sedative effects of benzodiazepines, but the amnestic effect was not affected, suggesting that benzodiazepine-induced amnesia is independent of sedation.[122,164] It has also been demonstrated that some benzodiazepines selectively impaired explicit memory (e.g., recall of a word list), but left other aspects of memory intact.[163] In this way, benzodiazepines have been used as pharmacological tools to identify distinct memory processes.

Roy-Byrne et al.[165] reported that diazepam (10 mg) impaired attentional processes during auditory presentation of a word list and immediate recognition of words that had been presented twice; however, naming examples of a category, such as vegetables (semantic memory), and self-evaluation of memory performance (meta-cognition) were not affected. Triazolam (0.25 to 0.5 mg) impaired free recall of a word list, but had no effect on implicit (memory without awareness of the source of information) or semantic memory.[166,167] Linnoila et al.[143] reported that adinazolam (15 or 30 mg) impaired attention during list presentation, but had no effect on delayed (1 min) free recall of words. Using a battery of tests that assessed numerous memory functions, Bishop et al.[124] reported that lorazepam (1 and 2 mg) impaired explicit (free recall), semantic, and implicit memory, but had no effect on working memory (manipulation of information for less than 30 s) and procedural memory (knowledge required for skills reflected as improved performance with practice). Similarly, a higher dose of lorazepam (2.5 mg) disrupted several memory processes (delayed recall, implicit and semantic memory), but did not affect short-term memory.[168] Such selective drug effects on memory and similarly selective clinical amnestic syndromes resulting from brain injury or disease[163] have allowed a greater understanding of cognitive functioning and the processes subserving learning and memory.

A large number of studies have investigated the effect of acute benzodiazepine administration on either immediate or delayed recall or recognition of word lists, numbers, or pictures in healthy volunteers. Impaired memory has been reported for adinazolam (20 to 30 mg),[140] alprazolam (0.5 to 2 mg),[129,144,169] diazepam (5 to 15 mg),[157,170] estazolam (1 to 4 mg),[152] lorazepam (1 to 4 mg),[130,171] temazepam (15 to 60 mg),[150] and triazolam (0.25 to 0.75 mg).[132–135,150,152,172] Acute administration of triazolam[135] and lorazepam[131] has been observed to significantly impair working memory. In addition, Buchanan et al.[173] reported that triazolam (0.25 mg) interfered with the facilitating effect that emotional stimuli have on long-term memory (both delayed recall and recognition). Diazepam (15 mg) also was reported to produce impairments in facial emotional recognition.[174] Testing subjects with histories of sedative abuse, Roache and Griffiths[136,142] reported that immediate and delayed recall and recognition of digits and symbols were impaired by diazepam (40 or 80 mg), lorazepam (1.5 to 9 mg), and triazolam (1 or 2 mg). After 5 days of dosing healthy subjects with either alprazolam (0.5 mg) or lorazepam (1 mg), anterograde amnesia was observed for word lists.[138] Hindmarch et al.[120] examined the effects of several benzodiazepines on the Sternberg memory test, which measures scanning and retrieval from short-term memory. They reported that acute administration of flunitrazepam (1 mg), lormetazepam (1 to 2 mg), and triazolam (0.5 mg) significantly slowed response time on the test and that performance remained impaired the next day with lormetazepam and triazolam. However, Kelly et al.[156] reported no effect of diazepam (5 and 10 mg) on the Sternberg test.

The effect of a number of benzodiazepines has been investigated on the repeated acquisition and performance of response sequences task, which comprises separate acquisition (learning) and performance components.[175] This task thus allows independent assessment of drug effects on acquisition of new information and performance of already learned information. In general, doses of benzodiazepines that increased errors in the acquisition component did not impair the performance component, although high doses decreased response rate and increased errors in both components. Impairment of acquisition of the response sequence has been reported following acute administration of alprazolam (1 to 3 mg),[175] diazepam (5 to 30 mg),[11,175,176] estazolam (1 to 4 mg),[152] lorazepam (2.8 to 5.6 mg),[149] temazepam (15 to 60 mg),[150] and triazolam (0.375 to 0.75 mg).[150-152,175,176] In these studies, only the highest doses impaired the performance component of the task. In one of the few studies to examine the chronic effects of benzodiazepines on cognitive processes, Bickel et al.[177] administered diazepam (80 mg daily) for 3 days to sedative abusers and found increased errors and decreased response rate in the acquisition component on day 1 that decreased on days 2 and 3, suggesting the development of tolerance. In the performance component, response rate was decreased on day 1; the magnitude of effect decreased over days. Performance error rate was relatively unaffected.

Few studies have examined the effects of benzodiazepines on other cognitive abilities. Rusted et al.[170] reported that 5 and 10 mg diazepam impaired performance on a logical reasoning test, but had no effect on a mental rotation task. Judd et al.[178] found that 30 mg flurazepam, but not 15 mg midazolam, impaired arithmetic (addition) abilities the day after drug administration. In contrast, flurazepam had no effect on reading comprehension.

4.1.4.5 Summary

When administered acutely to nontolerant, healthy volunteers, therapeutic doses of benzodiazepines produce sedation, which typically impairs most aspects of performance in a dose-dependent manner. In patients taking benzodiazepines medically and in individuals who abuse benzodiazepines recreationally, both of whom have developed tolerance, it is necessary to increase the dose of benzodiazepine to observe impaired performance. Benzodiazepines have been shown to decrease CFF threshold, a direct indication of CNS depression, and to impair ocular performance. Motor abilities are impaired by benzodiazepines, including fine (finger tapping) and gross (balance, circular lights, and body sway) motor coordination. Numerous studies have documented that benzodiazepines impair tests requiring focused, selective, divided, and sustained attention. One of the best-studied cognitive effects of benzodiazepines is their ability to produce anterograde amnesia, memory loss for information presented after drug administration. It has been demonstrated that these memory deficits are not secondary to benzodiazepine-induced sedation and that explicit memory (free recall of presented stimuli) functions are typically impaired, whereas other memory processes can remain unaffected. Benzodiazepines have also been shown to impair the acquisition (learning) of new information.

4.1.5   Opioid Analgesics and Anesthetics

The class of drugs referred to as opioids consists of a wide range of naturally occurring derivatives from the opium poppy, *Papaver somniferum*, such as morphine and codeine; semisynthetic derivatives from opium, such as heroin and hydromorphone; and completely synthetic opioids, such as meperidine and fentanyl. The primary pharmacological effect of all opioids is analgesia; a common side effect is sedation. At high doses, respiratory depression occurs, which is the usual cause of death from acute opioid overdose. The full range of clinical pain can be effectively treated with various opioids, and fentanyl and related synthetic congeners (sufentanil, alfentanil) are generally used clinically as anesthetics, but are also used for postoperative analgesia.

Opioids can be classified according to their pharmacological actions into those that function like morphine, producing their agonist effects primarily through the mu opioid receptor, and those that produce mixed effects, such as agonist-antagonists or partial agonists.[179] Mixed agonist-antagonists function as agonists at one type of opioid receptor (e.g., delta or kappa) and as an antagonist at other (e.g., mu) receptors. Partial agonists produce only limited effects at a given receptor. Morphine-like opioids are used clinically for moderate to severe pain, whereas agonist-antagonists and partial agonists produce less analgesia and are thus useful in the treatment of mild pain.

Previous reviews have concluded that opioids produce minimal impairment of human performance even at high doses.[179,180] However, more recent reviews[16,181] challenge this benign notion. In healthy, nontolerant research subjects, opioids impair psychomotor performance to a greater extent than cognitive abilities. Typically, opioids slow responses in tests requiring speed, but do not impair test accuracy. In contrast, individuals who have developed tolerance to opioids, such as patients suffering chronic pain[181] or persons maintained on methadone,[180] generally show little or no behavioral impairment after administration of their maintenance dose. The time required for tolerance to develop to any performance-impairing effects of methadone has been estimated at 3 to 4 weeks in methadone-maintained patients.[180] The studies reviewed here report the performance effects of opioids in nontolerant research volunteers, unless otherwise indicated.

4.1.5.1   *Sensory Abilities*

Studies investigating the effects of morphine, meperidine, buprenorphine, and nalbuphine on CFF threshold have, in general, found impaired functioning, consistent with the CNS depressant effect of opioids.[16] Veselis et al.[182] targeted fentanyl plasma concentrations of 1.0, 1.5, and 2.5 ng/ml using continuous IV infusion and found that CFF threshold was decreased at 1.5 ng/ml, whereas other performance measures were affected only at concentrations greater than 2.5 ng/ml. Morphine (10 mg, PO) was also found to decrease CFF threshold.[183] In contrast, pentazocine (30 mg) had no effect on CFF threshold;[184] however, other studies using higher doses of pentazocine have reported decreased CFF threshold.[16]

Zacny and colleagues have examined the effects of several opioids on the Maddox Wing test, a measure of ocular muscle imbalance indicating divergence of the eyes. Administration of morphine (2.5 to 10 mg, IV),[185] butorphanol (0.5 to 2.0 mg, IV),[186] dezocine (2.5 to 10 mg, IV),[187] pentazocine (30 mg, IM),[184] hydromorphone (1.3 mg, IV),[188] nalbuphine (2.5 to 10 mg, IV),[189] and an anesthetic combination of propofol and alfentanil[190] impaired performance on the Maddox Wing test in a dose-related manner. In contrast, fentanyl (25 to 100 μg, IV)[191] and meperidine (0.25 to 1.0 mg, IV)[192] were found to have no effect on Maddox Wing performance. Additionally, fentanyl (50 μg, IV)[193] and an IV combination of fentanyl (50 μg) plus propofol (35 mg),[194] an IV anesthetic, had no effect on the Maddox Wing test. Thus, many opioids have been shown to decrease CFF threshold, a measure of overall CNS arousal, whereas some, but not all, opioids impaired ocular muscle balance.

4.1.5.2 Motor Abilities

Compared with other measures of performance, few studies have investigated the effects of opioids on pure motor abilities, such as finger tapping and coordination.[16] Kerr et al.[195] used individually tailored steady-state infusions to target several plasma concentrations of morphine (20, 40, and 80 ng/ml). They found that only the high dose of morphine impaired finger tapping and the ability to maintain low constant levels of isometric force, which required precise motor control. Finger tapping rate was decreased in a group of patients with cancer who had received an increase of greater than 30% in their dose of opioid (morphine, hydromorphone, oxycodone, or codeine) compared to a group of patients who did not receive a dosage increase.[196] Finger tapping rate was also decreased following a short term anesthetic regimen of propofol and alfentanil.[190] In contrast, pentazocine (30 mg) had no effect on finger tapping.[184] Butorphanol (0.5 to 2 mg, IV) and nalbuphine (2.5 to 10 mg, IV) were shown to impair a measure of eye–hand coordination.[189] Slightly over half the studies investigating the effect of opioids on body sway, a measure of gross motor coordination, reported impairment.[16]

4.1.5.3 Attentional Abilities

A relatively large number of studies have investigated the effects of opioids on tests requiring focused attention. Morphine (2.5 to 10 mg, IV)[185] and propofol (70 mg, IV)[193] impaired an auditory simple reaction time test, and fentanyl (1 to 2.5 ng/ml, IV)[182] impaired a visual choice reaction time test. Jenkins et al.[197] reported that IV (3 to 20 mg) and smoked (2.6 to 10.5 mg) heroin impaired performance on a simple visual reaction time task. However, other studies reported no effect of butorphanol (0.5 to 2.0 mg, IV),[186] fentanyl (25 to 100 µg, IV),[191] meperidine (0.25 to 1.0 mg, IV),[192] and nalbuphine (2.5 to 10 mg, IV)[189] on an auditory simple reaction time test. It may be that visual reaction time tests are more sensitive than auditory tests to the effects of opioids, which would be consistent with opioid-induced impairment on the Maddox Wing test, discussed in the preceding section.

Numerous studies have reported that performance on the DSST was impaired by various opioids, including morphine (2.5 to 10 mg),[185,198] fentanyl (1 to 2.5 ng/ml),[182] pentazocine (30 mg),[184] butorphanol (0.5 to 2 mg),[186] dezocine (2.5 to 10 mg),[187] propofol (22 to 70 mg),[193,199] nalbuphine (2.5 to 10 mg, IV),[189] and the combination of fentanyl (50 µg) plus propofol (35 mg).[194] In contrast, meperidine was found to have no effect on the DSST.[192] Because the DSST is a timed test, it would appear that opioids slow speeded responses in a fairly consistent manner in opioid-naive subjects. However, in opioid abusers or opioid-dependent persons, Preston and colleagues have reported no effect on DSST performance of several opioids, including morphine (7.5 to 30 mg, IM),[200] hydromorphone (0.125 to 3 mg, IM),[201] buprenorphine (0.5 to 8 mg, IM),[202] pentazocine (7.5 to 120 mg, IM),[203] butorphanol (0.375 to 1.5 mg, IV),[204] and nalbuphine (3 to 24 mg, IM).[205]

Many of these same studies have also reported opioid-induced impairment of a 1-min tracking test in which subjects tracked a randomly moving target on a video monitor with a mouse-controlled cursor. This task measures visual-motor coordination and focused attentional abilities and was impaired by fentanyl (25 to 100 µg, IV),[191,193] meperidine (0.25 to 1.0 mg, IV),[192] butorphanol (0.5 to 2 mg, IV),[186] dezocine (2.5 to 10 mg, IV),[187] and propofol (0.08 to 0.32 mg/kg, IV) alone[199] and in combination with fentanyl (50 µg, IV).[194] Morphine (2.5 to 10 mg, IV) had no effect on the same tracking task.[185] In one of the few studies to investigate the effects of opioids on divided attention, pentazocine (30 mg, IM) was shown to impair the choice reaction time component, but had no effect on the tracking component of a divided attention test.[184] Fentanyl (100 µg, IV) slowed reaction time and movement time in a driving simulator.[206] However, patients suffering noncancer pain receiving transdermal fentanyl for at least 2 weeks showed no impairment on a battery of computerized tests designed to assess driving ability.[207] Further, Galski et al.[208] showed that patients on chronic opioid treatment were not impaired in off-road tests and in a driving simulator. Some studies with morphine have documented impaired sustained attention; however, the few studies that have been conducted with other opioids found no effect on a variety of vigilance tasks.[16,183]

4.1.5.4 Cognitive Abilities

A relatively large number of studies have examined the effects of opioids on memory and other cognitive functions; a minority of these studies have reported impairment.[16] Kerr et al.[195] found that steady-state levels of morphine (20 to 80 ng/ml, IV) slowed reading time of prose passages. When asked questions about the passage immediately after reading, subjects' recall was not impaired, but delayed questioning revealed impaired comprehension. In methadone-maintained patients, a single methadone dose equal to 100% of their daily stabilization dose impaired delayed recall of a prose passage, whereas 50% of their daily dose slightly improved recall.[209] Fentanyl (1 to 2.5 ng/ml, IV) was shown to impair a range of memorial abilities, including auditory-verbal recall of common words, picture recall, and digit recall.[182] In a group of patients with cancer whose opioid (morphine, hydromorphone, oxycodone, or codeine) dose was increased by at least 30%, decreases were observed in an arithmetic test, backward digit span, and a test of visual memory.[196] Propofol (0.08 to 0.32 mg/kg, IV) impaired delayed, but not immediate, recall of a word list only at the highest dose level.[199] In another study, propofol (70 mg, IV), but not fentanyl (50 μg, IV) impaired immediate free recall of words.[193] Walker et al.[189] reported that butorphanol (0.5 to 2 mg, IV), but neither nalbuphine nor pentazocine, slowed responding on a test of logical reasoning.

4.1.5.5 Summary

Administration of acute, therapeutic doses of opioids to nontolerant research subjects produces effects typical of CNS depressant drugs, including decreased CFF threshold. Many, but not all, opioids produce ocular muscle imbalance as assessed in the Maddox Wing test. Finger tapping and gross motor coordination were found to be impaired in some, but not all, studies. A relatively large number of studies have reported that opioids produce decrements in brief tests requiring focused attention and fine motor coordination, such as visual reaction time, DSST, and visual-motor tracking. Very few studies have examined the effects of opioids on selective, divided, and sustained attention. The effects of opioids on cognitive functioning are mixed, with the majority of studies indicating no impairment, but some well-designed studies showing decrements in memory. When administered to opioid-tolerant individuals, such as opioid abusers or patients with chronic pain, opioids typically produce little or no performance impairment, including impairment of skills related to driving.

4.1.6 Marijuana

Marijuana consists of the dried and crushed leaves and stems of the plant *Cannabis sativa*, which grows worldwide. In the U.S., marijuana is typically rolled in cigarettes (joints) or cigar wrappers (blunts) and smoked. In various parts of the world, other preparations of the cannabis plant are eaten or fumes from the ignited plant material are inhaled. The acute effects of smoked marijuana and Δ[9]-tetrahydrocannabinol (THC), the primary psychoactive constituent of marijuana, have been investigated in numerous studies over the past several decades.[10,11] One of the most reliable behavioral effects of acute marijuana is impairment of memory processes; less consistent impairment has been reported for motor and attentional tests. Documenting the effects of chronic marijuana use has been somewhat elusive, with early studies reporting no impairment of cognitive functioning;[210] however, more recent studies have shown chronic marijuana users to be impaired in perceptual-motor abilities,[211] attention,[212,213] mathematical and verbal skills,[214] and learning and memory.[213,215]

Unless otherwise noted, the studies reviewed here examined the acute effects of marijuana and were conducted with experienced marijuana users who smoked standard marijuana cigarettes provided by the National Institute on Drug Abuse (NIDA). These marijuana cigarettes resemble in size an unfiltered tobacco cigarette, weigh 700 to 900 mg, and are assayed by NIDA to determine the percentage of THC by weight. Doses are typically manipulated by using cigarettes that differ in THC content or by varying the number of puffs administered to subjects (five to eight puffs are equivalent to one cigarette). Placebo cigarettes have had active THC removed chemically from the plant material, but when burned, smell identical to an active marijuana cigarette.

Over the years, an intriguing research question with important practical implications has been whether marijuana impairs performance beyond the period of acute intoxication, which typically lasts 2 to 6 h after smoking one or two cigarettes. Studies have documented performance decrements 12 to 24 h after smoking marijuana.[216] One series of studies reported that 24 h after smoking a single marijuana cigarette (2.2% THC), experienced aircraft pilots were impaired attempting to land a plane in a flight simulator;[217,218] however, a third study failed to replicate this next-day effect.[219] In another series of studies, a comprehensive battery of tests revealed that only time estimation[220] and memory[221] were impaired 9 to 17 h after smoking two marijuana cigarettes (2.1 to 2.9% THC), leading the authors to conclude that evidence for next-day performance effects of marijuana was weak. Yet another series of studies found next-day impairment on tests of memory and mental arithmetic after smoking two or four marijuana cigarettes (2.6% THC) over a 4-h period,[222] but not after smoking one marijuana cigarette.[222,223] Thus, residual impairment after acute marijuana dosing appears to be a dose-related phenomenon, with effects more likely to be observed at higher marijuana doses.

Recently, two studies have examined the residual effects of long-term marijuana use.[224,225] In both studies, marijuana smokers were abstinent for 28 days during which time a battery of neuropsychological tests was repeatedly administered. Daily, chronic smokers were compared to less frequent smokers. Bolla et al.[224] reported that daily smokers were impaired on tests of memory, executive functioning, and psychomotor skills after 28 days of marijuana abstinence. In contrast, Pope et al.[225] found neuropsychological impairment during the first week of abstinence, but by day 28, there were no differences between daily smokers and control subjects. Both studies found that daily smokers evidenced greater impairment than less frequent smokers, which is consistent with the dose-related effect noted above for acute marijuana studies.

Another controversial issue has been the amotivational syndrome supposedly caused by heavy, chronic marijuana use. This syndrome has been characterized by feelings of lethargy and apathy and an absence of goal-directed behavior.[226,227] However, studies conducted in countries where segments of the population use marijuana heavily[228–230] and laboratory-based studies in the U.S.[231,232] have not found empirical support for an amotivational syndrome.

4.1.6.1 Sensory Abilities

Few studies have investigated the effects of marijuana on CFF threshold. Block et al.[233] reported that one marijuana cigarette (2.6% THC) decreased CFF threshold compared to placebo. However, Liguori et al.[234] found no effect of marijuana (1.8 and 4.0% THC) on CFF threshold. Although more a perceptual process than a sensory ability, a commonly reported effect of marijuana is to increase the subjective passage of time relative to clock time. This typically results in subjects either overestimating an experimenter-generated time interval[220] or underproducing a subject-generated interval.[235] However, Heishman et al.[236] reported that marijuana (3.6% THC; 4, 8, or 16 puffs) had no effect on either time estimation or production.

4.1.6.2 Motor Abilities

In their review, Chait and Pierri[11] indicated that marijuana produced moderate impairment of balance (increased body sway) and hand steadiness. Consistent with this motor impairment, one marijuana cigarette decreased postural balance as subjects attempted to maintain balance while standing on a platform that moved at random intervals,[237] impaired equilibrium in a computerized test of body sway,[234] and impaired balance in subjects attempting to stand on one leg.[238] Cone et al.[239] found that two marijuana cigarettes (2.8% THC) impaired performance on the circular lights task; however, Heishman et al.[240] reported no effect of marijuana (1.3 and 2.7% THC, two cigarettes) on circular lights performance. Marijuana impaired performance in a test of perceptual motor speed and accuracy.[241] In contrast, several studies have shown that marijuana did not influence finger tapping rate.[11]

4.1.6.3 Attentional Abilities

A relatively large number of studies have investigated the effects of marijuana on focused attention, including reaction time tests and the DSST. Marijuana (1.8 and 3.6% THC) was shown to slow responding on a simple, visual reaction time task;[242] however, others have not found marijuana to impair simple reaction time performance.[11,40,236] Similarly, some studies have shown that marijuana impairs complex or choice reaction time tasks,[11,233] whereas others have shown no effect.[234] O'Leary et al.[243] found no effect of a 20-mg marijuana cigarette on reaction time in a dichotic listening task.

In general, marijuana also impaired performance on the DSST. In concentrations ranging from 1.8 to 3.6% THC, marijuana has been shown to decrease number of attempted responses (speed) and/or decrease number of correct responses (accuracy) on the DSST.[235,236,238,240,242,244–246] Oral THC (10 and 20 mg) also impaired DSST performance.[247] However, other studies have reported no effect of marijuana (1.3 to 3.6% THC) on the DSST.[40,220,248] The reasons for a lack of effect in these latter studies is unclear given that doses of marijuana were comparable and, in one study,[248] task presentation was identical to those studies reporting impairment. Marijuana (1.2% THC) also impaired selective attention as evidenced by slower responding and greater interference scores in the Stroop color naming test.[249]

Divided attention has generally been shown to be impaired by marijuana. Many divided attention tests consist of a central or primary task and a secondary or peripheral task. Several studies have shown that marijuana impaired detection accuracy and/or stimulus reaction time in one or both test components.[235,245,250] Hart et al.[251] reported that oral THC (20 mg, q.i.d.) and smoked marijuana (3.1% THC, q.i.d.) decreased tracking speed in a divided attention task. Kelly et al.[252] used a complex, 5-min divided attention test, in which an arithmetic task (addition and subtraction of three-digit numbers) was presented in the center of the video monitor and three other stimulus detection tasks were presented in the corners of the monitor. Performance was impaired in a dose-related manner after smoking one marijuana cigarette (2.0 or 3.5% THC). This finding illustrates that marijuana readily disrupts performance in complex tasks requiring continuous monitoring and the ability to shift attention rapidly between various stimuli.

These same attentional abilities are required when operating a motor vehicle. Not surprisingly, laboratory tests that model various components of driving[241] and standardized tests used by law enforcement officials to determine whether a person can safely drive[253,254] have been shown to be impaired by marijuana. Liguori et al.[234] reported that smoked marijuana (1.8 and 4.0% THC) increased braking latency in a driving simulator. Finally, tests of on-road driving found that marijuana moderately increased lateral movement of the vehicle within the driving lane on a highway.[255,256]

Marijuana also impairs sustained attention. In a 30-min vigilance task, hashish users exhibited more false alarms than non-using control subjects.[257] This finding is consistent with the observation that the impairing effects of marijuana on sustained attention are most evident in tests that last 30 to 60 min; tests with durations of 10 min are not adversely affected by marijuana.[11]

4.1.6.4 Cognitive Abilities

Marijuana has been shown to impair learning in the repeated acquisition and performance of response sequences tasks. Increased errors in the acquisition phase were reported after smoked marijuana (2.0 and 3.5% THC)[244] and oral THC (10 and 20 mg).[247] However, other studies[40,52] have found no effect of smoked marijuana on this test, and one study[251] reported that oral THC (20 mg, q.i.d.) increased the number of completed trials. Block et al.[233] reported that one marijuana cigarette (2.6% THC) impaired paired-associative learning.

As stated previously, one of the most reliable effects of marijuana is the impairment of memory processes. Numerous studies have found that smoked marijuana decreased the number of words or digits recalled and/or increased the number of intrusion errors in either immediate or delayed tests of free recall after presentation of information to be remembered.[220,222,233,236,245,246,249,252] Curran et al.[258] reported that oral THC (15 mg) impaired explicit memory and a selective reminding task, but had no effect on implicit and working memory. Using an extensive battery of cognitive tests, Block et al.[233] reported that marijuana (2.6% THC) slowed response time for producing word associations, slowed reading of prose, and impaired tests of reading comprehension, verbal expression, and mathematics. Heishman et al.[222] also found that simple addition and subtraction skills were impaired by smoking one, two, or four marijuana cigarettes (2.6% THC). Finally, Kelly et al.[252] reported that marijuana (2.0 and 3.5% THC) slowed response time in a spatial orientation test requiring subjects to determine whether numbers and letters were displayed normally or as a mirror image when they were rotated between 90° and 270°. In contrast to these findings, Hart et al.[259] reported that although smoked marijuana (1.8 and 3.9% THC) slowed responding on several measures, it had no effect on accurate performance of tasks measuring cognitive flexibility, arithmetic skills, and reasoning ability.

4.1.6.5 Summary

Laboratory studies in which subjects smoked marijuana have documented that marijuana impaired sensory-perceptual abilities by reducing CFF threshold and by increasing the subjective passage of time relative to clock time. Marijuana impaired gross motor coordination as measured by body sway and postural balance. However, inconsistent findings have been reported for fine motor control; hand steadiness was impaired, whereas several studies have shown no effect of marijuana on finger tapping. Marijuana has been shown to impair complex, but not simple, reaction time tests. A majority of studies have found that marijuana disrupted performance on the DSST. Complex divided attention tests, including driving a vehicle, were readily impaired by marijuana, as were tests requiring sustained attention for more than 30 min. Numerous studies have documented that smoked marijuana and oral THC impaired learning, memory, and other cognitive processes.

4.1.7 Conclusion

It is evident that a large body of literature exists concerning the effects of psychomotor stimulants, nicotine and tobacco, benzodiazepines, opioids, and marijuana on human performance. As a result, we know much in general about the effects of these psychoactive drugs on sensory, motor, attentional, and cognitive abilities. However, there are some gaps in this literature that need to be filled with data from well-designed, well-controlled studies. For example, few studies have investigated the effects of D-amphetamine or cocaine on cognitive abilities, and, for all drugs, sensory and perceptual processes have received little research attention compared with other aspects of behavior. It is also important to continue investigating specific mechanisms underlying general effects of drugs on behavior. For example, we are beginning to understand the differential effects of benzodiazepines on various components of memory;[124,163] similar studies should be conducted examining the effects of marijuana on memory or the effects of nicotine on cognitive processes. Not only will we learn more about the potentially deleterious effects of drugs on human performance, but drugs can be used as tools to further our understanding of basic processes of performance and cognition.

Two other approaches for future research include the measurement of plasma drug concentrations concomitant with performance and a greater number of drug interaction studies. Very few of the studies reviewed in this chapter provided data on the amount of drug actually delivered to subjects. This is especially critical in studies with tobacco and marijuana because the large variability in smoking behaviors (e.g., length of puffs and depth of inhalations)[246,260] and the low bioavailability of smoked drugs[6,261] result in highly variable delivered drug doses.[262] Virtually none of the tobacco studies and only a few of the marijuana studies reviewed reported plasma drug concentrations. Such data are necessary to relate performance impairment with a known drug concentration. Relatively few studies have investigated the interactive effects of drugs on human behavior.[40,144,151,235] Such basic information is critically needed because the simultaneous use of drugs with different pharmacological effects (e.g., ethanol and marijuana; nicotine and all drugs) is common practice today. It is likely that the combined effect of two or more drugs is very different from that of each drug alone.

Last, laboratory research emphasizing applications of performance effects of psychoactive drugs to the workplace remains relatively uncharted (see Kelly et al., Chapter 4.2 of this volume). Performance assessment batteries need to be tested in the laboratory to determine their validity, reliability, and generalizability to the workplace. Although few performance measures have undergone such rigorous laboratory testing, the methodology exists for assessing the validity, reliability, and sensitivity of a performance task.[263–265] Because much of drug-induced impairment observed in the workplace will be subtle in nature, laboratory studies should pay greater attention to long-lasting (next day) drug effects and drug withdrawal effects. Additionally, controlled laboratory studies can provide important information concerning a drug's time course of action and its interaction with other drugs.

Acknowledgment

Drs. Heishman and Myers were supported by the NIH Intramural Research Program, NIDA.

REFERENCES

1. Hollingworth, H.L., The influence of caffeine on mental and motor efficiency, *Arch. Psychol.*, 22, 1, 1912.
2. Bates, R.L., The effects of cigarettes and cigarette smoking on certain psychological and physical functions, *J. Comp. Psychol.*, 2, 371, 1922.
3. Weiss, B. and Laties, V.G., Enhancement of human performance by caffeine and the amphetamines, *Pharmacol. Rev.*, 14, 1, 1962.
4. Koelega, H.S., Stimulant drugs and vigilance performance: a review, *Psychopharmacology*, 111, 1, 1993.
5. McNair, D.M., Antianxiety drugs and human performance, *Arch. Gen. Psychiatry*, 29, 611, 1973.
6. Heishman, S.J., Taylor, R.C., and Henningfield, J.E., Nicotine and smoking: a review of effects on human performance, *Exp. Clin. Psychopharmacol.*, 2, 345, 1994.
7. Foltin, R.W. and Evans, S.M., Performance effects of drugs of abuse: a methodological survey, *Hum. Psychopharmacol. Clin. Exp.*, 8, 9, 1993.
8. Hindmarch, I., Psychomotor function and psychoactive drugs, *Br. J. Clin. Pharmacol.*, 10, 189, 1980.
9. Nicholson, A.N. and Ward, J., Eds., Psychotropic drugs and performance, *Br. J. Clin. Pharmacol.*, 18, 1S, 1984.
10. Beardsley, P.M. and Kelly, T.H., Acute effects of cannabis on human behavior and central nervous system function, in *The Health Effects of Cannabis*, Kalant, H., Corrigall, W., Hall, W., and Smart, R., Eds., Addiction Research Foundation, Toronto, 1999, 127.
11. Chait, L.D. and Pierri, J., Effects of smoked marijuana on human performance: a critical review, in *Marijuana/Cannabinoids: Neurobiology and Neurophysiology*, Murphy, L. and Bartke, A., Eds., CRC Press, Boca Raton, FL, 1992, 387.
12. Curran, H.V., Benzodiazepines, memory and mood: A review, *Psychopharmacology*, 105, 1, 1991.
13. Ghoneim, M.M. and Mewaldt, S.P., Benzodiazepines and human memory: a review, *Anesthesiology*, 72, 926, 1990.
14. Koelega, H.S., Benzodiazepines and vigilance performance: a review, *Psychopharmacology*, 98, 145, 1989.

15. Sherwood, N., Effects of nicotine on human psychomotor performance, *Hum. Psychopharmacol. Clin. Exp.*, 8, 155, 1993.

16. Zacny, J.P., A review of the effects of opioids on psychomotor and cognitive functioning in humans, *Exp. Clin. Psychopharmacol.*, 3, 432, 1995.

17. Montoya, A.G. et al., Long-term neuropsychiatric consequences of "ecstasy" (MDMA): a review, *Harvard Rev. Psychiatry,* 10, 212, 2002.

18. Parrott, A.C., Human psychopharmacology of ecstasy (MDMA): a review of 15 years of empirical research, *Hum. Psychopharmacol. Clin. Exp,* 16, 557, 2001.

19. Gavin, F.H. and Ellinwood, E.H., Cocaine and other stimulants: actions, abuse, and treatment, *N. Engl. J. Med.*, 318, 1173, 1988.

20. Jaffe, J.H., Drug addiction and drug abuse, in *The Pharmacological Basis of Therapeutics*, Gilman, A.G., Rall, T.W., Nies, A.S., and Taylor, P., Eds., Pergamon Press, New York, 1990, 522.

21. Fischman, M.W. and Schuster, C.R., Cocaine self-administration in humans, *Fed. Proc.*, 41, 241, 1982.

22. Woolverton, W.L., Kandel, D., and Schuster, C.R., Tolerance and cross-tolerance to cocaine and D-amphetamine, *J. Pharmacol. Exp. Ther.*, 205, 525, 1978.

23. Derlet, R.W. et al., Amphetamine toxicity: experience with 127 cases, *J. Emerg. Med.*, 7, 157, 1989.

24. Myerson, A., Effect of benzedrine sulphate on mood and fatigue in normal and in neurotic persons, *Arch. Neurol. Psychiatry*, 36, 816, 1936.

25. Smith, J.M. and Misiak, H., Critical Flicker Frequency (CFF) and psychotropic drugs in normal human subjects — a review, *Psychopharmacology*, 47, 175, 1976.

26. Farre, M. et al., Alcohol and cocaine interactions in humans, *J. Pharmacol. Exp. Ther.*, 266, 1364, 1993.

27. Peck, A.W. et al., A comparison of bupropion hydrochloride with dexamphetamine and amitriptyline in healthy subjects, *Br. J. Clin. Pharmacol.*, 7, 469, 1979.

28. Bye, C. et al., A comparison of the effects of 1-benzylpiperazine and dexamphetamine on human performance tests, *Eur. J. Clin. Pharmacol.*, 6, 163, 1973.

29. Evans, M.A. et al., Effects of marihuana-dextroamphetamine combination, *Clin. Pharmacol. Ther.*, 20, 350, 1976.

30. Hamilton, M.J., Smith, P.R., and Peck, A.W., Effects of bupropion, nomifensine and dexamphetamine on performance, subjective feelings, autonomic variables and electroencephalogram in healthy volunteers, *Br. J. Clin. Pharmacol.*, 15, 367, 1983.

31. Higgins, S.T. and Stitzer, M.L., Monologue speech: effects of D-amphetamine, secobarbital and diazepam, *Pharmacol. Biochem. Behav.*, 34, 609, 1989.

32. Heishman, S.J. and Stitzer, M.L., Effects of D-amphetamine, secobarbital, and marijuana on choice behavior: social versus nonsocial options, *Psychopharmacology*, 99, 156, 1989.

33. Kinchla, R.A., Attention, *Annu. Rev. Psychol.*, 43, 711, 1992.

34. Warm, J.S., Ed., *Sustained Attention in Human Performance*, Wiley, New York, 1984.

35. McLeod, D.R. et al., An automated version of the digit symbol substitution task (DSST), *Behav. Res. Meth. Instr.*, 14, 463, 1982.

36. Holdstock, L. and de Wit, H., Individual difference in responses to ethanol and D-amphetamine: a within-subject study, *Alcohol. Clin. Exp. Res.*, 25, 540, 2001.

37. Higgins, S.T. et al., Effects of intranasal cocaine on human learning, performance and physiology, *Psychopharmacology*, 102, 451, 1990.

38. Higgins, S.T. et al., Acute behavioral and cardiac effects of cocaine and alcohol combinations in humans, *Psychopharmacology,* 111, 285, 1993.

39. Rush, C.R. and Baker, R.W., Behavioral pharmacological similarities between methylphenidate and cocaine in cocaine abusers, *Exp. Clin. Psychopharmacol.*, 9, 59, 2001.

40. Foltin, R.W. et al., Behavioral effects of cocaine alone and in combination with ethanol or marijuana in humans, *Drug Alcohol Depend.*, 32, 93, 1993.

41. Jenkins, A.J. et al., Correlation between pharmacological effects and plasma cocaine concentrations after smoked administration, *J. Anal. Toxicol.*, 26, 382, 2002.

42. Rush, C.R. et al., Reinforcing and subject-rated effects of methylphenidate and D-amphetamine in non-drug-abusing humans, *J. Clin. Psychopharmacol.*, 21, 273, 2001.

43. Cousins, M.S., Stamat, H.M., and de Wit, H., Acute doses of D-amphetamine and buproprion increase cigarette smoking, *Psychopharmacology*, 157, 243, 2001.

44. Fillmore, M.T., Rush, C.R., and Hays, L., Acute effects of oral cocaine on inhibitory control of behavior in humans, *Drug Alcohol Depend.*, 67, 157, 2002.

45. de Wit, H., Crean, J., and Richards, J.B., Effects of D-amphetamine and ethanol on a measure of behavioral inhibition in humans, *Behav. Neurosci.*, 114, 830, 2000.

46. McKetin, R. et al., Changes in auditory selective attention and event-related potentials following oral administration of D-amphetamine in humans, *Neuropsychopharmacology*, 21, 380, 1999.

47. Servan-Schreiber, D. et al., Dopamine and the mechanisms of cognition: Part II. D-amphetamine effects in human subjects performing a selective attention task, *Biol. Psychiatry*, 43, 723, 1998.

48. Perez-Reyes, M. et al., Interaction between ethanol and dextroamphetamine: effects on psychomotor performance, *Alcohol. Clin. Exp. Res.*, 16, 75, 1992.

49. Mills, K.C. et al., The influence of stimulants, sedatives, and fatigue on tunnel vision: risk factors for driving and piloting, *Hum. Factors*, 43, 310, 2001.

50. Kelly, T.H., Foltin, R.W., and Fischman, M.W., The effects of repeated amphetamine exposure on multiple measures of human behavior, *Pharmacol. Biochem. Behav.*, 38, 417, 1991.

51. Higgins, S.T. et al., Effects of cocaine and alcohol, alone and in combination, on human learning and performance, *J. Exp. Anal. Behav.*, 58, 87, 1992.

52. Foltin, R.W. and Fischman, M.W., The effects of combinations of intranasal cocaine, smoked marijuana, and task performance on heart rate and blood pressure, *Pharmacol. Biochem. Behav.*, 36, 311, 1990.

53. Foltin, R.W. et al., Effects of cocaine, alone and in combination with task performance, on heart rate and blood pressure, *Pharmacol. Biochem. Behav.*, 31, 387, 1988.

54. Soetens, E., D'Hooge, R., and Hueting, J.E., Amphetamine enhances human-memory consolidation, *Neurosci. Letters*, 161, 9, 1993.

55. Mattay, V.S. et al., Effects of dextroamphetamine on cognitive performance and cortical activation, *NeuroImage*, 12, 268, 2000.

56. Glennon, R.A., Titeler, M., and McKenney, J.D., Evidence for 5-HT2 involvement in the mechanism of action of hallucinogenic agents, *Life Sci.,* 35, 2505, 1984.

57. McGuire, P., Long term psychiatric and cognitive effects of MDMA use, *Toxicol. Lett.*, 112–113, 153, 2000.

58. Kalant, H., The pharmacology and toxicology of "ecstasy" (MDMA) and related drugs, *Can. Med. Assoc. J.*, 165, 917, 2001.

59. Vollenweider, F.X. et al., Opposite effects of 3,4-methylenedioxymethamphetamine (MDMA) on sensorimotor gating in rats versus healthy humans, *Psychopharmacology*, 143, 365, 1999.

60. Thomasius, R. et al., Mood, cognition and serotonin transporter availability in current and former ecstasy (MDMA) users, *Psychopharmacology*, 167, 85, 2003.

61. Cami, J. et al., Human pharmacology of 3,4-methylenedioxymethamphetamine ("Ecstasy"): psychomotor performance and subjective effects, *J. Clin. Psychopharmacol.*, 20, 455, 2000.

62. McCann, U.D. et al., Cognitive performance in (±) 3,4-methylenedioxymethamphetamine (MDMA, "ecstasy") users: a controlled study, *Psychopharmacology*, 143, 417, 1999.

63. Gouzoulis-Mayfrank, E. et al., Impaired cognitive performance in drug free users of recreational ecstasy (MDMA), *J. Neurol. Neurosurg. Psychiatry*, 68, 719, 2000.

64. Jacobsen, L.K. et al., Preliminary evidence of hippocampal dysfunction in adolescent MDMA ("ecstasy") users: possible relationship to neurotoxic effects, *Psychopharmacology*, 2003 Nov 28 [Epub ahead of print].

65. Gamma, A. et al., No difference in brain activation during cognitive performance between ecstasy (3,4-methylenedioxymethamphetamine) users and control subjects: a [H215O]-positron emission tomography study, *J. Clin. Psychopharmacol.*, 21, 66, 2001.

66. Parrott, A.C. and Lasky, J., Ecstasy (MDMA) effects upon mood and cognition: before, during and after a Saturday night dance, *Psychopharmacology*, 139, 261, 1998.

67. Parrott, A.C. et al., Cognitive performance in recreational users of MDMA or "ecstasy": evidence for memory deficits, *J. Psychopharmacol.*, 12, 79, 1998.

68. Morgan, M.J. et al., Ecstasy (MDMA): are the psychological problems associated with its use reversed by prolonged abstinence? *Psychopharmacology*, 159, 294, 2002.

69. Verkes, R.J. et al., Cognitive performance and serotonergic function in users of ecstasy, *Psychopharmacology*, 153, 196, 2001.

70. Reneman, L. et al., Cortical serotonin transporter density and verbal memory in individuals who stopped using 3,4-methylenedioxymethamphetamine (MDMA or "Ecstasy"), *Arch. Gen. Psychiatry,* 58, 901, 2001.

71. Wareing, M., Fisk, J.E., and Murphy, P.N., Working memory deficits in current and previous users of MDMA ("ecstasy"), *Br. J. Psychol.,* 91, 181, 2000.

72. Rodgers, J., Cognitive performance amongst recreational users of "ecstasy," *Psychopharmacology,* 151, 19, 2000.

73. Croft, R.J. et al., The relative contributions of ecstasy and cannabis to cognitive impairment, *Psychopharmacology,* 153, 373, 2001.

74. Johnston, L.D., O'Malley, P.M., and Bachman, J.G., National survey results on drug use from the Monitoring the Future Study, 1975–1994 (NIH Publication No. 95-4026). U.S. Government Printing Office, Washington, D.C., 1995.

75. Sherwood, N., Kerr, J.S., and Hindmarch, I., Psychomotor performance in smokers following single and repeated doses of nicotine gum, *Psychopharmacology,* 108, 432, 1992.

76. Hindmarch, I., Kerr, J.S., and Sherwood, N., Effects of nicotine gum on psychomotor performance in smokers and non-smokers, *Psychopharmacology,* 100, 535, 1990.

77. Jones, G.M.M. et al., Effects of acute subcutaneous nicotine on attention, information processing and short-term memory in Alzheimer's disease, *Psychopharmacology,* 108, 485, 1992.

78. Kerr, J.S., Sherwood, N., and Hindmarch, I., Separate and combined effects of the social drugs on psychomotor performance, *Psychopharmacology,* 104, 113, 1991.

79. Foulds, J. et al., Cognitive performance effects of subcutaneous nicotine in smokers and never-smokers, *Psychopharmacology,* 127, 31, 1996.

80. Perkins, K.A. et al., Behavioral performance effects of nicotine in smokers and nonsmokers, *Pharmacol. Biochem. Behav.,* 37, 11, 1990.

81. Perkins, K.A. et al., Chronic and acute tolerance to subjective, behavioral and cardiovascular effects of nicotine in humans, *J. Pharmacol. Exp. Ther.,* 270, 628, 1994.

82. West, R.J. and Jarvis, M.J., Effects of nicotine on finger tapping rate in non-smokers, *Pharmacol. Biochem. Behav.,* 25, 727, 1986.

83. Heishman, S.J. and Henningfield, J.E., Tolerance to repeated nicotine administration on performance, subjective, and physiological responses in nonsmokers, *Psychopharmacology,* 152, 321, 2000.

84. Le Houezec, J. et al., A low dose of subcutaneous nicotine improves information processing in non-smokers, *Psychopharmacology,* 114, 628, 1994.

85. Griesar, W.S., Zajdel, D.P., and Oken, B.S., Nicotine effects on alertness and spatial attention in non-smokers, *Nicotine Tob. Res.,* 4, 185, 2002.

86. Snyder, F.R. and Henningfield, J.E., Effects of nicotine administration following 12 h of tobacco deprivation: assessment on computerized performance tasks, *Psychopharmacology,* 97, 17, 1989.

87. Parrott, A.C. and Craig, D., Cigarette smoking and nicotine gum (0, 2 and 4 mg): effects upon four visual attention tasks, *Neuropsychobiology,* 25, 34, 1992.

88. Stroop, J.R., Studies of interference in serial verbal reactions, *J. Exp. Psychol.,* 18, 643, 1935.

89. Wesnes, K. and Revell, A., The separate and combined effects of scopolamine and nicotine on human information processing, *Psychopharmacology,* 84, 5, 1984.

90. Provost, S.C. and Woodward, R., Effects of nicotine gum on repeated administration of the Stroop test, *Psychopharmacology,* 104, 536, 1991.

91. Heishman, S.J., Snyder, F.R., and Henningfield, J.E., Performance, subjective, and physiological effects of nicotine in nonsmokers, *Drug Alcohol Depend.,* 34, 11, 1993.

92. Wesnes, K. and Warburton, D.M., Effects of smoking on rapid information processing performance, *Neuropsychobiology,* 9, 223, 1983.

93. Parrott, A.C. and Winder, G., Nicotine chewing gum (2 mg, 4 mg) and cigarette smoking: comparative effects upon vigilance and heart rate, *Psychopharmacology,* 97, 257, 1989.

94. Michel, C. et al., Cardiovascular, electrocortical, and behavioral effects of nicotine chewing gum, *Klin. Wochenschr.,* 66 (Suppl. 11), 72, 1988.

95. Herbert, M., Foulds, J., and Fife-Schaw, C., No effect of cigarette smoking on attention or mood in non-deprived smokers, *Addiction,* 96, 1349, 2001.

96. Wesnes, K., Warburton, D.M., and Matz, B., Effects of nicotine on stimulus sensitivity and response bias in a visual vigilance task, *Neuropsychobiology,* 9, 41, 1983.

97. Wesnes, K. and Revell, A., The separate and combined effects of scopolamine and nicotine on human information processing, *Psychopharmacology*, 84, 5, 1984.

98. Wesnes, K. and Warburton, D.M., Effects of scopolamine and nicotine on human rapid information processing performance, *Psychopharmacology*, 82, 147, 1984.

99. Levin, E.D. et al., Transdermal nicotine effects on attention, *Psychopharmacology*, 140, 135, 1998.

100. Andersson, K. and Post, B., Effects of cigarette smoking on verbal rote learning and physiological arousal, *Scand. J. Psychol.*, 15, 263, 1974.

101. Colrain, I.M. et al., Effects of post-learning smoking on memory consolidation, *Psychopharmacology*, 108, 448, 1992.

102. Warburton, D.M., Rusted, J.M., and Fowler, J., A comparison of the attentional and consolidation hypotheses for the facilitation of memory by nicotine, *Psychopharmacology*, 108, 443, 1992.

103. Warburton, D.M., Rusted, J.M., and Muller, C., Patterns of facilitation of memory by nicotine, *Behav. Pharmacol.*, 3, 375, 1992.

104. Rusted, J., Graupner, L., and Warburton, D., Effects of post-trial administration of nicotine on human memory: evaluating the conditions for improving memory, *Psychopharmacology*, 119, 405, 1995.

105. Rusted, J.M. et al., Effortful processing is a requirement for nicotine-induced improvements in memory, *Psychopharmacology*, 138, 362, 1998.

106. Phillips, S. and Fox, P., An investigation into the effects of nicotine gum on short-term memory, *Psychopharmacology*, 140, 429, 1998.

107. Krebs, S.J., Petros, T.V., and Beckwith, B.E., Effects of smoking on memory for prose passages, *Physiol. Behav.*, 56, 723, 1994.

108. Houlihan, M.E., Pritchard, W.S., and Robinson, J.H., Effects of smoking/nicotine on performance and event-related potentials during a short-term memory scanning task, *Psychopharmacology*, 156, 388, 2001.

109. West, R. and Hack, S., Effect of cigarettes on memory search and subjective ratings. *Pharmacol. Biochem. Behav.*, 38, 281, 1991.

110. Rusted, J. and Eaton-Williams, P., Distinguishing between attentional and amnestic effects in information processing: The separate and combined effects of scopolamine and nicotine on verbal free recall, *Psychopharmacology*, 104, 363, 1991.

111. Houston, J.P., Schneider, N.G., and Jarvik, M.E., Effects of smoking on free recall and organization, *Am. J. Psychiatry*, 135, 220, 1978.

112. Newhouse, P.A. et al., Intravenous nicotine in Alzheimer's disease: a pilot study, *Psychopharmacology*, 95, 171, 1988.

113. Sakurai, Y. and Kanazawa, I., Acute effects of cigarettes in non-deprived smokers on memory, calculation and executive functions, *Hum. Psychopharmacol. Clin. Exp.*, 17, 369, 2002.

114. Dunne, M.P., MacDonald, D., and Hartley, L.R., The effects of nicotine upon memory and problem solving performance, *Physiol. Behav.*, 37, 849, 1986.

115. Johnson, L. and Chernik, D.A., Sedative-hypnotics and human performance, *Psychopharmacology*, 76, 101, 1982.

116. Griffiths, R.R. and Wolf, B., Relative abuse liability of different benzodiazepines in drug abusers, *J. Clin. Psychopharmacol.*, 10, 237, 1990.

117. Woods, J.H., Katz, J.L., and Winger, G., Abuse liability of benzodiazepines, *Pharmacol. Rev.*, 39, 251, 1987.

118. de Wit, H. and Griffiths, R.R., Testing the abuse liability of anxiolytic and hypnotic drugs in humans, *Drug Alcohol Depend.*, 28, 83, 1991.

119. Kunsman, G.W. et al., The use of microcomputer-based psychomotor tests for the evaluation of benzodiazepine effects on human performance: A review with emphasis on temazepam, *Br. J. Clin. Pharmacol.*, 34, 289, 1992.

120. Hindmarch, I., Sherwood, N., and Kerr, J.S., Amnestic effects of triazolam and other hypnotics, *Prog. Neuropsychopharmacol. Biol. Psychiatry*, 17, 407, 1993.

121. Blom, M.W. et al., The effects of alprazolam, quazepam and diazepam on saccadic eye movements, parameters of psychomotor function and the EEG, *Fund. Clin. Pharmacol.*, 4, 653, 1990.

122. Curran, H.V. and Birch, B., Differentiating the sedative, psychomotor and amnesic effects of benzodiazepines: a study with midazolam and the benzodiazepine antagonist, flumazenil, *Psychopharmacology*, 103, 519, 1991.

123. Kerr, J.S., Hindmarch, I., and Sherwood, N., Correlation between doses of oxazepam and their effects on performance of a standardised test battery, *Eur. J. Clin. Pharmacol.*, 42, 507, 1992.

124. Bishop, K.I., Curran, H.V., and Lader, M., Do scopolamine and lorazepam have dissociable effects on human memory systems? A dose-response study with normal volunteers, *Exp. Clin. Psychopharmacol.*, 4, 292, 1996.

125. Saano, V., Hansen, P.P., and Paronen, P., Interactions and comparative effects of zoplicone, diazepam and lorazepam on psychomotor performance and on elimination pharmacokinetics in healthy volunteers, *Pharmacol. Toxicol.*, 70, 135, 1992.

126. Curran, H.V., Schifano, F., and Lader, M., Models of memory dysfunction? A comparison of the effects of scopolamine and lorazepam on memory, psychomotor performance and mood, *Psychopharmacology*, 103, 83, 1991.

127. Rettig, H.C. et al., Effects of hypnotics on sleep and psychomotor performance: a double-blind randomized study of lormetazepam, midazolam and zopiclone, *Anaesthesia*, 45, 1079, 1990.

128. Bond, A., Silveira, J.C., and Lader, M., Effects of single doses of alprazolam and alcohol alone and in combination on physiological performance, *Hum. Psychopharmacol. Clin. Exp.*, 6, 219, 1991.

129. Evans, S.M., Troisi, J.R., and Griffiths, R.R., Tandospirone and alprazolam: comparison of behavioral effects and abuse liability in humans, *J. Pharmacol. Exp. Ther.*, 271, 683, 1994.

130. Preston, K.L. et al., Subjective and behavioral effects of diphenhydramine, lorazepam and methocarbamol: Evaluation of abuse liability, *J. Pharmacol. Exp. Ther.*, 262, 707, 1992.

131. Mintzer, M.Z. and Griffiths, R.R., Lorazepam and scopolamine: a single-dose comparison of effects on human memory and attentional processes, *Exp. Clin. Psychopharmacol.*, 11, 56, 2003.

132. Evans, S.M., Funderburk, F.R., and Griffiths, R.R., Zolpidem and triazolam in humans: behavioral and subjective effects and abuse liability, *J. Pharmacol. Exp. Ther.*, 255, 1246, 1990.

133. Kirk, T., Roache, J.D., and Griffiths, R.R., Dose-response evaluation of the amnestic effects of triazolam and pentobarbital in normal subjects, *J. Clin. Psychopharmacol.*, 10, 160, 1990.

134. Roache, J.D. et al., Differential effects of triazolam and ethanol on awareness, memory, and psychomotor performance, *J. Clin. Psychopharmacol.*, 13, 3, 1993.

135. Mintzer, M.Z. and Griffiths, R.R., Triazolam-amphetamine interaction: dissociation of effects on memory versus arousal, *J. Psychopharmacol.*, 17, 17, 2003.

136. Roache, J.D. and Griffiths, R.R., Diazepam and triazolam self-administration in sedative abusers: concordance of subject ratings, performance and drug self-administration, *Psychopharmacology*, 99, 309, 1989.

137. Stoops, W.W. and Rush, C.R., Differential effects in humans after repeated administrations of zolpidem and triazolam, *Am. J. Drug Alcohol Abuse*, 29, 281, 2003.

138. Kumar, R. et al., Anxiolytics and memory: a comparison of lorazepam and alprazolam, *J. Clin. Psychiatry*, 48, 158, 1987.

139. Tobler, I. et al., Effects of night-time motor activity and performance in the morning after midazolam intake during the night, *Arzneimittelforschung*, 41, 581, 1991.

140. Fleishaker, J.C. et al., Psychomotor and memory effects of two adinazolam formulations assessed by a computerized neuropsychological test battery, *J. Clin. Pharmacol.*, 33, 463, 1993.

141. Ingum, J. et al., Relationship between drug plasma concentrations and psychomotor performance after single doses of ethanol and benzodiaepines, *Psychopharmacology*, 107, 11, 1992.

142. Roache, J.D. and Griffiths, R.R., Lorazepam and meprobamate dose effects in humans: behavioral effects and abuse liability, *J. Pharmacol. Exp. Ther.*, 243, 978, 1987.

143. Linnoila, M. et al., Effects of adinazolam and diazepam, alone and in combination with ethanol, on psychomotor and cognitive performance and on autonomic nervous system reactivity in healthy volunteers, *Eur. J. Clin. Pharmacol.*, 38, 371, 1990.

144. Linnoila, M. et al., Effects of single doses of alprazolam and diazepam, alone and in combination with ethanol, on psychomotor and cognitive performance and on autonomic nervous system reactivity in healthy volunteers, *Eur. J. Clin. Pharmacol.*, 39, 21, 1990.

145. Moskowitz, H., Linnoila, M., and Roehrs, T., Psychomotor performance in chronic insomniacs during 14-day use of flurazepam and midazolam, *J. Clin. Psychopharmacol.*, 10, 44S, 1990.

146. Pompeia, S. et al., Lorazepam induces an atypical dissociation of visual and auditory event-related potentials, *J. Psychopharmacol.*, 17, 31, 2003.

147. Ellinwood, E.H. et al., Comparative pharmacokinetics and pharmacodynamics of lorazepam, alprazolam and diazepam, *Psychopharmacology*, 86, 392, 1985.
148. Roache, J.D. et al., Benzodiazepine-induced impairment of matching-to-sample performance in humans, *Pharmacol. Biochem. Behav.*, 36, 945, 1990.
149. Rush, C.R. et al., Acute behavioral effects of lorazepam and caffeine, alone and in combination, in humans, *Behav. Pharmacol.*, 5, 245, 1994.
150. Rush, C.R. et al., A comparison of the acute behavioral effects of triazolam and temazepam in normal volunteers, *Psychopharmacology*, 112, 407, 1993.
151. Rush, C.R. et al., Acute behavioral effects of triazolam and caffeine, alone and in combination, in humans, *Exp. Clin. Psychopharmacol.*, 2, 211, 1994.
152. Rush, C.R., Madakasira, S., and Goldman, N.H., Acute behavioral effects of estazolam and triazolam in non-drug-abusing volunteers, *Exp. Clin. Psychopharmacol.*, 4, 300, 1996.
153. Rush, C.R. and Baker, R.W., Behavioral pharmacological similarities between methylphenidate and cocaine in cocaine abusers, *Exp. Clin. Psychopharmacol.*, 9, 59, 2001.
154. Freidman, H. et al., Pharmacokinetics and pharmacodynamics of oral diazepam: effect of dose, plasma concentration, and time, *Clin. Pharmacol. Ther.*, 52, 139, 1992.
155. Dowd, S.M. et al., The behavioral and cognitive effects of two benzodiazepines associated with drug-facilitated sexual assault, *J. Forensic Sci.*, 47, 1101, 2002.
156. Kelly, T.H. et al., Behavioral response to diazepam in a residential laboratory, *Biol. Psychiatry*, 31, 808, 1992.
157. Brown, G.G., Rich, J.B., and Simkins-Bullock, J., Correlated changes in focused attention and associative encoding following diazepam ingestion, *Exp. Clin. Psychopharmacol.*, 4, 114, 1996.
158. Volkerts, E.R. et al., A comparative study of on-the-road and simulated driving performance after nocturnal treatment with lormetazepam 1 mg and oxazepam 50 mg, *Hum. Psychopharmacol. Clin. Exp.*, 7, 297, 1992.
159. Brookhuis, K.A., Volkerts, E.R., and O'Hanlon, J.F., Repeated dose effects of lormetazepam and flurazepam upon driving performance, *Eur. J. Clin. Pharmacol.*, 39, 83, 1990.
160. Kuitunen, T., Drug and ethanol effects on the clinical test for drunkenness: single doses of ethanol, hypnotic drugs and antidepressant drugs, *Pharmacol. Toxicol.*, 75, 91, 1994.
161. Roache, J.D., Spiga, R., and Burt, D.B., Triazolam and ethanol effects on human matching-to-sample performance vary as a function of pattern size and discriminability, *Drug Alcohol Depend.*, 32, 219, 1993.
162. Mills, K.C., et al., The influence of stimulants, sedatives, and fatigue on tunnel vision: risk factors for driving and piloting, *Hum. Factors,* 43, 310, 2001.
163. Danion, J.N. et al., Pharmacology of human memory and cognition: illustrations from the effects of benzodiazepines and cholinergic drugs, *J. Psychopharmacol.*, 7, 371, 1993.
164. Hommer, D., Weingartner, H., and Breier, A., Dissociation of benzodiazepine-induced amnesia from sedation by flumazenil pretreatment, *Psychopharmacology*, 112, 455, 1993.
165. Roy-Byrne, P.P. et al., Effects of diazepam on cognitive processes in normal subjects, *Psychopharmacology*, 91, 30, 1987.
166. Weingartner, H.J. et al., Selective effects of triazolam on memory, *Psychopharmacology*, 106, 341, 1992.
167. Weingartner, H.J. et al., Specific memory and sedative effects of the benzodiazepine triazolam, *J. Psychopharmacol.*, 7, 305, 1993.
168. Matthews, A., Kirkby, K.C., and Martin, F., The effects of single-dose lorazepam on memory and behavioural learning, *J. Psychopharmacol.*, 16, 345, 2002.
169. Barbee, J.G., Black, F.W., and Todorov, A.A., Differential effects of alprazolam and buspirone upon acquisition, retention, and retrieval processes in memory, *J. Neuropsychiatry Clin. Neurosci.*, 4, 308, 1992.
170. Rusted, J.M., Eaton-Williams, P., and Warburton, D.M., A comparison of the effects of scopolamine and diazepam on working memory, *Psychopharmacology*, 105, 442, 1991.
171. Schifano, F. and Curran, H.V., Pharmacological models of memory dysfunction? A comparison of the effects of scopolamine and lorazepam on word valence ratings, priming and recall, *Psychopharmacology*, 115, 430, 1994.
172. Bixler, E.O. et al., Next-day memory impairment with triazolam use, *Lancet*, 337, 827, 1991.

173. Buchanan, T.W., Karafin, M.S., and Adolphs, R., Selective effects of triazolam on memory for emotional, relative to neutral, stimuli: differential effects on gist versus detail, *Behav. Neurosci.*, 117, 517, 2003.

174. Coupland, N.J. et al., Effects of diazepam on facial emotion recognition, *J. Psychiatry Neurosci.*, 28, 452, 2003.

175. Bickel, W.K., Hughes, J.R., and Higgins, S.T., Human behavioral pharmacology of benzodiazepines: effects on repeated acquisition and performance of response chains, *Drug Dev. Res.*, 20, 53, 1990.

176. Bickel, W.K., Higggins, S.T., and Hughes, J.R., The effects of diazepam and triazolam on repeated acquisition and performance of response sequences with an observing response, *J. Exp. Anal. Behav.*, 56, 217, 1991.

177. Bickel, W.K., Higgins, S.T., and Griffiths, R.R., Repeated diazepam administration: effects on the acquisition and performance of response chains in humans, *J. Exp. Anal. Behav.*, 52, 47, 1989.

178. Judd, L.L., Ellinwood, E., and McAdams, L.A., Cognitive performance and mood in patients with chronic insomnia during 14-day use of flurazepam and midazolam, *J. Clin. Psychopharmacol.*, 10, 56S, 1990.

179. Jaffe, J.H. and Martin, W.R., Opioid analgesics and antagonists, in *The Pharmacological Basis of Therapeutics*, Gilman, A.G., Rall, T.W., Nies, A. S., and Taylor, P., Eds., Pergamon Press, New York, 1990, 485.

180. Chesher, G.B., Understanding the opioid analgesics and their effects on skills performance, *Alcohol Drugs Driving*, 5, 111, 1989.

181. Chapman, S.L., Byas-Smith, M.G., and Reed, B.A., Effects of intermediate- and long-term use of opioids on cognition in patients with chronic pain, *Clin. J. Pain*, 18, S83, 2002.

182. Veselis, R.A. et al., Impaired memory and behavioral performance with fentanyl at low plasma concentrations, *Anesth. Analg.*, 79, 952, 1994.

183. O'Neill, W.M. et al., The cognitive and psychomotor effects of morphine in healthy subjects: a randomized controlled trial of repeated (four) oral doses of dextropropoxyphene, morphine, lorazepam and placebo, *Pain*, 85, 209, 2000.

184. Saarialho-Kere, U., Mattila, M.J., and Seppala, T., Parenteral pentazocine: effects on psychomotor skills and respiration, and interactions with amitriptyline, *Eur. J. Clin. Pharmacol.*, 35, 483, 1988.

185. Zacny, J.P. et al., A dose–response analysis of the subjective, psychomotor and physiological effects of intravenous morphine in healthy volunteers, *J. Pharmacol. Exp. Ther.*, 268, 1, 1994.

186. Zacny, J.P. et al., Comparing the subjective, psychomotor and physiological effects of intravenous butorphanol and morphine in healthy volunteers, *J. Pharmacol. Exp. Ther.*, 270, 579, 1994.

187. Zacny, J.P., Lichtor, J.L., and de Wit, H., Subjective, behavioral, and physiologic responses to intravenous dezocine in healthy volunteers, *Anesth. Analg.*, 74, 523, 1992.

188. Hill, J.L. and Zacny, J.P., Comparing the subjective, psychomotor, and physiological effects of intravenous hydromorphone and morphine in healthy volunteers, *Psychopharmacology*, 152, 31, 2000.

189. Walker, D.J. et al., Subjective, psychomotor, and physiological effects of cumulative doses of mixed-action opioids in healthy volunteers, *Psychopharmacology*, 155, 362, 2001.

190. Haavisto, E. and Kauranen, K., Psychomotor performance after short-term anaesthesia, *Eur. Acad. Anaesthesiol.*, 19, 436, 2002.

191. Zacny, J.P. et al., Subjective and behavioral responses to intravenous fentanyl in healthy volunteers, *Psychopharmacology*, 107, 319, 1992.

192. Zacny, J.P. et al., Subjective, behavioral and physiologic responses to meperidine in healthy volunteers, *Psychopharmacology*, 111, 306, 1993.

193. Thapar, P. et al., Using alcohol as a standard to assess the degree of impairment induced by sedative and analgesic drugs in ambulatory surgery, *Anesthesiology*, 82, 53, 1995.

194. Thapar, P. et al., Objective and subjective impairment from often-used sedative/analgesic combinations in ambulatory surgery, using alcohol as a benchmark, *Ambul. Anesth.*, 80, 1092, 1995.

195. Kerr, B. et al., Concentration-related effects of morphine on cognitive and motor control in human subjects, *Neuropsychopharmacology*, 5, 157, 1991.

196. Bruera, E. et al., The cognitive effects of the administration of narcotic analgesics in patients with cancer pain, *Pain*, 39, 13, 1989.

197. Jenkins, A.J. et al., Pharmacokinetics and pharmacodynamics of smoked heroin, *J. Anal. Toxicol.*, 18, 317, 1994.

198. Marsch, L.A. et al., Effects of infusion rate of intravenously administered morphine on physiological, psychomotor, and self-reported measures in humans, *J. Pharmacol. Exp. Ther.*, 299, 1056, 2001.

199. Zacny, J.P. et al., Subjective and psychomotor effects of subanesthetic doses of propofol in healthy volunteers, *Anesthesiology*, 76, 696, 1992.

200. Preston, K.L., Bigelow, G.E., and Liebson, I.A., Comparative evaluation of morphine, pentazocine and ciramadol in postaddicts, *J. Pharmacol. Exp. Ther.*, 240, 900, 1987.

201. Preston, K.L., Liebson, I.A., and Bigelow, G.E., Discrimination of agonist-antagonist opioids in humans trained on a two-choice saline-hydromorphone discrimination, *J. Pharmacol. Exp. Ther.*, 261, 62, 1992.

202. Strain, E.C. et al., Acute effects of buprenorphine, hydromorphone and naloxone in methadone-maintained volunteers, *J. Pharmacol. Exp. Ther.*, 261, 985, 1992.

203. Strain, E.C. et al., Precipitated withdrawal by pentazocine in methadone-maintained volunteers, *J. Pharmacol. Exp. Ther.*, 267, 624, 1993.

204. Preston, K.L., Bigelow, G.E., and Liebson, I.A., Discrimination of butorphanol and nalbuphine in opioid-dependent humans, *Pharmacol. Biochem. Behav.*, 37, 511, 1990.

205. Preston, K.L., Bigelow, G.E., and Liebson, I.A., Antagonist effects of nalbuphine in opioid-dependent human volunteers, *J. Pharmacol. Exp. Ther.*, 248, 929, 1989.

206. Stevenson, G.W. et al., Driving ability after fentanyl or diazepam: a controlled double-blind study, *Invest. Radiol.*, 21, 717, 1986.

207. Sabatowski, R., Driving ability under long-term treatment with transdermal fentanyl, *J. Pain Symptom Manage.*, 25, 38, 2003.

208. Galski, T., Williams, J.B., and Ehle, H.T., Effects of opioids on driving ability, *J. Pain Symptom Manage.*, 19, 200, 2000.

209. Curran, H.V. et al., Effects of methadone on cognition, mood and craving in detoxifying opiate addicts: a dose–response study, *Psychopharmacology*, 154, 153, 2001.

210. Schaeffer, J., Andrysiak, T., and Ungerleider, J.T., Cognition and long-term use of ganja (cannabis), *Science*, 213, 465, 1981.

211. Varma, V.K. et al., Cannabis and cognitive functions: a prospective study, *Drug Alcohol Depend.*, 21, 147, 1988.

212. Huestegge, L. et al., Visual search in long-term cannabis users with early age of onset, in *Progress in Brain Research*, Hyona, J., Munoz, D.P., Heide, W., and Radach, R., Eds., Elsevier, New York, 2002, 377.

213. Solowij, N. et al., Cognitive functioning of long-term heavy cannabis users seeking treatment, *J. Am. Med. Assoc.*, 287, 1123, 2002.

214. Block, R.I. and Ghoneim, M.M., Effects of chronic marijuana use on human cognition, *Psychopharmacology*, 110, 219, 1993.

215. Pope, H.G. and Yurgelun-Todd, D., The residual cognitive effects of heavy marijuana use in college students, *J. Am. Med. Assoc.*, 275, 521, 1996.

216. Pope, H.G., Gruber, A.J., and Yurgelun-Todd, D., The residual neuropsychological effects of cannabis: the current status of research, *Drug Alcohol Depend.*, 38, 25, 1995.

217. Leirer, V.O., Yesavage, J.A., and Morrow, D.G., Marijuana carry-over effects on aircraft pilot performance, *Aviat. Space Environ. Med.*, 62, 221, 1991.

218. Yesavage, J.A. et al., Carry-over effects of marijuana intoxication on aircraft pilot performance: a preliminary report, *Am. J. Psychiatry*, 142, 1325, 1985.

219. Leirer, V.O., Yesavage, J.A., and Morrow, D.G., Marijuana, aging, and task difficulty effects on pilot performance, *Aviat. Space Environ. Med.*, 60, 1145, 1989.

220. Chait, L.D., Fischman, M.W., and Schuster, C.R., "Hangover" effects the morning after marijuana smoking, *Drug Alcohol Depend.*, 15, 229, 1985.

221. Chait, L.D., Subjective and behavioral effects of marijuana the morning after smoking, *Psychopharmacology*, 100, 328, 1990.

222. Heishman, S.J. et al., Acute and residual effects of marijuana: Profiles of plasma THC levels, physiological, subjective, and performance measures, *Pharmacol. Biochem. Behav.*, 37, 561, 1990.

223. Fant, R.V. et al., Acute and residual effects of marijuana in humans, *Pharmacol. Biochem. Behav.*, 60, 777, 1998.

224. Bolla, K.I. et al., Dose-related neurocognitive effects of marijuana use, *Neurology*, 59, 1337, 2002.

225. Pope, H.G. et al., Neuropsychological performance in long-term cannabis users, *Arch. Gen. Psychiatry*, 58, 909, 2001.

226. McGlothin, W.H. and West, L.J., The marihuana problem: an overview, *Am. J. Psychiatry*, 125, 370, 1968.

227. Kupfer, D.J. et al., A comment on the "amotivational syndrome" in marijuana smokers, *Am. J. Psychiatry*, 130, 1319, 1973.

228. Comitas, L., *Cannabis* and work in Jamaica: a refutation of the amotivational syndrome, *Ann. N.Y. Acad. Sci.*, 282, 24, 1976.

229. Stefanis, C., Dornbush, R., and Fink, M., *Hashish: Studies of Long-Term Use*, Raven Press, New York, 1977.

230. Page, J.B., The amotivational syndrome hypothesis and the Costa Rica study: relationship between methods and results, *J. Psychoactive Drugs*, 15, 261, 1983.

231. Mendelson, J.H. et al., Operant acquisition of marihuana in man, *J. Pharmacol. Exp. Ther.*, 198, 42, 1976.

232. Kelly, T.H. et al., Multidimensional behavioral effects of marijuana, *Prog. Neuropsychopharmacol. Biol. Psychiatry*, 14, 885, 1990.

233. Block, R.I., Farinpour, R., and Braverman, K., Acute effects of marijuana on cognition: relationships to chronic effects and smoking techniques, *Pharmacol. Biochem. Behav.*, 43, 907, 1992.

234. Liguori, A., Gatto, C.P., and Robinson, J.H., Effects of marijuana on equilibrium, psychomotor performance, and simulated driving, *Behav. Pharmacol.*, 9, 599, 1998.

235. Chait, L.D. and Perry, J.L., Acute and residual effects of alcohol and marijuana, alone and in combination, on mood and performance, *Psychopharmacology*, 115, 340, 1994.

236. Heishman, S.J., Arasteh, K., and Stitzer, M.L., Comparative effects of alcohol and marijuana on mood, memory, and performance, *Pharmacol. Biochem. Behav.*, 58, 93, 1997.

237. Greenberg, H.S. et al., Short-term effects of smoking marijuana on balance in patients with multiple sclerosis and normal volunteers, *Clin. Pharmacol. Ther.*, 55, 324, 1994.

238. Greenwald, M.K. and Stitzer, M.L., Antinociceptive, subjective and behavioral effects of smoked marijuana in humans, *Drug Alcohol Depend.*, 59, 261, 2000.

239. Cone, E.J. et al., Acute effects of smoking marijuana on hormones, subjective effects and performance in male human subjects, *Pharmacol. Biochem. Behav.*, 24, 1749, 1986.

240. Heishman, S.J., Stitzer, M.L., and Bigelow, G.E., Alcohol and marijuana: comparative dose effect profiles in humans, *Pharmacol Biochem. Behav.*, 31, 649, 1988.

241. Kurzthaler, I. et al., Effect of cannabis use on cognitive functions and driving ability, *J. Clin. Psychiatry*, 60, 395, 1999.

242. Wilson, W.H. et al., Effects of marijuana on performance of a computerized cognitive-neuromotor test battery, *Psychiatry Res.*, 51, 115, 1994.

243. O'Leary, D.S. et al., Effects of smoking marijuana on brain perfusion and cognition, *Neuropsychopharmacology*, 26, 802, 2002.

244. Kelly, T.H., Foltin, R.W., and Fischman, M.W., Effects of smoked marijuana on heart rate, drug ratings and task performance by humans, *Behav. Pharmacol.*, 4, 167, 1993.

245. Azorlosa, J.L. et al., Marijuana smoking: effect of varying [9]-tetrahydrocannabinol content and number of puffs, *J. Pharmacol. Exp. Ther.*, 261, 114, 1992.

246. Heishman, S.J., Stitzer, M.L., and Yingling, J.E., Effects of tetrahydrocannabinol content on marijuana smoking behavior, subjective reports, and performance, *Pharmacol. Biochem. Behav.*, 34, 173, 1989.

247. Kamien, J.B. et al., The effects of [9]-tetrahydrocannabinol on repeated acquisition and performance of response sequences and on self-reports in humans, *Behav. Pharmacol.*, 5, 71, 1994.

248. Azorlosa, J.L., Greenwald, M.K., and Stitzer, M.L., Marijuana smoking: effects of varying puff volume and breathhold duration, *J. Pharmacol. Exp. Ther.*, 272, 560, 1995.

249. Hooker, W.D. and Jones, R.T., Increased susceptibility to memory intrusions and the Stroop interference effect during acute marijuana intoxication, *Psychopharmacology*, 91, 20, 1987.

250. Marks, D.F. and MacAvoy, M.G., Divided attention performance in cannabis users and non-users following alcohol and cannabis separately and in combination, *Psychopharmacology*, 99, 397, 1989.

251. Hart, C.L. et al., Comparison of smoked marijuana and oral [9]-tetrahydrocannabinol in humans, *Psychopharmacology*, 164, 407, 2002.

252. Kelly, T.H. et al., Performance-based testing for drugs of abuse: dose and time profiles of marijuana, amphetamine, alcohol, and diazepam, *J. Anal. Toxicol.*, 17, 264, 1993.

253. Heishman, S.J., Singleton, E.G., and Crouch, D.J., Laboratory validation study of Drug Evaluation and Classification program: ethanol, cocaine, and marijuana, *J. Anal. Toxicol.*, 20, 468, 1996.

254. Heishman, S.J., Singleton, E.G., and Crouch, D.J., Laboratory validation study of Drug Evaluation and Classification program: alprazolam, D-amphetamine, codeine, and marijuana, *J. Anal. Toxicol.*, 22, 503, 1998.

255. Robbe, H.W.J., *Influence of Marijuana on Driving*, University of Limburg Press, Maastricht, 1994.

256. Ramaekers, J.G., Robbe, H.W.J., and O'Hanlon, J.F., Marijuana, alcohol and actual driving performance, *Hum. Psychopharmacol. Clin. Exp.*, 15, 551, 2000.

257. Bahri, T. and Amir, T., Effect of hashish on vigilance performance, *Percept. Mot. Skills*, 78, 11, 1994.

258. Curran, H.V. et al., Cognitive and subjective dose–response effects of acute oral ^{9}-tetrahydrocannabinol (THC) in infrequent cannabis users, *Psychopharmacology*, 164, 61, 2002.

259. Hart, C.L. et al., Effects of acute smoked marijuana on complex cognitive performance, *Neuropsychopharmacology*, 25, 757, 2001.

260. Herning, R.I., Jones, R.T., Bachman, J., and Mines, A.H., Puff volume increases when low-nicotine cigarettes are smoked, *Br. Med. J.*, 283, 1, 1981.

261. Ohlsson, A. et al., Plasma delta-9-tetrahydrocannabinol concentrations and clinical effects after oral and intravenous administration and smoking, *Clin. Pharmacol. Ther.*, 28, 409, 1980.

262. Huestis, M.A., Henningfield, J.E., and Cone, E.J., Blood cannabinoids. I. Absorption of THC and formation of 11-OH-THC and THCCOOH during and after smoking marijuana, *J. Anal. Toxicol.*, 16, 276, 1992.

263. Parrott, A.C., Performance tests in human psychopharmacology (1): Test reliability and standardization, *Hum. Psychopharmacol. Clin. Exp.*, 6, 1, 1991.

264. Parrott, A.C., Performance tests in human psychopharmacology (2): Content validity, criterion validity, and face validity, *Hum. Psychopharmacol. Clin. Exp.*, 6, 91, 1991.

265. Parrott, A.C., Performance tests in human psychopharmacology (3): Construct validity and test interpretation, *Hum. Psychopharmacol. Clin. Exp.*, 6, 197, 1991.

4.2 PERFORMANCE-BASED ASSESSMENT OF BEHAVIORAL IMPAIRMENT IN OCCUPATIONAL SETTINGS

Thomas H. Kelly, Ph.D.,[1] **Richard C. Taylor, M.A.,**[2] **Stephen J. Heishman, Ph.D.,**[2] **and Jonathan Howland, Ph.D.**[3]

[1] Department of Behavioral Science, University of Kentucky College of Medicine, Lexington, Kentucky
[2] Clinical Pharmacology and Therapeutics Branch, National Institute on Drug Abuse, National Institutes of Health, Department of Health and Human Services, Baltimore, Maryland
[3] Social and Behavioral Sciences Department, Boston University School of Public Health, Boston, Massachusetts

4.2.1 Introduction

A number of technologies for the assessment of performance impairment have emerged in recent years.[1] These technologies, which include biological sample testing, neuropsychological assessment, personality assessment, and performance testing, are designed to identify risks to safety and/or productivity (e.g., poor health, sleep deprivation, use of behaviorally active drugs/medications), to alter behaviors associated with the development of these risks (e.g., health promotion, reducing drug-taking behavior), and to support the development and evaluation of interventions designed to enhance safety and productivity.[2] Each of these technologies has strengths and limitations.

Biological sample testing is highly specific for the assessment of risk factors associated with the presence of drugs and/or neurotoxins. The primary advantage of biological sample testing is the reliability and validity with which the presence of these risk factors can be detected (e.g., published standards for the development and implementation of drug-testing programs are available).[3] If the integrity of testing procedures is maintained, these technologies can provide accurate information regarding prior exposure to a wide variety of agents. There are a number of disadvantages associated with these technologies, however. The costs associated with development and maintenance of testing programs can be substantial. The collection of biological samples can be invasive. The time required to produce a result following collection of a biological sample can be impractical in applications in which immediate results are necessary. Perhaps the most complicated disadvantage associated with biological sample testing technologies available at the current time is that they provide uncertain information regarding performance effects. Drugs (and their metabolites) remain in biological samples for many hours/days after exposure, well beyond the period of time that is associated with performance-impairing effects. The detection of metabolites in biological samples, therefore, does not always provide sufficient information to determine whether or not a drug is producing effects on human performance.

Neuropsychological testing technologies attempt to measure neurological and behavioral function. These technologies generally involve one-time measurements of physiological and behavioral responses to tests, and clinical interpretations of the results of the tests are based, in part, on comparisons with scores (i.e., norms) collected from populations of individuals with similar characteristics (e.g., age, gender, race).[4] The reliability and validity of neuropsychological testing technologies are regularly and repeatedly tested, and these procedures can be used to assess the acute and long-term effects of environmental perturbations, such as injuries, disease states, and drug exposure, on human capabilities. An appropriately trained professional should conduct neuropsychological test battery administration and interpretation, and as such, the efficiency and expense of this technology may limit its use in applied settings. On the other hand, while designed for acute clinical assessment, many components of neuropsychological test batteries can be administered in a reliable manner on a repeated basis as part of an automated performance testing system. Additional research is needed to determine the validity of the use of components of neuropsychological test batteries in this manner.

Personality testing technologies attempt to identify and measure personality dimensions that differentiate individuals who have increased safety and/or productivity risks (e.g., drug users) from those who do not. Examples of such screening tools include integrity tests, attitude tests, and the measurement of risk factor profiles. Personality testing technologies have been evaluated most critically when used for pre-employment screening; their use in repeated assessments of workers has received less attention. A major concern with regard to this technology is the high rate of false positives (i.e., identification of an individual as being at risk when the individual is, in fact, not at any risk) that has been associated with its use.[5] Concerns regarding whether these approaches will ever achieve a sufficient level of accuracy to effectively measure performance impairment have been raised.[1]

In contrast to neuropsychological testing technologies that are designed for acute clinical assessment, performance testing technologies are designed for repeated measurement of an individual's performance under standardized testing conditions. Clinical evaluations of performance on these tests can be based on population norms (as is the case with many neuropsychological testing technologies) or on deviations from individually determined performance standards established through repeated measurements of an individual's performance (i.e., change from baseline performance). Most performance testing technologies have emerged from laboratory-based research that has occurred over the past three decades (e.g., see Heishman and Myers, Chapter 4.1 of this volume). The development and evaluation of performance testing technologies have proliferated in parallel with the availability of the personal computer, and a wide array of tests and systems are available for which significant information regarding reliability and validity exists. The major advantages of performance testing technologies for the detection of performance impairment are the wide variety of options that are available (i.e., the face validity of performance testing can be addressed through careful selection and modification of existing performance tests), the immediate availability of results, and the non-invasive manner in which tests can be administered (relative to biological sample testing). Disadvantages include the lack of specificity with regard to test results (i.e., many factors can alter test performance), and the cost of technology development and implementation. The high costs of performance testing technology development and implementation stem, in part, from a lack of information regarding the optimal use of performance tests in occupational settings. In addition, while the reliability and validity of performance tests have been repeatedly demonstrated in controlled laboratory settings, little evidence regarding the reliability and validity of these procedures in applied settings has been published in peer-reviewed journals. As such, the utility of these procedures has not been clearly established.

The focus of this chapter is on issues associated with the use of performance testing technologies for the detection of drug-induced impairment. Since performance tests are not selectively sensitive to the effects of drugs, alone, discussion will focus on the detection of the effects of risk factors, including drug use, sleep deprivation, or adverse physical or mental health, on performance. It is important to note, however, that while this chapter specifically addresses performance testing as a means of impairment detection, no direct or implied recommendation for exclusive development of performance testing technologies for impairment testing is suggested. It is likely that no single technology will be universally effective in all settings or situations. A combination of technologies, based on the availability of resources needed to support those technologies, will likely enhance the effectiveness of any impairment testing system.[1,6]

4.2.2 Issues in the Selection and Implementation of Performance Testing Technologies

The presence of risk factors, such as adverse physical and emotional health, use of behaviorally active drugs/medication, and sleep deprivation, may compromise performance safety and productivity. However, the presence of such risk factors may or may not have implications for how an individual will perform his or her work. An important consideration in the selection of an impairment testing technology is the purpose for which such testing is intended.[7] Impairment testing can be designed to detect the influence of risk factors on performance, regardless of whether or not the effects are related to the individual's work performance. However, impairment testing can also be designed to detect deviations from optimal work performance, regardless of the presence or absence of risk factors.

While the presence of risk factors may or may not have a direct effect on job performance under normal day-to-day operating conditions, it is often assumed that these factors can have an adverse impact on an individual's performance when there is a change from the normal conditions associated with job performance (e.g., the ability to respond safely and effectively to an emergency). If so, the detection of any change in normal performance (e.g., altered performance during a computerized assessment task) signals a change in an individual's capacity that could have adverse implications for job performance. If detection of risk factors is the objective of impairment testing, finding a technology that is reliable and sensitive to many risk factors may be a useful strategy, and concerns regarding reliability and validity in this pursuit become of paramount importance.

On the other hand, detection of the effects of risk factors on performance may have little to say about the likelihood with which an individual will effectively perform an appointed task. From this perspective, risk factors are relevant only if they have adverse effects on normal job performance (i.e., job performance is the relevant metric for impairment testing, not performance on assessment tasks). If the objective of impairment testing is to assess the normal job performance, considerations of the relationship between performance during impairment testing and job performance become a primary concern, and criterion validity issues must be carefully considered. Job simulation tests, such as video-disc simulators for emergency rooms,[8] are examples of performance tests designed to maximize the assessment of on-the-job performance.[2] One advantage of this approach is that employees more easily accept and comply with impairment testing when the ecological or face validity of the testing procedures is apparent.[9] On the other hand, the development costs of simulations can be substantial.

Although it is important to decide on the purpose(s) for performance impairment testing, practical issues must also be considered. Several reviews of practical considerations associated with the selection and implementation of impairment testing technologies have been published, and many details may be obtained from these sources.[4,9–11] However, one primary consideration is the manner in which performance tests will be administered. Performance assessment measures can be administered by trained observers, such as is the common practice with law enforcement personnel who administer field sobriety tests designed to detect the influence of drugs on driving ability, by computers under standardized conditions, or by some combination of these two approaches. The use of trained observers to administer performance impairment tests provides maximum flexibility and minimizes the amount of training and practice required of the test population. However, there are no well-validated observation systems that are currently available, and the reliability of testers will always be a concern, unless reliability and validity assessment can be incorporated into the standard testing protocol. In addition, the recurring personnel costs associated with such testing procedures can be substantial, given the need for repeated test administration.

Automation provides a solution for many of the concerns associated with trained observers. When trained observers are not available, time for testing is limited, or immediate results are needed, automated performance test administration procedures should be considered. It is also possible to standardize the presentation of stimulus materials and data collection with automated testing devices, thereby enhancing the reliability of the testing procedure. Initial development and start-up costs, which are based on the number of testing sites required and the amount of back-up support that is needed, can be substantial, but other than maintenance are not recurring costs. However, clinical interpretation of test results is limited when testing is completely automated and evaluations are based strictly on algorithms that are established as part of the testing system. Even the most automated systems will benefit from human interface for maintenance and set-up support, in addition to data management and interpretation. Given the clear advantages with regard to cost and efficiency, this chapter focuses on automated performance testing technologies.

4.2.2.1 Selecting a Performance Testing System

When selecting a performance testing system, issues that could affect the practicality, accuracy, and general utility of the system include the specific performance tests that are included in the system, the availability of norms upon which performance can be evaluated (and upon which decisions regarding readiness to perform are based), the reliability and validity of the measures, the accuracy of the measurement, the user interface, and the administrative interface. The relevance of each of these issues is discussed, as are some of the specific questions that merit some consideration when evaluating performance testing systems.

Selection of Individual Tests

Performance on various tests is thought to reflect the involvement of selective, and in some cases, isolated dimensions of human capacity, such as sensory and motor ability, attention, and elements of cognition (Heishman and Myers, Chapter 4.1). Drug effects have also been shown to vary as a function of behavioral mechanisms sustaining performance, including reinforcement contingencies and stimulus context. The use of multiple tests sampling a wide variety of human capacities under a variety of conditions has proved most effective for differentiating among the effects of drugs on behavior.[12] A general description of individual tests is beyond the scope of this chapter, but such descriptions are available elsewhere.[4,12,13] It is important to note that the task parameters and behavioral mechanisms can vary among similar tests when used in different assessment systems; it is critical to consider these variables when interpreting the dimensions of performance being measured within an assessment system.

Sensory tests measure ability to differentiate between objects varying along a stimulus dimension, such as auditory or visual intensity or frequency, or light flicker rate. The critical flicker frequency test is a commonly used type of sensory test.

Motor ability tests focus on measures associated with motor control. The most common examples of motor tasks are finger tapping tests, tracking tests, and hand steadiness tests.

Attention tests include tests of focused attention, in which performance is measured for short durations (typically less than 10 min); selective attention, which involve responding to selected stimuli among a variety of distracting or irrelevant stimuli; divided attention, which require attention to two or more tasks presented simultaneously; and sustained attention, in which some aspect of the previous three measures of attention are required over longer durations (typically 10 min or longer). Focused attention tests include measures of simple and choice reaction time, pursuit tracking, symbol substitution, encoding/decoding, time estimation, continuous performance (i.e., vigilance), visual monitoring, sequence comparisons, and visual monitoring. Clearly, performance on these tasks includes both sensory and motor components. Selective attention tasks include the Stroop test, Neisser tests, letter and number cancellation tests, dichotic listening tests, and switching or shifting attention tests.

Cognitive tests focus on measures of acquisition, memory, other performance that demonstrates effective use of language and logic, and measures of self-control or inhibition. Acquisition tests include serial and repeated acquisition, and associative learning. Memory tests include immediate and delayed free-recall and recognition tests, matching-to-sample and Sternberg tests, pattern comparison, sequence memory, selective reminding, text memory, the misplaced objects test, facial memory, and digit-span (i.e., digit-recall) or character-recall tests. Other language- or logic-based cognitive performance tests include spatial rotation, pattern matching, the Manikin test, logical reasoning, mental arithmetic, linguistic processing, vocabulary, and the Raven Progressive Matrices test. Measures of self-control include the card-perseveration and Stop/Go tests.

These tests have been used frequently for detection of the effects of risk factors on human performance. The greater the number of tests used in a system, the more comprehensive the assessment, and the more likely it will be that the adverse effects of any risk factor are detected. However, the cost of testing (i.e., test-taking time and training) is also directly related to the number of tests that are included. Many of these tests can be modified to simulate more carefully work-related activities (e.g., digit-recall tasks can be reformulated as telephone number–recall tasks) or incorporated into simulation tasks. Performance impairment test systems use varying combinations of these and other tests; however, there is no commonly agreed-upon strategy for selecting the number or diversity of tasks that are used in a test system. Selection of a system, or collection of tests, must be related to the needs of the testing organization and to the objectives of impairment testing.

Reliability and Validity

The selection of performance impairment test systems should also include a thorough consideration of the reliability and validity of the systems. Reliability refers to the consistency of results on the test across repeated testing, and validity refers to the effectiveness with which the test accomplishes its intended purpose, be that identification of the effects of risk factors or the detection of individuals who are at risk for reduced safety and/or productivity in the workplace.

Many performance impairment test systems are based on face validity, or the degree to which the tests appear to accomplish their intended purposes. While face validity is an important consideration with regard to the acceptance of a testing system by management and the workforce, it is, by itself, insufficient for demonstrating the evidence needed to ensure that the test system is indeed accomplishing its intended purposes. Few commercially available performance impairment systems provide adequate evidence of validity, and the evidence that is provided is often limited by the context under which the evidence was collected (i.e., does not generalize to different worksites — ecological validity). It is advised that information regarding the validity of performance testing systems be collected in a proactive manner when the systems are introduced, as there is not sufficient information available to justify even global statements regarding the validity of performance impairment testing systems at the present time.

Evaluation Norms

Another important consideration in the selection of an impairment testing system is whether norm-based decision criteria will be used to evaluate readiness to perform an assignment, and if so, whether such norms are currently available. It is important that such norms address both *decrements* and *improvements* in performance, as improved performance may also signal the influence of a risk factor. For example, stimulant medications may have minimal effect on performance of most tasks, but under test conditions requiring sustained attention, enhanced performance may be noted.[14] These same doses of stimulant medication may have important implications for more complex dimensions of human behavior,[15,16] so the detection of enhanced performance may signal an increased risk for detrimental effects on other more complex behaviors that are not directly measured during testing.

Two approaches to the establishment of norms have been proposed.[11] The first approach stresses the development of standards of performance that are universally applied to all individuals, and evaluation of test performance is based on whether an individual performs above or below a given standard. The second approach utilizes the results of prior performance of an individual to establish a baseline upon which to evaluate future performance.

The use of a fixed performance standard has appeal in that simple and consistent criteria may be uniformly applied to all individuals who are taking the test. If these criteria are closely linked with minimal standards of successful work performance, both workers and management can easily recognize and accept the utility of the testing procedure. However, a number of shortcomings with this strategy are also apparent. There are substantial individual differences in performance on most tests, and the routine performance of some individuals may fall below the standard criterion, regardless of risk factors. In addition, performance on tests may change over time, for example, through normal aging processes. An individual who has routinely met performance standards may, over time, exhibit gradually decreasing levels of proficiency that may eventually result in substandard performance. If standardized criteria are used, legal issues associated with discrimination must also be considered,[9] and the inclusion of the test during initial employment evaluations is recommended. The utility of minimal performance standards also presupposes that test performance is a valid indicator of effective work performance (as opposed to a valid indicator of the effect of a risk factor). The evidence needed to support such a supposition is rarely available. Under such conditions, the potential for misuse or abuse of performance test results must be considered.

Change from an individual's own baseline as determined by past performance is the more commonly used criterion for evaluation of the effects of risk factors on performance. Performance measures from previous tests can be evaluated with standardized algorithms to establish objective criteria for evaluating an individual's current or future performance on the same tests under similar test conditions. However, even when baseline measures are used, the establishment of criteria upon which to make decisions regarding whether changes from baseline performance are clinically relevant are oftentimes arbitrary. For example, if a user routinely completed 5.5 trials per minute during a test, what degree of change would be needed to be certain that the performance was influenced by some risk factor, rather than the result of chance variation in normal performance? Individualized variability criteria, which take into account a user's "normal" variance in performance, can be computed, as well, and used as a standard by which to evaluate change from baseline. The efficacy of this approach, however, presupposes that the user will provide samples of performance that are independent of the presence of any risk factor during baseline determinations; if baselines are established while an individual is using drugs, for example, the performance of the individual under the influence of a drug will become the norm. Additional research is needed to establish strategies for the development of effective standards of performance evaluation.[17]

Another complication of the baseline approach concerns the interpretation of relative performance among users. It is quite possible, when using baseline criteria, that the identification of a clinically significant decrement in performance from the normal baseline of one user may occur under conditions in which the level of performance of that user is higher than the performance of another user who is performing at baseline level. Interpretation of changes from baseline is a complicated process, and few standards are currently available.

One issue that is routinely associated with the degree of acceptability of testing programs to the workforce is the consequence of poor performance on a test.[9–11] The establishment of policies regarding the response of management to test failures requires careful consideration. Trice and Steele[9] suggest that coordination between performance testing and employee assistance programs will enhance the utility of both resources in the overall effort to reduce drug use by the workforce, and will enhance the acceptability of programs to both management and the workforce.

Questions have been raised about the feasibility of establishing evaluation norms that can be used across different populations and settings, or with similar tests used on different computer test systems. Certainly, situational factors influence performance on computerized performance tests. In addition, epidemiological factors, such as gender and age, have been demonstrated to influence performance on these tests. Due to mechanical and electronic differences across computer systems, as well as differences in software control techniques, it is perhaps impossible to provide norms that can be used across differing testing platforms. No universally accepted norms for the evaluation of task performance are currently available, and it is highly recommended that a scheduled evaluation of the validity of existing norms be planned in a proactive manner whenever these existing norms are used in new setting.

Administrative Interface

The ease and flexibility of the use of performance impairment test systems can be influenced by the interface between the software and test administrator. Characteristics that might be considered include the flexibility in organizing the tests to be delivered, making changes in test parameters, and in the manner in which data are presented, analyzed, and stored for future access.

Another consideration with regard to the administrative interface, as discussed previously, is the degree to which test delivery can be automated. The need for an administrator to be on site for test delivery has cost and efficiency implications. If the test is completely automated, procedures for maintaining accurate identification regarding test sessions (e.g., participant I.D., date, time, etc.) must be established.

User Interface

The cost of test delivery can also be influenced by the availability of user interfaces. The user interface can provide access to a variety of support resources to the user, including general instructions and support during training. If an instruction module is available, it should be designed to provide clear, complete, and standardized information and instructions concerning the operation of the test equipment and the completion of task components. One useful feature of an instruction module would be the inclusion of a section designed to assess whether users understood the instructions, particularly if these instructions are important determinants of user performance. This can be accomplished with a series of questions designed to provide additional information when users do not answer questions accurately. The training module should be designed to administer the tests and to provide feedback to users in a manner that enhances the development of stable and reliable performance.

4.2.2.2 Testing Platform

Hardware considerations for automated performance testing systems generally include the computer, software, monitor, and input devices. These features can be provided on multiple testing platforms, including personal computers, handheld personal digital assistants, Internet-based systems, or on platforms that are specially designed to simulate occupational contexts.

Personal Computers

Many government and commercial impairment testing systems can be implemented on standard commercially available personal computer platforms (e.g., PC, Macintosh). Despite software and hardware advancements that have minimized the differences across platforms, it is still important to consider carefully the hardware and software requirements needed to support a system, as these specifications may have important implications for the accuracy of stimulus presentation and the precision of performance measures. In addition, there may be differential costs associated with the hardware and software specifications. The speed of the computer processor is one important specification that requires careful consideration. Other concerns include the amount of memory that is needed to present the test and record the results, the manner in which the data are to be stored, the size and portability of the computer, and the video-display requirements. Some systems may also require additional components, such as joysticks, keyboards, mouse, touch-sensitive monitors, light pens and drawing boards, or response panels.

In general, the processor speeds and memory capacities of modern personal computers are sufficient to support most systems (e.g., milliseconds timing resolution and response monitoring requirements). However, running these systems on older computers having a slower processing speed and limited memory capacity could have a detrimental impact on the accuracy of the test, so caution is recommended.

There are a number of advantages associated with the use of personal computers for supporting performance testing systems. Given the ubiquity of personal computers, personal computers afford a fair amount of flexibility for equipment support and maintenance. If new equipment is acquired, personal computers can support a variety of services when not needed for performance testing. Finally, the availability of numerous personal computer vendors helps to assure reasonable prices and adequate product availability.

There are also some disadvantages associated with the use of personal computers. Desktop computers have limited mobility. Portable personal computers are typically more expensive, have more limited capabilities than desktop machines, and present greater security concerns. Data management can be more complicated if results from different testing occasions are required in a central database or if an individual is tested in multiple settings with different computers.

Handheld Personal Digital Assistants

Rapid advances in software and electronic capabilities of personal digital assistants have supported the proliferation of handheld data collection technologies.[18,19] Since these devices are typically less expensive than personal computers, the use of handheld personal digital assistants (PDA) for performance testing reduces the equipment cost of these systems. Like personal computers, these devices can support a variety of services when not needed for performance testing, particularly if each user is provided with his or her own device. The portability of the devices permits testing to occur in a greater variety of contexts and times, thereby enhancing the flexibility and reducing the cost of data collection.

There are disadvantages to the use of handheld devices, as well. Most importantly, the video display and response input capabilities of these devices are much more limited than for personal computers. Stimulus and response requirements are critical elements of many tasks, and as such,

PDAs may limit the range of tasks that can be included in a performance testing system. Security concerns are even greater than those presented by portable computers, and data management can be an even greater challenge than with personal computers, given the limitations in data exchange options associated with these devices.

Web-Based Systems

Although not yet available, it is likely that Web-based performance testing systems will become available in the near future. Web-based systems will permit selected tasks to be presented on computers equipped with appropriate Web browser software. Hardware requirements include internet access and appropriate memory and software to support Web-based applications. Depending on the design of the Web-based system, it is could be possible to tailor the specific tasks presented for the performance testing system from a menu of options. Alternatively, testing systems consisting of a standardized array of tasks can also be chosen. As such, the start-up costs of Web-based systems should be lower than with personal or handheld computer systems. Subject identification, date, and time can be recorded at the start of a test, and data from multiple subjects and test occasions can be stored in a central file for easy access to the data.

There are some clear disadvantages associated with Web-based systems, as well. The most important limitation is that the flexibility of the performance test systems is necessarily restricted to the range of tasks and associated parameters that are available through the Web-based software. While individualized software could be requested, it is likely that there will be additional time and monetary costs associated with each request. Second, stimulus presentation and response inputs may be variable across test sites unless standardized systems are used to access the Web-based software. It may also be difficult to use standardized norms to evaluate task performance, due to variable stimulus and response conditions that may exist across test sites. Finally, although the start-up costs may be reduced, there will be greater recurrent costs associated with repeated use of the Web-based software.

4.2.2.3 Test Implementation

In addition to considerations of impairment testing systems and the equipment and platform to administer the systems, the implementation of the testing system must also be considered. Test cost, frequency of administration, maintenance of stable patterns of performance (i.e., motivation), and worker acceptance are among the issues that merit consideration.[11] In addition, concerns regarding the legal status of performance test systems, the manner in which labor unions and arbitrators might view such test systems, and whether or not there is a potential for misuse of the test system could affect system implementation.[9]

Cost

Test costs include the initial expense of acquiring the test equipment and providing a test space, the time required to complete the test, and administrative costs (e.g., record keeping, test set-up, maintenance and replacement of equipment). However, test costs may be complicated by the presence of hidden factors, as well.[10] For example, cost of training the users may be substantial. Based on the consequences of test failure, lost work time may also be factored in, particularly under conditions in which the false positive rate (i.e., identification of the influence of a risk factor on a user's performance when none, in fact, exists) is high. There are additional costs associated with initial negotiations between management and workers concerning the appropriateness of a testing program and the consequences of test failure, and potential costs associated with litigation, should it occur.

Test Frequency

No clear landmarks exist for making decisions regarding test frequency. In general, tests are administered before an individual begins an assigned work activity. However, risk factors can emerge at any time, and are not limited to activities that occur before work activities begin. For example, the effects of fatigue, illness, and drug use can all occur after work has begun, and would not be measured by tests occurring only at the beginning of a work activity. In addition, it is not clear whether the frequency of test administration influences the reliability of test performance. If tests are administered on a regular basis, or if rest intervals (e.g., weekends) separate successive tests, motivational changes may influence performance.

Maintenance of Performance Stability

Repeated administration of tests, without contingencies designed to maintain motivation, invariably result in decrements in performance over time. Considerations of the maintenance of motivated performance across repeated administration of a test is an important consideration during the implementation of an impairment testing system. It is generally assumed that under conditions in which access to assigned work activities, and financial compensation for that work, is contingent on suitable test performance, motivated performance is likely to be maintained across repeated testing.[10] However, there have not been adequate investigations of this assumption, and it is likely that emotional behavior would also occur if access to work were denied as a result of poor performance on a test. The use of additional contingencies that target performance stability might be helpful, in addition to the seemingly punitive consequence of loss of work opportunities associated with poor performance. It has been suggested that the use of more complex or varied testing procedures may also help eliminate changes in motivation over time. Clearly, additional research on these issues is needed.

User Acceptance

Another important consideration with regard to the implementation of an impairment testing system is the acceptance of the test system by the workforce. Worker acceptance is influenced by the comfort in taking the tests, as well as by test relevance, or face validity, availability, and accuracy.[11] Comfort refers to the degree to which worker performance on these tests is acceptable under routine testing conditions, and may be inversely related to the likelihood of false positive outcomes. Relevance, or face validity, is associated with the extent to which workers report that performance during the test will reflect performance of their assigned work tasks. Availability refers to the reliability of the test equipment — if the tests cannot be administered when scheduled, confidence in the accuracy of the test system is questioned. Accuracy refers to the extent to which the test results are related to risk factors. Workers receive direct or indirect feedback on test systems (i.e., pass or fail). Rates of false positives (failures given the absence of any risk factor) and false negatives (passes given worker recognition of the influence of a potential risk factor, such as drug use) influence worker estimates of test accuracy.

Legal Issues

No clear guidelines exist with regard to the legal status of performance impairment test systems. In comparison with employee selection criteria, Trice and Steele[9] suggest that the legality of these test systems may be related to the degree to which their use results in discriminatory outcomes. They cite Klein's[20] description of an 80% rule as a workable strategy for assessing discriminatory practices. If the pass rate obtained when testing of any race, sex, or ethnic group is less than 80% of the group with the highest pass rate, then the test system has an adverse impact. Trice and Steele[9] also indicate that the absence of information regarding a cause of test failure could have a negative impact on considerations of the legality of test systems, because under such conditions employees might feel unduly compelled to reveal details of their personal lives.

The status of performance impairment test systems with regard to fair-labor practices is also undetermined at the present time. Trice and Steele[9] suggest that since biological sample testing approaches to the detection of drug use have been ruled in the past to be a mandatory labor practice, and as such, require bargaining with labor or unions prior to implementation, performance test systems would likely be viewed in a similar manner. However, they also note that, because performance tests are less invasive than biological sample testing procedures, and can be demonstrated to have greater job relatedness, employers could make the case that performance impairment test systems can be implemented unilaterally without bargaining.

Potential for Misuse of Test Systems

Misuse of performance impairment tests is related to the consequences of worker performance. Test systems can be implemented with the sole purpose of providing feedback to workers regarding their level of performance (i.e., no consequences associated with work activities are imposed). The objective of such testing procedures is to provide workers with information to use to adjust their own on-work and off-work behavior in an attempt to more accurately monitor their own levels of safety and productivity. For example, in describing a feasibility study of the implementation of a performance testing system, truck drivers adjusted their own rest behavior based on feedback they received during performance testing, even though that feedback was unrelated to drivers' work eligibility.[21] On the other hand, systems that use the results of performance on impairment tests to influence work eligibility (and possibly employment status) are more likely to involve some risk for test misuse.

No clear guidelines exist for the appropriate use of performance impairment test systems for work eligibility. There is general agreement that in situations in which worker or public safety is potentially influenced by a worker's performance, impairment test systems are justified. However, no clear criteria for identifying safety issues are available.[9] The use of such tests as a means of managing worker productivity is less universally accepted, and if used as an employee evaluation criterion, such tests should be given careful scrutiny.

4.2.3 Applications of Impairment Testing Technologies

Currently, application of laboratory-based performance assessment technologies occurs in at least three settings. The most frequent utilization of this technology is in the law-enforcement setting. Law enforcement personnel have varying amounts of training and experience in the administration of performance tests and in the interpretation of the behavior of individuals during test performance. In addition, law enforcement personnel have limited opportunities to compare their own evaluations of performance on field sobriety tests with the results of drug assays from blood tests taken concurrently with the tests in order to monitor the accuracy of their evaluations. Under these conditions, the reliability and validity of the field sobriety test remain largely unknown, in spite of its widespread utilization. Results from recent assessments of the reliability and validity of performance-based drug evaluation programs, such as sobriety testing, are presented here.

A second application of laboratory-based performance assessment technologies has been in the field of fitness-for-duty assessment, primarily supported by military and other government agencies. A varied number of fitness-for-duty assessment batteries have been developed; several of these are reviewed here. A major strength of these fitness-for-duty assessment batteries is the availability of a substantial database on the reliability and validity with which these batteries can detect changes in performance related to a number of manipulations, including drug administration, sleep deprivation, and exposure to extreme environments.

A third application of laboratory-based performance assessment technologies has been in the field of readiness-to-perform assessment in workplace settings. Many of the approaches to readiness-to-perform assessment that are being used in workplace settings have evolved from strategies that are currently in use in government-sponsored performance assessment batteries or laboratory settings, but, in general, these approaches have been subjected to reliability and validity assessment with less consistency. Several assessment technologies that have been subjected to some reliability and validity assessment are described here.

4.2.3.1 Law Enforcement Applications: Drug Evaluation and Classification Program

Background

Motor vehicle accidents are the leading cause of death in the U.S. for people aged 1 to 34.[22] Studies investigating the prevalence rate of drugs other than alcohol in fatally injured drivers have reported varied results, ranging from 6 to 37%.[23–27] Among individuals stopped for reckless driving who were judged to be clinically intoxicated, urine drug testing indicated 85% were positive for cannabinoids, cocaine metabolites, or both.[28] These relatively high prevalence rates reinforce the general assumption that psychoactive drugs are capable of impairing driving,[29,30] although drug prevalence rates do not imply impaired driving.[31,32] Because certain drugs reliably degrade psychomotor and cognitive performance in the laboratory (Heishman and Myers, Chapter 4.1), many drug-related vehicular accidents and DUI/DWI arrests probably involve impaired behaviors critical for safe driving.

Currently, the only standardized procedure for detecting drug-induced impairment is the Drug Evaluation and Classification (DEC) program,[33] which is used by police departments throughout the nation. The DEC program consists of a standardized evaluation conducted by a trained police officer (Drug Recognition Examiner, DRE) and the toxicological analysis of a biological specimen. The evaluation involves a breath alcohol test, examination of the suspect's appearance, behavior, eye movement, and nystagmus, field sobriety tests, vital signs, and questioning of the suspect. From the evaluation, the DRE concludes (1) if the suspect is behaviorally impaired such that he or she is unable to operate a motor vehicle safely, (2) if the impairment is drug-related, and (3) the drug class(es) likely causing the impairment. The toxicological analysis either confirms or refutes the DRE's drug class opinion.

Several field studies have indicated that DREs' opinions were confirmed by toxicological analysis in 74 to 92% of cases when DREs concluded suspects were impaired.[17,34–38] These studies attest to the validity of the DEC program as a measurement of drug-induced behavioral impairment in the field. However, the validity of the DEC evaluation has not been rigorously examined under controlled laboratory conditions. Heishman, Singleton, and Crouch[39,40] have examined the validity of the individual measures of the DEC evaluation in predicting whether research volunteers were administered various drugs of abuse. A synopsis of these studies is presented.

Method

Research volunteers were recruited from the community. Before the study, participants were given psychological and physical examinations to determine whether they were healthy and capable of participating in the study. At each test session, a single drug dose or placebo was administered under double-blind conditions. Sessions were separated by 48 to 72 h. In Study 1, participants received oral ethanol (0, 0.28, 0.52 g/kg); intranasal cocaine (4, 48, 96 mg/70 kg); and smoked marijuana (0, 1.75, 3.55% ⁹-tetrahydrocannabinol [THC], 16 puffs). In Study 2, participants received oral alprazolam (0, 1, 2 mg); oral D-amphetamine (0, 12.5, 25 mg); codeine (0, 60, 120 mg); and smoked marijuana (0, 3.58% THC, 8 puffs). Dosing of the various drugs was staggered so that the DEC evaluation occurred during peak drug effect.

The DEC evaluation began with an ethanol breath test. DREs measured pulse and recorded information about physical defects, corrective lenses, appearance of the eyes, and visual impairment. DREs also assessed eye tracking and nystagmus, pupillary size, and condition of eyelids. The next segment involved examination of the eyes and performance of four field sobriety tests (FST). Subjects' eyes were tested for horizontal gaze nystagmus, vertical nystagmus, and convergence. The FST were Romberg Balance (RB), Walk and Turn (WT), One Leg Stand (OLS), and Finger to Nose (FN). The RB assessed body sway and tremor while subjects stood for 30 s with feet together, arms at sides, head tilted back, and eyes closed. The WT test required subjects to take nine heel-to-toe steps along a straight line marked on the floor, turn, and return with nine heel-to-toe steps. The OLS assessed balance by having subjects stand on one leg, with the other leg elevated in a stiff-leg manner 15 cm off the floor for 30 s. Subjects were given a brief rest between right and left leg testing. In the FN test, subjects stood as in the RB and brought the tip of the index finger of the left or right hand (as instructed) directly to the tip of the nose. DREs then measured pulse, blood pressure, and oral temperature.

The final portion involved further examination of the eyes. DREs estimated the diameter of each pupil to the nearest 0.5 mm under conditions of ambient room light, nearly total darkness, indirect light, and direct light. While illuminating the eyes under direct light from a penlight for 15 s, DREs assessed constriction of the pupils and fluctuation of pupillary diameter. Last, DREs measured pulse and assessed muscle tone, attitude, coordination, speech, breath odor, and facial appearance.

Results

The 76 variables derived from the DEC evaluation were first analyzed using stepwise discriminant analysis to determine the variables that best predicted the presence or absence of each drug. This subset of best-predictor variables was then subjected to a discriminant function analysis that predicted and classified whether subjects were dosed or not dosed with drug. The resulting data were classified as true positive, true negative, false positive, or false negative. These parameters were then used to calculate several measures of predictive accuracy of the DEC evaluation, including sensitivity, specificity, and efficiency.

In Study 1, the stepwise discriminant analysis resulted in a subset of 17 variables that were the best predictors of ethanol. The discriminant function comprising these 17 variables predicted the presence or absence of ethanol with extremely high accuracy. The model was equally accurate in predicting the presence (sensitivity = 94.4%) and absence of ethanol (specificity = 92.6%); overall predictive efficiency was 93.3%. The analysis also resulted in a subset of 17 variables that were the best predictors of dosing with cocaine. The discriminant function predicted the presence or absence of cocaine with high accuracy. The model had greater specificity (96.3%) than sensitivity (88.9%), and efficiency was 93.3%. The stepwise discriminant analysis resulted in a subset of 28 variables that best predicted the presence or absence of marijuana. The discriminant function comprising these 28 variables predicted the presence (sensitivity = 100%) and absence (specificity = 98.1%) of marijuana with extremely high accuracy; predictive efficiency was 98.8%.

In Study 2, the stepwise discriminant analysis resulted in a subset of seven variables that were the best predictors of alprazolam. The model was more accurate in predicting the absence of alprazolam (specificity = 96.7%) than its presence (sensitivity = 78.3%), and predictive efficiency was 90.4%. The analysis resulted in a subset of three variables that were the best predictors of dosing with D-amphetamine. As with alprazolam, the model's predictions had greater specificity (92.5%) than sensitivity (75.0%), and efficiency of the model was high (86.5%). The discriminant analysis resulted in a subset of two variables that were the best predictors of codeine. The model's predictions had much greater specificity (92.4%) than sensitivity (34.8%), and efficiency was moderate (73.2%). The discriminant analysis resulted in a subset of seven variables that were the best predictors of marijuana. The model predicted with greater accuracy the absence (specificity = 93.3%) of marijuana than its presence (sensitivity = 61.4%); predictive efficiency was 82.7%.

Conclusion

The validity of the DEC evaluation was examined by developing mathematical models based on discriminant functions that identified the subsets of variables that best predicted whether subjects were dosed with placebo or active drug. The data clearly indicated that a subset of variables of the DEC evaluation accurately predicted acute administration of various psychoactive drugs across several pharmacological classes, including alprazolam, D-amphetamine, marijuana, ethanol, cocaine, and to a lesser extent, codeine. These findings suggest that predictions of impairment and drug use may be refined if DREs focused on a subset of variables associated with each drug class, rather than the entire DEC evaluation.

4.2.3.2   Government Application: Tests of Fitness for Duty

Background

Much of the early interest in the area of human performance testing was funded and manned by several branches of the U.S. Military. The successful military mission depends on optimal performance by its personnel. Hostile and hazardous environments may have subtle to profound influences on a soldier's performance.[41] The goal of military human performance research was to identify those environments and agents that cause a deterioration in ability, and to what degree. With this knowledge, military personnel could attempt to compensate for, or avoid, undesirable environments or agents. A comprehensive review of many assessment batteries used by government agencies, which includes a review of evidence related to the reliability and validity of the batteries, can be found elsewhere.[4,7]

Computerized Performance Test Batteries

Most government-sponsored computerized performance test batteries are compilations of computer performance tests that were originally developed and tested in controlled laboratory settings. The purpose of many of these tests is to determine the effects of risk factors on fitness for government duty, and to assess the efficacy of countermeasures designed to offset the performance effects of these risk factors.

Unified Tri-Service Cognitive Performance Assessment Battery — The Unified Tri-Service Cognitive Performance Assessment Battery (UTC-PAB) was constructed by the Tri-Service Working Group on Drug Dependent Degradation of Military Performance, which eventually became known as the Office of Military Performance Assessment Technology (OMPAT).[42] OMPAT, which was headed by Fred Hegge, included representatives from the U.S. Navy, Air Force, and Army. The group developed a standardized laboratory tool to assess cognitive performance using repeated measures in a tri-service chemical-defense biomedical drug-screening program.[43] All the tasks in the test battery were designed to run on standard MS DOS platform computers with graphical presentation and keyboard responding.

The UTC-PAB is a library of cognitive tests that can be modified into smaller subsets or batteries for a specific purpose. The original UTC-PAB consisted of 25 tasks that were chosen due to their construct validity, reliability, and sensitivity to levels of cognitive functioning. Several of the commonly known subsets or variations include the Testor's Workbench/Automated Neuropsychological Assessment Metrics (TWB/ANAM) or (ANAM) battery, the Naval Medical Research Institute Performance Assessment Battery (NMRI-PAB), the UTC-PAB/NATO AGARD STRES Battery, and the Criterion Task Set (CTS).[43]

The UTC-PAB's modular design offered the investigator the freedom of customized batteries by combining any number of the tasks, and in any order. This enabled researchers to utilize only

Table 4.2.1   Task Components of the Unified Tri-Service Cognitive Performance Assessment Battery (UTC-PAB)

Focused Attention

Complex Reaction Time
Visual-Motor Tracking
Substitution (Symbol-Digit or Code)
Time Estimation
Continuous Performance
Sequence Comparison
Visual Monitoring

Selective Attention

Stroop
Nessier
Dichotic Listening

Divided Attention

Acquisition

Repeated Acquisition

Memory

Match/Nonmatch to Sample
Sternberg Memory
Pattern Comparison
Sequence Memory

Other Cognitive Performance

Spatial Rotation-Sequential
Pattern Matching
Manikin
Grammatical/Logical Reasoning
Arithmetic Computation
Serial Add/Subtract
Linguistic Processing

those tasks that best suited the needs of each protocol or evaluation. Accuracy and response time were automatically measured and the data collection updated for any of the tasks that were selected. Numerous parameters of the individual tasks could be modified such as stimulus duration; inter-trial interval; number of stimulus presentations; and length of the task. Instruction screens and help files could be modified as well. The default parameter settings for the UTC-PAB tasks were patterned from the North Atlantic Treaty Organization AGARD-STRES Battery.[44]

Table 4.2.1 contains the individual tasks of the UTC-PAB. These tasks measure a variety of human cognitive and psychomotor functioning, including focused attention, selective attention, divided attention, memory, and a variety of additional task components.[4,7]

Walter Reed Army Institute Performance Assessment Battery — The Walter Reed Army Institute Performance Assessment Battery (WRPAB) was designed by Dr. David Thorne, Fred Hegge, and colleagues at the Walter Reed Army Institute of Research, Division of Neuropsychiatry, Department of Behavioral Biology. This battery was also supported by OMPAT, but was designed to measure changes in performance over time as a function of acute perturbations (e.g., drugs, fatigue, sleep deprivation) as opposed to serving as a screening tool.[45]

The WRPAB was designed to offer investigators a menu of individual cognitive, perceptual, and psychomotor tests from which investigators could choose specific tests to best support a given

Table 4.2.2 Task Components of the Walter Reed Army Institute Performance Assessment Battery (WRPAB)

Focused Attention

Complex Reaction Time
Substitution (Symbol-Digit or Code)
Encoding/Decoding
Time Estimation

Selective Attention

Stroop
Nessier

Acquisition

Associative Learning

Memory

Match/Nonmatch to Sample
Sternberg Memory
Pattern Comparison
Sequence Memory

Other Cognitive Performance

Manikin
Grammatical/Logical Reasoning
Arithmetic Computation
Serial Add/Subtract

application. Table 4.2.2 lists the individual tasks of the WRPAB. These tasks assess focused attention, selective attention, acquisition, memory, and a variety of additional task components.[45] A user-friendly building routine allows for the development of smaller, individualized PABs. Options are available to adjust the software to match the testing equipment and for specifying the characteristics of the data output, and individual task parameters can be adjusted by using documentation that accompanies the software. The software operates on the MS DOS platform with graphic screen presentation on a local or remote monitor with responding performed on a standard keyboard.[45] Installation of a timer card may be necessary to ensure precise timing.

As mentioned earlier, the WRPAB is best suited for experiments with repeated measures designs involving treatments, dosages, or differing environments. Specific tasks in the WRPAB have been found to be sensitive to certain psychoactive drugs. Several government agencies have implemented the WRPAB as a research tool. For example, the National Institute on Drug Abuse Intramural Research Program has studied the effects of nicotine and nicotine replacement on smokers' and nonsmokers' cognitive abilities and attention processes using the Two-[46,47] and Six-Letter Search.[46] Cognitive abilities were also measured using the WRPAB Digit Recall and Logical Reasoning tasks.[46,47]

Naval Medical Research Institute Performance Assessment Battery — The Naval Medical Research Institute Performance Assessment Battery (NMRI-PAB) was developed to measure the effects of a wide variety of military environments upon the technically oriented tasks of Marine and Naval personnel. The battery's methodology was based on a tri-service methodology in an attempt to standardize measurement of human performance in military environments.[41] The NMRI-PAB, like the WRPAB and UTC-PAB, is a menu-driven, microcomputer-based assessment tool that comprises individual tasks.

The NMRI-PAB consists of eight individual tasks that measure different aspects of human functioning (Table 4.2.3). The software controller allows the experimenter to modify certain aspects

Table 4.2.3   Task Components of the Naval Medical Research Institute Performance Assessment Battery (NMRI-PAB)

Focused Attention

Continuous Performance

Selective Attention

Stroop

Memory

Match/Nonmatch to Sample
Sternberg Memory
Pattern Comparison

Other Cognitive Performance

Spatial Rotation-Sequential
Manikin
Grammatical/Logical Reasoning

of task presentation. The software collects detailed information about subject's accuracy and speed of responding. Since the NMRI-PAB is microcomputer based, multiple subjects can participate simultaneously and in different locations. The software runs on standard MS DOS platform with graphical screen presentation and keyboard responding. The design of this assessment tool allows for repeated measures testing. The individual tasks of the NMRI-PAB measure the following areas of human cognitive functioning, including focused attention, selective attention, memory, and a variety of additional task components.[4]

Advisory Group for Aerospace Research and Development–Standardized Test for Research with Environmental Stressors Battery — The Advisory Group for Aerospace Research and Development–Standardized Test for Research with Environmental Stressors Battery (AGARD-STRES) was developed to investigate the effects of environmental stress on human performance.[44] After receiving funding from the U.S. Air Force, the Advisory Group for Aerospace Research and Development (AGARD) set out to construct a standardized performance assessment battery using tests that had proved successful in stress research. The group utilized seven of the individual tests from the UTC-PAB.[44] The AGARD-STRES battery was designed to provide a standardized method of task presentation (e.g., the seven tests are presented in a predetermined order, and the task parameters are designed to remain constant) in order to more effectively compare performance on these tasks across subject populations and settings. The software runs on standard MS DOS platform with graphical screen presentation with keyboard input. This would facilitate standardization and allow researchers to compare all administrations of the battery equally. This assessment tool is well suited for repeated measures research.

Table 4.2.4 presents the individual tests of the AGARD-STRESS battery. Focused attention, divided attention, and memory categories of tasks are included in this battery, in addition to a variety of other tasks.

Automated Neuropsychological Assessment Metrics — The Automated Neuropsychological Assessment Metrics assessment battery (ANAM) is a modified version of the AGARD STRES battery. The ANAM was developed primarily as a screening tool for assessing neuropsychological functioning and has been used in military and commercial aviation applications. This battery has added pursuit tracking, which requires a mouse for completion, and has eliminated tracking, dual task, and reaction time tasks from the AGARD STRES battery because these tasks engendered

Table 4.2.4 Task Components of the Advisory Group for Aerospace Research and Development — Standardized Test for Research with Environmental Stressors Battery (AGARD-STRESS)

Focused Attention

Complex Reaction Time
Visual-Motor Tracking

Divided Attention: Memory

Sternberg Memory

Other Cognitive Performance

Spatial Rotation-Sequential
Grammatical/Logical Reasoning
Serial Add/Subtract

Table 4.2.5 Task Components of the Automated Neuropsychological Assessment Metrics (ANAM)

Focused Attention

Complex Reaction Time
Visual-Motor Tracking

Memory

Sternberg Memory
Character/Number Recall

Other Cognitive Performance

Spatial Rotation
Spatial Rotation-Sequential
Grammatical/Logical Reasoning
Serial Add/Subtract

---

unsuitably variable performance. A tracking test, running memory test, the Walter Reed mood scale, and the Stanford sleepiness scale were substituted.

Table 4.2.5 presents the various tasks of the ANAM battery assess. Focused attention and memory categories of tasks are included in this battery, as well as a variety of additional task components.

The Spaceflight Cognitive Assessment Tool (S-CAT) is a variant of the ANAM that was compiled by NASA's Behavioral Health and Performance Group (BHPG) to assist in behavioral monitoring and assessment of flight crew health.[48] The battery was designed to assess memory, sustained concentration, working memory, and recall and was developed for use aboard the Space Station Mir and the International Space Station, as well as to support future prolonged space missions.

Another variant is the ANAM Readiness Evaluation System (ARES), a multiple-user cognitive testing system designed to run on PDAs using the Palm OS.[49] This system also incorporates many of the features of the ANAM. ARES is shipped with three standard test batteries. The NeuroCog battery is primarily used for monitoring the recovery of individuals with CNS damage. It is designed for use by neuropsychologists with ANAM interpretation experience. The ARES Commander is a self-monitoring battery that assesses concentration, working memory, and mental efficiency. The ARES Warrior is designed as a neurocognitive screening tool, which can be used by medical personnel during field operations. Custom batteries can also be created with provided support software.[49]

Table 4.2.6   Task Components of Neurobehavioral Evaluation System 2 (NES2)

Motor Ability Tests

Finger Tapping

Focused Attention

Simple Reaction Time
Substitution (Symbol-Digit or Code)
Continuous Performance

Selective Attention

Switching/Shifting Attention

Acquisition

Serial Acquisition
Associative Learning

Memory

Pattern Comparison
Character/Number Recall

Other Cognitive Performance

Pattern Matching
Grammatical/Logical Reasoning
Arithmetic Computation
Vocabulary

Neurobehavioral Evaluation System 2 — The Neurobehavioral Evaluation System 2 (NES2) is a neurobehavioral evaluation system designed to facilitate screening of populations at risk of nervous system damage due to environmental agents. This evaluation system is administered on a microcomputer. Epidemiologic research influenced the sets of tests that were included in this battery. An expert committee convened by the World Health Organization (WHO) and the National Institute for Occupational Safety and Health (NIOSH) proposed a set of core tests for this battery. Many of the core tests that were chosen are adaptations of preexisting clinical instruments that have been recognized as valuable tools in investigating neurotoxin exposure.[50]

Table 4.2.6 presents the individual tests of the NES2 battery. Motor ability, focused attention, selective attention, acquisition, and memory categories of tasks are included in this battery, in addition to a variety of other tasks. The battery is made up of separate tasks; performance on combinations of these tasks is potentially altered by exposure to neurotoxic agents such as pesticides, solvents, or carbon monoxide. Many of the tasks are suitable for repeated testing of any individual. Five of the tests are similar to the core tests of the WHO battery.[50]

The NES2 software was developed using IBM Advanced BASIC. The software is menu-driven and allows the interviewer to choose the individual tasks that are presented at any one session. The software was designed to run on IBM PC-compatible hardware with a standard DOS operating system. Response inputs occur through a joystick with a pair of push-buttons.[50]

Baker and colleagues[50] found that the validity and stability of three tests in the NES2 were comparable to five previously validated traditional interviewer-administered neuropsychological instruments. High correlations were reported between individual trials of the same interviewer-administered task. Stability on four of the computerized tests was supported by high correlations between scores when research subjects were tested on four separate days.

Automated Portable Test System — The Performance Evaluation Tests for Environmental Research Program (PETER), jointly sponsored by the U.S. Navy and NASA, attempted to identify measures of human cognitive, perceptual, and motor abilities that would be sensitive to environmental perturbations that are associated with decrements in safety and productivity. An extensive collection of literature yielded more than 140 tests that were rated for reliability and sensitivity. The PETER Program incorporated those tasks that were most suitable for repeated-measures applications. Inclusion criteria were met if a task's inter-trial correlations were unchanging and variances were homogenous across baselines.[51]

The Automated Portable Test System (APTS) evaluation system is an outgrowth of the work of the PETER Program. The PETER program had identified tests that were reliable, stable, and sensitive to environmental and toxic stressors. Kennedy and his colleagues[52] adopted and computerized a core set of 18 tasks from the PETER Program's recommended list of performance tasks suitable for repeated measures application. Those tasks are listed in Table 4.2.7.

Table 4.2.7   Task Components of the Automated Portable Test System (APTS)

Motor Ability Tests

Finger Tapping

Focused Attention

Simple Reaction Time
Complex Reaction Time
Substitution (Symbol-Digit or Code)
Time Estimation
Continuous Performance
Sequence Comparison
Visual Monitoring

Selective Attention

Stroop
Neisser

Acquisition

Associative Learning

Memory

Sternberg Memory
Pattern Comparison
Sequence Memory
Character/Number Recall

Other Cognitive Performance

Spatial Rotation
Spatial Rotation-Sequential
Pattern Matching
Manikin
Grammatical/Logical Reasoning
Arithmetic Computation
Serial Add/Subtract
Linguistic Processing
Spatial Visualization

**Table 4.2.8   Task Components of the Memory
Assessment Clinics Battery (MAC)**

Focused Attention

Complex Reaction Time

Divided Attention

Acquisition

Associative Learning

Memory

Match/Nonmatch to Sample
Selective Reminding
Text Memory
Misplaced Objects
Facial Memory
Character/Number Recall

The APTS was designed for portability works on IBM PC compatible systems running on a standard MS DOS operating system.[53] The battery measures abilities of motor function, focused attention, selective attention, acquisition, and memory, as well as spatial perception and reasoning, mathematical calculation, and other language skills.[4,7] Similar to most of the computerized performance assessment batteries, additions and deletions of individual components have occurred as the battery has matured and been used in different applications.

Memory Assessment Clinics Battery — The Memory Assessment Clinics Battery (MAC) was designed to assess the effects of pharmacological treatments on simulated memory tasks.[54] Intended to study potentially cognitive-enhancing pharmaceutical compounds, the battery is also used to assess age-related memory differences in ongoing clinical trials. Initial testing of the MAC Battery was administered on an AT&T 6300 computer utilizing color graphic presentation, laser-disk technology, and touch-screen responding along with other custom-made manipulanda.

The battery mimics real-life memory and recognition demands, such as remembering a 7- or 10-digit telephone number, or associating a name with a face. Table 4.2.8 presents the individual tasks of the MAC battery. Focused attention, divided attention, acquisition, and memory categories of tasks are included in this battery.

Synwork — Many performance batteries involve the administration of varied tasks, each of which requires the focused application of a limited number of cognitive or motor skills, in a sequential manner. One concern that has repeatedly been raised regarding the use of sequential laboratory tests as a system for measuring performance impairment is that such systems do not assess all human capabilities, including some that are critically dependent for job performance. For example, while performance tests may assess specific abilities, such as reaction time, or learning ability, it may be unusual in job settings for such activities to be required in a sequential manner. Elsmore and colleagues[55] contend that real-world human behaviors or operations may consist of two or more of these attributes and abilities occurring concurrently. Effective job performance may require the ability to engage in multiple tasks in a simultaneous or continuous manner, adjusting between task requirements as priorities change. It is unclear whether such higher-order performance requirements are effectively assessed in sequential performance test systems.

In contrast to PAB-like tasks involving the sequential presentation of individual performance tasks, Synwork attempts to emulate the simultaneous or continuous task demands of real-world jobs by requiring subjects to perform four individual tasks presented concurrently in one of four quadrants of a screen.[55] The tasks are presented on a standard IBM PC compatible computer with DOS operating platform. Subjects interact with the software by manipulating a standard mouse.

The individual tasks of the Synwork software measure attention and working memory (Sternberg Memory Task); mathematical calculations (Arithmetic task); spatial perception and reasoning (Visual Monitoring); and auditory perception and reasoning (Auditory Monitoring). A more detailed account of the Synwork software can be found in Elsmore et al.[56]

Elsmore and colleagues,[55] while examining the impairing effects of sleep deprivation, demonstrated that subjects find Synwork to be more interesting and demanding than a sequentially administered PAB-like version, but performance engendered by Synwork is less sensitive to the effects of sleep deprivation than the same tasks presented simultaneously.

Psychomotor Vigilance Task — The Walter Reed Army Institute of Research's Department of Behavioral Biology has developed a field-deployable version of a commercial Psychomotor Vigilance Task (PVT) that has been widely used in sleep research. The software runs on handheld PDAs running the Palm Operating System (Palm OS). It is modeled after the simple reaction time task of Wilkinson and Houghton,[57] as modified by Dinges and Powell.[58] The Palm OS version incorporates additional stimulus, feedback, control, and data options developed by Dr. Thorne. In laboratory studies, performance on the PDA task has been shown to be sensitive to time-on-task fatigue effects, sleep deprivation, and circadian variation.[18] Field studies have utilized the PVT to measure the efficacy of caffeine gum as a sleep loss countermeasure.

MiniCog — A Palm OS-based cognitive testing system, called MiniCog, is currently under development by the National Space Biomedical Research Institute's (NSBRI) neurobehavioral and psychosocial factors team. It will contain cognitive tasks that assess attention, (vigilance, divided attention, and filtering), motor control, verbal and spatial working memory, and verbal and spatial reasoning. The development team has designed this testing system for both spaceflight and ground-based research. MiniCog project development is currently obtaining norms from healthy subjects in a laboratory setting.[19]

4.2.3.3 Occupational Application: Readiness To Perform Tests

Background

Given the complex nature of many commercial work environments, as well as the reciprocal interactions between employers and employees, factors associated with the development and implementation of performance impairment test systems in commercial environments become equally complex. In addition to the selection of test systems that are reliable and valid indicators of performance impairment, it is equally important to consider issues associated with worker acceptance of the testing system, time associated with the test, and the economic implications of use and non-use of impairment test systems. Substantial research into the use of impairment testing systems has been conducted over the past decade; however, the vast majority of this work is available only in company reports and/or technical monographs; with few exceptions (e.g., Delta), little information is available in peer-reviewed scientific publications.

Performance Tests in Applied Settings

Four applications of laboratory-based performance impairment test systems are described. These systems have been chosen to be presented for two reasons. First, they provide examples of the use of test systems for the measurement of performance impairment in commercial settings. Second, some information regarding the reliability and validity of these systems is available.

NovaScan, Nova Technology, Inc. — The NovaScan is a testing paradigm, rather than a fixed performance test, in that the system represents a method of presenting selected tests in a manner that standardizes the attentional requirements of the test user. The paradigm also allows for measurement of elements of attention allocation. The testing paradigm is designed to present any combination of a subset of 30 individual tasks originally developed and validated through the UTC-PAB project, described above. The tasks that are presented can be selected based on the specific needs of the test application (e.g., different combinations of tests have been used for different commercial applications, based on the specific needs/interests of the company employing the NovaScan). The resulting test system is designed to assess a variety of job-related skills, as well as generic attentional processes associated with the completion of the tasks, in a time-efficient manner.

The NovaScan is presented on a PC-compatible computer equipped with standard memory and visual capabilities, and is run on a DOS-based operating system. A customized response apparatus, including a joystick, control keys, and a keypad, is recommended. Trials of the tasks chosen to be included in the test system are displayed on the computer monitor in a random manner, thereby eliminating the need for the user to focus attention among simultaneously presented tests. However, divided attention components can be added, if needed. The length of the test (i.e., number of trials presented) can be adjusted based on the demands of the test environment. Performance is evaluated in an automated fashion using a change-from-baseline approach, and the test can be administered in an automated or supervisor-controlled manner.

The NovaScan has received substantial testing in a number of laboratory and applied settings. Performance on the NovaScan has been demonstrated to be sensitive to the effects of alcohol, marijuana, diazepam, amphetamine, scopolamine, and an over-the-counter antihistamine.[6,59,60] In addition, epidemiological differences in performance associated with gender, age, and occupation has been considered. Variations of the testing paradigm have been used in a number of commercial settings.

Delta, Essex Corporation — Delta, a commercial performance impairment testing system produced by the Essex Corporation, was derived from the Automated Portable Test System (APTS) evaluation system, which, in turn, was based on the work of the Performance Evaluation Tests for Environmental Research Program (PETER), a jointly sponsored U.S. Navy and NASA program designed to identify measures of human cognitive, perceptual, and motor abilities that would be sensitive to environmental perturbations that are associated with decrements in safety and productivity.

The Delta system contains many of the same tests contained in the APTS system, including those that monitor motor function, reaction time, attention and working memory, learning and memory, spatial perception and reasoning, mathematical calculation, and language (Table 4.2.1). More complete descriptions of the psychometric and validity studies supporting the utility of this testing system are available elsewhere.[61,62]

Performance on the Delta system has been demonstrated to be sensitive to the effects of alcohol, amphetamine, scopolamine, chemoradiotherapy, and hypoxia.[63–66] The Delta test system has been used in a number of applied settings, including airplane and tank operator training sites.[61,62]

Performance-on-Line, SEDIcorp — Performance-on-Line is a software-based cognitive and psychomotor divided-attention task designed to evaluate tunnel vision, a rapid change in visual system activity in response to stress, that at elevated levels is associated with driving risk.[67] The task was derived from the hardware-based Simulated Evaluation of Driver Impairment (SEDI) distributed by SEDICorp. SEDI was found to generate performance that was highly reliable and sensitive to the effects of alcohol and marijuana.[68,69] SEDI used numeric displays that were novel to some subjects, and the memory-intensive instructions were found to be difficult to remember for some individuals. The hardware-based SEDI was also costly, and subjects frequently reported eye-muscle fatigue after its use.[70]

The Performance-on-Line software was designed to include language-free graphics and instructions that were not memory-intensive. Central and peripheral targets that are presented simultaneously require independent visual discrimination and responding. The software is designed to run on any computer using a DOS operating system. It supports a color graphic display and utilizes keyboard response inputs. The test is self administered, provides on-screen instructions, and has five independent levels of difficulty. An administrative interface allows for parametric modifications, such as whether or not performance feedback is provided to participants. The data are stored in formatted files that allow for easy use with other commercial spreadsheet or data analysis programs.[70] The Performance-on-Line software predicts driving performance[71] and engenders behavior that is sensitive to the effects of sleep deprivation, alcohol, and other drugs.[72]

CogScreen-Aeromedical Edition — In the late 1980s the Federal Aviation Administration (FAA) supported the development of a computer-based cognitive screening tool, CogScreen.[4] The goal of the FAA was to create a testing system that was sensitive to changes in cognitive function. If left unnoticed, cognitive dysfunction may result in poor pilot judgment or slow reaction time in critical operational situations.[73] Several phases of task selection and normative data collection yielded a cognitive testing system comprised of 11 tasks.[4] The current version, CogScreen-Aeromedical Edition (CogScreen-AE), is used during the medical re-certification evaluation of aviators suspected and/or known to have neurological or psychiatric conditions. This cognitive testing system detects changes in attention, immediate- and short-term memory, visual perceptual functions, sequencing functions, logical problem solving, calculation skills, reaction time, simultaneous information processing abilities, and executive functions.

4.2.3.4 *Occupational Applications: Simulation*

Background

An occupational simulation is a representation that approximates the actual operating conditions of a job.[2] Different scenarios can be used to represent specific sets of conditions developed for the purpose of assessing discrete sets of occupational skills within specified contexts.[74] Although initially developed for training purposes, they have evolved as tools for assessing skills for educational or formal certification purposes and are being used more frequently for evaluating occupational fitness. Simulation has most often been used to evaluate workers' ability to use machinery or drive vehicles. It has been more challenging to assess the job performance of other professionals, such as lawyers, doctors, and managers, with computer-based simulation, because their tasks are varied and complex. Recent developments in the use of actors in defined roles have expanded the use of simulation in a broader array of professions.

In those cases where simulation is possible, it can offer some important advantages. Simulation allows participants to perform job functions under a range of circumstances without risk of injury or adverse economic consequences. For example, within a given scenario, it is possible to monitor performance within contexts that approach or reach catastrophe (e.g., pilot response to problems during flight; account representative management of competition). Safety is an important attribute of simulation. A second advantage of simulation is that it permits the repeated assessment with specified scenarios, thereby supporting the assessment of reliability. High reliability is a necessary attribute for any effective performance assessment method, a threat when assessment is conducted in natural settings. A third advantage is that simulation can provide consistency in assessment procedures, which, in turn, allows for the comparison of performance across individuals or across worksites when individuals or groups are measured repeatedly over time. A simulated assessment exercise can also be recorded and played back. This provides an opportunity for participants to repeatedly observe their own performance within the context of a given scenario. Another advantage of simulation is that it supports assessment in rare or unusual contexts. The true measure of an employee may lie in performance during the low-probability real-world conditions with major safety or economic implications. Simulation provides a means to evaluate performance in low-probability but significant contexts. A final advantage of simulation is that the complexity and difficulty can be systematically altered within a given scenario. Employee ability to maintain effectiveness and efficiency as complications escalate is an important measure of performance capacity.

There are important limitations to simulation that deserve consideration, as well. As with all assessment strategies, validity should be questioned. Clearly, performance assessment that takes place in the occupational setting while work is actually performed is the most valid approach. Simulations can make employees feel as if they are operating under normal conditions; however, it is also clear that job performance expressed in a simulator is not "real." With regard to capturing the workplace context, simulators are still superior to computerized performance batteries. Nonetheless, performance assessment using computerized batteries can offer a greater degree of control over contextual variables that can influence performance, and can provide more precise measurement of specific functions, such as cognition, reaction time, divided attention, and memory, than is possible during simulation. Simulation provides a gross measure of overall job performance, whereas computerized batteries offer precise assessment of more elementary dimensions of performance. As simulators try to incorporate key elements of the workplace context, they become vulnerable to unknown confounding due to these contextual representations.

Simulations in Experimental Settings

Howland and colleagues[75] used maritime simulators that replicated merchant ship operation to test the effects of low-dose alcohol exposure in two separate scenarios. Maritime cadets were randomly assigned to receive either 0.00 (placebo) or 0.04 g% blood alcohol concentration, or BAC (a relatively low dose equivalent to two to three commercial cocktails). Significant alcohol-induced impairment was observed on simulated power plant operation and piloting.[76] The testing of simulated ship operation the day after random dosing at 0.10 g% BAC (five or more commercial cocktails) is ongoing. These experimental studies using a single occupational model are consistent with the adverse associations of heavy alcohol use derived from large-scale cross-sectional surveys of worker performance.[77] Simulation picked up subtle effects of low-dose alcohol sedation on work performance that are not visible in surveys. Furthermore, the merchant ship experiments could not have been conducted ethically without the use of simulators.

Automobile and truck simulators have also been used in randomized studies to demonstrate the impairing effects of various doses of alcohol.[78–80] Similar studies have been conducted using flight simulators.[81–85] In addition, both types of simulators have been used to assess the effects of marijuana, nicotine, and other sedative medications.[86–88] Simulations have also been used to examine other environmental perturbations, including sleep deprivation and elevated carbon dioxide levels.[89,90]

4.2.4   Conclusion

This chapter focused on issues associated with the use of performance testing technologies for the detection of performance impairment. While the application of this technology remains largely untested, the evidence presented in this chapter strongly suggests that this technology shows promise as a component of performance impairment testing systems. A substantial database regarding the reliability and validity of performance tests for measuring the effects of risk factors on human performance has been established, and initial efforts at developing performance testing systems made effective use of this database. Limitations with regard to the predictive validity of these tests continue to be addressed in modifications to existing testing systems, as well in the development of more sophisticated simulation testing systems. Issues regarding the selection and implementation of performance testing systems have been addressed in recent publications.[4,9–11] Clearly, careful and systematic evaluations of the use of these systems in applied settings is warranted.

It is important to note, however, that while this chapter specifically addressed performance testing as means of impairment detection, there is no evidence to suggest that performance testing systems are more effective than other impairment testing systems. Trice and Steele[9] suggest that performance testing systems may have practical advantages over more common biological sample testing systems, including potentially being more widely accepted by the workforce, requiring less invasive testing requirements, and interfacing more efficiently with existing employee assistance programs, but no evidence to support such claims is available, due to the limited information regarding the use of these systems. It is likely that no single technology will be universally effective in all settings, or even on one setting across all individuals over time. The combination of technologies, based on the availability of resources needed to support those technologies, will likely enhance the effectiveness of any impairment testing system.

Acknowledgment

Mr. Taylor and Dr. Heishman were supported by the NIH Intramural Research Program, NIDA.

REFERENCES

1. Normand, J., Lempert, R.O., and O'Brien, C.P., Under the Influence? Drugs and the American Work Force, National Academy Press, Washington, D.C., 1994, chap. 6.
2. Howland, J., Mangione, T.W., and Laramie, A., Simulation for measurement of occupational performance, unpublished data, 2004.
3. Finkle, B.S., Blanke, R.V., and Walsh, M.J., Technical, Scientific and Procedural Issues of Employee Drug Testing, U.S. Department of Health and Human Services, Washington, D.C., 1990.
4. Kane, R.L. and Kay, G.G., Computerized assessment in neuropsychology: a review of tests and test batteries, Neuropsychol. Rev., 3, 1, 1992.
5. Murphy, K.R., Honesty in the Workplace, Brooks Cole, Pacific Grove, CA, 1993.
6. Kelly, T.H. et al., Performance-based testing for drugs of abuse: dose and time profiles of marijuana, amphetamine, alcohol and diazepam, J. Anal. Toxicol., 17, 264, 1993.
7. Gilliland, K. and Schlegel, R.E., Readiness to perform testing: A critical analysis of the concept and current practices, U.S. Department of Transportation, National Technical Information Service, Springfield, VA, 1993.
8. Gerber, B., Simulating reality, Training, 27, 41, 1990.
9. Trice, H.M. and Steele, P.D., Impairment testing: issues and convergence with employee assistance programs, J. Drug Issues, 25, 471, 1995.
10. Gilliland, K. and Schlegel, R.E., Readiness-to-perform testing and the worker, Ergon. Des., January, 14, 1995.
11. Miller, J.C., Fit for duty? Performance testing tools for assessing public safety and health workers' readiness for work, Ergon. Des., April, 11, 1996.
12. Heishman, S.J., Taylor, R.C., and Henningfield, J.E., Nicotine and smoking: a review of effects on human performance, Exp. Clin. Psychopharmacol., 2, 345, 1994.
13. Zacny, J.P., A review of the effects of opioids on psychomotor and cognitive functioning in humans, Exp. Clin. Psychopharmacol., 3, 432, 1995.
14. Fischman, M.W., Cocaine and the amphetamines, in Psychopharmacology: The Third Generation of Progress, Meltzer, H.Y., Ed., Raven Press, New York, 1987, 1543.
15. Fischman, M.W., Kelly, T.H., and Foltin, R.W., Residential laboratory research: a multidimensional evaluation of the effects of drugs on behavior, in Drugs in the Workplace: Research and Evaluation Data, Vol. II, NIDA Research Monograph 100, Gust, S.W., Walsh, J.M., Thomas, L.B., and Crouch, D.J., Eds., U.S. Government Printing Office, Washington, D.C., 1991, 113.
16. Kelly, T.H., Foltin, R.W., and Fischman, M.W., Effects of alcohol on human behavior: implications for the workplace, in Drugs in the Workplace: Research and Evaluation Data, Vol. II, NIDA Research Monograph 100, Gust, S.W., Walsh, J.M., Thomas, L.B., and Crouch, D.J., Eds., U.S. Government Printing Office, Washington, D.C., 1991, 129.
17. Preusser, D.F., Ulmer, R.G., and Preusser, C.W., Evaluation of the impact of the drug evaluation and classification program on enforcement and adjudication, National Highway Traffic Safety Administration, DOT HS 808 058, U.S. Department of Transportation, Washington, D.C., 1992.

18. Thorne, D.R. et al., The Walter Reed Palm-held Psychomotor Vigilance Test, *Sleep*, 26(Suppl.), 182, 2002.
19. Kosslyn, S., Quick assessment of basic cognitive function: blood pressure cuffs for the mind. Technical Summary of Neurobehavioral and Psychosocial Factors Team Project, National Space Biomedical Research Institute, Houston, TX, 2002.
20. Klein, A. The current legal status of employment tests, *Los Angel. Lawyer*, July/August, 35, 1987.
21. Miller, J.C., Kim, H.T., and Parseghian, Z., Feasibility of carrier-based fitness-for-duty testing of commercial drivers: Final report, ESI-TR-94-003, Evaluation Systems, El Cajon, CA, 1994.
22. Morbidity and Mortality Weekly Report, Update: alcohol-related traffic fatalities — United States, 1982–1993, *Morb. Mortal. Wkly. Rep.*, 43, 861, 1994.
23. Terhune, K.W. et al., The incidence and role of drugs in fatally injured drivers, National Highway Traffic Safety Administration, U.S. Department of Transportation, DOT HS 808 065, Washington, D.C., 1992.
24. Williams, A.F. et al., Drugs in fatally injured young male drivers, *Public Health Rep.*, 100, 19, 1985.
25. Soderstrom, C.A. et al., Marijuana and alcohol use among 1023 trauma patients, *Arch. Surg.*, 123, 733, 1988.
26. Budd, R.D., Muto, J.J., and Wong, J.K., Drugs of abuse found in fatally injured drivers in Los Angeles County, *Drug Alcohol Depend.*, 23, 153, 1989.
27. Marzuk, P.M. et al., Prevalence of recent cocaine use among motor vehicle fatalities in New York City, *J. Am. Med. Assoc.*, 263, 250, 1990.
28. Brookoff, D. et al., Testing reckless drivers for cocaine and marijuana, *N. Engl. J. Med.*, 331, 518, 1994.
29. O'Hanlon, J.F. and de Gier, J.J., *Drugs and Driving*, Taylor & Francis, London, 1986.
30. Marowitz, L.A., Drug arrests and drunk driving. *Alcohol Drugs Driving*, 11, 1, 1995.
31. Consensus Development Panel, Drug concentrations and driving impairment, *J. Am. Med. Assoc.*, 254, 2618, 1985.
32. Bates, M.N. and Blakely, T.A., Role of cannabis in motor vehicle crashes, *Epidemiol. Rev.*, 21, 222, 1999.
33. National Highway Traffic Safety Administration, Drug evaluation and classification program, U.S. Department of Transportation, Washington, D.C., 1991.
34. Preusser Research Group, Inc., Drug evaluation and classification program: history and growth, National Highway Traffic Safety Administration, Letter Report, U.S. Department of Transportation, Washington, D.C., 1995.
35. Compton, R.P., Field evaluation of the Los Angeles Police Department drug detection procedure, National Highway Traffic Safety Administration, Report DOT HS 807 012, U.S. Department of Transportation, Washington, D.C., 1986.
36. Adler, E.V. and Burns, M., Drug recognition expert (DRE) validation study, Final Report to Governor's Office of Highway Safety, State of Arizona, 1994.
37. Kunsman, G.W. et al., Phencyclidine blood concentrations in DRE cases, *J. Anal. Toxicol.*, 21, 498, 1997.
38. Tomaszewski, C. et al., Urine toxicology screens in drivers suspected of driving while impaired from drugs, *Clin. Toxicol.*, 34, 37, 1996.
39. Heishman, S.J., Singleton, E.G., and Crouch, D.J., Laboratory validation study of Drug Evaluation and Classification program: ethanol, cocaine, and marijuana, *J. Anal. Toxicol.*, 468, 1996.
40. Heishman, S.J., Singleton, E.G., and Crouch, D.J., Laboratory validation study of Drug Evaluation and Classification program: alprazolam, *d*-amphetamine, codeine, and marijuana, *J. Anal. Toxicol.*, 22, 503, 1998.
41. Thomas, J.R. and Schrot, J., Naval Medical Research Institute performance assessment battery (NMRI PAB) documentation, Naval Medical Research Institute (NMRI 88-7), Bethesda, MD, 1988.
42. Hegge, F.W. et al., The Unified Tri-Service Cognitive Performance Assessment Battery (UTC-PAB), 11: Hardware Software Design and Specification, U.S. Army Medical Research and Development Command, Fort Detrick, MD, 1985.
43. Reeves, D., Schlegel, R., and Gililand, K., The UTCIPAB and the NATO AGARD STRES Battery: Results from standardization studies, Medical Defense Biosciences Review, Aberdeen, MD, 1991.
44. Santucci, G. et al., AGARDograph #308, Human Performance Assessment Methods, North Atlantic Treaty Organization Advisory Group for Aerospace Research and Development, Working Group 12, Seine, France, 1989.
45. Thorne, D. et al., The Walter Reed Performance Assessment Battery, *Neurobehav. Toxicol. Teratol.*, 7, 415, 1985.

46. Snyder, F.R and Henningfield, J.E., Effects of nicotine administration following 12 h of tobacco deprivation: assessment on computerized performance tasks, *Psychopharmacology*, 97, 17, 1989.

47. Heishman, S.J., Synder, F.R., and Henningfield, J.E., Performance, subjective and physiological effects of nicotine in non-smokers, *Drug Alcohol Depend.*, 34, 11, 1993.

48. Flynn, C. et al., Spaceflight Cognitive Assessment Tool for Lunar-Mars Life Support Test Project Phase III Test, in *Isolation: NASA Experiments in Closed-Environment Living*, Vol. 104, Lane, S.W., Sauer, R., and Feeback, D.L., Eds., Unicelt, Inc., San Diego, 2002, 155.

49. Elsmore, T.F., Reeves, D.L., and Reeves, A.N., ANAM™ for Palm OS Handheld Computers: the ARES® test system for Palm OS Handheld Computers, unpublished data, 2004.

50. Baker, E.L. et al., A computer-based neurobehavioral evaluation system for occupational and environmental epidemiology: methodology and validation studies, *Neurobehav. Toxicol. Teratol.*, 7, 369, 1985.

51. Bittner, A.C., Jr. et al., Performance Evaluation Tests for Environmental Research (PETER): evaluation of 114 measures, *Percep. Mot. Skills*, 63, 683, 1986.

52. Kennedy, R.S. et al., Development of an automated performance test system for environmental and behavioral toxicology studies, *Percep. Mot. Skills*, 65, 947, 1987.

53. Kennedy, R.S. et al., Psychology of computer use: IX. Menu of self administered microcomputer-based neurotoxicology tests, *Percep. Mot. Skills*, 68, 1255, 1989.

54. Larrabee, G.J. and Crook, T., A computerized everyday memory battery for assessing treatment effects, *Psychopharmacol. Bull.*, 24, 695, 1988.

55. Elsmore, T.F. et al., A comparison of the effects of sleep deprivation on synthetic work performance and a conventional performance assessment battery, Naval Health Research Center, San Diego, CA/Naval Medical Research and Development Command (Report No. 95-6), Bethesda, MD, 1995.

56. Elsmore, T.F. et al., Performance Assessment Under Operational Conditions Using a Computer-Based Synthetic Work Task, U.S. Army Research Institute of Environmental Medicine, Natick, MA, 1991.

57. Wilkinson, R.T. and Houghton, D., Field test of arousal: a portable reaction timer with data storage, *Hum. Factors*, 224, 487, 1982.

58. Dinges, D.F. and Powell, J.W., Microcomputer analyses of performance on a portable, simple visual RT task during sustained operations, *Behav. Res. Methods Instrum. Comput.*, 17, 652, 1985.

59. NTI, Inc., The effects of alcohol and fatigue on an FAA Readiness-To-Perform test, U.S. Department of Transportation/Federal Aviation Administration document DOT/FAA/AM-95/24, Office of Aviation Medicine, Washington, D.C., 1995.

60. O'Donnell, R.D., *The NOVASCAN™ Test Paradigm: Theoretical Basis and Validation*, Nova Technologies, Inc, Dayton, OH, 1992.

61. Turnage, J.J. and Kennedy, R.S., The development and use of a computerized human performance test battery for repeated-measures applications, *Hum. Perform.*, 5, 265, 1992.

62. Turnage, J.J. et al., Development of microcomputer-based mental acuity tests, *Ergonomics*, 35, 1271, 1992.

63. Kennedy, R.S. et al., Indexing cognitive tests to alcohol dosage and comparison to standardized field sobriety tests, *J. Stud. Alcohol*, 55, 615, 1994.

64. Parth, P. et al., Motor and cognitive testing of bone marrow transplant patients after chemoradiotherapy, *Percep. Mot. Skills*, 68, 1227, 1989.

65. Kennedy, R.S. et al., Differential effects of scopolamine and amphetamine on microcomputer-based performance tests, *Aviat. Space Environ. Med.*, 61, 615, 1990.

66. Kennedy, R.S. et al., Cognitive performance deficits occasioned by a simulated climb of Mount Everest: Operation Everest II, *Aviat. Space Environ. Med.*, 60, 99, 1989.

67. Mills, K.C., Tunnel vision: lifeline or killer? Some research on why training to "keep your cool" is valuable, *Law Order*, 11, 80, 2000.

68. Mills, K.C. and Bisgrove, E.Z., Cognitive impairment and perceived risk from alcohol: laboratory, self-report and field assessments, *J. Stud. Alcohol*, 44, 26, 1983.

69. Perez-Reyes, M. et al., Interaction between marihuana and ethanol: effects on psychomotor performance, *Alcohol. Clin. Exp. Res.*, 12, 269, 1988.

70. Mills, K.C., Parkman, K.M., and Spruill, S.E., A PC-based software test for measuring alcohol and drug effects in human subjects. *Alcohol. Clin. Exp. Res.*, 20, 1582, 1996.

71. Mills, K.C. et al., Prediction of driving performance through computerized testing: high-risk-driver assessment and training, Transportation Research Record 1689, Transportation Research Board, National Research Council, Washington, D.C., 1999.

72. Mills, K.C. et al., The influence of stimulants, sedatives and fatigue on tunnel vision: risk factors for driving and piloting, *Hum. Factors*, 43, 310, 2001.

73. Engelberg, A.C., Gibbons, H.L., and Doege, T.C., A review of the medical standards for civilian airmen: synopsis of a two-year study. *J. Am. Med. Assoc.*, 225, 1589, 1986.

74. National Research Council, Simulated Voyages: Using Simulation Technology to Train and License Mariners, National Academy Press, Washington, D.C., 1996.

75. Howland J. et al., Effects of low-dose alcohol exposure on simulated merchant ship piloting by maritime cadets, *Accid. Anal. Prevent.*, 33, 257, 2001.

76. Howland J. et al., Effects of low-dose alcohol exposure on simulated merchant ship power plant operation by maritime cadets, *Addiction*, 95, 719, 2000.

77. Mangione T.W. et al., Employee drinking practices and work performance, *J. Stud. Alcohol*, 60, 261, 1999.

78. Laurell, H., Effects of small doses of alcohol on driver performance in emergency traffic situation. *Accid. Anal. Prevent.*, 9, 191, 1977.

79. Liguori, A. et al., Alcohol effects on mood, equilibrium, and simulated driving, *Alcohol. Clin. Exp. Res.*, 23, 815, 1999.

80. Tornos, J. and Laurell, H., Acute and hangover effects of alcohol on simulated driving performance, *Blutalkohol*, 28, 24, 1991.

81. Morrow, D., Alcohol, age, and piloting; Judgement, mood, and actual performance, *Int. J. Addict.*, 26, 669, 1991.

82. Morrow, D., Leirer, V., and Yesavage, J., The influence of alcohol and aging on radio communication during flight, *Aviat. Space Environ. Med.*, 61, 12, 1990.

83. Ross, L.E. and Mundt, J.C., Multiattribute modeling analysis of the effects of low blood alcohol level on pilot performance, *Hum. Factors*, 30, 293, 1988.

84. Yesavage, J., Dolhert, N., and Taylor, J., Flight simulator performance of younger and older aircraft pilots: effects of age and alcohol, *J. Am. Geriat. Soc.*, 42, 577, 1994.

85. Yesavage, J. and Leirer, V., Hangover effects on aircraft pilots 14 hours after alcohol ingestion: a preliminary report, *Am. J. Psychiatry*, 143, 1546, 1986.

86. Mumenthaler, M.S. et al., Influence of nicotine on simulator flight performance in non-smokers, *Psychopharmacology*, 140, 38, 1998.

87. Vermeeren, A. and O'Hanlon, J.F., Fexofenadine's affects, alone and with alcohol, on driving and psychomotor performance, *J. Allerg. Clin. Immunol.*, 101, 306, 1998.

88. Weiler, J.M. et al., Effects of fexofenadine, diphenhydramine, and alcohol on driving performance, *Ann. Intern. Med.*, 132, 354, 2000.

89. Collins, W.E., Performance effects of alcohol intoxication and hangover at ground level and at simulated altitude, *Aviat. Space Environ. Med.*, 51, 327, 1980.

90. Traffinder, N.J. et al., Effect of sleep deprivation on surgeons' dexterity on laparoscopy simulator, *Lancet*, 352, 1191, 1998.

4.3 PUPILLOMETRY AND EYE TRACKING AS PREDICTIVE MEASURES OF DRUG ABUSE

Wallace B. Pickworth, Ph.D.[1] **and Rudy Murillo, B.A.**[2]
[1] Battelle Centers for Public Health Research and Evaluation, Baltimore, Maryland
[2] Clinical Pharmacology and Therapeutics Branch, National Institute on Drug Abuse, National Institutes of Health, Department of Health and Human Services, Baltimore, Maryland

4.3.1   Introduction

Measurements of pupillary diameter, eye tracking, and the pupillary response to a flash of light are readily available, non-invasive indices of central nervous system function. Recently, such parameters have been used by law enforcement personnel, employers, and primary care and emergency room physicians to make a rapid and initial assessment of recent drug ingestion. In this chapter, the physiological basis for the control of pupil size and the light reflex and the instruments used to measure pupillary responses are briefly reviewed. The results of a residential, within-subject study of the effects of various drugs of abuse on pupillary size and the light reflex are described. A summary of the literature on the effects of abused drugs on pupillary measures is given. An outpatient study analyzing the effects of polydrug use on pupillary responses is also presented. The advent of new classes of pupillometers that measure eye position and gaze is also included. These new instruments hold great promise for revealing subjective effects of drugs and drug withdrawal through a psychophysiologic measure. The chapter concludes with a discussion of the utility and limitations of pupillometry in the detection of abused drugs.

4.3.2 Physiological Basis of Pupil Size and the Light Reflex

4.3.2.1 Pupil Size

The human pupil ranges in diameter from 1.5 mm at full miosis to 8.0 mm at full mydriasis. The most powerful determinant of pupil size is the ambient light level. Pupil size is also influenced by several factors including subject age, iris pigmentation, gender, state of arousal, and time of day.[1] Newborns have very small pupils because the pupillary dilator muscle develops well after birth. Pupil size is maximal during adolescence and decreases in older age. People with a lightly pigmented iris (blue eyes) generally have larger pupils than those with a heavily pigmented iris (brown eyes). Pupil diameter tends to decrease over the course of the day.[2] About 17% of the population have pupils of unequal size (aniscoria), but differences exceeding 0.5 mm occur in only about 4% of the population.

4.3.2.2 Instrumentation

Pupil size can be estimated from direct observation. A variety of cards and scales are available whereby the experimenter compares the size of the pupil to standard patterns and scales. The simplest and most often used card is the Haab pupil gauge. This consists of a card with black circles graduated in size between 2 and 10 mm in 0.5 mm increments. The card is held on the temporal side of the eye out of the subject's vision (to reduce accommodation miosis). Pupil size can be determined to an accuracy of 0.2 mm. A disadvantage of this method is the inability to make measurements in the dark and the possibility that the subject's eyes will react to the test or its administration.

The Polaroid close-up camera has been used to photograph the eye of subjects before and after the administration of opiates and other psychoactive drugs.[3,4] Pupil size can be estimated to within 0.1 mm by means of calipers and a magnified scale that is concomitantly photographed. Disadvantages of this method are the possibility that the flash used in the photography can reduce pupil size, the expense of the film, and the possibility that the subject may focus on the camera, thereby inducing accommodation miosis. Recently, digital cameras have been used to determine pupil size.[5]

Sequential photographs can be used to monitor pupil size over an extended time. If the pupil is illuminated with infrared light and infrared sensitive film is used, recordings can be made in total darkness. Although this method was used in seminal studies of the pupillary light reflex and other dynamic applications,[6,7] it is seldom used today because of the high cost of film, processing time, and limited temporal resolution.

Other pupillometers usually employ infrared illumination of the eye and a television or computer. These instruments sample pupil diameter at rates up to 60 images per second. Pupillometers offer the advantage of accurate sampling across a wide range of ambient light. They can record pupil diameter over extended times, enabling the investigator to quantify dynamic aspects of the light reflex and fluctuations of pupil size (hippus). These instruments are extensively used to determine the effects of drugs, fatigue, stress, autonomic reactivity, and level of anesthesia. Instruments produced by Eye Dynamics (Torrance, CA) and Pulse Medical Instruments (Bethesda, MD) use short programmed trials to evaluate pupil diameter, light reflex measures, and saccadic or smooth pursuit eye tracking.

Modern pupillometers have the added ability to track eye position and movement. Pupillometers such as the I-Portal (Neuro Kinetics, Inc, Pittsburgh, PA), the Eye Link II (SR Research, Ontario, CA), and the EyeTrace 300X (Applied Science Laboratories, Bedford, MA) have sampling speeds of up to 600 samples/second. Their ability to track eye position and gaze fixation enables these pupillometers to be used to study components of drug abuse, such as drug seeking, stimulus relevance, and cue reactivity, which cannot be assessed with conventional pupillometry. One experiment of particular interest would be to study the time it takes drug users to find illicit drugs or drug paraphernalia within a matrix of control objects using eye tracking technology. In the following section aspects of the pupillary light reflex measured with modern pupillometers are discussed.

4.3.2.3 Light Reflex

When the retinal rods and cones are stimulated with light in the visual wavelength, there is constriction of the pupil. A major factor in determining the intensity of the reflex is the adaptation state of the retina because the rate of change of retinal illumination evokes the response. Other factors influence the light reflex. The retinal area that is stimulated is differentially sensitive; the fovea and macular areas are most sensitive and the periphery is least sensitive. The subject's state of arousal[8] and anxiety[9] and the wavelength of the stimulus light and its direction all may influence the reflex.[10,11]

As shown in Figure 4.3.1, there are several components of the light reflex that may be evaluated with dynamic pupillometers. From studies in cats, monkeys, and rabbits, Lowenstein and Lowenfeld[12] identified the components of the light reflex that were controlled by parasympathetic and sympathetic innervation of the smooth muscles controlling pupil diameter. They concluded that the parasympathetic nervous system must be intact to observe the light reflex; the sympathetic nervous system influences the shape of the reflex. For example, in the absence of sympathetic innervation, the constriction velocity is increased and the dilation velocity is decreased. Conversely, in situations of increased sympathetic tone, the constriction is sluggish and incomplete, and the pupil slowly returns to its baseline size. The effects of abused drugs on these and other components of the light reflex were studied in the experiment described below.

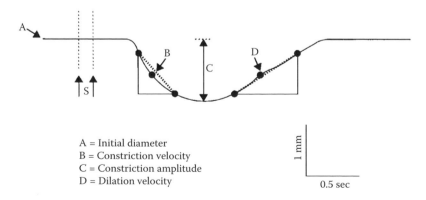

A = Initial diameter
B = Constriction velocity
C = Constriction amplitude
D = Dilation velocity

1 mm

0.5 sec

Figure 4.3.1 Pupil diameter before (A) and after a light stimulus (S). Constriction (B) and dilation (D) velocities are determined from a least square fit of the slope. Amplitude of constriction (C) represents the maximal difference in diameter before and after the flash.

4.3.3 Laboratory Study of Pupillary Effects of Abused Drugs in Humans

In an effort to understand and quantify the effects of several classes of abused drugs on human pupillary response, a study, briefly described below, was conducted on the residential unit of the Intramural Research Program of the National Institute on Drug Abuse (NIDA). Further methodological details and results are published elsewhere.[13]

4.3.3.1 Methods

Subjects

Eight healthy male subjects with a mean age of 34.1 years volunteered for this study. During their participation in the study, they resided on a clinical research unit. The subjects had extensive histories of illicit drug use that included recent ingestion (within the past 2 years) of opiates, marijuana, stimulants, alcohol, and sedative-hypnotics, although they were not dependent on any drug (except nicotine).

Study Design

All the subjects received each of the treatments. Neither the subjects nor the technician knew the identity of the treatment at the time of the experiment. The treatments were randomly presented a minimum of 48 hr apart. On study days subjects swallowed three opaque capsules, drank a large cold tonic drink (480 ml, in 15 min) with 2 ml 95% ethanol floating on top, and smoked a cigarette (either marijuana or placebo) according to a paced puffing procedure: 8 puffs per cigarette, 20 s puff retention, 40 s interpuff interval.[14] On any experimental day all of the dosage forms could have been a placebo (no active drugs) or one of the dosage forms could have contained an active drug. The active drug conditions were marijuana 1.3 and 3.9% THC; ethanol 0.3 and 1.0 g/kg; hydromorphone (Dilaudid) 1 and 3 mg; pentobarbital 150 and 450 mg; and amphetamine 10 and 30 mg. Drugs were administered at the same time each day (9:45 A.M.).

Pupillary Measures

Measures of pupillary diameter and parameters of the light reflex were made using a Pupilscan (Fairville Medical Optics) handheld pupillometer.[15] The sampling rate was 10 diameters (in pixels)/s; the light reflex was evoked with a 0.1-s, 20 Lumen/ft^2, 565 nm (green) stimulus light. Initial (prestimulus) pupil diameter and the following parameters of the light reflex were derived from the data collected on a personal computer: constriction and dilation velocities and the amplitude of constriction.[2,16] Pupillary measures were collected from the left eye before drug administration and at 30, 105, 180, and 300 min after the drug.

Subjective Measures

Subjective effects of the experimental drugs were estimated from scores on several standardized tests and computer-delivered 100 mm visual analog scales that measured drug symptoms, "strength" and "liking." The 100-mm scale was anchored with the terms "not at all" (0 mm) and extremely (100 mm). The subjects rated subjective effects at about the same times of the pupillary measures.

Performance Measures

Before beginning the experimental series, subjects trained to a consistent level of performance on several tests of cognitive performance including the Digit Symbol Substitution Test (DSST). In the DSST a random digit appeared on the computer screen. The subject used the numeric keypad of the computer to reproduce a geometric pattern (three keystrokes) that was uniquely associated with the displayed digit. The dependent measure used was the number of correct responses during the two-minute task.[17] In the circular lights task the subject pushed lighted buttons on a wall-mounted board. At the start of the task, one of the 33 buttons was illuminated. Pushing that button added a point to the score and lighted another button at a random position. The score was the total number of points (hits) in the 1-min task.[18]

Statistical Analyses

Repeated measures analyses of variance (ANOVA)[19] were conducted on the pupillary, subjective, and performance variables. The main factors were drug (12 levels) and time (5 or 6 levels). Using *a priori* tests, data points after drug administration were compared to baseline values and placebo values. The pupillary effects were correlated with subjective effects (visual analog rating of "high" and "strong") and performance effects (DSST, number correct; circular lights, hits) by means of the Pearson's product-moment correlation.

4.3.3.2 Results

Pupillary Measures

Pupil Diameter — The experimental drugs caused significant changes in pupillary diameter measured before the presentation of the light flash (Figure 4.3.2). One-way ANOVAs on the peak change indicated significant differences among the treatment conditions. A two-way ANOVA indicated significant differences among drug conditions and time of measurement, as well as a significant drug by time interaction. As shown in Table 4.3.1, high doses of ethanol, marijuana, hydromorphone, and pentobarbital decreased pupil size, whereas amphetamine caused an increase. Although the changes were statistically significant, their magnitude was not large. Pupil size decreased by 0.7, 0.5, 1.4, and 1.0 mm after the high doses of ethanol, marijuana, hydromorphone, and pentobarbital, respectively. The maximal increase after the high dose of amphetamine averaged 0.4 mm.

Constriction Amplitude — The constriction amplitude of the light reflex differed significantly among the treatment conditions (Figure 4.3.2). A two-way ANOVA indicated significant differences among drug conditions and time of measurement, as well as a significant drug by time interaction. As summarized in Table 4.3.1, constriction amplitude was significantly decreased by high doses of ethanol, marijuana, and hydromorphone. The magnitude of the effect was small and the maximal changes occurred at the time of the maximal change in pupillary size.

Constriction Velocity — The velocity of pupillary constriction changed significantly as a function of the drug treatment (Figure 4.3.2). A two-way ANOVA indicated significant differences among drug conditions and time of measurement, as well as a significant drug by time interaction. As shown in Table 4.3.1, constriction velocity decreased after high doses of ethanol, marijuana, hydromorphone, and pentobarbital. The high doses of marijuana, hydromorphone, and pentobarbital reduced the constriction velocity by 1.2, 0.6, and 1.3 mm/s, respectively, changes that represented reductions of 26, 14, and 27% of control velocities.

Dilation Velocity — As summarized in Table 4.3.1, only the high dose of marijuana significantly changed (reduced) the velocity of dilation of the pupil during the recovery phase of the light reflex.

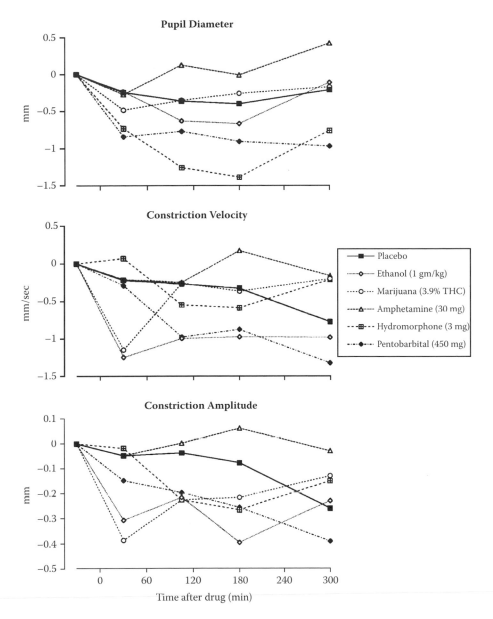

Figure 4.3.2 After high doses of the experimental drugs, changes (from baseline) in initial (prestimulus) pupil diameter, constriction velocity, and constriction amplitude varied as a function of the drug condition and time.

Subjective Measures

Visual analog scale scores on the strength of drug effect were significantly different as a function of drug condition and time of measurement (Figure 4.3.3). There was also a significant drug by time interaction (Figure 4.3.3). Similarly, scores on the drug liking visual analog scale differed significantly among the drug conditions. These data indicate the subjects perceived the high doses of the experimental drugs as being strong and being liked. The positive endorsement of questions of drug liking and strength by experienced drug users indicate that such drugs have a high abuse potential.[20]

Table 4.3.1 Pupillary Effects of Experimental Drugs

Drug	Dose	Pupil Diameter	Constriction Amplitude	Constriction Velocity	Dilation Velocity
Ethanol	1 g/kg	↓	↓	↓	NC
Marijuana	cigarette 3.9% THC	↓	↓	↓	↓
Hydromorphone	3 mg	↓	↓	↓	NC
Pentobarbital	450 mg	↓	↓	NC	NC
Amphetamine	30 mg	↑	NC	NC	NC

Note: Arrows indicate direction of significant changes from baseline values; NC indicates there was no significant change.

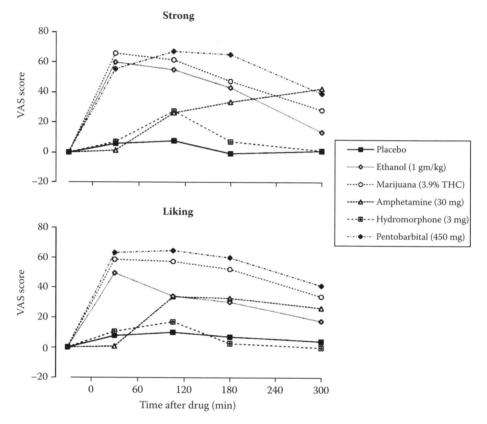

Figure 4.3.3 High doses of the experimental drugs increased scores (from baseline levels) on drug strength and drug liking. The effects varied as a function of the drug administered and the time after administration.

Performance Measures

Digit Symbol Substitution Task — ANOVAs on the number of correct responses on the DDST indicated there were significant differences among drug conditions, time of measurement, and a significant drug by time interaction (Figure 4.3.4). Performance was significantly impaired after high doses of marijuana, ethanol, pentobarbital, and hydromorphone.

Circular Lights Task — High doses of ethanol and pentobarbital significantly decreased the number of hits on the circular lights task (Figure 4.3.4). The other experimental drugs caused no significant change in this measure of performance.

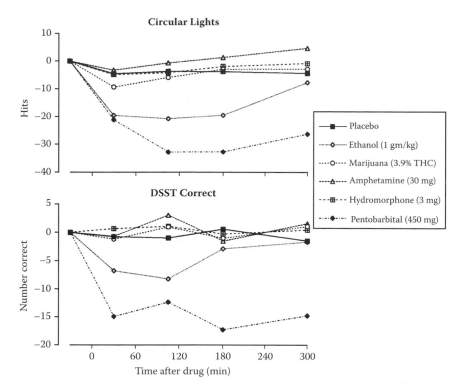

Figure 4.3.4 High doses of the experimental drugs caused changes (from baseline) in performance on the circular lights and DSST tasks. The effects varied as a function of the administered drug and the time after administration.

Correlational Analyses

A visual comparison of the pupillary, subjective, and performance effects of the experimental drug (Figures 4.3.2 through 4.3.4) indicates that in most instances the maximal change in each parameter occurred at the same time. Furthermore, the time of maximal effect was related to the dosage form. For example, smoked marijuana produced maximal subjective and performance effects 30 min after drug administration, whereas the capsules (pentobarbital, hydromorphone, and amphetamine) produced significant maximal changes 120 min or longer after drug administration. Correlational analyses were performed to determine if performance and subjective changes varied as a function of pupillary change. Correlations between the change in pupil diameter and the changes in the subjective and performance measures (total of 176 correlations) were statistically significant in only 15 cases (7 at the high dose condition). Furthermore, only 3 of the significant correlations in the high dose conditions occurred during the time of the maximal pupillary change. These results indicate there is a very weak relationship among the pupillary, performance, and subjective effects of these experimental drugs. Furthermore, pupillary changes, even under ideal laboratory conditions, do not predict changes in performance of experimental tasks. However, as discussed below, changes in pupillary measures may be useful in predicting performance in the workplace environment.

4.3.4 Effects of Abused Drugs on Pupillary Measures

4.3.4.1 Opiates

In early clinical studies, it was shown that morphine caused miosis and morphine withdrawal caused mydriasis.[21] In humans, most opiates caused pupillary constriction and diminished the constriction and dilation velocities of the light reflex.[22] The results of the above study confirm that hydromorphone, a potent orally active opiate, decreased pupil size and diminished the constriction velocity and amplitude of the light reflex. Buprenorphine, a partial opiate agonist, also decreased pupil size, constriction and dilation velocities, and the constriction amplitude of the light reflex.[23,24] On buprenorphine withdrawal there was a significant increase in pupil size and parameters of the light reflex.[16] Mixed agonists-antagonists caused less constriction than full agonists. For example, cyclazocine caused a small but reliable miotic response in human volunteers.[25]

4.3.4.2   Stimulants

As was demonstrated in the experiment above and elsewhere, amphetamine[26] and its derivatives and cocaine[26,27] significantly increased pupil size through an activation of the sympathetic nerve innervation of the iris. Evidence from an animal study indicated that amphetamine-induced mydriasis is partially mediated through actions in the brain where it inhibits the parasympathetic output of the oculomotor nucleus.[28] Tennant[29] also reported that cocaine and amphetamine-type stimulants increased pupil diameter and diminished the pupil reaction to light.

4.3.4.3   Barbiturates

In the laboratory experiment described above, pentobarbital (450 mg) caused a small but significant decrease in pupil size and a reduction in the constriction velocity of the light reflex. The maximal effect was measured 300 min after oral drug administration. Nystagmus (rhythmical oscillation of the eyeballs) and ptosis (drooping of the upper eyelid) are the eye signs that are most often attributed to ingestion of barbiturates, benzodiazepines, ethanol, and other CNS depressants.[26,30,31]

4.3.4.4   Ethanol

As shown in the above experimental results, ethanol caused a small but significant decrease in pupil size and a reduction in the response to a flash of light. In a review of the effects of abused drugs on pupillary and ocular measures, Tennant[29] reported that ethanol caused no change in pupil size but diminished the light reflex. Nystagmus is a well-known sign of ethanol intoxication.[26]

4.3.4.5   Marijuana

The high dose of marijuana decreased pupil diameter in all subjects in the experiment described above. The peak response occurred 30 min after smoking. There were significant decreases in the constriction and dilation velocities of the light reflex. Tennant[29] reported that marijuana obtunded the light reflex without changes in pupil size. In a subsequent study, marijuana smoking obtunded the light reflex and caused decrements in smooth pursuit eye tracking.[32]

4.3.4.6   Hallucinogens

Both indoleamine (e.g., lysergic acid diethylamide, LSD; psilocybin) and phenethylamine hallucinogens (e.g., mescaline) increased pupil diameter.[26] There have been no systematic studies of the effects of these drugs on dynamic measures of the light reflex. Phencyclidine (PCP) does not cause marked changes in pupil size or light reflex. However, subjects intoxicated with PCP often show horizontal and vertical nystagmus.[26]

4.3.4.7 Nicotine

Cigarette smoking has been reported to increase pupil size during the time the cigarette is being smoked.[33] Pupil size returned to baseline values within 45 s after smoking a single cigarette. Pupil diameter of smokers was smaller (mean = 5.1 mm) than that of nonsmokers (mean = 6.0 mm) suggesting that chronic cigarette smoking may persistently decrease pupil size.[34]

4.3.4.8 Club Drugs

MDMA (3,4-methylenedioxymethamphetamine), otherwise known as "ecstasy," causes significant mydriasis.[35,36] Cami et al.[35] reported significant mydriasis (increases of 3.5 mm) in subjects given doses above 50 mg. Ketamine, also known as "Special K," also causes mydriasis.[37] Other drugs such as gamma hydroxybutyrate (GHB) and flunitrazepam, Rophynol ("Roofie") are more difficult to study using pupillometry because they tend to render the users unconscious, although flunitrazepam has been found to cause mydriasis.[38] More research must be done to understand more fully the pupillary effects of this relatively new class of abused drugs.

4.3.5 Pupillary Effects of Concomitant Drug Use

Although a high percentage of drug users tend to abuse more than one drug at a time, no studies had analyzed the pupillary effects of poly-drug use. In a recent study[39] we measured the pupillary effects of polydrug use in an outpatient population undergoing methadone treatment. The purpose of this study was to determine if pupillary changes occurred when subjects co-administered illicit drugs while they were maintained on methadone or buprenorphine.

4.3.5.1 Methods

Participants

Patients (*n* = 37) already enrolled in studies at the NIDA Archway Clinic were invited to participate. The subject population included 21 males and 16 females; 68% of the participants were African Americans and 32% were Caucasian. The average age of the participants was 41.9 years. The participants had extensive drug abuse histories that included current opioid dependence, chronic cocaine use, and frequent use of other illicit drugs. Most (*n* = 35) were maintained on methadone in doses that ranged from 70 to 100 mg/day; two participants were maintained on buprenorphine (16 mg/day).

Study Design

After agreeing to participate, and signing an informed consent form, the operation of the pupillometer, FIT 2000 (Pulse Medical Instruments (PMI), Rockville, MD), was explained and demonstrated to the research volunteers. They were allowed to practice the test sequence in the presence of the administrator until they obtained a successful test sequence. This single exposure was the only supervised orientation the participants received.

Participants used the pupillometer three occasions each week, on days when they provided a urine sample for drug testing. Urine was analyzed on-site for: amphetamines, barbiturates, benzodiazepines, cocaine, marijuana metabolites, phencyclidine, and opiates. Subjects were compensated for successful pupillary tests with a $2 coupon redeemable at a fast food restaurant chain.

Study Measures

On study days, room lights were kept at a constant illumination. The participant stood comfortably in front of the instrument and looked through the viewing lens with one eye (left) while the other eye was open at all times. The pupillary test sequence was initiated when the participant pressed a start button. A green LED target quickly moved horizontally across the viewing screen. Saccadic velocity (SV) data were collected at a rate of 750 Hz during this phase. The target then paused in the middle of the viewing field, and a series of light flashes ensued. Initial pupillary diameter (ID) (measured before the flashes), constriction amplitude (CA), and constriction latency (CL) were collected at a rate of 60 Hz. If the instrument lost eye tracking or for any reason that data could not be collected, a low tone sounded, a fault message was given, and the test was aborted. After a fault message the participant could re-initiate a test sequence. A successful test sequence lasted about 30 s. Subjects repeated the test sequence until they obtained a successful result.

Statistical Analyses

The data were analyzed to determine the feasibility for use in this patient population. The number and percentage of successful and unsuccessful (faults) tests were summarized for each participant. Pupillary data from days when there was no evidence of other recent drug use (urine negative for abused drugs) were compared to days when there was evidence of recent drug use (urine positive). These comparisons were done using both within-subject and between-subject tests. A drug-free baseline was determined for subjects who provided negative urine on more than 10 days. The four parameters were used to determine the goodness-of-fit calculation as follows:

$$\text{Index} = \left(\frac{\mu_{ID} - ID}{\sigma_{ID}}\right)^2 + \left(\frac{\mu_{CL} - CL}{\sigma_{CL}}\right)^2 + \left(\frac{\mu_{CA} - CA}{\sigma_{CA}}\right)^2 + \left(\frac{\mu_{SV} - SV}{\sigma_{SV}}\right)^2$$

where ID, CL, CA, and SV are the value of the parameters on any particular pupillary screening, μ represents the mean baseline value, and σ is the baseline standard deviation of each parameter. After a baseline was established for each participant (FIT index), a chi square analysis with 4 degrees of freedom was calculated for subsequent drug positive days. This result was referenced against the critical chi square values table ($p < 0.1$, $\chi^2 = 7.78$, $p < 0.01$, $\chi^2 = 13.28$). These calculations yielded the probability that the particular reading differed from the established baseline. Finally, pupillary parameters in participants who always gave negative urine were compared to those who always gave positive urine to determine if there was more stability of measures among those who only ingested the treatment medication.

4.3.5.2 Results

Fault Analyses

The overall success rate for correct use of the pupillometer by participants ($n = 37$) was 92.9%; that is, nearly every time participants attempted a trial they were eventually successful. The success rate (percentage obtaining a successful sequence on the first try of each study day) in participants after minimal experience (2 weeks or about 6 exposures) was 72%, and if the four participants who had trouble obtaining stability were eliminated, the overall success rate further increased to 81%. Thus, even minimally trained patients maintained on methadone[4] or buprenorphine,[16] drugs known to produce miosis, obtained reliable pupillary measures.

Table 4.3.2 Participants (n = 6) with >10 days When Urine Was Positive or Negative for the Presence of Illicit Drugs

	Urine Negative	Urine Positive
Pupil diameter (ID) (mm)	5.7 ± 0.51	5.9 ± 0.68
Constriction amplitude (CA) (mm)	0.8 ± 0.12	0.8 ± 0.3
Constriction latency (CL) (mm/s)	297.9 ± 12.1	301.5 ± 14.6
Saccadic velocity (SV) (mm/s)	80.9 ± 7.22	82.8 ± 11.1

Note: Values shown are mean ± standard deviation of the four FIT parameters.

Table 4.3.3 Comparison of Pupillary Measures in Participants (n = 4) with Urine Samples Consistently Negative for Illicit Drugs and Participants (n = 20) with Consistently Positive Urines

	Urine Negative	Urine Positive
Pupil diameter (ID) (mm)	5.2 ± 0.31	5.9 ± 0.81
Constriction amplitude (CA) (mm)	0.9 ± 0.14	0.7 ± 0.13
Constriction latency (CL) (ms)	301.2 ± 9.86	314 ± 22.9
Saccadic velocity (SV)(mm/s)	75.0 ± 6.46	76.0 ± 10.1

Note: Values shown are mean ± standard deviation of the four FIT parameters.

Pupillary Reactions on Drug-Positive and Drug-Negative Days

Shown in Table 4.3.2 are the mean and standard deviation of the four parameters collected on subjects (n = 6) on days (minimum of 10) when their urine was negative for drugs of abuse compared to days when their urine was positive for abused drugs. Although the mean values are similar, the variability increased (larger standard deviation) for ID, CL, and SV on urine-positive days. The variability in the measures obtained for constriction amplitude was similar regardless of the presence of illicit drugs in the urine.

Comparison of Individuals Always Positive or Negative for Illicit Drugs

Many of the participants (n = 20) were never able to provide ten or more drug-free urine samples, and a few (n = 4) always gave urine samples that were drug negative. The data from these subjects were not useful for the comparisons illustrated in Table 4.3.2, but examination of the variation of the parameters in Table 4.3.3 revealed a similar pattern. Specifically, the standard deviation of the mean of ID, SV, and CL was larger in the group with the positive urine samples.

Fit Equation

Participants with 10 or more clean days were analyzed using the FIT equation. A baseline was established from pupillary data on days when the urine was negative for illicit drugs. The pupillary measures from days when the urine was positive for drugs were inserted into the FIT equation to determine probabilities between $p < 0.1$ and $p < 0.01$. For example, one participant had baseline values of 5.35 (± 0.68), 0.97 (± 0.12), 281.52 (± 8.0), and 78.2 (± 9.8) for ID, CA, CL, and SV, respectively. On a day when the urine was positive for cocaine and methamphetamines, the values for the four parameters were 6.31, 0.79, 305.1, and 91.23. When inserted into the equation this generated a FIT index of 14.69, a value well above the critical values for the $p < 0.1$ (7.78) and $p < 0.01$ (13.28). Using this methodology, concomitant drug use was detected 29% of the time at the $p < 0.1$ level. There was a high variability of detection among participants. At the p 0.1 level, drug positive urines were detected 53% of the time on three participants. However, in another three participants, detection averaged only 10%.

4.3.6 Utility and Limitations of Pupillary Testing for Abused Drugs

In some circumstances the use of pupillometry in drug detection appears reasonable. However, based on the experimental evidence cited above and a review of the literature, there are reservations about the use of pupillometry to detect recent ingestion of abused drugs. Several areas of concern and the limitations of the methodology are discussed below.

4.3.6.1 Subject Variability

The size of the pupil and its responsiveness to a light stimulus vary considerably across subjects. Normal pupil diameter ranges between 2 and 8 mm in the extremes of ambient light. In conditions of controlled, low-level (4 ft cd) ambient light, pupil size ranged from 3.5 to 8 mm, and there were similarly large variations in constriction and dilation velocities of the light reflex.[2] Fosnaugh et al.[2] recorded pupil measures on 4 consecutive days and found very little within-subject variation in pupil size and parameters of the light reflex. These findings have practical and theoretical importance. The wide variability between subjects indicates that a single examination of the pupils and the light reflex is unlikely to be highly predictive of recent drug ingestion. On the other hand, the small within-subject, day-to-day variability indicates that a relatively small change in pupil measures in an individual may be an indicator of recent drug ingestion. These suggestions emphasize the importance of having verifiable, drug-free baseline data (both mean and variation is important) for individuals enrolled in testing programs. As demonstrated in the polydrug study, a baseline with minimal variation is the best way to assure detection of differences.

4.3.6.2 Conditions of Measurement

The ambient light present when pupillary measures are made clearly influences the values obtained. For example, Fosnaugh et al.[2] determined the effects of ambient light on pupil size and measures of the light reflex. As ambient light varied between less than 0.1 to 200 ft cd, pupil size decreased from 6.5 to 2.5 mm; constriction and dilation velocities decreased from 6.0 to 1.5 mm/sc and from 2.5 to 1.5 mm/s, respectively. The ranges in the Fosnaugh et al.[2] experiment are similar to those reported elsewhere.[11,40] In the high ambient light conditions pupil diameter and constriction and dilation velocities increased when an opaque patch was placed over the contralateral eye.[2] These findings indicate that the design of pupillometers should incorporate features to assure that the ambient light is constant and that the subject consistently opens (or closes) the contralateral eye as the measures are made. In pupillometers where the subject is required to focus or gaze at a near object, accommodation-induced miosis will change pupil size and may diminish the sensitivity of the pupil to a light flash.

4.3.6.3 Effect of Fatigue, Disease, and Legal Drugs

Fatigue tends to decrease pupil size and diminish the response to light through diminished inhibition of the Edinger Westphal nucleus.[6] Subjects with diabetes mellitus have smaller pupils and a sluggish light reflex.[41] Schizophrenia and other psychiatric diagnoses are associated with sluggish pupillary response to a light flash and other pupillary abnormalities.[42] The light reflex is obtunded in anxious subjects.[9]

The ingestion of many widely used drugs changes pupillary diameter and the responsiveness to light.[26,30,43] For example, the following drug classes increase pupil size: anticholinergics (e.g., atropine, scopolamine), sympathomimetics (e.g., epinephrine, ephedrine), and antihistamines (diphenhydramine). Other drug classes decrease pupil diameter: cholinomimetics (physostigmine, pilocarpine), sympatholytics (e.g., reserpine, guanethidine, alpha-methyldopa), and chlorpromazine. The wide range of drugs that affect pupillary measures represents a challenge to the application of pupillometry in the detection of illegal drugs.

4.3.7 Conclusions

The proposal that pupillary measures could be used to distinguish classes of drugs likely to impair automobile driving performance[29] stimulated interest in the use of pupillometry for drug detection applications. More recently pupillometry has been applied to other fitness-for-duty applications on the assumption that small changes in static and dynamic indices of pupillary functions predict CNS impairment. The impairment may be induced by fatigue, disease, or stress. The literature reviewed and the results of the controlled, clinical studies presented in this chapter indicate that several classes of commonly abused drugs have specific, dose-related effects of pupil size and measures of the light reflex. The application of pupillometry for the detection of drugs of abuse is theoretically possible, but the practical utility is limited. Because of the large between-subject variation in pupillary measures, one must know baseline values and ordinary variations for the tested subject. This limits the use of the technique to workplace, military, or institutional applications. The profound influence of ambient light on pupillary measures dictates that the conditions under which measures are made be carefully controlled. Other drugs, fatigue, and some diseases also influence measures of the light reflex and may increase the number of false positive readings. Finally, the magnitude of the effects of the drugs studied are small and transient and often do not exceed the within-subject variability. These considerations challenge the use of pupillometry as a drug detection application.

Acknowledgments

Mr. Ed Hotchkiss (PMI) provided the pupillometer used in the Archway study and collaborated in analyzing results. We are grateful for the help of Ed Bunker and Reginald Fant for their efforts in the previous edition of this chapter and to the students who contributed to these studies: Heide York, Michelle Fank, and Sharifeh Farasat. This research was supported in part, by the NIH Intramural Research Program, NIDA.

REFERENCES

1. Alexandridis, E., *The Pupil*, Springer-Verlag, New York, 1985.
2. Fosnaugh, J.S., Bunker, E.B., and Pickworth, W.B., Daily variation and effects of ambient light and circadian factors on the human light reflex, *Meth. Find. Clin. Exp. Pharmacol.*, 14, 545, 1992.
3. Marquardt, W.G., Martin, W.R., and Jasinski, D.R., The use of the Polaroid CU camera in pupillography, *Int. J. Addict.*, 2, 301, 1967.
4. Jasinski, D.R. and Martin, W.R., Evaluation of a new photographic method for assessing pupil diameters, *Clin. Pharmacol. Ther.*, 8, 271, 1967.
5. Greenwald, M.K., Johanson, C.E., and Schuster, C.R., Opioid reinforcement in heroin-dependent volunteers during outpatient buprenorphine maintenance, *Drug Alcohol Depend.*, 56, 191, 1999.
6. Lowenstein, O. and Lowenfeld, I.E., The pupil, in *The Eye*, Davson, H., Ed., Academic Press, New York, 1969, 255.
7. Lowenstein, O. and Lowenfeld, I., Electronic pupillography, *Arch. Ophthalmol.*, 59, 352, 1958.
8. Newman, J. and Boughton, R., Pupillometric assessment of excessive daytime sleepiness in narcolepsy-cataplexy, *Sleep*, 14, 121, 1991.
9. Bakes, A., Bradshaw, C.M., and Szabadi, E., Attenuation of the pupillary light reflex in anxious patients, *Br. J. Clin. Pharmacol.*, 30, 377, 1990.
10. Zinn, K.M., *The Pupil*, Charles C Thomas, Springfield, 1972.

11. Ellis, C.J., The pupillary light reflex in normal subjects, *Br. J. Ophthalmology*, 65, 754, 1981.
12. Lowenstein, O. and Lowenfeld, I.E., Mutual role of sympathetic and parasympathetic in shaping of the pupillary reflex to light, *Arch. Neurology Psychiatry* (Chicago), 64, 341, 1950.
13. Pickworth, W.B., Rohrer M.S., and Fant, R.V., Effects of abused drugs on psychomotor performance, *Exp. Clin. Pharmacol.*, 5, 3, 1997.
14. Heishman, S.J., Stitzer, M.L., and Bigelow, G.E., Alcohol and marijuana: comparative dose effect profiles in humans, *Pharmacol. Biochem. Behav.*, 31, 649, 1988.
15. Radzius, A. et al., A portable pupilometer system for measuring pupillary size and light reflex, *Behav. Res. Method Instrum. Comput.*, 21, 611, 1989.
16. Pickworth, W.B., Lee, H., and Fudala, P.J., Buprenorphine-induced pupillary effects in human volunteers, *Life Sci.*, 47, 1269, 1990.
17. Heishman, S.J. et al., Acute and residual effects of marijuana: profiles of plasma THC levels, physiologic, subjective and performance measures, *Pharmacol. Biochem. Behav.*, 37, 561, 1990.
18. Pickworth, W.B. et al., Acetaminophen fails to inhibit ethanol-induced subjective effects in human volunteers, *Pharmacol. Biochem. Behav.*, 41, 189, 1991.
19. Winer, B.J., Brown, D.R., and Michels, K.M., *Statistical Principles in Experimental Design,* 3rd ed., McGraw-Hill, New York, 1991.
20. Jasinski, D.R., Johnson, R.E., and Henningfield, J.E., Abuse liability assessment in human subjects, *Trends Pharmacol. Sci.*, 5, 196, 1984.
21. Himmelsbach, C.K., The morphine abstinence syndrome, its nature and treatment, *Ann. Intern. Med.,* 15, 829, 1941.
22. Pickworth, W.B. et al., Opiate-induced pupillary effects in humans, *Meth. Find. Exp. Clin. Pharmacol.,* 11, 759, 1989.
23. Pickworth, W.B. et al., Intravenous buprenorphine reduces pupil size and the light reflex in humans, *Life Sci.*, 49, 129, 1991.
24. Pickworth, W. B. et al., Subjective and physiologic effects of intravenous buprenorphine in humans, *Clin. Pharmacol. Ther.*, 53, 570, 1993.
25. Pickworth, W.B et al., A laboratory study of hydromorphone and cyclazocine on smoking behavior in residential polydrug users, *Pharmacol. Biochem. Behav.,* 77, 711, 2004.
26. Urey, J.C., Some ocular manifestations of systemic drug abuse, *J. Am. Optometr. Assoc.,* 62, 832, 1991.
27. Rothman, R.B. et al., Lack of evidence for context-dependent cocaine-induced sensitization in humans: Preliminary studies, *Pharmacol. Biochem. Behav.*, 49, 583, 1994.
28. Sharpe, L.G., Pickworth W.B., and Martin W.R., Actions of amphetamine and antagonists on pupil diameter in the chronic sympathectomized dog, *Psychopharmacology*, 53, 115, 1977.
29. Tennant, F., The rapid eye test to detect drug abuse, *Postgrad. Med.,* 84, 108, 1988.
30. Koetting, J.F., The use of drugs for behavior modification as it relates to the practice of optometry — part 2, *J. Am. Optometr. Assoc.,* 48, 213, 1977.
31. McLane, N.J. and Carroll, D.M., Ocular manifestations of drug abuse, *Surv. Ophthalmol.*, 30, 298, 1986.
32. Fant, R.V. et al., Acute and residual effects of marijuana in humans, *Pharmacol. Biochem. Behav.*, 60, 4, 1998.
33. Roberts, J.D. and Adams, A.J., Short term effects of smoking on ocular accommodation and pupil size, *J. Am. Optometr. Assoc.*, 40, 528, 1969.
34. Pickworth, W.B. et al., Effects of mecamylamine on spontaneous EEG and performance in smokers and non-smokers, *Pharmacol. Biochem. Behav.*, 56, 81, 1997.
35. Mas, M. et al., Cardiovascular and neuroendocrine effects and pharmacokinetics of 3,4-methylenedioxymethamphetamine in humans, *J. Pharmacol. Exp. Ther.*, 290, 136, 1999.
36. Torre, R. et al., Pharmacology of MDMA in humans, *Ann. N.Y. Acad. Sci.*, 914, 225, 2000.
37. Pun, M.S. et al., Ketamine anaesthesia for paediatric ophthalmology surgery, *Br. J. Ophthalmol.*, 87, 535, 2003.
38. Raymon, L.P., Steele, B.W., and Walls, H.C., Benzodiazepines in Miami-Dade County, Florida driving under the influence (DUI) cases (1995–1998) with an emphasis on Rohypnol: GC-MS confirmation, patterns of use, psychomotor impairment, and results of Florida legislation, *J. Anal. Toxicol.*, 23, 490, 1999.
39. Murillo, R. et al., Pupillometry in the detection of concomitant drug use in opioid maintained patients, *Methods Find. Exp. Clin. Pharmacol.*, 26, 271, 2004.

40. Taniguchi, H. et al., Pupillary light reflex in healthy subjects, *Kobe J. Med. Sci.*, 34, 189, 1988.
41. Lanting, P. et al., The cause of increased pupillary light reflex latencies in diabetic patients: the relationship between pupillary light reflex and visual evoked potential latencies, *EEG Clin. Neurophysiol.*, 78, 111, 1991.
42. Steinhauer, S.R. and Hakerem, G., The pupillary response in cognitive psychophysiology and schizophrenia, in Psychophysiology and Experimental Psychopathology: A Tribute to Samuel Sutton, Friedman, D. and Bruder, G., Eds., *Ann. N.Y. Acad. Sci.*, 658, 182, 1992.
43. Turner, P., The human pupil as a model for clinical pharmacological investigations, *J. R. Coll. Physicians.* (London), 9, 165, 1975.

4.4 ABUSE OF MARKETED MEDICATIONS

Kenzie L. Preston, Ph.D.,[1] David H. Epstein, Ph.D.,[1] John P. Schmittner, M.D.,[1] and Sharon L. Walsh, Ph.D.[2]

[1] Clinical Pharmacology and Therapeutics Branch, National Institute on Drug Abuse, National Institutes of Health, Department of Health and Human Services, Baltimore, Maryland
[2] Department of Behavioral Science, Center on Drug and Alcohol Research, University of Kentucky College of Medicine, Lexington, Kentucky

4.4.1 Overview of the Problem

The abuse* of marketed medications has been at the forefront of public awareness in recent years, mostly due to widespread reports concerning OxyContin and hydrocodone.[1] While these are highly regulated, prescription-only medications with recognized potential for abuse, even some over-the-counter (OTC) medications have become problematic, either because of their own effects (e.g., ephedrine) or because they are used in the manufacture of other abused substances (e.g., pseudoephedrine, used to make methamphetamine).[2,3]

The increase in concern seems to reflect a true increase in incidence. The numbers of new nonmedical users of the four major classes of prescription-type drugs (narcotic pain relievers, tranquilizers, stimulants, and sedatives) increased between 1991 and 2001.[4] There were substantially more new users for narcotic pain relievers than for the other three drug categories — an increase from 628,000 initiates in 1990 to 2.4 million in 2001.[5] This increase in new users was accompanied by a 76% increase between 1997 and 2000 in the number of primary treatment admissions for narcotic-analgesic abuse.[6] Initiation of nonmedical tranquilizer use also increased steadily during the 1990s, from 373,000 initiates in 1990 to 1.1 million in 2001.[5]

With reports of increasing abuse has come increasing tension between the need to prevent diversion (illicit use of marketed medication) and the need to keep effective medications available. This tension has been most visible in the realm of opioid analgesics. The need for adequate treatment of pain (e.g., References 7 through 9) coexists uneasily with some state and federal regulatory policies, and with prosecutions of physicians by the Drug Enforcement Agency (DEA) for reported overprescribing; these efforts at control may deter *appropriate* prescribing.[10–12] A similar effect has been suggested with regard to state-legislated triplicate-prescription requirements and the appropriate prescription of benzodiazepines for agitation and anxiety.[13] Scheduled analgesics are also understocked at some pharmacies, especially in nonwhite neighborhoods.[14] Underavailability or underprescription of effective medication, resulting in inadequate treatment, may itself be a type of misuse of medication. For the sake of optimal patient care, an appropriate balance must be struck between the opposing needs for availability and control.

* Throughout this chapter, the term *abuse* is used in its broadest sense, referring to any nonmedical or not-as-prescribed use.

It is appropriate to recognize that some medications are more susceptible to abuse than others. If two medications are equally effective for a given indication, the one with lower abuse liability* would obviously be preferred. Information on abuse liability is necessary for the appropriate regulation of medications and provides a basis for education of physicians, patients, and the public. In this chapter we describe the control of marketed medications, abuse-liability assessment procedures for premarketing testing in laboratory animals and humans, considerations of the formulation properties, and postmarketing surveillance of abuse. Finally, we provide three "case studies" of marketed medications that have been abused.

4.4.2 Control of Marketed Medications

In the U.S., substances can be "scheduled" (controlled) under federal law if they are found to have the potential for abuse. Medications being proposed for approval by the U.S. Food and Drug Administration (FDA) may be required to undergo abuse-liability testing and scheduling review. Compounds deemed to have some liability for abuse can be scheduled at one of five levels reflecting how stringently their manufacture and distribution will be regulated. Compounds with high abuse liability and no medically recognized use in the U.S. are placed in Schedule I. (Some Schedule I compounds are used medically in other countries; for example, heroin is approved for analgesia in England.[15]) Compounds whose medical utility is recognized are placed in one of the other four schedules (II to V), with higher numbers reflecting less stringent control.

Scheduling serves as a warning to physicians and patients that a particular medication has the potential to be abused. However, the primary purpose of scheduling is to deter diversion and to provide a mechanism for detection if diversion should occur. To that end, requirements for many aspects of the manufacture and distribution of controlled substances are defined in the Controlled Substances Act.[16] The drugs in each schedule are listed, along with the requirements for labeling and packaging, security, storage, record maintenance, manufacturing quotas, and registration requirements both for persons who manufacture, distribute, dispense, import, or export the substances and for places where the substances are manufactured, distributed, dispensed, imported, or exported. Also regulated are the issuance of prescriptions by physicians, dispensing by pharmacists, and prescription labeling, filing, and refilling. For example, prescriptions for drugs in Schedule II cannot be refilled; prescriptions for drugs in Schedules III and IV cannot be refilled more than five times.

Eight criteria for a drug's scheduling, or exemption from scheduling, are outlined in Section 811 of the Controlled Substances Act:[17] (1) its actual or relative potential for abuse; (2) scientific evidence of its pharmacological effect, if known; (3) the state of current scientific knowledge regarding the substance; (4) its history and current pattern of abuse; (5) the scope, duration, and significance of abuse; (6) what, if any, risk there is to the public health; (7) its psychological or physiological dependence liability; (8) whether the substance is an immediate precursor of a substance already controlled.

Several of these factors (such as 1, 2, 3, and 7) are amenable to premarketing abuse-liability testing. Most abuse-liability testing is targeted to assess the pharmacological entity without regard to its formulation. The past decade has demonstrated that new formulations of old medications add a potentially dangerous twist to assessment of abuse liability.

4.4.3 Premarketing Abuse-Liability Testing

4.4.3.1 Assessment of Pharmacological Entity

Standardized experimental procedures have been developed to evaluate pharmacological entities according to actual or relative potential for abuse, pharmacological effects, and psychological or

---

* The term *abuse liability*, although standard in behavioral pharmacology, may have unintended implications to clinicians, for whom the word *liability* can connote a threat of litigation. In some contexts, *abuse potential* may be preferable.

physiological dependence liability. One indicator of abuse potential is the extent to which a drug produces reinforcing effects. This is typically estimated in self-administration studies by use of operant-conditioning paradigms that measure the ability of the drug to act as a reinforcer in laboratory animals or sometimes humans. Methods for measuring discriminative-stimulus and subjective effects have been developed to estimate the extent of similarity of the pharmacologic profile of novel compounds to prototypic compounds of a drug class that are already scheduled. In drug-discrimination studies, laboratory animals or human subjects are trained to discriminate the presence or absence of a prototypic drug, and novel drugs are tested for their ability to substitute for the prototypic drug. Subjective-effects studies are conducted with human participants. A novel drug is administered over a range of doses, and its subjective effects are measured on a battery of questionnaires and compared to those of prototypic drugs of abuse. In physical-dependence studies, the test drug is administered repeatedly and then withdrawn; physiological, behavioral, and, in the case of humans, subjective effects are measured. The capacity to produce physical dependence not only can increase the likelihood of abuse but also can increase the adverse consequences of abuse, although physical dependence alone is neither necessary nor sufficient for abuse potential.

The toxicity of abused substances is considered because misuse has the potential to create public-health problems and because the presence or absence of toxic effects can limit abuse liability. Toxicity data can be obtained in studies designed specifically for that purpose as well as from studies of other pharmacological effects such as those listed above.

Self-Administration

The self-administration paradigm is a model of drug abuse widely used to assess the reinforcing efficacy of drugs. In this model, research subjects, usually laboratory animals, are given access to a drug under controlled experimental conditions, and their drug-taking behavior is evaluated. A drug is considered to be reinforcing if the frequency of a designated behavioral response (e.g., a lever press) is increased when drug delivery is contingent on the performance of that response in comparison to the frequency of responses in the absence of the drug. The capacity of a drug to reinforce behavior and, thus, maintain self-administration under experimental conditions is associated with a significant likelihood of abuse by human drug abusers. Since the early 1960s, hundreds of drugs have been tested in operant self-administration paradigms. Drug self-administration has been demonstrated by various routes of administration (intravenous, oral, intragastric, intracranial, intracerebroventricular, intramuscular, and inhalation) and in a wide variety of species (pigeons, mice, rats, cats, dogs, non-human primates, and humans) (for review see Reference 18). The self-administration paradigm is complex; only a brief summary of methods is outlined below. For a more detailed discussion, interested readers are referred to one of the numerous reviews on this topic.[18–20]

To establish a drug's relative reinforcing efficacy in a self-administration paradigm, a number of procedures can be used: response-rate analysis, concurrent or second-order schedules, progressive-ratio (PR) schedules, and discrete-trial choice.[20] The most widely used method, response-rate analysis, employs an operant schedule of reinforcement that defines the work requirement for, or the temporal availability of, the drug, such as a fixed-ratio schedule (FR schedule; a given number of responses is required to obtain the reinforcer) or a fixed-interval schedule (FI schedule; the reinforcer is contingent on the first response emitted after a fixed time interval). Dependent measures typically include the rate of responding (responses/time), temporal response pattern, and the number of drug administrations per session. Duration of access to the drug is an important variable that can be manipulated. Access is typically confined to a limited and predetermined time period (e.g., a 3-h session) in which multiple small unit doses may be obtained. Using fixed access periods, FR and FI schedules generate reliable and reproducible patterns of responding for most drugs.

Self-administration studies can be initiated in one of two ways: direct self-administration or substitution. In the direct self-administration procedure, inexperienced subjects are given access to a test drug, and the extent to which self-administration is initiated and maintained is measured and can be compared to the rate of behavior observed when placebo and/or other drugs are available. In the more commonly used substitution procedure, self-administration of a standard or prototypic abused drug is established first; the test drug is then substituted for the standard drug, and changes in self-administration behavior are measured.

While self-administration has proved very useful in abuse-liability assessment, several issues must be considered when interpreting the results. One is the reliance on response rate as an index of reinforcing efficacy or reinforcement strength.[21] Drugs produce a constellation of effects, only a portion of which may be directly related to their reinforcing efficacy. Drug self-administered at the beginning of an experimental session can alter the subject's ability to make the required responses for self-administration later in the session. Thus, nonspecific behavioral effects must be ruled out. One control for nonspecific effects is to incorporate another operant task (such as responding for food) within the experimental session. Another approach is to use more complex schedules of reinforcement (such as second-order and concurrent schedules) (see Reference 20). Another complexity stems from the nonlinear relationship between dose and response rate or drug delivery. The dose–response function generated from self-administration studies is typically shaped as an inverted U. The relationship between dose and response rate or drug delivery is positive at low doses (thus forming the ascending limb of the dose–response curve) and negative at high doses (thus forming the descending limb). In some cases where there is an inverse relationship between unit dose (i.e., dose per injection) and the number of drug deliveries, the total intake of drug can actually be constant across the descending limb of the dose-response curve.[22,23] Consequently, response rate *per se* may not be a valid index of relative reinforcing strength or efficacy.

Alternatives to response-rate analysis include the progressive-ratio (PR) paradigm and the choice procedure. In the progressive-ratio paradigm, subjects are initially trained to complete a low requirement (e.g., FR-1) for the delivery of a given dose of drug, and then the response requirement is systematically increased until the subject fails to complete it. The last response requirement completed before cessation of responding is known as the "breakpoint"; this serves as the primary measure of the relative strength of the reinforcer. In general, there is an orderly relationship between PR breakpoint and drug dose. In the choice procedure, subjects are trained to respond on at least two separate manipulanda, each associated with its own distinctive conditioned stimulus (e.g., different colored lights). The subject is initially trained on a simple task in which a choice is made between two discriminable drug stimuli such as saline vs. a dose of cocaine. During subsequent testing, the subject is first given an opportunity to sample each choice, and then is required to make a preference choice between the two available manipulanda. In this task, the measure of reinforcing efficacy is the number of drug choices made in a given session and may be expressed as the total percentage of choices for a given drug.

Despite the numerous complexities of self-administration procedures, the data generated from these studies are invaluable for predicting the abuse liability of drugs. When self-administration studies are conducted with the appropriate experimental controls, orderly relationships can be obtained both across and within drug classes. For example, for drugs within the same class, those with higher abuse liability engender more self-administration behavior in the laboratory than related drugs with lower abuse liability. Based on the vast published self-administration literature and epidemiologic reports of drug abuse, self-administration behavior is considered a reliable and strong predictor of the abuse liability of drugs in humans.[18,24,25]

Self-administration is predominantly used in the animal laboratory, although our review of the literature suggests that an increasing number of self-administration studies are being conducted with human volunteers. As more of the parameters are worked out, it is likely that human self-administration studies will gain even wider use in abuse-liability assessment.

Drug Discrimination

Drug discrimination is an experimental paradigm used to classify drugs based on their interoceptive stimulus effects (i.e., effects occurring within the subject) using a behavioral criterion.[26]

The drug-discrimination paradigm and the types of data it generates have been reviewed in detail.[27–30] The paradigm has been used extensively to study pharmacology and to assess abuse liability in humans and nonhumans.[31–34] In drug-discrimination studies, differential reinforcement is used to establish discriminative control by two or more drugs: subjects are trained to emit one response in the presence of a training drug and to emit an alternate response in the absence of the training drug, while other environmental conditions are held constant. For example, in one training session, a drug dose is administered and responses on only one of two (or more) levers produce reinforcer delivery. In another training session, vehicle or no drug is administered, and responses on an alternate lever produce reinforcer delivery. Repeated reinforcement of correct identifications generally leads to stable discrimination.

After the discrimination is acquired, generalization or substitution testing with novel drug stimuli can be conducted. Doses of a test drug are administered in place of the training drug, and the distribution of responses on the drug-appropriate or vehicle-appropriate lever is recorded. If the novel drug produces predominantly drug-appropriate responses (usually 80% or greater), the novel drug is said to substitute completely and, thus, produce stimuli like those of the training drug. If the novel drug produces responses predominantly on the vehicle or no drug-appropriate lever, the novel drug is characterized as not substituting for the training drug. Intermediate degrees of responding are characterized as partial substitution. Drugs within the same pharmacological class that share interoceptive effects can be differentiated from drugs in other pharmacological classes; even within drug classes, discrimination procedures can differentiate among drugs having activity at different receptor subtypes.[27]

While drug discrimination has been predominantly used in animal studies, it is also used with humans.[35] The procedures used to study drug discrimination in humans are quite similar to those used in laboratory animals, but adapted to the unique capabilities of humans. In the discrimination-training phase, training drugs are paired with letter codes as identifying labels. Drugs are given under double-blind conditions and are not identifiable by appearance or volume, and money typically serves as the reinforcer for correct responses. Most human studies include the concurrent collection of questionnaire data on subjective effects, which has been invaluable in evaluating the interrelationship of behavioral discrimination and subjective effects.

Drug discrimination is not a direct measure of reinforcing efficacy. Although virtually all abused drugs can be trained as discriminative stimuli, most psychoactive drugs, including those that are not self-administered, are discriminable from vehicle or no drug.[35] Thus, discriminability in and of itself is not evidence of abuse liability; rather abuse liability may be inferred from the relative similarity of a drug's stimulus effects to those of a known standard or prototypical abused drug. However, there is substantial concordance between discriminative stimulus effects and subjective effects in humans[35,36] and self-administration behavior in laboratory animals.[27]

An important caveat in interpreting drug-discrimination data is that results must be considered in the context of the training drug. For example, in subjects trained to discriminate cocaine from saline, D-amphetamine fully substitutes for cocaine while pentobarbital and morphine do not, even though all four drugs have significant abuse potential.[37,38] Training dose is critical; with higher training doses, generalization dose–response curves tend to be shifted to the right so that higher doses of test drug are needed to produce full substitution. A drug with partial-agonist properties may substitute for a low training dose but fail to substitute for a higher training dose of a full agonist.[27] Lower training doses generally produce less pharmacologic specificity than higher training doses, increasing the likelihood of generalization between pharmacologically dissimilar drugs.[30]

Subjective Effects

Subjective-effect measures have been recognized as a critical element in abuse-liability assessment in humans for several decades.[39,40] Subjective effects are feelings, perceptions, and moods personally experienced by an individual. Drugs of abuse produce characteristic subjective effects or interoceptive stimuli that are perceived as positive and desirable to some individuals; drugs that produce these positive mood effects are often described as euphoriants.[40] Because subjective effects are not accessible to observers for public validation, they can only be obtained through self-reports from the individual experiencing them. Subjective-effect measures in the form of questionnaires have been developed to determine whether a drug produces perceptible effects and to determine the quantitative and qualitative characteristics the drug user experiences. They may be used to collect individual self-reports that are consistent across individuals, studies, and situations, can be combined across subjects, can provide reliable and replicable data, and are meaningful to outside observers. Such questionnaires are scientifically useful for assessing a drug's pharmacologic properties, including time course and potency, and can be used to measure the degree of similarity between a test drug and a known standard for abuse-liability assessment. In general, the critical element is the assessment of whether participants like the effects of the drug. Abuse-liability studies, however, usually incorporate multiple questionnaires in order to gather a comprehensive profile of a drug's subjective effects.

The most commonly used questionnaires are scales of global drug effects, subscales of the Addiction Research Center Inventory (ARCI), Profile of Mood States (POMS), Adjective Rating Scales, and the Drug-Class Questionnaire. On measures of global drug effects, participants are asked to integrate the different aspects of a drug's effects and to rate the "overall strength" of those effects, the participants' "liking" of the drug, and the degree to which the drug produces any "good" effects or "bad" effects. The ARCI is a 550-item true/false questionnaire that was developed empirically to assess a range of physical, emotive, and subjective effects of drugs from several pharmacological classes.[41,42] The ARCI can be tailored to study a particular drug by including only those subscales that are appropriate. The most frequently used scales in abuse-liability studies of acute drug effects are the Morphine-Benzedrine Group (MBG; an index of euphoria), the Pentobarbital-Chlorpromazine-Alcohol Group (PCAG; an index of apathetic sedation), and the Lysergic Acid Diethylamide Group (LSD; an index of dysphoria or somatic discomfort). Increases in the MBG scale, or euphoria scale as it is sometimes called, are associated with significant abuse potential. The Profile of Mood States (POMS) questionnaire is a 65- or 72-item standardized adjective rating scale developed to measure changes in mood in psychiatric populations.[43] The POMS does not contain drug-liking or euphoria scales; its utility in abuse-liability assessment derives from determinations of similarity to a standard drug of abuse and from identification of possible aversive effects.[44] Adjective rating scales are questionnaires on which participants rate symptoms describing global drug effects (e.g., high, strength of drug effect), mood effects (e.g., anxious, depressed), and physical symptoms (e.g., itchy, nausea). In the Drug-Class Questionnaire, participants are asked to indicate which among a list of drugs/drug classes was most similar to the test drug. Experienced abusers can reliably distinguish placebo from active drug and can reliably distinguish among the major drug classes when tested with adequate doses.[45]

Subjective-effect studies require consideration of several experimental factors and control procedures. Participants must be able to comprehend and respond appropriately to questionnaires. Drugs should be administered under double-blind conditions to avoid the introduction of bias into participants' reports. The participants' prior drug exposure could influence responding; most studies assessing abuse potential have used participants with histories of illicit drug use, though a number of studies have been conducted in healthy volunteers without histories of drug abuse.[40,44–47]

Subjective measures can be used to qualitatively characterize the effects of the drug, and these tend to be consistent across drug classes. Each of the major pharmacological classes has been characterized using the questionnaires described above. Drugs of different pharmacological classes generally produce profiles of subjective effects that are unique to that class of drugs and that are recognizable to individuals. This can be of value to the extent that pharmacological class predicts abuse liability. It can also be useful when testing novel drug classes, for example, when testing drugs that act at newly identified receptors and for which no prototypic drugs are known.

As one might expect, global subjective-effect measures such as "liking" and "disliking" tend not to differentiate between different pharmacological classes of drugs, although they do provide quantitative information regarding the overall magnitude of drug effects. Actually, "liking" has especially good concordance with rates of abuse (i.e., highly abused drugs produce dose-related increases in ratings of liking while nonabused drugs do not[40]) and is therefore probably the single most important subjective-effect measure in human abuse-liability assessment.

Physical-Dependence Capacity

Repeated administration of some drugs can result in tolerance and physical dependence. With the development of tolerance, the effect of a drug decreases if the dose is held constant. Tolerance to the desired effect often leads to escalation of the doses self-administered by abusers. Use of higher doses in turn increases the risk of adverse effects, such as physiological toxicity, psychomotor impairment, and physical dependence. Physical dependence becomes evident when reduction or termination of drug administration is followed by withdrawal signs and symptoms, which can manifest as physiological, psychological, and/or behavioral changes. The biological mechanisms of tolerance and physical dependence have been reviewed elsewhere (see, for example, References 48 and 49).

Physical dependence is no longer considered necessary or sufficient for abuse potential.[45,50] Nonetheless, physical dependence can contribute to the perpetuation of drug use (as dependent individuals seek drugs to avoid unpleasant withdrawal) and to the cost to the public health, in terms of both human suffering and the expense of medical treatment associated with withdrawal. Physical dependence, and the consequent abstinence syndrome, is significant for some drug classes such as opiates, barbiturates, and benzodiazepines, but less prominent with other highly abusable drugs including cocaine and the amphetamines. In addition, alleviation of the symptoms associated with physical dependence and withdrawal is not effective as a sole treatment for drug dependence.[50]

Physical-dependence capacity can be determined by direct addiction, substitution, or suppression studies. In direct-addiction studies, a test drug is administered repeatedly over time; doses are initially low and then gradually increased as tolerance develops to toxic effects. After subjects have been stabilized at a specified dose, tolerance and other effects of chronic drug administration are evaluated; methods for evaluating tolerance have been described in detail elsewhere.[20,51] Physical dependence can then be documented by abrupt discontinuation of drug administration or by administration of a selective antagonist for the appropriate receptor type (e.g., naloxone during chronic administration of an opioid). Subjects are observed for signs of an abstinence syndrome. With human subjects, self-report measures can also be included to gain qualitative information about the characteristics of the abstinence syndrome, including dysphoric effects. Drug-seeking behavior can also be monitored, either by recording requests for test drug or other medication during the withdrawal period (for example, see Reference 52), or by giving subjects the opportunity to self-administer drug.[53,54]

The substitution and suppression procedures, variations on direct addiction, have also been used to evaluate physical-dependence capacity. These procedures have chiefly been used with the opioids[45,52] and are described only briefly here. In suppression studies, subjects are initially made physically dependent on a prototypical opioid agonist, for example, morphine administered in four injections/day. In test sessions, agonist administration is abruptly withdrawn, and at the peak of withdrawal (e.g., approximately 30 h after the last morphine dose) test medications are administered and evaluated for their ability to suppress withdrawal. The ability of opioid agonists to suppress the abstinence syndrome was documented using this methodology. In substitution studies, the maintenance drug is replaced with doses of test drug or placebo. The ability of the test drug to prevent the onset of the withdrawal syndrome is assessed over a specified period of time (for example, 24 h). This procedure enables crossover studies with multiple drugs or multiple dose levels of a test drug; subjects are restabilized on the maintenance medication between experimental test sessions.

4.4.3.2 Assessment of Preparation

Pharmacokinetics

The abuse liability of a drug is influenced by its pharmacokinetic properties and the numerous factors that determine its distribution, metabolism, and excretion. One important factor is the speed with which a drug is delivered to the central nervous system. In general, abuse potential is enhanced by speeding the delivery of drug to the brain, and this closely corresponds with the rate of rising drug concentration in arterial blood (see also Reference 55). Increased speed of delivery shortens the interval between drug administration and the perceived onset of the drug's pharmacodynamic effects, a behavioral feature considered critical to abuse potential.[56] Routes of drug administration that provide a more rapid delivery are associated with greater abuse liability. Because route of administration largely determines the speed of delivery, one of the simplest means of modifying the speed of drug delivery is to change the route of administration. For most drugs the rank order for routes of administration from fastest to slowest delivery are typically as follows: inhalation (e.g., smoking) > intravenous > intramuscular ≈ subcutaneous > intranasal > oral. Cocaine is an example of a drug with abuse potential that increases across routes of administration, with oral having the lowest dependence potential and intravenous and smoked having the highest.[57–62] The relationship between speed of onset and abuse potential has also been shown for pentobarbital and diazepam.[63,64] There are some exceptions to these rules; these include drugs that are themselves inactive but produce active metabolites (i.e., prodrugs) and drugs with particularly poor bioavailability when administered by a specific route.

Capacity to Be Made into More Abusable Preparation

Because faster onset of action is associated with higher potential for abuse, abuse-liability assessment should include consideration of whether a formulation can be altered to increase the speed of onset. There are numerous examples of abuse of a medication by a route other than that intended by the manufacturer. The sustained-release oral form of oxycodone, designed to deliver an initial rapid dose followed by slow release, has been widely abused by chewing the tablet, thus releasing the entire content of the tablet at once.[65] There is also evidence for intravenous use of sublingual buprenorphine tablets.[66] Transdermal systems developed to deliver medication slowly for extended periods of time have been prime targets for misuse,[67] as discussed below in the case study of fentanyl.

A wide range of possible uses and misuses must be considered in both the development of formulations and in regulatory decisions. Formulations need to be tested as they might be used, not just as they are meant to be used. While it is possible to develop formulations that lower the abuse potential of a pharmacological constituent, every effort must be made to challenge the formulation to substantiate such a claim.

Availability

The availability of a marketed medication is a key determinant of its abuse liability. A highly abusable medication may have a low rate of abuse if it can only be obtained, for example, in hospital settings. Even within hospital settings, the degree to which availability and, thus, opportunity play a role in incidence of abuse is illustrated by the greater incidence of substance abuse among anesthesiologists than among other physician groups.[68,69] Increasing the availability of a medication with a low rate of abuse can substantially increase the incidence of abuse. Two examples of this phenomenon are described below in the case studies: abuse of both fentanyl (an agonist opioid with high abuse liability) and butorphanol (an agonist-antagonist opioid with moderate abuse liability) increased when each drug was approved for prescribed use in outpatients, despite the use of formulations that might have been expected to minimize abuse liability.

Even drugs with low potential for abuse can have periodic increases in abuse if they are widely available, as discussed below in the case study of the OTC cough suppressant dextromethorphan. Other examples include anticholinergics[70,71] and antihistamines.[72] Abuse of these drugs tends to be mostly limited to particular populations — patient populations in the case of anticholinergics, and youth in the case of dextromethorphan. That the abuse liability of a drug may differ across populations, and that different populations may abuse a drug for different reasons, is a possibility that needs consideration when selecting participants and outcome measures for abuse-liability studies. Abuse-liability testing has come to focus on assessment of euphoriant effects in experienced drug abusers rather than patterns of use in the clinical populations for whom the drug is intended or in other populations,[73] and while this approach is probably appropriate in most cases,[74] it does not always suffice (as illustrated below in the case studies).

In summarizing the relationship between availability and abuse, we need to recognize that there is no formula to predict exactly how much abuse will occur, and that the relationship may wax and wane over time, as discussed below in the case studies. Still, there are a few "rules of thumb." Given equal availability, drugs that produce more positive mood effects are more likely to be abused than those with less positive effects. However, all psychoactive drugs, even those with minimal positive mood effects, have the potential for abuse, even if only for their mood-altering effects. Increasing the availability of a drug will likely increase the absolute numbers of abuse incidents. Finally, acute toxicity has the opposing effects of decreasing the likelihood of abuse while increasing the adverse consequences if abuse should occur.

4.4.4 Postmarketing Surveillance

Postmarketing surveillance is a continuation of the risk assessment conducted during drug development.[75–78] Postmarketing surveillance is necessary because the number of patients exposed to a new drug during premarket testing is usually too small to detect low-incidence adverse events and determine statistically whether those events are caused by the new drug. In addition, patients selected to participate in clinical trials often have more limited ranges of medical conditions and concomitant medications than those who are prescribed the medication after marketing. In the U.S., the FDA maintains the MedWatch program to collect adverse-event reports on marketed medications and to provide safety information for health-care professionals and the public.[79] Pharmaceutical companies often establish their own monitoring programs for adverse events.

Surveillance systems also exist for drug abuse (for review, see Reference 80). Through the Substance Abuse and Mental Health Services Administration (SAMHSA), of the Department of Health and Human Services, the U.S. federal government maintains the Drug Abuse Warning Network (DAWN),[81] which monitors trends in drug-related emergency-department visits and deaths (although the quality of its data has been questioned[82]). SAMHSA also conducts several surveys on drug use and treatment.[83] One SAMHSA survey, the National Survey on Drug Use & Health, formerly called the National Household Survey of Drug Abuse (NHSDA/NSDUH), is administered annually to a statistically representative sample to collect data on the use of illicit drugs, the nonmedical use of licit drugs, and the use of alcohol and tobacco products. Another SAMHSA survey, the Drug and Alcohol Services Information System (DASIS), collects data on treatment facilities for substance abuse, including services offered, numbers of individuals treated, and the characteristics of individuals admitted to treatment. Two of the data sets within DASIS are the Treatment Episode Data Set (TEDS) and the National Survey of Substance Abuse Treatment Services (N-SSATS, formerly known as UFDS). TEDS has demographic and drug-history information about individuals admitted to treatment, primarily by providers receiving public funding.

N-SSATS is an annual census of U.S. treatment facilities registered with SAMHSA and contains information on their location, organization, structure, services, and utilization.

While these surveys are very informative about national trends in drug use, they probably have limited utility as early-warning systems for abuse of newly marketed medications. Ideally, detection of an emerging abuse problem would occur before the numbers of affected individuals grew large enough to be measurable on national surveys. More directed postmarketing surveillance has been used to monitor for diversion and abuse for two recently marketed medications, tramadol and sibutramine.[80] The tramadol surveillance program included spontaneous reports to the manufacturer and adverse-event data from MedWatch, but also used a key-informant network of treatment researchers who completed quarterly questionnaires. Proactive surveillance via the informant network increased the detection of cases of physical dependence, diversion, and abuse compared to the spontaneous-reporting systems.[84–86] In the sibutramine surveillance program, an anonymous questionnaire was completed by individuals in community- and university-based treatment programs every 6 months for 3 years.[80,87] The questionnaire requested information on experiences with sibutramine, phentermine (a scheduled anorectic agent), and a drug with a fabricated name. Early detection of clinically important diversion or abuse of a marketed medication through postmarketing surveillance could enable reconsideration of scheduling decisions before serious problems develop.

4.4.5 Case Studies

In practice, the regulatory status of a marketed drug rarely emerges in a tidy way from experimentally obtained abuse-liability data. In this section, we examine the histories of three drugs (butorphanol, fentanyl, and dextromethorphan) chosen because the prediction of abuse liability for each drug has been imperfect for different reasons. For each drug, we reviewed three types of information: abuse-liability studies in laboratory animals and humans; case reports and news items concerning diversion, abuse, addiction, or overdose; and news items and official documents concerning changes in regulatory or commercial status. Sources included papers found through the Medline and PsycInfo databases (1966 through 2003) supplemented with references cited in the papers themselves; items from the popular press found through the Lexis/Nexis database (early 1970s through 2003); and the Web sites of the FDA and the DEA.

For each drug, the prevalence of abuse was partly attributable to its absolute availability — for example, the over-the-counter status of dextromethorphan (DXM) or the expansion of fentanyl and butorphanol from inpatient to outpatient use. But the pattern of abuse for each drug was distinctive and probably could not have been predicted from the available experimental abuse-liability data.

4.4.5.1 Butorphanol

Table 4.4.1 shows a selective timeline of the evaluation, abuse, and regulation of butorphanol, an opioid with mixed activity at mu and kappa receptors. The most salient aspects of the drug's recent history can be summed up in terms of two questions:

Who abused it? Most of the reports have concerned patients experiencing iatrogenic physical dependence, especially after 1991, when the drug was approved for outpatient use in a nasal-spray formulation. Reports seemed especially to increase when the drug was marketed for a new indication, migraine — a disorder with recurrent symptoms and the possibility of rapid rebound of symptoms if medication is overused.[88] Anecdotally, the modal pattern of abuse seemed to be escalation of use in patients with legitimate prescriptions,[89] even though some patients reported that the acute effects of the drug were extremely unpleasant.[90] There have been very few reports of diversion or abuse by nonpatients, and essentially no reports of use for euphoriant properties or for the avoidance of withdrawal from other opiates such as heroin.

Why was this pattern not predicted? Published abuse-liability studies with butorphanol have generally been conducted in experienced abusers of mu-agonist opioids, and have generally focused

Table 4.4.1 Butorphanol Timeline

Year	Animal Data	Human Lab Data/Clinical Trials	Case Reports/Case Series/Surveys	News Items	Regulatory/Commercial Developments
1975		s.c.: Doses up to 8 mg do not precipitate morphine withdrawal; doses over 8 mg psychotomimetic[119]			
1976–1978		s.c.: Lower abuse potential than codeine or propoxyphene; no increase in liking w/doses 4–48 mg/day over a month, unlike pentazocine[120–122]			
1978		i.m.: No drug-seeking noted in participants in Bristol Labs Phase III trials after abrupt termination of drug[91]			i.m.: FDA's Drug Abuse Advisory Committee (DAAC) votes 12–2 to schedule butorphanol; recommendation not followed; scheduled in only one state (Oklahoma)[89]
1980					i.m.: FDA maintains position against scheduling due to absence of evidence of abuse; DAAC votes 9–4 in support of FDA[89]
1981	In rats, produces only mild withdrawal syndrome (similar to other partial agonists), but tends to precipitate withdrawal from morphine[123]				
1982	Baboons self-administer butorphanol, as well as nalbuphine and pentazocine (finding published 4 years after presentation)[124]				

Table 4.4.1   Butorphanol Timeline *(Continued)*

Year	Animal Data	Human Lab Data/Clinical Trials	Case Reports/Case Series/Surveys	News Items	Regulatory/Commercial Developments
1983			i.m.: Case report of diversion from hospital in Michigan[125]		DAAC votes 10–2 against scheduling of theoretical oral form; FDA considers diversion reports not of great significance[89]
1984	Physical dependence clearly shown in rats[94]		i.m.: 5 male teens in Mississippi using i.v. with antihistamine to get high; minor withdrawal syndrome; 1 fatal OD[126]		
1985			i.m.: Frequent diversion in hospitals;[127,128] some patients escalating use[129]		i.m.: Some hospitals indicate having tightened controls to Schedule II–IV level; some exclude drug from formulary[127]
1988		i.m.: In 3-choice discrimination in methadone patients: butorphanol more like naloxone than saline or hydromorphone; very little abuse liability[133]			
1989	In morphine-maintained rhesus monkeys: butorphanol discriminated as saline, not as naltrexone[132]				
ca. late 1980s			Nasal spray: 18 healthy volunteers in Bristol-Myers "first time in humans" study; withdrawal not seen when drug discontinued after 16 days[92]		

Year			
1990	i.m.: Very little abuse liability in methadone patients[133]	Nasal spray: Bristol-Myers clinical trial in post-Caesarian-section pain; no assessment of abuse liability or withdrawal[93]	Nasal spray: FDA approves nonscheduled, despite DAAC concerns (e.g., that clinical trials were insensitive to abuse liability)[89]
1991	In rats, naloxone-induced withdrawal is just as severe for butorphanol as for morphine[95]	Nasal spray: Very little abuse liability in male opioid abusers[134] i.m.: In 2-choice discrimination: butorphanol more like hydromorphone than like saline; withdrawal both morphine-like and kappa-like; but subjects choose sedative, not more butorphanol, for relief; increases liking, but not MBG; sometimes identified as barbiturate[135]	
1992			Nasal spray advertised for use in migraine; no published clinical trials on spray in migraine; Texas increases control amid reports of spray users unable to stop[89] Nasal spray: MedWatch reports increase[89]
1993–1994		Nasal spray: Chicago-area neurologist writes that of his 24 migraine patients, 13 had had ADRs; "extremely stoned," "stuporous"; 6 said it was worst experience of their lives; no withdrawal mentioned[90]	

Table 4.4.1 Butorphanol Timeline (Continued)

Year	Animal Data	Human Lab Data/Clinical Trials	Case Reports/Case Series/Surveys	News Items	Regulatory/Commercial Developments
1994	In cynomolgus monkeys, butorphanol acts only as an agonist[136]	i.m.: Male postaddicts; 3-choice discrimination: On VAS scales: increases High, Liking, Good, and Not Bad, but on ARCI, increased PCAG, not MBG; Drug class: ID'd as sedative, not opiate; Conclusion: more kappa than mu effects[137] i.v.: Healthy volunteers; on VAS, increases Sedated (also Liking, but not dose-related); on ARCI, increases PCAG and LSD; main difference from effects in opiate abusers: psychomotor impairment[138]	Nasal spray: Review of headache treatments acknowledges possibility of symptom rebound and dependence with overuse of analgesics, including spray[88]		
1995				Nasal spray: in August, suicide by gunshot during withdrawal (not widely reported until 1997)[139]	FDA survey: 39 of 47 states report diversion or abuse; 7 have tried to schedule butorphanol; more than half have special controls at hospitals; most-abused form is nasal spray. FDA leaves regulation to states[89] Nasal spray: in April, Bristol-Myers asks FDA to control[140]
1996					Nasal spray: Chicago-area pharmacists are said to dilute it to limit its abuse liability[89]
1997		i.v.: In healthy volunteers, butorphanol-induced ratings of "elated" (though not liking) actually increase during cold-water pain[96]		Nasal spray: Reports of addiction associated with rebound migraine[139] *Neurology* publishes historical review[89] coauthored by father of 1995 suicide	Nasal spray: FDA recommends scheduling to DEA, but decides against sending Dear Doctor letter[141] DEA places butorphanol in Schedule IV

Year			
1998	i.m.: Disliked by heroin/opiate abusers[142,143]	Nasal spray: Wrongful-death suits filed[144]	
2000	i.m.: Opioid chippers; hydromorphone vs. not hydromorphone discrimination; with these instructions, butorphanol does not substitute for hydromorphone at any dose; VAS: increases both Good and Bad, not Liking; no effects on ARCI[145]	Nasal spray: Scattered news reports of addiction continue[146]	
2001	i.m.: Heroin chippers; butorphanol compared with a selective kappa agonist (enadoline) and a selective mu agonist (hydromorphine) and was more mu-like than kappa-like on most measures[147]	Nasal spray: First news report of recreational use: fatal OD in teen girl[148]	Nasal spray: FDA gives Mylan abbreviated NDA for generic
2002	i.m.: Methadone-maintained humans; trained on "naloxone vs. placebo vs. novel" discrimination; butorphanol produces 70% naloxone responding, 29% novel responding[149]	Nasal spray: Another news report of an addicted provider[150]	Nasal spray: FDA approves generic form Roxane

Note: Abbreviations used in tables: ADR, Adverse Drug Reaction; ARCI, Addiction Research Center Inventory; DAAC, Drug Abuse Advisory Committee; DEA, Drug Enforcement Administration; DO, dextrorphan (active metabolite of dextromethorphan); DSM-IIIR, *Diagnostic and Statistical Manual*, 3rd ed. revised; DXM, dextromethorphan; FDA, Food and Drug Administration; ID, identification; i.m., intramuscular; i.v., intravenous; NDA, New Drug Application; OD, overdose; OTC, over the counter; PCP, phencyclidine; s.c., subcutaneous; VAS, Visual Analog Scales; WHO, World Health Organization.

on whether butorphanol produces liking or euphoria and on whether it has morphine-like properties. The absence of such findings may have contributed to the nonscheduled status of the drug (until it was placed in Schedule IV in 1997). One review article[91] summarizes "data on file" at Bristol Laboratories from 1978 as follows: "During Phase III clinical trials, [injectable] butorphanol was administered chronically at therapeutic doses to patients for as long as 9 months and then abruptly terminated. No withdrawal symptoms or compulsive drug-seeking behavior were precipitated." The patient population is unspecified; it seems unlikely that it consisted largely of patients with migraine or that they had the opportunity to self-administer the drug more frequently or in larger doses. Similarly, the later clinical trials supporting the nasal-spray formulation[92,93] did not include patients with migraine and would not have been able to detect a cycle of rebound headache and dose escalation.

Comments. The clearest lesson from the butorphanol experience is that when a drug is introduced to a new population, it is important to determine whether extant abuse-liability studies will generalize to that population. If not, then clinical trials should be designed to detect signs of abuse in that population, and careful postmarketing surveillance should occur. The goal is not to prevent patient access to necessary medications, but to ensure that providers and patients have adequate information about the risks of such medications.

One of the risks of butorphanol, its physical-dependence potential, emerged in animal studies[94,95] more clearly than in human abuse-liability studies. It is also interesting to note that the human experimental data that seem most consistent with marketing experience did not appear until 1997, when it was shown that the modest euphoriant effects of butorphanol are more prominent in the presence of a painful stimulus (a finding opposite to what has been observed with most morphine-like drugs).[96] Each of these findings shows, of course, that relevant abuse-liability data are easiest to pick out in hindsight. Still, future marketing and regulatory decisions may benefit from increased attention to the multiplicity of ways in which a drug could be prone to abuse.

4.4.5.2 *Fentanyl*

Table 4.4.2 shows a selective timeline of the evaluation, abuse, and regulation of fentanyl, a potent agonist at mu-opioid receptors. Again, the most salient aspects of the drug's recent history can be summed up with two questions:

Who abused it? In contrast to butorphanol, fentanyl has been abused primarily by nonpatients who had access to the drug. There have been numerous reports (far too many to include in the timeline) of diversion and abuse of fentanyl for its euphoriant properties. Until 1990, these reports usually involved health-care providers with access to the intravenous formulation in hospital settings. After 1990, when a transdermal-patch formulation became available to outpatients, abuse spread to a much broader population. Yet only a very small proportion of the reports concerned patients for whom legitimate prescriptions had been written — again in contrast to butorphanol. The modal pattern of abuse was through illegitimate access to patches (taken from trash cans, removed from nursing-home patients, or, in one twice-published case,[97,98] removed from a dead body), followed by inhalation, ingestion, or injection of their contents.[99–103]

Why was this pattern not predicted? The highly euphorogenic nature of fentanyl was actually clear in abuse-liability studies as early as 1965,[104] and the drug was accordingly placed in Schedule II of the 1970 Controlled Substances Act; this was the most restrictive possible placement that still permitted medical use. What was apparently not foreseen, when the patch formulation was approved for outpatient use in 1990, was that its slow-release properties would be defeated by individuals seeking intoxication. The published literature appears to contain no abuse-liability studies for the patch formulation.

Comments: The obvious lesson of the fentanyl experience is that abuse-liability studies must take into account the possibility that an intended slow-release system will be subverted by users. How to respond to this possibility is a difficult question. Sometimes it may be possible to develop a formulation that is more difficult to subvert, such as a subcutaneous implant. But it is also

Table 4.4.2 Fentanyl Timeline

Year	Human Lab Data/Clinical Trials	Case Reports/Case Series/Surveys	News Items	Regulatory/Commercial Developments
1965	i.v.: In postaddicts, more euphorogenic than morphine[104]			
early 1970s				i.v.: Sublimaze and Innovar introduced in U.S.; for hospital use only; on Schedule II
mid-1970s		i.v.: Abuse reported among health-care providers[151]		
1980s			i.v.: Scattered reports of diversion by health-care providers;[152,153] also some reports of illicitly manufactured powder[154]	
1989			Lozenge: Some controversy over appropriateness of "lollipop" formulation during multisite trials[155]	
1990				Patch: FDA approves Duragesic; no abuse-liability studies for patch in published literature
1991–1993		Patch: Scattered reports of misuse and ODs[103,156]		
1992			Illicit fentanyl: Many reports of fatal ODs on powder sold as "Tango & Cash;"[157] referred to as a "serial killer"[108,158]	Illicit fentanyl: Bill introduced in Congress to equate possession penalties with those for heroin possession[159]
1993				Lozenge: FDA approves Oralet for hospital use
1994			Lozenge: More controversy over appropriateness of "lollipop" formulation[160–162]	Patch: FDA sends Dear Doctor letter
1995			i.v.: Medical student in New York City dies from self-injected fentanyl[163]	
1996	i.v.: In healthy volunteers, euphoriant effects blunted during pain[106]			
1997				Lozenge: FDA DAAC recommends approving Actiq for outpatient use
1998				Lozenge: FDA approves Actiq for outpatient use
2000–2003		Patch: another case series on abuse and OD[164]	Patch: More stories on diversion and OD[165–167]	
			Lozenge: fatal OD with use of 3 simultaneously[105]	

Note: See Table 4.4.1 for abbreviations.

important that the drug be available in formulations that patients need, such as the fentanyl lozenge approved in 1998 for breakthrough pain in patients with cancer — despite the likelihood that these formulations will be abused. (There has already been a newspaper report implicating fentanyl lozenges in the death of a man who used three lozenges simultaneously.[105]) Higher scheduling of fentanyl would make the drug completely unavailable for medical use. The regulatory response to fentanyl abuse at the federal level has been to maintain close FDA monitoring of advertising claims, commercial manufacture of new formulations, and imports through Internet pharmacies. Additional measures, such as tighter prescription tracking, have been considered by individual states such as Florida.

As mentioned above, most reports of fentanyl abuse have not involved iatrogenic addiction in patients. As with butorphanol, the human experimental data most consistent with this did not appear until 1996, when it was shown that the euphoriant effects of fentanyl are blunted in the presence of a painful stimulus.[106] Clearly, however, low incidence of iatrogenic addiction or abuse may not predict the likelihood of abuse in nonpatient populations.

Earlier in the chapter, we pointed out that the relationship between drug availability and abuse may wax and wane over time. In the case of fentanyl, this can be seen in the differing results of two published analyses. In the first analysis, from 1990 to 1996, fentanyl prescriptions increased 1168% while an index of overdose admissions (DAWN mentions of fentanyl, including both licitly and illicitly manufactured fentanyl) actually decreased 59%.[107] But in the second analysis, from 1994 to 2001, both measures increased, with the largest relative increase in DAWN mentions occurring in 1997.[1] This pattern may be partly attributable to negative news coverage of both illicit and diverted fentanyl, which, based on our Lexis/Nexis search, peaked from 1991 through 1993, then declined from 1994 to 1999, perhaps permitting some "forgetting" of the drug's risks. Negative publicity, or lack thereof, is likely to have complex effects on a drug's abuse liability; according to one newspaper report, when police used bullhorns to warn of the lethal potency of a batch of illicitly manufactured fentanyl being sold under the name Tango & Cash, local attempts to purchase the drug actually increased.[108]

Among the other trends we noticed in press coverage of fentanyl was that, although reports of overdoses from illicitly manufactured fentanyl tended to be lurid (often referring to the drug or its manufacturers as "serial killers"), this line of reportage rarely influenced the tone of stories about pharmaceutically used formulations. Even as reports of street-fentanyl fatalities peaked in the early 1990s, several newspapers ran positive pieces on the therapeutic potential of the fentanyl patch. Although there are several different ways in which this can be viewed, it is probably encouraging that abuse of fentanyl in one form did not automatically lead to the derogation of other forms.

4.4.5.3 Dextromethorphan

Table 4.4.3 shows a selective timeline of the evaluation, abuse, and regulation of DXM, a nonnarcotic cough suppressant with activity at sigma and PCP receptors. Unlike butorphanol and fentanyl, it has never been scheduled in the Controlled Substances Act, and it is available without a prescription in various over-the-counter formulations.

Who abused it? Most reports of abuse have involved teenagers either specifically seeking a dissociative/hallucinogenic experience or simply seeking any intoxicating effect. The pattern of abuse has generally been sporadic since the introduction of DXM in the 1950s, but reports of abuse have been more frequent and widespread since the mid-1990s, coinciding with the more rapid spread of information on the Internet.

Why was this pattern not predicted? As with butorphanol, initial abuse-liability studies were generally conducted in experienced abusers of mu-agonist opioids, and generally focused on whether DXM produced liking or euphoria and on whether it had morphine-like properties.[109,110] Participants in the first study[109] seemed completely insensitive to the acute dissociative effects of large single oral doses (up to 800 mg), and even when larger doses were used (up to 1800 mg),

Table 4.4.3 Dextromethorphan (DXM) Timeline

Year	Animal Data	Human Lab Data/Clinical Trials	Case Reports/Case Series/Surveys	News Items	Regulatory/Commercial Developments
before 1956					Romilar tablets (DXM-only preparation) not controlled, but require prescription in U.S.[168]
1956					FDA moves Romilar tablets from prescription status to OTC[168]
1962		s.c. and oral: No acute subjective effects in postaddict prisoners; chronic subjective effects all aversive; also, no effects of active metabolite DO[109]			
1964–1969			Sporadic abuse outside U.S.[169–171]		
1970					DXM exempted from Controlled Substances Act[17]
1971		s.c. and oral: Acute psychotomimetic effects in postaddict prisoners, but no increase in VAS Liking or ARCI MBG; Drug ID: barbiturate or amphetamine; Subjective effects: similar to nalorphine[110]			
ca. 1973					Romilar taken off market after increase in abuse[172]

Table 4.4.3   Dextromethorphan (DXM) Timeline (Continued)

Year	Animal Data	Human Lab Data/Clinical Trials	Case Reports/Case Series/Surveys	News Items	Regulatory/Commercial Developments
1976					DO removed from Schedule II
1982					WHO concludes no evidence to warrant control[173]
1986					DXM made prescription-only in Sweden after reports of teen abuse there[174]
1988			First known fatal ODs, in Sweden: one suicide, one possible abuse[175]		
1990			Case of Robitussin-drinking dependence in U.S. meeting DSM-IIIR criteria; patient's initial attempts to seek help are met with disbelief (pharmacist says that getting high on cough syrup is impossible)[176]		Hearings by Pennsylvania drug board, then FDA; Penn. board was asked to put DXM on Penn.'s Schedule V (limiting it to pharmacy or physician dispensing and to patients over 18); FDA reviews reports of abuse from several states; decides to leave control to states[177]
1991	In rats: DO induces PCP-like behavior, but DXM does not[178]				
1992			Two case reports of DXM-associated mania[179,180]	First newspaper mention of recreational use in U.S., in advice column[181]	
1993			Case report of mania[182] Abuse by two teenage boys in southern U.S.[183]	Harper's piece says abuse of DXM cough syrup is well known among teens but rarely written about[184]	

Year	Regulatory / Product	News / Media	Case reports / Epidemiology	Clinical studies	Animal pharmacology
1994		Another advice-column mention[186]; November: William White's DXM FAQ appears on Web[115]			In rats, DXM itself has PCP-like discriminative-stimulus effects[185]
1995		News report that DXM-syrup fad among teens is already declining in popularity;[138] another advice-column mention[189]	Case report of massive long-term ingestion of cough syrup[187]		
1996	Drixoral Cough Caps apparently discontinued		School survey in rural Pennsylvania: DXM-cough-syrup abuse fairly well known, first heard of in 1987[190]; Two cases of mania with daily use[191]		
1997–1998		A few more news reports on abuse of cough syrups (e.g. [196]) and sale of DXM by mail order (e.g., [197])	Abuse in Korea[193,194]; Two nonfatal ODs in California[195]		In rats, DXM has sedative effects and DO has PCP-like effects[192]
1999	DEA official says that upswing in DXM abuse is "out of our realm [of jurisdiction]"[202]	Reports on sales of pure DXM over Internet[201]	Retrospective case series of ODs in Switzerland[199] and Texas; increase shown in Texas[200]		In rats and rhesus monkeys, "DXM has some PCP-like effects, but they are produced more reliably by DO"[198]
2000	FDA official says that DXM is not approved for use outside marketed formulations[208]	More OD reports in news, concerning both OTC formulations and pure DXM; Web sites criticized[204–207]		Oral in 9 detoxified alcoholics and 10 healthy controls, DXM (2 mg/kg) has ethanol-like effects, with higher scores in controls[203]	
2001	Local efforts to move DXM preparations behind the counter[211]	Fatal OD on Coricidin[209] Suspicion that teens are distilling pure DXM from cough syrup[210]			

Table 4.4.3 Dextromethorphan (DXM) Timeline *(Continued)*

Year	Animal Data	Human Lab Data/Clinical Trials	Case Reports/Case Series/Surveys	News Items	Regulatory/Commercial Developments
2002		Oral: in 10 methadone-maintained inpatients, DXM (120, 240, and 480 mg/day for 4 days each to reduce methadone tolerance) induced some drowsiness; no changes in subjective effects or ARCI; several patients reported intoxication at the highest dose[212]	Poisoning in a youth who tried to extract DXM from cough syrup with "Agent Lemon" procedure[213]	More local reports of abuse by teens, e.g., in New Hampshire;[214] increase shown in ODs near Chicago[215]	Failed bill in North Dakota to ban sale of cough medicine to minors;[216] more pharmacists move DXM behind the counter[217]
2003			Case of liver toxicity from abuse of Coricidin, due to acetaminophen[114]	More ODs, at least one fatal;[218] another acetaminophen poisoning from abuse of an OTC preparation[113]	Bill in Texas to ban sale of cough medicine to minors and outlaw abuse; in committee;[219] Palo Alto high-school resource officer on one-man "crusade" to make pharmacy chains change shelf placement of DXM products;[220] Pharmacist in Iowa City puts DXM products behind the counter[221]

Note: See Table 4.4.1 for abbreviations.

no dissociative effects emerged, perhaps because the outcome instruments had not been designed to detect them. The primary effect of single doses was drowsiness. Only chronic dosing produced strong effects, described as "confusion" and "loss of memory"; the participants found these effects frightening. The second study[110] found slightly stronger evidence for acute effects, such as increases on the PCAG (sedation) and LSD (dysphoria) scales of the ARCI, but again, no measures were used that would have specifically identified dissociative effects, and the participants did not report liking the drug.

Comments: The clearest lesson from the DXM experience is that when designing an abuse-liability study, it is important to consider all possible effects that can make a drug abusable, bearing in mind that effects to which a particular study sample is insensitive or averse may be desired effects in others.

In the case of DXM, however, the desirability of the intoxicating effects appears to be confined largely to individuals in their teens and twenties — an observation consistent with the finding that the use of hallucinogens peaks at age 19 and then declines rapidly, regardless of birth cohort.[111] As a result of the drug's limited appeal, outbreaks of abuse have usually been self-limiting. This may be among the reasons that DXM remains unscheduled by the DEA and retains its over-the-counter status by FDA regulations. Several states have seen legislative efforts to restrict the availability of DXM either fail or become stalled. However, in 2006, legislation passed in Illinois banned the sale of DXM in pure form. Some pharmacists have chosen to keep DXM-containing preparations behind the counter, but this approach has been criticized because it forces recreational users underground rather than giving pharmacists a chance to engage them.[112] (In one newspaper report, a pharmacist stated that he had been able to dissuade two teenagers from buying and abusing DXM-containing cough syrup by warning them of its risks.[113] Whether they obtained the drug elsewhere is not known.) The response of manufacturers has been to discontinue sales of DXM-only cough formulations; this may discourage abuse, but may also increase toxicity from other ingredients such as acetaminophen when abuse does occur.[114]

As mentioned above, outbreaks of DXM abuse seem to have increased with the rise of the Internet. Literature reviews and newspaper articles on DXM have frequently included pejorative or alarmist comments about the abundance and inaccuracy of DXM-related information found on the Internet. Yet the seminal Internet document about DXM, William White's DXM FAQ (Frequently Asked Questions)[115] — first posted to Usenet newsgroups in 1994, and made available on the Web in November of that year — was exhaustive (with scholarly interpretations of hundreds of studies from peer-reviewed journals) and balanced (with the risks of DXM abuse emphasized throughout). If the mid-to-late-1990s upswing in DXM abuse is to be attributed partly to the Internet's ability to spread information widely, perhaps it should also be attributed to the tendency of some readers not to absorb information thoroughly.

4.4.6 Further Reading

To avoid redundancy with several recently published reviews, we have limited our discussion of techniques for abuse-liability assessment. Interested readers are referred to these reviews,[73,74,116–118] which appear in a special issue of the journal *Drug and Alcohol Dependence*.

Acknowledgment

Drs. Preston, Epstein, and Schmittner were supported by the NIH Intramural Research Program, NIDA.

REFERENCES

1. Zacny, J. et al., College on Problems of Drug Dependence taskforce on prescription opioid non-medical use and abuse: position statement, *Drug Alcohol Depend.*, 69, 215, 2003.
2. Abourashed, E.A. et al., Ephedra in perspective — a current review, *Phytother. Res.*, 17, 703, 2003.
3. Cunningham, J.K. and Liu, L.M., Impacts of federal ephedrine and pseudoephedrine regulations on methamphetamine-related hospital admissions, *Addiction*, 98, 1229, 2003.
4. SAMHSA, Nonmedical use of prescription-type drugs among youths and young adults, http://www.samhsa.gov/oas/2k3/prescription/prescription.htm, 2003. Accessed January 9, 2004.
5. SAMHSA, Overview of Findings from the 2002 National Survey on Drug Use and Health, http://www.samhsa.gov/oas/NHSDA/2k2NSDUH/Results/2k2results.htm, 2003. Accessed January 9, 2004.
6. SAMHSA, The DASIS report: Treatment admissions involving narcotic painkillers, http://www.samhsa.gov/oas/2k3/painTX/painTX.htm, 2003. Accessed January 9, 2004.
7. Hockenberg, S.J., American Nurses Association position statement on promotion of comfort and relief of pain in dying patients, *Plast. Surg. Nurs.*, 12, 32, 1992.
8. Kalso, E. et al., Recommendations for using opioids in chronic non-cancer pain, *Eur. J. Pain*, 7, 381, 2003.
9. Jacob, E., Pain management in sickle cell disease, *Pain Manage. Nurs.*, 2, 121, 2001.
10. Nunnelley, P.P., Prosecution or persecution? *Kans. Med. Assoc. J.*, 89, 311, 1991.
11. Gilson, A.M. and Joranson, D.E., U.S. policies relevant to the prescribing of opioid analgesics for the treatment of pain in patients with addictive disease, *Clin. J. Pain*, 18, S91, 2002.
12. Ziegler, S.J. and Lovrich, N.P., Jr., Pain relief, prescription drugs, and prosecution: a four-state survey of chief prosecutors, *J. Law Med. Ethics*, 31, 75, 2003.
13. Reidenberg, M.M., Effect of the requirement for triplicate prescriptions for benzodiazepines in New York State, *Clin. Pharmacol. Ther.*, 50, 129, 1991.
14. Morrison, R.S. et al., "We don't carry that" — failure of pharmacies in predominantly nonwhite neighborhoods to stock opioid analgesics, *New Engl. J. Med.*, 342, 1023, 2000.
15. British National Formulary, Diamorphine, http://bnf.org/bnf/bnf/current/noframes/3521.htm, 2003. Accessed January 12, 2004.
16. DEA, Title 21 USC excerpts, subchapter 1, part C, http://www.deadiversion.usdoj.gov/21cfr/21usc/21icusct.htm, 2003. Accessed January 8, 2004.
17. DEA, 21 USC, Section 811, http://www.deadiversion.usdoj.gov/21cfr/21usc/811.htm, 2003. Accessed January 8, 2004.
18. Meisch, R.A. and Lemaire, G.A., Drug self-administration, in *Methods in Behavioral Pharmacology*, F. van Haaren, Ed., Elsevier, Amsterdam, 1993.
19. Bozarth, M.A., Ed., *Methods of Assessing the Reinforcing Properties of Abused Drugs*, Springer-Verlag, New York, 1987.
20. Brady, J.V. and Lukas, S.E., Testing Drugs for Physical Dependence Potential and Abuse Liability. NIDA Research Monograph 52, 1984.
21. Brady, J.V. and Griffiths, R.R., Behavioral procedures for evaluating the relative abuse potential of CNS drugs in primates, *Fed. Proc.*, 35, 2245, 1976.
22. Woods, J. and Schuster, C.R., Reinforcement properties of morphine, cocaine and SPA as a function of unit dose, *Int. J. Addict.*, 3, 231, 1968.
23. Wilson, M.C., Hitomi, M., and Schuster, C.R., Psychomotor stimulant self-administration as a function of dosage per injection in the rhesus monkey, *Psychopharmacologia*, 22, 271, 1971.
24. Griffiths, R.R., Bigelow, G.E., and Henningfield, J.E., Similarities in animal and human drug-taking behavior, in *Advances in Substance Abuse*, N.K. Mello, Ed., JAI Press, Greenwich, CT, 1980, 1.
25. Woolverton, W. and Nader, M., Experimental evaluation of the reinforcing effects of drugs, *Mod. Meth. Pharmacol.*, 6, 165, 1990.
26. Stolerman, I.P. and Shine, P.J., Trends in drug discrimination research analysed with a cross-indexed bibliography, 1982–1983, *Psychopharmacology*, 86, 1, 1985.
27. Young, A., Discriminative stimulus profiles of psychoactive drugs, in *Advances in Substance Abuse*, N.K. Mello, Ed., Jessica Kingsley Publishers, London, 1991, 140.
28. Overton, D.A., Applications and limitations of the drug discrimination method for the study of drug abuse, in *Methods of Assessing the Reinforcing Properties of Abused Drugs*, M.A. Bozarth, Ed., Springer-Verlag, New York, 1987, 291.

29. Stolerman, I., Measures of stimulus generalization in drug discrimination experiments, *Behav. Pharmacol.*, 2, 265, 1991.

30. Stolerman, I., Drug discrimination, in *Methods in Behavioral Pharmacology*, F. van Harden, Ed., Elsevier Science, Amsterdam, 1993, 217.

31. Balster, R.L., Drug abuse potential evaluation in animals, *Brit. J. Addict.*, 86, 1549, 1991.

32. Holtzman, S.G., Discriminative stimulus effects of drug: relationship to abuse liability, in *Testing and Evaluation of Drugs of Abuse*, M.W. Adler and A. Cowan, Eds., Wiley-Liss, New York, 1990.

33. Kamien, J. et al., Drug discrimination by humans compared to nonhumans: current status and future directions, *Psychopharmacology*, 111, 259, 1993.

34. Bigelow, G.E. and Preston, K.L., Drug discrimination: methods for drug characterization and classification, *NIDA Res. Mon.*, 92, 101, 1989.

35. Preston, K.L. and Bigelow, G.E., Subjective and discriminative effects of drugs, *Behav. Pharmacol.*, 2, 293, 1991.

36. Evans, S.M. and Johanson, C., Amphetamine-like effects of anorectics and related compounds in pigeons, *J. Pharmacol. Exp. Ther.*, 241, 817, 1987.

37. Dykstra, L. et al., Discriminative stimulus properties of cocaine alone and in combination with buprenorphine, morphine and naltrexone, *Drug Alcohol Depend.*, 30, 227, 1992.

38. Garza, R.D. and Johanson, C.E., The discriminative stimulus properties of cocaine in the rhesus monkey, *Pharmacol. Biochem. Behav.*, 19, 145, 1983.

39. Jasinski, D.R., History of abuse liability testing in humans, *Br. J. Addict.*, 86, 1559, 1991.

40. Jasinski, D., Johnson, R., and Henningfield, J., Abuse liability assessment in human subjects, *Trends Pharmacol. Sci.*, 5, 196, 1984.

41. Haertzen, C., Development of scales based on patterns of drug effects, using the addiction research center inventory (ARCI), *Psychol. Rep.*, 18, 163, 1966.

42. Haertzen, C.A. and Hickey, J.E., Addiction Research Center Inventory (ARCI): measurement of euphoria and other drug effects, in *Methods for Assessing the Reinforcing Properties of Abused Drugs*, M.A. Bozarth, Ed., Springer-Verlag, New York, 1987.

43. McNair, D.M., Lorr, M., and Droppleman, L.F., *Manual for the Profile of Mood States,* Educational and Industrial Testing Service, San Diego, 1971.

44. de Wit, H. and Griffiths, R.R., Testing the abuse liability of anxiolytic and hypnotic drugs in humans, *Drug Alcohol Depend.*, 28, 83, 1991.

45. Jasinski, D.R., Assessment of the abuse potentiality of morphinelike drugs (methods used in man), in *Drug Addiction 1: Morphine, Sedative/Hypnotic and Alcohol Dependence*, W.R. Martin, Ed., Springer-Verlag, Berlin, 1977.

46. Johanson, C., Discriminative stimulus effects of buspirone in humans, *Exp. Clin. Psychopharmacol.*, 1, 173, 1993.

47. Zacny, J.P. and Goldman, R.E., Characterizing the subjective, psychomotor, and physiological effects of oral propoxyphene in non-drug-abusing volunteers, *Drug Alcohol Depend.*, 73, 133, 2004.

48. Koob, G.F. and Bloom, F.E., Cellular and molecular mechanisms of drug dependence, *Science*, 242, 715, 1988.

49. Haefely, W., Biological basis of drug-induced tolerance, rebound, and dependence. Contribution of recent research on benzodiazepines, *Pharmacopsychiatry*, 19, 353, 1986.

50. Wise, R.A. and Bozarth, M.A., A psychomotor stimulant theory of addiction, *Psychol. Rev.*, 94, 469, 1987.

51. Branch, M.N., Behavioral factors in drug tolerance, in *Methods in Behavioral Pharmacology*, F. van Haaren, Ed., Elsevier, Amsterdam, 1993.

52. Jasinski, D.B. and Mansky, P.A., Evaluation of nalbuphine for abuse potential, *Clin. Pharmacol. Ther.*, 13, 78, 1972.

53. Mello, N.K. and Mendelson, J.H., Buprenorphine suppresses heroin use by heroin addicts, *Science*, 207, 657, 1980.

54. Preston, K.L., Bigelow, G.E., and Liebson, I.A., Self-administration of clonidine, oxazepam, and hydromorphone by patients undergoing methadone detoxification, *Clin. Pharmacol. Ther.*, 38, 219, 1985.

55. Oldendorf, W.H., Some relationships between addiction and drug delivery to the brain, *NIDA Res. Mon.*, 120, 13, 1992.

56. Gossop, M. et al., Severity of dependence and route of administration of heroin, cocaine and amphetamines, *Br. J. Addict.*, 87, 1527, 1992.

57. Javaid, J.I. et al., Cocaine plasma concentration: Relation to physiological and subjective effects in humans, *Science*, 202, 227, 1978.

58. Van Dyke, C. et al., Oral cocaine: plasma concentrations and central effects, *Science*, 14, 211, 1978.

59. Perez-Reyes, M. et al., Free-base cocaine smoking, *Clin. Pharmacol. Ther.*, 32, 459, 1982.

60. Resnick, R.B., Kestenbaum, R.S., and Schwartz, L.K., Acute systemic effects of cocaine in man: a controlled study by intranasal and intravenous routes, *Science*, 195, 696, 1977.

61. Evans, S.M., Cone, E.J., and Henningfield, J.E., Arterial and venous cocaine plasma concentrations in human: relationship to route of administration, cardiovascular effects and subjective effects, *J. Pharmacol. Exp. Ther.*, 279, 1345, 1996.

62. Mayersohn, M. and Perrier, D., Kinetics of pharmacologic response to cocaine, *Res. Commun. Chem. Pathol.*, 22, 465, 1978.

63. de Wit, H., Bodker, B., and Ambre, J., Rate of increase of plasma drug level influences subjective response in humans, *Psychopharmacology*, 107, 352, 1992.

64. de Wit, H., Dudish, S., and Ambre, J., Subjective and behavioral effects of diazepam depend on its rate of onset, *Psychopharmacology*, 112, 324, 1993.

65. Cone, E.J. et al., Oxycodone involvement in drug abuse deaths: a DAWN-based classification scheme applied to an oxycodone postmortem database containing over 1000 cases, *J. Anal. Toxicol.*, 27, 57, 2003.

66. Vidal-Trecan, G. et al., Intravenous use of prescribed sublingual buprenorphine tablets by drug users receiving maintenance therapy in France, *Drug Alcohol Depend.*, 69, 175, 2003.

67. Roberge, R.J., Krenzelok, E.P., and Mrvos, R., Transdermal drug delivery system exposure outcomes, *J. Emerg. Med.*, 18, 147, 2000.

68. Talbott, G.D. et al., The Medical Association of Georgia's Impaired Physicians Program. Review of the first 1000 physicians: analysis of specialty, *J. Am. Med. Assoc.*, 257, 2927, 1987.

69. Gallegos, K.V. et al., Addiction in anesthesiologists: drug access and patterns of substance abuse, *QRB Qual. Rev. Bull.*, 14, 116, 1988.

70. Dose, M. and Tempel, H.D., Abuse potential of anticholinergics, *Pharmacopsychiatry*, 33, S43, 2000.

71. Buhrich, N., Weller, A., and Kevans, P., Misuse of anticholinergic drugs by people with serious mental illness, *Psychiatr. Serv.*, 51, 928, 2000.

72. Cox, D., Ahmed, Z., and McBride, A.J., Diphenhydramine dependence, *Addiction*, 96, 516, 2001.

73. Griffiths, R.R., Bigelow, G.E., and Ator, N.A., Principles of initial experimental drug abuse liability assessment in humans, *Drug Alcohol Depend.*, 70, S41, 2003.

74. Balster, R.L. and Bigelow, G.E., Guidelines and methodological reviews concerning drug abuse liability assessment, *Drug Alcohol Depend.*, 70, S13, 2003.

75. O'Neill, R.T., Biostatistical considerations in pharmacovigilance and pharmacoepidemiology: linking quantitative risk assessment in pre-market licensure application safety data, post-market alert reports and formal epidemiological studies, *Stat. Med.*, 17, 1851, 1998.

76. Hasford, J. and Lamprecht, T., Company observational post-marketing studies: drug risk assessment and drug research in special populations — a study-based analysis, *Eur. J. Clin. Pharmacol.*, 53, 369, 1998.

77. Corrigan, O.P., A risky business: the detection of adverse drug reactions in clinical trials and post-marketing exercises, *Soc. Sci. Med.*, 55, 497, 2002.

78. Ajayi, F.O., Sun, H., and Perry, J., Adverse drug reactions: a review of relevant factors, *J. Clin. Pharmacol.*, 40, 1093, 2000.

79. FDA, Medwatch home page, http://www.fda.gov/medwatch/index.html, 2004. Accessed January 8, 2004.

80. Arfken, C.L. and Cicero, T.J., Postmarketing surveillance for drug abuse, *Drug Alcohol Depend.*, 70, S97, 2003.

81. SAMHSA, DAWN: Drug Abuse Warning Network, http://dawninfo.samhsa.gov, 2004. Accessed January 8, 2004.

82. Roberts, C.D., Data quality of the Drug Abuse Warning Network, *Am. J. Drug Alcohol Abuse*, 22, 389, 1996.

83. SAMHSA, OAS data systems for alcohol, tobacco, and illegal drug use treatment, http://www.sam-hsa.gov/oas/p0000014.htm#NHSDA, 2003. Accessed January 9, 2004.

84. Woody, G.E. et al., An independent assessment of MEDWatch reporting for abuse/dependence and withdrawal from Ultram (tramadol hydrochloride), *Drug Alcohol Depend.*, 72, 163, 2003.

85. Senay, E.C. et al., Physical dependence on Ultram (tramadol hydrochloride): both opioid-like and atypical withdrawal symptoms occur, *Drug Alcohol Depend.*, 69, 233, 2003.

86. Cicero, T. et al., A postmarketing surveillance program to monitor Ultram (tramadol hydrochloride) abuse in the United States, *Drug Alcohol Depend.*, 57, 7, 1999.

87. Arfken, C.L., Schuster, C.R., and Johanson, C.E., Postmarketing surveillance of abuse liability of sibutramine, *Drug Alcohol Depend.*, 69, 169, 2003.

88. Markley, H.G., Chronic headache: appropriate use of opiate analgesics, *Neurology*, 44, S18, 1994.

89. Fisher, M.A. and Glass, S., Butorphanol (Stadol): a study in problems of current drug information and control, *Neurology*, 48, 1156, 1997.

90. Robbins, L., Stadol Nasal Spray — treatment for migraine? *Headache*, 33, 220, 1993.

91. Pachter, I.J. and Evens, R.P., Butorphanol, *Drug Alcohol Depend.*, 14, 325, 1985.

92. Shyu, W.C. et al., Multiple-dose phase I study of transnasal butorphanol, *Clin. Pharmacol. Ther.*, 54, 34, 1993.

93. Abboud, T. et al., Transnasal butorphanol: a new method for pain relief in post-cesarean section pain, *Acta Anaesth. Scand.*, 35, 14, 1991.

94. McCarthy, P.S. and Howlett, G.J., Physical dependence induced by opiate partial agonists in the rat, *Neuropeptides*, 5, 11, 1984.

95. Horan, P. and Ho, I.K., The physical dependence liability of butorphanol: a comparative study with morphine, *Eur. J. Pharmacol.*, 203, 387, 1991.

96. Conley, K.M. et al., Modulating effects of a cold water stimulus on opioid effects in volunteers, *Psychopharmacology*, 131, 313, 1997.

97. Flannagan, L.M., Butts, J.D., and Anderson, W.H., Fentanyl patches left on dead bodies — potential source of drug for abusers, *J. Forensic Sci.*, 41, 320, 1996.

98. Yerasi, A.B. and Butts, J.D., Disposal of used fentanyl patches, *Am. J. Health Syst. Ph.*, 54, 85, 1997.

99. Anderson, D.T. and Muto, J.J., Duragesic transdermal patch: postmortem tissue distribution of fentanyl in 25 cases, *J. Anal. Toxicol.*, 24, 627, 2000.

100. Marquardt, K.A. and Tharratt, R.S., Inhalation abuse of fentanyl patch, *Clin. Toxicol.*, 32, 75, 1994.

101. Arvanitis, M.L. and Satonik, R.C., Transdermal fentanyl abuse and misuse, *Am. J. Emerg. Med.*, 20, 58, 2002.

102. Purucker, M. and Swann, W., Potential for duragesic patch abuse, *Ann. Emerg. Med.*, 35, 314, 2000.

103. DeSio, J.M. et al., Intravenous abuse of transdermal fentanyl therapy in a chronic pain patient, *Anesthesiology*, 79, 1139, 1993.

104. Gorodetzky, C.W. and Martin, W.R., A comparison of fentanyl, droperidol, and morphine, *Clin. Pharmacol. Ther.*, 6, 731, 1965.

105. Shulte, F. and McVicar, N., Deputies investigate doctor in drug case, *Sun-Sentinel*, Fort Lauderdale, FL, p. 1B, March 22, 2003.

106. Zacny, J.P. et al., The effects of a cold-water immersion stressor on the reinforcing and subjective effects of fentanyl in healthy volunteers, *Drug Alcohol Depend.*, 42, 133, 1996.

107. Joranson, D.E. et al., Trends in medical use and abuse of opioid analgesics, *J. Am. Med. Assoc.*, 283, 1710, 2000.

108. Mahony, E., Stalking a "serial killer" narcotic from Boston to Wichita, *Hartford Courant*, Hartford, CT, p. A1, February 23, 1993.

109. Fraser, H. and Isbell, H., Human pharmacology and addictiveness of certain dextroisomers of synthetic analgesics, *B. Narcotics*, 14, 25, 1962.

110. Jasinski, D.R., Martin, W.R., and Mansky, P.A., Progress report on the assessment of the antagonists nalbuphine and GPA-2087 for abuse potential and studies of the effects of dextromethorphan in man, *CPDD*, 33, 143, 1971.

111. Chilcoat, H.D. and Schutz, C.G., Age-specific patterns of hallucinogen use in the U.S. population: an analysis using generalized additive models, *Drug Alcohol Depend.*, 43, 143, 1996.

112. Levy, S., How R.Ph.s can curb teens' abuse of cough and cold products, *Drug Topics*, 146, 31, 2002.

113. Leinwand, D., Latest trend in drug abuse: youths risk death for cough-remedy high, *USA Today*, p. 1A, December 29, 2003.

114. Kirages, T.J., Sule, H.P., and Mycyk, M.B., Severe manifestations of coricidin intoxication, *Am. J. Emerg. Med.*, 21, 473, 2003.

115. White, W.E., The dextromethorphan FAQ, http://www.erowid.org/chemicals/dxm/faq/, 1994. Accessed January 5, 2003.

116. Ator, N.A. and Griffiths, R.R., Principles of drug abuse liability assessment in laboratory animals, *Drug Alcohol Depend.*, 70, S55, 2003.

117. Mansbach, R.S. et al., Incorporating the assessment of abuse liability into the drug discovery and development process, *Drug Alcohol Depend.*, 70, S73, 2003.

118. Brady, K.T., Lydiard, R.B., and Brady, J.V., Assessing abuse liability in clinical trials, *Drug Alcohol Depend.*, 70, S87, 2003.

119. Jasinski, D.R. et al., Progress report on studies from the clinical pharmacology section of the addiction research center, *CPDD*, 121, 1975.

120. Jasinski, D.R. et al., Progress report on studies from the clinical pharmacology section of the addiction research center, *CPDD*, 112, 1976.

121. Jasinski, D.R. et al., Progress report from the clinical pharmacology section of the NIDA addiction research center, *CPDD*, 39, 133, 1977.

122. Jasinski, D., Pevnick, J., and Griffith, J., Human pharmacology and abuse potential of the analgesic buprenorphine, *Arch. Gen. Psychiatry*, 35, 501, 1978.

123. Howes, J.F., A simple, reliable method for predicting the physical dependence liability of narcotic antagonist analgesics in the rat, *Pharmacol. Biochem. Behav.*, 14, 689, 1981.

124. Lukas, S., Brady, J., and Griffiths, R., Comparison of opioid self-injection and disruption of schedule-controlled performance in the baboon, *J. Pharmacol. Exp. Ther.*, 238, 924, 1986.

125. Austin, R.P., Diversion of butorphanol, *Am. J. Hosp. Pharm.*, 40, 1306, 1983.

126. Smith, S.G. and Davis, W.M., Nonmedical use of butorphanol and diphenhydramine, *J. Am. Med. Assoc.*, 252, 1010, 1984.

127. Hoover, R.C. and Williams, R.B., Survey of butorphanol and nalbuphine diversion in U.S. hospitals, *Am. J. Hosp. Pharm.*, 42, 1111, 1985.

128. Evans, W.S. et al., A case of stadol dependence, *J. Am. Med. Assoc.*, 253, 2191, 1985.

129. Brown, G.R., Stadol dependence: another case, *J. Am. Med. Assoc*, 254, 910, 1985.

130. Preston, K. et al., Drug discrimination in human post-addicts: agonist/antagonist opioids, *NIDA Res. Mon.*, 81, 209, 1988.

131. Preston, K. et al., Drug discrimination in human postaddicts: agonist-antagonist opioids., *J. Pharmacol. Exp. Ther.*, 250, 184, 1989.

132. France, C. and Woods, J., Discriminative stimulus effects of naltrexone in morphine-treated rhesus monkeys, *J. Pharmacol. Exp. Ther.*, 250, 937, 1989.

133. Preston, K.L., Bigelow, G.E., and Liebson, I.A., Discrimination of butorphanol and nalbuphine in opioid-dependent humans, *Pharmacol. Biochem. Behav.*, 37, 511, 1990.

134. Sullivan, J.T. et al., Relative abuse liability and pharmacodynamics of transnasal and intramuscular butorphanol, *NIDA Res. Mon.*, 105, 452, 1991.

135. Preston, K.L. and Jasinski, D.R., Abuse liability studies of opioid agonist-antagonists in humans, *Drug Alcohol Depend.*, 28, 49, 1991.

136. Fukase, H. et al., Effects of morphine, naloxone, buprenorphine, butorphanol, haloperidol and imipramine on morphine withdrawal signs in cynomolgus monkeys, *Psychopharmacology*, 116, 396, 1994.

137. Preston, K.L. and Bigelow, G.E., Drug discrimination assessment of agonist-antagonist opioids in humans: a three-choice saline-hydromorphone-butorphanol procedure, *J. Pharmacol. Exp. Ther.*, 271, 48, 1994.

138. Zacny, J. et al., Comparing the subjective, psychomotor and physiological effects of intravenous butorphanol and morphine in healthy volunteers, *J. Pharmacol. Exp. Ther.*, 270, 579, 1994.

139. Knox, R.A., Complaints mount on migraine drug; nasal spray called highly addictive, *Boston Globe*, p. A1, May 27, 1997.

140. Anstett, P., A migraine drug's relief may come at a high price, *Detroit Free Press*, p. 1A, June 9, 1997.

141. Neergaard, L., Migraine drug Stadol said to be addictive, *Chattanooga Times*, p. A4, June 16, 1997.

142. Greenwald, M. and Stitzer, M., Butorphanol agonist effects and acute physical dependence in opioid abusers: comparison with morphine, *Drug Alcohol Depend.*, 53, 17, 1998.
143. Schlaepfer, T.E. et al., Site of opioid action in the human brain: mu and kappa agonists' subjective and cerebral blood flow effects, *Am. J. Psychiatry*, 155, 470, 1998.
144. Steele, K., Company faces wrongful-death suit, *Augusta Chronicle*, p. B2, April 18, 1998.
145. Preston, K.L. and Bigelow, G.E., Effects of agonist-antagonist opioids in humans trained in a hydro-morphone/not hydromorphone discrimination, *J. Pharmacol. Exp. Ther.*, 295, 114, 2000.
146. O'Hara, T., Deputy's pain imperils her job; the school resource officer called in a phony prescription for a painkiller to ease her migraines, *Sarasota Herald-Tribune*, p. B1, September 2, 2000.
147. Walsh, S.L. et al., Enadoline, a selective kappa opioid agonist: comparison with butorphanol and hydromorphone in humans, *Psychopharmacology*, 157, 151, 2001.
148. Vigoda, R., A young life cut short by an overdose, *Philadelphia Inquirer*, p. A1, November 1, 2001.
149. Oliveto, A. et al., Butorphanol and nalbuphine in opioid-dependent humans under a naloxone discrimination procedure, *Pharmacol. Biochem. Behav.*, 71, 85, 2002.
150. Smith, B., District court, *Patriot Ledger*, Quincy, MA, p. 16, April 9, 2002.
151. Poklis, A., Fentanyl: a review for clinical and analytical toxicologists, *Clin. Toxicol.*, 33, 439, 1995.
152. Lohmann, B., Drugged-out doctors find help among their peers, *Los Angeles Times*, p. 2, October 5, 1986.
153. Pekkanen, J., Doctors' horror stories of drug addiction, *Los Angeles Times*, p. 4, December 6, 1988.
154. Lewis, N., Navy lab chemist held in drug case; man linked to powerful heroin substitute, *Washington Post*, p. C1, September 11, 1986.
155. Hilts, P.J., Narcotic lollipop tested as pre-surgical sedative; critics say children get wrong message, *Washington Post*, p. A3, February 23, 1989.
156. Anonymous, Fentanyl patches are new drug on street, *Addict. Lett.*, 8, 3, 1992.
157. Leavitt, P., Potent, deadly heroin surfaces in 3 states, *USA Today*, p. 6A, February 4, 1991.
158. Tyre, P., "Serial Killers" made drug 1,000 times stronger than heroin, *The Gazette*, Montreal, p. A1, March 10, 1993.
159. Anonymous, Rangel bill would equate fentanyl with heroin, *Alcoholism Drug Abuse Week*, 4, 6, 1992.
160. Morris, S., Narcotic lollipop denounced; group urges FDA to block drug, says painkiller endangers kids' lives, *Chicago Tribune*, p. 1, January 26, 1994.
161. Hilts, P.J., A la-la pop for kids leaves a sour taste, *New York Times*, p. 2, January 30, 1994.
162. Braun, R., A special kind of lollipop, *Washington Post*, p. A18, February 12, 1994.
163. McQuillan, A., Drug OD killed med school star, *Daily News*, New York, p. 48, December 14, 1995.
164. Kuhlman, J.J., Jr. et al., Fentanyl use, misuse, and abuse: a summary of 23 postmortem cases, *J. Anal. Toxicol.*, 27, 499, 2003.
165. Anonymous, Woman gets 2-year term in nephew's drug death; man died after ingesting fentanyl, a pain medicine, *Baltimore Sun*, p. 5B, May 29, 2003.
166. Tomlinson, S., Assistant at nursing home accused in medicine thefts, *Oregonian*, p. B2, June 10, 2003.
167. Westmoore, P., Drugs evident in deaths of mother, son, *Buffalo News*, Buffalo, NY, p. B4, November 26, 2003.
168. Magurno, J.A.J. Personal communication to K.L. Preston, January 19, 1990.
169. Degkwitz, R., [Dextromethorphan (Romilar) as an Intoxicating Agent], *Nervenarzt*, 35, 412, 1964.
170. Dodds, A. and Revai, E., Toxic psychosis due to dextromethorphan, *Med. J. Australia*, 2, 231, 1967.
171. Bornstein, S., Czermak, M., and Postel, J., [Apropos of a case of voluntary drug poisoning dextromethorphan hydrobromide], *Ann. Med-Psychol.*, 1, 447, 1968.
172. Shulgin, A.T., Drugs of abuse in the future, *Clin. Toxicol.*, 8, 405, 1975.
173. Fleming, P.M., Dependence on dextromethorphan hydrobromide, *Br. Med. J.*, 293, 597, 1986.
174. Bem, J.L. and Peck, R., Dextromethorphan. An overview of safety issues, *Drug Saf.*, 7, 190, 1992.
175. Rammer, L., Holmgren, P., and Sandler, H., Fatal intoxication by dextromethorphan: a report on two cases, *Forensic Sci. Int.*, 37, 233, 1988.
176. Helfer, J. and Kim, O.M., Psychoactive abuse potential of Robitussin-DM, *Am. J. Psychiatry*, 147, 672, 1990.
177. FDA, Drug Abuse Advisory Committee, Open Session, Vol. 1, Public Health Service, Washington, D.C., 1990.

178. Szekely, J.I., Sharpe, L.G., and Jaffe, J.H., Induction of phencyclidine-like behavior in rats by dextrorphan but not dextromethorphan, *Pharmacol. Biochem. Behav.*, 40, 381, 1991.
179. Mendez, M.F., Mania self-induced with cough syrup, *J. Clin. Psychiatry*, 53, 173, 1992.
180. Craig, D.F., Psychosis with Vicks Formula 44-D abuse, *CMAJ*, 146, 1199, 1992.
181. Graedon, J. and Graedon, T., Some kids overdose on cough medicine, *St. Louis Post-Dispatch*, p. 3D, January 27, 1992.
182. Walker, J. and Yatham, L.N., Benylin (dextromethorphan) abuse and mania, *Br. Med. J.*, 306, 896, 1993.
183. Murray, S. and Brewerton, T., Abuse of over-the-counter dextromethorphan by teenagers, *South. Med. J.*, 86, 1151, 1993.
184. Hogshire, J., The electric cough-syrup acid test, *Harper's*, p. 24, June, 1993.
185. Holtzman, S., Discriminative stimulus effects of dextromethorphan in the rat, *Psychopharmacology*, 116, 249, 1994.
186. Graedon, J. and Graedon, T., Cough medicine shouldn't be taken for depression, *St. Louis Post-Dispatch*, p. 4E, March 21, 1994.
187. Wolfe, T.R. and Caravati, E.M., Massive dextromethorphan ingestion and abuse, *Am. J. Emerg. Med.*, 13, 174, 1995.
188. Hinderer, J., Teens misusing medicine to get high, *Bismarck Tribune*, North Dakota, p. 12A, February 8, 1995.
189. Graedon, J. and Graedon, T., Cough syrup may heighten delusions, *Austin American-Statesman*, Texas, p. F3, October 3, 1995.
190. Darboe, M.N., Keenan, G.R., Jr., and Richards, T.K., The abuse of dextromethorphan-based cough syrup: a pilot study of the community of Waynesboro, Pennsylvania, *Adolescence*, 31, 633, 1996.
191. Polles, A. and Griffith, J.L., Dextromethorphan-induced mania, *Psychosomatics*, 37, 71, 1996.
192. Dematteis, M., Lallement, G., and Mallaret, M., Dextromethorphan and dextrorphan in rats: common antitussives — different behavioural profiles, *Fund. Clin. Pharmacol.*, 12, 526, 1998.
193. Chung, H.S. et al., Demographic characteristics of zipeprol-associated deaths in Korea, *Arch. Pharm. Res.*, 21, 286, 1998.
194. Chung, H., Drug abuse trends and epidemiological aspects of drug associated deaths in Korea, *J. Toxicol. Sci.*, 23, S197, 1998.
195. Nordt, S.P., "DXM": a new drug of abuse? *Ann. Emerg. Med.*, 31, 794, 1998.
196. Warner, G., Parents credit facilities with saving son's life, *Buffalo News*, New York, p. 4B, April 12, 1997.
197. Anonymous, Homestead teen provided cough syrup ingredient to friend, who passed out, *Milwaukee Journal Sentinel*, p. 2, February 17, 1998.
198. Nicholson, K.L., Hayes, B.A., and Balster, R.L., Evaluation of the reinforcing properties and phencyclidine-like discriminative stimulus effects of dextromethorphan and dextrorphan in rats and rhesus monkeys, *Psychopharmacology*, 146, 49, 1999.
199. Betschart, T. et al., Dose-dependent toxicity of dextromethorphan overdose, *Clin. Toxicol.*, 38, 190, 2000.
200. Baker, S.D. and Borys, D.J., A possible trend suggesting increased abuse from Coricidin exposures reported to the Texas Poison Network: comparing 1998 to 1999, *Vet. Hum. Toxicol.*, 44(3), 169–171, 2002.
201. Fischer, M., Large amounts of a legal drug bought on the Web sickened four teenagers Wednesday, *Philadelphia Inquirer*, p. B1, January 8, 1999.
202. Smith, A.J., We're still losing the "drug war," *Ventura County Star*, California, p. B7, July 26, 1999.
203. Schutz, C.G. and Soyka, M., Dextromethorphan challenge in alcohol-dependent patients and controls, *Arch. Gen. Psychiatry*, 57, 291, 2000.
204. Blum, A., Cough syrup abuse on rise; Internet sites exacerbate problem, *Capital-Gazette*, Annapolis, MD, p. C1, January 6, 2000.
205. Goetz, K., Kids abuse cough pills, *Cincinnati Enquirer*, p. 1D, February 18, 2000.
206. Mangalindian, M., Alleged drug sale on Ebay raises liability issue, *Wall Street Journal*, p. B18, May 30, 2000.
207. Ochs, R., Cough-medicine high: a new worry in teenage drug abuse, *Newsday*, New York, p. C4, November 7, 2000.

208. Schultz, S. and Kleiner, C., Turning to anything, just to get that high, *U.S. News & World Report*, p. 60, June 5, 2000.
209. Branton, J., Police report: overdose of cold pills killed teen, tests say, *The Columbian*, Vancouver, WA, p. C3, January 4, 2001.
210. Parrish, A., DXM, Ritalin become drugs of choice for some BA students, *Tulsa World*, Oklahoma, p. February 3, 2001.
211. Anon., Monitoring of cough drug urged, *Wilkes Barre Times Leader*, p. 11A, November 4, 2001.
212. Cornish, J.W. et al., A randomized, double-blind, placebo-controlled safety study of high-dose dextromethorphan in methadone-maintained male inpatients, *Drug Alcohol Depend.*, 67, 177, 2002.
213. Roll, D. and Tsipis, G., "Agent lemon": a new twist on dextromethorphan toxicity, *Clin. Toxicol.*, 40, 655, 2002.
214. Anonymous, Police are alarmed by abuse of cold medication, *Union Leader*, Manchester, NH, p. B3, December 10, 2002.
215. Anon., Be alert to new teen drug threat, *Chicago Daily Herald*, p. 8, May 7, 2002.
216. Brown, K., Bill would ban cough medicine sales to minors, *Bismarck Tribune*, North Dakota, p. 7A, February 13, 2003.
217. Hall, S., Teen abuse of cold drug on the rise; many pharmacies relocate Coricidin behind the counter, *Detroit News*, p. 1A, March 14, 2002.
218. Simpson, K., Coroner's jury rules man's death accidental, *Pantagraph*, Bloomington, IL, p. A4, December 13, 2003.
219. Stone, R., Bill targets cough medicine abuse; intoxicant would be denied to teenagers, *San Antonio Express-News*, Texas, p. 4B, January 11, 2003.
220. Seyfer, J. and Wong, N.C., Cold medicine crusade, *San Jose Mercury News*, California, p. B1, February 17, 2003.
221. Fullerton, S., OTC drugs going BTC at pharmacy, *Iowa City Press-Citizen*, p. 11A, September 23, 2003.

CHAPTER 5

Alcohol

Edited by Alan Wayne Jones, D.Sc.

Department of Forensic Toxicology, University Hospital, Linköping, Sweden

CONTENTS

INTRODUCTION

This chapter provides an overview of clinical and forensic-medical aspects of man's favorite recreational drug, alcohol (ethanol or ethyl alcohol). Consumption of alcoholic beverages is increasing worldwide as are many of the undesirable consequences of heavy drinking and drunkenness. The effects produced by alcohol depend on the amounts consumed and the speed of drinking. Small quantities cause euphoria and feelings of well-being whereas large amounts and high blood-alcohol concentration (BAC) depress the central nervous system and cause a decrement in performance and behavior, especially when skilled tasks like driving are concerned.

The various sections of this chapter reflect different areas of interest for both forensic scientists and clinical and forensic toxicologists. The acute effects of alcohol are major concerns for motor and cognitive functioning, which is important for traffic safety because alcohol intoxication and drunkenness are incriminated in many fatal crashes. Enforcement of drinking and driving laws throughout the world depends to a large extent on the concentration of alcohol measured in a specimen of blood, breath, or urine obtained from the suspect. This kind of "chemical testing" to produce evidence for prosecution requires the use of highly reliable analytical methods to guarantee legal security for the individual. The widespread adoption of concentration per se laws for driving under the influence of alcohol tends to create a razor sharp difference in penalty for those close to the statutory limit. Small analytical or pre-analytical errors might make the difference between acquittal or punishment in borderline cases.

In addition to details of the analytical methods used to measure alcohol in body fluids, knowledge is also required about the disposition and fate of alcohol in the body and the factors influencing absorption, distribution, and elimination processes. Alcohol also tops the list of drugs encountered in post-mortem toxicology. Although the methods of analysis are the same as for living subjects, making a correct interpretation of the results is often problematic. When dealing with autopsy specimens, various artifacts can arise because of the poor quality of blood and body fluid specimen, post-mortem diffusion and redistribution, sampling site differences, and the risk of post-mortem synthesis owing to microbial activity.

Judging whether a person drinks too much alcohol is not always easy because many people deny that they have a drinking problem. This complicates making an early diagnosis and commencement of treatment for those at greatest risk of becoming dependent on alcohol. Clearly there is an urgent need to develop more objective ways to verify overconsumption of alcohol. Considerable research effort has been devoted to evaluate biochemical tests with enough sensitivity and specificity to detect hazardous drinking before this escalates to the point of causing organ and tissue damage. The final section of this chapter describes recent advances in the field of alcohol biomarkers that are intended to disclose both acute and chronic consumption of alcohol as well as relapse after a period of rehabilitation.

5.1 MEASURING ACUTE ALCOHOL IMPAIRMENT

Christopher S. Martin, Ph.D.
Western Psychiatric Institute and Clinic, Department of Psychiatry, University of Pittsburgh School of
Medicine, Pittsburgh, Pennsylvania

This section reviews impairment produced by alcohol consumption, and issues in the measurement of such impairment. Motor and cognitive impairment produced by alcohol intoxication has been noted for centuries, and is apparent to almost everyone who lives in an alcohol drinking society. The effects of alcohol consumption on behavior, cognition, and mood have been reviewed by several authors in the scientific literature.[1-4] Unlike previous reviews, this section focuses on medical and forensic aspects of the topic, with a particular emphasis on impairment testing.

Impairment and its consequences are major reasons for forensic and medical interest in alcohol consumption. The assessment of impairment caused by acute alcohol intoxication is important for forensic, research, and clinical applications. At the same time, the determinants of impaired performance are complex, and are influenced by numerous pharmacological, motivational, and situational factors. Impairment also is extremely variable between persons. While obvious at extreme levels, alcohol-related impairment raises a number of difficult measurement issues. Although many impairment tests have adequate properties in the laboratory, assessments used in field applications have important limitations.

This section begins with a review of the acute effects of alcohol on behavioral and cognitive functioning. Emphasis is given to the effects of alcohol on speech and on the functioning of the vestibular system, which is centrally involved in balance control and spatial orientation. Next, individual differences in impairment are examined. This is followed by a description of how impairment is related to the time course of alcohol ingestion. The effects of rising vs. falling blood alcohol concentrations (BACs) and acute tolerance are discussed. The behavioral correlates of a hangover are reviewed. Then we discuss the ideal characteristics of impairment tests, followed by a description of the actual characteristics of impairment tests when evaluated in laboratory and field settings.

5.1.1 Behavioral Correlates of Acute Intoxication

This section reviews the effects of alcohol on motor coordination and cognitive performance. Most "behavioral" correlates of intoxication involve both motor control and cognitive functioning. As will be seen, the effects of alcohol are not uniform; impairment varies across different types of behavioral functions. Two areas of functioning that are sensitive to alcohol impairment and assessed in field sobriety tests are described in some detail: speech and vestibular functioning. In addition, this section describes individual differences in alcohol impairment related to age, gender, and alcohol consumption practices.

5.1.1.1 Motor Control and Cognitive Functioning

Alcohol functions as a general central nervous system depressant, and affects a wide range of functions. To the observer, one of the most apparent effects of alcohol consumption is on motor control, particularly behaviors that require fine motor coordination. Other well-known effects of alcohol involve decrements in the cognitive control of behavioral functioning, especially the ability to perform and coordinate multiple tasks at the same time. Research has assessed the effects of alcohol on numerous performance tasks. Almost all of these tasks involve both cognitive and motor control components, although tasks differ in the complexity of the motor and cognitive functioning required for performance.

Reaction Time

Some of the most basic performance tasks investigated in the literature are simple reaction time (RT) tasks, in which subjects must push a button as quickly and accurately as possible in response to a stimulus. Baylor et al.[5] found no effects of alcohol on simple RT at BACs of 100 mg/dL, but did find effects at very high BACs near 170 mg/dL. Taberner[6] found no effect of a low dose of 0.15 g/kg alcohol, and a small effect at a dose of 0.76 g/kg alcohol. Maylor et al.[7] found a small effect of alcohol on simple RT at a dose of 0.64 g/kg alcohol. Linnoila et al.[8] did not find effects of alcohol on simple RT, even though other types of performance were impaired at this dose. Although the findings are somewhat variable, simple RT appears to be relatively insensitive to alcohol consumption.

Other research has examined choice RT tasks, in which subjects are required to respond using two or more buttons in response to different stimuli. Such tasks involve motor speed as well as cognitive functions involved in categorizing a stimulus and choosing a response. Few differences were seen by Fagan et al.[9] on a six-choice RT procedure. Golby[10] found no effects of alcohol on two different choice RT tasks. Other studies have found rather small or inconsistent effects of alcohol on choice RT.[7,11] Overall, there is not consistent evidence that alcohol affects the performance of choice RT tasks in the range of BACs studied in laboratory experiments.

The research literature contains a number of studies that have examined the effects of alcohol on tracking performance, that is, the ability of subjects to move a pointer to track a moving target. Tracking tasks require fine motor control and coordination of the hands and eyes at a rapid speed. There is consistent evidence that alcohol significantly impairs tracking performance. Beirness and Vogel-Sprott[12] found that alcohol affected tracking performance at BACs above 50 mg/dL; this effect has been replicated in numerous studies by Vogel-Sprott and colleagues. Wilson et al.[13] found that BACs peaking at 100 mg/dL produced tracking impairments for 120 minutes after drinking relative to placebo. The effects of alcohol on tracking performance have been found by several other authors.[8,11,14,15]

Dual-Task Performance

Alcohol impairment is found consistently during dual-task performance, when subjects are required to perform multiple tasks simultaneously. When subjects were required to perform a tracking task and an RT task at the same time, Connors and Maisto[11] found that alcohol reduced tracking but not RT performance. Using a similar procedure, Maylor et al.[14] found that alcohol affected RT but not tracking. Differences between these two studies in the task that was affected may have been due to instructions or task demands that led subjects to select one of the two tasks as primary, leading to performance deficits on the secondary task. Niaura et al.[16] combined an RT task with a task requiring the subject to circle target characters on a printed sheet, and found that alcohol produced deficits on both tasks relative to placebo. Other researchers have used computerized divided-attention tasks, which require subjects to perform multiple functions simultaneously. Mills and Bisgrove[17] found that divided-attention performance (responding to numbers on central and peripheral monitors by pushing different buttons) was impaired after 0.76 g/kg alcohol, but not after a lower dose of 0.37 g/kg alcohol.

The performance of multiple challenging tasks is thought to require the utilization of a large amount of attention, defined as limited-capacity cognitive resources that are required for effortful processing. The demonstration that alcohol produces dual-task performance deficits is consistent with the idea that alcohol produces impairment, in part, by reducing the available amount of limited-capacity attentional resources. A similar "attention allocation" model was proposed by Steele and Josephs.[18] These authors found that alcohol produced clear deficits in secondary task performance without affecting primary task performance, and suggested that alcohol serves to allocate a greater amount of attentional resources to a primary task, leading to fewer resources available for processing secondary sources of information.

Other studies of the behavioral impairment produced by alcohol have used tests designed to simulate complex real-world behaviors such as driving. Accident statistics consistently demonstrate that crash risk in the natural environment increases significantly when BACs are above 40 mg/dL.[19] Automobile simulator studies generally find that the information processing and lateral guidance demands of driving are adversely affected by alcohol. Several well-designed laboratory studies have demonstrated adverse affects of alcohol on skills related to driving, beginning with BACs as low as 30 to 40 mg/dL.[15,20] Other research with automobile simulators has examined the effects of alcohol on risk taking, defined by levels of speed, cars overtaken, and number of accidents during simulated driving. McMillen et al.[21] did not find effects of alcohol on risk taking during a driving simulation, whereas Mongrain and Standing[22] did find that alcohol increased risk taking, albeit at very high BACs near 160 mg/dL.

The effects of alcohol on performance have also been studied under conditions of actual driving. Attwood et al.[23] found that performance variables such as velocity and lane position together discriminated between intoxicated and sober drivers. Huntley found decreased lateral guidance during a driving task after alcohol.[24] Brewer and Sandow[25] studied real accidents using driver and witness testimony. Among persons who were in accidents, those with BACs above 50 mg/dL were much more likely to have been engaged in a secondary activity at the time of the accident, compared to drivers with BACs below 50 mg/dL. Overall, it appears that alcohol adversely affects several types of behavioral functions involved in driving. Driving performance is complex and determined by a number of individual and situational factors and roadway conditions. More research is needed to better understand alcohol's effects on driving performance.

5.1.1.2 Speech

It is well known to bartenders, law enforcement personnel, and the general public that alcohol consumption can produce changes in speech production often described as "slurred speech." Because speech production requires fine motor control, timing, and coordination of the lips, tongue, and vocal cords, it may be a sensitive index of impairment resulting from alcohol intoxication. Having subjects recite the alphabet at a fast rate of speed is a well-known field sobriety test. Laboratory research suggests that speech can be a valid index of alcohol consumption. After consuming 10 oz of 86-proof alcohol, alcoholics were found to take longer to read a passage and had more word, phrase, and sound interjections, word omissions, word revisions, and broken suffixes in their speech.[26] Other research with nonalcoholic drinkers found that under intoxication, subjects made more sentence-level, word-level, and sound-level errors during spontaneous speech.[27,28] Intoxicated talkers consistently lengthen some speech sounds, particularly consonants in unstressed syllables.[29] The overall rate of speech also slows when intoxicated talkers read sentences and paragraphs.[27,30]

Pisoni and Martin[30] examined the acoustic-phonetic properties of speech for matched pairs of sentences spoken by social drinkers when sober and after achieving BACs above 100 mg/dL. Sentence duration was increased after drinking, and pitch (loudness), while not consistently higher or lower, was more variable. The strongest effects of alcohol at the sound level were for speech sounds that require fine motor control and timing of articulation events in close temporal proximity. Intoxicated talkers displayed difficulty in controlling the abrupt closures and openings of the vocal tract required for stops and affricate closures. This resulted in long durations of closures before voiced stops (e.g., /d/, /b/), and the complete absence of closures before affricates (e.g., the /ch/ in "church"). These effects are consistent with what is known about the degree of precision of motor control mechanisms required for the articulation of different speech sounds. Pisoni and Martin[30] also found that listeners can reliably discriminate speech produced while sober and under intoxication. State Troopers showed higher discrimination levels than other listeners, suggesting that experience in detecting intoxication may increase perceptual abilities. The approach of some field sobriety tests that have persons recite the alphabet quickly may effectively capture the detrimental effects of alcohol on the articulation of speech sounds in close temporal proximity.

Despite the data showing effects of alcohol on speech, there are a number of limitations that make it difficult to use speech production as an index of alcohol impairment. Changes in speech have been reliably produced with blood alcohol levels above 100 mg/dL; however, the effects of lower doses have been variable;[27–29] it is not clear whether reliable effects are produced in most persons when BACs are lower. Other types of impairment are likely to occur before speech is noticeably affected. It is not clear from the literature how motivation to avoid the detection of intoxication would affect speech production. Furthermore, the specificity of speech changes to alcohol intoxication (rather than fatigue, stress, etc.) needs further study. Finally, there is extreme variability between persons in the acoustic-phonetic properties of speech, such that it is difficult to estimate the degree of impairment without comparison samples of sober speech.[31] Despite these limitations, the literature suggests that speech is likely to be a good screening test for impairment, which can then be determined using other measures.

5.1.1.3 Vestibular Functioning

The vestibular system serves to maintain spatial orientation and balance, and eye movements that support these functions. The vestibular system is comprised of two sets of interconnected canals that provide information about spatial orientation. Each canal is comprised of a membrane embedded with sensory hair cells, and a surrounding extracellular fluid. The otolithic canals provide information about the direction of gravity relative to the head, and thus are sensitive to lateral (side to side) head movements. This is accomplished by the fact that the membrane has a specific gravity that is twice that of the extracellular space in otoliths. Under normal conditions, the semicircular canals are sensitive to rotational movements of the head, and do not respond to lateral movements. In semicircular canals, the membrane and the extracellular fluid have the same exact specific gravity (i.e., weight by volume), such that the hair cells have neutral buoyancy and are not subject to gravitational influences.[32]

Positional Alcohol Nystagmus (PAN)

Alcohol's effects on the vestibular system are seen in measures that evaluate oculo-motor control, i.e., the functional effectiveness of eye movements under different conditions. During alcohol consumption, many persons show significant nystagmus (jerkiness) in eye movements when the head is placed in a sideways position: this effect is known as Positional Alcohol Nystagmus (PAN). There are two types of PAN. PAN I is characterized by a nystagmus to the right when the right side of the head is down, and to the left when the left side of the head is down. PAN I normally occurs during rising and peak BACs, beginning around 40 mg/dL.[33] PAN II normally appears between 5 and 10 hours after drinking, and is characterized by nystagmus in the opposite directions seen in PAN I.[34]

The mechanisms of PAN I and II have been convincingly demonstrated.[35] Both types of PAN are produced by the effects of alcohol on the semicircular canals, making hair cells on the membrane responsive to the effects of gravity. As alcohol diffuses throughout the water compartments of the body, it first enters the membrane space (which is richly supplied with capillary blood), and diffuses only gradually into the extracellular fluid. For a time, the alcohol concentration is greater in membrane than the surrounding fluid. Because alcohol is lighter than water, the specific gravity of the membrane will be lighter than that of the surrounding fluid during this time, making the semicircular canals responsive to gravity and producing PAN I. The faster the rate of drinking, the faster PAN I appears.[36]

There is a period during descending BACs in which neither PAN I nor PAN II is apparent; during this time the semicircular membrane and the surrounding fluid have achieved equilibrium, and have the same specific gravity. PAN II occurs during alcohol elimination and after the body has no measurable amounts of alcohol. During PAN II, alcohol in the semicircular canals is removed from the membrane faster than the surrounding fluid; this results in the membrane having a heavier specific gravity than the surrounding fluid, which in turn produces PAN II.

Both PAN I and II may overstimulate the semicircular canals in a manner similar to motion sickness.[35] It is possible that the effects of alcohol on the semicircular canals play a central role in many symptoms of intoxication, including feelings of dizziness, nausea, and the experience of vertigo known as the "bedspins." Laboratory studies have shown that the magnitude of PAN I is associated with higher BACs,[36] with greater impairment in postural control, and with higher subjective intoxication ratings.[37] As described later, it has been speculated that PAN II is associated with hangover.[35]

Horizontal Gaze Nystagmus (HGN)

Another type of nystagmus produced by alcohol is known as Horizontal Gaze Nystagmus (HGN). HGN is defined by jerkiness in eye movements as gaze is directed to the side, when the head is in an upright position. HGN has long been noted as an effect of alcohol, and usually becomes apparent when rising BACs reach about 80 mg/dL.[38] HGN is assessed by having a subject follow an object with their eyes at an increasingly eccentric angle, without moving the head; the smallest angle at which nystagmus first appears is used to assess intoxication. While nystagmus occurs in a sober state at more extreme angles of eccentric gaze, alcohol decreases the size of the angle at which it is first apparent.

As with PAN, it has been demonstrated that HGN is highly associated with the effects of alcohol, as seen in studies of oculo-motor control.[39] Lehti[40] reported high correlations of BACs and the angle at which nystagmus in eccentric gaze became apparent. Similar effects of alcohol have been seen when nystagmus is assessed during active and passive head movements.[41] Tharp et al.[42] quantified the slope of a regression line predicting angle of onset of nystagmus from BAC. The angle of nystagmus onset was predicted at 45° for BACs of 50 mg/dL; 40° for BACs of 100 mg/dL; and 35° for BACs of 150 mg/dL. The angle of horizontal nystagmus onset has been found to have a high level of sensitivity and specificity in predicting BACs above 100 mg/dL in an emergency room setting.[43] HGN appears to be pharmacologically specific to alcohol. This is not the case for other aspects of occular control such as smooth pursuit. Smooth pursuit eye movements have proven to be much more sensitive to alcohol compared with marijuana, which has very small effects.[44] However, smooth pursuit eye movements are significantly affected by benzodiazapines, barbiturates, and antihistamines,[45] and thus cannot be said to be pharmcologically specific to alcohol. Deficits in smooth pursuit in the absence of significant BACs may indicate that a person has taken sedative drugs.

Postural control tasks are some of the most widely used measures of alcohol-related impairment in the laboratory and in the field. It is likely that the functional effectiveness of the vestibular system is an important locus of the effects of alcohol on postural control. Numerous studies have demonstrated that alcohol consumption leads to increases in sway as measured on a variety of balance platforms and similar types of apparatus, appearing in many drinkers at BACs of 30 to 50 mg/dL.[9,13,46,47] Other research has shown that sway increases with alcohol dose,[17,48,49] and that heavier drinkers sway less after alcohol compared to lighter drinkers.[48] The effects of alcohol become greater as the postural control task becomes more difficult, such as with eyes closed, or when the feet are in a heel-to-toe position.[49] Thus, postural control appears to be a sensitive index of alcohol effects. However, body sway shows a great deal of individual variation in a sober condition. For this reason, the ability to detect impairment from measuring sway is limited in field settings in which sober performance measures are not available.

5.1.1.4 Individual Differences

There are large individual differences in the impairment produced by alcohol consumption. The first and most obvious difference is that persons differ in the BACs they achieve when drinking alcohol. Even when controlling for BAC, however, there are large differences between persons in their sensitivity to alcohol impairment. Perhaps the most important factor is drinking practices. Those who drink more often and in greater amounts tend to develop a greater amount of tolerance to the impairing effects of alcohol, i.e., have an acquired decrease in the degree of impairment across multiple drinking sessions. Greater impairment in light drinkers compared to heavier drinkers has been shown by numerous authors using a variety of performance tasks.[4,48,50]

There are also gender differences in some aspects of alcohol pharmacokinetics. On average, women achieve significantly higher BACs than men when drinking the same amount of alcohol because of mean gender differences in body weight and body fat,[50] and because females tend to have lower levels of gastric alcohol dehydrogenase.[51] Some research with women has found greater alcohol elimination rates[52] and greater sensitivity to alcohol effects[53,54] during the mid-luteal and ovulatory phases of the menstrual cycle compared to the follicular phase. Other research, however, has not replicated these findings.[16,55,56]

Some laboratory studies have examined whether males and females differ in their sensitivity to alcohol. Mills and Bisgrove[17] found no gender differences in a divided-attention task after a low dose of alcohol, but greater impairment in females at a higher dose. However, in this study women achieved higher BACs, and reported less alcohol consumption compared to men. Burns and Moskowitz[57] found no significant gender differences in a series of motor and cognitive impairment tasks. When controlling for BACs, Niaura et al.[11] found few gender differences in psychomotor and cognitive responses to alcohol. Other research that controlled for gender differences in BACs and drinking practices has found few gender differences in response to alcohol.[58] Overall, when controlling for BACs and drinking practices, gender differences in alcohol impairment have not been demonstrated.

Little research has examined differences in alcohol impairment that are related to age. Using groups with fairly equivalent drinking practices, Parker and Noble[59] found that older subjects (over 42 years old) had more deficits on abstracting and problem solving after alcohol consumption compared to younger subjects. Linnoila et al.[8] found a trend towards increased impairment in subjects who were 25 to 35 years old, compared to those 20 to 25 years old. Other studies have also found age-related increases in psychomotor impairment in humans,[60,61] and in animals,[62] even when BACs and drinking practices were equivalent in older and younger groups. Although there appears to be an increase in sensitivity to alcohol's effects with advancing age, there are few studies, and most suffer from small sample sizes. Because age effects appear to occur even when BACs and drinking practices are controlled, some have speculated that age-related increases in alcohol impairment reflect the effects of aging on vulnerability of the central nervous system to alcohol's effects.[62]

5.1.2 Time of Ingestion

The effects of alcohol tend to vary dramatically over the time course of a drinking episode. An analysis of how the effects of alcohol change over time provides a clearer understanding of alcohol-related impairment. This section reviews differences in the effects of alcohol during the rising and falling limbs of the BAC curve, the phenomenon of acute tolerance, and post-drinking hangover.

5.1.2.1   Rising and Falling Blood Alcohol Concentrations

Researchers and clinicians have long noted that alcohol's effects are often biphasic during a drinking episode.[63] "Biphasic" refers to the fact that stimulant effects of alcohol tend to precede sedative alcohol effects during a drinking episode.[64,65] There are substantial individual differences in the magnitude of stimulant effects of alcohol and the BACs at which they occur.[66,67] Alcohol's stimulant effects are reflected in increased motor activity, talkativeness, and euphoric or positive mood at lower doses and during rising BACs.[67,68] Stimulant effects have been assessed in humans using a variety of psychophysiological, motor activity, and self-report measures,[65,66,69] and in animals using measures such as spontaneous motor activity.[63,70] Stimulant effects are present in some drinkers at BACs as low as 20 to 30 mg/dL, and may persist on the rising BAC limb well past 100 mg/dL.[63,65] Some current theories hold that stimulant effects reflect alcohol's reinforcing qualities, and that the magnitude of stimulant effects will predict future drinking and the development of alcohol dependence.[71,72]

Some research suggests that the rate of change of rising BACs helps determine the degree of alcohol effects. A faster rise of ascending BACs is associated with greater euphoria and intoxication,[71,73-75] as well as increased behavioral impairment.[11,76] It is interesting to speculate that the drinking patterns shown by many heavy drinkers and alcoholics may reflect an attempt to produce a rapid rise in BACs. These patterns include gulping drinks, drinking on an empty stomach, and using progressively fewer mixers to dilute distilled spirits.

Sedative effects of alcohol usually occur at higher BACs and on the descending limb of the BAC curve. Sedation has been measured in humans using EEG patterns and self-reports of anesthetic sensations and dysphoric mood,[64,74,77] and in animals with low motor activity and the onset of alcohol-induced sleep.[78,79] Robust sedative effects tend to first appear at peak BACs near 60 to 80 mg/dL in many drinkers, although in persons with higher tolerance sedative effects are not apparent until BACs are above 100 mg/dL.[49,64,65] Sedative effects of alcohol are negatively correlated with drinking practices, and lower levels of sedation after alcohol consumption may characterize persons at increased risk for the future development of alcoholism.[79-81]

Research has clearly demonstrated that alcohol-related impairment is greater on the ascending compared to the descending limb of the BAC curve. This finding appears consistently across different doses and impairment tests. The most straightforward explanation for this effect is acute tolerance.

5.1.2.2   Acute Tolerance

There are many different types of tolerance identified by researchers.[50] Metabolic tolerance refers to an acquired increase in the rate of alcohol metabolism. Functional tolerance can be defined as an acquired decrease in an effect of alcohol at a given BAC. There are several different types of functional tolerance. Chronic tolerance refers to an acquired decrease in an effect of alcohol across multiple exposures to the drug. This section focuses on acute tolerance, defined as a decrease over time in an effect of alcohol within a single exposure to alcohol, which occurs independently of changes in BAC.

Acute tolerance is one of the most robust effects that occur in laboratory alcohol administration research. In 1919, Mellanby[82] demonstrated that effects of alcohol were greater during the rising compared to the falling limb of the BAC curve, a phenomenon known as the "Mellanby Effect." A number of laboratory studies in humans and animals have replicated the Mellanby effect using numerous measures, such as motor coordination, self-reported intoxication, sleep time, and body temperature.[12,83-85]

One early question raised about the Mellanby effect was whether it was the result of a methodological artifact in the measurement of alcohol concentration in blood. Venous BAC, which is sampled for alcohol measurement, is known to lag behind arterial BAC during the ascending limb of the BAC curve, before the distribution of alcohol throughout body water compartments is complete. It is arterial blood that is closest to brain levels of alcohol. Thus, some wondered whether the Mellanby effect was an artifact because it actually compared impairment at different concentrations of alcohol in the brain.

It has been established, however, that acute tolerance and the Mellanby effect occur beyond any differences between arterial and venous BAC. First, the Mellanby effect is robust when BACs are assessed via breath alcohol; breath measures are closer to arterial than to venous BACs during the ascending limb of the BAC curve. Second, researchers have demonstrated the presence of acute tolerance using numerous alternative methods. When BACs are at a steady state, acute tolerance has been demonstrated by decreases in the effects of alcohol that occur over time.[13,86] Furthermore, the rate of decrease in alcohol effects are significantly greater than the rate of decrease in descending BACs.[87–89] Another demonstration of acute tolerance comes from social drinkers who report themselves as feeling completely sober when descending BACs are substantial (e.g., 30 to 50 mg/dL).[87] Investigators have demonstrated that decreased effects over time within an exposure to alcohol are not due to practice or other repeated-measures effects.[90-92]

In some models, acute tolerance occurs in a linear fashion as a function of the passage of time, independent of alcohol concentration.[89] Others have proposed that acute tolerance is concentration dependent.[93] Even in this latter model, the passage of time is critical; alcohol concentration simply influences the rate of recovery over time. Martin and Moss[87] found that at both higher and lower doses of alcohol, the magnitude of the Mellanby effect was highly correlated with the amount of time between the ascending and descending limb measurements. Clearly, the amount of impairment and intoxication shown during a drinking episode is not only affected by the level of BAC, but also by the amount of time alcohol has been in a person's system.

Vogel-Sprott and colleagues have published a large body of research that demonstrates that the degree of acute tolerance development is influenced by rewards and punishments, i.e., the consequences of non-impaired and impaired performance.[94] These investigators have demonstrated that acute tolerance to the impairment produced by alcohol increases when non-impaired performance leads to financial reward or praise.[12,95] One way to interpret these findings is in terms of motivation to show non-impaired performance. When an intoxicated motorist is stopped for questioning and/or field sobriety tests, that person will be highly motivated to show non-impaired behavior. While such attempts at appearing sober will be unsuccessful when BACs are sufficiently high, it is likely that many motorists avoid the detection of intoxication at substantial BACs by being highly motivated. Unfortunately, the same motorists may again show substantially impaired performance after the immediate contingency of detection and arrest are removed. Most of the laboratory impairment studies reviewed here did not adequately control for or study the impact of high motivational levels on the obtained results. For this reason, it is likely that the magnitude of impairment observed in many laboratory studies is greater than would be obtained in a field setting.

5.1.2.3 *Hangover*

Hangover has received relatively little attention in the scientific literature, but it can certainly produce alcohol-related impairment. Hangover is an aversive state typically experienced the morning after a heavy drinking bout, which is characterized by dysphoric and irritable mood, headache, nausea, dizziness, and dehydration. Sufficiently heavy drinking produces self-reported hangover symptoms in most persons, but there appears to be large individual differences in the occurrence, severity, and time course of perceived hangover that are independent of drinking practices.[96]

Studies reported in the literature are contradictory concerning whether hangover is accompanied by behavioral impairment. Several early studies found no performance impairment when BACs were at or close to zero.[97,98] Myrsten and colleagues[99] tested a variety of behavioral impairment measures 12 hours after subjects consumed a dose of alcohol producing mean BACs near 120 mg/dL. Morning BACs in this study averaged 4 mg/dL. Most measures showed no impairment, but hand steadiness was detrimentally affected. Collins and Chiles[100] gave impairment tests before an evening drinking session, after alcohol consumption, and again after subjects had slept 4 to 5 hours. Subjects were affected on the performance tests during acute intoxication, and they reported significant levels of hangover during the morning session. Despite these methodological strengths, there were no clear-cut performance impairing effects of hangover in this study.

Some other research indicates that hangover is accompanied by impairment in behavioral and cognitive functioning. One experiment found that after high peak BACs of about 150 mg/dL, there was an average 20% decrement on a simulated driving task 3 hours after BACs had returned to zero.[101] Yesavage and Leirer[102] examined hangover effects in Navy aircraft pilots 14 hours after drinking enough alcohol to produce BACs of about 100 mg/dL, using a variety of flight simulator measures. Significant detrimental effects of hangover were found for 3 of 6 variance measures and 1 of 6 performance measures. Similarly, other studies have found impairment due to hangover on only some of the tests employed in the research.[103,104]

Some have speculated that the nausea and dizziness of hangover may be associated with PAN II, an eye movement nystagmus that occurs during falling BACs and after measurable alcohol has left the system.[35] PAN II reflects the sensitivity of semicircular canal receptors to gravity, which also produces feelings similar to motion sickness. More research is needed to address the role of vestibular functioning in hangover.

Inconsistencies in the hangover literature probably reflect the fact that behavioral impairment during hangover is influenced by numerous factors, including sleepiness, fatigue, mood, and motivation to behave in a non-impaired manner. Moreover, there are individual differences in the frequency and duration of hangover, even among persons with similar drinking practices. For many persons, the BACs required to produce subsequent hangover may be greater than those typically obtained in laboratory studies. Hangover effects are poorly characterized, and are an important topic for further research.

5.1.3 Impairment Testing

5.1.3.1 Ideal Characteristics of Impairment Tests

The strengths and weaknesses of impairment tests used in the laboratory and the field are best evaluated in contrast with their ideal properties. There are a number of concepts that can be used to describe the characteristics of impairment tests, including scaling of results, applicability to field settings, reliability, validity, sensitivity, and specificity.[105]

Impairment tests differ in the scaling of results, that is, the nature of the scores or outcomes of a test. Results may be binary (impaired or not), ordinal rankings (low, medium, or high impairment), or quantitative scores. The need for precision of results depends upon the testing application. When used primarily as a screening tool for other sobriety tests or a BAC assessment, binary scores or ordinal rankings may be adequate. In other instances, continuous scores are desirable because they inform about the level of impairment.

Applicability to field settings is important for any impairment test used in law enforcement. One requirement is that a test must have adequate measurement properties in a field setting. A test may have demonstrated reliability and validity in the laboratory, but these properties may or may not generalize to field settings. Field applications involve a loss of control over numerous variables that can influence testing. Reliability and validity properties in the field may be far different from the laboratory, in part because data from a known sober condition are not available for comparison.

There are several other important considerations in relation to field settings. Ideally, a test must be easily administered in a standard way by test administrators, and readily understood by test takers. The level of technical skill required for administering the test, collection of data and interpretation of results should be acquired with a reasonably short duration of training. Any required instrumentation should not require extensive maintenance, and should not be easily subject to interference by test takers. Importantly, impairment tests must have credibility with law enforcement officers and the wider criminal justice system. Whereas sobriety tests are often used as a preliminary screen for reasonable cause in BAC testing, they nevertheless must be generally acceptable to prosecutors, judges, and juries.

Reliability

Reliability refers to the extent to which a test provides a result that is stable or repeatable. That is, a reliable test is one that will yield a similar result across multiple testings in the same person (test-retest reliability), or across multiple test administrators or raters examining the same person (inter-rater reliability). An ideal impairment test should be reliable across testings in a sober person, i.e., it would reveal a stable baseline for non-impaired performance. Furthermore, an ideal test should show reliability across testings in an intoxicated person. That is, multiple tests taken at the same level of impairment would show relatively little variation in the obtained scores. Reliability is a key feature of any impairment test. If obtained scores are not reliable, the results may be caused by factors other than impairment, such as variation in test administration or scoring.

Validity

Validity concerns the extent to which a test accurately measures what it was intended to measure. The validity of impairment tests refers to the extent to which these tests assess alcohol-related impairment, rather than other factors. Face validity refers to the extent to which law enforcement personnel and test takers believe that a test does measure alcohol impairment; many field sobriety tests have high levels of face validity. Concurrent validity refers to the extent to which an impairment test shows expected associations with other tests known to measure impairment, and with BACs. Construct validity refers to the adequacy and explanatory power of scientific concepts such as alcohol impairment. If alcohol-related impairment is highly variable across different behaviors, this will reduce the validity of any one test in measuring such a diffuse concept.

A test can be reliable but not valid. For example, a person's height can be measured in a highly reliable fashion, but the observed results would be an invalid index of alcohol impairment. In contrast, some level of reliability is needed in order for a test to show validity. If an impairment test has no reliability, it cannot be valid. The degree to which reliability is imperfect tends to place an upper limit on the degree of validity that can be shown by a test.[106]

Sensitivity

Sensitivity refers to the ability of a test to detect impairment, and can be defined as the proportion of impaired persons (as determined by some other established measure) who are classified as impaired by a test. Thus, insensitive tests can allow persons who are impaired to escape detection (a false negative test result). Whereas signs of intoxication are evident from test results in almost all persons when BACs become sufficiently high, many measures do not detect impairment when BACs are below 100 mg/dL. Among some heavy drinkers, many tests will be insensitive to BACs well above 100 mg/dL. In some cases, there probably is little impairment to detect when a test does not reveal impairment. In other cases, however, impaired performance is likely present, but a test is not sensitive enough to detect it.

Specificity

The specificity of an impairment test refers to the extent to which the results reflect alcohol impairment and not other factors such as fatigue, stress, and individual differences in cognitive and motor skills. A highly specific test will not be much influenced by changes in parameters other than alcohol impairment. An example of high test specificity in biological measurement is seen for BACs, where existing instrumentation allows assessment of alcohol in blood and breath that is not affected by closely related chemical compounds such as acetate, acetaldehyde, or acetone. Tests with low levels of specificity will lead to a high proportion of false positive test identifications. That is, results for a non-specific test will often suggest that a person is impaired when they actually are not impaired (as measured by BAC or other tests). Thus, low specificity in impairment testing can lead to an inefficient expenditure of law enforcement resources.

An important issue in evaluating the sensitivity and specificity of impairment tests is whether measures of sober performance are available. Many tests show large individual differences in sober performance.[13,94] In laboratory research tests, sensitivity and specificity are evaluated by comparing a subject's performance at different BACs with their test performance when sober, usually before drinking begins. However, sensitivity and specificity are more difficult to achieve in the field, when sober baseline performance data are not available. Therefore, tests that are known to have less variation among sober persons are preferable for field settings.

When developing cutoff scores on impairment tests, increased sensitivity almost always comes at the expense of decreased specificity, and vice versa. The "best" cutoff score for the definition of impairment depends upon the relative importance of sensitivity and specificity in a given application, as well as the estimated base rate of impairment in the population that will be tested.[106] The choice of an appropriate cutoff score for an impairment test must be based on an understanding of these factors.

5.1.3.2 Characteristics of Existing Field Sobriety Tests

This section focuses on three field sobriety tests (FSTs) that have been standardized by the National Highway Traffic Safety Administration,[107] and which are widely used in the U.S. and elsewhere. In the one-leg stand test, subjects must raise one foot at least 6 in. off the ground and stand on the other foot for 30 seconds, while keeping their arms at their sides. Performance is scored on a 4-point scale, using items such as showing significant sway, using arms for balance, hopping, and putting down the raised foot. In the walk-and-turn test, subjects must balance with feet heel-to-toe and listen to test instructions. Then, subjects must walk nine steps heel-to-toe on a straight line, turn 180 degrees, and walk nine additional steps heel-to-toe, all the time counting their steps, watching their feet and keeping their hands at their sides. Performance is scored on an 8-point scale, using items such as starting before instructions are finished, stepping off the line, maintaining balance with arm movements, and taking an incorrect number of steps. The gaze nystagmus test assesses horizontal gaze nystagmus. The angle of onset of nystagmus is assessed for each eye. Performance is scored on a 6-point scale (3 possible points for each eye).

Some research has examined the properties of these three FSTs. In a laboratory study, Tharp et al.[42] used 297 drinking volunteers with BACs from 0 to 180 mg/dL who were tested by police officers trained in the use of FSTs. Inter-rater reliability correlations for the FSTs ranged from 0.60 to 0.80, indicating an adequate level of reliability across test administrators. Test-retest correlations, examining the correspondence of FST scores on two separate occasions at similar BACs, ranged from about 0.40 to 0.75, indicating adequate test-retest reliability. All of the FSTs correlated significantly with BACs. Using all three FST test scores, officers were able to classify 81% of persons in terms of whether their BACs were above or below 100 mg/dL. Similar results using these standard FSTs in a field setting were obtained by Anderson et al.[108] However, neither of these reports provided data on the specificity and sensitivity of individual FSTs.

Few studies have reported the characteristics of individual FSTs in field settings. One study found that HGN, specifically the angle of horizontal nystagmus onset, had high levels of sensitivity and specificity in predicting BACs above 100 mg/dL in an emergency room setting.[43] Perrine et al.[109] examined the reliability and validity of the National Highway Traffic Safety Administration FSTs in a field setting with 480 subjects, using police officers and other trained individuals as test administrators. Inter-rater reliability was adequate for all three FSTs. All of the FSTs were significantly correlated with BAC; however, the magnitude of these correlations was low in the case of the walk-and-turn and the one-leg stand tests. Perrine et al.[109] provided data on the sensitivity and specificity of each FST as a function of different levels of BAC. The data indicated that the horizontal gaze nystagmus test had excellent sensitivity and specificity characteristics. Only 3% of subjects with a zero BAC failed the horizontal gaze nystagmus test (i.e., specificity was high when referenced to a zero BAC). Sensitivity was 100% for those with BACs over 150 mg/dL, and was 81% for subjects with BACs ranging from 100 mg/dL to 149 mg/dL.

However, Perrine et al.[109] found that prediction of BAC was much worse using the walk-and-turn and the one-leg stand test. For the walk-and-turn test, specificity was low, in that about half of those with a zero BAC were classified as impaired. While sensitivity was fairly high (78%) at BACs above 150 mg/dL, this parameter fell below 50% for those with BACs between 80 mg/dL and 100 mg/dL. For the one-leg stand test, 30% of those with a zero BAC were classified as impaired, indicating only moderate specificity. Sensitivity was only 50% for those with BACs between 100 mg/dL and 150 mg/dL, but improved to 88% for those with BACs above 150 mg/dL.

The literature suggests that overall, FSTs such as the walk and turn, one leg stand, and horizontal gaze nystagmus test, have adequate properties for detecting impairment in field settings. These tests meet the requirements of applicability to the field, in that they can be administered in a standardized fashion, have face validity, and are understood by test takers. Training of test administrators can occur in a reasonable period of time. Results suggest that these tests can be administered reliably, and have validity in the sense that they do measure impairment due to alcohol. However, horizontal gaze nystagmus performs much better at predicting BAC than the walk-and-turn and the one-leg stand tests. While they are worthwhile, the latter two FSTs have significant limitations when used in field settings. More research is needed to determine if improved testing procedures or different cutoff scores can improve the performance of the walk-and-turn and the one-leg stand tests.

It is important to note that the properties of FSTs depend upon the threshold BACs they are supposed to detect. FSTs can be used to test impairment that occurs at BACs below a legal limit, but much of their utility depends upon their ability to determine whether a person has a BAC above that allowed by law. The FSTs described above were designed and tested in the context of the limits of 100 mg/dL that exist throughout most of the U.S. However, the limit is currently 80 mg/dL in California, and is 50 mg/dL or 20 mg/dL in many European countries. It is likely that the performance of FSTs decreases as the BAC limit decreases. More research is needed to determine whether FSTs have utility when used to detect lower BAC threshold limits.

5.1.4 Conclusions

While it is clear that alcohol impairs performance, the presence and degree of impairment depends upon a large number of individual, situational, and pharmacological factors. Moreover, impairment is not uniform across all types of behavioral and cognitive functioning. Simple behaviors, such as reaction time tasks performed in isolation, are generally insensitive to alcohol consumption. Well-practiced behaviors tend to be insensitive to alcohol except at very high doses.

Impairment is seen consistently in tasks requiring the simultaneous processing of multiple sources of information. The results from dual-performance and divided-attention tasks suggest that alcohol reduces the amount of limited-capacity attentional resources available for coordinating multiple tasks. These results provide an important view of how alcohol can produce accidents and injuries. For example, the intoxicated motorist may perform with only moderate impairment on a well-known route with little traffic. However, when a situation arises that requires the simultaneous processing of multiple sources of information, such as avoiding an unexpected obstacle in traffic, large performance deficits may occur.

Alcohol also produces deficits in activities that require fine motor control at high rates of speed. One of the most sensitive behavioral measures of impairment found in the literature is tracking performance, which requires rapid small adjustments in the muscles of the hands and eyes, and a high level of hand-eye coordination. Tracking performance is an important aspect of impairment, in part, because it is central to the lateral guidance of a motor vehicle. Another type of behavior sensitive to alcohol is speech, which requires fine motor control, timing, and coordination among the lips, tongue, and vocal cords at a high rate of speed.

Impairments in eye movements and balance after drinking primarily reflect alcohol's effects on the brain's vestibular system. Alcohol is a small water-soluble molecule that readily diffuses throughout the brain, and impairment is often described in terms of alcohol's general depressant effects on all neural functions. However, impairment in vestibular functioning provides an example of specificity in alcohol's effects. The mechanisms of vestibular impairment have been fairly well characterized, and relate to how alcohol effects the specific physiology of this system. Vestibular functioning is relatively sensitive to alcohol's effects and important for behavioral functioning, and therefore is a logical focus of impairment testing.

There are large individual differences in the impairment produced by alcohol consumption, even when controlling for level of BAC. Several sources of these individual differences have been identified. Perhaps the most important factor is drinking practices. Those who drink more often and in greater amounts tend to develop a greater degree of chronic tolerance to the impairing effects of alcohol, i.e., have an acquired decrease in the degree of impairment across multiple drinking sessions. However, by definition, heavy drinkers tend to consume more and will be more likely to have higher BACs when tested in forensic settings. Thus, heavier drinking practices are probably not predictive of less impairment in field settings because individual differences in BACs are not controlled. Impairment tends to be greater in older adults as compared to younger adults; this effect is likely a combination of increased neural vulnerability with aging and differences in drinking practices between young and old. When controlling for BACs and drinking practices, gender differences in impairment have not been demonstrated.

The impairment produced by alcohol depends upon the time course of a drinking episode. Alcohol's effects have been described as biphasic, with initial euphoria and stimulant effects during early rising BACs, followed by dysphoria and sedative effects later on. Numerous measures of impairment are greater on the ascending compared to the descending limb of the BAC curve. This change in impairment due to limb of the BAC curve most likely reflects the phenomenon of acute tolerance, in which alcohol effects decrease over time within a drinking episode. In the prediction of impairment, the amount of time elapsed since alcohol has been in the system can be as important a variable as BAC itself.

The time course of alcohol's effects do not always end when BACs fall to zero. Sufficient drinking can produce hangover in many persons. Hangover is accompanied by impairment in behavioral functioning in some studies. Other research, however, has not found consistent effects of hangover on performance. There appear to be large individual differences in the degree of hangover effects, and their duration. Hangover effects are poorly characterized compared to other effects of alcohol, and are an important topic for further research. The demonstration of significant impairment related to hangover would suggest the need for a longer period of abstinence from alcohol use before job performance in some professions, similar to the rules often applied to airline pilots.

Field sobriety tests, such as the walk and turn, one-leg stand, and horizontal gaze nystagmus tests, can be administered in a standardized fashion and meet the requirements of applicability to the field. These tests have adequate levels of validity, in that they reliably assess functions known to reflect alcohol impairment, and correlate with BACs and other impairment measures. Levels of sensitivity and specificity appear to be fairly high for the horizontal gaze nystagmus test. On the other hand, levels of test sensitivity and specificity are adequate but somewhat low for the walk-and-turn and the one-leg stand. That is, many persons with positive BACs, including those over 100 mg/dL, will be classified as not impaired using these tests, and many persons with low or zero BACs will be classified as impaired. Furthermore, the validity of FSTs for detecting lower threshold BACs such as 50 mg/dL or 20 mg/dL remains to be established. The development of new field sobriety tests that increase the accurate assessment of impairment would be of great benefit in forensic applications.

REFERENCES

1. Carpenter, J. A., Effects of alcohol on some psychological processes, *Quarterly Journal of Studies on Alcohol*, 23, 274, 1980.
2. Levine, J. M., Kramer, J., Levine, E., Effects of alcohol on human performance, *Journal of Applied Psychology*, 60, 508, 1975.
3. Finnigan, F., Hammersley, R., The effects of alcohol on performance, in *Handbook of Human Performance*, Volume 2, Smith, A., Jones, D., Eds., Academic Press Ltd, Orlando, FL, 1992, p. 73.
4. Goldberg, L., Quantitative studies on alcohol tolerance in man. The influence of ethyl alcohol on sensory, motor, and psychological functions referred to blood alcohol in normal and habituated individuals, *Acta Physiol. Scand.,* 5 (Suppl. 16): 1, 1943.
5. Baylor, A. M., Layne, C. S., Mayfield, R. D., Osborne, L., Spirduso, W. W., Effects of ethanol on human fractionated response times, *Drug and Alcohol Dependence,* 23, 31, 1989.
6. Taberner, P. V., Sex differences in the effects of low doses of ethanol on human reaction time, *Psychopharmacology,* 70, 283, 1980.
7. Maylor, E. A., Rabbitt, P. M., James, G. H., Kerr, S. A., Effects of alcohol and extended practice on divided-attention performance, *Perception and Psychophysics*, 48, 445, 1990.
8. Linnoila, M., Erwin, C. W., Ramm, D., Cleveland, W. P., Effects of age and alcohol on psychomotor performance of men, *Journal of Studies on Alcohol*, 41, 488, 1980.
9. Fagan, D., Tiplady, B., Scott, D. B., Effects of ethanol on psychomotor performance, *British Journal of Anaesthesia*, 59, 961, 1987.
10. Golby, J., Use of factor analysis in the study of alcohol-induced strategy changes in skilled performance on a soccer test, *Perceptual and Motor Skills*, 68, 147, 1989.
11. Connors, G. J., Maisto, S. A., Effects of alcohol instructions and consumption rate on motor performance, *Journal of Studies on Alcohol*, 41, 509, 1980.
12. Beirness, D., Vogel-Sprott, M., Alcohol tolerance in social drinkers: operant and classical conditioning effects, *Psychopharmacology*, 84, 393, 1984.
13. Wilson, J., Erwin, G., McClearn, G., Effects of ethanol, II. Behavioral sensitivity and acute behavioral tolerance, *Alcoholism: Clinical and Experimental Research*, 8, 366, 1984.
14. Maylor, E. A., Rabbitt, P. M., Connolly, S. A., Rate of processing and judgment of response speed: comparing the effects of alcohol and practice, *Perception and Psychophysics*, 45, 431, 1989.
15. Moskowitz, H., Burns, M. M., Williams, A. F., Skilled performance at low blood alcohol levels, *Journal of Studies on Alcohol*, 46, 482, 1985.
16. Niaura, R. S., Nathan, P. E., Frankenstein, W., Shapiro, A. P., Brick, J., Gender differences in acute psychomotor, cognitive, and pharmacokinetic response to alcohol, *Addictive Behaviors*, 12, 345, 1987.
17. Mills, K., & Bisgrove, E., Body sway and divided attention performance under the influence of alcohol: dose-response differences between males and females, *Alcoholism: Clinical and Experimental Research*, 7, 393, 1983.
18. Steele, C. M., Josephs, R. A., Drinking your troubles away: II. An attention-allocation model of alcohol's effects on stress, *Journal of Abnormal Psychology*, 97, 196, 1988.
19. Zador, P. L., Alcohol-related relative risk of fatal driver injuries in relation to driver age and sex, *Journal of Studies on Alcohol*, 52, 302, 1991.
20. Hindmarch, I., Bhatti, J. Z., Starmer, G. A., Mascord, D. J., Kerr, J. S., Sherwood, N., The effects of alcohol on the cognitive function of males and females and on skills relating to car driving, *Human Psychopharmacology*, 7, 105, 1992.
21. McMillen, D. L., Smith, S. M., Wells-Parker, E., The effect of alcohol, expectancy, and sensation seeking on driving risk taking, *Addictive Behaviors*, 14, 477, 1989.
22. Mongrain, S., Standing, L., Impairment of cognition, risk-taking, and self-perception by alcohol, *Perceptual and Motor Skills*, 69, 199, 1989.
23. Attwood, D. A., Williams, R. D., Madill, H. D., Effects of moderate blood alcohol concentrations on closed-course driving performance, *Journal of Studies on Alcohol*, 41, 623, 1980.

24. Huntley, M. S., Centybear, T. M., Alcohol, sleep deprivation and driving speed effects upon control use during driving, *Human Factors*, 16, 19, 1974.
25. Brewer, N., Sandow, B., Alcohol effects on driver performance under conditions of divided attention, *Ergonomics*, 23, 185, 1980.
26. Sobell, L. C., Sobell, M. B., Effects of alcohol on the speech of alcoholics, *Journal of Speech and Hearing Research*, 15, 861, 1972.
27. Sobell, L. C., Sobell, M. B., Coleman, R. F., Alcohol-induced dysfluency in nonalcoholics, *Folia Phoniatrica*, 34, 316, 1982.
28. Trojan, F., Kryspin-Exner, K., The decay of articulation under the influence of alcohol and paraldehyde, *Folia Phoniatrica*, 20, 217, 1968.
29. Lester, L., Skousen, R., The phonology of drunkenness, in *Papers from the Parasession on Natural Phonology*, Bruck, A., Fox, R. A., LaGay, M. W., eds., Chicago, Chicago Linguistic Society, 1974, Chapter 8.
30. Pisoni, D. B., Martin, C. S., Effects of alcohol on the acoustic-phonetic properties of speech: perceptual and acoustic analyses, *Alcoholism: Clinical and Experimental Research*, 13, 577, 1989.
31. Johnson, K., Pisoni, D. B., Bermacki, R. H., Do voice recordings reveal whether a person is intoxicated? A case study, *Phonetica*, 47, 215, 1990.
32. Iurato, S., *Submicroscopic Structure of the Inner Ear*, London, Pergamon Press, 1967, p 216.
33. Money, K. E., Johnson, W. H., Corlett, B. M., Role of semicircular canals in positional alcohol nystagmus, *American Journal of Physiology*, 208, 1065, 1965.
34. Nito, Y., Johnson, W. H., Money, K. E., The non-auditory labyrinth and positional alcohol nystagmus. *Acta Otolaryngology*, 58, 65, 1964.
35. Money, K. E., Myles, W. S., Hoffert, B. M., The mechanism of positional alcohol nystagmus, *Canadian Journal of Otolaryngology*, 3, 302, 1974.
36. Aschan, G., Gergstedt, M., Positional alcoholic nystagmus (PAN) in man following repeated alcohol doses, *Acta Otolaryngology*, Suppl. 330, 15, 1975.
37. Fregly, A. R., Bergstedt, M., Graybiel, A., Relationships between blood alcohol, positional alcohol nystagmus, and postural equilibrium, *Quarterly Journal of Studies on Alcohol*, 28, 11, 1967.
38. Aschan, G., Different types of alcohol nystagmus, *Acta Otolarnygology*, Suppl. 140, 69, 1958.
39. Behrens, M. M., Nystagmus, *Journal of Opthalmological Clinics*, 18, 57, 1978.
40. Lehti, H., The effect of blood alcohol concentration on the onset of gaze nystagmus, *Blutalkohol*, 13, 411, 1976.
41. Barnes, G.R., Crombie, J.W., Edge, A., The effects of ethanol on visual-vestibular interaction during active and passive head movements, *Aviation, Space, and Environmental Medicine*, July 1985, p. 695.
42. Tharp, V. K., Burns, M., Moskowitz, H., *Development and field test of psychophysical tests for DWI arrest: final report*, technical report DOT-HS-805-864, Washington, D.C., National Highway Traffic Safety Administration, 1981.
43. Goding, G. S., Dobie, R. A., Gaze nystagmus and blood alcohol, *Laryngoscope*, 96, 713, 1986.
44. Baloh, R. W., Sharma, S., Moskowitz, H., Griffith, R., Effect of alcohol and marijuana on eye movements, *Aviation, Space, and Environmental Medicine*, p. 18, January 1979.
45. Gentles, W., Llewellyn-Thomas, E., Effect of benzodiazepines upon saccadic eye movements in man, *Clinical Pharmacology and Theraputics*, 12, 563, 1971.
46. Niaura, R.S., Wilson, G.T., Westrick, E., Self-awareness, alcohol consumption, and reduced cardiovascular reactivity, *Psychosomatic Medicine*, 50, 360, 1988.
47. Lipscomb, T. R., Nathan, P. E., Wilson, G. T., Abrams, D. B., Effects of tolerance on the anxiety-reducing functions of alcohol, *Archives of General Psychiatry*, 37, 577, 1980.
48. Lipscomb, T. R., Nathan, P. E., Effect of family history of alcoholism, drinking pattern, and tolerance on blood alcohol level discrimination, *Archives of General Psychiatry*, 37, 576, 1980.
49. O'Malley, S. S., Maisto, S. A. Factors affecting the perception of intoxication: dose, tolerance, and setting, *Addictive Behaviors*, 9, 111, 1984.
50. Goldstein, D. B., *Pharmacology of Alcohol*, New York, Oxford University Press, 1983.
51. Frezza, M., DiPadova, C., Pozzato, G., Terpin, M., Baraona, E., Lieber, C., High blood alcohol levels in women: the role of decreased gastric alcohol dehydrogenase activity and first-pass metabolism, *New England Journal of Medicine*, 322, 95, 1990.

52. Sutker, P. B., Goist, K., King, A., Acute alcohol intoxication in women: relationship to dose and menstrual cycle phase, *Alcoholism: Clinical and Experimental Research*, 11, 74, 1987.

53. Brick, J., Nathan, P. E., Shapiro, A. P., Westrick, E., Frankenstein, W., The effect of menstrual cycle on blood alcohol levels and behavior, *Journal of Studies on Alcohol*, 47, 472, 1986.

54. Sutker, P. B., Goist, K., Allain, A. N., Bugg, F., Acute alcohol intoxication: sex comparisons on pharmacokinetic and mood measures, *Alcoholism: Clinical and Experimental Research*, 11, 507, 1987.

55. Cole-Harding, S., Wilson, J., Ethanol metabolism in men and women, *Journal of Studies on Alcohol*, 48, 380, 1987.

56. Jones, B. M., Jones, M. K., Alcohol effects in women during the menstrual cycle, *Annals of the New York Academy of Sciences*, 273, 576, 1976.

57. Burns, M., Moskowitz, H., Gender-related differences in impairment of performance by alcohol, in *Currents in Alcoholism, Volume 3: Biological, Biochemical and Clinical Studies,* F. Sexias, Ed., New York: Grune & Stratton, 1978, p. 479.

58. Sutker, P. B., Allain, A. N., Brantley, P. S., Randall, C. L., Acute alcohol intoxication, negative affect, and autonomic arousal in women and men, *Addictive Behaviors*, 7, 17, 1982.

59. Parker, E. S., Noble, E. P., Alcohol and the aging process in social drinkers, *Journal of Studies on Alcohol*, 41, 170, 1980.

60. Jones, M. K., Jones, B. M., The relationship of age and drinking habits to the effects of alcohol on memory in women, *Journal of Studies on Alcohol*, 41, 179, 1980.

61. Vogel-Sprott, M., Barrett, P., Age, drinking habits, and the effects of alcohol, *Journal of Studies on Alcohol*, 45, 517, 1984.

62. York, J. L., Increased responsiveness to ethanol with advancing age in rats, *Pharmacology, Biochemistry, and Behavior*, 19, 687, 1983.

63. Pohorecky, L. A., Biphasic action of ethanol, *Biobehavioral Reviews*, 1, 231, 1977.

64. Martin, C. S., Earleywine, M., Musty, R. E., Perrine, M. W., Swift, R. M., Development and validation of the biphasic alcohol effects scale, *Alcoholism: Clinical and Experimental Research*, 17, 140, 1993.

65. Tucker, J., Vuchinich, R., Sobell, M., Alcohol's effects on human emotions: A review of the stimulation/depression hypothesis, *International Journal of the Addictions*, 17, 155, 1982.

66. deWit, H., Uhlenguth, E., Pierri, J., Johanson, C., Individual differences in behavioral and subjective responses to alcohol, *Alcoholism: Clinical and Experimental Research*, 11, 52, 1987.

67. Nagoshi, C., Wilson, J., One-month repeatability of emotional responses to alcohol, *Alcoholism: Clinical and Experimental Research*, 12, 691, 1988.

68. Freed, E., Alcohol and mood: an updated review. *International Journal of the Addictions*, 13, 173, 1978.

69. Newlin, D., Thomson, J, Chronic tolerance and sensitization to alcohol in sons of alcoholics, *Alcoholism: Clinical and Experimental Research*, 15, 399, 1991.

70. Waller, M., Murphy, J., McBride, W., Effect of low dose ethanol on spontaneous motor activity in alcohol-preferring and non-preferring lines of rats. *Pharmacology, Biochemistry, and Behavior*, 24, 617, 1986.

71. Stewart, J., deWit, H., Eikelboom, R., Role of unconditioned and conditioned drug effects in the self-administration of opiates and stimulants, *Psychological Review*, 91, 251, 1984.

72. Wise, R., Bozarth, M., A psychomotor stimulant theory of addiction, *Psychological Review*, 94, 469, 1987.

73. Connors, G. J., Maisto, S. A., Effects of alcohol instructions and consumption rate on affect and physiological sensations, *Psychopharmacology*, 62, 261, 1979.

74. Lukas, S., Mendelson, J., Benedikt, R., Instrumental analysis of ethanol-induced intoxication in human males, *Psychopharmacology*, 89, 89, 1986.

75. Martin, C. S., Earleywine, M., Ascending and descending rates of change of blood alcohol concentrations and subjective intoxication ratings, *Journal of Substance Abuse*, 2, 345, 1990.

76. Moskowitz, H., Burns M., Effects of rate of drinking on human performance, *Journal of Studies on Alcohol*, 37, 598, 1976.

77. Wilson, J., Nagoshi, C., Adult children of alcoholics: cognitive and psychomotor characteristics, *British Journal of Addiction*, 83, 809, 1988.

78. Engel, J., Liljequist, S., The involvement of different central neurotransmitters in mediating stimulatory and sedative effects of ethanol, in *Stress and Alcohol Use*, Pohorecky, L. A., Brick, J., Eds., New York: Elsevier Biomedical, 153, 1983.

79. Tabakoff, B., Hoffman, P., Tolerance and the etiology of alcoholism: hypothesis and mechanism, *Alcoholism: Clinical and Experimental Research*, 12, 184, 1988.

80. Gabrielli, W., Nagoshi, C., Rhea, S., Wilson, J., Anticipated and subjective sensitivities to alcohol, *Journal of Studies on Alcohol*, 52, 205, 1991.

81. Schuckit, M., Subjective responses to alcohol in sons of alcoholics and control subjects, *Archives of General Psychiatry*, 41, 879, 1984.

82. Mellanby, E., *Alcohol: Its Absorption and Disappearance from the Blood under Different Conditions*, London, Her Majesty's Statistical Office, Great Britain Medical Research Council, 1919.

83. Gilliam, D., Alcohol absorption rate affects hypothermic response in mice: evidence for acute tolerance, *Alcohol*, 6, 357, 1989.

84. Martin, C. S., Rose, R. J., Obremski, K. M., Estimation of blood alcohol concentrations in young male drinkers, *Alcoholism: Clinical and Experimental Research*, 15, 494, 1990.

85. Waller, M., McBride, W., Lumeng, L., Li, T. K., Initial sensitivity and acute tolerance to ethanol in the P and NP lines of rats, *Pharmacology, Biochemistry, and Behavior*, 19, 683, 1983.

86. Kaplan, H., Sellers, E., Hamilton, C. Is there acute tolerance to alcohol at a steady state?, *Journal of Studies on Alcohol*, 46, 253, 1985.

87. Martin, C. S., Moss, H. B., Measurement of acute tolerance to alcohol in human subjects, *Alcoholism: Clinical and Experimental Research*, 17, 211, 1993.

88. Nagoshi, C., Wilson, J., Long-term repeatability of alcohol metabolism, sensitivity, and acute tolerance, *Journal of Studies on Alcohol*, 50, 162, 1989.

89. Radlow, R., Hurst, P., Temporal relations between blood alcohol concentration and alcohol effect: an experiment with human subjects. *Psychopharmacology*, 85, 260, 1985.

90. Benton, R., Banks, W., Vogler, R., Carryover of tolerance to ethanol in moderate drinkers, *Journal of Studies on Alcohol*, 42, 1137, 1982.

91. Hurst, P., Bagley, S., Acute adaptation to the effects of alcohol, *Journal of Studies on Alcohol*, 33, 358, 1972.

92. LeBlanc, A., Kalant, H., Gibbons, R., Acute tolerance to ethanol in the rat, *Psychopharmacolgia*, 41, 43, 1975.

93. Kalant, H., LeBlanc, A., Gibbons, R., Tolerance to, and dependence on, some non-opiate psychotropic drugs, *Pharmacology Review*, 23, 135, 1971.

94. Vogel-Sprott, M., *Alcohol tolerance and social drinking: learning the consequences*, New York, Guilford Press, 1992.

95. Vogel-Sprott, M., Kartchner, W., McConnell, D., Consequences of behavior influence the effect of alcohol, *Journal of Substance Abuse*, 1, 369, 1989.

96. Newlin, D. B., Pretorious, M., Sons of alcoholics report greater hangover symptoms than sons of non-alcoholics: a pilot study, *Alcoholism: Clinical and Experimental Research*, 14, 713, 1990.

97. Collins, W. E., Schroeder, D. J., Gilson, R. D., Guedry, F. E., Effects of alcohol ingestion on tracking performance during angular acceleration, *Journal of Applied Psychology*, 55, 559, 1971.

98. Eckman, G., Frankenhaeuser, M., Goldberg, L., Hagdahl, R., Myrsten, A. L., Subjective and objective effects of alcohol as functions of dosage and time, *Psychopharmacologia*, 6, 399, 1964.

99. Kelly, M., Myrsten, A. L., Neri, A., Rydberg, U., Effects and after-effects of alcohol on psychological and physiological functions in man — a controlled study, *Blutalkohol*, 7, 422, 1970.

100. Collins, W. E., Chiles, W. D., Laboratory performance during acute alcohol intoxication and hangover, *Human Factors*, 22, 445, 1980.

101. Laurell, H., Tornros, J., Franck, D. H., If you drink, don't drive: the motto now applies to hangovers as well, *Journal of the American Medical Association Medical News*, October 7, 1983, p. 1657.

102. Yesavage, J. A., Leirer, V. O., Hangover effects on aircraft pilots 14 hours after alcohol ingestion: a preliminary report, *American Journal of Psychiatry*, 143, 1546, 1986.

103. Karvinen, E., Miettinen, A., Ahlman, K., Physical performance during hangover, *Quarterly Journal of Studies on Alcohol*, 23, 208, 1962.

104. Takala, M., Siro, E., Tiovainen, Y., Intellectual functions and dexterity during hangover, *Quarterly Journal of Studies on Alcohol*, 19, 1, 1958.

105. Allen, J. P., Litten, R. Z., Anton, R., Measures of alcohol consumption in perspective, in Litten, R. Z., Allen, J. P. (Eds.) *Measuring alcohol consumption: psychosocial and biochemical methods*, Totowa, NJ, Humana Press, 1992, p. 205.

106. Meehl, P. E., Rosen, A., Antecedent probability and the efficiency of psychometric signs, patterns, or cutting scores, *Psychological Bulletin*, 52, 194, 1952.

107. National Highway Traffic Safety Administration, DWI detection and standardized field sobriety testing: administrators guide, DOT-HS-178/RI/90, Washington, D.C., National Highway Traffic Safety Administration.

108. Anderson, T. E., Schweitz, R. M., Snyder, M. B., *Field evaluation of a behavioral test battery for DWI*, DOT-HS-806-475, Washington, D.C., National Highway Traffic Safety Administration.

109. Perrine, M. W., Foss, R. D., Meyers, A. R., Voas, R. B., Velez, C., Field sobriety tests: reliability and validity, in *Alcohol, Drugs and Traffic Safety-T92*, Utzelmann, H. D., Berghaus, G., Kroj, G., Eds., Verlag TUV Rheinland, Cologne, Germany, 1993.

5.2 UPDATE ON CLINICAL AND FORENSIC ANALYSIS OF ALCOHOL

Alan Wayne Jones, Dr.Sc.[1] and Derrick J. Pounder, M.D.[2]
[1] Department of Forensic Toxicology, University Hospital, Linköping, Sweden
[2] Department of Forensic Medicine, University of Dundee, Scotland, U.K.

5.2.1   Introduction

Alcohol is the world's favorite recreational drug and moderate drinking has few untoward effects on a person's health and well-being.[1] Indeed, drinking small amounts of alcohol helps to relax people and relieve their inhibitions.[2] Moreover, scores of studies testify to the efficacy of small doses of alcohol, such as one to two glasses of red wine daily, as an effective prophylactic treatment for cardiovascular diseases such as ischemic stroke and heart failure.[1,3,4] In contrast, heavy drinking and drunkenness constitute major public health problems for both the individual and society.[5,6] Binge drinking is the cause of deviant behavior and is closely linked to family violence. Many of those who seek help from hospital casualty and emergency units are under the influence of alcohol.[7–10] High blood alcohol concentrations (BACs) are a common finding in all out-of-hospital deaths, especially in victims of suicide and drowning.[11–13] Accordingly, the determination of alcohol in body fluids is the most frequently requested service from forensic science and toxicology laboratories worldwide.[14–17]

The role of alcohol intoxication in traffic crashes and deaths on the roads is well recognized, which has led to the creation of punishable BAC limits for driving.[18–21] Measuring a person's blood- or breath-alcohol concentration (BrAC) furnishes compelling evidence for the prosecution case and, if above the legal limit, a guilty verdict is virtually guaranteed.[20,21] People who perform skilled tasks like operating machinery or other safety-sensitive work should avoid drinking alcohol for obvious reasons. Indeed, alcohol use in the workplace is regulated by statute in the U.S. (1991 Omnibus Transportation Employee Testing Act), and similar legislation can be expected in other countries.[22] The threshold BAC in connection with workplace testing is set at 20 mg/dL (0.02 g/210 L in breath), below which no action is taken. However, drinking on duty or having a BAC above 40 mg/dL (0.04 g/210 L of breath) is prohibited and the offending individual will be removed from participating in safety-sensitive work and risks being dismissed.[22]

The punishment for driving under the influence of alcohol (DUI) includes a stiff fine, suspension of the driving license, and sometimes a period of imprisonment. Moreover, the validity of accident and insurance claims might be null and void if a person has been drinking and the BAC was above some threshold limit. The statutory alcohol limits for driving differ from country to country and

Table 5.2.1 Statutory BAC Limits for Driving in Different Parts of the World Expressed in Different Concentration Units

Country	g/100 mL	g/L (mg/mL)	mg/100 mL	mmol/L[a]
U.S. and Canada	0.08	0.80	80	17.3
Australia (most states)	0.05	0.50	50	10.9
U.K. and Ireland	0.08	0.80	80	17.3
Sweden and Norway[b]	0.02	0.20	20	4.3
Most EU countries	0.05	0.50	50	10.9

[a] Derived as [(mg/L)/46.07], where 46.07 is the molecular weight of ethanol to give mmol/L.

[b] The concentration unit mass/mass is used (mg/g or g/kg) so 0.02 mg/g = 0.21 mg/mL because the density of whole blood is 1.055 g/mL on average.

this seems to depend more on political forces rather than traffic safety research and studies of crash risk as a function of BAC.[20,21] Table 5.2.1 lists the current legal alcohol limits in blood for driving in various parts of the world. These critical values are so-called per se concentration limits and additional proof that the person was under the influence of alcohol is unnecessary for a successful prosecution.[20]

The evolution of methods for determination of alcohol in body fluids has a long history and the first wet-chemical oxidation procedures were introduced more than 100 years ago.[17,23,24] Because of ease of collection and the larger volumes available, urine was the first biological specimen to be used for analysis of alcohol in clinical investigations. Finding a high concentration of alcohol in a sample of urine was a more objective test to verify clinical signs and symptoms of drunkenness. Moreover, many studies showed that the concentration of alcohol was highly correlated with subjective and objective measures of alcohol influence and performance decrement. The methods available for analysis of alcohol in biological specimens have become considerably refined and exhibit high sensitivity, specificity, accuracy, and precision.[14,15,25]

Fast and reliable analytical methods are needed in emergency situations, such as when a patient is admitted unconscious smelling of alcohol. One needs to distinguish gross intoxication from head trauma, which might require immediate surgery to remove intracranial blood clots.[26–28] Analytical methods used at hospital clinical laboratories need to differentiate ethanol intoxication from the impairment caused by drinking more dangerous alcohols like methanol and ethylene glycol.[29–31]

Table 5.2.2 gives basic chemical information about the alcohols most commonly encountered in clinical and forensic toxicology, namely, ethanol, methanol, and ethylene glycol. Depending on the concentration of methanol and ethylene glycol in blood, the emergency physician has to make a life saving decision to treat the poisoned patient with invasive therapy and antidotes.[32–34] This might entail administration of ethanol by intravenous infusion of a 10% solution to reach a BAC of 100 to 120 mg/dL and maintain this level for several hours. More recently the drug fomepizole (4-methyl pyrazole) has been introduced as an alternative treatment and is more suitable for use in young children or those with liver dysfunction.[32,35] Both ethanol and fomepizole function as competitive inhibitors of hepatic alcohol dehydrogenase (ADH), and help to prevent the conversion of methanol and ethylene glycol into their toxic metabolites, formaldehyde and formic acid and glycolic and oxalic acids, respectively.[35,36] The methanol and ethylene glycol remaining unmetabolized can be removed from the blood by hemodialysis and bicarbonate is usually administered to counteract acidosis caused by the acid metabolites of these more toxic alcohols.[33] The various treatment strategies currently available for dealing with methanol and ethylene glycol poisoning have been extensively reviewed.[29–36]

The diagnosis of drunkenness has broad social-medical ramifications and great care is needed when forensic practitioners and others are called upon to interpret results of analysis and draw conclusions about the degree of alcohol influence and the consequences for behavioral impairment. This chapter provides an update of clinical and forensic-medical aspects of alcohol analysis in body fluids, and research into the disposition and fate of alcohol in the body are also covered. In post-

Table 5.2.2   Characteristic Features of Three Common Aliphatic Alcohols (Methanol, Ethanol and Ethylene Glycol) Often Encountered in Forensic and Clinical Toxicology

Property	Methanol	Ethanol	Ethylene Glycol
CAS-number[a]	65-46-1	64-17-5	107-21-1
Molecular weight	32.04	46.07	62.07
Molecular formula	C_2H_4O	C_2H_6O	$C_2H_6O_2$
Chemical formula	CH_3OH	CH_3CH_2OH	$(CH_2OH)_2$
Structure	Primary aliphatic alcohol	Primary aliphatic alcohol	Dihydroxy aliphatic alcohol (diol)
Structural formula			
Common name	Wood alcohol	Beverage or grain alcohol	Antifreeze solvent
Boiling point, °C	64.7	78.5	197
Melting point, °C	−95.8	−114.1	−13
Density, at 20°C	0.791	0.789	1.11
Water solubility	Mixes completely	Mixes completely	Mixes completely
Main metabolites	Formaldehyde and formic acid	Acetaldehyde and acetic acid	Glycolaldehyde, glycolic, glyoxylic and oxalic acid

[a] CAS, Chemical Abstract Service Registry Number.

mortem toxicology, the choice of specimens, the preservation and storage, and particularly the interpretation of the results require special considerations. The role of alcohol in post-mortem toxicology with main focus on interpreting the analytical findings is covered in more detail in Chapter 5.3.

5.2.2   Specimens for Clinical and Forensic Analysis of Alcohol

5.2.2.1   Concentration Units

Unfortunately, there is no generally accepted way of reporting the results of alcohol analysis in body fluids and it is seemingly impossible to reach a consensus among scientists, scientific journals, and forensic practitioners on this issue.[37,38] Most clinical chemistry laboratories use the International system of units (SI system) established by broad international agreement. According to this system, the standard for the unit of mass is the kilogram, the unit of volume is the liter, and the amount of substance is the mole. The concentrations of endogenous or exogenous substances in serum or plasma are therefore reported as mmol/L or μmol/L. By contrast, forensic science and toxicology laboratories report their analytical results in mass per unit volume units (mg/dL, g/L, g/dL or mg/mL) or in mass per unit mass units (g/kg or mg/g) when aliquots are weighed. The mass/mass unit is numerically less than the mass/volume unit by about 5.5% owing to the specific weight of whole blood, which is 1.055 g/mL on the average (1 mL whole blood weighs 1.055 g).[39] This means that a BAC of 100 mg/dL is the same as ~95 mg/100 g or 21.7 mmol/L.

5.2.2.2   Water Content of Serum and Whole Blood

The blood specimens received by forensic science and toxicology laboratories for analysis might be hemolyzed and are sometimes clotted. In contrast, the specimens analyzed at clinical laboratories usually consist of plasma or serum, that is, with the cellular elements, mainly red cells (erythrocytes), removed.[40] Because the water content of serum and plasma is higher than that of whole blood, the concentration of alcohol is also higher after removal of the red cells. Water content is a key factor controlling the distribution of alcohol in body fluids and this was recently the subject of a multicenter study in Germany.[41] The results reported by the three participating

Table 5.2.3   Mean, SD, CV%, and Range of Water Content of Serum (A) and Whole Blood (B) and the Serum/Blood Ratio of Water Contents (C) Based on Measurements Made at Three Different Laboratories in Germany

Laboratory	N	Mean g%	SD g%	CV%	Range g%
(A) Serum					
Kiel	230	90.49	0.86	0.95	87.2–93.3
Köln	503	90.71	0.54	0.59	88.6–92.2
Münster	100	90.75	0.61	0.67	89.1–92.8
Combined	833	90.66	0.66	0.72	87.2–93.3
(B) Whole blood					
Kiel	230	78.35	1.44	1.83	74.8–82.9
Köln	503	78.41	1.11	1.41	75.7–83.0
Münster	100	78.14	1.28	1.63	74.9–83.3
Combined	833	78.36	1.23	1.57	74.8–83.3
(C) Serum/Blood Ratio					
Kiel	230	1.156	0.0184	1.59	1.11–1.21
Köln	503	1.157	0.0145	1.25	1.10–1.20
Münster	100	1.162	0.0187	1.61	1.08–1.20
Combined	833	1.157	0.0163	1.40	1.08–1.21

laboratories are compared in Table 5.2.3 and the values are given in mass/mass units, namely, g water per 100 g specimen.

Because this work was done at three different laboratories each using highly reliably methods based on desiccation and gravimetric analysis, there is high confidence in the results reported.[42] To convert the results into mass/volume units, the values in Table 5.2.3 need to be multiplied by 1.055 (average density of whole blood is 1.055 g/mL).[39] The average serum/blood distribution ratio of water in this study was 1.157:1 and the standard deviation was 0.0163 ($N = 833$) with minimum and maximum values of 1.08 and 1.25. These results can be considered representative of people who drink and drive in Germany. Dividing the concentration of ethanol in serum by 1.16:1 gives the concentration expected in whole blood. Because plasma and serum contain the same amount of water, one expects the plasma/whole blood ratio of alcohol to be the same as the serum/whole blood ratio, as was shown empirically.[43] The results of alcohol analysis done at clinical chemistry laboratories should not be cited in drunken driving trials or other legal proceedings without an appropriate correction being made for the water content of the specimens or seeking expert help with interpretation of the results.[44,45]

The mean and standard deviation of the serum/whole blood distribution ratios of water from the German study[41] can be used to derive a 95% range of expected values in the relevant population as $1.16 \pm (1.96 \times 0.0163)$. Accordingly, 2.5% of individuals will have a serum/whole blood ratio above 1.19 and 2.5% will have a ratio below 1.12. Depending on requirements, more conservative values can be obtained by using the minimum and maximum values given in Table 5.2.3, namely 1.08 and 1.21.[41]

5.2.2.3   Blood Hematocrit and Hemoglobin

Hematocrit is defined as the percentage in a volume of whole blood represented by the red blood cells (erythrocytes) and is determined by centrifugation. The hematocrit is sometimes referred to as the packed red cell volume, and a common reference interval for healthy men is 39 to 49% compared with 35 to 45% for healthy women with wider ranges in young and elderly individuals.[40]

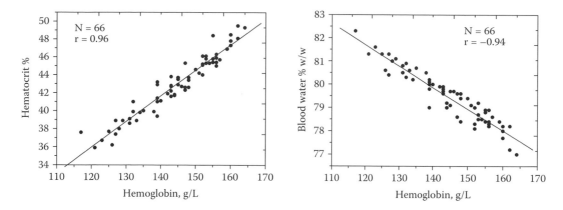

Figure 5.2.1 Strong positive correlation between hematocrit and hemoglobin content of venous blood samples (left plot) and strong negative correlation between water content and hemoglobin (right plot).

Because the water content of plasma is greater than that of whole blood and erythrocytes, one can expect that a blood specimen with high hematocrit (e.g., donated by a male subject) will contain less water than a blood specimen from a female with low hematocrit.[46] Extreme values in hematocrit and hemoglobin are likely to be found in conditions such as anemia (low values) or polycythemia (high values).[40,46]

Figure 5.2.1 (left graph) shows a strong positive correlation ($r = 0.96$) between blood hematocrit and hemoglobin content of whole blood specimens. The right plot shows a strong negative correlation ($r = -0.94$) between water content of whole blood and the hemoglobin content. These interrelationships will have a bearing on the plasma/whole blood and serum/whole-blood distribution ratios of alcohol in any individual case.

5.2.2.4   Alcohol Concentrations in Plasma and Whole Blood

Figure 5.2.2 shows mean concentration-time profiles of ethanol in plasma and whole blood after nine healthy men fasted overnight before drinking a bolus dose of ethanol (0.3 g/kg) diluted

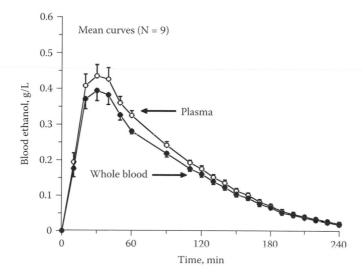

Figure 5.2.2 Mean concentration-time profiles of ethanol in specimens of whole blood and plasma from nine healthy men who drank a bolus dose of ethanol 0.30 g/kg mixed with orange juice in 15 min after an overnight fast.

Table 5.2.4   **Relationships between the Concentrations of Ethanol in Serum and the Expected Concentrations in Whole Blood Using Conversion Factors Based on Water Content of Serum and Whole Blood[41] (the 95% range and the minimum and maximum values are also calculated)**

Serum Alcohol[a] mg/100 mL	Blood Alcohol Mean mg/100 mL	Blood Alcohol 95% Range	Blood Alcohol min; max
20	17.2	16.7–17.7	16.5; 18.5
50	43.1	41.9–44.3	41.3; 46.3
80	68.9	67.1–70.9	66.1; 74.1
100	86.2	83.9–88.6	82.6; 92.6
150	129.3	125.8–132.9	123.9; 138.9
200	172.4	167.7–177.3	165.3; 185.1

[a] Mean serum/blood alcohol ratio 1.16:1, standard deviation 0.0163, and minimum and maximum values 1.08 and 1.21 (see Table 5.2.3).

with orange juice.[47,48] The plasma curves run systematically above the whole-blood curves as expected from the difference in water content of the specimens. In this study, the experimentally determined plasma/whole-blood ratios of alcohol ranged from 1.08 to 1.19.[47] In a study with drinking drivers, a mean distribution ratio of ethanol between plasma and whole blood was reported to be 1.14:1 (standard deviation 0.041).[49]

Table 5.2.4 compares the alcohol concentrations in plasma or serum with values calculated by assuming a mean ratio of 1.16 and minimum and maximum values of 1.08 and 1.21 according to the above-referenced study from Germany (Table 5.2.3). The results are reported for ethanol concentrations ranging from 20 to 200 mg/100 mL.[41]

As discussed by Rainey,[44] whenever the concentration of alcohol in plasma or serum is used to estimate the concentration in whole blood for law enforcement purposes, it is advisable to consider the inherent variations in plasma/blood ratio of alcohol. He recommended that a conversion factor of 1.22:1 should be used, thus corresponding to mean + 2 SD from the various studies cited. This higher conversion factor seems more appropriate in forensic casework instead of using a mean value and will give a more conservative estimate of the person's BAC. In criminal law, a beyond-a-reasonable-doubt standard is necessary, whereas in civil litigation a preponderance of the evidence is sufficient to determine the outcome.

5.2.2.5   Allowing for Analytical Uncertainty

When blood samples are submitted for forensic alcohol analysis, it is a standard practice to make the determinations in replicate, always duplicate, and sometimes in triplicate.[50–52] Finding a close agreement between the two measurements (high precision) gives added assurance that no mishaps have occurred during sample handling and analysis. Besides reporting the average result, an allowance is necessary to compensate for uncertainty (random and systematic error) in the analytical method used.[25,51,52] This is easily done by making a deduction from the mean result to give a lower 95, 99, or 99.9% confidence interval depending on requirements.

In connection with prosecution for DUI in Sweden, besides the mean alcohol concentration, it is standard practice to report the lowest concentration of alcohol in the specimen analyzed with a probability of 99.9%.[25] The suspect's true BAC is therefore not less than this value with confidence of 99.9% or, in other words, there is a risk of 1:1000 of being unfair to the accused. The amount deducted from the mean of a duplicate determination is given by $[3.09 \times (SD/2^{1/2})]$ where SD is the standard deviation for a single determination using an analytical system demonstrated to be under statistical control.[25,51] The factor 3.09 is obtained from statistical tables of the normal distribution. Although the mean result of analysis is the best estimate of a person's BAC, the deduction compensates for factors beyond the suspect's control and gives the benefit of the doubt in those instances when the true BAC is close to the legal limit for driving. In such borderline cases, the risk of reporting a result, which in reality was just below the legal limit, as being above the limit is only 1 in 1000. The use of a deduction has practical significance only for individuals with a BAC at or near the critical legal limit for driving.

This use of a deduction is not customary in clinical chemistry laboratories, where single analyses are usually made.[53,54] Instead, most clinical chemistry laboratories compare their results with established reference ranges derived from previous experiences with specimens from healthy individuals depending on age and gender.[53] The result for the patient sample is compared with a so-called "normal range" in a comparable population of healthy individuals.[54] The imprecision of the analytical methods are monitored from the expected coefficient of variation (CV%) derived from analysis of calibration standards or spiked biological specimens analyzed along with the unknowns.[40,53]

5.2.3 Measuring Alcohol in Body Fluids

5.2.3.1 Chemical Oxidation Methods

The first quantitative method of blood-alcohol analysis to gain general international acceptance in forensic science and toxicology was published in 1922[55] and became known as the Widmark micromethod (developed by Erik M.P. Widmark of Sweden). A specimen of capillary blood (100 mg) was sufficient for making a single determination and this could be obtained by pricking a fingertip or earlobe. Ethanol was determined by wet-chemistry oxidation with a mixture of potassium dichromate and sulfuric acid in excess. The amount of oxidizing agent remaining after the reaction was determined by iodometric titration.[55] Specially designed diffusion flasks permitted extraction of ethanol from the biological matrix by heating in a water bath for a few hours at 50°C. Ethanol and other volatiles were removed from the biological matrix by vaporization and oxidized within the flask and after cooling and addition of potassium iodide the final titrimetric analysis was done in the same flask. However, Widmark's method was not totally specific for determination of blood ethanol because other volatiles, if these were present, such as acetone, methanol or ether, were also oxidized by the reagents and gave false high ethanol readings. The likelihood of potential interfering substances (e.g., acetone) could be tested by making a qualitative analysis of urine by adding various chemical reagents and looking for any characteristic color change such as that seen with high levels of ketones.[56]

By the 1950s the chemical oxidation methods were improved by monitoring the end point by photometry rather than by volumetric titration.[17,56] Today, analytical procedures based on wet-chemistry oxidation reactions are virtually obsolete in clinical and forensic laboratories for determination of alcohol in body fluids.[14] The history, development, and application of chemical oxidation methods of alcohol analysis have been well covered in several review articles.[17,57-59]

5.2.3.2 Enzymatic Methods

Shortly after the enzyme alcohol dehydrogenase (ADH) was purified from horse liver and yeast in the early 1950s the way was clear for developing biochemical methods to determine alcohol in body fluids.[60-63] These methods offered milder oxidation conditions and analytical selectivity was enhanced compared with wet-chemistry oxidation procedures. The ADH derived from human or animal liver proved less selective for oxidation of ethanol compared with the enzyme obtained from yeast.[62] Other aliphatic alcohols (methanol, isopropanol, and n-propanol) were oxidized by mammalian ADH but not acetone, which was the most problematic substance for the older wet-chemical methods.[64] By optimizing the test conditions in terms of pH, reaction time, and temperature, methanol was not oxidized by yeast ADH and this source of the enzyme is still used today for clinical and forensic alcohol analysis.[62,63]

A typical manual ADH method might entail precipitation of plasma proteins by adding per-
chloric acid and then adjusting the pH of the supernatant to 9.6 with semicarbazide buffer.[62] The
purpose of the latter reagent, besides adjusting pH, was to trap the acetaldehyde produced during
ethanol oxidation and thus drive the reaction to completion. The buffer is usually pre-mixed with
the coenzyme NAD^+ before adding to the alcohol-containing supernatant, and finally the ADH
enzyme is added to start the reaction. The amount of NAD^+ that becomes reduced to NADH is
directly proportional to the concentration of ethanol in the original sample. After allowing the
mixture to stand at room temperature for about 1 h to reach an end point, the NADH formed was
determined by measuring absorption of ultraviolet (UV) light at a wavelength of 340 nm.

Later developments in ADH methods for analysis of alcohol tended to focus on separation of
proteins from the blood by semipermeable membranes (dialysis) or by micro-distillation to obtain
an aqueous ethanol solution for analysis.[65,66] With this modification and a Technicon® AutoAnalyzer
device, several hundred blood samples could be analyzed daily.[65] Scores of publications have
appeared describing diverse modifications and improvements to the original ADH method and
dedicated "reagent kits" are commercially available. These kits were ideal for use at hospital
laboratories and elsewhere where the throughput of samples was relatively low. Otherwise, most
efforts were directed toward automating the sample preparation and dispensing reagents to increase
sample throughput, and several batch analyzers or reaction rate analyzers appeared including a
micro-centrifugal analyzer using fluorescence light scattering for quantitative analysis.[67,68]

Enzymatic methods for determination of alcohol in body fluids are still used today in part
owing to the widespread availability of multichannel analyzers for testing urine for drugs of
abuse.[69] These procedures make use of a technique known as enzyme multiplied immunoassay
(EMIT), whereby an enzyme-labeled antigen reacts with ethanol or another drug and the change
in color after adding a substrate is measured by spectrophotometry.[69] The color-intensity is related
to the concentration of ethanol in the original specimen. Fluorescence polarization immunoassay
(FPIA) and the spin-off technology radiative energy attenuation (REA) are other examples of
analytical procedures developed to meet the increasing demand for drugs of abuse testing in urine
and therapeutic drug monitoring.[70–73] In several comparative studies, excellent agreement was
found for ethanol determined by REA and by gas chromatography in terms of accuracy and
precision.[70,73] The principles and practice of various immunoassay systems suitable for clinical
laboratory analysis were recently reviewed.[69]

Figure 5.2.3 shows a scatter plot comparing ethanol concentrations in urine determined by an
automated ADH method and also by headspace gas chromatography. The correlation was excellent:
$r = 0.99$. This kind of conventional $x–y$ scatter plot is best redrawn and displayed as a Bland and
Altman plot (Figure 5.2.4), whereby the difference in ethanol concentration by the two methods
(GC–ADH) is plotted against the average concentration [(GC + ADH)/2]. The mean difference
between the two methods indicates whether any bias exists between the two methods, which is a
measure of accuracy. The SD of the differences gives the magnitude of scatter or variability of the
individual differences and are referred to as limits of agreement between the two methods (±1.96
× SD), shown as dotted horizontal lines on the plot. This Bland and Altman plot has gained
considerable popularity for use in method comparison studies and makes it a lot easier to locate
outlier values.[74] Three such outliers are circled and indicated on the plot; note that these occurred
at very high BACs.

Despite many new developments in analytical technology for the analysis of alcohol in body
fluids, particularly EMIT, FPIA, and REA methods, gas chromatography still dominates the
instrument park at forensic toxicology laboratories owing to its superior selectivity. Indeed, some
recent work has shown that elevated concentrations of serum lactate and lactate dehydrogenase
might interfere with the analysis of alcohol by ADH methods.[75–77] This problem was traced to
various side reactions whereby the coenzyme NAD^+ was reduced to NADH by endogenous
substances and this could not be distinguished from NADH produced during the oxidation of

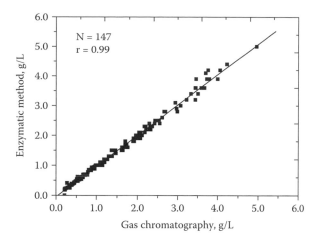

Figure 5.2.3 Conventional *x-y* scatter plot showing a high correlation between the concentrations of ethanol in urine determined by an automated enzymatic (ADH) method and by headspace gas chromatography (GC).

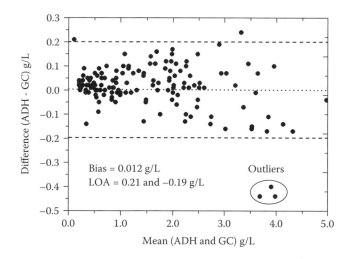

Figure 5.2.4 Bland and Altman plot of differences in results between the ADH and GC methods of analysis and the mean result of analysis by the two methods (data from Figure 5.2.3).

ethanol. This resulted in undesirable false positive results when plasma specimens from alcohol-free patients were analyzed.[76,77]

5.2.3.3 Gas Chromatographic Methods

In the early 1960s, physical-chemical methods began to be used for analysis of alcohol in body fluids such as infrared spectrometry, electrochemical oxidation, and gas-liquid chromatography (GLC).[78–83] Since then, GLC has become the method of choice for analysis of biological liquids in clinical and forensic laboratories. For determination of ethanol in breath, electrochemistry and infrared methods are widely used.[17] The first GLC methods required that the ethanol was extracted from blood by use of a solvent (e.g., *n*-propyl acetate) or by distillation, which was cumbersome and time-consuming.[78,79] Later developments meant that the blood was simply diluted (1:5 or 1:10) with an aqueous solution of an internal standard (*n*-propanol or *t*-butanol).[82,86] The five to ten times dilution with internal standard meant that matrix effects were eliminated and that aqueous alcohol standards could be used for calibration and standardization of the detector response.[82] The use of an internal standard also ensured that any unexpected variations in the GLC operating conditions during an analysis influenced the ethanol and the standard alike so the ratio of peak heights or peak areas (ethanol/standard) remained constant.[82]

The standard procedure entailed injecting 1 to 5 µL of the diluted blood into a heated chamber and any volatiles in the sample were mixed in a stream of helium or nitrogen, the carrier gas or mobile phase, which flowed through a glass or metal column with dimensions such as 2 m long by 0.3 mm inside diameter (i.d.). The column contained the liquid or stationary phase spread as a thin film over an inert solid support material, thus furnishing a large surface area. The volatile components of a mixture were distributed between the moving phase (carrier gas) and the liquid phase and depending on their physicochemical properties such as boiling point, functional groups present, and the relative solubility in the liquid phase, either partial or complete separation occurred during passage through the column. Polar stationary phases were an obvious choice for the analysis of alcohols and polyethylene glycol with average molecular weights of 400, 600, 1500, etc. became widely available and were known as Carbowax phases.[83–86] Otherwise, porous polymer materials such as Poropak Q and S were useful as packing materials for the separating columns when low-molecular-weight, volatile-like alcohols were being analyzed.[86]

A quantitative analysis of ethanol required monitoring the effluent from the column as a function of time originally with a thermal conductivity (TC) detector,[78] but this was later replaced with a flame ionization detector (FID), which was more sensitive and gave only a very small response to water vapor in body fluids.[81,82] The ethanol concentration in blood was calculated by comparing the detector response (peak height or peak area) with results of analyzing known strength aqueous alcohol standards and making a calibration plot. Methodological details of many of the older GC methods of blood-alcohol analysis have been reviewed elsewhere.[84–86]

Figure 5.2.5 is a schematic diagram of the headspace gas chromatographic (GC-HS) analysis, which has become the method of choice in forensic science and toxicology laboratories for determination of ethanol and other volatiles in body fluids.[87–91] HS-GC requires that the blood samples and aqueous standards are first diluted (1:5 or 1:10) with an aqueous solution of an internal standard and the mixture kept airtight in a small glass vial with crimped-on rubber septum. The vials are then heated to 50 or 60°C for about 30 min to achieve equilibrium between concentrations in gas (C_G) and liquid (C_L) phases for all volatiles in the specimen. Care is needed not to heat the sample for too long at 60°C, otherwise some of the ethanol might be oxidized into acetaldehyde by a non-enzymatic oxidation reaction involving oxyhemoglobin.[92] This undesirable effect can be avoided by pretreating the blood specimen with sodium azide or sodium dithionite, chemicals that block this oxidation reaction.[89,92] However, it is simpler to work with a lower equilibrium temperature (40 or 50°C), which also prevents this oxidation reaction.[89]

The headspace vapor can be injected into the gas chromatograph manually with the aid of a gas-tight syringe or, as is more usual, an automated sampling procedure. Automation is preferred because this gives a much more reproducible injection and thus a higher analytical precision. Dedicated equipment for GC headspace analysis has been available since the early 1960s and the U.S. company Perkin-Elmer has dominated the market. Various versions of its headspace instruments have appeared over the years and in chronological order these were called Multifract HS-40, HS-42, and HS-45, the numbers indicating the number of vials in the headspace carousel. A later version was called HS-100, and this was mounted on a Sigma 2000 gas chromatograph allowing automated analysis of up to 100 specimens. The AutoSystem XL GC is the most recent development and works together with TurboMatrix 110 headspace sampler. This arrangement permits overnight batch analysis of up to 110 specimens in a single run.

Packed, wide-bore, and capillary columns are feasible together with headspace gas chromatography and for high resolution work, such as when complex mixtures are being analyzed, capillary columns are essential.[93,94] Traditional packed columns made of glass or stainless steel are, however, more robust and are still widely used in some laboratories for routine blood-alcohol analysis. Figure

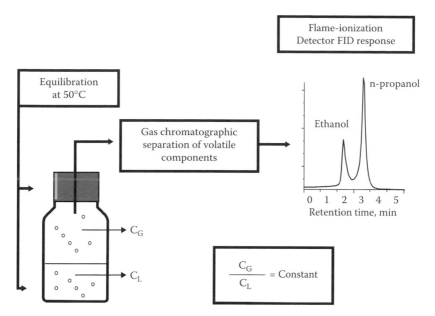

Figure 5.2.5 Schematic diagram of headspace gas chromatography. The blood or urine sample is first diluted 1:10 with an aqueous solution of an internal standard (*n*-propanol) directly into a glass vial made airtight with a crimped-on rubber membrane stopper. After reaching an equilibration at 50°C for 20 to 30 min, a sample of the vapor in equilibrium with the diluted specimen is removed either with a gas-tight syringe or by some automated sampling procedure and injected into the carrier gas (N_2) for transport through the chromatographic column to the detector. The resulting trace (chromatogram) shows a peak for ethanol followed by a peak for the internal standard (*n*-propanol). C_G is the ethanol concentration in the gas or air phase and C_L is the corresponding concentration in the liquid (blood or urine) phase at equilibrium.

5.2.6 gives examples of gas chromatographic traces obtained by headspace analysis of an aqueous mixture of volatiles commonly encountered in forensic toxicology. The column was made of capillary glass designed and marketed especially for blood-alcohol analysis (RtX-BAC1 and RtX-BAC2) and purchased from Restek Corporation (Bellefonte, PA, U.S.A.). The ethanol response is well resolved from potential interfering substances in an isothermal run lasting for 2 min. Table 5.2.5 gives retention times relative to *n*-propanol as internal standard for a wider range of low molecular volatiles under normal HS-GC conditions.

Sampling and analysis of the vapor in equilibrium with the blood specimen has the advantage that non-volatile constituents of the biological matrix (fats, proteins, etc.) do not clog the syringe or the column packing material. Sensitivity of the assay can be enhanced and matrix effects eliminated in another way, namely, by saturating the blood samples and aqueous ethanol standards with an inorganic salt such as NaCl, K_2CO_3, or Na_2SO_4, e.g., 0.5 mL blood + 1 g salt.[86,89] A salting-out technique is useful when trace concentrations of volatiles are analyzed in blood such as endogenous alcohols or alcoholic beverage congeners.[95–98]

More recently, the headspace vapor in equilibrium with blood or other body fluid can also be removed and transferred to a GC instrument with a solid phase micro-extraction probe.[99–100] The needle of the probe contains a porous polymer material and this is inserted into the headspace vapor to attain equilibrium with any volatiles in the flask. The probe is then withdrawn from the vial and introduced into the heated injection port of the gas chromatograph. This sampling technique is well suited for analysis of a wide range of volatile agents such as aliphatic and aromatic hydrocarbons as well as many water-soluble alcohols and ketones.[99]

Another modification of the standard headspace analysis involved inclusion of a cryofocusing step prior to GC analysis with a liquid nitrogen freeze trap.[101] This serves to concentrate the specimen prior to chromatographic analysis of volatiles with a capillary or wide-bore column. This was the

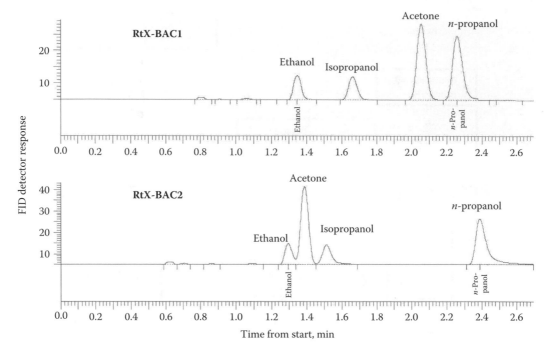

Figure 5.2.6 Gas chromatographic traces obtained from analysis of an aqueous mixture containing several volatile substances often encountered in forensic blood samples. The analysis was done by headspace gas chromatography using commercially available capillary columns (Restek Corporation) RtX-BAC1 and RtX-BAC2.

Table 5.2.5 Relative Retention Times (min) for Analysis of Volatile Compounds by Headspace Gas Chromatography Using Two Different Stationary Phases

Substance	Stationary Phase RtX-BAC1	Stationary Phase RtX-BAC2
Acetaldehyde	0.53	0.34
Acetone	0.91	0.57
Acetonitrile	0.91	0.81
1-Butanol	2.05	2.20
2-Butanone	1.37	1.04
t-Butanol	0.88	0.69
Ethanol	0.59	0.53
Isopropanol	0.74	0.62
Methanol	0.47	0.40

Note: Times are relative to n-propanol as internal standard and all determinations were made with a Perkin-Elmer AutoSystem XL gas chromatograph in isothermal mode and a TurboMatrix 110 headspace sampler.

approach used to measure trace amounts of endogenous volatile alcohols in blood samples or to establish the congener profile in blood after ingesting different kinds of alcoholic beverages.[97,98,101]

Gas chromatographic methods of analysis have the unique advantage that they combine a qualitative screening analysis of the components of a mixture based on their relative retention time after injection to appearance of the peak with a simultaneous quantitative analysis by measuring the detector response as reflected in the height or area of the resulting peak response.[102] Several comprehensive reviews have dealt with forensic applications of gas chromatography including applications for blood-alcohol analysis.[14,17,86,103,104] One of these reviews looked at more general applications of headspace analysis when applied to biological specimens for determination of organic volatile substances, including alcohols.[104]

In forensic work, it is advisable to use two different column packing materials, thus furnishing different retention times for ethanol and other volatiles that might be encountered in forensic blood samples. This becomes important whenever blood or tissue samples are putrefied and therefore might contain interfering substances with the same retention times as ethanol on a single stationary phase. The risk of obtaining coincident retention times on two or more stationary phases is reduced considerably. Otherwise, two different methodologies such as GC and chemical oxidation or GC and enzymatic oxidation could be used to analyze duplicate aliquots from the same blood sample.[105] HS-GC with two different detectors (flame ionization and electron capture) has been used to screen biological fluids for a large number of volatiles.[106] Such a dual-detector system was recommended for use in clinical toxicology to aid in the diagnosis of acute poisoning when a host of unknown substances might be responsible for the patient's condition.[107]

5.2.3.4 Other Methods

A multitude of other analytical methods exist for blood-alcohol analysis, but none of these can match HS-GC, which is considered the gold standard in forensic and clinical toxicology laboratories. Instead of a flame ionization detector, electrochemical sensing[108] or a metal oxide semiconductor device[109] has been applied to headspace analysis of blood samples. However, lack of a chromatographic separation step meant that neither of these procedures was sufficiently selective when interfering substances might be present. Some authorities recommend making a rapid screening of biological samples by ADH methods to eliminate those that do not contain any alcohol.[66] All positives are later run by the usual headspace analysis and gas chromatography. This same approach proved suitable for measuring the strength of alcoholic beverages and gave good results compared with a standard gas chromatographic method.[110]

Several novel methods for alcohol analysis make use of biosensors prepared from immobilized enzymes or bioelectrodes, and these have found applications in clinical chemistry laboratories.[111–115] The end point of the enzymatic reactions can be monitored either by amperometric, colorimetric, or spectrophotometric methods.[113,114] The enzyme alcohol oxidase has attracted attention for analysis of alcohol in body fluids and gives reasonably good semiquantitative results.[115–118] These systems are similar in principle to measuring blood glucose with a glucose oxidase electrode and open the possibility for self-testing applications such as the glucose dipstick technology.

Fourier transform infrared spectrometry (FTIR) was recently applied to the determination of alcohol in beer,[119] and when a purge-and-trap capillary GC separation stage was included, FTIR could also be adopted to measure a wide range of low-molecular-weight volatiles including ethanol.[120] A method based on proton nuclear magnetic resonance spectroscopy proved suitable for use in pharmacokinetic studies to analyze ethanol, acetone, and isopropanol in plasma samples.[121,122]

In clinical and emergency medicine, depression of freezing point (osmometry) has a long history as a screening test for certain pathological conditions.[123,124] Diabetes mellitus and uremia are often associated with abnormally high concentrations of plasma-glucose and plasma-urea, respectively. These common conditions cause discrepancies between the osmolality expected from the inorganic ions Na^+ and K^+ and the values measured by depression of the freezing point. Dedicated equipment for osmometry is available at most hospital laboratories and only about 0.2 mL of plasma is needed to measure freezing-point depression. Moreover, the method is nondestructive, which means that the same specimen of plasma can be used later for making a confirmatory toxicological analysis if necessary.[124]

The osmolal gap is defined as the difference between the measured serum osmolality determined by freezing point depression and the calculated serum molarity, from known osmotically active substances in the serum specimen (sodium, potassium urea, glucose, and ethanol).[40] Indeed, in emergency medicine, ethanol is the commonest cause of finding a high serum osmolality.[124–126] Ethanol carries an appreciable osmotic effect because of its low molecular weight (46.05), high solubility in water, and the fact that large quantities are ingested to produce gross intoxication.[126] Finding a normal osmolal gap speaks against the presence of a high concentration of ethanol but a high osmolal gap does not necessarily rule out that this was caused by ethanol. Other toxic solvents in serum such as acetone, methanol, isopropanol, and ethylene glycol will increase the serum or plasma osmolality as revealed by freezing point depression.[126] The principal limitation of using osmolal gap as a rapid test for high serum ethanol is the lack of selectivity because other toxic alcohols and non-electrolytes if present will be falsely reported as ethanol. Nevertheless, papers continue to be published dealing with the principles and practice of freezing point osmometry in emergency toxicology.[127]

Considerable interest has developed in point-of-care or near patient testing and in this connection non-invasive methods are preferred. Near-infrared spectrometry is a technique with huge potential for non-invasive analysis of various substances (e.g., tissue glucose) and more recently also tissue ethanol.[128,129] A light with fixed wavelength is beamed through a subject's fingertip or arm and after processing the absorption bands of the emitted light into their specific wavelengths various constituents in the tissue water can be identified and for some substances a quantitative analysis is possible. However, disentangling the signals of interest from the background noise generated by other biological molecules has proved a challenging problem. Progress is rapidly being made with the aid of sophisticated computer-aided pattern recognition techniques. Near-infrared spectroscopy has already been successfully applied to the analysis of glucose,[130] and a recent publication described the application of a similar technique for analysis of alcohol in tissue in a completely non-invasive way.[129] The future of such technology in clinical and forensic work remains to be seen.

The feasibility of combining gas chromatography (GC) to separate the volatile components in a mixture and mass spectrometry (MS) as the detector was demonstrated many years ago.[131] GC-MS provides an unequivocal qualitative analysis of ethanol from its three major mass fragments: m/z 31 (base peak), m/z 45, and m/z 46 (molecular ion).[132] Isotope-dilution GC-MS is of course feasible if instead of n-propanol as internal standard d_5-ethnaol is used ($C^2H_3{}^2H_2OH$).[133] Selected ion monitoring and deuterium-labeled ethanol was also used to distinguish between ethanol formed post-mortem by the action of bacteria on blood glucose using an animal model.[134,135] In a clinical pharmacokinetic study, unlabeled ethanol was administered mixed with its deuterium labeled analogue to investigate the bioavailability of ethanol and the role of first-pass metabolism in the gut.[136]

5.2.4 Breath-Alcohol Analysis

The smell of alcohol on the breath of a drinker has always been recognized as a sign of excess alcohol consumption. Quantitative studies demonstrate that only about 1 to 2% of the alcohol ingested is expelled unchanged in the breath. Breath-alcohol instruments were developed to provide a fast and non-invasive way of monitoring alcohol concentration in the blood. A large body of literature has dealt with the principles and practice of breath-alcohol analysis and the associated technology for applications in research, clinical practice, and law enforcement.[137–142] Analysis of a person's expired air furnishes an indirect way of monitoring volatile endogenous substances in the pulmonary blood and this approach has many interesting applications in clinical and diagnostic medicine.[143,144] However, the main application of breath-alcohol instruments is in the field of traffic-law enforcement for testing drunk drivers and more recently also for workplace alcohol testing.[137,141,142] Two categories of instrument for breath-alcohol analysis can be distinguished depending on whether the results are intended as a qualitative screening test for alcohol or as binding evidence for prosecution of drunk drivers (Table 5.2.6).

5.2.4.1 Handheld Screening Instruments

Various handheld devices are available for roadside pre-arrest screening of drinking drivers to indicate whether a certain threshold concentration of alcohol has been surpassed.[141,142] Such screen-

Table 5.2.6   Classification of Currently Available Instruments for Breath-Alcohol Analysis According to the Main Area of Application and the Analytical Principle Used

Instrument	Main Area of Application	Analytical Principle
Alcolmeter	Roadside screening of motorist, also in the workplace and at hospital casualty departments	Electrochemical oxidation (fuel cell)
Alco-Sensor*	Roadside screening of motorist, also in the workplace and at hospital casualty departments	Electrochemical oxidation (fuel cell)
Alcotest*	Roadside screening of motorist, also in the workplace and at hospital casualty departments	Electrochemical oxidation (fuel cell)
Lifeloc	Roadside screening of motorist, also in the workplace and at hospital casualty departments	Electrochemical oxidation (fuel cell)
Alcotest 7110	Evidence for prosecution of drinking drivers	Electrochemical oxidation and infrared (9.5 µm)
Intoxilyzer 8000	Evidence for prosecution of drinking drivers	Infrared analysis at 3.4 µm and 9.5 µm
BAC Datamaster	Evidence for prosecution of drinking drivers	Infrared analysis at three wavelengths close to 3.4 µm
Intoximeter EC/IR	Evidence for prosecution of drinking drivers	Electrochemical oxidation

* Also being used for roadside evidential testing in some U.S. states.

ing tests are usually conducted at the roadside, and for evidential purposes, a more controlled breath-alcohol analysis is usually mandatory. The instruments for evidential purposes are larger, more sophisticated, and include ways to check accurate calibration, analyze alcohol-free room air, and to produce a printed record of the results. In short, they furnish a quantitative analysis of BrAC and serve as binding evidence for prosecuting drunk drivers.[145,146] Breath-alcohol instruments have also found applications in clinical pharmacokinetic studies of ethanol and drug-alcohol interactions.[147,148] Handheld breath-alcohol analyzers are also very practical for use in emergency medicine as a quick and easy way to monitor whether a patient's behavior and signs and symptoms of impairment can be attributed to alcohol influence.[149–151]

The analytical principles for measuring ethanol in the exhaled air depend in part on the area of application, that is, whether results are intended for qualitative screening or evidential purposes.[148] Most handheld screening devices incorporate electrochemical "fuel-cell" sensors that oxidize ethanol to acetaldehyde and in the process produce free electrons. The electric current generated is directly proportional to the amount of ethanol consumed by the cell (Table 5.2.6). Acetone, which is the most abundant endogenous volatile exhaled in breath, is not oxidized at the electrode surface so elevated concentrations of this ketone (e.g., in untreated diabetes) will not cause a false-positive response.[152] However, if high concentrations of methanol or isopropanol are present in exhaled breath, these also undergo electrochemical oxidation although at different rates compared with ethanol.[151] Care is needed when test results with fuel-cell instruments are interpreted because isopropanol, under some circumstances, can be formed in the body by reduction of endogenous acetone.[153] The concentration of acetone in blood reaches abnormally high levels during food deprivation, prolonged fasting (dieting), or during diabetic ketoacidosis.[152]

5.2.4.2 Evidential Breath-Testing Instruments

Most of the evidential breath-testing instruments used today identify and measure the concentration of alcohol by its absorption of infrared energy at wavelengths of 3.4 or 9.5 µm, which corresponds to the C–H and C–O vibration stretching in the ethanol molecules, respectively (Table 5.2.6).[17,154–156] Selectivity for identifying ethanol is enhanced by combining infrared absorption at 9.5 µm and electrochemical oxidation within the same unit and the Alcotest 7110 features this dual-sensor technique.[141,142] Another example from the latest generation of breath-test instruments

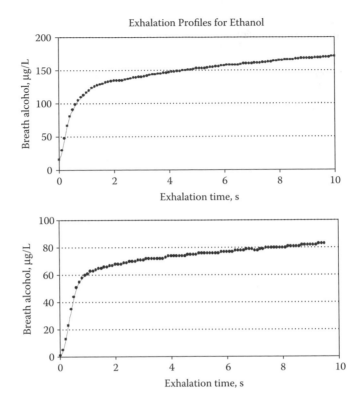

Figure 5.2.7 Breath-alcohol profiles during a prolonged exhalation by two test subjects.

is the Intoxilyzer 8000, which makes use of infrared wavelengths at 3.4 and 9.5 μm for identification and analysis of ethanol. This reduces considerably the risk of other breath volatiles, if any exist, being reported as ethanol.

Modern evidential breath-alcohol instruments are equipped with microprocessors that control the entire breath-test sequence including the exhaled volume and alcohol concentration and the exact shape of the BrAC–time profile is monitored and stored in the computer. Examples of exhalation profiles for two individuals tested with a state-of-the-art evidential breath-alcohol analyzer are given in Figure 5.2.7. One notices a rapid rise in the concentration of exhaled ethanol, and after just a few seconds of starting the exhalation, 70% of the final value is reached. Thereafter, the BrAC continues to increase although this occurs much more gradually until the person reaches the end of the exhalation after 9 to 10 s. Note that a BrAC plateau is never reached.

The rules and regulations governing evidential breath-alcohol tests stipulate the need for an observation and deprivation period of at least 15 min before starting the test.[157–159] Immediately after finishing a drink and for some time afterwards, the concentration of alcohol in the mucous surfaces of the mouth will be higher than that expected from the coexisting BAC. Time is needed for the alcohol to dissipate, and many studies have shown that this takes 15 to 20 min even after gargling with whisky or mouthwash.[160,161] The latest generation of breath-alcohol analyzers is equipped with algorithms that monitor the shape of the BrAC exhalation profile to help disclose abnormalities that might be caused by mouth alcohol. Besides the problem with alcohol in the mouth from a recent drink, the operator of the breath instrument should also ensure the person does not hiccup, burp, belch, or regurgitate stomach contents just before testing. This might result in a more dangerous form of mouth alcohol that is not so easily detected by monitoring the slope of the exhalation profile.[162]

Reporting results of breath-alcohol analysis can be a bit confusing and depends on whether the testing was done for clinical or traffic law enforcement purposes. In hospitals, it is standard practice

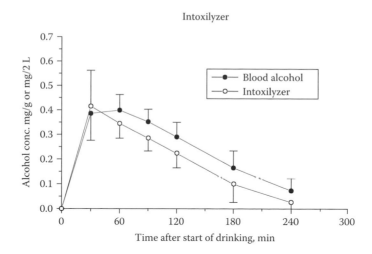

Figure 5.2.8 Relationship between the concentrations of ethanol in venous blood and end-expired breath determined with Intoxilyzer 5000, a quantitative infrared analyzer.

to translate the measured BrAC into the presumed concentration in venous blood, which requires use of a calibration factor. This is referred to as the blood/breath ratio and the instrument gives results directly in terms of BAC derived as [BrAC × ratio = BAC]. The value of the blood/breath ratio is generally taken to be 2100:1 (U.S. and Canada) although values of 2300:1 (U.K., Ireland, and Holland) and 2000:1 (Germany, France, Spain) are accepted. For legal purposes the BrAC is not converted to BAC but instead as g/210 L breath in U.S. so the 2100:1 blood/breath ratio is affirmed by statute.[159,160] However, many blood-alcohol and breath-alcohol comparisons show that a factor of 2100:1 gives a generous margin of safety to the individual.

Direct comparisons have shown that the concentration of alcohol in venous blood is about 10 to 15% higher compared with BrAC (× 2100) when samples are taken in the post-absorptive phase.[153] A closer agreement between the two methods of measurement is obtained using a 2300:1 factor for calibration purposes.[154] This is illustrated in Figure 5.2.8, which compares mean concentration-time profiles in venous blood and end-exhaled breath in ten subjects after they drank 0.4 g ethanol per kg body weight at about 2 h after their last meal.[156] The breath-alcohol instrument in this study was an Intoxilyzer 5000, which has been widely used for legal purposes in the U.S. and elsewhere.[153,155,163]

5.2.4.3 Blood/Breath Ratio of Alcohol

Studies have shown that the BAC/BrAC ratio of alcohol changes as a function of the time after drinking depending on whether tests were made on the absorption or the post-absorptive part of the alcohol curve.[164-166] The blood-to-breath alcohol ratio tends to be less than 2100:1 (1800 to 2000) during the absorption phase and greater than 2100:1 (2200 to 2400) in the post-absorptive phase. One reason for this temporal variation stems from the fact that venous instead of arterial blood was used for determination of alcohol.[167,168] The alcohol concentration in pulmonary blood reaching the air sacs (alveoli) of the lungs runs closer to the concentration in arterial blood transporting alcohol to tissue water compared with venous blood returning blood to the heart.

Figure 5.2.9 shows mean concentration–time profiles of alcohol derived from blood samples drawn from indwelling catheters in a radial artery at the wrist and a cubital vein at the elbow on the same arm.[167] The volunteers were healthy men who drank a moderate bolus dose of ethanol (0.6 g/kg body weight) 5 to 15 min before providing specimens of venous and arterial blood nearly simultaneously at various times after drinking ended. The concentration of alcohol in arterial blood samples exceeded venous blood samples during the first 90 min post-dosing whereas at all later

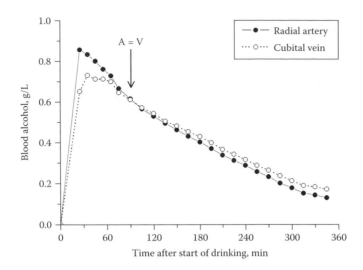

Figure 5.2.9 Mean blood-alcohol curves comparing the concentrations of ethanol in blood from a radial artery and a cubital vein on the same arm. The curves depict nine healthy men who drank 0.6 g ethanol per kg body weight in 2 to 15 min. Standard error bars are omitted for clarity.

times the venous blood was slightly higher than arterial blood. The arterial and venous concentrations were the same at only one time point at about 90 min post-drinking.

Note that for clinical applications, the breath-alcohol instruments are calibrated to estimate the alcohol concentration in whole blood and not the concentration in plasma or serum. This is often overlooked by clinicians who fail to appreciate the difference between whole blood and plasma concentrations of alcohol. To derive the concentration of alcohol in plasma or serum indirectly by analysis of breath, the instrument would need to be calibrated with a plasma/breath factor of about 2600:1 because whole blood contains about 15% less alcohol than the same volume of plasma or serum (Table 5.2.3).

When breath-alcohol testing is used for traffic law enforcement the results are almost always reported as the concentration of alcohol in the breath analyzed without considering the person's BAC. This avoids making any assumptions about the blood/breath ratio and its variability between and within individuals. Statutory limits for driving in many countries are therefore written in terms of threshold BAC and BrAC depending on the specimen analyzed.[166] Evidential breath-alcohol tests should be done in duplicate and the protocol should include analysis of room air blank and a known strength air–alcohol mixture as a control standard.[169,170] Results from all breath and control tests along with the date and time of testing as well as positive identification of the suspect should be available as a print-out and also stored online for later downloading to a central computer network.[169,170]

5.2.5 Quality Assurance Aspects of Alcohol Analysis

Much has been written about quality assurance of clinical laboratory analysis including concepts such as precision, accuracy, linearity, recovery, sensitivity, and limits of detection and quantitation of the method.[171] In addition, when results are used as evidence in criminal and civil litigation, the chain of custody record of the specimens is extremely important to document. This chain must be maintained intact from the moment of sampling to the moment results are reported, and each person involved in handling, transport, analysis, and storage of the specimen must be traceable from the written records. The entire analytical procedure including the actual chromatographic traces as well as proof that the instrument was properly calibrated on the day the blood specimens were analyzed might need to be verified at a later date. Participation in nationally or internationally recognized external proficiency tests is another essential element of quality assurance of laboratory results.[172]

The important concepts in development and validation of analytical methods include accuracy, precision, linearity, range, specificity/selectivity, limit of detection, and quantitation, and these terms are explained in brief below.[170,171]

Accuracy is defined as the closeness of agreement of the analytical result with a known reference or assigned value. Accuracy is therefore a measure of the exactness of the method. The difference if any between the true value and the value found is called analytical bias.

Precision describes the magnitude of random error as reflected in the closeness of agreement of multiple determinations on the same specimen. If the replicate measurements are made within the same analytical run, the calculated precision estimated is referred to as repeatability of the method. When replicates are made in different runs or at different laboratories by different people, then the analytical precision is referred to as reproducibility of the method. In mathematical terms, precision is reflected in the standard deviation (SD) of at least ten replicate measurements at a certain concentration of the target analyte. For obvious reasons, reproducibility can be expected to be poorer than repeatability. For blood-ethanol assay, the SD tends to increase as concentration in the specimen increases, and therefore precision is often expressed as a coefficient of variation (SD/mean) × 100, which tends to decrease slightly as the concentration of ethanol increases.

The terms **sensitivity** and **specificity** are often used interchangeably and they generally refer to a method's ability to distinguish between different analytes in a mixture and allow a response for just the substance of interest, that is, without interference from potential endogenous or exogenous compounds.

Linearity is the ability of a method to give results that are directly proportional to concentration of the target analyte or can be expressed by a well-defined mathematical transformation and shown to be a function of concentration over a certain range.

The **range** is the interval between the upper and lower concentrations of analyte that can be determined with sufficient accuracy, precision, and linearity.

The **limit of detection** (LOD) is the lowest concentration of analyte in a specimen that can be distinguished from background signals or instrument noise. Mathematically LOD is defined as 3 × the SD obtained from analysis of a blank specimen.

The **limit of quantitation** (LOQ) is the concentration of analyte in a sample that can be determined with certainty. Mathematically LOD is defined as 10 × the SD obtained from analysis of a blank specimen.

The most important features of pre-analytical, analytical, and post-analytical aspects of blood-alcohol analysis are presented below.

5.2.5.1 Pre-Analytical Factors

The subject or patient should be informed of the reason for taking a blood sample and, when necessary, informed written consent obtained. The equipment used for drawing blood is normally an evacuated tube (5- or 10-mL Vacutainer tubes) with sterile needle attachment. The blood is taken from an antecubital vein, and if necessary a tourniquet is applied to make it easier to visualize a suitable vein. The volume of blood drawn depends on the requirements and number of substances to be analyzed whether only ethanol or ethanol and other drugs of abuse. Even though in the case of ethanol only a few hundred microliters of blood are needed for each assay, the Vacutainer tubes should be filled with as much blood as possible. Sufficient blood should be available to allow making several determinations of the ethanol concentration and any retesting that might be necessary as well as common drugs of abuse. The specimen tubes should be gently inverted a few times immediately after collection to facilitate mixing and dissolution of the chemical preservatives; sodium fluoride (10 mg/mL) to inhibit the activity of various enzymes, microorganisms, and yeasts, and potassium oxalate (5 mg/mL) as an anticoagulant. The tubes of blood should be labeled with the person's name, the date and time of sampling, and the name of the person who took the sample should also be recorded. The Vacutainer tubes containing blood should be sealed in such a way as to prevent unauthorized handling or tampering and special adhesive paper strips are available for this purpose. The blood samples and other relevant paperwork should then be secured with tape so that any deliberate manipulating or adulteration is easily detected by laboratory personnel after shipment. After taking the samples, the tubes of blood should be stored in a cold room before being sent to the laboratory by express courier mail service.

The question of a deficient blood volume in the Vacutainer tubes sent for analysis of alcohol and the influence this might have on accuracy of HS-GC analysis was recently investigated in two separate publications.[173,174] It was alleged that a very small volume of blood meant an excess amount of sodium fluoride and that this increased the ethanol concentration in the headspace flask by a salting-out effect. This led to an acquittal in a drunken driving case trial in the court of appeals in the U.K., and the prosecution failed to rebut the argument with expert testimony. The new studies showed that an abnormally high concentration of NaF increased not only the concentration of ethanol in the headspace but also the concentration of the n-propanol internal standard. Because the ratio of responses EtOH/PrOH is used for quantitative analysis, the resulting ethanol concentration should be unchanged. In reality, it was shown that n-propanol was salted-out slightly more effectively than ethanol with the net result that the blood-ethanol concentration reported was lower than expected and was thus to the suspect's benefit.

Although pre-analytical factors are probably more important to consider when endogenous substances are analyzed such as in clinical chemistry laboratories, a standardized sampling protocol is also important for forensic blood-alcohol analysis.[175,176] Two tubes of blood should be drawn in rapid succession and the skin cleaned with soap and water and not with an organic solvent such as ether, isopropanol, or ethanol. Obviously, the blood samples should not be taken from veins into which intravenous fluids are being administered.[177] This kind of emergency treatment is often given as a first-aid to counteract shock or trauma as a result of involvement in traffic accidents. The blood samples should be taken only by trained personnel such as a phlebotomist, registered nurse, or physician.

5.2.5.2 *Analytical Factors*

The blood specimens must be carefully inspected when they arrive at the laboratory making a note whether or not the seals on the package as well as the individual tubes of blood are intact. If the specimen seems unusually dilute or if there are blood clots, then this should be noted. There are two ways to deal with clotted samples: (1) either centrifuge the specimen and use an aliquot of the supernatant for analysis and then report the results as a serum concentration or (2) homogenize the clot and analyze an aliquot of the hemolyzed blood specimen. Details of any mishaps occurring during transport of specimens such as breakage of the packaging, leakage of blood, etc., as well as the date and time of arrival should be recorded. Information written on the Vacutainer tubes should be compared with other documentation to ensure the suspect's name and the date and time of sampling are correct. The same unique identification number or barcode should be added to all paperwork and biological specimens received and this number used to monitor passage of the specimens through the laboratory. Ensure that the erythrocytes and plasma fractions are adequately mixed before removing aliquots of whole blood for analysis of ethanol. Replicate determinations can be made with different chromatographic systems and preferably by different technicians working independently. Any unidentified peaks on the gas chromatograms should be noted because these might indicate the presence of other volatiles in the blood sample.

5.2.5.3 *Post-Analytical Factors*

Quality assurance of individual results can be controlled by looking at critical differences (range) between replicate determinations.[170] The size of the difference will be larger, the higher the concentration of ethanol in the blood specimen because precision tends to decrease with an increase in the concentration of ethanol. Control charts offer a useful way to monitor day-to-day performance in the laboratory; one chart is used to depict random errors or precision and another chart to show systematic errors or bias derived by analysis of known strength standards together with unknowns.[178,179] These charts make it easy to detect sudden deterioration in analytical performance as shown by the scatter of individual values and the number of outliers.[178]

The rate of loss of alcohol during storage needs to be established under refrigerated conditions (+4°C) and also when specimens are kept deep frozen.[180–182] If necessary, corrections can be applied to blood specimen reanalyzed after prolonged periods of storage. In our experience, the blood-ethanol concentration decreases only slightly during storage at 4°C at a rate of 1 to 2 mg/dL per month.[148] Chromatographic traces and other evidence corroborating the analytical results such as calibration plots or response factors all need to be carefully labeled and stored in fire-proof cabinets. Today it is virtually mandatory that a forensic science or toxicology laboratory be accredited for the tasks they perform.[183,184] Participation in external proficiency trials of analytical performance is also a mandatory requirement to build confidence in the analytical reports.[172,185] When analytical results are used for criminal prosecution, information of the kind discussed above must be open to discovery and needs to be available for scrutiny.

5.2.5.4 Interlaboratory Proficiency Tests

Two papers looked at the results from interlaboratory proficiency tests of blood-alcohol analysis at clinical chemistry laboratories.[172,185] In one study, originating from Sweden, all participants were clinical chemistry laboratories and all used gas chromatographic analysis of plasma-ethanol. The coefficients of variation (CVs) between laboratories were within the range 10 to 17%.[172] In a similar study among U.K. laboratories, the corresponding CVs depended in part on the kind of methodology used for determination alcohol and immunoassays generally performed worse than gas chromatographic methods (liquid injection and headspace technique) and the CVs ranged from 8 to 20%.[185] It should be noted that determination of toxicological substances such as ethanol in blood is not the primary concern of clinical chemistry laboratories.

Table 5.2.7 presents results from an interlaboratory comparison of blood-alcohol analysis at specialist forensic toxicology laboratories in the Nordic countries (Denmark, Finland, Iceland, Norway, and Sweden). All participants used headspace gas chromatography for the determinations and the blood samples were obtained from apprehended drinking drivers. The CV between labo-

Table 5.2.7 Results of a Declared Interlaboratory Proficiency Test of Blood-Alcohol Analysis at Specialist Forensic Toxicology Laboratories In the Nordic Countries

Laboratory	Blood-1	Blood-2	Blood-3	Blood-4	Blood-5	Blood-6
1	0.46	1.01	2.15	1.62	0.74	1.75
2	0.47	1.01	2.27	1.70	0.78	1.83
3	0.46	1.01	2.26	1.67	0.77	1.81
4	0.47	1.00	2.17	1.66	0.78	1.81
5	0.48	1.01	2.15	1.66	0.78	1.79
Mean	0.47	1.01	2.20	1.66	0.77	1.80
SD	0.008	0.005	0.060	0.029	0.017	0.030
CV%	1.7%	0.49%	2.7%	1.7%	2.2%	1.7%

Notes: Venous blood samples were taken from apprehended drinking drivers in sterile tubes containing sodium fluoride and potassium oxalate as preservatives. The blood was portioned out into other tubes and sent to participating laboratories as a declared proficiency trial. As seen, the CVs between-laboratories were always less than 3% and the corresponding within-laboratory CVs were mostly less than 1% (data not shown).

ratories was always less than 3% regardless of the concentration of alcohol present, which testifies to highly reproducible analytical work. The corresponding CVs within laboratories were mostly 1% or less based on three to six determinations per sample. If the overall mean BAC in each sample is taken as the target value, then all laboratories showed accuracy to within ±5% of the attributed concentration.

5.2.6   Fate of Alcohol in the Body

Ethanol is a small polar molecule with a low molecular weight (46.07) and carries weak charge (see Table 5.2.2), which facilitates easy passage through biological membranes.[186,187] After ingestion, absorption of ethanol starts already in the stomach but this process occurs much faster from the upper part of the small intestine where the available surface area is much larger owing to the presence of microscopic villi covering the mucosal cells. Both the rate and extent of absorption is delayed if there is food in the stomach before drinking.[188,189] The blood that drains the gastrointestinal tract leads to the portal vein where any alcohol present must pass through the liver, and then via the hepatic vein on to the heart and the systemic circulation. After passage through the liver, ethanol distributes uniformly throughout all body fluids and tissue without binding to plasma proteins. Indeed, it is possible to determine total body water by the ethanol dilution method.[187]

The peak BAC reached after drinking (C_{max}) and the time required to reach the peak (t_{max}) vary widely from person to person and depend on many factors.[187] After 48 healthy male volunteers drank 0.68 g ethanol/kg body weight as neat whisky on an empty stomach, the peak concentration in capillary (fingertip) blood was reached at exactly 10, 40, 70, and 100 min after the end of drinking for 23, 14, 8, and 3 subjects, respectively.[190] The amount of alcohol consumed, the rate of drinking, the dosage form (beer, wine, spirits, cocktails), and most importantly the rate of gastric emptying will influence the speed of ethanol absorption.[187] The concentrations of ethanol in body fluids and tissues after reaching equilibration depend primarily on the water contents of these fluids and tissues and the ratio of blood flow to tissue mass.[187] Figure 5.2.10 shows the mean concentration–time profiles of ethanol in blood, breath, urine, and saliva obtained in experiments with healthy male volunteers who drank 0.68 g/kg as neat whisky in 20 min after an overnight fast.[187,191] Note that the concentrations in breath have been multiplied by an assumed average blood/breath ratio of 2100:1.

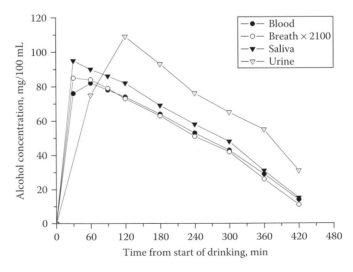

Figure 5.2.10   Mean concentration–time profiles of ethanol in venous blood, end-expired breath (×2100), saliva, and urine from experiments with healthy men who ingested 0.68 g ethanol per kg body weight as neat whisky in the morning after an overnight fast. Standard error bars are omitted for clarity.

The bulk of the dose of alcohol (95 to 98%) is eliminated by oxidative metabolism, which occurs via enzymatic reactions in the liver catalyzed by class I enzymes of alcohol dehydrogenase (ADH).[186,187] Between 2 and 5% of the dose is excreted unchanged in breath, urine, and sweat and a very small fraction (~0.1%) is conjugated with glucuronic acid and removed via the kidney.[192] Small amounts of alcohol are thought to undergo pre-systemic oxidation in the gastric mucosa or the liver or both organs but the practical significance of first-pass metabolism (FPM) is dose dependent and is not easy to quantify.[193]

At moderate BAC (>60 mg/dL), the microsomal enzymes (P4502E1), which have a higher k_m for oxidation of ethanol (60 to 80 mg/dL) compared with ADH ($k_m = 2$ to 5 mg/dL), become engaged in the metabolism of ethanol.[194–196] The P450 enzymes are also involved in the metabolism of many drugs and environmental chemicals, which raises the potential for drug–alcohol interactions, which might explain the toxicity of ethanol in heavy drinkers and alcoholics.[197–202] Moreover, the activity of P4502E1 enzymes increases after a period of continuous heavy drinking owing to a faster *de novo* synthesis of the enzyme and metabolic tolerance develops as reflected in twofold to threefold faster rates of elimination of alcohol from the bloodstream in alcoholics undergoing detoxification.[200–204]

The detrimental effects of ethanol on performance and behavior are complex and involve interaction with the membrane receptors in the brain associated with the inhibitory neurotransmitters glutamate and gamma aminobutyric acid (GABA).[205–208] The behavioral effects of ethanol are dose-dependent and after drinking small amounts the individual relaxes, experiences mild euphoria, and becomes more talkative. As drinking continues and the blood-ethanol concentration increases toward 150 to 200 mg/dL, impairment of body functioning becomes pronounced. Many of the pharmacological effects of ethanol can be explained by an altered flux of ions through the chloride channel activated by the neurotransmitter GABA.[206] The link between ethanol impairment and neurotransmission at the $GABA_A$ receptor also helps to explain observations about cross-tolerance with other classes of depressant drugs like benzodiazepines and barbiturates, which also bind to the $GABA_A$ receptor complex to open a chloride ion-channel to alter brain functioning.[200]

Although there is a reasonably good correlation between degree of ethanol-induced impairment and the person's BAC, there are large variations in response at the same BAC in different individuals who drink the same amount of alcohol within the same time frame. The reasons for this are twofold; first, larger people tend to have more body water so the same dose of alcohol enters a larger volume resulting in lower BAC compared with lighter people with less body water. This phenomenon is known as consumption tolerance and stems from variations in body weight and the relative amount of adipose tissue, which is influenced by age, gender, and ethnicity.[209,210] The second reason for interindividual differences in ethanol-induced performance decrement is called concentration tolerance, which is linked to a gradual habituation of brain cells to the presence of alcohol during repeated exposure to the drug.[210,211] Besides the development of acute tolerance (Mellanby effect), which appears during a single exposure (see Chapter 5.1), a chronic tolerance develops after a period of continuous heavy drinking. Among the mechanisms accounting for chronic tolerance are long-term changes in the composition of cell membranes particularly, the cholesterol content, the structure of the fatty acids, and also the arrangement of proteins and phospholipids making up the lipid bilayer.[210,211]

In occasional drinkers, the impairment effects of ethanol appear gradually, becoming more exaggerated as BAC increases. The various clinical signs and symptoms of intoxication are usually classified as a function of BAC from sober to dead drunk as was first proposed by Bogen.[212] This scheme has subsequently been developed further and improved upon by others. For example, at a BAC of 10 to 30 mg/dL alterations in a person's performance and behavior are insignificant and can only be discerned using highly specialized tests such as divided attention tasks. Between 30 and 60 mg/dL, most people experience euphoria, becoming more talkative and sociable owing to disinhibition. At a BAC between 60 and 100 mg/dL euphoria is more marked, often causing excitement with partial or complete loss of inhibitions and in some individuals judgment and control are seriously impaired. When the BAC is between 100 and 150 mg/dL, which are concentrations seldom reached during moderate social drinking, psychomotor performance deteriorates markedly and poor articulation and speech impediment is obvious. Between 150 and 200 mg/dL ataxia is pronounced and drowsiness and confusion are evident in most people. The relationship between BAC and clinical impairment is well documented in drunk drivers who often reach very high BACs of 350 mg/dL or more, but most of these individuals are obviously chronic alcoholics.[213,214] In two recent studies of forensic autopsies, the average BAC when death was attributed to acute alcohol poisoning was 360 mg/dL.[215,216]

It is important to note that the impairment effects of alcohol depend to a great extent on the dose and the speed of drinking and whether the person starts from zero BAC or not.[217,218] The person's age and experience with alcohol are important owing to the development of central nervous system tolerance.[219] People who are capable of functioning with a very high BAC, such as drunk drivers, e.g., 200 to 300 mg/dL, have probably been drinking continuously for several days or even weeks so that a chronic tolerance to alcohol has had time to develop. Drinking a large volume of neat spirits in a short time results in nausea, gross behavioral impairment, and marked drunkenness, and an inexperienced drinker runs the risk of losing consciousness and suffering acute alcohol poisoning. Drinking too much too fast is dangerous, and if gastric emptying is rapid, the BAC rises with such a velocity that a vomit reflex in the brain is triggered. This physiological response to acute alcohol ingestion has probably saved many lives.

Conducting controlled studies with people who drink to reach very high BAC are difficult to motivate for ethical reasons. One exceptional study was reported by Zink and Reinhardt,[220] who allowed healthy male volunteers to consume very large quantities of alcohol, either as beer or spirits or both, continuously for 8 to 10 h under social conditions. The BAC profiles were established unequivocally by frequent blood sampling from indwelling catheters every 15 to 20 min for up to 10 h. Some of the subjects reached abnormally high BAC of over 3.0 g/kg (300 mg/dL) and all developed a high degree of tolerance to the effects of alcohol. Figure 5.2.11 gives examples of the blood-concentration time profiles for four of the men who participated in this German study. Note that BAC is given in mass/mass (g/kg) as is customary in Germany and not weight/volume.

5.2.7 Clinical Pharmacokinetics of Ethanol

Clinical pharmacokinetics deals with the way that drugs and their metabolites are absorbed, distributed, and metabolized in the body and how these processes can be described in quantitative terms.[221–224]

5.2.7.1 Widmark Model

The clinical pharmacokinetics of ethanol has been investigated extensively since the 1930s thanks to the early availability of a reliable method of analysis in small volumes of blood.[209] Figure 5.2.12 shows a typical BAC–time profile after a healthy male subject drank 0.68 g/kg ethanol as neat whisky in the morning on an empty stomach. Before any pharmacokinetic evaluation of this curve is attempted, the data points on the post-absorptive phase should be carefully inspected and shown to fit well on a straight line. One indication of this is a high correlation coefficient ($r > 0.98$) for the concentration–time data points. The rectilinear declining phase is then extrapolated back to the ordinate (y-axis) or the time of starting to drink to give the C_0 parameter. This represents the concentration of ethanol in blood if the entire dose was absorbed and distributed in all body fluids and tissues without any metabolism occurring. The ratio of dose (g/kg) to C_0 (g/L) gives the ratio of body alcohol concentration to BAC and is known as the apparent volume of distribution, denoted "r" by Widmark or more recently V_d in units of L/kg. Inspection of this parameter allows a check on the validity of the experiment and the kinetic analysis because V_d can only take certain values. The value expected corresponds to the ratio of water in the whole body (60%) to the water content

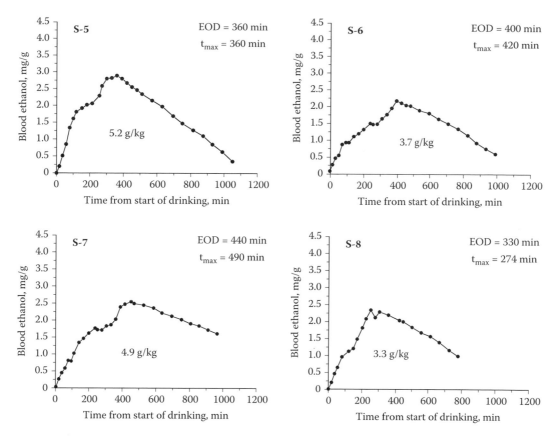

Figure 5.2.11 Concentration–time profiles of ethanol in four subjects (S-5 to S-8) who consumed very large quantities of alcohol (3.3 to 5.2 g/kg body weight) during a drinking time of 8 to 10 hours under controlled social conditions. EOD is time to end of drinking and t_{max} is time to reach the maximum BAC. Curves are redrawn from information published by Zink and Reinhardt.[220]

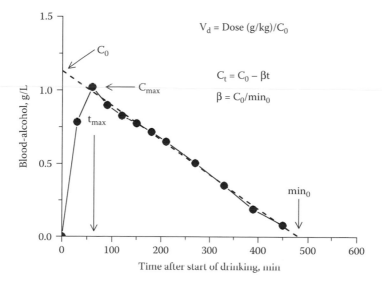

Figure 5.2.12 Blood-alcohol profile typically obtained after ingestion of a moderate dose of alcohol (0.68 g/kg) as neat whisky in 20 min after an overnight fast. Key pharmacokinetic parameters and how these are calculated are shown on the graph (see text for details).

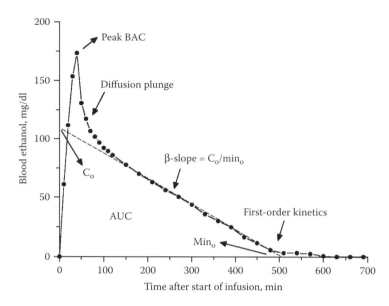

Figure 5.2.13 Concentration–time profile of ethanol in venous blood after one subject received 0.8 g ethanol per kg body weight by constant rate intravenous infusion over 40 min. The pharmacokinetic parameters are defined on this graph (see text for details).

of the blood (80%) and thus a ratio of 0.6 to 0.7 L/kg for a healthy male and 0.5 to 0.6 L/kg for a female.[209]

Alcohol can also be administered intravenously, which is sometimes desirable in research and clinical investigations to avoid problems with variable gastric emptying and to avoid first-pass metabolism occurring in the stomach or the liver or both organs.[224] In the example shown in Figure 5.2.13, the test subject received 0.80 g/kg as a 10% w/v solution in saline at a constant rate for 40 min. The peak BAC now coincides with the end of the infusion period and this is followed by a diffusion plunge, during which time ethanol equilibrates between the well-perfused central blood compartment and poorly perfused resting skeletal muscle tissues. At about 90 min post-infusion, the BAC starts to decrease at a constant rate per unit time in accordance with zero-order kinetics and the slope of this rectilinear disappearance phase is commonly referred to as the alcohol burn-off rate or β-slope. However, specialist textbooks in pharmacokinetics refer to the zero-order elimination slope as k_0 instead of β.[224] When the blood concentration decreases below about 10 mg/dL or after about 450 min post-dosing in Figure 5.2.13, the linear declining phase becomes curvilinear for the remainder of time alcohol is still measurable in the blood.[223,224] The elimination of alcohol now follows first-order kinetics and the rate constant is denoted k_1 Some studies showed that the half-life of this terminal phase was about 15 min.[225]

The first person to make a comprehensive mathematical analysis of BAC profiles was Erik M.P. Widmark and details of his life and work have been published.[226] Widmark introduced the following equation to represent the elimination kinetics of alcohol from blood in the post-absorptive phase.

$$C_t = C_0 - \beta t \tag{1}$$

where C_t = blood alcohol concentration at some time t on the post-absorptive part of the curve, C_0 = blood alcohol concentration extrapolated to the time of starting to drink, β = rate of elimination of alcohol from blood, and t = time in minutes.

The rate of elimination of alcohol from the blood in moderate drinkers falls within the range 10 to 20 mg/dL/h with a mean value of about 15 mg/dL/h.[197,209,225] Higher values are seen in drinking drivers (mean 19 mg/dL/h)[227] and in alcoholics undergoing detoxification (mean 22 mg/dL/h).[228–231]

The faster burn-off rates seen in heavy drinkers is probably one consequence of enzyme induction, which boosts the activity of the microsomal P4502E1 system during prolonged exposure to high concentrations of ethanol.[196,230,232] The P4502EI enzymes have a higher K_m (60 to 80 mg/dL) compared with ADH (2 to 5 mg/dL) and the slope of the elimination phase tends to be steeper when starting from a higher initial BAC, such as in alcoholics compared with moderate social drinkers.[230] In a controlled study with alcoholics undergoing detoxification, the mean β-slope was 22 mg/dL/h with a range from 13 to 36 mg/dL/h.[228] Liver disorders such as alcoholic hepatitis and cirrhosis did not seem to influence the rate of disposal of alcohol in these individuals.[228] When recently drinking alcoholics with high rates of alcohol elimination from blood were allowed to sober up for a few days and dosed again with a moderate amount of alcohol, the elimination rate was now in the range expected for moderate drinkers, namely, 15 mg/dL/h.[230]

The rate of elimination of alcohol from the blood was not much influenced by the time of day when 0.75 g/kg was administered at 9 A.M., 3 P.M., 9 P.M., and 3 A.M., according to an investigation into chrono-pharmacokinetics of ethanol.[233] However, gastric emptying seems to occur faster in the morning as reflected in a 32% higher peak BAC and an earlier time of its occurrence when ethanol (1.1 g/kg body weight) was consumed between 7.15 and 7.45 A.M., compared with the same time in the evening.[234] Smoking cigarettes slows gastric emptying and as a consequence delays the absorption of a moderate dose (0.50 g/kg) of ethanol resulting in a lower peak BAC in smokers.[235]

By extrapolating the rectilinear elimination phase back to the time of starting to drink, one obtains the y-intercept (C_0), which corresponds to the theoretical BAC expected if the entire dose was absorbed and distributed without any metabolism occurring (Figure 5.2.13). The empirically determined value of C_0 will always be greater than the ratio of dose/body weight because whole blood is 80% w/w water compared with the body, which is 60% w/w on average for men and 50% for women. The apparent volume of distribution (V_d) of alcohol is given by the ratio of dose (g/kg) divided by C_0 and in clinical pharmacology textbooks this is referred to as V_d with units of L/kg.[221–223] However, because BAC in Widmark's studies was reported in units of mg/g or g/kg, dividing the dose by C_0 gives a ratio without any dimensions. This needs to be considered whenever BAC is reported as weight/volume units (e.g., g/L) as is more usual today. The density of whole blood is 1.055 g/mL, which means there is an expected difference of 5.5% compared with values of V_d reported by Widmark.[209]

Values of the distribution factor "r" differ between individuals depending on age and body composition particularly the proportion of fat to lean body mass.[236] Obviously, the value of "r" will also depend on whether whole blood or plasma specimens were analyzed and used to plot the concentration–time profile when back-extrapolation is done to determine C_0. As shown in Figure 5.2.2, the plasma–alcohol curves run on a higher level compared with whole blood–alcohol curves because of the differences in water content as discussed earlier. This means that C_0 is higher for plasma curves compared with whole-blood curves.[47]

According to Widmark's second equation, the relationship between alcohol in the body and alcohol in the blood at equilibrium can be represented by the following equations:

$$A/(p \times r) = C_0 \tag{2}$$

$$A = C_0 \times (p \times r) \tag{3}$$

where A = amount of alcohol in grams absorbed and distributed in all body fluids, p = body weight of the person in kg, r = Widmark's "r" factor, and C_0 = y-intercept (Figure 5.2.13).

These equations make it is easy to calculate the amount of alcohol in the body from the concentration determined in a sample of blood provided that the value of "r" is known and that absorption and distribution of ethanol were complete at the time of sampling blood. However, in reality 100% absorption of the dose is only achieved when ethanol is given by intravenous infusion. Thus, the above equation will tend to overestimate the person's true BAC because part of an orally administered dose might be cleared by first-pass metabolism occurring either in the stomach or liver or in both places. Although the above equation has been much used in forensic alcohol calculations, it should not be applied to other drugs and narcotics and especially not in post-mortem toxicology, owing to problems with variation in drug concentrations in different sampling sites (see Section 5.2.3).

In the fasting state, the factor "r" will depend on age, gender, and body composition and Widmark reported mean values of 0.68 for 20 men (range 0.51 to 0.85) and 0.55 for 10 women (range 0.49 to 0.76).[209] However, in many later studies, which included more volunteer subjects, it was found that average values of "r" were closer to 0.70 L/kg for men and 0.60 L/kg for women with 95% confidence limits of about ±20%.[237]

The two separate Widmark equations for β and "r" can be easily combined by eliminating C_0 to give the following equation:

$$A = pr(C_t + \beta t) \tag{4}$$

The above equation is useful to estimate the total amount of alcohol absorbed from the gastrointestinal tract since the beginning of drinking or by rearrangement, the BAC (C_t) expected after intake of a known amount of alcohol.

$$C_t = (A/pr) - \beta t \tag{5}$$

When calculating BAC from the dose administered, or vice versa, it is necessary to assume that systemic availability is 100% and that absorption and distribution of alcohol into total body water is complete at the time of sampling blood. Furthermore, individual variations in β and "r" introduce uncertainty in the calculated dose (A) or BAC (C_t) when average values are applied to random subjects from the population. Various modifications or improvements have been suggested, such as by using estimates of total body water, lean body mass, or nomograms based on body mass index.[236–238] The individual variation has been estimated to ±20% for 95% confidence limits in tests involving more than 100 subjects who drank alcohol on an empty stomach.[237] However, in the entire population of drinking drivers, these limits can be expected to be much wider.

5.2.7.2 Michaelis–Menten Model

Because the class I ADH enzymes have a low k_m (2 to 5 mg/dL) for ethanol they become saturated with substrate after one to two drinks.[221,222] The rate of disappearance of ethanol from blood therefore follows zero-order kinetics over a large segment of the post-absorptive elimination phase (Figure 5.2.13).[236,237] When the BAC decreases below about 10 mg/dL, the ADH enzymes are no longer saturated and the curve changes to a curvilinear disappearance phase (first-order kinetics).[221–223,239] However, these low BACs are not very relevant when forensic science aspects of ethanol are concerned.

It was first demonstrated by Lundquist and Wolthers[240] that the entire post-absorptive elimination phase (zero-order and first-order stages) might be rationalized by an alternative pharmacokinetic model, namely, that of saturation kinetics.[223,239] Thanks to the availability of a highly sensitive ADH method of analysis, much lower blood-alcohol concentration (<10 mg/dL) could be reliably determined. These investigators from Denmark fitted their BAC–time data to the Michaelis–Menten (M-M) equation and from its integrated form they arrived at the parameters V_{max} and k_m that described the enzymatic reaction.[240] This application of nonlinear saturation kinetics of ethanol was thereafter strongly advocated by many specialists in pharmacokinetics, among others, Wagner, Wilkinson, and their colleagues[221,222,241–243] and values of 22 mg/dL/h and 5 mg/dL were suggested for V_{max} and k_m, respectively.[222] Although the use of M-M kinetics has found some support among forensic scientists,[243,244] others have not considered this necessary for actual casework because so many other variable factors and uncertainties influence the absorption, distribution, and elimination pattern of ethanol.[244] Moreover, the mathematical concepts needed to understand and apply M-M kinetics are much more challenging than those necessary to derive the Widmark equation. Explaining the scientific principles of pharmacokinetic multicompartment models and nonlinear kinetics to a judge and jury is a daunting task. Moreover, the idea of multiple enzyme systems being involved in the metabolism of ethanol including racial and ethnic differences and polymorphism might overly complicate the situation.[245,246] The contribution of various isozymes of ADH as well as the higher k_m microsomal CYP2E1 pathway for disposal of ethanol after chronic ingestion (metabolic tolerance) explains the faster rate of clearance from blood in binge drinkers.[201,204] Furthermore, the contribution from several enzyme systems is not strictly compatible with the conditions assumed to apply for application of the classical M-M equation.

5.2.7.3 First-Pass Metabolism and Gastric ADH

About 20 years ago, considerable attention was drawn to the possibility that metabolism of ethanol occurred also pre-systemically in the gastric mucosa.[247–252] Accordingly, part of the dose of ethanol ingested was broken down before reaching the systemic circulation and this was thought to involve an enzymatic oxidation process taking place in the gastric mucosa. Pre-systemic removal of an administered drug is important to understand and has implications for therapeutic efficacy. However, the liver, which contains most of the metabolizing enzymes, was considered the primary site for first-pass metabolism (FPM) of ethanol to occur. The magnitude of FPM tended to exhibit large intersubject variations and was dose dependent and strikingly influenced by speed of gastric emptying as well as fed–fasted state.[252] FPM was more pronounced after very small doses of ethanol (0.15 to 0.3 g/kg) when this was consumed about 1 h after eating a meal.[248,249] Food tends to delay stomach emptying thus allowing more time for ethanol metabolism by enzymes located in the gastric mucosa.

Distinguishing between pre-systemic oxidation of ethanol occurring in the stomach as opposed to the liver proved a very difficult task and much debate arose about the significance of gastric ADH compared with hepatic ADH as the site for FPM.[136,250–252] Some workers were adamant about the importance of gastric FPM of ethanol whereas others challenged its importance in the overall disposition of ethanol in the body.[250 253] The argument against rested in part on the fact that gastric ADH represented only a small fraction of the total amount of hepatic ADH and also the complex nature of M-M kinetics especially at the low BAC reached after small doses were ingested.[250] The main advocates of gastric ADH and its role in FPM of ethanol had failed to consider the critical importance of stomach emptying and effective clearance of ethanol at low substrate concentrations.[250–252] Factors that influence the rate of absorption of alcohol (food, drugs, type of beverage, posture, time of day) also influence the concentration of alcohol entering the portal venous blood and the degree of saturation of ethanol-metabolizing enzymes in the liver.[245–252]

Interest in FPM and gastric ADH escalated considerably when several publications appeared showing that commonly used medications, such as aspirin and H_2-receptor antagonists (cimetidine and ranitidine), when combined with small amounts of alcohol, resulted in higher C_{max} and area under the curve (AUC) compared with no-drug or placebo control treatment.[253–256] These drugs were shown to block activity of gastric ADH under *in vitro* conditions (e.g., in biopsies from the stomach) but the effects *in vivo* were less clear-cut.[257] Proponents of the role of gastric ADH in FPM of alcohol argued that this represented a protective barrier against some of the toxic effects of ethanol that cause organ and tissue damage.[258] If this barrier was weakened or removed by various common medications, this would result in greater exposure of inner organs to ethanol and a higher than expected C_{max} and, accordingly, a more pronounced impairment of body functions.[253–256,258] Because the activity of gastric ADH was lower in women, Asian populations, and also in alcoholics, these groups of people were thought to be more vulnerable to the toxic effects of moderate drinking.[249,259] This conclusion proved too hasty because a flood of articles appeared challenging the notion of drug-induced effects on gastric FPM of ethanol.[260–265] Indeed, these newer studies incorporated an improved experimental design with many more volunteer subjects and a wider range of alcohol doses, times of day, and intake with or without food.[260–265]

What did emerge from this new wave of interest in the clinical pharmacokinetics of ethanol was strong and convincing information for large inter- and intra-individual variations in the pharmacokinetic profiles of ethanol especially when small doses (0.15 to 0.3 g/kg) were ingested after a meal.[266–268] The biological variation in blood-alcohol profiles was particularly evident when small doses of alcohol were ingested together with or after a meal.[269,270]

5.2.7.4 Food and Pharmacokinetics of Ethanol

The presence of food in the stomach before drinking retards the absorption of ethanol from the gut by delaying gastric emptying.[271–273] After a meal, the C_{max} was considerably lower and the impairment effects of ethanol diminished compared with drinking the same dose on an empty stomach.[273] The reduced bioavailability of ethanol did not seem to depend on the composition of the meal in terms of its protein, fat, or carbohydrate content.[274–276] The altered bioavailability of ethanol with food in the stomach before drinking obviously has consequences when the apparent volume of distribution of ethanol and other kinetic parameters are evaluated, such as AUC. The dramatic lowering of C_0 in the fed state means that the ratio dose/C_0 might increase to reach an impossible nonphysiological result (>1.0) compared with the value expected of 0.7 in men and 0.6 in women. The notion of a "loss of ethanol" when drinking occurred after a meal was observed by Widmark,[109] and he proposed that the mechanism might involve chemical reaction of ethanol with constituents of the food. However, a more modern explanation for this food-induced lowering in the bioavailability of ethanol is presystemic oxidation by gastric and/or hepatic ADH.[274,275]

Figure 5.2.14 shows individual BAC curves after 12 male subjects drank 0.8 g/kg in the morning after an overnight fast.[268] Both C_{max} and t_{max} varied widely between individuals. The time to reach the C_{max} ranged from 0 to 150 min after the end of drinking. Those subjects with very slow rates

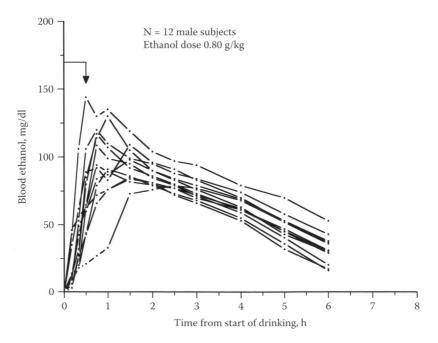

Figure 5.2.14 Individual concentration–time profile of ethanol in venous blood for 12 healthy men who drank 0.80 g ethanol per kg body weight in 30 min after an overnight fast.

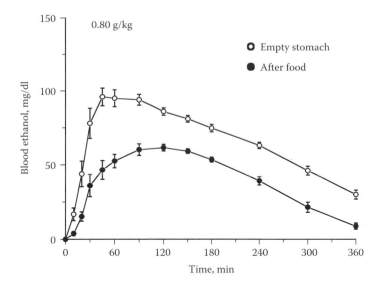

Figure 5.2.15 Mean blood-alcohol profiles after eight healthy men drank alcohol (0.80 g/kg in 30 min) either on an empty stomach or immediately after eating breakfast.

of absorption might have experienced a pyloric spasm so that the absorption took place through the stomach as opposed to the duodenum and jejunum where rapid absorption occurs.

The impact of food and body composition on BAC–time profiles for various drinking scenarios was recently the subject of a comprehensive review by Kalant.[277] Ingestion of food immediately before or together with alcohol resulted in a lower C_{max} compared with drinking the same dose on an empty stomach. This lowering effect does not seem to be related to the composition of the meal in terms of macronutrients (protein, fat, or carbohydrate), but instead the size of the meal is seemingly more important.[274] The delayed gastric emptying meant a slower delivery of alcohol into the small intestine, the site of rapid absorption into the portal blood, and therefore a longer exposure to gastric mucosal ADH thus enhancing the changes of gastric FPM of alcohol. Moreover, the role of FPM, whether gastric or hepatic, is small and highly variable and much depends on the dose of alcohol administered. After very small doses (<0.3 g/kg) FPM is more pronounced compared with moderate social drinking when BACs in the forensic relevant range (50 to 80 mg/dL) are reached.[277]

The BAC traces shown in Figure 5.2.15 demonstrate a marked effect of eating a meal before drinking. Both the C_{max} and also the area under the concentration–time profile are considerably lowered compared with drinking the same dose on an empty stomach.[189] Here the subjects drank 0.8 g ethanol per kg either after an overnight (10 h) fast or immediately after eating a standardized breakfast. Drinking in the fed state also results in a faster metabolism of ethanol as reflected in the shorter time of 1 to 2 h needed to reach zero BAC.[189] This accelerating effect of a meal on the elimination rate of alcohol from blood was confirmed even when the alcohol was given intravenously.[278,279] The mechanism of food-induced acceleration of ethanol metabolism might be related to an enhanced hepatic enzyme activity in a well-nourished organism. Furthermore, eating a meal is known to increase liver blood flow, which also facilitates a more rapid clearance of ethanol from the bloodstream at low ethanol concentrations.[275,276,278]

5.2.8 Concluding Remarks

Harmful and hazardous consumption of alcohol is increasing worldwide owing to, among other things, the lowering of excise taxation in some countries and longer opening times for bars and restaurants in others.[6] History has shown that deaths attributable to overconsumption of alcohol generally increase as a function of total consumption of alcohol in a population.[5,6] Chronic heavy drinking eventually leads to a wide spectrum of disease states and health disorders particularly liver diseases including hepatitis, cirrhosis, and death.[280] Acute inflammation of the pancreas is another consequence of heavy drinking, not to mention a host of unintentional injuries associated with drunkenness that require emergency medical treatment.[280] Drinking five drinks or more on one occasion is considered binge drinking, and might result in acute intoxication and drunkenness and trigger different kinds of reckless behavior, such as unsafe sex, drunk driving, aggressiveness, and family violence.[7-10] There is not the slightest doubt that testing for alcohol will remain the most frequently requested procedure from toxicology laboratories for a long time to come.

Few substances can be measured with such a high degree of accuracy, precision, and selectivity as the concentration of ethanol in a person's blood.[17] The method of headspace gas chromatography is the gold standard and can be used to analyze a wide range of volatile substances in body fluids besides ethanol.[281,282] Making duplicate determinations is an effective safeguard against various mishaps that might occur during sample preparation and analysis. The aliquots of blood should whenever possible be taken from two separate Vacutainer tubes, which will help to minimize the risk of sample mix-up during processing. To enhance the analytical selectivity, the duplicates should be run on different chromatographic systems, thus yielding different retention times for the substances of interest.[17,23-25] Alternatively, an independent analytical method such as enzymatic or chemical oxidation or mass spectrometry might be used in parallel with HS-GC to enhance specificity for ethanol.[131-133]

More attention should be given to pre-analytical factors that might influence precision and accuracy of the results of ethanol determination. This includes preparation of the subject, the way the blood sample was drawn including the sampling site and the skin disinfection used, as well as the kind of Vacutainer tubes and the preservatives they might contain. Things like the ambient temperature conditions, the mode and duration of transportation of blood specimens to the laboratory, and the condition of the blood sample on arrival (volume submitted and whether coagulated or not) are of concern. The situation is compounded when blood samples are taken from victims of traffic accidents who might require emergency hospital treatment including the administration of drugs or intravenous fluids to counteract shock. It is important to remember that the result of a chemical or biochemical test is only as good as the sample received for analysis. When the analytical result is close to the legal limit for driving, small errors that creep into the analytical procedures might make the difference between punishment or acquittal in borderline cases. Thus, pre-analytical factors are just as important to control and document as analytical factors.

In forensic casework when the BAC exceeds 0.2 g/L (20 mg/100 mL), the elimination of alcohol from blood occurs at a constant rate per unit time (zero-order kinetics) as was first proposed by Widmark.[190,209] From knowledge about the distribution volume of ethanol and the measured BAC, it is easy to calculate the amount of alcohol absorbed and distributed in the body at the time of blood sampling. Also if the time of starting to drink is known, then the total amount of alcohol consumed can be calculated by adding on the amount of alcohol eliminated through metabolism.[283] A good rule of thumb is that the rate of ethanol elimination from the whole body for a moderate drinker is approximately 0.1 g/kg body weight per h and this rate seems to be independent of gender.[284,285] Making a back-extrapolation of a person's BAC from the time of sampling to the time of driving is a dubious practice.[286] Without knowledge of the prior drinking scenario, including the timing and quantity of alcohol in the last drink, it is difficult to predict with certainty when C_{max} occurs. Consideration should also be given to inter- and intra-individual variations in the pharmacokinetic parameters of ethanol, especially the rate of alcohol disappearance from the bloodstream.[186,187]

Warnings about adverse drug–alcohol interactions and the risk of experiencing an unexpectedly high BAC after moderate drinking owing to concomitant use of medication such as aspirin and antacids (ranitidine and cimetidine) have been much exaggerated.[200] The magnitude of such an effect measured in percent was greatest after drinking very small doses of alcohol 1 h after subjects ate a fatty meal.[248,249] However, it is worth reiterating that small absolute increases in C_{max} between drug-treated and control group (e.g., 5 mg/dL) yield large percentage differences when the denominator of the ratio is low (e.g., 15 mg/dL); this corresponds to a 33% change. When subjects drank small doses of ethanol (0.15 g/kg), repetitively (four times) over a few hours, which is more like social drinking conditions, after medication with Zantac (ranitidine), both the C_{max} and AUC were higher compared with a placebo control treatment.[287] However, this observation still needs to be confirmed by other investigators. The authors of the study, which was published in a reputable scientific journal, concluded that social drinkers who might be medicated with ranitidine should be warned of the risk of developing unexpected functional impairment after drinking amounts of alcohol they might normally consider safe. Unfortunately, tests of functional impairment were not included in the study design so the warning is speculative and unfounded.[287]

The inter- and intra-individual differences in pharmacokinetics of alcohol were recently reviewed with major focus on Michaelis–Menten and multicompartment models.[288] Some investigators advocate use of more complex three-compartment models to explore the disposition and fate of alcohol in the body and to explain these processes in quantitative terms.[289–292] Within the forensically relevant range of BAC (20 to 300 mg/dL), the zero-order kinetics of ethanol first introduced by Widmark roughly 70 years ago still remains valid. Age and gender differences in the pharmacokinetics of ethanol are largely accounted for by differences in total body water (TBW) and therefore the distribution volume of ethanol (Widmark's r factor or V_d).[277] The notion of a significant gastric first-pass metabolism, including racial- and gender-related differences, has been much exaggerated and is only relevant after tiny doses of alcohol (<0.3 g/kg) are ingested in the fed state.[250–252] After moderate doses of alcohol consumed on an empty stomach, the bioavailability of ethanol is close to 100% and under these conditions TBW can be calculated by ethanol dilution, which speaks against any significant first-pass metabolism.[47,190,277] Ethanol's special physicochemical and physiological properties means that a person's BAC can be interpreted in relation to the amount of alcohol ingested.[283] Such calculations are not feasible for other drugs of abuse.

This overview has made it abundantly clear that ethanol is no simple drug, neither in terms of its pharmacokinetics nor its pharmacodynamics and mechanism of action on the brain. The costs to society for treatment and rehabilitation of people with alcohol problems are astronomical.[293] The entire field of biomedical alcohol research with the main focus on alcohol-related pathology was recently published in three volumes.[280] This comprehensive handbook is the latest rendition of basic and clinical aspects of the alcohol research literature and is well worth referencing.[280]

REFERENCES

1. Klatsky, A.L., Drink to your health. *Sci. Am.,* 288, 62–69, 2003.
2. Murphy, J.G., McDevitt-Murphy, M.E., and Barnett, N.P., Drink and be merry? Gender, life satisfaction and alcohol consumption among college students. *Psychol. Addict. Behav.,* 19, 184, 2005.
3. Gibbons, B., Alcohol — the legal drug. *Natl. Geogr.,* 181, 3, 1992.
4. Mukamal, K.J., Conigrave, K.M., Mittleman M.A., Camargo, C.A., Jr., Stampfer, M.J., Willett, W.C., and Rimm, E.B., Roles of drinking pattern and type of alcohol consumed in coronary heart disease in men. *N. Engl. J. Med.,* 348, 109, 2003.
5. Saitz, R., Unhealthy alcohol use. *N. Engl. J. Med.,* 352, 596, 2005.
6. Room, R., Babor, T., and Rehm, J., Alcohol and public health. *Lancet,* 365, 519, 2005.
7. Cherpitel, C.J., Alcohol and casualties — a comparison of emergency room and coroner data. *Alc. Alcohol.,* 29, 211, 1994.
8. Cherpitel, C.J., Injury and the role of alcohol; county-wide emergency room data. *Alcohol Clin. Exp. Res.,* 18, 679, 1994.
9. Stewart, S.H., Alcohol abuse in individuals exposed to trauma; a critical review. *Psychol. Bull.,* 120, 83, 1996.
10. VonMoreau, K.B., Mueller, P., Drirsch, D., Osswald, B., and Seitz, H.K., Alcohol and trauma. *Alcohol Clin. Exp. Res.,* 16, 141, 1992.
11. Driscoll, T.R., Harrison, J.A., and Steenkamp, M., Review of the role of alcohol in drowning associated with recreational aquatic activity. *Inj. Prev.,* 10, 107, 2004.

12. Cummings, P. and Quan, L., Trends in unintentional drowning: the role of alcohol and medical care. *J. Am. Med. Assoc.,* 281, 2198, 1999.

13. Chen, L.H., Baker, S.P., and Li, G., Drinking history and risk of fatal injury: comparison among specific injury causes. *Accid. Anal. Prev.,* 37, 245, 2005.

14. Jones, A.W., Forensic sciences; determination of alcohol in body fluids, in *Encyclopedia of Analytical Sciences,* Academic Press, New York, 1995, 1585.

15. Wright, J.W., Alcohol and the laboratory in the United Kingdom. *Ann. Clin. Biochem.,* 28, 212, 1991.

16. Garriott, J., *Medicolegal Aspects of Alcohol,* Lawyers & Judges, Tucson, 2004.

17. Jones, A.W., Measuring alcohol in blood and breath for forensic purposes — a historical review. *Forensic Sci. Rev.,* 8, 13, 1996.

18. Quinlan, K.P., Brewer, R.D., Sigel, P., Sleet, D.A., et al., Alcohol-impaired driving among US adults 1993–2002. *Am. J. Prev. Med.,* 28, 346, 2005.

19. Ferrara, S.D., Low blood-alcohol concentrations and driving impairment. A review of experimental studies and international legislation. *Int. J. Legal Med.,* 106, 169, 1994

20. Jones, A.W., Enforcement of drink-driving laws by use of "per se" legal alcohol limits; Blood and/or breath alcohol concentration as evidence of impairment. *Alc. Drugs Driving,* 4, 99, 1988.

21. Ziporyn, T., Definition of impairment essential for prosecuting drunken drivers. *J. Am. Med. Assoc.,* 253, 3509, 1985.

22. Dubowski, K.M. and Caplan Y., Alcohol testing in the workplace, in Garriott, J., Ed., *Medicolegal Aspects of Alcohol,* Lawyers & Judges, Tucson, 1996, 439.

23. Dubowski, K.M., Recent developments in alcohol analysis. *Alc. Drugs Driving,* 2, 13, 1986.

24. Dubowski, K.M., Alcohol determination in the clinical laboratory. *Am. J. Clin. Pathol.,* 74, 747, 1980.

25. Jones, A.W., and Schuberth, J.O., Computer-aided headspace gas chromatography applied to blood-alcohol analysis; Importance of on-line process control. *J. Forensic Sci.,* 34, 1116, 1989.

26. Kelly, D.F., Alcohol and head injury, an issue revisited. *J. Neurotrauma,* 12, 883, 1995.

27. Rutherford, W.H., Diagnosis of alcohol ingestion in mild head trauma. *Lancet,* 1, 1021, 1977.

28. Quaghebeur, G. and Richards, P., Comatose patients smelling of alcohol. *Br. Med. J.,* 299, 410, 1989.

29. Pappas, S.C. and Silverman M., Treatment of methanol poisoning with ethanol and hemodialysis. *CMA J.,* 15, 1391, 1982.

30. Jacobsen, O. and McMartin, K.E., Methanol and ethylene glycol poisoning; mechanisms of toxicity, clinical course, diagnosis and treatment. *Med. Toxicol.,* 1, 309, 1986.

31. Walder, A.D. and Tyler, C.K.G., Ethylene glycol antifreeze poisoning. *Anaesthesia,* 49, 964, 1994.

32. Egarbane, B., Borron, S.W., and Baud, F.J. Current recommendations for treatment of severe toxic alcohol poisonings, *Intensive Care Med.,* 31, 189, 2005.

33. Flanagan, R.J. and Jones, A.L., *Antidotes,* Taylor & Francis, London, 2001.

34. Youssef, G.M. and Hirsch, D.J., Validation of a method to predict required dialysis time for cases of methanol and ethylene glycol poisoning. *Am. J. Kidney Dis.,* 46, 509, 2005.

35. Brent, J., McMartin, K., Phillips, S., Aaron, C., and Kulig, K., Fomepizole for the treatment of methanol poisoning. *N. Engl. J. Med.,* 344, 424, 2001.

36. Eder, A.F., McGrath, C.M., Dowdy, Y.G., Tomaszewski, J.E., and Rosenberg, F.M. et al., Ethylene glycol poisoning: toxicokinetics and analytical factors affecting laboratory diagnosis. *Clin. Chem.,* 44, 168, 1998.

37. Flanagan, R.J., SI units — common sense not dogma is needed. *Br. J. Clin. Pharmacol.,* 39, 589, 1995.

38. Flanagan, R.J., Guidelines for the interpretation of analytical toxicology results and unit of measurement conversion factors. *Ann. Clin. Biochem.,* 35, 261, 1998.

39. Lentner, C., *Geigy Scientific Tables,* Vol., *Units of Measurement, Body Fluids, Composition of the Body, Nutrition,* CIBA-GEIGY, Basel, 1981.

40. Burtis, C.A. and Ashwood, E.R., Eds., *Tietz Fundamentals of Clinical Chemistry,* 5th ed., W.B. Saunders, Philadelphia, 2001.

41. Iffland, R., West, A., Bilzer, N., and Schuff, A., Zur Zuverlässigkeit der Blutalkoholbestimmung. Das Verteilungsverhältnis des Wassers zwischen Serum und Vollblut. *Rechtsmedizin,* 9, 123, 1999.

42. De Jong, G.M.Th., Huizenga, J.R., and Gips, C.H., Evaluation of gravimetric assays of the H2= concentration in human serum and urine. *Clin. Chim. Acta,* 163, 153, 1987.

43. Winek, C.L. and Carfagna, M., Comparison of plasma, serum, and whole blood ethanol concentrations. *J. Anal. Toxicol.,* 11, 267, 1987.

44. Rainey, P.M., Relation between serum and whole blood ethanol concentrations. *Clin. Chem.,* 39, 2288, 1993.

45. Frajola, W.J., Blood alcohol testing in the clinical laboratory: Problems and suggested remedies. *Clin. Chem.,* 39, 377, 1993.

46. Harmenina, D.M., Ed., *Clinical Hematology and Fundamentals of Hemostasis,* 4th ed., F.A. Davis, Philadelphia, 2002.

47. Jones, A.W., Hahn, R.G., and Stalberg, H.P., Pharmacokinetics of ethanol in plasma and whole blood: estimation of total body water by the dilution principle. *Eur. J. Clin. Pharmacol.,* 42, 445, 1992.

48. Jones, A.W., Hahn, R.G., Stalberg, H.P., Distribution of ethanol and water between plasma and whole blood; inter- and intra-individual variations after administration of ethanol by intravenous infusion. *Scand. J. Clin. Lab. Invest.,* 50, 775, 1990.

49. Charlebois, R.C., Corbett, M.R., and Wigmore, J.G., Comparison of ethanol concentrations in blood, serum, and blood cells for forensic applications. *J. Anal. Toxicol.,* 20, 171, 1996.

50. Fung, W.K., Chan, K.L., Mok, V.K.K., Lee, C.W., and Choi, V.M.F., The statistical variability of blood alcohol concentration measurements in drink-driving cases. *Forensic Sci. Int.,* 110, 207, 2000.

51. Jones, A.W., Dealing with uncertainty in chemical measurements. *IACT Newsl.,* 14, 6, 2003.

52. Walls, H.J. and Brownlie, A.R., *Drink, Drugs and Driving,* 2nd ed., Sweet & Maxwell, London, 1985.

53. Fraser, C.G., *Interpretation of Clinical Chemistry Laboratory Data.* Blackwell Scientific, Oxford, 1986.

54. Kratz, A., Ferraro, M.J., Sluss, P.M., and Lewandrowski, K.B., Laboratory reference values. *N. Engl. J. Med.,* 351, 1548, 2004.

55. Widmark, E.M.P., Eine Mikromethode zur Bestimmung von Äthylalkohol im Blut. *Biochem. Z.,* 131, 473, 1922.

56. Friedemann, T.E. and Dubowski, K.M., Chemical testing procedures for the determination of ethyl alcohol. *J. Am. Med. Assoc.,* 170, 47, 1959.

57. Lundquist, F., The determination of ethyl alcohol in blood and tissue, in *Methods of Biochemical Analysis,* Vol. VII, D. Glick, Ed., Interscience, New York, 1959, 217.

58. Smith, H.W., Methods for determining alcohol, in *Methods of Forensic Science*, A.S. Curry, Ed., Interscience, New York, 1965, 3.

59. Jain, N.C. and Cravey, R.H., Analysis of alcohol. I: A review of chemical and infrared methods. *J. Chromatogr. Sci.,* 10, 257, 1972.

60. Bonnichsen, R.K. and Wassén, A., Crystalline alcohol dehydrogenase from horse liver. *Arch. Biochem.,* 18, 361, 1948.

61. Bonnichsen, R.K. and Theorell, H., An enzymatic method for the microdetermination of ethanol. *Scand. J. Clin. Lab. Invest.,* 3, 58, 1951.

62. Bücher, Th. and Redetzki, H., Eine spezifische photometrische Bestimmung von Äthylalkohol auf fermentivem Wege. *Klin. Wochnschr.,* 29, 615, 1951.

63. Redetzki, H. and Johannsmeier, K., Grundlagen und Ergebnisse der enzymatischen Äthylalkohol-bestimmung. *Arch. Toxikol.,* 16, 73, 1957.

64. Vasiliades, J., Pollock, J., and Robinson, A., Pitfalls of the alcohol dehydrogenase procedure for the emergency assay of alcohol: A case study of isopropanol overdose. *Clin. Chem.,* 24, 383, 1978.

65. Buijten, J.C., An automated ultra-micro distillation technique for determination of ethanol in blood and urine. *Blutalkohol,* 12, 393, 1975.

66. Kristoffersen, L., Skuterud, B., Larssen, B.R., Skurtveit, S., and Smith-Kielland, A., Fast quantitation of ethanol in whole blood specimens by the enzymatic alcohol dehydrogenase method. Optimization by experimental design. *J. Anal. Toxicol.,* 29, 66, 2005.

67. Whitehouse, L.W. and Paul, C.J., Micro-scale enzymatic determination of ethanol in plasma with a discrete analyzer, the ABA-100. *Clin. Chem.,* 25, 1399, 1979.

68. Hadjiioannou, T.P., Hadjiioannou, S.I., Avery, J., and Malmstedt, H.V., Automated enzymatic determination of ethanol in blood serum and urine with a miniature centrifugal analyzer. *Clin. Chem.,* 22, 802, 1976.

69. Siagle, K.M. and Ghosen, S.J., Immunoassays: Tools for sensitive, specific, and accurate test results. *Lab. Med.,* 27, 177, 1996.

70. Caplan, Y. and Levine, B., The analysis of ethanol in serum, blood, and urine: a comparison of the TDx REA ethanol assay with gas chromatography. *J. Anal. Toxicol.,* 10, 49, 1986.

71. Urry, F.M., Kralik, M., Wozniak, E., Crockett, H., and Jennison, T.A., Application of the Technicon Chem 1 + chemistry analyzer to the Syva Emit ethyl alcohol assay in plasma and urine. *J. Anal. Toxicol.,* 17, 287, 1993.

72. Hannak, D. and Engel, C.H., Schnellbestimmung des Blutalkohols mit der ADH/REA methode: Methodenvergleich und Bewertung. *Blutalkohol,* 22, 371, 1985.

73. Alt, A. and Reinhardt, G., Die Genauigkeit der Blutalkoholbestimmung mit Head-Space GC, ADH und dem REA Ethanol Assay für das AXSYM System — ein Methodenvergleich. *Blutalkohol,* 33, 209, 1996.

74. Bland, J.M. and Altman, D.G. Statistical methods for assessing agreement between two methods of clinical measurement. *Lancet,* I, 307, 1986.

75. Nine, J.S., Moraca, M., Virji, M.A., and Rao, K.N., Serum-ethanol determination: comparison of lactate and lactate dehydrogenase interference in three enzymatic assays. *J. Anal. Toxicol.,* 19, 192, 1995.

76. Sloop, G., Hall, M., Simmondon, G.T., and Robinson, C.A., False positive postmortem EMIT drugs of abuse due to lactate dehydrogenase and lactate in urine. *J. Anal. Toxicol.,* 19, 554, 1995.

77. Badcock, N.R. and O'Reilly, D.A., False positive EMIT-st ethanol screen with infant plasma. *Clin. Chem.,* 38, 434, 1992.

78. Cadman, W.J. and Johns, T., Application of the gas chromatography in the laboratory of criminalistics. *J. Forensic Sci.,* 5, 369, 1960.

79. Fox, J.F., Gas chromatographic analysis of alcohol and certain other volatiles in biological material for forensic purposes. *Proc. Soc. Exp. Biol. Med.,* 97, 236, 1958.

80. Chundela, B. and Janak, J., Quantitative determination of ethanol besides other volatile substances in blood and other body liquids by gas chromatography. *J. Forensic Med.,* 7, 153, 1960.

81. Parker, K.D., Fontan, C.R., Yee, J.L., and Kirk, P.L., Gas chromatographic determination of ethyl alcohol in blood for medicolegal purposes; separation of other volatiles from blood or aqueous solution. *Anal. Chem.,* 34, 1234, 1962.

82. Curry, A.S., Walker, G.W., and Simpson, G.S., Determination of alcohol in blood by gas chromatography. *Analyst,* 91, 742, 1966.

83. Machata, G., The advantages of automated blood alcohol determination by head space analysis. *Z. Rechtsmedizin.,* 75, 229, 1975.

84. Jain, N.C. and Cravey, R.H., Analysis of alcohol. II: A review of gas chromatographic methods. *J. Chromatogr. Sci.,* 10, 263, 1972.

85. Cravey, R.H. and Jain, N.C., Current status of blood alcohol methods. *J. Chromatogr. Sci.,* 12, 209, 1974.

86. Dubowski, K.M., Manual for Analysis of Alcohol in Biological Liquids. U.S. Department of Transportation Report DOT-TSC-NHTSA-76-4, 1977.

87. Machata, G., Über die gaschromatographische Blutalkoholbestimmung Analyse der Dampfphase. *Microchim. Acta,* 262, 1964.

88. Anthony, R.M., Suthejmer, C.A., and Sunshine, I., Acetaldehyde, methanol, and ethanol analysis by headspace gas chromatography. *J. Anal. Toxicol.,* 4, 43, 1980.

89. Christmore, D.S., Kelly, R.C., and Doshier, L.A., Improved recovery and stability of ethanol in automated headspace analysis. *J. Forensic. Sci.,* 29, 1038, 1984.

90. Watts, M.T. and McDonald, O.L., The effect of specimen type on the gas chromatographic headspace analysis of ethanol and other volatile compounds. *Am. J. Clin. Pathol.,* 87, 79, 1987.

91. Watts, M.T. and McDonald, O.L., The effect of sodium chloride concentration, water content, and protein on the gas chromatographic headspace analysis of ethanol in plasma. *Am. J. Clin. Pathol.,* 93, 357, 1990.

92. Smalldon, K.W. and Brown, G.A., The stability of ethanol in stored blood samples: Part II, The mechanism of ethanol oxidation. *Anal. Chim. Acta,* 66, 285, 1973.

93. Macchia, T., Mancinelli, R., Gentilli, S., Lugaresi, E.C., Raponi, A., and Taggi, F., Ethanol in biological fluids: headspace GC measurement. *J. Anal. Toxicol.,* 19, 241, 1995.

94. Zilly, M., Langmann, P., Lenker, U., Satzinger, V. et al., Highly sensitive gas chromatographic determination of ethanol in human urine samples. *J. Chromatogr. B,* 798, 179, 2003.

95. Iffland, R. and Jones, A.W. Evaluating alleged drinking after driving — the hip-flask defence. Part 2. Congener analysis. *Med. Sci. Law,* 43, 39, 2003.

96. Krause, D. and Wehner, H.D., Blood alcohol/congeners of alcoholic beverages. *Forensic Sci. Int.,* 144, 177, 2004.

97. Bonte, W., *Begleistoffe alkoholischer Getränke,* Arbeitsmethoden der medizinischen und naturwissenschaftlichen Kriminalistik, Bd 17, Schmidt-Römhild, Lübeck, 1989.

98. Lachenmeier, D.W. and Musshoff, F., Begleitstoffgehalte alkoholischer Getränke Verlaufskontrollen, Chargenvergleich und aktuelle Konzentrationsbereiche. *Rechtsmedizin,* 14, 454, 2004.

99. Zuba, D., Parczewski, A., and Reichenbacher, M., Optimization of solid-phase microextraction conditions for gas chromatographic determination of ethanol and other volatile compounds in blood. *J. Chromatogr. B,* 773, 75, 2002.

100. De Martinis, B.S. and Martin, C.C., Automated headspace solid-phase micro-extraction and capillary gas chromatography analysis of ethanol in postmortem specimens. *Forensic Sci. Int.,* 128, 115, 2002.

101. Kuhnholz, B. and Bonte, W., Methodische Untersuchungen zur Verbesserung des fuselalkoholnachweises in Blutproben. *Blutalkohol,* 20, 399, 1983.

102. Logan, B.K., Analysis of alcohol and other volatiles, in *Gas Chromatography in Forensic Science,* J. Tebbett, Ed., Elsevier, Amsterdam, 1992, chap 4.

103. Tagliaro, F., Lubli, G., Ghielmi, S., Franchi, D., and Marigo, M., Chromatographic methods for blood alcohol determination. *J. Chromatogr.,* 580, 161, 1992.

104. Seto, E., Determination of volatile substances in biological samples by headspace gas chromatography. *J. Chromatogr.,* 674, 25, 1994.

105. Purdon, E.A., Distinguishing between ethanol and acetonitrile using gas chromatography and modified Widmark methods. *J. Anal. Toxicol.,* 17, 63, 1993.

106. Streete, P.J., Ruprah, M., Ramsey, J.D., and Flanagan, R.J., Detection and identification of volatile substances by headspace capillary gas chromatography to aid the diagnosis of acute poisoning. *Analyst,* 117, 1111, 1992.

107. Zuba, D., Piekoszewski, W., Pach, J., Winnik, L., and Parczewski, A., Concentrations of ethanol and other volatile compounds in the blood of acutely poisoned alcoholics. *Alcohol,* 26, 17, 2002.

108. Jones, A.W., A rapid method for blood alcohol determination by headspace analysis using an electrochemical detector. *J. Forensic Sci.,* 23, 283, 1978.

109. Dubowski, K.M., Method for alcohol determination in biological liquids by sensing with a solid-state detector. *Clin. Chem.,* 22, 863, 1976.

110. Criddle, W.J., Parry, K.W., and Jones, T.P., Determination of ethanol in alcoholic beverages using headspace procedure and fuel cell sensor. *Analyst,* 111, 507, 1986.

111. Kricka, L.J. and Thorpe, G.H.G., Immobilized enzymes in analysis. *Trends Biotechnol.,* 4, 253, 1986.

112. Varadi, M. and Adanyi, N., Application of biosensors with amperometric detection for determining ethanol. *Analyst,* 119, 1843, 1994.

113. Blaedel, W.J. and Engström, R.C., Reagentless enzyme electrodes for ethanol, lactate, and maleate. *Anal, Chem.,* 52, 1691, 1980.

114. Cheng, F.S. and Christian, G.D., Enzymatic determination of blood ethanol, with amperometric measurement of rate of oxygen depletion. *Clin. Chem.,* 24, 621, 1978.

115. Gulberg, E.L. and Christian, G.D., The use of immobilized alcohol oxidase in the continuous flow determination of ethanol with an oxygen electrode. *Anal. Chim. Acta,* 123, 125, 1981.

116. Gibson, T.D. and Woodward, J.R., Automated determination of ethanol using the enzyme alcohol oxidase. *Anal. Proc. Chem. Soc.,* 23, 360, 1986.

117. Gullbault, G.G., Danielsson, B., Mandenius, C.F., and Mosbach, K., Enzyme electrode and thermistor probes for determination of alcohols with alcohol oxidase. *Anal. Chem.,* 55, 1582, 1983.

118. Cenas, N., Rozgaite, J., and Kulys, J., Lactate, pyruvate, ethanol, and glucose-6-phosphate determination by enzyme electrode. *Biotech. Bioeng.,* 26, 551, 1984.

119. Gallignani, M., Garrigues, S., and Guardia, de la M., Derivative Fourier transform infrared spectrometric determination of ethanol in beer. *Analyst,* 119, 1773, 1994.

120. Ojanperä, I., Hyppölä, R., and Vuori, E., Identification of volatile organic compounds in blood by purge and trap PLOT-capillary gas chromatography coupled with Fourier transform infrared spectroscopy. *Forensic Sci. Int.,* 80, 201, 1996.

121. Pappas. A.A., Thompson, J.R., Porter, W.H., and Gadsden, R.H., High resolution proton nuclear magnetic resonance spectroscopy in the detection and quantitation of ethanol in human serum. *J. Anal. Toxicol.,* 17, 230, 1993.

122. Monaghan, M.S., Olsen, K.M., Ackerman, B.H., Fuller, G.L., Porter, W.H., and Pappas, A.A., Measurement of serum isopropanol and acetone metabolite by proton nuclear magnetic resonance: application to pharmacokinetic evaluation in a simulated overdose model. *Clin. Toxicol.,* 33, 141, 1995.

123. Robinson, A.G. and Loeb, J.N., Ethanol ingestion — commonest cause of elevated plasma osmolality. *N. Engl. J. Med.,* 284, 1253, 1971.

124. Hoffman, R.S., Smilkstein, M.J., Howland, M.A., and Goldfrank, L.R., Osmol gaps revisited: normal values and limitations. *Clin. Toxicol.,* 31, 81, 1993.

125. Osterloh, J.D., Kelly, T.J., Khayam-Bashi, H., and Romeo, R., Discrepancies in osmolal gaps and calculated alcohol concentrations. *Arch. Pathol. Lab. Med.,* 120, 637, 1996.

126. Purssell, R.A., Lynd, L.D., and Koga, Y., The use of osmole gap as a screening test for the presence of exogenous substances. *Toxicol. Rev.,* 23, 189, 2004.

127. Koga, Y., Purssell, R.A., and Lynd, L.D., The irrationality of the present use of the osmole gap: applicable physical chemistry principles and recommendations to improve the validity of current practices. *Toxicol. Rev.,* 23, 203, 2004.

128. Amato, I., Race quickens for non-stick blood monitoring technology. *Science,* 258, 892, 1992.

129. Ridder, T.D., Hendee, S.P., and Brown, C.D., Noninvasive alcohol testing using diffuse reflectance near-infrared spectroscopy. *Appl. Spectrosc.,* 59, 181, 2005.

130. Pan, S., Chung, H., Arnold, M.A., and Small, G.W., Near-infrared spectroscopic measurement of physiological glucose levels in variable matrices of protein and triglycerides. *Anal. Chem.,* 68, 1124, 1996.

131. Bonnichsen, R.K. and Ryhage, R., Determination of ethyl alcohol by computerized mass spectrometry. *Z. Rechsmed.,* 71, 134, 1972.

132. Jones, A.W., Mårdh, G., and Änggård, E., Determination of endogenous ethanol in blood and breath by gas chromatography-mass spectrometry. *Pharmacol. Biochem. Behav.,* 18(Suppl. 1), 267, 1983.

133. Dean, R.A., Thomasson, H.R., Dumaual, N., Amann, D., and Li, T.K., Simultaneous measurement of ethanol and ethyl-d5 alcohol by stable isotope gas chromatography-mass spectrometry. *Clin. Chem.,* 42, 367, 1996.

134. Takayasu, T., Ohshima, T., Tanaka, N., Maeda, H., Kondo, T., Nishigami, J., Ohtsuji, M., and Nagano, T., Experimental studies on postmortem diffusion of ethanol-d6 using rats. *Forensic Sci. Int.,* 76, 179, 1995.

135. Takayasu, T., Ohshima, T., Tanaka, N., Maeda, H., Kondo, T., Nishigami, J., and Nagano, T., Post-mortem degradation of administered ethanol-d6 and production of endogenous ethanol experimental studies using rats and rabbits. *Forensic Sci. Int.,* 76, 129, 1995.

136. Ammon, E., Schäfer, C., Hofmann, U., and Klotz, U., Disposition and first-pass metabolism of ethanol in humans: Is it gastric or hepatic and does it depend on gender. *Clin. Pharmacol. Ther.,* 59, 503, 1996.

137. Dubowski, K.M., The Technology of Breath-Alcohol Analysis. U.S. Department. of Health and Human Services, DHHS Publ. (ADM) 92-1728, 1992.

138. Wilson, H.K., Breath-analysis; Physiological basis and sampling techniques. *Scand. J. Work Environ. Health,* 12, 174, 1986.

139. Jones, A.W., Physiological aspects of breath-alcohol analysis. *Alc. Drug Driving,* 6, 1, 1990.

140. Mason, M. and Dubowski, K.M., Breath-alcohol analysis: uses, methods and some forensic problems — review and opinion. *J. Forensic Sci.,* 21, 9, 1976.

141. Harding, P., Breath-alcohol methods, in Garriott, J., *Medicolegal Aspects of Alcohol.* Lawyers & Judges, Tucson, 2004.

142. Gullberg, R.G., Breath alcohol analysis, in *Encyclopedia of Forensic and Legal Medicine,* J. Payne-James, R.W. Byard, T.S. Corey, and C. Henderson, Eds., Elsevier Science, Amsterdam, 2005, 21.

143. Manolis, A., The diagnostic potential of breath analysis. *Clin. Chem.,* 29, 5, 1983.

144. Phillips, M., Breath tests in medicine. *Sci. Am.,* 270, 52, 1992.

145. Jain, N.C. and Cravey, R.H., A review of breath alcohol methods. *J. Chromatogr. Sci.,* 12, 214, 1974.

146. Moynham, A., Perl, J., and Starmer, G.A., Breath-alcohol testing. *J. Traffic Med.,* 18, 167, 1990.

147. Jones, A.W., Pharmacokinetics of ethanol in saliva; comparison with blood and breath alcohol profiles, subjective feelings of intoxication and diminished performance. *Clin. Chem.,* 39, 1837, 1993.

148. Jones, A.W., Measurement of alcohol in blood and breath for legal purposes, in *Human Metabolism of Alcohol*, K.E. Crow and R.D. Batt, Eds., CRC Press, Boca Raton, FL, 1989, 71.

149. Evans, R.P. and McDermott, F.T., Use of an Alcolmeter in a casualty department. *Med. J. Aust.,* 1, 1032, 1977.

150. Gibbs, K.A., Johnston, C.C., and Martin, S.D., Accuracy and usefulness of a breath-alcohol analyzer. *Ann. Emerg. Med.,* 13, 516, 1984.

151. Falkensson, M., Jones, A.W., and Sörbö, B., Bedside diagnosis of alcohol intoxication with a pocket-size breath-alcohol device sampling from unconscious subjects and specificity for ethanol. *Clin. Chem.,* 35, 918, 1989.

152. Frank, J.F. and Flores, A.L., The likelihood of acetone interference in breath alcohol measurement. *Alc. Drugs Driving,* 3, 1, 1987.

153. Jones, A.W. and Andersson, L., Biotransformation of acetone to isopropanol observed in a motorist involved in a sobriety check. *J. Forensic Sci.,* 40, 686, 1995.

154. Emerson, V.J., Holleyhead, R., Isaacs, D.J., Fuller, N.A., and Hunt, D.J., The measurement of breath alcohol. *J. Forensic Sci. Soc.,* 20, 1, 1980.

155. Harte, R.A., An instrument for the determination of ethanol in breath in law enforcement practice. *J. Forensic Sci.,* 16, 167, 1971.

156. Fransson, M., Jones, A.W., and Andersson, L., Laboratory evaluation of a new evidential breath-alcohol analyzer designed for mobile testing. *Med. Sci. Law,* 45, 61, 2005.

157. Caddy, G.R., Sobell, M.B., and Sobell, L.C., Alcohol breath tests: Criterion times for avoiding contamination by mouth alcohol. *Behav. Res. Methods Instrum.,* 10, 814, 1978.

158. Gullberg, R.G., The elimination rate of mouth alcohol. Mathematical modeling and implications in breath alcohol analysis. *J. Forensic Sci.,* 37, 1363, 1992.

159. Langille, R.M. and Wigmore, J.G., The mouth alcohol effect after a mouthful of beer under social conditions. *Can. J. Forensic Sci. Soc.,* 33, 193, 2000.

160. Buczer, Y. and Wigmore, J.G., The significance of breath sampling frequency on the mouth alcohol effect. *Can. J. Forensic Sci. Soc.,* 35, 185, 2002.

161. Modell, J.G., Taylor, J.P., and Lee, J.Y., Breath alcohol values following mouthwash use. *J. Am. Med. Assoc.,* 270, 2955, 1993.

162. Jones, A.W., Reflections on the GERD defense. *DWI J. Law Sci.,* 20, 3, 2005.

163. Harding, P.M., Lacssig, R.H., and Ficld, P.H., Field performance of the Intoxilyzer 5000: a comparison of blood- and breath-alcohol results in Wisconsin drivers. *J. Forensic Sci.,* 35, 1022, 1990.

164. Jones, A.W. and Andersson, L., Comparison of ethanol concentrations in venous blood and end-expired breath during a controlled drinking experiment. *Forensic Sci. Int.,* 132, 18, 2003. 2003.

165. Jones, A.W., Variability of the blood-breath alcohol ratio *in vivo. J. Stud. Alcohol,* 39, 1931, 1978.

166. Jones, A.W., Medicolegal alcohol determination — blood and/or breath-alcohol concentration. *Forensic Sci. Rev.,*12, 23, 2000.

167. Jones, A.W., Lindberg, L., and Olsson, S.G., Magnitude and time course of arterio-venous differences in blood-alcohol concentration in healthy men. *Clin. Pharmacokinet.,* 43, 1157, 2004.

168. Martin E., Moll, M., Schmid P. et al., The pharmacokinetics of alcohol in human breath, venous and arterial blood after oral ingestion. *Eur. J. Clin. Pharmacol.,* 26, 619, 1984.

169. Dubowski, K.M., Quality assurance in breath-alcohol analysis. *J. Anal. Toxicol.,* 18, 306, 1994.

170. Gullberg, R.G., Methodology and quality assurance in forensic breath alcohol analysis. *Forensic Sci. Rev.,* 12, 23, 2000.

171. Taylor, J.K., *Quality Assurance of Chemical Measurements.* Lewis, Chelsea, MI, 1987.

172. Jones, A.W., Edman-Falkensson, M., and Nilsson, L., Reliability of blood alcohol determinations at clinical chemistry laboratories in Sweden. *Scand. J. Clin. Lab. Invest.,* 35, 463, 1995.

173. Jones, A.W. and Fransson, M., Blood analysis by headspace gas chromatography: does a deficient sample volume distort ethanol concentrations? *Med. Sci. Law,* 43, 241, 2003.

174. Miller, B.A., Day, S.M., Vasquest, T.E., and Evans, F.M., Absence of salting out effects in forensic blood alcohol determination at various concentrations of sodium fluoride using semi-automated headspace gas chromatography. *Sci. Justice,* 44, 73, 2004.

175. Narayanan, S., The preanalytical phase — an important component of laboratory medicine. *Am. J. Clin. Pathol.,* 113, 429, 2000.

176. Matlow, A.G. and Berte, L.M., Sources of error in laboratory medicine. *Lab. Med.,* 35, 331, 2004.

177. Riley, D., Wigmore, J.G., and Yen, B., Dilution of blood collected for medicolegal alcohol analysis by intravenous fluids. *J. Anal. Toxicol.,* 20, 330, 1996.

178. Gullberg, R.G., The application of control charts in breath alcohol measurement systems. *Med. Sci. Law,* 33, 33, 1993.

179. Paulson, R. and Wachtel, M., Using quality control charts for quality assurance. *Lab. Med.,* 26, 409, 1995.

180. Winek, T., Winek, C.L., and Wahba, W.W., The effect of storage at various temperatures on blood alcohol concentration. *Forensic Sci. Int.,* 78,179, 1996.

181. Meyer, T., Monge, P.K., and Sakshaug, J., Storage of blood samples containing alcohol. *Acta Pharmacol. Toxicol.,* 45, 282, 1979.

182. Dubowski, K.M., Gadsden, R.H., and Poklis, A., The stability of ethanol in human whole blood controls: an interlaboratory evaluation. *J. Anal. Toxicol.,* 21, 486, 1997.

183. Burnett, D., *Understanding Accreditation in Laboratory Medicine.* ACD Venture Publications, London, 1996.

184. Jones, G.R., Accreditation — toxicology, in *Encyclopedia of Forensic and Legal Medicine,* J. Payne-James, R.W. Byard, T.S. Corey, and C. Henderson, Eds., Elsevier Science, Amsterdam, 2005, 13.

185. Wilson, J.F. and Barnett, K., External quality assessment of techniques for assay of serum ethanol. *Ann. Clin. Biochem.,* 32, 540, 1993.

186. Jones, A.W., Biochemistry and physiology of alcohol: applications to forensic science and toxicology, in *Medicolegal Aspects of Alcohol,* Garriott, J., Ed. Lawyers & Judges, Tucson, 1996, 85.

187. Jones, A.W., Disposition and fate of ethanol in the body, in *Medicolegal Aspects of Alcohol,* 4th ed., Garriott, J., Ed. Lawyers & Judges, Tucson, 2003, 85.

188. Sedman, A.J., Wilkinson, P.K., Sakmar, E., Weidler, D.J., and Wagner, J.G., Food effect on absorption and metabolism of ethanol. *J. Stud. Alcohol,* 37, 1197, 1976.

189. Jones, A.W. and Jönsson, K.Å., Food-induced lowering of blood alcohol profiles and increased rate of elimination immediately after a meal. *J. Forensic Sci.,* 39, 1084, 1994.

190. Jones, A.W., Inter-individual variations in the disposition and metabolism of ethanol in healthy men. *Alcohol,* 1, 385, 1984.

191. Jones, A.W., Quantitative relationships among ethanol concentrations in blood, breath, saliva, and urine during ethanol metabolism in man, in *Proc. 8th Int. Conf. Alcohol, Drugs, and Traffic Safety,* L. Goldberg, Ed., Almqvist & Wiksell, Stockholm, 1981, 550.

192. Schmitt, G., Aderjan, R., Keller, T., and Wu, M., Ethyl Glucuronide: an unusual ethanol metabolite in humans, synthesis, and analytical data. *J. Anal. Toxicol.,* 19, 91, 1995.

193. Sato, N. and Kitamura, T. First-pass metabolism of ethanol: a review. *Gastroenterology,* 111, 1143, 1996.

194. Park, B.K., Pirmohamed, M., and Kitteringham, N.R., The role of cytochrome P450 enzymes in hepatic and extrahepatic human drug toxicity. *Pharmacol. Ther.,* 68, 385, 1995.

195. Teschke, P. and Gellert, J., Hepatic microsomal ethanol oxidizing systems (MEOS): metabolic aspects and clinical implications. *Alcohol Clin. Exp. Res.,* 10, 20S, 1986.

196. Lieber, C.S., The discovery of the microsomal ethanol oxidizing system and its physiologic and pathologic role. *Drug Metab. Rev.,* 36, 511, 2004.

197. Jones, A.W., Disappearance rate of ethanol from the blood of human subjects; implications in forensic toxicology. *J. Forensic Sci.,* 38, 104, 1993.

198. Lieber, C.S., Mechanisms of ethanol induced hepatic injury. *Pharmacol. Ther.,* 46, 1, 1990.

199. Lee, W.M., Drug-induced hepatotoxicity. *N. Engl. J. Med.,* 333, 1118, 1995.

200. Jones, A.W., Alcohol and drug interactions, in *Handbook of Drug Interactions: A Clinical and Forensic Guide,* A. Mozayani and L.P. Raymond, Eds., Humana Press, Totowa, NJ, 2003, 395.

201. Hu, Y., Ingelman-Sundberg, M., and Lindros, K.O., Inductive mechanisms of cytochrome P450 2E1 in liver: interplay between ethanol treatment and starvation. *Biochem. Pharmacol.,* 50, 155, 1995.

202. Slattery, J.T., Nelson, S.D., and Thummel, K.E., The complex interaction between ethanol and acetaminophen. *Clin. Pharm. Ther.,* 60, 241, 1996.

203. Ahmed, F.E., Toxicological effects of ethanol on human health. *C. R. Toxicol.,* 25, 347, 1995.

204. Oneta, C.M., Lieber, C.S., Li, J., Ruttimann, S. et al., Dynamics of cytochrome P4502E1 activity in man: induction by ethanol and disappearance during withdrawal. *J. Hepatol.,* 36, 47, 2002.

205. Nevo, I. and Hamon, M., Neurotransmitter and neuromodulatory mechanisms involved in alcohol abuse and alcoholism. *Neurochem. Int.,* 26, 305, 1995.

206. Mehta, A.K. and Ticka, M.K., An update on GABA$_A$ receptors. *Brain Res. Rev.,* 29, 196, 1999.

207. Bormann, J., The ABC of GABA receptors. *TIPS,* 21, 16, 2000.

208. Krystal, J.H., Petrakis, I.L., Mason, G., Trevisan, L., and D'Souza, D.C., *N*-Methyl-D-aspartate glutamate receptors and alcoholism: reward, dependence, treatment, and vulnerability. *Pharm. Ther.,* 99, 79, 2003.

209. Widmark, E.M.P., *Die theoretischen Grundlagen und die praktische Verwendbarkeit der gerichtlich-medizinischen Alkoholbestimmung.* Urban und Schwarzenberg, Berlin, 1932, 1–140.

210. Kalant, H., Current state of knowledge about the mechanisms of alcohol tolerance. *Addiction Biol.,* 1, 133, 1996.

211. Hoffman, P.L. and Tabakoff, B., Alcohol dependence: a commentary on mechanisms. *Alc. Alcohol,* 31, 333, 1996.

212. Bogen, E., The human toxicology of alcohol, *Alcohol and Man,* Emerson, H., Ed., Macmillan, New York, 1932, chap. 6.

213. Penttilä, A. and Tenhu, M., Clinical examination as medicolegal proof of alcohol intoxication. *Med. Sci. Law,* 16, 95, 1976.

214. Kataja, M., Penttilä, A., and Tenhu, M., Combining the blood alcohol and clinical examination for estimating the influence of alcohol. *Blutalkohol,* 12, 108, 1975.

215. Jones, A.W. and Holmgren, P., Comparison of blood-ethanol concentrations in deaths attributed to acute alcohol poisoning and chronic alcoholism. *J. Forensic Sci.,* 48, 874, 2003.

216. Koski, A., Ojanpera I., and Vuori, E., Alcohol and benzodiazepines in fatal poisonings. *Alcohol Clin. Exp. Res.,* 26, 956, 2002.

217. Jones, B.M. and Vega, A., Fast and slow drinkers; blood alcohol variables and cognitive performance. *J. Stud. Alc.,* 34, 797, 1973.

218. Moskowitz, H. and Burns, M., Effects of rate of drinking on human performance. *J. Stud. Alcohol,* 37, 598, 1976.

219. Jones, A.W. and Neri, A. Age-related differences in blood-ethanol parameters and subjective feelings of intoxication in healthy men. *Alc. Alcohol,* 20, 45, 1985.

220. Zink, P. and Reinhardt, G., Der Verlauf der Blutalkoholkurve bei großen Trinkmengen. *Blutalkohol,* 21, 422, 1984.

221. Wilkinson, P.K., Pharmacokinetics of ethanol. *Alcohol Clin. Exp. Res.,* 4, 6, 1980.

222. Holford, N.H.G., Clinical pharmacokinetics of ethanol. *Clin. Pharmacokinet.,* 13, 273, 1987.

223. Ludden, T.M., Nonlinear pharmacokinetics — clinical implications. *Clin. Pharmamcokinet.,* 20, 429, 1991.

224. Roland, M. and Tozer, T.N., *Clinical Pharmacokinetics: Concepts and Applications.* Lea & Febiger, Philadelphia, 1980.

225. Jones, A.W., *Forensic Science Aspects of Ethanol Metabolism,* in *Forensic Science Progress,* A. Mahley and R.L. Williams, Eds., Springer Verlag, New York, 1991, 33.

226. Andreasson, R. and Jones, A.W., The life and work of Erik M.P. Widmark. *Am. J. Forensic Med. Pathol.,* 17, 177, 1996.

227. Jones, A.W. and Andersson, L., Influence of age, gender, and blood-alcohol concentration on rate of alcohol elimination from blood in drinking drivers. *J. Forensic Sci.,* 41, 922, 1996.

228. Jones, A.W. and Sternebring, B., Kinetics of ethanol and methanol in alcoholics during detoxification. *Alc. Alcohol,* 27, 647, 1992.

229. Bogusz, M., Pach, J., and Stasko, W., Comparative studies on the rate of ethanol elimination in acute poisoning and in controlled conditions. *J. Forensic Sci.,* 22, 446, 1977.

230. Keiding, S., Christensen, N.J., Damgaard, S.E., Dejgård, A. et al., Ethanol metabolism in heavy drinkers after massive and moderate alcohol intake. *Biochem. Pharmacol.,* 20, 3097, 1983.

231. Haffner, H.T., Besserer, K., Stetter, F., and Mann, K., Die Äthanol-Eliminations-geschwindigkeit bei Alkoholikern unter besonderer Berücksichtigung der Maximalwertvarianyte der forensischsen BAK-Rückrechnung. *Blutalkohol,* 28, 46, 1991.

232. Conney, A.II., Induction of drug-metabolizing enzymes: a path to the discovery of multiple cytochromes P450. *Annu. Rev. Pharmacol.,* 43, 1, 2003.

233. Yap, M., Mascord, D.J., Starmer, G.A., and Whitfield, J.B., Studies on the chrono-pharmacokinetics of ethanol. *Alc. Alcohol,* 28, 17, 1993.

234. Lötterle, J., Husslein, E.M., Bolt, J., and Wirtz, P.M., Tageszeitliche Unterschiede der Alkoholresorption. *Blutalkohol,* 26, 369, 1989.

235. Johnson, R.D., Horowitz, M., Maddox, A.F., Wishart, J.M., and Shearman, D.J.C., Cigarette smoking and rate of gastric emptying: effect on alcohol absorption. *Br. Med. J.,* 302, 20, 1991.

236. Watson, P.E., Watson, I.D., and Batt, R.D., Prediction of blood alcohol concentration in human subjects; updating the Widmark equation. *J. Stud. Alcohol,* 42, 547, 1981.

237. Gullberg, R.G. and Jones, A.W., Guidelines for estimating the amount of alcohol consumed from a single measurement of blood alcohol concentration; re-evaluation of Widmark's equation. *Forensic Sci. Int.,* 69, 119, 1994.

238. Oneta, C.M., Pedrosa, M., Ruttimann, S., Russell, R.M., and Seitz, H.K., Age and bioavailability of alcohol. *Z. Gastroenterol.,* 39, 783, 2001.

239. Tozer, T.N. and Rubin, G.M., Saturable kinetics and bioavailability determination, in *Pharmacokinetics; Regulatory, Industrial, Academic Perspectives.* Vol. 33, *Drugs and the Pharmaceutical Sciences,* P.G. Welling and F.L.S. Tse, Eds., Marcel Dekker, New York, 1988, 473.

240. Lundquist, F. and Wolthers, H., The kinetics of alcohol elimination in man. *Acta Pharmacol. Toxicol.,* 14, 265, 1958.

241. Wilkinson, P.K., Sedman, A.J., Sakmar, E., Kay, D.R., and Wagner, J.G., Pharmacokinetics of ethanol after oral administration in the fasting state. *J. Pharmacokinet. Biopharm.,* 5, 207, 1977.

242. Wagner, J.G., Wilkinson, P.K., and Ganes, D.A., Parameters V_m and k_m for elimination of alcohol in young male subjects following low doses of alcohol. *Alc. Alcohol,* 24, 555, 1989.

243. Lewis, M.J., Blood alcohol: the concentration-time curve and retrospective estimation of level. *J. Forensic Sci. Soc.,* 26, 95, 1985.

244. Forrest, A.R.W., Non-linear kinetics of ethyl alcohol metabolism. *J. Forensic Sci. Soc.,* 26, 121, 1986.

245. Bosron, W.F. and Li, T.K., Genetic polymorphism of human liver alcohol and aldehyde dehydrogenases, and their relationship to alcohol metabolism and alcoholism. *Hepatology,* 6, 502, 1986.

246. Li, T.K., Yin, S.J., Crabb, D.W., O'Connor, S., and Ramchandani, V.A., Genetic and environmental influences on alcohol metabolism in humans. *Alcohol Clin. Exp. Res.,* 25, 136, 2001.

247. Oneta, C.M., Simanowski, U.A., Martinez, M., Allali-Hassani, A. et al., First pass metabolism of ethanol is strikingly influenced by the speed of gastric emptying. *Gut,* 43, 612, 1998.

248. Gentry, R.T., Baraona, E., and Lieber, C.S., Gastric first pass metabolism of alcohol. *J. Lab. Clin. Med.,* 123, 21, 1994.

249. Fressa, M., DiPadova, C., Pozzato, G., Terpin, M., Baraona, E., and Lieber, C.S., High blood alcohol levels in women; the role of decreased gastric alcohol dehydrogenase activity and first pass metabolism. *N. Engl. J. Med.,* 322, 95, 1990.

250. Levitt, M.D., The case against first-pass metabolism of ethanol in the stomach. *J. Lab. Clin. Med.,* 123, 28, 1994.

251. Levitt, M.D., Lack of clinical significance of the interaction between H_2-receptor antagonists and ethanol. *Aliment. Pharmacol. Ther.,* 7, 131, 1993.

252. Levitt, M.D. and Levitt, D.G., The critical role of the rate of ethanol absorption in the interpretation of studies purporting to demonstrate gastric metabolism of ethanol. *J. Pharmacol. Ther.,* 269, 297, 1994.

253. Arora, S., Baraona, E., and Lieber, C.S., Alcohol levels are increased in social drinkers receiving rantitidne. *Am. J. Gastroenterol.,* 95, 208, 2000.

254. DiPadova, C., Roine, R., Fressa, M., Gentry, T.R., Baraona, E., and Lieber, C.S., Effects of ranitidine on blood alcohol levels after ethanol ingestion. *J. Am. Med. Assoc.,* 267, 83, 1992.

255. Roine, R., Gentry, T., Hernandez-Munoz, R. et al., Aspirin increases blood alcohol concentration in humans after ingestion of alcohol. *J. Am. Med. Assoc.,* 264, 2406, 1990.

256. Amir, I., Anwar, N., Baraona, E., and Lieber, C.S., Ranitidine increases the bioavailability of imbibed alcohol by accelerating gastric emptying. *Life Sci.,* 58, 511, 1996.

257. Palmer, R.H., Frank, W.O., Nambi, P., Wetherington, J.D., and Fox, M.J., Effects of various concomitant medications on gastric alcohol dehydrogenase and its first-pass metabolism of ethanol. *Am. J. Gastroenterol.,* 86, 1749, 1991.

258. Lieber, C.S., Alcohol and the liver: 1994 update. *Gastroenterology.* 106, 1085, 1994.

259. Seitz., H.K., Egerer, G., Simanowski, U.A., Eckey, R., Agarwal, D.P., Goedde, H.W., and Von Wartburg, J.P., Human gastric alcohol dehydrogenase activity: effect of age, sex, and alcoholism. *Gut,* 34, 1433, 1993.

260. Raufman, J.P., Notar-Francesco, V., Raffaniello, R.D., and Straus, E.W., Histamine-2 receptor antagonists do not alter serum ethanol levels in fed, nonalcoholic men. *Ann. Intern. Med.,* 118, 488, 1983.

261. Kendall, M.J., Spannuth, F., Wait, R.P., Gibson, G.J. et al., Lack of effect of H2-receptor antagonists on the pharmacokinetics of alcohol consumed after food at lunchtime. *Br. J. Clin. Pharmacol.,* 37, 371, 1994.

262. Toon, S., Khan, A.Z., Holt, B.I., Mullins, F.G.P., Langley, S.J., and Rowland, M.M., Absence of effect of ranitidine on blood alcohol concentrations when taken morning, midday, or evening with or without food. *Clin. Pharmacol. Ther.,* 55, 385, 1994.

263. Bye, A., Lacey, L.F., Gupta, S., and Powell, J.R., Effect of ranitidine hydrochloride (150 mg twice daily) on the pharmacokinetics of increasing doses of ethanol (0.15, 0.3, 0.6 g/kg). *Br. J. Clin. Pharmacol.,* 41, 129, 1996.

264. Jönsson, K.Å., Jones, A.W., Boström, H., and Andersson, T., Lack of effect of omeprazole, cimetidine, and ranitidine, on the pharmacokinetics of ethanol in fasting male volunteers. *Eur. J. Clin. Pharmacol.,* 42, 209, 1992.

265. Melander, O., Liden, A., and Melander, A., Pharmacokinetic interaction of alcohol and acetylsalicylic acid. *Eur. J. Clin. Pharmacol.,* 48, 151, 1995.

266. Passananti, G.T., Wolff, C.A., and Vesell, E.S., Reproducibility of individual rates of ethanol metabolism in fasting subjects. *Clin. Pharmacol. Ther.,* 47, 389, 1990.

267. Fraser, A.G., Rosalki, S.B., Gamble, G.D., and Pounder, R.E., Inter-individual and intra-individual variability of ethanol concentration-time profiles: comparison of ethanol ingestion before or after an evening meal. *Br. J. Clin. Pharmacol.,* 40, 387, 1995.

268. Jones, A.W. and Jönsson, K.Å., Between subject and within subject variations in the pharmacokinetics of ethanol. *Br. J. Clin. Pharmacol.,* 37, 427, 1994.

269. Welling, P.G., Lyons, L.L., Elliot, R., and Amidon, G.L., Pharmacokinetics of alcohol following single low doses to fasted and nonfasted subjects. *J. Clin. Pharmacol.,* 199, 1977.

270. Welling, P.G., How food and fluid affect drug absorption. *Postgrad. Med.,* 62, 73, 1977.

271. McFarlane, A., Pooley, L., Welch I., Rumsey, R.D.E., and Read, N.W., How does dietary lipid lower blood alcohol concentrations? *Gut,* 27, 15, 1986.

272. Winstanley, P.A. and Orme, M.L.E., The effects of food on drug bioavailability. *Br. J. Clin. Pharmacol.,* 28, 621, 1989.

273. Millar, K., Hammersley, R.H., and Finnigan, F., Reduction of alcohol-induced performance by prior ingestion of food. *Br. J. Psychol.,* 83, 261, 1992.

274. Jones, A.W., Jönsson K.Å., and Kechagias, S., Effect of high-fat, high-protein and high-carbohydrate meals on the pharmacokinetics of a small dose of alcohol. *Br. J. Clin. Pharmacol.,* 44, 521, 1997.

275. Ramachandani, V.A., Kwo, P.Y., and Li, T.K., Effect of food and food composition on alcohol elimination rates in healthy men and women. *J. Clin. Pharmacol.,* 41, 1345, 2001.

276. Ramachandani, V.A., Bosron, W.T., and Li, T.K., Research advances in ethanol metabolism. *Pathol. Biol.,* 49, 676, 2001.

277. Kalant, H., Effects of food and body composition on blood alcohol levels, in *Comprehensive Handbook of Alcohol Related Pathology,* V.R. Preedy and R.R. Watson, Eds., Elsevier, Academic Press, Amsterdam, 2005, 87.

278. Hahn, R.G., Norberg, Å., Gabrielsson, J., Danielsson, A., and Jones, A.W., Eating a meal increases the clearance of ethanol given by intravenous infusion. *Alc. Alcohol,* 29, 673, 1994.

279. Pedrosa, M.C., Russell, R.M., Saltzman, J.R., Golner, B.B., Dallal, G.E., Sepe, T.E., Oats, E., Egerer, G., and Seitz, H.K., Gastric emptying and first-pass metabolism of ethanol in elderly subjects with and without atrophic gastritis. *Scand. J. Gastroenterol.,* 31,671, 1996.

280. Preedy, V.R. and Watson, R.R., Eds., *Comprehensive Handbook of Alcohol Related Pathology.* Elsevier Academic Press, London, 2004.

281. O'Neal, C.L., Wolf, C.E., Levine, B., Kunsman, G., and Poklis, A., Gas chromatographic procedures for determination of ethanol in postmortem blood using *t*-butanol and methyl ethyl ketone as internal standard. *Forensic Sci. Int.,* 83, 31, 1996.

282. Hunsaker, D.M. and Hundsaker, J.C., III, Blood and body fluid analysis, in *Encyclopedia of Forensic and Legal Medicine,* J. Payne-James, R.W. Byard, T.S. Corey, and C. Henderson, Eds., Elsevier Science, Amsterdam, 2005, 29.

283. Wagner, J.G., Wilkinson, P.K., and Ganes, D.A., Estimation of the amount of alcohol ingested from a single blood alcohol concentration. *Alc. Alcohol,* 25, 379, 1990.

284. Kwo, P.Y., Ramchandani, V.A., O'Connor, S., Amann, D., Carr, L.G., Sandrasgaran, K., Kopecky, K.K., and Li, T.K., Gender differences in alcohol metabolism: relationship to liver volume and effect of adjusting for body composition. *Gastroenterology,* 115, 1552, 1998.

285. Li, T.K, Beard, J.D., Orr, W.E., Kwo, P.Y., Ramchandani, V.A., and Thomasson, H.R., Variation in ethanol pharmacokinetics and perceived gender and ethnic differences in alcohol elimination. *Alcohol Clin. Exp. Res.,* 24, 415, 2000.

286. Jackson, P.R., Tucker, G.T., and Woods, H.F., Backtracking booze with Bayes — the retrospective interpretation of blood alcohol data. *Br. J. Clin. Pharmacol.,* 31, 55, 1991.

287. Arora, S., Bararona, E., and Lieber, C.S., Alcohol levels are increased in social drinkers receiving ranitidine. *Am. J. Gastroenterol.,* 95, 208, 2000.

288. Norberg, Å., Jones, A.W., Hahn, R.G., and Gabrielsson, J., and Role of variability in explaining ethanol pharmacokinetics. *Clin. Pharmacokinet.,* 42, 1, 2003.

289. Smith, G.D., Shaw, L.J., Maini, P.K., Ward, R.J., Peters, T.J., and Murray, J.D., Mathematical modelling of ethanol metabolism in normal subjects and chronic alcohol misusers. *Alc. Alcohol,* 28, 25, 1993.

290. Komura, S., Fujimiya, T., and Yoshimoto, K., Fundamental studies on alcohol dependence and disposition. *Forensic Sci. Int.,* 80, 99, 1996.

291. Fujimiya, T., Uemura, K., Ohbora, Y., and Komura, S., Problems in pharmacokinetic analysis of alcohol disposition: a trial of the Bayesian Least-Squares method. *Alcohol Clin. Exp. Res.,* 20, 2A, 1996.

292. Pieters, J. E., Wedel, M., and Schaafsma, G., Parameter estimation in a three-compartment model for blood alcohol curves. *Alc. Alcohol,* 25, 17, 1990.

293. Kosten, T.R. and O'Connor, P.G., Management of drug and alcohol withdrawal. *N. Engl. J. Med.,* 348, 1786, 2003.

5.3 POST-MORTEM ALCOHOL — ASPECTS OF INTERPRETATION

Derrick J. Pounder, M.D.[1] **and Alan Wayne Jones, D.Sc.**[2]

[1] Department of Forensic Medicine, University of Dundee, Scotland, U.K.
[2] Department of Forensic Toxicology, University Hospital, Linköping, Sweden

5.3.1 Introduction

In post-mortem toxicology, the sample most commonly submitted for analysis is blood and the most frequently encountered substance is alcohol. The technical details and procedures for measuring ethanol in blood and other body fluids obtained from a corpse are essentially the same as those used when analyzing specimens from the living. However, the interpretation of the analytical results obtained from autopsy samples is confounded by problems such as the lack of homogeneity of blood samples, microbial alcohol production post-mortem, alcohol diffusion from gastric residue and contaminated airways, and the lack of or unreliability of information on the clinical condition of the person immediately prior to death. On the other hand, autopsy offers opportunities for sampling body fluids and tissues not accessible or not readily available in the living. Sampling of blood from multiple vascular sites, the vitreous humor of the eye, gastric contents, sequestered hematomas, as well as bile, brain, skeletal muscle, cerebrospinal fluid, and liver are all possible. Nevertheless, multiple sampling at autopsy can only partly compensate for the increased interpretative difficulties created by the various post-mortem confounding factors. As a result it is necessary to apply a greater degree of caution in the interpretation of post-mortem ethanol analyses and to take into account the totality of the available information, which should always include not only the results of the autopsy examination but also the scene of death examination and anamnestic data. A single autopsy blood ethanol concentration is commonly uninterpretable without concurrent vitreous humor and urine ethanol concentrations, as well as information gleaned from the scene of death and case history.

5.3.2 Post-Mortem Specimens for Alcohol Analysis

Within a few hours of death the blood within the vascular system clots and simultaneously there is clot lysis. The effectiveness of the clot lysis will determine whether a blood sample obtained at autopsy is clotted, or completely fluid, or partly clotted and partly fluid. The fibrin clots invariably entrap large numbers of red blood cells so that the resulting clot is relatively red cell rich and serum poor. Occasionally the heart and great vessels may contain a large two-layered clot, the lower part typically red clot and the upper part pale yellow rubbery clot largely devoid of red cells (so called "chicken fat"). Consequently "blood samples" obtained at autopsy are variable in their red cell and protein content and this will have some influence on the measured ethanol concentration since ethanol is distributed in the water portion of blood. Blood obtained from limb vessels is most likely to be fluid and largely devoid of clots and therefore provides as homogeneous a sample for analysis as can be hoped for. The presence of blood clots will not necessarily have a negative influence on the accuracy of the blood alcohol analysis using headspace gas chromatography.[1]

Serum and plasma contains approximately 10 to 15% more water than whole blood. Since ethanol is distributed in the water portion of blood it can be expected that the concentration in plasma is approximately 10 to 15% higher than the corresponding whole blood concentration. This should be borne in mind whenever alcohol has been measured in serum or plasma in hospital prior to death or where a pre-mortem hospital sample of serum or plasma is subsequently analyzed for alcohol.

In 134 blood samples from healthy men and women[2] the mean blood alcohol concentration (BAC) was 105 mg/dL (range 22 to 155) and the mean serum alcohol concentration was 121 mg/dL (range 25 to 183) with a mean serum:blood ratio of 1.15 (range 1.10 to 1.25, standard deviation, SD, 0.02); 3 of the 134 serum:blood ratios were between 1.21 and 1.25. A larger study on 235 subjects[3] produced a similar mean serum:blood ratios of 1.14 with a range of 1.04 to 1.26 and a normal distribution with SD of 0.041. Ethanol concentration in red blood cells was reported in 167 of these subjects and ratio red cells:blood ethanol ranged from 0.66 to 1.00 with a mean of 0.865 and a negatively skewed distribution with an SD of 0.065. Given these data it is evident that there may be significant differences in ethanol concentrations between different blood samples obtained at the same time from the same corpse, since an autopsy "blood" sample may range in composition from being largely red cells at one extreme to largely plasma at the other. However, in practice, most autopsy blood samples will tend to be plasma rich rather than red blood cell rich because autopsy sampling procedures tend to avoid clots and favor clot-free fluid.

The water content of whole blood decreases post-mortem, and because ethanol is distributed only in the water phase of the body, this will cause the BAC to decrease. In a study of 71 cadavers[4] with a blood sample taken within 10 h of death (mean 2.1 h, range 0 to 9.6 h) the water content ranged between 72.4 and 89.3%, mean 80.4%, which is closely similar to the water content of blood from living persons (79.9 to 82.3% for women and 77.5 to 80.6% for men). Second samples taken from the same cadavers from 8 to 229 h post-mortem had a lower water content ranging between 64.4 and 88.0%, mean 74.0%. However, differences in blood ethanol concentration between the two sampling times was more strongly influenced by other post-mortem factors, such as putrefaction, rather than by water content changes, so that correcting a post-mortem blood alcohol for water content is not generally recommended.

5.3.3 Blood Alcohol Concentration

Ethanol is a central nervous system depressant drug exerting its effects in part via the $GABA_A$ inhibitory receptor. At very high BACs, stupor is followed by coma and then paralysis of the respiratory center in the brain stem so that breathing stops and death ensues. The lethal range of blood ethanol concentration is based on published case reports of human fatalities and the experimentally derived LD_{50} values of 500 to 550 mg/dL in rats, guinea pigs, chickens, and dogs.[5] However, a review of actual cases suggests that a concentration of 250 mg/dL might be potentially lethal rather than the higher figures commonly quoted.[6] In a retrospective review of 693 deaths attributed to acute alcohol poisoning, the mean BAC in femoral venous blood at autopsy was 360 mg/dL and the 5th and 95th percentiles were 220 and 500 mg/dL.[7] (For fatal blood ethanol levels in various series, see Niyogi.[8]) The often quoted lethal blood ethanol range of above 400 or 450 mg/dL may only apply to uncomplicated deaths as a result of acute alcohol poisoning in inexperienced drinkers. The complexity of interpreting the significance of high blood ethanol concentrations at autopsy is illustrated by a review[9] of fatalities with blood ethanol above 300 mg/dL. This study disclosed 502 cases attributable to acute ethanol poisoning alone but 24 resulting from well-documented natural causes, 260 from obvious trauma or violence, and 28 with a combination of a high blood ethanol and additional contributing or related abnormalities. An unusual form of sexual gratification involved self-administration of an alcohol-containing enema (klezmomania), which proved fatal with a BAC of 400 mg/dL found at autopsy following a wine enema.[10]

In a series of 115 deaths attributed to acute alcoholism 59% showed some asphyxial element, either postural asphyxia (positional asphyxia) or inhalation of vomit.[6] Since acute alcohol intoxication may induce vomiting and also suppresses the gag reflex, as part of its cerebral depressant effect, there is a high risk of inhalation of vomit. Alcohol-related deaths associated with an asphyxial element may show considerably lower BACs than uncomplicated alcohol poisonings. For this reason it is particularly important to have accurate documentation of the position of the body as found and any evidence of inhalation of vomitus at the scene of death, since passive regurgitation of gastric contents and contamination of the airways may occur post-mortem during removal of the body to the mortuary. In many of these deaths in which asphyxia is a contributing factor the urine alcohol is considerably higher than the blood alcohol suggesting that the mechanism of death was coma resulting from a high BAC and subsequent respiratory embarrassment and anoxia. In such fatalities the BAC observed at autopsy is not necessarily the same that caused death owing to ongoing metabolism up to the time of death.[6] The diagnostic features of accidental postural asphyxia are a body position that compromises breathing, such as abnormal neck flexion or limitation of chest movement, together with evidence of the accidental adoption of that position and an explanation for failure to escape, such as alcohol intoxication, in the absence of another explanation for the death.[11] Acute alcohol intoxication is a significant risk factor for this mode of death accounting for 22 of 30 cases in one study.[12]

A high autopsy blood ethanol concentration, although indicating chemical intoxication at the time of death, does not necessarily imply that there were observable clinical manifestations of drunkenness and this is particularly so in chronic alcoholics.[13] Alcohol abusers develop tolerance to alcohol to the extent that they can maintain very high blood ethanol concentrations in the potentially lethal range. In an Australian study[14] blood alcohol levels were determined in chronic alcoholics presenting to a detoxification service. Of the 32 subjects, all appeared affected by alcohol with 23 showing altered mood or behavior, 6 appearing confused, and 3 drowsy but none was stuporous or comatose. All displayed ataxia and dysarthria of varying degrees. The blood ethanol concentration ranged from 180 to 450 mg/dL with a mean of 313 mg/dL and 26 of the 32 were above 250 mg/dL. A similar Swedish study[15] identified 24 patients who attended a hospital casualty department and were found to have blood ethanol concentrations above 500 mg/dL. Of the 16 patients for whom there were complete data available, 8 were either awake or could be aroused by nonpainful stimuli. All left the hospital alive within 24 h. It is suggested that this tolerance to high blood ethanol levels seen in chronic alcoholics is primarily the result of neuronal adaptation. Physical dependence on ethanol, as demonstrated by the development of withdrawal signs and symptoms on stopping drinking, similarly indicates the existence of an adaptation process.

There are anecdotal descriptions of alcoholics surviving remarkably high levels of blood alcohol. In one instance,[16] a 24-year-old female chronic alcoholic presented at the hospital with abdominal pain. She was agitated and slightly confused but alert, responsive to questioning, and orientated to person and place, though unclear as to time. Her serum ethanol was 1510 mg/dL, which corresponds to a concentration in whole blood of about 1313 mg/dL (1510/1.15). After 12 h treatment with intravenous fluids, electrolyte replacement, chlordiazepoxide, and intensive care monitoring, she felt well, and was symptomless at discharge 2 days later. Similarly, a 52-year-old, 66-kg male was found unconscious in a bar with a blood ethanol concentration of 650 mg/dL and survived with minimum treatment comprising protection against aspiration and the occasional use of oxygen.[17] A 23-year-old, 57-kg female chronic alcoholic, who was admitted to the hospital in a comatose state with a blood ethanol level of 780 mg/dL, had apparently consumed 390 mL of absolute alcohol in the form of a bottle of bourbon. She was discharged 11 h later with a blood ethanol level of 190 mg/dL; the disappearance of ethanol from her blood seemingly followed a logarithmic function.[18] Two further case reports describe more stormy clinical courses but with survival, one with a serum ethanol level of 1127 mg/dL,[19] another with a blood ethanol level of 1500 mg/dL.[20] One individual arrested in Sweden for drunk-driving had a BAC of 545 mg/dL.[21] This tolerance to high blood ethanol concentrations seen in chronic alcoholics makes it difficult to interpret the significance of a blood ethanol level obtained at autopsy from such a person.

On the other hand, nonlethal levels of ethanol may be of particular significance in some types of death. Ethanol adversely affects thermal regulation and, depending upon the ambient temperature, may cause either hypothermia or hyperthermia.[22] There is a large body of experimental and clinical data available regarding the hypothermic effect of alcohol on both animals and humans at different degrees of cold exposure. In deaths related to acute alcohol poisoning, a mean BAC of 170 mg/dL in hypothermia-associated deaths contrasted with a much higher mean BAC of 360 mg/dL in deaths without associated hypothermia.[23] Alcohol consumption accelerates body heat loss by inducing dilatation of peripheral blood vessels and relaxing muscles, thereby inhibiting shivering thermogenesis. Heat loss is further facilitated by behavioral effects consequent on a feeling of warmth and comfort, and central nervous system depression. At a biochemical level, alcohol may inhibit the protective acute ketogenesis induced by the effects of hypothermia and so shorten the survival time.[24] Deaths from hypothermia associated with sobriety or a BAC of less than 100 mg/dL have a higher frequency of the macroscopic autopsy signs of hypothermia — bright red lividity, violet patches over the knees and elbows, acute gastric mucosa erosions, pancreatitis, and paradoxical undressing — than cases with a BAC greater than 100 mg/dL, suggesting that intoxication is associated with more rapid death before visible pathological signs develop.[24] The importance of ethanol in hyperthermic deaths is less well appreciated but illustrated by Finnish sauna fatalities. In a series of 228 hyperthermic deaths (221 sauna related) alcohol had been consumed in 192 cases and the consumption was categorized as "heavy" in 61.[25] Similarly, complex cerebral dysfunctions induced by alcohol are thought to be significant in the syndrome of sudden, alcohol-associated, cranio-facial traumatic death.[26] In this syndrome individuals who have collapsed and died at the scene of an assault are found at autopsy to have facial trauma insufficient to account for the death together with a high but nonlethal BAC.

The simultaneous presence of another drug with ethanol further complicates the interpretation of the concentrations measured at autopsy. Investigations into drug–alcohol interactions are complex because these interactions are influenced by the timing of administration of alcohol relative to the drug and the specific dosages. As well as being oxidized by alcohol dehydrogenase (ADH), ethanol is metabolized to acetaldehyde by a microsomal enzyme, cytochrome P4502E1 (CYP2E1). This same enzyme is involved in oxidative metabolism of a wide range of endogenous and exogenous substances, including therapeutic drugs, with the result that an important mechanism for drug–alcohol interactions involves either an inhibition or induction of this enzyme. After taking a large acute dose of alcohol, the ethanol molecules compete with other drugs for detoxification enzymes. On the other hand, chronic consumption of large amounts of alcohol causes induction of the enzyme system so that alcoholics acquire an enhanced capacity for the metabolism of drugs via this system. Alcoholics are more prone to suffer from hepato-toxicity from taking acetaminophen (paracetamol) owing to their more active CYP2E1 detoxification enzymes, which convert acetaminophen into a chemically reactive and toxic intermediate compound, N-acetyl-p-benzoquinone imine (NAPQI).[27]

Chloral hydrate, one of the oldest sedative hypnotic drugs, has a complex interaction with ethanol. In the liver, chloral hydrate is rapidly reduced to its pharmacologically active metabolite 2,2,2-trichloroethanol, and this reaction is facilitated by the excess NADH (nicotinamide adenine dinucleotide) produced in the liver during the metabolism of ethanol. The pharmacologically active trichloroethanol is either conjugated with glucuronic acid and then excreted in the urine or is oxidized by ADH to an inactive metabolite, trichloroacetic acid. This latter ADH reaction is inhibited by the presence of ethanol, which competes for binding sites on the enzyme. The net result of both of these interactions with alcohol is that the effect of chloral hydrate on the individual is more intense and prolonged.[27]

Ethanol is a central nervous system depressant and a similar synergistic effect is found for other hypnotic drugs as well as antidepressants and narcotic analgesics so that allowance for ethanol–drug synergism is necessary when blood concentrations measured at autopsy are interpreted.[28] In general, any drug or chemical agent with psychoactive properties, that is, with its site of action in the central nervous system, has the potential for pharmacodynamic interaction with ethanol. The toxicity of the painkiller propoxyphene is enhanced in alcohol abusers and binge drinkers. Although the mechanism of the interaction with ethanol is not completely understood, it appears to be related to synaptic activity at GABA and opiate receptors with additive effects on the depression of respiration. Sedative-hypnotic drugs, which are widely prescribed, are obvious candidates for interaction with ethanol, owing to the similar mechanism and sites of action in the brain, namely, the GABA receptor complex. Examples of sedative-hypnotics exerting a pharmacodynamic interaction with ethanol include barbiturates and benzodiazepines. Deaths resulting from the combined use of large doses of alcohol and barbiturates are well recognized. However, in case of fatalities it has proved difficult to establish an added toxic effect from the concurrent use of diazepam with alcohol, so that in cases of acute alcohol poisoning the blood ethanol concentration is about the same, with or without the presence of diazepam.[29]

The alcohol flush reaction exhibited by many Japanese and other Asians when they drink alcoholic beverages is a direct consequence of acetaldehyde accumulation in the blood. Acetaldehyde reacts with β-adrenergic receptors of the autonomic nervous system leading to violent and unpleasant vasomotor responses. These individuals inherit a defective form of the enzyme acetaldehyde dehydrogenase (ALDH) and as a result are genetically prone to react strongly after drinking small amounts of alcohol, so that in effect they are equipped with a natural aversion to alcohol. A fatality has been reported in a Japanese subject with this inherited defect resulting in abnormally high concentrations of acetaldehyde after consumption of ethanol.[30] Disulfiram (tetraethylthiuram disulfide or Antabuse®) inhibits ALDH and is used in aversion therapy for treating alcoholics, although its clinical effectiveness has been debated. In a person taking the drug, subsequent ingestion of alcohol produces numerous unpleasant symptoms as a result of the toxic accumulation of acetaldehyde. Fatalities have been reported after reaching relatively low blood ethanol concentrations and with acetaldehyde in blood at concentrations between 12 and 41 mg/L.[31] When the edible inky cap mushroom (*Coprinus atramentarius*) is mistakenly eaten at the same time alcohol is consumed, the result is an Antabuse-like reaction owing to the presence of an unusual amino acid protoxin, coprine (N5-1-hydroxycyclopropyl-L-glutamine), which is broken down in the body to 1-aminocyclopropanol, an inhibitor of hepatic ALDH. Enzyme inhibition generally persists for about 72 h but may continue for 5 days, so consumption of ethanol during this period might produce an unpleasant Antabuse-like reaction. Metronidazole has been reported to cause death when taken with ethanol as a consequence of an Antabuse-like reaction,[32] but others have suggested that there might be an allergic reaction to the drug modified by the presence of alcohol.[33] Other prescription drugs that might produce an Antabuse-like reaction are chlorpropamide and tolbutamide, both oral hypoglycemic agents used to treat diabetes.

Cocaethylene is biosynthesized during the metabolism of cocaine in individuals with elevated BACs. This compound passes the blood–brain barrier to exert its pharmacological effects through the dopamine receptor thus enhancing the feelings of euphoria. Since the elimination half-life of cocaethylene is longer than for cocaine, it prolongs the effects of the drug on the individual. Several studies have suggested that when cocaine is taken together with ethanol, the risk of cardiotoxicity[34,35] and a fatal outcome[36] is increased. It has been suggested that ethanol enhances the acute toxicity of heroin and that ethanol use indirectly influences fatal heroin overdose through its association with infrequent (non-addictive) heroin use and thus a reduced tolerance to the acute toxic effects of heroin.[37] Although it has been proposed that carbon monoxide and ethanol may have an additive affect there is no conclusive evidence of this.

5.3.4 Vitreous Alcohol

Analysis of vitreous humor (VH) is useful to corroborate a post-mortem BAC and this helps to distinguish ante-mortem intoxication from post-mortem synthesis of alcohol. VH can serve also as an alternative post-mortem specimen for alcohol analysis if for some reason blood is unavailable or contaminated. In most cases, the specimen of eye fluid is easily obtained and can be sampled without a full autopsy. Vitreous humor is a clear, serous fluid which is easy to work with analytically. Its anatomically isolated position protects it from bacterial putrefaction. In microbiological studies of vitreous obtained from 51 cadavers between 1 and 5 days post-mortem it was found that none of the samples contained large numbers of bacteria and only one contained fungi.[38]

The predictive value of a known vitreous humor alcohol concentration (VHAC) in estimating an unknown BAC in an individual case remains contentious, despite many studies.[39–50] Various formulae have been proposed, including a simple conversion factor, to predict BAC from VHAC but these do not take into account the uncertainty of the prediction for an individual subject. In one case series[51] simple linear regression was applied with BAC as outcome y variable and VHAC as predictor x variable (range 1 to 705 mg/dL). The regression equation was BAC = 3.03 + 0.852 VHAC with 95% prediction interval ± 0.019 $\sqrt{[7157272 + (VHAC - 189.7)^2]}$.

The practical application of the regression equation is shown in Table 5.3.1. Set out are the VHAC values that predict key BAC values of 80 and 150 mg/dL as the mean, or the minimum value at either the 95% or 99% prediction interval for the determination of a single BAC value. The prediction interval is too wide to be of much practical use. In addition, reanalysis of the raw data from previous publications gave significantly different regression equations in most instances. From an evidential viewpoint it would be unreasonable to give an estimate of the mean BAC based on the VHAC without also providing the 95% prediction interval, which is a measure of the degree of confidence attached to the estimate in an individual case.[52–54] Data from another large study suggest that dividing the VHAC by 2.0 would provide a very conservative estimate of the BAC, which is less than the true value with a high degree of confidence.[55]

Blood has a lower water content than vitreous, which is approximately 98 to 99% water v/v, so the expectation is that the blood:vitreous alcohol ratio will be less than unity. In cases where the ratio of blood alcohol to vitreous humor alcohol concentration exceeds 1.0, the most likely explanation is that death occurred before diffusion equilibrium had been attained, which might have forensic significance.[41] Animal studies[56,57] indicate that, following intraperitoneal or intravenous injections of ethanol, BAC:VHAC ratios may be greater than 0.95 for 30 min or longer. A study of 43 fatalities[45] disclosed a bimodal distribution of blood:vitreous alcohol ratios with the first mode from 0.72 to 0.90 and a positively skewed distribution from 0.94 to 1.37. It seems that

Table 5.3.1   Prediction of Critical Values of BAC (as
             mean, or lower limit of 95% and 99%
             prediction intervals) from VHAC (mg/dL)[51]

| Observed VHAC | | Predicted BAC mg/dL | |
mg/dL	Mean	95% PI	99% PI
90	80	29–131	13–147
150	131	80–182	64–198
169	147	96–198	80–214
173	150	100–201	83–217
232	201	150–251	134–268
251	217	166–268	150–284

Note: PI = prediction interval for the determination of a
       single BAC value. Thus for an observed VHAC of
       90 mg/dL the best estimate of BAC is 80 mg/dL;
       there is a 95% probability that the true value of
       BAC is between 29 and 131 mg/dL; and a 99%
       probability that the true value is between 13 and
       147 mg/dL.

the first mode of the distribution ratio represents the elimination phase of the blood alcohol curve and that the second mode represents the absorption phase prior to equilibrium being established.

A second study of 86 cases confirmed this bimodal distribution and suggested that a blood:vitreous ratio greater than 0.95 indicates that death had occurred before equilibrium was achieved, and therefore in the early absorptive phase. [48] The blood:vitreous ratio during this early phase had a mean of 1.09 (SD = 0.38) in contrast to the late absorptive and elimination phases where the mean was 0.80 (SD = 0.09). Others[47] failed to reproduce this bimodal distribution. However, most deaths occur during the elimination phase, and it is clear that the observation of a bimodal distribution of blood:vitreous alcohol ratios in any study depends on the inclusion of cases dying in the absorptive phase. It is likely that the proportion of absorptive phase cases included in published series has varied considerably and that this accounts, at least in part, for the differences in published BAC:VHAC ratios.

It seems reasonable to assume that ethanol may diffuse into or out of the vitreous post-mortem. The chemical constituents of embalming fluid may diffuse into the vitreous humor after a body has been embalmed. Fortunately almost all commercial embalming fluids are free of ethyl alcohol, although they commonly contain methanol. A comparison of ethanol concentrations in 38 corpses both pre- and post-embalming suggested that there was no significant change in the vitreous humor ethanol concentration in the immediate aftermath of embalming.[58] However, in one case the embalmer cleaned the globus of the eye with ethanol on a cotton swab prior to placing an eye cap into position and this caused an elevation of vitreous ethanol from 0 to 340 mg/dL. In another fatality, an unusually high VHAC was attributed to prolonged post-mortem exposure of the eye surface to alcohol-containing vomit.[59] Conversely, prolonged submersion of a body in water may result in diffusion of alcohol out of the vitreous. This was the proposed explanation for finding a zero ethanol concentration in vitreous but concentrations of 370 mg/dL in urine and 223 mg/dL in blood (blood acetone 46 mg/dL) in a man submerged in cold fresh water for about 6 weeks. In a rabbit model that duplicated these circumstances the vitreous ethanol level fell from a mean of 196 to 30 mg/dL over the 6-week period.[60]

5.3.5   Urinary Alcohol

The ureteral urine, which is the urine as it is being formed, has a concentration of alcohol approximately 1.3 times that of whole blood. In fatalities the urine sample obtained is pooled bladder urine, which has accumulated over an unknown time interval between last urination and death. Consequently, the bladder urine alcohol concentration (UAC) does not necessarily reflect the BAC existing at the time of death. Instead it reflects the average BAC prevailing during the period that urine accumulates in the bladder since it was last emptied.

Several studies have examined the range of ratios between BAC and pooled bladder UAC at autopsy. One study[61] reported an average UAC:BAC ratio of 1.28:1 with a wide range of 0.21 to 2.66. In another study[44] the mean UAC:BAC ratio was 1.21:1 with a range from 0.22 to 2.07 using a direct injection gas chromatography (GC) technique and a mean ratio of 1.16:1 with a range of 0.20 to 2.10 with the more widely used headspace GC technique. In a large case series, simple linear regression analysis with BAC as outcome variable and autopsy bladder UAC as predictor variable (n = 435, range 3 to 587 mg/dL) gave the regression equation BAC = −5.6 + 0.811UAC.[62] The 95% prediction interval around the regression line was given by the equation $\pm 0.026\sqrt{[9465804 + (UAC - 213.3)^2]}$. This shows that a BAC of 80 mg/dL was predicted with 95% certainty by a UAC of 204 mg/dL and similarly a BAC of 150 mg/dL by a UAC of 291 mg/dL. The prediction interval is very wide so that autopsy UAC has limited usefulness in predicting an unknown BAC for forensic purposes. Although an autopsy UAC should not be translated into a presumed BAC, it is possible to make a conservative estimate of the BAC existing during the time the urine was being produced and accumulated in the bladder, by dividing the observed autopsy UAC by 1.35 (or multiplying by three quarters). However, if the BAC profile was rising, which might be the case if death occurred soon after drinking ended, the calculation UAC/1.35 underestimates the coexisting BAC.

When both urine and blood specimens are available at autopsy, then the UAC:BAC ratio may be of interpretive value, by giving an indication of the state of alcohol absorption and elimination in the body at the time of death.[63] A ratio less than unity or not more than 1.2 suggests, but does not prove, the existence of a rising BAC. If the UAC:BAC ratio exceeds 1.3, this suggests that the subject was in the post-absorptive stage at the time of death. The UAC:BAC ratio in 628 deaths from acute ethanol poisoning was 1.18 (SD = 0.182) and in 647 chronic alcoholic deaths was 1.30 (SD = 0.29), suggesting that the former group died typically before complete absorption and distribution of alcohol while the latter group died typically after complete absorption and distribution.[64] However, establishing whether a deceased had consumed alcohol immediately prior to death is most easily achieved by obtaining a sample of stomach contents at autopsy and analyzing this for alcohol. A gastric contents concentration less than 500 mg/dL has been taken to indicate a post-absorptive state.[43] Unusually high UAC:BAC ratios reflect urine accumulation over a long period of time and extreme ratios are well recognized as occurring in delayed deaths from acute alcohol poisoning.[65] In delayed traumatic deaths post-mortem urine ethanol concentrations may help establish or exclude the role of alcohol. Urine ethanol content of 200 mg/dL may be found with no alcohol present in the blood.[66]

5.3.6 Alternative Biological Samples

There have been many attempts to correlate post-mortem BACs with the concentrations of alcohol measured in a creative variety of specimens. In addition to the usual urine and vitreous humor these specimens have included saliva, cerebrospinal fluid, brain, liver, kidney, bone marrow, and skeletal muscle. All show a very wide range of variation in the ratio of the ethanol content in the target tissue or fluid compared with that in blood, making them of little value in practice. Since ethanol distribution in the body follows the distribution of body water, the ethanol content of these unconventional specimens is influenced by their water content. Cerebrospinal fluid is 98 to 99% water w/w and therefore generally will have a higher ethanol content than blood, whereas muscle, brain, liver, and kidney, with a water content of 75 to 78% w/w, will have lower concentrations of alcohol than blood. Moreover, the continuing post-mortem enzymatic activity within liver and kidney may reduce their ethanol content.

For blood alcohol levels greater than 40 mg/dL the average liver:heart blood ratio in 103 cases was 0.56, SD 0.30, with a range of 0 to 1.40.[67] However, liver is not recommended as a suitable sample for post-mortem ethanol analysis because it is rapidly invaded by gut microorganisms and provides abundant glycogen as substrate for ethanol production by fermentation, as well as being subject to post-mortem diffusion from gastric residue. For bile, in 89 cases with blood ethanol ranging from 46 to 697 mg/dL the bile:blood ratio averaged 0.99, range 0.48 to 2.04. Bile has been suggested as superior to vitreous humor in the estimation or corroboration of a blood alcohol level,[68] but, unfortunately, bile is vulnerable to post-mortem diffusion of unabsorbed alcohol in the stomach.[69] For cerebrospinal fluid ($n = 54$, blood ethanol range 46 to 697 mg/dL) the average ratio was 1.14 and range 0.79 to 1.64.[43]

Since ethanol impairs body functioning by its effects on the brain, it would seem logical to analyze brain tissue for alcohol at autopsy. This is not the practice for two reasons. First, the analysis of post-mortem blood is more helpful as it allows comparison with data available from living persons. Second, the brain is extremely heterogeneous so that within the brain the ethanol concentration may vary twofold to threefold between different regions; highest concentrations are found in the cerebellum and pituitary and lowest concentrations in the medulla and pons.[70] Brain tissue obtained from the frontal lobe ($n = 33$ blood ethanol range 72 to 388 mg/dL) gave an average brain:blood ratio of 0.86 with a range of 0.64 to 1.20.[43]

5.3.7   Residual Gastric Alcohol

Opinions vary as to how much alcohol may be found in the stomach post-mortem in case material. In one series[71] the highest concentration found was 2.95 g/dL and the author quoted a similar high of 5 g/dL in a previous study. In another series[72] only 1 of 60 cases had a concentration as high as 5.1 g/dL. In a small study[73] the highest concentration observed was 8.7 g/dL and this was in a suicidal hanging. Given that alcohol is rapidly absorbed from the stomach, it seems likely that death must occur within about an hour or less of ingesting substantial amounts of alcohol to detect a significant residue in the stomach post-mortem.

Researchers in the 1940s and 1950s debated the suitability of heart blood for quantitative analysis of ethanol on the grounds of possible artifactual elevation resulting from post-mortem diffusion of alcohol present in the stomach at the time of death.[74–80] Later investigations by Plueckhahn[71,81–86] led to the conclusion that post-mortem ethanol diffusion from the stomach into the pericardial sac and left pleural cavity was significant and could contaminate blood samples allowed to pool there, but cardiac chamber blood, as such, was not susceptible to this diffusion artifact to any significant extent. However, more recent case studies and a cadaver model have shown that cardiac chamber, aortic, and other torso blood samples may be significantly affected by gastric diffusion artifact.[73]

In one study[87] blood was obtained from the right atrium, ascending aorta, and the inferior vena cava in 307 subjects without significant decomposition and in whom the blood ethanol concentration was not less than 50 mg/dL in any sample. A total of 104 (33.9%) had one blood ethanol value 20% lower than the highest value. The most striking differences were found when gastric ethanol concentrations were greater than or equal to 800 mg/dL and with associated evidence of aspiration. In a second study[72] blood was obtained from the femoral vein, the aortic root, and the right atrium in 60 cases with blood ethanol concentrations of 50 mg/dL or greater and no gross trauma or significant decomposition. Although the mean alcohol concentrations for the different samples were not significantly different, there were wide variations in alcohol concentration among the various blood sample sites in a number of individual cases. Of the cases, 20 (33.3%) had within-case blood alcohol differences greater than 25%; 4 had differences greater than 50%, with 1 of these cases exceeding 400%. Indeed 3 of the 4 latter cases had gastric alcohol concentrations between 1 and 5.1 g/dL and the fourth had a concentration between 0.5 and 1 g/dL, whereas, for the 60 cases as a whole, 22 were between 0.5 and 1 g/dL and 11 were above 1 g/dL. In a third study[73] of nine fatalities with known alcohol consumption shortly before death, two showed marked variations in blood ethanol concentrations in samples from ten sites, with ranges (mg/dL) of 97 to 238 and 278 to 1395; pericardial fluid 1060 and 686; vitreous humor 34 and 225; stomach contents 300 mL at 5.5 g/dL and 85 mL at 1.9 g/dL, respectively. These studies[72,73,87] suggest that post-mortem diffusion of alcohol from the stomach into the blood may be a significant, although uncommon problem.

The above findings were corroborated by a human cadaver model[73] with multiple blood site sampling after introducing 400 mL of alcohol solution (5%, 10%, 20%, or 40% weight/volume in water) into the stomach by esophageal tube. The pattern of ethanol diffusion showed marked between-case variability but typically concentrations were highest in pericardial fluid and, in decreasing order, in left pulmonary vein, aorta, left heart, pulmonary artery, superior vena cava, inferior vena cava, right heart, right pulmonary vein, and femoral vein. Diffusional flux was broadly proportional to the concentration of ethanol used, was time dependent (as assessed by 24-h and 48-h sampling), and was markedly inhibited by refrigeration at 4°C. After gastric instillation of 400 mL of 5% ethanol for 48 h at room temperature in paired cadavers, the concentrations (mg/dL) were as follows: pericardial fluid 135, 222; aorta 50, 68; left heart 77, 26; right heart 41, 28; femoral vein 0, 0. With a 10% solution of ethanol in the stomach, concentrations (mg/dL) were pericardial fluid 401, 255; aorta 129, 134; left heart 61, 93; right heart 31, 41; femoral vein 5, 7. The very high concentrations of alcohol found in the pericardial fluid emphasize the potential for serious contamination of any blood sample allowed to pool in the pericardial sac. Introducing 50 mL of 10% alcohol solution into the esophagus after esophago-gastric junction ligation produced similar aortic blood ethanol concentrations to those seen after gastric instillation. This suggests that post-mortem gastro-esophageal reflux and diffusion from the esophagus is one mechanism for artifactual elevation of aortic blood ethanol.

Post-mortem relaxation of the gastro-esophageal sphincter permits passive regurgitation of gastric contents into the esophagus, if body position and the volume of gastric contents permit. Thereafter manipulation of the body during removal and transport might easily lead to contamination of the airways by gastric material, simulating agonal aspiration of vomitus. Alcohol in this gastric material could diffuse from the airways into the blood. An experimental study[88] demonstrated that a relatively small amount of ethanol introduced into the trachea of cadavers was readily absorbed into cardiac blood and also that there was direct diffusion from the trachea into both the aorta and superior vena cava.

5.3.8   Post-Mortem Stability and Synthesis of Alcohol

Alcohol loss from body tissues and fluids may occur post-mortem as a result of evaporation, shifts in the water content of tissues, enzymatic breakdown, and bacterial degradation. Following the death of an individual, many of the cells of the body survive for a variable time, providing the window of opportunity for tissue and organ transplantation from non-beating-heart donors. During this period of cellular life following somatic death, cellular enzymatic activity continues, ethanol is metabolized and ethanol concentrations may fall slightly. Later bacterial invasion of tissues may result in further ethanol loss from bacterial degradation of ethanol. Ethanol is both utilized and produced by microorganisms, so that bodies with high initial levels may show a decrease, and bodies with low initial levels may show an increase.[89] However, in practice it is ethanol production by bacteria that represents the principal effect and this view is supported by an animal model.[90] Determining whether ethanol identified in post-mortem blood represents alcohol ingested prior to death or was formed post-mortem as a result of microbial activity is a common problem. Ethanol formation may occur in blood putrefying in a cadaver or in blood putrefying *in vitro*. It appears that ethanol is not formed post-mortem except by microbial action. Germ-free mice do not putrefy because of the absence of microorganisms,[91] and post-mortem autolysis of germ-free mice produces low levels of acetone and acetaldehyde but no ethanol. By contrast, putrefying conventional mice also produced ethanol, propionic acid, isopropyl alcohol, and *n*-propyl alcohol.[91]

Ethanol production in corpses[92] takes place by a pathway opposite to that of ethanol catabolism in the living body. The necessary alcohol dehydrogenase and acetaldehyde dehydrogenase enzymes are provided by the microorganisms associated with putrefaction while the carbohydrate substrates are present in blood and tissues. The level of tissue glycogen available for post-mortem glycolysis and subsequent microbial ethanol production varies considerably between tissues. Human liver contains about 1 to 8 g glycogen/100 g wet tissue; skeletal muscle 1 to 4 g/100 g, brain from a variety of animals 70 to 130 mg/100 g and retina (ox) 90 mg/100 g (all figures calculated from dry weight assuming 75% water).[93] Anaerobic glycolysis produces pyruvate, the main substrate for ethanol production. Besides glucose, lactate is a source of pyruvate through the action of lactate dehydrogenase. Since lactate is found in relatively high concentrations in all post-mortem tissues (about 150 to 650 mg/100 g),[90] it may well be an important source of ethanol. A study *in vitro* with putrefying post-mortem blood under anaerobic conditions at room temperature demonstrated that ethanol formation occurred not only by way of glycolysis but also from lactate via conversion into pyruvate.[93] There is also evidence that ethanol might be produced by bacterial catabolism of amino acids and fatty acids.[94]

Escape of large numbers of bacteria from the gut occurs in the first instance via the lymphatics and portal venous system, within a few hours after death. At room temperature bacterial contamination of the systemic circulation occurs after about 6 h, and after 24 h there is direct bacterial penetration of the intestinal wall. Generally the tissues remain relatively free of viable bacteria during the first 24 h. Trauma immediately prior to death, intestinal lesions and neoplastic disease, generalized infection, and gangrene are all conditions associated with early spread of bacteria post-mortem.[90] In a living person, ethanol may be produced by gut bacteria present in the infected intraperitoneal fluid associated with a peritonitis following a stabbing.[95] A wide variety of bacteria normally present in the gut and responsible for putrefaction can generate ethyl alcohol in blood, brain, liver, and other tissues.[96] As well as bacteria, yeasts such as *Candida albicans* may be responsible for post-mortem alcohol production.[97] *Candida* overgrowth in the gut in the living may cause intra-gastrointestinal alcohol fermentation syndrome, a rare condition described in Japan.[98] *Candida* colonization of the gut, stagnation of food, and a high carbohydrate diet allow fermentation to produce sufficient alcohol to cause intoxication to the point of illness, with a BAC of 254 mg/dL reported in one case.[98]

There is considerable evidence that ethanol can be produced in corpses at levels up to 150 mg/dL after they have been stored for a few days at room temperature. In a study of 130 decomposing bodies,[99] there were 23 with presumed post-mortem ethanol production. Of these, 19 of 23 had blood ethanol concentrations of 70 mg/dL or less and the other 4 had levels of 110, 120, 130, and 220 mg/dL. Since both bacterial growth and enzyme activity is temperature dependent it is reasonable to assume that post-mortem ethanol production is inhibited by refrigeration. For example, a series of 26 in-hospital deaths refrigerated within 1 h of death and stored at 6°C for 3 to 27 h before autopsy showed no evidence of post-mortem ethanol production despite positive blood cultures in 13 cases, 7 of whom had blood glucose in excess of 20 mg/dL.[100] Chemical inhibitors of bacterial growth, such as sodium fluoride, prevents the production of ethanol in post-mortem specimens. As with all blood specimens intended for ethanol analysis it is recommended that post-mortem specimens should be preserved with 2% w/v sodium fluoride and that storage at temperatures above 4°C should be minimized.

Circumstances that can be expected to provide fertile ground for post-mortem ethanol production include prolonged exposure to a high environmental temperature, terminal hyperglycemia, and death from infectious disease with septicemia, natural disease such as ischemia affecting the large bowel, abdominal trauma, and severe trauma with wound contamination. Body disruption of a severity that commonly occurs in aviation accidents is associated with extensive microbial contamination and a resultant higher probability of post-mortem ethanol production. In a series of 975 victims of fatal aircraft accidents[101] the BAC exceeded 40 mg/dL in 79 cases and of these it was considered, based on ethanol distribution in urine, vitreous humor, and blood, that 27% represented post-mortem production and 28% ingestion, but 45% were unresolved. In such traumatic cases blood concentrations as high as 300 mg/dL might be synthesized post-mortem. In the *USS Iowa* explosion the highest ethanol concentration attributed to post-mortem fermentation was 190 mg/dL.[102]

In establishing whether there is post-mortem production or *in vivo* ingestion of alcohol, circumstantial evidence and corroborative analyses of vitreous humor and urine is of considerable assistance. Although vitreous contains glucose and lactate, both substrates for bacterial production of alcohol, it is protected by its remoteness from invasion by putrefactive bacteria spreading from the gut through the vascular system. Urine is useful because it normally contains little or no substrate for bacterial conversion to ethanol. An exception occurs if the urine contains sufficient suitable substrate, such as glucose, as a consequence of some pathological abnormality, particularly diabetes mellitus.[103]

After the early post-mortem period, when decomposition begins, the problem of production of ethanol increases because both decomposition and synthesis of ethanol are the result of microorganism spread and proliferation. This putrefactive phase starts about 2 or 3 days after death in a temperate climate but varies considerably depending on environmental conditions, primarily temperature. In early putrefaction when a sample of vitreous humor is still obtainable the presence of ethanol in this fluid is the best indicator of ethanol ingestion ante-mortem. The presence of ethanol in the urine, if it is available, is also a good indicator of ethanol ingestion. Once decomposition has progressed so that the vitreous is no longer available, due to collapse of the eyeballs, and blood cannot be obtained because the blood vessels are filled with putrefactive gases, then no reliance can be placed upon any sample, and interpretation of analytical results is hazardous if not impossible. In these cases anamnestic data may be more reliable than analytical data. In around 20% of decomposed bodies the ethanol detected is probably derived from endogenous sources based on its presence in blood but absence in vitreous or urine, but in many cases endogenous production cannot be distinguished from ingestion.[99] Post-mortem ethanol production in decomposed bodies results in blood or putrefactive fluid concentrations less than 150 mg/dL in over 95% of cases, but this general observation does not assist in evaluating a higher level found in an individual case.[99,104] In decomposing bodies endogenous ethanol production may occur in the bile as well as the blood and this might be particularly marked in the sanguineous putrefactive fluid, which accumulates in the pleural cavities.[104]

The importance of measuring ethanol concurrently in vitreous, urine, and blood samples was demonstrated in the assessment of low post-mortem BACs. A series of 381 cases with autopsy BACs less than 50 mg/dL were evaluated using the presence of ethanol in the vitreous and/or urine as indicators of ingestion rather than post-mortem production.[105] When the BAC was 10 to 19 mg/dL, the investigators found that 54% of cases had positive vitreous or urine ethanol concentrations (greater than 10 mg/dL); when the BAC was 20 to 29 mg/dL this percentage increased to 63%; when the BAC was 30 to 39 mg/dL the percentage was 73%, and when the BAC was 40 to 49 mg/dL, 92% of the cases had an alternative specimen positive for ethanol. Of the 165 cases where both vitreous and urine were available, more than 90% demonstrated consistent results; however, in 14 cases, there was an unexplained inconsistency with one specimen positive and the other negative.

Bacterial production of ethyl alcohol is associated with the production of other volatile compounds such as isoamyl alcohol, formaldehyde, n-propyl alcohol, isopropyl alcohol, propionic acid, acetone, acetic acid, acetaldehyde, n-butanol, sec-butanol, tert-butanol, n-butyric acid and iso-butyric acid. Of these n-butyric acid and iso-butyric acid are said to be the most common associates of ethanol produced by putrefactive bacteria. [96] Others have advocated measuring n-propanol as a marker of microbial fermentation. [106] However, variability in metabolic pathways between microorganisms leads to variability in the final products of glucose fermentation. Furthermore, there is no reliable quantitative relationship between these volatiles and ethanol produced post-mortem. This limits considerably the potential usefulness of measuring these other volatile products to distinguish between alcohol ingestion and post-mortem production.

A variety of biochemical approaches to the assessment of post-mortem synthesis of alcohol have been proposed. The major enzymatic pathway for disposal of ethanol is oxidative metabolism with

Class I isozymes of ADH to produce acetaldehyde and this toxic metabolite is oxidized further by ALDH to acetic acid. Very small amounts of ingested ethanol (<1%) undergo non-oxidative metabolism by three different reaction mechanisms. Like many drug molecules with hydroxyl groups, ethanol undergoes a conjugation reaction catalyzed by liver enzymes to produce ethyl glucuronide (EtG) and ethyl sulfate (EtS).[107,108] Thus, EtG and EtS are specific metabolites of ethanol and these have proved very useful as markers of prior ethanol ingestion because elimination half-lives are much longer than for ethanol itself.[107,108] Analytical methods for ethyl glucuronide have been considerably improved in recent years such as by using liquid chromatography–mass spectrometry.[109]

Ethanol also reacts with a membrane-bound phospholipid to form phosphatidylethanol, and a third reaction is esterification with short-chain fatty acids to produce the corresponding esters.[110–112] These non-oxidative metabolites are measurable in blood and tissues and are excreted in urine with half-lives longer than ethanol itself.[112] Finding these non-oxidative metabolites, e.g., in urine taken at autopsy, is a strong indication that the deceased had consumed alcohol some time before death. The sensitivity of these markers compared with EtG and EtS remains to be established.

Another biochemical approach is based on the metabolic interaction between ethanol and the biogenic amine serotonin (Figure 5.3.1).[112] Without any consumption of alcohol, serotonin (5-hydroxytryptamine) undergoes oxidative deamination to 5-hydroxyindolealdehyde (5-HIALD).[112–114] This short-lived intermediate is rapidly oxidized to 5-hydroxyindoleacetic acid (5-HIAA) and a very small fraction (~1%) is reduced to 5-hydroxytryptophol (5-HTOL). Formation of the carboxylic acid (5-HIAA) is the dominant reaction and the 5HTOL/5-HIAA ratio in urine is normally very low (<15 nmol/μmol). However, after a person drinks alcohol the 5-HTOL/5-HIAA ratio increases appreciably owing to competitive inhibition for ALDH, which is now engaged in the metabolism of acetaldehyde derived from ethanol.[112–114] Measuring the 5-HTOL/5-HIAA ratio in urine has therefore found applications in clinical medicine to disclose consumption of alcohol, e.g., in alcohol and drug abusers, who must refrain from drinking as part of their treatment.[112] The ratio of serotonin metabolites can also be used to differentiate between ante-mortem ingestion of ethanol and post-mortem microbial synthesis.[113–115] Finding an elevated concentration

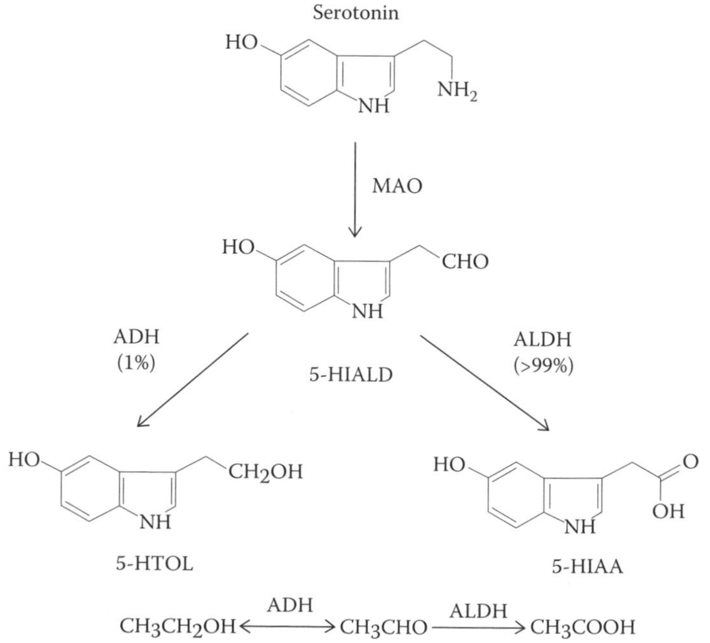

Figure 5.3.1 Serotonin and ethanol catabolism.

Table 5.3.2 Ethanol in Sequestered Hematomas

| Ref. | Survival Interval, h | Post-Mortem Ethanol Concentrations, mg/dL | | | |
		Cardiac Blood	Peripheral Blood	Urine	SDH
118	12	0		120	
	13	20		310	190
	6–12	160		310	300
	12–15	200			230 (R)
					360 (L)
	>4	160		250	300
	UK	260		370	320
121	10	23	29	265	132
	1.5	121	121	232	206
	UK	58	47	226	104
	UK	151		322	192
119	13	0			120
	26	0			260
	9	40			100
	UK	50			150
	UK	40			1110

Note: UK = unknown; SDH = subdural hematoma.

of ethanol in urine but with a 5-HTOL/5-HIAA ratio below 15 nmol/μmol strongly suggests that microbial synthesis of ethanol has occurred.[115–117] However, the question of whether an elevated concentration of ethanol in a post-mortem specimen partly reflects microbial synthesis and partly ante-mortem ingestion cannot be resolved using these kinds of biochemical markers.

5.3.9 Sequestered Hematomas

That ethanol might be measured in sequestered hematomas was first suggested by Hirsch and Adelson,[118] although they claimed no originality, explaining that it is one of the "tricks of the trade." It has been most commonly applied to cases of head trauma with subdural or epidural hematomas,[118–121] but also to intracerebral clots.[122,123] Although primarily used for ethanol, any toxicant might be measured in the hematoma. From the accumulated case data (Table 5.3.2), it is clear that concentrations of ethanol in subdural hematomas may be markedly different from autopsy peripheral blood. In interpreting the significance of the results several possibilities should be considered. The hematoma may have developed rapidly at the time of injury, or it may have been delayed and not developed for some hours, or it may have evolved over a period of time as the result of continuous or intermittent bleeding. If the hematoma accumulates over a period of hours, then its ethanol content will reflect a changing blood ethanol concentration during that time. Furthermore, the hematoma might not be perfectly sequestered and ethanol may diffuse both out of it and into it. An animal model[121] has provided good experimental evidence that the current approach to determination of ethanol in sequestered hematomas is well founded.

In cases of head trauma associated with subdural or extradural hematomas and with a prolonged survival time, the autopsy blood ethanol concentration may be very low or even zero whereas the ethanol concentration in the hematoma may be substantial, thus providing evidence that the deceased may have been intoxicated at the time of injury. In a study of 75 cases in which ethanol was measured in subdural hematomas and cardiac blood,[119] the analysis provided useful new information only in those cases with survival times greater than 9 h since it was these cases in which the blood ethanol had diminished markedly or been fully metabolized. In another case series consisting of 15 fatalities from penetrating and nonpenetrating head injuries,[120] there was a pre-mortem blood ethanol measurement available. Findings in nonpenetrating injuries (Table 5.3.3) and penetrating injuries were similar in that concentrations of ethanol in intracranial hematoma did not accurately

Table 5.3.3   Ethanol in Ante-Mortem Blood and Sequestered Hematomas[120]

Time (h)		Ethanol (mg/dL)		
Injury to Pre-Mortem Sample	Pre-Mortem Sample to Death	Pre-Mortem	Post-Mortem	SDH
1	21	535	0	170
3	7	486	130	190
5	8.5	183	0	90
3	41	161	0	40
1 1/2	4.5	164	70	110
2	18	93	0	120
1	25.5	240	0	110
1	58	101	0	40

Note: SDH = subdural hematoma.

reflect circulating blood concentrations at the time of injury. Therefore, quantitative interpretations must be cautious.

After suffering trauma, the development of an intracranial hemorrhage, either subdural or intracerebral, may be delayed. If the victim was intoxicated at the time of injury, then this delay may be sufficient to allow clearance of ethanol from the blood. The intracranial hematoma will then contain no ethanol despite the history of injury when intoxicated. This apparent conflict between the history of the circumstances of injury and the absence of ethanol in the hematoma has been used to provide corroboration that development of the hematoma had been delayed.[124]

5.3.10   Alcoholic Ketoacidosis

Sudden death in a chronic alcoholic with a subsequent negative autopsy is a common problem. At autopsy such cases have only the stigmata of alcoholism, such as a fatty liver, and an inconsequential blood alcohol level. The mechanism behind these "fatty liver deaths" is obscure,[125] and recently the syndrome of alcoholic ketoacidosis (AKA) has been suggested as having a role.[126,127] The clinical literature on AKA is scant, and probably belies the true frequency of the syndrome,[128–135] but it does suggest that AKA is typically a relatively benign condition and only fatal when associated with some other disease process. The combination of starvation and alcohol abuse together precipitate the syndrome of AKA,[128] which is characterized by a metabolic acidosis, malnutrition, and binge drinking superimposed upon chronic alcohol abuse.[131] The typical clinical picture is that of an alcohol debauch terminated by anorexia with cessation of both food and alcohol intake, and finally, a variable period of hyperemesis. By the time AKA develops there is no measurable blood alcohol. The common symptoms of nausea, vomiting, and abdominal pain are accompanied by few objective physical findings and mental status is usually normal or only slightly impaired, but severe obtundation or coma occasionally occurs.[132]

Although the pathophysiology of AKA is complex, it seems that the pivotal variable is probably a relative deficiency of insulin. This results from starvation with consequent hepatic glycogen depletion, the inhibition of gluconeogenesis by an increased NADH/NAD+ ratio resulting from metabolism of alcohol, and extracellular fluid volume depletion with α-adrenergic inhibition of insulin secretion.[133] Individuals with higher insulin levels would probably present with the syndrome of alcohol-induced hypoglycemia without ketoacidosis. Possibly the major factor separating AKA from alcohol-induced hypoglycemia is the dehydration and the starvation-induced α-adrenergic inhibition of insulin secretion in the former.

Extremely high free fatty acid levels in blood, ranging from 1800 to 3800 μEq/L have been a consistent finding in clinical cases of AKA.[128,129] Beta-oxidation of these fatty acids generates acetyl-CoA, which is the precursor of ketones. Two critical enzymes in the ketogenesis pathway to acetoacetate are found in liver mitochondria only, [130] so that the liver is the only appreciable site of ketone body production. Excess acetoacetate in liver is converted into β-hydroxybutyrate and extrahepatic tissues can convert β-hydroxybutyrate back into acetoacetate and utilize both of these ketone bodies as respiratory substrates. Acetone is thought to be the product of a non-enzymatic decarboxylation of acetoacetate. Acetone production is therefore a function of the level of acetoacetate and the duration of its elevation, so that the presence of acetone is indicative of a sustained severe ketoacidosis.[134] However, the extent, if any, of post-mortem conversion of acetoacetate to acetone is not known and it is advisable and convenient to make a combined analysis of these two ketones in autopsy samples.[127] For convenience, the term "ketone bodies" is used to include only acetone, acetoacetate, and β-hydroxybutyrate. While this terminology is convenient because all three compounds are metabolically related, it is inaccurate because it excludes other biologically important ketones, e.g., pyruvate, but includes β-hydroxybutyrate, which does not have a ketone structure, although it is part of ketone metabolism.

The biochemical hallmark of AKA is ketoacidosis without marked hyperglycemia,[132] while by contrast diabetic ketoacidosis is defined by the triad of hyperglycemia, acidosis, and ketosis. In AKA the ratio of serum β-hydroxybutyrate to acetoacetate, which is normally 1:1, is increased to between 2:1 and 9:1, a ratio higher than that generally found in diabetic ketoacidosis.[135] The clinical diagnosis of AKA is hampered because the nitroprusside test (Acetest) for ketones in the urine is sensitive to acetoacetate but not to β-hydroxybutyrate.[129] In fasting subjects the concentration of acetoacetate in plasma might range up to 0.23 mmol/L, and that of β-hydroxybutyrate up to 0.65 mmol/L. In comparison, in AKA the corresponding concentrations of acetoacetate have range up to 7.5 mmol/L and of β-hydroxybutyrate up to 20.5 mmol/L.[127] In one autopsy study,[126] total ketones (mmol/L) in 71 non-alcoholics were as follows: vitreous 0.19 to 3.35, median 0.49; pericardial fluid 0.02 to 1.54, median 0.35; and femoral blood 0.23 to 8.08, median 1.00. The significantly high levels found in this autopsy series likely reflect deaths from chronic disease or prolonged agonal periods. Among 22 alcoholics, 18 had ketone levels not statistically different from non-alcoholics but there were 4 with femoral blood total ketone levels of 129.9 (also diabetic), 39.4 (no anatomical cause of death), 38.5 (suicidal hanging), and 18.6 (hypothermia), suggesting that while alcoholic ketoacidosis may be a previously overlooked potential cause of death, interpretation must be guarded and made within the total case context. This is in keeping with the clinical consensus that AKA is fatal only when associated with some other illness.

In the present state of knowledge it is uncertain whether AKA alone is sufficient to account for death, but it seems that very high levels of ketones (>10 mmol/L in femoral blood and >5 mmol/L in vitreous) are indicative of profound AKA, and these values can be expected in about 10% of all alcoholics subjected to a medicolegal autopsy. Both vitreous and pericardial fluid ketone levels are lower than those in post-mortem blood, possibly because they are less affected by any agonal or post-mortem changes. Alcoholic ketoacidosis can be diagnosed at autopsy by measurement of total ketone bodies (acetone, acetoacetate, and β-hydroxybutyrate) in vitreous humor, pericardial fluid, or peripheral blood. Finding significantly elevated levels is associated with a typical history of an alcoholic binge followed by a day or more of anorexia, and consequently an insignificant BAC. In alcoholics in whom the autopsy is negative (so-called fatty liver deaths), AKA may be an explanation for sudden death as a result of profound acidosis, with a critical fall in blood pH to around 7.0, precipitating vascular collapse.

5.3.11 Post-Mortem Markers for Alcohol Abuse

The prevalence of alcoholism in the forensic autopsy population varies between jurisdictions but can be as high as 10% or more. Poor hygiene and multiple bruises of different ages are more common in chronic alcoholics than in the general forensic autopsy population, and raise the index of suspicion in an individual case. The traditional method of diagnosing chronic alcoholism post-mortem is to evaluate the BAC and liver histology in the light of the available medical history. However, the presence of alcohol in the blood merely indicates alcohol ingestion prior to death and almost half of all alcoholics die with a zero BAC. Also, the pathological features of alcoholic liver disease are relatively nonspecific and the extent of liver disease in many alcoholics is no worse than in the general forensic autopsy population.

The spectrum of alcoholic liver disease includes hepatomegaly, steatosis with or without lipogranulomas, alcoholic hepatitis, and cirrhosis.[136] This complete spectrum, including alcoholic-type hepatitis, can be perfectly mimicked by a few non-alcohol-related conditions such as obesity with or without dieting, jejuno-ileal bypass for obesity, diabetes mellitus, and perhexilline maleate toxicity. Hepatic steatosis is the most common form of alcoholic liver disease seen at necropsy, and significant steatosis may be induced by the amounts of alcohol consumed by many social drinkers. Following the withdrawal of alcohol, the mobilization of this accumulated fat begins in 1 to 2 days and is complete in 4 to 6 weeks even in severe cases. While hepatic steatosis is potentially reversible, alcoholic hepatitis is thought by some to represent the point of no return within the spectrum, for once this stage is reached the disorder tends to progress to cirrhosis. Even so, a person with alcoholic hepatitis may be symptom-free and performing normal social functions. In general, there is not always a good correlation between symptoms and morphological findings in alcoholic hepatitis. Histologically, alcoholic hepatitis is characterized by liver cell necrosis with a predominantly neutrophil polymorph reaction and peri-cellular fibrosis. The hepatitis is mainly centrilobular in distribution and classically associated with the presence of Mallory's hyaline. More than half of all cases of cirrhosis coming to autopsy are the result of alcohol abuse. The classical alcoholic cirrhosis is micronodular and fatty, but this is not necessarily so since it may not be fatty and may evolve into a macronodular cirrhosis. Persons abusing alcohol frequently abuse other drugs and may develop drug-related hepatotoxicity, in particular late acetaminophen (paracetamol) toxicity from excessive, but not suicidal, doses of this antipyretic drug.

The search for a corroborative post-mortem biochemical marker for chronic alcoholism has taken as a starting point those clinical studies on the value of biochemical markers of alcoholism in the living. The serum enzyme γ-glutamyltransferase (GGT) is one of the most frequently used clinical markers and has a reported sensitivity of 39 to 87% but a specificity of only 11 to 50%.[137] This poor specificity is mainly the result of interference by various hepatic and other diseases, and drug therapy. At autopsy the difficulties are greater because GGT is subject to significant post-mortem changes. GGT levels in right heart blood may be two to eight times greater than in femoral venous blood owing to post-mortem diffusion of GGT from the liver. Furthermore, post-mortem hemolysis interferes with some quantitative enzymatic GGT methods. More recently, carbohydrate-deficient transferrin (CDT) has been used as a clinical marker of alcoholism, offering 83 to 90% sensitivity and 99% specificity.[137] CDT is thought to become elevated at the threshold of hazardous drinking, which is generally accepted as being 50 to 80 g/day. An assessment of the value of CDT in diagnosing chronic alcoholism at autopsy concluded that it might have a sensitivity of 70% and a specificity of 85% if the cut-off value for the diagnosis of alcohol abuse post-mortem was raised above the accepted clinical cut-off value.[138] This suggests that both CDT and GGT are likely to be subject to post-mortem changes.

Trace amounts of methanol (less than 1.0 mg/L) are produced in the body in the course of intermediary metabolism and the endogenous levels increase during a period of heavy drinking. Ingestion of methanol as a congener in various alcohol beverages adds to this accumulation.[139] When alcoholics consume alcohol over a period of several days or weeks reaching blood ethanol concentrations of 150 to 450 mg/dL, then the methanol levels in blood and urine progressively increase to 20 to 40 mg/L. The elimination of methanol lags behind ethanol by 12 to 24 h and follows approximately the same time course as ethanol withdrawal symptoms leading to speculation on the role of methanol and/or its metabolites in alcohol withdrawal and hangover.[139] Below a blood ethanol concentration of about 10 mg/dL, hepatic ADH is no longer saturated with its preferred substrate and the metabolism of methanol can therefore commence. At this low concentration the elimination of ethanol follows first-order kinetics with a half life of 15 min.[139] The half-life of methanol, however, is about ten times longer. As a result elevated concentrations of methanol will persist in blood for about 10 h after ethanol has reached endogenous levels and can serve as a marker of recent heavy drinking.[139]

Blood methanol levels in 24 teetotalers ranged from 0.1 to 0.8 mg/L with a mean of 0.44 mg/L so that these levels can be regarded as physiological. By contrast, blood methanol concentrations in samples taken on admission of 20 chronic alcoholics to hospital ranged from 0.22 to 20.1 mg/L.[140] The general extent to which methanol may accumulate in the blood of chronic alcoholics can be gauged from a study of ethanol and methanol in blood samples from 519 drunk-driving suspects.[139] The concentration of ethanol ranged from 0.01 to 3.52 mg/g and the concentration of methanol in the same sample ranged from 1 to 23 mg/L with a mean of 7.3 (SD 3.6) and a positively skewed distribution. By contrast, in 15 fatalities following hospital admission for methanol poisoning the concentrations of methanol in post-mortem blood from the heart ranged from 23 to 268 mg/dL.[141]

5.3.12 Methanol

Methanol (wood alcohol) is used as antifreeze, photocopier developer, a paint remover, a solvent in varnishes, a denaturant of ethanol, and is readily available as methylated spirit. It may be used also as a substitute for ethanol by alcoholics.[142] The distribution of methanol in body fluids (including vitreous humor) and tissues was reported as similar to that of ethanol, but there may be preferential concentration in liver and kidney.[143,144] The lethal dose of methanol in humans shows pronounced individual differences ranging from 15 to 500 mL. Clusters of poisonings are seen secondary to consumption of adulterated beverages.[141,145,146]

Acute methanol poisoning produces a distinct clinical picture with a latent period of several hours to days between consumption and the appearance of first symptoms. A combination of blurred vision with abdominal pain and vomiting is found in the majority of victims within the first 24 h after presentation. Visual disturbances, pancreatitis, metabolic acidosis, and diffuse encephalopathy may be seen in severe cases.[145] The characteristic delay between ingestion and onset of symptoms is thought to reflect the delayed appearance of metabolites (formaldehyde and formic acid), which are more toxic than methanol itself.

Methanol poisoning is characterized by a metabolic acidosis with an elevated anion gap. The serum anion gap is defined as (sodium + potassium) to (bicarbonate + chloride), and represents the difference in unmeasured cations and unmeasured anions, which includes organic acids. Both formic acid, produced by methanol catabolism, and lactic acid, resulting from disturbed cellular metabolism, are responsible for the metabolic acidosis.[147] The severity of the poisoning correlates with the degree of metabolic acidosis more closely than with the blood concentration of methanol.[148] Measuring formic acid concentrations may be of some value in assessing methanol poisoning. Reported formic acid levels in two methanol fatalities were 32 and 23 mg/dL in blood and 227 and 47 mg/dL in urine.[149] One well-documented outbreak of methanol poisoning[150] involved 59 people, 8 of whom died outside hospital while 51 were hospitalized, and of these a further 9 died in hospital, 5 survived with sequelae, and 1 died a year later of cerebral sequelae. In the 51 hospitalized victims, who had a median age of 53 years, the serum concentration of methanol (range 10 to 470 mg/dL, median 80 mg/dL) proved a poor predictor of survival or visual sequelae. Respiratory arrest or coma on hospital admission was associated with 75 and 67% mortality, respectively. Overall, prognosis was closely correlated with the degree of metabolic acidosis, so that a fatal outcome was associated with a pH < 6.9 and base deficit > 28 mmol/L, with an inadequate ability to compensate for the metabolic acidosis by hyperventilation being reflected in an increased blood pCO_2.

Methanol poisoning has a high mortality mainly because of delay in diagnosis and treatment.[150] The standard treatment includes the competitive inhibition of methanol oxidation by the intravenous administration of ethanol, thus preventing the formation of toxic metabolites, formaldehyde and formic acid. Both methanol and ethanol are substrates for hepatic ADH, although the affinity of the enzyme is much higher for ethanol than for methanol by about 10:1.[151] Consequently, the biotransformation of methanol into its toxic metabolites can be blocked by the administration of ethanol.[152] One disadvantage of ethanol is that it exerts its own depressant effect on the central nervous system at the steady-state concentration of 100 to 120 mg/dL in blood, which must be maintained for many hours.[152,153] A more modern, and expensive, antidote for methanol poisoning is fomepizole (4-methyl pyrazole or Antizol®), which also acts as a competitive inhibitor of alcohol dehydrogenase.[154,155] This drug is preferred to ethanol for treating children and adults with known liver dysfunction.[156] During fomepizole treatment, the concentration of formate in blood may be a better prognostic indicator than the methanol concentration.[157]

5.3.13 Isopropyl Alcohol

Isopropyl alcohol (isopropanol) is used as a substitute for ethanol in many industrial processes and in home cleaning products, antifreeze, and skin lotions. A 70% solution is sold as "rubbing alcohol" and may be applied to the skin and then allowed to evaporate, as a means of reducing body temperature in a person with fever. Isopropanol has a characteristic odor and a slightly bitter taste. Although much less dangerous than methanol, deaths have been reported following accidental ingestion of isopropanol, e.g., in alcoholics who use it as an ethanol substitute.[158] Fatalities may occur rapidly as a result of central nervous system depression or may be delayed, when the presence or absence of shock with hypotension is the most important single prognostic factor.

Isopropyl alcohol has an apparent volume of distribution of 0.6 to 0.7 L/kg, being similar to that of ethanol and with distribution complete within about 2 h.[159,160] Elimination most closely approximates first-order kinetics although this is not well defined ($t_{1/2}$ = 4 to 6 h).[161] This secondary alcohol is metabolized to acetone, predominantly by liver alcohol dehydrogenase, and approximately 80% is excreted as acetone in the urine with 20% excreted unchanged.[161,162] The acetone causes a sweet ketonic odor on the breath. The elimination of both isopropanol and its major metabolite acetone obeyed apparent first-order kinetics with half-lives of 6.4 and 22.4 h, respectively, in a 46-year-old non-alcoholic female with initial serum isopropanol and acetone concentrations of 200 and 12 mg/dL, respectively.[161]

In a review of isopropanol deaths, 31 were attributed to isopropanol poisoning alone, and the blood isopropanol concentrations ranged from 10 to 250 mg/dL, mean 140 mg/dL, and acetone ranged from 40 to 300 mg/dL, mean 170 mg/dL.[163] Four cases with low blood isopropanol levels (10 to 30 mg/dL) had very high acetone levels (110 to 200 mg/dL). For this reason both acetone and isopropanol should be measured in suspected cases of isopropanol poisoning.

High blood levels of acetone may be found in diabetes mellitus and starvation ketosis, which opens the possibility that ADH might reduce acetone to isopropyl alcohol. This is the suggested explanation for the detection of isopropyl alcohol in the blood of persons not thought to have ingested this compound. In 27 such fatalities blood isopropyl alcohol ranged from less than 10 to 44 mg/dL with a mean of 14 mg/dL, and in only 3 cases was the concentration greater than 20 mg/dL. Acetone levels ranged up to 56 mg/dL and in no individual case did the combined isopropanol and acetone levels come close to those seen in fatal isopropyl alcohol poisoning.[164]

5.3.14 Concluding Remarks

Blood ethanol concentration can be expected to be positive in around one half of all unnatural deaths so that routine screening of such deaths for ethanol is highly desirable. For natural deaths as a whole, the return of positives is not sufficiently high to justify screening, unless there is a history of chronic alcoholism or of recent alcohol ingestion. The autopsy blood sample should never be obtained from the heart, aorta, or other large vessels of the chest or abdomen or from blood permitted to pool at autopsy in the pericardial sac, pleural cavities, or abdominal cavity. If by mischance such a specimen is the only one available, then its provenance should be clearly declared and taken into account in the interpretation of the analytical results. Blind needle puncture of the chest to obtain a "cardiac" blood sample or a so-called "subclavian stab" is not recommended because at best it produces a chest cavity blood sample of unknown origin and at worst a contaminated sample. The most appropriate routine autopsy blood sample for ethanol analyses, as well as other drug analyses, is one obtained from either the femoral vein or the external iliac vein using a needle and syringe after clamping or tying off the vessel proximally. The sample should be obtained early in the autopsy and prior to evisceration. Samples of vitreous humor and urine, if the latter is available, should also be taken. The interpretation of the significance of the analytical results of these specimens must, of necessity, take into account the autopsy findings, circumstances of death, and recent history of the decedent. To attempt to interpret the significance of an alcohol level in an isolated autopsy blood sample without additional information is to invite a medicolegal disaster.

REFERENCES

1. Senkowski, C.M., Senkowski, B.S., and Thompson, K.A., The accuracy of blood alcohol analysis using headspace gas chromatography when performed on clotted samples, *J. Forensic Sci.*, 35, 176, 1990.
2. Hodgson, B.T. and Shajani, N.K., Distribution of ethanol: plasma to the whole blood ratios, *Can. Soc. Forensic Sci. J.*, 18, 73, 1985.
3. Hak, E.A., Gerlitz, B.J., Demont, P.M., and Bowthorpe, W.D., Determination of serum alcohol: blood alcohol ratios, *Can. Soc. Forensic Sci. J.*, 28, 123, 1995.
4. Felby, S. and Nielsen, E., The postmortem blood alcohol concentration and the water content, *Blutalkohol,* 31, 24, 1994.
5. Wallgren, H. and Barry, H., *Actions of Alcohol,* Elsevier, Amsterdam, 1970.
6. Johnson, H.R.M., At what blood levels does alcohol kill, *Med. Sci. Law,* 25, 127, 1985.
7. Jones, A.W. and Holmgren, P., Comparison of blood-ethanol concentration in deaths attributed to acute alcohol poisoning and chronic alcoholism, *J. Forensic Sci.*, 48, 874, 2003.
8. Niyogi, S.K., Drug levels in cases of poisoning, *Forensic Sci.*, 2, 67, 1973.
9. Taylor, H.L. and Hudson, R.P.J., Acute ethanol poisoning: a two-year study of deaths in North Carolina, *J. Forensic Sci.,* 639, 1977.
10. Wilson, C.I., Ignacio, S.S., and Wilson, G.A., An unusual form of fatal ethanol intoxication, *J. Forensic Sci.,* 50, 676, 2005.
11. Padosch, S.A., Schmidt, P.H., Kroner, L.U., and Madea, B., Death due to positional asphyxia under severe alcoholisation: pathophysiologic and forensic considerations, *Forensic Sci. Int.,* 149, 67, 2005.
12. Bell, M.D., Rao, V.J., Wetli, C.V., and Rodriguez, R.N., Positional asphyxiation in adults, *Am. J. Forensic Med. Pathol.,* 13, 101, 1992.
13. Perper, J.A., Twerski, A., and Wienand, J.W., Tolerance at high blood alcohol concentrations: a study of 110 cases and review of the literature, *J. Forensic Sci.,* 31, 212, 1986.
14. Davis, A.R. and Lipson, A.H., Central nervous system tolerance to high blood alcohol levels, *Med. J. Aust.,* 144, 9, 1986.
15. Lindblad, B. and Olsson, R., Unusually high levels of blood alcohol? *J. Am. Med. Assoc.,* 236, 1600, 1976.
16. Johnson, R.A., Noll, E.C., and MacMillan Rodney, W., Survival after a serum ethanol concentration of 1 1/2%, *Lancet,* 1394, 1982.
17. Poklis, A. and Pearson, M.A., An unusually high blood ethanol level in a living patient, *Clin. Toxicol.,* 10, 429, 1977.
18. Hammond, K.B., Rumack, B.H., and Rodgerson, D.O., Blood ethanol: a report of unusually high levels in a living patient, *J. Am. Med. Assoc.,* 226, 63, 1973.
19. Berild, D. and Hasselbalch, H., Survival after a blood alcohol of 1127 mg/dL, *Lancet,* 383, 1981.
20. O'Neill, S., Tipton, K.F., Prichard, J.S., and Quinlan, A., Survival after high blood alcohol levels: association with first-order elimination kinetics, *Arch. Intern. Med.,* 144, 641, 1984.
21. Jones, A.W., The drunkest drinking driver in Sweden: blood-alcohol concentration 545%, *J. Stud. Alcohol.,* 60, 400, 1999.
22. Kortelainen, M., Drugs and alcohol in hypothermia and hyperthermia related deaths: a respective study. *J. Forensic Sci.,* 32, 1704, 1987.

23. Teige, B. and Fleischer, E., Blodkonsentrasjoner ved akutte forgiftningsdodsfall, *Tidsskr. Nor. Laege-foren.*, 103, 679, 1983.

24. Teresinki, G., Buszewicz, G., and Madro, R., Biochemical background of ethanol-induced cold susceptibility, *Legal Med*, 7, 15, 2005.

25. Kortelainen, M., Hyperthermia deaths in Finland in 1970–86. *Am. J. Forensic Med. Pathol.*, 12, 115, 1991.

26. Ramsay, D.A. and Shkrum, M.J., Homicidal blunt head trauma, diffuse axonal injury, alcoholic intoxication, and cardiorespiratory arrest: a case report of a forensic syndrome of acute brainstem dysfunction. *Am. J. Forensic Med. Pathol.*, 16, 107, 1995.

27. Jones, A.W., Alcohol and drug interactions, in *Handbook of Drug Interactions*, Mozayani, A. and Raymon, L.P., Eds., Humana Press, Totowa, NJ, 2003, 395.

28. King, L.A., Effect of ethanol on drug levels in blood in fatal cases, *Med. Sci. Law*, 22, 233, 1982.

29. Holmgren, P. and Jones, A.W., Coexistence and concentrations of ethanol and diazepam in post-mortem blood specimens: risk for enhanced toxicity? *J. Forensic Sci.*, 48, 1416, 2003.

30. Yamamoto, H., Tangegashima, A., Hosoe, H., and Fukunaga, T., Fatal acute alcohol intoxication in an ALDH2 heterozygote, *Forensic Sci. Int.*, 112, 201, 2000.

31. Heath, M.J., Pachar, J.V., Perez Martinez, A.L., and Toseland, P.A., An exceptional case of lethal disulfiram-alcohol reaction, *Forensic Sci. Int.*, 56, 45, 1992.

32. Cina, S.J., Russell, R.A., and Conradi, S.E., Sudden death due to metronidazole-ethanol interaction, *Am. J. Forensic Med. Pathol.*, 17, 343, 1996.

33. Williams, C.S. and Woodcock, K.R., Do ethanol and metronidazole interact to produce a disufiram-like reaction? *Ann. Pharmacother.*, 34, 255, 2000.

34. Jatlow, P., Cocaethylene. Pharmacologic activity and clinical significance, *Ther. Drug Monitor.*, 15, 533, 1993.

35. Jatlow, P., McChance, E.F., Bradberry, C.W., Elsworth, J.D., Taylor, J.R., and Roth, R.H., Alcohol plus cocaine: the whole is more than the sum of its parts, *Ther. Drug Monitor.*, 18, 460, 1996.

36. Tardiff, K., Marzuk, M.P., Leon, A.C., Hirsch, C.S., Stajic, M., Portera, L., and Hartwell, N., Cocaine, opiates, and ethanol in homicides in New York City: 1990 and 1991, *J. Forensic Sci.*, 40, 387, 1995.

37. Ruttenber, A.J., Kalter, H.D., and Santinga, P., The role of ethanol abuse in the etiology of heroin-related death. *J. Forensic Sci.*, 35, 891, 1990.

38. Harper, D.R., A comparative study of the microbiological contamination of postmortem blood and vitreous humour samples taken for ethanol determination, *Forensic Sci. Int.*, 43, 37, 1989.

39. Sturner, W.Q., and Coumbis, R.J., The quantitation of ethyl alcohol in vitreous humor and blood by gas chromatography, *Am. J. Clin. Pathol.*, 46, 349, 1966.

40. Leahy, M.S., Farber, E.R., and Meadows, T.R., Quantitation of ethyl alcohol in the postmortem vitreous humor, *J. Forensic Sci.*, 13, 498, 1968.

41. Felby, S. and Olsen, J., Comparative studies of postmortem ethyl alcohol in vitreous humor, blood, and muscle, *J. Forensic Sci.*, 14, 93, 1969.

42. Coe, J.I. and Sherman, R.E., Comparative study of postmortem vitreous humor and blood alcohol, *J. Forensic Sci.*, 15, 185, 1970.

43. Backer, R.C., Pisano, R.V., and Sopher, I.M., The comparison of alcohol concentrations in postmortem fluids and tissues, *J. Forensic Sci.*, 25, 327, 1996.

44. Winek, C.L. and Esposito, F.M., Comparative study of ethanol levels in blood versus bone marrow, vitreous humor, bile and urine, *Forensic Sci. Int.*, 17, 27, 1981.

45. Caughlin, J.D., Correlation of postmortem blood and vitreous humor alcohol concentration, *Can. Soc. Forensic Sci. J.*, 16, 61, 1983.

46. Stone, B.E. and Rooney, P.E., A study using body fluids to determine blood alcohol, *J. Anal. Toxicol.*, 8, 95, 1984.

47. Jollymore, B.D., Fraser, A.D., Moss, M.A., and Perry, R.A., Comparative study of ethyl alcohol in blood and vitreous humor, *Can. Soc. Forensic Sci. J.*, 17, 50, 1984.

48. Yip, D.C. and Shum, B.S., A study on the correlation of blood and vitreous humour alcohol levels in the late absorption and elimination phases, *Med. Sci. Law*, 30, 29, 1990.

49. Caplan, Y.H. and Levine, B., Vitreous humor in the evaluation of postmortem blood ethanol concentrations, *J. Anal. Toxicol.*, 14, 305, 1990.

50. Neil, P., Mills, A.J., and Prabhakaran, V.M., Evaluation of vitreous humor and urine alcohol levels as indices of blood alcohol levels in 75 autopsy cases, *Can. Soc. Forensic Sci. J.,* 18, 97, 1985.

51. Pounder, D.J. and Kuroda, N., Vitreous alcohol is of limited value in predicting blood alcohol, *Forensic Sci. Int.,* 65, 73, 1994.

52. Pounder, D.J. and Kuroda, N., Vitreous alcohol: the author's reply, *Forensic Sci. Int.,* 73, 159, 1995.

53. Kraut, A., Vitreous alcohol, *Forensic Sci. Int.,* 73, 157, 1995.

54. Yip, D.C.P., Vitreous humor alcohol, *Forensic Sci. Int.,* 73, 155, 1995.

55. Jones, A.W. and Holmgren, P., Uncertainty in estimating blood ethanol concentrations by analysis of vitreous humour, *J. Clin. Pathol.,* 54, 699, 2001.

56. Olsen, J.E., Penetration rate of alcohol into the vitreous humor studied with a new in vivo technique, *Acta Ophthalmol. Copenh.,* 49, 585, 1971.

57. Fernandez, P., Lopez-Rivadulla, M., Linares, J.M., Tato, F., and Bermejo, A.M., A comparative pharmacokinetic study of ethanol in the blood, vitreous humour and aqueous humour of rabbits, *Forensic Sci. Int.,* 41, 61, 1989.

58. Scott, W., Root, R., and Sanborn, B., The use of vitreous humor for determination of ethyl alcohol in previously embalmed bodies, *J. Forensic Sci.,* 913, 1974.

59. Singer, P.P. and Jones, G.R., Very unusual ethanol distribution in a fatality, *J. Anal. Toxicol.,* 21, 506, 1997.

60. Basu, P.K., Avaria, M., Jankie, R., Kapur, B.M., and Lucas, D.M., Effect of prolonged immersion on the ethanol concentration of vitreous humor, *Can. Soc. Forensic Sci. J.,* 16, 78, 1983.

61. Kaye, S. and Cardona, E., Errors of converting a urine alcohol value into a blood alcohol level, *Am. J. Clin. Pathol.,* 52, 577, 1969.

62. Kuroda, N., Williams, K., Pounder, D.J., Estimating blood alcohol from urinary alcohol at autopsy, *Am. J. Forensic Med. Pathol.,* 16, 219, 1995.

63. Levine, B. and Smialek, J.E., Status of alcohol absorption in drinking drivers killed in traffic accidents, *J. Forensic Sci.,* 45, 3, 2000.

64. Jones, A.W. and Holmgren, P., Urine/blood ratios of ethanol in deaths attributed to acute alcohol poisoning and chronic alcoholism, *Forensic Sci. Int.,* 135, 206, 2003.

65. Kaye, S. and Hag, H.B., Terminal blood alcohol concentrations in ninety-four fatal cases of acute alcoholism, *J. Am. Med. Assoc.,* 451, 1957.

66. Alha, A.R. and Tamminen, V., Fatal cases with an elevated urine alcohol but without alcohol in the blood, *J. Forensic Med.,* 11, 3, 1964.

67. Jenkins, A.J., Levine, B.S., and Smialek, J.E., Distribution of ethanol in postmortem liver. *J. Forensic Sci.,* 40, 611, 1995.

68. Stone, B.E. and Rooney, P.A., A study using body fluids to determine blood alcohol, *J. Anal. Toxicol.,* 8, 95, 1984.

69. Pounder, D.J., Fuke, C., Cox, D.E., Smith, D., and Kuroda, N., Postmortem diffusion of drugs from gastric residue, *Am. J. Forensic Med. Pathol.,* 17, 1, 1996.

70. Christopoulos, G., Kirch, E.R., and Gearien, J.E., Determination of ethanol in fresh and putrefied postmortem tissues, *J. Chromatogr.,* 87, 455, 1973.

71. Plueckhahn, V.D., Alcohol levels in autopsy heart blood, *J. Forensic Med.,* 15, 12, 1968.

72. Briglia, E.J., Bidanset, J.H., Dal Cortivo, L.A., The distribution of ethanol in postmortem blood specimens, *J. Forensic Sci.,* 37, 991, 1992.

73. Pounder, D.J. and Smith, D.R.W., Postmortem diffusion of alcohol from the stomach, *Am. J. Forensic Med. Pathol.,* 16, 89, 1995.

74. Bowden, K.M. and McCallum, N.E.W., Blood alcohol content: some aspects of its post-mortem uses, *Med. J. Aust.,* 2, 76, 1949.

75. Gifford, H. and Turkel, H.W., Diffusion of alcohol through stomach wall after death: a cause of erroneous postmortem blood alcohol levels, *J. Am. Med. Assoc.,* 161, 866, 1956.

76. Turkel, H.W. and Gifford, H., Erroneous blood alcohol findings at autopsy; avoidance by proper sampling technique, *J. Am. Med. Assoc.,* 164, 1077, 1957.

77. Turkel, H.W. and Gifford, H., Blood alcohol [letter]), *J. Am. Med. Assoc.,* 165, 1993, 1957.

78. Heise, H.A., Erroneous postmortem blood alcohol levels [letter], *J. Am. Med. Assoc.,* 165, 1739, 1957.

79. Muehlberger, C.W., Blood alcohol findings at autopsy [letter], *J. Am. Med. Assoc.,* 165, 726, 1957.

80. Harger, R.N., Heart blood vs. femoral vein blood for postmortem alcohol determinations [letter], *J. Am. Med. Assoc.,* 165, 725, 1957.

81. Plueckhahn, V.D., The significance of blood alcohol levels at autopsy, *Med. J. Aust.,* 15, 118, 1967.

82. Plueckhahn, V.D. and Ballard, B., Factors influencing the significance of alcohol concentrations in autopsy blood samples, *Med. J. Aust.,* 1, 939, 1968.

83. Plueckhahn, V.D., The evaluation of autopsy blood alcohol levels, *Med. Sci. Law,* 8, 168, 1968.

84. Plueckhahn, V.D. and Ballard, B., Diffusion of stomach alcohol and heart blood alcohol concentration at autopsy, *J. Forensic Sci.,* 12, 463, 1967.

85. Plueckhahn, V.D., Postmortem blood chemistry — the evaluation of alcohol (ethanol) in the blood, in *Recent Advances in Forensic Pathology,* Camps, F.E., Ed., Churchill, London, 1969, 197.

86. Plueckhahn, V.D., The significance of alcohol and sugar determinations in autopsy blood, *Med. J. Aust.,* 10, 46, 1970.

87. Marraccini, J.V., Carroll, T., Grant, S., Halleran, S., and Benz, J.A., Differences between multisite postmortem ethanol concentrations as related to agonal events, *J. Forensic Sci.,* 35, 1360, 1990.

88. Pounder, D.J. and Yonemitsu, K., Postmortem absorption of drugs and ethanol from aspirated vomitus — an experimental model, *Forensic Sci. Int.,* 51, 189, 1991.

89. Corry, J.E., Possible sources of ethanol ante- and post-mortem: its relationship to the biochemistry and microbiology of decomposition, *J. Appl. Bacteriol.,* 44, 1, 1978.

90. Takayasu, T., Ohshima, T., Tanaka, N., Maeda, H., Kondo, T., Nishigami, J., and Nagano, T., Postmortem degradation of administered ethanol-d6 and production of endogenous ethanol: experimental studies using rats and rabbits, *Forensic Sci. Int.,* 76, 129, 1995.

91. Davis, G.L., Leffert, R.L., and Rantanon, N.W., Putrefactive ethanol sources in postmortem tissues of conventional and germ-free mice, *Arch. Pathol.,* 94, 71, 1972.

92. Nanikawa, R., Moriya, F., and Hashimoto, Y., Experimental studies on the mechanism of ethanol formation in corpses, *Z. Rechtsmed.,* 101, 21, 1988.

93. Bogusz, M., Guminska, M., and Markiewicz, J., Studies on the formation of endogenous ethanol in blood putrefying *in vitro, J. Forensic Med.,* 17, 156, 1970.

94. de Lima, I.V. and Midio, A.F., Origin of blood ethanol in decomposed bodies, *Forensic Sci. Int.,* 106, 157, 1999.

95. Moriya, F. and Ishizu, H., Can micro-organisms produce alcohol in body cavities of a living person? *J. Forensic Sci.,* 39, 883, 1994.

96. Blackmore, D.J., The bacterial production of ethyl alcohol, *J. Forensic Sci. Soc.,* 8, 73, 1968.

97. Gormsen, H., Yeasts and the production of alcohol postmortem, *J. Forensic Med.,* 1, 170, 1954.

98. Kaji, H., Asanuma, Y., Yahara, O., Shibue, H., et al., Intragastrointestinal alcohol fermentation syndrome: report of two cases and review of the literature, *J. Forensic Sci. Soc.,* 24, 461, 1984.

99. Zumwalt, R.E., Bost, R.O., and Sunshine, I., Evaluation of ethanol concentrations in decomposed bodies, *J. Forensic Sci.,* 27, 549, 1982.

100. Clark, M.A. and Jones, J.W., Studies on putrefactive ethanol production: I: Lack of spontaneous ethanol production in intact human bodies, *J. Forensic Sci.,* 27, 366, 1982.

101. Canfield, D.V., Kupiec, T., and Huffine, E., Postmortem alcohol production in fatal aircraft accidents. *J. Forensic Sci.,* 38, 914, 1993.

102. Mayes, R., Levine, B., Smith, M.L., Wagner, G.N., and Froede, R., Toxicological findings in the *USS Iowa* disaster, *J. Forensic Sci.,* 37, 1352, 1992.

103. Ball, W. and Lichtenwalner, M., Ethanol production in infected urine, *N. Engl. J. Med.,* 301, 614, 1979.

104. Gilliland, M.G.F. and Bost, R.O., Alcohol in decomposed bodies: postmortem synthesis and distribution. *J. Forensic Sci.,* 38, 1266, 1993.

105. Levine, B., Smith, M.L., Smialek, J.E., and Caplan, Y.H., Interpretation of low postmortem concentrations of ethanol. *J. Forensic Sci.,* 38, 663, 1993.

106. Nanikawa, R., Ameno, K., Hashimoto, Y., and Hamada, K., Medicolegal studies on alcohol detected in dead bodies — alcohol levels in skeletal muscle, *Forensic Sci Int.,* 20, 133, 1982.

107. Wurst, F.M., Kempter, C., Metzger, J., Seidl, S., and Alt, A., Ethyl glucuronide: a marker of recent alcohol consumption with clinical and forensic implications, *Alcohol,* 20, 111, 2000.

108. Droenner, P., Schmitt, G., Aderjan, R., and Zimmer, H., A kinetic model describing the pharmacokinetics of ethyl glucuronide in humans, *Forensic Sci. Int.,* 126, 24, 2002.

109. Helander, A. and Beck, O., Mass spectrometric identification of ethyl sulphate as an ethanol metabolite in humans, *Clin. Chem.,* 50, 936, 2004.

110. Hansson, P., Varga, A., Krantz, P., and Alling, C., Phosphatidylethanol in post-mortem blood as a marker of previous heavy drinking, *Int. J. Legal Med.,* 115, 158, 2001.

111. Refaai, M.A., Nguyen, P.N., Steffensen, T.S., Evans, R.J. et al., Liver and adipose tissue fatty acid ethyl esters obtained at autopsy are post-mortem markers for pre-mortem ethanol intake, *Clin. Chem.,* 48, 77, 2002.

112. Helander, A., Biological markers in alcoholism, *J. Neural Transm.,* 66(Suppl.), 15, 2003.

113. Helander, A., Beck, O., and Jones, A.W., Distinguishing ingested ethanol from microbial formation by analysis of urinary 5-hydroxytryptophol and 5-hydroxyindoleacetic acid, *J. Forensic Sci.,* 40, 95, 1995.

114. Helander, A., Beck, O., and Jones, A.W., Urinary 5HTOL/5HIAA as biochemical marker of postmortem ethanol synthesis, *Lancet,* 340, 1159, 1992.

115. Johnson, R.D., Lewis, R.J., Canfield, D.V., and Blank, C.L., Accurate assignment of ethanol origin in post-mortem urine: liquid chromatographic-mass spectrometric determination of serotonin metabolites, *J. Chromatogr. B,* 805, 223, 2004.

116. Lewis, R.J., Johnson, R.D., Angier, M.K., and Vu, N.T., Ethanol formation in unadulterated post-mortem tissues, *Forensic Sci. Int.,* 146, 17, 2004.

117. Johnson, R.D., Lewis, R.J., Canfield, D.V., Dubowski, K.M., and Blank, C.L., Utilizing the urinary 5-HTOL/5-HIAA ratio to determine ethanol origin in civil aviation accident victims, *J. Forensic Sci.,* 50, 670, 2005.

118. Hirsch, C.S. and Adelson, L., Ethanol in sequestered hematomas, *Am. J. Clin. Pathol.,* 59, 429, 1973.

119. Buchsbaum, R.M., Adelson, L., and Sunshine, I., A comparison of post-mortem ethanol levels obtained from blood and subdura specimens, *Forensic Sci. Int.,* 41, 237, 1989.

120. Eisele, J.W., Reay, D.T., and Bonnell, H.J., Ethanol in sequestered hematomas: quantitative evaluation, *Am. J. Clin. Pathol.,* 81, 352, 1984.

121. Nanikawa, R., Ameno, K., and Hashimoto, Y., Medicolegal aspects on alcohol detected in autopsy cases — alcohol levels in hematomas [in Japanese], *Jpn. J. Leg. Med.,* 31, 241, 1977.

122. Freireich, A.W., Bidanset, J.H., and Lukash. L., Alcohol levels in intracranial blood clots, *J. Forensic Sci.,* 20, 83, 1975.

123. Smialek, J.E., Spitz, W.U., and Wolfe, J.A., Ethanol in intracerebral clot: report of two homicidal cases with prolonged survival after injury, *Am. J. Forensic Med. Pathol.,* 1, 149, 1980.

124. Cassin, B.J. and Spitz, W.U., Concentration of alcohol in delayed subdural hematoma, *J. Forensic Sci.,* 28, 1013, 1983.

125. Randall, B., Fatty liver and sudden death, *Hum. Pathol.,* 11, 147, 1980.

126. Pounder, D.J., Stevenson, R.J., and Taylor, K.K., Alcoholic ketoacidosis at autopsy, *J. Forensic Sci.,* 43, 812, 1998.

127. Kanetake, J., Kanawaku, Y., Mimasaka, S. et al., The relationship of a high level of serum beta-hydroxybutyrate to cause of death, *Legal Med.,* 7, 169, 2005.

128. Jenkins, D.W., Eckel, R.E., and Craig, J.W., Alcoholic ketoacidosis, *J. Am. Med. Assoc.,* 217, 177, 1971.

129. Levy, L.J., Duga, J., Girgis, M., and Gordon E.E., Ketoacidosis associated with alcoholism in nondiabetic subjects, *Ann. Intern. Med.,* 78, 213, 1973.

130. Bremer, J., Pathogenesis of ketonemia, *Scand. J. Clin. Lab. Invest.,* 23, 105, 1969.

131. Wrenn, K.D., Slovis, C.M., Minion, G.E., and Rutkowski, R., The syndrome of alcoholic ketoacidosis, *Am. J. Med.,* 91, 119, 1991.

132. Palmer, J.P., Alcoholic ketoacidosis: clinical and laboratory presentation, pathophysiology and treatment, *Clin. Endocrinol. Metab.,* 12, 381, 1983.

133. Halperin, M.L., Hammeke, M., Josse, R.G., and Jungas, R.L., Metabolic acidosis in the alcoholic: a pathophysiologic approach, *Metabolism,* 32, 308, 1983.

134. Cahill, G.F., Ketosis, *Kidney Int.,* 20, 416, 1981.

135. Isselbacher, K.H., Metabolic and hepatic effects of alcohol, *N. Engl. J. Med.,* 296, 612, 1977.

136. Pounder, D.J., Problems in the necropsy diagnosis of alcoholic liver disease, *Am. J. Forensic Med. Pathol.,* 5, 103, 1984.

137. Mihas, A.A. and Tavaossli, M., Laboratory markers of ethanol intake and abuse: a critical appraisal, *Am. J. Med. Sci.,* 303, 415, 1992.

138. Sadler, D.W., Girela, E., and Pounder, D.J., Post mortem markers of chronic alcoholism, *Forensic Sci. Int.,* 82, 153, 1996.

139. Jones, A.W. and Lowinger, H., Relationship between the concentration of ethanol and methanol in blood samples from Swedish drinking drivers, *Forensic Sci. Int.,* 37, 277, 1987.

140. Markiewicz, J., Chlobowska, Z., Sondaj, K., and Swiegoda, C., Trace quantities of methanol in blood and their diagnostic value, *Z. Zagadnien. Nauk. Sadowych.,* 33, 9, 1996.

141. Hashemy Tonkabony, S.E., Post-mortem blood concentration of methanol in 17 cases of fatal poisoning from contraband vodka, *Forensic Sci.,* 6, 1, 1975.

142. MacDougall, A.A., Clasg, M.A., and MacAulay, K., Addiction to methylated spirit, *Lancet,* Special Articles, 498, 1956.

143. Wu Chen, N.B., Donoghue, E.R., and Schaffer, M.I., Methanol intoxication: Distribution in postmortem tissues and fluids including vitreous humor, *J. Forensic Sci.,* 30, 213, 1985.

144. Pla, A., Hernandez, A.F., Gil, F., Garcia-Alonso, M., and Villanueva, E., A fatal case of oral ingestion of methanol. Distribution in postmortem tissues and fluids including pericardial fluid and vitreous humor, *Forensic Sci. Int.,* 49, 193, 1991.

145. Naraqi, S., Dethlefs, R.F., Slobodniuk, R.U., and Sairere, J.S., An outbreak of acute methyl alcohol intoxication, *Aust. N.Z. Med.,* 9, 65, 1979.

146. Swartz, R.D.M., McDonald, J.R., Millman, R.P., Billi, J.E., Bondar, N.P., Migdal, S.D., Simonian, S.K., Monforte, J.R., McDonald, F.D., Harness, J.K., and Cole, K.L., Epidemic methanol poisoning: clinical and biochemical analysis of a recent episode, *Medicine,* 60, 373, 1996.

147. Shahangian, S. and Owen Ash, K., Formic and lactic acidosis in a fatal case of methanol intoxication, *Clin. Chem.,* 32, 395, 1996.

148. Jacobsen, D., Jansen, H., Wiik-Larsen, E., Bredesen, J.E., and Halvorsen, S., Studies on methanol poisoning, *Acta Med. Scand.,* 212, 5, 1982.

149. Tanaka, E., Honda, K., Horiguchi, H., and Misawa, S., Postmortem determination of the biological distribution of formic acid in methanol intoxication, *J. Forensic Sci.,* 36, 936, 1991.

150. Houvda, K.E., Hunderi, O.H., Tafjord, A.B., Dunlop, O., Rudberg, N., and Jacobsen, D., Methanol outbreak in Norway 2002–2004: epidemiology, clinical features and prognostic signs, *J. Intern. Med.,* 258, 181, 2005.

151. Mani, J. C., Pietruszko, R., and Theorell, H., Methanol activity of alcohol dehydrogenase from human liver, horse liver, and yeast, *Arch. Biochem. Biophys.,* 140, 52, 1970.

152. Jacobsen, D. and McMartin, K.E., Antidotes for methanol and ethylene glycol poisoning, *Clin. Toxicol.,* 35, 127, 1997.

153. Barceloux, D.G., Bond, G.R., Krenzelok, E.P., Cooper, H., and Vale, J.A., American Academy of Clinical Toxicology practice guidelines on the treatment of methanol poisoning, *J. Toxicol. Clin. Toxicol.,* 40, 415, 2002.

154. Mycyk, M.B. and Leikin, J.B., Antidote review: fomepizole for methanol poisoning, *Am. J. Ther.,* 10, 68, 2003.

155. Brent, J., McMartin, K., Phillips, S., Aaron, C., and Kulig, K., Fomepizole for the treatment of methanol poisoning, *N. Engl. J. Med.,* 344, 424, 2001.

156. De Brabander, N., Wojciechowski, M., De Decker, K., De Weerdt, A., and Jorens, P.G., Fomepizole as a therapeutic strategy in paediatric methanol poisoning. A case report and review of the literature, *Eur. J. Pediatr.,* 164, 158, 2005.

157. Hovda, K.E., Andersson, K.S., Utdal, P., and Jacobsen, D., Methanol and formate kinetics during treatment with fomepizole, *Clin. Toxicol.,* 43, 221, 2005.

158. Adelson, L., Fatal intoxication with isopropyl alcohol (rubbing alcohol), *Am. J. Clin. Pathol.,* 38, 144, 1962.

159. Lacouture, P.G., Wason, S., Abrams, A., and Lovejoy, F.H., Acute isopropyl alcohol intoxication, *Am. J. Med.,* 75, 680, 1996.

160. Baselt, R.C. and Cravey, R.H., *Disposition of Toxic Drugs and Chemicals in Man.* 4th ed., Chemical Toxicology Institute, Foster City, CA, 1995.

161. Natowicz, M., Donahue, J., Gorman, L., Kane, M., and McKissick, J., Pharmacokinetic analysis of a case of isopropanol intoxication, *Clin. Chem.,* 31, 326, 1985.

162. Jones, A.W., Elimination half-life of acetone in humans: case-report and review of the literature, *J. Anal. Toxicol.,* 24, 8, 2000.

163. Alexander, C.B., McBay, A.J., and Hudson, R.P., Isopropanol and isopropanol deaths — ten years' experience, *J. Forensic Sci.,* 27, 541, 1982.

164. Lewis, G.D., Laufman, A.K., McAnalley, B.H., and Garriot, J.C., Metabolism of acetone to isopropyl alcohol in rats and humans, *J. Forensic Sci.,* 29, 541, 1996.

5.4 RECENT ADVANCES IN BIOCHEMICAL TESTS FOR ACUTE AND CHRONIC ALCOHOL CONSUMPTION

Anders Helander, Ph.D.[1] and Alan Wayne Jones, D.Sc.[2]

[1] Department of Clinical Neuroscience, Karolinska Institute and Karolinska University Hospital, Stockholm, Sweden

[2] Department of Forensic Toxicology, University Hospital, Linköping, Sweden

5.4.1 Introduction

Most people enjoy a drink and, for the vast majority of individuals, alcohol is a harmless, socially accepted recreational drug.[1] However, for about 10% of the population, especially among men, moderate drinking eventually leads to alcohol abuse and dependence with serious consequences for the individual and society.[2,3] Overconsumption of alcohol is a major public health hazard and a cause of premature death and morbidity.[4,5] Binge drinking, which is usually defined as consumption of five or more drinks on one occasion, is often associated with acute intoxication, hooliganism, drunk driving, and other deviant behavior with negative consequences for the person's family and friends.[6,7]

Statistics show that alcohol consumption is increasing worldwide in both sexes and this legal drug creates enormous costs for society in terms of treatment and rehabilitation of those who abuse alcohol.[8–10] Early recognition of problem drinkers in the society is therefore important to ensure adequate treatment strategies.[11] According to the American Medical Association, the difference between moderate use, abuse, and alcohol dependence ("alcoholism") are summarized as follows:

1. The consumption of alcohol in amounts considered harmless to health entails drinking at most one to two drinks per day (~10 to 20 g ethanol), and never first thing in the morning or on an empty stomach and the resulting blood alcohol concentration (BAC) should not exceed 0.2 g/L (0.02 g%) on any drinking occasion.

2. Abuse of alcohol is a pattern of drinking that is accompanied by one or more of the following problems: (a) failure to fulfill major work, school, or home responsibilities because of drinking, (b) drinking in situations that are physically dangerous, such as driving a car or operating machinery, (c) recurring alcohol-related legal problems, such as being arrested for driving under the influence of alcohol or for physically hurting someone while drunk, and (d) having social or relationship problems that are caused by or worsened by the effects of alcohol.

3. Alcohol dependence is a more severe pattern of drinking that includes the problems of alcohol abuse and persistent drinking in spite of obvious physical, mental, and social problems caused by alcohol. Also typical are (a) loss of control and inability to stop drinking once begun, (b) withdrawal symptoms associated with stopping drinking such as nausea, sweating, shakiness, and anxiety, and (c) tolerance to alcohol, needing increased amounts of alcohol in order to feel drunk.

Denial of drinking practices has always been a major stumbling block in the effective treatment of alcohol abuse and dependence.[12] Drinking histories are notoriously unreliable and this tends to complicate early detection and treatment of the underlying alcohol problem.[13,14] Much research effort has therefore focused on developing more objective ways to disclose excessive drinking, so that help

Table 5.4.1   Examples of Biochemical Markers of Alcohol Use and Abuse, and Possible Predisposition to Alcohol Dependence

Classification	Examples of Biochemical Markers
Acute Markers	Ethanol
	5-Hydroxytryptophol (5HTOL)
	Ethyl glucuronide (EtG)
	Ethyl sulfate (EtS)
	Fatty-acid ethyl esters (FAEE)
State Markers	γ-Glutamyl transferase (GGT)
	Alanine aminotransferase (ALT)
	Aspartate aminotransferase (AST)
	Mean corpuscular volume (MCV)
	Carbohydrate-deficient transferrin (CDT)
	Phosphatidylethanol (PEth)
Trait Markers	Monoamine oxidase (MAO)
	Adenylyl cyclase (AC)
	Neuropeptide Y (NPY)

can be given to those at risk of becoming dependent on alcohol.[15] In this connection, the use of various clinical laboratory tests is a useful complement to self-report questionnaires, such as the MAST and CAGE,[16,17] which are intended to divulge the quantity and frequency of alcohol consumption as well as various social-medical problems associated with alcohol abuse and dependence.

Accordingly, a multitude of biochemical markers have been developed to provide more objective ways of diagnosing overconsumption of alcohol and risk for alcohol-induced organ and tissue damage.[18–21] The liver is particularly vulnerable to heavy drinking and damage to liver cells is often reflected in an increased activity of various enzymes in the bloodstream, such as γ-glutamyl transferase (GGT) and alanine and aspartate aminotransferase (ALT and AST).[22,23] However, it seems that some individuals can drink excessively for months or years without displaying abnormal results with this kind of biochemical test, which implies a low *sensitivity* for detecting hazardous drinking. By contrast, some biological markers yield positive results in people suffering from non-alcohol-related liver problems, or after taking certain kinds of medication, which implies a low *specificity* for detecting alcohol abuse.

Nevertheless, interest in the use of biochemical tests or biomarkers for screening those individuals at most risk of developing problems with alcohol consumption has expanded greatly.[21,24,25] Besides many applications in clinical practice, such as in the rehabilitation of alcoholics and in drug-abuse treatment programs,[26] biochemical markers have found uses in occupational medicine,[27,28] forensic science,[29–32] and experimental alcohol research.[33,34] In general, three major classes of biochemical markers have been distinguished (examples are given in Table 5.4.1):

1. Tests sufficiently sensitive to detect even a single intake of alcohol, known as *acute markers* or *relapse markers.*
2. Tests that indicate disturbed metabolic processes or malfunctioning of body organs and/or tissue damage caused by long-term exposure to alcohol. This is reflected in altered hematological and/or biochemical parameters in blood or other body fluids. Such tests are referred to as *state markers* of hazardous alcohol consumption.
3. Tests that indicate whether a person carries a genetic predisposition for heavy drinking, abuse of alcohol, and development of alcohol dependence. Such tests are known as *trait markers* and often rely on identifying an abnormal enzyme or receptor pattern at the molecular level. Those prone to develop into heavy drinkers exhibit at an early age marked personality disorders, including sensation-seeking behavior, binge drinking, and abuse of other drugs.

In this chapter, we present an update of research dealing with laboratory markers for both acute and chronic drinking. The advantages and limitations of various laboratory tests are discussed and suggestions are made for their rational use in clinical and forensic medicine.

5.4.2 Diagnostic Sensitivity and Specificity

Biochemical markers are usually evaluated in terms of diagnostic sensitivity and specificity. *Sensitivity* refers to the ability of a test to detect the presence of the trait in question, whereas *specificity* refers to its ability to exclude individuals without the trait. Consequently, a marker with high sensitivity yields relatively few false negative results and one with high specificity gives few false positives. The ideal marker should, of course, be both 100% sensitive and specific, but this is never achieved because reference ranges for normal and abnormal values always tend to overlap. Instead, a cutoff, or threshold limit, is established for what is considered normal. These limits are usually determined empirically as the mean plus or minus two standard deviations (SD) of the test results for a healthy control population. Accordingly, 2.5% of individuals will be above the upper limit and 2.5% below the lower limit and the test specificity will always be less than 100%.

To obtain a sufficiently high specificity for routine purposes, the sensitivity of some markers has to be gradually reduced. On the other hand, most tests aimed at indicating liver damage caused by prolonged alcohol abuse often suffer from low specificity, because many liver diseases have non-alcoholic origin. So-called receiver-operating characteristic (ROC) curves are widely used for evaluating utility of biochemical markers and for comparing different analytical methods.[35] ROC curves are graphic illustrations created by plotting the relation between sensitivity (i.e., the percentage of true positives) against 1-specificity (i.e., the percentage of false positives) at different cutoff limits between normal and abnormal values.[36]

Most studies aimed at evaluating the sensitivity and specificity of alcohol biomarkers rely heavily on patient self-reports about drinking as the gold standard. However, considering that many patients fail to provide an accurate history of their true alcohol consumption, this creates a validity problem. Hence, besides the use of sensitive and specific markers of excessive alcohol consumption, there is also a need to develop and evaluate laboratory tests to monitor recent alcohol consumption in a more objective way.

5.4.3 Tests for Acute Alcohol Ingestion

5.4.3.1 Measuring Ethanol in Body Fluids and Breath

Ethanol and water mix together in all proportions and, after drinking alcoholic beverages, the ethanol distributes into all body fluids and tissues in proportion to the amount of water in these fluids and tissues. The body water in men makes up about 60% of their body weight and the corresponding figure for women is ~50%, although there are large inter-individual differences in these average figures, depending on age and, especially, the amount of adipose tissue. Accordingly, the most specific and direct way to demonstrate that a person has been drinking alcohol is to analyze a sample of blood, breath, urine, or saliva. However, because concentrations of ethanol in these body fluids decrease over time, owing to metabolism and excretion processes, the time frame for positive identification is rather limited.[37,38]

The smell of alcohol on the breath is perhaps the oldest and most obvious indication that a person has been drinking. But many alcoholics use breath fresheners or can regulate their intake so that the BAC is low or zero when they are examined by a physician.[39] A more objective way to disclose recent alcohol consumption is to measure the concentration of ethanol in the exhaled air. Several kinds of handheld breath alcohol analyzers are available for this purpose, such as Alcolmeter SD-400, AlcoSensor IV, or Alcotest 4010. The ethanol in a sample of breath is oxidized with an electrochemical sensor and the magnitude of the response is directly proportional to the concentration of ethanol present.[40] Studies have shown that these breath analyzers are accurate, precise, and selective for their intended purpose. Endogenous breath volatiles, such as acetone, are not oxidized under the same conditions and therefore does not interfere with the selectivity of the test for ethanol.

Breath alcohol concentration (BrAC) tests should become a standard procedure, if a patient is required to refrain from drinking as part of rehabilitation or treatment or because of workplace regulations concerning the use of alcohol.[41] However, a positive breath test needs to be confirmed by making a repeat test not less than 15 min later, to rule out the presence of ethanol in the mouth from recent drinking. Most of the currently available handheld breath alcohol analyzers have an analytical sensitivity of about 0.05 mg ethanol per liter breath, which corresponds to a blood ethanol equivalent of 10 mg/dL (~2.2 mmol/L). The result of a breath alcohol test appears immediately after capturing the sample and results are reported in units of g/210 L (U.S.) or mg/L (Sweden) or μg/100 mL (U.K.). Alternatively, the result of the test is translated into the presumed coexisting BAC and for this application the breath alcohol instrument is precalibrated with a blood/breath conversion factor, usually assumed to be 2100:1 or 2300:1. Careful control of calibration and maintenance of these breath test instruments is important to ensure obtaining valid and reliable results.

Measuring the concentration of ethanol in whole blood or plasma/serum will also provide reliable information about recent drinking. However, obtaining a sample of blood is an invasive procedure and the concentration of ethanol, if any, is not obtained immediately after sampling. The analysis of ethanol in blood or plasma is therefore less practical than breath testing, for clinical purposes, as a rapid screening test for recent drinking. The sensitivity of methods for blood alcohol analysis (e.g., gas chromatography; GC) is higher than breath test instruments and a BAC as low as 1 mg/dL can be measured. However, for clinical applications, it is wise to use a higher cutoff (i.e., decision limit) such as 5 or 10 mg/dL, to avoid discussions and debate that the ethanol came from some dietary constituent, such as fresh fruits or soft drinks.

After absorption and distribution of ethanol in body fluids and tissues is complete, there is a close correlation between the concentrations in saliva, blood, and urine. The equilibration of ethanol between blood and saliva is fairly rapid, which makes saliva sampling more suitable than urine for clinical purposes.[42,43] A number of devices have been developed for measuring ethanol in saliva and these have proved useful for alcohol screening purposes in clinical settings. A saliva-test device called QED has been evaluated extensively and gives on-the-spot results as to whether a person has consumed alcohol. The QED test incorporates alcohol dehydrogenase (ADH) to oxidize ethanol with the coenzyme NAD+ at pH 8.6. Ethanol is converted into acetaldehyde and the NADH is formed in direct proportion to the concentration of ethanol present. The acetaldehyde is trapped with semicarbazide to drive the reaction to completion. The NADH is then re-oxidized to produce a colored end product, by reaction with the enzyme diaphorase and a tetrazolium salt incorporated on a solid phase support. The length of the resulting blue-colored bar is directly proportional to the concentration of ethanol in the saliva sample and permits a direct readout of the test result about 1 min later. Saliva alcohol concentrations determined with QED agreed well with BAC and BrAC in controlled drinking experiments.[44,45]

Numerous studies have compared concentrations of ethanol in blood and urine sampled at various times after end of drinking.[46,47] In the post-absorptive phase, the urine-alcohol concentration (UAC) and the BAC are highly correlated ($r > 0.95$). Some have tried to estimate BAC indirectly from UAC, assuming a population average UAC/BAC, such as 1.3:1. However, there are large inter- and intra-individual variations in this relationship, which means that the estimated BAC will have a considerable uncertainty in any individual case.

One expects to find a higher concentration of ethanol in urine compared with blood, because of the difference in water content of these body fluids, namely, 100% vs. 80%. This suggests a UAC/BAC ratio of 1.25:1 for freshly produced urine. In reality, however, the UAC/BAC ratio also depends on the time after drinking, when the bladder was last voided, and how frequently the person urinates. Urine is stored but not metabolized in the bladder, whereas the BAC changes continuously, depending on the stage of metabolism and the rate of hepatic oxidation. Shortly after drinking during the absorption phase, the UAC and BAC are not well correlated, whereas in the post-peak phase, when BAC is decreasing at a constant rate of about 15 mg/dL/h, a good correlation exists between BAC and UAC.

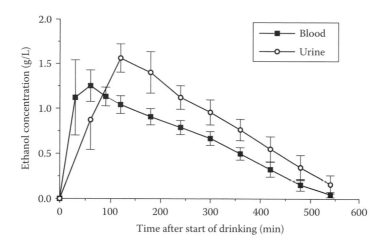

Figure 5.4.1 Mean concentration-time profiles of ethanol in blood and urine in 30 healthy men who drank 0.85 g/kg body weight after an overnight fast. The bladder was emptied before the start of drinking and alcohol was taken in the form of neat whisky.

The average curves for venous blood and urine concentration–time profiles of ethanol are compared in Figure 5.4.1. One notes that UAC and BAC curves are shifted in time, as a consequence of the time-lag between ethanol being absorbed into the bloodstream, reaching the kidney, and passing into the glomerular filtrate, and its storage in the bladder until voided. Shortly after the end of drinking, the UAC is less than the BAC (UAC/BAC < 1.0). After the peak BAC is reached, the two curves cross and the UAC has a higher C_{max} compared with the BAC. In the post-absorptive phase, the UAC is always higher than the corresponding BAC by a factor of 1.3 to 1.4. Note that the UAC reflects the average BAC prevailing during the time that urine was produced and stored in the bladder since the previous void. The UAC in a random void does not reflect the BAC at the time of emptying the bladder and, in this respect, is less useful than blood, saliva, or breath as a test of alcohol influence. Instead, the UAC reflects the BAC during production and storage of urine in the bladder. The UAC remains elevated for about 1 h after the BAC has already reached zero. Accordingly, the first morning void after an evening's drinking might be positive for ethanol, although the concentrations in blood or breath have already reached zero.[48] This relationship suggests that the BAC has reached zero sometime during the night and any ethanol already in the urine gets diluted with ethanol-free urine produced after complete metabolism of the alcohol consumed. Metabolism of ethanol does not occur in the urinary bladder, and back-diffusion of ethanol into the bloodstream is negligible, owing to the limited blood circulation.

Small quantities of ethanol are excreted through the skin by passive diffusion and also secreted through the sweat glands. The transdermal elimination of ethanol corresponds to about 0.5 to 1% of the dose ingested.[49] However, this route of excretion has found applications in clinical medicine, as a way to monitor alcohol consumption over periods of several weeks or months. This approach might be useful to control if alcoholics and others manage to remain abstinent, and has led to the introduction of a procedure known as transdermal dosimeter or, more simply, the sweat-patch test.[50,51] Although the first attempts to monitor alcohol consumption in this way were not very successful, owing to technical difficulties with the equipment used for collecting sweat, the procedures are now much improved and can be used to analyze other drugs of abuse as well.[52,53] The test person wears a tamper-proof and water-proof pad, positioned on an arm or leg, and the low-molecular substances that pass through the skin are collected during the time the patch remains intact. Ethanol and other volatiles are extracted with water and the concentration determined provides a cumulative index of alcohol exposure. The ethanol collected in the cotton pad can be determined in a number of ways, such as by extraction with water and GC analysis or by headspace

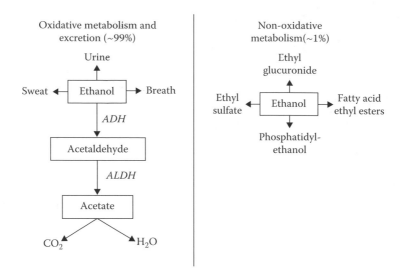

Figure 5.4.2 Fate of alcohol in the body illustrating both the oxidative and non-oxidative pathways of ethanol metabolism.

vapor analysis with a handheld electrochemical sensor, which was originally designed for breath alcohol testing.[54] A miniaturized electronic device for continuous sampling and monitoring of transcutaneous ethanol has recently been introduced.[55,56]

5.4.3.2 *Metabolism of Ethanol*

The disposition and fate of ethanol in the body has been studied extensively since the 1930s and our knowledge about this legal drug exceeds that of other abused substances. Ethanol is cleared from the bloodstream by both oxidative and non-oxidative metabolic pathways (Figure 5.4.2).

The minor non-oxidative pathway of alcohol metabolism has received considerable research interest since the first edition of this book appeared and this topic is covered later in this chapter. The main alcohol-metabolizing enzymes are located in the liver, the kidney, and the gastric mucosa. The bulk of the alcohol a person consumes undergoes hepatic metabolism by the action of Class I ADH, which exists in various molecular forms, so-called isozymes. Ethanol is metabolized in a two-stage process, first to acetaldehyde and this primary metabolite is rapidly converted to acetate (acetic acid) by the action of low K_m aldehyde dehydrogenase (ALDH2) located in the mitochondria. The end products of the oxidation of ethanol are carbon dioxide and water (see Figure 5.4.2).

Hepatic ADH is not specific for oxidation of ethanol, and other aliphatic alcohols, if present in the blood, as well as a number of endogenous substances (e.g., prostaglandins and hydroxysteroids), also serve as substrates. The substrate specificity of ADH toward aliphatic alcohols differs widely, and the rate of oxidation of methanol is considerably slower than that of ethanol by a factor of about 10:1.[57] The biotransformation of ethanol and methanol and the various metabolic products formed are compared in Figure 5.4.3.

Raised concentrations of the intermediary products of ethanol oxidation have been proposed as a way to test for recent drinking.[56] However, measuring acetaldehyde is not very practical, because of the extremely low concentrations present (<1% of the ethanol concentration), and also the fact that the necessary analytical procedures are much more challenging than those for the analysis of ethanol.[58] Acetaldehyde is rapidly converted to acetate, and the concentration of free acetaldehyde in peripheral venous plasma is further reduced owing to a more or less specific binding to various endogenous molecules such as proteins (see also Section 5.4.4.6). An additional problem arises if the blood contains ethanol, because acetaldehyde is formed after sampling resulting in

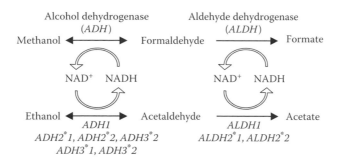

Figure 5.4.3 Schematic diagram comparing the metabolism of ethanol and methanol via the alcohol dehydrogenase pathway: NAD+ = oxidized form of the coenzyme nicotinamide adenine dinucleotide; NADH = reduced form of the coenzyme. The various isozymes of alcohol dehydrogenase (ADH) and aldehyde dehydrogenase (ALDH) are indicated.

falsely high results.[58,59] Measuring acetaldehyde in breath instead of blood has been suggested as an alternative approach, although even breath testing is not without its problems.[60]

The concentration of acetate in blood depends on the rate of ethanol oxidation and utilization of the acetate formed by peripheral tissues. The blood acetate concentration appears to be independent of the blood-ethanol concentration, and instead increases with the development of metabolic tolerance to alcohol (i.e., rate of ethanol elimination).[61,62] Measuring blood acetate was suggested as a marker of chronic abuse of alcohol,[63,64] and the sensitivity and specificity of this test was significantly higher than for GGT.[63] It should be emphasized, however, that blood-acetate remains elevated only as long as ethanol is being metabolized and, moreover, the rate of ethanol metabolism exhibits large inter-individual variations even in moderate drinkers.

5.4.3.3 Analysis of Methanol in Body Fluids

Ethanol and methanol are examples of endogenous alcohols and are normally present in biological specimens, albeit at extremely low concentrations (<1 mg/L). Moreover, trace quantities of the free alcohols or their esters might be ingested with certain foodstuffs or might be contained in soft drinks, such as fruit juices and sodas, or they could be formed by fermentation of dietary carbohydrates through the action of microorganisms inhabiting the gut.[65–68]

During the end stages of carbohydrate metabolism, trace amounts of acetaldehyde are produced from pyruvate and, after reduction via the ADH/NAD+ pathway, lead to small amounts of ethanol being present in body fluids.[69] The trace amounts of the endogenous alcohols produced in the gut are rapidly cleared from the portal venous blood, as it passes through the liver for the first time. The existence of an effective first-pass metabolism ensures that only vanishingly small concentrations of ethanol and methanol reach the peripheral circulation. With the use of highly sensitive and specific analytical methods, the concentrations of ethanol and methanol in body fluids obtained from healthy abstaining individuals ranges from 0.04 to 0.1 mg/dL.[70,71]

Ethanol and methanol compete for binding sites on the Class I isozymes of ADH, which show a stronger preference for the oxidation of ethanol.[57] As a consequence, during metabolism of ethanol, the concentration of methanol in blood increases and remains on a more or less constant level, until blood ethanol decreases below 20 mg/dL (~4.3 mmol/L) (Figure 5.4.4). Thereafter, methanol is cleared with a half-life of 2 to 3 h, which means that methanol can be detected in body fluids long after the concentration of ethanol has returned to baseline or endogenous levels.[37,72–74] This protracted wash-out of methanol opens the possibility of verifying recent drinking for several hours after ethanol has been cleared from the body.

Analysis of blood and urine methanol is included in some forensic investigations, when accountability for road traffic and workplace accidents are investigated.[38] Besides the acute effects of

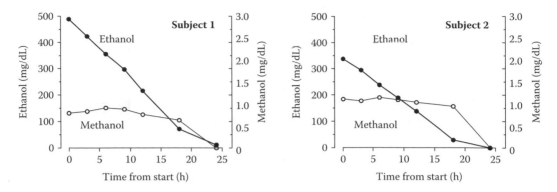

Figure 5.4.4 Elimination kinetics of ethanol and methanol in two alcoholics during detoxification. Note that the concentration of methanol in blood remains fairly constant at about 1 mg/dL until the ethanol concentration decreases toward zero.

alcohol on performance and behavior, many people are impaired the morning after an evening's heavy drinking; these post-intoxication effects of heavy drinking are known as hangover (see Chapter 5.1).

The higher affinity of ADH for oxidation of ethanol compared with methanol also explains the mechanism behind the therapeutic usefulness of ethanol in treating methanol poisoning. Ethanol is given by intravenous infusion to reach and maintain a blood ethanol concentration of about 100 to 120 mg/dL, which effectively blocks the metabolism of methanol into its toxic metabolites formaldehyde and formic acid.[75] In the meantime, the more dangerous methanol is removed from the blood by dialysis and bicarbonate can be administered to counteract metabolic acidosis.[76] However, there are some reservations against the continued use of this antidote, because ethanol exerts a pronounced effect on the central nervous system and should not be used in treating children who inadvertently ingest methanol (wood alcohol).[77] The antidote currently in vogue for treating people poisoned with methanol is 4-methyl pyrazole (fomepizole), a competitive inhibitor of ADH.[78,79]

Although alcoholic beverages are primarily mixtures of ethanol and water, they also contain a multitude of other chemical compounds, albeit at extremely low concentrations. These other substances, which are produced as by-products of the fermentation process, are collectively known as congeners and impart the smell and flavor to the alcoholic beverage.[80] Methanol is a ubiquitous congener and is present in beer (0.1 to 1 mg/dL), red and white wines (2 to 10 mg/dL), gin and whisky (0.1 to 20 mg/dL), and brandies and cognac (20 to 200 mg/dL).[81] Accordingly, a raised concentration of methanol in blood and other body fluids after drinking alcoholic beverages could partly be explained by its presence as a congener, and also because of the metabolic interaction with ethanol via competitive inhibition of ADH.[82] Finding a blood methanol concentration above 1 mg/dL suggests accumulation during a period of long-term heavy drinking (days or weeks), and some feel this furnishes a test for chronic alcohol abuse (see also Section 5.4.4.7).[83–85] However, care is needed to ensure that the alcoholic beverage consumed does not contain abnormally high concentrations of methanol.[81,86,87]

5.4.3.4 Conjugates of Ethanol Metabolism

The glucuronidation pathway of drug metabolism, including the conjugation of hydroxyl groups in aliphatic alcohols, was discovered more than a century ago.[88] Shortly after, it was found that ethanol was converted into ethyl glucuronide (EtG) and this minor metabolite was identified in urine.[89] However, interest in this non-oxidative pathway of ethanol metabolism was hampered, owing to the complexity of the analytical methods needed to determine reliably EtG concentrations in body fluids.[90,91] The advent of modern analytical techniques, such as the highly sensitive and

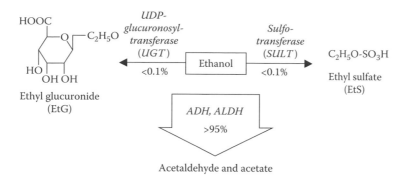

Figure 5.4.5 Schematic diagram illustrating the relative importance of the oxidation (phase I) and non-oxidative conjugation (phase II) elimination pathways for ethanol in the human body.

specific gas and liquid chromatography combined with mass spectrometry (GC-MS and LC-MS),[92] radically changed the situation and spawned in a new area of biomedical alcohol research. Careful studies showed that only a very small fraction of the ingested ethanol (<0.1%) undergoes phase II conjugation reactions with glucuronic acid or sulfuric acid to produce EtG and ethyl sulfate (EtS), respectively (Figure 5.4.5).[93,94] These soluble non-oxidative metabolites of ethanol are excreted with the urine, for several hours longer than ethanol itself.[93,95–97]

After acute alcohol ingestion, there is no accumulation of EtG in body fluids,[98] although it may be retained in hair.[99] The advantage of hair over other body media for drug analysis is the extended window of detection offered, and, based on segmental analysis and an average growth rate, some idea can be obtained as to when the drug was last being used.[100] Determination of EtG in urine provides a means to verify whether a person has recently been drinking alcohol, for much longer than ethanol is detectable in body fluids. The resulting higher sensitivity of the EtG test, compared with analysis of ethanol itself, has obvious practical advantages as an acute marker of alcohol consumption.

The availability of improved analytical methods for EtG based on mass spectrometry (GC-MS and LC-MS)[95,101,102] has allowed several research groups to make detailed studies of this trace metabolite of ethanol as a sensitive and specific biomarker of acute alcohol consumption.[21,103] However, as expected from knowledge of glucuronides in general, EtG is sensitive to urine dilution. The EtG concentration in urine can be lowered markedly by drinking large amounts of fluid prior to voiding, whereas this does not influence the EtG/creatinine ratio.[93] Furthermore, EtG is sensitive to enzymatic hydrolysis, so if biological samples are contaminated with certain bacteria containing β-glucuronidase (e.g., *Escherichia coli* which is common in urinary tract infections), this represents another reason for obtaining falsely low or false-negative results.[104]

Another phase II metabolic pathway, namely, sulfate conjugation, produces EtS and this minor metabolite of ethanol (<0.1%) is also excreted in urine.[94,97] EtS shows similar excretion kinetics to EtG,[94,97,105,106] but, in contrast to EtG, it is apparently not sensitive to bacterial hydrolysis.[104] Other minor metabolites of ethanol with potential use as alcohol biomarkers include ethyl nitrite and ethyl phosphate.[107]

5.4.3.5 *Fatty-Acid Ethyl Esters*

Fatty acid ethyl esters (FAEE), such as ethyl palmitate and ethyl oleate, are esterification products of fatty acids and ethanol synthesized through the action of the enzyme FAEE synthase. The presence of these short-chain esters in samples of blood, tissue, or hair has been proposed as a biomarker of alcohol intake with clinical and forensic applications.[100,108–110] After alcohol intake, the serum concentration of FAEE initially closely parallels that of ethanol (e.g., similar time for peak concentrations) but, because of a very slow terminal elimination phase, FAEE persists in the blood for some time after ethanol is no longer detectable.[111,112] The elimination rate of FAEE is faster than for some other acute alcohol biomarkers, implying a lower sensitivity for recent drinking.[112,113] Increasing evidence indicates that FAEE may be toxic metabolites and, as such, possible mediators of ethanol-induced organ damage.[114]

5.4.3.6 *Metabolites of Serotonin*

Studies have shown that the metabolic interaction between ethanol and serotonin (5-hydroxytryptamine) can help to detect recent alcohol consumption. 5-Hydroxytryptophol (5HTOL) is normally a minor metabolite of serotonin, but the proportion of this metabolite increases dramatically in a dose-dependent manner after drinking alcohol. At the same time, 5-hydroxyindole-3-acetic acid (5HIAA), the major metabolite under normal conditions, is concomitantly decreased.[115,116] Experiments with liver homogenates suggest that the shift in serotonin metabolism occurs because of competitive inhibition of ALDH by the acetaldehyde derived from oxidation of ethanol.[117] Furthermore, during the metabolism of ethanol and acetaldehyde, the reduced coenzyme NADH is present in excess and the redox state of the liver shifts to a more reduced potential, both in the cytosol and mitochondria compartments. This alters the equilibrium between several other endogenous NAD-dependent reactions, such as lactate:pyruvate and β-hydroxybutyrate:acetoacetate. The combined influences of a competitive inhibition of ALDH and altered redox state of the liver promote formation of 5HTOL at the expense of 5HIAA.[118,119] Most importantly, however, the urinary excretion of 5HTOL will not normalize until several hours after blood and urinary ethanol reaches zero (Figure 5.4.6).[116] On the basis of this time lag, an increased urinary concentration of 5HTOL was suggested and used as a sensitive biochemical marker of recent drinking.[120–122]

Expressing 5HTOL as a ratio 5HTOL/5HIAA, rather than 5HTOL/creatinine, improves test accuracy because dietary serotonin (high amounts in banana, pineapple, kiwi fruit, and walnuts) might otherwise cause false-positive results, owing to a general increase in the urinary output of both serotonin metabolites.[123] This device also compensates for variations in the concentration of 5HTOL caused by urine dilution after drinking fluids. To discriminate between a normal and elevated urinary ratios of 5HTOL/5HIAA, a cutoff limit of 15 nmol/μmol (i.e., 1.5%) is recommended for use in clinical practice.[122] This threshold value is based on studies with alcohol-free subjects of both Caucasian and Asian origin.[124] The 5HTOL/5HIAA ratio remains stable both within-days and between-days during periods of abstinence, and the metabolites are also relatively uninfluenced during transport, handling, and long-term storage of the urine specimens. Neither

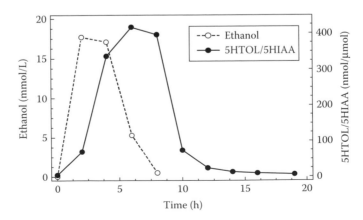

Figure 5.4.6 Time course of concentrations of ethanol and the ratio of 5-hydroxytryptophol (5HTOL) to 5-hydroxyindole-3-acetic acid (5HIAA) in urine after a healthy volunteer drank a single moderate dose of ethanol. The longer recovery time for the 5HTOL/5HIAA ratio is clearly evident.

gender nor genetic variations in ADH and ALDH isozyme patterns seem to influence the baseline ratio of 5HTOL/5HIAA.[37,124]

An increased urinary 5HTOL/5HIAA furnishes a specific and more sensitive laboratory test of recent drinking than measuring the concentration of ethanol or methanol in body fluids.[37,74] The major advantage of 5HTOL/5HIAA over ethanol and methanol is that a raised serotonin metabolite ratio persists for several hours longer, thereby improving the ability to detect covert drinking. Furthermore, in contrast to methanol, the baseline ratio of 5HTOL/5HIAA is not elevated after prolonged intermittent alcohol intake and can therefore identify recent drinking in moderate as well as chronic drinkers.[98] Apart from alcohol ingestion, the only factor known to increase the 5HTOL/5HIAA ratio is treatment with the ALDH inhibitors disulfiram (Antabuse) and cyanamide.[125] Another drawback is that urinary 5HTOL testing at present requires rather sophisticated analytical techniques based on GC-MS or LC-MS.[122,126,127]

Testing of urinary 5HTOL has, for example, been used in clinical practice, to detect alcohol use and single lapses during treatment of alcohol-dependent subjects in an outpatient setting,[128,129] in heroin addicts on methadone maintenance,[39] and in surgical patients with chronic alcohol abuse.[130] Furthermore, testing for 5HTOL/5HIAA has applications in forensic medicine, to distinguish ingested from microbially formed ethanol, which might occur in post-mortem specimens or in urine from individuals with diabetes or others with urinary tract infections.[29,30,32,131] The 5HTOL/5HIAA ratio has also been recommended for use during official forensic investigations of aviation crashes,[132] where the risk for post-mortem synthesis of ethanol is exaggerated.[126,133]

5.4.4 Tests of Chronic Alcohol Ingestion

5.4.4.1 Gamma-Glutamyl Transferase

For many years, the activity of the enzyme gamma-glutamyl transferase (GGT) in serum has been the most widely used biochemical test for alcohol abuse.[134] GGT is a membrane-bound glycoprotein widely distributed in various organs, and plays an important role in glutathione synthesis, amino acid transport, and peptide nitrogen storage. Only trace amounts are normally present in serum from healthy subjects. However, in liver damage, for example, resulting from continuous heavy drinking, a significant elevation in serum GGT occurs.[135,136] Although the mechanisms responsible are not known exactly, damage to hepatocytes and/or induction of hepatic GGT may cause the enzyme to leak into the blood.[137,138] After withdrawal from ethanol, GGT returns to normal levels within approximately 4 to 5 weeks.

The determination of GGT is routinely included in blood-chemistry profiles on admission to hospital. The major disadvantage of GGT is that the serum level is raised by a variety of other conditions besides alcohol misuse, thereby reducing its diagnostic specificity.[134,139,140] For example, several common medications, such as barbiturates and antiepileptics, and various liver disorders of non-alcohol origin, also elevate serum GGT. Moreover, accepted normal ranges depend on nutritional status, body weight, age, and gender of the individual. Different threshold limits depicting abnormal values need to be applied for women and men separately. Although GGT has limited utility as a single screening test for hazardous alcohol consumption in nonselected populations,[141] many of the confounding factors are well known and can often be excluded or controlled for in clinical situations. The major advantage of GGT as a marker of alcohol abuse is its ready availability at low cost from most clinical laboratories.

5.4.4.2 Aspartate and Alanine Aminotransferase

Other standard tests of liver dysfunction caused by hazardous drinking include raised serum levels of the transaminases aspartate (AST) and alanine aminotransferase (ALT), which are enzymes involved in amino acid metabolism. Like GGT, certain medical conditions other than alcohol abuse can cause abnormal AST and ALT values, and both these markers are typically less sensitive, though somewhat more specific, than GGT.[142,143] The ALT-to-AST ratio,[139] as well as the proportion of mitochondrial to total AST,[144,145] has been suggested as a way to discriminate alcohol-induced from non-alcoholic liver disease, but this has not been confirmed in studies in unselected populations.[146,147] The transaminases may be useful in combination with other biochemical tests,[148] and for follow-up of patients with already established alcoholic liver disease.[149]

5.4.4.3 *Erythrocyte Mean Corpuscular Volume*

Mean corpuscular volume (MCV) is included as part of a routine blood count and indicates the size of the red blood cells (erythrocytes). An elevated MCV is often observed in alcoholic patients,[150] and this parameter has been widely used as a marker of excessive alcohol consumption.[151] The underlying cause of swelling of the red cells is unknown, but may be a direct toxic effect of ethanol or the alcohol-mediated deficiency of folic acid. The sensitivity of MCV as a biochemical marker of heavy drinking is much too low to motivate its use as a sole indicator of this condition.[152] There are other explanations for elevated MCV besides continuous heavy drinking, such as smoking, which is very common in alcoholics.[153,154] However, MCV shows a higher specificity than GGT,[148,151,155,156] and it is often used in combination with other biochemical parameters and offers the added advantage that it takes longer (several months) for MCV to recover to normal values after cessation of heavy drinking.

5.4.4.4 *Carbohydrate-Deficient Transferrin*

The presence of an abnormal glycoform pattern of the iron transport glycoprotein transferrin in serum, named carbohydrate-deficient transferrin (CDT), has emerged as the most reliable routine method for detection of continuous high alcohol consumption for 2 or more weeks.[157] The discovery of CDT as a marker of heavy drinking dates back more than 20 years.[158] The finding of an abnormal transferrin pattern in blood serum appears to be fairly specific for overconsumption of alcohol and recovers to normal during periods of abstinence with a half-life of ~1.5 to 2 weeks.[158,159]

Normal variations in transferrin glycoform patterns could stem from genetic polymorphism, the degree of iron saturation, or the number of terminal sialic acid residues in the two *N*-linked oligosaccharide chains (*N*-glycans).[160–162] The most abundant glycoform in serum is tetrasialotransferrin, containing two biantennary carbohydrate chains making a total of four terminal sialic acid residues. Studies have shown that after prolonged heavy drinking, the abundance of transferrin molecules lacking one or both of the entire *N*-glycans (disialo- and asialotransferrin, respectively) increases appreciably (Figure 5.4.7).[163–165] The underlying mechanism that causes elevation of CDT may involve acetaldehyde-mediated inhibition of the enzymes responsible for glycosyl transfer.[166–168]

CDT is a much more specific indicator of excessive drinking than any of the other currently used laboratory tests, and it is also assumed to have better sensitivity for early detection of alcohol abuse compared to GGT.[158,169,170] However, it should be noted that a person typically needs to drink ~50 to 80 g ethanol or more daily over a period of at least 1 to 2 weeks before abnormal CDT values develop.[158,171,172] Falsely high or low CDT results are obtained in cases of uncommon genetic transferrin variants,[162,173–175] and in rare congenital disorders of glycosylation (CDG).[176,177] It is generally agreed that the CDT content should be expressed in relation to total transferrin (i.e., %CDT), instead of as an absolute amount (e.g., mg/L). This device has an analytical advantage, because an abnormally high or low serum transferrin concentration may otherwise render falsely high or low CDT results.[178–180]

Because the disialo- and asialotransferrin glycoforms lacking 2 or 4 terminal sialic acid residues are less negatively charged, and thereby have higher isoelectric points, than tetrasialotransferrin (pI

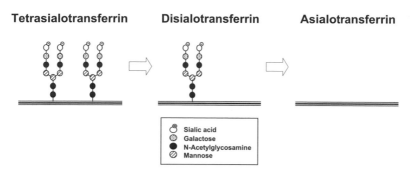

Tetrasialotransferrin   **Disialotransferrin**   **Asialotransferrin**

Sialic acid
Galactose
N-Acetylglycosamine
Mannose

Figure 5.4.7 Schematic illustration of the changes in transferrin glycosylation pattern caused by heavy alcohol consumption. Tetrasialotransferrin is normally the major glycoform (~75 to 80%), but prolonged heavy drinking results in increased levels of transferrin molecules lacking one or both of the entire *N*-glycans (disialo- and asialotransferrin, respectively).

~ 5.4), they are readily separated by techniques such as isoelectric focusing (IEF), capillary electrophoresis (CE), and ion-exchange chromatography (e.g., HPLC).[159,161,181–183] Although all these methods are laborious and rather time-consuming for routine use, especially when a large number of samples must be analyzed daily, an advantage is the visible documentation and, therefore, the reduced risk of obtaining false-positive results owing to genetic variations or other chromatographic interferences.[162] The first direct immunoassay for determination of %CDT was recently introduced, which at the same time appears to be insensitive to genetic transferrin variants.[184,185]

5.4.4.5 Phosphatidylethanol

Another non-oxidative pathway of ethanol elimination is the reaction with membrane phospholipids to produce phosphatidylethanol (PEth). PEths are unique phospholipids formed in cell membranes only in the presence of ethanol,[186,187] and have been proposed as a highly specific marker of chronic heavy drinking within the previous week(s). After alcoholic patients, with a self-reported daily intake of 60 to 300 g ethanol for at least 1 week, were admitted to a detoxification program, PEth was detectable in their blood for another 2 weeks.[188,189] Moreover, the sensitivity of PEth was reported to be greater than, or at least equal to, that of CDT.[190] Improved analytical procedures for quantitation of PEth will allow for routine clinical use of this biomarker.[191] However, a recently recognized problem, interfering with the specificity of PEth as a biomarker of prolonged heavy drinking, is the risk of artifact formation of PEth during storage if the blood sample contains ethanol.[192]

5.4.4.6 Acetaldehyde Adducts

Acetaldehyde, the proximate metabolite of ethanol oxidation, is a highly reactive chemical species and forms adducts with various biomolecules, including DNA, phospholipids, and proteins.[193–195] The binding of acetaldehyde to hepatocellular macromolecules has been suggested as the underlying cause of alcoholic liver injury.[196–198] Measurement of "whole blood-associated" acetaldehyde, acetaldehyde-hemoglobin adducts, or antibodies that recognize acetaldehyde-modified structures, have emerged as possible biochemical markers of excessive drinking.[199–202] However, some of these positive results were obtained *in vitro* after nonphysiological concentrations of acetaldehyde were administered, and the relevance of these findings *in vivo* has been a matter of debate. Although analysis of various forms of bound acetaldehyde have shown promising results, and, indeed, were found to be more sensitive for the detection of chronic excessive drinking than GGT and MCV,[203,204] more work is needed to determine the reliability and diagnostic potential for identification of heavy drinking in unselected populations. Moreover, most of the currently used methods for quantification of acetaldehyde adducts are probably too complex for routine purposes.

5.4.4.7 Other Potential Tests or Markers of Chronic Drinking

Numerous other candidate biochemical tests of alcohol use and abuse have been evaluated over the years, but only a few have gained general acceptance.[18,19] The major deficiencies are either poor sensitivity or specificity for alcohol abuse, or requiring laborious and time-consuming assay procedures. Some markers have not been tested in sufficiently large enough cohorts of subjects with use of appropriate control groups.

Several studies have reported that alcoholics after a recent or ongoing chronic drinking binge develop a lower blood, or erythrocyte, ALDH activity compared to healthy controls.[205] However, there is a considerable inter-individual overlap between heavy and moderate consumers of alcohol in this respect, and even between heavy drinkers and teetotalers.[206,207] Consequently, to obtain sufficient sensitivity, the specificity of this enzyme marker must be very low (see Section 5.4.2). In addition, several drugs, including the alcohol-sensitizing agents disulfiram (Antabuse) and cyanamide, as well as environmental factors like smoking, may cause long-lasting depression of the ALDH activity in blood.[205]

An increased level of the lysosomal enzyme β-hexosaminidase has been observed in serum from alcoholics, and was proposed as a more sensitive marker of heavy drinking than GGT.[208,209] In a study on patients undergoing detoxification, the B-isoforms of the enzyme compared well with CDT in terms of sensitivity and disappearance rate from the circulation during the alcohol withdrawal phase.[210] However, the sensitivity is much lower when unselected populations are examined,[211] and it should be noted that serum β-hexosaminidase is elevated not only after alcohol abuse but also in non-alcoholic liver disease, diabetes, hypertension, and pregnancy,[212] implying a low specificity for alcohol.

As mentioned earlier in this chapter (Section 5.4.3.3), trace amounts (~ 0.1 mg/dL) of both methanol and ethanol are produced naturally in the body during the course of intermediary metabolism or via bacteria in the colon acting on dietary carbohydrates. When the blood-ethanol concentration exceeds 20 mg/dL, the hepatic Class I isozymes of ADH are saturated and therefore fully engaged in the clearance of ethanol from the body. Methanol, however, continues to be produced from endogenous substrates and its oxidation is hindered, because of a competition with ethanol for available ADH enzymes. Furthermore, the concentration of methanol in blood increases during the drinking spree, owing to the congener content of the alcoholic beverages consumed. Recent studies have shown that this metabolic interaction between methanol and ethanol can help to distinguish between acute and chronic drinking practices.[213] After acute intake of ethanol, the BAC rarely exceeds 150 mg/dL and the corresponding blood methanol is generally below 0.5 mg/dL. However, if the BAC reaches 250 mg/dL, this suggests a period of continuous heavy drinking and the concentration of methanol now tends to increase in body fluids.[214] Depending on the intensity and duration of the drinking spree, as well as the methanol content of the drinks consumed,[81] the concentration of methanol in blood might increase appreciably and sometimes exceeds 1 mg/dL. Indeed, this concentration threshold (>1 mg/dL) is assumed to indicate continuous heavy drinking and therefore has been used as a marker of chronic alcoholism.[213] Because the metabolism of methanol is blocked after BAC exceeds 20 mg/dL (see Figure 5.4.3), the longer lasting the drinking spree so that BAC never drops below 20 mg/dL, the higher will be the steady-state concentration of methanol. The analysis of methanol as well as other biochemical markers of alcohol abuse has been used in Germany, to decide on re-granting of driving licenses and whether a convicted drunk driver should receive treatment or punishment for this traffic crime.[213]

5.4.5   Routine Clinical Use of Biochemical Tests for Excessive Drinking

5.4.5.1   Single Tests or Test Combinations?

As already indicated, most of the currently available standard laboratory tests lack sufficient sensitivity and/or specificity to warrant their use as sole evidence of heavy drinking. To increase diagnostic sensitivity, various combinations of markers have therefore been evaluated, such as two or more of GGT, MCV, AST, ALT, and CDT, as well as many others.[215–217] Even though combinations of markers tend to increase diagnostic sensitivity, at the same time this approach might reduce diagnostic specificity.[218–220] Furthermore, using multiple markers tends to complicate the interpretation of results and also increases the overall costs.

Nevertheless, a useful approach is to combine markers each independently associated with heavy drinking.[26] Whereas a strong association is usually obtained between liver function tests like GGT, AST, and ALT, this is not the case for GGT and CDT.[221–223] Rather, in one study, several of the highest CDT levels were observed in alcoholic subjects possessing normal or only moderately elevated GGT values, and vice versa.[222] This was further confirmed by another study in which a negative correlation between CDT and the severity of liver disease was reported.[224] It seems that the combined use of GGT and CDT significantly improves identification of heavy drinkers and those at risk of becoming dependent on alcohol.[219,222,223]

A combination of short-term and long-term markers of alcohol consumption has also been used successfully during outpatient treatment of alcohol-dependent subjects.[128,129] Finding an increased CDT suggests the person has returned to continuous heavy drinking after a period of abstinence, whereas normal CDT but instead a positive morning breath alcohol test or, preferably, other more sensitive biomarkers of acute alcohol intake, such as urinary 5HTOL, EtG or EtS, will identify single lapses.

5.4.5.2   Screening for Excessive Drinking in Unselected Populations

Many biochemical screening markers used for the early detection of harmful consumption of alcohol give excellent results (i.e., high sensitivity and specificity), when studies are carried out on selected populations, e.g., alcoholics undergoing detoxification as compared to moderate drinkers or teetotalers. By contrast, in studies on single individuals, and when screening people from the general population, most tests are less satisfactory, mainly because of a considerable overlap between the values obtained for heavy and moderate drinkers. Furthermore, because certain medical and environmental conditions may influence the test results, false positives are not uncommon. An example illustrates this point. Assuming that the prevalence of excessive drinking is 10%, a marker with 90% sensitivity and specificity will correctly identify 9 of 10 heavy drinkers in a study population of 100, but, at the same time, incorrectly identify 9 of 90 healthy subjects as having drinking problems. Thus, the chance of a correct classification under these conditions is only 50% (the positive predictive value). For most of the currently available laboratory markers of alcohol abuse, a single abnormal test result may thus be difficult to interpret in an unequivocal way, unless confirmed in a repeated test or by complementary testing to exclude other potential causes.

Another important issue is the time delay between drinking and sampling. Because different alcohol biomarkers have different life spans, the time since the last drink should always be considered, when evaluating the sensitivity of a test. The most widely used markers GGT and CDT, for example, have biological half-lives of ~2 to 3 weeks, so the specimen should preferably be collected no later than 1 week after admission to hospital or during alcohol withdrawal; otherwise the sensitivity of the test will be reduced considerably.

5.4.5.3 Treatment Follow-Up of Alcohol-Dependent Patients

Monitoring changes over time in a number of biomarkers of excessive drinking, such as CDT and GGT, during a 2- to 4-week period of alcohol withdrawal (e.g., during hospitalization or other inpatient treatment, or treatment with disulfiram), allows the most sensitive single marker to be identified.[222,225] If values normalize on withdrawal, this confirms that alcohol was most likely the cause of the abnormal test results. After discharge from the hospital, monitoring excessive drinking should continue on a routine basis in connection with return visits to the clinic. This facilitates early identification of relapse,[226] when combined with an early morning breath alcohol test or a more sensitive biomarker of acute drinking such as 5HTOL, EtG, and EtS.[26] The optimal testing frequency depends in part on the life span of the marker in question.[227] Giving feedback to patients about the results of the tests, for example, by presenting these graphically, can be very informative and may also improve self-report and treatment outcome.[228,229] However, if this strategy is used, it is imperative that the results are reliable (i.e., using highly specific tests); otherwise patients may become demoralized and lose faith in the use of laboratory markers.

The use of repeated testing also makes it possible to use individualized instead of population-based reference limits for each biomarker, thereby improving considerably the reliability of results.[129,149] The recommended cutoff limits between normal and abnormal are usually based on a Gaussian distribution in healthy controls. However, because of inter-individual variations, some subjects with very low baseline values probably need to drink much larger amounts of alcohol than those with considerably higher baseline values, in order to exceed the critical threshold limit. Therefore, by introducing individualized cutoffs, detection of relapse drinking can be significantly improved.[129,230]

5.4.6 Trait Markers of Alcohol Dependence

Eugenic studies conducted during the late 1800s demonstrated that excessive drinking, drunkenness, and alcohol dependence run in families. Unequivocal evidence for a genetic component in alcoholism and addiction came from the widely publicized adoption and twin studies.[231,232] Later research dealing with the inheritance of alcohol dependence led to the definitions of *type 1* and *type 2* subtypes, which have become widely accepted.[233] It seems that some people are more predisposed to becoming dependent on alcohol when they start to drink regularly, and, for this reason, efforts have been made to develop trait markers of alcohol dependence.[234–236]

Examples of such genetic or trait markers of a vulnerability to develop alcohol dependence include various neurotransmitter systems, such as the dopamine D_2 receptor gene, the activity of monoamine oxidase (MAO), and adenylyl cyclase (AC) enzymes and the serotonin transporter (5HTT), as well as the neuropeptides (e.g., neuropeptide Y, NPY), which are all involved in various aspects of compulsive, impulsive, and addictive behavior, including pleasure seeking and reward areas of the brain.[236,237] A significantly lower activity of MAO in blood platelets of alcoholics compared to controls was reported,[238] although concerns have been raised about the exact mechanism causing this difference.[239] Tobacco use, for example, which is common in alcoholics, can also lower MAO activity.[240]

Hitherto, the only clear-cut evidence linking alcohol use and abuse to genetics is the polymorphisms observed for ADH and ALDH enzymes in Japanese and some other Asian populations.[241] The presence of an inactive mitochondrial ALDH2 isozyme makes these individuals hypersensitive to acetaldehyde, which reaches an abnormally high concentration in blood even after drinking small amounts of alcohol. This inborn Antabuse-like reaction creates an aversion to alcohol, which influences drinking behavior and decreases the risk of becoming dependent on alcohol and developing alcoholic liver disease.[242]

5.4.7 Conclusions

Alcohol abuse and dependence are major risk factors for serious ill-health, social, and economic problems, and excessive drinking is a common cause of injuries and premature death.[243] Early identification of those who overindulge in drinking enhances the possibility of finding a successful treatment. However, obtaining accurate information about a person's drinking habits represents one of the major problems in the detection of excessive alcohol consumption. Self-reports of drinking practices during interview or in diagnostic questionnaires are widely used by clinicians for this purpose. Experience has shown that people with alcohol-related problems may deliberately deny or underreport the actual amounts they consume, at least in the early stages of misuse. For this reason, erroneous classification and underdiagnosis of alcohol abuse is fairly common.[146,244,245] To rectify this problem, efforts have been made to discover biochemical and hematological abnormalities associated with excessive drinking. These markers need to be sufficiently sensitive and specific to identify heavy drinkers, even when the person refrains from drinking prior to visiting a physician.

The perfect biochemical test should be specific for alcohol and also exhibit high sensitivity to hazardous drinking habits. Furthermore, the test should be inexpensive and yield rapid results with easily available specimens such as urine, saliva, or blood. Measuring ethanol in body fluids or breath is of course the most highly specific alcohol test, but, because ethanol is eliminated fairly rapidly from the body, the sensitivity of this test is low. Most of the currently available laboratory markers perform well, when selected high-risk populations are being compared, but they are less satisfactory in randomly selected individuals. An alcohol breath test is simple to perform but this needs to be combined with a battery of more sensitive biochemical indicators, as discussed in this chapter, such as GGT and CDT. When the aim is to test for acute alcohol intake or relapse, the recommended markers besides ethanol are 5HTOL, EtG, or EtS.

Alcohol is a legal, socially accepted, recreational drug, although the patterns of alcohol consumption, in terms of quantity and the choice of beverage, differ widely between individuals and nations. Furthermore, a pattern of drinking that might be harmless to one individual might damage health in another, owing to various genetic influences and risk of becoming dependent on alcohol (see Chapter 5.1). Over the past 10 to 15 years, considerable interest has developed in using biochemical markers to document alcohol use and abuse in a more objective way, compared with clinical interviews and screening questionnaires about the negative consequences and experiences after a drinking spree. Identifying people at greatest risk for developing alcohol problems is a challenge, and positive findings will ensure adequate and early treatment and rehabilitation programs. In this connection, biochemical markers have emerged as essential tools to verify abstinence and to detect relapse drinking in patients undergoing treatment for alcoholism.

REFERENCES

1. Doll, R., The benefit of alcohol in moderation. *Drug Alcohol Rev.*, 17, 353, 1998.
2. Hanson, G.R. and Li, T.K., Public health implications of excessive alcohol consumption. *J. Am. Med. Assoc.*, 289, 1031, 2003.
3. Room, R., Babor, T., and Rehm, J., Alcohol and public health. *Lancet*, 365, 519, 2005.
4. Cherpitel, C.J., Drinking patterns and problems and drinking in the injury event: an analysis of emergency room patients by ethnicity. *Drug Alcohol Rev.*, 17, 423, 1998.
5. Connor, J., Norton, R., Ameratunga, S., and Jackson, R., The contribution of alcohol to serious car crash injuries. *Epidemiology*, 15, 337, 2004.
6. Richardson, A. and Budd, T., Young adults, alcohol, crime and disorder. *Crim. Behav. Ment. Health*, 13, 5, 2003.
7. Brewer, R.D. and Swahn, M.H., Binge drinking and violence. *J. Am. Med. Assoc.*, 294, 616, 2005.

8. Serdula, M.K., Brewer, R.D., Gillespie, C., Denny, C.H., and Mokdad, A., Trends in alcohol use and binge drinking, 1985–1999: results of a multi-state survey. *Am. J. Prev. Med.,* 26, 294, 2004.

9. Borges, G., Cherpitel, C., and Mittleman, M., Risk of injury after alcohol consumption: a case-crossover study in the emergency department. *Soc. Sci. Med.,* 58, 1191, 2004.

10. Hall, W., British drinking: a suitable case for treatment? *Br. Med. J.,* 331, 527, 2005.

11. Meyerhoff, D.J., Bode, C., Nixon, S.J., de Bruin, E.A., Bode, J.C., and Seitz, H.K., Health risks of chronic moderate and heavy alcohol consumption: how much is too much? *Alcohol Clin. Exp. Res.,* 29, 1334, 2005.

12. Jellinek, E.M., *The Disease Concept of Alcoholism,* Hillhouse Press, New Haven, CT, 1960.

13. Fuller, R.K., Lee, K.K., and Gordis, E., Validity of self-report in alcoholism research: results of a Veterans Administration cooperative study. *Alcohol Clin. Exp. Res.,* 12, 201, 1988.

14. Ness, D.E. and Ende, J., Denial in the medical interview: recognition and management. *J. Am. Med. Assoc.,* 272, 1777, 1994.

15. Wilson, R.S., *Diagnosis of Alcohol Abuse,* CRC Press, Boca Raton, FL, 1989.

16. Mayfield, D., McLeod, G., and Hall, P., The CAGE questionnaire: validation of a new alcoholism screening instrument. *Am. J. Psychiatry,* 131, 1121, 1974.

17. Selzer, M.L., The Michigan Alcoholism Screening Test: the quest for a new diagnostic instrument. *Am. J. Psychiatry,* 127, 89, 1981.

18. Mihas, A.A. and Tavassoli, M., Laboratory markers of ethanol intake and abuse: a critical appraisal. *Am. J. Med. Sci.,* 303, 415, 1992.

19. Goldberg, D.M. and Kapur, B.M., Enzymes and circulating proteins as markers of alcohol abuse. *Clin. Chim. Acta,* 226, 191, 1994.

20. Conigrave, K.M., Saunders, J.B., and Whitfield, J.B., Diagnostic tests for alcohol consumption. *Alcohol Alcohol.,* 30, 13, 1995.

21. Helander, A., Biological markers in alcoholism. *J. Neural Transm.,* 66(Suppl.), 15, 2003.

22. Salaspuro, M., Characteristics of laboratory markers in alcohol-related organ damage. *Scand. J. Gastroenterol.,* 24, 769, 1989.

23. Rosman, A.S. and Lieber, C.S., Diagnostic utility of laboratory tests in alcoholic liver disease. *Clin. Chem.,* 40, 1641, 1994.

24. Wilson, R.S., Mohs, M.E., Eskelson, C., Sampliner, R.E., and Hartmann, B., Identification of alcohol abuse and alcoholism with biological parameters. *Alcohol Clin. Exp. Res.,* 10, 364, 1986.

25. Sharpe, P.C., Biochemical detection and monitoring of alcohol abuse and abstinence. *Ann. Clin. Biochem.,* 38, 652, 2001.

26. Helander, A., Biological markers of alcohol use and abuse in theory and practice, in *Alcohol in Health and Disease,* Agarwal, D.P. and Seitz, H.K., Eds., Marcel Dekker, New York, 2001, 177.

27. Hermansson, U., Helander, A., Huss, A., Brandt, L., and Rönnberg, S., The Alcohol Use Disorders Identification Test (AUDIT) and carbohydrate-deficient transferrin (CDT) in a routine workplace health examination. *Alcohol Clin. Exp. Res.,* 24, 180, 2000.

28. Hermansson, U., Knutsson, A., Brandt, L., Huss, A., Rönnberg, S., and Helander, A., Screening for high-risk and elevated alcohol consumption in day and shift workers by use of the AUDIT and CDT. *Occup. Med.* (London), 53, 518, 2003.

29. Helander, A., Beck, O., and Jones, A.W., Distinguishing ingested ethanol from microbial formation by analysis of urinary 5-hydroxytryptophol and 5-hydroxyindoleacetic acid. *J. Forensic Sci.,* 40, 95, 1995.

30. Helander, A. and Jones, A.W., 5-HTOL — a new biochemical alcohol marker with forensic applications. *Lakartidningen,* 99, 3950, 2002.

31. Bergström, J., Helander, A., and Jones, A.W., Ethyl glucuronide concentrations in two successive urinary voids from drinking drivers: relationship to creatinine content and blood and urine ethanol concentrations. *Forensic Sci. Int.,* 133, 86, 2003.

32. Jones, A.W., Eklund, A., and Helander, A., Misleading results of ethanol analysis in urine specimens from rape victims suffering from diabetes. *J. Clin. Forensic Med.,* 7, 144, 2000.

33. Balldin, J., Berglund, M., Borg, S., Månsson, M., Bendtsen, P., Franck, J., Gustafsson, L., Halldin, J., Nilsson, L.H., Stolt, G., and Willander, A., A 6-month controlled naltrexone study: combined effect with cognitive behavioral therapy in outpatient treatment of alcohol dependence. *Alcohol Clin. Exp. Res.,* 27, 1142, 2003.

34. Anton, R.F., Moak, D.H., Latham, P., Waid, L.R., Myrick, H., Voronin, K., Thevos, A., Wang, W., and Woolson, R., Naltrexone combined with either cognitive behavioral or motivational enhancement therapy for alcohol dependence. *J. Clin. Psychopharmacol.,* 25, 349, 2005.

35. Zweig, M.H. and Campbell, G., Receiver-operating characteristic (ROC) plots: a fundamental evaluation tool in clinical medicine. *Clin. Chem.,* 39, 561, 1993.

36. Henderson, A.R., Assessing test accuracy and its clinical consequences: a primer for receiver operating characteristic curve analysis. *Ann. Clin. Biochem.,* 30, 521, 1993.

37. Helander, A., Beck, O., and Jones, A.W., Laboratory testing for recent alcohol consumption: comparison of ethanol, methanol, and 5-hydroxytryptophol. *Clin. Chem.,* 42, 618, 1996.

38. Jones, A.W. and Helander, A., Disclosing recent drinking after alcohol has been cleared from the body. *J. Anal. Toxicol.,* 20, 141, 1996.

39. Helander, A., von Wachenfeldt, J., Hiltunen, A., Beck, O., Liljeberg, P., and Borg, S., Comparison of urinary 5-hydroxytryptophol, breath ethanol, and self-report for detection of recent alcohol use during outpatient treatment: a study on methadone patients. *Drug Alcohol Depend.,* 56, 33, 1999.

40. Jones, A.W., Measuring alcohol in blood and breath for forensic purposes: a historical review. *Forensic Sci. Rev.,* 8, 13, 1996.

41. Dubowski, K.M. and Caplan, Y.H., Alcohol testing in the workplace, in *Medicolegal Aspects of Alcohol,* Garriott, J.C., Ed., Lawyers & Judges, Tucson, 1996, 439.

42. Haeckel, R. and Hanecke, P., Application of saliva for drug monitoring. An *in vivo* model for transmembrane transport. *Eur. J. Clin. Chem. Clin. Biochem.,* 34, 171, 1996.

43. Toennes, S.W., Kauert, G.F., Steinmeyer, S., and Moeller, M.R., Driving under the influence of drugs — evaluation of analytical data of drugs in oral fluid, serum and urine, and correlation with impairment symptoms. *Forensic Sci. Int.,* 152, 149, 2005.

44. Jones, A.W., Measuring ethanol in saliva with the QED enzymatic test device: comparison of results with blood and breath-alcohol concentration. *J. Anal. Toxicol.,* 19, 169, 1995.

45. Degutis, L.C., Rabinovici, R., Sabbaj, A., Mascia, R., and D'Onofrio, G., The saliva strip test is an accurate method to determine blood alcohol concentration in trauma patients. *Acad. Emerg. Med.,* 11, 885, 2004.

46. Jones, A.W., Norberg, A., and Hahn, R.G., Concentration-time profiles of ethanol in arterial and venous blood and end-expired breath during and after intravenous infusion. *J. Forensic Sci.,* 42, 1088, 1997.

47. Jones, A.W., Reference limits for urine/blood ratios of ethanol in two successive voids from drinking drivers. *J. Anal. Toxicol.,* 26, 333, 2002.

48. Bendtsen, P., Jones, A.W., and Helander, A., Urinary excretion of methanol and 5-hydroxytryptophol as biochemical markers of recent drinking in the hangover state. *Alcohol Alcohol.,* 33, 431, 1998.

49. Pawan, G.L.S. and Grice, K., Distribution of alcohol in urine and sweat after drinking. *Lancet,* 2, 1016, 1968.

50. Swift, R.M., Martin, C.S., Swette, L., LaConti, A., and Kackley, N., Studies on a wearable, electronic, transdermal alcohol sensor. *Alcohol Clin. Exp. Res.,* 16, 721, 1992.

51. Phillips, M., Greenberg, J., and Andrzejewski, J., Evaluation of the Alcopatch, a transdermal dosimeter for monitoring alcohol consumption. *Alcohol Clin. Exp. Res.,* 19, 1547, 1995.

52. Cone, E.J., Hillsgrove, M.J., Jenkins, A.J., Keenan, R.M., and Darwin, W.D., Sweat testing for heroin, cocaine, and metabolites. *J. Anal. Toxicol.,* 18, 298, 1994.

53. Huestis, M.A., Cone, E.J., Wong, C.J., Umbricht, A., and Preston, K.L., Monitoring opiate use in substance abuse treatment patients with sweat and urine drug testing. *J. Anal. Toxicol.,* 24, 509, 2000.

54. Phillips, M., Sweat patch test for alcohol consumption: rapid assay with an electrochemical detector. *Alcohol Clin. Exp. Res.,* 6, 532, 1982.

55. Swift, R., Davidson, D., and Fitz, E., Transdermal alcohol detection with a new miniaturized sensor, the miniTAS. *Alcohol Clin. Exp. Res.,* 20, 45A, 1996.

56. Swift, R., Direct measurement of alcohol and its metabolites. *Addiction,* 98(Suppl. 2), 73, 2003.

57. Mani, J.C., Pietruszko, R., and Theorell, H., Methanol activity of alcohol dehydrogenase from human liver, horse liver, and yeast. *Arch. Biochem. Biophys.,* 140, 52, 1970.

58. Eriksson, C.J.P. and Fukunaga, T., Human blood acetaldehyde (update 1992). *Alcohol Alcohol.,* 2(Suppl.), 9, 1993.

59. Helander, A., Löwenmo, C., and Johansson, M., Distribution of acetaldehyde in human blood: effects of ethanol and treatment with disulfiram. *Alcohol Alcohol.*, 28, 461, 1993.

60. Jones, A.W., Measuring and reporting the concentration of acetaldehyde in human breath. *Alcohol Alcohol.*, 30, 271, 1995.

61. Lundquist, F., Production and utilization of free acetate in man. *Nature,* 193, 579, 1962.

62. Nuutinen, H., Lindros, K., Hekali, P., and Salaspuro, M., Elevated blood acetate as indicator of fast ethanol elimination in chronic alcoholics. *Alcohol,* 2, 623, 1985.

63. Korri, U.-M., Nuutinen, H., and Salaspuro, M., Increased blood acetate: a new laboratory marker of alcoholism and heavy drinking. *Alcohol Clin. Exp. Res.,* 9, 468, 1985.

64. Roine, R.P., Korri, U.-M., Ylikahri, R., Pentillä, A., Pikkarainen, J., and Salapuro, M., Increased serum acetate as a marker of problem drinking among drunken drivers. *Alcohol Alcohol.,* 23, 123, 1988.

65. Goldberger, B.A., Cone, E.J., and Kadehjian, L., Unsuspected ethanol ingestion through soft drinks and flavored beverages. *J. Anal. Toxicol.,* 20, 332, 1996.

66. Logan, B.K. and Distefano, S., Ethanol content of various foods and soft drinks and their potential for interference with a breath-alcohol test. *J. Anal. Toxicol.,* 22, 181, 1998.

67. Logan, B.K. and Jones, A.W., Endogenous ethanol "auto-brewery syndrome" as a drunk-driving defence challenge. *Med. Sci. Law,* 40, 206, 2000.

68. Ostrovsky, Y.M., Endogenous ethanol — its metabolic, behavioral and biomedical significance. *Alcohol,* 3, 239, 1986.

69. Krebs, H.A. and Perkins, J.R., The physiological role of liver alcohol dehydrogenase. *Biochem. J.,* 118, 635, 1970.

70. Sprung, R., Bonte, W., Rüdell, E., Domke, M., and Frauenrath, C., Zum Problem des endogenen Alkohols. *Blutalkohol,* 18, 65, 1981.

71. Haffner, H.-T., Graw, M., Besserer, K., Blicke, U., and Henssge, C., Endogenous methanol: variability in concentration and rate of production. Evidence of a deep compartment? *Forensic Sci. Int.,* 79, 145, 1996.

72. Jones, A.W., Elimination half-life of methanol during hangover. *Pharmacol. Toxicol.,* 60, 217, 1987.

73. Haffner, H.-T., Wehner, H.D., Scheytt, K.D., and Besserer, K., The elimination kinetics of methanol and the influence of ethanol. *Int. J. Leg. Med.,* 105, 111, 1992.

74. Helander, A. and Eriksson, C.J., Laboratory tests for acute alcohol consumption: results of the WHO/ISBRA Study on State and Trait Markers of Alcohol Use and Dependence. *Alcohol Clin. Exp. Res.,* 26, 1070, 2002.

75. Jacobsen, D., Jansen, H., Wiik-Larsen, E., Bredesen, J.-E., and Halvorsen, S., Studies on methanol poisoning. *Acta. Med. Scand.,* 212, 5, 1982.

76. Prabhakaran, V., Ettler, H., and Mills, A., Methanol poisoning: two cases with similar plasma methanol concentrations but different outcomes. *Can. Med. Assoc. J.,* 148, 981, 1993.

77. Hantson, P., Wittebole, X., and Haufroid, V., Ethanol therapy for methanol poisoning: duration and problems. *Eur. J. Emerg. Med.,* 9, 278, 2002.

78. Jacobsen, D. and McMartin, K.E., Antidotes for methanol and ethylene glycol poisoning. *J. Toxicol. Clin. Toxicol.,* 35, 127, 1997.

79. Brent, J., McMartin, K., Phillips, S., Aaron, C., and Kulig, K., Fomepizole for the treatment of methanol poisoning. *N. Engl. J. Med.,* 344, 424, 2001.

80. McAnalley, B.H., Chemistry of alcoholic beverages, in *Medicolegal Aspects of Alcohol*, Garriott, J.C., Ed., Lawyers & Judges, Tucson, 1996, 1.

81. Gilg, T., Alkoholbedingte Fahruntuchtigkeit. *Rechtsmedizin,* 15, 97, 2005.

82. Majchrowicz, E. and Mendelson, J.H., Blood methanol concentrations during experimentally induced ethanol intoxication in alcoholics. *J. Pharmacol. Exp. Ther.,* 179, 293, 1971.

83. Iffland, R., New ways to use biochemical indicators of alcohol abuse to regrant licences in a fairer manner after drunken driving in Germany. *Alcohol Alcohol.,* 31, 619, 1996.

84. Haffner, H.T., Banger, M., Graw, M., Besserer, K., and Brink, T., The kinetics of methanol elimination in alcoholics and the influence of ethanol. *Forensic Sci. Int.,* 89, 129, 1997.

85. Graw, M., Haffner, H.T., Althaus, L., Besserer, K., and Voges, S., Invasion and distribution of methanol. *Arch. Toxicol.,* 74, 313, 2000.

86. Taucher, J., Lagg, A., Hansel, A., Vogel, W., and Lindinger, W., Methanol in human breath. *Alcohol Clin. Exp. Res.,* 19, 1147, 1995.

87. Lindinger, W., Taucher, J., Jordan, A., Hansel, A., and Vogel, W., Endogenous production of methanol after the consumption of fruit. *Alcohol Clin. Exp. Res.,* 21, 939, 1997.

88. Bachmann, C. and Bickel, M.H., History of drug metabolism: the first half of the 20th century. *Drug Metab. Rev.,* 16, 185, 1985.

89. Neubauer, O., Uber Glukuronsaure paarung bei Stoffen der Fettreihe. *Arch. Exp. Pathol. Pharmacol.,* 46, 133, 1901.

90. Kamil, I.A., Smith, J.N., and Williams, R.T., A new aspect of ethanol metabolism: isolation of ethyl glucuronide. *Biochem. J.,* 51, 32, 1952.

91. Jaakonmaki, P.I., Knox, K.L., Horning, E.C., and Horning, M.G., The characterization by gas-liquid chromatography of ethyl β-D-glucosiduronic acid as a metabolite of ethanol in rat and man. *Eur. J. Pharmacol.,* 1, 63, 1967.

92. Hanai, T., Chromatography and computational chemical analysis for drug discovery. *Curr. Med. Chem.,* 12, 501, 2005.

93. Dahl, H., Stephanson, N., Beck, O., and Helander, A., Comparison of urinary excretion characteristics of ethanol and ethyl glucuronide. *J. Anal. Toxicol.,* 26, 201, 2002.

94. Helander, A. and Beck, O., Mass spectrometric identification of ethyl sulfate as an ethanol metabolite in humans. *Clin. Chem.,* 50, 936, 2004.

95. Schmitt, G., Aderjan, R., Keller, T., and Wu, M., Ethyl glucuronide: an unusual ethanol metabolite in humans. Synthesis, analytical data, and determination in serum and urine. *J. Anal. Toxicol.,* 19, 91, 1995.

96. Schmitt, G., Droenner, P., Skopp, G., and Aderjan, R., Ethyl glucuronide concentration in serum of human volunteers, teetotalers, and suspected drinking drivers. *J. Forensic Sci.,* 42, 1099, 1997.

97. Helander, A. and Beck, O., Ethyl sulfate: a metabolite of ethanol in humans and a potential biomarker of acute alcohol intake. *J. Anal. Toxicol.,* 29, 270, 2005.

98. Sarkola, T., Dahl, H., Eriksson, C.J., and Helander, A., Urinary ethyl glucuronide and 5-hydroxytryptophol levels during repeated ethanol ingestion in healthy human subjects. *Alcohol Alcohol.,* 38, 347, 2003.

99. Skopp, G., Schmitt, G., Potsch, L., Dronner, P., Aderjan, R., and Mattern, R., Ethyl glucuronide in human hair. *Alcohol Alcohol.,* 35, 283, 2000.

100. Yegles, M., Labarthe, A., Auwarter, V., Hartwig, S., Vater, H., Wennig, R., and Pragst, F., Comparison of ethyl glucuronide and fatty acid ethyl ester concentrations in hair of alcoholics, social drinkers and teetotallers. *Forensic Sci. Int.,* 145, 167, 2004.

101. Stephanson, N., Dahl, H., Helander, A., and Beck, O., Direct quantification of ethyl glucuronide in clinical urine samples by liquid chromatography-mass spectrometry. *Ther. Drug Monit.,* 24, 645, 2002.

102. Nishikawa, M., Tsuchihashi, H., Miki, A., Katagi, M., Schmitt, G., Zimmer, H., Keller, T., and Aderjan, R., Determination of ethyl glucuronide, a minor metabolite of ethanol, in human serum by liquid chromatography-electrospray ionization mass spectrometry. *J. Chromatogr. B Biomed. Sci. Appl.,* 726, 105, 1999.

103. Seidl, S., Wurst, F.M., and Alt, A., Ethyl glucuronide — a biological marker for recent alcohol consumption. *Addict. Biol.,* 6, 205, 2001.

104. Helander, A. and Dahl, H., Urinary tract infection: a risk factor for false-negative urinary ethyl glucuronide but not ethyl sulfate in the detection of recent alcohol consumption. *Clin. Chem.,* 51, 1728, 2005.

105. Schneider, H. and Glatt, H., Sulpho-conjugation of ethanol in humans *in vivo* and by individual sulphotransferase forms *in vitro. Biochem. J.,* 383, 543, 2004.

106. Dresen, S., Weinmann, W., and Wurst, F.M., Forensic confirmatory analysis of ethyl sulfate — a new marker for alcohol consumption — by liquid-chromatography/electrospray ionization/tandem mass spectrometry. *J. Am. Soc. Mass. Spectrom.,* 15, 1644, 2004.

107. Deng, X.S., Bludeau, P., and Deitrich, R.A., Formation of ethyl nitrite *in vivo* after ethanol administration. *Alcohol,* 34, 217, 2004.

108. Lange, L.G. and Sobel, B.E., Myocardial metabolites of ethanol. *Circ. Res.,* 52, 479, 1983.

109. Laposata, M., Hasaba, A., Best, C.A., Yoerger, D.M., McQuillan, B.M., Salem, R.O., Refaai, M.A., and Soderberg, B.L., Fatty acid ethyl esters: recent observations. *Prostaglandins Leukot. Essent. Fatty Acids,* 67, 193, 2002.

110. Kaphalia, B.S., Cai, P., Khan, M.F., Okorodudu, A.O., and Ansari, G.A., Fatty acid ethyl esters: markers of alcohol abuse and alcoholism. *Alcohol,* 34, 151, 2004.

111. Soderberg, B.L., Salem, R.O., Best, C.A., Cluette-Brown, J.E., and Laposata, M., Fatty acid ethyl esters. Ethanol metabolites that reflect ethanol intake. *Am. J. Clin. Pathol.,* 119(Suppl.), S94, 2003.

112. Bisaga, A., Laposata, M., Xie, S., and Evans, S.M., Comparison of serum fatty acid ethyl esters and urinary 5-hydroxytryptophol as biochemical markers of recent ethanol consumption. *Alcohol Alcohol.,* 40, 214, 2005.

113. Borucki, K., Schreiner, R., Dierkes, J., Jachau, K., Krause, D., Westphal, S., Wurst, F.M., Luley, C., and Schmidt-Gayk, H., Detection of recent ethanol intake with new markers: comparison of fatty acid ethyl esters in serum and of ethyl glucuronide and the ratio of 5-hydroxytryptophol to 5-hydroxyindole acetic acid in urine. *Alcohol Clin. Exp. Res.,* 29, 781, 2005.

114. Nanji, A.A., Su, G.L., Laposata, M., and French, S.W., Pathogenesis of alcoholic liver disease — recent advances. *Alcohol Clin. Exp. Res.,* 26, 731, 2002.

115. Davis, V.E., Brown, H., Huff, J.A., and Cashaw, J.L., The alteration of serotonin metabolism to 5-hydroxytryptophol by ethanol ingestion in man. *J. Lab. Clin. Med.,* 69, 132, 1967.

116. Helander, A., Beck, O., Jacobsson, G., Löwenmo, C., and Wikström, T., Time course of ethanol-induced changes in serotonin metabolism. *Life Sci.,* 53, 847, 1993.

117. Lahti, R.A. and Majchrowicz, E., Ethanol and acetaldehyde effects on metabolism and binding of biogenic amines. *Q. J. Stud. Alc.,* 35, 1, 1974.

118. Feldstein, A. and Williamson, O., 5-Hydroxytryptamine metabolism in rat brain and liver homogenates. *Br. J. Pharmacol.,* 34, 38, 1968.

119. Svensson, S., Some, M., Lundsjö, A., Helander, A., Cronholm, T., and Höög, J.O., Activities of human alcohol dehydrogenases in the metabolic pathways of ethanol and serotonin. *Eur. J. Biochem.,* 262, 324, 1999.

120. Voltaire, A., Beck, O., and Borg, S., Urinary 5-hydroxytryptophol: a possible marker of recent alcohol consumption. *Alcohol Clin. Exp. Res.,* 16, 281, 1992.

121. Helander, A., Beck, O., and Borg, S., The use of 5-hydroxytryptophol as an alcohol intake marker. *Alcohol Alcohol.,* Suppl. 2, 497, 1994.

122. Beck, O. and Helander, A., 5-Hydroxytryptophol as a marker for recent alcohol intake. *Addiction,* 98(Suppl. 2), 63, 2003.

123. Helander, A., Wikström, T., Löwenmo, C., Jacobsson, G., and Beck, O., Urinary excretion of 5-hydroxyindole-3-acetic acid and 5-hydroxytryptophol after oral loading with serotonin. *Life Sci.,* 50, 1207, 1992.

124. Helander, A., Walzer, C., Beck, O., Balant, L., Borg, S., and Wartburg, J.-P.V., Influence of genetic variation in alcohol and aldehyde dehydrogenase on serotonin metabolism. *Life Sci.,* 55, 359, 1994.

125. Beck, O., Helander, A., Carlsson, S., and Borg, S., Changes in serotonin metabolism during treatment with the aldehyde dehydrogenase inhibitors disulfiram and cyanamide. *Pharmacol. Toxicol.,* 77, 323, 1995.

126. Johnson, R.D., Lewis, R.J., Canfield, D.V., and Blank, C.L., Accurate assignment of ethanol origin in postmortem urine: liquid chromatographic-mass spectrometric determination of serotonin metabolites. *J. Chromatogr. B Anal. Technol. Biomed. Life Sci.,* 805, 223, 2004.

127. Stephanson, N., Dahl, H., Helander, A., and Beck, O., Determination of urinary 5-hydroxytryptophol glucuronide by liquid chromatography-mass spectrometry. *J. Chromatogr. B Anal. Technol. Biomed. Life Sci.,* 816, 107, 2005.

128. Voltaire Carlsson, A., Hiltunen, A.J., Beck, O., Stibler, H., and Borg, S., Detection of relapses in alcohol-dependent patients: comparison of carbohydrate-deficient transferrin in serum, 5-hydroxytryptophol in urine, and self-reports. *Alcohol Clin. Exp. Res.,* 17, 703, 1993.

129. Borg, S., Helander, A., Voltaire Carlsson, A., and Högstrom Brandt, A.M., Detection of relapses in alcohol-dependent patients using carbohydrate-deficient transferrin: improvement with individualized reference levels during long-term monitoring. *Alcohol Clin. Exp. Res.,* 19, 961, 1995.

130. Spies, C.D., Herpell, J., Beck, O., Muller, C., Pragst, F., Borg, S., and Helander, A., The urinary ratio of 5-hydroxytryptophol to 5-hydroxyindole-3-acetic acid in surgical patients with chronic alcohol misuse. *Alcohol,* 17, 19, 1999.

131. Helander, A., Beck, O., and Jones, A.W., Urinary 5HTOL/5HIAA as biochemical marker of postmortem ethanol synthesis. *Lancet,* 340, 1159, 1992.

132. Hagan, R.L. and Helander, A., Urinary 5-hydroxytryptophol following acute ethanol consumption: clinical evaluation and potential aviation applications. *Aviat. Space Environ. Med.,* 68, 30, 1997.

133. Johnson, R.D., Lewis, R.J., Canfield, D.V., Dubowski, K.M., and Blank, C.L., Utilizing the urinary 5-HTOL/5-HIAA ratio to determine ethanol origin in civil aviation accident victims. *J. Forensic Sci.,* 50, 670, 2005.

134. Rosalki, S.B. and Rau, D., Serum gamma-glutamyl transpeptidase activity in alcoholism. *Clin. Chim. Acta,* 39, 41, 1972.

135. Rosalki, S.B., gamma-Glutamyl transpeptidase. *Adv. Clin. Chem.,* 17, 53, 1975.

136. Nemesánszky, E. and Lott, J.A., gamma-Glutamyltransferase and its isoenzymes: progress and problems. *Clin. Chem.,* 31, 797, 1985.

137. Shaw, S. and Lieber, C.S., Mechanism of increased gamma glutamyl transpeptidase after chronic alcohol consumption: hepatic microsomal induction rather than dietary imbalance. *Substance Alcohol Actions/Misuse,* 1, 423, 1980.

138. Wu, A., Slavin, G., and Levi, A.J., Elevated serum gamma-glutamyl-transferase (transpeptidase) and histological liver damage in alcoholism. *Am. J. Gastroenterol.,* 65, 318, 1976.

139. Salaspuro, M., Use of enzymes for the diagnosis of alcohol related organ damage. *Enzyme,* 37, 87, 1987.

140. Nilssen, O. and Forde, O.H., Seven-year longitudinal population study of change in gamma-glutamyltransferase: the Tromsø study. *Am. J. Epidemiol.,* 139, 787, 1994.

141. Penn, R. and Worthington, L.J., Is serum gamma-glutamyltransferase a misleading test? *Br. Med. J.,* 286, 531, 1983.

142. Nalpas, R., Vassault, A., Charpin, S., Lacour, B., and Berthelot, P., Serum mitochondrial aspartate aminotransferase as a marker of chronic alcoholism: diagnostic value and interpretation in a liver unit. *Hepatology,* 6, 608, 1986.

143. Gluud, C., Andersen, I., Dietrichson, O., Gluud, B., Jacobsen, A., and Juhl, E., gamma-Glutamyltransferase, aspartate aminotransferase and alkaline phosphatase as marker of alcohol consumption in outpatient alcoholics. *Eur. J. Clin. Invest.,* 11, 171, 1981.

144. Nalpas, B., Vassault, A., Le Guillou, A., Lesgourgues, B., Ferry, N., Lacour, B., and Berthelot, P., Serum activity of mitochondrial asparate aminotransferase: a sensitive marker of alcoholism with or without alcoholic hepatitis. *Hepatology,* 5, 893, 1984.

145. Nalpas, R., Poupon, R.E., Vassault, A., Hauzanneau, P., Sage, Y., Schellenberg, F., Lacour, B., and Berthelot, P., Evaluations of mAST/tAST ratio as a marker of alcohol misuse in a non-selected population. *Alcohol Alcohol.,* 24, 415, 1989.

146. Nilssen, O., Huseby, N.E., Hoyer, G., Brenn, T., Schirmer, H., and Forde, O.H., New alcohol markers — how useful are they in population studies: the Svalbard Study 1988-89. *Alcohol Clin. Exp. Res.,* 16, 82, 1992.

147. Schiele, F., Artur, Y., Varasteh, A., Wellman, M., and Siest, G., Serum mitochondrial aspartate aminotransferase activity: not useful as marker of excessive alcohol consumption in an unselected population. *Clin. Chem.,* 35, 926, 1989.

148. Sillanaukee, P., Seppä, K., Lof, K., and Koivula, T., CDT by anion-exchange chromatography followed by RIA as a marker of heavy drinking among men. *Alcohol Clin. Exp. Res.,* 17, 230, 1993.

149. Irwin, M., Baird, S., Smith, T.L., and Schuckit, M., Use of laboratory tests to monitor heavy drinking by alcoholic men discharged from a treatment program. *Am. J. Psychiatry,* 145, 595, 1988.

150. Wu, A., Chanarin, I., and Levi, A.J., Macrocytosis in chronic alcoholism. *Lancet,* 1, 829, 1974.

151. Chick, J., Kreitman, N., and Plant, M., Mean cell volume and gamma-glutamyltranspeptidase as markers of drinking in working men. *Lancet,* 1, 1249, 1981.

152. Stimmel, B., Kurtz, D., Jackson, G., and Gilbert, H.S., Failure of mean red cell volume to serve as a biologic marker for alcoholism in narcotic dependence. *Am. J. Med.,* 74, 369, 1983.

153. Whitehead, T.P., Robinson, D., Allaway, S.L., and Hale, A.C., The effects of cigarette smoking and alcohol consumption on blood haemoglobin, erythrocytes and leucocytes: a dose related study on male subjects. *Clin. Lab. Haematol.,* 17, 131, 1995.

154. DiFranza, J.R. and Guerrera, M.P., Alcoholism and smoking. *J. Stud. Alcohol,* 51, 130, 1990.

155. Behrens, U.J., Worner, T.M., Braly, L.F., Schaffner, F., and Lieber, C.S., Carbohydrate-deficient transferrin, a marker for chronic alcohol consumption in different ethnic populations. *Alcohol Clin. Exp. Res.,* 12, 427, 1988.

156. Bell, H., Tallaksen, C.M., Try, K., and Haug, E., Carbohydrate-deficient transferrin and other markers of high alcohol consumption: a study of 502 patients admitted consecutively to a medical department. *Alcohol Clin. Exp. Res.,* 18, 1103, 1994.

157. Salaspuro, M., Carbohydrate-deficient transferrin as compared to other markers of alcoholism: a systematic review. *Alcohol,* 19, 261, 1999.

158. Stibler, H., Carbohydrate-deficient transferrin in serum: a new marker of potentially harmful alcohol consumption reviewed. *Clin. Chem.,* 37, 2029, 1991.

159. Jeppsson, J.O., Kristensson, H., and Fimiani, C., Carbohydrate-deficient transferrin quantified by HPLC to determine heavy consumption of alcohol. *Clin. Chem.,* 39, 2115, 1993.

160. de Jong, G., van Dijk, J.P., and van Eijk, H.G., The biology of transferrin. *Clin. Chim. Acta,* 190, 1, 1990.

161. Arndt, T., Carbohydrate-deficient transferrin as a marker of chronic alcohol abuse: a critical review of preanalysis, analysis, and interpretation. *Clin. Chem.,* 47, 13, 2001.

162. Helander, A., Eriksson, G., Stibler, H., and Jeppsson, J.O., Interference of transferrin isoform types with carbohydrate-deficient transferrin quantification in the identification of alcohol abuse. *Clin. Chem.,* 47, 1225, 2001.

163. Landberg, E., Påhlsson, P., Lundblad, A., Arnetorp, A., and Jeppsson, J.-O., Carbohydrate composition of serum transferrin isoforms from patients with high alcohol consumption. *Biochem. Biophys. Res. Commun.,* 210, 267, 1995.

164. Flahaut, C., Michalski, J.C., Danel, T., Humbert, M.H., and Klein, A., The effects of ethanol on the glycosylation of human transferrin. *Glycobiology,* 13, 191, 2003.

165. Peter, J., Unverzagt, C., Engel, W. D., Renauer, D., Seidel, C., and Hösel, W., Identification of carbohydrate deficient transferrin forms by MALDI-TOF mass spectrometry and lectin ELISA. *Biochim. Biophys. Acta,* 1380, 93, 1998.

166. Stibler, H. and Borg, S., Glycoprotein glycosyltransferase activities in serum in alcohol-abusing patients and healthy controls. *Scand. J. Clin. Lab. Invest.,* 51, 43, 1991.

167. Lieber, C.S., Carbohydrate deficient transferrin in alcoholic liver disease: mechanisms and clinical implications. *Alcohol,* 19, 249, 1999.

168. Sillanaukee, P., Strid, N., Allen, J.P., and Litten, R.Z., Possible reasons why heavy drinking increases carbohydrate-deficient transferrin. *Alcohol Clin. Exp. Res.,* 25, 34, 2001.

169. Allen, J.P., Litten, R.Z., Anton, R.F., and Cross, G.M., Carbohydrate-deficient transferrin as a measure of immoderate drinking: remaining issues. *Alcohol Clin. Exp. Res.,* 18, 799, 1994.

170. Conigrave, K.M., Degenhardt, L.J., Whitfield, J.B., Saunders, J.B., Helander, A., and Tabakoff, B., CDT, GGT, and AST as markers of alcohol use: the WHO/ISBRA collaborative project. *Alcohol Clin. Exp. Res.,* 26, 332, 2002.

171. Salmela, K.S., Laitinen, K., Nyström, M., and Salaspuro, M., Carbohydrate-deficient transferrin during 3 weeks' heavy alcohol consumption. *Alcohol Clin. Exp. Res.,* 18, 228, 1994.

172. Lesch, O.M., Walter, H., Antal, J., Heggli, D.E., Kovacz, A., Leitner, A., Neumeister, A., Stumpf, I., Sundrehagen, E., and Kasper, S., Carbohydrate-deficient transferrin as a marker of alcohol intake: a study with healthy subjects. *Alcohol Alcohol.,* 31, 265, 1996.

173. Kamboh, M.I. and Ferrell, R.E., Human transferrin polymorphism. *Hum. Hered.,* 37, 65, 1987.

174. Stibler, H., Borg, S., and Beckman, G., Transferrin phenotype and level of carbohydrate-deficient transferrin in healthy individuals. *Alcohol Clin. Exp. Res.,* 12, 450, 1988.

175. Bean, P. and Peter, J.B., Allelic D variants of transferrin in evaluation of alcohol abuse: differential diagnosis by isoelectric focusing-immunoblotting-laser densitometry. *Clin. Chem.,* 40, 2078, 1994.

176. Marquardt, T. and Denecke, J., Congenital disorders of glycosylation: review of their molecular bases, clinical presentations and specific therapies. *Eur. J. Pediatr.,* 162, 359, 2003.

177. Jaeken, J., Komrower Lecture. Congenital disorders of glycosylation (CDG): it's all in it! *J. Inherit. Metab. Dis.,* 26, 99, 2003.

178. Sorvajärvi, K., Blake, J.E., Israel, Y., and Niemelä, O., Sensitivity and specificity of carbohydrate-deficient transferrin as a marker of alcohol abuse are significantly influenced by alterations in serum transferrin: comparison of two methods. *Alcohol Clin. Exp. Res.,* 20, 449, 1996.

179. Helander, A., Absolute or relative measurement of carbohydrate-deficient transferrin in serum? Experiences with three immunological assays. *Clin. Chem.,* 45, 131, 1999.

180. Keating, J., Cheung, C., Peters, T.J., and Sherwood, R.A., Carbohydrate deficient transferrin in the assessment of alcohol misuse: absolute or relative measurements? A comparison of two methods with regard to total transferrin concentration. *Clin. Chim. Acta,* 272, 159, 1998.

181. Stibler, H., Borg, S., and Joustra, M., A modified method for the assay of carbohydrate-deficient transferrin (CDT) in serum. *Alcohol Alcohol.,* Suppl. 1, 451, 1991.

182. Helander, A., Husa, A., and Jeppsson, J.O., Improved HPLC method for carbohydrate-deficient transferrin in serum. *Clin. Chem.,* 49, 1881, 2003.

183. Helander, A., Wielders, J.P., te Stroet, R., and Bergström, J.P., Comparison of HPLC and capillary electrophoresis for confirmatory testing of the alcohol misuse marker carbohydrate-deficient transferrin. *Clin. Chem.,* 51, 1528, 2005.

184. Helander, A., Dahl, H., Swanson, I., and Bergström, J., Evaluation of Dade Behring N Latex CDT: a novel homogenous immunoassay for carbohydrate-deficient transferrin. *Alcohol Clin. Exp. Res.,* 28(Suppl.), 33A, 2004.

185. Kraul, D., Hackler, R., and Althaus, H., A novel particle-enhanced assay for the immuno-nephelometric determination of carbohydrate-deficient transferrin. *Alcohol Clin. Exp. Res.,* 28(Suppl.), 34A, 2004.

186. Alling, C., Gustavsson, L., and Änggård, E., An abnormal phospholipid in rat organs after ethanol treatment. *FEBS Lett.,* 152, 24, 1983.

187. Mueller, G.C., Fleming, M.F., LeMahieu, M.A., Lybrand, G.S., and Barry, K.J., Synthesis of phosphatidylethanol — a potential marker for adult males at risk for alcoholism. *Proc. Natl. Acad. Sci. U.S.A.,* 85, 9778, 1988.

188. Hansson, P., Caron, M., Johnson, G., Gustavsson, L., and Alling, C., Blood phosphatidylethanol as a marker of alcohol abuse: levels in alcoholic males during withdrawal. *Alcohol Clin. Exp. Res.,* 21, 108, 1997.

189. Varga, A., Hansson, P., Johnson, G., and Alling, C., Normalization rate and cellular localization of phosphatidylethanol in whole blood from chronic alcoholics. *Clin. Chim. Acta,* 299, 141, 2000.

190. Varga, A., Hansson, P., Lundqvist, C., and Alling, C., Phosphatidylethanol in blood as a marker of ethanol consumption in healthy volunteers: comparison with other markers. *Alcohol Clin. Exp. Res.,* 22, 1832, 1998.

191. Tolonen, A., Lehto, T.M., Hannuksela, M.L., and Savolainen, M.J., A method for determination of phosphatidylethanol from high density lipoproteins by reversed-phase HPLC with TOF-MS detection. *Anal. Biochem.,* 341, 83, 2005.

192. Aradottir, S., Seidl, S., Wurst, F.M., Jonsson, B.A., and Alling, C., Phosphatidylethanol in human organs and blood: a study on autopsy material and influences by storage conditions. *Alcohol Clin. Exp. Res.,* 28, 1718, 2004.

193. Stevens, V.J., Fantl, W.J., Newman, C.B., Sims, R.V., Cerami, A., and Peterson, C.M., Acetaldehyde adducts with hemoglobin. *J. Clin. Invest.,* 67, 361, 1981.

194. Tuma, D.J. and Casey, C.A., Dangerous byproducts of alcohol breakdown — focus on adducts. *Alcohol Res. Health,* 27, 285, 2003.

195. Niemelä, O. and Parkkila, S., Alcoholic macrocytosis — is there a role for acetaldehyde and adducts? *Addict. Biol.,* 9, 3, 2004.

196. Sorrell, M.F. and Tuma, D.J., Hypothesis: alcoholic liver injury and the covalent binding of acetaldehyde. *Alcohol Clin. Exp. Res.,* 9, 306, 1985.

197. Niemelä, O., Distribution of ethanol-induced protein adducts in vivo: relationship to tissue injury. *Free Radical Biol. Med.,* 31, 1533, 2001.

198. Lieber, C.S., Alcoholic fatty liver: its pathogenesis and mechanism of progression to inflammation and fibrosis. *Alcohol,* 34, 9, 2004.

199. Hoerner, M., Behrens, U.J., Worner, T., and Lieber, C.S., Humoral immune response to acetaldehyde adducts in alcoholic patients. *Res. Commun. Chem. Pathol. Pharmacol.,* 54, 3, 1986.

200. Peterson, K.P., Bowers, C., and Peterson, C.M., Prevalence of ethanol consumption may be higher in women than men in a university health service population as determined by a biochemical marker: whole blood-associated acetaldehyde above the 99th percentile for teetotalers. *J. Addict. Dis.,* 17, 13, 1998.

201. Itälä, L., Seppä, K., Turpeinen, U., and Sillanaukee, P., Separation of hemoglobin acetaldehyde adducts by high-performance liquid chromatography-cation-exchange chromatography. *Anal. Biochem.,* 224, 323, 1995.

202. Viitala, K., Israel, Y., Blake, J.E., and Niemelä, O., Serum IgA, IgG, and IgM antibodies directed against acetaldehyde-derived epitopes: relationship to liver disease severity and alcohol consumption. *Hepatology,* 25, 1418, 1997.

203. Sillanaukee, P., Seppä, K., Koivula, T., Israel, Y., and Niemelä, O., Acetaldehyde-modified hemoglobin as a marker of alcohol consumption: comparison of two new methods. *J. Lab. Clin. Med.,* 120, 42, 1992.

204. Halvorsen, M.R., Campbell, J.L., Sprague, G., Slater, K., Noffsinger, J.K., and Peterson, C.M., Comparative evaluation of the clinical utility of three markers of ethanol intake: the effect of gender. *Alcohol Clin. Exp. Res.,* 17, 225, 1993.

205. Helander, A., Aldehyde dehydrogenase in blood: distribution, characteristics and possible use as marker of alcohol misuse. *Alcohol Alcohol.,* 28, 135, 1993.

206. Johnson, R.D., Bahnisch, J., Stewart, B., Shearman, D.J.C., and Edwards, J.B., Optimized spectro-photometric determination of aldehyde dehydrogenase activity in erythrocytes. *Clin. Chem.,* 38, 584, 1992.

207. Hansell, N.K., Pang, D., Heath, A.C., Martin, N.G., and Whitfield, J.B., Erythrocyte aldehyde dehy-drogenase activity: lack of association with alcohol use and dependence or alcohol reactions in Australian twins. *Alcohol Alcohol.,* 40, 343, 2005.

208. Kärkkäinen, P., Poikolainen, K., and Salaspuro, M., Serum β-hexosaminidase as a marker of heavy drinking. *Alcohol Clin. Exp. Res.,* 14, 187, 1990.

209. Hultberg, B., Isaksson, A., Berglund, M., and Moberg, A.-L., Serum β-hexosaminidase isoenzyme: a sensitive marker for alcohol abuse. *Alcohol Clin. Exp. Res.,* 15, 549, 1991.

210. Hultberg, B., Isaksson, A., Berglund, M., and Alling, C., Increases and time-course variations in beta-hexosaminidase isoenzyme B and carbohydrate-deficient transferrin in serum from alcoholics are similar. *Alcohol Clin. Exp. Res.,* 19, 452, 1995.

211. Nyström, M., Peräsalo, J., and Salaspuro, M., Serum β-hexosaminidase in young university students. *Alcohol Clin. Exp. Res.,* 15, 877, 1991.

212. Hultberg, B. and Isaksson, A., Isoenzyme pattern of serum β-hexosaminidase in liver disease, alcohol intoxication and pregnancy. *Enzyme,* 30, 166, 1983.

213. Iffland, R. and Grassnack, F., Untersuchung zum CDT und anderen Indikatoren für Alkoholprobleme im Blut alkoholauffälliger Pkw-Fahrer. *Blutalkohol,* 32, 26, 1995.

214. Haffner, H.-T., Batra, A., Wehner, H.D., Besserer, K., and Mann, K., Methanolspiegel und Metha-nolelimination bei Alkoholikern. *Blutalkohol,* 30, 52, 1993.

215. Hollstedt, C. and Dahlgren, L., Peripheral markers in the female "hidden alcoholic." *Acta Psychiatr. Scand.,* 75, 591, 1987.

216. Harasymiw, J. and Bean, P., The combined use of the early detection of alcohol consumption (EDAC) test and carbohydrate-deficient transferrin to identify heavy drinking behaviour in males. *Alcohol Alcohol.,* 36, 349, 2001.

217. Javors, M.A. and Johnson, B.A., Current status of carbohydrate deficient transferrin, total serum sialic acid, sialic acid index of apolipoprotein J and serum beta-hexosaminidase as markers for alcohol consumption. *Addiction,* 98(Suppl. 2), 45, 2003.

218. Sillanaukee, P., Aalto, M., and Seppä, K., Carbohydrate-deficient transferrin and conventional alcohol markers as indicators for brief intervention among heavy drinkers in primary health care. *Alcohol Clin. Exp. Res.,* 22, 892, 1998.

219. Sillanaukee, P. and Olsson, U., Improved diagnostic classification of alcohol abusers by combining carbohydrate-deficient transferrin and gamma-glutamyltransferase. *Clin. Chem.,* 47, 681, 2001.

220. Bell, H., Tallaksen, C., Sjåheim, T., Weberg, R., Räknerud, N., Örjasaeter, H., Try, K., and Haug, E., Serum carbohydrate-deficient transferrin as a marker of alcohol consumption in patients with chronic liver diseases. *Alcohol Clin. Exp. Res.,* 17, 246, 1993.

221. Gjerde, H., Johnsen, J., Bjørneboe, A., Bjørneboe, G.E., and Mørland, J., A comparison of serum carbohydrate-deficient transferrin with other biological markers of excessive drinking. *Scand. J. Clin. Lab. Invest.,* 48, 1, 1988.

222. Helander, A., Carlsson, A.V., and Borg, S., Longitudinal comparison of carbohydrate-deficient trans-ferrin and gamma-glutamyl transferase: complementary markers of excessive alcohol consumption. *Alcohol Alcohol.,* 31, 101, 1996.

223. Randell, E., Diamandis, E.P., and Goldberg, D.M., Changes in serum carbohydrate-deficient transferrin and gammaglutamyl transferase after moderate wine consumption in healthy males. *J. Clin. Lab. Anal.,* 12, 92, 1998.

224. Niemelä, O., Sorvajärvi, K., Blake, J. E., and Israel, Y., Carbohydrate-deficient transferrin as a marker of alcohol abuse: relationship to alcohol consumption, severity of liver disease, and fibrogenesis. *Alcohol Clin. Exp. Res.,* 19, 1203, 1995.

225. Helander, A. and Carlsson, S., Carbohydrate-deficient transferrin and gamma-glutamyl transferase levels during disulfiram therapy. *Alcohol Clin. Exp. Res.,* 20, 1202, 1996.

226. Rosman, A.S., Basu, P., Galvin, K., and Lieber, C.S., Utility of carbohydrate-deficient transferrin as a marker of relapse in alcoholic patients. *Alcohol Clin. Exp. Res.,* 19, 611, 1995.

227. Keso, L. and Salaspuro, M., Laboratory tests in the follow-up of treated alcoholics: how often should testing be repeated? *Alcohol Alcohol.,* 25, 359, 1990.

228. Kristenson, H., Öhlin, H., Hulten-Nosslin, M.B., Trell, E., and Hood, B., Identification and intervention of heavy drinking in middle-aged men: results and follow-up of 24–60 months of long-term study with randomized controls. *Alcohol Clin. Exp. Res.,* 7, 203, 1983.

229. Kristenson, H. and Jeppsson, J.O., Drunken driver examinations. CD-transferrin is a valuable marker of alcohol consumption. *Lakartidningen,* 95, 1429, 1998.

230. Anton, R.F., Lieber, C., and Tabakoff, B., Carbohydrate-deficient transferrin and gamma-glutamyl-transferase for the detection and monitoring of alcohol use: results from a multisite study. *Alcohol Clin. Exp. Res.,* 26, 1215, 2002.

231. Goodwin, D.W., Schulsinger, F., Hermanssen, L., Guze, S.H., and Windkure, G., Alcohol problems in adoptees raised apart from alcoholic biological parents. *Arch. Gen. Psychiatry,* 28, 238, 1973.

232. Cloninger, C.R., Bohman, M., and Sigvardsson, S., Inheritance of alcohol abuse: cross fostering analysis of adopted men. *Arch. Gen. Psychiatry,* 38, 861, 1981.

233. Cloninger, C.R., Neurogenetic adaptive mechanisms in alcoholism. *Science,* 236, 410, 1987.

234. Devor, E.J. and Cloninger, C.R., Genetics of alcoholism. *Annu. Rev. Genet.,* 23, 19, 1989.

235. Ball, D.M. and Murray, R.M., Genetics of alcohol misuse. *Br. Med. Bull.,* 50, 18, 1994.

236. Ratsma, J.E., Van Der Stelt, O., and Gunning, W.B., Neurochemical markers of alcoholism vulnerability in humans. *Alcohol Alcohol.,* 37, 522, 2002.

237. Cowen, M.S., Chen, F., and Lawrence, A.J., Neuropeptides: implications for alcoholism. *J. Neurochem.,* 89, 273, 2004.

238. von Knorring, A.L., Bohman, M., von Knorring, L., and Oreland, L., Platelet MAO activity as a biological marker in subgroups of alcoholism. *Acta Psychiat. Scand.,* 72, 51, 1985.

239. Begleiter, H., The collaborative study on the genetics of alcoholism. *Alcohol Health Res. World,* 19, 228, 1995.

240. Fowler, J.S., Volkow, N.D., Wang, G.-J., Pappas, N., Logan, J., MacGregor, R., Alexoff, D., Shea, C., Schlyer, D., Wolf, A. P., Warner, D., Zezulkova, I., and Cliento, R., Inhibition of monoamine oxidase B in the brains of smokers. *Nature,* 379, 733, 1996.

241. Agarwal, D.P., Molecular genetic aspects of alcohol metabolism and alcoholism. *Pharmacopsychiatry,* 30, 79, 1997.

242. Chen, C.C., Lu, R.B., Chen, Y.C., Wang, M.F., Chang, Y.C., Li, T.K., and Yin, S.J., Interaction between the functional polymorphisms of the alcohol-metabolism genes in protection against alcoholism. *Am. J. Hum. Genet.,* 65, 795, 1999.

243. Glucksman, E., Alcohol and accidents. *Br. Med. Bull.,* 50, 76, 1994.

244. Midanik, L., The validity of self-reported alcohol consumption and alcohol problems: a literature review. *Br. J. Addict.,* 77, 357, 1982.

245. Del Boca, F.K. and Darkes, J., The validity of self-reports of alcohol consumption: state of the science and challenges for research. *Addiction,* 98(Suppl. 2), 1, 2003.

CHAPTER 6

Neurochemistry of Drug Abuse

Edited by Julie K. Staley, Ph.D. and Kelly P. Cosgrove, Ph.D.

Department of Psychiatry, Yale University School of Medicine, New Haven, Connecticut and VA Connnecticut Healthcare System, West Haven, Connecticut

CONTENTS

6.1 THE DOPAMINE TRANSPORTER AND ADDICTION

William M. Meil, Ph.D.[1] and John W. Boja, Ph.D.[2]

[1] Department of Psychology, Indiana University of Pennsylvania, Indiana, Pennsylvania
[2] U.S. Consumer Product Safety Commission, Directorate for Health Sciences, Bethesda, Maryland

Dopamine transporter (DAT) is a distinctive feature of dopaminergic neurons, discovered more than 20 years ago.[1–5] DAT is the major mechanism for the removal of released dopamine (DA). DA is actively transported back into dopaminergic neurons via a sodium- and energy-dependent mechanism.[6–8] Like other uptake carriers, DAT is regulated by a number of drugs including cocaine, amphetamine, some opiates, and ethanol. It is this interaction with DAT and the resulting increase in synaptic DA levels that have been suggested to be the basis for the action of several drugs of abuse. The dopaminergic hypothesis of drug abuse has been proposed by a number of researchers.[9,10] Di Chiara and Imperato[11] observed the effects of several drugs of abuse on DA levels in the nucleus accumbens and caudate nucleus using microdialysis. Drugs such as cocaine, amphetamine, ethanol, nicotine, and morphine were all observed to produce an increase in DA, especially in the nucleus accumbens. Drugs that are generally not abused by humans, such as bremazocine, imipramine, diphenhydramine, or haloperidol, decreased DA or increased DA in the caudate nucleus only. It was, therefore, concluded[11] that drugs abused by humans preferentially increase brain DA levels in the nucleus accumbens, whereas psychoactive drugs not abused by humans do not. By employing this hypothesis of drug reward as a starting point, this chapter reviews evidence regarding the function of DAT and the interaction of several drugs of abuse on DAT.

6.1.1 Dopamine Uptake

The uptake of DA depends on a number of factors[4–6,12–15] including temperature, sodium,[16–19] potassium,[6,16] chloride[7,20] but not calcium.[6] Krueger[21] suggested that dopamine transport occurred by means of two sodium ions and one chloride ion carrying a net positive charge into the neuron, which is utilized to drive DA against its electrochemical gradient. More recently, McElvain and Schenk[22] proposed a multisubstrate model of DA transport. In this model it was proposed that either one molecule of DA or two sodium ions bind to DAT in a partially random mechanism. Chloride binds next and it is only then that the DAT translocates from the outside of the neuron to the inside (Figure 6.1.1). Cocaine inhibition of DA transport occurs with cocaine binding to the sodium-binding site and changing the conformation of the chloride-binding site, thus preventing the binding of either and ultimately inhibiting dopamine uptake. DA uptake by cocaine appeared to be uncompetitive inhibition whereas the binding of sodium and chloride are competitively inhibited. This action is present only with neuronal membrane-bound DAT because cocaine does not appear to inhibit the reuptake of DA to the vesicles via the vesicular transporter.[23] Moreover, site-directed mutations of DAT hydrophobic regions[24] or the carboxyl-terminal tail[25] have resulted in differential effects on cocaine analogue binding and dopamine uptake.

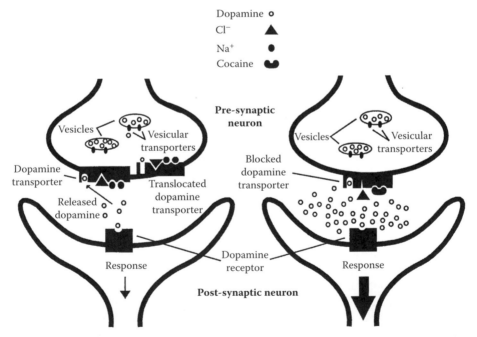

Figure 6.1.1 The dopamine transporter terminates the action of released dopamine by transport back into the presynaptic neuron. Dopamine transport occurs with the binding of one molecule of dopamine, one chloride ion, and two sodium ions to the transporter; the transporter then translocates from the outside of the neuronal membrane into the inside of the neuron.[22] Cocaine appears to bind to the sodium ion binding site. This changes the conformation of the chloride ion binding site; thus dopamine transport does not occur. This blockade of dopamine transport potentiates dopaminergic neurotransmission and may be the basis for the rewarding effects of cocaine.

A recent review of the literature on the amino acid structure of DAT stated that uptake of dopamine is dependent on multiple functional groups of amino acids within DAT.[26] The authors suggested that the amino acid functional groups of Phe[69], Phe[105], Phe[114], Phe[155], Thr[285], Phe[319], Phe[311], Pro[394], Phe[410], Ser[527], Phe[520], Tyr[533], and Ser[538] in rat DAT and Val[55] and Ser[528] in human DAT appear to be involved in DAT uptake.

6.1.2 Abused Drugs and the Dopamine Transporter

6.1.2.1 Cocaine

Cocaine has several mechanisms of action: inhibition of DA, norepinephrine, and serotonin reuptake, as well as a local anesthetic effect. While the stimulating and reinforcing effects of cocaine have been recognized for quite some time, it was not until recently that the mechanism for these effects was elucidated. The stimulatory effects of cocaine were first associated with the ability of cocaine to inhibit the reuptake of DA.[27,28] Saturable and specific binding sites for [³H] cocaine were then discovered by Reith using whole mouse brain homogenates.[29] When striatal tissue was utilized as the sole tissue source, Kennedy and Hanbauer[30] were able to correlate the pharmacology of [³H]cocaine binding and [³H]DA uptake inhibition and, thereby, hypothesized that the binding site for [³H]cocaine was in fact DAT. By using the data from binding experiments, it has been possible to correlate the strong reinforcing properties of cocaine with blockade of DAT rather than inhibition of either the serotonin (SERT) or norepinephrine transporters (NET).[31,32]

By using radiolabeled cocaine[33–35] or analogues of cocaine such as WIN 35,065-2,[30] WIN 35,428,[33,34] RTI-55,[35–43] and RTI-121,[44,45] it is possible to visualize the distribution of these drugs within the brain; the pattern of binding demonstrated by cocaine and its analogues appears to coincide with the distribution of dopamine within the brain. Areas of the brain with the greatest amount of dopaminergic innervation, such as the caudate, putamen, and nucleus accumbens, also demonstrate the greatest amount of binding, whereas moderate amounts of binding are observed in the substantia nigra and ventral tegmental areas. Recently specific antibodies to the DAT have been developed.[46] Visualization of the distribution of DAT within the brain using these antibodies demonstrated that there was a good correlation with cocaine binding.

Several unrelated compounds have been demonstrated to bind to the DAT, such as [³H]mazindol,[47] [³H]nomifensine,[48] and [³H]GBR 12935.[49] However, while these compounds also inhibit the reuptake of DA, they do not share the powerful reinforcing properties of cocaine. The question of why these compounds are non-addictive while cocaine is quite addictive remains unanswered. Several possibilities exist: Schoemaker et al.[50] observed that [³H]cocaine binds to both a high- and low-affinity site on the DAT, whereas other ligands such as [³H]mazindol,[47] [³H]nomifensine,[48] and [³H]GBR 12935[49] bind solely to a single high-affinity site. This does not indicate that the two binding sites demonstrated by cocaine and its analogues[43,44,51–54] represent two distinct sites, however, because both the high- and low-affinity sites arise from a single expressed cDNA for the DAT.[55] Another difference may be the pattern of binding, in that [³H]mazindol binds to different sites in the brain than those observed for [³H]cocaine.[54] In addition, the rate of entry into the brain is different for these different compounds. Mazindol and GBR 12935 have been demonstrated to enter the brain and occupy receptors much more slowly than cocaine.[57,58] At the present time it is still unclear which of these or other possible factors promote the strong reinforcing properties of cocaine.

Recently, mice lacking the gene for DAT have been developed;[59] DA is present in the dopaminergic extracellular space of the homozygous mice almost 100 times longer than it is present in the normal mouse. The homozygous mice were hyperactive compared to normal mice and, as expected, cocaine did not produce any effect in the locomotor activity of the homozygous mice. These results provide further evidence to support the concept of the DAT as a cocaine receptor. However, mice lacking DAT do show cocaine reinforcement.[60–63] Possible explanations for this observation include a role of SERT[60,62] or NET in the psychoactive effects of cocaine.

6.1.2.2 Amphetamine

Amphetamine and its analogues, including but not limited to methamphetamine, methylenc-dioxyamphetamine (MDA), and methylenedioxymethamphetamine (MDMA), increase brain DA levels.[64–76] Amphetamine has been postulated to increase brain DA levels either by increasing DA release or by blocking DA reuptake. Hadfield[77] observed amphetamine blockade of DA reuptake; however, reuptake inhibition occurred only at doses of amphetamine ($ED_{50} = 65$ mg/kg) that were much higher than the doses observed to increase release. While reuptake blockade may play a role in the ability of amphetamine to elevate DA, blockade occurs only at doses near those that produce stereotypy or toxicity. On the other hand, amphetamine-stimulated DA release occurs at much lower doses. Amphetamine-stimulated DA release has been postulated to occur by two mechanisms: one involves the interaction of amphetamine with the DAT, which then produces a reversal of the DAT so that DA is transported out of neuron while amphetamine is transported out of the neuron.[77–85] The other proposes passive diffusion of amphetamine-mediated alteration of vesicular pH.[84] Using human DAT-transfected EM4 cells, Kahlig[86] observed both a fast and slow efflux of dopamine following amphetamine stimulation suggesting that amphetamine releases DA via the DAT in a quantum-like manner resulting in a slow DA release and in a faster channel-like manner.

Besides this purported action on DAT, amphetamine has also been suggested to act upon the vesicular transporter as well. Pifl et al.[87] examined COS cells transfected with cDNA for either DAT or the vesicular transporter, or both. A marked increase in DA release was noted in cells that expressed both DAT and the vesicular transporter when compared to the release from cells that express only DAT or the vesicular transporter. The mechanism of action for amphetamine was further defined with the work of Giros et al.[59] In transgenic mice lacking the DAT, amphetamine did not produce hyperlocomotion or release DA.

In summary, the DAT appears to be the primary site of action for amphetamine-induced DA release via its activity on the DAT because amphetamine appears to employ DAT to transport DA out of the neuron while, at the same time, amphetamine may be sequestered in the neuron. The sequestered amphetamine then may release vesicular DA by altering vesicular pH or via interactions with the vesicular transporter.

6.1.2.3 Opiates

Opiate drugs share the ability to elevate extracellular DA concentrations in the nucleus accumbens,[88–90] possibly implicating mesolimbic DA activity in the abuse liability of these compounds. Whereas the locomotor[91] and reinforcing effects[92,93] of opiates may occur through DA-independent pathways, there is also evidence for dopaminergic mediation of these effects.[94,95] Lesions of dopaminergic neurons[96,97] or neuroleptic blockade of DA receptors[98,99] attenuate opiate reward as measured by intracranial electrical self-stimulation, conditioned place preference, and intravenous self-administration. In contrast to cocaine's ability to augment DA concentrations through direct action at DAT,[100] opiates appear to enhance DA concentrations primarily by indirectly stimulating DA neurons.[101,102]

However, evidence suggests that some opiates also act at DAT. Das et al.[103] reported that U50-488H, a synthetic κ opiate agonist, and dynorphin A, an endogenous κ ligand, dose-dependently inhibit [³H]DA uptake in synaptosomal preparations from the rat striatum and nucleus accumbens. Inhibition of [³H]DA uptake by U50-488H was not reversed by pretreatment with the opiate antagonists naloxone and nor-binaltorphine, suggesting that this effect is mediated through direct action at DAT rather than an indirect effect at κ receptors. However, the effects of another κ opiate agonist, U69593, do not appear mediated by the DAT since U69593 failed to attenuate GBR 12909- and WIN 35,428-induced cocaine seeking behavior.[104]

Meperidine, an atypical opiate receptor agonist with cocaine-like effects, has been shown to act at the DAT.[105] Meperidine inhibited [³H]DA uptake in rat caudate putamen with a maximal effect less than that achieved with cocaine. This suggests that meperidine may predominantly act at the high-affinity transporter site. Meperidine also displaced [³H]WIN 35,428 binding in a manner consistent with a single site affinity. Because meperidine shares key structural features with the phenyltropane analogues of cocaine, it is possible that these common structural features account for the cocaine-like actions of meperidine rather than any characteristics intrinsic to opiates. Similarly, fentanyl, a μ opiate agonist structurally related to meperidine, decreased [¹²³I]β-CIT binding in the basal ganglia of a single human subject and in rats, supporting the direct action of some opiates on dopamine reuptake.[106] In contrast, selective μ and opiate agonists failed to inhibit [³H]DA uptake in the striatum and nucleus accumbens across the same range of doses. Morphine, a μ opiate agonist, also did not inhibit [³H]DA uptake or displace [³H]WIN 35,428 binding in the striatum[105] or displace [³H]GBR 12935 binding in basal forebrain.[107] Conditioned place preference to morphine is increased in DAT knockout mice.[108]

Although opiates and psychostimulants may possess different sites of action, it has been suggested that cross-sensitization of their addictive properties may result from overlapping neural targets. Examining the localization of κ-opioid receptor and DAT antisera in nucleus accumbens shell of the rat, κ-opioid receptor labeling was seen primarily in axon terminals and DAT labeling was observed exclusively in axon terminals. Thus, opiate agonists in the nucleus accumbens shell may modulate DA release primarily via control of presynaptic neurotransmitter secretion that may influence or be influenced by intracellular DA.[109]

Although morphine appears to lack direct action at DAT, research suggests that chronic morphine may alter DAT expression. Repeated, but not acute administration of morphine to rats decreased the B_{max} of [³H]GBR12935 binding in the anterior basal forebrain, including the nucleus accumbens, but not the striatum.[107] However, radioligand affinity was not different in either brain region. Neither acute nor chronic morphine administration inhibited binding at the serotonin transporter in the striatum or anterior basal forebrain, suggesting that transporter down-regulation was selective for brain regions important for the reinforcing and/or motivational properties of opiates. Because daily cocaine administration in rats also attenuates DA uptake in the nucleus accumbens, and not the striatum,[110] chronic elevation of DA release and a subsequent reduction in DAT expression within the nucleus accumbens may prove important in the development of drug addiction. The effects of chronic morphine administration on DAT activity may also be related to withdrawal status of the animal. Rats implanted with morphine pellets for 7 days and examined with the pellets intact showed [³H] GBR 12935 binding was increased in the hypothalamus and decreased in the striatum. Rats examined 16 h after removal of the pellets showed increased binding in both the hypothalamus and hippocampus.[111] However, recent research has demonstrated that twice daily escalating doses of morphine for 7 days altered mRNA levels for several dopamine receptors (D$_2$R and D$_3$R) but not the DAT in discrete regions of the rat brain.[112] Also, post-mortem examination of the striatum of nine chronic heroin users revealed modest reductions in measures of dopamine function but levels of vesicular monoamine transporters were comparable to controls.[113]

6.1.2.4 Phencyclidine

Both systemic and local infusions of phencyclidine (PCP) enhance extracellular DA concentrations in the nucleus accumbens[114,115] and prefrontal cortex.[116] PCP-induced elevations of extracellular DA concentrations may result from both indirect and direct effects on the dopaminergic system. NMDA receptors exert a tonic inhibitory effect upon basal DA release in the prefrontal cortex[116,117] and in the nucleus accumbens through inhibitory effects on midbrain DA neurons.[118–120] Thus, PCP antagonism of NMDA receptors[121] may facilitate DA release by decreasing the inhibition of central dopaminergic activity.

PCP also increases calcium-independent [³H]DA release from dissociated rat mesencephalon cell cultures[122] and striatal synaptosomes.[123] PCP has been found to be a potent inhibitor of [³H]DA uptake in rat striatum,[124–127] to competitively inhibit binding of [³H]BTCP, a PCP derivative and potent DA uptake inhibitor in rat striatal membranes,[128] and to inhibit [3H]cocaine binding.[129] In addition, (trans)-4-PPC, a major metabolite of PCP in humans,[130] inhibits [3H]DA uptake in rat striatal synaptosomes with comparable potency to PCP and thus it may be involved in the psychotomimetic effects of PCP.[124] Recently it was reported that PCP exerts some direct actions at the DAT in the primate striatum using positron emission tomography. Moreover, it was suggested that GABA may also modulate PCP-induced augmentation of DA in the primate striatum.[131]

Despite the profound effect PCP exerts on mesolimbic DA activity, evidence suggests that the reinforcing properties of PCP are not dopamine dependent. Carlezon and Wise[132] have reported that rats will self-administer PCP into the ventromedial region of the nucleus accumbens, as well as NMDA receptor antagonists that do not inhibit DA reuptake. Co-infusion of the DA antagonist sulpiride into the nucleus accumbens inhibits intracranial self-administration of nomifensine, but not PCP. Moreover, rats self-administer PCP into the prefrontal cortex, an area that will not maintain self-administration of nomifensine.[133] Therefore, the reinforcing effects of PCP in the nucleus accumbens and prefrontal cortex appear to be related to PCP blockade of NMDA receptor function rather than its dopaminergic actions. Instead, PCP-induced elevations of extracellular DA may mediate other behavioral effects of PCP, such as its stimulant effects on locomotor activity.[134] The differential effects on locomotor activation of PCP and cocaine do not appear mediated though direct action at the DAT.[135]

6.1.2.5 Marijuana

Recent progress has greatly expanded our knowledge of the endocannabinoid system and the ways in which Δ^9-tetrahydrocannabinol (Δ^9-THC), the primary psychoactive component of marijuana, acts upon this system. Advances have included the identification of central cannabinoid receptors (CB_1) as abundant primarily presynaptic G protein–coupled receptors sensitive to endogenous transmitters (anandamide, 2-AG) that function as retrograde transmitters and alter presynaptic neurotransmitter release.[136] The identification of synthetic ligands that act as agonists and antagonists at the CB_1 receptor has also greatly furthered our understanding of the endocannabinoid system and the effects of Δ^9-THC in the brain.[137]

Activation of dopaminergic circuits known to play a pivotal role in mediating the reinforcing effects of other abused drugs also results from cannabinoid administration.[138] Systemic or local injections of Δ^9-THC enhance extracellular dopamine concentrations in the rat prefrontal cortex,[139,140] caudate,[141] nucleus accumbens,[142,143] and ventral tegmental.[144,145] In addition, Δ^9-THC augments both brain stimulation of reward and extracellular DA concentrations in the nucleus accumbens in Lewis rats, linking dopaminergic activity with the rewarding properties of marijuana.[143]

Recent research is beginning to define the interactions between DA and endocannabinoids in regions critical for our understanding of the reinforcing effects of Δ^9-THC. Activity-dependent release of endocannabinoids from the ventral tegmental area appears to serve as a regulatory feedback mechanism to inhibit synaptic inputs in response to DA neuron bursting and thus regulating firing patterns that may fine-tune DA release from afferent terminals.[146] Similarly, DA neurons in the prefrontal cortex have been suggested to release endocannabinoids to shape afferent activity and ultimately their own behavior.[147] Research has also begun to shed light on the intracellular signaling pathways activated by THC. Acute administration of Δ^9-THC produces phosphorylation of the mitogen-activated protein kinase/intracellular signal-regulated kinase (MAP/ERK) in the dorsal striatum and nucleus accumbens. This activation, corresponding to both neuronal cell bodies and the surrounding neuropil, is blocked by pretreatment with DA D_1, and to a lesser extent DA D_2 and NMDA glutamate, antagonists.[148] Given that ERK inhibition was found to block conditioned place preference for Δ^9-THC, these findings suggest dopaminergic influence of Δ^9-THC intracellular effects is important for the rewarding effects of Δ^9-THC.[148]

Facilitation of dopaminergic activity by Δ^9-THC may result from multiple mechanisms. Δ^9-THC increases DA synthesis[149] and release[150] in synaptosomal preparations. In addition, using in vivo techniques, Δ^9-THC has been reported to augment potassium-evoked DA release in the caudate[141] and increase calcium-dependent DA efflux in the nucleus accumbens.[142] However, whereas Δ^9-THC produces a dose-dependent augmentation of somatodendritic DA release in the ventral tegmental area, it fails to simultaneously alter accumbal DA concentrations.[144] Because local infusions of Δ^9-THC through a microdialysis probe did elevate nucleus accumbens DA concentrations, modulation of DA activity in the nucleus accumbens is likely to result from presynaptic effects.

Δ^9-THC also acts directly at the DAT to affect DA uptake. At low concentrations Δ^9-THC stimulates uptake of [^{3}H]DA in synaptosomal preparations of rat brain striatum and hypothalamus.[150] Similarly, mice injected with Δ^9-THC showed increased [^{3}H]DA uptake into striatal synaptosomes and, to a greater extent, in cortical synaptosomes.[151] At higher concentrations Δ^9-THC inhibits uptake of [^{3}H]DA in rat striatal[150,152,153] and hypothalamic[150] synaptosomes. Also consistent with the hypothesis that Δ^9-THC blocks DA uptake, using *in vivo* electrochemical techniques, it has been reported that Δ^9-THC and the DA-reuptake blocker nomifensine produce identical augmentation of voltammetric signals corresponding to extracellular DA.[141] While Δ^9-THC has a similar biphasic effect on norepinephrine uptake in hypothalamic and striatal synaptosomes[150] and increases uptake of 5-HT and GABA in cortical synaptosomes,[151] the psychoactive effects of Δ^9-THC are most likely related to dopaminergic activity because less potent and nonpsychoactive THC derivatives show much less effect on DA uptake than does Δ^9-THC.[151] It is only recently that the effects of Δ^9-THC exposure on human DAT levels have been examined and while it appears that postmortem DAT levels in the caudate of individuals with schizophrenia may be influenced by Δ^9-THC, this result may be of limited generalizability given that people suffering schizophrenia tend to show reduced DAT levels regardless of history of THC use.[154]

Δ^9-THC clearly has profound effects on dopaminergic activity in areas important to the maintenance of the reinforcing effects of other abused compounds. Research relating the persistence of Δ^9-THC-induced ventral tegmental DA neuron firing in animals chronically treated with Δ^9-THC to the lack of tolerance to marijuana's euphoric effects further bolsters this link.[155] The ability of Δ^9-THC to facilitate intracranial electrical self-stimulation in the median forebrain bundle has long been established,[156] however, only recently have the reinforcing effects of Δ^9-THC been clearly demonstrated using conditioned place preference[148,157] and drug self-administration[157,158] procedures. With advances in our understanding of the endocannabinoid system and the further establishment of animal models of Δ^9-THC-induced reinforcement, increased understanding of marijuana's abuse liability can be expected in coming years. The observation that CB_1 receptor antagonism attenuates the reinstatement of heroin self-administration has also implicated the endocannabinoid system in the mechanisms underlying addiction and suggests a potential therapeutic niche for cannabinoid ligands.[159]

6.1.2.6 *Ethanol*

Ethanol also alters the dopaminergic system. Administration of ethanol has been shown to release DA *in vivo*[160–162] and *in vitro*.[163–171] The mechanism(s) by which ethanol increases brain DA levels are slowly beginning to be understood and may involve modulation of DAT activity. Tan et al.[172] examined [^{3}H]DA uptake in brain synaptosomes prepared from rats in various stages of intoxication. [^{3}H]DA uptake was inhibited by ethanol for as long as 16 h following the withdrawal of ethanol. A potential mechanism by which ethanol might work to increase DAT function may involve regulation of DAT expression on the cell surface as [^{3}H]DA has been shown to accumulate following ethanol administration in human DAT expressing *Xenopus* oocytes in parallel with cell surface DAT binding measured by [^{3}H]WIN 35,428.[173] Moreover, sites on the second intracellular loop of the DAT have been identified that appear important for ethanol modulation of DAT activity.[174] However, further research on the effects of ethanol on DAT function is needed given that recent research suggests acute ethanol attenuates DAT function in rat dorsal striatum and ventral striatum of anesthetized rats and tissue suspensions.[175]

Ethanol also increased both spontaneous release and Ca^{2+}-stimulated release of DA, but decreased the amount of K^+-stimulated released DA in rat striatum.[160,172] The increased amount of DA release is not due to nonspecific disruption of the neuronal membrane because acetylcholine levels are not altered.[162] Thus, it appears that ethanol can affect both the release and reuptake of DA via a specific mechanism. However, research investigating ethanol-induced DA release in rat nucleus accumbens slices suggests the mechanism is different from that underlying the effects of depolarization with electrical stimulation or high potassium levels and implicate nonexocytotic mechanisms.[177] Using no net flux microdialysis methodology to examine the effects of intraperitoneal injections of ethanol-induced increases in DA in the rat nucleus accumbens, it was suggested the primary mechanism by which ethanol augments extracellular DA levels is by facilitating release from terminals rather than by blocking the DAT.[178] However, research showing attenuated ethanol preference and consumption in female DAT knockout mice suggests ethanol's action on DAT may be relevant to ethanol-induced reward.[179]

A transesterification product of ethanol and cocaine has been discovered. Benzoylecgonine ethyl ester or cocaethylene was first described by Hearn et al.[180] Cocaethylene possessed similar affinity for the DAT as cocaine and also inhibited DA uptake[180–183] and increased *in vivo* DA levels.[185,185] Cocaethylene has lower affinity for the serotonin transporter than cocaine. Cocaethylene produces greater lethality in rats, mice, and dogs than cocaine[186–189] and may potentiate the cardiotoxic effects and tendency toward violence from cocaine or alcohol in humans.[190] While showing a similar pharmacological and behavioral profile as cocaine, cocaethylene appears less potent than cocaine in human subjects.[191] Anecdotal reports from human addicts and experimental results with animal subjects support the hypothesis that alcohol is often ingested with cocaine in order to attenuate the negative aftereffects of cocaine.[192]

6.1.2.7 Nicotine

Nicotine increased DA levels both *in vivo*[11,193] and *in vitro*.[194–196] Nicotine[197] and its metabolites[198] were found to both release and inhibit the reuptake of DA in rat brain slices, with uptake inhibition occurring at a lower concentration than that required for DA release. In addition, the (–) isomer was more potent than the (+) isomer.[197] However, the effects of nicotine upon DA release and uptake were only apparent when brain slices were utilized because nicotine was unable to affect DA when a synaptosomal preparation was utilized.[197] These results indicate that nicotine exerts its effects upon the DAT indirectly, most likely via nicotine acetylcholine receptors. This finding was supported by the results of Yamashita et al.[199] in which the effect of nicotine on DA uptake was examined in PC12 and COS cells transfected with rat DAT cDNA. Nicotine inhibited DA uptake in PC12 cells that possess a nicotine acetylcholine receptor. This effect was blocked by the nicotinic antagonists hexamethonium and mecamylamine. Additionally, nicotine did not influence DA uptake in COS cells, which lack nicotinic acetylcholine receptors.

Interestingly, a series of cocaine analogues that potently inhibited cocaine binding also inhibited [^{3}H]nicotine and [^{3}H]mecamylamine binding.[200] It was concluded that the inhibition by these cocaine analogues involves its action on an ion channel on nicotinic acetylcholine receptors. Recently several studies have further investigated the ability of nicotine to regulate DAT function. In slices from rat prefrontal cortex, but not the striatum or nucleus accumbens, nicotine enhances amphetamine-stimulated [^{3}H]DA release via the DAT. Moreover, the nicotinic acetylcholine receptors responsible for mediating amphetamine-induced [^{3}H]DA release in the prefrontal cortex were found to be at least partially localized on nerve terminals.[201,202] However, nicotine was found to augment DA clearance in the striatum and prefrontal cortex in a mecamylamine-sensitive manner, suggesting nicotinic acetylcholine receptors also modulate striatal DAT function.[203] Chronic nicotine and passive cigarette smoke exposure increase DAT mRNA in the ventral tegmental area in the rat[204] and other data suggest that changes in DAT numbers following repeated nicotine exposure may be behaviorally relevant since increases in DAT and D_3 receptors in the nucleus accumbens appear to be at least partially responsible for gender differences in behavioral sensitization to nicotine.[205]

6.1.3   Abused Drugs and Genetic Polymorphism of the Dopamine Transporter

Familial, twin, and adoption studies suggest there may be a genetic predisposition toward drug addiction.[206] Genetic polymorphisms across several neurotransmitter systems, including the dopaminergic system, have been linked to the development of drug addiction.[207] In humans the DAT gene (DAT1) has a variable number of tandem repeats (VNTR) in the 3′-untranslated region known to influence gene expression.[208] Most research suggests the longer 10-repeat allele yields greater DAT1 expression than the 9-repeat allele.[209] According to the reward deficiency syndrome hypothesis alterations in various combinations of genes, including DAT1, may provide some individuals with an underactive reward system and increase the likelihood that they will seek stimulation from the environment including stimulation from abused drugs.[210]

Research has implicated DAT polymorphisms to numerous effects of addictive drugs and addictive liability. Cocaine users with the 9/9 and 9/10 genotypes appear more susceptible to cocaine-induced paranoia than those with the 10/10 genotype.[211] Recently Lott et al.[212] reported that healthy volunteers with the 9/9 genotype have a diminished responsiveness to acute amphetamine injections on measures of global drug effect, feeling high, dysphoria, anxiety, and euphoria. These results may be significant given a diminished response to alcohol has been linked to future development of alcoholism.[213] However, another study found no significant associations between DAT polymorphism and clinical variations in a population of methamphetamine abusers.[214] Genetic polymorphisms across opioid and monoaminergic systems have also been linked to the development of opiate addiction.[215] Genetic polymorphisms in both the SERT and the DAT were found to be related to opiate addiction.[216] Homozygosity at the serotonin transporter (especially 10/10) was related to the development of opiate addiction whereas the genotype 12/10 appeared to be protective against opiate addiction. The DAT1, genotype 9/9 was associated with early opiate addiction. Opiate abuse under the age of 16 was also predicted by a combination of the serotonin transporter genotype 10/10 and the DAT1 genotype 10/10.[216] Studies have also begun to assess whether the risk of alcoholism may be mediated by genetic polymorphism in a variety of genetic targets, including the dopaminergic system, although conflicting results remain to be clarified. According to some research DAT polymorphism has not clearly been identified as a risk factor for the development of alcoholism,[217] but it has been associated with the development of severe alcohol withdrawal symptoms.[218] However, other research has suggested that DAT polymorphism is related to the development of alcoholism but not alcohol withdrawal.[219] The role of DAT polymorphism in nicotine addiction has received the most attention. Although there have been some conflicting reports,[220] most studies suggest the 9-repeated allele of the DAT is related to a decreased likelihood of being a smoker, a lower likelihood of smoking initiation prior to age 16, and longer periods of abstinence among smokers.[221–223] This latter finding is consistent with the reward deficiency syndrome hypothesis since individuals with the 9-repeated allele would be expected to have decreased DAT expression leading to higher levels of intracellular DA and therefore a reduced need for novelty and external reward including cigarettes. Clearly genetic polymorphism across a number of neurotransmitter systems plays a role in the development of drug addiction. However, several studies now implicate genetic variation at DAT as being a potential contributor to this mixture.

6.1.4   Conclusions

The dopaminergic system plays a role in the abuse liability for some, if not most, drugs. The stimulants, opiates, marijuana, nicotine, and ethanol, all interact directly or indirectly with the dopaminergic system, and most of these have actions on the DAT (Table 6.1.4). Numerous lines of evidence suggest the positive reinforcement, or DA hypothesis, of addiction falls short in

Table 6.1.4 Comparison of the Self-Administration of Various Drugs and the Effect That Drug Has on DAT

Drug	Self-Administered	Increases DA via DAT	Ref.
Cocaine	+	+	27, 28, 224
Amphetamine	+	+	78, 224
MDMA	+	+	73, 225
DMT	?	–	226
Mescaline	–	–	224, 227
LSD	–	–	224, 227, 228
Opiates	+	+	103, 224
Barbiturates	+	–	229
Benzodiazepines	+	?	229–232
Alcohol	+	+	172, 224
Caffeine	+	–	224, 233
Nicotine	+	(Indirect)	194–199, 234
Marijuana	+	+	150, 157, 158
PCP	+	+	124–127, 235

accounting for all aspects of addiction.[236] While many believe the elevation of DA within the mesolimbic DA system is a contributing factor to the abuse liability of drugs, considerable evidence supports the notion that neuroadaptive changes resulting from chronic drug use is what actually drives addictive behavior.[237] An understanding of the role of the DAT in the addictive process will likely involve the understanding of how drugs initially interact with the DAT as well as the effects of chronic drug exposure on DAT expression and function.

DAT occupancy alone does not impart a drug with addictive properties. Some drugs that interact with the DAT, such as cocaine, are quite addictive, while other drugs, such as mazindol, are not. There appears to be a temporal component in that, while mazindol interacts with the dopaminergic system, its entry into the brain is slow compared to that of cocaine.[56,57] The importance of the rate at which transporter occupancy occurs is also underscored by the observation that routes of drug administration, like smoking or intravenous injection, that lead to rapid entry into the brain, and for some drugs rapid DAT occupancy, are more likely to produce an intense "high" and have greater addictive potential than drug administration via oral or nasal routes, which are associated with delayed drug action in the brain.[238,239] In addition, baseline DA activity within the mesolimbic pathway may also be an important influence on psychostimulant-induced "high." The subjective high produced by methylphenidate appears related to both DAT occupancy and basal DA activity of the subject.[240,241] This result hints at the potential importance of genetic polymorphism within the dopaminergic system on addictive liability. Given that genetic polymorphism of the DAT has been tentatively linked to the addictive potential of several drugs, a better understanding of the contribution that genetic polymorphism of the DAT plays in the development of addiction will be valuable.

The cloning of the DAT[242,244] and its subsequent transfection into cells have allowed for the study of DAT in much greater detail. Moreover, the development of transgenic mice that lack DAT has now afforded the study of the mechanisms of action for many drugs.[59] Using these and other powerful new tools, in the future we may be better able to understand the role of DAT in the mechanisms of action for addictive drugs, the addictive process, and individual differences in a person's predisposition toward drug addiction.

REFERENCES

1. Glowinski, J. and Iversen, L. L., Regional studies of catecholamines in the rat brain. I. The disposition of [³H]norepinephrine, [³H]dopamine and [³H]dopa in various regions of the brain, *J. Neurochem.*, 13, 655, 1996.

2. Snyder, S.J. and Coyle, J.T., Regional differences in [³H]norepinephrine and [³H]dopamine uptake into rat brain homogenates, *J. Pharmacol. Exp. Ther.*, 165, 78, 1969.

3. Kuhar, M.J., Neurotransmitter uptake: a tool in identifying neurotransmitter-specific pathways, *Life Sci.*, 13, 1623, 1973.

4. Horn, A.S., Characteristics of neuronal dopamine uptake, in *Dopamine. Advances in Biochemical Psychopharmacology,* Roberts, P.J., Woodruff, G.N., and Iversen, L.L., Eds., Vol. 19, Raven Press, New York, 1978, 25.

5. Horn, A.S., Dopamine uptake: a review of progress in the latest decade, *Prog. Neurobiol.*, 34, 387, 1990.

6. Holz, K.W. and Coyle, J.T., The effects of various salts, temperature and the alkaloids veratridine and batrachotoxin on the uptake of [³H]-dopamine into synatosomes from rat striatum, *Mol. Pharmacol.*, 10, 746, 1974.

7. Kuhar, M.J. and Zarbin, M.A., Synaptosomal transport: a chloride dependence for choline, GABA, glycine, and several other compounds, *J. Neurochem.*, 30, 15, 1978.

8. Cao, C.J., Shamoo, A.E., and Eldefrawi, M.E., Cocaine-sensitive, ATP-dependent dopamine uptake in striatal synaptosomes, *Biochem. Pharmacol.*, 39, 49, 1990.

9. Koob, G.F. and Bloom, F.E., Cellular and molecular mechanisms of drug dependence, *Science*, 242, 715, 1988.

10. Kuhar, M.J., Ritz, M.C., and Boja, J.W., The dopamine hypothesis of the reinforcing properties of cocaine, *Trends Neurosci.*, 14, 299, 1991.

11. DiChiara, G. and Imperato, A., Drugs abused by humans preferentially increase synaptic dopamine concentrations in the mesolimbic system of freely moving rats, *Proc. Natl. Acad. Sci. U.S.A.*, 85, 5274, 1988.

12. Coyle, J.T. and Snyder, S.H., Catecholamine uptake by synaptosomes in homogenates of rat brain: stereospecificity in different areas, *J. Pharmacol. Exp. Ther.*, 170, 221, 1969.

13. Iversen, L.L., Uptake processes for biogenic amines, in *Biochemistry of Biogenic Amines*, Plenum Press, New York, 3, 381, 1975.

14. Horn, A.S., Characteristics of transport in dopamine neurons, in *The Mechanism of Neuronal and Extraneuronal Transport of Catecholamines*, D.M. Paton, Ed., Raven Press, New York, 195, 1976.

15. Amara, S. and Kuhar, M.J., Neurotransmitter transporters: recent progress, *Annu. Rev. Neurosci.*, 16, 73, 1993.

16. Harris, J.E. and Baldessarini, R.J., The uptake of [³H]dopamine by homogenates of rat corpus striatum: effects of cations, *Life Sci.*, 13, 303, 1973.

17. Horn, A.S., in *The Neurobiology of Dopamine*, Horn, A.S., Korf, J., and Westerink, B.H.C., Eds., Academic Press, New York, 1979, 217.

18. Zimanyi, I., Lajitha, A., and Reith, M.E.A., Comparison of characteristics of dopamine uptake and mazindol binding in mouse striatum, *Naunyn-Schmiedeberg's Arch. Pharmacol.*, 240, 626, 1989.

19. Shank, R.P., Schneider, C.R., and Tighe, J.J., Ion dependence of neurotransmitter uptake: inhibitory effects of ion substrates, *J. Neurochem.*, 49, 381, 1978.

20. Amejdki-Chab, N., Costentin, J., and Bonnet, J.J., Kinetic analysis of the chloride dependence of the neuronal uptake of dopamine and effect of anions on the ability of substrates to compete with the binding of the dopamine uptake inhibitor GBR 12783, *J. Neurochem.*, 58, 793, 1992.

21. Krueger, B.K., Kinetics and block of dopamine uptake in synaptosomes from rat caudate nucleus, *J. Neurochem.*, 55, 260, 1990.

22. McElvain, J.S. and Schenk, J.O., A multisubstrate mechanism of striatal dopamine uptake and its inhibition by cocaine, *Biochem. Pharmacol.*, 43, 2189, 1992.

23. Rostene, W., Boja, J.W., Scherman, D., Carroll, F.I., and Kuhar, M.J., Dopamine transport: pharma-cological distinction between the synaptic membrane and vesicular transporter in rat striatum, *Eur. J. Pharmacol.*, 281, 175, 1992.

24. Kitayama, S., Shimada, S., Xu, H., Markham, L., Donovan, D.M., and Uhl, G.R., Dopamine transporter site-directed mutations differentially alter substrate transport and cocaine binding, *Proc. Natl. Acad. Sci. U.S.A.*, 89, 7782, 1992.

25. Lee, F.J.S., Pristupa, Z.B., Ciliax, B.J., Levey, A.L., and Niznik, H.B., The dopamine transporter carboxyl-terminal tail. Truncation/substitution mutants selectively confer high affinity dopamine uptake while attenuating recognition of the ligand binding domain, *J. Biol. Chem.*, 271, 20885, 1996.

26. Volz, T.J. and Schenk, J.O., A comprehensive atlas of the topography of functional groups of the dopamine transporter, *Synapse*, 58, 72, 2005.

27. Heikkila, R.E., Cabbat, F.S., and Duviosin, R.C., Motor activity and rotational behavior after analogs of cocaine: correlation with dopamine uptake blockade, *Commun. Psychopharm.*, 3, 285, 1979.

28. Heikkila, R.E., Manzino, L., and Cabbat, F.S., Stereospecific effects of cocaine derivatives on ^{3}H-dopamine uptake: correlations with behavioral effects, *Subst. Use Misuse*, 2, 115, 1981.

29. Reith, M.E.A., Sershen, H., and Lajtha, A., Saturable [3H]cocaine binding in central nervous system of the mouse, *Life Sci.*, 27, 1055, 1980.

30. Kennedy, L.T. and Hanbauer, I., Sodium-sensitive cocaine binding to rat striatal membrane: possible relationship to dopamine uptake sites, *J. Neurochem.*, 41, 172, 1983.

31. Ritz, M.C., Lamb, R.J., Goldberg, S.R., and Kuhar, M.J., Cocaine receptors on dopamine transporters are related to self-administration of cocaine, *Science*, 237, 1219, 1987.

32. Bergman, J., Madras, B.K., Johnson, S.E., and Spealman, R.D., Effects of cocaine and related drugs in nonhuman primates. III. Self-administration by squirrel monkeys, *J. Pharmacol. Exp. Ther.*, 251, 150, 1989.

33. Scheffel, U., Boja, J.W., and Kuhar, M.J., Cocaine receptors: *in vivo* labeling with [3]H-(-) cocaine, ^{3}H-WIN 35,065-2 and [3]H-35,428, *Synapse*, 4, 390, 1989.

34. Fowler, J.S., Volkow, N.D., Wolf, A.P., Dewey, S.L., Schlyer, D.J., MacGregor, R.R., Hitzmann, R., Logan, J., Bendriem, B., Gatley, S.J., and Christman, D.R., Mapping cocaine binding sites in human and baboon brain *in vivo*, *Synapse*, 4, 371, 1989.

35. Volkow, N.D., Fowler, J.S., Wolf, A.P., Wang, G.J., Logan, J., MacGregor, D.J., Dewey, S.L., Schlyer, D.J., and Hitzmann, R., Distribution and kinetics of carbon-11-cocaine in the human body measured with PET, *J. Nucl. Med.*, 33, 521, 1992.

36. Scheffel, U., Pogun, S., Stathis, A., Boja, J.W., and Kuhar, M.J., *J. Pharmacol. Exp. Ther.*, 257, 954, 1992.

37. Cline, E.J., Scheffel, U., Boja, J.W., Mitchell, W.M., Carroll, F.I., Abraham, P., Lewin, A.H., and Kuhar, M.J., *In vivo* binding of [^{125}I]RTI-55 to dopamine and serotonin transporters in rat brain, *Synapse*, 12, 37, 1992.

38. Scheffel, U., Dannals, R.F., Cline, E.J., Ricaurte, G.A., Carroll, F.I., Abraham, P., Lewin, A.H., and Kuhar, M.J., [[123/125]I]RTI-55, an *in vivo* label for the serotonin transporter, *Synapse*, 11, 134, 1992.

39. Carroll, F.I., Rahman, M.A., Abraham, P., Parham, K., Lewin, A.H., Dannals, R.F., Shaya,, E., Scheffel, U., Wong, D.F., Boja., J.W., and Kuhar, M.J., [^{123}I]3-4(-iodophenyl)tropan-2-caroxylic acid methyl ester (RTI-55), a unique cocaine receptor ligand for imaging the dopamine and serotonin transporters *in vivo*, *Med. Chem. Res.*, 1, 289, 1991.

40. Neumeyer, J.L., Wang, S., Milius, R.M., Baldwin, R.M., Zea-Ponce, Y., Hoffer, P.B., Sybirska, E., Al-tikriti, M., Charney, D.S., Malison, R.T., Laruelle, M., and Innis, R.B., [^{123}I]-2-carbomethoxy-3-(-4-iodophenyl)tropane: high affinity SPECT radiotracer of monoamine reuptake sites in brain, *J. Med. Chem.*, 34, 3144, 1991.

41. Innis, R., Baldwin, R.M., Sybirska, E., Zea, Y., Laruelle, M., Al-Tikriti, M., Charney, D., Zoghbi, S., Wisniewski, G., Hoffer, P., Wang, S., Millius, R., and Neumeyer, J., Single photon emission computed tomography imaging of monoamine uptake sites in primate brain with [^{123}I]CIT, *Eur. J Pharmacol.*, 200, 369, 1991.

42. Shaya, E.K., Scheffel, U., Dannals, R.F., Ricaurte, G.A., Carroll, F.I., Wagner, Jr., H.N., Kuhar, M.J., and Wong, D.F., *In vivo* imaging of dopamine reuptake sites in the primate brain using single photon emission computed tomography (SPECT) and iodine-123 labeled RTI-55, *Synapse*, 10, 169, 1992.

43. Boja, J.W., Mitchell, W.M., Patel, A., Kopajtic, T.A., Carroll, F.I., Lewin, A.H., Abraham, P., and Kuhar, M.J., High affinity binding of [^{125}I]RTI-55 to dopamine and serotonin transporters in rat brain, *Synapse*, 12, 27, 1992.

44. Boja, J.W., Cadet, J.L., Kopajtic, T.A.., Lever., J, Seltzman, H.H., Wyrick, C.D., Lewin, A.H., Abraham, P., and Carroll, F.I., Selective labeling of the dopamine transporter by the high affinity ligand 3-(4-[^{125}I]iodophenyltropane-2-carboxylic acid isopropyl ester, *Mol. Pharmacol.*, 47, 779, 1995.

45. Staley, J.K., Boja, J.W., Carroll, F.I., Seltzman, H.H., Wyrick, C.D., Lewin, A.H., Abraham, P., and Mash, D.C., Mapping dopamine transporters in the human brain with novel selective cocaine analog [^{125}I]RTI-121, *Synapse*, 21 364, 1995.

46. Ciliax, B.J., Heilman, C., Demchyshyn, L.L., Pristupa, Z.B., Ince, E., Hersch, S.M., Niznik, H.B., and Levey, A.I., The dopamine transporter: immunochemical characterization and localization in brain, *J. Neurosci.*, 15, 1714, 1995.

47. Javitch, J.A., Blaustein, R.O., and Snyder, S.H., [³H]Mazindol binding associated with neuronal dopamine and norepinphrine uptake sites, *Mol. Pharmacol.*, 26, 35, 1984.

48. Dubocovich, M.L. and Zahniser, N.R., binding characteristics of dopamine uptake inhibitor [³H]nomifensine to striatal membranes, *Biochem. Pharmacol.*, 34, 1137, 1985.

49. Anderson, P.H., Biochemical and pharmacological characterization of [³H]GBR 12935 binding *in vitro* to rat striatal membranes: labeling of the dopamine uptake complex, *J. Neurochem.*, 48, 1887, 1987.

50. Schoemaker, H., Pimoule, C., Arbilla, S., Scatton, B., Javoy-Agid, F., and Langer, S.Z., Sodium dependent [³H]cocaine binding associated with dopamine uptake sites in the rat striatum and human putamen decrease after dopamine denervation and in Parkinson's disease, *Naunyn-Schmiedeberg's Arch. Pharmacol.*, 329, 227, 1985.

51. Calligaro, D.O. and Eldefraei, M.E., High affinity stereospecific binding of [³H]cocaine in striatum and its relationship to the dopamine transporter, *Membr. Biochem.*, 7, 87, 1988.

52. Madras, B.K., Fahey, M.A., Bergman, J., Canfield, D.R., and Spealman, R.D., Effects of cocaine and related drugs in nonhuman primates. I. [³H]Cocaine binding sites in caudate-putamen, *J. Pharmacol. Exp. Ther.*, 251, 131, 1989.

53. Ritz, M.C., Boja, J.W., Zaczek, R., Carroll, F.I., and Kuhar, M.J., ³H WIN 35,065-2: a ligand for cocaine receptors in striatum, *J. Neurochem.*, 55, 1556, 1990.

54. Madras, B.K., Spealman, R.D., Fahey, M.A., Neumeyer, J.L., Saha, J.K., and Milius, R.A., Cocaine receptors labeled by [³H]2-carbomethoxy-3-(4-fluorophenyl)tropane, *Mol. Pharmacol.*, 36, 518, 1989.

55. Boja, J.W., Markham, L., Patel, A., Uhl, G., and Kuhar, M.J., Expression of a single dopamine transporter cDNA can confer two cocaine binding sites, *Neuroreport*, 3, 247, 1992.

56. Madras, B.K. and Kaufman, M.J., Cocaine accumulates in dopamine-rich regions of primate brain after I.V. administration: comparison with mazindol distribution, *Synapse*, 18, 261, 1994.

57. Pögün, S., Scheffel, U., and Kuhar, M.J., Cocaine displaces [³H]WIN 35,428 binding to dopamine uptake sites *in vivo* more rapidly than mazindol or GBR 12909, *Eur. J. Pharmacol.*, 198, 203, 1991.

58. Stathis, M., Scheffel, U., Lever, S.Z., Boja, J.W., Carroll, F.I., and Kuhar, M.J., Rate of binding of various inhibitors at the dopamine transporter *in vivo*, *Psychopharmacology*, 119, 376, 1995.

59. Giros, B., Jaber, M., Jones., S.R., Wightman, R.M., and Caron, M.G., Hyperlocomotion and indifference to cocaine and amphetamine in mice lacking the dopamine transporter, *Nature*, 379, 606, 1996.

60. Sora, I., Hall., F.S., Andrews, A.M., Itokawa, M., Li, X., Wei, H., Wichems, C., Lesch, K., Murphy, D.L., and Uhl, G.R., Molecular mechanisms of cocaine reward: combined dopamine and serotonin transporter knockouts eliminate cocaine place preference, *PNAS*, 98, 5300, 2001.

61. Carboni, E., Spielewoy, C., Vacca, C., Norten-Bertrand, M., Giros, B., and DiChiara, G., Cocaine and amphetamine increase extracellular dopamine in the nucleus accumbens of mice lacking the dopamine transporter gene, *J. Neurosci.*, 21, 1, 2001.

62. Mead, A.N., Rocha, B.A., Donovan, D.M., and Katz, J.L., Intravenous cocaine induced-activity and behavioral sensitization in norepinephrine-, but not dopamine-transporter knockout mice, *Eur. J. Neurosci.*, 16, 514, 2002.

63. Hall, F.S., Sora, I., Drgonova, J., Li, X.F., Goeb, M., and Uhl, G.R., Molecular mechanisms underlying the rewarding effects of cocaine, *Ann. N.Y. Acad. Sci.*, 1025, 47, 2004.

64. Ungerstedt, U., Striatal dopamine release after amphetamine or nerve degeneration revealed by rotational behavior, *Acta Physiol. Scand.*, 367, 49, 1971.

65. Masuoka, D.T., Alcaraz, A.F., and Schott, H.F., [³H]Dopamine release by d-amphetamine from striatal synaptosomes of reserpinized rats, *Biochem. Pharmacol.*, 31, 1969, 1982.

66. Kuczenski, R., Biochemical actions of amphetamine and other stimulants, in *Stimulants: Neurochemical, Behavioral, and Clinical Perspectives*, I. Creese, Ed., Raven Press, New York, 1983, 31.

67. Bowyer, J.F., Spuler, K.P., and Weiner, N., Effects of phencyclidine, amphetamine and related compounds on dopamine release from and uptake into striatal synaptosomes, *J. Pharmacol. Exp. Ther.*, 229, 671, 1984.

68. Moghaddam, B., Roth, R.H., and Bunny, B.S., Characterization of dopamine release in the rat medial prefrontal cortex as assessed by *in vivo* microdialysis: comparison to the striatum, *Neuroscience*, 36, 669, 1990.

69. Robertson, G.S., Damsma, G., and Fibiger, H.C., Characterization of dopamine release in the sub-stantia nigra by *in vivo* microdialysis in freely moving rats, *J. Neurosci.*, 11, 2209, 1991.

70. Schmidt, C.J. and Gibb, J.W., Role of the dopamine uptake carrier in the neurochemical response to methamphetamine: effects of amfonelic acid, *Eur. J. Pharmacol.*, 109, 73, 1985.

71. Johnson, M.P., Hoffman, A.J., and Nichols, D.E., Effects of the enantimers of MDA, MDMA, and related analogues of [³H]serotonin and [³H]dopamine release from superfused rat brain slices, *Eur. J. Pharmacol.*, 132, 269, 1986.

72. Steele, T.D., Nichols, D.E., and Yim, G.K., Stereochemical effects of 3,4-methylendioxymethamphet-amine (MDMA) and related amphetamine derivatives on inhibition of uptake of [³H]monoamines into synaptosomes from different regions of rat brain, *Biochem. Pharmacol.*, 36, 2297, 1987.

73. Yamamoto, B.K., and Spanos, L.J., The acute effects of methylenedioxymethamphetamine on dopam-ine release in awake-behaving rat, *Eur. J. Pharmacol.*, 148, 195, 1988.

74. Nash, J.F. and Nichols, D.E., Microdialysis studies on 3,4-methylenedioxyamphetamine and structur-ally related analogues, *Eur. J. Pharmacol.*, 200, 53, 1991.

75. Johnson, M.P., Conarty, P.F., and Nichols, D.E., [³H]Monoamine releasing and uptake inhibition properties of 3,4-methylenedioxymethamphetamine and *p*-chloroamphetamine analogues, *Eur. J. Pharmacol.*, 200, 9, 1991.

76. Azzaro, A.J., Ziance, R.J., and Rutledge, C.O., The importance of neuronal uptake of amines for amphetamine-induced release of ³H-norepinephrine from isolated brain tissue, *J. Pharmacol. Exp. Ther.*, 189, 110, 1974.

77. Hadfield, M.G., A comparison of *in vivo* and *in vitro* amphetamine on synaptosomal uptake of dopamine in mouse striatum, *Res. Commun. Chem. Mol. Pathol. Pharmacol.*, 48, 183, 1985.

78. Arnold, E.B., Molinoff, P.B., and Rutledge, C.O., The release of endogenous norepinephrine and dopamine from cerebral cortex by amphetamine, *J. Pharmacol. Exp. Ther.*, 202, 544, 1977.

79. Fisher, J.F. and Cho, A.K., Chemical release of dopamine from striatal homogenates: evidence for an exchange diffusion model, *J. Pharmacol. Exp. Ther.*, 208, 203, 1979.

80. Liang, N.Y. and Rutledge, C.O., Comparison of the release of [³H]dopamine from isolated corpus striatum by amphetamine, fenfluramine and unlabeled dopamine, *Biochem. Pharmacol.*, 31, 983, 1982.

81. Zaczek, R., Culp, S., and De Souza, E.B., Intrasynaptosomal sequestration of [³H]amphetamine and [³H]methylenedioxyamphetamine: characterization suggests the presence of a factor responsible for maintaining sequestration, *J. Neurochem.*, 54, 195, 1990.

82. Zaczek, R., Culp, S., and De Souza, E.B., Interactions of [³H]amphetamine with rat brain synapto-somes. II. Active, *J. Pharmacol. Exp. Ther.*, 257, 830, 1991.

83. Jacocks, H.M. and Cox, B.K., Serotonin-stimulated [³H]dopamine via reversal of the dopamine trans-porter in rat striatum and nucleus accumbens: a comparison with release elicited by potassium, N-methyl-D-aspartic acid, glutamic acid and D-amphetamine, *J. Pharmacol. Exp. Ther.*, 262, 356, 1992.

84. Sulzer, D., Maidment, N.T., and Rayport, S., Amphetamine and other weak bases act to promote reverse transport of dopamine in ventral midbrain neurons, *J. Neurochem.*, 60, 527, 1993.

85. Eshleman, A.J., Henningsen, R.A., Neve, K.A., and Janowsky, A., Release of dopamine via the human transporter, *Mol. Pharmacol.*, 45, 312, 1994.

86. Kahlig, K.M., Binda, F., Khoshbouei, H., Blakely, R.D., McMahon, D.G., Javitch, J.A., and Galli, A., Amphetamine induces dopamine efflux through a dopamine transporter channel, *PNAS*, 102, 3495, 2005.

87. Pifl, C., Drobny, H., Reither, H., Hornykiewicz, O., and Singer, E.A., Mechanism of the dopamine-releasing actions of amphetamine and cocaine: plasmalemmal dopamine transporter versus vesicular monoamine transporter, *Mol. Pharmacol.*, 47, 368, 1995.

88. Di Chiara, G. and Imperato, A., Opposite effects of mu and kappa opiate agonists on dopamine release in the nucleus accumbens and in the dorsal caudate of freely moving rat, *J. Pharmacol. Exp. Ther.*, 244, 1067, 1988b.

89. Di Chiara, G. and Imperato, A., Opposite effects of mu and kappa opiate agonists on dopamine release in the nucleus accumbens and in the dorsal caudate of freely moving rat, *J. Pharmacol. Exp. Ther.*, 244, 1067, 1988b.

90. Hurd, Y.L., Weiss, F., Koob, G., and Ungerstedt, U., Cocaine reinforcement and extracellular dopamine overflow in the rat nucleus accumbens: an *in vivo* microdialysis study, *Brain Res.*, 498, 199, 1989.

91. Kalivas, P.W., Winderlov, E., Stanley, D., Breese, G.R., and Prange, A.J., Jr., Enkephalin action on the mesolimbicdopamine system: a dopamine-dependent and dopamine-independent increase in locomotor activity, *J. Pharmacol. Exp. Ther.*, 227, 229, 1983.

92. Pettit, H.O., Ettenberg, A., Bloom, F.E., and Koob, G.F., Destruction of dopamine in the nucleus accumbens selectively attenuates cocaine but not heroin self-administration in rats, *Psychopharmacology*, 84, 167, 1984.

93. Sellings, L.H. and Clarke, P.B., Segregation of amphetamine reward and locomotor stimulation between nucleus accumbens medial shell and core, *J. Neurosci.*, 23, 6295, 2003.

94. Di Chiara, G. and North, A.R., Neurobiology of opiate abuse, *TIPS*, 13, 185, 1992.

95. Koob, G.F., Drugs of abuse: anatomy, pharmacology and function of reward pathways, *TIPS*, 13, 177, 1992.

96. Spyraki, C., Fibiger, H.C., and Phillips, A.G., Attenuation of heroin reward in rats by disruption of the mesolimbic dopamine system, *Psychopharmacology*, 79, 278, 1983.

97. Zito, K.A., Vickers, G., and Roberts, D.C.S., Disruption of cocaine and heroin self-administration following kianic acid lesions of the nucleus accumbens, *Pharmacol. Biochem. Behav.*, 23, 1029, 1985.

98. Bozarth, M.A. and Wise, R.A., Heroin reward is dependent on a dopaminergic substrate, *Life Sci.*, 29, 1881, 1981.

99. Kornetsky, C. and Porrino L.J., Brain Mechanisms of drug-induced reinforcement, in *Addictive States*, O'Brien, C.P. and Jaffe, J.H., Eds., Raven Press, New York, 1992, 59.

100. Reith, M.E.A., Meisler, B.E., Sershen, H., and Lajtha, A., Structural requirements for cocaine congeners to interact with dopamine and serotonin uptake sites in mouse brain and to induce stereotyped behavior, *Biochem. Pharmacol.*, 35, 1123, 1986.

101. Gysling, K. and Wang, R.Y., Morphine-induced activation of A10 dopamine neurons in the rat brain, *Brain Res.*, 277, 119, 1983.

102. Matthews, R.T. and German, D.C., Electrophysiological evidence for excitation of rat ventral tegmental area dopamine neurons by morphine, *Neuroscience*, 11, 617, 1984.

103. Das, D., Rogers, J., and Michael-Titus, A.T., Comparative study of the effects of mu, delta and kappa opioid agonists on 3H-dopamine uptake in the rat striatum and nucleus accumbens, *Neuropharmacology*, 33, 221, 1994.

104. Schenk, S., Partridge, B., and Shippenberg, T.S., Reinstatement of extinguished drug-taking behavior in rats: effect of the kappa-opioid receptor agonist, U69593, *Psychopharmacology*, 151, 85, 2000.

105. Izenwasser, S., Newman A.H., Cox, B.M., and Katz, J.L., The cocaine-like behavioral effects of meperidine are mediated by activity at the dopamine transporter, *Eur. J. Pharmacol.*, 297, 9, 1996.

106. Bergstrom, K.A., Jolkkonen, J., Kuikka, J.T., Akerman, K.K., Viinamaki, H., Airaksinen, O., Lansimies, E., and Tiihonen, J., Fentanyl decreases beta-CIT binding to the dopamine transporter, *Synapse*, 29, 413, 1998.

107. Simantov, R., Chronic morphine alters dopamine transporter density in the rat brain: possible role in the mechanism of drug addiction, *Neurosci. Lett.*, 163, 121, 1993.

108. Spielwoy, C., Gonon, F., Roubert, C., Fauchey, V., Jaber, M., Caron, M.G., Roques, B.P., Hamon, M., Betancur, C., Maldonado, R., and Giros, B., Increased rewarding properties of morphine in dopamine-transporter knockout mice, *Eur. J. Neurosci.*, 12, 1827, 2000.

109. Svingos, A.L., Clarke, C.L., and Pickel, V.M., Localization of delta-opioid receptor and dopamine transporter in the nucleus accumbens shell: implications for opiate and psychostimulant cross sensitization, *Synapse*, 34, 1, 1999.

110. Izenwasser, S. and Cox, B.M., Daily cocaine treatment produces a persistent reduction of [3H]dopamine uptake *in vitro* in the rat nucleus accumbens but not the striatum, *Brain Res.*, 531, 338, 1990.

111. Gudehithlu, K.P. and Bhargava, H.N., Modification of characteristics of dopamine transporter in brain regions and spinal cord of morphine tolerant and abstinent rats, *Neuropharmacology*, 35, 169, 1996.

112. Spangler, R., Goddard, N.L., Avena, N.M., Hoebel, B.G., and Leibowitz, S.F., Elevated D3 dopamine receptor mRNA in dopaminergic and dopaminoceptive regions of the rat brain in response to morphine, *Brain Res. Mol. Brain Res.*, 111, 74, 2003.

113. Kish, S.J., Kalasinsky, K.S., Derach, P., Schmunk, G.A., Guttman, M., Ang, L., Adams, V., Furukawa, Y., and Haycock, J.W., Striatal dopaminergic and serotonergic markers in human heroin users, *Neuropsychopharmacology*, 24, 561, 2001.

114. Carboni, E., Imperato, A., Perezzani, L., and DiChiara, G., Amphetamine, cocaine, phencyclidine and nomifensine increase extracellular dopamine concentrations preferentially in the nucleus accumbens of freely moving rats, *Neuroscience,* 28, 653, 1989.

115. Hernandez, L., Auerbach, S., and Hoebel, B.G., Phencyclidine (PCP) injected into the nucleus accumbens increases extracellular dopamine and serotonin as measured by microdialysis, *Life Sci.,* 42, 1713, 1988.

116. Hondo, H., Yonezawa, Y., Nakahara, T., Nakamura, K., Hirano, M., Uchimura, H., and Tashiro, N., Effect of Phencyclidine on dopamine release in the rat prefrontal cortex; an *in vivo* microdialysis study, *Brain Res.,* 633, 337, 1994.

117. Hata, N., Nishikawa, T., Umino, A., and Takahashi, K., Evidence for involvement of N-methyl-D-aspartate receptor in tonic inhibitory control of dopaminergic transmission in the rat medial frontal cortex, *Neurosci. Lett.,* 120, 101, 1990.

118. Freeman, A.S. and Bunney, B.S., The effects of phencyclidine and N-allynormetazocine on mid-brain dopamine neuronal activity, *Eur. J. Pharmacol.,* 104, 287, 1984.

119. Gariano, R.F. and Groves, P.M., Burst firing induced in mid-brain dopamine neurons by stimulation of the medial prefrontal and anterior cingulate cortices, *Brain Res.,* 462, 194, 1988.

120. Suaad-Chagny, M.F., Chergui, K., Chouvet, G., and Gonon, F., Relationship between dopamine release in the rat nucleus accumbens and the discharge activity of dopaminergic neurons during local *in vivo* application of amino acids in the ventral tegmental area, *Neuroscience,* 49, 63, 1992.

121. Fagg, G.E., Phencyclidine and related drugs bind to the activated N-methyl-D-aspartate receptor-channels complex in rat membranes, *Neurosci. Lett.,* 76, 221, 1987.

122. Mount, H., Boksa, P., Chadieu, I., and Quirion, R., Phencyclidine and related compounds evoked [3H] dopamine release from rat mesencephalon cell cultures by mechanisms independent of the phencyclidine receptor, sigma binding site, or dopamine uptake site, *Can. J. Physiol. Pharmacol.,* 68, 1200, 1990.

123. Bowyer, J.F., Spuhler, K.P., and Weiner, N., Effects of phencyclidine, amphetamine, and related compounds on dopamine release from and uptake into striatal synaptosomes, *J. Pharmacol. Exp. Ther.,* 229, 671, 1984.

124. Baba, A., Yamamoto, T., Yamamoto, H., Suzuki, T., and Moroji, T., Effects of the major metabolite of phencyclidine, the trans isomer of 4-phenyl-4-(l-piperidinyl) cyclohexanol, on [3H]N-(1-[2-thie-nyl]cyclohexyl)-3,4-piperidine([3H}TPC) binding and [3H] dopamine uptake in the rat brain, *Neurosci. Lett.,* 182, 119, 1994.

125. Garey, R.E. and Heath, R.G., The effects of phencyclidine on the uptake of 3H-catecholamines by rat striatal and hypothalamic synaptosomes, *Life Sci.,* 18, 1105, 1976.

126. Smith, R.C., Meltzer, H.Y., Arora, R.C., and Davis, J.M., Effects of phencyclidine on H-catecholamines and H-serotonin uptake in synaptosomal preparations from the rat brain, *Biochem. Pharmacol.,* 26, 1435, 1977.

127. Gerhardt, G.A., Pang, K., and Rose, G.M., *In vivo* electrochemical demonstration of presynaptic actions of phencyclidine in rat caudate nucleus, *J. Pharmacol. Exp. Ther.,* 241, 714, 1987.

128. Vignon, J., Pinet, V., Cerruti, C., Kamenka, J., and Chicheportiche, R., [3H]N-1(2-Benzo(b)thiophenyl)cyclohexyl]piperidinme ([3H]BTCP): a new phencyclidine analog selective for the dopamine uptake complex, *Eur. J. Pharmacol.,* 148, 427, 1988.

129. Kuhar, M.J., Boja, J.W., and Cone, E.J., Phencyclidine binding to striatal cocaine receptors, *Neuropharmacology,* 29, 295, 1990.

130. Cook, C.E., Perez, R.M., Jeffcoat, A.R., and Brine, D.R., Phencyclidine disposition in humans after small doses of radiolabeled drug, *Fed. Proc.,* 42, 2566, 1983.

131. Schiffer, W.K., Logan, J., and Dewey, S.L., Positron emission tomography studies of potential mechanisms underlying phencyclidine-induced alterations in striatal dopamine, *Neuropharmacology,* 28, 2192, 2003.

132. Carlezon, Jr., W.A. and Wise, R.A., Rewarding actions of phencyclidine and related drugs in the nucleus accumbens shell and frontal cortex, *J. Neurosci.,* 16, 3112, 1996.

133. Carlezon, Jr., W.A. and Wise, R.A., Habit-forming actions of nomifensine in the nucleus accumbens, *Psychopharmacology,* 122, 194, 1995.

134. Steinpreis, R.E. and Salamone, J.D., The role of nucleus accumbens dopamine in the neurochemical and behavioral effects of phencyclidine: a microdialysis and behavioral study, *Brain Res.,* 612, 263, 1993.

135. Hanania, T. and Zahniser, N.R., Locomotor activity induced by noncompetitive NMDA receptor antagonists versus dopamine transporter inhibitors: opposite strain differences in inbred long-sleep and short-sleep mice, *Alcohol Clin. Exp. Res.*, 26, 431, 2002.

136. Nicoll, R.A. and Alger B.E., The brain's own marijuana, *Sci. Am.*, 291, 68, 2005.

137. Chaperon, F. and Thiebot, M.H., Behavioral effects of cannabinoid agents in animals, *Crit. Rev. Neurobiol.*, 13, 243, 1999.

138. Ameri, A., The effects of cannabinoids on the brain, *Prog. Neurobiol.*, 59, 315, 1999.

139. Chen, J., Paredes, W., Lowinson, J.H., and Gardner, E.L., Δ^9-Tetrahydrocannabinol enhances presynaptic dopamine efflux in the medial prefrontal cortex, *Eur. J. Pharmacol.*, 190, 259, 1990.

140. Pistis, M., Ferraro, L., Flore, G., Tanganelli, S., Gessa, G.L., and Devoto, P., Delta(9)-tetrahydrocannabinol decreases extracellular GABA and increases extracellular glutamate and dopamine levels in the prefrontal cortex: an *in vivo* microdialysis study, *Brain Res.*, 948, 155, 2002.

141. Ng Cheong Ton, J.M., Gerhardt, G.A., Friedmann, M., Etgen, A.M., Rose, G.M., Sharpless, N.S., and Gardner, E.L., Effects of Δ^9-tetrahydrocannabinol on potassium-evoked release of dopamine in the rat caudate nucleus: an *in vivo* electrochemical and *in vivo* microdialysis study, *Brain Res.*, 451, 59, 1988.

142. Chen, J., Paredes, W., Li, J., Smith, D., Lowinson, J., and Gardner, E.L., *In vivo* brain microdialysis studies of Δ^9-tetrahydrocannabinol on presynaptic dopamine efflux in nucleus accumbens of the Lewis rat, *Psychopharmacology*, 102, 156, 1990.

143. Chen, J., Paredes, W., Lowinson, J.H., and Gardner, E.L., Strain-specific facilitation of dopamine efflux by Δ^9-tetrahydrocannabinol in the nucleus accumbens of a rat: an *in vivo* microdialysis study, *Neurosci. Lett.*, 129, 136, 1991.

144. Chen, J., Marmur, R., Pulles, A., Paredes, W., and Gardner, E.L., Ventral tegmental microinjection of Δ^9-tetrahydrocannabinol enhances ventral tegmental somatodendritic dopamine levels but not forebrain dopamine levels: evidence for local neural action by marijuana's psychoactive ingredient, *Brain Res.*, 621, 65, 1993.

145. French, E.D., Dillion, K., and Wu, X., Cannabinoids excite dopamine neurons in the ventral tegmentum and substantia nigra, *Neuroreport*, 8, 649, 1997.

146. Riegel, A.C. and Lupica, C.R., Independent presynaptic and postsynaptic mechanisms regulate endocannabinoid signaling at multiple synapses in the ventral tegmental area, *J. Neurosci.*, 24, 11070, 2004.

147. Melis, M., Perra, S., Muntoni, A.L., Pillolla, G., Lutz, B., Marsicano, G., Di Marzo, V., Gessa, G.L., and Pistis, M., Prefrontal cortex stimulation induces 2-arachidonoyl-glycerol-mediated suppression of excitation in dopamine neurons, *J. Neurosci.*, 24, 10707, 2004.

148. Valjent, E., Pages, C., Rogard, M., Besson, M.J., Maldonado, R., and Caboche, J., Delta 9-tetrahydrocannabinol-induced MAPK/ERK and Elk-1 activation *in vivo* depends on dopaminergic transmission, *Eur. J. Neurosci.*, 14, 342, 2001.

149. Bloom, A.S., Effect of delta-9-tetrahydrocannabinol on the synthesis of dopamine and norepinephrine in mouse brain synaptosomes, *J. Pharmacol. Exp. Ther.*, 221, 97, 1982.

150. Poddar, M.K. and Dewey, W.L., Effects of cannabinoids on catecholamine uptake and release in hypothalamic and striatal synaptosomes, *J. Pharmacol. Exp. Ther.*, 214, 63, 1980.

151. Hershkowitz, M. and Szechtman, H., Pretreatment with Δ^1 tetrahydrocannabinol and psychoactive drugs: effects on uptake of biogenic amines and on behavior, *Eur. J. Pharm.*, 59, 267, 1979.

152. Banerjee, S.P., Snyder, S.H., and Mechoulam, R., Cannabinoids: influence on neurotransmitter uptake in rat brain synaptosomes, *J. Pharmacol. Exp. Ther.*, 194, 74, 1975.

153. Sakurai-Yamashita, Y., Kataoka, Y., Fujiwara, M., Mine, K., and Ueki, S., Delta 9-tetrahydrocannabinol facilitates striatal dopaminergic transmission, *Pharmacol. Biochem. Behav.*, 33, 397, 1989.

154. Dean, B., Bradbury, R., and Copolov, D.L., Cannabis-sensitive dopaminergic markers in postmortem central nervous system: changes in schizophrenia, *Biol. Psychiatry*, 53, 585, 2003.

155. Wu, X. and French, E.D., Effects of chronic delta9-tetrahydrocannabinol on rat midbrain dopamine neurons: an electrophysiological assessment, *Neuropharmacology*, 39, 391, 2000.

156. Gardner, E.L., Paredes, W., Smith, D., Donner, A., Milling, C., Cohen, D., and Morrison, D., Facilitation of brain stimulation reward by Δ^9-tetrahydrocannabinol, *Psychopharmacology*, 96, 142, 1988.

157. Braida, D., Losue, S., Pegorini, S., and Sala, M., Delta9-tetrahydrocannabinol-induced conditioned place preference and intracerebroventricular self-administration in rats, *Eur. J. Pharmacol.*, 506, 63, 2004.

158. Justinova, Z., Tanda, G., Redhi, G.H., and Goldberg, S.R., Self-administration of delta(9)-tetrahydro-cannabinol (THC) by drug naïve squirrel monkeys, *Psychopharmacology,* 169, 135, 2003.

159. Fattore, L., Spano, S., Gregorio, C., Deiana, S., Fadda, P., and Fratta, W., Cannabinoid CB1 antagonist SR 141716A attenuates reinstatement of heroin self-administration in heroin-abstinent rats, *Neuropharmacology,* 48, 1097, 2005.

160. Samuel, D., Lynch, M.A., and Littleton, J.M., Picrotoxin inhibits the effect of ethanol on the spontaneous efflux of [^{3}H]-dopamine from superfused slices of rat corpus striatum, *Neuropharmacology,* 22, 1412, 1983.

161. Shier, W.T., Koda, L.Y., and Bloom, F.E., Metabolism of [^{3}H]dopamine following intracerebroventricular injection in rats pretreated with ethanol or choral hydrate, *Neuropharmacology,* 22, 279, 1983.

162. Russell, V.A., Lamm, M.C., and Taljaard, J.J., Effects of ethanol on [^{3}H]dopamine release in rat nucleus accumbens and striatal slices, *Neurochem. Res.,* 13, 487, 1988.

163. Strombom, U.H. and Liedman, B., Role of dopaminergic neurotransmission in locomotor stimulation by dexamphetamine and ethanol, *Psychopharmacology,* 78, 271, 1982.

164. Murphy, J.M., McBride, W.J., Lumeng, L., and Li, T.K., Monoamine and metabolite levels in CNS regions of the P line of alcohol-preferring rats after acute and chronic ethanol treatment, *Pharmacol. Biochem. Behav.,* 19, 849, 1983.

165. Di Chiara, G. and Imperato, A., Ethanol preferentially stimulates dopamine release in the nucleus accumbens of freely moving rats, *Eur. J. Pharmacol.,* 115, 131, 1985.

166. Imperato, I. and Di Chiara, G., Preferential stimulation of dopamine release in the nucleus accumbens of freely moving rats by ethanol, *J. Pharmacol. Exp. Ther.,* 239, 219, 1986.

167. Yoshimoto, K., McBride, W.J., Lumberg, L., and Li, T.K., Ethanol enhances the release of dopamine and serotonin in the nucleus accumbens, *Alcohol,* 9, 17, 1992.

168. McBride, W.J., Murphy, J.M., Gatto, G.J., Levy, A.D., Yoshimoto, K., Lumeng, L., and Li, T.K., CNS mechanisms of alcohol self-administration, *Alcohol Alcohol.,* Suppl. 2, 463, 1993.

169. Samson, H.H. and Hodge, C.W., The role of the mesoaccumbens dopamine system in ethanol reinforcement: studies using the techniques of microinjection and voltammetry, *Alcohol Alcohol.,* Suppl., 2, 469, 1993.

170. Weiss, F., Lorang, M.T., Bloom, F.E., and Koob, G.F., Oral alcohol self-administration stimulates dopamine release in the nucleus accumbens: genetic and motivational determinants, *J. Pharmacol. Exp. Ther.,* 267, 250, 1993.

171. Kiianmaa, K., Nurmi, M., Nykanen, I., and Sinclair, J.D., Effect of ethanol on extracellular dopamine in the nucleus accumbens of alcohol-preferring AA and alcohol-avoiding ANA rats, *Pharmacol. Biochem. Behav.,* 52, 29, 1995.

172. Tan, A.Y., Dular, R., and Innes, I.R., Alcohol feeding alters [^{3}H]dopamine uptake into rat cortical and brain stem synaptosomes, *Prog. Biochem. Pharmacol.,* 18, 224, 1981.

173. Mayfield, R.D., Maiya, R., Keller, D., and Zahniser, N.R., Ethanol potentiates the function of the human dopamine transporter expressed in *Xenopus* oocytes, *J. Neurochem.,* 79, 1070, 2001.

174. Maiya, R., Buck, K.J., Harris, R.A., and Mayfield, R.D., Ethanol-sensitive sites on the human dopamine transporter, *J. Biol. Chem.,* 277, 30724, 2002.

175. Robinson, D.L., Volz, T.J., Schenk, J.O., and Wightman, R.M., Acute ethanol decreases dopamine transporter velocity in rat striatum: *in vivo* and *in vitro* electrochemical measurements, *Alcohol Clin. Exp. Res.,* 29, 746, 2005.

176. Lynch, M.A., Samuel, D., and Littleton, J.M., Altered characteristics of [^{3}H]dopamine release from superfused slices of corpus striatum obtained from rats receiving ethanol *in vivo, Neuropharmacology,* 24, 479, 1985.

177. Yan, Q.S., Ethanol-induced nonexocytotic [^{3}H]dopamine release from rat nucleus accumbens slices, *Alcohol,* 27, 127, 2002.

178. Yim, H.J. and Gonzales, R.A., Ethanol-induced increase in dopamine extracellular concentrations in rat nucleus accumbens are accounted for by increased release and not uptake inhibition, *Alcohol,* 22, 107, 2000.

179. Savelieva, K.V., Caudle, W.M., Findlay, G.S., Caron, M.G., and Miller, G.W., Decreased ethanol preferences and consumption in dopamine transporter female knock-out mice, *Alcohol. Clin. Exp. Res.,* 26, 2002.

180. Hearn, W.L., Flynn, D.D., Hime, G.W., Rose, S., Cofino, J.C., Mantero-Atienza, E., Wetli, C.V., and Mash, D.C., Cocaethylene; a unique metabolite displays high affinity for the dopamine transporter, *J. Neurochem.*, 56, 698, 1991.

181. Jatlow, P., Elsworth, J.D., Bradberry, C.W., Winger, G., Taylor, J.R., Russell, R., and Roth, R.H., Cocaethylene: a neuropharmacologically active metabolite associated with concurrent cocaine-ethanol ingestion, *Life Sci.*, 48, 1781, 1991.

182. Woodward, J.J., Mansbach, R., Carroll, F.I., and Balster, R.L., Cocaethylene inhibits dopamine uptake and produces cocaine-like actions in drug discrimination studies, *Eur. J. Pharmacol.*, 197, 235, 1991.

183. Lewin, A.H., Gao, Y., Abraham, P., Boja, J.W., Kuhar, M.J., and Carroll, F.I., The effect of 2-substitution on binding affinity at the cocaine receptor, *J. Med. Chem.*, 35, 135, 1992.

184. Bradberry, C.W., Nobiletti, J.B., Elsworth, J.D., Murphy, B., Jatlow, P., and Roth, R.H., Cocaine and cocaethylene; microdialysis comparison of brain drug levels and effects on dopamine and serotonin, *J. Neurochem.*, 60, 1429, 1993.

185. Iyer, R.N., Nobiletti, J.B., Jatlow, P.I., and Bradberry, C.W., Cocaine and cocaethylene: effects of extracellular dopamine in the primate, *Psychopharmacology,* 120, 150, 1995.

186. Katz, J.I., Terry, P., and Witkin, J.M., Comparative behavioral pharmacology and toxicology of cocaine and its ethanol-derived metabolite, cocaine ethyl-ester (cocaethylene), *Life Sci.*, 50, 1351, 1992.

187. Hearn, W.L., Rose, S.L., Wagner, J., Ciarleglio, A.C., and Mash, D.C., Cocaethylene is more potent than cocaine in mediating lethality, *Pharmacol. Biochem. Behav.*, 39, 531, 1991.

188. Meehan, S.M. and Schechter, M.D., Cocaethylene-induced lethality in mice is potentiated by alcohol, *Alcohol,* 12, 383, 1995.

189. Wilson, L.D., Jeromin, J., Garvey, L., and Dorbandt, A., Cocaine, ethanol, and cocaethylene cardiotoxicity in an animal model of cocaine and ethanol abuse, *Acad. Emerg. Med.,* 8, 211, 2001.

190. Pennings, E.J., Leccese, A.P., and Wolff, F.A., Effects of concurrent use of alcohol and cocaine, *Addiction,* 97, 773, 2002.

191. Hart, C.L., Jatlow, P., Sevarino, K.A., and McCance-Katz, E.F., Comparison of intravenous cocaethylene and cocaine in humans, *Psychopharmacology,* 149, 153, 2001.

192. Knackstedt, L.A., Samimi, M.M., and Ettenberg, A., Evidence for opponent-process actions of intravenous cocaine and cocaethylene, *Pharmacol. Biochem. Behav.,* 72, 931, 2002.

193. Damsma, G., Westernik, B.H., de Vries, J.B., and Horn, A.S., The effect of systemically applied cholinergic drugs on the striatal release of dopamine and its metabolites, as determined by automated microdialysis in conscious rats. *Neurosci. Lett.,* 89, 349, 1988.

194. Westfall, T.C., Effect of nicotine and other drugs on the release of ^{3}H-norepinephrine and ^{3}H-dopamine from rat brain slices, *Neuropharmacology,* 13, 693, 1974.

195. Marien, M., Brien, J., and Jhamandas, K., Regional release of [^{3}H]dopamine from rat brain *in vitro*: effects of opioids on release induced by potassium nicotine, and L-glutamic acid, *Can. J. Physiol. Pharmacol.,* 61, 43, 1983.

196. Rapier, C., Lunt, G.G., and Wonnacott, S., Stereoselective nicotine-induced release of dopamine from striatal synaptosomes: concentration dependence and repetitive stimulation, *J. Neurochem.,* 50, 1123, 1988.

197. Izenwasser, S., Jacocks, H.M., Rosenberger, J.G., and Cox, B.M., Nicotine indirectly inhibits [^{3}H]dopamine uptake at concentrations that do not directly promote [^{3}H]dopamine release in rat striatum, *J. Neurochem.,* 56, 603, 1991.

198. Dwoskin, L.P., Leibee, L.L., Jewell, A.L., Fang, Z., and Crooks, P.A., Inhibition of [^{3}H]dopamine uptake into rat striatal slices by quaternary *N*-methylated nicotine metabolites, *Life Sci.,* 50, PL-223, 1992.

199. Yamashita, H., Kitayama, S., Zhang, Y.X., Takahashi, T., Dohi, T., and Nakamura, S., Effect of nicotine on dopamine uptake in COS cells possessing the rat dopamine transporter and in PC12 cells, *Biochem. Pharmacol.,* 49, 742, 1995.

200. Lerner-Marmarosh, N., Carroll, F.I., and Abood, L.G., Antagonism of nicotine's action by cocaine analogs, *Life Sci.,* 56, PL67, 1995.

201. Drew, A.E., Derbez, A.E., and Werling, L.L., Nicotinic receptor-mediated regulation of transporter activity in the rat prefrontal cortex, *Synapse,* 38, 10, 2000.

202. Drew, A.E. and Werling, L.L., Nicotinic receptor-mediated regulation of the dopamine transporter in rat prefrontocortical slices following chronic *in vivo* administration of nicotine, *Schizophr. Res.*, 65, 47, 2003.

203. Middleton, L.S., Cass, W.A., and Dwoskin, L.P., Nicotinic receptor modulation of dopamine transporter function in rat striatum and medial prefrontal cortex, *J. Pharmacol. Exp. Ther.*, 308, 367, 2003.

204. Li, S., Kim, K.Y., Kim, J.H., Kim, J.H., Park, M.S., Bahk, J.Y., and Kim, M.O., Chronic nicotine and smoking treatment increases dopamine transporter mRNA expression in the rat midbrain, *Neurosci. Lett.*, 363, 29, 2004.

205. Harrod, S.B., Mactutus, C.F., Bennett, K., Hasselrot, U., Wu, G., Welch, M., and Booze, R.M., Sex differences and repeated intravenous nicotine: behavioral sensitization and dopamine receptors, *Pharmacol. Biochem. Behav.*, 78, 581, 2004.

206. Batra, V., Patkar, A.A., Berrettini, W.H., Weinstein, S.P., and Leone, F.T., The genetic determinants of smoking, *Chest*, 123, 1730, 2003.

207. Arinami, T., Ishiguro, H., and Onaivi, E.S., Polymorphism in genes involved in neurotransmission in relation to smoking, *Eur. J. Pharmacol.*, 410, 221, 2000.

208. Vandenbergh, D.J., Persico, A.M., Hawkins, A.L., Griffin, C.A., Li, X., Jabs, E.W et al., Human dopamine transporter gene (DAT1) maps to chromosome 5p15.3 and displays VNTR, *Genomics*, 14, 1104, 1992.

209. Fuke, S., Suo, S., Takahashi, N., Koike, H., Sasagawa, N., and Ishuiri, S., The VNTR polymorphism of the human dopamine transporter (DAT1) gene affects gene expression, *Pharmacogenom. J.*, 1, 152, 2001.

210. Comings, D.E. and Blum, K., Reward deficiency syndrome: genetic aspects of behavioral disorders, *Prog. Brain Res.*, 126, 325, 2000.

211. Gelernter, J., Kranzler, H.R., Satel, S.L., and Rao, P.A., Genetic association between dopamine transporter protein alleles and cocaine induced paranoia, *Neuropsychopharmacology*, 11, 195, 1994.

212. Lott, D.C., Kim, S., Cook, E.H., and de Wit, H., Dopamine transporter gene associated with diminished subjective response to amphetamine, *Neuropharmacology*, 1, 2004.

213. Schuckit, M.A., Low level of response to alcohol as predictor of alcoholism, *Am. J. Psychol.*, 151, 184, 1994.

214. Liu, H., Lin, S., Liu, S., Chen, S., Hu, C., Chang, J., and Leu, S., DAT polymorphism and diverse clinical manifestations in methamphetamine abusers, *Psychiatr. Gen.*, 14, 33, 2004.

215. Kreek, M.J., Bart, G., Lilly, C., LaForge, K.S., and Nielsen, D.A., Pharmacogenetic and human molecular genetics of opiate and cocaine addictions and their treatments, *Pharmacol. Rev.*, 57, 1, 2005.

216. Galeeva, A.R., Greeva, A.E., Yur'ev, E.B., and Khusnutdinova, E.K., VNTR polymorphism of the serotonin transporter and dopamine transporter genes in male opiate addicts, *Mol. Biol.*, 36, 462, 2002.

217. Foley, P.F., Loh, E.W., Innes, D.J., Williams, S.M., Tannenberg, A.E., Harper, C.G., and Dodd, P.R., Association studies of neurotransmitter gene polymorphisms in alcoholic Caucasians, *Ann. N.Y. Acad. Sci.*, 1025, 39, 2004.

218. Gorwood, P., Limosin, F., Batel, P., Hamon, M., Ades, J., and Boni, C., The A9 allele of the dopamine transporter gene is associated with delirium tremens and alcohol-withdrawal seizure, *Biol. Psychiatry*, 53, 85, 2003.

219. Kohnke, M.D., Batra, A., Kolb, W., Kohnke, A.M., Lutz, U., Schick, S., and Gaertner, I., Association of the dopamine transporter gene with alcoholism, *Alcohol*, 40(5), 339, 2005.

220. Jorm, A.F., Henderson, A.S., Jacob, P.A., Christensen, H., Korten, A. E., Rodgers, B., Tan, X., and Easteal, S., Association of smoking and personality with polymorphism of the dopamine transporter gene: results from a community survey, *Am. J. Med. Gen.*, 96, 331, 2000.

221. Lerman, C., Caporaso, N.E., Audrain, J., Main, D., Bowman, E.D., Lockshin, B., Boyd, N.R., and Shields, P.G., Evidence suggesting the role of specific genetic factors in cigarette smoking, *Health Psychol.*, 18, 14, 1999.

222. Sabol, S.Z., Nelson, M.L., Fisher, C., Gunzerath, L., Brody, C.L., Hu, S., Sirota, L.A., Marcus, S.E., Greenberg, B.D., Lucas, F.R., IV, Benjamin, J., Murphy, D.L., and Hamer, D.H., A genetic association for cigarette smoking behavior, *Health Psychol.*, 18, 7, 1999.

223. Ling, D., Niu, T., Feng, Y., Xing, H., and Xu, X., Association between polymorphism of the dopamine transporter gene and early smoking onset: an interaction risk on nicotine dependence, *J. Hum. Genet.*, 49, 35, 2004.

224. Deneau, G., Yanagita, T., and Seevers, M.H., Self-administration of psychoactive substances by the monkey, *Psychopharmacologia,* 16, 30, 1969.

225. Beardsley, P.M., Balster, R.L., and Harris, L.S., Self-administration of methylendioxymethamphetamine (MDMA) by rhesus monkeys, *Drug Alcohol Depend.,* 18, 149, 1986.

226. Spampinato, U., Espisito, E., and Samainin, R., Serotonin agonists reduce dopamine synthesis in the striatum only when the impulse flow of nigro-striatal neurons is intact, *J. Neurochem.,* 45, 980, 1985.

227. Hetey, L., Schwitzlowsky, R., and Oelssner, W., Influence of psychotomimetics and lisuride on synaptosomal dopamine release in the nucleus accumbens of rats, *Eur. J. Pharmacol.,* 93, 213, 1983.

228. Hetey, L. and Quirling, K., Synaptosomal uptake and release of dopamine and 5-hydroxytryptamine in the nucleus accumbens *in vitro* following *in vivo* administration of lysergic acid diethlamide in rats, *Acta Biol. Med. Ger.,* 39, 889, 1980.

229. Ator, N.A. and Ator, R.R., Self-administration of barbiturates and benzodiazepines: a review, *Pharmacol. Biochem. Behav.,* 27, 391, 1987.

230. Murai, T., Koshikawa, N., Kanayama, T., Takada, K., Tomiyama, K., and Kobayashi, M., Opposite effects of midazolam and beta-carboline-3-carboxylate ethyl ester on the release of dopamine from rat nucleus accumbens measured by *in vivo* microdialysis, *Eur. J. Pharmacol.,* 261, 65, 1994.

231. Finlay, J.M., Damsma, G., and Fibiger, H.C., Benzodiazepine-induced decreases in extracellular concentration of dopamine in the nucleus accumbens after acute and repeated administration, *Psychopharmacology,* 106, 202, 1992.

232. Louilot, A., Le Moal, M., and Simon, H., Presynaptic control of dopamine metabolism in the nucleus accumbens. Lack of effect of buspirone as demonstrated using *in vivo* voltammetry, *Life Sci.,* 40, 2017, 1987.

233. Reith, M.E.A., Sershen, H., and Lajtha, A., effects of caffeine on monoaminergic systems in mouse brain, *Acta Biochem. Biophys. Hung.,* 22, 149, 1987.

234. Corrigall, W.A. and Coen, K.M., Nicotine maintains robust self-administration in rats on a limited access schedule, *Psychopharmacology,* 99, 473, 1989.

235. Balster, R.L., Johanson, C.E., Harris, R.T., and Schuster, C.R., Phencyclidine self-administration in the rhesus monkey, *Pharmacol. Biochem. Behav.,* 1, 167, 1973.

236. Robinson, T.E. and Berridge, K.C., The neural basis of drug craving: An incentive-sensitization theory of addiction, *Brain Res. Rev.,* 18, 247, 1993.

237. Koob, G.F. and Le Moal, M., Drug abuse: Hedonic homeostatic dysregulation, *Science,* 278, 52, 1997.

238. Volkow, N.D., Wang, G.-J., Fowler, J.S., Gatley, S.J., Logan, J., Ding, Y.-S., Hitzeman, R., and Pappas, N., Dopamine transporter occupancies in the human brain induced by therapeutic doses of oral methylphenidate, *Am. J. Psychiatry,* 155, 1325, 1998.

239. Volkow, N.D., Wang, G.-J., Fischman, M.W., Foltin, R., Fowler, J.S., Franceschi, D., Fraceschi, M., Logan, J., Gatley, S.J., Wong, C., Ding, Y.-S., Hitzeman, R., and Pappas, N., Effects of route of administration on cocaine induced dopamine transporter blockade in the human brain, *Life Sci.,* 67, 1507, 2000.

240. Volkow, N.D., Wang, G.-J., Fowler, J.S., Logan, J., Gatley, S.J., Wong, C., Hitzeman, R., and Pappas, N., Reinforcing effects of psychostimulants in humans are associated with increases in brain dopamine and occupancy of D^2 receptors, *J. Pharmacol. Exp. Ther.,* 291, 409, 1999.

241. Volkow, N.D., Wang, G.-J., Fowler, J.S., Gatley, S.J., Logan, J., Ding, Y.-S., Dewey, S.L., Hitzeman, R., Gifford, A.N., and Pappas, N., Blockade of striatal dopamine transporters by intravenous methylphenidate is not sufficient to induce self-reports of "high," *J. Pharmacol. Exp. Ther.,* 288, 14, 1999.

242. Shimada, S., Kitayama, S., Lin, C.-L., Patel, A., Nathankumar, E., Gregor, P., Kuhar, M.J., and Uhl, G., Cloning and expression of a cocaine-sensitive dopamine transporter complementary DNA, *Science,* 254, 576, 1991.

243. Amara, S. and Kuhar, M.J., Neurotransmitter transporters: recent progress, *Annu. Rev. Neurosci.,* 16, 73, 1993.

244. Giros, B. and Caron, M.G., Molecular characterization of the dopamine transporter, *TIPS,* 14, 43, 1993.

6.2 NEUROCHEMISTRY OF NICOTINE DEPENDENCE

Darlene H. Brunzell, Ph.D.

Department of Psychiatry, Yale University School of Medicine, New Haven, Connecticut

Tobacco use is the leading preventable cause of death in North America and a growing medical problem in developing countries throughout the world. In the Western world, the rising cost of cigarettes, social mores, and public policy against smoking have led to appreciable decreases in cigarette use over the last 25 years.[1,2] In recent years, however, smoking prevalence has appeared to reach asymptote at approximately 25%.[3,4] Those with schizophrenia, a history of depression, alcoholism or polydrug use, and those who have difficulty quitting with the help of currently available cessation methods continue to smoke.[3,5] Until recently, there were only two FDA-approved treatments for tobacco cessation: nicotine replacement therapy and bupropion. In May 2006, the FDA approved the use of a nicotinic receptor partial agonist, varenicline, for treatment of tobacco dependence. Whereas these therapies have realized some success, there remains an apparent need for novel treatments for nicotine and tobacco dependence. Nicotine is believed to be a major psychoactive component in cigarettes and smokeless tobacco. Advancing our understanding of the neurochemical mechanisms of nicotine use and how nicotine-associated changes in neurochemistry relate to behaviors that support addiction will not only lead to novel treatments for tobacco cessation, but might also lead to advanced therapies for diseases that have high comorbidity with tobacco use. This chapter reviews nicotinic receptor composition, followed by a systems overview of how various nicotinic receptor subtypes are thought to contribute to nicotine reinforcement and incentive motivational processes. Because nicotine dependence is thought to reflect changes in communication between areas of the brain that control motivation, cognition, and reward, candidate intracellular signaling proteins thought to promote nicotine-dependent neuroplasticity are discussed, and finally the promise of novel compounds for tobacco cessation and their potential clinical applications are discussed.

6.2.1 Nicotinic Receptor Composition

Nicotine action is mediated through the nicotinic acetylcholine receptors (nAChRs). Although slightly different in subunit composition, most of our notions about neuronal nAChR structure and function are derived from exquisite work on nAChRs in the torpedo electric organ and at the neuromuscular junction (for detailed review, see References 6 through 9). Members of the ligand-gated superfamily of receptors, nAChRs respond endogenously to acetylcholine (ACh) in the periphery and central nervous system (CNS).[6] There are two general classes of nAChRs in the brain, both pentameric in structure. Neuronal nAChRs are either heteropentameres, made up of a combination of five α_2–α_6 and β_2–β_4 receptor subunits, or are homomeric in structure, made up of five α_7 subunits (Figure 6.2.1). Each subunit contains an N-terminal agonist binding domain, four transmembrane domains (M1 to M4), a large cytoplasmic loop between M3 and M4, and an extracellular C-terminus.[10,11] The nAChRs exist in a variety of functional states including a closed, resting state, an open, activated state, a desensitized, unresponsive state, and an irreversible, inactive state.[12] When activated, the M2 domain of the nAChR undergoes a conformational change making the ion pore of the receptor permeable to cations (e.g., Na^+ and Ca^{2+};[10,13,14]) that lead to cellular activation, modification of second messenger signaling, and enhancement of neurotransmitter release.

The nAChR subtypes vary in response to pharmacological manipulation. The α_7 receptors have a low affinity for nicotine and are sensitive to α-bungarotoxin (α-BTX) antagonism whereas the heteromeric nAChRs are not.[14] The β_2 containing (β_2*: asterisk denotes the presence of additional subunits) nAChRs have the highest affinity for nicotine binding and some selectivity for antagonism

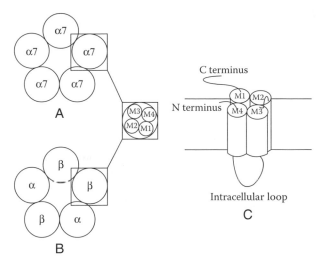

Figure 6.2.1 Diagram of nicotinic acetylcholine receptor (nAChR) structure. A top view of (A) an α_7 nAChR and (B) a β_2*nAChR shows that homomeric and heteromeric classes of nAChRs are both pentameric in structure. Each subunit is made up of four transmembrane domains with the M2 domain making up the ion pore. (C) A side view of the four transmembrane regions shows the N-terminus, C-terminus, and large M3–M4 intracellular loop that make up each nAChR subunit. The extracellular loops are available for binding to ligands and the intracellular loop is available for regulation of the nAChR by intracellular signaling proteins.

with dihydro-beta-erythroidine (DHβE),[15] and the α_3* and α_6*nAChRs are the only subtypes known to respond to α-conotoxin MII.[16–21] After some period of nAChR stimulation, there are conformational changes in the receptors[22,23] that cause them to become transiently unavailable for activation by nicotinic agonists,[24] sometimes irreversibly.[25] This desensitization of the receptors is thought to be regulated by calcium-mediated protein kinases at the intracellular loop between M3 and M4,[22,26] providing negative feedback to the nAChRs. The variability in sequence homology between nAChR subtypes at the intracellular loop may be responsible for the different rates of desensitization identified for the α_7 and β_2*nAChRs.[27–29] Once bound by acetylcholine or nicotinic agonists, nAChR effects on neurochemistry depend on the conformation of the receptor, neuroanatomical localization of the receptor subtype, and the intracellular consequences of nAChR activation.

6.2.2   Neurochemical Systems That Support Nicotine Use

The prevailing belief in the drug addiction field is that with repeated drug use, neuroplasticity occurs within areas of the brain that modulate motivation, impulsivity, and reward.[30–32] These neurochemical changes are thought to support addictive behaviors and to transform the non-addicted brain into an addicted one. Much of the animal work to date has focused on the neurochemical mechanisms of nicotine reinforcement. Drug reinforcement is not included in the DSM-IV addiction criteria for good reason. A person can enjoy the pleasurable properties of a glass of wine without having any particular risk for alcoholism. If a drug such as nicotine is not positively or negatively reinforcing, however, it will not be sufficiently administered in order for nicotine dependence to develop. In this context, understanding the mechanisms of nicotine reinforcement might help identify genetic vulnerabilities for or protection from developing an addictive phenotype.[33] *Nicotine dependence* is a much more complex behavioral phenomenon. Following repeated use, incentive motivational processes (e.g., craving) come to regulate drug intake even in the absence of drug reinforcement or relief of symptoms of withdrawal.[34,35] Repeated association of cues with a primary reinforcer, such as nicotine, results in the ability of those cues to reinforce behaviors like drug seeking.[16]

6.2.2.1 Nicotine Reinforcement

The Mesocorticolimbic Dopamine System

Like other drugs of abuse, the reinforcing effects of nicotine are modulated, in large part, via the mesocorticolimbic dopamine (DA) system. Animal studies have shown that systemic and ventral tegmental area (VTA) administration of nicotine results in DA release to the nucleus accumbens (NAc).[36–38] Accumbens DA release increases with repeated nicotine exposure.[36] This neuroplasticity, termed sensitization, coincides with nicotine reinforcement[39–41] and locomotor activating effects of nicotine.[36,37] Both blockade of VTA nicotinic receptors[42,43] and destruction of DA inputs to the NAc[44] greatly reduces nicotine self-administration and conditioned place preference (CPP)† in rats. Unlike other psychostimulants, which enhance dopamine release via binding to dopamine transporters, nicotine regulation of dopamine is less direct. Although much evidence suggests that nAChRs act postsynaptically to enhance DA neuron activity,[45,46] emerging evidence indicates that VTA and NAc nAChRs act presynaptically to modulate neurotransmitter release[19,28,47] and regulate transporter function.[48]

An accumulation of data suggests that both the β_2^* and α_7 receptor subtypes contribute to nicotine-induced increases in DA release and associated nicotine-dependent behaviors.[28,39,40,42,43,49,50] In the VTA, α_7 and β_2^*nAChRs, respectively, reside on glutamatergic and GABAergic terminals. Electrophysiological data indicate that the higher affinity β_2^*nAChRs are the first to be activated by nicotine (Figure 6.2.2A). In the VTA slice preparation, the β_2^*nAChRs desensitize very quickly, becoming inactivated.[28,47] Because β_2^*nAChRs stimulate γ-aminobutyric acid (GABA) release, desensitization of these receptors results in disinhibition of VTA DA neurons. Removal of GABA release on DA neurons is coincident with activation of the lower-affinity α_7 nAChRs, which facilitate excitatory glutamatergic input to the DA neurons (Figure 6.2.2B), resulting in a net increase in DA neuron firing.[28] At the DA terminals, however, β_2^*nAChRs ($\alpha_4\beta_2$, $\alpha_6\beta_3\beta_2$, $\alpha_4\alpha_6\beta_3\beta_2$, $\alpha_4\alpha_5\beta_2$) and not α_7 nAChRs support nicotine-stimulated DA release.[19]

Studies in knockout mice indicate that the β_2^*nAChRs are necessary for nicotine self-administration, DA-dependent locomotor activation, and nicotine-associated enhancement of NAc DA release.[40,51–53] Combined with studies showing that antagonism of the high-affinity nAChRs block self-administration,[44,54] it would appear that β_2^*nAChRs are particularly critical for nicotine reinforcement. Unlike wild-type mice that self-administer both cocaine and nicotine, β_2^*nAChR-null mutant mice learn to self-administer cocaine normally, but stop bar pressing as though receiving saline when cocaine is switched to nicotine.[40] Self-administration of VTA nicotine and associated DA release is rescued, however, in β_2^*nAChR knockout mice with lentiviral-mediated expression of β_2 subunit DNA in the VTA.[55] Whereas several configurations of the β_2^*nAChRs exist at the level of the VTA, much data point to the $\alpha_4\beta_2$ nicotinic receptors as playing a primary role in nicotine reinforcement. Mice lacking the α_4^*nAChRs fail to show nicotine-dependent enhancements of DA release,[53] and a single nucleotide leucine-to-alanine α_4 mutation in the pore-forming M2 domain renders the α_4^*nAChRs hypersensitive to nicotine stimulation and promotes conditioned place preference at otherwise sub-optimal doses of nicotine.[56] Together, these data suggest that the β_2^*nAChRs are necessary and the α_4^*nAChRs are sufficient for nicotine reinforcement. Interestingly, the α_4^*nAChR knockout animals but not the β_2-null mutant mice show an increase in basal DA release to the NAc,[40,53] indicating that receptor conformations in addition to $\alpha_4\beta_2$ mediate DA input to the NAc.

Another candidate receptor subunit for nicotine reinforcement that has been less studied is α_6. The α_6 subunit associates with the β_2, β_3, and α_4 nAChR subunits in the CNS.[19,20,57,58] Unlike

---

† Conditioned place preference refers to a Pavlovian learning paradigm in which animals are repeatedly exposed to two novel adjacent chambers, one paired with nicotine administration and the other paired with saline injection. During the test the animal is allowed to cross between compartments. An increased amount of time spent in the drug-paired chamber is thought to reflect drug reinforcement and is defined as conditioned place preference.

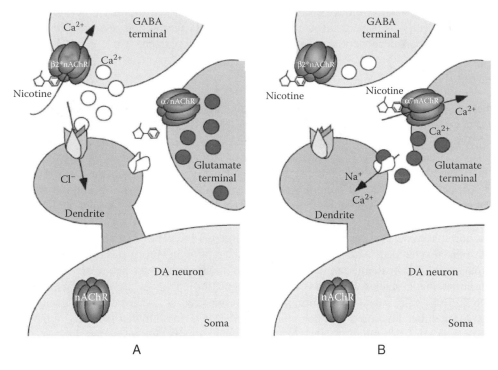

Figure 6.2.2 A presynaptic model of nicotine stimulation of ventral tegmental area DA neurons. (A) Nicotine first binds to the high-affinity β_2 containing nicotinic acetylcholine receptors (β_2*nAChRs), which reside on neuron terminals that release the inhibitory neurotransmitter GABA. Entry of calcium (Ca^{2+}) through the nAChR ion pore facilitates vesicle docking and neurotransmitter release. (B) The inhibitory GABA input to the DA neurons is short-lived, however, due to a fast desensitization of the β_2*nAChRs. As nicotine accumulates, it binds to the lower-affinity α_7 nAChRs that reside on the terminals of neurons that release the excitatory neurotransmitter, glutamate. Together nAChR-regulated disinhibition of GABA input and stimulation of glutamate input result in a net elevation of DA neuron activity and DA release in VTA projection areas.

$\alpha_4\beta_2$ nAChRs, which are ubiquitously expressed throughout the brain, α_6 mRNA is chiefly expressed in catecholaminergic nuclei,[58] with receptor expression on DA terminals in the striatum.[59] Although no direct link has been made regarding the role of this receptor subunit in nicotine reinforcement, α_6 is well suited to contribute to neuroplasticity associated with nicotine exposure. α_6*nAChRs are capable of modulating nicotine-associated DA release at striatal DA terminals[19,57] and are upregulated following chronic nicotine exposure,[60] suggesting that the α_6 subunit might contribute to nicotine-associated changes in DA release that correlate with locomotor activation and nicotine reinforcement.

As α_7 nAChRs are known to reside on glutamate terminals in the VTA,[61] the role of α_7 nAChRs in nicotine-elicited dopamine release is supported by studies that manipulate glutamate receptor function. Glutamate receptor antagonism in the VTA greatly reduces nicotine-associated increases in NAc DA release without affecting baseline levels of accumbens DA.[62] Behaviorally, NMDA glutamate receptor antagonism blocks nicotine locomotor sensitization in rats.[63] As the reports of α_7 antagonism on nicotine reinforcement are equivocal,[42,54,64] it is unclear what role the α_7 nAChRs play in nicotine reward. Local administration of 4 n*M* methyllycaconitine (MLA) into the VTA reverses nicotine-conditioned place preference,[42] and high doses of this putatively selective α_7 antagonist (3.9 and 7.8 mg/kg i.p.) attenuate nicotine self-administration in rats, suggesting that α_7 nAChRs contribute to nicotine reinforcement.[64] Similar doses of MLA achieved in brain,[65] however, block nicotine-stimulated DA release in striatal synaptosome preparations that do not contain α_7 nicotinic receptors,[19,66] bringing the selectivity of MLA for α_7 nAChRs into question at higher doses.[66] The fact that MLA blocks α conotoxin MII binding at behaviorally efficacious doses[20,67] raises the possibility that antagonism of α_3* or α_6*nAChRs in addition to α_7 nAChRs might be responsible for MLA-dependent attenuation of nicotine reinforcement.

Hindbrain Inputs to the VTA

Hindbrain regions including the pedunculopontine tegmental nucleus (PPT) and lateral dorsal tegmental nucleus (LDT) give rise to acetylcholinergic, GABAergic, and glutamatergic projections to the VTA that are thought to regulate drug reward.[68-70] Local infusion of GABA receptor agonists and lesions to the PPT result in a marked attenuation of nicotine-associated locomotor activation, nicotine CPP, and nicotine self-administration in rodents.[71-73] PPT administration of DHβE also greatly attenuates nicotine self-administration in rats,[72] suggesting that PPT-regulated nicotine reinforcement is mediated in part by high-affinity β_2*nAChRs. Nicotinic receptor antagonism also inhibits ACh release in PPT synaptosome preparation.[67]

Various studies suggest that basal forebrain cholinergic projections and accumbens ACh interneurons may also regulate behavior associated with the reinforcing properties of cocaine, morphine, and ethanol.[74-78] Whereas muscarinic ACh receptors might also meter behaviors associated with drug reinforcement, studies show that nAChR stimulation enhances and antagonism attenuates cocaine CPP. β_2-null mutant mice are also slightly impaired at cocaine CPP.[79] Given that ACh appears to modulate both drug aversion and reward,[42,76] it is possible that nAChRs in mesolimbic DA areas regulate motivational valence or learning and memory processes that underlie drug use and not drug reinforcement per se. There is very high comorbidity for tobacco use with substance use disorders.[3] The specific contributions of nAChRs to drug reinforcement, more broadly defined, remain to be determined.

Beyond the Role of DA in Nicotine Reinforcement

Although the research described thus far supports the tenet that nicotine reinforcement is regulated by the ability of nAChRs to enhance mesolimbic DA release, an accumulation of evidence questions the simplicity of this dogma. Despite treatment with neuroleptics that block DA receptor stimulation, the percentage of people with schizophrenia who smoke is several times greater than the population as a whole.[3,5] In rats, the effects of intra-VTA infusion of nicotine on behavior are dose dependent; animals display conditioned place aversion at low doses and CPP at steadily increasing doses of nicotine.[80] The experimenters found that intra-accumbens and systemic administration of the neuroleptic, α-flupenthixol, reversed the conditioned aversive but not rewarding effects of nicotine, concluding that NAc dopamine regulates nicotine aversion and not reward.[80] α-Flupenthixol, however, blocks both Gs-coupled, D_1- and Gi-coupled, D_2-type DA receptors, which are known to have opposite effects on the cAMP signaling pathway (Figure 6.2.3).[31] Recent evidence suggests that cAMP-responsive element-binding protein regulates both rewarding and aversive effects of morphine.[81] Together these data suggest that NAc DA and the cAMP pathway might serve to regulate motivational valence rather than drug reinforcement per se.

Electrophysiological data show that while pulses of ACh enhance DA neuron activity as one might expect with acute nicotine exposure, simulation of steady states of human nicotine concentrations[82] quickly result in desensitization of the midbrain nAChRs.[47] Indeed, striatal synaptosome preparation used to measure DA release show that much lower doses of nicotine are required for desensitization than for activation of nAChRs.[24,83] This acute tolerance might account for smoker reports that the first cigarette of the day is most pleasurable.[84] In human brain, β_2*nAChR binding is prolonged for as long as 5 h after a smoking episode,[85] begging the question as to why people continue to smoke throughout the day. Research using electrochemical cyclic voltammetry shows that nAChR regulation of DA release depends upon the state of the DA neuron during

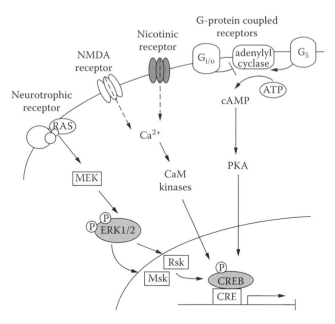

Figure 6.2.3 Mechanisms by which nicotine might affect ERK and CREB signaling. Nicotine stimulation of glutamate release or direct activation of nicotinic acetylcholine receptors (nAChRs) results in the influx of calcium (Ca^{2+}), among other cations, through NMDA glutamate and nAChRs. Intracellular Ca^{2+} can result in activation of Ca^{2+}/calmodulin-dependent protein kinases that lead to phosphorylation and activation of the transcription factor, cAMP-responsive element binding protein (CREB). Nicotine-associated changes in levels of growth factors result in changes in activation of neurotrophic receptors that stimulate extracellular regulated protein kinase (ERK) and downstream activation of CREB via protein kinases, ribosomal S6 kinase (Rsk) and mitogen- and stress-activated protein kinase (Msk). *In vitro* studies show that fast activation of ERK by nicotine is Ca^{2+}-dependent and mediated via voltage-gated Ca^{2+} channels;[119,120] however, the intracellular mechanism of Ca^{2+}-mediated ERK activation remains to be determined. Nicotine-stimulated elevations of DA release can lead to activation of G protein-coupled receptors, which in turn modify cAMP signaling and downstream activation of protein kinase A (PKA), a kinase known to directly phosphorylate CREB and promote CRE mediated transcription.

nicotine application.[86,87] When DA neurons are held in a tonic or "resting" state, nicotine decreases DA release, but when DA neurons are in a phasic state, as one would expect during the presentation of a reward,[88] nicotine enhances DA release.[86] Interestingly, DA neurons respond similarly to nicotine and nAChR antagonists, suggesting that nicotine's action on DA release is mediated by desensitization of the receptor.[86,87] Over time, cues come to elicit phasic activity of DA neurons where primary reinforcers once did.[88] These data may explain at an electrophysiological level how cigarette-associated cues maintain smoking behavior.

6.2.2.2 Neurochemistry of Cue-Driven Behaviors

Although the NAc has received the most attention for its role in nicotine reinforcement, other VTA projection areas including the hippocampus, prefrontal cortex, and amygdala contribute to the control that cues have over behavior, or conditioned reinforcement.[30,32] Such behaviors may represent changes in incentive motivation that perpetuate drug use even in the absence of drug reinforcement.[34] Sensory cues associated with the act of inhaling regulate the degree to which smokers find pleasure in smoking denicotinized cigarettes.[89,90] The VTA, NAc, amygdala, and prefrontal cortex are activated in humans during craving and the presentation of cigarette-associated cues,[91,92] indicating that these areas of the brain contribute to conditioned reinforcement associated with cigarette smoking.

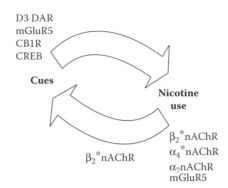

Figure 6.2.4 A perpetual learning model for nicotine dependence. Evidence shows that cues greatly enhance nicotine self-administration and that nicotine exposure augments conditioned reinforcement for natural and drug reinforcers. Although drug reinforcement does not necessarily lead to addiction, nicotine reinforcement most likely facilitates the development of nicotine dependence. Evidence suggests that the β_2^*, α_4^*, and α_7 nicotinic acetylcholine receptors (nAChRs) and metabotropic glutamate receptor 5 (mGluR5) glutamate receptors contribute to nicotine self-administration. The D_3 dopamine receptors (D3 DAR), CB_1 cannabinoid receptors (CB1R), mGluR5 glutamate receptors, and the transcription factor CREB appear to be involved in cue-associated changes in neuroplasticity and the control of nicotine-paired cues over nicotine-dependent behaviors. Nicotine-associated enhancement of conditioned reinforcement for cues paired with a natural reinforcer requires β_2^*nAChRs. β_2^*nAChRs might also serve to amplify the conditioned reinforcement properties of nicotine-associated cues.

Animal studies have shown that cues greatly enhance the degree to which animals will self-administer nicotine[34,93–95] and can support self-administration behavior for weeks after the removal of nicotine.[93,96] In rats, a nicotine-associated cue is a more efficient primer than nicotine itself at reinstating self-administration,[97] and a nicotine-paired context can elicit changes in immediate early gene activity in the prefrontal cortex,[98] suggesting that conditioned reinforcement for nicotine-associated cues occurs at a molecular level. Like other drugs of abuse, the control of nicotine-associated cues over behavior is likely mediated within areas of the brain that receive DA and glutamate stimulation.[32] One theory suggests that coincident activation of NAc neurons by DA and glutamate supports drug reinforcement and natural reward.[99] Blockade of metabotropic glutamate receptor 5 ($mGluR_5$) with the antagonist MPEP not only decreases nicotine self-administration and break points for nicotine,[100,101] but also significantly attenuates cue-induced reinstatement of nicotine self-administration.[102] Disruption of D_3 DA receptors, which are upregulated with repeated nicotine exposure,[103] significantly attenuates behavioral locomotor sensitization in response to a nicotine-paired context.[104] D_3 antagonists and partial agonists also block nicotine-conditioned place preference[105] suggesting that manipulation of D_3 receptors might be efficacious in reducing nicotine seeking or nicotine reinforcement. The efficacy of D_3 partial agonists and antagonists in blocking nicotine self-administration remains to be tested, however.

Not only do cues control nicotine use, but nicotine exposure also enhances conditioned reinforcement in rats and mice for weeks following exposure to nicotine[106–109] (Figure 6.2.4), and can act as an occasion setter to facilitate the association of cues with reward.[110] Studies in β_2-null mutant mice show that nicotine enhancement of conditioned reinforcement is dependent on the presence of the β_2^*nAChRs.[106] The cannabinoid receptor 1 (CB_1) antagonist, rimonabant, appears to curb both primary and incentive motivation processes affected by nicotine,[106] blocking control of conditioned reinforcers over nicotine intake and having potential to decrease weight gain associated with quit attempts.[111] Nicotine's ability to act as a primary reinforcer in addition to its ability to enhance learning and incentive motivational processes may explain why people and animals have difficulty abandoning behaviors associated with tobacco smoking and nicotine intake.

6.2.3 Nicotine-Associated Changes in Intracellular Signaling

At the cellular level, nicotine-induced changes in second messenger signaling are thought to support nicotine-associated changes in neurochemistry and behavioral phenotypes. Due to their putative roles in cellular processes underlying learning and memory (for detailed review, see References 112 and113), the extracellular regulated protein kinase (ERK) and cyclic AMP responsive element binding (CREB) signaling pathways have received the most attention for their potential roles in neuroplasticity underlying nicotine dependence (Figure 6.2.3).[114–117] In vitro studies have shown that ERK is activated by nicotine treatment[118] and is critical for nicotine-dependent activation of CREB[119,120] and tyrosine hydroxylase, the rate-limiting enzyme in DA synthesis.[121,122] In vivo studies show that regulation of ERK by nicotine is region and treatment specific.[114,116] Although acute administration of nicotine elevates levels of phosphorylated ERK (pERK) in the amygdala and prefrontal cortex,[116] chronic exposure to doses of nicotine known to have relevance for neural plasticity and locomotor activation[52,123] results in elevation of pERK in the prefrontal cortex, but leads to significant decreases in levels of ERK and pERK in the amygdala.[114] Amygdala changes in ERK protein expression following repeated nicotine exposure may support conditioned reinforcement processes; however, the role of ERK signaling in incentive motivation remains to be explored.

An accumulation of evidence suggests that the transcription factor CREB regulates the rewarding properties of nicotine. Unlike their wild-type counterparts, mice with a targeted mutation of CREB (CREB$^{\alpha\delta}$) fail to show nicotine-conditioned place preference following four pairings of a novel chamber with nicotine.[117] In wild-type mice, acute and four repeated exposures to nicotine both resulted in elevated levels of VTA pCREB,[117] suggesting that activation of CREB in the VTA might regulate the primary reinforcing properties of nicotine. Interestingly, the nicotine-paired chamber was also capable of eliciting an increase in pCREB,[117] showing that the nicotine-paired environment became a conditioned reinforcer capable of controlling intracellular signaling associated with nicotine exposure. Chronic and acute nicotine exposure and nicotine withdrawal have been shown to affect phosphorylation of CREB in the NAc, PFC, VTA, and amygdala.[114,115,117] NAc levels of pCREB differ between acute paradigms, where little to no change is observed,[114,117,124] and chronic exposure where marked decreases in NAc pCREB are evident.[114] Similarly, increases of pCREB in the prefrontal cortex are specific to chronic nicotine exposure in mice[114] and are observed to decrease in rats following nicotine withdrawal,[115] suggesting that CREB in the NAc and prefrontal cortex might regulate some conditioned emotive properties of nicotine reward or withdrawal. Nicotine withdrawal can precipitate an episode of depression[125] and inhibition of NAc CREB has antidepressant-like effects in rats.[126] More studies need to be done to clarify the contributions of the prefrontal cortex and NAc CREB in complex behaviors that support nicotine dependence.

6.2.4 Summary and Clinical Implications

Nicotine dependence is a complex biobehavioral phenomenon that is likely regulated by cue-driven incentive motivational processes. As suggested by the work described here, antagonism at mGluR$_5$ glutamate, D$_3$ DA, CB$_1$ cannabinoid, and β$_2$*nAChRs might have particular promise for promoting nicotine cessation. Preliminary trials indicate that quit rates for β$_2$*nAChR partial agonist varenicline are twice that reported for more traditional therapies.[127] Preclinical evidence suggests that even greater nicotine cessation outcomes might be achieved if varenicline is used in combination with behavioral therapies. If administered using techniques that enable local control of expression, CREB and ERK might serve as effective molecular targets for gene therapy. Other novel nicotine cessation treatments under consideration include those that reduce the function of mu opioid receptors in the brain. Evidence suggests that naltrexone, an opiate antagonist that has enjoyed some success as a treatment for alcohol cessation,[128] should be considered for "off-label" nicotine cessation use.[129–131] Mu opioid receptors in the VTA appear to promote nicotine reward[117] and may be one point of convergence for nicotine and alcohol abuse potential. Last, a nicotine vaccine that limits the bioavailability of nicotine in the brain has been shown to lead to significant reductions in nicotine intake in preclinical trials.[132]

Despite that a large number of smokers want to quit, few are able to do so with currently approved treatments for nicotine dependence. Among those who have particular difficulty quitting smoking are those who suffer from polydrug use, depression, and schizophrenia.[3,5] There is large individual variability in responsiveness to nicotine and reasons for smoking.[84] Parsing out the specific contributions of nAChRs and their downstream neurochemical targets to various behaviors that support nicotine dependence may lead to treatments for nicotine cessation that are effective in a broader spectrum of individuals.

REFERENCES

1. Mendez, D., Warner, K.E., Courant P.N. Has smoking cessation ceased? Expected trends in the prevalence of smoking in the United States. *Am. J. Epidemiol.* 148:249, 1998.
2. Stegmayr, B., Eliasson, M., Rodu, B. The decline of smoking in northern Sweden. *Scand. J. Public Health.* 33:321, 2005.
3. Kalman, D., Morissette, S.B., George, T.P. Co-morbidity of smoking in patients with psychiatric and substance use disorders. *Am. J. Addict.* 14:106, 2005.
4. Weintraub, J.M., Hamilton, W.L. Trends in prevalence of current smoking, Massachusetts and states without tobacco control programmes, 1990 to 1999. *Tob. Control.* 11(Suppl. 2):ii8, 2002.
5. Leonard, S., Adler L.E., Benhammou, K. et al. Smoking and mental illness. *Pharmacol. Biochem. Behav.* 70:561, 2001.
6. Le Novere, N., Changeux, J.P. Molecular evolution of the nicotinic acetylcholine receptor: an example of multigene family in excitable cells. *J. Mol. Evol.* 40:155, 1995.
7. Karlin, A. Emerging structure of the nicotinic acetylcholine receptors. *Nat. Rev. Neurosci.* 3:102, 2002.
8. Lindstrom, J.M. Nicotinic acetylcholine receptors of muscles and nerves: comparison of their structures, functional roles, and vulnerability to pathology. *Ann. N.Y. Acad. Sci.* 998:41, 2003.
9. Picciotto, M.R., Caldarone, B.J., Brunzell, D.H., Zachariou, V., Stevens, T.R., King, S.L. Neuronal nicotinic acetylcholine receptor subunit knockout mice: physiological and behavioral phenotypes and possible clinical implications. *Pharmacol. Ther.* 92:89, 2001.
10. Karlin, A., Akabas, M.H. Toward a structural basis for the function of nicotinic acetylcholine receptors and their cousins. *Neuron.* 15:1231, 1995.
11. Corringer, P.J., Le Novere, N., Changeux, J.P. Nicotinic receptors at the amino acid level. *Annu. Rev. Pharmacol. Toxicol.* 40:431, 2000.
12. Changeux, J.P., Devillers-Thiery, A., Chemouilli, P. Acetylcholine receptor: an allosteric protein. *Science.* 225:1335, 1984.
13. Leonard, R.J., Labarca, C.G., Charnet, P., Davidson, N., Lester, H.A. Evidence that the M2 membrane-spanning region lines the ion channel pore of the nicotinic receptor. *Science.* 242:1578, 1988.
14. Arias, H.R. Localization of agonist and competitive antagonist binding sites on nicotinic acetylcholine receptors. *Neurochem. Int.* 36:595, 2000.
15. Whiteaker, P., Marks, M.J., Grady, S.R. et al. Pharmacological and null mutation approaches reveal nicotinic receptor diversity. *Eur. J. Pharmacol.* 393:123, 2000.
16. Mackintosh, N. *The Psychology of Animal Learning.* Academic Press, New York, 1974.
17. Kulak, J.M., Nguyen, T.A., Olivera, B.M., McIntosh, J.M. alpha-Conotoxin MII blocks nicotine-stimulated dopamine release in rat striatal synaptosomes. *J. Neurosci.* 17:5263, 1997.
18. McIntosh, J.M., Azam, L., Staheli, S. et al. Analogs of alpha-conotoxin MII are selective for alpha6-containing nicotinic acetylcholine receptors. *Mol. Pharmacol.* 65:944, 2004.
19. Salminen, O., Murphy, K.L., McIntosh, J.M., et al. Subunit composition and pharmacology of two classes of striatal presynaptic nicotinic acetylcholine receptors mediating dopamine release in mice. *Mol. Pharmacol.* 65:1526, 2004.
20. Salminen, O., Whiteaker, P., Grady, S.R., Collins, A.C., McIntosh, J.M., Marks, M.J. The subunit composition and pharmacology of alpha-Conotoxin MII-binding nicotinic acetylcholine receptors studied by a novel membrane-binding assay. *Neuropharmacology.* 48:696, 2005.

21. Vailati, S., Moretti, M., Balestra, B., McIntosh, M., Clementi, F., Gotti, C. beta3 subunit is present in different nicotinic receptor subtypes in chick retina. *Eur. J. Pharmacol.* 393:23, 2000.

22. Fenster, C.P., Beckman, M.L., Parker, J.C. et al. Regulation of alpha4beta2 nicotinic receptor desensitization by calcium and protein kinase C. *Mol. Pharmacol.* 55:432, 1999.

23. Fenster, C.P., Hicks, J.H., Beckman, M.L., Covernton, P.J., Quick, M.W., Lester, R.A. Desensitization of nicotinic receptors in the central nervous system. *Ann. N.Y. Acad. Sci.* 868:620, 1999.

24. Grady, S.R., Marks, M.J., Collins, A.C. Desensitization of nicotine-stimulated [3H]dopamine release from mouse striatal synaptosomes. *J. Neurochem.* 62:1390, 1994.

25. Lukas, R.J. Effects of chronic nicotinic ligand exposure on functional activity of nicotinic acetylcholine receptors expressed by cells of the PC12 rat pheochromocytoma or the TE671/RD human clonal line. *J. Neurochem.* 56:1134, 1991.

26. Huganir, R.L., Delcour, A.H., Greengard, P., Hess, G.P. Phosphorylation of the nicotinic acetylcholine receptor regulates its rate of desensitization. *Nature.* 321:774, 1986.

27. Dani, J.A., Radcliffe, K.A., Pidoplichko, V.I. Variations in desensitization of nicotinic acetylcholine receptors from hippocampus and midbrain dopamine areas. *Eur. J. Pharmacol.* 393:31, 2000.

28. Mansvelder, H.D., Keath, J.R., McGehee, D.S. Synaptic mechanisms underlie nicotine-induced excitability of brain reward areas. *Neuron.* 33:905, 2002.

29. Wooltorton, J.R., Pidoplichko, V.I., Broide, R.S., Dani, J.A. Differential desensitization and distribution of nicotinic acetylcholine receptor subtypes in midbrain dopamine areas. *J. Neurosci.* 23:3176, 2003.

30. Jentsch, J.D., Taylor, J.R. Impulsivity resulting from frontostriatal dysfunction in drug abuse: implications for the control of behavior by reward-related stimuli. *Psychopharmacology* (Berlin). 146:373, 1999.

31. Nestler, E.J. Molecular basis of long-term plasticity underlying addiction. *Nat. Rev. Neurosci.* 2:119, 2001.

32. Robbins, T.W., Everitt, B.J. Limbic-striatal memory systems and drug addiction. *Neurobiol. Learn. Mem.* 78:625, 2002.

33. Lerman, C., Patterson, F., Berrettini, W. Treating tobacco dependence: state of the science and new directions. *J. Clin. Oncol.* 23:311, 2005.

34. Robinson, T.E., Berridge, K.C. Addiction. *Annu. Rev. Psychol.* 54:25, 2003.

35. Robinson, T.E., Berridge, K.C. The neural basis of drug craving: an incentive-sensitization theory of addiction. *Brain Res. Brain Res. Rev.* 18:247, 1993.

36. Benwell, M.E., Balfour, D.J. The effects of acute and repeated nicotine treatment on nucleus accumbens dopamine and locomotor activity. *Br. J. Pharmacol.* 105:849, 1992.

37. Di Chiara, G., Imperato, A. Drugs abused by humans preferentially increase synaptic dopamine concentrations in the mesolimbic system of freely moving rats. *Proc. Natl. Acad. Sci. U.S.A.* 85:5274, 1988.

38. Ferrari, R., Le Novere, N., Picciotto, M.R., Changeux, J.P., Zoli, M. Acute and long-term changes in the mesolimbic dopamine pathway after systemic or local single nicotine injections. *Eur. J. Neurosci.* 15:1810, 2002.

39. Epping-Jordan, M.P., Picciotto, M.R., Changeux, J.P., Pich, E.M. Assessment of nicotinic acetylcholine receptor subunit contributions to nicotine self-administration in mutant mice. *Psychopharmacology* (Berlin). 147:25, 1999.

40. Picciotto, M.R., Zoli, M., Rimondini, R. et al. Acetylcholine receptors containing the beta2 subunit are involved in the reinforcing properties of nicotine. *Nature.* 391:173, 1998.

41. Shoaib, M., Stolerman, I.P., Kumar, R.C. Nicotine-induced place preferences following prior nicotine exposure in rats. *Psychopharmacology* (Berlin). 113:445, 1994.

42. Laviolette, S.R., van der Kooy, D. The motivational valence of nicotine in the rat ventral tegmental area is switched from rewarding to aversive following blockade of the alpha7-subunit-containing nicotinic acetylcholine receptor. *Psychopharmacology* (Berlin). 166:306, 2003.

43. Corrigall, W.A., Coen, K.M., Adamson, K.L. Self-administered nicotine activates the mesolimbic dopamine system through the ventral tegmental area. *Brain Res.* 653:278, 1994.

44. Corrigall, W.A., Franklin, K.B., Coen, K.M., Clarke, P.B. The mesolimbic dopaminergic system is implicated in the reinforcing effects of nicotine. *Psychopharmacology* (Berlin). 107:285, 1992.

45. Klink, R., de Kerchove d'Exaerde, A., Zoli, M., Changeux, J.P. Molecular and physiological diversity of nicotinic acetylcholine receptors in the midbrain dopaminergic nuclei. *J. Neurosci.* 21:1452, 2001.

46. Wu, J., George, A.A., Schroeder, K.M. et al. Electrophysiological, pharmacological, and molecular evidence for alpha7-nicotinic acetylcholine receptors in rat midbrain dopamine neurons. *J. Pharmacol. Exp. Ther.* 311:80, 2004.

47. Pidoplichko, V.I., DeBiasi, M., Williams, J.T., Dani, J.A. Nicotine activates and desensitizes midbrain dopamine neurons. *Nature.* 390:401, 1997.

48. Middleton, L.S., Cass, W.A., Dwoskin, L.P. Nicotinic receptor modulation of dopamine transporter function in rat striatum and medial prefrontal cortex. *J. Pharmacol. Exp. Ther.* 308:367, 2004.

49. Pidoplichko, V.I., Noguchi, J., Areola, O.O. et al. Nicotinic cholinergic synaptic mechanisms in the ventral tegmental area contribute to nicotine addiction. *Learn. Mem.* 11:60, 2004.

50. Shoaib, M., Benwell, M.E., Akbar, M.T., Stolerman, I.P., Balfour, D.J. Behavioural and neurochemical adaptations to nicotine in rats: influence of NMDA antagonists. *Br. J. Pharmacol.* 111:1073, 1994.

51. Epping-Jordan, M.P., Watkins, S.S., Koob, G.F., Markou, A. Dramatic decreases in brain reward function during nicotine withdrawal. *Nature.* 393:76, 1998.

52. King, S.L., Caldarone, B.J., Picciotto, M.R. Beta2-subunit-containing nicotinic acetylcholine receptors are critical for dopamine-dependent locomotor activation following repeated nicotine administration. *Neuropharmacology.* 47(Suppl. 1):132, 2004.

53. Marubio, L.M., Gardier, A.M., Durier, S. et al. Effects of nicotine in the dopaminergic system of mice lacking the alpha4 subunit of neuronal nicotinic acetylcholine receptors. *Eur. J. Neurosci.* 17:1329, 2003.

54. Grottick, A.J., Trube, G., Corrigall, W.A. et al. Evidence that nicotinic alpha(7) receptors are not involved in the hyperlocomotor and rewarding effects of nicotine. *J. Pharmacol. Exp. Ther.* 294:1112, 2000.

55. Maskos, U., Molles, B.E., Pons, S. et al. Nicotine reinforcement and cognition restored by targeted expression of nicotinic receptors. *Nature.* 436:103, 2005.

56. Tapper, A.R., McKinney, S.L., Nashmi, R. et al. Nicotine activation of alpha4* receptors: sufficient for reward, tolerance, and sensitization. *Science.* 306:1029, 2004.

57. Champtiaux, N., Gotti, C., Cordero-Erausquin, M. et al. Subunit composition of functional nicotinic receptors in dopaminergic neurons investigated with knock-out mice. *J. Neurosci.* 23:7820, 2003.

58. Grinevich, V.P., Letchworth, S.R., Lindenberger, K.A. et al. Heterologous expression of human {alpha}6{beta}4{beta}3{alpha}5 nicotinic acetylcholine receptors: binding properties consistent with their natural expression require quaternary subunit assembly including the {alpha}5 subunit. *J. Pharmacol. Exp. Ther.* 312:619, 2005.

59. McCallum, S.E., Parameswaran, N., Bordia, T., McIntosh, J.M., Grady, S.R., Quik, M. Decrease in {alpha}3*/{alpha}6* nicotinic receptors but not nicotine-evoked dopamine release in monkey brain after nigrostriatal damage. *Mol. Pharmacol.* 68:737, 2005.

60. Parker, S.L., Fu, Y., McAllen, K. et al. Up-regulation of brain nicotinic acetylcholine receptors in the rat during long-term self-administration of nicotine: disproportionate increase of the alpha6 subunit. *Mol. Pharmacol.* 65:611, 2004.

61. Wonnacott, S., Kaiser, S., Mogg, A., Soliakov, L., Jones, I.W. Presynaptic nicotinic receptors modulating dopamine release in the rat striatum. *Eur. J. Pharmacol.* 393:51, 2000.

62. Schilstrom, B., Nomikos, G.G., Nisell, M., Hertel, P., Svensson, T.H. *N*-Methyl-D-aspartate receptor antagonism in the ventral tegmental area diminishes the systemic nicotine-induced dopamine release in the nucleus accumbens. *Neuroscience.* 82:781, 1998.

63. Shoaib, M., Schindler, C.W., Goldberg, S.R., Pauly, J.R. Behavioural and biochemical adaptations to nicotine in rats: influence of MK801, an NMDA receptor antagonist. *Psychopharmacology* (Berlin). 134:121, 1997.

64. Markou, A., Paterson, N.E. The nicotinic antagonist methyllycaconitine has differential effects on nicotine self-administration and nicotine withdrawal in the rat. *Nicotine Tob. Res.* 3:361, 2001.

65. Turek, J.W., Kang, C.H., Campbell, J.E., Arneric, S.P., Sullivan, J.P. A sensitive technique for the detection of the alpha 7 neuronal nicotinic acetylcholine receptor antagonist, methyllycaconitine, in rat plasma and brain. *J. Neurosci. Methods.* 61:113, 1995.

66. Mogg, A.J., Whiteaker, P., McIntosh, J.M., Marks, M., Collins, A.C., Wonnacott, S. Methyllycaconitine is a potent antagonist of alpha-conotoxin-MII-sensitive presynaptic nicotinic acetylcholine receptors in rat striatum. *J. Pharmacol. Exp. Ther.* 302:197, 2002.

67. Grady, S.R., Meinerz, N.M., Cao, J. et al. Nicotinic agonists stimulate acetylcholine release from mouse interpeduncular nucleus: a function mediated by a different nAChR than dopamine release from striatum. *J. Neurochem.* 76:258, 2001.

68. Garzon, M., Vaughan, R.A., Uhl, G.R., Kuhar, M.J., Pickel, V.M. Cholinergic axon terminals in the ventral tegmental area target a subpopulation of neurons expressing low levels of the dopamine transporter. *J. Comp. Neurol.* 410:197, 1999.

69. Kalivas, P.W. Neurotransmitter regulation of dopamine neurons in the ventral tegmental area. *Brain Res. Brain Res. Rev.* 18:75, 1993.

70. Omelchenko, N., Sesack, S.R. Laterodorsal tegmental projections to identified cell populations in the rat ventral tegmental area. *J. Comp. Neurol.* 483:217, 2005.

71. Corrigall, W.A., Coen, K.M., Zhang, J., Adamson, K.L. GABA mechanisms in the pedunculopontine tegmental nucleus influence particular aspects of nicotine self-administration selectively in the rat. *Psychopharmacology* (Berlin). 158:190, 2001.

72. Lanca, A.J., Adamson, K.L., Coen, K.M., Chow, B.L., Corrigall, W.A. The pedunculopontine tegmental nucleus and the role of cholinergic neurons in nicotine self-administration in the rat: a correlative neuroanatomical and behavioral study. *Neuroscience.* 96:735, 2000.

73. Laviolette, S.R., Alexson, T.O., van der Kooy, D. Lesions of the tegmental pedunculopontine nucleus block the rewarding effects and reveal the aversive effects of nicotine in the ventral tegmental area. *J. Neurosci.* 22:8653, 2002.

74. Alcantara, A.A., Chen, V., Herring, B.E., Mendenhall, J.M., Berlanga, M.L. Localization of dopamine D2 receptors on cholinergic interneurons of the dorsal striatum and nucleus accumbens of the rat. *Brain Res.* 986:22, 2003.

75. Berlanga, M.L., Olsen, C.M., Chen, V. et al. Cholinergic interneurons of the nucleus accumbens and dorsal striatum are activated by the self-administration of cocaine. *Neuroscience.* 120:1149, 2003.

76. Hikida, T., Kitabatake, Y., Pastan, I., Nakanishi, S. Acetylcholine enhancement in the nucleus accumbens prevents addictive behaviors of cocaine and morphine. *Proc. Natl. Acad. Sci. U.S.A.* 100:6169, 2003.

77. Nestby, P., Vanderschuren, L.J., De Vries, T.J. et al. Ethanol, like psychostimulants and morphine, causes long-lasting hyperreactivity of dopamine and acetylcholine neurons of rat nucleus accumbens: possible role in behavioural sensitization. *Psychopharmacology* (Berlin). 133:69, 1997.

78. Smith, J.E., Co, C., Yin, X. et al. Involvement of cholinergic neuronal systems in intravenous cocaine self-administration. *Neurosci. Biobehav. Rev.* 27:841, 2004.

79. Zachariou, V., Caldarone, B.J., Weathers-Lowin, A. et al. Nicotine receptor inactivation decreases sensitivity to cocaine. *Neuropsychopharmacology.* 24:576, 2001.

80. Laviolette, S.R., van der Kooy, D. Blockade of mesolimbic dopamine transmission dramatically increases sensitivity to the rewarding effects of nicotine in the ventral tegmental area. *Mol. Psychiatry.* 8:50, 2003.

81. Barrot, M., Olivier, J.D., Perrotti, L.I. et al. CREB activity in the nucleus accumbens shell controls gating of behavioral responses to emotional stimuli. *Proc. Natl. Acad. Sci. U.S.A.* 99:11435, 2002.

82. Benowitz, N.L., Porchet, H., Jacob, P., III. Nicotine dependence and tolerance in man: pharmacokinetic and pharmacodynamic investigations. *Prog. Brain Res.* 79:279, 1989.

83. Grady, S., Marks, M.J., Wonnacott, S., Collins, A.C. Characterization of nicotinic receptor-mediated [3H]dopamine release from synaptosomes prepared from mouse striatum. *J. Neurochem.* 59:848, 1992.

84. Russell, M.A. Subjective and behavioural effects of nicotine in humans: some sources of individual variation. *Prog. Brain Res.* 79:289, 1989.

85. Mitsis, E.M., van Dyck, C.H., Krantzler, E. et al. Prolonged occupancy of nicotinic acetylcholine receptors by nicotine in human brain: a preliminary study. Paper presented at the Annual Meeting of the Society for Research on Nicotine and Tobacco, 2006.

86. Rice, M.E., Cragg, S.J. Nicotine amplifies reward-related dopamine signals in striatum. *Nat. Neurosci.* 7:583, 2004.

87. Zhang, H., Sulzer, D. Frequency-dependent modulation of dopamine release by nicotine. *Nat. Neurosci.* 7:581, 2004.

88. Schultz, W. Getting formal with dopamine and reward. *Neuron.* 36:241, 2002.

89. Perkins, K.A., Gerlach, D., Vender, J., Grobe, J., Meeker, J., Hutchison, S. Sex differences in the subjective and reinforcing effects of visual and olfactory cigarette smoke stimuli. *Nicotine Tob. Res.* 3:141, 2001.

90. Rose, J.E., Behm, F.M. Extinguishing the rewarding value of smoke cues: pharmacological and behavioral treatments. *Nicotine Tob. Res.* 6:523, 2004.

91. Brody, A.L., Mandelkern, M.A., London, E.D. et al. Brain metabolic changes during cigarette craving. *Arch. Gen. Psychiatry.* 59:1162, 2002.

92. Due, D.L., Huettel, S.A., Hall, W.G., Rubin, D.C. Activation in mesolimbic and visuospatial neural circuits elicited by smoking cues: evidence from functional magnetic resonance imaging. *Am. J. Psychiatry.* 159:954, 2002.

93. Caggiula, A.R., Donny, E.C., Chaudhri, N., Perkins, K.A., Evans-Martin, F.F., Sved, A.F. Importance of nonpharmacological factors in nicotine self-administration. *Physiol. Behav.* 77, 683, 2002.

94. Caggiula, A.R., Donny, E.C., White, A.R. et al. Cue dependency of nicotine self-administration and smoking. *Pharmacol. Biochem. Behav.* 70:515, 2001.

95. Caggiula, A.R., Donny, E.C., White, A.R. et al. Environmental stimuli promote the acquisition of nicotine self-administration in rats. *Psychopharmacology* (Berlin). 163:230, 2002.

96. Cohen, C., Perrault, G., Griebel, G., Soubrie, P. Nicotine-associated cues maintain nicotine-seeking behavior in rats several weeks after nicotine withdrawal: reversal by the cannabinoid (CB1) receptor antagonist, rimonabant (SR141716). *Neuropsychopharmacology.* 30:145, 2005.

97. Lesage, M.G., Burroughs, D., Dufek, M., Keyler, D.E., Pentel, P.R. Reinstatement of nicotine self-administration in rats by presentation of nicotine-paired stimuli, but not nicotine priming. *Pharmacol. Biochem. Behav.* 79:507, 2004.

98. Schroeder, B.E., Binzak, J.M., Kelley, A.E. A common profile of prefrontal cortical activation following exposure to nicotine- or chocolate-associated contextual cues. *Neuroscience.* 105:535, 2001.

99. Kelley, A.E. Memory and addiction: shared neural circuitry and molecular mechanisms. *Neuron.* 44:161, 2004.

100. Paterson, N.E., Markou, A. The metabotropic glutamate receptor 5 antagonist MPEP decreased break points for nicotine, cocaine and food in rats. *Psychopharmacology* (Berlin). 179:255, 2005.

101. Paterson, N.E., Semenova, S., Gasparini, F., Markou, A. The mGluR5 antagonist MPEP decreased nicotine self-administration in rats and mice. *Psychopharmacology* (Berlin). 167:257, 2003.

102. Bespalov, A.Y., Dravolina, O.A., Sukhanov, I. et al. Metabotropic glutamate receptor (mGluR5) antagonist MPEP attenuated cue- and schedule-induced reinstatement of nicotine self-administration behavior in rats. *Neuropharmacology.* 49(Suppl.):167, 2005.

103. Le Foll, B., Diaz, J., Sokoloff, P. Increased dopamine D3 receptor expression accompanying behavioral sensitization to nicotine in rats. *Synapse.* 47:176, 2003.

104. Le Foll, B., Schwartz, J.C., Sokoloff, P. Disruption of nicotine conditioning by dopamine D(3) receptor ligands. *Mol. Psychiatry.* 8:225, 2003.

105. Le Foll, B., Sokoloff, P., Stark, H., Goldberg, S.R. Dopamine D3 receptor ligands block nicotine-induced conditioned place preferences through a mechanism that does not involve discriminative-stimulus or antidepressant-like effects. *Neuropsychopharmacology.* 30:720, 2005.

106. Brunzell, D.H., Chang, J.R., Schneider, B., Olausson, P., Taylor, J.R., Picciotto, M.R. β2-Subunit-containing nicotinic acetylcholine receptors are involved in nicotine-induced increases in conditioned reinforcement but not progressive ratio responding for food in C57BL/6 mice. *Psychopharmacology* (Berlin). 184:328, 2006.

107. Olausson, P., Jentsch, J.D., Taylor, J.R. Repeated nicotine exposure enhances reward-related learning in the rat. *Neuropsychopharmacology.* 28:1264, 2003.

108. Olausson, P., Jentsch, J.D., Taylor, J.R. Repeated nicotine exposure enhances responding with conditioned reinforcement. *Psychopharmacology* (Berlin). 173:98, 2004.

109. Olausson, P., Jentsch, J.D., Taylor, J.R. Nicotine enhances responding with conditioned reinforcement. *Psychopharmacology* (Berlin). 171:173, 2004.

110. Palmatier, M.I., Peterson, J.L., Wilkinson, J.L., Bevins, R.A. Nicotine serves as a feature-positive modulator of Pavlovian appetitive conditioning in rats. *Behav. Pharmacol.* 15:183, 2004.

111. Le Foll, B., Goldberg, S.R. Cannabinoid CB1 receptor antagonists as promising new medications for drug dependence. *J. Pharmacol. Exp. Ther.* 312:875, 2005.

112. Silva, A.J., Kogan, J.H., Frankland, P.W., Kida, S. CREB and memory. *Annu. Rev. Neurosci.* 21:127, 1998.

113. Sweatt, J.D. Mitogen-activated protein kinases in synaptic plasticity and memory. *Curr. Opin. Neurobiol.* 14:311, 2004.

114. Brunzell, D.H., Russell, D.S., Picciotto, M.R. *In vivo* nicotine treatment regulates mesocorticolimbic CREB and ERK signaling in C57Bl/6J mice. *J. Neurochem.* 84:1431, 2003.

115. Pandey, S.C., Roy, A., Xu, T., Mittal, N. Effects of protracted nicotine exposure and withdrawal on the expression and phosphorylation of the CREB gene transcription factor in rat brain. *J. Neurochem.* 77:943, 2001.

116. Valjent, E., Pages, C., Herve, D., Girault, J.A., Caboche, J. Addictive and non-addictive drugs induce distinct and specific patterns of ERK activation in mouse brain. *Eur. J. Neurosci.* 19:1826, 2004.

117. Walters, C.L., Cleck, J.N., Kuo, Y.C., Blendy, J.A. Mu-opioid receptor and CREB activation are required for nicotine reward. *Neuron.* 46:933, 2005.

118. Dineley, K.T., Westerman, M., Bui, D., Bell, K., Ashe, K.H., Sweatt, J.D. Beta-amyloid activates the mitogen-activated protein kinase cascade via hippocampal alpha7 nicotinic acetylcholine receptors: *in vitro* and *in vivo* mechanisms related to Alzheimer's disease. *J. Neurosci.* 21:4125, 2001.

119. Chang, K.T., Berg, D.K. Voltage-gated channels block nicotinic regulation of CREB phosphorylation and gene expression in neurons. *Neuron.* 32:855, 2001.

120. Nakayama, H., Numakawa, T., Ikeuchi, T., Hatanaka, H. Nicotine-induced phosphorylation of extracellular signal-regulated protein kinase and CREB in PC12h cells. *J. Neurochem.* 79:489, 2001.

121. Griffiths, J., Marley, P.D. Ca^{2+}-dependent activation of tyrosine hydroxylase involves MEK1. *Neuroreport.* 12:2679, 2001.

122. Haycock, J.W. Multiple signaling pathways in bovine chromaffin cells regulate tyrosine hydroxylase phosphorylation at Ser19, Ser31, and Ser40. *Neurochem. Res.* 18:15, 1993.

123. Sparks, J.A., Pauly, J.R. Effects of continuous oral nicotine administration on brain nicotinic receptors and responsiveness to nicotine in C57Bl/6 mice. *Psychopharmacology* (Berlin). 141:145, 1999.

124. Pluzarev, O., Pandey, S.C. Modulation of CREB expression and phosphorylation in the rat nucleus accumbens during nicotine exposure and withdrawal. *J. Neurosci. Res.* 77:884, 2004.

125. Markou, A., Kenny, P.J. Neuroadaptations to chronic exposure to drugs of abuse: relevance to depressive symptomatology seen across psychiatric diagnostic categories. *Neurotox. Res.* 4:297, 2002.

126. Newton, S.S., Thome, J., Wallace, T.L. et al. Inhibition of cAMP response element-binding protein or dynorphin in the nucleus accumbens produces an antidepressant-like effect. *J. Neurosci.* 22:10883, 2002.

127. Kuehn, B.M. FDA speeds smoking cessation drug review. *JAMA* 8:295(6), 614, 2006.

128. O'Malley, S.S., Krishnan-Sarin, S., Farren, C., Sinha, R., Kreek, M.J. Naltrexone decreases craving and alcohol self-administration in alcohol-dependent subjects and activates the hypothalamo-pituitary adrenocortical axis. *Psychopharmacology* (Berlin). 160:19, 2002.

129. Krishnan-Sarin, S., Meandzija, B., O'Malley, S. Naltrexone and nicotine patch smoking cessation: a preliminary study. *Nicotine Tob. Res.* 5:851, 2003.

130. Krishnan-Sarin, S., Rosen, M.I., O'Malley, S.S. Naloxone challenge in smokers. Preliminary evidence of an opioid component in nicotine dependence. *Arch. Gen. Psychiatry.* 56:663, 1999.

131. Rukstalis, M., Jepson, C., Strasser, A. et al. Naltrexone reduces the relative reinforcing value of nicotine in a cigarette smoking choice paradigm. *Psychopharmacology* (Berlin). 180:41, 2005.

132. Lesage, M.G., Keyler, D.E., Hieda, Y. et al. Effects of a nicotine conjugate vaccine on the acquisition and maintenance of nicotine self-administration in rats. *Psychopharmacology* (Berlin). 1, 2005.

6.3 NEUROCHEMICAL SUBSTRATES OF HABITUAL TOBACCO SMOKING

Irina Esterlis, Ph.D., Suchitra Krishnan-Sarin, Ph.D., and Julie K. Staley, Ph.D.
Department of Psychiatry, Yale University School of Medicine, New Haven, Connecticut and VA Connecticut Healthcare System, West Haven, Connecticut

Tobacco is the most widely abused substance in our society today. Not only are cigarettes highly addictive and the source of a multitude of social, economic, and medical consequences, but also their abuse is most prevalent among psychiatric populations, including persons afflicted with schizophrenia, bipolar, major depressive, anxiety, and substance abuse disorders. Cigarette smoking kills more Americans than accidents, alcoholism, fires, illegal drugs, AIDS, murder, and suicide combined, and is responsible for approximately 400,000 premature deaths per year in the U.S. and 4.83

million premature deaths per year worldwide.[1] The medical, social, and economic consequences of cigarette smoking cost the U.S. society approximately $100 billion annually.[2] Despite the overwhelming evidence of the medical risks associated with cigarette smoking, about 20% of the U.S. population continues to smoke. These devastating costs to society underscore the need for research into the neurochemical mechanisms underlying the development and maintenance of the addiction to cigarette smoking. By understanding the neurochemical substrates promoting the addiction to cigarettes, better treatments for this destructive and costly brain disorder may be developed.

6.3.1   Cholinergic Adaptations in Smokers

The nicotinic acetylcholine receptor (nAChR) is the initial site of action of nicotine. With the advent of *in vivo* imaging methods, such as single photon emission computed tomography (SPECT), the amount of nicotine occupying nAChR in brain after smoking a cigarette may be measured. The occupancy of nAChR containing the β_2-subunit by nicotine after smoking one and two cigarettes has recently been determined using the nicotinic agonist radioligand [123I]5-IA-85380 and SPECT. Occupancy of β_2-nAChR after smoking one cigarette ranged from 34 to 62%, while, after two cigarettes, the range was from 35 to 56%, both in a region-dependent manner. Interestingly, nicotine continually occupied β_2-nAChR 1.8 to 6 h after smoking a cigarette even in the presence of continued radiotracer infusion (see Figure 6.3.1). The long-lasting occupancy of the β_2-nAChR by nicotine raises important questions about the frequency of cigarette smoking. Specifically, why do smokers smoke cigarettes every 1 to 2 h if the receptor remains occupied by nicotine, a pharmacologically active metabolite or endogenous acetylcholine for up to 6 h after smoking? One hypothesis is that the long-lasting occupancy may render this subset of receptors inactive, thus promoting the upregulation of receptors and agonist-binding sites as has been noted in post-mortem brain and peripheral lymphocytes from smokers. [3H]nicotine binding is higher in peripheral blood cells of smokers vs. nonsmokers and, interestingly, correlates with the number of cigarettes smoked per day.[3] [3H]nicotine binding is higher in the gyrus rectus (Brodman area 11), hippocampus, thalamus, midbrain,[4,5] striatum, entorhinal cortex, and cerebellum,[6] and [3H]epibatidine binding is higher in prefrontal and temporal cortex and hippocampus[7] in post-mortem brain from human

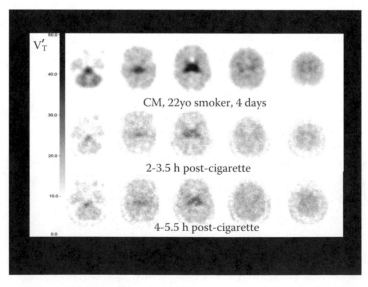

Figure 6.3.1   Transaxial parametric images in units of V_T' show regional [123I]5-IA binding to β_2-nAChR prior to and 2 to 3.5 h and 4 to 5.5 h after smoking a single cigarette. The bar at the right illustrates shades of gray corresponding to V_T' values.

smokers. Studies in animals treated chronically with nicotine have demonstrated that the upregulation in nAChR is due solely to the effects of nicotine.[8,9]

The mechanism of the upregulation in nicotine binding sites is not well understood. It has been established that, in contrast to the classic pharmacological dogma, which states that a desensitized receptor has lower affinity for agonists, the desensitized inactivated nAChR[10] exhibits higher binding affinity for agonists compared to the closed "resting" state and the open "activated" state.[11] When an endogenous agonist (e.g., acetylcholine), or an exogenous agonist (e.g., nicotine) binds to β_2-nAChR in its closed "resting" state, the channel undergoes a conformational change to the "open" state where ions influx. Subsequently, the ion channel undergoes a second conformational change to the "desensitized" state that corresponds to the closing of the channel. With prolonged desensitization, the β_2-nAChR enters an "inactivated" state.[12] The state of nAChR receptor is determined by agonist concentration, and the time course of agonist administration.[11] It is well established that the agonist-induced conformational change of the nAChR to the desensitized state occurs rapidly (i.e., within milliseconds).[13] However, in animals the nAChR upregulation has been mapped at time points only as early as 7 to 24 h post-nicotine.[14,15] Thus, while it is known that the desensitized state of the receptor exhibits higher affinity for agonist that may give an appearance of an acute increase in β_2-nAChR, it appears that the increase in agonist binding to nAChR occurs only after prolonged inactivation of the receptor.[16] In contrast, a recent study demonstrated that increased high-affinity nicotine binding was paralleled by a twofold increase in acetylcholine-evoked currents that were less sensitive to desensitization. The differential reports relating function to increased binding may be due to different subunit combinations that all demonstrate increased agonist binding but differ in the effects on function. In keeping, Lindstrom and colleagues[17] recently demonstrated that doses of nicotine that activate $\alpha_3\beta_2$ block the channel, whereas the nicotine dose that maximally activates the $\alpha_4\beta_2$ combination does not block the channel. Increased nicotinic agonist binding is not associated with changes in β_2-nAChR mRNA,[10,18,19] and the role of protein synthesis is not clear (e.g., no effect).[20,21] There is increasing evidence that the upregulation results from a combination of increased receptor expression on the cell surface[22] and decreased receptor turnover,[10,23] and that this change is associated with persistent functional inactivation that occurs via distinct post-translational mechanisms and at rates and magnitudes that are nAChR-subtype specific.[12] Moreover, the magnitude of the effect of nicotine to upregulate nAChR agonist binding sites may be genetically determined. Feng and colleagues,[24,25] who studied the gene expression of α_4 and β_2 subunits in 901 male siblings from 222 families, noted a strong association between the severity of nicotine dependence and haplotypes of the α_4 and β_2 subunits in men. While more studies are needed, these preliminary findings suggest that the propensity to develop nicotine dependence may be genetically determined, which may explain why some smokers are able to smoke "casually" while others develop severe dependence.

Another important question relates to how long the receptor upregulation lasts. In rodents, [^{3}H]nicotine binding is elevated in brain for up to 3 days, and normalizes to baseline values within 7 days of nicotine withdrawal,[26] whereas in living human tobacco smokers abstinent for 4 to 9 days, nAChR measured using [^{123}I]5-IA-85380 are elevated compared to age-matched never smokers suggesting that the receptor has not yet normalized at 1 week of abstinence.[27] In post-mortem human brain, high-affinity nicotine binding in ex-smokers (>2 months) is similar to that of the nonsmokers, suggesting that the receptor normalized within a 2-month period of time.[4–6] In a preliminary sample of living human smokers, this time frame is similar.[28] Thus, while the time period necessary for normalization is still unclear, it is apparent that the time frame for normalization in humans is longer than that noted in rodents.

An important consideration for measuring the nicotine binding site on nAChR in living humans is the time interval since the last cigarette required for residual nicotine to clear from brain so that it does not interfere with binding of the radioligand. Studies in nonhuman primates indicated that approximately 7 days would be required for nicotine to clear.[29] Thus, measurements of nAChR levels in humans should be obtained within a time interval in which the upregulation is still evident, but yet, sufficient time for nicotine to clear has been achieved. An important note is that plasma nicotine levels, which have a half-life of approximately 2 h, are a poor indicator of clearance of nicotine or pharmacologically active metabolites from brain. In our studies of both nonhuman primates chronically administered nicotine and human tobacco smokers, we have found urine cotinine levels to be a reliable predictor of nicotine clearance from brain.

6.3.2 Dopaminergic Adaptations in Smokers

Alterations in dopamine (DA) levels are associated with the rewarding effects of abused substances including cigarettes. Specifically, the mesolimbic DA pathway, which originates in the ventral tegmental area (VTA) and projects to nucleus accumbens, is believed to be the primary reward pathway in brain.[30] nAChRs containing the alpha7 subunit (α_7-nAChR) are abundant in the VTA. Stimulation of these receptors by nicotine or by endogenous acetylcholine, whose release was induced by nicotine or other components of cigarette smoke, produces an increase in glutamate concentrations which in turn stimulate N-methyl-D-aspartate receptors (NMDARs) on DA-containing neurons in the VTA, facilitating DA release and enhancing dopaminergic function in this critical brain reward area.[31] α_7-nAChRs are localized on glutamatergic terminals along with β_2-nAChRs on gamma-aminobutyric acid (GABA) nerve terminals postsynaptic to DA neurons within the VTA. Additionally, β_2-nAChRs are localized to DA cell bodies within the VTA. Nicotine actions on each of these strategically localized nAChRs are likely responsible for the interactions of nicotine with the DA reward pathway that mediates the development and maintenance of habitual tobacco smoking.[32]

In human tobacco smokers, synaptic DA levels increase in response to smoking a single cigarette.[33] [^{11}C]raclopride binding to DA D_2 receptors is sensitive to endogenous DA levels and, thus, DA release may be determined by measuring the change in [^{11}C]raclopride binding to D_2 receptors after smoking a cigarette. After smoking a cigarette, [^{11}C]raclopride binding was reduced by 25.9 to 36.6% compared to the 0 to 13.6% decrease observed in smokers who did not smoke a cigarette, demonstrating that smoking a cigarette causes significant DA release in the striatal reward areas. Moreover, DA levels positively correlated with craving in left ventral caudate/nucleus accumbens ($r = 0.49$, $p = 0.04$) and in putamen ($r = 0.65$, $p = 0.004$) suggesting that the larger DA release provided a greater relief from craving. In a similar study design in nonhuman primates, nicotine caused a 5 to 6% reduction in [^{11}C]raclopride binding to D_2 receptors after a nicotine infusion in nonhuman primates.[34] The lower amount of DA release from nicotine challenge compared to a smoking challenge is not surprising and suggests that other chemical(s) in tobacco smoke may be contributing to the reinforcing properties of smoking by enhancing nicotine-induced DA release. Fowler and colleagues[35] have elegantly demonstrated that monoamine oxidase B (MAO-B, the primary catabolic enzyme for DA in the brain) is lower throughout the brain of living smokers (basal ganglia, thalamus, cerebellum, cingulate gyrus, and frontal cortex). Similar decreases have been noted in post-mortem brain of tobacco smokers where lower [^{3}H]azabemide binding to MAO-B in amygdala was observed.[36] Because nicotine does not inhibit MAO-B,[37] it appears that the lower MAO-B levels in smoker's brain is due to chronic inhibition by other components of tobacco smoke. For example, tobacco smoke contains harmala alkaloids, including harmon and norharmon, that are potent monoamine oxidase inhibitors (MAOIs),[38] and Villegier[39] observed behavioral sensitization induced by repeated injections of nicotine in rats is short-lasting, but was prolonged upon the co-injection of a MAOI. These findings imply that behavioral effects of nicotine are transient and insufficient to induce long-term behavioral sensitization in the absence of MAOIs, suggesting that MAOIs contribute to the addictive properties of tobacco smoking. Collectively, these studies lead to the conclusion that the rewarding properties of tobacco smoking are mediated by the combined effects of nicotine and harmala alkaloids on DA release.

In addition to the acute effects of tobacco smoking on dopaminergic function in the striatal reward areas, there is significant evidence suggesting that the smoker's brain is in a chronic hyperdopaminergic state. Uptake of L-dopa (the precursor to DA) is higher in smokers vs. non-smokers, suggesting DA biosynthesis is accelerated in smokers. In keeping, the striatal homovanillic acid (HVA)/DA ratio is lower in post-mortem brain of smokers compared to nonsmokers due to higher DA levels (as opposed to lower HVA).[6] It is interesting to note that tyrosine hydroxylase (TH), the rate-limiting enzyme for DA biosynthesis, has been associated with vulnerability to develop nicotine dependence. Specifically, smokers that have the K4 allele of the TH enzyme are about 85% less likely to smoke in a dependent manner.[40] On the other hand, those carrying the K1 allele or three single nucleotide polymorphisms (SNPs) at the TH locus were not protected from developing nicotine dependence upon smoking. While the relationship of the K4 allele to TH expression and function is unclear, one may speculate that individuals with the K4 allele may synthesize DA at a slower rate, resulting in a smaller increase in DA in response to smoking and in turn decreasing reward salience and vulnerability to developing nicotine dependence.

The DA transporter has been suggested to be a critical dopaminergic substrate for habitual tobacco smoking because of its innate function — to regulate intrasynaptic DA availability and dopaminergic neurotransmission — and also because it has been genetically linked to nicotine dependence and age of smoking onset.[41] However, studies of DA transporter availability in post-mortem human brain from elderly tobacco smokers[6] and also in a younger population of living smokers did not detect a significant difference in striatal DA transporter availability. Moreover, there appears to be no significant relationship between DA transporter availability and smoking behavior.[42] Interestingly, the vesicular monoamine transporter (VMAT$_2$), an intraneuronal carrier among all monoaminergic systems, is decreased in platelets of habitual smokers vs. nonsmokers.[43]

With regards to DA receptors, postsynaptic DA D$_1$ receptors are decreased in living smokers as evidenced by lower [^{11}C]SCH 23390 binding in smokers compared to nonsmokers in the striatum, and most specifically in the nucleus accumbens.[44] Since [^{11}C]SCH 23390 binding to striatal D$_1$ receptors is insensitive to acute changes in extracellular DA concentration *in vivo*, it is likely that the decrease truly reflects altered D$_1$ receptor availability in smokers. Of note, the only study that has assessed D$_1$ receptors in post-mortem human brain of smokers compared to nonsmokers did not note any differences in D$_1$ receptor number.[6] The discrepancy between the post-mortem and *in vivo* study in living smokers may be due to age differences in the subject populations studied, or may reflect confounds associated with studies in post-mortem tissue including length of storage time and post-mortem interval. Lower D$_{1\text{-like}}$ receptor availability as observed in living smokers is a logical compensatory adaptive response to prolonged repeated perturbations in elevated synaptic DA levels. Alternatively, lower D$_{1\text{-like}}$ receptor availability may be genetically determined. Currently, there is no evidence for a genetic relationship between the D$_1$ receptor genotype and smoking behaviors; however, preliminary evidence suggests that the T allele of the closely related D$_5$ receptor is protective against smoking initiation.[45] Because there are no drugs available that pharmacologically distinguish between D$_1$ and D$_5$ receptors, the relationship between D$_{1/5}$ genotypes and receptor availability is unclear. However, it may be hypothesized that smokers smoke in effort to enhance dopaminergic signaling of an innately lower dopaminergic state that would make them more vulnerable to developing an addiction to tobacco smoking.

D$_2$ receptor function also appears to be aberrant in smokers as demonstrated by reduced growth hormone response to apomorphine challenge compared with nonsmokers. Interestingly, there was no difference between response to apomorphine during *ad libitum* smoking and 12 h of abstinence. These findings suggest that regardless of whether or not nicotine is on board, D$_2$ receptor sensitivity to DA agonists is reduced in smokers.[46] Importantly, D$_2$ receptor sensitivity to apomorphine was inversely correlated with cotinine serum levels and severity of nicotine dependence as measured by the Fagerstrom Tolerance Nicotine Dependence questionnaire (FTND). Reduced sensitivity of D$_2$ receptors to agonist stimulation likely reflects uncoupling of G proteins from the D$_2$ receptors, which would decrease the sensitivity to agonist stimulation but would not demonstrate a difference in D$_2$ receptor numbers measured using a radiolabeled antagonist.[6] Further support for the D$_2$ receptor as a neurochemical substrate of smoking is provided by evidence demonstrating that smokers carrying the A1 allele of the D_2 receptor have reduced P300 amplitude compared to nonsmokers[47] and carriers of the rare B1 allele for the D_2 receptor gene are more likely to be ever smokers.[48] In addition, the D_4 VNTR polymorphism moderates reactivity to smoking cues. Specifically, carriers of the DRD_4 L polymorphism demonstrate greater craving, attention, and arousal in response to smoking cues.[49] In contrast, individuals carrying the D_4 S allele do not demonstrate reactivity to smoking cues. Collectively, these studies support the D_2-like receptors as critical substrate for vulnerability to tobacco smoking.

6.3.3   GABAergic Adaptations in Smokers

GABA is a major neurotransmitter in the mammalian brain and controls neuronal excitability. It has been implicated in the addictive and withdrawal processes of nicotine dependence. Nicotine stimulates GABA release via modulation of nAChR on GABAergic neurons, which could lead to a decrease in inhibitory tone from GABAergic stimulation of $GABA_B$ autoreceptors.[50] Alternatively, nicotine-induced alterations in the levels of neurosteroids that regulate $GABA_A$ receptors could also potentially lead to altered levels of GABA.[51] Changes in GABA might also occur through nicotine's actions at the nAChR, which increases GABA release. Nicotine-induced GABA release is blocked by mecamylamine and dihydro-β-erythroidine and the effect is lost in the β_2 knockout mice, suggesting that β_2-nAChR mediate GABA release. The α_7 nAChR antagonist, alpha bungarotoxin, did not alter release.[52,53] Nicotine-induced GABA release has been demonstrated in the thalamus, hippocampus, and throughout the cerebral cortex.[54–60] The differential effects of nicotine on GABA release may be due to regional differences in nAChR subunit combinations in different regions.

Cortical GABA is also dysregulated in disorders associated with affective instability,[61] including premenstrual dysphoric disorder. Since nicotine modulates GABA function, Epperson and colleagues[62] suggest it is possible that nicotine modulates mood.[62] In a magnetic resonance spectroscopy (MRS) study of men and women smokers abstinent for 48 h, cortical GABA levels were decreased in women smokers imaged during the follicular phase (when hormone levels are similar to those in men) as compared to men. Furthermore, there were no differences in GABA levels between men smokers and nonsmokers but there was a drastic decrease in GABA levels in women smokers compared to women nonsmokers during the follicular phase of the menstrual cycle. These findings suggested that the phasic differences in cortical GABA levels evident in women nonsmokers are suppressed in women smokers. Since menstrual cycle phase was confirmed by serum estradiol and progesterone levels, changes in GABA levels cannot be attributed to lack of hormonal cyclicity.

The acute or chronic regulatory effects of nicotine treatment or tobacco smoking on cortical $GABA_A$-benzodiazepine receptors ($GABA_A$–BZR) are poorly studied. To date, only one animal study has examined effects of chronic nicotine and has demonstrated increased $GABA_A$–BZ receptors.[63] In addition to nicotine, tobacco smoke also contains the β-carbolines harman and norharman,[64] which are well known as MAOIs,[65,66] but may also be inverse agonists at the $GABA_A$–BZ receptor.[67] Currently, it is not clear what the combined effects of nicotine and β-carbolines are on $GABA_A$–BZR.

There is some evidence for a role for $GABA_B$ receptors as a neurochemical substrate of tobacco smoking. $GABA_{B1}$ receptors appear to be regulated by nicotine. Li[50] demonstrated a significant reduction of $GABA_B$ receptor mRNA in the hippocampus in rats chronically treated with nicotine. $GABA_B$ receptors primarily function to modulate release of neurotransmitters including GABA, glutamate, acetylcholine, noradrenalin, and serotonin that in the hippocampus are important for cognitive processes including attention and memory. Thus, nicotine-induced alterations in $GABA_B$ receptor expression in the hippocampus, a widely accepted site for learning and memory in both humans and animals, may be implicated in cognitive properties of tobacco smoke on cognition. A genetic linkage between $GABA_{B2}$ and nicotine dependence has been demonstrated in African American and European Americans.[68]

6.3.4 Opioidergic Adaptations in Smokers

The endogenous opioid system is believed to be the primary common pathway for all drugs of abuse. However, the role of the opioid system in habitual tobacco smoking has only recently become of interest. Using the short-acting mu-opioid antagonist naloxone, some studies have found decreases in smoking behavior in short-term laboratory paradigms[69,70] while others have reported no effect of naloxone on smoking behavior.[71] The long-acting mu-opioid antagonist naltrexone has been studied more extensively and has been shown to reduce smoking behavior and craving for cigarettes.[72,73] When used in combination with the nicotine patch, naltrexone has been shown to reduce smoking behavior and tobacco craving[74] and craving in response to cues,[75] as well as to block some effects of nicotine.[76] Evidence from clinical trials of naltrexone is equivocal with both positive[74,77] and negative findings.[78,79] Preclinical evidence suggests that the effects of naltrexone on cigarette smoking may be mediated by its ability to differentially alter expression and function of the α_7 and $\alpha_4\beta_2$ nAChRs in the central nervous system.[80]

Nicotine administration causes release of the endogenous opioid peptide beta-endorphin.[81] Preclinical evidence suggests that the mu opioid receptors are involved in nicotine reward.[82] Nicotine induced sufficient beta-endorphin to displace binding of the mu opioid receptor agonist [^{11}]C-carfentanil in brain in recently abstinent male smokers. Importantly, Scott and colleagues[83] used [^{11}C]carfentanil and positron emission tomography (PET) to demonstrate that nicotine, but not denicotinized cigarettes, induced endogenous opioid release in the thalamus and amygdala but reduced release in the anterior cingulate suggesting that nicotine was the sole chemical in tobacco smoke responsible for activation of the opioid reward pathway in the thalamus, amygdala, and cingulate. This suggests opioid changes in the cingulate mediate craving for nicotine while the opioidergic changes in the thalamus and amygdala may mediate the feelings of "satisfaction" after smoking a cigarette.

Lerman and colleagues[84] proposed that OPRM1 (mu-opioid receptor gene) may be responsible for efficacy of the type of nicotine replacement therapy and examined the relationship of the OPRM1 in relation to response to different nicotine replacement therapies. Smokers carrying the less common OPRM1 Asp40 variant were significantly more likely than those homozygous for the wild-type Asn40 variant to be abstinent at the end of nicotine replacement phase, with the effect being significant for the transdermal nicotine vs. nicotine nasal spray therapies. Furthermore, individuals with Asp40 variant treated by transdermal nicotine exhibited a significantly higher rate of recovery from short smoking lapses than those with Asn40 variant and significantly less negative side effects of smoking cessation (e.g., weight gain and withdrawal symptoms). These findings suggest that nicotine replacement therapies will be more efficacious in carriers of the Asp40 variant for the opioid receptor.

6.3.5 Serotonergic Adaptations in Smokers

Serotonin (5-HT) regulates many bodily functions, including appetite[85] and sleep (i.e., modulation of REM latency)[86] and may be involved in initiation and maintenance of tobacco smoking. Drugs that enhance 5-HT levels facilitate smoking cessation in highly dependent smokers.[87–89] In turn, nicotine has been shown to elevate 5-HT levels by stimulating 5-HT release through binding to the nAChR[90] and inhibiting 5-HT reuptake.[90,91] 5-HT levels are further enhanced in the smoker's brain as a consequence of decreased monoamine oxidase-A (MAO-A; the neuronal enzyme which serves to degrade 5-HT) activity.[35] Similar decreases in MAO activity have been noted in platelets of smokers[92] and support reports of twofold higher platelet 5-HT levels in smokers as compared to nonsmokers.[93] In addition, nicotine has been shown to decrease platelet 5-HT release and inhibit 5-HT uptake.[94] Active smokers excrete approximately 30% more 5-HT and 5-hydroxyindoleacetic acid (5-HIAA) as compared to never smokers and former smokers.[95] In the central nervous system, nicotine and its primary metabolite cotinine both decrease 5-HT turnover in rat brain, which results in a net enhancement in 5-HT neurotransmission. The 5-HT transporter (5HTT) regulates magnitude and duration of serotonergic neurotransmission. Chronic exposure to nicotine is associated with reduction in 5HTT sites in the brain[96] and nicotine dependence (as assessed using FTND questionnaire) has been found to be inversely correlated with densities of platelet 5HTT.[97,98] In brain, diencephalon 5-HT transporter availability is not altered in living human tobacco smokers.[42] However, there is a trend for higher brain stem 5-HT transporter availability in smokers vs. nonsmokers (10% higher in smokers), which appears to be more evident in men than women smokers. The perturbations in 5-HT function induced by nicotine may in part contribute to the reinforcing properties of cigarette smoking. In keeping, smoking cessation is facilitated by enhancing 5-HT function by administration of the MAO-A inhibitor moclobemide in highly dependent smokers.[99]

5-HT$_{1A}$ receptor gene expression is higher in DG, C1, and C3 subfields of the hippocampus after 2 and 24 h nicotine administration in rodents,[100] suggesting that nicotine is capable of modulating 5-HT$_{1A}$ receptor expression in some cortical and limbic brain regions. Rasmussen and Szachura[101] examined the effects of 5-HT$_{1A}$ agonist 8-OH-DPAT on the single-unit activity of serotonergic neurons in anesthetized rats undergoing nicotine withdrawal. They demonstrated a significant increase in the DRN to the 5-HT$_{1A}$ agonist 8-OH-DPAT during nicotine withdrawal, which led to an enhanced startle response. They report an increase in sensitivity develops over time with significance at days 3 and 4, and dropping to baseline by day 7. This finding may suggest that pre- and post-synaptic 5-HT$_{1A}$ antagonist drugs may be useful in attenuating some of the symptoms of nicotine withdrawal, therefore contributing to smoking cessation in humans. 5-HT$_{2A}$ receptors play a role in schizophrenia and alcohol dependence, both of which are associated with high prevalence of smoking behavior. However, the specific role of this receptor in smoking has not been widely studied. One study showed an association between 5-HT$_{2A}$ and maintenance of smoking but not smoking initiation.[102]

6.3.6   Implications for Smoking Cessation Treatments

Tobacco smoking is currently the most prevalent and deadly addiction. While there are numerous treatments currently available, there is a lot of room for improvement. Two types of pharmacological therapies have been approved by the U.S. Food and Drug Administration (FDA) — nicotine replacement therapies including gum, transdermal patch, lozenge, and inhaler, which deliver nicotine without the tar, and non-nicotine-based therapy such as bupropion hydrochloride (Zyban). There is significant between-subject variability in the efficacy of nicotine and non-nicotine-based pharmacotherapies, which could play a role in individual ability to quit and abstain from tobacco smoking. Factors such as genetic susceptibility, including family history, are currently being investigated in an effort to enhance the effectiveness of pharmacotherapies for smoking cessation. Because of the critical roles in drug reward, DA and opioid substrates are candidates for smoking cessation pharmacotherapies. Stimulation of D$_2$ receptors via bromocriptine decreases smoking, whereas D$_2$ receptor antagonism via haloperidol facilitates smoking. Zyban (bupropion), an atypical anti-depressant, has demonstrated efficacy for promoting long-term abstinence by reducing nicotine-related withdrawal symptoms,[103] negative affect,[104] and craving.[105] Zyban's mechanism of action for reducing smoking is believed to be inhibition of DA and norepinephrine reuptake, enhancement of norepinephrine and 5-HT neuronal activity, as well as noncompetitive inhibition of $\alpha_3\beta_2$, $\alpha_4\beta_2$, and α_7 nAChRs. However, Zyban is not equally effective in all smokers. For example, David and colleagues[106] demonstrated that individuals with *DRD2-Taq1 A2/A3* experience less craving upon smoking cessation, and reduced anxiety and impatience as compared to those with *DRD2-Taq1 A1/A2* or *A1/A1* who demonstrated no reduction in withdrawal symptoms.

Several other clinically available pharmacological agents have been tested for their potential to facilitate smoking cessation, although they are not approved by the FDA for this purpose. For example, tricyclic antidepressants, which inhibit reuptake of noradrenaline and 5-HT, promote smoking cessation in conjunction with behavioral treatment in some individuals.[107] However, these medications are limited because of their significant side effects. 5-HT-selective reuptake inhibitors (SSRIs) are believed to be a safer class of antidepressants but have not demonstrated effectiveness in smoking cessation.[108]

Cohen proposed that there may be a third way to treat nicotine dependence.[109] Since smokers still experience withdrawal symptoms with bupropion, and nicotine replacement therapies are not fully effective, Cohen and colleagues examined the effect of using a nicotinic receptor agonist in order to aid in smoking cessation. A novel nAChR ligand SSR591813 was employed due to its selective $\alpha_4\beta_2$ partial agonist activity. SSR591813 reduced the number of nicotine infusions on day 2 and 3 of treatment. Unlike mecamylamine, SSR591813 did not precipitate withdrawal signs in nicotine-exposed rats but prevented withdrawal signs precipitated by mecamylamine. Cohen and colleagues suggest these results imply $\alpha_4\beta_2$ involvement in the nicotine withdrawal syndrome. Since the SSR591813 may moderate nicotine withdrawal symptoms, which have been shown to cause enough distress to individuals that they relapse, it is important to continue investigation in its use for smoking cessation.

Acknowledgments

This work was supported by R01DA015577 and Transdisciplinary Tobacco Research Center (P50AA15632).

REFERENCES

1. Ezzati, M., Lopez, A. Estimates of global mortality attributable to smoking in 2000. *Lancet.* 362:847, 2003.
2. NIDA. NIDA InfoFacts: Cigarettes and Other Nicotine Products; 2005.
3. Benhammou, K.L.M., Strook, M.A., Sullivan, B., Logel, J., Raschen, K., Gotti, C., Leonard, S. [^{3}H]nicotine binding in peripheral blood cells of smokers is correlated with the number of cigarettes smoked per day. *Neuropharmacology.* 39:2818, 2000.
4. Benwell, M., Balfour, D., Anderson, J. Evidence that tobacco smoking increases the density of (-)-[^{3}H]nicotine binding site in human brain. *J. Neurochem.* 50:1243, 1988.
5. Breese, C., Marks, M., Logel, J. et al. Effect of smoking history on [3H]nicotine binding in human postmortem brain. *J. Pharmacol. Exp. Ther.* 282:7, 1997.
6. Court, J., Lloyd, S., Thomas, N. et al. Dopamine and nicotinic receptor binding and the levels of dopamine and homovanillic acid in human brain related to tobacco use. *Neuroscience.* 87:63, 1998.
7. Perry, D., Dávila-García, M., Stockmeier, C., Kellar, K. Increased nicotinic receptors in brains from smokers: Membrane binding and autoradiography studies. *J. Pharmacol. Exp. Ther.* 289:1545, 1999.
8. Bhat, R., Turner, S., Selvaag, S., Marks, M., Collins, A. Regulation of brain nicotinic receptors by chronic agonist infusion. *J. Neurochem.* 56:1932, 1991.
9. Mochizuki, T., Villemagne, V., Scheffel, U. et al. Nicotine induced up-regulation of nicotinic receptors in CD-1 mice demonstrated with an *in vivo* radiotracer: gender differences. *Synapse.* 30:116, 1998.
10. Peng, X., Gerzanich, V., Anand, R., Whiting, P., Lindstrom, J. Nicotine-induced increase in neuronal nicotinic receptor results from a decrease in the rate of receptor turnover. *Mol. Pharmacol.* 46:523, 1994.
11. Dani, J., Heinemann, S. Molecular and cellular aspects of nicotine abuse. *Neuron.* 16:905, 1996.
12. Ke, L., Eisenhour, C., Bencherif, M., Lukas, R. Effects of chronic nicotine treatment on expression of diverse nicotinic acetylcholine receptor subtypes. I. Dose- and time-dependent effects of nicotine treatment. *J. Pharmacol. Exp. Ther.* 286:825, 1998.
13. Ochoa, E., Chattopadhyay, A., McNamee, M. Desensitization of the nicotinic acetylcholine receptor: Molecular mechanisms and effect of modulators. *Cell Mol. Neurobiol.* 9:141, 1989.
14. Marks, M., Stitzel, J., Collins, A. Time course study of the effects of chronic nicotine infusion on drug response and brain receptors. *J. Pharmacol. Exp. Ther.* 235:619, 1985.
15. Nasrallah, H., Coffman, J., Olson, S. Structural brain imaging findings in affective disorders: an overview. *J. Neuropsychiatr. Clin. Neurosci.* 1:21, 1989.

16. Wonnacott, S. The paradox of nicotinic acetylcholine receptor upregulation by nicotine. *Trends Pharmacol. Sci.* 11:216, 1990.

17. Rush, R., Kuryatov, A., Nelwon, M., Lindstrom, J. First and second transmembrane segments of α_3, α_4, β_2 and β_4 nicotinic acetylcholine receptor subunits influence the efficacy and potency of nicotine. *Mol. Pharmacol.* 61:1416, 2002.

18. Marks, M., Pauly, J., Gross, S. et al. Nicotine binding and nicotinic receptor subunit RNA after chronic nicotine treatment. *J. Neurosci.* 2765, 1992.

19. Zhang, X., Gong, Z.-H., Hellstrom-Lindahl, E., Nordberg, A. Regulation of $\alpha_4\beta_2$ nicotinic acetylcholine receptors in M10 cells following treatment with nicotinic agents. *Neuroreport.* 6:313, 1994.

20. Buisson, B., Bertrand, D. Chronic exposure to nicotine upregulates the human $\alpha_4\beta_2$ nicotinic acetylcholine receptor function. *J. Neurosci.* 21:1819, 2001.

21. Gopalakrishnan, M., Molinari, E., Sullivan, J. Regulation of human $\alpha_4\beta_2$ neuronal nicotinic acetylcholine receptors by cholinergic channel ligands and second messenger pathways. *Mol. Pharmacol.* 52:524, 1997.

22. Harkness, P., Millar, N. Changes in conformation and subcellular distribution of a4b2 nicotinic acetylcholine receptors revealed by chronic nicotine treatment and expression of subunit chimeras. *J. Neurosci.* 22:10172, 2002.

23. Wang, F., Nelson, M., Kuryatov, A. et al. Chronic nicotine treatment upregulates human $\alpha_3\beta_2$ but not $\alpha_3\beta_4$ acetylcholine receptors stably transfected in human embryonic kidney cells. *J. Biol. Chem.* 1998:28721, 1998.

24. Feng, Y.N.T., Xing, H., Xu, Xin, Chen, C., Peng, S., Wang, L., Xu, Xiping. A common haplotype of the nicotine acetylcholine receptor alpha-4 subunit gene is associated with vulnerability to nicotine addiction in men. *Am. J. Hum. Genet.* 75:112, 2004.

25. Feng, Y., Niu, T., Xing, H. et al. A common haplotype of the nicotine acetylcholine receptor α_4 subunit gene is associated with vulnerability to nicotine addiction in men. *Am. J. Hum. Genet.* 75:112, 2004.

26. Pietila, K., Lahde, T., Attila, M., Ahtee, L., Nordberg, A. Regulation of nicotinic receptors in the brain of mice withdrawn from chronic oral nicotine treatment. *Naunyn-Schmiedeberg's Arch. Pharmacol.* 357:176, 1998.

27. Staley, J., Krishnan-Sarin, S., Cosgrove, K. et al. β_2* Nicotinic acetylcholine receptor availability in recently abstinent smokers. *J. Neurosci.* Accepted.

28. Cosgrove, K.P., Frohlich, E.B., Krantzler, E. et al. SPECT imaging of beta 2 nicotine acetylcholine receptors in tobacco smokers during acute and prolonged withdrawal. Paper presented at the Annual Meeting for the Society of Research on Nicotine and Tobacco, 2006.

29. Cosgrove, K., Ellis, S., Al-Tikriti, M. et al. Assessment of the effects of chronic nicotine on β_2-nicotinic acetylcholine receptors in nonhuman primate using [I-123]5-IA-85830 and SPECT. Paper presented at: Sixty-Sixth Annual Scientific Meeting of the College on Problems of Drug Dependence, 2004; San Juan, Puerto Rico.

30. Walters, C.L., Kuo, Y.C., Blendy, J.A. Differential distribution of CREB in the mesolimbic dopamine reward pathway. *J. Neurochem.* 87:1237, 2003.

31. Nomikos, G.G., Schilstrom, B., Hilderbrand, B.E., Panagis, G., Grenhoff, J., Svensson, T.H. Role of alpha7 nicotinic receptors in nicotine dependence and implications for psychiatric illness. *Behav. Brain Res.* 113:97, 2000.

32. Pich, E., Pagliusi, S., Tessari, M., Talabot-Ayer, D., Huijsduijnen, R.H.v., Chiamulera, C. Common neural substrates for the addictive properties of nicotine and cocaine. *Science.* 275:83, 1997.

33. Brody, A.L., Olmstead, R.E., London, E.D., Farahi, J., Meyer, J.H., Grossman, P., Lee, G.S., Huang, J., Hahn, E.L., Mandelkern, M.A. Smoking-induced ventral striatum dopamine release. *Am. J. Psychiatry.* 161:1211, 2004.

34. Marenco, S., Carson, R., Berman, K., Herscovitch, P., Weinberger, D. Nicotine-induced dopamine release in primates measured with [^{11}C]raclopride PET. *Neuropsychopharmacology.* 259, 2004.

35. Fowler, J., Volkow, N., Wang, G.-J. et al. Brain monoamine oxidase A inhibition in cigarette smokers. *Proc. Natl. Acad. Sci. U.S.A.* 93:14065, 1996.

36. Karolewicz, B., Klimek, V., Zhu, H., Szebeni, K., Nail, E., Stockmeier, C.A., Johnson, L., Ordway, G.A. Effects of depression, cigarette smoking, and age on monoamine oxidase B in amygdaloid nuclei. *Brain Res.* 1043:57, 2005.

37. Fowler, J., Volkow, N., Wang, G. et al. Neuropharmacological actions of cigarette smoke: brain monoamine oxidase B (MAO B) inhibition. *J. Addictive Dis.* 17:23, 1998.

38. Nelson, D., Herbet, A., Glowinski, J., Harmon, M. [3H]Harmaline as a specific ligand of MAO A-- II. Measurement of the turnover rates of MAO A during ontogenesis in the rat brain. *J. Neurochem.* 32:1829, 1979.

39. Villegier, A.S., Blanc, G., Glowinski, J., Tassin, J.P. Transient behavioral sensitization to nicotine becomes long-lasting with monoamine oxidases inhibitors. *Pharmacol. Biochem. Behav.* 76:267, 2003.

40. Anney, R.J.L., Olsson, C.A., Lotfi-Miri, M., Patton, G.C., Williamson, R. Nicotine dependence in a prospective population-based study of adolescents: the protective role of a functional tyrosine hydroxylase polymorphism. *Pharmacogenetics.* 14:73, 2004.

41. Ling, D., Niu, T., Feng, Y., Xing, H., Xu, X. Association between polymorphism of the dopamine transporter gene and early smoking onset: an interaction risk on nicotine dependence. *J. Hum. Genet.* 49:35, 2004.

42. Staley, J., Krishnan-Sarin, S., Zoghbi, S. et al. Sex differences in [123I]beta-CIT SPECT measures of dopamine and serotonin transporter availability in healthy smokers and nonsmokers. *Synapse.* 41:275, 2001.

43. Schwartz, K., Weizman, A., Rehavi, M. Decreased platelet vesicular monoamine transporter density in habitual smokers. *Eur. Neuropsychopharmacol.* 15:235, 2005.

44. Dagher, A., Bleicher, C., Aston, J.A.D., Gunn, R.N., Clarke, P.B.S., Cumming, P. Reduced dopamine D1 receptor binding in the ventral striatum of cigarette smokers. *Synapse.* 42:48, 2001.

45. Sullivan, P.F., Neale, M.C., Silberman, M.A., Harris-Kerr, C., Myakishev, M., Wormley, B., Webb, B.T., Ma, Y., Kendler, K.S., Straub, R.E. An association study of DRD5 with smoking initiation and progression to nicotine dependence. *Am. J. Med. Genet..* 105:259, 2001.

46. Smolka, M.N., Budde, H., Karow, A.C., Schmidt, L.G. Neuroendocrinological and neuropsychological correlates of dopaminergic function in nicotine dependence. *Psychopharmacology.* 175:374, 2004.

47. Anokhin, A.P., Torodov, A.A., Madden, P.A.F., Grant, J.D., Heath, A.C. Brain event-related potentials, dopamine D2 receptor gene polymorphism, and smoking. *Genet. Epidemiol.* 17(Suppl. 1):S37, 1999.

48. Spitz, M.R., Shi, H., Yang, F. et al. Case-control study of the D2 dopamine receptor gene and smoking status in lung cancer patients [see comment]. *J. Natl. Cancer Inst.* 90:358, 1998.

49. Hutchison, K.E., LaChance, H., Niaura, R., Bryan, A., Smolen, A. The DRD4 VNTR polymorphism influences reactivity to smoking cues. *J. Abnormal Psychol.* 111:134, 2002.

50. Li, S., Park, M., Bahk, J., Kim, M. Chronic nicotine and smoking exposure decreases $GABA_{B1}$ receptor expression in the rat hippocampus. *Neurosci. Lett.* 334:135, 2002.

51. Porcu, P., Sogliano, C., Cinus, M., Purdy, R.H., Biggio, G., Concas, A. Nicotine induced changes in cerebrocortical neuroactive steroids and plasma corticosterone concentrations in the rat. *Pharmacol. Biochem. Behav.* 74:683, 2003.

52. Lena, C., Changeux, J.-P. Role of Ca^{2+} ions in nicotinic facilitation of GABA release in mouse thalamus. *J. Neurosci.* 17:576, 1997.

53. Lu, Y., Grady, S., Marks, M., Picciotto, M., Changeux, J.-P., Collins, A. Pharmacological characterization of nicotinic receptor stimulated GABA release from mouse brain synaptosomes. *J. Pharmacol. Exp. Ther.* 287:648, 1998.

54. Meshul, C.K., Kamel, D., Moore, C., Kay, T.S., Krentz, L. Nicotine alters striatal glutamate function and decreases the apomorphine-induced contralateral rotations in 6-OHDA-lesioned rats. *Exp. Neurol.* 175:257, 2002.

55. Mansvelder, H.D., Keath, J.R., McGehee, D.S. Synaptic mechanisms underlie nicotine-induced excitability of brain reward areas. *Neuron.* 33:905, 2002.

56. Erhardt, S., Schwieler, L., Engberg, G. Excitatory and inhibitory responses of dopamine neurons in the ventral tegmental area to nicotine. *Synapse.* 43:227, 2002.

57. Reid, M.S., Fox, L., Ho, L.B., Berger, S.P. Nicotine stimulation of extracellular glutamate levels in the nucleus accumbens: neuropharmacological characterization. *Synapse.* 35:129, 2000.

58. Fedele, E., Varnier, G., Ansaldo, M.A., Raiteri, M. Nicotine administration stimulates the *in vivo* N-methyl D aspartate receptor/nitric oxide/cyclic GMP pathway in rat hippocampus through glutamate release. *Br. J. Pharmacol.* 125:1042, 1998.

59. Domino, E.F., Minoshima, S., Guthrie, S.K. et al. Effects of nicotine on regional cerebral glucose metabolism in awake resting tobacco smokers. *Neuroscience.* 101:277, 2000.

60. Ghatan, P.H., Ingvar, M., Eriksson, L. et al. Cerebral effects of nicotine during cognition in smokers and non-smokers. *Psychopharmacology.* 136:179, 1998.

61. Shiah, I.S.Y.L. GABA function in mood disorders: an update and critical review. *Life*. 63:1289, 1998.
62. Epperson, C.N.O.M.S., Czarkowski, K.A., Gueorguieva, R., Jatlow, P., Sanacora, G., Rothman, D.L., Krystal, J.H., Mason, G.F. Sex, GABA, and nicotine: the impact of smoking on cortical GABA levels across the menstrual cycle as measured with proton magnetic resonance. *Biol. Psychiatry*. 57:44, 2005.
63. Magata, Y., Kitano, H., Shiozaki, T. et al. Effect of chronic (-) nicotine treatment on rat cerebral benzodiazepine receptors. *Nuclear Med. Biol*. 27:57, 2000.
64. Poindexter, E., Carpenter, R. The isolation of harmane and norharmane from tobacco and cigarette smoke. *Phytochemistry*. 1:215, 1962.
65. McIsaac, W., Estevez, V. Structure-action relationship of beta-carbolines as monoamine oxidase inhibitors. *Biochem. Pharmacol*. 15:1625, 1966.
66. Buckholtz, N., Boggan, W. Monoamine oxidase inhibition in brain and liver produced by b-carbolines: structure activity relationships and substrate specificity. *Biochem. Pharmacol*. 26:1991, 1977.
67. Rommelspacher, H., Nanz, C., Borbe, H., Fehske, K., Muller, W., Wollert, U. Benzodiazepine antagonism by harmane and other β-carbolines *in vitro* and *in vivo*. *Eur. J. Pharmacol*. 70:409, 1981.
68. Beuten, J.M.J., Payne, T.J., Dupont, R.T., Crews, K.M., Somes, G., Williams, N.J., Elston, R.C., Li, M.D. Single- and multilocus allelic variants within the $GABA_B$ receptor subunit 2 ($GABA_{B2}$) gene are significantly associated with nicotine dependence. *Am. J. Hum. Genet*. 76:859, 2005.
69. Karras, A., Kane, J. Naloxone reduces cigarette smoking. *Life Sci*. 27:1541, 1980.
70. Gorelick, D.A.R.J., Jarvik, M.E. Effect of naloxone on cigarette smoking. *J. Subst. Abuse*. 1:153, 1988.
71. Nemeth-Coslett, R., Griffiths, R.R. Naloxone does not affect cigarette smoking. *Psychopharmacology*. 89:261, 1986.
72. Sutherland, G., Stapleton, J., Russell, M., Feyerabend, C. Naltrexone, smoking behaviour and cigarette withdrawal. *Psychopharmacology*. 120:418, 1995.
73. King, A., Meyer, P. Naltrexone alteration of acute smoking response in nicotine-dependent subjects. *Pharmacol. Biochem. Behav*. 66:563, 2000.
74. Krishnan-Sarin, S., Meandzija, B., O'Malley, S. Naltrexone and nicotine patch in smoking cessation: a preliminary study. *Nicotine Tob. Res*. 5:851, 2003.
75. Hutchison, K., Monti, P., Rohsenow, D. et al. Effects of naltrexone with nicotine replacement on smoking cue reactivity: preliminary results. *Psychopharmacology*. 142:139, 1999.
76. Brauer, L., Behm, F., Westman, E., Patel, P., Rose, J. Naltrexone blockade of nicotine effects in cigarette smokers. *Psychopharmacology*. 143:339, 1999.
77. King, A. Role of naltrexone in initial smoking cessation: preliminary findings. *Alcohol. Clin. Exp. Res*. 26:1942, 2002.
78. Covey, L., Glassman, A., Stetner, F. Naltrexone effects on short-term and long-term smoking cessation. *J. Addict. Dis*. 18:31, 1999.
79. Wong, G., Wolter, T., Croghan, G., Croghan, I., Offord, K., Hurt, R. A randomized trial of naltrexone for smoking cessation. *Addiction*. 94:1227, 1999.
80. Almeida, L.E.P.E., Alkondon, M., Fawcett, E.P., Randall, W.R., Albuquerque, E.X. The opioid antagonist naltrexone inhibits activity and alters expression of alpha7 and alpha4beta2 receptors in hippocampal neurons: implications for smoking cessation programs. *Neuropharmacology*. 39:2740, 2000.
81. Boyadjieva, N.I.S.D. The secretory response of hypothalamic beta-endorphin neurons to acute and chronic nicotine treatments and following nicotine withdrawal. *Life Sci*. 61:PL59, 1997.
82. Berrendero, R., Kieffer, B., Maldonado, R. Attenuation of nicotine-induced antinociception, rewarding effects and dependence in mu-opioid receptor knock out mice. *J. Neurosci*. 22:10935, 2002.
83. Scott, D., Heitzeg, M., Ni, L., Domino, E., Zubieta, J. Endogenous opioid neurotransmission and tobacco smoking behavior: a PET study. Paper presented at: Society for Neuroscience, 2004; San Diego, CA.
84. Lerman, C.W.E., Patterson, F., Rukstalis, M., Audrain-McGovern, J., Restine, S., Shields, P.G., Kaufmann, V., Redden, D., Benowitz, N., Berrettine, W.H. The functional mu opioid receptor (OPRM1) Asn40Asp variant predicts short-term response to nicotine replacement therapy in a clinical trial. *Pharmacogenomics J*. 4:184, 2004.
85. Bever, K., Perry, P. Dexfenfluramine hydrochloride: an anorexigenic agent. *Am. J. Health Syst. Pharm*. 54:2059, 1976.
86. Fornal, C.R.M. Sleep suppressant action of fenfluramine in rats. I. Relation to postsynaptic serotonergic stimulation. *J. Pharmacol. Exp. Ther*. 225:667, 1953.

87. Berlin, I.S.S., Spreux-Varoquaux, O., Launay, J.M., Olivares, R., Millet, V., Lecrubier, Y., Puech, A.J. A reversible monoamine oxidase A inhibitor (moclobemide) facilitates smoking cessation and abstinence in heavy, dependent smokers. *Clin. Pharmacol. Ther.* 58:444, 1995.

88. Berlin, I., Said, S., Spreux-Varoquaux, O. et al. A reversible monoamine oxidase A inhibitor (moclobemide) facilitates smoking cessation and abstinence in heavy, dependent smokers. *Clin. Pharmacol. Ther.* 58:444, 1995.

89. Cornelius, J., Salloum, I., Ehler, J. et al. Double-blind fluoxetine in depressed alcoholic smokers. *Psychopharmacol. Bull.* 33:165, 1997.

90. Rausch, J., Fefferman, M., Ladisich-Rogers, D., Menard, M. Effect of nicotine on human blood platelet serotonin uptake and efflux. *Prog. Neuropsychopharmacol. Biol. Psychiatry.* 13:907, 1989.

91. Schievelbein, H., Werle, H. Mechanism of the release of amines by nicotine. *Ann. N.Y. Acad. Sci.* 142:72, 1967.

92. Berlin, I., Spreux-Varoquaux, O., Said, S., Launay, J. Effects of past history of major depression on smoking characteristics, monoamine oxidase-A and -B activities and withdrawal symptoms in dependent smokers. *Drug Alcohol Depend.* 45:31, 1997.

93. Racke, K., Schworer, H., Simson, G. Effects of cigarette smoking or ingestion of nicotine on platelet 5-hydroxytryptamine (5-HT) levels in smokers and non-smokers. *Clin. Invest.* 70:201, 1992.

94. Pfueller, S.L., Burns, P., Mak, K., Firkin, B.G. Effects of nicotine on platelet function. *Haemostasis.* 18:163, 1988.

95. Sparrow, D., O'Connor, G., Young, J., Rosner, B., Weiss, S. Relationship of urinary serotonin excretion to cigarette smoking and respiratory symptoms. *Chest.* 101:976, 1992.

96. Xu, Z., Seidler, F.J., Ali, S.F., Slikker, W., Jr., Slotkin, T.A. Fetal and adolescent nicotine administration: effects on CNS serotonergic systems. *Brain Res.* 914:166, 2001.

97. Batra, V., Patkar, A., Berrettini, W., Weinstein, S., Leone, F. The genetic determinants of smoking. *Chest.* 123:1730, 2003.

98. Patkar, A.A.G.R., Berrettini, W.H., Weinstein, S.P., Vergare, M.J., Leone, F.T. Differences in platelet serotonin transporter sites between African-American tobacco smokers and non-smokers. *Psychopharmacology.* 166:221, 2003.

99. Berlin, I., Said, S., Spreux-Varoquaux, O., Olivares, R., Launay, J.-M., Peuch, A. Monoamine oxidase A and B activities in heavy smokers. *Biol. Psych.* 38:756, 1995.

100. Kenny, P.J.F.S., Rattray, M. Nicotine regulates 5-HT$_{1A}$ receptor gene expression in the cerebral cortex and dorsal hippocampus. *Eur. J. Neurosci.* 13:1267, 2001.

101. Rasmussen, K.C.J. Nicotine withdrawal leads to increased sensitivity of serotonergic neurons to the 5-HT$_{1A}$ agonist 8-OH-DPAT. *Psychopharmacology.* 133:343, 1997.

102. do Prado-Lima, P.A.S.C.J., Ataufer, M., Oliveira, G., Silveira, E., Neto, C.A., Haggstram, F., Bodanese, L.C., da Cruz, I.B.M. Polymorphism of 5HT$_{2A}$ serotonin receptor gene is implicated in smoking addiction. *Am. J. Med. Genet. B.* 128B:90, 2004.

103. Shiffman, S.J.J., Kharallah, M., Elash, C.A., Gwaltney, C.J., Paty, J.A., Gnys, M., Evoniuk, G., DeVeaugh-Geiss, J. The effect of bupropion on nicotine cravings and withdrawal. *Psychopharmacology.* 148:33, 2000.

104. Lerman, C.R.D., Kaufmann, V., Audrain, J., Hawk, L., Liu, A., Niaura, R., Epstein, L. Mediating mechanisms for the impact of bupropion in smoking cessation treatment. *Drug Alcohol Depend.* 67:219, 2002.

105. Durcan, M.J.D.G., White, J, Johnston, J.A., Gonzales, D., Niaura, R., Rigotti, N., Sachs, D.P. The effect of bupropion sustained-release on cigarette craving after smoking cessation. *Clin. Ther.* 24:540, 2002.

106. David, S.P.N.R., Papandonatos, G.D., Shadel, W.G., Burkholder, G.J., Britt, D.M., Day, A., Stumpff, J., Hutchinson, K., Murphy, M., Johnstone, E., Griffiths, S.E., Walton, R.T. Does the DRD2-Taq1 A polymorphism influence treatment response to bupropion hydrochloride for reduction of the nicotine withdrawal syndrome? *Nicotine Tob. Res.* 5:935, 2003.

107. Hall, S., Reus, V., Munoz, R. et al. Nortriptyline and cognitive-behavioral therapy in the treatment of cigarette smoking. *Arch. Gen. Psychiatry.* 55:683, 1998.

108. Schneider, N.G.O.R., Steinberg, C., Sloan, K., Daims, R.M., Brown, H.V. Efficacy of buspirone in smoking cessation: a placebo-controlled trial. *Clin. Pharmacol. Ther.* 60:568, 1996.

109. Cohen, C.B.E., Galli, F., Lochead, A.W., Jegham, S., Biton, B., Leonardon, J., Avenet, P., Sgard, F., Besnard, F., Graham, D., Coste, A., Oblin, A., Curet, O., Voltz, C., Gardes, A., Caille, D., Perrault, G., George, P., Soubrie, P., Scatton, B. SSR591813, a novel selective and partial α4β2 nicotinic receptor agonist with potential as an aid to smoking cessation. *J. Pharmacol. Exp. Ther.* 306:407, 2003.

6.4 NEUROCHEMICAL AND NEUROBEHAVIORAL CONSEQUENCES OF METHAMPHETAMINE ABUSE

Colin N. Haile, Ph.D.
Department of Psychiatry, Yale University School of Medicine, New Haven, Connecticut and VA Connecticut Healthcare System, West Haven, Connecticut

Methamphetamine (METH) is a highly addictive and potent central nervous system (CNS) stimulant. Its rapid and escalating abuse in the U.S. has highlighted deficiencies in our understanding of the neurobiological mechanisms that underlie its powerful reinforcing effects. Availability of the drug facilitated through technological advances in synthesis and drug trafficking from other countries has also contributed to its rapid dissemination. According to the National Survey on Drug Use and Health, 12.3 million Americans have tried METH at least once, an increase of 40% from 2000 and 156% over 1996 numbers.[1] Although METH abuse was originally concentrated in the western part of the U.S. (Hawaii, California) recent statistics indicate a dramatic shift in its use to rural Midwest States. The National Clandestine Laboratory Database notes that the number of small-scale labs producing METH increased substantially in the Midwest (Illinois, Michigan, Ohio, Pennsylvania)[2] indicative of the redistribution of METH production and abuse in the U.S.[3] Availability of the drug, in turn, has resulted in substantial increases in substance abuse treatment admissions. Moreover, METH use is often associated with high-risk behaviors for transmitting HIV and other diseases. Because METH abuse has a profound impact on the health of the individual and society at large it is paramount that we gain a better understanding of its effects on the human brain and its medical consequences.

6.4.1 Military, Medical Use, and Eventual Abuse of METH

METH is a derivative of amphetamine (AMPH) and both have many similarities in their effects on brain chemistry and behavior. They also share a common use history. AMPH was originally synthesized by Lazar Edeleanu in 1887 and again independently synthesized in 1927 by Gordon Alles.[4] It was eventually introduced commercially for the treatment of a myriad of ailments ranging from schizophrenia to hiccups.[5] AMPH has been used by the military to enhance concentration and vigilance ever since the Spanish Civil War. In World War II, American, German, British, and Japanese fighter pilots were administered the drug to stave off fatigue on long missions, a common use even today.[6] First synthesized by the Japanese pharmacologist Nagayoshi Nagai in the late 1800s, METH was also used during World War II to reduce soldier fatigue during military action and by civilians working in factories supporting the war effort. Similar to AMPH, METH was eventually sold over the counter in Japan beginning in 1941 as *Philopon* and *Sedrin*. Following the end of World War II, availability of METH increased further due to army surplus flooding the market. This initiated what has been called the "First Epidemic" (1945–1957) of METH abuse in Japan. Soon over half a million individuals were heavily abusing the drug, including 5% of the population between the ages of 16 and 25.[7] Strict laws were implemented in the 1950s to help deal with the problem. A "Second Epidemic" occurred in the 1970s when METH use increased among blue-collar workers, students, and housewives.[8] At present, METH abuse continues to be a serious problem in Japan and has remained the most popular illicit drug for the last 10 years.[9] In the U.S., underground METH labs appeared in California Bay Area in the 1960s. Recognizing the profitability of METH, motorcycle gangs began distributing the drug along the West Coast. METH abuse was so rampant it was the topic of a popular book at the time.[10] Drug enforcement crackdowns on gang activity and limitation of precursor chemicals for the synthesis of METH quelled the distribution to a certain degree. At present, however, the bulk of the West Coast drug supply — and the Midwest — appears to be coming from Mexican "super labs" with a minor percentage produced by small-scale establishments or so called "mom-and-pop" laboratories.[3]

6.4.2 Characteristics and Patterns of Use and Abuse

METH has been available legally in the U.S. for many years as a therapeutic drug (trade name Desoxyn) used to treat obesity and attention-deficit/hyperactivity disorder (ADHD). Illegal street forms are commonly known as "speed" or "meth," which can be self-administered via injection, smoking, nasal inhalation ("snorting"), or oral ingestion. In its highly pure smokable form it is referred to as "crystal," "ice," "crank," or "glass." When ingested, the lipophilic compound efficiently penetrates the CNS,[11] increasing concentrations of monoamines (particularly dopamine, DA) through multiple mechanisms (see below).[12] The intensity of the "high" and mood alteration produced from METH ingestion is route dependent. Smoking and injection results in an almost immediate euphoria or "rush," whereas the effect is less intense and rapid when administered via "snorting" (effects felt within 3 to 5 min) or oral ingestion (15 to 20 min).[1] The half-life of METH is an impressive 10 h in humans (compared to 90 min for cocaine).[13-15] METH abusers tend to self-administer the drug in a "binge and crash" pattern. "Binges" or "Runs" may last for 1 to 3 days or more followed by a period of abstinence. Because of the long half-life of METH in humans, "binge" administration results in successive accumulation of residual drug in the system. Tolerance to many — but not all — of the peripheral and central effects of METH occurs almost immediately.[16,17] Acute METH intoxication results in powerful stimulation of the sympathetic nervous system resulting in mydriasis (pupil dilation), hypertension, tachycardia, diaphoresis, and hyperthermia. The reinforcing or positive effects of acute administration include euphoria, increased energy, heightened attentiveness, hypersexuality, and decreased anxiety.[18,19] Upon withdrawal from METH the individual is said to "crash," which is discernible by the presence of depression, anhedonia, irritability, anxiety, fatigue, hypersomnia, poor concentration, intense craving, and aggression.[19-22] In certain respects, symptoms are more intense and distinguishable from amphetamine and cocaine withdrawal.[21,23,24] Individuals who have been consuming METH frequently and for long periods of time show severe psychiatric disturbances or METH "psychosis," which has many characteristics in common with schizophrenia.[9,25-28]

6.4.3 Neurochemistry of METH: Mechanisms of Action and Reinforcement

6.4.3.1 Dopamine

METH is similar to other drugs of abuse in that its reinforcing effects are mediated through multiple sites and mechanisms in the brain. It is well established that drugs of abuse — and natural reinforcers such as food — exert their effects, in part, by activation of the mesolimbic DA system.[29-31] This system consists of DA cell bodies in the ventral tegmental area (VTA) and their forebrain terminals in the prefrontal cortex (PFC) and nucleus accumbens (NAC). Drugs abused by humans evoke DA release in the PFC and NAC, the latter a crucial brain substrate that mediates the reinforcing or addictive aspects of drugs of abuse.[32] It is hypothesized that DA release in these areas increases the saliency or attractiveness of rewarding stimuli contributing to the addiction process.[33] Addictive drugs including METH are self-administered under controlled conditions[34,35] and activate mesolimbic DA in humans.[36] Lesions at different loci of this system alter the behavioral effects of drugs of abuse in animals.[37,38] Released DA from terminal regions subsequently binds to a number of DA receptor subtypes such as D_1-like (D_1, D_5) or D_2-like (D_2, D_3, D_4), which are classified based on molecular and pharmacological characteristics. DA neurotransmission is then terminated by sequestration of the transmitter into the presynaptic neuron through the dopamine transporter (DAT).[39,40] Depending on the behavioral paradigm, drugs that block DA receptors alter the behavioral effects of drugs of abuse to varying degrees.[30]

In animals, repeated intermittent psychostimulant administration (i.e., cocaine, AMPH, METH) enhances locomotor behavior over time. This phenomenon is referred to as behavioral sensitization. Sensitization is considered a key characteristic in the development of drug addiction and believed by some to be a model of psychosis or schizophrenia.[41-43] Induction of sensitization appears to be related to enhancement of DA neurotransmission in the mesolimbic DA system although other neurotransmitters such as glutamate (GLU), serotonin (5-HT), and norepinephrine (NE) are involved.[44] Drugs that block behavioral sensitization may have pharmacotherapeutic potential. Another important concept in addiction is tolerance. Tolerance is the decrease in behavioral response to the same dose of the drug over time and most likely plays a role in the increasing amounts of ingested drug over time by drug addicts.[45]

Similar to cocaine and AMPH, METH has strong effects at the DAT, which are likely responsible for its potent addictive properties. In fact, cocaine's reinforcing effects are related to its ability to enhance extraneuronal DA concentrations by blocking the DAT.[46] Likewise, AMPH increases DA levels by primarily reversing the DAT and inducing transmitter release into the extracellular space.[47,48] Strong evidence supporting this assumption comes from finding that neither cocaine nor AMPH is effective in genetically modified mice lacking this transporter.[49] Acute administration of METH also potently increases DA concentrations in reward circuitry[50-52] via an exchange diffusion mechanism independent of neuronal depolarization[53] and by redistributing cytosolic DA to areas in the neuron for quick fusion and discharge.[54,55] Systemic treatment for 7 days with METH enhances the response of mesolimbic VTA cell body neurons to subsequent administrations of the drug. This effect is antagonized with Ca^{2+} channel blockers.[56] A similar treatment regimen (5 days) results in hypersensitivity of VTA neurons altering the maximum amplitude and the ED_{50} value of D_2 receptor mediated hyperpolarization.[57] Hyperpolarization (i.e., inhibition) of DA neurons in the VTA may be a compensatory mechanism engaged to decrease excessive DA release in the NAC. However, an attenuation of DA release in this terminal region results in sensitized DA receptors, which is perhaps also compensatory. Consistent with this notion, *in vitro* intracellular recording in brain slices from rats pretreated with METH show supersensitized D_1 receptor-mediated hyperpolarizations in the NAC.[58]

The exact mechanisms responsible for the ability of METH to increase extracellular DA are fairly well delineated and are, in part, due to facilitation of DA discharge and inactivation of the DAT. For instance, the release of massive quantities of DA facilitates the formation of reactive oxygen species via auto-oxidation of DA[59] that, in turn, inactivates DAT.[60,61] Inactivation of DAT increases synaptic DA by preventing reuptake into the presynaptic neuron. Other reactive species such as superoxide or peroxynitrite also inactivate DA by oxidization, transforming it into highly reactive DA quinones that can also compromise DAT function.[62,63] Indeed, experiments show that acute and chronic administrations of METH cause a rapid and reversible decrease in the DAT.[64,65] Remarkably, a single METH injection dose-dependently decreases [^{3}H]dopamine uptake into striatal synaptosomes 1 h after treatment, suggesting rapid deleterious effects on DAT function.[64] DAT inactivation is blocked by depleting DA using the tyrosine hydroxylase inhibitor α-methyl-*p*-tyrosine[66] and by pretreatment with D_1 and D_2 antagonists and DAT blockers.[66-68] This suggests that abnormally high levels of DA evoked by METH may be the causative agent underlying DAT inactivation. Yet, studies also demonstrate that the potent hyperthermic effects of METH aid in enhanced production of reactive oxygen species that may further contribute to the inactivation of DAT.[63,69] Neutralizing METH-induced increases in body temperature[66] blocks its effects on the DAT, suggesting that inactivation involves a multicomponent process.

As DA is taken back up into the presynaptic neuron, it is sequestered into synaptic vesicles and repackaged for storage and subsequent re-release, a process mediated by the vesicular monoamine transporter (VMAT-2) in monoaminergic neurons. Once inside the neuron, DA is protected against oxidation, which could produce reactive oxygen species implicated in DAT inactivation.[70] Indeed, acute and multiple administrations of METH rapidly and persistently (up to 24 h) alter (within 60 min) vesicular [^{3}H]DA uptake as assessed in vesicles purified from striatum.[71,72] Pretreatment with the DA D_2 antagonist eticlopride but not the D_1 antagonist (SCH23390) prevents decreases in vesicular DA uptake by METH.[73] These data implicate D_2 receptors in METH-induced decreases of VMAT-2. As mentioned previously and consistent with other transmitter releasing compounds,[47] METH administration redistributes vesicles within the nerve terminal for immediate release, interestingly, in a fashion opposite to that of cocaine.[74] The distinctive difference between the two drugs may contribute to differences in their neurotoxic and behavioral profiles. Subcellular fraction preparations from striatum in rats analyzed at 24 h after METH administration show reduced overall VMAT-2 protein suggesting actual degradation occurs.[75] Taken together, VMAT-2 inactivation would hypothetically lead to increased cytosolic DA levels and potential formation of reactive oxygen species by auto-oxidation or by monoamine oxidase (MAO) leading to neurotoxicity,[76] a prominent feature of chronic METH consumption.[77]

6.4.3.2 Serotonin

In a number of ways, the effects of METH on serotonin (5-HT) are similar to those on DA. For example, repeated METH injections increase hippocampal (250%, over controls)[78] and nucleus accumbal (900%) extracellular 5-HT levels.[52] Long-lasting deficits in 5-HT metabolite parameters occur in the striatum, hippocampus, and frontal cortex in response to multiple administrations of METH.[79,80] A single high dose of METH (15 mg/kg) decreases tryptophan hydroxylase — the rate limiting enzyme in 5-HT synthesis — in the NAC and caudate.[81] Previous studies confirm these effects and posit that — similar to DA — inactivation may be caused by reactive oxygen species formed inside 5-HT terminals oxidizing the enzyme and causing deleterious effects to the neuron.[79,82,83] Acute and multiple injections of METH (10 mg/kg) result in reversible decreases in 5-HT transporter (SERT) function *in vivo*[68,84] whereas high doses of fenfluramine, cocaine, or methylphenidate do not.[85] High (15 mg/kg) but not low (7.5 mg/kg) doses of METH administered repeatedly reduces the binding of [^{3}H]cyanoimipramine ([^{3}H]CN-IMI) to serotonin uptake sites assessed by quantitative autoradiography.[86] Similar to DA, studies have shown that inactivation of SERT may also be due to the production of reactive oxygen species such as the endotoxin tryptamine-4,5-dione, a by-product of oxidized 5-HT.[87] Acute METH administration blocks SERT function in the striatum but not in the hippocampus. This effect appears to be mediated through DAergic pathways and partly by the hyperthermic effects of METH. Decreasing METH-induced increases in body temperature, depleting striatal DA with α-methyl-*p*-tyrosine, or pretreatment with D_1 and D_2 antagonists (SCH23390 and eticlopride) blocks the ability of METH to decrease SERT activity in the striatum but not in the hippocampus.[88] These results suggest that the action of METH on SERT localized in the striatum is predominantly mediated through DA and that hyperthermia also plays a role. Hippocampal changes appear to be dependent on 5-HTergic pathways. In addition, like DAT blockers, SERT blockers (citalopram and chlorimipramine) are also neuroprotective.[82,89]

6.4.3.3 Norepinephrine

Evidence from human and animal studies highlights a unique role for norepinephrine (NE) in the neurobiological effects of METH. For example, METH increases extracellular NE divergently in the caudate and hippocampus of rodents as measured by microdialysis.[90] Depletion of NE with the selective neurotoxin *N*-(-2-chloroethyl)-*N*-ethyl-2-bromobenzylamine (DSP-4) (50 mg/kg) significantly enhances METH-induced striatal DA depletion in rodents.[91] Pharmacological blockade of NE with clonidine, a drug that shuts down NE release via presynaptic α_2 adrenergic autoreceptors, potentiates METH-induced effects, whereas blockade of α_2 with antagonists (e.g., yohimbine), which enhances release, reduces the drug's deleterious effects.[91] These results suggest that NE may help attenuate alterations in neurochemistry attributed to DA. An early study also demonstrated that METH-induced increases in tryptophan hydroxylase activity are blocked with the NE antagonist propranolol indicating NE and 5-HT coordinate in some unknown way.[92] Unlike DAT and SERT, however, NET appears to be less vulnerable to the adverse effects of METH. METH treatment does decrease NET activity in synaptosomes; however, these changes are due to a direct effect of the drug on the transporter and not by indirect inactivation via reactive oxygen species seen with DA and 5-HT. Indeed, the aberrant effects on NETs can be reversed by simply rinsing the *in vitro* preparation of residual METH.[93] In addition, high doses of METH administered over a 2-week period results in depletion of DA and 5-HT but not NE in nonhuman primate brain.[94] Similarly, single or repeated METH administration reduces many neurochemical metabolic parameters associated with DA and 5-HT but not NE in the striatum-accumbens and thalamus-hypothalamus in mice.[95] Although it appears that NE plays a minimal role in the action of METH on the brain, there is evidence NE may be important. An *in vitro* study has recently shown that oral doses of psychostimulants, including METH, which produce subjective effects in humans, correlate with their potency to release NE not DA or 5-HT,[96] and prazosin, an α_1 adrenergic antagonist, blocks cocaine-induced reinstatement in an animal model of relapse.[97] Moreover, human METH abusers who develop spontaneous recurrence of METH psychosis show markedly elevated NE plasma levels, indicating that this neurotransmitter may be of prime importance.[98]

6.4.4   Neurobehavioral and Neuropharmacological Effects of METH: Pharmacotherapeutic Targets

Experiments in rodents and other animals allow us to closely examine the complex interplay between the drive or motivation to consume addictive drugs and behavior. This information has helped determine the neurobiological substrates that are responsible for the reinforcing or addictive effects of drugs of abuse.[99] Accumulating evidence suggests that the robust abnormal drug-seeking behavior seen in the addicted state is due, in part, to drug-induced alterations in neural sensitivity, neurotransmitter levels, and neural plasticity that is heavily embedded in learning.[100,101] Teasing out the mechanisms behind drug-induced alterations in brain proteins in areas that mediate these addictive states is of prime importance. Likewise, drugs that reverse or block these changes may serve as useful pharmacotherapies. Therefore, the effects of METH in the context of motivation and drug-induced changes in reinforcement-related brain circuits and possible drug therapy targets are reviewed below.

6.4.4.1   *Dopamine's Vital Contributions to METH-Induced Reinforcement*

Similar to cocaine and AMPH, acute administration of METH (2 mg/kg) potently increases DA in the NAC 1000% over baseline levels.[102,103] METH administration also leads to the development of behavioral sensitization[95,104] that is heavily dependent on dose and drug regimen.[105,106] As a testament to the reinforcing properties of METH, and like other psychostimulants, the drug is readily self-administered across a number of species.[107–112] In fact, self-administration of METH in combination with other drugs of abuse such as heroin makes it even more reinforcing.[113] Consistent with the action of METH on the DA system, drugs that modulate DA in one way or another alter METH-induced behaviors. For example, co-treatment with either a D_1 (SCH23390) or a D_2 (YM-09151-2) antagonist blocks the development and expression of METH-induced (4 mg/kg) behavioral sensitization in rats over 14 days of treatment.[104] Correspondingly, Witkin et al.[104a] demonstrated that pretreatment with the highly selective D_1 antagonist SCH39166 or the D_2 antagonist spiperone blocks the behavioral activation of METH (0.3 mg/kg) in mice. METH-induced behavioral sensitization in animals is used as a model of psychosis and drugs that antagonize this effect may be useful in treating disorders such as schizophrenia.[43] Particular attention has been focused on the D_4 receptor subtype when it was discovered that the atypical antipsychotic clozapine blocks this receptor among its many other actions.[114] Pretreatment with a selective D_4 antagonist (NRA 0160) blocks METH-induced hyperactivity in mice to a similar degree to that of clozapine.[115] It is unknown if clozapine would prove a useful treatment for METH abuse.

Given that METH, and other psychostimulants, readily bind and modulate SERT, DAT, and NET to varying degrees, compounds acting on these transporters in unison may prove therapeutic. Indatraline, a compound that binds to 5-HT, NET, and DAT, was recently shown to inhibit METH-induced DA release *in vitro*.[116] In a rat model of relapse, priming injections of indatraline marginally reinstated previously extinguished cocaine-seeking behavior (lever pressing for drug) as measured by self-administration yet failed to alter overall drug intake.[117] Along these lines, the 3-phenyltropane analogue RTI 111 that is marginally selective for the DAT, yet also has proclivity for the other transporters, increases the potency of self-administered METH in nonhuman primates.[118] Although counterintuitive, other drugs that enhance the effects of psychostimulants such as cocaine to the point at which they are aversive have proven efficacious.[119] However, RTI 111 is readily self-administered in a manner similar to cocaine and thus may possibly be abused itself. Other drugs that are more selective for the DAT, such as GBR12909, have been tested. GBR12909 inhibits AMPH transport into striatal synaptosomes suggesting that it could attenuate the behavioral effects of its cousin METH.[120] Similar to RTI 111, however, GBR 12909 co-treatment with METH potentiates the discriminative stimulus effects of METH in rats, a behavioral model that tests the subjective effects of drugs.[121] Moreover, priming injections of GBR 12909 reinstated previously extinguished cocaine-seeking behavior as measured by self-administration.[117] The results mentioned above emphasize the fact that experimental results attained *in vitro* are poor predictors for how the drug will behave *in vivo*. Nevertheless, a recent study with a long-lasting version of GBR12909 shows promise as a treatment for METH addiction in preclinical models.[52] Whether compounds targeting the DAergic system will produce optimal treatments for METH remains to be seen.

6.4.4.2 Serotonin Modulation of the Reinforcing Effects of METH

Aside from the known contribution of DA, preclinical studies indicate 5-HT plays a role in the reinforcing effects of drugs of abuse. For instance, mice lacking 5-HT_{1B} receptors are hypersensitive to the behavioral activating effects of cocaine.[122] Lesions of forebrain 5-HTergic tracts increase amphetamine self-administration suggesting that 5-HT regulates DA-mediated effects to a degree.[123] Indeed, it is well known that stimulating 5-HT by various means can augment DA neurotransmission.[124,125] Although the contribution of 5-HT in the effects of METH is not fully known, METH does indeed potently activate the 5-HTergic system[84] enhancing release[126] and increasing extracellular levels in brain.[90] Munzar et al.[127] demonstrated that the powerful 5-HT-releaser fenfluramine initially decreases METH self-administration. However, due to unknown mechanisms, tolerance developed to this effect after repeated dosing.[127] Results from drug discrimination experiments in that same study found that various 5-HT compounds targeting a number of receptor subtypes modulate and/or generalize to the discriminative stimulus effects elicited by METH.[127] These results are consistent with other studies demonstrating the modulatory effects of 5HT on METH-induced behaviors. For example, pretreatment with 5-HT_{1A} (NAN-190), $5\text{-HT}_{1B/1D}$ (methiothepin), and 5-HT_{2C} (mianserin) antagonists attenuates the acute locomotor stimulating effects of METH, whereas $5\text{-HT}_{2A/2B}$ (methyserigide) and 5-HT_3 (ondansetron) antagonists potentiate the METH effects.[128,129] The mechanisms that underlie the ability of different 5 HTergic compounds to divergently alter the behavioral effects of METH are unknown. Taken together, however, these data suggest that 5-HT likely plays more of a modulatory role than that of DA in METH-induced behaviors.[130] Drugs acting on this system may prove useful treatments especially for abnormalities in mood and aggression associated with METH withdrawal.

6.4.4.3 Glutamate and METH-Induced Behaviors

Glutamate (GLU) is the most abundant neurotransmitter in the brain and clearly has an important position in addiction. Indeed, GLU is essential in psychostimulant-induced sensitization[131] and reinforcement[132,133] by possibly altering DA neurotransmission in the PFC.[134] Remarkably, mice genetically lacking the metabotropic GLU receptor GluR5 are immune to the locomotor and reinforcing effects of cocaine.[135] Compounds that block this receptor also attenuate the reinforcing effects of other drugs of abuse.[136] Although METH and AMPH are similar and share common biochemical and behavioral effects, METH administration increases GLU levels in the PFC to a greater extent compared to AMPH.[103] The direct consequences of this difference in GLU-releasing ability are not known but may be important in terms of drug-associated neuroplasticity and treatment.

Consistent with the notion that GLU is important in the behavioral effects of METH, compounds that block AMPA-type glutamatergic receptors (NBQX) [137,138] or NMDA receptors (NPC 12626) decrease METH-induced locomotion. However, only high doses of NPC 12626 that disrupt normal locomotor behavior are effective,[138] indicating that the METH effects are most likely mediated largely through the AMPA receptor subtype. Similarly, drugs that facilitate removal of METH-induced increases of GLU from the extracellular space block its rewarding effects[139] as measured by a place conditioning paradigm.[140] The clinical implications for METH-induced increases of GLU in the context of drug abuse are not known. However, current evidence suggests individuals with obsessive-compulsive behavior or disorder (OCD) show hyperglutamatergic activity in the PFC.[141] Obsessive-compulsive behavior is akin to uncontrollable drug-seeking and individuals with OCD have an increased likelihood of drug abuse.[142]

6.4.4.4 Novel Therapeutic Targets for METH Addiction

A number of studies have tested compounds that home in on other novel neurotransmitter systems and reveal important clues to the action of METH. Initially classified as an opioid receptor, sigma (σ) receptors (sigma-1 and sigma-2) have been implicated in a variety of psychiatric disorders including depression, anxiety, schizophrenia[143,144] and, more recently, psychostimulant addiction.[145] Interestingly, sigma receptors are strategically localized in the nucleus accumbens and other areas within limbic circuitry.[145] Studies have demonstrated that psychostimulants bind to sigma receptors[146] and sigma (1) antagonists block many of the behavioral effects of cocaine and AMPH.[147,148]

Like other psychostimulants, *in vitro* binding studies show that METH also preferentially binds to sigma-1 receptors and pretreatment with sigma-1 receptor antagonists, such as BD1063 or BD1047, attenuates its acute behavioral activating effects.[148] Similarly, antisense oligodeoxynucleotides aimed at sigma-1 receptors, acting as a molecular antagonist, attenuate the locomotor-stimulating effects of METH. Evidence shows that psychostimulants either increase the number or sensitivity of sigma receptors *in vivo* and this also appears to be the case for METH. Indeed, rats previously sensitized to METH are significantly more responsive to the sigma receptor agonist (+)3-(3-hydroxyphenyl)-*N*-(1-propyl)piperidine ((+)-3-PPP).[149] Repeated administration of METH increases binding of the sigma ligand [^{3}H](+)pentazocine in a number of brain areas in rodents.[150] Sigma-1 receptors are also upregulated (protein and mRNA) in rats that self-administer but not in those that passively received METH.[151] Most importantly, sigma-1 antagonists block METH-induced behavioral sensitization.[152,153] The exact mechanism through which sigma-1 receptors are responsible for neutralizing the action of METH is unknown. However, experiments show that sigma-1 receptors mediate cellular restructuring via cholesterol and cytoskeletal trafficking from the endoplasmic reticulum to the plasma membrane and nucleus.[154,155] It is likely, then, that sigma-1 receptors may be involved in psychostimulant-induced neuroplasticity related to uncontrollable drug intake and by blocking these receptors may interrupt this process.[156] Although details are still emerging, these studies suggest a crucial role for the sigma receptor in the behavioral effects of METH and may prove a useful drug treatment target.

Early studies provided support for an alkaloid (*ibogaine*) found in the root bark of the African shrub *Tabernanthe iboga* having anti-addictive properties. Concerns of toxicity associated with *ibogaine* led to the development of the *iboga* alkaloid congener 18-MC (18-methoxycoronaridine).[157] Experiments in rodents show that 18-MC *enhances* METH-induced locomotion[158] and reduces METH self-administration.[159] These results are consistent with recent reports showing that disulfiram, a clinically efficacious compound for the treatment of cocaine addiction,[119] enhances the development and expression of cocaine-induced behavioral sensitization in rats.[160] Binding studies *in vitro* determined that *ibogaine* and 18-HC act as potent antagonists at $\alpha_3\beta_4$ nicotinic acetylcholine receptors with less potency seen at $\alpha_4\beta_2$, NMDA, or 5-HT$_3$ receptors.[161] Drugs such as mecamylamine and dextromethorphan that also antagonize $\alpha_3\beta_4$ block METH self-administration, lending further support for this receptor as a novel therapeutic target.[161,162] Indeed, lobeline, the lipophilic alkaloid obtained from the herb *Lobelia inflata*, also blocks $\alpha_3\beta_2$ and $\alpha_4\beta_2$ nicotinic neuronal receptors and has demonstrated great potential as a possible treatment for psychostimulant abuse. Lobeline pretreatment inhibits METH-induced locomotion, blocks the discriminative stimulus cue elicited by METH,[163] and decreases self-administration in rats.[164] Surprisingly, increasing the dosage of METH does not surmount the antagonism by lobeline suggesting good pharmacotherapeutic potential. How lobeline is able to block the powerful reinforcing effects of METH is unknown, although studies indicate that the ability of lobeline to block the METH effects is not due to preventing METH-induced elevations of DA but more likely due to its ability to prevent decreases in VMAT-2 and induction of hyperthermia.[75] Yet, lobeline also interacts with DAT[165] and increases 5-HT release that may involve SERT and contribute toward its anti-addictive effects.[166] Analogues of lobeline for the treatment of psychostimulant abuse are being developed.[167] Other preclinical studies testing possible novel treatments for METH abuse have targeted GABA,[168] cannabinoid,[169,170] and histamine receptors.[171] As has been attempted for cocaine addiction, a monoclonal antibody vaccine against METH is also in the developmental phase.[172]

6.4.4.5 METH-Induced Alterations in Intracellular Messenger Systems Related to Reinforcement

Recent research has focused on alterations in intracellular messenger systems and regulation of gene expression in response to drugs of abuse.[173–175] Similar to changes at the neurotransmitter level, molecular alterations occur in areas of the brain that mediate the reinforcing aspects of drug addiction and are long-lasting.[176] Drug-induced alterations are well thought of as a form of neural plasticity.[156] This neural plasticity occurs in response to modified gene expression that eventually leads to changes in neurotransmitter–receptor dynamics. In fact, every major drug of abuse produces long-term neuroplasticity in, for example, the VTA.[177] Understanding these alterations at the cellular level will inevitably improve our understanding of the underlying neural adaptations that govern addiction.

The first intracellular pathway to be thoroughly examined in the context of drug abuse was the cAMP/PKA/CREB cascade.[178] Neurotransmitters or drugs that activate D$_1$ receptors facilitate (acting through G$_{\alpha s}$ stimulatory G proteins) whereas neurotransmitters or drugs that activate D$_2$ (acting through G$_{\alpha i}$ inhibitory G proteins) decrease the formation of cyclic adenosine 3,5-monophosphate (cAMP). cAMP, in turn, affects cAMP-dependent protein kinase (PKA). The formation of cAMP is dependent on adenylyl cyclase and is degraded by various phosphodiesterase enzymes in the cytoplasm.[179] Drugs of abuse alter the dynamics of this intracellular messenger system. For example, repeated psychostimulant administration results in decreases in inhibitory G proteins (G$_{\alpha i}$) linked to D$_2$ receptors,[180,181] and elevated tyrosine hydroxylase[181–183] in the VTA. A number of persistent neuroadaptations are seen in the NAC in response to drug exposure. These include psychostimulant induced supersensitivity of D$_1$-mediated effects,[184] decreased levels of G$_{\alpha i}$, but no effect on Gs G proteins,[185,186] increased adenylyl cyclase, cAMP-dependent protein kinase (PKA),[185] and immediate-early gene expression of fos-associated proteins such as ΔFosB.[187–189] Enhancing cAMP activity in the VTA potentiates psychostimulant sensitization and inactivation of PKA blocks this effect.[190] Infusion of cAMP analogues, Rp- and Sp-cAMPS, bilaterally into the NAC, that block and facilitate PKA, respectively, induce and prevent relapse of cocaine seeking behavior.[191] Of primary importance is recent work on cAMP-response element-binding protein (CREB), a transcription factor localized in the nucleus that plays a crucial role in gene expression and plasticity associated events.[192,193] CREB has been implicated in a number of behavioral processes in particular, drug-induced sensitization,[194] and reinforcement.[175,195,196]

Elevating cAMP/PKA levels in the NAC enhances, whereas blocking PKA attenuates, the expression of cocaine-induced locomotor sensitization.[197] Likewise, recent reports demonstrate that the behavioral activating effects of METH can be antagonized by indirectly increasing cAMP levels with rolipram, a selective inhibitor of cAMP-specific phosphodiesterase 4 that degrades cAMP.[198] Co-treatment with systemic rolipram (4 mg/kg) blocks METH-induced activation in rats following a sensitizing treatment regimen (4 mg/kg × 5 days, 1 week withdrawal, then a 2 mg/kg METH challenge). Rolipram does not alter METH-induced increases in extracellular levels of DA in the striatum suggesting that the antagonism of the behavioral effects of METH were most likely due to increases in cAMP.[199] These data are in complete agreement with Mori et al.[199a] showing rolipram co-treatment blocks METH and morphine's locomotor activating effects but not those elicited by phencyclidine. The authors found that very high doses of rolipram (10 mg/kg) only partially attenuated SKF81297-induced (D_1 agonist) locomotion. Therefore, these data suggest that METH effects were likely blocked by increasing cAMP through inhibitory D_2 receptors. Post-mortem findings in METH abusers support this notion (see below).

Activated through the D_1 receptor pathway, DA and cAMP-regulated phosphoprotein 32kDa (DARPP-32) is a substrate for PKA found in the striatum and is involved in molecular adaptations that occur in response to drugs of abuse.[200] Phosphorylation by PKA converts DARPP-32 into an efficient inhibitor of PP1 (protein phosphatase-1). Consistent with the known fact that psychostimulants alter cellular responses acutely and long-term, PP1 has been shown to modulate AMPA channels involved in neuronal plasticity.[201–203] Once activated by PKA, however, DARPP-32 then affects a variety of downstream physiological effectors.[200] Studies in genetically modified mice lacking DARPP-32 show altered responses to psychostimulants.[204,205] Like cocaine, acute METH administration (20 mg/kg) increases DARPP-32 immunoreactivity and phosphorylation of various residues associated with GLU receptor subtypes in the neostriatum in wild-type but not in DARPP-32 knockout mice.[206] This effect was also shown in vitro and in vivo in the striatum of rats sensitized to METH.[207,208] DARPP-32 is also phosphorylated by a cyclin-dependent kinase (cdk5) that reverts the protein into a PKA inhibitor.[209] Interestingly, intra-NAC injections of roscovitine, a cdk5 inhibitor, attenuates METH-induced locomotor sensitization.[208] Moreover, recent evidence has connected cdk5 with ΔFosB, a transcription factor implicated in long-term adaptations to drugs of abuse.[210] However, whether METH induces the expression of ΔFosB is not known. METH also affects ARPP-21, a cAMP-regulated phosphoprotein of 21 kDa that is also phosphorylated by PKA and enriched in limbic structures.[211] Acute administration of METH or cocaine increases ARPP-21 phosphorylation in rodents.[212] What role these proteins play in METH-induced behavioral effects such as reinforcement is unclear.

Intracellular signaling is heavily dependent on Ca^{2+}, and drug-induced alterations could have profound effects on normal neuronal function. Indeed, chronic METH decreases kinases associated with Ca^{2+} such as Ca^{2+}/calmodulin (CaM)-dependent protein kinase II (CaM-kinase II) specifically in the VTA-NAC pathway that is blocked by the D1 antagonist SCH23390 and MK801, a GLU antagonist.[213,214] Other Ca^{2+}-associated proteins are also affected by METH, for example, calmodulin, a calcium-binding protein also implicated in the effects of other drugs of abuse.[215] Similar to the effects seen on CaM-kinase II, chronic METH (4 mg/kg × 14 days, 28 day withdrawal and a 4mg/kg challenge) significantly decreases calmodulin mRNA in the NAC and VTA. Comparable decreases have been seen in calcineurin in the striatum of rats sensitized to METH.[207] It is not known, however, whether these decreases affect neuronal function in a manner associated with drug sensitization or reinforcement. However, reduced activity of Ca^{2+} proteins involved in intracellular trafficking would undoubtedly have effects on several substrate proteins that are important for proper neuronal functioning.

Experiments conducted *in vitro* using immunofluorescence and mobility shift assays reveal that acute application leads to accumulation of METH in cytosol and vesicular compartments (4 to 6 h) and eventual translocation into the nucleus. In the nucleus, METH increases activator protein-1 (AP-1) and CREB DNA binding activity.[216,217] Pre-incubation with an anti-METH antibody prevents the enhancement of these DNA-binding proteins.[218] Experimental evidence shows that METH-evoked enhancement of AP-1 and CREB binding but not of other transcription factors (NF-KB, SP-1, STAT1, STAT3) is dose-dependent and is apparent in brain areas involved in reinforcement such as the frontal cortex and hippocampus.[219] METH (4 mg/kg) administration for 2 weeks with a 1 week interval and a final challenge — a treatment that produces drug sensitization — results in significant increases in cFos, CREB, and pCREB (phosphorylated form of CREB) immunoreactivity in rat striatum.[220] Animals learn preferences for places (place preference) where they have previously experienced a reward. Drugs that are more rewarding induce robust place preferences. In contrast, drugs that are not rewarding may produce aversion.[221] Recent studies show that CREB plays a primary role in the rewarding effects of psychostimulants. For example, Carlezon et al.[221a] demonstrated using viral transfer techniques that overexpression of CREB in the NAC makes cocaine aversive whereas blocking CREB enhances the rewarding attributes of the drug. Whether modulating CREB in the NAC will alter METH-induced reward is not known.

While the role of molecular adaptations in response to drugs of abuse affecting the cAMP/PKA/CREB signaling cascade has been thoroughly investigated, less attention has been paid to other intracellular pathways. For example, the mitogen-activated protein kinase (MAPK) pathway plays an important role in cell growth, differentiation, proliferation,[222] and neural plasticity associated with learning and memory.[223] Evidence suggests that drug-induced maladaptive forms of neural plasticity in areas of the brain involved in reward learning[101,156] may underlie the uncontrolled drug-seeking and drug intake seen in addiction.[224] For example, changes in plasticity-related genes in response to METH include tissue plasminogen activator,[225] activity-regulated cytoskeleton-associated protein,[226] synaptophysin, and stathmin[227] and MAP kinase phosphatases.[228] A number of other gene-products associated with this pathway are altered in METH-induced sensitized animals.[229] METH-evoked expression of genes involved in neuronal remodeling in limbic brain areas could contribute to drug-reward processes. For example, a number of studies in rodents implicate MAPK pathway in psychostimulant-induced sensitization and reward learning.[230–232] Consistent with these results, Mizoguchi et al.[232a] provide definitive evidence involving MAPK and METH-induced reward conditioning. Results show hyperphosphorylation of MAPK/ERK1/2 in the NAC and striatum but not in other areas in rats that had previously undergone METH-induced place conditioning. Pretreatment with both D_1 (SCH23390) and D_2 (raclopride) antagonists and PD98059 (a selective MAPK inhibitor) directly infused into the NAC blocks METH-induced place preference conditioning and ERK1/2 activation. This suggests a critical involvement of the MAPK/ERK signaling cascade in METH-evoked reward learning.

6.4.4.6   *METH-Induced Alterations in Intracellular Messenger Systems in Humans*

Results from post-mortem human studies addressing METH-induced changes in receptors and intracellular messenger systems are generally in line with changes seen in animal studies (Figure 6.4.1). For example, inhibitory G proteins, $G_{\alpha i1}$ and $G_{\alpha i2}$, and $G_{\alpha o}$ levels are reduced (32 to 49%) in the NAC of METH (and heroin) abusers.[233] These results are consistent with rodent studies showing that cocaine and heroin decrease inhibitory G protein levels in the NAC.[185,186] Experiments exploring the effects of METH specifically on G protein levels have not been conducted in animals. Although the lower inhibitory G protein levels could represent a preexisting deficit it is more likely that they are the result of neural adaptations employed to restore balance in response to chronic

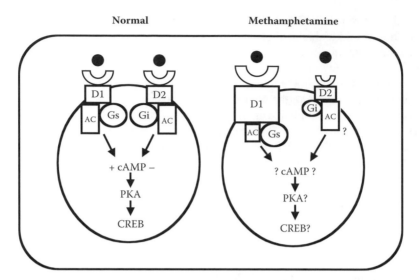

Figure 6.4.1 Hypothetical schematic diagram depicting cellular changes in the NAC based on post-mortem analysis of human brain. Normally, DA stimulates D_1 receptors coupled to the G_s G protein that stimulates the formation of cAMP via adenylyl cyclase (AC). The D_2 receptor is coupled to the inhibitory $G_{\alpha i}$ G protein that inhibits the formation of cAMP by AC. Accumulation of cAMP frees the catalytic subunits of cAMP-dependent protein kinase (PKA) to enter the nucleus and phosphorylate CREB. Most all drugs of abuse alter this cascade to an extent. Although evidence is limited, methamphetamine abusers show increased D_1 receptor protein levels and decreased DA stimulated AC (indicated by the increased and reduced size, respectively). D_2 receptor protein levels are marginally decreased and $G_{\alpha i}$ and $G_{\alpha o}$ G proteins are significantly decreased in METH abusers. These changes may represent adaptations aimed at regaining homeostasis. Decreases in D_2 receptors and inhibitory G proteins may compensate for overstimulation with METH-induced supraphysiological levels of extracellular DA. Increased D_1 receptor levels could also be considered compensatory for the cellular effects rendered through overstimulated D_2 receptors. However, D_1-stimulated AC activity is impaired in human METH abusers. These results indicate possible downregulation or tolerance in both pathways by different mechanisms.

METH stimulation. Inhibitory G proteins are linked to a number of receptors including D_2. A compensatory down-regulation of the D_2 receptor pathway, or D_2 receptors specifically, is consistent with imaging studies showing that this receptor is significantly decreased in METH abusers.[234] Moreover, D_1 receptor protein is significantly increased, whereas D_2 receptors are marginally decreased in the NAC of METH abusers.[235] The increase in D_1 receptors could also be part of the compensatory homeostatic mechanism engendered to oppose overstimulation of the D_2 pathway. Indeed, this scenario is supported by findings in a number of animal studies.[179,185,191] Yet, although total D_1 receptor protein is increased, evidence shows that DA stimulation of adenylyl cyclase activity is decreased by 25 to 30% in the NAC of human METH abusers.[236] These results call for caution in predicting functional abnormalities based on receptor and G protein concentrations. Additional studies in human brain are needed to further characterize intracellular neuroadaptive changes in the addicted state.

6.4.5 Neurotoxicity Associated with METH Consumption

Evidence from rodent, nonhuman primate, and post-mortem human studies indicates that METH is highly toxic to the CNS. This section briefly reviews neurotoxicity associated with METH abuse with particular attention on monoamines. Excellent and detailed reviews have been published elsewhere.[77,237–242]

METH-evoked neurotoxicity in the striatal DA system has been characterized in a number of species. For example, acute and chronic administration leads to striatal DA depletion, damaged nerve terminals,[243–246] and altered DAT,[64,243,247,248] tyrosine hydroxylase,[249,250] and VMAT.[76,251,252] The hyperthermic-inducing effects of METH play a role in toxicity. Experiments in rats show that blocking METH-facilitated increases in body temperature[66] is neuroprotective[253,254] perhaps by decreasing damage caused by reactive oxygen species formed from supraphysiological levels of extracellular DA.[66] Further, evidence indicates that terminal regions of the nigrostriatal DA system are especially susceptible to the toxic effects of METH,[255] whereas the VTA–NAC reward pathway is less affected.[256] Similar to DA, acute and chronic METH exposure decreases tryptophan hydroxylase, SERT, and depletes 5-HT.[82,251]

Analogous to most rodent studies, nonhuman primate studies show METH-induced deficits in DAT, VMAT, and DA.[256–258] Interestingly, long-term experiments indicate that some of these effects reverse over time[259,260] particularly when METH dosage regimen resembles the "binge"-like intake patterns seen in humans. Correspondingly, rodent and primate studies suggest that metabolite parameters in DA and 5-HT neurotransmitter systems and behavior appear to normalize over time; however, the extent of recovery depends on dose and length of drug exposure.[259,261–264]

Post-mortem human studies *partially* confirm preclinical findings in animals. METH abusers have decreased striatal tyrosine hydroxylase, DA, and DAT in the NAC and striatum.[265] Yet presynaptic markers VMAT and DOPA decarboxylase are not altered.[266] These findings suggest that there is no permanent damage to neurons in humans and confirms the results of one study in monkeys showing that nigral cell bodies are preserved following recovery.[255] However, evidence from imaging studies indicate, no matter the length of time of recovery, deficits remain[267] (see below). A number of factors, however, may explain these discrepant results between animal and post-mortem studies such as dose, duration of abuse, young vs. old population, and past drug histories. Taken together, post-mortem evidence supports that the human brain is susceptible to METH-induced alterations in DAergic parameters.

6.4.5.1 Oxidative Stress: A Possible Cause of METH-Induced Neurotoxicity

The exact mechanisms responsible for METH-induced neurotoxicity have not been fully defined. As mentioned previously, however, a large body of work implicates oxidative stress inflicted by reactive oxygen species in damaging neurons. Although GLU plays a significant role in the destructive effects of METH,[268] it is clear that excess DA is required for neurotoxicity to occur. Reactive species can form from oxidation of DA, DA auto-oxidation, and disruption of mitochondria.[77] Pretreatment with DA-synthesis inhibitors prevents METH-induced damage in both DA and 5-HT systems and L-dopa reverses this effect.[82,269–271] METH administration also induces the formation of an endogenous neurotoxin 6-hydroxydopamine (6-OHDA), used experimentally to induce DA-specific lesions.[272,273] Further, studies in genetically modified mice have shown that the degree of damage is mediated, in part, by a number of enzymes. Mice over-expressing the reducing enzyme superoxide dismutase (SOD) show reduced METH-induced neurotoxicity.[274–277] In contrast, mice devoid of the reactive-species-producing enzyme nitrous oxide synthase are resistant to the toxic effects of METH.[278] METH abnormally redistributes DA into the oxidizing environment of the neuron's cytoplasm from the reducing environment of the synaptic vesicles leading to possible damage to the neuron. Support for this assumption comes from experiments in which mice lacking the VMAT-2, which sequesters DA into synaptic vesicles, show exacerbated METH-induced damage in the DA system.[279] Also consistent with this notion, antioxidants including ascorbic acid,[280] vitamin E,[274] nicotinamide,[281] melatonin,[282,283] and selenium[284–286] attenuate METH-induced neurotoxicity.

6.4.5.2 METH-Induced Effects in Human Brain: Imaging Studies

Advances in imaging techniques have furthered our knowledge of the neural circuits involved in addiction. Positron emission tomography (PET), single photon emission tomography (SPECT), and function magnetic resonance imaging (fMRI), among others, allow measurement of relevant neuropharmacological parameters in the living brain. Recent studies using these techniques in

METH abusers reveal a number of abnormalities. For example, a PET [^{18}F]fluorodeoxyglucose (a marker of brain glucose metabolism) study in detoxified METH abusers showed hypermetabolism in the parietal cortex and hypometabolism in the striatum (caudate and putamen) suggesting a dysregulation between DAergic and non-DAergic mechanisms.[267] Compared to controls, current METH abusers undergoing a vigilance task exhibit lower metabolism in areas of the brain implicated in mood (anterior cingulate, insula and orbitofrontal area, middle and posterior cingulate, amygdala, ventral striatum, and cerebellum) as also measured by PET [^{18}F]fluorodeoxyglucose.[287] Two additional SPECT ^{99m}Tc-hexamethylpropylene-amine-oxime (HMPAO) studies corroborated with PET results show abnormal perfusion profiles in METH abusers.[288,289] Greater thalamic but not striatal (caudate and NAC) metabolism is apparent in METH abusers abstinent <6 months compared to 12 to 17 months.[290] The persistent decrease in striatal metabolism suggests long-lasting changes. Consistent with findings in post-mortem human brain, individuals with METH abuse histories have significant decreases in binding of the PET DAT radioligand [^{11}C]WIN-35,428 in the caudate and putamen.[291] Other PET studies using compounds targeting the DAT have confirmed decreased DAT binding in the caudate and putamen in current abusers,[292] recently detoxified subjects,[293] and in those abstinent for upwards of 11 months.[234] Studies have also linked abnormalities in D$_2$ receptors and substance abuse given that lower levels are found in alcoholics,[294] and cocaine[295] and heroin[296] abusers. In line with these data, D$_2$ receptor levels are lower in the caudate and putamen of METH abusers, as measured by PET [^{11}C]raclopride[267] (but see Reference 293). Taken together, these data clearly show abnormal brain function in METH abusers. Future studies are needed to determine permanent neurochemical deficits through longitudinal studies and possible therapies to reverse these deficits.

6.4.6 Conclusions

METH continues to be a major public health concern in the U.S. and other parts of the world. The dramatic increase in METH patient admissions and untoward effects on social, community, and familial sectors underscores the need for effective treatments. Yet despite significant advances in our understanding of the neurobiological mechanisms that govern its addictive properties, effective pharmacotherapies have not emerged.[297,298] Long-term social support and pharmacological treatments aimed at relieving the protracted anhedonia, dysphoria, anxiety, severe craving from METH withdrawal, and maladaptive drug-seeking are badly needed. Campaigns to alert the health care community of the importance in identification and proper treatment of the METH-addicted patient are paramount. It is hoped that further studies on the neurobiology of METH bring a clearer understanding of the mechanisms that underlie its deleterious effects.

REFERENCES

1. NIDA. NIDA Research Report: Methamphetamine: Abuse and Addiction, NIDA Research Report, Vol. 2005, 2002.
2. DEA. Total of All Meth Clandestine Laboratory Incidents, Calendar Year 2003, Vol. 2005, Domestic Strategic Intelligence Unit (NDAS) of the Office of Domestic Intelligence, 2003.
3. DEA. Drug Trafficking in the United States, Vol. 2005, Domestic Strategic Intelligence Unit (NDAS) of the Office of Domestic Intelligence, 2001.
4. Alles, G.A. The comparative physiological actions of the DL-beta-phenylisopropylamines. I. Pressor effect and toxicity. *J. Pharmacol. Exp. Ther.* 47:339, 1933.
5. Miller, M.A., Hughes, A.L. Epidemiology of amphetamine use in the United States, in Cho, A.K., Segal, D.S., Eds., *Amphetamine and Its Analogs.* Academic Press, San Diego, 1994, 503.
6. Caldwell, J.A., Caldwell, J.L., Darlington, K.K. Utility of dextroamphetamine for attenuating the impact of sleep deprivation in pilots. *Aviat. Space Environ. Med.* 74:1125, 2003.

7. Fukui, S., Wada, K., Iyo, M. Epidemiology of amphetamine abuse in Japan and its social implications, in Cho, A.K., Segal, D.S., Eds., *Amphetamine and Its Analogs*. Academic Press, San Diego, 1994, 503.

8. Anglin, M.D., Burke, C., Perrochet, B., Stamper, E., Dawud-Noursi, S. History of the methamphetamine problem. *J. Psychoactive Drugs* 32:137, 2000.

9. Ujike, H., Mitsumoto, S. Clinical features of sensitization to methamphetamine observed in patients with methamphetamine dependence and psychosis. *Ann. N.Y. Acad. Sci.* 1025:279, 2004.

10. Thompson, H.S. *Hell's Angels*. Ballantine Books, New York, 1966.

11. Lake, C.R., Quirk, R.S. CNS stimulants and the look-alike drugs. *Psychiatr. Clin. North Am.* 7:689, 1984.

12. Sulzer, D., Sonders, M.S., Poulsen, N.W., Galli, A. Mechanisms of neurotransmitter release by amphetamines: a review. *Prog. Neurobiol.* 75:406, 2005.

13. Cook, C.E., Jeffcoat, A.R., Hill, J.M. et al. Pharmacokinetics of methamphetamine self-administered to human subjects by smoking S-(+)-methamphetamine hydrochloride. *Drug Metab. Dispos.* 21:717, 1993.

14. Cook, C.E., Jeffcoat, A.R., Sadler, B.M. et al. Pharmacokinetics of oral methamphetamine and effects of repeated daily dosing in humans. *Drug Metab. Dispos.* 20:856, 1992.

15. Cho, A.K., Melega, W.P., Kuczenski, R., Segal, D.S. Relevance of pharmacokinetic parameters in animal models of methamphetamine abuse. *Synapse.* 39:161, 2001.

16. Fischman, M.W., Schuster, C.R. Tolerance development to chronic methamphetamine intoxication in the rhesus monkey. *Pharmacol. Biochem. Behav.* 2:503, 1974.

17. Perez-Reyes, M., White, W.R., McDonald, S.A. et al. Clinical effects of daily methamphetamine administration. *Clin. Neuropharmacol.* 14:352, 1991.

18. Martin, W.R., Sloan, J.W., Sapira, J.D., Jasinski, D.R. Physiologic, subjective, and behavioral effects of amphetamine, methamphetamine, ephedrine, phenmetrazine, and methylphenidate in man. *Clin. Pharmacol. Ther.* 12:245, 1971.

19. Gawin, F.H., Ellinwood, E.H.J. Cocaine and other stimulants. Actions, abuse, and treatment. *N. Engl. J. Med.* 318:1173, 1988.

20. Cretzmeyer, M., Sarrazin, M.V., Huber, D.L., Block, R.I., Hall, J.A. Treatment of methamphetamine abuse: research findings and clinical directions. *J. Subst. Abuse Treat.* 24:267, 2003.

21. Newton, T.F., Kalechstein, A.D., Duran, S., Vansluis, N., Ling, W. Methamphetamine abstinence syndrome: preliminary findings. *Am. J. Addict.* 13:248, 2004.

22. Rawson, R.A., Huber, A., Brethen, P. et al. Status of methamphetamine users 2–5 years after outpatient treatment. *J. Addict. Dis.* 21:107, 2002.

23. Cantwell, B., McBride, A.J. Self-detoxification by amphetamine-dependent patients: a pilot study. *Drug Alcohol Depend.* 49:157, 1998.

24. Weddington, W.W., Brown, B.S., Haertzen, C.A. et al. Changes in mood, craving, and sleep during short-term abstinence reported by male cocaine addicts. A controlled, residential study. *Arch. Gen. Psychiatry.* 47:861, 1990.

25. Yui, K., Goto, K., Ikemoto, S. et al. Neurobiological basis of relapse prediction in stimulant-induced psychosis and schizophrenia: the role of sensitization. *Mol. Psychiatry.* 4:512, 1999.

26. Srisurapanont, M., Ali, R., Marsden, J. et al: Psychotic symptoms in methamphetamine psychotic inpatients. *Int. J. Neuropsychopharmacol.* 6:347, 2003.

27. Yui, K., Ikemoto, S., Ishiguro, T., Goto, K. Studies of amphetamine or methamphetamine psychosis in Japan: relation of methamphetamine psychosis to schizophrenia. *Ann. N.Y. Acad. Sci.* 914:1, 2000.

28. Akiyama, K., Kanzaki, A., Tsuchida, K., Ujike, H. Methamphetamine-induced behavioral sensitization and its implications for relapse of schizophrenia. *Schizophrenia Res.* 12:251, 1994.

29. Heffner, T.G., Hartman, J.A., Seiden, L.S. Feeding increases dopamine metabolism in the rat brain. *Science.* 208:1168, 1980.

30. Wise, R.A., Rompre, P.P. Brain dopamine and reward, in Rosenzweig, M., Porter, L., Eds. *Annual Review of Psychology*. Annual Review, Inc., Palo Alto, CA, 1989, 191.

31. Roberts, D.C., Koob, G.F. Disruption of cocaine self-administration following 6-hydroxydopamine lesions of the ventral tegmental. *Pharmacol. Biochem. Behav.* 17:901, 1982.

32. DiChiara, G., Imperato, A. Drugs abused by humans preferentially increase synaptic dopamine concentrations in the mesolimbic system of freely moving rats. *Proc. Natl. Acad. Sci. U.S.A.* 85:5274, 1988.

33. Robinson, T.E., Berridge, K.C. Addiction. *Annu. Rev. Psychol.* 54:75, 2003.
34. Hart, C.L., Ward, A.S., Haney, M., Foltin, R.W., Fischman, M.W. Methamphetamine self-administration by humans. *Psychopharmacology.* 157:75, 2001.
35. Fischman, M.W., Schuster, C.R. Cocaine self-administration in humans. *Fed. Proc.* 41:241, 1982.
36. Vollm, B.A., deAraujo, I.E., Cowen, P.J. et al. Methamphetamine activates reward circuitry in drug naive human subjects. *Neuropsychopharmacology.* 29:1715, 2004.
37. Pettit, H.O., Ettenberg, A., Bloom, F.E., Koob, G.F. Destruction of dopamine in the nucleus accumbens selectively attenuates cocaine but not heroin self-administration in rats. *Psychopharmacology.* 84:167, 1984.
38. Zito, K.A., Vickers, G., Roberts, D.C. Disruption of cocaine and heroin self-administration following kainic acid lesions of the nucleus accumbens. *Pharmacol. Biochem. Behav.* 23:1029, 1985.
39. Glowinski, J., Iversen, L.L. Regional studies of catecholamines in the rat brain. I. The disposition of [^{3}H]norepinephrine, [^{3}H]dopamine and [^{3}H]dopa in various regions of the brain. *J. Neurochem.* 13:655, 1966.
40. Snyder, S.H., Coyle, J.T. Regional differences in ^{3}H-norepinephrine and ^{3}H-dopamine uptake into rat brain homogenates. *J. Pharmacol. Exp. Ther.* 165:78, 1969.
41. Robinson, T.E., Becker, J.B. Enduring changes in brain and behavior produced by chronic amphetamine administration: a review and evaluation of animal models of amphetamine psychosis. *Brain Res. Rev.* 11:157, 1986.
42. Robinson, T.E., Berridge, K.C. The neural basis of drug craving: an incentive-sensitization theory of addiction. *Brain Res. Rev.* 18:247, 1993.
43. Ellinwood, E.H., Sudilovski, A., Nelson, L.J. Evolving behavior in the clinical and experimental amphetamine (model) psychosis. *Am. J. Psychiatry.* 34:1088, 1974.
44. Pierce, R.C., Kalivas, P.W. A circuitry model of the expression of behavioral sensitization to amphetamine-like psychostimulants. *Brain Res. Rev.* 25:192, 1997.
45. Koob, G.F., LeMoal, M. Drug addiction, dysregulation of reward, and allostasis. *Neuropsychopharmacology.* 24:97, 2001.
46. Ritz, M.C., Lamb, R.J., Goldberg, S.R., Kuhar, M.J. Cocaine receptors on dopamine transporters are related to self-administration of cocaine. *Science.* 237:1219, 1987.
47. Sulzer, D., Sonders, M.S., Poulsen, N.W., Galli, A. Mechanisms of neurotransmitter release by amphetamines: a review. *Prog. Neurobiol.* 75:406, 2005.
48. Liang, N.Y., Rutledge, C.O. Comparison of the release of [3H]dopamine from isolated corpus striatum by amphetamine, fenfluramine and unlabelled dopamine. *Biochem. Pharmacol.* 31:983, 1982.
49. Giros, B., Jabar, M., Jones, S.R., Wightman, R.M., Caron, M.G. Hyperlocomotion and indifference to cocaine and amphetamine in mice lacking the dopamine transporter. *Nature.* 379:606, 1996.
50. Kashihara, K., Hamamura, T., Okumura, K., Otsuki, S. Methamphetamine-induced dopamine release in the medial frontal cortex of freely moving rats. *Jpn. J. Psychiatry Neurol.* 45:677, 1991.
51. Melega, W.P., Williams, A.E., Schumitz, D.A., DiStefano, E.W., Cho, A.K. Pharmacokinetic and pharmacodynamic analysis of the actions of D-amphetamine and D-methamphetamine on the dopamine terminal. *J. Pharmacol. Exp. Ther.* 274:90, 1995.
52. Baumann, M.H., Ayestas, M.A., Sharpe, L.G., et al. Persistent antagonism of methamphetamine-induced dopamine release in rats pretreated with GBR12909 decanoate. *J. Pharmacol. Exp. Ther.* 301:1190, 2002.
53. Fischer, J., Cho, A. Chemical release of dopamine from striatal homogenates: evidence for an exchange diffusion model. *J. Pharmacol. Exp. Ther.* 208:203, 1979.
54. Jones, S.R., Gainetdinov, R.R., Wightman, R.M., Caron, M.G. Mechanisms of amphetamine action revealed in mice lacking the dopamine transporter. *J. Neurosci.* 18:1979, 1998.
55. Cubells, J.F., Rayport, S., Raygendran, G., Sulzer D. Methamphetamine neurotoxicity involves vacuolation of endocytic organelles and dopamine-dependent intracellular oxidative stress. *J. Neurosci.* 14:2260, 1994.
56. Uramura, K., Yada, T., Muroya, S. et al. Methamphetamine induces cytosolic Ca^{2+} oscillations in the VTA dopamine neurons. *NeuroReport* 11:1057, 2000.
57. Amano, T., Maztsubayashi, H., Seki, T., Sasa, M., Sakai, N. Repeated administration of methamphetamine causes hypersensitivity of D_2 receptor in rat ventral tegmental area. *Neurosci. Lett.* 347:89, 2003.

58. Higashi, H., Inanaga, K., Nishi, S., Uchimura, N. Enhancement of dopamine actions on rat nucleus accumbens neurones *in vitro* after methamphetamine pre-treatment. *J. Physiol.* 408:587, 1989.

59. Chiueh, C.C., Miyake, J., Peng, M.T. Role of dopamine autoxidation, hydroxyl radical generation, and calcium overload in underlying mechanisms involved in MPTP-induced parkinsonism. *Adv. Neurol.* 60:251, 1993.

60. Berman, S.B., Zigmond, M.J., Hastings, T.G. Modification of dopamine transporter function: effect of reactive oxygen species and dopamine. *J. Neurochem.* 67:593, 1996.

61. Fleckenstein, A.E., Metzger, R.R., Beyeler, M.L., Gibb, J.W., Hanson, G.R. Oxygen radicals diminish dopamine transporter function in rat striatum. *Eur. J. Pharmacol.* 334:111, 1997.

62. Fornstedt, B., Carlsson, A. A marked rise in 5-S-cysteinyl-dopamine levels in guinea-pig striatum following reserpine treatment. *J. Neural Transm.* 76:155, 1989.

63. LaVoie, M.J., Hastings, T.G. Dopamine quinone formation and protein modification associated with the striatal neurotoxicity of methamphetamine: evidence against a role for extracellular dopamine. *J. Neurosci.* 19:1484, 1999.

64. Fleckenstein, A.E., Metzger, R.R., Wilkins, D.G., Gibb, J.W., Hanson, G.R. Rapid and reversible effects of methamphetamine on dopamine transporters. *J. Pharmacol. Exp. Ther.* 282:834, 1997.

65. Kokoshka, J.M., Vaughan, R.A., Hanson, G.R., Fleckenstein, A.E. Nature of methamphetamine-induced rapid and reversible changes in dopamine transporters. *Eur. J. Pharmacol.* 361:269, 1998.

66. Metzger, R.R., Haughey, H.M., Wilkins, D.G. et al. Methamphetamine-induced rapid decrease in dopamine transporter function: role of dopamine and hyperthermia. *J. Pharmacol. Exp. Ther.* 295:1077, 2000.

67. Broening, H.W., Morford, L.L., Vorhees, C.V. Interactions of dopamine D_1 and D_2 receptor antagonists with D-methamphetamine-induced hyperthermia and striatal dopamine and serotonin reductions. *Synapse.* 56:84, 2005.

68. Hanson, G.R., Gibb, J.W., Metzger, R.R., Kokoshka, J.M., Fleckenstein, A.E. Methamphetamine-induced rapid and reversible reduction in the activities of tryptophan hydroxylase and dopamine transporters: oxidative consequences? *Ann. N.Y. Acad. Sci.* 844:103, 1998.

69. Giovanni, A., Liang, L.P., Hastings, T.G., Zigmond, M.J. Estimating hydroxyl radical content in rat brain using systemic and intraventricular salicylate: impact of methamphetamine. *J. Neurochem.* 64:1819, 1995.

70. Liu, Y., Edwards, R.H. The role of vesicular transport proteins in synaptic transmission and neural degeneration. *Annu. Rev. Neurosci.* 20:125, 1997.

71. Brown, J.M., Hanson, G.R., Fleckenstein, A.E. Methamphetamine rapidly decreases vesicular dopamine uptake. *J. Neurochem.* 74:2221, 2000.

72. Hogan, K.A., Staal, R.G., Sonsalla, P.K. Analysis of VMAT2 binding after methamphetamine or MPTP treatment: disparity between homogenates. *J. Neurochem.* 74:2217, 2000.

73. Brown, J.M., Riddle, E.L., Sandoval, V. et al. A single methamphetamine administration rapidly decreases vesicular dopamine uptake. *J. Pharmacol. Exp. Ther.* 302:497, 2002.

74. Riddle, E.L., Topham, M.K., Haycock, J.W., Hanson, G.R., Fleckenstein, A.E. Differential trafficking of the vesicular monoamine transporter-2 by methamphetamine and cocaine. *Eur. J. Pharmacol.* 449:71, 2002.

75. Eyerman, D.J., Yamamoto, B.K. Lobeline attenuates methamphetamine-induced changes in vesicular monoamine transporter 2 immunoreactivity and monoamine depletions in the striatum. *J. Pharmacol. Exp. Ther.* 312:160, 2005.

76. Fleckenstein, A.E., Hanson, G.R. Impact of psychostimulants on vesicular monoamine transporter function. *Eur. J. Pharmacol.* 479:283, 2003.

77. Davidson, C., Gow, A.J., Lee, T.H., Ellinwood, E.H. Methamphetamine neurotoxicity: necrotic and apoptotic mechanisms and relevance to human abuse and treatment. *Brain Res. Rev.* 36:1, 2001.

78. Rocher, C., Gardier, A.M. Effects of repeated systemic administration of *d*-fenfluramine on serotonin and glutamate release in rat ventral hippocampus: comparison with methamphetamine using *in vivo* microdialysis. *Naunyn Schmiedeberg's Arch. Pharmacol.* 363:422, 2001.

79. Bakhit, C., Morgan, M.E., Peat, M.A., Gibb, J.W. Long-term effects of methamphetamine on the synthesis and metabolism of 5-hydroxytryptamine in various regions of the rat brain. *Neuropharmacology.* 20:1135, 1981.

80. Morgan, M.E., Gibb, J.W. Short-term and long-term effects of methamphetamine on biogenic amine metabolism in extra-striatal dopaminergic nuclei. *Neuropharmacology.* 19:989, 1980.

81. Haughey, H.M., Fleckenstein, A.E., Hanson, G.R. Differential regional effects of methamphetamine on the activities of tryptophan and tyrosine hydroxylase. *J. Neurochem.* 72:661, 1999.

82. Hotchkiss, A.J., Morgan, M.E., Gibb, J.W. The long-term effects of multiple doses of methamphetamine on neostriatal tryptophan hydroxylase, tyrosine hydroxylase, choline acetyltransferase and glutamate decarboxylase activities. *Life Sci.* 25:1373, 1979.

83. Hanson, G.R., Rau, K.S., Fleckenstein, A.E. The methamphetamine experience: a NIDA partnership. *Neuropharmacology.* 47:92, 2004.

84. Kokoshka, J.M., Metzger, R.R., Wilkins, D.G. et al. Methamphetamine treatment rapidly inhibits serotonin, but not glutamate, transporters in rat brain. *Brain Res.* 799:78, 1998.

85. Fleckenstein, A.E., Haughey, H.M., Metzger, R.R. et al. Differential effects of psychostimulants and related agents on dopaminergic and serotonergic transporter function. *Eur. J. Pharmacol.* 382:45, 1999.

86. Kovachich, G.B., Aronson, C.E., Brunswick, D.J. Effects of high-dose methamphetamine administration on serotonin uptake sites in rat brain measured using [3H]cyanoimipramine autoradiography. *Brain Res.* 505:123, 1989.

87. Wrona, M.Z., Dryhurst, G. Oxidation of serotonin by superoxide radical: implications to neurodegenerative brain disorders. *Chem. Res. Toxicol.* 11:639, 1998.

88. Haughey, H.M., Fleckenstein, A.E., Metzger, R.R., Hanson, G.R. The effects of methamphetamine on serotonin transporter activity: role of dopamine and hyperthermia. *J. Neurochem.* 75:1608, 2000.

89. Schmidt, C.J., Gibb, J.W. Role of the serotonin uptake carrier in the neurochemical response to methamphetamine: effects of citalopram and chlorimipramine. *Neurochem. Res.* 10:637, 1985.

90. Kuczenski, R., Segal, D.S., Cho, A.K., Melega, W. Hippocampus norepinephrine, caudate dopamine and serotonin, and behavioral responses to the stereoisomers of amphetamine and methamphetamine. *J. Neurosci.* 15:1308, 1995.

91. Fornai, F., Alessandri, M.G., Torracca, M.T. et al. Noradrenergic modulation of methamphetamine-induced striatal dopamine depletion. *Ann. N.Y. Acad. Sci.* 844:166, 1998.

92. Bakhit, C., Morgan, M.E., Gibb, J.W. Propranolol differentially blocks the methamphetamine-induced depression of tryptophan hydroxylase in various rat brain regions. *Neurosci. Lett.* 99, 1981.

93. Haughey, H.M., Brown, J.M., Wilkins, D.G., Hanson, G.R., Fleckenstein, A.E. Differential effects of methamphetamine on Na(+)/Cl(−)-dependent transporters. *Brain Res.* 863:59, 2000.

94. Preseton, K.L., Wagner, G.C., Schuster, C.R., Seiden, L.S. Long-term effects of repeated methylamphetamine administration on monoamine neurons in the rhesus monkey brain. *Brain Res.* 338:243, 1985.

95. Kitanaka, N., Kitanaka, J., Takemura, M. Behavioral sensitization and alteration in monoamine metabolism in mice after single versus repeated methamphetamine administration. *Eur. J. Pharmacol.* 474:63, 2003.

96. Rothman, R.B., Baumann, M.H., Dersch, C.M. et al. Amphetamine-type central nervous system stimulants release norepinephrine more potently than they release dopamine and serotonin. *Synapse.* 39:32, 2001.

97. Zhang, X.Y., Kosten, T.A. Prazosin, an alpha-1 adrenergic antagonist, reduces cocaine-induced reinstatement of drug-seeking. *Biol. Psychiatry.* 57:1202, 2005.

98. Yui, K., Goto, K., Ikemoto, S. The role of noradrenergic and dopaminergic hyperactivity in the development of spontaneous recurrence of methamphetamine psychosis and susceptibility to episode recurrence. *Ann. N.Y. Acad. Sci.* 1025:296, 2004.

99. Wise, R.A. Dopamine, learning and motivation. *Nat. Rev. Neurosci.* 5:483, 2004.

100. Robbins, T.W., Everitt, B.J. Limbic-striatal memory systems and drug addiction. *Neurobiol. Learn. Mem.* 78:625, 2002.

101. Jones, S., Bonci, A. Synaptic plasticity and drug addiction. *Curr. Opin. Pharmacol.* 5:20, 2005.

102. Zetterstrom, T., Sharp, T., Collin, A.K., Ungerstedt, U. *In vivo* measurement of extracellular dopamine and DOPAC in rat striatum after various dopamine-releasing drugs; implications for the origin of extracellular DOPAC. *Eur. J. Pharmacol.* 148:327, 1988.

103. Shoblock, J.R., Sullivan, E.B., Maisonneuve, I.M., Glick, S.D. Neurochemical and behavioral differences between d-methamphetamine and d-amphetamine in rats. *Psychopharmacology.* 165:359, 2003.

104. Ujike, H., Onoue, T., Akiyama, K., Hamamura, T., Otsuki, S. Effects of selective D-1 and D-2 dopamine antagonists on development of methamphetamine-induced behavioral sensitization. *Psychopharmacology.* 98:89, 1989.

104a. Witkin, J.M., Savtchenko, N., Mashkovsky, M., Beekman, M., Munzar, P., Gasior, M., Goldberg, S.T., Ungard, J.T., Kim, J., Shippenberg, T., Chefer, V. Behavioral, toxic, and neurochemical effects of sydnocarb, a novel psychomotor stimulant: comparisons with methamphetamine. *J. Pharmacol. Exp. Ther.* 288:1298, 1999.

105. Post, R.M. Intermittent versus continuous stimulation: effect of time interval on the development of sensitization. *Life Sci.* 26:1275, 1980.

106. Davidson, C., Lee, T.H., Ellinwood, E.H. Acute and chronic continuous methamphetamine have different long-term behavioral and neurochemical consequences. *Neurochem. Int.* 46:189, 2005.

107. Yokel, R.A., Pickens, R. Self-administration of optical isomers of amphetamine and methylamphetamine by rats. *J. Pharmacol. Exp. Ther.* 187:27, 1973.

108. Balster, R.L., Schuster, C.R. A comparison of *d*-amphetamine, *l*-amphetamine, and methamphetamine self-administration in rhesus monkeys. *Pharmacol. Biochem. Behav.* 1:67, 1973.

109. Balster, R.L., Kilbey, M.M., Ellinwood, E.H.J. Methamphetamine self-administration in the cat. *Psychopharmacologia.* 46:229, 1976.

110. Woolverton, W.L., Cervo, L., Johanson, C.E. Effects of repeated methamphetamine administration on methamphetamine self-administration in rhesus monkeys. *Pharmacol. Biochem. Behav.* 21:737, 1984.

111. Stefanski, R., Ladenheim, B., Lee, S.H., Cadet, J.L., Goldberg, S.R. Neuroadaptations in the dopaminergic system after active self-administration but not after passive administration of methamphetamine. *Eur. J. Pharmacol.* 371:123, 1999.

112. Stefanski, R., Lee, S.H., Yasar, S., Cadet, J.L., Goldberg, S.R. Lack of persistent changes in the dopaminergic system of rats withdrawn from methamphetamine self-administration. *Eur. J. Pharmacol.* 439:59, 2002.

113. Ranaldi, R., Wise, R.A. Intravenous self-administration of methamphetamine-heroin (speedball) combinations under a progressive-ratio schedule of reinforcement in rats. *Neuroreport.* 11:2621, 2000.

114. Wong, A.H.C., VanTol, H.H.M. The dopamine D_4 receptors and mechanisms of antipsychotic atypicality. *Prog. Neuropsychopharmacol. Biol. Psychiatry.* 27:1091, 2003.

115. Okuyama, S., Kawashima, N., Chaki, S. et al. A selective dopamine D_4 receptor antagonist, NRA0160: a preclinical neuropharmacological profile. *Life Sci.* 65:2109, 1999.

116. Rothman, R.B., Partilla, J.S., Baumann, M.H. et al. Neurochemical neutralization of methamphetamine with high-affinity nonselective inhibitors of biogenic amine transporters: a pharmacological strategy for treating stimulant abuse. *Synapse.* 35:222, 2000.

117. Schenk, S. Effects of GBR 12909, WIN 35,428 and indatraline on cocaine self-administration and cocaine seeking in rats. *Psychopharmacology.* 160:263, 2002.

118. Ranaldi, R., Anderson, K.G., Carroll, F.I., Woolverton, W.L. Reinforcing and discriminative stimulus effects of RTI 111, a 3-phenyltropane analog, in rhesus monkeys: interaction with methamphetamine. *Psychopharmacology.* 53:103, 2000.

119. Carroll, K.M., Fenton, L.R., Ball, S.A. et al. Efficacy of disulfiram and cognitive behavior therapy in cocaine-dependent outpatients: a randomized placebo-controlled trial. *Arch. Gen. Psychiatry.* 61:264, 2004.

120. Zaczek, R., Culp, S., DeSouza, E.B. Interactions of [3H]amphetamine with rat brain synaptosomes. II. Active transport. *J. Pharmacol. Exp. Ther.* 257:830, 1991.

121. Holtzman, S.G. Differential interaction of GBR 12909, a dopamine uptake inhibitor, with cocaine and methamphetamine in rats discriminating cocaine. *Psychopharmacology.* 155:180, 2001.

122. Rocha, B.A., Scearce-Levie, K., Lucas, J.J. et al. Increased vulnerability to cocaine in mice lacking the serotonin-1B receptor. *Nature.* 393:175, 1998.

123. Leccese, A.P., Lyness, W.H. The effects of putative 5-hydroxytryptamine receptor active agents on D-amphetamine self-administration in controls and rats with 5,7-dihydroxytryptamine median forebrain bundle lesions. *Brain Res.* 303:153, 1984.

124. Parsons, L.H., Justice, J.B. Perfusate serotonin increases extracellular dopamine in the nucleus accumbens as measured by *in vivo* microdialysis. *Brain Res.* 606:195, 1993.

125. Yeghiayan, S.K., Kelley, A.E., Kula, N.S., Campbell, A., Baldessarini, R.J. Role of dopamine in behavioral effects of serotonin microinjected into rat striatum. *Pharmacol. Biochem. Behav.* 56:251, 1997.

126. Berger, U.V., Gu, X.F., Azmitia, E.C. The substituted amphetamines 3,4-methylenedioxymethamphet-amine, methamphetamine, *p*-chloroamphetamine and fenfluramine induce 5-hydroxytryptamine release via a common mechanism blocked by fluoxetine and cocaine. *Eur. J. Pharmacol.* 215:153, 1992.

127. Munzar, P., Laufert, M.D., Kutkat, S.W., Novakova, J., Goldberg, S.R. Effects of various serotonin agonists, antagonists, and uptake inhibitors on the discriminative stimulus effects of methamphetamine in rats. *J. Pharmacol. Exp. Ther.* 291:239, 1999.

128. Ginawi, O.T., Al-Majed, A.A., Al-Suwailem, A.K., El-Hadiyah, T.M. Involvement of some 5-HT recep-tors in methamphetamine-induced locomotor activity in mice. *J. Physiol. Pharmacol.* 55:357, 2004.

129. Ginawi, O.T., Al-Majed, A.A., Al-Suwailem, A.K. NAN-190, a possible specific antagonist for meth-amphetamine. *Regul. Toxicol. Pharmacol.* 41:122, 2005.

130. Czoty, P.W., Ramanathan, C.R., Mutschler, N.H., Makriyannis, A., Bergman, J. Drug discrimination in methamphetamine-trained monkeys: effects of monoamine transporter inhibitors. *J. Pharmacol. Exp. Ther.* 311:720, 2004.

131. Rockhold, R.W. Glutamatergic involvement in psychomotor stimulant action. *Prog. Drug Res.* 50:155, 1998.

132. Carlezon, W.A.J., Wise, R.A. Rewarding actions of phencyclidine and related drugs in nucleus accumbens shell and frontal cortex. *J. Neurosci.* 16:3112, 1996.

133. Carlezon, W.A.J., Boundy, V.A., Haile, C.N. et al. Sensitization to morphine induced by viral-mediated gene transfer. *Science.* 277:812, 1997.

134. Feenstra, M.G., Botterblom, M.H., van Uum, J.F. Behavioral arousal and increased dopamine efflux after blockade of NMDA-receptors in the prefrontal cortex are dependent on activation of glutamater-gic neurotransmission. *Neuropharmacology.* 42:752, 2002.

135. Chiamulera, C., Epping-Jordan, M.P., Zocchi, A. et al. Reinforcing and locomotor stimulant effects of cocaine are absent in mGluR5 null mutant mice. *Nat. Neurosci.* 4:873, 2001.

136. Tessari, M., Pilla, M., Andreoli, M., Hutcheson, D.M., Heidbreder, C.A. Antagonism at metabotropic glutamate 5 receptors inhibits nicotine- and cocaine-taking behaviours and prevents nicotine-triggered relapse to nicotine-seeking. *Eur. J. Pharmacol.* 19:121, 2004.

137. Larson, J., Quach, C.N., LeDuc, B.Q. et al. Effects of an AMPA receptor modulator on methamphet-amine-induced hyperactivity. *Brain Res.* 738:353, 1996.

138. Witkin, J.M. Blockade of the locomotor stimulant effects of cocaine and methamphetamine by glutamate antagonists. *Life Sci.* 53:PL405, 1993.

139. Nakagawa, T., Fujio, M., Ozawa, T., Minami, M., Satoh, M. Effect of MS-153, a glutamate transporter activator, on the conditioned rewarding effects of morphine, methamphetamine and cocaine in mice. *Behav. Brain Res.* 156:233, 2005.

140. Haile, C.N., GrandPre, T., Kosten, T.A. Chronic unpredictable stress, but not chronic predictable stress, enhances the sensitivity to the behavioral effects of cocaine in rats. *Psychopharmacology.* 154:213, 2001.

141. Carlsson, M.L. On the role of cortical glutamate in obsessive-compulsive disorder and attention-deficit hyperactivity disorder, two phenomenologically antithetical conditions. *Acta Psychiatr. Scand.* 102:401, 2000.

142. Compton, W.M., Cottler, L.B., BenAbdallah, A. et al. Substance dependence and other psychiatric disorders among drug dependent subjects: race and gender correlates. *Am. J. Addict.* 9:113, 2000.

143. Guitart, X., Codony, X., Monroy, X. Sigma receptors: biology and therapeutic potential. *Psychophar-macology.* 174:301, 2004.

144. Hayashi, T., Su, T.P. Sigma-1 receptor ligands: potential in the treatment of neuropsychiatric disorders. *CNS Drugs.* 18:269, 2004.

145. Matsumoto, R.R., Liu, Y., Lerner, M., Howard, E.W., Brackett, D.J. Sigma receptors: potential medications development target for anti-cocaine agents. *Eur. J. Pharmacol.* 469:1, 2003.

146. Sharkey, J., Glen, K.A., Wolfe, S., Kuhar, M.J. Cocaine binding at sigma receptors. *Eur. J. Pharmacol.* 49:171, 1988.

147. Maurice, T., Martin-Fardon, R., Romieu, P., Matsumoto, R.R. Sigma(1) (sigma(1)) receptor antagonists represent a new strategy against cocaine addiction and toxicity. *Neurosci. Biobehav. Rev.* 26:499, 2002.

148. Nguyen, E.C., McCracken, K.A., Liu, Y., Pouw, B., Matsumoto, R.R. Involvement of sigma (sigma) receptors in the acute actions of methamphetamine: receptor binding and behavioral studies. *Neuropharmacology.* 3:00, 2005.

149. Ujike, H., Okumuma, K., Zushi, Y., Akiyama, K., Otsuki, S. Persistent supersensitivity of s receptors develops during repeated methamphetamine treatment. *Eur. J. Pharmacol.* 211:323., 1992.

150. Itzhak, Y. Repeated methamphetamine-treatment alters brain receptors. *Eur. J. Pharmacol.* 230:243, 1993.

151. Stefanski, R., Justinova, Z., Hayashi, T. et al. Sigma1 receptor upregulation after chronic methamphetamine self-administration in rats: a study with yoked controls. *Psychopharmacology.* 175:68, 2004.

152. Takahashi, S., Miwa, T., Horikomi, K. Involvement of sigma-1 receptors in methamphetamine-induced behavioral sensitization in rats. *Neurosci. Lett.*289:21, 2000.

153. Ujike, H., Kanzaki, A., Okumuma, K., Akiyama, K., Otsuki, S. Sigma antagonist BMY 14802 prevents methamphetamine-induced sensitization. *Life Sci.* 50:PL129, 1992.

154. Hayashi, T., Su, T.-P. Regulating ankyrin dynamics: roles of sigma-1 receptors. *Proc. Natl. Acad. Sci. U.S.A.* 98:491, 2001.

155. Hayashi, T., Su, T.-P. Sigma-1 receptors (sigma-1 binding sites) form raft-like microdomains and target lipid droplets on the endoplasmic reticulum: roles in endoplasmic reticulum lipid compartmentalization and export. *J. Pharmacol. Exp. Ther.* 306:718, 2003.

156. Robinson, T.E., Kolb, B. Structural plasticity associated with exposure to drugs of abuse. *Neuropharmacology.* 47:33, 2004.

157. Maisonneuve, I.M., Glick, S.D. Anti-addictive actions of an iboga alkaloid congener: a novel mechanism for a novel treatment. *Pharmacol. Biochem. Behav.* 75:607, 2003.

158. Szumlinski, K.K., Herrick-Davis, K., Teitler, M., Maisonneuve, I.M., Glick, S.D. Interactions between iboga agents and methamphetamine sensitization: studies of locomotion and stereotypy in rats. *Psychopharmacology.* 151:234, 2000.

159. Glick, S.D., Maisonneuve, I.M., Dickinson, H.A. 18-MC reduces methamphetamine and nicotine self-administration in rats. *Neuroreport.* 11:2013, 2000.

160. Haile, C.N., During, M.J., Jatlow, P.I., Kosten, T.R., Kosten, T.A. Disulfiram facilitates the development and expression of locomotor sensitization to cocaine in rats. *Biol. Psychiatry.* 54:915, 2003.

161. Glick, S.D., Maisonneuve, I.M., Kitchen, B.A., Fleck, M.W. Antagonism of alpha 3 beta 4 nicotinic receptors as a strategy to reduce opioid and stimulant self-administration. *Eur. J. Pharmacol.* 438:99, 2002.

162. Jun, J.H., Schindler. C.W. Dextromethorphan alters methamphetamine self-administration in the rat. *Pharmacol. Biochem. Behav.* 67:405, 2000.

163. Miller, D.K., Crooks, P.A., Teng, L. et al. Lobeline inhibits the neurochemical and behavioral effects of amphetamine. *J. Pharmacol. Exp. Ther.* 296:1023, 2001.

164. Harrod, S.B., Dwoskin, L.P., Crooks, P.A., Klebaur, J.E., Bardo, M.T. Lobeline attenuates *d*-methamphetamine self-administration in rats. *J. Pharmacol. Exp. Ther.* 298:172, 2001.

165. Dwoskin, L.P., Crooks, P.A. A novel mechanism of action and potential use for lobeline as a treatment for psychostimulant abuse. *Biochem. Pharmacol.* 63:89, 2002.

166. Lendvai, B., Sershen, H., Lajtha, A. et al. Differential mechanisms involved in the effect of nicotinic agonists DMPP and lobeline to release [3H]5-HT from rat hippocampal slices. *Neuropharmacology.* 35:1769, 1996.

167. Miller, D.K., Crooks, P.A., Zhang, G. et al. Lobeline analogs with enhanced affinity and selectivity for plasmalemma and vesicular monoamine transporters. *J. Pharmacol. Exp. Ther.* 310:1035, 2004.

168. Ranaldi, R., Poeggel, K. Baclofen decreases methamphetamine self-administration in rats. *Neuroreport.* 13:1107, 2002.

169. Vinklerova, J., Novakova, J., Sulcova, A. Inhibition of methamphetamine self-administration in rats by cannabinoid receptor antagonist AM 251. *J. Psychopharmacol.* 16:139, 2002.

170. Anggadiredja, K., Nakamichi, M., Hiranita, T. et al. Endocannabinoid system modulates relapse to methamphetamine seeking: possible mediation by the arachidonic acid cascade. *Neuropsychopharmacology.* 29:1470, 2004.

171. Munzar, P., Tanda, G., Justinova, Z., Goldberg, S.R. Histamine h3 receptor antagonists potentiate methamphetamine self-administration and methamphetamine-induced accumbal dopamine release. *Neuropsychopharmacology.* 29:705, 2004.

172. McMillan, D.E., Hardwick, W.C., Li, M. et al. Effects of murine-derived anti-methamphetamine monoclonal antibodies on (+)-methamphetamine self-administration in the rat. *J. Pharmacol. Exp. Ther.* 309:1248, 2004.

173. Bailey, C.P., Connor, M. Opioids: cellular mechanisms of tolerance and physical dependence. *Curr. Opin. Pharmacol.* 5:60, 2005.

174. Pandey, S.C. The gene transcription factor cyclic AMP-responsive element binding protein: role in positive and negative affective states of alcohol addiction. *Pharmacol. Ther.* 104:47, 2004.

175. Nestler, E.J. Molecular mechanisms of drug addiction. *Neuropharmacology.* 47:24, 2004.

176. Robinson, T.E., Kolb, B. Persistent structural modifications in nucleus accumbens and prefrontal cortex neurons produced by previous experience with amphetamine. *J. Neurosci.* 17:8491, 1997.

177. Saal, D., Dong, Y., Bonci, A., Malenka, R.C. Drugs of abuse and stress trigger a common synaptic adaptation in dopamine neurons. *Neuron.* 37:577, 2003.

178. Nestler, E.J. Historical review: Molecular and cellular mechanisms of opiate and cocaine addiction. *Trends Pharmacol. Sci.* 25:210, 2004.

179. Nestler, E.J. Molecular neurobiology of addiction. *Am. J. Addict.* 10:201, 2001.

180. Self, D.W., Nestler, E.J. Molecular mechanisms of drug reinforcement and addiction. *Annu. Rev. Neurosci.* 18:463, 1995.

181. Haile, C.N., Hiroi, N., Nestler, E.J., Kosten, T.A. Differential behavioral responses to cocaine are associated with dynamics of mesolimbic dopamine proteins in Lewis and Fischer 344 rats. *Synapse.* 41:179, 2001.

182. Beitner-Johnson, D., Nestler, E.J. Morphine and cocaine exert common chronic actions on tyrosine hydroxylase in dopaminergic brain reward regions. *J. Neurochem.* 57:344, 1991.

183. Sorg, B.A., Chen, S.Y., Kalivas, P.W. Time course of tyrosine hydroxylase expression after behavioral sensitization to cocaine. *J. Pharmacol. Exp. Ther.* 266:424, 1993.

184. Henry, D.J., White, F.J. Repeated cocaine administration causes persistent enhancement of D1 dopamine receptor sensitivity within the rat nucleus accumbens. *J. Pharmacol. Exp. Ther.* 258:882, 1991.

185. Terwilliger, R.Z., Beitner-Johnson, D., Sevarino, K.A., Crain, S.M., Nestler, E.J. A general role for adaptations in G-proteins and the cyclic AMP system in mediating the chronic actions of morphine and cocaine on neuronal function. *Brain Res.* 548:100, 1991.

186. Striplin, C.D., Kalivas, P.W. Robustness of G protein changes in cocaine sensitization shown with immunoblotting. *Synapse.* 14:10, 1993.

187. Chen, J., Nye, H.E., Kelz, M.B. et al. Regulation of delta FosB and FosB-like proteins by electroconvulsive seizure and cocaine treatments. *Mol. Pharmacol.* 48:880, 1995.

188. Hiroi, N., Brown, J.R., Haile, C.N. et al. FosB mutant mice: loss of chronic cocaine induction of Fos-related proteins and heightened sensitivity to cocaine's psychomotor and rewarding effects. *Proc. Natl. Acad. Sci. U.S.A.* 94:10397, 1997.

189. Kelz, M.B., Chen, J., Carlezon, W.A.J. et al. Expression of the transcription factor deltaFosB in the brain controls sensitivity to cocaine. *Nature.* 401:272, 1999.

190. Tolliver, B.K., Ho, L.B., Reid, M.S., Berger, S.P. Evidence for involvement of ventral tegmental area cyclic AMP systems in behavioral sensitization to psychostimulants. *J. Pharmacol. Exp. Ther.* 278:411, 1996.

191. Self, D.W., Genova, L.M., Hope, B.T. et al. Involvement of cAMP-dependent protein kinase in the nucleus accumbens in cocaine self-administration and relapse of cocaine-seeking behavior. *J. Neurosci.* 18:1848, 1998.

192. Shaywitz, A.J., Greenberg, M.E. CREB: a stimulus-induced transcription factor activated by a diverse array of extracellular signals. *Annu. Rev. Biochem.* 68:821, 1999.

193. Mayr, B., Montminy, M. Transcriptional regulation by the phosphorylation-dependent factor CREB. *Nat. Rev. Mol. Cell. Biol.* 2:599, 2001.

194. Turgeon, S.M., Pollack, A.E., Fink, J.S. Enhanced CREB phosphorylation and changes in c-Fos and FRA expression in striatum accompany amphetamine sensitization. *Brain Res.* 749:120, 1997.

195. Carlezon, W.A., Duman, R.S., Nestler E.J. The many faces of CREB. *Trends Neurosci.* 28:436, 2005.

196. Kelley, A.E. Memory and addiction: shared neural circuitry and molecular mechanisms. *Neuron.* 44:161, 2004.

197. Miserendino, M.J., Nestler, E.J. Behavioral sensitization to cocaine: modulation by the cyclic AMP system in the nucleus accumbens. *Brain Res.* 674:299, 1995.

198. Wachtel, H. Characteristic behavioural alterations in rats induced by rolipram and other selective adenosine cyclic 3´, 5´-monophosphate phosphodiesterase inhibitors. *Psychopharmacology.* 77:309, 1982.

199. Iyo, M., Bi, Y., Hashimoto, K., Inada, T., Fukui, S. Prevention of methamphetamine-induced behavioral sensitization in rats by a cyclic AMP phosphodiesterase inhibitor, rolipram. *Eur. J. Pharmacol.* 312:163, 1996.

199a. Mori, M., Baba, J., Ichimaru, Y., Suzuki, T. Effects of rolipram, a selective inhibitor of phosphodiesterase 4, on hyperlocomotion induced by several abused drugs in mice. *Jpn. J. Pharmacol.* 83:113, 2000.

200. Greengard, P., Allen, P.B., Nairn, A.C. Beyond the dopamine receptor: the DARPP-32/protein phosphatase-1 cascade. *Neuron.* 23:435, 1999.

201. Walaas, S.I., Aswad, D.W., Greengard, P. A dopamine- and cyclic AMP-regulated phosphoprotein enriched in dopamine-innervated brain regions. *Nature.* 301:69, 1983.

202. Ouimet, C.C., daCruz, E., Silva, E.F., Greengard, P. The alpha and gamma 1 isoforms of protein phosphatase 1 are highly and specifically concentrated in dendritic spines. *Proc. Natl. Acad. Sci. U.S.A.* 92:3396, 1995.

203. Yan, Z., Hsieh-Wilson, L., Feng, J. et al. Protein phosphatase 1 modulation of neostriatal AMPA channels: regulation by DARPP-32 and spinophilin. *Nat. Neurosci.* 2:13, 1999.

204. Hiroi, N., Fienberg, A.A., Haile, C.N. et al. Neuronal and behavioural abnormalities in striatal function in DARPP-32-mutant mice. *Eur. J. Neurosci.* 11:1114, 1999.

205. Fienberg, A.A., Hiroi, N., Mermelstein, P.G. et al. DARPP-32: regulator of the efficacy of dopaminergic neurotransmission. *Science.* 281:838, 1998.

206. Snyder, G.L., Allen, P.B., Fienberg, A.A. et al. Regulation of phosphorylation of the GluR1 AMPA receptor in the neostriatum by dopamine and psychostimulants *in vivo. J. Neurosci.* 20:4480, 2000.

207. Lin, X.H., Hashimoto, T., Kitamura, N. et al. Decreased calcineurin and increased phosphothreonine-DARPP-32 in the striatum of rats behaviorally sensitized to methamphetamine. *Synapse.* 44:181, 2002.

208. Chen, P.C., Chen, J.C. Enhanced Cdk5 activity and p35 translocation in the ventral striatum of acute and chronic methamphetamine-treated rats. *Neuropsychopharmacology.* 30:538, 2005.

209. Bibb, J.A., Snyder, G.L., Nishi, A. et al. Phosphorylation of DARPP-32 by Cdk5 modulates dopamine signalling in neurons. *Nature.* 402:669, 1999.

210. McClung, C.A., Ulery, P.G., Perrotti, L.I. et al. DeltaFosB: a molecular switch for long-term adaptation in the brain. *Brain Res. Mol. Brain Res.* 132:146, 2004.

211. Ouimet, C.C., Hemmings, H.C.J., Greengard, P. ARPP-21, a cyclic AMP-regulated phosphoprotein enriched in dopamine-innervated brain regions. II. Immunocytochemical localization in rat brain. *J. Neurosci.* 9:865, 1989.

212. Caporaso, G.L., Bibb, J.A., Snyder, G.L. et al. Drugs of abuse modulate the phosphorylation of ARPP-21, a cyclic AMP-regulated phosphoprotein enriched in the basal ganglia. *Neuropharmacology.* 39:1637, 2000.

213. Akiyama, K., Suemaru, J. Effect of acute and chronic administration of methamphetamine on calcium-calmodulin dependent protein kinase II activity in the rat brain. *Ann. N.Y. Acad. Sci.* 914:263, 2000.

214. Suemaru, J., Akiyama, K., Tanabe, Y., Kuroda, S. Methamphetamine decreases calcium-calmodulin dependent protein kinase II activity in discrete rat brain regions. *Synapse.* 36:155, 2000.

215. Cheung, W.Y. Calmodulin plays a pivotal role in cellular regulation. *Science.* 207:19, 1980.

216. Ishihara, T., Akiyama, K., Kashihara, K. et al. Activator protein-1 binding activities in discrete regions of rat brain after acute and chronic administration of methamphetamine. *J. Neurochem.* 67:708, 1996.

217. Bronstein, D.M., Pennypacker, K.R., Lee, H., Hong, J.S. Methamphetamine-induced changes in AP-1 binding and dynorphin in the striatum: correlated, not causally related events? *Biol. Signals.* 317, 1996.

218. Asanuma, M., Hayashi, T., Ordonex, S.V., Ogawa, N., Cadet, J.L. Direct interactions of methamphetamine with the nucleus. *Brain Res. Mol. Brain Res.* 80:237, 2000.

219. Lee, Y.W., Son, K.W., Flora, G., et al. Methamphetamine activates DNA binding of specific redox-responsive transcription factors in mouse brain. *J. Neurosci. Res.* 70:82, 2002.

220. Muratake, T., Toyooka, K., Hayashi, S. et al. Immunohistochemical changes of the transcription regulatory factors in rat striatum after methamphetamine administration. *Ann. N.Y. Acad. Sci.* 844:21, 1998.

221. Tzschentke, T.M. Measuring reward with the conditioned place preference paradigm: a comprehensive review of drug effects, recent progress and new issues. *Prog. Neurobiol.* 56:613, 1998.

221a. Carlezon, W.A., Thome, J., Olson, V.G., Lane-Ladd, S.B., Brodkin, E.S., Hiroi, N., Duman, R.S., Neve, R.L., Nestler, E.J. Regulation of cocaine reward by CREB. *Science* 282:2272, 1998.

222. Thomas, G.M., Huganir, R.L. MAPK cascade signaling and synaptic plasticity. *Nat. Rev. Neurosci.* 5:173, 2004.

223. Sweatt, J.D. Mitogen-activated protein kinases in synaptic plasticity and memory. *Curr. Opin. Neurobiol.* 14:311, 2004.

224. Wolf, M.E., Sun, X., Mangiavacchi, S., Chao, S.Z. Psychomotor stimulants and neuronal plasticity. *Neuropharmacology.* 47:61, 2004.

225. Hashimoto, T., Kajii, Y., Nishikawa, T. Psychotomimetic-induction of tissue plasminogen activator mRNA in corticostriatal neurons in rat brain. *Eur. J. Neurosci.* 10:3387, 1998.

226. Kodama, M., Akiyama, K., Ujike, H. et al. A robust increase in expression of arc gene, an effector immediate early gene, in the rat brain after acute and chronic methamphetamine administration. *Brain Res.* 796:273, 1998.

227. Takaki, M., Ujike, H., Kodama, M. et al. Increased expression of synaptophysin and stathmin mRNAs after methamphetamine administration in rat brain. *Neuroreport.* 12:1055, 2001.

228. Takaki, M., Ujike, H., Kodama, M. et al. Two kinds of mitogen-activated protein kinase phosphatases, MKP-1 and MKP-3, are differentially activated by acute and chronic methamphetamine treatment in the rat brain. *J. Neurochem.* 79:679, 2001.

229. Ujike, H., Takaki, M., Kodama, M., Kuroda, S. Gene expression related to synaptogenesis, neuritogenesis, and MAP kinase in behavioral sensitization to psychostimulants. *Ann. N.Y. Acad. Sci.* 965:55, 2002.

230. Berhow, M.T., Hiroi, N., Nestler, E.J. Regulation of ERK (extracellular signal regulated kinase), part of the neurotrophin signal transduction cascade, in the rat mesolimbic dopamine system by chronic exposure to morphine or cocaine. *J. Neurosci.* 16:4707, 1996.

231. Pierce, R.C., Pierce-Bancroft, A.F., Prasad, B.M. Neurotrophin-3 contributes to the initiation of behavioral sensitization to cocaine by activating the Ras/Mitogen-activated protein kinase signal transduction cascade. *J. Neurosci.* 19:8685, 1999.

232. Valjent, E., Corvol, J.C., Pages, C. et al. Involvement of the extracellular signal-regulated kinase cascade for cocaine-rewarding properties. *J. Neurosci.* 20:8701, 2000.

232a. Mizoguchi, H., Yamada, K., Mizuno, M., Nitta, A., Noda, Y., Nabeshima, T. Regulations of methamphetamine reward by extracellular signal-regulated kinase 1/2/ets-like gene-1 signaling pathway via the activation of dopamine receptors. *Mol. Pharmacol.* 65:1293, 2004.

233. McLeman, E.R., Warsh, J.J., Ang, L. et al. The human nucleus accumbens is highly susceptible to G protein down-regulation by methamphetamine and heroin. *J. Neurochem.* 74:2120, 2000.

234. Volkow, N.D., Chang, L., Wang, G.J. et al. Association of dopamine transporter reduction with psychomotor impairment in methamphetamine abusers. *Am. J. Psychiatry.* 158:377, 2001.

235. Worsley, J.N., Moszczynska, A., Falardeau, P. et al. Dopamine D1 receptor protein is elevated in nucleus accumbens of human, chronic methamphetamine users. *Mol. Psychiatry.* 5:664, 2000.

236. Tong, J., Ross, B.M., Schmunk, G.A. et al. Decreased striatal dopamine D1 receptor-stimulated adenylyl cyclase activity in human methamphetamine users. *Am. J. Psychiatry.* 160:896, 2003.

237. Frost, D.O., Cadet, J.-L. Effects of methamphetamine-induced neurotoxicity on the development of neural circuitry: a hypothesis. *Brain Res. Rev.* 34:103, 2000.

238. Cho, A.K., Melega, W.P. Patterns of methamphetamine abuse and their consequences. *J. Addict. Dis.* 21:21, 2002.

239. Cadet, J.-L., Jayanthi, S., Deng, X. Speed kills: cellular and molecular bases of methamphetamine-induced nerve terminal degeneration and neuronal apoptosis. *FASEB J.* 17:1775, 2003.

240. Kita, T., Wagner, G.C., Nakashima, T. Current research on methamphetamine-induced neurotoxicity: animal models of monoamine disruption. *J. Pharmacol. Sci.* 92:178, 2003.

241. Itzhak, Y., Achat-Mendes, C. Methamphetamine and MDMA (Ecstasy) neurotoxicity: "of mice and men." *IUBMB Life.* 56:249, 2004.

242. Meredith, C.W., Jaffe, C., Ang-Lee, K., Saxon, A.J. Implications of chronic methamphetamine use: a literature review. *Harvard Rev. Psychiatry.* 13:141, 2005.

243. Wagner, G.C., Ricaurte, G.A., Seiden, L.S. et al. Long-lasting depletions of striatal dopamine and loss of dopamine uptake sites following repeated administration of methamphetamine. *Brain Res.* 181:151, 1980.

244. Ricaurte, G.A., Guillery, R.W., Seiden, L.S., Schuster, C.R., Moore, R.Y. Dopamine nerve terminal degeneration produced by high doses of methylamphetamine in the rat brain. *Brain Res.* 235:93, 1982.

245. Ricaurte, G.A., Guillery, R.W., Seiden, L.S., Schuster, C.R. Nerve terminal degeneration after a single injection of D-amphetamine in iprindole-treated rats: relation to selective long-lasting dopamine depletion. *Brain Res.* 291:378, 1984.

246. Eisch, A.J., Marshall, J.F. Methamphetamine neurotoxicity: dissociation of striatal dopamine terminal damage from parietal cortical cell body injury. *Synapse.* 30:433, 1998.

247. Brunswick, D.J., Benmansour, S., Tejani-Butt, S.M., Hauptmann, M. Effects of high-dose methamphetamine on monoamine uptake sites in rat brain measured by quantitative autoradiography. *Synapse.* 11:287, 1992.

248. Villemagne, V., Yuan, J., Wong, D.F. et al. Brain dopamine neurotoxicity in baboons treated with doses of methamphetamine comparable to those recreationally abused by humans: evidence from [11C]WIN-35,428 positron emission tomography studies and direct *in vitro* determinations. *J. Neurosci.* 18:419, 1998.

249. Koda, L.Y., Gibb, J.W. Adrenal and striatal tyrosine hydroxylase activity after methamphetamine. *J. Pharmacol. Exp. Ther.* 185:42, 1973.

250. Trulson, M.E., Cannon, M.S., Faegg, T.S., Raese, J.D. Effects of chronic methamphetamine on the nigral-striatal dopamine system in rat brain: tyrosine hydroxylase immunochemistry and quantitative light microscopic studies. *Brain Res. Bull.* 15:569, 1985.

251. Ricaurte, G.A., Schuster, C.R., Seiden, L.S. Long-term effects of repeated methylamphetamine administration on dopamine and serotonin neurons in the rat brain: a regional study. *Brain Res.* 193:153, 1980.

252. Frey, K., Kilbourn, M., Robinson, T. Reduced striatal vesicular monoamine transporters after neurotoxic but not after behaviorally-sensitizing doses of methamphetamine. *Eur. J. Pharmacol.* 334:273, 1997.

253. Bowyer, J.F., Tank, A.W., Newport, G.D. et al. The influence of environmental temperature on the transient effects of methamphetamine on dopamine levels and dopamine release in rat striatum. *J. Pharmacol. Exp. Ther.* 260:817, 1992.

254. Ali, S.F., Newport, G.D., Holson, R.R., Slikker, W.J., Bowyer, J.F. Low environmental temperatures or pharmacologic agents that produce hypothermia decrease methamphetamine neurotoxicity in mice. *Brain Res.* 58:33, 1994.

255. Harvey, D.C., Lacan, G., Tanious, S.P., Melega, W.P. Recovery from methamphetamine induced long-term nigrostriatal dopaminergic deficits without substantia nigra cell loss. *Brain Res.* 871:259, 2000.

256. Harvey, D.C., Lacan, G., Melegan, W.P. Regional heterogeneity of dopaminergic deficits in vervet monkey striatum and substantia nigra after methamphetamine exposure. *Exp. Brain Res.* 133:349, 2000.

257. Seiden, L.S., Fischman, M.W., Schuster, C.R. Long-term methamphetamine induced changes in brain catecholamines in tolerant rhesus monkeys. *Drug Alcohol Depend.* 1:215, 1976.

258. Melega, W.P., Lacan, G., Harvey, D.C., Huang, S.C., Phelps, M.E. Dizocilpine and reduced body temperature do not prevent methamphetamine-induced neurotoxicity in the vervet monkey: [11C]WIN 35,428-positron emission tomography studies. *Neurosci. Lett.* 258:17, 1998.

259. Woolverton, W.L., Ricaurte, G.A., Forno, L.S., Seiden, L.S. Long-term effects of chronic methamphetamine administration in rhesus monkeys. *Brain Res.* 486:73, 1989.

260. Melega, W.P., Raleigh, M.J., Stout, D.B. et al. Recovery of striatal dopamine function after acute amphetamine- and methamphetamine-induced neurotoxicity in the vervet monkey. *Brain Res.* 766:113, 1997.

261. Cass, W.A., Manning, M.W. Recovery of presynaptic dopaminergic functioning in rats treated with neurotoxic doses of methamphetamine. *J. Neurosci.* 19:7653, 1999.

262. Cass, W.A. Attenuation and recovery of evoked overflow of striatal serotonin in rats treated with neurotoxic doses of methamphetamine. *J. Neurochem.* 74:1079, 2000.

263. Friedman, S.D., Castaneda, E., Hodge, G.K. Long-term monoamine depletion, differential recovery, and subtle behavioral impairment following methamphetamine-induced neurotoxicity. *Pharmacol. Biochem. Behav.* 61:35, 1998.

264. Melega, W.P., Quintana, J., Raleigh, M.J. et al. 6-[18F]Fluoro-L-DOPA-PET studies show partial reversibility of long-term effects of chronic amphetamine in monkeys. *Synapse.* 22:63, 1996.

265. Moszczynska, A., Fitzmaurice, P., Ang, L. et al. Why is parkinsonism not a feature of human methamphetamine users? *Brain.* 127:363, 2003.

266. Wilson, J.M., Kalasinsky, K.S., Levey, A.I. et al. Striatal dopamine nerve terminal markers in human, chronic methamphetamine users. *Nat. Med.* 2:699, 1996.

267. Volkow, N.D., Chang, L., Wang, G.J. et al. Higher cortical and lower subcortical metabolism in detoxified methamphetamine abusers. *Am. J. Psychiatry.* 158:383, 2001.

268. Sonsalla, P.K., Nicklas, W.J., Heikkila, R.E. Role for excitatory amino acids in methamphetamine-induced nigrostriatal dopaminergic toxicity. *Science.* 243:398, 1989.

269. Gibb, J.W., Kogan, F.J. Influence of dopamine synthesis on methamphetamine-induced changes in striatal and adrenal tyrosine hydroxylase activity. *Naunyn Schmiedeberg's Arch. Pharmacol.* 310:185, 1979.

270. Schmidt, C.J., Ritter, J.K., Sonsalla, P.K., Hanson, G.R., Gibb, J.W. Role of dopamine in the neurotoxic effects of methamphetamine. *J. Pharmacol. Exp. Ther.* 233:539, 1985.

271. Johnson, M., Stone, D.M., Hanson, G.R., Gibb, J.W. Role of the dopaminergic nigrostriatal pathway in methamphetamine-induced depression of the neostriatal serotonergic system. *Eur. J. Pharmacol.* 135:231, 1987.

272. Seiden, L.S., Vosmer, G. Formation of 6-hydroxydopamine in caudate nucleus of the rat brain after a single large dose of methylamphetamine. *Pharmacol. Biochem. Behav.* 21:29, 1984.

273. Axt, K.J., Commins, D.L., Vosmer, G., Seiden, L.S. alpha-Methyl-*p*-tyrosine pretreatment partially prevents methamphetamine-induced endogenous neurotoxin formation. *Brain Res.* 515:269, 1990.

274. DeVito, M.J., Wagner, G.C. Methamphetamine-induced neuronal damage: a possible role for free radicals. *Neuropharmacology.* 28:1145, 1989.

275. Cadet, J.L., Sheng, P., Ali, S. et al. Attenuation of methamphetamine-induced neurotoxicity in copper/zinc superoxide dismutase transgenic mice. *J. Neurochem.* 62:380, 1994.

276. Hirata, H., Ladenheim, B., Carlson, E., Epstein, C., Cadet, J.L. Autoradiographic evidence for methamphetamine-induced striatal dopaminergic loss in mouse brain: attenuation in CuZn-superoxide dismutase transgenic mice. *Brain Res.* 714:95, 1996.

277. Maragos, W.F., Jakel, R., Chesnut, D. et al. Methamphetamine toxicity is attenuated in mice that overexpress human manganese superoxide dismutase. *Brain Res.* 878:218, 2000.

278. Itzhak, Y., Gandia, C., Huang, P.L., Ali, S.F. Resistance of neuronal nitric oxide synthase-deficient mice to methamphetamine-induced dopaminergic neurotoxicity. *J. Pharmacol. Exp. Ther.* 284:1040, 1998.

279. Fumagalli, F., Gainetdinov, R.R., Wang, Y.M. et al. Increased methamphetamine neurotoxicity in heterozygous vesicular monoamine transporter 2 knock-out mice. *J. Neurosci.* 19:2424, 1999.

280. Wagner, G.C., Carelli, R.M., Jarvis, M.F. Ascorbic acid reduces the dopamine depletion induced by methamphetamine and the 1-methyl-4-phenyl pyridinium ion. *Neuropharmacology.* 25:559, 1986.

281. Huang, N.K., Wan, F.J., Tseng, C.J., Tung, C.S. Nicotinamide attenuates methamphetamine-induced striatal dopamine depletion in rats. *Neuroreport.* 8:1883, 1997.

282. Ali, S.F., Martin, J.L., Black, M.D., Itzhak, Y. Neuroprotective role of melatonin in methamphetamine- and 1-methyl-4-phenyl-1,2,3,6-tetrahydropyridine-induced dopaminergic neurotoxicity. *Ann. N.Y. Acad. Sci.* 890:119, 1999.

283. Hirata, H., Asanuma, M., Cadet, J.L. Melatonin attenuates methamphetamine-induced toxic effects on dopamine and serotonin terminals in mouse brain. *Synapse.* 30:150, 1998.

284. Imam, S.Z., Newport, G.D., Islam, F., Slikker, W.J., Ali, S.F. Selenium, an antioxidant, protects against methamphetamine-induced dopaminergic neurotoxicity. *Brain Res.* 18:575, 1999.

285. Imam, S.Z., Ali, S.F. Selenium, an antioxidant, attenuates methamphetamine-induced dopaminergic toxicity and peroxynitrite generation. *Brain Res.* 855:186, 2000.

286. Kim, H.C., Jhoo, W.K., Choi, D.Y. et al. Protection of methamphetamine nigrostriatal toxicity by dietary selenium. *Brain Res.* 851:76, 1999.

287. London, E.D., Simon, S.L., Berman, S.M. et al. Mood disturbances and regional cerebral metabolic abnormalities in recently abstinent methamphetamine abusers. *Arch. Gen. Psychiatry.* 61:73, 2004.

288. Iyo, M., Namba, H., Yanagisawa, M. et al. Abnormal cerebral perfusion in chronic methamphetamine abusers: a study using 99MTc-HMPAO and SPECT. *Prog. Neuropsychopharmacol. Biol. Psychiatry.* 21:789, 1997.

289. Alhassoon, O.M., Dupont, R.M., Schweinsburg, B.C., et al. Regional cerebral blood flow in cocaine- versus methamphetamine-dependent patients with a history of alcoholism. *Int. J. Neuropsychopharmacol.* 4:105, 2001.

290. Wang, G.J., Volkow, N.D., Chang, L. et al. Partial recovery of brain metabolism in methamphetamine abusers after protracted abstinence. *Am. J. Psychiatry.* 31:313, 2004.

291. McCann, U.D., Wong, D.F., Yokoi, F. et al. Reduced striatal dopamine transporter density in abstinent methamphetamine and methcathinone users: evidence from positron emission tomography studies with [11C]WIN-35,428. *J. Neurosci.* 18:8417, 1998.

292. Sekine, Y., Iyo, M., Ouchi, Y. et al. Methamphetamine-related psychiatric symptoms and reduced brain dopamine transporters studied with PET. *Am. J. Psychiatry.* 58:1206, 2001.

293. Iyo, M., Sekine, Y., Mori, N. Neuromechanism of developing methamphetamine psychosis: a neuroimaging study. *Ann. N.Y. Acad. Sci.* 1025:288, 2004.

294. Volkow, N.D., Wang, G.J., Fowler, J.S. et al. Decreases in dopamine receptors but not in dopamine transporters in alcoholics. *Alcohol Clin. Exp. Res.* 20:1594, 1996.

295. Volkow, N.D., Fowler, J.S., Wolf, A.P. et al. Effects of chronic cocaine abuse on postsynaptic dopamine receptors. *Am. J. Psychiatry.* 147:740, 1990.

296. Wang, G.J., Volkow, N.D., Fowler, J.S. et al. Dopamine D2 receptor availability in opiate-dependent subjects before and after naloxone-precipitated withdrawal. *Neuropsychopharmacology.* 16:174, 1997.

297. Rawson, R.A., Gonzales, R., Brethen, P. Treatment of methamphetamine use disorders: an update. *J. Subst. Abuse Treat.* 23:145, 2002.

298. Cretzmeyer, M., Sarranzin, M.V., Huber, D.L., Block, R.I., Hall, J.A. Treatment of methamphetamine abuse: research findings and clinical directions. *J. Subst. Abuse Treat.* 24:267, 2003.

6.5 NEUROCHEMICAL ADAPTATIONS AND COCAINE DEPENDENCE

Kelly P. Cosgrove, Ph.D. and Julie K. Staley, Ph.D.

Department of Psychiatry, Yale University School of Medicine, New Haven, Connecticut and the VA Connecticut Healthcare System, West Haven, Connecticut

Cocaine addiction is a disease of the brain that is characterized by compulsive drug-taking behavior that may be a consequence of an altered neurochemical state. Cocaine use by inhalation or injection produces a rapid, intense, euphoric "rush," which leads to repeated use. The repeated use of cocaine causes long-lasting changes in brain receptors and transporters that perpetuate drug use and the resulting dysphoria or depression. Furthermore, regulatory changes in neurochemical targets that have occurred as a compensatory response to "oppose" or "neutralize" the pharmacological effects of the drug persist after the drug has cleared from the brain, and may underlie the craving and dysphoria associated with cocaine withdrawal and relapse. Revolutionary advances in basic neuroscience have catalyzed extraordinary efforts toward the discovery and development of novel central nervous system (CNS) drugs effective for the treatment of cocaine dependence. These advances have included the molecular cloning and characterization of many of the receptors and transporters implicated in the rewarding effects of and dependence on cocaine. Understanding how and which receptors and transporters are altered by chronic cocaine use may identify targets for the development of drugs that will alleviate the symptoms associated with the initiation and perpetuation of drug-taking behavior. Current drug discovery efforts have taken multiple approaches toward the development of cocaine pharmacotherapies.

Many of the novel pharmacological agents currently under development are directed toward a single molecular target related to or regulated by cocaine. Some pharmacotherapies currently under evaluation are directed toward multiple distinct receptor and/or transporter populations known to modulate the activity of the drug reward circuit. Several approaches have been taken to develop medications to treat cocaine dependence. Cocaine "substitute" medications are drugs that act via a similar mechanism as cocaine but with a more limited abuse potential. This strategy seeks to alleviate some of the withdrawal effects and reduce craving and is similar to nicotine replacement therapy for tobacco smoking or methadone maintenance for heroin addiction. Cocaine antagonists block the effects of cocaine or block the binding of cocaine to the dopamine transporter and thus attenuate the reinforcing effects of cocaine and reduce the likelihood of cocaine use. This is similar to naltrexone therapy for heroin addiction in which naltrexone, a mu-opioid receptor antagonist, blocks the binding of heroin or other opiates to the mu-opioid receptor. This strategy may also target other receptor systems that modulate dopaminergic activity to functionally antagonize the effects of cocaine. The cocaine vaccine interferes with the pharmacokinetics of cocaine by blocking or slowing cocaine's uptake into the brain, thus eliminating its reinforcing effects. Thus far, several promising treatments have been developed yet no truly effective medications exist and none is approved specifically for the treatment of cocaine dependence. This chapter reviews recent research studies that have identified neurochemical targets regulated by chronic cocaine use and their implications for the development of pharmacotherapies for cocaine dependence.

6.5.1 Neurochemistry of Cocaine Dependence

Many drugs with abuse liability including cocaine have been shown to enhance dopaminergic neurotransmission in the mesolimbic drug reward circuits. Cocaine, an indirect-acting dopaminergic agonist, binds to recognition sites on the plasma membrane dopamine (DA) transporter and increases dopamine levels by preventing the reuptake of released dopamine.[1-3] Intravenous injection of cocaine has been shown to significantly inhibit dopamine reuptake within 4 s.[4] The reinforcing effects of cocaine are initiated by the interactions of dopamine with pre- and postsynaptic DA receptors. Two classes of DA receptors have been classified including the D_1 receptor family (D_1, D_{1a}, and D_5/D_{1b} receptor subtypes) and the D_2 receptor family (D_2, D_3, and D_4 receptor subtypes).[5] The DA receptor subtypes are distinguished by their distinct anatomical, molecular, pharmacological, and signal transduction properties.[5] When cocaine is present, extracellular dopamine levels are elevated resulting in chronic stimulation of the DA receptors.[3] This persistent interaction of dopamine with its receptors alters the DA receptor signaling, which may, in part, underlie the reinforcing properties of cocaine.[3] Furthermore, postsynaptic DA receptors have been localized to other neurotransmitter-containing pathways including GABAergic, glutamatergic, and cholinergic projections indicating that additional neurochemical pathways may undergo compensatory adaptive changes in response to the persistent activation of DA receptors. The effects of cocaine in brain are widespread in the mesolimbic system including the ventral tegmental area, ventral striatum, and prefrontal cortex.

Recently, considerable evidence has accumulated suggesting that other neurochemical substrates (i.e., glutamatergic, serotonergic, GABAergic, and opioidergic) also play a role in the development of cocaine dependence. The anatomical organization of these neurochemical systems within the drug reward circuit suggests that functional interactions may occur between dopaminergic systems and neighboring neural pathways. Nigrostriatal dopaminergic neurons and corticostriatal glutamatergic neurons colocalize on common GABAergic medium spiny dendrites in the striatum suggesting the potential for interdependency between the two circuits.[6] Glutamate antagonists that act at the NMDA receptor complex block stereotypy and locomotor activation in animal models of cocaine dependence indicating that the glutamatergic pathway may be critical to the expression of these psychomotor stimulant behaviors.[6,7] Serotonergic projections to the ventral tegmental area input onto dopamine cell bodies suggesting that serotonin modulates mesolimbic DA neurotransmission by direct stimulation (i.e., cocaine increases extracellular serotonin by blocking reuptake) or by indirect modulatory feedback mechanisms from DA nerve terminal activation.[8] Mesolimbic DA neurotransmission is modulated in part by tonic activation of the μ- and κ-opioid receptors located in the vicinity of the DA cell bodies and DA nerve terminals, respectively. Activation of μ-opioid receptors in the ventral tegmental area increases dopamine release in the nucleus accumbens, whereas activation of the κ-opioid receptors in the nucleus accumbens inhibits dopamine release.[9–11] Cross-talk between opioids, serotonin, glutamate, GABA, and dopamine may lead to a sequence of neuroadaptive processes that contribute to the behavioral and physiological manifestations associated with cocaine dependence. Additionally, understanding of the neuroadaptive changes involved in cocaine dependence may lead to the development of effective medications for the treatment of the disorder.

6.5.2 DA Transporter and Cocaine Dependence

6.5.2.1 Regulation of the Dopamine Transporter (DAT) by Cocaine

The addictive liability of cocaine and other DA-enhancing psychostimulants may be related to compensatory adaptation of the dopamine transporter (DAT) to chronic elevations of intrasynaptic DA. The DAT is a protein on neuronal membranes that is involved in synaptic transmission by transporting DA from the extracellular space to the neuron.[12] There is a wealth of evidence suggesting that cocaine mediates its powerful reinforcement by binding to recognition sites on the DAT. Interestingly, mice lacking the DAT (DAT-KO) still self-administer cocaine[13] and show cocaine-induced conditioned place preference,[14] indicating that cocaine exerts strong reinforcing effects via alternative neurotransmitter systems. Persistent inhibition of DA reuptake by cocaine has been shown to alter the number of cocaine recognition sites associated with the DAT. Chronic treatment of rats with intermittent doses of cocaine resulted in a two- to fivefold increase in the apparent density of [^{3}H]cocaine and [^{3}H]BTCP binding in the striatum.[15] Significant increases in striatal [^{3}H]WIN 35,428 binding were observed in rats allowed to self-administer cocaine in a chronic unlimited access paradigm,[16] rats treated intermittently and continuously with cocaine,[17] and rabbits treated with intermittent cocaine injections.[18] Chronic cocaine exposure in nonhuman primates resulted in significantly increased DAT binding sites compared to binding in drug-naïve control monkeys in the ventral striatum measured with [^{3}H]WIN 35,248.[19] Consistently, in post-mortem brain from human cocaine users, striatal DAT binding sites were significantly increased compared to controls using [^{3}H]WIN 35,248.[20,21] DAT densities detected using [^{125}I]RTI-55 and [^{3}H]WIN 35,248 were elevated throughout the caudate, putamen, and nucleus accumbens of cocaine-related deaths[22] and fatal cocaine overdose victims (Figure 6.5.1).[22–25] Furthermore, Rosenthal plots of the saturation binding data demonstrated that the increase of [^{3}H]WIN 35,428 binding observed in the cocaine overdose victims was due to an elevation in the apparent density of the high-affinity cocaine recognition site on the DAT.[24] While most studies indicate chronic cocaine results in increased DAT binding sites, some have reported a decrease[26] or no change.[27] Further, it was reported that administration of GBR 12909 (also called vanoxerine) but *not* cocaine resulted in a decrease in DAT density in caudate putamen and nucleus accumbens[28] highlighting that while GBR 12909 is a selective DA reuptake blocker, cocaine's effect involves other transporter systems. Importantly, elevations in DAT demonstrated in the post-mortem brains of human cocaine abusers are supported by *in vivo* SPECT imaging in human cocaine-dependent subjects.[29] Here, the striatal uptake of [^{123}I]β-CIT (also called RTI-55) was significantly elevated (25%) in acutely abstinent (≥96 h) cocaine-dependent subjects. These studies suggest that the high-affinity cocaine binding sites are upregulated in the striatal reward centers with chronic cocaine use as a compensatory response to elevated synaptic levels of DA. It was hypothesized that this upregulation of cocaine recognition sites associated with

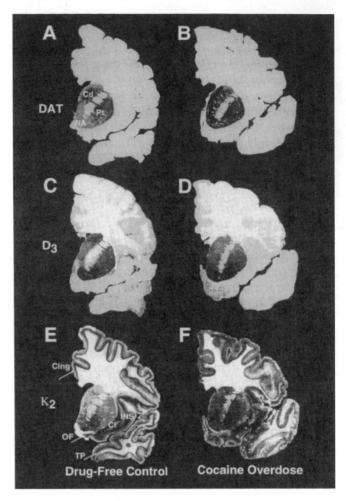

Figure 6.5.1 Visualization of the distribution of the DA transporter, D_3 receptor, and κ_2-opioid receptor in the human brain of a drug-free control subject and a representative cocaine overdose victim. (A, B) The DA transporter was measured using [3H]WIN 35,428 (2 n*M*) as described previously. (C, D) The D_3 receptor was measured using [3H]-(+)-7-OH-DPAT (1 n*M*) in the presence of GTP (300 m*M*) to enhance the selective labeling of the D_3 receptor subtype over the D_2 receptor subtype as described previously. (E, F) The κ_2-opioid receptor subtype was measured using [125I]IOXY on tissue sections pretreated with BIT and FIT to occlude binding to the μ- and δ-opioid receptors, respectively.

the DAT may reflect an increased ability of the protein to transport DA. As the transporter elevates its apparent density in the nerve terminal to clear DA from the synapse, more cocaine will be needed to experience cocaine's reinforcing effects and euphoria.[24] This neuroadaptive regulation of the DAT may occur as a result of the direct interaction of cocaine with the DAT, or, alternatively, may be due to feedback mechanisms that are activated as a consequence of prolonged elevation concentrations of DA. Recent evidence suggests that chronic cocaine may also lead to increased DAT function. Mash and colleagues[30] reported increased [3H]WIN 34,428 binding and [3H]dopamine uptake in post-mortem human striatal synaptosomes from cocaine addicts compared to age-matched controls, indicating that chronic cocaine functionally upregulates DAT. Additionally, evidence from cell cultures suggests that the increase in DAT transport activity from chronic cocaine may be due to the concurrent increase in DAT cell surface expression.[31,32] The direct regulation of DAT by cocaine suggest that the DAT is an ideal target for the development of anti-cocaine medications.

6.5.2.2   Rate of Interaction of Cocaine with the DAT and Cocaine Reinforcement

An alternative neurochemical hypothesis for the reinforcing efficacy of cocaine at the DAT is related to the rate of entry of cocaine into the brain, coupled with its ability to rapidly bind to the DAT, inhibit DA uptake, and enhance dopaminergic neurotransmission.[3] This hypothesis is based on the knowledge that other drugs known to block DA uptake, such as mazindol, GBR 12909, and methylphenidate, are not as reinforcing as cocaine[33] and exhibit a slower rate of entry into the brain and a slower onset of action.[34] Furthermore, GBR 12909, methylphenidate, bupropion, and mazindol displace the *in vivo* binding of the radiolabeled cocaine congener [³H]WIN 35,428 at a considerably slower rate than cocaine.[35] In humans, methylphenidate demonstrates a lower abuse liability as compared to cocaine, but enters the CNS with a rate similar to cocaine. An *in vivo* study determined that the potency of methylphenidate vs. cocaine at the DAT is similar and thus unlikely to underlie the differences in abuse potential.[36] However, methylphenidate is cleared more slowly than cocaine and has a longer duration of side effects, and both factors may underlie its decreased rate of administration and abuse liability.[37] Imaging studies have shown that, in general, while the level of DAT blockade is important in determining the intensity of the euphoric effects or "high," the rate at which substances block DAT determines the perceived "high."[38] For example, in monkeys, a PET study showed that cocaine and GBR 12909 affected DA synthesis and DAT availability with different time courses; e.g., GBR 12909 decreased [¹¹C]β-CFT binding for a longer time than did cocaine.[39] These studies suggest that pharmacological interventions that decrease the rate of entry into or clearance of cocaine from the brain, or alternatively block or slow cocaine's interaction with the DA transporter may be useful for the treatment of cocaine dependence.

6.5.2.3   The DAT as a Target for Cocaine Pharmacotherapies

One pharmacotherapy strategy for the treatment of cocaine dependence that has received significant attention is the development of drugs that antagonize or substitute for cocaine at its site of action in the brain.[40,41] Hypothetically, the "ideal cocaine antagonist" would manifest high-affinity binding to cocaine recognition sites on the DAT, slow dissociation from these binding sites, minimal inhibition of substrate binding and uptake, a long biological half-life, and low abuse liability.[40–42] The DA reuptake inhibitor, GBR 12909 appears to satisfy several of these criteria.[40–42] At low doses, GBR 12909 binds to the DAT with high affinity, dissociates slowly, causes only a modest increase in extracellular DA, and partially antagonizes the increase in extracellular DA evoked by local perfusion of cocaine into the striatum and the nucleus accumbens.[40,41] However, at high doses, GBR 12909 produces locomotor activation, stereotypy, behavioral sensitization, and cross-sensitizes with cocaine.[42] Importantly, behavioral studies indicate that GBR 12909 reduces cocaine-maintained behaviors in rats[43] and in nonhuman primates.[44] The dose of GBR 12909 that reduced cocaine self-administration in rhesus monkeys[44] was quantified *in vivo* in baboon and results indicated that GBR 12909 must occupy at least 50% of DAT to translate into behavioral efficacy, e.g., reduce responding for cocaine.[45] This is consistent with the finding that doses of cocaine that are reliably self-administered by rhesus monkeys occupy 53 to 87% of DAT.[46] These studies suggest that the development of a cocaine antagonist is plausible; however, efficacy as a cocaine antagonist may be dose-related. At some doses GBR 12909 has also been shown to *increase* or reinstate cocaine-seeking behavior,[43] but it is unclear whether this would translate into high abuse liability in a human clinical population. Other DAT inhibitors that have been shown to reduce the self-administration of cocaine in animals include PTT, RTI 113, and HD-23.[47–49] Molecular characterization studies of DAT, which used chimeric dopamine-norepinephrine transporters, delineated discrete domains for substrate and cocaine interactions.[50,51] These studies support the development of a cocaine antagonist devoid of uptake blockade activity for the clinical management of cocaine addiction. Current drug discovery efforts have focused on the development of compounds using cocaine as the core structure, in an effort to find a drug that blocks cocaine interactions with the DAT, but does not block the normal uptake function of the transporter. While these studies are in the early stages, it is anticipated that this approach may lead to the development of an efficacious anti-cocaine medication.

6.5.2.4 Cocaine Vaccines

An alternative pharmacotherapy for cocaine dependence currently under investigation is use of a cocaine vaccine to blunt the reinforcing effects of cocaine.[51–60] The basis of this pharmacotherapy is to decrease the rate of entry of cocaine into the CNS (and therefore the onset of action), by either binding cocaine with antibody generated by active immunization with a stable cocaine conjugate or by using an enzymatically active antibody specific for cocaine.

Because cocaine is a small molecule (MW = 303 g/mol) it is unlikely that it will be immunogenic and therefore must be conjugated to a carrier molecule such as KLH (keyhole limpet hymacyanin), polyethylene glycol, diphtheria, or tetanus toxoids to enhance its immunogenicity.[53–55] While early attempts to make a cocaine vaccine did not demonstrate significant efficacy for blocking the effects of cocaine in the CNS,[55] recent studies have been more successful.[56,57] Active immunization with a stable cocaine-KLH conjugate lowered cocaine levels in the brain by 80% in immunized vs. control rats, enough to decrease cocaine-induced hyperlocomotion and stereotypic behavior.[56] However, while the active immunization approach to cocaine pharmacotherapy appears promising, its success will be hindered if the addict administers large enough quantities of cocaine to override the antibody-induced blockade.[57] Active immunization with the cocaine immunogen GNC-KLH significantly reduced cocaine-induced reinstatement in rats and resulted in an eightfold rightward shift in the cocaine dose–effect curve, indicating that surmountability of the vaccine occurred at a dose of cocaine that was eight times higher than a dose necessary to maintain cocaine responding.[61] Subsequently, a second-generation hapten 3 (GND) was synthesized and, in rats, active immunization with GND-KLH resulted in robust decreases in cocaine-induced ambulatory and stereotypic behaviors.[62]

Use of a catalytic cocaine antibody may bypass this potential downfall of the active immunization approach. The enzymatically active catalytic cocaine antibody cleaves cocaine into two inactive metabolites: ecognine methyl ester and benzoic acid. The two metabolites are released from the catalytic antibody rendering the antibody free to degrade more cocaine. Because the catalytic antibodies are not depleted, it is impossible for the cocaine abuser to "override" the presence of the antibody by administering higher doses of cocaine.[58] Catalytic antibodies have been generated against transition state analogues of cocaine[58–60] and a catalytic antibody was shown to reduce cocaine-induced toxicity and block the self-administration of cocaine in rats.[63] While this strategy to blunt the reinforcing effects of cocaine is promising, the antibody will not alleviate the craving, dysphoria, anxiety, or depression often linked to relapse. Thus, although the cocaine antibodies may prevent cocaine reinforcement, they will not block the reinforcing effects of other psychostimulants that an addict may administer to relieve withdrawal symptoms.[64] In addition, the success of the catalytic antibody may be hindered if the antibody is perceived as foreign, and idiotypic antibodies are produced that will interact with the cocaine antibody, rendering it enzymatically inactive.

The safety of the cocaine vaccine TC-CD in former cocaine abusers has been evaluated in a Phase I clinical trial, and it was determined that the vaccine was well tolerated with dose-related increases in antibody levels.[65] Two Phase II clinical trials have now been conducted.[66,67] The vaccine was again well tolerated and subjects reported a reduction in cocaine's reinforcing effects. The antibody levels were detectable after the second dose, peaked at 8 to 12 weeks, and remained elevated for up to 6 months; preliminary findings indicated a negative association between antibody level and cocaine use. Other anti-cocaine vaccines in development include a blocking antibody (ITAC-cocaine) and a monoclonal catalytic antibody (15A10).

6.5.3   DA Receptors and Cocaine Dependence

The rewarding effects of dopamine are mediated by five DA receptor subtypes distinguished by their unique molecular and pharmacological properties and distinct anatomical locations. Repeated and prolonged elevations in synaptic dopamine levels that result from the binge use of cocaine may result in alterations in the affinity, number, or coupling state of the DA receptors. At present, the relative contribution of each of the DA receptor subtypes to the rewarding effects of cocaine is not clear. Dopamine agonists that interact with receptors belonging to both the D_1 and D_2 receptor families function as positive reinforcers, while both D_1-like and D_2-like receptor antagonists decrease the reward value of psychostimulants.[68,69] Stimulation of D_1 or D_2 receptors in the ventral tegmental area enhances the rewarding effect for brain stimulation.[70] These findings suggest that compensatory changes in DA receptor number or signaling may contribute to the development of cocaine dependence.

6.5.3.1   *Cocaine-Induced D_1 Receptor Adaptations*

The reinforcing effects of cocaine are mediated, in part, by the D_1 receptors in the nucleus accumbens and the central nucleus of the amygdala.[71] In preclinical animal studies, administration of the D_1 receptor antagonist SCH 23390 prevents reinstatement to cocaine-induced conditioned place preference,[72] reduces reinstatement to cocaine-seeking behavior,[73] and SCH 23390 when administered in combination with cocaine prevents the development of cocaine sensitization.[74,75] While cocaine self-administration is increased in the presence of D_1 receptor antagonists,[68,76–79] which is likely a compensatory response, it has recently been demonstrated that, under some schedules of reinforcement, low doses of benzazepine D_1 receptor antagonists block cocaine self-administration.[80] Additionally, a variety of D_1 receptor agonists (SKF 82958, SKF 81297, SKF 83959) and an antagonist (ecopipam) reduced reinstatement of cocaine-seeking in nonhuman primates.[81] Further, SCH 23390 reversed the attenuating effects of SKF 81297 on cocaine-seeking behavior but not cue-induced reinstatement in rats[82] indicating that the reductions in cocaine-seeking behavior are not due simply to behavioral disruption. These findings suggest that the state of the D_1 receptor population may dictate the ability of D_1 receptor antagonists to enhance or to block the reinforcing effects of cocaine. D_1 receptor mRNA levels, receptor number, and receptor sensitivity are altered as a consequence of protracted cocaine exposure and may, in part, account for some of the D_1 receptor-mediated behavioral responses to cocaine. D_1 receptor mRNA is not altered in the striatum, nucleus accumbens, or substantia nigra of human cocaine abusers;[83] however, elevations in D_1 receptor mRNA were observed in the striatum of rats chronically treated with cocaine.[84] The D_1 receptor is also critical for mediating cocaine-induced expression of certain genes (the fos and Jun family immediate early genes which encode transcription factors) and molecules such as brain-derived neurotrophic factor, β-catenin, and Gαolf, which are implicated in mediating cocaine's actions in the nucleus accumbens and caudate putamen.[85] Increased D_1 receptor density was reported in the nucleus accumbens and olfactory tubercle in rat brain following twice-daily injections of cocaine.[86] Chronic cocaine treatment results in an adaptive increase in D_1 receptor number in olfactory tubercle, nucleus accumbens, central pallidum, and substantia nigra, which normalized within 1 day[87] and remained at baseline values for up to 3 days[88] and 30 days[89] after cocaine treatment. Conversely, decreased striatal D_1 receptor densities that persisted for at least 2 weeks after the last administration of cocaine have been observed.[84] Chronic cocaine exposure in monkeys resulted in increased D_1 receptor density in striatum.[90] Electrophysiological sensitivity of D_1 receptors in the nucleus accumbens neurons is enhanced in rats 2 weeks post-cocaine administration,[91,92] suggesting that despite the number of D_1 receptors detected, adaptation in the D_1 receptor signaling cascade may occur to enhance D_1-receptor-mediated dopamine transmission. When these findings are viewed collectively, it is difficult to ascertain precisely the regulatory adaptations that the D_1 receptor undergoes in response to protracted cocaine use. The differences may be due to a variety of factors including variations in dose, frequency, and route of administration. These factors have been shown to influence the adaptive responses of dopaminergic synaptic markers; therefore, the differences may be attributed to distinct drug administration protocols.[17] Regardless of the adaptive response observed, it is evident from these studies that the adaptations of the D_1 receptor may be integral to the development of cocaine dependence and therefore may be a useful target for the development of cocaine pharmacotherapies.

6.5.3.2 Cocaine-Induced Adaptations in D_2 Receptors

The actions of cocaine on D_2 receptors have been shown to be essential to the development of cocaine dependence. The D_2 receptor antagonist haloperidol inhibits the development of behavioral sensitization to cocaine.[74] Sensitization is believed to play an important role in drug craving and the reinstatement of compulsive drug-taking behavior;[93,94] thus, altered regulation of D_2 receptors may contribute to the reinforcing potential of cocaine. D_2 mRNA levels were not altered in the striatum of human cocaine abusers[83] or rats treated with cocaine.[95,96] D_2 receptor mRNA levels were decreased in the olfactory tubercle of rats treated with a single injection of cocaine,[95] whereas D_2 receptor mRNA levels were transiently elevated in rats treated chronically with cocaine.[84] A transient increase in the binding of [³H]raclopride in the olfactory tubercle and rostral nucleus accumbens and caudate-putamen was observed after binge administration of cocaine[97] and elevations in [³H]spiperone and [¹²⁵I]spiperone binding were seen in the nucleus accumbens, olfactory tubercle, and substantia nigra after intermittent cocaine administration.[87] In contrast, D_2 receptor densities were not significantly affected in the rat striatum 3 days post-cocaine administration.[88] In monkeys, chronic cocaine exposure resulted in a significant decrease in D_2 receptor density throughout the striatum measured with [³H]raclopride.[90] Furthermore, [¹⁸F]N-methylspiroperidol labeling in living cocaine abusers demonstrated decreased D_2 receptor densities after a 1 week detoxification[98] and quantitative immunoblotting of post-mortem brain samples demonstrated a decrease in protein levels of D_2 receptors in the nucleus accumbens of cocaine users compared to controls.[99] Viewed collectively, these studies suggest that the D_2 receptor may undergo a transient elevation in the response to acute cocaine administration, which normalizes upon cocaine abstinence. However, caution should be taken in the interpretation of these data because these radioligands do not discriminate between D_2 and D_3 receptors and, therefore, identity of the regulated D_2 receptor subtype is not known.

6.5.3.3 Cocaine-Induced Adaptations in D_3 Receptors

Cocaine-induced adaptations at the D_3 receptor may mediate some of the reinforcing effects of cocaine. D_3 receptor-preferring agonists, although not self-administered by drug-naïve monkeys, are self-administered by monkeys previously trained to self-administer cocaine.[100] D_3 receptor-preferring agonists substitute for the discriminative stimulus effects of cocaine and produce place preference in rats and monkeys indicating that the D_3 receptor may mediate some of the subjective effects of cocaine.[101–103] These studies suggest that adaptations in the affinity, density, or molecular expression of the D_3 receptor induced by chronic cocaine use may underlie, in part, the development of cocaine dependence.

The D_3 receptor-preferring agonist [³H]-(+)-7-OH-DPAT has been used in quantitative *in vitro* autoradiography studies to assess the status of D_3 receptors in human cocaine overdose (CO) victims[104] (Figure 6.5.1). Binding of [³H]-(+)-7-OH-DPAT was elevated one- to threefold in the nucleus accumbens and ventromedial sectors of the caudate and putamen in CO victims as compared to drug-free and age-matched control subjects. D_3 receptor/cyclophilin mRNA ratios were also increased sixfold in the nucleus accumbens in CO vs. control subjects indicating that cocaine exposure effects D_3 receptor mRNA expression. These findings were confirmed by saturation analysis of the $[^3H]$-(+)-7-OH-DPAT binding in membranes from the nucleus accumbens. The affinity for $[^3H]$-(+)-7-OH-DPAT binding was not different in the CO victims or the "Excited Delirium" (ED) victims as compared to drug-free control subjects. However, the saturation binding density for the CO victims (4.4 ± 0.4 pmol/g) when compared to the drug-free control subjects (3.1 ± 0.2 pmol/g) was significantly elevated.[105]

Interestingly, after 1-day withdrawal from chronic treatment with cocaine, increased D_3 receptor densities were observed in the striatum, while decreased D_3 receptor densities were observed in the nucleus accumbens of the rat brain.[106] In another study D_3 receptor binding was increased in the nucleus accumbens and ventral caudate putamen at 31 days after the last cocaine delivery but not at the 2-day or 8-day time points compared to controls.[107] Additionally, the density of D_3 receptors was increased in animals exposed to cocaine-associated stimuli.[108] It should be noted, however, that in the first study mentioned[106] the densities of the D_3 receptors were high in the dorsal striatum, as compared to the nucleus accumbens, which contrasts with the intense localization of the D_3 receptor mRNA in the nucleus accumbens of rat and human brain[109,110] and the higher D_3 receptor densities in the ventral striatum and the nucleus accumbens of the human brain.[105] In another study, D_3 receptor mRNA expression was not altered in human cocaine abusers.[111] These findings suggest that D_3 receptor mRNA and binding sites may be differentially regulated by cocaine exposure. A single cocaine exposure was recently shown to increase brain-derived neurotrophic factor (BDNF) mRNA in the prefrontal cortex of rats and was associated with a long-lasting increase in D_3 mRNA and D_3 protein in the nucleus accumbens.[112] Chronic treatment of C_6 glioma cells transfected with the D_3 receptor cDNA with DA agonists increased D_3 receptor densities, but did not change D_3 mRNA abundance.[113] The upregulation in D_3 receptor densities was blocked by treatment with cycloheximide, suggesting that the increase was mediated by increased protein synthesis. Changes in proteins, mRNA, and BDNF in addition to changes in D_3 density are likely associated with long-lasting cocaine-conditioned and cocaine-seeking behavior.

Alternatively, increased $[^3H]$-(+)-7-OH-DPAT binding may reflect a selective increase in one of the D_3 receptor isoforms. The D_3 receptor specific probes may have hybridized to multiple alternative splice variants, including the truncated D_3 receptors.[114] Because DAergic ligands do not bind to the proteins generated from the truncated splice variants, regulation of message levels and binding site densities would be dissociated. The relative abundance of specific D_3 receptor isoforms may vary also with alterations in DA neurotransmission. While the biological significance and function of the D_3 receptor splice variants are not understood, it has been suggested that alternative splicing may regulate the relative abundance of the different D_3 receptor isoforms to differentially modulate D_3 receptor-mediated signaling.[115] Therefore, it may be suggested that the elevation in D_3 receptor density after chronic cocaine use may reflect a selective increase in one of the D_3 receptor isoforms. Additional studies are needed to determine if this regulatory pattern occurs in the human brain. D_3 receptor adaptations that result from repeated activation of the DA neurotransmission due to chronic "binge" use of cocaine may contribute to the development of cocaine dependence. This adaptive increase in the D_3 receptor may enhance the reinforcing effects of cocaine and contribute to the development of cocaine dependence. Recent development of potential *in vivo* agents for imaging the D_3 receptor in living humans will advance our understanding of the role of D_3 receptors in cocaine dependence.[116]

6.5.3.4 *DA Receptors as Targets for Cocaine Pharmacotherapies*

The search for pharmacotherapies for cocaine dependence has focused on drugs that target the DA receptors. Cocaine's reinforcing properties result from its ability to prolong the action of dopamine at the DA receptors in brain reward regions.[3] From this perspective it has been suggested that DA antagonists may block cocaine use by preventing the interaction of dopamine with its receptors, and therefore block reinforcement. In animal self-administration studies, both D_1 receptor (SCH 23390[68,76]) and D_2 receptor antagonists (pimozide,[117,118] sulpiride,[118] chlorpromazine,[119] spiperone,[76] metoclopramide,[118] pherphenazine[120]) increase cocaine self-administration by decreasing the reinforcing potential of cocaine. However, recent studies have shown that low doses of benza-zepine D_1 receptor antagonists attenuate cocaine self-administration under certain schedules of reinforcement.[80] These findings suggest that certain doses of D_1 receptor antagonists may be efficacious for the treatment of cocaine dependence. Flupentixol, a dopamine antagonist with high affinity for the D_1 receptor, has demonstrated some efficacy for decreasing craving and increasing treatment retention in human cocaine abusers.[121] D_2 receptor antagonists (haloperidol and chlor-promazine) have been efficacious for the treatment of paranoia and psychosis but not craving in human cocaine abusers.[122,123] D_2 receptor antagonists also elicit significant adverse side effects such as abnormal movements and are not effective at reducing cocaine use even at high doses.[124] While DA antagonists may block the reinforcing efficacy of cocaine, use of DA antagonists as pharma-cotherapies may be hampered by their propensity to enhance cocaine withdrawal symptoms.[64] Furthermore, compliance is hindered by the dysphoric and extrapyramidal side effects associated with the blockade of DA neurotransmission.[125]

DA receptor agonists also have been suggested as anti-cocaine medications because of their propensity to reduce craving that occurs during cocaine withdrawal. A recent study using pergolide, a D_2/D_3 receptor agonist, has demonstrated some efficacy for decreasing craving.[126] Bromocriptine, a D_2-like agonist, has undergone extensive evaluation as a treatment for cocaine dependence and appears to reduce craving in cocaine abusers.[127] However, its efficacy as a pharmacotherapy for cocaine dependence was weak.[128] Furthermore, studies using an indirect-acting DA agonist, aman-tadine, were not as successful as anticipated.[129] The poor outcome of these studies, which were conducted in the late 1980s, may be explained by a recent preclinical study which demonstrated that D_2-like agonists actually enhance cocaine-seeking behavior or "prime" the addict to initiate another binge use of cocaine[125,130] and D_2 receptor agonists are typically no longer developed as potential medications for cocaine dependence. However, cabergoline, a long-acting D_2 receptor agonist, has recently been evaluated in a Phase II trial for cocaine dependence and was more effective than placebo in reducing cocaine use as measured by negative urine screens for cocaine metabolites.[131] D_1-like agonists oppose cocaine-seeking behavior induced by cocaine itself [130] suggesting that D_1-like receptor agonists may be efficacious for the treatment of craving in cocaine dependence. However, while D_1-like agonists may attenuate the craving associated with cocaine withdrawal and relapse and may not enhance cocaine-seeking behavior, they may be reinforcing and therefore at risk to be abused themselves.

The close association of the D_3 receptor with the striatal reward pathways and its selective distribution in the mesolimbic dopamine system suggests that drugs that target the D_3 receptor subtype may decrease the reinforcing effects of cocaine. Because D_3 receptors' densities elevate as cocaine dependence develops, this upregulation of D_3 receptors may contribute to the reinforcing effects of cocaine.[105] From this perspective, the development of drugs that block D_3 receptor function may be useful for the treatment of cocaine dependence. In keeping with this hypothesis, the D_3-selective antagonists (–)DS 121[125] and SB-277011A[132] attenuate cocaine self-administration in rats and block cocaine reinstatement.[133,134] Alternatively, agents that act as D_3 agonists or partial agonists may be used as substitutes to treat cocaine dependence.[135] The compound BP 897, a highly selective D_3 agonist, reduced cocaine seeking behavior in rats;[136] however, BP 897 also demonstrates antag-onist properties at human D_3 and D_2 receptors,[137] suggesting that the cocaine-reducing effects may be due to antagonism at these sites. While these studies are encouraging, additional research is necessary to confirm the efficacy of either D_3 receptor antagonists or agonists as clinically useful pharmacotherapies. Several other agents that act within the dopamine system are being evaluated in clinical trials. These include disulfiram, which may act by increasing brain levels of dopamine and decreasing levels of norepinephrine, selegiline, which is an irreversible MAO inhibitor, and reserpine, a Rauwolfia alkaloid currently used as an antihypertensive agent, which acts to deplete dopamine, norepinephrine, and serotonin in presynaptic vesicles; see Gorelick et al.[138] for review.

6.5.4 Kappa-Opioid Receptors

The endogenous opioidergic system has been implicated as a primary mediator of the behavioral and reinforcing effects of cocaine.[94] (See Reference 139 for more information on the interaction of cocaine with the opioid system including the mu- and delta-opioid receptors). Pharmacological and molecular cloning studies have recently reported the existence of at least three subtypes of κ-opioid receptors.[140–147] Receptor mapping studies have demonstrated that both κ_1-opioid receptor and κ_2-opioid receptor subtypes are prevalent throughout the mesocorticolimbic pathways in the human brain.[26,148,149] One striking difference in the localization of the two subtypes is reflected by the intense localization of the κ_2-opioid receptor subtype in the ventral or "limbic" sectors of the striatum and the nucleus accumbens in the human brain.[149] Conversely, the κ_1-opioid receptor subtype may preferentially localize to the dorsal or "sensorimotor" areas of the human striatum.[26] Based on their neuroanatomical distribution in the human striatum, it may be hypothesized that the κ_1-opioid receptor subtype modulates motor functions, while the κ_2-opioid receptor subtype mediates emotional behaviors and affect. The anatomical localization of the κ-opioid receptor subtypes and their intimate association with dopaminergic reward pathways suggests that regulatory alterations in both κ_1- and κ_2-opioid receptors may be important in cocaine dependence.

6.5.4.1 Regulation of Kappa-Opioid Receptors by Cocaine

At present, the functional significance and relevance of each of the κ-opioid receptor subtypes in the CNS and their role in modulating the brain reward pathways with chronic substance abuse is not well understood. An adaptive increase in the density of κ-opioid receptors in guinea pig brain after chronic cocaine treatments was detected using the κ_1-selective radioligand [^{3}H]U69,593.[150] Furthermore, elevations in [^{125}I]Tyr^1-D-Pro^{10}-dynorphin A binding to κ-opioid receptors were observed within the dorsal and "motor" sectors of the striatum of human cocaine abusers.[26] Dynorphin A demonstrates higher affinity to the κ_1-opioid receptor subtype as compared to the κ_2-opioid receptor subtype; therefore, it may be suggested on the basis of occupancy that the elevated binding of [^{125}I]Tyr^1-D-Pro^{10}-dynorphin A observed in these studies may be due to recognition of the κ_1-opioid receptor subtype.[147,151,152] These findings combined with animal behavioral studies (e.g., cocaine place preference and self-administration) suggest a definitive role for the $_1$-opioid receptor in cocaine dependence. While these studies are reasonably conclusive, other studies are not, due to the use of radioligands, which lack selectivity between κ-opioid receptor subtypes. After chronic continuous exposure to cocaine,[153] elevated binding of the nonselective opioid agonist and antagonist ([^{3}H]bremazocine and [^{3}H]naloxone, respectively) were observed in the nucleus accumbens. Thrice daily injections of cocaine in rats resulted in increased κ-opioid receptor density in cingulate cortex, nucleus accumbens, and caudate putamen.[86] Furthermore, in rats treated with cocaine using a binge-administration paradigm, binding of [^{3}H]bremazocine to κ-opioid receptors was increased.[154] Binding density of [^{3}H]U-69593, a selective κ-opioid receptor ligand, was significantly higher in caudate putamen and nucleus accumbens after chronic cocaine infusion[155] indicating increased numbers of κ-opioid receptors in brain areas associated with drug craving and reward.

It is interesting that in the same animal model, κ-opioid receptor mRNA was decreased in the substantia nigra, but not in the ventral tegmental area of cocaine treated rats.[156] A recent study also reported κ-opioid receptor mRNA levels are decreased after cocaine self-administration in rats in the nucleus accumbens and ventral tegmental area.[157] The reasons for this disconnect between κ-opioid receptor binding and the κ-opioid receptor mRNA are not known. However, the discrepancy may be due to the detection of multiple κ-opioid receptor mRNAs or binding sites or to the binding of the [^{3}H]bremazocine to a κ-opioid receptor subtype distinct from the κ-opioid receptor message that was measured. While the interpretation of these studies with regards to which κ-opioid receptor subtype was measured and the regulation of each subtype by cocaine is difficult at this time, recent

advances in the cloning of these receptor subtypes and the development of subtype-specific radioligands will clarify these issues in the near future.

Recently, pharmacological binding assays to selectively label the κ_2-opioid receptor subtype
have been developed using the opioid antagonist [^{125}I]IOXY in the presence of drugs occluding
binding to the μ- and κ-opioid receptor subtypes.[151] This strategy was used in ligand binding and
in vitro autoradiography assays to assess the regulation of the κ_2-opioid receptor subtype after
cocaine exposure in post-mortem human brain (death was from cocaine overdose) (Figure
6.5.1).[149,158] Quantitative region-of-interest densitometric measurements of [^{125}I]IOXY binding demonstrated a twofold elevation in the anterior and ventral sectors of the caudate and putamen and in
the nucleus accumbens of human cocaine overdose victims as compared to drug-free and age-
matched control subjects. In subjects who experienced paranoia and agitation prior to their death,
κ_2-opioid receptors were also elevated in the amygdala.[104,158]

The regulation of κ_2-opioid receptor numbers in the striatal reward centers suggests that adaptations in the κ_2-opioid receptors may also contribute to the development of cocaine dependence.
κ-opioid agonists do not generalize to cocaine cues in drug discrimination paradigms;[159,160] however,
κ-opioid agonists suppress the stimulus effects of cocaine in monkeys.[161] Therefore, it is unlikely
that κ-opioid receptors play a direct role in the stimulus of euphoric effects of cocaine. The elevation
of the κ_2-opioid receptor subtype along with its discrete localization to the "limbic" or "emotional"
striatum indicates that compensatory adaptation in this subtype may underlie the "affective" or
"emotional" effects associated with cocaine dependence. Shippenberg and colleagues[162] have suggested that "conditioned aversive effects" associated with hyperactivity of κ-opioidergic neurons
in the ventral striatum may underlie the "motivational incentive" to use cocaine. Furthermore, the
subjective effects of κ-opioid agonists mimic the symptoms of cocaine withdrawal suggesting that
excessive activity of the opioidergic system may, in part, contribute to the aversive effects associated
with cocaine withdrawal. Because protracted exposure to cocaine alters the DA-mediated reward
systems, κ-opioidergic systems may undergo adaptations in an effort to re-establish the balance
between the reward system and the opposing aversive system. However, when cocaine is withdrawn
and the dopaminergic reward circuit is no longer activated, the κ_2-opioid receptor numbers may
remain elevated, and may contribute to the unpleasant feelings and dysphoria associated with
withdrawal from cocaine.

6.5.4.2 *Kappa-Opioid Receptor Drugs as Cocaine Pharmacotherapies*

There is considerable evidence supporting a critical role for κ-opioid receptors in the development of cocaine dependence. Co-administration of κ-opioid agonists with cocaine inhibits
cocaine self-administration,[163] cocaine-induced place preference,[162] and the development of sensitization to the rewarding effects of cocaine.[93,94,164] In rats, U-69593, a κ-opioid receptor agonist,
reduced cocaine self-administration and cocaine seeking behavior[165] and the reinstatement to
cocaine self-administration.[166] Further, daily administration of the mixed κ-opioid antagonist and
partial μ-opioid agonist buprenorphine reduces cocaine self-administration by rhesus monkeys[167]
and prevents the reinstatement of cocaine-reinforced responding in rats.[168] κ-opioid agonist drugs
such as bremazocine also reduce cocaine self-administration in rhesus monkeys.[169,170] These potent
anti-cocaine effects exhibited by κ-opioid receptor agents in preclinical animal studies suggest that
κ-opioid receptors may be a useful target for the pharmacotherapeutic treatment of cocaine dependence. One κ-opioid agonist, enadoline, has recently been examined in clinical trials. While the
drug was well-tolerated it did not reduce the acute subjective effects in a laboratory study.[171]
Buprenorphine has demonstrated some efficacy in decreasing cocaine abuse in heroin abusers[172,173]
and the combination of buprenorphine and naloxone, a μ-opioid antagonist, is currently used for
the treatment of heroin and other opiate addiction.[174] As a medication for cocaine addiction,
buprenorphine has been studied in cocaine abusers with concurrent opioid dependence and was
found to reduce cocaine use.[175] The development of pharmacotherapeutic κ-opioid agonists has

been hindered by reports that, in humans, administration of κ-opioid agonists elicits aversive and psychotomimetic effects.[176–178] The recent identification of multiple subtypes of κ-opioid receptors with distinct pharmacological and molecular properties[140–147] has led to the hypothesis that different κ-opioid receptor subtypes may mediate distinct actions of κ-opioid agonists.[151,152,178] Therefore, it may be possible to develop κ-opioid drugs that lack and/or inhibit the dysphoric properties and yet maintain efficacy for blocking cocaine administration. At present, distinct "sensorimotor" vs. "limbic" striatum may, in part, mediate the feelings of dysphoria and craving associated with cocaine withdrawal distress. The similarity between symptoms associated with cocaine withdrawal and the subjective effects of kappa-opioid agonist administration suggests that increased activity in the kappa opioid receptor system during cocaine withdrawal may underlie the dysphoric effects. The extent that the κ_2-opioid receptor subtype specifically mediates the dysphoric properties of κ-opioid agonists will not be known until selective κ_2-opioid agonists are developed. However, if the κ_2-opioid receptor does not mediate dysphoria during cocaine withdrawal, then selective κ_2-opioid receptor antagonists may be useful for the treatment of the dysphoria that underlies relapse and the perpetuation of cocaine misuse.

6.5.5   Serotonin Transporter and Cocaine Dependence

Cocaine binds with high affinity to the serotonin (5-HT) transporter and inhibits 5-HT uptake.[2,179] Serotonergic neurons project from the dorsal raphe to the ventral tegmental area where they modulate mesolimbic DA neurotransmission. Inhibition of 5-HT uptake in the dorsal raphe nucleus by cocaine decreases the firing of the raphe neurons by feedback activation of the 5-HT$_{1A}$ autoreceptors,[180–182] an effect that is blocked by pretreatment with a 5-HT synthesis inhibitor p-chlorophenylalanine.[181] With chronic cocaine treatment, these mechanisms become sensitized probably as a result of a compensatory upregulation of [^{3}H]imipramine binding to the 5-HT transporter in the dorsal raphe, frontal cortex, medial, and sulcal prefrontal cortex of cocaine treated rats.[182] These studies suggest that adaptations in the serotonergic neurotransmission may contribute in part to the expression of cocaine-induced behaviors. While an enhancement of serotonin neurotransmission is believed to be inhibitory to the expression of cocaine-mediated behaviors or to have minimal effect,[183,184] there is some evidence that 5-HT may play a role in the mood-elevating effects of acute cocaine. Interestingly, depletion of tryptophan (the precursor to 5-HT) severely attenuated the subjective high experienced by cocaine-dependent subjects.[185] Furthermore, withdrawal from chronic cocaine use has been associated with symptoms of depression[186] due to cocaine-induced alterations in 5-HT neurotransmission.[187] Together, these studies suggest that regulatory alterations in serotonergic signaling play a role in cocaine dependence. Furthermore, drugs that antagonize these alterations in serotonergic systems may be efficacious for the treatment of cocaine dependence.

6.5.5.1   The 5-HT Transporter as a Target for Cocaine Pharmacotherapy

The effects of cocaine may be antagonized by 5-HT-mediated inhibition of mesolimbic DA neurotransmission.[188] Thus, increased 5-HT neurotransmission that results from blocking presynaptic 5-HT uptake may decrease cocaine administration. In keeping, preclinical animal studies have demonstrated that enhancement of serotonergic neurotransmission by administration of the selective 5-HT uptake inhibitors citalopram and fluoxetine attenuates the discriminative stimulus effects of cocaine in monkeys.[189] Furthermore, fluoxetine inhibits cocaine self-administration[190] and reduces the breakpoints on a progressive ration schedule reinforced by cocaine.[191] Conversely, depletion of 5-HT enhances cocaine self-administration.[192] Several 5-HT reuptake inhibitors have been evaluated for the treatment of cocaine dependence. Fluoxetine significantly decreased subjective ratings of cocaine's positive mood effects on several visual analog measures and attenuated the mydriatic effect of cocaine in human cocaine abusers.[193] Fluoxetine has been suggested to decrease craving and cocaine use in methadone-maintained cocaine users.[194–196] While the efficacy of fluoxetine may be related to its ability to reduce craving,[197,198] it is likely that its effects are more related to its ability to reverse the symptoms of depression that are associated with cocaine withdrawal. Another 5-HT transporter inhibitor, sertraline, was not shown to be more effective than placebo in reducing cocaine use in recent clinical trials.[199]

6.5.6 Glutamate Receptors and Cocaine Dependence

There is increasing evidence supporting a role for glutamate receptors including the NMDA (*N*-methyl-D-aspartate) and AMPA receptors in the neural and behavioral changes resulting from chronic cocaine administration.[7] Glutamate is the major excitatory neurotransmitter found mainly in cortical and limbic neurons, which project to the nucleus accumbens. Preclinical studies with the noncompetitive NMDA receptor antagonist MK-801 have linked excitatory glutamatergic synapses with the development of cocaine sensitization, a cardinal feature of cocaine dependence. Simultaneous administration of low doses of MK-801 prevented the development of sensitization to the stereotypic and locomotor stimulant effects of cocaine.[200–205] Alternatively, when MK-801 was administered prior to cocaine, the stimulating effects of cocaine were enhanced.[206] The competitive NMDA antagonist CPP partially prevented the development of cocaine sensitization.[204] MK-801 decreased the incidence of seizures and mortality caused by cocaine.[207–209] The AMPA receptor antagonist NBQX produced dose-dependent decreases in cocaine-induced locomotor stimulation.[203] Dopaminergic neurons in the ventral tegmental area of cocaine-treated rats were more responsive to glutamate while nucleus accumbens neurons were less sensitive.[210] Cortical NMDA receptors are upregulated after cocaine treatment[211] and GluR1 (an AMPA receptor subunit) and NMDAR1 (an NMDA receptor subunit) are upregulated in the ventral tegmental area[212] suggesting that compensatory adaptation of the glutamate receptors may result from or contribute to enhanced glutamatergic neurotransmission. Alterations in the mesocorticolimbic glutamate transmission may in part contribute to the development of cocaine sensitization.[210] Recent evidence suggests that neuroadaptive changes in amygdaloid glutamate receptors, which are involved in cocaine seeking and craving, are apparent during cocaine withdrawal.[213]

6.5.6.1 *Glutamate Receptors as Targets for Cocaine Pharmacotherapies*

Since NMDA receptors mediate the development of sensitization to cocaine's reinforcing effects, they may serve as a target for cocaine pharmacotherapies.[214] However, while both competitive and noncompetitive NMDA receptor antagonists block the development of cocaine sensitization, they appear to be ineffective once sensitization has developed. NMDA receptor antagonists do not alter the acute stimulant effects of cocaine.[7,200] Acute pretreatment with MK-801 caused a loss of discriminative responding; however, it did not block cocaine self-administration.[214] Furthermore, many drugs that act at the NMDA receptors produce phencyclidine-like behavioral effects.[203] Together, these preclinical studies do not offer significant support for NMDA receptor antagonists as cocaine pharmacotherapies. However, AMPA receptor antagonists do not appear to produce phencyclidine-like behavioral effects, and they block cocaine-induced locomotor stimulation. While additional preclinical studies are necessary, it has been suggested that non-NMDA glutamate receptor antagonists, such as agents acting at the metabotropic glutamate receptor 5 (mGluR5), may be a target for the development of pharmacotherapies for the treatment of cocaine dependence.

6.5.7 GABA Receptors and Cocaine Dependence

The GABAergic system in concert with the dopaminergic and glutamatergic systems are involved in cocaine addiction. Dopamine and glutamate terminals synapse on GABA spiny cells in the brain reward area of the nucleus accumbens[215] and there are GABA projections to the nucleus accumbens.[216] There are many similarities in the projections of dopamine and GABA suggesting that GABA may modulate the effects of cocaine within the dopaminergic system. For example, treatment with the dopamine agonist pramipexole was associated with increased GABA levels in the prefrontal cortex of cocaine dependent subject after 8 weeks of treatment.[217] Additionally, acute cocaine use increased dopamine together with increased GABA transmission in the prefrontal cortex,[218] while repeated cocaine use decreased dopamine D_2 receptor and $GABA_B$ receptor function.[219] These changes could ultimately result in lower GABA levels in cocaine-dependent individuals, and, therefore, medications that increase GABA levels may be useful in treating cocaine addiction.

6.5.7.1 GABA Receptors as Targets for Cocaine Pharmacotherapies

Preclinical and clinical studies have examined the effects of GABA agents on cocaine-seeking behaviors. In animals, gamma-vinyl gamma-aminobutyric acid (GVG), a GABA agonist, reduced cocaine self-administration,[220] and a combination of muscimol, a $GABA_A$ agonist, and baclofen, a $GABA_B$ agonist, blocked the reinstatement of cocaine[221] and decreased cocaine self-administration.[222,223] In humans, the GABA agonists topiramate,[224] tiagabine,[199] and baclofen[225] decreased cocaine use. Baclofen has also been shown to reduce limbic activation in response to cocaine craving.[225] The use of $GABA_B$ agonists as treatments has been slowed by the adverse side effects including sedation and motor impairment. Recently, positive allosteric modulators at the $GABA_B$ receptor have been developed, which do not have intrinsic activity but interact with already present GABA to enhance its effect.[226] Further research is necessary to determine whether GABA receptor agonists, positive allosteric GABA modulators, or possibly a combination will be clinically useful.

6.5.8 Multitarget Pharmacotherapeutic Agents

Many of the novel pharmacotherapeutic agents currently under development are directed toward a single molecular target related to cocaine or known to be regulated by cocaine. Although this strategy has been somewhat beneficial, the development of an effective treatment for cocaine dependence may require multisite targeting of distinct neuroreceptor populations that are known to modulate the activity of the drug reward circuit. Cocaine interacts with at least three distinct neurochemical systems in the brain including the dopaminergic, serotonergic, and noradrenergic systems. Cocaine enhances the neurotransmission of each of these systems by blocking the presynaptic reuptake. Chronic perturbations of monoaminergic neurotransmission that result from protracted use of cocaine may, in turn, alter cholinergic and glutamatergic neurotransmission by indirect actions. The ability of cocaine to alter signaling of multiple neurochemical pathways in the brain suggests that a multitarget pharmacotherapy may be an optimal approach for the treatment of cocaine dependence.

6.5.8.1 Ibogaine: The Rain Forest Alkaloid

Ibogaine, the principal alkaloid of the African rain forest shrub Tabernanthe iboga (Apocynaceae family), is currently being evaluated as an agent to treat psychostimulant addiction.[227] Anecdotal reports of ibogaine treatments in opiate-dependent or cocaine-dependent humans describe alleviation of drug "craving" and physical signs of opiate withdrawal after a single administration of ibogaine, which in some subjects contributes to drug-free periods lasting several months thereafter. This has recently been confirmed in a preliminary study reporting that ibogaine significantly reduced craving for both cocaine and heroin and significantly improved depressive symptoms in an inpatient detoxification setting.[228] In drug self-administration studies, ibogaine and related iboga alkaloids reduced intravenous self-administration of cocaine 1 h after treatment. This suppression on cocaine intake was evident 1 day later, and in some rats a persistent decrease was noted for as long as several weeks.[229] Ibogaine also effectively blocks morphine self-administration[229] and reduces preference for cocaine consumption in a mouse cocaine-preference drinking model.[230] And, cocaine-induced stereotypy and locomotor activity were significantly lower in ibogaine-treated mice.

The mechanism of action for ibogaine may be resolved in part by defining high-affinity pharmacological targets for ibogaine. The receptor binding profile for ibogaine suggests that multiple neurochemical pathways may be responsible for ibogaine's anti-addictive properties. Ibogaine binds to μ- and κ_1-opioid receptors, α-1 adrenergic receptors, M_1 and M_2 muscarinic receptors, serotonin 5-HT$_2$ and 5-HT$_3$ receptors, and voltage-dependent sodium channels with micromolar affinities.[231] Ibogaine completely displaced [^{3}H]MK-801 binding[232,233] and blocked NMDA-depolarizations in frog motor neurons.[233] Ibogaine demonstrated moderate affinity for binding to cocaine recognition sites on the DA transporter[231] and on the 5-HT transporter.[234] Ibogaine, which blocks access of cocaine to the DA transporter, may[235] or may not restrict substrate uptake.[236] Because ibogaine displays lower affinity for the DA transporter compared to cocaine, it may meet some of the criteria for the "ideal cocaine antagonist."

The anti-addictive properties of ibogaine may, in part, be mediated by a pharmacologically active metabolite. Recently, the principal metabolite of ibogaine was isolated from biological specimens of subjects administered ibogaine using GC/MS.[234,237] The metabolite that results from O-demethylation of the parent drug was identified as 12-hydroxyibogamine (noribogaine). Preliminary pharmacokinetic studies have suggested that noribogaine is generated rapidly and exhibits a slow clearance rate.[234] The relatively long half-life of noribogaine suggests that the long-term biological effects of ibogaine may, in part, be mediated by its metabolite. Similar to ibogaine, noribogaine binds to the μ- and κ_1-opioid receptors with micromolar potency.[238,239] The most striking finding has been the demonstration that noribogaine binds to the cocaine recognition site on the 5-HT transporter with a nanomolar potency,[234,239] and elevates extraneuronal 5-HT in a dose-dependent manner.[234,236] Given the recent evidence that serotonin uptake blockers alleviate some of the symptoms associated with psychostimulant "craving," these findings suggest that the effects of noribogaine on the 5-HT transmission may account, in part, for the potential of ibogaine to interrupt drug-seeking behavior in humans. Overall, it may be suggested that the putative efficacy of ibogaine as a pharmacotherapy for cocaine dependence may be attributed to the combined actions of the parent and the metabolite at multiple CNS targets.[233,239]

6.5.9   Conclusions

Significant advances have been made in understanding the neurochemical consequences of cocaine dependence in the past decade. Integration of the findings observed for cocaine's effects on behavior, together with the identification of the receptors and transporters that undergo compensatory adaptations to neutralize cocaine's effects, has led to the identification of several potential neurochemical targets for the development of cocaine pharmacotherapies. Pharmacotherapies that target one or more of the neurochemical systems that have been altered by protracted cocaine use may alleviate the dysphoria, depression, and anxiety that underlie relapse and compulsive cocaine use.

Acknowledgments

This work was supported by the M.I.R.E.C.C. and the NIMH Biological Sciences Training Program.

REFERENCES

1. Ritz M., Lamb S., Goldberg S., Kuhar M. Cocaine receptors on dopamine transporters are related to self-administration of cocaine. *Science.* 237:1219, 1987.

2. Reith M., Kramer H., Sershen H., Lajtha A. Cocaine completely inhibits catecholamine uptake into brain synaptic vesicles. *Res. Commun. Subst. Abuse.* 10:205, 1989.

3. Kuhar M., Ritz M., Boja J. The dopamine hypothesis of the reinforcing properties of cocaine. *Trends Neurosci.* 14:299, 1991.

4. Mateo Y., Budygin E.A., Morgan D., Roberts D.C., Jones S.R. Fast onset of dopamine uptake inhibition by intravenous cocaine. *Eur. J. Neurosci.* 20:2838, 2004.

5. Gingrich J., Caron M. Recent advances in the molecular biology of dopamine receptors. *Annu. Rev. Neurosci.* 16:299, 1993.

6. Karler R., Calder L., Thai L., Bedingfield J. A dopaminergic-glutamatergic basis for the action of amphetamine and cocaine. *Brain Res.* 8:658, 1994.

7. Trujillo K., Akil H. Excitatory amino acids and drugs of abuse: a role for *N*-methyl-D-aspartate receptors in drug tolerance, sensitization and physical dependence. *Drug Alcohol Depend.* 38:139, 1995.

8. Chen N., Reith M. Autoregulation and monoamine interactions in the ventral tegmental area in the absence and presence of cocaine: a microdialysis study in freely moving rats. *J. Pharmacol. Exp. Ther.* 271:1597, 1994.

9. DiChiara G., Imperato A. Opposite effects of my and kappa opiate agonists on dopamine release in the nucleus accumbens and in the dorsal caudate of freely moving rats. *J. Pharmacol.* 244:1067, 1988.

10. Spanagel R., Herz A., Shippenberg T. The effects of opioid peptides on dopamine release in the nucleus accumbens: an *in vivo* microdialysis study. *J. Neurochem.* 55:1734, 1990.

11. Spanagel R., Herz A., Shippenberg T. Opposing tonically active endogenous opioid systems modulate the mesolimbic dopaminergic pathway. *Proc. Natl. Acad. Sci. U.S.A.* 89:2046, 1992.

12. Vaughan R.A., Parnas M.L., Gaffaney J.D. et al. Affinity labeling the dopamine transporter ligand binding site. *J. Neurosci. Methods.* 143:33, 2005.

13. Rocha B.A., Fumagalli F., Gainetdinov R.R. et al. Cocaine self-administration in dopamine-transporter knockout mice. *Nat. Neurosci.* 1:132, 1998.

14. Sora I., Hall F.S., Andrews A.M. et al. Molecular mechanisms of cocaine reward: combined dopamine and serotonin transporter knockouts eliminate cocaine place preference. *Proc. Natl. Acad. Sci. U.S.A.* 98:5300, 2001.

15. Alburges M., Narang N., Wamsley J. Alterations in the dopaminergic receptor system after chronic administration of cocaine. *Synapse.* 14:314, 1993.

16. Wilson J., Nobrega J., Carroll M. et al. Heterogenous subregional binding patterns of ^{3}H-WIN 35,428 and ^{3}H-GBR 12,935 are differentially regulated by chronic cocaine self-administration. *J. Neurosci.* 14:2966, 1994.

17. Hitri A., Little K., Ellinwood D. Effect of cocaine on dopamine transporter receptors depends on routes of chronic cocaine administration. *Neuropsychopharmacology.* 14:205, 1996.

18. Aloyo V., Pazalski P., Kirifides A., Harvey J. Behavioral sensitization, behavioral tolerance, and increased [^{3}H]WIN 35,428 binding in rabbit caudate nucleus after repeated injections of cocaine. *Pharmacol. Biochem. Behav.* 52:335, 1995.

19. Letchworth S.R., Nader M.A., Smith H.R., Friedman D.P., Porrino L.J. Progression of changes in dopamine transporter binding site density as a result of cocaine self-administration in rhesus monkeys. *J. Neurosci.* 21:2799, 2001.

20. Little K., McLaughlin D., Zhang L. et al. Brain dopamine transporter messenger RNA and binding sites in cocaine users. *Arch. Gen. Psychiatry.* 55:793, 1998.

21. Little K., Zhang L., Desmond T., Frey K., Dalack G., Cassin B. Striatal dopaminergic abnormalities in human cocaine users. *Am. J. Psychiatry.* 156:238, 1999.

22. Little K., Kirkman J., Carroll F., Clark T., Duncan G. Cocaine use increases [^{3}H]WIN 35, 428 binding sites in human striatum. *Brain Res.* 628:17, 1993.

23. Staley J., Basile M., Wetli C. et al. Differential regulation of the dopamine transporter in cocaine overdose deaths. *Natl. Inst. Drug Abuse Res. Monogr.* 32, 1994.

24. Staley J., Hearn W., Ruttenber A., Wetli C., Mash D. High affinity cocaine recognition sites on the dopamine transporter are elevated in fatal cocaine overdose victims. *Pharmacol. Exp. Ther.* 271:1678, 1994.

25. Staley J., Wetli C., Ruttenber A., Dearn W., Mash D. Altered dopaminergic synaptic markers in cocaine psychosis and sudden death. *Natl. Inst. Drug Abuse Res. Monogr.* 153:491, 1995.

26. Hurd Y., Herkenham M. Molecular alterations in the neostriatum of human cocaine addicts. *Synapse.* 13:357, 1993.

27. Wilson J., Levey A., Bergeron C. et al. Striatal dopamine, dopamine transporter, and vesicular monoamine transporter in chronic cocaine users. *Ann. Neurol.* 40:428, 1996.

28. Kunko P.M., Loeloff R.J., Izenwasser S. Chronic administration of the selective dopamine uptake inhibitor GBR 12,909, but not cocaine, produces marked decreases in dopamine transporter density. *Naunyn Schmiedeberg's Arch. Pharmacol.* 356:562, 1997.

29. Malison R. SPECT imaging of DA transporters in cocaine dependence with [^{123}I]B-CIT. *Natl. Inst. Drug Abuse Res. Monogr.* 152, 1995.

30. Mash D., Pablo J., Ouyang Q., Hearn W., Izenwasser S. Dopamine transport function is elevated in cocaine users. *J. Neurochem..* 81:292, 2002.

31. Daws L., Callaghan P., Morom J. et al. Cocaine increases dopamine uptake and cell surface expression of dopamine transporters. *Biochem. Biophys. Res. Commun.* 290:1545, 2002.

32. Little K., Elmer L., Zhong H., Scheys J., Zhang L. Cocaine induction of dopamine transporter trafficking to the plasma membrane. *Mol. Pharmacol.* 61:436, 2002.

33. Chiat L. Reinforcing and subjective effects of methylphenidate in humans. *Behav. Pharmacol.* 5:281, 1994.

34. Pogun S., Scheffel U., Kuhar M. Cocaine displaces [^{3}H]WIN 35,428 binding to dopamine uptake sites *in vivo*, more rapidly than mazindol or GBR 12,909. *Eur. J. Pharmacol.* 198:203, 1991.

35. Stathis M., Sheffel U., Lever S., Boja J., Carroll F., Kuhar M. Rate of binding of various inhibitors at the dopamine transporter *in vivo*. *Psychopharmacology.* 119:376, 1995.

36. Volkow N., Wang G., Fowler J. et al. Methylphenidate and cocaine have a similar *in vivo* potency to block dopamine transporters in the human brain. *Life Sci.* 65:7, 1999.

37. Volkow N., Ding Y., Fowler J. et al. Is methylphenidate like cocaine? *Arch. Gen. Psychiatry.* 52:456, 1995.

38. Volkow N., Fowler J., Wang G. Imaging studies on the role of dopamine in cocaine reinforcement and addiction in humans. *J. Psychopharmacol.* 13:337, 1999.

39. Tsukada H., Harada N., Nishiyama S., Ohba H., Kakiuchi T. Dose-response and duration effects of acute administrations of cocaine and GBR12909 on dopamine synthesis and transporter in the conscious monkey brain: PET studies combined with microdialysis. *Brain Res.* 860:141, 2000.

40. Rothman R., Glowaw J. A review of the effects of dopaminergic agents on human, animals, and drug-seeking behavior, and its implications for medication development. *Mol. Neurobiol.* 10:1, 1995.

41. Rothman R. High affinity dopamine reuptake inhibitors as potential cocaine antagonists: a strategy for drug development. *Life Sci.* 46:PL17, 1990.

42. Baumann M., Char G., Costa B.D., Rice K., Rothman R. GBR 12909 attenuates cocaine-induced activation of mesolimbic dopamine neurons in the rat. *J. Pharmacol. Exp. Ther.* 271:1216, 1994.

43. Schenk S. Effects of GBR 12909, WIN 35,428 and indatraline on cocaine self-administration and cocaine seeking in rats. *Psychopharmacology* (Berlin). 160:263, 2002.

44. Glowa J., Fantegrossi W., Lewis D., Matecka D., Rice K., Rothman R. Sustained decrease in cocaine-maintained responding in rhesus monkeys with 1-[2]-bis(4-flourophenyl)methoxy[ethyl]-4-(3-hydroxy-3-phenylpropyl)piperazinyldecanoate, a long-acting ester derivative of GBR 12909. *J. Med. Chem.* 39:4689, 1996.

45. Villemagne V., Rothman R., Yokoi F. et al. Doses of GBR 12909 that suppress cocaine self-administration in nonhuman primates substantially occupy dopamine transporters as measured by [^{11}C]WIN 35,428 PET scans. *Synapse.* 32:44, 1999.

46. Howell L., Wilcox K. The dopamine transporter and cocaine medication development: drug self-administration in nonhuman primates. *J. Pharmacol. Exp. Ther.* 298:1, 2001.

47. Dworkin S.I., Lambert P., Sizemore G.M., Carroll F.I., Kuhar M.J. RTI-113 administration reduces cocaine self-administration at high occupancy of dopamine transporter. *Synapse.* 30:49, 1998.

48. Sizemore G.M., Davies H M., Martin T.J., Smith J.E. Effects of 2beta-propanoyl-3beta-(4-tolyl)-tropane (PTT) on the self-administration of cocaine, heroin, and cocaine/heroin combinations in rats. *Drug Alcohol Depend.* 73:259, 2004.

49. Roberts D.C., Jungersmith K.R., Phelan R., Gregg T.M., Davies H.M. Effect of HD-23, a potent long acting cocaine-analog, on cocaine self-administration in rats. *Psychopharmacology* (Berlin). 167:386, 2003.

50. Giros B., Wang Y., Sutter S., McLeskey S., Pfil C., Caron M. Delineation of discrete domains for substrate, cocaine, and tricyclic antidepressant interactions using chimeric dopamine-norepinephrine transporters. *J. Biol. Chem.* 15985, 1994.

51. Buck K., Amara S. Chimeric dopamine-norepinephrine transporters delineate structural domains influencing selectivity for catecholamines and 1-methyl-4-phenylpyridinium. *Proc. Natl. Acad. Sci. U.S.A.* 91:12584, 1994.

52. Christenson J. Radioimmunoassay for benzoyl ecogine. U.S. patent 4. 102:979, 1978.

53. Leute R., Bolz G. Nitrogen derivates of benzoyl ecgonine. U.S. patent 3888:866, 1975.

54. Mule S., Jukofshy D., Kogan M., Pace A., De Verebey K. Evaluation of the radioimmunoassay for benzoylecgonine (a cocaine metabolite) in human urine. *Clin. Chem.* 23:796, 1977.

55. Bagasra O., Forman L., Howeedy A., Whittle P. A potential vaccine for cocaine abuse prophylaxis. *Immunopharmacology.* 23:173, 1992.

56. Carrera M., Ashley J., Parsons L., Wirschung P., Koob G. Suppression of psycho-active effects of cocaine by active immunization. *Nature.* 378:727, 1995.

57. Slusher B., Jackson P. A shot in the arm for cocaine addiction. *Nat. Med.* 2:26, 1996.

58. Landry D., Zhao K., Yang G.-Q., Glickman M., Georgiadis T. Antibody-catalyzed degradation of cocaine. *Science.* 259:1899, 1993.

59. Basmadjian G., Singh S., Sastrodjojo B. et al. Generation of polyclonal catalytic antibodies against cocaine using transition state analogs of cocaine conjugated to diphtheria toxoid. *Chem. Pharm. Bull.* 43:1902, 1995.

60. Berkman C., Underiner G., Cahsman J. Synthesis of an immunogenic template for the generation of catalytic antibodies for (–) cocaine hydrolysis. *J. Org. Chem.* 61:5686, 1996.

61. Rocio M., Carrera A., Ashley J. et al. Cocaine vaccines: Antibody protection against relapse in a rat model. *PNAS.* 97:6202, 2000.

62. Rocio M., Carrera A., Ashley J., Wirsching P., Koob G., Janda K. A second-generation vaccine protects against the psychoactive effects of cocaine. *PNAS.* 98:1988, 2001.

63. Mets B., Winger G., Cabrera C. et al. A catalytic antibody against cocaine prevents cocaine's reinforcing and toxic effects in rats. *Proc. Natl. Acad. Sci. U.S.A.* 95:10176, 1998.

64. Self D. Cocaine abuse takes a shot. *Nature.* 378:666, 1995.

65. Kosten T., Rosen M., Bond J. et al. Human therapeutic cocaine vaccine: safety and immunogenicity. *Vaccine.* 20:1196, 2002.

66. Kosten T., Owens S.M. Immunotherapy for the treatment of drug abuse. *Pharmacol. Ther.* 108:76, 2005.

67. Martell B.A., Mitchell E., Poling J., Gonsai K., Kosten T.R. Vaccine pharmacotherapy for the treatment of cocaine dependence. *Biol. Psychiatry.* 58:158, 2005.

68. Robledo P., Maldonado-Lopez R., Koob G. Role of the dopamine receptors in the nucleus accumbens in the rewarding properties of cocaine. *Ann. N.Y. Acad. Sci.* 654:509, 1992.

69. Pulvirenti L., Koob G. Dopamine receptor agonists, partial agonists and psychostimulant addiction. *Trends Pharmacol. Sci.* 15:374, 1994.

70. Ranaldi R., Beninger R. The effects of systemic and intracerebral injections of D_1 and D_2 agonists on brain stimulation reward. *Brain Res.* 651:283, 1994.

71. Caine S., Heinrichs S., Coffin V., Koob G. Effects of the dopamine D-1 antagonist SCH23390 microinjected into the accumbens, amygdala or striatum on cocaine self-administration in the rat. *Brain Res.* 692:47, 1995.

72. Sanchez C.J., Bailie T.M., Wu W.R., Li N., Sorg B.A. Manipulation of dopamine d1-like receptor activation in the rat medial prefrontal cortex alters stress- and cocaine-induced reinstatement of conditioned place preference behavior. *Neuroscience.* 119:497, 2003.

73. Anderson S.M., Bari A.A., Pierce R.C. Administration of the D1-like dopamine receptor antagonist SCH-23390 into the medial nucleus accumbens shell attenuates cocaine priming-induced reinstatement of drug-seeking behavior in rats. *Psychopharmacology* (Berlin). 168:132, 2003.

74. Tella S. Differential blockade of chronic versus acute effects of intravenous cocaine by dopamine receptor antagonists. *Pharmacol. Biochem. Behav.* 48:151, 1994.

75. Shippenberg T., Heidbreder C. Sensitization to the conditioned rewarding effects of cocaine: pharmacological and temporal characteristics. *J. Pharmacol. Exp. Ther.* 273:808, 1995.

76. Hubner C., Moreton J. Effect of selective D_1 and D_2 dopamine antagonists on cocaine self-administration in the rat. *Psychopharmacology.* 105:151, 1991.

77. Woolverton W. Effects of D_1 and D_2 dopamine antagonists on the self-administration of cocaine and piribedil by rhesus monkeys. *Pharmacol. Biochem. Behav.* 24, 1986.

78. Koob G., Le H., Creese I. The D_1 dopamine antagonist SCH 23390 increases cocaine self-administration in the rat. *Neurosci. Lett.* 79:315, 1987.

79. Eglimez Y., Jung M., Lane J., Emmett-Oglesby M. Dopamine release during cocaine self-administration in the rat: effect of SCH 23390. *Brain Res.* 701:142, 1995.

80. Caine S., Koob G. Effects of dopamine D-1 and D-2 antagonists on cocaine self-administration under different schedules of reinforcement in the rat. *J. Pharmacol. Exp. Ther.* 270:209, 1994.

81. Khroyan T.V., Platt D.M., Rowlett J.K., Spealman R.D. Attenuation of relapse to cocaine seeking by dopamine D1 receptor agonists and antagonists in non-human primates. *Psychopharmacology* (Berlin). 168:124, 2003.

82. Alleweireldt A.T., Kirschner K.F., Blake C.B., Neisewander J.L. D1-receptor drugs and cocaine-seeking behavior: investigation of receptor mediation and behavioral disruption in rats. *Psychopharmacology* (Berlin). 168:109, 2003.

83. Meador-Woodruff J., Little K., Damask S., Mansour P., Watson S. Effects of cocaine on dopamine receptor gene expression: A study in the postmortem human brain. *Biol. Psychiatry.* 34:348, 1993.

84. Laurier L., Corrigall C., George S. Dopamine receptor density, sensitivity and mRNA levels are altered following self-administration of cocaine in the rat. *Brain Res.* 634:31, 1994.

85. Zhang D., Zhang L., Lou D.W., Nakabeppu Y., Zhang J., Xu M. The dopamine D1 receptor is a critical mediator for cocaine-induced gene expression. *J. Neurochem.* 82:1453, 2002.

86. Unterwald E.M., Kreek M.J., Cuntapay M. The frequency of cocaine administration impacts cocaine-induced receptor alterations. *Brain Res.* 900:103, 2001.

87. Peris J., Boyson S., Cass W. et al. Persistence of neurochemical changes in dopamine systems after repeated cocaine administration. *J. Pharmacol. Exp. Ther.* 253:35, 1990.

88. Claye L., Akunne H., Davis M., DeMattos S., Soliman K. Behavioral and neurochemical changes in the dopaminergic system after repeated cocaine administration. *Mol. Neurobiol.* 11:55, 1995.

89. Zeigler S., Lipton J., Toga A., Ellison G. Continuous cocaine administration produces persisting changes in the brain neurochemistry and behavior. *Brain Res.* 552:27, 1991.

90. Nader M.A., Daunais J.B., Moore T. et al. Effects of cocaine self-administration on striatal dopamine systems in rhesus monkeys: initial and chronic exposure. *Neuropsychopharmacology.* 27:35, 2002.

91. Henry D., White F. Repeated cocaine administration causes persistent enhancement of D_1 dopamine receptor sensitivity within the rat nucleus accumbens. *J. Pharmacol. Exp. Ther.* 258:882, 1991.

92. Henry D.J., White F.J. The persistence of behavioral sensitization to cocaine parallels enhanced inhibition of nucleus accumbens neurons. *J. Neurosci.* 15:6287, 1995.

93. Shippenberg T., Heidbreder C. Kappa opioid receptor agonists prevent sensitization to the rewarding effects of cocaine. *NIDA Res. Monogr.* 153:456, 1994.

94. Shippenberg T., LeFevour A., Heidbreder C. K-opioid receptor agonists prevent sensitization to the conditioned rewarding effects of cocaine. *J. Pharmacol. Exp. Ther.* 276:545, 1996.

95. Spyraki C., Sealfon S. Regulation of dopamine D2 receptor mRNA expression in the olfactory tubercle by cocaine. *Mol. Brain Res.* 19:313, 1993.

96. Przewlocka B., Lason W. Adaptive changes in the proenkephalin and D_2 dopamine receptor mRNA expression after chronic cocaine in the nucleus accumbens and striatum of the rat. *Neuropsychopharmacology.* 5:464, 1995.

97. Unterwald E., Ho A., Rubenfeld J., Kreek M. Time course of the development of behavioral sensitization and dopamine receptor up-regulation during binge cocaine administration. *J. Pharmacol. Exp. Ther.* 270:1387, 1994.

98. Volkow N., Fowler J., Wolf A. et al. Effects of chronic cocaine abuse on postsynaptic dopamine receptors. *Am. J. Psychiatry.* 147:719, 1990.

99. Worsley J.N., Moszczynska A., Falardeau P. et al. Dopamine D1 receptor protein is elevated in nucleus accumbens of human, chronic methamphetamine users. *Mol. Psychiatry.* 5:664, 2000.

100. Nader M., Mach R. Self-administration of the dopamine D_3 agonist 7-OH-DPAT in rhesus monkeys is modified by prior cocaine exposure. *Psychopharmacology.* 125:13, 1996.

101. Acri J., Carter S., Alling K. et al. Assessment of cocaine-like discriminative stimulus effects of dopamine D_3 receptor ligands. *Eur. J. Pharmacol.* 281:R7, 1995.

102. Mallet P., Beninger R. 7-OH-DPAT produced place conditioning in rats. *Eur. J. Pharmacol.* 261:R5, 1994.

103. Lamas X., Negus S., Nader M., Mello N. Effects of the putative dopamine D_3 receptor agonist 7-OH-DPAT in rhesus monkeys trained to discriminate cocaine from saline. *Psychopharmacology.* 124:306, 1996.

104. Mash D.C., Staley J.K. D3 dopamine and kappa opioid receptor alterations in human brain of cocaine-overdose victims. *Ann. N.Y. Acad. Sci.* 877:507, 1999.

105. Staley J., Mash D. Adaptive increase in D_3 dopamine receptors in the brain reward circuits of human cocaine fatalities. *J. Neurosci.* 16:6100, 1996.

106. Wallace D., Mactutus C., Booze R. Repeated intravenous cocaine administrations: locomotor activity and dopamine D_2/D_3 receptors. *Synapse.* 19, 1996.

107. Neisewander J.L., Fuchs R.A., Tran-Nguyen L.T., Weber S.M., Coffey G.P., Joyce J.N. Increases in dopamine D3 receptor binding in rats receiving a cocaine challenge at various time points after cocaine self-administration: implications for cocaine-seeking behavior. *Neuropsychopharmacology.* 29:1479, 2004.

108. Le Foll B., Frances H., Diaz J., Schwartz J.C., Sokoloff P. Role of the dopamine D3 receptor in reactivity to cocaine-associated cues in mice. *Eur. J. Neurosci.* 15:2016, 2002.

109. Landwehrmeyer B., Mengod G., Palacios J. Differential visualization of dopamine D_2 and D_3 receptor sites in the rat brain. A comparative study using in situ hybridization histochemistry and ligand binding autoradiography. *Eur. J. Neurosci.* 5:145, 1993.

110. Landwehrmeyer B., Mengod G., Palacios J. Dopamine D_3 receptor mRNA and binding site in human brain. *Mol. Brain Res.* 18:187, 1993.

111. Meador-Woodruff J., Little K., Damask S., Watson S. Effects of cocaine on D_3 and D_4 receptor expression in the human striatum. *Biol. Psych.* 38:263, 1995.

112. Le Foll B., Diaz J., Sokoloff P. A single cocaine exposure increases BDNF and D3 receptor expression: implications for drug-conditioning. *Neuroreport.* 16:175, 2005.

113. Cox B., Rosser M., Kozlowski M., Duwe K., Neve R., Neve K. Regulation and functional characterization of a rat recombinant dopamine D_3 receptor. *Synapse.* 21:1, 1995.

114. Fishburn C., Belleli D., David C., Carmon S., Fuchs S. A novel short isoform of the D_3 dopamine receptor generated by alternative splicing in the third cytoplasmic loop. *J. Biol. Chem.* 268:5872, 1993.

115. Sokoloff P., Giros B., Martres M. et al. Localization and function of the D_3 dopamine receptor. *Arzneim. Forsch. Drug Res.* 42:224, 1992.

116. Grundt P., Carlson E.E., Cao J., et al. Novel heterocyclic trans olefin analogues of N-{4-[4-(2,3-dichlorophenyl)piperazin-1-yl]butyl}arylcarboxamides as selective probes with high affinity for the dopamine D_3 receptor. *J. Med. Chem.* 48:839, 2005.

117. DeWit H., Wise R. Blockade of cocaine reinforcement in rats with the dopamine receptor blocker pimozide, but not the noradrenergic blockers phentolamine and phenobenzamine. *Can. J. Psychol.* 31:195, 1977.

118. Roberts D., Vickers G. Atypical neuroleptics increase self-administration of cocaine: an evaluation of a behavioral screen for antipsychotic activity. *Psychopharmacology.* 82:1135, 1984.

119. Wilson M., Schuster C. The effects of chlorpromazine on psychomotor stimulant self-administration in rhesus monkeys. *Psychopharmacologia.* 26:115, 1972.

120. Johansen C., Kandel D., Bonese K. The effect of perphenazine on self-administration behavior. *Pharmacol. Biochem. Behav.* 4:427, 1976.

121. Gawin F., Allen D., Humblestone B. Outpatient treatment of "crack" cocaine smoking with flupentixol decanoate. *Arch. Gen. Psychiatry.* 46:322, 1989.

122. Gawin F. Neuroleptic reduction of cocaine-induced paranoia, but not euphoria? *Psychopharmacology.* 90:142, 1986.

123. Crosby R., Halikas J., Carlson G. Pharmacotherapeutic interventions for cocaine abuse: present practices and future directions. *J. Addict. Dis.* 10:13, 1991.

124. Grabowski J., Rhoades H., Silverman P. et al. Risperidone for the treatment of cocaine dependence: randomized, double-blind trial. *J. Clin. Psychopharmacol.* 20:305, 2000.

125. Roberts D., Ranaldi R. Effect of dopaminergic drugs on cocaine reinforcement. *Clin. Neuropharmacol.* 18:S84, 1995.

126. Malcolm R., Hutto B., Philips J., Ballenger J. Pergolide mesylate treatment of cocaine withdrawal. *J. Clin. Psychiatry.* 52:39, 1991.

127. Dackis C., Golf M., Sweeney D., Byron J., Climko R. Single dose bromocriptine reverses cocaine craving. *Psychiatry Res.* 20:261, 1987.

128. Tennant F., Sagherian A. Double-blind comparison of amantadine and bromocriptine for ambulatory withdrawal from cocaine dependence. *Arch. Intern. Med.* 147:109, 1987.

129. Handelsman L., Chordia P., Escovar I., Marion I., Lowinson J. Amantadine for treatment of cocaine dependence in methadone-maintained patients. *Am. J. Psychiatry.* 145:533, 1988.

130. Self D., Barnhart W., Lehman D., Nestler E. Opposite modulation of cocaine-seeking behavior by D1- and D2-like dopamine receptor agonists. *Science.* 271:1586, 1996.

131. Shoptaw S., Watson D.W., Reiber C. et al. Randomized controlled pilot trial of cabergoline, hydergine and levodopa/carbidopa: Los Angeles Cocaine Rapid Efficacy Screening Trial (CREST). *Addiction.* 100(Suppl. 1):78, 2005.

132. Xi Z.X., Gilbert J.G., Pak A.C., Ashby C.R., Jr., Heidbreder C.A., Gardner E.L. Selective dopamine D3 receptor antagonism by SB-277011A attenuates cocaine reinforcement as assessed by progressive-ratio and variable-cost-variable-payoff fixed-ratio cocaine self-administration in rats. *Eur. J. Neurosci.* 21:3427, 2005.

133. Gilbert J.G., Newman A.H., Gardner E.L., et al. Acute administration of SB-277011A, NGB 2904, or BP 897 inhibits cocaine cue-induced reinstatement of drug-seeking behavior in rats: role of dopamine D_3 receptors. *Synapse.* 57:17, 2005.

134. Xi Z.X., Gilbert J., Campos A.C., et al. Blockade of mesolimbic dopamine D_3 receptors inhibits stress-induced reinstatement of cocaine-seeking in rats. *Psychopharmacology* (Berlin). 176:57, 2004.

135. Le Foll B., Schwartz J.C., Sokoloff P. Dopamine D_3 receptor agents as potential new medications for drug addiction. *Eur. Psychiatry.* 15:140, 2000.

136. Pilla M., Perachon S., Sautel F. et al. Selective inhibition of cocaine-seeking behaviour by a partial dopamine D_3 receptor agonist. *Nature.* 400:371, 1999.

137. Wood M.D., Boyfield I., Nash D.J., Jewitt F.R., Avenell K.Y., Riley G.J. Evidence for antagonist activity of the dopamine D_3 receptor partial agonist, BP 897, at human dopamine D_3 receptor. *Eur. J. Pharmacol.* 407:47, 2000.

138. Gorelick D.A., Gardner E.L., Xi Z.X. Agents in development for the management of cocaine abuse. *Drugs.* 64:1547, 2004.

139. Unterwald E.M. Regulation of opioid receptors by cocaine. *Ann. N.Y. Acad. Sci.* 937:74, 2001.

140. Clark J., Liu L., Price M., Hersh B., Edelson M., Pasternak G. Kappa opiate receptor multiplicity: evidence for two U50-488-sensitive K_1 subtypes and a novel K_3 subtype. *J. Pharmacol. Exp. Ther.* 251:461, 1989.

141. Rothman R., France C., Bykov V. et al. Pharmacological activities of optically pure enantiomers of the K opioid agonist, U50,488 and its *cis* diastereomer: evidence for three K receptor subtypes. *Eur. J. Pharmacol.* 167:345, 1989.

142. Rothman R., Bykov V., Coasta R.D., Jacobsen A., Rice K., Brady L. Evidence for four opioid kappa binding sites in guinea pig brain. Presented at International Narcotics Research Conference (INRC) '89. 9, 1990.

143. Wollemann M., Benhye S., Simon J. The kappa-opioid receptor: evidence for the different subtypes. *Life Sci.* 52:599, 1993.

144. Nishi M., Takeshima H., Fukada K., Kato S., Mori K. cDNA cloning and pharmacological characterization of an opioid receptor with high affinities for kappa-subtype selective ligands. *FEBS Lett.* 330:77, 1993.

145. Pan G., Standifer K., Pasternak G. Cloning and functional characterization through antisense mapping of a K_3-related opioid receptor. *Mol. Pharmacol.* 47:1180, 1995.

146. Raynor K., Kong H., Chen Y. et al. Pharmacological characterization of the cloned kappa- delta- and mu-opioid receptors. *Mol. Pharmacol.* 45:330, 1993.

147. Simonin F., Gaveriaux-Ruff C., Befort K. et al. k-Opioid receptor in humans: cDNA and genomic cloning, chromosomal assignment, functional expression, pharmacology, and expression pattern in the central nervous system. *Proc. Natl. Acad. Sci. U.S.A.* 92:7006, 1995.

148. Quirion R., Pilapil C., Magnan J. Localization of kappa opioid receptor binding sites in human forebrain using [^{3}H]U69,593: Comparison with [^{3}H]bremazocine. *Cell Mol. Neurobiol.* 7:303, 1987.

149. Staley J., Rothman R., Partilla J. et al. Cocaine upregulates kappa opioid receptors in human striatum. *Natl. Inst. Drug Abuse Res. Monogr.* 162:234, 1996.

150. Itzhak Y. Differential regulation of brain opioid receptors following repeated cocaine administration to guinea pigs. *Drug Alcohol Depend.* 3:53, 1993.

151. Ni Q., Xu H., Partilla J., Costa B.D., Rice K., Rothman R. Selective labeling of K_2 opioid receptors in rat brain by [125I]IOXY: interactions of opioid peptides and other drugs with multiple K_{2a} binding sites. *Peptides.* 14:1279, 1993.

152. Ni Q., Xu H., Partilla J., et al. Opioid peptide receptor studies. Interaction of opioid peptides and other drugs with four subtypes of the K_2 receptor in guinea pig brain. *Peptides.* 16:1083, 1995.

153. Hammer R. Cocaine alters opiate receptor binding in critical brain reward regions. *Synapse.* 3:55, 1989.

154. Unterwald E., Rubenfeld J., Kreek M. Repeated cocaine administration upregulates kappa and mu but not gamma opioid receptors. *Neuroreport.* 5:1613, 1994.

155. Collins S.L., Kunko P.M., Ladenheim B., Cadet J.L., Carroll F.I., Izenwasser S. Chronic cocaine increases kappa-opioid receptor density: lack of effect by selective dopamine uptake inhibitors *Synapse.* 45:153, 2002.

156. Spangler R., Bo A., Zhou Y., Maggos C., Yuferov V., Kreek M. Regulation of kappa opioid receptor mRNA in the rat brain by "binge" pattern cocaine administration and correlation with preprodynorphin mRNA. *Mol. Brain Res.* 38:71, 1996.

157. Rosin A., Lindholm S., Franck J., Georgieva J. Downregulation of kappa opioid receptor mRNA levels by chronic ethanol and repetitive cocaine in rat ventral tegmentum and nucleus accumbens. *Neurosci. Lett.* 275:1, 1999.

158. Staley J.K., Rothman R.B., Rice K.C., Partilla J., Mash D.C. Kappa2 opioid receptors in limbic areas of the human brain are upregulated by cocaine in fatal overdose victims. *J. Neurosci.* 17:8225, 1997.

159. Broadbent J., Gaspard T., Dworkin S. Assessment of the discriminative stimulus effects of cocaine in the rat: lack of interaction with opioids. *Pharmacol. Biochem. Behav.* 51:379, 1995.

160. Ukai M., Mori E., Kameyama T. Effects of centrally administered neuropeptides on discriminative stimulus properties of cocaine in the rat. *Pharmacol. Biochem. Behav.* 51:705, 1995.

161. Spealman R., Bergman J. Modulation of the discriminative stimulus effects of cocaine by mu and kappa opioids. *J. Pharmacol. Exp. Ther.* 261:607, 1992.

162. Shippenberg T., Herz A., Spanagel R., Bals-Kubik R., Stein C. Conditioning of opioid reinforcement: Neuroanatomical and neurochemical substrates. *Ann. N.Y. Acad. Sci.* 654:347, 1992.

163. Glick S., Maisonneuve I., Raucci J., Archer S. Kappa opioid inhibition of morphine and cocaine self-administration in rats. *Brain Res.* 681:147, 1995.

164. Heidbreder C., Goldberg S., Shippenberg T. The kappa-opioid receptor agonist U-69,593 attenuates cocaine-induced behavioral sensitization in the rat. *Brain Res.* 616:335, 1993.

165. Schenk S., Partridge B., Shippenberg T.S. U69593, a kappa-opioid agonist, decreases cocaine self-administration and decreases cocaine-produced drug-seeking. *Psychopharmacology* (Berlin). 144:339, 1999.

166. Schenk S., Partridge B., Shippenberg T.S. Reinstatement of extinguished drug-taking behavior in rats: effect of the kappa-opioid receptor agonist, U69593. *Psychopharmacology* (Berlin). 151:85, 2000.

167. Mellow N., Kamein J., Lukas S., Mendelson J., Drieze J., Sholar J. Effects of intermittent buprenorphine administration of cocaine self-administration by rhesus monkeys. *J. Pharmacol. Exp. Ther.* 264:530, 1993.

168. Comer S., Lac S., Curtis L., Carroll M. Effects of buprenorphine and naltrexone on reinstatement of cocaine-reinforced responding in rats. *J. Pharmacol. Exp. Ther.* 267:1470, 1993.

169. Cosgrove K., Carroll M. Effects of bremazocine on self-administration of smoked cocaine base and orally delivered ethanol, phencyclidine, saccharin, and food in rhesus monkeys: a behavioral economic analysis. *J. Pharmacol. Exp. Ther.* 301:Jun 2002, 2002.

170. Mello N.K., Negus S.S. Effects of kappa opioid agonists on cocaine- and food-maintained responding by rhesus monkeys. *J. Pharmacol. Exp. Ther.* 286:812, 1998.

171. Walsh S.L., Geter-Douglas B., Strain E.C., Bigelow G.E. Enadoline and butorphanol: evaluation of kappa-agonists on cocaine pharmacodynamics and cocaine self-administration in humans. *J. Pharmacol. Exp. Ther.* 299:147, 2001.

172. Kosten T. Pharmacological approaches to cocaine dependence. *Clin. Neuropharmacol.* 15(Suppl. 70A), 1992.

173. Fudala P., Johnson R., Jaffe J. Outpatient comparison of buprenorphine and methadone maintenance. II. Effects of cocaine usage, retention time in study and missed clinical visits. In Harrison L., Ed. Problems of Drug Dependence. *Natl. Inst. Mental Health Res. Monogr.* 105:587, 1991.

174. Wesson D.R. Buprenorphine in the treatment of opiate dependence: its pharmacology and social context of use in the U.S. *J. Psychoactive Drugs.* Suppl. 2:119, 2004.

175. Montoya I.D., Gorelick D.A., Preston K.L. et al. Randomized trial of buprenorphine for treatment of concurrent opiate and cocaine dependence. *Clin. Pharmacol. Ther.* 75:34, 2004.

176. Pfeiffer A., Brandt V., Herz A. Psychotomimesis mediated by kappa opiate receptors. *Science.* 233:774, 1986.

177. Kumor K., Haertzen C., Johnson R., Kocher T., Jasinski D. Human psychopharmacology of ketocyclazocine as compared with cyclazocine, morphine and placebo. *J. Pharmacol. Exp. Ther.* 238:960, 1986.

178. Herz A. Implications of the multiplicity of opioid receptors for the problem of addiction. *Drug Alcohol Depend.* 25:125, 1990.

179. Koe B. Molecular geometry of inhibitors of the uptake of catecholamines and serotonin in synaptosomal preparations of rat brain. *J. Pharmacol. Exp. Ther.* 199:649, 1976.

180. Pitts D., Marwah J. Cocaine modulation of central momoaminergic neurotransmission. *Pharmacol. Biochem. Behav.* 26:453, 1987.

181. Cunningham K., Lakoski J. The interaction of cocaine with serotonin dural raphe neurons. Single unit extracellular recording studies. *Neuropsychopharmacology.* 3:41, 1990.

182. Cunningham K., Paris J., Goeders N. Chronic cocaine enhances serotonin autoregulation and serotonin uptake binding. *Synapse.* 11:112, 1992.

183. Reith M., Fischette C. Sertraline and cocaine-inducted locomotion in mice. II. Chronic studies. *Psychopharmacology.* 103:306, 1991.

184. Reith M., Wiener H., Fischette C. Sertraline and cocaine-induced locomotion in mice. I. Acute studies. *Psychopharmacology.* 103:306, 1991.

185. Aronson S., Black J., McDougle C. et al. Serotonergic mechanisms of cocaine effects in humans. *Psychopharmacology.* 119:179, 1995.

186. Zeidonis D., Kosten T. Depression as a prognostic factor for pharmacological treatment of cocaine dependence. *Psychopharmacol. Bull.* 27:337, 1991.

187. Parsons L., Koob G., Weiss F. Serotonin dysfunction in the nucleus accumbens of rats during withdrawal after unlimited access to intravenous cocaine. *J. Pharmacol. Exp. Ther.* 274:1182, 1995.

188. Galloway M. Regulation of dopamine and serotonin synthesis by acute administration of cocaine. *Synapse.* 6:63, 1990.

189. Spealman R. Modification of behavioral effect of cocaine by selective serotonin and dopamine uptake inhibitors in squirrel monkeys. *Psychopharmacology.* 112:93, 1993.

190. Carroll M., Lac S., Asencio M., Kragh R. Fluoxetine reduces intravenous cocaine self-administration in rats. *Pharmacol. Biochem. Behav.* 35:237, 1990.

191. Richardson N., Roberts D. Fluoxetine pre-treatment reduced breaking points on a progressive ratio schedule reinforced by intravenous cocaine administration in the rat. *Life Sci.* 49:833, 1991.

192. Lyness W., Friedle N., Moore K. Increased self-administration of d-amphetamine, self-administration. *Pharmacol. Biochem. Behav.* 12:937, 1980.

193. Walsh S., Preston K., Sullivan J., Fromme R., Bigelow G. Fluoxetine alters the effects of intravenous cocaine in humans. *J. Clin. Psychopharmacol.* 14:396, 1994.

194. Batki S., Washburn A., Manfredi L. et al. Fluoxetine in primary and secondary cocaine dependence: outcome using quantitative benzoylecgonine concentration. *Natl. Inst. Drug Abuse Res. Monogr.* 141:140, 1994.

195. Batki S., Manfredi L., Jacob P., Jones R. Fluoxetine for cocaine dependence in methadone maintenance: quantitative plasma and urine cocaine/benzoylecgonine concentrations. *J. Clin. Psychopharmacol.* 13:243, 1993.

196. Pollack M., Rosenbaum J. Fluoxetine treatment of cocaine abuse in heroin addicts. *J. Clin. Psychiatry.* 52:31, 1991.

197. Satel S. Craving for and fear of cocaine: A phenomenologic update on cocaine craving and paranoia. In Kosten T., Kleber H., Eds. *Clinician's Guide to Cocaine Addiction.* Guilford Press, New York, 1992, 172.

198. Satel S., Krystal J., Delgado P., Kosten T., Charney D. Tryptophan depletion and attenuation of cue-induced craving for cocaine. *Am. J. Psychiatry.* 152:778, 1995.

199. Winhusen T.M., Somoza E.C., Harrer J.M. et al. A placebo-controlled screening trial of tiagabine, sertraline and donepezil as cocaine dependence treatments. *Addiction.* 100(Suppl. 1):68, 2005.

200. Karler R., Calder L., Chaudhry I., Turkanis S. Blockade of 'reverse tolerance' to cocaine and amphetamine by MK-801. *Life Sci.* 45:599, 1989.

201. Pudiak C., Bozarth M. L-NAME and MK-801 attenuate sensitization to the locomotor-stimulating effect of cocaine. *Life Sci.* 53:1517, 1993.

202. Wolf M., Jeziorski M. Coadministration of MK-801 with amphetamine, cocaine or morphine prevents rather than transiently masks the development of behavioral sensitization. *Brain Res.* 613:291, 1993.

203. Witkin J. Blockade of the locomotor stimulant effects of cocaine and methamphetamine by glutamate antagonists. *Life Sci.* 53:PL 405, 1993.

204. Haracz J., Belanger S., MacDonall J., Sircar R. Antagonists of N-methyl-D-aspartate receptors partially prevent the development of cocaine sensitization. *Life Sci.* 57:2347, 1995.

205. Ida I., Aami T., Kuribara H. Inhibition of cocaine sensitization by MK-801 a noncompetitive N-methyl-D-aspartate (NMDA) receptor antagonist: evaluation by ambulatory activity in mice. *Jpn. J. Pharmacol.* 69:83, 1995.

206. Carey R., Dai H., Krost M., Huston J. The NMDA Receptor and cocaine: evidence that MK-801 can induce behavioral sensitization effects. *Pharmacol. Biochem. Behav.* 51:901, 1995.

207. Rockhold R., Oden G., Ho I., Andrew M., Farley J. Glutamate receptor antagonists block cocaine-induced convulsions and death. *Brain Res. Bull.* 27:721, 1991.

208. Itzhak Y., Stein I. Sensitization to the toxic effects of cocaine in mice is associated with regulation of N-methyl-D-aspartate receptors in the cortex. *J. Pharmacol. Exp. Ther.* 262:464, 1992.

209. Shimosato K., Marley R., Saito T. Differential effects of NMDA receptor and dopamine receptor antagonists on cocaine toxicities. *Pharmacol. Biochem. Behav.* 51, 1995.

210. White F., Hu X., Zhang X., Wolf M. Repeated administration of cocaine or amphetamines alters neuronal responses to glutamate in the mesoaccumbens dopamine system. *J. Pharmacol. Exp. Ther.* 273:445, 1995.

211. Itzhak Y. Modulation of the PCP/NMDA Receptor complex and sigma binding by psychostimulants. *Neurotoxicol. Teratol.* 16:363, 1994.

212. Fitzgerald L., Oritz J., Hamedani A., Nestler E. Drugs of abuse and stress increase the expression of GluR1 and NMDAR1 glutamate receptor subunits in the rat ventral tegmental area: common adaptations among cross-sensitizing agents. *J. Neurosci.* 16.274, 1996.

213. Lu L., Dempsey J., Shaham Y., Hope B.T. Differential long-term neuroadaptations of glutamate receptors in the basolateral and central amygdala after withdrawal from cocaine self-administration in rats. *J. Neurochem.* 94:161, 2005.

214. Schenk S., Valadez A., McNamara C. et al. Development and expression of sensitization to cocaine's reinforcing properties: role of NMDA receptors. *Psychopharmacology.* 111:332, 1993.

215. Sesack S.R., Pickel V.M. In the rat medial nucleus accumbens, hippocampal and catecholaminergic terminals converge on spiny neurons and are in apposition to each other. *Brain Res.* 527:266, 1990.

216. Pennartz C.M., Groenewegen H.J., Lopes da Silva F.H. The nucleus accumbens as a complex of functionally distinct neuronal ensembles: an integration of behavioural, electrophysiological and anatomical data. *Prog. Neurobiol.* 42:719, 1994.

217. Streeter C.C., Hennen J., Ke Y. et al. Prefrontal GABA levels in cocaine-dependent subjects increase with pramipexole and venlafaxine treatment. *Psychopharmacology* (Berlin). 1, 2005.

218. Dackis C.A., O'Brien C.P. Cocaine dependence: a disease of the brain's reward centers. *J. Subst. Abuse Treat.* 21:111, 2001.

219. Jayaram P., Steketee J.D. Effects of cocaine-induced behavioural sensitization on GABA transmission within rat medial prefrontal cortex. *Eur. J. Neurosci.* 21:2035, 2005.

220. Stromberg M.F., Mackler S.A., Volpicelli J.R., O'Brien C.P., Dewey S.L. The effect of gamma-vinyl-GABA on the consumption of concurrently available oral cocaine and ethanol in the rat. *Pharmacol. Biochem. Behav.* 68:291, 2001.

221. McFarland K., Kalivas P.W. The circuitry mediating cocaine-induced reinstatement of drug-seeking behavior. *J. Neurosci.* 21:8655, 2001.

222. Campbell U.C., Lac S.T., Carroll M.E. Effects of baclofen on maintenance and reinstatement of intravenous cocaine self-administration in rats. *Psychopharmacology* (Berlin). 143:209, 1999.

223. Roberts D.C., Andrews M.M., Vickers G.J. Baclofen attenuates the reinforcing effects of cocaine in rats. *Neuropsychopharmacology.* 15:417, 1996.

224. Kampman K.M., Pettinati H., Lynch K.G. et al. A pilot trial of topiramate for the treatment of cocaine dependence. *Drug Alcohol Depend.* 75:233, 2004.

225. Brebner K., Childress A.R., Roberts D.C. A potential role for GABA(B) agonists in the treatment of psychostimulant addiction. *Alcohol Alcohol.* 37:478, 2002.

226. Roberts D.C. Preclinical evidence for GABA(B) agonists as a pharmacotherapy for cocaine addiction. *Physiol. Behav.* 86:18, 2005.

227. Sanchez-Ramos J., Mash D. Ibogaine Human Phase I Pharmacokinetic and Safety Trial. FDA IND. 3968, 1993 (revised 1995).

228. Mash D.C., Kovera C.A., Pablo J. et al. Ibogaine: complex pharmacokinetics, concerns for safety, and preliminary efficacy measures. *Ann. N.Y. Acad. Sci.* 914:394, 2000.

229. Glick S., Kuehne M., Caucci J. et al. Effects of iboga alkaloids on morphine and cocaine self-administration in rats: relationship to tremorigenic effects and to effects on dopamine release in nucleus accumbens and striatum. *Brain Res.* 657:14, 1994.

230. Sershen H., Hashim A., Lajtha A. Ibogaine reduces preference for cocaine consumption in C57BL/6By mice. *Pharmacol. Biochem. Behav.* 47:13, 1994.

231. Sweetnam P., Lancaster J., Snowman A. et al. Receptor binding profile suggests multiple mechanisms of action are responsible for ibogaine's putative anti-addictive activity. *Psychopharmacology.* 118:369, 1995.

232. Popik P., Layer R., Skolnik P. The putative anti-addictive drug ibogaine is a competitive inhibitor of [^{3}H]MK-801 binding to the NMDA receptor complex. *Psychopharmacology.* 114:672, 1994.

233. Mash D., Staley J., Pablo J., Holohean A., Hackman J., Davidoff R. Properties of ibogaine and its principal metabolite (12-hydroxyibogamine) at the MK-801 binding site of the NMDA complex. *Neurosci. Lett.* 192:53, 1995.

234. Mash D., Staley J., Baumann M., Rothman R., Hearn W. Identification of a primary metabolite of ibogaine that targets serotonin transporters and elevates serotonin. *Life Sci.* 57:PL45, 1995.

235. Baumann M. Personal communication.

236. Broderick P., Phelan F., Eng F., Wechsler R. Ibogaine modulates cocaine responses which are altered due to environmental habituation: *In vivo* microvoltammetric and behavioral studies. *Pharmacol. Biochem. Behav.* 49:711, 1994.

237. Hearn W., Pablo J., Hime G., Mash D. Identification and quantitation of ibogaine and an *O*-demethylated metabolite in brain and biological fluids using gas chromatography mass spectrometry. *J. Anal. Toxicol.* 19:427, 1995.

238. Pearl S., Herrick-Davis K., Teitler M., Glick S. Radioligand binding study of noribogaine a likely metabolite of ibogaine. *Brain Res.* 675:342, 1995.

239. Staley J., Ouyang Q., Pablo J. et al. Pharmacological screen for activities of 12-hydroxyibogamine: a primary metabolite of the indole alkaloid ibogaine. *Psychopharmacology.* 127:10, 1996.

6.6 NEUROPSYCHIATRIC CONSEQUENCES OF CHRONIC COCAINE ABUSE

Deborah C. Mash, Ph.D.
Departments of Neurology and Molecular and Cellular Pharmacology, University of Miami, Miller School of Medicine, Miami, Florida

Mortality data have indicated that deaths involving psychostimulant drugs stem not only from overdose, but also from drug-induced mental states that may lead to serious injuries.[1] The arrival of inexpensive smokable "crack" cocaine has radically changed the nature of the epidemic and revealed the great addictive potential of cocaine. Cocaine, particularly smoked "crack" cocaine, is known to be one of the most widely abused psychoactive substances in the U.S. With the increased use of cocaine in its various forms over the past 15 years, researchers and clinicians have focused on the definition of cocaine dependence and withdrawal.[2] Cocaine was not thought to be addictive prior to the 1980s, as neither chronic use nor its cessation resulted in the physiological tolerance or withdrawal observed in opiate dependence. The progression of occasional use to compulsive use,[3] and the description of a cocaine abstinence syndrome,[4] has led to the definition of diagnostic criteria for cocaine dependence. Clinical experience has fostered the view that persons with psychiatric disorders tend to have high rates of substance abuse, and vice versa.[5,6] Epidemiological studies demonstrate that a large portion of the population experiences both mental and addictive disorders.[7] These studies have underscored the gravity of the problem of dual diagnoses of mental health and substance abuse disorders.

6.6.1 Differential Diagnosis of Psychotic Disorders

Drug use is a major complicating factor in psychosis, it renders the management of psychotic disorders more difficult, and adverse reactions to recreational drugs may mimic psychosis.[8] The differential diagnosis of psychotic disorders in the young routinely includes "drug induced psychosis." This diagnostic category has not had consistent definition and the relationship between drug use and psychotic symptoms is controversial. Adverse psychiatric effects associated with acute cocaine intoxication include extreme agitation, irritability or affective liability, impaired judgment, paranoia, hallucinations (visual or tactile), and, sometimes, manic excitement. Medical and psychiatric symptoms caused by acute cocaine intoxication are a common reason for presentation to the emergency department. Psychiatric symptoms of cocaine intoxication usually subside within 24 h, but some patients may require benzodiazepines for acute agitation. Neuroleptics are often used for the treatment of unremitting paranoid psychosis, hallucinations, and delusions. The transient paranoid state is a common feature of cocaine dependence, with affected persons possessing an obvious predisposition to this drug-induced state.[9] Psychiatric complications of cocaine intoxication include cocaine-induced paranoia, agitated delirium, delusional disorder, and the depressed mood and dysphoria associated with abrupt cocaine withdrawal (Table 6.6.1).

Extended behavioral signs of cocaine psychosis usually imply the presence of an underlying major psychopathology in susceptible individuals.[9] Cocaine-induced psychosis typically manifests as an intense hypervigilance (paranoia) accompanied by marked apprehension and fear. Auditory and tactile hallucinations, formal thought disorder, and ideas of reference frequently noted with chronic use of amphetamines are not prevalent in cocaine abusers. Paranoid experience secondary to cocaine use is usually limited to a drug episode, which dissipates by the time the user awakens from the "crash," usually about 8 to 36 h after the cessation of the cocaine "binge."[10] In a sample of 100 cocaine-dependent males, none reported cocaine paranoia extending beyond the crash phase.[10]

In contrast to the effects of cocaine, amphetamine has greater and longer-acting psychotogenic properties.[11] Angrist[11] has suggested that high rates of cocaine use that cause sustained elevations in plasma levels may be necessary for the development or kindling of an episode of cocaine psychosis. In keeping with this suggestion, certain cocaine-induced effects are known to become progressively more intense after repeated administration, a phenomenon referred to as sensitization. However, Satel and co-workers[10] have provided data to suggest that instances of cocaine-induced paranoia or psychosis lasting more than several days most likely indicate the presence of an underlying primary psychotic disorder.

Table 6.6.1 Behavioral Signs of Acute Psychostimulant Toxicity

Excitability
Restlessness
Delusions
Hallucinations
Paranoia
Panic Attacks
Agitated Delirium

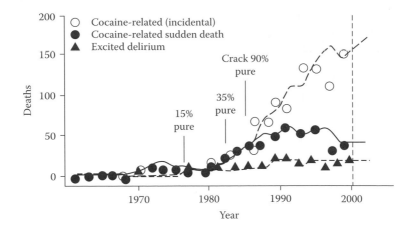

Figure 6.6.1 Tracking the incidence of cocaine overdose deaths in Dade County, FL. Medicolegal investigations of the deaths were conducted by forensic pathologists. Forensic pathologists evaluate the scene environment and circumstances of death and autopsied the victim in order to determine the cause and manner of death. The circumstances of death and toxicology results were reviewed before classifying a death due to cocaine toxicity with or without preterminal delirium. There was a sharp increase in the incidence of cocaine-related and cocaine overdose cases with the arrival of "crack" cocaine in Dade County. The incidence of cocaine delirium victims is shown by year, from the first report in 1982.

6.6.2 Cocaine Delirium

Delirium symptoms suggest dysfunction of multiple brain regions.[12] Clinical subtypes of delirium with unique and definable phenomenological or physical characteristics are not widely accepted. At present, very little information is known about the neuropathogenesis of cocaine delirium. While various neurotransmitter alterations may converge to result in a delirium syndrome or subtype thereof, an excess of the neurotransmitter dopamine (DA) has been implicated as a cause of cocaine delirium.

In 1985, a case series of cocaine overdose victims who died following a syndrome of excited delirium was first described.[13] It was not clear whether this type of cocaine toxicity represented a new syndrome that was associated with cocaine use alone, or whether there were other causes or underlying genetic risk factors. The cocaine delirium syndrome comprises four components that appear in sequence: hyperthermia, delirium with agitation, respiratory arrest, and death. An episode of cocaine delirium is most often seen at the end of one or more days of drug use.[14] Compared with other accidental cocaine toxicity deaths, a larger proportion of victims of cocaine delirium survive longer after the onset of the overdose. This factor probably accounts for the lower blood cocaine concentrations reported for cocaine delirium victims.[15] The incidence of this disorder is not known with any certainty, but the number of cases has increased markedly since the beginning of the epidemic of "crack" cocaine use in Dade County, FL (Figure 6.6.1).

In the original report of Wetli and Fishbain,[13] they described the cocaine delirium syndrome in seven cases, and all had somewhat stereotyped histories. A typical example of a cocaine delirium victim was the case of a 33-year-old man, who in an agitated state started pounding on the door of his former house. He was shouting that he wanted to see his wife and daughter. The occupants informed him that nobody by that name resided there; yet he continued. Four bystanders finally restrained him and assisted police units upon their arrival. The subject was handcuffed and put into a police car, whereupon he began to kick out the windows of the vehicle. The police subsequently restrained his ankles and attached the ankle restraints and handcuffs together. He was then transported to a local hospital. While en route, the police officers noted that he became tranquil. Upon

Table 6.6.2   Common Traits Associated with the Fatal Cocaine Delirium Syndrome

Male
Extreme Agitation
Hyperthermia (>103°F)
High body mass index
Survive longer than 1 h after the onset of symptoms
Die in police custody

arrival at the hospital approximately 45 min after the onset of the agitated delirium, the subject was discovered to be in a respiratory arrest.

A post mortem examination and a rectal temperature of 41°C (106°F) were recorded. He had needle marks typical of intravenous drug abuse and pulmonary and cerebral edema. Abrasions and contusions of the ankles and wrists were evident from his struggling. Lidocaine was not administered to the victim during the resuscitative attempts. The clinical presentation of cocaine delirium is different from that of nonpsychotic cocaine abusers with sudden death or massive drug overdose. The cocaine delirium victims are almost always men, they are more likely to die in custody, and are more likely to survive for more than 1 h after the onset of symptoms (Table 6.6.2).

In the epidemiological tracking of agitated delirium victims in Metropolitan Dade County, men with preterminal delirium comprised approximately 10% of the annual number of cocaine overdose deaths. The demographic trends show that the proportion of these cases remains consistent throughout the epidemic of cocaine abuse and tends to track the annual frequency of cocaine-related sudden deaths. This observation suggests that a certain percentage of cocaine addicts may be at risk for cocaine delirium with chronic abuse.

Cocaine delirium deaths are seasonal and tend to cluster during the late summer months. Core body temperatures are markedly elevated, ranging from 104°C to 108°C. Based on a review of the constellation of psychiatric symptoms associated with this disorder, Kosten and Kleber[16] have termed agitated delirium as a possible cocaine variant of neuroleptic malignant syndrome. Neuroleptic malignant syndrome (NMS) is a highly lethal disorder seen in patients taking dopamine (DA) antagonists or following abrupt withdrawal from DAergic agonists.[17,18] NMS is usually associated with muscle rigidity, while the cocaine variant of the syndrome presents with brief onset of rigidity immediately prior to respiratory collapse.[19]

At present it is not clear whether extreme agitation, delirium, hyperthermia, and rhabdomyolysis are effects of cocaine that occur independently and at random among cocaine users, or whether these features are linked by common toxicologic and pathologic processes.[20] Ruttenber and colleagues[20] have examined excited delirium deaths in a population-based registry of all cocaine-related deaths in Dade County. This study has led to clear description of the cocaine delirium syndrome, its pattern of occurrence in cocaine users over time, and has identified a number of important risk factors for the syndrome.

Cocaine delirium deaths are defined as accidental cocaine toxicity deaths that occurred in individuals who experienced an episode of bizarre behavior prior to death. Bizarre behavior is defined as hyperactivity accompanied by incoherent shouting, aggression (fighting with others or destroying property), or evidence of extreme paranoia as described by witnesses and supported by scene evidence. The results of this study demonstrate that victims are more likely to be male, black and younger than other cocaine overdose toxicity deaths. The most frequent route of administration was injection for the excited delirium victims as compared to inhalation for the other accidental cocaine toxicity deaths. The frequency of smoked "crack" cocaine was similar for both groups. Of the excited delirium victims, 39% died in police custody as compared with only 2% for the comparison group of accidental cocaine toxicity cases.[20] A large proportion of these individuals survive between 1 and 12 h after the onset of the syndrome.

The most striking feature of the excited delirium syndrome is the extreme hyperthermia. The epidemiological data[20] provide some clues for the etiology of the elevated body temperature. Victims of cocaine excited delirium have higher body mass indices. This finding suggests that muscle mass and adiposity may contribute to the generation of body heat. Temporal clustering in summer months[13] supports the hypothesis that abnormal thermoregulation is an important risk factor for death in people who develop the syndrome. Being placed in police custody prior to death can also raise body temperature through increased psychomotor activity if the victim struggles in the process of restraint. Descriptions of the circumstances around death suggest that police officers frequently had to forcibly restrain these victims. Positional asphyxia and a restraint-induced increase in catecholamines have been hypothesized as contributing causes of cocaine delirium.[21]

6.6.3 Neurochemical Pathology of Cocaine Delirium

The mesolimbic dopaminergic (DAergic) system is an important pathway mediating reinforcement and addiction to cocaine and other psychostimulants.[22] Cocaine potentiates DAergic neurotransmission by binding to the DA transporter and blocking neurotransmitter uptake, leading to marked elevations in synaptic DA (for review, see Reference 23). Long-term cocaine abuse leads to neuroadaptive changes in the signaling proteins that regulate DA homeostasis. DA transporter binding site densities have been shown to be upregulated *in vitro* in the post-mortem brain of cocaine addicts,[24–27] and *in vivo* in acutely abstinent cocaine-dependent individuals.[28]

A number of different studies point to a possibility of a defective interaction of cocaine with the DA transporter in the etiology of cocaine delirium. The effects of chronic, intermittent cocaine treatment paradigms on the labeling of the cocaine recognition sites on the DA transporter have been investigated in rat studies. Neuroadaptive changes in the DA transporter have been characterized with a number of different radioligands, including [^{3}H]cocaine, the cocaine congeners [^{3}H]WIN 35,428 and [^{125}I]RTI-55, and more recently with [^{125}I]RTI-121 (for review, see Reference 29). In contrast to the classic DA transport inhibitors ([^{3}H]mazindol, [^{3}H]GBR 12935, and [^{3}H]nomifensine), the cocaine congeners ([^{3}H]WIN 35,428, [^{125}I]RTI-55, and [^{125}I]RTI-121) label multiple sites with a pharmacological profile characteristic of the DA transporter in rat, primate, and human brain.[30–32] Chronic treatment of rats with intermittent doses of cocaine demonstrated a twofold to fivefold increase in the apparent density of [^{3}H]cocaine binding sites in the striatum.[33] Rats that were allowed to self-administer cocaine in a chronic unlimited access paradigm had significant increases in [^{3}H]WIN 35,428 binding sites when the animals were sacrificed on the last day of cocaine access.[34] Rabbits treated with cocaine (4 mg/kg i.v. 2 × per day for 22 days) show an elevation in the density of [^{3}H]WIN 35,428 binding sites in the caudate.[35] A progression of changes were observed in cocaine self-administering monkeys, which had marked elevations in DA transporter binding sites in the more limbic sectors of the striatum (ventromedial putamen and nucleus accumbens) in monkeys exposed to cocaine for 3 months to 1 year.[36] Taken together, these results demonstrate that cocaine exposure leads to an increase in the density of cocaine binding sites on the DA transport carrier.

Cocaine congeners label high- and low-affinity sites on the cloned and native human DA transporter, one of which appears to overlap with the functional state of the carrier protein.[37] In cocaine overdose victims, high-affinity cocaine recognition sites on the DA transporter were upregulated significantly in the striatum as compared to age-matched and drug-free control subjects (Figure 6.6.2). If this regulatory change in high affinity [^{3}H]WIN 35,428 binding sites on the human DA transporter reflects an increased ability of the protein to transport DA, it may help to explain the addictive liability of cocaine. In synaptosomes isolated from cryoprotected brain specimens, DA uptake function was elevated twofold in the ventral striatum from cocaine users as compared to age-matched drug-free control subjects.[27] In contrast, the levels of [^{3}H]DA uptake were not elevated in victims of excited cocaine delirium, who experienced paranoia and marked agitation prior to death. In keeping with the increase in DA transporter function, radioligand binding

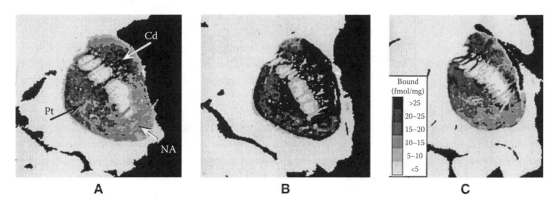

Figure 6.6.2 *In vitro* autoradiographic maps of [³H]WIN 35,428 labeling of the DA transporter in coronal sections of the striatum. (A) Representative age-matched and drug-free subject, (B) cocaine overdose victim, and (C) cocaine delirium victim. The brain maps illustrate the adaptive increase in DA transporter density over the striatum in the cocaine overdose victim. Note the lack of any apparent elevation for the victim presenting with agitated delirium. Since the DA transporter regulates the synaptic concentration of neurotransmitter, the lack of a compensatory upregulation may result in a DA overflow following a cocaine "binge." Elevated synaptic DA with repeat exposures may kindle the emergence of the agitated delirium syndrome. Gray scale codes are shown in panel B (black = high densities; gray = intermediate; light gray to white = low densities). Abbreviations: Cd, caudate; NA, nucleus accumbens, Pt, putamen.

to the DA transporter was increased in the cocaine users, but not in the victims of excited delirium. These results demonstrate that long-term cocaine abuse leads to neuroadaptive changes in the signaling proteins that regulate dopamine homeostasis, including elevated DA transporter function and binding sites.

Since cocaine potentiates dopaminergic neurotransmission by binding to DA transporter and blocking reuptake, persisting increases in DA transporter function after cocaine levels have fallen in blood and brain may result in an acute decrease in the intrasynaptic concentration of DA and lower DAergic tone. As the transporter carrier upregulates its apparent density in the nerve terminal to more efficiently transport DA back into the presynaptic nerve terminal, more cocaine will be needed to experience cocaine's reinforcing effects and euphoria. During acute abstinence from cocaine, enhanced function of the DA transporter could lead to net depletion in synaptic DA. This depletion of DA may serve as a biological substrate for anhedonia, the cardinal feature of cocaine withdrawal symptomatology.

Unlike the results seen in cases of accidental cocaine overdose,[24] the density of high-affinity cocaine recognition sites on the DA transporter measured in the striatum from cocaine delirium victims fails to demonstrate a compensatory increase with chronic abuse.[27] Since the concentration of synaptic DA is controlled by the reuptake mechanism(s), the lack of compensatory increase in cocaine recognition sites could be the defect in DAergic transmission that explains the paranoia and agitation associated with this syndrome. Paranoia in the context of cocaine abuse is common and several lines of evidence suggest that this phenomenon may be related to the function of the DA transporter protein.[38] Genetic differences in the makeup of individuals who abuse cocaine may also underlie some of these differences in susceptibility to the development of adverse neuropsychiatric effects with chronic cocaine abuse, that appear to result from a defective regulation of the DA transporter protein.[38] In addition to the adverse neuropsychiatric sequalae, cocaine delirium victims are distinguished from other accidental cocaine overdose deaths by the premorbid occurrence of hyperthermia. Body temperature has a high correlation to a disordered CNS, leading to the loss of thermal regulation. DA receptors are known to play a role in regulating core body temperature. Since hyperthermia is a clinical feature of cocaine delirium, Kosten and Kleber[16] have speculated that death occurred due to a malfunction in DAergic control of thermoregulation. Hypothermia receptors are known to be downregulated by high levels of intrasynaptic DA. Direct application of intracerebral DA at first lowers body temperature; however, a subsequent "rebound" in body temperature occurs about 1 h after discontinuing this stimulation.[39,40]

When cocaine is repeatedly administered, DAergic receptor numbers are altered.[40,41] The likelihood of hyperthermia may be increased with chronic cocaine abuse if the DAergic receptors involved in thermoregulation are undergoing adaptive changes with chronic cocaine exposure. In keeping with this hypothesis, cocaine delirium victims had a different profile of D_2 receptor binding within the thermoregulatory centers of the hypothalamus as compared to cocaine overdose deaths.[25,42] The density of the D_2 DA receptor subtype in the anterior and preoptic nuclei of the hypothalamus in the cocaine delirium subgroup of cocaine overdose deaths were decreased significantly ($p < 0.05$). These results may be relevant to an understanding of the contribution of selective alterations in D_1 and D_2 receptor subtypes in central DAergic temperature regulation. D_1 and D_2 receptors mediate opposite effects on thermoregulation, with the D_1 receptor mediating a prevailing increase in core body temperature, while the D_2 receptor mediates an opposing decrease in temperature.[42] Thus, the selective downregulation in the density of the D_2 DAergic receptor subtype within the hypothalamus may explain the loss of temperature regulation in cocaine delirium victims.

6.6.4 Conclusions

Cocaine abuse is associated with neuropsychiatric disorders, including acute psychotic episodes, paranoid states, and delirium. The mechanistic basis of these brain states is not fully known. The advent of new tools from the neurosciences and molecular genetics has led to a proliferation of research approaches aimed at defining the neurobiological consequences of chronic cocaine use. The development of radioligands with high specific activity and selectivity for neurotransmitter carriers and receptor subtypes has made it possible to map and quantify the neurochemical pathology in the brains of cocaine abusers. Since the DA transport carrier is a key regulator of DAergic neurotransmission, alterations in the numbers of these reuptake sites by cocaine may affect the balance in DAergic signaling. Understanding the influence of cocaine's effects on DAergic neurotransmission may shed light on the etiology of neuropsychiatric syndromes associated with cocaine abuse and dependence.

Acknowledgments

The authors acknowledge the expert technical assistance of Margaret Basile, M.S., and Qinjie Ouyang, B.A. This work was supported by USPHS Grant DA06627.

REFERENCES

1. Baker, S.P. *The Injury Fact Book.* 2nd ed. Oxford University Press, New York, 1992.
2. Gawin, F.H., Cocaine addiction: psychology and neurophysiology. *Science.* 251: 1580, 1991.
3. Chitwood, D. Patterns and consequences of cocaine use. *Natl. Inst. Drug Abuse Res. Monogr.* Ser. 61: 111, 1985.
4. Gawin, F.H. and Kleber, H.D. Abstinence symptomatology and psychiatric diagnosis in cocaine abusers. *Arch. Gen. Psychiatry.* 43: 107, 1986.
5. Crawford, V. Comorbidity of substance misuse and psychiatric disorders. *Curr. Opin. Psychiatry.* 9: 231, 1996.
6. Kilbey, M.M., Breslau, N., and Andreski, P. Cocaine use and dependence in young adults: associated psychiatric disorders and personality traits. *Drug Alcohol Depend,* 29: 283, 1992.
7. Reiger, D.A., Farmer, M.E., Rae, D.S., Locke, B.Z., Keith, S.J., Judd, L.L., and Goodwin, F.K., Comorbidity of mental disorders with alcohol and other drug abuse. *J. Am. Med. Assoc.* 264: 2511, 1990.
8. Poole, R. and Brabbins, C. Drug induced psychosis. *Br. J. Psychiatry.* 168: 135, 1996.

9. Satel, S.L., Seibyl, J.P., and Charney, D.S. Prolonged cocaine psychosis implies underlying major psychopathology. *J. Clin. Psychiatry.* 52: 8, 1991.

10. Satel, S.L., Southwick, S.M., and Gawin, F.H. Clinical Features of cocaine-induced paranoia. *Am. J. Psychiatry*; 148: 495, 1991.

11. Angrist, B.M. Cocaine in the context of prior central nervous system stimulant epidemics. In Volkow, N., Swann, A.C., Eds. *Cocaine in the Brain* (Mind in Medicine Series). Rutgers University Press, New Brunswick, NJ, 1990, 7.

12. Tucker, G.J. Delirium. *Semin. Clin. Neuropsychiatry.* 5: 63–255, 2000.

13. Wetli, C.V. and Fishbain D.A. Cocaine-induced psychosis and sudden death in recreational cocaine users. *J. Forensic. Sci..* 30: 873, 1985.

14. Stephens, B.G., Baselt, R., Jentzen, J.M., Karch, S., Mash, D.C., and Wetli, C.V. Criteria for the interpretation of cocaine levels in human biological samples and their relation to cause of death. *J. Forensic Med. Pathol.* 25: 1, 2004.

15. Stephens, B.G., Jentzen, J.M., Karch, S., Wetli, C.V., and Mash, D.C. National Association of Medical Examiners position paper on the certification of cocaine-related deaths. *J. Forensic Med. Pathol.* 25: 11, 2004.

16. Kosten, T. and Kleber, H.D., Sudden death in cocaine abusers: relation to neuroleptic malignant syndrome. *Lancet.* 1: 1198, 1987.

17. Friedman, J.H., Feinberg, S.S., and Feldman, R.G. A neuroleptic malignant like syndrome due to levodopa therapy withdrawal. *J. Am. Med. Assoc.* 254: 2792, 1985.

18. Levison, J. Neuroleptic malignant syndrome. *Am. J. Psychiatry.* 142: 1137, 1985.

19. Kosten, T.R. and Kleber, H.D. Rapid death during cocaine abuse: a variant of neuroleptic malignant syndrome. *Am J. Drug Alcohol Abuse* 14: 335, 1988.

20. Ruttenber, A.J., Lawler-Haevener, J., Wetli, C.V., Hearn, W.L., and Mash, D.C., Fatal excited delirium following cocaine use: epidemiologic findings provide evidence for new mechanisms of cocaine toxicity. *J. Forensic Toxicol.* 42: 25, 1997.

21. O'Halloran, R.L. and Lewman, L.V., Restraint asphyxiation in excited delirium. *Am J. Forensic Med. Pathol.* 14: 289, 1993.

22. Self, D.W. and Nestler, E.J. Relapse to drug-seeking: neural and molecular mechanisms. *Drug Alcohol Depend.* 51: 49, 1998.

23. Giros, B. and Caron, M.G. Molecular characterization of the dopamine transporter. *Trends. Pharmacol. Sci.* 14: 43, 1993.

24. Staley, J.K., Hearn, W.L., Ruttenber, A.J., Wetli, C.V., and Mash, D.C. High affinity cocaine recognition sites on the dopamine transporter are elevated in fatal cocaine overdose victims. *J. Pharmacol. Exp. Ther.* 271: 1678, 1995.

25. Staley, J.K., Wetli, C.V., Ruttenber, A.J., Hearn, W.L., Kung, H.F., and Mash, D.C. Dopamine transporter and receptor autoradiography in cocaine psychosis and sudden death. *Biol. Psychiatry.* 37: 656, 1995.

26. Little, K.Y., Zhang, L., McLaughlin, D.P., Desmond, T., Frey, K.A., Dalack, G.W., and Cassin, B.J. Striatal dopaminergic abnormalities in human cocaine users. *Am. J. Psychiatry.* 156: 238, 1999.

27. Mash, D.C., Pablo, J., Ouyang, Q., Hearn, W.L., and Izenwasser, S. Dopamine transport function is elevated in cocaine users. *J. Neurochem.*, 81: 292, 2002.

28. Malison, R.T., Best, S.E.; van Dyck, C.H., McCance, E.F., Wallace, E.A., Laruelle, M. Baldwin, R.M. Seibyl, J.P., Price, L.H., Kosten, T.R., and Innis, R.B. Elevated striatal dopamine transporters during acute cocaine abstinence as measured by [^{123}I]β-CIT SPECT. *Am. J. Psychiatry.* 155: 832, 1998.

29. Boja, J.W., Carroll, F.I., Rahman, M.A., Philip, A., Lewin, A.H. and Kuhar, M.J.: New, potent cocaine analogs: ligand binding and transport studies in rat striatum. *Eur. J. Pharmacol.* 184: 329, 1990.

30. Staley, J.K., Boja, J.W., Carroll, F.I., Seltzman, H.H., Wyrick, C.D., Lewin, A.H., Abraham, P., and Mash, D.C. Mapping dopamine transporters in the human brain with novel selective cocaine analog [^{125}I]RTI-121. *Synapse.* 21: 364, 1995.

31. Madras, B.K., Spealman, R.D., Fahey, M.A., Neumeyer, J.L., Saha, J.K., and Milius, R.A. Cocaine receptors labeled by [^{3}H]2B-carbomethoxy-3β-(4-fluorophenyl)tropane. *Mol. Pharmacol.* 36: 518, 1989.

32. Mash, D.C. and Staley, J.K. Cocaine recognition sites on the human dopamine transporter in drug overdose victims. In *Neurotransmitter Transporter: Structure and Function*, M.E.A. Reith, Ed. Humana, New York, 1996, 56.

33. Alburges, M.E., Narang, N., and Wamsley, J.K. Alterations in the dopaminergic receptor system after chronic administration of cocaine. *Synapse.* 14: 314, 1993.

34. Wilson, J.M., Nobrega, J.N., Carroll, M.E., Niznik, H.B., Shannak, K., Lac, S.T., Pristupa, Z.B. Dixon, L.M., and Kish, S.J. Heterogenous subregional binding patterns of ^{3}H-WIN 35,428 and ^{3}H-GBR 12,935 are differentially regulated by chronic cocaine self-administration. *J. Neurosci.* 14: 2966, 1994.

35. Aloyo, V.J., Harvey, J.A., and Kirfides, A.L. Chronic cocaine increases WIN 35428 binding in rabbit caudate. *Soc. Neurosci. Abstr.* 19: 1843, 1994.

36. Letchworth, S.R., Nader, M., Smith, H., Friedman, D.P., and Porrino, L.J. Progression of changes in dopamine transporter binding site density as a result of cocaine self-administration in rhesus monkeys. *J. Neurosci.* 21: 2799, 2001.

37. Pristupa, Z.B., Wilson, J.M., Hoffman, B.J., Kish, S.J., and Niznik, H.B. Pharmacological heterogeneity of the cloned and native human dopamine transporter: dissociation of [^{3}H]WIN 35,428 and [^{3}H]GBR 12935 binding. *Mol. Pharmacol.* 45, 125, 1994.

38. Gelernter, J., Kranzler, H.R., Satel, S.L., and Rao, P.A. Genetic association between dopamine transporter protein alleles and cocaine-induced paranoia. *Neuropsychopharmacology.* 11: 195, 1994.

39. Costentin, J., Duterte-Boucher, D., Panissaud, C., and Michael-Titus, A. Dopamine D_1 and D_2 receptors mediate opposite effects of apomorphine on the body temperature of reserpinized mice. *Neuropharmacology.* 29: 31, 1990.

40. Meller, E., Hizami, R., and Kreuter, L. Hypothermia in mice: D_2 dopamine receptor mediation and absence of spare receptors. *Pharmacol. Biochem. Behav.* 32: 141, 1989.

41. Kleven, M.S., Perry, B.D., Woolverton, W.L., and Seiden, L.S. Effects of repeated injections of cocaine on D_1 and D_2 dopamine receptors in rat brain. *Brain Res.* 532: 265, 1990.

42. Wetli, C.V., Mash, D.C., and Karch, S. Agitated delirium and the neuroleptic malignant syndrome. *Am. J. Emerg. Med.* 14: 425, 1996.

6.7 NEUROBIOLOGY OF 3,4-METHYLENEDIOXYMETHAMPHETAMINE (MDMA, OR "ECSTASY")

Michael H. Baumann, Ph.D. and Richard B. Rothman, M.D., Ph.D.
Clinical Psychopharmacology Section, Intramural Research Program, National Institute on Drug Abuse, National Institutes of Health, Department of Health and Human Services, Baltimore, Maryland

3,4-Methylenedioxymethamphetamine (MDMA, or "Ecstasy") is an illicit drug used by young adults who attend "rave" dance parties in the U.S., Europe, and elsewhere. The allure of MDMA is related to its unique psychoactive effects, which include amphetamine-like stimulant actions, coupled with feelings of increased emotional sensitivity and closeness to others.[1,2] Epidemiological data indicate that MDMA misuse among children and adolescents is widespread in the U.S.[3,4] In a recent sampling of high school students, 10% of 12th graders reported using MDMA at least once.[5] As shown in Figure 6.7.1, MDMA-related emergency room visits have risen more than 20-fold in recent years, consistent with the increasing popularity of the drug. Serious adverse effects of acute MDMA intoxication include cardiac arrhythmias, hypertension, hyperthermia, serotonin (5-HT) syndrome, hyponatremia, liver problems, seizures, coma and, in rare cases, death.[6] Accumulating evidence indicates that long-term MDMA abuse is associated with cognitive impairments and mood disturbances, which can last for months after cessation of drug intake.[7,8]

Despite the potential risks associated with illicit MDMA use, a growing number of clinicians believe the drug could have therapeutic potential in the treatment of psychiatric disorders.[9] For example, adjunct therapy with MDMA might prove useful for alleviating the anxiety that accompanies post-traumatic stress disorder (PTSD) or end-stage terminal illness. Indeed, clinical trials aimed at testing the efficacy of MDMA for the treatment of PTSD are under way.[10] MDMA has been administered to human subjects in controlled research settings, and few side effects are

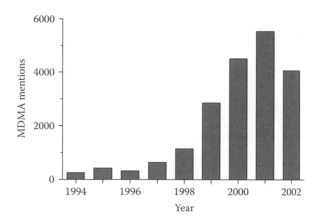

Figure 6.7.1 Emergency department mentions of MDMA from 1994–2002. (Adapted from Office of Applied Studies, SAMSHA, Drug Abuse Warning Network, 2002; updated 03/2003.)

observed under these conditions, supporting the relative safety of the drug.[11,12] The aforementioned considerations provide compelling reasons to evaluate the neurobiology of MDMA and related compounds. In this chapter, we review the acute and long-term effects of MDMA administration on central nervous system (CNS) function. The chapter focuses on results obtained from rats since most preclinical MDMA research has been carried out in this animal model. Experimental data from our laboratory at NIDA are included to supplement literature reports, and clinical data are mentioned in certain instances to note similarities or differences between rats and humans.

6.7.1 MDMA Interacts with Monoamine Transporters

6.7.1.1 In Vitro Studies

Figure 6.7.2 shows that MDMA is a ring-substituted analogue of methamphetamine, and "Ecstasy" tablets ingested by humans contain a racemic mixture of (+) and (–) isomers of the drug.[13,14] Upon systemic administration, MDMA is N-demethylated via first-pass metabolism in the liver to yield (+) and (–) isomers of the amphetamine analogue, 3,4-methylenedioxyamphetamine (MDA).[15,16] Initial pharmacological studies carried out in the 1980s revealed that isomers of MDMA and MDA stimulate efflux of 5-HT, and to a lesser extent dopamine (DA), in brain tissue preparations.[17–19] Subsequent investigations demonstrated that MDMA is a substrate for

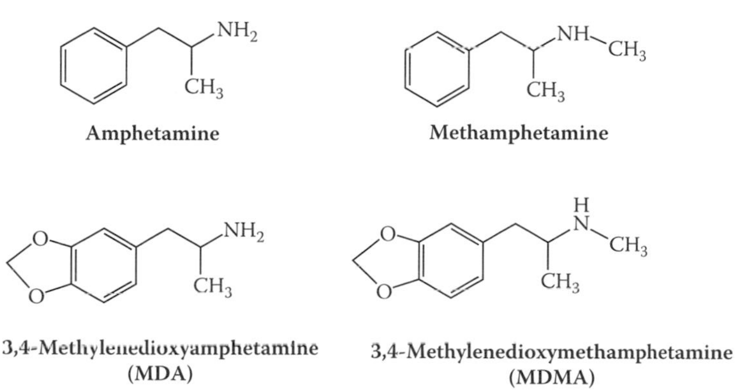

Amphetamine

Methamphetamine

3,4-Methylenedioxyamphetamine
(MDA)

3,4-Methylenedioxymethamphetamine
(MDMA)

Figure 6.7.2 Chemical structures of MDMA and related compounds.

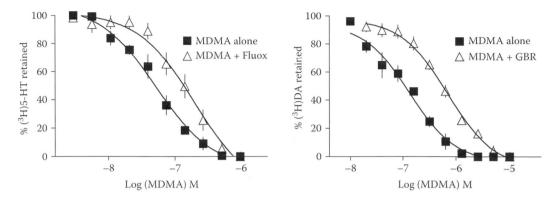

Figure 6.7.3   Dose–response effects of MDMA on the release of preloaded [³H]5-HT (left panel) and [³H]DA (right panel) from synaptosomes *in vitro*. [³H]Transmitter release is expressed as percent of tritium retained in tissue. Various concentrations of MDMA were incubated with or without the 5-HT uptake blocker fluoxetine (10 n*M*) in [³H]5-HT assays, whereas various concentrations of MDMA were incubated with or without the DA uptake blocker GBR12909 (10 n*M*) in [³H]DA assays. Data are mean ± SD for three separate experiments, each performed in triplicate. See Baumann et al.[39] for methods.

monoamine transporter proteins, evoking the non-exocytotic release of 5-HT, DA, and norepinephrine (NE) from nerve terminals.[20-22]

Like other substrate-type releasers, MDMA and MDA bind to plasma membrane monoamine transporters and are subsequently translocated into the cytoplasm.[23] The ensuing transmitter release occurs by a two-pronged mechanism: (1) transmitter molecules exit the cell along their concentration gradient via a diffusion-exchange process that involves reversal of normal transporter flux, and (2) cytoplasmic concentrations of transmitter are increased due to drug-induced disruption of vesicular storage.[24,25] This latter action serves to markedly increase the pool of cytoplasmic transmitter available for diffusion-exchange release. Because substrate-type releasing drugs must be transported into cells to promote transmitter release, transporter uptake inhibitors can block the effects of releasers. Figure 6.7.3 depicts data from our laboratory showing MDMA produces a dose-dependent release of preloaded [³H]5-HT and [³H]DA from rat brain synaptosomes. In these experiments, the "release" of preloaded radiolabeled transmitter is expressed as a reduction in the amount of tritium retained in tissue. Reserpine is added to the incubation medium to prevent the trapping of radiolabeled transmitter in vesicles.[26,27] MDMA-induced release of [³H]5-HT is antagonized by co-incubation with the selective 5-HT uptake inhibitor fluoxetine, whereas release of [³H]DA is antagonized by the selective DA uptake inhibitor GRB12909. These findings support the hypothesis that MDMA stimulates 5-HT and DA release *in vitro* via interactions at 5-HT transporters (SERT) and DA transporters (DAT), respectively.

The data in Table 6.7.1 summarize structure–activity relationships for MDMA, MDA, and related drugs, with respect to monoamine release from rat brain synaptosomes.[28,29] Stereoisomers of MDMA and MDA are substrates for SERT, DAT, and NE transporters (NET), with (+) isomers exhibiting greater potency as releasers. In particular, (+) isomers of MDMA and MDA are much more effective DA releasers than their corresponding (–) isomers. It is noteworthy that (+) isomers of MDMA and MDA are rather nonselective in their ability to stimulate monoamine release *in vitro*. When compared to other amphetamines, the major effect of methylenedioxy ring-substitution is enhanced potency for 5-HT release and reduced potency for DA release. For example, (+)-MDMA releases 5-HT (EC_{50} = 70.8 n*M*) about ten times more potently than (+)-methamphetamine (EC_{50} = 736 n*M*), whereas (+)-MDMA releases DA (EC_{50} = 142 n*M*) about six times less potently than (+)-methamphetamine (EC_{50} = 24 n*M*).

Table 6.7.1 **Profile of MDMA and Related Compounds as Monoamine Transporter Substrates**

Drug	5-HT Release EC$_{50}$ (nM ± SD)	NE Release EC$_{50}$ (nM ± SD)	DA Release EC$_{50}$ (nM ± SD)
(+)-Methamphetamine	736 ± 45	12 ± 0.7	24 ± 2
(−)-Methamphetamine	4640 ± 240	29 ± 3	416 ± 20
(±)-MDMA	74.3 ± 5.6	136 ± 17	278 ± 12
(+)-MDMA	70.8 ± 5.2	110 ± 16	142 ± 6
(−)-MDMA	337 ± 34	564 ± 60	3682 ± 178
(+)-Amphetamine	1765 ± 94	7.1 ± 1.0	25 ± 4
(±)-MDA	159 ± 12	108 ± 12	290 ± 10
(+)-MDA	99.6 ± 7.4	98.5 ± 6.1	50.0 ± 8.0
(−)-MDA	313 ± 21	287 ± 23	900 ± 49

Sources: The data are taken from Partilla et al.[28] and Setola et al.[29] Details concerning *in vitro* methods can be found in these papers.

6.7.1.2 *In Vivo Microdialysis Studies*

The technique of *in vivo* microdialysis allows continuous sampling of extracellular fluid from intact brain, and dialysate samples can be assayed for monoamine transmitters using various analytical methods.[30] Microdialysis studies in rats demonstrate that systemic administration of MDMA increases extracellular levels of 5-HT and DA in the brain, consistent with the *in vitro* results noted above.[31–34] Pretreatment with 5-HT uptake inhibitors can block the rise in dialysate 5-HT produced by MDMA, suggesting the involvement of SERT.[33,35] Interestingly, the effect of MDMA administration on dialysate DA appears to be more complex and entails at least two processes: (1) a tetrodotoxin-insensitive mechanism that involves substrate interaction at DAT proteins,[36,37] and (2) a tetrodotoxin-sensitive mechanism that involves activation of 5-HT$_{2A}$ receptor sites by endogenous 5-HT.[33,38] Findings from our laboratory, illustrated in Figure 6.7.4, reveal that intravenous (i.v.) MDMA administration causes dose-related elevations in extracellular levels of 5-HT and DA in rat nucleus accumbens.[39] In these experiments, drugs were administered to conscious rats undergoing *in vivo* microdialysis. Dialysate levels of 5-HT and DA were determined by high-performance liquid chromatography coupled to electrochemical detection (HPLC-ECD). We found

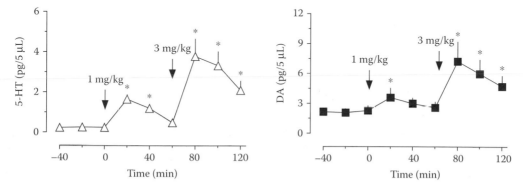

Figure 6.7.4 Dose–response effects of MDMA on extracellular levels of endogenous 5-HT (left panel) and DA (right panel) in rat nucleus accumbens. Male rats undergoing *in vivo* microdialysis received i.v. injections of 1 and 3 mg/kg MDMA at 0 and 60 min, respectively. Dialysate levels of 5-HT and DA were assayed by HPLC-ECD. Data are mean ± SEM, expressed as pg/5 μl sample, for N = 6 rats/ group. Baseline levels of 5-HT and DA were 0.22 ± 0.03 and 1.44 ± 0.24 pg/5 μl, respectively. *Significant with respect to pre-injection control (P < 0.05 Duncan's). See Baumann et al.[39] for methods.

that MDMA has greater effects on *in vivo* 5-HT release when compared to DA release, and this observation has been confirmed in brain regions such as cortex and striatum. At the 1 mg/kg i.v. dose of MDMA, extracellular 5-HT was elevated approximately sixfold above baseline whereas extracellular DA was elevated approximately twofold.

6.7.2 Acute Effects of MDMA

6.7.2.1 In Vivo Pharmacological Effects of MDMA

The acute CNS effects of MDMA administration are mediated by the release of monoamine transmitters, with the subsequent activation of presynaptic and postsynaptic receptor sites.[40] As specific examples in rats, MDMA suppresses 5-HT cell firing, evokes neuroendocrine secretion, and stimulates locomotor activity. MDMA-induced suppression of 5-HT cell firing in the dorsal and median raphe involves activation of presynaptic 5-HT$_{1A}$ autoreceptors by endogenous 5-HT.[41,42] Neuroendocrine effects of MDMA include secretion of prolactin from the anterior pituitary and corticosterone from the adrenal glands.[43] Evidence supports the notion that these MDMA-induced hormonal effects are mediated via postsynaptic 5-HT$_2$ receptors in the hypothalamus, which are activated by released 5-HT. MDMA elicits a unique profile of locomotor effects characterized by forward locomotion and elements of the 5-HT behavioral syndrome such as flattened body posture, Straub tail, and forepaw treading.[44–46] The complex motor effects of MDMA are dependent on monoamine release followed by activation of multiple postsynaptic 5-HT and DA receptor subtypes in the brain,[47] but the precise role of specific receptor subtypes is still under investigation.

In our laboratory, we carried out *in vivo* microdialysis in rats that were housed in chambers equipped with photo-beams to allow automated assessment of motor activity. Under these conditions, i.v. MDMA administration increases motor activity in conjunction with elevations in extracellular 5-HT and DA (see Figure 6.7.4). The data in Figure 6.7.5 demonstrate that MDMA increases forward locomotion (i.e., ambulation) and repetitive movements (i.e., stereotypy) in a dose-dependent fashion. Stereotypy produced by i.v. MDMA consists predominately of lateral side-to-side head weaving and reciprocal forepaw treading. We discovered that MDMA-induced 5-HT release in the nucleus accumbens and caudate nucleus is significantly correlated with stereotypic movements, whereas DA release in these brain regions is correlated with ambulation. These data suggest

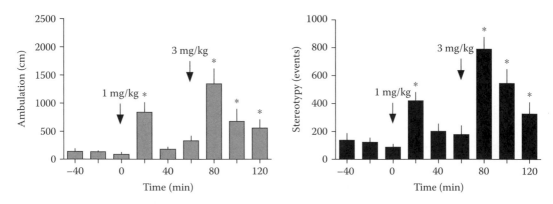

Figure 6.7.5 Dose–response effects of MDMA on ambulation (left panel) and stereotypy (right panel) in rats undergoing *in vivo* microdialysis. Male rats received i.v. injections of 1 and 3 mg/kg MDMA at 0 and 60 min, respectively. Ambulation (i.e., forward locomotion) and stereotypy (i.e., repetitive movements) were measured by photo-beam break analysis. Data are mean ± SEM, expressed as centimeters traveled for ambulation and number of events for stereotypy, with $N = 6$ rats/ group. *Significant with respect to pre-injection control ($P < 0.05$ Duncan's). See Baumann et al.[39] for methods.

that 5-HT and DA systems influence MDMA-induced motor activation in a region-specific and modality-specific manner.

Adverse effects of high-dose MDMA intoxication, including cardiovascular stimulation and elevated body temperature, are thought to involve monoamine release from sympathetic nerves in the periphery or nerve terminals in the CNS.[48] MDMA increases heart rate and mean arterial pressure in conscious rats;[49,50] this cardiovascular stimulation is probably related to MDMA-induced release of peripheral NE stores, similar to the effects of amphetamine.[51] MDMA is reported to have weak agonist actions (i.e., $IC_{50} > 1$ μM) at α_2-adrenoreceptors and 5-HT$_2$ receptors, which might influence its cardiac and pressor effects.[52–54] Moreover, the MDMA metabolite MDA is a potent 5-HT$_{2B}$ agonist, and this property could contribute to adverse cardiovascular effects.[29] The ability of MDMA to elevate body temperature is well characterized in rats,[35,43,46,55] and this response has long been considered a 5-HT-mediated process. However, a recent study by Mechan et al.[35] provides convincing evidence that MDMA-induced hyperthermia in rats involves activation of postsynaptic D$_1$ receptors by released DA.

6.7.2.2 MDMA Metabolism

MDMA is extensively metabolized in humans and other species.[56] Figure 6.7.6 depicts the major pathway of MDMA biotransformation in humans, which entails: (1) O-demethylation catalyzed by cytochrome P450 2D6 (CYP2D6) and (2) O-methylation catalyzed by catechol-O-methyltransferase (COMT). CYP2D6 and COMT are both polymorphic in humans; the differential expression of CYP2D6 isoforms leads to marked inter-individual variations in the metabolism of serotonergic medications (e.g., SSRIs).[57] Interestingly, CYP2D6 is not present in rats, and this species expresses a homologous but functionally distinct cytochrome P450 2D1 that metabolizes MDMA.[58,59] A minor pathway of MDMA biotransformation in humans involves N-demethylation

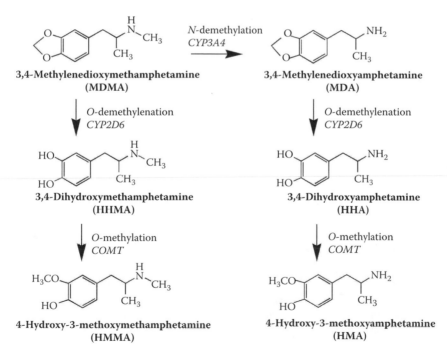

Figure 6.7.6 Metabolism of MDMA in humans. Abbreviations: *CYP2D6*, cytochrome P450 2D6; *CYP3A4*, cytochrome P450 3A4; *COMT*, catechol-O-methyltransferase. (Adapted from de la Torre and co-workers.[56])

of MDMA to form MDA, which is subsequently O-demethylenated and O-methylated as described above. The N-demethylation pathway represents a more important mechanism for biotransformation of MDMA in rats when compared to humans.[60]

As noted above, MDA is a potent stimulator of monoamine release (see Table 6.7.1), and recent reports indicate that a number of MDMA metabolites are bioactive. For example, Forsling et al.[61] showed that the metabolite 4-hydroxy-3-methoxymethamphetamine (HMMA) is more potent than MDMA as a stimulator of vasopressin secretion from rat posterior pituitaries *in vitro*. The neuroendocrine effects produced by *in vivo* administration of MDMA metabolites have not been examined. Monks et al.[62] demonstrated that catechol metabolites of MDMA and MDA, namely, 3,4-dihydroxymethamphetamine (HHMA) and 3,4-dihydroxyamphetamine (HHA), exhibit neurotoxic properties when oxidized and conjugated with glutathione. Further characterization of the biological effects of MDMA metabolites is an important area of research.

The findings of de la Torre et al.[63] have shown that MDMA displays nonlinear kinetics in humans such that administration of increasing doses, or multiple doses, leads to unexpectedly high plasma levels of the drug. Enhanced plasma and tissue levels of MDMA are most likely related to auto-inhibition of MDMA metabolism, mediated via formation of a metabolite-enzyme complex that irreversibly inactivates CYP2D6.[64] Because of the nonlinear kinetics, repeated MDMA dosing could produce serious adverse consequences due to unusually high blood and tissue levels of the drug. The existing database of MDMA pharmacokinetic studies represents a curious situation where clinical findings are well documented, whereas preclinical data even in rodents are lacking. Specifically, few studies in animals have assessed the relationship between pharmacodynamic and pharmacokinetic effects of MDMA after single or repeated doses (although see Reference 65). No studies have systematically characterized the nonlinear kinetics of MDMA in rodent or nonhuman primate models.

6.7.3 Long-Term Effects of MDMA

6.7.3.1 Long-Term Effects of MDMA on 5-HT Neurons

The adverse effects of MDMA on 5-HT systems have been widely publicized, as many studies in animals show that high-dose MDMA administration produces persistent reductions in markers of 5-HT nerve terminal integrity.[66] Table 6.7.2 summarizes the findings of investigators who first demonstrated that MDMA causes long-term (>2 weeks) inhibition of tryptophan hydroxylase activity, depletion of brain tissue 5-HT, and reduction in SERT binding and function.[67–70] Immunohistochemical analysis of 5-HT in the CNS reveals an apparent loss of 5-HT axons and terminals in MDMA-treated rats, especially the fine-diameter projections arising from the dorsal raphe nucleus.[71,72] Moreover, the 5-HT axons and terminals remaining after MDMA treatment appear swollen and fragmented, suggesting structural damage. Time-course studies indicate that MDMA-induced 5-HT depletion occurs in a biphasic manner, with a rapidly occurring acute phase followed

Table 6.7.2 Long-Term Effects of MDMA on 5-HT Neuronal Markers in Rats

5-HT Deficit	Dose	Survival Interval	Ref.
Depletions of 5-HT in forebrain regions as measured by HPLC-ECD	10–40 mg/kg, s.c., twice daily, 4 days	2 weeks	Commins et al.[68]
Reductions in tryptophan hydroxylase activity in forebrain regions	10 mg/kg, s.c., single dose	2 weeks	Stone et al.[70]
Loss of [³H]-paroxetine-labeled SERT binding sites in forebrain regions	20 mg/kg, s.c., twice daily, 4 days	2 weeks	Battaglia et al.[67]
Deceased immunoreactive 5-HT in fine axons and nerve terminals	20 mg/kg, s.c., twice daily, 4 days	2 weeks	O'Hearn et al.[72]

by a delayed long-term phase.[69,70] In the acute phase, which lasts for the first few hours after drug administration, massive depletion of brain tissue 5-HT is accompanied by inactivation of tryptophan hydroxylase. By 24 h later, tissue 5-HT recovers to normal levels but tryptophan hydroyxylase activity remains diminished. In the long-term phase, which begins within 1 week and lasts for months, depletion of 5-HT is accompanied by sustained inactivation of tryptophan hydroxylase and loss of SERT binding and function.[73,74]

The findings in Table 6.7.2 have been replicated by many investigators, and the spectrum of decrements produced by MDMA administration is typically described as 5-HT "neurotoxicity." Possible mechanisms underlying MDMA-induced 5-HT deficits are not completely understood, but evidence suggests the involvement of free radicals, oxidative damage, and metabolic stress.[75–77] As noted above, there are increasing data to support a role for toxic MDMA metabolites in mediating the long-term serotonergic effects of the drug.[60,62] Most studies examining MDMA neurotoxicity in rats have employed intraperitoneal (i.p.) or subcutaneous (s.c.) injections of 10 mg/kg or higher, either as single or repeated treatments. Such MDMA dosing regimens are known to produce significant hyperthermia, which exacerbates 5-HT deficits.[78,79]

There are some caveats to the hypothesis that MDMA produces 5-HT neurotoxicity. O'Hearn et al.[71,72] showed that MDMA has no effect on 5-HT cell bodies in the dorsal raphe despite profound loss of 5-HT in forebrain projection areas. Accordingly, the effects of MDMA on 5-HT neurons are often referred to as "axotomy," to account for the fact that perikarya arc not damaged. MDMA-induced reductions in 5-HT levels and SERT binding eventually recover,[73,74] suggesting that 5-HT terminals are not destroyed. Many drugs used clinically produce effects similar to MDMA. For instance, reserpine causes sustained depletions of brain tissue 5-HT; yet reserpine is not considered a neurotoxin.[80] Chronic administration of 5-HT selective reuptake inhibitors (SSRIs), like paroxetine and sertraline, leads to a marked loss of SERT binding and function analogous to MDMA, but these agents are important therapeutic drugs rather than neurotoxins.[81,82] In fact, Frazer and Benmansour[83] have suggested that sustained downregulation of SERT binding and function underlies the efficacy of SSRIs in the treatment of depression and other mood disorders. Finally, high-dose administration of SSRIs produces swollen, fragmented, and abnormal 5-HT terminals, which are indistinguishable from the effects of high-dose MDMA and other substituted amphetamines.[84]

The above-mentioned caveats raise a number of questions with regard to MDMA neurotoxicity. Of course, the most important question is whether MDMA abuse causes neurotoxic damage to 5-HT systems in humans. This complex issue is a matter of ongoing debate, which has been addressed by recent papers.[85–87] Clinical studies designed to critically evaluate the long-term effects of MDMA are hampered by a range of factors including comorbid psychopathology and polydrug abuse among MDMA users. Animal models afford the unique opportunity to evaluate the potential neurotoxic effects of MDMA administration without many of these complicating factors.

6.7.3.2 Long-Term Effects of MDMA on Markers of Neurotoxicity

It is well accepted that MDMA produces 5-HT depletions in rat CNS, but much less attention has been devoted to the effects of MDMA on established markers of neurotoxicity such as cell death, silver-positive staining, and reactive gliosis. Support for the hypothesis of MDMA-induced axotomy relies heavily on immunohistochemical analysis of 5-HT levels, which could produce misleading results if not validated by other methods. For example, MDMA-induced loss of 5-HT could be due to persistent adaptive changes in gene expression or protein function, reflecting a state of metabolic quiescence rather than neurotoxic damage. Table 6.7.3 summarizes the effects of MDMA on hallmark measures of neurotoxicity.

Anatomical evidence reveals that MDMA does not damage 5-HT cell bodies, and functional studies support this notion. 5-HT neurons in the dorsal raphe exhibit pacemaker-like firing, which can be recorded using electrophysiological techniques.[41,42] High-dose MDMA administration (20 mg/kg, s.c., twice daily, 4 days) has no lasting effects on 5-HT cell firing or action potential

Table 6.7.3 Effects of MDMA on Established Markers of Neurotoxicity in Rats

CNS Marker	Dosing Regimen	Survival Interval	Ref.
No change in 5-HT cell firing in raphe nuclei	20 mg/kg, s.c., twice daily, 4 days	2 weeks	Gartside et al.[88]
Increased silver-positive staining in degenerating neurons	80 mg/kg, s.c., twice daily, 4 days 25–150 mg/kg, s.c., twice daily, 2 days	15–48 h 2 days	Commins et al.[68] Jensen et al.[92]
No reactive astrogliosis, as measured by a lack of change in levels of GFAP	10–30 mg/kg, s.c., twice daily, 7 days 20 mg/kg, s.c., twice daily, 4 days 7.5 mg/kg, i.p., 3 doses	2 days 3 days, 1 week 2 days, 2 weeks	*O'Callaghan et al.[96] *Pubill et al.[98] *Wang et al.[97,99]

* These investigators found no effect of MDMA on GFAP expression, at doses that significantly depleted 5-HT levels in brain tissue.

characteristics, when recordings are carried out 2 weeks after drug pretreatment.[88] The electrophysiological data in MDMA-pretreated rats differ from the effects produced by the neurotoxin 5,7-dihydroxytryptamine (5,7-DHT). In 5,7-DHT-pretreated rats, 5-HT cell firing is dramatically decreased in the dorsal raphe, in conjunction with loss of 5-HT immunofluorescence.[89,90] Thus, 5,7-DHT produces reductions in 5-HT cell firing that are attributable to cell death, but MDMA does not.

Silver staining techniques are commonly used to identify neuronal degeneration,[91] and two studies have examined the ability of MDMA to affect silver-positive staining (i.e., argyrophilia) in rat CNS. Commins et al.[68] administered single or multiple s.c. doses of 80 mg/kg MDMA to male rats, whereas Jensen et al.[92] gave twice daily s.c. injections of 50 to 250 mg/kg. In both cases, MDMA-pretreated rats displayed dose-dependent increases in the number of silver-positive nerve terminals, axons, and cell bodies in various brain areas, with the most severe degeneration observed in frontoparietal cortex. These results provide direct strong support for MDMA-induced neurotoxicity, but certain factors must be considered when interpreting the data. First, massive daily doses of MDMA ranging from 80 to 500 mg/kg were utilized, and these doses far exceed those producing 5-HT depletions in rats (see Table 6.7.2). Second, both investigations noted the presence of argyrophilic cell bodies in the cortex of MDMA-treated rats. Because 5-HT cell bodies are not present in the cortex,[93] these damaged cells must be nonserotonergic. Finally, the pattern of MDMA-induced silver staining does not correspond to the pattern of 5-HT innervation or the pattern of 5-HT depletions. It seems that sufficiently high doses of MDMA can increase silver-positive staining but this does not reflect 5-HT neurotoxicity per se.

A universal response to cell damage in the CNS is hypertrophy of astrocytes.[94] This "reactive gliosis" is accompanied by enhanced expression of glial-specific structural proteins, like glial fibrillary acidic protein (GFAP). O'Callaghan et al.[95] verified that a wide range of neurotoxic chemicals increase the levels of GFAP in rat CNS, indicating this protein can be used as a sensitive marker of neuronal damage. These investigators administered twice daily s.c. injections of 10 to 30 mg/kg MDMA to rats for 7 consecutive days; under these conditions, MDMA produced large 5-HT depletions in forebrain without any changes in GFAP expression.[96] Effects of MDMA on GFAP expression have been compared to the effects of 5,7-DHT.[96,97] At doses of MDMA and 5,7-DHT that cause comparable 5-HT depletions, only 5,7-DHT increases GFAP. Several recent reports from our laboratory and others confirm that MDMA-induced 5-HT depletions are not associated with increased GFAP expression.[97–99] Taken together, the majority of data from rats indicate that doses of MDMA causing significant 5-HT depletions (i.e., single or repeated doses of 10 to 20 mg/kg) do not induce cell death, silver-positive staining, or glial activation, suggesting these doses may not cause neuronal damage.

6.7.4 Interspecies Scaling and MDMA Dosing

6.7.4.1 Allometric Scaling and MDMA Dosing Regimens

A major point of controversy relates to the relevance of MDMA doses administered to rats when compared to those self-administered by humans (see References 40 and 48). As noted above, MDMA regimens that produce 5-HT depletions in rats involve administration of one or more doses of 10 to 20 mg/kg, whereas the amount of "Ecstasy" abused by humans is one or two tablets of 80 to 100 mg, about 1 to 3 mg/kg. Based on principles of "interspecies scaling," some investigators have proposed that high noxious doses of MDMA in rats correspond to recreational doses in humans.[100] The concept of interspecies scaling is based on shared biochemical mechanisms among eukaryotic cells (e.g., aerobic respiration), and was initially developed to describe variations in basal metabolic rate (BMR) in animal species of different sizes.[101,102] In the 1930s, Kleiber derived what is now called the "allometric equation" to describe the relationship between BMR and body weight. The generic form of the allometric equation is $Y = aW^b$, where Y is the variable of interest, W is the body weight, a is the allometric coefficient, and b is the allometric exponent. In the case where Y is BMR, b is accepted to be 0.75. In agreement with predictions of the allometric equation, smaller animals are known to have faster metabolism, heart rates, and circulation times, leading to faster clearance of exogenously administered drugs.

Unfortunately, the allometric equation is not always a valid predictor of drug dosing across species, especially for those compounds that are extensively metabolized in the liver.[103,104] As outlined previously, MDMA is readily metabolized *in vivo* (see Figure 6.7.6).[56,59] There are significant species differences in the expression level and functional activity of cytochrome P450 isoforms involved in the metabolism of MDMA.[59,60] The potential for nonlinear kinetics complicates comparative aspects of MDMA metabolism, and no information is available concerning this phenomenon in diverse species. Additionally, brain tissue uptake of substituted amphetamines is much greater in rats than in humans,[105] suggesting rats could be more sensitive than humans to the effects of MDMA, rather than vice versa. Collectively, the available information indicates that allometric scaling can be used to extrapolate *physiological* variables across species, but this method cannot be used to predict idiosyncratic distribution and metabolism of exogenously administered MDMA in a given animal model.

6.7.4.2 Effect Scaling and MDMA Dosing Regimens

The limitations of allometric scaling led us to investigate the method of "effect scaling" as an alternative strategy for matching equivalent doses of MDMA in rats and humans. In this approach, the lowest dose of drug that produces specific pharmacological responses is determined for rats and humans, and subsequent dosing regimens in rats are calculated with reference to the predetermined threshold dose. Table 6.7.4 shows the doses of MDMA that produce comparable CNS effects in rats and humans. Remarkably, the findings reveal that doses of MDMA in the range of 1 to 2 mg/kg produce pharmacological effects that are equivalent in both species.

Administration of MDMA at doses of 1 to 3 mg/kg causes marked elevations in extracellular 5-HT and DA in rat brain, as determined by *in vivo* microdialysis.[33,34,39] Although it is impossible to directly measure 5-HT and DA release in living human brain, clinical studies indicate that subjective effects of MDMA (1.5 mg/kg, p.o.) are antagonized by SSRIs, suggesting the involvement of transporter-mediated release of 5-HT.[1,106] Nash et al.[43] showed that i.p. injections of 1 to 3 mg/kg of MDMA stimulate prolactin and corticosterone secretion in rats, and similar oral doses increase plasma prolactin and cortisol in human drug users.[11,12] The dose of MDMA discriminated by rats and humans is identical: 1.5 mg/kg, i.p., for rats[107,108] and 1.5 mg/kg, p.o., for humans.[109] Schenk et al.[110] demonstrated that rats can be trained to self-administer MDMA using i.v. doses ranging

Table 6.7.4 Comparative Neurobiological Effects of MDMA Administration in Rats and Humans

CNS Effect	Dose in Rats	Dose in Humans
In vivo release of 5-HT and DA	2.5 mg/kg, i.p., Gudelsky et al.[33] 1 mg/kg, s.c., Kankaanpaa et al.[34]	*1.5 mg/kg p.o., Leichti et al.[1,106]
Secretion of prolactin and glucocorticoids	1–3 mg/kg, i.p., Nash et al.[43]	125 mg, p.o., Mas et al.[11] 1.5 mg/kg, p.o., Harris et al.[12]
Drug discrimination	1.5 mg/kg, i.p., Schechter[108] 1.5 mg/kg, i.p., Glennon and Higgs[107]	1.5 mg/kg, p.o., Johanson et al.[109]
Drug self-administration	1 mg/kg, i.v., Schenck et al.[110]	**1–2 mg/kg, p.o., Tancer and Johanson[111]

* Subjective effects were attenuated by 5-HT uptake blockers, suggesting the involvement of transporter-mediated 5-HT release.
** Reinforcing effects were determined based on a multiple choice procedure.

from 0.25 to 1.0 mg/kg, indicating these doses possess reinforcing efficacy. Tancer and Johanson[111] reported that 1 and 2 mg/kg doses of MDMA have reinforcing properties in humans that resemble those of (+)-amphetamine. The findings summarized in Table 6.7.4 indicate there is no need to use interspecies scaling to "adjust" MDMA doses between rats and humans.

Based on this analysis, we devised a repeated MDMA dosing regimen in rats to mimic a one-time recreational binge in humans. Male rats weighing 300 to 350 g served as subjects and were double-housed in plastic shoebox cages. In our initial studies, 3 i.p. injections of 1.5 or 7.5 mg/kg MDMA were administered, one dose every 2 h, to yield cumulative doses of 4.5 or 22.5 mg/kg, respectively. Control rats received saline vehicle according to the same schedule. Rats were removed from their cages to receive i.p. injections, but were otherwise confined to their home cages. The 1.5 mg/kg dose was used as a low "behavioral" dose whereas the 7.5 mg/kg dose was used as a high "noxious" dose (i.e., a dose fivefold greater than threshold). Our repeated dosing regimen was designed to account for the common practice of sequential dosing (i.e., "bumping) used by human subjects during rave parties. During the MDMA dosing procedure, rectal temperatures were recorded and 5-HT-mediated behaviors were scored every hour. Rats were decapitated 2 weeks after dosing, brain regions were dissected, and tissue levels of 5-HT and DA were determined by HPLC-ECD as described previously.[112]

Data in Figure 6.7.7 illustrate that repeated i.p. doses of 7.5 mg/kg MDMA elicit persistent hyperthermia on the day of treatment, whereas repeated doses of 1.5 mg/kg do not. As shown in Figure 6.7.8, high-dose MDMA treatment produces long-term depletions of tissue 5-HT in a number of brain regions (~50% reductions), but the low-dose group displays 5-HT concentrations similar to saline controls. Transmitter depletion is selective for 5-HT neurons since tissue DA levels are unaffected. The magnitude of 5-HT depletions depicted in Figure 6.7.8 is similar to that observed by others.[67–70] Our findings demonstrate that repeated injections of MDMA at a threshold behavioral dose do not cause acute hyperthermia or long-term 5-HT depletions. In contrast, repeated injections of MDMA at a dose that is fivefold higher than the behavioral dose induce both of these adverse effects. The data are consistent with those of O'Shea et al.[113] who reported that high-dose MDMA (10 or 15 mg/kg, i.p.), but not low-dose MDMA (4 mg/kg, i.p.), causes acute hyperthermia and long-term 5-HT depletion in Dark Agouti rats. Thus, our data confirm that acute hyperthermia produced by MDMA is an important factor contributing to the mechanism underlying subsequent long-term 5-HT depletion.

6.7.5 Consequences of MDMA-Induced 5-HT Depletions

As noted above, high-dose MDMA administration causes persistent inactivation of tryptophan hydroxylase, which leads to inhibition of 5-HT synthesis and long-term loss of 5-HT.[70,72] Moreover, MDMA-induced reduction in the density of SERT binding sites leads to decreased capacity for reuptake of [³H]5-HT in nervous tissue.[67–69] Regardless of whether these deficits reflect neurotoxic

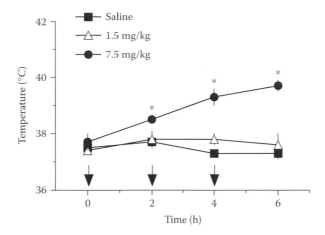

Figure 6.7.7 Acute effects of MDMA on core body temperature in rats. Male rats received three sequential i.p. injections of 1.5 or 7.5 mg/kg MDMA, one dose every 2 h (i.e., injections at 0, 2, and 4 h). Saline was administered on the same schedule. Core temperature was recorded via a rectal thermometer probe every 2 h. Data are mean ± SEM expressed as degrees Celsius for N = 5 rats/group. *Significant with respect to saline-injected control at each time point (P < 0.05 Duncan's).

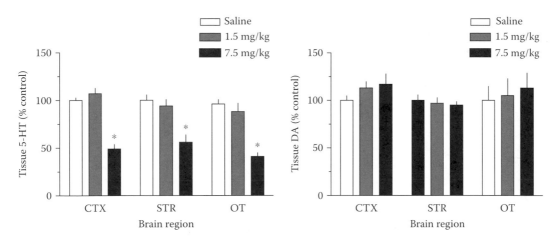

Figure 6.7.8 Long-term effects of MDMA on tissue levels of 5-HT (left panel) and DA (right panel) in brain regions. Male rats received three i.p. injections of 1.5 or 7.5 mg/kg MDMA, one dose every 2 h. Saline was administered on the same schedule. Rats were killed 2 weeks after injections, brain regions were dissected, and tissue 5-HT and DA were assayed by HPLC-ECD.[112] Data are mean ± SEM expressed as percent of saline-treated control values for each region, N = 5 rats/group. Control values of 5-HT and DA were 557 ± 24 and 28 ± 4 pg/mg tissue for frontal cortex (CTX), 429 ± 36 and 10,755 ± 780 pg/mg tissue for striatum (STR), and 1174 ± 114 and 4545 ± 426 pg/mg tissue for olfactory tubercle (OT). * Significant compared to saline-injected control for each region (P < 0.05 Duncan's).

damage or long-term adaptation, such changes would be expected to have discernible *in vivo* correlates. Many investigators have examined functional consequences of high-dose MDMA administration, and a comprehensive review of this subject is beyond the scope of the present review.[48] Nonetheless, the following discussion will consider long-term effects of MDMA (i.e., >2 weeks) on *in vivo* indicators of 5-HT function in rats, as measured by microdialysis sampling, neuroendocrine secretion, and specific aspects of behavior. A number of key findings are summarized in Table 6.7.5. In general, few published studies have been able to relate the magnitude of MDMA-induced 5-HT depletion to the degree of specific functional impairment. MDMA administration rarely causes persistent changes in baseline measures of neural function, and deficits are most readily demon-

Table 6.7.5   Long-Term Effects of MDMA on Functional Indices of 5-HT Transmission in Rats

CNS Effect	Dosing Regimen	Survival Interval	Ref.
Reductions in evoked 5-HT release in vivo	20 mg/kg, s.c., twice daily, 4 days 10 mg/kg, i.p., twice daily, 4 days	2 weeks 1 week	Series et al.[114] Shankaran and Gudelsky [115]
Changes in corticosterone and prolactin secretion	20 mg/kg, s.c. 20 mg/kg, s.c., twice daily, 4 days	2 weeks 4, 8, and 12 months	Poland et al.[124,125] Poland et al.[125]
Impairments in short-term memory	10–20 mg/kg, s.c., twice daily, 3 days	2 weeks	*Marston et al.[134]
Increased anxiety-like behaviors	5 mg/kg, s.c., 1 or 4 doses, 2 days 7.5 mg/kg, s.c., twice daily, 3 days	3 months 2 weeks	**Morley et al.[135]; McGregor et al.[138] **Fone et al.[137]

* Most studies show no effect of MDMA on learning and memory in rats (see text).
** These investigators noted marked increases in anxiogenic behaviors in the absence of significant MDMA-induced 5-HT depletion in brain.

strated by provocation of the 5-HT system by pharmacological (e.g., drug challenge) or physiological means (e.g., environmental stress).

6.7.5.1   In Vivo Microdialysis Studies

In vivo microdialysis has been used to evaluate the persistent neurochemical consequences of MDMA exposure in rats.[88,114–116] Series et al.[114] carried out microdialysis in rat frontal cortex 2 weeks after a 4-day regimen of 20 mg/kg s.c. MDMA. Prior MDMA exposure did not affect baseline extracellular levels of 5-HT, but decreased levels of the 5-HT metabolite, 5-hydroxyindoleacetic acid (5-HIAA), to ~30% of control. Moreover, the ability of (+)-fenfluramine to evoke 5-HT release was markedly blunted in MDMA-pretreated rats. In an analogous investigation, Shankaran and Gudelsky[115] assessed neurochemical effects of acute MDMA challenge in rats that had previously received 4 doses of 10 mg/kg i.p. MDMA. A week after MDMA pretreatment, baseline levels of dialysate 5-HT and DA in striatum were not altered even though tissue levels of 5-HT were depleted by 50%. The ability of MDMA to evoke 5-HT release was severely impaired in MDMA-pretreated rats while the concurrent DA response was normal. In this same study, effects of MDMA on body temperature and 5-HT syndrome were attenuated in MDMA-pretreated rats, suggesting drug tolerance.

Taken together, the microdialysis data reveal several important consequences of MDMA administration: (1) baseline levels of dialysate 5-HT are unaltered, despite depletion of tissue indoles, (2) baseline levels of dialysate 5-HIAA are consistently decreased, and (3) stimulated release of 5-HT is blunted in response to pharmacological or physiological provocation. The microdialysis findings in MDMA-pretreated rats resemble those obtained with 5,7-DHT, in which drug-pretreated rats display normal baseline extracellular 5-HT but decreased 5-HIAA.[117–119] In a representative study, Kirby et al.[117] performed microdialysis in rat striatum 4 weeks after intracerebroventricular 5,7-DHT. These investigators found that reductions in baseline dialysate 5-HIAA and impairments in stimulated 5-HT release are highly correlated with the degree of tissue 5-HT depletion, whereas baseline dialysate 5-HT is not. In fact, depletions of brain tissue 5-HT up to 90% did not affect baseline levels of dialysate 5-HT. Clearly, adaptive mechanisms serve to maintain normal concentrations of synaptic 5-HT, even under conditions of severe transmitter depletion. A comparable situation exists after lesions of the nigrostriatal DA system in rats where baseline levels of extracellular DA are maintained in the physiological range despite substantial loss of tissue DA.[120] In the case of high-dose MDMA treatment, it seems feasible that reductions in 5-HT uptake (e.g., less functional SERT protein) and metabolism (e.g., decreased monoamine oxidase activity) can compensate for 5-HT depletions in order to keep optimal concentrations of 5-HT bathing nerve cells. On the other hand, deficits in the ability to release 5-HT are readily demonstrated in MDMA-pretreated rats when 5-HT systems are taxed by drug challenge or stressors.

6.7.5.2 Neuroendocrine Challenge Studies

5-HT neurons projecting to the hypothalamus provide stimulatory input for the secretion of adrenocorticotropin (ACTH) and prolactin from the anterior pituitary.[121] Accordingly, 5-HT releasers (e.g., fenfluramine) and 5-HT receptor agonists increase plasma levels of these hormones in rats and humans.[122] Neuroendocrine challenge experiments have identified changes in serotonergic responsiveness in rats treated with MDMA.[123–125] In the most comprehensive study, Poland et al.[125] examined effects of high-dose MDMA on hormone responses elicited by acute fenfluramine challenge. Rats received injections of 20 mg/kg s.c. MDMA and were tested 2 weeks later. Prior MDMA exposure did not alter baseline levels of circulating ACTH or prolactin. However, in MDMA-pretreated rats, fenfluramine-induced ACTH secretion was reduced while prolactin secretion was enhanced. The MDMA dosing regimen caused significant depletions of tissue 5-HT in various brain regions, including hypothalamus. In a follow-up time-course study, rats exposed to multiple doses of 20 mg/kg MDMA displayed blunted ACTH responses that persisted for 12 months, even though tissue levels of 5-HT were not depleted at this time point. The data show that high-dose MDMA can cause functional abnormalities for up to 1 year, and such changes are not necessarily coupled to 5-HT depletions.

In our laboratory, we wished to further explore the long-term neuroendocrine consequences of MDMA administration. Utilizing the "effect scaling" regimen described previously, male Sprague-Dawley rats received 3 i.p. injections of 1.5 or 7.5 mg/kg MDMA, one dose every 2 h. Control rats received saline vehicle according to the same schedule. A week after MDMA treatment, rats were fitted with indwelling jugular catheters under pentobarbital anesthesia. After 1 week of recovery from surgery (i.e., 2 weeks after MDMA or saline), rats were brought into the testing room, i.v. doses of 1 and 3 mg/kg MDMA were administered, and blood samples were withdrawn. Plasma levels of corticosterone and prolactin were measured by radioimmunoassay methods.[126] The data depicted in Figure 6.7.9 show that MDMA pretreatment did not alter baseline levels of either hormone. Acute

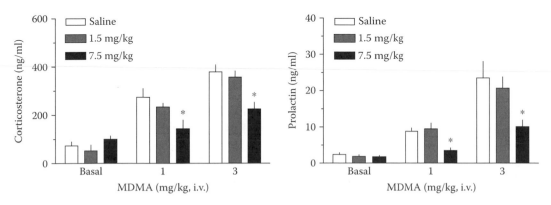

Figure 6.7.9 Effects of MDMA pretreatment on secretion of corticosterone (left panel) and prolactin (right panel) evoked by acute MDMA challenge. Male rats received three i.p. injections of 1.5 or 7.5 mg/kg MDMA, one dose every 2 h. Saline was administered on the same schedule. Then 2 weeks later rats received i.v. injections of 1 and 3 mg/kg MDMA. Blood samples were drawn via indwelling catheters; plasma corticosterone and prolactin were measured by RIA.[126] Data are mean ± SEM, expressed as ng/ml of plasma for $N = 8$ rats/group. Baseline corticosterone and prolactin levels were 73 ± 18 and 2.4 ± 0.6 ng/ml of plasma, respectively. *Significant compared to saline-pretreated control group ($P < 0.05$ Duncan's).

administration of MDMA elicited dose-dependent elevations in circulating corticosterone and pro-lactin as shown by others.[43] Rats exposed to high-dose MDMA pretreatment displayed significant reductions in corticosterone and prolactin secretion in response to acute MDMA challenge, whereas hormone responses in the low-dose MDMA rats were indistinguishable from controls.

Our neuroendocrine results are consistent with the development of tolerance to hormonal effects of MDMA. These findings do not agree completely with the data of Poland et al.[125] discussed above. However, our findings are consistent with previous data showing blunted hormonal responses to fenfluramine in rats with fenfluramine-induced 5-HT depletions.[126] Perhaps more importantly, the data shown in Figure 6.7.9 are strikingly similar to clinical findings in which cortisol and prolactin responses to acute (+)-fenfluramine administration are reduced in human MDMA users.[85,127,128] Indeed, Gerra et al.[128] reported that (+)-fenfluramine-induced prolactin secretion is blunted in abstinent MDMA users for up to 1 year after cessation of drug use. The mechanism(s) underlying altered sensitivity to (+)-fenfluramine and MDMA are not known, but it is tempting to speculate that MDMA-induced impairments in evoked 5-HT release are involved, as shown by *in vivo* microdialysis studies. While some investigators have cited neuroendocrine changes in human MDMA users as evidence for 5-HT neurotoxicity, Gouzoulis-Mayfrank et al.[85] provide a compelling argument that endocrine abnormalities in MDMA users could be related to cannabis use rather than MDMA. Further experiments will be required to resolve the precise nature of neuroendocrine changes in MDMA users.

6.7.5.3 Behavioral Assessments

One of the more serious and disturbing clinical findings is that MDMA causes persistent cognitive deficits in human users.[7,8,87] Numerous studies have examined the effects of MDMA treatment on learning and memory in rats, and most studies failed to identify persistent impairments — even when extensive 5-HT depletions were present.[45,129–133] While an exhaustive review of this literature is not possible here, representative findings will be mentioned. In an extensive series of experiments, Seiden et al.[129] evaluated the effects of high-dose MDMA on a battery of tests including open-field behavior, schedule-controlled behavior, one-way avoidance, discriminated two-way avoidance, forced swim, and radial maze performance. Male rats received twice daily s.c. injections of 10 to 40 mg/kg MDMA for 4 days, and were tested beginning 2 weeks after treatment. Despite large depletions of brain tissue 5-HT, MDMA-pretreated rats exhibited normal behaviors in all paradigms. Likewise, Robinson et al.[130] found that MDMA-induced depletion of cortical 5-HT up to 70% did not alter spatial navigation, skilled forelimb use, or foraging behavior in rats. In contrast, Marston et al.[134] reported that MDMA administration produces persistent deficits in a delayed non-match to performance (DNMTP) procedure when long delay intervals are employed (i.e., 30 s). The authors theorized that delay-dependent impairments in the DNMTP procedure reflect MDMA-induced deficits in short-term memory consolidation, possibly attributable to 5-HT depletion.

With the exception of the findings of Marston et al., the collective behavioral data in rats indicate that MDMA-induced depletions of brain 5-HT have little or no effect on cognitive processes. There are several potential explanations for this apparent paradox. First, high-dose MDMA administration produces only partial depletion of 5-HT in the range of 40 to 60% in most brain areas. This level of 5-HT loss may not be sufficient to elicit behavioral alterations, as compensatory adaptations in 5-HT neurons could maintain normal physiological function. Second, MDMA appears to selectively affect fine diameter fibers arising from the dorsal raphe, and it seems possible that these 5-HT circuits may not subserve the behaviors being monitored. Third, the behavioral tests utilized in rat studies might not be sensitive enough to detect subtle changes in learning and memory processes. Finally, the functional reserve capacity in the CNS might be sufficient to compensate for even large depletions of a single transmitter.

While MDMA appears to have few long-term effects on cognition in rats, a growing body of evidence demonstrates that MDMA administration can cause persistent anxiety-like behaviors in this species.[135–137] Morley et al.[135] first reported that MDMA induces long-term anxiety in male rats. These investigators administered one or 4 i.p. injections of 5 mg/kg MDMA on 2 consecutive days, then tested rats 3 months later in a battery of anxiety-related paradigms including elevated plus maze, emergence, and social interaction tests. Rats receiving single or multiple MDMA injections displayed marked increases in anxiogenic behaviors in all three tests. In a follow-up study, Gurtman et al.[136] replicated the original findings of Morley et al. using rats pretreated with 4 i.p. injections of 5 mg/kg MDMA for 2 days — persistent anxiogenic effects of MDMA were associated with depletions of 5-HT in the amygdala, hippocampus, and striatum. Interestingly, Fone et al.[137] showed that administration of MDMA to adolescent rats caused anxiety-like impairments in social interaction, even in the absence of 5-HT depletions or reductions in [^{3}H]-paroxetine-labeled SERT binding sites. These data suggest that MDMA-induced anxiety does not require 5-HT deficits.

In an attempt to determine potential mechanisms underlying MDMA-induced anxiety, McGregor et al.[138] evaluated effects of the drug on anxiety-related behaviors and a number of post-mortem parameters including autoradiography for SERT and 5-HT receptor subtypes. Rats received moderate (5 mg/kg, i.p., 2 days) or high (5 mg/kg, i.p., 4 injections, 2 days) doses of MDMA, and tests were conducted 10 weeks later. This study confirmed that moderate doses of MDMA can cause protracted increases in anxiety-like behaviors without significant 5-HT depletions. Furthermore, the autoradiographic analysis revealed that anxiogenic effects of MDMA may involve long-term reductions in 5-HT$_{2A/2C}$ receptors rather than reductions in SERT binding. Additional work by Bull et al.[139,140] suggests that decreases in the sensitivity of 5-HT$_{2A}$ receptors, but not 5-HT$_{2C}$ receptors, could underlie MDMA-associated anxiety. Clearly, more investigation into this important area of research is warranted.

6.7.6 Conclusions

The findings reviewed here allow a number of tentative conclusions to be made with regard to MDMA neurobiology. (1) MDMA is a substrate for monoamine transporters, and non-exocytotic release of 5-HT, NE, and DA underlies pharmacological effects of the drug. While MDMA is often considered a selective serotonergic agent, many actions including cardiovascular stimulation and hyperthermia likely involve NE and DA mechanisms. (2) MDMA produces long-term changes in 5-HT neurons, as exemplified by sustained depletions of forebrain 5-HT in rats. Emerging evidence indicates that 5-HT deficits are not synonymous with neuronal damage, however, since doses of MDMA that cause marked 5-HT depletions (e.g., 10 to 20 mg/kg) are not associated with cell death, silver-positive staining, or reactive gliosis. Like many other psychotropic agents, MDMA is capable of producing *bona fide* neurotoxicity at sufficient doses (e.g., >30 mg/kg) and damage is not confined to 5-HT neurons. (3) There appears to be no scientific rationale for using interspecies scaling to adjust doses of MDMA between rats and humans because behaviorally active doses are similar in both species (e.g., 1 to 2 mg/kg). Nonetheless, the complex metabolism of MDMA needs to be examined in various animal species to permit comparison with clinical literature and to validate appropriate preclinical models. (4) MDMA-induced 5-HT depletions in rats are accompanied by abnormalities in evoked 5-HT release, neuroendocrine secretion, and specific behaviors. The clinical relevance of preclinical findings is uncertain, but the fact that MDMA can produce persistent increases in anxiety-like behaviors in rats without measurable 5-HT deficits suggests even moderate doses may pose risks.

Acknowledgments

This research was generously supported by the NIDA Intramural Research Program. The authors are indebted to John Partilla, Chris Dersch, Mario Ayestas, Robert Clark, Fred Franken, and John Rutter for their expert technical assistance during these studies.

REFERENCES

1. Liechti, M.E. and Vollenweider, F.X., Which neuroreceptors mediate the subjective effects of MDMA in humans? A summary of mechanistic studies, *Hum. Psychopharmacol.* 16(8), 589–598, 2001.

2. Vollenweider, F.X., Gamma, A., Liechti, M., and Huber, T., Psychological and cardiovascular effects and short-term sequelae of MDMA ("ecstasy") in MDMA-naive healthy volunteers, *Neuropsychopharmacology* 19(4), 241–251, 1998.

3. Landry, M.J., MDMA: a review of epidemiologic data, *J. Psychoactive Drugs* 34(2), 163–9, 2002.

4. Yacoubian, G.S., Jr., Tracking ecstasy trends in the United States with data from three national drug surveillance systems, *J. Drug Educ.* 33(3), 245–258, 2003.

5. Banken, J.A., Drug abuse trends among youth in the United States, *Ann. N.Y. Acad. Sci.* 1025, 465–471, 2004.

6. Schifano, F., A bitter pill. Overview of ecstasy (MDMA, MDA) related fatalities, *Psychopharmacology* (Berlin) 173(3–4), 242–248, 2004.

7. Morgan, M.J., Ecstasy (MDMA): a review of its possible persistent psychological effects, *Psychopharmacology* (Berlin) 152(3), 230–248, 2000.

8. Parrott, A.C., Recreational Ecstasy/MDMA, the serotonin syndrome, and serotonergic neurotoxicity, *Pharmacol. Biochem. Behav.* 71(4), 837–844, 2002.

9. Doblin, R., A clinical plan for MDMA (Ecstasy) in the treatment of posttraumatic stress disorder (PTSD): partnering with the FDA, *J. Psychoactive Drugs* 34(2), 185–94, 2002.

10. Check, E., Psychedelic drugs: the ups and downs of ecstasy, *Nature* 429(6988), 126–128, 2004.

11. Mas, M., Farre, M., de la Torre, R., Roset, P.N., Ortuno, J., Segura, J., and Cami, J., Cardiovascular and neuroendocrine effects and pharmacokinetics of 3,4-methylenedioxymethamphetamine in humans, *J. Pharmacol. Exp. Ther.* 290(1), 136–145, 1999.

12. Harris, D.S., Baggott, M., Mendelson, J.H., Mendelson, J.E., and Jones, R.T., Subjective and hormonal effects of 3,4-methylenedioxymethamphetamine (MDMA) in humans, *Psychopharmacology* (Berlin) 162(4), 396–405, 2002.

13. Bell, S.E., Burns, D.T., Dennis, A.C., and Speers, J.S., Rapid analysis of ecstasy and related phenethylamines in seized tablets by Raman spectroscopy, *Analyst* 125(3), 541–544, 2000.

14. Huang, Y.S., Liu, J.T., Lin, L.C., and Lin, C.H., Chiral separation of 3,4-methylenedioxymethamphetamine and related compounds in clandestine tablets and urine samples by capillary electrophoresis/fluorescence spectroscopy, *Electrophoresis* 24(6), 1097–1104, 2003.

15. Cho, A.K., Hiramatsu, M., Distefano, E.W., Chang, A.S., and Jenden, D.J., Stereochemical differences in the metabolism of 3,4-methylenedioxymethamphetamine *in vivo* and *in vitro*: a pharmacokinetic analysis, *Drug Metab. Dispos.* 18(5), 686–691, 1990.

16. Lim, H.K. and Foltz, R.L., *In vivo* and *in vitro* metabolism of 3,4-(methylenedioxy)methamphetamine in the rat: identification of metabolites using an ion trap detector, *Chem. Res. Toxicol.* 1(6), 370–378, 1988.

17. Nichols, D.E., Lloyd, D.H., Hoffman, A.J., Nichols, M.B., and Yim, G.K., Effects of certain hallucinogenic amphetamine analogues on the release of [³H]serotonin from rat brain synaptosomes, *J. Med. Chem.* 25(5), 530–535, 1982.

18. Johnson, M.P., Hoffman, A.J., and Nichols, D.E., Effects of the enantiomers of MDA, MDMA and related analogues on [³H]serotonin and [³H]dopamine release from superfused rat brain slices, *Eur. J. Pharmacol.* 132(2–3), 269–276, 1986.

19. Schmidt, C.J., Levin, J.A., and Lovenberg, W., *In vitro* and *in vivo* neurochemical effects of methylenedioxymethamphetamine on striatal monoaminergic systems in the rat brain, *Biochem. Pharmacol.* 36(5), 747–755, 1987.

20. Fitzgerald, J.L. and Reid, J.J., Interactions of methylenedioxymethamphetamine with monoamine transmitter release mechanisms in rat brain slices, *Naunyn Schmiedeberg's Arch. Pharmacol.* 347(3), 313–323, 1993.

21. Berger, U.V., Gu, X.F., and Azmitia, E.C., The substituted amphetamines 3,4-methylenedioxymethamphetamine, methamphetamine, *p*-chloroamphetamine and fenfluramine induce 5-hydroxytryptamine release via a common mechanism blocked by fluoxetine and cocaine, *Eur. J. Pharmacol.* 215(2–3), 153–160, 1992.

22. Crespi, D., Mennini, T., and Gobbi, M., Carrier-dependent and Ca(2+)-dependent 5-HT and dopamine release induced by (+)-amphetamine, 3,4-methylenedioxymethamphetamine, *p*-chloroamphetamine and (+)-fenfluramine, *Br. J. Pharmacol.* 121(8), 1735–1743, 1997.

23. Rothman, R.B. and Baumann, M.H., Therapeutic and adverse actions of serotonin transporter substrates, *Pharmacol. Ther.* 95(1), 73–88, 2002.

24. Rudnick, G. and Wall, S.C., The molecular mechanism of "ecstasy" [3,4-methylenedioxy-methamphetamine (MDMA)]: serotonin transporters are targets for MDMA-induced serotonin release, *Proc. Natl. Acad. Sci. U.S.A.* 89(5), 1817–1821, 1992.

25. Schuldiner, S., Steiner-Mordoch, S., Yelin, R., Wall, S.C., and Rudnick, G., Amphetamine derivatives interact with both plasma membrane and secretory vesicle biogenic amine transporters, *Mol. Pharmacol.* 44(6), 1227–1231, 1993.

26. Rothman, R.B., Baumann, M.H., Dersch, C.M., Romero, D.V., Rice, K.C., Carroll, F.I., and Partilla, J.S., Amphetamine-type central nervous system stimulants release norepinephrine more potently than they release dopamine and serotonin, *Synapse* 39(1), 32–41, 2001.

27. Rothman, R.B., Partilla, J.S., Baumann, M.H., Dersch, C.M., Carroll, F.I., and Rice, K.C., Neurochemical neutralization of methamphetamine with high-affinity nonselective inhibitors of biogenic amine transporters: a pharmacological strategy for treating stimulant abuse, *Synapse* 35(3), 222–227, 2000.

28. Partilla, J.S., Dersch, C.M., Yu, H., Rice, K.C., and Rothman, R.B., Neurochemical neutralization of amphetamine-type stimulants in rat brain by the indatraline analog (–)-HY038, *Brain Res. Bull.* 53(6), 821–826, 2000.

29. Setola, V., Hufeisen, S.J., Grande-Allen, K.J., Vesely, I., Glennon, R.A., Blough, B., Rothman, R.B., and Roth, B.L., 3,4-Methylenedioxymethamphetamine (MDMA, "Ecstasy") induces fenfluramine-like proliferative actions on human cardiac valvular interstitial cells *in vitro*, *Mol. Pharmacol.* 63(6), 1223–1229, 2003.

30. Baumann, M.H. and Rutter, J.J., Application of *in vivo* microdialysis methods to the study of psychomotor stimulant drugs, in *Methods in Drug Abuse Research, Cellular and Circuit Level Analysis*, Warerhouse, B.D. CRC Press, Boca Raton, FL, 2003, 51–86.

31. Nash, J.F. and Nichols, D.E., Microdialysis studies on 3,4-methylenedioxyamphetamine and structurally related analogues, *Eur. J. Pharmacol.* 200(1), 53–58, 1991.

32. Yamamoto, B.K., Nash, J.F., and Gudelsky, G.A., Modulation of methylenedioxymethamphetamine-induced striatal dopamine release by the interaction between serotonin and gamma-aminobutyric acid in the substantia nigra, *J. Pharmacol. Exp. Ther.* 273(3), 1063–1070, 1995.

33. Gudelsky, G.A. and Nash, J.F., Carrier-mediated release of serotonin by 3,4-methylenedioxymethamphetamine: implications for serotonin-dopamine interactions, *J. Neurochem.* 66(1), 243–249, 1996.

34. Kankaanpaa, A., Meririnne, E., Lillsunde, P., and Seppala, T., The acute effects of amphetamine derivatives on extracellular serotonin and dopamine levels in rat nucleus accumbens, *Pharmacol. Biochem. Behav.* 59(4), 1003–1009, 1998.

35. Mechan, A.O., Esteban, B., O'Shea, E., Elliott, J.M., Colado, M.I., and Green, A.R., The pharmacology of the acute hyperthermic response that follows administration of 3,4-methylenedioxymethamphetamine (MDMA, "ecstasy") to rats, *Br. J. Pharmacol.* 135(1), 170–180, 2002.

36. Nash, J.F. and Brodkin, J., Microdialysis studies on 3,4-methylenedioxymethamphetamine-induced dopamine release: effect of dopamine uptake inhibitors, *J. Pharmacol. Exp. Ther.* 259(2), 820–825, 1991.

37. Shankaran, M., Yamamoto, B.K., and Gudelsky, G.A., Mazindol attenuates the 3,4-methylenedioxymethamphetamine-induced formation of hydroxyl radicals and long-term depletion of serotonin in the striatum, *J. Neurochem.* 72(6), 2516–2522, 1999.

38. Schmidt, C.J., Sullivan, C.K., and Fadayel, G.M., Blockade of striatal 5-hydroxytryptamine2 receptors reduces the increase in extracellular concentrations of dopamine produced by the amphetamine analogue 3,4-methylenedioxymethamphetamine, *J. Neurochem.* 62(4), 1382–1389, 1994.

39. Baumann, M.H., Clark, R.D., Budzynski, A.G., Partilla, J.S., Blough, B.E., and Rothman, R.B., N-substituted piperazines abused by humans mimic the molecular mechanism of 3,4-methylenedioxymethamphetamine (MDMA, or "Ecstasy"), *Neuropsychopharmacology* 30(3), 550–560, 2005.

40. Cole, J.C. and Sumnall, H.R., The pre-clinical behavioural pharmacology of 3,4-methylenedioxymethamphetamine (MDMA), *Neurosci. Biobehav. Rev.* 27(3), 199–217, 2003.

41. Sprouse, J.S., Bradberry, C.W., Roth, R.H., and Aghajanian, G.K., MDMA (3,4-methylene-dioxymethamphetamine) inhibits the firing of dorsal raphe neurons in brain slices via release of serotonin, *Eur. J. Pharmacol.* 167(3), 375–383, 1989.

42. Gartside, S.E., McQuade, R., and Sharp, T., Acute effects of 3,4-methylenedioxymethamphetamine (MDMA) on 5-HT cell firing and release: comparison between dorsal and median raphe 5-HT systems, *Neuropharmacology* 36(11–12), 1697–703, 1997.

43. Nash, J.F., Jr., Meltzer, H.Y., and Gudelsky, G.A., Elevation of serum prolactin and corticosterone concentrations in the rat after the administration of 3,4-methylenedioxymethamphetamine, *J. Pharmacol. Exp. Ther.* 245(3), 873–879, 1988.

44. Gold, L.H., Koob, G.F., and Geyer, M.A., Stimulant and hallucinogenic behavioral profiles of 3,4-methylenedioxymethamphetamine and N-ethyl-3,4-methylenedioxyamphetamine in rats, *J. Pharmacol. Exp. Ther.* 247(2), 547–555, 1988.

45. Slikker, W., Jr., Holson, R.R., Ali, S.F., Kolta, M.G., Paule, M.G., Scallet, A.C., McMillan, D.E., Bailey, J.R., Hong, J.S., and Scalzo, F.M., Behavioral and neurochemical effects of orally administered MDMA in the rodent and nonhuman primate, *Neurotoxicology* 10(3), 529–542, 1989.

46. Spanos, L.J. and Yamamoto, B.K., Acute and subchronic effects of methylenedioxymethamphetamine [(+/–)MDMA] on locomotion and serotonin syndrome behavior in the rat, *Pharmacol. Biochem. Behav.* 32(4), 835–840, 1989.

47. Bankson, M.G. and Cunningham, K.A., 3,4-Methylenedioxymethamphetamine (MDMA) as a unique model of serotonin receptor function and serotonin-dopamine interactions, *J. Pharmacol. Exp. Ther.* 297(3), 846–852, 2001.

48. Green, A.R., Mechan, A.O., Elliott, J.M., O'Shea, E., and Colado, M.I., The pharmacology and clinical pharmacology of 3,4-methylenedioxymethamphetamine (MDMA, "ecstasy"), *Pharmacol. Rev.* 55(3), 463–508, 2003.

49. O'Cain, P.A., Hletko, S.B., Ogden, B.A., and Varner, K.J., Cardiovascular and sympathetic responses and reflex changes elicited by MDMA, *Physiol. Behav.* 70(1–2), 141–148, 2000.

50. Badon, L.A., Hicks, A., Lord, K., Ogden, B.A., Meleg-Smith, S., and Varner, K.J., Changes in cardiovascular responsiveness and cardiotoxicity elicited during binge administration of Ecstasy, *J. Pharmacol. Exp. Ther.* 302(3), 898–907, 2002.

51. Fitzgerald, J.L. and Reid, J.J., Sympathomimetic actions of methylenedioxymethamphetamine in rat and rabbit isolated cardiovascular tissues, *J. Pharm. Pharmacol.* 46(10), 826–832, 1994.

52. Lyon, R.A., Glennon, R.A., and Titeler, M., 3,4-Methylenedioxymethamphetamine (MDMA): stereoselective interactions at brain 5-HT1 and 5-HT2 receptors, *Psychopharmacology* (Berlin) 88(4), 525–526, 1986.

53. Battaglia, G. and De Souza, E.B., Pharmacologic profile of amphetamine derivatives at various brain recognition sites: selective effects on serotonergic systems, *NIDA Res. Monogr.* 94, 240–258, 1989.

54. Lavelle, A., Honner, V., and Docherty, J.R., Investigation of the prejunctional alpha2-adrenoceptor mediated actions of MDMA in rat atrium and vas deferens, *Br. J. Pharmacol.* 128(5), 975–980, 1999.

55. Dafters, R.I., Hyperthermia following MDMA administration in rats: effects of ambient temperature, water consumption, and chronic dosing, *Physiol. Behav.* 58(5), 877–882, 1995.

56. de la Torre, R., Farre, M., Roset, P.N., Pizarro, N., Abanades, S., Segura, M., Segura, J., and Cami, J., Human pharmacology of MDMA: pharmacokinetics, metabolism, and disposition, *Ther. Drug Monit.* 26(2), 137–144, 2004.

57. Charlier, C., Broly, F., Lhermitte, M., Pinto, E., Ansseau, M., and Plomteux, G., Polymorphisms in the CYP 2D6 gene: association with plasma concentrations of fluoxetine and paroxetine, *Ther. Drug Monit.* 25(6), 738–742, 2003.

58. Malpass, A., White, J.M., Irvine, R.J., Somogyi, A.A., and Bochner, F., Acute toxicity of 3,4-methylenedioxymethamphetamine (MDMA) in Sprague-Dawley and Dark Agouti rats, *Pharmacol. Biochem. Behav.* 64(1), 29–34, 1999.

59. Maurer, H.H., Bickeboeller-Friedrich, J., Kraemer, T., and Peters, F.T., Toxicokinetics and analytical toxicology of amphetamine-derived designer drugs ("Ecstasy"), *Toxicol. Lett.* 112–113, 133–142, 2000.

60. de la Torre, R. and Farre, M., Neurotoxicity of MDMA (ecstasy): the limitations of scaling from animals to humans, *Trends Pharmacol. Sci.* 25(10), 505–508, 2004.

61. Forsling, M.L., Fallon, J.K., Shah, D., Tilbrook, G.S., Cowan, D.A., Kicman, A.T., and Hutt, A.J., The effect of 3,4-methylenedioxymethamphetamine (MDMA, "ecstasy") and its metabolites on neurohypophysial hormone release from the isolated rat hypothalamus, *Br. J. Pharmacol.* 135(3), 649–656, 2002.

62. Monks, T.J., Jones, D.C., Bai, F., and Lau, S.S., The role of metabolism in 3,4-(+)-methylenedioxyamphetamine and 3,4-(+)-methylenedioxymethamphetamine (ecstasy) toxicity, *Ther. Drug Monit.* 26(2), 132–136, 2004.

63. de la Torre, R., Farre, M., Ortuno, J., Mas, M., Brenneisen, R., Roset, P.N., Segura, J., and Cami, J., Non-linear pharmacokinetics of MDMA ("ecstasy") in humans, *Br. J. Clin. Pharmacol.* 49(2), 104–109, 2000.

64. Wu, D., Otton, S.V., Inaba, T., Kalow, W., and Sellers, E.M., Interactions of amphetamine analogs with human liver CYP2D6, *Biochem. Pharmacol.* 53(11), 1605–1612, 1997.

65. Chu, T., Kumagai, Y., DiStefano, E.W., and Cho, A.K., Disposition of methylenedioxymethamphet amine and three metabolites in the brains of different rat strains and their possible roles in acute serotonin depletion, *Biochem. Pharmacol.* 51(6), 789–796, 1996.

66. Lyles, J. and Cadet, J.L., Methylenedioxymethamphetamine (MDMA, Ecstasy) neurotoxicity: cellular and molecular mechanisms, *Brain Res. Brain Res. Rev.* 42(2), 155–168, 2003.

67. Battaglia, G., Yeh, S.Y., O'Hearn, E., Molliver, M.E., Kuhar, M.J., and De Souza, E.B., 3,4-Methylenedioxymethamphetamine and 3,4-methylenedioxyamphetamine destroy serotonin terminals in rat brain: quantification of neurodegeneration by measurement of [^{3}H]paroxetine-labeled serotonin uptake sites, *J. Pharmacol. Exp. Ther.* 242(3), 911–916, 1987.

68. Commins, D.L., Vosmer, G., Virus, R.M., Woolverton, W.L., Schuster, C.R., and Seiden, L.S., Biochemical and histological evidence that methylenedioxymethylamphetamine (MDMA) is toxic to neurons in the rat brain, *J. Pharmacol. Exp. Ther.* 241(1), 338–345, 1987.

69. Schmidt, C.J., Neurotoxicity of the psychedelic amphetamine, methylenedioxymethamphetamine, *J. Pharmacol. Exp. Ther.* 240(1), 1–7, 1987.

70. Stone, D.M., Merchant, K.M., Hanson, G.R., and Gibb, J.W., Immediate and long-term effects of 3,4-methylenedioxymethamphetamine on serotonin pathways in brain of rat, *Neuropharmacology* 26(12), 1677–1683, 1987.

71. Molliver, M.E., Berger, U.V., Mamounas, L.A., Molliver, D.C., O'Hearn, E., and Wilson, M.A., Neurotoxicity of MDMA and related compounds: anatomic studies, *Ann. N.Y. Acad. Sci.* 600, 649–661; discussion 661–664, 1990.

72. O'Hearn, E., Battaglia, G., De Souza, E.B., Kuhar, M.J., and Molliver, M.E., Methylenedioxyamphetamine (MDA) and methylenedioxymethamphetamine (MDMA) cause selective ablation of serotonergic axon terminals in forebrain: immunocytochemical evidence for neurotoxicity, *J. Neurosci.* 8(8), 2788–2803, 1988.

73. Battaglia, G., Yeh, S.Y., and De Souza, E.B., MDMA-induced neurotoxicity: parameters of degeneration and recovery of brain serotonin neurons, *Pharmacol. Biochem. Behav.* 29(2), 269–274, 1988.

74. Scanzello, C.R., Hatzidimitriou, G., Martello, A.L., Katz, J.L., and Ricaurte, G.A., Serotonergic recovery after (+/−)3,4-(methylenedioxy) methamphetamine injury: observations in rats, *J. Pharmacol. Exp. Ther.* 264(3), 1484–1491, 1993.

75. Sprague, J.E., Everman, S.L., and Nichols, D.E., An integrated hypothesis for the serotonergic axonal loss induced by 3,4-methylenedioxymethamphetamine, *Neurotoxicology* 19(3), 427–441, 1998.

76. Kuhn, D.M. and Geddes, T.J., Molecular footprints of neurotoxic amphetamine action, *Ann. N.Y. Acad. Sci.* 914, 92–103, 2000.

77. Gudelsky, G.A. and Yamamoto, B.K., Neuropharmacology and neurotoxicity of 3,4-methylenedioxymethamphetamine, *Methods Mol. Med.* 79, 55–73, 2003.

78. Malberg, J.E. and Seiden, L.S., Small changes in ambient temperature cause large changes in 3,4-methylenedioxymethamphetamine (MDMA)-induced serotonin neurotoxicity and core body temperature in the rat, *J. Neurosci.* 18(13), 5086–5094, 1998.

79. Green, A.R., O'Shea, E., and Colado, M.I., A review of the mechanisms involved in the acute MDMA (ecstasy)-induced hyperthermic response, *Eur. J. Pharmacol.* 500(1–3), 3–13, 2004.

80. Carlsson, A., The contribution of drug research to investigating the nature of endogenous depression, *Pharmakopsychiatr. Neuropsychopharmakol.* 9(1), 2–10, 1976.

81. Benmansour, S., Cecchi, M., Morilak, D.A., Gerhardt, G.A., Javors, M.A., Gould, G.G., and Frazer, A., Effects of chronic antidepressant treatments on serotonin transporter function, density, and mRNA level, *J. Neurosci.* 19(23), 10494–10501, 1999.

82. Benmansour, S., Owens, W.A., Cecchi, M., Morilak, D.A., and Frazer, A., Serotonin clearance *in vivo* is altered to a greater extent by antidepressant-induced downregulation of the serotonin transporter than by acute blockade of this transporter, *J. Neurosci.* 22(15), 6766–6772, 2002.

83. Frazer, A. and Benmansour, S., Delayed pharmacological effects of antidepressants, *Mol. Psychiatry* 7(Suppl. 1), S23–S28, 2002.

84. Kalia, M., O'Callaghan, J.P., Miller, D.B., and Kramer, M., Comparative study of fluoxetine, sibutramine, sertraline and dexfenfluramine on the morphology of serotonergic nerve terminals using serotonin immunohistochemistry, *Brain Res.* 858(1), 92–105, 2000.

85. Gouzoulis-Mayfrank, E., Becker, S., Pelz, S., Tuchtenhagen, F., and Daumann, J., Neuroendocrine abnormalities in recreational ecstasy (MDMA) users: is it ecstasy or cannabis? *Biol. Psychiatry* 51(9), 766–769, 2002.

86. Kish, S.J., How strong is the evidence that brain serotonin neurons are damaged in human users of ecstasy? *Pharmacol. Biochem. Behav.* 71(4), 845–855, 2002.

87. Reneman, L., Designer drugs: how dangerous are they? *J. Neural Transm. Suppl.* 66, 61–83, 2003.

88. Gartside, S.E., McQuade, R., and Sharp, T., Effects of repeated administration of 3,4-methylenedioxymethamphetamine on 5-hydroxytryptamine neuronal activity and release in the rat brain *in vivo*, *J. Pharmacol. Exp. Ther.* 279(1), 277–283, 1996.

89. Aghajanian, G.K., Wang, R.Y., and Baraban, J., Serotonergic and non-serotonergic neurons of the dorsal raphe: reciprocal changes in firing induced by peripheral nerve stimulation, *Brain Res.* 153(1), 169–175, 1978.

90. Hajos, M. and Sharp, T., A 5-hydroxytryptamine lesion markedly reduces the incidence of burst-firing dorsal raphe neurones in the rat, *Neurosci. Lett.* 204(3), 161–164, 1996.

91. Switzer, R.C., III, Application of silver degeneration stains for neurotoxicity testing, *Toxicol. Pathol.* 28(1), 70–83, 2000.

92. Jensen, K.F., Olin, J., Haykal-Coates, N., O'Callaghan, J., Miller, D.B., and de Olmos, J.S., Mapping toxicant-induced nervous system damage with a cupric silver stain: a quantitative analysis of neural degeneration induced by 3,4-methylenedioxymethamphetamine, *NIDA Res. Monogr.* 136, 133–149; discussion 150–154, 1993.

93. Steinbusch, H.W., Distribution of serotonin-immunoreactivity in the central nervous system of the rat-cell bodies and terminals, *Neuroscience* 6(4), 557–618, 1981.

94. O'Callaghan, J.P. and Sriram, K., Glial fibrillary acidic protein and related glial proteins as biomarkers of neurotoxicity, *Expert Opin. Drug Saf.* 4(3), 433–442, 2005.

95. O'Callaghan, J.P., Jensen, K.F., and Miller, D.B., Quantitative aspects of drug and toxicant-induced astrogliosis, *Neurochem. Int.* 26(2), 115–124, 1995.

96. O'Callaghan, J.P. and Miller, D.B., Quantification of reactive gliosis as an approach to neurotoxicity assessment, *NIDA Res. Monogr.* 136, 188–212, 1993.

97. Wang, X., Baumann, M.H., Xu, H., and Rothman, R.B., 3,4-Methylenedioxymethamphetamine (MDMA) administration to rats decreases brain tissue serotonin but not serotonin transporter protein and glial fibrillary acidic protein, *Synapse* 53(4), 240–248, 2004.

98. Pubill, D., Canudas, A.M., Pallas, M., Camins, A., Camarasa, J., and Escubedo, E., Different glial response to methamphetamine- and methylenedioxymethamphetamine-induced neurotoxicity, *Naunyn Schmiedeberg's Arch. Pharmacol.* 367(5), 490–499, 2003.

99. Wang, X., Baumann, M.H., Xu, H., Morales, M., and Rothman, R.B., ({+/–})-3,4-Methylenedioxymethamphetamine administration to rats does not decrease levels of the serotonin transporter protein or alter its distribution between endosomes and the plasma membrane, *J. Pharmacol. Exp. Ther.* 314(3), 1002–1012, 2005.

100. Ricaurte, G.A., Yuan, J., and McCann, U.D., (+/–)3,4-Methylenedioxymethamphetamine ("Ecstasy")-induced serotonin neurotoxicity: studies in animals, *Neuropsychobiology* 42(1), 5–10, 2000.

101. White, C.R. and Seymour, R.S., Allometric scaling of mammalian metabolism, *J. Exp. Biol.* 208(9), 1611–1619, 2005.

102. West, G.B. and Brown, J.H., The origin of allometric scaling laws in biology from genomes to ecosystems: towards a quantitative unifying theory of biological structure and organization, *J. Exp. Biol.* 208(9), 1575–1592, 2005.

103. Lin, J.H., Applications and limitations of interspecies scaling and *in vitro* extrapolation in pharmacokinetics, *Drug Metab. Dispos.* 26(12), 1202–1212, 1998.

104. Mahmood, I., Allometric issues in drug development, *J. Pharm. Sci.* 88(11), 1101–1106, 1999.

105. Campbell, D.B., The use of toxicokinetics for the safety assessment of drugs acting in the brain, *Mol. Neurobiol.* 11(1–3), 193–216, 1995.

106. Liechti, M.E. and Vollenweider, F.X., The serotonin uptake inhibitor citalopram reduces acute cardiovascular and vegetative effects of 3,4-methylenedioxymethamphetamine ("Ecstasy") in healthy volunteers, *J. Psychopharmacol.* 14(3), 269–274, 2000.

107. Glennon, R.A. and Higgs, R., Investigation of MDMA-related agents in rats trained to discriminate MDMA from saline, *Pharmacol. Biochem. Behav.* 43(3), 759–763, 1992.

108. Schechter, M.D., Serotonergic-dopaminergic mediation of 3,4-methylenedioxymethamphetamine (MDMA, "ecstasy"), *Pharmacol. Biochem. Behav.* 31(4), 817–824, 1988.

109. Johanson, C.E., Kilbey, M., Gatchalian, K., and Tancer, M., Discriminative stimulus effects of 3,4-methylenedioxymethamphetamine (MDMA) in humans trained to discriminate among *d*-amphetamine, meta-chlorophenylpiperazine and placebo, *Drug Alcohol Depend.* 81, 27–36, 2006.

110. Schenk, S., Gittings, D., Johnstone, M., and Daniela, E., Development, maintenance and temporal pattern of self-administration maintained by ecstasy (MDMA) in rats, *Psychopharmacology* (Berlin) 169(1), 21–27, 2003.

111. Tancer, M. and Johanson, C.E., Reinforcing, subjective, and physiological effects of MDMA in humans: a comparison with *d*-amphetamine and mCPP, *Drug Alcohol Depend.* 72(1), 33–44, 2003.

112. Baumann, M.H., Ayestas, M.A., Dersch, C.M., and Rothman, R.B., 1-(*m*-chlorophenyl)piperazine (mCPP) dissociates *in vivo* serotonin release from long-term serotonin depletion in rat brain, *Neuropsychopharmacology* 24(5), 492–501, 2001.

113. O'Shea, E., Granados, R., Esteban, B., Colado, M.I., and Green, A.R., The relationship between the degree of neurodegeneration of rat brain 5-HT nerve terminals and the dose and frequency of administration of MDMA ("ecstasy"), *Neuropharmacology* 37(7), 919–926, 1998.

114. Series, H.G., Cowen, P.J., and Sharp, T., *p*-Chloroamphetamine (PCA), 3,4-methylenedioxy-methamphetamine (MDMA) and *d*-fenfluramine pretreatment attenuates *d*-fenfluramine-evoked release of 5-HT *in vivo*, *Psychopharmacology* (Berlin) 116(4), 508–514, 1994.

115. Shankaran, M. and Gudelsky, G.A., A neurotoxic regimen of MDMA suppresses behavioral, thermal and neurochemical responses to subsequent MDMA administration, *Psychopharmacology* (Berlin) 147(1), 66–72, 1999.

116. Matuszewich, L., Filon, M.E., Finn, D.A., and Yamamoto, B.K., Altered forebrain neurotransmitter responses to immobilization stress following 3,4-methylenedioxymethamphetamine, *Neuroscience* 110(1), 41–48, 2002.

117. Kirby, L.G., Kreiss, D.S., Singh, A., and Lucki, I., Effect of destruction of serotonin neurons on basal and fenfluramine-induced serotonin release in striatum, *Synapse* 20(2), 99–105, 1995.

118. Romero, L., Jernej, B., Bel, N., Cicin-Sain, L., Cortes, R., and Artigas, F., Basal and stimulated extracellular serotonin concentration in the brain of rats with altered serotonin uptake, *Synapse* 28(4), 313–321, 1998.

119. Hall, F.S., Devries, A.C., Fong, G.W., Huang, S., and Pert, A., Effects of 5,7-dihydroxytryptamine depletion of tissue serotonin levels on extracellular serotonin in the striatum assessed with *in vivo* microdialysis: relationship to behavior, *Synapse* 33(1), 16–25, 1999.

120. Zigmond, M.J., Abercrombie, E.D., Berger, T.W., Grace, A.A., and Stricker, E.M., Compensations after lesions of central dopaminergic neurons: some clinical and basic implications, *Trends Neurosci.* 13(7), 290–296, 1990.

121. Van de Kar, L.D., Neuroendocrine pharmacology of serotonergic (5-HT) neurons, *Annu. Rev. Pharmacol. Toxicol.* 31, 289 320, 1991.

122. Levy, A.D., Baumann, M.H., and Van de Kar, L.D., Monoaminergic regulation of neuroendocrine function and its modification by cocaine, *Front. Neuroendocrinol.* 15(2), 85–156, 1994.

123. Series, H.G., le Masurier, M., Gartside, S.E., Franklin, M., and Sharp, T., Behavioural and neuroen-docrine responses to *d*-fenfluramine in rats treated with neurotoxic amphetamines, *J. Psychopharmacol.* 9, 214–222, 1995.

124. Poland, R.E., Diminished corticotropin and enhanced prolactin responses to 8-hydroxy-2(di-*n*-propy-lamino)tetralin in methylenedioxymethamphetamine pretreated rats, *Neuropharmacology* 29(11), 1099–1101, 1990.

125. Poland, R.E., Lutchmansingh, P., McCracken, J.T., Zhao, J.P., Brammer, G.L., Grob, C.S., Boone, K.B., and Pechnick, R.N., Abnormal ACTH and prolactin responses to fenfluramine in rats exposed to single and multiple doses of MDMA, *Psychopharmacology* (Berlin) 131(4), 411–419, 1997.

126. Baumann, M.H., Ayestas, M.A., and Rothman, R.B., Functional consequences of central serotonin depletion produced by repeated fenfluramine administration in rats, *J. Neurosci.* 18(21), 9069–9077, 1998.

127. Gerra, G., Zaimovic, A., Giucastro, G., Maestri, D., Monica, C., Sartori, R., Caccavari, R., and Delsignore, R., Serotonergic function after (+/–)3,4-methylene-dioxymethamphetamine ("Ecstasy") in humans, *Int. Clin. Psychopharmacol.* 13(1), 1–9, 1998.

128. Gerra, G., Zaimovic, A., Ferri, M., Zambelli, U., Timpano, M., Neri, E., Marzocchi, G.F., Delsignore, R., and Brambilla, F., Long-lasting effects of (+/–)3,4-methylenedioxymethamphetamine (ecstasy) on serotonin system function in humans, *Biol. Psychiatry* 47(2), 127–136, 2000.

129. Seiden, L.S., Woolverton, W.L., Lorens, S.A., Williams, J.E., Corwin, R.L., Hata, N., and Olimski, M., Behavioral consequences of partial monoamine depletion in the CNS after methamphetamine-like drugs: the conflict between pharmacology and toxicology, *NIDA Res. Monogr.* 136, 34–46; discussion 46–52, 1993.

130. Robinson, T.E., Castaneda, E., and Whishaw, I.Q., Effects of cortical serotonin depletion induced by 3,4-methylenedioxymethamphetamine (MDMA) on behavior, before and after additional cholinergic blockade, *Neuropsychopharmacology* 8(1), 77–85, 1993.

131. Ricaurte, G.A., Markowska, A.L., Wenk, G.L., Hatzidimitriou, G., Wlos, J., and Olton, D.S., 3,4-Methylenedioxymethamphetamine, serotonin and memory, *J. Pharmacol. Exp. Ther.* 266(2), 1097–1105, 1993.

132. McNamara, M.G., Kelly, J.P., and Leonard, B.E., Some behavioural and neurochemical aspects of subacute (+/–)3,4-methylenedioxymethamphetamine administration in rats, *Pharmacol. Biochem. Behav.* 52(3), 479–484, 1995.

133. Byrne, T., Baker, L.E., and Poling, A., MDMA and learning: effects of acute and neurotoxic exposure in the rat, *Pharmacol. Biochem. Behav.* 66(3), 501–508, 2000.

134. Marston, H.M., Reid, M.E., Lawrence, J.A., Olverman, H.J., and Butcher, S.P., Behavioural analysis of the acute and chronic effects of MDMA treatment in the rat, *Psychopharmacology* (Berlin) 144(1), 67–76, 1999.

135. Morley, K.C., Gallate, J.E., Hunt, G.E., Mallet, P.E., and McGregor, I.S., Increased anxiety and impaired memory in rats 3 months after administration of 3,4-methylenedioxymethamphetamine ("ecstasy"), *Eur. J. Pharmacol.* 433(1), 91–99, 2001.

136. Gurtman, C.G., Morley, K.C., Li, K.M., Hunt, G.E., and McGregor, I.S., Increased anxiety in rats after 3,4-methylenedioxymethamphetamine: association with serotonin depletion, *Eur. J. Pharmacol.* 446(1–3), 89–96, 2002.

137. Fone, K.C., Beckett, S.R., Topham, I.A., Swettenham, J., Ball, M., and Maddocks, L., Long-term changes in social interaction and reward following repeated MDMA administration to adolescent rats without accompanying serotonergic neurotoxicity, *Psychopharmacology* (Berlin) 159(4), 437–444, 2002.

138. McGregor, I.S., Clemens, K.J., Van der Plasse, G., Li, K.M., Hunt, G.E., Chen, F., and Lawrence, A.J., Increased anxiety 3 months after brief exposure to MDMA ("Ecstasy") in rats: association with altered 5-HT transporter and receptor density, *Neuropsychopharmacology* 28(8), 1472–1484, 2003.

139. Bull, E.J., Hutson, P.H., and Fone, K.C., Reduced social interaction following 3,4-methylene-dioxymethamphetamine is not associated with enhanced 5-HT 2C receptor responsivity, *Neuropharmacology* 44(4), 439–448, 2003.

140. Bull, E.J., Hutson, P.H., and Fone, K.C., Decreased social behaviour following 3,4-methylene-dioxymethamphetamine (MDMA) is accompanied by changes in 5-HT2A receptor responsivity, *Neuropharmacology* 46(2), 202–210, 2004.

CHAPTER 7

Addiction Medicine

Edited by Kim Wolff, Ph.D.
King's College London, Institute of Psychiatry, National Addiction Centre, London, U.K.

CONTENTS

INTRODUCTION

Substance misuse is often considered to be an unpopular subject with many doctors, partly because of the frequent relapse experienced by addicts and partly because of the behavioral problems that can occur when drug users interact with substance misuse treatment services.

Many clinical drug treatment services are dominated by the prescribing of methadone to those dependent on heroin (diacetylmorphine). Methadone maintenance treatment (MMT) has been the most rapidly expanded treatment for heroin dependence over the last 30 years with increasingly large numbers of countries providing such treatment for extensive treatment populations. Even more recently buprenorphine, a partial agonist, has been introduced into drug treatment services and has provided an alternative to methadone. Many doctors involved with addiction problems will see themselves as having only a prescribing role whereas specialists in the field will, in addition, require a repertoire of psychotherapy skills.

Prescribing for patients who may have a dependence on a number of drugs, who may wish to conceal the extent of their substance use, and who may have a marked tolerance to some classes of drug is discussed in order to help inform the practitioner.

This chapter is divided into six sections, mainly intended to provide an overview for the non-specialist. The first section explains the psychology of addiction, as opposed to the neurochemistry of addiction discussed in Chapter 6. Overviews are provided of substitute prescribing, an increasingly accepted practice. Considerable discussion is devoted to the identification and management of withdrawal syndromes, whether sedative or stimulant. The final section briefly discusses toxicological testing, primarily for the purpose of assessing compliance. Additional information on this subject can be found in Chapters 1, 3, and 11.

7.1 THE PRINCIPLES OF ADDICTION MEDICINE

Duncan Raistrick, M.B.B.S.
The Leeds Addiction Unit, Leeds, U.K.

Many doctors involved with addiction problems will see themselves as having only a prescribing role whereas specialists in the field will, in addition, require a repertoire of psychotherapy skills.

Prescribing for patients who may have a dependence on a number of drugs, who may wish to conceal the extent of their substance use, and who may have a marked tolerance to some classes of drug presents difficulties for the unwary or ill-informed doctor. In order to prescribe safely and effectively doctors must:

1. Understand the nature of dependence
2. Understand the dependence-forming potential of drugs
3. Understand the importance of motivation

7.1.1 Understanding the Nature of Dependence

In the U.K. and North America, the understanding of addiction has been dominated by the disease theory and the social learning theory. Heather[1] succinctly describes the history and development of thinking underpinning these theories. Other theories or, perhaps more correctly, models of addiction have been popular in particular cultures or where partial explanations have utility; for example, psychoanalytical interpretations of addictive behavior are common in some European countries, and equally, religious or moral failures are attractive reasons to account for addictive behavior where spiritual values are important as in many Asian and Indian communities.

The important implications of the disease theory depend on the notion that addiction is caused by some irreversible deficiency or pathology and that treatment is, therefore, primarily a medical concern. Certain conclusions inevitably follow from such a premise: (1) abstinence is the only treatment goal, (2) loss of control is the hallmark feature, (3) patients are not responsible for their illness, (4) therapists tend to be medical practitioners, and, finally, (5) community-based prevention will be ineffective.

In formulating a description of alcohol and later other drug dependence, Edwards and Gross[2] argued against the disease model in favor of a biopsychosocial construction of dependence, which was identified as belonging to a separate dimension from substance-related harms. This formulation has been adopted in the International Classification of Diseases, ICD-10.[3] The important implications of social learning theory are: a range of treatment goals is possible, the ability to control substance use is emphasized, users are active participants in treatment, therapists tend to be nonmedical, and fiscal and other control measures will be effective.

The biopsychosocial description of dependence has been criticized for placing unwarranted emphasis on withdrawal symptoms. While the anticipation or experience of withdrawal may indeed be a potent source of negative reinforcement for drinking, it is not the only source of reinforcement, and it may be that the positive reinforcement of a pharmacological (drug) effect is more important whether or not an individual also experiences withdrawal. To take account of this, Raistrick et al.[4] have proposed a modified description of the dependence syndrome and developed the idea of substance dependence as a purely psychological phenomenon where tolerance and withdrawal are understood as consequences of regular drinking, rather than being a part of dependence. The withdrawal symptoms themselves are one step removed from the cognitive response to the symptoms, which may or may not include thoughts about drinking. If withdrawal symptoms were themselves a defining element of dependence, then different drugs would be associated with different kinds of dependence, but this is not a widely held view. Rather, it is believed that dependence can readily shift from one substance to another.[5] The markers of substance dependence translate the neuroadaptive elements of the biopsychosocial description of dependence into cues that condition cognitions and behaviors and are therefore of more universal application. There are ten markers of substance dependence:

1. Preoccupation with drinking or taking drugs
2. Salience of substance use behavior
3. Compulsion to start using alcohol or drugs
4. Planning alcohol- or drug-related behaviors

5. Maximizing the substance effect
6. Narrowing of substance use repertoire
7. Compulsion to continue using alcohol and drugs
8. Primacy of psychoactive effect
9. Maintaining a constant state (of intoxication)
10. Expectations of need for substance use

In summary, the most complete account of addictive behaviors comes from a synthesis of physiology, pharmacology, psychology, sociology, and social learning. Dependence exists along a continuum of severity implying the need for different treatments and outcome goals. Substance-related
harms in physical, psychological, and social spheres belong to a separate domain. *Addiction* has
become a term without precise meaning, but is generally taken to include dependence, problem
use, and any related harms. While social learning allows that anyone may become dependent on
psychoactive substances and may also unlearn their dependence, it does not preclude the possibility
that substance use may cause deficiencies of endogenous neurotransmitters, which are usually
reversible, or permanent damage to receptor structure and connectivity. Indeed, it is likely that such
changes occur.

7.1.2   Understanding the Dependence-Forming Potential of Drugs

7.1.2.1   *Potency of Psychoactive Effect*

In humans, the reinforcing properties of psychoactive substances, which combine to generate
the umbrella construct dependence, are complex: a prominent view attaches importance to the
positive reinforcing effects of inducing pleasurable mood states and the negative reinforcement of
avoiding painful affects. Pervin[5] explores this very issue in a study of four polydrug users: subjects
were asked to describe situations (1) where they wanted to use drugs, (2) after they had used drugs,
(3) where they wanted to use drugs but could not, and (4) unrelated to drug use, and then to
associate affects from a prepared list with the four situations they described. A factor analysis
produced three factors accounting for 44% of the variance: the first factor, Wish, was characterized
as being tense, helpless, jittery, lonely; the second factor, After Drugs, was characterized as lonely,
empty, inhibited, angry; and the third factor, Taking Drugs, included confidence, relaxed, high,
secure, strong, satisfied. The results also indicated that subjects discriminated between drugs suited
to dealing with different effects.

In two complementary reports, Johanson and Uhlenbuth[6,7] compared changes in mood among
normal volunteers in a choice experiment between placebo, diazepam, and amphetamine. Amphetamine 5 mg was chosen significantly more often than placebo, 81% of possible choices, with
increased scores for vigor, friendliness, elation, arousal, positive mood, and decreased scores for
confusion. In contrast, diazepam 5 and 10 mg were chosen significantly less often than placebo,
28 and 27% of choices, respectively, with decreased scores on vigor and arousal and increased
scores on confusion and fatigue. The point to underline here is that normal subjects are likely to
have different effects to patient groups and the reinforcing potential of different substances will
therefore vary between such groups: within matched subjects the reinforcing properties of different
substances will also vary in strength.

At a clinical level, most doctors are wary of addictive drugs: for example, long-term methadone
prescribing is intended to achieve pharmacological stability, at least partially block the effect of
other opioids, and prevent withdrawal symptoms. However, Bickel et al.[8] suggest that, although
methadone is seen as a low tariff drug, treatment retention is, in part, associated with its reinforcing
properties. Using a choice paradigm, subjects maintained on methadone 50 mg daily, identified to
subjects as capsule A, had the option of taking capsule B, which, in different trials, contained either
methadone 50, 60, 70, or 100 mg, in place of Capsule A. Capsule B was chosen on 50, 73, 87,
and 97%, respectively, of occasions: at the highest dose, subjects identified an opioid effect and a

liking for the drug but no high or withdrawal was reported. The clinical implications are quantified by McGlothlin and Anglin[9] in a 7-year follow-up of patients attending high- vs. low-dose methadone maintenance programs: the high-dose program performed better in terms of retention, significantly fewer arrests and periods of incarceration, less criminal activity, and less supplementary drug use. In a similar type of study, Hartnoll et al.[10] followed up addicts randomly allocated to an injectable heroin or oral methadone program: at 1-year follow-up, 74% of the heroin group against 29% of the methadone group were still in treatment but only 10% against 30% had achieved abstinence from illicit drugs. So, the dilemma is that prescriptions most liked by addicts, namely, those that are more reinforcing, achieve good program retention and a degree of stability, but at the cost of slowing movement away from substance use and the associated subculture.

The potency of psychoactive effect is not simply a function of dose or plasma level, but also depends on receptor uptake characteristics. For example, Chiang and Barnett[11] have shown that immediately after intravenous tetrahydrocannabinal a rising plasma concentration of approximately 45 ng/ml relates to a subjective high of 10% whereas the same falling plasma concentration 15 min later relates to a high of nearly 80% on a self-rating 0 to 100% scale. This phenomenon is accounted for by a slow uptake of THC at the receptors. Active metabolites may spuriously suggest the same phenomenon.

Similarly, the partial agonist buprenorphine has a high, but slow, binding affinity at the opiate mu receptor: it has the potential to act as antagonist against pure opioid agonists and itself appears to have a ceiling effect at about 1 mg subcutaneously for subjective response. Although addicts identify buprenorphine as having an opioid effect and therefore potential for misuse, its binding affinity at the mu receptor and antagonist activity confer a quite different reinforcement profile to pure agonists such as diamorphine (heroin).

The clinical significance is demonstrated by Johnson et al.[12] who substituted heroin for buprenorphine in ascending daily doses of 2, 4, and 8 mg: using this regimen, diamorphine withdrawal symptoms were avoided and, overall, subjects reported a feeling of well-being. Withdrawal from buprenorphine 8 mg daily does not precipitate an opiate withdrawal syndrome.

7.1.2.2 *Pharmacokinetics*

The previous section argued that the mood-altering effects of psychoactive drugs may, depending on the pre-drug mental state, have both positive and negative reinforcing properties. Psychoactive effect alone is insufficient explanation of within-drug-group differences of dependence forming potential: different pharmacokinetics is important. The benzodiazepines and opioids are the most fruitful source of investigation here because both drug groups contain many different compounds that are widely used and misused. However, it is difficult to conduct studies that control for confounding factors such as absorption rate, potency, purity, half-life, or street availability (and likelihood of supplementing). It is perhaps not surprising that researchers are parsimonious with conclusions.

There are ethical problems in conducting laboratory experiments with potent drugs such as heroin and to avoid this problem Mello et al.[13] investigated the reinforcing efficacy in primates for three opioids: they found buprenorphine and methadone to have similar strength but heroin to be more powerful. Equally in humans heroin is preferred to other opiates including morphine.[14] Since heroin is converted to morphine within the central nervous system (CNS), it can be concluded that its faster rate of CNS availability accounts for the difference. Absorption rate and, therefore, immediacy of effect have similarly been shown to be important for benzodiazepines. Funderburk et al.[15] compared the effects of equipotent oral doses of lorazepam (0, 1.5, 3, and 6 mg) and diazepam (0, 10, 20, and 40 mg) in recreational benzodiazepine users: the drug liking ratings were similar for both drugs, suggesting that the absorption rate, which is similar for the two drugs, is more important than the elimination half-life, which is much shorter for lorazepam even though subjective ratings of effect persist much longer for this compound. Learning theory predicts the importance of absorption rate in that the most immediate positive consequence of a behavior (drug taking) is the most reinforcing. While potency and the speed of onset of effect are particularly important for initiating dependence, elimination rate assumes greater importance in building and maintaining dependence. As a rule, the more quickly a drug is metabolized, the sooner the user experiences a loss of effect and possibly also withdrawal symptoms. Both of these consequences become cues for further drug use.

7.1.2.3 Plasticity

Plasticity is defined as the degree to which the effect of a drug is independent of internal environment (e.g., mood, thirst) and external environment (e.g., with friends, comfort). Edwards[16] has described substances as existing along a continuum: highly plastic substances, that is, those where the content of the effect is markedly influenced by environment, exist at one end (e.g., solvents, LSD), and substances with very predictable content (e.g., heroin, cocaine) exist at the opposite end. Plasticity has a bearing on the dependence-forming potential of substances; where the content of a drug effect is uncertain, repeated use is unlikely. In contrast, a very predictable effect may not suit the variety of uses demanded of a recreational substance, but yet be powerfully reinforcing, that is, addictive. It is interesting that the most popular recreational drugs, alcohol and cannabis, fall around the middle of the plasticity continuum, perhaps signaling a point that allows an agreeable interaction between drug and expectation effects. In summary, the dependence-forming potential of a drug is a function of:

1. Potency of effect
2. Speed of entering the CNS
3. Speed of joining with receptors
4. Elimination rate
5. Predictability of effect

7.1.3 Understanding the Importance of Motivation

The measurement of dependence and the identification of substance-related problems tell the clinician what outcome goals are likely to be successful and how much treatment is needed; alongside this an understanding of motivation informs what kind of treatment is needed. The Model of Change described by Prochaska and DiClemente[17] is a motivational model widely used in the addiction field. The purpose of using the model is twofold: first, to understand what is going on for a patient at a given time; second, to inform the patient of the choice of interventions. People who are not motivated to change their substance use are said to be at the pre-contemplation stage, which is characterized by denial and rationalization of substance use and its consequences. There are two strands to treatment strategy at this stage: one is to minimize harm without expecting to change the substance use behavior (for example, by giving nutritional supplements or substitute prescribing). The second is to introduce conflict about the substance use (for example, by making links with untoward life events and thereby creating motivation for change). The temptation is to offer treatments aimed at changing substance use behavior before the patient is ready to change. In such circumstances the treatment will always fail.

The experience of significant conflict about substance use (for example, when an arrest is felt to be incompatible with a self-image of being a sensible and responsible person) or when the cost of substance use is causing family hardship indicates movement into the contemplation stage. At this stage, motivational interventions, which may involve the use of simple clinical tools (for example, the decision matrix), or may draw on more sophisticated skills (for example, motivational interviewing),[18] are indicated. At this stage substitute prescribing or agonist prescribing may be helpful.

The action stage is reached when conflict is resolved and there is a commitment to change. A number of things will have happened at a psychological level: the person will believe that life will be better on stopping or controlling their substance use (positive outcome expectancy), they are able to change (self-efficacy), and they will know how to change (skills learning). Elective detoxification is the most common medical intervention at the action stage.

The maintenance stage follows behavioral change. This is the achievement of abstinence or controlled substance use. Maintenance of behavior change for alcohol misuse may be assisted by prescribing a sensitizing agent such as disulfiram or, for opiate misuse, prescribing an antagonist such as naltrexone. Pharmacological interventions are no more than an adjunct to the main task of achieving lifestyle change. Successful exit from the maintenance stage, recovery, requires that the patient has confidence and skills to deal with substance use cues. Achieving the right mix of pharmacology and psychology is more art than science, but an understanding of the underlying brain mechanisms, reviewed for clinicians by Nutt,[19] and a parallel understanding of motivation will help achieve safe and effective prescribing.

7.1.4   Prescribing in Context

Addiction problems are everyone's business: the sociologist, the politician, the biochemist, the doctor, the police officer, the parent, the pharmacist, the taxpayer, the drug dealer, and the public. The list is long; such is the diversity of interests vested in substance use and misuse. Everyone will have opinions about addiction including opinions about what doctors should prescribe. Doctors should seek the widest possible clinical freedom to manage addiction patients and to secure this freedom. It follows that prescribers must be sensitive to the prevailing medicopolitical views on what constitutes good practice. People who misuse substances, particularly illicit substances, may have particularly forceful views about what doctors should prescribe, but these views are likely to change depending on where a person is within his or her addiction career. It follows that prescribers must have an understanding of addictive behaviors and characteristics of addictive substances. The Model of Change (described above) is a simple, commonly used tool that offers a framework for prescribing and other interventions.

For most people who have developed a moderate or severe dependence, pharmacotherapy will, at some time, be an important part of treatment. However, prescribing alone will never be sufficient. It follows that prescribers must have a repertoire of skills, including behavior therapy and psychotherapy or, alternatively, must work with a co-therapist. When working with a co-therapist, the doctor must be satisfied with the reasons for prescribing and take responsibility for the prescription given.

7.1.5   General Precautions

Doctors who are inexperienced in the field of addiction often feel pressured to prescribe beyond their knowledge and skills, and as a result may issue inappropriate prescriptions. In contrast, specialists are likely to be circumspect about the place of pharmacotherapy and especially so when this means prescribing addictive drugs.[20] The precautions listed below are applicable to any prescribing; however, patients who misuse both prescribed and illicit drugs are especially at risk, not least because prescriptions are often for potent preparations in doses higher than normally recommended. Doctors may be required to justify their prescribing to a variety of authorities and are more likely to fall afoul of legal action or audit because of precipitate rather than delayed prescribing. Having established the appropriateness of prescribing, the following checklist will ensure the safety of a prescription:

Prescribe drugs with low dependence-forming potential.
Prescribe drugs with low injection potential.

Prescribe drugs with low "street value."
Prescribe inherently stabilizing drugs.
Assess:
    Risk of overdose by patient
    Risk of overdose by others living with patient
    Risk of diversion for profit or misuse
    Risk of failing to control use as prescribed
Assess tolerance before prescribing potentially lethal doses.
Check other prescribed medication.
Check on co-existing medical conditions.
Monitor compliance.

Safety of prescribing needs to be balanced against a regimen that is convenient for the patient and which will therefore achieve the best results in terms of retention and compliance.[21,22] Before finally giving a prescription, it is crucial to ensure that both the doctor and the patient understand the purpose of the prescription.[23] There should be agreement on how to monitor whether or not the intended purpose is being achieved; if the purpose is not achieved then the prescription should be reviewed and possibly discontinued. This does not imply an end to therapy but rather consideration of a shift to an alternative, possibly nonpharmacological treatment.

7.2 SUBSTITUTE PRESCRIBING

Kim Wolff, Ph.D.
King's College London, Institute of Psychiatry, National Addiction Centre, London, U.K.

Substitute prescribing is the prescription of the main drug of misuse or a drug from the same pharmacological group but of lower dependence potential to a dependent individual. The main purpose of substitute prescribing is to stabilize a person's substance use and offer a period of time to work on non-drug-focused interventions. Slow reduction or detoxification can occur at any time during substitute prescribing. Recipients of substitute prescribing may fall into one or more of the following categories:

1. Diagnosis of opioid, cocaine, amphetamine, or benzodiazepine dependence
2. Minimum 6-month history of regular use
3. Regular injecting, especially if high risk, of whatever duration
4. Failed attempts to achieve abstinence
5. At time of initial assessment, likely to be at the pre-contemplation or contemplation stage of change

Evidenced-based guidelines for providing substitute treatment for drug misusers have been reported[23–25] and, in brief, aim to bring about:

Short term:
    Attract patients into treatment
    Relieve withdrawal symptoms
Long term:
    Retain in treatment
    Reduce injecting behavior
    Stabilize drug use
    Stabilize lifestyle

Reduce criminal behavior
Reduce human immunodeficiency virus (HIV), HBV, and HBC transmission
Reduce death rate

7.2.1 Opioid-Specific Prescribing

Maintenance prescribing differs from substitute prescribing only in that there is no active effort to bring about change in a person's drug use or psychological state. The majority of clinical drug misuse services are concerned principally with the prescription of methadone to heroin users. American reviews tend to cite methadone as a direct pharmacological treatment in the way that insulin is used for diabetes. Many Europeans, however, would view methadone more as a substitute treatment whereby the improvements that are seen result from removing individuals from the process of using street drugs.[24]

7.2.1.1 Methadone Maintenance Prescribing

Methadone, a synthetic opioid first reported as a maintenance (long-term, fixed-dose) treatment for opiate dependence by Dole and Nyswander,[26] is the most widely used pharmacological treatment for this type of addiction in Britain and North America. Methadone first appeared in Europe in the late 1960s in response to an emerging use of heroin and was officially introduced into Britain in 1968.[27] Today methadone remains the preferred drug of choice for the treatment of heroin dependence,[28] dominating the substitute prescribing market.[29]

Substantial evidence exists in the international literature to support the effectiveness of methadone maintenance treatment (MMT), particularly with regard to reduction in intravenous drug misuse,[30,31] less crime,[32,33] reemployment,[34] social rehabilitation,[35] overall health status,[34] improved quality of lifestyle,[36] and safety and cost effectiveness compared to other (drug-free) alternatives.[37] The National Treatment Outcome Research Study (NTORS) reported similar findings in Britain.[38] Retention in treatment is the key, however, and discernible treatment effects are only seen when patients remain in treatment for longer than 1 year.[39] The available evidence indicates that it is methadone per se that retains patients in treatment.[40]

Following a move toward a harm minimization (rather than abstinence) in response to the perceived threat from the HIV, there was a rapid expansion of methadone treatment in Britain, the U.S., and Australia.[41] Methadone treatment continues to play an important role in the prevention of the transmission of HIV infection among injectors of heroin.[42,43]

7.2.1.2 Treatment Compliance

Studies of treatment response have shown that patients who comply with the recommended course of treatment have favorable outcomes during treatment and longer-lasting post-treatment benefits. Thus, it is discouraging for many practitioners that opiate users are frequently poorly compliant or noncompliant and subsequently resume substance use.[44] Insufficient methadone dose has been identified as a major cause of therapeutic failure and relapse to re-abuse drugs,[40] affecting behavior above and beyond individual differences in motivation and severity of drug dependence.

Despite more than 35 years of clinical use of methadone for the treatment of heroin dependence, appropriate dosing remains controversial. However, a consistent relationship between higher doses of the drug, less illicit opioid use, and retention in treatment has been frequently observed.[50,51] Previous research indicates that an insufficient dose (inadequate for the prevention of withdrawal symptoms for the total duration of the dosing interval, 24 h) is a major problem for opioid users during treatment.[52] Unfortunately, the likelihood of success is offset by the fact that many patients do not remain in treatment until they are rehabilitated, and those who drop out usually return (relapse) to drug misuse.[53]

7.2.1.3 *Therapeutic Drug Monitoring for Methadone*

Many different parameters have been investigated to help assess the efficacy of methadone maintenance treatment. Randomized controlled trials to investigate methadone treatment have been advocated recently.[32] A randomized-controlled trial of methadone maintenance treatment in 593 Australian prisoners indicated that heroin use was significantly lower among treated prisoners than control subjects at follow up.[54,55]

The usual procedure for assessing opioid users at clinics involves urinalysis screening for drugs of abuse (see Chapter 7.6). Urinalysis drug screening is an important way of assessing drug misuse by patients undergoing methadone treatment, but sheds no light on patient compliance, i.e., whether the patient is taking medication as prescribed. It is essential to know if a patient is taking all of their medication (at the correct time and in the correct amount) and to find out whether the patient is using extra methadone (obtained illicitly) or selling some of the prescription, perhaps to other users. Urinalysis will only indicate whether or not a patient has taken some of the medication. Dosage alterations based on interpretation of plasma measurements may help more patients do well on methadone.[56–58]

Scientific measurements, in addition to urinalysis and report systems, are clearly needed to evaluate patients. It was found that plasma measurements of methadone filled the gap and provided much needed evidence on compliance. Compliance in methadone maintenance patients has been measured using a pharmacological indicator to "estimate" plasma methadone concentrations. The study showed that many patients took their medication haphazardly (incorrect self-administration), whereas others supplemented their dose with illicit methadone.[59]

The success or failure of patients in methadone treatment may be related to the determination of an appropriate daily oral dose,[60] identifying patients who respond poorly to treatment,[61] and ensuring compliance to the dosage regimen. Such tasks are difficult as clinicians are currently without an accurate, convenient, and objective therapeutic tool for therapeutic drug monitoring.

Blood is the primary biological sample for pharmacokinetic analyses, as both parent and metabolite concentrations can be quantified and samples cannot be adulterated by the donor.[62] Methadone plasma concentration has been correlated to oral dose when compliance is good[61,63,64] and plasma methadone concentration can be used to determine an appropriate oral dose.

Studies have reported that there is a robust linear relationship between plasma methadone concentration and oral dose, when patients are on a constant dose, and compliance is good.[64,65] This relationship can be demonstrated over a wide range of dosages (3 to 100 mg), and the correlation has been reported at $r = 0.89$.[64]

7.2.1.4 *Indications for Plasma Methadone Monitoring*

Take-home methadone: Initially attendance at a methadone dispensing clinic is required on a daily basis to consume medication under staff supervision. This requirement becomes impractical when the patient is assuming responsibility and trying to engage in work, rehabilitation, education programs, or responsible homemaking. Shared-care may be a sensible solution. A collaborative relationship between the prescribing doctor, community pharmacist, and specialist drug treatment center has been advocated as good practice as a means to allow flexibility with prescribing. Unfortunately, the practice of permitting take-home supplies for unsupervised self-administration have contributed problems, including:[66]

1. Accidental ingestion of methadone by nontolerant persons, especially children
2. Methadone toxic reactions
3. Overdose fatalities
4. Diversion for illicit sale

5. Redistribution to other heroin users suffering from withdrawal symptoms
6. Redistribution to drug users seeking a new euphoriant

Monitoring the concentration of methadone in patients who take the drug away from the clinic is advisable to confirm that the prescribed dose is being consumed in the correct amount and at the correct time.

Methadone is metabolized by a specific cytochrome P450 pathway, but as a predominantly oral drug absorption is a prerequisite for its activity. The absorption process is affected by many factors, not least the degree of intestinal first-pass metabolism, which occurs by cytochrome P4503A (CYP3A) and the active extrusion of absorbed drug by the multidrug efflux pump, *P*-glycoprotein (P-gr).

Measuring *N*-demethylation activity or depletion in human liver microsomes and recombinant P450 isoform showed the highest contribution for CYP3A4.[67,68] However, the metabolism of methadone is complex and has been shown to be subject to *N*-demethylation by CYP2B6, 2CI9, 2D6, and 2C9.[69] Accordingly, CYP3A4 selective inhibitors or monoclonal human anti-CYP3A4 antibodies are able to inhibit the foundation of the main metabolic product EDDP by up to 80%,[70] and CYP3A4 inducers produce a similar reaction in the opposite direction.

Hence many compounds may affect methadone kinetics. Concomitant administration of enzyme-inducing (or inhibiting) drugs is said to be a factor influencing methadone kinetics. Reports suggest that rifampicin,[71,72] phenytoin,[73] barbiturates,[74] and disulfiram[75] are associated with unexpectedly low plasma methadone concentrations. Similar affects have been reported with zidovudine (azidothymidine; AZT), fucidic acid,[76] and amitriptyline,[77] which are not known enzyme inducers. Reports of the effect of drug inhibitors on the kinetics of methadone are less apparent clinically, but the effect has been demonstrated for fluconzole.[78] Diazepam appears to inhibit the metabolism of methadone,[79] but not with therapeutic (<40 mg\day diazepam\day) dosing.[80] Interaction between methadone and medications used to treat HIV infection are other examples.[81]

Physiological state: Other factors said to influence the clearance of methadone include excessive alcohol consumption[82] and physiological states such as pregnancy.[83] To conclude, when compliance is good, plasma methadone concentrations can be used to validate dosing regimes. Conversely, plasma methadone measurements can also be used to assess compliance.

7.2.2 Buprenorphine Maintenance Prescribing

Nick Lintzeris, M.B.B.S., Ph.D.
National Addiction Centre, South London and Maudsley NHS Trust, London, U.K.

Generally, the more efficacious the drug is at producing its pharmacological effect, the greater the addiction potential and value as an illicit drug. Drugs with lower efficacy are called partial agonists. Buprenorphine (BPN) is a partial agonist for opioid receptors. The pharmacological profile of partial agonists is such that they are useful in substitution therapy because they provide some reinforcement of the opiate effect but should also reduce illicit heroin use.

BPN, a derivative of the morphine alkaloid thebaine, is a partial agonist at the μ opiate receptor, resulting in milder, less euphoric, and less sedating opiate effects than full opioid agonists such as heroin, morphine, or methadone. In adequate doses, BPN exerts sufficient opiate effects to diminish cravings for heroin and prevent opiate withdrawal features. BPN also has a high affinity for μ receptors, binding more tightly than full agonists such as heroin or methadone, and through this mechanism reduces the effects of any additional heroin (or other opiate) use.

BPN is also an antagonist at the κ opiate receptor, which may be associated with some antidysphoric[84-86] and antipsychotic properties[87] in certain individuals. Further research is required in this area, and BPN is not currently indicated for these conditions.

7.2.2.1 Pharmacokinetics

BPN undergoes extensive first-pass metabolism when taken orally and has more potent effects when injected or taken sublingually. Contemporary preparations in addiction treatment utilize sublingual tablets.* Peak plasma concentrations are achieved 1 to 2 h after sublingual administration. BPN is principally metabolized by two hepatic pathways: conjugation with glucuronic acid and N-dealkylation by the CP450 3A4 enzyme system to nor-BPN, an active metabolite that appears not to cross the blood–brain barrier and therefore is of minor clinical importance. Metabolites are excreted in the biliary system with enterohepatic cycling, and the majority of the drug is excreted in feces and urine.

BPN has a relatively short half-life, however, and can exert a considerably longer duration of action, due to its high affinity for μ opiate receptors and its high lipophilicity (accumulation in fat with chronic dosing). Peak effects are described within 1 to 4 h after sublingual administration, with continued effects for up to 12 h at low doses (e.g., 2 mg) to as long as 72 h at higher doses (such as 16 or 32 mg).[91] The prolonged duration at high doses enables alternate day, 3-day, and even 4-day dispensing regimens in many patients.[88,89]

BPN has an advantageous safety profile due to ceiling dose–response effects, such that high doses (16 mg or more) do not produce substantially greater peak opiate effects than lower doses (8 or 12 mg)[90] and do not result in significant respiratory depression even in non-opiate-dependent individuals. As with methadone, there are concerns regarding the safety of BPN in combination with other sedatives (alcohol, benzodiazepines), and a number of deaths have occurred under such circumstances. Many patients describe less sedation with BPN than methadone. As with other opiates, constipation, disturbed sleep, drowsiness, headaches, sweating, and nausea are the more common side effects[91] with most side effects subsiding as tolerance develops.

The partial agonist properties of BPN and prolonged duration of action are thought to account for a milder opiate withdrawal syndrome following the cessation of BPN compared to heroin, morphine, or methadone.[92] The cessation of long-term BPN results in opiate withdrawal peaking 3 to 14 days after cessation, with mild symptoms persisting for weeks. Cessation of short BPN courses (e.g., 1 to 2 weeks) appears to be associated with only minor withdrawal discomfort of several days duration.

Precipitated withdrawal is caused by the high affinity of BPN displacing other opiates (e.g., methadone, heroin) from opiate receptors, but having less opiate activity (partial agonist). This rapid reduction in opiate effects can be experienced as precipitated withdrawal, typically occurring within 1 to 3 h after the first BPN dose, peaking in severity over the first 3 to 6 h, and then subsiding. Precipitated withdrawal is of concern if a patient has recently used heroin (e.g., <6 h previously) or methadone (<24 h previously) prior to his or her BPN dose. Transferring from high-dose methadone (e.g., above 60 mg) to BPN increases the risk of precipitated withdrawal, due to methadone's long duration of action (Table 7.2.1).

Objectively, there was no significant difference between the two groups on measures of opiate withdrawal symptoms. The group receiving alternate-day treatment reported subtle withdrawal symptoms subjectively whereas the daily treatment group reported no such problems.[93] A 24-h dosage interval is most commonly recommended. Opiate-dependent subjects find BPN an accept-

---

* Most studies using sublingual buprenorphine have used a liquid solution in 30% aqueous ethanol. However, commercial sublingual preparations (e.g., Subutex, Suboxone) are tablets with approximately 50% bioavailability of the ethanol solution.

Table 7.2.1   Pharmacological Properties and Clinical Implications of BPN

Pharmacological Property	Clinical Implication
Partial agonist producing mild opiate effects	Reduces cravings for heroin and increases treatment retention Less sedating than full agonists (heroin, morphine, or methadone)
Alleviates opiate withdrawal	Can be used for maintenance or detoxification
High receptor affinity diminishes the effects of additional opiate use	Diminishes heroin use Complicates attempts at analgesia with other opioids (e.g., morphine)
Long duration of action	Allows for once-a-day, to three times a week dosing schedules
Ceiling dose–response effects	Safer in overdose
Sublingual preparation	More time involved in supervised dispensing
Comparable affinity for mu receptors to opioid antagonists	Treatment with naltrexone can be commenced within 24 h of BPN
Side-effect profile similar to other opiates	Generally well tolerated by heroin users, with most side effects transient

able treatment for their dependence and report a "morphine-like" effect. It is possible to convert people from heroin or methadone to BPN with minimal withdrawal problems.[94]

Due to its wide therapeutic index, BPN is relatively safe in overdose. It has been shown that there is a ceiling effect at higher doses of BPN. This is due to its intrinsic opiate antagonist activity and means that it is possible for a nondependent person to tolerate a single dose of BPN up to 70 times the recommended analgesic dose without life-threatening consequences.[95] Sublingual preparations have been shown to be as effective as subcutaneous preparations and to have a similar profile of effects in opiate-dependent subjects.[96]

As with methadone, effective BPN maintenance treatment requires regular monitoring and review, structured dispensing arrangements, access to psychosocial services, and long-term treatment retention. A key goal during BPN induction is to prevent precipitated withdrawal, which can usually be achieved by patient education; delaying the first BPN dose until the patient is in mild opiate withdrawal; and commencing with a low first BPN dose (e.g., 4 mg). After ensuring precipitated withdrawal has been averted, the BPN dose should be rapidly titrated upwards, achieving effective doses (e.g., 12 to 24 mg for most patients) within 3 days of commencing treatment. Maintenance BPN doses should be titrated against treatment objectives for each patient. Doses of between 12 and 24 mg/day are often required in order for patients to cease unsanctioned opiate use. Low doses (less than 8 mg/day) are more commonly associated with ongoing heroin use. In treatment settings where BPN dosing is predominately supervised, the frequency of dispensing (and hence inconvenience and costs) can be reduced for most patients by alternate- and 3-day dosing. A dose intended for 48 h interval is approximately twice a daily dose, and a 3-day dose is approximately 2.5 to 3 times a daily dose. Withdrawal from BPN maintenance treatment should only be recommended for stable patients who have ceased substance abuse, are medically, socially, and psychiatrically stable, and who wish to withdraw from maintenance treatment. A gradual reduction over weeks is usually recommended, with 2 mg dose reductions every 2 to 4 weeks as tolerated.

7.2.3   Stimulant Specific

Substitute prescribing for amphetamine usually takes the form of dexamphetamine sulfate tablets whereas there is no obvious alternative for cocaine dependence. However, prescriptions of this kind are only appropriate for a very small minority of patients. It is more likely to be the case that prescribing for stimulant dependence takes the form of an agonist of a different pharmacological group to the main drug of misuse but having its action at the same receptors or in the same neurochemical pathways (replacement prescribing). Typically these agents are used to reduce cravings associated with the cessation of stimulant use. Replacement prescribing is addressed in detail in Chapter 7.4.

7.2.4 Benzodiazepine Specific

Little attention has thus far been paid to the extent to which benzodiazepines are abused primarily as the drug of choice. It seems that benzodiazepines are frequently abused on the illicit drug scene in combination with other drugs, particularly alcohol,[97] stimulants,[98] and opiates.[99] However, there appear to be a number of features that indicate benzodiazepine abuse: two key factors appear to be supra therapeutic dosage to extremely high levels and intermittent binge usage. Substitution prescribing usually takes the form of a long-acting alternative, most commonly diazepam, which has the effect of stabilizing drug use. More recently, chlordiazepoxide has been used to substitute for the benzodiazepine of choice because of its low abuse potential, low street value, and long elimination half-life.

7.2.5 Outcomes for Substitute Prescribing

The Department of Health[23] has selected hierarchies of outcomes for substitute prescribing in the areas of drug use, physical and psychological health, and social functioning, as follows:

Drug use:
1. Abstinence from drugs
2. Near abstinence from drugs
3. Reduction in the quantity of drugs consumed
4. Abstinence from street drugs
5. Reduced use of street drugs
6. Change in drug taking behavior from injecting to oral consumption
7. Reduction in the frequency of injecting

Physical and psychological health:
1. Improvement in physical health
2. No deterioration in physical health
3. Improvement in psychological health
4. Reduction in sharing injection equipment
5. Reduction in sexual risk-taking behavior

Social functioning and life context:
1. Reduction in criminal activity
2. Improvement in employment status
3. Fewer working/school days missed
4. Improved family relationships
5. Improved personal relationships
6. Domiciliary stability/improvement

7.3 TREATMENT OF WITHDRAWAL SYNDROMES

Joanna Banbery, M.B.B.S.
The Leeds Addiction Unit, Leeds, U.K.

7.3.1 Understanding Withdrawal Syndromes

A withdrawal syndrome is the constellation of physiological and behavioral changes that are directly related to the sudden cessation (or reduction in use) of a psychoactive drug to which the body has become adapted. The *Diagnostic and Statistical Manual of the American Psychiatric*

Association in its revised fourth edition (DSM-IV-R)[100] requires three criteria to be fulfilled before a diagnosis of substance withdrawal can be made. For each drug or group of drugs it lists the symptoms and signs that must be present:

Criterion 1: The development of a syndrome (which is substance specific) due to the cessation of or reduction in substance use. The substance use must be heavy and prolonged.

Criterion 2: The withdrawal syndrome must cause clinically significant distress or impairment in social and/or occupational functioning.

Criterion 3: The symptoms caused must not be due to any other medical or mental condition.

Dependence has been discussed in the introduction to this chapter. Withdrawal symptoms were described as a consequence of regular drug use rather than as a fundamental element. On a cellular level, dependent use of a drug will cause a state of adaptation in which the presence of the drug is necessary for normal functioning and in which the removal of the drug will cause some abnormality of function.[101] Drug-induced alterations to function include alteration of the fluidity of the cell membrane, or alteration in neurotransmitters and receptor changes. Each group of drugs will produce its own characteristic withdrawal syndrome, which will be dependent on specific alterations to the above systems. These have already been well reviewed.[102]

Although the basis of withdrawal lies in the cellular and receptor changes, it is important not to forget that there is a significant psychological component. Changes at the tissue level give rise to symptoms and signs. These are then interpreted in a way that will depend on a person's situation and expectations about withdrawal together with his or her emotional state. These reactions then feedback and may magnify the original changes or help to reduce them. Psychologists have found that withdrawal symptoms will behave as conditioned responses. They will develop more quickly if associated with a cue and can be evoked by environmental stimuli when the drug has not been used for some time.[103] This helps to explain why the clinical symptoms presented by patients are very variable both from time to time and place to place. The time it takes to develop a withdrawal effect will depend on the pharmacokinetics of the drug, so that withdrawal from methadone, which has a long half-life, will not become evident for 24 to 36 h, whereas withdrawal from heroin, with a shorter half-life, will occur within 6 to 8 h of the last dose. This is of clinical importance in planning a detoxification.

7.3.1.1 Detoxification

When drug use ceases, the nervous system will begin to undergo a return to normal functioning. During this time, abnormal responses will be evident in the form of withdrawal symptoms, and the patient will be vulnerable both physically and psychologically. Detoxification is the process of rapidly and successfully achieving a drug-free state and will usually involve both the prescription of drugs to attenuate withdrawal symptoms and the attention to the relief of other stressors.

It is an appropriate intervention for those patients who are at the "action" stage of change,[17] that is, those patients who have demonstrated a commitment to change their substance use, believe they are able to change, and have acquired the necessary skills to enable them to sustain change. Detoxification will also be necessary for other patients as an expedience in situations such as emergency hospitalization or rapidly deteriorating mental or physical health.

The goal of achieving abstinence with the minimum amount of discomfort should be agreed upon with the patient. Adequate preparation is essential; the patient must be informed of the expected symptoms, their likely duration, medication that will be used to relieve symptoms and its likely effects. Consideration should be given to the setting for the detoxification. Home, outpatient, or inpatient facilities may all be suitable. The physician and the patient will need to agree upon an environment that is comfortable, nonthreatening, and safe. If the detoxification is to be undertaken at home, there must be confidence that any withdrawal symptoms will not be severe and that adequate support is available.

The appearance of withdrawal symptoms should be carefully monitored with consideration being given to the use of assessment scales.[104] If an outpatient detoxification is being performed the patient may attend on a daily basis for an objective assessment of withdrawal symptoms to be made. The severity of the syndrome will influence the dosage and frequency of medication given to alleviate them. Physicians should have an awareness of which drugs will cause severe or dangerous withdrawal symptoms and may require particularly careful assessment. Increasingly, patients present with polydrug use, which requires extra vigilance and may require adaptations of usual prescribing regimens.

Patients who are to be detoxified will require a thorough medical examination usually with routine blood tests. These patients are at high risk of an underlying medical problem related either to specific drug-related harm, e.g., intravenous users at risk of abscesses, endocarditis, etc., or related to lifestyle, such as malnutrition or tuberculosis. An assessment of mental state is important and this should be monitored during detoxification. Patients may present, for example, with confusion or lowering of mood with suicidal ideation. These symptoms usually do not require anything beyond symptomatic relief and resolve as withdrawal progresses; however, the appropriate level of nursing care and support must be assessed.

Other therapies play an important role in detoxification and can minimize the need for medication. Relaxation training has been said to be a useful way to reduce stress particularly in benzodiazepine withdrawal, and complementary therapies such as massage have also been used to reduce discomfort. Controlled studies of their efficacy are awaited. Competent nursing care is also important. The patient's condition should be assessed accurately, and it has been shown that this can in itself reduce withdrawal symptom scores.[105] Reassurance and attention to nutrition and sleeping patterns also play their part. Any medication prescribed will either substitute for the drug that has been withdrawn or treat the symptoms of the withdrawal syndrome. Consideration must be given to the dosage and the length of time of prescribing.

It has been said that the three most common errors in the management of withdrawal syndromes are (1) failure to diagnose, (2) prescription of too much for too long, and (3) failure to use psychological means to abate withdrawal.[106] The physician must have adequate knowledge both of the symptoms, signs, and duration of the common withdrawal syndrome and of their treatment to guard against all of these.

7.3.2   Opiate-Specific Withdrawal Syndrome

DSM-IV-R[100] describes opioid withdrawal following cessation or reduction in heavy and prolonged use of either illicit drugs or prescribed medication. The syndrome described consists of craving for the drug and three or more of the following symptoms: dysphoric mood, nausea or vomiting, lachrymation and rhinnarhea, muscle aches, pupillary dilatation, piloerection, diarrhea, yawning, or insomnia. The signs and symptoms should develop acutely within days of cessation of drug use and be severe enough to impair a patient's functioning. In addition to this, body temperature and blood pressure may be slightly elevated with a variable effect on pulse. As discussed earlier, the onset of a withdrawal syndrome will depend on the quantity of the drug used and the route of administration,[107] as well as the frequency of usage, and the half-life of the drug. Heroin withdrawal normally begins 6 to 8 h after last use, symptoms peak at 2 to 3 days, and have usually resolved within a week. Withdrawal from other opiates is similar but will exhibit different time scales and intensities, e.g., methadone withdrawal may last for several weeks and not commence for 36 to 48 h. Opioid withdrawal can also be precipitated by an antagonist such as naloxone, which will produce a severe withdrawal with peak intensity about 30 min from administration.

The opiate withdrawal syndrome is very rarely life-threatening and has been described as being similar to having influenza. It is, however, experienced as sufficiently unpleasant for it to be avoided whenever possible by users and for its successful negotiation to be the necessary first step toward abstinence. For this reason it is important that it is properly managed by the clinician.

The essential judgment in a planned detoxification is about its speed. A rapid detoxification will produce more severe withdrawal symptoms than a slower one, but it may be easier to maintain motivation. There are a number of different pharmacological approaches that may be used and tailored to the individual's requirements. A brief review of the use of methadone, alpha-2-agonists, and buprenorphine in detoxification is given.

7.3.2.1 Detoxification Using Methadone

A wide variety of different regimens has been used and there is some lack of clarity between those that are long-term slow reductions and merge with methadone maintenance therapy (MMT) and those that are short term and aimed at immediate abstinence. In clinical practice patients who are on methadone maintenance treatment will usually have their methadone dose reduced gradually, commonly at a rate of 5 mg every 2 weeks to a daily dose of 20 to 30 mg. Reductions then occur in smaller increments to zero. In the U.K. there is no recommended time for this process of reduction to continue. In the U.S. the FDA regulations permit extended opioid detoxification for up to 6 months.

Various time scales for withdrawal have been studied.[108] It is important to inform patients about what to expect during detoxification as almost everyone undergoing methadone reduction will experience withdrawal symptoms. These have been shown to be a major factor in precipitating relapse. However, data from the literature are hardly comparable; programs vary widely with regard to duration,[108] design,[109] and treatment objectives, impairing the application of meta-analysis. A recent review by Amato[110] confirmed that slow tapering with temporary substitution of long acting opioids (methadone), accompanied by medical supervision and ancillary medications can reduce withdrawal severity. Nevertheless the majority of patients relapsed to heroin use.

Negotiation between prescriber and patient about rates of reduction together with the understanding that extra psychological support will be available during detoxification are also important. The setting for detoxification should be given consideration.[111] Opioid users are likely to live in environments with other drug users, which makes abstinence difficult to achieve. It may be appropriate to consider the initial reductions of methadone as an outpatient and then admit the patient to finally achieve a drug-free state.

Methadone reduction regimens have been de rigueur in many clinical settings but in practice it is often difficult to achieve abstinence by this method, with patients often becoming "stuck" when low doses of methadone (15 mg/day) are reached. Indeed it has been said that "most methadone treatment is maintenance treatment because most patients fail detoxification."[112] Although it is a common clinical problem, the cause is not clear. It may be that the withdrawal symptoms become intolerable. Another explanation is that the drug user wants to seek a drug effect which is lost at lower dosages. Current practice suggests that methadone reduction should be attempted in combination with other psychological interventions and other pharmacological agents (buprenorphine).

7.3.2.2 Detoxification Using Buprenorphine

There is an emerging evidence base for the use of buprenorphine (BPN) in detoxification regimens. For detoxification, most comparative randomized trials have been against symptomatic medications (e.g., clonidine, benzodiazepines). The evidence suggests that BPN is more effective in reducing withdrawal severity, increasing detoxification completion rates, and increasing uptake of post-detoxification (e.g., naltrexone maintenance) treatment. There is less research directly comparing BPN and methadone reductions, although the evidence suggests there is less "rebound" withdrawal (symptoms after stopping medication) following short courses of BPN compared to methadone.

Table 7.3.1 Selecting Medications: Advantages and Disadvantages of BPN Compared to Methadone

Advantages	Disadvantages
Greater blockade of heroin use	Blockade not desired by some patients
Smoother opiate effect and less sedating than methadone	Some patients do better with sedating effects of high-dose methadone
Safer in overdose than methadone	Tablets easily abused if not supervised
	Safety in pregnancy not yet established
Milder withdrawal than methadone	Mild withdrawal may make it too easy to "jump off"
3 or 4 times a week supervised dosing possible for most clients (~66%)	Supervised dispensing more time-consuming
Some clients prefer BPN	Some clients prefer methadone

BPN can be used in brief detoxification regimens over 1 to 2 weeks in inpatient or outpatient settings to assist individuals detoxifying from heroin; or in more gradual outpatient reduction regimens lasting several weeks to months. Longer-term reduction regimens appear to be associated with more "rebound withdrawal," but do allow a greater opportunity for the patient to "stabilize" while in treatment. As in any detoxification program, a key aspect is to facilitate patients continuing in ongoing treatment for their dependence. This may entail naltrexone treatment, counseling, or rehabilitation programs for those aiming to achieve abstinence, or continuing in maintenance BPN treatment for those unable to immediately achieve long-term abstinence.

The milder withdrawal syndrome associated with BPN compared with methadone suggests that transfer to BPN may be one option for stable patients who are ready to cease maintenance substitution treatment, but are experiencing difficulties withdrawing off methadone.[113] There have been a number of fixed-dose and flexible-dose Phase III randomized trials comparing BPN to methadone maintenance treatment, recently reviewed in a systematic Cochrane review.[114] Fixed dose studies suggest comparable efficacy when used in equivalent doses (low dose, 20 to 35 mg, methadone is broadly equivalent to low dose, 2 to 4 mg, BPN), although to date there have been no trials comparing "gold standard" high dose (e.g., 80 to 120 mg) methadone to high dose (e.g., 16 to 32 mg) BPN treatment. Flexible dosing studies have identified greater early treatment dropout among BPN patients, which may reflect the slow BPN induction regimens used in these trials.

The increased range of opioid pharmacotherapies potentially allows for better tailoring of medications to suit the patient's treatment objectives. While research suggests comparable efficacy between the two medications, it is yet to provide a clear indication of which individuals will benefit most from maintenance treatment with either BPN or methadone. Without a clear evidence base, clients and clinicians must consider a range of factors when selecting a pharmacotherapy, including a patient's past history of response to a medication, individual variation in pharmacokinetics (e.g., rapid methadone metabolizers), adverse events, logistics of participating in treatment (such as costs, accessibility of services), and patient (and clinician) expectancy. Particular issues in selecting BPN and methadone are shown in Table 7.3.1.

Substitution treatment (such as methadone) has historically been confined to specialist clinic-based programs. Recent decades have seen the expansion of substitution maintenance and detoxification treatment into primary care (general practice and community pharmacy) settings in many countries in order to "normalize" addiction treatment, reduce treatment costs, and increase the accessibility of services. This trend has extended to the U.S., where trained and accredited physicians can deliver BPN treatment outside of clinic settings ("office based prescribing"). Increasingly, the role of specialist services is to target patients with more complex treatment needs (e.g., polydrug dependence, severe social dysfunction, or medical or psychiatric comorbidity).

A number of studies have examined the acceptability and effectiveness of BPN in the treatment of opiate dependence. It has been shown that BPN treatment is as effective as methadone in the detoxification of heroin users.[115] BPN has been shown to attenuate self-administration of illicit opiates in opiate-dependent individuals. The study used a daily dose of 8 mg of subcutaneous BPN and recorded a 69 to 98% suppression of heroin self-administration, which compares favorably to the opiate antagonist naltrexone.[116] Treatment with opiate antagonists (e.g., naltrexone) can be commenced as soon as 24 h after the cessation of BPN without precipitating severe opiate withdrawal; in comparison, naltrexone usually precipitates severe withdrawal if initiated within days of heroin or methadone use.

There are a number of different pharmacological options available for the treatment of opiate withdrawal and it is important to tailor detoxification to suit each individual. As Seivewright and Greenwood[24] point out, a 17-year-old who has been using heroin for 6 months with few social problems will require treatment different from a 35-year-old injector of heroin with a long history of dependence and failed previous detoxifications. The first patient may do best being detoxified using lofexidine; the second may need a long-term methadone reduction program. There is a need for further research to establish precisely which group of patients is likely to do best with which treatment.

7.3.2.3 Detoxification Using Adrenergic Agonists

A subgroup of the adrenergic agonists are the alpha-2 agonists clonidine and lofexidine, which are being increasingly used in opiate detoxification. Chronic administration of opiate drugs results in tolerance to the effects mediated by opiate receptors such as euphoria, and tolerance to the effects of opiates on the automatic nervous system, which is mediated by noradrenergic pathways. The locus coerulus in the dorsal pons is the origin of much of the central nervous system noradrenergic activity. It is associated with opiate and presynaptic alpha-2-noradrenergic receptors, which are inhibiting.

Chronic opiate intake leads to tolerance and to stimulation of the opiate receptors. Abrupt withdrawal leads to an escape from this inhibition and a rebound rapid firing of the neurons. A "noradrenergic storm" results and is responsible for many of the opiate withdrawal symptoms.[117] Clonidine and lofexidine act as presynaptic alpha-2-adrenergic agonists, which inhibit this and therefore are able to attenuate symptoms. However, those experiencing the most severe withdrawal symptoms are not well controlled by clonidine and the symptoms of arthralgia, myalgia, anergia, and insomnia were not alleviated. Its use has also been limited because of its potentially serious side effects, which include hypotension, sedation, and psychiatric symptoms in those who are vulnerable.

Lofexidine is a newer alpha-2-adrenergic agonist (licensed in the U.K. since 1992), which appears not to have the same problems with side effects and which has gained in popularity as a non-opiate for use in detoxification in a variety of settings. Lofexidine when used to withdraw patients from methadone demonstrated good completion rates, and there were no reports of significant lowering of blood pressure or sedation. However, residual withdrawal symptoms with insomnia, lethargy, and bone pain mentioned and were observed in users stabilized on relatively low doses of methadone.

Bearn et al.[118] conducted the first randomized double-blind study comparing methadone and lofexidine detoxification in 86 polydrug-abusing opioid addicts. The lofexidine group experienced more severe symptoms from day 3 to day 7 and by day 20 both groups showed a similar progressive decline in symptoms. The two treatments had similar effects on blood pressure and treatment completion.

7.3.2.4 Naltrexone-Assisted Detoxification

In an attempt to reduce the duration of the opiate withdrawal syndrome, particularly from long-acting opioids such as methadone, combinations of compounds have been used. A rapid process using scopolamine with naltrexone and naloxone has been reported.[119]

More recently interest has been shown in very rapid (<48 h) opiate detoxification, using opiate antagonists and general anesthesia. However, this method is expensive and adds a risk of death to a nonfatal condition. Reports of delirium from rapid opioid detoxification have also emerged.[120]

The addition of other medications to lofexidine in detoxification (such as hypnotics, muscle relaxants, and antidiarrheal medication) may need to be considered on an individual basis. Other short-acting opioids such as dihydrocodeine have been used in detoxification regimens although there is little evidence for their efficacy. One regimen employed involves a crossover period from low dose (30 mg or less) methadone to the equivalent dose of dihydrocodeine over 7 to 10 days and then a reduction of dihydrocodeine over the following 7 days.[122]

7.3.3 Stimulant-Specific Withdrawal Syndrome

Withdrawal symptoms of these drugs, manifest in broad terms as the inverse of the stimulant effects, can be explained by the neurochemical changes that they induce. The existence of a withdrawal syndrome was for some time controversial because of the lack of physical withdrawal symptoms and signs. During the 1980s, the use of cocaine in the form of crack increased dramatically in North America and this has led to an increase in clinical and research evidence about its dependence-forming properties and withdrawal syndrome. DSM-IV-R[100] defines both amphetamine and cocaine withdrawal in the same way.

The symptoms are characterized by a constellation of signs and symptoms that appear within a few hours to several days after either cessation or reduction in heavy or prolonged use of the drugs. The symptoms must not be due to another medical or mental disorder and must cause impairment of functioning. It is described as consisting of dysphoric mood and two or more of the following: fatigue, vivid and unpleasant dreams, insomnia or hypersomnia, increased appetite, and either psychomotor retardation or agitation. Drug craving and anhedonia may also be present. Cocaine withdrawal has been reported to reach its peak in 2 to 4 days, with symptoms such as lowering of mood, fatigue, and general malaise lasting for several weeks. Amphetamine withdrawal is also reported to peak within 2 to 4 days with the most characteristic symptoms being lowering of mood and associated suicidal ideation.

Most of the recent studies looking at stimulant withdrawal have investigated cocaine. However, given the different pharmacokinetics of amphetamine and cocaine it would be reasonable to expect quite different time courses for the appearance, peak, and duration of the respective withdrawal syndromes. The half-life of cocaine is approximately 1 h, with the onset of action between 8 s and 30 min depending on the route of administration. The duration of effect is reported to be between 5 and 90 min.[123] Conversely, the half-life of amphetamine is about 10 to 15 h, with its onset of action and duration of effect two to eight times as long as cocaine. This would lead to the expectation that amphetamine withdrawal would have a slower onset on action, last longer, and be less intense than cocaine withdrawal. Further controlled studies in humans need to be done to confirm this. Our current concepts of amphetamine withdrawal are based largely on clinical impressions and animal studies.

The main physical and psychological effects of cocaine and crack have been recently reviewed. Users feel stronger, more alert and energetic, confident and physically strong. Common physical effects include dry mouth, sweating, loss of appetite, and increased heart rate. When snorted, cocaine produces a slow wave of euphoria followed by a plateau and a "comedown." Smoked as crack, the drug has a much more intense and immediate effect. Excessive doses can cause severe medical problems including death from pulmonary edema, heart failure, and myocardial infarction.

Substantial numbers of people who are cocaine dependent will not report or have clinically evident withdrawal symptoms even after cessation of heavy and prolonged use.[124] This, combined with clinical observations, suggests that stimulant withdrawal is associated with considerable heterogeneity. It has been said to depend on dose of drug, pattern of use, duration of history, and pre-withdrawal psychopathology.[125] Patterns of use may vary from daily use to a common pattern of using for several days at a time followed by days of abstinence. This will have an effect on the appearance of withdrawal symptoms and their severity.

Stimulants do not produce dangerous physical withdrawal syndromes, and because of this there is no advantage to a gradual withdrawal of the drug. Patients should be advised to discontinue the drug abruptly. Advice and information should be given about the likely effects of cessation and consideration given to the setting for detoxification. Those patients who present with mild symptoms that last a matter of hours or days usually are not a management problem. Symptomatic treatment for agitation or anxiety with a drug of low abuse potential such as thioridazine may be necessary.

More severe withdrawal symptoms may require admission. Close observation will be necessary for those expressing suicidal ideas. Symptomatic relief for other symptoms such as anxiety and insomnia may be required. Having achieved abstinence, the next phase is to identify psycho-social problems and initiate interventions designed to maintain a drug-free state and deal with drug craving. A number of different pharmacological treatments have been used mainly in cocaine dependence to treat the dysphoric symptoms associated with withdrawal and to attempt to reduce craving. These are reviewed in Chapter 7.4.

The small numbers of studies, the absence of physical withdrawal symptoms, and the variation in patterns of drug use make stimulant withdrawal more difficult to characterize than with other groups of drugs. Cocaine has been studied because of the "crack" epidemic of the 1980s, and has led to an increase in our understanding of both the symptoms and the underlying neurochemistry of withdrawal. Numerous different agents have been used to attempt to treat the drug craving and mood disorders associated with withdrawal, all with limited success. Less is published about amphetamine withdrawal and details of ecstasy withdrawal are scarce. Any comparisons with cocaine should not forget the differences in the drugs' properties and pharmacokinetics.

7.3.4 Hypnotic and Sedative Withdrawal Syndrome

In practice it is the benzodiazepines that dominate the market for both hypnotics and anxiolytics. Barbiturates such as secobarbital, pentobarbital, and amobarbital are under the same federal controls as morphine in the U.S. and in the U.K., and they are rarely prescribed.

DSM-IV-R[100] criteria for sedative, hypnotic, or anxiolytic withdrawal require two or more of the following to be present:

1. Autonomic hyperactivity (e.g., sweating or pulse rate greater than 100)
2. Increased hand tremor
3. Insomnia
4. Nausea or vomiting
5. Transient visual, tactile, or auditory hallucinations or illusions
6. Psychomotor agitation
7. Anxiety
8. Grand mal seizures

Physicians can then specify if perceptual disturbances are present. As in other classes of drug, the withdrawal symptoms are the opposite of the drug effects and are explained by the underlying changes in neurophysiology largely via the gamma aminobutyric acid (GABA) system. GABA is the most widely distributed inhibitory neurotransmitter in the central nervous system. Close to its receptors are specific receptors for the benzodiazepines and the barbiturates. When these are activated, the action of the GABA system is potentiated causing further inhibition. With continued drug use, the number of GABA receptors falls due to downregulation.

When GABA binds with its receptor it causes hyperpolarization of the neuron as the chloride channel is activated and hyperpolarization is reversed by increased entry of calcium to the cell. If drug use ceases, the increased intraneuronal calcium produces a state of hyperexcitability. The reduction in the number of GABA receptors has the effect of reducing the overall effect of the main inhibiting system resulting in the symptoms previously listed.

Benzodiazepines dependence is not a single entity and varying different classifications have been proposed. Perhaps the most useful division within the context of drug abuse is the division between high-dose and normal-dose dependence. Non-abusers who are dose dependent take their benzodiazepines within the recommended therapeutic range and remain on this regimen long term. These people may want to do without their medication but feel unable to because of the withdrawal symptoms experienced upon cessation of their medication. In high-dose misuse, up to ten times the normal recommended dosage may be consumed on a regular basis.

Benzodiazepine withdrawal can be classified in several ways. A division between minor and major withdrawal is sometimes used and this emphasizes the severity of the symptoms. Symptoms associated with low-dose withdrawal are nausea, vomiting, tremor, incoordination, restlessness, blurred vision, sweating, and anorexia. Depersonalization, heightened perceptions, and illusions are also described. In a review of recent studies, Alexander and Perry[126] concluded that symptoms occurred in 50% of those withdrawn from therapeutic doses of benzodiazepines with an average use of 3 years and most symptoms were mild to moderate.

Discontinuing high doses of benzodiazepines can produce all the minor symptoms discussed, but patients are also at risk of seizures, psychosis, and depression. Early studies indicate a high risk of severe withdrawal when high doses are discontinued. The incidence and the severity of withdrawal symptoms can be predicted to some extent by the dose and duration of use. The time course is influenced by the half-life of the drug. Those with a short action may begin to produce mild withdrawal symptoms within 1 to 5 days of ceasing use and usually disappear over 2 to 4 weeks. Drugs with a longer half-life may not produce withdrawal symptoms for 1 to 2 weeks after use ceases and they are likely to be less severe, but more prolonged.

7.3.4.1 Management of Withdrawal

Sudden withdrawal of benzodiazepines is not advised. For an uncomplicated low-dose withdrawal, a gradual tapering of the drug is recommended. If patients are on a short-acting drug, then they may be switched to a longer-acting drug with the rationale that less severe withdrawal symptoms occur with long-acting drugs. Diazepam has been the most widely studied, and conversion data from common benzodiazepines are available. Once stabilized this can then be reduced. A number of different schemes are available. The tapering dose can be calculated by dividing the total dose by 5 and reducing by this amount weekly. Most patients can be reduced to zero in 4 to 8 weeks. Slower withdrawal may be necessary toward the end of the reduction and consideration should be given to admission if withdrawal symptoms become very intense.

In high-dose withdrawal, the picture is often complicated by other illicit drug or alcohol use. A conversion to diazepam may be difficult because of problems in establishing dosage and frequency of use. Concomitant use of alcohol is particularly common. Most clinicians would withdraw the alcohol after establishing the patient on a stable dose of a long-acting benzodiazepine. Benzodiazepines are also commonly taken by opiate users to boost the opioid effect.[127] In North America it has been found that alprazolam was replacing diazepam as the drug of choice in this population. For those patients where an accurate and reliable history of drug intake is not available, then admission is indicated for tolerance testing performed to assess tolerance and severity of withdrawal before planning a detoxification regimen.

7.4 REPLACEMENT PRESCRIBING

Kim Wolff, Ph.D.
King's College London, Institute of Psychiatry, National Addiction Centre, London, U.K.

7.4.1 Opioid-Specific Prescribing

Antagonists have zero efficacy and as such are very effective blockers of agonists. Their main limitations are that they can precipitate withdrawal in physically dependent drug users, and because they do not provide any reinforcement, there is little incentive for those dependent on illicit drugs to be compliant. Naltrexone is a long-acting, orally effective competitive antagonist at opioid receptors. It displaces any agonist present at the receptors and blocks the effects of any opioid subsequently administered. Naltrexone is predominantly metabolized by the liver and its major metabolite, 6-beta-naltrexol, is also an active opioid antagonist. The opiate-blocking effects of naltrexone last between 48 and 72 h. Naltrexone has not been shown to produce tolerance and therefore does not lead to physical dependence.[128]

Oral administration of naltrexone to an opioid-dependent individual results in the immediate appearance of a severe opioid withdrawal syndrome. It is therefore necessary to be completely detoxified from opioid prior to commencing naltrexone treatment. It is necessary to discontinue short-acting opioids such as heroin for approximately 5 to 7 days prior to commencing naltrexone. Longer-acting opioids such as methadone need to be discontinued for approximately 10 to 14 days before naltrexone can be successfully commenced. In the event of naltrexone being given prior to the end of detoxification, it is likely that withdrawal symptoms will appear. This, in turn, makes it much less likely that the individual will agree to taking naltrexone at any point subsequently despite reassurance from the prescribing doctor.

Successful naltrexone treatment depends on careful selection of individuals and understanding that naltrexone treatment is only a small part of the relapse prevention package. Psychological treatment looking at issues, such as craving, drug-refusal skills, and making appropriate lifestyle changes, should be administered at the same time as naltrexone. A positive outcome is more likely in those who are well supported by friends or family members and those who had good pre-morbid adjustment in terms of education, employment, and social class. Naltrexone treatment is contraindicated in people with acute hepatitis or liver failure. It is necessary to check liver function tests both prior to and during naltrexone treatment.

Individuals who are due to start on naltrexone should be informed of the possible side effects, which include gastrointestinal disturbances such as nausea, vomiting, abdominal pains, and diarrhea. They should also be warned of the potential dangers of trying to overcome the naltrexone blockade by taking large doses of opioids. This can lead to respiratory depression and death. It is also important for those prescribed naltrexone to understand that they will be unable to use opioid analgesics for mild pain. They should be advised about non-opiate alternatives. If opioid analgesia is required, this should be administered in a hospital setting under the supervision of trained staff. Naltrexone should be discontinued 72 h prior to elective surgery and reinstated once the surgical procedure has been performed.[129]

Prior to prescribing naltrexone for the first time, it is necessary to confirm that an individual is abstinent from opioids. This can be done by means of urine toxicology or by performing a "naloxone challenge." This involves the intravenous or intramuscular administration of the short-acting opiate antagonist naloxone. If opioid withdrawal symptoms are not precipitated, then it is appropriate to commence naltrexone approximately 1 h later. If opioid withdrawal symptoms are present, then naltrexone treatment should be deferred until the naloxone challenge has been repeated without the appearance of withdrawal symptoms.

Naltrexone (25 mg) should be given on the first day, followed by daily dosing of 50 mg thereafter. A dose of 50 mg naltrexone blocks the effects of 25 mg of heroin for up to 48 h, 150 mg of naltrexone blocks the effects for 72 h. To supervise the swallowing of naltrexone tablets and improve compliance, it is possible to prescribe naltrexone three times per week (i.e., 100 mg on Monday and Wednesday, 150 mg on Friday). Due to the variable nature of opioid dependence, the length of time that people are required to take naltrexone varies between individuals. Naltrexone prescribing should continue, in the absence of complications or contraindications, until the individual is confident that it is possible to resist the temptation to return to dependent use of opioid drugs. This time span may be only a few weeks but can be as long as a few years in some cases.

In summary, naltrexone is a competitive opioid antagonist that displaces opioid agonists from the opioid receptors and blocks the effects of opioid agonists subsequently administered. It is a useful adjunct to psychological relapse prevention methods in well-motivated individuals receiving treatment for opioid dependence.

7.4.2 Stimulant-Specific Prescribing

A useful pharmacotherapy for stimulant (cocaine and amphetamine) dependence remains elusive. As a rule, symptoms of stimulant withdrawal are not medically dangerous. Detoxification from these substances requires no treatment other than abstinence. However, many users find the symptoms of cocaine withdrawal intensely dysphoric and immediately relapse and reuse cocaine in order to fend off the symptoms. The addictive nature of stimulants, particularly crack, the freebase form of cocaine, is, in part, the result of their effects on the neurochemistry of the brain. Stimulant drugs act directly on the so-called brain reward pathways.

One of cocaine's primary effects in the brain is to block the presynaptic reuptake of dopamine, norepinephrine, and serotonin, whereas amphetamine and methamphetamine increase the release of these neurotransmitters. Chronic use of cocaine results in dopamine depletion through the increased activity of catechol-*o*-methyl transferase, and supersensitivity of the dopamine, norepinephrine, and serotonin receptors, while both catecholamine and indolamine transmitters are depleted. Chronic use of cocaine seems to compromise the body's ability to regenerate these neurotransmitters causing withdrawal symptoms when the user stops. Withdrawal symptoms manifest as the inverse of the stimulant's effects. Acute tolerance, rebound depression (or the crash), and craving for stimulant drugs have been specifically attributed to dopamine depletion and receptor supersensitivity. Neurochemical changes also explain the withdrawal syndrome, which includes lethargy, depression, oversleeping, overeating, and craving for more cocaine. Extinguishing drug craving is one of the most difficult aspects of treating stimulant dependence.

7.4.2.1 Neurochemical Approach: Dopaminergic Agents and Selective Serotonin-Reuptake Inhibitors

The involvement of multiple neurotransmitter systems during stimulant use have complicated the search for pharmacological agents to address dependence. A variety of data suggest that dopamine is an important mediator for stimulant self-administration. As a result, drugs that modify dopaminergic neurotransmission are of interest as potential treatments for stimulant use. Both agonists and antagonists have been studied in this regard, agonists because they mimic the effects and act as a stimulant substitute, theoretically reducing or eliminating drug intake and antagonists because they might reduce the reinforcing properties of stimulants and facilitate abstinence. However, a review of evidence shows little or no support for the clinical use of dopamine agonists, mazindol, phenytoin, nimodine, amantadine, bromocriptine, carbamazepine, buproprion (Zyban), and chlordiazepoxide in the treatment of cocaine dependence.[130]

Dopamine Agonists

Bromocriptine (Parlodel) is an agonist at the D_2 receptor. It acts by stimulating dopamine receptors in the brain and was thought to reduce some symptoms of cocaine withdrawal, have anticraving effects, and was effective as an antidepressant, alleviating the low mood that accompanies the cocaine crash. However, other more recent studies using a controlled approach have not supported the general usefulness of this drug.[131]

Amantadine (Symmetrel) is an indirect dopamine agonist. Open-label pilot studies in primary cocaine users and methadone-maintained cocaine users have indicated that amantadine might reduce cravings for cocaine.[132] The lack of efficacy of amantadine for the reduction of craving or cocaine recently reported by Hendelson[133] is consistent with those of other placebo-controlled clinical trials in methadone-maintained patients.[134] Amantadine, while well tolerated, is not particularly efficacious for the reduction of cocaine use or cocaine craving.[135]

Methylphenidate (Ritalin) may reduce cocaine cravings in patients with attention-deficit disorder, possibly because of its ability to stimulate the central nervous system. However, the abuse potential of this drug severely limits its, and other similar drugs', usefulness as a treatment for cocaine misuse.

Dopamine Antagonists

Flupenthixol, a dopamine antagonist, has also shown promise in treating cocaine withdrawal; however, Spiperone has not reduced the effects of cocaine in mice, rats, or dogs.[136]

Dopamine Partial Agonists

Aminoergolines (Terguride and SD208911), medications that act as partial agonists at the dopamine receptor, may be candidates for normalizing dopamine transmission. The efficacy of the partial agonist depends on the level of occupancy of a given receptor by full agonists, such as dopamine. Consequently, partial agonists function as antagonists during pharmacological stimulation due to stimulant use when transmitter activity is high. By occupying dopamine receptors and exerting low intrinsic activity, partial agonists might represent a novel antipsychotic agent. However, human self-administration studies have yet to be performed.

Buprenorphine: Recent evidence suggests that the dopamine reward system of the brain is also stimulated by μ-opiate agonists. Over the past 5 years there has been significant interest in buprenorphine, a partial agonist, as a potential treatment agent for cocaine abuse. Preclinical primate work suggests that buprenorphine might modulate dopaminergic systems to the degree of altering the reinforcing properties of cocaine. However, there may be inherent problems in prescribing a medication with opiate agonist properties to opiate-naive individuals in an effort to treat cocaine dependence, particularly in a population with a known vulnerability for addiction to substances with a demonstrated abuse liability.[137]

Selective Serotonin-Reuptake Inhibitors

In addition to the blockade of dopamine reuptake, cocaine is thought to produce an increase in serotonergic tone. Therefore, it was felt that drugs that modify serotonergic neurotransmission may also alter the behavioral effects of cocaine and be potentially useful as therapies for cocaine users. However, fluoxetine (Prozac) and lofepramine are important only if underlying depression is confirmed. Selective serotonin-reuptake inhibitors (SSRIs) should be used with caution if cocaine use persists because of the rare occurrence of the "serotonergic syndrome," which is characterized by changes in autonomic neuromotor and cognitive-behavioral function triggered by increased serotonergic stimulation.[138]

7.4.2.2 Clinical Approach, Tricyclic Antidepressants, and Antisensitizing Agents

The other main approach for the treatment of stimulant dependence is clinical because the clinical syndrome that evolves after the discontinuation of cocaine or amphetamine resembles a depressive disorder. And it is widely held that antidepressant medications may have clinical utility in alleviating drug craving and self-administration. Neurochemical and clinical rationales are not mutually exclusive, and an antidepressant agent that reduces the clinical phenomena observed after cessation of cocaine might also have significant dopaminergic activity that would be consistent with a neurochemical approach to treating cocaine use.

Tricyclic Antidepressants

Since chronic tricyclic antidepressant treatment has been shown to downregulate adrenergic and dopaminergic receptor sensitivities, it has been suggested that antidepressant agents could reverse the neuroreceptor adaptations to cocaine abuse.

Desipramine (Pertofran) has been studied as an adjunct to reducing cocaine use in patients because of its high degree of selective noradrenergic activity and inhibition of the norepinephrine transporter.

Imipramine (Tofranil): Tricyclics generally exert only modest anticraving and antieuphoriant effects, which may translate into reduced cocaine use and this is certainly the case with imipramine. Carroll[139] found that the antidepressant, anti-self-medication effect of imipramine was better in depressed users. Intravenous and freebase crack users showed poor outcome with imipramine. It seems likely that tricyclics such as imipramine are most effective in specific subgroups, e.g., nasal users who are exposed to less cocaine, or patients with comorbid depression, where depression plays a role in initiating or perpetuating cocaine use.

7.4.3 New Approaches

Immunopharmacotherapy is a new strategy to treat cocaine use. It has been developed in rodents by Carrera et al.,[140] who proposed generating an active immunization to cocaine to block the actions of the drug. Active immunization against cocaine is accomplished by linking stable cocaine-like conjugates with a foreign carrier protein to stimulate the immune system to produce antibodies that subsequently recognize and bind the drug preventing it from entering the central nervous system and thereby exerting psychoactive effects. However, there are many problems to be addressed before immunization is to be effective in preventing or treating cocaine addiction in humans.

The National Institute on Drug Abuse (NIDA) is currently looking at ways to neutralize the drug in the bloodstream and reduce the amount available for brain uptake. Scientists are trying to develop catalytic antibodies, synthetic molecules that will target and break down cocaine molecules more quickly than the body's natural enzyme systems and, therefore, limit the amount of drug crossing the blood–brain barrier. The literature reveals no pharmacological agent that has been demonstrated in large double-blind studies to be significantly better than placebo for stimulant dependence in men and women. While several medications appear promising and will require more extensive investigation, many of the positive clinical reports are anecdotal and uncontrolled. At present, it remains difficult to justify routine clinical use of a single pharmacological agent.

7.5 MANAGEMENT OF COMORBIDITY

Duncan Raistrick, M.B.B.S.
The Leeds Addiction Unit, Leeds, U.K.

7.5.1 Understanding Comorbidity

Comorbidity is defined as the coexistence of two or more psychiatric or psychological conditions; for the purposes of this section, one of these conditions will be substance misuse or substance dependence. It is usual to take ICD-10 or the *American Diagnostic and Statistical Manual*, now in version DSM-IV-R,[100] as the descriptive classification of these conditions. Practitioners are usually concerned with current comorbidity, but from the point of view of understanding etiology and deciding upon rational treatment approaches it may be more useful to think in the longer term. Estimates of comorbidity will be influenced by methodological factors including the diagnostic criteria, time frame, and the population sample: there will be marked differences, for example, between general population and treatment population samples, or even between groups assigned to different treatment programs. In spite of these difficulties, some general conclusions are evident.

Wittchen et al.[141] looked at key international studies of comorbidity in community population samples and concluded that there were strong similarities between different countries; summarizing two large studies from the U.S., they state: (1) over half of those individuals who have a substance misuse problem have also experienced other mental disorders within their lifetime, (2) dependence on, rather than misuse of, alcohol or other drugs is more likely to be associated with a mental disorder, (3) major depression, anxiety disorders, phobias, mania, schizophrenia, and conduct disorder in adolescence or adult antisocial behavior are all strongly associated with substance dependence, and (4) social phobia and adolescent conduct disorder are also associated with alcohol or drug misuse.

The National Comorbidity Survey of the general adult population in the U.S. studied lifetime and 12-month comorbidity in more than 8000 subjects: the lifetime prevalence for any substance misuse or dependence disorder was 26.6% and 12-month prevalence was 11.3%, with males having approximately twice the rates of women.[142] These data imply considerable variation and possibly substitution of mental disorders, one with another, over time. The stability of substance-related comorbidity is of importance in determining treatment regimens. Clinicians generally underestimate the presence of psychiatric and psychological disorders when assessing patients with substance misuse problems. Clinicians expect high levels of morbidity and often assume that symptoms are due to withdrawal, transient physical problems, or dependence itself. To determine the true prevalence of comorbidity in a treatment population, Driessen et al.[143] studied 100 inpatients' post-alcohol detoxification: they found 3% to have schizophrenia or schizoaffective disorders, 13% affective disorders, 22% phobic disorders, and 2% general anxiety. Alcohol dependence was judged to be secondary to the psychiatric condition in 60% of patients with schizophrenia, 48% with depression, and 72% with phobic disorder. This does not necessarily mean that a psychiatric condition that antedates substance misuse will persist beyond detoxification, or that there is any causal relationship.

It is important for the clinician to know what is driving an individual's substance use. Comorbidity does not imply cause and effect, but is one of several possibilities:

- Substance use and psychiatric disorder may coexist by chance.
- Substance use may cause psychiatric disorder.
- Psychiatric disorder may cause substance use.
- A third factor may mediate both substance use and psychiatric disorder.

Where a psychiatric disorder is seen to be of primary importance and driving the substance use, the psychiatric disorder should be the focus of treatment. However, a psychiatric disorder that initiated substance misuse or precipitated a relapse may be superseded by dependence driving the maintenance of substance use.

7.5.2 Making Prescribing Decisions

As a matter of general principle there are several reasons doctors should be reserved when prescribing for people who misuse alcohol or other drugs: for those who also have a mental health problem there is a risk that prescribing sends out a message that taking drugs, prescribed or otherwise, is an appropriate way to deal with psychological distress. When undertaking a mental state examination, the doctor tries to balance benefits of pharmacotherapy against risk; risk is a function not only of the medication but also the treatment setting. In assessing risk, it is the ephemeral nature of psychological distress coexisting with substance misuse that is perhaps the most compelling reason to wait until a patient is drug free or stable before prescribing, and also a reason to consider hospital admission solely for the purpose of establishing a psychiatric diagnosis.

With a focus on alcohol, Allan[144] has recommended that patients presenting with anxiety and alcohol dependence should first be detoxified and reassessed after 6 weeks when only an expected 10% will be found to have persistent symptoms amounting to an anxiety state. The persistent anxiety can then be treated using conventional pharmacological or behavioral methods. She points out that patients may resist such an approach, preferring to deal with their psychological distress before tackling their substance use. People who are dependent on alcohol or other drugs usually succumb to a number of financial, family, health, and relationship problems, and it is not surprising that many will complain of depression; again it is not surprising that 80% or more will recover within a few weeks of abstinence without recourse to antidepressant treatment.

While abstinence may enforce an acceptance of problems accumulated while drinking or taking other drugs and this might be anticipated to increase depression, abstinence is also an opportunity to build self-efficacy and self-esteem, both powerful psychological antidepressants. Pharmacological antidepressants should be avoided unless there is unequivocal evidence of a biological depression of mood. The key point is that diagnoses of mental illness and substance use comorbidity made in haste will often evaporate. Nonetheless, it may be that the severity of symptoms is so severe when a patient presents as to indicate immediate symptomatic prescribing without the benefit of a diagnosis. Equally, it may be that a provisional diagnosis, for example, alcoholic delirium or Wernicke encephalopathy, demands urgent treatment.

The general principle to observe and "wait and see" can be a difficult course to follow, and in addition to cases of obvious florid psychosis, there are times when urgent action (usually not pharmacotherapy) is required. For example, suicidal ideation is a common emergency for doctors specializing in addiction. Alcohol and other drugs are commonly found on toxicological screening of subjects who have committed suicide. Depressant drugs in particular are likely to impair judgment and, therefore, increase both the risk of any suicide attempt, but especially suicides involving violence or impulse, such as driving into a bridge or jumping in front of a train.

Murphy[145] has identified seven risk factors for suicide in "alcoholics":

- Depression
- Suicidal thoughts
- Poor social support
- Physical illness
- Unemployment
- Living alone
- Recent interpersonal loss

The risks accumulate over a number of years, suggesting that there is scope for preventive social and health care. In short, people who misuse alcohol or other drugs are at increased risk of committing suicide: pharmacological treatment risks providing a means of suicide and active, social therapy is more likely to be effective. Other psychiatric conditions may be less urgent than a suicide threat, but nonetheless complex in terms of reaching prescribing decisions.

Insomnia, which may result from psychological distress and may be a symptom of recreational drug use or may be part of a withdrawal syndrome, is ubiquitous and merits special mention. Alcohol and other sedatives increase slow wave sleep and reduce REM and are therefore effective hypnotics. Short-acting hypnotics and alcohol are, in normal amounts, metabolized through the night, causing rebound arousal and wakenings. For people who misuse depressant drugs, including alcohol, the rebound of REM may cause vivid nightmares and sleep disturbance, which persists for months after achieving abstinence. The use of stimulant drugs causes a similar overarousal.

Patients with addiction problems are often reluctant to accept nonpharmacological approaches to insomnia; however, advice to reduce smoking and coffee drinking in the evening and to exercise during the day should at least accompany any prescribing of hypnotics.

In summary, for many people who suffer from psychiatric or psychological disorders, substance use and misuse has utility. It is often the case that traditional medicine has less to offer than the patient's own self-medication regimen and that social rather than pharmacological interventions are really what is needed. It is particularly important for doctors to be clear about the purpose of their prescribing and to monitor its effectiveness. Where substance misuse and psychiatric disorder coexist, the case for not prescribing, even for psychiatric illness, should always be vigorously explored.

7.6 TOXICOLOGIC ISSUES

Kim Wolff, Ph.D.

King's College London, Institute of Psychiatry, National Addiction Centre, London, U.K.

7.6.1 Heat and Drug Stability

The variety of different body matrices that can be analyzed to determine the presence or absence of different psychoactive substances is extensive, ranging from semen to cerumen. There are, however, practical limitations to the extent to which different biological samples can be used, and the mechanism of collection and supervision of samples are critical to the procedure. This chapter focuses on those biological samples that are commonly used for testing within various drug treatment settings, namely, urine, saliva, blood, and hair. Urinalysis is routinely used in hospital-based services, blood in forensic environments, hair analysis for medicolegal cases, and saliva tests have been used in the prison services and outreach units.

Many would advocate that the assessment of psychoactive drug use could reliably be achieved using self-report from the drug user (client). However, there are issues around the method of inquiry — the context, purpose, interviewer characteristics, etc.[146] that may bias self-report. Circumstances where the drug user sees the self-report to the inquirer about drug use as influential on his own continued treatment or possible loss of privileges are particular examples.

The drug being tested for and the period of time that the clinician wishes to consider influence the choice of body fluid. Blood and, to a lesser degree, saliva are likely to give the most accurate measurement of drugs currently active in the system, whereas urine provides a somewhat broader time period, but with less quantitative accuracy. Hair provides a substantially longer time frame.[147]

The routine drug testing strategy most widely adopted is to send urine samples to a laboratory for an initial screen to detect psychoactive drugs of interest. Analysis is performed using a semi-automated commercially available immunoassay or thin layer chromatography (TOXILAB) test. Several types of the former test exist and include radioimmunoassay, RIA:Europ/DPC, enzyme-mediated immunoassay test, Syva:EMIT, and fluorescence polarization immunoassay, FPIA. Recently, several rapid detection devices (near patient test, NPT) for drugs of abuse screening have been marketed in the U.K. Such tests offer a more rapid turnaround of results to aid clinical decision making.[148] However, all initial drug screen tests are nonspecific and identify only in a nonquantitative fashion the class of drug present, e.g., opiates, amphetamines, or benzodiazepines, etc.

Ideally, any positive test result should then be confirmed by a second test working on different physicochemical principles to the screening test. Gas and liquid chromatography with mass spectrometric detection are regarded as the "gold standard" and are favored where legally defensible results are required. It cannot be overemphasized that the confirmation of drug screening test results is essential. For amphetamine-specific immunoassays, the confirmation test provides the opportunity to differentiate legitimate medicines. For instance, pseudoephedrine and phentermine give a positive test result (cross-react) with tests for illicit drugs like amphetamine and 3,4-methylene-dioxymethamphetamine, MDMA. For opiate drugs, initial immunoassay tests for morphine cross-react with codeine, dihydrocodeine, pholcodeine, 6-monoactetylmorphine (6-MAM), morphine-3-glucuronide, and morphine-6-glucuronide. Consequently, if more than one of these substances is present in a urine sample, the test result will relate to the concentration of the sum of all these opiates and their metabolites. In this way an inaccurate picture of the window-of-detection of opiate drugs in urine may be concluded. The clinical benefit of the confirmation test is that it is able to verify the specific substance(s) present. For example, a confirmation test can detect the presence of 6-MAM, the only specific indicator (metabolite) of heroin use

Table 7.6.1 Checks for Urine Sample Adulteration

Problem	Check to Confirm
Dilution	Creatinine <20 mg/dl (1.77 mmol/L)
	Specific gravity <1.003
Substitution	Creatinine 5 mg/dl (0.44 mmol/L)
	Specific gravity 1.001 or 1.020
Concentration	pH values of <4 and >8 are abnormal
Temperature	Values <32°C and >38°C are abnormal
Adulteration (bleach, nitrate)	Sample will not smell like urine
	Nitrite level >500 g/ml

7.6.2 Analysis Using Other Body Fluids

The advantages of urine sampling for detecting drugs of abuse are the higher drug concentrations; the large volume of urine; the opportunity to concentrate urine samples, which in turn, increases drug concentrations, and thus the possibility of detection; and the fact that urine collection is a non-invasive procedure. Urine testing is the most reliable and interpretable process available to the clinician and is the technique universally supported by laboratories across the country. Urine testing is recommended as essential to help confirm opiate dependence before commencing substitute prescribing with methadone or buprenorphine. Random urine tests are also used to monitor illicit drug use during treatment. Hair testing is more common in occupational health setting and for medicolegal cases where a longer history of drug use is required. Providing the client's hair is of sufficient length (hair grows at a rate of 1 cm/month) and thickness (50 to 100 strands are needed), a drug history covering a 3-month period may be obtained. Cannabis use, however, is very difficult to detect in hair and different rates of drug deposition in the hair strand have been identified for different races, treated (bleached hair), and in blond compared to black-haired people. Blood (and possibly saliva) provides an accurate picture of the immediate situation and is best suited for therapeutic drug monitoring, which has been reported for methadone treatment.

Sample integrity has frequently been an issue with urinalysis and every effort should be made to avoid substitution or adulteration of specimens. Simple observational checks of foaming, color, and temperature are valuable. Collection cups with temperature indicator strips are available for immediate monitoring of specimen temperature. For workplace or pre-employment testing, medicolegal work and sport testing, chain-of-custody procedures, tamper-free collection vesicles, and documentation to accompany each sample are required.

Dilution is a commonly reported problem. The U.K. National External Quality Assessment Scheme (UKNEQAS) for drugs of abuse screening in urine reported that 86% of samples found adulterated had been diluted.[149] As it is possible to drink large volumes of water and lower urine drug concentrations below the positive cutoff, thresholds for tests of urine creatinine and specific gravity have been proposed (Table 7.6.1).

There has been a huge growth in the development of NPT kits. Most are predominantly for urine sample collection and have the advantage of offering rapid results. Such tests include FRONT-LINE (Boehringer Mannheim) and Rapi Tests (Morwell Diagnostics), EZ-Screen (for cannabis and cocaine), Triage (for benzodiazepines, methadone, and cocaine; Biosite Diagnostic), Abuscreen ONTRAK (for cannabis and morphine; Roche Diagnostics), ONTRAK TESTCUP (for opiates; Roche Diagnostics). There have been many reported limitations for these immunoassay test devices. For cannabinoids, the accuracy varies from 52 to 90%; for opiates 37 to 90%; for amphetamines 44 to 83%, and for cocaine 72 to 92%.[150] Another reported failing of the NPT kits has been the lack of available information about cross-reactivity,[151] which is important in drug treatment services where poly substance use is commonplace. Urine samples for use with NPT kits also have the same issues with authenticity as those collected for laboratory-based testing and in addition concern has been raised that without onsite staff training the number of false-positive and false-negative test results could be unacceptably high. Confirmation of the test result with all initial tests is recommended as good practice.

Most recently, oral fluid immunoassay test kits have also become available (Cozart RapiScan, www.cozart.co.uk) offering a less invasive testing procedure. Oral fluid screening is, however, subject to contamination of the buccal cavity from drugs taken intranasally or sublingually, i.e., cannabis and buprenorphine, respectively. Additionally, the pH of saliva (the main component of oral fluid) can be changed during the sample collection procedure by chewing, which may alter (reduce) the diffusion of the drugs of interest into the oral fluid sample. This could result in false-negative test results. Cost is also prohibitive and currently there is little evidence-based information about these products.[152]

Accurate interpretation of the drug-screening test within a clinical setting, alongside other relevant information, remains the key to the usefulness of any test.

REFERENCES

1. Heather, N. and Robertson, I., *Problem Drinkers,* Oxford: Oxford University Press, 1989.
2. Edwards, G. and Gross, M.M., Alcohol dependence: provisional description of a clinical syndrome, *Br. Med. J.,* 1, 1058, 1976.
3. World Health Organisation, *The ICD-10 Classification of Mental and Behavioural Disorders: Clinical Descriptions and Diagnostic Guidelines,* Geneva: World Health Organisation, 1992.
4. Raistrick, D.S., Bradshaw, J., Tober, G., Weiner, J., Allison, J., and Healey, C., Development of the Leeds Dependence Questionnaire, *Addiction,* 89, 563, 1994.
5. Pervin, L.A., Affect and addiction, *Addict. Behav.,* 13, 83, 1988.
6. Johanson, C.E. and Uhlenhuth, E.H., Drug preference and mood in humans: diazepam, *Psychopharmacology,* 71, 269, 1980.
7. Johanson, C.E. and Uhlenhuth, E.H., Drug preference and mood in humans: d-amphetamine, *Psychopharmacology,* 71, 275, 1980.
8. Bickel, W.K., Higgins, S.T., and Stitzer, M.L., Choice of blind methadone dose increases by methadone maintenance patients, *Drug Alcohol Depend.,* 18, 165, 1986.
9. McGlothlin, W.H. and Anglin, D., Long-term follow-up of clients of high and low-dose methadone programs, *Arch. Gen. Psychiatry,* 38, 1055, 1981.
10. Hartnoll, R.L., Mitcheson, M.C., Battersby, A., Brown, G., Ellis, M., Fleming, P., and Hedley, N., Evaluation of heroin maintenance in controlled trial, *Arch. Gen. Psychiatry,* 37, 877, 1980.
11. Chiang, C.W. and Barnett, G., Marijuana effect and delta-9-tetrahydrocannabinol plasma levels, *Clin. Pharmacol. Ther.,* 36, 234, 1984.
12. Johnson, R.E., Cone, E.J., Henningfield, J.E., and Fudala, P.J., Use of buprenorphine in the treatment of opiate addiction. I. Physiologic and behavioural effects during a rapid dose induction, *Clin. Pharmacol. Ther.,* 46, 335, 1989.
13. Mello, N.K., Lukas, S.E., Bree, M.P., and Mendekson, J.H., Progressive ration performance maintained by buprenorphine, heroin and methadone in macaque monkeys, *Drug Alcohol Depend.,* 21, 81, 1988.
14. Stimson, G.V. and Oppenheimer, E., *Heroin Addiction: Treatment and Control in Britain,* London: Tavistock Publications, 1982.
15. Funderburk, F.R., Griffiths, R.R., McLeod, D.R., Bigelow, G.E., Mackenzi, A., Liebson, I.A., and Nemeth-Coslett, R., Relative abuse liability of lorazepam and diazepam: an evaluation in "recreational" drug users, *Drug Alcohol Depend.,* 22, 215, 1988.
16. Edwards, G., Drug dependence and plasticity, *Q. J. Stud. Alcohol,* 35, 176, 1974.
17. Prochaska, J.O. and DiClemente, C.C., *The Transtheoretical Approach: Crossing Traditional Boundaries of Therapy,* Homewood, IL: Dow Jones-Irwin, 1984.
18. Tober, G., Motivational interviewing with young people, in Miller, W. and Rollnick, S., Eds., *Motivational Interviewing: Preparing People to Change,* New York: Guildford, 1991.
19. Nutt, D.J., Addiction: brain mechanisms and their treatment implications, *Lancet,* 347, 31, 1996.
20. Finn, P., Program administrator and medical staff attitudes toward six hypothetical medications for substance abuse treatment, *J. Psychoactive Drugs,* 28, 161, 1996.

21. Pani, P.P., Piratsu, R., Ricci, A., and Gessa, G.L., Prohibition of take-home dosages: negative conse-quences on methadone maintenance treatment, *Drug Alcohol Depend.,* 41, 81, 1996.

22. Greenfield, L., Brady, J.V., Besteman, K.J., and De Smet, A., Patient retention in mobile and fixed-site methadone maintenance treatment, *Drug Alcohol Depend.,* 42, 125, 1996.

23. Department of Health. *Drug Misuse and Dependence: Guidelines in Clinical Management.* London: HMSO, 1999.

24. Seivewright, N.A. and Greenwood, J., What is important in drug misuse treatment. *Lancet,* 347, 373, 1996.

25. Lingford-Hughes, A.R., Welch, S., and Nutt, D.J., Evidence-based guidelines for the pharmacological management of substance misuse addiction and co-morbidity: recommendations from the British Association for Psychopharmacology, *J. Psychopharmacol.,* 18, 293, 2004.

26. Dole, V.P. and Nyswander, M., A medical treatment for diacetylmorphine (heroin) addiction, *J. Am. Med. Assoc.,* 193, 80, 1965.

27. Solberg, U., Burkhaut, G., and Nilson, M., An overview of opiate substitution treatment in the European Union and Norway. *Int. J. Drug Policy,* 8, 575, 2002.

28. Verster, A. and Buning, E., *European Methadone Guidelines,* Amsterdam, the Netherlands: Euro-Methwork, 2000.

29. Corkery, J.M., Schifano, F., Ghodse, A.H., and Oyefeso, A., The effects of methadone and its role in fatalities. *Hum. Psychopharmacol. Clin. Exp.,* 19, 565, 2004.

30. Schuster, C.R., The National Institute on Drug Abuse and methadone maintenance treatment, *J. Psychoactive Drugs,* 23, 111, 1991.

31. Gossop, M., Marsden, J., Stewart, D., and Kidd, T., Reduction or cessation of injecting behaviours? Treatment outcomes at 1 year follow-up, *Addict. Behav.,* 28, 785, 2003.

32. Hall, W., Bell, J., and Carless, J., Crime and drug use among applicants for methadone maintenance, *Drug Alcohol Depend.,* 31, 123, 1993.

33. Gossop, M., Marsden, J., and Stewart, D., NTORS after five years: changes in substance use, health and criminal behaviour during the five years after intake, London: Department of Health, 2001.

34. Ball, J.C., Lange, W.R., Myers, C.P., and Friedman, S.R., Reducing the risk of AIDS through meth-adone maintenance treatment, *J. Health Social Behav.,* 29, 214, 1988.

35. Ward, J., Mattick, R., and Hall, W., *Key Issues in Methadone Maintenance Treatment,* University of New South Wales Press, Sydney, Australia, 1992.

36. Reno, R.R. and Aiken, L.S., Life activities and life quality of heroin addicts in and out of treatment, *Int. J. Addict.,* 28, 211, 1993.

37. Glass, R.M., Methadone maintenance: new research on a controversial treatment [editorial], *J. Am. Med. Assoc.,* 269, 1995, 1993.

38. Gossop, M., Marsden, J., Edwards, C., Stewart, D., Wilson, A., Segar, G., and Lehmann, P., *The National Treatment Outcome Study (NTORS): Summary of the Project, the Clients, and Preliminary Findings,* London: Department of Health, 1996.

39. D'Aunno, T. and Vaughn, T.E., Variations in methadone treatment practice, *J. Am. Med. Assoc.,* 267, 253, 1992.

40. Caplehorn, J.R.M., Bell, J., Kleinbaum, D.G., and Gebski, V.J., Methadone dose and heroin use during maintenance treatment, *Addiction,* 88, 119, 1993.

41. Kang, S.-Y. and De Leon, G., Correlates of drug injection behaviours among methadone outpatients, *Am. J. Drug Alcohol Abuse,* 19, 107, 1993.

42. Thiede, H., Hagan, H., and Murrill, C.S., Methadone treatment and HIV and Hepatitis B and C: risk reduction in the Seattle area, *J. Urban Health,* 77, 331, 2000.

43. Wong, K.H., Lee, S.S., Lim, W.I., and Low, H.K., Adherence to methadone is associated with a lower level of HIV related risk behaviour in drug users, *J. Subst. Abuse Treat.,* 24, 233, 2003.

44. Wolff, K., Hay, A., Raistrick, D., Calvert, R., and Feely, M., Measuring compliance in methadone maintenance patients: use of pharmacological indicator to "estimate" methadone plasma levels, *Clin. Pharmacol. Ther.,* 50, 199, 1991.

45. Gerstein, D.R., The effectiveness of drug treatment, in *Addictive States,* O'Brien, C.P. and Jaffe, J.H., Eds., New York: Raven Press, 1992, 235.

46. Strain, E.C., Bigelow, G.E., Liebson, I.A., and Stitzer, M.L., Moderate versus high dose methadone in the treatment of opioid dependence; a randomized trial, *J. Am. Med. Assoc.,* 281, 1000, 1999.

47. Faggiano, F., Vigana-Tagliati, F.E., and Lemma, P., Methadone Maintenance at Different Doses, The Cochrane Library, Chichester, U.K.: John Wiley & Sons, 1, 37, 2004.

48. Wolff, K., Hay, A.W.M., and Raistrick, D., Plasma methadone measurements and their role in methadone detoxification programmes, *Clin. Chem.*, 38, 420, 1992.

49. Ball, J.C. and Ross, A., *The Effectiveness of Methadone Maintenance Treatment*, New York: Springer, 1991.

50. Ling, W. and Wessan, D.R., Methadyl acetate and methadone as maintenance treatments for heroin addicts. A Veterans Administration cooperative study, *Arch. Gen. Psychiatry*, 232, 149, 2003.

51. Barnett, P.G., Rodgers, J.H., and Bloch, D.A., A meta analysis comparing buprenorphine to methadone for treatment of opiate dependence, *Addiction*, 96, 683, 2001.

52. Wolff, K. and Hay, A.W.M., Plasma methadone monitoring with methadone maintenance treatment, *Drug Alcohol Depend.*, 36, 69, 1994.

53. Wolff, K., Sanderson, M., and Hay, A.W.M., Methadone concentrations in plasma and their relationship to drug dosage, *Clin. Chem.*, 37, 205, 1991.

54. Wolff, K., Hay, A.W.M., Raistrick, D., and Calvert, R., Steady state pharmacokinetics of methadone in opioid addicts, *Eur. J. Clin. Pharmacol.*, 44, 189, 1993.

55. Kreek, M.J., Gutjahr, C.R., Garfield, J.W., Bowen, D.V., and Field, F.H., Drug interactions with methadone, *Ann. N.Y. Acad. Sci.*, 281, 350, 1976.

56. Liu, S.J. and Wang, R.I.H., Case report of barbiturate-induced enhancement of methadone metabolism and withdrawal syndrome, *Am. J. Psychiatry*, 141, 1287, 1984.

57. Dole, V.P., Implications of methadone maintenance for theories of narcotic addiction, *J. Am. Med. Assoc.*, 260, 3025, 1988.

58. Blaine, J.D., Renault, P.F., Levine, G.L., and Whysner, J.A., Clinical use of LAAM, *Ann. N.Y. Acad. Sci.*, 311, 214, 1978.

59. Kreek, M.J., Garfield, J.N., Gutjahr, C.L., and Giusti, L.M., Rifampicin induced methadone withdrawal, *N. Engl. J. Med.*, 294, 1104, 1976.

60. Caplehorn, J., Bell, J., Kleinbaum, D., and Gebski, V., Methadone dose and heroin use during maintenance treatment, *Addiction*, 88, 119, 1993.

61. Dyer, K.R., Foster, D.J.R., White, J.M., Somogyi, A.A., Menelaou, A., and Bochner, F., Steady-state pharmacokinetics and pharmacodynamics in methadone maintenance patients: comparison of those who do and do not experience withdrawal and concentration-effect relationships, *Clin. Pharmacol. Ther.*, 65, 685, 1999.

62. Fishman, S.M., Wilsey, B., Yang, J., Reisfield, G.M., Bandman, T.B., and Borsook, D., Adherence monitoring and drug surveillance in chronic opioid therapy, *J. Pain Sympt. Manage.*, 20, 293, 2000.

63. Eap, C.B., On the usefulness of therapeutic drug monitoring of methadone, *Eur. Addict. Res.*, 6, 31, 2000.

64. Wolff, K., Hay, A., Raistrick, D., Calvert, R., and Feely, M., Measuring compliance in methadone maintenance patients: use of a pharmacologic indicator to "estimate" methadone plasma levels, *Clin. Pharmacol. Ther.*, 50, 199, 1999.

65. Torrens, M., Castillo, C., San, L., del Moral, E., González, M.L., and de la Torre, R., Plasma methadone concentrations as an indicator of opioid withdrawal symptoms and heroin use in a methadone maintenance program, *Drug Alcohol Depend.*, 52, 193, 1998.

66. Wolff, K., Rostami-Hodjegan, A., Hay, A.W., Raistrick, D., and Tucker, G., Population-based pharmacokinetic approach for methadone monitoring of opiate addicts: potential clinical utility, *Addiction*, 95, 1771, 2000.

67. Foster, D.J., Somogyi, A.A., White, J.M., and Bochner, F., Population pharmacokinetics of (R)-, (S)- and rac-methadone in methadone maintenance patients, *Br. J. Clin. Pharmacol.*, 57, 742, 2004.

68. Iribarne, C., Berthou, F., Baird, S., Dreano, Y., Picart, D., Bail, J.P., Beaune, P., and Menez, J., Involvement of cytochrome P450 3A4 enzyme in the N-demethylation of methadone in human liver microsomes, *Chem. Res. Toxicol.*, 9, 365, 1996.

69. Gerber, J.G., Rosenkraz, S., Segal, Y., Aberg, J., D'Amico, R., Mildvan, D., Gulick, R., Hughes, V., Vlexner, C., Aweeka, F., Hsu, A., Gal, J., and ACTG 401 Study Team, Effect of ritonavir/saquinavir on stereoselective pharmacokinetics of methadone: results of AIDS Clinical Trials Group (ACTG) 401, *J. Acquir. Immune Defic. Syndr.*, 27, 153, 2001.

70. Foster, D.J., Somogyi, A.A., and Bochner, F., Methadone N-demethylation in human liver microsomes: lack of stereoselectivity and involvement of CYP3A4, *Br. J. Clin. Pharmacol.*, 47, 403, 1999.

71. Raistrick, D., Hay, A., and Wolff, K., Methadone maintenance and tuberculosis treatment, *Br. Med. J.*, 313, 925, 1996.
72. Tong, T.G., Pond, S.M., Kreek, M.J., Jaffery, N.F., and Benowitz, N.L., Phenytoin induced methadone withdrawal, *Ann. Intern. Med.*, 94, 349, 1981.
73. Liu, S.-J. and Wang, R.I.H., Case report of barbiturate-induced enhancement of methadone metabolism and withdrawal syndrome, *Am. J. Psychiatry*, 141, 1287, 1984.
74. Tong, T.G., Benowitz, N.N.L., and Kreek, M.J., Methadone-disulfiram interaction during methadone maintenance, *J. Clin. Pharmacol.*, 10, 506, 1980.
75. Mertins, L., Brockmeyer, N.H., Daecke, C., and Goos, M., Pharmacokinetic interaction of antimicrobial agents with levomethadon (L) elimination in drug addicted AIDS patients [abstr.], presented at 2nd European Conference on Clinical Aspects of HIV Infection, March 8/9, 1990.
76. Plummer, J.L., Gourlay, G.K., Cousins, C., and Cousins, M.J., Estimation of methadone clearance: application in the management of cancer pain, *Pain*, 33, 313, 1988.
77. Spaulding T.C., Minimum, L., Kotake, A.N., and Takemori, A.E., The effects of diazepam on the metabolism of methadone by the liver of methadone dependent rats, *Drug Metab. Dispos.*, 2, 458, 1974.
78. Pond, S.M., Tong, T.G., Benowitz, N.L., Jacob, P., and Rigod, J., Lack of effect of diazepam on methadone metabolism in methadone maintained addicts, *Clin. Pharmacol. Ther.*, 31, 139, 1982.
79. Nilsson, M.-I., Grönbladh, L., Widerlöv, E., and Ånggård, E., Pharmacokinetics of methadone in methadone maintenance treatment: characterization of therapeutic failures, *Eur. J. Clin. Pharmacol.*, 25, 497, 1983.
80. Perret, G., Deglon, J.J., Kreek, M.J., Ho, A., and La Harpe, R., Lethal methadone intoxications in Geneva, Switzerland, from 1994 to 1998, *Addiction*, 95, 1647, 2000.
81. Gourevitch, M.N. and Friedland, G.H., Interactions between methadone and medications used to treat HIV infection: a review, *Mt. Sinai J. Med.*, 67, 429, 2000.
82. Kreek, M.J., Metabolic interactions between opiates and alcohol, *Ann. N.Y. Acad. Sci.*, 362, 36, 1981.
83. Wolff, K., Boys, A., Hay, A.W.M., and Raistrick, D., Methadone kinetics in pregnancy, *Eur. J. Clin. Pharmacol.*, 61, 763, 2005.
84. Emrich, H.M., Vogt, P., and Herz, A., Possible antidepressant effects of opioids: action of buprenorphine, *Ann. N.Y. Acad. Sci.*, 398, 108, 1982.
85. Kosten, T.R., Morgan, C., and Kosten, T.A., Depressive symptoms during buprenorphine treatment of opioid abusers, *J. Subst. Abuse Treat.*, 7, 51, 1990.
86. Mongan, L. and Callaway, E., Buprenorphine responses, *Biol. Psychiatry*, 28, 1065, 1990.
87. Groves, S. and Nutt, D.J. Buprenorphine and schizophrenia, *Hum. Psychopharmacol.*, 6, 71, 1991.
88. Kosten, T., Krystal, J.H., Charney, D.S., Price, L.H., Morgan, C.H., and Kleber, H.D., Opioid antagonist challenges in buprenorphine maintained patients, *Drug Alcohol Depend.*, 25, 73, 1990.
89. Johnson, R.E., Cone, E.J., Henningfield, J.E., and Fudala, P.J., Use of buprenorphine in the treatment of opiate addiction. I. Physiologic and behaviour effects during a rapid dose induction, *Clin. Pharmacol. Ther.*, 46, 335, 1989.
90. Cowan, A., Lewis, J.W., and MacFarlane, I.R., Agonist and antagonist properties of buprenorphine, *Br. J. Pharmacol.*, 60, 537, 1977.
91. Amass, L., Bickel, W.K., Higgins, S.T., and Badger, G.J., Alternate day dosing during buprenorphine treatment of opioid dependence, *Br. J. Pharmacol.*, 60, 537, 1994.
92. Walsh, S.L., Preston, K.L., Stitzer, M.L., Cone, E.J., and Bigelow, G.E., Clinical pharmacology of buprenorphine: ceiling effects at high doses, *Clin. Pharmacol. Ther.*, 55, 569, 1994.
93. Jasinski, D.R., Fudala, P.J., and Johnson, R.E., Sublingual versus subcutaneous buprenorphine in opiate abusers, *Clin. Pharmacol. Ther.*, 45, 513, 1989.
94. Perera, K.M.H., Tulley, M., and Jenner, F.A., The use of benzodiazepines among drug addicts, *Br. J. Addict.*, 82, 511, 1987.
95. Strang, J., Seivewright, N., and Farrell, M., Oral and intravenous abuse of benzodiazepines, in *Benzodiazepine Dependence*, Hallstrom, C., Ed. Oxford: Oxford Medical Publications, 1993, 9.
96. Busto, U., Sellers, E.M., Naranjo, C.A., Kappell, H.D., Sanchez-Craig, M., and Simpkins, J., Patterns of benzodiazepine abuse and dependence, *Br. J. Addict.*, 81, 87, 1986.
97. Johnson, S.M. and Fleming, W.W., Mechanisms of cellular adaptive sensitivity changes: applications to opioid tolerance and dependence, *Pharmacol. Rev.*, 41, 435, 1989.
98. Foy, A., Drug withdrawal: a selective review, *Drug Alcohol Rev.*, 10, 203, 1991.

99. Paulos, C.X. and Cappell, H., Conditioned tolerance to the hypothermic effect of ethyl alcohol, *Science*, 206, 1109, 1979.

100. Whitfield, C.L. et al., Detoxification of 1,024 alcoholic patients without psychoactive drugs, *J. Am. Med. Assoc.*, 239, 1409, 1974.

101. American Psychiatric Association, *Diagnostic and Statistical Manual of Mental Disorders*, 4th ed. Washington, D.C.: Author, 1994.

102. Smolka, M. and Schmidt, L.G., The influence of heroin dose and route of administration on the severity of opiate withdrawal syndrome, *Addiction*, 94, 1191, 1999.

103. Gossop, M., Bradley, M., and Philips, G., An investigation of withdrawal symptoms shown by opiate addicts during and subsequent to a 21 day in-patient methadone detoxification procedure, *Addict. Behav.*, 12, 1, 1987.

104. Gossop, M., Bradley, M., and Strang, J., Opiate withdrawal symptoms in response to 10 day and 21 day methadone withdrawal programs, *Br. J. Psychiatry*, 154, 560, 1989.

105. Amato, L., Davoli, M., Minozzi, S., Ali, R., and Ferri, M., Methadone at tapered doses for the management of opioid withdrawal, *Cochrane Database Syst. Rev.*, July 20, 2005.

106. Hughes, J.R., Higgens, S.T., and Bickel, K.W., Common errors in pharmacologic treatment of drug dependence and withdrawal, *Comprehensive Ther.*, 20, 89, 1994.

107. Cook, C.C.H., Scannell, T.D., and Lepsedge, M.S., Another clinical trial that failed, *Lancet*, 524–525, 1988.

108. Bearn, J., Gossop, M., and Strang, J., Randomised double-blind comparison of lofexidine and methadone in the in-patient treatment of opiate withdrawal, *Drug Alcohol Depend.*, 43, 87, 1996.

109. Yang, G., Zhao, W., and Xu, K., The combined use of scopolamine, naltrexone, and naloxone as a rapid safe, effective detoxification treatment for heroin addicts, *Zhonghua Yi Xue Za ZHI*, 79, 679, 1999.

110. Golden, S.A. and Sakhrani, D.I., Unexpected delirium during Rapid Opioid Detoxification (ROD), *J. Addict. Dis.*, 23, 65, 2004.

111. Mello, N.K., Mendelson, J.H., and Keuhnle, J.C., Buprenorphine effects on human heroin self administration: an operant analysis, *J. Pharmacol. Exp. Ther.*, 223, 30, 1982.

112. Kosten, T.R., Morgan, C., and Kleber, H.D., Clinical trials of buprenorphine: detoxification and induction onto naltrexone, in Baline, J.D., Ed., *Buprenorphine: An Alternative Treatment for Opioid Dependence*, NIDA Research Monograph Series, 121, 101, 1994.

113. Gawin, F.H. and Kleber, H.D., Abstinence symptomology and psychiatric diagnosis in cocaine observers: clinical observations, *Arch. Gen. Psychiatry*, 43, 107, 1986.

114. Ellinwood, E.H., Jr. and Lee, T.H., Amphetamine abuse, in *Drugs of Abuse*, Balieres Clinical Psychiatry, 2, 3, 1996.

115. Alexander, B. and Perry, P., Detoxification from benzodiazepines, schedules and strategies, *J. Subst. Abuse Treat.*, 8, 9, 1991.

116. McDuff, D., Schwartz, R., Tommasello, M.S., Threpal, S., Donovan, T., and Johnson, J., Out-patient benzodiazepine detoxification procedure for methadone patients, *J. Subst. Abuse Treat.*, 10, 297, 1993.

117. Tyrer, P., Rutherford, D., and Huggett, T., Benzodiazepine withdrawal symptoms and propanolol, *Lancet*, 1, 520, 1981.

118. Kleber, H.D., Naltrexone, *J. Subst. Abuse Treat.*, 2, 117, 1985.

119. Pfohl, D.N., Allen, A.I., Atkinson, R.L., Knoppman, D.S., Malcolm, R.J., Mitchell, J.E., and Morley, J.E., Naltrexone hydrochloride: a review of serum transaminase elevations at high dosage, *NIDA Res. Monogr. Ser.*, 67, 66, 1986.

120. Weddington, W.W., Brown, B.S., Haertzen, C.A., Hess, J.M., Mahaffey, J.R., Kolar, A.F., and Jaffe, J.H., Comparison of amantadine and desipramine combined with psychotherapy for treatment of cocaine dependence, *Am. J. Drug Alcohol Abuse*, 17, 137, 1991.

121. Kranzler, H.R. and Bauer, L.O., Bromocriptine and cocaine cue reactivity in cocaine dependent patients, *Br. J. Addict.*, 87, 1537, 1992.

122. Alterman, A.I., Droba, M., Antelo, R.E., Cornish, J.W., Sweeney, K.K., Parikh, G.A., and O'Brien, C.P., Amantadine may facilitate detoxification of cocaine addicts, *Drug Alcohol Depend.*, 31, 19, 1992.

123. Gawin, F.H., Allen, D., and Humblestone, B., Outpatient treatment of crack cocaine smoking with flupenthixol decanoate, *Arch. Gen. Psychiatry*, 46, 322, 1989.

124. Handelsman, L., Limpitlaw, L., Williams, D., Schmeidler, J., Paris, P., and Stimmel, B., Amantadine does not reduce cocaine use or craving in cocaine-dependent methadone maintenance patients, *Drug Alcohol Depend.*, 39, 173, 1995.

125. Lima, M.S., Pharmacological treatment of cocaine dependence: a systematic review, *Arch. Gen. Psychiatry*, 49, 900, 1992.

126. Kosten, T.R., Morgan, C.M., Falcione, J., and Schottenfeld, R.S., Pharmacotherapy for cocaine abusing methadone maintained patients using amantadine and despiramine, *Arch. Gen. Psychiatry*, 49, 894, 1992.

127. Kolar, A.F., Brown, B.S., Weddington, W.W., Haertzen, C.C., Michaelson, B.S., and Jaffe, J.H., Treatment of cocaine dependence in methadone maintained clients: a pilot study comparing the efficacy of desipramine and amantadine, *Int. J. Addict.*, 27, 849, 1992.

128. Mello, N.K., Kamien, J.B., and Lukas, S.E., The effects of intermittent buprenorphine administration on cocaine self-administration by rhesus monkeys, *J. Pharmacol. Exp. Ther.*, 264, 530, 1993.

129. Carroll, K.M., Rounsaville, B.J., Nich, C., Gordon, L.T., Wirtz, P.W., and Gawin, F., One-year follow-up of psychotherapy and pharmacotherapy for cocaine dependence: delayed emergence of psychotherapy effects, *Arch. Gen. Psychiatry*, 51, 989, 1994.

130. Compton, P.A., Ling, W., Charuvastra, V.C., and Wesson, D.R., Buprenorphine as a pharmacotherapy for cocaine abuse: a review of the evidence, *J. Addict. Dis.*, 14, 97, 1995.

131. Sternbach, H., Serotonin syndrome: how to avoid it, identify and treat dangerous interactions, *Curr. Psych. Online*, 2, 5, 2002.

132. Extin, I.X. and Gold, M.S., The treatment of cocaine addicts: bromocriptine or desipramine, *Psychiatric Annals*, 18, 535, 1988.

133. Arndt, L., Desipramine treatment of cocaine dependence in MMT, *Arch. Gen. Psychiatry*, 49, 888, 1992.

134. Arndt, I.O., Dorozynsky, L., Woody, G., McLellan, A.T., and O'Brien, C.P., Desipramine treatment of cocaine dependence in methadone-maintained patients, *Arch. Gen. Psychiatry*, 49, 888, 1992.

135. Nunes, E.V., McGrath, P.J., Quitkin, F.M., Welikson, K.O., Stewart, J.E., Koenig, T., Wager, S., and Klein, D.F., Imipramine treatment of cocaine abuse: possible boundaries of efficacy, *Drug Alcohol Depend.*, 39, 185, 1995.

136. Carrera, M.R.A., Ashley, J.A., Parsons, L.H., Wirsching, P., Koob, G.F., and Janda, K.D., Suppression of psychoactive effects of cocaine by active immunisation, *Nature*, 378, 727, 1995.

137. Wittchen, H., Perkonigg, A., and Reed, V., Comorbidity of mental disorders and substance use disorders, *Eur. Addict. Res.*, 2, 36, 1996.

138. Kessler, R.C., McGonagle, K.A., Shanyang, Z., Nelson, C.B., Hughes, M., Eshleman, S., Wittchen, H., and Kendler, K.S., Lifetime and 12 month prevalence of DSM-III-R psychiatric disorders in the United States, *Arch. Gen. Psychiatry*, 51, 8, 1994.

139. Penick, E.C., Powell, B.J., Liskow, B.I., Jackson, J.O., and Nickel, E.J., The stability of coexisting psychiatric syndromes in alcoholic men after one year, *J. Stud. Alcohol*, 49, 395, 1988.

140. Driessen, M., Arolt, V., John, U., Veltrup, C., and Dilling, H., Psychiatric comorbidity in hospitalized alcoholics after detoxification treatment, *Eur. Addict. Res.*, 2, 17, 1996.

141. Allan, C.A., Alcohol problems and anxiety disorders — a critical review, *Alcohol Alcohol.*, 30, 145, 1995.

142. Ohberg, A., Vuori, E. Ojanperä, I., and Lonnqvist, J., Alcohol and drugs in suicides, *Br. J. Psychiatry*, 169, 75, 1996.

143. Murphy, G.E., *Suicide in Alcoholism*, New York: Oxford University Press, 1992.

144. Krausz, M., Haasen, C., Mass, R., Wagner, H.-B., Peter, H., and Freyberger, H.J., Harmful use of psychotropic substances by schizophrenics: coincidence, patterns of use and motivation, *Eur. Addict. Res.*, 2, 11, 1996.

145. Stradling, J.R., Recreational drugs and sleep, *Br. Med. J.*, 306, 573, 1993.

146. Eisen, J., MacFarlane, J., and Shapiro, C.M., Psychotropic drugs and sleep, *Br. Med. J.*, 306, 1331, 1993.

147. Magura, S., Casriel, C., Goldsmith, D.S., Strug, D.L., and Lipton, D.S., Contingency contracting with poly drug-abusing methadone patients, *Addict. Behav.*, 13, 113, 1988.

148. Wells, R. and McKay, B., Review of funding of methadone programmes in Australia. Report to the Department of Community Services and Health, 1989.

149. Braithwaite, R.A., Jarvie, D.R., Minty, P.S.B., Simpson, D., and Widdop, B., Screening for drugs of abuse. I: Opiates, amphetamines and cocaine, *Ann. Clin. Biochem.*, 32, 123, 1995.

150. Decrease, R., Magura, A., Lifshitz, M., and Tilson, J., *Drug Testing in the Workplace,* American Society of Clinical Pathologists, Chicago, 1989, 1–11.
151. American Association for Clinical Chemistry, Protocol issues in urinalysis of abused substances: report of the Substance-abuse Testing Committee, *Clin. Chem.,* 34, 605, 1989.
152. Strang, J., Marsh, A., and Desouza. N., Hair analysis for drugs of abuse, *Lancet,* 1, 740, 1990.
153. Harkey, M.R. and Henderson, G.L., Hair analysis for drugs of abuse, *Adv. Anal. Toxicol.,* 298, 1989.
154. Fraser, A.D., Clinical toxicology of drugs used in the treatment of opiate dependency, *Clin. Toxicol. I Clin. Lab. Med.,* 10(2), 375, 1990.

CHAPTER 8

Medical Complications of Drug Abuse

Edited by Neal L. Benowitz, M.D.
Division of Clinical Pharmacology and Experimental Therapeutics, University of California,
San Francisco, California

CONTENTS

8.1 MEDICAL ASPECTS OF DRUG ABUSE

Shoshana Zevin, M.D.,[1] **and Neal L. Benowitz, M.D.**[2]
[1] Department of Internal Medicine, Shaare Zedek Medical Center, Jerusalem, Israel
[2] Division of Clinical Pharmacology and Experimental Therapeutics, University of California, San Francisco, California

Drug abuse is associated with many medical problems and complications stemming both from regular use and from overdoses. Another serious medical complication arising from drug abuse is the withdrawal syndrome, which manifests during abstinence from the drug (see Chapter 7 for a more detailed discussion of withdrawal syndromes).

Drug abuse affects a number of organ systems. Central nervous system (CNS) symptoms can range from headaches and altered mental status to life-threatening situations like coma and seizures (Table 8.1.1 and Table 8.1.2). Cardiovascular manifestations of drug abuse include alterations in blood pressure, heart rate, as well as arrhythmias and organ ischemia. Respiratory arrest, pulmonary edema, and pneumothorax may occur. Metabolic effects such as alterations in body temperature, electrolytes, and acid–base disturbances are commonly seen (Table 8.1.3). Reproductive consequences, ranging from impaired fertility to intrauterine growth retardation, premature births, and neonatal syndromes, may also occur.

Infectious complications from intravenous drug use include viral infections such as HIV and hepatitis B, as well as bacterial infections including bacterial endocarditis, osteomyelitis, and abscesses.

In this chapter we describe the specific clinical syndromes associated with drugs of abuse.

Table 8.1.1 Drugs of Abuse Commonly Causing Altered Mental Status

Agitation	Amphetamines
	Cocaine
	Phencyclidine
	Phenylpropanolamine
Hallucinations	Khat
	LSD
	Marijuana
	Mescaline
	Phencyclidine
	Solvents
Psychosis	Amphetamines
	Khat
	LSD
	Phencyclidine
	Phenylpropanolamine
Stupor/Coma	Barbiturates
	Benzodiazepines
	Ethanol
	Opiates
	Phencyclidine
	"Crash" after binging on cocaine or amphetamines

Table 8.1.2 Drugs of Abuse Commonly Causing Seizures

Amphetamines
Cocaine
Meperidine
Phencyclidine
Phenylpropanolamine
Propoxyphene
Ethanol and sedative–hypnotic drug withdrawal

Table 8.1.3 Drugs of Abuse Commonly Causing Temperature Disturbances

Hyperthermia	Amphetamines
	Cocaine
	LSD
	Phencyclidine
	Ethanol and/or sedative–hypnotic drugs withdrawal
Hypothermia	Barbiturates
	Benzodiazepines
	Opiates

8.1.1 Stimulants

Stimulant drugs act primarily through activation of the sympathetic nervous system. In moderate doses they result in an elevated mood, increased energy and alertness, and decreased appetite. During intoxication they have profound central nervous system, cardiovascular system, and metabolic effects (Table 8.1.4).

8.1.1.1 Cocaine

Cocaine is one of the most frequent causes of medical complications of drug abuse.[1–3] Its actions include blockade of reuptake of catecholamines and dopamine by the neurons, release and/or blockade of the reuptake of serotonin, and centrally mediated neural sympathetic activa-

Table 8.1.4   Effects of Stimulant Intoxication

CNS Effects	Cardiovascular Effects	Metabolic Effects	Respiratory Effects
Irritability	Tachycardia[a]	Hyperthermia	Respiratory arrest
Euphoria	Hypertension	Rhabdomyolysis	
Insomnia	Cardiovascular collapse		
Anxiety			
Aggressiveness			
Delirium (agitated)			
Psychosis			
Stupor			
Coma			
Seizures			

[a] Except alpha-adrenergic agonists, which cause reflex bradycardia.

tion.[4,5] In addition to stimulating the sympathetic nervous system, cocaine also has a local anesthetic effect due to blockade of fast sodium channels in neural tissue and the myocardium.

Cocaine may be injected intravenously, smoked, snorted, or orally ingested. Its half-life is approximately 60 min. After intravenous injection or smoking there is a rapid onset of CNS manifestations; the effects may be delayed 30 to 60 min after snorting, mucosal application, or oral ingestion. The duration of cocaine effect is dependent on the route of administration, and is usually about 90 min after oral ingestion. Acute cocaine intoxication usually resolves after about 6 h, but some manifestations, such as myocardial infarction and stroke, may occur many hours after use, and a cocaine "crash" syndrome may last for several days after cocaine binging.

Most of the toxic manifestations of cocaine are due to excessive central and sympathetic nervous system stimulation. CNS stimulation causes behavioral changes, mood alterations, and psychiatric abnormalities. Autonomic stimulation causes cardiovascular system abnormalities, such as alterations in blood pressure, heart rate, arrhythmias, and hyperthermia (Table 8.1.5). Some of these manifestations, especially in CNS and cardiovascular system, can be life-threatening.

Central Nervous System

In moderate doses cocaine produces arousal and euphoria, but also anxiety and restlessness. Acute intoxication may result in severe psychiatric disturbances, such as acute anxiety, panic attacks, delirium, or acute psychosis.[6] Chronic cocaine intoxication can produce paranoid psychosis, similar to schizophrenia.[7] There is evidence suggesting that chronic cocaine use may lead to permanent neurological abnormalities. Brain atrophy, particularly in the frontal cortex and basal ganglia, has been found in chronic cocaine abusers, as well as cerebral blood perfusion deficits in frontal, periventricular, and temporal areas.[7,8] Abnormalities in cerebral glucose metabolism, as well as reduction in β-ATP/Pi ratios in cerebral cortex, were found in chronic cocaine addicts. These changes are similar to those observed after cerebral hypoxia.[9]

Headache: Headache is quite common in cocaine users, and has been reported in 13 to 50% of the users surveyed. In some patients the headaches were triggered by cocaine, whereas others reported them in association with cocaine withdrawal.[8,10] Some patients experienced migraine headaches. In some instances, headaches may be induced by hypertension. Persistent headaches, despite normalization of blood pressure, should raise concern about a possible stroke.

Stroke and transient neurologic defects: A variety of neurologic signs have been reported in patients with cocaine intoxication, among them dizziness, vertigo, tremor, and blurred vision. Transient hemiparesis has also been observed, and may be the result of cerebral vasospasm.[11,12] Strokes are being increasingly recognized in cocaine abuse, particularly in young patients. In one case-control study, the odds ratio for women aged 15 to 44 years who used cocaine or amphetamines was 7.[13] Among the patients with strokes, about 50% have cerebral hemorrhage, 30% subarachnoid

Table 8.1.5 Medical Complications of Cocaine Intoxication and Abuse

CNS	Headache
	Stroke (ischemic and hemorrhagic)
	Transient neurological deficit
	Subarachnoid hemorrhage
	Seizures
	Toxic encephalopathy
	Coma
Cardiovascular	Hypertension
	Aortic dissection
	Arrhythmia (sinus tachycardia, supraventricular tachycardia, ventricular tachycardia/fibrillation)
	Shock
	Sudden death
	Myocarditis
	Myocardial ischemia and infarction
	Other organ ischemia: renal infarction, intestinal infarction, limb ischemia
Respiratory	Pulmonary edema
	Respiratory arrest
	"Crack lung"
	Pneumothorax
	Pneumomediastinum
Metabolic	Hyperthermia
	Rhabdomyolysis
	Renal failure (myoglobinuria)
	Coagulopathy
	Lactic acidosis
Reproductive/Neonatal	Spontaneous abortion
	Placental abruption
	Placenta previa
	Intrauterine growth retardation
	"Crack baby syndrome"
	Cerebral infarction
Infectious	HIV/AIDS[a]
	Hepatitis B[a]
	Infectious endocarditis[a]
	Frontal sinusitis with brain abscess[b]
	Fungal cerebritis[a]
	Wound botulism
	Tetanus

[a] Associated with contaminated needles.
[b] Associated with intranasal insufflation.

Source: Modified from Benowitz.[24]

hemorrhage, and 20% ischemic stroke.[8,10,14] This distribution differs from the one found in the general population, where ischemia and not hemorrhage accounts for the majority of strokes. There was also a report of acute subdural hematoma associated with cocaine use.[15] The mechanism of stroke is thought be an acute elevation of blood pressure induced by increased sympathetic activity, which may cause rupture of cerebral aneurysm; or vasospasm or cerebral vasoconstriction.[16] Interestingly, anticardiolipin antibodies, which are associated with an increased risk of stroke, were found in 27% of asymptomatic cocaine users, and in 5 of 7 cocaine users with thromboembolism.[17] Chronic cocaine abuse has been associated with acute dystonic reactions, which in some cases have been precipitated by neuroleptics, and in others without neuroleptics. Acute dystonia was reported after cocaine use as well as during cocaine withdrawal.[18,19] Choreoathetoid movements lasting up to 6 days have also been described.[20]

Seizures: Seizures are seen in about 1.4 to 2.8% of cocaine abusers admitted to a hospital.[8,10,18,21,22] They are usually generalized, tonic-clonic in character, and may occur soon after taking cocaine, or after a delay of several hours. Seizures may be associated with recreational cocaine use, but are more common in intoxication or "body packer" syndrome.[8,21] Children can have seizures as a first manifestation of cocaine exposure.[10] The mechanism of cocaine-related seizures is not clear, and may be related to its local anesthetic properties.

Toxic encephalopathy and coma: Often patients present after several days of cocaine binge; at first they may experience severe anxiety, hyperactivity, and paranoia, which last for about 6 to 8 h, and then may become hypersomnolent and depressed. This latter phase can last 2 to 3 days.

Other complications associated with cocaine abuse are frontal sinusitis and brain abscess after chronic cocaine snorting.[23] Cocaine snorting is also associated with atrophy of nasal mucosa, necrosis, and perforation of the nasal septum.[18]

Cardiovascular System

Blood pressure: Intense sympathetic stimulation induced by cocaine results in hypertension and tachycardia. Hypertension is a combined result of increased cardiac output and increased systemic vascular resistance. Hypertension may cause stroke, aortic dissection, and acute pulmonary edema.

Myocardial ischemia: Myocardial infarction has been well documented in cocaine abuse. It is the end result of a combination of several factors including coronary vasospasm, increased myocardial oxygen demand due to increased myocardial work load, and thrombosis.[24–27] Most patients with cocaine-related ischemia present within 1 h of cocaine use, when the plasma concentrations of cocaine are the highest; however, some patients present hours after cocaine use. The late presentation may be caused by delayed coronary vasoconstriction induced by major cocaine metabolites.[26,28] However, only between 4 and 6% of patients presenting to emergency room with cocaine-associated chest pain have acute coronary syndrome.[26,29] Ambulatory electrocardiographic (ECG) monitoring of chronic cocaine users during the first week of cocaine withdrawal demonstrated recurrent episodes of ST segment elevation, probably due to vasospasm.[30] Myocarditis presenting as patchy myocardial necrosis has been observed after acute cocaine intoxication, and is believed to result from intense catecholamine stimulation.[24,30] Clinically, this results in ST segment elevations and/or T wave inversions, with elevated CPK-MB fraction. In chronic cocaine use, the result may be myocardial fibrosis and cardiomyopathy. Other organs may be affected by ischemia resulting from vasoconstriction, including renal infarction and ischemic colitis and mesenteric ischemia,[31–33] which can be life-threatening. These patients usually present with intense flank or diffuse abdominal pain.

Arrhythmia: Arrhythmia is common in cocaine intoxication; in acute intoxication it results from sympathetic stimulation; and later it may be the result of myocardial ischemia or myocarditis. The most common arrhythmia is sinus tachycardia; other arrhythmias include atrial tachycardia and fibrillation, ventricular tachycardia, including *torsade de pointes* and conduction disturbances due to local anesthetic effects of cocaine, with wide complex tachycardia.[30] Ventricular fibrillation can be a cause of sudden death, and asystole has also been reported. QT prolongation was observed in patients after cocaine exposure.[34]

Shock: Shock may develop in patients with cocaine intoxication as a result of reduced cardiac output due to myocardial ischemia, direct myocardial depression, myocarditis, or arrhythmia, and as a result of vasodilatation due to either local anesthetic effects of cocaine on blood vessels, or its effects on brain stem. Hypovolemia may also be present in agitated and/or hyperthermic patients.

Sudden Death: Most deaths occur within minutes to hours of acute cocaine intoxication, and most are the result of arrhythmia due to either massive catecholamine release or ischemia. Many convulse prior to death. Another syndrome associated with sudden death during cocaine intoxication is "excited delirium," in which the victim manifests aggressive and bizarre behavior accompanied by hyperthermia, and then suddenly dies.[35–38] Death due to medical reasons related to cocaine intoxication accounts for about 11% of all cocaine-related deaths; the majority of cocaine-related deaths are due to trauma and homicide.[14,39]

Pulmonary: Pulmonary edema is a common finding at autopsies of victims of cocaine intoxication. It can occur in acute intoxication either because of myocardial dysfunction or as a result of a massive increase in the afterload due to vasoconstriction. Noncardiogenic pulmonary edema has also been reported.[24] A syndrome called "crack lung" has been described, and consists of fever, pulmonary infiltrates, bronchospasm, and eosinophilia.[40-42] Alveolar macrophages from crack cocaine smokers were deficient in cytokine production and in their ability to kill bacteria and tumor cells.[43] Respiratory arrest can occur as a result of CNS depression. Pneumomediastinum and pneumothorax have been described in patients who snort or smoke cocaine, presumably due to increased airway pressure during a Valsalva maneuver.

Metabolic complications: Severe hyperthermia has been described in patients with acute cocaine intoxication; the mechanism probably is muscular hyperactivity due to agitation or seizures and increased metabolic rate. However, cocaine, even in small doses, was shown to impair sweating and cutaneous vasodilatation, as well as heat perception.[44] Consistent with these findings, it was found that on hot days (with ambient temperature above 31°C), the number of deaths from accidental cocaine overdose was 33% higher compared to that on days with lower temperatures.[45] Hyperthermia is also part of the "agitated delirium" syndrome, where it accompanies extremely violent and agitated behavior, in sometimes fatal cocaine intoxications.[36,37] Victims of the "agitated delirium" syndrome were more likely to be young, male, and black, compared to the victims of accidental cocaine overdose.[37,38] Hyperthermia, if untreated, can result in brain damage, rhabdomyolysis with renal failure, coagulation abnormalities, and death. Rhabdomyolysis in acute cocaine intoxication is most often the result of muscular hyperactivity and hyperthermia, but can also be due to muscular ischemia due to vasoconstriction. It presents as muscular pains, which can also occur in the chest wall, and must be distinguished from the pain of myocardial ischemia. Lactic acidosis may be a complication of prolonged muscular hyperactivity.

Reproductive/neonatal: Cocaine use during pregnancy can result in an increased incidence of spontaneous abortion, placenta previa, and abruption of the placenta. Placental ischemia results in intrauterine growth retardation.[46,47] Neonates born to cocaine-addicted mothers have various neurologic abnormalities, including irritability, tremulousness, poor feeding, hypotonia or hypertonia, and hyperreflexia. This syndrome may last for 8 to 10 weeks.[24,47] There is a dose–response relationship between adverse neonatal effects and maternal cocaine exposure.[47]

Withdrawal: Abstinence after prolonged use of cocaine can result in a "cocaine crash," manifesting as anxiety, depression, exhaustion, and craving for cocaine. Suicidal ideation is common. The symptoms can last for several weeks to several months after the cessation of use.[48]

8.1.1.2 Natural Stimulants

Ephedrine and khat belong to a group of natural stimulants. Ephedrine is found in a variety of plants, as well as in many Chinese medicines and is part of many nonprescription decongestants. Khat shrub grows in Ethiopia, and khat leaves are chewed in East African countries, particularly in Yemen and Somalia.[18,49] The active ingredient in khat leaves is (–)cathinone. Both ephedrine and cathinone resemble amphetamine in structure.

Ephedrine

Ephedrine acts directly on alpha and beta-adrenergic receptors, and also stimulates the release of norepinephrine. It exhibits fewer CNS effects compared to amphetamine. Pseudoephedrine is a dextro isomer of ephedrine, and has similar alpha, but less beta-adrenergic activity. Both drugs are marketed as nonprescription medications for nasal decongestion, and are ingredients in many cold medications and bronchodilators. Ephedrine-containing dietary supplements (also known as ma-huang) are widely used for weight loss and energy enhancement. The main manifestations of ephedrine intoxication are cardiovascular, with elevation of blood pressure and heart rate.[50] Hypertension due to ephedrine intoxication, even if moderate, can result in neurologic complications including headache, confusion, seizures, and stroke, both ischemic and hemorrhagic.[51] There have also been reports of intracerebral vasculitis and hemorrhage associated with ephedrine abuse.[52] Severe headache, focal neurologic deficit, or changes in mental status in ephedrine intoxication should raise the possibility of stroke. Fatalities may result from myocardial infarction, arrhythmia, seizures, or stroke.[53]

Use of dietary supplements containing ephedrine (ma-huang), even in doses recommended by the manufacturer, has been associated with severe cardiovascular events, including myocardial infarction, sudden death, and stroke.[54,55] Many of the adverse effects occurred in young people without risk factors for cardiovascular disease.

Another, little recognized complication of chronic use of ephedra-containing products is kidney stones, which have been found to contain ephedrine and pseudoephedrine.[56]

Khat

Khat has CNS effects quite similar to amphetamine; but due to the bulkiness of the plant the actual amounts of the active ingredient, cathinone, which is actually ingested, are usually not large. Social use of khat causes increase in energy level and alertness, but also mood lability, anxiety, and insomnia.[57] Khat abuse may result in mania-like symptoms, paranoia, and acute schizophrenia-like psychosis. In most cases of khat-induced psychosis, heavy khat consumption preceded the episodes.[49,57,58] Most of the cases are resolved within weeks with cessation of khat use. There is one case report of leukoencephalopathy associated with heavy khat use.[59] No specific physical withdrawal syndrome is recognized, but there is a psychological withdrawal characterized by depression, hypersomnia, and loss of energy.[49,57]

Khat intoxication may result in cardiovascular toxicity with hypertension and tachycardia, but severe hypertension has not been observed.[57,60] Khat chewing may be a precipitating factor for myocardial infarction, probably due to its catecholamine-releasing properties. As compared to non-chewers, khat chewers presenting with acute myocardial infarction were more likely to be young and without cardiovascular risk factors, and were more likely to present during or immediately after khat-chewing sessions.[61]

There is an association between khat use and gastric ulcers, and also between its use and constipation, although causation is not clear.[57]

Babies born to khat-chewing mothers are likely to suffer from intrauterine growth retardation. Long-term chewing of khat (for more than 25 years) was found to be strongly associated with oral cancer.[49]

8.1.1.3 Synthetic Stimulants

Amphetamine, along with its analogues methamphetamine and methylphenidate, are sympathomimetics; they act by releasing biogenic amines from storage sites both in the CNS and the peripheral nervous system as well as by directly stimulating alpha- and beta-adrenergic receptors. Thus, they produce CNS stimulation and arousal, and serious mental changes and cardiovascular effects during intoxication.

Amphetamine

Amphetamine is one of the most potent CNS stimulators. It exists as a racemic solution, but dextroamphetamine (D-isomer) is three to four times more potent than levoamphetamine with regard to CNS stimulation. It is mainly administered orally or intravenously. Clinically amphetamine effects are very similar to those of cocaine, but amphetamine has a longer half-life compared to cocaine (10 to 15 h), and the duration of amphetamine-induced euphoria is four to eight times longer than for cocaine.

CNS effects: During acute intoxication with amphetamines, patients commonly present with euphoria, restlessness, agitation, and anxiety.[18,62] Suicidal ideation, hallucinations, and confusion are seen in 5 to 12% of the patients with acute intoxication. In one sample of drug users, 55% of amphetamine users reported having at least one adverse effect (anxiety, depression, paranoia, sleep and appetite disturbances).[3] Seizures may occur in about 3% of the patients presenting in the hospital with amphetamine intoxication.[22,62] Stroke has been reported in patients with amphetamine intoxication; it is usually hemorrhagic and results from hypertension.[13,63,64] There have also been reports of cerebral vasculitis and hemorrhage with chronic abuse of amphetamine.[65-67] Chronic amphetamine abuse may precipitate psychiatric disturbances, such as paranoia and psychosis that can persist for weeks.[68,69]

Movement disorders: Chronic high-dose amphetamine use is associated with stereotypic behavior, dyskinesias, and also with chorea, especially in patients with preexisting basal ganglia disorders. Amphetamines exacerbate tics in patients who already have them, and may induce tics, although the causation is unclear.[18]

Cardiovascular effects: The major effects seen during acute intoxication are hypertension and tachycardia. Arrhythmia can occur, including ventricular fibrillation. Myocardial ischemia and infarction have been reported; the underlying mechanisms are increased myocardial oxygen demand and/or coronary vasospasm.[25,62,70,71] Chronic abuse has been reported to result in cardiomyopathy.[72] Systemic necrotizing vasculitis, resembling periarteritis nodosa, has been associated with chronic amphetamine abuse.[73]

Metabolic and other effects: Acute amphetamine intoxication can manifest with sweating, tremor, muscle fasciculations, and rigidity. Hyperthermia can develop and may be life-threatening if not treated promptly.[74] The mechanisms underlying hyperthermia are muscle hyperactivity and seizures. The same mechanisms may also cause rhabdomyolysis with attendant renal failure. Chronic amphetamine abuse can result in weight loss of up to 20 to 30 lb and malnutrition.[18]

Withdrawal: Amphetamine withdrawal peaks in 2 to 4 days of abstinence, and can last several weeks. The main symptom is depression, occasionally with suicidal ideation.[48]

Methamphetamine

Methamphetamine is an amphetamine analogue; it has an increased CNS penetration and a longer half-life; its effects may persist for 6 to 24 h longer than amphetamine. It can be ingested orally, smoked, or snorted.[75] Methamphetamine produces more CNS stimulation with fewer peripheral effects compared to amphetamine,[76] but large doses may result in hypertension. Stroke, both ischemic and hemorrhagic, has been reported with methamphetamine abuse, and in some cases the stroke was delayed by 10 to 12 h after last use.[77,78] The mechanisms may be hypertension, thrombosis, vasospasm, and vasculitis. Rhabdomyolysis has also been described in association with methamphetamine abuse.[79]

Methylphenidate

Methylphenidate is structurally related to amphetamine; in therapeutic doses it is a mild CNS stimulant, with more mental than motor effects, and it has minimal peripheral effects in therapeutic doses. It is used clinically for the treatment of attention-deficit disorder and narcolepsy. However, when abused and used in high doses it may cause generalized CNS stimulation with symptoms similar to amphetamine, including seizures. A case of cerebral vasculitis associated with therapeutic doses of methylphenidate was reported.[80]

Phenylpropanolamine

Phenylpropanolamine (PPA) is primarily an alpha-adrenergic agonist, both direct and indirect through release of norepinephrine. It is structurally related to amphetamine. Phenylpropanolamine is an ingredient in many cold and anorectic agents. Phenylpropanolamine combined with caffeine has been sold as a look-alike "amphetamine." PPA has a low therapeutic index, and doses two to three times in excess of recommended may result in toxicity. Susceptible individuals, particularly those suffering from hypertension or autonomic insufficiency with attendant denervation hypersensitivity of adrenergic receptors, may experience adverse effects even with therapeutic doses. The main manifestations of phenylpropanolamine toxicity are cardiovascular; however, CNS stimulant effects usually appear at higher doses.

Cardiovascular effects: The main effect of phenylpropanolamine is hypertension due to its alpha-adrenergic properties. Because it has only slight beta-adrenergic activity, there is no tachycardia; rather, a reflex bradycardia is usually present.[81] Patients with phenylpropanolamine-induced hypertension are at risk for stroke, both ischemic and hemorrhagic.[81–83] A strong association was found between the risk of hemorrhagic stroke in women aged 18 to 49 years and use of phenylpropanolamine-containing appetite suppressants and cold medications. No increase in risk was found in men.[84] These findings prompted the FDA to remove phenylpropanolamine from over-the-counter medications.[85,86] Headache is a common feature, and may reflect an acutely elevated blood pressure, or may be the first manifestation of stroke. Patients with a severe headache, altered mental status, or neurologic deficit should be evaluated for stroke even if their blood pressure is not elevated. There are also case reports of chest pain, myocardial infarction, and ECG repolarization abnormalities.[81] The duration of intoxication is about 6 h.

CNS effects: When taken in large doses and/or chronically abused, phenylpropanolamine causes symptoms similar to amphetamine, including anxiety, agitation and psychosis.[81,87] There are individuals at risk for psychiatric side effects from phenylpropanolamine even at therapeutic doses: these are individuals with past psychiatric history, children younger than 6 years, and post-partum women.[88,89] Seizures have also been reported, though often when phenylpropanolamine was combined with other drugs, such as caffeine. Case reports of cerebral vasculitis and hemorrhage with phenylpropanolamine use have been described.[90]

8.1.2 Hallucinogens

The primary effects of hallucinogenic drugs are altered perception and mood. The specific effects differ in different drug classes. They are also accompanied by autonomic changes (Table 8.1.6). Most hallucinogens do not induce physical dependence. The specific mechanisms of action are not known for many of the drugs, but there are indications that they act as adrenergic and serotoninergic agonists. The changes in mood and perception are probably related to their serotoninergic actions.[91,92] After prolonged or high-dose use of the drugs, there is evidence of depletion of serotonin and dopamine in the neurons in the brain. The psychiatric effects may be quite severe, and require medication. Sometimes the psychosis may be prolonged long beyond the presence of the drug in the body, and there may be chronic psychiatric impairment and memory disturbances, possibly related to damage to serotoninergic neurons in the brain.

8.1.2.1 Phenylethylamine Derivatives

Mescaline

Mescaline is a phenylethylamine derivative. Its use probably dates from as long as 5700 years ago.[93] It is found in peyote cactus, and can be ingested orally or intravenously. It is structurally related to epinephrine. The precise mechanism of action is unknown, but it is thought to alter the activity of serotonin, norepinephrine, and dopamine receptors.[76] The signs of intoxication appear within 30 min of ingestion, peak at 4 h, and last 8 to 14 h. The psychic phase lasts about 6 h.[94] There are both physiological and psychological manifestations of mescaline.

Physiological effects: These are mainly manifestations of autonomic adrenergic activation: dilated pupils, increased sweating, elevated systolic blood pressure and temperature. Large doses of mescaline may induce hypotension, bradycardia, and respiratory depression.[95] Some users may

Table 8.1.6 Manifestations of Hallucinogen Intoxication and Abuse

Neuropsychiatric:	
Acute	Euphoria
	Altered time perception
	Heightened visual and color perception
	Anxiety
	Disorientation
	Delirium
	Panic attacks
	Suicidal ideation
	Hallucinations
Chronic	Depression
	Drowsiness
	Anxiety
	Panic disorder
	Psychosis
	Impaired memory
	Flashbacks (LSD)
Medical	Hypertension
	Tachycardia
	Nausea
	Vomiting
	Muscle pains
	Trismus (MDMA)
	Flushing
	Arrhythmia (MDMA)
	Cardiovascular collapse
	Respiratory arrest
	Stroke (MDMA)
	Hyperthermia
	Seizures
	Hepatotoxicity (MDMA)
	SIADH (MDMA)

experience nausea, vomiting, or dizziness, which usually resolve within an hour.[96] A fatal case of Mallory–Weiss lacerations has been described after mescaline ingestion.[97] Peyote ceremonial tea, which had been stored for a prolonged time, was contaminated with botulism.[98]

Psychological effects: These begin several hours after the ingestion. Typically there is a feeling of euphoria, a sense of physical power, and distortion of sensation. There is an increased color perception.[95,99] Sometimes there are visual hallucinations, especially of vivid colors. Users may also experience feelings of depersonalization, disorientation, anxiety, emotional lability, and/or emotional outbursts.[96] There is no physical dependence for mescaline.[95,99]

TMA-2 (2,4,5-Trimethoxyamphetamine)

TMA is a synthetic analogue of mescaline and amphetamine. It is more potent than mescaline, but resembles mescaline in the effects.[100]

DOM/STP (4-Methyl-2,5-Dimethoxyamphetamine)

This is another amphetamine analogue. It has a narrow therapeutic index. Low doses of 2 to 3 mg cause perceptual distortion and mild sympathetic stimulation, but doses two to three times that produce hallucinations and more severe sympathetic stimulation.[76,101]

PMA (para-Methoxyamphetamine)

This is a very potent hallucinogen and CNS stimulant. Overdose may present with severe sympathetic stimulation including seizures, hyperthermia, coagulopathy, and rhabdomyolysis (like in amphetamine intoxication) and can result in fatalities.[102–104] PMA is a more potent CNS stimulant compared to other amphetamines, and there were reports of fatalities where PMA was substituted for MDMA.[104]

DOB (4-Bromo-2,5-Dimethoxyamphetamine)

DOB, otherwise called bromo-DOM, is one of the most potent phenylethylamine derivatives; it has about 100 times the potency of mescaline. It is long-acting, with effects starting within an hour, reaching their full strength after 3 to 4 h, and lasting up to 10 h.[105] The manifestations of intoxication are mood enhancement with visual distortion. There are case reports of severely intoxicated patients with hallucinations, agitation, and sympathetic stimulation.[106] DOB, when ingested in large doses, can have an ergot-like effect, and cause severe generalized peripheral vasospasm with tissue ischemia.[76]

MDA (3,4-Methylenedioxyamphetamine)

MDA is an amphetamine derivative included in the category of "designer drugs." While in small doses it produces mild intoxication with a feeling of euphoria, large doses can cause hallucinations, agitation, and delirium.[76] It also can produce intense sympathetic stimulation, with hypertension, tachycardia, seizures, and hyperthermia. Death has been reported after MDA use, usually as a result of seizures or hyperthermia.[107]

MDMA (3,4-Methylenedioxymethamphetamine)

MDMA is one of the most popular "designer drugs" today, and is used recreationally by a large number of young people.[108] It is also known as "Ecstasy," "Adam," and "M&M." It was "rediscovered" in the 1970s as an adjunct to psychotherapy, but its use for this purpose has since diminished.

Psychological effects: After ingestion of 75 to 150 mg, users experience a sense of euphoria, heightened awareness, improved sense of communication, but also some impairment in the performance of psychomotor tasks.[95,109] Women tend to have more intense psychoactive effects of MDMA compared to men.[110] Acute neuropsychiatric complications have been reported, and include anxiety, insomnia, depression, paranoia, confusion, panic attacks, and psychosis.[109,111–113] Adverse effects during the 24 h following use include lack of energy, restlessness, insomnia, lack of appetite, and difficulty concentrating.[114] Chronic effects of MDMA abuse include depression, drowsiness, anxiety, panic disorder, aggressive outbursts, psychosis, and memory disturbance.[115–117] The memory disturbance and impaired cognitive performance were found in chronic users who were abstinent, as well as in former users as long as a year after stopping.[118–123] Although the exact mechanism of action is not known, there is some evidence from animal studies, as well as from human subjects, that MDMA can cause damage to serotoninergic neurons in the brain.[109,124,125] Chronic users of MDMA were found to have lower density of 5-HT transporters in cortex compared to nonusers; there was a dose–response with the extent of use.[120,126,127] These effects were more pronounced in women compared to men.[127]

Medical effects: Stimulatory effects of MDMA are apparent even in mild intoxication, and include increased blood pressure and heart rate, decreased appetite, and dry mouth. The recreational doses of MDMA significantly increased heart rate and blood pressure.[128,129] Also common are nausea, vomiting, trismus (jaw clenching), teeth grinding, hyperreflexia, muscle aches, hot and cold flushes, and nystagmus. Additional side effects reported include paresthesias, blurred vision, and motor ticks. There are several reports of MDMA-induced arrhythmias, asystole, and cardiovascular collapse. Other potentially fatal complications include seizures, hyperthermia, and rhabdomyolysis with acute renal failure.[118,130] There are several case reports of hepatotoxicity, including hepatic failure requiring transplantation, following MDMA ingestion,[130–134] and several cases of inappropriate antidiuretic hormone secretion (SIADH) with severe hyponatremia and seizures.[135–139] CNS complications including stroke (ischemic and hemorrhagic), subarachnoid hemorrhage, and cerebral venous sinus thrombosis have been reported following MDMA ingestion. One syndrome of MDMA intoxication has been reported specifically in the setting of crowding and vigorous dancing, such as in "raves" or clubs. It includes several manifestations: hyperthermia, dehydration, seizures, rhabdomyolysis, disseminated intravascular coagulation, and acute renal failure.[118,140] This is thought to be the consequence of the combination of sympathomimetic effects including cutaneous vasoconstriction and extreme physical exertion in hot and poorly ventilated conditions, although some features are those of serotonin syndrome.[141] There are two case reports of MDMA intoxication, one of them fatal, after regular recreational doses in HIV patients on ritonavir therapy.[142,143] The mechanism is probably inhibition of CYP2D6, which metabolizes amphetamines, by ritonavir.

Reproductive/neonatal effects: A prospective study following 136 women exposed to MDMA during pregnancy found a significantly increased risk (15.4%) of congenital defects, particularly cardiovascular and musculosceletal anomalies.[144]

MDEA (3,4-Methylenedioxyethamphetamine)

This is an analogue of MDMA, with effects similar to those of MDMA.

8.1.2.2 Lysergic Acid Diethylamide

Lysergic acid diethylamide (LSD) is a synthetic ergoline, and it is the third most-frequently used drug among adolescents, after alcohol and marijuana.[145,146] The main site of action of LSD is serotoninergic receptor 5-HT$_2$.[147] The effects of LSD, psychological and physical, are dose-related. With oral doses of 20 to 50 µg the onset of effects is after 5 to 10 min, with peak effects occurring 30 to 90 min post-ingestion. Duration of the effects may be 8 to 12 h, and recovery lasts between 10 and 12 h, when normal cognition alternates with altered mood and perception. Cognitive effects include distortion of time and altered visual perception with very vivid color perception. Euphoria and anxiety may be experienced. There are also signs of sympathetic stimulation, with dilated pupils, tachycardia, elevated blood pressure and temperature, and facial flushing. Tremors and hyperreflexia are also common.[95,148] A "bad trip" may be experienced during LSD intoxication: terrifying hallucinations, which precipitate panic attack, disorientation, delirium, or depression with suicidal ideation. A "bad trip" may occur with first-time use, as well as after recurrent use. Five major categories of psychiatric adverse effects have been described: anxiety and panic attacks, self-destructive behavior, such as attempting to jump out of the window, hallucinations, acute psychosis, and major depressive reactions.[148] Patients who have taken very high doses of LSD have presented with manifestations of intense sympathetic stimulation including hyperthermia, coagulopathy, circulatory collapse, and respiratory arrest.[149] Another danger of LSD abuse is accidents and trauma while trying to drive during intoxication, or during the recovery phase.

There may be chronic toxic effects associated with LSD abuse. Effects that have been described include:

1. Prolonged psychosis, especially among users with preexisting psychiatric morbidity
2. Prolonged or intermittent major depression
3. Disruption of personality
4. Post-hallucinogen perceptual disorder (PHPD)

The last syndrome is characterized by flashbacks, when imagery experienced during LSD intoxication returns without taking the drug. Flashbacks may occur months, and even years, after LSD use. It has been reported that 50% of users experienced flashbacks during the 5 years after their last use of LSD.[148–150] In most cases flashbacks occur after LSD has been used more than ten times.[149] Rarely, the flashbacks may be frightening hallucinations; in extreme cases these have been associated with homicide or suicide. Flashbacks may be triggered by stress, illness, and marijuana and alcohol use.[95,148]

8.1.2.3 Disassociative Anesthetics

Phencyclidine

Phencyclidine (PCP) was developed as an anesthetic, but its psychiatric side effects precluded its use in humans. In the1960s PCP became a popular street drug. It is most commonly smoked, but can also be ingested orally, snorted, or injected intravenously. PCP is also commonly used as an additive to other drugs, such as marijuana, mescaline, and LSD. The mechanisms of action of PCP include anesthesia without depression of ventilation, and its main site of action is probably blockade of cationic channel of NMDA receptor, as well as sigma opioid receptors.[151,152] It also inhibits the reuptake of dopamine and norepinephrine, and has direct alpha-adrenergic effects. The effects of PCP are dose-dependent (Table 8.1.7). Smoking causes a rapid onset of effects; the half-life of PCP may range from 11 to 51 h.[153]

Psychiatric effects: At low doses of 1 to 5 mg, PCP produces euphoria, relaxation, and a feeling of numbness. There may also be a feeling of altered body image and sensory distortion. At higher doses there may be agitation, bizarre behavior, and psychosis resembling paranoid schizophrenia. The patients may alternate between agitation and catatonic-like state. There is also analgesia, which may lead to self-injury.[153,154]

Physical effects: In mild intoxication the most prominent sign is nystagmus, both vertical and horizontal, and numbness in extremities. In severe intoxication there are signs of adrenergic stimulation, with hypertension, tachycardia, flushing, and hyperthermia sometimes complicated by rhabdomyolysis and acute renal failure, and also of cholinomimetic stimulation with sweating,

Table 8.1.7 Manifestations of Phencyclidine Intoxication

Mild (≤5 mg)	Confusional state
	Uncommunicative
	Agitated, combative
	Bizarre behavior
	Nystagmus
	Ataxia
	Myoclonus
	Muscle rigidity or catalepsy
	Hypertension
Severe (≤20 mg)	Coma
	Eyes may be open
	Myosis
	Nystagmus
	Muscle rigidity
	Extensor posturing, opisthotonus
	Increased deep tendon reflexes
	Hypertension
	Hyperthermia
	Seizures
Massive (500 mg)	Prolonged coma
	Hypoventilation
	Respiratory arrest
	Hypertension
	Prolonged and fluctuating confusional state upon recovery from coma

Source: Modified from Benowitz.[186]

hypersalivation, and miosis, and dystonic reactions, ataxia, and myoclonus may also occur. With high doses PCP causes seizures, coma with extensor posturing, respiratory arrest, and circulatory collapse.[154,155] The eyes may remain open during coma. Coma may be prolonged, even up to several weeks. Death may result directly from intoxication (seizures, hyperthermia) or from violent behavior. Chronic effects of PCP abuse include memory impairment, personality changes, and depression, which may last up to a year after stopping. There is probably no physical dependence on PCP, but after stopping there is craving.

8.1.3 Marijuana

Marijuana is obtained from the *Cannabis sativa* plant; it is a mixture of crushed leaves, seeds, and twigs from the plant. There are many active ingredients in the plant, but the ingredient accounting for the majority of the effects is delta-9-tetrahydrocannabinol (THC). There is a great variability in the amount of THC in different plants and in different batches of marijuana. Hashish is a resinous sap of the *Cannabis* plant, and typically contains 20 to 30 times the amount of THC compared to the equal weight of marijuana. THC exerts its effects through binding to G protein type CB_1 cannabinoid receptors in the brain (CB_2 cannabinoid receptors have been identified in the spleen macrophages and other immune cells). Endogenous cannabinoids, including anandamide and 2-arachidonylglycerol, have been identified.[156–158] The endogenous cannabinoids produce effects similar to those of THC when administered to animals. Their physiological functions are not yet fully understood, and probably involve neuromodulation of pain and stress and immunomodulation.

Today marijuana is the most commonly used illicit drug in the U.S.[159–161] Marijuana is usually smoked; one "joint" typically contains 10 to 30 mg of THC; the onset of action is within 10 to 20 min, and the effects last up to 2 to 3 h.[153] However, during the past 20 years improved cultivation techniques resulted in a greatly increased potency of cannabis products. Today a joint may contain up to 150 mg of THC.[158,162] Acute effects of marijuana include relaxation and sometimes euphoria, and also perceptual changes, such as enhanced vividness of colors, music, and emotions.[158,162] There may be a feeling of depersonalization. These effects may last for 2 h or more, depending on the dose. There is impairment of concentration, psychomotor performance, and problem solving. Driving skills may be affected. High doses of THC may cause hallucinations, anxiety, panic, and psychosis.[153,163,164] These effects can last for several days. Physical effects include impairment of balance, conjunctival infection, increased heart rate, orthostatic hypotension, peripheral vasoconstriction with cold extremities, dry mouth, and increased appetite.[158,162] There are reports of intravenously injected marijuana extract, which results in rapid onset of nausea, vomiting, fever, and diarrhea, and is followed by hypotension, acute renal failure, thrombocytopenia, and rhabdomyolysis.[165]

Chronic users of marijuana have been reported to experience an amotivation syndrome, in which apathy, lack of energy, and loss of motivation persist for days or longer.[163] Chronic and heavy users of marijuana exhibit impaired performance on tests of memory and attention even after 19-h abstinence.[166–169] The impaired performance was significantly correlated with the duration of cannabis use.[166] However, it is not clear whether there is any permanent neurological damage, or whether the impairment is due to prolonged release of cannabis from tissues.[168,169] Chronic use of marijuana may result in inhibition of secretion of reproductive hormones, and cause impotence in men and menstrual irregularities in women.[170] No clear association was found between maternal cannabis use during pregnancy and adverse perinatal outcomes or birth defects, when cigarette smoking and other drug use were taken into account.[162,171] However, there is a suggestion that *in utero* exposure to marijuana led to deficits in sustained attention and memory between ages 4 and 9.[172]

Chronic smokers of marijuana are at risk for chronic obstructive lung disease, and marijuana tar is carcinogenic and appears to be associated with development of respiratory tract carcinoma and head and neck cancer in young adults.[41,43,173–177] There are also reports of spontaneous pneumothorax in daily marijuana smokers, although the patients smoked tobacco as well. The mechanism is sustained Valsalva maneuver during forced inhalation.[178]

Table 8.1.8 Opiate Receptor Subtypes

Receptor Subtype	Prototype Drug	Major Action
μ_1	All opiates and most opioid peptides	Supraspinal analgesia Prolactin release Catalepsy
μ_2	Morphine	Respiratory depression Gastrointestinal transit Growth hormone release Cardiovascular effects
δ	Enkephalins	Spinal analgesia Growth hormone release
κ	Dynorphin Ketocyclazocine	Spinal analgesia Sedation Inhibition of vasopressin release
ϵ	β-Endorphin	?
σ	N-allylnormetazocine	Psychotomimetic effects

Source: Modified from Olson et al.[257]

Chronic cannabis use has been shown to lead to the development of tolerance and dependence, and withdrawal syndrome has been demonstrated. About 8 to 10% of cannabis users will develop dependence.[158,179–182] Cannabis withdrawal syndrome is characterized by restlessness, anxiety, insomnia, anorexia, muscle tremors, and craving for marijuana.[158,183,184]

8.1.4 Opioids

Opioids have been used and abused since ancient times. They are indispensable in clinical use for pain management, and are also used as cough suppressants and antidiarrheal agents. They are abused for their mood-altering effects, and tolerance and physical and psychological dependence account for continued abuse. Patients who use narcotic analgesics for pain relief may develop physical dependence, but rarely develop psychological dependence on the drug. Opioids are a diverse group of drugs, among them derivatives of the naturally occurring opium (morphine, heroin, codeine), synthetic (methadone, fentanyl), and endogenous compounds (enkephalins, endorphins, and dynorphins). Morphine-like analgesic drugs are also known as narcotics. There are several subtypes of opiate receptors (mu, delta, and kappa), which differ in their affinity to different agonists and antagonists, and in their effects (Table 8.1.8). Opiate receptors are present in different concentrations in different regions of the nervous system. Some of the receptors involved in analgesia are located in the periaqueductal gray matter; the receptors believed to be responsible for reinforcing effects are in the ventral tegmental area and the nucleus acumbens. There are opiate receptors in locus ceruleus, which plays an important role in control of autonomic activity; their activation results in inhibition of locus ceruleus firing. After opiate withdrawal there is an increase in locus ceruleus neuronal firing, resulting in autonomic hyperactivity characteristic of opiate withdrawal. Tolerance develops to many of the opiate effects, but differentially to different effects.[185,186]

In general, opioids cause analgesia and sedation, respiratory depression, and slowed gastrointestinal transit. Severe intoxication results in coma and respiratory depression, which may progress to apnea and death (Table 8.1.9).[187] Adverse side effects from opiates are seen in drug abusers who take an overdose (intentional or unintentional), but also in medical patients who are treated with opiates. Morphine, heroin, methadone, propoxyphene, and fentanyl-derivatives account for about 98% of all opiate deaths and hospital admissions.[188] In the 1990s there was a significant increase in the medical use of opioid analgesics in the U.S. (particularly morphine, fentanyl, hydromorphone, and oxycodone); however, no increase was seen in the emergency department admissions due to abuse of these drugs.[189]

Table 8.1.9 Medical Complications of Opiate Intoxication and Withdrawal

Intoxication	
CNS	Stupor or coma
	Myosis
	Seizures (propoxyphene, meperidine)
Respiratory	Hypoventilation
	Cough suppression
	Respiratory arrest
	Pulmonary edema
Cardiovascular	Hypotension
	Bradycardia
	Conduction abnormalities (propoxyphene)
Metabolic	Hypothermia
	Cool, moist skin
Withdrawal	Anxiety
	Insomnia
	Chills
	Myalgias, arthralgias
	Nausea, vomiting
	Anorexia
	Diarrhea
	Yawning
	Midriasis
	Tachycardia
	Diaphoresis, lacrimation

Even though different opioid drugs have similar effects, the cross-tolerance is not complete. This is explained by the discovery of different subtypes of mu and delta receptors with differential binding of opioid agonists.[190–192]

8.1.4.1 Opiate Effects

Analgesic Effects

Opioid receptors mu_1 play a major role in analgesia; analgesic effects are mediated through central, spinal, and peripheral mechanisms. Analgesia is dose-dependent, and in high doses opioids produce anesthesia. Tolerance to analgesic effects develops less rapidly compared to tolerance to mood or respiratory effects.[185]

Mental Effects

Mood: Opiate drugs have reinforcing properties, possibly mediated through dopaminergic neuron activation in the ventral tegmental area and nucleus acumbens. Usually, the effect on the mood is relaxation and euphoria; although patients who take opiates for pain relief more often report dysphoria after taking the drug. Tolerance to euphoria-inducing effects develops rapidly.

Sedation: Sedation is dose-dependent, and is often accompanied by stereotypic dreaming.[185] Tolerance develops rapidly. Sedation is a first sign of opiate intoxication; respiratory depression does not occur unless the patient is sedated.

Gastrointestinal Effects

Nausea and vomiting: Nausea and vomiting are prominent side effects of opiates, resulting from their actions on the chemoreceptor trigger zone in the medulla. However, tolerance usually develops to these effects. Different opiates have different likelihood for causing nausea.

Constipation: Opioid drugs decrease gastrointestinal motility and peristalsis, acting in the spinal cord and gastrointestinal tract, thus causing constipation. Tolerance does not develop to this effect, and so constipation persists even in chronic users.[193] The constipating effect of opiates is used for symptomatic treatment of diarrhea.

Respiratory Effects

Respiratory depression: Respiratory depression is the most serious adverse effect of opiates; it is dose-dependent, and respiratory arrest is almost always the cause of death from opiate overdose. Respiratory arrest occurs within minutes of the intravenous overdose. After overdose from oral, intramuscular, or subcutaneous route, sedation almost always precedes respiratory arrest. Tolerance to respiratory depression develops, but is lost rapidly after abstinence. All opioid agonists produce the same degree of respiratory depression given the same degree of analgesia. The mechanism is through mu_2 receptor stimulation in respiratory centers in the brain stem.[194] Opioids are medically used for the relief of dyspnea in terminally ill patients with cancer; this effect may be also mediated by opioid receptors in the bronchioles and alveolar walls.[187]

Pulmonary edema: Pulmonary edema occurs with several opioid drugs, and is noncardiogenic. The precise mechanisms are unknown but probably involve hypoperfusion with tissue injury and cytokine-induced pulmonary capillary endothelial injury. Pulmonary edema is particularly common with heroin intoxication, and may be precipitated by the administration of naloxone (which reverses venodilation and redistributes blood to the central circulation).

Cough suppression: Opiates cause cough suppression by acting in the medulla; the doses needed are usually lower than for analgesia.

Other Effects

Pupillary constriction: Miosis is invariably present in opiate intoxication, unless anoxic brain damage is present.

Pruritus: Pruritis is very common in patients receiving opiates, as well as in addicts. It is caused by histamine release mediated by the mu receptors.[195]

Urinary retention: This effect is mediated through spinal cord opiate receptors.[196]

Individual narcotic agents have specific effects, which are discussed below.

8.1.4.2 Specific Narcotic Agents

Morphine: Morphine has an elimination half-life of 1.7 h, but its 6-glucuronide metabolite is also pharmacologically active. Morphine can be administered by intravenous, subcutaneous, oral, and rectal routes. While well absorbed, morphine undergoes significant first-pass metabolism when given orally, and thus requires high doses to achieve the desired effects. Although the oral route is the accepted route of administration for pain control in patients with chronic pain, it is not often utilized by drug addicts. Neuroexcitatory side effects, not mediated by opioids receptors, including delirium, myoclonus, seizures, hyperalgesia, and allodynia, have occurred with morphine, and are probably related to the accumulation of metabolites such as morphine-3-glucuronide.[197,198]

Heroin: Heroin (diacetyl-morphine) is a synthetic derivative of morphine. In the body, it is rapidly converted to 6-acetylmorphine, and then to morphine. The conversion to morphine occurs within minutes. In addition to the effects common to all opiates, there have been reports of acute rhabdomyolysis with myoglobinuria during heroin intoxication.[199,200] In some case the patients have been comatose, lying with pressure on their muscles, but in other cases rhabdomyolysis occurred with alert patients, accompanied by muscle pains, weakness, and swelling.[201,202] Chronic abuse of heroin has been associated with progressive nephrotic syndrome resulting in renal failure.[203] The histopathology is focal segmental glomerulosclerosis. There is a broad spectrum of neuropathological changes in the brains of heroin abusers. Some are related to prolonged anoxia or vasculitis. Spongiform leukoencephalopathy has been described following inhalation of pre-heated heroin. Two cases of delayed-onset spongiform leukoencephalopathy following intravenous heroin overdose were also reported.[201,202,204,205] There was also a report of extrapyramidal toxicity after recovery from intranasal heroin overdose.[206]

Codeine: Codeine, one of the substances found in opium, is about 20% as potent as morphine as an analgesic. It is mostly used as a cough suppressant, and as an ingredient in pain medications. To be effective as an analgesic, codeine must be converted to morphine; this reaction is performed by the isozyme CYP2D6 of the P450 enzymes. The majority of the dose is glucuronidated, and the glucuronide is inactive as an analgesic. The enzyme converting codeine to morphine is subject to genetic polymorphism. About 10% of Caucasians are poor metabolizers, meaning that they do not convert codeine to morphine, and thus do not derive therapeutic benefit from codeine. Inhibition of CYP2D6 resulted in diminished effects of codeine, and caused codeine-dependent patients to use less codeine.[207,208]

Methadone: Methadone is a synthetic long-acting opiate agonist. It is well absorbed orally, and does not undergo significant first-pass metabolism. It has a half-life of approximately 35 h. Methadone is mainly used as a maintenance therapy for heroin addicts, but occasionally is also used to treat chronic pain. There have been reports of deaths associated with methadone treatment, mostly as a result of too rapid dose increases in subjects who may have lost their tolerance.[209]

Propoxyphene: Propoxyphene is a derivative of methadone, but unlike methadone, it is only a mild analgesic. It has a half-life of about 15 h, but is metabolized to norpropoxyphene, a potentially toxic metabolite with a longer half-life (about 30 h). Propoxyphene has been associated with a high incidence of toxicity, because in addition to being a respiratory depressant, it also acts as a local anesthetic, and has potent membrane-stabilizing effects. Propoxyphene is an ingredient in many compound analgesics, but it is also abused.[210] The main cause of death in propoxyphene intoxication is cardiac abnormalities[211] resulting from its membrane-stabilizing effects. Conduction abnormalities with wide QRS that respond to sodium bicarbonate, and cardiovascular collapse have been described.[212] Seizures have also been associated with propoxyphene intoxication.[211] Unlike respiratory depression, cardiac abnormalities and seizures do not respond to naloxone, since these effects are not mediated through opiate receptors.

Fentanyl: Fentanyl and related drugs are synthetic opioid agonists structurally related to meperidine. Fentanyl is 50 to 100 times more potent than morphine, and has a half-life of about 4 h. Fentanyl is administered intravenously and transdermally, and is used for surgical anesthesia, especially for cardiac surgery; transdermal fentanyl is used for post-operative analgesia and for chronic pain management.[213] Fentanyl derivatives that are "street-synthesized" belong to a group of "designer drugs," and include alpha-methyl-fentanyl ("China White") and 3-methyl-fentanyl (3MF). Due to the very high potency of fentanyl and related drugs, respiratory depression may occur very rapidly. There are some reports of seizures associated with fentanyl anesthesia,[214] and a syndrome of delayed respiratory depression with truncal muscular rigidity occurring after recovering from fentanyl anesthesia has been reported.[215]

Hydromorphone: This is a synthetic derivative of morphine that is seven to ten times more potent compared to morphine. Its half-life is 2.5 h. Hydromorphone intoxication presents with all the signs of typical opiate intoxication.

Hydrocodone: Hydrocodone is almost identical to codeine. It is converted in the body to hydromorphone. Like other opiates, it can cause respiratory depression and death.

Oxycodone: This compound is a codeine derivative. Its potency and half-life are comparable to those of morphine. Deaths due to respiratory depression following oxycodone ingestion have been reported.[216]

Oxymorphone: This compound is seven to ten times more potent than morphine. It produces all the signs of classic opiate intoxication.

Meperidine: Meperidine is a synthetic opiate. Its half-life is about 3 h, but its metabolite, normeperidine, has a half-life of 15 to 34 h, and thus accumulates in plasma with repeated dosing.

In patients with renal failure the half-life of normeperidine may be as long as 3 to 4 days. Normeperidine is pharmacologically active, and has both mu-mediated effects as well as other effects not mediated by opioid receptors. Acute intoxication with meperidine presents like morphine intoxication, with respiratory depression, and can be reversed with naloxone. Patients treated with high doses of meperidine, or patients with renal failure, may accumulate high levels of normeperidine resulting in a syndrome characterized by irritability, myoclonus, and seizures.[217–220] Because of the side effects on the one hand, and lack of any specific benefits on the other, meperidine use has been declining since the 1990s.[189]

Pentazocine: Pentazocine is both an opiate agonist and an antagonist. It is an agonist for kappa, delta, and sigma receptors,[221] but antagonizes mu receptors. This renders pentazocine less likely to be abused. Pentazocine produces analgesia in nontolerant patients, but may produce withdrawal in tolerant individuals. The action on sigma and kappa receptors probably mediates a psychotomimetic reaction.[222] Pentazocin also potentiates the release of catecholamines from adrenal glands, and in high doses can cause elevated blood pressure and tachycardia.[188] There are two case reports of fibrous myopathy following intramuscular pentazocine abuse.[223,224]

8.1.4.3 Opiate Withdrawal

Abstinence after prolonged use of opiates results in the opiate withdrawal syndrome (Table 8.1.9). The severity of the symptoms depends on the duration of use and the daily dose of the opiates taken before the cessation of use; it is usually more severe in drug abusers than in patients taking opiates for pain relief. Opiate withdrawal can be precipitated by naloxone, and can occur even after a single dose of an opiate. Acute withdrawal after naloxone usually results in nausea and vomiting, profuse sweating, diarrhea, fatigue, and aches and pains, which may last up to 12 h.[225] During unassisted opiate withdrawal the patient will experience craving for the drug, usually 4 to 6 h after the last administered dose of short-acting opiates such as morphine or heroin (the interval may be 12 to 24 h for methadone). If no drug is administered at this point, there will be a feeling of intense discomfort, with anxiety, agitation, myalgias, sweating, and increased bowel movement. The symptoms will increase over the next 36 to 48 h, reach their peak at 36 to 72 h, and resolve over the next 7 to 10 days. The withdrawal symptoms are not life-threatening. They can be treated specifically with opiate replacement (usually methadone) in doses that will make the patient comfortable, and/or with supportive treatment including clonidine (a central alpha-agonist with some opiate-like effects), or benzodiazepines for anxiety.

8.1.5 Sedative–Hypnotics

8.1.5.1 Benzodiazepines

Benzodiazepines belong to the category of CNS depressant drugs, and are used in clinical practice as sedative–hypnotic and anxiolytic agents. Some benzodiazepines are also used as anti-epileptics and anesthetics. Their principal mechanism of action is potentiation of gamma-aminobu-tyric acid (GABA) — an inhibitory neurotransmitter — activity in the brain. GABA binds to the receptor opening chloride channels. The influx of chloride ions hyperpolarizes the cell membrane and prevents its firing. Benzodiazepines bind to a different site on the GABA receptor, potentiating the effects of GABA on chloride flux and enhancing the inhibitory effects of GABA.[226] Prolonged use of benzodiazepines results in tolerance. The possible mechanisms are downregulation of the GABA receptors, and configurational changes of the receptor-agonist complex resulting in dimin-ished agonist sensitivity.[227–229]

There are many drugs in the benzodiazepine class, which share the same pharmacodynamic properties. They differ in their pharmacokinetics, and the differences in elimination half-life and in duration of action indicate their different uses (Table 8.1.10A). Benzodiazepines are classified as

Table 8.1.10A Commonly Used Benzodiazepines

Drug	Elimination Half-Life (h)
Very short-acting	
Triazolam	1.5–3
Midazolam	2–5
Short-acting	
Alprazolam	10–20
Lorazepam	10–20
Oxazepam	5–10
Temazepam	10–17
Intermediate-acting	
Chlordiazepoxide	10–29
Clonazepam	20–30
Diazepam	30–60
Nitrazepam	15–24
Long-acting	
Clorazepate	50–80
Flurazepam	50–100

Table 8.1.10B Commonly Used Barbiturates

Drug	Elimination Half-Life (h)	Duration of Effect (h)
Ultrashort-acting		
Thiopental	8–10	<0.5
Methohexital	3–5	<0.5
Short-acting		
Pentobarbital	15–50	>3–4
Secobarbital	15–50	>3–4
Intermediate-acting		
Amobarbital	10–40	>4–6
Aprobarbital	14–34	>4–6
Butabarbital	35–50	>4–6
Long-acting		
Phenobarbital	80–120	>6–12
Mephobarbital	10–70	>6–12

Source: Adapted from Olson.[333]

very short acting (midazolam), short acting (triazolam), intermediate acting (alprazolam), long acting (diazepam), and very long acting (flurazepam). Most of the benzodiazepines, except oxazepam and lorazepam, which are glucuronidated, are metabolized by liver cytochrome P450 and have active metabolites. Tolerance usually develops to benzodiazepines' effects after continuous use, slowly for long-acting drugs (after about 1 month or more) and more rapidly for short-acting ones. Most users of benzodiazepines obtain the drugs by prescription. Benzodiazepines are abused usually by people who abuse other drugs as well.[230,231] However, inappropriate chronic use by patients is also common.[231,232] Because benzodiazepines cause physical and psychological dependence, they are generally recommended for limited periods of time (several weeks) and the doses carefully titrated.[230,233,234] Side effects of use include daytime drowsiness, aggravation of depression, and memory impairment, especially anterograde amnesia.[233,235–238] Benzodiazepine use in elderly individuals has been associated with falls and hip fractures, due to drowsiness and ataxia.[239] Chronic benzodiazepine exposure in elderly individuals was associated with functional impairment similar to that caused by medical conditions.[234] However, discontinuation of benzodiazepines results in normalization of memory and psychomotor performance.[240,241] Short-acting benzodiazepines, in particular triazolam, have been associated with withdrawal symptoms during treatment. The symptoms include rebound insomnia and anxiety when the drug is stopped. The use of triazolam as a hypnotic has also been associated with global amnesia[242] and affective and psychiatric disturbances.[236]

Intoxication with benzodiazepines results in CNS depression. In general, they have a very high toxic-therapeutic ratio, and doses 15 to 20 times the therapeutic dose may not cause serious side

Table 8.1.11   Manifestations of Sedative–Hypnotic Drug Intoxication
               and Withdrawal

Intoxication	
Mild	Sedation
	Disorientation
	Slurred speech
	Ataxia
	Nystagmus
Moderate	Coma, arousable by painful stimuli
	Hypoventilation
	Depressed deep tendon reflexes
Severe	Coma, unarousable
	Absent corneal, gag, and deep tendon reflexes
	Hypoventilation, apnea
	Hypotension, shock
	Hypothermia
Withdrawal	Anxiety
	Insomnia
	Irritability
	Agitation
	Anorexia
	Tremor
	Seizures (short-acting benzodiazepines and barbiturates)

Source: Modified from Benowitz.[186]

effects. With high doses the patients present with lethargy, ataxia, or slurred speech (Table 8.1.11). With very high doses, and especially when there is co-ingestion of alcohol or barbiturates, coma and respiratory depression may occur. Rapid intravenous injection of diazepam and midazolam may cause respiratory arrest. Respiratory depression has also been reported with short-acting benzodiazepines, particularly triazolam.

Withdrawal: Withdrawal usually occurs after sudden cessation of benzodiazepines; it is usually associated with a prolonged use of high doses, but also after therapeutic doses when the drug was used for several months. The symptoms include anxiety, panic attacks, insomnia, irritability, agitation, tremor, and anorexia (Table 8.1.11). Withdrawal from high doses of benzodiazepines and from short-acting benzodiazepines is usually more severe, and may result in seizures and psychotic reactions.[243] The time course of the withdrawal syndrome depends on the half-life of the specific compound.

8.1.5.2 Barbiturates

Barbiturates are clinically used as sedative–hypnotic drugs, and also for the treatment of epilepsy and induction of anesthesia. They modulate GABA receptor binding sites and potentiate the effects of the inhibitory neurotransmitter GABA. In high concentrations the barbiturates may enhance chloride ion flux independently.[244] There are several classes of barbiturates based on their elimination half-life (Table 8.1.10B). The commonly used antiepileptic agent phenobarbital has a half-life of 80 to 120 h. Serious toxicity may occur when the ingested dose is five to ten times the therapeutic. Intoxication with barbiturates results in progressive encephalopathy and coma. Mild intoxication may present as oversedation, slurred speech, ataxia, and nystagmus. Severe intoxication may present with coma, absent reflexes, hypothermia, hypotension, and respiratory depression. Apnea and shock may occur. The time course of intoxication depends on the pharmacokinetics of the specific drug; for phenobarbital coma may last for 5 to 7 days. Barbiturates are usually abused as a "treatment" for unpleasant symptoms of stimulant intoxication; in this context, short-acting drugs, such as pentobarbital and secobarbital, are often used.[245]

Withdrawal: Withdrawal symptoms upon cessation of barbiturates occur after prolonged use even of therapeutic doses, although severe withdrawal is seen most commonly in polydrug abusers.

The presentation is similar to that of benzodiazepines withdrawal, but there may be a greater risk of seizures with barbiturates withdrawal (Table 8.1.11).

8.1.5.3 Solvents

Solvent abuse has been a problem for many years, particularly among adolescents. The most frequently abused agents are glues, paint thinners, nail lacquer removers, lighter fluids, cleaning solutions, aerosols, and gasoline.[246,247] The most frequently encountered chemical is toluene, which is an ingredient in glues, paint thinners, and some petroleum products. Other chemicals are acetone in nail lacquer remover, naphtha, fluorinated hydrocarbons, trichloroethylene, and others. The methods of inhalation are breathing the substance from a plastic bag placed directly over the nose or the mouth, inhaling directly from the container or from impregnated rags, and spraying aerosols directly into the mouth. All the solvents are lipid-soluble, and thus easily cross the blood–brain barrier and cell membranes. They typically produce similar effects.

The acute effects of solvent inhalation begin within minutes, and last 15 to 45 min after inhalation. Habitual abusers of solvents may have a rash around the nose and mouth from inhaling, and may have the odor of solvent on their breath.[248] The typical effects are feelings of euphoria, disinhibition, and dizziness (Table 8.1.12). There may be also slurred speech, lack of coordination, and impaired judgment.[248,249] More severe intoxication may result in nausea and vomiting, diarrhea, tremor, ataxia, paresthesia, diffuse pains, and hallucinations. Seizures and coma may ensue.[247–250] The acute intoxication usually resolves quickly. Toluene abuse has been associated with renal tubular acidosis and severe hypokalemia, as well as interstitial nephritis, and acute tubular necrosis.[251] There are deaths associated with acute solvent abuse, about half of them the result of accidents such as asphyxiation from the plastic bag. Almost all the rest are thought to be from cardiac causes, including ventricular fibrillation and pulmonary edema.[249] Persistent toxic effects have been reported in chronic frequent abusers of volatile substances (Table 8.1.12). These include cerebellar syndrome, parkinsonism, and peripheral neuropathy and cognitive impairments. On magnetic resonance imaging (MRI), cerebral atrophy is seen, particularly in the areas of corpus callosum and cerebellar vermis; SPECT studies have demonstrated areas of hypoperfusion in the brain.[252–254] Cerebellar syndrome is associated mainly with toluene abuse and presents with nystagmus, ataxia, and tremor. It may be reversible with continued abstinence.[248] However, MRI changes demonstrating cerebral and cerebellar atrophy were found.[254] There was a report of parkinsonism in a young patient who

Table 8.1.12 Manifestations of Solvent Intoxication and Abuse

Mild	Euphoria
	Disinhibition
	Dizziness
	Slurred speech
	Lack of coordination
	Sneezing and coughing
Moderate	Lethargy, stupor
	Hallucinations
	Nausea, vomiting
	Diarrhea
	Ataxia
	Tremors
	Myalgias
	Paresthesias
Severe	Coma
	Seizures
Chronic	Cerebellar syndrome: ataxia, nystagmus, tremor (toluene)
	Parkinsonism (toluene)
	Peripheral neuropathy: symmetrical, motor, mainly involving hands and feet (n-hexene, naphtha)

chronically abused lacquer thinner; the symptoms persisted for more than 3 months after cessation of use.[255] Peripheral neuropathy, predominantly motor and symmetrical, is associated with n-hexene and naphtha. Symptoms usually start weeks after the first exposure, and the deterioration may continue for several months after the cessation of solvents. There are reports of hepatitis and liver failure, renal failure, and aplastic anemia associated with chronic solvent abuse.[256]

Acknowledgments

The authors acknowledge the support of NIH Grant DD01696.

REFERENCES

1. Gawin FH, Ellinwood EH, Jr. Cocaine and other stimulants. Actions, abuse, and treatment. *N Engl J Med* 1988;318(18):1173–82.
2. Boghdadi MS, Henning RJ. Cocaine: pathophysiology and clinical toxicology. *Heart Lung* 1997;26(6):466–83.
3. Williamson S, Gossop M, Powis B, Griffiths P, Fountain J, Strang J. Adverse effects of stimulant drugs in a community sample of drug users. *Drug Alcohol Depend* 1997;44(2–3):87–94.
4. Fleckenstein AE, Gibb JW, Hanson GR. Differential effects of stimulants on monoaminergic transporters: pharmacological consequences and implications for neurotoxicity. *Eur J Pharmacol* 2000;406(1):1–13.
5. Ramamoorthy S, Blakely RD. Phosphorylation and sequestration of serotonin transporters differentially modulated by psychostimulants. *Science* 1999;285(5428):763–6.
6. Lowenstein DH, Massa SM, Rowbotham MC, Collins SD, McKinney HE, Simon RP. Acute neurologic and psychiatric complications associated with cocaine abuse. *Am J Med* 1987;83(5):841–6.
7. Majewska MD. Cocaine addiction as a neurological disorder: Implications for treatment. *NIDA Res Monogr* 1996;163:1–26.
8. Daras M. Neurologic complications of cocaine. *NIDA Res Monogr* 1996;163:43–65.
9. Christensen JD, Kaufman MJ, Levin JM, Mendelson JH, Holman BL, Cohen BM, et al. Abnormal cerebral metabolism in polydrug abusers during early withdrawal: a 31P MR spectroscopy study. *Magn Reson Med* 1996;35(5):658–63.
10. Mueller PD, Benowitz NL, Olson KR. Cocaine. *Emerg Med Clin North Am* 1990;8(3):481–93.
11. Rowbotham MC. Neurologic aspects of cocaine abuse [clinical conference]. *West J Med* 1988;149(4):442–8.
12. Effiong C, Ahuja TS, Wagner JD, Singhal PC, Mattana J. Reversible hemiplegia as a consequence of severe hyperkalemia and cocaine abuse in a hemodialysis patient. *Am J Med Sci* 1997;314(6):408–10.
13. Petitti DB, Sidney S, Quesenberry C, Bernstein A. Stroke and cocaine or amphetamine use. *Epidemiology* 1998;9(6):596–600.
14. Tardiff K, Gross E, Wu J, Stajic M, Millman R. Analysis of cocaine-positive fatalities. *J Forensic Sci* 1989;34(1):53–63.
15. Keller TM, Chappell ET. Spontaneous acute subdural hematoma precipitated by cocaine abuse: case report. *Surg Neurol* 1997;47(1):12–4.
16. Kaufman MJ, Levin JM, Ross MH, Lange N, Rose SL, Kukes TJ, et al. Cocaine-induced cerebral vasoconstriction detected in humans with magnetic resonance angiography. *JAMA* 1998;279(5):376–80.
17. Fritsma GA, Leikin JB, Maturen AJ, Froelich CJ, Hryhorczuk DO. Detection of anticardiolipin antibody in patients with cocaine abuse. *J Emerg Med* 1991;9 Suppl 1:37–43.
18. Sanchez-Ramos JR. Psychostimulants. *Neurol Clin* 1993;11(3):535–53.
19. Catalano G, Catalano MC, Rodriguez R. Dystonia associated with crack cocaine use. *South Med J* 1997;90(10):1050–2.
20. Daras M, Koppel BS, Atos Radzion E. Cocaine-induced choreoathetoid movements ("crack dancing"). *Neurology* 1994;44(4):751–2.

21. Winbery S, Blaho K, Logan B, Geraci S. Multiple cocaine-induced seizures and corresponding cocaine and metabolite concentrations. *Am J Emerg Med* 1998;16(5):529–33.
22. Zagnoni PG, Albano C. Psychostimulants and epilepsy. *Epilepsia* 2002;43 Suppl 2:28–31.
23. Naveen RA. Brain abscess: A complication of cocaine inhalation. *NY State J Med* 1988;88:548–50.
24. Benowitz NL. Clinical pharmacology and toxicology of cocaine [published erratum appears in *Pharmacol Toxicol* 1993 Jun;72(6):343]. *Pharmacol Toxicol* 1993;72(1):3–12.
25. Ghuran A, Nolan J. Recreational drug misuse: Issues for the cardiologist. *Heart* 2000;83(6):627–33.
26. Lange RA, Hillis LD. Cardiovascular complications of cocaine use. *N Engl J Med* 2001;345(5):351–8.
27. Benzaquen BS, Cohen V, Eisenberg MJ. Effects of cocaine on the coronary arteries. *Am Heart J* 2001;142(3):402–10.
28. Mittleman MA, Mintzer D, Maclure M, Tofler GH, Sherwood JB, Muller JE. Triggering of myocardial infarction by cocaine. *Circulation* 1999;99(21):2737–41.
29. Feldman JA, Fish SS, Beshansky JR, Griffith JL, Woolard RH, Selker HP. Acute cardiac ischemia in patients with cocaine-associated complaints: results of a multicenter trial. *Ann Emerg Med* 2000;36(5):469–76.
30. Nademanee K. Cardiovascular effects and toxicities of cocaine. *J Addict Dis* 1992;11(4):71–82.
31. Boutros HH, Pautler S, Chakrabarti S. Cocaine-induced ischemic colitis with small-vessel thrombosis of colon and gallbladder. *J Clin Gastroenterol* 1997;24(1):49–53.
32. Linder JD, Monkemuller KE, Raijman I, Johnson L, Lazenby AJ, Wilcox CM. Cocaine-associated ischemic colitis. *South Med J* 2000;93(9):909–13.
33. Niazi M, Kondru A, Levy J, Bloom AA. Spectrum of ischemic colitis in cocaine users. *Dig Dis Sci* 1997;42(7):1537–41.
34. Gamouras GA, Monir G, Plunkitt K, Gursoy S, Dreifus LS. Cocaine abuse: Repolarization abnormalities and ventricular arrhythmias. *Am J Med* Sci 2000;320(1):9–12.
35. Mirchandani HG, Rorke LB, Sekula-Perlman A, Hood IC. Cocaine-induced agitated delirium, forceful struggle, and minor head injury. A further definition of sudden death during restraint. *Am J Forensic Med Pathol* 1994;15(2):95–9.
36. Wetli CV, Mash D, Karch SB. Cocaine-associated agitated delirium and the neuroleptic malignant syndrome. *Am J Emerg Med* 1996;14(4):425–8.
37. Ruttenber AJ, McAnally HB, Wetli CV. Cocaine-associated rhabdomyolysis and excited delirium: Different stages of the same syndrome. *Am J Forensic Med Pathol* 1999;20(2):120–7.
38. Ruttenber AJ, Lawler Heavner J, Yin M, Wetli CV, Hearn WL, Mash DC. Fatal excited delirium following cocaine use: epidemiologic findings provide new evidence for mechanisms of cocaine toxicity. *J Forensic Sci* 1997;42(1):25–31.
39. Marzuk PM, Tardiff K, Leon AC, Hirsch CS, Stajic M, Portera L, et al. Fatal injuries after cocaine use as a leading cause of death among young adults in New York City. *N Engl J Med* 1995;332(26):1753–7.
40. Kissner DG, Lawrence WD, Selis JE, Flint A. Crack lung: pulmonary disease caused by cocaine abuse. *Am Rev Respir Dis* 1987;136(5):1250–2.
41. Tashkin DP. Airway effects of marijuana, cocaine, and other inhaled illicit agents. *Curr Opin Pulm Med* 2001;7(2):43–61.
42. Albertson TE, Walby WF. Respiratory toxicities from stimulant use. *Clin Rev Allergy Immunol* 1997;15(3):221–41.
43. Baldwin GC, Tashkin DP, Buckley DM, Park AN, Dubinett SM, Roth MD. Marijuana and cocaine impair alveolar macrophage function and cytokine production. *Am J Respir Crit Care Med* 1997;156(5):1606–13.
44. Crandall CG, Vongpatanasin W, Victor RG. Mechanism of cocaine-induced hyperthermia in humans. *Ann Intern Med* 2002;136(11):785–91.
45. Marzuk PM, Tardiff K, Leon AC, Hirsch CS, Portera L, Iqbal MI, et al. Ambient temperature and mortality from unintentional cocaine overdose. *JAMA* 1998;279(22):1795–800.
46. Bateman DA, Chiriboga CA. Dose–response effect of cocaine on newborn head circumference. *Pediatrics* 2000;106(3):E33.
47. Chiriboga CA, Brust JC, Bateman D, Hauser WA. Dose–response effect of fetal cocaine exposure on newborn neurologic function. *Pediatrics* 1999;103(1):79–85.

48. Lago JA, Kosten TR. Stimulant withdrawal. *Addiction* 1994;89(11):1477–81.

49. Yousef G, Huq Z, Lambert T. Khat chewing as a cause of psychosis. *Br J Hosp Med* 1995;54(7):322–6.

50. Battig K. Acute and chronic cardiovascular and behavioural effects of caffeine, aspirin and ephedrine. *Int J Obes Relat Metab Disord* 1993;17 Suppl 1:S61–4.

51. Bruno A, Nolte KB, Chapin J. Stroke associated with ephedrine use. *Neurology* 1993;43(7):1313–6.

52. Wooten MR, Khangure MS, Murphy MJ. Intracerebral hemorrhage and vasculitis related to ephedrine abuse. *Ann Neurol* 1983;13(3):337–40.

53. MMWR. Adverse events associated with ephedrine-containing products — Texas, December 1993–September 1995. *MMWR Morb Mortal Wkly Rep* 1996;45(32):689–93.

54. Haller CA, Benowitz NL. Adverse cardiovascular and central nervous system events associated with dietary supplements containing ephedra alkaloids. *N Engl J Med* 2000;343(25):1833–8.

55. Samenuk D, Link MS, Homoud MK, Contreras R, Theohardes TC, Wang PJ, et al. Adverse cardiovascular events temporally associated with ma huang, an herbal source of ephedrine. *Mayo Clin Proc* 2002;77(1):12–6.

56. Powell T, Hsu FF, Turk J, Hruska K. Ma-huang strikes again: Ephedrine nephrolithiasis. *Am J Kidney Dis* 1998;32(1):153–9.

57. Luqman W, Danowski TS. The use of khat (*Catha edulis*) in Yemen. Social and medical observations. *Ann Intern Med* 1976;85(2):246–249.

58. Pantelis C, Hindler CG, Taylor JC. Use and abuse of khat (*Catha edulis*): A review of the distribution, pharmacology, side effects and a description of psychosis attributed to khat chewing. *Psychol Med* 1989;19(3):657–68.

59. Morrish PK, Nicolaou N, Brakkenberg P, Smith PE. Leukoencephalopathy associated with khat misuse. *J Neurol Neurosurg Psychiatry* 1999;67(4):556.

60. Hassan NA, Gunaid AA, Abdo Rabbo AA, Abdel Kader ZY, al Mansoob MA, Awad AY, et al. The effect of Qat chewing on blood pressure and heart rate in healthy volunteers. *Trop Doct* 2000;30(2):107–8.

61. Al Motarreb A, Al Kebsi M, Al Adhi B, Broadley KJ. Khat chewing and acute myocardial infarction. *Heart* 2002;87(3):279–80.

62. Derlet RW, Rice P, Horowitz BZ, Lord RV. Amphetamine toxicity: Experience with 127 cases. *J Emerg Med* 1989;7(2):157–61.

63. Agaba EA, Lynch RM, Baskaran A, Jackson T. Massive intracerebral hematoma and extradural hematoma in amphetamine abuse. *Am J Emerg Med* 2002;20(1):55–7.

64. El Omar MM, Ray K, Geary R. Intracerebral haemorrhage in a young adult: consider amphetamine abuse. *Br J Clin Pract* 1996;50(2):115–6.

65. Matick H, Anderson D, Brumlik J. Cerebral vasculitis associated with oral amphetamine overdose. *Arch Neurol* 1983;40(4):253–4.

66. Shaw HE, Jr., Lawson JG, Stulting RD. *Amaurosis fugax* and retinal vasculitis associated with methamphetamine inhalation. *J Clin Neuroophthalmol* 1985;5(3):169–76.

67. Buxton N, McConachie NS. Amphetamine abuse and intracranial haemorrhage. *J R Soc Med* 2000;93(9):472–7.

68. Harris D, Batki SL. Stimulant psychosis: symptom profile and acute clinical course. *Am J Addict* 2000;9(1):28–37.

69. Flaum M, Schultz SK. When does amphetamine-induced psychosis become schizophrenia? *Am J Psychiatry* 1996;153(6):812–5.

70. Costa GM, Pizzi C, Bresciani B, Tumscitz C, Gentile M, Bugiardini R. Acute myocardial infarction caused by amphetamines: A case report and review of the literature. *Ital Heart J* 2001;2(6):478–80.

71. Waksman J, Taylor RN, Jr., Bodor GS, Daly FF, Jolliff HA, Dart RC. Acute myocardial infarction associated with amphetamine use. *Mayo Clin Proc* 2001;76(3):323–6.

72. Smith HJ, Roche AH, Jausch MF, Herdson PB. Cardiomyopathy associated with amphetamine administration. *Am Heart J* 1976;91(6):792–7.

73. Welling TH, Williams DM, Stanley JC. Excessive oral amphetamine use as a possible cause of renal and splanchnic arterial aneurysms: a report of two cases. *J Vasc Surg* 1998;28(4):727–31.

74. Callaway CW, Clark RF. Hyperthermia in psychostimulant overdose. *Ann Emerg Med* 1994;24(1):68–76.

75. Albertson TE, Derlet RW, Van Hoozen BE. Methamphetamine and the expanding complications of amphetamines. *West J Med* 1999;170(4):214–9.

76. Buchanan JF, Brown CR. 'Designer drugs.' A problem in clinical toxicology. *Med Toxicol Adverse Drug Exp* 1988;3(1):1–17.

77. Rothrock JF, Rubenstein R, Lyden PD. Ischemic stroke associated with methamphetamine inhalation. *Neurology* 1988;38(4):589–92.

78. Perez JA, Jr., Arsura EL, Strategos S. Methamphetamine-related stroke: four cases. *J Emerg Med* 1999;17(3):469–71.

79. Richards JR, Johnson EB, Stark RW, Derlet RW. Methamphetamine abuse and rhabdomyolysis in the ED: A 5-year study. *Am J Emerg Med* 1999;17(7):681–5.

80. Schteinschnaider A, Plaghos LL, Garbugino S, Riveros D, Lazarowski A, Intruvini S, et al. Cerebral arteritis following methylphenidate use. *J Child Neurol* 2000;15(4):265–7.

81. Pentel P. Toxicity of over-the-counter stimulants. *JAMA* 1984;252(14):1898–903.

82. Kikta DG, Devereaux MW, Chandar K. Intracranial hemorrhages due to phenylpropanolamine. *Stroke* 1985;16(3):510–2.

83. Edwards M, Russo L, Harwood-Nuss A. Cerebral infarction with a single oral dose of phenylpropanolamine. *Am J Emerg Med* 1987;5(2):163–4.

84. Kernan WN, Viscoli CM, Brass LM, Broderick JP, Brott T, Feldmann E, et al. Phenylpropanolamine and the risk of hemorrhagic stroke. *N Engl J Med* 2000;343(25):1826–32.

85. Mersfelder TL. Phenylpropanolamine and stroke: the study, the FDA ruling, the implications. *Cleve Clin J Med* 2001;68(3):208–9, 213–9, 223.

86. SoRelle R. FDA warns of stroke risk associated with phenylpropanolamine; cold remedies and drugs removed from store shelves. *Circulation* 2000;102(21):E9041–3.

87. Mueller SM. Neurologic complications of phenylpropanolamine use. *Neurology* 1983;33(5):650–2.

88. Goodhue A, Bartel RL, Smith NB. Exacerbation of psychosis by phenylpropanolamine. *Am J Psychiatry* 2000;157(6):1021–2.

89. Lake CR, Masson EB, Quirk RS. Psychiatric side effects attributed to phenylpropanolamine. *Pharmacopsychiatry* 1988;21(4):171–81.

90. Glick R, Hoying J, Cerullo L, Perlman S. Phenylpropanolamine: An over-the-counter drug causing central nervous system vasculitis and intracerebral hemorrhage. Case report and review. *Neurosurgery* 1987;20(6):969–74.

91. Aghajanian GK, Marek GJ. Serotonin model of schizophrenia: emerging role of glutamate mechanisms. *Brain Res Brain Res Rev* 2000;31(2–3):302–12.

92. Aghajanian GK, Marek GJ. Serotonin and hallucinogens. *Neuropsychopharmacology* 1999;21(2 Suppl):16s–23s.

93. Bruhn JG, De Smet PAGM, El Seedi HR, Beck O. Mescaline use for 5700 years. *Lancet* 2002;359(9320):1866.

94. Hollister LE, Hartman AM. Mescaline, lysergic acid diethylamide and psilocybin: comparison of clinical syndromes, effects on color perception and biochemical measures. *Comprehensive Psychiatry* 1962;3:235–241.

95. Leikin JB, Krantz AJ, Zell-Kanter M, Barkin RL, Hryhorczuk DO. Clinical features and management of intoxication due to hallucinogenic drugs. *Med Toxicol Adverse Drug Exp* 1989;4(5):324–50.

96. Kapadia GJ, Fayez MB. Peyote constituents: chemistry, biogenesis, and biological effects. *J Pharm Sci* 1970;59(12):1699–727.

97. Nolte KB, Zumwalt RE. Fatal peyote ingestion associated with Mallory-Weiss lacerations. *West J Med* 1999;170(6):328.

98. Hashimoto H, Clyde VJ, Parko KL. Botulism from peyote. *N Engl J Med* 1998;339(3):203–4.

99. Mack RB. Marching to a different cactus: peyote (mescaline) intoxication. *N C Med J* 1986;47(3):137–8.

100. Shulgin AT. Profiles of psychedelic drugs: TMA-2. *J Psychedelic Drugs* 1976;8:169.

101. Shulgin AT. Profiles of psychedelic drugs: STP. *J Psychedelic Drugs* 1977;9:171–172.

102. James RA, Dinan A. Hyperpyrexia associated with fatal paramethoxyamphetamine (PMA) abuse. *Med Sci Law* 1998;38(1):83–5.

103. Kraner JC, McCoy DJ, Evans MA, Evans LE, Sweeney BJ. Fatalities caused by the MDMA-related drug paramethoxyamphetamine (PMA). *J Anal Toxicol* 2001;25(7):645–8.

104. Byard RW, Gilbert J, James R, Lokan RJ. Amphetamine derivative fatalities in South Australia — is "Ecstasy" the culprit? *Am J Forensic Med Pathol* 1998;19(3):261–5.

105. Shulgin A. Profiles of psychedelic drugs: DOB. *J Psychoactive Drugs* 1981;13(1):99.

106. Buhrich N, Morris G, Cook G. Bromo-DMA: the Australasian hallucinogen? *Aust NZ J Psychiatry* 1983;17(3):275–9.

107. Simpson DL, Rumack BH. Methylenedioxyamphetamine. Clinical description of overdose, death, and review of pharmacology. *Arch Intern Med* 1981;141(11):1507–9.

108. Strote J, Lee JE, Wechsler H. Increasing MDMA use among college students: results of a national survey. *J Adolesc Health* 2002;30(1):64–72.

109. Steele TD, McCann UD, Ricaurte GA. 3,4-Methylenedioxymethamphetamine (MDMA, "Ecstasy"): pharmacology and toxicology in animals and humans. *Addiction* 1994;89(5):539–51.

110. Liechti ME, Gamma A, Vollenweider FX. Gender differences in the subjective effects of MDMA. *Psychopharmacology* (Berlin) 2001;154(2):161–8.

111. McCann UD, Ricaurte GA. MDMA ("ecstasy") and panic disorder: induction by a single dose. *Biol Psychiatry* 1992;32(10):950–3.

112. Alciati A, Scaramelli B, Fusi A, Butteri E, Cattaneo ML, Mellado C. Three cases of delirium after "ecstasy" ingestion. *J Psychoactive Drugs* 1999;31(2):167–70.

113. Vaiva G, Boss V, Bailly D, Thomas P, Lestavel P, Goudemand M. An "accidental" acute psychosis with ecstasy use. *J Psychoactive Drugs* 2001;33(1):95–8.

114. Vollenweider FX, Gamma A, Liechti M, Huber T. Psychological and cardiovascular effects and short-term sequelae of MDMA ("ecstasy") in MDMA-naive healthy volunteers. *Neuropsychopharmacology* 1998;19(4):241–51.

115. Morgan MJ, McFie L, Fleetwood H, Robinson JA. Ecstasy (MDMA): Are the psychological problems associated with its use reversed by prolonged abstinence? *Psychopharmacology* (Berlin) 2002;159(3):294–303.

116. MacInnes N, Handley SL, Harding GF. Former chronic methylenedioxymethamphetamine (MDMA or ecstasy) users report mild depressive symptoms. *J Psychopharmacol* 2001;15(3):181–6.

117. Gerra G, Zaimovic A, Ampollini R, Giusti F, Delsignore R, Raggi MA, et al. Experimentally induced aggressive behavior in subjects with 3,4-methylenedioxy-methamphetamine ("Ecstasy") use history: psychobiological correlates. *J Subst Abuse* 2001;13(4):471–91.

118. McCann UD, Slate SO, Ricaurte GA. Adverse reactions with 3,4-methylenedioxymethamphetamine (MDMA; "Ecstasy"). *Drug Saf* 1996;15(2):107–115.

119. Ricaurte GA, McCann UD. Assessing long-term effects of MDMA (Ecstasy). *Lancet* 2001;358(9296):1831–2.

120. Reneman L, Lavalaye J, Schmand B, de Wolff FA, van den Brink W, den Heeten GJ, et al. Cortical serotonin transporter density and verbal memory in individuals who stopped using 3,4-methylene-dioxymethamphetamine (MDMA or "ecstasy"): preliminary findings. *Arch Gen Psychiatry* 2001;58(10):901–6.

121. Gouzoulis Mayfrank E, Daumann J, Tuchtenhagen F, Pelz S, Becker S, Kunert HJ, et al. Impaired cognitive performance in drug free users of recreational ecstasy (MDMA). *J Neurol Neurosurg Psychiatry* 2000;68(6):719–25.

122. Parrott AC, Sisk E, Turner JJ. Psychobiological problems in heavy "ecstasy" (MDMA) polydrug users. *Drug Alcohol Depend* 2000;60(1):105–10.

123. Verkes RJ, Gijsman HJ, Pieters MS, Schoemaker RC, de Visser S, Kuijpers M, et al. Cognitive performance and serotonergic function in users of ecstasy. *Psychopharmacology* (Berlin) 2001;153(2):196–202.

124. McCann UD, Ridenour A, Shaham Y, Ricaurte GA. Serotonin neurotoxicity after (+/–)3,4-methyl-enedioxymethamphetamine (MDMA; "Ecstasy"): a controlled study in humans. *Neuropsychopharmacology* 1994;10(2):129–38.

125. Kish SJ, Furukawa Y, Ang L, Vorce SP, Kalasinsky KS. Striatal serotonin is depleted in brain of a human MDMA (Ecstasy) user. *Neurology* 2000;55(2):294–6.

126. McCann UD, Szabo Z, Scheffel U, Dannals RF, Ricaurte GA. Positron emission tomographic evidence of toxic effect of MDMA ("Ecstasy") on brain serotonin neurons in human beings. *Lancet* 1998;352(9138):1433–7.

127. Reneman L, Booij J, de Bruin K, Reitsma JB, de Wolff FA, Gunning WB, et al. Effects of dose, sex, and long-term abstention from use on toxic effects of MDMA (ecstasy) on brain serotonin neurons. *Lancet* 2001;358(9296):1864–9.

128. Lester SJ, Baggott M, Welm S, Schiller NB, Jones RT, Foster E, et al. Cardiovascular effects of 3,4-methylenedioxymethamphetamine. A double-blind, placebo-controlled trial. *Ann Intern Med* 2000;133(12):969–73.

129. Mas M, Farre M, de la Torre R, Roset PN, Ortuno J, Segura J, et al. Cardiovascular and neuroendocrine effects and pharmacokinetics of 3, 4-methylenedioxymethamphetamine in humans. *J Pharmacol Exp Ther* 1999;290(1):136–45.

130. Henry JA. Ecstasy and the dance of death. *Br Med J* 1992;305(6844):5–6.

131. Milroy CM, Clark JC, Forrest AR. Pathology of deaths associated with "ecstasy" and "eve" misuse. *J Clin Pathol* 1996;49(2):149–53.

132. Jones AL, Simpson KJ. Review article: mechanisms and management of hepatotoxicity in ecstasy (MDMA) and amphetamine intoxications. *Aliment Pharmacol Ther* 1999;13(2):129–33.

133. Brauer RB, Heidecke CD, Nathrath W, Beckurts KT, Vorwald P, Zilker TR, et al. Liver transplantation for the treatment of fulminant hepatic failure induced by the ingestion of ecstasy. *Transpl Int* 1997;10(3):229–33.

134. Garbino J, Henry JA, Mentha G, Romand JA. Ecstasy ingestion and fulminant hepatic failure: liver transplantation to be considered as a last therapeutic option. *Vet Hum Toxicol* 2001;43(2):99–102.

135. Maxwell DL, Polkey MI, Henry JA. Hyponatraemia and catatonic stupor after taking "ecstasy" [see comments]. *Br Med J* 1993;307(6916):1399.

136. Satchell SC, Connaughton M. Inappropriate antidiuretic hormone secretion and extreme rises in serum creatinine kinase following MDMA ingestion. *Br J Hosp Med* 1994;51(9):495.

137. Forsling M, Fallon JK, Kicman AT, Hutt AJ, Cowan DA, Henry JA. Arginine vasopressin release in response to the administration of 3,4-methylenedioxymethamphetamine ("ecstasy"): Is metabolism a contributory factor? *J Pharm Pharmacol* 2001;53(10):1357–63.

138. Henry JA, Fallon JK, Kicman AT, Hutt AJ, Cowan DA, Forsling M. Low-dose MDMA ("ecstasy") induces vasopressin secretion. *Lancet* 1998;351(9118):1784.

139. Wilkins B. Cerebral oedema after MDMA ("ecstasy") and unrestricted water intake. Hyponatraemia must be treated with low water input. *Br Med J* 1996;313(7058):689–90.

140. Williams H, Dratcu L, Taylor R, Roberts M, Oyefeso A. "Saturday night fever": Ecstasy related problems in a London accident and emergency department. *J Accid Emerg Med* 1998;15(5):322–6.

141. Mueller PD, Korey WS. Death by "ecstasy": The serotonin syndrome? *Ann Emerg Med* 1998;32(3 Pt 1):377–80.

142. Henry JA, Hill IR. Fatal interaction between ritonavir and MDMA. *Lancet* 1998;352(9142):1751–2.

143. Harrington RD, Woodward JA, Hooton TM, Horn JR. Life-threatening interactions between HIV-1 protease inhibitors and the illicit drugs MDMA and gamma-hydroxybutyrate. *Arch Intern Med* 1999;159(18):2221–4.

144. McElhatton PR, Bateman DN, Evans C, Pughe KR, Thomas SH. Congenital anomalies after prenatal ecstasy exposure. *Lancet* 1999;354(9188):1441–2.

145. Webb E, Ashton CH, Kelly P, Kamali F. Alcohol and drug use in UK university students. *Lancet* 1996;348(9032):922–5.

146. Golub A, Johnson BD, Sifaneck SJ, Chesluk B, Parker H. Is the U.S. experiencing an incipient epidemic of hallucinogen use? *Subst Use Misuse* 2001;36(12):1699–729.

147. Jacobs BL. How hallucinogenic drugs work. *Am Sci* 1987;75:386–392.

148. Schwartz RH. LSD. Its rise, fall, and renewed popularity among high school students. *Pediatr Clin North Am* 1995;42(2):403–13.

149. Abraham HD, Aldridge AM. Adverse consequences of lysergic acid diethylamide. *Addiction* 1993;88(10):1327–34.

150. Kawasaki A, Purvin V. Persistent palinopsia following ingestion of lysergic acid diethylamide (LSD). *Arch Ophthalmol* 1996;114(1):47–50.

151. Contreras PC, Monahan JB, Lanthorn TH, Pullan LM, DiMaggio DA, Handelmann GE, et al. Phencyclidine. Physiological actions, interactions with excitatory amino acids and endogenous ligands. *Mol Neurobiol* 1987;1(3):191–211.

152. Sonders MS, Keana JF, Weber E. Phencyclidine and psychotomimetic sigma opiates: recent insights into their biochemical and physiological sites of action. *Trends Neurosci* 1988;11(1):37–40.

153. Brust JC. Other agents. Phencyclidine, marijuana, hallucinogens, inhalants, and anticholinergics. *Neurol Clin* 1993;11(3):555–61.

154. McCarron MM, Schulze BW, Thompson GA, Conder MC, Goetz WA. Acute phencyclidine intoxication: Clinical patterns, complications, and treatment. *Ann Emerg Med* 1981;10(6):290–7.

155. Aniline O, Pitts FN, Jr. Phencyclidine (PCP): a review and perspectives. *Crit Rev Toxicol* 1982;10(2):145–77.

156. Martin BR, Mechoulam R, Razdan RK. Discovery and characterization of endogenous cannabinoids. *Life Sci* 1999;65(6–7):573–95.

157. Ameri A. The effects of cannabinoids on the brain. *Prog Neurobiol* 1999;58(4):315–48.

158. Ashton CH. Pharmacology and effects of cannabis: a brief review. *Br J Psychiatry* 2001;178:101–6.

159. Gruber AJ, Pope HG, Jr. Marijuana use among adolescents. *Pediatr Clin North Am* 2002;49(2):389–413.

160. Gledhill Hoyt J, Lee H, Strote J, Wechsler H. Increased use of marijuana and other illicit drugs at US colleges in the 1990s: results of three national surveys. *Addiction* 2000;95(11):1655–67.

161. Harris D, Jones RT, Shank R, Nath R, Fernandez E, Goldstein K, et al. Self-reported marijuana effects and characteristics of 100 San Francisco medical marijuana club members. *J Addict Dis* 2000;19(3):89–103.

162. Hall W, Solowij N. Adverse effects of cannabis. *Lancet* 1998;352(9140):1611–6.

163. Johns A. Psychiatric effects of cannabis. *Br J Psychiatry* 2001;178:116–22.

164. Nunez LA, Gurpegui M. Cannabis-induced psychosis: a cross-sectional comparison with acute schizophrenia. *Acta Psychiatr Scand* 2002;105(3):173–8.

165. Farber SJ, Huertas VE. Intravenously injected marijuana syndrome. *Arch Int Med* 1976;136:337–339.

166. Solowij N, Stephens RS, Roffman RA, Babor T, Kadden R, Miller M, et al. Cognitive functioning of long-term heavy cannabis users seeking treatment. *JAMA* 2002;287(9):1123–31.

167. Pope HG, Jr., Yurgelun Todd D. The residual cognitive effects of heavy marijuana use in college students. *JAMA* 1996;275(7):521–7.

168. Pope HG, Jr., Gruber AJ, Hudson JI, Huestis MA, Yurgelun Todd D. Neuropsychological performance in long-term cannabis users. *Arch Gen Psychiatry* 2001;58(10):909–15.

169. Pope HG, Jr. Cannabis, cognition, and residual confounding. *JAMA* 2002;287(9):1172–4.

170. Hollister LE. Health aspects of cannabis. *Pharmacol Rev* 1986;38(1):1–20.

171. Fergusson DM, Horwood LJ, Northstone K. Maternal use of cannabis and pregnancy outcome. *BJOG* 2002;109(1):21–7.

172. Fried PA, Smith AM. A literature review of the consequences of prenatal marihuana exposure. An emerging theme of a deficiency in aspects of executive function. *Neurotoxicol Teratol* 2001;23(1):1–11.

173. Taylor FMd. Marijuana as a potential respiratory tract carcinogen: a retrospective analysis of a community hospital population. *South Med J* 1988;81(10):1213–6.

174. Wu TC, Tashkin DP, Djahed B, Rose JE. Pulmonary hazards of smoking marijuana as compared with tobacco. *N Engl J Med* 1988;318(6):347–51.

175. Taylor DR, Poulton R, Moffitt TE, Ramankutty P, Sears MR. The respiratory effects of cannabis dependence in young adults. *Addiction* 2000;95(11):1669–77.

176. Van Hoozen BE, Cross CE. Marijuana. Respiratory tract effects. *Clin Rev Allergy Immunol* 1997;15(3):243–69.

177. Zhang ZF, Morgenstern H, Spitz MR, Tashkin DP, Yu GP, Marshall JR, et al. Marijuana use and increased risk of squamous cell carcinoma of the head and neck. *Cancer Epidemiol Biomarkers Prev* 1999;8(12):1071–8.

178. Feldman AL, Sullivan JT, Passero MA, Lewis DC. Pneumothorax in polysubstance-abusing marijuana and tobacco smokers: three cases. *J Subst Abuse* 1993;5(2):183–6.

179. von Sydow K, Lieb R, Pfister H, Hofler M, Sonntag H, Wittchen HU. The natural course of cannabis use, abuse and dependence over four years: a longitudinal community study of adolescents and young adults. *Drug Alcohol Depend* 2001;64(3):347–61.

180. Swift W, Hall W, Teesson M. Characteristics of DSM-IV and ICD-10 cannabis dependence among Australian adults: results from the National Survey of Mental Health and Wellbeing. *Drug Alcohol Depend* 2001;63(2):147–53.

181. Rosenberg MF, Anthony JC. Early clinical manifestations of cannabis dependence in a community sample. *Drug Alcohol Depend* 2001;64(2):123–31.
182. Coffey C, Carlin JB, Degenhardt L, Lynskey M, Sanci L, Patton GC. Cannabis dependence in young adults: an Australian population study. *Addiction* 2002;97(2):187–94.
183. Budney AJ, Hughes JR, Moore BA, Novy PL. Marijuana abstinence effects in marijuana smokers maintained in their home environment. *Arch Gen Psychiatry* 2001;58(10):917–24.
184. Kouri EM, Pope HG, Jr. Abstinence symptoms during withdrawal from chronic marijuana use. *Exp Clin Psychopharmacol* 2000;8(4):483–92.
185. Foley KM. Opioids. *Neurol Clin* 1993;11(3):503–22.
186. Benowitz NL. Substance abuse: dependence and treatment. In: Melmon KL, Morrelli HF, Hoffman BB, Nierenberg DW, Eds. *Clinical Pharmacology.* 3 ed: New York: McGraw-Hill; 1992. p. 763–786.
187. Zebraski SE, Kochenash SM, Raffa RB. Lung opioid receptors: pharmacology and possible target for nebulized morphine in dyspnea. *Life Sci* 2000;66(23):2221–31.
188. Karch SB. *The Pathology of Drug Abuse.* Boca Raton, FL: CRC Press; 1993.
189. Joranson DE, Ryan KM, Gilson AM, Dahl JL. Trends in medical use and abuse of opioid analgesics. *JAMA* 2000;283(13):1710–4.
190. Pasternak GW. Insights into mu opioid pharmacology: the role of mu opioid receptor subtypes. *Life Sci* 2001;68(19–20):2213–9.
191. Pasternak GW. The pharmacology of mu analgesics: from patients to genes. *Neuroscientist* 2001;7(3):220–31.
192. Zaki PA, Bilsky EJ, Vanderah TW, Lai J, Evans CJ, Porreca F. Opioid receptor types and subtypes: the delta receptor as a model. *Annu Rev Pharmacol Toxicol* 1996;36:379–401.
193. Pappagallo M. Incidence, prevalence, and management of opioid bowel dysfunction. *Am J Surg* 2001;182(5A Suppl):11s–18s.
194. Ling GS, Spiegel K, Lockhart SH, Pasternak GW. Separation of opioid analgesia from respiratory depression: evidence for different receptor mechanisms. *J Pharmacol Exp Ther* 1985;232(1):149–55.
195. Ballantyne JC, Loach AB, Carr DB. Itching after epidural and spinal opiates. *Pain* 1988;33(2):149–60.
196. Dray A. Epidural opiates and urinary retention: new models provide new insights [editorial]. *Anesthesiology* 1988;68(3):323–4.
197. Smith MT. Neuroexcitatory effects of morphine and hydromorphone: evidence implicating the 3-glucuronide metabolites. *Clin Exp Pharmacol Physiol* 2000;27(7):524–8.
198. Mercadante S. Opioid rotation for cancer pain: rationale and clinical aspects. *Cancer* 1999;86(9):1856–66.
199. Chan P, Lin TH, Luo JP, Deng JF. Acute heroin intoxication with complications of acute pulmonary edema, acute renal failure, rhabdomyolysis and lumbosacral plexitis: a case report. *Chung Hua I Hsueh Tsa Chih* (Taipei) 1995;55(5):397–400.
200. Richter RW. Muscle damage in heroin addicts. *N Engl J Med* 1971;284(15):920.
201. Klockgether T, Weller M, Haarmeier T, Kaskas B, Maier G, Dichgans J. Gluteal compartment syndrome due to rhabdomyolysis after heroin abuse. *Neurology* 1997;48(1):275–6.
202. Rice EK, Isbel NM, Becker GJ, Atkins RC, McMahon LP. Heroin overdose and myoglobinuric acute renal failure. *Clin Nephrol* 2000;54(6):449–54.
203. Dubrow A, Mittman N, Ghali V, Flamenbaum W. The changing spectrum of heroin-associated nephropathy. *Am J Kidney Dis* 1985;5(1):36–41.
204. Niehaus L, Meyer BU. Bilateral borderzone brain infarctions in association with heroin abuse. *J Neurol Sci* 1998;160(2):180–2.
205. Buttner A, Mall G, Penning R, Weis S. The neuropathology of heroin abuse. *Forensic Sci Int* 2000;113(1–3):435–42.
206. Schoser BG, Groden C. Subacute onset of oculogyric crises and generalized dystonia following intranasal administration of heroin. *Addiction* 1999;94(3):431–4.
207. Kathiramalainathan K, Kaplan HL, Romach MK, Busto UE, Li NY, Sawe J, et al. Inhibition of cytochrome P450 2D6 modifies codeine abuse liability. *J Clin Psychopharmacol* 2000;20(4): 435–44.
208. Romach MK, Otton SV, Somer G, Tyndale RF, Sellers EM. Cytochrome P450 2D6 and treatment of codeine dependence. *J Clin Psychopharmacol* 2000;20(1):43–5.
209. Drummer OH, Opeskin K, Syrjanen M, Cordner SM. Methadone toxicity causing death in ten subjects starting on a methadone maintenance program. *Am J Forensic Med Pathol* 1992;13(4):346–50.

210. Ng B, Alvear M. Dextropropoxyphene addiction — a drug of primary abuse. *Am J Drug Alcohol Abuse* 1993;19(2):153–8.

211. Lawson AA, Northridge DB. Dextropropoxyphene overdose. Epidemiology, clinical presentation and management. *Med Toxicol Adverse Drug Exp* 1987;2(6):430–44.

212. Stork CM, Redd JT, Fine K, Hoffman RS. Propoxyphene-induced wide QRS complex dysrhythmia responsive to sodium bicarbonate — A case report. *J Toxicol Clin Toxicol* 1995;33(2):179–83.

213. Yee LY, Lopez JR. Transdermal fentanyl. *Ann Pharmacother* 1992;26(11):1393–9.

214. Sprung J, Schedewie HK. Apparent focal motor seizure with a jacksonian march induced by fentanyl: a case report and review of the literature. *J Clin Anesth* 1992;4(2):139–43.

215. Caspi J, Klausner JM, Safadi T, Amar R, Rozin RR, Merin G. Delayed respiratory depression following fentanyl anesthesia for cardiac surgery. *Crit Care Med* 1988;16(3):238–40.

216. Drummer OH, Syrjanen ML, Phelan M, Cordner SM. A study of deaths involving oxycodone. *J Forensic Sci* 1994;39(4):1069–75.

217. Stock SL, Catalano G, Catalano MC. Meperidine associated mental status changes in a patient with chronic renal failure. *J Fla Med Assoc* 1996;83(5):315–9.

218. Hassan H, Bastani B, Gellens M. Successful treatment of normeperidine neurotoxicity by hemodialysis. *Am J Kidney Dis* 2000;35(1):146–9.

219. Kussman BD, Sethna NF. Pethidine-associated seizure in a healthy adolescent receiving pethidine for postoperative pain control. *Paediatr Anaesth* 1998;8(4):349–52.

220. Latta KS, Ginsberg B, Barkin RL. Meperidine: a critical review. *Am J Ther* 2002;9(1):53–68.

221. Zabetian CP, Staley JK, Flynn DD, Mash DC. [3H]-(+)-Pentazocine binding to sigma recognition sites in human cerebellum. *Life Sci* 1994;55(20):L389–95.

222. Pfeiffer A, Brantl V, Herz A, Emrich HM. Psychotomimesis mediated by kappa opiate receptors. *Science* 1986;233(4765):774–6.

223. Das CP, Thussu A, Prabhakar S, Banerjee AK. Pentazocine-induced fibromyositis and contracture. *Postgrad Med J* 1999;75(884):361–2.

224. Sinsawaiwong S, Phanthumchinda K. Pentazocine-induced fibrous myopathy and localized neuropathy. *J Med Assoc Thai* 1998;81(9):717–21.

225. Farrell M. Opiate withdrawal. *Addiction* 1994;89(11):1471–5.

226. Tallman JF, Gallager DW, Mallorga P, Thomas JW, Strittmatter W, Hirata F, et al. Studies on benzodiazepine receptors. *Adv Biochem Psychopharmacol* 1980;21:277–83.

227. Miller LG, Greenblatt DJ, Roy RB, Summer WR, Shader RI. Chronic benzodiazepine administration. II. Discontinuation syndrome is associated with upregulation of gamma-aminobutyric acidA receptor complex binding and function. *J Pharmacol Exp Ther* 1988;246(1):177–82.

228. Lader M. Biological processes in benzodiazepine dependence. *Addiction* 1994;89(11):1413–8.

229. Bateson AN. Basic pharmacologic mechanisms involved in benzodiazepine tolerance and withdrawal. *Curr Pharm Des* 2002;8(1):5–21.

230. Woods JH, Winger G. Current benzodiazepine issues. *Psychopharmacology* (Berlin) 1995;118(2):107–15; discussion 118, 120–1.

231. Griffiths RR, Weerts EM. Benzodiazepine self-administration in humans and laboratory animals — implications for problems of long-term use and abuse. *Psychopharmacology* (Berlin) 1997;134(1):1–37.

232. Michelini S, Cassano GB, Frare F, Perugi G. Long-term use of benzodiazepines: tolerance, dependence and clinical problems in anxiety and mood disorders. *Pharmacopsychiatry* 1996;29(4):127–34.

233. Ashton H. Guidelines for the rational use of benzodiazepines. When and what to use. *Drugs* 1994;48(1):25–40.

234. Nelson J, Chouinard G. Guidelines for the clinical use of benzodiazepines: pharmacokinetics, dependency, rebound and withdrawal. Canadian Society for Clinical Pharmacology. *Can J Clin Pharmacol* 1999;6(2):69–83.

235. Vgontzas AN, Kales A, Bixler EO. Benzodiazepine side effects: role of pharmacokinetics and pharmacodynamics. *Pharmacology* 1995;51(4):205–23.

236. Fraser AD. Use and abuse of the benzodiazepines. *Ther Drug Monit* 1998;20(5):481–9.

237. Buffett Jerrott SE, Stewart SH. Cognitive and sedative effects of benzodiazepine use. *Curr Pharm Des* 2002;8(1):45–58.

238. Buffett Jerrott SE, Stewart SH, Teehan MD. A further examination of the time-dependent effects of oxazepam and lorazepam on implicit and explicit memory. *Psychopharmacology* (Berlin) 1998;138(3–4):344–53.

239. Wysowski DK, Baum C, Ferguson WJ, Lundin F, Ng MJ, Hammerstrom T. Sedative–hypnotic drugs and the risk of hip fracture. *J Clin Epidemiol* 1996;49(1):111-3.

240. Rickels K, Lucki I, Schweizer E, Garcia Espana F, Case WG. Psychomotor performance of long-term benzodiazepine users before, during, and after benzodiazepine discontinuation. *J Clin Psychopharmacol* 1999;19(2):107–13.

241. Kilic C, Curran HV, Noshirvani H, Marks IM, Basoglu M. Long-term effects of alprazolam on memory: a 3.5 year follow-up of agoraphobia/panic patients. *Psychol Med* 1999;29(1):225–31.

242. Morris HHd, Estes ML. Traveler's amnesia. Transient global amnesia secondary to triazolam. *JAMA* 1987;258(7):945–6.

243. Petursson H. The benzodiazepine withdrawal syndrome. *Addiction* 1994;89(11):1455–9.

244. Ito T, Suzuki T, Wellman SE, Ho IK. Pharmacology of barbiturate tolerance/dependence: GABAA receptors and molecular aspects. *Life Sci* 1996;59(3):169–95.

245. Coupey SM. Barbiturates. *Pediatr Rev* 1997;18(8):260–4.

246. Kurtzman TL, Otsuka KN, Wahl RA. Inhalant abuse by adolescents. *J Adolesc Health* 2001;28(3):170–80.

247. Brouette T, Anton R. Clinical review of inhalants. *Am J Addict* 2001;10(1):79–94.

248. Ron MA. Volatile substance abuse: a review of possible long-term neurological, intellectual and psychiatric sequelac. *Br J Psychiatry* 1986;148:235–46.

249. al-Alousi LM. Pathology of volatile substance abuse: a case report and a literature review. *Med Sci Law* 1989;29(3):189–208.

250. Meadows R, Verghese A. Medical complications of glue sniffing. *South Med J* 1996;89(5):455–62.

251. Crowe AV, Howse M, Bell GM, Henry JA. Substance abuse and the kidney. *QJM* 2000;93(3):147–52.

252. Rosenberg NL, Grigsby J, Dreisbach J, Busenbark D, Grigsby P. Neuropsychologic impairment and MRI abnormalities associated with chronic solvent abuse. *J Toxicol Clin Toxicol* 2002;40(1):21–34.

253. Kucuk NO, Kilic EO, Ibis E, Aysev A, Gencoglu EA, Aras G, et al. Brain SPECT findings in long-term inhalant abuse. *Nucl Med Commun* 2000;21(8):769–73.

254. Kamran S, Bakshi R. MRI in chronic toluene abuse: low signal in the cerebral cortex on T2-weighted images. *Neuroradiology* 1998;40(8):519–21.

255. Uitti RJ, Snow BJ, Shinotoh H, Vingerhoets FJ, Hayward M, Hashimoto S, et al. Parkinsonism induced by solvent abuse. *Ann Neurol* 1994;35(5):616–9.

256. Schuckit MA. *Drug and Alcohol Abuse*. 3 ed. New York: Plenum Press; 1989.

257. Olson KR, Pentel PR, Kelly MT. Physical agreement and differential diagnosis of the poisoned patient. *Med Toxicol* 1987;2:52–81.

258. Albertson TE. Barbiturates. In: Olson KR, Ed. *Poisoning and Drug Overdose*. 3 ed. Stamford, CT: Appleton & Lange; 1999.

8.2 EMERGENCY MANAGEMENT OF DRUG ABUSE

Brett A. Roth, M.D.,[1] Neal L. Benowitz, M.D.,[2] and Kent R. Olson, M.D.[2]
[1] University of Texas Southwestern Medical Center, Dallas, Texas
[2] Division of Clinical Pharmacology and Experimental Therapeutics, University of California, San Francisco, California

The management of complications from drug abuse demands a variety of skills from airway management to control of seizures and shock. Several reviews have addressed the issues of general resuscitation[1-3] and toxidromes.[4-8] The purpose of this chapter is to present a series of management strategies for the emergency physician or other clinical personnel caring for patients with acute complications from drug abuse. Immediate interventions (e.g., resuscitation and stabilization), secondary interventions (e.g., emergency care after the patient is stable), as well as diagnostic workup (e.g., laboratory data, imaging), and disposition of the patient are discussed. This chapter proposes a variety of treatment approaches based on a review of the pertinent literature and clinical experience. A general treatment approach based on symptom complex (i.e., seizures, coma, hyperthermia) is presented since initial management decisions frequently have to be made without the benefit of a reliable history. This is followed by a brief review of the each particular drug of abuse (i.e., psychostimulants, opiates, hallucinogens). The reader is referred to the previous chapter, Medical Aspects of Drug Abuse, for a detailed description of the clinical toxicology associated with each drug of abuse.

It should be emphasized that the adverse reaction to a drug may depend on the unique characteristics of an individual (i.e., presence of cardiovascular disease) as well as the type of drug abused. These protocols serve as guidelines only and an individualized approach to management should be made whenever possible.

8.2.1   Decreased Mental Status: Coma, Stupor, and Lethargy

8.2.1.1   General Comments

In the setting of drug overdose, coma usually reflects global depression of the brain's cerebral cortex. This can be a direct effect of the drug on specific neurotransmitters or receptors or an indirect process such as trauma or asphyxia. Treatment deals largely with maintaining a functional airway, the administration of potential antidotes, and evaluation for underlying medical conditions. The following section describes the appropriate use of antidotes and the approach to the patient with a decreased level of consciousness from drug abuse.

Level vs. content of consciousness: It is often useful to distinguish between the *level* and the *content* of consciousness. Alertness and wakefulness refer to the level of consciousness; awareness is a reflection of the content of consciousness.[9] In referring to coma, stupor, and lethargy here we address the level of consciousness as it applies to the drug-abusing patient along a clinical spectrum with deep coma on one end, stupor in the middle, and lethargy representing a mildly decreased level of consciousness. Agitation, delirium, and psychosis is addressed in a subsequent section with a greater focus on *content* of consciousness, i.e., presence or absence of hallucinations, paranoia, severe depression, etc.

Attributes of a good antidote: The ideal antidote should be safe, effective, rapidly acting, and easy to administer. It should also have low abuse potential, and act as long as the intoxicating drug. The following standard antidotes are of potentially great benefit and little harm in all patients.

Thiamine: Thiamine is an important cofactor for several metabolic enzymes that are vital for the metabolism of carbohydrates and for the proper function of the pentose–phosphate pathway.[10] When thiamine is absent or deficient, Wernicke's encephalopathy, classically described as a triad of oculomotor abnormalities, ataxia, and global confusion, may result. Although Wernicke's is rare, empiric treatment for this disease is safe,[11] inexpensive (wholesale price of 100 mg of thiamine is approximately $1), and cost-effective.[12]

Dextrose: Hypoglycemia is a common cause of coma or stupor and should be assessed or treated empirically in all patients with deceased level of consciousness. Concerns about 50% dextrose causing an increase in infarct size and mortality in stroke,[13–15] as well as increasing serum hypertonicity in hyperosmolar patients, have been raised when arguing the benefits of routine administration of 50% dextrose. Animal models of stroke[16] that showed worse outcomes associated with hyperglycemic subjects used large doses of dextrose (approximately 2 mg/kg) as opposed to the 0.3 g/kg (25 g in a 70-kg adult) routinely given as part of the coma cocktail. Also, one ampoule of 50% dextrose in water should only raise the serum glucose level of a 70-kg patient by about 60 mg/dl (0.3 mOsm) if it distributes into total body water prior to any elimination or metabolism.[17]

Naloxone: A 19th-century method for treating opiate overdose:

The surface of the body may be stimulated by whipping,... the patient should be made to walk around for 6–8 hours[18]

Shoemaker, 1896

Fortunately, the use of modern antidotes such as naloxone can provide a more effective and less abusive reversal of opiate-induced narcosis. In addition to reversing respiratory depression and eliminating the need for airway interventions, naloxone may assist in the diagnosis of opiate overdose and eliminate the need for diagnostic studies such as lumbar puncture and computed tomography (CT) scanning. Despite its advances over 19th-century treatments for narcotic overdose, naloxone may not always be the best approach to management. The risk of "unmasking," or exposing the effects of dangerous co-ingestions such as cocaine or PCP[19] and of precipitating opiate withdrawal must be considered. The main effects of naloxone include the reversal of coma and respiratory depression induced by *exogenous* opiates, but it also reverses miosis, analgesia, bradycardia, and gastrointestinal stasis.[20] Presumably related to the reversal of the effects of *endogenous* opioid peptides, such as endorphins and enkephalins, naloxone has also been reported to have nonspecific benefit (e.g., reversing properties) for the treatment of ethanol, clonidine, captopril, and valproic acid.[21–24] These "nonspecific" responses are usually not as complete as a true reversal of opiate-induced coma by naloxone. The current literature raises many serious concerns about the safety of naloxone. Pulmonary edema,[25–30] hypertension,[31–33] seizures,[34] arrhythmias,[33,35] and cardiac arrest[36] have been reported following naloxone administration. In addition, reversing the sedating effects of a drug like heroin may produce acute withdrawal symptoms,[37] which, although they are not life-threatening, can cause the patient to become agitated, demanding, or even violent.[38] Considering the great number of patients who have received large doses of naloxone as part of controlled trials for shock,[39–42] stroke,[43–46] and spinal cord injuries,[47–49] as part of healthy volunteer studies,[50,51] and for overdose management,[52,53] all without significant complications, the use of naloxone appears relatively safe.[17] Opioid withdrawal symptoms commonly occur in addicted patients given naloxone.[37] While withdrawal symptoms are treatable, the best approach is avoidance. Withdrawal symptoms may be avoided either by (1) withholding opioid antagonists from known drug addicts and supporting the airway with traditional methods (e.g., endotracheal intubation) or (2) by titrating the dose of naloxone slowly such that enough antidote is given to arouse the patient but not to precipitate withdrawal. The latter can be done by administering small doses (0.2 to 0.4 mg) intravenously in a repetitive manner. While conjunctival[54] and nasal[55,56] testing for opioid addiction have been described, these tests are impractical in the patient with altered mental status in whom immediate action is necessary.

Nalmefene: Nalmefene ($t_{1/2}$ = 8 to 9 hours) is a methylene analogue of naltrexone that, like naloxone, is a pure opioid antagonist. It was developed to address concerns about the short duration of action of naloxone (~60 min). Studies have proved it to be as safe and effective with a duration of action at least twice as long as naloxone.[57] Other reports suggest a duration of action of up to 4 h.[57–59] However, 4 h is still not long enough to safely manage patients who have overdosed on long-lasting opiates such as methadone ($t_{1/2}$ up to 48 h) or propoxyphene ($t_{1/2}$ of active metabolite up to 36 h), or in those patients with delayed absorption. The use of nalmefene may potentially be advantageous due to (1) less risk of recurrent respiratory depression in the patient who leaves the emergency department against medical advise, (2) fewer doses of antagonist needed, cutting down on nursing time, and (3) fewer complications resulting from fluctuations in levels of consciousness (e.g., sedation, aspiration, occult respiratory insufficiency).[60] The dose is 0.25 to 1.0 mg IVP, with the lower dose recommended to avoid opiate withdrawal. The disadvantage of nalmefene is its cost (average wholesale price of nalmefene is $31.21/1 mg versus $5.52/0.4 mg of naloxone). Current use of nalmefene has been limited to the reversal of procedural sedation,[61] alcohol dependence,[62] and avoidance of opiate side effects in patients receiving epidural analgesia.[63]

Flumazenil: Flumazenil is a highly selective competitive inhibitor of benzodiazepines at the GABA/benzodiazepine-receptor complex.[64] Like naloxone it is a pure antagonist lacking agonist properties or abuse potential. It has been shown to be safe and effective for the reversal of benzodiazepine-induced sedation in volunteer studies[65] and in patients undergoing short procedures such as endoscopy.[66–70] There has been some debate about the role of flumazenil in the treatment of patients presenting with an acute drug overdose. Although initially recommended with caution for this population,[71,72] recent advice would be to administer it only when there is a reliable history of benzodiazepine ingestion and the likelihood of a significant proconvulsant or proarrhythmic coingestion or benzodiazepine dependency is limited. Adverse effects including precipitation of benzodiazepine withdrawal,[73,74] seizures,[75–78] ballism,[79] arrhythmias,[80,81] and even death[82,83] have occurred. In a review of 43 cases of seizure activity associated with flumazenil administration, 42% of the patients had ingested overdoses of cyclic antidepressants.[75] In addition to patients with concurrent cyclic antidepressant poisoning, *high-risk populations* include patients who have been receiving benzodiazepines for a seizure disorder or an acute convulsive episode, patients with concurrent major sedative–hypnotic drug withdrawal, patients who have recently been treated with repeated doses of parenteral benzodiazepines, and overdose patients with myoclonic jerking or seizure activity before flumazenil administration.[75] To minimize the likelihood of a seizure, it is recommended that flumazenil not be administered to patients who have used benzodiazepines for the treatment of seizure disorders or to patients who have ingested drugs that place them at risk for the development of seizures[75] (e.g., cyclic antidepressants, cocaine, amphetamines, diphenhydramine, lithium, methylxanthines, isoniazid, propoxyphene, buproprion HCl, etc.). As with naloxone, flumazenil may also uncover the effects of a more serious intoxication such as cocaine making the patient unmanageable. Because benzodiazepine overdoses are associated with only rare mortality[84] and only mild morbidity (the major complication being aspiration pneumonia),[85] a conservative approach with supportive airway maneuvers (e.g., endotracheal intubation) seems safest. Despite concerns over side effects, the use of flumazenil in patients with acute overdose is justified under certain circumstances. When there is a reliable history of a single drug ingestion supported by clinical manifestations consistent with benzodiazepine intoxication, and the likelihood of a significant proconvulsant or proarrhythmic co-ingestion or benzodiazepine dependency is limited, reversal of sedation may be warranted.[17] One case report described continuous flumazenil infusion for 16 days without adverse effects for clonazepam-induced sedation.[86] Errors can be avoided by obtaining a thorough history and by performing a thorough physical examination as well as a screening electrocardiogram to exclude the possibility of significant cyclic antidepressant intoxication; correction of hypoxia, hypotension, acidosis, and arrhythmias; and then by administering the agent slowly. Greenblatt[85] showed that of 99 cases in which patients overdosed on benzodiazepines only 12 were known to ingest benzodiazepines alone. Given the high incidence of co-ingestions in the drug-abusing population the risk for unmasking proconvulsants such as cocaine or amphetamine must be considered high. It is interesting that flumazenil has been credited with the reversal of paradoxical benzodiazepine-induced agitation[87] and hepatic encephalopathy[88] and that it is being investigated as a treatment aid for benzodiazepine withdrawal.[89]

8.2.1.2   Stepwise Approach to Management

Immediate Interventions

1. Airway, Breathing, Circulation: Maintain the airway and assist ventilation if necessary. Administer supplemental oxygen. Treat hypotension, and resuscitate as per previous reviews.[2,90]

2. Thiamine: Administer thiamine,100 mg IVP over 2 min to all the following patients:

a. Patients with altered mental status if the patient has signs or symptoms of Wernicke's encephalopathy

   b. Patients who are malnourished[91]
   c. Patients with a history of alcoholism[10]
   d. Patients with prolonged history of vomiting[92]
   e. Patients who are chronically ill[93]

Comment: There is no need to withhold hypertonic dextrose (D_{50}, D_{25}) until thiamine administration since thiamine uptake into cells is slower than the entry of dextrose into cells.[94] Previous reports describing adverse reactions to IV thiamine[95] have recently been disputed. In a review by Wrenn et al.[11] the incidence of adverse reactions to IV thiamine ($n = 989$) was 1.1% and consisted of transient local irritation in all patients except one who developed generalized pruritis. Thiamine may also be administered intramuscularly (IM) or by mouth (po).

3. Dextrose

Bedside fingerstick glucose level: Perform rapid bedside testing in all patients. If hypoglycemia is detected then the patient should receive hypertonic dextrose (25 g of 50% hypertonic dextrose solution IVP).

Comment: This approach avoids giving dextrose solution to patients who do not need it (eliminating concerns that hyperglycemia impairs cerebral resuscitation) and detects the vast majority of hypoglycemic patients. Relying on physical signs and symptoms such as tachycardia and diaphoresis in combination with a history of diabetes mellitus is an unreliable way to predict hypoglycemia, missing up to 25% of hypoglycemic patients.[17]

Borderline rapid assay results: In any patient with borderline rapid assay results (60 to 100 mg/dl) a decision on whether or not to treat should be based on the clinical suspicion of hypoglycemia and a repeat rapid assay. Alternatively, simply treat all patients with borderline blood sugar results.

Comment: Rapid reagent assays for blood glucose may, at times, be inaccurate. Failure to detect hypoglycemia has been described in 6 to 8% of patients tested in the prehospital setting,[96,97] but results are generally more accurate inside of the hospital. False-negative results have also been reported in neonatal populations[98] and in patients with severe anemia.[99] False-positive tests (false hypoglycemia) has occurred in patients with severe peripheral vascular disease,[100] shock,[101] and hyperthermia.[102] Because most errors occur in patients with borderline glucose readings (60 to 100 mg/dl),[17] the recommendation to treat borderline glucose values is made. This also makes sense in light of recent reports that describe individual variability in response to borderline hypoglycemia;[103] e.g., patients with poorly controlled diabetes mellitus may experience clinical symptoms of hypoglycemia at greater glucose concentrations than nondiabetics.

Empiric treatment: In patients where rapid bedside testing for serum glucose is not available, administer 25 g of 50% hypertonic dextrose solution IVP after collecting a specimen of blood for glucose analysis at a later time.

4. Naloxone/Nalmefene:

   a. **Restraint:** Consider restraining and disrobing the patient prior to administration.
   b. **Antidote:** All patients with classic signs (RR < 12, pupils miotic, needle marks) and symptoms of opioid intoxication should receive naloxone.

      Comment: Because of nalmefene's expense, naloxone is generally recommended. Nalmefene may be advantageous in the patient who leaves the emergency department against medical advice or if close monitoring of the patient is not possible. The usual initial dose is 0.25 mg IV followed by repeated doses until adequate response is achieved.

      Comment: Hoffman et al.,[104] using a clinical criteria of respiratory rate less than 12 breaths/min, circumstantial evidence of opioid abuse, or miosis, decreased the use of naloxone by 75 to 90% while still administering it to virtually all naloxone responders who had a final diagnosis of opiate overdose.

   c. **Initial Doses:** Small doses (0.2 to 0.4 mg IV of naloxone) should be given to patients who are breathing, and at possible risk for withdrawal. If no response, repeat or titrate the same dose IV every minute until 2.0 mg of naloxone or 1.0 mg of nalmefene have been given or the patient wakes up.

Table 8.2.1   Half-Lives and Observation Times Required after Acute Narcotic Overdose

Opioid	Duration of Action via IV Route	$t_{1/2}$	Observation Time (h)
Propoxyphene (Darvon, Doloxene)	May be >24 h	6-12[a]	24
Methadone (Dolophine, Amidone)	May be days	15[b]–72[c]	24–36 or longer
Morphine	Usually 2–4 h	3	6
Heroin	Usually 2–4 h	Very short[d]	6
Fentanyl (Sublimaze)	Minutes	4	6
Codeine	2–4 h (oral)	3[d]	6
Meperidine (Demerol)	2–4 h	2.5	6
Pentazocine (Talwin)	2–4 h	2	6
Dextromethorphan	2–4 h (oral)	6–29	4

Note: Generally, if patients remain asymptomatic 6 h after the administration of naloxone, they may be discharged.

[a] About 1/2 of dose is metabolized to norproxyphene, an active metabolite with a $t_{1/2}$ of 30–36 h.
[b] Single dose.
[c] Repeated dosing.
[d] Rapidly deacetylated to morphine.

Comment: If the patient is not suspected to be at risk for opiate withdrawal (i.e., most children) and there is no risk of unmasking a dangerous co-intoxicant such as cocaine or phencyclidine (PCP), 2.0 mg of naloxone may be given initially.

d. **High-dose antidote:** If there is still no response to a total of 2.0 mg of naloxone and opiate overdose is highly suspected by history or clinical presentation, one can give 10 to 20 mg of naloxone in one bolus dose. Certain opiates (i.e., propoxyphene, pentazocine, diphenoxylate, butorphanol, nalbuphine, codeine) may require larger doses of naloxone due to higher affinity for the kappa receptors.[105]

Comment: Reversal of opioid toxicity, once achieved, will be sustained for approximately 20 to 60 min ($t_{1/2}$ = 1 h). Because the duration of action of most opioids exceeds the duration of action of naloxone, the patient may require repeated bolus doses or to be started on a continuous infusion at a dose sufficient to prevent the reappearance of respiratory depression (see Section 8.2.10.2 on opiates).

Comment: A true response to naloxone or nalmefene is a dramatic improvement. Anything less should be considered a sign of a coexisting intoxication or illness, a nonspecific improvement from the reversal of endogenous opiates, or the presence of anoxic encephalopathy from prolonged respiratory depression. If dramatic improvement is noted, further management depends on the type on narcotic involved and the amount taken (Table 8.2.1).

e. **Dose in respiratory arrest:** Patients with respiratory arrest should either be given larger does (0.4 to 2.0 mg of naloxone) or endotracheally intubated and artificially ventilated.

Comment: Naloxone is easily administered via the IV, IM, intratracheal,[105] intralingual,[106] or even the intranasal[56] routes. The intravenous route is preferred since it allows more exact titration and because it provides for a rapid onset of action (about 1 min) and predictable delivery of drug. The intramuscular route (1.0 to 2.0 mg) usually works within minutes, but makes titration more difficult and takes longer to work (5 to 10 min). It may be advantageous in the prehospital setting. The intralingual route, with antidote given near the venous plexus on the ventral lateral tongue, may work as rapidly as the intravenous route, but does not allow for titration of dosage.

f. **Aspiration:** Guard against aspiration.

5. Flumazenil

a. **Caution:** Because of a higher incidence of severe adverse effects flumazenil should be used only under the limited circumstances described previously.

b. **Restraint:** Consider restraining and disrobing the patient prior to administering antidote.

c. **Antidote:** If a pure benzodiazepine overdose is suspected, treat hypoxia, hypotension, acidosis, and arrhythmias and check a 12-lead electrocardiogram (ECG) for QRS widening. If the ECG is normal, and the patient has no known seizure disorders, *and* is not taking proconvulsant medications, flumazenil may be administered.

   Comment: Generally flumazenil should be used only to reverse serious respiratory depression. Its use is not advised to waken a stable, mildly somnolent patient. If serious respiratory depression does exist, consider endotracheal intubation and mechanical ventilation as an alternative to flumazenil.

   Comment: In a study of 50 patients treated with flunitrazepam ($t_{1/2}$ = 20 to 29 h) Claeys et al.[107] showed that 90 min after administration of flumazenil significant recurrent sedation was observed in healthy patients undergoing orthopedic surgery. Because the binding of flumazenil to the benzodiazepine-receptor complex is competitive, and because flumazenil has a much shorter duration of action ($t_{1/2}$ = 40 to 80 min) than most benzodiazepines, patients should be closely monitored for resedation.

d. **Dose:** Give flumazenil 0.2 mg over 30 s, to be followed 30 s later by 0.3 mg if the patient does not respond. Subsequent doses of 0.5 mg may also be given although most patients respond to less than 1.0 mg.[108] Although the manufacturers recommend the administration of up to 3 mg we recommend a maximal dosage of 1.0 mg in the drug-abusing patient at high risk for withdrawal.

   Comment: As long as flumazenil is administered slowly with a total dose of less than 1 mg, only 50% of benzodiazepine receptors will be occupied by the drug.[109] In theory, this should prevent the severe manifestations of withdrawal associated with higher doses.[17]

Secondary Interventions

1. Reassess: If the patient remains comatose, stuporous, or lethargic despite antidotes, reassess for underlying medical causes (meningitis, trauma, epilepsy, etc.) and admit to hospital.

2. Monitor: Maintain continuous monitoring (cardiac status, oxygen saturation, blood pressure) at all times.

Comment: This is particularly important since the duration of action of most narcotics and benzodiazepines of abuse is much longer than the duration of action of their respective antidote.

3. CT/lumbar puncture: Consider CT and lumbar puncture if the patient is febrile or has persistently decreased level of consciousness or focal neurological findings.

4. ECG: Perform an ECG on all elderly patients.

5. Laboratory Data: For patients who respond to antidotes and return to their baseline mental status within an observation period of several hours, no laboratory testing may be necessary given a normal physical examination on reassessment. If the patient remains persistently altered or has significantly abnormal vital signs check electrolytes, CBC, CPK, CPK-MB, renal function, and possibly hepatic function. While the use of toxicology screens of blood and urine are generally overutilized,[5] they are recommended if the diagnosis remains questionable.

6. Disposition

   Admission: All patients who have required more than one dose of antidote to maintain their mental status should be admitted for further evaluation and therapy including possible infusion of naloxone or flumazenil.

   Comment: Infusions should be maintained in an *intensive care setting* and patients should be closely monitored any time the infusion is stopped. Duration of observation depends on the route of drug administration, the drug ingested, the presence or absence of liver dysfunction, and the possibility of ongoing drug absorption from the gastrointestinal tract. Usually 6 h is adequate.

   Flumazenil infusion: Infuse 0.2 to 0.5 h in maintenance fluids (D5W, D51/2NS, 1/2NS, NS), adjusting rate to provide the desired level of arousal. Hojer et al.[110] demonstrated that infusions of 0.5 mg/h were well tolerated and that this dose prevented patients with severe benzodiazepine poisoning from relapsing into coma after arousal with a single bolus injection.

   Naloxone infusion: Goldfrank et al.[111] suggest taking two thirds the amount of naloxone required for the patient to initially wake up and administering that amount at an hourly rate in the patient's maintenance IV (D5W, D51/2NS, 1/2NS, NS). Based on the half-life of naloxone this regimen will maintain the plasma naloxone levels at or greater than those that would have existed 30 min after the bolus dose.[111,112]

Example: The patient responds to 3 mg of naloxone initially. Add 20 mg naloxone to 1 L maintenance fluids and run at 100 cc/h thus delivering 2 mg naloxone/h (e.g., 2/3 the initial dose per hour).

7. Discharge: Stable patients who have regained normal mental status and have normal (or near normal) laboratory data may be observed for a period of time, which depends on the drug ingested (see Table 8.2.1 for recommended observation period after opioid overdose) and underlying conditions. Usually if the patient is awake and alert *6 h* after administration of antidote, the patient may be safely discharged if there is no further drug absorption from the gastrointestinal tract.

8.2.2   Agitation, Delirium, and Psychosis

8.2.2.1   *General Comments*

Confounders: Rapid control of drug-induced agitation, delirium, or psychosis is one of the most difficult skills to master when dealing with complications of drug abuse. The use of sedation and restraints is fraught with a host of ethical and legal issues.[113–116] Safety issues for the patient as well as the medical staff must be considered. Numerous reports of injuries to emergency department personnel[117,118] exist. Diagnostic confusion may occur since agitation or delirium may be the result of a drug overdose alone, or may be from a medical problem combined with drug intoxication (i.e., myocardial infarction from cocaine abuse), or simply a medical problem masquerading as drug abuse (i.e., meningitis). Finally, failing to understand the differences between agitation, psychosis, and delirium (see following discussion) often leads to incorrect management schemes. Regardless of the cause, effective, compassionate, and rapid control of agitation is necessary to decrease the incidence of serious complications and to provide a thorough evaluation of the patient. One can never safely say that the patient was "too agitated" or "too uncooperative" to assess.

Delirium vs. psychosis with and without agitation: Altered sensorium (disorientation and confusion) and visual hallucinations are characteristic of *delirium*. In contrast, *psychosis* is associated with paranoia, auditory hallucinations, and usually an intact sensorium.[5] *Agitation* (physical or psychic perturbation) may complicate either delirium or psychosis and is commonly seen in patients with stimulant overdose. Differentiating between delirium and psychosis with or without agitation and agitation alone is useful because it may suggest specific groups of drugs and potentially, specific treatment.[5] For example, a patient with anticholinergic poisoning from Jimson weed typically has delirium with confusion and disorientation, while an amphetamine- or cocaine-intoxicated person usually has paranoid psychosis with agitation, but is oriented. Physostigmine is useful in the diagnosis of anticholinergic syndrome,[119] but would not be helpful for amphetamine- or cocaine-induced agitation. Agitation from stimulants should be treated with benzodiazepines, while psychosis alone can be treated with haloperidol with or without benzodiazepines.

Benzodiazepines vs. neuroleptics: There is significant controversy regarding the optimal choice of sedating agents. Much research has dealt directly with agitated patients in the psychiatric setting,[120–122] but no controlled clinical studies of benzodiazepines or neuroleptic medications in treating strictly drug-induced agitation have been described. Animal research[123–125] and human experience[126] support the use of *benzodiazepines* for cocaine-induced agitation as well as generalized anxiety.[127,128] Neuroleptics (e.g., haloperidol) have been shown to decrease the lethal effects of amphetamines in rats[129–131] and chlorpromazine was found to be effective in treating a series of 22 children with severe amphetamine poisoning.[132] Many of the children exhibited seizures before receiving chlorpromazine, but ongoing motor activity was reduced in all cases. These data are consistent with the observation that chlorpromazine antagonizes cocaine-induced seizures in dogs.[123] Callaway et al.[133] argue that neuroleptics have been used safely in other patient populations at risk for seizures, such as the treatment of alcoholic hallucinosis during alcohol withdrawal.[134] Concerns about neuroleptics potentiating drug-induced seizures may therefore be exaggerated. Butyrophenone neuroleptics such as haloperidol have less effect on seizure thresholds than do phenothiazines such as chlorpromazine[135] and also produce less interference with sweat-mediated evaporative cooling (e.g., anticholinergic effect) in cases of drug-induced hyperthermia.[133] Hoffman[136] has argued against the use of haloperidol for cocaine intoxication on the basis of controlled animal studies showing haloperidol failed to improve survival, and *possibly* increased lethality.[137] He also argues that haloperidol causes a variety of physiologic responses that limit heat loss. These include (1) presynaptic dopamine-2 (D_2) receptor blockage, causing a loss of inhibition of norepinephrine release and increased central and peripheral adrenergic activity; (2) hypothalamic D_2 blockade causing direct inhibition of central heat dissipating mechanisms; and (3) anticholinergic effects causing loss of evaporative cooling via loss of sweat. The risk of a dystonic reaction, which has been associated with fatal laryngospasm[138,139] and rhabdomyolysis,[140] is also of concern. Acute dystonia, which is more common in young males,[141] could severely impair a resuscitation attempt and may aggravate hyperthermia. Interestingly, the incidence of dystonic reactions from neuroleptic agents has been shown to be dramatically reduced when benzodiazepines are coadministered.[142] Recently the use of the atypical antipsychotic agent ziprazidone has been recommended for controlling acute psychotic agitation. Although study populations are mixed, they are primarily composed of psychiatric patients with functional, as opposed to drug-induced psychosis. Nevertheless, ziprazidone has not been associated with hyperthermia, dystonia, nor the anticholinergic effects of haloperidol. Studies suggest beneficial effects similar to lorazepam or haloperidol with less sedation.[143–145]

Recommendations: Because of the complex neuropharmacology associated with agitation, delirium, and psychosis in the drug abusing patient our preference is a selective approach based on symptom complex:

> **Severe agitation:** In cases of severe agitation, regardless of underlying delirium or psychosis, we recommend starting with benzodiazepines due to their proven safety and known ability to increase the seizure threshold. They should be given in incremental doses until the patient is appropriately sedated and large doses should not be withheld as long as the blood pressure remains stable and the airway is secure. If respiratory depression occurs, the patient should be endotracheally intubated and mechanically ventilated.[136]

> **Psychosis:** If severe agitation includes marked psychotic features or there is known amphetamine or amphetamine-derivative overdose (i.e., 3,4-methylenedioxymethamphetamine or MDMA), or if the major symptom complex has psychotic features, then haloperidol may be used. Due to synergistic effects[122] and to decrease the incidence of dystonic reactions,[142] haloperidol should be administered in combination with a benzodiazepine. Anticholinergic agents (i.e., benztropine) reduce the incidence of dystonic reactions;[146] however, because of the potential to confuse an anticholinergic syndrome with psychosis[147] and because anticholinergic agents limit heat dissipation, they are not routinely recommended.

> **Delirium:** As long as agitation is not prominent the administration of low dose benzodiazepines, or observation alone, is usually adequate to control symptoms of mild delirium until drug effects wear off. Intramuscular ziprazidone may also be considered in this setting. In selected anticholinergic poisonings involving uncontrollable agitation or severe hyperthermia, physostigmine (0.5 to 1.0 mg slow IV push) should be considered.[148] Physostigmine may potentiate the effects of depolarizing neuromuscular-blocking agents (e.g., succinylcholine decamethonium)[149,150] and may have additive depressant effects on cardiac conduction in patients with cyclic antidepressant overdose.[151,152] Its use is therefore contraindicated in patients with tricyclic antidepressant poisoning and poisoning that impairs cardiac conduction. Physostigmine may induce arousal in patients with benzodiazepine or sedative-hypnotic intoxication[153] due to its nonspecific analeptic effects.

> **A word of caution:** Control of agitation, delirium, and psychosis is important, but even more important is the treatment of the underlying cause. Algorithms for detecting hypoxia, hypotension, and hypoglycemia still apply. In the mentally unstable patient, who will not allow evaluation or examination, physical restraint and the liberal use of benzodiazepines (see below) may be necessary.

8.2.2.2 Stepwise Approach to Management

Immediate Interventions

1. Airway, Breathing, Circulation: Maintain the airway and assist ventilation if necessary. Administer supplemental oxygen. Treat hypotension, and resuscitate as per previous reviews.[90]

2. Antidotes: Administer appropriate antidotes, including 25 g dextrose IV if the patient is hypoglycemic, as per the section on coma. If the patient does not allow assessment and stabilization, proceed as follows (once the patient is under control, reassess the need for antidotes).

3. Reduction of environmental stimuli: If possible attempt calming the patient by eliminating excessive noise, light, and physical stimulation. Generally, this is all that is necessary for the treatment of panic attacks from mild cocaine overdose, or from certain hallucinogens such as LSD or marijuana.[148,154] Talk to the patient and attempt to address the patient's immediate needs (minor pain, anxiety, need to use the bathroom). An offer of food or water may calm the patient and avoid further confrontation. Gay et al.[154] from the Haight-Ashbury Free Medical Clinics, in San Francisco, have described the "ART" technique as a way of establishing credibility with the intoxicated patient:

> *A = Acceptance.* Acceptance disarms patients who may already be experiencing fear of their surroundings or paranoid ideation.
>
> *R = Reduction of stimuli, rest, and reassurance.* If patients are stable and symptoms are mild, place them in a quiet surrounding, and reassure them that they are going to be all right as you proceed to assess them. If patients are dangerous or seriously ill, control them with physical and/or medical restraints (see following section). When stable, proceed to eliminate any source of obvious distraction or distress (too many people in the resuscitation room, bright lights, loud noises, etc.).
>
> *T = Talkdown technique.* Use verbal sincerity, concern, and a gentle approach since drug abusers can misinterpret insincere and/or abrupt actions as being hostile. If patients are obviously beyond reason or dangerous *do not attempt to "talk them down."* Generally, this step should be restricted to patients who are oriented and simply frightened. It is also *not* recommended for patients who have taken phencyclidine (PCP) due to the unpredictable effects of this drug.[155] Staff members should be careful to never position themselves with a potentially violent or distraught patient between them and the door.

4. Sedation: Medical management may be necessary if the patient remains uncooperative. Explain to the patient your intention to use medications.

5. Paralysis: If significant hyperthermia occurs as a result of excessive muscular hyperactivity, or if significant risk for spinal injury is present, consider early skeletal muscle paralysis (see discussion under hyperthermia). Procedures for the rapid sequence induction for airway management and paralysis are reviewed elsewhere.[2]

6. Physical restraints: Restraint has proven efficacy in reducing injury and agitation.[156] If the patient continues to be uncooperative, rapidly gain control of the individual using several trained staff and physical restraints (Table 8.2.2 on restraining technique and Table 8.2.3 on universal precautions). Empty the room of all extraneous and/or potentially dangerous objects and apply the restraints in a humane and professional manner.[157] The method of restraint should be the least restrictive necessary for the protection of the patient and others.[113]

Secondary Interventions

1. Insert IV, monitor: Once the patient is restrained insert an intravenous line, and assess vital signs.

2. Assess underlying medical conditions: Draw blood and assess for serious medical conditions. Rule out metabolic disturbances (e.g., hypoxia, hypoglycemia, hyponatremia, thyrotoxicosis,

Table 8.2.2   Patient Management with Use of Restraints

A. Rehearse strategies before employing these techniques.

B. Use restraints sooner rather than later and thoroughly document all actions.

C. Remember universal precautions (see Table 8.2.3).

D. Use restraints appropriately. The use of overwhelming force will often be all that is necessary to preclude a fight.

    1. When it is time to subdue the patient, approach him or her with at least five persons, each with a prearranged task.

    2. Grasp the clothing and the large joints to attempt to "sandwich" the patient between two mattresses.

    3. Place the patient on the stretcher face down to reduce leverage and to make it difficult for the patient to lash out.

    4. Remove the patient's shoes or boots.

    5. In exceptional circumstances, as when the patient is biting, grasp the hair firmly.

    6. Avoid pressure to the chest, throat, or neck.

E. The specific type of restraint used (hands, cloth, leather, etc.) is determined by the amount of force needed to subdue (i.e., use hard restraints for PCP-induced psychoses).

F. Keep in mind, when using physical restraints, that the minimum amount of force necessary is the maximum that ethical practice allows. The goal is to restrain, not to injure. Restraining ties should be adequate but not painfully constricting when applied (being able to slip your finger underneath is a good standard). The restrained patient should be observed in a safe, quiet room away from the other patients; however, the patient must be reevaluated frequently, as the physical condition of restrained patients could deteriorate.

Source: From Wasserberger, J. et al., *Top. Emerg. Med.*, 14, 71, 1992. With permission.

Table 8.2.3   Universal Precautions

1. Appropriate barrier precautions should be routinely used when contact with blood or other body fluids is anticipated. Wear gloves. Masks and eye protection are indicated if mucous membranes of the mouth, eyes, and nose may be exposed to drops of blood or other body fluids. Gowns should be worn if splashes of blood are likely.

2. Hands and skin should be washed immediately if contaminated. Wash hands as soon as gloves are removed.

3. Exercise care in handling all sharps during procedures, when cleaning them, and during disposal. Never recap or bend needles. Carefully dispose of sharps in specially designed containers.

4. Use a bag-valve-mask to prevent the need for mouth-to-mouth resuscitation. Such devices should be readily available.

5. Health care workers with weeping dermatitis should avoid direct patient care until the condition resolves.

6. Because of the risk of perinatal HIV transmission, pregnant health care workers should strictly adhere to all universal precautions.

Note: In its 1987 recommendations, the Centers for Disease Control (CDC) stated that universal precautions "should be used in the care of all patients, especially including those in emergency-care settings in which the risk of blood exposure is increased and the infection status of the patient is usually unknown." The CDC stipulated the six basic universal precautions above.

uremia), alcohol or sedative-hypnotic withdrawal, CNS infection (e.g., meningitis, encephalitis) or tumor, hyperthermia, postictal state, trauma, etc.

    3. Frequent reassessment: Any patient left in physical restraints must have frequent reassessments of vital signs, neurological status, and physical examination.[113] Sudden death, and asphyxiation, have occurred in individuals while in restraints.[115,158–160]

    4. Documentation: The patient's danger to him- or herself, degree of agitation, specific threats, and verbal hostilities should all be documented in case of future charges by the patient that the patient was improperly restrained against his or her will (i.e., battery). Documentation should include the reasons for, and means of, restraint and the periodic assessment (minimum of every 20 min) of the restrained patient. Legal doctrines pertinent to involuntary treatment have been reviewed elsewhere.[116]

    5. Medications: Sedation is necessary for patients struggling vigorously against restraints, or for patients who are persistently agitated, hyperthermic, panicking, or hyperadrenergic. Consider one of the following sedatives or combinations: See previous discussion under general comments.

Lorazepam	0.05–0.10 mg (2–7 mg) IM or IV initially over 1–2 min	May repeat doses every 5 min until sedation is achieved
Diazepam	to 0.20 mg/kg (5–10 mg) IV initially over 1–2 min	May repeat doses every 5 min until sedation is achieved Diazepam is not recommended in patients >60 years old due to prolonged duration of action in this group
Haloperidol	0.1–0.2 mg/kg (5–10 mg) IM or IV initially over 1–2 min	May repeat dosing 5 mg every 15 min until sedation is achieved Probably safe in most overdoses although more studies are necessary to confirm
Ziprasidone	10–20 mg IM	Studies still pending for use in patients with drug-induced agitation

6. Reassess medical condition: For persistently altered mental status perform CT of the head and consider lumbar puncture. Cases involving body packers[161–163] or stuffers[164] with ongoing absorption of drug, or certain drugs that delayed absorption (i.e., belladonna alkaloids in Jimson weed[165]) may have prolonged duration of symptoms.

7. Laboratory Data: Electrolytes, CBC, BUN, Cr, CPK, CPK with MB fraction if myocardial infarction or ischemia is suspected. Consider liver function studies including PT/ PTT in severely ill patients. Rule out coagulopathy with a disseminated intravascular coagulation (DIC) panel. Obtain blood and urine cultures if hyperthermic. While the use of toxicology screens of blood and urine are generally overutilized,[5] they are recommended if the diagnosis remains questionable.

8. Disposition: Consider discharging patients who meet all the following criteria after an appropriate period of observation:

    a. Normal vital signs and mental status
    b. Normal or near normal laboratory data

Patients who have a chronically altered mental status, e.g., schizophrenia, or organic psychosis, and who are not at risk to themselves or others may be considered for discharge with appropriate psychological counseling and follow up. Patients with true delirium, or escalating agitation, or abnormal vital signs must be either admitted to the hospital or observed for further improvement.

8.2.3 Seizures

8.2.3.1 General Comments

Seizures from drug abuse have been known to be lethal[166–168] or cause permanent neurological injury.[169–171] Primate studies using baboons[172] have shown that 82 min of induced status epilepticus produced visible neuropathological injury in nonparalyzed ventilated animals. Results were similar if the baboons were paralyzed and ventilated first. In addition to the potential for direct brain injury, prolonged seizure activity may cause or aggravate hyperthermia, which can further injury to the brain and produce rhabdomyolysis.

Mechanisms: Drugs may precipitate seizures through several distinct mechanisms (Table 8.2.4). A direct CNS stimulant effect is probably the mechanism in most cocaine-, phencyclidine-, and amphetamine-induced seizures.[173,174] Seizures from these drugs generally occur *at the time of use* while seizures associated with other drugs such as alcohol, benzodiazepines, and barbiturates, generally occur during *a time of withdrawal* from chronic, high doses of the drug.[173] Other *indirect* causes of seizures exist. Cerebral infarction or hemorrhage may precipitate seizures in patients abusing cocaine or amphetamines.[175,176] Vasculitis has been associated with amphetamine and cocaine abuse and may result in seizures.[177] Intravenous drug-abusing (IVDA) patients with acquired immune deficiency syndrome (AIDS) are susceptible to CNS infections such as toxoplasmosis, cryptococcus, viral encephalitis, and syphilis or lymphoma, which can precipitate seizures. IVDA also is frequently complicated by bacterial endocarditis, septic cerebral emboli, and seizures.

Table 8.2.4 Mechanisms of Drug-Related Seizures

1. Direct CNS toxicity: Cocaine, phencyclidine, amphetamines
2. CNS hyperactivity after cessation of drug: Alcohol, barbiturates, benzodiazepines
3. Indirect CNS toxicity
    a. Trauma: subdural, epidural hematoma due to blunt force
    b. Stroke: cerebral infarct, hemorrhage, or vasculitis
    c. Infection of CNS
    d. Foreign materials (e.g., talc), other drug adulterants (see Tables 8.2.5 to 8.2.7)
    e. Systemic metabolic problems (e.g., hypoglycemia, liver, or renal failure)
    f. Post-traumatic epilepsy, or epilepsy exacerbated by drug abuse
    g. Epilepsy additional to drug use

Foreign material (e.g., talc or cotton) emboli and toxic drug by-products or expanders have been implicated[178] (Table 8.2.5 through Table 8.2.7) as well as brain trauma or closed head injury. Finally, chronic alcohol abuse often leads to systemic medical problems such as hypoglycemia, liver failure, sepsis, or meningitis, all of which may precipitate seizure activity.

Benzodiazepines: Benzodiazepines are the preferred choice for the initial control of the actively seizing patient.[179] Accordingly, pharmacological studies demonstrated that cocaine-induced seizures

Table 8.2.5 Cocaine Additives

Pharmacologically Active	Inert
Lidocaine	Inositol
Cyproheptidine	Mannitol
Methephedrine	Lactose
Diphenhydramine	Dextrose
Benzocaine	Starch
Mepivacaine	Sucrose
Aminopyrine	Sodium bicarbonate
Methapyrilene	Barium carbonate
Tetracaine	Mannose
Nicotinamide	
Ephedrine	**Volatile Compounds**
Phenylpropanolamine	
Acetaminophen	Benzene
Procaine base	Methyl ethyl ketone
Caffeine	Ether
Acetophenetidin	Acetone
1-(1-Phenylcyclohexyl)pyrrolidine	
Methaqualone	
Dyclonine	
Pyridoxine	
Codeine	
Stearic acid	
Piracetum	
Rosin (colophonum)	
Fencanfamine	
Benzoic acid	
Phenothiazines	
L-Threonine	
Heroin	
Boric acid	
Aspirin	
Dibucaine	
Propoxyphene	
Heroin[a]	
Amphetamine[a]	
Methamphetamine[a]	

[a] Considered frequent additives/coinjectants; absolute frequency unknown.

Source: Shesser, R. et al., *Am. J. Emerg. Med.* 9, 336, 1991. With permission.

Table 8.2.6   Phencyclidine Additives

Active	Inert
Phenylpropanolamine	Magnesium sulfate
Benzocaine	Ammonium chloride
Procaine	Ammonium hydroxide
Ephedrine	Phenyllithium halide
Caffeine	Phenylmagnesium halide
Piperidine	
PCC (1-piperidinocyclohexanecarbonitrile)	**Volatile**
TCP (1-[1-(2-thienyl)cyclohexyl]-piperdine)	
PCE (cyclohexamine)	Ethyl ether
PHP (phenylcyclohexylpyrrolidine)	Toluene
Ketamine	Cyclohexanol
	Isopropanol

Source: Shesser, R. et al., *Am. J. Emerg. Med.* 9, 336, 1991. With permission.

Table 8.2.7   Heroin Additives

Alkaloids	Inert
Thebaine	Starch
Acetylcodeine	Sugar
Papaverine	Calcium tartrate
Noscapine	Calcium carbonate
Narceine	Sodium carbonate
Active Nonalkaloids	Sucrose
Tolmectin	Dextrin
Quinine	Magnesium sulfate
Phenobarbital	Dextrose
Methaqualone	Lactose
Lidocaine	Barium sulfate
Phenolphthalein	Silicon dioxide
Caffeine	Vitamin C
Dextromoramide	
Chloroquine	**Volatile**
Diazepam	
Nicotinamide	Rosin
N-Phenyl-2-naphthylamine	Toluene
Phenacetin	Methanol
Acetaminophen	Acetaldehyde
Fentanyl	Ethanol
Doxepin	Acetone
Naproxen	Diethyl ether
Promazine	Chloroform
Piracetem	Acetic Acid
Procaine	
Diphenhydramine	
Aminopyrine	
Allobarbital	
Indomethacin	
Glutethimide	
Scopolamine	
Sulfonamide	
Arsenic	
Strychnine	
Cocaine[a]	
Amphetamine[a]	
Methamphetamine[a]	

[a] Considered frequent additives/coinjectants; absolute frequency unknown.

Source: Shesser, R. et al., *Am. J. Emerg. Med.* 9, 336, 1991. With permission.

were efficiently inhibited by $GABA_A$ receptor agonists and NMDA receptor antagonists, whereas sodium and calcium channel blockers were ineffective.[174] Benzodiazepines, unlike MNDA receptor antagonists, are readily available, require no prolonged loading, and are quite safe from a cardiovascular standpoint.[180–182] The main disadvantages are excessive sedation and respiratory depression, especially when given with barbiturates such as phenobarbital. Lorazepam is also quite viscous and must be refrigerated and diluted before infusion.[179] Diazepam is irritating to veins and after intramuscular dosing absorption is unpredictable.

Which Benzodiazepine?: Of the benzodiazepines lorazepam has the longest anticonvulsant activity[183] (4 to 6 h) and is considered the agent of first choice. Lorazepam has a tendency to persist in the brain while agents like diazepam and midazolam both redistribute out of the brain more rapidly and thus have a shorter protective effect.[184] Leppik et al.[185] found no significant statistical difference between diazepam and lorazepam in clinical efficacy for initial control of convulsive status. It was found, however, that lorazepam provided seizure control in 78% of patients with the first intravenous dose while diazepam provided seizure control after the first injection only 58% of the time. Levy and Kroll[186] found that the average dose of lorazepam to control status epilepticus in a study of 21 patients was 4 mg and all patients responded within 15 min. Chiulli et al. reported on a retrospective study of 142 equally matched children given benzodiazepines and phenytoin for control of seizures.[530] The intubation rate for those given lorazepam (mean dose 2.7 mg) was 27% while 73% of those given diazepam (mean dose 5.2 mg) had to be intubated. This study had an overall intubation rate that was quite high (45%), raising the question why so many children needed to be intubated.[179] Interestingly, lorazepam is not FDA-approved for seizure control. Midazolam may be used alternatively and has the advantage of rapid IM absorption in patients without venous access. In one study it was found to have a stronger influence on electroencephalographic measures,[187] and may be more effective in status epilepticus than diazepam or lorazepam.[188]

Barbiturates: Barbiturates are associated with a higher incidence of hypotension than benzodiazepines,[189–191] and as a result should not be administered in the hypotensive patient. Furthermore, they require time-consuming loading (greater than 30 min). Although phenobarbital may be administered at an IV rate of 100 mg/min (requiring only 10 min to fully load a 70-kg patient with 15 mg/kg) most nursing protocols require the physician to institute phenobarbital loading or to give no more than 60 mg/min IV.[179] Finally, barbiturates frequently cause prolonged sedation (especially after the co-administration of benzodiazepines) thus hindering the ability of the physician to perform serial examinations. Barbiturates do have an advantage of lowering intracranial pressure[190] in the head-injured patient and are helpful for treating withdrawal symptoms in patients with sedative–hypnotic addiction.[192,193] Barbiturates (i.e., phenobarbital) are considered second-line agents after the use of benzodiazepines (i.e., lorazepam) for seizures caused by drugs of abuse.

Fosphenytoin: Phenytoin is a poorly soluble anticonvulsant that is mixed with propylene glycol to enhance its solubility. The propylene glycol, not the phenytoin, is a cardiac depressant and may cause hypotension and cardiovascular collapse if administered too rapidly. Fosphenytoin was recently introduced to eliminate the poor aqueous solubility and irritant properties of intravenous phenytoin and to eliminate the need for the propylene glycol solvent. Fosphenytoin is rapidly converted to phenytoin after intravenous or intramuscular administration and unlike phenytoin does not require prolonged administration of a loading dose on a cardiac monitor. In clinical studies, this prodrug showed minimal evidence of adverse events and no serious cardiovascular or respiratory adverse reactions.[194] Unlike phenobarbital and benzodiazepines, which elevate the seizure threshold, phenytoin exerts its anticonvulsant effects mainly by limiting the spread of seizure activity and reducing seizure propagation. Because phenytoin does not elevate the seizure threshold, it is less effective against drug induced seizures.[195] Animal models[196] of cocaine-induced seizures and human studies[197] of alcohol withdrawal seizures have supported this claim. Cardiac toxicity of phenytoin was suggested by Callaham et al.[198] who showed an increased incidence of ventricular tachycardia in dogs intoxicated with amitriptyline treated with phenytoin. Fosphenytoin and phenytoin are thus considered third-line agents for drug-induced seizures. They may be considered more useful for the drug-abusing patient with epilepsy whose seizures have responded to phenytoin in the past.

General anesthesia: Pentobarbital or thiopental anesthesia may be used as a last resort, usually with the aid of an anesthesiologist, to induce general anesthesia.[199,200] If paralysis is used, the patient must be intubated and mechanically ventilated. It is important to remember that when patients having seizures are paralyzed with neuromuscular blockers such that seizure activity is not readily apparent, they may continue to have electrical seizure activity, which results in persistent cerebral hypermetabolism and the continued risk of brain injury.[172] Munn and Farrell[201] reported on a 14-year-old girl who was pharmacologically paralyzed during 14 h of unrecognized status epilepticus. The originally healthy girl suffered persistent, serious cognitive impairment and subsequent epilepsy. An EEG should be used to monitor in all patients paralyzed for a seizure disorder to determine the need for further anticonvulsant therapy.

8.2.3.2 Stepwise Approach to Management

Immediate Interventions

1. Airway, Breathing, Circulation: Maintain the airway and assist ventilation if necessary. Administer supplemental oxygen. Treat hypotension, and resuscitate as per previous reviews.[90]

2. Antidotes: Administer appropriate antidotes, including 25 g dextrose IV if the patient is hypoglycemic. Administer naloxone only if seizures are thought to be caused by hypoxia resulting from narcotic-associated respiratory depression.

3. Anticonvulsants: Administer one of the drugs listed in the tabulation below.

Comment: As noted above the authors have a strong preference for benzodiazepines (i.e., lorazepam). If lorazepam is chosen, most seizures stop after 2 to 4 mg, but there are no clear dose–response data available.[179] Some authorities stop if 4 mg is unsuccessful, but it seems reasonable to give up to 10 to 12 mg of lorazepam before switching to an alternative therapy. Neurologists generally recommend the aggressive use of a single drug before switching to another drug. Switching too quickly frequently results in the underdosing of both drugs. Respiratory depression should not keep one from using large doses of benzodiazepines[179] (as has been done safely with delirium tremens[202]), especially in the drug-abusing patient with status epilepticus. If large doses of benzodiazepines are used, patients frequently require intubation and mechanical ventilation.

Drugs Used for Seizure Control

Lorazepam	0.05–0.10 mg/kg IV over 2 min	May repeat as necessary, may give intramuscularly (IM) although IV route preferred
Midazolam	0.05 mg/kg IV over 2 min	May repeat as necessary
Diazepam	0.10 mg/kg IV over 2 min	May repeat as necessary
Phenobarbital	15–20 mg/kg IV over 20 min	Watch for hypotension, prolonged sedation
Fosphenytoin	15–20 mg/kg IV given at 100–150 mg/min (7–14 min)	Generally not as effective as benzodiazepines or barbiturates, may give IM although IV route preferred
Pentobarbital	5–6 mg/kg IV, slow infusion over 8–10 min, then continuous infusion at 0.5–3.0 mg/kg/h titrated to effect	Use as inducing agent for general anesthesia, watch for hypotension, continuous EEG monitoring necessary after general anesthesia

4. Reassess temperature: Immediately check the rectal temperature and cool the patient rapidly if the temperature is above 40°C (104°F) (see Section 8.2.4 on hyperthermia).

5. Lumbar puncture: Perform lumbar puncture if the patient is febrile to rule out meningitis. Do not wait for CT results or laboratory analysis of cerebral spinal fluid (CSF) to initiate therapy with appropriate antibiotics (i.e., a third-generation cephalosporin) if meningitis is suspected. Perform CT prior to lumbar puncture if the patient is at risk for having a CNS mass lesion.

Table 8.2.8 High-Risk Seizures

Neurological deficit
Evidence of head trauma
Prolonged postictal state
Focal seizures or focal onset with secondary generalization[a]
Seizures occurring after a period of prolonged abstinence[a]
Onset of seizures before age 30 if alcohol only involved
Mental illness or inability to fully evaluate the patient's baseline mental function

[a] High risk for having a positive CT result requiring intervention.

6. Gastric decontamination: Consider gastrointestinal decontamination if the patient is a body packer or stuffer or if the patient has ingested large quantities of drug (see Section 8.2.9, gastric decontamination).

7. Laboratory Data: Electrolytes, glucose, calcium, magnesium, and biochemical screens for liver and renal disease are generally recommended.[173] Check creatine kinase levels to detect evidence of rhabdomyolysis. Although the use of urine and blood toxicologic screens are generally overutilized,[5] they are recommended in the case of new onset seizures to avoid an inappropriate diagnosis of idiopathic epilepsy.

Secondary Interventions

1. Computerized Tomography (CT): Earnest et al.[178] documented a 16% incidence of "important intracranial lesions on CT scan" in a series of 259 patients with first alcohol-related seizures, and Pascual-Leone et al.[203] found CT scan lesions in 16% ($n = 44$) of cocaine-induced seizures. Cocaine-induced thrombosis and hypertension have been implicated as the cause of stroke in patients with seizures.[204–206] Considering these studies and also the high incidence of traumatic, hemorrhagic, and infectious injuries associated with drug abuse, a CT of the brain (with contrast) is recommended for new-onset seizures or for any high-risk seizures (Table 8.2.8). In a smaller study Holland et al.[207] performed a retrospective review of 37 cocaine-associated seizures and concluded that CT scanning was not necessary regardless of the patient's previous seizure history if the patient suffered a brief, generalized, tonic–clonic seizure and had normal vital signs, physical examination, and a postictal state lasting 30 min or less. We await larger studies to confirm the Holland et al. findings prior to making similar recommendations.

2. Monitor: Monitor neurological and cardiovascular status as well as hydration and electrolyte balance.

3. Anticonvulsant therapy: Chronic anticonvulsant or other specific treatment of alcohol- or drug-related seizures rarely is indicated. For patients who present with multiple seizures, status epilepticus, or high-risk seizures (Table 8.2.8) continued outpatient therapy may be indicated.

4. Disposition: Only patients with normal vital signs, and physical examination; after a brief isolated seizure; with a normal evaluation (i.e., CT scan, laboratory data, etc.) should be considered for discharge from the emergency department.

8.2.4 Hyperthermia/Heat Stroke

8.2.4.1 General Comments

While mild hyperthermia is usually benign, in the setting of drug overdose it may be a sign of impending disaster. Severe hyperthermia (>40.5°C) is a well-recognized cause of major morbidity and mortality, regardless of the cause. Classic heat stroke, for example, characterized by a core temperature of 40.5°C or higher, and severe CNS dysfunction has been associated with mortality rates of up to 80% as well as with a high likelihood of disabling neurologic sequelae.[208] Although no study has documented the incidence of death as it relates to drug abuse per se, a case series by Rosenberg et al.[209] described 12 patients who presented with temperatures 40.5°C or greater for at least 1 h. Five of 12 patients died and four had severe permanent neurologic sequelae. Clinical signs common to patients who went on to develop severe hyperthermia were increased muscular activity and absence of sweating.

Classic vs. drug-induced heat stroke: If a patient with apparent environmental heat illness has a continuing rise in temperature even after removal from ambient heat and ongoing exertion, drug-induced hyperthermia must be strongly considered. Rosenberg et al. reported a 3 to 12 h delay to the onset of severe hyperthermia in 7 of 12 patients with drug-induced hyperthermia.[209] A variety of drugs[133,210–213] and toxins[171] can cause hyperthermia, and this may initially be overlooked while the more familiar manifestations (i.e., seizures) of the intoxication are being managed. Patients with hyperthermia and altered mental status may be diagnosed as having environmental or exertional heat stroke while the potential contribution of drugs is neglected.[209] Clues to drug-induced hyperthermia from the history and physical examination must be aggressively pursued.

Mechanisms: Mechanisms of drug-induced hyperthermia are varied. Most commonly, excessive heat production results from muscular hyperactivity (sympathomimetic and epileptogenic agents) or metabolic hyperactivity (salicylates). Heat dissipation is often impaired by inhibition of sweating (anticholinergic agents), cutaneous vasoconstriction (sympathomimetic agents), and/or by interference with central thermoregulation (phenothiazines, cocaine, amphetamines).[209,214–216] When healthy, cocaine-naive persons are subjected to passive heating, pretreatment with even a small dose of intranasal cocaine impairs sweating and cutaneous vasodilation (the major autonomic adjustments to thermal stress) and heat perception (the key trigger for behavioral adjustments).[217] The combined serotonin-releasing and dopamine-releasing drug MDMA produces lethal hyperthermia more potently than amphetamine,[218] supporting a synergistic role for serotonergic with dopamine in drug-induced hyperthermia.[133] *Phencyclidine* is a sympathetic nervous system stimulant, and may also have anticholinergic properties,[219] which inhibit sweating. This property plus the tendency to generate unrestrained outbursts of violent activity and seizures have resulted in hyperthermia and rhabdomyolysis and death.[220] Of 1000 cases of PCP intoxication reviewed by McCarron et al.[221] 26 had temperatures over 38.9°C and four had temperatures over 41°C. Large overdoses of *LSD* have been associated with severe hyperthermia.[222,223] This has been suggested to be due to its serotonergic effects[210] and a tendency to provoke panic. A patient retrained in a straitjacket after becoming violent after LSD ingestion developed hyperthermia to 41.6°C, hypotension, rhabdomyolysis, renal failure, and died.[224] Specific mechanisms may dictate the specific form of hyperthermic syndrome although classically five syndromes are described: malignant hyperthermia, neuroleptic malignant syndrome, anticholinergic poisoning, sympathomimetic poisoning, and serotonin syndrome.

Malignant hyperthermia: Less commonly, drug-induced hyperthermia may develop as a form of malignant hyperthermia. Although hyperthermia associated with cocaine and PCP have been ascribed this diagnosis,[225,226] malignant hyperthermia is a rare complication that is usually associated with exposure to volatile anesthetic agents or depolarizing muscle relaxants.[171] The primary defect is felt to be an alteration in cellular permeability, which results in an inability to regulate calcium concentrations *within* the skeletal muscle fibers.[227] As a result neuromuscular paralysis (acting at the *neuromuscular junction*) is not effective in controlling the severe muscular rigidity and heat generation seen with malignant hyperthermia. Dantrolene (1 to 2 mg/kg rapidly IV) is the most effective treatment for malignant hyperthermia. While dantrolene has been suggested to diminish hyperthermia associated with amphetamine[228,229] and LSD[230] overdose, it has not been shown in any controlled study to be effective and confirmation of its usefulness for these indications requires further evaluation.

Neuroleptic malignant syndrome: Neuroleptic malignant syndrome (NMS) is another uncommon cause of drug-induced hyperthermia associated with the use of haloperidol and certain other neuroleptic agents. It has been reviewed in depth elsewhere.[212,231,232] Muscular rigidity, autonomic instability, and metabolic disturbances are presumed to occur due to neurotransmitter imbalances.

Neuromuscular paralysis and routine external cooling measures are generally effective for treatment of the severe rigidity and hyperthermia in this condition. In case reports NMS has been attributed to cocaine[233,234] and LSD,[230] although exertional hyperthermia seems a more probable diagnosis in these instances. Treatment includes the use of bromocriptine (5.0 mg per nasogastric tube every 6 h),[235] and supportive care.

Serotonin syndrome: A clinical syndrome associated with increased free serotonin levels; usually the result of a prescription drug interaction such as selective serotonin-reuptake inhibitor with cocaine or amphetamines. Muscle rigidity is not as prominent as with NMS and sweating and gastrointestinal complaints are much more common. Symptoms of hyperthermia hyperreflexia, agitation, and an exaggerated tremor predominate.[214–216]

Importance of paralysis and cooling: Zalis et al.[236,237] showed that hyperthermia was directly related to mortality in mongrel dogs with *amphetamine* overdose. Paralysis was shown to stop muscle hyperactivity, reduce hyperthermia, and decrease mortality.[238] Davis et al.[239] showed that dogs treated with toxic doses of *PCP* exhibited toxicity, which was diminished by paralysis and cooling measures.[239] Animal studies also indicate a key role for hyperthermia in complications associated with *cocaine* overdosage. Catravas and Waters[123] demonstrated that dogs given otherwise lethal *cocaine* infusions survived if severe hyperthermia was prevented. In this study temperature correlated better with survival than did pulse or blood pressure. Measures to prevent hyperthermia have included paralysis with pancuronium, sedation with chlorpromazine or diazepam, and external cooling.

Prognosis: Prognosis for severe hyperthermia depends on the *duration of temperature elevation*, the *maximum temperature* reached, and the affected individual's *underlying health*.[240] Coagulopathy was reported to be associated with death in four of five cases in one report[209] and has been shown to correlate with mortality in other studies.[241] *Seizures* are also associated with a poor prognosis.[209] This may in part be because they are often resistant to treatment in the hyperthermic individual. Any *delay in cooling* has been associated with a significantly increased incidence of mortality as well.[242]

8.2.4.2   Stepwise Approach to Management

It does not take long either to boil an egg or to cook neurons.[243]

Immediate Interventions

1. Airway, Breathing, Circulation: Maintain the airway and assist ventilation if necessary. Administer supplemental oxygen. Treat hypotension, and resuscitate as per previous reviews.[1–3]

2. Antidotes: Administer appropriate antidotes, including 25 g dextrose IV if the patient is hypoglycemic, as per the section on coma.

3. Control seizures and muscular hyperactivity: See Section 8.2.3, seizures, and Section 8.2.2, agitation.

4. Cooling: The fastest cooling techniques reported in the literature have usually been implemented in a research laboratory environment, utilizing animal models and equipment and techniques that are not universally available. In clinical practice, a technique that allows easy patient access and is readily available is preferable to a technique that may be more effective, but is difficult to perform. A comparison of the cooling rates achieved in several animal and human models with various cooling techniques is shown in Table 8.2.9. The advantages and disadvantages are summarized in Table 8.2.10. We favor evaporative cooling as the technique of choice. Evaporative cooling combines the advantages of simplicity and noninvasiveness with the most rapid cooling rates that can be achieved with any external techniques.[244] Some authors advocate the use of strategically placed ice packs although there are no controlled studies demonstrating their effectiveness and ice packs may contribute to shivering, which may further increase heat generation. In the authors' experience with exercise-induced heat stroke, ice packs placed at the groin and axillae do not causing shivering if they were used when the temperature is high (>40°C) and removed as the

Table 8.2.9   Cooling Rates Achieved with Various Cooling Techniques

Technique	Author/Year	Species	Rate °C/min
Evaporative	Weiner/1980[520]	Human	0.31
	Barner/1984[521]	Human	0.04
	Al-Aska/1987[522]	Human	0.09
	Kielblock/1986[523]	Human	0.034
	Wyndam/1959[524]	Human	0.23
	White/1987[525]	Dog	0.14
	Daily/1948[526]	Rat	0.93
Immersion (ice water)	Weiner/1980[520]	Human	0.14
	Wyndam/1959[524]	Human	0.14
	Magazanik/1980[527]	Dog	0.27
	Daily/1948[526]	Rat	1.86
Icepacking (whole body)	Kielblock/1986[523]	Human	0.034
	Bynum/1978[528]	Dog	0.11
Strategic ice packs	Kielblock/1986[523]	Human	0.028
Evaporative and strategic ice packs	Kielblock/1986[523]	Human	0.036
Cold gastric lavage	Syverud/1985[529]	Dog	0.15
	White/1987[525]	Dog	0.06
Cold peritoneal lavage	Bynum/1978[528]	Dog	0.56

Source: Helmrich, D.E. and Syverud, S.A., Roberts, J.R. and Hedges, J.R., Eds., *Clinical Procedures in Emergency Medicine,* 2nd ed. Philadelphia: Saunders, 1991. With permission.

Table 8.2.10   Various Cooling Techniques

Technique	Advantages	Disadvantages
Evaporative	Simple, readily available Noninvasive Easy monitoring and patient access Relatively more rapid	Constant moistening of skin surface required to maximize heat loss
Immersion	Noninvasive Relatively more rapid	Cumbersome Patient monitoring and access difficult — inability to defibrillate Shivering Poorly tolerated by conscious patients
Ice packing	Noninvasive Readily available	Shivering Poorly tolerated by conscious patients
Strategic ice packs	Noninvasive Readily available Can be combined with other techniques	Relatively slower Shivering Poorly tolerated by conscious patients
Cold gastric lavage	Can be combined with other techniques	Relatively slower Invasive May require airway protection Human experience limited Invasive
Cold peritoneal lavage	Very rapid	Invasive Human experience limited

Source: Helmrich, D.E., Syverud, S.A., Roberts, J.R. and Hedges, J.R., Eds., *Clinical Procedures in Emergency Medicine,* 2nd ed. Philadelphia: Saunders, 1991. With permission.

patient cools. Gastric lavage with cold water or saline is an effective and rapid central cooling technique that can be used in combination with evaporation in severe cases. Neuromuscular paralysis is recommended in all severe cases in which temperature is persistently greater than 40°C. Cooling technique is as follows:

a. Completely remove *all* clothing.
b. Place cardiac monitor leads on the patient's back so that they adhere to the skin during the cooling process.
c. Wet the skin with lukewarm tap water with a sponge or spray bottle (plastic spray bottles work the best).

d. Position *large high-speed fan(s)* close to the patient and turn them on.
e. Place ice pack to the groin and axillae (optional).
f. If shivering occurs, treat with diazepam, 0.1 to 0.2 mg/kg IV, or midazolam, 0.05 mg/kg IV.
g. Treat continued muscular hyperactivity, i.e., either severe shivering, rigidity, or agitation, with neuromuscular paralysis (vecuronium, 0.1 mg/kg IVP) with endotracheal intubation and mechanical ventilation.
h. Employ vigorous fluid replacement to correct volume depletion and to facilitate thermoregulation by sweating.
i. If the patient continues to exhibit muscle rigidity despite administration of neuromuscular blockers, give dantrolene, 1 mg/kg rapid IV push. Repeat as necessary up to 10 mg/kg.
j. Place a Foley catheter and monitor urine output closely.
k. Monitor the rectal or esophageal temperature and discontinue cooling when the temperature reaches 38.5°C to avoid hypothermia.

Comments:

Immersion: Immersion in an ice water bath is also a highly effective measure to reduce core temperatures, but limits the health care provider's access to the patient, and requires more equipment and preparation.

Thermometry: Unfortunately, most standard measurements of body temperature differ substantially from actual core temperature. Oral thermometry is affected by mouth breathing and is a poor approximation of core temperature. Rectal thermometry is less variable, but responds to changes in core temperature slowly. Thermistors that are inserted 15 cm into the rectum offer continuous monitoring of temperature with less variability and, although slower to respond to changes in core temperature than tympanic temperature readings, are not biased by head skin temperature. Temperatures taken using infrared thermometers that scan the tympanic membrane are of variable reliability and reproducibility.[245–248] Studies have shown that infrared tympanic membrane thermometers may be influenced by patient age,[249] measuring technique,[250] the presence or absence of cerumen,[245,251] and head skin temperature as noted above.[252] If a patient has a Swan-Ganz catheter, pulmonary arterial temperature may be measured precisely with a thermistor catheter. An esophageal thermistor positioned adjacent to the heart closely correlates with core temperature as well. It is the least invasive, most accurate method available in the emergency department and is recommended (although rectal thermistors will suffice for most cases). Thermistors attached to urinary catheters may work equally well.

Circulatory support: Usually, fluid requirements are modest, averaging 1200 ml of Ringer's lactate or saline solution in the first 4 h.[253,254] This is because a major factor in the hypotensive state is peripheral vasodilation.[171] With cooling there may be a sudden rise in systemic vascular resistance, and pulmonary edema may be caused, or exacerbated, by overzealous fluid administration.[255,256] Insertion of a Swan-Ganz catheter or central venous pressure monitor is indicated whenever necessary to guide fluid therapy. Patients with low cardiac output and hypotension should not be treated with α-adrenergic agents since these drugs promote vasoconstriction without improving cardiac output or perfusion, decrease cutaneous heat exchange, and perhaps enhance ischemic renal and hepatic damage.[257] One case report described excellent results using low-dose continuous isoproterenol infusion (1 μg/min).[253]

Shivering: Since shivering may occur with rapid cooling, and thus generate more heat, some authors[257,258] recommend chlorpromazine as an adjunct measure. Chlorpromazine is felt to act as a muscle relaxant and vasodilator promoting heat exchange at the skin surface. Phenothiazines, however, *may* aggravate hypotension, and have anticholinergic properties. They are also associated with serious dystonic reactions that may exacerbate hyperthermia. Distinct subtypes of dopamine receptors have been identified, including D_1 and D_2 receptors. Chlorpromazine and haloperidol are *D_2 receptor antagonists* and rat studies have shown that specific *D_1 receptor antagonist*, but not D_2 receptor antagonists reduced the hyperthermic response to cocaine infusion.[259] Dopamine is also known to participate in core temperature regulation, but it is unclear whether a predominance of D_1 or D_2 receptor activation results in hyperthermia or hypothermia.[260] Until more is understood about the exact role of the dopaminergic system in hyperthermia, the use of chlorpromazine and other dopamine blockers in the management of hyperthermia victims is not recommended.

Other pharmacologic interventions: Pharmacologic interventions aimed specifically at hyperthermia (i.e., dantrolene) have been suggested for such drugs as MDMA (i.e., ecstasy)[228] but have not been proven to be of any benefit.[229,261] Antipyretics are of no specific benefit[262] and salicylates may aggravate bleeding tendencies.[263] Alcohol sponge baths are not recommended, particularly in small children, since alcohol may be absorbed through dilated cutaneous blood vessels and inhaled, producing isopropanol poisoning and coma.[264]

Secondary Interventions

1. Laboratory Data: Send blood for complete blood count, platelet count, PT, PTT, electrolytes, calcium, CPK, cardiac enzymes, BUN, creatinine, and liver function tests. Type and cross-match blood and send blood cultures. For severely ill patients send lactic acid level, and ABG. Check serum CPK and urine for myoglobin. If rhabdomyolysis is suspected, see Section 8.2.5 on rhabdomyolysis. Although urine and blood toxicologic screens are generally overutilized,[5] they should be sent if the diagnosis is in question. Send salicylate levels on all cases with an unknown cause of hyperthermia.

2. CT: Consider CT of brain for persistently altered mental status, focal neurological deficit.

3. Lumbar puncture: Perform lumbar puncture and send cerebral spinal fluid for analysis if patient has signs or symptoms of meningitis. Do not wait for results before administering empiric antibiotics.

4. Cardiac evaluation: ECG, CXR.

5. Disposition: All patients with serious hyperthermia or heat stroke should be admitted to the hospital. Patients with normal or mildly abnormal laboratory values who become normothermic in the emergency department may be admitted to the medical floor. All others require intensive monitoring.

8.2.5   Rhabdomyolysis

8.2.5.1   General Comments

Rhabdomyolysis is defined as a syndrome of skeletal muscle injury or necrosis with release of muscle cell contents into the blood.[265] It has been associated with all drugs of abuse.[133,224,266–277] Since the classic signs and symptoms of nausea, vomiting, myalgias, muscle swelling, tenderness, and weakness are present in only a minority of cases (13% in one study[278]), the diagnosis depends on laboratory evaluation and a high clinical suspicion. Elevated levels of serum CK, in the absence of CK from other sources (brain or heart), is the most sensitive indicator of muscle injury[265] with most authors recognizing a CK level of more than fivefold that of the upper limit of normal as diagnostic. The diagnosis may also be suspected with a positive urine dipstick for heme: if no red blood cells are present on the urine microscopic examination, the positive orthotolidine reaction may be attributed to myoglobin (or hemoglobin). Because myoglobin is cleared from the plasma in 1 to 6 h by renal excretion and by metabolism to bilirubin,[265] the urine dipstick test for myoglobin may occasionally be negative due to rapid clearance.[279,280] Gabow et al.[265] reported that in the absence of hematuria, only 50% of patients with rhabdomyolysis had urine that was orthotolidine-positive.

The diagnosis of rhabdomyolysis is important because it may produce life-threatening hyperkalemia and myoglobinuric renal failure; it is often associated with disseminated intravascular coagulation (DIC), and acute cardiomyopathy from serious underlying conditions such as heat stroke or severe acidosis.[265,277,280–282] Myoglobinuric renal failure may frequently be prevented by vigorous treatment.

Case in point: In 1984, Ron and colleagues[283] described seven patients at very high risk for developing renal failure as a result of extensive crush injuries, severe rhabdomyolysis, and gross myoglobinurea following the collapse of a building. Their treatment goal was to rapidly obtain a urine pH of 6.5 and to maintain diuresis of 300 ml/h or more. Crystalloid infusions were begun at the scene and continued during transport to the hospital. If urine output did not rise to 300 ml/h and the central venous pressure rose by more than 4 cm H_2O, the infusion was halted and 1 g mannitol/kg body weight as a 20% solution was administered IV. Sodium bicarbonate (44 mEq) was added to every other bottle of 500-ml crystalloid solution. The electrolyte composition of IV solutions was adjusted to maintain a serum sodium concentration of 135 to 145 mmol/L and a serum potassium concentration between 3.5 and 4.5 mmol/L. Repeated doses of mannitol (1 g/kg body wt) were given if the urine output fell below 300 ml/h for 2 consecutive hours and if the central venous pressure rose by more than 4 cm H_2O. Further does of bicarbonate were given if the urine pH fell below 6.5. Acetazolamide was given intravenously if plasma pH approached 7.45. Despite peak creatinine kinase (CK) levels exceeding 30,000 IU/dl none of the seven patients developed renal failure.

Assessing risk for developing acute renal failure: Several heterogeneous studies have attempted to identify which patients will progress to myoglobinuric renal failure based on their laboratory values. Unfortunately, there are no prospective studies with standardized treatment regimens to determine which patients are at risk. A study of 200 victims of severe beatings in South Africa found that base deficit, delay in treatment, and CK levels were significant risk factors for the development of ARD and death.[284] Ward et al.,[284a] in another retrospective study ($n = 157$) found that the factors predictive of renal failure included (1) a peak CK level greater than 16,000 IU/dl (58% of patients with CK above 16,000 IU/dl vs. 11% of patients with CK below 16,000 IU/dl developed renal failure), (2) a history of hypotension, (3) *dehydration*, (4) older age, (5) sepsis, and (6) hyperkalemia. A retrospective review of 93 patients with "severe" rhabdomyolysis (serum CK greater than 5000 U/L) found that patients with a peak CK level of greater than 15,000 U/L had significantly higher rates of acute renal dysfunction (72% vs. 38%).[285] A recent analysis of 372 patients with crush syndrome after the 1995 earthquake in Kobe, Japan, demonstrated that patients with a peak CK level greater than 75,000 U/L had a higher rate of acute renal failure and mortality than those with a peak CK less than 75,000 U/L (84% vs. 39% and 4% vs. 17%, respectively).[286] Eneas et al.[287] found that only patients with a peak CK greater than 20,000 U/L failed to respond to a mannitol–bicarbonate diuresis and went on to require dialysis. The nonresponders also had significantly higher serum phosphate levels and hematocrit readings upon admission, indicative of more severe muscle injury and hemoconcentration. Several studies have attempted to predict the development of renal failure using serum or urine myoglobin levels. A prospective study of eight patients by Feinfeld[288] found that four of five patients with urine myoglobin levels greater than 1000 ng/ml (normal = <10 ng/ml) developed acute renal dysfunction, while none of the three patients with urine myoglobin levels less than 300 ng/ml developed it. Another report found that elevated urine myoglobin levels greater than 20,000 ng/ml were associated with a significantly increased risk of renal dysfunction.[289]

Prognosis: Approximately 10% of patients with rhabdomyolysis presenting to hospitals develop myoglobinuric renal failure[277] and major reports of patient series indicate that approximately 5% of patients with serious rhabdomyolysis die.[265,268,280,281,290] Death is often due not to rhabdomyolysis or one of its complications but to a complication of the primary disorder associated with the rhabdomyolysis (i.e., traumatic injury, or sepsis). With temporary support from hemodialysis acute myoglobinuric renal failure has a good prognosis, and full recovery should be expected.[280,281,291]

Crystalloids: Less controversy exists behind the need for volume replacement in the setting of rhabdomyolysis than it does for the use of bicarbonate, mannitol, or furosemide. In reviews of myoglobinuric renal failure,[265,268,280,283,292–295] hypovolemia is a consistent finding among all evaluated risk factors. Myoglobinuric renal failure seen in military recruits and bodybuilders has an especially strong association with dehydration.[296–298] Recently, Zurovsky et al.[299] demonstrated that, in rats, mortality and renal failure increased from both chronic dehydration (24 to 72 h) and acute dehydration from sucrose-induced diuresis or hemorrhage. The role of dehydration appears to implicate renal ischemia and perhaps acidosis and/or aciduria as necessary cofactors in the development of myoglobinuric acute renal failure.[300]

Alkalinization: The purpose of alkalinization of urine is to prevent the dissociation of myoglobin into globin and hematin.[277] Dissociation has been shown to occur below a pH of 5.6.[301] The nephrotoxic effect of hematin has been ascribed to the production of free hydroxy radicals.[302] Dog studies have shown that the infusion of free hematin causes significantly greater renal dysfunction than does myoglobin.[303] Furthermore, in urine below pH 5.0, the solubility of myoglobin decreases markedly causing myoglobin cast formation and an increase in the percentage of myoglobin retained in renal tubules This process has been shown to have a high correlation with the development of acute renal failure.[304] Rabbit studies by Perri et al.[305] showed that animals with a urinary pH of less than 6 invariably develop renal failure after infusions of myoglobin, whereas those with a urine pH of more than 6 do not develop renal insufficiency. Despite well-performed animal studies, no controlled human studies have evaluated the effectiveness of alkalinization for rhabdomyolysis. For this reason, as well as certain concerns about hypernatremia, hypervolemia, and hypocalcemia, some authors[306] do not recommend bicarbonate therapy. We feel that the preponderance of evidence favors the use of bicarbonate and that with adequate monitoring of volume, electrolyte, and calcium levels bicarbonate therapy is safe is likely to be of benefit.

Mannitol: Three major mechanisms have been proposed to explain the protective action of mannitol. The first suggests that a diuresis may simply dilute nephrotoxic agents in urine (e.g., hematin, urate) and "flush out" partial obstructed tubules.[307] Knochel points out that renal tubular oxygen consumption is closely coupled to sodium reabsorption[282] and by preventing sodium reabsorption, mannitol or furosemide may decrease oxygen requirements of renal tubules. This may allow the tubules to survive the metabolic insult produced by hematin.[277] Finally, mannitol may simply convert oliguric renal failure to non-oliguric renal failure. Studies have demonstrated a lower morbidity and mortality in nonoliguric renal failure than in oliguric renal failure.[308,309] Wilson et al.[310] showed that mannitol plus saline almost totally prevented the development of azotemia after glycerol-induced rhabdomyolysis in rats. As with bicarbonate, mannitol has not been shown to be more effective in prospective, controlled trials than saline alone. In selected cases in which urinary output is low (see following recommendations) and where hemodynamic status is stable, we believe potential benefits of mannitol administration outweigh the potential risks.

Furosemide: Loop diuretics such as furosemide have also been used in an attempt to prevent acute renal failure. As with mannitol and bicarbonate no controlled human studies on its efficacy have been done. Furosemide may work similarly to mannitol to decrease sodium reabsorption and thus conserve renal tubule energy expenditure, thus decreasing the risk of ischemia. It may also simply convert oliguric renal failure to non-oliguric renal failure. Furosemide has the advantage of not increasing serum osmolality to the extent that mannitol does, but may exacerbate hypovolemia if not used with caution.

Recommendation: Based on the report by Ron and co-workers,[283] animal studies, and personal experience with the treatment of more than 100 cases of documented rhabdomyolysis, Curry et al.[277] proposed a treatment regimen that we recommend with adjustments under a stepwise approach to management. Using this treatment approach Curry et al. report only two instances of myoglobinuric renal failure out of 100 patients presenting with evidence of rhabdomyolysis. One was in a woman with severe salicylate poisoning who had established renal failure and anuria at the time of admission. The second was a woman who had sepsis and anoxic encephalopathy after seizures and cardiac arrest from IV cocaine.[277] While this regimen has not been tested prospectively it has suggestive benefit and if volume, serum osmolarity, and electrolyte status are monitored it is quite safe. Patients lacking nephrotoxic risk factors such as dehydration and acidosis, with only mild elevations of CK (<16,000 IU/dl) and no ongoing muscle injury may not require the full course of therapy recommended here. Any patient not treated by the full protocol should have CK levels monitored closely (i.e., every 12 h) and should be able to drink large amounts of fluids to maintain a brisk *urine output*.

8.2.5.2 Stepwise Approach to Management

Immediate Interventions

1. Airway, Breathing, Circulation, Antidotes: Maintain the airway and assist ventilation if necessary. Administer supplemental oxygen. Treat hypotension, and resuscitate as per previous reviews.[3] Administer appropriate antidotes, including 25 g dextrose IV if the patient is hypoglycemic, as per the section on coma.

2. Crystalloid: If cardiac/volume status is stable, initiate a fluid bolus of 1 L normal saline and continue until hypovolemia is corrected. Assuming that larger volumes are not needed for other reasons, crystalloid infusion is then administered at a rate of 2.5 ml/kg body weight per hour. Monitor urine output closely.

3. Bicarbonate: If urinary pH is <5.6 (the pH at which myoglobin dissociates into globin and hematin), administer sodium bicarbonate IV in boluses of 1 mmol/kg body weight until the arterial blood pH is about 7.45 or the urinary pH rises to 5.6.

Comment: *Urinary* pH, not arterial pH, has been found to correlate with precipitation of myoglobin within renal tubules,[304,305] and as a result the primary concern should be to increase urinary pH. Because of metabolic complications that may exist at a higher arterial pH (hypokalemia, and the shifting of the oxygen-hemoglobin saturation curve to the left), bicarbonate should not be used if serum pH is already >7.45.

Secondary Interventions

1. Reassess: Check serum sodium and potassium concentrations, and urine pH frequently.

Comment: If large volumes of normal saline are required for resuscitation, or sodium bicarbonate is used, check sodium every 6 to 8 h; otherwise check every 12 to 24 h. Check arterial pH every few hours if the patient is significantly acidotic (pH < 7.3) or if large amounts of sodium bicarbonate are used.

2. Potassium: Potassium may help to maintain a more alkaline urine. If urine pH falls below 5.6 in the presence of alkalemia and serum potassium is less than 4.0 mEq/L, then administer additional potassium until the urine pH rises above 6.0 or until the serum potassium concentration reaches 5 mmol/L.

Comment: The kidney of patients with hypokalemia will spare potassium and excrete hydrogen ions resulting in a decrease of urinary bicarbonate, thus maintaining aciduria. Acidic urine increases myoglobin precipitation and increases the risk of myoglobinuric renal failure. There are no controlled studies demonstrating the role of potassium in the treatment of rhabdomyolysis, but it is of little harm and may be beneficial. One study showed that during active work, potassium may act as a vasodilator and increase blood flow to working muscle.[311] Knochel et al.[312] have presented data demonstrating that skeletal muscle of potassium-depleted dogs releases very little potassium during exertion and that exertion is not accompanied by an increase in blood flow. This may result in localized muscle ischemia and persistent rhabdomyolysis.

3. Acetazolamide: Acetazolamide, like potassium, may assist in producing a more alkaline urine. If the patient is persistently aciduric despite alkalemia and normal serum potassium concentrations, Curry et al.[277] recommend the use of 250 mg of acetazolamide IV to increase urinary pH. There is, however, no evidence that acetazolamide is efficacious for treatment of rhabdomyolysis.

Comment: In general, acetazolamide should not be given to a patient suffering from salicylate poisoning since it acidifies blood and alkalinizes CSF, increasing the volume of distribution of salicylate and trapping salicylate in the CNS.[313–315] In animal models of salicylate poisoning, the administration of acetazolamide markedly increases mortality rate.[315]

4. Decreased urine output below 1.5 to 2.0 ml/kg/h with objective hemodynamic parameters of either normovolemia or hypovolemia: Administer more crystalloid (500 cc fluid bolus) and consider increasing crystalloid infusion rate to 3.5 cc/kg/h.

5. Decreased urine output below 1.5 to 2.0 ml/kg/h with objective hemodynamic parameters of hypervolemia (Mannitol): Give a single dose of 1 g/kg body weight IV over 30 min, administer any additional doses 0.5 g/kg IV over 15 min. Monitor serum osmolality if repeated doses are required. Mannitol may be administered every 6 h if serum osmolality remains below 300 mOsm/L.

Comment: Watch for pulmonary edema and monitor serum osmolality. Mannitol should also not be used in the presence of hemorrhagic shock or hypovolemia.

6. Furosemide: If urine output does not respond to fluids or mannitol, then administer furosemide. Start with 10 mg IVP.

7. Discontinuation of therapy: Continue the above treatment protocol until the urine is consistently orthotolidine-negative, laboratory signs of continued rhabdomyolysis are no longer present, and renal function is improving or normal. Stop fluids, mannitol, and bicarbonate if oliguria or anuria are refractory to therapy.

8. Hemodialysis: Those who do go on to develop acute tubular necrosis may require hemodialysis or peritoneal dialyses for several days or weeks until renal function returns.[265,277,280,281] Indications for hemodialysis include serious electrolyte abnormalities (e.g., hyperkalemia), clinically significant acidosis resistant to conventional therapy, and volume overload. A moderate elevation of BUN and creatinine levels without other clinical effects is not an indication for dialysis.[306]

9. Hyperkalemia: Sodium bicarbonate, glucose and insulin, sodium polystyrene, calcium, and dialysis may be required in severe cases.[265,281]

10. Hypocalcemia: Hypocalcemia is common in patients with severe rhabdomyolysis[277] but even with calcium levels less than 8.0 mEq/L, hypocalcemia rarely causes symptoms.[282,316,317] Treatment of asymptomatic hypocalcemia has been discouraged because it theoretically could increase deposition of calcium due to precipitation with phosphate in damaged muscle, further augmenting rhabdomyolysis.[316]

11. Laboratory Data: CBC, electrolytes, BUN, creatinine, calcium, phosphorus, urinalysis, urine dip for blood (orthotolidine test), CK (MM and MB fractions), and arterial blood gas (if sodium bicarbonate to be used) (Figure 8.2.1).

12. Disposition: Patients with drug overdose who present with mild elevations of their CK (less than 3000 U/L) may be considered for discharge if all of the following conditions are met:

    a. The patient must have normal vital signs.
    b. There is no evidence of ongoing muscle injury.
    c. The patient has normal renal function.
    d. The patient is well hydrated and not acidotic, with normal electrolytes.
    e. The patient can take fluids by mouth and is not at risk for dehydration.
    f. Follow up is easily arranged for repeat CK in 12 to 24 h.
    g. A repeat serum CK level 6 to 8 h after the first shows a decreasing trend.

All other patients should be admitted to the hospital for aggressive fluid therapy as described above.

8.2.6 Hypertensive Emergencies

8.2.6.1 General Comments

Hypertension: Drug-induced hypertension is of concern because it can cause stroke (usually cerebral hemorrhage), acute myocardial infarction, pulmonary edema, dissecting aneurysm, and/or hypertensive encephalopathy.[319–321] Phenylpropanolamine, in particular, has been associated with

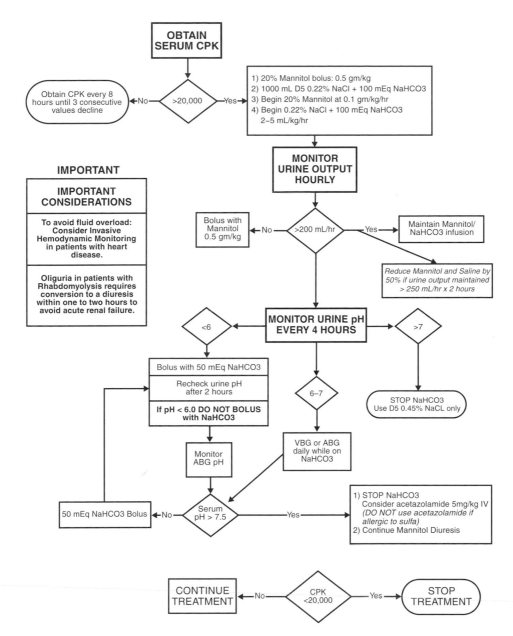

Figure 8.2.1 Treatment algorithm by Malinoski et al.,[318] which is a slightly more aggressive alternative to the protocol recommended above, advocating the use of mannitol and sodium bicarbonate in all patients.

cerebral hemorrhage when blood pressure was not rapidly lowered.[322–324] In patients with hypertension associated with amphetamines or cocaine, benzodiazepines may be successful in controlling the hypertension (and possibly dysrhythmias) by reducing the central sympathetic stimulus[123–125] and related catecholamine release.[325,326] If a stable, previously normotensive patient, without evidence of end organ damage, has extremely high blood pressure (>120 mm Hg diastolic) despite sedation, one should consider the use of a vasodilator such as nitroglycerin or phentolamine, or possibly a calcium channel blocker.[327] In contrast to patients with chronic hypertension, most young patients with drug-induced hypertension do not have chronic compensatory changes in their cerebral and cardiovascular system. For this reason blood pressure in previously normotensive individuals may be reduced rapidly to normal levels.[328]

Hypertensive emergencies: Hypertensive emergencies, defined as an increase in blood pressure that causes functional disturbances of the CNS, the heart, or the kidneys,[329] require a more aggressive approach.[330–332] Evidence of hypertensive encephalopathy, acute heart failure, aortic dissection, or coronary insufficiency requires rapid reduction of blood pressure (usually within 60 min) in a controlled fashion. Direct arteriolar dilating agents such as nitroglycerin, or nitroprusside, a pure alpha-adrenergic blocking agent such as phentolamine, or a calcium antagonist[333] may be used.

Stroke: Hypertension in the presence of a stroke is a more complicated issue, since hypertension may be a homeostatic response to maintain intracerebral blood flow in the presence of intracranial hypertension.[334] In this case blood pressure should not be lowered, or, if there is ongoing evidence of sympathomimetic drug intoxication, lowered gradually to a diastolic blood pressure no less than the 100 to 110 mm Hg range.

Beta-blockers: In animal models of cocaine intoxication associated with hemodynamic dysfunction and mortality, propanolol has been shown to be protective,[335] to have no effect,[336] or to increase mortality.[337,338] The reasons for the differences in these experimental results are unclear but may be related to the different doses of cocaine or the type of beta-adrenergic antagonist utilized.[339] Human studies, however, have been more consistent. In a randomized, double-blinded, placebo-controlled trial, Lange et al.[340] administered intranasal cocaine to 30 stable volunteers referred for cardiac catheterization. In this study it was found that intracoronary propranolol administration caused no change in arterial blood pressure but decreased coronary sinus blood flow and increased coronary vascular resistance. Several case reports have also documented an aggravation of hypertension when nonselective beta-adrenergic antagonists have been used in the treatment of acute cocaine intoxication.[341–343]

Labetalol: The exacerbation of hypertension and coronary vasospasm when nonselective beta-adrenergic antagonists are administered to cocaine-intoxicated patients may result from blockade of beta-2 receptor-induced vasodilation causing an "unopposed" peripheral alpha-adrenergic vasoconstriction.[339] It has therefore been suggested that labetalol, which has both alpha-adrenergic and beta-adrenergic antagonist activity, may be safer.[154,342] Controversy exists since the beta-adrenergic antagonist potency of labetalol is seven times greater than its relatively weak alpha antagonist potency,[344] and studies of hypertension in cocaine-intoxicated animals are conflicting: some have shown hemodynamic improvement[345] while others show no hemodynamic effect.[346] Mortality data are difficult to decipher as studies have shown decreased mortality,[335] increased mortality,[337,338] or no change in mortality.[336] The human experience (case reports) with labetalol has been better than with propanolol,[342,347,348] but in two unusual cases involving catecholamine excess that physiologically resemble cocaine intoxication (one involving pheochromocytoma,[349] and the other an accidental epinephrine overdosage[350]), hypertension was exacerbated by the administration of labetalol. In a study similar to that of Lange et al.,[351] Boehrer et al.[352] evaluated 15 patients referred for cardiac catheterization and found that while labetalol reversed the cocaine-induced rise in mean arterial pressure *it did not* alleviate cocaine-induced coronary vasoconstriction. An interesting case report described the induction of life-threatening hyperkalemia in a dialysis patient with hypertensive emergency treated with labetalol.[353]

Esmolol: Esmolol, an ultra-short acting ($t_{1/2} = 9$ min), easily titrated, beta-1 selective, adrenoreceptor blocking agent, has been used successfully in the treatment of cocaine-induced adrenergic crises.[126,343,354] However, the effects of esmolol on coronary vasoconstriction have not been evaluated. Its use may be most appropriate to control heart rate in the setting of acute aortic dissection[355] induced by hypertension from stimulant abuse. If esmolol is used, it is recommended that vasodilators such as nitroglycerin be given simultaneously since nitroglycerin is known to alleviate stimulant-induced vasoconstriction.[356] Pollan et al.[354] reported a case of a 64-year-old man who became hypertensive and tachycardic after the administration of cocaine for nasal polyp removal. This patient had *resolution* of ST segment depression after the administration of 20 mg IV of esmolol with good control of hemodynamic parameters. Esmolol has also been used in the management of pheochromocytoma with a rapid decrease in systolic blood pressure without effect on diastolic pressure.[357,358]

8.2.6.2 Stepwise Approach to Management

Immediate Interventions

1. Airway, Breathing, Circulation: Maintain the airway and assist ventilation if necessary. Administer supplemental oxygen. Resuscitate as per previous reviews.[3]

2. Antidotes: Administer appropriate antidotes, including 25 g dextrose IV if the patient is hypoglycemic, as per Section 8.2.1.

3. Agitation or Seizures: Administer a benzodiazepine such as lorazepam (0.05 to 0.10 mg/kg) and control agitation as described under Section 8.2.2.

4. Medications: If the patient is persistently hypertensive and a hypertensive emergency exists, then administer one of the following drugs:

Treatment for Drug-Induced, Hypertensive Emergency

Drug	Dose	Onset	Mechanism of Action
Sodium nitroprusside	0.25–10 µg/kg/min as IV infusion	2–5 min	Direct arterial and venous vasodilator
Nitroglycerin	5–100 µg as IV infusion	2–5 min	Direct arterial and venous vasodilator
Esmolol	Load with 500 µg/kg/min over 1 min Maintenance infusion: 50–200 µg/kg/min	2–5 min	B$_1$ adrenoreceptor blocker
Phentolamine	5–10 mg IVP	2–5 min	Alpha-adrenergic blocker

The treatment goal is to lower the blood pressure to a level that is "normal" for that patient within 30 to 60 min in a controlled, graded manner.[329] Although there is a broad range of normal blood pressures for an individual, if the patient's normal blood pressure is unknown, the diastolic blood pressure should be lowered to a minimum of 120 mm Hg or until there is no evidence of ongoing organ injury. The use of nitroprusside generally requires continuous intra-arterial blood pressure monitoring.

Comment: Phenylpropanolamine, an indirect sympathomimetic and direct alpha agonist, is frequently substituted for stimulants such as amphetamine and cocaine. The combination of severe hypertension with reflex bradycardia is a clue to vasoconstriction from the direct alpha-stimulation from phenylpropanolamine. Hypertension from phenylpropanolamine is usually best treated with phentolamine.

5. Laboratory data/imaging: For patients with hypertensive emergencies: Draw electrolytes, CK, CK-MB, BUN, creatinine, and PT/PTT. Perform EKG, and CXR. For apparently uncomplicated hypertension: Laboratory data may be done at the discretion of the physician. An ECG is recommended to rule out silent ischemia.

Secondary Interventions

1. Monitoring: Continue close monitoring of patient's blood pressure and cardiac status with frequent manual blood pressure readings. Consider placing an arterial line for better monitoring in patients with persistently labile hypertension or for those who have hypertension that is difficult to control.

2. CT of brain: Patients with severe headaches that do not resolve after the control of hypertension should undergo CT of the head to rule out intracranial bleeding.

3. Lumbar puncture: If CT of head is negative and the patient continues to have symptoms of severe headache and/or nuchal rigidity, perform lumbar puncture to rule out small subarachnoid hemorrhage.

4. Disposition: All patients that meet the following conditions may be considered for discharge from the emergency department:

a. Moderate uncomplicated hypertension controlled with sedation or a single dose of antihypertensive agents
b. Normal vital signs after a period of observation of 4 to 6 h
c. Normal ECG
d. Normal physical examination

All patients with hypertensive emergencies should be admitted to the hospital regardless of response to initial therapy.

8.2.7   Cardiac Care

8.2.7.1   General Comments

Almost all drugs of abuse can be associated with acute cardiac complications ranging from benign supraventricular tachycardia to ventricular fibrillation, sudden death, and myocardial infarction. Cocaine is a prototype cardiac toxin among drugs of abuse. As such, most of this section pertains directly to cocaine. Other stimulants (i.e., amphetamines,[359,360] phenylpropanolamine,[361,362] and methylphenidate[363,364]) may be associated with cardiac complications as well, and management should proceed in a fashion similar to that of the cocaine-intoxicated patient. One should also consider the likely possibility that cocaine has been mixed with or substituted for other stimulants (see Table 8.2.5 to Table 8.2.7).[365] If cardiac complications occur from drugs of abuse other than stimulants (i.e., heroin, barbiturates) cardiac care parallels current advanced cardiac life support guidelines,[366] with a few exceptions.

Mechanisms: The ability of cocaine to increase myocardial oxygen demand secondary to induction of hypertension and tachycardia, while decreasing coronary blood flow through vasoconstriction, and induction of coronary thromboses (the latter due to enhancement of platelet aggregation) makes it an ideal precipitant of myocardial ischemia and infarction.[367,368]

Benzodiazepines: In experiments in animals, benzodiazepines attenuate the cardiac and CNS toxicity of cocaine.[123,124,369] Perhaps through their anxiolytic effects, benzodiazepines reduce blood pressure and heart rate, thereby decreasing myocardial oxygen demand.[367] They are recommended as first-line agents for treatment of cocaine-intoxicated patients with myocardial ischemia who are anxious, have tachycardia, and/or are hypertensive.

Aspirin: Aspirin should be administered to help prevent the formation of thrombi in patients with suspected ischemia. This recommendation is based on theoretical considerations (e.g., decreasing platelet aggregation),[370-372] the drug's good safety profile, and the extensive investigation of aspirin in patients with ischemic heart disease unrelated to cocaine. There are, however, no clinical data on the use of aspirin in patients with cocaine-associated myocardial ischemia.[367]

Nitroglycerin: Nitroglycerin is recommended as first-line therapy for cocaine-induced cardiac ischemia based on studies that show a reversal of cocaine-induced coronary artery vasoconstriction[356] and reports of its ability to relieve cocaine-associated chest pain.[373]

Calcium-channel blockers: In studies of cocaine intoxication in animals, calcium-channel blockers prevent malignant arrhythmias,[374] blunt negative ionotropic effects,[375] limit the increase in systemic vascular resistance,[375] and protect against myocardial infarction.[336] However, one study by Derlet et al.[376] showed that calcium-channel blockers may increase CNS toxicity and mortality.[376] This study, which was performed on rats, has been criticized on the basis that the cocaine was administered intraperitoneally and that pretreatment with a calcium antagonist might have accelerated peritoneal absorption.[377] Another study by Nahas et al.[378] showed that nitrendipine (a calcium antagonist with good CNS penetration) protected rats against cocaine-induced seizures and lethality. Verapamil reverses cocaine-induced coronary artery vasoconstriction[379] and may play a role in the treatment of refractory myocardial ischemia secondary to cocaine use.

Phentolamine: Phentolamine, an alpha-adrenergic antagonist, reverses cocaine-induced coronary artery vasoconstriction,[351] and electrocardiographic resolution of ischemia has been documented in some patients.[367] The use of a low dose (1 mg) may avoid the hypotensive effects of the drug while maintaining the anti-ischemic effects.[380]

Beta-blockers: Because of their association with coronary vasoconstriction and conflicting animal studies (see previous section on hypertension), beta-adrenergic blockers are not routinely recommended for the treatment of cocaine-associated ischemic chest pain. However, esmolol is indicated for severe adrenergic crisis associated with tachycardia and hypertension. Esmolol or metoprolol may play a role in the treatment of cocaine-induced malignant ventricular ectopy if lidocaine and defibrillation fail[380] (see section below on arrhythmias).

Thrombolytic therapy: Biogenic amines such as serotonin and epinephrine, which are released in large quantities by drugs such as cocaine, stimulate platelet aggregation. Stimulated platelets release thromboxane A2, which exacerbates ischemia by increasing vasoconstriction. The activation of the coagulation cascade and the formation of thrombin clot may follow. Thus, thrombolytic therapy seems rational in the setting of cocaine-induced myocardial infarction. However, the safety of thrombolysis has been questioned by Bush[381] after one patient died of an intracerebral hemorrhage. A larger study by Hollander et al.[382] noted no such complications among 36 patients who received thrombolytic therapy. Although thrombolytic agents may be safe, several concerns persist among clinicians: First, the mortality from cocaine-associated myocardial infarction is extremely low in patients who reach the hospital alive (0/136 patients in one study).[383] Second, the clinical benefit of thrombolytic therapy in cocaine-induced coronary thrombosis has not been demonstrated.[382] Finally, young patients with cocaine-associated chest pain have a high incidence of early repolarization (a variant of the normal ECG[384,385]); as a result they may inadvertently receive thrombolysis when it is not necessary.[381,384,385] Because of these concerns as well as the belief by some[386] that the major mechanism of cocaine-mediated infarction is vasospasm, thrombolytic therapy is only recommended under the following circumstances: (1) when percutaneous coronary intervention and angioplasty is not available; (2) in acute myocardial infarction with an electrocardiogram with >2 mm ST-segment elevation in two or more contiguous *precordial leads*, or >1 mm ST-segment elevation in two or more contiguous *limb leads*; and (3) when no contraindications to thrombolytic therapy exist (Table 8.2.11). It is interesting to note that studies have shown significant coronary artery disease (i.e., stenosis > 50%) is present in up to 77% of patients with cocaine induced myocardial infarction.[387]

Lidocaine: Lidocaine, a sodium channel blocker, was initially thought to increase the risk of arrhythmias and seizures in patients with cocaine intoxication, based on studies in Sprague-Dawley rats.[388] Recent evidence from dog[389] and guinea pig hearts[390] suggests that lidocaine competes with cocaine for binding sites at the sodium channels and is then rapidly released from the sodium channel without harmful effects. A retrospective review of 29 patients who received lidocaine in the context of cocaine-associated dysrhythmias showed no adverse outcomes.[391] Cautious use of lidocaine to treat ventricular arrhythmias occurring after cocaine use therefore seems reasonable. Ventricular arrhythmias that occur within a few hours after the use of cocaine may be the result of sodium channel blockade (e.g., quinidine-like effects) or from excessive levels of circulating catecholamines. For this reason cardioselective beta-blockers and/or sodium bicarbonate may be effective as well.[392]

Arrhythmias: Arrhythmias that occur after cocaine abuse may be associated with myocardial infarction, excessive catecholinergic surge, and/or sodium channel blockade (e.g., "quinidine-like" effects).[393]

Table 8.2.11   Contraindications to Thrombolytic Therapy

Absolute Contraindications

Active internal bleeding
Altered consciousness
Cerebrovascular accident (CVA) in the past 6 months or *any* history of hemorrhagic CVA
Intracranial or intraspinal surgery within the previous 2 months
Intracranial or intraspinal neoplasm, aneurysm, or arteriovenous malformation
Known bleeding disorder
Persistent, severe hypertension (systolic BP > 200 mm Hg and/or diastolic BP > 120 mm Hg)
Pregnancy
Previous allergy to a streptokinase product (this does not contraindicate tPA administration)
Recent (within 1 month) head trauma
Suspected aortic dissection
Suspected pericarditis
Trauma or surgery within 2 weeks that could result in bleeding into a closed space

Relative Contraindications

Active peptic ulcer disease
Cardiopulmonary resuscitation for > 10 min
Current use of oral anticoagulants
Hemorrhagic ophthalmic conditions
History of chronic, uncontrolled hypertension (diastolic BP > 100 mm Hg), treated or untreated
History of ischemic or embolic CVA > 6 months ago
Significant trauma or major surgery > 2 weeks ago but < 2 months ago
Subclavian or internal jugular venous cannulation

Source: Adapted from National Heart Attack Alert Program Coordinating Committee 60 Minutes to Treatment Working Group, NIH Publication No. 93-3278. September 1993, p. 19.

Supraventricular arrhythmias: Supraventricular arrhythmias due to cocaine include paroxysmal supraventricular tachycardia, rapid atrial fibrillation, and atrial flutter.[394] These arrhythmias are usually short-lived and if the patient is hemodynamically stable do not require immediate therapy.[395–397] Benzodiazepines modulate the stimulatory effects of cocaine on the CNS[154,170,398] and may blunt the hypersympathetic state driving the arrhythmia. Patients with persistent supraventricular arrhythmias should be treated initially with a benzodiazepine (i.e., lorazepam or diazepam), and then if necessary with a cardioselective beta-blocker such as esmolol (see discussion under stepwise approach to management). Unstable supraventricular rhythms should be managed in accordance with the American Heart Association's American Cardiac Life Support (ACLS) protocols.

Ventricular arrhythmias (stable): As with supraventricular arrhythmias from cocaine, ventricular ectopy and short runs of ventricular tachycardia (VT) are usually transient, and most often resolve with careful observation supplemented by titrated doses of a benzodiazepine.[366] In cases with persistent ventricular ectopy, cardioselective beta-blockers (i.e., metoprolol or esmolol) may reverse excessive catecholaminergic stimulation and suppress the ectopy. Lidocaine may also be of benefit.[123,399,400]

Ventricular arrhythmias (unstable): Ventricular fibrillation (VF) and malignant VT (VT) with hypotension, or evidence of congestive heart failure, or ischemia, should initially be treated as recommended by the ACLS algorithm. Lidocaine (1.0 to 1.5 mg/kg) may be given with caution as previously discussed. Defibrillation should proceed as usual.[366]

Epinephrine: Concerns about epinephrine have been raised since it has similar cardiovascular effects as cocaine and may even mediate many of its effects. There is, however, no good evidence to suggest eliminating the initial epinephrine dose in treating cocaine-induced VF. Clinicians should, however, increase the interval between subsequent doses of epinephrine to every 5 to 10 min and avoid high-dose epinephrine (greater than 1 mg per dose) in refractory patients.[366]

Propranolol or other beta-blocker: Propranolol continues to be recommended by the Committee on Emergency Cardiac Care for the treatment of malignant cocaine-induced VF and VT. This recommendation is based on animal data and empiric reports but is not supported by any human studies.[154,369,401,402] The risk of beta-blockade in cocaine toxicity is that of unopposed alpha-stimulation resulting in severe hypertension, as well as coronary vasoconstriction.[341] This is of less concern with the use of a cardioselective beta-blocker such as esmolol or metoprolol.

8.2.7.2 Stepwise Approach to Management

Immediate Interventions

1. Airway, Breathing, Circulation: Maintain the airway and assist ventilation if necessary. Administer supplemental oxygen. Treat hypotension, and resuscitate as per previous reviews.[3,366]

2. Antidotes: Administer appropriate antidotes, including 25 g dextrose IV if the patient is hypoglycemic, as per the Section 8.2.1 on coma.

3. IV, Monitor, O_2: Administer oxygen by nasal cannula at 4 L/min, monitor cardiac status (obtain ECG) and start a peripheral intravenous line. Hang normal saline to keep vein open.

4. Benzodiazepines: Administer a benzodiazepine (i.e., 0.25 to 0.5 mg, or 2 to 4 mg IVP lorazepam) if the patient is anxious, hypertensive, or is experiencing cardiac chest pain or transient arrhythmias.

5. Sublingual and transdermal nitroglycerin/aspirin: If hemodynamically stable but chest pain persists, administer nitroglycerin sublingually (up to three tablets or three sprays of 0.4 mg each). Apply a nitroglycerin paste, 1 in., to the chest. Give one aspirin (325 mg) by mouth.

6. IV nitroglycerin: If chest pain is present and the patient is hemodynamically stable, begin a nitroglycerin drip starting at 8 to 10 μg/min. Titrate upward to control of pain if blood pressure remains stable.

7. Calcium-channel blocker: Consider the use of calcium-channel blocker such as verapamil (5.0 mg IV over 2 min, with a repeat 5 mg dose IV if symptoms persist) or diltiazem (0.25 mg/kg IV over 2 min, with repeat dose of 0.35 mg/kg IV over 2 min if symptoms persist) for resistant myocardial ischemia. Consider administration of **morphine sulfate** for chest pain if hemodynamically stable (2.0 mg IVP with additional doses titrated to control pain and anxiety).

8. Phentolamine: Use phentolamine, 1.0 to 5.0 mg IVP for resistant chest pain.

9. Thrombolytics: If ECG shows new ST segment elevation (greater than 2 mm in two consecutive leads) that persist despite nitrates or calcium-channel blockers, no contraindications exist (Table 8.2.11), and percutaneous coronary intervention is not readily available, administer a thrombolytic agent (Table 8.2.12, dosing). See previous reviews for comprehensive guide to thrombolytics.[403–406]

Comment: Establish two peripheral IVs, and perform a 12-lead ECG q 30 min until infusion completed. Avoid all unnecessary venous and arterial sticks and beware that automated blood pressure cuffs, nasogastric tubes, Foley catheters, and central lines are associated with increased bleeding.[407]

10. Arrhythmias:

Supraventricular arrhythmias: See discussion above. Generally, treatment parallels ACLS guidelines with the use of benzodiazepines and beta-blockers in the doses recommended below.

Ventricular arrhythmias: If stable ventricular tachycardia does not respond to benzodiazepines (i.e., lorazepam 0.25 to 0.50 mg/kg or 2 to 4 mg IVP) it should be treated with lidocaine (1.5 mg/kg IVP) and/or beta-blockers (metoprolol 5.0 mg IV every 5 min, to a total of 15 mg; or esmolol, load with 500 μg/kg/min over 1 min and run a maintenance infusion at 50 to 200 μg/kg/min; or propranolol, 1.0 mg IV every 5 min to a total of 3 mg). Esmolol has the advantage of being a beta-1, cardioselective agent with a short half life ($t_{1/2}$ = 9 min) allowing it to be rapidly discontinued in the event of an adverse reaction. Unstable ventricular tachycardia should be treated with immediate cardioversion or defibrillation (see ACLS recommendations on VT, VF) along with the administration of lidocaine, beta-blockers, and benzodiazepines. Patients should be reshocked after each administration of lidocaine or beta-blocker.[366] The quinidine-like effects of cocaine are man-

Table 8.2.12   Current Thrombolytic Agents and Their Dosing in the Acute MI Patient

Drug	Dose	Comments
Streptokinase (SK) (Cost $300)[a]	1.5 million units IV over 60 min	SK is antigenic; allergic reaction and rarely anaphylaxis (<1% incidence) may occur. Administration may cause hypotension, necessitating a slower infusion rate than that recommended. SK may not be effective if administered 5 days to 6 months after prior SK therapy or 12 months after APSAC therapy or a streptococcal infection.
APSAC (Anistreplase) (Cost $1675)[a]	30 units IV over 2–5 min	APSAC is also antigenic and its administration may be complicated by hypotension (see above). APSAC may not be effective if administered 5 days to 12 months after prior SK or APSAC therapy or a streptococcal infection.
Reteplase (Retavase) (Cost $3200)[a]	10 units IV over 2 min, followed by a second dose of 10 units IV over 2 min, 30 min after the first dose	Fast, convenient double-bolus dosing. Unlike SK and APSAC, reteplase is not antigenic. Hypotension complicating infusion is less likely than with either SK or APSAC. A slightly higher incidence of cerebral hemorrhage has been noted compared with SK.
tPA (Alteplase) (Cost $3200)[a]	"Front-loaded" dosing: 15 mg IV over 2 min, followed by 0.75 mg/kg (50 mg maximum) IV over 30 min, followed by 0.5 mg/kg (35 mg maximum) IV over 60 min	Do not exceed the maximum dose of 100 mg. Unlike SK and APSAC, tPA is not antigenic. Hypotension complicating infusion is less likely than with either SK or APSAC. A slightly higher incidence of cerebral hemorrhage has been noted compared with SK.
Tenecteplase (TNKase) (Cost $2850)	A single bolus dose should be administered over 5 s based on patient weight (30–50 mg)	Ease of administration, but may not stop infusion once given. Similar efficacy and complication rate as tPA.

[a] Average wholesale price to the pharmacy.

ifested by a wide complex sinus rhythm and frequently respond to boluses of sodium bicarbonate (50 mEq IV, repeat every 5 min to a total of 150 mEq). A bicarbonate drip (made by adding two to three ampoules of sodium bicarbonate in one liter of D5W) may be run simultaneously at 200 cc/h.

Comment: Caution should be taken to avoid hypernatremia or hypervolemia and resulting pulmonary edema from overzealous sodium bicarbonate administration. Also, class IA and IC antiarrhythmic agents (i.e., procainamide, dysopyramide, quinidine, propafenone) are contraindicated in the setting of drug-induced conduction blockade as is occasionally seen with cocaine.[390,392,408]

Secondary Interventions

1. **Repeat ECG:** Repeat ECG if chest pain worsens or recurs.

2. **Chest radiograph:** To further assess for congestive heart failure or evidence of cardiomyopathy; also to assess for pneumothorax, or pneumomediastinum.

3. **Monitoring:** A minimum of 12 h of cardiac monitoring is recommended for patients with chest pain associated with cocaine use (see section on disposition).

4. **Coronary Stress Testing:** Because patients with cocaine-associated chest pain have a 1-year survival of 98% and an incidence of late myocardial infarction of only 1%, urgent cardiac evaluation is probably not necessary for patients in whom acute myocardial infarction has been ruled out.[367] However, keep in mind that patients who rule in for cocaine-induced myocardial infarction, despite an average age of 32 to 38 years, have a 31 to 67% incidence of significant underlying coronary artery disease.

5. **Laboratory Data:** Baseline laboratory data should include a CBC, PT/PTT, cardiac isoenzymes including creatine kinase MB, troponin T, as well as electrolytes. Repeat isoenzymes every 8 to 12 h.

Comment: Rhabdomyolysis may complicate cocaine intoxication and as a result increased concentrations of myoglobin, creatine kinase, and creatine kinase MB may occur even in the absence of myocardial infarction.[409] After using cocaine, approximately 50% of patients have elevations in the serum creatine kinase concentration whether or not they are experiencing a myocardial infarction.[410] If the patient has a continuously rising enzyme concentration this is much more likely to represent a true myocardial infarction.[383,410] The immunoassay for cardiac troponin I has no detectable cross-reactivity with human skeletal muscle troponin I, making it a more specific test than that for creatine kinase MB in assessing myocardial injury when skeletal-muscle injury also exists.[411,412] However, troponin I is a late marker for myocardial infarction with improved sensitivity after 12 h (95 to 100%) vs. CK-MB, which is usually elevated within 6 to 8 h.[413]

6. Disposition

a. **Intensive care unit**: All patients with evidence of acute myocardial infarction, or any unstable patient.

b. **Telemetry:** Hemodynamically stable patients without ongoing chest pain, ECG changes, or elevated cardiac isoenzymes to a monitored observation unit for a minimum of 12 h of monitoring and serial creatine-kinase MB measurements and repeat ECGs. Patients who have no evidence of ongoing chest pain with normal ECG and cardiac isoenzymes after 12 h may be discharged.

c. **Home:** Selected patients who have normal ECG, cardiac enzymes, and no evidence of ongoing ischemia may be discharged after a period of 9 to 12 h.

Comment: Observation periods to 9 to 12 h to rule out myocardial infarction in low-risk patients with chest pain unrelated to cocaine use have become more common.[414–416] Similar observation periods may be appropriate for many patients with cocaine-associated chest discomfort since these patients appear to have a low incidence of cardiovascular complications, whether or not they have myocardial infarction.[417] Of patients with cocaine-associated chest pain, approximately 6% will have a myocardial infarction.[384,410,418] Of those patients with cocaine-associated myocardial infarction, 36% will go on to develop cardiovascular complications.[383] Of those who develop cardiovascular complications 94–100% can be detected by the use of ECG, serial creatine kinase MB measurements, and observation for 12 h.[383]

8.2.8 Stroke

8.2.8.1 General Comments

Any physician treating a patient who has suffered a stroke must consider drug abuse in the differential diagnosis, especially if the patient is young.[419–424] In a study done at San Francisco General Hospital, drug abuse was identified as the most common predisposing condition among patients under 35 years of age presenting with stroke.[425] Most patients had either infective endocarditis (13/73) or stroke occurring soon after the use of a stimulant (34/73). Kaku and Lowenstein[425] estimated that the relative risk for stroke among drug abusers after controlling for other stroke risk factors was 6.5.

Mechanism: Acute stroke associated with drugs of abuse may result from hemorrhage, vasoconstriction, severe hypertension, hypotension, embolism of foreign materials (i.e., talc, ground up tablets, etc.; see Table 8.2.5 through Table 8.2.7) via a patent foramen ovale, vasculitis, cardiac thrombi, endocarditis, and opportunistic infection.[426] Among patients with stroke from cocaine abuse about 50% have cerebral hemorrhage, 30% subarachnoid hemorrhage, and 20% have ischemic stroke.[427,428] The pathophysiologic mechanisms involved are thus much different than for the general population, where the overwhelming majority of strokes are ischemic (80%) in origin and only 10% result from hemorrhage.[429] This difference makes the treatment of drug-induced stroke significantly different. Instead of anticoagulation or internal carotid artery surgery, the drug-abusing patient may be more appropriately treated with steroids for vasculitis, antibiotics for endocarditis, or calcium-channel blockers for vasospasm.

Thrombolytics: There is substantial disagreement in the literature regarding the safety and efficacy of thrombolytic therapy for ischemic strokes. Data from the five completed randomized trials evaluating the use of intravenous thrombolytics in the treatment of ischemic strokes (ECASS,[430] MAST-I,[431] NINDS,[432] MAST-E,[433] and ASK[434]) involve a total of more than 2500 patients, but these studies used two different thrombolytic agents — tissue plasminogen activator (tPA) and streptokinase (SK) — that were given at different doses, with different adjunctive treatments, and with very different inclusion criteria. Thus it is impossible to pool the data for meta-analysis. Analyzing the studies individually, however, reveals that all three of the SK trials found excess mortality in the SK group that was both statistically and clinically significant, as did one of the two studies that used tPA. The fifth study, the NINDS trial, is the only one of the five to find outcome benefit in treated patients. The patients in the NINDS study all received thrombolytics within a 3-h time interval, which required rapid CT and radiologist review of the results before treatment could begin. These strict exclusion criteria would result in the treatment of only a very small percentage of stroke victims[434a] (less than 5%). Furthermore, the increased risk of bleeding associated with thrombolytics would be imposed upon a number of patients who did not require treatment. Libman and colleagues[435] reported that about 20% of the time when members of the trained acute stroke intervention team at their institution diagnosed stroke on clinical grounds prior to CT scan, the ultimate diagnosis proved to be different. Although treatment depended on CT results, in over half of the patients misdiagnosed clinically the CT scan also returned a result entirely compatible with stroke. Of these, 13 patients were postictal, 13 had systemic infections as the cause of their "stoke mimic," and 10 had an ultimate diagnosis of toxic-metabolic cause. Because of the controversy surrounding ischemic strokes, and because of the increased risk of intracerebral hemorrhage (from uncontrolled hypertension; seizures; cerebral aneurysms, and vasculitis), thrombolytics are not recommended at this time for the treatment of drug-induced stroke.

Heparin: Although heparin has been recommended for the treatment of crescendo transient ischemic attacks (TIAs), strokes with a cardioembolic source, and posterior circulation strokes,[436–438] it should be used with extreme caution in patients with drug-induced strokes because of the higher potential for hemorrhage (i.e., ~50%).

Antibiotics: Stroke complicates approximately 20% of all cases of endocarditis, with an overall mortality rate for endocarditis-associated strokes of 20%.[439,440] Fortunately, the risk of recurrent embolism is low when infection is controlled (0.3%/day),[440] obviating the need for anticoagulation despite that most endocarditis-related stokes are due to embolism from cardiac vegetations.[439,440] Present recommendations for empiric antibiotic treatment are nafcillin 2.0 g q 4 h IV + gentamicin 1.0 mg/kg q 8 h IM or IV. If the patient is penicillin allergic give vancomycin 1.0 g q 12 h IV + gentamicin 1.0 mg/kg q 8 h IM or IV.

Surgery: Foreign body emboli most often have followed injection of crushed tablet preparations meant for oral use, especially methylphenidate (Ritalin) and pentazocine plus tripelennamine ("T's and Blues").[441,442] Patients dissolve tablets or capsules in water and filter them to varying extents, and then inject them. Showers of insoluble fillers (principally talc) enter the circulation[419] and lodge in the lung, forming granulomas. Granulomas may also form in the lung and brain (possibly due to the passage of foreign materials through a patent foramen ovale), and may require surgical intervention. Surgery may also be required for decompression of cerebral hematomas, repair of ruptured aneurysms, and the removal of abscesses.

Nimodipine: Cocaine is known to decrease reuptake of serotonin, which is believed to play a role in cocaine-induced headaches and may be associated with cocaine-induced vasoconstriction.[443–445] Rothrock et al.[446] reported on three cases of amphetamine-related stroke: in one case a 35-year-old abuser had 20 episodes of transient right hemiparesis occurring within minutes of inhaling methamphetamine; later he developed permanent right hemiparesis. In animal studies, intravenous methamphetamine administration has resulted in narrowing of the middle cerebral artery branches within 19 min.[447] While the pharmacologic approaches to cerebral vasospasm are varied, the calcium-channel blocker nimodipine has been used widely with proven efficacy in preventing vasospasm associated with hemorrhagic stroke.[448,449] No studies looking at this issue in the setting of drug-induced hemorrhagic stroke exists. Although two animal studies[450,451] found that nimodipine potentiated the toxicity of cocaine and amphetamines in rats, it is felt that in selected patients the risk–benefit ratio may favor nimodipine administration. Such populations may include the drug-abusing patient who is experiencing transient ischemic attacks closely temporally related to substance abuse or who has had a documented subarachnoid hemorrhage associated with cerebral vasospasm. Recent reports suggest no benefit of nifedipine in ischemic strokes of any type.[452]

Glucocorticoids/cyclophosphamide (vasculitis): Vasculitis has been associated with nearly every drug of abuse (ephedrine,[453] pentazocine and tripelennamine,[442] amphetamines,[447,454,455] phenylpropanolamine,[456] heroin,[457,458] methylphenidate,[459] pseudoephedrine,[323] and cocaine[460–463]). In the case of drug-induced vasculitis, removal and discontinuance of the offending agent is essential. While not considered emergency therapy, the combination of cyclophosphamide and prednisone may be of benefit in the treatment of drug-induced vasculitis and resulting stroke. Salanova[464] and Glick[323] reported on two cases of amphetamine- and phenylpropanolamine-induced vasculitis that had improvement documented angiographically with combination cyclophosphamide and prednisone This combination therapy is also recommended for the treatment of other life-threatening vasculitides including polyarteritis nodosa (PAN) and Wegener's granulomatosis.[464]

Comment: Many reports of drug-induced vasculitis are based on angiographic findings of segmental narrowing and dilations of distal intracerebral arteries. Although such signs are characteristic of cerebral vasculitis, they are nonspecific features of vascular injury, and can also be caused by vasospasm (secondary to a drug's action or to subarachnoid hemorrhage), fibromuscular dysplasia, atherosclerosis, and cerebral emboli.[465] Biopsy is recommended to determine which patients should receive appropriate therapy.

Acute hypertension: Acute, severe hypertension from stimulants such as cocaine and amphetamines can increase vascular intraluminal pressures, cause turbulent blood flow, and weaken the endothelium, leading to hemorrhage and thrombosis. Severe hypertension should therefore be controlled (see Section 8.2.6 on hypertension). Moderate hypertension, however, may be a homeostatic response designed to maintain intracerebral blood flow in the presence of intracranial hypertension. In this case, blood pressure should not be lowered, or, if there is ongoing evidence of sympathomimetic drug intoxication, it should be lowered gradually to a diastolic blood pressure in the 100 to 110 mm Hg range. Clinical judgment should be used in this setting since decreasing blood flow to "watershed" areas or borderline ischemic zones with poor collateral circulation may lead to larger neurological deficits.[466–468]

8.2.8.2 Stepwise Approach to Management

Immediate Interventions

1. Airway, Breathing, Circulation: Maintain the airway and assist ventilation if necessary. Administer supplemental oxygen. Treat hypotension, and resuscitate as per previous reviews.[3,366] If the patient requires rapid sequence intubation consider using an agent such as pentobarbital, 5 mg/kg, or thiopental, 3 to 5 mg/kg, that will both lower intracranial pressure and decrease risk of seizures. Do not give barbiturates to a hypotensive patient. Lidocaine, 100 mg, prior to intubation is helpful in attenuating the rise in intracranial pressure seen with laryngoscopy.[469,470]

2. Antidotes: Administer appropriate antidotes, including 25 g dextrose IV if the patient is hypoglycemic, as per Section 8.2.1 on coma. Even focal findings may be caused by hypoglycemia; a focal neurologic finding occurs in about 2.5% of hypoglycemic patients.[471]

3. IV, Monitor, O$_2$: Administer oxygen by nasal cannula at 4 L/min. Monitor cardiac status (obtain ECG) and start a peripheral intravenous line. Hang normal saline to keep vein open.

4. Herniation and increased intracranial pressure: Hyperventilation (to a pCO_2 of 30 to 35 mm Hg), mannitol (0.5 g/kg over 20 min IV), and possibly furosemide (10 mg IV) are indicated for evidence of *progressive* mass effect, shift, or herniation. Limit IV fluids to avoid cerebral edema.

5. Control agitation: An agitated patient with ongoing sympathomimetic effects of stimulants (delirium, psychosis, and agitation) should be sedated with benzodiazepines as discussed in Section 8.2.2. Straining, struggling, or arguing could elevate intracranial pressure and increase the risk of exacerbating a hemorrhagic stroke. Neuromuscular paralysis with endotracheal intubation and mechanical ventilation may be necessary.

6. Control seizure activity: Due to their ability to lower intracranial pressure barbiturates may be preferred for seizure control if the patient has evidence of increased intracranial pressure. Benzodiazepines are still recommended for the rapid initial management (Section 8.2.3, seizures).

7. Control nausea and vomiting: For the same reasons discussed above. Use something that will not lower the seizure threshold such as prochlorperizine. Instead, try metoclopramide 10 to 50 mg IVP.

8. Hypertension: Antihypertensive therapy is not usually necessary in the emergency department. Exceptions may be patients in whom acute ongoing drug intoxication is apparent. It should be kept in mind that the more severe the stroke, the greater the homeostatic, hypertensive response.

9. CT of the brain: Perform a CT of the brain without contrast on all the following patients:

a. Patients with focal neurological deficits
b. Patients with altered mental status that does not rapidly return to normal after a brief period of observation
c. Patients who complain of severe rapid onset of headache that persists after sedation, and minor pain medications

10. Laboratory Data: Baseline laboratory data should include CBC, platelets, PT/PTT, electrolytes, and sedimentation rate. Perform CPK isoenzymes if the patient has chest pain, or is obtunded to rule out myocardial infarction. Draw blood cultures if endocarditis is suspected. While the use of toxicology screens of blood and urine are generally overutilized,[5] they are recommended if diagnosis remains questionable.

Secondary Interventions

1. Monitor and reassess: Closely monitor neurological status for signs of deterioration.

2. ECG: Perform ECG to determine underlying cardiac rhythm.

3. Seizure prophylaxis: Phenobarbital 15 mg/kg IV over 20 min, as prophylaxis in hemorrhagic strokes. Fosphenytoin may be considered as an alternative although is considered less effective for drug related seizures.

4. Autonomic instability: Extreme fluctuations in blood pressure and heart rate are often the result of excessive autonomic discharge associated with hemorrhagic stroke and may, in severe cases, be treated with esmolol or labetalol (see hypertension).

5. Echocardiogram, blood cultures: Transthoracic echocardiography is a useful noninvasive diagnostic test for endocarditis, which is approximately 80% sensitive in finding vegetations on native and bioprosthetic valves.[472] Transesophogeal echocardiography (not usually available in the emergency department) is preferred for the detection of valvular vegetations due to increased sensitivity, especially if the patient has mechanical prosthetic valves that may produce artifact from the metallic components.[473] Obtain three blood cultures to increase sensitivity to greater than 95% in the febrile patient.[474]

6. Thrombolytics/heparin: Avoid thrombolytics and use heparin sparingly (e.g., only in those patients with evidence of cressendo transient ischemia in consultation with a neurologist, in patients who have had hemorrhagic stroke ruled out).

7. Angiogram: If the stroke is hemorrhagic or if the patient has evidence of endocarditis, consider performing a cerebral angiogram to rule out vasculitis/aneurysm.

8. Nimodipine: Nimodipine, 60 mg PO q 6 h should be considered in all patients with subarachnoid hemorrhage and others with evidence of recent drug abuse and stuttering onset or progression of symptoms suggestive of acute vasospasm.

9. Biopsy: Surgical biopsy should be performed when the diagnosis of *vasculitis* is suggested by angiogram and yet still remains in question. Alternatively, if the patient requires surgery for any other reason (i.e., intracerebral hematoma) a biopsy can be done at that time. Because there seems to be discernible histological differences between drug-induced and primary CNS vasculitis, leptomeningeal biopsy may be the definitive means of differentiating these two entities.[323]

10. Disposition: All patients with drug-induced stroke should be admitted to the hospital for thorough evaluation. Likewise all patients with drug-induced TIAs should be admitted to the hospital.

8.2.9 Ingestions and Decontamination

8.2.9.1 *General Comments*

Ingestion vs. "packing" or "stuffing": Definitions of the terms ingestion, packing, and stuffing are required to understand the different approaches to decontamination that are recommended here. *Ingestions* occur when drugs of abuse are taken orally as a method of inducing a "high" or as a suicidal attempt. *Body packing* refers to the use of the human gastrointestinal (GI) tract for purposes of drug smuggling.[475–477] Smugglers or "mules" ingest a drug, usually cocaine or heroin, in carefully wrapped high-grade latex, aluminum foil, or condoms designed to prevent leakage. Case reports even describe the use of children who are forced to consume large numbers of drug-containing packets.[478] Each packet typically contains potentially lethal amounts of drug (a typical packet of cocaine contains 5 to 7 g; lethal dose = 1.0 to 1.2 g in a human). *Body stuffing* refers to the act of swallowing poorly wrapped "baggies," vials, or other packages filled with illegal drugs in an attempt to conceal them from the police. Baggies or vials may or may not contain lethal amounts of drug. A variant of body stuffing is the ingestion of drugs to produce an acute medical condition that could necessitate medical intervention, thereby deferring incarceration[479] (see Table 8.2.13).

Methods of decontamination:

Gastric lavage: Gastric lavage has been a widely accepted medical treatment for ingested poisons.[480] Opposed to this practice are four large prospective, randomized, controlled studies in humans involving a total of 2476 patients, which have consistently failed to support the routine use of gut emptying. Kulig et al.[481] demonstrated that poisoned patients receiving charcoal alone without prior gut emptying had no significant difference in clinical outcome compared to patients who were treated with both gastric lavage and activated charcoal. The exception was a small subset ($n = 16$) of patients who were obtunded on presentation and were lavaged within 1 h of ingestion. Albertson et al.[482] compared the clinical effectiveness of syrup of ipecac and activated charcoal to that of activated charcoal alone in the treatment of 200 patients with mild to moderate toxic ingestions. Patients receiving only activated charcoal were discharged from the emergency department in significantly less time than those receiving both syrup of ipecac plus activated charcoal. Merigian et al.[483] evaluated 808 patients with ingestions and found no benefit from gastric emptying with administration of activated charcoal compared to activated charcoal alone. Moreover, gastric lavage was associated with a higher incidence of medical intensive care unit admissions and aspiration pneumonia in this study. Most recently, Pond et al.[484] performed a prospective, controlled study of 876 patients and concluded that gastric emptying is unnecessary in the treatment of acute overdose regardless of severity of intoxication and promptness of presentation.

Recommendation: Based on these studies, there is little support for routine use of gastric lavage in the drug abusing patient who presents to the emergency department after an ingestion. An exception

Table 8.2.13   Comparison of Body Packers and Body Stuffers

	Body Packer	**Body Stuffer**
Profile	Returning from trip abroad; found in airports or at border crossings	Encountered on street or in drug raid, often arrested for dealing or other charge; may be chronic drug abuser or known drug dealer
How brought to attention	Deny drug ingestion; serious symptoms (seizure, respiratory arrest) or asymptomatic; diagnosis by radiograph or physical examination; likely to have a diagnostic radiograph or rectal examination	Seen taking drugs, or found symptomatic in jail; radiograph tends to be of little diagnostic help
Drugs involved	High-profit drug (e.g., cocaine or heroin)	Any drug sold on street, including hallucinogens or sedatives; often involves more than one drug
Packaging material	High-grade latex, aluminum foil, or condoms designed to prevent leakage Large amount of drugs per package.	Loosely wrapped in paper or foil; single doses or free drug
Treatment	Usually observation; surgery for intestinal obstruction; value of charcoal or cathartic unknown; treat if symptoms develop	Gastric emptying and activated charcoal and cathartic; observe and treat symptomatically
Clinical course	Rupture of single package may be fatal because of the large amount of drug per package; specific toxic syndromes may be present, e.g., narcotic or cocaine toxicity	Variable symptoms, often from a mixed drug overdose; may have acute laryngeal obstruction

may be the patient who has swallowed an extremely large quantity of drug and presents within 30 to 60 min.

Activated charcoal: Activated charcoal given orally has been proved to be as effective as gastric emptying followed by activated charcoal in the studies described above. In other studies involving volunteers, activated charcoal was shown to be superior to ipecac-induced emesis, or gastric lavage.[485,486] A dose of 50 to 100 g of activated charcoal is generally sufficient to bind the drug and prevent absorption, although this may vary depending on the drug and the amount that was taken. This 50 to 100 g dose was based on a study in which healthy volunteers were given up to 5 g of para-aminosalicylate (PAS).[487] The fraction of unadsorbed PAS decreased from 55 to 3% as the charcoal-to-PAS ratio increased from 1:1 to 10:1. Activated charcoal is relatively safe, although vomiting and diarrhea are seen commonly when cathartics such as sorbitol are added, and constipation can result if cathartics are withheld. Serious adverse effects include pulmonary aspiration of activated charcoal along with gastric contents;[488–490] significant morbidity from spillage of activated charcoal in the peritoneum after perforation from gastric lavage;[491] and intestinal obstruction and pseudo-obstruction,[492–494] especially following repeated doses of activated charcoal in the presence of dehydration.

Recommendation: Activated charcoal is recommended in all cases of orally administered drug intoxication except if the drug is not bound by charcoal (e.g., lithium, iron, alcohols).

Multiple-dose activated charcoal: Multiple-dose activated charcoal (MDAC), sometimes referred to as "gastrointestinal dialysis," is thought to produce its beneficial effect by interrupting the enteroenteric and in some cases, the enterohepatic re-circulation of drugs.[495] In addition, any remaining unabsorbed drug may be adsorbed to the repeated doses of activated charcoal. Phenobarbital is the only drug of abuse for which there is evidence from both clinical and experimental studies in animals and volunteers that drug elimination is increased by the use of MDAC.[495] Pharmacokinetic data would also support the use of MDAC for carbamazepine, theophylline, aspirin, dapsone, and quinine ingestions.[495] Pond et al.[496] performed a controlled trial of ten comatose patients who overdosed on phenobarbital. In this study, the control and treatment groups both received 50 g activated charcoal on presentation and, in addition, patients in the treatment group were given 17 g activated charcoal together with sorbitol every 4 h until they could be extubated. Although the mean elimination half-life of phenobarbital was shortened (36 ± 13 h vs. 93 ± 52 h), the length of time the patients in each group required mechanical ventilation or stayed in the hospital did not differ significantly. This study suggested that acute tolerance to the effects of the drug obviated the benefit of faster drug elimination. Another study looking at a series of six patients given charcoal in larger doses and without cathartic showed enhanced elimination of phenobarbital, and also decreased time to recovery.[497] Beware of inducing aspiration with MDAC. Other adverse effects including obstipation and appendicitis have been described with MDAC.[498]

Recommendation: MDAC is recommended in cases in which there may be large quantities of drug in the intestinal tract (i.e., body packers or body stuffers) and in selected cases of phenobarbital overdose (i.e., comatose patients who have not received hemoperfusion).

Whole bowel irrigation: Whole bowel irrigation (WBI) involves the administration of large volumes (2 L/h in an adult, 0.5 L/h in a child) of polyethylene glycol electrolyte lavage solution (PEG-ELS) per nasogastric tube to flush out the gastrointestinal tract and decrease the time available for drug to be absorbed. It has been used effectively in the management of iron,[499–501] sustained-release theophylline,[502] sustained-release verapamil,[503,504] sustained release fenfluramine,[505] zinc sulfate,[504] and lead,[506] and for body packers.[475,507] Because of its balanced electrolyte content and iso-osmolor nature, PEG-ELS use results in minimal net water and electrolyte shifts, and is safe and effective under the right circumstances. In the case of body packers, the excellent bowel cleansing from WBI may reduce morbidity should bowel perforation occur or surgery be required.[475] In a case described by Utecht et al.[507] 10-g packets of heroin wrapped in electrician's tape appeared to be dissolved by 8 L of PEG-ELS solution. Endoscopy showed this patient to have only electrician's tape left in his stomach after WBI, suggesting the heroin initially present had been dissolved by the WBI solution. Polyethylene glycols are used extensively in pharmaceutical manufacturing as solubilizing agents and it has been shown that PEG 4000, a water-soluble polymer comparable to the polymer used in PEG-ELS, can increase the dissolution rates of poorly water-soluble drugs.[508] Alkaloidal heroin is poorly water soluble; 1 g dissolves in 1700 ml of water.[509] Therefore, the large amount of heroin, 10 g in each package, would not have been solubilized in the stomach by water alone. The patient had continuing absorption of heroin despite the administration of multiple doses of activated charcoal. Rosenberg[510] has shown that the antidotal efficacy of oral activated charcoal was markedly diminished by PEG-ELS in volunteers treated with aspirin. Tenenbein[511] likewise reported that PEG-ELS binds to charcoal and that this interferes with aspirin adsorption by activated charcoal.

Recommendation: WBI is recommended in cases involving body packers. WBI is also recommended in situations in which large amounts of drug may still be present in the gastrointestinal tract due to concretions (common with gluthethimide, and meprobamate) or when a sustained release preparation (i.e., sustained release morphine) has been ingested. Because WBI may solubilize heroin and may diminish the efficacy of activated charcoal the use of activated charcoal and cathartics is preferred over WBI for treatment of heroin body packers.

8.2.9.2 Stepwise Approach to Management

Immediate Interventions

1. Airway, Breathing, Circulation: Maintain the airway and assist ventilation if necessary. Administer supplemental oxygen. Treat hypotension, and resuscitate as per previous reviews.[3, 90]

2. IV, Monitor, O$_2$: Administer oxygen by nasal cannula at 4 L/min, monitor cardiac status (obtain ECG), and start a peripheral intravenous line. Hang normal saline to keep vein open.

3. Gastric lavage: Not recommended unless patient has ingested massive quantities and arrives within 30 min to 1 h of ingestion.

4. Activated charcoal: Administer activated charcoal 50 to 100 g PO. Try to obtain a 10:1 ratio of activated charcoal to drug by weight if possible. If unable to administer enough activated charcoal on the first dose repeat the dose in 4 h. Multiple-dose activated charcoal: give 12.5 g/h or 25 g every 3 to 4 h. Studies have shown that the administration of hourly activated charcoal produces a shorter half-life than less frequent dosing, even though the same dose was administered over the same treatment period.[512,513]

Comment: Administer MDAC for (1) the rare phenobarbital overdoses (as discussed above), (2) for the body packer or body stuffer (see below), and (3) for the patient suspected of taking a sustained release preparation. If the patient has difficulty tolerating activated charcoal because of drug-induced vomiting, smaller doses of activated charcoal administered more frequently may reduce the likelihood of vomiting. It may, however, be necessary to give either IV metoclopramide (10 to 50 mg IVP) or ondansetron (4 to 8 mg IVP) to ensure satisfactory administration of charcoal.[495]

5. Guard against aspiration: Do not force patients who are nauseated to take activated charcoal. If nausea exists, treat with metoclopramide as above. Patients who do not have a gag reflex should have their airways protected with endotracheal intubation (although this does not guarantee protection) and elevation of the head of the bed to 45°.

6. Laboratory Data: Baseline laboratory data should be guided by clinical presentation. If the patient is asymptomatic no laboratory is immediately essential. Perform a CBC, and electrolytes with CPK isoenzymes if the patient is obtunded or has chest pain, to rule out occult metabolic/infectious disease and/or myocardial infarction. While the use of toxicology screens of blood and urine are generally overutilized,[5] they are recommended if diagnosis remains questionable.

Comment: The use of urine toxicology screening may be particularly misleading in the case of a body packer or stuffer and should not be used to determine if the patient ingested any drugs. Recreational use of the drug prior to "stuffing" could lead to a false positive test. On the other hand, no prior drug usage without rupture of packets could lead to a false negative test. In one study of 50 body packers 64% had positive urine toxicology screens for drugs of abuse.[514]

Secondary Interventions

1. The body stuffer: Some authors recommend that the asymptomatic body packer or stuffer should be observed for a period of at least 48 to 72 h and treated with repeated dose-activated charcoal and cathartics.[479] This approach may be better suited to the treatment of body packers who have a lethal amount of drug in their intestinal tract. In the asymptomatic body stuffer the administration of activated charcoal and observation seems more appropriate but has not been carefully studied. In a series of more than 100 cocaine body packers, those who went on to develop serious complications became symptomatic within 6 h.[515] A recommended treatment approach follows:

  a. **Activated charcoal:** Give activated charcoal, 1 g/kg.
  b. **Observation:** If asymptomatic, observe for 6 h and repeat activated charcoal.
  c. **Discharge:** At this time it is felt that there is too little evidence to guide a well-supported recommendation for the release of these patients from the hospital. Clinical judgment should be used based on the type and the amount of drug ingested. Some recommend discharge after an observation period of greater than 6 h if the patient is asymptomatic.
  d. **WBI:** If symptomatic and large amount of drug has been ingested or sustained-release preparations are involved, consider whole bowel irrigation with 2 L/h of polyethylene glycol (PEG) after the first dose of activated charcoal.

2. The body packer: Treatment is as per the body stuffer and it is wise to admit these patients until all packets are passed and accounted for.

  a. **X-rays:** A plain upright abdominal film can detect a large percentage of packets (e.g., false negative rate of 17 to 19% in two series[516,517]) and is recommended to determine location and amount of drug ingested. However, a negative x-ray does not rule out body packing.
  b. **WBI:** The use of electrolyte bowel preparation solutions such as polyethylene glycol (e.g., GOLYTELY) has aided foreign body passage[475,518] and is recommended in all cases except those involving heroin. Give 2 L/h for adults and 500 cc/h for children.
  c. **Cathartic:** An alternative to whole bowel irrigation is a cathartic, such as 3% sodium sulfate solution (250 to 500 ml), given orally with the activated charcoal. Cathartics such as sodium sulfate do not eliminate packets as rapidly as WBI. This may allow more time for the packets to dissolve. Conversely, a gentler approach with less risk of damage to the packets is provided. Use of cathartics

without WBI is recommended in uncooperative patients (unless a court order is obtained), those who body-pack heroin (due to the reported possibility of increasing solubility of heroin in poly-ethylene glycol[507]), and in those known to have packets that are weakly wrapped (due to theoretical concerns about breaking open packets with vigorous irrigation and increased peristalsis[507]). Further studies are needed to validate these recommendations.

d. **Enemas:** If foreign bodies are located in the colon, low-volume phosphasoda enemas or high-volume normal saline enemas may be helpful.[507]

e. **Suppository:** One Dulcolax suppository per rectum to empty the rectum.

f. **Gastrointestinal series:** Following the passage of the "last" packet, a Gastrograffin upper gastrointestinal series with small bowel follow-through may be performed to ensure that the gut has been purged of all containers.[519]

g. **Surgery:** In the presence of a leaking or a ruptured package, decisions about surgical removal should be made on an individual basis; laparotomy is indicated if this is intestinal obstruction.

Comment: Because of risk of packet rupture avoid attempts to remove packages via gastroscopy or colonoscopy.[519] Syrup of ipecac or gastric lavage are ineffective due to the large size of the packets, and may cause packages to break.

3. Disposition: Patients may be discharged from the emergency department if they meet the following criteria:

a. Normal vital signs
b. Normal physical exam, including the presence of bowel sounds
c. Normal or near normal laboratory data
d. Ingestion known to be nontoxic
e. Psychiatric referral
f. Stable family environment

Comment: As noted previously more studies are needed to support any recommendations for the safe discharge of body stuffers.

8.2.10 Management of Specific Drugs of Abuse

8.2.10.1 Psychostimulants

Drug	Unique Characteristics	Key Management Issues
Cocaine	Stimulant associated with more serious complications than any other; affects all organ systems; no longer confined to affluent sectors of society	Adrenergic crisis, hyperthermia, hypertension, cardiac ischemia and arrhythmias, seizures, stroke, panic attacks, psychosis, rhabdomyolysis
Amphetamines and methamphetamine	Frequently associated with paranoid psychosis after chronic abuse. Lead poisoning has been described (lead is used as a reagent in illicit laboratories)	Same as cocaine with lower incidence of cardiac ischemia, stroke
MDMA, MDEA/MDA ("Ecstasy")	Designer amphetamine widely used at dance parties or "raves"; affects serotonin more than other amphetamines, leading to hallucinations; possibly linked to the serotonin syndrome	Same as cocaine with lower incidence of cardiac ischemia, stroke; severe hyperthermia in dehydrated dancers has led to death. Rehydrate and control hyperthermia
Methcathinone ("CAT")	Designer amphetamine with intoxicating effects that may last up to 6 days; more common in former Soviet Union	Same as amphetamines

Continued.

Drug	Unique Characteristics	Key Management Issues
Pemoline/methylph enidate	Principal therapeutic use is in children and adults with attention-deficit disorder; commonly associated with abnormal involuntary movements	Same as amphetamines
DOB	Strong hallucinogenic effects that are long-lasting (up to 10 h); may have an ergot-like effect	Same as amphetamines, severe hypertension, or evidence of ischemia (digital, mesenteric) should be treated with phentolamine and anticoagulation
TMA-2, DOM/STP	Designer amphetamines with less sympathetic stimulation in usual doses; prominent hallucinogenic effects	Adequate treatment is usually possible by calming hallucinations with benzodiazepines and removal to a quiet setting
Ephedrine	Recently removed from over-the-counter sale; amphetamine-like substance less potent than amphetamines	Same as amphetamines
Phenylpropanol-amine	Primarily an β-adrenergic agonist, as a result hypertension with reflex bradycardia is common, also associated with cerebral hemorrhage	May treat hypertension with an β-blocker such as phentolamine; do not treat bradycardia with atropine since this will exacerbate hypertension
Mescaline	Phenylethylamine derivative found in peyote cactus, associated with strong hallucinogenic properties due to effects on the serotonergic system	Adequate treatment is usually possible by calming hallucinations with benzodiazepines and removal to a quiet setting
PCP, PHP, and derivatives	Associated with erratic, violent behavior; intoxicated patients prone to sustaining significant injuries due to dissociative, anesthetic properties	As with other psychostimulants with greater emphasis on controlling behavioral toxicity since this is the major cause of death

Abbreviations: MDMA-3,4-methylenedioxymethamphetamine; MDEA-3,4 methylenedioxyethamphetamine; MDA-3,4-methylenedioxyamphetamine; DOB-4-bromo-2,5-dimethoxyamphetamine; TMP-2-2,4,5-trimethoxyamphetamine; DOM/STP-4-methyl-2,5-dimethoxyamphetamine; PCP-Phencyclidine; PHP-phenylcyclohexlpyrrolidine.

Contraindications: Nonselective beta-blockers should not be administered to patients with chest pain if a psychostimulant has been ingested although cardioselective beta-blockers may be used for certain tachyarrhythmias. Acidification of urine may slightly hasten the elimination of PCP and amphetamines but it is not recommended due to an increased risk of myoglobinuric renal failure.

8.2.10.2 Opiates

Drug	Unique Characteristics	Key Management Issues
Diacetylmorphine (heroin)	Prototype opiate of abuse, rapidly metabolized to morphine, more lipid soluble	Respiratory depression, coma, anoxic encephalopathy, pulmonary edema, withdrawal, compartment syndromes
Methadone (Dolophine)	Slow onset and long duration of action (half-life 15–72 h)	As with heroin; may require a naloxone infusion (see below) and prolonged monitoring
Designer Opiates: Fentanyl (Sublimaze), Sufentanil (Sufenta), Alfentanil (Alfenta)	Most potent opiates (16–700× morphine), with rapid onset and short duration of action (minutes)	As with heroin May accumulate in body fat necessitating observation periods similar to heroin overdose (12 h); may see negative screen for opiates

Continued.

Drug	Unique Characteristics	Key Management Issues
Propoxyphene (Darvon)	High mortality, sudden death reported, convulsions and cardiac arrhythmias due to metabolite (norpropoxyphene), fat soluble so may have prolonged duration of action	As with heroin Prolonged observation required after overdose (see Table 8.2.1) Wide complex tachycardia may respond to bicarbonate, may be resistant to naloxone, check acetaminophen level
Pentazocine (Talwin)	Agonist-antagonist, dysphoria, no cases of pulmonary edema reported	As with heroin May be resistant to naloxone
Dextromethorphan/ codeine	Less respiratory depression, possible serotonin-releasing effects	As with heroin Usually less serious in overdose than other opiates, check acetaminophen level if codeine ingested
Meperidine (Demerol)	Synthetic opiate associated with seizures in large doses due to metabolite (normeperidine)	As with heroin
Hydromorphone (Dilaudid)	Similar to morphine but more potent and shorter duration of action	As with heroin
Morphine (MS-contin)	Sustained-release, oral chewing converts to rapidly acting agents	As with heroin Prolonged observation required after overdose (see Table 8.2.1)

Contraindications: Administration of high dose (>2.0 mg) naloxone in any patient at risk for opiate withdrawal.

Naloxone infusion: Take two-thirds the amount of naloxone required for the patient to initially wake up and give that amount at an hourly rate. Mix the naloxone in the patient's maintenance IV (D5W, D51/2NS, 1/2NS, NS, etc.). Infusions should be maintained in an intensive care setting. Patients should be closely watched any time the infusion is stopped. Duration of observation depends on the route of drug administration, the drug ingested, the presence or absence of liver dysfunction, and the possibility of ongoing drug absorption from the gastrointestinal tract. Usually 6 h is adequate.

8.2.10.3 Sedative–Hypnotic Agents

Drug	Unique Characteristics	Key Management Issues
Benzodiazepines	High therapeutic index makes death unlikely unless coingestions involved; memory impairment common	Respiratory depression, coma, compartment syndromes; severe withdrawal; use flumazenil in selected cases only; supportive care usually all that is required
GHB	Common at "raves," associated with profound coma that rapidly resolves within 2 h, increased muscle tone with jerking	Supportive care, rarely requires endotracheal intubation, guard against aspiration
Long-lasting barbiturates (i.e., phenobarbital); duration of action = 10–12 h	Phenobarbital ($t_{1/2}$ = 24–140 h) may induce prolonged deep coma (5–7 days) mimicking death; pneumonia is a common complication due to prolonged coma; hypothermia	As with benzodiazepines, although cardiac depression and hypotension are more common and may necessitate cardiac support; alkalinization of urine may increase elimination; MDAC in selected cases (see discussion); hemoperfusion in selected cases
Other barbiturates: Intermediate acting (i.e., amobarbital) Short acting (i.e., secobarbital) Ultrashort acting (i.e., thiopental)	Commonly abused barbiturates; chronic drowsiness, psychomotor retardation; hypothermia	As above, although alkalinization, MDAC not helpful; hemoperfusion in selected cases; major withdrawal may necessitate hospitalization

Continued.

Drug	Unique Characteristics	Key Management Issues
Ethchlorvynol (Placidyl)	Pungent odor sometimes described as pearlike, gastric fluid often has a pink or green color, noncardiac pulmonary edema	See barbiturates
Glutethimide (Doriden)	Prominent anticholinergic side effects including mydriasis Prolonged cyclic or fluctuating coma (average 36–38 h); often mixed with codeine as a heroin substitute	See barbiturates
Meprobamate (Miltown)	Forms concretions, hypotension is more common than with other sedative-hypnotics, prolonged coma (average 38–40 h)	If concretions suspected, WBI or gastroscopic or surgical removal of drug may be necessary; hemoperfusion useful in severe cases
Methqualone (Quaalude)	Muscular hypertonicity, clonus, and hyperpyrexia, popular as an "aphrodisiac" or "cocaine downer"; no longer manufactured in the U.S.	Charcoal hemoperfusion increases clearance and may be useful in severe cases; diazepam may be necessary to treat severe muscular hypertonicity or "seizures"
Chloral hydrate	Metabolized to trichloroethanol which may sensitize the myocardium to the effects of catecholamines, resulting in cardiac arrhythmias	Tachyarrhythmias may respond to propranolol, 1–2 mg IV or esmolol; flumazenil has been reported to produce dramatic reversal of coma in one case; amenable to hemodialysis

Note: Catecholamines (especially dopamine and epinephrine) are relatively contraindicated in cases of chloral hydrate-induced tachyarrhythmias.

Abbreviations: GHB, gammahydroxybuterate; MDAC, multiple-dose activated charcoal; WBI, whole bowel irrigation.

8.2.10.4   Hallucinogens

Drug	Unique Characteristics	Key Management Issues
LSD	Potent agent associated with panic attacks, acute psychotic reaction, and flashbacks in chronic users; vital signs are usually relatively normal; hallucinations for 1–8 h	Patients usually respond to benzodiazepines and seclusion in a quiet environment; toxicology screen negative; in extremely agitated patients watch for hyperthermia, rhabdomyolysis
Marijuana	Commonly used, associated with conjunctival injection, stimulation of appetite, orthostatic hypotension, and mild tachycardia; duration of effect: 3 h	Usually respond to simple reassurance and possible adjunctive benzodiazepine
Ketamine	Dissociative anesthetic with hallucinations characterized by profound analgesia, amnesia, and catalepsy Increasingly common as drug of abuse; duration of effect: 1–3 hours	Provide supportive care until drug effects wear off; cardiovascular parameters are usually well preserved
Atropine, hycosyamine, scopolamine (*Datura stramonium* or Jimson weed)	Anticholinergic syndrome with true delirium, symptoms may continue for 24–48 h because of delayed GI motility	Usually supportive care only, consider activated charcoal; physostigmine for uncontrolled agitation, hyperthermia

Continued.

Drug	Unique Characteristics	Key Management Issues
Solvents	Products of petroleum distillation abused by spraying them into a plastic bag or soaking a cloth and then deeply inhaling; cardiac sensitization may result in malignant arrhythmias, low viscosity agents (i.e., gasoline) are associated with aspiration); chronic exposure associated with hepatitis and renal failure	Usually hallucinogenic effects are short lived; removing the patient from the offending agent and providing fresh air are all that is necessary; treat aspiration by supporting airway; arrhythmias may respond to beta-blockers, epinephrine may worsen arrhythmias
Psilocybin	From the Stropharia and Conocybe mushrooms; suppresses serotonergic neurons, less potent than LSD with hallucinations that last from 2–8 h, patients may exhibit destructive behavior; hallucinations for 1–6 h	As with LSD

Note: Epinephrine is contraindicated in cases of solvent-induced tachyarrhythmias.

Abbreviations: LSD, lysergic acid diethylamide, GI, gastrointestinal.

REFERENCES

1. Barnes, T.A., et al., Cardiopulmonary resuscitation and emergency cardiovascular care. Airway devices. *Ann Emerg Med*, 2001. 37(4 Suppl): p. S145–51.

2. Blanda, M. and U.E. Gallo, Emergency airway management. *Emerg Med Clin North Am*, 2003. 21(1): p. 1–26.

3. Kern, K.B., H.R. Halperin, and J. Field, New guidelines for cardiopulmonary resuscitation and emergency cardiac care: changes in the management of cardiac arrest. *JAMA*, 2001. 285(10): p. 1267–9.

4. Krenzelok, E.P. and J.B. Leikin, Approach to the poisoned patient. *Dis Mon*, 1996. 42(9): p. 509–607.

5. Olson, K.R., P.R. Pentel, and M.T. Kelley, Physical assessment and differential diagnosis of the poisoned patient. *Med Toxicol*, 1987. 2(1): p. 52–81.

6. Proudfoot, A., Practical management of the poisoned patient. *Ther Drug Monit*, 1998. 20(5): p. 498–501.

7. Riordan, M., G. Rylance, and K. Berry, Poisoning in children 1: general management. *Arch Dis Child*, 2002. 87(5): p. 392–6.

8. Mokhlesi, B., et al., Adult toxicology in critical care: part I: general approach to the intoxicated patient. *Chest*, 2003. 123(2): p. 577–92.

9. Peterson, J., Coma, in *Emergency Medicine, Concepts and Clinical Practice*, P. Rosen and R.M. Barkin, Eds. 1992, Mosby Year Book: St Louis. p. 1728–1751.

10. Guido, M.E., W. Brady, and D. DeBehnke, Reversible neurological deficits in a chronic alcohol abuser: a case report of Wernicke's encephalopathy. *Am J Emerg Med*, 1994. 12(2): p. 238–40.

11. Wrenn, K.D., F. Murphy, and C.M. Slovis, A toxicity study of parenteral thiamine hydrochloride. *Ann Emerg Med*, 1989. 18(8): p. 867–70.

12. Centerwall, B.S. and M.H. Criqui, Prevention of the Wernicke–Korsakoff syndrome: a cost-benefit analysis. *N Engl J Med*, 1978. 299(6): p. 285–9.

13. Kagansky, N., S. Levy, and H. Knobler, The role of hyperglycemia in acute stroke. *Arch Neurol*, 2001. 58(8): p. 1209–12.

14. Parsons, M.W., et al., Acute hyperglycemia adversely affects stroke outcome: a magnetic resonance imaging and spectroscopy study. *Ann Neurol*, 2002. 52(1): p. 20–8.

15. Lindsberg, P.J. and R.O. Roine, Hyperglycemia in acute stroke. *Stroke*, 2004. 35(2): p. 363–4.

16. Dietrich, W.D., O. Alonso, and R. Busto, Moderate hyperglycemia worsens acute blood–brain barrier injury after forebrain ischemia in rats. *Stroke*, 1993. 24(1): p. 111–6.

17. Hoffman, R.S. and L.R. Goldfrank, The poisoned patient with altered consciousness. Controversies in the use of a "coma cocktail." *JAMA*, 1995. 274(7): p. 562–9.

18. Fowkes, J. Opiates in the Emergency Department, in *Toxicology and Infectious Disease in Emergency Medicine*. 1992. San Diego, CA.

19. Osterwalder, J.J., Naloxone — for intoxications with intravenous heroin and heroin mixtures — harmless or hazardous? A prospective clinical study. *J Toxicol Clin Toxicol*, 1996. 34(4): p. 409–16.

20. Meissner, W. and K. Ullrich, Re: naloxone, constipation and analgesia. *J Pain Symptom Manage*, 2002. 24(3): p. 276–7; author reply 277–9.

21. Dole, V.P., et al., Arousal of ethanol-intoxicated comatose patients with naloxone. *Alcohol Clin Exp Res*, 1982. 6(2): p. 275–9.

22. Wedin, G.P. and L.J. Edwards, Clonidine poisoning treated with naloxone [letter]. *Am J Emerg Med*, 1989. 7(3): p. 343–4.

23. Alberto, G., et al., Central nervous system manifestations of a valproic acid overdose responsive to naloxone. *Ann Emerg Med*, 1989. 18(8): p. 889–91.

24. Varon, J. and S.R. Duncan, Naloxone reversal of hypotension due to captopril overdose. *Ann Emerg Med*, 1991. 20(10): p. 1125–7.

25. Harrington, L.W., Acute pulmonary edema following use of naloxone: a case study. *Crit Care Nurse*, 1988. 8(8): p. 69–73.

26. Schwartz, J.A. and M.D. Koenigsberg, Naloxone-induced pulmonary edema. *Ann Emerg Med*, 1987. 16(11): p. 1294–6.

27. Partridge, B.L. and C.F. Ward, Pulmonary edema following low-dose naloxone administration [letter]. *Anesthesiology*, 1986. 65(6): p. 709–10.

28. Prough, D.S., et al., Acute pulmonary edema in healthy teenagers following conservative doses of intravenous naloxone. *Anesthesiology*, 1984. 60(5): p. 485–6.

29. Taff, R.H., Pulmonary edema following naloxone administration in a patient without heart disease. *Anesthesiology*, 1983. 59(6): p. 576–7.

30. Flacke, J.W., W.E. Flacke, and G.D. Williams, Acute pulmonary edema following naloxone reversal of high-dose morphine anesthesia. *Anesthesiology*, 1977. 47(4): p. 376–8.

31. Wasserberger, J. and G.J. Ordog, Naloxone-induced hypertension in patients on clonidine [letter]. *Ann Emerg Med*, 1988. 17(5): p. 557.

32. Levin, E.R., et al., Severe hypertension induced by naloxone. *Am J Med Sci*, 1985. 290(2): p. 70–2.

33. Azar, I. and H. Turndorf, Severe hypertension and multiple atrial premature contractions following naloxone administration. *Anesth Analg*, 1979. 58(6): p. 524–5.

34. Mariani, P.J., Seizure associated with low-dose naloxone. *Am J Emerg Med*, 1989. 7(1): p. 127–9.

35. Michaelis, L.L., et al., Ventricular irritability associated with the use of naloxone hydrochloride. Two case reports and laboratory assessment of the effect of the drug on cardiac excitability. *Ann Thorac Surg*, 1974. 18(6): p. 608–14.

36. Cuss, F.M., C.B. Colaco, and J.H. Baron, Cardiac arrest after reversal of effects of opiates with naloxone. *Br Med J* (Clin Res Ed), 1984. 288(6414): p. 363–4.

37. Lubman, D., Z. Koutsogiannis, and I. Kronborg, Emergency management of inadvertent accelerated opiate withdrawal in dependent opiate users. *Drug Alcohol Rev*, 2003. 22(4): p. 433–6.

38. Gaddis, G.M. and W.A. Watson, Naloxone-associated patient violence: an overlooked toxicity? *Ann Pharmacother*, 1992. 26(2): p. 196–8.

39. Rock, P., et al., Efficacy and safety of naloxone in septic shock. *Crit Care Med*, 1985. 13(1): p. 28–33.

40. Groeger, J.S., G.C. Carlon, and W.S. Howland, Naloxone in septic shock. *Crit Care Med*, 1983. 11(8): p. 650–4.

41. Gurll, N.J., et al., Naloxone without transfusion prolongs survival and enhances cardiovascular function in hypovolemic shock. *J Pharmacol Exp Ther*, 1982. 220(3): p. 621–4.

42. Groeger, J.S. and C.E. Inturrisi, High-dose naloxone: pharmacokinetics in patients in septic shock. *Crit Care Med*, 1987. 15(8): p. 751–6.

43. Olinger, C.P., et al., High-dose intravenous naloxone for the treatment of acute ischemic stroke. *Stroke*, 1990. 21(5): p. 721–5.

44. Baskin, D.S., C.F. Kieck, and Y. Hosobuchi, Naloxone reversal and morphine exacerbation of neurologic deficits secondary to focal cerebral ischemia in baboons. *Brain Res*, 1984. 290(2): p. 289–96.

45. Baskin, D.S. and Y. Hosobuchi, Naloxone and focal cerebral ischemia [letter]. *J Neurosurg*, 1984. 60(6): p. 1328–31.

46. Baskin, D.S. and Y. Hosobuchi, Naloxone reversal of ischaemic neurological deficits in man. *Lancet*, 1981. 2(8241): p. 272–5.

47. Flamm, E.S., et al., A phase I trial of naloxone treatment in acute spinal cord injury. *J Neurosurg*, 1985. 63(3): p. 390–7.

48. Young, W., et al., Pharmacological therapy of acute spinal cord injury: studies of high dose methyl-prednisolone and naloxone. *Clin Neurosurg*, 1988. 34: p. 675–97.

49. Bracken, M.B., et al., A randomized, controlled trial of methylprednisolone or naloxone in the treatment of acute spinal-cord injury. Results of the Second National Acute Spinal Cord Injury Study [see comments]. *N Engl J Med*, 1990. 322(20): p. 1405–11.

50. Cohen, M.R., et al., High-dose naloxone infusions in normals. Dose-dependent behavioral, hormonal, and physiological responses. *Arch Gen Psychiatry*, 1983. 40(6): p. 613–9.

51. Cohen, R.M., et al., High-dose naloxone affects task performance in normal subjects. *Psychiatry Res*, 1983. 8(2): p. 127–36.

52. Gerra, G., et al., Clonidine and opiate receptor antagonists in the treatment of heroin addiction. *J Subst Abuse Treat*, 1995. 12(1): p. 35–41.

53. Stine, S.M. and T.R. Kosten, Use of drug combinations in treatment of opioid withdrawal. *J Clin Psychopharmacol*, 1992. 12(3): p. 203–9.

54. Creighton, F.J. and A.H. Ghodse, Naloxone applied to conjunctiva as a test for physical opiate dependence. *Lancet*, 1989. 1(8641): p. 748–50.

55. Loimer, N., P. Hofmann, and H.R. Chaudhry, Nasal administration of naloxone for detection of opiate dependence. J *Psychiatr Res*, 1992. 26(1): p. 39–43.

56. Kelly, A.M. and Z. Koutsogiannis, Intranasal naloxone for life threatening opioid toxicity. *Emerg Med J*, 2002. 19(4): p. 375.

57. Wilhelm, J.A., et al., Duration of opioid antagonism by nalmefene and naloxone in the dog. A nonparametric pharmacodynamic comparison based on generalized cross-validated spline estimation. *Int J Clin Pharmacol Ther*, 1995. 33(10): p. 540–5.

58. Barsan, W.G., et al., Duration of antagonistic effects of nalmefene and naloxone in opiate-induced sedation for emergency department procedures. *Am J Emerg Med*, 1989. 7(2): p. 155–61.

59. Kaplan, J.L. and J.A. Marx, Effectiveness and safety of intravenous nalmefene for emergency depart-ment patients with suspected narcotic overdose: a pilot study. *Ann Emerg Med*, 1993. 22(2): p. 187–90.

60. Ellenhorn, M., *Ellenhorn's Medical Toxicology*. 2nd ed., M. Ellenhorn, Ed. 1997, New York: Elsevier Science Publishing Company. p. 437–8.

61. Chumpa, A., et al., Nalmefene for elective reversal of procedural sedation in children. *Am J Emerg Med*, 2001. 19(7): p. 545–8.

62. Nalmefene for alcohol dependence. *Harv Ment Health Lett*, 2000. 16(9): p. 7.

63. Rosen, D.A., et al., Nalmefene to prevent epidural narcotic side effects in pediatric patients: a pharmacokinetic and safety study. *Pharmacotherapy*, 2000. 20(7): p. 745–9.

64. Kearney, T., Flumazenil, in *Poisoning and Drug Overdose*, Olson, K.R., Ed. 1994, Appleton & Lange: Englewood Cliffs, NJ. p. 340–1.

65. Dunton, A.W., et al., Flumazenil: U.S. clinical pharmacology studies. *Eur J Anaesthesiol Suppl*, 1988. 2: p. 81–95.

66. Jensen, S., L. Knudsen, and L. Kirkegaard, Flumazenil used in the antagonizing of diazepam and midazolam sedation in out-patients undergoing gastroscopy. *Eur J Anaesthesiol Suppl*, 1988. 2: p. 161–6.

67. Kirkegaard, L., et al., Benzodiazepine antagonist Ro 15-1788. Antagonism of diazepam sedation in outpatients undergoing gastroscopy. *Anaesthesia*, 1986. 41(12): p. 1184–8.

68. Sewing, K.F., The value of flumazenil in the reversal of midazolam-induced sedation for upper gastrointestinal endoscopy [letter; comment]. *Aliment Pharmacol Ther*, 1990. 4(3): p. 315.

69. Bartelsman, J.F., P.R. Sars, and G.N. Tytgat, Flumazenil used for reversal of midazolam-induced sedation in endoscopy outpatients. *Gastrointest Endosc*, 1990. 36(3 Suppl): p. S9–12.

70. Davies, C.A., et al., Reversal of midazolam sedation with flumazenil following conservative dentistry. *J Dent*, 1990. 18(2): p. 113–8.

71. Chern, T.L., et al., Diagnostic and therapeutic utility of flumazenil in comatose patients with drug overdose. *Am J Emerg Med*, 1993. 11(2): p. 122–4.

72. Weinbroum, A., P. Halpern, and E. Geller, The use of flumazenil in the management of acute drug poisoning — a review. *Intensive Care Med*, 1991. 17 Suppl 1: p. S32–8.

73. Weinbroum, A., et al., Use of flumazenil in the treatment of drug overdose: a double-blind and open clinical study in 110 patients. *Crit Care Med*, 1996. 24(2): p. 199–206.

74. Thomas, P., C. Lebrun, and M. Chatel, De novo absence status epilepticus as a benzodiazepine withdrawal syndrome. *Epilepsia*, 1993. 34(2): p. 355–8.

75. Spivey, W.H., Flumazenil and seizures: analysis of 43 cases. *Clin Ther*, 1992. 14(2): p. 292–305.

76. Chern, T.L. and A. Kwan, Flumazenil-induced seizure accompanying benzodiazepine and baclofen intoxication [letter]. *Am J Emerg Med*, 1996. 14(2): p. 231–2.

77. McDuffee, A.T. and J.D. Tobias, Seizure after flumazenil administration in a pediatric patient. *Pediatr Emerg Care*, 1995. 11(3): p. 186–7.

78. Mordel, A., et al., Seizures after flumazenil administration in a case of combined benzodiazepine and tricyclic antidepressant overdose. *Crit Care Med*, 1992. 20(12): p. 1733–4.

79. Kim, J.S., et al., Flumazenil-induced ballism. *J Korean Med Sci*, 2003. 18(2): p. 299–300.

80. Lheureux, P., et al., Risks of flumazenil in mixed benzodiazepine-tricyclic antidepressant overdose: report of a preliminary study in the dog. *J Toxicol Clin Exp*, 1992. 12(1): p. 43–53.

81. Treatment of benzodiazepine overdose with flumazenil. The Flumazenil in Benzodiazepine Intoxication Multicenter Study Group. *Clin Ther*, 1992. 14(6): p. 978–95.

82. Haverkos, G.P., R.P. DiSalvo, and T.E. Imhoff, Fatal seizures after flumazenil administration in a patient with mixed overdose. *Ann Pharmacother*, 1994. 28(12): p. 1347–9.

83. Lim, A.G., Death after flumazenil [letter] [published erratum appears in BMJ 1989 Dec 16;299(6714):1531] [see comments]. *BMJ*, 1989. 299(6703): p. 858–9.

84. Serfaty, M. and G. Masterton, Fatal poisonings attributed to benzodiazepines in Britain during the 1980s [see comments]. *Br J Psychiatry*, 1993. 163: p. 386–93.

85. Greenblatt, D.J., et al., Acute overdosage with benzodiazepine derivatives. *Clin Pharmacol Ther*, 1977. 21(4): p. 497–514.

86. Guglielminotti, J., et al., Prolonged sedation requiring mechanical ventilation and continuous flumazenil infusion after routine doses of clorazepam for alcohol withdrawal syndrome. *Intensive Care Med*, 1999. 25(12): p. 1435–6.

87. Saltik, I.N. and H. Ozen, Role of flumazenil for paradoxical reaction to midazolam during endoscopic procedures in children. *Am J Gastroenterol*, 2000. 95(10): p. 3011–2.

88. Reichen, J., Review: flumazenil leads to clinical and electroencephalographic improvement in hepatic encephalopathy in patients with cirrhosis. *ACP J Club*, 2003. 138(1): p. 15.

89. Gerra, G., et al., Intravenous flumazenil versus oxazepam tapering in the treatment of benzodiazepine withdrawal: a randomized, placebo-controlled study. *Addict Biol*, 2002. 7(4): p. 385–95.

90. Proceedings of the Guidelines 2000 Conference for Cardiopulmonary Resuscitation and Emergency Cardiovascular Care: An International Consensus on Science. *Ann Emerg Med*, 2001. 37(4 Suppl): p. S1–200.

91. Harper, C., et al., An international perspective on the prevalence of the Wernicke–Korsakoff syndrome. *Metab Brain Dis*, 1995. 10(1): p. 17–24.

92. Peeters, A., et al., Wernicke's encephalopathy and central pontine myelinolysis induced by hyperemesis gravidarum. *Acta Neurol Belg*, 1993. 93(5): p. 276–82.

93. Boldorini, R., et al., Wernicke's encephalopathy: occurrence and pathological aspects in a series of 400 AIDS patients. *Acta Biomed Ateneo Parmense*, 1992. 63(1–2): p. 43–9.

94. Tate, J.R. and P.F. Nixon, Measurement of Michaelis constant for human erythrocyte transketolase and thiamin diphosphate. *Anal Biochem*, 1987. 160(1): p. 78–87.

95. Reuler, J.B., D.E. Girard, and T.G. Cooney, Current concepts. Wernicke's encephalopathy. *N Engl J Med*, 1985. 312(16): p. 1035–9.

96. Cheeley, R.D. and S.M. Joyce, A clinical comparison of the performance of four blood glucose reagent strips. *Am J Emerg Med*, 1990. 8(1): p. 11–5.

97. Jones, J.L., et al., Determination of prehospital blood glucose: a prospective, controlled study. *J Emerg Med*, 1992. 10(6): p. 679–82.

98. Wilkins, B.H. and D. Kalra, Comparison of blood glucose test strips in the detection of neonatal hypoglycaemia. *Arch Dis Child*, 1982. 57(12): p. 948–50.

99. Barreau, P.B. and J.E. Buttery, The effect of the haematocrit value on the determination of glucose levels by reagent-strip methods. *Med J Aust*, 1987. 147(6): p. 286–8.

100. Tanvetyanon, T., M.D. Walkenstein, and A. Marra, Inaccurate glucose determination by fingerstick in a patient with peripheral arterial disease. *Ann Intern Med*, 2002. 137(9): p. W1.

101. Atkin, S.H., et al., Fingerstick glucose determination in shock. *Ann Intern Med*, 1991. 114(12): p. 1020–4.

102. Fazel, A., et al., Influence of sample temperature on reflectance photometry and electrochemical glucometer measurements. *Diabetes Care*, 1996. 19(7): p. 771–4.

103. Boyle, P.J., et al., Plasma glucose concentrations at the onset of hypoglycemic symptoms in patients with poorly controlled diabetes and in nondiabetics. *N Engl J Med*, 1988. 318(23): p. 1487–92.

104. Hoffman, J.R., D.L. Schriger, and J.S. Luo, The empiric use of naloxone in patients with altered mental status: a reappraisal. *Ann Emerg Med*, 1991. 20(3): p. 246–52.

105. Weisman, R., Naloxone, in *Goldfrank's Toxicologic Emergencies*, Goldfrank, L.R., Lewin, N.A., et al., Eds. 1994, Appleton & Lange: Englewood Cliffs, NJ. p. 784.

106. Maio, R.F., B. Gaukel, and B. Freeman, Intralingual naloxone injection for narcotic-induced respiratory depression. *Ann Emerg Med*, 1987. 16(5): p. 572–3.

107. Claeys, M.A., et al., Reversal of flunitrazepam with flumazenil: duration of antagonist activity. *Eur J Anaesthesiol Suppl*, 1988. 2: p. 209–17.

108. Martens, F., et al., Clinical experience with the benzodiazepine antagonist flumazenil in suspected benzodiazepine or ethanol poisoning. *J Toxicol Clin Toxicol*, 1990. 28(3): p. 341–56.

109. Persson, A., et al., Imaging of [11C]-labelled Ro 15-1788 binding to benzodiazepine receptors in the human brain by positron emission tomography. *J Psychiatr Res*, 1985. 19(4): p. 609–22.

110. Hojer, J., et al., A placebo-controlled trial of flumazenil given by continuous infusion in severe benzodiazepine overdosage. *Acta Anaesthesiol Scand*, 1991. 35(7): p. 584–90.

111. Goldfrank, L., et al., A dosing nomogram for continuous infusion intravenous naloxone. *Ann Emerg Med*, 1986. 15(5): p. 566–70.

112. Mofenson, H.C. and T.R. Caraccio, Continuous infusion of intravenous naloxone [letter]. *Ann Emerg Med*, 1987. 16(5): p. 600.

113. Use of patient restraint. American College of Emergency Physicians. *Ann Emerg Med*, 1996. 28(3): p. 384.

114. Shanaberger, C.J., What price patient restraint? *Orwick v. Fox. J Emerg Med Serv JEMS*, 1993. 18(6): p. 69–71.

115. Stratton, S.J., C. Rogers, and K. Green, Sudden death in individuals in hobble restraints during paramedic transport. *Ann Emerg Med*, 1995. 25(5): p. 710–2.

116. Lavoie, F.W., Consent, involuntary treatment, and the use of force in an urban emergency department. *Ann Emerg Med*, 1992. 21(1): p. 25–32.

117. Gunnels, M., Violence in the emergency department: a daily challenge. *J Emerg Nurs*, 1993. 19(4): p. 277.

118. Cembrowicz, S.P. and J.P. Shepherd, Violence in the accident and emergency department. *Med Sci Law*, 1992. 32(2): p. 118–22.

119. Rumack, B.H., Editorial: Physostigmine: rational use. *JACEP*, 1976. 5(7): p. 541–2.

120. Lenox, R.H., et al., Adjunctive treatment of manic agitation with lorazepam versus haloperidol: a double-blind study. *J Clin Psychiatry*, 1992. 53(2): p. 47–52.

121. Cavanaugh, S.V., Psychiatric emergencies. *Med Clin North Am*, 1986. 70(5): p. 1185–202.

122. Stevens, A., et al., Haloperidol and lorazepam combined: clinical effects and drug plasma levels in the treatment of acute schizophrenic psychosis. *Pharmacopsychiatry*, 1992. 25(6): p. 273–7.

123. Catravas, J.D. and I.W. Waters, Acute cocaine intoxication in the conscious dog: studies on the mechanism of lethality. *J Pharmacol Exp Ther*, 1981. 217(2): p. 350–6.

124. Guinn, M.M., J.A. Bedford, and M.C. Wilson, Antagonism of intravenous cocaine lethality in non-human primates. *Clin Toxicol*, 1980. 16(4): p. 499–508.

125. Derlet, R.W. and T.E. Albertson, Diazepam in the prevention of seizures and death in cocaine-intoxicated rats. *Ann Emerg Med*, 1989. 18(5): p. 542–6.

126. Merigian, K.S., et al., Adrenergic crisis from crack cocaine ingestion: report of five cases. *J Emerg Med*, 1994. 12(4): p. 485–90.

127. Shephard, R.A., Behavioral effects of GABA agonists in relation to anxiety and benzodiazepine action. *Life Sci*, 1987. 40(25): p. 2429–36.

128. Norman, T.R. and G.D. Burrows, Anxiety and the benzodiazepine receptor. *Prog Brain Res*, 1986. 65: p. 73–90.

129. Derlet, R.W., T.E. Albertson, and P. Rice, The effect of haloperidol in cocaine and amphetamine intoxication. *J Emerg Med*, 1989. 7(6): p. 633–7.

130. Derlet, R.W., T.E. Albertson, and P. Rice, Antagonism of cocaine, amphetamine, and methamphetamine toxicity. *Pharmacol Biochem Behav*, 1990. 36(4): p. 745–9.

131. Derlet, R.W., T.E. Albertson, and P. Rice, Protection against d-amphetamine toxicity. *Am J Emerg Med*, 1990. 8(2): p. 105–8.

132. Espelin, D., Amphetamine poisoning: Effectiveness of clorpromazine. *N Engl J Med*, 1968. 278: p. 1361–5.

133. Callaway, C.W. and R.F. Clark, Hyperthermia in psychostimulant overdose. *Ann Emerg Med*, 1994. 24(1): p. 68–76.

134. Soyka, M., C. Botschev, and A. Volcker, Neuroleptic treatment in alcohol hallucinosis: no evidence for increased seizure risk. *J Clin Psychopharmacol*, 1992. 12: p. 66–7.

135. Lipka, L.J. and C.M. Lathers, Psychoactive agents, seizure production, and sudden death in epilepsy. *J Clin Pharmacol*, 1987. 27(3): p. 169–83.

136. Hoffman, R.S., Cocaine intoxication considerations, complications and strategies: point and counterpoint. *Emerg Med*, 1992. 1: p. 1–6.

137. Witkin, J., S.R. Godberg, and J.L. Katz, Lethal effects of cocaine are reduced by the dopamine-1 receptor antagonist SCH 23390 but not by haloperidol. *Life Sci*, 1989. 44: p. 1285–91.

138. Pollera, C.F., et al., Sudden death after acute dystonic reaction to high-dose metoclopramide [letter]. *Lancet*, 1984. 2(8400): p. 460–1.

139. Barach, E., et al., Dystonia presenting as upper airway obstruction. *J Emerg Med*, 1989. 7(3): p. 237–40.

140. Cavanaugh, J.J. and R.E. Finlayson, Rhabdomyolysis due to acute dystonic reaction to antipsychotic drugs. *J Clin Psychiatry*, 1984. 45(8): p. 356–7.

141. Addonizio, G. and G.S. Alexopoulos, Drug-induced dystonia in young and elderly patients. *Am J Psychiatry*, 1988. 145(7): p. 869–71.

142. Menza, M.A., et al., Controlled study of extrapyramidal reactions in the management of delirious, medically ill patients: intravenous haloperidol versus intravenous haloperidol plus benzodiazepines. *Heart Lung*, 1988. 17(3): p. 238–41.

143. Yildiz, A., G.S. Sachs, and A. Turgay, Pharmacological management of agitation in emergency settings. *Emerg Med J*, 2003. 20(4): p. 339–46.

144. Brook, S., J.V. Lucey, and K.P. Gunn, Intramuscular ziprasidone compared with intramuscular haloperidol in the treatment of acute psychosis. Ziprasidone I.M. Study Group. *J Clin Psychiatry*, 2000. 61(12): p. 933–41.

145. Brook, S., Intramuscular ziprasidone: moving beyond the conventional in the treatment of acute agitation in schizophrenia. *J Clin Psychiatry*, 2003. 64 Suppl 19: p. 13–8.

146. Spina, E., et al., Prevalence of acute dystonic reactions associated with neuroleptic treatment with and without anticholinergic prophylaxis. *Int Clin Psychopharmacol*, 1993. 8(1): p. 21–4.

147. Shenoy, R.S., Pitfalls in the treatment of jimsonweed intoxication [letter]. *Am J Psychiatry*, 1994. 151(9): p. 1396–7.

148. Hurlbut, K.M., Drug-induced psychoses. *Emerg Med Clin North Am*, 1991. 9(1): p. 31–52.

149. Kopman, A.F., G. Strachovsky, and L. Lichtenstein, Prolonged response to succinylcholine following physostigmine. *Anesthesiology*, 1978. 49(2): p. 142–3.

150. Manoguerra, A.S. and R.W. Steiner, Prolonged neuromuscular blockade after administration of physostigmine and succinylcholine. *Clin Toxicol*, 1981. 18(7): p. 803–5.

151. Pentel, P. and C.D. Peterson, Asystole complicating physostigmine treatment of tricyclic antidepressant overdose. *Ann Emerg Med*, 1980. 9(11): p. 588–90.

152. Newton, R.W., Physostigmine salicylate in the treatment of tricyclic antidepressant overdosage. *JAMA*, 1975. 231(9): p. 941–3.

153. Nattel, S., L. Bayne, and J. Ruedy, Physostigmine in coma due to drug overdose. *Clin Pharmacol Ther*, 1979. 25(1): p. 96–102.

154. Gay, G.R., Clinical management of acute and chronic cocaine poisoning. *Ann Emerg Med*, 1982. 11(10): p. 562–72.

155. Khantzian, E.J. and G.J. McKenna, Acute toxic and withdrawal reactions associated with drug use and abuse. *Ann Intern Med*, 1979. 90(3): p. 361–72.

156. Fisher, W.A., Restraint and seclusion: a review of the literature. *Am J Psychiatry*, 1994. 151(11): p. 1584–91.

157. Splawn, G., Restraining potentially violent patients. *J Emerg Nurs*, 1991. 17(5): p. 316–7.

158. Wetli, C.V. and D.A. Fishbain, Cocaine-induced psychosis and sudden death in recreational cocaine users. *J Forensic Sci*, 1985. 30(3): p. 873–80.

159. O'Halloran, R.V. and L.V. Lewman, Restraint asphyxiation in excited delirium [see comments]. *Am J Forensic Med Pathol*, 1993. 14(4): p. 289–95.

160. Miles, S.H., Restraints and sudden death [letter; comment]. *J Am Geriatr Soc*, 1993. 41(9): p. 1013.

161. Introna, F., Jr. and J.E. Smialek, The "mini-packer" syndrome. Fatal ingestion of drug containers in Baltimore, Maryland. *Am J Forensic Med Pathol*, 1989. 10(1): p. 21–4.

162. Simon, L.C., The cocaine body packer syndrome. *West Indian Med J*, 1990. 39(4): p. 250–5.

163. Geyskens, P., L. Coenen, and J. Brouwers, The "cocaine body packer" syndrome. Case report and review of the literature. *Acta Chir Belg*, 1989. 89(4): p. 201–3.

164. Pollack, C.V., Jr., et al., Two crack cocaine body stuffers [clinical conference]. *Ann Emerg Med*, 1992. 21(11): p. 1370–80.

165. Jimson weed poisoning — Texas, New York, and California, 1994. *MMWR Morb Mortal Wkly Rep*, 1995. 44(3): p. 41–4.

166. Wetli, C.V. and R.K. Wright, Death caused by recreational cocaine use. *JAMA*, 1979. 241(23): p. 2519–22.

167. Simpson, D.L. and B.H. Rumack, Methylenedioxyamphetamine. Clinical description of overdose, death, and review of pharmacology. *Arch Intern Med*, 1981. 141(11): p. 1507–9.

168. Campbell, B.G., Cocaine abuse with hyperthermia, seizures and fatal complications. *Med J Aust*, 1988. 149(7): p. 387–9.

169. Olson, K.R., et al., Seizures associated with poisoning and drug overdose [corrected and republished article originally printed in *Am J Emerg Med* 1993 Nov;11(6):565–8]. *Am J Emerg Med*, 1994. 12(3): p. 392–5.

170. Jonsson, S., M. O'Meara, and J.B. Young, Acute cocaine poisoning. Importance of treating seizures and acidosis. *Am J Med*, 1983. 75(6): p. 1061–4.

171. Olson, K.R. and N.L. Benowitz, Environmental and drug-induced hyperthermia. Pathophysiology, recognition, and management. *Emerg Med Clin North Am*, 1984. 2(3): p. 459–74.

172. Meldrum, B.S., R.A. Vigouroux, and J.B. Brierley, Systemic factors and epileptic brain damage. Prolonged seizures in paralyzed, artificially ventilated baboons. *Arch Neurol*, 1973. 29(2): p. 82–7.

173. Earnest, M.P., Seizures. *Neurol Clin*, 1993. 11(3): p. 563–75.

174. Lason, W., Neurochemical and pharmacological aspects of cocaine-induced seizures. *Pol J Pharmacol*, 2001. 53(1): p. 57–60.

175. Jacobs, I.G., et al., Cocaine abuse: neurovascular complications. *Radiology*, 1989. 170(1 Pt 1): p. 223–7.

176. Auer, J., R. Berent, and B. Eber, Cardiovascular complications of cocaine use. *N Engl J Med*, 2001. 345(21): p. 1575; author reply 1576.

177. Rumbaugh, C.L., et al., Cerebral angiographic changes in the drug abuse patient. *Radiology*, 1971. 101(2): p. 335–44.

178. Earnest, M.P., et al., Neurocysticercosis in the United States: 35 cases and a review. *Rev Infect Dis*, 1987. 9(5): p. 961–79.

179. Roberts, J.R., Initial therapeutic strategies for the treatment of status epilepticus. *Emerg Med News*, 1996. 10: p. 2, 14–5.

180. Finder, R.L. and P.A. Moore, Benzodiazepines for intravenous conscious sedation: agonists and antagonists. *Compendium*, 1993. 14(8): p. 972, 974, 976–80 passim; quiz 984–6.

181. Roth, T. and T.A. Roehrs, A review of the safety profiles of benzodiazepine hypnotics. *J Clin Psychiatry*, 1991. 52 Suppl: p. 38–41.

182. Dement, W.C., Overview of the efficacy and safety of benzodiazepine hypnotics using objective methods. *J Clin Psychiatry*, 1991. 52 Suppl: p. 27–30.

183. Treiman, D.M., The role of benzodiazepines in the management of status epilepticus. *Neurology*, 1990. 40(5 Suppl 2): p. 32–42.

184. Kyriakopoulos, A.A., D.J. Greenblatt, and R.I. Shader, Clinical pharmacokinetics of lorazepam: a review. *J Clin Psychiatry*, 1978. 39(10 Pt 2): p. 16–23.

185. Leppik, I.E., et al., Double-blind study of lorazepam and diazepam in status epilepticus. *JAMA*, 1983. 249(11): p. 1452–4.

186. Levy, R.J. and R.L. Krall, Treatment of status epilepticus with lorazepam. *Arch Neurol*, 1984. 41(6): p. 605–11.

187. Bebin, M. and T.P. Bleck, New anticonvulsant drugs. Focus on flunarizine, fosphenytoin, midazolam and stiripentol. *Drugs*, 1994. 48(2): p. 153–71.

188. Kumar, A. and T.P. Bleck, Intravenous midazolam for the treatment of refractory status epilepticus. *Crit Care Med*, 1992. 20(4): p. 483–8.

189. Schalen, W., K. Messeter, and C.H. Nordstrom, Complications and side effects during thiopentone therapy in patients with severe head injuries. *Acta Anaesthesiol Scand*, 1992. 36(4): p. 369–77.

190. Singbartl, G. and G. Cunitz, [Pathophysiologic principles, emergency medical aspects and anesthesiologic measures in severe brain trauma]. *Anaesthesist*, 1987. 36(7): p. 321–32.

191. Lee, T.L., Pharmacology of propofol. *Ann Acad Med Singapore*, 1991. 20(1): p. 61–5.

192. Sellers, E.M., Alcohol, barbiturate and benzodiazepine withdrawal syndromes: clinical management. *Can Med Assoc J*, 1988. 139(2): p. 113–20.

193. Sullivan, J.T. and E.M. Seller, Treating alcohol, barbiturate, and benzodiazepine withdrawal. *Ration Drug Ther*, 1986. 20(2): p. 1–9.

194. Ramsay, R.E. and J. DeToledo, Intravenous administration of fosphenytoin: options for the management of seizures. *Neurology*, 1996. 46(6 Suppl 1): p. S17–9.

195. Staff, *Clinical Pharmacology: An Electronic Drug Reference and Teaching Guide*. 1.5 ed, S. Reents, Ed. 1995, Gainesville, FL: Gold Standard Multimedia.

196. Derlet, R.W. and T.E. Albertson, Anticonvulsant modification of cocaine-induced toxicity in the rat. *Neuropharmacology*, 1990. 29(3): p. 255–9.

197. Alldredge, B.K., D.H. Lowenstein, and R.P. Simon, Placebo-controlled trial of intravenous diphenylhydantoin for short-term treatment of alcohol withdrawal seizures. *Am J Med*, 1989. 87(6): p. 645–8.

198. Callaham, M., H. Schumaker, and P. Pentel, Phenytoin prophylaxis of cardiotoxicity in experimental amitriptyline poisoning. *J Pharmacol Exp Ther*, 1988. 245(1): p. 216–20.

199. Appleton, R., T. Martland, and B. Phillips, Drug management for acute tonic-clonic convulsions including convulsive status epilepticus in children. *Cochrane Database Syst Rev*, 2002(4): p. CD001905.

200. Lowenstein, D.H., Treatment options for status epilepticus. *Curr Opin Pharmacol*, 2003. 3(1): p. 6–11.

201. Munn, R.I. and K. Farrell, Failure to recognize status epilepticus in a paralyzed patient. *Can J Neurol Sci*, 1993. 20(3): p. 234–6.

202. Wolf, K.M., A.F. Shaughnessy, and D.B. Middleton, Prolonged delirium tremens requiring massive doses of medication [see comments]. *J Am Board Fam Pract*, 1993. 6(5): p. 502–4.

203. Pascual-Leone, A., et al., Cocaine-induced seizures. *Neurology*, 1990. 40(3 Pt 1): p. 404–7.

204. Brown, E., et al., CNS complications of cocaine abuse: prevalence, pathophysiology, and neuroradiology. *AJR Am J Roentgenol*, 1992. 159(1): p. 137–47.

205. Daras, M., A.J. Tuchman, and S. Marks, Central nervous system infarction related to cocaine abuse. *Stroke*, 1991. 22(10): p. 1320–5.

206. Tuchman, A.J. and M. Daras, Strokes associated with cocaine use [letter]. *Arch Neurol*, 1990. 47(11): p. 1170.

207. Holland, R.W.D., et al., Grand mal seizures temporally related to cocaine use: clinical and diagnostic features [see comments]. *Ann Emerg Med*, 1992. 21(7): p. 772–6.

208. Sarnquist, F. and C.P. Larson, Jr., Drug-induced heat stroke. *Anesthesiology*, 1973. 39(3): p. 348–50.

209. Rosenberg, J., et al., Hyperthermia associated with drug intoxication. *Crit Care Med*, 1986. 14(11): p. 964–9.

210. Sporer, K.A., The serotonin syndrome. Implicated drugs, pathophysiology and management. *Drug Saf*, 1995. 13(2): p. 94–104.

211. Walter, F.G., et al., Marijuana and hyperthermia. *J Toxicol Clin Toxicol*, 1996. 34(2): p. 217–21.

212. Ebadi, M., R.F. Pfeiffer, and L.C. Murrin, Pathogenesis and treatment of neuroleptic malignant syndrome. *Gen Pharmacol*, 1990. 21(4): p. 367–86.

213. Lecci, A., et al., Effect of psychotomimetics and some putative anxiolytics on stress-induced hyperthermia. *J Neural Transm Gen Sect*, 1991. 83(1–2): p. 67–76.

214. Halloran, L.L. and D.W. Bernard, Management of drug-induced hyperthermia. *Curr Opin Pediatr*, 2004. 16(2): p. 211–5.

215. Hadad, E., A.A. Weinbroum, and R. Ben-Abraham, Drug-induced hyperthermia and muscle rigidity: a practical approach. Eur *J Emerg Med*, 2003. 10(2): p. 149–54.

216. McGregor, I.S., et al., Increased anxiety and "depressive" symptoms months after MDMA ("ecstasy") in rats: drug-induced hyperthermia does not predict long-term outcomes. *Psychopharmacology* (Berlin), 2003. 168(4): p. 465–74.

217. Crandall, C.G., W. Vongpatanasin, and R.G. Victor, Mechanism of cocaine-induced hyperthermia in humans. *Ann Intern Med*, 2002. 136(11): p. 785–91.

218. Gordon, C.J., et al., Effects of 3,4-methylenedioxymethamphetamine on autonomic thermoregulatory responses of the rat. *Pharmacol Biochem Behav*, 1991. 38(2): p. 339–44.

219. Aniline, O. and F.N. Pitts, Jr., Phencyclidine (PCP): a review and perspectives. *Crit Rev Toxicol*, 1982. 10(2): p. 145–77.

220. Eastman, J.W. and S.N. Cohen, Hypertensive crisis and death associated with phencyclidine poisoning. *JAMA*, 1975. 231(12): p. 1270–1.

221. McCarron, M.M., et al., Acute phencyclidine intoxication: incidence of clinical findings in 1,000 cases. *Ann Emerg Med*, 1981. 10(5): p. 237–42.

222. Friedman, S.A. and S.E. Hirsch, Extreme hyperthermia after LSD ingestion. *JAMA*, 1971. 217(11): p. 1549–50.

223. Klock, J.C., U. Boerner, and C.E. Becker, Coma, hyperthermia and bleeding associated with massive LSD overdose. A report of eight cases. *West J Med*, 1974. 120(3): p. 183–8.

224. Mercieca, J. and E.A. Brown, Acute renal failure due to rhabdomyolysis associated with use of a straitjacket in lysergide intoxication. *Br Med J* (Clin Res Ed), 1984. 288(6435): p. 1949–50.

225. Armen, R., G. Kanel, and T. Reynolds, Phencyclidine-induced malignant hyperthermia causing submassive liver necrosis. *Am J Med*, 1984. 77(1): p. 167–72.

226. Loghmanee, F. and M. Tobak, Fatal malignant hyperthermia associated with recreational cocaine and ethanol abuse. *Am J Forensic Med Pathol*, 1986. 7(3): p. 246–8.

227. Zorzato, F., et al., Role of malignant hyperthermia domain in the regulation of Ca2+ release channel (ryanodine receptor) of skeletal muscle sarcoplasmic reticulum. *J Biol Chem*, 1996. 271(37): p. 22759–63.

228. Singarajah, C. and N.G. Lavies, An overdose of ecstasy. A role for dantrolene [see comments]. *Anaesthesia*, 1992. 47(8): p. 686–7.

229. Watson, J.D., et al., Exertional heat stroke induced by amphetamine analogues. Does dantrolene have a place? *Anaesthesia*, 1993. 48(12): p. 1057–60.

230. Behan, W., A.M.O. Bakheit, P.W. Hegan, and I.A.R. More, The muscle findings in the neuroleptic malignant syndrome associated with lysergic acid deithylamide. *J Neurol Neurosurg Psychiatry*, 1991. 54: p. 741–743.

231. Woodbury, M.M. and M.A. Woodbury, Neuroleptic-induced catatonia as a stage in the progression toward neuroleptic malignant syndrome. *J Am Acad Child Adolesc Psychiatry*, 1992. 31(6): p. 1161–4.

232. Totten, V.Y., E. Hirschenstein, and P. Hew, Neuroleptic malignant syndrome presenting without initial fever: a case report. *J Emerg Med*, 1994. 12(1): p. 43–7.

233. Daras, M., et al., Rhabdomyolysis and hyperthermia after cocaine abuse: a variant of the neuroleptic malignant syndrome? *Acta Neurol Scand*, 1995. 92(2): p. 161–5.

234. Wetli, C.V., D. Mash, and S.B. Karch, Cocaine-associated agitated delirium and the neuroleptic malignant syndrome. *Am J Emerg Med*, 1996. 14(4): p. 425–8.

235. SFPCC, *Poisoning & Drug Overdose. A Lange Clinical Manual*, K. Olson, Ed. 1994, Norwalk, CT: Appleton & Lange.

236. Zalis, E.G. and G. Kaplan, The effect of aggregation on amphetamine toxicity in the dog. *Arch Int Pharmacodyn Ther*, 1966. 159(1): p. 196–9.

237. Zalis, E.G., G.D. Lundberg, and R.A. Knutson, The pathophysiology of acute amphetamine poisoning with pathologic correlation. *J Pharmacol Exp Ther*, 1967. 158(1): p. 115–27.

238. Zalis, E.G., G.D. Lundberg, and R.A. Knutson, Acute lethality of the amphetamines in dogs and its antagonism by curare. *Proc Soc Exp Biol Med*, 1965: p. 557.

239. Davis, W.M., et al., Factors in the lethality of i.v. phencyclidine in conscious dogs. *Gen Pharmacol*, 1991. 22(4): p. 723–8.

240. Tek, D. and J.S. Olshaker, Heat illness. *Emerg Med Clin North Am*, 1992. 10(2): p. 299–310.

241. Callaham, M., Tricyclic antidepressant overdose. *JACEP*, 1979. 8(10): p. 413–25.

242. Sprung, C.L., Heat stroke; modern approach to an ancient disease. *Chest*, 1980. 77(4): p. 461–2.

243. Hamilton, D., Heat stroke. *Anaesthesia*, 1976. 32: p. 271.

244. Walker, J. and M.V. Vance, Heat emergencies, in *Emergency Medicine: A Comprehensive Study Guide*, J. Tintinalli, Ruiz, E, Krome, R.L., Eds. 1996, McGraw-Hill: New York. p. 850–856.

245. Rabinowitz, R.P., et al., Effects of anatomic site, oral stimulation, and body position on estimates of body temperature. *Arch Intern Med*, 1996. 156(7): p. 777–80.

246. Hooker, E.A., et al., Subjective assessment of fever by parents: comparison with measurement by noncontact tympanic thermometer and calibrated rectal glass mercury thermometer. *Ann Emerg Med*, 1996. 28(3): p. 313–7.

247. Yaron, M., S.R. Lowenstein, and J. Koziol-McLain, Measuring the accuracy of the infrared tympanic thermometer: correlation does not signify agreement. *J Emerg Med*, 1995. 13(5): p. 617–21.

248. Craig, J.V., et al., Infrared ear thermometry compared with rectal thermometry in children: a systematic review. *Lancet*, 2002. 360(9333): p. 603–9.

249. Selfridge, J. and S.S. Shea, The accuracy of the tympanic membrane thermometer in detecting fever in infants aged 3 months and younger in the emergency department setting. *J Emerg Nurs*, 1993. 19(2): p. 127–30.

250. White, N., S. Baird, and D.L. Anderson, A comparison of tympanic thermometer readings to pulmonary artery catheter core temperature recordings. *Appl Nurs Res*, 1994. 7(4): p. 165–9.

251. Doezema, D., M. Lunt, and D. Tandberg, Cerumen occlusion lowers infrared tympanic membrane temperature measurement. *Acad Emerg Med*, 1995. 2(1): p. 17–9.

252. Cabanac, M. and H. Brinnel, The pathology of human temperature regulation: thermiatrics. *Experientia*, 1987. 43(1): p. 19–27.

253. O'Donnell, T.F., Jr. and G.H. Clowes, Jr., The circulatory abnormalities of heat stroke. *N Engl J Med*, 1972. 287(15): p. 734–7.

254. O'Donnell, T.F., Jr. and G.H. Clowes, Jr., The circulatory requirements of heat stroke. *Surg Forum*, 1971. 22: p. 12–4.

255. Seraj, M.A., et al., Are heat stroke patients fluid depleted? Importance of monitoring central venous pressure as a simple guideline for fluid therapy. *Resuscitation*, 1991. 21(1): p. 33–9.

256. Zahger, D., A. Moses, and A.T. Weiss, Evidence of prolonged myocardial dysfunction in heat stroke. *Chest*, 1989. 95(5): p. 1089–91.

257. Clowes, G.H., Jr. and T.F. O'Donnell, Jr., Heat stroke. *N Engl J Med*, 1974. 291(11): p. 564–7.

258. Gottschalk, P.G. and J.E. Thomas, Heat stroke. *Mayo Clin Proc*, 1966. 41(7): p. 470–82.

259. Rockhold, R.W., et al., Dopamine receptors mediate cocaine-induced temperature responses in spontaneously hypertensive and Wistar-Kyoto rats. *Pharmacol Biochem Behav*, 1991. 40(1): p. 157–62.

260. Kosten, T.R. and H.D. Kleber, Rapid death during cocaine abuse: a variant of the neuroleptic malignant syndrome? *Am J Drug Alcohol Abuse*, 1988. 14(3): p. 335–46.

261. Fox, A.W., More on rhabdomyolysis associated with cocaine intoxication [letter]. *N Engl J Med*, 1989. 321(18): p. 1271.

262. Travis, S.P., Management of heat stroke. *J R Nav Med Serv*, 1988. 74(1): p. 39–43.

263. Rumack, B.H., Aspirin versus acetaminophen: a comparative view. *Pediatrics*, 1978. 62(5 Pt 2 Suppl): p. 943–6.

264. McFadden, S. and J.E. Haddow, Coma produced by topical application of isopropanol. *Pediatrics*, 1969. 43: p. 622.

265. Gabow, P.A., W.D. Kaehny, and S.P. Kelleher, The spectrum of rhabdomyolysis. *Medicine*, 1982. 61: p. 141–52.

266. Bogaerts, Y., N. Lameire, and S. Ringoir, The compartmental syndrome: a serious complication of acute rhabdomyolysis. *Clin Nephrol*, 1982. 17: p. 206–11.

267. Akisu, M., et al., Severe acute thinner intoxication. *Turk J Pediatr*, 1996. 38(2): p. 223–5.

268. Akmal, M., et al., Rhabdomyolysis with and without acute renal failure in patients with phencyclidine intoxication. *Am J Nephrol*, 1981. 1(2): p. 91–6.

269. Anand, V., G. Siami, and W.J. Stone, Cocaine-associated rhabdomyolysis and acute renal failure [see comments]. *South Med J*, 1989. 82(1): p. 67–9.

270. Bakir, A.A. and G. Dunea, Drugs of abuse and renal disease. *Curr Opin Nephrol Hypertens*, 1996. 5(2): p. 122–6.

271. Chan, P., et al., Acute heroin intoxication with complications of acute pulmonary edema, acute renal failure, rhabdomyolysis and lumbosacral plexitis: a case report. *Chung Hua I Hsueh Tsa Chih* (Taipei), 1995. 55(5): p. 397–400.

272. Chan, P., et al., Fatal and nonfatal methamphetamine intoxication in the intensive care unit. *J Toxicol Clin Toxicol*, 1994. 32(2): p. 147–55.

273. Cogen, F.C., et al., Phencyclidine-associated acute rhabdomyolysis. *Ann Intern Med*, 1978. 88(2): p. 210–2.

274. Henry, J.A., K.J. Jeffreys, and S. Dawling, Toxicity and deaths from 3,4-methylenedioxymethamphetamine ("ecstasy") [see comments]. *Lancet*, 1992. 340(8816): p. 384–7.

275. Melandri, R., et al., Myocardial damage and rhabdomyolysis associated with prolonged hypoxic coma following opiate overdose. *J Toxicol Clin Toxicol*, 1996. 34(2): p. 199–203.

276. Tehan, B., R. Hardern, and A. Bodenham, Hyperthermia associated with 3,4-methylenedioxyethamphetamine ("Eve"). *Anaesthesia*, 1993. 48(6): p. 507–10.

277. Curry, S.C., D. Chang, and D. Connor, Drug- and toxin-induced rhabdomyolysis. *Ann Emerg Med*, 1989. 18(10): p. 1068–84.

278. Welch, R.D., K. Todd, and G.S. Krause, Incidence of cocaine-associated rhabdomyolysis. *Ann Emerg Med*, 1991. 20(2): p. 154–7.

279. Knochel, J.P., Rhabdomyolysis and myoglobinuria. *Annu Rev Med*, 1982. 33: p. 435–443.

280. Koffler, A., R.M. Friedler, and S.G. Massry, Acute renal failure due to nontraumatic rhabdomyolysis. *Ann Intern Med*, 1976. 85: p. 23–28.

281. Grossman, R.A., et al., Nontraumatic rhabdomyolysis and acute renal failure. *N Engl J Med*, 1974. 291(16): p. 807–11.

282. Knochel, J.P., Rhabdomyolysis and myoglobinuria. *Semin Nephrol*, 1981. 1: p. 75–86.

283. Ron, D., et al., Prevention of acute renal failure in traumatic rhabdomyolysis. *Arch Intern Med*, 1984. 144(2): p. 277–80.

284. Knottenbelt, J.D., Traumatic rhabdomyolysis from severe beating — experience of volume diuresis in 200 patients. *J Trauma*, 1994. 37(2): p. 214–9.

285. Veenstra, J., et al., Relationship between elevated creatine phosphokinase and the clinical spectrum of rhabdomyolysis. *Nephrol Dial Transplant*, 1994. 9(6): p. 637–41.

286. Oda, J., et al., Analysis of 372 patients with crush syndrome caused by the Hanshin-Awaji earthquake. *J Trauma*, 1997. 42(3): p. 470–5; discussion 475–6.

287. Eneas, J.F., P.Y. Schoenfeld, and M.H. Humphreys, The effect of infusion of mannitol-sodium bicarbonate on the clinical course of myoglobinuria. *Arch Intern Med*, 1979. 139(7): p. 801–5.

288. Feinfeld, D.A., et al., A prospective study of urine and serum myoglobin levels in patients with acute rhabdomyolysis. *Clin Nephrol*, 1992. 38(4): p. 193–5.

289. Loun, B., et al., Adaptation of a quantitative immunoassay for urine myoglobin. Predictor in detecting renal dysfunction. *Am J Clin Pathol*, 1996. 105(4): p. 479–86.

290. Thomas, M.A. and L.S. Ibels, Rhabdomyolysis and acute renal failure. *Aust NZ J Med*, 1985. 15(5): p. 623–8.

291. Cadnapaphornchai, P., S. Taher, and F.D. McDonald, Acute drug-associated rhabdomyolysis: an examination of its diverse renal manifestations and complications. *Am J Med Sci*, 1980. 280(2): p. 66–72.

292. Knochel, J.P., Catastrophic medical events with exhaustive exercise: "white collar rhabdomyolysis." *Kidney Int*, 1990. 38(4): p. 709–19.

293. Kageyama, Y., Rhabdomyolysis: clinical analysis of 20 patients. *Nippon Jinzo Gakkai Shi*, 1989. 31(10): p. 1099–103.

294. Ellinas, P.A. and F. Rosner, Rhabdomyolysis: report of eleven cases. *J Natl Med Assoc*, 1992. 84(7): p. 617–24.

295. Ward, M.M., Factors predictive of acute renal failure in rhabdomyolysis. *Arch Intern Med*, 1988. 148(7): p. 1553–7.

296. Gardner, J.W. and J.A. Kark, Fatal rhabdomyolysis presenting as mild heat illness in military training. *Mil Med*, 1994. 159(2): p. 160–3.

297. Morocco, P.A., Atraumatic rhabdomyolysis in a 20-year-old bodybuilder. *J Emerg Nurs*, 1991. 17(6): p. 370–2.

298. Uberoi, H.S., et al., Acute renal failure in severe exertional rhabdomyolysis [see comments]. *J Assoc Physicians India*, 1991. 39(9): p. 677–9.

299. Zurovsky, Y., Effects of changes in plasma volume on fatal rhabdomyolysis in the rat induced by glycerol injections. *J Basic Clin Physiol Pharmacol*, 1992. 3(3): p. 223–37.

300. Sinert, R., et al., Exercise-induced rhabdomyolysis. *Ann Emerg Med*, 1994. 23(6): p. 1301–6.

301. Bunn, H.F. and J.H. Jandi, Exchange of heme analogue hemoglobin molecules. *Proc Natl Acad Sci USA*, 1977. 56: p. 974–8.

302. Paller, M.S., Hemoglobin- and myoglobin-induced acute renal failure in rats: role of iron in nephrotoxicity. *Am J Physiol*, 1988. 255(3 Pt 2): p. F539–44.

303. Anderson, W.A.D., D.B. Morrison, and E.F. Williams, Pathologic changes following injection of ferrihemate (hematin) in dogs. *Arch Pathol*, 1942. 33: p. 589–602.

304. Garcia, G., et al., Nephrotoxicity of myoglobin in the rat: Relative importance of urine pH and prior dehydration (abstract). *Kidney Int*, 1981. 19: p. 200.

305. Perri, G.C. and P. Gerini, Uraemia in the rabbit after injection of crystalline myoglobin. *Br J Exp Pathol*, 1952. 33: p. 440–4.

306. POISONDEX(R) Editorial Staff and K. Kulig, Rhabdomyolysis. 1992, POISONDEX(R): Treatment protocols.

307. Eneas, J.F., P.Y. Schoenfeld, and M.H. Humphreys, The effect of infusion of mannitol-sodium bicarbonate on the clinical course of myoglobinuria. *Arch Intern Med*, 1979. 139: p. 801–5.

308. Lameire, N., et al., Pathophysiology, causes, and prognosis of acute renal failure in the elderly. *Renal Fail*, 1996. 18(3): p. 333–46.

309. Druml, W., Prognosis of acute renal failure 1975–1995. *Nephron*, 1996. 73(1): p. 8–15.

310. Wilson, D.R., et al., Glycerol induced hemoglobinuric acute renal failure in the rat. 3. Micropuncture study of the effects of mannitol and isotonic saline on individual nephron function. *Nephron*, 1967. 4(6): p. 337–55.

311. Kjellmer, I., Potassium ion as a vasodilator during muscular exercise. *Acta Physiol Scand*, 1965: p. 466–8.

312. Knochel, J.P. and E.M. Schlein, On the mechanism of rhabdomyolysis in potassium depletion. *J Clin Invest*, 1972. 51(7): p. 1750–8.

313. Temple, A.R., Acute and chronic effects of aspirin toxicity and their treatment. *Arch Intern Med*, 1981. 141(3 Spec No): p. 364–9.

314. Javaheri, S., Effects of acetazolamide on cerebrospinal fluid ions in metabolic alkalosis in dogs. *J Appl Physiol*, 1987. 62(4): p. 1582–8.

315. Kaplan, S.A. and F.T. Del Carmen, Experimental salicylate poisoning. Observation on the effects of carbonic anhydrase inhibitor and bicarbonate. *Pediatrics*, 1958. 21: p. 762–70.

316. Lijnen, P., et al., Biochemical variables in plasma and urine before and after prolonged physical exercise. *Enzyme*, 1985. 33(3): p. 134–42.

317. Davis, A.M., Hypocalcemia in rhabdomyolysis [letter] [published erratum appears in *JAMA* 1987 Oct 9;258(14):1894]. *JAMA*, 1987. 257(5): p. 626.

318. Malinoski, D.J., M.S. Slater, and R.J. Mullins, Crush injury and rhabdomyolysis. *Crit Care Clin*, 2004. 20(1): p. 171–92.

319. Qureshi, A.I., et al., Cocaine use and hypertension are major risk factors for intracerebral hemorrhage in young African Americans. *Ethn Dis*, 2001. 11(2): p. 311–9.

320. Brecklin, C.S. and J.L. Bauman, Cardiovascular effects of cocaine: focus on hypertension. *J Clin Hypertens* (Greenwich), 1999. 1(3): p. 212–7.

321. Eagle, K.A., E.M. Isselbacher, and R.W. DeSanctis, Cocaine-related aortic dissection in perspective. *Circulation*, 2002. 105(13): p. 1529–30.

322. Brown, C., Phenylpropanolamine — an ongoing problem. *Clin Toxicol Update*, 1987. 9(2): p. 5–8.

323. Glick, R., et al., Phenylpropanolamine: an over-the-counter drug causing central nervous system vasculitis and intracerebral hemorrhage. Case report and review. *Neurosurgery*, 1987. 20(6): p. 969–74.

324. Jackson, C., A. Hart, and M.D. Robinson, Fatal intracranial hemorrhage associated with phenylpropanolamine, pentazocine, and tripelennamine overdose. *J Emerg Med*, 1985. 3(2): p. 127–32.

325. Nahas, G.G., R. Trouve, and W.M. Manger, Cocaine, catecholamines and cardiac toxicity. *Acta Anaesthesiol Scand Suppl*, 1990. 94: p. 77–81.

326. Rothman, R.B., et al., Amphetamine-type central nervous system stimulants release norepinephrine more potently than they release dopamine and serotonin. *Synapse*, 2001. 39(1): p. 32–41.

327. McDonald, A.J., D.M. Yealy, and S. Jacobson, Oral labetalol versus oral nifedipine in hypertensive urgencies in the ED. *Am J Emerg Med*, 1993. 11(5): p. 460–3.

328. Benowitz, N.L., Discussion over hypertension in drug abuse, 1996. Personal communication.

329. Rahn, K.H., How should we treat a hypertensive emergency? *Am J Cardiol*, 1989. 63(6): p. 48C–50C.

330. Somberg, J.C., The therapeutics of hypertensive emergency. *Am J Ther*, 1996. 3(11): p. 741.

331. Vidt, D.G., Emergency room management of hypertensive urgencies and emergencies. *J Clin Hypertens* (Greenwich), 2001. 3(3): p. 158–64.

332. Kumar, A.M., E.S. Nadel, and D.F. Brown, Case presentations of the Harvard Emergency Medicine Residency. Hypertensive crisis. *J Emerg Med*, 2000. 19(4): p. 369–73.

333. Haft, J.I., Use of the calcium-channel blocker nifedipine in the management of hypertensive emergency. *Am J Emerg Med*, 1985. 3(6 Suppl): p. 25–30.

334. Benowitz, N.L., Central nervous system manifestations of toxic disorders, in *Metabolic Brain Dysfunction in Systemic Disorders*, A.L. Arieff and R.C. Griggs, Ed. 1992, Boston: Little, Brown. p. 409–36.

335. Derlet, R.W. and T.E. Albertson, Acute cocaine toxicity: antagonism by agents interacting with adrenoceptors. *Pharmacol Biochem Behav*, 1990. 36(2): p. 225–31.

336. Trouve, R. and G.G. Nahas, Antidotes to lethal cocaine toxicity in the rat. *Arch Int Pharmacodyn Ther*, 1990. 305: p. 197–207.

337. Murphy, D.J., et al., Effects of adrenergic antagonists on cocaine-induced changes in respiratory function. *Pulm Pharmacol*, 1991. 4(3): p. 127–34.

338. Smith, M., D. Garner, and J.T. Niemann, Pharmacologic interventions after an LD$_{50}$ cocaine insult in a chronically instrumented rat model: are beta-blockers contraindicated? *Ann Emerg Med*, 1991. 20(7): p. 768–71.

339. Hessler, R., Cardiovascular principles, in *Goldfrank's Toxicologic Emergencies*, L.R. Goldrank, N.E. Flomenbaum, and N.A. Lewin, Eds. 1992, Norwalk, CT: Appleton & Lange. p. 181–204.

340. Lange, R.A., et al., Potentiation of cocaine-induced coronary vasoconstriction by beta-adrenergic blockade [see comments]. *Ann Intern Med*, 1990. 112(12): p. 897–903.

341. Ramoska, E. and A.D. Sacchetti, Propranolol-induced hypertension in treatment of cocaine intoxication. *Ann Emerg Med*, 1985. 14(11): p. 1112–3.

342. Dusenberry, S.J., M.J. Hicks, and P.J. Mariani, Labetalol treatment of cocaine toxicity [letter]. *Ann Emerg Med*, 1987. 16(2): p. 235.

343. Sand, I.C., et al., Experience with esmolol for the treatment of cocaine-associated cardiovascular complications. *Am J Emerg Med*, 1991. 9(2): p. 161–3.

344. Darmansjah, I., et al., A dose-ranging study of labetalol in moderate to moderately severe hypertension. *Int J Clin Pharmacol Ther*, 1995. 33(4): p. 226–31.

345. Kenny, D., P.S. Pagel, and D.C. Warltier, Attenuation of the systemic and coronary hemodynamic effects of cocaine in conscious dogs: propranolol versus labetalol. *Basic Res Cardiol*, 1992. 87(5): p. 465–77.

346. Schindler, C.W., S.R. Tella, and S.R. Goldberg, Adrenoceptor mechanisms in the cardiovascular effects of cocaine in conscious squirrel monkeys. *Life Sci*, 1992. 51(9): p. 653–60.

347. Karch, S.B., Managing cocaine crisis [comment]. *Ann Emerg Med*, 1989. 18(2): p. 228–30.

348. Gay, G.R. and K.A. Loper, The use of labetalol in the management of cocaine crisis [see comments]. *Ann Emerg Med*, 1988. 17(3): p. 282–3.

349. Briggs, R.S., A.J. Birtwell, and J.E. Pohl, Hypertensive response to labetalol in phaeochromocytoma [letter]. *Lancet*, 1978. 1(8072): p. 1045–6.

350. Larsen, L.S. and A. Larsen, Labetalol in the treatment of epinephrine overdose. *Ann Emerg Med*, 1990. 19(6): p. 680–2.

351. Lange, R.A., et al., Cocaine-induced coronary-artery vasoconstriction [see comments]. *N Engl J Med*, 1989. 321(23): p. 1557–62.

352. Boehrer, J.D., et al., Influence of labetalol on cocaine-induced coronary vasoconstriction in humans. *Am J Med*, 1993. 94(6): p. 608–10.

353. Hamad, A., et al., Life-threatening hyperkalemia after intravenous labetolol injection for hypertensive emergency in a hemodialysis patient. *Am J Nephrol*, 2001. 21(3): p. 241–4.

354. Pollan, S. and M. Tadjziechy, Esmolol in the management of epinephrine- and cocaine-induced cardiovascular toxicity. *Anesth Analg*, 1989. 69(5): p. 663–4.

355. O'Connor, B. and J.B. Luntley, Acute dissection of the thoracic aorta. Esmolol is safer than and as effective as labetalol [letter; comment]. *BMJ*, 1995. 310(6983): p. 875.

356. Brogan, W.C.D., et al., Alleviation of cocaine-induced coronary vasoconstriction by nitroglycerin. *J Am Coll Cardiol*, 1991. 18(2): p. 581–6.

357. Gray, R.J., et al., Comparison of esmolol and nitroprusside for acute post-cardiac surgical hypertension. *Am J Cardiol*, 1987. 59(8): p. 887–91.

358. de Bruijn, N.P., et al., Pharmacokinetics of esmolol in anesthetized patients receiving chronic beta blocker therapy. *Anesthesiology*, 1987. 66(3): p. 323–6.

359. Bashour, T.T., Acute myocardial infarction resulting from amphetamine abuse: a spasm-thrombus interplay? *Am Heart J*, 1994. 128(6 Pt 1): p. 1237–9.

360. Ragland, A.S., Y. Ismail, and E.L. Arsura, Myocardial infarction after amphetamine use. *Am Heart J*, 1993. 125(1): p. 247–9.

361. Burton, B.T., M. Rice, and L.E. Schmertzler, Atrioventricular block following overdose of decongestant cold medication. *J Emerg Med*, 1985. 2(6): p. 415–9.

362. Pentel, P.R., J. Jentzen, and J. Sievert, Myocardial necrosis due to intraperitoneal administration of phenylpropanolamine in rats. *Fundam Appl Toxicol*, 1987. 9(1): p. 167–72.

363. Lucas, P.B., et al., Methylphenidate-induced cardiac arrhythmias [letter]. *N Engl J Med*, 1986. 315(23): p. 1485.

364. Jaffe, R.B., Cardiac and vascular involvement in drug abuse. *Semin Roentgenol*, 1983. 18(3): p. 207–12.

365. Lewin, N.G., L.R., and R.S. Hoffman, Cocaine, in *Goldfrank's Toxicologic Emergencies*, L. Goldfrank, Ed. 1994, Norwalk, CT: Appleton & Lange. p. 847–62.

366. Guidelines 2000 for Cardiopulmonary Resuscitation and Emergency Cardiovascular Care. Part 6: advanced cardiovascular life support: section 6: pharmacology II: agents to optimize cardiac output and blood pressure. The American Heart Association in collaboration with the International Liaison Committee on Resuscitation. *Circulation*, 2000. 102(8 Suppl): p. I129–35.

367. Hollander, J.E., The management of cocaine-associated myocardial ischemia. *N Engl J Med*, 1995. 333(19): p. 1267–72.

368. Benowitz, N.L., Clinical pharmacology and toxicology of cocaine [published erratum appears in *Pharmacol Toxicol* 1993 Jun;72(6):343]. *Pharmacol Toxicol*, 1993. 72(1): p. 3–12.

369. Catravas, J.D., et al., Acute cocaine intoxication in the conscious dog: pathophysiologic profile of acute lethality. *Arch Int Pharmacodyn Ther*, 1978. 235(2): p. 328–40.

370. Togna, G., et al., Platelet responsiveness and biosynthesis of thromboxane and prostacyclin in response to *in vitro* cocaine treatment. *Haemostasis*, 1985. 15(2): p. 100–7.

371. Schnetzer, G.W.D., Platelets and thrombogenesis — current concepts. *Am Heart J*, 1972. 83(4): p. 552–64.

372. Rezkalla, S.H., et al., Effects of cocaine on human platelets in healthy subjects. *Am J Cardiol*, 1993. 72(2): p. 243–6.

373. Hollander, J.E., et al., Nitroglycerin in the treatment of cocaine associated chest pain — clinical safety and efficacy. *J Toxicol Clin Toxicol*, 1994. 32(3): p. 243–56.

374. Billman, G.E., Effect of calcium channel antagonists on cocaine-induced malignant arrhythmias: protection against ventricular fibrillation. *J Pharmacol Exp Ther*, 1993. 266(1): p. 407–16.

375. Knuepfer, M.M. and C.A. Branch, Calcium channel antagonists reduce the cocaine-induced decrease in cardiac output in a subset of rats. *J Cardiovasc Pharmacol*, 1993. 21(3): p. 390–6.

376. Derlet, R.W. and T.E. Albertson, Potentiation of cocaine toxicity with calcium channel blockers. *Am J Emerg Med*, 1989. 7(5): p. 464–8.

377. Hoffman, R., Comment to calcium channel blockers may potentiate cocaine toxicity. AACT clinical toxicology update, 1990 (March).

378. Nahas, G., et al., A calcium-channel blocker as antidote to the cardiac effects of cocaine intoxication [letter]. *N Engl J Med*, 1985. 313(8): p. 519–20.

379. Negus, B.H., et al., Alleviation of cocaine-induced coronary vasoconstriction with intravenous verapamil. *Am J Cardiol*, 1994. 73(7): p. 510–3.

380. Hollander, J.E., W.A. Carter, and R.S. Hoffman, Use of phentolamine for cocaine-induced myocardial ischemia [letter]. *N Engl J Med*, 1992. 327(5): p. 361.

381. Bush, H.S., Cocaine-associated myocardial infarction. A word of caution about thrombolytic therapy [see comments]. *Chest*, 1988. 94(4): p. 878.

382. Hollander, J.E., et al., Cocaine-associated myocardial infarction. Clinical safety of thrombolytic therapy. Cocaine Associated Myocardial Infarction (CAMI) Study Group. *Chest*, 1995. 107(5): p. 1237–41.

383. Hollander, J.E., et al., Cocaine-associated myocardial infarction. Mortality and complications. Cocaine-Associated Myocardial Infarction Study Group. *Arch Intern Med*, 1995. 155(10): p. 1081–6.

384. Gitter, M.J., et al., Cocaine and chest pain: clinical features and outcome of patients hospitalized to rule out myocardial infarction [see comments]. *Ann Intern Med*, 1991. 115(4): p. 277–82.

385. Hollander, J.E., et al., "Abnormal" electrocardiograms in patients with cocaine-associated chest pain are due to "normal" variants. *J Emerg Med*, 1994. 12(2): p. 199–205.

386. Keller, K.B. and L. Lemberg, The cocaine-abused heart. *Am J Crit Care*, 2003. 12(6): p. 562–6.

387. Kontos, M.C., et al., Coronary angiographic findings in patients with cocaine-associated chest pain. *J Emerg Med*, 2003. 24(1): p. 9–13.

388. Derlet, R.W., T.E. Albertson, and R.S. Tharratt, Lidocaine potentiation of cocaine toxicity. *Ann Emerg Med*, 1991. 20(2): p. 135–8.

389. Liu, D., R.J. Hariman, and J.L. Bauman, Cocaine concentration-effect relationship in the presence and absence of lidocaine: evidence of competitive binding between cocaine and lidocaine. *J Pharmacol Exp Ther*, 1996. 276(2): p. 568–77.

390. Winecoff, A.P., et al., Reversal of the electrocardiographic effects of cocaine by lidocaine. Part 1. Comparison with sodium bicarbonate and quinidine. *Pharmacotherapy*, 1994. 14(6): p. 698–703.

391. Shih, R.D., et al., Clinical safety of lidocaine in patients with cocaine-associated myocardial infarction. *Ann Emerg Med*, 1995. 26(6): p. 702–6.

392. Beckman, K.J., et al., Hemodynamic and electrophysiological actions of cocaine. Effects of sodium bicarbonate as an antidote in dogs. *Circulation*, 1991. 83(5): p. 1799–807.

393. Goel, P. and G.C. Flaker, Cardiovascular complications of cocaine use. *N Engl J Med*, 2001. 345(21): p. 1575–6.

394. Barth, C.W.d., M. Bray, and W.C. Roberts, Rupture of the ascending aorta during cocaine intoxication. *Am J Cardiol*, 1986. 57(6): p. 496.

395. Brody, S.L., C.M. Slovis, and K.D. Wrenn, Cocaine-related medical problems: consecutive series of 233 patients [see comments]. *Am J Med*, 1990. 88(4): p. 325–31.

396. Derlet, R.W. and T.E. Albertson, Emergency department presentation of cocaine intoxication. *Ann Emerg Med*, 1989. 18(2): p. 182–6.

397. Rich, J.A. and D.E. Singer, Cocaine-related symptoms in patients presenting to an urban emergency department. *Ann Emerg Med*, 1991. 20(6): p. 616–21.

398. Silverstein, W., N.A. Lewin, and L. Goldfrank, Management of the cocaine-intoxicated patient [letter]. *Ann Emerg Med*, 1987. 16(2): p. 234–5.

399. Kloner, R.A., et al., The effects of acute and chronic cocaine use on the heart. *Circulation*, 1992. 85(2): p. 407–19.

400. Isner, J.M., et al., Acute cardiac events temporally related to cocaine abuse. *N Engl J Med*, 1986. 315(23): p. 1438–43.

401. Cregler, L.L. and H. Mark, Medical complications of cocaine abuse. *N Engl J Med*, 1986. 315(23): p. 1495–500.

402. Robin, E.D., R.J. Wong, and K.A. Ptashne, Increased lung water and ascites after massive cocaine overdosage in mice and improved survival related to beta-adrenergic blockage. *Ann Intern Med*, 1989. 110(3): p. 202–7.

403. Ouriel, K., Comparison of safety and efficacy of the various thrombolytic agents. *Rev Cardiovasc Med*, 2002. 3 Suppl 2: p. S17–24.

404. Baker, W.F., Jr., Thrombolytic therapy. *Clin Appl Thromb Hemost*, 2002. 8(4): p. 291–314.

405. Baker, W.F., Jr., Thrombolytic therapy: clinical applications. *Hematol Oncol Clin North Am*, 2003. 17(1): p. 283–311.

406. Nordt, T.K. and C. Bode, Thrombolysis: newer thrombolytic agents and their role in clinical medicine. *Heart*, 2003. 89(11): p. 1358–62.

407. Williams, M.L. and D.A. Tate, *Emergency Medicine: A Comprehensive Study Guide*. 4th ed, J. Tintinalli, E. Ruiz, and R.L. Krome, Eds. 1996, New York: McGraw-Hill. p. 344–54.

408. Grawe, J.J., et al., Reversal of the electrocardiographic effects of cocaine by lidocaine. Part 2. Concentration-effect relationships. *Pharmacotherapy*, 1994. 14(6): p. 704–11.

409. Tokarski, G.F., et al., An evaluation of cocaine-induced chest pain [see comments]. *Ann Emerg Med*, 1990. 19(10): p. 1088–92.

410. Hollander, J.E., et al., Prospective multicenter evaluation of cocaine-associated chest pain. Cocaine Associated Chest Pain (COCHPA) Study Group. *Acad Emerg Med*, 1994. 1(4): p. 330–9.

411. Adams, J.E., 3rd, et al., Cardiac troponin I. A marker with high specificity for cardiac injury. *Circulation*, 1993. 88(1): p. 101–6.

412. Kontos, M.C., et al., Utility of troponin I in patients with cocaine-associated chest pain. *Acad Emerg Med*, 2002. 9(10): p. 1007–13.

413. Wu, A.H., et al., Comparison of myoglobin, creatine kinase-MB, and cardiac troponin I for diagnosis of acute myocardial infarction. *Ann Clin Lab Sci*, 1996. 26(4): p. 291–300.

414. Graff, L., et al., American College of Emergency Physicians information paper: chest pain units in emergency departments — a report from the Short-Term Observation Services Section. *Am J Cardiol*, 1995. 76(14): p. 1036–9.

415. Lee, T.H., et al., Ruling out acute myocardial infarction. A prospective multicenter validation of a 12-hour strategy for patients at low risk. *N Engl J Med*, 1991. 324(18): p. 1239–46.

416. Weber, J.E., et al., Validation of a brief observation period for patients with cocaine-associated chest pain. *N Engl J Med*, 2003. 348(6): p. 510–7.

417. Hollander, J.E. and R.S. Hoffman, Cocaine-induced myocardial infarction: an analysis and review of the literature. *J Emerg Med*, 1992. 10(2): p. 169–77.

418. Zimmerman, J.L., R.P. Dellinger, and P.A. Majid, Cocaine-associated chest pain. *Ann Emerg Med*, 1991. 20(6): p. 611–5.

419. Kokkinos, J. and S. Levine, Stroke. *Neurol Clin*, 1993. 11(3): p. 577–90.

420. Petitti, D.B., et al., Stroke and cocaine or amphetamine use. *Epidemiology*, 1998. 9(6): p. 596–600.

421. Qureshi, A.I., et al., Cocaine use and the likelihood of nonfatal myocardial infarction and stroke: data from the Third National Health and Nutrition Examination Survey. *Circulation*, 2001. 103(4): p. 502–6.

422. Friedman, E.H., Cocaine-induced stroke. *Neurology*, 1993. 43(9): p. 1864–5.

423. Tolat, R.D., et al., Cocaine-associated stroke: three cases and rehabilitation considerations. *Brain Inj*, 2000. 14(4): p. 383–91.

424. Riggs, J.E. and L. Gutmann, Crack cocaine use and stroke in young patients. *Neurology*, 1997. 49(5): p. 1473–4.

425. Kaku, D. and D.H. Lowenstein, Emergence of recreational drug abuse as a major risk factor for stroke in young adults. *Ann Intern Med*, 1990. 113: p. 821.

426. Konzen, J.P., S.R. Levine, and J.H. Garcia, Vasospasm and thrombus formation as possible mechanisms of stroke related to alkaloidal cocaine. *Stroke*, 1995. 26(6): p. 1114–8.

427. Tardiff, K., et al., Analysis of cocaine-positive fatalities. *J Forensic Sci*, 1989. 34(1): p. 53–63.

428. Mueller, P.D., N.L. Benowitz, and K.R. Olson, Cocaine. *Emerg Med Clin North Am*, 1990. 8(3): p. 481–93.

429. Barsan, W.G. and M. Bain, Stroke, in *Emergency Medicine: Concepts and Clinical Practice*, P. Rosen and R.M. Barkin, Eds. 1992, St. Louis: Mosby Year Book. p. 1825–41.

430. Hacke, W., et al., Intravenous thrombolysis with recombinant tissue plasminogen activator for acute hemispheric stroke. The European Cooperative Acute Stroke Study (ECASS). *JAMA*, 1995. 274(13): p. 1017–25.

431. Randomised controlled trial of streptokinase, aspirin, and combination of both in treatment of acute ischaemic stroke. Multicentre Acute Stroke Trial — Italy (MAST-I) Group. *Lancet*, 1995. 346(8989): p. 1509–14.

432. Tissue plasminogen activator for acute ischemic stroke. The National Institute of Neurological Disorders and Stroke rt-PA Stroke Study Group. *N Engl J Med*, 1995. 333(24): p. 1581–7.

433. Thrombolytic therapy with streptokinase in acute ischemic stroke. The Multicenter Acute Stroke Trial — Europe Study Group. *N Engl J Med*, 1996. 335(3): p. 145–50.

434. Donnan, G.A., et al., Streptokinase for acute ischemic stroke with relationship to time of administration: Australian Streptokinase (ASK) Trial Study Group. *JAMA*, 1996. 276(12): p. 961–6.

434a. Hoffman, J.R., Should physicians give tPA to patients with acute ischemic stroke? *West J Med*, 2000. 173: p. 149–50.

435. Libman, R.B., et al., Conditions that mimic stroke in the emergency department. Implications for acute stroke trials. *Arch Neurol*, 1995. 52(11): p. 1119–22.

436. Turpie, A.G., R. Bloch, and R. Duke, Heparin in the treatment of thromboembolic stroke. *Ann N Y Acad Sci*, 1989. 556: p. 406–15.

437. Sage, J.I., Stroke. The use and overuse of heparin in therapeutic trials. *Arch Neurol*, 1985. 42(4): p. 315–7.

438. Korczyn, A.D., Heparin in the treatment of acute stroke. *Neurol Clin*, 1992. 10(1): p. 209–17.

439. Salgado, A.V., et al., Neurologic complications of endocarditis: a 12-year experience. *Neurology*, 1989. 39(2 Pt 1): p. 173–8.

440. Hart, R.G., et al., Stroke in infective endocarditis. *Stroke*, 1990. 21(5): p. 695–700.

441. Showalter, C.V., T's and blues. Abuse of pentazocine and tripelennamine. *JAMA*, 1980. 244(11): p. 1224–5.

442. Caplan, L.R., C. Thomas, and G. Banks, Central nervous system complications of addiction to "T's and Blues." *Neurology*, 1982. 32(6): p. 623–8.

443. Lipton, R.B., M. Choy-Kwong, and S. Solomon, Headaches in hospitalized cocaine users. *Headache*, 1989. 29(4): p. 225–8.

444. Benowitz, N.L., How toxic is cocaine? *Ciba Found Symp*, 1992. 166: p. 125–43; discussion 143–8.

445. Satel, S.L. and F.H. Gawin, Migrainelike headache and cocaine use. *JAMA*, 1989. 261(20): p. 2995 6.

446. Rothrock, J.F., R. Rubenstein, and P.D. Lyden, Ischemic stroke associated with methamphetamine inhalation. *Neurology*, 1988. 38(4): p. 589–92.

447. Rumbaugh, C.L., et al., Cerebral vascular changes secondary to amphetamine abuse in the experimental animal. *Radiology*, 1971. 101(2): p. 345–51.

448. Wadworth, A.N. and D. McTavish, Nimodipine. A review of its pharmacological properties, and therapeutic efficacy in cerebral disorders. *Drugs Aging*, 1992. 2(4): p. 262–86.

449. Rickels, E. and M. Zumkeller, Vasospasm after experimentally induced subarachnoid haemorrhage and treatment with nimodipine. *Neurochirurgia* (Stuttgart), 1992. 35(4): p. 99–102.

450. Ansah, T.A., L.H. Wade, and D.C. Shockley, Effects of calcium channel entry blockers on cocaine and amphetamine-induced motor activities and toxicities. *Life Sci*, 1993. 53(26): p. 1947–56.

451. Derlet, R.W., C.C. Tseng, and T.E. Albertson, Cocaine toxicity and the calcium channel blockers nifedipine and nimodipine in rats. *J Emerg Med*, 1994. 12(1): p. 1–4.

452. Kaste, M., et al., A randomized, double-blind, placebo-controlled trial of nimodipine in acute ischemic hemispheric stroke. *Stroke*, 1994. 25(7): p. 1348–53.

453. Wooten, M.R., M.S. Khangure, and M.J. Murphy, Intracerebral hemorrhage and vasculitis related to ephedrine abuse. *Ann Neurol*, 1983. 13(3): p. 337–40.

454. Rumbaugh, C.L., et al., Cerebral microvascular injury in experimental drug abuse. *Invest Radiol*, 1976. 11(4): p. 282–94.

455. Citron, B.P., et al., Necrotizing angiitis associated with drug abuse. *N Engl J Med*, 1970. 283(19): p. 1003–11.

456. Loizou, L.A., J.G. Hamilton, and S.A. Tsementzis, Intracranial haemorrhage in association with pseudoephedrine overdose. *J Neurol Neurosurg Psychiatry*, 1982. 45(5): p. 471–2.

457. Brust, J.C. and R.W. Richter, Stroke associated with addiction to heroin. *J Neurol Neurosurg Psychiatry*, 1976. 39(2): p. 194–9.

458. Woods, B.T. and G.J. Strewler, Hemiparesis occurring six hours after intravenous heroin injection. *Neurology*, 1972. 22(8): p. 863–6.

459. Trugman, J.M., Cerebral arteritis and oral methylphenidate [letter]. *Lancet*, 1988. 1(8585): p. 584–5.

460. Fredericks, R.K., et al., Cerebral vasculitis associated with cocaine abuse. *Stroke*, 1991. 22(11): p. 1437–9.

461. Krendel, D.A., et al., Biopsy-proven cerebral vasculitis associated with cocaine abuse. *Neurology*, 1990. 40(7): p. 1092–4.

462. Kaye, B.R. and M. Fainstat, Cerebral vasculitis associated with cocaine abuse. *JAMA*, 1987. 258(15): p. 2104–6.

463. Nalls, G., et al., Subcortical cerebral hemorrhages associated with cocaine abuse: CT and MR findings. *J Comput Assist Tomogr*, 1989. 13(1): p. 1–5.

464. Salanova, V. and R. Taubner, Intracerebral haemorrhage and vasculitis secondary to amphetamine use. *Postgrad Med J*, 1984. 60(704): p. 429–30.

465. Cerebral vasculitis associated with cocaine abuse or subarachnoid hemorrhage? [letter]. *JAMA*, 1988. 259(11): p. 1648–9.

466. Powers, W.J., Acute hypertension after stroke: the scientific basis for treatment decisions. *Neurology*, 1993. 43(3 Pt 1): p. 461–7.

467. Kenton, E.J., III, Diagnosis and treatment of concomitant hypertension and stroke. *J Natl Med Assoc*, 1996. 88(6): p. 364–8.

468. Shephard, T.J. and S.W. Fox, Assessment and management of hypertension in the acute ischemic stroke patient. *J Neurosci Nurs*, 1996. 28(1): p. 5–12.

469. Brucia, J.J., D.C. Owen, and E.B. Rudy, The effects of lidocaine on intracranial hypertension. *J Neurosci Nurs*, 1992. 24(4): p. 205–14.

470. Lev, R. and P. Rosen, Prophylactic lidocaine use preintubation: a review. *J Emerg Med*, 1994. 12(4): p. 499–506.

471. Malouf, R. and J.C. Brust, Hypoglycemia: causes, neurological manifestations, and outcome. *Ann Neurol*, 1985. 17(5): p. 421–30.

472. Swartz, M.H., L.E. Teichholz, and E. Donoso, Mitral valve prolapse: a review of associated arrhythmias. *Am J Med*, 1977. 62(3): p. 377–89.

473. Savage, D.D., et al., Mitral valve prolapse in the general population. 3. Dysrhythmias: the Framingham Study. *Am Heart J*, 1983. 106(3): p. 582–6.

474. Washington, J.A.D., The role of the microbiology laboratory in the diagnosis and antimicrobial treatment of infective endocarditis. *Mayo Clin Proc*, 1982. 57(1): p. 22–32.

475. Hoffman, R.S., M.J. Smilkstein, and L.R. Goldfrank, Whole bowel irrigation and the cocaine body-packer: a new approach to a common problem. *Am J Emerg Med*, 1990. 8(6): p. 523–7.

476. Duenas-Laita, A., S. Nogue, and G. Burillo-Putze, Body packing. *N Engl J Med*, 2004. 350(12): p. 1260–1; author reply 1260–1.

477. Bulstrode, N., F. Banks, and S. Shrotria, The outcome of drug smuggling by 'body packers' — the British experience. *Ann R Coll Surg Engl*, 2002. 84(1): p. 35–8.

478. Traub, S.J., et al., Pediatric "body packing." *Arch Pediatr Adolesc Med*, 2003. 157(2): p. 174–7.

479. Roberts, J.R., et al., The bodystuffer syndrome: a clandestine form of drug overdose. *Am J Emerg Med*, 1986. 4(1): p. 24–7.

480. Olson, K.R., Is gut emptying all washed up? [editorial]. *Am J Emerg Med*, 1990. 8(6): p. 560–1.

481. Kulig, K., et al., Management of acutely poisoned patients without gastric emptying. *Ann Emerg Med*, 1985. 14(6): p. 562–7.

482. Albertson, T.E., et al., Superiority of activated charcoal alone compared with ipecac and activated charcoal in the treatment of acute toxic ingestions [see comments]. *Ann Emerg Med*, 1989. 18(1): p. 56–9.

483. Merigian, K.S., et al., Prospective evaluation of gastric emptying in the self-poisoned patient. *Am J Emerg Med*, 1990. 8(6): p. 479–83.

484. Pond, S.M., et al., Gastric emptying in acute overdose: a prospective randomised controlled trial [see comments]. *Med J Aust*, 1995. 163(7): p. 345–9.

485. Curtis, R.A., J. Barone, and N. Giacona, Efficacy of ipecac and activated charcoal/cathartic. Prevention of salicylate absorption in a simulated overdose. *Arch Intern Med*, 1984. 144(1): p. 48–52.

486. Tenenbein, M., S. Cohen, and D.S. Sitar, Efficacy of ipecac-induced emesis, orogastric lavage, and activated charcoal for acute drug overdose. *Ann Emerg Med*, 1987. 16(8): p. 838–41.

487. Olkkola, K.T., Effect of charcoal-drug ratio on antidotal efficacy of oral activated charcoal in man. *Br J Clin Pharmacol*, 1985. 19(6): p. 767–73.

488. Pollack, M.M., et al., Aspiration of activated charcoal and gastric contents. *Ann Emerg Med*, 1981. 10(10): p. 528–9.

489. Menzies, D.G., A. Busuttil, and L.F. Prescott, Fatal pulmonary aspiration of oral activated charcoal. *BMJ*, 1988. 297(6646): p. 459–60.

490. Givens, T., M. Holloway, and S. Wason, Pulmonary aspiration of activated charcoal: a complication of its misuse in overdose management. *Pediatr Emerg Care*, 1992. 8(3): p. 137–40.

491. Mariani, P.J. and N. Pook, Gastrointestinal tract perforation with charcoal peritoneum complicating orogastric intubation and lavage. *Ann Emerg Med*, 1993. 22(3): p. 606–9.

492. Ray, M.J., et al., Charcoal bezoar. Small-bowel obstruction secondary to amitriptyline overdose therapy [published erratum appears in *Dig Dis Sci* 1988 Oct;33(10):1344]. *Dig Dis Sci*, 1988. 33(1): p. 106–7.

493. Watson, W.A., K.F. Cremer, and J.A. Chapman, Gastrointestinal obstruction associated with multiple-dose activated charcoal. *J Emerg Med*, 1986. 4(5): p. 401–7.

494. Longdon, P. and A. Henderson, Intestinal pseudo-obstruction following the use of enteral charcoal and sorbitol and mechanical ventilation with papaveretum sedation for theophylline poisoning. *Drug Saf*, 1992. 7(1): p. 74–7.

495. Bradberry, S.M. and J.A. Vale, Multiple-dose activated charcoal: a review of relevant clinical studies. *J Toxicol Clin Toxicol*, 1995. 33(5): p. 407–16.

496. Pond, S.M., et al., Randomized study of the treatment of phenobarbital overdose with repeated doses of activated charcoal. *JAMA*, 1984. 251(23): p. 3104–8.

497. Boldy, D.A., J.A. Vale, and L.F. Prescott, Treatment of phenobarbitone poisoning with repeated oral administration of activated charcoal. *Q J Med*, 1986. 61(235): p. 997–1002.

498. Eroglu, A., et al., Multiple dose-activated charcoal as a cause of acute appendicitis. *J Toxicol Clin Toxicol*, 2003. 41(1): p. 71–3.

499. Everson, G.W., E.J. Bertaccini, and J. O'Leary, Use of whole bowel irrigation in an infant following iron overdose. *Am J Emerg Med*, 1991. 9(4): p. 366–9.

500. Turk, J., et al., Successful therapy of iron intoxication in pregnancy with intravenous deferoxamine and whole bowel irrigation. *Vet Hum Toxicol*, 1993. 35(5): p. 441–4.

501. Bock, G.W. and M. Tenenbein, Whole bowel irrigation for iron overdose [letter]. *Ann Emerg Med*, 1987. 16(1): p. 137–8.

502. Janss, G.J., Acute theophylline overdose treated with whole bowel irrigation. *S D J Med*, 1990. 43(6): p. 7–8.

503. Buckley, N., et al., Slow-release verapamil poisoning. Use of polyethylene glycol whole-bowel lavage and high-dose calcium. *Med J Aust*, 1993. 158(3): p. 202–4.

504. Burkhart, K.K., K.W. Kulig, and B. Rumack, Whole-bowel irrigation as treatment for zinc sulfate overdose. *Ann Emerg Med*, 1990. 19(10): p. 1167–70.

505. Melandri, R., et al., Whole bowel irrigation after delayed release fenfluramine overdose. *J Toxicol Clin Toxicol*, 1995. 33(2): p. 161–3.

506. Roberge, R.J. and T.G. Martin, Whole bowel irrigation in an acute oral lead intoxication. *Am J Emerg Med*, 1992. 10(6): p. 577–83.

507. Utecht, M.J., A.F. Stone, and M.M. McCarron, Heroin body packers. *J Emerg Med*, 1993. 11(1): p. 33–40.

508. Niazi, S., Effect of polyethylene glycol 4000 on dissolution properties of sulfathiazole polymorphs. *J Pharm Sci*, 1976. 65(2): p. 302–4.

509. Diacetylmorphine, in *Merck Index*. 1984, Rahway, NJ: Merck & Co, Inc. p. 429.

510. Rosenberg, P.J., D.J. Livingstone, and B.A. McLellan, Effect of whole-bowel irrigation on the antidotal efficacy of oral activated charcoal. *Ann Emerg Med*, 1988. 17(7): p. 681–3.

511. Tenenbein, M., Whole bowel irrigation and activated charcoal [letter]. *Ann Emerg Med*, 1989. 18(6): p. 707–8.

512. Ilkhanipour, K., D.M. Yealy, and E.P. Krenzelok, The comparative efficacy of various multiple-dose activated charcoal regimens. *Am J Emerg Med*, 1992. 10(4): p. 298–300.

513. Park, G.D., et al., Effects of size and frequency of oral doses of charcoal on theophylline clearance. *Clin Pharmacol Ther*, 1983. 34(5): p. 663–6.

514. Marc, B., et al., Managing drug dealers who swallow the evidence. *BMJ*, 1989. 299(6707): p. 1082.

515. Sporer, K., Cocaine body stuffers. 1997, unpublished data.

516. McCarron, M.M. and J.D. Wood, The cocaine 'body packer' syndrome. Diagnosis and treatment. *JAMA*, 1983. 250(11): p. 1417–20.

517. Caruana, D.S., et al., Cocaine-packet ingestion. Diagnosis, management, and natural history. *Ann Intern Med*, 1984. 100(1): p. 73–4.

518. Farmer, J.W. and S.B. Chan, Whole body irrigation for contraband bodypackers. *J Clin Gastroenterol*, 2003. 37(2): p. 147–50.

519. Jeanmarie, P., Cocaine, in *Emergency Medicine, A Comprehensive Study Guide*, J. Tintinalli, Ed. 1996, New York: McGraw-Hill. p. 777–778.

520. Weiner, J.S. and M. Khogali, A physiological body-cooling unit for treatment of heat stroke. *Lancet*, 1980. 1(8167): p. 507–9.

521. Barner, H.B., et al., Field evaluation of a new simplified method for cooling of heat casualties in the desert. *Mil Med*, 1984. 149(2): p. 95–7.

522. Al-Aska, A.K., et al., Simplified cooling bed for heatstroke. *Lancet*, 1987. 1(8529): p. 381.

523. Kielblock, A.J., J.P. Van Rensburg, and R.M. Franz, Body cooling as a method for reducing hyperthermia. An evaluation of techniques. *S Afr Med J*, 1986. 69(6): p. 378–80.

524. Wyndham, C.H., N.B. Strydom, and H.M. Cooke, Methods of cooling subjects with hyperpyrexia. *J Appl Physiol*, 1959. (14): p. 771.

525. White, J.D., et al., Evaporation versus iced gastric lavage treatment of heatstroke: comparative efficacy in a canine model. *Crit Care Med*, 1987. 15(8): p. 748–50.

526. Daily, W.M. and T.R. Harrison, A study of the mechanism and treatment of experimental heat pyrexia. *Am J Med Sci*, 1948. 215: p. 42.

527. Magazanik, A., et al., Tap water, an efficient method for cooling heatstroke victims — a model in dogs. *Aviat Space Environ Med*, 1980. 51(9 Pt 1): p. 864–6.

528. Bynum, G., et al., Peritoneal lavage cooling in an anesthetized dog heatstroke model. *Aviat Space Environ Med*, 1978. 49(6): p. 779–84.

529. Syverud, S.A., et al., Iced gastric lavage for treatment of heatstroke: efficacy in a canine model. *Ann Emerg Med*, 1985. 14(5): p. 424–32.

530. Chiulli, D.A., T.E. Terndrup, and R.K. Kaufer, The influence of diazepam or lorazepam on the frequency of endotracheal intubation in childhood status epilepticus. *J Emerg Med*, 1991. 9: p. 13–17.

CHAPTER 9

Sports

Edited by Marc D. Bollmann, M.D.[1] and Martial Saugy, Ph.D.[2]
[1] University Institute of Legal Medicine, Lausanne, Switzerland
[2] Swiss Laboratory for Doping Analyses, University Institute of Legal Medicine, Lausanne, Switzerland

CONTENTS

Doping contravenes the ethics of both sport and medical science. It consists of the administration of substances belonging to prohibited classes of pharmacological agents, and/or the use of various prohibited methods.

WADA — *IOC Definition, 2004*

Doping is not a new phenomenon. Ancient Greek athletes tried to enhance performance by ingestion of alcoholic drinks and sheep testicles. The term "doping" is said to have its roots in the Dutch word *Dop*, which, in South Africa, referred to an alcoholic drink used as a stimulant by the Zulus in ceremonial dancing. At the end of 19th century, athletes experimented with cocaine, heroin, and strychnine. In the 1904, Thomas Hicks nearly died using strychnine in combination with brandy during a bicycle race. Today modern drugs have replaced alcohol as doping agent, although strychnine is still rarely reported. These examples illustrate that misuse of drugs by athletes has been a problem since the beginning of sports history. About 35 years ago, after the first widely reported doping scandals, health and sports ethics became a major concern of the medical commission of the International Olympic Commission (IOC) and also of the individual sport federations. Doping has also become a problem even in recreational sports. Thus, the fight against doping began.

The medical commission of the IOC has created a list of forbidden substances and prohibited methods, which is included in the IOC's medical code. Doping control is performed by a network of IOC accredited laboratories, which analyze urine samples collected after or out of competition. Following the World Anti-Doping Conference in Lausanne in 1999, sports authorities and governments decided to produce a World anti-doping code (Code) and to fund a World Anti-Doping Agency (WADA). The main aim of WADA is to harmonize the fight against doping around the world. The anti-doping Code works in conjunction with four International Standards aimed at harmonization among anti-doping organizations:

1. Prohibited List of substances and methods
2. International standards for testing
3. International standards for laboratories
4. Therapeutic use exemptions (TUES)

These standards have been the subject of lengthy consultation among the WADA stakeholders and are mandatory for all signatories of the World Anti-Doping Code.

Prohibited List of Substances and Methods

The Prohibited List (List) was first published in 1963 under the leadership of the International Olympic Committee. Since 2004, it had been updated and published by the WADA. The List is the cornerstone of the Code and a key component of harmonization. It lists substances and methods prohibited in and out of competition, as well as substances prohibited for particular disciplines. The use of prohibited substances can be authorized for medical reasons by virtue of a TUES.

Prohibited Substance Classes:

1. S1. Anabolic Agents
   Anabolic Androgenic Steroids (AAS), e.g., testosterone, nandrolone, methandienone, stanozolol, etc.
   Other anabolic agents, e.g., Clenbuterol
2. S2. Hormones and related substances
   Erythropoietin (EPO)
   Growth hormone (GH), insulin-like growth factor (IGF-1), mechano growth factors (MGFs)
   Gonadotrophins (LH, HCG)
   Insulin
   Corticotrophins
3. S3. Beta-2-agonists
4. S4. Agents with anti-estrogenic activity
   Aromatase inhibitors, including anastrazole, letrozole, etc.
   Selective estrogen receptor modulators (SERMs), including tamoxifène, toremifene, etc.
   Other anti-estrogenic substances, including clomiphene, cyclofenyl, etc.
5. S5. Diuretics and other masking agents
   Masking agents, including epitestosterone, probenecid, plasma expanders
   Diuretics, including acetazolamide, furosemide, etc.
6. S6. Stimulants
   Examples: Amphetamine, ethylefrine, modafinil, ephedrine, cathine, methylephedrine, etc.
   Note: For ephedrine, methylephedrine, and cathine a cutoff urine concentration has been defined
7. S7. Narcotics
   Examples: Buprenorphine, fentanyl, methadone, etc.
8. S8. Cannabinoids
9. S9. Glucocorticoids
10. P1. Alcohol and P2. Beta-blockers are prohibited in some specific sports

Table 9.1   General Statistics for 2004

Sports	Samples Analyzed	Adverse Analytical Findings	% Adverse of Total
Olympic	128,591	2,145	1.67
Non-Olympic	40,596	764	1.88
Total	169,187	2,909	1.72

Table 9.2   Number of Substances Identified for 2004

Substance Group	No.	% of All Adverse Analytical Findings
Anabolic agents	1191	36.0
Glucocorticoids	548	16.6
Cannabinoids	518	15.7
Stimulants	382	11.6
beta-2-Agonists	381	11.5
Masking agents	157	4.8
Peptide hormones	78	2.4
beta-Blockers	25	0.8
Narcotics	15	0.5
Anti-Estrogens	8	0.2
Blood transfusion	2	0.1
Total	3305	

Prohibited Methods:

1. M1. Enhancement of oxygen transfer
   Blood doping, for example, homologous or autologous blood transfusion
   Artificial transport of oxygen, for example, PFCs, modified hemoglobins, etc.
2. M2. Chemical and physical manipulation
   Tampering with the sample
   Intravenous infusions
3. M3. Gene doping

International Standards for Testing

The purpose of the International Standards for Testing is to plan for effective testing and to maintain the integrity and identity of samples throughout the testing process, from notifying the athlete to transport of the samples for analysis.

International Standard for Laboratories

The purpose of the International Standard for Laboratories (ISL) is to ensure production of valid test results and evidentiary data, and to achieve uniform and harmonized results and reporting from all accredited laboratories. The ISL includes requirements for WADA accreditation of doping laboratories, operating standards for laboratory performance, and description of the accreditation process.

WADA publishes annually an overview of the results reported by its accredited laboratories.[1] The 2004 statistics include analyses conducted by WADA-accredited laboratories for in- and out-of-competition testing (Table 9.1 through Table. 9.3). When looking at the statistics of 2004, anabolic steroids are still the most often reported doping agents, as it has been the case every year since the beginning of the 1990s. Surprisingly, the glucocorticoids and cannabinoids are nowadays at second and third place. The large number of testosterone cases should be taken with caution

Table 9.3 The 12 Most Identified Substances for 2004

	Substance	Group	No.
1	Cannabis	Cannabinoids	518
2	Testosterone[a]	Anabolic steroids	392
3	Nandrolone	Anabolic steroids	339
4	Salbutamol[b]	beta-2-Agonists	251
5	Triamcinolone Ac.[b]	Glucocorticoids	246
6	Stanozolol	Anabolic steroids	226
7	Betamethasone[b]	Glucocorticoids	121
8	Amphetamine	Stimulants	112
9	Ephedrine	Stimulants	102
10	Terbutaline[b]	beta-2-Agonists	78
11	Cocaine	Stimulants	75
12	Methandienone	Anabolic steroids	62

[a] These are adverse analytical findings reported from laboratories. Some of these results can be due to naturally elevated testosterone levels.
[b] beta-2-Agonist and glucocorticoid adverse analytical findings could have been justified by therapeutic use exemption (TUE).

because the differentiation between a naturally elevated concentration of the endogenous hormone and abuse of testosterone esters cannot always be done.

International Standard for Therapeutic Use Exemptions

The purpose of the International Standard for TUE is to ensure that the process of granting TUEs is harmonized across sports and countries. But what is a TUE? Athletes, like all others, may have illnesses or conditions that require them to take particular medications. If the medication happens to fall under the Prohibited List, a TUE authorizes the athlete to take the needed drug.

The criteria to grant a TUE are:

The athlete would experience significant health problems without taking the prohibited substance or method
The therapeutic use of the substance would not produce significant enhancement of performance
There is no reasonable therapeutic alternative to the use of the prohibited substance or method.

Under the World Anti-Doping Code, WADA has issued an International Standard for the granting of TUEs. The standard states that all International Federations and National Anti-Doping Organizations must have a process in place whereby athletes with documented medical conditions can request a TUE. A panel of independent physicians called the Therapeutic Use Exemption Committee (TUEC) examines the request. International Federations and National Anti-Doping Organizations are responsible for granting or declining such applications. There are two types of TUEs: abbreviated and standard.

Abbreviated TUE: Only for glucocorticosteroids by nonsystemic routes (topical application) and beta-2 agonists (formoterol, salbutamol, salmeterol, and terbutaline) by inhalation. Dermatological applications are not prohibited and do not require any TUE. A notification is sent to the athlete by the relevant organization upon receipt of a duly completed request. The athlete can begin treatment as soon as the form has been received by the relevant organization.

Standard TUE: For any treatment involving a substance or a method on the Prohibited List that does not qualify for an abbreviated TUE, the prescription must be reviewed by a TUEC. If approved, the athlete may begin treatment only after receiving the authorization notice from the relevant organization (except in rare cases of an acute life-threatening condition for which a retroactive approval may be considered).

9.1 TESTOSTERONE AND SYNTHETIC ANABOLIC STEROIDS

Christophe Saudan, Ph.D. and Norbert Baume, Ph.D.
Swiss Laboratory for Doping Analyses, University Institute of Legal Medicine, Lausanne, Switzerland

9.1.1   Introduction

Anabolic steroids are synthetic derivatives of testosterone modified to enhance the anabolic rather than the androgenic actions of the hormone. Testosterone is hormone-synthesized in the human body from cholesterol. It serves distinct functions at different stages of life. During embryonic life, androgen action is central to the development of the male phenotype. At puberty, the hormone is responsible for the secondary sexual characteristics that transform boys into men. Testosterone intervenes in many physiological processes in the adult male including muscle protein metabolism, sexual and cognitive functions, erythropoiesis, plasma lipids, and bone metabolism (Figure 9.1.1).

9.1.2   Pharmaceutical Action of Anabolic Steroids

Testosterone is virtually inactive when taken orally. After oral ingestion, testosterone is absorbed from the small intestine and passes via the portal vein to the liver where it is rapidly metabolized, mostly to inactive compounds. Accordingly, chemical modifications of testosterone have been made to alter the relative anabolic–androgenic potency, slow the rate of inactivation, and change the pattern of metabolism. Most orally anabolic-androgenic steroids (AAS) preparations are 17-β alkylated derivatives of testosterone that are relatively resistant to hepatic inactivation. Esterification of the 17-β hydroxyl group makes the molecule more soluble in lipid vesicles for injection. This slows the release of the injected steroid into the circulation. Commonly used 17-β alkyl and 17-β ester derivatives are:

  17-β alkyl derivatives: Stanozolol, danazol, fluoxymesterone, methyltestosterone, methandrostenolone, oxandrolone, and oxymetholone
  17-β ester derivatives: Nandrolone decanoate, boldenone, trenbolone, methenolone, and testosterone enanthate

Evidence suggests that with normal male physiological plasma levels of testosterone, the androgen receptors, to which testosterone and dihydrotestosterone (DHT, an active metabolite of testosterone) bind, are fully saturated. *In vitro* studies have demonstrated that the dose–response relationship of testosterone and skeletal muscle growth reaches a plateau once the physiological concentration is exceeded. It has been suggested that when anabolic steroids are abused by athletes, the drugs exert their effects by another receptor mechanism that is unsaturated or unaffected by normal plasma

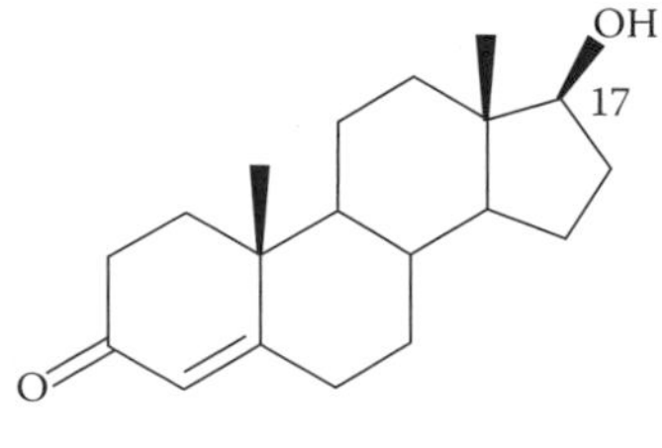

Figure 9.1.1 Molecular structure of testosterone.

testosterone and DHT levels. Indeed, it is believed that the effects of supraphysiological doses of testosterone on muscle are mediated through an antiglucocorticoid action, independent of the androgen receptor. Glucocorticoids such as cortisol and corticosterone are hormones that influence glucose synthesis and protein catabolism. Stimulation of glucocorticoid receptor will lead to an enhancement of protein breakdown in muscle. According to one theory the high doses of anabolic steroids used by many athletes displace glucocorticoids from glucocorticoid receptor and inhibit muscle protein catabolism, leading overall to an anabolic or muscle-building effect.[2]

9.1.3 Therapeutic Uses

A number of clinical studies using a variety of experimental designs have shown that the potent anabolic effects of AAS have a positive effect on various pathological conditions.[3] Physiologic replacement doses of testosterone have been used to stimulate sexual development in cases of delayed puberty, and to substitute for the hormone after surgical removal of a testis. The first major clinical use of anabolic steroids was to inhibit the loss of protein and aid muscle regeneration after major surgery. Anabolic steroids may also be used to increase growth in prepubertal boys who have failed to reach their expected minimal height for their age.

9.1.4 Athletic Use

For many years, the medical community fought AAS use by denying that they had any effects on the lean body mass. Early studies were flawed and did not reflect the way AAS are actually used. Athletes "cycle" on and off compounds, switching from one to another to avoid developing tolerance. They "stack" AAS, taking several different steroids at the same time to lower the dose of each, and to activate different steroid receptors. The scientific basis for stacking is, however, highly questionable and has not been proved.

AAS are generally accepted as having the desired anabolic effects, provided athletes also have an adequate protein supply and exercise intensely. In a randomized controlled trial, those taking 600 mg testosterone intramuscular injections weekly for 10 weeks had significantly increased muscle mass, muscle strength, and fat-free mass compared to those taking a placebo. However, not all studies have found such strength gains.

9.1.5 Anabolic Testing

The latest list of prohibited substances, established by the WADA for 2005, includes two types of steroids: (1) typically exogenous steroids, main examples of which have been given previously, and (2) typically endogenous steroids, e.g., androstenediol, androstendione, dehydroepiandrosterone (DHEA), dihydrotestosterone (DIIT), testosterone, and related substances.

Testing for anabolic agents in the urine of athletes was first implemented on a large scale during the 1976 Montreal Olympic Games. Testing was mainly based on radioimmunoassay (RIA) techniques. The techniques for the identification and characterization of steroids and their metabolites in urine have improved considerably during the last three decades. This improvement is largely due to the use of gas chromatography-mass spectrometry (GC-MS) techniques. Today, most anti-doping laboratories use techniques that are based on the solid-phase extraction of the urine sample, followed by chemical modifications prior to GC-MS analysis.[4] The confirmation procedure for the unequivocal identification of an anabolic doping agent consists in matching GC and MS data of the supposed substance and/or its metabolites with pure standards, or matching the metabolite profile of the sample with reference urine originating from an excretion study.

The detection of exogenous substances requires the identification of a parent compound and/or at least one metabolite. However, with endogenously produced substances, such as testosterone, the presence of the substance alone cannot be considered as an offense. Moreover, a cutoff value for testosterone concentration cannot be used because of large inter-individual and intra-individual urinary concentrations of the hormone.[5] However, the intake of testosterone causes characteristic changes in the pattern of steroids excreted in the urine. In 1983, based on studies performed on athletes, the IOC adopted a ratio of testosterone to epitestosterone (T/E) of up to 6.0, as a criterion for the administration of testosterone. Epitestosterone formation seems to parallel testosterone formation,[6] but it does not increase to the same extent as testosterone after exogenous testosterone administration, resulting in an increase of the T/E ratio.

In populations of athletes, a mean T/E ratio of less than 2.0 is observed. For that reason the IOC rules clearly state that a T/E ratio greater than 6.0 constitutes an offense, unless there is evidence that the result is due to an extraordinary physiological or pathological condition (e.g., low epitestosterone excretion, androgen producing tumor, and enzyme deficiencies). Before a sample is declared positive, further investigations are conducted as a confirmational study.[7] As a first step, a comparison with previous values is made. After that, or if no previous values are available, several additional urine samples are analyzed over a short period. This longitudinal study may represent a useful tool to detect false-positive results (naturally elevated T/E ratios).

WADA suggested in 2004 that urine samples should now be submitted to isotopic ratio mass spectrometry (IRMS) if the T/E is greater than or equal to 4.0, and testosterone, testosterone metabolites, epitestosterone, and DHEA concentrations are greater than fixed cutoff concentrations.[8] Even if additional studies of the particular athlete suggest the potential steroid profile manipulation, there is a lack of definitive proof for the exogenous application of natural steroids. This problem can be solved by the determination of the ratio of the two stable carbon isotopes $^{13}C/^{12}C$, which allow the differentiation of natural and synthetic steroids. As exogenous testosterone or precursors contain less ^{13}C than their endogenous homologues, a lower urinary $^{13}C/^{12}C$ ratio can be expected if steroids have been administered.

The method for determining the isotopic composition of the relevant analyte includes GS, a subsequent combustion to CO_2, and, finally, MS analysis of the gas in a special multicollector mass spectrometer (isotope-ratio-mass-spectrometry, IRMS). The $^{13}C/^{12}C$ ratio of testosterone or its metabolites is measured and compared to urinary reference steroids within the sample.[9] It should be emphasized that the $^{13}C/^{12}C$ ratio of these endogenous reference compounds should not be affected by steroid administration.[10] The result will be reported as consistent with the administration of a steroid, if a significant difference is observed between the $^{13}C/^{12}C$ values of testosterone metabolites and the endogenous reference compound. According to population studies, the WADA Laboratory Committee has stated a difference cutoff for positivity in 2004. If the IRMS study does not clearly indicate exogenous administration, an inconclusive result may be reported and further longitudinal studies can be performed.[8]

Nandrolone, or 19-nortestosterone, is a synthetic AAS, a member of the norsteroids family derived from the testosterone molecule. A small chemical modification (on the carbon atom 19) gives nandrolone more anabolic rather than androgenic properties. Some nandrolone-positive cases with low levels of metabolites (19-norandrosterone and 19-noretiocholanolone) are encountered in several sports such as football, judo, and tennis. A debate about the capability of the human body to endogenously produce traces of nandrolone metabolites, without any intake of forbidden substances, was initiated a decade ago. Research projects on the effects of nandrolone and on its metabolism were performed and provided the following results:

Endogenous production of nandrolone has been observed. It is due to enzymatic transformation of endogenous testosterone to endogenous 19-nortestosterone (nandrolone).[11]
A possible exogenous source is the intake of nutritional supplements and/or over-the-counter drugs, which have previously been intentionally or accidentally contaminated by nandrolone precursors.[12–14]
Physical exercise may also influence the excretion of nandrolone, but studies on this subject have produced mixed results.[15–18]

9.2 STIMULANTS

Lidia Avois-Mateus, Ph.D.
Swiss Laboratory for Doping Analyses, University Institute of Legal Medicine, Lausanne, Switzerland

9.2.1 Introduction

These drugs stimulate the central nervous system (CNS) and may be used to reduce fatigue, as well as increase alertness, competitiveness, and aggression. They are considered to have a performance-enhancing effect in explosive power activities and endurance events, since the capacity to exercise strenuously is increased and sensitivity to pain is reduced. Because of their short half-life, stimulants are mostly used on the day of a competition. They may also be used in training, to allow an increase in intensity of the training session. Testing for stimulants is done in-competition only. Because stimulants can increase an athlete's aggression toward other competitors or officials, their misuse in contact sports may be dangerous. Relatively high doses are needed to reduce fatigue, and performance may be reduced by side effects such as tremor.

The stimulant class includes psychomotor stimulants, sympathomimetics, and miscellaneous CNS stimulants.[19,20] Specific examples of this class include caffeine, amphetamines, ephedrines, and cocaine (Figure 9.2.1).

9.2.2 Caffeine

Caffeine is the pharmacologically active substance found in tea, coffee, and cola. The amount of caffeine present varies according to the type of drink and the way it has been prepared. In addition, caffeine may be an ingredient of some common medications (e.g., against the common cold, pain relievers), but usually in quantities of less than 100 mg per dose. Caffeine produces mild CNS stimulation, similar to that of amphetamines, reducing fatigue and increasing concentration and alertness. Physiological effects include increased cardiac output, and increased metabolic rate and urine production. High doses can cause anxiety, insomnia, and nervousness.[20] Since 2004, caffeine has been removed from the list of prohibited substances and included, instead, in the Monitoring Program. The Monitoring Program is concerned with substances that are not on the Prohibited List, but which WADA wishes to monitor in order to detect patterns of misuse in sport (WADA Code 4.5).

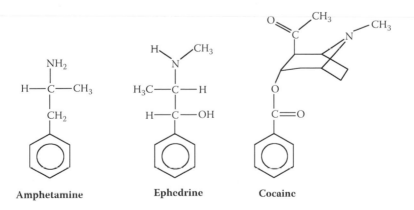

Amphetamine   Ephedrine   Cocaine

Figure 9.2.1 Common stimulants.

9.2.3   Amphetamine

Amphetamine was synthesized in 1920 and used to reduce fatigue and increase alertness in soldiers during World War II. Many derivatives have since been elaborated, such as methamphetamine, dimethamphetamine, methylendioxyamphetamine (MDA), methylendioxymethamphetamine (MDMA, "ecstasy"), selegiline, etc. They are all forbidden in the practice of sport. Amphetamine was used as a nasal decongestant, antidepressant, and appetite suppressant, but its powerful CNS stimulant properties were soon discovered. It acts primarily by enhancing the brain activity of norepinephrine and dopamine, resulting in intensification of alertness, concentration, and self-confidence. Amphetamines may induce dependence, and generally fall under the drug legislation of the athlete's own country.

9.2.3.1   Metabolism of Amphetamines

Amphetamine is readily absorbed, mainly from the small intestine, and the peak concentration occurs 1 to 2 h following administration. Absorption is usually complete in 2.5 to 4 h and is accelerated by food intake. The metabolism of amphetamine has been difficult to investigate because of the wide variation between species in its metabolic effects. The principal amphetamine metabolites are *p*-hydroxyephedrine and *p*-hydroxyamphetamine. Amphetamine is eliminated by renal filtration. For the detection of amphetamine use in sport, the urine is analyzed for the parent compound amphetamine. After a single dose of amphetamine, it can be found in the first void urine and continues to be detectable for at least 48 h after the intake of the drug. The peak urine concentration is quite variable and occurs between 3 and 12 h after the intake of the drug. Amphetamine excretion may be accelerated by acidification of the urine — this property has been used in the treatment of amphetamine overdose.

9.2.3.2   Amphetamine Action

Amphetamine's positive effects include an increase in physical energy and an improvement in some mental skills, but there are also increased talkativeness, restlessness, and excitement. Subjects taking amphetamine also report that they feel confident, efficient, ambitious, and that their food intake is reduced. Other negative effects of amphetamine — which can be dose-dependent — are anxiety, indifference, slowness in reasoning, irresponsible behavior, irritability, dry mouth, tremors, insomnia, and, following withdrawal, depression.

Tolerance develops rapidly to many of the effects of the amphetamines. Amphetamines induce dependence and the amphetamine-dependent person may become psychotic, aggressive, and antisocial. Withdrawal of amphetamines is associated with mental and physical depression. Other major side effects of amphetamine administration include confusion, delirium, sweating, palpitations, mydriasis, tachypnea, hypertension, tachycardia, tremors, as well as muscle and joint pain. Chronic amphetamine administration is also associated with myocardial pathology and possibly with growth retardation in adolescents. High chronic doses may lead to a variety of persistent personality changes, paranoid delusions, and tactile hallucinations called *amphetamine psychosis*. Transient changes indistinguishable from schizophrenia were commonly reported during the 1950s, when amphetamine abuse was very widespread.

9.2.3.3   Amphetamine in Sport

The action of amphetamine on sporting performance was first investigated in 1959 and it has been concluded that it enhances anaerobic performances while having little or no effect on aerobic activity. Since then, amphetamine has been studied in attempts to enhance performance in various disciplines. It might improve reaction time when fatigued, increase muscular strength and endurance, increase acceleration, increase lactic acid level at maximal exercise, increase anaerobic endurance capacity, and stimulate metabolism with loss of body fat. Dosage seems to be important depending on the desired effect. Aggressiveness increases with high dosage, whereas alertness is enhanced with lower quantities.

All amphetamines are banned by the WADA and IOC codes. No quantification is necessary, as the qualitative demonstration of the substance is sufficient to declare the case an analytical adverse finding. The presence of amphetamine in urine is considered a severe doping offense, because amphetamine has no medical indication any more and its use is prohibited in many countries.

9.2.4 Cocaine

Cocaine is the most potent stimulant of natural origin. Unlike amphetamines, which are synthetic compounds, cocaine is obtained from naturally occurring *Coca* species, although it can be produced synthetically. Its current notoriety belies the fact that people have used the drug as a stimulant for thousands of years. In the past cocaine was used in a number of patent medicines and even in soft drinks. Except for head and neck surgery, where it is still used as a local anesthetic (because it is a vasoconstrictor in addition to being an anesthetic), its therapeutic indications are now mostly obsolete, as much safer drugs have been produced. Cocaine can be snorted, smoked, or injected.

9.2.4.1 Cocaine's Actions

Physical effects of cocaine use include vasoconstriction, thermogenesis, increased heart rate, and increased blood pressure. Cocaine also increases motor activity, talkativeness, and is a potent euphoriant. Users feel an initial "rush" or sense of well-being, of having more energy, and of being more alert. The duration of cocaine's immediate euphoric effects, which include hyperstimulation, reduced fatigue, and increased mental clarity, depends on the route of administration, but generally is very short.

9.2.4.2 Cocaine in Sport

Despite popular myth, cocaine does not really enhance performance whether at work, in sports, at school, or with sex. On the contrary, long-term use can lead to loss of concentration, irritability, loss of memory, paranoia, loss of energy, anxiety, and a loss of interest in sex. Several studies have demonstrated that cocaine has no beneficial effect on running times and reduces endurance performance. Furthermore, at all doses, cocaine significantly increases glycogen utilization and plasma lactate concentration, without producing consistent changes in plasma catecholamine levels.

The controlling effect cocaine has on an addict's life can lead to exclusion of all other facets of life. Nevertheless, despite these apparently detrimental effects, cocaine continues to be abused in sport. The reason may be that cocaine has positive ergogenic effect on activities of short duration requiring a burst of high-intensity energy output. The activities associated with the drug's CNS stimulatory effect may be more important than its action on peripheral metabolism. It has been suggested that it is precisely because of central heightened arousal and increased alertness, achieved principally at low doses, that cocaine is used in sport.

Cocaine can currently be administered by a doctor for legitimate medical uses, such as local anesthetic for some eye, ear, and throat surgeries. Both WADA and IOC ban cocaine, including its use as a local anesthetic. A recent report showed positive urine test results for benzoylecgonine (metabolite of cocaine) within 24 h in subjects after ingestion of a 250 ml infusion of Mate de Coca tea.[21] Cocaine, like amphetamine, is part of the category S6 of the prohibited substances in competition and its — and/or its metabolites — presence in urine can be considered a severe doping offense.

9.2.5 Ephedrine

Ephedra alkaloids, which are popular components of many nutritional supplements, are naturally occurring CNS stimulants, which may be obtained from several *Ephedra* plant species. Naturally occurring *Ephedra* plants contain ephedrine, pseudoephedrine, norephedrine, methylephedrine, norpseudoephedrine, and methylpseudoephedrine. Phenylpropanolamine is a synthetic compound with effects similar to ephedra-alkaloids. Methylephedrine is a very widely used cough suppressant, popular in Asia. Historically, ephedra-alkaloids have been used for both asthma and allergies in China for more than 5000 years. The structure of ephedrine is closely related to methamphetamine, although its effects on the CNS are much less potent and longer acting than those of the amphetamines. Its peripheral stimulant actions are similar to but less powerful than those of epinephrine (also called adrenaline), a hormone produced in the body by the adrenal glands.

9.2.5.1 Ephedrine Action

Ephedrine is a mixed sympathomimetic agent that acts as a stimulant in the CNS by enhancing the release of norepinephrine from sympathetic neurons and stimulating alpha- and beta-receptors. Ephedrine is the most potent thermogenic agent of the ephedra alkaloids. It increases heart rate, but only by an average of 8 to 10 beats per minute, and thereby cardiac output. In multiple controlled studies it has been found to cause minimal effect on systolic pressure and no effect or even a decrease in diastolic pressure (the phenomenon known as diastolic runoff). When given as an intravenous bolus it causes peripheral vasoconstriction resulting in an increase of peripheral resistance that may lead to a sustained rise in blood pressure, which is why it is still very widely used to counter the hypotensive effects of spinal anesthesia. Ephedrine relaxes bronchial smooth muscle and is used as a decongestant and for temporary relief of shortness of breath caused by asthma, although it quickly loses its effect because of beta-receptor downregulation. It is present in numerous nutritional and dietary supplements, such as energy stimulants and anorexic agents, although its use in the U.S. has now been banned. Pseudoephedrine can be found in many over-the-counter preparations for respiratory infections or allergies. Phenylpropanolamine, similarly to pseudoephedrine, has still been used recently in over-the-counter diet pills. Ephedrine is excreted largely unchanged in the urine and the usual elimination half-life is 3 to 6 h, which can be prolonged with increased urine pH.

9.2.5.2 Ephedrine in Sport

With their stimulant properties and sympathomimetic actions, ephedra-alkaloids have been perceived as potential performance-enhancing substances, offering unfair advantages to athletes, even if used in supplement forms.[22] It appears, through various studies, that the isolated use of ephedrine, pseudoephedrine, and phenylpropanolamine at the usual dosages has an inconsistent, and probably insignificant, ergogenic benefit for power, endurance, strength, or speed. Other studies looking at the use of ephedrine combined with vitamins, minerals, or caffeine have, nevertheless, supported potential ergogenic effects. Many athletes indeed use food supplements containing ephedra alkaloids because of supposed energy increase and potential increase of metabolism with fat loss and increased muscular strength. A number of placebo-controlled studies have evaluated the effects of ephedrine in combination with caffeine. They demonstrated a prolonged time until exhaustion and a decreased perception of exhaustion on cycle ergometry.

WADA and IOC tolerate the medical use of ephedrine at therapeutic levels. Nevertheless, an ephedrine urine concentration of higher than 10 µg/ml is considered as positive result. Unlike amphetamine and cocaine, even if ephedrine is part of the category S6 of the prohibited substances in competition, its presence in urine is not considered as a severe doping offense and the sanctions are often milder or submitted to discussion.

9.3 ERYTHROPOIETIN — BLOOD DOPING

Neil Robinson, Ph.D.
Swiss Laboratory for Doping Analyses, University Institute of Legal Medicine, Lausanne, Switzerland

9.3.1 Introduction to Erythropoiesis

Erythropoiesis is part of the larger process of hematopoiesis, which involves the production of mature cells found in the blood and lymphoid organs. Hematopoiesis is continuously required because of normal turnover in the cell populations in the blood and lymphoid organs. In the normal adult human, the daily turnover of erythrocytes exceeds 10^{11} cells. In case of acute erythrocyte loss due to hemolysis or hemorrhage, the production of erythrocytes increases rapidly and markedly.

In hematopoiesis, rare hematopoietic stem cells in the bone marrow proliferate and differentiate so as to give rise to all the cellular components of the blood and the lymphoid system. During this process, an individual hematopoietic cell undergoes an apparent random process called commitment. When a cell undergoes commitment, its proliferation becomes limited and its potential to develop into multiple types of mature cells is restricted. Thus, these hematopoietic cells are termed committed, lineage-specific progenitor cells.

The major stages of differentiation in mammalian erythropoiesis are the following: The most immature stage of committed erythroid progenitors is the burst-forming unit-crythroid (BFU-E). The next major stage of erythroid progenitor cell development is the colony-forming unit-erythroid (CFU-E). A continuum of erythroid progenitor stages exists between the BFU-E and CFU-E, with decreasing proliferative potential as the progenitors approach the CFU-E stage. The descendant cells of the CFU-E are termed erythroid precursor cells. The erythroid precursors are proerythroblasts, basophilic erythroblasts, polychromatophilic erythroblasts, and orthochromatic erythroblasts. The orthochromatic erythroblasts do not divide but they enucleate, forming the nascent erythrocyte called the reticulocyte.

9.3.2 Production of Erythropoietin

EPO is a 30,400 D glycoprotein hormone produced mainly in the kidney, in the liver (<10%), and, in very small quantities, in the brain. The physiological stimulus for EPO production is tissue hypoxia, which, in the large majority of instances, is directly related to the number of circulating erythrocytes. Thus, EPO and erythropoiesis are part of a negative-feedback cycle that keeps tissue oxygen delivery within a narrow range by controlling the number of erythrocytes circulating in the blood. In a normal individual, any loss of erythrocytes, such as by bleeding or hemolysis, decreases delivery of oxygen to the tissues. When tissue hypoxia is sensed by cells capable of producing EPO in the kidney and liver, they produce and secrete EPO into the plasma. EPO is carried to the bone marrow, where it binds to specific cell-surface receptors on its target cells — the CFU-E, proerythroblasts, and basophilic erythroblasts. The binding of EPO by these cells increases their ability to survive and reach the reticulocyte stage and thereby contribute to the population of circulating erythrocytes. The increased numbers of circulating erythrocytes in turn deliver more oxygen to the tissues. This increased oxygen delivery is sensed by the EPO-producing cells, which then reduce EPO production so that the normal steady-state number of erythrocytes exists.

The response of the kidneys to hypoxia is exponential. That is, in individuals with a normal capacity to produce EPO, a linear decline in hematocrit is accompanied by an exponential increase in plasma EPO levels. This exponential increase is not based on the release of stored, pre-formed EPO. Rather, the hypoxia is sensed by an intracellular molecule that interacts with an enhancer element of the EPO gene and thereby induces transcription of the gene. The increase in EPO production in the hypoxic kidney is achieved by recruitment of more cells to produce EPO. The EPO-producing cells of the kidney are a minor subset of cortical interstitial cells. Under normal conditions, only a few scattered cells produce EPO. When a threshold level of hypoxia is achieved, those cells capable of producing EPO do so at a maximal rate. The greater the areas of renal cortex in which the hypoxia threshold has been met, the greater the number of cells that produce EPO.

9.3.3 Mechanism of Erythropoietin Action

In the bone marrow, EPO binds to receptors displayed on the cell surface of CFU-E, proeryth-roblasts, and basophilic erythroblasts. The mature EPO receptor is an approximately 72,000 D, transmembrane glycoprotein that is a member of a much larger family of receptors of cytokines and hematopoietic growth factors. The effect of EPO binding to its receptor, in terms of cellular physiology, is the prevention of programmed cell death (apoptosis). In multiple systems of eryth-ropoiesis, EPO has repeatedly been shown to be a survival factor for the erythroid cells in the later stages of differentiation from the CFU-E through basophilic erythroblasts. Although an effect of EPO on mitosis has been reported for BFU-E and an EPO-dependent cell lines, EPO is required only for the stages of CFU-E and later; apoptosis appears to result when EPO signaling cannot occur.

9.3.4 Detecting Recombinant EPO (rHuEPO) Abuse in Sports

As soon as rHuEPO became available in 1987, it was clear that this ergogenic hormone would be used illicitly in endurance sports. Therefore, the IOC Medical Commission decided specifically to ban it in 1990, even though all forms of blood doping had already been officially banned since 1984. Two approaches were developed for the detection of rHuEPO abuse. The first was based on the detection of indirect blood markers, and the second one was based on the direct detection of rHuEPO in urine. The rationale for using secondary blood markers was mainly based on the fact that they could be used to detect rHuEPO injections that had been given more than a week prior, and also because they could be used to detect all kinds of erythropoietic stimulators such as erythropoietin alpha, beta, omega, and Darbepoitin, as well as mimetic peptides. At the same time, scientists were working on methods for the direct detection of rHuEPO in blood or urine. This latter approach had the advantage of identifying the drug itself (or metabolites), but had the disadvantage of being expensive, not very sensitive, and delicate to perform.

9.3.4.1 Indirect Methods

In 1993, with the introduction of sophisticated hematological analyzers, some scientists proposed a model based on the analysis of the percentage of red blood cells having a hemoglobin concentration below 28 pg (MCH) and a volume above 128 fl (MCV). These red blood cells were called macrocytic hypochromatic erythrocytes. This test had the advantage of being fast and cheap (as long as the laboratory was equipped with this special analyzer) and was very selective. Unfortunately, the test was limited by a relatively poor sensitivity; 50% of the rHuEPO samples were not detected.

In 1996, another approach for the detection of rHuEPO-abuse, based on the determination of the soluble-transferrin-receptor (sTFR)/ferritin ratio. The results obtained during a trial involving healthy subjects demonstrated that regular rHuEPO injections significantly increased the sTFR concentration. Ferritin was used as a denominator mainly to prevent hydration level variations. Unfortunately, during this trial, the ferritin level declined, because the subjects did not receive an adequate iron supply. Knowing that iron supplementation was a common practice among athletes (especially intravenous iron injections), the sTFR/ferritin ratio was modified into a new ratio taking into account the possible exercise-induced hemoconcentration, the sTFR/total protein.

The lack of sensitivity of some of the secondary blood markers, as well as the lack of specificity of some others, fostered the idea of combining them together, and produce a mathematical model

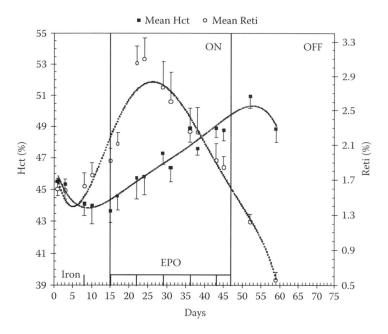

Figure 9.3.1 Model showing the profile of mean hematocrit and reticulocyte count (SEM) during a continuous rHuEPO treatment with regular intravenous iron injections (see vertical bars). The study included three periods: baseline, treatment (ON), and post-treatment (OFF) periods.

to discriminate rHuEPO abusers from healthy sportsmen. Following a double-blind study with regular rHuEPO injections (continuous treatment), the Australian Institute of Sport together with the Australian Sports Drug Testing Laboratory designed an anti-doping test using multiple secondary blood markers such as the hematocrit level, the reticulocyte hematocrit, serum sTFR and EPO concentrations, and finally the percentage of macrocytic cells. Different mathematical models allowing the identification of athletes under rHuEPO treatment (ON-model) and those who took rHuEPO in the past days (OFF-model) were developed. In August 2000, the IOC Medical Commission approved the ON-model to be used during the Sydney 2000 Olympic Games. As the direct method capable of discriminating endogenous EPO from rHuEPO was published in spring 2000, the ON-model was only used as a screening test to determine which urine samples had to be collected to perform the urinary test.[23]

At the same time the study was performed in Australia, the WADA accredited laboratory of Lausanne did a very similar controlled, randomized, double-blind trial, except that the importance of iron supplementation was recognized, and it was given intravenously to simulate the situation in cycling. Therefore, the behavior of secondary blood markers was different during the continuous treatment. Unlike the Australian study, the Swiss study found that some of the secondary blood markers (hematocrit, hemoglobin, and reticulocyte count) could be used as part of a screening test, but in no case could the multifactorial approach be used for anti-doping purposes (Figure 9.3.1).[24]

9.3.4.2 Direct Methods

Endogenous EPO and rHuEPO are slightly different, and these differences stem from the glycosilation of rHuEPO, which takes place in Chinese hamster ovary (CHO) cells but not in human cells. Post-translational modifications are species and tissue dependent and also depend on the cell culture conditions. Therefore, it is possible to separate the endogenous from the exogenous EPO isoforms thanks to the differences of charges carried by the different sugar structures. This technique

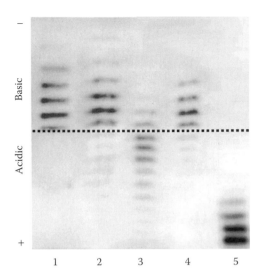

Figure 9.3.2 Anti-doping urine analysis demonstrating the presence of rHuEPO in urine (see lane 4). 1. rHuEPO standard. 2. Positive urine (control). 3. Negative urine (control). 4. Sample declared positive. 5. Darbepoïétine (Aranesp standard).

proved to be very reliable in urine and in blood, but only as long as the biological samples were collected within 24 h after the last rHuEPO injection. By 3 days after injection, less than 50% of the treated subjects could be declared positive. By 7 days after the last rHuEPO injection, none of the samples showed any traces of rHuEPO.

A few months before the Summer Olympic Games in Sydney, the French anti-doping laboratory in Paris published a paper in *Nature* describing a novel test based on the isoelectric focusing patterning and a double blotting protocol. Because the exogenous isoforms of rHuEPO are less acidic than endogenous EPO, it was possible to separate them using the isoelectric focusing method. This test was designed to separate alpha, omega, and beta rHuEPO (Figure 9.3.2).[25]

9.3.4.3 Abnormal Blood Profiles

For approximately 2 years, laboratories have been encountering abnormal blood profiles in individuals with no traces of rHuEPO in their urine. This meant either that the athletes were doping with undetectable compounds or that they had returned to "ancient" doping techniques such as blood transfusion. Blood transfusion was common practice in the 1970s, used to enhance oxygen transport with the increase of red blood cell mass. This type of doping virtually disappeared with the arrival of rHuEPO at the end of the 1980s, because it is a much easier way to use the hormone (easy to store and use and cheaper). When direct testing of urine rHuEPO began in 2000, an unintended side effect was the return to blood transfusions.

Repeated and regular measurements of some blood parameters such as hematocrit, haemoglobin, and reticulocyte count showed that some athletes had abnormal blood parameters although rHuEPO could not be detected in urine. This indicated a return to blood transfusion practices. As erythrocytes differ from one person to another by membrane proteins, the Swiss Antidoping Laboratory (LAD) performed antidoping tests in blood for the first time in the summer of 2004. The analyses of some specific red blood cell membrane proteins in combination with flow cytometry showed that some abnormal blood profiles were due to homologous blood transfusion. Federations having introduced blood testing have a powerful tool to follow all athletes potentially abusing rHuEPO or blood transfusion.[26] Therefore, they need to focus their anti-doping tests mainly on those demonstrating abnormal blood profiles. This targeting aid also enables the federations to determine the prevalence of doping methods, before any validated anti-doping test is on the market. In this way, for example, it was possible to determine that HBOC (hemoglobin based oxygen carrier) abuse was not a major problem, because none of the athletes tested had abnormal hematological indices.

9.3.5 Conclusion

It is nowadays possible to accurately detect blood doping and rHuEPO abuse complete detection. The necessity to take blood samples to screen and test for that type of doping habit has become obvious for sport authorities. But there is still a need for more research and coordination with other anti-doping panels in order to better target the use of blood manipulation. Hematological follow-up of the athlete is certainly one of the solutions for this targeting. In addition, new biochemical investigations should allow scientists to improve the tools for direct detection blood doping.

9.4 HUMAN GROWTH HORMONE

Martial Saugy, Ph.D.
Swiss Laboratory for Doping Analyses, University Institute of Legal Medicine, Lausanne, Switzerland

9.4.1 Introduction

Growth hormone (GH) is a naturally occurring peptide hormone secreted by the pituitary gland. Even if the hormone in the body is rather heterogeneous, the major component is made of 191 amino acids, stabilized by two disulfide bonds and reaching the molecular weight of 22 kD. Previously, the only source of GH was human cadavers, but the contamination of treated patients with a prion disease (Creutzfeldt–Jakob disease) made this form of treatment obsolete. Since the late 1980s, recombinant human GH (rGH) has been developed, and is available for the treatment of GH-deficient patients. This form of GH has an identical sequence to the naturally occurring 22-kDa peptide. Its abuse by athletes was suspected because of its anabolic properties. Some athletes claimed that the use of GH effectively increased the lean body mass and decreased fat content.

Today, the use of GH in sport is not only based on its anabolic properties, but also on its effect on the metabolism of carbohydrates and fat. Recombinant GH was detected in swimming and also during the Tour de France 1998.

International federations and the IOC included GH in the list of forbidden compounds in 1989, as it appeared quite obvious that recombinant GH would be more and more accessible, because of the new biotechnological methods making manufacture easier.

9.4.2 Growth Hormone and Exercise

The effect of acute exercise on growth hormone production in the body has been widely described in specialized literature.[27–32] The GH concentration in blood increases with time for a given work intensity and can increase tenfold during prolonged moderate exercise. During a more intensive exercise with accumulation of lactate at 70% of VO_2-max for a short-term period (10 to 20 min), the increase of GH will increase by fivefold to tenfold. Furthermore, it seems that GH response is more closely related to the peak intensity of exercise than to the total work output.[33,34] Apart from the increase related to exercise itself, GH secretion can be increased by hypoglycemia, high temperature, and stress. The administration of exogenous GH cannot be differentiated from the physiological variations by observing GH levels alone.

9.4.3 Physiological Action of GH

GH is secreted by somatotrope cells in the anterior pituitary gland. Its secretion is pulsatile and is regulated by two hypothalamic peptides, growth hormone releasing hormone (GHRH), which stimulates GH secretion, and somatostatin, which inhibits GH secretion.[35] Women secrete slightly more GH than men and the highest levels are observed at puberty.[36] There is a decrease in GH secretion with age, by about 14% per decade. Moreover, its secretion is variable and higher GH levels have been observed during slow wave sleep, with exercise, stress, fever, and fasting.[37] Some specific drugs such as clonidine, L-dopa, and GHB (gamma-hydroxybutyrate) increase its secretion as well as androgens and estrogens. GH binds to specific receptors, which are omnipresent throughout the whole body.

9.4.4 Therapeutic Use of GH

GH is mainly used to treat GH deficiency and children with Turner syndrome. GH is also used in high doses to relieve the symptoms of excessive burns or thermal injuries. Major studies of GH-therapy in GH-deficient adults have demonstrated that rGH treatment for a period of 4 to 6 months has favorable effects on body composition, exercise aptitude, renal and cardiac functions, and generally improves quality of life. In long-term experiments, an increase of the bone mass with persistence of the above-mentioned effects has been observed. The positive effects on the body composition are essentially due to the anabolic, lipolytic, and anti-natriuretic properties. Doses in adults are generally individualized, but the mean dose is 1 to 2 IU/day applied subcutaneously every evening. No adverse side effects have been observed with therapeutic doses.

9.4.5 GH as a Doping Agent

Growth hormone has been considered an ergogenic drug since the late 1980s. Since that time, official and non-official sources report that its abuse in sport has steadily increased. The popularity of GH is based on widespread knowledge of its efficiency, difficult detection, and the fact that few side effects have been reported with conservative dosing. A survey reported GH abuse in 5% of male American high school students.[38] We do not know how popular GH is among female athletes, but some cases have been reported. One reason for a woman to use GH might be the absent risk of androgenic side effects in contrast to anabolic steroids.

The frequency of use and the dosage are difficult to evaluate. Underground sources stated doses of 10 to 25 IU per day, three to four times a week. Mean doses are probably about 4 IU/day and mostly combined with other doping agents (e.g., with anabolic steroids in power sports, or with EPO in endurance sports). The treatment is often applied in cycles of 4 to 6 weeks as for anabolic steroids in bodybuilding. In endurance sport, very little is known about the optimal use of GH. The doses involved are certainly adapted to the discipline, to the charge of training, and to the regimen of other ergogenic substances absorbed simultaneously.

The effectiveness of rGH for improving sport performance is still a subject of debate among abusers. The positive effects described in GH-deficient adults are not so evident for athletes. Many underground reports describe some positive effect on the muscle mass. The interpretation of such reports is difficult because of the combined use with other substances (e.g., anabolic steroids) leading to positive effects, and inefficient products on the market with no effect at all. Moreover, controlled studies did not confirm the spectacular effects described in underground reports from abusers, the efficiency of high dose GH being generally less impressive under controlled conditions.[39] The anabolic effect of GH is not the only one explored by athletes, as GH is also used in endurance sport in combination with oxygen transport enhancing methods.

It is difficult to draw any conclusions regarding the effects of excessive GH administration on skeletal muscle function. It must be also stressed that, today, GH may be used for purposes other than just increasing the muscle mass.

9.4.6 Detection of GH Doping

Until the Athens 2004 Olympic Games, GH was considered undetectable. Several factors complicate the detection of doping with GH:

GH is a peptide with a very short half-life in blood, and low concentration in urine.
GH is a peptide and to measure it the analyst must use nonclassic technologies.
The amino acid sequence of the recombinant molecule is identical to the major 22-kDa isoform, secreted by pituitary gland.
GH is not a glycoprotein like erythropoietin. Thus, the post-transcription modification of the molecule cannot be used to differentiate between the recombinant and the natural state.
Secretion of GH by the pituitary gland is pulsatile, leading to highly fluctuating levels in circulation, influenced by factors such as sleep, nutritional status, exercise, and emotion.
Secretion of GH shows high intra- and inter-individual variability.

9.4.6.1 The Urine Strategy

Anti-doping urine samples are mostly collected out of competition or after effort. Because of their availability in high volume, convenient collection, and longer detection time window in contrast to blood, attempts for peptide detection were made in urine. This was successful for EPO, but much less so for GH. In urine, the average concentration of GH is between 100 and 1000 times lower than in blood. An extremely sensitive immune test was used to quantify the total amount of the hormone in urine, but lack of sensitivity and specificity of the result made the urinary test less promising than blood testing.[40]

More stable serum parameters, such as those implied in the biological cascade produced by GH secretion or application, may provide the best route for detection of GH. Growth factor (IGF-1), or some of its transport proteins (IGFBP-3), has been proposed as a possible candidate for indirect detection of GH doping.[41] But their inter-individual variability is also quite high and makes a quantitative cutoff level hard to define precisely.

9.4.6.2 The Indirect and Direct Approaches in Blood

Two main strategies are currently being followed to detect GH doping in blood.[42]

The Indirect Approach

Increasing knowledge about the naturally occurring variability of several GH-dependent parameters, such as the growth factor IGF-1, the different IGF binding proteins (IGFBPs), and several markers of bone turnover,[43] may provide data for establishing individualized normal ranges for concentration and normal constellation of these parameters. This approach did not, however, bring a final solution for detection of GH doping. The indirect approach still may be useful for screening and targeting purposes that allow for the identification of probable GH abusers.[44]

The Direct Approach

The Strasburger-Bidlingmaier group in Munich developed a so-called direct method for the detection of GH doping.[45] Two specific immunoassays allow the quantification of the several GH isoforms. Recombinant GH consists exclusively of the 22-kDa form, whereas physiological GH is present in several forms, as shown Table 9.4.1.

When the recombinant form is injected in the body, a transient increase of the 22-kDa form will be observed, modifying its ratio in comparison to the other circulating forms. Moreover, long-term treatment will inhibit the endogenous secretion of GH by a classical feedback regulation,

Table 9.4.1   Relative Abundance of GH Molecular
              Forms in Circulation (the percentages
              are approximate)

Isoforms	%
22-kDa monomer	48
20-kDa monomer	9
Modified GH (dimers and oligomers)	30
Acidic GH (desaminated and acylated forms)	7
Fragmented GH (17, 12, 5, 30KDa)	Variable

Source: Adapted from Bidlingmaier et al.[45]

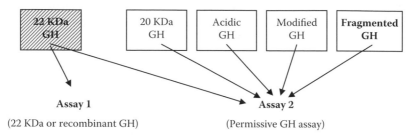

Figure 9.4.1   Molecular basis of direct detection of GH abuse by differential immunoassay: A ratio is calculated
between the signals given by the Assay 1 to the signal given by the Assay 2. Two of these double
tests must be performed in case of positive result in order to confirm the diagnostic. (Adapted
from Bidlingmaier et al.[45])

resulting in an even bigger relative increase of the 22-kDa form. This test was used during the
Olympic Games in Athens. To fulfill the requirements of the WADA Code, and the standards for
laboratories, two double tests have been applied successively to serum samples: the first test is for
quantifying specifically the 22-kDa form, and the second is a comprehensive assay measuring all
forms present in the serum. The ratio was then calculated and a cutoff-level has been defined to
differentiate the normal subjects (negative samples) from those having a significantly higher
proportion of 22-kDa GH (positive samples) (Figure 9.4.1). A second double test was used for
confirmation purposes.

Depending on the dosage, the detection window for these tests is between 24 to 36 hours after
the last injection. This test may act as a deterrent if applied in and out of competition. It has been
shown also that this direct test is not influenced by environmental parameters such as exercise or
stress. The example illustrates that the fight against doping must evolve in new analytical techniques
and new strategies based on different biological matrices.

9.5 CANNABINOIDS

Christian Giroud, Ph.D.
University Institute of Legal Medicine, Lausanne, Switzerland

The relative high incidence of cannabinoids detected in urine (see Tables 9.2 and 9.3 above)
reflects the high prevalence of cannabis use among young adults. Various studies carried out in
Europe and elsewhere have shown an impressive increase in the frequency and quantity of consumption, essentially in the younger population, with an ever earlier onset of use. According to the

report of the European Monitoring Center for Drugs and Drug Addiction (2005), 1.2 to 16% of young people aged 15 to 24, from 18 European countries, indicated cannabis consumption during the last month while 16% of young U.S. adults aged 18 to 25 reported past month use of cannabis (Substance Abuse and Mental Health Service Administration report, 2004).

Because cannabis smoking impairs cognition, psychomotor, and exercise performance, it is considered an ergolytic drug. Renaud and Cormier[46] have shown that marijuana smoking reduces maximal exercise performance: when 12 healthy young adults cycled to exhaustion 10 min after smoking, exercise duration was shortened from 16 to 15 min. Driving and piloting skills are also negatively affected, pointing out the danger of cannabis exposure when high levels of alertness and quick reflexes are required such as in automobile sports.[47] It can be inferred from the psychological effects of marijuana that cannabis may be efficient in allowing the athlete to relax and to escape from social pressures. The main features of recreational use of cannabis are a feeling of euphoria, decreased anxiety, and increased sociability, which may alleviate the stress generated by competition. However, cannabis can also produce dysphoric reactions, including severe anxiety[48] and panic disorders, paranoia, and psychosis.[49,50]

These unwanted reactions are more common in naïve, anxious subjects and psychologically vulnerable individuals and appear more frequently after ingestion than after smoking. Cannabis diminishes alertness and has relaxing and sedative properties; it may therefore be used to improve sleeping time and quality. Lorente and co-workers[51] reported that relaxation, feelings of well-being, and improved sleep were the main effects that motivate the use of cannabis in French sport science universities. Athletes engaged in "X-treme" sports are more prone to cannabis use. A relationship between drug use and "sensation seeking" behavior has been often reported. Competition level is also considered as a risk factor for cannabis use, with a view to coping with stress and anxiety.[52]

According to the IOC, urine samples are considered positive for cannabis exposure if the sum of the concentrations of free and conjugated carboxy-THC is greater than 15 ng/ml (when determined by GC/MS). This threshold value distinguishes active users from passive smokers.[53] It also reduces the risk of a positive result due to commercial food products containing traces of cannabinoids.[54,55] Since the mid-1990s, the use of food products containing seeds or hemp seed oil has increased considerably in several Western countries. However, several countries have enacted THC regulatory limits for foodstuffs and beverages lowering THC intake from hemp food and reducing the risk of a positive urine test. Regulations in Canada, the main supplier of hemp seeds to the U.S., limit THC levels in hemp seed products to 10 parts per million (ppm) (Industrial Hemp Regulations, Schedule No. 1089, Canada).

Several other problems should be mentioned in relation to carboxy-THC analysis in urine. First, the relevance of the 15 ng/ml cutoff value could be improved by normalizing the urine concentration to the creatinine level. Through this approach, quantitative results are corrected for urine dilution and possible adulteration. Prediction of repetitive or new marijuana use by analyzing the urinary cannabinoid-to-creatinine ratio in two consecutive urine samples collected at least 24 h apart are also possible.[56] Quantification of carboxy-THC in urine does not allow deducing the time of last marijuana use and there is no relationship between urine concentrations and psychomotor effects. Huestis and co-workers[57] have shown that occasional users of marijuana had positive urine specimens for 3 to 4 days after receiving a defined dose of marijuana. In heavy smokers, urine specimens remained positive for 4 to 28 days (median value: 16.6 days) after last drug use.[58] Ellis et al.[59] reported an average time until the last positive result of 31.5 days (4 to 77 days) in urine for THC metabolites screened by immunoassay with a cutoff value of 20 ng/ml. According to Manno et al.,[60] determination of the time of last cannabis use is possible by measuring total THC in urine. Significant levels of THC could be measured by using a hydrolysis step in the extraction protocol. A concentration greater than 2 ng/ml would suggest marijuana use within a 5-h time window, a time during which psychological and performance effects are known to occur.

9.6 ETHANOL USE IN SPORT AND INTERACTION WITH OTHER DOPING AGENTS

Alcohol (ethanol) is prohibited in-competition only, in a limited number of sports (e.g., automobile, archery, modern pentathlon for disciplines involving shooting). Sport federations have set up cutoff limits in blood, which are regularly updated. They range between 0.1 and 0.3 g/L for 2006. The basis of the ban is the antitremor effect of low-dose ethanol that may enhance shooting performance.[61] Even at low concentrations, alcohol disrupts many motor performances and can interfere with complex activities such as skiing or driving. Alcohol is therefore prohibited for obvious safety reasons. Because, there have been cases of athletes using alcohol to boost their aggressiveness and confidence, alcohol is prohibited in some fighting sports (karate). Alcohol is often ingested because of its exhilarating and anxiolytic effects: drinking after the game is considered as a good way to unwind. Ethanol is also known to interact with a large array of pharmacological active substances, including steroids, analgesics, and stimulants.[62,63] Combination of AAS with ethanol may contribute to the increase in aggressive behavior.

9.7 MORBIDITY OF DOPING

Marc D. Bollmann, M.D. and Patrice Mangin, Ph.D.
University Institute of Legal Medicine, Lausanne, Switzerland

The clinical and pathological findings are often difficult to associate with a specific drug for numerous reasons. On one hand the tissue reaction to different forms of injury is rather uniform (e.g., chemical, physical, hypoxic, immunological), ending in inflammation and fibrosis. On the other hand the end-stage mechanism of abused substances is often similar (e.g., stimulant catecholamine toxicity). The following examples illustrate the adverse effects of some commonly abused substances.[64,65]

9.7.1 Anabolic-Androgenic Steroids (AAS)

AAS are widely used and effective in enhancing athletic performance, even in recreational sports. In a survey of 1881 schoolchildren aged from 13 to 17 years in Georgia, 6% of boys and 2% of girls reported taking androgens without a physician's prescription. The trade-off, however, is the occurrence of adverse side effects and even sudden death, reported mostly among weightlifters and bodybuilders.[66–68] In general, the orally administered AAS have more adverse effects than parenterally administered AAS. In addition, the type of AAS is not only important for the beneficial effects, but also for the adverse effects. AAS containing a 17-alkyl group have more potential to exert adverse effects, in particular in relation to the liver. One of the problems with athletes, in particular strength athletes and bodybuilders, is the use of oral and parenteral AAS at the same time ("stacking"), and in dosages that may be several times (up to 40) the recommended therapeutic dose. The frequency and severity of side effects are quite variable. It depends on several factors such as type of drug, dosage, duration of use, and the individual sensitivity and response. Since AAS have effects on almost all organ systems, myriad side effects can be found.

9.7.1.1 Cardiovascular

Chronic administration of anabolic steroids causes a reversible reduction in serum high-density lipoprotein (HDL) levels. Since HDL binds cholesterol and renders it inert, reduced HDL levels

Table 9.7.1 Summary of Case Reports Concerning Anabolic Steroid Abuse Associated with Sudden Death

Ref.	Year	Age	Body Weight	Heart Weight	LVT[a]	Findings
Luke et al.[72]	1990	21	97	530	16	Necrosis, fibrosis
Ferenchick[73]	1991	22				Thrombus
Lyndberg[74]	1991	27	91	423	17	Fibrosis
Kennedy et al.[68]	1993	18		410	13	Disarray fibrosis
Kennedy et al.[68]	1993	24		440	17	Fibrosis
Dickerman et al.[75]	1995	20		515		Concentric hypertrophy
Hausman et al.[76]	1998	23		500		Focal necrosis, fibrosis
Fineschi et al.[77]	2001	32	90	450	14	Subacute infarct
Fineschi et al.[77]	2001	29	72	390	19	Necrosis
Madea et al.[66]	1998	41	90	470	18	Fibrosis, old infarct
Madea et al.[66]	1998	28	136	800		Fibrosis
Lausanne case	2000	51	78	400	16	Coronary occlusion

[a] LVT = left ventricular thickness.

are associated with arteriosclerosis and enhance the risk of coronary heart disease.[69,70] AAS can enhance the vascular responsiveness to catecholamines and may favor effort-triggered arrhythmia.[71] The effects on protein synthesis may involve the myocardium and can lead to hypertrophy and shortage in oxygen delivery. The cardiac afterload may increase by water retention, which represents another source of cardiac hypertrophy. The combination of these effects can lead to a higher oxygen demand with less oxygen delivery and consequently myocardial cell death and scars, with the inherent risk of lethal reentry tachyarrhythmia. Table 9.7.1 shows a summary of case reports concerning anabolic steroid abuse associated with sudden death. Left ventricular hypertrophy is encountered in almost all of these cases.

9.7.1.2 Hepatic

AAS may exert a profound adverse effect on the liver. This is particularly true for orally administered AAS. Less adverse effects are reported for parenterally administered AAS. In this respect testosterone cypionate, testosterone enanthate, and other injectable anabolic steroids seem to have little adverse effects on the liver. However, lesions of the liver have been reported after parenteral nortestosterone administration, and also occasionally after injection of testosterone esters. The influence of AAS on liver function has been studied extensively. The majority of the studies involve hospitalized patients who are treated for prolonged periods for various diseases, such as anemia, renal insufficiency, impotence, and dysfunction of the pituitary gland. In clinical trials, treatment with anabolic steroids resulted in a decreased hepatic excretory function. Even liver neoplasia has been reported,[69] but the number of cases is few and causality remains uncertain.

9.7.1.3 Endocrine/Reproductive

Exogenous AAS reduce serum testosterone levels, which may decrease male fertility. In one study, sperm count fell by 73%, and in three individuals aspermia (complete absence of sperm) was found, when high doses of anabolic steroids were taken chronically. In-depth interviews with 110 AAS users revealed that 56% of the males reported testicular atrophy; 62% of the females had menstrual irregularities. Gynecomastia occurs because testosterone is converted to estradiol via the action of the aromatase enzyme complex, so that high doses of testosterone result in high serum estradiol concentrations. Other side effects have been reported including baldness, virilization and premature epiphyseal fusion and stunting of growth. The effects on the coagulation system are controversial.

9.7.1.4 Psychological

Administration of AAS may affect behavior. Increased testosterone levels in the blood are associated with masculine behavior, aggressiveness, and increased sexual desire. Increased aggressiveness may be beneficial for athletic training, but may also lead to overt violence outside the gym or the track. There are reports of violent, criminal behavior in individuals taking AAS. Other reported side effects of AAS are euphoria, confusion, sleeping disorders, pathological anxiety, paranoia, hypomania, or major depression.[78]

9.7.1.5 Tendon Injuries

Tendon rupture has been linked with AAS use on the basis of a small number of published case reports, and it has been suggested that these drugs predispose the tendon rupture by altering collagen structure. It is also possible that the rapid increase of skeletal muscle produced by AAS is not matched by the slower adapting tendon structures, making tendons the weakest link in the chain.

9.7.2 Stimulants

Stimulants are the second big group of currently abused drugs. Amphetamine was widely ignored until the 1960 Olympics, when the Danish cyclist Knut Jensen died of a speed-induced heart attack during a race. During the 1967 Tour de France, the British cyclist Tom Simpson collapsed and died. A vial of methamphetamine was found in his pocket at the time of his death. The impact of his death was extensive, in part because it was the first "doping death" to be televised.

One should suspect stimulant abuse in cases of hyperthermia, dehydration and all forms of overtaxing the body. Elite athletes are also at risk for out-of-competition stimulant (especially cocaine) abuse, partly because of the constant pressure they live under and the confrontation with celebrity, news media, and fans, for which they are often unprepared. Cocaine should be tested for in every case of sport-related sudden death.

9.7.2.1 Amphetamine

Some side effects of amphetamine are particularly important in athletes and do not only include headaches, sleeplessness, and anxiety. Indeed, amphetamine use may carry significant health risks for the sportsman, as evidenced by several amphetamine-linked deaths in sport. Two of the major risks are the amphetamine-induced heatstroke and cardiac arrest. Hyperthermia may be attributed to an increase in physical activity and peripheral vasoconstriction, making it difficult for the body to cool down. The ability of amphetamine to obscure painful injuries has enabled athletes in some sports to compete by exacerbating their injuries. The side effects of amphetamine on behavior are another important factor in sport. Amphetamine administered to promote aggression and euphoria, while weakening the sensation of fatigue, has led to misjudgments and major fouls on the pitch.

9.7.2.2 Cocaine

Classical physical effects of cocaine use include peripherical vasoconstriction, mydriasis, thermogenesis, and increased heart rate and blood pressure. These symptoms lead to an overall higher workload for the heart, and increase its oxygen demand. On the other hand, vasoconstriction of coronary arteries may make it impossible to meet the oxygen demand. This may lead to acute arrhythmia, favored additionally by an altered excitability of the cardiomyocytes (e.g., QT-prolongation), and/or structural damage (e.g., fibrosis and microvascular disease) to the heart.[79–81] A number of dramatic fatalities associated with coronary occlusion have occurred in cocaine abusing athletes, usually those who have been exercising following drug administration. Cocaine abuse is strongly associated with cerebrovascular accidents arising from either the rupture or spasm of cerebral blood vessels.[82]

Cocaine is highly addictive, and with increasing doses, it may lead to a state of irritability, restlessness, anxiety, and paranoia. Cocaine is often consumed in combination with other drugs, enhancing the toxic effects, especially on the heart. Some fatalities have also occurred when cocaine has been combined with alcohol or anabolic steroids.

9.7.2.3 Ephedrine

Common side effects of ephedrine are qualitatively similar to those produced by amphetamines, but are generally milder: headache, dizziness, irritability, anxiety, tremor and psychosis. Higher doses (overdose) can cause restlessness and anxiety, dizziness, insomnia, tremor, rapid pulse, sweating, respiratory difficulties, confusion, hallucinations, delirium and convulsions. The most dangerous symptoms of overdose are arterial hypertension peaks and cardiac arrhythmia. Finally, a number of instances of psychosis, clinically similar to amphetamine psychosis, have resulted from chronic high-dose abuse.

There are serious doubts about the safety of food supplements containing ephedra-alkaloids. Because supplements are not considered therapeutic, they are not under the same strict surveillance as prescribed and over-the-counter medications. Because of recent highly publicized tragedies, various athletic associations have focused on further evaluations of the use of these substances and are trying to warn athletes about the potential health risks associated with their use.

9.7.3 Erythropoietin

Erythropoietin is still a widely used and efficient doping method. An interesting illustration of the problem may be the industrial production of erythropoietin covering about 10 times the medical needs.[83] In theory the main risk of erythropoietin abuse would be thrombosis because of the increased viscosity of the blood. Only one case of a survived cerebral sinus thrombosis in a professional cyclist has been reported after admitted erythropoietin abuse.[84]

9.7.4 Human Growth Hormone (GH)

The long-term risks due to utilization of GH are not well known. Acromegaly, describing a pathological increased endogenous production from a pituitary tumor, would be expected after excessive use of GH. The major symptoms are the swelling of the hands and feet, coarsened facial appearance, dentition problems, arthralgia, fluid retention, and excessive sweating. Acromegalic patients have increased risk for diabetes mellitus and hypertension defined in total by premature mortality from cardiovascular diseases. There are also risks of developing osteoporosis, menstrual irregularities, and impotence. Arthralgia and myalgia have, however, been reported in more than 50% of treated subjects.[85] Some of these side effects are certainly reversible after withdrawal of the drug. Furthermore, GH abuse can disturb lipid pattern with decreased HDL-cholesterol.

Epidemiological data regarding that type of treatment in healthy sportsmen are missing as well as scientific reports about the mentioned side effects. Reports of oversize shoes in tennis players and swimmers are anecdotic.

Since GH is administered by injection, there is a great risk of cross infections such as HIV and hepatitis if syringes are contaminated. GH was once extracted from human bodies, which implied a risk of Creutzfeldt-Jakob disease[86] characterized by a progressive dementia.

9.8 MORTALITY OF DOPING — SUDDEN DEATH IN ATHLETES

Marc D. Bollmann, M.D.
University Institute of Legal Medicine, Lausanne, Switzerland

Athletes are thought to represent the healthiest segment of our society and they are highly visible. For these reasons, the sudden death of an athlete has a large impact and receives much attention. The incidence of sudden death in athletes is estimated 2.5 times higher than in non-athletes.[87] It has also been shown that almost every single case of sudden death in athletes was due to an underlying hereditary or acquired heart disease, in which effort might trigger arrhythmia.[87–89] In only about 1% of the examined cases could drug abuse be confirmed. The main pathologies accounting for more than 80% of sudden deaths in young athletes are the following:

Hypertrophic cardiomyopathy (HCM)[90] is a relatively common genetic cardiac disease (1 in 500), with heterogeneous clinical, morphologic, and genetic expression. To date 12 disease-causing loci have been identified, mostly encoding for thick filament components in cardiomyocytes. The heart action may be normal or even more vigorous; this may also explain the high incidence of the disease in athletes. The morphological characteristics of the disease are an asymmetrical, hypertrophied, and non-dilated left ventricle, disorganized myocardial architecture, and replacement scarring. Some variations are, however, not easily diagnosed. When in doubt, the medical history of a victim and his or her family can be helpful to differentiate an athlete's heart from an HCM. If the left ventricular wall thickness exceeds 13 mm, an underlying pathology and/or substance abuse must be suspected, even in a young population of well-trained athletes.[91] Genetic analysis can be performed for known mutations.[92,93] Hypertrophy alone may, however, be drug induced (e.g., by anabolic steroids).

Arrhythmogenic right ventricular cardiomyopathy (ARVC) also accounts for numerous sudden deaths in athletes.[94] The right heart muscle is replaced with fatty and fibrous tissue, altering conductivity and leading to fatal arrhythmia. Sudden death is often the first symptom. So far five genes have been identified as containing mutations for ARVC. The first one is the cardiac ryanodine receptor, which regulates intracellular Ca^{2+}. A dysfunction in the same receptor is held responsible for catecholaminergic polymorphic ventricular tachycardia, which is characterized by exercise-induced fatal arrhythmias without any morphologic heart disease.[95] For reasons that remain unexplained, this syndrome is reported with much greater frequency in Europe than in the U.S.

Long-QT syndrome and Brugada syndrome are two common hereditary channelopathies. Fatal arrhythmia can occur, and drugs of many kinds can facilitate or induce it.

Congenital malformations such as mitral valve prolapse or anomalies of coronary arteries (especially those in which the anomalous coronary artery makes an acute bend and courses between the pulmonary artery and aorta).

A problem with the mentioned studies, however, is the often missing or incomplete toxicological analysis. So even if a possible or probable cause of death is found at the autopsy, there remains doubt about a substance-triggered or facilitated sudden death (e.g., coronary thrombosis with evidence of EPO abuse, stimulants, and channelopathy). Another factor to bear in mind is the growing analytical possibilities, which may place many old cases of natural death in a new context. For all the above reasons toxicological investigation should be carried out in every case of sudden death in athletes. In the news-media-driven environment of sports, the suspicion of doping will sooner or later come up anyway.

Substance abuse as sole cause of death in athletes is, however, very rare (in spite of the mainly historic cases of lethal cocaine, strychnine, or amphetamine levels). Doping and substance abuse should rather be considered supplementary risk factors for sudden death because they permit one to overtax the organism and may contribute to structural disease. Another mechanism is the modification of cellular excitability and/or induction of an acquired long-QT interval (e.g., cocaine induced).[80] Combined with other factors like acquired and/or hereditary heart disease, adverse weather conditions (heat with dehydration and electrolyte disorder), or simply effort, a high-risk situation for lethal arrhythmia can arise. If substance abuse is involved in the mechanism of death, an investigation of the circumstances should be carried out. As efficient doping practice is only possible with a close medical follow-up, one should also look for possible medical malpractice.

The sudden death of an athlete is difficult to solve and requires a multidisciplinary approach and careful investigation. Athletes are considered the healthiest segment of society, and so the sudden death of an athlete has considerable impact and the hypothesis of doping is easily advanced. However, most cases of sudden death in athletes are related to an underlying hereditary cardiovascular disease. The possibilities to diagnose hereditary heart disease are now growing steadily. Genetic testing may also be helpful to provide advice and lower the risk for the relatives of the victim. Preventive measures have been taken to prevent morbidity and mortality in athletes, for example, using medical follow-up and screening, carried out by team-independent physicians. Athletes at high risk of sudden death may be excluded from competition. Some international and national sports federations have already taken steps in this direction.

Drug abuse is widespread in sports and the already large arsenal of analytical methods should be used and improved. Reports about dangerous side effects alone do not act as a deterrent. In a survey conducted by *Sports Illustrated*, athletes were asked if they would take a performance-enhancing drug if they would win and not be caught. Of 198, 195 answered "yes." A second question asked them if they would take a substance making them win every competition for 5 years, but with the drawback of dying of its side effects. Still more than 50% answered "yes."[96]

9.9 THE FUTURE OF DOPING: NEW DRUGS AND GENETIC DOPING

Christian Giroud, Ph.D.[1] and Marc D. Bollmann, M.D.[2]
[1] Swiss Laboratory for Doping Analyses, University Institute of Legal Medicine, Lausanne, Switzerland
[2] University Institute of Legal Medicine, Lausanne, Switzerland

The pharmaceutical industry is continuously looking for new blockbusters and "smart" drugs. New areas of research include the production of drugs able to alter the aging process, and maintain muscle integrity. Both would be possible candidates for future doping agents. Peroxisome proliferator-activated receptor ligands (PPAR) are new drugs that are now being investigated for using against cardiovascular disease and syndrome-X. They increase fat burning and may enhance sports performance by changing fast glucose-burning muscle fibers into fat-burning muscle.[97] Wang et al.[98] have shown that activation of PPAR-δ in mice leads to muscle fiber transformation, and enhances physical performance and exercise endurance. According to Azzazy et al.,[99] the main candidates of gene doping are erythropoietin, human growth hormone, insulin-like growth factor-1, PPAR-δ, myostatin inhibitor genes, and hypoxia-inducible factors. Genes encoding for analgesic opioids such as endorphins and enkephalins constitute another valuable target. Altering behavior, alertness, anxiety, and psychological resistance to stress may be possible with gene transfer in the limbic system of the brain.[100] The roots of gene doping lie in gene therapy, for which only very few therapeutic successes have been achieved to date (December 2005). Nine French infants suffering from severe combined immune deficiency (X-SCID) were cured by gene therapy of their own bone marrow cells. However, due to proviral insertional oncogenesis, two individuals developed T-cell leukemia more than 2 years after the gene transfer.[101] The paucity of successful results and the high incidence of serious side effects cast doubt on the use of genetic engineering methods in sports in the near future. It should also be noted that genetic doping is detectable by existing techniques as recently demonstrated by Lasne and co-workers.[102]

REFERENCES

1. WADA. WADA Laboratory statistics 2004, 2005.
2. Evans NA. Current concepts in anabolic-androgenic steroids. *Am J Sports Med* 2004;32(2):534–42.
3. Mottram DR, George AJ. Anabolic steroids. *Baillieres Best Pract Res Clin Endocrinol Metab* 2000;14(1):55–69.
4. Saugy M, Cardis C, Robinson N, Schweizer C. Test methods: anabolics. *Baillieres Best Pract Res Clin Endocrinol Metab* 2000;14(1):111–33.
5. van de Kerkhof DH, de Boer D, Thijssen JH, Maes RA. Evaluation of testosterone/epitestosterone ratio influential factors as determined in doping analysis. *J Anal Toxicol* 2000;24(2):102–15.
6. Starka L. Epitestosterone. *J Steroid Biochem Mol Biol* 2003;87(1):27–34.
7. Catlin DH, Hatton CK, Starcevic SH. Issues in detecting abuse of xenobiotic anabolic steroids and testosterone by analysis of athletes' urine. *Clin Chem* 1997;43(7):1280–8.
8. WADA. WADA Technical Document: reporting and evaluation guidance for testosterone, epitestosterone, T/E ratio and other endogenous steroids. 2004.
9. Saudan C, Baume N, Mangin P, Saugy M. Urinary analysis of 16(5alpha)-androsten-3alpha-ol by gas chromatography/combustion/isotope ratio mass spectrometry: implications in anti-doping analysis. *J Chromatogr B Anal Technol Biomed Life Sci* 2004;810(1):157–64.
10. Saudan C, Desmarchelier A, Sottas PE, Mangin P, Saugy M. Urinary marker of oral pregnenolone administration. *Steroids* 2005;70(3):179–83.
11. Bricout V, Wright F. Update on nandrolone and norsteroids: how endogenous or xenobiotic are these substances? *Eur J Appl Physiol* 2004;92(1–2):1–12.
12. Green GA, Catlin DH, Starcevic B. Analysis of over-the-counter dietary supplements. *Clin J Sport Med* 2001;11(4):254–9.
13. Kamber M, Baume N, Saugy M, Rivier L. Nutritional supplements as a source for positive doping cases? *Int J Sport Nutr Exerc Metab* 2001;11(2):258–63.
14. Uralets VP, Gillette PA. Over-the-counter delta5 anabolic steroids 5-androsen-3,17-dione; 5-androsten-3beta, 17beta-diol; dehydroepiandrosterone; and 19-nor-5-androsten-3,17-dione: excretion studies in men. *J Anal Toxicol* 2000;24(3):188–93.
15. Baume N, Avois L, Sottas PE, et al. Effects of high-intensity exercises on 13C-nandrolone excretion in trained athletes. *Clin J Sport Med* 2005;15(3):158–66.
16. Le Bizec B, Monteau F, Gaudin I, Andre F. Evidence for the presence of endogenous 19-norandrosterone in human urine. *J Chromatogr B Biomed Sci Appl* 1999;723(1–2):157–72.
17. Robinson N, Taroni F, Saugy M, Ayotte C, Mangin P, Dvorak J. Detection of nandrolone metabolites in urine after a football game in professional and amateur players: a Bayesian comparison. *Forensic Sci Int* 2001;122(2–3):130–5.
18. Schmitt N, Flament MM, Goubault C, Legros P, Grenier-Loustalot MF, Denjean A. Nandrolone excretion is not increased by exhaustive exercise in trained athletes. *Med Sci Sports Exerc* 2002;34(9):1436–9.
19. Verroken M. Drug use and abuse in sport. *Baillieres Best Pract Res Clin Endocrinol Metab* 2000;14(1):1–23.
20. George AJ. Central nervous system stimulants. *Baillieres Best Pract Res Clin Endocrinol Metab* 2000;14(1):79–88.
21. Turner M, McCrory P, Johnston A. Time for tea, anyone? *Br J Sports Med* 2005;39(10):e37.
22. Bohn AM, Khodaee M, Schwenk TL. Ephedrine and other stimulants as ergogenic aids. *Curr Sports Med Rep* 2003;2(4):220–5.
23. Parisotto R, Gore CJ, Emslie KR, et al. A novel method utilising markers of altered erythropoiesis for the detection of recombinant human erythropoietin abuse in athletes. *Haematologica* 2000;85(6):564–72.
24. Robinson N, Saugy M, Buclin T, Gremion G, Mangin P. The interpretation of secondary blood markers can get hazardous in case of a discontinuous rhEPO treatment. *Haematologica* 2002;87(6):ELT28.
25. Lasne F, de Ceaurriz J. Recombinant erythropoietin in urine. *Nature* 2000;405(6787):635.
26. Nelson M, Ashenden M, Langshaw M, Popp H. Detection of homologous blood transfusion by flow cytometry: a deterrent against blood doping. *Haematologica* 2002;87(8):881–2.

27. Lassarre C, Girard F, Durand J, Raynaud J. Kinetics of human growth hormone during submaximal exercise. *J Appl Physiol* 1974;37(6):826–30.

28. Felsing NE, Brasel JA, Cooper DM. Effect of low and high intensity exercise on circulating growth hormone in men. *J Clin Endocrinol Metab* 1992;75(1):157–62.

29. Shephard RJ, Sidney KH. Effects of physical exercise on plasma growth hormone and cortisol levels in human subjects. *Exerc Sport Sci Rev* 1975;3:1–30.

30. Vanhelder WP, Goode RC, Radomski MW. Effect of anaerobic and aerobic exercise of equal duration and work expenditure on plasma growth hormone levels. *Eur J Appl Physiol Occup Physiol* 1984;52(3):255–7.

31. Kanaley JA, Weltman JY, Veldhuis JD, Rogol AD, Hartman ML, Weltman A. Human growth hormone response to repeated bouts of aerobic exercise. *J Appl Physiol* 1997;83(5):1756–61.

32. Galbo H. Endocrinology and metabolism in exercise. *Curr Probl Clin Biochem* 1982;11:26–44.

33. Godfrey RJ, Madgwick Z, Whyte GP. The exercise-induced growth hormone response in athletes. *Sports Med* 2003;33(8):599–613.

34. Sartorio A, Agosti F, Marazzi N, et al. Gender-, age-, body composition- and training workload-dependent differences of GH response to a discipline-specific training session in elite athletes: a study on the field. *J Endocrinol Invest* 2004;27(2):121–9.

35. Parker ML, Utiger RD, Daughaday WH. Studies on human growth hormone. II. The physiological disposition and metabolic fate of human growth hormone in man. *J Clin Invest* 1962;41:262–8.

36. Veldhuis JD. Neuroendocrine control of pulsatile growth hormone release in the human: relationship with gender. *Growth Horm IGF Res* 1998;8 Suppl B:49–59.

37. Muller EE, Locatelli V, Cocchi D. Neuroendocrine control of growth hormone secretion. *Physiol Rev* 1999;79(2):511–607.

38. Rickert VI, Pawlak-Morello C, Sheppard V, Jay MS. Human growth hormone: a new substance of abuse among adolescents? *Clin Pediatr* (Philadelphia) 1992;31(12):723–6.

39. Berggren A, Ehrnborg C, Rosen T, Ellegard L, Bengtsson BA, Caidahl K. Short-term administration of supraphysiological recombinant human growth hormone (GH) does not increase maximum endurance exercise capacity in healthy, active young men and women with normal GH-insulin-like growth factor I axes. *J Clin Endocrinol Metab* 2005;90(6):3268–73.

40. Saugy M, Cardis C, Schweizer C, Veuthey JL, Rivier L. Detection of human growth hormone doping in urine: out of competition tests are necessary. *J Chromatogr B Biomed Appl* 1996;687(1):201–11.

41. Di Luigi L, Guidetti L. IGF-I, IGFBP-2, and -3: do they have a role in detecting rhGH abuse in trained men? *Med Sci Sports Exerc* 2002;34(8):1270–8.

42. Rigamonti AE, Cella SG, Marazzi N, Di Luigi L, Sartorio A, Muller EE. Growth hormone abuse: methods of detection. *Trends Endocrinol Metab* 2005;16(4):160–6.

43. Minuto F, Barreca A, Melioli G. Indirect evidence of hormone abuse. Proof of doping? *J Endocrinol Invest* 2003;26(9):919–23.

44. Ehrnborg C, Bengtsson BA, Rosen T. Growth hormone abuse. *Baillieres Best Pract Res Clin Endocrinol Metab* 2000;14(1):71–7.

45. Bidlingmaier M, Wu Z, Strasburger CJ. Test method: GH. *Baillieres Best Pract Res Clin Endocrinol Metab* 2000;14(1):99–109.

46. Renaud AM, Cormier Y. Acute effects of marihuana smoking on maximal exercise performance. *Med Sci Sports Exerc* 1986;18(6):685–9.

47. Menetrey A, Augsburger M, Favrat B, et al. Assessment of driving capability through the use of clinical and psychomotor tests in relation to blood cannabinoids levels following oral administration of 20 mg dronabinol or of a cannabis decoction made with 20 or 60 mg delta9-THC. *J Anal Toxicol* 2005;29(5):327–38.

48. Favrat B, Menetrey A, Augsburger M, et al. Two cases of "cannabis acute psychosis" following the administration of oral cannabis. *BMC Psychiatry* 2005;5(1):17.

49. Ashton CH. Adverse effects of cannabis and cannabinoids. *Br J Anaesth* 1999;83(4):637–49.

50. Ashton CH. Pharmacology and effects of cannabis: a brief review. *Br J Psychiatry* 2001;178:101–6.

51. Lorente FO, Peretti-Watel P, Grelot L. Cannabis use to enhance sportive and non-sportive performances among French sport students. *Addict Behav* 2005;30(7):1382–91.

52. Arvers P, Choquet M. [Sporting activities and psychoactive substance use. Data abstracted from the French part of the European School Survey on Alcohol and other Drugs (ESPAD 99)]. *Ann Med Intern* (Paris) 2003;154 Spec No 1:S25–34.

53. Cone EJ, Johnson RE, Darwin WD, et al. Passive inhalation of marijuana smoke: urinalysis and room air levels of delta-9-tetrahydrocannabinol. *J Anal Toxicol* 1987;11(3):89–96.

54. Leson G, Pless P, Grotenhermen F, Kalant H, ElSohly MA. Evaluating the impact of hemp food consumption on workplace drug tests. *J Anal Toxicol* 2001;25(8):691–8.

55. ElSohly MA. Practical challenges to positive drug tests for marijuana. *Clin Chem* 2003;49(7):1037–8.

56. Huestis MA, Cone EJ. Differentiating new marijuana use from residual drug excretion in occasional marijuana users. *J Anal Toxicol* 1998;22(6):445–54.

57. Huestis MA, Mitchell JM, Cone EJ. Urinary excretion profiles of 11-nor-9-carboxy-delta 9-tetrahydrocannabinol in humans after single smoked doses of marijuana. *J Anal Toxicol* 1996;20(6):441–52.

58. Smith-Kielland A, Skuterud B, Morland J. Urinary excretion of 11-nor-9-carboxy-delta9-tetrahydrocannabinol and cannabinoids in frequent and infrequent drug users. *J Anal Toxicol* 1999;23(5):323–32.

59. Ellis GM, Jr., Mann MA, Judson BA, Schramm NT, Tashchian A. Excretion patterns of cannabinoid metabolites after last use in a group of chronic users. *Clin Pharmacol Ther* 1985;38(5):572–8.

60. Manno JE, Manno BR, Kemp PM, et al. Temporal indication of marijuana use can be estimated from plasma and urine concentrations of delta9-tetrahydrocannabinol, 11-hydroxy-delta9-tetrahydrocannabinol, and 11-nor-delta9-tetrahydrocannabinol-9-carboxylic acid. *J Anal Toxicol* 2001;25(7):38–49.

61. Catlin DH, Murray TH. Performance-enhancing drugs, fair competition, and Olympic sport. *JAMA* 1996;276(3):231–7.

62. Lukas SE. CNS effects and abuse liability of anabolic-androgenic steroids. *Annu Rev Pharmacol Toxicol* 1996;36:333–57.

63. Lewis MJ, June HL. Synergistic effects of ethanol and cocaine on brain stimulation reward. *J Exp Anal Behav* 1994;61(2):223–9.

64. Karch SB. *Karch's Pathology of Drug Abuse*. 3rd ed. Boca Raton, FL: CRC Press; 2002.

65. Brinkmann B, Madea B. *Handbuch gerichtliche Medizin*. Berlin: Springer; 2003.

66. Madea B, Grellner W, Musshoff F, Dettmeyer R. Medico-legal aspects of doping. *J Clin Forensic Med* 1998;5(1):1–7.

67. Parssinen M, Kujala U, Vartiainen E, Sarna S, Seppala T. Increased premature mortality of competitive powerlifters suspected to have used anabolic agents. *Int J Sports Med* 2000;21(3):225–7.

68. Kennedy MC, Lawrence C. Anabolic steroid abuse and cardiac death. *Med J Aust* 1993;158(5):346–8.

69. Hartgens F, Kuipers H. Effects of androgenic-anabolic steroids in athletes. *Sports Med* 2004;34(8):513–54.

70. Hartgens F, Rietjens G, Keizer HA, Kuipers H, Wolffenbuttel BH. Effects of androgenic-anabolic steroids on apolipoproteins and lipoprotein (a). *Br J Sports Med* 2004;38(3):253–9.

71. Sullivan ML, Martinez CM, Gennis P, Gallagher EJ. The cardiac toxicity of anabolic steroids. *Prog Cardiovasc Dis* 1998;41(1):1–15.

72. Luke JL, Farb A, Virmani R, Sample RH. Sudden cardiac death during exercise in a weight lifter using anabolic androgenic steroids: pathological and toxicological findings. *J Forensic Sci* 1990;35(6):1441–7.

73. Ferenchick G, Schwartz D, Ball M, Schwartz K. Androgenic-anabolic steroid abuse and platelet aggregation: a pilot study in weight lifters. *Am J Med Sci* 1992;303(2):78–82.

74. Lyngberg KK. [Myocardial infarction and death of a body builder after using anabolic steroids]. *Ugeskr Laeger* 1991;153(8):587–8.

75. Dickerman RD, Schaller F, Prather I, McConathy WJ. Sudden cardiac death in a 20-year-old body-builder using anabolic steroids. *Cardiology* 1995;86(2):172–3.

76. Hausmann R, Hammer S, Betz P. Performance enhancing drugs (doping agents) and sudden death — a case report and review of the literature. *Int J Legal Med* 1998;111(5):261–4.

77. Fineschi V, Baroldi G, Monciotti F, Paglicci Reattelli L, Turillazzi E. Anabolic steroid abuse and cardiac sudden death: a pathologic study. *Arch Pathol Lab Med* 2001;125(2):253–5.

78. Pope HG, Jr., Katz DL. Psychiatric and medical effects of anabolic-androgenic steroid use. A controlled study of 160 athletes. *Arch Gen Psychiatry* 1994;51(5):375–82.

79. Fineschi V, Silver MD, Karch SB, et al. Myocardial disarray: an architectural disorganization linked with adrenergic stress? *Int J Cardiol* 2005;99(2):277–82.

80. Karch SB. Cocaine cardiovascular toxicity. *South Med J* 2005;98(8):794–9.

81. Knuepfer MM. Cardiovascular disorders associated with cocaine use: myths and truths. *Pharmacol Ther* 2003;97(3):181–222.

82. Buttner A, Mall G, Penning R, Sachs H, Weis S. The neuropathology of cocaine abuse. *Leg Med* (Tokyo) 2003;5 Suppl 1:S240–2.

83. Bourgat M. *Tout savoir sur le dopage*. Lausanne: Favre; 1999.

84. Lage JM, Panizo C, Masdeu J, Rocha E. Cyclist's doping associated with cerebral sinus thrombosis. *Neurology* 2002;58(4):665.

85. Van Loon K. Safety of high doses of recombinant human growth hormone. *Horm Res* 1998;49 Suppl 2:78–81.

86. Sartorio A, Arosio M, Faglia G, Resentini M, Morabito F. Human growth hormone treatment and Creutzfeldt-Jakob disease. *J Endocrinol Invest* 1986;9(5):439.

87. Corrado D, Basso C, Rizzoli G, Schiavon M, Thiene G. Does sports activity enhance the risk of sudden death in adolescents and young adults? *J Am Coll Cardiol* 2003;42(11):1959–63.

88. Maron BJ, Carney KP, Lever HM, et al. Relationship of race to sudden cardiac death in competitive athletes with hypertrophic cardiomyopathy. *J Am Coll Cardiol* 2003;41(6):974–80.

89. Maron BJ, Roberts WC, McAllister HA, Rosing DR, Epstein SE. Sudden death in young athletes. *Circulation* 1980;62(2):218–29.

90. Maron BJ. The young competitive athlete with cardiovascular abnormalities: causes of sudden death, detection by preparticipation screening, and standards for disqualification. *Card Electrophysiol Rev* 2002;6(1–2):100–3.

91. Pelliccia A, Maron BJ, Spataro A, Proschan MA, Spirito P. The upper limit of physiologic cardiac hypertrophy in highly trained elite athletes. *N Engl J Med* 1991;324(5):295–301.

92. Fatkin D, Graham RM. Molecular mechanisms of inherited cardiomyopathies. *Physiol Rev* 2002;82(4):945–80.

93. Roberts R. Molecular genetics and its application to cardiac muscle disease. *Sports Med* 1997;23(1):1–10.

94. Corrado D, Basso C, Schiavon M, Thiene G. Screening for hypertrophic cardiomyopathy in young athletes. *N Engl J Med* 1998;339(6):364–9.

95. Taur Y, Frishman WH. The cardiac ryanodine receptor (RyR2) and its role in heart disease. *Cardiol Rev* 2005;13(3):142–6.

96. Bamberger M YD. Over the edge. *Sports Illus* 1997(14):62–72.

97. Ewan S. From fat to fit. *Drug Discov Today* 2005;10(11):744.

98. Wang YX, Zhang CL, Yu RT, et al. Regulation of muscle fiber type and running endurance by PPARdelta. *PLoS Biol* 2004;2(10):e294.

99. Azzazy HM, Mansour MM, Christenson RH. Doping in the recombinant era: Strategies and counter-strategies. *Clin Biochem* 2005;38(11):959–65.

100. Sapolsky RM. Altering behavior with gene transfer in the limbic system. *Physiol Behav* 2003;79(3):479–86.

101. Gaspar HB, Thrasher AJ. Gene therapy for severe combined immunodeficiencies. *Expert Opin Biol Ther* 2005;5(9):1175–82.

102. Lasne F, Martin L, de Ceaurriz J, Larcher T, Moullier P, Chenuaud P. "Genetic Doping" with erythropoietin cDNA in primate muscle is detectable. *Mol Ther* 2004;10(3):409–10.

CHAPTER 10

Workplace Testing

Edited by Yale H. Caplan, Ph.D., DABFT,[1] and Marilyn A. Huestis, Ph.D.[2]*

[1] National Scientific Services, Baltimore, Maryland
[2] Chemistry and Drug Metabolism Section, Intramural Research Program, National Institute on Drug Abuse, National Institutes of Health, Department of Health and Human Services, Baltimore, Maryland

CONTENTS

---

* Dr. Huestis contributed to this book in her personal capacity. The views expressed are her own and do not necessarily represent the views of the National Institutes of Health or the U.S. government.

10.1 DRUGS IN THE WORKPLACE

Yale H. Caplan, Ph.D., DABFT,[1] and Marilyn A. Huestis, Ph.D.[2]*
[1] National Scientific Services, Baltimore, Maryland
[2] Chemistry and Drug Metabolism Section, Intramural Research Program, National Institute on Drug Abuse, National Institutes of Health, Baltimore, Maryland

Substance abuse has been a mainstay of society for the past few millennia. Epidemics come and go in somewhat predictable cycles and the problem has never been resolved. Over the past century, as this cyclic equilibrium has shifted, the magnitude of the problem has generally intensified. The number of euphoric substances has grown and their enhanced distribution has increased abuse. Technology has increased the potency of euphoric compounds, i.e., the synthesis of natural opium to heroin and the *de novo* synthesis of non-natural substances such as PCP, LSD, MDMA, and others. Cocaine has been concentrated and modified from the coca plant to produce freebase and crack cocaine. Improvement in horticulture techniques has increased the content of marijuana to 10 to 15% tetrahydrocannabinol (THC).

Workplace drug and alcohol testing is the latest component to be added to the discipline of forensic toxicology, which now comprises the triad fields of post-mortem, human performance, and workplace drug testing toxicology. Since drug testing is conducted as a deterrent to drug abuse, and society seeks to protect the rights of individuals in the workplace, every effort is necessary to prevent harm to persons through false accusation. Drug testing is a multifaceted process. The accuracy and validity of analysis and the use and application of the reported results are concerns. Multiple factors include the methodologies (initial and confirmatory), cutoff concentrations, administrative or legally mandated rules, and the influence of prescribed drugs or environmental exposure.

Acquiring a full understanding of workplace drug testing is necessary for practitioners (toxicologists, physicians, and others). The tenets of forensic science and regulatory requirements influence workplace drug testing. The right questions must be asked and proper caveats applied. Traditionally in medical practice, the test result is only one part of the diagnostic paradigm that also includes history and physical examination. In workplace testing, the test result is the primary and paramount element. There is no diagnostic paradigm and the result must stand alone evaluated only after the test event by medical personnel identified as a medical review officer (MRO).

Workplace testing is employed to ensure safety and productivity in the workplace. It is complex with myriad elements vital to its success. This chapter and those to follow will overview workplace drug testing including its background and current status, its regulatory basis, its application in the U.S. and abroad, analytical approaches, the use of urine and other biological matrices, quality

* Dr. Huestis contributed to this book in her personal capacity. The views expressed are her own and do not necessarily represent the views of the National Institutes of Health or the U.S. government.

control and validity testing, the role of the MRO, and associated legal issues. Although alcohol testing and on-site (point of collection) testing are practiced in the workplace, they are not included in this chapter; rather, they are discussed in other sections of this book.

10.1.1 History

Workplace drug testing has grown at a steady rate over the last 20 years. It is recognized that employee/applicant drug testing has become a standard business practice in the U.S. It is likely that almost half of the American workforce will be tested for illegal drugs this year. A more detailed history was provided in the earlier edition of this book.[1]

The workplace drug-testing phenomenon did not occur overnight, but rather evolved slowly during the 1980s. At the outset, workplace drug testing began in the U.S. military with most of the testing done in military laboratories by military personnel. Testing was highly regimented; however, even within the military programs (Army, Navy, and Air Force), procedures, equipment, and standards varied considerably. As the use of the new immunoassay-based drug-testing technology spread to the private sector in 1982–1983, there were no regulations, no certified laboratories, no standardized procedures, and many of the devices marketed for testing were not cleared by the U.S. Food and Drug Administration. Medical and scientific questions concerning the accuracy and reliability of drug testing were raised continuously by those who opposed testing and often formed the basis of lengthy litigation. As interest in workplace drug testing increased in the public and private sectors, the need for regulations to establish the appropriate science, technology, and practice became obvious.

The beginnings of regulated testing were initiated in 1983 when the National Transportation Safety Board (NTSB) sent a series of specific recommendations to the Secretary of Transportation demanding action in regard to alcohol- and drug-related accidents, particularly in the railroad industry. The report indicated that seven train accidents occurring between June 1982 and May 1983 involved alcohol or other drugs. In response to the NTSB recommendations, the Federal Railroad Administration (FRA) with the assistance of the National Institute on Drug Abuse (NIDA) began to develop the first Department of Transportation (DOT) drug regulations in 1983. However, it was not until early 1986 that legal obstacles were cleared and the rule went into effect and was fully implemented. During the 1983–1986 timeframe, many companies in the oil, chemical, transportation, and nuclear industries voluntarily implemented drug-testing programs. Without standards and recognized procedures, almost every action incurred controversy. Lawsuits and arbitration caseloads mounted rapidly. Reports of laboratory errors in the massive military program raised concerns that the application of this state-of-the-art technology might be premature. Allegations of employees stripped naked and forced to provide specimens in view of other employees were often repeated and added justification for regulations.

In 1986, the federal government became involved in employee drug testing in a significant way. In March 1986, President Reagan's Commission on Organized Crime issued its final report. Among the recommendations were the following:

> The President should direct the heads of all Federal agencies to formulate immediately clear policy statements, with implementing guidelines, including suitable drug testing programs, expressing the utter unacceptability of drug abuse by Federal employees. State and local governments and leaders in the private sector should support unequivocally a similar policy that any and all use of drugs is unacceptable. Government contracts should not be awarded to companies that fail to implement drug programs, including suitable drug testing. Government and private sector employers who do not already require drug testing of job applicants and current employees should consider the appropriateness of such a testing program.

NIDA convened a conference in March 1986. The conference was designed to discuss and achieve consensus on drug-testing issues. Prior to the release of the President's Commission on

Organized Crime report, the NIDA position advocating testing for critical and sensitive positions was viewed as radical. However, once the recommendation for widespread testing of everyone employed in both the public and private sectors was proposed by the President's Commission, the NIDA position became one of reasonable accommodation. The conference thus focused on prescribing the conditions under which testing could be conducted. After lengthy discussions, consensus was reached on the following points:

1. All individuals tested must be informed.
2. All positive results on an initial screen must be confirmed through the use of an alternate methodology.
3. The confidentiality of test results must be assured.
4. Random screening for drug abuse under a well-defined program is appropriate and legally defensible in certain circumstances.

The consensus reached at this meeting in 1986 on technical, medical, legal, and ethical issues truly served to provide the foundation for the development of the federal regulations that were to evolve over the next decade and continue to evolve. The responsibility for developing technical and scientific guidelines for these drug-testing programs was assigned to the Secretary of Health and Human Services (HHS) and was delegated to NIDA. An informal advisory group produced the initial set of guidelines in a matter of months. On February 19, 1987, HHS Secretary Dr. Otis Bowen issued the required set of technical and scientific guidelines for federal drug-testing programs. Several months later Congress passed a new law (Public Law 100-71 section 503) that set the stage for the widespread regulation of employee drug testing. Enacted on July 7, 1987, the law permitted the President's *Drug Free Federal Workplace* program to go forward only if a number of administrative prerequisites were met. Among the list of required administrative actions was that the Secretary of Health and Human Services publish the HHS technical and scientific guidelines in the *Federal Register* for notice and comment, and to expand the "Guidelines" to include standards for laboratory certification. The NIDA advisory group had been working on the concept of laboratory accreditation since early in 1986 anticipating the eventuality of laboratory certification. This allowed NIDA to revise the "guidelines" quickly and include a proposed scheme of laboratory certification, which was published in the *Federal Register* on August 13, 1987, less than 6 weeks after the passage of the law.

The HHS Guidelines included procedures for collecting urine samples for drug testing, procedures for transmitting the samples to testing laboratories, testing procedures, procedures for evaluating test results, quality control measures applicable to the laboratories, record keeping and reporting requirements, and standards and procedures for HHS certification of drug-testing laboratories. The basic intent of the guidelines was and remains to safeguard the accuracy and integrity of test results and the privacy of individuals who are tested. Following comment and revision, the scientific and technical aspects of the guidelines remained intact as drafted and were published in the *Federal Register* as the "Mandatory Guidelines for Federal Workplace Drug Testing Programs" on April 11, 1988. In July 1988, utilizing the certification standards developed as part of the "Mandatory Guidelines," a National Laboratory Certification Program was implemented by HHS/NIDA and was administered under contract by the Research Triangle Institute. More than 100 laboratories have been certified in this program since 1988 with approximately 50 remaining certified in 2006.

The U.S. DOT published an interim final rule on November 21, 1988 establishing drug-testing procedures applicable to drug testing for transportation employees under six DOT regulations. These six regulations were published on that same date by the Federal Aviation Administration (FAA), Federal Highway Administration (FHWA), Federal Railroad Administration, U.S. Coast Guard, Urban Mass Transportation Administration, and Research and Special Programs Administration. The interim final rule (49 CFR part 40) followed closely the HHS regulation entitled "Mandatory Guidelines for Federal Workplace Drug Testing Programs." DOT issued its final rule on December 1, 1989 with an implementation date of January 2, 1990. These regulations brought the rest of the transportation modes in line with the railroad industry and, in most aspects, standardized the procedures across the industry. The Congress later passed the Omnibus Transportation Employee Drug Testing Act of 1991. This Act was an extremely important piece of legislation that broadly expanded drug testing in the transportation industry. The impetus for the legislation was a very visible subway accident in New York City where the engineer was found to be under the influence of alcohol. The Act required DOT to prescribe regulations within 1 year to expand the existing DOT drug regulations in aviation, rail, highway, and mass transit industries to cover intrastate as well as interstate transportation and to expand the drug-testing program to include alcohol. Final DOT rules were published in the *Federal Register* in February 1994, which continued to incorporate the HHS "Guidelines" and required implementation by January 1, 1995 for large employers (i.e., >50 covered employees) and January 1, 1996 for small employers. Currently the DOT regulations cover more than 12 million transportation workers nationwide.

Drug testing in the workplace has changed considerably over the last 20 years and the changes have improved the program. The development and scope of regulations related to testing have had an important effect not only to improve the accuracy and reliability of employee drug testing but also to establish the credibility of the testing process and the laboratories' capabilities to routinely perform these tests. The stringent laboratory certification standards imposed on forensic drug-testing laboratories have influenced clinical laboratory medicine, with dramatic improvement over the last decade. A real concern is that the federal regulations may have become too rigid, precluding technological advances. The Substance Abuse and Mental Health Services Administration (SAMHSA), which was mandated oversight of workplace drug testing in 1992, has regularly modified regulations and, most recently, proposed new adaptations in technology in a broad sweeping proposal to include the testing of hair, sweat, and oral fluid in addition to urine specimens. It also proposes the use of on-site tests of urine and oral fluid at the collection site, the establishment of instrumented initial test facilities, and changes in operational standards.[2]

10.1.2 Incidence of Drugs in the Workplace

Good comprehensive statistics regarding drug use and testing incidence have not been developed. The National Household Survey (2003) shows that 19.5 million people over 12 years of age used drugs during the past month. Of these 54.6% used marijuana, 20.6% marijuana and other drugs, and 24.8% used other drugs. Use was predominately in the 14- to 29-year-old age group as follows: 10.9% (14–15), 19.2% (16–17), 23.3% (18–20), 18.3% (21–25), 13.4% (26–29), and 14.9% (all others).

The only comprehensive compilation of drug test data is published by Quest Diagnostics. Its Drug Testing Index is compiled semiannually. Quest Diagnostics is one of the largest providers of workplace drug tests performing more than 12 million tests annually. Its results are the best available statistical indication of trends in the field. Over the years the drug positivity rates have gone from a high in 1988 (13.6%) when drug-testing programs started to 4.5% in 2004. The number of positives has been relatively consistent since 1997 (5.0 to 4.5%); see Table 10.1.1. The positivity rates by drug category for the combined workforce for the last 5 years (2000 to 2004) is shown in Table 10.1.2. Updated revisions and more specific breakdowns of these statistics may be found on the Quest Diagnostics Web site www.questdiagnostics.com.

Table 10.1.1 Annual Positivity Rates for Combined U.S. Workforce (more than 7.2 million tests from January to December 2004)

Year	Drug Positive Rate
1988	13.6%
1989	12.7%
1990	11.0%
1991	8.8%
1992	8.8%
1993	8.4%
1994	7.5%
1995	6.7%
1996	5.8%
1997	5.0%
1998	4.8%
1999	4.6%
2000	4.7%
2001	4.6%
2002	4.4%
2003	4.5%
2004	4.5%

Source: Courtesy of Quest Diagnostics.

Table 10.1.2 Positivity Rates by Drug Category for Combined U.S. Workforce as a Percentage of All Positives (more than 7.2 million tests from January to December 2004)

Drug Category	2004	2003	2002	2001	2000
Acid/base	0.13%	0.18%	0.27%	0.24%	0.08%
Amphetamines	10.2%	9.3%	7.1%	5.9%	5.1%
Barbiturates	2.5%	2.5%	2.6%	2.9%	3.2%
Benzodiazepines	4.5%	4.7%	4.5%	4.5%	3.9%
Cocaine	14.7%	14.6%	14.6%	13.9%	14.4%
Marijuana	54.8%	54.9%	57.6%	60.6%	62.8%
Methadone	1.5%	1.4%	1.1%	0.88%	0.82%
Methaqualone	0.00%	0.00%	0.00%	0.00%	0.00%
Opiates	6.2%	6.4%	5.5%	5.8%	5.4%
Oxidizing adulterants (incl. nitrites)	0.09%	0.19%	0.52%	0.54%	0.92%
PCP	0.38%	0.61%	0.58%	0.59%	0.56%
Propoxyphene	4.4%	4.5%	5.1%	3.5%	2.3%
Substituted	0.66%	0.73%	0.68%	0.51%	0.58%

Source: Courtesy of Quest Diagnostics.

REFERENCES

1. Walsh, J.M., Development and scope of regulated testing. In Workplace Testing, Y.H. Caplan, Ed., *Drug Abuse Handbook,* S.B. Karch, Ed. in Chief. CRC Press, Boca Raton, FL, 1998, 729–736.
2. Department of Health and Human Services, Substance Abuse and Mental Health Services Administration, Proposed Revisions to Mandatory Guidelines for Workplace Drug Testing Programs (69 FR 19673), April 13, 2004.

10.2 FEDERAL REGULATION OF WORKPLACE DRUG
AND ALCOHOL TESTING

10.2.1 An Overview of the Mandatory Guidelines for Federal Workplace Drug Testing Programs

Donna M. Bush, Ph.D., DABFT
Drug Testing Team Leader, Division of Workplace Programs, Center for Substance Abuse Prevention, Substance Abuse and Mental Health Services Administration, Rockville, Maryland

10.2.1.1 History

"The Federal Government, as the largest employer in the world, can and should show the way towards achieving drug-free workplaces through a program designed to offer drug users a helping hand." These words are part of President Reagan's Executive Order (EO) Number 12564,[1] issued September 15, 1986, which served to launch the Federal Drug-Free Workplace Program. This EO authorized the Secretary of Health and Human Services (HHS) to promulgate scientific and technical guidelines for drug testing programs, and required agencies to conduct their drug testing programs in accordance with these guidelines once promulgated. This Federal Drug-Free Workplace Program covers approximately 1.8 million federal employees. Of this total number, approximately 400,000 federal employees and job applicants work in health- and safety-sensitive positions identified as Testing Designated Positions, and are subject to urine drug testing.

The Supplemental Appropriations Act of 1987 (Public Law 100-71, Section 503) outlined the general provisions for drug testing programs within the federal sector, and directed the Secretary of the Department of Health and Human Services (DHHS) to set comprehensive standards for all aspects of laboratory drug testing. The authority to develop and promulgate these standards was delegated to the National Institute on Drug Abuse (NIDA), an institute within the Alcohol, Drug Abuse and Mental Health Administration (ADAMHA). Following the ADAMHA Reorganization Act (Public Law No. 102–321) in 1992, the authority for this oversight now resides within the Center for Substance Abuse Prevention (CSAP), Substance Abuse and Mental Health Services Administration (SAMHSA). The Division of Workplace Programs (DWP) in CSAP, SAMHSA, administers and directs the National Laboratory Certification Program (NLCP), which certifies laboratories to perform drug testing in accordance with the "Mandatory Guidelines for Federal Workplace Drug Testing Programs" (Guidelines). These Guidelines were first published by the Secretary of HHS in the *Federal Register* on April 11, 1988,[2] and were revised and published in the *Federal Register* on June 9, 1994[3] and again on November 13, 1998.[4] Another revision was recently published in the *Federal Register* on April 13, 2004, and now includes specific urine specimen validity testing (SVT) requirements.[5] The intent of these Guidelines is to ensure the accuracy, reliability, and forensic supportability of drug and SVT results as well as protect the privacy of individuals (federal employees) who are tested.

Subpart B of these Guidelines sets scientific and technical requirements for drug testing and forms the framework for the NLCP. Subpart C focuses on specific laboratory requirements and certification of laboratories engaged in drug testing for federal agencies. The Guidelines cover requirements in many aspects of analytical testing, standard operating procedures, quality assurance, and personnel qualifications.

Requirements for a comprehensive drug-free workplace model outlined in the Guidelines[1–5] include:

1. A policy that clearly defines the prohibition against illegal drug use and its consequences
2. Employee education about the dangers of drug use

3. Supervisor training concerning their responsibilities in a Drug-Free Workplace Program
4. A helping hand in the form of an Employee Assistance Program for employees who have a drug problem
5. Provisions for identifying employees who are illegal drug users, including drug testing on a controlled and carefully monitored basis

Several different types of drug testing are performed under federal authority. These include job applicant, accident/unsafe practice, reasonable suspicion, follow-up to treatment, random, and voluntary testing.

Under separate authority and public law, the U.S. Departments of Transportation (DOT) also conducts a similar Drug-Free Workplace Program that applies to more than 250,000 regulated industry employers who employ more than 12 million workers. The Nuclear Regulatory Commission conducts a similar Drug-Free Workplace Program that applies to about 104,000 employees working for its licensees. Both of these programs require that any drug testing performed as part of these Drug-Free Workplace Programs be conducted in a laboratory certified by the U.S. DHHS to perform testing in accordance with the scientific and technical requirements in the Guidelines.

In December 1988, the first ten laboratories were certified by DHHS through the NLCP to perform urine drug testing in accordance with the requirements specified in the Guidelines. As of July 2005, there are 49 certified laboratories in the NLCP. The largest number of laboratories certified at any one time was 91 in 1993. Even though there are fewer NLCP-certified laboratories today, the testing capability of the laboratories overall has greatly increased. This reflects the evolution of the business of drug testing, which includes laboratory chains and individual large-scale laboratories that can consistently and accurately test more than 10,000 specimens/day in accordance with the requirements of the mandatory Guidelines. In 2004, more than 6.5 million specimens were tested under federal requirements.

10.2.1.2 Specimen Collection

It is important to ensure the integrity, security, and proper identification of a donor's urine specimen. The donor's specimen is normally collected in the privacy of a bathroom stall or other partitioned area. Occasionally, a donor may try to avoid detection of drug use by tampering with, adulterating, or substituting their urine specimen. Precautions taken during the collection process include, but are not limited to the following:

1. Placing a bluing (dye) agent in the toilet bowl to deter specimen dilution with toilet bowl water
2. Requiring photo identification of the donor to prevent another individual from providing the specimen
3. Requiring the donor to empty his or her pockets and display the items to the collector
4. Requiring the donor to wash his or her hands prior to the collection
5. Collector remaining close to the donor to deter tampering, adulterating, or substituting by the donor
6. Taking the temperature of the specimen within 4 min of collection

A label that is made of tamper-evident material is used to seal the specimen bottle, and a standardized Federal Custody and Control Form (CCF) is used to identify the individuals who handled the specimen, for what purpose, and when they had possession of the specimen.

The entire collection process must be able to withstand the closest scrutiny and challenges to its integrity, especially if a specimen is reported positive for a drug or metabolite, substituted, adulterated, or invalid.

To ensure uniformity among all federal agency and federally regulated workplace drug testing programs, the use of an OMB-approved federal CCF is required. Based on the experiences of using the current federal CCF for the past several years, SAMHSA and DOT initiated a joint effort to develop a new federal CCF that was easier to use and that more accurately reflected both the collection process and how results were reported by the drug testing laboratories. The federal CCF is a five-page carbonless document, with copies distributed to all parties involved in specimen collection, testing, and reporting.

Copy 1 is the Laboratory Copy and accompanies the specimen(s) to the testing laboratory; Copy 2 is the Medical Review Officer (MRO) Copy and is sent directly to the MRO; Copy 3 is the Collector Copy and is retained by the specimen collector for a period of time; Copy 4 is the Employer Copy and is sent to the Agency representative; Copy 5 is given to the donor when the collection is completed.

An image of Copy 1 is shown in Figure 10.2.1. The entire form, including instructions, may be viewed at http://workplace.samhsa.gov.

Briefly, the Instruction for Completing the Federal Drug Testing Custody and Control Form is as follows:

A. The collector ensures that the name and address of the drug testing laboratory appear on the top of the CCF and the Specimen I.D. number on the top of the CCF matches the Specimen I.D. number on the labels/seals.

B. The collector provides the required information in STEP 1 on the CCF. The collector provides a remark in STEP 2 if the donor refuses to provide his/her SSN or Employee I.D. number.

C. The collector gives a collection container to the donor for providing a specimen.

D. After the donor gives the specimen to the collector, the collector checks the temperature of specimen within 4 minutes and marks the appropriate temperature box in STEP 2 on the CCF. The collector provides a remark if the temperature is outside the acceptable range.

E. The collector checks the split or single specimen collection box. If no specimen is collected, that box is checked and a remark is provided. If it is an observed collection, that box is checked and a remark is provided. If no specimen is collected, Copy 1 is discarded and the remaining copies are distributed as required.

F. The donor watches the collector pouring the specimen from the collection container into the specimen bottle(s), placing the cap(s) on the specimen bottle(s), and affixing the label(s)/seal(s) on the specimen bottle(s).

G. The collector dates the specimen bottle label(s) after they are placed on the specimen bottle(s).

H. Donor initials the specimen bottle label(s) after the label(s) have been placed on the specimen bottle(s).

I. The collector turns to Copy 2 (MRO Copy) and instructs the donor to read the certification statement in STEP 5 and to sign, print name, date, provide phone numbers, and date of birth after reading the certification statement. If the donor refuses to sign the certification statement, the collector provides a remark in STEP 2 on Copy 1.

J. The collector completes STEP 4 (i.e., provides signature, printed name, date, time of collection, and name of delivery service), immediately places the sealed specimen bottle(s) and Copy 1 of the CCF in a leak-proof plastic bag, releases specimen package to the delivery service, and distributes the other copies as required.

DWP publishes a Urine Specimen Collection Handbook for Federal Agency Workplace Drug Testing Programs, available at http://workplace.samhsa.gov, which provides additional guidance to those who will be collecting federal employee urine specimens in accordance with the Guidelines.[6]

10.2.1.3 *Specimen Testing*

The procedures described in the Guidelines include, but are not limited to, collecting a urine specimen, transporting specimens to the laboratories, drug and validity testing of the specimen, evaluating test results by qualified personnel, specifying quality control measures within the labo-

FEDERAL DRUG TESTING CUSTODY AND CONTROL FORM

||||| ||||||| || ||||||| ||||||
1234567

SPECIMEN ID NO.   1234567

STEP 1: COMPLETED BY COLLECTOR OR EMPLOYER REPRESENTATIVE

A. Employer Name, Address, I.D. No.	B. MRO Name, Address, Phone and Fax No.

OMB No. 0930-0158

C. Donor SSN or Employee I.D. No. _____

D. Reason for Test: ☐ Pre-employment ☐ Random ☐ Reasonable Suspicion/Cause ☐ Post Accident
☐ Return to Duty ☐ Follow-up ☐ Other (specify) _____

E. Drug Tests to be Performed: ☐ THC, COC, PCP, OPI, AMP ☐ THC & COC Only ☐ Other (specify) _____

F. Collection Site Address:

Collector Phone No. _____

Collector Fax No. _____

STEP 2: COMPLETED BY COLLECTOR

Read specimen temperature within 4 minutes. Is temperature between 90° and 100° F? ☐ Yes ☐ No, Enter Remark	Specimen Collection: ☐ Split ☐ Single ☐ None Provided (Enter Remark)	Observed (Enter Remark)

REMARKS

PRESS HARD - YOU ARE MAKING MULTIPLE COPIES

STEP 3: Collector affixes bottle seal(s) to bottle(s). Collector dates seal(s). Donor initials seal(s). Donor completes STEP 5 on Copy 2 (MRO Copy)

STEP 4: CHAIN OF CUSTODY - INITIATED BY COLLECTOR AND COMPLETED BY LABORATORY

I certify that the specimen given to me by the donor identified in the certification section on Copy 2 of this form was collected, labeled, sealed and released to the Delivery Service noted in accordance with applicable Federal requirements.

X _____ AM PM ► **SPECIMEN BOTTLE(S) RELEASED TO:**

Signature of Collector   Time of Collection

_____ (PRINT) Collector's Name (First, MI, Last)   Date (Mo./Day/Yr.) ► _____ Name of Delivery Service Transferring Specimen to Lab

RECEIVED AT LAB:

X _____ ►

Signature of Accessioner

Primary Specimen Bottle Seal Intact
☐ Yes
☐ No, Enter Remark Below

SPECIMEN BOTTLE(S) RELEASED TO:

_____ (PRINT) Accessioner's Name (First, MI, Last)   Date (Mo./Day/Yr.) ►

STEP 5a: PRIMARY SPECIMEN TEST RESULTS - COMPLETED BY PRIMARY LABORATORY

☐ NEGATIVE ☐ POSITIVE for: ☐ MARIJUANA METABOLITE ☐ CODEINE ☐ AMPHETAMINE ☐ ADULTERATED
☐ DILUTE ☐ COCAINE METABOLITE ☐ MORPHINE ☐ METHAMPHETAMINE ☐ SUBSTITUTED
☐ REJECTED FOR TESTING ☐ PCP ☐ 6-ACETYLMORPHINE ☐ INVALID RESULT

REMARKS _____

TEST LAB (if different from above) _____

I certify that the specimen identified on this form was examined upon receipt, handled using chain of custody procedures, analyzed, and reported in accordance with applicable Federal requirements.

X _____ _____ _____
Signature of Certifying Scientist   (PRINT) Certifying Scientist's Name (First, MI, Last)   Date (Mo./Day/Yr.)

STEP 5b: SPLIT SPECIMEN TEST RESULTS - (IF TESTED) COMPLETED BY SECONDARY LABORATORY

| Laboratory Name | ☐ RECONFIRMED ☐ FAILED TO RECONFIRM - REASON _____ I certify that the split specimen identified on this form was examined upon receipt, handled using chain of custody procedures, analyzed, and reported in accordance with applicable Federal requirements. | |
| Laboratory Address | X _____ Signature of Certifying Scientist | _____ (PRINT) Certifying Scientist's Name (First, MI, Last) | Date (Mo./Day/Yr.) |

||||| ||||||| || ||||||| ||||||
PEFI 1234567   A
SPECIMEN ID NO.

PLACE OVER CAP

1234567
SPECIMEN BOTTLE SEAL

Date (Mo. Day Yr.)
Donor's Initials

||||| ||||||| || ||||||| ||||||
PEFI 1234567   B (SPLIT)
SPECIMEN ID NO.

PLACE OVER CAP

1234567
SPECIMEN BOTTLE SEAL

Date (Mo. Day Yr.)
Donor's Initials

COPY 1 - LABORATORY COPY

Figure 10.2.1 Copy 1 of federal CCF.

ratory, specifying record keeping and reporting of laboratory results to an MRO, and standards for certification of drug testing laboratories by SAMHSA.

The cornerstone of the analytical testing requirements specified in the Guidelines is the "two-test" concept: (1) an initial test is performed for each class of drugs tested and a drug(s) for creatinine, pH, and oxidizing adulterants; if an initial test is positive for drugs or outside defined limits for SVT, (2) a confirmatory test using a different chemical principle is performed on a different aliquot of the original specimen. Specifically, the initial test technology requires an immunoassay for drugs and colorimetric test for creatinine, pH, and oxidizing adulterants. The confirmatory testing technology requires gas chromatography/mass spectrometry (GC/MS) for drugs, and potentiometry using a pH meter, multiwavelength spectrophotometry, ion chromatography, atomic absorption spectrophotometry, inductively coupled plasma mass spectrometry, capillary electrophoresis, or GC/MS for SVT.

The initial test cutoffs as published in the Guidelines[5] are as follows:

Drug Class	Cutoff (ng/ml)
Marijuana metabolites	50
Cocaine metabolites	300
Opiate metabolites	2000
Phencyclidine	25
Amphetamines	1000

The confirmatory test cutoffs as published in the Guidelines[5] are as follows:

Drug	Cutoff (ng/ml)
Marijuana metabolite[a]	15
Cocaine metabolite[b]	150
Opiates	
Morphine	2000
Codeine	2000
6-Acetylmorphine[c]	10
Phencyclidine	25
Amphetamines	
Amphetamine	500
Methamphetamine[d]	500

[a] delta-9-Tetrahydrocannabinol-9-carboxylic acid.
[b] Benzoylecgonine.
[c] 6-Acetylmorphine tested when the morphine concentration is greater than or equal to 2000 ng/ml.
[d] Specimen must also contain 200 ng/ml amphetamine.

SVT for federal employee specimens collected under the Guidelines is required as of November 1, 2004. This includes, but is not limited to, determining creatinine concentration, the specific gravity of every specimen for which the creatinine concentration is less than 20 mg/dl, pH, and performing one or more validity tests for oxidizing adulterants. A much more complete discussion of specimen testing and reporting results can be found in the Guidelines.[6]

As part of an overall quality assurance program, there are three levels of quality control (QC) required of each certified laboratory:

1. Internal open and blind samples constituting 10% of the daily, routine sample workload (these are constructed by the laboratory as part of their daily testing protocols).
2. External open performance testing samples, which are distributed quarterly (these are prepared by the government under contract).
3. Double-blind QC samples, which constitute 1% of the total number of specimens submitted to the laboratory for analysis, not to exceed 100 per quarter; 80% of these samples are negative for drugs.
4. Federal agencies are required to procure and submit these samples from reputable suppliers.

10.2.1.4 Laboratory Result Reporting to and Review of Laboratory Results by an MRO

After accurate and reliable urine drug test results are completed by a SAMHSA-certified laboratory, the Guidelines require these results to be reported to an agency's MRO. As defined in the Guidelines, the MRO is a licensed physician responsible for receiving laboratory results generated by an agency's drug testing program who has knowledge of substance abuse disorders and who has appropriate medical training to interpret and evaluate an individual's positive test result together with the medical records provided to the MRO by the donor, his or her medical history, and any other relevant biomedical information. The MRO must contact the donor when the donor's specimen is reported by the laboratory as drug positive, adulterated, substituted, or invalid, and give the donor the opportunity to discuss the results prior to making a final decision to verify the test result. The donor is given the opportunity to request a retest when his or her specimen is reported as positive, substituted, or adulterated. The retest (i.e., an aliquot of the single specimen collection or Bottle B of a split specimen collection) is performed at a second certified laboratory, with specific procedures applied, depending on the results reported by the first testing laboratory.

A positive test result does not automatically identify an individual as an illegal drug user. The MRO evaluates all relevant medical information provided to him or her by the donor who tested positive. If there was a legitimate, alternative medical explanation for the presence of the drug(s) in the donor's urine, the test result is reported as negative to the employer; if there is no alternative medical explanation for the presence of drug(s) in the donor's urine, the MRO reports the result as positive to the agency/employer. Additional instruction and guidance for evaluating adulterated, substituted, and invalid test results for federal employee specimens is provided in the MRO Manual for Federal Agency Drug Testing Programs.[7]

It is also necessary that negative laboratory results be reviewed by an MRO. Laboratory results for double blind performance test samples (many of which are negative) are reported to the MRO in the same manner as results for donor specimens. In this manner, negative laboratory results are evaluated as part of ongoing quality control programs initiated prior to specimen submission to the laboratory.

10.2.1.5 Laboratory Participation in the National Laboratory Certification Program

Application

A laboratory applying to become part of the NLCP must complete a comprehensive application form, which reflects in detail each section of the Laboratory Information Checklist and General Laboratory Inspection Reports. Evaluation of this completed application must show that the laboratory is equipped and staffed in a manner to test specimens in compliance with the Guidelines' requirements in order for the laboratory to proceed with the initial certification process.

In essence, the Guidelines promulgate forensic drug testing standards for the evaluation of a specimen provided by a federal employee, on which critical employment decisions will be made. The processes that govern this testing are regulatory in nature, designed to ensure that this testing is accurate, reliable, and forensically supportable.

Performance Testing

As part of the initial certification process, the applicant laboratory must successfully analyze three sets of 25 samples (minimum), in a sequential order. The progress of this phase of the certification process is determined by the successful identification and quantification of analytes by the laboratory. If the first two sets of 25 samples are successfully completed, the third set of 25 samples is scheduled for receipt, accessioning, and analysis during the initial laboratory inspection site visit. As part of the maintenance certification process, each certified laboratory must successfully analyze a set of 25 samples (20 drug related and 5 SVT related) sent on a quarterly basis by the NLCP. There are five different types of samples developed by the NLCP to ensure accurate and reliable analyte identification and quantification for drugs and validity testing:

1. Routine samples, which may contain an analyte specified in the Guidelines, and are screened and confirmed in accordance with established cutoffs
2. Routine negative samples, which may contain a drug analyte specified in the Guidelines, but at a concentration less than or equal to 10% of cutoff
3. Routine plus samples, which may contain an analyte specified in the Guidelines and interfering and/or cross-reacting substances
4. Routine retest samples
5. Retest samples with interfering substances

For details on the evaluation of the performance test results, please refer directly to Section 3.18 of the April 13, 2004 Guidelines.[5]

Laboratory Inspection

The laboratory facility must be inspected and found acceptable in accordance with the conditions stated in the Guidelines and further detailed in the Laboratory Information Checklist, General Laboratory Inspection Report, Computer Systems Report, and Records Audit Report. Inspectors are trained by the NLCP staff (SAMHSA/DWP technical staff and their contractors) in the use of the detailed NLCP Laboratory Information Checklist and Reports, and the NLCP Manual for Laboratories and Inspectors.

Prior to the inspection, the laboratory is required to submit detailed information concerning its operations. This information is provided to the inspectors prior to the actual inspection. In this way, the inspectors become familiar with the laboratory operation prior to arrival. A brief description of each section completed by the laboratory follows:

A. Instructions to Laboratory
B. Laboratory Information — Physical aspects of the laboratory such as location, hours of operation, staffing, specimen testing throughput, and licenses
C. Laboratory Procedures — Type of analytical equipment, calibration procedures, reagent kits, derivatives and ions monitored for each drug analyte, as well as similar information relating to validity testing

In addition, there are questions relating to certification and reporting of results, electronic reporting of results, as well as a description of the Laboratory Information Management System (LIMS).

In the past few years, a number of significant updates have been implemented in the NLCP inspection program. These improvements were the result of a careful review of the program experience over several years and also reflected the reality of market consolidation and growth that significantly increased the number of specimens tested under the Guidelines. This workload increase made it difficult for inspectors to review sufficient non-negative test results (i.e., positive, adulterated, invalid, and substituted) during the scheduled laboratory inspection. To address this issue, the NLCP increased the number of inspectors and hours of inspections for some of the laboratory inspection categories. By increasing the number of inspectors, the percentage of non-negative test results reviewed by each inspection team was enhanced in the larger laboratories. The number of inspectors for Categories I and II remained unchanged. That is, a Category I inspection consisted of two inspectors (one checklist inspector and one data auditor) performing a 2-day inspection, and a Category II inspection consisted of three inspectors (one checklist inspector and two data auditors) performing a 2-day inspection. For the larger laboratories (i.e., Categories III to V) the NLCP increased the number of inspectors, and greatly enhanced the percentage of non-negative test results reviewed by the inspection teams. A Category III inspection now requires a team of four inspectors (two checklist inspectors and two data auditors, rather than the three inspectors previously inspecting this category of laboratory) conducting a 3-day inspection. A Category IV inspection has a team of five inspectors (two checklist inspectors and three data auditors) conducting a 3-day inspection. A new Category V inspection was established for laboratories with large workloads, usually testing more than 2000 regulated specimens per day. A Category V inspection has a team of nine inspectors (three checklist inspectors and six data auditors) conducting a 3-day inspection.

For those laboratories that use corporate LIMS not under the direct day-to-day observation and control of the responsible persons (RPs) of the laboratories that it serves, there will be a special inspection of the LIMS at the facility where the LIMS is located. This special inspection will be a 1-day inspection using two inspectors, with one a LIMS professional. Each corporate LIMS facility will undergo this inspection regardless of the number of laboratories that it serves. This new approach began in January 2005.

Historically, the NLCP has primarily focused the inspection on the procedures of the laboratory. The NLCP has now balanced that focus with an increased examination of the laboratory's forensic product. To accomplish this, a major audit component has been incorporated into NLCP inspections. To facilitate these audits, HHS requires each laboratory to submit a list to the NLCP staff of the non-negative (i.e., drug positive, adulterated, invalid, substituted, and rejected for testing) primary specimens and split specimens reported for a 6-month period prior to an inspection. Specific guidance on the format and information to be included on the list is provided to the laboratories. For each of the following specimen categories, the laboratory must submit a *separate* spreadsheet in a workbook to the NLCP:

1. Positive for delta-9-tetrahydrocannabinol-9-carboxylic acid
2. Positive for benzoylecgonine
3. Positive for opiates (morphine, codeine, and/or 6-acetylmorphine)
4. Positive for amphetamines (amphetamine and/or methamphetamine and d-methamphetamine if performed)
5. Positive for phencyclidine
6. Adulterated
7. Invalid test
8. Substituted
9. Rejected for testing

NLCP technical staff direct the laboratory to make available all the batch data and documentation for a selected number of those non-negative and split specimen test results to facilitate review by the inspectors. A specific number of non-negative specimens (NNS) are identified for in-depth review consisting of all analytical test records and chain of custody documentation. The number of NNSs selected for this in-depth information review is determined by the category of the laboratory and is as follows: 40 for Category I, 120 for Category II, 200 for Category III, 310 for Category IV, and 650 for Category V laboratories. Additionally, the same in-depth information review for 40 PT samples is conducted at each laboratory regardless of category.

As a key part of updating the NLCP laboratory inspection system, the inspector cadre was reviewed with the goal of using a smaller core group of inspectors, each of whom has committed to participating in multiple inspections per year. This has significantly enhanced the consistency and uniformity in the NLCP inspection process. NLCP inspectors now are required to perform at least two to three inspections per year, to document active participation in forensic toxicology/workplace drug testing/regulated drug testing, and to attend mandatory NLCP inspector training on an annual basis.

The document previously known as the Laboratory Inspection Checklist was reorganized into two documents, from which two reports are generated by the inspection team. These two reports are the General Laboratory Inspection Report and the Records Audit Report. There were also some significant changes in the roles and configurations of NLCP inspection teams that represent the combined observations of the individual team members. Although each inspector does not complete a separate checklist, all team members tour the laboratory and participate in documenting/verifying any checklist deficiencies.

Inspectors assigned to the roles of "Lead Inspector" and "Inspector" use the General Laboratory Inspection Report to inspect the laboratory's current standard operating procedures (SOP) and forensic operations and may aid in the review of the NLCP PT records, and method validation. The Lead Inspector has the responsibility to finalize and submit the team's summary General Laboratory Inspection Report to RTI, Research Triangle Park, NC, the contractor currently handling the technical and logistical aspects of the National Laboratory Certification Program for SAMHSA/HHS. Inspectors assigned to the roles of "Lead Auditor" and "Auditor" use the Data Audit Inspection Report and review a number of non-negative test results (i.e., positive, adulterated, invalid, and substituted), NLCP PT records, and method validation records. The Lead Auditor has the responsibility to finalize and submit the team's summary Data Audit Inspection Report and NNS Review List to the NLCP.

The checklist inspector(s) review and document all aspects of forensic urine drug testing processes and procedures at that laboratory for program review and evaluation for compliance with the minimum standards of the Guidelines. The lead checklist inspector prepares a summary report reflecting the 12 sections of the inspection checklist and one section of the Computer System checklist reviewed during their site visit along with an Inspection Evaluation Summary. A brief description of each section follows:

D. Chain of Custody — Assesses laboratory practices to verify specimen identity, maintain specimen integrity, secure specimens, and maintain chain of custody during specimen receiving/accessioning, aliquoting, initial drug testing, SVT, confirmation testing, and specimen and aliquot disposal

E. Accessioning — Assesses laboratory practices to accept or reject specimens, evaluate specimen integrity, handle split specimens, maintain specimen integrity

F. Security — Assesses laboratory practices to control and document specimen and record access

G. Quality Control Materials and Reagents — Assess laboratory practices to prepare or procure and verify drug or SVT QC samples, properly identify them, and establish acceptable performance limits

H. Quality Assurance: Review of QC Results — Assess laboratory practices to review control results so as to detect assay problems

I. Equipment and Maintenance — Assess laboratory practices for checking and maintaining all laboratory equipment

J. Specimen Validity Tests — Assess laboratory practices for handling of aliquots of specimens during validity testing, performing initial and confirmatory testing as required (at a minimum a test for creatinine, pH, and oxidizing adulterant on all specimens), applying appropriate cutoffs, analyzing appropriate QC samples for both initial and confirmatory testing as required

K. Initial Drug Tests — Assess laboratory practices to analyze specimens with specific immunoassay methods and analyze appropriate QC samples

L. Confirmatory Drug Tests — Assess laboratory practices to analyze specimens with appropriate GC/MS procedures and analyze appropriate QC samples

M. Certification and Reporting — Assess laboratory practices to report negative and non-negative results to the MRO with both the federal CCF, and electronically if so desired

N. Standard Operating Procedures, Procedures Manual — Assess laboratory procedure manual for content, comprehensiveness, agreement with day-to-day observed operations of the laboratory, determine availability to staff as a routine reference, and any modifications made to reflect changes in current practice in the laboratory

O. Personnel — Assess qualifications of the RP, scientists who certify the accuracy and reliability of results, and supervisory staff; assesses staffing adequacy of these personnel in relationship to the number of specimens analyzed

P. Laboratory Computer Systems — Assess laboratory policies and procedures for the validation and security of the LIM system, the handling of electronic records and reports, the ability to provide audit trails, monitoring the LIM system, and responding to incidents and providing disaster recovery, as well as documenting the qualifications of the LIMS personnel

The auditor(s) extensively review the laboratory's chain of custody documentation, analytical data, and reported results for non-negative specimens (i.e., positive, adulterated, substituted, invalid, rejected for testing) reported in the defined 6-month period (1 month prior to the last inspection to 1 month prior to the current inspection). The lead auditor prepares a summary report reflecting the four sections of the records audit report along with an Inspection Evaluation Summary and Summary of Issues. A brief description of each section follows:

R. Specimen Records — Review and evaluate specimen records for completion of chain of custody documents, for identity of specimens, calibrators and controls, for the individuals performing and reviewing the testing, evidence that the certifying scientists who reported the results to the MROs reviewed all appropriate information

S. Method Validation, Periodic Re-Verification — Review and evaluate revised test methods, and both SVT and confirmatory drug assays for periodic re-verification for levels of detection, linearity, and specificity

T. NLCP Performance Test Records — Review and evaluate the NLCP PT records to determine if they support the reported results and if all remediation to PT errors was taken and acceptable

U. Reports — Review and evaluate non-negative specimen reports, both hard copy and electronic, to determine if they are in accordance with NLCP guidance

The laboratory's first (initial) inspection is performed by two NLCP-trained inspectors. Prior to their arrival at the laboratory site, the inspectors are provided copies of the information supplied by the laboratory concerning its operations, its standard operating procedures, and its testing procedures.

The inspectors complete sections of the checklist similar to those completed by the inspection team for a maintenance inspection and submit the completed document to the NLCP. A summary, or critique, is prepared from the report by an individual independent of that laboratory's inspection. The items in the critique are then evaluated for compliance with the minimum requirements of the Guidelines. It is necessary that a laboratory's operation be consistent with good forensic laboratory practice. Once all requirements are met, the laboratory is certified by the Secretary, DHHS, as being able to perform drug testing of federal employees' specimens in compliance with the Guidelines. A letter is sent to the laboratory conveying its certification in the NLCP.

Then, 3 months after its initial certification, the laboratory is again inspected, with a broadened focus, now evaluating both practice and the results reported by the laboratory. A critique developed from the individual checklist and audit reports is developed by an individual independent of that laboratory's inspection. The issues in the critique are then evaluated for compliance with the minimum requirements of the Guidelines. It is necessary that a laboratory's operation be consistent with good forensic laboratory practice. If all requirements are met or there are minor easily correctable deficiencies, the inspection critique is sent to the laboratory. A cover letter may also be included, which outlines issues that must be addressed within a defined timeframe. After successful completion of this inspection, a 6-month cycle of site inspections begins. The number of inspectors sent to the laboratory for an inspection depends on the resources necessary to adequately evaluate the laboratory's operation. These resources are allocated based on the laboratory's personnel involved in accessioning and certification, the number of specimens performed under the laboratory's certification, and the number of non-negative specimens reported by the laboratory.

During the maintenance phase of a laboratory's certification, if all requirements are met or there are minor easily correctable deficiencies, the inspection critique is sent to the laboratory. A cover letter may also be included, which outlines issues that must be addressed within a defined time frame. A laboratory continues its certified status as long as its operation is in compliance with the Guidelines and consistent with good forensic laboratory practice. Since participation in the NLCP is a business decision on the part of a laboratory and is voluntary, a laboratory may choose to withdraw from the NLCP. Upon such voluntary withdrawal from the NLCP, a laboratory must inform its clients that it is no longer certified in the NLCP and cease to advertise itself as an NLCP-certified laboratory.

Suspension of Certification

If significant deficiencies in the laboratory's procedures are found, an evaluation of these deficiencies is performed by the NLCP, the program staff in the DWP, and the Office of the General Counsel. A report is prepared for the Director, DWP. If it is determined that there is imminent harm to the government and its employees, action may be taken by the Secretary to immediately suspend the laboratory's certification to perform drug testing of federal, federally regulated, and private sector specimens tested in accordance with the Guidelines. The period and terms of suspension depend on the facts and circumstances of the suspension and the need to ensure accurate and reliable drug testing of federal employees.

Revocation of Certification

Several factors may be considered by the Secretary in determining whether revocation is necessary. Among these are (1) unsatisfactory performance of employee drug testing, (2) unsatisfactory results of performance testing and/or laboratory inspections, (3) federal drug testing contract violations, (4) conviction for any criminal offense committed incident to operation of the laboratory, and (5) other causes that affect the accuracy and reliability of drug test results from that laboratory.

10.2.1.6 Conclusion

Illicit drug use and abuse continues to affect safety and security in the American workplace. Data from the 1995 National Household Survey on Drug Abuse[8] reveal that there were 12.8 million current (or past month) users of illicit drugs. Since that time, there has been an increase in drug use and abuse. In 2003, the last year for which this report is available,[9] the number of individuals, 12 or older, indicating current drug use was 19.4 million individuals.

Tragic events serve as examples of how drug abuse in the workplace can affect society and cause long-term environmental and economic consequences. Examples of such tragedies where substance abuse in the workplace was responsible for death and destruction include the 1986 railroad accident in Chase, MD, the 1991 subway accident in New York City, and the 1989 environmental disaster in Prince William Sound, AK, caused by the grounding of the *Exxon Valdez* oil tanker.

REFERENCES

1. Executive Order 12564, Drug-Free Federal Workplace, *Federal Register*, 51(180), 32889–32893, September 15, 1986, available at http://workplace.samhsa.gov.

2. Mandatory Guidelines for Federal Workplace Drug-Testing Programs, *Federal Register,* 53(69), 11970–11989, April 11, 1988, available at http://workplace.samhsa.gov.

3. Mandatory Guidelines for Federal Workplace Drug-Testing Programs, *Federal Register,* 59(110), 29908–29931, June 9, 1994, available at http://workplace.samhsa.gov.

4. Mandatory Guidelines for Federal Workplace Drug-Testing Programs, *Federal Register,* 63(219), 63483–63484, November 14, 1998, available at http://workplace.samhsa.gov.

5. Mandatory Guidelines and Proposed Revisions to Mandatory Guidelines for Federal Workplace Drug-Testing Programs, *Federal Register,* 69(71), 19644–19673, April 13, 2004, available at http://workplace.samhsa.gov.

6. Urine Specimen Collection Handbook for Federal Workplace Drug Testing Programs, Division of Workplace Programs, Center for Substance Abuse Prevention, Substance Abuse and Mental Health Services Administration, U.S. Department of Health and Human Services, available at http://workplace.samhsa.gov.

7. Medical Review Officer Manual for Federal Employee Drug Testing Programs, Division of Workplace Programs, Center for Substance Abuse Prevention, Substance Abuse and Mental Health Services Administration, U.S. Department of Health and Human Services, available at http://workplace.samhsa.gov.

8. National Household Survey on Drug Abuse: Main Findings 1995, Office of Applied Studies, Substance Abuse and Mental Health Services Administration, DHHS Publication Number (SMA) 97-3127, 1997, available at http://www.oas.samhsa.gov.

9. National Survey on Drug Use and Health: Main Findings 2003, Office of Applied Studies, Substance Abuse and Mental Health Services Administration, DHHS Publication Number (SMA) 04-3964, 2004, available at http://www.oas.samhsa.gov.

10.2.2 The Department of Transportation's Workplace Testing Program

Kenneth C. Edgell, M.S.
Past Director (2001–2004), Office of Drug and Alcohol Policy and Compliance, U.S. Department of Transportation, Washington, D.C.

The Department of Transportation (DOT) oversees the largest drug- and alcohol-testing program in the country. The DOT rules affect more than 12 million transportation employees across the U.S. The program also has international impact in that all motor carriers and some railroad workers whose work brings them into the U.S., either from Canada or Mexico, are subject to the same testing requirements as their American counterparts.

The overall responsibility for management and coordination of the DOT program resides with the Office of the Secretary of Transportation (OST), an Executive Cabinet position appointed by the president. Compliance and enforcement within the different transportation industries are the responsibility of the DOT agency that has regulatory authority over the particular industry. Those DOT agencies are the Federal Aviation Administration (FAA), Federal Motor Carrier Safety Administration (FMCSA), Federal Railroad Administration (FRA), Federal Transit Administration (FTA), and Pipeline and Hazardous Materials Safety Administration (PHMSA).

Safety has been the highest priority for the Secretary of Transportation since Congress established the department in 1966. One of the means used by the Secretary to ensure DOT maintains the highest degree of safety possible is to subject transportation workers to drug and alcohol testing. The workers who are tested have direct impact on the safety of the traveling public or the safety of those potentially affected by the transportation of hazardous products, such as gas and oil pipeline operations. Any worker, who has a positive test, or other drug and alcohol violation, becomes ineligible to continue performing the duties of his or her safety job. In order for the individual to return to a safety job in transportation, that person must satisfactorily complete certain DOT return-to-duty requirements.

Since the outset of the DOT program, there have been a number of legal challenges from those who oppose drug testing. However, because safety is its sole reason for existing, court decisions have allowed the testing to continue without any major setbacks. The Supreme Court, in fact, found a compelling government need "in an industry that is regulated pervasively to ensure safety."[1] So, the program continues. As might be expected, most states that have developed statutes regarding nonregulated testing have referred to the DOT program as the standard of practice they would also follow.

10.2.2.1 Background

The Department of Transportation drug and alcohol testing rules were an outgrowth of a highly visible and tragic transportation accident that occurred in 1987. The investigation of the accident revealed that employees in safety jobs, regulated by DOT (in this case train crew members), admitted using marijuana and alcohol prior to the accident. In response to the findings of the accident investigation, Senators Earnest Hollings (D-SC) and John Danforth (R-MO) sponsored legislation requiring drug and alcohol testing in the rail, aviation, and trucking industries. DOT, feeling the obvious impact of the accident and the duty to respond to the public, did not wait for the passage of the bill, but instead implemented drug testing under its own authority in 1989.

The action of DOT appeared to have been insightful in the years to follow. In August 1991, another deadly transportation accident occurred. Barely 2 months later, the Hollings-Danforth bill, which had been stymied in Congress for more than 4 years, was passed and signed into law by then-President George H.W. Bush. That legislation, cited as the "Omnibus Transportation Employee Testing Act of 1991" (OTETA),[2] required drug and alcohol testing of employees occupying safety-sensitive jobs in the transportation industries of aviation, trucking, railroads, and mass transit "in the interests of safety." While the gas and oil pipeline industry and the U.S. Coast Guard's (USCG) maritime industry were not mentioned in OTETA, testing within those industries also began, and continues, under the authority granted to DOT as a government agency with regulatory responsibility.

Like most laws, OTETA provided a general overview of what Congress expected to occur. It provided high-level instructions on who would be tested and for what reasons, how the tests would be conducted, and what would happen if and when someone tested positive. With that basic guidance, the statute put the burden of prescribing the remainder of the detail (i.e., the regulations) on the Secretary of Transportation. To fully meet the requirements of OTETA — and develop regulations that were as consistent as possible across all of DOT — the Secretary established the Office of Drug and Alcohol Policy and Compliance (ODAPC) to manage the development effort for workplace drug and alcohol testing.

ODAPC is a "small" office (staffing has never exceeded more than ten people) whose mission is to ensure that the drug and alcohol testing policies and goals of the Secretary are developed and carried out in a consistent, efficient, and effective manner within the transportation industries for the ultimate safety and protection of the traveling public. This is accomplished through program review, compliance evaluation, and the issuance of consistent guidance material for DOT Operating Administrations (OAs) and for their regulated industries. The director of ODAPC is a "political appointee," in that as the administration changes, the director changes; the staff are career employees. Information about this office, along with the most current updates of program documents, can be found at the ODAPC Web site: www.dot.gov/ost/dapc/.

49 CFR Part 40, the "Procedures for Transportation Workplace **Drug** and **Alcohol Testing** Programs,"[3] was developed by ODAPC. With this document, DOT set the standard by which all of its required drug and alcohol testing would be conducted. Such a standard assures that whether the employee is an airline pilot, truck driver, or railroad engineer, their drug and alcohol tests are conducted and reviewed using the same procedures. This regulation also sets the criteria that must be met before a person can return to safety-sensitive work after a drug or alcohol violation. Better

Table 10.2.1   Number of Federally Regulated Employers and
Employees Subject to Testing

Industry	Government Agency	No. Employers	No. Employees
Aviation	FAA	7,200	525,000
Highway	FMCSA	650,000	10,941,000
Railroad	FRA	650	97,000
Transit	FTA	2,600	250,000
Pipeline	PHMSA	2,450	190,000
Maritime	USCG[5]	12,000	132,000
Totals		674,900	12,135,000

known simply as "Part 40," this regulation, or rule (the terms are used interchangeably) has become the standard for drug and alcohol testing in the workplaces across the U.S. ODAPC is responsible for providing any authoritative interpretations, if and when they are necessary, on Part 40.

In 1994, also in response to OTETA, six agencies (or "modes," as they are known) within DOT also published testing regulations.[4] These regulations covered who would be subject to drug and alcohol tests, when and why those tests would occur, and what responsibilities the transportation employers would bear in ensuring that the program was implemented properly. By the end of calendar year 2005, the scope of DOT testing covered approximately 12.1 million transportation workers (Table 10.2.1). It is estimated that out of this total population about 7,000,000 drug tests are conducted each year under DOT authority. This figure represents approximately 20% of the drug tests conducted in this country on an annual basis. The remaining 80% of the testing falls under "non-regulated" status, where companies of their own volition, not due to any government mandate, conduct tests. The number of alcohol tests conducted each year under DOT authority is far less than the number of drug tests; this number could be as little as 1,000,000 tests per year.

10.2.2.2   DOT Relationship with Health and Human Services

DOT drug testing follows the guidelines established by the Department of Health and Human Services (HHS). HHS was tasked[6] during, the Reagan Administration's "War on Drugs," to develop standards for conducting drug tests on federal employees who occupied positions of a safety- or security-related nature. Ultimately, HHS determined which drugs to test for and how laboratories should conduct the tests, including what cutoffs to use. HHS also established specific standards for certifying the laboratories to conduct drug tests for federal agencies. This material is published in an oddly titled regulation called the "Mandatory Guidelines."[7] More detail on the content of the HHS Guidelines can be found in elsewhere in this volume (see Section 10.2.1).

OTETA required DOT to "develop requirements that, for laboratories and testing procedures for controlled substances, incorporate the Department Health and Human Services scientific and technical guidelines dated April 11, 1988, and any amendments to those guidelines, including mandatory guidelines." With that direction, DOT has taken most of the testing requirements contained in the HHS Guidelines, either by reference or by actually repeating the language, and incorporated them into Part 40 for those entities subject to DOT rules. This approach may seem a little repetitious, but it does allow those having to implement the programs not to have to maintain proficiency with two sets of drug testing rules issued by two government agencies.

The DOT drug-testing program is a laboratory-based urine-testing program, exclusively. While much ado was made of an "alternative specimen" proposal issued by HHS in 2004, which proposed allowing federal agencies to collect and test specimens other than urine (i.e., hair, oral fluid, and sweat), those specimens are not allowed for use under the DOT rules. Neither is any sort of "on-site" test. In fact, the HHS proposal does not apply to DOT.

For the record: Regardless of what conclusion HHS comes to with respect to "alternative specimens," the DOT drug test program will not change until DOT issues a change to its rule — 49 CFR Part 40. Changing any government rule takes time and includes a public notice that seeks public comment. Prior to issuing a final rule, DOT will publish a Notice of Proposed Rulemaking (NPRM). (The NPRM is the document that will solicit public comment.) Complicated rulemaking, which would be the case if additional specimens were required for use by the DOT program, could take several years to finalize. Bottom line: Any utilization of alternative specimens in DOT drug testing is uncertain at this time. It may be an appropriate subject for a future edition of this text.

The remainder of this section provides a general summary of Part 40. For further understanding or more detailed information on a particular subject, especially for the purposes of trying to implement a DOT program, the reader should obtain a copy of the rule. It is written in what the government refers to as "plain language," rather than gobbledygook, a style of writing more reminiscent of past federal offerings. The regulation is divided into functional sections and, while somewhat lengthy, is fairly easy to follow and understand.

10.2.2.3 *Program Responsibility*

The responsibility to assure that drug and alcohol testing is carried out according to the requirements of DOT lies with the transportation employers. Sometimes referred to as an "unfunded mandate," the U.S. Congress, through the OTETA statute, mandated drug and alcohol testing for certain transportation industries, and instructed the Secretary of Transportation to develop the rules under which each industry must abide. However, neither DOT nor any of its agencies provides funding to transportation employers to offset any of the program costs. The DOT rules instruct transportation employers to implement this very comprehensive program and then hold the employers responsible for compliance. Employers are expected to absorb the costs; the benefit is a safer workplace.

Transportation employers are free to contract out any portion of the drug and alcohol testing program functions; however, employers cannot outsource their compliance responsibilities. *Service agents* is the term given to those who contract directly or indirectly with employers to accomplish the tasks set forth in DOT rules. Service agents include collectors, laboratories, medical review officers (MROs), breath alcohol technicians, consortia/third party administrators, and substance abuse professionals.

10.2.2.4 *Safety-Sensitive Employees*

OTETA required each DOT administration to specify those under its regulatory purview who are subject to testing. These individuals occupy positions known as "covered functions," or, more universally, as "safety-sensitive" positions (Table 10.2.2). A person who occupies a safety-sensitive job and performs its functions, whether on a full-time, part-time, or intermittent basis, is subject to testing.

Table 10.2.2   Government Agencies and Safety-Sensitive Job Positions

Industry (Mode)	Safety-Sensitive Job Positions
Aviation (FAA)	Flight crew members, flight attendants, flight instructors, air traffic controllers, aircraft dispatchers, maintenance personnel, and screening and ground security coordinator personnel
Highways (FMCSA)	Commercial motor vehicle operators
Railroads (FRA)	Hours-of-service employees (engine, train and signal services, dispatchers, and operators)
Mass Transit (FTA)	Vehicle operators, dispatchers, mechanics, and safety personnel (carrying firearms)
Oil and Gas Pipeline (PHMSA)	Pipeline operations and maintenance personnel, and emergency response personnel
Maritime (USCG)	Maritime crew members (operating a commercial vessel)

10.2.2.5 *Reasons for Testing*

The DOT drug-testing program is a deterrence-based program, testing for prohibited use of illegal drugs regardless of when the employee might use the drugs. The DOT alcohol-testing program is more a fitness-for-duty program; testing for prohibited use of a legal substance in and around the time a person is working. Drug tests may be conducted at any time the employee is at work, while alcohol tests are only conducted prior to, during, or just after the performance of safety-sensitive functions. OTETA requires DOT to have specific categories of testing, or "reasons for test." There are six testing categories: pre-employment, post-accident, random, reasonable suspicion, return-to-duty, and follow-up.

Pre-employment tests may be conducted before an applicant is hired or after an offer to hire. These tests must be conducted prior to the actual first-time performance of the individual's safety-sensitive functions. Pre-employment tests are also required when employees transfer to a safety-sensitive position from a non-safety-sensitive position within the same company. All DOT modes require new employees to take (and pass) a pre-employment drug test before they begin work. Pre-employment alcohol tests are authorized, but not mandated by all modes. DOT leaves the decision to conduct pre-employment alcohol tests to each individual transportation employer.

Post-accident testing is conducted after qualifying accidents or where the performance of the employee could have contributed to the accident. Each administration determines what "qualifying" means, with respect to an accident within its particular industry. Obviously, aviation accidents are drastically different from highway accidents. Referencing the rule that corresponds to one of the six administrations would be necessary to determine the criteria for a qualifying accident and subsequent requirements for testing. Contributing to an accident could be seen, for example, in a citation given to a driver by law enforcement after a moving traffic violation. All modes do require that post-accident alcohol tests be conducted within 8 h, and post-accident drug tests be conducted within 32 h of the occurrence of the accident.

Random tests are conducted on a random, unannounced basis. Random testing rates are established in a consistent manner at the beginning of each year, but can be different from mode to mode. Each administration sets the annual random testing rate, one for drugs and one for alcohol, based on the industry's respective random positive rate for the previous year. There are two possible annual rates for random drug testing — 25 or 50%; random alcohol testing has three possible rates of testing — 10, 25, and 50%.

If an industry has a random drug-positive rate of 1% or less for 2 consecutive years, the administrator may reduce the random testing rate to 25% per year for that industry. If the random positive rate is greater than 1% for any year, the random testing rate must move back to 50% per year. Like random drug testing, a random alcohol testing rate is calculated for each industry based on that industry's positive rate for the past 1 to 2 years. If the industry's positive rate is less than 0.5% for 2 consecutive years, the modal administrator can set the resulting alcohol testing rate at 10%. Between 0.5 and 1% for 2 consecutive years, the administrator can set the rate at 25%. When the industry positive rate goes above 1%, the random testing rate is set at 50%. A mode must hold a random positive rate within the above ranges for 2 consecutive years in order for the testing rate to be reduced; a 1-year increase returns the industry to the next higher testing rate. Employees in the pipeline industry, under PHMSA, and employees in the maritime industry, under USCG, are not subject to random alcohol testing. The best explanation for this difference is that neither industry was mentioned in OTETA.

Reasonable suspicion testing is conducted when a supervisor, previously trained in the signs and symptoms of drug abuse and alcohol misuse, observes behavior or appearance that is characteristic of drug or alcohol abuse of the employee. The test must be based on observations that are specific, contemporaneous, and articulable. A rumor of "a big party" over the weekend is not reason enough to conduct a reasonable suspicion test.

Return-to-duty and *follow-up* testing is conducted when an individual, who has a drug or alcohol violation (e.g., positive test), returns to the workplace to resume his or her safety-sensitive work. Initially, a return-to-duty test is given. After passing the return-to-duty test, the employee is eligible to return to safety work. Upon returning to work, the person will be placed back in the company's random testing pool. At the same time, the person must also be subject to unannounced follow-up testing to be conducted at least six times within the first 12 months of returning to work.

10.2.2.6 Consequences of a Drug or Alcohol Violation

All workers committing a violation of the DOT drug or alcohol rules must be removed immediately from their safety-sensitive job and are ineligible to return until they satisfactorily complete the DOT return-to-duty requirements. A DOT drug or alcohol violation includes:

- Alcohol tests with a result of 0.04 or higher alcohol concentration
- Verified positive drug tests
- Refusals to be tested (including verified adulterated or substituted drug test results)
- Other violations of DOT agency drug and alcohol testing regulations (such as, using or possessing alcohol or illicit drugs while on duty, or using alcohol within 4 h–8 h for flight crews and flight attendants — of reporting for duty, or using alcohol within 8 h after an accident or prior to a post-accident test being conducted, whichever comes first)

10.2.2.7 Specimen Collections

DOT has established a specific set of procedures for collecting a urine specimen. Precautions are built into the process to help ensure the control and integrity of the collection. The detail that DOT has devoted to collecting the specimen will serve to minimize the collection errors and maximize the probability that the employer will be able to rely on the test result, regardless of its outcome. DOT has built the model system, but it is the individual diligence of each collector upon which that system relies. Obviously, a problem occurring during the collection has the potential to "ripple" and affect the test outcome.

A DOT urine specimen must be collected using a standard collection kit, documented with a standard form, and conducted by a trained collector. All DOT specimens are collected as "split specimens." The standard kit consists of a single-use collection container that has an attached temperature strip for reading the urine temperature, two sealable plastic bottles for the "split specimens," a leak-resistant plastic bag with two separate pouches (one for the bottles and the other for the collection paperwork), absorbent material, and a shipping container to protect the specimen during transit to the laboratory (Figure 10.2.2).

The standard form for all DOT collections is the Federal Drug Testing Custody and Control Form, or CCF. The CCF is a five-part form. DOT requires the same form for collections as is used within the federal program, under the purview of HHS. Figure 10.2.1 in the previous section presents an illustration of the CCF.

The collector is the person who is in charge of and assists with the collection and has been trained under the provisions of DOT's Part 40 and the DOT Urine Specimen Collection Guidelines,[8] written by ODAPC. Collectors need to be trained prior to collecting their first specimen.

All DOT collections allow the donor to provide the specimen in the privacy of a bathroom stall unless there is a suspicion of tampering, on the part of the donor, or preexisting conditions allow an exception (i.e., return-to-duty and follow-up). The exception would be to conduct the collection under direct-observation procedures, whereby a same-sex collector watches the specimen flow directly from the donor's body and into the collection cup.

DOT has broken down the specimen collection procedure into some 23 different steps in the Collection Guidelines. In general, the donor will present for a urine collection and provide the

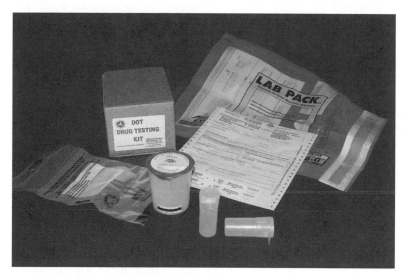

Figure 10.2.2 Example of DOT Standard Urine Collection Kit.

collector with a form of identification that includes a picture ID. The collector will briefly explain the collection process to the donor emphasizing that, once the collection begins, the donor cannot leave the collection site until excused by the collector. DOT directs collectors to obtain a minimum of 45 ml of urine in one single void; 30 ml is for the primary specimen and 15 ml is for the "split" specimen. Generally collections take less than 15 min to complete.

Donors will be informed that their collection period will be extended up to 3 h in order to obtain the requisite volume of urine should the donor be unable to provide the full 45 ml in a single void. During the additional time period, the donor will be encouraged to drink up to 40 oz. of fluid. After 3 h, if the donor fails to provide the required amount, the collector will inform the donor's employer. The employer must then send the employee for a physical examination. The finding of the examination must be that the individual has a current physical, or a pre-documented psychiatric, condition, or the final result will be deemed a "refusal to test." This expanded collection, with the follow-on physical examination, is referred to as the "shy bladder" process.

During the instruction phase of the collection, the collector will also instruct the donor that the failure to follow any of the collector's instructions could result in the collector stopping the testing process and informing the donor's employer that the donor has "refused to test."

The collection procedures include precautions to guard against possible tampering, such as toilet-water bluing and having donors empty their pockets to reveal any adulterating-type products. Donor are also required to wash their hands before entering the bathroom stall. When the donor presents the collector with the specimen, the collector will examine the specimen for signs of tampering and check the temperature to make sure it is within the acceptable range (90 to 100°F). Any attempt by the donor to adulterate the specimen, which is detected by the collector (e.g., a blue specimen), will result in a second collection to follow immediately. That collection will be conducted using the direct-observation procedures. Should the donor refuse to permit the same-sex, direct-observation collection to occur, the collector will stop the collection and inform the donor that the donor has refused to test. "Refusals to test" are final results of record, and are DOT violations.

Assuming that the collection has gone without incident, the collector will divide, or "split," the specimen into two separate specimen bottles and seal and label both bottles with uniquely numbered tampering evident labels that are an integral part of the CCF. This is an important step and must be witnessed by the donor. The CCF paperwork is completed with both the donor and collector filling out their specific sections, and then the split specimens and one copy of the CCF are placed in the leak-proof plastic bag, which is sealed and ready to be sent to the laboratory.

It is the responsibility of the collector to secure the specimens until they are sent to the laboratory. The final duty of the collector is to distribute the remaining copies of the CCF to the appropriate parties (i.e., MRO, collector, employer, and employee).

Even though DOT has developed specific training requirements for all collectors, with more than 7,000,000 collections each year, collection errors still occur. This is perhaps inevitable since the position of *collector* is still an entry-level position in most companies and, thus, subject to high turnover. Lack of proper training or training that is administered in a hurried manner is another cause of collection errors. However, any collector who makes an error that results in a test being canceled must be retrained.

10.2.2.8 *Laboratory Testing*

DOT makes exclusive use of laboratories certified under the HHS National Laboratory Certification Program. HHS publishes a listing of certified laboratories (each month in the *Federal Register*) of those meeting the criteria set forth in the HHS Guidelines. Currently, the vast majority of these laboratories are located in the U.S.; there are a couple in Canada, but none in Mexico. DOT follows HHS criteria for both drug testing and specimen validity testing. The criteria are specified in detail in Section 10.2.1 of this text. Therefore, only general references are made to DOT test criteria in this text section.

All laboratories receive, unpackage, and enter a DOT specimen into the testing process. This is called *accessioning.* All DOT specimens are tested for the five drugs of abuse: marijuana, cocaine, opiates, amphetamines, and phencyclidine. The drug panel has not changed since the outset of the program. DOT follows the protocols set up by HHS. Some of the test criteria, such as the cutoffs for initial or confirmation tests, have changed over the years. As testing technology advances and drug-use tendencies change, it is quite possible that similar changes may occur again in the future. It is also possible that additional drugs could be added to the test panel. However, such changes are not made without first being proposed to the public, in order that the public may comment on the recommendations, and then issuing a change to the HHS and DOT rules.

All DOT specimens also undergo "specimen validity" testing. This is a relatively new category of tests brought on in the late 1990s by attempts of individuals to beat the test by tampering with the specimen (e.g., adding a substance to the urine specimen in hopes of altering the test result).

Specimen validity testing (SVT) consists of measuring creatinine and specific gravity to detect a *diluted* or *substituted* specimen. pH is measured as one criterion established to detect an *adulterated* specimen. HHS has developed criteria to be used in testing for specific adulterants such as nitrites, chromates, surfactants, and other active chemical compounds. Substituted or adulterated specimen results are DOT rule violations and have the same weight as a positive test.

Sometimes neither drug testing nor SVT can produce a result that is conclusive. The laboratory may be able to determine only that the specimen has some abnormal reaction. Testing the specimen reveals that it has definitely not met criteria to be reported as negative, however, criteria are not met to call it positive, substituted, or adulterated. This result is classified as *invalid.* Most invalid test results are recollected using directly observed collection procedures.

All results fall into one of two categories: negative and non-negative. *Negative* specimens are those that prove to be negative for drugs and do not have any specimen-validity issues. Negative results may also show that the specimen was *dilute.* (Dilute specimen results are not violations; however, DOT allows employers to have a policy of recollecting specimens from employees who have dilute results.) Approximately 95% of all DOT specimens are negative. Negative results are reached in less (laboratory) time than non-negative results. DOT gives laboratories the authority to report negative results using only computer-generated reports.

Non-negative specimens are all other results — positive, substituted, adulterated, and invalid. Since some of these results will require that the employee be removed from his safety-sensitive job, and possibly terminated, DOT requires more documentation be included with these test reports.

The laboratory must also provide a copy of the corresponding CCF, generated at the time of the collection and completed by the certifying laboratory scientist who verifies the laboratory results, when the report is released.

DOT test results may only be reported to a physician who will review the drug test. This physician is called the Medical Review Officer. DOT prohibits laboratories from reporting results to anyone other than the MRO (e.g., consortia/third-party administrators, employers).

10.2.2.9 Medical Review Officer

The MRO has been designated by DOT as the "gatekeeper" of the drug-testing program. "MROs" are physicians (a doctor of medicine or osteopathy) who receive all drug test results and make determinations whether the employee has committed a drug violation (e.g., verified positive test result), while maintaining the confidentiality for the employee during an interview process. MROs are required to have knowledge and clinical experience in substance abuse disorders, to be trained on Part 40, and to pass a written examination. Chasing paperwork, listening to far-fetched stories as to why a person was positive or how the specimen became adulterated, and dealing with employers anxious to put people to work are all part of the MRO's duties.

Laboratories *certify* drug test results, while MROs *verify* drug test results. The MRO receives all DOT drug test results directly from the laboratory. Employers or third-party administrators are not authorized to receive the drug test results or act as an intermediary to the MRO. Staff, under the supervision of the MRO, may assist with paperwork duties, establishing donor contact, and reporting results to employers. However, only the MRO can conduct the interview with the donor to determine if there is a legitimate medical explanation for the positive, substituted, or adulterated test result.

"Legitimate medical explanations," while rare for these test results, are possible. Recognizing what is acceptable and what is not is subject-matter training for MROs in the DOT-required MRO training courses. Generally, such explanations are limited to prescriptions or medical procedures where drugs are introduced to the donor and can subsequently be verified by the MRO. Additionally, special studies may be set up to prove that the donor can naturally produce a substituted or adulterated urine specimen. To date, there has been one such case for the former (substituted specimen), but none for the latter (adulterated specimen). In fact, as of this writing, there is no known adulterant, introduced *in vivo,* that can interfere with a laboratory's analytical procedure. All adulterants that have an effect on the analytical process or can be detected by laboratory analysis are introduced into the specimen cup — by the donor — *in vitro.*

When the MRO gets a result that is positive, substituted, adulterated, or invalid, the donor will be contacted and interviewed by telephone. Through the interview, if the MRO determines that there is a legitimate medical reason for the donor's test result, the MRO has the discretion to "downgrade" the result (from positive) to negative and forward that result to the employer. The process devised by DOT gives the MRO latitude to downgrade the final result to negative and still provide a safety warning to the employer if the donor is using a medication that would medically disqualify the donor under agency rules or where continued use would pose a safety risk, even though the medication was obtained with a valid prescription.

For those individuals for whom the MRO determines that the reported result will be positive, substituted, or adulterated, the MRO will also provide the donor with the opportunity of having the split specimen tested at another HHS-certified laboratory. However, the employer will immediately remove the donor from the safety job being performed on the initial report by the MRO. If the split specimen result does not confirm the initial specimen result, the result reported to the employer will be canceled by the MRO — as if the test never occurred — and the donor will undergo a second collection where the process starts over from scratch. If the split confirms the initial result, which is what normally occurs, the employer and the donor are so notified.

MROs may also be called upon for consultation during the post-violation assessment process that the donor must undergo in order to return to the transportation workplace. MROs are encouraged to cooperate with this part of the process, which usually involves providing only drug quantitations that may be helpful during the assessment. MROs may also be asked to assist the donor in obtaining test records from the laboratory that conducted the testing. DOT requires laboratories to interface with MROs, not donors. Donors are entitled to any records produced as a result of their drug test, and having the MRO act as the intermediary keeps it simple. Likewise, donors have access to MRO records, pertaining to their test, as well as laboratory records.

10.2.2.10 Alcohol Testing

OTETA mandated that alcohol tests be part of the dual-testing program. For the first time in the workplace setting, alcohol tests would be conducted alongside drug tests. This new territory presented especially difficult challenges for the DOT.

Alcohol, unlike the drugs that DOT tests for, is a legal substance. While it could not be tolerated in the safety-sensitive workplace, parameters had to be established for off-duty use occurring near the time when the employee would report for duty. Additionally, consideration needed to be given to the period after accidents, but prior to a test being conducted.

Originally the DOT interpreted OTETA language as requiring alcohol testing for all reasons-for-test: pre-employment, random, reasonable suspicion, post-accident, return-to-duty, and follow-up. The 1994 testing rules issued by DOT included requirements for all six test categories. Eventually, the 4th Circuit Court of Appeals ruled that pre-employment testing was problematic as a routine, mandated test. It was subsequently reverted back to DOT for resolution. DOT decided to "authorize" employers to conduct pre-employment alcohol tests as a condition of employment, and definitively modified the rules in 2001. Today, alcohol testing is authorized for pre-employment and mandated for other test reasons (except random testing) in the same manner as drug tests. Random alcohol tests are not required under PHMSA and USCG rules.

Personnel who conduct alcohol tests are called screening test technicians (STT) and breath alcohol technicians (BAT). Most of the tests are conducted by "BATs," as they are called. Both

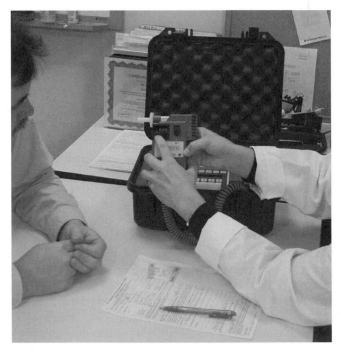

Figure 10.2.3 DOT Breath Alcohol Testing in process.

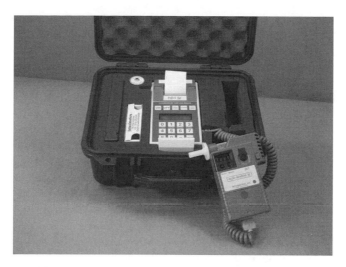

Figure 10.2.4   Example of Evidential Breath Testing device.

technicians need to be trained and only use instruments for the test that have been approved by DOT. All alcohol test devices approved for DOT use are certified by DOT's National Highway Traffic Safety Administration (NHTSA) and placed on a use approved listing,[9] which is published in the *Federal Register*.

Alcohol tests (Figure 10.2.3), like drug tests, use a standard form and a specific set of procedures,[10] both designed and developed by DOT. Unlike drug testing, when alcohol was mandated by OTETA, DOT did not have the luxury of following HHS guidelines — no other branch of the government tests for alcohol. Procedures for workplace alcohol testing had to be developed by DOT.

Alcohol tests, like drug tests, use a two-test procedure. The first test, or initial test, can use either breath or saliva testing devices, and may be non-evidential in nature. The second test can only use an Evidential Breath Testing (EBT) device (Figure 10.2.4). This device produces a printed record documenting all aspects of the test (e.g., time of test, specific device, breath alcohol concentration). Any individual who shows the presence of alcohol at a concentration of 0.02 or higher on the initial test must be subjected to a second test, or confirmation test. Prior to conducting the second test, the BAT will wait at least 15 min, but not more than 30 min, before proceeding. This 15-min waiting period allows any alcohol that may be in the person's mouth to dissipate. "Mouth alcohol" can be attributed to mouthwash or breath lozenges. The waiting period is precautionary to protect the person being tested. During this wait period, the BAT will also conduct an "air blank" on the EBT to show that the device does not contain any residual alcohol.

The result of the second test becomes the result of record. An alcohol concentration of 0.04 or higher is a DOT violation (e.g., similar to a positive drug test); an alcohol concentration between 0.02 and 0.039 is prohibited conduct, and the person cannot perform safety-sensitive work while testing within this range.

The services of an MRO, to review an alcohol test, are not required. The reason is that there is no legitimate medical explanation for alcohol in one's system. Alcohol is alcohol. Whether its source was from beer, whiskey, or mouthwash, the effect is still the same. The BAT will report the result immediately to the employer and the employer will respond by removing the person from duty.

10.2.2.11   *Substance Abuse Professional*

OTETA requires that an opportunity for treatment be made available to covered employees. In order to implement this mandate, an employer must refer any transportation worker, who has engaged in conduct prohibited by DOT drug or alcohol rules, for evaluation and treatment. Modeled with the substance abuse profession in mind, the DOT rules require substance abuse professionals, or SAPs, to have certain credentials, possess specific knowledge, receive training, and achieve a passing score on an examination. There is also a continuing education requirement. The SAP Guidelines,[11] written by ODAPC, supplement Part 40.

The primary safety objective of the DOT rules is to prevent, through deterrence and detection, alcohol and controlled substance users from performing transportation industry safety-sensitive functions. The SAP is responsible for several duties important to the evaluation, referral, and treatment of employees identified through breath and urinalysis testing as positive for alcohol and controlled substance use, or who refuse to be tested, or who have violated other provisions of the DOT rules.

A SAP's fundamental responsibility is to provide a comprehensive face-to-face assessment and clinical evaluation to determine what level of assistance the employee needs in resolving problems associated with alcohol use or prohibited drug use. Following the evaluation, education and/or treatment is recommended, whereby the employee must demonstrate successful compliance in order to return to DOT safety-sensitive duty.

Prior to the employee's return to safety-sensitive duties, the SAP conducts a face-to-face follow-up evaluation with the employee to determine if the individual has demonstrated successful compliance with recommendations of the initial evaluation. This evaluation must be accomplished before an employer can consider the employee for return to safety-sensitive functions. Therefore, the evaluation serves to provide the employer with assurance that the employee has made appropriate clinical progress sufficient to return to work.

The SAP also develops and directs a follow-up testing plan for the employee returning to work following successful compliance, specifying the number and frequency of unannounced follow-up tests. If polysubstance use has been indicated, the follow-up testing plan should include testing for drugs as well as alcohol, even though a violation of both was not the original offense.

If the MRO is considered the "gatekeeper" in the drug-testing process, then the metaphor is equally appropriate for the SAP in the return-to-duty process.

10.2.2.12   Confidentiality and Release of Information

Part 40 is very clear about what information is to be generated, where it goes, and who is authorized to receive it. Beyond the Part 40 instruction, service agents and employers participating in the DOT drug or alcohol testing process are prohibited from releasing individual test results or medical information about an employee to third parties without the employee's specific written consent.

A "third party" is any person or organization that the rule (Part 40) does not explicitly authorize or require the transmission of information from in the course of the drug or alcohol testing process. "Specific written consent" means a statement signed by the employee agreeing to the release of a particular piece of information to a particular, explicitly identified, person or organization at a particular time. "Blanket releases," in which an employee agrees to a release of a category of information (e.g., all test results) or to release information to a category of parties (e.g., other employers who are members of a C/TPA, companies to which the employee may apply for employment), are prohibited by DOT.

Information pertaining to an employee's drug or alcohol test may be released in certain legal proceedings without the employee's consent. These include a lawsuit (e.g., a wrongful discharge action), grievance (e.g., an arbitration concerning disciplinary action taken by the employer), or administrative proceeding (e.g., an unemployment compensation hearing) brought by, or on behalf of, an employee and resulting from a positive DOT drug or alcohol test or a refusal to test. Also included are criminal or civil actions resulting from an employee's performance of safety-sensitive duties, in which a court of competent jurisdiction determines that the drug or alcohol test information sought is relevant to the case and issues an order directing the employer to produce the information. For example, in personal injury litigation following a truck or bus collision, the court could determine that a post-accident drug test result of an employee is relevant to determining whether the driver or the driver's employer was negligent. The employer is authorized to respond to the court's order to produce the records.

DOT instructs employers and service agents to notify the employee in writing of any information released without the employee's written consent.

Lastly, release of DOT program information is not in conflict with the HHS Health Insurance Portability and Accountability (HIPAA) rules.[12] HIPAA rules do not conflict with the DOT drug and alcohol-testing program for employer and service agent responsibilities under Part 40 and operating administration drug and alcohol testing rules. Information may be generated and flow to its intended parties, as required by Part 40, without the employee signing a HIPAA-type consent.

10.2.2.13 *Consortium/Third-Party Administrators*

In the early days of the DOT testing program, the department believed that employers might pool their resources or band together to help each other accomplish the things the testing rules required. This did not happen. What did happen was that the DOT program created an entire "cottage industry" of *service agents*, including consortia/third-party administrators (C/TPA), and substance abuse providers, who contract directly or indirectly with employers to accomplish the tasks set forth in DOT rules. In short, a C/TPA will handle all of the administrative processes for an employer's testing program. The types of services typically offered by C/TPAs are:

- Urine collections, including permanent and mobile facilities
- Laboratory testing
- Random selections
- Background checks on new hires
- Policy and procedures
- Supervisory training
- Providing MRO test review and SAP referrals
- Maintaining records and preparing statistical data
- Assisting employers preparing for DOT audits

Employers are allowed to contract with C/TPAs (service agents) to get the job done. Service agents are obligated to do the work they have signed on to do as if they were the employer. However, even though the department has a method to rid the testing community of a "bad" service agent, the employer is still held responsible for the actions of the service agent.

10.2.2.14 *Public Interest Exclusion*

Service agents perform the bulk of drug and alcohol testing services for transportation employers. Employers, particularly small employers, necessarily rely on service agents to comply with their testing obligations. Employers are ultimately responsible for all aspects of the program. However, in good faith, they may hire a service agent who purposely does not comply with the rules. These employers often do not have the expertise in testing matters that would enable them to evaluate independently the quality, or even the regulatory compliance, of the work that service agents perform for them. Subpart R of Part 40 provides a mechanism to help ensure that service agents will be held accountable for serious noncompliance with DOT rules. The *public interest exclusion* (PIE) is based in concept on the existing DOT non-procurement suspension and debarment rule[13] and permits DOT to suspend a service agent for willful noncompliance with the drug and alcohol testing rules. The mechanism, both for policy and resource reasons, is only used in cases of serious misconduct.

An employer's compliance with DOT regulations is largely dependent on its service agents' performance. If a service agent makes a serious mistake that results in the employer being out of compliance with a DOT rule, accountability must be addressed. The employer may be subject to civil penalties from a DOT agency. The employer can be subject to litigation resulting from personnel action it took on the basis of the service agent's noncomplying services. Most importantly, the employer's efforts to ensure the safety of its operations may be damaged, e.g., as when an employee who apparently uses drugs is returned to duty because of a service agent's noncompliance.

The standard of proof in a PIE proceeding is "the preponderance of the evidence." There is no policy or legal basis apparent for raising this burden to the higher "clear and convincing evidence" level. A PIE could apply to all the divisions, organizational elements, and types of services provided by the service agent involved, unless the director limited the scope of the proceeding. Under some circumstances, affiliates and individuals could also be subject to a PIE. The intent of the PIE is to protect the public from the misconduct of an organization. As of mid-2006, the DOT had not suspended any service agents.

10.2.2.15 Conclusion

The history of the DOT drug- and alcohol-testing program is a relatively short one. The benefits of the last 10-plus years of program implementation are not fully known. However, data on illegal drug use by transportation employees, accidents related to use, and changes in attitudes about workplace safety and substance abuse are encouraging. The ultimate success of OTETA and the employer-based programs that it mandates will be measured over time in terms of lives saved, injuries prevented, and property losses reduced. OTETA is not a cure-all for safety problems or problem workers. Only everyday due diligence on the part of all safety workers will help in that area.

NOTES

1. *Skinner v. Railway Executives' Association*, 489 U.S. 616-617 (1989); and *National Treasury Employees Union v. Von Robb*, 489 U.S. 656, 674-675 (1989).
2. Public Law 102-143, October 28, 1991, Title V — Omnibus Transportation Employee Testing, 105 Stat. 952-965; 49 U.S.C. 45104(2).
3. Title 49, Code of Federal Regulations (CFR), Part 40, Procedures for Transportation Workplace Drug and Alcohol Testing Programs, Office of the Secretary of Transportation, Department of Transportation.
4. Federal Aviation Administration (FAA): 14 CFR Part 121, Appendix I & J; Federal Motor Carrier Safety Administration (FMCSA): 49 CFR Part 382; Federal Railroad Administration (FRA): 49 CFR Part 219; Federal Transit Administration (FTA): 49 CFR Part 655; Pipeline and Hazardous Materials Safety Administration (PHMSA): 49 CFR Part 199; and U.S. Coast Guard (USCG); 46 CFR Part 16 and 46 CFR Part 4.
5. The USCG transferred to the Department of Homeland Security in March 2003, but still conducts drug testing under DOT rules.
6. Executive Order 12564, Drug-Free Federal Workplace, September 15, 1986.
7. Mandatory Guidelines for Federal Workplace Drug Testing Programs, Division of Workplace Programs (DWP), Substance Abuse and Mental Health Services Administration (SAMHSA), Department of Health and Human Services (HHS).
8. Urine Specimen Collection Guidelines, Office of Drug and Alcohol Policy and Compliance, DOT, Version 1.01, August 2001.
9. Conforming Products Listing, National Highway Traffic Safety Administration, 69 FR 42237.
10. DOT Model Course for Breath Alcohol Technicians and Screening Test Technicians, Office of Drug and Alcohol Policy and Compliance, DOT, August 2001.
11. Substance Abuse Professional Guidelines, Office of Drug and Alcohol Policy and Compliance, DOT, August 2001.
12. Health Insurance Portability and Accountability Act of 1996 (HIPAA), Department of Health and Human Services, 45 CFR Part 164.
13. 49 CFR Part 29, Governmentwide Debarment and Suspension (Nonprocurement), Office of the Secretary, DOT.

10.2.3 Drug Testing in the Nuclear Power Industry: The NRC Fitness-for-Duty Rules

Theodore F. Shults, **J.D., M.S.**
Chairman, American Association of Medical Review Officers, Research Triangle Park, North Carolina

10.2.3.1 Background

The private nuclear power generating industry in the U.S. is highly regulated. The primary federal regulator is the Nuclear Regulatory Commission (NRC). The NRC has a great deal of oversight, inspection responsibilities, safety analysis, and involvement in every aspect of the operation of a nuclear generating facility. The nuclear industry has been highly sensitive to the public safety aspect of its operations and recognizes that in addition to the fundamental engineering issues involved in maintaining the safe operation and security of a reactor and its fuel, a great deal of attention must be paid to the basic human performance issues as well. In this industry careful consideration is given to who has access to the facility, their background, their health and their behavior — particularly in respect to illegal drug use and alcohol abuse.

The rules that govern drug and alcohol testing in the nuclear industry are called the *Fitness-for-Duty Rules* (FFD) and are found in Title 10 Code of Federal Regulations, Section 26, or ubiquitously known in the industry as 10 CFR 26. The initial Fitness-for-Duty rule was published in 1989. This rule requires that each nuclear power plant licensee establish a Fitness-for-Duty program. The NRC crafted these rules at the same time that the HHS Mandatory Guidelines were put together. The NRC adopted the fundamental requirement of using MROs, certified laboratories, and many of the procedural safeguards.

There were, however, a few fundamental differences in philosophy and goals between the HHS Mandatory Guidelines and the NRC fitness-for-duty programs. The NRC had an interest in deterrence of illegal drugs, but the NRC and the industry as a whole also was deeply interested in the concept of overall "fitness" of the employee, the safety of operations, the overall security of the facility and "trustworthiness" of individuals who had access to nuclear plants and facilities. As a result of these considerations, the NRC program that was adopted back in 1988 looked similar to the HHS procedures but contained a number of radically different elements.

First, the NRC gave the individual nuclear electric generating plant (called a licensee) a great deal of flexibility. For example, whereas HHS Mandatory Guidelines restrict drug testing to five categories of drugs, the NRC allows the licensee to test for additional drugs and to test for drugs at lower cutoff levels than specified and required in the HHS Mandatory Guidelines. The NRC also allowed for the on-site testing for specimen validity at the collection site, and allowed the licensee to have an on-site immunoassay screening laboratory for initial screening of urine specimens. The NRC also adopted a modified stand-down provision that a licensee can use. All these deviations from HHS provisions were controversial at the time, but they have worked for the nuclear power industry.

Another fundamental difference is that unlike the DOT/HHS testing model, the NRC does not require the MRO to receive all of the laboratory results from the certified laboratory, or even to review the negative results. (Everything in the nuclear industry is reviewed about ten times — but not by the MRO.) The results typically go to a fitness-for-duty coordinator, who again typically has access to all the testing information, including the MRO records. This is a very different process than seen in DOT testing. On the other hand, the MRO in the nuclear industry often has to play an expanded role in respect to management of the health, qualifications, and prescription drug use of the employees in the program.

In 1995, the NRC published a proposed update to its Fitness-for-Duty Regulations. These proposed rules were open for comment in 1996, were debated, and then went into a state of regulatory limbo. Meanwhile, utilities continued to follow the existing rules and modify and update their programs within the regulatory framework of 10 CFR 26. While the proposed rules were in limbo, a lot happened in other areas of testing. HHS implemented program documents giving laboratories guidelines on how to test for adulterants, and subsequently adopted a mandatory specimen validity rule. DOT has rewritten its drug and alcohol testing rules, adopted procedures for managing insufficient urine volume (shy bladder), and established procedures for testing of adulterated and substituted urine. During this time the nuclear industry was going through a challenging period of reorganization in order to adapt to a new "deregulated" industry of gyrating market conditions.

In 2000, prior to establishing an implementation date for the 1995 "new" rule to go into effect, the NRC held a meeting for the industry to provide any additional clarifications. It was a difficult meeting for all parties. What became clear was that many aspects of what were viewed as enhancements in 1995 looked stale in 2000. In 1995, the regulatory language was still of the old school, as opposed to the new question-and-answer format used by DOT and HHS.

The world changed in September 2001, and the NRC refocused its efforts on counterterrorism and security. In the fitness-for-duty area there was more emphasis and interest in managing fatigue and enhancing background checks. The NRC staff was continuing to work on updating the fitness-for-duty rules, and the industry recognized the benefit of incorporating the DOT and HHS experience with respect to managing specimen validity. The NRC and the nuclear industry also took the opportunity to develop a comprehensive rule (framed as amendments to the existing rules) that better addresses the issues of adulteration, emerging technologies, drug and alcohol abuse, and safety in a less cumbersome way and to integrate a decade and a half of experience from well-run programs.

Thus, after a 10-year period of struggle and at times a mind-numbing regulatory process, the NRC pre-released a proposed new rule in April 2005. This new proposal represents countless hours of work on the part of all of the stakeholders, and a significant catch-up and enhancement of the existing program. True to its original intent, the "fitness-for-duty" rules include the procedures and requirements for the management of "fatigue," which are outlined below.

10.2.3.2   The 2005 Proposed Amendments to the NRC Fitness-for-Duty Rules

On May 16, 2005, the NRC published in the *Federal Register* a notice that stated that it intended to propose:

> A rule (that) would amend the Commission's regulations to ensure compatibility with the Department of Health and Human Services guidelines, eliminate or modify unnecessary requirements in some areas, clarify the Commission's original intent of the rule, and improve overall program effectiveness and efficiency and establish threshold for the control of working hours at nuclear power plants to ensure that working hours in excess of the thresholds are controlled through a risk-informed deviation process. Because of the issues raised in response to the earlier affirmed (fitness for duty) rule, a new proposed rule will be published, including provisions to provide significantly greater assurance that worker fatigue does not adversely affect the operational safety of nuclear power plants. This new proposed rule is scheduled to be provided to the Commission by June 1, 2005.*

This new fitness-for-duty rule is available on the NRC Web site.† It is awaiting approval from the Office of Management and Budget, which should take some additional time. The rule when published will provide at least 120 days before going into effect.

As could be anticipated in updating a 10-year-old drug and alcohol testing rule, the proposed fitness-for-duty rule contains a significant number of changes to the existing program. The following

---

* The NRC is reviewing the public comments and projects that the rule will become final in January 2007.
† Go to nrc.gov and use the search feature to find "fitness for duty." The searcher should find the old rule, the history of the rule, a wealth of background material, and the new rule in its pre-published form.

are some of the most significant changes that deal directly with drug and alcohol testing. The proposed new *fitness-for-duty* rule would:

- Add requirements for validity tests on urine specimens to determine if a specimen has been adulterated, diluted, or substituted. At the request of stakeholders, the rule would permit licensee testing facilities to perform validity screening tests using non-instrumented testing devices, as proposed by HHS on April 13, 2004 (69 FR 19672), but not yet incorporated into final HHS guidelines.
- Add a requirement that assays used for testing for drugs in addition to those specified in this part, or testing at more stringent cutoff levels than those specified in this part, would be evaluated and certified by an independent forensic toxicologist. (§26.31(d))
- Add a requirement that cutoff levels would be applied equally to all individuals subject to testing. (§26.31(d))
- Establish a process for determining whether there is a medical reason that a donor is unable to provide a urine specimen of at least 30 ml. (§25.119)

Alcohol Testing

With respect to alcohol testing the new provisions would:

- Add requirements for the use of oral fluids (i.e., saliva) as acceptable specimens for initial alcohol tests.
- Lower the blood alcohol concentration (BAC) at which a confirmatory test is required from 0.04 to 0.02%. (§26.31(d)) This is a significant change. One of the reasons for the change has been the observation of the occasional donors who had been on the job for a few hours and still had a breath alcohol test above 0.03%.
- Eliminate blood testing for alcohol. (§26.31(d)) Blood testing is allowed under the existing program as a "voluntary procedure" for individuals who had tested positive on two sequential evidentiary breath testing devices. This extraordinary provision allowing a positive donor to obtain a blood alcohol result was incorporated in an abundance of caution and concern over defending the results in respect to an individual's challenge of the EBT alcohol testing results. The elimination of this provision is recognition that having not just one but two evidential breath testing devices is overkill.

Sanctions

As distinguishable from the general DOT rules (with a few notable exceptions in the FAA rules), the NRC does specify employment sanctions for violations of the fitness-for-duty rule. The sanctions are made more severe under the new provisions. Significantly, they include:

- Require unfavorable termination of authorization for 14 days for a first confirmed positive drug or alcohol test result. (§26.75(e))
- Increase the authorization denial period for a second confirmed positive drug or alcohol test result from 3 to 5 years. (§26.75(e))
- Add permanent denial of authorization for additional FFD violations following any previous denial for 5 years. (§26.75(g))
- Require permanent denial of authorization for refusing to be tested or attempting to subvert the testing process. (§26.75(b))
- Add a 5-year denial of authorization for resignation to avoid removal for an FFD violation. (§26.75(d))

Catch-Up Provisions

The new rule also proposes a number of "catch-up" provisions that incorporate standards already established in DOT and HHS rules. These provisions include such items as:

- Add cutoff levels for initial validity tests of urine specimens at licensee testing facilities and certified laboratories, and require tests for creatinine, pH, and one or more oxidizing adulterants. The rule would not allow licensees and other entities to establish more stringent cutoff levels for validity testing, and would also specify the criteria for determining that a specimen must be forwarded to an HHS-certified laboratory for further testing. (§26.131)
- Replace and amend cutoff levels for initial tests for drugs and drug metabolites to be consistent with HHS cutoff levels. (Decrease the cutoff level for marijuana metabolites from 100 to 50 ng/ml. Increase the cutoff level for opiate metabolites from 300 to 2,000 ng/ml.) (§26.133)

Provisions for MROs

With respect to MROs, the following provisions are being proposed:

- Clarify requirements concerning donor requests to test the specimen in Bottle B of a split sample. (§26.135)
- Clarify and expand the requirements relating to qualifications, relationships, and responsibilities of the MRO.
- Add a requirement that the MRO pass a certification examination within 2 years of rule implementation. (§26.183)
- Add specific prohibitions concerning conflicts of interest. (§26.183)
- Specify MRO programmatic responsibilities. (§26.183)
- Establish the requirements and responsibilities of the MRO staff.
- Add a requirement for the MRO to be directly responsible for the activities of individuals who perform MRO staff duties. (§26.183)
- Add a requirement that MRO staff duties must be independent from any other activity or interest of the licensee or other entity. (§26.183)
- Prohibit the MRO from delegating his or her responsibilities for directing MRO staff activities to any individual or entity other than another MRO. (§26.183)
- Specify the job duties that MRO staff may and may not perform. (§26.183)
- Clarify and expand MRO responsibilities for verifying an FFD violation.
- Make the MRO responsible for assisting the licensee or other entity in determining whether the donor has attempted to subvert the testing process. (§26.185)
- Provide detailed guidance on circumstances in which the MRO may verify a non-negative test result as an FFD policy violation without prior discussion with the donor. (§26.185)
- Clarify MRO responsibilities when the HHS-certified laboratory reports that a specimen is invalid. (§26.185)
- Specify actions the MRO may take if he or she has reason to believe that the donor may have diluted a specimen in a subversion attempt, including confirmatory testing of the specimen at the assay's lowest level of detection for any drugs or drug metabolites. (§26.185)
- Add requirements for the MRO to determine whether a donor has provided an acceptable medical explanation for a specimen that the HHS-certified laboratory reported as adulterated or substituted. (§26.185)
- Incorporate HHS recommendations on verifying a positive drug test for opiates. (§26.185)
- Incorporate federal policy prohibiting acceptance of an assertion of consumption of a hemp food product or coca leaf tea as a legitimate medical explanation for a prohibited substance or metabolite in a specimen. (§26.185)
- Provide detailed requirements for evaluation of whether return-to-duty drug test results indicate subsequent drug use. (§26.185)

Return to Duty

In respect to return-to-duty provisions the new proposed rule would:

- Add a new position, substance abuse expert (SAE), to the minimum requirements for FFD programs and specify the qualifications and responsibilities of the SAE. (§26.187) This SAE may or may not be defined as the SAP is defined in DOT regulations. Nevertheless, the change in the acronym is a significant improvement.

- Specify the role of the SAE in making determinations of fitness and the return-to-duty process, including the initial evaluation, referrals for education and/or treatment, the follow-up evaluation, continuing treatment recommendations, and the follow-up testing plan. The rule would specify the role of the SAE in determinations of fitness based on the types of professional qualifications possessed by the SAE. (§26.189)

Managing Fatigue

The new rule integrates fatigue management and fitness for duty. It is a logical association, but the development of sound fatigue rules that are not burdensome on the industry is a daunting challenge. In summary, the proposed rules:

- Establish program requirements for fatigue management at nuclear power plants.
- Codify a process for workers to self-declare that they are not fit for duty because of fatigue. (§26.197)
- Require training for workers and supervisors on symptoms of and contributors to fatigue and on fatigue countermeasures. (§26.197)
- Require licensees to include fatigue management information in the annual FFD program performance report that would be required under §26.217, including the number of waivers of the individual limits and break requirements that were granted, the collective work hours of any job duty group that exceeded the group average limit in any averaging period, and certain details of fatigue assessments conducted. (§26.197)

10.2.3.3 Conclusion

This is just an outline of the significant differences. Overall, the NRC has had an exceptional record of performance, even while working with a rule that was clearly long in the tooth. A key to the success of the NRC fitness-for-duty program has been a combination of the rigorous analysis that nuclear managers bring to the table in respect to safety concerns as well as some degree of regulatory flexibility.

One can also anticipate that there may be some changes between the pre-published amendments and what becomes final law, and no doubt the NRC will be evaluating the final rule that HHS is expected to publish with respect to the effectiveness of alternative drug testing technologies. It is also safe to assume that it will be unlikely that the NRC will fall behind again in the race for effective management of substance abuse and employee fitness.

10.3 WORKPLACE DRUG TESTING OUTSIDE THE U.S.

Anya Pierce, M.Sc., M.B.A.
Toxicology Department, Beaumont Hospital, Dublin, Ireland, U.K.

10.3.1 Introduction

Although workplace drug testing (WDT) began in the U.S., it is increasingly prevalent in all parts of the globe.[1] A major contributor to its spread was U.S. multinational corporations introducing the practice internationally. The amount of WDT performed is still minimal compared to the U.S. but it is steadily increasing.

WDT began in the U.S. military and this trend has continued worldwide, with armed forces everywhere adopting the practice. It is impossible to obtain accurate statistics for most countries, and even when statistics are available, there often is no agreement about what constitutes WDT. For example, many countries include prison testing programs in their statistics.

There is an aura of secrecy about WDT in Europe, as if it were somehow shameful for companies to admit involvement. This is hard to understand because WDT in Europe and Australia is led by health and safety concerns. The greater prevalence of trade unions in Europe appears to inhibit the acceptance of WDT. There is also much greater use of point-of-care testing (POCT) outside the U.S., with its consequent problems of little or no elements of quality assurance.

10.3.2 Scope

This section covers the state of workplace drug testing and the development of regulations, both in place or proposed, accepted methods, and cutoffs in Europe, Australia, and other international arenas.

10.3.3 Workplace Drug Testing in Europe

10.3.3.1 History

In 1989, Spain held the presidency of the European Economic Community (EEC) and made the following proposals concerning drug testing:

- Examine the criteria currently used for reporting positive results, including the need to distinguish between screening and confirmation results.
- Examine the existing quality assurance programs.
- Examine the validity of certified reference materials for illicit drugs and their metabolites.

This work was followed by a questionnaire to collect information on:

- Substances tested
- Cutoff values
- Test methods
- Need for duplicate samples
- Interpretation and transmission of results
- External quality assurance practices

Last, a survey on quality and reliability was distributed. This led to the formation of an expert group under the aegis of Marie Therese Van der Venne of DG VI of the European Commission. Several meetings were held in Luxembourg with one or two representatives from each EEC country. This culminated in a 2-day meeting in Barcelona with original representatives and additional experts. Recommendations[2] were finalized and published in journals nominated by the experts from each country under the following categories:

- Sample handling and chain of custody
- Cutoff values
- Analytical methodology
- Educational requirements
- External quality assurance and accreditation

These recommendations met with a great deal of opposition. Some thought they were too limited, while others thought they were too restrictive. Some disliked the specific cutoffs selected. Different countries had widely varying attitudes, socially and legally, to drug use.

10.3.3.2 European Workplace Drug Testing Society

The sponsor in the European Commission died suddenly and workplace testing guidelines failed to progress until a meeting entitled "Drug Testing at the Workplace" was held in Huddinge Hospital in Stockholm, Sweden. This meeting led to the formation of the European Workplace Drug Testing Group (EWDTG) on March 1, 1998. The group consisted of one or two members from each EU country and representatives from Norway and Switzerland. From this core group the European Workplace Drug Testing Society (EWDTS) developed.

The mission of the EWDTS is to ensure that workplace drug testing in Europe is performed to a defined quality standard, in a legally secure manner, and to provide an independent forum for discussion of all aspects of workplace drug testing. Guidelines for urine testing are published and are discussed below. Guidelines for other matrices are under development.

The EWDTS objectives are to:

- Provide the source of expertise on WDT in Europe
- Function as the primary advisor to the European Commission
- Develop relevant literature and dispense information via the EDWTS Web site
- Train medical review officers (MROs)
- Train sample collectors

There is no specific legislation regarding WDT in any country in Europe. Finland had planned to introduce it, but at the last minute deleted the section from the relevant act.

Industries that perform WDT are mainly in:

- Transport
- Information technology
- Petrochemicals
- Shipping
- Pharmaceuticals
- Customer support (call) centers

Testing occurs predominantly at the pre-employment level, although in transport it is also routinely performed after an accident. Government employees outside the U.S. are not tested.

10.3.3.3 Sweden

In 1995, the Swedish government evaluated WDT and found no need for legislation. Instead, it was found preferable for the labor market to regulate this issue itself. In 1998, 23,997 people were tested, of whom 2.3% were positive.

A person working as a cleaner in a non-safety critical area of a nuclear power plant objected to drug testing. The case was referred to the European Court of Human Rights. The court handed down a judgment on March 9, 2004 rejecting the application, saying it was impractical to differentiate employees and that drug testing of all its employees was a proportionate measure that did not violate Article 8.2 of the European Convention on Human Rights. This is the only case law in Europe at present.

10.3.3.4 The Netherlands

Interestingly, the only laws referring to WDT in the EU are in the Netherlands, where pre-employment testing is prohibited. There is also opposition from trade unions and occupational health specialists, who believe that it is an infringement of individual privacy. In companies that do drug testing, it cannot be obligatory and employees have the right to refuse.

Only one laboratory performs WDT. It is located in Rotterdam with a client-base of petrochemical and shipping industries, many of whose employees work offshore. About 20,000 tests are performed annually. Amsterdam, renowned for its coffee shops where small amounts of cannabis can be purchased, has almost no WDT.

10.3.3.5 Spain and Portugal

In a 1994 survey of companies in the Lisbon district with more than 50 workers, Vitòria[3] estimated that 20% were doing drug testing. Pinheiro et al.[4] found that 14% of the largest Portuguese companies (with a workforce greater than 1000) were performing tests in 1997, the majority without correct chain of custody or confirmation.

No statistics are available from Spain. The majority of WDT on the Iberian Peninsula is done by the military. The most representative (and probably sole) indicators of WDT activity are those of the Portuguese army, where positive results have decreased from 17% in 1986 to 5.8% in 1995. Positive cannabis and opiate tests accounted for 4.1 and 1.4% of total positive tests.

10.3.3.6 Luxembourg

Some private companies are performing on-site testing for drugs of abuse, and some companies are sending urine specimens to special laboratories. Again, there are no firm statistics.

10.3.3.7 France

Air France and the automobile industry do the majority of drug testing. Private laboratories provide these services. In August 2004 the Department of Transport allowed occupational physicians in the railroad industry to drug test workers in safety-critical positions.

10.3.3.8 Germany

There is very little WDT in Germany. Most of the major companies in transport and manufacture do not test. Generally, WDT is perceived as an invasion of privacy, although some companies, mainly around Frankfurt, have begun testing.

10.3.3.9 Greece

WDT is done only in Thessaloniki, at the Aristotelian University.[5] Specimens for analysis come from:

- District attorney offices for testing of prisoners' specimens
- Directorate of Transportation for drivers seeking the reinstatement of driving licenses revoked for previous drug abuse
- Private individuals during pre-employment testing
- Security services under a law passed in 1997
- Prostitutes and housekeepers at houses of prostitution under a law passed in November 1999

10.3.3.10 Ireland

Ireland has a large number of nonindigenous pharmaceutical and information technology companies. The majority of them test at the pre-employment level and use the policies of their parent companies. The armed forces began random testing in September 2002, although they have performed pre-employment testing for many years. Some companies use laboratories in other countries. The use of POCT is widespread; it is estimated that 50,000 tests are performed annually.

In 2006 the Health and Safety Authority enacted into law the Safety, Health and Welfare at Work Act 2005. One of the more controversial sections states as follows:

An employee shall, while at work —

(a) comply with the relevant statutory provisions, etc.

(b) ensure that he or she is not under the influence of an intoxicant to the extent that he or she is in such a state as to endanger his or her own safety, health or welfare at work or that of any other person.

(c) if reasonably required by his or her employer, submit to any appropriate reasonable and proportionate tests, by or under the supervision of a registered medical practitioner who is a competent person, as may be prescribed. This is the first such law in Europe. It still has to be fine tuned to decide which occupations are considered safety critical and what drugs are to be looked for.

10.3.3.11   U.K.

Testing became more prevalent in the 1980s and is growing. The discovery of oil and the opening of oil rigs in the North Sea and chemical and transport industries have increased testing demand. At present, it is estimated that more than 500,000 tests are performed annually. It is not known how many of the analyses are generated from outside the U.K.

The Railway & Transport Safety Act covers air/road/rail and sea, which includes any person in charge of a vehicle and means they can be tested. The rail sector is the most rigorous with pre-employment "with cause" testing for all and random testing for those in safety-critical positions, and education and help for anyone who discloses a problem. Overall, there is a trend of taking a risk assessment approach to drugs and alcohol, and looking at business-critical as well as safety-critical issues.

10.3.3.12   Belgium

The main users of WDT are in transport and the automobile industry. There are again no reliable statistics. The General Medical Council established strict guidelines in 1993: analysis may only be performed in a laboratory, drug testing is only allowed if clinical examination of impairment is not possible, and positive results must be confirmed by another laboratory. A recent (2002) initiative to amend these rules was not successful.

10.3.3.13   Finland

An Act on the Protection of Privacy in Working Life, which was recently enacted into law, covers several aspects of workplace drug testing. The Finnish guidelines on drug testing are the European Workplace Drug Testing (EWDTS) guidelines. WDT in Finland is mostly pre-employment testing, but random testing is increasing. WDT is usually part of health screening and the employer may often be told only that the applicant has failed the medical examination, with no further details provided.

10.3.3.14   Denmark

There is no legislation regarding WDT in Denmark. It is organized at the local level and mainly for the transport sector, offshore workers, and the police force. Persistent findings indicate that up to 12% of the workforce is influenced by one or more drugs.

Approximately 10,000 tests per year are performed, mainly random testing or cluster testing, with very few pre-employment tests. Approximately 90% of all drug tests are performed as on-site testing (immunoassay screening) by health professionals, who also play a role in developing drug-free workplace programs.

10.3.4 Attitude Surveys

10.3.4.1 U.K. CIPD Survey

A 2001 survey of 281 organizations by the Chartered Institute of Personnel and Development reported[6] that:

20% of the organizations were considered safety-critical, 38% partly so
56% have an alcohol and drug policy
18% carry out drug testing
12% perform drug testing when drug use is suspected
9% test for pre-employment
7% test for post-accident evaluation
6% perform random testing
6% do post-rehabilitation testing
2% test prior to promotion

10.3.4.2 Drug Testing in Prisons

Drug testing in prisons varies within and between countries. Positive tests tend to result in loss of privileges only. A split sample is taken, and re-screening and confirmation are available in some countries upon receipt of payment from the prisoner. The U.K. has a mix of mandatory and voluntary testing. Sweden also tests for anabolic steroids.

10.3.4.3 Employee Attitudes Survey

A survey was conducted in Sweden, Portugal, and Ireland in 2000 to acquire knowledge about attitudes toward drug testing in the workplace.[7] Questionnaires were given to people who were tested for drugs at pre-employment. The answers were voluntary and anonymous. The questions asked were:

Do you think that drug testing can be a good method to achieve a more drug free workplace?
Do you consider donating a urine sample for this purpose in any way offensive?
If you had a choice, what matrix would you prefer?
Do you think that narcotics are a problem in our society?
What are your views on the use of recreational drugs such as cannabis or ecstasy?

The results showed little difference between countries with the Swedish most certain of the benefits of WDT and the Portuguese the least. The Irish preferred urine as a matrix with very few countries in favor of sweat testing. Individuals under 20 and those over 40 saw the least danger in the use of recreational drugs. The main problem with the survey was that the number of participants was small, self-selecting, and the survey should have involved more countries. Interestingly, a number of people who responded had reservations about the failure to differentiate between cannabis and ecstasy use. They felt that ecstasy was much more dangerous and should have been treated separately.

10.3.5 European Laboratory Guidelines for Legally Defensible Workplace Drug Testing

10.3.5.1 Introduction

The EWDTS guidelines[8] are based on the U.K. WDT guidelines. Urine is the only matrix included at present, although it is planned to introduce breath, oral fluid, hair, etc. The guidelines

Table 10.3.1   European Screening Cutoffs

Drug	ng/ml
Amphetamine	300
Benzodiazepines	200
Cannabis metabolites	50
Cocaine metabolites	300
Opiates (total)	300
Methadone/metabolites	300
Barbiturates	200
Phencyclidine	25
Buprenorphine/metabolites	5
LSD/metabolites	1
Propoxyphene/metabolites	300
Methaqualone	300

represent best practice, which can withstand legal scrutiny, and are intended to provide a common standard throughout Europe. The guidelines have now been accepted by the European Accreditation (EA) body as the benchmark for WDT.

The guidelines include:

- Specimen collection
- Laboratory organization
- Laboratory analysis
- Quality control and quality assurance
- Medical review officer

10.3.5.2   Screening Cutoffs

Table 10.3.1 presents European screening cutoffs.

10.3.5.3   Confirmation Cutoffs

Table 10.3.2 presents European confirmation cutoffs.

10.3.6   U.S.–EU Comparison

Neither the individual European governments nor the EU parliament has shown real interest in WDT compared to the U.S. government. The U.S. has legally enforceable guidelines, while the European guidelines have no legal standing. In Europe, there is greater use of POCT and small non-accredited laboratories. In the U.S., testing is performed in a small number of large laboratories that are accredited and operated under very strict controls. Testing in the U.S. is mandatory for federal employees, which is not the case in Europe.

10.3.7   WDT in Australia and New Zealand

10.3.7.1   Standards

WDT is increasing in Australia. Although mining is the main industry to embrace WDT, other industries are also testing, including:

- Metalliferous
- Quarrying

- Transport
- Construction

Neither transport nor construction industries have introduced a systematic procedure to measure the extent of drug use within their workforce. Some transport industries across Australia do have *ad hoc* testing. Similar to Europe, drug testing in Australia is conducted as part of an overall Occupational Health and Safety policy. Thus, there are many safeguards for employees who test positive. They are not dismissed, but instead are referred to a rehabilitation program. Only after repeatedly testing positive are individuals liable for dismissal.

Many unions and even Employee Assistance Providers do not support drug testing. In general, within the workforce, the most common drugs of abuse identified are cannabis and methamphetamine. The most common drugs detected are therapeutic codeine and pseudoephedrine. Tables 10.3.3 and 10.3.4 present Australia/New Zealand screening and confirmatory cutoffs.

10.3.7.2 The Australian Mining Industry

This industry is the leader in the introduction of drug and alcohol testing of its workforce. Drug testing is carried out as part of occupational health and safety requirements.

The mining industries in Western Australia, Queensland, and New South Wales are in the forefront. Policies, including compulsory drug and alcohol testing, usually require that an employee

Table 10.3.2   European Confirmation Cutoffs

Amphetamine	200
Methylamphetamine	200
MDA	200
MDMA	200
MDEA	200
Other amphetamines	200
Temazepam	100
Oxazepam	100
Desmethyldiazepam	100
Other benzodiazepines	TBA
11-Nor-9-tetra hydrocannabinol-9-carboxylic acid	15
Benzoylecgonine	150
Morphine	300
Codeine	300
Dihydrocodeine	300
6-Monoacetylmorphine	10
Methadone/metabolites	250
Barbiturates	150
Phencyclidine	25
Buprenorphine/metabolite	5
LSD/metabolites	1
Propoxyphene/metabolite	300
Methaqualone	300

Table 10.3.3   Australian/New Zealand (AS/NZS 4308) Screening Cutoffs

Drug	ng/ml
Opiates	300
Sympathomimetic amines	300
Cannabis	50
Cocaine	300
Benzodiazepines	200

Table 10.3.4   Australian/New Zealand (AS/NZS 4308) Confirmation Cutoffs

Drug	ng/ml
Morphine, codeine	300
Amphetamine, methamphetamine, MDMA	300
Phentermine, ephedrine, pseudoephedrine	500
Carboxytetrahydrocannabinol	15
Benzoylecgonine, ecognine methyl ester	150
Oxazepam, temazepam, diazepam, nordiazepam, 7-aminoclonazepam, 7-aminonitrazepam, 7-aminoflunitrazepam	150

is not impaired due to the ingestion of illicit drugs. This wording has created problems, as it is impossible to prove impairment, particularly in the case of a positive cannabis test. There is a lobby to increase the cannabis cutoff to reduce this perceived problem. Unfortunately, policy makers have used terminology from established alcohol testing for drug testing. Even though drug testing has been introduced under health and safety regulations, the unions have concerns. They defend an individual's right to privacy, are concerned about the accuracy of drug testing, and state that individuals should not be penalized for using cannabis on their own time.

Each Australian state has its own mining legislation. In effect, it is the duty of mine managers to ensure that no person is impaired by alcohol or drugs while on site. On-site drug testing is well established. Accredited laboratories perform confirmation analyses. Although there are no legal requirements, most companies select laboratories that are accredited by the National Association of Testing Authorities (NATA) to conduct analyses according to Australian/New Zealand Standards AS/NZS 4308.

More recently, drug and alcohol testing has been extended to include contractors to the mining industry. To date, contractors present a greater risk for impairment than do employees of a company. In due course, it is expected that testing will significantly reduce the incidence of recreational drugs by workers, either employed full time or contracted to the mining industry.

10.3.7.3 New Zealand

Laboratories perform WDT work to the standards of the AS/NZS 4308.[9] The 2001 standard is currently being updated to include a section for use of "on-site" screening devices. Standards Australia is also developing an Oral Fluid Standard.

The number of tests is rising each year. In 1998/1999, about 3000 urine specimens were tested. This rose to an estimated 50,000 in 2005/2006.

The industries that test are divided as follows (2005/2006):

Road/Horizontal Construction	21%
Forestry	15%
Transport	13%
Meat/Poultry	11%
Dairy	10%
Fishing/Shipping	6%
Aluminum Smelting	4%
Power/Oil	3%
Manufacturing	2%
Vertical Construction	2%
Mining	<2%
Personnel Consulting	<2%

The majority of testing (78%) is at pre-employment, followed by random (15%). Only 2% of the tests are performed after an accident/incident or for "just cause."

Percentage positives in 2005/2006 were 8% (pre-employment), 13% (random testing), and 30% (post-accident or just cause).

10.3.8 WDT in South America

10.3.8.1 Introduction

Workplace drug testing is not a common practice in South America. Most countries do not have established guidelines or policies. Generally, it is performed because the company (usually North American based) requires it as part of a global policy of WDT. The most notable case is Exxon, which requires all of its employees to undergo testing. The tests are mainly performed in a U.S. laboratory and conform to SAMHSA/NIDA guidelines.

10.3.8.2 Brazil

WDT began in 1992 with oil companies and has broadened to include transport and car manufacture, as well as the state police. Since 1992, more than 40,000 tests have been performed and they conform to SAMSHA/NIDA requirements. Over 80% of these tests have been done in the past 3 years. Tests are mainly in urine, but can include hair and oral fluid. Positive tests are handled according to the individual company's drug prevention program. This may include outright dismissal, but the vast majority of companies adopt a more tolerant approach with rehabilitation and treatment. An individual is usually allowed up to three positive drug tests prior to dismissal.

This latter approach has yielded positive results, with many employees voluntarily seeking help for their drug/alcohol problems. When employees perceive that they will receive adequate and sympathetic treatment, rather than dismissal, they are more prone to accept rehabilitation.

The rate of companies adopting a drug prevention policy with testing is increasing at the rate of 5 to 7% a year. Government policy is neither for nor against WDT. It is seen as one important step in the antidrug campaign: it promotes issues of occupational health and safety.

10.3.8.3 Other South American Countries

Argentina: There is no national program and only one company (Exxon) requires it.
Bolivia: There is no official drug-testing program apart from companies that require testing as part of a global program.
Chile: It is starting to develop policies but without any testing so far.
Colombia: Again only one oil company (Exxon) has a WDT program.
Paraguay: A WDT program is beginning, but the tests will be performed in Brazil.
Venezuela: Some major oil companies have WDT programs with testing performed abroad. According to Dr. Lilia Scott (M.D.), there is great difficulty in implementing such programs in the country, as the government does not endorse WDT.
Ecuador, Peru, Uruguay, Guyanas (Guyana, Suriname, and French Guyana). There are no reports of WDT in these countries.

10.3.9 Conclusion

WDT is minimally performed around the world compared to in the U.S. It is not envisaged that it ever will become as prevalent. In the U.S., there are rigid regulations for all aspects of drug testing from collection to reporting. The rest of the world does not have the same safeguards. There is much more use of POCT with all the attendant problems of correct use of the device. Some companies do not inform the employee or presumptive employee that he or she is being tested. Often there is no confirmation test. The use of alternative matrices for WDT is also increasing.

Acknowledgments

Dr. John Lewis, Toxicology Unit, Pacific Laboratory Medical Services, Sydney, NSW, Australia.
Prof. Alain Verstraete, Klinische Biologie, University of Ghent, Belgium
Dr. Anthony Wong, Maxilab Diagnósticos, Brazil
Dr. Leendert Mostert, Deltalab, Rotterdam, the Netherlands
Mr. Per Bjorklov, Huddinge Hospital, Stockholm, Sweden
Prof. Robert Wennig, Centre Universitaire, Luxembourg
Ms. Satu Suoimen, Helsinki, Finland
Prof. Gerold Kauert, Centre of Legal Medicine, Frankfurt, Germany
Dr. Cesar Fernandez, Toxscreen, Barcelona, Spain
Ms. Lindsay Hadfield, Medscreen, London, U.K.
Mr. Leo Rebsdorf, ScanScreen ApS, Kolding, Denmark

REFERENCES

1. Verstraete, A.G. and Pierce, A., Workplace drug testing in Europe, *Forensic Sci. Int.*, 121(1–2), 2–6, 2001.
2. de la Torre, R., Segura, J., de Zeeuw, R., Williams, J. et al., Recommendations for the reliable detection of illicit drugs in urine in the European Union, with special attention to the workplace, *Ann. Clin. Biochem.*, 34, 1997.
3. Vitoria, P.D., Consumo de alcool e drogas ilegais em empresas do distrito de Lisboa. Fundacao Portuguesa para o Estudo, Prevencao e Tratamento da Toxicodependencia, Cascais, 1994.
4. Pinheiro, J., Pinheiro, R., Marques, E.P., and Vieira, D.N., O consumo de substãncias nas maiores empresas portuguesas. 4° Forum de Medicina do Trabalho, Lisboa, 1997.
5. Tsoukali, H., Raikos, N., Kovatsi, L., Kotrotsi, E., Athanasaki, R., and Psaroulis, D., Workplace drug testing in Northern Greece during the period 2000–2002, presented at 3rd European Symposium on Workplace Drug Testing, Barcelona, Spain, 2003.
6. Survey on alcohol and drug policies in U.K. organisations, Chartered Institute of Personnel and Development, www.cipd.co.uk.
7. Pinheiro, J., Pierce, A., and Bjorklov, P., Employee Attitude Survey, presented at 2nd EWTDS Symposium, Rimini, Italy, 2000.
8. European Laboratory Guidelines for legally defensible Workplace Drug Testing, www.ewdts.org.
9. Nolan, S. and Turner, S., Workplace & Prison Inmate Drug Testing Programmes in New Zealand over a ten year period, presented at TIAFT 41st International Meeting, Melbourne, Australia, 2003.

10.4 ANALYTICAL CONSIDERATIONS AND APPROACHES FOR DRUGS

Daniel S. Isenschmid, Ph.D.[1] and Bruce A. Goldberger, Ph.D.[2]
[1] Toxicology Laboratory, Wayne County Medical Examiner's Office, Detroit, Michigan
[2] University of Florida College of Medicine, Gainesville, Florida

Although recent national surveys have reported declines in overall drug use, more than 11 million Americans still reported using one or more illicit drug in 1992.[1] In addition, results from several studies targeting specific populations, particularly students in high school and college, show that this downward trend has started to reverse itself.[2,3] In response to the numerous reports on the incidence of alcohol and drug abuse in the workplace, many employers have introduced substance abuse programs, one component of which is urine drug testing.[1,4,5] There are several very important differences between this type of testing and the laboratory testing performed for medical reasons:

- The test is not performed on a patient; instead, a specimen is collected from a donor.
- The test result is not used to support a diagnosis; it is a single collection that is used in decisions relating to hiring, suspension from employment, referral to employee assistance programs (EAP), and occasionally, dismissal of the employee. Unlike a true clinical test, it has no medical data to support its veracity and, except in rare circumstances, the collection cannot be repeated.
- For regulated industries in which drug testing is required, the laboratory has to be certified by the Department of Health and Human Services.[6,7] This certification from the Substance Abuse and Mental Health Services Administration (SAMHSA, formerly the National Institute on Drug Abuse) has become the "standard of care" for all drug testing, including that performed for the nonregulated industry. This certification mandates that the laboratory use certain analytical procedures, including gas chromatography mass spectrometry (GC/MS), for confirming immunoassay results, and that it follows rigid chain-of-custody, quality assurance, and data review guidelines.
- The result may be used in a legal environment to support disciplinary action.

Workplace urine drug testing is performed by many laboratories. Because of the strict chain-of-custody and security requirements, most drug testing laboratories are "stand-alone" laboratories, either secured separately from other specialties in larger laboratories or as distinct entities. More recently, there has been a trend toward "mega-laboratories." These are single locations dedicated to workplace drug testing, processing thousands of specimens per shift. Both service expectations and the economics of drug testing have caused the evolution of such facilities. Today's expectations are that negative results will be available within 24 h of collection of the specimen, and that positives will be available within another 24 h. Obviously these expectations, together with the desire to decrease costs, will play an increasing part in the choice of the analytical procedures used. Increasing emphasis is being placed on the ease of automation of such procedures.

This chapter outlines the analytical protocols used in such programs. Since there may be significant penalties if a person tests positive for a drug of abuse, it is critical that individuals are not falsely accused of drug use. It is, therefore, important that drug tests are precise and accurate, utilizing validated methodologies. The validity of a drug test is defined as the ability of an assay to detect drug and/or its metabolites in biological fluids following drug administration. This definition encompasses a variety of factors including: assay characteristics such as sensitivity and specificity; and metabolic and pharmacological variables such as dose, route of administration, biological fluid pH, and intersubject variability in absorption, metabolism, and excretion.[8] Typical urine drug and drug metabolite detection times are given in Table 10.4.1.

10.4.1 Immunoassay Testing

When testing urine specimens for drugs of abuse, laboratories usually screen specimens utilizing a nonspecific immunoassay. These assays may detect classes of drugs, such as the opiates, rather than specific drugs within a class, such as morphine. Since the majority of specimens will test negative, this eliminates the need to do more costly additional testing.

Immunoassays are based on the principle of competition between labeled and unlabeled antigen (drug) for binding sites on a specific antibody. The label may be an enzyme (homogeneous enzyme immunoassays or heterogeneous enzyme-linked immunosorbant assays), a radioisotope (radioimmunoassay), a fluorophore (fluorescence polarization immunoassay), or latex microparticles (particle immunoassay). Immunoassays are characterized by several variables including specificity and sensitivity.

Specificity is the ability of an assay to distinguish the target analyte(s) from other compounds including those with and without structural similarity. Specificity data are typically provided by manufacturers of immunoassays in the form of a package insert. The specificity requirements and design of a particular assay are critical, and may be dependent on the metabolism of the specific drug. For example, since cocaine is rapidly metabolized, all cocaine immunoassays are formulated to detect the primary cocaine metabolite in urine (benzoylecgonine). Furthermore,

Table 10.4.1   Typical Urine Drug and Drug Metabolite Detection Times*

Drug Class	Detection Times[a]
Amphetamines	1–3 days
Barbiturates	Short-acting, 1 day; intermediate- and long-acting, 1–3 weeks
Benzodiazepines	5–7 days
Cannabinoids	1–3 days; greater (several weeks) with chronic use
Cocaine	1–3 days
LSD	Less than 1 day
Methadone	1–3 days
Methaqualone	1–2 weeks
Opiates	1–3 days
Phencyclidine	Up to 3 days
Propoxyphene	1 2 days

[a] Detection times vary with method of detection, dose, route of administration, frequency of use, and individual factors.

Sources: Substance-Abuse Testing Committee, 1988; Baselt and Cravey, 1995.

Table 10.4.2   Immunoassay Cutoff Concentrations (ng/ml)

Drug Group	Target Antigen	Cutoff
Amphetamines	D-amphetamines, D-methamphetamine or both	300 or 1000*
Barbiturates	Secobarbital	200 or 300
Benzodiazepines	Oxazepam or nordiazepam	100, 200, or 300
Cannabinoids	THCA	20, 25, 50*, or 100
Cocaine	Benzoylecgonine	150 or 300*
Methadone	D-Methadone or D,L-methadone	300
Methaqualone	Methaqualone	300
Opiates	Morphine	300 or 2000*
Phencyclidine	Phencyclidine	25* or 75
Propoxyphene	D-Propoxyphene	300

* Cutoffs used in the SAMHSA Guidelines and the regulated programs.

assays are often designed to be drug class specific (rather than analyte specific) in order that several analytes within a drug class, such as opiates, may be detected with a single assay. Immunoassay performance may be affected by "adulterants," which may be added to a urine specimen in an effort to subvert the testing process. A discussion on specimen adulteration is presented elsewhere in this volume.

Very early in the evolution of workplace drug testing, it was decided, after considerable debate, that there was a need for assay "cutoffs" to ensure some standardization and equality among the various programs. The "cutoff" is an administrative breakpoint used to distinguish positive and negative specimens. When utilizing assay cutoff concentrations, any specimen that contains drug at a concentration at or above the cutoff will be reported as positive, and any specimen that is less than the cutoff will be reported as negative. Immunoassay screening cutoff concentrations are summarized in Table 10.4.2.

When selecting an immunoassay, there are several factors to consider. These include (1) specificity of the kit to the drug group or drug being tested for, (2) the stability of the immunoassay over time, (3) the ability of the immunoassay either to detect adulterants or to be resistant to them, and (4) the ability of the immunoassay to be automated.

10.4.1.1   Radioimmunoassay

The first laboratory assays developed for the detection of drugs of abuse and their metabolites in urine were based on the radioimmunoassay technique. Heterogeneous radioimmunoassays are based upon the competitive binding of ^{125}I-radiolabeled antigen and unlabeled antigen for antibody. Analyte antibody and radiolabeled antigen are added to the specimen and the analyte present in the specimen competes with radiolabeled antigen for antibody sites. After precipitation of the antigen–antibody complex with a second antibody reagent, the supernatant is removed and the pellet containing bound antigen is counted using a gamma counter. The amount of radioactivity is inversely related to the concentration of analyte in the specimen.

Radioimmunoassays are very sensitive, generally more so than non-isotopic enzyme immunoassays. Radioimmunoassays have been developed for all common drugs of abuse and have been designed to produce qualitative and semiquantitative results. The disadvantages of radioimmunoassays include limited reagent shelf-life due to the short half-life of ^{125}I, the requirement for additional laboratory safety precautions due to radioisotope use, and considerable technician involvement. They are infrequently used in the urine drug testing industry today, although they are still used for drug testing in alternative matrices, especially blood and hair, as they are less susceptible to matrix effects than many enzyme immunoassays.

10.4.1.2 Enzyme Immunoassay

Enzyme immunoassays for the detection of drugs of abuse in urine initially developed during the early 1970s by Syva Company under the trade name EMIT™ (enzyme multiplied immunoassay technique) are now also available from a variety of manufacturers. At the time of its introduction, the EMIT technology offered several advantages over other available procedures for drug testing. The technique provided moderate sensitivity, eliminated a separation stage, utilized reagents with longer shelf-life, could be performed rapidly, and was easily adaptable to manual and automated spectrophotometer-based laboratory instrumentation. The principle of the EMIT assay is based on competition between drug in the specimen and drug labeled with the enzyme glucose-6-phosphate dehydrogenase for antibody binding sites. The enzyme activity decreases following binding to the antibody; therefore, the drug concentration in the specimen can be measured in terms of enzyme activity. In practice, when free analyte is present in the specimen, the displaced free enzyme will convert nicotinamide adenine dinucleotide (NAD) to NADH resulting in a change in absorbance, which is measured spectrophotometrically. The resultant increase in absorbance is proportional to the concentration of the analyte in the specimen.

More recently, this technology has been applied to enzyme-linked immunosorbent assays (ELISA). These assays differ from liquid enzyme immunoassays in that the assays are heterogeneous and are performed on a microtiter plate and are therefore less subject to the matrix effects than are homogeneous enzyme immunoassays. In ELISA diluted specimens and drug-labeled enzyme are incubated in microplate wells coated with fixed amounts of oriented polyclonal antibody. The enzyme (horseradish peroxidase)-drug complex competes for antibodies with the free antigen (drug). After incubation, the wells are washed and a chromogenic substrate (tetramethylbenzidine) is added. Tetramethylbenzidine is converted to a colored product by the unbound drug-enzyme complex. The color reaction is stopped by adding dilute acid. Plates are then read at 450 nm with the intensity of color inversely proportional to the concentration of drug in the sample. These assays offer all of the advantages of radioimmunoassays without radioactive disposal issues and in addition are more amenable to automation using robotic pipettor-diluters, plate washers, and spectrophotometric readers. In addition, as the assay uses an enzyme as a label, shelf-lives are much longer than for radioimmunoassays. Although enzyme-linked immunoassays are not commonly used in very high volume urine drug testing laboratories, they are used in high-volume oral fluid drug testing laboratories and for blood drug testing. Many manufacturers now offer these types of assays.

In the mid-1990s, Microgenics Corporation introduced a new homogeneous assay system for drugs of abuse in urine called cloned enzyme donor immunoassay, or CEDIA®. The CEDIA assay is based on the genetically engineered bacterial enzyme β-galactosidase that consists of two inactive fragments. These fragments spontaneously associate to form an active enzyme that cleaves a substrate, chlorophenol red β-galactopyranoside, producing a color change that is measured spectrophotometrically. In the assay, analyte in the specimen competes with analyte conjugated to one inactive fragment of β-galactosidase for antibody binding site. If analyte is present in the specimen, it will bind to antibody, leaving the inactive enzyme fragments free to form active enzyme. The amount of active enzyme formed and resultant increase in absorbance are proportional to the amount of analyte present in the specimen.

10.4.1.3   Fluorescence Polarization Immunoassay

Fluorescence polarization immunoassays (FPIA) were initially developed by Abbott Laboratories for use by laboratories performing therapeutic drug monitoring and were subsequently adapted for detection of drugs of abuse in urine specimens. The Abbott FPIA system employs a fluorescein-analyte labeled tracer. The tracer, when excited by linearly polarized light, emits fluorescence with a degree of polarization inversely related to its rate of rotation. The analyte of interest, if present in the specimen, competes for a limited number of antibody binding sites with the labeled tracer. If the tracer molecules become bound to its specific antibody, the rotation of the tracer assumes that of the larger antibody molecule, which is significantly less than the unbound tracer molecule, and the subsequent polarization is high. The remaining unbound tracer becomes randomly oriented and rotates rapidly; the subsequent polarization is low. The degree of fluorescence polarization is inversely related to the concentration of analyte in the specimen.

The Abbott FPIA abused drug assays offer laboratories several options that are not available with other systems. All FPIAs utilize a six-point calibration curve, in conjunction with nonlinear regression data manipulation, to estimate unknown specimen drug concentrations. Assay cutoff concentrations can be programmed by the laboratory between the assay sensitivity limit and the highest calibrator concentration. Also, the data printout can be programmed to include either qualitative or semiquantitative results. The assays are amenable to the analysis of other matrices, are very stable, and are resistant to a number of adulterants.

10.4.1.4   Particle Immunoassay

In the early 1990s, Roche Diagnostic Systems introduced the Abuscreen ONLINE® (immunoassay system known as the kinetic interaction of microparticles in solution, or KIMS®). The assay is based on the competition of analyte in a specimen for free antibody with analyte-microparticle conjugate. Particle aggregation occurs in the absence of analyte when free antibody binds to the analyte-microparticle conjugate. The formation of an aggregate scatters light, which results in a reduction of light transmission that can be measured spectrophotometrically. The absorbance change is inversely related to the analyte concentration. The assays can be run on many automated clinical chemistry analyzers, have good stability, and are resistant to a number of adulterants.

10.4.1.5   On-Site Drug Testing

A new market of drug testing devices has grown in recent years due to the desire to decrease turnaround time and cut costs. These "on-site" drug testing kits are typically used at the specimen collection site and are self-contained devices utilizing immunoassay technology for drug testing. The use of these devices has increased in recent years due to their simplicity, ease of performance, and no requirement for expensive equipment or skilled personnel. Minimal operator training is required, results are typically obtained within 10 to 15 min of specimen application, and the presence or absence of a color is the most common method of reading the results. The cost saving occurs in that only those specimens that test positive by this screening assay will be sent to a laboratory for confirmation by an alternative analytical technique. Depending on the specific device and the number of drugs assayed, the cost per test may range between $3.00 and $25.00.[9]

The kits may be used in emergency rooms, physician offices, drug treatment centers, probation services, and by employers for pre-employment and random or reasonable cause drug testing to provide preliminary qualitative results. The majority of the devices have built-in validation controls. If the testing is performed for forensic purposes, all positive specimens must be confirmed by an alternative technique. These tests utilize urine as the drug testing matrix and are available to test several drug classes. There are many manufacturers of these devices and their efficacy, as with all assays, depends on their validity in the detection of drugs of abuse. There are several reports of validity assessment studies of these devices.[9–20]

10.4.1.6 Testing for HHS-Regulated Drugs by Immunoassay

Amphetamines

Amphetamines are sympathomimetic phenethylamine derivatives with potent central nervous system stimulant activity. Amphetamine and methamphetamine are extensively metabolized and can be detected in urine specimens for up to 3 days. Because methamphetamine is metabolized to amphetamine, amphetamine and methamphetamine-amine are present in urine after methamphetamine ingestion.

In workplace testing, the detection of amphetamines by immunoassay is commonly performed using a kit designed to detect the D-isomers of amphetamine and/or methamphetamine, and not kits designed to detect the amphetamine group. However, there are amphetamine class assays available for clinical toxicology laboratories and others interested in detecting relatively low concentrations of other sympathomimetic amines. Many of these agents, including ephedrine, pseudoephedrine, phentermine, phenylpropanolamine, and phenylephrine, are found in popular nonprescription over-the-counter, cold, allergy, and diet medications. Even though the kits designed to detect the D-isomers of amphetamine and/or methamphetamine have low cross-reactivity to these other sympathomimetic amines, their concentrations in urine may still be high enough to trigger a false-positive test result.

There are important differences between the kits most widely used for amphetamine detection. They all share a 1000 ng/ml cutoff, but some use D-methamphetamine as a calibrator, whereas others use D-amphetamine. When comparing tests for amphetamines, three important questions must be answered: (1) are all assays equivalent in detecting the abuse or use of D-methamphetamine or D-amphetamine, (2) are all assays stereospecific to the D-isomers or will they detect use of L-isomers (Vicks Inhaler) or drugs metabolized to L-isomers (Selegiline), and (3) if the illicit form of methamphetamine used is a racemic mixture, can all assays detect the use? As one might expect, the answers to these questions vary significantly.

The EMIT and CEDIA enzyme assays have good cross-reactivity toward D-amphetamine (the metabolite of D-methamphetamine), and therefore, if the specimen contains 500 ng/ml of D-methamphetamine and 500 D-amphetamine, one would expect the response to be equal to or greater than that of 1000 ng/ml of the calibrator. It should be noted that for the EMIT d.a.u., which uses D-methamphetamine as calibrator, the response would be greater because of the cross-reactivity of D-amphetamine. In fact, one of the claims made about this kit is that 300 ng/ml of D-amphetamine is equivalent to 1000 ng/ml of D-methamphetamine.

A different situation exists with FPIA. Here the calibrator is D-amphetamine and the cross-reactivity toward D-methamphetamine varies, depending on its concentration. In this case there is an increased response toward mixtures of amphetamine and methamphetamine such that combined concentrations of less than 1000 ng/ml may test positive.

A similar situation exists with the KIMS assay, which was specifically designed to satisfy the federal reporting requirement, which states that in order to report a confirmed positive result for methamphetamine in urine (at or above 500 ng/ml), amphetamine must also be present at or above 200 ng/ml.[7] The assay has little cross-reactivity with pure methamphetamine but enhanced cross-reactivity when amphetamine is present with methamphetamine. This creates two potential scenarios: (1) the assay may detect specimens that contain less than 1000 ng/ml methamphetamine when amphetamine is present and (2) proficiency specimens containing only methamphetamine that are designed to test the laboratories' ability to follow reporting requirements may not produce a positive test result. For practical purposes using donor specimens, the assay has been found to be equivalent to the EMIT assays in detecting positive specimens from methamphetamine users.[21]

An examination of the cross-reactivities of the different tests toward *l*-methamphetamine might lead one to the conclusion that therapeutic use of Vicks Inhaler would not result in a positive response using these kits. Fitzgerald et al.[22] reported concentrations of methamphetamine as high as 6000 ng/ml following use of this decongestant, and these would certainly not be expected to elicit a positive response. He also reported *l*-amphetamine concentrations as high as 455 ng/ml. However, the situation is not as clear as it first seems. The College of American Pathologists, in its Forensic Urine Drug Testing Program, challenged laboratories with a specimen containing approximately 9000 ng/ml of *l*-methamphetamine and 2000 ng/ml of *l*-amphetamine. Greater than 80% of the respondents reported the drugs as positive. Given that the majority, if not all, of the respondents used one of the immunoassays mentioned above, there is likely an additive response in the presence of *l*-methamphetamine and *l*-amphetamine (as there would be for the D-isomers). One obvious outcome of this is that the physician reviewing drug test results should routinely request the separation of stereoisomers by GC/MS.

Methamphetamine can be synthesized by different routes and some of these may lead to the formation of D,*l*-methamphetamine rather than D-methamphetamine.[23] If the donor has used this racemic mixture, then the urine will be less reactive than if he or she had used the pure D-isomer. Under these conditions, 1000 ng/ml of D,L-amphetamine may not trigger a positive response using the immunoassays; the exact response will depend on the amount of methamphetamine and amphetamine present and the additive response of the kit to this mixture.

From this discussion, it is apparent that the exact response of a specimen containing various amounts of amphetamines and varying ratios of the stereoisomers cannot be predicted with any certainty and that the various commercially available immunoassays will react differently. Is this important? It is unlikely that any of these kits are failing to detect the majority of methamphetamine abusers; however, the possibility exists that specimens from some abusers are not being detected and that specimens from users of Vicks Inhaler are being reported as positive (particularly outside of the regulated programs). Without a standardization of the various kits used (for example, requiring them to detect 500 ng/ml of D-methamphetamine and 500 ng/ml of D-amphetamine on a 1:1 basis), the situation will remain as varied as it is today.

Recently there has been significant attention given to the illicit stimulants 3,4-methylenedioxymethamphetamine (MDMA, also known as "Ecstasy") and 3,4-methylenedioxyamphetamine (MDA, also known as the "love pill"). Currently, HHS regulations do not allow for the testing of these drugs. However, some immunoassays designed for testing for amphetamines possess considerable cross-reactivity to these drugs. Immunoassay kits designed specifically to detect these agents are available as well. For example, some ELISA assays (e.g., Immunalysis) have kits specifically designed for the analysis of either D-methamphetamine (and MDMA) or D-amphetamine (and MDA). Both kits have very low cross-reactivity to the L-isomers of methamphetamine and amphetamine, respectively. However, as methamphetamine kit has low cross-reactivity to amphetamine and the amphetamine kit has low cross-reactivity to methamphetamine, these types of kits would not be particularly well suited for drug testing under the HHS Guidelines. A similar situation is encountered for several radioimmunoassays as well.

Cannabinoids

Marijuana is a popular, potent hallucinogen used primarily for its euphoric effects. The psychoactive constituent in marijuana is δ-9-tetrahydrocannabinol (THC). THC is metabolized to 11-

hydroxy-δ-9-tetrahydrocannabinol, which is rapidly metabolized to 11-nor-δ-9-tetrahydrocannab-inol-9-carboxylic acid (THCA). THCA may be detected in urine specimens for variable periods of time and potentially for up to several weeks depending on the frequency of use.

Immunoassay techniques are designed to detect cannabinoids in urine specimens utilizing THCA as the target analyte. Other non-cannabinoid analytes usually do not cross-react with the cannabinoid assays. Marinol®, synthetic THC, used for the treatment of anorexia associated with AIDS, will produce positive test results. The original formulation of the EMIT cannabinoid assay was subject to false-positive test results in the presence of ibuprofen. The assay was reformulated in 1986, and is no longer affected by ibuprofen.

Cannabinoid immunoassay cutoff concentrations will affect the percentage of nonconfirmable positive screening results, especially in specimens with urinary concentrations of THCA between 50 and 100 ng/ml. Further, it is difficult to correlate immunoassay response with GC/MS confir-mation results for THCA since immunoassay results reflect total cannabinoid metabolite concen-tration, rather than THCA concentration only.[27]

A problem associated with the interpretation of urine cannabinoid test results is that positive tests may occur from passive inhalation of marijuana smoke. The presence of cannabinoid metab-olites in urine specimens due to passive inhalation is a function of environmental conditions, duration and frequency of exposure, and THC content of the smoked marijuana.[25–28] Although passive inhalation studies have shown that individuals exposed to marijuana cigarette smoke under typical conditions would not test positive for cannabinoids, in order to avoid interpretive problems, the federally mandated THCA cutoff concentration was initially set at 100 ng/ml. The cutoff concentration was lowered to 50 ng/ml in 1994.[7] However, passive inhalation studies were per-formed with marijuana cigarettes containing low concentration of THC (less than 4.0%). Cigarettes seized by law enforcement personnel in recent years have demonstrated THC concentrations exceeding 20%, clearly demonstrating the need to reinvestigate passive inhalation issues.

Cocaine (Metabolite)

Cocaine is a potent central nervous system stimulant and local anesthetic. It is rapidly hydro-lyzed to benzoylecgonine and ecgonine methyl ester by metabolic and chemical reactions. Ben-zoylecgonine, the primary cocaine metabolite in urine, is readily detected for 1 to 3 days. Following chronic use of cocaine, benzoylecgonine may be detected for longer periods of time.

Immunoassay techniques are designed to detect cocaine metabolites in urine specimens utilizing benzoylecgonine as the target analyte. Cross-reactivity with other non-cocaine compounds such as lidocaine, benzocaine, and procaine does not occur and will not produce false-positive test results.

In the mid-1980s it was found that Health Inca Tea, which was sold in U.S. health food stores, contained trace amounts of cocaine. The U.S. Food and Drug Administration has since banned the importation of any tea containing residual cocaine. Yet several studies performed with Health Inca Tea and other teas imported from South American countries clearly show that even very low amounts of cocaine in a beverage can result in a positive urine drug test. Health Inca Tea has been reported to contain an average of 4.8 mg of cocaine/bag[29] and between 1.87 and 2.15 mg of cocaine/cup of prepared tea.[30,31] In four subjects ingesting one cup of Health Inca Tea containing 1.87 mg of cocaine, peak urinary benzoylecgonine concentration ranged from 1400 to 2800 ng/ml 4 to 11 h after ingestion, well above the 300 ng/ml regulated immunoassay cutoff concentration.[31] In another study where one subject drank a cup of tea containing 2.15 mg of cocaine, the peak urinary benzoylecgonine concentration of 1280 ng/ml occurred 2 h after tea ingestion.[30] In a study where 6 oz. of Coca-Cola fortified with 25 mg cocaine HCl was consumed by a 165-lb male, peak urinary concentrations of benzoylecgonine (7940 ng/ml) were obtained at 12 h.[32] Urine benzoylecgonine concentrations remained in excess of 300 ng/ml for 48 h.

These studies demonstrate that very small amounts of cocaine, <5.0 mg or about one fifth of a typical intranasal dose (or line), when added to or contained in a beverage, are sufficient to produce a positive drug test in an unsuspecting subject for cocaine metabolites in urine. In such cases, the detection of unique cocaine metabolites, such as methylecgonidine or ecgonidine, produced after smoking crack cocaine, may prove to be useful in refuting alleged oral ingestion of cocaine after a positive drug test for benzoylecgonine; however, testing for these analytes is not currently permitted under federal drug testing guidelines. Instead, the guidelines provided to Medical Review Officers (MROs) state that unknowing ingestion of cocaine is not an alternative medical explanation for the presence of benzoylecgonine in the donor's urine.

Opiates

Opiates are potent drugs that are routinely utilized as analgesics to treat moderate to severe pain. Legitimate pharmaceutical sources of opiates include morphine and codeine. Heroin, an illicit substance, is most often abused for production of euphoria and avoidance of withdrawal symptoms. Heroin is rapidly metabolized to 6-acetylmorphine, which is further metabolized to morphine. Codeine is also metabolized to morphine. Opiates may be detected in urine specimens for up to 24 h or for several days, depending on the amount and agent administered.

Immunoassay techniques are designed to detect opiates and their metabolites (primarily morphine, codeine, and their glucuronide metabolites) in urine specimens using morphine as the target analyte. Most opiate assays are generally nonspecific and cross-react with many opiate compounds. Under the federal drug testing program, only morphine, codeine, and 6-acetylmorphine may be reported. In nonregulated testing, other opiates, especially hydrocodone, hydromorphone, and oxycodone, are frequently included as part of the opiate panel, although it should be noted that oxycodone frequently has limited cross-reactivity in general opiate immunoassays. Oxycodone-specific immunoassays are available.

Morphine and codeine have been identified in urine specimens of individuals who have ingested poppy seeds and/or poppy seed cakes. Opiate immunoassays are sufficiently sensitive to detect morphine and morphine conjugates in these specimens days following ingestion. These results are true positives, even though not indicative of opiate abuse. Therefore, in the case of a positive opiate test result, additional testing may be required to differentiate the heroin user from the poppy seed consumer.[25,33] In an attempt to address this issue, in 1997 the mandatory guidelines were changed to increase the initial and confirmatory testing cutoffs for morphine and codeine from 300 to 2000 ng/ml.[34] In addition, the requirement for testing for 6-acetylmorphine (cutoff concentration 10 ng/ml) when morphine is present at concentrations at or above 2000 ng/ml was added. These changes were implemented on December 1, 1998.

Phencyclidine

Phencyclidine (commonly known as PCP), a hallucinogen and dissociative anesthetic, is readily detected in urine specimens for up to several days following administration. Immunoassay techniques are designed to detect phencyclidine in urine specimens utilizing phencyclidine as the target analyte. Cross-reactivity with other non-phencyclidine-related compounds is not usually observed except for high concentrations of thioridazine in some assays.[35]

10.4.1.7 Testing for Other Drugs by Immunoassay

Barbiturates

Barbiturates are central nervous system depressants and are utilized as sedative-hypnotic and anticonvulsant agents. There are many barbiturate derivatives that constitute this class of drugs and are classified as ultrashort-, short-, intermediate-, and long-acting agents. Detection of a specific barbiturate in urine depends upon the type of barbiturate ingested, and ranges from 24 h (short-acting) to several weeks (long-acting).

All immunoassay techniques are designed to detect the majority of short-, intermediate-, and long-acting barbiturates in urine specimens using secobarbital as the target analyte. A positive test result indicates the presence of barbiturates in the urine specimen. Additional testing utilizing a chromatographic technique is necessary to identify the specific barbiturate(s) present.

Benzodiazepines

Benzodiazepines are central nervous system depressants utilized for their anxiolytic, seda-tive–hypnotic, anticonvulsant, and muscle relaxant properties. There are many benzodiazepines that constitute this class of drugs, and they are classified as ultrashort-, short-, and long-acting agents. Detection of a specific benzodiazepine in urine depends on the type of benzodiazepine ingested and ranges from 5 to 7 days.

Immunoassay techniques are designed to detect benzodiazepine compounds and their metabo-lites in urine specimens utilizing oxazepam or nordiazepam as the target analyte. A positive test result requires further testing utilizing a chromatographic technique to identify the specific benzo-diazepine compound and/or metabolite(s) present in the specimen. Depending on the immunoassay technique, other benzodiazepines, such as alprazolam, clonazepam, lorazepam, and triazolam, may be difficult to detect.

Methadone

Methadone is a synthetic opioid that has analgesic actions and potency similar to morphine. Although its primary use has been in the detoxification and maintenance of heroin addiction, its use is also indicated for treatment of severe pain. This latter use has become much more common in the past few years and reports of methadone abuse and methadone-related fatalities are increas-ing.[36] Methadone is readily detected in urine specimens for up to 72 h after administration.

Immunoassay techniques are designed to detect methadone in urine specimens using methadone as the target analyte. Although the methadone assays usually do not cross-react with compounds structurally unrelated to methadone, the presence of metabolites in urine specimens from individuals administered L-alpha-acetylmethadol (LAAM), a long-acting methadone analogue, may produce positive test results.

Methaqualone

Methaqualone is a central nervous system depressant. Although methaqualone was a popular drug during the 1970s and early 1980s, its use has been replaced by other drugs such as benzodi-azepines. Methaqualone is not currently available legally in the U.S. Following administration, methaqualone can be detected in urine specimens for up to 14 days. Immunoassay techniques are designed to detect methaqualone in urine specimens using methaqualone as the target analyte. Cross-reactivity with other non-methaqualone-related compounds is not usually observed.

Propoxyphene

Propoxyphene is a synthetic opioid that has analgesic actions and potency similar to codeine. Its use is indicated for the treatment of moderate to severe pain. Propoxyphene and its primary metabolite, norpropoxyphene, are present in urine specimens for several days. Immunoassay tech-niques are designed to detect propoxyphene and norpropoxyphene in urine specimens utilizing propoxyphene as the target analyte. Cross-reactivity with other non-propoxyphene-related com-pounds is not usually observed.

Table 10.4.3   GC/MS Cutoff Concentrations

Drug Group	Common Analyte(s)	Cutoff Concentration (ng/ml)
Amphetamines	Amphetamine, methamphetamine	300 or 500[a],*
Barbiturates	Amobarbital, butalbital, pentobarbital, phenobarbital, secobarbital	200 or 300
Benzodiazepines	alpha-Hydroxyalprazolam, nordiazepam, oxazepam, temazepam	100, 200, or 300
Cannabinoids	THCA	10 or 15*
Cocaine	Benzoylecgonine	150*
Methadone	Methadone	100 or 300
Methaqualone	Methaqualone	300
Opiates	Codeine, morphine (6-acetylmorphine)	300 or 2000* (10*)
Phencyclidine	Phencyclidine	25* or 75
Propoxyphene	Propoxyphene and/or norpropxyphene	300

[a] 200 ng/ml amphetamine must be present to report methamphetamine positive.
* Cutoffs used in the SAMHSA Guidelines and the regulated programs.

10.4.2   Confirmatory Testing

Before the introduction of the HHS Guidelines[6] there was considerable discussion among forensic toxicologists regarding the appropriate analytical procedures to be used to confirm immunoassay results. There was a recognition that these had to be based on a different chemical principle than immunoassay, but there was not a consensus that this needed to be GC/MS. However, the Guidelines mandated that GC/MS be used to confirm presumptive positives from immunoassay testing and its use was further incorporated into the College of American Pathologist's FUDT inspection program. It has now become the standard of practice in workplace drug testing to confirm all initial immunoassay results by GC/MS. Common cutoff concentrations are listed in Table 10.4.3.

Not only was there considerable discussion on the need for GC/MS, there was also considerable debate about the suitability of selected ion monitoring for the identification of drugs and/or their metabolites. Several well-respected forensic toxicologists argued that full scan GC/MS was necessary before a specimen could be reported as positive. Although this argument is still heard today, there is a broad consensus of opinion that selected ion monitoring is an accurate and reliable procedure for identification of these substances. The analytical principles of GC/MS have been well covered by other authors.[37,38] The HHS Guidelines[6,7] required certified drug testing laboratories to be inspected every 6 months, and it is this inspection process that has driven the improvement in the confirmation procedures. This section examines some of the quality assurance/quality control procedures that have become common practice in certified drug testing laboratories and briefly discusses some analytical issues.

10.4.2.1   Quality Assurance

To provide adequate control and verification of the analytical process, laboratories must implement appropriate policies and procedures regarding GC/MS analysis. This section is intended to discuss the quality control and quality assurance requirements pertinent to the regulated drug-testing laboratory, although many of the components specified below are directly applicable to any laboratory performing drug testing in biological specimens. Much of the information in this section has been condensed from a comprehensive review of commonly practiced quality control and quality assurance procedures in forensic urine drug testing laboratories.[39]

Method Validation

Method validation is a process of documenting or proving that an analytical method is acceptable for its intended purpose. For analytical methods to be implemented in laboratory-based regulatory drug testing programs, the laboratory must be able to demonstrate that the chosen analytical method has the ability to provide *accurate* and *reliable* data. At a minimum, the key assay characteristics to be established and evaluated should include the accuracy, precision, linearity, specificity, sensitivity, carryover potential, and ruggedness of the analytical method. Additional characteristics to be evaluated may include the stability of the analyte under various analytical and storage conditions, identification and concentration of the internal standard(s) for the method, validation of use of partial (diluted) sample volumes, and estimated recovery of the analyte from the matrix.

Accuracy and Precision — Two of the most important assay characteristics to be determined during method validation are accuracy and precision. Together, accuracy and precision determine the error of an analytical measurement. The accuracy of a method refers to the closeness of the measured value to the true value for the sample. Precision, on the other hand, refers to the variability of measurements within a set. It is most often used to demonstrate scatter or dispersion between numeric values in a set of measurements that have been determined under the same analytic parameters.

The accuracy and precision of an assay can be determined by comparing test results utilizing laboratory-prepared standards and controls with those obtained with an established reference method or by analysis of standard reference materials. Secondary checks may involve reanalysis of specimens whose concentrations are already known to be accurate (e.g., patient or proficiency samples analyzed by reference laboratories using a validated method).

Accuracy is generally expressed as the percentage difference from the actual value. The assessment of accuracy must be carried out on mean values that have been calculated from replicate measurements of reference materials containing known concentration of analyte. It has been recommended that accuracy be assessed using a minimum of nine determinations over a minimum of three concentrations (i.e., 3 concentrations/3 replicates each).[40,41]

Accuracy acceptability ranges in forensic urine drug testing laboratories should not exceed 20% (by convention) of the target concentration. Many laboratories routinely use lower ranges, such as 10%. It should be noted that the acceptable accuracy range selected for initial method validation may differ from that selected for routine use (batch acceptance criteria). For example, a laboratory may require that accuracy be within 10% of the known concentration during method validation, and then choose to increase the acceptable range to 20% for routine daily analysis.[42]

Precision of an analytical method is usually assessed in two ways: analysis of multiple measurements during a single analytical run (within-run precision) and analysis of single, or mean, measurements over many runs (between-run precision). Precision is expressed as the percentage relative standard deviation or coefficient of variation (CV). Within-run precision can be considered a measure of the precision of an analytical method under optimal conditions. The between-run precision, however, is a better representation of the precision one might observe during routine use of the assay. The precision of an assay should be determined at concentrations below, at, and above the assay cutoff concentration for that assay. This can be accomplished by repeated analyses of quality control samples on a within- and between-batch basis. Precision should be determined not only when validating the methods, but on an ongoing basis. The SAMHSA guidelines currently require annual review of accuracy and precision. Generally, within-run and between-run CV values of less than <15% are considered acceptable.[43–45] However, greater variability is to be expected as analyte concentrations approach the limit of detection (LOD) of the analytical method and the laboratory might choose to increase the acceptability criterion to 20% at its lowest measured concentrations.[46]

Linearity and Sensitivity of the Analytical Method — The linear range of a method should be established during initial assay characterization and periodically thereafter with specimens containing drug analytes over a wide range of concentrations. In forensic urine drug testing, linearity should be established via evaluation of a plot of instrument response (y) as a function of analyte concentration (x) using least-squares analysis.[47,48] Using a series of calibrators that have been prepared at various known concentrations of analyte, the individual concentrations of each calibrator are "reverse calculated" using the regression line generated. Acceptable linearity is demonstrated when the correlation coefficient exceeds a defined value, such as 0.990, and quantitative concentration of each point falls within ±20% of the target value. For purposes of forensic urine drug testing, the limit of quantitation and upper limit of linearity of the assay are typically defined as the lowest and highest concentrations, respectively, where all quantitative *and* qualitative quality control criteria are met. The limit of detection of the assay is the lowest concentration for which qualitative quality control criteria are met. Other approaches (e.g., signal/noise ratios) may be used to establish these parameters and have been reviewed elsewhere.[39]

The laboratory uses this information to establish the range, or concentration interval, which it will routinely use for analysis of samples. Validating the method over a wider range than that used in daily practice provides increased confidence that the routine standard concentrations are well removed from nonlinear response concentrations.

Specificity of the Analytical Method (Interference Studies) — Specificity refers to the ability of the analytical method to accurately measure an analyte response in the presence of all potential sample components. All methods should at a minimum be investigated for potential interference by endogenous matrix components, as well as common compounds that are structurally similar to the analyte of interest.

The potential interference of endogenous urine components with the assay is most frequently assessed by evaluation of urine specimens from several sources (donors) that are known to be drug-free for the analyte of interest. Assessment of interference from structurally-related compounds can be determined by fortification of urine with high concentrations (e.g., 1 mg/ml) of potentially interfering analytes and cutoff concentrations of target analytes, or with concentrations of analyte that are expected under therapeutic conditions. For example, possible interference with the measurement of amphetamine and methamphetamine may occur due to the presence of sympathomimetic amines such as ephedrine, pseudoephedrine, phenylpropanolamine, and phentermine.[49] Further, interference with the measurement of morphine and codeine due to the presence of opiate metabolites and synthetic 6-keto-opioids such as dihydrocodeine, hydromorphone, hydrocodone, oxymorphone, and oxycodone has also been described.[50]

The problem of interfering substances may be addressed by employing more selective extraction methods, chromatographic separations, or detection methods. For example, to eliminate potential false-positive amphetamine/methamphetamine results due to the presence of other sympathomimetic amines, aliquots of specimens can be treated with a solution of 0.035 M sodium periodate at room temperature, then subjected to extraction. In the presence of periodate, α-hydroxyamines undergo oxidative cleavage removing the potential interferent.[51] It is recommended that periodate oxidation be conducted at pH 7 or lower to prevent possible formation of low levels of amphetamine from extremely high levels of methamphetamine that may be present in the specimen.[52]

Carryover — The term *carryover* is used to refer to the contamination of a sample by a sample analyzed immediately prior to it.[53,54] In the urine drug testing laboratory, the term *carryover limit* is used to delineate the concentration of analyte in a sample above which contamination may reasonably be expected to occur. There is at least one common approach to performing such studies that involves the analysis of standards prepared at increasingly higher concentrations of analyte, preferably reflecting the highest concentrations that a laboratory typically encounters during routine analysis of samples. Each standard should be injected separately, followed by injection of a blank or solvent to determine if a signal (response) characteristic of the analyte is present in the sample above a pre-established limit (typically the limit of detection). Once the concentration at which carryover occurs is determined, the laboratory establishes its carryover limit at the next lowest concentration that did *not* have evidence of carryover in the blank or solvent. More precisely, upon completion of carryover studies, a laboratory should define the range of analyte concentrations at which carryover does not occur. The laboratory should also ensure that the quantitative value for the carryover limit established in the carryover study falls within the linearity of the assay to ensure that the quantitative value is accurate.

It is also advisable to evaluate carryover of an assay on each instrument system, including autosamplers, on which the method is to be performed, although there is no general consensus on this issue. This is to ensure that the established carryover limit is properly applied to data obtained on each system routinely used in the laboratory. It is important that criteria be established for evaluating the acceptability of solvent blanks or negative quality control samples that have been inserted to assess possible carryover.[55] If carryover is suspected, a potentially contaminated specimen should be reextracted, rather than reinjected, because the extract vial may have been contaminated.

Other Factors — Other factors include selection of a derivatizing reagent, selection of the internal standard(s) for the assay, and selection of ions to monitor for selected-ion monitoring or full-scan analysis. These topics are considered in Section 10.4.2.4 (Analytical Issues).

Another important parameter to assess during the method validation phase is that of stability of the analyte. This includes stability of stock solutions of analyte, as well as stability of the analyte in biological matrix. Stability studies will typically be performed to assess stability under different temperatures (storage conditions) and different lengths of time (in-process stability and long-term stability). It is recommended that the laboratory at least establish analyte stability under its own anticipated storage and processing conditions. While there are many different approaches to the performance of stability studies, a common approach is to use quality control materials prepared at known concentrations to assess stability.[43]

10.4.2.2   Calibrators and Controls

Assay Calibration

In forensic urine drug testing laboratories, assay calibration is necessary to determine whether an analyte is present in an unknown sample at or above a preestablished administrative cutoff value, as well as to determine the accurate quantitative concentration of the analyte under certain circumstances.[56] Calibrators are prepared from a mixture of different amounts of known concentrations of analyte standards with a fixed amount of internal standard. The two most common approaches to assay calibration in forensic urine drug testing laboratories are multipoint calibration curves and single-point calibrations.

Multipoint calibration curves must include calibrators that bracket the cutoff concentration. Although many laboratories include a calibrator at the cutoff concentration, it is not required.[56] For each calibrator, specific ion-abundances are measured for the analyte and internal standard. A ratio is calculated for each calibrator and a calibration curve is generated using a simple least-squares regression model. Generally accepted criteria for acceptable linearity using deuterated internal standards for calibration include a correlation coefficient of at least 0.990, and a y-intercept close to zero, although slightly positive or negative y-intercept values are also acceptable. For assay calibration, the laboratory must also establish whether the regression line will be forced through the origin (a "no-intercept" model) or will not be forced through the origin (an "intercept" model). Selection of a no-intercept model implies that the assay limit of detection is *zero*, which is usually not the case for GC/MS urine drug testing assays. Therefore, in most instances regression through the origin should not be used in assay calibration. Finally, the calculated concentration of all standards against the constructed calibration curve should be within ±20% of their respective target concentrations.

Single-point calibrations utilize a calibrator containing analyte at the assay cutoff concentration. Laboratories then include quality control materials at concentrations below, at, and above and below the cutoff concentration to demonstrate linearity. The quantitative results for the quality control materials used in single-point calibration must fall within 20% of their respective target concentrations.

During assay calibration, the laboratory also establishes acceptance ranges for retention time and ion ratios. Acceptance ranges are established to evaluate each calibrator, control, and unknown specimen in the batch. For single-point calibration assays, the acceptable limits are determined from the calibrator at the cutoff. For multipoint calibration curves, acceptable limits may be determined from either the calibrator at the cutoff *or* from the average of all the calibrators analyzed. The laboratory must apply the acceptable ranges consistently to all calibrators, controls, and specimens in the batch. (See Section 10.4.2.3, Criteria for Designating a Positive Result.)

Chromatographic Performance

The chromatographic performance of an assay should also be assessed before the analysis of specimens. This is achieved readily by the injection of an unextracted performance standard including analyte(s) and internal standard(s). Use of an unextracted standard removes sources of variation due to the extraction procedure and matrix interferences. In addition to permitting evaluation of the quality of the chromatographic system, the analysis of an unextracted standard serves to verify that the analyte(s) of interest elute at the expected retention time, that all MS acquisition windows are appropriately set, and that no unexpected adsorptive system losses have occurred. Evaluation criteria in the standard operating procedure manual should include a thorough description of peak shape, resolution, and signal abundance requirements. A complete review of methods for evaluation of chromatographic performance is beyond the scope of this chapter; however, acceptable alternative criteria for evaluation of chromatographic acceptability can be found in many textbooks and other reference materials.[54,57–61]

Quality Control

Under the HHS guidelines each assay batch must include a minimum total of 10% open and blind positive and negative quality control samples in an appropriate urine matrix.[6,7] Quality control samples may be purchased commercially or prepared from a different source or lot of standard material than that used to prepare calibrators. The target concentration at one control must be within approximately 125% of the cutoff concentration; other controls should be prepared at appropriate concentrations in order to regularly access accuracy below and/or above the assay cutoff concentration. It is recommended that a highly concentrated control sample be diluted in a similar manner as diluted specimens during aliquoting in order to verify the accuracy of the dilution technique, if one is routinely used to prepare presumptive positive specimens for confirmation.[56]

To evaluate the efficiency of the hydrolysis process, cannabinoid and opiate control samples containing conjugated THCA and morphine-glucuronide, respectively, should be assayed. Negative urine samples spiked with these reference materials can be prepared, or as an alternative, hydrolysis control samples can be prepared from a combined urine pool of previously confirmed specimens (which would otherwise be discarded). An additional quality control that includes potentially interfering substances (such as a control-containing phenylpropanolamine, ephedrine, phentermine, and/or pseudoephedrine) is also recommended.

Verification of Quality Control Materials — Prior to the use of reference materials to prepare calibrator, control, or internal standard material in the laboratory, the laboratory is required to verify that its chemical identity is correct and that it is of acceptable purity and concentration *independently* from the supplier. At a minimum, most laboratories perform a full-scan GC/MS analysis to verify the chemical identity and purity of the material and compare the obtained spectra with that of available library spectra to determine that significant impurities are not present in the material which might interfere with the method. The isotopic purity of the internal standard can also be verified with this procedure. Additional methods for verification of chemical identity and purity may involve measurement of physical constants, such as melting point or refractive index, as well as use of other analytical techniques (HPLC, IR, NMR, TLC, or UV/VIS) to detect nonpolar or nonvolatile impurities.[54] Verification of concentration is most often evaluated indirectly by preparation of calibrators or controls at known concentrations and analysis in routine batches. The laboratory must establish specific evaluation criteria for reference materials, such as spectral match requirements, percent isotopic purity required, and quantitative results. The laboratory must retain documentation of all verification procedures performed.[56] The laboratory may then use the reference material to prepare calibrators for controls for routine use. Of course, these new calibrators and controls must then be themselves validated for concentration (e.g., ±20% of the target concentration) prior to routine use.

Evaluation of Quality Control Results — In forensic urine drug testing, the most common approach to the evaluation of quality control results is through the use of a fixed-criterion quantitative acceptance range, usually ±20% of the target concentration. The laboratory's standard operating procedure (SOP) manual must thoroughly describe the quality control evaluation criteria to be used and must include a policy for the required course of corrective action if quality control sample results fail to meet acceptance criteria. To assess laboratory performance, all control data, including out-of-limit data, should be recorded in the quality control log in Levey–Jennings or Shewart chart format.[56,62–67] Out-of-limit data should include documentation of required corrective action. It may be acceptable to reinject a quality control sample one additional time. If the results are still unacceptable, other minimally acceptable protocols include (1) reinjection of calibrators, followed by reprocessing of *all* quality control samples and routine specimen data against the new calibration, *if* the time since the last injection is not excessive and the instrument has not been retuned; (2) reinjection of all calibrators, quality control samples, and routine specimens; and (3) acceptance of negative test results that are less than the LOD and reextraction of all other specimens in the batch.

10.4.2.3   Criteria for Designating a Positive Test Result

Qualitative Criteria

Criteria for designating a positive test result include chromatographic and spectral identification. Chromatographic identification of an analyte requires comparison of the retention time of the specimen with that of a calibrator at the cutoff or the average of multiple calibrators. Generally, the retention time of the analyte should be within ±2% of the retention time as established by the calibrator(s).[56,68,69]

Further, identification of an analyte requires comparison of ion ratios or full-scan mass spectra, respectively. Acceptable ion ratios for the analyte and its corresponding internal standard are usually calculated using ion abundance data obtained for the cutoff calibrator or by determining the mean ion ratios for all calibrators. It has been demonstrated statistically that while full-scan mass spectrometric provides the maximum confidence for analyte identification, a minimum of three structurally significant ions generated under electron ionization conditions appear to provide adequate information for an identification.[68,70] If the regulated urine drug testing laboratory uses electron ionization, it is currently required to use a minimum of two ion ratios for identification of the analyte and at least one ion ratio for the internal standard.[56]

The ion ratios for the analyte and its corresponding internal standard obtained for the unknown should not differ by more than ±20% of the target ion ratio and acceptance criteria must be uniformly applied to all specimens within the batch.[62] The establishment of this 20% acceptance criteria for ion abundance ratios has been determined to be appropriate based on ion statistics.[68–70] Different ion ratio criteria cannot be applied to different specimens, calibrators, or controls within the batch.

Quantitative Criteria

Regardless of the detection technique, to be designated as positive, the measured concentration of a specimen must be equal to or exceed the established assay cutoff concentration. Quantitative results around the cutoff must be truncated, rather than rounded up to the nearest whole number, so that the statistical bias is toward a "negative" result. Specimens directed for GC/MS retest analyses are not subject to cutoff concentrations and are reported as reconfirmed if the concentration is equal to or greater than the LOD of the method. The specimen retest must also meet all other criteria for designating a positive test result.

If the specimen concentration exceeds the upper limit of linearity for the assay, quantitative reports must state that the concentration of the analyte is "greater than *the established upper limit of linearity*" or be reanalyzed using an appropriate dilution. Also, all criteria for designating a positive test result must be satisfied, including chromatographic performance, ion ratios, and retention time data.

Data Review

All data must be thoroughly reviewed by a minimum of two individuals to verify compliance with the methods specified in the laboratory's procedure manual and to identify clerical and analytical errors. Batch acceptance criteria include within-range standards and controls and acceptable MS tune, chromatographic performance, ion abundance (adequate signal-to-noise ratio), and ion ratios or mass spectral match quality. Also, the laboratory may choose to monitor the consistency (reproducibility) of the ion abundance for the internal standard to ensure that it has been added appropriately, and at the correct concentration, to each calibrator, control, and unknown in confirmatory analyses. Furthermore, an acceptable calibration curve must be obtained, a lack of carryover must be demonstrated, and chain-of-custody documentation must be in order.

The SOP must also address the handling and reporting of results when duplicate extracts are assayed, or diluted and undiluted extracts are analyzed. Acceptance criteria for duplicates must specify minimum correlation of quantitative results, usually ±20% if both results fall within the assay's linear range. Both of the results must be equal to or greater than the mandated cutoff concentration. If reporting quantitative results, the least diluted sample within the assay's linear range is typically reported. Review of specimen data should include comparison of the initial immunoassay response with the GC/MS result, an evaluation of chromatographic performance including presence of interfering or extraneous peaks, retention time, minimum ion abundance, ion ratios or mass spectral match quality, quantitation, extraction efficiency, potential for carryover, and chain-of-custody documentation.

10.4.2.4 Analytical Issues

It is far beyond the scope of this section to discuss specific analytical procedures for confirmation of drugs. Methods are readily available in the literature and have been described for urine as well as other matrices. However, it is important to discuss a few of the specific analytical issues that the laboratory will need to face when performing confirmation testing for drugs of abuse by GC/MS.

Selection of a Derivative

Selection of a suitable derivative is a critical component of an assay when required. There are at least three major reasons for using a derivatized compound. First, the analyte can often be made sufficiently volatile to allow its introduction to the mass spectrometer by gas chromatography, permitting optimal separation of the analyte from possible interfering substances. Second, the

Table 10.4.4   Derivatization Procedures

Drug Group	Drugs Commonly Included	Derivatizing Procedure	Ref.
Amphetamines	Amphetamine Methamphetamine	Acylation Silylation	23, 84–86
Barbiturates	Amobarbital Butabarbital Pentobarbital Phenobarbital Secobarbital	Alkylation	87
Benzodiazepines	Nordiazepam Oxazepam	Silylation	88–90
Cannabinoids	THCA	Acylation/esterification Alkylation Silylation	91–94
Cocaine	Benzoylecgonine	Alkylation Silylation	95, 96
Opiates	Codeine Morphine 6-Acetylmorphine[a]	Alkylation Acylation Silylation	97–100

[a] See discussion in text.

stability of the analyte during storage, isolation, and thermal volatilization can be enhanced via formation of the derivatized product. Third, the increase in molecular mass resulting from derivatization on the fragmentation may be beneficial, providing ions which, by virtue of their higher mass, are more specific for the analyte.[71,72] The ideal derivatization procedure should be convenient and rapid to perform, form a consistent and stable product in high yield, require small volumes, be selective for the analyte of interest, be safe to handle, and should not form by-products that interfere with the analysis.[73–77]

Table 10.4.4 summarizes the numerous choices of derivatizing reagents available to today's drug testing laboratory. Table 10.4.4 does not include all the analytes that can be included under each drug group. For example, the amphetamines assay can be modified to include MDMA, MDA, and MDE, the benzodiazepines to include α-hydroxyalprazolam, α-hydroxytriazolam, diazepam, and N-desalkylflurazepam, and the opiates to include hydrocodone and hydromorphone. Detailed information about these procedures is available in the references listed. However, there are issues associated with a number of the assays that do deserve discussion.

Amphetamines — In the early 1990s, it was discovered that during certain GC/MS procedures, and under certain conditions, methamphetamine can be formed from large concentrations of ephedrine (or pseudoephedrine). Consequently, HHS introduced a requirement that for a specimen to be reported as positive for methamphetamine, it must not only contain at least 500 ng/ml of methamphetamine but also at least 200 ng/ml of amphetamine.[7] This prevented the reporting of false-positive methamphetamines as there was no evidence of the formation of amphetamine during the GC/MS process. This rule does not apply to nonregulated testing, and there may be noncertified laboratories that have not incorporated the reporting rule into their procedures.

A more reliable procedure for eliminating the potential for false-positive results is to incorporate a pre-oxidation step into the extraction.[51] In this protocol, oxidation with sodium periodate destroys hydroxylated sympathomimetics before the extraction, thereby preventing their conversion to methamphetamine during derivatization or GC/MS. If this procedure is used, then good laboratory practices require the laboratory to analyze a control containing the amphetamines together with high concentrations of the sympathomimetics as part of their standard protocols.

In the initial discussion of immunoassay testing for amphetamines, it was mentioned that under certain conditions L-methamphetamine (together with L-amphetamine) will cause a positive amphetamines response. Because of this, it is important that laboratories incorporate procedures to separate the stereoisomers into their protocols. Such procedures are based on derivatization with an optically pure derivative of an amino acid.[22] Interpretation of these GC/MS results is usually straightforward: specimens from Vick's Inhaler users contain greater than 90% of the L-isomer and those from users of D-methamphetamine contain greater than 90% of the D-isomer.

Benzodiazepines — Over the past 5 years numerous publications have focused on this GC/MS assay for benzodiazepines. Historically, it was possible to convert the parent drugs and their metabolites to benzophenones by acid hydrolysis;[78] however, this procedure does not allow for the confirmation of α-hydroxyalprazolam or α-hydroxytriazolam, metabolites of two of the newer, and most commonly prescribed, benzodiazepines. Using this procedure it is also not possible to differentiate the use of certain benzodiazepines, leading to potential interpretative difficulties.

For these reasons, acid hydrolysis has fallen out of favor and been replaced with procedures involving GC/MS analysis of the parent drug or their metabolites. Because a number of benzodiazepines and their metabolites are metabolized by glucuronidation, it is necessary to perform a hydrolysis step before extraction. Unlike the hydrolysis used for opiates, which can be either acid or enzymatic, only enzymatic ones can be used in the extraction of the benzodiazepines. Because of the polar nature of the benzodiazepines it is necessary to derivatize them; normally the trimethylsilyl derivatives are formed.

The major issue surrounding benzodiazepine testing is the cutoff to be used for confirmation. Historically, either a 200 or 300 ng/ml cutoff has been used; however, this is inappropriate for many of today's benzodiazepines. For example, to confirm many of the immunoassay positives resulting from alprazolam or flunitrazepam use it is necessary to lower this cutoff to 100 ng/ml. As the potency of these drugs increases it will be necessary to constantly monitor whether the confirmation (and the screening) assays are appropriate for their detection. Even in today's environment it is surprising how many laboratories continue to confirm only nordiazepam and oxazepam.

Opiates — Although morphine and codeine have been confirmed by GC/MS for a number of years, this assay continues to cause laboratories problems. One of the underlying issues is whether to use acid or enzymatic hydrolysis. Although studies have shown that acid hydrolysis is more efficient in releasing the parent drug from its conjugate, it has the disadvantage of resulting in a "dirty" hydrolysate that can cause problems in either solid-phase or liquid-liquid extractions. For this reason (as well as for safety ones) most laboratories use enzymatic methods, and with the correct choice of enzyme and conditions, hydrolysis can occur quickly and efficiently. Finally, acid hydrolysis will destroy 6-acetylmorphine in a specimen whereas enzymatic hydrolysis is more "gentle." However, most laboratories utilize a different analytical procedure altogether when testing for the presence of 6-acetylmorphine as hydrolysis is not required and there are other issues relating to its analysis (see below).

A second issue associated with opiate confirmation is the separation and identification of hydrocodone and hydromorphone in the presence of morphine and codeine. This problem is confounded by norcodeine. One of the most common procedures used involves silylation as the derivatization procedure. When this technique is used, the separation of the trimethylsilyl derivatives of codeine from hydrocodone and those of morphine and hydromorphone can be difficult, particularly when it is required to have greater than 90% resolution. It is true that the derivatives can be clearly identified by choosing the appropriate ions to monitor; however, it is still necessary to use common ions. Under normal conditions, the separation of trimethylsilyl derivatives of morphine and norcodeine is almost impossible to achieve.

Therefore, the confirmation of morphine after codeine use can be impractical if the laboratory uses silylation as a derivatization. Under normal conditions, when the donor has only taken codeine, this may not be important; however, if the donor has taken heroin and codeine a negative report for morphine is extremely misleading. The easiest way to resolve this problem is to use a different derivatizing procedure. Either acylation or acetylation is suitable; however, acyl derivatives are notoriously unstable. Acetylation with acetic anhydride or propionic anhydride is recommended. Although it is more time-consuming from an extraction point of view, the derivatives are well separated chromatographically.

For the analysis of 6-acetylmorphine, silylation is the method of choice although other methods have been used. It is obviously inappropriate to use acetylation as this will acetylate both 6-acetylmorphine and morphine back to heroin, therefore no positive morphine specimens would ever be negative for 6-acetylmorphine! As the regulated laboratory is required to detect 6-acetylmorphine at a cutoff concentration of 10 ng/ml compared with 2000 ng/ml for morphine and codeine, linearity considerations make simultaneous analysis for the determination of morphine, codeine, and 6-acetylmorphine impractical.

Selection of an Internal Standard

The selection of a suitable internal standard is highly linked to the appropriate selection of a derivative (if needed) for the assay as well the particular ions to be monitored for analyte identification and quantitation. An ideal internal standard behaves identically to the analyte throughout the extraction, chromatographic separation, and ionization processes. Deuterium-labeled analogues are the most frequently used stable isotope internal standards in urine drug testing laboratories. Several factors are important to consider when selecting the deuterium isotope-labeled internal standard to be used in an assay. The isotope should not undergo exchange under any of the conditions under which it will be used, such as the extraction, derivatization, or chromatographic separation procedures, as well as the mass spectrometer source.[79]

In addition, the isotope must be stable under routine storage conditions, so that exchange of deuterium and hydrogen does not occur.[80] The isotopic variant selected should have a molecular weight three or more mass units greater than the unlabeled compound because the naturally occurring heavy isotope content of organic compounds in general produces ions of significant intensity at one or two mass units above each carbon-containing compound in the analyte's mass spectrum.[79,81–83] It is therefore critical that the isotopic variant is of high purity (>99%) to prevent interference with the analyte of interest during the analysis. Also, the labeling of the isotope should be in such a manner that it is located in the molecular structure so that, after the fragmentation or ionization process, a sufficient number and intensity of high-mass ions that retain the label are present and will not interfere with the intensity measurement of the corresponding ions derived from the analyte.[83] The laboratory must carefully evaluate the concentration of internal standard used in its assay to ensure that there is no contribution to analyte signal itself. Generally, ions of high, even mass-to-charge ratios have fewer possible origins and are therefore more likely to be characteristic of a particular analyte. It is recommended that laboratories using selected-ion monitoring utilize at least three characteristic ions for the analyte of interest, and a minimum of two characteristic ions for the internal standard.[56]

Selection of Ions

There has been considerable discussion regarding the choice of ions to monitor and whether they are suitable for identification purposes. For most analytes of interest this is not a problem; however, for some it is. Analytes that clearly fall into the first category include benzoylecgonine, the opiates, and THCA.

Amphetamines — Unless amphetamine and methamphetamine are derivatized, their base peaks in the electron impact mode are 58 and 44 m/z, respectively. These two masses are certainly not diagnostic as they represent a dimethylamine and a methylamine fragment, respectively. Second, monitoring such low ions can lead to a loss of chromatographic selectivity because of the potential for co-extracted interfering compounds with low mass ions. Derivatization with a perfluoroacyl reagent (e.g., heptafluorobutyric anhydride, HFBA]) will result in ions of considerably higher mass and generally much "cleaner" ion chromatograms. However, there is still need for caution in the GC/MS confirmation of amphetamines because of the potential for interferences from other sympathomimetics as was previously discussed.

Barbiturates — The barbiturates (amobarbital, butabarbital, butalbital, pentobarbital, phenobarbital, and secobarbital) are frequently included in nonregulated drug testing programs. Their confirmation presents some difficulty because of the similarity of electron impact mass spectra of certain barbiturates and the absence of a clearly defined third ion for the analyte. For example, the mass spectra of amobarbital, butabarbital, and pentobarbital include two major ions, at 141 and 156 m/z. A similar situation exists with butalbital and secobarbital (167 and 168 m/z). In addition these five barbiturates elute closely together on the majority of capillary columns used today. Phenobarbital has two distinctly different ions (and is well separated chromatographically) at 204 and 232 m/z. Therefore, laboratories performing this confirmation without a derivatization step are, in essence, basing their identification of the barbiturates more on retention time than on the ions monitored. One solution to this problem is to derivatize the barbiturates before GC/MS. This results in more diagnostic ions and improves the chromatographic separation. In our laboratory, alkyl derivatives are formed using Meth Elute.

Benzodiazepines — As previously discussed, GC/MS confirmation of this group of drugs is difficult; however, one of the issues with developing a procedure for these drugs is the choice of ions to monitor. All of the benzodiazepines contain a halogen (fluorine, chlorine, or bromine). If the choice is to monitor a fragment containing chlorine or bromine, the laboratory should be careful not to choose a second fragment that is simply one containing a chlorine or bromine isotope.

Methadone and Propoxyphene — Assays for these two drugs are based on confirming the presence of the parent drug, and are faced with the same problems as those designed to confirm the presence of underivatized amphetamine and methamphetamine: the base peak in the electron impact mass spectra represents an alkyl amine moiety. It is therefore necessary to choose ions of low intensity for monitoring purposes, or to establish assays based on the metabolites (EDDP for methadone and norpropoxyphene for propoxyphene).

Phencyclidine — Most confirmation assays for this drug monitor the following ions: 200, 242, and 243 m/z. Obviously 243 m/z is simply the carbon isotope fragment corresponding to the 242 m/z ion. However, in this case there are no other suitable diagnostic ions. Fortunately, the 243 ion arises from a different molecular fragment and does not arise solely as result an isotope of the 243 ion.

Acknowledgments

Portions of this chapter were adapted from:

Peat, M. and Davis, A.E., Analytical considerations and approaches for drugs, in Karch, S.B., *Handbook of Drug Abuse*, 1st ed., CRC Press, Boca Raton, FL, 1998, chap. 10.3.

Goldberger, B.A., Huestis, M.A., and Wilkins, D.G., Commonly practiced quality control and quality assurance procedures for gas chromatography/mass spectrometry analysis in forensic urine drug-testing laboratories. *Forensic Sci. Rev.,* 9, 59, 1997.

Goldberger, B.A. and Jenkins, A.J., Drug toxicology, in *Sourcebook on Substance Abuse: Etiology, Epidemiology, Assessment, and Treatment*, Allyn & Bacon, Boston, 1999, 184–196.

REFERENCES

1. 1992 National Household Survey on Drug Abuse. Advance Report 3. Substance Abuse and Mental Health Services Administration (SAMHSA), Office of Applied Studies, DHHS, Rockville, MD, 1993.

2. Monitoring the Future Survey. College Students. National Institute on Drug Abuse, DHHS, Rockville, MD, 1993.

3. Monitoring the Future Survey. High School Students. National Institute on Drug Abuse. DHHS, Rockville, MD, 1993.

4. Anthony, J.C., Eaton, W.W., Garrison, R., and Mandell, W., Psychoactive drug dependence and abuse: more common in some occupations than others. *J. Employee Assistance Res.,* 1, 148, 1992.

5. Harris, M.M. and Heft, L.L., Alcohol and drug abuse in the workplace: issues, controversies and directions for future research. *J. Manage.,* 18, 239, 1992.

6. Mandatory Guidelines for Federal Workplace Testing Programs. *Fed. Register,* 53, 11970, 1988.

7. Mandatory Guidelines for Federal Workplace Testing Programs. *Fed. Register,* 59, 29908, 1994.

8. Gorodetzky, C.W., Detection of drugs of abuse in biological fluids, in Born, G.V.R., Eichler, O., Farah, A., Herken, H., and Welch, A.D., Eds., *Handbook of Experimental Pharmacology.* Springer-Verlag, Berlin, 1977.

9. Wu, A.H.B., Near-patient and point-of-care testing for alcohol and drugs of abuse. Therapeutic Drug Monitoring and Toxicology In-Service Training and Continuing Education Program, American Association for Clinical Chemistry, 16, 227, 1995.

10. Jenkins, A.J., Mills, L.C., Darwin, W.D., Huestis, M.A., Cone, E.J., and Mitchell, J.M., Validity testing of the EZ-SCREEN® cannabinoid test. *J. Anal. Toxicol.,* 17, 292, 1993.

11. Jenkins, A.J., Darwin, W.D., Huestis, M.A., Cone, E.J., and Mitchell, J.M., Validity testing of the *accu*PINCH™ THC test. *J. Anal. Toxicol.,* 19, 5, 1995.

12. Kadehjian, L.J., Performance of five non-instrumented urine drug-testing devices with challenging near-cutoff specimens. *J. Anal. Toxicol.,* 25,870, 2001.

13. Crouch, D.J., Frank, J.F., Farrell, L.J., Karsh, H.M., and Klaunig, J.E., A multiple-site laboratory evaluation of three on-site urinalysis drug-testing devices. *J. Anal. Toxicol.,* 22, 493, 1998.

14. Peace, M.R., Tarnai, L.D., and Poklis, A., Performance evaluation of four on-site drug-testing devices for detection of drugs of abuse in urine. *J. Anal. Toxicol.,* 24, 589, 2000.

15. Peace, M.R., Poklis, J.L., Tarnai, L.D., and Poklis, A., An evaluation of the OnTrak Testcup® on-site urine drug-testing device for drugs commonly encountered from emergency departments. *J Anal. Toxicol.,* 26, 500, 2002.

16. Crouch, D.J., Hersch, R.K., Cook, R.F., Frank, J.F., and Walsh, J.M., A field evaluation of five on-site drug-testing devices. *J. Anal. Toxicol.,* 26, 493, 2002.

17. Crouch, D.J., Cheever, M.L., Andrenyak, D.M., Kuntz, D.J., and Loughmiller, D.L., A comparison of ONTRAK TESTCUP, abuscreen ONTRAK, abuscreen ONLINE, and GC/MS urinalysis test results. *J. Forensic Sci.,* 43, 35, 1998.

18. Taylor, E.H., Oertli, E.H., Wolfgang, J.W., and Mueller, E., Accuracy of five on-site immunoassay drugs-of-abuse testing devices. *J. Anal. Toxicol.,* 23, 119, 1999.

19. Wu, A.H.B., Wong, S.S., Johnson, K.G., Callies, J., Shu, D.X., Dunn, W.E., and Wong, S.H.Y., Evaluation of the Triage system for emergency drugs-of-abuse testing in urine. *J. Anal. Toxicol.,* 17, 241, 1993.

20. Gronholm, M. and Lillsunde, P., A comparison between on-site immunoassay drug-testing devices and laboratory results. *Forensic Sci. Int.,* 121, 37, 2001.

21. Baker, D.P., Murphy, M.S., Shepp, P.F., Royo, V.R., Calderone, M.E., Escoto, B., and Salamone, S.J., Evaluation of the Abuscreen OnLine assay for amphetamines on the Hitachi 737: comparison with EMIT and GCMS methods. *J. Forensic Sci.,* 40, 108, 1995.

22. Fitzgerald, R.L., Ramos, Jr., J.M., Bogema, S.C., and Poklis, A., Resolution of methamphetamine stereoisomers in urine drug testing: urinary excretion of R (–)-methamphetamine following use of nasal inhalers. *J. Anal. Toxicol.,* 12, 255, 1988.

23. Cody, J.T., Important issues in testing for amphetamines, in *Handbook of Workplace Drug Testing,* Liu, R.H and Goldberger, B.A., Eds., AACC Press, Washington, D.C., 1995, chap. 10.

24. Liu, R.H., Evaluation of commercial immunoassay kits for effective workplace drug testing, in *Handbook of Workplace Drug Testing,* Liu, R.A. and Goldberger, B.A., Eds., AACC Press, Washington, D.C., 1995.

25. ElSohly, M.A. and Jones, A.B., Drug testing in the workplace: could a positive test for one of the mandated drugs be for reasons other than illicit use of the drug? *J. Anal. Toxicol.,* 19, 450, 1995.

26. Huestis, M.A. and Cone, E.J., Drug test findings resulting from unconventional drug exposure, in *Handbook of Workplace Drug Testing,* Liu, R.A. and Goldberger, B.A., Eds., AACC Press, Washington, D.C., 1995.

27. Cone, E.J., Johnson, R.E., Darwin, W.D., Yousefnejad, D., Mell, L.D., Paul, B.D., and Mitchell, J., Passive inhalation of marijuana smoke: urinalysis and room air levels of delta-9-tetrahydrocannabinol. *J. Anal. Toxicol.* 11, 89, 1987.

28. Hayden, J.W., Passive inhalation of marijuana smoke: a critical review. *J. Subst. Abuse* 3, 85, 1991.

29. Siegel, R.K., ElSohly, M.A., Plowman, T., Rury, P.M., and Jones, R.T., Cocaine in herbal tea. *J. Am. Med. Assoc.,* 255, 40, 1986.

30. ElSohly, M.A., Stanford, D.F., and ElSohly, H.N., Coca tea and urinalysis for cocaine metabolites. *J. Anal. Toxicol.,* 10, 256, 1986.

31. Jackson, G.F., Saady, J.J., and Poklis, A., Urinary excretion of benzoylecgonine following ingestion of Health Inca Tea. *Forensic Sci. Int.,* 49, 57, 1991.

32. Baselt, R.C and Chang, R., Urinary excretion of cocaine and benzoylecgonine following oral ingestion in a single subject. *J. Anal. Toxicol.,* 11, 81, 1987.

33. ElSohly, M.A. and Jones, A.B., Origin of morphine and codeine in biological specimens, in *Handbook of Workplace Drug Testing,* Liu, R.A. and Goldberger, B.A., Eds., AACC Press, Washington, D.C., 1995.

34. Changes to the testing cut-off levels for opiates for federal workplace drug testing programs. *Fed. Register,* 62, 51118, 1997.

35. Emit d.a.u. phencyclidine assay package insert; Dade-Behring, May 1997.

36. Information from Drug Abuse Warning Network: http://dawninfo.samhsa.gov/.

37. Watson, J.T., *Introduction to Mass Spectrometry,* Raven Press, New York, 1985.

38. Deutsch, D.G., Gas chromatography/mass spectrometry using table top instruments, in *Analytical Aspects of Drug Testing*, Deutsch, D.G., Ed., John Wiley & Sons, New York, 1989, chap. 4.

39. Goldberger, B.A., Huestis, M.A., and Wilkins, D.G., Commonly practiced quality control and quality assurance procedures for gas chromatography/mass spectrometry analysis in forensic urine drug-testing laboratories. *Forensic Sci. Rev.,* 9, 59, 1997.

40. The Draft Guideline on Validation of Analytical Procedures, *Fed. Register,* 62, 9315, 1996.

41. Stevenson, R., An open letter to the Food and Drug Administration, *Am. Lab.,* 28, 4, 1996.

42. Karnes, H.T., Shiu, G. and Shah, V.P., Review. Validation of bioanalytical methods. *Pharm. Res.,* 8, 421, 1991.

43. Dadgar, D., Burnett, P.E., Choc, M.G., Gallicano, K., and Hooper, J.W., Application issues in bioanalytical method validation, sample analysis and data reporting. *J. Pharm. Biomed. Anal.,* 13, 89, 1995.

44. Arnoux, P. and Morrison, R., Drug analysis of biological samples: a survey of validation approaches in chromatography in the United Kingdom pharmaceutical industry. *Xenobiotica,* 22, 757, 1992.

45. Inman, E.L., Frishmann, J.K., Jimenez, P.J., Winkel, G.D., Persinger, M.L., and Rutherford, B.S., General method validation guidelines for pharmaceutical samples. *J. Chrom. Sci.,* 25, 252, 1987.

46. Karnes, H.T. and March, C., Precision, accuracy, and data acceptance criteria in biopharmaceutical analysis. *Pharm. Res.* 10, 1420, 1993.

47. Bonate, P.L., Concepts in calibration theory, Part I: Regression; *LC-GC,* 10, 310, 1992.

48. Bonate, P.L., Concepts in calibration theory, Part II: Regression through the origin — when should it be used? *LC-GC,* 10, 378, 1992.

49. Hornbeck, C.L., Carrig, J.E., and Czarny, R.J., Detection of a GC/MS artifact peak as methamphetamine. *J. Anal. Toxicol.,* 17, 257, 1993.

50. Fenton, J., Mummert, J., and Childers, M., Hydromorphone and hydrocodone interference in GC/MS assays for codeine and morphine. *J. Anal. Toxicol.,* 18, 159, 1994.

51. ElSohly, M.A., Stanford, D.F., Sherman, D., Shah, H., Bernot, D., and Turner, C.E., A procedure for eliminating interferences from ephedrine and related compounds in the GC/MS analysis of amphetamine and methamphetamine. *J. Anal. Toxicol.,* 16, 109, 1992.

52. Paul, B.D., Past, M.R., McKinley, R.M., Foreman, J.D., McWhorter, L.K., and Snyder, J.J., Amphetamine as an artifact of methamphetamine during periodate degradation of interfering ephedrine, pseudoephedrine, and phenylpropanolamine: an improved procedure for accurate quantitation of amphetamines in urine. *J. Anal. Toxicol.,* 18, 331, 1994.

53. Kaplan, L.A. and Pesce, A.J., *Clinical Chemistry: Theory, Analysis, and Correlation.* C.V. Mosby, St. Louis, MO, 1984.

54. Smith, R.V. and Stewart, J.T., *Textbook of Biopharmaceutic Analysis.* Lea & Febiger, Philadelphia, 1981.

55. Wu Chen, N.B., Cody, J.T., Garriott, J.C., Foltz, R.L., Peat, M.A., and Schaffer, M.I., Report of the 1988 Ad Hoc Committee on Forensic GC/MS: Recommended guidelines for forensic GC/MS procedures in toxicology laboratories associated with offices of medical examiners and/or coroners. *J. Forensic Sci.,* 35, 236, 1990.

56. Guidance Document for Laboratories and Inspectors, U.S. Department of Health and Human Services, National Laboratory Certification Program, Revised August, 29, 1994.

57. Kaplan, A. and Szabo, L., *Clinical Chemistry: Interpretation and Techniques,* 2nd ed., Lea & Febiger, Philadelphia, 1983.

58. Moffat, A.C., Jackson, J.V., Moss, M.S., and Widdop, B., Eds., *Clarke's Isolation and Identification of Drugs,* 2nd ed., Pharmaceutical Press, London, 1986.

59. Poole, C.F. and Shuette, S., *Contemporary Practice of Chromatography,* Elsevier, New York, 1984.

60. Grob, K., Grob, G., and Grob, K., Jr., Testing capillary gas chromatographic columns. *J. Chromatogr.,* 219, 13, 1981.

61. McNair, H.M., Method development in gas chromatography. *LC-GC,* 11, 94, 1993.

62. Cembrowski, G.S. and Carey, R.N., *Laboratory Quality Management.* ASCP Press, Chicago, IL, 1989.

63. Westgard, J.O., Better quality control through microcomputers. *Diagn. Med.,* 61, 741, 1982.

64. Westgard, J.O., Barry, P.L., Hunt, M.R., and Groth, T., A multi-rule Shewart chart for quality control in clinical chemistry. *Clin. Chem.,* 27, 493, 1981.

65. Westgard, J.O. and Barry, P.L., *Cost-Effective Quality Control: Managing the Quality and Productivity of Analytical Processes.* AACC Press, Washington, D.C., 1986.

66. Shewhart, W.A., *Statistical Method from the Viewpoint of Quality Control.* Dover, New York, 1986.

67. Garfield, F.M., *Quality Assurance Principles for Analytical Laboratories,* AOAC International, Gaithersburg, MD, 1991.

68. Cairns, T., Siegmund, E.G., and Stamp, J.J., Evolving criteria for confirmation of trace level residues in food and drugs by mass spectrometry. Part I. *Mass Spectrom. Rev.,* 8, 93, 1989.

69. Cairns, T., Siegmund, E.G., and Stamp, J.J., Evolving criteria for confirmation of trace level residues in food and drugs by mass spectrometry. Part II. *Mass Spectrom. Rev.,* 8, 127, 1989.

70. Sphon, J.A., Use of mass spectrometry for confirmation of animal drug residues. *J. Assoc. Off. Anal. Chem.,* 61, 1247, 1978.

71. Garland, W.A. and Barbalas, M.P., Applications to analytic chemistry: An evaluation of stable isotopes in mass spectral drug assays. *J. Clin. Pharm.,* 26, 412, 1986.

72. Lawson, A.M., Gaskell, S.J., and Hjelm, M., Methodological aspects on quantitative mass spectrometry used for accuracy control in clinical chemistry. International Federation of Clinical Chemistry (IFCC), Office for Reference Methods and Materials (ORMM). *J. Clin. Chem. Clin. Biochem.,* 23, 433, 1985.

73. Knapp, D.R., *Handbook of Analytical Derivatization Reactions,* John Wiley & Sons, New York, 1979.

74. Blau, K. and King, G.S., Eds., *Handbook of Derivatives for Chromatography.* Heyden & Son, London, 1978.

75. Blau, K. and Halket, J.M., Eds., *Handbook of Derivatives for Chromatography,* 2nd ed. John Wiley & Sons, New York, 1993.

76. Knapp, D.R., Chemical derivatization for mass spectrometry. *Methods Enzymol.,* 193, 314, 1990.

77. Moore, J.M., The application of chemical derivatization in forensic drug chemistry for GC and HPLC methods of analysis. *Forensic Sci. Rev.,* 2, 80, 1990.

78. Seno, H., Suzuki, O., and Kumazawa, T., Rapid isolation with Sep-Pak C18 cartridges and wide-bore capillary gas chromatography of benzophenones, the acid-hydrolysis products of benzodiazepines. *J. Anal. Toxicol.,* 15, 21, 1991.

79. Foltz, R.L., Fentiman, A.F., and Foltz, R.B., GC/MS Analysis for Abused Drugs in Body Fluids, NIDA Research Monograph 32, August 1980.

80. Millard, B.J., *Quantitative Mass Spectrometry.* Heyden, London, 1978.

81. Liu, R.H., Baugh, D.L., Allen, E.E., Salud, S.C., Fentress, J.G., Chadha, H., and Walia, A.S., Isotopic analogue as the international standard for quantitative determination of benzoylecgonine: concerns with isotopic purity and concentration level. *J. Forensic Sci.* 34, 986, 1989.

82. Liu, R.H., McKeehan, A.M., Edwards, C., Foster, G., Bensley, W.D., Langner, J.G., and Walia, A.S., Improved gas chromatography/mass spectrometry analysis of barbiturates in urine using centrifuge-based solid-phase extraction, methylation with d5-pentobarbital as internal standard. *J. Forensic Sci.*, 39, 1501, 1994.

83. Liu, R.H., Foster, G., Cone, E.J., and Kumar, S.D., Selecting an appropriate isotopic internal standard for gas chromatography/mass spectrometry analysis of drugs of abuse — pentobarbital example. *J. Forensic Sci.*, 40, 983, 1995.

84. Thurman, E.M., Pedersen, M.J., Stout, R.L., and Martin, T., Distinguishing sympathomimetic amines from amphetamine and methamphetamine in urine by gas chromatography/mass spectrometry. *J. Anal. Toxicol.*, 16, 19, 1992.

85. Hughes, R.O., Bronner, W.E., and Smith, M.L., Detection of amphetamine and methamphetamine in urine by gas chromatography/mass spectrometry following derivatization with (–)-methyl chloroformate. *J. Anal. Toxicol.*, 15, 256, 1991.

86. Melgar, R. and Kelly, R.C., A novel GC/MS derivatization method for amphetamines. *J. Anal. Toxicol.*, 17, 399, 1993.

87. Mule, S.J. and Casella, G.A., Confirmation and quantitation of barbiturates in human urine by gas chromatography/mass spectrometry. *J. Anal. Toxicol.*, 13, 13, 1989.

88. Dickson, P.H., Markus, W., McKernan, J., and Nipper, H.C., Urinalysis of alpha-hydroxyalprazolam, alpha-hydroxytriazolam, and other benzodiazepine compounds by GC/EIMS. *J. Anal. Toxicol.*, 16, 67, 1992.

89. Fitzgerald, R.L., Rexin, D.A., and Herold, D.A., Benzodiazepine analysis by negative ion chemical ionization gas chromatography/mass spectrometry. *J. Anal. Toxicol.*, 17, 342, 1993.

90. Black, D.A., Clark, G.D., Haver, V.M., Garbin, J.A., and Saxon, A.J., Analysis of urinary benzodiazepines using solid-phase extraction and gas chromatography-mass spectrometry. *J. Anal. Toxicol.*, 18, 185, 1994.

91. Kemp, P.M., Abukhalaf, I.K., Manno, J.E, Manno, B.R., Alford, D.D., and Abusada, G.A., Cannabinoids in humans. I. Analysis of delta-9-tetrahydrocannabinol and six metabolites in plasma and urine using GC-MS. *J. Anal. Toxicol.*, 19, 285, 1995.

92. Kemp, P.M., Abukhalaf, I.K., Manno, J.E, Manno, B.R., Alford, D.D., Mcwilliams, M.E., Nixon, F.E., Fitzgerald, M.J., Reeves, R.R., and Wood, M.J., Cannabinoids in humans. II. The influence of three methods of hydrolysis on the concentration of THC and two metabolites in urine. *J. Anal. Toxicol.*, 19, 292, 1995.

93. Joern, W.A., Detection of past and recurrent marijuana use by a modified GC/MS procedure. *J. Anal. Toxicol.*, 11, 49, 1987.

94. Paul, B.D., Mell, L.D., Mitchell, J.M., and McKinley, R.M., Detection and quantitation of urinary 11-nor-delta-9-tetrahydrocannabinol-9-carboxylic acid, a metabolite of tetrahydrocannabinol by capillary gas chromatography and electron impact mass fragmentography. *J. Anal. Toxicol.*, 11, 1, 1987.

95. Cone, E.J., Hillsgrove, M., and Darwin, W.D., Simultaneous measurement of cocaine, cocaethylene, their metabolites and "crack" pyrolysis products by gas chromatography-mass spectrometry. *Clin. Chem.*, 40, 1299, 1994.

96. Mule, S.J. and Casella, G.A., Confirmation and quantitation of cocaine, benzoylecgonine, ecgonine methyl ester in human urine by GC/MS. *J. Anal. Toxicol.*, 12, 153, 1988.

97. Goldberger, B.A., Darwin, W.D., Grant, T.M., Allen, A.C., Caplan, Y.H., and Cone, E.J., Measurement of heroin and its metabolites by isotope-dilution electron-impact mass spectrometry. *Clin. Chem.*, 39, 670, 1993.

98. Mitchell, J.M, Paul, B.D., Welch, P., and Cone, E.J., Forensic drug testing for opiates. II. Metabolism and excretion rate of morphine in humans after morphine administration *J. Anal. Toxicol.*, 15, 49, 1991.

99. Cone, E.J., Welch, P., Mitchell, J.M., and Paul, B.D., Forensic drug testing of opiates. I. Detection of 6-acetylmorphine in urine as an indicator of recent heroin exposure. Drug and assay considerations and detection times. *J. Anal. Toxicol.*, 15, 1, 1991.

100. ElSohly, H.N., ElSohly, M.A., and Stanford, D.F., Poppy seed ingestion and opiate urinalysis: a closer look. *J. Anal. Toxicol.*, 14, 308, 1990.

10.5 ANALYTICAL APPROACHES FOR DRUGS IN BIOLOGICAL MATRICES OTHER THAN URINE

Pascal Kintz, Pharm.D., Ph.D., Marion Villain, M.S., and Vincent Cirimele, Ph.D.
ChemTox Laboratory, Illkirch, France

It is generally accepted that chemical testing of biological fluids is the only objective means of diagnosis of drug use. The presence of a drug analyte in a biological specimen can be used as evidence of exposure. The standard procedure in drug testing is the immunoassay screening, followed by the gas chromatographic/mass spectrometric (GC/MS) confirmation conducted on a urine sample.[1,2] More recently, a variety of body specimens other than urine, such as oral fluid, sweat, or hair, have been proposed to document drug exposure. It appears that the value of alternative specimen analysis for the identification of drug users is steadily gaining recognition. This can be seen from its growing use in pre-employment screening, in forensic sciences, and in clinical applications.[3–5]

The advantage of these samples over traditional media like urine and blood is that collection is almost non-invasive, relatively easy to perform, and may be achieved under close supervision to prevent adulteration or substitution of the sample. Tools for the detection of drugs in alternative specimens utilize traditional technology, although some limitations are imposed that require special attention:

1. The specimen volume or mass is often small.
2. The target analytes are different from urine.
3. The analyte concentration is lower than in urine.
4. The sample preparation for drug analysis can be more difficult.

Although remarkable advances in sensitive analytical techniques enable drug confirmation in oral fluid, sweat and hair today,[6] limited progress has been made in the development of commercial collection devices, on-site and laboratory-based commercial screening assays, quality control materials, proficiency-testing programs, and regulatory guidelines for utilization of alternative matrices in drug testing.

REFERENCES

1. Substance Abuse and Mental Health Administration, Mandatory guidelines for Federal workplace drug testing programs. *Fed. Regis.*, 53, 11970, 1988.
2. de la Torre, R. et al., Recommendations for the reliable detection of illicit drugs in urine in the European Union with special attention to the workplace, *Ann. Clin. Biochem.*, 34, 339, 1997.
3. Caplan, Y.H. and Goldberger, B.A., Alternative specimens for workplace drug testing, *J. Anal. Toxicol.*, 25, 396, 2001.
4. UNDCP, *Guidelines for Testing under International Control in Hair, Sweat and Saliva*, United Nations, New York, 1998.
5. Cone, E., Legal, workplace, and treatment drug testing with alternate biological matrices on a global scale, *Forensic Sci. Int.*, 21, 7, 2001.
6. Kintz, P. and Samyn N., Unconventional samples and alternative matrices. In *Handbook of Analytical Separations: Forensic Science,* M. Bogusz, Ed., Elsevier, Amsterdam, 2000, 459.

10.5.1 Hair

In the 1960s and 1970s, hair analysis was used to evaluate exposure to toxic heavy metals, such as arsenic, lead, or mercury. This was achieved using atomic absorption spectroscopy that allowed detection in the nanogram range. At that time, examination of hair for organic substances, especially drugs, was not possible because analytical methods were not sensitive enough. Examination by means of drugs marked with radioactive isotopes, however, established that these substances can move from blood to hair and are deposited there. Ten years after these first investigations, it was possible to demonstrate the presence of various organic drugs in hair by means of radioimmunoassay (RIA). In 1979, Baumgartner and colleagues[1] published the first report on the detection of morphine in the hair of heroin abusers using RIA. They found that differences in the concentration of morphine along the hair shaft correlated with the time of drug use. Today, GC/MS is the method of choice for hair analysis and this technology is routinely used to document repetitive drug exposure in forensic science, traffic medicine, occupational medicine, clinical toxicology, and more recently in sports.

The major practical advantage of hair testing compared to urine or blood testing for drugs is that it has a larger surveillance window (weeks to months, depending on the length of the hair shaft, against 2 to 4 days for most drugs). For practical purposes, the two tests complement each other. Urinalysis and blood analysis provide short-term information of an individual's drug use, whereas long-term histories are accessible through hair analysis. While analysis of urine and blood specimens often cannot distinguish between chronic use and single exposure, hair analysis can offer the distinction.

10.5.1.1 Hair Collection

Collection procedures for hair analysis for drugs have not been standardized. In most published studies, the samples are obtained from random locations on the scalp. Hair is best collected from the area at the back of the head, called the *vertex posterior*. Compared with other areas of the head, this area has less variability in the hair growth rate, the number of hairs in the growing phase is more constant, and the hair is less subject to age- and sex-related influences. Hair strands are cut as close as possible from the scalp, and their location on the scalp must be noted. Once collected, hair samples may be stored at ambient temperature in aluminum foil, an envelope, or a plastic tube. The sample size taken varies considerably among laboratories and depends on the drug to be analyzed and the test methodology. For example, when fentanyl or buprenorphine are investigated, a 100-mg sample is recommended. Sample sizes reported in the literature range from a single hair to 200 mg, cut as close to the scalp as possible. When sectional analysis is performed, the hair is cut into segments of about 1, 2, or 3 cm, which corresponds to about 1, 2, or 3 months' growth.

10.5.1.2 Decontamination Procedures

Contaminants of hair would be a problem if they were drugs of abuse or their metabolites or if they interfered with the analysis and interpretation of the test results. It is unlikely that anyone would intentionally or accidentally apply anything to their hair that would contain a drug of abuse. The most crucial issue facing hair analysis is the avoidance of technical and evidentiary false positives. Technical false positives are caused by errors in the collection, processing, and analysis of specimens, while evidentiary false-positives are caused by passive exposure to the drug. Approaches for preventing evidentiary false positives due to external contamination of the hair specimens have been described.[2]

Most but not all laboratories use a wash step; however, there is no consensus or uniformity in the washing procedures. Among the agents used in washing are detergents such as shampoo, surgical scrubbing solutions, surfactants such as 0.1% sodium dodecylsulfate, phosphate buffer, or organic solvents such as acetone, diethyl ether, methanol, ethanol, dichloromethane, hexane, or pentane of various volumes for various contact times. Generally, a single washing step is used; although a second identical wash is sometimes performed. If external contamination is found by analyzing the wash solution, the washout kinetics of repeated washing can demonstrate that contamination is rapidly removed. According to Baumgartner and Hill,[2] the concentration of drug in the hair after washing should exceed the concentration in the last wash by at least ten times. It has also been proposed that hair should be washed three times with phosphate prior to analysis to remove any possible external contamination and that the total concentration of any drug present in the three phosphate washes should be greater than 3.9 times the concentration in the last wash.

Detection of drug metabolites in hair, whose presence could not be explained by hydrolysis or environmental exposure, would unequivocally establish that internal drug exposure had occurred.[3] Cocaethylene and nor-cocaine would appear to meet these criteria, as these metabolites are formed only when cocaine is metabolized. Because these metabolites are not found in illicit cocaine samples, they would not be present in hair as a result of environmental contamination, and thus their presence in hair could be considered a marker of cocaine exposure. This procedure can be extended to other drugs. However, there is still a great controversy about the potential risk of external contamination, particularly for crack, cannabis, and heroin when smoked as several authors have demonstrated that it is not possible to fully remove the drugs.[4,5] In conclusion, although it is highly recommended to include a decontamination step, there is no consensus on which procedure performs best and each laboratory must validate its own technique.

10.5.1.3 Drug Solubilization

To determine the amount of a drug remaining in hair after washing, it is necessary to solubilize the drugs in the hair. Solubilization must be such that the analytes are not altered or lost. Care is necessary to prevent the conversion of cocaine to benzoylecgonine or 6-monoacetylmorphine to morphine, for example.

The hair sample can be pulverized in a ball-mill prior to testing, cut into segments, or the entire hair dissolved. The preparation techniques are generally based on one of the following procedures:

- Incubation in an aqueous buffer and analysis with immunological techniques, mostly RIA
- Incubation in an acidic or basic solution followed by liquid–liquid extraction or solid-phase extraction and analysis with chromatographic techniques, mostly GC/MS
- Incubation in an organic solvent (generally methanol with or without hydrochloric acid), liquid extraction or solid-phase extraction and analysis with chromatographic techniques, mostly GC/MS
- Digestion in an enzymatic solution, liquid extraction or solid-phase extraction and analysis with chromatographic techniques, mostly GC/MS

10.5.1.4 Drug Analysis

The first publication dealing with the analysis of morphine in hair for determining the history of opiate abuse reported the use of RIA.[1] This paper was followed by a great number of procedures, which mostly used RIA and/or GC/MS. Chromatographic procedures are a powerful tool for the identification and quantification of drugs in hair, owing to their separation ability and their detection sensitivity and specificity, particularly when coupled with MS. Proposed cutoff concentrations and expected concentrations for drugs of abuse in hair are presented in Table 10.5.1.

Table 10.5.1 Proposed Cutoff Concentrations (when tested by GC/MS) and Expected Concentrations for Drugs of Abuse in Hair

Drug	GC/MS Cutoff Concentration	Expected Concentrations
Heroin	0.5 ng/mg of 6-acetylmorphine	0.5–100 ng/mg, in most cases <15 ng/mg
Cocaine	0.5 ng/mg of cocaine	0.5–100 ng/mg, in most cases <50 ng/mg, in crack abusers >300 ng/mg is possible
Amphetamine, MDMA	0.5 ng/mg for both drugs	0.5–50.0 ng/mg
Cannabis	0.05 ng/mg for THC 0.5 pg/mg for THC-COOH	THC: 0.05–10 ng/mg, in most cases <3 ng/mg THC-COOH: 0.5–50 pg/mg, in most cases <5 pg/mg

Table 10.5.2 Screening Procedures for the Detection of Controlled Drugs in Hair (see Reference 9)

Method	Kauert	Moeller	Kintz
Analytes	Heroin, 6-MAM, dihydrocodeine, codeine, methadone, THC, cocaine, amphetamine, MDMA, MDEA, MDA	6-MAM, dihydrocodeine, codeine, methadone, THC, cocaine, amphetamine, MDMA, MDEA, MDA	6-MAM, codeine, methadone, cocaine, amphetamine, MDMA, MDEA, MDA, most pharmaceuticals
Decontamination step	Ultrasonic 5 min each 5 ml H_2O 5 ml acetone 5 ml petroleum ether	20 ml H_2O (2×) 20 ml acetone	5 ml dichloromethane (2 × 5 min)
Homogenization	100 mg hair cut into small sections in a 30-ml vial	Ball mill	Ball mill
Extraction	4 ml methanol, ultrasonic 5 h, 50°C	20–30 mg powdered hair, 2 ml acetate buffer + β-glucuronidase/aryl-sulfatase, 90 min/40°C	50 mg powdered hair, 1 ml 0.1 N HCl, 16 h/56°C
Clean-up	None	$NaHCO_3$; SPE (C18), elution with 2 ml acetone/dichloromethane (3:1)	$(NH_4)_2HPO_4$; extraction 10 ml chloroform/2-propanol/n-heptane (50:17:33); organic phase purified with 0.2 N HCl; HCl phase to pH 8.4; re-extraction with $CHCl_3$
Derivatization	Propionic acid anhydride	1000 μl PFPA/75 μl PF-n-propanol; 30 min/60°C; N_2/60°C; 50 μl ethylacetate	40 μl BSTFA + 1% TMCS or HFBA; 20 min/70°C

Radioimmunoassay is the most common screening test for hair. Kits, generally designed for urine, can be used without any modification, at pH values above 7. Calibration curves are obtained either from the controlled urines in the kit or from extracts of drug-free hair samples spiked with the drugs. Duplicate determinations are recommended. The RIA results should be confirmed by GC/MS. In the absence of a second independent method, RIA detection must be interpreted with caution. However, even the high sensitivity of GC/MS is sometimes not sufficient to detect drugs, especially when starting with a small quantity of hair. For these reasons, it may be necessary to carry out immunological analysis of drugs in hair using RIA reagents that are specific for the selective estimation of a drug like fentanyl, lysergide (LSD), or buprenorphine.

Chromatographic methods have been used as screening and confirming tests. Moreover, they allow quantification of the drugs and drug metabolites. Some classic GC/MS procedures are given in detail in Table 10.5.2. There are very few papers that present data using high-performance liquid chromatography/MS (HPLC/MS), except for buprenorphine, diuretics, and corticosteroids.

10.5.1.5 Drug Identification

Opiates

As heroin samples always contain codeine, codeine is also detected in cases of heroin abuse. Morphine is a metabolite of codeine and can be detected when codeine is abused. The quantification of both drugs was proposed to differentiate between codeine and heroin abuse.[6] If the morphine concentration is clearly higher than the codeine concentration in the hair sample, heroin or morphine abuse is highly probable. If the codeine concentration is higher than the morphine level, then it may be assumed that codeine has been ingested. However, the discrimination of heroin users from individuals exposed to other sources of morphine alkaloids can be achieved by identifying directly heroin or 6-monoacetylmorphine.[7,8] In this case, alkaline hydrolysis must not be used in order to avoid hydrolysis. In most samples, it was demonstrated that 6-monoacetylmorphine concentrations exceeded those of morphine, which is a less lipophilic compound. Other opioids have been detected, including dihydrocodeine, pholcodine, ethylmorphine, dextromoramide, methadone, fentanyl, sufentanyl, pentazocine, zipeprol, and buprenorphine.

Cocaine

Procedures for the detection of cocaine have been published in several papers.[9,10] There is considerable variety in the workup and derivatization conditions. In most cases, cocaine is found in higher concentrations than benzoylecgonine and methylecgonine.[11,12] The determination of the pyrolysis product of cocaine, anhydroecgonine methylester (AEME), is helpful to distinguish cocaine from crack users. Kintz found AEME in the range 0.2 to 2.4 ng/mg for seven crack users.[13] An important study with controlled doses of cocaine-d_5 was published in 1996.[14] The deuterium-labeled cocaine was administered intravenously and/or intranasally in doses of 0.6 to 4.2 mg/kg under controlled conditions. A single dose could be detected for 2 to 6 months; the minimum detectable dose appeared to be between 22 and 35 mg.

Amphetamines

Papers dealing with amphetamine and methamphetamine have been published.[15] The workup (liquid–liquid extraction after acid or alkaline hydrolysis) and derivatization procedures (trifluoro-acetic anhydride, TFA) are similar in most of the publications. After methamphetamine intake, its major metabolite, amphetamine, can be detected in hair samples and the differentiation between methamphetamine and amphetamine intake can be achieved by reviewing the ratio between the drugs. In 1992, methylenedioxy-*N*-methamphetamine (MDMA or ecstasy) was first detected in the hair of an abuser at the concentration of 0.6 ng/mg.[16] In Europe, MDMA is one of the most frequently identified drugs. Since the first screening procedure in 1995, different methods have been published.[17,18] These procedures permit the determination of amphetamine, methylamphet-amine, methylenedioxyamphetamine, methylenedioxymethamphetamine, methylenedioxyetham-phetamine, and *N*-methylbenzodioxazolybutanamine (MBDB) by electron impact GC/MS.

Cannabis

In 1995 the first results on cannabis in hair by using GC/MS and the determination in the same run of ^{9}-tetrahydrocannabinol (THC) and its major metabolite 11-nor-^{9}-THC carboxylic acid (THC-COOH) were reported.[19] The measured concentrations were low, particularly in comparison with other drugs. Some authors suggested the use of negative chemical ionization[20] to target the drugs or the application of tandem mass spectrometry.[21] More recently, a simpler method was proposed,[22] based on the simultaneous identification of cannabinol (CBN), cannabidiol (CBD), and THC. This procedure is a screening method that is rapid, economic, and does not require derivatization prior to analysis. To avoid potential external contamination (as THC, CBD, and CBN are present in smoke), the endogenous metabolite, THC-COOH, should be looked for to confirm drug use. The concentrations measured are very low, particularly for THC-COOH (pg/mg range).

10.5.1.6 *Place of Hair*

Although there are still controversies on how to interpret the results, particularly concerning external contamination, cosmetic treatments, genetic considerations, and drug incorporation, pure analytical work in hair analysis has reached a sort of plateau, having solved almost all the analytical problems. Although GC/MS is the method of choice in practice, GC/MS/MS or LC/MS are today used in several laboratories, even for routine cases, particularly to target low-dosage compounds, such as THC-COOH, fentanyl, flunitrazepam, or buprenorphine. Electrophoretic/electrokinetic analytical strategies, chiral separation, or application of ion mobility spectrometry constitute the latest new developments of the analytical tools reported to document the presence of drugs in hair. Quality assurance is a major issue of drug testing in hair. Since 1990, the National Institute of Standards and Technology (Gaithersburg, MD) has developed interlaboratory comparisons, recently followed by the Society of Hair Testing (Strasbourg, France). At the moment, some laboratory guidelines concerning hair analysis are under preparation, both by the U.S. Substance Abuse Mental Health Services Administration (SAMHSA) Mandatory Guidelines and the Society of Hair Testing; however, final publication has not yet materialized.

By providing information on exposure to drugs over time, hair analysis may be useful in verifying self-reported histories of drug use in any situation in which a history of past rather than recent drug use is desired, as in pre-employment and employee drug testing. In addition, hair analysis may be especially useful when a history of drug use is difficult or impossible to obtain, such as from psychiatric patients. During control tests of hair fragments, a drug addict is not able to hide the fact that drugs have been used whereas intermittent drug use may be difficult to detect if urine or blood tests alone are undertaken, even when the tests are repeated. There are essentially three types of problems with urine drug testing: false positives when not confirmed with GC/MS, the embarrassment associated with observed urine collection, and evasive maneuvers, including adulteration. These problems can be greatly mitigated or eliminated through hair analysis. It is always possible to obtain a fresh, identical hair sample if there is any claim of a specimen mix-up or breach in the chain of custody. This makes hair analysis essentially fail-safe, in contrast to urinalysis, since an identical urine specimen cannot be obtained at a later date.

Another potential use of hair analysis is to verify accidental or unintentional ingestion of drinks or food that has been laced with drugs. In case of a single use, the hair will not test positive. For example, ingestion of poppy seeds appears to be sufficient for the creation of a positive urine result, while ingestion of up to 30 g of poppy seeds did not result in a positive hair identification (Sachs, personal communication, 1994). The greatest use of hair analysis, however, may be in identifying false negatives, since neither abstaining from a drug for a few days nor trying to "beat the test" by diluting urine will alter the concentration in hair. Urine does not indicate the frequency of drug intake in subjects who might deliberately abstain for several days before drug screenings. While analysis of urine specimens cannot distinguish between chronic use and single exposure, hair analysis offers the potential to make this distinction.

REFERENCES

1. Baumgartner, A.M. et al., Radioimmunoassay of hair for determining opiate-abuse histories, *J. Nuclear Med.*, 20, 748, 1979.
2. Baumgartner, W.A. and Hill, V.A., Hair analysis for drugs of abuse: decontamination issues. In *Recent Developments in Therapeutic Drug Monitoring and Clinical Toxicology,* Sunshine, I., Ed., Marcel Dekker, New York, 1992, 577.
3. Cone, E.J. et al., Testing human hair for drugs of abuse. II. Identification of unique cocaine metabolites in hair of drug abusers and evaluation of decontamination procedures, *J. Anal. Toxicol.*, 15, 250, 1991.
4. Blank, D.L. and Kidwell, D.A., Decontamination procedures for drugs of abuse in hair: are they sufficient? *Forensic Sci. Int.*, 70, 13, 1995.
5. Romano, G. et al., Determination of drugs of abuse in hair: evaluation of external heroin contamination and risk of false positives, *Forensic Sci. Int.*, 131, 98, 2003.
6. Sachs, H. and Arnold, W., Results of comparative determination of morphine in human hair using RIA and GC/MS, *J. Clin. Chem. Clin. Biochem.*, 27, 873, 1989.
7. Sachs, H. and Uhl, M., Opiat-Nachweis in Haar-Extrakten mit Hilfe von GC/MS/MS und Supercritical Fluid Extraction, *Toxichem. Krimtech.*, 59, 114, 1992.
8. Nakahara, Y. et al., Hair analysis for drugs of abuse. IV. Determination of total morphine and confirmation of 6-acetylmorphine in monkey and human hair by GC/MS, *Arch. Toxicol.*, 66, 669, 1992.

9. Sachs, H. and Kintz, P., Testing for drugs in hair. Critical review of chromatographic procedures since 1992, *J. Chromatogr. B,* 713, 147, 1998.
10. Moeller, M.R., Drug detection in hair by chromatographic procedures, *J. Chromatogr.,* 580, 125, 1992.
11. Henderson, G.L., Harkey, M.R., and Zhou, C., Cocaine and metabolite concentrations in hair of South American coca chewers, *J. Anal. Toxicol.,* 16, 199, 1992.
12. Moeller, M.R., Fey, P., and Rimbach, S., Identification and quantitation of cocaine and its metabolites, benzoylecgonine and ecgonine methylester in hair of Bolivian coca chewers by GC/MS, *J. Anal. Toxicol.,* 16, 291, 1992.
13. Kintz, P. et al., Testing human hair and urine for anhydroecgonine methylester, a pyrolysis product of cocaine, *J. Anal. Toxicol.,* 19, 479, 1995.
14. Henderson, G.L. et al., Incorporation of isotopically labeled cocaine and metabolites into human hair. 1. Dose–response relationships, *J. Anal. Toxicol.,* 20, 1, 1996.
15. Nakahara, Y. et al., Hair analysis for drug abuse, Part II. Hair analysis for monitoring of methamphetamine abuse by isotope dilution GC/MS, *Forensic Sci. Int.,* 46, 243, 1990.
16. Moeller, M.R., Maurer, H.H., and Roesler, M., MDMA in blood, urine and hair: a forensic case. In *Proceedings of the 30th Meeting of TIAFT,* Nagata, T., Ed., Yoyodo Printing Kaisha, Fukuoka, 1992, 347.
17. Kintz, P. et al., Simultaneous determination of amphetamine, methamphetamine, MDA and MDMA in human hair by GC/MS, *J. Chromatogr. B,* 670, 162, 1995.
18. Rothe, M. et al., Hair concentrations and self-reported abuse history of 20 amphetamine and ecstasy users, *Forensic Sci. Int.,* 89, 111, 1997.
19. Cirimele, V., Kintz, P., and Mangin, P., Testing human hair for cannabis, *Forensic Sci. Int.,* 70, 175, 1995.
20. Kintz, P., Cirimele, V., and Mangin, P., Testing human hair for cannabis. II. Identification of THC-COOH by GC/MS/NCI as an unique proof, *J. Forensic Sci.,* 40, 619, 1995.
21. Uhl, M., Determination of drugs in hair using GC/MS/MS, *Forensic Sci. Int.,* 84, 281, 1997.
22. Cirimele, V. et al., Testing human hair for cannabis. III. Rapid screening procedure for the simultaneous identification of THC, cannabinol and cannabidiol, *J. Anal. Toxicol.,* 20, 13, 1996.

10.5.2 Oral Fluid

Oral fluid has been increasingly used as an analytical tool in pharmacokinetic studies, therapeutic drug monitoring, and the detection of illicit drugs. More recently, particular interest in oral fluid has been expressed by law enforcement agencies for roadside testing of intoxicated drivers or in occupational medicine. The presence of metabolites of drugs in urine of potentially impaired drivers can be interpreted as evidence of relatively recent exposure, except for cannabis. However, this does not necessarily mean that the subject was under the influence at the time of sampling. It has been claimed that the concentrations of many drugs in oral fluid correlate well with blood concentrations, which suggests that qualitative measurements in saliva may be a valuable technique to determine the current degree of exposure to a definite drug at the time of sampling.

10.5.2.1 Oral Fluid Sampling

Several methods have been described for the collection of mixed saliva. Based on a recommendation of a working group of the Drug Testing Advisory Board in the U.S., the term *oral fluid* is preferred. Saliva stands for the secretion of the salivary glands, while the testing fluid also contains mucosal transsudate and crevicular fluid.

Oral fluid is usually collected by spitting into a collection vial or wiping the oral cavity with a swab. Many different stimuli will cause salivation. Spitting itself is usually a sufficient stimulus to elicit a flow of about 0.5 ml/min. However, there are a number of limitations: in an on-site situation "dry mouth" was often reported;[1] moreover, the salivary flow is decreased after intake of certain drugs, e.g., some tricyclic antidepressants and amphetamines. Individuals often collect more froth than actual liquid providing a viscous sample with a small sample size, which complicates the analysis. Many researchers have found it advantageous to stimulate salivation by placing sour candy or citric acid crystals in the mouth prior to collection, or chewing an inert material like Teflon. Substances like Parafilm® should be avoided because they may absorb highly lipophilic drugs. The individual should allow saliva to accumulate in the mouth and then expectorate into a suitable container. Some special devices have been designed to facilitate the sampling of saliva. The use of a dental cotton roll to collect saliva has been improved and is nowadays available as the Salivette® (Sarstedt, Germany). Other commercialized devices include Accu-sorb®, SmartClip®, and Intercept®.

The effect of collection methods on drug concentrations in oral fluid is not well described in the scientific literature. However, caution has to be taken. As the oral fluid flow rate increases, the concentration of bicarbonate ions increases. This may alter the saliva–plasma ratio in a pH-dependent manner, especially for weakly basic drugs with a pK_a approaching the oral fluid pH, e.g., cocaine and opioids.[2] Kato et al.[3] observed that the concentrations of cocaine, benzoylecgonine, and ecgonine methylester were substantially greater in nonstimulated mixed saliva than after stimulation with citric acid. A controlled clinical study designed to determine the effects of selected collection protocols on oral fluid codeine concentrations was published recently.[4] Concentrations at different time points averaged 3.6 times higher after spitting without stimulation (= control method) than with acidic stimulation. The control method showed 1.3 to 2.0 times higher concentrations than concentrations in specimens collected by chewing a sugarless gum or using the Salivette or the Finger Collector containing Accu-Sorb® (Avitar Technologies Inc., Canton, MA, U.S.A.). A second issue influencing the use of oral fluid as a drug testing matrix is the contamination of the buccal cavity depending on the route of administration, e.g., for several hours after smoking or sniffing certain drugs. After smoking a cannabis cigarette, the cannabinoids in the smoke are sequestered in the mouth. THC concentrations obtained after direct extraction of a Salivette (positioned between gum and cheek for 1 to 2 min) exceeded the concentrations of THC in samples obtained by spitting by a factor 10 to 100.

10.5.2.2 Screening Tests for Oral Fluid

Before oral fluid can be used for rapid screening and especially for on-site testing, the following criteria should be met: (1) a fast, simple, and validated sampling procedure; (2) a test that needs a small sample volume (100 µl); (3) an antibody targeted to the parent molecules rather than the metabolites; (4) a sensitivity adapted to the expected concentrations in oral fluid; (5) screening cutoff values that meet the requirements for high sensitivity and specificity; (6) an electronic reader.

Some prototypes of on-site tests have been investigated during the course of the ROSITA project.[5] Unfortunately, none of the present devices is satisfactory in terms of sensitivity and reliability. However, many development efforts are under way and the involved companies are improving the ease of use and the accuracy of their tests.

The results of the first large-scale database on oral fluid testing in private industry were published in 2002.[6] About 77,000 specimens were screened by the Intercept immunoassay at manufacturer's recommended cutoff values for five drug classes (cannabis, opiates, amphetamines, cocaine, and phencyclidine). Presumptive positive specimens were confirmed by GC/MS/MS.

The screening cutoffs will depend on the specificity of the antibodies, and the presence of other cross-reacting metabolites in oral fluid. Quite recently, SAMHSA cutoff values have been proposed for the screening and confirmation of most illicit drugs in oral fluid.

10.5.2.3 Analytical Procedures

Oral fluid can be extracted and analyzed as other biological fluids such as blood. In general, there will be less interference from endogenous compounds than with blood or urine. An oral fluid sample collected with a special device usually provides the analyst with a clean specimen. However, a sample collected by spitting contains cell debris, food particles, and strings of mucus; centrifugation is difficult because of the high viscosity. The specimen has to be stored at –4°C and measured as soon as possible because of possible bacterial and fungal growth. The cocaine concentration in saliva, stored in a plastic recipient without addition of citric acid or other stabilizers, remains unaltered at –4°C for 1 week. Freezing of the sample lowers the viscosity substantially so that centrifugation can be performed after thawing. This ensures better handling of the sample and a high stability for most analytes for a long period of time except for THC. Sometimes, the addition of sodium fluoride is reported, e.g., for cannabis and benzodiazepines.

A selection of various chromatographic procedures for drugs of abuse in saliva has been published recently.[2] Quantitation is usually performed with the common GC/MS procedures for drugs of abuse in blood, using electron impact mode and the appropriate deuterated standards. Since oral fluid contains the parent drugs, it is important to add internal standards for the quantification of THC, cocaine, and 6-MAM. Due to the smaller sample volume of an oral fluid specimen in comparison to a blood sample, analytical procedures using MS in chemical ionization mode, tandem MS/MS confirmation, or LC-MS are being developed.

Amphetamines

It has been shown recently[1] that the concentrations of amphetamine and MDMA in oral fluid, either obtained by spitting or with a Salivette, exceed the corresponding plasma concentrations 10 to 100 times. Oral contamination after sniffing of the drug can account for only some of the high concentrations during the first hours. Oral fluid samples can also be extracted using the common solid-phase extraction procedures for amphetamines in blood. Proposed SAMHSA screening cutoff values are 50 ng/ml for D-methamphetamine as the target analyte and confirmation cutoff values are 50 ng/ml for D-amphetamine and 50 ng/ml for D-methamphetamine.

A first innovative approach to the problem of low sample volumes is the use of LC-MS-MS with a minimum sample workup. Detection limits are in the range of 2 ng/ml for amphetamine and the designer amphetamines, using only 50 µl of oral fluid.[7] A simple precipitation of the proteins with methanol followed by centrifugation or even dilution of the saliva sample followed by direct injection allows the analyst to process a high number of oral fluid samples with a small sample size.

Cannabis

Although there is very little transport for THC from blood to saliva, the usual administration routes (smoking, ingestion) provide detectable levels of THC for several hours with different techniques (HPLC, GC-ECD, GC-MS; limit of quantification 1 to 20 ng/ml). It is obvious that the higher THC concentrations after smoking are due to contamination of the buccal cavity. Calculation of S/P ratios in these circumstances is of little value but the detection of cannabinoids in saliva is a better indication of recent use than detection of the metabolite in urine.

The analytes of interest are THC, cannabinol, and cannabidiol.[1] SAMHSA proposes a screening cutoff of 4 ng/ml for THC as the target analyte for the initial screen and 4 ng/ml of THC in the confirmation analysis. Extraction from an oral fluid sample can be done with a mixture of hexane/ethylacetate (9/1) (v/v) after acidification; derivatization is performed by methylation with tetramethylammoniumhydroxide and iodomethane and subsequent extraction into isooctane. The limit of detection can be increased by pulsed splitless injection of 4 µl of the derivatized extract; linearity is observed in the range 0.5-50 ng/ml, with a LOD of 0.1 ng/ml.

It has been demonstrated[8] that the cotton from the Salivette adsorbs 90% of the THC content of a spiked saliva sample. After centrifugation, no THC could be detected in the recovered fluid. Extraction of the dry cotton with methanol or with hexane/ethylacetate (9/1) (v/v) after addition of THC-d₃ to the roll resulted in THC concentrations exceeding 100 ng/salivette in drivers showing impairment and providing a positive blood sample.[5]

Cocaine

Numerous reports have documented the excretion of cocaine and metabolites in saliva. Cocaine appeared in saliva rapidly following intravenous injection, inhalation, and intranasal administration to volunteers. Contamination of the oral cavity after smoking and sniffing was variable but significant during the first 2 h after dosing. Anhydroecgonine methyl ester was detectable in saliva after smoking, but it was quickly cleared. Benzoylecgonine and ecgonine methyl ester levels were only comparable with cocaine concentrations at times when those had declined to below 100 ng/ml. However, the concentrations of the metabolites will be higher in chronic users. Proposed SAMHSA screening cutoff values are 20 ng/ml for benzoylecgonine as the target analyte, 8 ng/ml for the confirmation.

Generally, cocaine and its metabolites can be detected in saliva using a simple solid-phase extraction procedure: the sample is diluted with acetate buffer pH 4.0 and brought on a conditioned Bond Elut Certify® column; washing is performed with water, buffer pH 4.0, and acetonitrile, and elution occurs with dichloromethane/isopropanol/ammonia (80/20/2) (v/v/v). Replacing the buffer with 0.1 N HCl allows a washing step with methanol instead of acetonitrile because of the ionary binding of benzoylecgonine to the column. Derivatization is often performed with BSTFA but pentafluoropropionic anhydride in combination with pentafluoropropanol provides a better sensitivity for benzoylecgonine. Limits of detection are in the range 1 to 5 ng/ml.

Opiates

Heroin is rapidly metabolized to 6-MAM in blood, which is in turn converted to morphine. After intravenous injection, the saliva/plasma ratio for heroin and 6-MAM can be lower than one, depending on the salivary pH. After smoking or sniffing of heroin, the concentrations of the analytes in saliva remain higher than in plasma for 2 to 3 h due to a contamination of the buccal cavity. SAMHSA proposed cutoff values are 40 ng/ml morphine for the initial screen and 40 ng/ml of morphine and 4 ng/ml of 6-MAM for the confirmation. Detection of morphine, codeine, and 6-MAM in saliva is based on similar analytical procedures as for cocaine. However, a washing step with a strong acid will result in the hydrolysis of 6-MAM, so acetate buffer pH 4.0 is preferred for opioids. GC-MS data after silylation show similar results as for the PFP derivatives.

Codeine was detected in oral fluid for 12 to 24 h after oral intake of 30 mg of liquid codeine phosphate depending on the individual and on the collection protocol.[4] After solid-phase extraction, derivatization occurred with TFAA and GC-MS analysis was performed using positive-ion chemical ionization. The limit of quantification was 5 ng/ml, limit of detection 1.0 ng/ml. Substantially different pharmacokinetic parameters were detected after spitting, with or without stimulation, using a Salivette or the Finger collector containing Accu-Sorb®. Moreover, *in vitro* studies showed that more than 90% of codeine and morphine could be recovered from the Salivette after centrifugation and only 60% from the Finger collector after milking the foam.

REFERENCES

1. Samyn, N., and van Haeren, C., On-site testing of saliva and sweat with Drugwipe, and determination of concentrations of drugs of abuse in saliva, plasma and urine of suspected users, *Int. J. Legal Med.*, 113, 150, 2000.
2. Samyn, N. et al., Analysis of drugs of abuse in saliva, *Forensic Sci. Rev.*, 11, 1, 1999.
3. Kato, K. et al., Cocaine and metabolite excretion in saliva under stimulated and nonstimulated conditions, *J. Anal. Toxicol.*, 17, 338, 1993.
4. O'Neal, C.L. et al., The effects of collection methods on oral fluid codeine concentrations, *J. Anal. Toxicol.*, 24, 536, 2000.
5. Verstraete, A. and Puddu, M., Deliverable D4: evaluation of different roadside drug tests. ROSITA Contract DG VII RO 98-SC.3032, 2000. http://www.rosita.org.

6. Cone, E.J. et al., Oral fluid testing for drugs of abuse: positive prevalence rates by Intercept immu-
    noassay screening and GC-MS/MS confirmation and suggested cut-off concentrations, *J. Anal. Tox-
    icol.*, 26, 541, 2002.
7. Wood, M. et al., Development of a rapid and sensitive method for the quantitation of amphetamines
    in human plasma and oral fluid by LC-MS-MS, *J. Anal. Toxicol.*, 27, 78, 2003.
8. Kintz, P., Cirimele, V., and Ludes, B., Detection of cannabis in oral fluid (saliva) and forehead wipes
    (sweat) from impaired drivers, *J. Anal. Toxicol.*, 24, 557, 2000.

10.5.3 Sweat

Researchers have known for more than a century[1] that drugs are excreted in sweat. Although
it is still poorly understood how nonvolatile chemicals exit the body through the skin, significant
advances in sweat analyses have been made during the past few years with the development of the
sweat-patch technology.[2] Over a period of 1 to 7 days, sweat will saturate the pad located in the
center of the patch and will slowly concentrate, and drugs present in the perspiration fluid will be
retained. Sweat appears to offer the advantage of being a non-invasive means of obtaining a
cumulative estimate of drug exposure over 1 week. Sweat testing has found applications in monitoring of individuals in drug rehabilitation or in probation/parole programs.[3,4]

The term *sweat-testing* is misleading, because drugs are not only excreted by sweat glands; the
excretion of drugs through the skin is also possible by sebaceous glands or transdermal liquid transport.

Sweat is a liquid secreted by the sweat glands, originating deep within the skin. Water (99%)
is the major component. Na^+ and Cl^- are the major ions, present in variable concentrations, ranging
from 5 to 80 mmol/L. Amino acids, biogenic amines, and vitamins are only present in trace amounts.
The pH (4 to 6) is strongly associated with the amount of lactic acid excreted. Apocrine glands
secrete a more viscous, cloudy, yellow-white liquid, which is primarily sterile and odorless, and
rich in cholesterol (75%), triglycerides, and fatty acids (20%).

Sebaceous glands are associated with hair follicles and located everywhere except on palms
and soles; they are particularly abundant on the scalp and forehead. They produce a viscous, yellow-
white liquid oily sebum that consists of triglycerides (60%) and wax esters. Excreted sweat and
sebum cannot be examined separately.

Sweat secretion is an important homeostatic mechanism for maintaining a constant core body
temperature. At temperatures above 31°C, body heat is dissipated by the release of sweat on the
skin surface resulting in evaporative heat loss. Between 300 to 700 ml/day of *insensible* sweat is
produced over the whole body, likely caused by diffusion through the skin, whereas 2 to 4 L/h of
sensible sweat may be produced for short periods by extensive exercise. The amount of sweat that
is produced is thus affected by body location, ambient temperature, body temperature, and relative
humidity of the environment and by emotional, mental, and physical stress. The variability of these
factors and the uneven distribution of the sweat glands make it difficult to obtain specimens of
sweat systematically.

10.5.3.1 Sweat Collection

Almost all studies obtain mixed secretions of sweat and sebum, which is incorrectly referred
to as sweat. Methods to collect drugs in sweat have included the use of gauze, cotton, towel, or
filter paper to absorb sweat and the collection of liquid sweat in rubber gloves or plastic body
bags.[2,5] Thermal[6] or pharmacological stimulations such as with pilocarpine[7] were proposed to secrete
an unusually large amount of sweat.

Patches, similar to bandages, have been developed to wear for extended periods of time. Early
patches were made of absorbent cotton pads sandwiched between a waterproof, polyurethane outer
layer and a porous inner layer that is placed against the skin. They have been successfully applied
to the detection of ethanol in sweat.[8]

Significant advances have been made during the past few years to develop a non-occlusive sweat collection device, which has been marketed as the PharmChek™ sweat patch. The device consists of an adhesive layer on a thin transparent film of surgical dressing to which a rectangular absorbent pad is attached. The sweat patch acts as a specimen container for nonvolatile and liquid components of sweat, including drugs. Nonvolatile substances from the environment cannot penetrate the transparent film, which is a semipermeable membrane over the pad that allows oxygen, water, and carbon dioxide to pass through the patch, leaving the skin underneath healthy. Over a period of 1 to 10 days, sweat saturates the pad and the water content of the perspiration is volatilized by the body's heat; drugs present in sweat are retained. The region of the skin where the patch will be applied is thoroughly decontaminated with 50% of isopropanol. Subjects can wear one patch with minimal discomfort for at least 1 week. Normal hygiene practices can be achieved. Attempts to remove the patch prematurely are readily visible to personnel trained to monitor the sweat patch.

An alternative collection for epidemiological surveys and for testing of potentially impaired drivers consists of wiping the skin with a cosmetic pad moistened with isopropanol.[9] This procedure allows rapid collection of drugs that may arise both from sweat evaporating on the surface of the skin and from external contamination.

10.5.3.2 *Drug Detection without a Patch Collection*

By using some of the early "home-made" collection methods, it was possible to identify various drugs, including methadone, phenobarbital, morphine, cocaine, THC, and methamphetamine.[10] Sweat samples that are collected on gauze or cotton by wiping the surface of the skin are eluted with water and extracted by liquid–liquid methods.

Kidwell et al.[11] investigated an alternative collection of sweat to detect cocaine prevalence in a university population. Sampling of hands and forehead was performed with a cotton pad (skin wipe) moistened with 500 µl of 90 or 70% isopropanol. LODs of the GC-MS-CI confirmatory method were 1.2 to 2.2 ng/wipe for cocaine and benzoylecgonine. A skin swab test may provide a rapid way to gather data on drug use/exposure in a certain population without the embarrassment often felt when obtaining urine samples and the concern for cosmetic damage often expressed when individuals are asked to take hair samples. Skin wipes detect drugs excreted in sweat/sebum more rapidly than a device (patch) that needs to collect pure sweat over an extended period of time.

Sweat, as a forehead specimen, was obtained from injured drivers[9] by wiping the forehead with a commercial pad spiked with 0.5 ml of water/isopropanol (50:50). After extraction of the pad with hexane/ethyl acetate (90:10) and methylation, THC was detectable by GC/MS between 4 to 152 ng/pad, with the risk of environmental contamination. Neither 11-hydroxy-THC nor THC-COOH was identified.

10.5.3.3 *Drug Detection with a Patch Collection*

Controlled experimental studies using the Pharmchek™ sweat patch have been performed for cocaine,[2,12] heroin,[13] and amphetamine derivatives, such as methamphetamine,[14] MBDB,[15] and MDMA.[16]

Administration of low doses of cocaine (about 1 to 5 mg) produced detectable amounts of cocaine in sweat.[12] Sweat patches were applied to the back and abdomen of subjects prior to and periodically after drug administration. Before affixing the patches, the skin area was cleaned with an isopropyl alcohol (70%) swab. The absorbent pad was extracted with 2.5 ml of a mixture of 0.1% Triton X-100 in 0.2 *M* acetate buffer, in the presence of deuterated internal standards. After agitation and centrifugation, the filtered extract solution was purified by SPE and submitted to GC/MS. LODs for cocaine and metabolites were approximately 1 ng/patch. Within- and between-run coefficients of variation were less than or equal to 10%. It was observed that the parent drug was the predominant analyte with cocaine levels (ng/patch) being much higher than the concentrations of the metabolites benzoylecgonine and ecgonine methyl ester. After a single 25-mg IV injection, 42-mg smoked, and 32-mg intranasal administration, cocaine appeared in sweat within 2 h after drug administration and peaked within 24 h with maximum concentrations varying from as low as 15 to as high as 70 ng cocaine/patch. Inter-subject variability was high whereas intra-subject variability was relatively low.

More recent work has focused on the applications of the "Fast Patches" requiring only 30 min for sweat collection because they employ heat-induced sweat stimulation and a larger cellulose pad for increased drug collection.[2] Sweat was collected periodically for 48 h following subcutaneous administration of 75 or 150 mg of cocaine hydrochloride/70 kg. Torso Fast Patches were applied to the abdomen or flank, and Hand-held Fast Patches were affixed to the palm of the nondominant hand and elution of the patch was performed with 0.5 M sodium acetate buffer (pH 4.0). Peak cocaine concentrations (4.5 to 24 h after dosing) ranged from 33 to 3579 ng/patch for the Hand-held Patch and from 22 to 1463 ng/patch for the Torso Fast Patch. Cocaine could be detected for at least 48 h after dosing. Drug concentrations were considerably higher than those reported for the Pharmchek sweat patch. Cocaine concentrations in the Hand-held Patch were more than twofold greater than those found in the Torso Fast Patch.

In a study conducted during a heroin maintenance program, 14 subjects were injected with two or three doses of heroin hydrochloride ranging from 80 to 1000 mg/day. The sweat patches were applied before the first dosage and removed after 24 h, minutes before the next dosage.[13] Patches were extracted with acetonitrile before GC-MS analysis. Concentrations (ng/patch) ranged from 2.1 to 96.3 for heroin, 0 to 24.6 for 6-MAM, and 0 to 11.2 for morphine. There was no correlation between the doses of heroin administered and the concentrations of heroin measured in sweat.

An enzyme immunoassay screening test was described for methamphetamine in eluates of sweat patches, with a cross-reactivity of 144% for MDMA, 30% for amphetamine, and 21% for MDA. Diagnostic sensitivity and specificity were 84.5 and 93.2%, respectively, when comparing to the GC-MS results and applying a cutoff value of 10 ng/ml amphetamine equivalents (using methamphetamine calibrators). The clinical sensitivity and specificity of the overall analysis system were 85 and 100%, respectively, using known methamphetamine dosing of volunteers as the reference standard. Drug doses given were probably lower than a street drug dose.[14]

N-Methyl-1-(3,4-methylenedioxyphenyl)-2-butanamine (MBDB) was detected in the methanolic extract from the Pharmchek sweat patch with concentrations increasing during the first 36 h following a single dose of 100 mg MBDB.[15] Peak concentrations of MBDB and its metabolite 3,4-methylene-dioxyphenyl-2-butanamine (BDB) were 44 and 23 ng/patch, respectively.

In a recent study,[16] sweat was collected for up to 24 h with the PharmChek sweat patches from recreational users of MDMA who received a single 100-mg dose of the drug. After SPE and derivatization, analytes were tested by GC/MS. MDMA was detected in sweat as early as 1.5 h after administration and peaked at 24 h. In all the nine subjects, an on-site test with the Drugwipe immunochemical strip test was positive at 1.5 h.

As a result of the poor passive diffusion from plasma, it was necessary to use very sensitive techniques to detect some drugs in sweat. Ion trap GC/MS/MS was reported as useful for cannabis.[17] THC was identified in sweat of nine cannabis users after wearing a patch for 5 days (4-38 ng/patch).[3]

REFERENCES

1. Tachau, H., Uber den Ubergang von Arzneimitteln in der Schweiss, *Arch. Exp. Pathol. Pharmakol.*, 66, 224, 1911.

2. Huestis, M. et al., Sweat testing for cocaine, codeine and metabolites by gas chromatography-mass spectrometry, *J. Chromatogr. B,* 733, 247,1999.

3. Kintz, P. et al., Sweat testing in opioid users with a sweat patch, *J. Anal. Toxicol.,* 20, 393, 1996.

4. Huestis, M.A. et al., Monitoring opiate use in substance abuse treatment patients with sweat and urine drug testing, *J. Anal. Toxicol.,* 24, 509, 2000.

5. Inoue, T. and Seta, S., Analysis of drugs in unconventional samples, *Forensic Sci. Rev.,* 4, 90, 1992.

6. Fox, R.H. et al., The nature of the increase in sweating capacity produced by heat acclimatization, *J. Physiol.,* 171, 368, 1964.

7. Balabanova, S. et al., Die Bedeutung der Drogenbestimmung in Pilocarpinschweiss für den Nachweis eines zurückliegendes Drogenkonsum, *Beitr. Gerichtl. Med.,* 50 111, 1992.

8. Phillips, M., Sweat-patch testing detects inaccurate self-reports of alcohol consumption, *Alcohol. Clin. Exp. Res.,* 8, 51, 1984.

9. Kintz, P., Cirimele, V., and Ludes, B., Detection of cannabis in oral fluid (saliva) and forehead wipes (sweat) from impaired drivers, *J. Anal. Toxicol.,* 24, 557, 2000.

10. Kidwell, D.A., Holland, J.C., and Athanaselis, S., Testing for drugs of abuse in saliva and sweat, *J. Chromatogr. B,* 713, 111, 1998.

11. Kidwell, D.A., Blanco, M.A., and Smith, F.P., Cocaine detection in a university population by hair analysis and skin swab testing, *Forensic Sci. Int.,* 84, 75, 1997.

12. Cone, E.J. et al., Sweat testing for heroin, cocaine and metabolites, *J. Anal. Toxicol.,* 18, 298, 1994.

13. Kintz, P. et al., Sweat testing for heroin and metabolites in a heroin maintenance program, *Clin. Chem.,* 43, 736, 1997.

14. Fay, J. et al., Detection of methamphetamine in sweat by EIA and GC-MS, *J. Anal. Toxicol.,* 20, 398, 1996.

15. Kintz, P., Excretion of MBDB and BDB in urine, saliva, and sweat following single oral administration, *J. Anal. Toxicol.,* 21, 570, 1997.

16. Pichini, S. et al., Usefulness of sweat testing for the detection of MDMA after a single-dose administration, *J. Anal. Toxicol.,* 27, 294, 2003.

17. Ehorn, C., Fretthold, D., and Maharaj, M., Ion trap GC/MS/MS for analysis of THC from sweat. In *Proceedings of the TIAFT-SOFT Congress 1994,* Tampa, FL, abstr. 11.

10.5.4 General Conclusion

It appears that the value of alternative specimen analysis for the identification of drug users is steadily gaining recognition. This can be seen from its growing use in pre-employment screening, in forensic sciences, and in clinical applications.

Saliva and sweat will probably be used in the near future in roadside testing both for epidemiological and screening purposes.

Hair analysis may be a useful adjunct to conventional drug testing in toxicology. Methods for evading urinalysis do not affect hair analysis.

Specimens of saliva or sweat can be more easily obtained with less embarrassment than for urine, and hair can provide a more accurate history of drug use. However, due to a lack of suitable screening tools, costs are too high for routine use (because the analyses require hyphenated chromatographic procedures) but the generated data are extremely helpful to document positive urine cases. These new matrices may find useful applications in the near future, for example, in occupational medicine, roadside testing, or doping control or for law enforcement agencies to document illicit drug use.

10.6 INTERPRETING ALTERNATIVE MATRIX TEST RESULTS

Edward J. Cone, Ph.D.,[1] Angela Sampson-Cone, Ph.D.,[1] and Marilyn A. Huestis, Ph.D.[2]*

[1] ConeChem Research, Severna Park, Maryland
[2] Chemistry and Drug Metabolism Section, Intramural Research Program, National Institute on Drug Abuse, National Institutes of Health, Baltimore, Maryland

10.6.1　Drug Testing with Alternative Matrices

Significant advances in analytical technology over the last decade have provided the analytical toxicologist with the means of testing for drugs of abuse and their metabolites in biologic matrices with ultrahigh sensitivity and specificity. Conclusive identification and measurement of drug residues in tissues provide important information on an individual's past drug use and exposure history. Such evidence can be important in many types of forensic investigations, e.g., workplace testing, accident investigations, health assessments, diagnosis, treatment and monitoring of drug abusers, and whether drug use was a contributory factor in civil and criminal acts. Many centrally acting drugs produce significant physiologic and behavioral impairment. Frequently, when accidents and loss of life and property occur, medical personnel and toxicologists are called upon to interpret toxicology results. This evidence may support or refute the presence of drug-induced behavioral changes in an individual. In addition, results may indicate whether drug use or drug exposure occurred, the frequency and route of drug use, and the probable level of exposure.

Many different types of biologic specimens can be tested for drug residues. The most frequently collected types are urine, oral fluid, sweat, hair, and blood. Circumstances often determine the type of specimen collected. Whereas post-mortem testing traditionally involves collection of blood and tissue specimens, accident and criminal investigations most frequently involve urine and blood. Workplace and treatment programs generally test urine specimens but, more recently, some have begun to test oral fluid, hair, and sweat as alternative or complementary specimens. Urine and sweat are utilized most commonly in the legal community, e.g., parolee monitoring.

The growing use of different biological specimens presents an array of challenges to those involved in forensic and clinical interpretation. The unique properties of each biological specimen offer somewhat different information on past drug use, and it is becoming increasingly important to understand these differences. In some cases, test results from diverse biological specimens may not agree. The reasons for agreement or disagreement may be complex. Forensic interpretation of specimen test results must be based on an understanding of the chemical and pharmacologic properties of the drug, performance characteristics of analytical methods, and the unique physiological properties of the biological specimens.

This chapter examines the similarities and differences of drug disposition in blood, urine, oral fluid, sweat, and hair specimens. The primary focus is on the chemical and physiologic properties of different specimens and the time course of drug disposition into and out of the biologic matrix. Differences in the physicochemical properties of drugs add to the complexity of interpretation of results. Cocaine is used as the primary model compound in this chapter to illustrate similarities and differences in specimen types. Understanding the "uniqueness" of drug disposition in biological matrices will guide interpretation of similar and disparate results from multiple biological specimens.

---

* Dr. Huestis contributed to this book in her personal capacity. The views expressed are her own and do not necessarily represent the views of the National Institutes of Health or the U.S. government.

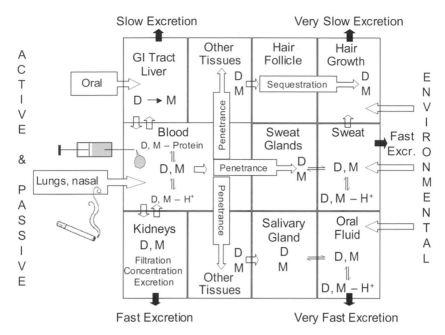

Figure 10.6.1 Disposition of drug (D) and metabolite (M) in blood and tissues following active and passive drug administration and environmental exposure. The rate of excretion of drug and metabolite is indicated as "Very Fast" (minutes), "Fast" (minutes to hours), "Slow" (hours to days), and "Very Slow (days to months). Abbreviations: D = drug; M = metabolite; D,M–Protein = protein-bound drug or metabolite; D, M–H+ = ionized drug or metabolite.

10.6.2 Drug Disposition in Alternative Matrices

10.6.2.1 Circumstances of Drug Exposure

Drug exposure takes place under many different circumstances. Active drug use can involve a variety of routes of administration including oral ingestion, inhalation, parenteral administration, and absorption through skin and mucosal membranes. Passive drug exposure can occur through inhalation of drug smoke, vapor, or dust, by external contamination of the skin, hair, and mucous membranes, and by oral ingestion, e.g., doping. "Active" drug administration is defined generally as intentional drug self-administration by the individual undergoing testing, whereas "passive drug exposure" is defined as unintentional drug exposure. Figure 10.6.1 provides a graphic illustration of the complex rate processes involved in drug use and exposure and in transfer into and out of different bodily tissues.

Regardless of how drug use or exposure occurs, the consequences of a positive test may be highly detrimental to the donor. Understanding how drugs penetrate and reside in different tissues is an important component in the development and use of biological specimens for drug testing.

10.6.2.2 Absorption and Distribution

During the process of penetrance into the body, drugs may be altered by metabolic and chemical processes. Drug metabolism that occurs during absorption, distribution, and elimination processes can result in the production of metabolites with substantially different properties than the parent drug. The pharmacologic activity of metabolites may be enhanced, reduced, or totally eliminated by molecular alteration. Once drug penetrance into the bloodstream occurs, the route of administration becomes less important to drug disposition. Depending on the chemical properties of the drug, metabolism may occur immediately in blood, but more commonly occurs following uptake into the liver and other organs. Arterial blood carries drugs and metabolites to tissues and venous blood transports them away. The transfer of drug and metabolites into tissues is governed by factors such as the chemical properties of the drug, degree of tissue perfusion, protein binding, and characteristics of the tissue membrane. Drug uptake into tissues is generally rapid and equilibrium between highly perfused tissues and venous blood is quickly established. The rate of drug uptake is dependent on the rate of blood flow and the tissue/blood partition coefficient. Accumulation of drug by organ tissues occurs in the extracellular fluid. Some drugs also cross cell membranes into intracellular water. Long-term accumulation of lipid-soluble drugs may occur in fatty tissues.

10.6.2.3 Clearance and Elimination

Most drugs are cleared from the body through the processes of metabolism and excretion. The liver is the major site of drug metabolism and the type of metabolite produced is based on the enzymatic processes involved. A drug may be subject to hydrolytic cleavage, oxidation, reduction, and conjugation reactions, depending upon its molecular structure. Frequently, these reactions produce metabolites with greater water-solubility and less pharmacologic activity than the parent molecule. Such reactions primarily are irreversible and serve to clear active drug from the body. The enhanced water-solubility of metabolites facilitates their removal by excretory processes.

Nonvolatile drugs and metabolites are generally excreted in urine and feces. Other pathways of drug elimination include excretion in bile, saliva, sweat, milk (via lactation), sebum, other bodily fluids, skin (via desquamation), and hair. Some processes, such as excretion into bile and saliva, may be circulatory in nature and reabsorption into the bloodstream may occur during transit through the gastrointestinal tract.

10.6.3 Physiologic Considerations

10.6.3.1 Blood

Although blood is infrequently collected in workplace testing, it is important to understand drug disposition in this matrix. The primary mode of entry of drugs and metabolites into other biological specimens is from blood. On average, an adult human male weighing 70 kg has a blood volume of approximately 5 L. Blood is composed of two parts, plasma, the fluid portion, and formed elements that include blood cells and platelets that are suspended in the fluid. There are more than 60 proteins in plasma that fight infection, transport lipids, and prevent uncontrolled bleeding. Albumin is a major component of plasma protein and undergoes reversible binding with many drugs. Binding to protein has a major influence on a drug's disposition in the body. Protein-bound drug is a large molecular complex that cannot easily cross membranes. An equilibrium exists between protein-bound drug and free drug. Consequently, drug distribution to other tissues is limited to the portion of drug that exists as free unbound drug.

Drug molecules dissolved in blood are transported through a network of fine capillaries to the tissues. The rate of passage of drugs across cell membranes is dependent on the drug's chemical properties and the properties of the cell membrane. Capillary wall membranes are generally highly porous, whereas other membranes may be considerably more complex and less porous, e.g., unique endothelial cells of the blood–brain barrier and the multilayered epithelial cell layers of the dermis and epidermis. Lipid-soluble drugs generally diffuse more easily across membranes than polar, water-soluble drugs, metabolites, and highly protein-bound drugs.

Following drug absorption into the bloodstream, changes in blood concentrations initially reflect changes that occur as a result of distribution and uptake by tissues. At some point after administration, drug concentration in plasma approaches equilibrium with drug sequestered in tissues. Once

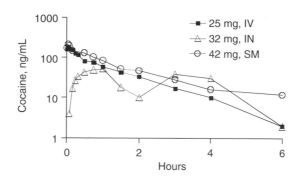

Figure 10.6.2   Plasma concentrations of cocaine in a subject (Subject I) after intravenous (IV), intranasal (IN), and smoked (SM) administration of single doses of cocaine.

equilibrium is established, drug concentration declines as a result of metabolic and elimination processes. Most drug concentrations decline at a rate proportional to the amount of drug remaining in the body. The elimination half-life ($t_{1/2}$) of a drug is the time required for the plasma concentration to be reduced by one half. The half-life of a particular drug generally is constant for an individual across a broad range of dosages; however, some drugs exhibit nonlinear kinetics when dosages overwhelm enzymatic and/or elimination processes.

An illustration of the decline of plasma cocaine concentrations of one subject (Subject I) following intravenous, intranasal, and smoked administration of 25 mg of cocaine hydrochloride is shown in Figure 10.6.2. Cocaine exhibited a plasma half-life of approximately 1.4 h after either intravenous or smoked administration. The decline in cocaine concentration following intranasal administration was biphasic, likely as a result of irregular absorption.

The appearance of drug metabolites in blood is influenced by the route of administration. The liver is the major site of drug metabolism. When drug is ingested, absorption of virtually all drugs is faster from the small intestine than from the stomach due to its large surface area. Therefore, gastric emptying is a rate-limiting step. The intraluminal pH is 4 to 5 in the duodenum, but becomes progressively more alkaline, approaching a pH of 8 in the lower ileum. Absorption of drugs from the gastrointestinal tract depends on the drug's ability to pass across intestinal cell membranes and resist destruction in the liver (first-pass effect). In most cases, drugs pass through intestinal membranes by simple diffusion, from an area of high concentration (inside the lumen) to an area of lower concentration (bloodstream). During absorption, significant metabolism may occur, so that only a fraction of the drug may survive intact. Metabolites formed in the liver may be excreted into the feces via bile, or may be released into the bloodstream at the same time as parent drug. Hence, following oral administration, the initial appearance of a metabolite in the bloodstream may be rapid with concentrations sometimes exceeding that of the parent drug.

Drug administration by other routes, e.g., parenteral, transmucosal, and inhalation, may partially or totally bypass the liver and avoid the "first-pass effect" of oral ingestion. Once drug enters the bloodstream, it is immediately distributed to all parts of the body. Approximately 25% of cardiac output is directed to the liver, where drug may be extracted from blood. A variety of processes may affect the ability of the liver to extract drug from blood, including the degree of drug-protein binding (only free, unbound drug may be extracted), solubility of the drug in the hepatic membrane, and metabolic processes occurring in the hepatocytes. Once formed, metabolite(s) may be transported into bile and released into the gastrointestinal tract or be returned to the bloodstream.

In contrast to oral administration, initial appearance of metabolites following parenteral and mucosal administration may be delayed. As an example, Figure 10.6.3 illustrates the appearance in plasma of cocaine and benzoylecgonine (BZE), a metabolite of cocaine, following intravenous administration. BZE was initially detected at 10 min and rose to a maximum concentration in

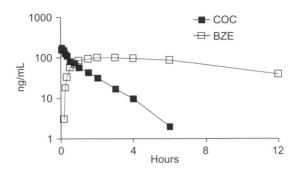

Figure 10.6.3 Plasma concentrations of cocaine (COC) and benzoylecgonine (BZE) in a subject (Subject I) after intravenous administration of a single 25-mg dose of cocaine.

approximately 1 h following cocaine administration. Thereafter, BZE declined slowly with an approximate half-life of 6.3 h. The rapid formation and slow disappearance of BZE relative to cocaine indicates that elimination, rather than metabolism, was the rate-limiting step for BZE. When the half-life of a metabolite is longer than that of the parent drug, accumulation of the metabolite can occur with repeated, frequent administrations, as occurs with BZE.

10.6.3.2 Urine

Approximately 20 to 25% of the blood from cardiac output, or 1200 mL/min, goes to the kidney. Blood enters the glomerulus for nonselective filtering of the plasma. Most drug molecules with low molecular weights can pass through the filter forming an ultrafiltrate with a concentration similar to plasma; however, only the unbound portion of the drug can be filtered. Consequently, drugs that are highly bound to plasma protein generally undergo a longer renal elimination period than drugs that are less highly bound. In addition, some drugs undergo active renal secretion, a carrier-mediated system. If the carrier has greater affinity for the free drug than plasma protein, then active renal secretion can increase the rate of elimination despite protein binding.

The glomerulus receives blood first and filters about 125 mL/min of plasma containing substances with molecular weights less than 20,000 Da. The plasma ultrafiltrate flows through the proximal convoluted tubule, loop of Henle, distal tubule, and continues through the collecting duct to the bladder. During transit through the nephron, electrolytes, nutrients, and water are reabsorbed and returned to the bloodstream. Excess water and waste products, such as urea, organic substances (including drugs and metabolites), and inorganic substances, are eliminated from the body. Normally, water is reabsorbed reducing urine flow to less than 1 to 2 mL/min. The daily amount and composition of urine vary widely depending upon many factors such as fluid intake, diet, health, drug effects, and environmental conditions. The volume of urine produced by a healthy adult in a 24-h period ranges from 1 to 2 L with a pH range of 5 to 7.5, but normal values outside these limits may be encountered.

As a consequence of extensive water reabsorption in the kidney, drugs and metabolites concentrate in urine. Indeed, if a drug or metabolite exists largely in the unbound state in plasma, its relative concentration could be up to 100 times greater in urine. Figure 10.6.4 illustrates the concentrations of cocaine and BZE in urine compared to plasma in a subject following intravenous administration of cocaine. Urine cocaine and BZE concentrations were approximately 15 and 100 times higher than in plasma, respectively. These findings suggest that BZE is less highly bound to protein than cocaine or alternately that cocaine is reabsorbed by the kidney during renal excretion. It is important to note that despite the large concentration differences observed in plasma as compared to urine, estimation of elimination half-lives were similar for both drugs in plasma and urine.

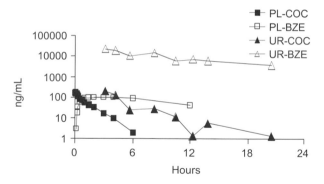

Figure 10.6.4   Plasma (PL) and urine (UR) concentrations of cocaine (COC) and benzoylecgonine (BZE) in a subject (Subject I) after intravenous administration of a single 25-mg dose of cocaine.

10.6.3.3   Oral Fluid

Oral fluid is a composite specimen that consists primarily of saliva, gingival crevicular fluid (fluid from the gingival crevice), and cellular debris. The bulk of fluid in the oral cavity originates from the submandibular and parotid glands and gingival crevicular fluid. During resting conditions, about 71% of oral fluid is supplied by the submandibular glands, approximately 25% originates from the parotid glands, and the remaining 4% is produced by other minor glands.[1] With stimulation, the fluid contribution from the parotid gland rises to about 41%. Salivary glands are innervated by both sympathetic and parasympathetic nerves. Saliva production occurs in response to neurotransmitter release. The volume of saliva varies considerably from approximately 500 to 1500 mL/day. The pH of saliva is generally acidic, but may range from 6.0 to 7.8, depending on the rate of saliva flow. As saliva flow increases, levels of bicarbonate increase, thus increasing pH.[2]

Saliva glands, as they are highly perfused, have a high blood flow. Drug in plasma is distributed rapidly to salivary glands and may appear in saliva within minutes of parenteral drug administration.[3] Figure 10.6.5 illustrates the rapid appearance of cocaine and BZE in oral fluid compared to plasma. Cocaine concentrations in oral fluid generally exceeded those of plasma by a factor of approximately two. The acidic nature of oral fluid compared to plasma and cocaine's lipophilicity favor excretion in oral fluids and account for its higher concentration. BZE also appeared in oral fluid simultaneously with its appearance in plasma, but was present at approximately one third of its plasma concentration. The greater water solubility and lower lipid solubility of BZE apparently accounts

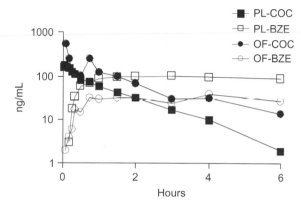

Figure 10.6.5   Plasma (PL) and oral fluid (OF) concentrations of cocaine (COC) and benzoylecgonine (BZE) in a subject (Subject I) after intravenous administration of a single 25-mg dose of cocaine.

for its lower concentration in oral fluid relative to plasma. However, the longer half-life of BZE compared to cocaine leads to prolonged appearance in oral fluid, in this case, exceeding the concentration of cocaine within 4 to 6 h. With multiple cocaine doses and accumulation of BZE, testing for BZE in oral fluid is likely to be of greater utility for the detection of cocaine use.

Other drugs of abuse such as opiates, amphetamines, phencyclidine, and designer drugs that contain basic nitrogen moieties exhibit similar distribution patterns in oral fluid compared to plasma.[4] In contrast, tetrahydrocannabinol (THC), the major active ingredient of cannabis, is a non-nitrogen-containing compound that is highly fat soluble. Deposition of THC in the oral cavity during smoking and oral ingestion most likely accounts for its presence in oral fluid. Fortunately, the residence time of THC in the oral cavity is sufficient for detection over a similar time course as its presence in plasma. Indeed, detection rates for cannabis use by oral fluid testing appear to be similar to those seen in urine testing.[5]

10.6.3.4   Sweat

Sweat secretion is an important mechanism for maintaining a constant core body temperature. Following sympathetic nerve stimulation, sweat is excreted onto the surface of the skin and evaporated to release body heat. Sweat is secreted from two types of sweat glands: eccrine and apocrine glands. These glands originate deep within the skin dermis and terminate in excretory ducts emptying onto the skin or developing hair follicles. Eccrine glands are located on most skin surfaces, while apocrine glands are restricted to skin of the axilla, genitalia, and anus. Water is the primary constituent of sweat accounting for approximately 99% of its bulk,[6] and sodium chloride is the most concentrated solute. Sweat also contains albumin, gamma globulins, waste products, trace elements, drugs, and many other substances found in blood. The rate of sweating is highly dependent on the environmental temperature. Above 31°C, humans begin to sweat and may excrete as much as 3 L/h over short periods of time. The average pH of sweat of resting individuals is reported to be 5.82.[7] Following exercise, the pH increases with increasing flow rates and is reported to be between 6.1 and 6.7.[8] Approximately 50% of sweat is generated by the trunk of the body, 25% from the legs, and the remaining 25% from the head and upper extremities.[8]

Blood flow delivers drug and metabolite to sweat glands, i.e., eccrine and apocrine glands, where diffusion of unbound drug and metabolite occurs through membranes. The rate of passage of drug from blood to sweat via the sweat gland epithelium appears to be proportional to the oil/water partition coefficient of the unionized drug.[9] This process would be facilitated for drugs that demonstrate low degrees of ionization at physiological pH. For lipid-soluble, basic drugs with high pKa values, excretion in sweat is further enhanced by the acidic nature of sweat. For example, cocaine generally is excreted in sweat in higher concentrations than found in plasma. Figure 10.6.6 illustrates the excretion of cocaine in sweat following intravenous, intranasal, and smoked routes of administration. Plasma cocaine concentrations are also shown following intravenous administration. After 2 h, sweat cocaine concentrations were considerably higher in sweat than in plasma. Despite the longer half-life of BZE, it was present in only trace concentrations (not shown).

10.6.3.5   Hair

Hair consists of five morphological components: cuticle, cortex, medulla, melanin granules, and cell membrane complex. Each is distinct in morphology and chemical composition. The number of human head hair follicles ranges from 80,000 to 100,000 follicles, but this decreases with age.[10] Hair follicles are embedded in the dermis of skin and are highly vascularized to nourish the growing hair root or bulb.[11] The bulb at the base of the follicle contains matrix cells that give rise to the layers of the hair shaft including the cuticle, cortex, and medulla. Matrix cells undergo morphological and structural changes as they move upward during growth to form different layers of the hair shaft. These layers can often be distinguished by qualitative and quantitative differences in

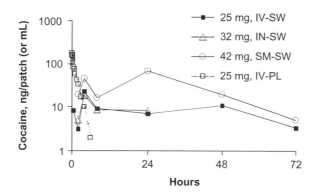

Figure 10.6.6 Sweat (SW) patch concentrations of cocaine in a subject (Subject I) after intravenous (IV), intranasal (IN), and smoked (SM) administration of single doses of cocaine. For comparison, plasma (PL) cocaine concentrations after IV administration are also shown (dotted line). Sweat patches were applied and removed between each collection point.

their proteins and pigments.[10] Hair is composed of approximately 65 to 95% protein, 1 to 9% lipid, and small quantities of trace elements, polysaccharides, and water.[11] The durability and strength of the hair shaft is determined by the proteins synthesized within the matrix cells. Matrix cells also may acquire pigment or melanin during differentiation into individual layers of hair. The pigment present in hair cells determines the color of the hair shaft. The primary structure of hair consists of two or three α-keratin chains wound into strands called microfibrils. Microfibrils are organized into larger bundles of macrofibrils that comprise the bulk of the cortex. Hair strands are stabilized and shaped by disulfide and hydrogen bonds giving the microfibrils a semi-crystalline structure. Cytochrome P450 and other enzymes have been identified in the hair follicle providing evidence that drug metabolism may occur within this structure; however, as hair becomes fully keratinized in 3 to 5 days, this capability is presumed to be greatly reduced.[11]

A protective layer of epithelial cells called the cuticle surrounds the cortex. The cuticle is the outermost layer of hair, the innermost region is the medulla, and the hair cortex lies between these components. The overlapping cuticle cells protect the cortex from the environment. As hair ages, there is a gradual degeneration of the cuticle along the shaft due to exposure to ultraviolet radiation, chemicals, and mechanical stresses. The cuticle may be partially or totally missing in cases of damaged hair.[12] Hair damaged by cosmetic treatments and/or ultraviolet radiation may influence the deposition and stability of drug in the hair.[13]

Hair follicles continue to grow for a number of years and undergo different phases during a normal growth cycle of several years. Approximately 85 to 90% of the hair is in the anagen or growth phase at any single time.[10] A small portion of mature hair then enters the catagen phase, in which there is a rapid reduction in growth rate. This phase lasts for a period of 2 to 3 weeks and is immediately followed by the telogen phase, the resting phase of hair. During this phase, no growth occurs. Approximately 10 to 15% of head hair is usually in the telogen phase. The hair strand may not be shed for several months prior to replacement by a new strand. Hair growth rates vary according to body location, sex, and age.

Head hair grows at an average rate of 1.3 cm/month although there is some variation according to sex, age, and ethnicity.[14] Mangin and Kintz[15] determined morphine and codeine concentrations in human head, axillary, and pubic hair from heroin overdose cases. Morphine concentrations were highest in pubic hair followed by head and axillary hair. Codeine to morphine ratios ranged from 0.054 to 0.273. The slower growth rate of pubic hair and possible drug contribution from sweat or urine were presumed to account for the differences in drug concentration in the different hair samples.

There are multiple possible pathways for drug incorporation into hair, including (1) passive diffusion from blood into the hair follicle; (2) excretion onto the surface of hair from sweat and sebum; (3) passage from skin to hair; and (4) from external contamination. Henderson[16] suggested

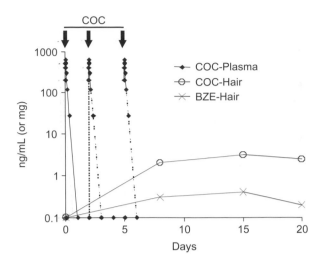

Figure 10.6.7 Cocaine (COC) concentrations in plasma and cocaine and benzoylecgonine (BZE) concentrations in human head hair after 150 mg/kg cocaine administration by the subcutaneous route. Data represent the mean average for five subjects. Three separate cocaine administrations occurred on days 0, 2, and 5. The dotted lines for cocaine plasma represent simulated plasma concentrations (not measured). (Data adapted from References 18 and 19.)

that drugs may enter hair from multiple sites, via multiple mechanisms, and at various times during the hair growth cycle. Drugs and their metabolites are distributed throughout the body primarily by passive diffusion from blood. Distribution across membranes is generally facilitated by high lipid solubility, low protein binding, and physicochemical factors that favor the unionized form of the drug in blood. Diffusion of drug from arterial blood capillaries to matrix cells in the base of the follicle is considered a primary means for drug deposition in hair. Presumably, drug binds to components in the matrix and to pigments. As the cells elongate and age, they gradually die and coalesce, forming the nonliving hair fiber. Drug that may be present is embedded in the hair matrix.

Drug entering hair via blood from the capillary plexus of the follicle is not detectable by standard hair cutting methods until hair grows to the skin surface. With daily sampling of beard, the time course for morphine and codeine to appear was reported to be in the range of 7 to 10 days.[17] In controlled dosing studies with cocaine and codeine, these drugs were detectable in "unwashed" human head hair approximately 8 days after the first drug administration.[18] Peak drug concentrations occurred in approximately 15 days. BZE concentrations were detectable over the same time course at approximately one tenth the concentration of cocaine. Figure 10.6.7 illustrates mean concentrations of cocaine in plasma and cocaine and BZE in hair.[18,19] Of special interest in these studies was the finding that solvent washes removed 50 to 55% of cocaine and codeine in the first hair specimens collected after drug dosing, but minimal drug was removed by solvent washing of specimens collected in later weeks. It was concluded that early deposition of drug on hair by sweat accounted for the differences observed in solvent washing and that multiple mechanisms may be involved in drug deposition in hair. Environmental contamination also has been reported to a potential route of cocaine entry into hair.[20,21]

10.6.4 Pharmacokinetic, Chemical, and Analytical Considerations

The pattern of disposition of drugs in alternative matrices is influenced by time of collection relative to dosing, frequency of drug use, chemical and physiological differences between alternative matrices, and chemical differences between drugs and between parent drug and metabolites. The relative abundance of parent drug and metabolites is a dynamic process, especially over the first

12 to 24 h after drug administration. Generally, parent drug concentrations are highest in biological tissues during this time. Some drugs, such as heroin, may be metabolized so quickly that their presence in tissues like blood and urine may be extremely short-lived. In contrast, heroin sequestration in hair and in sweat (sweat patch) may have a stabilizing effect and preserve the molecule intact for detection for long intervals after use. Metabolic processes and distribution to tissues proceeds rapidly, thereby altering relative abundances of parent drug and metabolites. Multiple dosing also can exert significant influences on the pattern of drug disposition. Frequently, drug metabolites have a longer half-life than the parent, resulting in accumulation of metabolites to concentrations exceeding those of the parent drug. In some cases, metabolites are the only detectable analytes. Table 10.6.1 presents a summary of metabolic and chemical influences on drug and metabolite distribution in alternative matrices.

Development of drug testing methodologies for alternative matrices involves consideration of the spectrum of target analyte(s) and acceptable cutoff concentration(s) for useful detection windows. Table 10.6.2 provides a summary of target analytes, pharmacokinetic considerations, references for analysis of each drug, and for interpretation of results. Each alternative matrix has unique characteristics that influence test outcomes. Some generalities are useful as guides to alternative matrices testing:

Detection methods for drugs in urine:
- Frequently target end-stage metabolites
- Frequently require a hydrolysis step to measure conjugated metabolites
- Demand only moderate to high sensitivity due to the concentrating ability of the kidneys

Detection methods for drugs in oral fluid and blood:
- Have similarities in target analyte distribution and time course of detection, except for cannabis where detection in oral fluid is primarily due to sequestration of THC in the oral cavity
- Frequently measure active parent drug
- Require ultrasensitive methodology due to low concentrations

Detection methods for drugs in sweat and hair:
- Generally have similar distribution of parent drug and metabolites
- Require ultrasensitive methodology due to low concentrations

10.6.5 Interpretation of Alternative Matrices

10.6.5.1 Time Course of Detection in Alternative Matrices

The time course of detection of drugs and metabolites in alternative matrices varies from hours to months depending on the type of biological specimen being tested. Generally, drug detection times follow the following order: blood < oral fluid < urine < sweat < hair. A general scheme for drug detection in different matrices is shown in Figure 10.6.8. Drug detection in blood and oral fluid generally follows the same time course. Drugs of abuse are generally detected in blood and oral fluid from 1 to 3 days depending on the pattern of drug usage and cutoff concentration.

Single doses of most drugs of abuse are detected in urine for 1 to 3 days.[22] Multiple dosing extends the detection window for cocaine, opiates, and amphetamines by 1 to 2 days, whereas multiple dosing of cannabis and phencyclidine may result in positive urine test results for up to 27 days.[23] A short lag time (hours) may be observed for drug appearance in urine following drug administration. For example, in some individuals, delays up to 4 h have been noted for the appearance of cannabinoids in urine following marijuana smoking.[24]

Studies on sweat testing with the Sweat Patch showed that it takes approximately 2 to 8 h following drug administration for sufficient drug to be deposited in the patch for detection. Additional cocaine use, while the patch is being worn, results in further deposition. Cocaine use 24 to

Table 10.6.1   Metabolic and Chemical Influences on Drug and Metabolite Distribution in Alternate Matrices

Drug	Blood	Urine	Oral Fluid	Sweat	Hair
Cannabis	THC highly lipid soluble and rapidly distributed to tissues resulting in a short detection period; THCCOOH formed rapidly from THC; significant accumulation of THCCOOH may occur from frequent use	THCCOOH conjugated and rapidly excreted; accumulation after multiple dosing significantly extends detection period	THC sequestered in oral cavity after smoking and ingestion providing basis for detection; sequestered THC in oral mucosa may influence blood THC	THC found in low concentrations (<2 ng/patch), after controlled drug administration of up to 27 mg; THC in sweat from frequent users can be >100 ng/patch or Drugwipe	THC and THCCOOH sequestered in hair matrix; identification of THCCOOH considered evidence of active use; THCCOOH present in extremely low concentrations
Cocaine	COC rapidly converted to BZE and EME; hydrolysis to BZE continues to occur after collection unless chemically stabilized	COC and BZE rapidly excreted; rate of COC excretion may be influenced by urine pH; BZE has longer half-life	Acidic pH of oral fluid concentrates COC compared to blood; acidic pH enhances stability of COC; BZE concentration < blood	Acidic pH of sweat enhances stability of COC, but hydrolysis to BZE in collection device may occur	Cocaine binding to hair matrix enhances stability; hydrolysis to BZE may occur; BZE/COC ratio >0.1, cocaethylene or norcocaine considered evidence of active use
Heroin/morphine	HER rapidly hydrolyzed to 6-AM and MOR; lipid solubility of heroin and 6-AM facilitates rapid uptake into tissues as compared to morphine; MOR extensively conjugated	MOR and conjugated MOR rapidly excreted; 6-AM excreted in small amounts for a few hours after heroin administration	Acidic pH of oral fluid enhances 6-AM concentration compared to blood; pH enhances stability of 6-AM	Acidic pH of sweat enhances stability of heroin and 6-AM, but hydrolysis to MOR in collection device may occur	HER and 6-AM binding to hair matrix enhances stability; hydrolysis to MOR may occur
Codeine	COD rapidly and extensively metabolized by conjugation; forms small amounts of active metabolite (MOR) considered responsible for effects; genetic variability in O-demethylation activity	COD, conjugated COD, MOR and conjugated MOR rapidly excreted	Acidic pH of oral fluid enhances COD concentration compared to blood	Acidic pH of sweat likely enhances COD concentration	COD bound to hair matrix; no further metabolic changes considered likely to occur
PCP	PCP highly lipid soluble and rapidly distributed to tissues	Rate of excretion influenced by urine pH	Acidic pH of oral fluid likely enhances concentration compared to blood	Acidic pH of sweat likely enhances concentration	PCP bound to hair matrix; no further metabolic changes considered likely to occur
Amphetamine	AMP lipid soluble and rapidly distributed to tissues	Rate of excretion influenced by urine pH	Acidic pH of oral fluid enhances concentration	Acidic pH of sweat likely enhances concentration	AMP bound to hair matrix; no further metabolic changes considered likely to occur
Methamphetamine	METH lipid soluble and rapidly distributed to tissues; limited metabolism to AMP	Rate of excretion influenced by urine pH; presence of AMP generally required for confirmation	Acidic pH of oral fluid enhances concentration	Acidic pH of sweat enhances concentration	METH bound to hair matrix; no further metabolic changes considered likely to occur

Abbreviations: THC = tetrahydrocannabinol; THCCOOH = 11-nor-9-carboxy-Δ9-tetrahydrocannabinol; COC = cocaine; BZE = benzoylecgonine; EME = ecgonine methyl ester; HER = heroin; 6-AM = 6-acetylmorphine; MOR = morphine; COD = codeine; PCP = phencyclidine; METH = methamphetamine; AMP = amphetamine.

Table 10.6.2 Relative Abundances of Target Analytes in Alternative Matrices, Pharmacokinetic Considerations, and Selected References to Aid Interpretation of Results

Drug	Blood/Plasma/Serum	Urine	Oral Fluid	Sweat	Hair
Cannabis					
Target analytes	THCCOOH > THC	THCCOOH-G > THCCOOH	THC	THC	THC > THCCOOH
PK effects	Collection time, multiple dosing and long $t_{1/2}$ of THCCOOH alters THCCOOH/THC ratio[44–50]	Multiple dosing and long $t_{1/2}$ of THCCOOH produces accumulation and prolongs detection[23,51–68]	Multiple dosing may produce accumulation and prolonged detection[35,69–73]	Multiple dosing may produce accumulation and prolonged detection[71,74–78]	Multiple dosing may be necessary for detection; metabolite identification important to eliminate environmental contamination[79–86]
Cocaine					
Target analytes	BZE > COC > EME > NCOC; CE (with ethanol)	BZE > COC	BZE > COC	COC > BZE	COC > BZE > NCOC; CE (with ethanol)
PK effects	Collection time, multiple dosing and long $t_{1/2}$ of BZE alters BZE/COC ratio; COC in combination with ethanol forms CE[3,19,87–104]	Collection time, multiple dosing and long $t_{1/2}$ of BZE alters COC/BZE ratio; COC in combination with ethanol forms CE[25,60,87,89–91,93–95,105–117]	Collection time, multiple dosing and long $t_{1/2}$ of BZE alters COC/BZE ratio; COC in combination with ethanol forms CE[92,94–96,105,118–124]	Collection time, multiple dosing and long $t_{1/2}$ of BZE alters COC/BZE ratio; COC in combination with ethanol forms CE[25,32,76,125,126]	Metabolite identification, e.g., NCOC, important to eliminate environmental contamination; presence of CE indicates systemic COC and ethanol exposure[18,83,87,97,118,127–140]
Heroin/morphine					
Target analytes	MOR-G > MOR > 6-AM > HER	MOR-G > MOR > 6-AM > HER	6-AM MOR > HER	6-AM MOR > HER	6-AM > MOR
PK effects	Collection time, multiple dosing and long $t_{1/2}$ of MOR alters MOR-G/MOR/6-AM ratios; HER and 6-AM frequently not detected[17,96,97,141–148]	Collection time, multiple dosing and long $t_{1/2}$ of MOR alters MOR-G/MOR/6-AM ratios; HER and 6-AM frequently not detected[17,87,143,144,149–163]	6-AM and MOR most frequently detected; HER may also be detected[17,75,87,96,141,142,150,159,164–166]	6-AM and MOR most frequently detected; HER also may be detected[74–76,125,126,163,167–169]	Multiple dosing may be necessary for detection; 6-AM and MOR most frequently detected, but HER also may be detected[17,83,87,97,127,128,130–135,139,142,143,165,170–174]
Codeine					
Target analytes	COD-G > COD > MOR > NCOD	COD-G > COD > MOR > NCOD	COD > MOR	COD > MOR	COD > MOR> NCOD
PK effects	Collection time, multiple dosing may alter COD-G/COD/MOR/NCOD ratios[17,19,142,175–178]	Collection time, multiple dosing may alter COD-G/COD/MOR/NCOD ratios; MOR may exceed COD late in excretion phase[17,149,160,179–184]	Collection time, multiple dosing may alter COD/MOR ratio; MOR may not be detected[17,123,142,166,175,177,178,185–188]	Collection time, multiple dosing may alter COD/MOR ratio[32,123,189,190]	Multiple dosing may be necessary for detection[17,18,127,142,191–197]

Continued

Table 10.6.2 Relative Abundances of Target Analytes in Alternative Matrices, Pharmacokinetic Considerations, and Selected References to Aid Interpretation of Results (Continued)

Drug	Blood/Plasma/Serum	Urine	Oral Fluid	Sweat	Hair
PCP					
Target analytes	PCP	PCP > HO-PCP	PCP	PCP	PCP
PK effects	Multiple dosing may substantially increase detection time[198–207]	Multiple dosing may substantially increase detection time[202,208–211]	Multiple dosing may substantially increase detection time[212,213]	Multiple dosing may substantially increase detection time[76]	Multiple dosing may be necessary for detection[136,214–219]
Amphetamine					
Target analytes	AMP	AMP	AMP	AMP	AMP
PK effects	Multiple dosing may increase detection time[204,220–224]	Multiple dosing may increase detection time[221,225–242]	Multiple dosing may increase detection time[35,36,75,223,224,241,243,244]	Multiple dosing may increase detection time[35,75,243,245]	Multiple dosing may be necessary for detection[36,38,82,97,128,131,222,243,246–255]
Methamphetamine					
Target analytes	METH > AMP	METH > AMP	METH > AMP	METH > AMP	METH > AMP
PK effects	Multiple dosing may increase detection time[204,220,221,243,256–260]	Collection time, multiple dosing may alter METH/AMP ratio[221,226,229,231–233,235,237,241–243,258,261–268]	Collection time, multiple dosing may alter METH/AMP ratio[241,243,244,269]	Collection time, multiple dosing may alter METH/AMP ratio[243,269,270]	Multiple dosing may be necessary for detection; AMP present in lower amounts[243,248,249,251–255,269,271–275]
MDA/MDMA/MDEA					
Target analytes					
PK effects	MDMA demonstrates nonlinear rise in plasma levels with increasing dose; poor CYP2D6 metabolizers may be at risk of toxicity[276–281]	Rapidly excreted primarily as parent drug, N-desmethyl-metabolites, and hydroxyl-metabolites[233,279–285]	Acidic pH of oral fluid enhances concentration compared to blood[277,281]	Detectable in sweat for 2–12 h after administration[286,287]	MDA/MDMA/ MDEAMDMA concentrations usually exceed MDA (metabolite)[135,219,247–249, 251–253,288–292]

Abbreviations: THC = tetrahydrocannabinol; THCCOOH = 11-nor-9-carboxy-Δ9-tetrahydrocannibinol; THCCOOH-G = 11-nor-9-carboxy-Δ9-tetrahydrocannibinol-glucuronine; COC = cocaine; BZE = benzoylecgonine; EME = ecgonine methyl ester; NCOC = norcocaine; CE = cocaethylene; MOR-G = morphine glucuronide; MOR = morphine; HER = heroin; 6-AM = 6-acetylmorphine; COD-G = codeine glucuronide; COD = codeine; PCP = phencyclidine; HO-PCP = hydroxyphencyclidine; METH = methamphetamine; AMP = amphetamine; MDA = methylenedioxyamphetamine; MDMA = methylenedioxymethamphetamine; MDEA = methylenedioxyethylamphetamine.

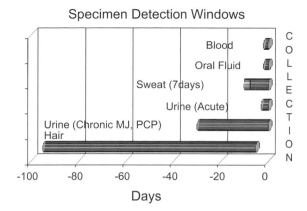

Figure 10.6.8   General detection times for drugs in blood, oral fluid, urine, sweat, and hair. Lighter shaded area of sweat indicates possible detection of drug use that occurred 24–48 h prior to application of sweat patch.

48 h prior to application of the patch may also produce positive results.[25] However, drug use just prior to patch removal is not likely to be detected because of the delay in appearance of drug in sweat.

Multiple mechanisms for drug entry into hair may account for the confusion regarding the beginning of the drug detection window.[18,26,27] Drug excreted in sweat may appear on hair within hours after use, but also may be more difficult to detect if washing procedures efficiently remove the bulk of drug residue. A period of hair growth estimated to be 3 to 5 days[14] must occur for drug in hair to appear at the skin surface, thereby accounting for the "lag" period (days) in its detection window.

Changes in analytical sensitivity and specificity, e.g., antibody changes in the screening assay, may result in enhanced or diminished detection times for all types of specimens. Also, administrative changes in recommended cutoff concentrations could have a similar effect.

10.6.5.2   Multiple Specimen Testing

Continued development, approval, and use of alternative matrices in drug testing programs may present interesting problems in interpretation of results. In the past, it was rare to have test results from more than one type of specimen, particularly in workplace testing. The financial costs of testing more than one type of biological specimen almost certainly will force most drug testing programs to choose a single type of specimen best suited to their needs; however, there are likely to be instances when individuals and even entire drug testing programs decide to test more than one biological specimen. Already, individuals informed of positive test results may request additional testing; e.g., an individual who tested positive in a urine testing program may choose to undergo hair testing. Medical Review Officers may also request additional testing if there is reasonable doubt concerning the validity of a test result. Post-accident testing calls for the highest scrutiny regarding the potential role of drugs as causative factors; hence, multiple specimens may become the norm in this type of testing arena. In addition, drug testing authorities may want information on test comparability, e.g., urine vs. oral fluid testing, prior to switching to a new matrix. Consequently, it is quite likely that there will be many instances where multiple test results from different biological matrices will be collected and require interpretation.

10.6.5.3   Guidance in Interpretation of Alternative Matrices Results

Considerable guidance information is available for interpretation of positive urine test results.[22,28] Although there is less information available for alternative matrices, a number of reviews are helpful in this regard.[1,2,4,29–43] When multiple test results from different matrices are available, interpretation may be considerably more complex, particularly for disparate results. There are a number of legitimate reasons why one might obtain disparate results. Each type of biological specimen has unique physiological and chemical properties that may alter the pattern of drug disposition. For example, renal excretion processes favor elimination of water soluble metabolites, whereas excretion of drug into oral fluid favors parent drugs capable of rapid passive diffusion across membranes. Sweat excretion processes also appear to favor parent drug. The acidic nature of oral fluid and sweat favors excretion and trapping of drugs containing basic nitrogen moieties. Although the complex mechanisms for drug binding to hair pigment and proteins have not been fully elucidated, it is clear that these binding processes exhibit greater affinity for drugs containing basic nitrogen moieties. Residence times in each matrix also differ substantially, yielding wide variability in windows of detection.

The many differences in physiological and chemical properties of alternative matrices undoubtedly result in production of occasional disparate test results when more than one type of biological specimen is utilized for testing. There are many possible explanations for disparate results. For example, testing two different matrices, e.g., urine and oral fluid, may result in two equivalent or two disparate results. When one considers the possible combinations of results that could arise from testing of blood, urine, oral fluid, sweat, and hair, there are 20 possible disparate results if only two matrices are tested. The different scenarios of disparate results for two specimens and some of the possible explanations are depicted in Table 10.6.3. It will become the responsibility of the Medical Review Officer and forensic toxicologists to provide interpretation of such results. Clearly, much information must be available to provide a scientific basis for the interpretation of alternative matrices' results.

Table 10.6.3   Disparate Results from Testing Two Different Biological Matrices and Possible Explanations

Scenario	Blood	Urine	Oral Fluid	Sweat	Hair	Possible Explanations for Disparate Results
1	Positive	Negative				Time of urine collection too close to time of drug use
2	Positive		Negative			Highly protein-bound drugs may be poorly distributed to oral fluid, e.g., benzodiazepines
3	Positive			Negative		Low drug dose; sampling time outside detection "window"
4	Positive				Negative	Low drug dose; low binding affinity to hair matrix; hair treatments, e.g., bleaching, straighteners; sampling time outside detection "window"
5	Negative	Positive				Long interval after dosing; concentration effect by kidney
6		Positive	Negative			Long interval after dosing; concentration effect by kidney; highly protein-bound drug; sampling time outside detection "window"
7		Positive		Negative		Concentration effect by kidney; sampling time outside detection "window"
8		Positive			Negative	Concentration effect by kidney; low dose; low binding affinity to hair matrix; sampling time outside detection "window"
9	Negative		Positive			Insufficient time for drug absorption; "depot" effect
10		Negative	Positive			Insufficient time for drug absorption, metabolism and excretion; "depot" effect
11			Positive	Negative		Insufficient time for drug absorption, metabolism and excretion; "depot" effect; sampling time outside detection "window"
12			Positive		Negative	Low drug dose; low binding affinity to hair matrix; insufficient time for drug absorption, metabolism and excretion; sampling time outside detection "window"
13	Negative			Positive		Sampling time outside detection "window"
14		Negative		Positive		Sampling time outside detection "window"
15			Negative	Positive		Sampling time outside detection "window"
16				Positive	Negative	Low drug dose; low binding affinity to hair matrix; insufficient time for drug absorption, metabolism and excretion; sampling time outside detection "window"
17	Negative				Positive	Sampling time outside detection "window"
18		Negative			Positive	Sampling time outside detection "window"
19			Negative		Positive	Sampling time outside detection "window"
20				Negative	Positive	Sampling time outside detection "window"

REFERENCES

1. R. Haeckel. Factors influencing the saliva/plasma ratio of drugs. *Ann. N. Y. Acad. Sci.* 694: 128–142 (1993).

2. N. Samyn, A. Verstraete, C. van Haeren, and P. Kintz. Analysis of drugs of abuse in saliva. *Forensic Sci. Rev.* 11: 1–19 (1999).

3. E.J. Cone. Pharmacokinetics and pharmacodynamics of cocaine. *J. Anal. Toxicol.* 19: 459–478 (1995).

4. E.J. Cone. Saliva testing for drugs of abuse. *Ann. N. Y. Acad. Sci.* 694: 91–127 (1993).

5. E.J. Cone, L. Presley, M. Lehrer, W. Seiter, M. Smith, K. Kardos, D. Fritch, S. Salamone, and R.S. Niedbala. Oral fluid testing for drugs of abuse: Positive prevalence rates by Intercept™ immunoassay screening and GC–MS–MS confirmation and suggested cutoff concentrations. *J. Anal. Toxicol.* 26: 541–546 (2002).

6. S. Robinson and A.H. Robinson. Chemical composition of sweat. *Psychol. Rev.* 34: 202–220 (1954).

7. W.C. Randall. The physiology of sweating. *Am. J. Phys. Med.* 32: 292–318 (1953).

8. D. Doran, J. Terney, M. Varano, and S. Ware. A study of the pH of perspiration from male and female subjects exercising in the gymnasium. *J. Chem. Educ.* 70: 412–414 (1993).

9. H.L. Johnson and H.I. Maibach. Drug excretion in human eccrine sweat. *J. Invest. Dermatol.* 56: 182–188 (1971).

10. L. Potsch. On physiology and ultrastructure of human hair. In *Hair Analysis in Forensic Toxicology: Proceedings of the 1995 International Conference and Workshop*, R.A. de Zeeuw, I. Al Hosani, S. Al Munthiri, and A. Maqbool, Eds. Organizing Committee of the Conference, Abu Dhabi, 1995, 1–27.

11. M.R. Harkey. Anatomy and physiology of hair. *Forensic Sci. Int.* 63: 9–18 (1993).

12. *Human Hair Volume I: Fundamentals and Methods for Measurement of Elemental Composition,* CRC Press, Boca Raton, FL, 1988, 1–88.

13. L. Potsch, R. Aderjan, G. Skopp, and M. Herbold. Stability of opiates in the hair fibers after exposures to cosmetic treatment and UV radiation. In *Proceedings of the 1994 JOINT TIAFT/SOFT International Meeting*, V. Spiehler, Ed. TIAFT/SOFT Joint Congress, 1994, 65–72.

14. M. Saitoh, M. Uzuka, and M. Sakamoto. Rate of hair growth. In *Advances in Biology of Skin*, Vol. IX. *Hair Growth*, W. Montagna and R.L. Dobson, Eds. Pergamon, Oxford, 1969, 183–201.

15. P. Mangin and P. Kintz. Variability of opiates concentrations in human hair according to their anatomical origin: head, axillary and pubic regions. *Forensic Sci. Int.* 63: 77–83 (1993).

16. G.L. Henderson. Mechanisms of drug incorporation into hair. *Forensic Sci. Int.* 63: 19–29 (1993).

17. E.J. Cone. Testing human hair for drugs of abuse. I. Individual dose and time profiles of morphine and codeine in plasma, saliva, urine, and beard compared to drug-induced effects on pupils and behavior. *J. Anal. Toxicol.* 14: 1–7 (1990).

18. R.E. Joseph, Jr., K.M. Hold, D.G. Wilkins, D.E. Rollins, and E.J. Cone. Drug testing with alternative matrices II. Mechanisms of cocaine and codeine disposition in hair. *J. Anal. Toxicol.* 23: 396–408 (1999).

19. R.E. Joseph, J.M. Oyler, A.T. Wstadik, C. Ohuoha, and E.J. Cone. Drug testing with alternative matrices I. Pharmacological effects and disposition of cocaine and codeine in plasma, sebum, and stratum corneum. *J. Anal. Toxicol.* 22: 6–17 (1998).

20. W.L. Wang and E.J. Cone. Testing human hair for drugs of abuse. IV. Environmental cocaine contamination and washing effects. *Forensic. Sci. Int.* 70: 39–51 (1995).

21. G. Romano, N. Barbera, and I. Lombardo. Hair testing for drugs of abuse: evaluation of external cocaine contamination and risk of false positives. *Forensic Sci. Int.* 123: 119–129 (2001).

22. M. Vandevenne, H. Vandenbussche, and A. Verstraete. Detection time of drugs of abuse in urine. *Acta Clin. Belg.* 55: 323–333 (2000).

23. A. Smith-Kielland, B. Skuterud, and J. Morland. Urinary excretion of 11-nor-9-carboxy-delta9-tetrahydrocannabinol and cannabinoids in frequent and infrequent drug users. *J. Anal. Toxicol.* 23: 323–332 (1999).

24. R.S. Niedbala, K.W. Kardos, D.F. Fritch, S. Kardos, T. Fries, J. Waga, J. Robb, and E.J. Cone. Detection of marijuana use by oral fluid and urine analysis following single-dose administration of smoked and oral marijuana. *J. Anal. Toxicol.* 25: 289–303 (2001).

25. K.L. Preston, M.A. Huestis, C.J. Wong, A. Umbricht, B.A. Goldberger, and E.J. Cone. Monitoring cocaine use in substance-abuse-treatment patients by sweat and urine testing. *J. Anal. Toxicol.* 23: 313–322 (1999).

26. D.A. Kidwell and D.L. Blank. Mechanisms of incorporation of drugs into hair and the interpretation of hair analysis data. In *Hair Testing for Drugs of Abuse: International Research on Standards and Technology*, E.J. Cone, M.J. Welch, and M.B. Grigson Babecki, Eds. NIH Pub. 95-3727, National Institute on Drug Abuse, Rockville, MD, 1995, 19–90.

27. M.R. Harkey and G.L. Henderson. Hair analysis for drugs of abuse. In *Advances in Biomedical Analytical Toxicology*, Vol. II, R.C. Baselt, Ed. Biomedical Publishers, Chicago, 1989, 298–329.

28. Medical Review Officer Manual for Federal Workplace Drug Testing Programs, W.F. Vogl and D.M. Bush, Eds. Department of Health and Human Services, Washington, D.C., 1997, 1–72.

29. B. Caddy. Saliva as a specimen for drug analysis. In *Advances in Analytical Toxicology*, R.C. Baselt, Ed. Biomedical Publications, Foster City, 1984, 198–254.

30. Y.H. Caplan and B.A. Goldberger. Alternative specimens for workplace drug testing. *J. Anal. Toxicol.* 25: 396–399 (2001).

31. Y. Gaillard and G. Pepin. Testing hair for pharmaceuticals. *J. Chromatogr. B.* 733: 231–246 (1999).

32. M.A. Huestis, J.M. Oyler, E.J. Cone, A.T. Wstadik, D. Schoendorfer, and R.E. Joseph, Jr. Sweat testing for cocaine, codeine and metabolites by gas chromatography-mass spectrometry. *J. Chromatogr. B Biomed. Sci. Appl.* 733: 247–264 (1999).

33. O.R. Idowu and B. Caddy. A review of the use of saliva in the forensic detection of drugs and other chemicals. *J. Forensic Sci. Soc.* 22: 123–135 (1982).

34. D.A. Kidwell, E.H. Lee, and S.F. DeLauder. Evidence for bias in hair testing and procedures to correct bias. *Forensic Sci. Int.* 107: 39–61 (2000).

35. D.A. Kidwell, J.C. Holland, and S. Athanaselis. Testing for drugs of abuse in saliva and sweat. *J Chromatogr. B* 713: 111–135 (1998).

36. P. Kintz and N. Samyn. Use of alternative specimens: drugs of abuse in saliva and doping agents in hair. *Ther. Drug Monit.* 24: 239–246 (2002).

37. P. Mangin. Drug analyses in nonhead hair. In *Drug Testing in Hair*, P. Kintz, Ed. CRC Press, Boca Raton, FL, 1996, 279–287.

38. M.R. Moeller. Hair analysis as evidence in forensic cases. *Ther. Drug Monit.* 18: 444–449 (1996).

39. J.C. Mucklow, M.R. Bending, G.C. Kahn, and C.T. Dollery. Drug concentration in saliva. *Clin. Pharmacol. Ther.* 24: 563–570 (1978).

40. H. Sachs. Forensic applications of hair analysis. In *Drug Testing in Hair*, P. Kintz, Ed. CRC Press, Boca Raton, FL, 1996, 211–222.

41. W. Schramm, R.H. Smith, P.A. Craig, and D.A. Kidwell. Drugs of abuse in saliva: a review. *J. Anal. Toxicol.* 16: 1–9 (1992).

42. G. Skoand and L. Potsch. Perspiration versus saliva — basic aspects concerning their use in roadside drug testing. *Int. J. Leg. Med.* 112: 213–221 (1999).

43. V. Spiehler. Hair analysis by immunological methods from the beginning to 2000. *Forensic Sci. Int.* 107: 249–259 (2000).

44. S.J. Heishman, M.A. Huestis, J.E. Henningfield, and E.J. Cone. Acute and residual effects of marijuana: profiles of plasma THC levels, physiological, subjective, and performance measures. *Pharmacol. Biochem. Behav.* 37: 561–565 (1990).

45. E.J. Cone and M.A. Huestis. Relating blood concentrations of tetrahydrocannabinol and metabolites to pharmacologic effects and time of marijuana usage. *Ther. Drug Monit.* 15: 527–532 (1993).

46. M.A. Huestis, J.E. Henningfield, and E.J. Cone. Blood cannabinoids. I. Absorption of THC and formation of 11-OH-THC and THCCOOH during and after smoking marijuana. *J. Anal. Toxicol.* 16: 276–282 (1992).

47. M.A. Huestis, J.E. Henningfield, and E.J. Cone. Blood cannabinoids. II. Models for the prediction of time of marijuana exposure from plasma concentrations of delta-9-tetrahydrocannabinol (THC) and 11-nor-9-carboxy-delta-9-tetrahydrocannabinol (THCCOOH). *J. Anal. Toxicol.* 16: 283–290 (1992).

48. M.A. Huestis, A.H. Sampson, B.J. Holicky, J.E. Henningfield, and E.J. Cone. Characterization of the absorption phase of marijuana smoking. *Clin. Pharmacol. Ther.* 52: 31–41 (1992).

49. D.E. Moody, L.F. Rittenhouse, and K.M. Monti. Analysis of forensic specimens for cannabinoids I. comparison of RIA and GC/MS analysis of blood. *J. Anal. Toxicol.* 16: 297–301 (1992).

50. D.E. Moody, K.M. Monti, and D.J. Crouch. Analysis of forensic specimens for cannabinoids. II. Relationship between blood delta-9-tetrahydrocannabinol and blood and urine 11-nor-delta-9-tetrahydrocannabinol-9-carboxylic acid concentrations. *J. Anal. Toxicol.* 16: 302–306 (1992).

51. M.A. Huestis and E.J. Cone. Urinary excretion half-life of 11-nor-9-carboxy-delta9-tetrahydrocannabinol in humans. *Ther. Drug Monit.* 20: 570–576 (1998).

52. P.M. Kemp, I.K. Abukhalaf, J.E. Manno, B.R. Manno, D.D. Alford, M.E. McWilliams, F.E. Nixon, M.J. Fitzgerald, R.R. Reeves, and M.J. Wood. Cannabinoids in humans. II. The influence of three methods of hydrolysis on the concentration of THC and two metabolites in urine. *J. Anal. Toxicol.* 19: 292–298 (1995).

53. P.C. Painter, J.H. Evans, J.D. Greenwood, and W.W. Fain. Urine cannabinoids monitoring. *Diagn. Clin. Testing* 27: 29–33 (1989).

54. G.M. Ellis, M.A. Mann, B.A. Judson, N.T. Schramm, and A. Tashchian. Excretion patterns of cannabinoid metabolites after last use in a group of chronic users. *Clin. Pharmacol. Ther.* 38: 572–578 (1985).

55. P.M. Kemp, I.K. Abukhalaf, J.E. Manno, B.R. Manno, D.D. Alford, and G.A. Abusada. Cannabinoids in humans. I. Analysis of delta-9-tetrahydrocannabinol and six metabolites in plasma and urine using GC-MS. *J. Anal. Toxicol.* 19: 285–291 (1995).

56. M.A. Huestis, J.M. Mitchell, and E.J. Cone. Lowering the federally mandated cannabinoid immunoassay cutoff increases true-positive results. *Clin. Chem.* 40: 729–733 (1994).

57. E.J. Cone and R.E. Johnson. Contact highs and urinary cannabinoid excretion after passive exposure to marijuana smoke. *Clin. Pharmacol. Ther.* 40: 247–254 (1986).

58. R.J. Bastiani. Urinary cannabinoid excretion patterns. In *The Cannabinoids: Chemical, Pharmacologic, and Therapeutic Aspects*, S. Agurell, W.L. Dewey, and R.E. Willette, Eds. Academic Press, Orlando, FL, 1984, 263–280.

59. E.J. Cone, R.E. Johnson, B.D. Paul, L.D. Mell, and J. Mitchell. Marijuana-laced brownies: behavioral effects, physiologic effects, and urinalysis in humans following ingestion. *J. Anal. Toxicol.* 12: 169–175 (1988).

60. E.J. Cone, R. Lange, and W.D. Darwin. *In vivo* adulteration: Excess fluid ingestion causes false-negative marijuana and cocaine urine test results. *J. Anal. Toxicol.* 22: 460–473 (1998).

61. A. Costantino, R.H. Schwartz, and P. Kaplan. Hemp oil ingestion causes positive urine tests for delta9-tetrahydrocanabinol carboxylic acid. *J. Anal. Toxicol.* 21: 482–485 (1997).

62. M.A. Huestis, J.M. Mitchell, and E.J. Cone. Urinary excretion profiles of 11-nor-9-carboxy-Δ9-tetrahydrocannabinol in humans after single smoked doses of marijuana. *J. Anal. Toxicol.* 20: 441–452 (1996).

63. M.A. Huestis, J.M. Mitchell, and E.J. Cone. Detection times of marijuana metabolites in urine by immunoassay and GC-MS. *J. Anal. Toxicol.* 19: 443–449 (1995).

64. M.A. Huestis and E.J. Cone. Differentiating new marijuana use from residual drug excretion in occasional marijuana users. *J. Anal. Toxicol.* 22: 445–454 (1998).

65. D.S. Isenschmid and Y.H. Caplan. Incidence of cannabinoids in medical examiner urine specimens. *J. Forensic Sci.* 33(6): 1421–1431 (1988).

66. R.C. Meatherall and R.J. Warren. High urinary cannabinoids from a hashish body packer. *J. Anal. Toxicol.* 17: 439–440 (1993).

67. C. Tomaszewski, M. Kirk, E. Bingham, B. Saltzman, R. Cook, and K. Kulig. Urine toxicology screens in drivers suspected of driving while impaired from drugs. *Clin. Toxicol.* 34(1): 37–44 (1996).

68. R.A. Gustafson, B. Levine, P.R. Stout, K.L. Klette, M.P. George, E.T. Moolchan, and M.A. Huestis. Urinary cannabinoid detection times after controlled oral administration of delta9-tetrahydrocannabinol to humans. *Clin. Chem.* 49: 1114–1124 (2003).

69. M.A. Huestis, S. Dickerson, and E. J. Cone. Can saliva THC levels be correlated to behavior? In *American Academy of Forensic Science*, Fittje Brothers, Colorado Springs, 1992, 190.

70. N. Fucci, N. De Giovanni, M. Chiarotti, and S. Scarlata. SPME-GC analysis of THC in saliva samples collected with "EPITOPE" device. *Forensic Sci. Int.* 119: 318–321 (2001).

71. P. Kintz, V. Cirimele, and B. Ludes. Detection of cannabis in oral fluid (saliva) and forehead wipes (sweat) from impaired drivers. *J. Anal. Toxicol.* 24: 557–561 (2000).

72. D.B. Menkes, R.C. Howard, G.F.S. Spears, and E.R. Cairns. Salivary THC following cannabis smoking correlates with subjective intoxication and heart rate. *Psychopharmacology* 103: 277–279 (1991).

73. A. Jehanli, S. Brannan, L. Moore, and V.R. Spiehler. Blind trials of an onsite saliva drug test for marijuana and opiates. *J. Forensic Sci.* 46: 1214–1220 (2001).

74. P. Kintz, A. Tracqui, P. Mangin, and Y. Edel. Sweat testing in opioid users with a sweat patch. *J. Anal. Toxicol.* 20: 393–397 (1996).

75. N. Samyn and C. van Haeren. On-site testing of saliva and sweat with Drugwipe and determination of concentrations of drugs of abuse in saliva, plasma and urine of suspected users. *Int. J. Legal Med.* 113: 150–154 (2000).

76. D.J. Crouch, R.F. Cook, J.V. Trudeau, D.C. Dove, J.J. Robinson, H.L. Webster, and A.A. Fatah. The detection of drugs of abuse in liquid perspiration. *J. Anal. Toxicol.* 25: 625–627 (2001).

77. L.K. Thompson and E.J. Cone. Determination of delta-9-tetrahydrocannabinol in human blood and saliva by high-performance liquid chromatography with amperometric detection. *J. Chromatogr.* 421: 91–97 (1987).

78. P. Kintz. Drug testing in addicts: a comparison between urine, sweat, and hair. *Ther. Drug Monit.* 18: 450–455 (1996).

79. V. Cirimele, H. Sachs, P. Kintz, and P. Mangin. Testing human hair for cannabis. III. Rapid screening procedure for the simultaneous identification of delta9-tetrahydrocannabinol, cannabinol, and cannabidiol. *J. Anal. Toxicol.* 20: 13–16 (1996).

80. D. Wilkins, H. Haughey, E. Cone, M.A. Huestis, R. Foltz, and D. Rollins. Quantitative analysis of THC, 11-OH-THC, and THCCOOH in human hair by negative ion chemical ionization mass spectrometry. *J. Anal. Toxicol.* 19: 483–491 (1995).

81. T. Cairns, D. J. Kippenberger, H. Scholtz, and W. A. Baumgartner. Determination of carboxy-THC in hair by mass spectrometry. In *Hair Analysis in Forensic Toxicology: Proceedings of the 1995 International Conference and Workshop*, R.A. de Zeeuw, I. Al Hosani, S. Al Munthiri, and A. Maqbool, Eds. Organizing Committee of the Conference, Abu Dhabi, 1995, 185–193.

82. V. Cirimele. Cannabis and amphetamine determination in Human Hair. In *Drug Testing in Hair*, P. Kintz, Ed. CRC Press, Boca Raton, FL, 1996, 181–189.

83. C. Jurado, M.P. Gimenez, M. Menendez, and M. Repetto. Simultaneous quantification of opiates, cocaine and cannabinoids in hair. *Forensic Sci. Int.* 70: 165–174 (1995).

84. P. Kintz, V. Cirimele, and P. Mangin. Testing human hair for cannabis II. Identification of THC-COOH by GC-MS-NCI as a unique proof. *J. Forensic Sci.* 40: 619–622 (1995).

85. P. Kintz, V. Cirimele, and P. Mangin. Testing human hair for cannabis. Identification of natural ingredients of cannabis sativa metabolites of THC. In *Hair Analysis in Forensic Toxicology: Proceedings of the 1995 International Conference and Workshop*, R.A. de Zeeuw, I. Al Hosani, S. Al Munthiri, and A. Maqbool, Eds. Organizing Committee of the Conference, Abu Dhabi, 1995, 194–202.

86. S. Strano-Rossi and M. Chiarotti. Solid-phase microextraction for cannabinoids analysis in hair and its possible application to other drugs. *J. Anal. Toxicol.* 23: 7–10 (1999).

87. W.L. Wang, W.D. Darwin, and E.J. Cone. Simultaneous assay of cocaine, heroin and metabolites in hair, plasma, saliva and urine by gas chromatography-mass spectrometry. *J. Chromatogr.* 660: 279–290 (1994).

88. A.J. Jenkins, R.M. Keeenan, J.E. Henningfield, and E.J. Cone. Correlation between pharmacological effects and plasma cocaine concentrations after smoked administration. *J. Anal. Toxicol.* 26: 382–392 (2002).

89. R.H. Williams, J.A. Maggiore, S.M. Shah, T.B. Erickson, and A. Negrusz. Cocaine and its major metabolites in plasma and urine samples from patients in an urban emergency medicine setting. *J. Anal. Toxicol.* 24: 478–481 (2000).

90. E.T. Shimomura, G.D. Hodge, and B.D. Paul. Examination of postmortem fluids and tissues for the presence of methylecgonidine, ecgonidine, cocaine, and benzoylecgonine using solid-phase extraction and gas chromatography-mass spectrometry. *Clin. Chem.* 47: 1040–1047 (2001).

91. M.W. Linder, G.M. Bosse, M.T. Henderson, G. Midkiff, and R. Valdes. Detection of cocaine metabolite in serum and urine: frequency and correlation with medical diagnosis. *Clin. Chim. Acta* 295: 179–185 (2000).

92. E.T. Moolchan, E.J. Cone, A. Wstadik, M.A. Huestis, and K.L. Preston. Cocaine and metabolite elimination patterns in chronic cocaine users during cessation: plasma and saliva analysis. *J. Anal. Toxicol.* 24: 458–466 (2000).

93. J.C. Garriott, R.G. Rodriguez, and J.L. Castorena. Cocaine metabolites in urine and blood after ingestion of Health Inca Tea. *SWAFS* (1988).

94. R.A. Jufer, A. Wstadik, S.L. Walsh, B.S. Levine, and E.J. Cone. Elimination of cocaine and metabolites in plasma, saliva, and urine following repeated oral administration to human volunteers. *J. Anal. Toxicol.* 24: 467–477 (2000).

95. W. Schramm, P.A. Craig, R.H. Smith, and G.E. Berger. Cocaine and benzoylecgonine in saliva, serum, and urine. *Clin. Chem.* 39: 481–487 (1993).

96. A.J. Jenkins, J.M. Oyler, and E.J. Cone. Comparison of heroin and cocaine concentrations in saliva with concentrations in blood and plasma. *J. Anal. Toxicol.* 19: 359–374 (1995).

97. R. Kronstrand, R. Grundin, and J. Jonsson. Incidence of opiates, amphetamines, and cocaine in hair and blood in fatal cases of heroin overdose. *Forensic Sci. Int.* 92: 29–38 (1998).

98. D.N. Bailey. Serial plasma concentrations of cocaethylene, cocaine, and ethanol in trauma victims. *J. Anal. Toxicol.* 17: 79–83 (1993).

99. G.W. Hime, W.L. Hearn, S. Rose, and J. Cofino. Analysis of cocaine and cocaethylene in blood and tissues by GC-NPD and GC-ion trap mass spectrometry. *J. Anal. Toxicol.* 15: 241–245 (1991).

100. M. Perez-Reyes and A.R. Jeffcoat. Ethanol/cocaine interaction: cocaine and cocaethylene plasma con-
     centrations and their relationship to subjective and cardiovascular effects. *Life Sci.* 51: 553–563 (1992).
101. P.R. Puopolo, P. Chamberlin, and J.G. Flood. Detection and confirmation of cocaine and cocaethylene
     in serum emergency toxicology specimens. *Clin. Chem.* 38: 1838–1842 (1992).
102. R.M. Smith. Ethyl esters of arylhydroxy-and arylhydroxymethoxycocaines in the urines of simulta-
     neous cocaine and ethanol users. *J. Anal. Toxicol.* 8: 38–42 (1984).
103. J. Sukbuntherng, A. Walters, H.-H. Chow, and M. Mayersohn. Quantitative determination of cocaine,
     cocaethylene (ethylcocaine), and metabolites in plasma and urine by high-performance liquid chro-
     matography. *J. Pharm. Sci.* 84(7): 799–804 (1995).
104. A.H.B. Wu, T.A. Onigbinde, K.G. Johnson, and G.H. Wimbish. Alcohol-specific cocaine metabolites
     in serum and urine of hospitalized patients. *J. Anal. Toxicol.* 16: 132–136 (1992).
105. J. Leonard, M. Doot, C. Martin, and W. Airth-Kindree. Correlation of buccal mucosal transudate
     collected with a buccal swab and urine levels of cocaine. *J. Addict. Dis.* 13: 27–33 (1994).
106. M.A. ElSohly, D.F. Stanford, and H.N. ElSohly. Coca tea and urinalysis for cocaine metabolites. *J.
     Anal. Toxicol.* 10: 256–256 (1986).
107. A.J. Jenkins, T. Llosa, I. Montoya, and E.J. Cone. Identification and quantitation of alkaloids in coca
     tea. *Forensic Sci. Int.* 77: 179–189 (1996).
108. K.L. Preston, D.H. Epstein, E.J. Cone, A.T. Wtsadik, M.A. Huestis, and E.T. Moolchan. Urinary
     elimination of cocaine metabolites in chronic cocaine users during cessation. *J. Anal. Toxicol.* 26:
     393–400 (2002).
109. K.L. Preston, K. Silverman, C.R. Schuster, and E.J. Cone. Assessment of cocaine use with quantitative
     urinalysis and estimation of new uses. *Addiction* 92: 717–727 (1997).
110. K.M. Kampman, A.I. Alterman, J.R. Volpicelli, I. Maany, E.S. Muller, D.D. Luce, E.M. Mulholland,
     A.F. Jawad, G.A. Parikh, F.D. Mulvaney, R.M. Weinrieb, and C.P. O'Brien. Cocaine withdrawal
     symptoms and initial urine toxicology results predict treatment attrition in outpatient cocaine depen-
     dence treatment. *Psychol. Addict. Behav.* 15: 52–59 (2001).
111. D.M. Jacobson, R. Berg, G.F. Grinstead, and J.R. Kruse. Duration of positive urine for cocaine
     metabolite after ophthalmic administration: implications for testing patients with suspected Horner
     syndrome using ophthalmic cocaine. *Am. J. Ophthalmol.* 131: 742–747 (2001).
112. E.J. Cone, A. Tsadik, J. Oyler, and W.D. Darwin. Cocaine metabolism and urinary excretion after
     different routes of administration. *Ther. Drug Monit.* 20: 556–560 (1998).
113. E.J. Cone, S.L. Menchen, B.D. Paul, L.D. Mell, and J. Mitchell. Validity testing of commercial urine
     cocaine metabolites assays: I. Assay detection times, individual excretion patterns, and kinetics after
     cocaine administration to humans. *J. Forensic Sci.* 34: 15–31 (1989).
114. J. Ambre, T.I. Ruo, J. Nelson, and S. Belknap. Urinary excretion of cocaine, benzoylecgonine, and
     ecgonine methyl ester in humans. *J. Anal. Toxicol.* 12: 301–306 (1988).
115. F.K. Rafla and R.L. Epstein. Identification of cocaine and its metabolites in human urine in the presence
     of ethyl alcohol. *J. Anal. Toxicol.* 3: 59–63 (1979).
116. R. de La Torre, M. Farre, J. Ortuno, J. Cami, and J. Segura. The relevance of urinary cocaethylene
     following the simultaneous administration of alcohol and cocaine. *J. Anal. Toxicol.* 15: 223 (1991).
117. D.L. Phillips, I.R. Tebbett, and R.L. Bertholf. Comparison of HPLC and GC-MS for measurement
     of cocaine and metabolites in human urine. *J. Anal. Toxicol.* 20: 305–308 (1996).
118. F.P. Smith and D.A. Kidwell. Cocaine in hair, saliva, skin swabs, and urine of cocaine users' children.
     Forensic Sci. Int. 83: 179–189 (1996).
119. E.J. Cone, J. Oyler, and W.D. Darwin. Cocaine disposition in saliva following intravenous, intranasal,
     and smoked administration. *J. Anal. Toxicol.* 21: 465–475 (1997).
120. K. Kato, M. Hillsgrove, L. Weinhold, D.A. Gorelick, W.D. Darwin, and E.J. Cone. Cocaine and
     metabolite excretion in saliva under stimulated and nonstimulated conditions. *J. Anal. Toxicol.* 17:
     338–341 (1993).
121. R.S. Niedbala, K. Kardos, T. Fries, A. Cannon, and A. Davis. Immunoassay for detection of
     cocaine/metabolites in oral fluids. *J. Anal. Toxicol.* 25: 62–68 (2001).
122. E.J. Barbieri, G.J. DiGregorio, A.P. Ferko, and E.K. Ruch. Rat cocaethylene and benzoylecgonine
     concentrations in plasma and parotid saliva after the administration of cocaethylene. *J. Anal. Toxicol.*
     18: 60–61 (1994).

123. P. Kintz, V. Cirimele, and B. Ludes. Codeine testing in sweat and saliva with the Drugwipe. *Int. J. Leg. Med.* 111: 82–84 (1998).

124. P. Campora, A.M. Bermejo, M.J. Tabernero, and P. Fernandez. Quantitation of cocaine and its major metabolites in human saliva using gas chromatography-positive chemical ionization-mass spectrometry (GC-PCI-MS). *J. Anal. Toxicol.* 27: 270–274 (2003).

125. M.A. Huestis, E.J. Cone, C.J. Wong, K. Silverman, and K.L. Preston. Efficacy of sweat patches to monitor cocaine and opiate use during treatment. Problems of Drug Dependence 1997: Proceedings of the 59th Annual Scientific Meeting, NIDA Monograph 187, p. 223, NIH Pub. No. 98-43051, National Institute of Drug Abuse, Rockville, MD (1997).

126. E.J. Cone, M.J. Hillsgrove, A.J. Jenkins, R.M. Keenan, and W.D. Darwin. Sweat testing for heroin, cocaine, and metabolites. *J. Anal. Toxicol.* 18: 298–305 (1994).

127. K.M. Hold, D.G. Wilkins, D.E. Rollins, R.E. Joseph, and E.J. Cone. Simultaneous quantitation of cocaine, opiates, and their metabolites in human hair by positive ion chemical ionization gas chromatography-mass spectrometry. *J. Chromatogr. Sci.* 36: 125–130 (1998).

128. M.R. Moeller, P. Fey, and R. Wennig. Simultaneous determination of drugs of abuse (opiates, cocaine and amphetamine) in human hair by GC/MS and its application to a methadone treatment program. *Forensic Sci. Int.* 63: 185–206 (1993).

129. E.J. Cone, D. Yousefnejad, W.D. Darwin, and T. Maquire. Testing human hair for drugs of abuse. II. Identification of unique cocaine metabolites in hair of drug abusers and evaluation of decontamination procedures. *J. Anal. Toxicol.* 15: 250–255 (1991).

130. D. Garside and B. A. Goldberger. Determination of cocaine and opioids in hair. In *Drug Testing in Hair*, P. Kintz, Ed. CRC Press, Boca Raton, FL, 1996, 151–177.

131. P. Kintz and P. Mangin. Determination of gestational opiate, nicotine, benzodiazepine, cocaine and amphetamine exposure by hair analysis. *J. Forensic Sci. Soc.* 33: 139–142 (1993).

132. S. Magura, R.C. Freeman, Q. Siddiqi, and D.S. Lipton. The validity of hair analysis for detecting cocaine and heroin use among addicts. *Int. J. Addict.* 27: 51–69 (1992).

133. G. Pepin and Y. Gaillard. Concordance between self-reported drug use and findings in hair about cocaine and heroin. *Forensic Sci. Int.* 84: 37–41 (1997).

134. S. Strano-Rossi, A.B. Barrera, and M. Chiarotti. Segmental hair analysis for cocaine and heroin abuse determination. *Forensic Sci. Int.* 70: 211–216 (1995).

135. F. Tagliaro, R. Valentini, G. Manetto, F. Crivellente, G. Carli, and M. Marigo. Hair analysis by using radioimmunoassay, high-performance liquid chromatography and capillary electrophoresis to investigate chronic exposure to heroin, cocaine and/or ecstasy in applicants for driving licenses. *Forensic Sci. Int* 107: 121–128 (2000).

136. T. Cairns, D.J. Kippenberger, and A.M. Gordon. Hair analysis for detection of drugs of abuse. *Handbook of Analytical Therapeutic Drug Monitoring and Toxicology*, S.H.Y. Wong and I. Sunshine, Eds. CRC Press, Boca Raton, FL, 1997, 237–251.

137. A.C. Gruszecki, C.A. Robinson, Jr., J.H. Embry, and G.G. Davis. Correlation of the incidence of cocaine and cocaethylene in hair and postmortem biologic samples. *Am. J. Forensic Med. Pathol.* 21: 166–171 (2000).

138. K. Janzen. Concerning norcocaine, ethylbenzoylecgonine, and the identification of cocaine use in human hair. *J. Anal. Toxicol.* 16: 402 (1992).

139. J. Segura, C. Stramesi, A. Redon, M. Ventura, C.J. Sanchez, G. Gonzalez, L. San, and M. Montagna. Immunological screening of drugs of abuse and gas chromatographic-mass spectrometric confirmation of opiates and cocaine in hair. *J. Chromatogr. B Biomed. Sci. Appl.* 724: 9–21 (1999).

140. G.L. Henderson, M.R. Harkey, C. Zhou, R.T. Jones, and P. Jacob III. Incorporation of isotopically labeled cocaine and metabolites into human hair: 1. Dose–response relationships. *J. Anal. Toxicol.* 20: 1-12 (1996).

141. E.A. Kopecky, S. Jacobson, J. Klein, B. Kapur, and G. Koren. Correlation of morphine sulfate in blood plasma and saliva in pediatric patients. *Ther. Drug Monit.* 19: 530–534 (1997).

142. W. Piekoszewski, E. Janowska, R. Stanaszek, J. Pach, L. Winnik, B. Karakiewicz, and T. Kozielec. Determination of opiates in serum, saliva and hair addicted persons. *Przegl. Lek.* 58: 287–289 (2001).

143. M.R. Moeller and C. Mueller. The detection of 6-monoacetylmorphine in urine, serum and hair by GC/MS and RIA. *Forensic Sci. Int.* 70: 125–133 (1995).

144. L.W. Hayes, W.G. Krasselt, and P.A. Mueggler. Concentrations of morphine and codeine in serum and urine after ingestion of poppy seed. *Clin. Chem.* 33: 806–808 (1987).

145. A.J. Jenkins, R.M. Keenan, J.E. Henningfield, and E.J. Cone. Pharmacokinetics and pharmacodynamics of smoked heroin. *J. Anal. Toxicol.* 18: 317–330 (1994).

146. B.A. Goldberger, W.D. Darwin, T.M. Grant, A.C. Allen, Y.H. Caplan, and E.J. Cone. Measurement of heroin and its metabolites by isotope-dilution electron-impact mass spectrometry. *Clin. Chem.* 39: 670–675 (1993).

147. M.J. Burt, J. Kloss, and F.S. Apple. Postmortem blood free and total morphine concentrations in medical examiner cases. *J. Forensic Sci.* 46: 1138–1142 (2001).

148. G. Ceder and A.W. Jones. Concentration ratios of morphine to codeine in blood of impaired drivers as evidence of heroin use and not medication with codeine. *Clin. Chem.* 47: 1980–1984 (2001).

149. L.H. Yong and N.T. Lik. The human urinary excretion pattern of morphine and codeine following the consumption of morphine, opium, codeine and heroin. *Bull. Narcotics* 29: 45–74 (1977).

150. G.S. Yacoubian, Jr., E.D. Wish, and D.M. Perez. A comparison of saliva testing to urinalysis in an arrestee population. *J. Psychoactive Drugs* 33: 289–294 (2001).

151. S.J. Mule and G.A. Casella. Rendering the "poppy-seed defense" defenseless: Identification of 6-monoacetylmorphine in urine by gas chromatography/mass spectroscopy. *Clin. Chem.* 34: 1427–1430 (1988).

152. M.L. Smith, E.T. Shimomura, J. Summers, B.D. Paul, D. Nichols, R. Shippee, A.J. Jenkins, W.D. Darwin, and E.J. Cone. Detection times and analytical performance of commercial urine opiate immunoassays following heroin administration. *J. Anal. Toxicol.* 24: 522–529 (2000).

153. A.C. Spanbauer, S. Casseday, D. Davoudzadeh, K.L. Preston, and M.A. Huestis. Detection of opiate use in a methadone maintenance treatment population with the CEDIA 6-acetylmorphine and CEDIA DAU opiate assays. *J. Anal. Toxicol.* 25: 515–519 (2001).

154. E.J. Cone, R. Jufer, and W.D. Darwin. Forensic drug testing for opiates. VII. Urinary excretion profile of intranasal (snorted) heroin. *J. Anal. Toxicol.* 20: 379–391 (1996).

155. E.J. Cone, P. Welch, J.M. Mitchell, and B.D. Paul. Forensic drug testing for opiates: I. Detection of 6-acetylmorphine in urine as an indicator of recent heroin exposure; Drug and assay considerations and detection times. *J. Anal. Toxicol.* 15: 1–7 (1991).

156. H.J.G.M. Derks, K.V. Twillert, and G. Zomer. Determination of 6-acetylmorphine in urine as a specific marker for heroin abuse by high-performance liquid chromatography with fluorescence detection. *Anal. Chim. Acta* 170: 13–20 (1985).

157. C.L. O'Neal and A. Poklis. The detection of acetylcodeine and 6-acetylmorphine in opiate positive urines. *Forensic Sci. Int.* 95: 1–10 (1998).

158. J.M. Mitchell, B.D. Paul, P. Welch, and E.J. Cone. Forensic drug testing for opiates. II. Metabolism and excretion rate of morphine in humans after morphine administration. *J. Anal. Toxicol.* 15: 49–53 (1991).

159. I.M. Speckl, J. Hallbach, W.G. Guder, L.V. Meyer, and T. Zilker. Opiate detection in saliva and urine — a prospective comparison by gas chromatography-mass spectrometry. *J. Toxicol. Clin. Toxicol.* 37: 441–445 (1999).

160. E.J. Cone, S. Dickerson, B.D. Paul, and J.M. Mitchell. Forensic drug testing for opiates. V. Urine testing for heroin, morphine, and codeine with commercial opiate immunoassays. *J. Anal. Toxicol.* 17: 156–164 (1993).

161. J. Fehn and G. Megges. Detection of O6-monoacetylmorphine in urine samples by GC/MS as evidence for heroin use. *J. Anal. Toxicol.* 9: 134–138 (1985).

162. G. Fritschi and W.R. Prescott, Jr. Morphine levels in urine subsequent to poppy seed consumption. *Forensic Sci. Int.* 27: 111–117 (1985).

163. M.A. Huestis, E.J. Cone, C.J. Wong, A. Umbricht, and K.L. Preston. Monitoring opiate use in substance abuse treatment patients with sweat and urine drug testing. *J. Anal. Toxicol.* 24: 509–521 (2000).

164. L. Presley, M. Lehrer, W. Seiter, D. Hahn, B. Rowland, M. Smith, K.W. Kardos, D. Fritch, S. Salamone, R.S. Niedbala, and E.J. Cone. High prevalence of 6-acetylmorphine in morphine-positive oral fluid specimens. *Forensic Sci. Int.* 133: 22–25 (2003).

165. J. Jones, K. Tomlinson, and C. Moore. The simultaneous determination of codeine, morphine, hydrocodone, hydromorphone, 6-acetylmorphine, and oxycodone in hair and oral fluid. *J. Anal. Toxicol.* 26: 171–175 (2002).

166. R.S. Niedbala, K. Kardos, J. Waga, D. Fritch, L. Yeager, S. Doddamane, and E. Schoener. Laboratory analysis of remotely collected oral fluid specimens for opiates by immunoassay. *J. Anal. Toxicol.* 25: 310–315 (2001).

167. P. Kintz, R. Brenneisen, P. Bundeli, and P. Mangin. Sweat testing for heroin and metabolites in a heroin maintenance program. *Clin. Chem.* 43: 736–739 (1997).

168. J.A. Levisky, D.L. Bowerman, W.W. Jenkins, and S.B. Karch. Drug deposition in adipose tissue and skin: evidence for an alternative source of positive sweat patch tests. *Forensic Sci. Int.* 110: 35–46 (2000).

169. D.A. Kidwell and F.P. Smith. Susceptibility of PharmChek drugs of abuse patch to environmental contamination. *Forensic Sci. Int.* 116: 89–106 (2001).

170. S. Darke, W. Hall, S. Kaye, J. Ross, and J. Duflou. Hair morphine concentrations of fatal heroin overdose cases and living heroin users. *Addiction* 97: 977–984 (2002).

171. B. Ahrens, F. Erdmann, G. Rochholz, and H. Schutz. Detection of morphine and monoacetylmorphine (MAM) in human hair. *J. Anal. Chem.* 344: 559–560 (1992).

172. E.J. Cone, W.D. Darwin, and W.L. Wang. The occurrence of cocaine, heroin and metabolites in hair of drug abusers. *Forensic. Sci. Int.* 63: 55–68 (1993).

173. P. Kintz, C. Jamey, V. Cirimele, R. Brenneisen, and B. Ludes. Evaluation of acetylcodeine as a specific marker of illicit heroin in human hair. *J. Anal. Toxicol.* 22: 425–429 (1998).

174. B.A. Goldberger, Y.H. Caplan, T. Maguire, and E.J. Cone. Testing human hair for drugs of abuse. III. Identification of heroin and 6-acetylmorphine as indicators of heroin use. *J. Anal. Toxicol.* 15: 226–231 (1991).

175. C.L. O'Neal, D.J. Crouch, D.E. Rollins, A. Fatah, and M.L. Cheever. Correlation of saliva codeine concentrations with plasma concentrations after oral codeine administration. *J. Anal. Toxicol.* 23: 452–459 (1999).

176. M.K. Brunson and J.F. Nash. Gas-chromatographic measurement of codeine and norcodeine in human plasma. *Clin. Chem.* 21: 1956–1960 (1975).

177. I. Kim, A.J. Barnes, J.M. Oyler, R. Schepers, R.E. Joseph, Jr., E.J. Cone, D. Lafko, E.T. Moolchan, and M.A. Huestis. Plasma and oral fluid pharmacokinetics and pharmacodynamics after oral codeine administration. *Clin. Chem.* 48: 1486–1496 (2002).

178. R.J. Schepers, J.M. Oyler, R.E. Joseph, Jr., E.J. Cone, E.T. Moolchan, and M.A. Huestis. Methamphetamine and amphetamine pharmacokinetics in oral fluid and plasma after controlled oral methamphetamine administration to human volunteers. *Clin. Chem.* 49: 121–132 (2003).

179. E.J. Cone, P. Welch, B.D. Paul, and J.M. Mitchell. Forensic drug testing for opiates. III. Urinary excretion rates of morphine and codeine following codeine administration. *J. Anal. Toxicol.* 15: 161–166 (1991).

180. H.N. ElSohly, D.F. Stanford, A.B. Jones, M.A. ElSohly, H. Snyder, and C. Pedersen. Gas chromatographic/mass spectrometric analysis of morphine and codeine in human urine of poppy seed eaters. *J. Forensic Sci.* 33: 347–356 (1988).

181. P. Lafolie, O. Beck, Z. Lin, F. Albertioni, and L. Boreus. Urine and plasma pharmacokinetics of codeine in healthy volunteers: implications for drugs-of-abuse testing. *J. Anal. Toxicol.* 20: 541–546 (1996).

182. F. Mari and E. Bertol. Observations on urinary excretion of codeine in illicit heroin addicts. *J. Pharm. Pharmacol.* 33: 814–815 (1981).

183. J.M. Oyler, E.J. Cone, R.E. Joseph, Jr., and M.A. Huestis. Identification of hydrocodone in human urine following controlled codeine administration. *J. Anal. Toxicol.* 24: 530–535 (2000).

184. G. Ceder and A.W. Jones. Concentrations of unconjugated morphine, codeine and 6-acetylmorphine in urine specimens from suspected drugged drivers. *J. Forensic Sci*: 366–368 (2002).

185. M.E. Sharp, S.M. Wallace, K.W. Hindmarsh, and H.W. Peel. Monitoring saliva concentrations of methaqualone, codeine, secobarbital, diphenhydramine and diazepam after single oral doses. *J. Anal. Toxicol.* 7: 11–14 (1983).

186. G.J. Di-Gregorio, A.J. Piraino, B.T. Nagle, and E.K. Knaiz. Secretion of drugs by the parotid glands of rats and human beings. *J. Dental Res.* 56: 502–509 (1977).

187. C.L. O'Neal, D.J. Crouch, D.E. Rollins, and A.A. Fatah. The effects of collection methods on oral fluid codeine concentrations. *J. Anal. Toxicol.* 24: 536–542 (2000).

188. G. Skopp, L. Potsch, K. Klinder, B. Richter, R. Aderjan, and R. Mattern. Saliva testing after single and chronic administration of dihydrocodeine. *Int. J. Legal Med.* 114: 133–140 (2001).

189. P. Kintz, A. Tracqui, C. Jamey, and P. Mangin. Detection of codeine and phenobarbital in sweat collected with a sweat patch. *J. Anal. Toxicol.* 20: 197–201 (1996).

190. A. Tracqui, P. Kintz, B. Ludes, C. Jamey, and P. Mangin. The detection of opiate drugs in nontraditional specimens (clothing): a report of ten cases. *J. Forensic Sci.* 40: 263–265 (1995).

191. D.E. Rollins, D.G. Wilkins, G.G. Krueger, M.P. Augsberger, A. Mizuno, C. O'Neal, C.R. Borges, and M.H. Slawson. The effect of hair color on the incorporation of codeine into human hair. *J. Anal. Toxicol.* 27: 545–551 (1999).

192. V. Cirimele, P. Kintz, and P. Mangin. Drug concentrations in human hair after bleaching. *J. Anal. Toxicol.* 19: 331 (1995).

193. S.P. Gygi, R.E. Joseph, Jr., E.J. Cone, D.G. Wilkins, and D.E. Rollins. Incorporation of codeine and metabolites into hair. Role of pigmentation. *Drug Metab. Dispos.* 24: 495–501 (1996).

194. R. Kronstrand, S. Forstberg-Peterson, B. Kagedal, J. Ahlner, and G. Larson. Codeine concentration in hair after oral administration is dependent on melanin content. *Clin. Chem.* 45: 1485–1494 (1999).

195. H. Sachs, R. Denk, and I. Raff. Determination of dihydrocodeine in hair of opiate addicts by GC/MS. *Intl. J. Legal. Med.* 105: 247–250 (1993).

196. M. Scheller and H. Sachs. The detection of codeine abuse by hair analysis. *Dtsch. Med. Wochenschr.* 115: 1313–1315 (1990).

197. D.G. Wilkins, H.M. Haughey, G.G. Krueger, and D.E. Rollins. Disposition of codeine in female human hair after multiple-dose administration. *J. Anal. Toxicol.* 19: 492–498 (1995).

198. D.N. Bailey and J.J. Guba. Gas-chromatographic analysis for phencyclidine in plasma, with use of a nitrogen detector. *Clin. Chem.* 26: 437–440 (1980).

199. D.N. Bailey. Phencyclidine abuse. Clinical findings and concentrations in biological fluids after nonfatal intoxication. *Am. J. Clin. Pathol.* 72: 795–799 (1979).

200. D.N. Bailey, R.F. Shaw, and J.J. Guba. Phencyclidine abuse: Plasma levels and clinical findings in casual users and in phencyclidine-related deaths. *J. Anal. Toxicol.* 2: 233–237 (1978).

201. C.E. Cook, D.R. Brine, A.R. Jeffcoat, J.M. Hill, M.E. Wall, M. Perez-Reyes, and S.R. DiGuiseppi. Phencyclidine disposition after intravenous and oral doses. *Clin. Pharmacol. Ther.* 31: 625–634 (1982).

202. E.F. Domino and A.E. Wilson. Effects of urine acidification on plasma and urine phencyclidine levels in overdosage. *Clin. Pharmacol. Ther.* 22: 421–424 (1977).

203. J.O. Donaldson and R.C. Baselt. CSF phencyclidine. *Am. J. Psychiatry* 136: 1341–1342 (1979).

204. S. Kerrigan and J.W. Phillips, Jr. Comparison of ELISAs for opiates, methamphetamine, cocaine metabolite, benzodiazepines, phencyclidine, and cannabinoids in whole blood and urine. *Clin. Chem.* 47: 540–547 (2001).

205. G.W. Kunsman, B. Levine, A. Costantino, and M.L. Smith. Phencyclidine blood concentrations in DRE cases. *J. Anal. Toxicol.* 21: 498–502 (1997).

206. A.L. Misra, R.B. Pontani, and J. Bartolomeo. Persistence of phencyclidine (PCP) and metabolites in brain and adipose tissue and implications for long-lasting behavioural effects. *Res. Commun. Chem. Path. Pharmacol.* 24: 431–445 (1979).

207. A.E. Wilson and E.F. Domino. Plasma phencyclidine pharmacokinetics in dog and monkey using a gas chromatography selected ion monitoring assay. *Biomed. Mass Spectrom.* 5: 112–116 (1978).

208. D.N. Bailey. Percutaneous absorption of phencyclidine hydrochloride in vivo. *Res. Commun. Subst. Abuse* 1: 443–450 (1980).

209. W. Bronner, P. Nyman, and D. von Minden. Detectability of phencyclidine and 11-nor-delta-9-tetrahydrocannabinol-9-carboxylic acid in adulterated urine by radioimmunoassay and fluorescence polarization immunoassay. *J. Anal. Toxicol.* 14: 368–371 (1990).

210. E.J. Cone, D.B. Vaupel, and D. Yousefnejad. Monohydroxymetabolites of phencyclidine (PCP): activities and urinary excretion by rat, dog, and mouse. *J. Pharm. Pharmacol.* 34: 197–199 (1982).

211. C.C. Stevenson, D.L. Cibull, G.E. Platoff, D.M. Bush, and J.A. Gere. Solid phase extraction of phencyclidine from urine followed by capillary gas chromatography/mass spectrometry. *J. Anal. Toxicol.* 16: 337–339 (1992).

212. D.N. Bailey and J.J. Guba. Measurement of phencyclidine in saliva. *J. Anal. Toxicol.* 4: 311–313 (1980).

213. M.M. McCarron, C.B. Walberg, J.R. Soares, S.J. Gross, and R.C. Baselt. Detection of phencyclidine usage by radioimmunoassay of saliva. *J. Anal. Toxicol.* 8: 197–201 (1984).

214. W.A. Baumgartner, V.A. Hill, and W.H. Blahd. Hair analysis for drugs of abuse. *J. Forensic Sci.* 34: 1433–1453 (1989).

215. T. Sakamoto and A. Tanaka. Determination of PCP and its major metabolites, PCHP and PPC, in rat hair after administration of PCP. In *Proceedings of the 1994 JOINT TIAFT/SOFT International Meeting*, V. Spiehler, Ed. TIAFT/SOFT Joint Congress, 1994, 215–224.

216. D.A. Kidwell. Analysis of phencyclidine and cocaine in human hair by tandem mass spectrometry. *J. Forensic Sci.* 38: 272–284 (1993).

217. Y. Nakahara, K. Takahashi, T. Sakamoto, A. Tanaka, V.A. Hill, and W.A. Baumgartner. Hair analysis for drugs of abuse XVII. Simultaneous detection of PCP, PCHP, and PCPdiol in human hair for confirmation of PCP use. *J. Anal. Toxicol.* 21: 356–362 (1997).

218. T. Sakamoto, A. Tanaka, and Y. Nakahara. Hair analysis for drugs of abuse XII. Determination of PCP and its major metabolites, PCHP and PPC, in rat hair after administration of PCP. *J. Anal. Toxicol.* 20: 124–130 (1996).

219. Y. Nakahara, R. Kikura, T. Sakamoto, T. Mieczkowski, F. Tagliaro, and R. L. Foltz. Findings in hair analysis for some hallucinogens (LSD, MDA/MDMA and PCP). In *Hair Analysis in Forensic Toxicology: Proceedings of the 1995 International Conference and Workshop*, R.A. de Zeeuw, I. Al Hosani, and S. Al Munthiri, Eds. Organizing Committee of the Conference, Abu Dhabi, 1995, 161–184.

220. H. Gjerde, I. Hasvold, G. Pettersen, and A.S. Christophersen. Determination of amphetamine and methamphetamine in blood by derivatization with perfluorooctanoyl chloride and gas chromatography/mass spectrometry. *J. Anal. Toxicol.* 17: 65–68 (1993).

221. S. Cheung, H. Nolte, S.V. Otton, R.F. Tyndale, P.H. Wu, and E.M. Sellers. Simultaneous gas chromatographic determination of methamphetamine, amphetamine and their *p*-hydroxylated metabolites in plasma and urine. *J. Chromatogr.* 690: 77–87 (1997).

222. Y. Gaillard, F. Vayssette, and G. Pepin. Compared interest between hair analysis and urinalysis in doping controls. Results for amphetamines, corticosteroids and anabolic steroids in racing cyclists. *Forensic Sci. Int* 107: 361–379 (2000).

223. S.B. Matin, S.H. Wan, and J.B. Knight. Quantitative determination of enantiomeric compounds. I:- Simultaneous measurement of the optical isomers of amphetamine in human plasma and saliva using chemical ionization mass spectrometry. *Biomed. Mass Spectrom.* 4: 118–121 (1977).

224. F.P. Smith. Detection of amphetamine in bloodstains, semen, seminal stains, saliva, and saliva stains. *Forensic Sci. Int.* 17: 225–228 (1981).

225. J.M. Davis, I.J. Kopin, L. Lemberger, and J. Axelrod. Effects of urinary pH on amphetamine metabolism. *Ann. N. Y. Acad. Sci.* 179: 493–501 (1971).

226. B.D. Paul, M.R. Past, R.M. McKinley, J.D. Foreman, L.K. McWhorter, and J.J. Snyder. Amphetamine as an artifact of methamphetamine during periodate degradation of interfering ephedrine, pseudoephedrine, and phenylpropanolamine: an improved procedure for accurate quantitation of amphetamines in urine. *J. Anal. Toxicol.* 18: 331–336 (1994).

227. G.A. Alles and B.B. Wisegarver. Amphetamine excretion studies in man. *Toxicol. App. Pharmacol.* 3: 678–688 (1961).

228. A.H. Beckett and M. Rowland. Determination and identification of amphetamine in urine. *J. Pharm. Pharmacol.* 17: 59–60 (1965).

229. J. D'Nicuola, R. Jones, B. Levine, and M.L. Smith. Evaluation of six commercial amphetamine and methamphetamine immunoassays for cross-reactivity to phenylpropanolamine and ephedrine in urine. *J. Anal. Toxicol.* 16: 211–213 (1992).

230. A.H. Beckett and M. Rowland. Urinary excretion kinetics of amphetamine in man. *J. Pharm. Pharmacol.* 17: 628–638 (1965).

231. D.E. Blandford and P.R.E. Desjardins. Detection and identification of amphetamine and methamphetamine in urine by GC/MS. *Clin. Chem.* 40: 145–147 (1994).

232. J.T. Cody and S. Valtier. Detection of amphetamine and methamphetamine following administration of benzphetamine. *J. Anal. Toxicol.* 22: 299–309 (1998).

233. B.K. Gan, D. Baugh, R.H. Liu, and A.S. Walia. Simultaneous analysis of amphetamine, methamphetamine, and 3,4-methylenedioxymethamphetamine MDMA in urine samples by solid-phase extraction, derivatization, and gas chromatography/mass spectrometry. *J. Forensic Sci.* 36: 1331–1341 (1991).

234. L.M. Gunne. The urinary output of d-and l-amphetamine in man. *Biochem. Pharmacol.* 16: 863–869 (1967).

235. S.J. Mule and G.A. Casella. Confirmation of marijuana, cocaine, morphine, codeine, amphetamine, methamphetamine, phencyclidine by GC/MS in urine following immunoassay screening. *J. Anal. Toxicol.* 12: 102–107 (1988).

236. A. Nice and A. Maturen. False-positive urine amphetamine screen with Ritodrine. *Clin. Chem.* 35: 1542– (1989).

237. J.L. Valentine, G.L. Kearns, C. Sparks, L.G. Letzig, C.R. Valentine, S.A. Shappell, D.F. Neri, and C.A. DeJohn. GC/MS determination of amphetamine and methamphetamine in human urine for 12 hours following oral administration of dextro-methamphetamine: Lack of evidence supporting the established forensic guidelines for methamphetamine confirmation. *J. Anal. Toxicol.* 19: 581–590 (1995).

238. M.R. Peace, L.D. Tarnai, and A. Poklis. Performance evaluation of four on-site drug-testing devices for detection of drugs of abuse in urine. *J. Anal. Toxicol.* 24: 589–594 (2000).

239. A. Poklis and K.A. Moore. Response of EMIT amphetamine immunoassays to urinary desoxyephedrine following Vicks inhaler use. *Ther. Drug Monit.* 17: 89–94 (1995).

240. A. Smith-Kielland, B. Skuterud, and J. Morland. Urinary excretion of amphetamine after termination of drug abuse. *J. Anal. Toxicol.* 21: 325–329 (1997).

241. H. Vapaatalo, S. Karkkainen, and K.E.O. Senius. Comparison of saliva and urine samples in thin-layer chromatographic detection of central nervous stimulants. *Int. J. Clin. Pharmacol.* 1: 5–8 (1984).

242. E.M. Thurman, M.J. Pedersen, R.L. Stout, and T. Martin. Distinguishing sympathomimetic amines from amphetamine and methamphetamine in urine by gas chromatography/mass spectrometry. *J. Anal. Toxicol.* 16: 19–27 (1992).

243. K. Takahashi. Determination of methamphetamine and amphetamine in biological fluids and hair by gas chromatography. *Dep. Legal Med.* 38: 319–336 (1984).

244. S.H. Wan, S.B. Matin, and D.L. Azarnoff. Kinetics, salivary excretion of amphetamine isomers, and effect of urinary pH. *Clin. Pharmacol. Ther.* 23: 585–590 (1978).

245. T.B. Vree, A.T. Muskens, and J.M. Van Rossum. Excretion of amphetamines in human sweat. *Arch. Int. Pharmacodyn. Ther.* 199: 311–317 (1972).

246. Y. Nakahara and R. Kikura. Hair analysis for drugs of abuse. XIII. Effect of structural factors on incorporation of drugs into hair: the incorporation rates of amphetamine analogs. *Arch. Toxicol.* 70: 841–849 (1996).

247. M. Rothe, F. Pragst, K. Spiegel, T. Harrach, K. Fischer, and J. Kunkel. Hair concentrations and self-reported abuse history of 20 amphetamine and ecstasy users. *Forensic Sci. Int.* 89: 111–128 (1997).

248. F. Musshoff, H.P. Junker, D.W. Lachenmeier, L. Kroener, and B. Madea. Fully automated determination of amphetamines and synthetic designer drugs in hair samples using headspace solid-phase microextraction and gas chromatography-mass spectrometry. *J. Chromatogr. Sci.* 40: 359–364 (2002).

249. F. Musshoff, D.W. Lachenmeier, L. Kroener, and B. Madea. Automated headspace solid-phase dynamic extraction for the determination of amphetamines and synthetic designer drugs in hair samples. *J. Chromatogr. A* 958: 231–238 (2002).

250. P. Kintz and V. Cirimele. Interlaboratory comparison of quantitative determination of amphetamine and related compounds in hair samples. *Forensic Sci. Int.* 84: 151–156 (1997).

251. D.L. Allen and J.S. Oliver. The use of supercritical fluid extraction for the determination of amphetamines in hair. *Forensic Sci. Int.* 107: 191–199 (2000).

252. P. Kintz, V. Cirimele, A. Tracqui, and P. Mangin. Simultaneous determination of amphetamine, methamphetamine, 3,4-methylenedioxyamphetamine and 3,4-methylenedioxymethamphetamine in human hair by gas chromatography-mass spectrometry. *J. Chromatogr.* 670: 162–166 (1995).

253. J. Rohrich and G. Kauert. Determination of amphetamine and methylenedioxy-amphetamine-derivatives in hair. *Forensic Sci. Int.* 84: 179–188 (1997).

254. O. Suzuki, H. Hattori, and M. Asano. Detection of methamphetamine and amphetamine in a single human hair by gas chromatography/chemical ionization mass spectrometry. *J. Forensic Sci.* 29: 611–617 (1984).

255. R. Kikura and Y. Nakahara. Distinction between amphetamine-like OTC drug use and illegal amphetamine/methamphetamine use by hair analysis. In *Proceedings of the 1994 JOINT TIAFT/SOFT International Meeting*, V. Spiehler, Ed. TIAFT/SOFT, 1994, 236–247.

256. B.K. Logan, C.L. Fligner, and T. Haddix. Cause and manner of death in fatalities involving methamphetamine. *J. Forensic Sci.* 43(1): 28–34 (1998).

257. B.K. Logan. Methamphetamine and driving impairment. *J. Forensic Sci.* 41: 457–464 (1996).

258. S. Rasmussen, R. Cole, and V. Spiehler. Methamphetamine in antemortem blood and urine by radioimmunoassay and GC/MS. *J. Anal. Toxicol.* 13: 263–267 (1989).

259. V.R. Spiehler, I.B. Collison, P.R. Sedgwick, S.L. Perez, S.D. Le, and D.A. Farnin. Validation of an automated microplate enzyme immunoassay for screening of postmortem blood for drugs of abuse. *J. Anal. Toxicol.* 22: 573–579 (1998).

260. R.C. Driscoll, F.S. Barr, B.J. Gragg, and G.W. Moore. Determination of therapeutic blood levels of methamphetamine and pentobarbital by GC. *J. Pharm. Sci.* 60(10): 1492–1495 (1971).

261. R.L. Fitzgerald, J.M. Ramos, S.C. Bogema, and A. Poklis. Resolution of methamphetamine stereoisomers in urine drug testing: Urinary excretion of R(–)-methamphetamine following use of nasal inhalers. *J. Anal. Toxicol.* 12: 255–259 (1988).

262. J.T. Cody. Determination of methamphetamine enantiomer ratios in urine by gas chromatography-mass spectrometry. *J. Chromatogr.* 580: 77–95 (1992).

263. J. Sukbuntherng, A. Hutchaleelaha, H.H. Chow, and M. Mayersohn. Separation and quantitation of the enantiomers of methamphetamine and its metabolites in urine by HPLC: precolumn derivatization and fluorescence detection. *J. Anal. Toxicol.* 19: 139–147 (1995).

264. C.L. Hornbeck, J.E. Carrig, and R.J. Czarny. Detection of a GC/MS artifact peak as methamphetamine. *J. Anal. Toxicol.* 17: 257–263 (1993).

265. M.R. Lee, S.C. Yu, C.L. Lin, Y.C. Yeh, Y.L. Chen, and S.H. Hu. Solid-phase extraction in amphetamine and methamphetamine analysis of urine. *J. Anal. Toxicol.* 21: 278–282 (1997).

266. K. McCambly, R.C. Kelly, T. Johnson, J.E. Johnson, and W.C. Brown. Robotic solid-phase extraction of amphetamines from urine for analysis by gas chromatography-mass spectrometry. *J. Anal. Toxicol.* 21: 438–444 (1997).

267. A. Poklis and K.A. Moore. Stereoselectivity of the TDxADx/FLx amphetamine/methamphetamine II amphetamine/methamphetamine immunoassays — Response of urine specimens following nasal inhaler use. *Clin. Toxicol.* 33: 35–41 (1995).

268. J.M. Oyler, E.J. Cone, R.E. Joseph, Jr., E.T. Moolchan, and M.A. Huestis. Duration of detectable methamphetamine and amphetamine excretion in urine after controlled oral administration of methamphetamine to humans. *Clin. Chem.* 48: 1703–1714 (2002).

269. S. Suzuki, T. Inoue, H. Hori, and S. Inayama. Analysis of methamphetamine in hair, nail, sweat, and saliva by mass fragmentography. *J. Anal. Toxicol.* 13: 176–178 (1989).

270. J. Fay, R. Fogerson, D. Schoendorfer, R.S. Niedbala, and V. Spiehler. Detection of methamphetamine in sweat by EIA and GC-MS. *J. Anal. Toxicol.* 20: 398–403 (1996).

271. Y.C. Yoo, H.S. Chung, H.K. Choi, and W.K. Jin. Determination of methamphetamine in the hair of Korean drug abusers by GC/MS. In *Proceedings of the 1994 JOINT TIAFT/SOFT International Meeting*, V. Spiehler, Ed. TIAFT/SOFT Joint Congress, 1994, 207–214.

272. I. Ishiyama, T. Nagai, and S. Toshida. Detection of basic drugs (methamphetamine, antidepressants, and nicotine) from human hair. *J. Forensic Sci.* 28: 380–385 (1983).

273. R. Kikura and Y. Nakahara. Hair analysis for drugs of abuse. IX. Comparison of deprenyl use and methamphetamine use by hair analysis. *Biol. Pharm. Bull.* 18: 267–272 (1995).

274. Y. Nakahara, R. Kikura, M. Yasuhara, and T. Mukai. Hair analysis for Drug Abuse XIV. Identification of substances causing acute poisoning using hair root. I. Methamphetamine. *Forensic Sci. Int.* 84: 157–164 (1997).

275. S. Suzuki, T. Inoue, T. Yasuda, T. Niwaguchi, H. Hori, and S. Inayama. Analysis of methamphetamine in human hair by fragmentography. *Eisei Kagaku* 30: 23–26 (1984).

276. M.R. Moeller and M. Hartung. Ecstasy and related substances — Serum levels in impaired drivers. *J. Anal. Toxicol.* 21: 501–501 (1997).

277. M. Navarro, S. Pichini, M. Farre, J. Ortuno, P.N. Roset, J. Segura, and R. de la Torre. Usefulness of saliva for measurement of 3,4-methylenedioxymethamphetamine and its metabolites: correlation with plasma drug concentrations and effect of salivary pH. *Clin. Chem.* 47: 1788–1795 (2001).

278. T.P. Rohrig and R.W. Prouty. Tissue distribution of methylenedioxymethamphetamine. *J. Anal. Toxicol.* 16: 52–53 (1992).

279. R. de la Torre, M. Farre, J. Ortuno, M. Mas, R. Brenneisen, P.N. Roset, J. Segura, and J. Cami. Nonlinear pharmacokinetics of MDMA ("ecstasy") in humans. *Br. J. Clin. Pharmacol.* 49: 104–109 (2000).

280. T. Kraemer and H.H. Maurer. Toxicokinetics of amphetamines: metabolism and toxicokinetic data of designer drugs, amphetamine, methamphetamine, and their *N*-alkyl derivatives. *Ther. Drug Monit.* 24: 277–289 (2002).

281. N. Samyn, G. De Boeck, M. Wood, C.T. Lamers, D. De Waard, K.A. Brookhuis, A.G. Verstraete, and W.J. Riedel. Plasma, oral fluid and sweat wipe ecstasy concentrations in controlled and real life conditions. *Forensic Sci. Int.* 128: 90–97 (2002).

282. A. Poklis, R.L. Fitzgerald, K.V. Hall, and J.J. Saady. EMIT-d.a.u. monoclonal amphetamine/methamphetamine assay. II. Detection of methylenedioxyamphetamine (MDA) and methylenedioxymethamphetamine (MDMA). *Forensic Sci. Int.* 59: 63–70 (1993).

283. G.W. Kunsman, B. Levine, J.J. Kuhlman, R.L. Jones, R.O. Hughes, C.I. Fujiyama, and M.L. Smith. MDA-MDMA concentrations in urine specimens. *J. Anal. Toxicol.* 20: 517–521 (1996).

284. J.M. Ramos, Jr., R.L. Fitzgerald, and A. Poklis. MDMA and MDA cross reactivity observed with Abbott TDx amphetamine/methamphetamine reagents. *Clin. Chem.* 34: 991– (1988).

285. H.H. Maurer, J. Bickeboeller-Friedrich, T. Kraemer, and F.T. Peters. Toxicokinetics and analytical toxicology of amphetamine-derived designer drugs ("Ecstasy"). *Toxicol. Lett.* 112–113: 133–142 (2000).

286. R. Pacifici, M. Farre, S. Pichini, J. Ortuno, P.N. Roset, P. Zuccaro, J. Segura, and R. de la Torre. Sweat testing of MDMA with the Drugwipe analytical device: a controlled study with two volunteers. *J. Anal. Toxicol.* 25: 144–146 (2001).

287. S. Pichini, M. Navarro, R. Pacifici, P. Zuccaro, J. Ortuno, M. Farre, P.N. Roset, J. Segura, and R. de la Torre. Usefulness of sweat testing for the detection of MDMA after a single-dose administration. *J. Anal. Toxicol.* 27: 294–303 (2003).

288. F. Tagliaro, Z. De Battisti, A. Groppi, Y. Nakahara, D. Scarcella, R. Valentini, and M. Marigo. High sensitivity simultaneous determination in hair of the major constituents of ecstasy (3,4-methylenedioxymethamphetamine, 3,4-methylenedioxyamphetamine and 3,4-methylene-dioxyethylamphetamine) by high-performance liquid chromatography with direct fluorescence detection. *J. Chromatogr. B Biomed. Sci. Appl.* 723: 195–202 (1999).

289. M. Uhl. Tandem mass spectrometry: a helpful tool in hair analysis for the forensic expert. *Forensic Sci. Int* 107: 169–179 (2000).

290. Y. Nakahara and R. Kikura. Hair analysis for drugs of abuse. XVIII. 3,4-Methylenedioxymethamphetamine (MDMA) disposition in hair roots and use in identification of acute MDMA poisoning. *Biol. Pharm. Bull.* 20: 969–972 (1997).

291. C. Girod and C. Staub. Analysis of drugs of abuse in hair by automated solid-phase extraction, GC/EI/MS and GC ion trap/CI/MS. *Forensic Sci. Int.* 107: 261–271 (2000).

292. R. Kikura, Y. Nakahara, T. Mieczkowski, and F. Tagliaro. Hair analysis for Drug Abuse XV. Disposition of 3,4-methylenedioxymethamphetamine (MDMA) and its related compounds into rat hair and application to hair analysis for MDMA abuse. *Forensic Sci. Int.* 84: 165–177 (1997).

10.7 SPECIMEN VALIDITY TESTING

Yale H. Caplan, Ph.D., DABFT
National Scientific Services, Baltimore, Maryland

Urine drug testing is, by its nature and the privacy considerations, decisions, and laws of the federal government and the states, an unobserved process. This is the standard practice unless there is specific individual suspicion that a specimen has been altered or substituted. Although the practice of tampering had been reported prior to the implementation of the federally regulated workplace drug-testing program, the problem became evident in the 1990s with the introduction of "Urine Aid" and later "Klear," products among others advertised to "Beat a Drug Test." Earlier methods were crude and often ineffective utilizing more commonly available products such as salt, bleach, soap, and vinegar and sharing information about such products by "word of mouth." Later a significant cottage industry grew through health food stores, advertisements in *High Times* and other magazines and extensive citation on the Internet.

How effective can a drug-testing program be if a magic potion priced at $20 to $30 can provide a person a means to evade detection? In a deterrent-based program, credibility can rapidly decline if users believe they can beat the test. The Department of Health and Human Services (HHS) and the Department of Transportation (DOT) developed countermeasures by causing laboratories to inspect and test specimens, verify their normal composition, and search for foreign chemicals. The term *specimen validity testing* (SVT) was coined to identify a sequence of testing designed to check if urine was really urine and if the urine was normal or adulterated. This task was not so simple. Laboratories developed credible tests for the five classes of drugs, substances of known composition and predictable outcome, and were now faced with developing tests for a variety of specimen characteristics and an array of unknown compounds. Indeed, the task of comprehensively searching for normal elements that comprise urine and ascertaining that no foreign materials have been added can be more complex and costly than the drug testing itself.

The intent of the donor is to subvert the drug testing procedure and create a false negative result. This can be accomplished in three ways: (1) by diluting the urine through excessive fluid intake, (2) by substituting other urine, hopefully drug free urine, in place of the donor's urine, and (3) adulterating the urine by adding a chemical to the specimen that either destroys the drug in the urine or otherwise interferes with the laboratory immunoassay tests.

10.7.1 Characteristics of Urine

Urine is an aqueous solution produced by the kidneys. A review of urine characterization with emphasis on workplace testing has been compiled.[1] Urine's major constituents are primarily electrolytes, metabolic excretory products, and other substances eliminated through the kidneys. The initial characterization of a urine specimen is based on its appearance. Color, clarity, odor, and foaming properties contribute to the appearance of urine.

The color of a urine specimen is related to the concentration of its various constituents, most notably urochromes, which exhibit yellow, brown, and red pigments. A normal first morning void has a distinct deep yellow color. It should not be colorless. The characteristic yellow color is predominately caused by the presence of urobilinogen, a hemoglobin breakdown product. After hydration, urine is usually straw-colored, indicating dilute urine. Very dilute urine is essentially colorless and has a water-like appearance.

A normal fresh void is clear and transparent. Freshly voided urine that is cloudy or turbid can indicate the presence of white blood cells, red blood cells, epithelial cells, or bacteria. Upon standing, flaky precipitates from urinary tract mucin may appear in the specimen. Aged alkaline urine may become cloudy because of crystal precipitation. After a lipid-rich meal, urine may also become alkaline and cloudy.

Freshly voided urine is normally odorless. With age, urine acquires a characteristic aromatic odor. As the constituents in the urine decompose, ammonia, putrefaction compounds, and hydrogen sulfide are detected. Certain foodstuffs, such as coffee, garlic, or asparagus, give a distinctive scent. Patients with poorly controlled diabetes produce ketone bodies such as acetone, which impart a fruity odor to urine.

Urine foaming is caused by the presence of protein in the specimen, and foam bubbles should not exhibit the rainbow appearance that is indicative of soap contamination.

10.7.2 Chemical Constituents and Other Characteristics of Urine

The kidneys filter plasma, reabsorb most of the dissolved substances that are filtered, secrete some of these substances back into its filtrate, and leave behind a concentrated solution of metabolic waste known as urine. Metabolic waste products are present in urine at high concentrations.

Creatinine is spontaneously and irreversibly formed from creatine and creatine phosphate in muscle. Creatinine, creatine's anhydride, is a metabolic waste product that is not reutilized by the body. Because there is a direct relationship between creatinine formation and muscle mass, creatinine production is considered constant from day-to-day provided that muscle mass remains unchanged. In view of this constant production, random creatinine results approximate 24-h collection reference intervals. Creatinine is freely filtered by the renal glomeruli and is not significantly reabsorbed by the renal tubules, but a small amount is excreted by active renal tubular secretion. Creatinine is excreted at a relatively constant rate relatively independent of diuresis, provided kidney function is not impaired. Creatinine production and excretion are age and sex dependent. Normal urine creatinine concentrations are greater than 20 mg/dl. Abnormal levels of creatinine may result from excessive fluid intake, glomerulonephritis, pyleonephritis, reduced renal blood flow, renal failure, myasthenia gravis, or a high meat diet.

Specific gravity assesses urine concentration, or amount of dissolved substances present in a solution. As increasing amounts of substances are added to urine, the concentration of these dissolved substances and the density, or the weight of the dissolved substances per unit volume of liquid, increase. Specific gravity varies greatly with fluid intake and state of hydration. Normal values for the specific gravity of human urine range from approximately 1.0020 to 1.0200. Decreased urine specific gravity values may indicate excessive fluid intake, renal failure, glomerulonephritis, pyelonephritis, or diabetes insipidus. Increased urine specific gravity values may result from dehydration, diarrhea, excessive sweating, glucosuria, heart failure, proteinuria, renal arterial stenosis, vomiting, and water restriction.

pH is the inverse logarithmic function of the hydrogen ion concentration. It serves as an indicator of the acidity of a solution. The two organs that are primarily responsible for regulating the extremely narrow blood pH range that is compatible with human life are the lungs and the kidneys. The kidneys maintain the blood pH range by eliminating metabolic waste products. The pH of the urine is used clinically to assess the ability of the kidneys to eliminate toxic substances. Urinary pH undergoes physiological fluctuations throughout the day. Urinary pH values are decreased in the early morning followed by an increase in the late morning and early afternoon. In the bacteria-contaminated urine specimen, pH will increase upon standing because of bacterial ammonia formation. Normal urinary pH values range from 4.5 to 9.0.

10.7.3 The Role of HHS and DOT in Specimen Validity Testing

HHS through its Mandatory Guidelines for Federal Workplace Drug Testing and other notices has directed laboratories in the conduct of specimen validity tests. The early guidelines permitted testing but did not define the characteristics. When the adulteration and substitution issues became more prominent, HHS and DOT issued guidance. These were considered voluntary.

HHS–SAMHSA Program Document (PD) 33
> Title: Testing Split (Bottle B) Specimen for Adulterants
> Dated: March 9, 1998
> Summary: The guidance established technical threshold "cutoff" values for pH and nitrates. It required laboratory testing for pH and nitrite concentration in any split specimen that failed to reconfirm. It also authorized additional adulteration testing for the presence of glutaraldehyde, surfactants, bleach, and other adulterants if indicated.

HHS–SAMHSA Program Document (PD) 35
> Title: Guidelines for Reporting Specimen Validity Test Results
> Dated: September 28, 1998
> Summary: PD 35 replaced the Category I, II, and III reporting protocols established in 1993 with more detailed laboratory test reporting protocols. It established unacceptable limits for nitrite concentration, pH, and substitution. It required further testing when a split specimen failed to reconfirm.

U.S. DOT–Office of Drug and Alcohol Policy and Compliance (ODAPC)
   Title: MRO Guidance for Interpreting Specimen Validity Test Results
   Dated: September 28, 1998
   Summary: This companion document to PD 35 contained formal regulatory guidance for MROs, detailing how they were to respond to the various laboratory reporting protocols.
HHS–SAMHSA Program Document (PD) 37
   Title: Specimen Validity Testing
   Dated: July 28, 1999
   Summary: PD 37 provided specific technical guidelines to the laboratories. The document notes that specimen validity testing **may** be conducted on Bottle A and *must* be conducted on Bottle B if Bottle B fails to reconfirm for the requested drug/analyte. Specimen validity tests *may* include, but are not limited to, tests for creatinine concentration, specific gravity, pH, nitrite concentration, pyridine, glutaraldehyde, bleach, and soap. These tests must be performed using methods that are validated by the laboratory.

Subsequently, DOT published its final rule, 49CFR Part 40, on December 19, 2000[2] and a technical amendment to the Final Rule on August 1, 2001.[3] The 2000 rule mandated validity testing but the 2001 amendment changed this to *authorized* but *not mandated* pending future HHS actions. The rule section 40.91 states:
What validity tests must laboratories conduct on primary specimens?

Creatinine and specific gravity (SG)
SG if Creatinine < 20 mg/dl
Measure pH
Substances that may be used to adulterate urine
Send to second laboratory if unable to confirm adulterant
New adulterant, report to DOT and HHS
Complete testing for drugs
Conserve specimen

Most recently HHS published its Revised Mandatory Guidelines for Workplace Drug Testing Programs on April 13, 2004 with an effective date of November 1, 2004.[4] It defined the final SVT requirements. Notably it included the following:

1. Creatinine concentration criterion defining a substituted specimen changed to <2 mg/dl
2. SG analysis with four decimal places required to report as substituted or as invalid based on creatinine and SG
3. Added definitions specifically associated with SVT
   • Initial drug test, initial validity test
   • Confirmatory drug test, confirmatory validity test
   • Dilute specimen, adulterated specimen
   • Donor empties pockets and displays for collector
4. Included all the reporting requirements to report a specimen adulterated, substituted, diluted, or as an invalid result
5. Added a requirement to report the actual numerical values (concentrations) for adulterated results, and the confirmatory creatinine concentration and confirmatory SG result for a substituted specimen
6. Added specimen retention requirements for the laboratory
7. Provided a list of fatal flaws and correctable flaws
8. Expanded retest requirements for drugs
9. Mandated agencies to have BQC that are adulterated or substituted
10. MRO review expanded to include adulterated and substituted specimens and reporting
11. Requires laboratories to conduct drug and validity testing at the same facility
12. Defined requirements for creatinine and SG:
    • Determine the creatinine on every specimen

- Determine the SG if creatinine < 20 mg/dl
- Determine SG to four decimal places if reporting a specimen as substituted or as invalid based on creatinine and SG
13. Determine the pH on every specimen
14. Perform one or more validity tests for oxidizing adulterants on every specimen
15. Perform additional validity tests when the following conditions are observed:
    - Abnormal physical characteristics
    - Reactions or responses characteristic of an adulterant during testing
    - Possible unidentified interfering substance or adulterant
16. May send to second laboratory if unable to confirm adulterant (laboratory and MRO decide)
17. If a new adulterant is identified, report to DOT and HHS
    - Complete testing for drugs
18. Conserve specimen

According to these guidelines:

Substituted is a specimen with
- Creatinine < 2 mg/dl and SG < 1.0010 or
- Creatinine < 2 mg/dl and SG > 1.0200
Dilute is a specimen with
- Creatinine 2 to <20 mg/dl and
- SG 1.0010 to 1.0030
Invalid is a specimen in which inconsistent creatinine concentration and SG results are obtained, i.e.,
- Creatinine less than 2 mg/dl on *both* the initial and confirmatory creatinine tests and SG greater than 1.0010 but less than 1.0200 on *either or both* the initial and confirmatory SG tests
- Creatinine greater than or equal to 2 mg/dl on *either or both* the initial or confirmatory creatinine tests and SG less than or equal to 1.0010 on both the initial and confirmatory SG tests
A urine specimen is reported adulterated when:
- pH < 3
- pH ≥ 11
- Nitrite concentration ≥ 500 µg/ml (two different tests required)
- Chromium (VI) concentration ≥ 50 µg/ml (two different tests required)
- Halogen is detected and confirmed, with a specific concentration ≥ the LOD of the confirmatory test on the second aliquot (two different tests required)
- Glutaraldehyde is detected and confirmed, with a concentration ≥ the LOD of the confirmatory test on the second aliquot (two different tests required)
- Pyridine is detected and confirmed, with a concentration ≥ the LOD of the confirmatory test on the second aliquot (two tests required)
- Surfactant is detected and confirmed, with a ≥100 µg/ml dodecylbenzene sulfonate-equivalent cutoff concentration on the second aliquot (two tests required)
- The presence of any other adulterant not specified is verified using an initial test on the first aliquot and a different confirmatory test on the second aliquot

The reporting requirements are summarized in Table 10.7.1. The table was provided by HHS as part of the Mandatory Guidelines effective November 1, 2004. It describes the conditions for positive and negative drug test results as well as adulterated and substituted SVT results; however, it expands the number of conditions for which a specimen is reported as invalid. The increased number of SVT tests plus many more tests that cannot be satisfactorily completed caused a significant increase in the number of invalid reports.

10.7.4 Role of the Medical Review Officer

Medical Review Officers are required to review tests reported as adulterated, substituted, and invalid. Although the HHS Mandatory Guidelines are in effect, there exist some differences between

Table 10.7.1   HHS Reporting Template

Effective 11-1-2004

Result Box(es) checked on Federal CCF (Step 5a) or Result indicated on Electronic Report	Note
Negative	All drug tests are negative and all specimen validity test results are acceptable
Negative and Dilute	For DOT-regulated specimens: provide Creatinine & SpGr numerical values (See Below)
Invalid Result	State reason for invalid result (See Below)
Positive, Specific Drug	No comment required
Positive, Specific Drug, and Dilute	No comment required
Positive, Specific Drug, and Adulterated	State reason for adulterated result (See Below)
Positive, Specific Drug, and Substituted	Provide Creatinine & SpGr numerical values (See Below)
Positive, Specific Drug, and Invalid Result	State reason for invalid result (See Below)
Adulterated	State reason for adulterated result (See Below)
Adulterated and Invalid Result	State reasons for adulterated & invalid results (See Below)
Adulterated and Substituted	State reason for adulterated result & provide Creatinine and SpGr numerical values (See Below)
Substituted	Provide Creatinine and SpGr numerical values (See Below)
Substituted and Invalid Result	Provide Creatinine and SpGr numerical values & state reason for invalid result (See Below)
Rejected for Testing	State reason for rejecting specimen (See Below)

Test Result	Specific Comment Required on Remarks Line (Step 5a) of the CCF and on Electronic Report	Note
Negative and Dilute	For DOT-Regulated specimens: Creatinine = (numerical value) mg/dL & SpGr = (numerical value)	
Substituted	Creatinine = (conf. test numerical value) mg/dL & SpGr = (conf. test numerical value)	
Adulterated	pH = (conf. test numerical value)	
	Nitrite = (conf. test numerical value) mcg/mL	
	Chromium (VI) = (conf. test numerical value) mcg/mL	
	(Specify Halogen) Present	
	Glutaraldehyde = (conf. test numerical value) mcg/mL	
	Pyridine = (conf. test numerical value) mcg/mL	
	Surfactant Present	
	(Specify Adulterant) Present	
Invalid Result	Creatinine < 2 mg/dL; SpGr Acceptable	SpGr >1.0010 & <1.0200
	SpGr ≤ 1.0010; Creatinine ≥ 2 mg/dL	
	Abnormal pH	
	Possible (Characterize as Oxidant, Halogen, Aldehyde, or Surfactant) Activity*	
	Immunoassay Interference*	
	GC/MS interference*	
	Abnormal Physical Characteristic - (Specify)*	
	Bottle A and Bottle B - Different Physical Appearance*	
Rejected for Testing	Fatal Flaw: Specimen ID number mismatch/missing	
	Fatal Flaw: No collector printed name & No signature	
	Fatal Flaw: Tamper-evident seal broken	If redesignation is not possible
	Fatal Flaw: Insufficient specimen volume	
	Uncorrected Flaw: Wrong CCF Used	Wait 5 business days before reporting flaw if uncorrected
	Uncorrected Flaw: Collector signature not recovered	

* Lab shall contact the MRO to discuss the Invalid Result   ➜   *Revised January 4, 2005*

DOT and HHS requirements. First HHS mandates SVT for the federal agencies it controls. DOT incorporates HHS requirements in its rules but at present they are not entirely compatible. DOT SVT testing is authorized but not mandated. In addition, DOT published an interim final rule on May 28, 2003,[5] changing the creatinine criterion to <2 from 5 mg/dl and an additional interim rule on November 9, 2004[6] to incorporate most of the HHS rule. The differences are as follows:

HHS — Laboratories report quantitative creatinine and SG values for adulterated and substituted only
DOT — Laboratories report quantitative creatinine and SG values for all negative dilute specimens

MROs are required to take the following actions if the creatinine is above 2 mg/dl:

HHS — No requirements
DOT — Creatinine 2 or greater but less than 5 mg/dl with appropriate SG: Recollect under direct observation
DOT — Creatinine 5 or greater but less than 20 mg/dl with appropriate SG: If negative (drug) may, but not required, to take another test immediately

10.7.5 Dilution/Substitution

A donor may attempt to decrease the concentration of drugs or drug metabolites that may be present in his or her urine by dilution. Deliberate dilution may occur *in vivo* by consuming large volumes of liquid or *in vitro* by adding water or another liquid to the specimen. Donors also have been known to substitute urine specimens with drug-free urine or other liquid during specimen collection. Due to donor privacy considerations, collections for federally regulated drug testing programs are routinely unobserved. Therefore, dilution and substitution may go undetected by collectors and thus provide a viable method for donors to defeat drug tests. There are many products available today purporting to "cleanse" the urine prior to a drug test; some of which are diuretics. Others are designed specifically for urine specimen substitution, including drug-free urine, additives, and containers/devices to aid concealment. Some devices have heating mechanisms to bring the substituted specimen's temperature within the range set by HHS to determine specimen validity at the time of collection (i.e., 32 to 38°C/90 to 100°F). Additional products include prosthetic devices to deceive the collector/observer even during a direct observed collection.

According to federal guidelines, a specimen is:

Dilute if the creatinine is < 20 mg/dl and the specific gravity is < 1.003, unless the criteria for a substituted specimen are met.

The concentration of drug metabolites in urine is a function of collection time (related to drug use) and relative water content. The goal of the suborner is to dilute the urine and the drugs in it to concentrations that are below the cutoff concentrations for the various drugs. Hydration simply reduces the detection time since last use. It may or may not be significant. Attempts to manage intentional hydration are limited by the fact that normal hydration and specific gravity are highly variable. One cannot unduly restrict water consumption on one hand, and demand an adequate volume of urine from a donor on the other.

There are currently no effective techniques to address the issue of dilution. Most dilute specimens probably occur as the result of hydration — donor drinking large quantities of fluids prior to the collection — rather than the external addition of water to a specimen after it has been provided. Heated water sources should not be available; hence, external hydration should result in detection through temperature checks. Other water sources should be blued with dye to facilitate detection if used.

The most appropriate solution to the dilution problem would be to lower the cutoff values when testing for drugs in dilute specimens. However, this is not allowed in most regulated testing programs (NRC is the exception). The procedures, although technically possible, are not standard-ized among laboratories in a manner that would assure appropriate uniformity. Such techniques may be valuable, however, in special circumstances for specific situations, especially in nonregu-lated testing programs.

Diuretics may have the same effect as hydration or dilution. One common belief is that herbal teas ("Golden Seal" is a common example) will effectively protect an individual from detection. There is some historical truth in this belief. In the days when thin-layer chromatography was used to screen for drugs, some material in the tea acted as a masking agent by blocking the visualization of morphine or other opiates. The belief is reinforced by the fact that pigments in the tea result in a change in urine color to a darker hue. With the current immunoassay techniques, there is no value to the teas except the related diuresis and the increased hydration that results.

10.7.6 The Science Underlying the Substituted Specimen

According to federal guidelines, a specimen is:

Substituted (i.e., the specimen does not exhibit the clinical signs or characteristics associated with normal human urine) if the creatinine concentration is < 2 mg/dl *and* the specific gravity is < 1.0010 or > 1.0200.

Specimens reported as "substituted" have creatinine and specific gravity values that are so dimin-ished or incongruent that they are not consistent with normal human urine. Since the establishment of the federal guidelines for "substituted" specimen criteria, there have been an increasing number of specimens that have been reported as substituted — even some that had apparently been collected under direct observation. Many of these met the "substituted" criteria by having creatinine concen-trations and specific gravity levels that were outside the acceptable range. More specifically these are "water-loaded" or "ultra-dilute" specimens.

What is the clinical basis for concluding that a urine specimen meets the current definition of "substituted"? Such a result is the administrative equivalent of an overt "refusal" to be tested or a "positive" drug test.

10.7.6.1 NLCP: State of the Science — Update 1

In February 2000, a technical review was published under the auspices of HHS/SAMHSA, entitled NLCP: "State of the Science – Update #1, Urine Specimen Validity Testing, Evaluation of the Scientific Data Used to Define a Urine Specimen as Substituted." Its purpose was to provide an overview of the published scientific literature that HHS used to develop the criteria for defining a specimen as substituted. The report's conclusion was as follows:

In order for a specimen to be reported as substituted, both creatinine and specific gravity must meet defined criteria; that is, urine creatinine < 5 mg/dl *and* urine specific gravity < 1.001 or > 1.020. This testing requirement provides both an analytical and physiological safeguard. The review of the scientific literature including random clinical studies, medical conditions resulting in severe overhy-dration or polyuria, and water loading studies confirms that the urine criteria of creatinine < 5 mg/dl *and* urine specific gravity < 1.001 or > 1.020 represent a specimen condition that is *not* consistent with normal human urine. In the deductive evaluation of 47 studies, no exception to the criteria defining a "substituted" specimen was reported.

However, the review cannot be interpreted as conclusive evidence that it is not possible for anyone to physiologically produce a "substituted" urine, since none of the studies cited was designed to look specifically at the amount of water it takes to produce a substituted specimen. Theoretical physiology suggests a lower value and nephrologists have more recently advised that on a mathematical basis individuals with low normal serum creatinine values may produce a urine creatinine value slightly below 5 mg/dl.

Later that same year, DOT performed a water-loading study that asked the question: How much water does it take to produce a substituted specimen? Or: How much water can a person consume and still not have a "substituted" specimen?

10.7.6.2 DOT Water Loading Study

The DOT study,[7] entitled "Paired Measurements of Creatinine and Specific Gravity after Water Loading," is more on point. The study used 40 female and 13 male volunteers. The first phase was to simulate the shy bladder procedure. The first morning void was collected; then all volunteers were given 40 oz of fluid and were asked to provide a specimen every hour for the first 3 h and to continue with an additional 40 oz or more over the next 3 h. The volunteers were asked to drink as much as they could. Two participants were unable to consume the minimum amount of fluid intended. On the other hand, 11 participants (5 men and 6 women) consumed more than 1 gal of fluid by the end of their test periods. The bottom line was that none of the 480 specimens were identified as "substituted." The maximal suppression of creatinine values (which is the critical function value) was seen in an individual who had consumed 1.5 gal of water by the 5-h mark. It was reported that the creatinine value approached but was not below 5 mg/dl. Then, interestingly enough, the individual consumed another liter, and in the final hour had an elevated creatinine. Overall, the data showed that many of the volunteers attained levels of specific gravity below the 1.001 threshold value, but did not attain creatinine levels below 5 mg/dl. It, therefore, appeared that individuals cannot consume enough water to have a "substituted" specimen although it may be theoretically possible to do so. The results suggest that it is not physiologically possible to "unintentionally" drink too much water and be confronted with a "refusal to test–substituted specimen." In the absence of a related medical condition, unintentional ingestion of water seems to be as unlikely as passive inhalation of drugs. (Can a person unintentionally drink 1 1/2 gal of water?)

10.7.6.3 FAA Workplace Urine Specimen Validity Testing Colloquium

In light of several witnessed and documented cases of individuals demonstrating a creatinine concentration slightly below 5 mg/dl, the FAA sponsored a "Workplace Urine Specimen Validity Testing Colloquium," February 4–6, 2003. The colloquium was organized in direct response to a Congressional mandate to the FAA to prepare a report on whether there were any particular medical conditions, dietary factors, or individual characteristics that could result in a urine specimen meeting the existing criteria of an adulterated or substituted specimen. Participants included, among others, distinguished toxicologists and specific technical experts from the relevant fields of medicine, science, drug testing, and law. The participants had experience in drug-testing programs, medical, and other related fields. Presentations and discussions centered on the physiological impact of medical issues, working conditions, and dietary habits on validity testing conducted on specimens submitted under the DOT workplace program.

In April 2004, FAA released its report with the following findings and conclusions:

1. Dietary habits, medical issues, and working conditions do not affect the validity of specimens.
2. The validity testing criteria as currently established for adulteration are appropriate.

Only a few substituted specimens are attributed to physiological concentrations of urine creatinine (a compound in urine) below the HHS established value. However, the established value for creatinine is not appropriate for all people.

It made the following recommendations:

1. Substitution: The creatinine level for determining substituted specimens should be lowered to less than 2 mg/dl. This will prevent any individual who can achieve this concentration through normal physiological means from being improperly labeled as providing a substituted urine specimen.
2. Dilution: The current creatinine and specific gravity levels for determining a dilute specimen are adequate. For federally regulated programs, specimens identified as dilute should be tested for drugs at lower cutoff values in order to overcome the efforts of individuals to hide the presence of drugs.
3. Adulteration: The levels established for pH (<3 or >11), chromium VI (cutoff concentration of 20 μg/ml or more) and nitrite (greater than or equal to 500 μg/ml) are satisfactory. However, all laboratory testing for adulterants should include two distinct chemical methods to determine the presence of adulterants in the specimens (i.e., one for initial testing and another to confirm the presence of the adulterant).
4. Role of the Medical Review Officer: Supplement current verification process for assessing individuals' claims that they can produce a specimen meeting the substituted criteria through physiological means. Provide additional guidelines and training for the changes in the verification process.

10.7.7 Adulteration

"Adulterated" is the term used for a specimen that has been altered by the donor in an attempt to defeat the drug test. The donor's goal in this regard is to affect the ability of the laboratory to properly test the specimen for drugs and/or to destroy any drug or drug metabolite that may be present in the specimen.[8–10] Many substances can be used to adulterate a urine specimen *in vitro*, including common household products, commercial chemicals, and commercial products developed specifically for drug test specimen adulteration. Adulterants are therefore readily available, may be easily concealed by the donor during the collection procedure, and can be added to a urine specimen without affecting the temperature or physical appearance of the specimen. To identify adulterated specimens, HHS requires certified laboratories to perform a pH test and a test for one or more oxidizing compounds on all regulated specimens. Laboratories are also allowed to test regulated specimens for any other adulterant, providing they use initial and confirmatory tests that meet the validation and quality control requirements specified by the HHS Guidelines.

An adulterant may interfere with a particular test method or analyte, but not affect others. For example, an adulterant may cause a false-negative marijuana (cannabinoids) result using a particular immunoassay reagent, but not affect the test results for other drugs. The same adulterant may not affect the test results obtained using a different immunoassay reagent or method. It is also possible for an adulterant to cause a false-positive drug test result, rather than the intended false negative. The initial drug test required for federal workplace programs (immunoassay) is more sensitive to adulterants than the required confirmatory drug test (gas chromatography/mass spectrometry, GC/MS). Currently, the GC/MS assays for marijuana metabolite (THCA) and opiates appear to be the most affected.

An adulterated specimen is defined in 49CFRPart 40.3 as "A specimen that contains a substance that is not expected to be present in human urine, or contains a substance expected to be present but is at a concentration so high that it is not consistent with human urine." An adulterated specimen may be reported by the laboratory as having a nitrite concentration that is too high, a pH level that is too high or too low, or identified as having a specific adulterant (such as glutaraldehyde) present.

The reference in the HHS guidelines to a general oxidant test is new. Most adulterants used are oxidizing agents and the early tests for nitrite and chromate were oxidant tests, although specifically named as either nitrite or chromate. Since the general characteristic of the adulterants was that of an oxidant, it is practical to use a comprehensive general test for screening purposes to be followed by specific confirmation tests, rather than do a series of similar and potentially cross-reacting tests to screen for adulterants.

HHS allows certified laboratories to test for any adulterant. It is not possible to provide specific program guidance for all substances that may be used as adulterants; however, HHS has included specific requirements in the Guidelines for pH analysis and for the analysis of some known adulterants that follow:

10.7.7.1 pH

The pH of human urine is usually near neutral (pH 7) although some biomedical conditions affect urine pH. HHS set the program cutoffs for pH based on a physiological range of approximately 4.5 to 9. Specimens with pH results outside this range are reported as invalid. An extremely low pH (i.e., less than 3) or an extremely high pH (i.e., at or above 11) is evidence of an adulterated specimen. Urine specimens that are found to have a pH <3 or >11 can be reported as "Specimen Adulterated: pH is too high (or too low)." The establishment and publication of these threshold limits ends the debate and uncertainty that has surrounded the issue of what is a normal urine pH and what margin of safety should be given to upper and lower levels.

To the average donor who may be contemplating the addition of a chemical substance to his to her urine, acids and bases seem like good choices. Battery acid and Drano have been used and are generally available. Such compounds have a significant impact on the pH of the specimen and include hydrochloric (muriatic) acid used for swimming pools. Commercial adulterants that affect pH include Amber-13 and THC-free. Amber-13 is a sulfur-smelling liquid sold in a glass vial. When 8 ml of Amber-13 is mixed with 50 to 150 ml of water it produces a pH of about 1. Urine will probably buffer this to some degree. THC-Free lists its formulation as water, muriatic acid, potassium chloride, phosphoric acid, and potassium hydrogen phosphate. One vial of THC-Free added to 50 m of urine will produce a pH of between 1 and 2.

10.7.7.2 Nitrite

Nitrite is an oxidizing agent that has been identified in various commercial adulterant products. Nitrite is produced by reduction of nitrate. Nitrite in high concentrations is toxic to humans, especially infants, causing methemoglobinemia by oxidizing the iron in hemoglobin. Nitrate and to a lesser extent nitrite are present in the environment. Nitrite may be normally present in human urine.

There has been a lot of confusion between nitrites and nitrates. It is important to understand the difference between the two compounds.

> *Nitrite* is NO_2 — Nitrites have a therapeutic use as a vasodilator (oral dose = 30 to 60 mg). Inorganic nitrite can be used in treatment of cyanide poisoning (intravenous dose = 300 to 500 mg). One example of an organic nitrite is nitroglycerin. Nitrite is toxic; after accidental ingestion of nitrite, toxic symptoms include weakness, nausea, numbness, shortness of breath, tachycardia, and cyanosis. One reported case of nitrite overdose resulted in a urine concentration of 340 mg/l.
>
> *Nitrate* is NO_3 — Nitrates have a widespread use as fertilizers, which can lead to accumulation in food plants and water supplies.

Both nitrites and nitrates are also used as curing agents in processed meats. They may legally be present in these products in the following concentrations: nitrites up to 200 ppm and nitrates up to 500 ppm. Some pathological conditions (infection, inflammation), medical treatments (cancer), and urinary tract infections may result in nitrites in urine.

In whole blood, nitrite is unstable. Whole-blood nitrite is almost completely converted to nitrate within 1 h. The nitrate that is formed is almost completely excreted in the urine. Normal nitrite concentrations in urine are very low and have been demonstrated in a variety of studies to generally be below 100-200 µg/ml.

Because low levels of nitrite may be present in human urine, HHS set a cutoff level of 500 µg/ml for adulteration and 200 µg/ml for invalid results. These concentrations are well above levels normally seen in human urine. Therefore, normal exposure does not explain a nitrite-adulterated result.

Drug testing laboratories began to study the effects of nitrite in detail when the product Klear came on the market in 1997. A urine specimen would screen positive and then fail confirmation. It would not just fail in the sense that no drug was identified, but it looked like something was destroying all of the organic compounds in the specimen.

Specimens adulterated with Klear were oxidizing THCA during the extraction process. When aliquots to be tested were acidified, the oxidation process exponentially accelerated. The mass ion peaks on the mass spectral chromatograms were absent. There is no drug and there is no internal standard either. The internal standard is a deuterated version of the drug or metabolite being tested. It is added as a control reference for the analysis and its destruction is diagnostic for an oxidizing adulterant.

Some commercial nitrite adulterants include Klear, Whizzies, and Randy's Klear (I). Klear is a product that comes in a small plastic vial containing 500 to 800 mg of white crystals (potassium nitrite). The cost of two tubes is $29.95. Whizzies (sodium nitrite) appears to be a knockoff product of Klear. It is sold as white powder contained in two vials each containing about 850 mg of the compound.

10.7.7.3 Chromium

Chromium exists in a number of chemical states. The zero valence state, Cr^0, is the metallic state. Chromium also exists in nature in a divalent [Cr^{2+}, Cr(II)], trivalent [Cr^{3+}, Cr(III)], and hexavalent [Cr^{6+}, Cr(VI)] state. Understanding the significant differences in the chemistry and toxicology is important in understanding and interpreting adulteration results. The divalent state is very unstable and is rapidly changed to Cr^{3+}. The biologically or toxicologically significant states are the trivalent Cr^{3+} and hexavalent Cr^{6+} states.

Trivalent chromium Cr^{3+} is an essential nutrient in diet. It plays a critical role in maintaining normal glucose tolerance. The trivalent chromium is the species found in the dietary supplement chromium picolinate. It is important to realize that even large doses of chromium picolinate will not produce any hexavalent chromium in the urine. It will, naturally, produce a small amount of trivalent chromium in the urine. A literature review shows levels in the low nanogram range. The highest concentration of trivalent chromium reported was 11 ng/ml. Those individuals took 400 μg/day of chromium picolinate for 3 days.

The hexavalent chromium Cr^{6+} is a strong oxidizing agent. Cr^{6+} is reduced to Cr^{3+}; however, Cr^{3+} is not converted to Cr^{6+}. Cr^{6+} is used in chrome plating, dyes and pigments, leather tanning, and wood preserving. Hexavalent chromium is present in the environment and is a carcinogen. It is a very toxic and irritating compound. In studies that looked at dietary or environmental exposure to hexavalent chromium, the maximum level reported was 690 ng/ml. In this instance, 10 mg/day of Cr^{6+} (in water) were ingested for 3 days. These levels are in stark contrast to what is seen with adulterated urine.

In summary, concentrations of Cr^{3+} in urine are small — in the nanogram per milliliter range. Concentrations of Cr^{6+} found in adulterated urine specimens are large — in the microgram per milliliter range. In addition, the laboratory adulteration assays are specific for Cr^{6+} and do not include Cr^{3+}. Urine concentrations of hexavalent chromium found in adulterated urine specimens exceed the highest toxic case reported. (The case was suicide by ingestion of chromic acid solution; 3 days after ingestion, urine contained 5.13 μg/ml. Death occurred 1 month later from injury.) The HHS reporting cutoff is 50 μg/ml.

Some chromium containing adulterants include Klear II, LL418, Sweet Pee's Spoiler (pyridium chlorochromate), UrineLuck, and Ultra Kleen (chromate).

Pyridinium chlorochromate is a strong oxidizing agent that has been the agent in some commercial adulterants. This compound is identified by urine drug testing laboratories using a confirmatory test for pyridine. Pyridine at any detectable level in a urine specimen is evidence of adulteration.

10.7.7.4 Hydrogen Peroxide and Peroxidase

The commercial adulterant Stealth comes in a packet that contains two plastic vials. One vial contains a tan solid that does not melt. The other vial contains about 1.7 ml of a clear liquid, with a measured pH of 4.5. The user is instructed to pour the solid into the collection cup, add urine, then add the liquid "activator." The tan solid contains a peroxidase, the enzyme that speeds the oxidation process. The liquid contains peroxide. Stealth goes to work quickly and oxidizes the THC metabolites in a matter of hours, then "self-destructs." Hence, the name Stealth.

10.7.7.5 Halogens

Halogens are the four elements fluorine, chlorine, bromine, and iodine. Halogen compounds have been used as adulterants. The term "halogen" (from the Greek *hals*, "salt," and *gennan*, "to form or generate") was given to these elements because they are salt formers. None of the halogens can be found in nature in its elemental form. They are found as salts of the halide ions (F^-, Cl^-, Br^-, and I^-). Fluoride ions are found in minerals. Chloride ions are found in rock salt ($NaCl$), the oceans, and in lakes that have a high salt content. Both bromide and iodide ions are found at low concentrations in the oceans, as well as in brine wells. The assays used by certified laboratories identify halogen compounds that act as oxidants. These do not include the halogen salts that may be present in a urine specimen. The presence of an oxidative halogen in a urine specimen is evidence of adulteration.

Iodine/Iodate is a recent adulterant in the halogen class. Molecular iodine (I_2) is a blue black solid that sublimes. Iodide (I^-) is generally found in the form of potassium or sodium salts (KI, NaI). Iodate (IO_3^-) also appears as potassium or sodium salts (KIO_3, $NaIO_3$) of iodic acid. Iodate is a strong oxidizing agent and is reduced to iodide. Iodide and iodate are used as food and salt additives, in antiradiation products and in thyroid hormones. Normal concentrations are approximately 600 µg/L.

10.7.7.6 Glutaraldehyde

Glutaraldehyde is a clear, colorless liquid with a distinctive pungent odor sometimes compared to rotten apples. One of the first effective commercial adulterants, UrinAid, was found to contain glutaraldehyde. Glutaraldehyde is used as a sterilizing agent and disinfectant, leather tanning agent, tissue fixative, embalming fluid, resin or dye intermediate, and cross-linking agent. It is also used in X-ray film processing, in the preparation of dental materials, and surgical grafts. Glutaraldehyde reacts quickly with body tissues and is rapidly excreted. The most common effect of overexposure to glutaraldehyde is irritation of the eyes, nose, throat, and skin. It can also cause asthma and allergic reactions of the skin.

Glutaraldehyde does not normally occur in urine and is readily detectable. It will interfere with the immunochemical screening tests. It may also interfere with the recovery of the drug in GC/MS analysis or it may destroy the metabolite. It is interesting to note that, although this product is sold as a way to guarantee a negative in the urine of marijuana users, it affects the analysis of other drugs as well. It has a chemical aldehyde smell and it will denature proteins in the urine, so that over a 1- or 2-day period of time a brown precipitate will appear. No matter what the preliminary basis may be for suspecting adulteration of a specimen by glutaraldehyde, the presence of glutaraldehyde should be confirmed by reliable chemical analysis such as GC/MS. Glutaraldehyde at any detectable level in a urine specimen is evidence of adulteration.

Clear Choice is another adulterant containing glutaraldehyde and squalene.

10.7.7.7 Other Chemicals and Household Products

Surfactants, including ordinary detergents, have been used to adulterate urine specimens. Surfactants have a particular molecular structure made up of a hydrophilic and a hydrophobic component. They greatly reduce the surface tension of water when used in very low concentrations.

Foaming agents, emulsifiers, and dispersants are surfactants that suspend an immiscible liquid or a solid, respectively, in water or some other liquid.

> Liquid Soap: Reported to cause false negatives in EIA procedures for THC and PCP. Its addition increases the pH of the specimen. A commercial adulterant called Mary Jane SuperClean 13 was reported to be primarily soap.
>
> Sodium Chloride: Reported to cause false negative in EIA procedures. Its addition increases the specific gravity and chloride ion content of the specimen.
>
> Bleach: Reported to cause a false negative in EIA procedures for all five drugs tested for by SAMHSA and in FPIA procedures for all but cocaine.
>
> Drano: Reported to cause false negatives in EIA procedures. Its addition increases the pH of the specimen.
>
> Sodium Bicarbonate: Reported to cause false negatives in EIA procedures for opiates and PCP. Its addition increases the pH of the specimen.

10.7.8 The Invalid Result

HHS describes an invalid result as follows:

> When a laboratory is unable to obtain a valid drug test result or when drug or specimen validity tests indicate a possible unidentified adulterant, the laboratory reports the specimen to the MRO as "invalid result."

This definition is not a comprehensive. Invalid results also include a category of specimens that can be described as having suspect or abnormal characteristics, such as pH out of the normal range, high nitrite levels, or unusual creatinine and specific gravity levels. It is true that "invalid" results can indicate a possible unidentified adulterant or substitution and that many invalid results could not be physiologically possible. But in many cases there is just an absence of conclusive scientific evidence that the specimen is not physiologically possible, and/or that the analytical method is not definitive, precise, or valid enough to withstand legal challenge.

When an MRO receives an "invalid" specimen report, it is incumbent upon him or her to discuss with the laboratory whether additional tests should be performed by the laboratory or by another certified laboratory. It may be possible to obtain definitive drug test results for the specimen using a different drug test method or to confirm adulteration using additional specimen validity tests. The choice of the second laboratory or additional tests will be dependent on the suspect adulterant and the validated characteristics of the different drug test. Laboratory staff should be knowledgeable of their tests' validated characteristics including effects of known interfering substances, and be able to recommend whether additional testing is worthwhile.

The current HHS specimen validity rules require screening of specimens for oxidants, but do not require the laboratory to confirm the screening results. The rationale is that requiring specific confirmation methods for a broad class of defined and undefined adulterants would represent a significant cost increase in laboratory services. The majority of laboratories have decided not to bother with confirming oxidant results, and simply report the screening results as "invalid." Somewhat unanticipated is that even laboratories that were confirming common oxidants such as nitrites have withdrawn from this practice. The specimen validity rule requires the laboratories to have more comprehensive and definitive confirmatory procedures for nitrites. This likely requires the acquisition of additional laboratory equipment. In addition, there is significant time involved in confirming results of any type. In the wake of increased litigation, there are lingering liability concerns at the laboratories. The end result is that only a small number of laboratories perform confirmatory procedures for nitrites and other oxidants as required by the current rules.

So today there have evolved three conceptual categories of laboratory results: the positive (drug, adulterated, and/or substituted), the invalid (everything in between), and the negative (dilute and non-dilute). Each requires the focus and attention of the laboratory and the MRO.

10.8 THE ROLE OF THE MEDICAL REVIEW OFFICER IN WORKPLACE DRUG TESTING

Joseph A. Thomasino, M.D., M.S., FACPM
JAT MRO, Inc., Jacksonville, Florida

10.8.1 The MRO as the "Gatekeeper" of the Workplace Drug Testing Program

A Medical Review Officer (MRO) has come to be defined in U.S. Department of Transportation (DOT) regulations (i.e., 49 CFR Part 40) as a licensed physician (Doctor of Medicine or Osteopathy) who is knowledgeable about and has clinical experience in controlled substance abuse disorders, including detailed knowledge of alternative medical explanations for laboratory confirmed drug test results. The MRO has become an integral part of the workplace drug testing process as federal regulations for workplace drug testing have been developed and implemented, at first for drug testing of federal employees, and then for millions of other workers in private industry for which drug testing was mandated by federal agencies such as the U.S. DOT, The U.S. Coast Guard, and the Nuclear Regulatory Commission. Beginning in the mid-1980s the MRO has been involved in an ever-growing number of drug tests. Federal regulatory requirements for workplace drug testing have expanded and these regulations have further defined and broadened the role of the MRO in the process. Programs for workplace drug testing requiring medical review have been implemented by various states (e.g., Florida, Georgia, others) in connection with worker compensation programs. Some states have required medical review of all workplace drug tests results collected in those states (e.g., Oklahoma and New York). Increasing numbers of private employers have been implementing drug testing programs that include medical review of results absent any regulatory requirement to do so. Although originally all workplace drug testing programs involved the collection of urine drug testing specimens, and most still do, other sampling media including hair, blood, saliva, sweat, and others are beginning to be accepted and used in workplace drug testing programs. All of these factors have led to the emergence of the MRO as the "gatekeeper" of the workplace drug testing process.

The identification of the MRO as the "gatekeeper" in the workplace drug testing process was first made in DOT regulations. It is an apt characterization of the overall role of the MRO in this process. One way to conceptualize this role is to consider that the MRO is an "equity agent." In a sense the MRO oversees all the elements of the process. The MRO ensures that the donor (i.e., the individual providing the drug testing specimen) has had the specimen collected properly, that it has been analyzed correctly, that the result has been reported to the MRO promptly and clearly, that alternative medical explanations for any positive or other non-negative results where appropriate have been sought, that the donor's technical questions have been answered and the donor's response to an adverse determination (e.g., a reconfirmation test, substance abuse professional evaluation, etc.) has been facilitated, and that a prompt and clear report of the final determination/verification has been made to the employer or other organization commissioning the drug test. By performing the above functions in reviewing each drug test the MRO helps confer legitimacy and fairness to a process that can become contentious as serious sanctions are often applied to donors with verified non-negative results. A verified positive result, or a determination that the donor has refused to provide an adequate specimen for drug testing, may result in denial or termination of employment, loss of other benefits, or other adverse outcomes for the donor. Thus the role of the MRO in allowing the donor due process to explain properly collected and technically valid drug testing results before an adverse determination is made has become vital in maintaining the integrity, value, and effectiveness of workplace drug testing programs.

10.8.2 The MRO and the Collection Process

Proper collection of drug testing specimens is the first and arguably the most critical step in the implementation of any workplace drug testing program. Important in this is that chain-of-custody procedures be established and followed in collecting drug testing specimens. Given the serious consequences for the donor that often follow adverse determinations, and the concomitant risk for the organization commissioning the test in applying those consequences inappropriately, it is clear that before becoming involved in the review of any drug test the MRO must be sure that appropriate chain of custody procedures were followed in the collection and further handling of the specimen as it is transported to and analyzed at the laboratory. Strict adherence to the appropriate collection protocol with close attention to properly establishing, maintaining, and documenting the chain of custody for each specimen is therefore vital to the overall success of any drug testing program.

The MRO is rarely, if ever, actually present at the time any specimen is collected. In most instances the MRO does not actually know, and has never met the collector for any given specimen. Therefore as the "gatekeeper" of the process the MRO must rely on review of the chain of custody and control form (CCF) that has been completed by the collector and the donor at the time the specimen is collected. Needless to say, prompt provision of a legible copy of the CCF to the MRO by the collector is absolutely vital for the proper management and promulgation of any drug testing program. Practically speaking, assuring that a legible copy of the CCF for each specimen is obtained as rapidly as possible after a specimen has been collected is a major activity for the MRO and staff. The success of most MRO practices, and the ability to gain and maintain clients by the MRO, is largely determined by how rapidly the MRO is able to provide reports of final determination/verification to the organization commissioning a test, once a test has been collected.

Once received, the CCF for each specimen is reviewed by the MRO or staff to ensure that it is legible and that it has been appropriately completed by the collector and the donor. The legible, properly completed CCF is then matched with the result received from the laboratory and the MRO and/or staff complete the review and make report to the organization commissioning the test. Any deficiencies in the CCF should be corrected, if possible, by the MRO before the final determination is made. Often deficiencies will have been detected and corrected by the laboratory before the result is reported to the MRO. However, if it becomes apparent that the laboratory has failed to detect or correct a deficiency it falls to the MRO to do so.

Certain flaws on the CCF are "fatal." The most common of these are quantity of specimen insufficient for testing; no collector printed name or collector signature in the collector certification portion of the CCF; tamper-evident seal broken or missing on the specimen container upon arrival at the laboratory; and donor identification on the specimen container not matching the donor identification on the CCF submitted with the specimen. When these "fatal" deficiencies or flaws are detected the laboratory will not perform the analysis. When this condition is reported to the MRO the final determination/verification must be that the test was canceled due to the flaw. However, for other deficiencies, if the laboratory has not corrected them, the MRO must do so. These include, among others, a CCF on which the collector's name is printed but the collector has failed to sign that section of CCF in which the collector certifies that the specimen was submitted by the donor in question and that the specimen was collected, labeled, and sealed in accordance with the appropriate protocol; the certifying scientist has failed to sign the laboratory copy of the CCF when reporting the result (this becomes apparent to the MRO only in the case of a non-negative result for which the laboratory copy of the CCF must be provided to and reviewed by the MRO prior to making a final determination/verification); and times and/or dates on the CCF missing or contradictory. There is at least one flaw or deficiency that cannot ordinarily be corrected by the laboratory prior to analysis. This is failure of the donor to sign that section of the CCF in which the donor certifies that the specimen was actually submitted by the donor, that it has not been adulterated or tampered with, that the specimen container was sealed with a tamper-evident seal in the donor's presence, and that the information on the CCF and the label affixed to the specimen container is correct. As the laboratory ordinarily does not receive a copy of the CCF that bears the donor's signature, it is the MRO's responsibility to check for and correct this deficiency when it arises. Unless the collector has noted in the remarks section of the CCF that the donor has refused to sign, or that the collector forgot to have the donor sign before leaving the collection site, an attempt should be made to correct the flaw. This flaw, like other flaws that can be corrected, is corrected by having the collector sign an affidavit, certificate of correction, or memorandum for record (these are synonymous terms). This document should indicate that despite the flaw, the specimen was, in fact, submitted by the donor in question, the specimen was otherwise collected, handled, and transported to the laboratory properly, and that this is a true and accurate statement on the part of the collector. Once the properly executed document is received by the MRO it is maintained with the other documentation for the specimen, and review proceeds as for any other specimen. If the deficiency is not corrected in a reasonable time, usually considered to be no more than 1 to 2 weeks from when the flaw was detected and the certificate of correction was presented to the collector, the specimen is reported as canceled due to the uncorrected flaw.

When "fatal" or uncorrected flaws result in the cancellation of a specimen, it is the responsibility of the MRO to document and point this out to the collector in question, urge the collector to ensure that the situation is not repeated, and suggest that if additional training or education is needed to address the situation and prevent recurrences that it be promptly obtained by the collector. Even minor deficiencies or administrative mistakes that do not cause cancellation of the test, or require formal correction per se, in order to make a final determination/verification, should be documented and pointed out to the collector for corrective action. Errors of this sort that have no significant adverse effect on the donor's ability to have a fair and accurate drug test include among others: failure of the collector to indicate whether the specimen temperature was read within 4 min of collection and/or whether or not the temperature was within range; minor mistakes in recording the donor identification number on the CCF; reason for test inappropriate or unmarked on the CCF; failure to directly observe a specimen in instances where observation was called for; and delay in the collection process.

By careful review of the CCF for each specimen the MRO helps ensure the integrity of the collection process, and by extension the entire drug testing process, as proper collection is the foundation of any successful workplace drug testing program. By correcting deficiencies that are detected and making collectors aware of them, the MRO strengthens and fosters this most important element of workplace drug testing programs.

10.8.3 The MRO and the Analytical Laboratory

In a sense the MRO is one of the main "customers" of the analytical laboratory performing toxicological testing in the drug testing process. Although the organization commissioning the test may actually originally arrange for and pay for drug testing, in most instances the analytical laboratory reports results directly to the MRO who makes a final verification of the results before reporting them to the organization commissioning the test that has engaged the MRO for this purpose. In most instances where an organization has engaged an MRO the organization is not made aware of the laboratory confirmed result by the laboratory and the laboratory will not reveal the laboratory confirmed result to the organization, insisting that the MRO report all results to the organization. This arrangement is required for federally mandated testing and by some state-sponsored testing programs, e.g., in Florida. In other states either all results or only laboratory confirmed positive results (e.g., in Maryland), must be reviewed by the MRO before they are reported to the organization commissioning the test. Therefore, in practice, the MRO and staff usually develop close working relationships with their counterparts at the analytical laboratories, i.e., the toxicologists, certifying scientists, and client service representatives. This is necessary to ensure prompt receipt of results by the MRO once analysis has been completed and for the MRO and staff to clarify and fully understand all aspects of the laboratory report.

As the "gatekeeper" in the drug testing process the MRO has a responsibility to correct any flaws in the testing process that may be discovered on the part of the analytical laboratory before making a final determination for any given test result. Failure of the certifying scientist to provide necessary documentation (e.g., the properly completed laboratory copy of the CCF for non-negative results on federal testing), failure of the certifying scientist to sign or otherwise fully and properly complete necessary documentation, and correction of flaws in the collection process not detected by the analytical laboratory prior to release of results to the MRO are examples of this.

The MRO has a responsibility to ensure that all aspects of the laboratory report are understood before making a final verification. This is particularly important when invalid drug test results are reported by the laboratory. In these instances, where for a variety of technical reasons the toxicologist does not feel that a reliable analysis can be made (e.g., presence of an interfering substance the exact nature of which is unknown, urine specimen colored blue or having some other unusual color or appearance, urine creatinine low with normal specific gravity, among others), the MRO must interview the donor to establish whether or not a legitimate medical explanation can be established to explain these circumstances. It is incumbent on the MRO to fully understand why the specimen was deemed unsuitable for analysis rendering the invalid result, and to consult with appropriate laboratory personnel in this regard, so as to properly direct the interview with the donor. Similarly, there are instances where it is not clear to the MRO whether a donor's explanation for any non-negative result would in fact explain the result. The MRO can and should consult with appropriate laboratory personnel in these instances and make reliance on the information and guidance they provide in these matters.

Finally, the MRO often has a responsibility to offer the donor the option to have a drug testing specimen with a non-negative result sent to a different analytical laboratory for reconfirmation testing after an adverse determination has been made for that result by the MRO. This is required for federally mandated drug testing, by some state sponsored drug testing programs, by state law in some states, and as a matter of organizational policy for some organizations commissioning drug testing. As the "gatekeeper" of this process, if a specimen fails to reconfirm for the result in question, the MRO has a responsibility to then amend the final determination/verification for that specimen. The MRO must also notify the donor and the organization commissioning the test of this, and depending on the type of testing, e.g., federally mandated, state sponsored, etc., may also have to make a report to a governmental or other body overseeing the drug testing process. Such a report may have serious consequences for the analytical laboratory found to have reported a "false positive" or other erroneous result in terms of the laboratory's ability to continue to provide drug testing services.

In practice the MRO and staff must develop and maintain good communications and close working relationships with their counterparts at the analytical laboratories. This is essential for the proper conduct of any drug testing program.

10.8.4 The MRO and the Verification of Drug Testing Results

The primary role of the MRO in workplace drug testing programs has always been to verify the results of the drug tests collected. When federally mandated drug testing programs were first implemented in the 1980s it was considered essential that donors with laboratory-confirmed positive drug testing results be afforded an opportunity to confidentially provide a legitimate alternative medical examination, if one existed, before the commissioning organization learned of the result. In the event that a legitimate alternative medical explanation could be established, the laboratory-confirmed positive result would be "downgraded," i.e., reported as negative to the commissioning organization by the MRO in such a way that it would appear to be no different from any other laboratory-confirmed negative result. As part of allowing "due process" before sanctions were applied to the donor as a result of a laboratory-confirmed positive result, the role of the MRO as the finder of fact, interpreter of information offered, and maker of the final determination was conceived.

A large portion of the time an MRO devotes to MRO practice is spent conducting and interpreting the results of interviews conducted with donors with laboratory-confirmed non-negative results. Originally, these were individuals with laboratory-confirmed positive results for the five drugs or classes of drugs tested for in federally mandated testing, i.e., amphetamine and methamphetamine, cocaine metabolites, marijuana metabolites, opiates (specifically codeine, morphine, and 6-acetylmorphine), and phencyclidine. As non-federally regulated drug testing programs were implemented, expanded, and in some cases tailored to the needs of individual organizations, other substances including alcohol, barbiturates, benzodiazepines, methadone, methaqualone, other opiates, propoxyphene, and others have been included in workplace drug testing programs, and naturally the MRO has had to deal with laboratory-confirmed positive results for these as well. In this process the MRO confidentially conducts and documents the interview; explains the result to the donor and the MRO's role in the process; allows the donor the opportunity to present an explanation; gives the donor reasonable time to develop and provide any evidence supporting any explanation offered; and promptly reviews, interprets, confirms, and verifies any information received before making the final determination/verification.

Besides laboratory-confirmed positive results, other non-negative results have also come to require an interview of the donor and interpretation of information gathered prior to verification by the MRO. For federally mandated testing, urine specimens that have been adulterated with a foreign substance that can be specifically and reliably identified are reported as such to the MRO by the laboratory. The MRO conducts an interview to determine if a legitimate alternative medical explanation can be established for the presence of the adulterant in the specimen. If this cannot be established, the result is reported as a "refusal to test" to the organization commissioning the test with resultant sanctions applied to the donor as prescribed in federal regulations. For federally mandated testing, urine specimens with extremely low creatinine levels (i.e., 2 mg/dl or less) and specific gravity of 1.001 or less or 1.020 or greater are reported as substituted (i.e., not consistent with normal human urine) to the MRO. Similar to adulterated specimens, for substituted specimens the MRO must also conduct an interview to determine if a legitimate alternative medical explanation can be established to explain these abnormal creatinine and specific gravity values. If it appears to the MRO that such an explanation may exist, the donor is then required to demonstrate under observed and controlled conditions that urine with these abnormal characteristics can once again be produced. The MRO reviews the results of this procedure in making the final determination. Once again, failure to establish an acceptable explanation or to demonstrate the production of urine meeting these criteria under observed and controlled circumstances will result in a final verification of the result and report to the commissioning organization as a "refusal to test." Invalid drug test results, as discussed above, also require an interview with the donor. In these if a legitimate alternative medical explanation can be established, the result is simply verified as canceled with no further action required unless a negative result is required (on federally mandated testing this is for pre-employment, return to duty, or follow-up testing). If a legitimate alternative medical explanation cannot be established, the test is verified as canceled but on federally mandated testing the organization commissioning the test is informed that an immediate re-collection directly observed by an individual of the same sexual gender as the donor must be conducted with minimal advance notice to the donor.

There are some additional circumstances that require review by the MRO of information not gathered directly from the donor or provided by the analytical laboratory. Results of evaluations conducted in response to substituted specimens were mentioned above. For opiate positive results (i.e., codeine or morphine) the MRO in some circumstances (6-acetylmorphine negative, and codeine or morphine level less than 15,000 ng/ml on federally mandated urine drug testing) the MRO must have clinical evidence of opioid abuse before making a final determination/verification that the test is positive. This involves in some cases a "hands on" physical examination conducted by the MRO, or review by the MRO of an examination conducted by another physician acceptable to the MRO, to establish whether or not there is clinical evidence of opioid abuse (e.g., needle marks or tracks, disturbance of the sensorium, neurological abnormalities, etc.) before making the final determination/verification. Individuals who do not provide sufficient urine for testing even when provided extra time and fluids to do so are putatively demonstrating so-called "shy bladder." In these cases, on federally mandated testing, the donor is required to undergo an examination by the MRO or other qualified physician acceptable to the MRO to establish whether or not an ascertainable physiologic condition (e.g., a urinary system dysfunction) or a documented preexisting psychological disorder had or with a high degree of probability could have prevented the donor from providing a sufficient quantity of urine for testing. The MRO must review the results of this evaluation, seriously consider the opinion of the examiner if the examination was conducted by another, and render a final determination. If there is an acceptable explanation established as a result of the examination the test is verified as canceled unless a negative result is required; if there is no acceptable explanation established it is reported as a "refusal to test." On federally mandated testing where a negative result is required and the test is canceled due to an established legitimate explanation, an additional examination of the donor is required to establish whether not clinical evidence of illicit drug use also exists. The results of this examination, conducted once again either by the MRO or another physician acceptable to the MRO, are reviewed by the MRO and a final determination is rendered. This evaluation may also include drug testing using another medium such as blood, saliva, hair, etc. If there is no evidence of illicit drug use, the test is verified as negative and is so reported to the organization commissioning the test. If there is evidence of illicit drug use, the test is reported as canceled and the evidence of illicit drug use is also reported to the organization commissioning the test.

Although the personal focus of the MRO is naturally on non-negative results, the vast majority of results reviewed by the MRO and staff are negative. The MRO has a responsibility to ensure that negative results are also properly reviewed and promptly verified and reported as negative. The concerns expressed above concerning collection and laboratory issues apply to negative results as well. Regular, periodic review by the MRO of negative results verified by staff is required for federally mandated testing, and is an essential element of good MRO practice in general.

The heart of the MRO's practice and professional responsibility is timely, accurate, and equitable review, verification, and reporting of drug testing results. The integrity, credibility, and success of this vital public safety and health program depend on the responsible and proper performance of this function by professionals dedicated to it.

10.8.5 The MRO and Safety Issues

Often, during the interviews conducted for non-negative results, the MRO will be informed by the donor, or will otherwise learn through other information provided as part of this process, of a condition the donor is suffering or a medication the donor is taking, that either renders the donor medically unqualified for safety-sensitive work in terms of the federal regulation in response to which drug testing is being conducted or which otherwise poses a potential safety hazard to the worker, co-workers, or the general public. Many of these federal regulations, e.g., those of the DOT, require the MRO to report these circumstances to the employer or other organization commissioning the drug test, without the consent of the donor. Some state-sponsored drug testing programs, e.g., the Florida Drug-Free Workplace Program, include similar provisions. In general, it is common for the MRO to feel obligated to report such circumstances to the organization commissioning drug testing even when not required or encouraged to do so by any extant federal or state law, regulation, or guideline.

Obviously, such a report will usually have serious consequences for the donor as it may result in the donor being prohibited from performing all or part of the donor's work duties until the situation is resolved. DOT regulations, for example, currently require the MRO to report the safety issue to the employer. However, these regulations also require the MRO to instruct the donor that if additional information is provided to the MRO in a timely fashion from the donor's treating health practitioner that modifies the situation the MRO must then share that with the employer for the employer's further consideration of the matter. A similar approach may be adopted by the MRO for non-federally mandated testing in an attempt to resolve these potentially serious and often contentious issues.

This issue has been complicated by the Health Insurance Portability and Accountability Act (HIPAA). Some information obtained during the MRO interview or other portions of the drug testing process may be considered "protected health information" and therefore under HIPAA would require specific consent or authorization from the donor before it was released by the MRO to the organization commissioning the test. The DOT has opined that such information gathered as part of the drug testing regulated by that agency is exempt from the provisions of HIPAA, and that the MRO, and other service providers, need no consent or authorization to release information gathered during this process in accordance with the federal regulation. However, for state-sponsored programs, or other non-federally mandated testing, it is not at all clear that "protected health information" gathered during the process of drug testing can be released by the MRO or other service providers to the organization commissioning the test in the absence of the consent or authorization of the donor without running afoul of HIPAA. In some states, for example, Maryland, certain information gathered as part of the drug testing process cannot be released to the organization commissioning the test without the donor's consent or authorization as a matter of state law, over and above any requirements imposed by HIPAA. Until this issue is clarified, and in some states regardless of any interpretations or modifications of HIPAA, it would appear most prudent for the MRO to obtain specific written consent from the donor before releasing "protected health information" to the organization commissioning the test, unless as is the case for DOT testing the issue has been specifically and definitively addressed. In practice, this may be accomplished *ad hoc* on a case-by-case basis as the need arises, or by advising the organization commissioning the test to require an appropriate written consent or authorization be executed by the donor before drug testing is performed.

10.8.6 The MRO and Other Administrative Functions in Workplace Drug Testing

The MRO may be called upon to perform a number of administrative functions beyond simply reviewing and reporting of results.

As discussed above, additional examinations of donors may be required before the MRO can make a final determination/verification in certain instances. For federally mandated testing donors with shy bladders (i.e., not able to produce a sufficient quantity of urine for testing), donors whose inability to produce a sufficient quantity of urine for testing is due to a permanent or long-term condition and for whom a negative result is required (i.e., on pre-employment, follow-up, or return to duty testing), those with adulterated or substituted specimens under certain circumstances, and donors for whom clinical evidence of opioid abuse must be obtained, will require the MRO to approve of the selection of the referral physician other than the MRO for these examinations, and in some instances help either the organization commissioning the test or the donor to locate a suitable examiner.

On federally mandated testing the MRO has a responsibility to cooperate with the Substance Abuse Professional (SAP) working with a donor for whom the MRO has verified a result as positive, or refusal to test. The MRO must also provide available information that the SAP requests, e.g., quantitative test results, information gathered during the MRO interview, etc.

The requirement on federally mandated testing for the MRO to report medical information to the organization commissioning the test that is likely to result in the donor being determined to be medically unqualified for safety-sensitive duties, or otherwise indicates that continued performance of safety-sensitive duties by the donor is like to pose a significant safety risk, has also been mentioned above. Prompt sharing of additional information received from the donor's physician that might modify such a situation with the organization commissioning the test is an important administrative function the MRO is called upon to perform.

For all forms of testing the MRO has a responsibility to preserve the confidentiality of all information gathered and maintain records of MRO activities for varying periods of time depending upon regulatory requirements, state laws, contractual obligations, and professional guidelines. The MRO may also be called upon to provide these records to individual donors and produce them in various court or other legal or administrative proceedings.

Finally, in practice, the MRO is often called upon as a general consultant source for all matters dealing with drug and alcohol testing, not only by employers, but also by labor organizations and individual donors with concerns about drug testing. The MRO may be called upon by the organization commissioning the test to help arrange and review specialized toxicological testing tailored to some particular circumstance or situation in the workplace. Perhaps the most important administrative function for the MRO is to be knowledgeable and available to employers and donors to address their questions and concerns so as to support the integrity and credibility of the drug testing process.

10.8.7 Emerging Issues for the MRO

A number of issues are currently emerging that will affect MRO practice. These include specimen validity issues, alternative testing matrices, expanding the scope of toxicological testing on federally mandated and other testing, and on-site testing.

Concerns have been raised as to the level of creatinine in the urine that when present with a specific gravity of 1.001 or less or 1.020 or greater is to be considered evidence of a substituted specimen, not consistent with normal human urine, and thus exposing the donor to sanctions if such a specimen is verified as a refusal to test on this basis. Formerly this level was 5 mg/dl or less. However, quite recently, in response to scientific review of this issue and demonstrated ability on the part of donors to produce creatinine levels of 3 to 4 mg/dl simply by ingesting fluids, with no underlying physiologic disorder, DOT has lowered the level at which the specimen is to be considered substituted by the MRO to 2 mg/dl. Formerly, negative specimens were considered substituted with levels of creatinine between 2 and 5 mg/dl. These required the MRO to interview the donor, and in the absence of conditions that would lead the MRO to believe there was a reasonable probability that such levels of creatinine and specific gravity could be produced physiologically by the donor, verify the result as a refusal to test. These are now to be verified by the MRO as negative and dilute with the requirement that the specimen be re-collected immediately under direct observation by an observer of the same gender as the donor. This issue will continue to be controversial and additional changes to the approach to the problem of ultradilute specimens may very well be forthcoming as experience and research expand. Needless to say, any such changes are bound to affect MRO practice.

As noted above, urine has been the traditional medium or matrix for drug testing. Most workplace drug testing programs still collect urine. Currently, federally mandated alcohol testing utilizes breath or oral fluid (i.e., saliva) specimens. At present, for federally mandated drug testing only urine specimens may be collected, with the exception of instances where the donor is unable to produce sufficient urine for testing due to a permanent or long-term medical condition and a negative result is required. However, additional matrices are emerging that are gaining greater acceptance and wider use. Blood has always been available, but the invasive collection method and the greater expenses involved have relegated it to a very minor role in workplace drug testing programs. More recently, hair testing has been implemented in a number of state-sponsored (e.g., Florida) or other unregulated programs. Oral fluid testing is being offered by analytical laboratories for unregulated testing and some companies are starting to adopt it. On the horizon are other matrices, including sweat, that may also emerge as practical media for drug testing. The MRO will have to become familiar with the pitfalls and nuances of interpretation of results obtained from these alternative matrices.

The scope of workplace drug testing has largely been confined to the ten drugs or classes of drugs mentioned above. However, changes in the drug of choice of some members of industrial populations over time are being noted and calls for an expansion of the drugs tested for on regulated and unregulated testing are being increasingly made by employers and other organizations commissioning testing. At present there is pressure to include methylenedioxymethamphetamine (MDMA or "ecstasy"), gamma-hydroxybutyric acid (GHB or "Georgia home boy"), Rohypnol (flunitrazepam or "the date rape drug"), OxyContin (oxycodone), and others in standard drug testing panels. Obviously as the scope of drug testing expands this will increase the challenges faced by the MRO.

Workplace drug testing has traditionally been based on collecting a specimen at or near the workplace. The specimen is then sent to an analytical laboratory distant from the workplace. The results of the analysis have then been reported to the MRO who has reviewed them before they are released to the employer or other organization commissioning the test. Currently, federally mandated drug testing must be done in this way. However, new systems of testing have been developed that permit reading of the result immediately after collection at the workplace. In practice, most organizations performing this on-site drug testing will immediately act on negative results without any further testing, e.g., permitting a pre-placement applicant to begin work immediately, etc. Specimens demonstrating non-negative results upon on-site testing are usually sent to an analytical laboratory for confirmatory testing. If results are confirmed as non-negative, definitive action is then taken in response to the confirmatory testing done off-site. The accuracy, sensitivity, and specificity of the various on-site testing systems currently available vary, and approach the accuracy, sensitivity, and specificity of traditional analytical laboratory testing to varying degrees depending on the system used. Depending on the design of the system there may be no role at all for the MRO in the review of negative results of on-site testing, with MRO review being reserved for non-negative results that are confirmed as non-negative as described above. To what degree and in what fashion the MRO is to be integrated in on-site testing will obviously be of great interest as use of on-site testing grows.

10.9 QUALITY PRACTICES IN WORKPLACE TESTING

John M. Mitchell, Ph.D. and Francis M. Esposito, Ph.D.
Health Science Unit, Science and Engineering Group, RTI International, Research Triangle Park, North Carolina

10.9.1 History

The roots of workplace drug testing lie in the U.S. military's drug testing program. The military began drug testing military personnel in response to the rise in drug abuse that accompanied the Vietnam War. Initially, it was designed to identify "at risk" individuals and to present an opportunity for treatment. By 1980, drug abuse in the U.S. military was rampant. A survey found that approximately 50% of enlisted personnel had used illicit drugs within the past 10 days.[1] It was obvious that more stringent measures were necessary. At first, the military turned to the resources available in the civilian laboratory community, but it soon recognized that the methodologies available for the testing of the large number of specimens needed to support military goals were woefully inadequate. A taskforce consisting of civilian advisors, testing industry representatives, and military personnel was organized to develop a system that would allow testing of large numbers of urine specimens in a forensically defensible manner. It was through these measures that modern-day forensic urine drug testing laboratories were created. These efforts are notable, because the military system established the basis for legal and scientific acceptance of the methods and procedures utilized in today's workplace drug testing. Important innovations in the military's program include random testing of personnel and instrumented on-site testing. This integrated program resulted in a reduction in drug use by enlisted personnel such that by 1982 a survey found that the number of personnel who used drugs in the past 30 days had dropped to less than 30%. By 1988, the number dropped to less than 10%.[2]

The military drug testing program was built upon the experience obtained from mass testing of biological samples in the clinical laboratory and forensic principles. While the primary purpose of the military's program was to maintain national security by removing personnel who were abusing drugs, it incorporated a quality system to protect service members from inaccurate results. The quality system that provided reliable testing included: observed collection of urine specimens, written standard operating procedures (SOPs), separate testing methods for initial and confirmatory tests, mass screening with immunoassay tests, confirmation of immunoassay positives by gas chromatography/mass spectrometry detector (GC/MS), utilization of deuterated analytes as internal standards for GC/MS procedures, internal and external quality control systems, independent assessment of laboratory performance by a team of experienced scientists, and the right of an accused to have a portion of the specimen retested.

Workplace programs mandated by the federal government and many state governments have incorporated most of the quality assurance components from the military's system. One component, routine observed collections, has not been incorporated into these systems, and this omission has proved to be a problem for "urine only" based workplace programs. Unobserved collections have fostered an industry dedicated to the subversion of these programs by the provision of synthetic urine, negative human urine, prosthetic devices for the delivery of substitution products, oxidants, fixatives, peroxidases, acids, bases, and other substances that are intended to interfere with the testing methods.

10.9.2   The Need for Quality Assurance

The necessity for maintaining quality in current workplace drug testing programs becomes apparent when the potential impact of this testing is considered. In 2002, laboratories certified by the Department of Health and Human Services (HHS) tested an estimated 6 million urine specimens collected from donors under federal mandate and an additional estimated 23 million specimens collected under other workplace programs (source: data supplied by federally regulated laboratories that participate in the National Laboratory Certification Program, NLCP). With estimated positive rates of 2.5% in regulated programs and 4.8% in nonregulated programs,[3] this would mean that in 2002, these laboratories reported an estimated 1 million results consistent with drug use. In order that innocent individuals do not lose their jobs, and are not denied gainful employment or placed under suspicion of drug use, the goal for quality assurance (QA) in workplace testing programs must be zero tolerance for errors. In the following sections, we review the parts of workplace drug testing programs that are critical to success, examine the programs and methods currently in place to measure the quality of the system, and provide some suggestions for future measurements.

10.9.3   Parts of the Workplace Drug Testing Quality System

To obtain a goal of zero errors, the quality system must encompass all parts of the workplace drug testing program. The people, the equipment and instruments, the materials, the methods, and the facilities utilized in all phases of the program must be considered.

10.9.3.1   The Employer

In workplace drug testing, the quality system begins and ends with the employer. Without proper planning, training, and guidance, the program developed by an employer may not meet the requirements mandated by law and other guidelines. The choices an employer makes in selecting collection sites, testing facilities, and Medical Review Officers (MROs) will undoubtedly influence program effectiveness. While cost is a consideration in making these selections, it should not be the only factor considered. It is important that each test result be supported by proper collection, accurate and legally supportable testing, and appropriate determination of drug abuse. Without these elements, the actions taken by the employer as a result of a drug test may not be in accordance with the law or other guidance, may place the employer in jeopardy, and may wrongly accuse a valued employee or a qualified candidate for employment.

10.9.3.2   The Donor

The donor is an important part of the quality process, but the controls that can be placed on the donor are limited in most programs by considerations of privacy and personal rights. While most donors are conscientious and trustworthy, the quality system must limit the opportunity for a small drug-using minority to subvert the test by substituting their specimen with another urine or other aqueous solution, diluting their specimen by adding water or drinking large amounts of water before collection, or adulterating the specimen with substances that are meant to interfere with testing.

10.9.3.3   The Collection

A specimen must be properly collected to ensure an accurate test. Quality practices need to be followed to ensure the identity and integrity of the specimen. The identity of the donor must be determined, and the link between the specimen and the donor must be maintained throughout the process. Once obtained, the specimen must be secure from tampering and handled under forensic guidelines. There should be no opportunity for subversion of the drug test by the donor, the collector, or the two in collusion. These practices apply to specimens collected for on-site testing or shipped to a testing facility.

Specimens collected for workplace drug testing must be closely scrutinized for the quality of the collection. A positive drug test or an abnormal specimen validity test must be able to withstand the challenges of an MRO, a donor, or a legal review. Components of a quality collection include the collector, collection site, collection materials, and collection protocol. One source of guidance for urine specimen collection may be found in the handbook published by the Substance Abuse and Mental Health Services Administration (SAMHSA).[4] Some of the information in this section was obtained from this handbook, with a focus on the items critical to the quality of the collection process.

The Collector

A key element in a quality performance by a collector is training. A collector may be responsible for collecting one or more specimen matrices (i.e., hair, urine, sweat, and oral fluid) and may conduct on-site tests on some of these matrices. Collectors must be thoroughly trained in the collection process for each matrix. They must be trained not only for the routine collection, but also for problems that might arise during the collection (e.g., unacceptable specimen temperature, apparent adulterated specimen, insufficient amount of specimen). For collectors also conducting on-site testing, training must be specific for each on-site testing device. The training should include when and how to conduct the test, demonstration of testing proficiency, actions to take for borderline results, how to package specimens for shipment to a testing facility for additional testing, completion of documentation, and reporting of negative results.

Proper collector training begins with a qualified trainer. For urine collection, which is the most common matrix in workplace testing, a supervisor of the collection facility with previous experience typically assumes this responsibility; however, there are organizations such as the Drug and Alcohol Testing Industry Association (DATIA) that will also provide a standard course on specimen collection. With the introduction of other matrices and on-site testing into federal and state programs, all training programs may require changes. New initiatives between the testing and collection industries and controlling agencies will become necessary to ensure the validity of the specimens and the results of on-site tests. Training will need to be provided for each specimen type and each on-site test device. Training should go beyond the standard classroom lecture format. Error-free mock collections should be demonstrated for each specimen type, and testing proficiency using blind controls should be demonstrated with each type of on-site testing device. Written exams may also be part of the training program.

All training must be documented in a manner that can be easily reviewed and understood by an outside auditor. Minimally, documentation would include a description of the training, time of conduction, identification of the trainer, results of all examinations, and criteria for acceptable performance.

Beyond the initial training, a collector should be monitored for performance. Errors that occur during specimen collection or with the use of on-site testing devices require error correction training. For example, the Department of Transportation (DOT) requires collector correction training when errors in the collection process of urine specimens cause a test to be canceled.[5] The DOT requires the collector to demonstrate proficiency in the collection procedure by completing one uneventful mock collection and two mock collections related to the error. The person providing the retraining attests in writing that the mock collections were performed correctly with no errors. However, this process fails to address frequency of errors, which is an indicator of the collector's overall performance and the potential for test-canceling errors.

Within the urine drug testing industry, the collection site is perceived to be the weak link in the quality system. To correct this perception, it is recommended that the performance of all collectors be monitored and training requirements be standardized. Within federal programs, one approach to monitoring collector performance would be to examine the chain-of-custody documents, commonly referred to as custody and control forms (CCF), completed by a collector. CCFs failing to conform to federal guidelines would initiate further assessment of the collector's performance and appropriate corrective actions. Examples of collector noncompliance would be submission of a single specimen when a split specimen is required, submission of two specimens with differing physical appearance as a split specimen collection, or submission of CCFs containing multiple administrative errors. Collectors for non-federal programs might be monitored by professional groups such as DATIA.

A collector's proficiency with on-site testing devices should be measured with periodic performance testing (PT) samples for each on-site device utilized, as well as routine submission of a percentage of the on-site negatives to a laboratory conducting instrumented immunoassay testing and confirmatory testing of immunoassay positives. Abnormal numbers of false negatives should then be investigated to determine if the cause is the on-site device or the performance of the tester. Federal programs should be able to monitor on-site devices and tester performance; however, other programs may have to rely on professional groups for this function.

Collection Site

A collection site must meet certain requirements to ensure a quality collection. The site must have restricted access. Collection materials, records, and specimens must be properly stored and secured from unauthorized individuals. Materials (e.g., controls, reagents, testing devices) must be kept in acceptable temperature and humidity conditions for proper performance. Secure storage must be provided for specimens until they are tested or shipped to a testing facility, and records must be retained as required by applicable regulations. As part of its records, a collection site must maintain copies of current and past SOPs, a copy of each CCF, log books or log sheets, temperature logs from storage areas for specimens and perishable supplies, inventory of supplies/materials, donor information, and chain-of-custody handling. These records should be retained for the length of time required by governing regulations, usually 2 years or more. Urine collection sites should place bluing agent in the toilet bowl and tank and restrict access to soap, water, cleaning agents, and other materials that could be used to adulterate a specimen.

Collection Materials

A quality collection requires a collection kit designed for the matrix to be collected. The kit should contain a single-use collection device, container(s) for shipment of the specimen to a testing facility, CCFs, and tamper-evident seal(s). Kits for some matrices may require additional materials (e.g., scissors for a hair collection, wipes for a sweat collection). If on-site testing is to be conducted, the kit may also contain an on-site device. All materials must be proved not to affect the testing of the specimen. Containers used for storage/shipment must be capable of holding a tamper-evident security seal at room and frozen temperatures. Additional security can be provided to transported specimens with the use of individual sealable bags or boxes. Shipping containers can be used to protect the specimen from physical damage during transport.

Collection Protocol

A detailed written protocol (SOP) must be followed for every type of specimen collection. The basic requirements of a collection are the following:

Preparation of the collection site (discussed above)
Verification of donor identity
Preparation of donor for specimen collection (e.g., removal of coats and hats for unobserved collections)
Inspection of the specimen to ensure proper amount (and correct temperature of urine) and inspect for evidence of adulteration or substitution
Preparation of the specimen for testing, storage, or shipment (e.g., sealing the specimen with tamper-evident labels)
Completion of the CCF

The CCF is used to identify the donor, collector, employer, and MRO; to provide a unique specimen identification number; to account for handling of the specimen; and to report results and remarks in a uniform manner.

10.9.3.4 *The Testing Facility*

Testing facilities should establish QA programs to ensure the quality of their processes. Central to the quality assurance program is an SOP manual that details all procedures and processes. This manual and the documentation generated from a QA program in a workplace drug testing facility must be available for review by client auditors, certification agencies, lawyers, judges, etc. Users of the testing services in these facilities need to be assured that the results are high quality and legally defensible. A comprehensive QA program must include the handling, testing, and reporting processes. Components of QA practices include training personnel; validating and maintaining analytical instruments, analytical equipment, and computer systems; validating analytical methods; monitoring chain-of-custody procedures; using quality control samples; and participating in PT programs.

Personnel

Testing facility personnel must be well trained and motivated. They must not be allowed to succumb to the routine nature of the procedures utilized in today's high-throughput facilities. They must be knowledgeable of the scientific principles underlying the analytical procedures, the capabilities and limitations of the equipment they utilize to perform their work, and the regulatory requirements related to their work. They must be well versed in forensic principles and procedures, and their qualifications, training, and proficiency must be well documented.

Equipment and Instrumentation

The equipment and instruments utilized to test specimens are an intrinsic part of the quality system. They must be appropriate for the task and proven to perform the tasks through validation processes. This also includes the facility's management information system (MIS) and other computer-controlled equipment.

Materials

The importance of quality materials is often overlooked until a problem develops. As with equipment, the quality of the materials must be proven, not assumed. Quality facilities should perform acceptance tests on materials prior to their use and monitor their performance as a part of routine operations.

Methods

The methods utilized by a facility for all aspects of specimen handling and testing are a critical part of the quality system. A facility may have the best equipment available, highly motivated and trained personnel, and proven materials, but if the method is poorly designed, it will fail more often than a scientifically sound, operationally rugged method. Analytical methods and procedures utilized in workplace drug testing must be validated and characterized to provide timely results that will withstand the scrutiny of legal and administrative proceedings. Their continued performance at the desired level must be monitored by internal and external quality systems.

Basic Quality Assurance Practices

Method Validation — The quality of an analytical procedure is documented during its validation. Performance parameters commonly determined during validation of initial test procedures are linearity, specificity, precision, accuracy, and carryover studies. Validation of quantitative confirmatory procedures also includes sensitivity, limits of detection, and quantitation and ruggedness. Validation samples are prepared in the matrix to be tested and within the concentration range of interest. At a minimum, these tests are performed annually and when major changes (e.g., change in extraction procedure, new instrumentation) are made to an existing method. Validation records must be organized for an auditor's review and should include the purpose, scientific principle, method, results, discussion, summary, and review with approval by the facility director.

Quality Control — Quality control (QC) is a subsection of QA. QC is used to determine if all components of an analytical process are performing correctly. QC samples of known content are analyzed with the test specimens. Their purpose is to monitor the performance of an analytical procedure within defined limits of variation.

Calibrators are samples of known content by which the identification and concentration of an analyte in a specimen is determined. Calibration of a device or instrument can be established with a single calibrator or a series of calibrators at varying concentrations. It is common to find initial and confirmatory workplace drug tests evaluated with a single calibrator, but this approach requires the concentration to be determined at the administrative cutoff concentration or decision point. Multiple calibrators can be used to extend the limits of accurate quantitation on an instrument.

Calibrators and controls (often referred to as QC samples) are routinely prepared in the matrix of interest to minimize matrix effects. A quality practice is to prepare QC samples from a reference material of documented purity and content. Additionally, calibrators and controls should be prepared with reference materials from different suppliers; otherwise, a bias may occur. If both types of QC samples must be prepared from a single reference material, then they must be prepared independently.

QC samples must be validated before they are placed into use. The quantitative criteria for acceptance of calibrators should be more stringent than the criteria applied to other QC samples. Typically, calibrators should not differ by more than 10% from the target value, whereas controls may differ up to 20%. The primary method of validating new QC samples is by parallel testing with QC samples in use. If available, externally certified reference samples should be included in the validation process. The history and use of QC samples should be documented with information that includes the lot number, date of preparation and first use, expiration date, individual preparing the sample, preparation procedure, and validation data.

Workplace drug testing utilizes administrative cutoffs. QC samples at concentrations above and below the cutoff are used to demonstrate linearity around the cutoff, allowing clear differentiation of positive and negative specimens. These controls should be within the linear range of the assay and near the cutoff (±25%). Analytical batches should also contain a negative control to demonstrate the response of the assay in the absence of an analyte and a blind sample to demonstrate that the analytical batch has been properly prepared and analyzed. Other controls may be included to demonstrate extended linearity, lack of carryover, completeness of hydrolysis steps, lack of interference from structurally related analytes, and adherence to dilution protocols. Typically, a minimum of 5 to 10% of QC samples are required in each batch of specimens, some of which should be distributed throughout the batch.

Internal standards are essential to accurate quantitative analysis of QC samples and donor specimens. Ideally, the concentration of the internal standard should be close to the cutoff. Deuterated analogues of the analyte of interest are best for GC/MS selected ion monitoring as they have similar fragmentation patterns. However, structurally similar analytes can serve as the internal standard if the available deuterated internal standards are unsuitable (e.g., coelute with the analyte of interest and have the same major ion fragments).

Quantitative and qualitative acceptance criteria for initial and confirmatory tests must be established and adhered to during analysis. QC results, acceptable and unacceptable, must be documented as a complete record of QC performance. Systems for monitoring QC results should be established to detect shifts, trends, and biases. Actions to be taken to correct these anomalies should be contained in the facility's SOP.

Physical Plant

The physical plant in which testing occurs must be sufficient to meet requirements for security, habitability, safety, and performance of the work required. It must provide security for the specimen, the testing, and the results such that the linkage of the result with a donor is never in doubt. It must provide adequate space, ventilation, and other features to ensure a safe environment for employees and an optimum environment to conduct testing. Errors can be introduced in the testing process when the physical plant is inadequate.

It is important that an alternative source of power be available during prolonged power outages. At a minimum, there must be a plan to ensure proper temperature conditions for stored specimens.

Management Information Systems

An MIS is designed to improve the reliability, efficiency, and productivity of the testing facility. It may exist as a centralized data system with workstations tied into analytical equipment or stand-alone personal computers. It is used to log in and track samples, order tests, receive and manage data, report results, and handle routine administrative tasks. The MIS must be independently validated before being utilized for any task associated with the receipt, handling, testing, data review, or result reporting. All software and hardware added after the initial validation should be validated prior to use. Security must be in place to prevent unauthorized access, inappropriate release of information, and introduction of unauthorized, unvalidated software. The MIS must be monitored for problems, and audit trails must be established for all functions. Backup and disaster recovery procedures should be in place to prevent loss of information entered into the system.

MIS procedures should be subjected to routine audits as part of an inspection process. An MIS SOP manual describing the items above must be established and available during inspections. The person responsible for management of the MIS may not be the testing facility director; however, the director must be knowledgeable of the functions performed by the MIS, have input into its functions, and ensure that the forensic testing is supported. The testing facility director and MIS manager must work together to establish procedures for requesting changes to the MIS, validate changes, and determine end-user acceptance.

10.9.3.5 The Medical Review Officer

Testing facilities in all federal and many nonregulated workplace programs report test results directly to an MRO. Both DOT regulations[5] and HHS Mandatory Guidelines[6] contain requirements for MROs. To meet these requirements, physicians may obtain training and certification from any one of three organizations: American Association of Medical Review Officers, American College of Occupational and Environmental Medicine, and American Society of Addiction Medicine. To correctly interpret test results, MROs use their medical knowledge and their understanding of the applicable laws and regulations, the testing process, the collection process, and information provided by the donor. The properly trained and motivated MRO must be willing to question not only the donor, but also the collection site and the testing facility to ensure that the employer is provided a determination that considers the applicable science and regulations. MROs are often called gate-keepers because they are able to query the entire process to ensure that the quality system was intact.

The MRO practice should have a detailed SOP to ensure the quality of the MRO process, consistency of procedures, and adherence to governing guidelines and regulations. A more complete description of the MRO practice is described elsewhere in this volume.

Currently, MROs are not routinely monitored for the quality of their review. One approach to an MRO review program could be based on the documentation received by testing facilities. CCFs containing results for specimens reported as adulterated, substituted, invalid, and drug positive could be audited to determine the final disposition of the test. Reviews that revealed noncompliance with regulations would require an in-depth audit of other non-negative results reported by that MRO. Reports of these reviews could then be provided to the employer and other agencies, as appropriate.

10.9.4 Measuring Quality in the Workplace System

Measuring the quality of workplace testing requires the establishment of standards against which the measurement may be performed. Currently, there are four programs that establish standards for testing facilities and conduct measurements against those standards. While there are programs that accredit or certify MROs and collectors, none conduct measurements beyond the initial certification or accreditation. Subsequent sections will describe some of the tools utilized by organizations to measure the quality of testing facilities.

10.9.4.1 Testing Facility Certifying and Accrediting Organizations

NLCP

The reliability of facilities that test specimens for drugs in the workplace will always be of concern. A high degree of certainty of results is required of drug testing facilities to prevent false accusations against those undergoing testing. For this reason, the "Mandatory Guidelines for Federal Workplace Drug Testing Programs"[6] were developed to provide guidance to federal agencies for the collection and analysis of urine specimens collected from federal employees. With these Guidelines, HHS established standards for certification that have made HHS-certified urine drug testing laboratories the "gold standard" in the drug testing industry. Regulations issued by the DOT for the drug testing of safety-sensitive private sector employees in its operating modes, as well as the Nuclear Regulatory Commission for fitness for duty employees require the use of HHS-certified laboratories to perform their mandated drug testing.

The NLCP was developed for the establishment of initial and ongoing certification of forensic urine drug testing laboratories. The NLCP is designed to examine laboratories for compliance to the Mandatory Guidelines. In doing so, it examines the laboratory quality practices discussed above. Two of the major components of the NLCP are the PT program and the inspection program. Other components of the NLCP are described elsewhere in this volume.

The NLCP PT program emphasizes the laboratory's ability to accurately quantify drug concentrations in urine and report the results following Federal requirements. Strict scoring policies mean that a certified laboratory's failure to successfully test the PT samples may result in suspension or revocation of its certification. The NLCP challenges laboratories with PT samples formulated to mimic real specimens from donors in order to identify problems and to ensure appropriate actions are taken to correct those problems. Laboratories are expected to investigate all PT errors and must submit documentation of investigation and completed corrective action, as directed.

The NLCP categorizes laboratories (Category 1–smallest to Category 5–largest), using an objective system based in part on laboratory size, regulated specimen workload, and number of non-negative specimens reported in a 6-month period. Depending on category, semiannual maintenance inspections last 2 or 3 days and consist of one or two inspectors performing a general inspection (i.e., reviewing procedures and observing practice) and one to six inspectors performing a records audit. The NLCP focuses inspections on the procedures of the laboratory and on examination of the laboratory's forensic product through the audit component. The teams use two checklists: the General Laboratory Procedures Checklist and the Records Audit Checklist. The inspection team submits two summary reports, one from the general inspectors and one from the auditors. The inspection reports are reviewed by the NLCP technical staff. An Inspection Final Report is returned to the laboratory listing the deficiencies. Major deficiencies require a remedial action plan within 5 business days. All others must complete the remedial process within 30 days. Remedial actions are reviewed at the next inspection.

College of American Pathologists

The College of American Pathologists (CAP) has developed a Forensic Urine Drug Testing (FUDT) Accreditation Program that parallels the NLCP but is directed at non-federal workplace drug testing. Although this is a voluntary program, many clients require this accreditation for their non-federal employee drug testing.

The CAP program requires completion of a self-inspection checklist between on-site inspections that are conducted by a group of volunteers in the forensic toxicology field. Inspectors, guided by a checklist, focus on laboratory procedures and processes that include specimen handling, analytical instruments and procedures, quality control, personnel, computer operations, safety, facilities, records, and reporting.

Laboratories are also required to participate in at least the Urine Drug Testing Confirmation PT program. Acceptable performance is based on correctly identifying and quantifying drugs and obtaining a minimum score of 80%. A false-positive drug report is a survey failure with accreditation probation. Continued failures result in loss of accreditation.

The FUDT program differs from the NLCP in that the laboratory is evaluated for drugs other than the illicit drugs used in the federal program. In addition, the laboratory may use initial and confirmatory cutoffs unlike those stated in the Mandatory Guidelines. A more detailed description of the FUDT program can be found in a previous edition of this textbook.[7]

State of Florida

The State of Florida has established a Drug-Free Workplace program similar to the HHS Program for Federal Employees.[8] It regulates workplace testing for state employees and private workplace drug testing programs seeking discounts on Florida workers' compensation insurance premiums. Oversight of the program is maintained by the State Agency for Health Care Administration.[9] It allows the testing of biological samples (primarily urine and hair) for ten drugs/drug classes and their metabolites and alcohol (blood). It requires laboratories to conduct initial and confirmatory testing of positive specimens using two different scientific methods, to participate in proficiency testing programs, and to report test results to an MRO. Laboratories must participate in a proficiency testing program that tests for all of the required drugs. Inspections of licensed laboratories are semiannual and are conducted by the state. An HHS-certified laboratory may request to substitute one of the state inspections with an NLCP inspection and is required to submit the results of all NLCP inspections. Blind PT specimens are not required as part of the QA program.

State of New York

The State of New York amended its public health laws in 1966 to require the licensure of clinical laboratories by establishing minimum qualifications for directors and by requiring that the performance of all procedures employed by clinical laboratories meet minimum standards accepted and approved by the state department of health.[10] The laboratory licensure program is managed by the state's public health laboratory for 27 specialties of laboratory science, including forensic toxicology. The laboratory director must hold a certificate of qualification from the state department of health; minimum qualifications include a doctoral degree and 4 years of postdoctoral laboratory experience, 2 of which must be in the toxicology specialty. Laboratories engaged in the toxicological analysis of biological specimens are required to participate successfully in the state's proficiency testing program and must be in substantial compliance with standards of practice as assessed through biennial inspections. Laboratory standards and proficiency testing performance requirements in the forensic toxicology specialty are comparable to those of the NLCP. However, the State of New York has not imposed limitations on the specimen matrix, the drugs to be tested for in workplace programs, or the assay cutoff concentrations. These service characteristics are established through laboratory-client contracts. Performance in proficiency testing is evaluated in the context of the assay cutoff concentrations that are reported to the program. The proficiency testing specimen matrix is urine. Blind PT specimens are not required as part of the laboratory licensure program.

10.9.4.2 *Methods of Measuring Quality*

There are four primary systems for measuring the quality of a drug testing program: inspections, PT, blind specimens, and retests of non-negative specimens (conducted under most programs at the request of the donor).

Inspections

The inspection process is essential for improving and maintaining the quality of a testing facility, collection site, collector, and MRO. An inspection should represent an independent review of operations and be conducted by trained and knowledgeable professionals. It provides a means of peer review and feedback. Inspections provide a snapshot of the operations at the time they are conducted and are not a substitute for other quality systems. Since each part of the workplace drug testing system is dynamic, constantly changing to improve quality, increase efficiency, and reduce expenses, it is important that inspections occur on a regular basis. Although accreditation/certification may not be mandatory or available for each part of the system, it would provide additional assurance to clients that quality services and results are being provided. Currently there are no provisions for routine inspections of collection sites, collectors, and MROs.

Typically, inspections of a testing facility are a requirement for initial accreditation or certification, as are periodic maintenance inspections by certifying or accreditation organizations such as those previously described. Technically and professionally qualified inspectors receive training and continuing education sponsored by those organizations. The inspectors review all of the relevant administrative and technical functions of the site to ensure they are in accordance with prescribed regulations and industry practices. Inspectors, guided by an inspection checklist, review and evaluate testing processes to include: SOP manual, specimen handling, analytical equipment and maintenance, computer operations, analytical procedures, review and reporting of results, QCs, and personnel qualifications and training. Inspectors also review records that include specimen data, method validation data, PT data, chain-of-custody documentation, and reports transmitting results to the client or MRO. Deficiencies noted during the inspection must be corrected and reviewed at the next inspection.

A critical issue in any testing facility inspection is the amount of data that should be reviewed. The data should be carefully selected to optimize the detection of possible administrative, technical, and forensic issues. This is best accomplished by reviewing documentation and results for specimens that were reported as non-negatives. Non-negative specimens include drug positives, abnormal specimens (i.e., adulterated, diluted, and substituted), and specimens received but not tested. The resources required for an inspection should be determined by the testing facility's workload, the number of non-negative results reported, and the amount of review necessary to determine that all procedures have been adequately evaluated. Inspections meeting these criteria consume large amounts of time and resources, but are essential to maintaining quality.

Proficiency/Performance Testing (PT)

Participation in PT programs is an important quality practice for all testing entities, including testing facilities and personnel conducting on-site tests. They provide a mechanism for assessing the accuracy of the handling, testing, and reporting processes. They can be used to identify and test modifications to operating procedures, methods, and equipment. Regulatory agencies now require testing facilities to maintain acceptable performance in designated PT programs as a condition for initial and continued accreditation/certification. Although there are no regulatory requirements for routine PTs for on-site tests in workplace drug testing, some on-site testing facilities are using available PT programs to monitor performance.

PT samples are prepared by fortifying the matrix of interest (e.g., urine, oral fluids, hair) to the desired drug analyte concentration. Within workplace drug testing, PT samples are normally formulated to determine the ability of the testing facility to accurately identify and quantify drug analytes alone or in the presence of possible interfering substances, to identify abnormal or adulterated specimens, and to determine the dynamic range of the testing methods.

PT samples should be handled in the same manner as donor specimens. This includes not using replicate analysis if routine samples are not run in replicate. Criteria used to identify and quantify specimens should be the same for donor and PT specimens. It is ideal for a testing facility to include PT samples among donor specimens when testing the samples.

Reported PT results from participating facilities are compared to a reference value (normally the average of all results excluding outliers) to determine acceptable quantitative performance. If different analytical methods are used, means for each method are sometimes determined for comparison. Appropriate ranges for each method's mean can be standard deviations, percentage from the mean, or both. Method means can be further used to determine acceptable methods and/or instrumentation when compared to established reference methods.

The number of specimens in a PT cycle is small in comparison to the total specimens analyzed in a facility. For this reason, a quality practice is to participate in as many PT programs as possible. It is desirable to spread these PT sets over the entire year.

Testing facilities should review the information returned by the PT program. Any trends that are developing should be examined. Unacceptable results are to be investigated and corrective action taken to prevent reoccurrence. For major errors (e.g., false positives, large variations from the reference value), immediate resolution of the error through remedial action should be required by the certifying/accreditation agency.

Do PT programs make a difference in performance? Analysis of data from the NLCP PT program indicates that a PT program can enforce an initial level of performance and over time improve the performance of conforming facilities. In Figure 10.9.1A, bar graphs depict, through average coefficients of variation (CV), the performance of laboratories that applied for certification and certified laboratories in 1990. The variation within the population of certified laboratories was less than that of the candidate population for all drug analytes. In Figure 10.9.1B, it can be seen that since 1990, the average CV for most drug analytes has decreased. Not shown are the average CVs for codeine and phencyclidine, which have remained at 9 to 12% since 1990.

Blind Specimens

QA specimens presented to a testing facility in the same manner as donor specimens are referred to as blind specimens. They are submitted with fictitious information on the required custody documents and specimen bottles. These specimens should not be readily identifiable as blind specimens. The drug content of a blind specimen should be validated before use.

The HHS Mandatory Guidelines and DOT regulations require that employers submit blind specimens to certified laboratories as part of their drug testing program. Many testing facilities have QA programs that submit blind specimens to the facility as part of their quality practices. Blind specimens provide an excellent means of monitoring all of a facility's procedures. In addition to checking the technical processes of a testing facility, blind samples submitted with broken seals, incomplete CCF, etc., can also challenge the facility's procedures for handling of administrative errors.

The results of blind specimens should be closely monitored, and an investigation should be initiated when the results are inconsistent with target analyte identification or concentration. This investigation should evaluate the supplier and testing facility, identify the source of the inconsistent results, and require corrective actions.

Retests of Non-Negative Specimens

In many programs, the donor of a specimen found to be non-negative may request that an aliquot of the original specimen, in the case of a single specimen collection, or the unopened bottle,

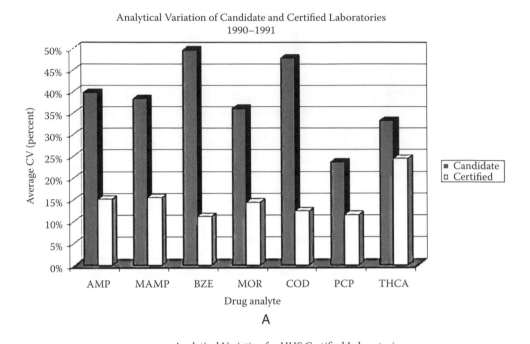

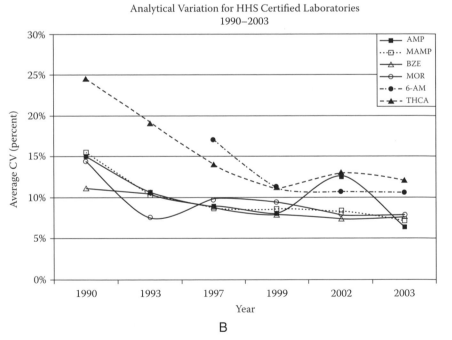

Figure 10.9.1   (A) Comparison of the average CV of GC/MS values reported by NLCP candidate and certified laboratories in 1990–1991 for amphetamine (AMP), methamphetamine (MAMP), benzoylecgonine (BZE), morphine (MOR), codeine (COD), phencyclidine (PCP), and 11-nor-9-carboxy THC (THCA). (B) Average CV for amphetamine (AMP), methamphetamine (MAMP), benzoylecgonine (BZE), morphine (MOR), 6-acetylmorphine (6-AM), and 11-nor-9-carboxy THC (THCA).

in the case of a split specimen collection, be retested. The retest is normally conducted at a testing facility different from the one reporting the non-negative result. Failure of the second testing facility to confirm the original result provides an opportunity to investigate the data from both facilities. Investigations of these incidences most often point to an issue with the collection process, usually the addition of an adulterant or a lack of a proper collection, rather than a testing facility error.

10.9.5 Conclusion

Workplace drug testing programs have become well established over the past 20-plus years. They have grown from a modest beginning in the military to become a program much larger than any imagined. The science and testing methodologies for urine drug testing have been well established. Now, it appears that the structure of workplace testing will change. The pressures from efforts to subvert a urine drug test have generated a need for solutions. Specimen validity testing cannot detect all efforts to suborn drug testing. Civil rights issues associated with observed collections make it clear that they can only be used under specific circumstances. Workplace drug testing using matrices such as hair, oral fluids, and sweat are being offered as a solution. While it would appear that these matrices are less subject to undetectable attempts to circumvent a valid test, there is still discussion within the scientific and legal communities about interpretation of results from these tests and their appropriate use. It is believed that these issues will be clarified and in the future the effectiveness of workplace drug testing will be enhanced as a result of their implementation. However, as a word of caution, this is possible only if the lessons learned about the quality requirements of the urine drug testing system are appropriately applied to the testing of new matrices.

Acknowledgments

The authors express their appreciation to Donna M. Bush, Ph.D., Walter F. Vogl, Ph.D., and Charles Lodico, M.S., of the Division of Workplace Programs, Center for Substance Abuse Prevention, Substance Abuse and Mental Health Services Administration, U.S. Department of Health and Human Services; Richard W. Jenny, Ph.D., of the State of New York Department of Health; and Patricia L. James, B.S., M.A., the State of Florida Agency for Health Care Administration for regulatory insight.

REFERENCES

1. Department of Defense. Urinalysis test results analysis. Naval Military Personnel Command Contract N00600-82-D-2956, October 22, 1982.
2. Brey, R.M. et al. Highlights of the 1988 worldwide survey of substance abuse and health behaviors among military personnel. Department of Defense Contract MDA903-87-C-0854, 1989.
3. Quest Diagnostics, Inc. 2003 drug testing index. http://www.questdiagnostics.com/.
4. Urine Specimen Collection Handbook for the New Federal Drug Testing Custody and Control Form. Division of Workplace Programs, Substance Abuse and Mental Health Services Administration, Department of Health and Human Services. http://www.drugfreeworkplace.gov/DrugTesting/SpecimenCollection/UrnSpcmnHndbk.html.
5. Procedures for Transportation Workplace Drug and Alcohol Testing Programs, 49 CFR Part 40, Department of Transportation, 65 *Federal Register* 79462, December 19, 2000 and 65 *Federal Register* 41944, August 9, 2001.
6. Mandatory Guidelines for Federal Workplace Drug Testing Programs, Substance Abuse and Mental Health Services Administration, Department of Health and Human Services, 59 *Federal Register* 29908, June 9, 1994.

7. Baenziger, J., The College of American Pathologists voluntary laboratory accreditation program, in *Drug Abuse Handbook*, Karch, S.B., Ed., CRC Press, Boca Raton, FL, 1998, chap. 10.2.2.
8. Florida Statutes Section 112.0455.
9. Florida Administrative Code Chapter 59A-24.
10. New York State Public Health Law Article 5, Title V.

10.10 CURRENT LEGAL ISSUES OF WORKPLACE DRUG TESTING

Theodore F. Shults, J.D., M.S.
Chairman, American Association of Medical Review Officers, Research Triangle Park, North Carolina

Over the 20-year life of modern workplace drug testing, a body of law has been created that is directly related to and directly influences its practice. It is an expansive body, stretching from the constitutional limits on the government's ability to require testing under the Fourth Amendment; it involves a large and expanding matrix of state drug testing laws and legal cases, and travels all the way down to local rules establishing how to introduce drug test results in an unemployment security case.[1] Over this timeframe, fundamental federal laws such as the Americans with Disabilities Act, the Omnibus Transportation Employee Testing Act of 1991, and more recently the Health Insurance Portability and Accountability Act (HIPAA) came into existence. All of these laws affect and shape drug testing practices, the drug testing industry, employment practices, and social policy.

There are a number of legal treatises that deal with employment drug testing and that cover federal and state drug testing laws. This chapter focuses on current key legal issues with a particular perspective of a drug testing service provider and employer. Regardless of the reader's knowledge of and facility with the specific laws of workplace drug testing, the following are broad issues that all employers and providers of drug testing services such as collectors, laboratories, third-party administrators, and medical review officers (MROs) will be dealing with directly in the years ahead.

10.10.1   Liability of Drug Testing

Over these 20 years or so of modern workplace drug testing there have been literally millions of drug tests performed, tens of thousands of positive tests reported, and relatively few lawsuits. There are many reasons for this, but perhaps the most significant is that the analytical procedures are reliable and defendable. Mistakes happen, and mistakes have happened, but there is a very low incidence of error considering the large number of tests performed. Other historical factors contributing to the relatively low level of litigation are that it is often difficult for a donor to bring an action against an employer or a service agent alleging negligence, and the damages of such alleged negligence are often low. One of the great concerns of drug testing has been the fact that often the only evidence of drug use is the laboratory test, and for many donors it is easier to deny illicit drug use and claim the results are a "false positive" than to acquiesce to the results and reality. Thus, there has always been a great deal of potential for litigation, which would cripple drug testing programs.

From the perspective of an employer, the greatest liability is not from drug testing but rather from the damages caused by an impaired employee to a third party. If an employee, acting within the scope of employment, causes injury to customers or to the public after consuming alcohol or drugs, liability may be imputed to the employer under the doctrine of *respondeat superior*. This vicarious liability can occur in commonplace situations, such as an accident caused by an impaired employee driving a company vehicle.[2] The actual costs of a drug- or alcohol-related accident can be astronomical, e.g., the *Exxon Valdez* environmental catastrophe and damage awards. Employers involved in hazardous or safety-sensitive work have understandable concern over the drug use, fitness, and qualifications of their employees.

One of the greatest misconceptions in drug testing is that employers who drug-test are at a great risk for lawsuits from employees over the results and adverse employment consequences. That's not true — or at least, it is an overstatement. Certainly, if an employer discriminates against an employee or applicant there are legal consequences, but courts do not want to get into routine hiring and firing decisions, or second-guessing business decisions. Thus, there is the judicial doctrine of *employment-at-will,* which broadly protects employers from direct suits from employees over drug testing.

Essentially, the employment-at-will doctrine stands for the premise that in the absence of an employment contract there is no "temporal" relationship between employer and employee. In other words, the employer–employee relationship can be terminated without notice, and without cause. Since there is no need for a reason to terminate the relationship, it is irrelevant whether the reason for the termination is reasonable, unreasonable, fair, unfair, right or wrong, as long as it is not illegal or against public policy. (An illegal reason is discrimination based on race, age, or sex, retaliation for filing a workers' compensation claim, or termination for certain types of "whistle-blowing.") Thus, in the absence of any state law to the contrary, employers have a great deal of insulation from lawsuits arising from employment decisions based on drug test results, even if the results are not accurate.

An important distinction is when there is a collective bargaining agreement (CBA). This is a type of employment contract. The key distinction between a CBA and employment-at-will is that an employer cannot terminate a covered employee unless there is a reason, which is usually phrased as "just cause."[3] With unionized employees, the union has a duty to defend its members, and there is a right to a grievance process and arbitration. The employer may have to reinstate a terminated employee following arbitration, and pay back wages, but there are no monetary damages.

From the service provider's perspective, liability issues are more complex. First, there is contractual liability, which is the service provider's responsibility for performing drug testing services appropriately for the client (the employer). For the laboratory, it involves the accurate handling, analysis, and reporting of specimens. For collectors, it is the proper performance of the collection process. For MROs, it is fulfilling the verification process correctly. But this contractual liability exists between the service providers and the client (i.e., the parties to the contract). There have been a few situations where employers have sought damages against a service provider for breach of contract, but this has been relatively rare.

Second, the doctrine of employment-at-will has not been extended to cover service agents, even though they are acting in many cases as the "agent" of an employer. What has historically protected service agents from lawsuits from donors is the fact that the law has not recognized a duty of care existing between the third-party service agent and the donor of a specimen. Historically, the service provider did not owe a "legal duty" to the donor. Thus, a donor who alleged that the specimen was mishandled or was a "false positive" could not bring a negligence claim against the service provider, because an essential element of negligence law is the existence of a legal duty. To be a bit more accurate, the donor *could* bring a suit against the service provider, but it would be quickly dismissed. That has been changing on a state-by-state basis since the mid-1990s. That historical protection or legal insulation is eroding, and has been eliminated in a number of jurisdictions.

A good illustration of how the law looks differently at employers and service providers is the case of *Jane Doe v. SmithKline.* In this 1994 case, the Quaker Oats Company made an offer to an applicant (Jane Doe) for a marketing job. The job offer was contingent on passing a drug test. The drug test was reported to Quaker as positive for a low level of morphine. Apparently there was no MRO verification, and no clinical evidence of abuse. When it learned that the laboratory had identified morphine in the specimen, Quaker simply withdrew the offer.[4] The applicant, who had quit her job and was in the process of relocating, brought suit against Quaker and the laboratory. Even though Quaker did not use an MRO and withdrew the offer of employment, the court quickly dismissed Quaker as a defendant under the employment-at-will doctrine. It was not so easy, however, for the lab. The trial court found that it was liable.

The Texas Court of Appeals ruled that, given these facts, a laboratory had a legal duty to warn test subjects of possible influences on results (e.g., poppy seed ingestion). The Texas Supreme Court, however, overruled this decision. The laboratory analysis was correct — there was morphine in the urine. That was what the laboratory was asked to determine, and it did. In the end, a divided court found that the laboratory has no legal duty to warn donors.[5]

The failure to mention poppy seeds to the employer, and the employer's reliance on the test results, may still be a basis for a suit alleging willful and intentional interference with the conditional offer of employment between the employer and employee.

No wrong goes without a right, as plaintiffs' lawyers like to say. Thus, with employment-at-will protecting the employer and with no legal duty attaching to the provider, the donor might not have any legal recourse. Naturally, with drug testing an almost universal employment practice, this insulation was not going to last forever. The law adapts, and it is in that process.

Over the past few years there has been a case-by-case, jurisdiction-by-jurisdiction expansion of what is essentially the scope of legal liability to cover various drug test providers. There is an expanding body of law that allows employees to bring direct actions against laboratories (and theoretically against MROs, third-party administrators, and specimen collectors).

In the first significant case, *Stinson v. Physicians Immediate Care, Limited*, Stinson alleged that the laboratory had been negligent in performing a drug test on him and had reported a false-positive result for cocaine. Stinson alleged that the test result was false or, in the alternative, the report of the test result was false. As is characteristic in this type of case, the allegations were general in nature. The plaintiff alleged the defendant was negligent.

The trial court dismissed Stinson's case on the grounds that a laboratory does not have any legal duty to the donor of the specimen. The appellate court in Illinois, however, reversed this decision and held that a drug testing laboratory owes a duty of reasonable care to persons whose specimens it tests for employers or prospective employers.

The appellate court view was that it is reasonably foreseeable that the tested person will be harmed if the laboratory negligently reports the test results to the employer, that the laboratory is in the best position to guard against injury, and that the laboratory is better able to bear the burden financially than an individual who is wrongly maligned by a false-positive report.

Thus a terminated employee, and presumably a frustrated applicant, has a basis to state a claim against a laboratory by alleging that the laboratory has a duty to the donor to act with reasonable care in collecting, handling, and testing the specimen, and reporting the results accurately. Several appellate decisions have defined the legal responsibility of laboratories.[6]

This expansion of legal duty is not limited to the laboratories. In November 1999, the Wyoming Supreme Court cited the *Stinson* case when it held not only that a collector (and a collection company) owes a duty of care to the donor, but that it also has a duty of care as a consultant, where the collection company recommended a urine alcohol test. (And this duty to the donor essentially extends to all of the service providers.)

The Wyoming case was *Duncan v. Afton, Inc.*[7] It is another example of a court finding that a drug test provider (in this case, a third-party administrator, a collector, a laboratory, and an MRO) owes a duty of care when collecting, handling, and processing urine specimens for the purpose of performing substance abuse testing. This duty is not only to the employer, but to employees and applicants as well.

All of the above cases deal with the duty of drug and alcohol service providers in regard to allegations of "false-positives" and protecting the donor's interests. A question that has been in the background is whether service providers such as MROs owe a duty to third parties for "false negatives" or "undue delay" in reporting results, or the failure to notify an employer that an employee may be unfit for a safety-sensitive position. In other words, is there exposure for a service provider who fails to report a "positive" test for whatever reason, and there is a drug-related catastrophic accident?

Such circumstances are rare, but one court case has dealt with such an occurrence. The case, *Turley v. Taylor Clinic*, went to trial in late 2005 in the Aniston, Alabama state court, the first reported case of a drug-related catastrophic accident occurring while the MRO verification process was under way. It is the first case where an MRO has been charged with causing harm to a "third party" — not the donor, but individuals harmed by the donor (a drug-impaired truck driver).

The case illustrates the relatively indefensible position the MRO and the MRO's employer, Taylor Clinic, were placed in by the failure of the regulations to address a fundamental flaw in drug testing analysis and the intrinsic regulatory conflict between "safety" and the prohibition of removing a presumptive positive donor from safety-sensitive tasks until the verification process is complete.

Methamphetamine exists in two forms called isomers, with significantly different clinical and pharmacological properties. Both forms look identical to a mass spectrometer. The *l* isomer, levmetamfetamine, is found in over-the-counter inhalers like Vicks Inhaler®. The *d* isomer is the form of methamphetamine that acts as a potent CNS stimulant and is the form that is a controlled substance and is abused. The *l* and *d* forms of methamphetamine can be differentiated analytically, but there is no regulatory requirement to do so. Therefore, most laboratories that must compete on price in this mandatory testing program do not do the analysis.

The risk to all MROs is that if they do not order the *d* and *l* test for a methamphetamine positive (in cases where there is no other medical explanation), the MRO is exposed to a future claim from the donor that the results were in fact due to legal use of a nasal inhaler.[8] The positive methamphetamine donor will allege that the MRO negligently or intentionally failed to order the isomer identification analysis. Thus, under the current regulatory scheme the laboratory's report of undifferentiated methamphetamine presents MROs with the Hobson's choice of either verifying a methamphetamine-positive without objective laboratory evidence of whether the drug reported is *d* methamphetamine or *l* levmetamfetamine, or delaying the verification to perform the *d* and *l* testing.

A regulatory conflict exists in addition to this technical deficiency. DOT regulations place a legal duty on MROs to remove donors who present safety risks, and yet also prohibit removal of a donor with a positive test until the result is verified by the MRO.[9]

What happened in the *Turley* case is that the laboratory reported a positive undifferentiated methamphetamine to the MRO. The MRO immediately contacted the truck driver. The truck driver first claimed that the result was due to prescription use of Didrex®, then to Adipex®.[10] He strongly denied use of illegal methamphetamine. The MRO determined that there was no prescription use and ordered the *d* and *l* analysis. The MRO promptly contacted the employer representative as soon as the laboratory analysis came back as *d* methamphetamine.

While the MRO was waiting for the *d* and *l* analysis, the truck driver was seen driving his rig erratically on a major highway. Before the state police could intercept him, the driver exited the highway and ran the stop sign at the end of the exit ramp. A pickup truck collided with the side of his tractor-trailer, resulting in the immediate death of the passenger and the subsequent death of the driver. The truck driver was uninjured.

The police arrested the driver, who could not stay awake. A police-requested blood test for drugs and alcohol was positive for methamphetamine. The truck driver was found to have grossly overextended his time on the road. He had doctored his logbooks and was suffering from fatigue. He pled guilty to vehicular homicide and was given an active jail sentence.

In the discovery process of the wrongful death suits filed against the trucking firm, the plaintiffs' attorneys discovered that the random DOT drug test for methamphetamine had not been reported to the employer at the time of the accident. To the plaintiffs, this simply looked like negligence. The plaintiffs alleged in their respective complaints that the MRO should have contacted the employer and had the driver removed the moment the lab result came in (although this would have violated DOT's regulations), and subsequently that the MRO should not have ordered the *d* and *l* isomer test, which caused a delay in reporting the result.[11]

What the plaintiffs presented at trial were the bad acts of the truck driver and his guilty plea for drug-related vehicular homicide. They pointed out to the jury that DOT regulations refer to the MRO as the "gatekeeper" for the program. This was creatively interpreted to mean the MRO is supposed to protect the public from illegal drug users — specifically, from methamphetamine-crazed truckers. The plaintiffs also read the provisions from Part 40 that state the donor has the "burden of proof" as meaning that if on the first telephone call the donor cannot prove he has an alternative medical explanation, he must be found to be positive and/or removed from service.

It mattered little that these were fundamental misinterpretations of the regulations. It did not seem to matter that the MRO role is also to protect individuals who are not illegal drug users from being falsely accused or losing employment because they use an over-the-counter inhaler. It was quite simple for the plaintiffs: local fellows are dead, an out-of-town doctor failed to report the results — bad outcome, bad MRO.

These issues could have been addressed. However, the defense was essentially forced to settle this case by following the informal guidance (or as it was described, the bombshell) that was dropped by DOT's Office of Drug and Alcohol Policy and Compliance (ODAPC). The defense counsel for Taylor Clinic asked ODAPC its view on the actions of the MRO and presented the office with a "hypothetical" synopsis of the facts. The defense counsel was surprised to learn from ODAPC that:

> ... the MRO had no compelling medical reason to order the d,l isomer test and delay reporting. The donor offered no medication or explanation in the hypothetical that gave a reason for delaying the final verification decision waiting for that particular additional test.

The new concept of requiring a *compelling medical reason* to order a *d* and *l* test is without any regulatory basis and is in frank conflict with the guidance DOT has given for over a decade.

It also raises the question of whether an MRO, in the absence of a compelling medical reason, should delay reporting of *any* positive results where the purported explanation is unlikely. For example, it is common for a donor to claim that he or she is positive for cocaine because his or her dentist used cocaine in a recent procedure. It is generally understood in the MRO community, the general medical community, and the dental community that cocaine is not used in routine dental procedures in the U.S. The standard of practice has been, however, for the MRO to give the donor some reasonable amount of time to get information from the dentist. Some MROs even contact the dentist directly to verify the information. If there is a drug-related accident or injury while this aspect of the verification process is under way, can it now be alleged that the MRO was negligent because there was *no compelling medical reason* to verify the donor's claim? DOT has certainly opened the door for such allegations.

ODAPC further exacerbated its guidance to Taylor Clinic in respect to verification of methamphetamine by subsequently proposing that MROs go ahead and report positive methamphetamine results without the *d* and *l* analysis. The MRO is then free to decide whether to order the additional test. In the event the *d* and *l* results are reported back as all *l* isomer, the MRO can issue a "revised" report. This sounds reasonable, except that in most cases the donor will have already been fired, and most employers who are not governed by collective bargaining agreements will be under no legal obligation to rehire them. It is doubtful that this "guidance" is even constitutional, as it is simply an unreasonable rule with unreasonable results. At the time of this writing, these concerns have been expressed to DOT without satisfactory response.

Turley v. Taylor Clinic is the worst-case scenario for an MRO and for the government. It all stems from the failure of the HHS Mandatory Guidelines to require laboratories to identify which form of methamphetamine they are reporting. If the trend is toward holding the service provider liable for the shortcomings of policy and regulatory schizophrenia, MRO verification of DOT results will begin to present unacceptable levels of risk. Some legislative relief would be appropriate.

10.10.2   Specimen Validity: Managing the Integrity of Specimens and the Question of Federal Preemption

Workplace drug testing has historically been based on the analysis of urine specimens. There are many advantages to using urine. There is sufficient quantity, it is easy for a laboratory to handle and manipulate the specimen, urine is mostly water, and the physiologic processes and kidneys provide a first pass at concentrating the metabolites and drugs of interest in the urine. The development of high-speed automated immunoassay instruments in the 1980s facilitated the ability to quickly and effectively screen urine specimens and made large-scale urinalysis programs practical. Urine gives a 2- to 3-day window of detection using typical workplace drug testing cutoff levels.

The disadvantage of urine is, frankly, that it is urine. Urine collection involves a personal and private process that requires a reasonable degree of privacy. A legal (and social) constraint of urinalysis testing is the premise that in the absence of individualized suspicion of adulteration or other subterfuge of the collection process, it is unreasonable to witness or directly observe the production of a urine specimen.[12] This "reasonable" degree of privacy in the collection process has provided a reasonable opportunity for a drug user to adulterate, substitute, or otherwise attempt to undermine the drug testing process, and many have. Adulteration and substitution have challenged the integrity, technology, and economics of urine drug testing. The very principles and legal foundation of drug testing have been challenged by the adulteration industry and their willing accomplices: drug users who have no interest in changing their behavior.

In 2004, HHS implemented a technical strategy that required certified laboratories to screen all specimens received from federal agencies for the presence of oxidants, check the pH, and determine the level of creatinine.[13] The new standard is known as the specimen validity testing (SVT) rule. It establishes a technical protocol that provides a level of screening and confirmation for adulterants and the identification of substituted specimens equivalent to the identification of prohibited drugs and metabolites.

The rule was framed as the ultimate solution for the war on adulterants. However, in developing its SVT rule, HHS made a fundamental policy decision to require only a generic screening for adulterants, and not to require any laboratory to have a confirmation procedure for the screen. A survey of laboratories in 2005 indicated that the certified laboratories have essentially abandoned the process of adulterant confirmation.[14] One presumes that the extent of the laboratory retreat from this area was unanticipated, but the consequence has been the precipitous drop in the number of adulterated specimen reports.

A specimen that meets the screening criteria for a tampered or suspect specimen is then reported as an "invalid" result. Following the implementation of the SVT rule, all adulterated specimens became invalids. These "invalid" results trigger requirements for the MRO to have discussions with the laboratory, call the donor to discuss the results, and in most every case call the donor back for an observed recollection. In addition, now the MRO must even "verify" that the observed collection was indeed observed.

This approach begs the question: What are the results of these second observed collections? How many are positive? No systematic data has been released to support the fundamental premise of the SVT rule. Is the return visit of the donor with an invalid any better than requiring a second drug test of anyone for no reason? Under this rule, the mandatory recollection of specimens under observed conditions is not productive.

Unfortunately, the HHS specimen validity testing rule has been implemented and serves as a standard and template for testing federal agency employees. It has become the *de facto* standard, being authorized under DOT and NRC for regulated industry. In late 2005, DOT formally proposed adopting these rules without modification.[15] However, DOT and NRC are still evaluating the merits of the overall approach, and may ultimately decide not to follow this protocol.

A recurring pattern of specimen validity testing has been that when laboratories begin to test for a particular adulterant, such testing has a profound impact on the use of the identified adulterant. In the 1990s glutaraldehyde was one of the more common urine adulterants. Its use dropped off sharply and in a relatively short period of time after the laboratories began to identify the compound. Unfortunately, this lesson has not been incorporated into the HHS SVT rule. There are now no more confirmed adulterated test results, only invalids.

Current thinking is that alternative tests such as oral fluid, sweat patches, and even hair testing provide a better specimen because the collection is essentially one that is observed. But the adulteration industry sees these "*alternative*" specimens merely as new markets and opportunities ahead. Adulteration products are already available to "clean toxins" out of hair. One can foresee a line of products to "detoxify" the mouth and breath and to purify sweat. Like so many products in this genre, the product does not have to work to be successfully sold in this market.

To date, the legal issues of specimen validity testing have not involved the question of whether it is appropriate to test for adulterants or for substitution. The focus has been on the integrity of the analysis and the validity of the cutoff levels.

Although laboratories are not actually performing confirmation testing of adulterants, they are reporting creatinine and specific gravity results. The creatinine cutoff level for a substituted specimen was initially established by HHS at 5 ng/ml. This was, however, found to be high enough for some individuals to achieve. In other words, it was not medically or physiologically impossible to produce a "substituted" specimen at or around this level. Although a donor could challenge the substituted results and engage what was called a "referral physician" and demonstrate their ability to produce creatinine at such low levels, it was a burdensome process.

In February 2003, a colloquium funded by Congress and hosted by the FAA Civil Aerospace Medical Institute (CAMI) specifically convened to assess the soundness of the specimen validity rules in effect at that time.[16] One result of the research and findings of this colloquium was the decision to lower the creatinine cutoff level for substituted specimens.

The change from 5 ng/ml creatinine to <2.0 ng/ml was made officially by DOT on May 28, 2003. DOT also directed that specimens that had been previously reported as substituted and had a creatinine between 5 and 2 were to be canceled. They are now reported as "dilute" and require a subsequent collection under direct observation.

A separate but related concern to determining the appropriate physiological cutoff values for creatinine and specific gravity is the issue of how accurately these can be measured. A lot was learned the hard way. In the early days of testing some of the analytical instruments designed for measuring creatinine levels had a feature of truncating results, or rounding down to the lower integer. This feature was buried in the software and no one really cared about the decimal place, until substitution became an issue. Dropping the fractional number turned out to have significant consequences.

The case that received the most attention in respect to truncating creatinine results was *Ishikawa v. Delta Air Lines, and LabOne, Inc.* On July 3, 2001, a federal district court jury in Portland, Oregon, found LabOne negligent under the state negligence law in the laboratory analysis of Yasuko Ishikawa's drug test. LabOne had reported Ms. Ishikawa's specimen as substituted to her employer, Delta Air Lines, and Delta had fired Ms. Ishikawa, who worked as a flight attendant. Her dismissal was based on Delta's policy to terminate employees who have been reported as having substituted or adulterated specimens. The laboratory found itself in the difficult position of not being able to prove conclusively that Ms. Ishikawa's urine did in fact meet the existing definition of a substituted specimen, primarily because of the software truncation of creatinine results. The laboratory was also placed in the difficult position of defending a federal standard for creatinine levels that was subsequently lowered.

In the end, Ms. Ishikawa was awarded $400,000 in compensatory damages. This verdict was appealed on the grounds that federal law, in particular the Federal Omnibus Employee Testing Act, which is the current statutory authority for the DOT regulations, "preempts" state law, including negligence law. The trial court did not accept that argument, and the case was appealed to the Ninth Circuit Court of Appeals. The Ninth Circuit took the opposite view and noted that if anything, Part 40 *preserved* the donor's right to sue. The court noted that the DOT regulations expressly provide: *"[t]he employee may not be required to waive liability with respect to negligence on the part of any person participating in the collection, handling, or analysis of the specimen."*[17,18]

The court deduced that since negligence is a state common law tort, it would make no sense for the DOT regulation to prohibit requiring the employee to waive negligence claims if those claims were preempted and could not be made. This regulation prohibiting required waivers of negligence claims implies that such claims exist and are not preempted.

On November 30, 2004, the Eighth Circuit followed this decision in *Chapman v. LabOne* and *Howell v. LabOne*. These two cases were consolidated on appeal. In both cases the federal district court judges ruled that the state negligence action against the laboratory was preempted. The district court in Iowa dismissed the *Chapman* case on the ground that the common law claims were preempted by the Federal Railroad Safety Act (FRSA), as amended by the Federal Omnibus Transportation Employee Testing Act of 1991 (FOTETA), and the Railway Labor Act (RLA). The district court in Nebraska ruled that removal of the *Howell* case was proper based on the doctrine of "complete preemption" under the FRSA and the FOTETA, and then dismissed the case on the ground that the FOTETA provided no private right of action.

The Eighth Circuit reversed both of these cases and noted:

> We agree with the Ninth Circuit that "[n]egligence is a state common law tort, and it would make no sense for the regulation to prohibit requiring the employee to waive negligence claims if those claims were preempted and could not be made."

This appears to be the current majority view, which essentially means service agents (not just laboratories) performing drug testing under the DOT program will be subject to state negligence law in respect to their work, in jurisdictions that have expanded the "duty of care" to donors. The legacy of the litigation surrounding specimen validity issues has resulted in a more rugged technological approach and numerous additional safeguards for specimen validity testing. It may also be a turning point in how the industry views the litigation risks of this endeavor.

10.10.3   2005 Congressional Interest in Adulteration and Substitution

On May 17, 2005, the House Energy and Commerce Oversight and Investigations Subcommittee held a public hearing to investigate the issue of the subversion of federal drug testing by adulteration and substitution. There had been growing interest in getting Congress involved in this problem, specifically seeking federal legislation to help curb the marketing and use of devices and chemicals designed to defeat drug tests.

The hearing came coincidentally on the heels of a widely covered story of Minnesota Vikings running back Onterrio Smith, who was detained by airport security who were curious about the freeze-dried urine in his carry-on luggage. No doubt they were also curious about the plastic prosthetic device that was also present. What Mr. Smith had was *The Whizzinator*, which has been on the market for a number of years. The Whizzinator consists of a prosthetic penis that will deliver a liquid at about 98.6°F. It is now sold with freeze-dried urine.

Thus, the Whizzinator became the media breakout product for the adulteration and substitution industry. But the Whizzinator is just one of approximately 400 products available today to defeat drug screening tests, according to the report by the U.S. Government Accountability Office (GAO) released at the hearing.

> The sheer number of these products, and the ease with which they are marketed and distributed through the Internet, present formidable obstacles to the integrity of the drug testing process.[19]

The GAO report was released as three major manufacturers and sellers of the adulterants and devices pleaded the Fifth Amendment, declining to answer questions at a hearing after receiving subpoenas from the House Energy and Commerce Oversight and Investigations Subcommittee.

At this time a bill has been introduced in the House of Representatives titled: The Drug Testing Integrity Act of 2005. The purpose of the bill is "To prohibit the manufacture, marketing, sale, or shipment in interstate commerce of products designed to assist in defrauding a drug test." It is a short bill that focuses on the manufacturers and distributors of these products, which are riper targets than users. Such federal legislation will not eliminate the problems of adulteration and substitution, but it will certainly help.

10.10.4   Expanding Technology: The Opportunity and Challenge of Hair, Oral Fluid, and Sweat Testing

There has been long-standing interest and research in testing other biological specimens, such as saliva (now referred to more accurately as oral fluid), hair, and sweat. One generic advantage of all these methods is that collection of the specimens can be witnessed by a collector. A witnessed collection greatly reduces the opportunity for adulteration or substitution. There are other advantages and disadvantages of these methods, and a somewhat new legal frontier is ahead.

In April 2004, HHS published a proposed rule to amend the current Mandatory Guidelines for Federal Workplace Drug Testing.[20] The amendment would have expanded federally mandated drug testing to include the collection and testing of hair, oral fluids, and sweat. It also would have expanded urine testing to include on-site testing, decentralized screening of urine, the testing of designer drugs, and lower cutoffs for amphetamine and cocaine.

Oral fluid is relatively easy to obtain from a donor. In what is referred to as laboratory-based oral fluid testing, a stick with an absorbent pad is placed in the mouth for a short time.[21] In one system, the device is sent to the laboratory for screening and confirmation. There is more and more evidence that oral fluids perform equally as well as current urine testing in terms of prevalence rates of positive drug tests. It is a very promising technology that is particularly attractive not only to employers, but also to school districts interested in drug testing students. On the other hand, there is some concern that the method has a relatively shorter detection time for marijuana use and paradoxically is more susceptible to "passive" or secondhand smoke.

Hair testing has been a controversial area of drug testing for more than a decade. It is clear that drugs and metabolites can be sequestered in the matrix of the hair and may be identified years after use. In workplace programs, only a relatively short section from the scalp is tested. This practice is to correlate the detection window to the past 90 days of hair growth, which will fall within the bounds of the "current use" definition of the Americans with Disabilities Act. One issue that remains somewhat unresolved is how well the laboratories can distinguish use of the parent drug from environmental contamination. Some laboratories are quite adamant that this is not an issue; other experts are not so sure.

Another complexity of hair testing is that there is large body of evidence that the sequestered amount of some drugs such as THC and cocaine is proportional to the darkness of hair. There is a good correlation of the amount of drug in hair and the amount of melanin. There is a somewhat charged debate in the toxicology community, and moving into the legal community, as to the significance of this color bias in respect to its possible disparate impact on African-Americans and Hispanics.

The use of sweat is not common in workplace drug testing programs because it involves the adherence of a sweat patch to donors for a period of at least a week. Its use is almost exclusively in monitoring treatment and abstinence.

The HHS proposed rule summarized 8 years of work by industry working groups and framed many of the critical issues. It was subject to public comment and was extensively critiqued as raising as many questions as answers. The 283 formal comments raised 2000 separate issues that needed to be addressed. In 2006, the Office of Management and Budget (OMB) announced on its list of 2006 completed rulemaking that these proposed amendments have been withdrawn.

Regardless of this misadventure, much was learned. These alternative technologies will continue to develop and grow in the private sector. Private employers are still faced with the challenge of assessing the technical and practical merits of each alternative technology.

Conceptually, the alternative biological specimens provide different types of information about drug use and drug exposure. An individual's current mental and physical status and recent use may be best assessed in terms of oral fluid testing results. Past history and pattern of use may be best revealed with hair. It is unlikely that a hair test would be used for a post-accident test, simply because hair tests do not typically reflect drug use in the past few days, and there is no peer-reviewed data showing a correlation between hair concentration and behavioral effects. Similarly, the use of an oral fluid test, which provides a relatively narrow window of detection of recent drug use, would be of less value than urine in assessing abstinence for the purposes of a return-to-duty test. Urine testing has been used for all types of drug tests: random, pre-employment, post-accident, for-cause testing, and return-to-duty. It is unlikely that any of the alternative tests would have such broad application.

In the years ahead, the courts will be dealing with all of these technologies in a variety of circumstances. In general, the legal issues and litigation will be similar to what has been seen with urine testing. Is the test accurate? Was the test, collection, or interpretation done correctly? Does the employer have the right to use these tests? Do the tests violate existing state privacy or drug testing law? Do the tests and the employer's policy violate the Americans with Disabilities Act? Do the tests discriminate against a protected class?

To the degree that alternative testing methods mimic the technical safeguards in urine testing, such as using approved and accepted screening and confirmation methods and having MRO verification, the legal cases should follow the same results that urine testing has produced.

The courts (and perhaps legislatures) may also be dealing with a relatively new issue that did not exist in a one-test universe of urinalysis. The new issue is whether the selection of a particular method is "fair." Is it fair to screen some employees with urine testing and others with hair? Or is it fair to have oral fluid testing for some post-accident testing and urine for others? Does the less-rigorous standard open the door for charging that an employer is not doing an adequate job of screening employees?

Employees have a strong sentiment that testing should be fair, although their definition of "fair" may not necessarily be rational. For example, employees may feel that for drug testing to be fair everyone has to be tested at the same time, or that employers have an obligation to provide assistance and/or treatment for substance abuse. Employers also have an interest in projecting fairness. The reality is, however, that life is not fair, and there is limited legal recourse for "fairness" for employees. Here is where state legislatures have stepped in — for better or worse, depending on one's perspective.

At the federal and state level, a more rigorous constitutional test is required when a government agency performs the tests or requires an employer to test as part of a regulation or law. It is premature to speculate on the legal significance of "fairness" in the federal program, other than to say that the U.S. Constitution requires reasonableness. At some point, *fair* and *reasonable* intersect.

The constitutional requirement of governmentally mandated testing also requires a showing of compelling governmental reason for testing by one of these novel methods, and that the testing is minimally invasive. If these tests are ever added to the federal program and the legal challenges are resolved, employers will have a firm basis for decision making.

With no federal standard in place for testing these biological specimens, all of these methods are currently being used by employers in the private sector in a trial-and-error approach. With an understanding of the technical limitations and weaknesses of each method and an appreciation of the legal risks in a particular employment environment, employers can make sound decisions and enhance their programs with the proper use of these technologies.

10.10.5   Managing Prescription Drugs: The Use/Abuse, Treatment/Risk Analysis

The focus of workplace drug testing has been on "illegal" drug use and alcohol misuse and abuse. The primary legal justification for focusing the government's drug testing program on illegal drugs has been in large part the concern for public safety. Private employers share this concern and have additional justifications for their interest and involvement in drug testing. What has become evident is that safety, performance, integrity, and addiction are also being significantly affected by the abuse of prescription drugs.

Workplace drug testing programs do not directly address the safety and performance issues of prescription drug abuse. The essence of the federal model for workplace drug testing programs is to establish a policy that prohibits the use of "illegal" drugs, tests for the presence of these drugs, confirms the presence, and then determines through a confidential dialogue with an MRO whether there is an "alternative medical explanation" for the presence of that drug or metabolite. *Alternative medical explanation* essentially means that the drug was obtained legally by means of direct administration by a physician, such as topical cocaine to a broken nose, or by prescription (e.g., codeine). Once it has been established that the drug was obtained legally, the results are reported as negative.

The existing model does not directly address the issue of whether prescription use is appropriate, such as the prescription for Marinol® for complaints like "nervousness," or the donor's multiple prescriptions for stimulants, or the donor's inappropriate dosing of codeine, or even the use of an old prescription.

The DOT and NRC programs have provisions for the MRO to determine whether a safety issue exists and to report it to the employer or to make an assessment. In the DOT program, this happens when the problem comes to the attention of the MRO, usually inadvertently. Many nonregulated employers are following this approach, and expanding on it by expanding the menu of drugs being tested. Typically the expanded drugs include the synthetic narcotics and benzodiazepines.

The challenge for employers (and society) is how to effectively manage the appropriate use of drugs that have abuse potential and present safety and productivity problems. Although the two largest categories of drugs of concern are historically the synthetic narcotics and the benzodiazepines, there are others.

There are a few cases where employers have taken some independent actions. In an interesting case, a large trucking firm automatically disqualified all applicants who reported that they were taking drugs that were on a list compiled by the firm's safety director. Any drug that was identified in the *Physician's Desk Reference* as requiring a warning about driving was added to the list. The court did not find this to be a violation of the Americans with Disabilities Act.

Testing is, however, only a part of the management of prescription drugs. Employers who are involved in safety-sensitive work have to develop comprehensive policies and procedures that require the disclosure of prescription drugs to a designated medical representative, who then can make an independent judgment in conjunction with the treating physician as to the performance of safety-sensitive functions. The disclosure of prescription drug use can be framed in such a way as not to violate the Americans with Disabilities Act, by avoiding adverse employment action and focusing on the safety issues. These procedures are best justified in clearly safety-sensitive environments, and some degree of employee education is also required. (There need not be any requirement to disclose drug use unless the drug has an effect on performance.)

A related issue has been the growing use of the Internet, not only for filling legitimate prescriptions, but also for obtaining questionable prescriptions for controlled substances. A number of MROs have noted that donors who have tested positive for amphetamines claim to have a prescription and to have obtained the amphetamine from an Internet pharmacy. The issue is not that the prescription was filled by an Internet pharmacy, but rather that the prescription itself was issued by a physician over the Internet, related to or referred from the pharmacy site.

The DEA position is that a prerequisite requirement for the issue of a prescription for a controlled substance is a doctor–patient relationship, and that such a relationship must be based on a face-to-face meeting. Unfortunately, in some states a doctor–patient relationship can be created over the telephone, and telemedicine is only expanding the exception to the face-to-face rule. It is these states that license Internet pharmacies, however, not the DEA.

The problem of Internet prescription writing is not unmanageable for the MRO. Under the DOT regulations the donor has the obligation (burden) to present sufficient evidence to the MRO that his or her drug use that resulted in a confirmed positive laboratory result was obtained by prescription. In the typical Internet case, the donor often has a hard time determining who the prescribing doctor is and establishing that he or she is a licensed physician, or establishing that the drug was dispensed in accordance with federal and state laws. It is highly unlikely that, if there is a physician involved, the physician can establish to whom he or she wrote the prescription. The Internet is anonymous. In these cases the donor cannot meet the minimal requirement of identifying the physician, and the physician cannot establish for whom the prescription was written. In the absence of a face-to-face meeting and any meaningful diagnosis, these cases are typically reported to employers as presenting a safety problem.

10.10.6   Medical Marijuana

Medical marijuana is not a prescription drug, but its use has been decriminalized in 11 states. Most of the state medical marijuana acts list the medical conditions for which the drug can be used and require the "recommendation" of a physician. Many states also have formal patient registries and other conditions of use. In the U.S., the federal government and the states share jurisdiction in respect to the control of legal and illegal drugs. There is usually symmetry in this dual jurisdictional approach, but not always, as seen in the controversy over medical marijuana.

Federal policy has been consistent in prohibiting MROs from accepting medical marijuana as a valid explanation for a positive THC test. Synthetic versions of THC (such as Marinol®, a Schedule III controlled drug) are, however, acceptable. The challenge has been for employers operating in states with medical marijuana acts to develop policies that are legally enforceable. Much of the legal uncertainty has been resolved by the courts.

The most significant court decision in this area is the well-publicized case of *Raich v. Ashcroft*. In *Raich*, the users and growers of marijuana for medical purposes under the California Compassionate Use Act sought a declaration that the Federal Controlled Substances Act (CSA) was unconstitutional as applied to them, in that this federal law is based on the commerce clause, and that growing marijuana legally for one's own use is not "commerce." The plaintiffs prevailed on this argument, which was then appealed to the Supreme Court.

In November 2004, the U.S. Supreme Court heard oral arguments in *Raich v. Ashcroft* (retitled *Raich v. Gonzales*). On June 14, 2005, the Supreme Court released its decision. The Court upheld the federal government's constitutional authority to prosecute the possession, sale, and manufacture of marijuana, regardless of conflicting state law.[22]

The government's brief in the *Raich* case stated:

The "home-grown" manufacturing, free distribution, and possession of controlled substances, whether for recreational or purported medicinal purposes, also pose an appreciable risk of diversion to others for further drug use or distribution, a result that further swells the illicit market. Local users may ultimately sell or divert the drug to others (for instance, should their production yield exceed their purported needs or should additional funds be required to finance their drug production or other activities).[23]

Justice Souter noted in oral arguments that there could be 100,000 medical marijuana patients just in California, based on the number of cancer/chemo patients. No one disagreed. He noted that carving out an exception for patients in the absence of any other control is *de facto* decontrol. Justice Souter's observation is correct, but the decision in this case, while maintaining the *status quo,* did not end the matter.

The Supreme Court decision did make it easier for employers in California and other states with medical marijuana acts to prohibit the use of native marijuana in any form, particularly for safety-sensitive jobs. But *Raich* did not deal directly with employment issues, and many employers remained worried over possible claims of disability, discrimination or wrongful termination. Those claims could quite easily be tried in a sympathetic state court with a sympathetic jury and a sympathetic sick employee using medical marijuana.

Employers' concerns over disability claims have been greatly reduced with a significant decision by the Oregon Supreme Court. That watershed case is *Washburn v. Columbia Forest Products,* which was decided in May 2006. The issue that was before the Oregon Supreme Court was whether the Oregon State Disabilities Act (which tracks with the Americans with Disabilities Act) requires an employer to make a disability-related accommodation for an employee who uses marijuana for medical purposes.

The plaintiff, Robert Washburn, was an employee of Columbia Forest Products, Inc. He was also a medical marijuana recipient who regularly used the drug before going to bed to counteract leg spasms that otherwise would keep him awake. After he tested positive for marijuana use, Columbia terminated his employment. Washburn brought action against Columbia, alleging a violation of state prohibitions against disability-related discrimination in the workplace. The trial court granted summary judgment for Columbia, holding, in part, that Washburn was not "disabled" under the pertinent Oregon statutes. The court of appeals disagreed with that conclusion and held that Columbia's summary judgment motion should not have been granted.[24]

Upon review, the Oregon Supreme Court concluded that Washburn was not "disabled." The court followed the U.S. Supreme Court's line of reasoning in previous cases that hold if a drug or corrective action corrects or mitigates the disability, the person is not "disabled" and there is no requirement to make any further accommodation.[25] Setting aside the somewhat circular reasoning of the courts, this decision provides solace to employers in states with medical marijuana laws.[26]

A separate concurring opinion in the case makes the more salient point that, although a state may choose to exempt medical marijuana users from the reach of state criminal law, it is not reasonable to require an employer to accommodate what federal law specifically prohibits.

Although there are employers in jurisdictions where medical marijuana has been excluded from state criminal law sanctions who accept medical marijuana as a legitimate excuse, these employers are making the accommodations more on the basis of employer–employee relations and community standards.

For MROs, the claim of medical marijuana is common in states with medical marijuana laws. MROs recognize that legitimate cases are mixed in with a significant number of bogus claims. Recommendations from physicians to use medical marijuana are not hard to obtain.

Effective management of medical marijuana in non-regulated, non-safety-sensitive employment situations requires some degree of collaboration between MROs and employers, and the establishment of sound employer policies on what is and what is not acceptable.

10.10.7 Screen-Only Drug Testing

On-site drug testing technology has progressed and diversified to the point where it appears that a broader definition of the term "on-site" is needed. On-site testing initially referred to bench-top automated immunoassay devices used outside of a formal laboratory setting. Over time, as immunoassay methods progressed, instrumental measurement of the immunoassay reaction could be replaced by visual inspection. Immunoassay impregnated on plastic cards became the new "on-site" technology, and the term "non-instrumented on-site testing" was adopted. A variety of different designs exists, from bottles with the immunoassay integrated into the side, to cards that are simply dipped into a urine specimen. Most of the technology is designed to produce a line when the specimen is negative for the specified drug, and the absence of a line indicates a "presumptive" positive test. Most current strip technology performs equally to laboratory screening in identifying negative tests. But like the laboratory-based immunoassay screening, it is not 100% conclusive of the presence of a prohibited drug.

Further, the distinction between instrumented and non-instrumented immunoassay on-site testing is also dissolving. Handheld instrumental devices are in development that will provide an "on-site" analysis of oral fluids and urine. Visual interpretation of a line or no line will be replaced by an automatic report or a simple display. Another innovation is the integration of an on-site instrument that objectively reads the immunoassay results and transmits the results over the Internet to a centralized facility. The computer at the central facility analyzes the results according to a software program and essentially determines whether the specimen should be sent to a laboratory for further testing (either as a non-negative or a random quality control). The final results are then reported to an MRO. This type of approach is a hybrid of centralized laboratory management and local collection and screening. The first such product, called *eScreen*, is already being marketed.

The open question in the utilization of inexpensive immunoassays is to what degree all of the safeguards of training, quality control, and technical management, which are required and used in a certified forensic drug testing laboratory, are applicable to on-site testing, and whether they are necessary.

It should go without saying that existing confirmatory testing requirements will continue to be required in the event that on-site technology becomes incorporated into federally mandated drug testing programs. Confirmatory testing is one of the essential constitutional requirements of federally mandated testing. In workplace drug testing, confirmatory testing has become synonymous with GC/MS technology. But in a broader sense, confirmatory tests can be conducted with LC/MS or MS/MS or comparable instrumentation. The essential element of confirmatory testing is the independent definitive nature of the analysis. It is the true technical foundation upon which sound decisions affecting employment can be made.

All manufacturers and distributors of on-site products are in the chorus recommending GC/MS confirmation and MRO review. However, it is not a foregone conclusion that either of these safeguards will be automatically included in private sector workplace drug testing programs, in the absence of a state law requiring them. Most employers do not have a legal duty or mandate to require confirmation testing, and the economics and apparent simplicity of screen-only results are seductive.

The employment-at-will doctrine is a pillar of labor and employment law in the U.S. The doctrine essentially states that either party to an employment relationship, the employer or the employee, can terminate the relationship for any reason, or for no reason. Thus, it is argued that an employer may terminate an employee based on a screen-only result, but it is an ill-advised practice. First, it is highly unlikely that a screen-only result will be persuasive in any employment proceeding, whether it is an unemployment security hearing, labor arbitration, or a workers' compensation hearing. Further, the employer's publication of a screen-only result to another employer may raise the issue of defamation. This is because for all practical purposes, 99% accuracy is simply not good enough. All screen-positives claim to be that 1%, and the law allows them to make that claim.

A collateral rule to the employment-at-will doctrine is that an employer is free to hire or not to hire applicants based on the employer's assessments, as long as the hiring criteria and decisions are not discriminatory in nature. Thus for many employers the use of a screening device for applicants that produces false-positives does not appear to present any significant legal repercussions.

There is essentially no "right" to any job. Applicant screening is the target market for many on-site testing devices. It is a very large market, and many employers do not perceive a need for confirmatory testing or for MROs. In the absence of any state prohibition against screen-only testing of applicants, the argument can be made that the employer who does screen-only testing could run afoul of the Americans with Disabilities Act. Applicants who have been denied a job without confirmation testing may bring an action claiming that they were discriminated against because the employer thought that they were illegal drug users and have a disability, and they do not use illegal drugs and do not have a disability. Although this argument may technically be true, it is not a strong discouragement of screen-only practices.

The broader danger of widespread screen-only practices will be the undermining of the public's acceptance of drug testing. The unwritten social pact is that drug testing is accurate and reliable, and that there will be no adverse impact on an individual who is not currently engaging in illegal drug use.

The open question is whether the incident rate of litigation will continue to remain low, or whether the industry will be faced with increased risk exposure and legal costs. It will not take too many cases for service providers to withdraw from this market.

NOTES

1. The "rules" of workplace drug testing vary considerably and are dependent on such things as who is being tested, why they are being tested, who is doing the testing, and where the test is being collected and performed. An employer in Maine must have a comprehensive program with all the safeguards in place approved by the state before testing, while the same employer in a state with no drug testing law can screen an applicant's urine with an unapproved on-site immunoassay device with impunity. There has been an ongoing process of state legislation that has generated hundreds of statutes that prescribe what is allowed in a particular state and what is not allowed. Today it is nearly impossible for a company to have a uniform drug and alcohol policy and procedure that can be rolled out nationally. This will be a continuing challenge as employers begin to adopt other testing methods.

2. *See,* e.g., *B & F Eng'g, Inc. v. Cotroneo*, 309 Ark. 175, 830 S.W.2d 835 (1992). The court noted that the negligence of impaired transportation workers, such as flight mechanics, bus drivers, or railroad switchmen, can cost an employer millions. *Mulroy v. Olberding*, 29 Kan. App. 2d 757, 30 P.3d 1050 (2001). *But see Beckendorf v. Simmons*, 539 S.W.2d 31 (Tenn. 1976). When the employer had repeatedly forbidden the employee to drive the vehicle, there was no liability.

3. In most collective bargaining agreements, the employer has agreed to provide assistance and a SAP evaluation and return-to-duty requirements for transgressions of the substance abuse policy.

4. The amount of morphine in the specimen was around 600 ng/ml, which is quite consistent with poppy seed ingestion.

5. *SmithKline Beecham Corp. v. Doe.* 903 S.W.2d 347 (Tex. 1995).

6. The following are the cases that reached the appellate level. Drug testing laboratory owes persons tested a duty to perform its services with reasonable care: *Willis v. Roche Biomedical Lab.,* 21 F.3d 1368, 1372-1375 (5th Cir. 1994); *Stinson v. Physicians Immediate Care, Ltd.,* 269 Ill. App.3d 659, 207 Ill. Dec. 96, 646 N.E.2d 930, 932-934 (1995). Laboratory owes prospective employee a duty not to contaminate sample and report a false result: *Nehrenz v. Dunn,* 593 So.2d 915, 917-918 (La.Ct.App. 1992). Laboratory owes employee a duty to perform test in a competent manner: *Elliott v. Laboratory Specialists,* 588 So.2d 175, 176 (La.Ct.App. 1991); writ denied, 592 So.2d 415 (La. 1992). Laboratory owes employee a duty to perform test in a scientifically reasonable manner: *Lewis v. Aluminum Co. of Am.,* 588 So.2d 167, 170 (La.Ct.App. 1991); writ denied, 592 So.2d 411 (La. 1992). Laboratory owes employee a duty to perform tests in a competent, non-negligent manner: See *Herbert v. Placid Ref. Co.,* 564 So.2d 371, 374 (La.Ct.App. 1990).

7. *Harvey J. Duncan, a/k/a Jim Duncan, Appellant (Plaintiff) v. Afton, Inc.,* a Tennessee corporation, d/b/a Healthcomp Evaluation Services Corporation, d/b/a National Ameritest, a/k/a Ameritest; and Leigh Ann Shears, an individual, Appellees (Defendants). No. 99-24. Supreme Court of Wyoming. Nov. 30, 1999. (Cite as: 1999 WL 1073434 (Wyo.).)

8. Claims have been made against MROs, and there have been significant settlements.

9. The general legal duty to remove individuals from safety-sensitive positions is found in 49 C.F.R. 40.23. The prohibition against removing an individual prior to MRO verification is found in 49 C.F.R. 40.21.

10. Didrex is a prescription drug that will cause a positive methamphetamine result. Adipex is a prescription drug that is used as an appetite suppressant; it will not cause a methamphetamine result.

11. It is worth noting that although the actual quantitative value for the methamphetamine was never reported, the initial laboratory result to the MRO reported the presence of methamphetamine only. This means that the amphetamine level was under 500 ng/ml, and such a laboratory result is consistent with inhaler use.

12. Such a practice of universal direct observation of miturition (the process of emptying the bladder) or even the suggestion of doing so, would quickly erode a great deal of public support for drug testing. It may also be viewed as unnecessarily invasive, and trigger various challenges to mandatory drug testing as being an unreasonable invasion of privacy. In fact, many state drug-free workplace statutes require privacy in providing urine specimens. DOT regulations are quite specific on this, and a number of courts have suggested that an observed collection of urine in the absence of individualized suspicion could be viewed as the tort of common law invasion of privacy (e.g., *Borse v. Piece Goods,* 963 F.2d 611 (3d Cir. 1992), applying Pennsylvania law). In *Borse,* the plaintiff was discharged for refusing to submit to urinalysis screening and to personal property searches at the workplace. The federal appellate court predicted that, if faced with the issue, the Pennsylvania Supreme Court would find a public policy exception to the employment-at-will doctrine based on the common law tort of invasion of privacy if the employer was going to require Mrs. Borse to provide urine under observed collection (in the absence of individualized suspicion).

13. Department of Health and Human Services Substance Abuse and Mental Health Services Administration, *Mandatory Guidelines for Federal Workplace Drug Testing Programs,* Tuesday, April 13, 2004 (69 FR 19644-01).

14. Edgell, K., Laboratory survey of adulterant testing, *MROAlert,* Volume XVI, No. 10 (December 2005).

15. U.S. Department of Transportation. Procedures for Transportation Workplace Drug and Alcohol Testing Programs, Notice of Proposed Rule Making, October 31, 2005 (70 FR 62276).

16. Federal Aviation Administration, Office of Aviation Medicine, *Workplace Urine Specimen Validity Testing Colloquium,* Tampa, Florida (February 4–6, 2003).

17. 1998 DOT regulations, 49 C.F.R. Subtitle A, §40.25(f)(22)(ii).

18. See also 2001 DOT §40.355: "What limitations apply to the activities of service agents? As a service agent, you are subject to the following limitations concerning your activities in the DOT drug and alcohol testing program. (a) You must not require an employee to sign a consent, release, waiver of liability, or indemnification agreement with respect to any part of the drug or alcohol testing process covered by this part (including, but not limited to, collections, laboratory testing, MRO, and SAP services). No one may do so on behalf of a service agent."

19. GAO-05-653T: "Drug Tests: Products to Defraud Drug Use Screening Tests Are Widely Available."

20. Department of Health and Human Services, Substance Abuse and Mental Health Services Administration. Proposed Revisions to Mandatory Guidelines for Federal Workplace Drug Testing Programs, April 13, 2004 (69 FR 19673-01).

21. On-site oral fluid testing devices are available but are essentially ineffective at identifying the parent drug THC in specimens. THC is the target for oral fluid testing since the amount of metabolite (THC-COOH) found in urine is found in very small quantities in the mouth.

22. *Alberto R. Gonzales, Attorney General, et al., Petitioners, v. Angel McClary Raich et al.* No. 03-1454. Supreme Court of the United States. Decided June 6, 2005. 125 S.Ct. 2195.

23. In the Supreme Court of the United States, *John D. Ashcroft, Attorney General, et al., Petitioners v. Angel McClary Raich, et al.* On Writ of Certiorari to the United States Court of Appeals for the Ninth Circuit, No. 03-1454. Brief for the Petitioners, Paul D. Clement, Acting Solicitor General.

24. *Washburn v. Columbia Forest Products, Inc.,* 197 Or App 104, 104 P3d 609 (2005).

25. The U.S. Supreme Court had held that a person is not disabled under federal disability law if a mitigating measure will alleviate an otherwise substantial limitation to a major life activity. *See, e.g., Sutton v. United Airlines, Inc.,* 527 US 471, 119 S Ct 2139, 144 L Ed 2d 450 (1999).

26. What appears circular in applying the mitigation rule to the use of medical marijuana is that the decision essentially prohibits the employee from taking advantage of the very medication that alleviates his purported disability.

CHAPTER 11

Point of Collection Drug Testing

Edited by Dennis J. Crouch, M.B.A.
Director, Sports Medicine Research and Testing Laboratory, and Co-Director, Center for Human
Toxicology, University of Utah, Salt Lake City, Utah, and Consulting Toxicologist, The Walsh Group, P.A.,
Bethesda, Maryland

CONTENTS

Point of collection testing (POCT) utilizes some of the least-sophisticated drug testing technology, yet has been quite controversial. The earliest on-site facilities used instrumented-immunoassay techniques for testing. Despite acceptance of the technology for laboratory testing, its use at the site of specimen collection was questioned due to scientific, ethical, and medicolegal concerns about confidentiality of the donor and donor results, the lack of confirmation, proficiency of the operators, security of the facilities, quality control, and a host of related issues. However, the demand for immediate drug test results from clinical, workplace, and criminal justice settings fueled the continued growth of POCT and POCT technologies. The introduction of non-instrumented and subjectively interpreted POCT devices has added to the controversy surrounding on-site testing, but has provided an innovative new approach to drug and alcohol detection. The scientific skepticism about the reliability of these devices was often warranted because early products had varying sensitivity, specificity, and accuracy. However, there has been an evolution of the technology, as discussed in Section 11.5, such that the products are more reliable and the technology more widely accepted. A primary motivator for product and technology development and improvement has been the criminal justice system. Here, as discussed in Section 11.2, testing is routinely performed in pretrial, pre-sentencing, probation, parole, incarceration, and drug treatment programs. In the identification of impaired drivers, POCT also evolved from instrumented breath alcohol testing instruments to handheld devices (see Section 11.4). Some of the most recent advances in POCT have involved the analysis of alcohol and other drugs in oral fluids. As discussed in Sections 11.1 and 11.4, instrumented and several non-instrumented devices are now available. Oral fluid collections are less invasive and problematic than urine collections, making POCT using this specimen a fertile area of product development and scientific research.

Federal, state, and local regulations have often changed the face of laboratory science. Based on pending regulations discussed in Section 11.3, oral fluid and urine testing devices, analysts, procedures, and facilities may soon be required to conform to standards similar to those imposed on conventional urinalysis drug testing. This is potentially a very significant development because (1) the previous urine regulations had a sweeping impact on drug testing and its allied industries, and (2) many of the scientific, ethical, and medicolegal concerns about POCT are addressed in the pending regulation.

11.1 POINT OF COLLECTION TESTING OF ALTERNATIVE SPECIMENS (OTHER THAN URINE)

Alain Verstraete, M.D., Ph.D.[1] and J. Michael Walsh, Ph.D.[2]
[1] Ghent University Hospital, Laboratory of Clinical Biology–Toxicology, Ghent, Belgium
[2] The Walsh Group, P.A., Bethesda, Maryland

In 1984, Rodgers et al.[1] developed an enzyme-channeling test strip immunoassay for the detection of cannabinoids in saliva. The limit of detection was 10 ng/ml of THCCOOH. The antibody had high cross-reactivity for THC, and the test was positive for 2 to 2.5 h after smoking. Since the mid-1990s, there has been a growing interest in POCT testing of alternative specimens for drugs.

Some authors and device manufacturers have attempted to use POCT tests (designed for urine) to test alternative matrices, but with mixed results. Indeed, in alternative matrices, the drug concentrations are often lower than in urine and the parent molecules are excreted, more than the metabolites. Therefore, antibodies with other target molecules must be used. Iwersen and Schmoldt[2] tried to adapt the Boehringer Frontline urine assay (which was subsequently used in the Drugwipe) for analysis of saliva. By increasing the contact time of the saliva specimen to the collection pad they could perform the analysis; however, up to 8 min was needed in some cases to obtain sufficient moistening of the pad. They observed no false-positive, but many false-negative cases. The sensitivity of the modified procedure was 73, 53, and 75% for cocaine, cannabis, and opiates, respectively.

The first on-site or point of collection testing (POCT) devices that were commercially available for oral fluid analysis were the Securetec Drugwipe® (that could be used for sweat as well), Avitar Oralscreen™, and Cozart Rapiscan. The European project Rosita[3] (Roadside Testing Assessment) was the first large-scale evaluation of POCT oral fluid and sweat testing devices and it provided a strong impetus for further development of POCT products for saliva/oral fluid and sweat.

Most POCT research and development efforts in the last 5 years have been directed toward testing of saliva/oral fluid. Although some testing of perspiration/sweat has been done, this has been done on a much more limited scale. To the authors' knowledge, no point-of-collection tests currently exist for hair or nails.

Table 11.1.1 gives possible applications of oral fluid POCT devices. The main applications are workplace and roadside drug testing. As of the beginning of 2004, POCT oral fluid tests are being used in prisons and some workplaces (mining, printing, transportation, and manufacturing). POCT roadside controls by police using alternative matrices such as oral fluid have generally only been performed on an experimental basis, although legislation introduced in December 2003 in the state of Victoria in Australia will eventually allow police to perform roadside oral fluid tests for cannabis and methamphetamine.[4]

In the U.K., the Cozart Rapiscan has been in use since 2001 by the Home Office to test for drugs of abuse (cocaine and heroin) in arrestees detained in police custody.[5]

Table 11.1.1   Possible Applications of Point-of-Collection Drug Testing Devices

Workplace drug testing
Roadside drug testing
Treatment centers
Prisons
Insurance physicals
Emergency departments
Autopsy rooms

Table 11.1.2 Overview of POCT Oral Fluid Drug Tests

Device	Manufacturer	Web Site (accessed Dec. 2003)
DrugTest	Dräger Safety, Lübeck, Germany	www.draeger.com
UPlink	OraSure Technologies, Inc., Bethlehem, PA 18015, USA	www.orasure.com
Drugwipe II	Securetec Detektions-Systeme AG, Ottobrunn, Germany	www.securetec.net
Impact test system	LifePoint Inc., Ontario, CA 91761, USA	www.lifepointinc.com
On-Site OraLab	Varian Inc., Lake Forest, CA, USA	varian-onsite.com
OraLine s.a.t. Test	Sun Biomedical Laboratories, Inc., Blackwood, NJ 08012, USA	www.sunbiomed.com
ORALscreen	Avitar, Inc., Canton, MA 02021, USA	www.avitarinc.com
Oratect	Branan Medical Corporation, Irvine, CA 92618, USA	www.brananmedical.com
RapiScan	Cozart Bioscience Limited, Abingdon, Oxfordshire, U.K.	www.cozart.co.uk
SalivaScreen	ulti med Products GmbH, Germany	www.ultimed.org www.salivascreen.de
SmartClip	EnviteC-Wismar GmbH, Wismar, Germany	www.envitec.com

11.1.1 Testing Devices/Techniques

11.1.1.1 Examples of Devices

During the Rosita project,[3] three POCT devices for saliva and one device for sweat were identified. However, by the end of 2003, ten different devices were commercially available (Table 11.1.2).

11.1.1.2 Principle of Example Testing Methods

Most rapid oral fluid and sweat tests use the lateral flow immunoassay technology, typically with visual evaluation of the results. However, some of the devices can be coupled to electronic readers and the results read automatically.

Another technology, the UPlink™ POCT *in vitro* diagnostic system, uses Up-Converting Phosphor Technology (UPT™). UPT particles are small ceramic nano-spheres composed of rare earth metals. These particles are similar to the particles excited by ultraviolet light that have been used for decades in television display screens and fluorescent tubes. However, unlike the particles used in television screens, UPT particles are excited by infrared light and they "up-convert" the energy to give a visible emission. The use of infrared light (rather than ultraviolet light) to create a colored signal is called up-conversion. Because no other materials in nature up-convert, biological specimens will not emit light when excited by infrared energy. Therefore, tests using these particles are unaffected by specimen background, resulting in a very sensitive assay system especially when linked to well-designed antibodies. In addition, just like current television display screens, UPT particles are available that emit different colors, which allows multiplexing. UPT labels have been incorporated into a rapid lateral flow test format and a portable, bench-top instrument was developed to read the lateral flow test strips using compact laser diodes.[6]

11.1.1.3 Operation (General)

One can divide the available POCT devices along a continuum of complexity of operation, from those very easy to operate devices to those that are more complex to operate. Three examples are discussed below: Branan Medical Oratect™ (Figure 11.1.1), Securetec Drugwipe (Figure 11.1.2), and OraSure Technologies Uplink™ (Figure 11.1.3).

Branan Medical Oratect (two steps, total analysis time about 5 to 10 min)

1. Collect an oral fluid sample by placing device inside the donor mouth on the inner cheek. The collection pad should touch the donor's cheek.

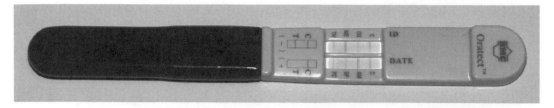

Figure 11.1.1   Branan Medical Oratect. The test shows the control line and a line in the area of the amphet-amines, methamphetamine, cannabis, cocaine, and opiates, which means that none of the tested drugs was found in the sample.

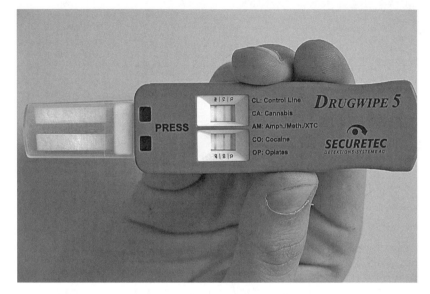

Figure 11.1.2   Securetec Drugwipe II. The test shows two control lines and a line in the area of the amphet-amines/methamphetamine/ecstasy, cannabis, cocaine, and opiates, which means that all of the tested drugs were found in the sample.

2. After 10 s, move the device to the bottom of the mouth under the tongue. Leave the device under the tongue until the colored lines appear in the viewing windows indicating that a sufficient volume of saliva has been collected, and then remove the device from the mouth.
3. Read the results visually within 9 to 11 min after removing the device. Do not read results after 11 min because the intensity of the colored line may change.

Securetec Drugwipe (three steps, total time is about 5 to 10 min)

1. Disconnect wiping section from the device.
2. Wipe the surface of the tongue or the body (if testing for drugs deposited on the skin) for approximately 10 s.
3. Reassemble the device, dip the absorbent pad into water, and remove after counting to 10.
4. Read the result visually after approximately 10 min.

OraSure Technologies Uplink/Dräger Safety Drugtest (eight steps, total analysis time is about 16 min)

1. Insert sample preparation cartridge (SPC) into the cassette.
2. Align lower tabs with notches on cassette and press until it "clicks."
3. Remove cap of SPC and store.

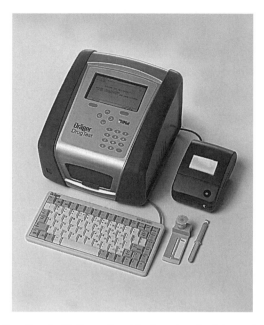

Figure 11.1.3 The Dräger DrugRead with the optional keyboard and printer and the sample collection device.

4. Collect an oral fluid sample with the collection sponge.
5. Express fluid from the sponge by pressing the collection device into SPC until it "cracks."
6. Remove collection device wand by twisting it counter-clockwise.
7. Replace cap on SPC until it is fully seated.
8. Incubate the sample for 4 min.
9. Twist SPC clockwise to align upper tabs with notches on cassette and press down until SPC wings contact test cassette rim.
10. Run test on the reader (this takes 8 min).

The total procedure takes 16 min.

11.1.1.4 Evaluations of Devices

The following is a compilation of information about field testing of the ten oral fluid/sweat POCT devices that we identified. Much of the information presented below comes from studies conducted by, or sponsored by, the device manufacturers. Some of the devices discussed are not yet commercially available (e.g., OraSure Uplink, Lifepoint Impact, and Envitec-Wismar Smartclip).

Three devices were evaluated during the first Rosita study.[3] The results (Table 11.1.3) show that their reliability was not sufficient, but differences in confirmation techniques and prevalence of positive samples made comparisons difficult. However, most of these devices have been significantly modified since the Rosita study to improve their sensitivity and reliability. Some of the POCT devices identified have already been extensively evaluated, while others have not. Recently, Walsh et al.[7] evaluated the performance of six devices with drug-fortified oral fluid samples. A summary of the detection limits for the different drugs is given in Table 11.14. For amphetamine, methamphetamine, and opiates testing, several devices could detect concentrations lower than the oral fluid cutoffs mentioned in draft 4 of the SAMHSA guidelines for workplace drug testing.[8] However, there were some problems in testing cocaine (most devices target benzoylecgonine) and no device could detect THC at the 4 ng/ml recommended cutoff.

The results of field evaluations of the individual POCT devices are given below.

Table 11.1.3   Summary of the Results Obtained with POCT Oral Fluid and Sweat Tests during the First Rosita Study[3]

Oral Fluid	RapiScan					Drugwipe					Oralscreen				
	n	Prev.	Sens.	Spec.	Acc.	n	Prev.	Sens.	Spec.	Acc.	n	Prev.	Sens.	Spec.	Acc.
Amphetamines	80	73%	83%	68%	79%	120	74%	87%	55%	78%					
Benzodiazepines	133	47%	17%	90%	56%										
Cannabinoids	9										190	2%	25%	84%	83%
Cocaine	33	0%	—	100%	100%	118	25%	59%	92%	84%	180	0%	—	99%	99%
Opiates	37	49%	61%	26%	43%	46	48%	41%	79%	61%	183	4%	57%	93%	91%
Sweat															
Amphetamines						63	92%	94%	67%	92%					
Cocaine						22	100%	77%	—	77%					
Opiates						9	100%	89%	—	89%					

Note: All POCT results were compared to GC-MS in oral fluid/sweat, except for benzodiazepines, where they were compared to blood.

Abbreviations: n: number of comparisons, Prev: prevalence of positive samples, Sens: sensitivity of the test, Spec: specificity of the test, Acc: accuracy of the test, = number of true positives and true negatives divided by the number of tests.

Table 11.1.4 Detection Limits (ng/ml) of Six POCT Tests in Spiked Oral Fluid Samples[7,32]

	Amphetamine	THC	Morphine	Cocaine	Methamphetamine
Drugwipe	500	50	20	200	100
Oratect	25	ND	20	40	25
Rapiscan	25	50	80	200	100
OraLab	500	100	80	10	500
Saliva screen	NT	ND	20	40	25
Uplink	25	20	20	200	25

NT: not tested; ND: no THC could be detected, even at 100 ng/ml.

Orasure Technologies Uplink/Dräger Safety Drugtest

After drinking 200 ml of Coca tea, benzoylecgonine could be detected during for 22.5 to 27.5 h. Using a GC-MS/MS limit of detection (LOD) of 0.4 ng/ml benzoylecgonine, the Dräger DrugTest demonstrated a sensitivity, specificity, and accuracy of 86, 87, and 86%, respectively.[9]

The Dräger DrugTest was also evaluated using samples from 92 patients in an addiction treatment program. The Dräger DrugTest results were compared to GC-MS/MS and the sensitivity, specificity, and accuracy were 95.2, 90.1, and 91.3% for THC; 87.5, 96.4, and 95.7% for cocaine; and 92.9, 84.4, and 87.0% for opiates.[10]

The Dräger DrugTest was further evaluated by the German police during drug controls during the Love Parade of 2003. The accuracy of the POCT device, compared to GC-MS or GC-MS/MS, was 91.5% for THC, 97.2% for cocaine, 100% for opiates, 95.8% for methamphetamine, and 74.6% for amphetamine (S. Steinmeyer, presented at the 41st TIAFT meeting, Melbourne, Australia, November 2003).

In a study using volunteers who smoked marijuana cigarettes, the Uplink rapid drug test was able to detect THC up to 24 h after smoking. The concentrations of THC collected by the Uplink collector ranged from 3.6 to 13,860 ng/ml over the 24-h period of the study. ROC (receiver operating characteristic[11]) analysis of the data showed a sensitivity of 90% and a specificity of 97.2% using an Uplink screening cutoff of 25 ng/ml with a 15 ng/ml confirmation cutoff. The concentrations in samples collected with the Uplink collector were high when compared to other commercially available devices. Also in passive smokers, a THC concentration of 25 ng/ml was observed. (S. Niedbala, presented at the 41st TIAFT meeting, Melbourne, Australia, November 2003).

Dräger Safety decided in August 2005 to discontinue the marketing of the Uplink/DrugTest system, but the company is developing a new 2nd Dräger DrugTest Generation for mobile drug screening applications.

Securetec Drugwipe

One of the first evaluations of the Securetec Drugwipe I was performed by Kintz et al.,[12] who administered 60 mg of codeine to six volunteers and analyzed their oral fluid (by wiping on the tongue) and sweat (by wiping the forehead) with the Drugwipe. The foreheads of the subjects were swabbed for 10 s at 1, 4, 9, and 24 h after codeine administration. In all subjects (except one) the Drugwipe tested positive for opiates. However, some false-negative results were observed. In the second part of the study, the tongues of the subjects were carefully wiped at specific times over a period of 24 h, and at the same times a specimen of saliva was collected. Although codeine could be detected using the Drugwipe, numerous false-negative results were observed compared to GC/MS. The authors attributed the false-negative results to the codeine concentrations being too low to be detected by Drugwipe, the presence of interfering substances in saliva, or to inadequate sampling procedures.

For sweat testing, the first-generation Drugwipe was introduced to routine work by the police in Baden-Württemberg (Germany) after a successful study. A preliminary evaluation of the amphetamine tests showed good sensitivity and reliability, especially for ecstasy.[13]

However, the police determined that the cannabis test showed poor reliability. After intake of 100 mg of MDMA by two volunteers, the Drugwipe could detect MDMA in sweat taken from the armpit in a time window of 2 and 12 h.[14]

With the use of the Drugread optical reader to read the Drugwipe results, MDMA could be determined in oral fluid quantitatively and could be detected for up to 24 h.[15]

Lifepoint Impact Test System

In an experimental setting, the limit of detection for THC was 5.5 ng/ml (Wang et al., poster at the SOFT meeting in Milwaukee, October 2000). No results of field evaluations have been published or presented at the time of writing. *Note:* Effective April 28, 2005, LifePoint assigned its assets in trust to the Insolvency Services Group, Inc.

Varian On-Site OraLab

No field evaluations have been presented or published.

Sun Biomedical Laboratories OraLine s.a.t. Test

No field evaluations have been presented or published.

Avitar ORALscreen

Barrett et al.[16] compared the ORALscreen to urine results in drug users in inpatient substance abuse clinics and in a probation department. The agreements with known positive results were 96, 96, 86, and 43% for cocaine, opiates, methamphetamine, and THC, respectively. For negative results, the agreements were 92, 96, 94, and 76%, respectively. After consumption of poppy-seed bread, the opiate results were positive for 1 h.

Branan Medical Corporation Oratect

With samples fortified at concentrations 300, 100, 75, 50, and 25% of the cutoff, the sensitivity was 80% for all assays, except morphine (90%), and the specificity was 97.1% for THC, PCP, amphetamine, and methamphetamine, and 98.6% for cocaine and morphine.[17] An evaluation of 40 oral fluid samples from donors with negative urine drug tests all showed negative Oratect results. In donors with positive urine drug tests, Oratect gave positive results in 12/13 cases for cocaine, 13/13 for morphine, 1/2 for methamphetamine, and 7/8 for THC.[18,19]

After administration of 10 mg of codeine to ten volunteers, all subjects tested positive up to 4 h with the Oratect (with a cutoff at 20 ng/ml). At 6 h, six out of ten volunteers tested positive. The Oratect results correlated well with the Intercept device showing low to undetectable opiate concentrations at 6 h.

An evaluation of the Oratect benzodiazepines assay using fortified samples and samples that were positive by GC-MS confirmed the cutoff of 15 ng/ml oxazepam. All samples that were positive by GC-MS were positive by Oratect. The detection limits varied between 5 ng/ml for temazepam, over 30 ng/ml for nordiazepam to 150 ng/ml for chlordiazepoxide (R. Wong, poster at the 41st TIAFT meeting in Melbourne, Australia, November 2003).

Cozart Bioscience Rapiscan

Jehanli et al.[20] evaluated the Cozart Rapiscan after administration of marijuana and 16 mg of codeine to human volunteers. Codeine could be detected for 9 h in all subjects and at 24 h in three out of five subjects, but marijuana could not be detected for more than 1 or 2 h (at the time of the evaluation, the detection limit was 150 ng/ml of THC in neat saliva) in the subjects.

Moore et al.[21] compared the Rapiscan methadone and opiates tests on 50 samples collected from patients attending a substance abuse clinic to EIA and GC-MS. Compared to GC-MS, the methadone test had 100% sensitivity and specificity, the opiate test had 100% sensitivity and 92% specificity.

De Giovanni et al.[22] evaluated the Rapiscan (except the cannabis test) on using drug-fortified saliva samples, samples from methadone treatment patients and young people at the exit of a discotheque. No false-positive results were obtained. In the drug-abusers group, no opiates and benzodiazepines were present and only one of three cocaine-positive cases was detected. For methadone, 15 of the 21 positives were detected. The three amphetamine cases were detected with the Rapiscan. In the discotheque goers, no opiates, methadone, or benzodiazepines were observed. All positive amphetamines and two of three cocaine cases were detected. All volunteers accepted the sampling without problems.

The Rapiscan cocaine and opiate assays were evaluated by the Forensic Science Service (an executive agency of the U.K. Home Office that supplies forensic services to police forces in England and Wales). Drugs could readily be detected for 24 to 36 h after last admitted use. For the cocaine assay, compared to EIA ($n = 1081$), 10.4% true positives, 86.5% true negatives, 0.6% false positives, and 2.5% false negatives were observed. With GC-MS, 80.6% of the positive samples were confirmed. For the opiates, compared to EIA ($n = 1060$), 50.5% true positives, 29.2% true negatives, 0.3% false positives, and 20.0% false negatives were observed. With GC-MS, 72.6% of the positive samples were confirmed. Reducing the Rapiscan cutoff by 5% would have decreased the number of false-negative results by more than half. Clinic staff and donors greatly preferred providing oral fluid specimens for drug testing compared to urine. The greatest criticism of oral fluid testing was the time taken to collect samples. In non-drug-using individuals, samples could normally be taken within 2 to 4 min. In regular drug users, sample collection times ranged between 5 and 15 min. In a small number of cases, collection was abandoned when insufficient sample had been collected after 15 min (D. Osselton, personal communication SOFT Annual meeting, October 2001).

Kolbrich et al.[23] evaluated the Rapiscan after controlled administration of cocaine. Compared to an 8 ng/ml cutoff by GC-MS, the Rapiscan had a sensitivity, specificity, and efficiency of 82.7, 94.5, and 87.6%, respectively.

A new collection device that allows for direct analysis (by the Cozart Rapiscan Instrument) of drugs in the oral fluid without the need to use dilution buffer, was evaluated in ten healthy volunteers (five males and five females). The new collector is designed so that collection of about 1.5 to 2.0 ml of oral fluid activates an electric circuit with a LED (light emitting diode). The volume collected from the volunteers varied between 1.3 and 2.0 ml. Completion of collection took a maximum of 5 min with the shortest time 45 s. No chemical stimulant is needed as the device itself is designed to stimulate salivation (A. Jehanli, presented at the 41st TIAFT meeting, Melbourne, Australia, November 2003).

ulti med Products Salivascreen

No field evaluations have been presented or published.

Envitec-Wismar SmartClip

The SmartClip was evaluated by German police forces (Thüringen) mainly in road-side testing from February to June 2003 (S. Fellner, personal communication). The handling procedure of the SmartClip was confirmed to be simple and hygienic. In several cases, additional buffer had to be added onto the collection sponge following oral fluid collection to ensure sufficient sample volume. The reading and interpretation of test results were found to be simple and unambiguous. A

preliminary analysis of the data (54 cases) showed that 13% (6 cases for amphetamine/metham-
phetamine and 1 case for morphine) of the reported test results were true positive and only 2% (1
case for amphetamine) of the reported test results were false positive. (S. Fellner, presented at the
41st TIAFT meeting, Melbourne, Australia, November 2003).

Noncommercial Assays

Cope et al.[24] described a disposable, 10-min, near-patient POCT saliva test to monitor cigarette
smoking. A plastic device contains the dried reagents that measure nicotine and its metabolites by
a colorimetric assay. The device can be used semiquantitatively by observing a color change and
comparing it to a reference chart or quantified by measuring the light absorbance with a colorimeter.
This method correlated with cotinine, as measured independently by radioimmunoassay ($r = 0.57$,
$P < 0.005$).

11.1.2 Specimens (Saliva/Sweat/Others)

In all oral fluid POCT devices, the sample is collected with a collector that is provided by the
manufacturer of the device. Experience has shown that it is important to use the collector that is
recommended by the manufacturer. Indeed, obtaining a good sample of oral fluid is one of the
most critical parts of testing.[25] People who have recently used drugs often have difficulty producing
saliva, and it may be very viscous. Some sampling techniques that work well with normal volunteers
do not work with drug users, and in this case, some stimulation and/or dilution with a buffer might
be needed. However, stimulation of the saliva and use of buffers may affect drug detection and
concentration.[25] THC is not excreted in saliva and the THC present in the mouth is the result of
oral contamination. Sampling devices that wipe the mucosa have a greater yield of THC.[26] Moreover,
THC also binds to the cotton of the sampling device, and extraction with a solvent might be needed
to improve recovery.

Many devices have a reservoir, so the remainder of the sample (that is not used for the POCT
testing) can be sent to a laboratory for confirmation by reference techniques.

For sweat, the Drugwipe is the only POCT device that has been used. Sampling is done by
wiping the pad over the skin of the forehead or the palm of the hand. No evaluations of the
reproducibility of the sampling process have been reported.

Quality Control, Quality Assurance, Proficiency Testing: Most POC immunoassay tests have
a built-in control line, and the result is "invalid" if the control line does not appear. In most instances,
an invalid result is because the sample volume is not sufficient or the sample is too viscous. There
have been some pilot oral fluid POC proficiency testing programs in the U.K. and the U.S. At this
time, no established programs exist for oral fluid and *a fortiori* for POCT tests.

Training: Use and interpretation of POCT oral fluid or sweat POC drug tests requires adequate
training. Some manufacturers will train and certify the operators of their devices.

Evidentiary Value: POC tests are immunoassays, with their known limitations, e.g., false-
positive results due to structurally analogous medications, like phentermine giving a false positive
amphetamine result.[20] They can only give a presumptive result that has to be confirmed by a
chromatographic technique coupled to mass spectrometry.

Advantages, Disadvantages, and Limitations: POC drug tests in alternative matrices have a
place in some situations where immediate measures need to be taken, e.g., in enforcing DUID
legislation.[27] There has been progress in the reliability and the detection limits of the devices, but
further improvement is needed. George and Braithwaite[28] have reviewed the advantages and disadvantages of using POCT testing for drugs of abuse. They made five recommendations:

1. All devices should be initially evaluated by professional laboratory staff.
2. A cost–benefit analysis should be performed, taking into account consumables and staff time.

3. Adequate training should be given and the operators should understand that they are responsible for any errors in interpretation of the results.
4. Quality control and quality assurance must be covered in addition to proper storage, maintenance, and calibration of the device.
5. Any device should undergo a rigorous evaluation to determine its suitability before it can be marketed.

11.1.3 Developing Technologies

In addition to lateral flow immunoassays and up-converting phosphor technology, some other technologies have been proposed for POCT drug testing in oral fluid.

Surface-enhanced Raman spectroscopy has been applied to analysis of amphetamines in oral fluid.[29]
Kidwell and Van Wie[30] developed a reusable, fieldable, and portable sensor for the detection of cocaine in oral fluid, based on ion selective electrodes for drugs. The data are transmitted by an infrared link to a palm computer. The detection limit was 50 ng/ml in buffered media.
Ion mobility spectroscopy has been tried for the detection of drugs in oral fluid, but to date this has not been successful (N. Samyn, personal communication). However, Skopp and Pötsch[31] report a preliminary study in which heroin and cocaine use could be detected in skin wipes (with a Salivette moistened with 70% ethanol) of the sternal or axillary region in cases where 6-acetylmorphine, morphine, or cocaine had been found by GC-MS. The skin swabs were directly blotted onto the filter pads and dried with a hairdryer.

11.1.4 Conclusions

There is a strong need for POC testing of alternative matrices, particularly for roadside testing. The use of, e.g., oral fluid has the advantage that the parent drug will be detected and that the presence of a drug in oral fluid may correlate better with impairment than the presence of drug metabolites in urine. Obtaining an oral fluid sample can be done under supervision and without embarrassment. But individuals who have recently consumed drugs often have very little and viscous oral fluid. Therefore, obtaining a suitable sample can take 15 to 20 min or be impossible. There has been tremendous progress in the performance of POC drug tests for alternative matrices; however, more research is needed on the influence of collection, adulterants, and other parameters that could violate the integrity of the specimen, the concentrations seen after passive exposure, and most importantly further research is needed to improve the sensitivity for detection of THC and benzodiazepines.

REFERENCES

1. Rodgers, R., Lee, R.H., Allen, M.P. et al., Detection of cannabis in saliva using a test strip immunoassay, in *TIAFT Proceedings,* Dunnett, N. and Kimber, K.J., Eds., TIAFT, Brighton, 1984, 215.
2. Iwersen, S. and Schmoldt, A., Frontline test sticks for drug testing in saliva? in *TIAFT Proceedings,* Sachs, H., Bernhard, W., and Jeger, A., Eds., TIAFT, Munich, 1996.
3. Verstraete, A.G. and Puddu, M., Evaluation of different roadside drug tests, in *Rosita. Roadside Testing Assessment,* A.G. Verstraete, Ed., Rosita Consortium, Gent, 2001, 167–232.
4. Parliament of Victoria. Road Safety (drug driving) Act 2003. 111/2003. 9-12-2003.
5. Second U.K. government contract for "Cozart Rapiscan," *Cozart Biz* 1, 2002.
6. Niedbala, R.S., Feindt, H., Kardos, K. et al., Detection of analytes by immunoassay using up-converting phosphor technology. *Anal. Biochem.* 293, 22–30, 2001.
7. Walsh, J.M., Flegel, R., Crouch, D.J. et al., An evaluation of rapid point-of-collection oral fluid drug-testing devices. *J. Anal. Toxicol.* 27, 429–439, 2003.
8. Substance Abuse and Mental Health Services Administration, Mandatory Guidelines for Federal Workplace Drug Testing Programs. Fed. Reg. 6, 19673–19732, 2004.

9. Steinmeyer, S., Saucedo, G., Polzius, R. et al., Nachweis von Cocain in Speichelproben nach Konsum von Bolivianischem Coca-Tee und Bestätigung mit GC/MSMS. *Toxichemt Krimtech* 70, 29, 2003.

10. Zorec-Karlovsek, M., Niedbala, R.S., Steinmeyer, S. et al., The suitability of oral fluid testing in outpatient clinics for treatment of drug addiction [abstr.]. *Forensic. Sci. Int.* 136, 310, 2003.

11. Zweig, M.H. and Campbell, G., Receiver-operating characteristic (ROC) plots: a fundamental evaluation tool in clinical medicine. *Clin. Chem.* 39, 561–577, 1993.

12. Kintz, P., Cirimele, V., and Ludes, B., Codeine testing in sweat and saliva with the Drugwipe. *Int. J. Legal Med.* 111, 82–84, 1998.

13. Sachs, H., Place of sweat in drugs of abuse testing., in *Proceedings of the 16th International Conference on Alcohol, Drugs and Traffic Safety,* Mayhew, D. and Dussault, C., Eds, Société de l'assurance automobile du Québec, Montréal, 2002 (CD-ROM).

14. Pacifici, R., Farre, M., Pichini, S. et al., Sweat testing of MDMA with the Drugwipe analytical device: a controlled study with two volunteers. *J. Anal. Toxicol.* 25, 144–146, 2001.

15. Pichini, S., Navarro, M., Farre, M. et al., On-site testing of 3,4-methylenedioxymethamphetamine (ecstasy) in saliva with Drugwipe and Drugread: a controlled study in recreational users. *Clin. Chem.* 48, 174–176, 2002.

16. Barrett, C., Good, C., and Moore, C., Comparison of point-of-collection screening of drugs of abuse in oral fluid with a laboratory-based urine screen. *Forensic. Sci. Int.* 122, 163–166, 2001.

17. Wong, R.C., Nguyen, P, Wong, B., and Wang, D., Development of an integrated oral fluid collection and testing drug screen device. *J. Anal. Toxicol.* 27(3), 185. 2003.

18. Cirimele, V., Kintz, P., and Mangin, P., Detection and quantification of lorazepam in human hair by GC-MS/NCI in a case of traffic accident. *Int. J. Legal Med.* 108, 265–267, 1996.

19. Wong, B., Wong, R.C., Fan, P., and Tran, M., Detection of abused drugs in oral fluid by an on-site one-step drug screen — Oratect™. *Clin. Chem.* 49(6 Suppl.), A125. 2003.

20. Jehanli, A., Brannan, S., Moore, L. et al., Blind trials of an onsite saliva drug test for marijuana and opiates. *J. Forensic. Sci.* 46, 1214–1220, 2001.

21. Moore, L., Wicks, J., Spiehler, V. et al., Gas chromatography-mass spectrometry confirmation of Cozart RapiScan saliva methadone and opiates tests. *J. Anal. Toxicol.* 25, 520–524, 2001.

22. De Giovanni, N., Fucci, N., Chiarotti, M. et al., Cozart Rapiscan system: our experience with saliva tests. *J. Chromatogr. B Anal. Technol. Biomed. Life. Sci.* 773, 1–6, 2002.

23. Kolbrich, E.A., Kim, I., Barnes, A.J. et al., Cozart RapiScan Oral Fluid Drug Testing System: an evaluation of sensitivity, specificity, and efficiency for cocaine detection compared with ELISA and GC-MS following controlled cocaine administration. *J. Anal. Toxicol.* 27, 407–411, 2003.

24. Cope, G., Nayyar, P., Holder, R. et al., Near-patient test for nicotine and its metabolites in saliva to assess smoking habit. *Ann. Clin. Biochem.* 37, 666–673, 2000.

25. O'Neal, C.L., Crouch, D.J., Rollins, D.E. et al., The effects of collection methods on oral fluid codeine concentrations. *J. Anal. Toxicol.* 24, 536–542, 2000.

26. Samyn, N., De Boeck, G., and Verstraete, A.G., The use of oral fluid and sweat wipes for the detection of drugs of abuse in drivers. *J. Forensic. Sci.* 47, 1380–1387, 2002.

27. Verstraete, A.G. and Puddu, M., General conclusions and recommendations, in *Rosita: Roadside Testing Assessment,* A.G. Verstraete, Ed., Rosita Consortium, Ghent, 2001, 393–397.

28. George, S. and Braithwaite, R.A., Use of on-site testing for drugs of abuse. *Clin. Chem.* 48, 1639–1646, 2002.

29. Lamping, S.L., Lacey, R.J., Head, L. et al., Investigating the presence of drugs of abuse in oral fluid using surface enhanced Raman spectroscopy (SERS) as a possible application for roadside screening device, in *Proceedings of the 16th International Conference on Alcohol, Drugs and Traffic Safety,* Mayhew, D. and Dussault, C., Eds., Société de l'assurance automobile du Québec, Montréal, 2002 (CD-ROM).

30. Kidwell, D.A. and Van Wie, B.J., A rapid, reusable, system to test for drugs of abuse in saliva. *Ther. Drug Monit.* 23, 489, 2001.

31. Skopp, G. and Potsch, L., Perspiration versus saliva — basic aspects concerning their use in roadside drug testing. *Int. J. Legal Med.* 112, 213–221, 1999.

32. Walsh, J.M., An evaluation of oral fluid point of collection testing devices phase 2. The Walsh Group, Bethesda, MD, 2003.

11.2 POINT OF COLLECTION TESTING IN CRIMINAL JUSTICE

Leo Kadehjian, Ph.D.
Biomedical Consulting, Palo Alto, California

11.2.1 Introduction

With the well-established association between drug use and crime, the criminal justice system is presented with a population with a high prevalence of drug users. Current (2000) data from the Arrestee Drug Abuse Monitoring program (ADAM) surveying arrestees in 35 cities across the U.S. indicate that more than half of all individuals brought into criminal justice systems have substance abuse problems. Of adult male arrestees, 64% tested positive by urinalysis for at least one drug (ranging from 52 to 80% between cities). For female arrestees, 63% tested positive for at least one drug (ranging from 31 to 80%). For juvenile arrestees, 56% of males and 40% of females tested positive for at least one drug.[1]

It is critical that the criminal justice system monitor those under its supervision to ensure that ongoing drug use is both detected and deterred. This is most effectively done through urine drug testing which has been demonstrated to be an objective and effective tool.[2–49] Such drug testing is often specifically mandated by law.

Accordingly, there has been a great demand for effective urine drug testing programs within criminal justice contexts. These urine drug testing programs have been implemented in a variety of criminal justice contexts including testing of arrestees before their initial appearance in court, testing imposed by the court as a condition of release pending trial,[16–39] pre-sentence testing, testing while on probation or parole,[40–43] and testing within jails and prisons.[44–49] Furthermore, drug testing is a cornerstone of effective specialized drug courts,[3] community corrections programs, and court-mandated treatment programs.

11.2.2 Point of Collection Drug Testing

By far, the drug testing technology most used in point of collection (POC) testing programs within the criminal justice setting is urine testing. This specimen has the benefit of large specimen volume allowing for multiple tests and retests, including the possibility to split the original specimen at the time of collection ensuring that a second untouched specimen is available in the event of challenges. Furthermore, there are well-established testing methodologies for both laboratory and POC use, and recognized testing procedures and laboratory standards. There is a large body of clinical and scientific literature addressing the detection of drugs in urine. In addition, urine benefits from having drug and/or metabolite concentrations generally 100 times those found in many other body specimens (e.g., blood, oral fluid, sweat, hair). However, urine does suffer from awkward specimen collection procedures and the possibility of specimen adulteration, substitution, and dilution. Nonetheless, urine remains the specimen of choice for drug testing within criminal justice contexts.

Criminal justice drug testing programs have historically utilized commercial laboratories, with trained and experienced scientists, providing assurance of quality results, but with often frustrating delays between specimen collection, transport to the laboratory, testing, reporting of the result, and ultimately responding to the substance user. With the availability of simple, robust, and accurate automated bench-top immunoassay analyzers, many testing programs established their own POC drug testing facilities. Since the first court-based testing laboratory was established in 1971 in the Superior Court of the District of Columbia a wide variety of POC testing programs have been

Table 11.2.1 Comparison between Instrumented and Non-Instrumented Drug Test Devices

Automated Bench-Top Analyzer	Non-Instrumented Devices
Objective read	Subjective read
Suitable for high volume	Suitable for low volume
Rapid turnaround time	Immediate turnaround time
Lower cost/test ($1/drug)	Higher cost/test ($1–3/drug)
Daily calibration/controls	No calibration/use internal control(s)
Established QC practices	Undefined QC requirements
Established proficiency testing programs	Proficiency testing programs available
Hardcopy print-out	No hardcopy print-out
Established case law	Little case law
Repeat testing often meets due process	Due process requirements uncertain

implemented nationwide. These programs have recognized the value of rapid drug test results with the benefit of immediate responses to ongoing drug use, as well as immediate positive reinforcement for not using drugs. For many of these criminal justice applications, POC bench-top automated immunoassay analyzers have been used successfully for many years. For example, within the U.S. federal courts, at least 20 pre-trial and probation drug testing programs use automated immunoassay analyzers, with a few even using sophisticated high-volume analyzers as found in clinical and commercial laboratories. Many of these POC testing programs using simple bench-top automated immunoassay analyzers have their testing competently performed by officers who have been trained and certified by the test system manufacturer, although they may have had no other formal laboratory training. In addition, these POC testing programs within the federal courts are subjected to rigorous on-site inspections, and participate in quarterly blind proficiency testing, demonstrating excellent performance. Test results from these POC testing programs have been repeatedly upheld in numerous legal challenges. A 1991 National Institute of Justice study of drug testing technologies recognized that on-site automated immunoassay analyzers demonstrated performance equal to commercial laboratory-based testing.[10]

Although POC bench-top automated analyzers offer the benefits of rapid turnaround time, objective hard copy results, reduced test costs (dependent on volume), and a proven track record of performance and admissibility in a variety of legal and administrative proceedings, not all criminal justice testing programs have either the budget or a sufficient number of specimens to justify having an automated analyzer at the point of collection. Furthermore, there may not be the availability of a dedicated and properly trained staff member to operate the analyzer.

However, as a result of impressive advancements in immunoassay technology, urine drug tests as performed on automated analyzers have now been made available in simple, rapid, easy to use, visually read test strips. Such non-instrumented test strips allow for rapid, accurate, and reliable testing in those sites that cannot justify an automated analyzer as well as in numerous field situations.

Some of the key comparative issues between on-site automated analyzers and non-instrumented drug testing devices within a criminal justice setting are shown in Table 11.2.1.

11.2.3 Non-Instrumented POC Drug Tests

There are a wide variety of non-instrumented drug test devices available, from simple dipsticks, which are briefly inserted into a specimen and then allowed to develop over a few minutes, to cassettes where a few drops of the specimen are added with a plastic pipette or calibrated syringe, and even specimen collections cups with the test strips incorporated directly into their walls or cap, which obviate any handling or pipetting of the specimen. Furthermore, many of the non-instrumented test devices are available in single drug assay or multidrug assay formats. For all of these devices, the test results are available in anywhere from 3 to 15 min. These devices utilize well-established immunoassay technologies (described in detail in other chapters of this section), with antigen–antibody reactions similar to the automated instrument homogeneous immunoassay technologies. However, for these test strips the antigen–antibody reaction occurs on chromatographic test strips and so they are considered solid-phase immunoassays. The immunoassay strips are labeled with antibodies directed to the specific drug and/or drug metabolites to be detected. The test results are read visually within a few minutes as the presence or absence of a colored line at a specified position on the strip pertaining to each drug in question. The test strips also have control lines so each test is in part internally controlled. The great interest in these devices is evidenced by the rapid proliferation of the wide variety of these devices, and numerous manufacturers and even more distributors.

However, there has been ongoing concern that these simple, visually read devices may not provide sufficient scientific or forensic accuracy for use in some of the above-mentioned criminal justice applications. The concerns of the accuracy of these devices are based mainly on the subjective nature of visually reading the test results as the presence or absence of a colored line. There has been a concern that specimens with drug concentrations at or near the specified test cutoff concentration may yield indeterminate lines challenging the reader to determine if the result should be called positive or negative. The device package inserts indicate that any such equivocal or borderline results should be reported as negative, taking a conservative approach. There even are a few POC testing devices that utilize a small electronic reader to provide an objective readout of the result. Such readers are available not only for POC urine test devices but also for POC oral fluid testing.

Since the introduction of POC non-instrumented urine drug testing strips in the 1980s, there have been numerous technological advancements and performance improvements such that many of these devices perform quite well. There have been numerous positive performance evaluations of these devices presented at scientific meetings and in peer-reviewed scientific publications (see References 50 to 53 and references cited therein). In 1996, the Administrative Office of the U.S. Courts commissioned a comprehensive study of the available non-instrumented urine drug testing devices. That study of 15 non-instrumented devices found that many of these devices performed amazingly well, especially considering a challenging specimen set, artificially weighted around the immunoassay cutoffs, with accuracies (against the gold standard of GC/MS confirmation) comparable to a commonly used automated bench-top analyzer. The non-instrumented devices demonstrated an overall accuracy of 71% (52 to 79%) vs. the automated analyzer's average of 80% (78 to 82%).[51]

A second similar comprehensive study was commissioned in 1998 by the Substance Abuse and Mental Health Services Administration (SAMHSA) with similar impressive results, with the 15 devices demonstrating an overall accuracy of 70% (61 to 78%) vs. automated analyzer 76%.[51]

It is important to remember that these studies used artificially weighted specimen sets with drug concentrations around the cutoffs to challenge the devices. With specimens that were drug-free or had much higher concentrations of drugs the accuracies of the devices were much higher. These devices are expected to demonstrate even higher accuracies with specimen populations actually encountered in routine criminal justice settings.

There are also concerns about accuracy since in a criminal justice setting the tests may likely be performed by nontechnical staff without formal laboratory experience. To address use of these devices by nonscientists, a more recent study, also utilizing challenging near cutoff specimens, had results independently read by both a scientist and a nonscientist with almost identical performance.[50]

It should be noted that some devices prove to be relatively "aggressive"; that is, they give positive results for specimens with amounts of drug just below the specified cutoff. It is important to note that these positive results should not be considered false positives when they have in fact correctly identified drug use. The device in fact may be correct in accurately identifying drug presence but simply at a concentration that may not always confirm when subjected to laboratory based testing, e.g., using SAMHSA GC/MS confirmation criteria. It should also be noted that some devices proved to be relatively "conservative," missing some specimens with drug concentrations at or slightly above the specified cutoff.[50]

Furthermore, the performance of these and other unit test devices have undergone regulatory review by numerous agencies: by the U.S. Food and Drug Administration (FDA) establishing regulatory criteria for clearance for marketing; by the SAMHSA for potential application in federally-regulated workplace drug testing programs;[54] by a wide variety of criminal justice agencies; and by laboratory accreditation and standards organizations such as the College of American Pathologists (CAP), the Center for Medicaid and State Operations (CLIA regulations), and the National Committee for Clinical Laboratory Standards (NCCLS).

In spite of the impressive performance of such simple, rapid, and easy-to-use devices, there appears to be a consensus within the laboratory community that the results of these devices alone should not be used to impose significant sanctions without some form of further confirmation testing. It is interesting to note that, although these devices are now being widely used in numerous settings, there is little significant case law where there has been detailed judicial scrutiny of the accuracy of these devices and whether use of these devices fulfills the due process requirements in each of the variety of criminal justice settings.

11.2.4 Detection of Adulteration/Dilution

One limitation to the use of urine as a specimen for drug testing is the potential for specimen adulteration, substitution, and dilution. Given that urine specimen collections in the criminal justice context are generally performed under direct observation, the possibility of adulteration or substitution is minimized. In fact, by performing the drug test immediately upon specimen collection, the opportunity for an adulterant to be effective may be minimized because often some time is required for the adulterant to perform its disruptive chemistry. However, specimen dilution through excess fluid ingestion is an issue that merits careful attention. To address these challenges to effective testing there are a variety of POC devices to assess specimen integrity. These include handheld refractometers to measure specific gravity, as well as simple dipsticks, which can assess a variety of adulterants, oxidants, pH, and creatinine. Some of the non-instrumented drug test devices actually incorporate such specimen validity tests in the test device. Non-instrumented devices may also offer indications of inappropriate specimens or failure of the test to perform properly through the use of built-in control lines.

11.2.5 Other Issues

There are some additional issues to consider when an officer is asked to perform drug testing in the presence of a defendant or offender. Officers may be resistant to taking on testing responsibilities as they may feel it is not part of their job function. The officers may also fear increased risk of exposure to infectious disease in handling urine specimens (although the 1991 OSHA Bloodborne Pathogen Regulations, 56 FR 64004, recognized the extremely low risk from casual exposure to urine specimens when not visibly contaminated with blood). There is also the potential for physical harm when confronting a potentially violent offender with a positive drug test result. It may be easier for the officer to deal with a confirmed positive report from a formal laboratory than with a presumptive positive test result from a non-instrumented device. Despite these concerns, there are clear benefits in the use of these non-instrumented drug test devices in front of the offender. Many offenders, when told of the accuracy of the device, will admit to drug use even as the test is being run. Furthermore, when faced with a positive test result many will admit to drug use. In contrast, it is rare for an offender to admit to drug use when the specimen is collected for shipment to an off-site laboratory. Also, when on-site test results are negative, the officer can provide immediate positive reinforcement for maintaining abstinence. When on-site test results are positive, the officer can confront the issue directly and immediately, rather than later dealing with "prior" drug use.

11.2.6 Other Technologies

There are several other specimens and technologies used within the criminal justice system to detect drug use. These include oral fluid testing, sweat patch testing, hair testing, oculomotor testing, and trace drug residue analysis. Hair testing and sweat patch testing are not considered POC testing technologies as the specimens must currently be sent to a laboratory for analysis.

Oral fluid testing is certainly getting attention as a specimen suitable for a variety of POC testing contexts, especially roadside testing.[55,56] There are both laboratory based methods as well as a few POC testing devices, similar to the POC urine testing cassettes. The main benefit of oral fluid is the ease and gender neutrality of specimen collection. That oral fluid as a specimen for drug testing has reached a level of scientific acceptance is manifested by the fact that SAMHSA has included oral fluid through four rounds of draft guidelines for updating federally regulated workplace testing programs.[54] Note also that saliva has been well recognized as a suitable specimen for alcohol testing and is allowed under the Department of Transportation's non-evidential on-site alcohol testing procedures.

Another recent technology being promoted to the criminal justice community is oculomotor testing.[57–59] With these devices, the eyes' response to a flash of light is objectively measured, and by comparison to the person's own baseline or population averages, a determination of exposure to drugs is made. It has been demonstrated that drug use can have detectable effects on various involuntary oculomotor function parameters. Numerous clinical studies examining the effects of drugs incorporate some of these ocular assessments. However, the ability of such oculomotor assessments to reliably and effectively detect drug *use* as opposed to *impairment* has not been convincingly demonstrated in the peer-reviewed scientific literature. Although these devices appear to have gained interest from the corrections community, there is little published literature from controlled-dose studies, neither are there epidemiological data from field studies, from which an accurate assessment of the performance of these devices can be made or a determination of their relative performance compared to other testing technologies such as urine or oral fluid testing. However, their ease of use certainly merits further research into their performance capabilities.

Another technology occasionally found within corrections settings is a device designed to detect trace amounts of drugs on persons, not only inmates, but also those visiting prisons and even prison staff.[60]

11.2.7 Regulatory Issues

There are few formal regulations specifically regarding drug testing technologies in criminal justice contexts. Although there are several statutory requirements regarding drug testing within corrections settings, these statutes are generally broadly worded leaving specifics about technologies up to those implementing the testing requirements. Generally, the major issues involve whether there must be confirmation testing (generally specified as GC/MS) before certain sanctions may occur.

The Federal Bureau of Prisons has a statutory requirement that, for those serving their sentence in a contract community treatment center, all positive test results be validated to substantiate the positive result (28 CFR §550.42(c)). The current federal probation regulations also require that if a probationer is to be returned to prison based on a drug test, it must be confirmed by GC/MS at a SAMHSA-certified laboratory. Otherwise corrections-based urine drug testing programs are generally not otherwise strictly regulated. However, in order to withstand legal scrutiny, such on-site testing programs should conform to standards of good laboratory practice, including quality control practices and participation in proficiency testing. The on-site testing programs of the U.S. federal courts utilizing automated analyzers have been following such practices for many years, including on-site inspections and participation in external proficiency testing. Quality control practices, external proficiency testing, and appropriate inspection criteria are now being developed for such programs within the federal courts utilizing non-instrumented drug testing devices.

Any criminal justice drug testing program should take into account any state or federal regulations regarding drug testing in other contexts, such as workplace testing, as these standards may be brought up in any challenge to the criminal justice testing program. However, due process issues are generally diminished within a criminal justice context, and accordingly drug testing programs and technologies may be held to a lower standard than in workplace testing. Another concern should be state and federal regulations addressing laboratories in general. These regulations typically apply to clinical laboratories, and corrections-based testing programs are generally not considered to be "clinical."

11.2.8 Legal Issues

There has been a long history of drug testing within corrections settings and, accordingly, ample case law regarding many aspects of such corrections-based testing programs. There is ample case law precedent in many criminal justice contexts for the admissibility of instrumented immunoassay urine drug testing, both when performed in a laboratory and when performed at the point of collection. Most of these cases uphold the use of repeat immunoassay testing as meeting the due process requirements for use in prison disciplinary hearings and even in probation revocations, without additional confirmation testing.

Currently, there have been few significant cases specifically addressing non-instrumented drug testing technologies, at least at the appellate court level. This may be in part because these tests are rarely being used alone for imposing sanctions without some form of confirmation testing. One area where legal challenges could occur would be the admissibility of the test results themselves, arguing that the testing technology is new and of either unproven or insufficient scientific validity. The aforementioned performance studies should be persuasive in demonstrating the scientific reliability and acceptance of these devices. A question that requires resolution is whether these non-instrumented devices are accurate enough to be used alone or with repeat testing, but without further confirmation testing by an alternative technique, such as GC/MS.

In order for non-instrumented drug test results be used in these various corrections contexts, not only must the inherent performance of the devices be demonstrated, but also whether the devices are properly used. Issues such as operator training, proper chain of custody, specimen handling, device and ancillary storage conditions, and record-keeping procedures must be documented. On-site inspection of these non-instrumented testing programs as well as participation in external proficiency testing programs will also be important components in assessing the admissibility and weight such non-instrumented drug testing evidence should receive. Within the federal courts' pre-trial and probation on-site testing programs, appropriate inspection checklists and proficiency testing programs are being developed and implemented for use of these non-instrumented drug test devices.

It must be recognized that the due process requirements vary depending on the corrections context, from a fairly low "some evidence" standard in prison disciplinary hearings, to a "beyond a reasonable doubt" standard in criminal cases, with these non-instrumented drug test devices demonstrating overall accuracies on the order of 70%, even in studies that generally meet even the preponderance of the evidence standard (>50%) and possibly even the higher "clear and convincing" evidence standard. Certainly this would be the case for assays for cannabis or cocaine, where cross-reacting substances are minimal and accordingly interpretation of test results is relatively straightforward. However, it is unlikely that these devices alone would be held to meet the beyond a reasonable doubt standard (95% or higher). It is important to note that these devices would be expected to demonstrate accuracies well beyond the 70% observed with near-cutoff specimens, when testing specimens within the criminal justice context with a less-challenging concentration distribution. Furthermore, when examining the performance of these devices against the criteria of drug presence or absence (rather than GC/MS confirmation cutoff criteria) these devices have demonstrated positive predictive values of virtually 1. That is, a positive on-site, non-instrumented drug test result, at least for cocaine or cannabinoids, can be relied on to indicate the presence of drug in the specimen, even though there may be insufficient amounts to be confirmed positive when using standard confirmation cutoffs.

11.2.9 Conclusions

There is no question that several of the non-instrumented drug testing devices are not only rapid and easy to use, but also are sufficiently accurate and reliable for use within a variety of criminal justice programs. There is ample peer-reviewed scientific literature supporting the accuracy of these devices as well as many studies demonstrating their utility within a wide variety of criminal justice settings. That they are being considered for use within the federally regulated workplace testing programs is also a testament to their level of scientific and regulatory acceptance. Furthermore, there is a growing body of case law addressing these devices' levels of accuracy and reliability and how they comport with various due process requirements. However, these devices will still likely need to be used with some form of confirmation testing if significant sanctions are to be imposed.

REFERENCES

1. 2000 Arrestee Drug Abuse Monitoring: Annual Report, National Institute of Justice, NCJ 193013, 2003. www.adam-nij.net.
2. Kadehjian, L. and Baer, J., *On-Site Testing Devices in the Criminal Justice System, On-Site Drug Testing,* Jenkins, A.J. and Goldberger, B.A., Eds., Humana Press, Totowa, NJ, 2002, chap. 5.
3. Robinson, J. and Jones, J., Drug Testing in a Drug Court Environment: Common Issues to Address, NCJ 181103, 2000.
4. Crowe, A. and Sydney, L., Ten Steps for Implementing a Program of Controlled Substance Testing of Juveniles, NCJ 178897, 2000.
5. Crowe, A. and Sydney, L., Developing a Policy for Controlled Substance Testing of Juveniles. June, NCJ 178896, 2000.
6. Torres, S., The use of a credible drug testing program for accountability and intervention, *Fed. Prob.,* 60(4), 18, 1996.
7. Carver, J.A., Using drug testing to reduce detention, *Fed. Prob.,* 57(1), 42, 1993.
8. The Impact of Systemwide Drug Testing in Multnomah County, Oregon, National Institute of Justice, 1995.
9. Stephens, R. and Feucht, T., Reliability of self-reported drug use and urinalysis in the drug use forecasting system, *Prison J.,* 73 (3–4), 279, 1993.
10. Visher, C. and McFadden, K., A Comparison of Urinalysis Technologies for Drug Testing in Criminal Justice, National Institute of Justice, 1991.
11. Wish, E. and Gropper, B., Drug Testing by the Criminal Justice System: Method, Research, and Application, in *Crime and Justice,* Vol. 13: *Drugs and Crime.* University of Chicago Press, Chicago, 1990.
12. BJA Monograph, Urinalysis as a Part of a Treatment Alternative to Street Crime Program, Bureau of Justice Assistance, NCJ 115416, 1988.
13. Wish, E., et al. Identifying Drug Users and Monitoring Them during Conditional Release, National Institute of Justice, NCJ 108560, 1988.
14. Carver, J., Drugs and Crime: Controlling Use and Reducing Risk through Testing, National Institute of Justice, 1986.
15. Wish, E., Drug Testing, National Institute of Justice, NCJ 104556, n.d.
16. Integrating Drug Testing into a Pretrial Services System: 1999 Update, NCJ 176340, 1999.
17. Henry, D. and Clark, J., Pretrial Drug Testing: An Overview of Issues and Practices, NCJ 176341, 1999.
18. Rhodes, W. et al., Predicting Pretrial Misconduct with Drug Tests of Arrestees. Evidence from Six Sites, National Institute of Justice, Research in Brief, NCJ 157108, 1996.

19. Rhodes, W. et al., Predicting pretrial misconduct with drug tests of arrestees: evidence from eight settings, *J. Quant. Criminol.*, 12(3), 315, 1996.

20. Drug Testing. Guidelines for Pretrial Release and Diversion, National Association of Pretrial Services Agencies, 1995.

21. BJA Monograph, Integrating Drug Testing into a Pretrial Services System, Bureau of Justice Assistance, NCJ 142414, 1993.

22. Jones, P.R. and Goldkamp, J.S., Implementing pretrial drug testing programs in two experimental sites: some deterrence and jail bed implications, *Prison J.*, 73(2), 199–219, 1993.

23. Britt, C.L., Gottfredson, M.R., and Goldkamp, J.S., Drug testing and pretrial misconduct: an experiment on the specific deterrent effects of drug monitoring defendants on pretrial release, *J. Res. Crime Delinquency,* 29(1), 62, 1992.

24. Goldkamp, J.S. and Jones, P.R., Pretrial drug testing experiments in Milwaukee and Prince George's County: the context of implementation, *J. Res. Crime Delinquency,* 29(4), 430–465, 1992.

25. Smith, D. and Polsenberg, C., Specifying the relationship between arrestee drug use test results and recidivism, *J. Crim. Law Criminol.*, 83(2), 364, 1992.

26. Visher, C., Pretrial drug testing: panacea or Pandora's box? *Ann. Am. Acad.,* 521, 112, 1992.

27. Visher, C., Pretrial Drug Testing, National Institute of Justice, 1992.

28. Carver, J., Pretrial drug testing: an essential step in bail reform, *B.Y.U. J. Pub. Law,* 5(2), 371, 1991.

29. Nielson, D., Consenting to searches after being arrested: pretrial drug testing, *B.Y.U. J. Pub. Law,* 5(2), 439, 1991.

30. Meyers, P., Pretrial drug testing: is it vulnerable to due process challenges? *B.Y.U. J. Pub. Law,* 5(2), 285, 1991.

31. Walton R., et al., Pretrial drug testing — an essential component of the national drug control strategy, *B.Y.U. J. Pub. Law,* 5(2), 341, 1991.

32. Jensen, C., Survey of current and prior pretrial drug testing sites, *B.Y.U. J. Pub. Law,* 5(2), 451, 1991.

33. Skousen, R., A special needs exception to the warrant and probable cause requirements for mandatory and uniform pre-arraignment drug testing in the wake of *Skinner v. Railway Labor Executives' Association and National Treasury Employees' Union v. Von Raab, B.Y.U. J. Pub. Law,* 5(2), 409, 1991.

34. Goldkamp, J.S., Gottfredson, M.R., and Weiland, D., Pretrial drug testing and defendant risk, *J. Crim. Law Criminol.*, 81(3), 585, 1990.

35. Visher, C., Using drug testing to identify high-risk defendants on release: a study in the District of Columbia, *J. Crim. Justice*, 18, 321, 1990.

36. Toborg, M. et al., Assessment of Pretrial Urine Testing in the District of Columbia, National Institute of Justice, 1989.

37. BJA Monograph, Estimating the Cost of Drug Testing for a Pretrial Services Program, Bureau of Justice Assistance, 1989.

38. Rosen, C. and Goldkamp, J., The constitutionality of drug testing at the bail stage, *J. Crim. Law Criminol.*, 80(1), 114, 1989.

39. Abell, R., Pretrial drug testing: expanding rights and protecting public safety, *Geo. Wash. Law Rev.*, 57(4), 943, 1989.

40. BJA Monograph, Drug Testing Guidelines and Practices for Adult Probation and Parole Agencies, Bureau of Justice Assistance, NCJ 129199, 1991.

41. Rosen, C., The Fourth Amendment implications of urine testing for evidence of drug use in probation, *Brooklyn Law Rev.*, 55, 1159, 1990.

42. delCarmen, R. and Sorensen, J., Legal Issues in Drug Testing Probation and Parole Clients and Employees, Department of Justice, National Institute of Corrections, 1989.

43. delCarmen, R. and Sorensen, J., Legal issues in drug testing probationers and parolees, *Fed. Prob.*, 19, 1988.

44. Wilson, D., Drug Use, Testing, and Treatment in Jails, NCJ 179999, 2000.

45. Bird, A. et al., Harm reduction measures and injecting inside prison versus mandatory drug testing: results of a cross sectional anonymous questionnaire survey, *Br. Med. J.*, 315, 21, 1997.

46. Gore, S. and Bird, A., Cost implications of random mandatory drug tests in prisons, *Lancet*, 348, 1124, 1996.

47. Gore, S. et al., Prison rights: mandatory drug tests and performance indicators for prisons, *Br. Med. J.*, 312, 1411, 1966.

48. Gore, S. and Bird, A., Mandatory drug tests in prisons, *Br. Med. J.*, 310, 595, 1995.

49. Epstein, R., Urinalysis testing in correctional facilities, *Boston Univ. Law Rev.*, 67, 475, 1987.

50. Kadehjian, L., Performance of five non-instrumented urine drug-testing devices with challenging near-cutoff specimens, *J. Anal. Toxicol.*, 25, 670, 2001.

51. Willette, R. and Kadehjian, L., *Drugs-of-Abuse Test Devices, in On-Site Drug Testing*, Jenkins, A.J. and Goldberger, B.A., Eds., Humana Press, Totowa, NJ, 2002, chap. 17.

52. Crouch, D. et al., A field evaluation of five on-site drug-testing devices, *J. Anal. Toxicol.*, 26, 493, 2002.

53. Yacoubian, G.S., Wish, E.D., and Choyka, J.D., A comparison of the ONTRAK TesTcup-5 to laboratory urinalysis among arrestees, *J. Psychoactive Drugs*, 34(3), 325, 2002.

54. Mandatory Guidelines for Federal Workplace Drug Testing Programs, SAMHSA, Draft 4, Sept. 5, 2001. www.workplace.samhsa.gov.

55. Walsh, J.M. et al., An evaluation of rapid point-of-collection oral fluid drug-testing devices, *J. Anal. Toxicol.*, 27, 429, 2003.

56. Yacoubian, G.S., Wish, E.D., and Perez, D.M., A comparison of saliva testing to urinalysis in an arrestee population, *J. Psychoactive Drugs*, 33(3), 289, 2001.

57. www.passpoint.org.

58. www.mcjeyecheck.com.

59. Crucilla, C. and Pickworth, W., Eye evaluations as pre-screening for drugs, presented at the College on Problems of Drug Dependence Annual Meeting, Scottsdale, AZ, June, 2001. Abstract available at http://views.vcu.edu/cpdd/index.htm.

60. Mieczkowski, T., The utilization of ion mobility spectrometry in a criminal justice field application, in *Drug Testing Technology. Assessment of Field Applications,* T. Mieczkowski, Ed., CRC Press, Boca Raton, FL, 1999, chap 4.

11.3 REGULATORY CONCERNS FOR POINT OF COLLECTION TESTING IN THE WORKPLACE

Michael R. Baylor, Ph.D., Craig A. Sutheimer, Ph.D., and Susan D. Crumpton, M.S.
Health Sciences Unit, Science and Engineering Group, RTI International, Research Triangle Park, North Carolina

11.3.1 Introduction

Point of collection (POC) testing is relatively new in workplace and other areas of forensic drug testing. As with laboratory-based workplace drug testing, POC test users must implement procedures that ensure accurate and reliable test results while protecting donor rights to privacy and confidentiality. Many procedures for the collection, handling, and reporting of workplace drug test specimens are common to both POC testing and laboratory-based testing. However, some aspects of POC testing are unique. These are further discussed below.

At the time of this writing, the federal government is revising the Department of Health and Human Services (HHS) Mandatory Guidelines for Federal Workplace Drug Testing Programs.[1,2] The purpose of the Guidelines is to ensure that the regulated drug testing programs under this umbrella meet stringent forensic and scientific/technical standards. The original Guidelines addressed only laboratory-based urine drug testing. With the new Guidelines, the government plans to allow POC testing, as well as testing of other specimen matrices (i.e., hair, oral fluid, sweat). The final revised Guidelines are to be published following public comment and any revisions made after consideration of those comments.

11.3.2 POC Testing Techniques

11.3.2.1 POC Testing Devices for Drugs of Abuse

POC devices for drugs of abuse were first available in the mid-1980s and early 1990s. POC devices include both non-instrumented devices with visually detected end points as well as semi-automated or automated instrumented testing devices with instrument-read end points. POC testing can be performed in the workplace with little or no prior notice and provides information that supports decisions about hiring or continued employment. Drug tests conducted with POC devices utilize a chromatographic migration of the specimen in addition to competitive binding immunoassays, the same general scientific principle used in the initial tests conducted by certified laboratories on their regulated specimens. The devices use either a negative indicating reaction (i.e., the absence of a band indicates a presumptive positive result) or a positive indicating reaction (i.e., the presence of a band indicates a presumptive positive result). There is a wide variation in the testing panels and cutoffs available for POC devices. Although their ability to perform at some administrative cutoffs has been questioned,[3] commercially available devices meet minimal technical requirements. A number of the devices have been cleared by the Food and Drug Administration (FDA). The FDA Center for Devices and Radiological Health provides information on test categorization and approval/clearance of test devices (searchable databases are available at http://www.fda.gov/cdrh/consumer/mda/index.html#databases).

Investigators, independent of the manufacturers, have evaluated urine non-instrumented POC devices and have found them to perform similarly to the instrumented immunoassay tests conducted in certified laboratories[3–6] using current cutoffs. The investigators conducted tests on both drug-free urine and donor specimens. The drug-free urine was tested with and without drug analytes and the donor specimens were selected from specimens that had previously been analyzed and determined to be drug-free or to contain varying amounts of target analyte. Little device performance difference was noted between tests conducted by laboratory technicians and laypersons who had been trained in the proper procedures for conducting and reading the test.[3,4]

To date, only one group of independent investigators[7] has evaluated non-instrumented POC devices for oral fluid. In their study, fortified oral fluids at concentrations consistent with the proposed HHS cutoffs were analyzed. The study found device variability and noted device difficulty in detecting cannabinoids. The investigators suggest that the rapid evolution of the device technology should be able to overcome any current problems relating to targeted analyte and manufacturer's cutoff and be able to provide assays consistent with proposed HHS cutoffs. The investigators felt that "there is every reason to be optimistic about the future for drug testing using the oral fluid matrix."

To date, independent evaluations of instrumented POC devices have not been available for review.

11.3.2.2 POC Testing Devices for Specimen Validity

Specimen validity test (SVT) POC devices for the detection of products used to suborn urine drug testing have become more widely used in the past several years. POC devices include non-instrumented devices with visually read end points as well as semiautomated instrumented testing devices with instrument-read end points. Specimen validity tests conducted with these devices utilize colorimetric assays, the same technology utilized by certified laboratories on their instrumented testing equipment used for at least initial SVT procedures.

Both independent investigators and manufacturers have evaluated urine non-instrumented SVT POC devices for the detection of abnormal urine specimens.[8–10] The studies evaluated drug-containing specimens to which were added adulterating chemicals or adulterants that had been purchased. Results from these preliminary studies were variable; however, the studies did demonstrate the ability of the varying devices to detect creatinine, as well as some oxidizing adulterants, and to measure pH.

11.3.3 Regulatory Issues for POC Testing

11.3.3.1 Evidentiary Value

POC testing must be scientifically and forensically sound. At this time, POC test results do not meet the forensic and scientific standards that have been deemed necessary for regulated workplace drug testing. The proposed HHS Guidelines allow POC testing to identify the absence of drugs or to identify a specimen as valid. According to the proposed Guidelines, only valid negative drug test results can be reported from a POC testing site by a trained tester. All presumptive non-negative specimens must be sent under chain-of-custody to a certified laboratory for initial and confirmatory testing. A POC test specimen is considered a presumptive non-negative specimen if the POC test result is positive or invalid (i.e., a specimen with an unacceptable POC SVT result, an abnormal POC drug test response, or an abnormal physical characteristic identified by the collector or trained tester).

11.3.3.2 Regulatory Oversight

It is anticipated that monitoring POC testing would necessitate an extensive program that cannot be easily managed by a single regulatory entity. While one regulatory body could retain overall responsibility for regulated testing, it might be necessary for other organizations, designated as POC Oversight Groups (POGs), to take an active part in the direct oversight of POC testing sites and trained testers. Possible oversight groups could be the individual federal agencies under whose regulations specimens are tested, a contractor, or a nongovernment training/certifying organization (e.g., industry group). In turn, the regulatory body could monitor the POG's procedures and records.

11.3.3.3 POC Devices

Certified laboratories are expected to validate their initial and confirmatory testing instruments and assays prior to use with regulated specimens. Their validation studies address variables that exist in and among laboratories. The variables include the instruments (e.g., manufacturer, model, condition, settings), analysts (e.g., variation in practices including measurement and pipetting techniques), quality control materials, and reagents (e.g., different materials and/or mixtures, as well as differences in preparation and/or storage conditions). Due to the multiple variables, the regulatory emphasis is on the user's validation, as well as the product manufacturer's validation.

The regulatory focus on POC test validation at least in part can be shifted from the user to the manufacturer of the device. POC testing involves discrete non-instrumented devices that have fewer testing variables than the instrumented assays used by laboratories. Unlike laboratory-based instrumented tests, an individual with little or no scientific/technical knowledge and experience can utilize a POC device, without extensive training. At least two published studies have documented comparable performance between individuals with nonscientific backgrounds and those with scientific/technical experience.[3,4] Non-instrumented POC devices are configured by the manufacturer and most include manufacturer's controls (i.e., QC integrated into the device or QC samples provided by the device manufacturer). This process should reduce variability in QC among testers, as opposed to QC samples prepared by individual users or purchased from various suppliers. POC devices require no specimen pretreatment (e.g., extraction) and no user-prepared reagents are needed for POC testing. The validation of POC devices by manufactured lot would be the basis for approved use in regulated drug testing programs.

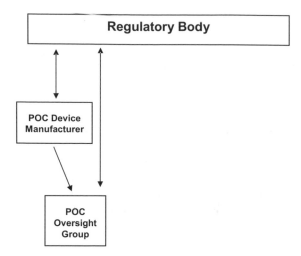

Figure 11.3.1 Regulatory Issues: POC device manufacturer, regulatory body and POG. POC manufacturer
submits application and device lot validation data to the regulatory body; regulatory body forwards
application and validation data to the POG for review; POG forwards PT set to the manufacturer;
manufacturer reports PT results to POG for review; if acceptable the POG recommends approval
of the device lot to the regulatory body; regulatory body places approved device lot on CPL.

To set some baseline level of performance, POC devices used in a regulated program must be
cleared by the FDA through its regulatory processes. These processes include review and evaluation
of the manufacturer's validation records for the device supporting the stated purpose (i.e., drug
detection). The forensic requirements of workplace drug testing necessitate evaluation beyond that
required by the FDA. This additional evaluation should involve review by the regulatory body or
a POG designated by the Body.

Under this evaluation structure, the POC device manufacturer would submit an application to
the regulatory body, along with data that support the manufactured lot's performance at and around
specified cutoffs, as well as data supporting the lot's specificity to detect the target analyte(s) in the
presence of analogous compounds. The regulatory body would forward the application and supporting data to the POG for technical review. The POG would send a performance testing (PT) set
to the manufacturer. The manufacturer would report PT results back to the POG for review. If the
application, validation data, and PT performance are found to be acceptable, the POG recommends
approval of the device lot to the regulatory body and requests that the manufacturer submit a
predetermined number of devices that could be used to assess problems that might arise during the
life of the device lot. The regulatory body would issue a certificate of acceptability and place the
device lot on a Conforming Products List (CPL) that would be published and updated periodically.

The relationships between the POC device manufacturer, POG, and regulatory body as described
above are schematically depicted in Figure 11.3.1.

11.3.3.4   Trained Testers and POC Testing Sites

The regulatory body should specify training and performance requirements for POC testers.
This training must address chain-of-custody documentation, confidentiality of test results and donor
information, record keeping, and testing procedures that ensure proper operation, storage, QC
procedures, result interpretation, and any maintenance procedures for each type of POC device
used. Individuals should also successfully complete a set of proficiency testing samples. A certificate
of qualification program would identify individuals allowed to test regulated specimens.

Individuals seeking certification for testing regulated specimens would be required to submit
an application and documentation of appropriate training to the regulatory body. Qualified applicants

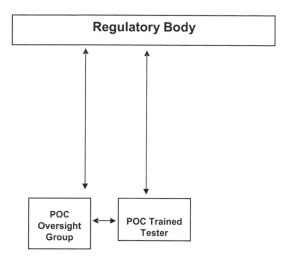

Figure 11.3.2 Regulatory Issues: POC trained testers, regulatory body, and POG. POC trained tester submits an application and training documentation to the regulatory body; regulatory body forwards application and training documentation to the POG for review; POG forwards PT set to the trained tester; trained tester reports PT results to the POG for review. If acceptable, the POG recommends certification of the trained tester to the regulatory body; regulatory body issues certificate to trained tester; trained tester provides copy of certification to the POG.

would be sent a set of proficiency samples by the POG. Individuals reporting acceptable results would be issued a trained tester certificate with a specified expiration date (e.g., 1 year). Prior to the expiration date, the POG would send a set of proficiency samples to the trained tester for certification renewal. Training records must be available for review, and should be maintained by the POG and updated as appropriate.

Ongoing compliance must also be monitored. Direct oversight of POC testing sites/trained testers could be accomplished by a POG in a manner similar to the current National Laboratory Certification Program (NLCP) for urine drug testing laboratories, with on-site inspections and PT challenges.

As is currently required of certified laboratories, the POC testing sites/trained testers must use a written standard operating procedures (SOP) manual that incorporates procedures required for regulated workplace testing. To ensure consistency among the various POC testing sites/trained testers, it may be practical for entities under whose regulations testing is performed (e.g., individual federal agencies) to write and distribute the SOP manuals.

Any procedural deficiencies or discrepant test results identified through the inspection, PT, or a specimen QA program (as described below) or reported by a Medical Review Officer (MRO) could be addressed through remediation by the POG with the POC testing site. Remediation would involve investigation and corrective actions to correct identified problems. Based on identified deficiencies, a POC testing site or a trained tester could be suspended from testing regulated specimens. Any errors attributed to a POC device itself could be referred for remediation by the POG with the POC device manufacturer. Based on identified deficiencies, a device lot could be removed from the CPL. The timing of the suspension or device lot removal would be dependent on the degree and imminence of harm to the tested population and general public.

The relationships between the trained tester, POG, and regulatory body as described above are outlined in Figure 11.3.2.

11.3.3.5 *Specimens*

As noted above, when the revised Guidelines go into effect, federal agencies and regulated employers will be allowed to test different specimen matrices (i.e., urine, hair, oral fluid, sweat) in their workplace drug testing programs. These matrices are already being tested in the private sector. The choice of specimen matrix depends on several factors, especially the drug detection time using a particular specimen matrix and the reason for the test (e.g., pre-employment, post-accident, reasonable suspicion, return to duty, follow-up, random). Currently, POC devices are available for testing urine or oral fluid specimens. Devices for other specimen matrices may be developed in the future.

POC testing of urine is most suited for situations that require quick, negative results such as in emergency/crisis management. It can be used for random, reasonable suspicion/cause, and post-accident testing if drug use occurred more than 3 h prior to the incident. This type of testing may be least suited for pre-employment, return-to-duty, and follow-up testing.

POC testing of oral fluid also is most suited for situations that require quick, negative results such as in emergency/crisis management. Therefore, in a workplace setting, it is most suited for reasonable suspicion/cause and post-accident testing. It may be least suited for random testing. Oral fluid is not suited for return-to-duty, follow-up, and pre-employment testing.

11.3.3.6 *Collection Sites and Specimen Collection*

Specimen collection requirements should closely parallel those procedures already established for laboratory-based workplace drug testing.[11,12] These procedures were developed to ensure a consistent, forensically defensible collection using strict chain-of-custody procedures, thereby ensuring that the integrity and identity of each specimen are maintained. A brief summary of specimen collection requirements follows.

A collection site may be a permanent or temporary facility. All sites where regulated specimens are collected must be equipped with security features limiting access to appropriate collection site personnel. A dedicated collection facility must be secured at all times. Temporary collection facilities, at a minimum, must be secured during collections.

Collection sites must tailor the facility and operations to the specimen type(s) collected. For example, oral fluid specimen collections require only direct observation. Urine specimen collections require facilities that provide donor privacy during collection and also enable observed collections. Measures must be taken to prevent specimen adulteration or substitution (e.g., turning off water supply or securing faucets, coloring the water in the toilet, preventing access to items that may be used to adulterate a specimen). All facilities must have a means for donors to wash their hands, preferably in the area where the collection takes place.

Essential elements of a proper collection include procedures for verifying donor identity; maintaining specimen identification and integrity throughout the collection process, subsequent storage, and transfers; documenting the collection and chain-of-custody using a standardized custody and control form (CCF); and examining the specimen for adequate volume and other characteristics (e.g., temperature of a urine specimen). Specimen containers should be sealed in the presence of the donor. The collection container must be tamper-evident and prevent contamination of the specimen. Some current POC devices are incorporated into the collection container. Collection site record-keeping procedures must ensure the accuracy, security, and confidentiality of drug test information.

11.3.3.7 *POC Testing Procedures and Reporting Results*

POC testing differs from laboratory-based testing in that the same individual may collect and test the specimen. To avoid confrontation, testing should not occur in the presence of the donor and the collector should not reveal any test results to the donor.

Presumptive non-negative specimens should be resealed with tamper-evident tape to ensure the integrity of the specimen. Both primary and split specimens should be placed into secured temporary

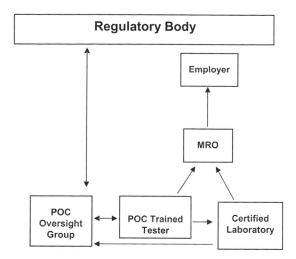

Figure 11.3.3 Regulatory Issues: POC non-negative confirmation testing, reporting results and quality assurance. Trained tester reports negative results to the MRO; trained tester forwards non-negative specimens to the laboratory for confirmation testing; a percentage of negative specimens are forwarded to laboratory for QA testing; laboratory reports non-negative results to the MRO; laboratory reports QA results to the POG; MRO reports results to the employer.

storage and be under chain-of-custody until the specimen is transferred to a certified laboratory for initial and confirmatory testing.

Specimens with negative POC drug test results and acceptable responses for POC specimen validity tests should be reported by the trained tester directly to the MRO. These specimens should be discarded immediately after testing (unless the negative specimen is to be sent to a certified laboratory for QA purposes). Valid negative results must be reported to the MRO by sending a completed CCF or electronic report. Measures must be taken to ensure the security and confidentiality of donor information.

The relationships between the trained testers, laboratory, MRO, and POG for reporting results from POC sites are depicted in Figure 11.3.3.

11.3.3.8 Quality Control/Quality Assurance

Due to the forensic aspects of workplace drug testing, QC requirements for workplace POC testing will be more stringent than those for nonregulated on-site testing in clinical environments (i.e., "point of care testing").[13] However, quality control requirements for POC testing will also differ from those required for laboratory-based instrumented tests in a regulated workplace testing program.

Certified laboratories are required to document the validity of specimen results in each initial and confirmatory test batch by analyzing a specified type and percentage of QC samples. POC testing using discrete POC devices has fewer testing variables. In addition, many, if not most, devices include a test line or control line that indicates proper test performance. Therefore, it would appear sufficient to document acceptable performance for each trained tester on each day that the individual tests specimens with a specific test device. As previously noted, POC testing will be used only as a screening test, with any presumptive non-negative specimens tested and confirmed in a certified laboratory in accordance with stringent QC policies.

The HHS Mandatory Guidelines for Workplace Drug Testing Programs require federally regulated programs to have an external QA program. Federal agencies and regulated employers are required to submit blind proficiency samples to certified laboratories (i.e., a specified percentage of the donor specimens they submit for testing) to demonstrate the laboratory's ability to obtain and report results correctly. A QA program for POC testing sites/trained testers could require a

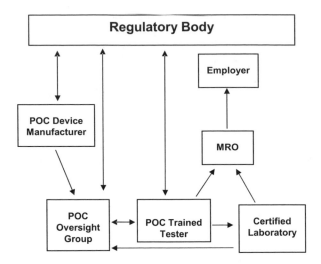

Figure 11.3.4 The regulatory oversight of POC testing: The interaction of all components.

specified percentage of POC test-negative donor specimens to be sent to a certified laboratory for testing (with donor identification and demographic information redacted). The laboratory would then report its results to the POG for review.

This QA process involving the interactions of the trained tester, laboratory, and POG is incorporated into Figure 11.3.4.

11.3.4 POC Testing Advantages and Disadvantages

The major advantage of POC testing is the almost immediate identification of negative test results. POC testing is performed as a discrete analysis, not requiring batch configuration, so individual specimens can be analyzed without delay.

Employer costs for negative POC test specimens are comparable to costs of laboratory-based testing. Due to the additional testing performed, it would appear that the employer costs for non-negative specimens will be greater than current costs for laboratory testing. POC test devices have a shelf life of 12 to 18 months. This relatively short time may be a major disadvantage to testing sites with a limited specimen volume to be analyzed, as the tendency of manufacturers to package devices in multiples could result in numbers of the devices expiring before use.

Another disadvantage of POC testing may be the fees associated with the complex oversight/regulatory program needed for an extremely decentralized population of sites/testers.

Procedural disadvantages that have been noted for POC testing in other fields, such as clinical testing,[14] would not appear to be of concern in a regulated workplace setting with POC testing used only as a presumptive test method. For example, the potential for misinterpretation of results would be unlikely. A POC device that is prone to inconclusive results probably would not meet criteria for placement on the CPL. Additionally, training requirements for testers and regulatory oversight as previously described (e.g., proficiency testing, QA program using POC test-negative specimens) should reveal systemic problems.

11.3.5 Role of the Medical Review Officer

The MRO plays an essential part in regulated workplace drug testing. In POC testing, the MRO would provide the final interpretation of test results and serve as the liaison among the various parties involved in a drug test (e.g., the regulatory body, federal agency, the employer, the donor, the collection site, the POC testing site and POC trained tester, and the laboratory). The MRO must report negative drug test results from a POC testing site to the employer/agency in the same manner as results obtained from a laboratory. Non-negative specimens must be treated by the MRO in the same manner regardless of whether they were first tested using POC tests or tested only by a laboratory.

MROs must be knowledgeable about the capabilities of the POC tests and laboratory-based test methods that were used for specimens that they review. The MRO must report any discrepant or erroneous test results to the regulatory body, so an investigation can be conducted to identify and address the cause of the problem.

Due to conflict of interest concerns, some relationships between MROs and certified laboratories are considered inappropriate and are prohibited (i.e., the MRO must not be an employee, agent of, or have any financial interest in a certified laboratory). Similar prohibitions should be instituted for the relationship between MROs and POC device manufacturers and for the relationship between MROs and POC testing sites for which the MRO reviews drug test results.

11.3.6 Regulatory Oversight

The unique challenges for the regulatory body are that the POC testing sites may be numerous and decentralized and that many trained testers may have little forensic background or training. As proposed, another oversight group (POG) could provide administrative and technical support to a regulatory body. It is conceived that delegated functions could include reviewing and approving POC devices, providing training (i.e., initial training for users or "train-the-trainer" courses), and maintaining administrative oversight of testers and POC testing sites. Records are an essential component in any forensic field. A POG could maintain the records for workplace drug testing programs such as a registry of trained testers, records of results by tester for each device as part of a QA program, and other documentation demonstrating the acceptability of testing, reporting, and record keeping.

POC testing has both technical-scientific issues and administrative-policy issues that need to be incorporated into the regulatory process.[15] The Substance Abuse and Mental Health Services Administration and the Department of Health and Human Services (SAMHSA/HHS) currently certifies laboratories to perform federal workplace urine drug testing and monitors federal workplace drug testing through the National Laboratory Certification Program (NLCP) via on-site inspections and quarterly PT challenges. Similar direct oversight may be required to ensure that regulated workplace drug testing using POC testing is conducted with the equivalent integrity and technical standards as testing in a certified laboratory. With proper safeguards and regulatory oversight in place, it is envisioned that POC testing has the potential to become a significant part of regulated workplace drug testing.

Acknowledgments

The authors express their appreciation to Donna M. Bush, Ph.D., Walter F. Vogl, Ph. D., and Charles LoDico, M.S. (Division of Workplace Programs, Center for Substance Abuse Prevention, SAMHSA) for regulatory insight and to Robert Dow (RTI staff member) for graphic and editorial support.

REFERENCES

1. Mandatory Guidelines for Workplace Drug Testing Programs, Substance Abuse and Mental Health Services Administration, Department of Health and Human Services, 59 Federal Register (FR) 29916 (June 9, 1994).
2. Draft 4, Department of Health and Human Services, Substance Abuse and Mental Health Services Administration, Mandatory Guidelines for Workplace Drug Testing Programs, September 5, 2001, available at URL http://www.workplace.samhsa.gov.

3. Kadehjian, L.J., Performance of five non-instrumented urine drug-testing devices with challenging near-cutoff specimens. *J. Anal. Toxicol.,* 25, 670, 2001.

4. Crouch, D.J. et al., A field evaluation of five on-site drug-testing devices. *J. Anal. Toxicol.,* 26, 493, 2002.

5. Peace, M.R, Tarnai, L.D., and Poklis, A., Performance evaluation of four on-site drug-testing devices for detection of drugs of abuse in urine. *J. Anal. Toxicol.,* 24, 589, 2002.

6. SAMHSA, On-site Testing: An Evaluation of Non-Instrumented Drug Test Devices, January 29, 1999, available at URL http://www.workplace.samhsa.gov.

7. Walsh, J.M. et. al., An evaluation of rapid point-of-collection oral fluid drug-testing devices. *J. Anal. Toxicol.,* 27, 429, 2003.

8. Peace, M.R. and Tarnai, L.D., Performance evaluation of three on-site adulterant detection devices for urine specimens. *J. Anal. Toxicol.*, 26, 464, 2002.

9. Wong, B. et. al., Adulterants: its detection and effects on urine drug screens. Abstract: Society of Forensic Toxicologists 2003 Meeting.

10. Wong, R. The effect of adulterants on urine screen for drugs of abuse: detection by an on-site dipstick device. *Am. Clin. Lab.,* 21, 37, 2002.

11. HHS, Urine Specimen Collection Handbook for the New Federal Drug Testing Custody and Control Form, OMB Number 0930-0158, Exp Date: June 30, 2003.

12. DOT Urine Specimen Collection Guidelines for the U.S. Department of Transportation Workplace Drug Testing Programs, 49 CFR Part 40, available at URL http://www.dot.gov/ost/index.html.

13. Wu, A.H.B., On-site tests for therapeutic drugs, in *On-Site Drug Testing,* Jenkins, A.J. and Goldberger, B.A., Eds., Humana Press, Totowa, NJ, 2002, chap. 2.

14. George, S. and Braithwaite, R., Use of on-site testing for drugs of abuse. *Clin. Chem.*, 48, 10, 2002.

15. Shults, T.F. and Caplan, Y.H., Program requirements, standards, and legal considerations for on-site drug testing devices in workplace testing programs, in *On-Site Drug Testing,* Jenkins, A.J. and Goldberger, B.A., Eds., Humana Press, Totowa, NJ, 2002, chap 4.

11.4 ALCOHOL DETERMINATION IN POINT OF COLLECTION TESTING

J. Robert Zettl, B.S., M.P.A., DABFE
Forensic Consultants, Inc., Centennial, Colorado

The section covers five topics: general considerations; pharmacology and toxicology of alcohol; organizational policies and procedures for specimen collection and testing; governmental regulations; and devices for testing of breath, saliva, and urine. A comprehensive discussion of alcohol pharmacology and toxicology and evidentiary breath testing can be found in other sections of this text. The material presented in those areas serves to assist the reader in understanding this chapter.

Devices used for human subject alcohol determination can be separated into four broad categories: (1) law enforcement — driving under the influence (DUI); (2) diagnostic for treatment or other medical purposes; (3) pre-employment and workplace for compliance; and (4) for cause and random for governmental compliance. This chapter focuses on devices used in the last two venues.

11.4.1 General Considerations

The primary focus of this section is alcohol point of collection test devices and procedures, but it is appropriate to discuss briefly how and why alcohol testing is important in point of collection testing.

According to information from the National Highway Traffic Safety Administration, there were 41,471 motor vehicle traffic fatalities in the U.S. in 2000.[1] Of those 41,471 fatalities, 15,935 or 38.4% were alcohol related. This represents an average of one alcohol-related fatality every 31 min.

The National Safety Council[2] estimates the economic loss to society from a single highway fatality to be $90,000, and the corresponding total economic loss exceeding $4 billion annually.[3] The drinking driver affects every one of us through increased taxes for additional law enforcement needs, medical facilities, incarceration, rehabilitation, social security and welfare for survivors, as well as increased insurance rates.

In the U.S., alcohol accounts for two thirds of all workplace substance abuse complaints and depletes a similar percentage from their health care benefit budgets. The results of a 2002 study[4] released by the Substance Abuse and Mental Health Services Administration (SAMHSA) showed drug use trends in the U.S. Of interest is that most alcohol and drug users are employed.

Alcohol abuse and its related problems cost society many billions of dollars each year.[5–8] Estimates of the economic costs of alcohol abuse attempt to assess in monetary terms the damage that results from the misuse of alcohol. These costs include expenditures on alcohol-related problems and opportunities that are lost because of alcohol. In a 1985 cost study, Rice and co workers[9] estimated that the cost to society of alcohol abuse was $70.3 billion. By adjusting cost estimates for the effects of inflation and the growth of the population over time, that cost today could be well over $100 billion.

11.4.2 Pharmacology and Toxicology of Alcohol

Alcohol is commonly ingested orally and passes from the mouth, through the esophagus, into the stomach, and then into the small intestine. From here, alcohol is absorbed into the blood and distributed by the circulatory system to all parts of the body. As alcohol is transported through the body by the blood flow, it passes through the liver, which is primarily responsible for its metabolism, then to the kidneys where it is eliminated into the urine, then to the brain where it elicits its primary effect, and finally to the lungs where some alcohol passes unaltered out of the body. This unaltered alcohol permits the determination of a breath alcohol concentration (BrAC) from the alveolar or deep lung air.[10]

Alcohol is a low-molecular-weight organic molecule that is sufficiently similar to water to be miscible with water in all proportions. In addition, alcohol is able to cross cell membranes by a simple diffusion process; therefore, it can quickly achieve equilibrium throughout the body. The result of these properties is that alcohol rapidly becomes associated with all parts of the body, *including oral fluid,* and concentrations of alcohol will be found in proportion to body water content.

11.4.3 Organizational Policies and Procedures

11.4.3.1 Collection and Testing

Although it is the quantity of alcohol present in the brain that actually affects a person's normal functions, practicality necessitates a specimen that is in equilibrium with the brain be used to reflect alcohol concentration.

Therefore, most studies center on the use of blood to correlate the degree of alcohol impairment; however, over the last 30-plus years, breath testing has supplemented blood as the specimen of choice. Due to the difficulty in the collection of urine, its use as a specimen has fallen into some disfavor. Blood is more likely to be used in defining driving under the influence of alcohol and blood and/or urine in defining driving under the influence of drugs.

Serum or plasma is often used in clinical situations where alcohol is tested. Since the water content of serum or plasma is greater than that of whole blood, serum/plasma alcohol concentrations are typically 10 to 20% greater than the corresponding blood specimen. Therefore, if serum/plasma tests are to be utilized where blood alcohol concentrations (BACs) define legal penalties, the serum/plasma concentrations must be corrected. Serum to blood ratios vary from 1.12 to 1.17 while plasma averages 1.18. A ratio of 1.16 is commonly used to make the conversion.[11]

Blood or urine is seldom used in alcohol point of collection testing (APOCT) because of difficulties that hinder their ease of collection. In most instances, existing regulations or statutes will dictate the choice of specimen. At present breath and saliva are the specimens collected in the majority of APOCT venues.[12]

11.4.3.2 Specimens for Analysis

The most commonly used specimen for APOCT is breath for the two venues covered in this chapter: (a) pre-employment and workplace for compliance and (2) for cause and random for governmental compliance. With recent technological advances, saliva is taking on a new dimension and is pressing breath as the "new" specimen of choice. Saliva can, with appropriate care in specimen procurement and application of the accepted distribution ratios, be correlated with blood and a blood alcohol equivalent can be reported.

11.4.4 Breath Testing for Alcohol

11.4.4.1 Principles

Breath tests to determine the alcohol concentration present in a person's body are by far the most frequently utilized tests in cases involving driving under the influence of alcohol. States today have universally adopted legislation that permits reporting of a subject's alcohol concentration in breath units of alcohol per 210 L of breath. Breath alcohol analysis is the method of choice of law enforcement and many others due to ease and operational simplicity of new generation breath testing equipment, speed with which analyses may be conducted, convenience of being able to perform the analysis at or near the scene of an incident, and the convenience of having the subjects' test results immediately available. (A complete discussion of breath alcohol testing can be found elsewhere in this volume.)

11.4.4.2 Breath Alcohol Testing Devices

Introduction

The National Highway Traffic Administration has established a conforming products list for instruments that conform to the "Model Specifications for Devices to Measure Breath Alcohol."[13] This list contains all devices currently approved to perform breath alcohol testing within the U.S. Although many of the devices found on the present conforming products list are no longer manufactured, many are still in use.

In 1995, Zettl in conjunction with the Colorado Department of Public Health and Environment conducted a national survey of alcohol programs.[14] Some "electronic" devices listed in the 1995 Colorado Department of Public Health survey are no longer manufactured and newer-generation devices have been introduced since that survey was completed. Refer to the National Highway Traffic Administration conforming products list for a complete listing of all "electronic" instruments that can be used for point of collection testing.

Electronic Devices — Evidentiary

Electronic devices are generally classified into two distinct categories: (1) tabletop devices, which are larger and more expensive units originally designed for use in DUI testing, and (2) handheld or preliminary breath (alcohol) testers (PBTs), which are smaller units originally designed for use as screening devices by law enforcement to determine a suspected DUI's approximate

BrAC level at the time of stop. PBTs are now used extensively as evidentiary units in workplace and DUI testing.

Both types of devices are designed to analyze a breath sample and determine the amount of alcohol present in such a manner that the results have a degree of scientific accuracy and specificity sufficient to be reliable for presentation in court as evidence. They are self-contained portable laboratories in which the underlying principle, mode of operation, and safeguards are such that the end user can effectively operate the instruments and develop reproducible results.

Electronic Tabletop Devices

Infrared (IR) technology utilizes the principle that alcohol present as a vapor in breath absorbs specific wavelengths of IR light. Alveolar air is trapped in a sample chamber. IR light is directed through the sample cell and finally reaches a detector that measures the amount of light absorbed. As the concentration of alcohol vapor increases in the chamber, the amount of IR energy reaching the detector falls in a predictable exponential manner; hence, IR devices measure alcohol by detecting the decrease in the intensity of IR energy as it passes through the chamber.

The Draeger Corporation, Breathalyzer Division (Durango, CO) and Intoximeters, Inc. (St. Louis, MO) have developed breath test instruments that incorporate IR technology combined with an electrochemical (EC) fuel cell. Use of dual technology enhances both the quality and integrity of the sample and the accuracy of the alcohol test result. Fuel cell technology is discussed later in this chapter under Electronic Handhelds.

The most recent device, the Intoxilyzer 8000, uses dual IR (two separate wavelengths), one for alcohol concentration and the other for interferent detection.

Electronic Gas Chromatographic Tabletop Devices

These devices are no longer being manufactured but may still be in use. They are the Gas Chromatograph Intoximeter (GCI) Mark II and Mark IV manufactured by Intoximeters, Inc. and the Alco-Analyzer Gas Chromatograph, models 1000, 2000, and 2100, manufactured by Luckey Laboratories and later US Alcohol Testing.

Although the instruments used different methods of detection, they were of equal specificity and accuracy. They could be used as either direct measurement devices or they could analyze collected samples such as blood, delayed breath, saliva, and urine by means of headspace chromatography. They were excellent for use in a centralized facility setting; that is, samples could be collected in the field and forwarded to a centralized processing facility where technical personnel conducted the testing.

Electronic Handheld Devices: PBTs

Handheld "electronic screening devices" are small, portable, relatively inexpensive, may cost only a few hundred dollars, and were originally designed to estimate the BAC or BrAC of an individual. Some of the devices may be prone to erroneous readings both falsely high and low. The electrical sensor instruments — fuel cell — are generally more accurate (±10% range or better) and some are more specific for alcohol than others with printer attachments to be used in evidential settings. As stated, they were originally intended to assist in quickly determining the approximate alcohol concentration in an individual and were referred to as PBTs. The devices are useful for monitoring and controlling alcohol abuse and or intoxication in various workplace, alcohol abuse programs, and correctional institutions.

Evidentiary handhelds utilize an EC sensor — generally a fuel cell — to measure the amount of alcohol present in the sample. All of the devices in this category use alveolar air and may be calibrated for BrAC concentration.

Table 11.4.1 Pass–Warn–Fail PBTs

1. B.A.T. III by Century Systems, Inc. uses catalytic combustion for alcohol analysis. Pointer indicates Warn or Fail.
2. Alcohalt Detector by Mine Safety Appliance Company uses catalytic combustion for alcohol analysis and two indicator lights for Pass or Fail.
3. A.L.E.R.T. Model J3AD by Alcohol Counter Measures, Inc. Uses a Taguchi semiconductor detector to analyze the alcohol and a series of green, amber, and red lights to indicate Pass, Warn, or Fail.
4. Older generation Alco-Sensor by Intoximeters, Inc. Used a cluster of light-emitting diodes to indicate Pass, Warn, Fail (later models use a digital display for a direct readout of the % alcohol present).

Table 11.4.2 Digital Display PBTs

1. Alco-Sensors II through IV by Intoximeters, Inc. The Alco Sensor IV is shown in Figure 11.4.1.
2. Phoenix by Life Loc. See Figure 11.4.2.
3. CMI Corporations S-D2 and Models 200, 300, and 400. See Figure 11.4.3 for the S-D2.
4. National Draeger's Alcotest 7410. See Figure 11.4.4.

Because the devices were originally intended for screening, they should be used carefully and only for their intended purpose by trained personnel. Some of the older-generation devices are not sufficiently accurate for evidentiary purposes and if the subject tested is placed at risk pending the results of such tests, then the initial "screening" test should be confirmed by an evidentiary test. PBTs are extremely useful because they are generally less expensive than tabletop units and training and upkeep is less involved. Newer-generation PBTs, when used according to manufacturer specifications, can yield an accurate BrAC.

Pass–Warn–Fail Devices

These devices are calibrated to determine into which of three likely broad-range categories of BrAC an individual will likely fall.

PASS — Alcohol concentration below a predetermined level. Usually a level at which the individual is considered able to drive safely. Usually less than 0.05% except for underage drinkers.
WARN — Alcohol concentration above the level where a person would pass but below a level where the individual is considered intoxicated. Usually at or above 0.05% but less than the state's legal limit for per se.
FAIL — Alcohol concentration above the level where the individual is considered intoxicated. Usually at or above 0.08% or 0.10%. Depends on the state's level for DUI.

The concentrations at each level may be arbitrarily set as desired. Refer to Table 11.4.1 for a listing of some of the Pass–Warn–Fail devices and Table 11.4.2 for a listing of some of the digital display devices.

Digital Display Devices

There are many digital display devices on the NHTSA conforming products list. Some are shown in Table 11.4.2 (Figures 11.4.1 through 11.4.4). All use a fuel cell to determine the amount of alcohol present and %BrAC is digitally displayed.

Handheld — Non-Evidentiary

According to the manufacturer's product information the Alco-Scan Model AL-2500 (Figure 11.4.5), is a very versatile device that measures %BAC. The user gently blows at the sensor's intake and within 2 s the LCD displays a BrAC. The AL2500 is a compact and ideal device for use in social gatherings and for group testing.[15]

Figure 11.4.1 Intoximeters, Alco Sensor IV.

Figure 11.4.2 Lifeloc, Phoenix.

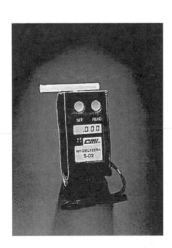

Figure 11.4.3 CMI SD-2.

Figure 11.4.4 Draeger 7410.

Figure 11.4.5   Alco-Scan Model AL-2500.

There are many devices like the Alco-Scan Model AL-2500, many priced under $100, but the end user should be cautioned that many are non-evidentiary and may not be suitable for some testing venues.

Screening Devices

NHTSA establishes which devices can be used as screening devices under its "Conforming Products List of Screening Devices to Measure Alcohol in Body Fluids.[16]"

11.4.4.3   Saliva-Based Technology

Analytical Principle

Saliva collection for alcohol testing is regularly employed in POCT facilities but is not used in DUI testing due to its practical constraints in court. Although saliva may be impractical for DUI enforcement because significant subject cooperation is needed to facilitate collection, recent advances in collection technology hold great promise for its use in POCT on-site (roadside) drug detection. For additional information, visit the RoadSIdeTestingAssessment Web site.[17]

Saliva alcohol results can be compared to the amount of alcohol contained in a person's blood. If collected properly by observing a waiting period after a person has consumed his or her last alcoholic beverage, usually 10 to 15 min, then any residual alcohol will have been absorbed, swallowed, or evaporated, and the person's mouth is "clear." According to one manufacturer's information the relationship between the amount of saliva alcohol and blood alcohol is 1:1 whereas with breath it is 000048:1, making saliva a more sensitive testing medium than breath.[18]

There are two prominent saliva-based alcohol test procedures. The QED saliva alcohol test procedure will not react with ketones often found in the saliva of patients with diabetes. Unlike some breath analyzers and other saliva tests, the QED is specific to ethyl alcohol and will not cross-react with acetone and ketones produced by diabetics.

The second type of disposable tester, strip test technology, does not have a great correlation between a person's true BAC and saliva alcohol concentration. Strip-based saliva testers are treated with an enzyme alcohol oxidase, which responds to alcohol in proportion to the concentration of alcohol in a mixed saliva sample placed on it. The user estimates the BAC by comparing the color change on the test strip patch to standard colors calibrated to correspond to different BACs. Although some saliva testers seem to indicate the presence of alcohol well, the enzyme alcohol oxidize used in these testers is easily affected by hot and cold temperatures. Hot temperatures will tend to indicate falsely high readings, while cold temperatures will tend to indicate falsely low readings.

Exposure to temperatures above 80°F or to ambient air will destroy the enzyme alcohol oxidase, rendering the tester useless. Most saliva testers give no indication if contamination has occurred, and if it has, they may not work effectively. Saliva testers generally have a shelf life of 1 year or less.

The technology and chemical reaction employed in the QED or the test strip technology is not as precise, accurate, or reliable as breath alcohol testing. Saliva-based alcohol tests require an evidential breath test (EBT) to confirm positive test results. Saliva alcohol testing is much less expensive to operate than a breath test, and unless a POCT facility conducts a very high volume of tests in a central location, then saliva testing instead of breath may be more cost-effective. Since most employees do not test positive for alcohol, simple screening is generally more cost-effective for POCT facilities.

Saliva-Based Devices

QED Saliva Alcohol Test — The QED (Figure 11.4.6) is a quantitative test device for the rapid determination of equivalent BAC using a non-invasive saliva sample. Approved by the Federal Department of Transportation (DOT) for commercial alcohol testing programs, the QED uses a unique patented lateral flow method to rapidly determine alcohol presence in saliva expressed as %BAC and milliliter per deciliter concentration. It is as simple as reading a thermometer.[19]

The QED Saliva Alcohol test uses a preset chemical reactive process that requires no user intervention; a color bar rises to the level of alcohol present in the system in much the same way as a mercury thermometer. In extensive clinical trials, saliva alcohol levels measured by the QED

Figure 11.4.6 QED Saliva Alcohol Test.

Saliva Alcohol test demonstrated a high correlation rate of 98% ($r = 0.98$) to blood analyzed by sophisticated laboratory gas chromatography methods.[20]

The QED Saliva Alcohol Test (Figure 11.4.6) is an easy-to-use diagnostic procedure with everything required contained in a sealed foil package. Total time required for the test is between 3 and 5 min. The three basic steps are as follows:

1. Using the cotton swab included, actively swab around the cheeks, gums, and tongue for 30 to 60 s or until the cotton swab is completely saturated with saliva.
2. Place the test device on a flat surface. Gently twist the swab with the collected saliva sample into the entry port and apply steady pressure to activate the capillary action until the pink fluid passes the QA Spot™ located at the top of the test device.
3. Allow the test device to develop for 2 min. A distinct purple bar will form within the marked scale region. The highest point of the purple bar represents the level of alcohol expressed either as a percentage or as grams per 100 ml or milligrams per deciliter concentration.

According to product information, the QED Saliva Alcohol Test will accurately measure a range of BAC of 0 to 145 mg/dl or 0.000% to 0.145% equivalent BAC.[20]

POCT facilities using the saliva alcohol test in very remote areas can comply with the DOT requirement that confirmation tests on positive screening tests must be conducted within 30 min. DOT will accept results of confirmation tests conducted more than 30 min after a positive screening test (49 CFR Part 40 section 40.65, paragraph (b)).[20] The DOT added a sentence, which directs the Breath Alcohol Technician (BAT) to simply explain "why?" if a confirmation test is done more than 30 min after a screening test.

Saliva-Based Test Strip — **Alco-Screen:** The ALCO-Screen™ (Figure 11.4.7) saliva alcohol test is intended for use as a rapid, highly sensitive method to detect the presence of alcohol in saliva and to provide a semiquantitative approximation of BAC. For applications where a quantitative determination of BAC is required, a positive ALCO-Screen result must be verified using an acceptable quantitative alcohol analysis procedure. ALCO-Screen requires no special training provided instructions are followed carefully. However, a qualified professional should perform

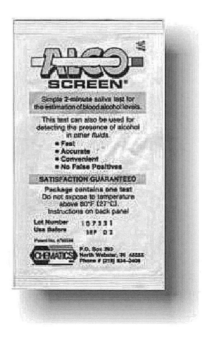

Figure 11.4.7 ALCO-Screen.

quantitative follow-up testing. ALCO-Screen is not intended as a measurement of mental or physical impairment but rather a screening test for the presence of alcohol in semiquantitative amounts. As with any saliva-based or breath alcohol tester, a deprivation period of at least 15 min must be observed before beginning the test. This includes non-alcoholic drinks, tobacco products, coffee, breath mints, food, etc. The ALCO-Screen is used by saturating a reactive pad with saliva from the test individual's mouth or sputum cup. At exactly 2 min, a change in color is observed in the reactive pad. A color change of green or blue indicates the presence of alcohol and a positive result. Results obtained after more than 2 min and 30 s (2.5 min) may be erroneous and should not be used. A BAC is estimated by comparing the color of the reactive pad to the color chart on the back of the test package (Figure 11.4.7). The ALCO-Screen produces a color change in the presence of saliva alcohol ranging from a light green-gray color at 0.02% BAC to a dark blue-gray color near 0.30% BAC. ALCO-Screen is designed and calibrated to be interpreted 2 min after saturation of the reactive pad. Waiting longer than 2 min to interpret the test can result in erroneous or false-positive results. ALCO-Screen is a visually interpreted test; as such, exact interpretation of results is not required in most cases. However, persons who are color blind or visually impaired may experience difficulty when a more specific interpretation is required. Furthermore, where test interpretation may be biased for whatever reason, it is suggested that another person's opinion of test results or color matching be obtained.[20]

ALCO Screen 2: ALCO-Screen 2 is a simple and cost-effective method of monitoring for alcohol consumption in a zero tolerance testing program. According to its product information, the ALCO-Screen 2 has been tested and approved by the U.S. DOT for required testing of all transportation and safety-sensitive employees for BACs above the federally mandated zero tolerance level of 0.02% (Figure 11.4.8). ALCO-Screen 2 is a simple one-step saliva-screening test that works in a clean, non-invasive manner and provides results in 4 min. Simply wet the test pad with saliva and wait 4 min. The development of a line on the test pad at 4 min indicates a BAC exceeding 0.02%. Any line, no matter how faint, developing on the reactive test pad at 4 min is a positive

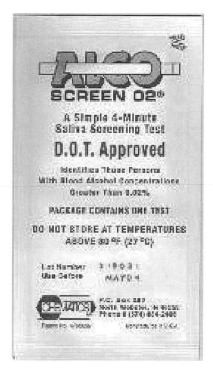

Figure 11.4.8 ALCO-Screen 2.

test. The Alco-Screen 2 is highly sensitive and can be used for evidentiary purposes. Completed test results can be photocopied for permanent filing.[20]

11.4.4.4 Chemical–Color-Change-Based Devices

Subcategories of screening devices, which are not electronic, make a determination of alcohol concentration by use of a chemical reaction. The first type of non-electronic device consists of either dichromate or permanganate salts in acid-impregnated crystals, which are placed in glass tubes. The individual being tested blows into a balloon or plastic bag or through the tube. After a certain volume of air or time has transpired, a measurement of the length of stain on the crystals in the tube (color change) is used to approximate the BrAC. The color change is a result of the chemical reaction occurring between alcohol and the chromate or permanganate salts in the crystals. Examples of older devices of this type include the Alcolyzer, several varieties distributed by Intoximeters, Inc., the Becton-Dickinson devices, Kitigawa Drunk-O-Tester by the Komo Chemical Industrial Company, Sober-Meters (Mobats) by US Alcohol and AlcoPro (Knoxville, TN). These screening devices use a mixed expired breath sample with the exception of the Becton-Dickinson device, which uses a two-chambered plastic bag to obtain alveolar air for the screening test. The results obtained from using these devices should be read according to time requirements expressed by the manufacturer. Other oxidizable components of breath will continue to react with the chemicals and may produce false positives.

Screening devices that utilize a color change reaction for alcohol detection are disposable and good for only one test whereas electronic devices have an extended life and can be used repeatedly after resetting; hence they may be more cost-effective if an agency is doing multiple testing.

One of the more popular disposable screeners is the BreathScan® Alcohol Detector (Figure 11.4.9).[20] According to the manufacturer's promotional material, "it is a disposable breath-alcohol indicator designed for one-time use" and according to its manufacturer it provides an accurate measure of the alcohol present in the exhaled breath of a test subject. By measuring the alcohol content in the breath, a reliable indication of the blood alcohol level is achieved. The BreathScan detector employs a new, patented technology for simple, on-the-spot screening for the presence of alcohol. The BreathScan tester can only be used once and then disposed of, minimizing contamination associated with repeated use of nondisposable units (no AIDS cross transmission).

The BreathScan's low cost and ease of use make the tester ideal for screening to determine whether an individual should submit to a forensic-quality blood test for confirmation. Just break the internal capsule, shake, and blow hard into the test cylinder of breath alcohol detector for a few seconds. Then read the color change of the chemical crystals in 2 min or less. Approved by the DOT, the detectors are available in five BAC levels for a complete range of sensitivity: 0.10%, 0.08%, 0.05%, 0.04%, and 0.02% (for zero tolerance testing), and they are very light and easy to carry around, weighing 0.16 oz each.

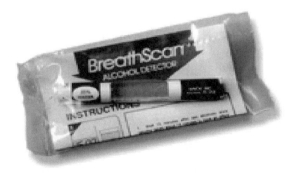

Figure 11.4.9 BreathScan Alcohol Detector.

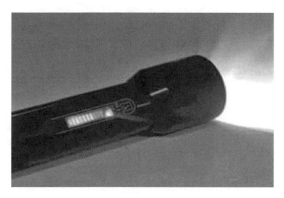

Figure 11.4.10 PAS IV "Sniffer."

11.4.4.5 *Passive Alcohol Sensor Devices*

"Passive" alcohol sensing (PAS) devices are designed to detect the presence of alcohol in a person's normally expelled breath; that is, the subject being tested is not required to blow into a mouthpiece as with conventional breath test devices. Passive alcohol sensing devices pull, through the use of a fan or other mechanical means, the vapor from the subject's normal breathing when the device is activated and held in close proximity to the subject's mouth. The device can also be held over open containers of an alcohol beverage to see if an underage person is drinking illegally. The present distributor of the PAS Systems is LLC (Fredericksburg, VA). It markets the PAS III, non-invasive alcohol-screening instrument, which has a built-in high-intensity flashlight (Figure 11.4.10). Their product information refers to the device as a "sniffer" for overt or covert alcohol detection. This device uses fuel cell technology for determining alcohol concentration. Another PAS device, the Alcometer, is currently available from Lions Laboratories (Cardiff, Wales, U.K.).

Passive alcohol sensors have had a varied history — first introduced in the early 1970s without much success. In a recent DOT/NHTSA study (DOT HS 807 394), one such device was able to discriminate among differing alcohol air samples under laboratory conditions. The user has to be cognizant that passive alcohol sensors are influenced by wind disturbances. Wind or any air movement tends to invalidate their proficiency.

11.4.5 Blood and Urine — Collection, Identification, and Preservation of Specimens

This issue is addressed only briefly here. Other treatises and handbooks can be found that will assist the reader in understanding this area of alcohol testing.[21,22] Blood or urine specimens must be collected in a manner to maintain the chain of custody as in any other forensic case. However, additional precautions are required since the specimens are biological in nature, namely, removal of blood by qualified medical persons in an alcohol-free manner, and preservation of the specimen to permit mailing and long-term storage. Before establishing a system for collection, one should consult with the certifying state or other agency in control of specimen collection and testing to prevent unnecessary problems.

11.4.6 Quality Assurance and Proficiency Testing

11.4.6.1 *Saliva*

Quality control (QC) requirements for the Saliva Alcohol test can be conducted using control checks, with the Saliva Alcohol Ethanol Control from OraSure Technologies.[23] Saliva alcohol ethanol control solutions should be run once per lot number of saliva alcohol tests.

Saliva-based devices such as the ALCO-Screen may be qualitatively verified using a test solution prepared by adding 4 drops of 80-proof distilled spirits to 8 oz (1 glass) of water. This solution should provide a color reaction equal to or higher (darker) than the 0.04% color block. The color reaction with alcohol in saliva is somewhat slower and less intense than with alcohol in aqueous solutions.

11.4.6.2 Body Fluids

A laboratory conducting blood alcohol determinations whether for clinical or forensic purposes should maintain an internal system designed to assure the reliability of all laboratory data and should participate in an external proficiency testing program, where available, that evaluates the laboratory on the basis of the comparability of its results with those of several reference laboratories analyzing the same sample.

The quality assurance program should include maintenance and periodic testing of equipment, validation and recalibration of methods, reagent evaluation, and surveillance of results. In-house reference calibrators and controls may be prepared from outdated whole human blood targeting concentrations of 0.000, 0.050, 0.100, 0.200, and 0.400% ethanol. Various reference materials are available to prepare or serve as standards, calibrators, and controls, e.g., the National Institute of Standards and Testing (NIST) material, SRM 1821 Ethanol (formerly National Bureau of Standards), and the College of American Pathologists (CAP) alcohol reference materials. Many states, private entities, and reagent manufacturers provide reference, calibrator, and control materials.

For standardization, calibrators are assayed in triplicate and an appropriate standard curve prepared. Standardization should be repeated periodically or as dictated by changes in operational protocol. One or more quality control blood specimens (0.080, 0.015%, etc.) should be prepared and the mean and standard deviation determined for a total of 20 samples analyzed over a period of 10 days. The quality control sample should then be analyzed with every run of unknown alcohol samples and the result should fall within 95% confidence limits. The American Academy of Forensic Sciences, Toxicology Section and the Society of Forensic Toxicologists, Inc. have approved a quality assurance program titled, "Forensic Toxicology Laboratory Guidelines."[24]

These same quality control procedures should be used for the testing of any other body fluids such as urine, serum, saliva, and post-mortem samples. An excellent resource for quality assurance can be found in Garriott's *Medicolegal Aspects of Alcohol*[22] or by obtaining the "Forensic Toxicology Laboratory Guidelines" from the American Academy of Forensic Sciences, Toxicology Section or the Society of Forensic Toxicologists, Inc.[24]

Duplicate aliquoting and testing of forensic biological specimens is an important part of any quality assurance procedure or program. In general, the results of the two independent tests should fall within a range of each other by ±10% or 0.02% BAC. Other accuracy or precision criteria may be used, but an increased degree of confidence in the reported results is achieved by duplicate testing.[25]

11.4.6.3 Breath

Although correlation between alcohol concentrations calculated using breath testing instruments and alcohol concentrations determined directly from blood have been well documented in the literature and accepted by the courts, it is necessary to have a method for the standardization and quality control of breath test devices. For scientific and legal reasons, it is necessary to demonstrate that a particular device was functioning properly at the time a subject was tested.

Wet Bath Breath Alcohol Simulation

The relationship between the concentration of alcohol in air as compared to blood at 34°C is discussed in other chapters of this text. The partition ratio for air/blood is greater than that of air/water; therefore, if an aqueous alcohol solution is heated to 34°C the amount of alcohol in the air space at equilibrium will be less than that of blood. To produce a breath sample that simulates a given BAC, it is therefore necessary that the aqueous (water and alcohol solution) be of an alcohol concentration greater than the expected reading value. If an expected BrAC of 0.100% at 34°C is required, then the aqueous water and alcohol concentration must be 0.121%.

Simulation Units for Breath Alcohol Testers

There are several manufactures of breath alcohol simulation devices. A complete list of companies and their devices can be obtained by contacting the National Highway Traffic Safety Administration, Office of Alcohol and State Programs, at 400 Seventh Street, S.W., Washington, D.C., 20590, (202) 366-5593 and asking for the current Model Specifications for Calibrating Units for Breath Alcohol Testers.

The Simulator maintains the temperature at a constant 34 ± 0.2°C. The simulator contains several basic components: the first is the jar that holds the solution; the second is the head, which serves as a seal to the jar and contains the thermostat, thermometer, propeller, and motor, an air inlet tube that is attached to a bubbler tube, an air outlet tube, and a wire mesh baffle to prevent the solution from escaping through the outlet tube.

The simulator solution is the most critical component. It should be carefully prepared and its accuracy checked by a competent laboratory and standardized by chemical and chromatographic analysis, comparing the results to a primary reference standard material (e.g., potassium dichromate, NIST Alcohol Standard).

Gas Breath Alcohol Simulation

Breath alcohol simulation is achieved by using a dry gas mixture. Several manufactures prepare or sell gaseous ethanol products. The device consists of a tank of pressurized air containing a specified alcohol concentration; a button is depressed and the alcohol/air mixture is released into the breath-testing device. These gaseous standards are useful if the breath test instrument utilizes a relatively small sample volume. For breath testing instruments with large sample volumes, use of these gaseous standards may or may not be practical. Any pressurized gas mixture of alcohol and air is subject to variation due to atmospheric pressure; hence, the mixture should be standardized against a wet solution of known alcohol concentration prior to use in a field situation.

For a complete listing of the dry gas ethanol manufactures, contact DOT/NHTSA and obtain its most recent listing of these units, contained in the conforming products list of calibrating units.[26]

11.4.7 Concluding Remarks

The abbreviation BAC refers to blood alcohol concentration, with concentrations expressed as percent weight to volume, % (w/v) or grams of alcohol per 100 ml of blood. The abbreviation BrAC refers to breath alcohol concentration expressed as percent weight to volume, % (w/v) or grams of alcohol per 210 L of deep lung or alveolar breath. The term alcohol refers to ethyl alcohol or ethanol. There are many excellent resources for forensic alcohol information; those by Garriott and Saferstein are especially helpful. In addition to printed documentation, numerous Internet sites are available. Table 11.4.3 provides a list of some of these.

Acknowledgments

The author thanks Yale Caplan, Ph.D., and the manufacturers of alcohol test equipment for providing assistance, information, and photographs.

Table 11.4.3 Alcohol and Traffic Safety-Related Sites on the Internet

Air Products	www.airproducts.com
American Academy of Forensic Sciences	www.aafs.org
AAA Foundation for Traffic Safety	www.aaafts.org
Alcohol Countermeasure Systems	www.acs-corp.com
Bureau of Transportation Statistics	www.bts.gov
Canadian Safety Council	www.safety-council.org
CMI, Inc.	www.alcoholtest.com
Drug and Alcohol Testing Industry Association	www.datia.com
Draeger Breathalyzer Division	www.drager-breathalyzer.com
Guth Laboratories	www.guthlabs.com
Health and Human Services Drug Testing	www.health.org/workpl.htm
Insurance Institute for Highway Safety	www.carsafety.org
International Association for Chemical Testing	www.iactonline.org
International Council on Alcohol, Drugs and Traffic Safety	raru.adelaide.edu.au/icadts/
Intoximeters, Inc.	www.intox.com
Lifeloc	www.lifeloc.com
Lion Laboratories	www.lionlaboratories.com
Mothers Against Drunk Driving	www.madd.org
National Clearinghouse for Alcohol and Drug Information	www.health.org
National Committee for Clinical Laboratory Standards	www.nccls.org
National Highway Traffic Safety Administration	www.nhtsa.dot.gov
National Institute of Health	www.nih.gov
National Institute on Alcohol Abuse and Alcoholism	www.niaaa.nih.gov
National Institute on Drug Abuse	www.nida.nih.gov
National Motorists Association	www.motorists.org
National Safety Council, Committee on Alcohol & Other Drugs	www.nsc.org
NPAS DataMaster	www.npas.com
PAS Systems International	www.sniffalcohol.com
Road Side Testing Assessment	www.rosita.org
Scott Specialty Gasses	www.scottgas.com
Society of Forensic Toxicologists	www.soft-tox.org
Substance Abuse and Mental Health Services Administration	www.samhsa.gov
Transportation Research Board	www.nas.edu/trb
U.S. Department of Health and Human Services	www.hhs.gov
U.S. Department of Transportation	www.dot.gov

REFERENCES

1. January 2000 Impaired Driving Program Update, National Highway Traffic Safety Administration, Traffic Safety Programs, Impaired Driving Division, Washington, D.C., 2000.
2. National Safety Council, 1121 Spring Lake Drive, Itasca, IL.
3. Colorado Association of Chiefs of Police, D.U.I. Enforcement Manual for the State of Colorado (August, 1977).
4. Results from the 2002 National Survey on Drug Use and Health: National Findings. Department of Health and Human Services, Substance Abuse and Mental Health Services Administration, Office of Applied Studies. Washington, D.C., 2002.
5. Berry, R.E., Boland, J.P., Smart, C., and Kanak, J., *The Economic Cost of Alcohol Abuse: 1975*. Policy Analysis, Brookline, MA, 1977.
6. Cruze, A.M., Harwood, H.J., Kristiansen, P.L., Collins, J.J., and Jones, D.C., *Economic Costs to Society of Alcohol and Drug Abuse and Mental Illness: 1977*. Research Triangle Institute, Research Triangle Park, NC, 1981.
7. Harwood, H.J., Napolitano, D.M., Kristiansen, P.L., and Collins, J.J., *Economic Costs to Society of Alcohol and Drug Abuse and Mental Illness: 1980*. Research Triangle Institute, Research Triangle Park, NC, 1984.

8. Rice, D.P., Estimating the Cost of Illness. Health Economics Series, No. 6. DHEW Pub. No. (PHS) 947-6, 1966. U.S. Department of Health, Education and Welfare, Rockville, MD, 1966.
9. Rice, D.P., Kelman, S., Miller, L.S., and Dunmeyer, S., *The Economic Costs of Alcohol and Drug Abuse and Mental Illness: 1985.* National Institute on Drug Abuse, Rockville, MD, 1990.
10. Zettl, J.R., Prosecution of driving while under the influence student manual, in Toxicology and the Forensic Analysis of Alcohol. American Prosecutors Research Institute, National Traffic Law Center, Washington, D.C. USDOT/NHTSA Project Number 004NTLC and 0922 Drug Driver.
11. Payne, J.P., Hill, D.W., and King, N.W., Observations on the distribution of alcohol in blood, breath and urine, *Br. Med. J.,* 1, 196, 1996.
12. Dubowski, K.M. and Caplan, Y.H., Alcohol testing in the workplace, in *Medicolegal Aspects of Alcohol,* 3rd ed., J.C. Garriott, Ed., Lawyers & Judges Publishing, Tucson, 1996, 439–475.
13. National Highway Traffic Safety Administration, Highway Safety Programs, Model specifications for devices to measure breath alcohol, amended, *Fed. Regis.,* 67(192), 2002.
14. Zettl, J.R., *Colorado Alcohol Test Program Survey — Update,* Colorado Department of Public Health and Environment, Laboratory and Radiation Services Division, February 27, 1997.
15. Advance Safety Devices, 21000 Osborne Street, Suite 4, Canoga Park, CA 91304.
16. National Highway Traffic Safety Administration, Highway Safety Programs, Conforming products list for screening devices to measure alcohol in body fluids, amended, *Fed. Regis.,* 66(87), 2001.
17. www.rosita.org//.
18. Craig Medical Distribution, Inc. 185 Park Center Drive, Building P, Vista, CA 92801.
19. OraSure Technologies, Inc. Bethlehem, PA (Formerly STC Technologies, Inc.).
20. STC Technologies, Inc. 1745 Eaton Avenue, Bethlehem PA 18018-1799.
21. Caplan, Y.A. and Zettl, J.R., The determination of alcohol in blood and breath, in *Forensic Science Handbook,* Vol. 1, 2nd ed., R.E. Saferstein, Ed., Prentice Hall, Upper Saddle River, NJ, 2001, chap. 12.
22. Garriott, J.C., Ed., *Medicolegal Aspects of Alcohol,* 3rd ed., Lawyers & Judges Publishing, Tucson, 1996.
23. OraSure Technologies, Inc. 220 East First Street Bethlehem, PA 18015.
24. *Forensic Toxicology Laboratory Guidelines,* American Academy of Forensic Sciences, Toxicology Section and Society of Forensic Toxicologists, Inc., 1997–98.
25. Jones, A.W. and Logan, B.K., DUI defenses, in *Drug Abuse Handbook,* S. Karch, Ed., CRC Press, Boca Raton, FL, 1998, 1006–1045.
26. Department of Transportation, National Highway Traffic Safety Administration, Model specifications for calibrating units for breath alcohol testers; conforming products list of calibrating units, *Fed. Regis.,* 62(156), August 13, 1997.

11.5 ON-SITE POINT-OF-COLLECTION DRUG TESTING: HISTORY, DEVELOPMENT, AND APPLICATIONS

Jane S.C. Tsai, M.D.
Roche Diagnostics, Indianapolis, Indiana

The advantage or projected benefit of prompt analytical investigations near the site of specimen collection has aggrandized the development of point-of-care products in diverse fields of *in vitro* diagnostics. POC is used in clinical or diagnostic tests as an abbreviation for point-of-care testing. A variety of descriptions have been used to describe diagnostic POC testing (POCT), including on-site testing, near patient testing (NPT), and decentralized testing. The term POC is also cited in the literature for drugs of abuse testing and clinical toxicology.[1-3] In contrast to general clinical diagnostic assays, testing for drugs of abuse involves the considerations of specimen collection, chain-of-custody, specimen validity, two-tier screening and confirmation testing, and the reporting process. Therefore, SAMHSA (Substance Abuse and Mental Health Services Administration) and

DTAB (Drug Testing Advisory Board) have adopted the term point of collection testing (POCT) for POC drug testing during the drafting process for the new "Mandatory Guidelines for Federal Workplace Drug Testing Programs."[4]

Although both the concept and practice of POCT have been evolving over an extended period of time, technological advances in the past two decades have greatly expanded the role of POCT in health care. An assortment of POC tests, ranging from urinalysis strips to handheld sensor systems and sophisticated bench-top analyzers, are currently in active use,[1] especially for applications that require fast turn-around time (TAT). In the areas where the availability of an immediate test result could influence the outcome management or patient care, the use of POCT is desirable even though there are important considerations regarding the reliability, accuracy, and cost-effectiveness of these tests.

Testing for drug abuse or misuse is an example of areas where the immediacy of a test result could contribute to enhance the efficiency of the testing program. Therefore, POCT has been applied in workplace drug testing programs to facilitate the decision-making process[5,6] and evaluated in the field for road-side testing or traffic safety.[7,8] POC drugs of abuse testing is also widely used in various compliance programs (e.g., criminal justice, psychiatric, rehabilitation, and drug treatment testing) to aid in behavior modification for higher admission of use and better sanctions of ongoing drug use.[9,10] When used appropriately, POC substance abuse testing can be utilized in clinics or the emergency department to help rule out or rule in drug exposure.[1,3]

In Subpart L of the draft of new mandatory guidelines,[4] POCT will be defined as "an initial test conducted at the collection site either to determine the presence of drugs and/or to determine the validity of a specimen." The proposed guidelines specify two types of POCT devices: (1) Non-instrumented for which the end-point result is obtained by visual evaluation (i.e., read by human eye); or (2) instrumented for which the result is obtained by instrumental evaluation (e.g., densitometer, spectrophotometer, fluorometer).

The majority of publications have used the expression "on-site" instead of "POC" for drugs of abuse testing. In addition to the terms "on-site," "point-of-care," and "point-of-collection," an assortment of terminology has been used to describe single-use, disposable, commercial immunoassay kits for drugs of abuse screening. Trade names that contain or imply the words "rapid," "quick," "fast," "instant," "express," "simple," "screen," "scan," "no-step," or "one-step" have been used in commercial drug POCT products.

11.5.1 Evolution of On-Site/POC Drug Testing

During the early phases of drug testing, "on-site" urine drug tests were carried out on the premises as compared to those sent to an "off-site" laboratory. The first court-based testing laboratory was established in 1971.[9] On-site urine drug testing using "instrumented" immunoassays could also be carried out in a clinic with immediate feedback of results to patients and staff. In 1977, Goldstein et al.[11] evaluated on-site vs. off-site urine testing in a methadone treatment program. The authors concluded that there were negligibly small differences between the on-site or off-site urine testing groups with respect to illicit drug use although other advantages might justify the adoption of on-site testing in methadone programs.

At the early stage of workplace drug testing implementation, the term "on-site" urine testing for drugs of abuse was generally used to refer to tests "done at the place of business."[12] In the 1986 NIDA Research monograph 73, Willette[12] wrote that "the first major consideration" to be reviewed when selecting a system for drug testing is to decide if testing will be done on-site or by an outside laboratory. The horizon of on-site drug testing has since been expanded far beyond the defined "on-site equipment at on-site testing area" to an array of "non-instrumented" devices used by various substance abuse testing programs. In the monograph, however, the described advantages and disadvantages of on-site vs. laboratory screening remain coetaneous considerations for current on-site drug testing.

The historical milestones for the development of the federal guidelines have been for laboratory drug testing, and the drafting of guidelines that will formally permit on-site testing[4] was still in process as of early 2004. Subsequent to the publication of the 1988 mandatory guidelines,[13] NIDA sponsored a "Consensus Conference" in 1989 to assess and evaluate such programs and to develop recommendations for change.[14] The seven working groups and the participants of this conference were able to reach a consensus as recorded in the Consensus Report.[14] The issue of on-site testing was one of four issues considered by multiple working groups. In this Consensus Report, the "on-site initial screening only testing facilities" should "only be allowed where safety issues demand the most rapid turn-around time, justifying the risk to the client inherent in unconfirmed tests, and the considerable difficulties in achieving accurate testing that such facilities create." It was agreed that on-site urine screening "can reliably identify negative specimens, provided appropriate safeguards are built into the procedure."

A NIDA-funded evaluation of 11 laboratory-based on-site drug testing facilities[15] concluded that on-site drug testing was technically possible for screening in the private sector, military, and criminal justice systems. However, recommendations were made to address the flaws identified in personnel, specimen handling, security, standard operating procedure manual, testing method, quality control and assurance programs, and policies.[15,16] It was recommended that guidelines should be developed to establish operational consistency and analytical accuracy among on-site drug testing facilities.

Meanwhile, the 1989 Nuclear Regulatory Commission (NRC) "Fitness for Duty" rule permitted NRC licensees to have their own on-site testing program.[17] Licensees were permitted to conduct initial screening tests of an aliquot before forwarding selected specimens to a laboratory certified by the Department of Health and Human Services (HHS), provided the licensee's and testing facilities meet the stated quality criteria for conducting the tests.. Similarly, a 1991 National Institute of Justice (NIJ) study on urinalysis technology comparison reported that on-site instrumented drug testing demonstrated equal performance to commercial laboratory-based testing.[9,18]

In parallel with instrumented testing, non-instrumented-based "on-site testing devices" that can be used without the need of a laboratory were launched into a few nonregulated drug testing fields but did not become a viable alternative of regulated workplace drug testing when the federal-mandated testing was initiated. The revision of mandatory guidelines in 1994[19] also did not specify rules for on-site testing; however, several departments of the U.S. government have since sponsored evaluations and working groups to assess the reliability of, and to address issues associated with, these on-site testing devices.[20–23] During the SAMHSA-sponsored On-Site Drug Testing Workgroup Meeting in 1999,[16] the consensus recommendations from 1989 were reviewed again. It was recognized that the main elements remain the same but the "grid" would be revised to take into consideration the non-instrumented-based and instrumented-based techniques, to add oral fluids, and to leave out "elements that are clearly laboratory based."

A laboratory for conducting "only instrumented initial drug and validity tests" will be called an Instrumented Initial Test Facility (IITF) as described in Subpart M of the draft of new mandatory guidelines.[4] Four types of specimen can be tested at an IITF (hair, oral fluid/saliva, sweat/patch, and urine). In comparison, a POCT will be "an initial test conducted at the collection site" using either non-instrumented or instrumented assays for urine or oral fluid drug testing.

In addition to the SAMHSA mandatory guidelines for workplace drug testing, several other organizations have developed their recommended "guidelines" for forensic, athletic, or clinical drug testing. The National Academy of Clinical Biochemistry (NACB) Laboratory Medicine Practice Guidelines addressed the "major limitations" of immunoassays for drug testing in emergency department and clinical laboratories to support the diagnosis and management of the poisoned patients.[24] Issues associated with the nature of antibody-based drug screening and the different cutoff requirements for workplace vs. compliance or clinical testing are applied to both laboratory-based and POC drug testing. Some of the countries that develop their drug testing guidelines take into consideration the different drug testing segments. For example, the Swiss guidelines for drug testing (non-legally binding) defined four areas of application: clinical sector, substitution or withdraw treatment, forensic investigations, and "non-traditional" environment (workplace, physicals, military, school).[25] The application of non-instrumental immunoassays in each of the four areas is addressed in the document; however, the use of rapid tests is generally not preferred.

Despite that on-site drug testing has not been permitted in mandated testing programs and is not preferred in many settings, there has been a significant growth of on-site drug testing in the past few years.[16,26] Compared to off-site urinalysis, on-site drug testing was shown to have lower variable costs, and total costs were lower once a threshold of 27 employees tested was attained.[27] Mastrovitch et al.[28] evaluated the POCT screening approach in an emergency department of a tertiary-care, urban medical center and showed at least 37.5% cost saving per analyte using POCT as compared to laboratory-based urine screening. The widespread interest in on-site drug testing can also be measured from the arrays of comparative studies conducted in the past decade that evaluated various combinations of "currently available on-site drug testing devices" under a variety of conditions.[20–23,29] The business models for on-site drug testing are very complex due to multiple customer types with multiple requirements and expectations. With few examples of federal agency preemption, on-site testing has been subject to different U.S. state laws and various levels of restrictions. The manner in which a drug testing program is managed in private sectors can be quite client-driven. The recent explosion of on-site testing products and the Internet has further complicated the fields of on-site drug testing. Therefore, the examples described in this chapter are general representations and are not all-inclusive for these very diverse fields.

11.5.2 History of Technology and Product Development

Significant strides in the development of technologies and products for competitive immunoassays of small molecules have been made in the past 30 years. There have also been substantial research and development investments in drug screening technologies. Generally, the instrumented immunoassays played a role in supporting the commercialization of non-instrumented immunoassays. One example of such can be demonstrated by the FDA (Food and Drug Administration) 510(k) pre-market clearance review process whereby a new product gains approval by demonstrating substantial equivalency to one or more "predicate devices" on the market. Confirmation technologies, especially GC/MS, are used as the gold reference for immunoassay studies for 510(k) submission and are occasionally used as the predicate methods. Although increasing numbers of test-strip products have obtained clearance utilizing similar test-strip products as predicate devices, the first phases of on-site products were comparatively evaluated with instrumented, laboratory-based immunoassays to attain FDA approval.

11.5.2.1 Instrumented Immunoassays

The early concept of the "two-stage field testing procedure" involved the on-site collection of samples that could be preserved and transported in a convenient way for completing the instrumented testing in a laboratory. For "field" application, the samples can be absorbed onto paper disks such as a paper loaded with cation-exchange resin, dried, and mailed to the laboratory for radioimmunoassay (RIA).[30] The locally collected, sample-treated paper with ion-exchange resin could also be tested with hemagglutination-inhibition and spectrophotofluorimetry.[31] In a 1976 review article, Cleeland et al.[32] reported that the RIAs appear to be equally applicable to detection of drugs in urine, blood, saliva, and tissues, and "can be used equally well for emergency (STAT) tests or mass screening."

Nonetheless, the most commonly utilized urine drug testing methodology for on-site facilities has been homogeneous immunoassays that can be easily performed using small automated analyzers. Reagents based on the principles of EMIT (enzyme multiplied immunoassay technique), and to a lesser degree, FPIA (fluorescent polarization immunoassay), and KIMS (kinetic interaction of particles in solution), have all been utilized in the context of on-site laboratory testing. Examples of bench-top analyzers or newer analyzer families that offer models suitable for small- to medium-size laboratories include Dade Behring (Deerfield, IL) ETS-Plus, Viva, 30Rand V-Twin; Abbott (Abbott Park, IL) TDx, TDxFLx; Olympus (Melville, NY) AU series, and Roche (Indianapolis, IN) Hitachi Systems, Cobas MIRA-Plus, and Cobas Integra systems.

11.5.2.2 Non-Instrumented Drug Testing Products

Microparticle-Based On-Site Immunoassays

The utilization of hemagglutination-inhibition methods to detect abused drugs was reported in 1971.[33] Early versions of a non-instrumented testing device for abused drugs included a latex agglutination-inhibition-based testing device (Abutex) made available for investigation by Hoffmann-La Roche in the 1970s. By 1981, several Roche Agglutex products for abused drug screening had received FDA 510(k) approval. The Agglutex assays were available from the mid-1970s until the early 1990s; the method was reported to be easy to use and could accommodate analysis of "approximately a hundred specimens per hour without sophisticated instrumentation" although the results were available after a 2-h incubation period.[34] By contrast, the next generation of latex agglutination-inhibition based products, Roche Abuscreen OnTrak,[35–44] produced results in approximately 4 min. The first wave of OnTrak products received FDA approval in 1988. A multianalyte agglutination assay was reported in 1993 by Abbott researchers[45] as a 10-min assay system for five classes of abused drugs.

Slide or capillary-flow microparticle-based POCT immunoassay products have the advantage of better-controlled reaction kinetics (liquid-phase, thorough reagent mixing, and incubation) and relatively easy visual interpretation of a positive or negative result. However, these assays are less versatile due to the requirements of liquid reagent storage and handling and were gradually replaced by membrane-based products in the past few years.

Membrane-Based Assays for Urine Drug Testing — One-Step Lateral Flow Immunochromatography

Paper strip-based immunochromatographic assays or "dipstick" assays have been explored for drug immunoassay development. The first application of lateral flow paper strip was disclosed in a 1978 patent that utilized immunochromatography to carry out an RIA.[46] In 1983, Litman et al.[47] reported "an internally referenced test strip immunoassay for morphine." Enzyme-channeling immunoassay that involved sequential incubation of the strip in the sample and developer solution could "score the test as positive or negative for drug" based on the ratio of the color formed on the indicator pad to that formed on the reference pad. An enzyme immunochromatography based on "the spatial distribution of enzyme label" for analyte quantification[48] was used in the Syva Accu-Level product for therapeutic drug monitoring.[49,50]

Earlier evaluations of paper chromatography tests for drugs of abuse screening in urine, such as the 1980 Technology Resources, Inc., TRI dipstick and the 1987 Keystone Diagnostic Inc. Quik Test, all indicated that the tests were inaccurate, unreliable, and unacceptable.[51–54] By the mid-1990s, approximately a dozen membrane-based on-site products for screening drugs of abuse in urine were launched either by established companies in the drug testing business or by new companies founded to enter POC or drug testing markets. Examples of products marketed or evaluated during this time period include (in alphabetical order) Abusign (Princeton Biomeditech, Princeton, NJ),[55,56] accu-PINCH (Hycor Biomedical Inc., Garden Grove, CA),[57] EZ-Screen (Environmental Diagnostics, Burlington, NC),[58–61] Frontline (Boehringer Mannheim/Roche),[62,63] microLine (DSSI, later Casco-Nerl, Portland, ME), OnTrak TesTcup and OnTrak TesTstik (Roche Diagnostics, now Varian, Inc., Irvine, CA),[64–71] Rapid Drug Screening (American Bio Medica Corp. Kinderhook, NY), Triage

(BioSite, San Diego, CA),[72–78] Verdict (Editek, Inc., now MedTox, Burlington, NC), Visualine (Sun Biomedical, Cherry Hill, NJ),[79] etc. Over time a number of POCT products or brands were either "on and off the market" — or completely changed product configurations.

From the late 1990s into the early 2000s, there has been a rapid proliferation in both the numbers and distributors of on-site drug testing products. Besides those in the U.S., the number of overseas manufacturers of POC drug testing products has also increased in recent years. Several of the on-site testing investigation projects either inventoried or evaluated the contemporaneous on-site testing products.[20–23,28] The reports list descriptions of selected products and some of the different products that are in fact identical products. From published information and government databases, it can be noted that many products either share the same strip manufacturer or are essentially the same devices under different packaging or labeling. For products marketed under different trade names, their package inserts typically contain the same data because no additional studies are needed for FDA "Add-to-file" approval for selling the device with different trade names or labeling.

Collectively, divergent factors have contributed to the explosion of the number and types of POC drug testing products. Among the contributing factors are increased acceptance of on-site testing by the marketplaces, more recognition of the on-site testing benefits, more new companies and new alliances, and more "menu configurations" comprising various combinations of single and panel tests. Conversely, the lack of mandated or standardized regulations, the significant price erosion, and the promulgation of the Internet also contributed to blurring the entry barriers into the on-site drug testing markets.

Membrane-Based Drug Assays for Alternative Matrices

In addition to urine drug testing, some of the on-site testing products were evaluated for blood or post-mortem blood testing following blood extraction or acetone precipitation.[80,81] However, the performance is different. In recent years, one-step lateral flow immunochromatography has also been the format of choice for most of the on-site drug testing for alternative matrices. Examples of on-site saliva testing products[82–89] include (in alphabetical order) Drugwipe and DrugwipeII (Securetec, Ottobrunn, Germany), OralLab (Varian, Inc., Irvine, CA), OralScreen (Avitar, Inc., Canton, MA), RapiScan Cozart Bioscience Ltd. (Cozart Bioscience Ltd., U.K.), and SalivaScreen (Ulti-Med, Ahrensberg, Germany). The Drugwipe products are also marketed for drug detection in sweat or on the skin. These products are discussed in another chapter of this section. However, with more of the on-site urine test manufacturers expanding into the oral fluid testing field, the number of oral fluid testing products is likely to increase in the coming years.

11.5.2.3 Hybrid of Instrumented and Non-Instrumented On-Site Drug Testing

The "hybrid" system usually consists of a handheld "reader" to help interpret the color development result of an on-site testing strip. There are bench-top readers that can integrate sample-handling or testing procedures. Many of the test strip developers have developed readers for internal use or for products; moreover, a few generic strip readers are commercially available. Nevertheless, not all companies make the commercialization decision. Examples of on-site tests that have to be used in conjunction with an instrument include RapiScan (Cozart Biosciences), eScreen (eScreen, Inc., Overland Park, KS), etc. Currently, there are companies that can offer connectivity and multivendor information management for POCT. Some of the on-site device or service providers may offer customized data management for the needs of chain-of-custody and data entry, reporting, and storage.

The sensitivity of the reader depends on the quality of the optical components, resulting in a trade-off between the quality, the price, and the portability of the readers. Instruments that employ light reflectance or optical scanners may not achieve greater sensitivity than the human eye. Because the "gray zone" of color reading (weakly positive vs. weakly negative) also falls on the analytical gray zone of the testing result (around cutoff region of the calibration curve), the overall interpretation accuracy is not significantly affected by human or machine reading. However, the human subjectivity and lighting issues can both be minimized by instrument reading. The instrument reading also offers benefits in result recording and processing, although it carries additional cost and handling and quality control of the readers. Therefore, the choice of adopting the hybrid system is at the discretion of the users for their drug testing program budget and goals.

Specific readers are required for assays that utilize fluorescence or phosphor particles to achieve lower detection limits for certain analytes, especially for oral fluid drug testing. The Uplink analyzer developed by OraSure Technologies, Inc. (OTI) is a portable instrument containing a laser source that "interrogates" the test strip based on Up-Converting Phosphor Technology (UPT).[90]

A few research reports have shown the feasibility of applying immunosensor technology to drug testing.[91,92] The future development of immunosensor-based on-site drug testing may potentially be applied to "smart" handheld devices with more digital capability in result processing, wireless transmission, and data management.

11.5.3 Principles of Detection Reactions

The majority of on-site drug testing products utilize microparticles to maximize reagent reaction surfaces and to allow detection of the outcome of the competitive immunoassays. Microparticle agglutination-inhibition assays such as Abuscreen OnTrak assays use relatively large white microparticles with coated drug-conjugate to bind antibody and produce visible latex aggregates in the absence of drugs. The presence of drugs above the designated cutoff level prevents the agglutination and produces a milky appearance, indicating a screening positive result. Membrane-based assays utilize smaller colored nanoparticles with attached antibody to bind pre-immobilized drug conjugate and produce a color signal. The binding can be inhibited by drugs in the sample so the absence of the color signal indicates a screening positive result.

Membranes such as nitrocellulose or nylon membrane have become the key component of POC immunoassays. In rapid POC immunoassays, membranes not only provide means for separation of the bound and unbound but also serve as solid-phase reaction chambers. There are two major forms of membrane-based tests: lateral-flow and flow-through. Lateral flow is the most commonly used "one-step assay" because of its ease of use. The "convective mass transfer" of the immunoreactant to the binding partner allows the assay to be performed upon the initiation of sample flow. However, immunoreactions in a lateral flow strip are not carried out under an equilibrium condition, which results in certain degree of compromise in reaction kinetics when compared with assays performed in an equilibrium mode. Various chemical, reagent, and process optimizations, most of them proprietary, have been actively sought to enhance performance and manufacturing consistency while maintaining the one-step advantage. The plastic housing for lateral flow test strips is typically a self-contained device that has all the reagents necessary to complete a test.

The flow-through tests typically involve the handling of liquid solution and require more than one step of user intervention. Thus the flow-through form can require more manual manipulation and need more time to carry out tests for the same groups of analytes; however, the trade-off allows incubation of immunoreaction components in liquid state until they reach a predetermined near-equilibrium state. The system with sequential incubations and washing may help to reduce residual nonspecific binding and can be more forgiving of potential sample matrix effects. The assembly of flow-through assays usually is a single device designed to allow for wicking of the sample and excess reagents.

11.5.3.1 One-Step Lateral Flow Immunochromatography

Typically, the basic test configuration comprises a nitrocellulose membrane strip with an immobilized capture reagent, which contains one member of the antigen–antibody binding pairs. The detection reagent consists of colored nanoparticles, which have been sensitized with the complementary binding partner. The strip also contains other components to modulate optimal immunore-actions. For drugs of abuse testing, the immobilized reagent is usually a drug derivative that has been covalently attached to a large molecular carrier protein (i.e., drug conjugate). There are two types of nanoparticles used in the reaction of visual-read lateral flow assays: metal sol (usually colloidal gold) or colored latex nanoparticles. The particle size and uniformity of colloidal gold require optimal manufacturing control with an ideal diameter of gold particles for lateral flow assays of around 40 nm. In contrast, the choice of colored uniform latex particles is typically in the 100- to 300-nm range.

The constructions of lateral flow strips have previously been described in detail, as the examples include a representative colloidal gold-based test strip configuration[93] and a blue latex-enhanced immunochromatography.[94] In brief, lateral flow immunoassays are based on competition between the drug, which may be present in the sample being tested, and the immobilized drug conjugate for binding to specific antibodies on the surface of the nanoparticles. If drug is present in the sample being tested, it binds with the antibody and inhibits the antibody reaction with the drug conjugate. Subsequently, no color is observed in the test results area. If the sample being tested contains drug below the cutoff concentration or is drug-free, the antibody is free to bind with the drug conjugate and a color band develops in the test results area. A second line, a control, may also be formed on the membrane by excess nanoparticles, indicating the test is complete or valid.

Lateral flow strips can be designed to test for one or more analytes in a single strip or for panel testing in a single housing containing several strips. For drugs of abuse assays, the test can be completed within 3 to 5 min of sample application. The results of colloidal gold-based strips need to be interpreted within a few minutes of assay completion (most package inserts specify the results reading time limits). The results of blue latex-based strips can stay stable for longer periods of time and the results can be read upon tester convenience for up to a few hours after assay completion.

Lateral flow assays have also been applied to use with up-converting phosphor reporters and the UPlink reader for detecting drugs in oral fluid.[90] UPT nanoparticles are lanthanide-containing ceramic particles that can absorb infrared light and emit visible light. The UPlink reader contains a miniaturized infrared laser and can measure the signal intensity of the lines for conversion to qualitative results.

11.5.3.2 *Multistep, Liquid Reagent, and Membrane-Based Assays*

One example of a membrane-based enzyme immunoassay is EZ-SCREEN.[61] The testing card contains antibody immobilized in the reactive area. Testing sample, along with positive and negative controls, is added to the reactive area as indicated on the card. Then the enzyme conjugate solution, wash reagent, and substrate reagents are added sequentially. The presence of drug in the testing sample competes with the drug–enzyme conjugate for binding to the membrane-embedded antibody and thereby reduces the color development after the substrate is added. The results are interpreted in 3 min by comparing color in the sample reaction site to that of the positive control site. The color differentiation of positive and negative control sites serves to indicate if the test is valid or not.

Another example is ASCEND MultImmunoAssay (AMIA) that employs two reaction phases and a wash step for Triage drug panel testing.[72,78] The first step involves the incubation of a pre-defined sample volume in a reaction well that contains three lyophilized reagent beads. After 10 min, the reaction mixture is transferred to a membrane solid phase with immobilized antibodies in discrete drug detection lines. The results can be interpreted visually after allowing the complete soaking of the reaction mixture and a subsequent wash of the membrane. The three reagent beads contain the set of antibodies for the analytes of interest, the corresponding drug derivative-colloidal gold conjugates, and reaction buffer, respectively. The drug conjugate competes with the corresponding drug in the donor urine for limited antibody binding sites. Competition of drug conjugate and drug in the urine for antibody binding occurs in the solution phase. When the reaction mixture is transferred to the testing area, freed drug conjugate can bind to its respective antibody on the test-plate membrane. After washing, positive result produces a reddish-colored bar in the drug detection zone adjacent to the drug name whereas negative sample produces no color. The results are read within 5 min of completion.

11.5.4 General Operational Considerations

11.5.4.1 Testing Flow and Confirmation

In general, workplace programs that use POCT are more likely to follow the same chain-of-custody and testing flow as laboratory-based drug testing programs. Depending on the industrial sectors, company size, and local and state regulations, however, the actual practice of workplace testing can vary dramatically. In contrast to workplace testing, NACB discourages the maintenance of chain-of-custody documentation for clinical toxicological purposes[24] unless it is known in advance that a specimen will likely be involved in a medicolegal matter. For compliance testing programs, the practice can range from those following regulated testing flow to those conducting tests in front of the person being tested.

All the drug testing immunoassays are required by the FDA to clearly emphasize on product labeling that screen results are only preliminary and a more specific alternative chemical method must be used to obtain a confirmed analytical result. For the diverse end users of on-site drug immunoassays, however, the decision to confirm is at user discretion. The two-tier screening and confirmation system has not yet been a "mandate" for non-federal-regulated testing programs; however, many of the workplace testing programs do establish the confirmation requirements. Testing programs that employ full-service providers can have service bundled from collection to confirmation and reporting. For clinical testing, however, NACB considers the need for obtaining STAT results as negating the value of confirmation in emergency cases and recommends against routinely performing confirmative analyses on positive screening results.[24] If the clinician anticipates subsequent involvement with medicolegal or social services or clinical need to identify a specific drug, the staff should notify the laboratory for a confirmation analysis.[24] In criminal justice and drug treatment programs, user admission of drug use following a positive on-site screening result may be sufficient to waive further confirmation. However, in many cases confirmation is required for legal reasons and specific regulations.

11.5.4.2 Training

Similar to other aspects of on-site drug testing, training for using the products and interpreting the results can vary from program to program. The most popular mode of training is for the manufacturers/device providers to develop the training materials, audio-visual aids, and documentations. The manufacturers provide the first tier of training directly or through a third-party organization. The customers may have the option to set up a "training the trainers" program. The training typically involves presentations and reading materials, live demonstrations, and hands-on training using known controls and blind samples. Written examinations and certificates are mechanisms to certify the completion of training. The manufacturers can also develop interactive web-based e-learning training. With the wide spectrum of device providers, however, the quality, delivery, and outcome of the training may vary considerably.

11.5.4.3 Quality Control and Quality Assurance

Unlike the instrumented laboratory-based immunoassays that employ on-board calibrations and controls, single-use POC test strips are precalibrated during the manufacturing process. Manufacturers that follow good manufacturing practices with validated procedures typically specify multiple steps of batch- and lot-based quality controls at both the test strip production phase and the finished-goods stage.

In theory, the majority of on-site drug testing devices have built-in procedural controls that should not be confused with analytical controls. One-step, competitive lateral flow assays contain one antigen–antibody pair of reagents and employ one control line downstream from the result zone. Multistep assays such as AMIA require two control lines to ensure that the test procedure is valid. In reality, these built-in controls do not verify the actual immunoreactions of the devices to target drug(s) and the only method of true "control" is via the use of externally prepared and validated drug-containing and drug-negative controls. The built-in test valid zones can be designed to visually correspond to the positive and negative results; however, the quality control recommendation in all device package inserts includes running external controls.

Quality assurance (QA) is a comprehensive program that provides constant surveillance of all aspects of a laboratory or a testing facility. Quality control is an important part of a QA program and is used to ensure the accuracy of the tests. The implementation of a QA program and the use of quality control for POC drug testing are both client-driven. Although Clinical Laboratory Improvement Amendments (CLIA) exempt drug testing, many clinical testing and some state workplace testing regulations have requirements that are equivalent to or stricter than CLIA. Most of the clinical testing and some of the testing programs require daily run of external positive and negative controls unless special exemption is granted. In nonclinical testing, the more typical practice is to run quality controls either at fixed time intervals or when starting to use a new shipment or new lot of devices. A number of testing programs and devices also participate in open and blind proficiency testing.

11.5.5 Product Comparison Studies

A number of studies have evaluated and compared the performance of rapid POC drug tests. Reports investigating the performance of POCT devices generally fall into five categories:

1. Detailed description and performance summary of one particular or two similar device types[34–40,43,49–54,51–80,82–88,95,96]
2. General comparative evaluation of a number of different on-site devices and/or laboratory-based immunoassays[28,41,42,44,55,81,89,97–101]
3. Comparative challenges of the devices with samples specifically selected to test the limits of immunoassay screens, such as near-cutoff performance or challenge of potential cross-reactivity issues[20,21,103,104]
4. General comments or reviews[3,5,9,10,27,105,106]
5. Field studies[7,8,22,23,29,102]

When comparing results from these studies, it is always crucial to recognize that different study goals, sample selections, and protocols can dramatically influence the outcome and interpretation of these studies. It is also important to take into consideration the target analyte and cutoff selections of the assays as well as the type and prevalence of the testing population. There are voluminous references but only examples of cutoff-challenge studies or field studies are briefly reviewed in this chapter.

11.5.5.1 Studies That Emphasized Near-Cutoff Challenges

In 1999, SAMHSA published a Division of Workplace Programs-sponsored evaluation of on-site testing that was designed to challenge 15 non-instrumented devices and an instrument-immunoassay on their accuracy near the cutoff.[20] The DWP-sponsored evaluation and its predecessor, a study carried out for the Administrative Office of the U.S. Courts, were subsequently published as a book chapter.[21] Although there are trade-offs of sensitivity vs. specificity when the majority of the samples evaluated are within ±25% of the cutoff values, the report stated that performance of most on-site devices was comparable to that of an instrument-based immunoassay. The overall accuracy of all drug test results vs. GC/MS (HHS cutoffs) ranged from 63% (PharmScreen DS) to 78% (OnTrak TesTstik), as compared to the accuracy of 76% for instrumented EMIT assays. The authors commented that the "favorable performance" of these devices was "encouraging." Moreover, "it is expected that specimens encountered in most workplace testing situations will have fewer specimens with drug concentrations near the cutoff."[20] Therefore, "a much higher percentage of confirmed positive results and fewer false negative results should occur during actual testing in the field."

With the similar principle of "using challenging clinical sample sets" containing drug concentrations close to the screening cutoffs, Kadehjian[104] compared the performance of five on-site drugs-of-abuse testing devices (microLine, TesTcup5, RapidTest, RapidCup, and Triage) and an instrumented test (Emit d.a.u.). In this study, 298 specimens were tested on each of five devices and each result was independently read by two operators. There was little difference in overall accuracy between the scientist and nonscientist readers. The percent borderline results ranged from 10% (RapidCup) to 32% (microLine), whereas the accuracy of borderline results ranged from 34% (Triage) to 82% (TesTcup). More importantly, the author reported that accuracy generally improved with all devices demonstrating predictive values between 0.98 and 1.0 when device performance was assessed according to drug presence/absence criteria.

11.5.5.2 Field Evaluations

In 2000, the U.S. DOT published a study sponsored by the National Highway Safety Administration (NHTSA), "Field Test of On-Site Drug Testing Devices."[22,23] In this study, 30 on-site products were identified and 16 devices were rated based on 14 criteria. From the rating results, five devices (AccuSign, TesTcup5, TesTstik, Rapid Drug Screen, and Triage) were selected to evaluate 800 samples in two high drug prevalence counties in New York and Texas. The study had police officers participate in the actual use of the devices. Samples that showed positive results for any assay from any of the devices and 5% of the samples that showed negative results on all devices were sent to a laboratory for confirmation. The unconfirmed positive rates as a percentage of all samples tested (drug present in concentrations below the MS confirmation cutoff) were as follows: 0.12% for amphetamines, 1.0 to 1.12% for cannabinoids, 0.5 to 1.37% for cocaine metabolites, 0.25 to 0.37% for opiates and PCP, respectively. The false negative rates were as follows: 0% for amphetamines, 0.25 to 0.87% for cannabinoids, 0.12 to 0.37% for cocaine metabolites, 0 to 0.12% for opiates, and 0 to 0.25% for PCP. The report indicated that, when cutoff concentration and additional drugs are taken into consideration, the POCT devices were accurate in identifying positive samples and rarely failed to identify a driver with the target drugs in urine. Participating police officers generally favored the use of on-site devices in the enforcement of impaired driving laws. Nonetheless, the use of these devices should not supplant the officer's judgment regarding impairment.

Another field evaluation of on-site, multi-analyte drug testing devices as tools to identify drivers under the influence of drugs was funded by HHS/NIDS and reported by Buchan et al.[8] During the 4-month study in a Florida county, voluntary and legal urine specimens were collected from suspects placed under arrest for suspicion of DUI and 303 samples contained a sufficient volume of urine for testing and confirmation. Specimens were tested in a university laboratory using four different POCT kits (AbuSign, TesTcup, Abuscreen OnTrak, and Triage). Results indicated that the accuracy ranged from 97.4 to 98.0% for THC, 97.4 to 98.0% for cocaine, and 99.7 to 100% for opiates. The authors observed that the four kits were in very close agreement on prevalence (15.5 to 15.8% for THC, all at 13.2% for cocaine, and all at 0.7% for opiates).

11.5.6 Examples of POC Drug Testing Applications

11.5.6.1 Testing in the Workplace

Technical standards established for federally mandated workplace testing have withstood a number of constitutional challenges and served as a model for some state statutes for Drug-Free Workplace and for voluntary employer drug testing programs. Ideally, POC workplace drug testing by and large should follow this model. The portable and qualitative nature of on-site drug testing devices, however, can be a serious challenge to the "safeguards" that were built into the mandated program. In private sector workplace testing, employers may use their discretion on how to conduct POC testing or to contract to third-party or comprehensive drug testing service providers. Regardless of where and how a test is performed, a reliable workplace testing program has to take into consideration specimen collection (site, personnel, device, and procedure), donor and specimen (integrity, security, privacy, chain-of-custody, storage or transfer), result (handling and reporting), quality (QC, QA), and outcome management (confirmation, medical review officer).

The most prominent example of large-scale application of on-site drug testing in the workplace has been the U.S. Postal Service (USPS) drug testing program.[16] USPS started a pilot program in 1997. The pilot study involved a variety of different validation studies using both clinical and spiked specimens that involved four collection sites and large numbers of side-by-side studies over several months. In 1999, USPS decided to make the pilot project a full-time program. USPS has now implemented POCT in more than 1000 collection sites nationwide. The USPS example demonstrates that a well-planned and well-structured on-site workplace drug testing program can be effective and sustainable even when it involves a large number of geographically diverse sites.

11.5.6.2 Testing in Clinical Settings

Controversies continue to exist regarding the value of urine drug testing in clinical settings. The cited reasons for the controversies include the drugs involved, the sample, the methods utilized to perform the tests, and the level of understanding of the physician using the data.[107] Despite the demand for rapid results in emergency situations, the immunoassays "are often designed for, or adapted from, workplace testing and are not necessarily optimized for clinical applications." The study authors concluded that "While the literature is replete with studies concerning new methods and a few regarding physician understanding, there are none that we could find that thoroughly, objectively, and fully addressed the issues of utility and cost-effectiveness."[107] Likewise, NACB considers that immunoassays, although rapid, have major limitations in sensitivity and specificity.[24]

Even so, the features of fast TAT and panel screening have helped POC drug testing to become a viable technology in clinical settings. In comparison to the SAMHSA-5 panel for workplace testing, on-site testing devices for the clinical settings contain additional assays for benzodiazepines, barbiturates, and/or tricyclic antidepressants. Although assays for cannabinoids and phencyclidine are considered not useful in general clinical testing, on-site products for the clinical market generally contain a menu of eight to ten assays. Examples of products evaluated for on-site clinical testing include the market leader Triage DOA panel as well as ABMC Rapid Drug Screen, Dade Behring RapidTest, Abbott Signify-ER, Roche TesTcard 9, TesTcup-ER, BioRad Tox-See, etc.[28,38–40,69,72–78,95–96] According to the Biosite promotional material, on-site drug testing has been used in over 2500 U.S. hospitals, indicating that on-site devices also can be effective and sustainable in the clinical market.

11.5.6.3 Testing in the Criminal Justice Systems

The utility of urine drug testing as an objective and effective tool to identify and treat substance abusers within the criminal justice systems has been well-recognized and is fully documented in another chapter of this section.[9] The major market segments for drug testing within the criminal justice systems include community corrections, institutions and prisons, rehabilitation, and law enforcement. Community corrections, such as probation and parole, security, pre-trial services, and drug courts, are among the largest of the four segments to adopt non-instrumented devices for POC drug testing.

Road-side drug testing and DUI programs can be categorized in the law enforcement segment. These applications have been thoroughly evaluated in studies sponsored by government or organizations such as DOT, HHS/NIDS, and ROSITA.[8,22,23,29,102]

11.5.6.4 *Other Applications — Testing at School, Home, and Direct Consumer Testing*

Examples of more recent uses of POCT include school and home testing. These applications are still evolving and will not be discussed at this time. Regardless of the sources of on-site testing devices (e.g., over-the-counter retails, pharmacy, or Internet), the direct consumer sales of both on-site drug testing device and drug testing adulterants signal an intriguing era of drug testing. Together with the drug and drug testing "knowledge" from Internet and multimedia information sources, people have the means to test themselves before reporting to a drug test or to titer or experiment with the use of both drugs and adulterants. There are a number of ethical questions regarding lay misuse of the devices and non-consent testing but the topics are beyond the scope of this chapter. Recently, the U.S. FDA established a specific Web site for home drug tests;[108] this is a resourceful online tool that provides clear yet comprehensive explanations of the two-step drugs of abuse tests.

11.5.7 Continuing Evolution and Future Trends

The evolution of on-site drug testing has truly come a long way. Since the 1980s, the challenges of exploring the "new" POCT markets have included the diverse marketing requirements, different laws and individual state legislation constraints, lack of permission in regulated testing, legal and interpretation considerations, and various market acceptance criteria and customer expectations. To date, some of the challenges remain critical but the tests continue to be popular for several reasons. The simple operation to produce visible results within a few minutes has been an attractive feature. Most importantly, the major products have had proven performance for customer needs that not only established customer and legislative acceptance but increased the practical utility of POCT as part of the drug testing programs. In general, these rapid assays can provide comparable performance with conventional immunoassays in most drug-screening settings. The near-cutoff precision is typically better with laboratory instrumented assays; however, on-site assays are useful for routine drug screening in the markets that demand rapid, qualitative determination. The trend of adopting POC drug testing appears to continue into the foreseeable future even though the market growth has been leveling off.

Considering the dynamics of the diagnostic industry and drug testing business, the description of POCT product development in this chapter is not an attempt to be all-inclusive. Companies often make business decisions concerning alliances, divestiture, and acquisition to best meet their strategic considerations and goals. Naturally the business activities will continue into the future and can influence not only existing products but also future development of on-site drug testing. In addition, the World Wide Web and globalization will continue to influence on-site drug testing. Besides regular e-commerce activities of product providers, there are plenty of independent Web sites selling assortments of trade-name and generic on-site drug testing devices on the Internet. Additionally, many drug testing "full service providers" and "re-sellers" (third-party administrators, labs, distributors, medical review officers) have bundled into their service on-site drug testing devices from a variety of device manufacturers. Ironically, the Internet era also considerably boosts the adulteration industry, and most of the Web sites that sell drug testing adulterants also sell on-site drug testing devices for self-titration of drug use and for user self-testing.

Because drug testing can have decisive medicolegal and social consequences, the industry is closely affected by regulatory and legislative issues and decisions. In general, most of the companies that are active in the on-site drug testing business are members of major industrial associations such as NOTA (National On-Site Testing Association) and DATIA (Drug and Alcohol Testing Industry Association). NOTA is an advocacy and resource center for on-site drug and alcohol testing. DATIA was founded in 1995 as the National Association of Collection Sites, and has since expanded its scope to represent the entire spectrum of drug and alcohol service providers, including collection sites, laboratories, consortiums/third party administrators, medical review officers, and testing equipment manufacturers. The two associations have worked independently or collaborated on behalf of on-site drug testing and will continue to play important roles in the future of on-site drug testing.

The limitations of immunoassay for drug screening apply to both laboratory-based instrumented testing and on-site testing. Because the understanding of antibody cross-reactivity issues and various cutoff decisions requires knowledge of immunoassay and drug testing, interpreting and reporting results can continue to be issues with on-site drug screening unless safeguard requirements are built into the testing program. There is more to a drug testing program than just results and the success of an on-site testing program relates to how it is structured and implemented. The draft for the next versions of SAMHSA federal guidelines takes into considerations many of these requirements for conducting POCT.[4] Meanwhile, the FDA is revising its guidance of pre-market submission for drugs of abuse screening tests by combining the previous drafts for prescription and over-the-counter drug screening into one draft.[109] These new regulatory developments both recognize the co-existence of conventional laboratory tests and on-site screening for drugs of abuse. All of these developments will continue to shape the future of on-site drug testing.

REFERENCES

1. Price, C.P. and Hicks, J.M., Eds., *Point-of-Care Testing*, AACC Press, Washington, D.C., 1999.
2. Bissell, M., Point-of-care testing at the millennium, *Crit. Care Nurs. Q.* 24, 39, 2001.
3. Yang, J.M., Toxicology and drugs of abuse testing at the point of care. *Clin. Lab. Med.* 21, 363, 2001.
4. Draft Mandatory Guidelines for Federal Workplace Drug Testing Programs, Draft 4, 2001. http://workplace.samhsa.gov/ResourceCenter/DT/FA/GuidelinesDraft4.htm.
5. Armbruster, D.A., On-site workplace drug testing, in *On-Site Drug Testing*, Jenkins, A.J. and Goldberger, B.A., Eds., Humana Press, Totowa, NJ, 2002, 25.
6. Shults, T.F. and Caplan, Y.H., Program requirements, standards, and legal considerations for on-site drug testing devices in workplace testing programs, in *On-Site Drug Testing*, Jenkins, A.J. and Goldberger, B.A., Eds., Humana Press, Totowa, NJ, 2002, 37.
7. Walsh, J.M., On-site testing devices and driving-under-the-influence cases, in *On-Site Drug Testing*, Jenkins, A.J. and Goldberger, B.A., Eds., Humana Press, Totowa, NJ, 2002, 67.
8. Buchan, B.J., Walsh, J.M. and Leaverton, P.E., Evaluation of the accuracy of on-site multi-analyte drug testing devices in the determination of the prevalence of illicit drugs in drivers, *J. Forensic Sci.* 43, 395, 1998.
9. Kadehjian, L.J. and Baer, J., On-site testing devices in the criminal justice system, in *On-Site Drug Testing*, Jenkins, A.J. and Goldberger, B.A., Eds., Humana Press, Totowa, NJ, 2002, 55.
10. Valentine, J.L., Clinical point-of-care testing for drugs of abuse, in *On-Site Drug Testing*, Jenkins, A.J. and Goldberger, B.A., Eds., Humana Press, Totowa, NJ, 2002, 1.
11. Goldstein, A., Horns, W.H., and Hansteen, R.W., Is on-site urine testing of therapeutic value in a methadone treatment program? *Int. J. Addict.* 12, 717, 1977.
12. Willette, R.E., Choosing a Laboratory, NIDA Res Monograph 73, Hawks, R.L. and Chiang, C.N., Eds., 1986, 13.

13. Mandatory guidelines for federal workplace drug testing programs, *Fed. Regis.* 53, 1988, 11970.

14. NIDA Technical, Scientific and Procedural Issues of Employee Drug Testing Consensus Report, Finkle, B.S., Blanke, R.V., and Walsh, J.M., Eds., NIDA, 1990.

15. Rollins, D., On-site drug testing in the workplace. Final Report to the National Institute on Drug Abuse. Division of Workplace Programs, 1992.

16. Transcript On-Site Drug Testing Workgroup Meeting, 1999. http://workplace.samhsa.gov/ResourceCenter/r382.htm.

17. U.S. Nuclear Regulatory Commissions Fitness-for-Duty Program, 10 CFR Part 26, 1989. http://www.nrc.gov/reading-rm/doc-collections/cfr/part026/full-text.html.

18. Visher, C. and McFadden, K., A comparison of urinalysis technologies for drug testing in criminal justice, National Institute of Justice, 1991.

19. Mandatory guidelines for federal workplace drug testing programs, 1994, *Fed. Regis.* 59, 29908 http://www.health.org/workplace/GDLNS-94.htm or http://workplace.samhsa.gov/fedprograms/MandatoryGuidelines/HHS09011994.pdf.

20. An Evaluation of Non-Instrumented Drug Test Devices, Substance Abuse and Mental Health Services Administration, Center for Substance Abuse Prevention, Division of Workplace Programs, 1999. http://workplace.samhsa.gov/ResourceCenter/r409.htm.

21. Willette, R.E. and Kadehjian, L.J., Drugs-of-abuse test devices: a review, in *On-Site Drug Testing*, Jenkins, A.J. and Goldberger, B.A., Eds., Humana Press, Totowa, NJ, 2002, 219.

22. DOT HS 809 192. Field test of on-site drug detection devices, 2000. http://www.nhtsa.dot.gov/ people/ injury/research/pub/onsitedetection/Drug_index.htm or http://www.nhtsa.dot.gov/people/injury/research/pub/onsitedetection/On-SiteDrugDetection.pdf.

23. Crouch, D.J., Hersch, R.K., Cook, R.F., Frank, J.F., and Walsh, J.M., A field evaluation of five on-site drug-testing devices, *J. Anal. Toxicol.* 26, 493, 2002.

24. Wu, A.H., McKay, C., Broussard, L.A., Hoffman, R.S., Kwong, T.C., Moyer, T.P., Otten, E.M., Welch, S.L., and Wax, P., National academy of clinical biochemistry laboratory medicine practice guidelines: recommendations for the use of laboratory tests to support poisoned patients who present to the emergency department, *Clin. Chem.* 49, 357, 2003.

25. AGSA Swiss Working Group for Drugs of Abuse Testing Guidelines. http://www.consilia-sa.ch/agsa/E/AGSA%20Guidelines_E_rev3.pdf.

26. Armbruster, D.A., On-site drug testing on the rise and growing strong, *MLO Med. Lab. Obs.* 29, 40, 1997.

27. Ozminkowski, R.J., Mark, T., Cangianelli, L., Walsh, J.M., Davidson, R., Blank, D., Flegel, R.R., and Goetzel, R.Z., The cost of on-site versus off-site workplace urinalysis testing for illicit drug use, *Health Care Manage.* (Frederick) 20, 59, 2001.

28. Mastrovitch, T.A., Bithoney, W.G., DeBari, V.A. and Nina, A.G., Point-of-care testing for drugs of abuse in an urban emergency department, *Ann. Clin. Lab. Sci.* 32, 383, 2002.

29. ROSITA Deliverable D2, Inventory of state-of-the-art roadside drug testing equipment, 1999. www.rosita.org.

30. Alexander, G.J. and Machiz, S., Simplified radioimmunoassay of urinary drugs of abuse adsorbed on ion-exchange papers, *Clin. Chem.* 23, 1921, 1977.

31. Alexander, G.J., A procedure for drug screening without the need to transport urines: use of ion exchange papers and hemagglutination inhibition, *Clin. Toxicol.* 9, 435, 1976.

32. Cleeland, R., Christenson, J., Usategui-Gomez, M., Heveran, J., Davis, R., and Grunberg, E., Detection of drugs of abuse by radioimmunoassay: a summary of published data and some new information, *Clin. Chem.* 22, 712, 1976.

33. Adler, F.L. and Liu, C.T., Detection of morphine by hemagglutination-inhibition, *J. Immunol.* 106, 1684, 1971.

34. Deom, A., Evaluation of a new latex agglutination inhibition test, Agglutex, for the demonstration of opiates in urine, *Ann. Biol. Clin.* (Paris), 42, 317, 1984.

35. Schwartz, J.G., Zollars, P.R., Okorodudu, A.O., Carnahan, J.J., Wallace, J.E., and Briggs, J.E., Accuracy of common drug screen tests, *Am. J. Emerg. Med.* 9, 166, 1991.

36. Armbruster, D.A. and Krolak, J.M., Screening for drugs of abuse with the Roche ONTRAK assays, *J. Anal. Toxicol.* 16, 172, 1992.

37. Welch, E., Fleming, L.E., Peyser, I., Greenfield, W., Steele, B.W., and Bandstra, E.S., Rapid cocaine screening of urine in a newborn nursery, *J. Pediatr.* 123, 468, 1993.

38. Westdorp, E.J., Salomone, J.A., III, Roberts, D.K., McIntyre, M.K., and Watson, W.A., Validation of a rapid urine screening assay for cocaine use among pregnant emergency patients, *Acad. Emerg. Med.* 2, 795, 1995.

39. Belfer, R.A., Klein, B.L., Boenning, D.A., and Soldin, S.J., Emergency department evaluation of a rapid assay for detection of cocaine metabolites in urine specimens, *Pediatr. Emerg. Care* 12, 113, 1996.

40. Birnbach, D.J., Stein, D.J., Grunebaum, A., Danzer, B.I., and Thys, D.M., Cocaine screening of parturients without prenatal care: an evaluation of a rapid screening assay, *Anesth. Analg.* 84, 76, 1997.

41. Crouch, D.J., Frank, J.F., Farrell, L.J., Karsch, H.M., and Klaunig, J.E., A multiple-site laboratory evaluation of three on-site urinalysis drug-testing devices, *J. Anal. Toxicol.* 22, 493, 1998.

42. Crouch, D.J., Cheever, M.L., Andrenyak, D.M., Kuntz, D.J., and Loughmiller, D.L., A comparison of ONTRAK TESTCUP, abuscreen ONTRAK, abuscreen ONLINE, and GC/MS urinalysis test results, *J. Forensic Sci.* 43, 35, 1998.

43. Farrell, L.J. Abuscreen ONTRAK tests for drugs of abuse, in *On-Site Drug Testing*, Jenkins, A.J. and Goldberger, B.A., Eds., Humana Press, Totowa, NJ, 2002, 153.

44. Schilling, R.F., Bidassie, B., and El-Bassel, N., Detecting cocaine and opiates in urine: comparing three commercial assays. *J. Psychoactive Drugs* 31, 305, 1999.

45. Parsons, R.G., Kowal, R., LeBlond, D., Yue, V.T., Neargarder, L., Bond, L., Garcia, D., Slater, D., and Rogers, P., Multianalyte assay system developed for drugs of abuse. *Clin. Chem.* 39, 1899, 1993.

46. Deutsch, M. and Mead, L.W., Test device U.S. patent, 4,094,647, 1978.

47. Litman, D.J., Lee, R.H., Jeong, H.J., Tom, H.K., Stiso, S.N., Sizto, N.C., and Ullman, E.F., An internally referenced test strip immunoassay for morphine. *Clin. Chem.* 29, 1598, 1983.

48. Zuk, R.F., Ginsberg, V.K., Houts, T., Rabbie, J., Merrick, H., Ullman, E.F., Fischer, M.M., Sizto, C.C., Stiso, S.N., and Litman, D.J. Enzyme immunochromatography — a quantitative immunoassay requiring no instrumentation, *Clin. Chem.* 31, 1144, 1985.

49. Opheim, K.E., Statland, B.E., Tillson, S.A., and Litman, D.J., Calibration, quality control, and stability of a quantitative enzyme immunochromatographic method for therapeutic drug monitoring, *Ther. Drug Monit.* 9, 190, 1987.

50. Morris, R.G. and Schapel, G.J., Phenytoin and phenobarbital assayed by the ACCULEVEL method compared with EMIT in an outpatient clinic setting, *Ther. Drug Monit.* 10, 469, 1988.

51. Jukofsky, D., Kramer, A., and Mule, S.J., Evaluation of the TRI "dipstick" test for the detection of drugs of abuse in urine, *J. Anal. Toxicol.* 5, 14, 1981.

52. Cone, E.J. and Menchen, S.L., Lack of validity of the KDI Quik Test Drug Screen for detection of benzoylecgonine in urine, *J. Anal. Toxicol.* 11, 276, 1987.

53. Kaplan, R.M., Fochtman, F., Brunett, P., White, C., and Heller, M.B., An analysis of clinical toxicology urine specimens using the KDI Quik test, *J. Toxicol. Clin. Toxicol.* 27, 369, 1989.

54. Schwartz, R.H., Bogema, S., and Thorne, M.M., Evaluation of the Keystone Diagnostic Quik Test. A paper chromatography test for drugs of abuse in urine, *Arch. Pathol. Lab. Med.,* 113, 363, 1989.

55. Ros, J.J., Pelders, M.G., and Egberts, A.C., Performance of Abusign drugs-of-abuse slide tests with particular emphasis on concentrations near the cutoff: comparison with FPIA-ADx and confirmation of results with GC-MS, *J. Anal. Toxicol.* 22, 40, 1998.

56. Ros, J.J.W. and Pelders, M.G., AccuSign drugs of abuse test, in *On-Site Drug Testing*, Jenkins, A.J. and Goldberger, B.A., Eds., Humana Press, Totowa, NJ, 2002, 111.

57. Jenkins, A.J., Darwin, W.D, Heustis, M.A., Cone, E.J., and Mitchell, J.M., Validity testing of the accuPINCHTM THC test, *J. Anal. Toxicol.* 19, 5, 1995.

58. Schwartz, R.H., Bogema, S., and Thorne, M.M., Evaluation of the EZ-SCREEN enzyme immunoassay test for detection of cocaine and marijuana metabolites in urine specimens, *Pediatr. Emerg. Care* 6, 147, 1990.

59. Jenkins, A.J., Mills, L.C., Darwin, W.D., Huestis, M.A., Cone, E.J., and Mitchell, J.M., Validity testing of the EZ-SCREEN cannabinoid test, *J. Anal. Toxicol.* 17, 292, 1993.

60. Kranzler, H.R., Stone, J., and McLaughlin, L., Evaluation of a point-of-care testing product for drugs of abuse; testing site is a key variable, *Drug Alcohol Depend.* 40, 55, 1995.

61. Ferrara, S.D., Tedeschi, L., and Castagna, F., The EZ-SCREEN and RapidTest devices for drugs of abuse, in *On-Site Drug Testing,* Jenkins, A.J. and Goldberger, B.A., Eds., Humana Press, Totowa, NJ, 2002, 123.

62. Wennig, R., Moeller, M.R., Haguenoer, J.M., Marocchi, A., Zoppi, F., Smith, B.L., de la Torre, R., Carstensen, C.A., Goerlach-Graw, A., Schaeffler, J., and Leinberger, R. Development and evaluation of immunochromatographic rapid tests for screening of cannabinoids, cocaine, and opiates in urine, *J. Anal. Toxicol.* 22, 148, 1998.

63. Schneider, S. and Wennig, R., Frontline testing for drugs of abuse, in *On-Site Drug Testing*, Jenkins, A.J. and Goldberger, B.A., Eds., Humana Press, Totowa, NJ, 2002, 143.

64. Towt, J., Tsai, S.C.J., Hernandez, M.R., Klimov, A.D., Kravec, C.V., Rouse, S.L., Subuhi, H.S., Twarowska, B., and Salamone, S.J., ONTRACT TESTCUP: A novel, on-site, multi-analyte screen for the detection of abused drugs, *J. Anal. Toxicol.* 19, 504, 1995.

65. Tsai, J.S.C., Towt, J., Kravec, C., Oades, B., Rashid, F., Talbot, L.A., Twarowska, B., and Salamone, S.J., ONTRAK TESTCUP-5: A multianalyte immunoassay device for onsite drug testing, *Proc. TIAFT* 35, 466, 1997.

66. Crouch, D.J.. The OnTrak TesTcup system, in *On-Site Drug Testing*, Jenkins, A.J. and Goldberger, B.A., Eds., Humana Press, Totowa, NJ, 2002, 163.

67. Birnbach, D.J., Browne, I.M., Kim, A., Stein, D.J., and Thys, D.M., Identification of polysubstance abuse in the parturient, *Br. J. Anaesth.* 87, 488, 2001.

68. Yacoubian, G.S., Jr., Wish, E.D., and Choyka, J.D., A comparison of the OnTrak Testcup-5 to laboratory urinalysis among arrestees, *J. Psychoactive Drugs* 34, 325, 2002.

69. Peace, M.R., Poklis, J.L., Tarnai, L.D., and Poklis, A., An evaluation of the OnTrak Testcup-er on-site urine drug-testing device for drugs commonly encountered from emergency departments, *J. Anal. Toxicol.* 26, 500, 2002.

70. Tsai, J.S.C., Oades, B., Demirtzoglou, D., Zhao, H., and Salamone, S., Simultaneous evaluation of OnTrak TesTstik Amphetamines Assay and TesTstik Methamphetamine Assay for the screening of amphetamines in urine, *Proc. TIAFT* 39, 160, 2001.

71. Salamone, S.J. and Tsai, J.S.C., OnTrak TesTstik device, in *On-Site Drug Testing*, Jenkins, A.J. and Goldberger, B.A., Eds., Humana Press, Totowa, NJ, 2002, 185.

72. Buechler, K.F., Moi, S., Noar, B., McGrath, D., Villela, J., Clancy, M., Shenhav, A., Colleymore, A., Valkirs, G., Lee, T., Bruni, J.F.., Walsh, M., Hoffman, R., Ahmuty, F., Nowakowski, M., Buechler, J., Mitchell, M., Boyd, D., Stiso, N., and Anderson, R., Simultaneous detection of seven drugs of abuse by the Triage panel for drugs of abuse, *Clin. Chem.* 38, 1678, 1992.

73. Wu, A.H., Wong, S.S., Johnson, K.G., Callies, J., Shu, D.X., Dunn, W.E., and Wong, S.H., Evaluation of the Triage system for emergency drugs-of-abuse testing in urine, *J. Anal. Toxicol.* 17, 241, 1993.

74. de la Torre, R., Domingo-Salvany, A., Badia, R., Gonzalez, G., McFarlane, D., San, L., and Torrens, M., Clinical evaluation of the Triage analytic device for drugs-of-abuse testing, *Clin. Chem.* 42, 1433, 1996.

75. Valentine, J.L. and Komoroski, E.M., Use of a visual panel detection method for drugs of abuse: clinical and laboratory experience with children and adolescents, *J. Pediatr.* 126, 135, 1995.

76. Poklis, A. and O'Neal, C.L., Potential for false-positive results by the TRIAGE panel of drugs-of-abuse immunoassay, *J. Anal. Toxicol.* 20, 209, 1996.

77. Poklis, A., Edinboro, L.E., Lee, J.S., and Crooks, C.R., Evaluation of a colloidal metal immunoassay device for the detection of tricyclic antidepressants in urine, *J. Toxicol. Clin. Toxicol.* 35, 77, 1997.

78. de la Torre, R., Triage device for drug analysis, in *On-Site Drug Testing*, Jenkins, A.J. and Goldberger, B.A., Eds., Humana Press, Totowa, NJ, 2002, 199.

79. Kuzdzal, S.A. and Nichols, J.H., Visualine II drugs-of-abuse test kits, in *On-Site Drug Testing*, Jenkins, A.J. and Goldberger, B.A., Eds., Humana Press, Totowa, NJ, 2002, 213.

80. Moriya, F. and Hashimoto, Y., Application of the Triage panel for drugs of abuse to forensic blood samples, *Nippon Hoigaku Zasshi* 50, 50, 1996.

81. Hino, Y., Ojanpera, I., Rasanen, I., and Vuori, E., Performance of immunoassays in screening for opiates, cannabinoids and amphetamines in post-mortem blood, *Forensic Sci. Int.* 131, 148, 2003.

82. Kintz, P., Cirimele, V., and Ludes, B., Codeine testing in sweat and saliva with the Drugwipe, *Int. J. Legal Med.* 111, 82, 1998.

108. U.S. Food and Drug Administration, Home use test, Drugs of abuse (two-step tests), 2003. http://www.fda.gov/cdrh/oivd/homeuse-drug-2step.html.

109. U.S. Food and Drug Administration, Draft Guidance: Premarket Submissions and Labeling Recommendations for Drugs of Abuse Screening Tests, 2003. http://www.fda.gov/cdrh/oivd/guidance/152.html.

CHAPTER 12

Post-Mortem Toxicology

Edited by Henrik Druid, M.D., Ph.D.
Associate Professor, Department of Forensic Medicine, Karolinska Institute, Stockholm, Sweden

CONTENTS

Due to the continuous increase in availability and use of pharmaceuticals and illicit drugs, post-mortem toxicology has become more and more important in death investigations. The introduction of new substances on the market requires a high awareness among pathologists and toxicologists and necessitates the development of methods that encompasses the newcomers. Fortunately, many important achievements have been made in methodology, and the application of novel techniques, such as modifications of solid phase extraction and LC/MS techniques, now offers better conditions for efficient and sensitive analyses of numerous substances.

Many important contributions regarding the impact of various post-mortem changes that may influence the toxicological results have been published. Pharmacogenetic analyses, e.g., to identify poor metablizers, may now be applied on post-mortem material and assist in the determination of the manner of death, and studies on post-mortem redistribution of drugs have resulted in a wide-spread appreciation of the influence of the specimen type on the drug concentrations.

In recent years, the specific detection of many compounds and their metabolites in various matrices has improved substantially. However, the interpretation of their concentrations remains a difficult task. Hence, despite the progress in post-mortem toxicology, information about previous drug use and the circumstances surrounding death, and the autopsy findings are still very important in order to arrive at correct conclusions when interpreting the analytical results. An intimate collaboration between toxicologists and pathologists is therefore desirable.

12.1 INTRODUCTION TO POST-MORTEM TOXICOLOGY

W. Lee Hearn, Ph.D.[1] and H. Chip Walls, B.S.[2]
[1] Director, Dade County Medical Examiner Toxicology Laboratory, Miami, Florida
[2] Department of Pathology, Forensic Toxicology Laboratory, University of Miami, Miami, Florida

12.1.1 Medicolegal Death Investigation

The medical examiner's office investigates sudden, violent, unnatural, or unexpected deaths,[1-3] and the medical examiner, coroner, or pathologist is responsible for determining the cause and manner of death. The cause of death is the injury, intoxication, or disease that initiates a process leading to death, and if that initial event had not occurred, the individual would not have died. Death may follow years after the causal event. The manner of death is the circumstances in which the cause of death occurred. Five classifications are used to categorize the manner of death: homicide, suicide, accident, natural, and undetermined. Anatomic findings elicited at autopsy are often insufficient to determine the manner of death.

To determine the manner of death, all available information pertaining to a particular case, including the terminal events, scene investigation, police reports, social and medical history, autopsy findings, and results of histologic and toxicologic testing, must be considered. The question "Did alcohol, other drugs, or poisons cause or contribute to this person's death?" must always be answered. Success in arriving at the correct conclusion depends on the combined efforts of the pathologist, the investigators, and the toxicologist. The process of death investigation and the role of the laboratory are outlined in Figure 12.1.1.

12.1.1.1 *The Role of Police and Medical Examiner Investigators*

When a death is reported to the medical examiner's office, a case investigator will obtain certain information to determine whether the case falls under the jurisdiction of the medical examiner. The following is a list of important topics to consider, which may vary according to jurisdiction:

Cases Requiring Medicolegal Death Investigation

1. Any death where any form of violence, whether criminal, suicidal, or accidental, was directly responsible or contributory.
2. Any death caused by an unlawful act or criminal neglect.
3. Any death occurring in a suspicious, unusual, or unexplained fashion.
4. Any death where there is no attending physician.
5. Any death of a person confined to a public institution.
6. The death of any prisoner even though both the cause and manner appear to be natural.
7. Any death caused by or contributed to by drugs or other chemical poisoning or overdose.
8. Any sudden death of a person in apparent good health.
9. Any death occurring during diagnostic or therapeutic procedures.
10. Any fetal stillbirth in the absence of a physician.
11. Any death where there is insufficient medical information to explain the individual's demise.

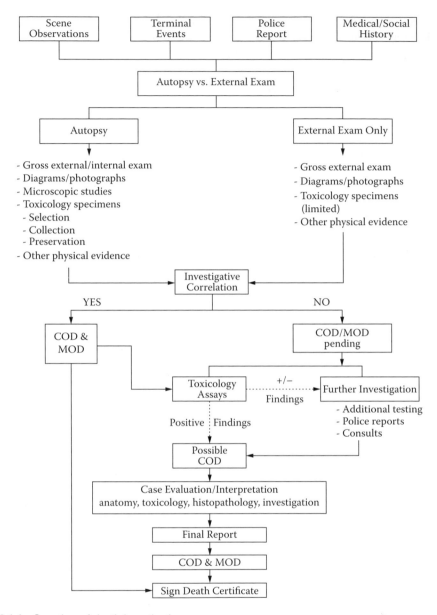

Figure 12.1.1 Overview of death investigation.

An unnatural death is any death that is not a direct result of a natural, medically recognized disease process. Any death where an outside, intervening influence, either directly or indirectly, is contributory to the individual's demise, or accelerates and exacerbates an underlying disease process to such a degree as to cause death, would also fall into the category of unnatural death.

Investigators are the eyes and ears of the medical examiner, especially in cases where the body is removed prior to the pathologist's involvement. The importance of an adequate investigation into past social and medical history cannot be overemphasized.

Police reports and investigations provide scene documentation. Typically, a report will include a description and identification of the body, time and place of death, eyewitness accounts, drugs present, and photographs. Investigators assigned by the medical examiner collect all items and information pertaining to establishing the cause and manner of death. Investigators contact the family and friends of the deceased for information regarding, for example, past medical and social history and prescribed medications. Many cases have histories of prescription drugs to guide the investigation. All medication bottles should be verified as to content and count, in addition to performing a routine pharmacy check of the person's medication usage. Medical examiner investigators must also contact hospitals and treating physicians to obtain copies of medical records and police agencies to obtain arrest records. Progressively, a file is assembled that contains all of the relevant background information to assist the pathologist in understanding the medical and social history of the deceased.

The medicolegal systems in countries outside the U.S. vary, but the selection of cases subjected to a forensic pathology examination is usually similar. However, in several countries the police are responsible for the investigation even in noncriminal cases. It is therefore important that the pathologists and toxicologists stay in good contact with the investigating police officer to obtain all relevant information outlined above.

12.1.1.2 Role of the Forensic Pathologist

The principal role of the forensic pathologist is to investigate sudden, unexpected, and violent deaths in order to determine the cause and manner of death. In suspected drug-related deaths or poisonings, the pathologist must both exclude traumatic or pathological mechanisms as possible causes of death *and* select and preserve appropriate specimens for toxicologic analysis. After autopsy, cases can often be divided into two categories: those with an anatomical cause of death and those without. Few drugs leave telltale signs so obvious that the pathologist can determine a manner and cause of death without additional testing. Obvious exceptions include liver necrosis caused by acetaminophen, or the severely hemorrhagic gastric mucosa and smell from cyanide exposure, or coronary artery disease and cardiac enlargement in a cocaine user. Negative findings require toxicological analyses.

Approximately 10% of the cases submitted for toxicology do not have any guiding features. However, many of the thousands of potential compounds that could have caused death will have already been eliminated after history and autopsy results are correlated. Since the majority of drugs and poisons do not produce characteristic pathological lesions, their presence in the body can be demonstrated only by chemical methods.

Collection and preservation of appropriate specimens is a critical component of the autopsy examination.[4-9] Just what is collected depends, at least partly, on the policy and finances of the department. The utility of these specimens depends not only on the condition of the body, but also on the pathologist's technique. Specimens must be large enough, the correct preservative must be used, and they must be placed in appropriate, clearly and correctly labeled containers.

Specimen collection is the first link in the chain of custody. Sample integrity within the chain of custody is an essential requirement for the rest of the forensic investigation. In cases where autopsy fails to determine a cause of death, or where there is an incomplete investigation, it is imperative to collect an adequate variety of specimens. Subsequent findings may modify or narrow the field of search, and make it unnecessary to examine each specimen, but they can always be discarded. However, many toxins are completely lost in the embalming process, so if the appropriate specimens are not collected at the time of the initial post-mortem examination, the cause of death may never be determined.

12.1.2 Certification of Death

Each state requires a medical and legal document known as the Death Certificate be filed with the Bureau of Vital Statistics. The certificate contains demographic information as well the cause and manner of death as determined by the medical examiner. Five different classifications are recognized: (1) homicide, (2) suicide, (3) accident, (4) natural, and (5) undetermined.

The results from toxicological analyses of post-mortem specimens are applied to determine whether drugs or toxins are a cause of death, or whether they may have been a contributing factor in the death. Negative toxicological results may be equally important as positive results, and sometimes even more meaningful as in the case of antiseizure medicines not detected in a suspected seizure death as compared to a positive marijuana test in the urine of a shooting victim.

12.1.3 The Role of Toxicology in Death Investigation

Most toxicology offices have established routines for specific types of cases, and the pathologist often provides some indication of what toxicological testing should be performed on each case (Figure 12.1.2). It would appear that cases of suspected homicide require much more thorough testing than obvious cases of accidental or natural death, but that is not really the case. Alcohol and other sedative hypnotic drugs, for example, are often detected in fire victims and may well have contributed to the cause of death.

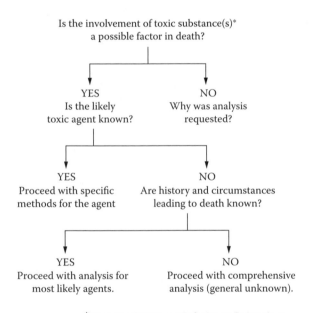

Is the involvement of toxic substance(s)*
a possible factor in death?

YES
Is the likely
toxic agent known?

NO
Why was analysis
requested?

YES
Proceed with specific
methods for the agent

NO
Are history and circumstances
leading to death known?

YES
Proceed with analysis for
most likely agents.

NO
Proceed with comprehensive
analysis (general unknown).

*<u>**Forensic Questions Relative to Poisoning:**</u>

1. Was the death or illness due to a poison?
2. What toxin produced the illness?
3. Was the substance employed capable of producing death?
4. Was a sufficient quantity taken to produce death or toxic results?
5. When and how was the toxin taken?
6. Could a poisoning have occurred and the poison either be or have become undetectable?
7. Could the detected poison have an origin other than in poisoning?
8. Was the poisoning SUICIDAL, ACCIDENTAL, OR HOMICIDAL?
9. Were the correct specimens collected and preserved, analyzed in such a manner to answer the question at hand?

Figure 12.1.2 Identification of a toxicology issue in the death investigation.

12.1.3.1 Homicides

The relationship between intoxication and violence is well recognized.[10-12] Toxicological studies in cases of traumatic homicide should include tests for alcohol, prescribed medications, and other drugs. Negative findings can be used in court to rebut assertions of self-defense against a "drug-crazed" attacker. Positive findings may help explain how the victim became involved in a physical altercation. In addition, results of drug screening provide information about the deceased's lifestyle that may prove useful to police as they search for the murderer. Toxicological investigations may also reveal evidence that a victim was drugged to incapacitation and then murdered.

12.1.3.2 Suicides

In cases of suicide, investigators try to discover an explanation for the act.[13-15] People may be driven to suicide by failing health, financial problems, loss of a loved one, severe mental depression, or other causes. Drugs that can potentiate or exacerbate depression are commonly detected in suicides. A well-recognized drawback with antidepressants is that they neutralize passivity and inhibition before they affect the mood, and thereby confer an increased risk for suicide during the first weeks of treatment.[16,17] Drugs commonly found in suicide victims include alcohol, sedatives (particularly benzodiazepines), analgesics, and hypnotics, and sometimes even illicit drugs. Therefore, toxicological investigations should encompass a large number of intoxicants. Occasionally, a suicide victim employs multiple means to reduce the chances of survival, implying that intake of drugs should not be overlooked even if another suicidal method is apparent.

12.1.3.3 Accidents

For fatal accidents, highway crashes immediately come to mind; however, accidental deaths occur in many other circumstances.[9,11,18-22] Drownings, falls, fires, electrocutions, boating accidents, and aircraft crashes, as well as accidental drug overdoses, are included in this classification. Accidents often result from carelessness or the impairment of mental or motor function on the part of the victim or another person. In apparent cases of accidental death, it is important to confirm or rule out alcohol- or other drug-induced impairment. Many insurance policies exclude death or injury resulting from the misuse of intoxicating substances, although in some cases quite the opposite is true. In those jurisdictions where drug deaths are considered accidents, double indemnity clauses may come into play. The families of victims dying from cocaine toxicity could, in some instances, be entitled to twice the face value of the decedent's life insurance.

Parties injured in an accident may litigate to recover damages. The sobriety or intoxication of the deceased can be a factor in efforts to assign blame. And, of course, apparent accidental deaths may actually turn out to be suicides, or they may be natural deaths occurring in circumstances that suggest an accident. When a driver becomes incapacitated by a heart attack, for example, and loss of control results in an accident, toxicological studies may play a part in the investigation. Detection of intoxicants, together with other evidence, may indicate that an apparent accident was actually intentional. For example, finding large quantities of a drug in a deceased person's stomach suggests that an overdose was intentional (i.e., suicide) rather than accidental.

If post-mortem investigation fails to detect carbon monoxide in the blood of a burn victim, or soot in the airway, it may be that the victim had already died when the fire started. Such cases may be deaths from natural causes, or attempts to destroy evidence of a murder. Further investigation may discover evidence of illness or trauma. Workplace accidents must always be investigated for the possible involvement of alcohol or other drugs, since there are likely to be insurance claims against the employer. If the victim is shown to have intoxicants in the body, the employer may be held blameless. Another aspect of workplace-related accidents concerns exposure to toxic chemicals. The potential for such exposures varies with the nature of the business. If exposure to a toxic chemical is alleged or suspected, investigators should obtain a list of chemicals in the workplace, and the toxicology laboratory of the medical examiner should analyze for those chemicals whose toxicity is consistent with the circumstances of death.

12.1.3.4 Natural Deaths

Apparent natural deaths may or may not require toxicological study. If the autopsy clearly reveals the cause of death, and no history of drug or alcohol misuse is known, the pathologist may decide that further toxicological study is not necessary.[23,25] Sometimes studies are ordered to evaluate compliance with required pharmacotherapy, such as measurement of anticonvulsant drug levels in an person with epilepsy who has a seizure and then dies. When the apparent cause of death may be related to drug or alcohol misuse, testing should be done to determine whether or not relevant drugs are present. For example, acute myocardial infarctions, cerebral hemorrhages, ruptured berry aneurysms, and dissecting aortic aneurysms are often associated with recent cocaine use. Such cases should be tested for cocaine and other drugs, particularly when this occurs in young people or when there is a history of drug use. A diagnosis of alcoholism should call for a blood alcohol analysis.

The diagnosis of sudden infant death syndrome (SIDS) is a diagnosis of exclusion. All apparent SIDS cases should be tested for alcohol and other drugs. Child abuse can include drugging a restless infant, where even a small dose of drug may be fatal.

When there is any uncertainty regarding the cause of death, testing should be done to rule out an overdose. Terminally ill people sometimes commit suicide, and hospice patients are occasionally poisoned by their caregivers. When samples for apparent natural deaths are submitted to the toxicology laboratory for testing, unrecognized poisoning cases are sometimes discovered.

12.1.3.5 Unclassified, Undetermined, or Pending

When the cause or manner of death remains elusive at the completion of investigations and autopsy, the case is left unclassified, pending further studies.[4,23] Additional inquiries, microscopic examinations, and toxicological studies are initiated to find sufficient evidence for a diagnosis. The primary goal for the toxicology laboratory is to determine whether or not toxic substances are present in the deceased in sufficient quantities to kill. If a probable toxic cause of death is identified, the laboratory gathers additional evidence to assist the pathologist in deciding how it was administered, and estimating how much was used, and how long before death. The results of toxicology testing are considered along with other evidence to formulate an opinion regarding the manner of death.

12.1.3.6 Pending Toxicology (Overdose)

Death by poisoning or overdose may be accidental, suicidal, or homicidal.[15,20,23,25–27] Various clues indicating poisoning may be observed during the autopsy. In some cases, a large amount of partially degraded medicinal tablets is found in the stomach, esophagus, mouth, and nostrils, or a typical strong smell of alcohol is noticed. However, other unusual odors or abnormal colors of stomach contents, urine, or tissues, and specific lesions may suggest to the experienced forensic pathologist that a drug or poison was the cause of death. Evidence from the death scene, such as a suicide note or empty containers, may point to a poisoning or drug overdose in some cases. However, most drug-related deaths do not leave such telltale markers as those found in heart attacks, cancer, or trauma. Often the only clue from the autopsy is pulmonary congestion and edema. The pathologist calls upon the toxicology laboratory to confirm the suspicion by identifying the poison or poisons and gathering enough quantitative data to support a conclusion that the detected poison was sufficient to cause death.

In addition, the laboratory may sometimes be able to shed light on the issues of how much was taken and the route of administration. The assignment of manner of death is based on the totality of the evidence, including the pharmacology and toxicology of the substance, the route of administration and quantity taken, the social and medical history of the deceased, and evidence collected from the death scene.[7,20,28,29] Drug-related death certification is by a process of compilation and evaluation of all findings during the death investigation, where elimination of a number of other possible causes of death (COD) is as important as the detection of a toxic substance in sufficient concentrations to have caused or contributed to the death.[28]

12.1.4 The Toxicology Examination

The toxicologic investigation typically begins with the preliminary identification of drugs or chemicals present in post-mortem specimens.[30–39] Confirmatory testing is then performed to conclusively identify the substance(s) present in the post-mortem specimens. In a forensic laboratory, positive identification must be established by at least two independent analyses, each based on a different analytic principle. The next step in the process is to determine the quantity of substance in the appropriate specimens. Identifying drugs in waste fluids, such as bile and urine, is a useful undertaking, but quantifying drugs in these fluids usually has limited interpretive value. Drug quantification in peripheral blood, along with quantification in samples from liver, gastric contents, or other specimens, as dictated by the case, provides more meaningful interpretive information. Therapeutic and toxic ranges have been established for many compounds,[28] but it should be recognized that "therapeutic" concentrations rarely can be determined in the post-mortem setting.[40]

All cases cannot be tested for all drugs. A number of factors, some not immediately obvious, determine what kind, and how many, tests will be done. The importance of the medicolegal classification of death and specimen collection has already been mentioned. But other factors, such as geographic patterns of drug use and laboratory capabilities, must also be considered.

Occasionally, mere detection of a drug is sufficient. But, in the case of some prescription medications, the actual amount present must be quantified. A request for "therapeutic" drug analysis may be made even if the autopsy has already determined the cause of death. If a history of seizure is obtained, the pathologist may request an antiepileptic drug screen to determine whether or not the person was taking any such medication. The same holds true for, e.g., theophylline in individuals with asthma. An individual who has committed suicide may have been prescribed therapeutic drugs for depression or other mental illness. A test for these drugs may indicate the degree of patient compliance. In forensic toxicology, a negative laboratory result carries the same weight as a positive result.

12.1.4.1 Poisons

Often the nature of a suspected toxin is unknown. This type of case is termed a "general unknown."[41,42] In cases of this nature, a full analysis of all available specimens by as many techniques as possible may be required to reach a conclusion. The most common approach involves first testing for volatile agents, and then performing drug screens. The drug screen is usually confined to those drugs that are commonly seen in the casework. When the most common substances have been ruled out, the laboratory proceeds to test for more exotic drugs and poisons.

12.1.4.2 Comprehensive Toxicology Screening

It is impossible to consider the topic of forensic toxicology without discussing analytical toxicology in detail.[43–46] Screening methods should provide presumptive identification, or at least class identification while also giving an indication of concentration. An adequate screening protocol, capable of detecting or eliminating the majority of the commonly encountered toxins, usually requires a combination of three or more chemically unrelated techniques. In general, some toxins are so common that, no matter the type of case, they should always be included for analysis; e.g., ethanol, salicylate, acetaminophen, sedatives, hypnotics, and other drugs such as cocaine, opiates, and antidepressants. All screening tests that are positive for substances relevant to the case must then be confirmed, and analytes of significance submitted for quantification in several tissues. Later sections in this chapter discuss testing methods and how they are combined to yield effective analytical strategies.

12.1.4.3 Case Review

During the toxicological investigation, each case is subjected to periodic review, its status evaluated, and the need for additional testing determined. Based on what is known about the death and the specimens available, a panel of screening tests is designed to quickly detect or rule out the most common drugs and, when appropriate, poisons.[33,37,38,43,47] New tests may be ordered to expand the initial search, or to confirm preliminary findings.

The flow of information in forensic toxicology must be in two directions[48] — from pathologist to laboratory, then back to the physician who will integrate all of the findings. Laboratory personnel must effectively communicate with the pathologist concerning the scope (and limitations) of the services they can provide, suggest the proper selection of specimens, and assist with interpretation of the results. In particular, when drug screens are used, the pathologist should know which drugs they cover — and which drugs will go undetected. To operate effectively, the toxicologist must be provided with enough information about the history and autopsy findings to rationally select the most appropriate tests.

12.1.4.4 Quality Assurance

Each laboratory must formulate and adhere to a quality assurance (QA) program. QA provides safeguards to ensure that the toxicology report contains results that are accurate and reproducible, and that the chain of custody has been preserved. A written QA plan sets out the procedures employed to ensure reliability, and provides the means to document that those procedures were correctly followed. The laboratory's strict adherence to a proper QA program induces confidence in the laboratory's work product and prevents or overcomes potential legal challenges. Before a new or improved method is introduced into a laboratory, it must be selected with care and its performance must be rigorously and impartially evaluated under laboratory conditions.

12.1.4.5 The Toxicology Report

When all toxicological testing is completed, the results are summarized in a report that is sent to the pathologist. This report becomes a part of the autopsy report. It specifies the name of the deceased, if known, and the medical examiner case number. The specimens tested, the substances detected in each specimen, and the measured concentrations of those substances are presented in tabular form. The report should also list substances tested for, but not found, especially if they were named in the toxicology request. If any drug was detected, but not confirmed, a note to that effect should be on the report. In addition, any information about the specimens, such as the date and time of collection of ante-mortem blood or any unusual condition of a specimen, should also be noted on the report. Because of the well-known difficulties associated with the post-mortem redistribution of many drugs, the report should always indicate where in the body the blood specimen was obtained. Toxicology reports are usually signed or initialed by the issuing toxicologist, and in some jurisdictions may be signed by the pathologist as well.

12.1.4.6   Toxicological Interpretation

All substances are poisons; there is none which is not a poison. The right dose differentiates a poison and a remedy.

Paracelsus (1493–1541)

Poisons and medicines are oftentimes the same substance given with different intents.

Peter Mere Latham (1789–1875)

The significance of the reported results must be explained, often to a jury.[5,28,43,48–51] The pharmacology, toxicology, local patterns of drug abuse, and post-mortem changes all can affect toxicological results. In any given case, a toxicologist may be asked the following questions (even though a definitive answer may not be possible in all instances):

1. What was taken, when and how?
2. Was the drug or combination of drugs sufficient to kill or to affect behavior?
3. What are its effects on behavior?
4. Does the evidence indicate if a substance was taken for therapeutic purposes, as a manifestation of drug misuse, for suicidal purposes or was it administered homicidally?
5. Was the deceased intoxicated at the time of the incident that caused death?
6. How would intoxication by the particular drug manifest?
7. Is there any alternative explanation for the findings?
8. What additional tests might shed light on the questions?

REFERENCES

1. Mason, J.K., Forensic medicine [review]. *Injury* 21: 325–327, 1990.
2. Prahlow, J.A. and Lantz, P.E., Medical examiner/death investigator training requirements in state medical examiner systems. *J. Forensic Sci.* 40: 55–58, 1995.
3. Gross, E.M., The Model Postmortem Examinations Act in the State of Connecticut, 1969–1974. *Legal Med. Annu.* 51–66, 1975.
4. Norton, L.E., Garriott, J.C., and DiMaio, V.J., Drug detection at autopsy: a prospective study of 247 cases. *J. Forensic Sci.,* 27: 66–71, 1982.
5. Margot, P.A., Finkle, B.S., and Peat, M.A., Analysis and problems of interpretation of digoxin in postmortem blood and tissues. *Proc. West. Pharmacol. Soc.* 26: 393–396, 1983.
6. Patel, F., Ancillary autopsy — forensic histopathology and toxicology. *Med. Sci. Law* 35: 25–30, 1995.
7. Prouty, R.W. and Anderson, W.H., The forensic science implications of site and temporal influences on postmortem blood-drug concentrations. *J. Forensic Sci.* 35: 243–270, 1990.
8. McCurdy, W.C., Postmortem specimen collection. *Forensic Sci. Int.* 35: 61–65, 1987.
9. Nagata, T., Significance of toxicological examination in the practice of forensic medicine [Japanese]. *Fukuoka Igaku Zasshi Fukuoka Acta Medica* 77: 173–177, 1986.
10. Garriott, J.C., Drug use among homicide victims. *Am. J. Forensic Med. Pathol.* 14: 234–237, 1993.
11. Ladewig, D. Drugs and violence [German]. *Ther. Umschau* 50: 194–198, 1993.
12. Poklis, A., Graham, M., Maginn, D., Branch, C.A., and Gantner, G.E., Phencyclidine and violent deaths in St. Louis, Missouri: a survey of medical examiners' cases from 1977 through 1986. *Am. J. Drug Alcohol Abuse* 16: 265–274, 1990.
13. Derby, L.E., Jick, H., and Dean, A.D., Antidepressant drugs and suicide. *J. Clin. Psychopharmacol.* 12: 235–240, 1992.
14. Nielsen, A.S., Stenager, E., and Brahe, U.B., Attempted suicide, suicidal intent, and alcohol. *Crisis* 14: 32–38, 1993.

15. Marzuk, P.M., Tardiff, K., and Leon, A.C., Final exit and suicide assessment in a forensic setting — reply. *Am. J. Psychiatry* 152: 1833, 1995.

16. Stahl, S.M., Nierenberg, A.A., and Gorman, J.M., Evidence of early onset of antidepressant effect in randomized controlled trials. *J. Clin. Psychiatry* 62(Suppl. 4): 17–23, discussion 37, 2001.

17. Licinio, J. and Wong, M.L., Depression, antidepressants and suicidality: a critical appraisal. *Nat. Rev. Drug Discov.* 4: 165–171, 2005.

18. Alleyne, B.C., Stuart, P., and Copes, R., Alcohol and other drug use in occupational fatalities. *J. Occup. Med.* 33: 496–500, 1991.

19. Caplan, Y.H., Ottinger, W.E., Park, J., and Smith, T.D., Drug and chemical related deaths: incidence in the state of Maryland — 1975 to 1980. *J. Forensic Sci.* 30: 1012–1021, 1985.

20. Hammersley, R., Cassidy, M.T., and Oliver, J., Drugs associated with drug-related deaths in Edinburgh and Glasgow, November 1990 to October 1992. *Addiction* 90: 959–965, 1995.

21. Marx, J., Alcohol and trauma. *Emerg. Med. Clin. North Am.* 8: 929–938, 1990.

22. Lewis, R.J. and Cooper, S.P., Alcohol, other drugs, and fatal work-related injuries. *J. Occup. Med.* 31: 23–28, 1989.

23. Mcginnis, J.M. and Foege, W.H., Actual causes of death in the United States [see comments]. *J. Am. Med. Assoc.* 270: 2207–2212, 1993.

24. Hanzlick, R., National Association of Medical Examiners Pediatric Toxicology (PedTox) Registry Report 3. *Am. J. Forensic Med. Pathol.* 16: 270–277, 1995.

25. Briglia, E.J., Davis, P.L., Katz, M., and Dal Cortivo, L.A., Attempted murder with pancuronium. *J. Forensic Sci.* 35: 1468–1476, 1990.

26. Bogan, J., Rentoul, E., Smith, H., and Weir, W.P., Homicidal poisoning by strychnine. *J. Forensic Sci. Soc.* 6: 166–169, 1966.

27. Moffat, A.C., Interpretation of post mortem serum levels of cardiac glycosides after suspected overdosage. *Acta Pharmacol. Toxicol.* 35: 386–394, 1974.

28. Stead, A.H. and Moffat, A.C., A collection of therapeutic, toxic and fatal blood drug concentrations in man. *Hum. Toxicol.* 2: 437–464, 1983.

29. Brettel, H.F. and Dobbertin, T., Multifactorial studies of 154 fatalities of psychotropic drug poisoning [German]. *Beitr. Gerichtl. Med.* 50: 127–130, 1992.

30. Sunshine, I., Basic toxicology. *Pediatr. Clin. North Am.* 17: 509–513, 1970.

31. Levine, B., Forensic toxicology [review]. *Anal. Chem.* 65: 272A–276A, 1993.

32. Jentzen, J.M., Forensic toxicology. An overview and an algorithmic approach. *Am. J. Clin. Pathol.* 92: S48–55, 1989.

33. Levine, B.S., Smith, M.L., and Froede, R.C., Postmortem forensic toxicology [review]. *Clin. Lab. Med.* 10: 571–589, 1990.

34. Flanagan, R.J., Widdop, B., Ramsey, J.D., and Loveland, M., Analytical toxicology [review]. *Hum. Toxicol.* 7: 489–502, 1988.

35. Chollet, D. and Kunstner, P., Fast systematic approach for the determination of drugs in biological fluids by fully automated high-performance liquid chromatography with on-line solid-phase extraction and automated cartridge exchange. *J. Chromatogr.* 577: 335–340, 1992.

36. Maurer, H.H., Systematic toxicological analysis of drugs and their metabolites by gas chromatography-mass spectrometry. *J. Chromatogr.* 580: 3–41, 1992.

37. Nagata, T., Fukui, Y., Kojima, T., Yamada, T., Suzuki, O., Takahama, K. et al., Trace analysis for drugs and poisons in human tissues [Japanese]. *Nippon Hoigaku Zasshi Jpn. J. Legal Med.* 46: 212–224, 1992.

38. Stewart, C.P. and Stollman, A., The toxicologist and his work, in *Toxicology: Mechanisms and Analytical Methods,* Stewart, C.P. and Stollman, A., Eds., Academic Press, New York, 1960, chap. 1.

39. Puopolo, P.R., Volpicelli, S.A., Johnson, D.M., and Flood, J.G., Emergency toxicology testing (detection, confirmation, and quantification) of basic drugs in serum by liquid chromatography with photodiode array detection. *Clin. Chem.* 37: 2124–2130, 1991.

40. Druid, H. and Holmgren, P., Compilations of therapeutic, toxic, and fatal concentrations of drugs, *J. Toxicol. Clin. Toxicol.* 36:133–134, 1998.

41. Wu Chen, N.B., Schaffer, M.I., Lin, R.L., Kurland, M.L, Donoghue, E.R., Jr., and Stein, R.J., The general toxicology unknown. I. The systematic approach. *J. Forensic Sci.* 28: 391–397, 1983.

42. Wu Chen, N.B., Schaffer, M.I., Lin, R.L., Kurland, M.L., Donoghue, E.R., Jr., and Stein, R.J., The general toxicology unknown. II. A case report: doxylamine and pyrilamine intoxication. *J. Forensic Sci.* 28: 398–403, 1983.

43. Osselton, M.D., Analytical forensic toxicology [review]. *Arch. Toxicol.* Suppl. 15: 259–267, 1992.

44. Drummer, O.H., Kotsos, A., and Mcintyre, I.M., A class-independent drug screen in forensic toxicology using a photodiode array detector. *J. Anal. Toxicol.* 17: 225–229, 1993.

45. Bailey, D.N., Comprehensive toxicology screening in patients admitted to a university trauma center. *J. Anal. Toxicol.* 10: 147–149, 1986.

46. Chen, J.S., Chang, K.J., Charng, R.C., Lai, S.J., Binder, S.R., and Essien, H., The development of a broad-spectrum toxicology screening program in Taiwan. *J. Toxicol. Clin. Toxicol.* 33: 581–589, 1995.

47. De Zeeuw, R.A., Procedures and responsibilities in forensic toxicology [letter]. *J. Forensic Sci.* 27: 749–753, 1982.

48. Stafford, D.T., Prouty, R.W., and Anderson, W.H., Current conundrums facing forensic pathologists and toxicologists [editorial]. *Am. J. Forensic Med. Pathol.* 4: 103–104, 1983.

49. Lokan, R.J., James, R.A., and Dymock, R.B., Apparent post-mortem production of high levels of cyanide in blood. *J. Forensic Sci. Soc.* 27: 253–259, 1987.

50. Heatley, M.K. and Crane, J., The blood alcohol concentration at post-mortem in 175 fatal cases of alcohol intoxication. *Med. Sci. Law* 30: 101–105, 1990.

51. Schulz, M. and Schmoldt, A., A compilation of therapeutic and toxic plasma drug concentrations. *Anaesthesist* 43: 835–844, 1994.

12.2 SPECIMEN SELECTION, COLLECTION, PRESERVATION, AND SECURITY

Bradford R. Hepler, Ph.D. and Daniel S. Isenschmid, Ph.D.
Toxicology Laboratory, Wayne County Medical Examiner's Office, Detroit, Michigan

Specimen selection, collection, preservation, and security place unique demands on the post-mortem forensic toxicologist. The quality of results expected from the post-mortem laboratory today is high and reflects the research advances and continued improvements in instrumentation and analytical methods seen since the origins of modern forensic toxicology in the early 20th century.[1–3] However, it must be recognized that — even with technological advances — accurate, forensically defensible results are predicated on the quality and type of specimens provided, and the documentation of each specimen's origin and history. As important are issues relating to security and evidence control during the collection and storage process. Finally, in considering data available from publications and databases, it is important to recognize that the quality and the "comparability" of data between institutions are only as good as the consistency of approach in specimen collection, storage, and analysis between these organizations.

Many major references in forensic pathology have, each in their own manner, sought to provide information about specimen collection issues.[1,4–9] More recently, the literature has focused on novel and more intriguing issues such as post-mortem release and/or redistribution of drugs from tissues into blood as mechanisms that can lead to legitimate debates about the meaning of a reported value.[10–17] Thus, even an analytically "accurate value" may be subject to misinterpretation when the drug concentration in a single blood specimen is used to explain the circumstances surrounding a drug intoxication death, particularly when the drug concentrations are not excessively high or low. This and other specimen collection and documentation issues are the subjects for discussion in this chapter.

12.2.1 Chain of Custody

One major difference between forensic and clinical toxicology is that institutions performing forensic work are held legally accountable for documenting the handling of specific evidence within the organization. This means that all evidence associated with a specific case must be kept in a secure area at all times and be accounted for during its lifetime by using a record or chain of custody (COC).

Documentation should include *who* handled the evidence, *what* evidence was handled, *when* and *why* the evidence was handled, and *where* the evidence was located at all times. This documentation is central to the demonstration that the evidence has remained intact, and not been adulterated, changed, mishandled, or misplaced in any fashion that would compromise its integrity. Evidence ties together people, places, actions, and things, which have important impact on circumstances surrounding events in which individuals are held legally accountable. In criminal actions the importance of the evidence may truly involve a "life or death" determination, while in civil litigation large sums of money or property may be at stake.

The biological specimens collected during the autopsy are evidence and must be legally accounted for. Specimens must be maintained in secure, limited-access areas at all times with access restricted to only those individuals designated in the institution's standard operating procedure. Specimen handling has been and will continue to be legally scrutinized by the courts. Properly maintained COC documentation rules out any period of time in which a specimen may be left vulnerable to adulteration or tampering. Failure to properly document the COC may compromise not only the integrity of the specimen, but also the credibility of the institution handling the specimen.

Labor-intensive documentation can be tedious and a natural deterrent to the consistent maintenance of records, including the COC. The use of computers for documenting COC and other specimen transactions within the post-mortem forensic toxicology laboratory has recently been demonstrated.[18-20] The ability of the computer to routinely maintain and monitor predictable and consistently occurring events make it an ideal tool for tracking of forensic events.

12.2.2 Specimen Collection

12.2.2.1 Specimen Containers

There are several unique challenges to collecting post-mortem forensic toxicology specimens compared with specimen collection in other forensic toxicology disciplines such as human performance toxicology and employment drug testing. Post-mortem specimen quality can be quite variable, making specimen collection and subsequent reproducibility in aliquoting of the specimen difficult at times. Specimen quantity, or availability, will vary considerably from one case to another, yet the laboratory must attempt to provide a comprehensive toxicological analysis for a general unknown. In the latter regard, detection limits are pressed, and trace findings may have a major bearing on issues of compliance and proper patient care in hospitalized or extended care facilities and the potential for civil litigation. The use of appropriate specimen containers and preservatives can be critical in the toxicologists' ability to ultimately identify a substance in a given specimen.

Usually, the best container to utilize when collecting and storing post-mortem biological fluids is glass.[1,9,21] Glass is inert, does not contain any plasticizer contaminants, and maximizes storage space. Plasticizer contamination is further reduced with Teflon-lined caps. If drug concentrations of less than 0.010 μg/mL are expected, silation of glassware may be indicated.[1] Disposable Pyrex glass culture tubes are suitable for long-term frozen storage and come in a variety of sizes. It is important that the container size chosen for each specimen will allow it to be as close to full as possible in order to minimize concerns about oxidative losses due to air trapped in the top of the container, volatile drug evaporation, and "salting-out" effects from preservatives that may be added to the tube.[1] Generally, 50-mL culture tubes represent the best choice for blood and urine specimens.

Smaller tubes (e.g., 15, 20, and 30 mL) can be used for the collection of small amounts of blood, vitreous humor, and bile specimens.

Most types of plastic containers are suitable for the collection of solid tissue specimens and gastric contents. The nature of solid tissue reduces direct contact with the plastic container, and the relative amount of drug(s) present in gastric contents will minimize the influence of plasticizer interference.

The principal argument that can be made against glass containers is the possibility of breakage. However, this can be minimized by using appropriate storage racks and carrying totes. Some laboratories have successfully used plastic containers by identifying a product that reduces plasticizer contribution and adsorption of drug to the container. Nalgene® containers have been recommended for collection of post-mortem biological fluids.[22] While drug stability in these containers was not determined to be a problem, the evaluation of contaminants was not reported. Whether a facility chooses glass or plastic, it is important that the laboratory carefully evaluate the container before routinely collecting specimens in it. The nature and potential for contamination can be evaluated by analyzing drug-negative biological fluids stored over time in the container. In addition, the plastic must be chosen carefully to ensure that it does not crack when frozen. For example, polystyrene is subject to cracking under these conditions whereas polypropylene is not.

12.2.2.2 Specimen Preservatives

Blood specimens should be preserved by adding 2% w/v sodium fluoride to the collection container. Sodium fluoride is added to inhibit microorganism conversion of glucose to ethanol, microorganism oxidation of ethanol,[23,24] post-mortem conversion of cocaine to ecgonine methyl ester by cholinesterases,[25] and enzymatic loss of other esters such as 6-acetylmorphine.[1,26] Esters, subject to alkaline hydrolysis, are more stable in post-mortem blood than ante-mortem blood because the pH of blood falls after death; therefore acidification of blood is not indicated. Some laboratories may choose to add an anticoagulant such as potassium oxalate, EDTA, or sodium citrate at a concentration of 5 mg/mL in addition to the fluoride preservative.[21,23,24] Preservatives and anticoagulants may be added to collection containers designated for blood ahead of time. However, if only a small amount of blood is collected, the excess fluoride may affect headspace volatile assays by altering the vapor pressure of the analyte.[11] Ideally, one preserved and one unpreserved blood specimen should be taken for comparison, if needed.[22]

Once collected, blood specimens should be stored in tightly sealed containers at low temperatures (4°C short term and –20°C long term). The low temperatures inhibit bacterial growth and generally slow reaction kinetics such as the conversion of ethanol to acetaldehyde.[25] In addition, an aliquot of preserved blood, sufficient in quantity to fill the secondary container, should be removed from the primary specimen at the time of specimen accessioning and stored at -20°C in a frost-free freezer. This aliquot should be saved for the quantitative confirmation of unstable analytes such as cocaine and olanzapine and for ethanol reanalysis, if needed.

Specimen preservatives are generally not required for other specimens (e.g., urine, bile, vitreous, tissues, etc.); however, to all samples subject to alcohol analysis, sodium (or potassium) fluoride should be added. As for blood, these specimens should be stored sealed at 4°C until testing is completed and then frozen at –20°C if long-term storage is required.

12.2.3 Sampling

Biological fluids are collected using new or chemically clean hypodermic syringes using appropriate needle gauges and lengths for the specimen to be collected. One needle and syringe should be used per specimen taken. If syringes and needles are to be reused, then care must be taken to scrupulously clean and disinfect these devices between uses. A typical cleansing procedure should include a minimum of 30 min of soaking in a disinfectant, e.g., 10% solution of household

Table 12.2.1   Guide to the Collection of Routine Toxicology Specimens

Specimen	Amount	When to Obtain	Comments
Blood, heart	50–100 mL	Always	Identify source; preserve with 2% sodium fluoride and potassium oxalate; reserve an aliquot without preservative, if possible
Blood, peripheral	5–10 mL	For complete toxicology testing	Identify source; use femoral or subclavian blood if possible
Blood, clot	Whole clot	Trauma cases	
Urine	All	Always	Submit any quantity, even if <1 mL, for immunoassay screening
Bile	All	Always	Tie off gallbladder to reduce contamination; collect prior to liver
Vitreous humor	All	Always	Combine fluid from both eyes into a single tube
Gastric contents	All	For complete toxicology testing	Tie off stomach to prevent contamination of other viscera; note total volume
Liver	50 g	Always	Identify source; deep right lobe preferred
Kidney	50 g	Metals, ethylene glycol	
Spleen	50 g	CO, CN	Very useful when blood not available in fire deaths
Brain, fat	50 g	Lipophilic drugs	Brain may be especially useful in infant drug deaths
Lung	50 g	Volatile poisons	Collect in sealed container; collect tracheal air as well
Hair	Pen-sized bundle	Drug history, metals	Identify distal and proximal ends

Note: Biological specimens should be kept at refrigerated temperatures (4°C) for short-term storage (up to 2 weeks) and at frozen temperatures (–20°C) for long-term storage. An aliquot of preserved blood should be frozen immediately for analysis and preservation of less stable compounds.

bleach in water (0.5% w/v sodium hypochlorite in water), followed by washing with a non-ionic detergent and rinsing with copious amounts of clean water. Additional disinfection can be performed using an autoclave operated under proper quality control guidelines. The College of American Pathologists recommends that instruments be autoclaved at the usual steam autoclave pressure of 15 lb for 45 min. These conditions are suitable for most pathogens; however, higher pressures and temperatures for longer times (approximately 2 h) are necessary if the rare Creutzfeldt–Jakob disease is of concern.[21] For all this effort, it would seem that disposable needles and syringes are the easiest and most time effective and efficient approach for sampling while reducing the possibility for specimen contamination.

Additionally, autopsy staff must maintain the cleanliness of the specimen container as they collect the specimen. All spillage on the outside of the container should be rinsed off and decontaminated using 10% bleach solution.

Collection techniques are discussed below by specimen type. Table 12.2.1 provides a summary of the information discussed in detail in the text.

12.2.3.1 Blood

Whenever possible, post-mortem blood specimens from two sites, heart and peripheral, should be collected at every autopsy. If no autopsy is performed, then only peripheral blood should be collected.

Heart blood specimens should be taken by needle aspiration using a suitable hypodermic syringe. To obtain a proper cardiac specimen, the pericardial sack must be opened, the pericardium removed, the heart dried, and the blood specimen removed by syringe. Blood from the right chamber is preferable, but regardless from where blood is collected it is essential to label the site from which it was taken.[21] At least 50 mL should be collected, more if possible.

Peripheral blood specimens are usually obtained from the femoral vein. Leg veins are preferred to veins of the head and neck due to the anatomical presence of a larger number of valves that resist blood movement from the intestines.[23] The peripheral blood specimen should be taken using a clean or new 10- to 20-mL hypodermic syringe. Do not "milk" the leg in order to increase specimen volume. If possible, up to 10 mL of peripheral blood should be collected. The source of the peripheral blood specimen should be noted on the specimen container.

As discussed elsewhere, blood clots should be collected in cases of head trauma or if other blood specimens are not available. Because of the strong possibility of contamination, thoracic and abdominal cavity blood should be avoided unless no other blood is available. If collected, they should clearly be labeled as to the source or origin.

12.2.3.2 Urine

During autopsy, urine specimens should be taken directly from the bladder by insertion of a clean/new hypodermic needle into the bladder. For non-autopsied cases the needle may be inserted directly through the lower abdominal wall, just above the pubic symphysis.[9] If possible, up to 100 mL of urine should be acquired. In cases where the bladder appears to be empty, it is important to aspirate as much urine as possible from the bladder and the ureter. Bladder washings using a minimum amount of clean water (or saline) would be desirable in the absence of any urine. The specimen container should clearly identify and indicate the nature of this specimen, and the amount of water/saline utilized. As little as 50 μl of urine can be useful for some applications such as chemical spot tests and immunoassay testing.

12.2.3.3 Bile

Following the removal of the organ block during the autopsy process, bile is aspirated from the gallbladder using a clean/new hypodermic syringe. If there is any possibility of contamination, the gallbladder should be tied off and removed from the organ block so that the bile may be collected away from the potential source of contamination. Up to 15 mL of bile should be collected and placed into a properly labeled screw-capped glass culture tube.

12.2.3.4 Vitreous Humor

Vitreous humor specimens are obtained by direct aspiration from each eye using a 5- to 10-mL syringe and 20-gauge needle. The needle should be inserted through the outer canthus, until its tip is placed centrally in the globe. Vitreous humor can be aspirated from the globe by application of gentle suction. Vacuum tubes and heavy suction should be avoided to prevent specimen contamination with retinal fragments and other tissue. With proper technique 2 to 3 mL of fluid can be removed from each eye in an adult, while up to about 1 mL of specimen may be removed from a newborn.[27] Once the vitreous specimen has been removed from the eye, an appropriate amount of saline can be injected back into the eye in order to reproduce the cosmetic integrity of the eye. Vitreous humor specimens obtained from both eyes may be combined in one properly labeled specimen container.

12.2.3.5 Gastric Contents

Because gastric contents are not homogeneous, and because the total volume of gastric fluid is critical in the interpretation of positive findings, the entire contents of the stomach should be collected. If this is not possible, then the total volume present must be noted and provided with the specimen to the laboratory. The prosector should tie off the stomach ends before removing it from the organ block. The stomach should be opened away from other specimens and tissues, in a manner to avoid contamination of other viscera.

12.2.3.6　Hair

Hair is preferably collected from the posterior vertex or the back of the skull, where the average hair growth rate is fairly constant, and has been extensively studied.[28] The size of the sample to be collected is dependent on the purpose of the analysis. If a segmental analysis is desired, hair from a 1×2 cm area will typically yield about 50 mg of hair/cm segments, which is the amount used for many GC/MS or LC/MS methods reported. Additional samples have to be collected if several analyses with different extraction techniques are desired. One strategy is to collect one sample for screening, and additional samples for confirmation analyses,[29] should the screening come out positive.

In cases with a suspicion of a recent poisoning, analysis of plucked hair may be rewarding, since there is an interval for most drugs during which blood, urine, and cut hair may all be negative, but where the intradermal portion of the hair may harvest traces of the drug. The most common scenario is, however, that the hair analysis is used as a supplementary tool to disclose or confirm previous drug use. Cut hair is then usually preferable since hair roots, often containing high amounts of drugs from an acute intake, are then excluded. Unfortunately, it is difficult to avoid disalignment of a hair sample no matter how carefully the hair is cut from the scalp. An easy way to align the hair strands is to put the sample collected into a small Eppendorff tube with the cut end first and use tweezers to adjust the hair strands. If the time for exposure is not an issue, this procedure is not necessary, and further, smaller hair samples may suffice.

Directly after collection, a convenient means to preserve the alignment, and to keep control of the scalp end, is to put the sample into a small piece of aluminum foil, which is folded once or twice. Putting hair into folded paper should be avoided, particularly regarding plucked hair, since the sticky hair roots will become fixed to the porous surface of the paper, and the strands will break at variable distances from the root. Hair that has been soaked with blood should first be washed with water and then dried before sampling. It is wise to make a note that such contamination has occurred if it turns out that the blood contains high levels of drugs.

12.2.3.7　Tissues

When collecting tissue, a minimum of 50 g should be collected. Each specimen collected should be put into its own properly labeled airtight container. If inhalants are suspected, it is important to collect and seal the specimen in a container as soon as possible after the body has been opened. Because of the possibility that portions of the liver can be contaminated by post-mortem diffusion of drugs from the gastric contents, only liver from deep within the right lobe should be collected.[30] Additionally, bile should be collected prior to the liver specimen, to prevent specimen contamination.

12.2.3.8　Labeling

The first step in the specimen collection process (including evidence collection) is ensuring that the specimen containers are labeled appropriately. Without attention to this detail all other activities that occur with the specimen(s) are suspect. First, the collector must only be working with one specimen at a time. Second, specimens collected should *never* be placed into an unlabeled container. The collector must ensure that the container is labeled so that it can be read prior to the placement of the specimen into the container. As a minimum, the label should include the following information: (1) institutional case number identifier; (2) name or other identifier; (3) date and time of collection; (4) signature or initials of the collector; (5) specimen type (blood, liver, kidney, etc.) and where collected, when applicable (heart blood, femoral blood, etc.). Finally, tamper-resistant tape with the collector's initials and the collection date should be placed over the specimen lid and container to document specimen integrity. Alternatively, all of the samples collected for a given case may be placed in a tamper-evident container labeled with the case number and name. This protocol is particularly useful in institutions with larger caseloads where specimens may not immediately be transferred to the toxicology laboratory.

12.2.4 Selection of Post-Mortem Specimens

The choice of specimens available in a post-mortem forensic toxicology investigation can be numerous and variable. Specimens may be selected based on case history, institutional policy, and availability for a given case. Generally, the specimens routinely collected from cases in which an autopsy was performed include blood from both peripheral and cardiac sources, all urine and bile available, vitreous humor, all available gastric contents, and tissues (particularly liver).[2] However, because the autopsy allows a one-time opportunity to collect as many specimens as may be needed to complete the toxicological investigation, it is suggested that as many specimens be obtained as is feasible for the institution.

In cases where no autopsy is performed, only peripheral blood, urine, and vitreous humor are collected. Heart blood should be avoided due to the potential of contamination by esophageal contents when performing a blind stick.[31,32]

On some occasions a medical examiner or coroner's case may have had a significant survival time in the hospital prior to death. In cases where hospital survival time exceeds 24 to 48 h, the value of post-mortem specimens diminishes considerably. This is especially true if there are allegations that a death may be drug related. Under these circumstances, hospital admission specimens (blood and urine) taken prior to significant therapeutic intervention can be invaluable in the documentation and support of this history. It is important that the post-mortem toxicology laboratory physically obtain these specimens (under COC) for reanalysis, since the results available from the hospital are frequently unconfirmed screening results.

Decomposed, skeletonized, or embalmed cases present unique challenges for the forensic toxicologist. The possibilities for specimens in some of these cases are limited only by availability, analytical capabilities, and sometimes imagination, of the toxicology laboratory. Some of these unusual specimens are discussed later in this section.

12.2.4.1 Blood

Blood is the specimen of choice for detecting, quantifying, and interpreting drug concentrations in post-mortem toxicology. Historically, most of the meaningful data derived from the literature was determined in blood.[33] Despite concerns about post-mortem redistribution of drugs from tissues to blood, some aspects of interpretation remain straightforward. A negative result below a defined limit of detection for a given analyte can be readily interpreted as lack of acute exposure to that analyte or noncompliance in the case of therapeutic agents. Conversely, blood drug concentrations that exceed therapeutic (or, for some drugs, toxic) concentrations by 10 to 20 times are still consistent with intoxication or death (barring an obvious contamination problem). In addition, the higher the parent drug-to-metabolite ratio, the more likely acute intoxication is a factor. This is especially the case when multiple drug analytes are involved, and in cases involving ethanol.

Interpretation becomes especially difficult in cases where drug analytes known to undergo post-mortem redistribution are determined to be present in a heart blood specimen at concentrations ranging between the upper therapeutic limit and the lower limit where intoxication or death has been reported. In these cases, analysis of a peripheral blood specimen may be critical in determining the role that the drug may have played in the decedent. Although drug concentrations in cardiac blood generally rise due to post-mortem drug redistribution, and peripheral blood drug concentrations tend to remain constant, this is not always the case.[13,34,35] Thus, results from a single post-mortem blood specimen, whether cardiac or peripheral, may be difficult if not impossible to interpret. Since cardiac blood is usually more plentiful than peripheral blood, many laboratories perform initial toxicological tests on cardiac blood, reserving the peripheral blood specimens for cases where additional context is needed for interpretation. Regardless of the blood samples available for analysis, it is important for the toxicologist to appreciate that the material collected as "blood" at autopsy is not the same specimen collected in an ante-mortem venipuncture and clinically based pharmacokinetic principles may not be applicable to post-mortem cases.

Following injury or trauma to the head, blood clots from the brain cavity (subdural, subarachnoid, and/or epidural) should be collected in properly identified containers and saved for the laboratory. These materials are potential "time capsules," which are generally poorly perfused, and may reflect drug or alcohol concentrations closer to the time of injury. These specimens become more important as accurate knowledge of the post-injury survival time increases. Blood clots may also be useful for documenting preexisting drug use prior to hospital therapy. Most laboratories routinely analyze alcohol on these specimens, reserving analysis for additional drugs if indicated. Thoracic and abdominal cavity blood should be collected for analysis only if blood or uncontaminated blood clots cannot be obtained from any other area. These "blood" specimens tend to be contaminated by and contain large numbers of microbes. Additional contamination from gastric contents is also possible. Nevertheless, qualitative documentation of presence of given analytes is of importance and value in death investigations with respect to compliance and exposure issues.

12.2.4.2 Urine

Urine collected at autopsy has the greatest potential of any specimen to provide the toxicologist with qualitative ante-mortem drug-exposure information. The urine matrix is generally devoid of circulating serum proteins, lipids, and other related large-molecular-weight compounds due to the renal filtration process, simplifying preparation of the specimen for analysis. The accumulation of drugs and their metabolites in urine results in relatively high drug concentrations, facilitating detection of an exposure to a potential poison. Immunoassays and non-instrumental spot tests can be performed directly on the urine specimen for the analysis of certain drug classes. Detection times for drugs in urine can vary from 24 h to as long as a month, depending on the drug. Thus, except for acute drug deaths where survival time is less than an hour and drugs may not yet have been excreted into the urine, urine provides an ideal matrix for the detection for the widest variety of compounds.

Positive identification of drugs in the urine indicates past drug use, but does not indicate when or how much drug was ingested. To interpret the context of exposure, blood should be tested for the analytes found in the urine. In cases where death is suspected to have occurred rapidly due to drug ingestion, as might be suggested by the presence of a needle in the decedent's arm at the time of death, negative urine drug findings may be consistent if blood drug concentrations are very high.

12.2.4.3 Bile

Bile is another fluid that should be collected at autopsy as a matter of course since many drugs and drug metabolites have been demonstrated to accumulate in this specimen.[1,9,21,36,37] The qualitative finding of the presence of drug and/or metabolites in this specimen is important, for documentation of historic exposures to specific agents and chronic drug-use history. In the absence of urine, bile has also been useful as an alternative specimen for alcohol analysis[38] and has been used in immunoassay screening after sample pretreatment[39] or without pretreatment using enzyme-linked immunosorbent immunoassays.[40] Historically, bile has most often been used in the determination of opiates in general and morphine in particular.[1,36,37] More recently, it has been noted that many drugs are found to accumulate at concentrations significantly higher then those in blood.[39] With an appropriate sample cleanup, bile is a useful specimen for the analysis of a wide variety of drugs and their metabolites, including benzodiazepines.

12.2.4.4 Vitreous Humor

Vitreous humor plays an important role in helping resolve many issues in a post-mortem examination. Because of this, it should be collected in all cases when possible, including cases where no autopsy is performed. Vitreous humor, by virtue of its protected environment inside the eye, is less subject to contamination and bacterial decomposition. As a result it may be used to distinguish ante-mortem alcohol ingestion from post-mortem alcohol formation and may provide the only opportunity to establish an ante-mortem ethanol concentration in embalmed bodies.[23,24,41–43] Additionally, because vitreous humor is contained in a peripheral compartment, there is a delay in both the uptake of drugs and alcohol into this fluid as well as a delay in the excretion process.

It has been observed that vitreous drug concentrations often reflect circulating blood concentrations 1 to 2 h prior to death and that any drug found in the blood will be detected in the corresponding vitreous specimen given analytical techniques of sufficient sensitivity.[9] Although these findings suggest that vitreous humor analysis following positive blood findings might be useful to aid in the interpretation of blood drug concentrations, more research needs to be performed. Studies comparing vitreous humor and blood ethanol concentrations yielded a wide variety of ratios of vitreous humor to blood ethanol.[42] If such diversity is seen for an analyte that demonstrates minimal post-mortem redistribution effects, attempting to use vitreous humor drug concentrations to aid in interpreting heart blood drug concentrations may prove difficult.[11] Despite these concerns, vitreous humor is the best specimen from which to evaluate post-mortem digoxin concentrations.[21] However, the analysis of femoral blood in addition to vitreous humor is still recommended to provide the best context for an appropriate interpretation of ante-mortem digoxin toxicity.[44]

Vitreous humor lacks the esterases that hydrolyze certain drugs and metabolites in blood and may be the specimen of choice to detect the metabolite of heroin, 6-acetylmorphine.[45–48] Because 6-acetylmorphine is quickly hydrolyzed *in vivo* and *in vitro* (especially without the presence of sodium fluoride) to morphine in blood, the analysis of vitreous humor may be helpful in establishing whether a death occurred after heroin use. Similarly, cerebrospinal fluid may also be useful.[48,49]

Vitreous humor has been shown to be particularly useful for the post-mortem analysis of glucose, urea nitrogen, uric acid, creatinine, sodium, and chloride. Measuring these analytes is important for documenting diabetes, degree of hydration, electrolyte balance, and the state of renal function prior to death. A recent article has reviewed the extent and breadth of chemistry analyte analysis applied to vitreous fluid, among other post mortem specimens.[27]

12.2.4.5 Gastric Contents

Oral ingestion is still the major route of drug administration for prescribed drugs and therefore a major compartment for the investigation of a potential poisoning. Drug overdoses, whether by accident or by intent, may readily be discovered through the analysis of gastric contents. In many cases undissolved capsules or tablets may be discovered, which may be useful for identification. In addition, illicit drugs are frequently smuggled by ingestion of balloons or condoms filled with the contraband. If these devices burst and an acute drug death occurs, evidence of these items may be seen in the gastric contents at autopsy.[50]

A large quantity of the parent drug in the gastric content, relative to a prescription dose, are indicative of an oral drug overdose when supported by blood and/or tissue findings.[51] However, the toxicologist is cautioned that low concentrations of drug in the stomach, especially drug metabolites and weak bases, may represent passive diffusion and/or ion trapping from the blood back into the stomach contents and may not be indicative of a recent oral ingestion of these agents. It is important to make a record of the total volume of gastric contents present in the decedent in order to calculate the total amount of the analyte present in the stomach. Since the gastric content is not a homogeneous specimen, ideally the entire specimen should be submitted to the toxicology laboratory for mixing before aliquoting.

The odor of gastric contents can potentially point to a specific agent that might otherwise elude routine detection in the toxicology laboratory. Cyanide ingestions produce stomach contents with the odor of bitter or burned almonds. Although not everyone is able to discern this odor, its presence is almost certainly indicative of a cyanide intoxication, and may be potentially hazardous in close quarters. Other characteristic odors include the "fruity-like" odor of ethanol and its congeners; the odor of airplane glue (xylene, toluene); cleaning fluid (halogenated hydrocarbons); carrots (ethchlorvynol);[32] and garlic (organophosphate insecticides).[32]

12.2.4.6 Tissues

Tissues commonly collected for post-mortem study include liver, kidney, brain, lung, and spleen. Tissues provide the best and most useful context with which to interpret blood findings. They may also be the only specimens available in decomposed cases. A large amount of data for drug findings in tissue exists, primarily for liver and kidney, and, to a lesser degree, brain, and lung.[33] Comparison is most often between heart blood findings and those in the liver, the site where many drugs are metabolized and for which the greatest amount of reference data is available. For example, in cases where the concentration of basic drugs in blood is high and ratios of liver to blood drug concentration exceed 10, a drug fatality is strongly suggested if no other interceding cause of death is present. Smaller ratios, even with high heart blood concentrations, tend to suggest a greater potential for post-mortem redistribution of drugs into the blood.

Analysis of tissue may be more appropriate than analysis of biological fluids for some analytes. In cases of heavy metal poisoning, kidney is a very useful specimen as heavy metals concentrate in it. In addition, structural damage to the kidney due to heavy metal or ethylene glycol exposure may be documented histologically. Spleen, an organ rich in blood, is useful for the analysis of compounds that bind to hemoglobin, such as carbon monoxide and cyanide. Frequently, in fire deaths where extensive charring is present, spleen may be the only useful specimen available to perform these assays. Lung tissue is particularly useful in cases where inhalation of volatile substances, such as solvents or Freon, is suspected. In addition, air may be collected directly from the trachea with a syringe and injected into a sealed vial to be used for headspace analysis.[52] Brain, due to its high fat content, tends to accumulate lipophilic substances, such as chlorinated hydrocarbons, and other organic volatiles. Additionally, there is evidence to suggest that ratios of brain to blood cocaine are high in cocaine fatalities; thus cocaine deaths may be more readily interpreted through the analysis of both matrices.[53] Finally, because the brain is in a protected environment, it also tends to be more resistant to post-mortem decomposition.

The analysis of tissue is performed by weight. Usually, 1 to 5 g of tissue is shredded and homogenized with four parts of water (or saline) to generate a final dilution factor of 5. Recovery of drug from this homogenate has been found to be consistent with recovery of drug from post-mortem blood.[54] Drilling through the tissue with a cork-borer allows tissue to be sampled and weighed while frozen.[55] This method is easier and more precise than sampling wet tissue and is less malodorous when handling decomposed specimens.

12.2.4.7 Hair

Hair has a long history as a useful specimen in forensic toxicology. Traditionally, hair, along with fingernails, was the specimen of choice in determining chronic heavy metal poisoning such as arsenic, mercury, and lead. Heavy metals bind to sulfhydryl groups on the cysteine molecule to form a covalent complex. Keratin, found in large amounts in hair and nails, is an excellent source of cysteine, and therefore an ideal specimen for determining chronic arsenic and mercury poisoning. Interpretation of positive findings can be augmented by segmentation of the hair strands to assist in determining the time of exposure.[56–58]

More recently, hair has been successfully used as a specimen from which chronic drug use may determined.[59] Numerous drugs have been identified in hair including drugs of abuse[60,61] and, more recently, various therapeutic agents.[62,63] The usefulness of hair analysis in determining compliance remains controversial.[64] However, in post-mortem toxicology, segmental analysis can offer a temporal mapping of the drug abuse pattern, and such information may prove useful to identify possible hazardous drug combinations and to detect periods of abstinence that might indicate reduced tolerance to particular groups of drugs. In extremely decomposed or skeletonized cases where no other specimens remain, positive findings for drugs in hair may at least corroborate a history of drug use. The use of hair in workplace drug testing is controversial due to issues such as environmental contamination,[65] washing techniques,[66] sex or ethnic bias,[67,68] the difficulty in performing quantitative analysis,[69] and establishing cutoff concentrations.[70] In the post-mortem setting these issues are not critical, and drug analysis for both pharmaceutical and illicit drugs in hair will most likely become more frequently applied following a growing appreciation of the supplemental information that such analysis may add to the interpretation of the routine toxicological results.

12.2.4.8 Bone and Bone Marrow

Bone marrow has not received a great deal of consideration as an alternative specimen in post-mortem toxicology. Because it is protected by bone, the highly vascularized tissue may be particularly useful when contamination of blood specimens is suspected in trauma cases. Research studies have been performed, primarily on rabbits, showing that linear relationships exist between bone marrow and peri-mortem blood drug concentrations for up to 24 h for many substances including tricyclic antidepressants, barbiturates, benzodiazepines, and ethyl alcohol.[71–74] However, these studies were performed when the bone marrow was still fresh and moist. Although putrefaction is delayed in bone marrow, usually bone marrow is not considered as an alternative specimen in post-mortem toxicology unless other specimens are unavailable. Typically, at this stage of decomposition the bone marrow has transformed from spongy red marrow to a brown viscous liquid or paste-like substance, and it is unknown if any interpretation can be made from quantitative data.[75] However, drugs have even been identified in the bone marrow of skeletonized remains,[76,77] and heavy metals have been identified in the bone itself.[78]

12.2.4.9 Skeletal Muscle

Skeletal muscle is an often-overlooked specimen with many potential applications in post-mortem forensic toxicology. It meets many of the criteria of an ideal forensic specimen: it is relatively homogeneous, almost always available, and not easily contaminated. Studies have shown that drug concentrations in thigh muscle reflect drug concentrations in blood for many common basic drugs and ethyl alcohol, except in cases of an acute drug death where muscle drug concentrations may be lower than blood due to inadequate time for tissue equilibration.[79] The analysis of thigh muscle may be especially useful in cases where drugs suspected of undergoing post-mortem release are detected in the heart blood.[79] It is important that extremity muscle be collected, where possible, as drug concentrations in other muscles, such as abdominal muscle, increase with time while remaining constant in thigh muscle.[80,81]

Because skeletal muscle is often well preserved despite advanced decomposition of other tissue, it may be useful as an indicator of post-mortem blood concentrations even in decomposed cases, although more studies need to be performed.[81,82] Surprisingly, even parent cocaine, which is known to be unstable in blood, has been identified in numerous cases of decomposed, dried skeletal muscle.[83]

The potentially useful data that may be obtained from the analysis of skeletal muscle have prompted some toxicologists to recommend that skeletal muscle be collected in all cases where drugs may be implicated in the cause of death.[81] One disadvantage to skeletal muscle is the need to homogenize the sample prior to analysis. However, this is true of many traditional specimens as well, such as liver and kidney. As more laboratories analyze skeletal muscle leading to the availability of additional data to aid in the interpretation of results, its potential advantages will outweigh any disadvantages.

12.2.4.10 Larvae

In cases of suspected poisoning where decomposition prevents traditional specimens from being obtained, homogenized fly larvae, usually of Calliphorid genus (blowfly), have proved to be useful alternative specimens in which drugs may be identified. Depending on temperature, larvae may be present as soon as 1 to 2 days after death. The first reported use of fly larvae in drug analysis occurred as recently as 1980 and involved a phenobarbital case.[84] Since then numerous drugs have been identified in fly larvae including barbiturates, benzodiazepines, and tricyclic antidepressants,[85] opiates,[86] cocaine,[87] and the organophosphate, malathion.[88]

The choice of where larvae are best collected from the body needs further study. Interpretation of positive findings seem to be most useful if the larvae are collected at the site of their food source, such as any remaining muscle or liver, under the premise that drugs detected in fly larvae feeding on a body can only have originated from the tissues of that body.[89] This assumption seems to be supported by one study where a quantitative relationship was suggested between the morphine concentrations in the larvae and the livers on which they fed.[90] By contrast, other studies suggest that the analysis of fly larvae provides only qualitative data.[85,86,91] However, in these studies larvae were collected from multiple sites and pooled before analysis. If larval drug concentrations are based on the tissue on which they fed,[89] these results are not surprising.

Studies using Calliphorid larvae have shown that the age of the larvae may also play a major role in determining whether drugs may be identified in them.[91,92] By collecting larvae over a period of up to 11 days in cases of known suicidal drug overdoses, it was demonstrated that drugs were readily detectable in larvae through the third instar stage, but a precipitous fall in drug concentration was associated with pupariation after their food ingestion ceases. Similarly, larvae that had been feeding on drug-laden muscle for 5 days demonstrated a significant loss in drug concentration within 1 day of being transferred to drug-free tissue. This suggests that Calliphorid larvae readily eliminate drugs when removed from a food source. Thus it appears to be critical that larvae collected for drug analysis from a decomposed body be frozen and analyzed as soon as possible after collection. Even under refrigerated conditions, when larvae are in a state of diapause, slow bioelimination of drugs still occurs over the course of several weeks.[93] In addition, to eliminate surface contamination as a possible source of interpretive error, larvae should be washed with deionized water prior to analysis.

12.2.4.11 Meconium

Meconium, the first fecal matter passed by a neonate, has recently been given much attention because it is a useful specimen in which to determine fetal drug exposure. Issues relating to the screening and confirmation of most drugs of abuse in meconium have been reviewed.[94] While meconium analysis has principally been performed to assess *in utero* drug exposure in newborns so that treatment may begin as early after birth as possible, it may also be useful in determining drug exposure in stillborn infants. One study demonstrated the presence of cocaine in the meconium of a 17-week-old fetus, suggesting that fetal drug exposure can be determined early in gestation.[95]

Unlike urine, which allows the detection of fetal drug exposure for only 2 to 3 days before birth, meconium extends this window to about 20 weeks. Most post-mortem toxicology laboratories are not currently performing meconium analysis. While potentially useful, there are several issues that must be considered. Because meconium forms layers in the intestine as it is being deposited, it is not a homogeneous specimen. As with other nonhomogeneous specimens, such as gastric contents, it is important that all available specimens be collected and thoroughly mixed before sampling. Consideration should also be given to the fact that infants do not metabolize some drugs the way adults do. If commercial immunoassay screening kits are used that target metabolites found in adult urine, the ability to detect some drugs in meconium may be compromised.[96]

12.2.4.12 Other Specimens

Many other specimens have been used in toxicological investigations. Any item with which a body or bodily fluid has been in contact is a potential candidate for the identification of drugs or poisons. Examples include tracheal air,[52] blood stains on clothing,[97] soil samples collected at the site of a skeleton or decomposed body,[98] and even cremation ash.[99] Even though positive findings in these specimens are qualitative, there is at least the potential that this information can be useful in determining the circumstances of a death.

12.2.5 Nonbiological Evidence

Evidence found at a scene may provide additional information to assist in the toxicological investigation. Drug paraphernalia (cocaine spoons, cookers, bhongs, syringes, poppers, whipped cream propellant canisters, butane lighters, etc.) is suggestive of a possible drug-related death, or at least a history of drug abuse. Prescription drugs at a scene may be useful for compiling a list of suspected drugs, attending physicians, and pharmacy phone numbers. However, this evidence may be misleading as drugs found a scene are frequently old, may not have been taken for years or due to patient compliance problems, or may be someone else's medication. Pain medication and tranquilizers, particularly important in drug deaths, are often prescribed to be taken on an as-needed basis, and thus subject to collecting in medicine cabinets. Counting the number of tablets or capsules in a prescription vial for consistency with the date of the prescription and dosage instructions may be useful, but has the potential for many variables including that of compliance. Additionally, empty medicine vials are not necessarily indicative of a drug overdose. Nevertheless, it is important that for a potential drug-related death, the role of the drugs found at the scene be ruled out by assaying for the agents of potential pharmacological significance.

Whether prescription vials are submitted to the toxicology laboratory is largely a matter of choice in a given jurisdiction. Since these items are evidence, it is often best that the police maintain them and provide a list to the laboratory. Unless the toxicology laboratory has specific experience in analyzing powders and syringes, or has jurisdiction over them, these items are best left for the crime laboratory to analyze, if needed.

In cases where poisoning is suspected, household products at the scene may provide key evidence for the toxicologist. Examples include aerosol containers in suspected inhalation deaths, rat and pest killers, insecticides and pesticides, caustics, windshield washer solvents, anti-freeze, Freon, etc. The garage, basement, or under-sink cabinets are common storage places for many of these items. Unlabeled containers holding solids or liquids, or more importantly, labeled containers that clearly hold a different product, may be the key to a poisoning case. These items, or an aliquot of them, should be provided to the toxicology laboratory, since they often contain analytes for which the toxicology laboratory does not test. The analysis of the product in question may provide mass spectral data and chromatographic information that can be correlated with findings in the biological matrix.

Suicide notes are often critical in determining whether drug intoxication is determined to be an accident or a suicide. However, the toxicologist is cautioned that if a suicide note identifies the suicidal agent or agents, toxicological analysis may reveal a different substance entirely.

REFERENCES

1. Moffat, A.C., Ed., *Clark's Isolation and Identification of Drugs in Pharmaceuticals, Body Fluids and Postmortem Material*, Pharmaceutical Press, London, 1986.
2. Levine, B.S., Smith, M.L., and Froede, R.C., Postmortem forensic toxicology, *Clin. Lab. Med.*, 10, 571–589, 1990.
3. Levine, B., Forensic toxicology, *Anal. Chem.*, 65, 272A–276A, 1993.
4. Adelson, L., *The Pathology of Homicide*, Charles C Thomas, Springfield, IL, 1974.
5. Stewart, C.P. and Stoleman, A., *Toxicology: Mechanisms and Analytical Methods*, Vol. I, Academic Press, New York, 1960.
6. Sunshine, I., Ed., *Methodology for Analytical Toxicology*, CRC Press, Cleveland, 1975.
7. Spitz, W.U. and Fisher, R.S. *Medicolegal Investigation of Death*, 2nd ed., Charles C Thomas, Springfield, IL, 1980.
8. Klaassen, C.D., Amdur, M.O., and Doull J., eds., *Casarett and Doull's Toxicology: The Basic Science of Poisons*, 3rd ed., Macmillan, New York, 1986.
9. DiMaio, D.J. and DiMaio, V.J.M., *Forensic Pathology*, CRC Press, Boca Raton, FL, 1993.
10. Jones, G.R. and Pounder, D.J., Site dependence of drug concentrations in postmortem blood — a case study, *J. Anal. Toxicol.*, 11, 186–189, 1987.
11. Prouty, R.W. and Anderson, W.H., A comparison of postmortem heart blood and femoral blood ethyl alcohol concentrations, *J. Anal. Toxicol.*, 11, 191–197, 1987.
12. Prouty, R.W. and Anderson, W.H., The forensic science implications of site and temporal influences on postmortem blood-drug concentrations, *J. Forensic Sci.*, 35, 243–270, 1990.
13. Anderson, W.H. and Prouty, R.W., Postmortem redistribution of drugs, in *Advances in Analytical Toxicology*, Vol. II, Baselt, R.C., Ed., Year Book Medical Publishers, Boca Raton, FL, 1989, 71–102.
14. Levine, B, Wu, S.C., Dixon, A., and Smialek, J.E., Site dependence postmortem blood methadone concentrations, *Am. J. Forensic Med. Pathol.*, 16, 97–100, 1995.
15. Logan, B.K. and Smirnow, D., Postmortem distribution and redistribution of morphine in man, *J. Forensic Sci.*, 41, 37–46, 1996.
16. Pelissier-Alicot, A., Gaulier, J., Champsaur, P., and Marquet, P., Mechanisms underlying postmortem redistribution: a review, *J. Anal. Toxicol.*, 27, 533–544, 2003.
17. Hepler, B.R., Isenschmid, D.S., and Schmidt, C.J., Postmortem redistribution: practical considerations in death investigation, presented at the American Academy of Forensic Sciences, Abstract K-14, Dallas, TX, 2004.
18. Cechner, R.L., Hepler, B.R., and Sutheimer, C.A., Improving information management in a metropolitan coroner's office, part I: design and implementation of a cost effective minicomputer system with initial application for the toxicology laboratory, *J. Forensic Sci.*, 35, 375–390, 1990.
19. Cechner, R.L. Hepler, B.R., and Sutheimer, C.A., Expert systems in the forensic toxicology laboratory, *Diagn. Clin. Testing*, 27, 42–45, 1989.
20. Hepler, B.R., Monforte, J.R., and Cechner, R.L., Use of the Toxlab-pc® in alcohol and drug incidence in Wayne County, *Ther. Drug Monit. Clin. Toxicol. Newsl.*, 8, 2–4, 1993.
21. Hutchens, G.M., Ed., *An Introduction to Autopsy Technique*, College of American Pathologists, Northfield, IL, 1994.
22. McCurdy, W.C. Postmortem specimen collection, *Forensic Sci. Int.*, 35, 61–65, 1987.
23. Harper, D.R. and Couy, J.E.L., Collection and storage of specimens for alcohol analysis, in *Medicolegal Aspects of Alcohol Determination in Biological Samples*, Garriott, J.C., Ed., Year Book Medical Publishers, Boca Raton, FL, 1988, 145–169.
24. Caplan, Y.H., Blood, urine and other fluid and tissue specimens for alcohol analysis, in *Medicolegal Aspects of Alcohol Determination in Biological Samples*, Garriott, J.C., Ed., Year Book Medical Publishers, Boca Raton, FL, 1988, 74–86.
25. Isenschmid, D.S., Levine, B.S., and Caplan, Y.H., A comprehensive study of the stability of cocaine and its metabolites, *J. Anal. Toxicol.*, 13, 250–256, 1989.
26. Isenschmid, D.S. and Hepler, B.R., Unpublished data.
27. Coe, J.I., Postmortem chemistry update: emphasis on forensic application, *Am. J. Forensic Med. Pathol.*, 14, 91–117, 1993.
28. Pounder, D. and Davies, J. Zopiclone poisoning, letter to the editor, *J. Anal. Toxicol.*, 20, 273, 1996.

29. Harkey, M.R., Anatomy and physiology of hair, *Forensic Sci. Int.,* 63, 9–18, 1993.

30. Kronstrand, R., Nystrom, I., Strandberg, J., and Druid, H., Screening for drugs of abuse in hair with ion spray LC-MS-MS, *Forensic Sci. Int.,* 145,183–90, 2004.

31. Logan, B.K. and Lindholm, G., Gastric contamination of postmortem blood samples during blind stick sample collection, *Am. J.. Forensic Med. Pathol.,* 17, 109–111, 1996.

32. Monforte, J.R., Methodology and interpretation of toxicological procedures, in *Medicolegal Investigation of Death,* 2nd ed., Spitz, W.U. and Fisher, R.S., Eds., Charles C Thomas, Springfield, IL, 1980, 571–589.

33. Baselt, R. and Cravey, R., *Disposition of Drugs and Toxic Chemicals in Man,* 4th ed., Chemical Toxicology Institute, Foster City, CA, 1995.

34. Hearn, W.L., Keran, E.E., Wei, H., and Hime, G., Site-dependent postmortem changes in blood cocaine concentrations, *J. Forensic Sci.,* 36, 673–684, 1991.

35. Logan, B.K., Smirnow, D., and Gullberg, R.G., Time dependent changes and site dependent difference in postmortem concentration of cocaine, benzoylecgonine and cocaethylene, presented at the American Academy of Forensic Sciences, Abstract K-32, Nashville, TN, 1996.

36. Stajic, M., The general unknown, in *Introduction to Forensic Toxicology,* Cravey, R.C. and Baselt, R.C., Eds., Biomedical Publications, Davis, CA, 1981, 169–181.

37. Agarwal, A. and Lemoc, M., Significance of bile analysis in drug induced deaths, *J. Anal. Toxicol.,* 20, 61–62, 1996.

38. Baselt, R.C. and Danhof, I.E., Disposition of alcohol in man, in *Medicolegal Aspects of Alcohol Determination in Biological Samples* Garriott, I.C., Ed., Year Book Medical Publishers, Boca Raton, FL, 1988, 55–73.

39. Hepler, B.R., Sutheimer, C.A., Sebrosky, G.F., and Sunshine, I., Combined enzyme immunoassay-LCEC method for the identification, confirmation and quantitation of opiates in biological fluids, *J. Anal. Toxicol.,* 8, 78, 1984.

40. Isenschmid, D.S., Patton, D.M., Hepler, B.R., and Schmidt, C.J., Use of the Immunalysis™ ELISA assays for the detection of drugs in postmortem specimens: a multiple matrix approach, presented at The International Association of Forensic Toxicologists, Poster Session 2, Paper 77, Melbourne, Australia, 2003.

41. O'Neal, C.L. and Poklis, A., Postmortem production of ethanol and factors that influence interpretation, *Am. J. Forensic Med. Pathol.,* 17, 8–20, 1996.

42. Caplan, Y.H. and Levine, B.S., Vitreous humor in the evaluation of postmortem blood ethanol concentrations, *J. Anal. Toxicol.,* 14, 305–307, 1990.

43. Scott, W., Root, I., and Sanborn, B., The use of vitreous humor for determination of ethyl alcohol in previously embalmed bodies, *J. Forensic Sci.,* 19, 913–196, 1974.

44. Vorpahl, T.E. and Coe, J.I., Correlation of antemortem and postmortem digoxin levels, *J. Forensic Sci.,* 23, 329–334, 1978.

45. Pragst, F., Spiegel, K., Leuschner, U., and Hager, A., Detection of 6-acetylmorphine in vitreous humor and cerebralspinal fluid — comparison with urinary analysis for proving heroin administration in opiate fatalities, *J. Anal. Toxicol.,* 23, 168–172, 1999.

46. Scott, K.S. and Oliver, J.S., Vitreous humor as an alternative sample to blood for the supercritical fluid extraction of morphine and 6-monoacetylmorphine, *Med. Sci. Law,* 39, 77–81, 1999.

47. Pearson, J.M. and Saady, J.J., Utility of vitreous humor in investigations of heroin-related deaths, *J. Anal. Toxicol.,* 27, 199, 2003.

48. Wyman, J. and Bultman, S., Post-mortem distribution of heroin metabolites in femoral blood, liver, cerebrospinal fluid, and vitreous humor, *J. Anal. Toxicol.,* 28, 260–263, 2004.

49. Jenkins, A.J. and Lavins, E.S., 6-Acetylmorphine detection in postmortem cerebrospinal fluid, *J. Anal. Toxicol.,* 22, 173–175, 1998.

50. Wetli, C.V. and Mittelman, R.E., The "body packer" syndrome — toxicity following ingestion of illicit drugs packaged for transportation, *J. Forensic Sci.,* 26, 492–500, 1981.

51. Freimuth, H.C., Guidelines for preservation of toxicological evidence, in *Medicolegal Investigation of Death,* 2nd ed., Spitz, W.U. and Fisher, R.S., Eds., Charles C Thomas, Springfield, IL, 1980, 556–564.

52. Isenschmid, D.S., Cassin, B.J., and Hepler, B.R., Acute tetrachloroethylene intoxication in an autoerotic fatality, presented at the American Academy of Forensic Sciences, Abstract K-20, Seattle, WA, 1995.

53. Karch, S.B., *The Pathology of Drug Abuse*, CRC Press, Boca Raton, FL, 1993, 42–43.

54. Hepler, B.R., Sutheimer, C.A., and Sunshine, I., Unpublished data.

55. Anderson, W.H. and Prouty, R.W., Personal communication.

56. Smith, H., Forshufvud, S., and Wassen, A., Distribution of arsenic in Napoleon's hair, *Nature,* 194, 725–726, 1962.

57. Grandjean, P., Lead poisoning: hair analysis shows the calendar of events, *Hum. Toxicol.,* 3, 223–228, 1984.

58. Poklis, A. and Saady, J.J., Arsenic poisoning: acute or chronic? *Am. J. Forensic Med. Pathol.,* 11, 236–232, 1990.

59. DuPont, R.L. and Baumgartner, W.A., Drug testing by urine and hair analysis: complementary features and scientific issues, *Forensic Sci. Int.,* 70, 63–76, 1995.

60. Baumgartner, W.A., Cheng, C., Donahue, T.D., Hayes, G.F., Hill, V.A., and Scholtz, H., Forensic drug testing by mass spectrometric analysis in hair, in *Forensic Applications of Mass Spectrometry,* Yinon, J., Ed., CRC Press, Boca Raton, FL, 1995, chap. 2.

61. Harkey, M.R. and Henderson, G.L., Hair analysis for drugs of abuse, in *Advances in Analytical Toxicology,* Vol. II, Baselt, R.C., Ed., Yearbook Medical Publishers, Chicago, 1989, chap. 10.

62. Couper, F.J., McIntyre, I.M., and Drummer, O.H., Detection of antidepressant and antipsychotic drugs in postmortem human scalp hair, *J. Forensic Sci.,* 40, 87–90, 1995.

63. Uematsu, T., Therapeutic drug monitoring in hair samples: principles and practice, *Clin. Pharmaco-kinetics*, 25, 83–87, 1993.

64. Tracqui, A., Kintz, P., and Mangin, P., Hair analysis: a worthless tool for therapeutic compliance monitoring, *Forensic Sci. Int.,* 70, 183–189, 1995.

65. Cone, E.J. and Wang, W.L., Testing human hair for drugs of abuse, IV, environmental cocaine contamination and washing effects, *Forensic Sci. Int.,* 70, 39–51, 1995.

66. Blank, D.L. and Kidwell, D.A., Decontamination procedures for drugs of abuse in hair: are they sufficient? *Forensic Sci. Int.,* 70, 13–38, 1995.

67. Joseph, R.E., Su, T., and Cone, E.J., Sex bias in hair testing for cocaine, presented at the American Academy of Forensic Sciences, Abstract K-10, Seattle, WA, 1995.

68. Joseph, R.E., Su, T., and Cone, E.J., Evaluation of *in vitro* binding of cocaine to lipids and melanin in hair, presented at the American Academy of Forensic Sciences, Abstract K-19, Nashville, TN, 1996.

69. Welch, M.J., Sniegoski, L.T., and Allgood, C.C., Interlaboratory comparison studies on the analysis of hair for drugs of abuse, *Forensic Sci. Int.,* 63, 295–303, 1993.

70. Kintz, P. and Mangin, P., What constitutes a positive result in hair analysis: proposal for the establishment of cut-off values, *Forensic Sci. Int.,* 70, 3–11, 1995.

71. Winek, C.L., Morris, E.M., and Wahba, W.W., The use of bone marrow in the study of postmortem redistribution of amitriptyline, *J. Anal. Toxicol.,* 17, 93, 1993.

72. Winek, C.L., Costantino, A.G., Wahba, W.W., and Collom, W.D., Blood versus bone marrow pento-barbital concentrations, *Forensic Sci. Int.,* 27, 15–24, 1985.

73. Winek, C.L. and Pluskota, M., Plasma versus bone marrow flurazepam concentrations in rabbits and humans, *Forensic Sci. Int.,* 19, 155–163, 1982.

74. Winek, C.L. and Esposito, F.M., Comparative study of ethanol levels in blood versus bone marrow, vitreous humor, bile and urine, *Forensic Sci. Int.,* 17, 27–36, 1981.

75. Winek, C.L., Matejczyk, R.J., and Buddie, E.G., Blood, bone marrow and eye fluid ethanol concentrations in putrefied rabbits, *Forensic Sci. Int.,* 22, 151–159, 1983.

76. Noguchi, T.T., Nakamura, G.R., and Griesemer, E.C., Drug analysis of skeletoninzing remains, *J. Forensic Sci.,* 23, 490–492, 1978.

77. Kojima, T., Okamoto, I., Miyazaki, T., Chikasue, F., Yashiki, M., and Nakamura, K., Detection of methamphetamine and amphetamine in a skeletonized body buried for 5 years, *Forensic Sci. Int.,* 31, 93–102, 1986.

78. Logemann, E., Krützfeldt, B., Kalkbrenner, G., and Schüle, W., Mercury in bones, presented at the Society of Forensic Toxicologists, Abstract 44, Tampa, FL, 1994.

79. Garriott, J.C., Skeletal muscle as an alternative specimen for alcohol and drug analysis, *J. Forensic Sci.,* 36, 60, 1991.

80. Kudo K., Nagata, T., Kimura, K., Imamura, T., and Urakawa, N., Postmortem changes of triazolam concentrations in body tissues, *Nippon Hoigaku Zasshi,* 46, 293, 1992.

81. Christensen, H., Steentoft, A., and Worm, K., Muscle as an autopsy material for evaluation of fatal cases of drug overdose, *J. Forensic Sci. Soc.*, 25, 191–206, 1985.

82. Garriot, J.C., Interpretive toxicology: drug abuse and drug abuse deaths, in *Forensic Pathology*, DiMaio, D.J. and DiMaio, V.J.M., Eds., CRC Press, Boca Raton, FL, 1993, chap. 21.

83. Manhoff, D.T., Hood, I., Caputo, F., Perry, J., Rosen, S., and Mirchandani, H.G., Cocaine in decomposed human remains, *J. Forensic Sci.*, 36, 1732, 1991.

84. Beyer, J.C., Enos, W.F., and Stajic, M., Drug identification through analysis of maggots, *J. Forensic Sci.*, 25, 411–413, 1980.

85. Kintz, P., Godelar, B., Tracqui, A., Mangin, P. Lugnier, A.A., and Chaumont, A.J., Fly larvae: a new toxicological method of investigation in forensic medicine, *J. Forensic Sci.*, 35, 204–207, 1990.

86. Kintz, P., Traqui, A., and Mangin, P., Analysis of opiates in fly larvae sampled on a putrefied cadaver, *J. Forensic Sci. Soc.*, 34, 95–97, 1994.

87. Nolte, K.B., Pinder, R.D., and Lord, W.D., Insect larvae used to detect cocaine poisoning in a decomposed body, *J. Forensic Sci.*, 37, 1179–1185, 1992.

88. Gunatilake, K. and Goff, L., Detection of organophosphate poisoning in a putrefying body analyzing arthropod larvae, *J. Forensic Sci.*, 34, 714–716, 1989.

89. Pounder, D.J., Forensic entomotoxicology, *J. Forensic Sci. Soc.*, 31, 469–472, 1991.

90. Introna, F., Lo Dico, C., Caplan, Y.H., and Smialek, J.E., Opiate analysis in cadaveric blowfly larvae as an indicator of narcotic intoxication, *J. Forensic Sci.*, 35, 118–122, 1990.

91. Kintz, P., Traqui, P., Ludes, B., Waller, J., Boukhabza, A., Mangin, P., Lugnier, A.A., and Chaumont, A.J., Fly larvae and their relevance in forensic toxicology, *Am. J. Forensic Med. Pathol.*, 11, 63–65, 1990.

92. Wilson, Z., Hubbard, S., and Pounder, D.J., Drug analysis in fly larvae, *Am. J. Forensic Med. Pathol.*, 14, 118–120, 1993.

93. Sadler, D.W., Fuke, C., Court, F., and Pounder, D.J., Drug accumulation and elimination in *Calliphora vicina* larvae, *Forensic Sci. Int.*, 71, 191–197, 1995.

94. Moore, C. and Negrusz, A., Drugs of abuse in meconium, *Forensic Sci. Rev.*, 7, 103–118, 1995.

95. Ostrea, E.M., Romero, A., Knapp, D.K., Ostrea, A.R., Lucena, J.E., and Utarnachitt, R.B., Postmortem drug analysis of meconium in early-gestation human fetuses exposed to cocaine, *J. Pediatr.*, 124, 477, 1994.

96. Steele, B.W., Bandstra, E.S., Wu, N.C., Hime G.W., and Hearn, W.L., *m*-Hydroxy-benzoylecgonine: an important contributor to the immunoreactivity in assays for benzoylecgonine in meconium, *J. Anal. Toxicol.*, 17, 348–351, 1993.

97. Tracqui, A., Kintz, P., Ludes, B., Jamey, C., and Mangin, P., The detection of opiate drugs in nontraditional specimens (clothing): a report of ten cases, *J. Forensic Sci.*, 40, 263–265, 1995.

98. Monforte, J.R., Personal communication.

99. Barchet, R., Harzer, K., Helmers, E., and Wippler, K., Arsenic content in cremation ash after lethal arsenic poisoning, in *Proceedings of the 1994 Joint TIAFT/SOFT International Meeting*, Spiehler, V., Ed., Newport Beach, CA, 1995, 315–319.

12.3 COMMON METHODS IN POST-MORTEM TOXICOLOGY

W. Lee Hearn, Ph.D.[1] **and H. Chip Walls, B.S.**[2]

[1] Director, Dade County Medical Examiner Toxicology Laboratory, Miami, Florida

[2] Department of Pathology, Forensic Toxicology Laboratory, University of Miami, Miami, Florida

12.3.1 Analytical Chemistry in Post-Mortem Toxicology

Analytical toxicology is an applied science.[1-4] Toxicologists must be familiar not only with the effects and toxic mechanisms involved in poisoning, but also with the metabolism of drugs, the chemical properties of parent drugs and their metabolites, and the composition of biological

Table 12.3.1 Comparison of Frequently Used Methods for Analysis of Biosamples

Method	Specificity	Sensitivity	Multiple Drugs	Identification: Structural Analysis (Qualitative)	Quantitative Analysis	Labor	Expertise
Color tests	+	+	Yes	+	Some	+	+
UV-VIS	+	+	No	++++	Yes	++	++
IA	++	++	Some	No	Some	+	+
GC	++	++	Yes	++	Yes	++	++
TLC	++	+	Yes	++	No	+++	+++
HPLC	++	++	Yes	++	Yes	++	++
GC/MS	++++	++++	Yes	++++	Yes	+++	++++
AAS	+++	+++	No	++	++++	+++	++++
ICP-MS	++++	++++	Yes	++++	++++	++++	++++

Key: Low = +; High = ++++; UV-VIS = ultraviolet-visible spectrophotometry; IA = immunoassay; GC = gas chromatography; TLC = thin-layer chromatography; HPLC = high performance liquid chromatography; GC/MS = gas chromatography mass spectrometry; AAS = atomic absorption spectrometry; ICP-MS = inductively coupled plasma mass spectrometry.

From Dolgin, J., Human Clinical Toxicology, in *CRC Handbook of Toxicology,* Derelanko, M.J. and Hollinger, M.A., Eds., CRC Press, Boca Raton, FL, 1995, 697.

samples. The detection and measurement of toxicologically relevant concentrations of potent new drugs requires the use of analytical techniques on the forefront of instrumental technology.[5–9]

Immunoassay technology, now a mainstay of drug screening protocols, first became commercially available only about 25 years ago.[10–14] At that time, classical thin-layer chromatography (TLC),[15–23] packed column gas chromatography,[24,25] strip chart recorders, and ultraviolet-visible spectrophotometry were the state of the art in toxicology laboratories.[26–29] Over the intervening years, capillary column gas chromatography,[30–44] solid-phase extraction technology,[46–53] nitrogen-phosphorus gas chromatography detectors,[42,43,54,55] high-performance liquid chromatography (HPLC),[56–74] ion trap mass spectrometry,[75–79] and computerized mass spectrometry have become essential to the practice of post-mortem toxicology.[80,99]

New technology is continually being introduced. Mass spectrometry is evolving to tandem mass spectrometry, and is being interfaced to liquid chromatographs.[92,100–106] Chemical ionization, in both positive and negative ion modes, is increasingly used in the mass spectral analysis of drugs and poisons.[107–119] Robotic technology is used to increase efficiency of sample processing while maintaining and documenting sample integrity.[120–123] At the same time, the proliferation of ever more powerful microcomputers, and sophisticated software applications, has vastly improved the processing and archiving of analytical data, control of instruments, laboratory management, and quality assurance monitoring.

While newer technologies have replaced many of the older, less sensitive, and less specific testing methods, some of the older tests, such as the microchemical tests, still have a place in the modern toxicology laboratory. But change is occurring so rapidly that today's technology may soon be obsolete. The best and most current guides to the innovations in testing methodologies are to be found in the scientific journals such as the *Journal of Forensic Science* and the *Journal of Analytical Toxicology*; the annual meetings of professional organizations such as the Society of Forensic Toxicologists and the American Academy of Forensic Sciences; and the annual meeting of the Pittsburgh Conference on Analytical Chemistry and Applied Spectroscopy. Table 12.3.1 compares the analytical techniques with respect to specificity, sensitivity, labor, cost, and applicability.

12.3.2 Simple Chemical Tests

Chemical tests were once the mainstay of post-mortem toxicology.[21,124–127] Today, many have been abandoned and replaced by automated broad range screening procedures. However, some are still useful as supplemental tests to rapidly and easily detect drugs and poisons that are not detected by the other screening tests.

Virtually all clinical and forensic toxicology laboratories utilize micro-color tests to indicate the possible presence of drugs or toxins; the so-called spot tests.[21,125,127–133] Micro-color tests are performed by adding a single or multiple reagents to a specimen or extract and observing the color produced. Color tests are specific examples of the more general method of qualitative organic chemistry, relying on functional group reactions with the reagents. These tests require some expertise and familiarity to use, but are inexpensive and relatively rapid. They are nonspecific. However, in conjunction with other confirmatory tests, they can be used as rapid diagnostic aids.

Color tests can be combined with visible or spectrophotometric methodologies for qualitative to semiquantitative answers. Drugs including phenothiazines, salicylates, acetaminophen, carbamates, ethchlorvynol, and imipramine may be detected by colorimetric methods. Positive test results are confirmed and quantified by another technique. The greatest advantage of color tests is their ease of use. They can be performed directly on urine or a protein-free filtrate of blood or tissues. A negative color test precludes the need for any further work on that drug, assuming the detection limit of the test is acceptable. For example, the color test for phenothiazines is useful if an overdose has occurred, but is not sensitive enough to test for patient compliance with the drug.

12.3.2.1 Useful Color Tests

Some or all of the following tests may be incorporated in a routine screening protocol or some may be reserved for cases requiring more comprehensive poison screening.

Trinder's Reagent

Trinder's test is a simple color test that detects salicylic acid in urine or serum. It does not detect acetylsalicylic acid in gastric contents without prior hydrolysis by boiling with dilute HCl. Trinder's reagent is a mixture of ferric nitrate and mercuric chloride in dilute hydrochloric acid. It immediately produces a violet color when mixed with an equal volume of sample containing salicylate. Phenothiazines also give a positive reaction.[125,126,129,133,134]

Fujiwara Test for Trichloro Compounds

A mixture of 1 mL 20% sodium hydroxide and 1 mL of pyridine at 100°C yields a red or pink color with chloral hydrate or other compounds with at least two halogens bound to one carbon.[124–126,131,135] Trichloroethanol gives a yellow color. Contamination of the laboratory atmosphere with chlorinated solvents will give "false" positive results. Metabolites of carbon tetrachloride may also give a positive result with this test, but carbon tetrachloride is only partially metabolized to trichloromethyl compounds and the test may fail to detect this agent. A blank sample and a control (trichloroacetic acid) should be tested at the same time, with both blank and control solutions treated in similar fashion to the sample.

Diphenylamine Test for Oxidizing Agents

A solution of 0.5% diphenylamine in 60% sulfuric acid added to the sample or sample filtrate in a porcelain spot plate or a test tube immediately gives an intense blue color if an oxidizing agent is present. This test detects hypochlorite, chlorate, bromate, iodate, chromate, dichromate, nitrate, nitrite, permanganate, vanadate, lead (IV), or manganese (III, IV, or VII).[125,126]

Ethchlorvynol (Placidyl) Test

In this test 1 mL of sample (urine or sample filtrate) is mixed with the reagent and allowed to stand for 20 min. If ethclorvynol is present, the solution turns red or pink. The reagent consists of 1 g diphenylamine dissolved in 50 mL concentrated sulfuric acid and added slowly with stirring to 100 mL of 50% (V/V) acetic acid. The test is sufficiently sensitive to detect therapeutic concentrations.[125,126,136]

12.3.2.2   Other Color Tests That May Be Included in a Screen

Other color tests that may be included in a screen can be found in various toxicology references.[124–128]

12.3.3   Reinsch Test for Heavy Metals

A spiral of copper wire is first cleaned with 35% nitric acid and washed. It is then immersed in 15 mL of sample, acidified with concentrated HCl (4 mL), heated for 1 h, and then examined. A silver colored deposit on the copper indicates mercury, while a dark colored or black deposit is produced by arsenic, antimony, bismuth, tellurium, selenium, and sulfur. Further differentiation can be made on the basis of color of the deposit, and its solubility characteristics in potassium cyanide solution.[128,137–141]

12.3.4   Microdiffusion Tests

12.3.4.1   Cyanide Test

In this test 2 mL of sample are placed in a screw cap culture tube. Disks are punched from a strip of Cyantesmo paper, available from Gallard-Schlessinger Chemical Mfg. Co. (Carle Place, New York), and one disk is stuck to the adhesive in the center of a 1-cm square of cellophane tape. The sample is acidified with H_2SO_4, the tape is placed over the mouth of the tube, with the adhesive and disk side down, and the tube is tightly capped. After 4 h at 35°C, the caps are removed and the color of the disk is compared with cyanide standards treated the same way. A pale green or yellow color is a negative result. Cyanide turns the disk blue in proportion to the concentration in the sample. Comparison of the color with standards from 0.2 to 5.0 mg/L cyanide can be used to estimate the concentration.

12.3.4.2   Carbon Monoxide

A simple test for carbon monoxide utilizes a procedure similar to the cyanide test described above, but using a disk of filter paper saturated with palladium chloride solution (1%) in 0.12 N HCl and dried. Carbon monoxide is released from hemoglobin by the addition of a solution containing lactic acid and potassium ferricyanide. Lead acetate is added to trap sulfide, which might interfere with the test. If carbon monoxide is present, the disk turns gray to black. While this test is simple, a faster and more effective method is to analyze the blood with a CO-Oximeter (Instrumentation Laboratories), which gives a result in % saturation of hemoglobin.

12.3.5   Other Simple Tests

12.3.5.1   Glucose, Ketones, Protein, and pH via a Diagnostic Reagent Strip (Dip-Stick)

Dip a strip briefly into the urine and read after 10 to 60 s. Elevated glucose may indicate diabetes. A positive result for ketones may indicate intoxication by acetone or isopropyl alcohol. This test may also be positive in starvation or in diabetic ketosis.

12.3.5.2   Odor, Color, and pH of Gastric Contents

Characteristic smells may indicate the presence of substances such as camphor, cresol, cyanide, ethanol and other organic solvents, ethchlorvynol, methyl salicylate, and paraldehyde. A high pH may indicate ingestion of alkali. A green or blue color suggests the presence of iron salts. Other colors may result from dissolution of colored pills or capsules. Intact tablets or capsules should be retrieved and examined separately.

12.3.6   Immunoassays

Immunoassays for post-mortem toxicology are sold commercially as kits. Often, they are exactly the same products as those used for urine drug screening in forensic urine drug testing programs.[142] Such products are standardized and validated by the manufacturer, and are approved by the U.S. Food and Drug Administration (FDA). They are intended and approved for the analysis of particular specimen types, such as urine or serum. When urine cannot be obtained, other tissue may be used. A number of publications have described effective techniques for precipitating/extracting drugs from blood or tissue homogenates. Generally, the technique involves use of a solvent, such as acetone or acetonitrile, followed by evaporation of the solvent/water mixture and reconstitution in a suitable reagent for assay, according to the procedure for urine. However, application to specimens other than urine requires validation[143–156]

Immunoassays are based upon the principle that antibodies can be produced that recognize and bind to specific chemicals by interacting with unique structural features of their molecules. The interaction is analogous to that of a lock and key. Some antibodies are so selective that they bind to only one substance, such as methamphetamine. Others interact with a variety of compounds with similar structures, such as amphetamine, methamphetamine, phentermine, ephedrine, pseudoephedrine, and others, though not with structurally dissimilar compounds such as morphine. For post-mortem screening, assays utilizing antibodies with broad selectivity for drugs within a particular class, such as sympathomimetic amines, are preferred over those with antibodies sensitive to one specific drug such as methamphetamine. Thus, a negative class selective assay can exclude all drugs with which it interacts, albeit with differing sensitivity for individual drugs. Conversely, a positive result requires further testing to distinguish among the possibilities. With few exceptions, all cross-reacting substances are of potential interest to the post-mortem toxicology laboratory.

Immunoassays used for drug screening utilize a competitive interaction between the drug in the specimen and a labeled drug in the reagent, for sites on an antibody specific to the drug being tested. The drug is detected by its ability to displace or block binding of a fixed amount of chemically labeled drug molecules that are included in the reagent. The label can be an enzyme, a fluorescent molecule, a radioactive isotope, or some other substance that can be detected by instrumental means. The object of the assay is to measure either the amount of antibody-bound or the amount of free labeled drug, which is related to the concentration of the targeted drug in the sample.

Some assays can distinguish between bound and free labeled drug in a mixture and are referred to as homogeneous immunoassays. Others require physical separation of bound and free label prior to making the measurement. These are called heterogeneous immunoassays. In general, homogeneous immunoassays are more readily automated and, thus, less labor intensive than heterogeneous immunoassays.

Various types of immunoassays use different detection principles, such as enzyme immunoassay (EIA), fluorescence polarization immunoassay (FPIA), radioimmunoassay (RIA), kinetic interaction of microparticulates in solution (KIMS), and enzyme-linked immunosorbent assay (ELISA). Each type has advantages and disadvantages in terms of cost, throughput, and time for analysis in post-mortem drug screening. The detection limit for various members of a class of drugs (e.g., opiates) or the degree of cross-reactivity for similar drugs (e.g., sympathomimetic amines) varies.

Each manufacturer of immunoassay reagents should be consulted for specific information regarding detection limits for various drugs within a class.

These assays are easy to perform, the results are "semiquantitative" (higher or lower than a predetermined calibrator cutoff concentration) rather than subjective (e.g., TLC), and they generally have low detection limits (0.02 to 1.0 μg/mL). Several non-isotopic immunoassays (e.g., EMIT™, CEDIA®, and FPIA) have been automated for post-mortem drug screening. Immunoassays complement chromatographic procedures (TLC and gas chromatography, GC) because they detect those drugs that would require hydrolysis prior to chromatography (e.g., morphine-3-glucuronide and oxazepam glucuronide), that may require a separate extraction (e.g., benzoylecgonine) or derivatization, or that have high TLC detection limits (e.g., phencyclidine). For abused drugs, immunoassays are the methods of choice for initial screening.

12.3.6.1 Enzyme Immunoassay

General

EIA reagents are available from several manufacturers. Spectrophotometric readings are used to measure the quantity of product produced by an enzyme-catalyzed reaction. The homogeneous EIAs are readily adaptable to automated clinical analyzers for rapid throughput of sample batches with minimal labor. Most are designed for screening urine samples, but they can be adapted for screening unhemolyzed serum or plasma. However, results depend on transmission of light through the reaction mixture, so these assays cannot be applied to turbid, highly colored, or opaque specimens, without first doing labor-intensive pre-extraction steps. The homogeneous EIA reagents are the most economical immunoassays for analysis of urine and stomach contents, although the extra labor required for their application to whole blood and other tissues may offset the reagent savings for those applications.[10–14,142,157–166]

CEDIA

CEDIA assays represent state-of-the-art technique, utilizing two genetically engineered enzymatically inactive fragments of beta-galactosidase as the basis for a homogeneous enzyme immunoassay.[167–173] Two separate genes are engineered to express two separate inactive polypeptide fragments: enzyme-donor (ED) and enzyme-acceptor (EA). These fragments can spontaneously recombine to form active beta-galactosidase enzyme. Ligands can be attached to the ED peptide in such a way that the degree of recombination is controlled by the binding of anti-ligand antibodies to the ED–ligand conjugate. CEDIA methodology is based on the competition between ligand in the sample and ED–ligand conjugate for a limited amount of antibody binding sites. The advantages of the CEDIA immunoassay system over conventional homogeneous EIAs include a linear calibration curve with high precision over the entire assay range, and lower limits of detection of analytes in human body fluids. Assay procedures can easily be automated and can be performed on most automated clinical chemistry analyzers.

ELISA

ELISA assays are heterogeneous enzyme immunoassays conducted in special multiwell (typically 96 wells) assay plates.[174–179] They are more labor intensive than the homogeneous EIAs if assayed manually, although robotic equipment is available to process plates in a semiautomated manner. They require specialized plate readers to measure the reaction products. Costs are somewhat higher than homogeneous EIA reagents; however, ELISA assays are manufactured for some drugs for which no other immunoassay is commercially available (e.g., haloperidol, methylphenidate, phenylbutazone, furosemide, phenothiazine, reserpine, and others). ELISA has the great advantage that it can be used with whole blood, typically diluted with water or buffer, and with proper validation even tissue homogenates.

12.3.6.2   Fluoresence Polarization Immunoassay

FPIA reagents were developed by Abbott Laboratories, and some are also available from Sigma Chemical Company.[99,149,161-164,166,180-194] They are homogeneous immunoassays that can be used only in specialized instruments that are capable of exciting the fluorescein label with polarized ultraviolet light, and then measuring the intensity of polarized fluorescent emissions. Because the sample is highly dilute in the reaction mixture and the instrument measures emitted, rather than transmitted, light, FPIA is less subject to interference by color or turbidity of the sample matrix than are EIAs.

Most hemolyzed or whole blood samples, as well as serum, plasma, and urine, can be analyzed directly without extraction. If the sample is too dark to be analyzed without pretreatment, it can usually be analyzed after diluting with buffer, although with less sensitivity. In addition to their application to drug screening, some of the FPIA assays can yield quantitative measurements, because of the high specificity of their antibodies. The major drawbacks of FPIAs are the high price of reagents and the limited sample capacity of the instruments. The latter problem is being addressed with the introduction of a new high-capacity instrument (Abbott AxSYM™).

12.3.6.3   Radioimmunoassay

RIA reagents are available from several manufacturers. They are heterogeneous immunoassays and, as such, are not readily automated. However, some RIAs have the antibody bound to the inside of the assay tube, which simplifies the separation and wash procedures. Most RIA reagents that are used in toxicology have ^{125}I as the label, and require a gamma counter to measure either bound or unbound label. Reagents are available for many drugs and drug classes, cost is reasonable, and sensitivity is excellent. The major drawbacks of RIA relate to the use of radioactive materials, i.e., the need for radioactive materials licensure and radioactive waste disposal, and the relatively short shelf life of the reagents.[79,145,150-152,161,162,165,174,182,195-202]

12.3.6.4   Kinetic Interaction of Microparticles in Solution

KIMS (OnLine) reagents are available only from Roche Diagnostics. They are homogeneous assays with microscopic particles as the label. In the absence of drug, the labeled drug is bound by antibody, forming light-scattering aggregates. The intensity of light transmitted through the sample is measured spectrophotometrically in an automated clinical analyzer. Light transmission increases with concentration of unlabeled drug in the sample. Reagents are stable and sensitivity is good, although price remains somewhat higher than the EIA reagents.[161,165,166,203-205]

12.3.6.5   Useful Immunoassays for Post-Mortem Toxicology Screening

Amphetamines (Class)

Polyclonal immunoassays for sympathomimetic amines including amphetamine, methamphetamine, phenylpropanolamine, ephedrine, pseudoephedrine, methylenedioxymethamphetamine (MDMA), phentermine, and related compounds are preferred over monoclonal assays for postmortem toxicology. Approximate detection times are 12 h to 3 days. Administrative detection cutoffs are 300 to 1000 ng/mL in urine based on amphetamines or methamphetamine. They may be less sensitive for other drugs within the class.[13,144,167,187,194,203,206-217]

Barbiturates (Class)

Most assays detect pentobarbital, secobarbital, amobarbital, butalbital, phenobarbital, thiopental, and related compounds. Normal detection times are 6 h to 2 days after administration. Detection cutoffs are 300 to 8000 ng/mL in urine depending on cross-reactivity.[145,196,218-221]

Benzodiazepines (Class)

Most benzodiazepine immunoassays use antibodies directed to oxazepam. Their cross-reactivity for other benzodiazepines varies considerably, but most detect diazepam, oxazepam, flurazepam metabolites, chlordiazepoxide metabolites, alprazolam, triazolam, and related compounds. Lorazepam, flunitrazepam metabolites, and some others may not be detected by some immunoassays. Normal detection times are 3 h to 2 weeks. Administrative detection cutoffs are 300 to 3000 ng/mL in urine.[144,146,173,176,181,188,191,192,222-234]

Benzoylecgonine

The cocaine metabolite assays are designed to detect benzoylecgonine, the principal urinary metabolite of cocaine. Cocaine and ecgonine methyl ester may also be detected if present in sufficient concentrations. Normal detection times are 6 h to 5 days. Administrative detection cutoffs are 300 ng/mL in urine.[149,178,179,235-250]

Opiates (Class)

These assays detect a variety of opiates including morphine, morphine-glucuronide, hydromorphone, codeine, hydrocodone, and heroin metabolites. High concentrations of meperidine and oxycodone may give positive test results. Normal detection times are 6 h to 3 days. Administrative detection cutoffs are 300 to 3000 ng/mL in urine.[12,144,154-156,160,165,167,173,202,204,215,245,251-257]

Phencyclidine

The phencyclidine (PCP) assays detect only PCP metabolites. Normal detection times are 24 h. Administrative detection cutoffs are 25 ng/mL in urine.[156,173,221-265]

Propoxyphene

The propoxyphene assays detect the parent drug and the metabolite norpropoxyphene. In abuse situations, methadone (a close structural similarity) and chlorpromazine can produce a false positive. Normal detection time is 24 h. The administrative detection cutoff is 300 ng/mL in urine.[156,226]

Cannabinoids

The cannabinoid assays interact with at least ten of the non-active metabolites of tetrahydrocannabinol (THC). Normal detection times range from hours to weeks, depending on the frequency, potency, dose, and route of administration. Administrative detection cutoffs for the principal urinary metabolites are 20 to 100 ng/mL in urine, depending on the assay.[61,79,148,155,160,161,165,167,205,267-277]

Cyclic Antidepressants (Class)

The immunoassay for tricyclic antidepressants detects amitriptyline, nortriptyline, imipramine, desipramine, and their hydroxy metabolites, clomipramine, doxepin, protriptyline, cyclobenzaprine, and certain phenothiazines. Administrative detection cutoffs are 300 to 2000 ng/mL in urine.[278-283]

12.3.7 Chromatography

Chromatographic drug screening techniques separate components of mixtures by partitioning them between a stationary phase, usually a solid or viscous liquid, and a mobile phase consisting of a gas or liquid. Under a given set of chromatographic conditions, the time required for a substance to traverse the chromatographic column (retention time) or the distance traveled on a TLC plate relative to the solvent front (R_f) is a constant. Separated analytes are detected and identified by a variety of techniques, and often quantitative measurements or semiquantitative estimates of analyte concentration may be made by reference to a standard curve. Chromatographic techniques that are currently used for screening purposes in post-mortem toxicology include TLC, GC, and HPLC.

12.3.7.1 Thin-Layer Chromatography

TLC is a versatile procedure that requires no instrumentation and thus is relatively simple and inexpensive to perform.[16–21,23,82,284–293] However, its application to drug screening requires considerable skill to recognize drug and metabolite patterns and the various detection color hues. TLC techniques employ silica gel or a chemically modified silica gel as the stationary phase. The mobile phase consists of a mixture of organic solvents, often with a small quantity of acid or base to convert acidic or basic drugs to nonionic species. After extraction and specimen spotting, the TLC plates are developed with appropriate solvents to achieve chromatographic resolution. After the chromatogram is developed, drug spots are visualized by chemical modification to colored products or by absorption or fluorescence in ultraviolet light. Drug identifications are based on R_f values, color reactions, and presence of expected metabolite patterns. Standards are included on each plate to compensate for variations in R_f values.

With TLC, a large number of drugs may be detected, and presumptively identified, with a single analysis. TLC may be used to analyze serum, gastric contents, or urine. Urine, however, is the specimen of choice, since most drugs and drug metabolites are present in urine in relatively high concentrations. Although the detection limit varies for each drug, and with the conditions of extraction and detection, it is generally on the order of 0.5 to 4.0 µg/mL. TLC is less sensitive than immunoassay techniques, but its use is not restricted to the detection of only the drug or drugs for which antibodies are available. Literally hundreds of drugs can be detected and identified.

TLC can be used as either a screening or a confirmation procedure in toxicology tests. Many laboratories use TLC as a first screening step, because a wide variety of drugs/toxins can potentially be detected and presumptively identified. When used to screen, confirmation of TLC results can be made by using a variety of other procedures, including GC, GC/mass spectrometry (GC/MS), immunoassay, and HPLC. In some situations, the spot can be scraped from the TLC plate, extracted from the solid phase and injected directly into a GC or GC/MS for confirmation.

TLC will usually produce a spot for any organic drug/toxin that is present in sufficient concentration in urine or other body fluid. The major disadvantage of this technique is its insensitivity. In addition, when urine is the extracted specimen, drug metabolites are often present, and evaluation of a chromatogram containing several drugs and their metabolites can be complicated. However, the presence of known metabolites, when interpreted properly, adds support to the identification of the parent drug. TLC also has the drawback of being subjective in interpretation. A color-blind technologist will have difficulty interpreting the results.

Toxi-Lab® TLC

Over the last 20 years, classical TLC has been largely replaced in the post-mortem toxicology laboratory by the Toxi-Lab® TLC system.[284,290–293] The Toxi-Lab system is a group of products produced by the AnaSys Corporation and marketed through major vendors of laboratory supplies and equipment. The Toxi-Lab TLC plates, Toxi-Grams®, are composed of glass fiber paper impregnated with silica gel or a C-8 (8 carbon aliphatic) reversed-phase sorbent. Drugs are extracted from urine, stomach contents, or other specimens in prepared Toxi-Tubes® containing buffer and an optimized extraction solvent mixture. Sample extracts are evaporated in disposable aluminum cups with small disks of the same material as the plates. As the evaporation proceeds, extracted drugs are adsorbed into the disk, which, when dry, is inserted into a matching hole at the bottom of the plate. Standards are contained in similar disks. Both prestandardized and unstandardized plates are available and standard impregnated disks are available separately.

The prepared plate is developed in a glass chamber with a solvent mixture designated by the manufacturer for each chromatography system. After developing, plates are dried, and then drugs are visualized by sequentially dipping the chromatogram into a series of tanks containing reagents and viewing under long-wave ultraviolet (UV) light. Colors and positions of spots are recorded at each visualization stage. Photographic illustrations of visualization stages and metabolite patterns are available in a compendium comprising more than 100 drugs with new drugs added as data are developed.

An available PC-compatible search program can help with data analysis, yielding statistical probability for identifications. Systems are available to screen for basic and neutral drugs, acidic and neutral drugs, tetrahydrocannabinol metabolites, and opiates, as well as the C-8 reversed-phase system that is used for further differentiating and confirming presumptive findings. In addition, confirmatory procedures for many drugs are described. The Toxi-Lab system is a powerful tool for screening urine and stomach contents. It is less effective for blood and other tissues due to interference from lipids and sensitivity limitations.

12.3.7.2 Gas Chromatography

GC is widely used for qualitative and quantitative drug analysis. It is relatively rapid, and capable of resolving a broad spectrum of drugs. Modern gas chromatography employs fused silica capillary columns that are coated on their inner wall with a liquid stationary phase consisting of a polymer chemically bonded to the silica.[45,80,294] The most common liquid phases are methyl silicones that contain 1, 5, or 50% phenyl side chains. The higher phenyl contents yield higher polarity liquid phases. Other polymers are used for special purposes.

The mobile phase is a gas, i.e., the carrier gas. Usually helium is used, although hydrogen, nitrogen, and gas mixtures may be preferred for some applications. The coiled column, which may be 10 to 60 m in length, is located in an oven having a precisely controlled programmable temperature capability. During a chromatographic analysis, the column temperature may be kept constant, raised at a selected constant rate, or programmed through a series of temperature ramps and isothermal intervals.

The separation capabilities of GC are determined by the polarity of the liquid phase, the flow rate and composition of the carrier gas, and the temperature program. Compounds are separated as a consequence of their different vapor pressures at the column temperature and their affinity for the liquid phase, which is related to their polarity.

In practice, the sample is injected manually or by an autosampler, either as an extract in a suitable organic solvent, or as a vapor of volatile analytes mixed with air or carrier gas. The sample is volatilized in the heated injection port and its constituents are swept into the column. As the analysis proceeds, some components move through the column faster than others, forming discrete bands that progress to the distal end and emerge into the detector, ideally in a pure state. GC detectors of various types recognize particular properties of substances, generating an electrical signal proportional to the quantity of the substance in the detector.

The resulting signal is electronically amplified and recorded on a moving chart or, more commonly, processed by a microcomputer to yield absolute and relative retention time, peak area, and height data for each detected component in the sample. Retention times of sample components, relative to a reference compound (internal standard) that is added to the sample, are constant for a given set of chromatographic conditions. Presumptive identifications are based on relative retention times corresponding with those produced by standards under identical conditions. For drug screening, some laboratories use dual column GCs with both columns originating at the same injection port. The sample is divided between the two columns and analyzed simultaneously on both. Agreement of relative retention times in two columns of differing polarities provides greater certainty of identification.

Some drugs do not chromatograph well with GC because they contain polar functional groups that adhere strongly to the liquid phase or depress the vapor pressure. Such problems can often be overcome by converting the active functional groups to less polar derivatives; such as esters from alcohols, phenols, or carboxylic acids, or amides from amines. Derivatives may be selected to give longer or shorter retention times while improving peak shape and sensitivity.[36,77,88,89,117,295–304]

Several types of detectors are used in post-mortem toxicology laboratories. Each has characteristics that allow for detection and quantification of some, but not all, of the drugs and poisons that are of concern to the post-mortem toxicologist.

Flame Ionization Detector

The flame ionization detector (FID) uses a hydrogen/air flame to oxidize sample components that emerge from the column. Substances containing carbon yield a charged plasma. Electrodes produce a high-voltage field that deflects the charged particles to a collector that produces an electric current with a magnitude proportional to the quantity of the component. The FID detects virtually all drugs that can be passed through the GC; however, lipids and other matrix-derived components interfere with the detection of drugs and limit practical sensitivity.

The FID, once the mainstay of GC in toxicology laboratories, is still used for the analysis of alcohols and other volatile substances in the GC equipped with an automated headspace sampler. Barbiturates and other acidic and neutral drugs are detected and quantified effectively with FID.[305–310] However, most GC basic drug screens typically employ nitrogen/phosphorus detectors (NPD), which provide better sensitivity and selectivity than FID.

Nitrogen/Phosphorus Detector

The NPD has some similarities to the flame ionization detector in that a hydrogen-air flame is used, but the collector is a ceramic bead coated with a rubidium salt. The NPD is insensitive to carbon when properly adjusted, but it responds with high sensitivity to compounds containing nitrogen or phosphorus. Furthermore, it can be tuned to maximize sensitivity to either element. The selectivity for nitrogen makes the NP detector ideal for screening basic drugs, which all contain amine functions.[30,42,43,55,311–314] Lipids and other non-nitrogenous matrix components do not interfere with the analysis.

Electron Capture Detector

The electron capture detector (ECD) contains a radioactive nickel-63 foil that emits high energy electrons (beta particles). The carrier gas is ionized by the radiation, forming anions that establish an ion current between two electrodes. Sample compounds, emerging from the GC column, extract electrons from the ionized gas, decreasing the current flow. The change in current is the signal produced by the detector.

Most substances do not capture electrons and are not detected by the ECD. However, the presence of two or more halogen atoms or a nitro or nitroso group in the molecule allows the substance to be detected. The outstanding sensitivity of the ECD for most polyhalogenated compounds is the reason for its use in the analysis of benzodiazepines.[232,315–317] A laboratory possessing a GC with ECD detector must have a radioactive materials license. A general license is sufficient for sealed detectors, but a specific license is required if the detector can be disassembled.

12.3.7.3 Gas Chromatography/Mass Spectrometry

GC/MS is a powerful analytical tool for identification of semivolatile organic compounds. It combines the separation efficiency of gas chromatography with the structure elucidating capabilities of mass spectrometry.[6,78–83,94,97,98,318–321] When it is used to identify unknown substances in a sample extract, the instrument may be programmed to automatically search for matches against a predefined library (target compound analysis) or it can acquire spectral data for later analysis. In the latter instance, the operator examines a chromatogram peak by peak, extracting background-subtracted spectra and searching spectral libraries by using a pattern-matching algorithm through the instrument's data system. If no acceptable match is found, the spectrum can be visually compared with printed compilations of mass spectral data. Considerable experience is required for effective and efficient substance identification by GC/MS. A chromatogram may consist of hundreds of peaks, most of which represent endogenous compounds. Recognition of frequently encountered patterns can save considerable time by avoiding unnecessary library searches. Conversely, the experienced operator will recognize the novel pattern as one that requires investigation. Nevertheless, a thorough search of a GC/MS data file can take an hour or more.

The price of GC/MS instrumentation has dropped to the point where many laboratories use it as a primary drug screening technique. However, some laboratories still rely on less definitive techniques such as TLC, GC, or class selective immunoassays for pre-screening.[80,255,256,269,297,319,322–324] When GC/MS is employed to identify unknown peaks from a GC analysis, the portion of the chromatogram that must be examined can be narrowed if the same type of column and same column temperature program are used in both instruments. The remaining extract from the GC analysis can be injected into the GC/MS. Knowing the relative retention time of the unknown, the operator can first locate the peak corresponding to the internal standard and then estimate the region of the GC/MS chromatogram where the unknown peak should be. That region is examined carefully to locate and identify a peak whose spectrum is inconsistent with expected endogenous compounds. With some instrumentation it is possible to simultaneously inject extracts onto a system with both MS and NP detector systems. This may be done either by connecting two columns to a single injector or by splitting the effluent from one column into two detectors (one MS, one NP).

In the identification of substances giving rise to unknown spots on TLC, an extract of the sample is analyzed in the GC/MS with a column temperature program extending from below the boiling point of the solvent to 300°C or higher. When the GC/MS run is complete, the entire chromatogram is examined. Time can be saved by initially examining the 20 or 30 largest peaks first. The GC/MS is much more sensitive than TLC, so any component that gives a visible spot should produce a large peak on the GC/MS. Alternatively, the operator may examine all peaks, and detect even substances missed by the TLC analysis. In most cases, such sensitivity is unnecessary for analyzing urine or gastric contents, but it can be useful when potent drugs such as fentanyl or haloperidol must be excluded.

An alternative approach to the identification of unknowns detected by TLC is to scrape the spot from a duplicate plate and analyze it by GC/MS. In practice, a second TLC plate is prepared and developed, but is not sprayed or dipped with color reagents. Instead, the area of the plate corresponding to the unknown spot is scraped (or cut from a Toxi-Gram), and the drug is eluted into a solvent. The solvent is evaporated, and the residue is redissolved and analyzed by GC/MS. This procedure should produce a single major peak on the GC/MS that corresponds to the unknown spot on the TLC plate. The spectrum of the major peak can then be searched to identify the unknown.

GC/MS is often used to identify the drug, or drugs, giving rise to a positive result in a class selective immunoassay test. Such analyses are most efficiently accomplished by methods that search an area of the chromatogram for patterns matching reference spectra in a computer library.

The library is generated by analyzing a standard of each of the targeted drugs and storing a representative spectrum in the data system.[92,199,256,325] The search can be programmed to take place automatically at the end of each data file acquisition. However, the data must be reviewed by the operator before reporting.

GC/MS data can be used for both identification and confirmation in drug screening.[318,320,321,325-327] However, for it to serve as a final confirmation test, the GC/MS analysis should be performed on a separate aliquot or a different specimen from that which yields the initial presumptive finding.

12.3.7.4 High-Performance Liquid Chromatography

HPLC utilizes a column filled with microscopic particles of silica, or resin particles bonded with a polymer whose side chains have specific functional groups.[57,59,64,69,328-332] The polymer is the stationary phase in HPLC, and the nature of the side chains determines the type of interactions the column will have with analytes. Various normal phases and reverse phases are available. Normal phases are characterized by polar side chains such as silica, diol, amino, and cyano, whereas reverse phases have nonpolar side chains such as 8 carbon (C-8) and 18 carbon (C-18) aliphatic and phenyl moieties. Anion and cation exchange phases are also available.

The mobile phase in HPLC is a mixed solvent containing a buffer to suppress or induce ionization of analytes as required for the intended separation. The solvent composition may be kept constant (isocratic) or the percentages of components may be varied (gradient) during the analysis. For instance, in reverse-phase HPLC, the mobile phase will start at higher polarity. As the run proceeds, the polarity is decreased, enabling the removal of any remaining nonpolar substances from the nonpolar reverse phase column, while decreasing the tendency toward broad peaks near the end of a run.

Ultraviolet Absorption Detectors

The most common detection systems for HPLC are UV absorption detectors.[56,64,72,331,332] The less expensive detectors measure absorption at a single wavelength which may be fixed (e.g., at 254 or 280 nm) or variable over a range of 190 to over 340 nm. The variable wavelength detectors are set to a desired wavelength by the operator, and some can be programmed to change wavelengths during the analysis. However, the time required to change wavelengths precludes using variable wavelength detectors for spectral scanning of peaks.

Diode Array Detectors

Photo diode array detectors simultaneously measure absorbance at many small wavelength increments over a broad wavelength band.[46,57,58,64,69,70,73,74,333-348] The detector uses a diffraction grating to break the light beam into a spectrum that is focused onto an array of UV-sensitive photo diodes. Thus, UV spectra of individual peaks can be recorded. A data processing system enables the instrument to determine peak purity by comparing spectra at the leading and tailing ends of a peak and to create and search libraries of target analyte spectra. The sensitivity of the diode array detector is poorer than that of the fixed or variable wavelength, but the availability of spectral data makes it a valuable tool for drug screening.

Fluorescence Detectors

Fluorescence detectors, with variable excitation and emission wavelengths, provide high sensitivity and specificity for the detection and quantification of fluorescent compounds, but they are more useful for quantification than for screening. Fluorescence detection could be used to provide a sensitive screen to target a single substance or a group of substances with similar fluorescence characteristics and different retention times.[56–59]

Advantages and Disadvantages of HPLC

HPLC systems can be equipped with autosamplers, manual injectors, or both. In general, the greatest screening efficiency is achieved through automation. Increased applications of HPLC for drug screening are likely. Substantially more definitive drug identification can be achieved by the use of a mass spectrometer as the HPLC detector. The relatively high cost of these liquid chromatograph/mass spectrometer-coupled instruments limits their current usage for general drug screening or confirmation, although their use is becoming increasingly more common.

HPLC is a more expensive and labor intensive and less sensitive analytical technique than GC, so it is less commonly used for screening. However, it can be used to detect many drugs and poisons that are thermolabile, too polar or lacking in sufficient volatility for analysis by GC. In addition to the qualitative information obtained from the chromatographic retention time, quantification can also be obtained. The signal generated by the detector is proportional to the amount of substance detected. Therefore, by preparing standards of known concentration and treating them in like fashion to the case specimen, the amount of toxin in the specimen can be quantified. The precision of the quantification can be enhanced by adding an internal standard at the beginning of the extraction. The internal standard is usually a compound with similar extraction and chromatographic characteristics to the analytes of interest. The presence of the internal standard permits the quantification to be based on the ratio of analyte to internal standard peak heights or areas. Because ratios are used instead of absolute amounts, the need for quantitative transfers in the extraction process is removed.

REMEDi HS™ HPLC

A commercial, completely automated HPLC system designed for drug screening is available (REMEDi HS; Bio-Rad Laboratories, Hercules, CA).[349–352] This system utilizes four columns in series and column switching techniques to extract, separate, and perform a spectral scan on eluted drugs. Identification of about 500 drugs and metabolites is based on computer matching of retention time and spectra with comparable data stored in the drug library.

Quantification of identified drugs may also be performed. REMEDi HS was developed for the clinical laboratory, but it can be adapted for post-mortem drug screening. Urine, serum, and plasma can be analyzed directly, but whole blood and tissues require manual extraction prior to analysis. Sensitivity for many drugs is not as good as GC with NPD, but should be sufficient for screening urine or stomach contents. If REMEDi HS is applied to screening blood or tissues, sensitivity may not be adequate to detect therapeutic or intoxicating concentrations of some important drugs, but should be adequate for detecting lethal concentrations.

The REMEDi HS system can be complementary to other drug screening techniques, detecting drugs that would otherwise be overlooked and providing corroborative evidence to confirm identifications.

12.3.8 Ultraviolet-Visible Spectrophotometry

Ultraviolet-visible (UV-Vis) spectrophotometry was one of the earliest instrumental techniques used in post-mortem forensic toxicology.[26–29] The use of ultraviolet and visible spectrophotometry as a screening tool is based on the fact that many drugs contain aromatic nuclei that absorb light in the UV and visible regions. Such drugs have absorption spectra with maxima and minima at characteristic wavelengths. Furthermore, the spectrum often changes with the ionization state of the drug in acidic or basic solutions. UV absorption maxima and entire spectra of drugs and poisons are available from various references.

Several limitations, however, affect the use of spectrophotometry. The major limitation is the lack of sensitivity required to detect many of today's therapeutic or misused drugs. Another drawback of spectrophotometry is the requirement that the drug be isolated in a form free from substances with overlapping spectra. Drug mixtures and impure extracts yield mixed spectra that may not be interpretable. In addition, spectrophotometry is not able to distinguish between the parent drug and metabolites. Some of a drug's metabolites may be active while others are inactive, and there is a need to distinguish between these compounds. In spite of these deficiencies, a role remains for spectrophotometric methods for some drug and toxicant analyses. UV spectrometry is especially useful for purity and concentration checks of primary and stock standards.

12.3.9 Spectroscopic Methods for Analysis of Toxic Metals and Metaloids

Toxicologists should be prepared to support investigations that involve toxic exposure to metals and metaloids. Proper sample collection and rigorous state-of-the-art analytical techniques are critical to prevent exogenous contamination.[353,354] A number of different techniques may be employed for the identification of such compounds: flame atomic absorption spectroscopy (FAAS),[355] graphite furnace atomic absorption spectroscopy (GF-AAS),[356,357] inductively coupled plasma-emission spectroscopy (ICPAES),[358] and inductively coupled plasma-mass spectrometry (ICP-MS)[358,359] may all be used. These are sensitive and specific techniques that provide the laboratory with the capability to measure a broad range of metals. An in-depth discussion of methods used for metal analysis is beyond the scope of this chapter.

12.3.10   Sample Preparation

12.3.10.1   Extraction Methods

There are two approaches to the screening of biofluids for drugs or poisons. One is the direct analysis of the specimen for the presence of a specific analyte or its class, without isolation or purification. The other is isolation of the analyte from the sample followed by instrumental analysis of the concentrated extract. The most common example of this is liquid-liquid extraction of an appropriately buffered sample with an immiscible organic solvent.[21,23,25,43,65,66,71,314,360-371] The proper choice of sample, pH, and solvent will effectively remove the target analytes from the aqueous sample matrix.[21,25,362,371-373] Separation of an analyte from interfering substances usually will require more involved techniques.

Liquid–Liquid Extraction

The liquid–liquid extraction technique dates to the mid-19th century when Stas and Otto developed extraction schemes for nonvolatile organic compounds. The method utilizes differences in the pH and solubility characteristics of various analytes. A basic compound is in the non-ionized form in alkaline pH; an acidic compound is in the ionized form in a similar medium. A compound in its non-ionized form prefers the lipophilic environment of an organic solvent to the aqueous environment of the biologic sample. It is on this basis that the separation of drugs from the biologic matrix occurs. The specimen is buffered according to the pH characteristics of the analyte of interest and mixed with an immiscible organic solvent. Commonly used solvents are hexane, toluene, diethyl ether, chlorobutane, dichloromethane, chloroform, or mixtures of these. Ionized compounds and many of the biologic components such as proteins remain in the aqueous layer while the un-ionized drug molecules are transferred to the organic solvent.

The extraction process can be illustrated by taking as an example a basic drug of pK 8, present in plasma. If the plasma is brought to pH 10 using a suitable alkali or alkaline buffer and is shaken with a suitable organic solvent, the drug will be removed from the aqueous into the organic phase.

Unfortunately, many endogenous bases and neutral compounds will also be extracted if they are soluble in the organic solvent. The organic phase is then separated from the aqueous phase (using a Pasteur pipette, for example). This is usually done after centrifugation, to completely separate the two phases.

For drugs that behave like strong acids and bases, a further purification step called back-extraction can be carried out. By shaking the organic phase with dilute acid, such as 0.1 N sulfuric, the basic drug will now be ionized and will no longer be as soluble in the organic phase: it will be extracted into the aqueous phase. Any neutral compounds will be left behind in the organic phase. Endogenous bases may also be co-extracted with the basic drug, but by carefully choosing the pH and the organic solvent the amounts of these bases can be reduced. The acidic aqueous phase is then made alkaline by the addition of a base, such as 2 N sodium hydroxide, and shaken with fresh organic solvent to take the drug into the organic phase. The organic phase can be separated, evaporated, reconstituted, and analyzed.

In many methods the organic phase, containing the drug, is washed with water, and the washings are discarded. This step must be carefully controlled. For example, if the drug is a moderate to strong base and the wash water is even slightly acidic, then some of the drug may be removed into the aqueous phase. If such a process takes place, then low and very erratic recoveries will result.

Before leaving the subject of solvent extraction a number of simple points should be emphasized:

1. In general the least polar solvent capable of extracting the drug in question should be used in order to reduce the possibility of co-extracting endogenous materials. The least polar solvents are the hydrocarbons, such as hexane, toluene, chlorinated hydrocarbons, and diethyl and related ethers. Ethyl acetate is more polar, and the short-chain alcohols are very polar and miscible with water to a greater or lesser degree.
2. Many drugs are so highly lipid soluble that they can be extracted into nonpolar solvents, even in the ionized state. For example, the β-adrenoreceptor blocking drug propranolol has a pK of about 9.5, and therefore in a pH 7.4 buffer it is more than 99% ionized. Since its partition coefficient, between n-octanol and pH 7.4 buffer at 37°C, is 20.2, this means that the ionized drug is highly soluble in n-octanol.
3. Many extraction procedures employ a ratio of solvent to aqueous phase greater than unity in order to reduce the possibility of emulsion formation during extraction. The ideal is a 10:1 solvent-to-sample ratio. There are, however, successful methods that use ratios very much less than unity. Troublesome emulsions can also be avoided or reduced by saturating the aqueous phase with an inorganic salt, such as sodium chloride, before extraction.
4. Recoveries can be increased by using mixed solvents such as hexane: butanol (9:1) or hexane-isoamyl alcohol (97:3). Such solvents are also mandatory to efficiently extract polar drugs or metabolites.
5. Extraction conditions should always be optimized using the relevant biological fluid. It should not be assumed that the extractability from water will exactly match that from blood or tissue homogenates.
6. When extraction conditions have been optimized, it is worthwhile to put a series of specimens through the complete procedure, half of them diluted approximately tenfold. Although this does not always succeed, it can result in cleaner extracts.
7. The multiple step liquid–liquid extraction process is quite effective in separating analytes from biologic specimens, but is also time-consuming. In an attempt to alleviate this time-related problem, solid-phase extraction (SPE) techniques have been developed.

Solid Phase Extraction

In SPE, the specimen is applied to a solid packing material, which is usually, but not exclusively, silica gel based. The sample is partitioned between the matrix and the solid phase, which provides the separation. The general process of SPE involves several steps: (1) column conditioning,

(2) addition of specimen, (3) column washing with solvents to remove interfering substances, and (4) analyte elution.[46–53,55,57,59,63,69,70,72,82,91,308,374–391] Each individual step depends on the analyte of interest, or the type of extraction column, and method development frequently involves a significant amount of trial and error. SPE is utilized in a vast number of analytical methods developed for drug analysis in human post-mortem materials.[392] The advantages of SPE procedures include decreased operator time, reduced solvent volumes, and increased extraction efficiency. In post-mortem toxicology, the availability of automated SPE systems has made this extraction technique attractive to forensic laboratories with a high throughput of post-mortem samples, where several extraction programs adjusted for different analytical methods can be run on the same system. For certain analyses, immunoaffinity SPE techniques may be employed, significantly improving the purity of the sample. This variant of the SPE technique has been used in the analysis of a large number of drugs.[393]

A little more than a decade ago, solid-phase microextraction (SPME) was introduced and the technique has since been extensively used in several areas, including analysis of drugs and endogenous compounds.[394,395] SPME has many advantages over other extraction methods; it is simple, rapid, efficient, and requires no solvent. All steps of sample preparation, i.e., extraction, concentration, derivatization, and transfer to the chromatograph, are integrated in one step and in one device. In forensic toxicology applications of this technique include analytical methods for barbiturates,[396] drug screening in hair,[397] organophosphates,[398] GHB,[399] and certain pharmaceutical drugs.[400] SPME is typically followed by GC/MS or LC/MS analysis, but may be combined with other methods. Recently, SPME has been applied in a methodological approach to determine the binding parameters of drugs to human serum albumin. From these parameters the concentrations of albumin, free drug, and total drug can be calculated in unknown mixtures.[401]

A closely related technique is solid-phase dynamic extraction (SPDE), based on an inside needle capillary absorption trap. An automated HS-SPDE-GC-MS procedure was developed and applied for analysis of drugs of abuse in hair, and was found to provide, compared with SPME, a higher extraction rate, in addition to a faster automated operation and greater stability of the device.[402]

Summing up, the development of the several different modifications of solid-phase extraction techniques in recent years is impressive, and is comparable to the rapid innovations in LC/MS instrumentation. It seems likely that we will face a large number of new methodological concepts and applications of SPE techniques that will resolve several analytical problems in forensic toxicology.

pH Adjustment for Extraction

Weakly acidic drugs, such as barbiturates, primidone, and phenytoin, can be separated from the specimen by using a liquid–liquid or solid-phase extraction at pH 5. This extraction also removes some neutral drugs, such as meprobamate, glutethimide, and carbamazepine. After solvent concentration, these drugs can be identified by TLC, GC, or HPLC.

The largest group of drugs that are normally encountered in the post-mortem laboratory are the organic bases. These include antiarrhythmics, antidepressants, antihistamines, benzodiazepines, cocaine, narcotic analgesics, nicotine, phencyclidine, phenothiazines, and sympathomimetic amines. These drugs all extract under alkaline conditions.

Amphoteric drugs such as morphine and benzoylecgonine require careful adjustment of pH for their efficient extraction by liquid–liquid procedures. Amphoteric compounds contain both acidic and basic functional groups. If the aqueous phase is too acidic or too basic, one of the functional groups will be ionized, and extraction will be inefficient. The pH must be close to the isoelectric point for high recovery by liquid–liquid extraction. Such compounds may be isolated by solid phase techniques, if a column with ion exchange functions is used. The pH is adjusted to completely ionize one of the functional groups in the analyte. The appropriate solid phase will capture ionized analyte as the sample passes through. The sorbent is washed to remove impurities, and then the analyte is recovered in either an acidic or basic elution solvent in order to reverse its ionization.

12.3.10.2 Hydrolysis to Release Drugs in Sample Pretreatment

Before extraction, tissues may be homogenized with a blender or an ultrasonic disruptor, or they may be hydrolyzed by enzymes such as Subtilysin Carlsburg or Protease K to produce a homogeneous fluid sample.[39,365,378,403] Conjugates can be cleaved by gentle but time-consuming enzymatic hydrolysis, or by rapid acid hydrolysis.[34,53,117,224,227,404,405] However, the formation of artifacts during the latter procedure must be considered.

12.3.10.3 Applications

Universal liquid–liquid extraction procedures are preferable for general unknown analysis because substances with very different physicochemical properties must be isolated from heterogeneous matrices. On the other hand, solid-phase extraction is preferable if target compounds must be selectively isolated from relatively homogeneous samples, such as urine for confirmation of a single drug, or metabolite, or a group of drugs with similar extraction properties.

REFERENCES

1. Jackson, J.V., Forensic toxicology, in *Clarke's Isolation and Identification of Drugs in Pharmaceuticals, Body Fluids, and Post-Mortem Material*, 2nd ed., Moffatt, A.C., Ed., Pharmaceutical Press, London, 1986, 35.
2. Jentzen, J.M., Forensic toxicology. An overview and an algorithmic approach, *Am. J. Clin. Pathol.*, 92, S48–55, 1989.
3. Stewart, C.P. and Martin, G.J., The mode of action of poisons, in *Toxicology: Mechanisms and Analytical Methods*, Vol. 2, Stewart, C.P. and Stolman, A., Eds., Academic Press, New York, 1960, 1–15.
4. Stewart, C.P. and Stolman, A., The toxicologist and his work, in *Toxicology: Mechanisms and Analytical Methods*, Stewart, C.P. and Stolman, A., Eds., Vol. 1, Academic Press, New York, 1960, 1–22.
5. Garriott, J.C., Drug analysis in postmortem toxicology, *Chem. Anal.* (New York), 85, 353–376, 1986.
6. Costello, C.E., GC/MS analysis of street drugs, particularly in the body fluids of overdose victims, in *Street Drug Analysis and Its Social and Clinical Implications*, John Wiley & Sons, New York, 1974, 67–78.
7. Walker, S. and Johnston, A., Laboratory screening of body fluids in self poisoning and drug abuse, *Ann. Acad. Med. Singapore*, 20, 91–94, 1991.
8. Duncan, W.P. and Deutsch, D.G., The use of GC/IR/MS for high-confidence identification of drugs, *Clin. Chem.*, 35, 1279–1281, 1989.
9. Kinberger, B., Holmen, A., and Wahrgren, P., A strategy for drug analysis in serum and urine. An application to drug screening of samples from drivers involved in traffic accidents, *Anal. Lett.*, 15, 937–951, 1982.
10. Rowley, G.L., Armstrong, T.A., Crowl, C.P., Eimstad, W.M., Hu, W.M., Kam, J.K. et al., Determination of THC and its metabolites by EMIT homogeneous enzyme immunoassay: a summary report, *NIDA Res. Monogr.*, 7, 28–32, 1976.
11. Walberg, C.B., Correlation of the "EMIT" urine barbiturate assay with a spectrophotometric serum barbiturate assay in suspected overdose, *Clin. Chem.*, 20, 305–306, 1974.
12. Cavanagh, K., Draisey, T.F., and Thibert, R.J., Assessment of the EMIT technique as a screening test for opiates and methadone for a methadone maintenance clinic and its calibration by Bayesian statistics, *Clin. Biochem.*, 11, 210–213, 1978.
13. Oellerich, M., Kulpmann, W.R., and Haeckel, R., Drug screening by enzyme immunoassay (EMIT) and thin-layer chromatography (Drug Skreen), *J. Clin. Chem. Clin. Biochem.*, 15, 275–283, 1977.
14. Fletcher, S.M., Urine screening for drugs by EMIT, *J. Forensic Sci. Soc.*, 21, 327–332, 1981.
15. Davidow, B., Li Petri, N., and Quame, B., A thin-layer chromatographic screening procedure for detecting drug abuse, *Tech. Bull. Registry Med. Technol.*, 38, 298–303, 1968.

16. Kaistha, K.K. and Jaffe, J.H., TLC techniques for identification of narcotics, barbiturates, and CNS stimulants in a drug abuse urine screening program, *J. Pharm. Sci.*, 61, 679–689, 1972.

17. Siek, T., Thin-layer and gas chromatography as identification aids in forensic science, *Analabs (Res. Notes)*, 13, 1–15, 1973.

18. Davidow, B., Quame, B., Abell, L.L., and Lim, B., Screening for drug abuse, *Health Lab. Sci.*, 10, 329–334, 1973.

19. Davidow, B. and Fastlich, E., The application of thin-layer chromatography and of other methods for the detection of drug abuse, *Prog. Clin. Pathol.*, 5, 85–98, 1973.

20. Masoud, A.N., Systematic identification of drugs of abuse. II: TLC, *J. Pharm. Sci.*, 65, 1585–1589, 1976.

21. Hackett, L.P. and Dusci, L.J., Rapid identification of drugs in the overdosed patient, *Clin. Toxicol.*, 11, 341–352, 1977.

22. Sunshine, I., *CRC Handbook Series in Clinical Laboratory Science: Section B: Toxicology,* Vol. I, CRC Press, West Palm Beach, FL, 1978, 3–269.

23. Warfield, R.W. and Maickel, R.P., A generalized extraction-TLC procedure for identification of drugs, *J. Appl. Toxicol.*, 3, 51–57, 1983.

24. Foerster, E.H., Hatchett, H., Garriott, J.C., A rapid, comprehensive screening procedure for basic drugs in blood or tissues by gas chromatography, *J. Anal. Toxicol.*, 2, 50–55, 1978.

25. Dusci, L.J. and Hackett, L.P., The detection of some basic drugs and their major metabolites using gas-liquid chromatography, *Clin. Toxicol.*, 14, 587–593, 1979.

26. Siek, T.J. and Osiewicz, R.J., Identification of drugs and other toxic compounds from their ultraviolet spectra. Part II: Ultraviolet absorption properties of thirteen structural groups, *J. Forensic Sci.*, 20, 18–37, 1975.

27. Siek, T.J., Osiewicz, R.J., and Bath, R.J., Identification of drugs and other toxic compounds from their ultraviolet spectra. Part III: Ultraviolet absorption properties of 22 structural groups, *J. Forensic Sci.*, 21, 525–551, 1976.

28. Feldstein, M., Spectrum analysis: B. Absorption spectra Part 1: The use of ultraviolet spectra in toxicological analysis, in *Toxicology: Mechanisms and Analytical Methods*, Vol. 1, Stewart, C.P. and Stolman, A., Eds., Academic Press, New York, 1960, 464–506.

29. Curry, S., Spectrum analysis: B. Absorption spectra Part 2: Ultraviolet spectrophotometry, in *Toxicology: Mechanisms and Analytical Methods*, Vol. 1, Stewart, C.P. and Stolman, A., Eds., Academic Press, New York, 1960, 507–555.

30. Demedts, P., De Waele, M., Van der Verren, J., and Heyndrickx, A., Application of the combined use of fused silica capillary columns and NPD for the toxicological determination of codeine and ethylmorphine in a human overdose case, *J. Anal. Toxicol.*, 7, 113–115, 1983.

31. Anderson, W.H. and Archuleta, M.M., The capillary gas chromatographic determination of trazodone in biological specimens, *J. Anal. Toxicol.*, 8, 217–219, 1984.

32. Francom, P., Andrenyak, D., Lim, H.K., Bridges, R.R., Foltz, R.L., and Jones, R.T., Determination of LSD in urine by capillary column gas chromatography and electron impact mass spectrometry, *J. Anal. Toxicol.*, 12, 1–8, 1988.

33. Feng, N., Vollenweider, F.X., Minder, E.I., Rentsch, K., Grampp, T., and Vonderschmitt, D.J., Development of a gas chromatography-mass spectrometry method for determination of ketamine in plasma and its application to human samples, *Ther. Drug Monit.*, 17, 95–100, 1995.

34. Meatherall, R., GC/MS confirmation of urinary benzodiazepine metabolites, *J. Anal. Toxicol.*, 18, 369–381, 1994.

35. Taylor, R.W., Greutink, C., and Jain, N.C., Identification of underivatized basic drugs in urine by capillary column gas chromatography, *J. Anal. Toxicol.*, 10, 205–208, 1986.

36. Christophersen, A.S., Biseth, A., Skuterud, B., and Gadeholt, G., Identification of opiates in urine by capillary column gas chromatography of two different derivatives, *J. Chromatogr.*, 422, 117–124, 1987.

37. Lee, X.P., Kumazawa, T., and Sato, K., Rapid extraction and capillary gas chromatography for diazine herbicides in human body fluids, *Forensic Sci. Int.*, 72, 199–207, 1995.

38. Seno, H., Suzuki, O., Kumazawa, T., and Hattori, H., Rapid isolation with Sep-Pak C18 cartridges and wide-bore capillary gas chromatography of benzophenones, the acid-hydrolysis products of benzodiazepines, *J. Anal. Toxicol.*, 15, 21–24, 1991.

39. Turcant, A., Premel-Cabic, A., Cailleux, A., and Allain, P., Screening for neutral and basic drugs in blood by dual fused-silica column chromatography with nitrogen-phosphorus detection [published erratum appears in *Clin. Chem.* 34(11):2370, 1988], *Clin. Chem.*, 34, 1492–1497, 1988.

40. Watts, V.W. and Simonick, T.F., Screening of basic drugs in biological samples using dual column capillary chromatography and nitrogen-phosphorus detectors, *J. Anal. Toxicol.*, 10, 198–204, 1986.

41. Anderson, W.H. and Fuller, D.C., A simplified procedure for the isolation, characterization, and identification of weak acid and neutral drugs from whole blood, *J. Anal. Toxicol.*, 11, 198–204, 1987.

42. Cox, R.A., Crifasi, J.A., Dickey, R.E., Ketzler, S.C., and Pshak, G.L., A single-step extraction for screening whole blood for basic drugs by capillary GC/NPD, *J. Anal. Toxicol.*, 13, 224–228, 1989.

43. Fretthold, D., Jones, P., Sebrosky, G., and Sunshine, I., Testing for basic drugs in biological fluids by solvent extraction and dual capillary GC/NPD, *J. Anal. Toxicol.*, 10, 10–14, 1986.

44. Perrigo, B.J., Peel, H.W., and Ballantyne, D.J., Use of dual-column fused-silica capillary gas chromatography in combination with detector response factors for analytical toxicology, *J. Chromatogr.*, 341, 81–88, 1985.

45. Bogusz, M., Bialka, J., Gierz, J., and Klys, M., Use of short, wide-bore capillary columns in GC toxicological screening, *J. Anal. Toxicol.*, 10, 135–138, 1986.

46. Theodoridis, G., Papadoyannis, I., Tsoukali-Papadopoulou, H., and Vasilikiotis, G., A comparative study of different solid phase extraction procedures for the analysis of alkaloids of forensic interest in biological fluids by RP-HPLC/diode array, *J. Liquid Chromatogr.*, 18, 1973–1995, 1973.

47. Taylor, R.W., Jain, N.C., and George, M.P., Simultaneous identification of cocaine and benzoylecgonine using solid phase extraction and gas chromatography/mass spectrometry, *J. Anal. Toxicol.*, 11, 233–234, 1987.

48. Casas, M., Berrueta, L.A., Gallo, B., and Vicente, F., Solid phase extraction conditions for the selective isolation of drugs from biological fluids predicted using liquid chromatography, *Chromatographia*, 34, 79–82, 1992.

49. Platoff, G.E., Jr. and Gere, J.A., Solid phase extraction of abused drugs from urine, *Forensic Sci. Rev.*, 3, 117–133, 1992.

50. Chen, X.H., Hommerson, A.L., Zweipfenning, P.G., Franke, J.P., Harmen-Boverhof, C.W., Ensing, K. et al., Solid phase extraction of morphine from whole blood by means of Bond Elut Certify columns, *J. Forensic Sci.*, 38, 668–676, 1993.

51. Dixit, V. and Dixit, V.M., Solid phase extraction of phencyclidine with GC/MS confirmation, *Indian J. Chem. Sect. B*, 30, 164–168, 1991.

52. Marko, V. and Bauerova, K., Study of the solid phase extraction of pentoxifylline and its major metabolite as a basis of their rapid low concentration gas chromatographic determination in serum, *Biomed. Chromatogr.*, 5, 256–261, 1991.

53. Huang, W., Andollo, W., and Hearn, W.L., A solid phase extraction technique for the isolation and identification of opiates in urine, *J. Anal. Toxicol.*, 16, 307–310, 1992.

54. Kintz, P., Tracqui, A., Mangin, P., Lugnier, A., and Chaumont, A., Subnanogram GC/NPD method for the determination of sparteine in biological fluids, *Methods Findings Exp. Clin. Pharmacol.*, 11, 115–118, 1989.

55. Taylor, R.W., Le, S.D., Philip, S., and Jain, N.C., Simultaneous identification of amphetamine and methamphetamine using solid-phase extraction and GC/NPD or GC/MS, *J. Anal. Toxicol.*, 13, 293–295, 1989.

56. Binder, S.R., Analysis of drugs of abuse in biological fluids by liquid chromatography, in *Advances in Chromatography*, Vol. 36, Brown, P. and Grushka, E., Eds., Marcel Dekker, New York, 1996.

57. Akerman, K.K., Jolkkonen, J., Parviainen, M., and Penttila, I., Analysis of low-dose benzodiazepines by HPLC with automated solid-phase extraction, *Clin. Chem.*, 42, 1412–1416, 1996.

58. Clauwaert, K.M., Vanbocxlaer, J.F., Lambert, W.E., and Deleenheer, A.P., Analysis of cocaine, benzoylecgonine, and cocaethylene in urine by HPLC with diode array detection, *Anal. Chem.*, 68, 3021–3028, 1996.

59. Bourque, A.J., Krull, I.S., and Feibush, B., Automated HPLC analyses of drugs of abuse via direct injection of biological fluids followed by simultaneous solid-phase extraction and derivatization with fluorescence detection, *Biomed. Chromatogr.*, 8, 53–62, 1994.

60. Gill, R., Moffat, A.C., Smith, R.M., and Hurdley, T.G., A collaborative study to investigate the retention reproducibility of barbiturates in HPLC with a view to establishing retention databases for drug identification, *J. Chromatogr. Sci.,* 24, 153–159, 1986.

61. Bogusz, M., Hill, D.W., and Rehorek, A., Comparability of RP-HPLC Retention indices of drugs in three databases, *J. Liquid Chromatogr. Relat. Technol.,* 19(8), 1291–1316, 1996.

62. Law, B., Williams, P.L., and Moffat, A.C., The detection and quantification of cannabinoids in blood and urine by RIA, HPLC/RIA and GC/MS, *Vet. Hum. Toxicol.,* 21, 144–147, 1979.

63. Moore, C., Browne, S., Tebbett, I., and Negrusz, A., Determination of cocaine and its metabolites in brain tissue using high-flow solid-phase extraction columns and HPLC, *Forensic Sci. Int.,* 53, 215–219, 1992.

64. Wong, A.S., An evaluation of HPLC for the screening and quantitation of benzodiazepines and acetaminophen in post mortem blood, *J. Anal. Toxicol.,* 7, 33–36, 1983.

65. Bernal, J.L., Delnozal, M.J., Rosas, V., and Villarino, A., Extraction of basic drugs from whole blood and determination by HPLC, *Chromatographia,* 38, 617–623, 1994.

66. Pawula, M., Barrett, D.A., and Shaw, P.N., An improved extraction method for the HPLC determination of morphine and its metabolites in plasma, *J. Pharm. Biomed. Anal.,* 11, 401–406, 1993.

67. Bogusz, M., Influence of elution conditions on HPLC retention index values of selected acidic and basic drugs measured in the 1-nitroalkane scale, *J. Anal. Toxicol.,* 15, 174–178, 1991.

68. Bogusz, M. and Erkens, M., Influence of biological matrix on chromatographic behavior and detection of selected acidic, neutral, and basic drugs examined by means of a standardized HPLC-DAD system, *J. Anal. Toxicol.,* 19, 49–55, 1995.

69. Logan, B.K., Stafford, D.T., Tebbett, I.R., and Moore, C.M., Rapid screening for 100 basic drugs and metabolites in urine using cation exchange solid-phase extraction and HPLC with diode array detection, *J. Anal. Toxicol.,* 14, 154–159, 1990.

70. Musshoff, F. and Daldrup, T., A rapid solid-phase extraction and HPLC/DAD procedure for the simultaneous determination and quantification of different benzodiazepines in serum, blood and post-mortem blood, *Int. J. Legal Med.,* 105, 105–109, 1992.

71. Mayer, F., Kramer, B.K., Ress, K.M., Kuhlkamp, V., Liebich, H.M., Risler, T. et al., Simplified, rapid and inexpensive extraction procedure for a high-performance liquid chromatographic method for determination of disopyramide and its main metabolite mono-*N*-dealkylated disopyramide in serum, *J. Chromatogr.,* 572, 339–345, 1991.

72. Ferrara, S.D., Tedeschi, L., Frison, G., and Castagna, F., Solid-phase extraction and HPLC-UV confirmation of drugs of abuse in urine, *J. Anal. Toxicol.,* 16, 217–222, 1992.

73. Bogusz, M. and Wu, M., Standardized HPLC/DAD system, based on retention indices and spectral library, applicable for systematic toxicological screening [published erratum appears in *J. Anal. Toxicol.,* 16(3), 16A, 1992], *J. Anal. Toxicol.,* 15, 188–197, 1991.

74. Tracqui, A., Kintz, P., and Mangin, P., Systematic toxicological analysis using HPLC/DAD, *J. Forensic Sci.,* 40, 254–262, 1995.

75. Wu, A.H., Onigbinde, T.A., Wong, S.S., and Johnson, K.G., Evaluation of full-scanning GC/ion trap MS analysis of NIDA drugs-of-abuse urine testing in urine, *J. Anal. Toxicol.,* 16, 202–206, 1992.

76. Schuberth, J., Volatile compounds detected in blood of drunk drivers by headspace/capillary gas chromatography/ion trap mass spectrometry, *Biol. Mass Spectrom.,* 20, 699–702, 1991.

77. McCurdy, H.H., Lewellen, L.J., Callahan, L.S., and Childs, P.S., Evaluation of the Ion Trap Detector for the detection of 11-nor-delta 9-THC-9-carboxylic acid in urine after extraction by bonded-phase adsorption, *J. Anal. Toxicol.,* 10, 175–177, 1986.

78. Hernandez, A., Andollo, W., and Hearn, W.L., Analysis of cocaine and metabolites in brain using solid phase extraction and full-scanning gas chromatography/ion trap mass spectrometry, *Forensic Sci. Int.,* 65, 149–156, 1994.

79. Moody, D.E., Rittenhouse, L.F., and Monti, K.M., Analysis of forensic specimens for cannabinoids. I. Comparison of RIA and GC/MS analysis of blood, *J. Anal. Toxicol.,* 16, 297–301, 1992.

80. Pettersen, J.E. and Skuterud, B., Application of combined GC/MS as compared to a conventional analytical system for identification of unknown drugs in acute drug intoxications, *Anal. Chem. Symp. Ser.,* 13, 111–129, 1983.

81. Ullucci, P.A., Cadoret, R., Stasiowski, D., and Martin, H.F., A comprehensive GC/MS drug screening procedure., *J. Anal. Toxicol.,* 2, 33–35, 1978.

82. Lillsunde, P. and Korte, T., Comprehensive drug screening in urine using solid-phase extraction and combined TLC and GC/MS identification, *J. Anal. Toxicol.*, 15, 71–81, 1991.

83. Finkle, B.S., Foltz, R.L., and Taylor, D.M., A comprehensive GC/MS reference data system for toxicological and biomedical purposes., *J. Chromatogr. Sci.*, 12, 304–328, 1974.

84. Clouette, R., Jacob, M., Koteel, P., and Spain, M., Confirmation of 11-nor-delta 9-tetrahydrocannabinol in urine as its t-butyldimethylsilyl derivative using GC/MS, *J. Anal. Toxicol.*, 17, 1–4, 1993.

85. Bellanca, J.A., Davis, P.L., Donnelly, B., Dal Cortivo, L.A., and Weinberg, S.B., Detection and quantitation of multiple volatile compounds in tissues by GC and GC/MS, *J. Anal. Toxicol.*, 6, 238–240, 1982.

86. Fehn, J. and Megges, G., Detection of O6-monoacetylmorphine in urine samples by GC/MS as evidence for heroin use, *J. Anal. Toxicol.*, 9, 134–138, 1985.

87. Dunemann, L. and Hajimiragha, H., Development of a screening method for the determination of volatile organic compounds in body fluids and environmental samples using purge and trap GC/MS, *Anal. Chim. Acta*, 283, 199–204, 1993.

88. West, R. and Ritz, D., GC/MS analysis of five common benzodiazepine metabolites in urine as tert-butyl-dimethylsilyl derivatives, *J. Anal. Toxicol.*, 17, 114–116, 1993.

89. Wimbish, G.H. and Johnson, K.G., Full spectral GC/MS identification of delta 9-carboxy-tetrahydrocannabinol in urine with the Finnigan ITS40, *J. Anal. Toxicol.*, 14, 292–295, 1990.

90. Zune, A., Dobberstein, P., Maurer, K.H., and Rapp, U., Identification of drugs using a gas chromatography-mass spectrometry system equipped with electron impact-chemical ionization and electron impact-field ionization field desorption combination sources, *J. Chromatogr.*, 122, 365–371, 1976.

91 Liu, R.H., McKeehan, A.M., Edwards, C., Foster, G., Bensley, W.D., Langner, J.G. et al., Improved GC/MS analysis of barbiturates in urine using centrifuge-based solid-phase extraction, methylation, with d5- pentobarbital as internal standard, *J. Forensic Sci.*, 39, 1504–1514, 1994.

92. Van Vyncht, G., Gaspar, P., DePauw, E., and Maguin-Rogister, G., Multi-residue screening and confirmatory analysis of anabolic steroids in urine by GC/MS/MS, *J. Chromatogr.*, A, 683, 67–74, 1994.

93. Maurer, H.H., On the metabolism and the toxicological analysis of methylenedioxyphenyl-alkylamine designer drugs by gas chromatography mass spectrometry, *Ther. Drug Monit.*, 18, 465–470, 1996.

94. Saady, J.J., Narasimhachari, N., and Blanke, R.V., Rapid, simultaneous quantification of morphine, codeine, and hydromorphone by GC/MS, *J. Anal. Toxicol.*, 6, 235–237, 1982.

95. Wu Chen, N.B., Cody, J.T., Garriott, J.C., Foltz, R.L., Peat, M.A., and Schaffer, M.I., Recommended guidelines for forensic GC/MS procedures in toxicology laboratories associated with offices of medical examiners and/or coroners, *J. Forensic Sci.*, 35, 236–242, 1990.

96. Moeller, M., Doerr, G., and Warth, S., Simultaneous quantitation of delta-9-tetrahydrocannabinol (THC) and 11-nor-9-carboxy-delta-9-tetrahydrocannabinol (THC-COOH) in serum by GC/MS using deuterated internal standards and its application to a smoking study and forensic cases, *J. Forensic Sci.*, 37, 969–983, 1992.

97 Gibb, R.P., Cockerham, H., Goldfogel, G.A., Lawson, G.M., and Raisys, V.A., Substance abuse testing of urine by GC/MS in scanning mode evaluated by proficiency studies, TLC/GC, and EMIT, *J. Forensic Sci.*, 38, 124–133, 1993.

98. Maurer, H.H., Systematic toxicological analysis of drugs and their metabolites by gas chromatography-mass spectrometry [review], *J. Chromatogr.*, 580, 3–41, 1992.

99. Maurer, H.H. and Kraemer, T., Toxicological detection of selegiline and its metabolites in urine using fluorescence polarization immunoassay (FPIA) and gas chromatography-mass spectrometry (GC/MS) and differentiation by enantioselective GC/MS of the intake of selegiline from abuse of methamphetamine or amphetamine, *Arch. Toxicol.*, 66, 675–678, 1992.

100. Covey, T.R., Lee, E.D., and Henion, J.D., High-speed LC/MS/MS for the determination of drugs in biological samples, *Anal. Chem.*, 58, 2453–2460, 1986.

101. Brotherton, H.O. and Yost, R.A., Determination of drugs in blood serum by MS/MS, *Anal. Chem.*, 55, 549–553, 1983.

102. Phillips, W.H., Jr., Ota, K., and Wade, N.A., Tandem mass spectrometry (MS/MS) utilizing electron impact ionization and multiple reaction monitoring for the rapid, sensitive, and specific identification and quantitation of morphine in whole blood, *J. Anal. Toxicol.*, 13, 268–273, 1989.

103. Kerns, E., Lee, M.S., Mayol, R., and Klunk, L.J., Comparison of drug metabolite identification methods: rapid MS/MS screening versus isolation and GC/MS analysis, presented at 38th ASMS Conference, Tucson, AZ, 1990.

104. Gilbert, J.D., Greber, T.F., Ellis, J.D., Barrish, A., Olah, T.V., Fernandez-Metzler, C. et al., The development and cross-validation of methods based on radioimmunoassay and LC/MS/MS for the quantification of the class III antiarrhythmic agent, MK-0499, in human plasma and urine, *J. Pharm. Biomed. Anal.*, 13, 937–950, 1995.

105. Henion, J., Crowthers, J., and Covey, T., An improved thermospray LC/MS system for determining drugs in urine, *Proc. ASMS*, 32, 203–204, 1984.

106. Verheij, E.R., van der Greef, J., La Vos, G.F., van der Pol, W., and Niessen, W.M., Identification of diuron and four of its metabolites in human postmortem plasma and urine by LC/MS with a moving-belt interface, *J. Anal. Toxicol.*, 13, 8–12, 1989.

107. Koves, E.M. and Yen, B., The use of gas chromatography/negative ion chemical ionization mass spectrometry for the determination of lorazepam in whole blood, *J. Anal. Toxicol.*, 13, 69–72, 1989.

108. Leloux, M. and Maes, R., The use of electron impact and positive chemical ionization mass spectrometry in the screening of beta blockers and their metabolites in human urine, *Biomed. Environ. Mass Spectrom.*, 19, 137–142, 1990.

109. Cailleux, A. and Allain, P., Superiority of chemical ionization on electron impact for identification of drugs by GC/MS, *J. Anal. Toxicol.*, 3, 39–41, 1979.

110. Harkey, M.R., Henderson, G.L., and Zhou, C., Simultaneous quantitation of cocaine and its major metabolites in human hair by gas chromatography/chemical ionization mass spectrometry, *J. Anal. Toxicol.*, 15, 260–265, 1991.

111. Ohno, Y. and Kawabata, S., Rapid detection of illicit drugs by direct inlet chemical ionization mass spectrometry, *Kanzei Chuo Bunsekishoho*, 27, 7–15, 1987.

112. Mulvana, D.E., Duncan, G.F., Shyu, W.C., Tay, L.K., and Barbhaiya, R.H., Quantitative determination of butorphanol and its metabolites in human plasma by gas chromatography electron capture negative-ion chemical ionization mass spectrometry, *J. Chromatogr. B Biomed. Appl.*, 682, 289–300, 1996.

113. Milne, G.W.A., Foles, H.M., and Axenrod, T., Identification of dangerous drugs by isobutane chemical ionization mass spectrometry, *Anal. Chem.*, 43, 1815–1820, 1971.

114. Wu, W.S., Szklar, R.S., and Smith, R., Gas chromatographic determination and negative-ion chemical ionization mass spectrometric confirmation of 4,4´-methylenebis(2-chloroaniline) in urine via thin-layer chromatographic separation, *Analyst*, 121, 321–324, 1996.

115. Saferstein, R., Manura, J.J., and De, P.K., Drug detection in urine by chemical ionization-mass spectrometry, *J. Forensic Sci.*, 23, 29–36, 1978.

116. Wolen, R.L., Ziege, E.A., and Gruber, C., Jr., Determination of propoxyphene and norpropoxyphene by chemical ionization mass fragmentography, *Clin. Pharmacol. Ther.*, 17, 15–20, 1975.

117. Fitzgerald, R.L., Rexin, D.A., and Herold, D.A., Benzodiazepine analysis by negative chemical ionization gas chromatography-mass spectrometry, *J. Anal. Toxicol.*, 17, 342–347, 1993.

118. Suzuki, O., Hattori, H., and Asano, M., Detection of methamphetamine and amphetamine in a single human hair by gas chromatography-chemical ionization mass spectrometry, *J. Forensic Sci.*, 29, 611–617, 1984.

119. Sosnoff, C.S., Ann, Q., Bernert, J.T., Jr., Powell, M.K., Miller, B.B., Henderson, L.O. et al., Analysis of benzoylecgonine in dried blood spots by liquid chromatography — atmospheric pressure chemical ionization tandem mass spectrometry, *J. Anal. Toxicol.*, 20, 179–184, 1996.

120. Vidal, D.L., Ting, E.J., Perez, S.L., Taylor, R.W., and Le, S.D., Robotic method for the analysis of morphine and codeine in urine, *J. Forensic Sci.*, 37(5), 1283–1294, 1992.

121. Lloyd, T.L., Perschy, T.B., Gooding, A.E., and Tomlinson, J.J., Robotic solid phase extraction and high performance liquid chromatographic analysis of ranitidine in serum or plasma, *Biomed. Chromatogr.*, 6, 311–316, 1992.

122. Taylor, R.W. and Le, S.D., Robotic method for the analysis of cocaine and benzoylecgonine in urine, *J. Anal. Toxicol.*, 15, 276–278, 1991.

123. de Kanel, J., Korbar, T., Robotics and the analysis of drugs of abuse, in *Analysis of Addictive and Misused Drugs*, Adamovics, J.A., Ed., Marcel Dekker, New York, 1995, 267–294.

124. Clarke, E. and Williams, M., Microcolor tests in toxicology, *J. Pharm. Pharmacol.*, 7, 255–262, 1955.

125. Stevens, H.M., Color tests, in *Clarke's Isolation and Identification of Drugs in Pharmaceuticals, Body Fluids and Postmortem Material*, Moffat, A.C., Ed., Pharmaceutical Press, London, 1986, 28–147.

126. Widdop, B., Hospital toxicology and drug abuse screening, in *Clarke's Isolation and Identification of Drugs in Pharmaceuticals, Body Fluids and Postmortem Material*, Moffat, A.C., Ed., Pharmaceutical Press, London, 1986, 4–6.

127. Masoud, A.N., Systematic identification of drugs of abuse. I: spot tests, *J. Pharm. Sci.*, 64, 841–844, 1975.

128. Berry, D.J. and Grove, J., Emergency toxicological screening for drugs commonly taken in overdose, *J. Chromatogr.*, 80, 205–220, 1973.

129. Trinder, P., Rapid determination of salicylates in biological materials, *Biochem. J.*, 57, 1954.

130. King, J.A., Storrow, A.B., and Finkelstein, J.A., Urine Trinder spot test: a rapid salicylate screen for the emergency department, *Ann. Emerg. Med.*, 26, 330–333, 1995.

131. Stair, E.L. and Whaley, M., Rapid screening and spot tests for the presence of common poisons, *Vet. Hum. Toxicol.*, 32, 564–566, 1990.

132. Hepler, B.R., Sutheimer, C.A., and Sunshine, I., The role of the toxicology laboratory in emergency medicine. II: Study of an integrated approach, *J. Toxicol. Clin. Toxicol.*, 22, 503–528, 1984.

133. Decker, W.J. and Treuting, J.J., Spot tests for rapid diagnosis of poisoning, *Clin. Toxicol.*, 4, 89–97, 1971.

134. Asselin, W.M. and Caughlin, J.D., A rapid and simple color test for detection of salicylate in whole hemolyzed blood, *J. Anal. Toxicol.*, 14, 254–255, 1990.

135. Reith, J.F., Ditmarsh, W.C., and DeRuiter, T., An improved procedure for application of the Fujiwara reaction in the determination of organic halides, *Analyst*, 99: 652–656, 1974.

136. Frings, C.S. and Cohen, S., Rapid colorimetric method for the quantitative determination of ethchlorvynol (placidyl) in serum and urine, *Am. J. Clin. Pathol.*, 54, 833, 1970.

137. Kaye, S., Arsenic, in *Methodology for Analytical Toxicology*, Vol. I, Sunshine, I., Eds., CRC Press, Boca Raton, FL, 1984, 30–31.

138. Stolham, A., Chemical tests for metallic poisons, in *Toxicology: Mechanisms and Analytical Methods*, Stewart, C.P. and Stolman, A., Eds., Academic Press, New York, 1960, 640–678.

139. Stollman, A. and Stewart, C.P., Metallic Poisons, in *Toxicology: Mechanisms and Analytical Methods*, Vol. 1, Stewart, C.P. and Stolman, A., Eds., Academic Press, New York, 1960, 202–222.

140. Kaye, S., Simple procedure for the detection of arsenic in body fluids, *Am. J. Clin. Pathol.*, 14, 36, 1944.

141. Gettler, A.O., Simple tests for mercury in body fluids and tissues, *Am. J. Clin. Pathol. (Tech. Suppl.)*, 7, 13, 1937.

142. Aziz, K., Drugs-of-abuse testing. Screening and confirmation [review], *Clin. Lab. Med.*, 10, 493–502, 1990.

143. Slightom, E.L., The analysis of drugs in blood, bile, and tissue with an indirect homogeneous enzyme immunoassay, *J. Forensic Sci.*, 23, 292–303, 1978.

144. Bogusz, M., Aderjan, R., Schmitt, G., Nadler, E., and Neureither, B., The determination of drugs of abuse in whole blood by means of FPIA and EMIT-dau immunoassays — a comparative study, *Forensic Sci. Int.*, 48, 27–37, 1990.

145. Mason, P.A., Law, B., Pocock, K., and Moffat, A.C., Direct radioimmunoassay for the detection of barbiturates in blood and urine, *Analyst*, 107, 629–633, 1982.

146. Goddard, C.P., Stead, A.H., Mason, P.A., Law, B., Moffat, A.C., McBrien, M. et al., An iodine-125 radioimmunoassay for the direct detection of benzodiazepines in blood and urine, *Analyst*, 111, 525–529, 1986.

147. Lewellen, L.J. and McCurdy, H.H., A novel procedure for the analysis of drugs in whole blood by homogeneous enzyme immunoassay (EMIT), *J. Anal. Toxicol.*, 12, 260–264, 1988.

148. Perrigo, B.J. and Joynt, B.P., Optimization of the EMIT immunoassay procedure for the analysis of cannabinoids in methanolic blood extracts, *J. Anal. Toxicol.*, 13, 235–237, 1989.

149. Maier, R.D., Erkens, M., Hoenen, H., and Bogusz, M., The screening for common drugs of abuse in whole blood by means of EMIT-ETS and FPIA-ADx urine immunoassays, *Int. J. Legal Med.*, 105, 115–119, 1992.

150. Henderson, L.O., Powell, M.K., Hannon, W.H., Miller, B.B., Martin, M.L., Hanzlick, R.L. et al., Radioimmunoassay screening of dried blood spot materials for benzoylecgonine, *J. Anal. Toxicol.*, 17, 42–47, 1993.

151. Appel, T.A. and Wade, N.A., Screening of blood and urine for drugs of abuse utilizing Diagnostic Products Corporation's Coat-A-Count radioimmunoassay kits, *J. Anal. Toxicol.,* 13, 274–276, 1989.
152. Spiehler, V. and Brown, R., Unconjugated morphine in blood by radioimmunoassay and gas chromatography/mass spectrometry, *J. Forensic Sci.,* 32, 906–916, 1987.
153. Asselin, W.M. and Leslie, J.M., Modification of EMIT assay reagents for improved sensitivity and cost effectiveness in the analysis of hemolyzed whole blood, *J. Anal. Toxicol.,* 16, 381–388, 1992.
154. Gjerde, H., Christophersen, A.S., Skuterud, B., Klemetsen, K., and Morland, J., Screening for drugs in forensic blood samples using EMIT urine assays, *Forensic Sci. Int.,* 44, 179–185, 1990.
155. Blum, L.M., Klinger, R.A., and Rieders, F., Direct automated EMIT d.a.u. analysis of *N,N*-dimethylformamide-modified serum, plasma, and postmortem blood for benzodiazepines, benzoylecgonine, cannabinoids, and opiates, *J. Anal. Toxicol.,* 13, 285–288, 1989.
156. Asselin, W.M., Leslie, J.M., and McKinley, B., Direct detection of drugs of abuse in whole hemolyzed blood using the EMIT d.a.u. urine assays [published erratum appears in *J. Anal. Toxicol.,* 12(6), 16A, 1988], *J. Anal. Toxicol.,* 12, 207–215, 1988.
157. Fraser, A.D., Clinical evaluation of the EMIT salicylic acid assay, *Ther. Drug Monit.,* 5, 331–334, 1983.
158. Gooch, J.C., Caldwell, R., Turner, G.J., and Colbert, D.L., Cost effective EMIT assays, for drugs of abuse in urine, using the Eppendorf EPOS analyser, *J. Immunoassay,* 13, 85–96, 1992.
159. Poklis, A., Jortani, S., Edinboro, L.E., and Saady, J.J., Direct determination of benzoylecgonine in serum by EMIT d.a.u. cocaine metabolite immunoassay, *J. Anal. Toxicol.,* 18, 419–422, 1994.
160. Armbruster, D.A., Schwarzhoff, R.H., Pierce, B.L., and Hubster, E.C., Method comparison of EMIT 700 and EMIT II with RIA for drug screening, *J. Anal. Toxicol.,* 18, 110–117, 1994.
161. Armbruster, D.A., Schwarzhoff, R.H., Hubster, E.C., and Liserio, M.K., Enzyme immunoassay, kinetic microparticle immunoassay, radioimmunoassay, and fluorescence polarization immunoassay compared for drugs-of-abuse screening [see comments], *Clin. Chem.,* 39, 2137–2146, 1993.
162. Camara, P.D., Velletri, K., Krupski, M., Rosner, M., and Griffiths, W.C., Evaluation of the Boehringer Mannheim ES 300 immunoassay analyzer and comparison with enzyme immunoassay, fluorescence polarization immunoassay, and radioimmunoassay methods, *Clin. Biochem.,* 25, 251–254, 1992.
163. Fraser, A.D., Bryan, W., and Isner, A.F., Urinary screening for alpha-OH triazolam by FPIA and EIA with confirmation by GC/MS, *J. Anal. Toxicol.,* 16, 347–350, 1992.
164. Meenan, G.M., Barlotta, S., and Lehrer, M., Urinary tricyclic antidepressant screening: comparison of results obtained with Abbott FPIA reagents and Syva EIA reagents, *J. Anal. Toxicol.,* 14, 273–276, 1990.
165. Armbruster, D.A., Schwarzhoff, R.H., Pierce, B.L., and Hubster, E.C., Method comparison of EMIT II and online with RIA for drug screening [see comments], *J. Forensic Sci.,* 38, 1326–1341, 1993.
166. Kintz, P., Machart, D., Jamey, C., and Mangin, P., Comparison between GC/MS and the EMIT II, Abbott ADx, and Roche OnLine immunoassays for the determination of THCCOOH, *J. Anal. Toxicol.,* 19, 304–306, 1995.
167. Armbruster, D.A., Hubster, E.C., Kaufman, M.S., and Ramon, M.K., Cloned enzyme donor immunoassay (CEDIA) for drugs-of-abuse screening, *Clin. Chem.,* 41, 92–98, 1995.
168. Coty, W.A., Loor, R., Bellet, N., Khanna, P.L., Kaspar, P., and Baier, M., CEDIA — homogeneous immunoassays for the 1990s and beyond [review], *Wiener Klin. Wochenschr. Suppl.,* 191, 5–11, 1992.
169. Engel, W.D. and Khanna, P.L., CEDIA *in vitro* diagnostics with a novel homogeneous immunoassay technique. Current status and future prospects, *J. Immunol. Methods,* 150, 99–102, 1992.
170. Fleisher, M., Eisen, C., and Schwartz, M.K., An evaluation of a non-isotopic homogeneous enzyme immunoassay (CEDIA assay) for cortisol and its clinical utility, *Wiener Klin. Wochenschr. Suppl.,* 191, 77–80, 1992.
171. Henderson, D.R., Friedman, S.B., Harris, J.D., Manning, W.B., and Zoccoli, M.A., CEDIA, a new homogeneous immunoassay system, *Clin. Chem.,* 32, 1637–1641, 1986.
172. Klein, G., Collinsworth, W., Courbe, A., Diez, O., Domke, I., Hanseler, E. et al., Results of the multicenter evaluation of the CEDIA Phenobarbital assay, *Wiener Klin. Wochenschr. Suppl.,* 191, 43–47, 1992.
173. Wu, A.H., Forte, E., Casella, G., Sun, K., Hemphill, G., Foery, R. et al., CEDIA for screening drugs of abuse in urine and the effect of adulterants, *J. Forensic Sci.,* 40, 614–618, 1995.
174. Gosling, J.P., A decade of development in immunoassay methodology, *Clin. Chem.,* 36, 1408–1427, 1990.

175. Roberts, C.J. and Jackson, L.S., Development of an ELISA using a universal method of enzyme-labelling drug-specific antibodies, *J. Immunol. Methods,* 181, 157–166, 1995.

176. Laurie, D., Mason, A.J., Piggott, N.H., Rowell, F.J., Seviour, J., Strachan, D. et al., Enzyme linked immunosorbent assay for detecting benzodiazepines in urine, *Analyst,* 121, 951–954, 1996.

177. Makowski, G.S., Richter, J.J., Moore, R.E., Eisma, R., Ostheimer, D., Onoroski, M. et al., An enzyme-linked immunosorbent assay for urinary screening of fentanyl citrate abuse, *Ann. Clin. Lab. Sci.,* 25, 169–178, 1995.

178. Aoki, K., Yoshida, T., and Kuroiwa, Y., Forensic immunochemistry, *Forensic Sci. Int.,* 80, 163–173, 1996.

179. Cone, E.J., Validity testing of commercial urine cocaine metabolite assays: III, *J. Forensic Sci.,* 34, 991–995, 1989.

180. Oeltgen, P.R., Shank, W., Jr., Blouin, R.A., and Clark, T., Clinical evaluation of the Abbott TDx fluorescence polarization immunoassay analyzer, *Ther. Drug Monit.,* 6, 360–367, 1984.

181. Becker, J., Correll, A., Koepf, W., and Rittner, C., Comparative studies on the detection of benzodiazepines in serum by means of immunoassays (FPIA), *J. Anal. Toxicol.,* 17, 103–108, 1993.

182. Alvarez, J.S., Sacristan, J.A., and Alsar, M.J., Comparison of a monoclonal antibody fluorescent polarization immunoassay with monoclonal antibody radioimmunoassay for cyclosporin determination in whole blood, *Ther. Drug Monit.,* 14, 78–80, 1992.

183. De la Torre, R., Badia, R., Gonzalez, G., Garcia, M., Pretel, M.J., Farre, M. et al., Cross-reactivity of stimulants found in sports drug testing by two fluorescence polarization immunoassays, *J. Anal. Toxicol.,* 20, 165–170, 1996.

184. Ferrara, S.D., Tedeschi, L., Frison, G., Brusini, G., Castagna, F., Bernardelli, B. et al., Drugs-of-abuse testing in urine: statistical approach and experimental comparison of immunochemical and chromatographic techniques, *J. Anal. Toxicol.,* 18, 278–291, 1994.

185. Karnes, H.T. and Beightol, L.A., Evaluation of fluorescence polarization immunoassay for quantitation of serum salicylates, *Ther. Drug Monit.,* 7, 351–354, 1985.

186. Beutler, D., Molteni, S., Zeugin, T., and Thormann, W., Evaluation of instrumental, nonisotopic immunoassays (fluorescence polarization immunoassay and enzyme-multiplied immunoassay technique) for cyclosporine monitoring in whole blood after kidney and liver transplantation, *Ther. Drug Monit.,* 14, 424–432, 1992.

187. Przekop, M.A., Manno, J.E., Kunsman, G.W., Cockerham, K.R., and Manno, B.R., Evaluation of the Abbott ADx Amphetamine/Methamphetamine II abused drug assay: comparison to TDx, EMIT, and GC/MS methods, *J. Anal. Toxicol.,* 15, 323–326, 1991.

188. Fraser, A.D. and Bryan, W., Evaluation of the Abbott TDx serum benzodiazepine immunoassay for the analysis of lorazepam, adinazolam, and N-desmethyladinazolam, *J. Anal. Toxicol.,* 19, 281–284, 1995.

189. AlFares, A.M., Mira, S.A., and el-Sayed, Y.M., Evaluation of the fluorescence polarization immunoassay for quantitation of digoxin in serum, *Ther. Drug Monit.,* 6, 454–457, 1984.

190. Caplan, Y.H., Levine, B., and Goldberger, B., Fluorescence polarization immunoassay evaluated for screening for amphetamine and methamphetamine in urine, *Clin. Chem.,* 33, 1200–1202, 1987.

191. Huang, W., Moody, D.E., Andrenyak, D.M., and Rollins, D.E., Immunoassay detection of nordiazepam, triazolam, lorazepam, and alprazolam in blood, *J. Anal. Toxicol.,* 17, 365–369, 1993.

192. Beck, O., Lafolie, P., Odelius, G., and Boreus, L.O., Immunological screening of benzodiazepines in urine: improved detection of oxazepam intake, *Toxicol. Lett.,* 52, 7–14, 1990.

193. Wong, S.H., Methodologies for antidepressant monitoring [review], *Clin. Lab. Med.,* 7, 415–433, 1987.

194. Ensslin, H.K., Kovar, K.A., and Maurer, H.H., Toxicological detection of the designer drug 3,4-methylenedioxyethylamphetamine (MDE, Eve) and its metabolites in urine by gas chromatography-mass spectrometry and fluorescence polarization immunoassay, *J. Chromatogr. B: Biomed. Appl.,* 683, 189–197, 1996.

195. Castro, A. and Malkus, H., Radioimmunoassays of drugs of abuse in humans: a review [review], *Res. Commun. Chem. Pathol. Pharmacol.,* 16, 291–309, 1977.

196. Budd, R.D., Yang, F.C., and Utley, K.O., Barbiturates — structure versus RIA reactivity, *Clin. Toxicol.,* 18, 317–352, 1981.

197. Weaver, M.L., Gan, B.K., Allen, E. et al., Correlations on RIA, FPIA, and EIA of *Cannabis* metabolites with GC/MS analysis of 11-nor-D9-THC acid in urine specimens, *Forensic Sci. Int.,* 49, 43–56, 1991.

198. Moeller, M.R. and Mueller, C., The detection of 6-monoacetylmorphine in urine, serum and hair by GC/MS and RIA, *Forensic Sci. Int.*, 70, 125–133, 1995.

199. Abercrombie, M.L. and Jewell, J.S., Evaluation of EMIT and RIA high volume test procedures for THC metabolites in urine utilizing GC/MS confirmation, *J. Anal. Toxicol.*, 10, 178–180, 1986.

200. Watts, V.W. and Caplan, Y.H., Evaluation of the Coat-A-Count 125I fentanyl RIA: comparison of ^{125}I RIA and GC/MS-SIM for quantification of fentanyl in case urine specimens, *J. Anal. Toxicol.*, 14, 266–272, 1990.

201. Kintz, P., Cirimele, V., Edel, Y., Jamey, C., and Mangin, P., Hair analysis for buprenorphine and its dealkylated metabolite by RIA and confirmation by LC/ECD, *J. Forensic Sci.*, 39, 1497–1503, 1994.

202. Budd, R.D., Leung, W.J., and Yang, F.C., RIA opiates: structure versus reactivity, *Clin. Toxicol.*, 17, 383–393, 1980.

203. Baker, D.P., Murphy, M.S., Shepp, P.F., Royo, V.R., Caldarone, M.E., Escoto, B. et al., Evaluation of the Abuscreen ONLINE assay for amphetamines on the Hitachi 737: comparison with EMIT and GC/MS methods, *J. Forensic Sci.*, 40, 108–112, 1995.

204. Hailer, M., Glienke, Y., Schwab, I.M., and von Meyer, L., Modification and evaluation of Abuscreen OnLine assays for drug metabolites in urine performed on a COBAS FARA II in comparison with EMIT d.a.u. Cannabinoid 20, *J. Anal. Toxicol.*, 19, 99–103, 1995.

205. Moody, D.E. and Medina, A.M., OnLine kinetic microparticle immunoassay of cannabinoids, morphine, and benzoylecgonine in serum, *Clin. Chem.*, 41, 1664–1665, 1995.

206. Budd, R.D., Amphetamine EMIT — structure versus reactivity, *Clin. Toxicol.*, 18, 91–110, 1981.

207. Bailey, D.N., Amphetamine detection during toxicology screening of a university medical center patient population, *J. Toxicol. Clin. Toxicol.*, 25, 399–409, 1987.

208. Budd, R.D., Amphetamine radioimmunoassay — structure versus reactivity, *Clin. Toxicol.*, 18, 299–316, 1981.

209. Kunsman, G.W., Manno, J.E., Cockerham, K.R., and Manno, B.R., Application of the Syva EMIT and Abbott TDx amphetamine immunoassays to the detection of 3,4-methylene-dioxymethamphetamine (MDMA) and 3,4-methylene-dioxyethamphetamin (MDEA) in urine, *J. Anal. Toxicol.*, 14, 149–153, 1990.

210. Turner, G.J., Colbert, D.L., and Chowdry, B.Z., A broad spectrum immunoassay using fluorescence polarization for the detection of amphetamines in urine, *Ann. Clin. Biochem.*, 28, 588–594, 1991.

211. D'Nicuola, J., Jones, R., Levine, B., and Smith, M.L., Evaluation of six commercial amphetamine and methamphetamine immunoassays for cross-reactivity to phenylpropanolamine and ephedrine in urine [see comments], *J. Anal. Toxicol.*, 16, 211–213, 1992.

212. Cody, J.T. and Schwarzhoff, R., Fluorescence polarization immunoassay detection of amphetamine, methamphetamine, and illicit amphetamine analogues, *J. Anal. Toxicol.*, 17, 23–33, 1993.

213. Levine, B.S. and Caplan, Y.H., Isometheptene cross reacts in the EMIT amphetamine assay, *Clin. Chem.*, 33, 1264–1265, 1987.

214. Poklis, A. and Moore, K.A., Response of EMIT amphetamine immunoassays to urinary desoxyephedrine following Vicks Inhaler use, *Ther. Drug Monit.*, 17, 89–94, 1995.

215. Braithwaite, R.A., Jarvie, D.R., Minty, P.S., Simpson, D., and Widdop, B., Screening for drugs of abuse. I: Opiates, amphetamines and cocaine [review], *Ann. Clin. Biochem.*, 32, 123–153, 1995.

216. Poklis, A. and Moore, K.A., Stereoselectivity of the TDx/ADx/FLx amphetamine/methamphetamine II immunoassay — response of urine specimens following nasal inhaler use, *J. Toxicol. Clin. Toxicol.*, 33, 35–41, 1995.

217. Moore, F.M., Jarvie, D.R., and Simpson, D., Urinary amphetamines, benzodiazepines and methadone: cost-effective detection procedures, *Med. Lab. Sci.*, 49, 27–33, 1992.

218. Law, B. and Moffat, A.C., The evaluation of an homogeneous enzyme immunoassay (EMIT) and radioimmunoassay for barbiturates, *J. Forensic Sci. Soc.*, 21, 55–66, 1981.

219. Spector, S. and Flynn, E.J., Barbiturates: radioimmunoassay, *Science*, 174, 1036–1038, 1971.

220. Jain, N.C., Mass screening and confirmation of barbiturates in urine by RIA/gas chromatography, *Clin. Toxicol.*, 9, 221–233, 1976.

221. Caplan, Y.H. and Levine, B., Abbott phencyclidine and barbiturates abused drug assays: evaluation and comparison of ADx FPIA, TDx FPIA, EMIT, and GC/MS methods, *J. Anal. Toxicol.*, 13, 289–292, 1989.

222. Frazer, A.D., Urinary screening for alprazolam, triazolam, and their metabolites with the EMIT d.a.u. benzodiazepine metabolite assay, *J. Anal. Toxicol.*, 11, 263–266, 1987.

223. Budd, R.D., Benzodiazepine structure versus reactivity with EMIT oxazepam antibody, *Clin. Toxicol.*, 18, 643–655, 1981.

224. Meatherall, R., Benzodiazepine screening using EMIT II and TDx: urine hydrolysis pretreatment required, *J. Anal. Toxicol.*, 18, 385–390, 1994.

225. Fitzgerald, R., Rexin, D., and Herold, D., Detecting benzodiazepines: immunoassays compared with negative chemical ionization gas chromatography/mass spectrometry, *Clin. Chem.*, 40, 373–380, 1994.

226. Beck, O., Lafolie, P., Hjemdahl, P., Borg, S., Odelius, G., and Wirbing, P., Detection of benzodiazepine intake in therapeutic doses by immunoanalysis of urine: two techniques evaluated and modified for improved performance, *Clin. Chem.*, 38, 271–275, 1992.

227. Simonsson, P., Liden, A., and Lindberg, S., Effect of beta-glucuronidase on urinary benzodiazepine concentrations determined by fluorescence polarization immunoassay, *Clin. Chem.*, 41, 920–923, 1995.

228. Manchon, M., Verdier, M.F., Pallud, P., Vialle, A., Beseme, F., and Bienvenu, J., Evaluation of EMIT-TOX Enzyme Immunoassay for the analysis of benzodiazepines in serum: usefulness and limitations in an emergency laboratory, *J. Anal. Toxicol.*, 9, 209–212, 1985.

229. Valentine, J.L., Middleton, R., and Sparks, C., Identification of urinary benzodiazepines and their metabolites — comparison of automated HPLC and GC/MS after immunoassay screening of clinical specimens, *J. Anal. Toxicol.*, 20, 416–424, 1996.

230. Huang, W. and Moody, D.E., Immunoassay detection of benzodiazepines and benzodiazepine metabolites in blood, *J. Anal. Toxicol.*, 19, 333–342, 1995.

231. Beyer, K.H. and Martz, S., [Immunologic studies of benzodiazepine — the effect of structural characteristics on cross-reactivity] [in German], *Arch. Pharm.*, 324, 933–935, 1991.

232. Schutz, H., Modern screening strategies in analytical toxicology with special regard to new benzodiazepines, *Z. Rechtsmed. J. Legal Med.*, 100, 19–37, 1988.

233. Fraser, A.D., Bryan, W., and Isner, A.F., Urinary screening for alprazolam and its major metabolites by the Abbott ADx and TDx analyzers with confirmation by GC/MS, *J. Anal. Toxicol.*, 15, 25–29, 1991.

234. Borggaard, B. and Joergensen, I., Urinary screening for benzodiazepines with radioreceptor assay: comparison with EMIT dau, *J. Anal. Toxicol.*, 18, 243–246, 1994.

235. Schramm, W., Craig, P.A., Smith, R.H., and Berger, G.E., Cocaine and benzoylecgonine in saliva, serum, and urine, *Clin. Chem.*, 39, 481–487, 1993.

236. Martinez, F., Poet, T.S., Pillai, R., Erickson, J., Estrada, A.L., and Watson, R.R., Cocaine metabolite (benzoylecgonine) in hair and urine of drug users, *J. Anal. Toxicol.*, 17, 138–142, 1993.

237. Foltz, R.L., Botelho, C., Reuschel, S.A., Kuntz, D.J., Moody, D.E., and Bristow, G.M., Comparison of immunoassays for semi-quantitative measurement of benzoylecgonine in urine, in NIDA Research Monograph 126, U.S. Government Printing Office, Rockville, MD, 1995, 110–117.

238. Moore, F.M. and Simpson, D., Detection of benzoylecgonine (cocaine metabolite) in urine: a cost-effective low risk immunoassay procedure, *Med. Lab. Sci.*, 47, 85–89, 1990.

239. Peterson, K.L., Logan, B.K., and Christian, G.D., Detection of cocaine and its polar transformation products and metabolites in human urine, *Forensic Sci. Int.*, 73, 183–196, 1995.

240. Poklis, A., Evaluation of TDx cocaine metabolite assay, *J. Anal. Toxicol.*, 11, 228–230, 1987.

241. Baugh, L.D., Allen, E.E., Liu, R.H., Langner, J.G., Fentress, J.C., Chadha, S.C. et al., Evaluation of immunoassay methods for the screening of cocaine metabolites in urine, *J. Forensic Sci.*, 36, 79–85, 1991.

242. De Kanel, J., Dunlap, L., and Hall, T.D., Extending the detection limit of the TDx fluorescence polarization immunoassay for benzoylecgonine in urine, *Clin. Chem.*, 35, 2110–2112, 1989.

243. Yee, H.Y., Nelson, J.D., and Papa, V.M., Measurement of benzoylecgonine in whole blood using the Abbott ADx analyzer, *J. Anal. Toxicol.*, 17, 84–86, 1993.

244. Steele, B.W., Bandstra, E.S., Wu, N.C., Hime, G.W., and Hearn, W.L., *m*-Hydroxybenzoylecgonine: an important contributor to the immunoreactivity in assays for benzoylecgonine in meconium, *J. Anal. Toxicol.*, 17, 348–352, 1993.

245. McCord, C.E. and McCutcheon, J.R., Preliminary evaluation of the Abbott TDx for benzoylecgonine and opiate screening in whole blood, *J. Anal. Toxicol.*, 12, 295–297, 1988.

246. Robinson, K. and Smith, R.N., Radioimmunoassay of benzoylecgonine in samples of forensic interest, *J. Pharm. Pharmacol.*, 36, 157–162, 1984.

247. Cone, E.J., Menchen, S.L., Paul, B.C., Mell, L.D., and Mitchell, J., Validity testing of commercial urine cocaine metabolite assays: I, *J. Forensic Sci.,* 34, 15–31, 1989.

248. Cone, E.J. and Mitchell, J., Validity testing of commercial urine cocaine metabolite assays: II. Sensitivity, specificity, accuracy, and confirmation by gas chromatography/mass spectrometry, *J. Forensic Sci.,* 34, 32–45, 1989.

249. Cone, E.J., Yousefnejad, D., and Dickerson, S.L., Validity testing of commercial urine cocaine metabolite assays: IV. Evaluation of the EMIT d.a.u. cocaine metabolite assay in a quantitative mode for detection of cocaine metabolite, *J. Forensic Sci.,* 35, 786–791, 1990.

250. Cone, E.J., Menchen, S.L., and Mitchell, J., Validity testing of the TDx Cocaine Metabolite Assay with human specimens obtained after intravenous cocaine administration, *Forensic Sci. Int.,* 37, 265–275, 1988.

251. Van der Slooten, E.P. and van der Helm, H.J., Comparison of the EMIT (enzyme multiplied immunoassay technique) opiate assay and a gas-chromatographic–mass-spectrometric determination of morphine and codeine in urine, *Clin. Chem.,* 22, 1110–1111, 1976.

252. Smith, M.L., Hughes, R.O., Levine, B., Dickerson, S., Darwin, W.D., and Cone, E.J., Forensic drug testing for opiates. VI. Urine testing for hydromorphone, hydrocodone, oxymorphone, and oxycodone with commercial opiate immunoassays and gas chromatography-mass spectrometry, *J. Anal. Toxicol.,* 19, 18–26, 1995.

253. Cone, E.J., Dickerson, S., Paul, B.D., and Mitchell, J.M., Forensic drug testing for opiates. V. Urine testing for heroin, morphine, and codeine with commercial opiate immunoassays, *J. Anal. Toxicol.,* 17, 156–164, 1993.

254. Cone, E.J., Dickerson, S., Paul, B.D., and Mitchell, J.M., Forensic drug testing for opiates. IV. Analytical sensitivity, specificity, and accuracy of commercial urine opiate immunoassays, *J. Anal. Toxicol.,* 16, 72–78, 1992.

255. Mitchell, J.M., Paul, B.D., Welch, P., and Cone, E.J., Forensic drug testing for opiates, *J. Anal. Toxicol.,* 15, 49–53, 1991.

256. Spichler, V.R. and Sedgwick, P., Radioimmunoassay screening and GC/MS confirmation of whole blood samples for drugs of abuse, *J. Anal. Toxicol.,* 9, 63–66, 1985.

257. Lee, J.W., Pedersen, J.E., Moravetz, T.L., Dzerk, A.M., Mundt, A.D., and Shepard, K.V., Sensitive and specific radioimmunoassays for opiates using commercially available materials, *J. Pharm. Sci.,* 80, 284–288, 1991.

258. Weingarten, H.L. and Trevias, E.C., Analysis of phencyclidine in blood by gas chromatography, radioimmunoassay, and enzyme immunoassay, *J. Anal. Toxicol.,* 6, 88–90, 1982.

259. Heveran, J.E., Anthony, M., and Ward, C., Determination of phencyclidine by radioimmunoassay, *J. Forensic Sci.,* 25, 79–87, 1980.

260. Fyfe, M.J., Chand, P., McCutchen, C., Long, J.S., Walia, A.S., Edwards, C. et al., Evaluation of enzyme immunoassay performance characteristics — phencyclidine example, *J. Forensic Sci.,* 38, 156–164, 1993.

261. Sneath, T.C. and Jain, N.C., Evaluation of phencyclidine by EMIT d.a.u. utilizing the ETS analyzer and a 25-ng/mL cutoff, *J. Anal. Toxicol.,* 16, 107–108, 1992.

262. Ragan, F., Jr., Hite, S.A., Samuels, M.S., Garey, R.E., Daul, G., and Schuler, R.E., Extended EMIT-DAU phencyclidine screen, *J. Clin. Psychiatry,* 47, 194–195, 1986.

263. Levine, B., Goldberger, B.A., and Caplan, Y.H., Evaluation of the Coat-a-Count radioimmunoassay for phencyclidine, *Clin. Chem.,* 34, 429, 1988.

264. Cary, P.L., Johnson, C.A., Folsom, T.M., and Bales, W.R., Immunoassay method validation for a modified EMIT phencyclidine assay, *J. Anal. Toxicol.,* 16, 48–51, 1992.

265. Budd, R.D., Phencyclidine (PCP)-structure versus reactivity, *Clin. Toxicol.,* 18, 1033–1041, 1981.

266. Kintz, P. and Mangin, P., Abbott propoxyphene assay: evaluation and comparison of TDx FPIA and GC/MS methods, *J. Anal. Toxicol.,* 17, 222–224, 1993.

267. Frederick, D.L., Green, J., and Fowler, M.W., Comparison of six cannabinoid metabolite assays, *J. Anal. Toxicol.,* 9, 116–120, 1985.

268. Budgett, W.T., Levine, B., Xu, A., and Smith, M.L., Comparison of Abbott fluorescence polarization immunoassay (FPIA) and Roche radioimmunoassay for the analyses of cannabinoids in urine specimens, *J. Forensic Sci.,* 37, 632–635, 1992.

269. Kaeferstein, H., Sticht, G., and Staak, M., Comparison of various immunological methods with GC/MS analysis in the detection of cannabinoids in urine, *Beitr. Gerichtl. Med.,* 47, 115–122, 1989.

270. Moore, F.M.L. and Simpson, D., Detection of cannabinoids in urine: a cost-effective low risk immunoassay procedure, *Med. Lab. Sci.,* 48, 76–79, 1991.

271. Colbert, D.L., Sidki, A.M., Gallacher, G., and Landon, J., Fluoroimmunoassays for cannabinoids in urine, *Analyst,* 112, 1483–1486, 1987.

272. McBurney, L.J., Bobbie, B.A., and Sepp, L.A., GC/MS and EMIT analyses for delta 9-tetrahydrocannabinol metabolites in plasma and urine of human subjects, *J. Anal. Toxicol.,* 10, 56–64, 1986.

273. King, D.L., Martel, P.A., and O'Donnell, C.M., Laboratory detection of cannabinoids [review], *Clin. Lab. Med.,* 7, 641–653, 1987.

274. Moyer, T.P., Palmen, M.A., Johnson, P., Charlson, J.R., and Ellefson, P.J., Marijuana testing — how good is it? *Mayo Clin. Proc.,* 62, 413–417, 1987.

275. Cook, C.E., Seltzman, H.H., Schindler, V.H., Tallent, C.R., Chin, K.M., and Pitt, C.G., Radioimmunoassays for cannabinoids, *NIDA Res. Monogr.,* 42, 19–32, 1982.

276. Gjerde, H., Screening for cannabinoids in blood using EMIT: concentrations of delta-9-tetrahydrocannabinol in relation to EMIT results, *Forensic Sci. Int.,* 50, 121–124, 1991.

277. Goodall, C.R. and Basteyns, B.J., A reliable method for the detection, confirmation, and quantitation of cannabinoids in blood, *J. Anal. Toxicol.,* 19, 419–426, 1995.

278. Ernst, R., Williams, L., Dalbey, M., Collins, C., and Pankey, S., Homogeneous enzyme immunoassay (EMIT) protocol for monitoring tricyclic antidepressants on the COBAS-BIO centrifugal analyzer, *Ther. Drug Monit.,* 9, 85–90, 1987.

279. Asselin, W.M. and Leslie, J.M., Direct detection of therapeutic concentrations of tricyclic antidepressants in whole hemolyzed blood using the EMITtox serum tricyclic antidepressant assay, *J. Anal. Toxicol.,* 15, 167–173, 1991.

280. Benitez, J., Dahlqvist, R., Gustafsson, L.L., Magnusson, A., and Sjoqvist, F., Clinical pharmacological evaluation of an assay kit for intoxications with tricyclic antidepressants, *Ther. Drug Monit.,* 8, 102–105, 1986.

281. Dorey, R.C., Preskorn, S.H., and Widener, P.K., Results compared for tricyclic antidepressants as assayed by liquid chromatography and enzyme immunoassay, *Clin. Chem.,* 34, 2348–2351, 1988.

282. Nebinger, P. and Koel, M., Specificity data of the tricyclic antidepressants assay by fluorescent polarization immunoassay, *J. Anal. Toxicol.,* 14, 219–221, 1990.

283. Vandel, S., Vincent, F., Prudhon, F., Nezelof, S., Bonin, B., and Bertschy, G., Results compared for tricyclic antidepressants as assayed by gas chromatography and enzyme immunoassay, *Therapie,* 47, 41–45, 1992.

284. Brunk, S.D., Thin-layer chromatography using Toxi-lab system, in *Analysis of Addictive and Misused Drugs,* Adamovics, J.A., Ed., Marcel Dekker, New York, 1995, 41–50.

285. Guebitz, G. and Wintersteiger, R., Identification of drugs of abuse by high-performance thin-layer chromatography, *J. Anal. Toxicol.,* 4, 141–144, 1980.

286. Singh, A.K., Granley, K., Ashraf, M., and Misha, U., Drug screening and confirmation by thin layer chromatography, *J. Planar Chromatogr. Mod. TLC,* 2, 410–419, 1989.

287. Wilson, J.F., Williams, J., Walker, G., Toseland, P.A., Smith, B.L., Richens, A. et al., Sensitivity and specificity of techniques used to detect drugs of abuse in urine, in *Recent Developments in Therapeutic Drug Monitoring and Clinical Toxicology,* Sunshine, I., Ed., Marcel Dekker, New York, 1992, 527–535.

288. Bogusz, M., Klys, M., Wijsbeek, J., Franke, J.P., and de Zeeuw, R.A., Impact of biological matrix and isolation methods on detectability and interlaboratory variations of TLC Rf-values in systematic toxicological analysis, *J. Anal. Toxicol.,* 8, 149–154, 1984.

289. Wolff, K., Sanderson, M.J., and Hay, A.W., A rapid horizontal TLC method for detecting drugs of abuse, *Ann. Clin. Biochem.,* 27, 482–488, 1990.

290. Jarvie, D.R. and Simpson, D., Drug screening: evaluation of the Toxi-Lab TLC system, *Ann. Clin. Biochem.,* 23, 76–84, 1986.

291. Nishigami, J., Ohshima, T., Takayasu, T., Kondo, T., Lin, Z., and Nagano, T., [Forensic toxicological application of TOXI-LAB screening for biological specimens in autopsy cases and emergency cares], *Nippon Hoigaku Zasshi Jpn. J. Legal Med.,* 47, 372–379, 1993.

292. Nadkarni, S., Faye, S., and Hay, A., Experience with the use of the Toxi-Lab TLC system in screening for morphine/heroin abuse, *Ann. Clin. Biochem.,* 24, 211–212, 1987.

293. Plavsic, F., Barbaric, V., Parag, M., Arambasin, M., Gjerek, J., and Stavljenic, A., Increased possibilities for detecting drugs by the Toxi-Lab screening test, *Ann. Clin. Biochem.*, 22, 324–326, 1985.

294. Caldwell, R. and Challenger, H., A capillary column GC method for the identification of drugs of abuse in urine samples, *Ann. Clin. Biochem.*, 26, 430–443, 1989.

295. Grinstead, G.F., A closer look at acetyl and pentafluoropropionyl derivatives for quantitative analysis of morphine and codeine by gas chromatography–mass spectrometry, *J. Anal. Toxicol.*, 15, 293–298, 1991.

296. Kataoka, H., Derivatization reactions for the determination of amines by gas chromatography and their applications in environmental analysis, *J. Chromatogr. A*, 733, 19–34, 1996.

297. Lho, D., Hong, J., Paek, H., Lee, J., and Park, J., Determination of phenolalkylamines, narcotic analgesics, and beta-blockers by gas chromatography-mass spectrometry, *J. Anal. Toxicol.*, 14, 77–83, 1990.

298. Sanchez, M.C., Colome, J., and Gelpi, E., Electron capture and multiple ion detection of benzodiazepine esters in pharmacokinetic studies, *J. Chromatogr.*, 126, 601–613, 1976.

299. Beck, O. and Faull, K.F., Extractive acylation and mass spectrometric assay of 3-methoxytyramine, normetanephrine, and metanephrine in cerebrospinal fluid, *Anal. Biochem.*, 149, 492–500, 1985.

300. Jain, N.C., Sneath, T.C., Budd, R.D., and Leung, W.J., Gas chromatographic/thin-layer chromatographic analysis of acetylated codeine and morphine in urine, *Clin. Chem.*, 21, 1486–1489, 1975.

301. Czarny, R.J. and Hornbeck, C.L., Quantitation of methamphetamine and amphetamine in urine by capillary GC/MS Part II. Derivatization with 4-carbethoxyhexafluorobutyryl chloride, *J. Anal. Toxicol.*, 13, 257–262, 1989.

302. Bowie, L.J. and Kirkpatrick, P.B., Simultaneous determination of monoacetylmorphine, morphine, codeine, and other opiates by GC/MS, *J. Anal. Toxicol.*, 13, 326–329, 1989.

303. Toyo'oka, T., Use of derivatization to improve the chromatographic properties and detection selectivity of physiologically important carboxylic acids, *J. Chromatogr. B Biomed. Appl.*, 671, 91–112, 1995.

304. Zamecnik, J., Use of cyclic boronates for GC/MS screening and quantitation of beta-blockers and some bronchodilators, *J. Anal. Toxicol.*, 14, 132–136, 1990.

305. Liu, F., Liu, Y.T., Feng, C.L., and Luo, Y., Determination of methaqualone and its metabolites in urine and blood by UV, GC/FID and GC/MS, *Yao Hsueh Hsueh Pao Acta Pharm. Sin.*, 29, 610–616, 1994.

306. Michalek, R.W., Rejent, T.A., and Spencer, R.A., Disopyramide fatality: case report and GC/FID analysis, *J. Anal. Toxicol.*, 6, 255–257, 1982.

307. Kintz, P., Mangin, P., Lugnier, A.A., and Chaumont, A.J., A rapid and sensitive gas chromatographic analysis of meprobamate or carisoprodol in urine and plasma, *J. Anal. Toxicol.*, 12, 73–74, 1988.

308. Qiu, F.H., Liu, L., Guo, L., Luo, Y., and Lu, Y.Q., [Rapid identification and quantitation of barbiturates in plasma using solid-phase extraction combined with GC-FID and GC/MS method], *Yao Hsueh Hsueh Pao Acta Pharm. Sin.*, 30, 372–377, 1995.

309. Kageura, M., Hara, K., Hieda, Y., Takamoto, M., Fujiwara, Y., Fukuma, Y. et al., [Screening of drugs and chemicals by wide-bore capillary gas chromatography with flame ionization and nitrogen phosphorus detectors]. [Japanese], *Nippon Hoigaku Zasshi Jpn. J. Legal Med.*,43(2), 161–165, 1989.

310. Ghittori, S., Fiorentino, M.L., and Imbriani, M., [Use of gas chromatography with flame ionization (GC-FID) in the measurement of solvents in the urine], *Giorn. Ital. Med. Lavoro*, 9, 21–24, 1987.

311. Verebey, K., Jukofsky, D., and Mule, S.J., Confirmation of EMIT benzodiazepine assay with GLC/NPD, *J. Anal. Toxicol.*, 6, 305–308, 1982.

312. Trinh, V. and Vernay, A., Evaluation of sample treatment procedure for the routine identification and determination at nanogram level of *O*-monoacetylmorphine in urine by capillary GC and dual NPD-FID, *J. High Resolution Chromatogr.*, 13, 162–166, 1990.

313. Verebey, K. and DePace, A., Rapid confirmation of enzyme multiplied immunoassay technique (EMIT) cocaine positive urine samples by capillary gas-liquid chromatography/nitrogen phosphorus detection (GLC/NPD), *J. Forensic Sci.*, 34, 46–52, 1989.

314. Balkon, J. and Donnelly, B., Determination of basic drugs in post mortem tissues: a microextraction technique utilizing GLC/NPD of effluents, *J. Anal. Toxicol.*, 6, 181–184, 1982.

315. Gaillard, Y., Gay-Montchamp, J.P., and Ollagnier, M., Simultaneous screening and quantitation of alpidem, zolpidem, buspirone and benzodiazepines by dual-channel gas chromatography using electron-capture and nitrogen-phosphorus detection after solid-phase extraction, *J. Chromatogr.*, 622, 197–208, 1993.

316. Japp, M., Garthwaite, K., Geeson, A.V., and Osselton, M.D., Collection of analytical data for benzo-diazepines and benzophenones, *J. Chromatogr.*, 439, 317–339, 1988.

317. Lillsunde, P. and Seppala, T., Simultaneous screening and quantitative analysis of benzodiazepines by dual-channel gas chromatography using electron-capture and nitrogen-phosphorus detection, *J. Chromatogr.*, 533, 97–110, 1990.

318. Kokanovich, J.D., Simonick, T.F., and Watts, V.W., High speed analysis of underivatized drugs by GC/MS, *J. High Resolution Chromatogr.*, 12, 45–48, 1989.

319. Lillsunde, P. and Korte, T., Thin-layer chromatographic screening and GC/MS confirmation in analysis of abused drugs, in *Analysis of Addictive and Misused Drugs*, Adamovics, J.A., Ed., Marcel Dekker, New York, 1995, 221–265.

320. Maurer, H. and Pfleger, K., Screening procedure for detection of antidepressants and their metabolites in urine using a computerized GC/MS technique, *J. Chromatogr.*, 305, 309–323, 1984.

321. Siren, H., Saarinen, M., Hainari, S., Lukkari, P., and Riekkola, M.L., Screening of beta-blockers in human serum by ion-pair chromatography and their identification as methyl or acetyl derivatives by GC/MS, *J. Chromatogr.*, 632, 215–227, 1993.

322. Needleman, S.B. and Porvaznik, M., Identification of parent benzodiazepines by gas chromotography/mass spectroscopy (GC/MS) from urinary extracts treated with B-glucuronidase, *Forensic Sci. Int.*, 73, 49–60, 1995.

323. Maurer, H. and Pfleger, K., Screening procedure for detection of phenothiazines and analogous neuroleptics and their metabolites in urine using a computerized GC/MS technique, *J. Chromatogr.*, 306, 125–145, 1984.

324. Fraser, A.D., Bryan, W., and Isner, A.F., Urinary screening for midazolam and its major metabolites with the Abbott ADx and TDx analyzers and the EMIT dau benzodiazepine assay with confirmation by GC/MS, *J. Anal. Toxicol.*, 15, 8–12, 1991.

325. Masse, R., Ayotte, C., and Dugal, R., An integrated GC/MS screening method for anabolic steroid urinary metabolites in man, in *Developments in Analytical Methods in Pharmaceutical, Biomedical, and Forensic Sciences*, Quebec, Canada, 1986.

326. Maurer, H.H., Identification and differentiation of barbiturates, other sedative-hypnotics and their metabolites in urine integrated in a general screening procedure using computerized GC/MS, *J. Chromatogr.*, 530, 307–326, 1990.

327. Maurer, H. and Pfleger, K., Identification and differentiation of alkylamine antihistamines and their metabolites in urine by computerized gas chromatography, mass spectrometry, *J. Chromatogr.*, 430, 31–41, 1988.

328. Gill, R., Lopes, A.A., and Moffat, A.C., Analysis of barbiturates in blood by high-performance liquid chromatography, *J. Chromatogr.*, 226, 117–123, 1981.

329. Kleinschnitz, M., Herderich, M., and Schreier, P., Determination of 1,4-benzodiazepines by high performance liquid chromatography electrospray tandem mass spectrometry, *J. Chromatogr. B Biomed. Appl.*, 676, 61–67, 1996.

330. Mangin, P., Lugnier, A.A., and Chaumont, A.J., A polyvalent method using HPLC for screening and quantification of 12 common barbiturates in various biological materials, *J. Anal. Toxicol.*, 11, 27–30, 1987.

331. Hill, D.W. and Langner, K.J., Screening with high performance liquid chromatography, in *Analytical Aspects of Drug Testing*, Deutsch, D.G., Ed., John Wiley & Sons, New York, 1989, 129–148.

332. Ng, L.L., Sample preparation by salts precipitation and quantitation by HPLC with UV detection of selected drugs in biological fluids, *J. Chromatogr.*, 257, 345–353, 1983.

333. Foukaridis, G.N., Muntingh, G.L., and Osuch, E., Application of diode array detection for the identification of poisoning by traditional medicines, *J. Ethnopharmacol.*, 41, 135–146, 1994.

334. Lambert, W.E., Piette, M., Van Peteghem, C., and De Leenheer, A.P., Application of high-performance liquid chromatography to a fatality involving azide, *J. Anal. Toxicol.*, 19, 261–264, 1995.

335. Dipietra, A.M., Gatti, R., Andrisano, V., and Cavrini, V., Application of high-performance liquid chromatography with diode-array detection and on-line post-column photochemical derivatization to the determination of analgesics, *J. Chromatogr.*, 729, 355–361, 1996.

336. Puopolo, P.R., Volpicelli, S.A., Johnson, D.M., and Flood, J.G., Emergency toxicology testing (detection, confirmation, and quantification) of basic drugs in serum by liquid chromatography with photodiode array detection, *Clin. Chem.*, 37, 2124–2130, 1991.

337. Koves, E.M. and Wells, J., Evaluation of a photodiode array/HPLC-based system for the detection and quantitation of basic drugs in postmortem blood, *J. Forensic Sci.*, 37, 42–60, 1992.

338. Tracqui, A., Kintz, P., and Mangin, P., High-performance liquid chromatographic assay with diode-array detection for toxicological screening of zopiclone, zolpidem, suriclone and alpidem in human plasma, *J. Chromatogr.*, 616, 95–103, 1993.

339. Balikova, M. and Vecerkova, J., High-performance liquid chromatographic confirmation of cocaine and benzoylecgonine in biological samples using photodiode-array detection after toxicological screening, *J. Chromatogr. B Biomed. Appl.*, 656, 267–273, 1994.

340. Wielbo, D., Bhat, R., Chari, G., Vidyasagar, D., Tebbett, I.R., and Gulati, A., High-performance liquid chromatographic determination of morphine and its metabolites in plasma using diode-array detection, *J. Chromatogr.*, 615, 164–168, 1993.

341. Li, S., Gemperline, P.J., Briley, K., and Kazmierczak, S., Identification and quantitation of drugs of abuse in urine using the generalized rank annihilation method of curve resolution, *J. Chromatogr. B Biomed. Appl.*, 655, 213–223, 1994.

342. Overzet, F., Rurak, A., van der Voet, H., Drenth, B.F., Ghijsen, R.T., and de Zeeuw, R.A., On-line diode array UV-visible spectrometry in screening for drugs and drug metabolites by high-performance liquid chromatography, *J. Chromatogr.*, 267, 329–345, 1983.

343. Balikova, M., Selective system of identification and determination of antidepressants and neuroleptics in serum or plasma by solid-phase extraction followed by high-performance liquid chromatography with photodiode-array detection in analytical toxicology, *J. Chromatogr.*, 581, 75–81, 1992.

344. Tracqui, A., Kintz, P., Kreissig, P., and Mangin, P., A simple and rapid method for toxicological screening of 25 antidepressants in blood or urine using high performance liquid chromatography with diode-array detection, *Ann. Biol. Clin.*, 50, 639–647, 1992.

345. Puopolo, P.R., Pothier, M.E., Volpicelli, S.A., and Flood, J.G., Single procedure for detection, confirmation, and quantification of benzodiazepines in serum by liquid chromatography with photodiode-array detection, *Clin. Chem.*, 37, 701–706, 1991.

346. Turcant, A., Premel-Cabic, A., Cailleux, A., and Allain, P., Toxicological screening of drugs by microbore high-performance liquid chromatography with photodiode-array detection and ultraviolet spectral library searches, *Clin. Chem.*, 37, 1210–1215, 1991.

347. Stanke, F., Jourdil, N., Lauby, V., and Bessard, G., Zopiclone and zolpidem quantification in human plasma by high performance liquid chromatography with photodiode-array detection, *J. Liquid Chromatogr. Relat. Technol.*, 19, 2623–2633, 1996.

348. Law, B. and Stafford, L.E., The use of ultraviolet spectra and chromatographic retention data as an aid to metabolite identification, *J. Pharm. Biomed. Anal.*, 11, 729–736, 1993.

349. Demedts, P., Wauters, A., Franck, F., and Neels, H., Evaluation of the REMEDi drug profiling system, *Eur. J. Clin. Chem. Clin. Biochem.*, 32, 409–417, 1994.

350. Ohtsuji, M., Lai, J.S., Binder, S.R., Kondo, T., Takayasu, T., and Ohshima, T., Use of REMEDi HS in emergency toxicology for a rapid estimate of drug concentrations in urine, serum, and gastric samples, *J. Forensic Sci.*, 41, 881–886, 1996.

351. Patel, V., McCarthy, P.T., and Flanagan, R.J., Disopyramide analysis using REMEDi: comparison with EMIT and conventional high performance liquid chromatographic methods, *Biomed. Chromatogr.*, 5, 269–272, 1991.

352. Poklis, A. and Edinboro, L.E., REMEDi drug profiling system readily distinguishes between cyclobenzaprine and amitriptyline in emergency toxicology urine specimens [letter], *Clin. Chem.*, 38, 2349–2350, 1992.

353. Christensen, J.M., Human exposure to toxic metals: factors influencing interpretation of biomonitoring results, *Sci. Total Environ.*, 166, 89–135, 1995.

354. Flanagan, R.J., The poisoned patient: the role of the laboratory [review], *Br. J. Biomed. Sci.*, 52, 202–213, 1995.

355. Van Ormer, D.G., Atomic absorption analysis of some trace metals of toxicological interest, *J. Forensic Sci.*, 20, 595–623, 1975.

356. Sotera, J.J., Dulude, G.R., and Stux, R.L., Determination of toxic elements in biological materials by furnace atomic absorption spectrometry, *Sci. Total Environ.*, 71, 45–48, 1988.

357. Solomons, E.T. and Walls, H.C., Analysis of arsenic in forensic cases utilizing a rapid, non-ashing technique and furnace atomic absorption, *J. Anal. Toxicol.*, 7, 220–222, 1983.

358. Yoshinaga, J., [Inductively coupled plasma atomic emission spectrometry and ICP mass spectrometry], *Nippon Rinsho Jpn. J. Clin. Med.,* 54, 202–206, 1996.

359. Kalamegham, R. and Ash, K.O., A simple ICP-MS procedure for the determination of total mercury in whole blood and urine, *J. Clin. Lab. Anal.,* 6, 190–193, 1992.

360. Inoue, T. and Suzuki, S., Comparison of extraction methods for methamphetamine and its metabolites in tissue, *J. Forensic Sci.,* 31, 1102–1107, 1986.

361. Bush, M.T., Design of solvent extraction methods, *Methods Enzymol.,* 77, 353–372, 1981.

362. Dusaci, L.J. and Hackett, L.P., Direct extraction procedure for the analysis of neutral drugs in tissue, *Clin. Toxicol.,* 11, 353–358, 1977.

363. Brooks, K.E. and Smith, N.B., Efficient extraction of basic, neutral, and weakly acidic drugs from plasma for analysis by gas chromatography-mass spectrometry [published erratum appears in *Clin. Chem.* 38(2), 323, 1992], *Clin. Chem.,* 37, 1975–1978, 1991.

364. Hyde, P.M., Evaluation of drug extraction procedures from urine, *J. Anal. Toxicol.,* 9, 269–272, 1985.

365. Osselton, M.D., Hammond, M.D., and Watchett, P.J., The extraction and analysis of benzodiazepines in tissues by enzymatic digestion and HPLC, *J. Pharm. Pharmacol.,* 29, 460–462, 1977.

366. Bailey, D.N. and Kelner, M., Extraction of acidic drugs from water and plasma: study of recovery with five different solvents, *J. Anal. Toxicol.,* 8, 26–28, 1984.

367. Chiarotti, M., Overview on extraction procedures [review], *Forensic Sci. Int.,* 63, 161–170, 1993.

368. Ford, B., Vine, J., and Watson, T.R., A rapid extraction method for acidic drugs in hemolyzed blood, *J. Anal. Toxicol.,* 7, 116–118, 1983.

369. Moore, C.M. and Tebbett, I.R., Rapid extraction of anti-inflammatory drugs in whole blood for HPLC analysis, *Forensic Sci. Int.,* 34, 155–158, 1987.

370. Stoner, R.E. and Parker, C., Single-pH extraction procedure for detecting drugs of abuse, *Clin. Chem.,* 20, 309–311, 1974.

371. Hackett, L.P. and Dusci, L.J., The use of buffered celite columns in drug extraction techniques and their proposed application in forensic toxicology, *J. Forensic Sci.,* 22, 376–382, 1977.

372. Siek, T.J., Effective use of organic solvents to remove drugs from biologic specimens, *Clin. Toxicol.,* 13, 205–230, 1978.

373. Dusci, L.J. and Hackett, L.P., A comparison of the borate-celite column screening technique with other extraction methods in forensic toxicology, *J. Forensic Sci.,* 22, 545–549, 1977.

374. Chen, X.H., Franke, J.P., Wijsbeek, J., and de Zeeuw, R.A., Isolation of acidic, neutral, and basic drugs from whole blood using a single mixed-mode solid-phase extraction column, *J. Anal. Toxicol.,* 16, 351–355, 1992.

375. Black, D.A., Clark, G.D., Haver, V.M., Garbin, J.A., and Saxon, A.J., Analysis of urinary benzodiazepines using solid-phase extraction and gas chromatography-mass spectrometry [see comments], *J. Anal. Toxicol.,* 18, 185–188, 1994.

376. Lensmeyer, G.L., Wiebe, D.A., and Darcey, B.A., Application of a novel form of solid-phase sorbent (Empore membrane) to the isolation of tricyclic antidepressant drugs from blood, *J. Chromatogr. Sci.,* 29, 444–449, 1991.

377. Chen, X.H., Franke, J.P., Wijsbeek, J., and de Zeeuw, R.A., Determination of basic drugs extracted from biological matrices by means of solid-phase extraction and wide-bore capillary gas chromatography with nitrogen-phosphorus detection, *J. Anal. Toxicol.,* 18, 150–153, 1994.

378. Huang, Z.P., Chen, X.H., Wijsbeek, J., Franke, J.P., and Dezeeuw, R.A., An enzymic digestion and solid-phase extraction procedure for the screening for acidic, neutral, and basic drugs in liver using gas chromatography for analysis, *J. Anal. Toxicol.,* 20, 248–254, 1996.

379. Leloux, M.S., de Jong, E.G., and Maes, R.A., Improved screening method for beta-blockers in urine using solid-phase extraction and capillary gas chromatography-mass spectrometry, *J. Chromatogr.,* 488, 357–367, 1989.

380. Anderson, R.E. and Nixon, G.L., Isolation of benzoylecgonine from urine using solid-phase extraction, *J. Anal. Toxicol.,* 17, 432–433, 1993.

381. Cosbey, S.H., Craig, I., and Gill, R., Novel solid-phase extraction strategy for the isolation of basic drugs from whole blood, *J. Chromatogr. B Biomed. Appl.,* 669, 229–235, 1995.

382. Matyska, M. and Golkiewicz, W., Quantitation of benzodiazepine hydrolysis products in urine using solid-phase extraction and high performance liquid chromatography, *J. Liquid Chromatogr.,* 14, 2769–2778, 1991.

383. Wright, A.W., Watt, J.A., Kennedy, M., Cramond, T., and Smith, M.T., Quantitation of morphine, morphine-3-glucuronide, and morphine-6-glucuronide in plasma and cerebrospinal fluid using solid-phase extraction and high-performance liquid chromatography with electrochemical detection, *Ther. Drug Monit.,* 16, 200–208, 1994.

384. Bouquillon, A.I., Freeman, D., and Moulin, D.E., Simultaneous solid-phase extraction and chromatographic analysis of morphine and hydromorphone in plasma by high-performance liquid chromatography with electrochemical detection, *J. Chromatogr.,* 577, 354–357, 1992.

385. Pocci, R., Dixit, V., and Dixit, V.M., Solid-phase extraction and GC/MS confirmation of barbiturates from human urine, *J. Anal. Toxicol.,* 16, 45–47, 1992.

386. Chen, X.-H., Franke, J.-P., and de Zeeuw, R.A., Solid-phase extraction for systematic toxicological analysis, *Forensic Sci. Rev.,* 4, 147–159, 1992.

387. Casas, M., Berrueta, L.A., Gallo, B., and Vicente, F., Solid-phase extraction of 1,4-benzodiazepines from biological fluids, *J. Pharm. Biomed. Anal.,* 11, 277–284, 1993.

388. Dixit, V., Solid-phase extraction of amphetamine and methamphetamine, *Am. Clin. Lab.,* 11, 6, 1992.

389. Scheurer, J. and Moore, C.M., Solid-phase extraction of drugs from biological tissues — a review, *J. Anal. Toxicol.,* 16, 264–269, 1992.

390. Chen, X.H., Franke, J.P., Wijsbeek, J., and de Zeeuw, R.A., Study of lot-to-lot reproducibilities of Bond Elut Certify and Clean Screen DAU mixed-mode solid-phase extraction columns in the extraction of drugs from whole blood, *J. Chromatogr.,* 617, 147–151, 1993.

391. Nakamura, G.R., Meeks, R.D., and Stall, W.J., Solid-phase extraction, identification, and quantitation of 11-nor-delta-9-tetrahydrocannabinol-9-carboxylic acid, *J. Forensic Sci.,* 35, 792–796, 1990.

392. Scheurer, J. and Moore, C.M., Solid-phase extraction of drugs from biological tissues — a review, *J. Anal. Toxicol.,* 16, 264–269, 1992.

393. Delaunay-Bertoncini, N. and Hennion, M.C., Immunoaffinity solid-phase extraction for pharmaceutical and biomedical trace-analysis-coupling with HPLC and CE-perspectives, *J. Pharm. Biomed. Anal.,* 34, 717–736, 2004.

394. Ulrich, S., Solid-phase microextraction in biomedical analysis, *J. Chromatogr. A,* 902, 167–194, 2000.

395. Pawliszyn, J., Solid phase microextraction, *Adv. Exp. Med. Biol.,* 488, 73–87, 2001.

396. Iwai, M., Hattori, H., Arinobu, T., Ishii, A., Kumazawa, T., Noguchi, H., Noguchi, H., Suzuki, O., and Seno, H., Simultaneous determination of barbiturates in human biological fluids by direct immersion solid-phase microextraction and gas chromatography-mass spectrometry, *J. Chromatogr. B Anal. Technol. Biomed. Life Sci.,* 806, 65–73, 2004.

397. Lachenmeier, D.W., Kroener, L., Musshoff, F., and Madea, B., Application of tandem mass spectrometry combined with gas chromatography and headspace solid-phase dynamic extraction for the determination of drugs of abuse in hair samples, *Rapid Commun. Mass Spectrom.,* 17, 472–478, 2003.

398. Musshoff, F., Junker, H., and Madea, B., Simple determination of 22 organophosphorous pesticides in human blood using headspace solid-phase microextraction and gas chromatography with mass spectrometric detection, *J. Chromatogr. Sci.,* 40, 29–34, 2002.

399. Frison, G., Tedeschi, L., Maietti, S., and Ferrara, S.D., Determination of gamma-hydroxybutyric acid (GHB) in plasma and urine by headspace solid-phase microextraction and gas chromatography/positive ion chemical ionization mass spectrometry, *Rapid Commun. Mass Spectrom.,* 14, 2401–2407, 2000.

400. Frison, G., Tedeschi, L., Maietti, S., and Ferrara, S.D., Determination of midazolam in human plasma by solid-phase microextraction and gas chromatography/mass spectrometry, *Rapid Commun. Mass Spectrom.,* 15, 2497–2501, 2001.

401. Musteata, F.M. and Pawliszyn, J., Study of ligand-receptor binding using SPME: investigation of receptor, free, and total ligand concentrations, *J. Proteome Res.,* 4, 789–800, 2005.

402. Musshoff, F., Lachenmeier, D.W., Kroener, L., and Madea, B., Automated headspace solid-phase dynamic extraction for the determination of cannabinoids in hair samples, *Forensic Sci. Int.,* 133, 32–38, 2003.

403. Bogusz, M., Bialka, J., and Gierz, J., Enzymic digestion of biosamples as a method of sample pretreatment before XAD-2 extraction, *Z. Rechtsmed. J. Legal Med.,* 87, 287–295, 1981.

404. Bogusz, M., Bialka, J., and Gierz, J., Enzymic hydrolysis of tissues before XAD-2 extraction in poisoning cases, *Forensic Sci. Int.,* 20, 27–33, 1982.

405. Romberg, R.W. and Lee, L., Comparison of the hydrolysis rates of morphine-3-glucuronide and morphine-6-glucuronide with acid and beta-glucuronidase, *J. Anal. Toxicol.,* 19, 157–162, 1995.

12.4 STRATEGIES FOR POST-MORTEM TOXICOLOGY INVESTIGATION

Edited and Revised by Henrik Druid, M.D., Ph.D.
Associate Professor, Department of Forensic Medicine, Karolinska Institute, Stockholm, Sweden

From the original by W. Lee Hearn, Ph.D.
Director, Dade County Medical Examiner Toxicology Laboratory, Miami, Florida

12.4.1 Screening Strategy

The first step in any case is to review the case history and autopsy findings. If the pathologist makes no specific requests for analysis, then responsibility for deciding which tests to do falls exclusively to the professional judgment of the toxicologist.[1-9]

Obviously, cases of suspected drug intoxication require the most comprehensive testing, typically on samples of blood, liver, gastric contents, and urine or bile.[10,11] Tests in the case of a drug-related homicide may include a blood-ethanol analysis, and a standard drug-of-abuse screen on urine, with the concentration of any identified drug being quantified in the blood.[12-18] Fatalities involving motor vehicle drivers require a blood-ethanol determination, and a comprehensive urine screen with any positive drug concentration quantified in the blood.[19-23] Fatalities resulting from a fire require blood-carbon monoxide and sometimes cyanide analyses in addition to alcohol and other drugs.[24-26]

12.4.2 General Concepts

Screening protocols should include tests capable of detecting as many drugs as possible, within the constraints imposed by the available specimens, the laboratory's workload, and requirements specific to the case (Figure 12.4.1).[5-9,27] Most laboratories lack the resources required to treat every case as a general unknown, applying test after test until all possible drugs and poisons are ruled out. Such an approach may occasionally be warranted when there is a high suspicion of poisoning, but usually several standardized protocols can be used to eliminate most of the substances that can realistically be expected in a sample.

A broad-spectrum screen, capable of detecting or eliminating most of the common drugs, usually requires a combination of three or more techniques.[1,2,11,28-88] Additional tests can be combined with standardized screening protocols, thereby expanding the screening capability to encompass additional drugs of concern based upon the specifics of the case. Table 12.4.1 shows test panels commonly employed for screening various types of cases.

The most effective strategies employ a combination of immunoassays, with chromatographic techniques, and chemical tests, in order to detect a wide range of substances. Immunoassays are used to test for classes of drugs with similar structures, while the chromatographic tests detect large groups of drugs with similar extraction characteristics, polarities, and detection characteristics. Chemical tests are selective for the chemical reactivity of substances with similar structures. The type of analysis required also depends on the type of biologic specimen to be analyzed. A putrefied liver specimen, for example, will require greater sample preparation than would a fresh urine specimen. Some drugs are present in much smaller concentrations than others and thus require more sophisticated detection techniques.

It is impossible to design a single analytical scheme that is capable of detecting all the available drugs and poisons while being suitable for the wide variety of specimen combinations that may be submitted. In general, a collection of about a dozen standard general screening methods is supplemented with as many special methods as required. Because the main objective is qualitative

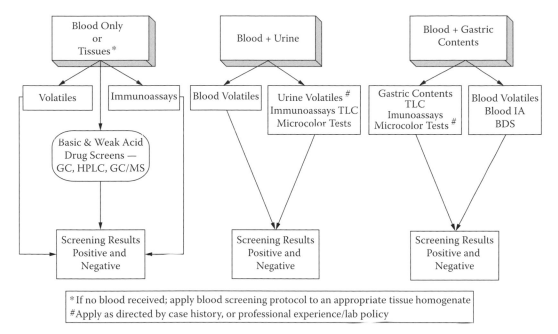

Figure 12.4.1 Post-mortem forensic toxicology screening protocols.

detection, rather than quantification, general screening methods are usually more flexible than special methods and can therefore be applied to a wider variety of materials. A good general method will provide a provisional identification, which can then be confirmed by the application of a quantitative directed analysis.

Often, the nature of a suspected toxin is unknown. The classic example is a person who has expired under suspicious circumstances and where the history, scene, and autopsy fail to disclose a definitive cause of death. In such cases, the screening strategy must be more extensive, since thousands of toxic drugs and chemicals are available on the market worldwide. A systematic procedure that allows the simultaneous detection of as many toxicants in biosamples as possible is necessary for a comprehensive toxicological analysis.[1,2,4,5,89–91]

12.4.3 Basic Strategies

In laboratories with small caseloads, each case may be reviewed individually by the director who assigns specific tests. Testing large numbers of samples proceeds more efficiently, and in a more organized fashion, when standardized assay panels are performed on batches of samples. Blood and urine are the specimens of choice to screen for drugs and poisons. Depending on the circumstances of the case, other samples include liver, stomach contents, or bile.

The blood volatiles screen detects and quantifies ethanol while simultaneously screening for methanol, isopropanol, and acetone as well as other volatiles, such as halogenated and non-halogenated hydrocarbons that are sometimes inhaled for purposes of intoxication.[46,70,92–95] Each of the immunoassay tests is used to detect substances that cannot easily be included in one or two chromatographic procedures, or for which routine chromatographic tests may be too insensitive, or where specialized extraction or derivatization conditions may be required.

12.4.3.1 Amphetamines

The amphetamines are relatively volatile, and can be lost by evaporation if the extract is not first acidified. In addition, they tend to give tailing peaks unless the gas chromatography (GC)

Table 12.4.1   Case Management by Manner of Death

	Volatiles	IA B/U	CO/ CN	BDS	WAN	TOXI- A/B	MCT	Specials
Accident								
MVA- pedestrian	X	X				X		
MVA-driver	X	X	X			X	X	
MVA- passenger	X	X	X			X		
Workplace	X	X	X			X	X	As required
Police investigation	X	X				X		As required
Aviation-crew	X	X	X	X	X	X		
Fire/Smoke	X	X	X			X	X	
Other	X	X	X			X	X	As required
Natural								
With a COD	X	X				X		
SIDS	X	X				X		APAP, ASA
Epileptics	X	X			X	X		
Asthmatics	X					X		As required
Homicides								
Active role	X	X				X	X	
Innocent victim	X	X				X		
Unknown role	X	X				X	X	
Suicide (non-drug)								
Trauma	X	X				X		
CO	X	X	X			X		As required
Pending pathology	X	X				X		
Pending toxicology	X	X	X	X	X	X	X	As required

Immunoassays imply the use of urine, however, if a urine specimen is unavailable, or "indicates the presence of" a drug, a blood analysis should follow. At a minimum, perform amphetamines, barbiturates, benzodiazepines, cocaine, opiates, PCP, and others as required by case type and history.

CO (carbon monoxide): Between the months of September and May, request on all MEO (medical examiner office) cases involving apparent natural death and pending cases occurring indoors.

MCTs: Require urine and gastric contents.

Key: IA= immunoassays; B/U = blood and/or urine; CO/CN = carbon monoxide and cyanide; BDS = basic drug screen; WAN = weak acid neutral drug screen; TOXI-A/B = commercial thin-layer chromatography acids and bases; MCT = microcolor tests; MVA = motor vehicle accident; COD = cause of death; SIDS = sudden infant death syndrome; APAP = acetaminophen; ASA = salicylates.

columns are well maintained, or the amphetamines are derivatized. However, ToxiLab can effectively detect and differentiate the sympathomimetic amines in urine, so the amphetamines immunoassay could be omitted if ToxiLab is used. If an amphetamines immunoassay is used, it should be one of broad class selectivity, not one of the newer and more specific monoclonal antibody assays, so that is has the chance of detecting the maximum number of amphetamines and related drugs (e.g., ephedrine, pseudoephedrine).[96–98]

12.4.3.2   Barbiturates

An immunoassay for barbiturates can eliminate the need for labor-intensive chromatographic screens of weakly acidic and neutral drugs in the majority of cases. Only those cases testing positive, or where phenytoin is indicated, need the chromatographic screen. The ToxiLab B system can help to differentiate barbiturates in urine, or the testing can proceed directly to a GC, HPLC, or GC-MS screen on an acidic drug extract of blood to identify the specific barbiturate(s) present in the body.[99–104]

12.4.3.3 Benzodiazepines

The benzodiazepines comprise a large class of drugs that are often detected in post-mortem cases. ToxiLab does not ordinarily detect them in urine at therapeutic doses, and a basic drug GC screen rarely detects the more potent drugs in this class, except in cases of overdose. Available immunoassays can yield positive results in urine for metabolites from most of the common benzodiazepines. Exceptions are lorazepam and flunitrazepam. GC with electron capture detection, or GC/mass spectrometry (GC/MS), may be applied to urine or blood to differentiate benzodiazepines and to detect those that are missed by immunoassays.[105–117] Whether or not to use these more labor intensive chromatographic tests in the absence of a positive immunoassay depends upon the potential significance of a benzodiazepine, if it were to be found, and on any indications from the investigation that one may have been taken. Several methods have also been published for the detection of a wide range of benzodiazepines by LC/MS or LC/MS/MS.

12.4.3.4 Cocaine

Cocaine should always be included in a post-mortem toxicology screen. Even infants and elderly individuals occasionally test positive. The most efficient way to screen for cocaine is to use an immunoassay for benzoylecgonine.[118–121] Although both ToxiLab A and basic drug GC screens can actually detect cocaine itself, special procedures are required for the chromatographic detection of benzoylecgonine. Cocaine may not always be found in the urine with benzoylecgonine, although benzoylecgonine is almost always found whenever cocaine is present.

12.4.3.5 Opiates

The common opiates include morphine, 6-monoacetylmorphine, codeine, hydromorphone, hydrocodone, and oxycodone. Routine ToxiLab A or basic drug GC screens detect codeine, hydrocodone, and oxycodone. These methods are less effective for morphine and hydromorphone, which are usually found in the urine as water-soluble conjugates of glucuronic acid. Immunoassays can detect both parent drug and metabolites. Differentiation of opiates is usually accomplished by GC/MS, using procedures that include hydrolysis of conjugates and derivatization for maximum sensitivity and specificity, or by LC/MS.[122–124]

12.4.3.6 Phencyclidine

Phencyclidine (PCP) is more commonly encountered in some regions, while not in others. It is a powerful dissociative anesthetic with significant effects on behavior at low doses, and should be included as part of the post-mortem drug screen. Both thin-layer chromatography (TLC) and GC detect PCP, although they may be insufficiently sensitive to reliably rule it out. Immunoassays capable of detecting PCP in urine down to 25 ng/mL provide a reliable screening test.[125,126]

12.4.3.7 Immunoassays for Other Illegal Drugs

Immunoassays have been developed to screen for the presence of other illegal drugs, including cannabinoids, LSD, and prescription drugs such as propoxyphene, methadone, and methaqualone. With the exception of cannabinoids and LSD, all of the analytes are readily detected by either ToxiLab A or GC basic drug screens. Cannabinoid and LSD assays may be included in a standard screening protocol or may be reserved for cases involving an issue of possible behavioral toxicity, since those are not known to contribute to either fatal intoxications or deaths attributable to natural causes.

12.4.3.8   Chromatographic Methods

Chromatographic methods are used to expand the range of a drug screen beyond those drugs detectable by the immunoassays. The extraction system should be selective for basic drugs, and neutral substances will also be extracted.[47,58,62,71–76,127–130]

ToxiLab A for Urine and Gastric Contents

The ToxiLab A system for basic drug detection is a powerful tool for drug screening in urine or gastric contents.[55–57,131] The four-stage visualization process, combined with R_f and detection of metabolite patterns, adds considerably to the confidence in drug identification. Sensitivity for many drugs is on the order of 0.5 to 1.0 mg/L, which is satisfactory for screening urine or gastric samples. The ToxiLab A can detect nearly 150 drugs and their metabolites.

Alternatives to ToxiLab

A screen for basic and neutral drugs by CG with a nitrogen/phosphorus detector (NPD) is an alternative to ToxiLab TLC for a laboratory having sufficient GC capacity.[47,71,74–76,82,127] GC is much more sensitive than TLC, having limits of detection on the order of 0.01 to 0.10 mg/L from 1 mL of sample. GC can be calibrated to presumptively identify hundreds of drugs and drug metabolites, and the NPD data can reveal other unidentified nitrogen-containing substances that may be characterized by additional analysis of the extract by GC/MS.

The Trinders test is added to the screen to detect salicylate from aspirin, a common drug and one that is sometimes taken for suicidal purposes. It may be eliminated if the screen is intended only to evaluate potential behavioral toxicity. The chemical tests for ethchlorvynol and chloral hydrate fill another gap in the screening protocol, since these drugs are not detected by immunoassay or in chromatographic screens for basic drug or volatiles. Figure 12.4.2 illustrates the analytical scheme for routine cases with both urine and blood submitted to the laboratory.

12.4.3.9   Gastric Contents vs. Urine

Often, urine is not available for testing because the bladder was empty at the time of autopsy. In such cases, an extract or filtrate of gastric contents may be substituted. However, a gastric drug screen alone may not be sufficient to exclude all potentially relevant substances. Drugs that are typically administered parenterally, smoked, or insufflated may not diffuse into the stomach in detectable amounts, so blood or plasma analysis with immunoassays for opiates and benzoylecgonine is often required to detect those substances.

Drugs taken hours before death may not remain in the stomach. However, some quantity of a basic drug will diffuse into the stomach from blood and become ionized, and thus remains there. The resulting concentration in the stomach contents is determined in part by the drug's concentration in blood and in part by its pKa. For optimum sensitivity, a gastric content drug screen may be combined with immunoassays on plasma, vitreous humor, or blood for barbiturates, benzodiazepines, benzoylecgonine, opiates, and a basic drug screen of blood by GC-NPD. The following protocols, which employ tests on gastric contents and blood (or plasma), can be used in place of a urine drug screen. The same blood test panel may be used when gastric contents are not available, or applied to tissue homogenates when blood is not available.

Immunoassays can usually be performed directly on unhemolyzed plasma or vitreous humor. Even hemolyzed plasma and post-mortem whole blood can be tested directly if FPIA or RIA is used.[50,52,132–145] If results are unsatisfactory, simple dilution with an equal volume of assay buffer is often sufficient to render an analyzable sample. If FPIA or RIA is not available in the laboratory, blood may be screened with spectrophotometry-based immunoassays, although hemoglobin and

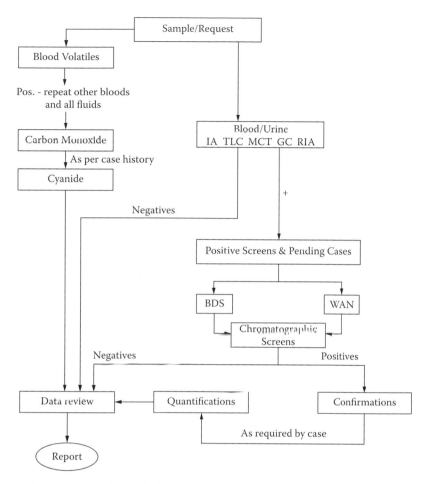

Figure 12.4.2 Flowchart for routine toxicology cases.

other proteins must first be precipitated by addition of acetone, methanol, or acetonitrile. The centrifuged supernatant from such treatment can be assayed against similarly prepared calibrators.[49–52,146–154] When applied to blood, plasma, or vitreous humor, immunoassays should be calibrated to a lower cutoff threshold than that used for urine screening. Cutoffs, on the order of 50 ng/mL (500 ng/mL for barbiturates) will yield some false positives. Considering the variations in cross-reactivity for analytes of interest (e.g., benzodiazepines), some false-positive immunoassay results may be acceptable in the interest of minimizing false negatives. Any positive immunoassay result must, of course, be confirmed if it is to be reported. If the case may involve lethal toxicity, immunoassays for acetaminophen and salicylate should be added to the panel.

12.4.3.10 Screening with Gas Chromatography

GC for basic drugs in blood is more sensitive than a basic drug screen on gastric contents, but is also more labor intensive. It may be included in a general drug screen whenever urine is not available or it may be reserved for cases where intoxication is indicated by the investigation, and gastric contents yield negative screening results. Figure 12.4.1 illustrates general screening protocols for various combinations of post-mortem samples.

When initial chromatographic screening tests reveal an unidentified spot on TLC or a response from GC that does not match any standard, extracts may be further screened by GC/MS in the full scan electron-impact ionization mode.[80,82,83,100,155–163] Reconstructed ion chromatograms are inspected for spectra that indicate exogenous (i.e., xenobiotic) substances. Suspect spectra are compared with the instrument's computerized libraries of drugs, poisons, and their metabolites. In addition, spectra may be visually compared with published compilations of mass spectral data.[164-169] Whenever a tentative identification is made, the unknown and reference spectra must be visually compared to verify their identity. GC/MS is the most complex method of screening for drugs and poisons, and also the most expensive. The analyst must have a considerable amount of training and experience to reliably perform GC/MS screening.

To provide adequate support for a medical examiner's office the toxicology laboratory should periodically assess the prevalence of drugs in the population served, and adjust its offering of routine tests accordingly. Certain drugs are more prevalent in various localities due to supply routes, ethnic practices, and demand. Changing patterns of drug use may be identified through crime laboratory statistics and various epidemiological monitoring programs, such as the Drug Abuse Warning Network (DAWN) and the community-based Drug Epidemiology Network. In Europe, the www.emcdda Web site offers similar information for the EU countries.

12.4.3.11   Screening with Liquid Chromatography

Many drugs that cannot be detected by GC can be detected by high-performance liquid chromatography (HPLC). HPLC separates analytes in solution, at or near ambient temperature, and therefore can be used for drugs that are too thermolabile or polar to be analyzed by GC. Furthermore, chemical derivatization is rarely, if ever, required prior to analysis of drugs by HPLC. While most, but not all drugs, absorb ultraviolet (UV) light sufficiently well to be detected by a UV detector, a UV spectrum usually does not give sufficient information on its own, for a forensically valid identification. Therefore, the preferred detector increasingly is becoming the mass spectrometer. However, LC/MS has not yet become widely accepted as a useful screening technique for two reasons. First, LC/MS instrumentation continues to cost approximately twice as much as a GC/MS instrument. Second, and more important, it has been very difficult to generate reference libraries that are universally useful. Although, perhaps arguably more useful than UV spectra, most LC/MS spectra lack the detail of typical electron impact (EI) GC/MS spectra, and worse, relative abundances across the spectrum can vary with pH and ionic strength.

12.4.4 The General Unknown

Cases in which a toxic cause of death is suspected but where a specified toxic agent is not known are referred to as general unknowns, and require an open-ended search for poisons. The first step in investigating a general unknown is to carefully examine the medical records, case history, autopsy findings, and scene observations for evidence of specific toxins, or of a toxic mechanism.[1-3,5-9,30,170,171]

The case history and medical records may describe symptoms characteristic of a particular pharmacologic category. Cardiac rhythm disturbances, respiratory rate and pattern, pupil size and responsiveness, condition of reflexes, convulsions, and any other pre-mortem symptoms may suggest a toxic mechanism that excludes some toxins from a long list of possible agents.

Autopsy findings may also provide guidance. The condition of the gastric and esophageal mucosa may suggest or exclude corrosive poisons. The presence of massive pulmonary edema may indicate preterminal respiratory depression. Hepatic necrosis may indicate acetaminophen or *Amanita* mushroom toxicity, among other agents. Needle punctures and, especially, "track marks" indicate possible intravenous drug overdose. These and other observations, properly interpreted, can narrow the focus of the analytical search.

Consideration of the place where death occurred, or where the terminal symptoms appeared, may suggest toxic agents. Scene investigation can yield valuable clues. For example, the death of a jewelry store employee may have resulted from exposure to cyanide, which is used in jewelry manufacture. Other employment settings have associated chemical hazards that should be recognized when planning a strategy for investigation of a workplace death.

In the home, other toxic exposures are more likely. Drugs, pesticides, and other chemical products for household use are possible agents. Also, drug misuse at home can result in accidents or fatal intoxication. Reports of witnesses can also give valuable clues. What was the deceased doing at the onset of illness? When was the deceased last seen alive? Was the deceased behaving normally, or was intoxication indicated? Was there a complaint of feeling sick? Eliciting such observations may make it possible to shorten the list of possible drugs.

The volatiles screen by headspace GC, while designed to test for the common alcohols and acetone, can also detect other volatile chemicals such as toluene and other solvents and volatile anesthetics. Drug screening tests are essential to rule out drug intoxication, and chromatographic screens can detect many other chemical substances besides drugs. GC/MS is a mainstay of screening protocols for general unknowns. Semivolatile organic compounds can be identified by computerized comparison of their mass spectra with libraries containing over 50,000 spectra of pesticides, drugs, and industrial chemicals. Figure 12.4.3 illustrates a strategy for analysis of cases where classification is pending the outcome of toxicology testing.

Tests for drugs and poisons not detected by the basic strategy can be added to the protocol for general unknowns. Selective immunoassays are available to test for cardiac glycosides, LSD, fentanyls, haloperidol, aminoglycoside antibiotics, and anticonvulsants. Clinical laboratories can provide assistance with tests for potassium, lithium, iron, and insulin or C-peptide. Toxic metals and nonmetals can be detected by atomic absorption spectrophotometry, and classical inorganic qualitative tests can be used to screen for toxic anions on a dialysate of urine, blood, or stomach contents. Other drugs that do not chromatograph well by GC may be detected by HPLC.

The following guidelines should be observed in approaching the general unknown:

1. If specimen selection and quantity are not limiting factors, then the objective should be the broadest screen possible with available technology.
2. The blood and vitreous fluid alcohol content should be determined before or simultaneously with other analyses.
3. Blood alcohol analyses should be performed by headspace GC, utilizing an internal standard. This does not preclude possible confirmation by some other procedure.
4. If carbon monoxide is to be determined, this should also be done prior to drug screening procedures.
5. In the absence of background information on a given case, the selected analytical scheme should provide the best chances of successfully finding a drug or poison. That is, the more commonly encountered drugs and poisons should be sought before the more rarely encountered ones are considered.
6. In the event that specimen selection and quantity are limited, it will be necessary to plan assays more carefully. Immunoassay procedures should be applied early in the scheme if proper samples are available.
7. All assays should be considered with the intent of subsequently confirming positive findings by another independent procedure. This means, for example, that if specimen size is a limiting factor, then different stages of a general screen should be performed sequentially rather than in parallel.

12.4.5 Confirmation

12.4.5.1 *What Confirmation Is Necessary, and Why*

Courts require that the opinions expressed by toxicologists be of a "reasonable scientific probability," that the identity of reported substances be known with "scientific certainty," and that quantitative values be accurate to a stated statistical probability. Screening tests provide tentative identification of drugs and poisons. The forensic standard for conclusive identification requires that their identity be confirmed by additional tests.[172]

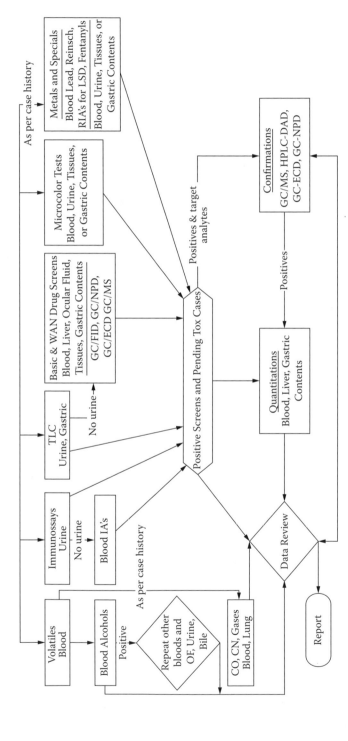

Figure 12.4.3 Analytical strategies for post-mortem toxicology screening in the pending tox case.

The first analytical indication of the presence of a particular drug is usually obtained from an immunoassay, a chromatographic screen (e.g., TLC), or a spot test. The initial test may point to a particular drug, or class of drugs, such as barbiturates, benzodiazepines, or opiates. The confirmatory test must clearly identify the specific drug and/or its metabolite(s). Confirmatory methods may include gas chromatography with flame ionization (GC-FID), electron capture (GC-ECD), and nitrogen-phosphorus (GC-NPD) detectors, HPLC, UV spectroscopy, GC/MS, and other hyphenated techniques such as MS/MS coupled to either a GC or LC sample introduction system.

Any chemical test can be subject to errors that may cause a false-positive result. Immunoassays can cross-react with substances other than the target drug. Chromatographic methods can have interfering substances that produce a signal or spot at the same time and place as a target analyte. Even GC/MS can yield false positive results if a sample is mislabeled or contaminated in process, or by carryover from a preceding injection, or if the spectrum does not have a unique fragmentation pattern. For example, amitriptyline and cyclobenzaprine have similar retention times and yield fragmentation patterns that are nearly identical. They may be confused if the molecular ion cannot be discerned.

In recognition of the possibility of a false-positive result from a single test, it is necessary that all potentially significant results be confirmed. Confirmation requires at least one additional test based on a different chemical detection principle, with high specificity and sensitivity at least equal to the initial test.[172] The essence of confirmation is to assemble a sufficient body of evidence such that a technically competent independent reviewer would agree with the conclusion.

The requirement for two or more chemically distinct methodologies is based on the concern that chemical similarity could cause a false-positive result in one type of test, and may also influence another test with a similar chemical principle. A radioimmunoassay cannot confirm enzyme immunoassay results since the chemical properties responsible for antibody binding may affect the antibodies in both tests similarly. Likewise, two similar GC columns such as 1 and 5% phenyl-methylsilicone (DB-1 and DB-5) would not serve to confirm one another, because the polarities of the two liquid phases and, hence, the elution orders of most drugs are similar.

A combination of less specific chromatographic procedures (e.g., TLC, GC-NPD/ECD, or HPLC) can be used to confirm screening results from immunoassay or spot test results. A second chromatographic method based on a different chemical principle may be used to confirm a presumptive finding from a chromatographic screening test (e.g., TLC and GLC or HPLC and GC-NPD/EC). Derivatization of the presumptively identified drug can alter its chromatographic behavior sufficiently to permit confirmation by reanalysis in the same chromatographic system. Some screening procedures, such as GC/MS, identify specific compounds. Even here, a second test on a separate aliquot should be performed to "verify" the analyte and ensure that no human error in sample handling or analyses has occurred. Re-injection of the same extract would not be sufficient. An exception to this rule would be limited sample volume precluding repeat analyses.

In post-mortem toxicology, confirmation tests are often applied to specimens other than the one used for screening. By employing a quantitative confirmatory method, the analyte is simultaneously confirmed and quantified. For example, a presumptive finding of diphenhydramine in urine by TLC may be confirmed by a quantitative GC procedure applied to blood.

Some additional illustrative examples of confirmation follow:

1. An immunoassay positive for opiates in urine, followed by a GC/MS analysis of urine to identify the specific drug(s).
2. An immunoassay positive for benzodiazepines in urine, followed by an analysis of blood by GC-ECD to identify the specific drug(s).
3. A drug such as amitriptyline detected by TLC in urine or gastric contents followed by GC-NPD analysis of blood with relative retention times matching the suspected drug, ideally on two columns of differing liquid phase. A quantification of the drug by HPLC would give additional confirmatory evidence as would detection of metabolites of the presumptively identified drug by TLC or GC.

4. Immunoassay positive for cocaine metabolite in urine or blood with detection of parent cocaine in blood by GC-NPD.
5. In some cases, such as blood volatiles analysis, GC headspace analysis can be correlated as relative retention times on two GC columns of differing polarity (giving a different elution order) to confirm an identification. However, novel or rarely detected analytes such as toluene or 1,1,1,-trichloroethane may require further confirmation by headspace GC/MS.

12.4.5.2 When Is Confirmation Necessary?

In general, any finding that could reasonably be questioned, or adversely affect insurance coverage or the reputation of the deceased, should be confirmed before it is reported. The greater the significance of a finding to the case, the more important it becomes to confirm that finding to absolute certainty by GC/MS, if possible.

- When the substance is potentially related to the cause and manner of death
- When the detected substance is an illicit drug such as marijuana, cocaine, methamphetamine, or PCP, since labeling an individual a possible drug abuser has serious sociologic and legal implications[173–176]
- Any prescription drug that is not known to have been prescribed for the deceased

12.4.5.3 When Is Confirmation Unnecessary?

When the substance presumptively detected has no relationship to the cause or manner of death, and when the detected substance carries no stigma, if reported, confirmation may not be needed. Over-the-counter medications, with no behavioral toxicity, usually do not require confirmation except when it is suspected that they may have contributed to toxicity. For example, salicylate or acetaminophen need not be confirmed in traumatic death cases, but should be confirmed in cases pending toxicology or suicidal intoxications.

Medications commonly administered during resuscitation, such as lidocaine and atropine, do not need confirmation if the deceased received such treatment before being pronounced dead. Prescribed medications that the deceased had been taking, and which are not related to the cause or manner of death, may not require confirmation either, since their presence in biological specimens is consistent with the history. Any substance reported without confirmation should be identified in the report as an unconfirmed presumptive finding.

12.4.6 Gas Chromatography-Mass Spectrometry

Today, GC/MS is generally accepted as unequivocal identification for most drugs, providing the best confirmatory information when performed correctly.[177,178] However, GC/MS assays can be performed in many ways, depending on the specific requirements and use of the results. Pharmacokinetic studies generally employ chemical ionization with single-ion monitoring to obtain optimum sensitivity. In such studies, the target drug is expected to be present, so criteria for identification need not be so rigorous, but single-ion monitoring is not usually considered sufficient for forensic purposes. GC/MS methods for the confirmation of illegal drugs of abuse in urine most often use electron impact ionization and multiple-ion monitoring to obtain conclusive results.[177–181] The more traditional MS identification criterion calls for matching retention times and full-scan electron impact mass spectra of the unknown with a standard.

Whether forensic samples should be analyzed by full-scan data acquisition, or by selected ion monitoring, is a matter of contention. The debate really comes down to one underlying question: How much spectral and chromatographic information is needed to provide a scientifically and legally defensible identification? Is a full-scan spectrum necessary? If selected ion monitoring is acceptable, how many ions must be monitored? Unfortunately, there are no simple answers. A good-quality, full-scan mass spectrum that matches a reference spectrum clearly constitutes a more definitive identification than ion current profiles of a few selected ions at the correct retention time.

Cody and Foltz have stated that the specificity of a GC/MS assay depends on many factors, including:

1. Choice of internal standard. The role of the internal standard in the overall analytical process cannot be overemphasized.[182-187]
2. Selectivity of the extraction procedure.
3. Choice of derivative, where appropriate.[188-190]
4. Efficiency of the GS separation.
5. Method of ionization.
6. Relative uniqueness of the analyte's mass spectrum or the chosen ions to be monitored.
7. Signal-to-noise ratio of the detected ions.[192]

Using GC/MS in the scanning mode, as both a screening and definitive identification methodology, has become quite common.[163] If the drug is an unknown, full-scan mode is the method of choice. Further comparison of the unknown's full mass spectrum with reference spectra will be necessary. Mass spectra are tentatively identified by a computerized library search and visually compared by an experienced analyst.[80,81,161-163]

GC/MS with selected ion monitoring (GC/MS-SIM) is commonly used to confirm the presence of drugs and/or metabolites in post-mortem samples.[180,191] A well-designed assay, involving the selected ion monitoring of three or more abundant and structurally diagnostic ions, combined with specific requirements for the analyte's retention time relative to a suitable internal standard or calibrator, is regarded as a reliable identification.[192] Even fewer ions can provide an acceptable identification if the assay employs a highly selective extraction procedure or selective mode of ionization, such as ammonia chemical ionization.

GC/MS-SIM assays are extremely useful to confirm or exclude the presence of a suspected analyte that may have been indicated by history or screening results. However, target compound analyses such as GC/MS-SIM will detect, or exclude, only a limited number of related chemical compounds or classes of drugs. A reference standard and control materials of the target analyte must be analyzed within the same batch. Selected ion monitoring typically provides signal intensities that are 10- to 100-fold greater than those from full-scan analysis performed on quadrupole instruments. SIM analyses are therefore better adapted for quantitative measurements. Selected ion monitoring is generally less susceptible to interferences from co-eluting compounds than an assay employing full-scan recording. However, unlike full-scan spectral acquisition, a selected ion monitoring assay will not detect unsuspected drugs that may be of toxicological significance.

Standards adopted for conclusive drug identification include (1) the appearance of the monitored ions at a correct retention time, (2) acceptable intensity ratios among those ions. The retention time and ion intensity ratios observed in the test sample are compared with those established from the calibrator(s) containing the target analyte, at a suitable concentration, incorporated in the same analytical batch.

12.4.6.1 Qualitative GC/MS-SIM Determination Criteria

To qualitatively identify a compound by selected ion monitoring (SIM), ion chromatograms are obtained from the reference compound for the primary ion and two or more qualifier ions. The criteria below must be met for a qualitative identification of an unknown:

1. The characteristic ions of the compound must be found at maxima in the same scan or within one scan of each other.
2. The retention time of the unknown compound's mass spectrum must be within ±2% of the retention time of the authentic compound or deuterated internal standard.

3. The ratios of the SIM peak areas must agree within ±20% with the ratios of the relative intensities for those ions in a reference mass spectrum from a calibrator analyzed on the same run by the GC/MS system.

These criteria should be kept in mind when making compound identification decisions. In addition Dr. Rodger Foltz has proposed the following helpful guidelines:[160,192–194]

1. Agreement among the relative ion intensities within a small mass range is more important than for those encompassing a wide mass range.
2. The higher mass ions are generally more diagnostic than those occurring at low mass.
3. No prominent ions in either spectrum (those with relative intensities above 10%) should be totally missing from the other spectrum, unless they can be attributed to an impurity.

12.4.6.2 Potential Problems with GC/MS Analyses

Several problems may be encountered in GC/MS analysis. The mass spectral library may give erroneous identifications when concentrations near the detection limit are analyzed, or when chromatographically interfering substances are present, or when isomers are analyzed. Even MS with a full fragmentation pattern may not provide adequate confirmation, either because several drugs have very similar fragmentation patterns, as the barbiturates, for example, or because the drug may exhibit only one major peak consisting of a low mass fragment ion in its mass spectrum, such as the tricyclic antidepressants.

When using the SIM mode, a considerable gain in GC/MS sensitivity can be achieved by focusing on the most abundant ion, and two or more other characteristic ions. However, many illegal drugs or metabolites (and numerous other commonly used drugs, e.g., antihistamines, local anesthetics, some beta-blocking agents, etc.) have similar EI mass spectra, showing a common base peak and weak molecular ion signals. Many elute over a wide range of retention times; others may have closely related retention indices.

The complexity of biological matrices encountered in post-mortem cases, such as "blood," tissues, gastric contents, and hair/nails, necessitates well-designed, and often multistep, sample treatment procedures.[195] This is especially true when utilizing procedures based on physicochemical properties of drug/metabolites. Suitable sample preparation is the most important prerequisite in the GC/MS of typical post-mortem samples. It involves isolation and, if necessary, cleavage of conjugates and/or derivatization of the drugs and their metabolites. Derivatization steps are necessary if relatively polar compounds such as metabolites are to be screened or confirmed.

12.4.7 Liquid Chromatography-Mass Spectrometry

LC/MS is fast becoming an important technique in forensic toxicology, despite its increased cost over GC/MS.[225–230] For a long time, the combination of HPLC and MS was not an alternative because of interface problems. Now when this obstacle has been overcome by different innovations, LC/MS has become increasingly popular both for screening purposes and for sensitive and specific confirmation analyses. Many drugs cannot be analyzed by GC/MS because they are either thermolabile, or are too polar or insufficiently volatile to chromatograph well, if at all. In contrast, virtually any drug can be analyzed by LC/MS after development of a suitable method. Other than the issue of cost, the only disadvantage of LC over GC is that LC separations usually require more development time than GC separations. The comments in Section 12.4.6, above, generally apply to LC/MS analysis, especially in regard to SIM analysis. As with GC/MS, so-called "hyphenated" techniques may be used, such as LC/MS/MS. Tandem MS-MS instruments have the enormous advantage of being able to provide a much higher degree of specificity than LC/MS alone. The first mass spectrometer in the LC/MS/MS system generates a conventional mass spectrum. One specific mass is then allowed to pass through into a separate collision cell where it can be ionized further. Either the entire mass spectrum of that chosen ion may be displayed, or a single ion isolated in SIM mode. Tandem MS techniques such as LC/MS/MS are particularly useful for post-mortem forensic work because they minimize interference from endogenous compounds such as putrefactive products. LC/MS/MS-TOF (time-of-flight) instruments offer a further degree of specificity because of the increased specificity imparted by the medium to high mass resolution of TOF instruments. Of course, the major drawbacks of LC/MS/MS and LC/MS/MS-TOF instruments are considerably increased cost, and complexity of operation, often requiring a dedicated operator. Having stated that, the development of a method for a particular analyte is generally easier with LC/MS than with GC/MS because standards with reference compounds can be directly injected and calibration curves can readily be constructed. A special feature that the operator must keep in mind is that a change in pH to adjust the chromatography will also affect the charge of the compounds at the time for ionization, and hence influence the mass spectrometric detection.

Different interface systems are available. The most utilized alternative is atmospheric pressure-positive electrospray ionization (API-ES), and a number of applications in forensic toxicology with this methodology has been reported.[231–235] Alternatively, atmospheric pressure-chemical ionization (APCI) can be used. Both these variants of LC/MS instrumentation cover a wider spectrum of polar and nonpolar drugs than GC/MS analysis can offer, and API-ES also allows for analysis of molecules with higher masses. APCI MS/MS has been shown to be useful for sensitive screening of certain classes of drugs such as benzodiazepines and hypnotics,[236] and beta-blockers.[237]

12.4.8 Method Validation

Bioanalytical methods, based on a variety of physicochemical and biological techniques, such as chromatography, immunoassay, and mass spectrometry, must all be individually validated prior to and during use to generate confidence in the results.[196–210] Method validation is discussed in Chapter 12.5.

12.4.9 Quantification of Drugs and Poisons

When you can measure what you are speaking about and express it in numbers, you know something about it; but when you cannot express it in numbers, your knowledge is of meagre and unsatisfactory kind.

— **Lord Kelvin (1824–1907)**

Screening and confirmation (qualitative) tests establish the presence of a specific substance; quantitative tests measure the amount of that substance in a particular specimen. Qualitative information alone can demonstrate that the deceased was exposed to the substance before death, and may even enable the toxicologist to offer an opinion regarding the ante-mortem interval in which the exposure probably took place. However, quantitative information is often required to form an opinion whether or not the exposure was sufficient to cause behavioral toxicity or death. Drug concentrations in post-mortem tissues, or fluids, must be related to reference values derived from other cases.[5,211–215]

12.4.9.1 What Should Be Quantified?

Substances should be quantified only when necessary for interpretation. Most quantitative assays are separate, labor-intensive procedures that measure only one drug or group of similar compounds. Quantifying substances that, by their nature, could have no conceivable bearing on the issues of the case is a waste of time and resources. For example, drugs with no psychoactivity, such as acetaminophen, should not be quantified in a motor vehicle accident driver victim, while diphen-hydramine, an antihistamine with sedative side effects, should. On the other hand, if the victim was a passenger, diphenhydramine would not require quantification. In deaths from asthma or epilepsy, the laboratory should quantify theophylline or anticonvulsant, respectively, to determine whether or not they were within or below the therapeutic concentration range.

In general, substances that can cause behavioral toxicity should be quantified. In most natural deaths, it is important to know that the concentration of a prescribed or therapeutic drug is not excessive. Semiquantitative information, derived from blood screening tests, is often sufficient to make the assessment. Only if the concentration estimate indicates an excessive amount would a quantitative assay be required. Poisons such as carbon monoxide, cyanide, and heavy metals should always be quantified in appropriate specimens. Tests for ethanol usually yield both qualitative and quantitative data, which should be reported if above the laboratory's administrative cutoff (usually 0.01%).

Cocaine should always be quantified. Its concentration is usually important and its instability in storage may prevent subsequent analysis if it is not quantified soon after detection. Other drugs or poisons that are unstable in storage should be quantified before their decomposition renders the analysis unreliable. In a case that is pending the outcome of toxicology testing, any detected drugs or poisons and their metabolites should be quantified, unless it is clear from the circumstances of the case that a particular substance did not play a role in the cause or manner of death.

When resuscitation has been attempted, lidocaine and atropine may be detected in post-mortem blood. Unless a medication error is suspected, or the quantity appears to be excessive, it is not necessary to quantify them. Nor is there any need to quantify caffeine and nicotine, unless toxicity is suspected or screening tests indicate that an abnormally large amount of either is present.

In most cases a drug's metabolites are just as important to quantify as the parent compound. The ratio of parent drug to its metabolite often indicates the state of pharmacokinetics in the individual case. For example, a ratio greater than 1 for amitriptyline/nortriptyline may indicate an acute ingestion or short interval from ingestion to death, while a ratio of 0.3 in a propoxyphene/norpropoxyphene case may indicate a chronic exposure.

Active or toxic metabolites of a drug or poison are always measured, but inactive metabolites may also be important. Their presence may shed light on the pattern of drug use. High concentrations of benzoylecgonine indicate accumulations from multiple doses. Low concentrations suggest that only a few doses were taken or that there has been a long interval since the last dose. Furthermore, there is some evidence that benzoylecgonine may be a vasoconstrictor, so it may contribute to the hypertensive effects of cocaine use.

12.4.9.2 *Specimens for Quantification of Drugs and Poisons*

The choice of the sample for quantitative analysis is very important.[216] Often it is sufficient to quantify drugs or poisons in blood only. If toxicity is not suspected, a blood quantification can verify that the drug was present, and that its concentration was consistent with therapeutic use. Also, when a drug concentration is clearly in the lethal range, and poisoning or overdose is suspected, a blood determination may be sufficient. It may not be necessary to quantify brain morphine levels in an intravenous heroin user, found dead with syringe, tourniquet, and "cooker" present, with autopsy evidence of pulmonary edema, and a high concentration of morphine in the blood, to support a conclusion that death was caused by a heroin overdose. Likewise, a 15 mg/L blood amitriptyline concentration, in a case accompanied by a suicide note, is sufficient to define overt toxicity, regardless of potential post-mortem diffusion.[216] Carbon monoxide should be measured in blood, its site of action. Other specimens are likely to give negative results. One exception, not related to drug abuse, is the analysis of skeletal muscle specimens for carbon monoxide to assist in the differentiation between entrance and exit gunshot wounds.

Tissues that selectively take up a particular drug class may have a much higher concentration than that found in blood. For example, volatile anesthetics, cocaine, marijuana, tricyclic antidepressants, and other lipid-soluble substances are preferentially absorbed into the fatty tissues of the brain and liver, while digoxin and other cardiac glycosides are taken up by cardiac muscle. Figure

12.4.2 and Figure 12.4.3 show the relationship of quantifications to the overall process of post-mortem toxicology analysis.

12.4.9.3 Quantification: Procedural Issues

Instruments

Many of the instruments used for screening tests can also provide accurate quantitative data. Immunoassays designed for therapeutic drug monitoring (TDM) (e.g., serum assays for phenobarbital, theophylline, and phenytoin) are specific, and yield accurate results with most post-mortem specimens.[144,217] GC, HPLC, GC/MS, and LC/MS are readily adapted for quantification. Spectrophotometric methods are useful for some analytes, such as ethchlorvynol and heavy metals.[1] However, their utility is limited because many drugs have metabolites or breakdown products with similar spectra (e.g., phenothiazines), so relative contributions of the parent drug, and active and inactive metabolites, to the signal cannot be segregated and assessed.

Sample Preparation

Blood and other fluids are usually extracted with no pretreatment other than dilution. GC screening tests can provide an estimate of the concentration of the analyte. If the estimated concentration is above the upper limit of linearity of the assay, the sample must be diluted with water, buffer, or negative control matrix and thoroughly mixed to bring the analyte concentration into the dynamic range of the assay. Homogenates of tissue samples are prepared in a blender or a tissue homogenizer in water or a buffer usually in a 1:2 to a 1:5 ratio. These homogenates deteriorate rapidly so they are usually used within 2 weeks or less, and the remainder discarded. Gastric contents are weighed or measured by volume, homogenized, and appropriately diluted.

With the exception of some immunoassays, samples are usually extracted with organic solvent to isolate the compounds of interest from the biological matrix. Often, liquid–liquid extraction is used, with back-extraction to eliminate lipid interference. Recent advances in solid-phase extraction technology have made possible the application of these techniques to the analysis of blood and tissues. The speed and efficiency of solid-phase extractions make them an attractive alternative to liquid–liquid extraction procedures, and their use is expanding in post-mortem toxicology. However, lot-to-lot inconsistencies in solid-phase extraction columns can cause quantitative methods to fail, due to poor recovery of analytes. Therefore, it is extremely important to evaluate each new batch of columns before risking wastage of, sometimes limited, samples.

Duplicate samples should be analyzed through the entire procedure to demonstrate the reproducibility of the result. If the difference between duplicate analyses is greater than the two standard deviations for the method, the analyst should suspect that an error occurred in one or both. Additional analyses should be performed to determine an accurate result with acceptable precision.

Internal Standard

Most quantitative procedures employ one or more internal standards to compensate for variations in extraction efficiency, injection volume, and changes in detector sensitivity. An internal standard is a substance with chemical properties similar to the target analyte. It is added in identical quantity to each sample and standard before the extraction process. The internal standard is extracted along with the analyte, so that any loss of analyte in the extraction process will be compensated for by a proportional loss of internal standard. The assumption is that the ratio of analyte to internal standard does not change. Selection and evaluation of the internal standards is a critical component for the development of a quantitative procedure.[184,218–222] Method development and validation and the selection of internal standards are discussed in Chapter 12.5.

12.4.10   The Review Process

Individual cases should be reviewed periodically to assess the status of the investigation and the quality of the acquired data. Reassessment may suggest the need for additional tests. Before a report is issued, the entire case file must be reviewed to ensure that results are forensically acceptable and that sufficient data have been gathered to determine whether, and to what extent, drugs or poisons influenced the cause and manner of death. When testing has been completed, the toxicologist reviews the file one final time to ensure that nothing has been overlooked.

12.4.11   Pending Toxicology Conference

In cases where the cause of death is not obvious, and determinations have been put on hold pending the results of toxicological testing, the toxicologist and pathologist together review the investigation, autopsy, and toxicology results. When both are satisfied that the toxicology results answer the questions pertinent to the case, a final toxicology report is issued. The need for communication and teamwork for an effective system cannot be overemphasized.[1–5,223,224] Refer to Figure 12.4.3 summarizing the analytic strategies for drug screening in "pending tox cases."

REFERENCES

1. Curry, A.S., Outline of a systematic search for an unknown poison in viscera, in *Mechanisms and Analytical Methods*, Vol. 1, Stewart, C.P. and Stolman, A., Eds., Academic Press, New York, 257–283, 1960.
2. Freimuth, H.C., Isolation and separation of poisons from biological material, in *Mechanisms and Analytical Methods*, Vol. 1, Stewart, C.P. and Stolman, A., Eds., Academic Press, New York, 285–302, 1960.
3. Stewart, C.P. and Martin, G.J., The mode of action of poisons, in *Mechanisms and Analytical Methods*, Stewart, C.P. and Stolman, A., Eds., Vol. 2, Academic Press, New York, 1–15, 1960.
4. Stewart, C.P. and Stolman, A., The toxicologist and his work, in *Toxicology: Mechanisms and Analytical Methods*, Vol. 1, Stewart, C.P. and Stolman, A., Eds., Academic Press, New York, 1–22, 1960.
5. Jackson, J.V., Forensic toxicology, in *Clarke's Isolation and Identification of Drugs in Pharmaceuticals, Body Fluids, and Post-Mortem Material*, 2nd ed., Moffatt, A.C., Ed., Pharmaceutical Press, London, 35, 1986.
6. Finkle, B.S., Forensic toxicology in the 1980's: the role of the analytical chemist, *Anal. Chem.*, 54, 433A–438A, 1982.
7. Levine, B., Forensic toxicology [review], *Anal. Chem.*, 65, 272A–276A, 1993.
8. Levine, B.S., Smith, M.L., and Froede, R.C., Postmortem forensic toxicology [review], *Clin. Lab. Med.*, 10(3), 571–589, 1990.
9. Osselton, M.D., Analytical forensic toxicology [review], *Arch. Toxicol. Suppl.*, 15, 259–267, 1992.
10. Kasantikul, V. and Kasantikul, D., Death following intentional overdose of psychotropic drugs, *J. Med. Assoc. Thailand*, 72, 109–111, 1989.
11. Costello, C.E., GC/MS analysis of street drugs, particularly in the body fluids of overdose victims, in *Street Drug Analysis and Its Social and Clinical Implications*, Marshman, J.A., Ed., Addiction Research Foundation, Toronto, 1974, 67–78.
12. Nashelsky, M.B., Dix, J.D., and Adelstein, E.H., Homicide facilitated by inhalation of chloroform, *J. Forensic Sci.*, 40, 134–138, 1995.
13. Tardiff, K., Marzuk, P.M., Leon, A.C., Hirsch, C.S., Stajic, M., Portera, L. et al., Cocaine, opiates, and ethanol in homicides in New York City: 1990 and 1991, *J. Forensic Sci.*, 40, 387–390, 1995.
14. Bailey, D.N. and Shaw, R.F., Cocaine- and methamphetamine-related deaths in San Diego County (1987): homicides and accidental overdoses, *J. Forensic Sci.*, 34, 407–422, 1989.
15. Budd, R.D., The incidence of alcohol use in Los Angeles County homicide victims, *Am. J. Drug Alcohol Abuse*, 9, 105–111, 1982.
16. Garriott, J.C., Di Maio, V.J., and Rodriguez, R.G., Detection of cannabinoids in homicide victims and motor vehicle fatalities, *J. Forensic Sci.*, 31, 1274–1282, 1986.

17. Garriott, J.C., Drug use among homicide victims, *Am. J. Forensic Med. Pathol.,* 14, 234–237, 1993.

18. Poklis, A., Graham, M., Maginn, D., Branch, C.A., and Gantner, G.E., Phencyclidine and violent deaths in St. Louis, Missouri: a survey of medical examiners' cases from 1977 through 1986, *Am. J. Drug Alcohol Abuse,* 16, 265–274, 1990.

19. Gerostamoulos, J. and Drummer, O.H., Incidence of psychoactive cannabinoids in drivers killed in motor vehicle accidents, *J. Forensic Sci.,* 38, 649–656, 1993.

20. Marzuk, P.M., Tardiff, K., Leon, A.C., Stajic, M., Morgan, E.B., and Mann, J.J., Prevalence of recent cocaine use among motor vehicle fatalities in New York City [see comments], *J. Am. Med. Assoc.,* 263, 250–256, 1990.

21. Perez-Reyes, M., Hicks, R.E., Bumberry, J., Jeffcoat, A.R., and Cook, C.E., Interaction between marihuana and ethanol: effects on psychomotor performance, *Alcohol. Clin. Exp. Res.,* 12, 268–276, 1988.

22. Garriott, J.C., DiMaio, V.J., Zumwalt, R.E., and Petty, C.S., Incidence of drugs and alcohol in fatally injured motor vehicle drivers, *J. Forensic Sci.,* 22, 383–389, 1977.

23. Deveaux, M., Marson, J.C., Goldstein, P., Lhermitte, M., Gosset, D., and Muller, P.H., [Alcohol and psychotropic drugs in fatal traffic accidents (the Nord-Pas-de-Calais region, France)] [in French], *Acta Med. Legal. Socialis,* 40, 61–70, 1990.

24. Balkon, J., Results of a multilaboratory checksample analysis program for carbon monoxide and cyanide, *J. Anal. Toxicol.,* 15, 232–236, 1991.

25. Risser, D. and Schneider, B., Carbon monoxide-related deaths from 1984 to 1993 in Vienna, Austria, *J. Forensic Sci.,* 40, 368–371, 1995.

26. Nowak, R. and Sachs, H., [Development of carbon monoxide and hydrocyanic acid in automobile fires and their forensic significance], *Versicherungsmedizin,* 45, 20–22, 1993.

27. Jentzen, J.M., Forensic toxicology. An overview and an algorithmic approach, *Am. J. Clin. Pathol.,* 92, S48–55, 1989.

28. Taylor, R.L., Cohan, S.L., and White, J.D., Comprehensive toxicology screening in the emergency department: an aid to clinical diagnosis, *Am. J. Emerg. Med.,* 3, 507–511, 1985.

29. Stair, E.L. and Whaley, M., Rapid screening and spot tests for the presence of common poisons, *Vet. Hum. Toxicol.,* 32, 564–566, 1990.

30. Bailey, D.N., Comprehensive toxicology screening: the frequency of finding other drugs in addition to ethanol, *J. Toxicol. Clin. Toxicol.,* 22, 463–471, 1984.

31. Berry, D.J. and Grove, J., Emergency toxicological screening for drugs commonly taken in overdose, *J. Chromatogr.,* 80, 205–219, 1973.

32. Kinberger, B., Holmen, A., and Wahrgren, P., A strategy for drug analysis in serum and urine. An application to drug screening of samples from drivers involved in traffic accidents, *Anal. Lett.,* 15, 937–951, 1982.

33. Ueki, M., [Drug screening in clinical toxicology and analytical doping control in sports] [review] [5 refs] [in Japanese], *Nippon Rinsho Jpn. J. Clin. Med.,* 1, 904–906, 1995.

34. Howarth, A.T. and Clegg, G., Simultaneous detection and quantitation of drugs commonly involved in self-administered overdoses, *Clin. Chem.,* 24, 804–807, 1978.

35. Jatlow, P.I., UV spectrophotometry for sedative drugs frequently involved in overdose emergencies, in *Methodology for Analytical Toxicology,* Vol. I, Sunshine, I., Ed., CRC Press, Boca Raton, FL, 414, 1984.

36. Christophersen, A.S. and Morland, J., Drug analysis for control purposes in forensic toxicology, workplace testing, sports medicine and related areas [review], *Pharmacol. Toxicol.,* 74, 202–210, 1994.

37. Chen, J.S., Chang, K.J., Charng, R.C., Lai, S.J., Binder, S.R., and Essien, H., The development of a broad-spectrum toxicology screening program in Taiwan, *J. Toxicol. Clin. Toxicol.,* 33, 581–589, 1995.

38. Bailey, D.N., Results of limited versus comprehensive toxicology screening in a university medical center [see comments], *Am. J. Clin. Pathol.,* 105, 572–575, 1996.

39. Tilson, H.A. and Moser, V.C., Comparison of screening approaches [review], *Neurotoxicology,* 13, 1–13, 1992.

40. Gambaro, V., Lodi, F., Mariani, R., Saligari, E., Villa, M., and Marozzi, E., [Systematic generic chemico-toxicological testing in forensic toxicology. IV. Application of a computer in a generic survey of substances of toxicological interest] [in Italian], *Farm. Ed. Pratica,* 38, 133–172, 1983.

41. Crouch, D.J., Peat, M.A., Chinn, D.M., and Finkle, B.S., Drugs and driving: a systematic analytical approach, *J. Forensic Sci.,* 28, 945–956, 1983.

42. Masoud, A.N., Systematic identification of drugs of abuse. I: spot tests, *J. Pharm. Sci.,* 64, 841–844, 1975.

43. Schepers, P.G., Franke, J.P., and de Zeeuw, R.A., System evaluation and substance identification in systematic toxicological analysis by the mean list length approach, *J. Anal. Toxicol.,* 7, 272–278, 1983.

44. Wennig, R., [Evaluation of a systematic analysis scheme used in clinical toxicology. Evaluation of 4 years' experience in a national health laboratory] [in French], *Rech. Eur. Toxicol.,* 5, 277–280, 1983.

45. Marozzi, E., Cozza, E., Pariali, A., Gambaro, V., Lodi, F., and Saligari, E., [Generic systematic chemico-toxicological research in forensic toxicology] [in Italian], *Farm. Ed. Pratica,* 33, 195–207, 1978.

46. Tagliaro, F., Lubli, G., Ghielmi, S., Franchi, D., and Marigo, M., Chromatographic methods for blood alcohol determination [review], *J. Chromatogr.,* 580, 161–190, 1992.

47. Cox, R.A., Crifasi, J.A., Dickey, R.E., Ketzler, S.C., and Pshak, G.L., A single-step extraction for screening whole blood for basic drugs by capillary GC/NPD, *J. Anal. Toxicol.,* 13, 224–228, 1989.

48. Simpson, D., Jarvie, D.R., and Heyworth, R., An evaluation of six methods for the detection of drugs of abuse in urine, *Ann. Clin. Biochem.,* 26, 172–181, 1989.

49. Gjerde, H., Christophersen, A.S., Skuterud, B., Klemetsen, K., and Morland, J., Screening for drugs in forensic blood samples using EMIT urine assays, *Forensic Sci. Int.,* 44, 179–185, 1990.

50. Maier, R.D., Erkens, M., Hoenen, H., and Bogusz, M., The screening for common drugs of abuse in whole blood by means of EMIT-ETS and FPIA-ADx urine immunoassays, *Int. J. Legal Med.,* 105, 115–119, 1992.

51. Diosi, D.T. and Harvey, D.C., Analysis of whole blood for drugs of abuse using EMIT d.a.u. reagents and a Monarch 1000 Chemistry Analyzer, *J. Anal. Toxicol.,* 17, 133–137, 1993.

52. Bogusz, M., Aderjan, R., Schmitt, G., Nadler, E., and Neureither, B., The determination of drugs of abuse in whole blood by means of FPIA and EMIT-dau immunoassays — a comparative study, *Forensic Sci. Int.,* 48, 27–37, 1990.

53. Masoud, A.N., Systematic identification of drugs of abuse II: TLC, *J. Pharm. Sci.,* 65, 1585–1589, 1976.

54. Machata, G., [Thin layer chromatography in systematic, toxicologic analysis processes] [in German], *Dtsch. Z. Ges. Gerichtl. Med.,* 59, 181–185, 1967.

55. Brunk, S.D., Thin-layer chromatography using Toxi-Lab system, in *Analysis of Addictive and Misused Drugs,* Adamovics, J.A., Ed., Marcel Dekker, New York, 41–50, 1995.

56. Jarvie, D.R. and Simpson, D., Drug screening: evaluation of the Toxi-Lab TLC system, *Ann. Clin. Biochem.,* 23, 76–84, 1986.

57. Nishigami, J., Ohshima, T., Takayasu, T., Kondo, T., Lin, Z., and Nagano, T., [Forensic toxicological application of TOXI-LAB screening for biological specimens in autopsy cases and emergency cares] [in Japanese], *Nippon Hoigaku Zasshi Jpn. J. Legal Med.,* 47, 372–379, 1993.

58. Warfield, R.W. and Maickel, R.P., A generalized extraction-TLC procedure for identification of drugs, *J. Appl. Toxicol.,* 3, 51–57, 1983.

59. Whitter, P.D. and Cary, P.L., A rapid method for the identification of acidic, neutral, and basic drugs in postmortem liver specimens by Toxi-Lab, *J. Anal. Toxicol.,* 10, 68–71, 1986.

60. Hackett, L.P., Dusci, L.J., and McDonald, I.A., Extraction procedures for some common drugs in clinical and forensic toxicology, *J. Forensic Sci.,* 21, 263–274, 1976.

61. Chen, X.H., Wijsbeek, J., van Veen, J., Franke, J.P., and de Zeeuw, R.A., Solid-phase extraction for the screening of acidic, neutral and basic drugs in plasma using a single-column procedure on Bond Elut Certify, *J. Chromatogr.,* 529, 161–166, 1990.

62. Chen, X.H., Franke, J.P., Wijsbeek, J., and de Zeeuw, R.A., Isolation of acidic, neutral, and basic drugs from whole blood using a single mixed-mode solid-phase extraction column, *J. Anal. Toxicol.,* 16, 351–355, 1992.

63. Foerster, E.H., Hatchett, C., and Garriott, J.C., A rapid, comprehensive screening procedure for basic drugs in blood or tissues by gas chromatography, *J. Anal. Toxicol.,* 2, 50–55, 1978.

64. Midha, K.K., Charette, C., McGilveray, I.J., Webb, D., and McLean, M.C., Application of GLC-alkali FID and GLC-MS procedures to analysis of plasma in suspected cases of psychotropic drug overdose, *Clin. Toxicol.,* 18, 713–729, 1982.

65. Griffiths, W.C., Oleksyk, S.K., and Diamond, I., A comprehensive gas chromatographic drug screening procedure for the clinical laboratory, *Clin. Biochem.,* 6, 124–131, 1973.

66. Eklund, A., Jonsson, J., and Schuberth, J., A procedure for simultaneous screening and quantification of basic drugs in liver, utilizing capillary gas chromatography and nitrogen sensitive detection, *J. Anal. Toxicol.*, 7, 24–28, 1983.

67. Marozzi, E., Gambaro, V., Lodi, F., and Pariali, A., [General systematic chemico-toxicological research in forensic toxicology. I. Considerations on the gas- chromatographic test in the general chemico-toxicological research] [in Italian], *Farm. Ed. Pratica*, 31, 180–211, 1976.

68. Drummer, O.H., Kotsos, A., and McIntyre, I.M., A class-independent drug screen in forensic toxicology using a photodiode array detector, *J. Anal. Toxicol.*, 17, 225–229, 1993.

69. Ojanpera, I., Rasanen, I., and Vuori, E., Automated quantitative screening for acidic and neutral drugs in whole blood by dual-column capillary gas chromatography, *J. Anal. Toxicol.*, 15, 204–208, 1991.

70. Premel-Cabic, A., Cailleux, A., and Allain, P., [A gas chromatographic assay of fifteen volatile organic solvents in blood (author's transl)] [in French], *Clin. Chim. Acta*, 56, 5–11, 1974.

71. Drummer, O.H., Horomidis, S., Kourtis, S., Syrjanen, M.L., and Tippett, P., Capillary gas chromatographic drug screen for use in forensic toxicology, *J. Anal. Toxicol.*, 18, 134–138, 1994.

72. Taylor, R.W., Greutink, C., and Jain, N.C., Identification of underivatized basic drugs in urine by capillary column gas chromatography, *J. Anal. Toxicol.*, 10, 205–208, 1986.

73. Ehresman, D.J., Price, S.M., and Lakatua, D.J., Screening biological samples for underivatized drugs using a splitless injection technique on fused silica capillary column gas chromatography, *J. Anal. Toxicol.*, 9, 55–62, 1985.

74. Turcant, A., Premel-Cabic, A., Cailleux, A., and Allain, P., Screening for neutral and basic drugs in blood by dual fused-silica column chromatography with nitrogen-phosphorus detection [published erratum appears in *Clin. Chem.*, 34(11), 2370, 1988], *Clin. Chem.*, 34, 1492 1497, 1988.

75. Watts, V.W. and Simonick, T.F., Screening of basic drugs in biological samples using dual column capillary chromatography and nitrogen-phosphorus detectors, *J. Anal. Toxicol.*, 10, 198–204, 1986.

76. Fretthold, D., Jones, P., Sebrosky, G., and Sunshine, I., Testing for basic drugs in biological fluids by solvent extraction and dual capillary GC/NPD, *J. Anal. Toxicol.*, 10, 10–14, 1986.

77. Chia, D.T. and Gere, J.A., Rapid drug screening using Toxi-Lab extraction followed by capillary gas chromatography/mass spectroscopy, *Clin. Biochem.*, 20, 303–306, 1987.

78. Fiers, T., Maes, V., and Sevens, C., Automation of toxicological screenings on a Hewlett Packard Chemstation GC/MS System, *Clin. Biochem.*, 29, 357–361, 1996.

79. Pettersen, J.E. and Skuterud, B., Application of combined GC/MS as compared to a conventional analytical system for identification of unknown drugs in acute drug intoxications, *Anal. Chem. Symp. Ser.*, 13, 111–129, 1983.

80. Maurer, H.H., Systematic toxicological analysis of drugs and their metabolites by gas chromatography-mass spectrometry [review], *J. Chromatogr.*, 580, 3–41, 1992.

81. Neill, G.P., Davies, N.W., and McLean, S., Automated screening procedure using gas chromatography-mass spectrometry for identification of drugs after their extraction from biological samples, *J. Chromatogr.*, 565, 207–224, 1991.

82. Brooks, K.E. and Smith, N.B., Efficient extraction of basic, neutral, and weakly acidic drugs from plasma for analysis by gas chromatography-mass spectrometry [published erratum appears in *Clin. Chem.*, 38(2), 323, 1992], *Clin. Chem.*, 37, 1975–1978, 1991.

83. Cailleux, A., Turcant, A., Premel-Cabic, A., and Allain, P., Identification and quantitation of neutral and basic drugs in blood by gas chromatography and mass spectrometry, *J. Chromatogr. Sci.*, 19, 163–176, 1981.

84. Maurer, H.H., Identification and differentiation of barbiturates, other sedative-hypnotics and their metabolites in urine integrated in a general screening procedure using computerized GC/MS, *J. Chromatogr.*, 530, 307–326, 1990.

85. Lambert, W.E., Meyer, E., Xue-Ping, Y., and De Leenheer, A.P., Screening, identification, and quantitation of benzodiazepines in postmortem samples by HPLC with photodiode array detection, *J. Anal. Toxicol.*, 19, 35–40, 1995.

86. Bogusz, M. and Wu, M., Standardized HPLC/DAD system, based on retention indices and spectral library, applicable for systematic toxicological screening [published erratum appears in *J. Anal. Toxicol.*, 16(3), 16A, 1992], *J. Anal. Toxicol.*, 15, 188–197, 1991.

87. Maier, R.D. and Bogusz, M., Identification power of a standardized HPLC/DAD system for systematic toxicological analysis, *J. Anal. Toxicol.*, 19, 79–83, 1995.

88. Chollet, D. and Kunstner, P., Fast systematic approach for the determination of drugs in biological fluids by fully automated high-performance liquid chromatography with on-line solid-phase extraction and automated cartridge exchange. Application to cebaracetam in human urine, *J. Chromatogr.*, 577, 335–340, 1992.

89. Wu Chen, N.B., Schaffer, M.I., Lin, R.L., Kurland, M.L., Donoghue, E.R., Jr., and Stein, R.J., The general toxicology unknown. I. The systematic approach, *J. Forensic Sci.*, 28, 391–397, 1983.

90. Wu Chen, N.B., Schaffer, M.I., Lin, R.L., Kurland, M.L., Donoghue, E.R., Jr., and Stein, R.J., The general toxicology unknown. II. A case report: doxylamine and pyrilamine intoxication, *J. Forensic Sci.*, 28, 398–403, 1983.

91. Maurer, H.H., Detection of anticonvulsants and their metabolites in urine within a "general unknown" analytical procedure using computerized GC/MS, *Arch. Toxicol.*, 64, 554–561, 1990.

92. Oliver, J.S. and Watson, J.M., Abuse of solvents "for kicks," *Lancet*, 1, 84–86, 1977.

93. Astier, A., Chromatographic determination of volatile solvents and their metabolites in urine for monitoring occupational exposure, *J. Chromatogr.*, 643, 389–398, 1993.

94. Jones, A.W., A rapid method for blood alcohol determination by headspace analysis using an electrochemical detector, *J. Forensic Sci.*, 23, 283–291, 1978.

95. Ghittori, S., Fiorentino, M.L., and Imbriani, M., [Use of gas chromatography with flame ionization (GC-FID) in the measurement of solvents in the urine], *Giorn. Ital. Med. Lavoro*, 9, 21–24, 1987.

96. Turner, G.J., Colbert, D.L., and Chowdry, B.Z., A broad spectrum immunoassay using fluorescence polarization for the detection of amphetamines in urine, *Ann. Clin. Biochem.*, 28, 588–594, 1991.

97. Kunsman, G.W., Manno, J.E., Cockerham, K.R., and Manno, B.R., Application of the Syva EMIT and Abbott TDx amphetamine immunoassays to the detection of 3,4-methylenedioxymethamphetamine (MDMA) and 3,4-methylenedioxyethamphetamine (MDEA) in urine, *J. Anal. Toxicol.*, 14, 149–153, 1990.

98. D'Nicuola, J., Jones, R., Levine, B., and Smith, M.L., Evaluation of six commercial amphetamine and methamphetamine immunoassays for cross-reactivity to phenylpropanolamine and ephedrine in urine [see comments], *J. Anal. Toxicol.*, 16, 211–213, 1992.

99. Mule, S. and Casella, G., Confirmation and quantitation of barbiturates in human urine by gas chromatography/mass spectrometry, *J. Anal. Toxicol.*, 13, 13–16, 1989.

100. Maurer, H.H., Identification and differentiation of barbiturates, other sedative-hypnotics and their metabolites in urine integrated in a general screening procedure using computerized gas chromatography-mass spectrometry, *J. Chromatogr.*, 530, 307–326, 1990.

101. Liu, R., McKeehan, A., Edwards, C., Foster, G., Bensley, W., Langner, J. et al., Improved gas chromatography-mass spectrometry analysis of barbiturates in urine using centrifuge-based solid-phase extraction, methylation, with d5-pentobarbital as internal standard, *J. Forensic Sci.*, 39, 1504–1514, 1994.

102. Mangin, P., Lugnier, A.A., and Chaumont, A.J., A polyvalent method using HPLC for screening and quantification of 12 common barbiturates in various biological materials, *J. Anal. Toxicol.*, 11, 27–30, 1987.

103. Jain, N.C., Mass screening and confirmation of barbiturates in urine by RIA/gas chromatography, *Clin. Toxicol.*, 9, 221–233, 1976.

104. Gill, R., Stead, A.H., and Moffat, A.C., Analytical aspects of barbiturate abuse: identification of drugs by the effective combination of gas-liquid, high-performance liquid and thin-layer chromatographic techniques, *J. Chromatogr.*, 204, 275–284, 1981.

105. Valentine, J.L., Middleton, R., and Sparks, C., Identification of urinary benzodiazepines and their metabolites — comparison of automated HPLC and GC/MS after immunoassay screening of clinical specimens, *J. Anal. Toxicol.*, 20, 416–424, 1996.

106. Schutz, H., Modern screening strategies in analytical toxicology with special regard to new benzodiazepines, *Z. Rechtsmed. — J. Legal Med.*, 100, 1937, 1988.

107. Black, D.A., Clark, G.D., Haver, V.M., Garbin, J.A., and Saxon, A.J., Analysis of urinary benzodiazepines using solid-phase extraction and gas chromatography-mass spectrometry [see comments], *J. Anal. Toxicol.*, 18, 185–188, 1994.

108. Jones, C.E., Wians, F.H., Jr., Martinez, L.A., and Merritt, G.J., Benzodiazepines identified by capillary gas chromatography-mass spectrometry, with specific ion screening used to detect benzophenone derivatives, *Clin. Chem.*, 35, 1394–1398, 1989.

109. Sioufi, A. and Dubois, J.P., Chromatography of benzodiazepines [review], *J. Chromatogr.,* 531, 459–480, 1990.

110. Drouet-Coassolo, C., Aubert, C., Coassolo, P., and Cano, J.P., Capillary GC/MS method for the identification and quantification of some benzodiazepines and their unconjugated metabolites in plasma, *J. Chromatogr.,* 487, 295–311, 1989.

111. Japp, M., Garthwaite, K., Geeson, A.V., and Osselton, M.D., Collection of analytical data for benzodiazepines and benzophenones, *J. Chromatogr.,* 439, 317–339, 1988.

112. Moore, C., Long, G., and Marr, M., Confirmation of benzodiazepines in urine as trimethylsilyl derivatives using gas chromatography-mass spectrometry, *J. Chromatogr. B Biomed. Appl.,* 655, 132–137, 1994.

113. Fitzgerald, R., Rexin, D., and Herold, D., Detecting benzodiazepines: immunoassays compared with negative chemical ionization gas chromatography-mass spectrometry, *Clin. Chem.,* 40, 373–380, 1994.

114. Joern, W.A., Confirmation of low concentrations of urinary benzodiazepines, including alprazolam and triazolam, by GC/MS: An extractive alkylation procedure., *J. Anal. Toxicol.,* 16, 363–367, 1992.

115. Needleman, S.B. and Porvaznik, M., Identification of parent benzodiazepines by gas chromotography-mass spectroscopy (GC/MS) from urinary extracts treated with B-glucuronidase, *Forensic Sci. Int.,* 73, 49–60, 1995.

116. McIntyre, I., Syrjanen, M., Crump, K., Horomidis, S., Peace, A., and Drummer, O., Simultaneous HPLC gradient analysis of 15 benzodiazepines and selected metabolites in postmortem blood, *J. Anal. Toxicol.,* 17, 202–207, 1993.

117. Lillsunde, P. and Seppala, T., Simultaneous screening and quantitative analysis of benzodiazepines by dual-channel gas chromatography using electron-capture and nitrogen-phosphorus detection, *J. Chromatogr.,* 533, 97–110, 1990.

118. Baugh, L.D., Allen, E.E., Liu, R.H., Langner, J.G., Fentress, J.C., Chadha, S.C. et al., Evaluation of immunoassay methods for the screening of cocaine metabolites in urine, *J. Forensic Sci.,* 36, 79–85, 1991.

119. Cone, E.J. and Mitchell, J., Validity testing of commercial urine cocaine metabolite assays: II. Sensitivity, specificity, accuracy, and confirmation by gas chromatography-mass spectrometry, *J. Forensic Sci.,* 34, 32–45, 1989.

120. Moore, F.M. and Simpson, D., Detection of benzoylecgonine (cocaine metabolite) in urine: a cost-effective low risk immunoassay procedure, *Med. Lab. Sci.,* 47, 85–89, 1990.

121. Mueller, M.A., Adams, S.M., Lewand, D.L., and Wang, R.I., Detection of benzoylecgonine in human urine, *J. Chromatogr.,* 144, 101–107, 1977.

122. Smith, M.L., Hughes, R.O., Levine, B., Dickerson, S., Darwin, W.D., and Cone, E.J., Forensic drug testing for opiates. VI. Urine testing for hydromorphone, hydrocodone, oxymorphone, and oxycodone with commercial opiate immunoassays and gas chromatography-mass spectrometry, *J. Anal. Toxicol.,* 19, 18–26, 1995.

123. Huang, W., Andollo, W., and Hearn, W.L., A solid phase extraction technique for the isolation and identification of opiates in urine, *J. Anal. Toxicol.,* 16, 307–310, 1992.

124. Cone, E.J., Dickerson, S., Paul, B.D., and Mitchell, J.M., Forensic drug testing for opiates. V. Urine testing for heroin, morphine, and codeine with commercial opiate immunoassays, *J. Anal. Toxicol.,* 17, 156–164, 1993.

125. Fyfe, M.J., Chand, P., McCutchen, C., Long, J.S., Walia, A.S., Edwards, C. et al., Evaluation of enzyme immunoassay performance characteristics — phencyclidine example, *J. Forensic Sci.,* 38, 156–164, 1993.

126. Ragan, F., Jr., Hite, S.A., Samuels, M.S., Garey, R.E., Daul, G., and Schuler, R.E., Extended EMIT-DAU phencyclidine screen, *J. Clin. Psychiatry,* 47, 194–195, 1986.

127. Chen, X.H., Franke, J.P., Wijsbeek, J., and de Zeeuw, R.A., Determination of basic drugs extracted from biological matrices by means of solid-phase extraction and wide-bore capillary gas chromatography with nitrogen-phosphorus detection, *J. Anal. Toxicol.,* 18, 150–153, 1994.

128. Balkon, J. and Donnelly, B., Determination of basic drugs in post mortem tissues: a microextraction technique utilizing GLC/NPD of effluents, *J. Anal. Toxicol.,* 6, 181–184, 1982.

129. Sharp, M.E., Evaluation of a screening procedure for basic and neutral drugs: *n*-butyl chloride extraction and megabore capillary gas chromatography, *J. Can. Soc. Forensic Sci.,* 19, 83–101, 1986.

130. Hyde, P.M., Evaluation of drug extraction procedures from urine, *J. Anal. Toxicol.,* 9, 269–272, 1985.

131. Plavsic, F., Barbaric, V., Parag, M., Arambasin, M., Gjerek, J., and Stavljenic, A., Increased possibilities for detecting drugs by the Toxi-Lab screening test, *Ann. Clin. Biochem.*, 22, 324–326, 1985.

132. Moody, D.E., Rittenhouse, L.F., and Monti, K.M., Analysis of forensic specimens for cannabinoids. I. Comparison of RIA and GC/MS analysis of blood, *J. Anal. Toxicol.*, 16, 297–301, 1992.

133. Law, B., Williams, P.L., and Moffat, A.C., The detection and quantification of cannabinoids in blood and urine by RIA, HPLC/RIA and GC/MS, *Vet. Hum. Toxicol.*, 21, 144–147, 1979.

134. Clatworthy, A., Oon, M., Smith, R., and Whitehouse, M., Gas chromatographic-mass spectrometric confirmation of radioimmunoassay results for cannabinoids in blood and urine, *Forensic Sci. Int.*, 46, 219–230, 1990.

135. Mason, P.A., Law, B., Pocock, K., and Moffat, A.C., Direct radioimmunoassay for the detection of barbiturates in blood and urine, *Analyst*, 107, 629–633, 1982.

136. Lafisca, S., Bolelli, G., Mosca, R., and Zanon, C., Radioimmunoassay of morphine and morphine-like substances in biological fluids and human tissues, *Ric. Clin. Lab.*, 7, 179–190, 1977.

137. Spiehler, V. and Brown, R., Unconjugated morphine in blood by radioimmunoassay and gas chromatography/mass spectrometry, *J. Forensic Sci.*, 32, 906–916, 1987.

138. Altunkaya, D. and Smith, R., Evaluation of a commercial radioimmunoassay kit for the detection of lysergide (LSD) in serum, whole blood, urine and stomach contents, *Forensic Sci. Int.*, 47, 113–121, 1990.

139. Owens, S.M., McBay, A.J., Reisner, H.M., and Perez-Reyes, M., 125I radioimmunoassay of delta-9-tetrahydrocannabinol in blood and plasma with a solid-phase second-antibody separation method, *Clin. Chem.*, 27, 619–624, 1981.

140. Teale, J.D., Forman, E.J., King, L.J., Piall, E.M., and Marks, V., The development of a radioimmunoassay for cannabinoids in blood and urine, *J. Pharm. Pharmacol.*, 27, 465–472, 1975.

141. Goddard, C.P., Stead, A.H., Mason, P.A., Law, B., Moffat, A.C., McBrien, M. et al., An iodine-125 radioimmunoassay for the direct detection of benzodiazepines in blood and urine, *Analyst*, 111, 525–529, 1986.

142. Yee, H.Y., Nelson, J.D., and Papa, V.M., Measurement of benzoylecgonine in whole blood using the Abbott ADx analyzer, *J. Anal. Toxicol.*, 17, 84–86, 1993.

143. Appel, T.A. and Wade, N.A., Screening of blood and urine for drugs of abuse utilizing Diagnostic Products Corporation's Coat-A-Count radioimmunoassay kits, *J. Anal. Toxicol.*, 13, 274–276, 1989.

144. Caplan, Y.H. and Levine, B., Application of the Abbott TDx lidocaine, phenytoin, and phenobarbital assays to postmortem blood specimens, *J. Anal. Toxicol.*, 12, 265–267, 1988.

145. Alvarez, J.S., Sacristan, J.A., and Alsar, M.J., Comparison of a monoclonal antibody fluorescent polarization immunoassay with monoclonal antibody radioimmunoassay for cyclosporin determination in whole blood, *Ther. Drug Monit.*, 14, 78–80, 1992.

146. Peel, H.W. and Perrigo, B.J., Detection of cannabinoids in blood using EMIT, *J. Anal. Toxicol.*, 5, 165–167, 1981.

147. Slightom, E.L., Cagle, J.C., McCurdy, H.H., and Castagna, F., Direct and indirect homogeneous enzyme immunoassay of benzodiazepines in biological fluids and tissues, *J. Anal. Toxicol.*, 6, 22–25, 1982.

148. Blum, L.M., Klinger, R.A., and Rieders, F., Direct automated EMIT d.a.u. analysis of N,N-dimethylformamide-modified serum, plasma, and postmortem blood for benzodiazepines, benzoylecgonine, cannabinoids, and opiates, *J. Anal. Toxicol.*, 13, 285–288, 1989.

149. Lewellen, L.J. and McCurdy, H.H., A novel procedure for the analysis of drugs in whole blood by homogeneous enzyme immunoassay (EMIT), *J. Anal. Toxicol.*, 12, 260–264, 198.

150. Asselin, W.M., Leslie, J.M., and McKinley, B., Direct detection of drugs of abuse in whole hemolyzed blood using the EMIT d.a.u. urine assays [published erratum appears in *J. Anal. Toxicol.*, 12(6), 16A, 1988], *J. Anal. Toxicol.*, 12, 207–215, 1988.

151. Asselin, W.M. and Leslie, J.M., Direct detection of therapeutic concentrations of tricyclic antidepressants in whole hemolyzed blood using the EMITtox serum tricyclic antidepressant assay, *J. Anal. Toxicol.*, 15, 167–173, 1991.

152. Perrigo, B.J. and Joynt, B.P., Optimization of the EMIT immunoassay procedure for the analysis of cannabinoids in methanolic blood extracts, *J. Anal. Toxicol.*, 13, 235–237, 1989.

153. Collins, C., Muto, J., and Spiehler, V., Whole blood deproteinization for drug screening using automatic pipettors, *J. Anal. Toxicol.*, 16, 340–342, 1992.

154. Slightom, E.L., The analysis of drugs in blood, bile, and tissue with an indirect homogeneous enzyme immunoassay, *J. Forensic Sci.,* 23, 292–303, 1978.

155. Klein, M., Mass spectrometry of drugs and toxic substances in body fluids, in *Forensic Mass Spectrometry,* Yinon, J., Ed., CRC Press, Boca Raton, FL, 1987, 51–86.

156. Gudzinowicz, B.J. and Gudzinowicz, M., *Analysis of Drugs and Metabolites by GC/MS,* Vol. 7, Marcel Dekker, New York, 1980.

157. Cone, E.J., Analysis of drugs in biological samples by combined GC/MS, *Drugs Pharm. Sci.,* 11A, 143–227, 1981.

158. Foltz, R.L., Applications of GC/MS in clinical toxicology, *Spectra,* 10, 8–10, 1985.

159. Finkle, B.S., Foltz, R.L., and Taylor, D.M., A comprehensive GC/MS reference data system for toxicological and biomedical purposes, *J. Chromatogr. Sci.,* 12, 304–328, 1974.

160. Wu Chen, N.B., Cody, J.T., Garriott, J.C., Foltz, R.L., Peat, M.A., and Schaffer, M.I., Recommended guidelines for forensic GC/MS procedures in toxicology laboratories associated with offices of medical examiners and/or coroners, *J. Forensic Sci.,* 35, 236–242, 1990.

161. Smith, N.B., Automated identification by computer of the mass spectra of drugs in urine or serum extracts, *J. Anal. Toxicol.,* 18, 16–21, 1994.

162. Ardrey, R.E., Mass spectrometry, in *Clarke's Isolation and Identification of Drugs in Pharmaceuticals, Body Fluids, and Post-Mortem Material,* 2nd ed., Moffatt, A.C., Ed., Pharmaceutical Press, London, 1986.

163. Gibb, R.P., Cockerham, H., Goldfogel, G.A., Lawson, G.M., and Raisys, V.A., Substance abuse testing of urine by GC/MS in scanning mode evaluated by proficiency studies, TLC/GC, and EMIT, *J. Forensic Sci.,* 38, 124–133, 1993.

164. Mills, T., Roberson, J.D., McCurdy, H.H., and Wall, W.H., *Instrumental Data for Drug Analysis* (5 vols.), 2nd ed., Elsevier, New York, 1992.

165. Pfleger, K., Maurer, H.H. and Weber, A., *Mass Spectral and GC Data of Drugs, Poisons, Pesticides, Pollutants and Their Metabolites,* 2nd ed., Vols. 1–3, 1992, Vol. 4, 2000, Wiley-VCH, New York, 2000.

166. Sunshine, I. and Caplis, M., *CRC Handbook of Mass Spectra of Drugs,* CRC Press, Boca Raton, FL, 1981.

167. Ardrey, R.E., Bal, T.S., Joyce, J.R. and Moffat, A.C., *Pharmaceutical Mass Spectra,* Pharmaceutical Press, London, 1985.

168. Hites, R.A., *Handbook of Mass Spectra of Environmental Contaminants,* 2nd ed., Lewis Publishers, Boca Raton, FL, 1992.

169. Cornu, A. and Massot, R., *Compilation of Mass Spectral Data,* Heyden & Son, London, 1966.

170. Reys, L.L. and Santos, J.C., Importance of information in forensic toxicology, *Am. J. Forensic Med. Pathol.,* 13, 33–36, 1992.

171. Stafford, D.T. and Logan, B.K., Information resources useful in forensic toxicology, *Fundam. Appl. Toxicol.,* 15, 411–419, 1990.

172. Forensic Toxicology Laboratory Guidelines, Society of Forensic Toxicologists/American Academy of Forensic Sciences, 2002. Available from the SOFT Web site http://www.soft-tox.org.

173. Osterloh, J.D. and Becker, C.E., Chemical dependency and drug testing in the workplace, *J. Psychoactive Drugs,* 22, 407–417, 1990.

174. Ng, T.L., Dope testing in sports: scientific and medico-legal issues [review], *Ann. Acad. Med. Singapore,* 22, 48–53, 1993.

175. DeCresce, R., Mazura, A., Lifshitz, M., and Tilson, J., *Drug Testing in the Workplace,* ASCP Press, Chicago, 1989.

176. McCunney, R.J., Drug testing: technical complications of a complex social issue, *Am. J. Indust. Med.,* 15, 589–600, 1989.

177. Gough, T.A., The analysis of drugs of abuse, in *The Analysis of Drugs of Abuse,* Gough, T.A., John Wiley & Sons, Chichester, U.K., 1991, 628.

178. Deutsch, D.G., Gas chromatography/mass spectrometry using tabletop instruments, in *Analytical Aspects of Drug Testing,* Deutsch, D.G., Ed., John Wiley & Sons, New York, 1989, 87–128.

179. Baselt, R.C., Ed., *Advances in Analytical Toxicology,* Vol. 1, Biomedical Publications, Foster City, CA, 1984, 275.

180. Lehrer, M., Application of gas chromatography-mass spectrometry instrument techniques to forensic urine drug testing, *Clin. Lab. Med.,* 10, 271–288, 1990.

181. Garland, W.A. and Powell, M.L., Quantitative selected ion monitoring (QSIM) of drugs and/or metabolites in biological matrices, *J. Chromatogr. Sci.,* 19, 392–434, 1981.

182. Gelpi, E., Bioanalytical aspects on method validation, *Life Sci.,* 41, 849–852, 1987.

183. Troost, J.R. and Olavesen, E.Y., Gas chromatographic-mass spectrometric calibration bias, *Anal. Chem.,* 68, 708–711, 1996.

184. ElSohly, M.A., Little, T.L., Jr., and Stanford, D.F., Hexadeutero-11-nor-delta 9-tetrahydrocannabinol-9-carboxylic acid: a superior internal standard for the GC/MS analysis of delta 9-THC acid metabolite in biological specimens, *J. Anal. Toxicol.,* 16, 188–191, 1992.

185. Giovannini, M.G., Pieraccini, G., and Moneti, G., Isotope dilution mass spectrometry: definitive methods and reference materials in clinical chemistry, *Ann. Istituto Superiore Sanita,* 27, 401–410, 1991.

186. Needleman, S.B. and Romberg, R.W., Limits of linearity and detection for some drugs of abuse, *J. Anal. Toxicol.,* 14, 34–38, 1990.

187. Liu, R.H., Foster, G., Cone, E.J., and Kumar, S.D., Selecting an appropriate isotopic internal standard for gas chromatography-mass spectrometry analysis of drugs of abuse — pentobarbital example, *J. Forensic Sci.,* 40, 983–989, 1995.

188. Carreras, D., Imaz, C., Navajas, R., Garcia, M.A., Rodriguez, C., Rodriguez, A.F. et al., Comparison of derivatization procedures for the determination of diuretics in urine by gas chromatography-mass spectrometry, *J. Chromatogr. A,* 683, 195–202, 1994.

189. Anderegg, R.J., Derivatization for GC/MS analysis, *Mass Spectrom. Rev.,* 7, 395, 1988.

190. Melgar, R. and Kelly, R.C., A novel GC/MS derivatization method for amphetamines, *J. Anal. Toxicol.,* 17, 399–402, 1993.

191. Goldberger, B.A. and Cone, E.J., Confirmatory tests for drugs in the workplace by gas chromatography-mass spectrometry, *J. Chromatogr. A,* 674, 73–86, 1994.

192. Cody, J.T. and Foltz, R.L., GC/MS analysis of body fluids for drugs of abuse, in *Forensic Applications of Mass Spectrometry,* Yinon, J., Ed., CRC Press, Boca Raton, FL, 1995, 1–59.

193. Foltz, R.L., Fentiman, A.F., Jr., and Foltz, R.B., GC/MS assays for abused drugs in body fluids [review], *NIDA Res. Monogr.,* 32, 1–198, 1980.

194. Foltz, R.L., High sensitivity quantitative analysis of drugs and metabolites by GC/MS, in *31st Annual Conference on Mass Spectrometry and Allied Topics,* Boston, May 8–13, 1983.

195. Bogusz, M., Wijsbeek, J., Franke, J.P., de Zeeuw, R.A., and Gierz, J., Impact of biological matrix, drug concentration, and method of isolation on detectability and variability of retention index values in gas chromatography, *J. Anal. Toxicol.,* 9, 49–54, 1985.

196. Hartmann, C., Massart, D.L., and McDowall, R.D., An analysis of the Washington Conference Report on bioanalytical method validation, *J. Pharm. Biomed. Anal.,* 12, 1337–1343, 1994.

197. Shah, V.P., Midha, K.K., Dighe, S., McGilveray, I.J., Skelly, J.P., Yacobi, A. et al., Analytical methods validation: bioavailability, bioequivalence and pharmacokinetic studies. Conference report, *Eur. J. Drug Metab. Pharmacokinet.,* 16, 249–55, 1991.

198. Mesley, R.J., Pocklington, W.D., and Walker, R.F., Analytical quality assurance — a review, *Analyst,* 116, 975–990, 1991.

199. Dadgar, D., Burnett, P.E., Choc, M.G., Gallicano, K., and Hooper, J.W., Application issues in bioanalytical method validation, sample analysis and data reporting [review], *J. Pharm. Biomed. Anal.,* 13, 89–97, 1995.

200. Pachla, L.A., Wright, D.S., and Reynolds, D.L., Bioanalytic considerations for pharmacokinetic and biopharmaceutic studies, *J. Clin. Pharmacol.,* 26, 332–335, 1986.

201. Karnes, H.T. and March, C., Calibration and validation of linearity in chromatographic biopharmaceutical analysis, *J. Pharm. Biomed. Anal.,* 9, 911–918, 1991.

202. Lang, J.R. and Bolton, S., A comprehensive method validation strategy for bioanalytical applications in the pharmaceutical industry. 2. Statistical analyses, *J. Pharm. Biomed. Anal.,* 9, 435–442, 1991.

203. Arnoux, P. and Morrison, R., Drug analysis of biological samples. A survey of validation approaches in chromatography in the UK pharmaceutical industry, *Xenobiotica,* 22, 757–764, 1992.

204. Passey, R.B. and Maluf, K.C., Foundations for validation of quantitative analytical methods in the clinical laboratory, *Arch. Pathol. Lab. Med.,* 116, 732–738, 1992.

205. Edwardson, P.A., Bhaskar, G., and Fairbrother, J.E., Method validation in pharmaceutical analysis, *J. Pharm. Biomed. Anal.,* 8, 929–933, 1990.

206. Buick, A.R., Doig, M.V., Jeal, S.C., Land, G.S., and McDowall, R.D., Method validation in the bioanalytical laboratory, *J. Pharm. Biomed. Anal.,* 8, 629–637, 1990.

207. Cardone, M.J., Willavize, S.A., and Lacy, M.E., Method validation revisited: a chemometric approach, *Pharm. Res.,* 7, 154–160, 1990.

208. Wieling, J., Hendriks, G., Tamminga, W.J., Hempenius, J., Mensink, C.K., Oosterhuis, B. et al., Rational experimental design for bioanalytical methods validation. Illustration using an assay method for total captopril in plasma, *J. Chromatogr. A,* 730, 381–394, 1996.

209. Braggio, S., Barnaby, R.J., Grossi, P., and Cugola, M., A strategy for validation of bioanalytical methods [review], *J. Pharm. Biomed. Anal.,* 14, 375–388, 1996.

210. Karnes, H.T., Shiu, G., and Shah, V.P., Validation of bioanalytical methods [review], *Pharm. Res.,* 8, 421–426, 1991.

211. Stead, A.H., Hook, W., Moffat, A.C., and Berry, D., Therapeutic, toxic and fatal blood concentration ranges of antiepileptic drugs as an aid to the interpretation of analytical data, *Hum. Toxicol.,* 2, 135–147, 1983.

212. Caplan, Y.H., Ottinger, W.E., and Crooks, C.R., Therapeutic and toxic drug concentrations in post mortem blood: a six year study in the State of Maryland, *J. Anal. Toxicol.,* 7, 225–230, 1983.

213. Baselt, R.C., Wright, J.A., and Cravey, R.H., Therapeutic and toxic concentrations of more than 100 toxicologically significant drugs in blood, plasma, or serum: a tabulation [review], *Clin. Chem.,* 21, 44–62, 1975.

214. Stead, A.H. and Moffat, A.C., A collection of therapeutic, toxic and fatal blood drug concentrations in man, *Hum. Toxicol.,* 2, 437–464, 1983.

215. Balselt, R.C. and Cravey, R.H., *Disposition of Toxic Drugs and Chemicals in Man,* 4th ed., Chemical Toxicology Institute, Foster City, CA, 1995.

216. Prouty, R.W. and Anderson, W.H., The forensic science implications of site and temporal influences on postmortem blood-drug concentrations, *J. Forensic Sci.,* 35, 243–270, 1990.

217. Othman, S., al-Turk, W.A., Awidi, A.S., Daradkeh, T.K., and Shaheen, O., Comparative determination of phenytoin in plasma by fluorescence polarization immunoassay and high performance liquid chromatography, *Drug Design Delivery,* 2, 41–47, 1987.

218. Valtier, S. and Cody, J.T., Evaluation of internal standards for the analysis of amphetamine and methamphetamine, *J. Anal. Toxicol.,* 19, 375–380, 1995.

219. Smith, N.B., Internal standards in gas-chromatographic analyses for ethylene glycol in serum [letter; comment], *Clin. Chem.,* 39, 2020, 1993.

220. Thomas, L.C. and Weichmann, W., Quantitative measurements via co-elution and dual-isotope detection by gas chromatography-mass spectrometry, *J. Chromatogr.,* 587, 255–262, 1991.

221. Pollak, P.T., A systematic review and critical comparison of internal standards for the routine liquid chromatographic assay of amiodarone and desethylamiodarone, *Ther. Drug Monit.,* 18, 168–178, 1996.

222. Claeys, M., Markey, S.P., and Maenhaut, W., Variance analysis of error in selected ion monitoring assays using various internal standards. A practical study case, *Biomed. Mass Spectr.,* 4, 122–128, 1977.

223. Tilstone, W.J. Pharmacokinetics metabolism, and the interpretation of results, in *Clarke's Isolation and Identification of Drugs in Pharmaceuticals, Body Fluids, and Postmortem Material,* 2nd ed., Moffatt, A.C., Ed., Pharmaceutical Press, London, 1986, 276.

224. Toseland, P.A., Samples and sampling, in *Clarke's Isolation and Identification of Drugs in Pharmaceuticals, Body Fluids, and Post-Mortem Material,* 2nd ed., Moffatt, A.C., Ed., Pharmaceutical Press, London, 1986, 111.

225. Bogusz, M.J., Hyphenated liquid chromatographic techniques in forensic toxicology, *J. Chromatogr. B,* 733, 65–91, 1999.

226. Lips, A.G., et al., Methodology for the development of a drug library based upon collision-induced fragmentation for the identification of toxicologically relevant drugs in plasma samples, *J. Chromatogr. B,* 759, 191–207, 2001.

227. Marquet, P., Is LC-MS suitable for a comprehensive screening of drugs and poisons in clinical toxicology? *Ther. Drug Monit.,* 24, 125–133, 2002.

228. Saint-Marcoux, F., Lachatre, G., and Marquet, P., Evaluation of an improved general unknown screening procedure using liquid chromatography-electrospray-mass spectrometry by comparison with gas chromatography and high-performance liquid-chromatography — diode array detection, *J. Am. Soc. Mass Spectrom.,* 14, 14–22, 2003.

229. Marquet, P., et al., Comparison of a preliminary procedure for the general unknown screening of drugs and toxic compounds using a quadrupole-linear ion-trap mass spectrometer with a liquid chromatography-mass spectrometry reference technique, *J. Chromatogr. B,* 789, 9–18, 2003.

230. Venisse, N. et al., A general unknown screening procedure for drugs and toxic compounds in serum using liquid chromatography-electrospray-single quadrupole mass spectrometry, *J. Anal. Toxicol.*, 27, 7–14, 2003.

231. Politi, L., Groppi, A., and Polettini, A., Applications of liquid chromatography-mass spectrometry in doping control, *J. Anal. Toxicol.*, 29(1), 1–14, 2005.

232. Maurer, H.H., Advances in analytical toxicology: the current role of liquid chromatography-mass spectrometry in drug quantification in blood and oral fluid, *Anal. Bioanal. Chem.*, 381, 110–118, 2005.

233. Weinmann, W., Schaefer, P., Thierauf, A., Schreiber, A., and Wurst, F.M., Confirmatory analysis of ethylglucuronide in urine by liquid-chromatography/electrospray ionization/tandem mass spectrometry according to forensic guidelines, *J. Am. Soc. Mass Spectrom.*, 15, 188–193, 2004.

234. Saint-Marcoux, F., Lachâtre, G., and Marquet, P., Evaluation of an improved general unknown screening procedure using liquid chromatography-electrospray-mass spectrometry by comparison with gas chromatography and high-performance liquid-chromatography — diode array detection, *J. Am. Soc. Mass Spectrom.*, 14, 14–22, 2003.

235. Marquet, P. and Lachâtre, G., Liquid chromatography-mass spectrometry: potential in forensic and clinical toxicology, *J. Chromatogr. B Biomed. Sci. Appl.*, 733, 93–118, 1999.

236. Kratzsch, C., Tenberken, O., Peters, F.T., Weber, A.A., Kraemer, T., and Maurer, H.H., Screening, library-assisted identification and validated quantification of 23 benzodiazepines, flumazenil, zaleplone, zolpidem and zopiclone in plasma by liquid chromatography/mass spectrometry with atmospheric pressure chemical ionization, *J. Mass Spectrom.*, 39(8), 856–872. 2004.

237. Maurer, H.H., Tenberken, O., Kratzsch, C., Weber, A.A., and Peters, F.T., Screening for library-assisted identification and fully validated quantification of 22 beta-blockers in blood plasma by liquid chromatography-mass spectrometry with atmospheric pressure chemical ionization, *J. Chromatogr. A*, 1058(1–2), 169–181, 2004.

12.5 QUALITY ASSURANCE IN POST-MORTEM TOXICOLOGY

Wilmo Andollo, B.S.

Quality Assurance Officer, Dade County Medical Examiner Department, Toxicology Laboratory, Miami, Florida

12.5.1 Introduction

The essence of the post-mortem forensic analysis is to characterize a subject's biological tissue in terms of toxic chemical content. Based on the analytical result, an opinion can then be formed about the influence the toxic substance may have had on the subject. Since the result of any chemical analysis carries with it an uncertainty that is inherent in all measurements, an attempt must be made to control and measure the factors that influence that uncertainty. Only when these factors are measured and controlled can the analytical results be deemed reliable.

The quality assurance program is established to ensure the public that the results generated by the laboratory are reliable. This is crucial in a forensic toxicology laboratory since the analytical results are closely scrutinized in a court of law, where truth and impartiality must be authenticated for the public good. A comprehensive quality assurance program will provide an expert witness with details concerning the measurable factors that affect the analytical result. These factors include personnel, the implements of measurement; the quality of materials used; the sample; the analytical method; the analytical instruments; data handling; and reporting.

The *quality assurance* program describes the steps taken to *document* the execution of the quality control procedures; the traceability of reported data to raw data; instrument status during analysis; quality control status; description of the analytical method; qualifications of the analysts; sample integrity and chain of custody; and the corrective actions undertaken for out-of-control situations. The *quality control* program sets forth the procedures to be taken to *measure* and *control* all sources of random and systematic errors so that limits of accuracy and precision can be established for all analytical methods. It also describes the technical operations undertaken to assure that the data obtained are within the established limits.

12.5.2 Standard Operating Procedures

The standard operating procedure is a written document that outlines in detail the mode of operation of the laboratory. It addresses the relationship of the laboratory with the institutions that it serves, the organizational structure of the laboratory, the quality assurance program, and the chemical hygiene plan. It must address every facet of the laboratory's operation and be available to all laboratory personnel and the public for consultation and review.

The standard operating procedures should address, as a minimum, the following aspects of the laboratory operation:

- Table of organization
- Personnel qualifications
- Precision implements
- Materials
- Sampling
- Analytical methods
- Instruments
- Data
- Reporting
- Proficiency program

The standard operating procedures manual is to be kept up to date and reviewed on a yearly basis to ensure that it typifies the actual operation and that it meets the needs of the laboratory. It is important to archive any old procedures, whether modified or omitted from the manual, so that they can be retrieved for future reference.

The rest of this chapter is devoted to expanding on the subjects that are deemed indispensable in a comprehensive quality assurance program and standard operating procedure manual.

12.5.3 Personnel

The table of organization should be represented by means of a flowchart or schematic diagram. It should include all positions in order of hierarchy, name of persons occupying each position, and accountability of each individual.

The subject of personnel in forensic toxicology laboratories is covered in detail in the SOFT/AAFS Forensic Laboratory Guidelines.[1]

12.5.3.1 Continuing Education

The laboratory director is responsible for providing access to continuing education to all employees. Continuing education is essential to the development of the laboratory in maintaining the reliability and integrity necessary in an ever challenging field. New and more potent drugs are being continuously developed along with more advanced analytical techniques and equipment necessary for their detection and identification. Keeping abreast of the new information, be it pharmacological or analytical, is of outmost importance for the subsistence of the forensic laboratory. Membership in professional forensic organizations, such as the American Academy of Forensic Sciences (AAFS), the Society of Forensic Toxicologists (SOFT), the California Association of Toxicologists (CAT), and The International Association of Forensic Toxicologists (TIAFT), provide the venue by which continuing education is not only available but relevant to the forensic laboratory.

12.5.4 Measuring Devices

Regardless of their simplicity, burets, pipettes, volumetric flasks, pipettors, pipettor-diluters, and the analytical balance are used in one way or another in nearly every chemical analysis. They impart the first sources of systematic errors in the analysis. For this reason, it is imperative that their quality, maintenance, and calibration be addressed in the standard operating procedures.

The selection and maintenance of chemical measuring devices and instruments is beyond the scope of this section, but is covered in detail in textbooks of quantitative chemical analysis and instrumental analysis.[2,3]

12.5.5 Reagents

Chemicals, reagents, solvents, and gases used in the process of executing the analytical procedures must meet minimum quality criteria as required by the analytical method. They should be properly stored, according to manufacturers' specifications or good chemical hygiene practice, in order to maintain their integrity and safety. Special care must be taken to record the receipt date and consider the stability of the reagent before use.

The determination of trace amounts of analytes in complex biological fluids or tissues often requires concentration of organic solvent extracts, which must be analyzed by very sensitive instruments. This circumstance creates a need for high-purity solvents, reagents, and gases to avoid introducing significant amounts of interferences during the analytical process. Commercially available solvents have been developed with special qualities applicable to specific purposes. Examples include solvents possessing low ultraviolet absorption, used in high-performance liquid chromatography and spectrophotometry, as well as solvents with negligible halogenated organic content, required for electron capture detectors or negative ion chemical ionization mass spectrometry. A post-mortem toxicology laboratory should procure the highest quality of reagent possible to minimize the potential for interferences with its analytical methods.

The use of inert, high-purity gases for gas-liquid chromatographs has been an essential part of the operation of gas chromatography since its inception as an analytical tool. The fragile nature of liquid phases in the presence of oxygen (air) at high temperatures and the development of very sensitive detectors such as nitrogen-phosphorus, electron capture, and mass spectrometers, among others, have made the gas quality a priority issue in the operation of the laboratory. Gases with 99.999% purities containing subpart-per-million quantities of air, moisture, and organic compounds are readily available at moderate cost. There are also a variety of products designed to remove or "scrub" contaminants from the gas stream before their introduction into the instrument, which can be utilized if high-purity gases are not readily available. These gas scrubbers should be monitored periodically for proper operation as part of the standard operating procedures.

The preparation of reagents, buffers, and mixtures should be conducted according to the specific instructions in the procedures manual. A reagent log book containing the preparation instructions for the most common solutions provides a convenient way to record their preparation with traceable information such as date of preparation, preparer, stock reagent lot number, and expiration date. This information should always be included in the reagent flask label along with the identification of the solution, its concentration, and any applicable safety recommendation.

12.5.6 Reference Materials

The accuracy of any quantitative analytical procedure depends directly on the purity of the standard used for calibrating the method. Therefore, the analyst must ascertain that the standards, or reference materials, used to prepare the calibrators are chemically pure. The subject of reference materials is discussed in the SOFT/AAFS Forensic Toxicology Laboratory Guidelines.[1]

12.5.6.1 *Calibrators*

Calibrators are materials with which the sample is compared in order to determine the concentration or other quantity.[6] Methods known to have acceptable accuracy because physical or matrix effects are negligible may be calibrated with certified reference solutions. However, procedural constraints and complex matrix effects of biological samples make the use of certified reference solutions impossible in many routine methods. The calibrators selected for such methods must simulate the physical and chemical properties of the samples in order to compensate for matrix effects during analysis and to be sensitive to important changes in analytical error conditions.

Assay values assigned to calibrators must be sufficiently accurate for the intended use. The uncertainty interval for the assigned concentration value must be small compared to the analytical precision of the method to be calibrated. That is, the absolute error calculated for the assigned value using dimensional analysis must be smaller than the absolute error obtained when the calibrator is analyzed multiple times by the method.[7]

In the forensic laboratory, three types of calibrators may be encountered. The first is use of a reference standard solution as a calibrator when the method has no procedural constraints and matrix effects are virtually non-existent. Certified standard solutions for this type of method can be obtained commercially or prepared in the laboratory with reference materials. This type of method, although rare in the forensic laboratory, can best be exemplified by the analysis of volatiles using headspace techniques with gas chromatography, and the percent purity determination of drug exhibits using ultraviolet spectrometry.

The second type of calibrators includes those obtained from commercial sources as kits to be used in self-contained analytical systems. They are matrix specific and manufactured in bulk under strict quality control. They are carefully designed to perform a specific task under rigorously controlled conditions and are provided with lot numbers and expiration dates. Assays of this type include quantitative techniques by radioactive, enzymatic, and fluorescent immunoassays.

The last type of calibrators encountered in the forensic laboratory are of most concern because they assume the most uncertainty. They are usually employed in analytical assays involving multistep extractions, concentration, derivatization, and complex instruments of analysis and data reduction. These working standards must be prepared in the laboratory from pure reference materials, be diluted with blank sample matrix to resemble the biological sample, and remain accurate enough to convey a reliable measurement when a sample is compared to them. For this reason, every effort should be made to ensure the quality of reference material, the proper maintenance of volumetric implements and balances, and the application of good analytical skills.

The preparation of a calibrator, or working standard, begins with the preparation of a stock solution from the reference drug material. A water-soluble organic solvent that readily dissolves the drug material without adverse reaction is the solvent of choice. Solvents that are not water soluble can be used, but they require additional steps to remove the solvent when further dilutions are made into aqueous biological fluids. A concentration of 1 mg of the un-ionized form of the drug per milliliter of solvent is convenient and adequate for most drugs analyzed. To keep the uncertainty of the calibrator below the variance of the method, it is desirable to know the exact concentration of the stock standard to at least three significant figures. The solutions stored in capped amber vials at −20°C can have long shelf lives if care is taken to allow the solutions to reach room temperature before opening, thus avoiding moisture condensation in the solution. The stability of these solutions must be established periodically. Calibration standards are discussed in the *CRC Handbook of Clinical Chemistry*.[7]

Multilevel Calibration

The calibration scheme used for the purpose of carrying out quantifications of unknown specimens is done with the preparation of a calibration graph that includes a minimum of three different concentrations and a blank. The concentrations of analyte used to prepare the graph must include the lower and upper limits of required linear response, since linearity must be demonstrated in every assay.

The recommended scheme for the preparation of a set of calibrators has been discussed in the Research Monograph Series of the National Institute on Drug Abuse.[8]

To control for the influence of matrix effects, it is recommended to add the same volume of working stock solution to each aliquot of biological matrix when preparing the calibrators. To do this, a fresh set of working stock solutions is prepared by serial dilutions from the stock solution. Mixtures of drugs and metabolites can also be included in the working stock solution sets.

The calibration graph is obtained by plotting the detector response against the assigned concentration of analyte in the working standard. Chromatographic assays that use internal standards are calibrated by plotting the detector response ratio of analyte to internal standard against the assigned concentration of analyte in the working standard. Using the statistical method of linear regression, the straight line that best fits the points can be determined. The slope of the line and the y-intercept are used to calculate the quantity of analyte in an unknown sample based on its detector response. Figure 12.5.1 shows a representative calibration curve for the analysis of fentanyl. Some calibrations are inherently nonlinear, and therefore it is acceptable to apply a quadratic curve fit rather than force a linear fit to data that is clearly not linear. It is up to the analyst, or as a matter of policy the laboratory, to determine when the degree of nonlinearity is clearly unacceptable. Furthermore, it is good practice for evaluation of the calibration to include reading each calibrator against the established curve. Most calibrators should read within ±20% of the target with perhaps a wider margin as the calibration approaches the origin.

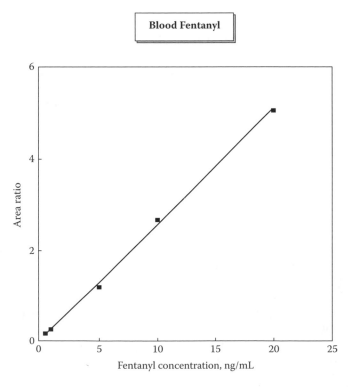

Figure 12.5.1 Multilevel calibration.

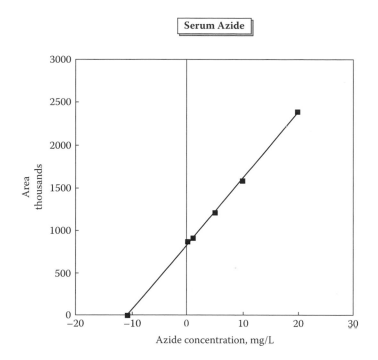

Figure 12.5.2 Calibration by method of additions.

Method of Addition

The method of additions is a very powerful calibration technique because the accuracy is independent of matrix effects. The technique requires that replicates of the specimen, instead of blank matrix, be fortified with the different levels of calibrators, along with an unspiked replicate of the specimen serving as the "blank." All the samples are analyzed by the analytical method as usual. A calibration graph is generated by plotting the detector response of the analyte (or response ratio if using internal standard) against the concentration of the calibrators and plotting the response of the unfortified specimen on the y-axis ($x = 0$). Using the statistical method of linear regression, the straight line that best fits the points is determined and the absolute value of the x-intercept represents the calculated concentration of the specimen. Figure 12.5.2 shows the calculation of azide in blood by the method of additions.

A disadvantage encountered in forensic analysis when using the method of additions is the requirement that multiple aliquots of the specimen be used when forensic samples are inherently limited in size. The use of this method of calibration, therefore, should be limited to situations where a rare analysis is being considered, controls are not available, or when dealing with a particularly difficult matrix.

12.5.6.2 Internal Standards

A suitable internal standard should be used in chromatographic assays such as gas chromatography, high-performance liquid chromatography, and gas chromatography-mass spectrometry. The internal standard can be defined as a substance that is added to all samples (specimens, standards, and controls) in a given assay before processing begins to correct for the many variations that occur in the manipulation of the samples during the entire analysis. Systematic errors affecting the quantity of analyte isolated from the sample will also affect the quantity of the internal standard in the same proportion. Therefore, the ratio of analyte to internal standard at the beginning of the procedure will remain unchanged throughout. For this concept to hold true, the internal standard must comply with certain qualifications.

First, the internal standard must have chemical and physical characteristics very similar to the analyte of interest. This quality ensures that extraction partition coefficients, formation of derivatives, chromatographic characteristics, and detector response are similar enough not to alter their weight ratio significantly. A compound such as difluorococaine, for example, is not a good internal standard choice for cocaine because its enhanced lipophilicity imparts a very different extraction partition ratio, a different chromatographic characteristic, and a dissimilar response to a nitrogen-phosphorus detector. A compound such as propylbenzoylecgonine, an analogue of cocaine containing a propyl ester instead of a methyl ester, is chemically and physically more satisfactory. From the point of view of extraction and derivatization properties the most appropriate internal standard is an analogue of the analyte that has been labeled with a stable isotope. These substances have identical chemical and physical characteristics to the analyte, so their weight ratio is not affected during the analysis. However, unless the chromatographic system can resolve the two components, these are only useful in analyses by gas chromatography-mass spectrometry.

In addition, it is important to add precisely the same amount of internal standard to each sample. It is not necessary to know exactly the weight amount added as long as it is exactly the same amount. The normal practice is to decide in advance the approximate quantity of internal standard to be added to each sample, since the ratio of analyte to internal standard can be measured most accurately when they are present in similar concentrations. The quantity of internal standard added to the samples, then, should give a concentration intermediate between the lowest and highest expected analyte concentrations. This concentration should be such that the lowest anticipated weight ratio of analyte to internal standard should approximately equal the inverse of the highest anticipated ratio. So, if one desires to measure concentrations of a drug over the range 1 to 1000 ng/mL, the amount of internal standard added should give a concentration of approximately 32 ng/mL (1:32 ~ 32:1000). Some analysts may favor the use of a lower concentration of internal standard to facilitate more accurate measurements of low levels of the drug, since low levels are more difficult to measure than high levels. On the other hand, higher amounts of internal standard can be used to act as a "carrier" to minimize losses of analyte due to adsorption at active sites on the surface of extraction vessels and within the chromatographic column.[9]

12.5.6.3 Controls

A control is a test sample of known concentration that is analyzed along with every batch of specimen to make certain that the analytical procedure performs within the expected limits of variation. Three types of controls can be defined: (1) the negative control, which is drug free and analyzed in qualitative and quantitative methods to show that the method is not introducing a contaminant that may construe a false positive, (2) a positive control, containing the drug at a concentration near the limit of detection and used in qualitative methods to demonstrate adequate performance, and (3) the analytical control(s), containing the drug at a meaningful level(s) and used to monitor the performance of the quantitative method. The intended use of controls is to monitor the performance of a method over a long period of time in an internal quality control program, never to calibrate a procedure. The level chosen for the analytical control should be of clinical and/or forensic importance, such as the significant therapeutic concentration of a drug or the legal intoxication level of ethanol. For assays where many samples are being analyzed, controls should be evenly distributed throughout the run, and one should be included at the end.

Control materials are useful only if applicable to the analytical method used. As is the case with calibrators, the control must simulate the physical and chemical properties of the samples to compensate for matrix effects during analysis and to monitor the performance characteristics of the method. They must be homogeneous to be sensitive to analytical imprecision and stable enough to detect system errors for meaningful periods of time.

The source of control materials and their applications have been discussed extensively in the literature as it pertains to clinical chemistry.[10–15] The principles discussed, although applicable to some extent to forensic analysis, do not conform to the unique complexity of the specimens encountered in post-mortem work, such as nails, hair, decomposed tissue, and unstable analytes. However, the need to measure the quality of the method's performance during an analysis is still imperative, and these obstacles must be overcome with analytically sound ingenuity and thorough documentation.

Commercial immunoassays and commercial thin-layer chromatography kits are provided with control materials specifically designed to be used for their intended purpose. These control materials are manufactured in bulk under strict quality control and are conveniently provided with the expected value, acceptable limits of variation, lot number, and expiration dates. However, it is good laboratory practice, where practical, to include at least one independently prepared positive control.

Control materials may be obtained from commercially available sources, although the cost can be high, especially if this is to be done for the very wide range of drugs typically analyzed by a typical post-mortem toxicology laboratory. These are usually supplied in the form of urine or lyophilized serum or plasma, with target concentrations, lot numbers, and expiration dates. Their stability may be short (5 to 30 days) once they have been reconstituted, but they remain stable for months if refrigerated in their lyophilized state. The drug selection available usually incorporates common drugs of abuse and of clinical therapeutic interest, which, albeit adequate, leaves the forensic laboratory with unaddressed needs. The matrices of these materials may not appropriately simulate the typical forensic sample under specific analytical conditions. Therefore, the suitability of these commercial control materials must be ascertained by evaluating them against properly selected calibrators under controlled conditions.

A reasonable source of control material is the pooling of excess laboratory specimens. This source is not very dependable, however, because of difficulties in obtaining unique drug selectivity, the uncontrolled degradation of biological fluids and drugs, biohazards, and increasing legal concerns regarding the use of human fluids and tissues for purposes other than strict determination of cause and manner of death of the individual from whom the specimens were collected.

An alternative is the preparation of controls in the laboratory using outdated whole blood or plasma from blood banks, voided urine, and tissue homogenates prepared from drug free sources. Some analysts in the field have successfully used bovine blood after adjusting the hematocrit to simulate human levels by diluting with water.[16] The only concern about "homemade" controls is that there is no independent way of qualifying the process. For this reason, every effort should be made to ensure the quality of reference material, the proper maintenance of volumetric implements and balances, and the execution of good analytical skills in the preparation of the in-house control.

The process begins with the preparation of a stock solution from a certified reference drug material. This stock solution must be distinct from the one used to prepare the calibrators. It is axiomatic that if the same reference solution is used to prepare both, the control is invalid. A water-soluble organic solvent that readily dissolves the drug material without adverse reaction is the solvent of choice. Solvents that are not water soluble can be used, but they require additional steps to remove the solvent when further dilutions are made into aqueous biological fluids. A concentration of 1 mg of the un-ionized form of the drug per milliliter of solvent is convenient and adequate for most drugs analyzed. The solutions stored in capped amber vials at $-20°C$ can have long shelf lives if care is taken to allow the solutions to reach room temperature before opening, thus avoiding moisture condensation in the solution. The stability of these solutions should be established periodically as described earlier in this chapter.

A decision must be made whether to prepare batches of control material for future use or to prepare a working stock solution from which fresh controls can be fashioned at the time of analysis. The decision to prepare large batches of control material for future use rests on the requirements that (1) the drug be stable for a reasonable period of time in the appropriately preserved matrix of choice, and (2) the control be used frequently enough to merit the effort of establishing the limits of variation for the batch. For example, assays that are used frequently, such as blood ethanol, are good candidates for this type of control material. An assay that is performed about two or three times a year does not merit a batch preparation, even if the control material is deemed stable for a period of years in a frozen state.

A batch is simply prepared by making a proper dilution of the stock solution into the desired volume of biological fluid and adding the required preservatives as outlined in the procedures manual for the specimens being simulated. The control material can be dispensed into labeled vials containing working aliquots and stored until needed under the same protocols used for samples.

Control materials fashioned at the time of analysis are preferred for many post-mortem toxicology analyses. They are prepared fresh at the time of analysis by spiking an aliquot of a working stock solution into the required amount of blank matrix. Hence, any fluid or tissue homogenate can be fortified with the control before processing, allowing the performance of the assay to be monitored for any tissue. The working stock solutions may remain stable for long periods of time because they are prepared in organic solvents. Therefore, a single working stock solution may be used repeatedly to monitor performance even for infrequently performed analyses. However, precautions must be taken to prevent or minimize evaporation of the solvent.

The working stock solution is prepared by diluting the stock solution to an intermediate concentration so that a small aliquot added to the required amount of blank matrix yields the desired control concentration. The solvent used must be water soluble and care must be taken that the volume of control solution chosen to spike the blank does not affect the matrix significantly. Keeping the solvent concentration of the matrix well below 10% is advisable to avoid protein precipitation.

Once a control material has been procured, it is identified with a lot number and, if applicable, an expiration date. Using control materials, the assay is evaluated to determine accuracy and precision expressed as standard deviation and coefficient of variation, which are evaluated by standard statistical methods. Where practical, this requires that the control be analyzed 20 to 30 times over a period of several days by all analysts who perform the assay using the variety of measuring devices that could conceivably be used to perform the assay. A smaller number of analyses may be more practical where the analyte is not routinely performed.

Occasionally, the forensic laboratory needs to perform a rare analysis for which a control has not been established (e.g., yohimbine, estazolam) or one for which a control is impractical to maintain (e.g., toluene, cyanide). In these situations, one can perform a "spike recovery" study to verify that the calculated result was not influenced by matrix differences between the specimen and the calibrators. This is accomplished by spiking a replicate of the specimen with one of the working stock calibrator solutions. The solution is chosen so that the amount added is not less than one tenth the existing concentration, nor more than ten times the existing concentration, and that the addition does not produce a concentration higher than the limits of linearity. The spiked sample is analyzed and the result is used to calculate the percent recovery as follows.

Recoveries that are outside the 20% margin allowed by this principle indicate that matrix effects are abnormally high and that the original concentration calculated for the specimen is inaccurate. If this is the case, the method of additions discussed in Section 12.5.6.1.6 can be pursued in the quest for an accurate result.

12.5.7 Samples and Sampling

Sampling is often called the basis of analysis because the analytical result is never better than the sample from which it is derived. The purpose of sampling is to provide the analyst with a representative part of the "object" that is suitable for the analysis. In forensic work, an appreciation of how the analytes may decompose and how contaminants may be introduced are important factors to consider.[17,18] The subject of samples and sampling is discussed in Chapter 12.2. The subject of safe handling of infectious materials has been treated in detail elsewhere.[19]

12.5.8 Analytical Methods and Procedures

The analytical method is the set of instructions detailing the entire procedure by which a particular analysis is performed. The instructions describe the preparation of reagents, standards, controls, and sample; the steps to isolate and concentrate the analyte; the instrumental requirements; and the data manipulation. It is in the execution of the method that most of the sources of error are introduced, so strict guidelines must be followed to control them.

12.5.8.1 Quality of an Analytical Procedure

An analytical challenge is approached by selecting the method that is most appropriate in terms of its quality features to tackle the chemical problem. The factors that govern the quality of an analytical procedure are the limit of detection, sensitivity, dynamic linear range, precision, accuracy, and selectivity. An in-depth discussion on the subject of quality of analytical procedures has been provided by Kateman and Pijpers.[20]

Limit of Detection

The limit of detection can be defined as the smallest detector response given by the analyte that can be reliably differentiated from background noise produced by the instrument or the procedure. This signal is not necessarily quantifiable, since most detectors are not linear at low response levels.

The classical determination for the method detection limit involves statistical analysis of the probability that the signal is produced by the analyte, and not the instrument, with given confidence limits. These methods, which have been treated extensively in the literature, are involved and require that the background noise be consistent from sample to sample.[21-23]

In methodologies that render irregular background noise from sample to sample it is commonly accepted to determine a signal-to-noise ratio of at least 3:1 to consider the signal as being produced by the analyte. Establishment of a higher signal-to-noise ratio as a decision guideline increases the confidence that the analyte is present at the expense of deciding it is absent at lower ratios. The benefit of doubt imparted to the decision at higher signal-to-noise ratios can be comforting from a forensic viewpoint.

Sensitivity and Linearity

The sensitivity of a method can be defined as the change in detector response given by a change in concentration. The detector response is composed of a part that depends on the concentration and a part that is independent of it (the blank). In addition, the detector response is not linearly proportional to the concentration over the entire range of possible values. The range of values for which the sensitivity is constant is called the "linear dynamic range," and methods should be developed so that this range is as large as possible.

The linear dynamic range, or linearity, is limited at the lower level by concentration values whose detector response cannot be distinguished from the detector noise, or by ambiguous values of sensitivity. The linear range is limited at the upper level by saturation of the detector signal.

Precision

Precision is a measure of the dispersion of results when an analytical procedure is repeated on one sample. Although the dispersion of results may be caused by many sources, it is usually implied that it is caused by random fluctuations in the procedure. If no bias exists, the results usually scatter around the expected value in a normal distribution, described by a Gaussian curve (Figure 12.5.3).

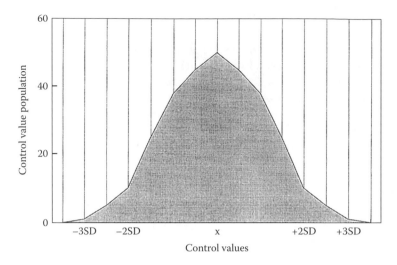

Figure 12.5.3 Gaussian curve.

The normal distribution of the population of results is characterized by the position of the mean (x), and the standard deviation (s). The precision of an analytical method is often expressed as the standard deviation or coefficient of variation (CV), and it is calculated and monitored by analysis of control materials (Section 12.5.6.3).

Accuracy

Although the concept of accuracy is vague and difficult to interpret, it has been defined as the difference (error or bias) between an individual result, or the mean of a set of results, and the value that is accepted as the true or correct value for the quantity measured.[24]

An accurate measurement is one that is free of bias, does not scatter when repeated, and results in the "true value." The true value, however, is unknown because it must be measured, and measurements are biased and imprecise. Nevertheless, the accuracy can be estimated by measuring properties that are related to the concept of "accurate." Precision can be measured and bias can be estimated. Youden[25] stated that the mean of the results obtained by a number of independent laboratories, using comparable methods of data presentation and data handling, can be assumed to be the "true value."

Selectivity and Specificity

Selectivity refers to the ability of an analytical procedure to produce correct results for various components of a mixture without any mutual interference among the components. Specificity refers to the ability of an analytical procedure to discriminate between components in a mixture by their ability to produce a detector signal.

12.5.8.2 Qualitative Methods

Qualitative methods characterize the sample in terms of the identity of its toxic constituents. The identity can be specific, as produced by mass or infrared spectra, or nonspecific, as produced by immunoassays and spot tests.

Qualitative methods require that all analytes that can be detected or ruled out in the analysis be known. For nonspecific assays, such as thin-layer or gas chromatography, this can be an ever increasing list as new drugs are introduced.

With each assay, a negative control and a control representative of the analytes being tested should be analyzed. The positive control should contain the analytes near their respective limit of detection, and both should be prepared in a matrix similar to the samples. Interferences that can adversely affect the result should be indicated in the written procedure.

12.5.8.3 Quantitative Methods

Quantitative methods characterize the sample in terms of the quantity of its toxic constituents. The measured quantity carries with it an inherent uncertainty that must be known in order to appraise its reliability. The accepted thresholds of uncertainty, or limits of variation, are determined by quantifying the factors that affect the quality of the method. Therefore, each quantitative technique must be validated by determining its limit of detection, dynamic linear range, precision, and accuracy.

12.5.8.4 Method Development and Validation

Guidelines for method development instituted in a comprehensive procedures manual provide an effective way to tackle the analytical challenges that are frequently encountered in the forensic laboratory. The considerations listed below provide the basis upon which an analytical method can be implemented:

- Establishment of the intended purpose of the method
- Identification of chemical problems that must be addressed to fulfill the intended purpose of the method
- Search of the literature for existing methods that can fulfill the intended purpose and be accommodated by the laboratory

Appendix IC provides literature sources for qualitative and quantitative assay procedures for most common drugs. The references should serve as a starting point for method development.

Once the basic characteristics of the method have been established, the method is developed by evaluating and documenting as much of the following information as possible:

- Analytical principle of the assay
- Brief description of toxic substances being analyzed
- Sample preparation requirements
- The sources of materials and the preparation of reagents, standards, and controls
- Quantitative statements about the stability of the reagents, standards, and controls
- Procedural steps to isolate and/or concentrate the analytes
- Instrumental requirements and settings
- Validation parameters; limit of detection and/or quantification, linear range, coefficient of variation, and recovery efficiency
- Interferences
- Data handling
- References to the source of the method

All analyses should be performed by the procedures set forth in the procedures manual, and carried out explicitly as described by the procedure whenever possible. Exceptions should be made only when special considerations are dictated by the character of the specimen (for example, interferences resulting from multidrug content). When modification to a method is necessary, the exercise of good analytical judgment and proper documentation are essential to impart confidence in the result.

12.5.9 Instruments

In analytical chemistry, information about the chemical composition of a sample is obtained by measuring some chemical or physical property that is characteristic of the component of interest. These measurements are made by various analytical instruments designed to measure specific properties.

To apply instrumentation most efficiently to the problems, the analyst must understand the fundamental relations of chemical species to their physical and chemical properties. The analyst must know the scope, applicability, and limitations of physical property measurement with respect to qualitative and quantitative analysis. Knowing this, the analyst can call upon the instrumentation for the measurement of the desired properties with the needed accuracy and precision.[26,27]

The instrument is a device that converts chemical information to a form that is more readily observable. It accomplishes this function in several steps that may include (1) generation of a signal, (2) transduction (transformation of the signal to one of a different nature, such as electrical), (3) amplification of the transformed signal, and (4) presentation of the signal by a scale, recorder, integrator, or printout. Some instruments also prepare the sample to a form that can be analyzed or perform separation of components for increased specificity. It is common to find a combination of instruments working in tandem to produce the desired results.

To ensure that the instrumental data are reliable, steps must be taken to control the proper function of the instrument. This can be accomplished by establishing standard operating procedures that address proper installation guidelines, a preventive maintenance program, periodic performance evaluations, and preanalysis checklists.

All documentation concerning instrument maintenance and checks should be kept in bound notebooks specific to each instrument. These are to be kept near the instrument for easy access and inspection by all analysts. With time, a history of the instrument will develop that will impart a great insight for effective and timely troubleshooting.

12.5.9.1 Installation

An effort should be made to install the instrument in a manner that is commensurate with the recommendations of the manufacturer. These usually include environmental, energy, and safety requirements that are necessary for the proper function and longevity of the instrument.

12.5.9.2 Preventive Maintenance

A preventive maintenance program can reduce the frequency of instrument failure during analysis. It also reduces the likelihood of major breakdowns and extended downtime. Preventive maintenance requirements and procedures are usually specified in the instrument operation manual. The time interval required between preventive maintenance services is dictated by the amount of use and environmental factors. Therefore, laboratories must establish their own protocols according to their needs.

12.5.9.3 Pre-Analysis Checklist

A review of vital instrument parameters before processing samples assures that the correct settings have been chosen for the analysis and that the instrument is in good working order. This becomes especially important when the instrument is used for multiple procedures by multiple analysts. Use of a checklist is the most effective way to ensure that no parameter is overlooked and produces documentation that pre-analysis checks were performed. The specific parameters to be checked and their proper settings will vary with the instrument.

12.5.10   Data

The American Academy of Forensic Sciences and the Society of Forensic Toxicologists recommend that before results are reported, each batch of analytical data should be reviewed by scientific personnel who are experienced with the analytical protocols used in the laboratory.[1] At a minimum this review should include chain of custody data, validity of analytical data and calculations, and quality control data. The review should be documented within the analytical record.

12.5.10.1   Chain-of-Custody Data

Review of the chain-of-custody documentation ensures that the analytical result represents the correct sample. The data necessary to accomplish this task include the dates and identification of individuals performing the sample collection and transportation to the laboratory; receipt; transfer of specimens or aliquots within the laboratory; chemical analysis; and analytical report.

12.5.10.2   Analytical Data

The first task of an analyst who wants to evaluate a procedure is to collect relevant data of measurements using that procedure. The second task is to reduce the number of measurements, remove irrelevant and erroneous data, and convert the measurements into statements pertaining to the condition of the procedure under control. To convert the data into a form that can be handled, data reduction procedures are applied.

Analytical instruments are usually equipped with data filters or data handlers that smooth and reduce the data collected, relieving the analyst of such arduous tasks. For this reason, the concepts of data production, information theory, data reduction, data handling, analysis of variance, pattern recognition, and system optimization are not discussed in this chapter. However, the analyst should have some understanding of how instruments perform data analysis. This knowledge will help the analyst identify corrupt data, correctly set thresholds for proper peak integration, and determine signal-to-noise ratios. A thorough discussion on data production and data reduction has been presented by Kateman and Pijpers.[28]

A thorough review by responsible supervisory personnel of the raw analytical data and the calculations derived therefrom should be performed before a report is issued.

12.5.10.3   Quality Control Data

A review of the results obtained from the analysis of control material is essential to evaluate the performance of the analysis. This is accomplished by deriving control charts for each control material so that control rules or decision criteria can be applied to determine whether the method performed within expected limits of variation.[29–32]

The control chart is a graphical representation of the arithmetic mean and the control limits calculated for the control material as described in Section 12.5.6.3. The x-axis is scaled to provide appropriate time period intervals. Horizontal lines are drawn corresponding to the mean (center) and multiples of the standard deviation above and below the mean, as shown in Figure 12.5.4. These graphs are sometimes referred to as Shewhart or Levey–Jennings charts.

The control rules or criteria described here are based on statistical properties arising from single control measurements, rather than replicate measurements, since they are more common. They provide a low level of false rejection, improved capability for detecting analytical errors, and some indication of the error type to aid in problem solving. Rejection of an analytical run occurs when the control value obtained violates one or more of the following rules, symbolized for brevity and convenience:

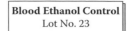

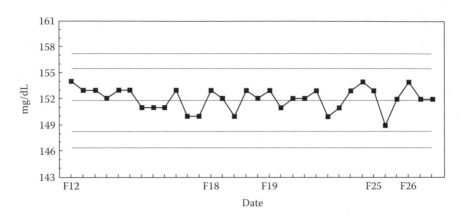

Figure 12.5.4   Quality control chart.

- (1₃ₛ) A value outside 3 standard deviations
- (2₂ₛ) Two consecutive values outside 2 standard deviations; one value outside 2 standard deviations should be considered a warning, requiring inspection of a second control
- (R₄ₛ) Two consecutive values that differ by 4 standard deviations or more
- (4₁ₛ) Four consecutive values on the same side of the mean that are more than 1 standard deviation from the mean
- (10ₓ) Ten consecutive values on the same side of the mean

The particular rule violated may give some indication of the type of analytical error occurring. Random error will most often be detected by the 13s and R4s rules. Systematic error will usually be detected by the 22s, 41s, or 10× rules and, when very large, by the 13s rule. However, these rules may be difficult or impossible to properly apply in forensic toxicology work where, with the exception of ethanol and a small number of drugs, the frequency of analysis is relatively low.

12.5.11   Reports

Post-mortem forensic laboratories are an integral part of, supported by, or associated with government agencies involved in medicolegal investigations. The laboratory must comply with the reporting requirements mandated by the agency to which the reports are submitted. Thus, a report format can be neither standardized nor recommended, since it will depend on the specific needs of the recipient. In general, however, the written report should include all information necessary to identify the case and its source, the test results, and the signature of the individual responsible for its contents. Forensic toxicology reporting is discussed in depth in the AAFS/SOFT Forensic Toxicology Laboratory Guidelines.[1]

12.5.12   Proficiency Programs

In addition to the laboratory's effort in implementing a quality control program to impart confidence to its analytical results, there is a requirement to scrutinize the analytical process by independent evaluation against peer laboratories. A proficiency testing program established by accrediting organizations or independent consultants provides laboratories with such an evaluation mechanism.

The proficiency program provides laboratories with chemically fortified samples simulating those encountered routinely by the laboratory for analysis. The program derives statistical data on the results reported by the participating laboratories and issues a summary of useful information about the results. When the result of a chemical analysis is compared to the results obtained by other laboratories on the same sample, the laboratory can make a responsible determination of the strengths and weaknesses of its overall operation. This information can be used to focus resources on those areas that need improvement, be it personnel, training, equipment, method development, reference materials, or the like. It also builds confidence in the methods that yield reliable results.

Forensic toxicology laboratories must participate in external proficiency testing programs that evaluate as many of the analytical tests in as many specimen types as possible. These programs are the only independent way to evaluate the reliability of the methods used and the overall operating procedures of the laboratory.

12.5.13   Accreditation Programs

Accreditation is playing an increasing role in the quality of work performed in forensic laboratories. It ensures that the laboratory has acceptable analytical methods, general procedures, and most important, that the standard operating procedures are followed. There are currently four organizations that offer accreditation in the field of forensic toxicology. The National Laboratory Certification Program (NLCP) is operated under private contract through the U.S. Substance Abuse and Mental Health Services Administration (SAMHSA).[33] That NLCP program applies only to U.S. federally regulated testing in the specific area of forensic urine drug testing for amphetamine and methamphetamine, cannabinoids, codeine and morphine, cocaine, and phencyclidine. The College of American Pathologists also operates a voluntary program for forensic urine drugs testing, but which covers a slightly greater range of drugs of abuse in urine.[34] However, the two major, broad-based accreditation programs that encompass forensic toxicology are run by the American Society of Crime Laboratory Directors Laboratory Accreditation Board (ASCLD/LAB), and the American Board of Forensic Toxicology (ABFT).[35,36] The ASCLD/LAB program covers all aspects of forensic laboratory management and operation, including forensic toxicology, whereas the ABFT program is focused on forensic toxicology, and specifically those laboratories performing post-mortem toxicology and human performance drug testing (e.g., driving under the influence of drugs).

REFERENCES

1. Joint Committee of the American Academy of Forensic Sciences (AAFS) and the Society of Forensic Toxicologists, Inc. (SOFT), *Forensic Toxicology Laboratory Guidelines*, Colorado Springs, 2002. Available online from www.soft-tox.org.
2. Ayres, G.H., The analytical balance and its use, in *Quantitative Chemical Analysis*, 2nd ed., Harper & Row, New York, 1968, chap. 2.
3. Schenk, G.H., Hahn, R.B., and Hartkopf, A.V., Fundamentals of weighing and related measurements, in *Quantitative Analytical Chemistry — Principles and Life Science Applications*, Allyn & Bacon, Boston, 1977, chap. 6.
4. Blanke, R.V., Validation of the purity of standards, Publication 87-0175, Abbott Laboratories, Diagnostics Division, Irving, TX, 1989.
5. Williams, S., Ed., *Official Methods of Analysis of the Association of Official Analytical Chemists*, 14th ed., Association of Official Analytical Chemists, Arlington, VA, 1984, 1007.
6. Buttner, J., Borth, R., Boutwell, J.H., and Broughton, P.M.G., Provisional recommendation on quality control in clinical chemistry. I. General principles and terminology, International Federation of Clinical Chemistry, *Clin. Chem.*, 22, 532, 1976.
7. Ross, J.W., Control materials and calibration standards, *CRC Handbook of Clinical Chemistry*, Vol. 1, CRC Press, Boca Raton, FL, 1989, 359.

8. Foltz, R.L., Fentiman, A.F., and Foltz, R.B., GC/MS Assays for Abused Drugs in Body Fluids, Research Monograph Series 32, National Institute on Drug Abuse, Bethesda, MD, 1980, 9–12.

9. Samuelsson, B., Hamberg, M., and Sweely, C.C., *Anal. Biochem.*, 38, 301, 1970.

10. Lawson, N.S. and Haven, G.T., Analyte stability in control and reference materials, in *CRC Handbook of Clinical Chemistry*, Vol. 1, CRC Press, Boca Raton, FL, 1989, 371.

11. Bowers, G.N., Burnett, R.W., and McComb, R.B., Selected method: preparation and use of human serum control materials for monitoring precision in clinical chemistry, *Clin. Chem.*, 21, 1830, 1975.

12. Approved Standard: ASC-2, *Calibration Reference Materials and Control Materials in Clinical Chemistry*, National Committee for Clinical Laboratory Standards, Villanova, PA, 1975.

13. Anido, G., Preparation of quality control materials in clinical chemistry and hematology, *Proc. R. Soc. Med.*, 68, 624, 1975.

14. Klugerman, M.R., and Boutwell, J.H., Commercial control sera in the clinical chemistry laboratory, *Clin. Chem.*, 7, 185, 1961.

15. Logan, J.E., and Allen, R.H., Control serum preparations, *Clin. Chem.*, 14, 437, 1968.

16. Wilkins, D., Ph.D., Associate Toxicologist and Quality Control Manager, Center for Human Toxicology, personal communication, AAFS Meeting, New Orleans, February 1992.

17. Kateman, G. and Pipjers, F.W., Sampling, in *Quality Control in Analytical Chemistry*, Vol. 60, John Wiley & Sons, New York, 1981, chap. 2.

18. Toseland, P.A., Samples and sampling, *Clarke's Isolation and Identification of Drugs in Pharmaceuticals, Body Fluids, and Post-Mortem Material*, 2nd ed., Pharmaceutical Press, London, 1986, 111.

19. Committee on Hazardous Biological Substances in the Laboratory; Board on Chemical Sciences and Technology; Commission on Physical Sciences, Mathematics, and Resources; National Research Council, Biosafety in the Laboratory — Prudent Practices for the Handling and Disposal of Infectious Materials, National Academy Press, Washington, D.C., 1989.

20. Kateman, G. and Pipjers, F.W., Analysis, in *Quality Control in Analytical Chemistry*, Vol. 60, John Wiley & Sons, New York, 1981, chap. 3.

21. Ingle, J.D., *J. Chem. Ed.,* 51(2), 100, 1974.

22. Glaser, J.A., Foerst, D.L., McKee, G.D., Quave, S.A., and Budde, W.L., Trace analysis for wastewaters, *Environ. Sci. Technol.*, 15, 1426, 1981.

23. Code of Federal Regulations Part 100-136, Protection of Environment, Definition and Procedure for the Determination of the Method Detection Limit, Part 136, Appendix B, July 1992.

24. Analytical chemistry, *Anal. Chem.*, 47, 2527, 1975.

25. Youden, W.J. and Steiner, E.H., *Statistical Manual of the Association of Official Analytical Chemists*, Association of Official Analytical Chemists, Washington, D.C., 1975.

26. Sandell, E.B. and Elving, P.J., in *Treatise on Analytical Chemistry,* Part 1, Vol. 1, Kothoff, I.M. and Elving, P.J., Ed., Interscience Publishers, New York, 1959, 17.

27. Skoog, D.A. and West, D.M., *Principles of Instrumental Analysis*, Holt, Rinehart & Winston, New York, 1971.

28. Kateman, G. and Pipjers, F.W., Data processing, in *Quality Control in Analytical Chemistry*, Vol. 60, John Wiley & Sons, New York, 1981, chap. 4.

29. Westgard, J.O., Barry, P.L., and Hunt, M.R., A multi-rule Shewhart chart of quality control in clinical chemistry, *Clin. Chem.*, 27(3), 493–501, 1981.

30. Levey, S. and Jennings, E.R., The use of control charts in the clinical laboratories, *Am. J. Clin. Pathol.*, 20, 1059–1066, 1950.

31. Westgard, J.O., Groth, T., and Aronsson, T., Performance characteristics of rules for internal quality control: probabilities for false rejection and error detection, *Clin. Chem.*, 23, 1857–1867, 1977.

32. Westgard, J.O. and Groth, T., Power functions for statistical control rules, *Clin. Chem.*, 25, 863–869, 1979.

33. Substance and Mental Health Services Administration (SAMHSA): http://workplace.samhsa.gov.

34. College of American Pathologists: http://www.cap.org.

35. American Society of Crime Laboratory Directors/Laboratory Accreditation Board: http://www.ascld-lab.org.

36. American Board of Forensic Toxicology: http://www.abft.org.

12.6 INTERPRETATION OF POST-MORTEM DRUG LEVELS

Graham R. Jones, Ph.D., DABFT
Office of the Chief Medical Examiner, Edmonton, Alberta, Canada

12.6.1 Introduction

In the early to mid-1900s, the practice of forensic toxicology was relatively limited in scope. Certainly, toxicologists could determine blood alcohol and a limited number of drugs with accuracy approaching that of today. However, the toxicological investigation was different in at least two respects. First, the sophistication of testing for drugs was limited, primarily relying on the efficiency of extraction techniques, followed by gravimetric and later spectrophotometric analysis. Second, with the exception of alcohol and a relatively limited number of drugs or poisons (e.g., salicylate, barbiturates, arsenic, heavy metals), there was a very limited database of reference drug concentrations available. The interpretation of quantitative results relied very heavily on the history and circumstances of the case, including the police investigation, witness accounts, and autopsy findings.

The development of gas chromatography (GC) and high-performance liquid chromatography (HPLC) during the early 1970s had a major influence on the development and growth of pharmacokinetics and therapeutic drug monitoring. As a result, the kinetics of drug absorption, distribution, metabolism, and excretion in clinical patients was easier to understand and predict. This coincided with a vast increase in the range of pure pharmaceuticals available, many of which were of lower absolute dosage compared with those previously available; for example, the replacement of barbiturates with low-dose benzodiazepines. It was logical that toxicologists started to use the pharmacokinetic data gained from living patients to interpret post-mortem blood concentrations, for example, to predict whether a given blood drug concentration was "in the therapeutic range," whether the blood level was "fatal," or even to predict the amount ingested prior to death. Experience has since shown that post-mortem drug concentrations must be interpreted from a perspective very different from for those in living patients. Many processes occur after death that can change drug and alcohol concentrations, sometimes to a very large extent.

The period of enthusiasm in the late 1970s and 1980s has given way to the realization that there are many unique aspects of post-mortem toxicology that must be considered when interpreting analytical results. It is no longer acceptable to interpret post-mortem toxicology results from tables of so-called therapeutic, toxic, and fatal ranges, without taking into consideration the medical history, the immediate circumstances of the death, and the various processes that can affect drug concentrations both before and after death. It is probably fair to say that many toxicologists and pathologists are less confident about interpreting post-mortem drug concentrations today — and with good reason — than they may have been 10 to 20 years ago.

It is important to remember that there are no "absolute" rules for the interpretation of toxicology results. The more information that is available to, and considered by the interpreter, the more likely are the conclusions reached to be accurate. In the courtroom, lawyers, judges, and jurors often view all science, including the forensic subspecialties, in absolute terms. Certainly, if the toxicologist does his or her job properly, the laboratory findings will have the required accuracy. However, the subsequent interpretation is in part based on the scope of the toxicology testing (not least including the range of specimens tested), in part on the quantitative results, and perhaps most importantly, on the history and circumstances surrounding the death. Attempts to interpret toxicology findings solely on the basis of so-called normal or reference ranges are irresponsible.

It is not the purpose of this chapter to teach anyone *how* to interpret post-mortem drug concentrations, but rather to outline some of the pre-mortem and post-mortem factors that should be taken into account when doing so.

12.6.2 General Considerations

12.6.2.1 The Analytical Result

It should be obvious that the interpretation of any toxicology test result will be no more reliable than the analytical result itself. The interpreter must be satisfied that the analysis is sufficiently accurate for the purpose, or at least know the limitations of the testing. Was the standard material used to prepare the calibrators pure and correctly identified? For example, was the salt or water of crystallization properly taken into account? Was the calibration properly prepared and valid in the range where the specimens were measured? Was the assay adequately verified by quality control samples? Was the assay sufficiently specific? Could endogenous substances or other drugs or metabolites have interfered with analysis of the specimen, either by obscuring the target analyte or by increasing the apparent concentration? If the specimen was analyzed only once, what was the potential for accidental contamination? Was there a matrix effect? For example, was recovery of the drug from the specimen the same, relatively, as from the calibrators? Using similar matrix calibrators (e.g., blood) is not necessarily a guarantee of that since post-mortem blood, by its nature, is variable from case to case, or even from site to site within the same cadaver. The extraction efficiency of drug or metabolite or internal standard from animal or outdated blood bank blood may sometimes be markedly different from decomposed case blood. Although it is practically impossible to know the "absolute" or true concentration of drug in a post-mortem specimen, the degree of confidence increases with the specificity of the analysis, with replication, or in some cases by applying multiple analytical methods of different physical or chemical principle.

The use of GC/mass spectrometry with multiple ion monitoring and stable isotope (e.g., deuterated) labeled internal standards will usually provide a higher degree of confidence in the accuracy of the analytical result, than, say, use of an immunoassay procedure. The completeness of the analysis should also be considered. It is never possible to test for every single drug during routine screening tests. However, a careful review of the medications or other potential poisons available to the deceased should assist the laboratory in determining whether any of these substances would have been detected if present in significant concentrations.

12.6.2.2 Post-Mortem Specimens

Relying on a toxicology result from a single specimen can be misleading, because of the post-mortem changes that can occur. The most commonly used specimen, blood, is not a homogeneous fluid. It is good forensic practice to have multiple specimens available, or at least blood specimens from different sites in the body, because of the potential difficulties in interpreting post-mortem toxicology results.

Blood

The concentrations of many drugs are affected by post-mortem redistribution through the vascular system from the major organs, by direct post-mortem diffusion from organ to organ, and sometimes by incomplete distribution. Sedimentation of blood after death may also affect the drug "blood" concentration obtained. For some drugs the distribution between blood and plasma is markedly uneven during life. However, toxicologists should be cautious about applying factors to "correct" for blood:plasma distribution unless it is known that the distribution is maintained after death. It may be found that the blood:plasma distribution that exists during life, due to active processes, decays after death occurs, for example, due to changes in pH and, therefore, protein binding.

Toxicologists should be cautious about inferring the exact source of a blood specimen from the labeled description. Blood, simply labeled as such, could come from almost anywhere, even collected as pooled blood at the scene. Most toxicologists and pathologists are well acquainted with the widely discouraged practice of drawing blood by a "blind stick" through the chest wall. Although such blood may be labeled as "heart blood," it may contain pericardial fluid, or worse, may be from the pleural cavity, and therefore potentially be contaminated by gastric contents, particularly if the death was traumatic or decomposition severe.[1] Even blood drawn from the "heart" after opening the body cavity at autopsy may contain blood from a number of sources. So-called "heart" blood may contain blood from one or more of the cardiac chambers — the ventricles and atria. However, it may equally contain blood that has drained from the pulmonary vein and artery (and hence the lungs), from the inferior vena cava (and hence from the liver), and from the aorta and subclavian veins. As a result, so-called heart blood is potentially one of the most nonhomogeneous specimens in the body. As described later, post-mortem redistribution and other factors can cause the concentrations of many drugs to vary markedly from site to site.[2–4] Even drug concentrations in blood drawn from the same site, but simply placed into different collection vials, can also sometimes differ by severalfold.

It is generally recommended that to avoid the effects of post-mortem redistribution or diffusion from the major organs, femoral blood should be sampled wherever possible. While this is certainly a good practice, interpreters should be cautioned that there is no such thing as "pure femoral blood"; it is simply blood drawn from the site of the femoral vein. Certainly, if the proximal part of the femoral vein is ligated prior to sampling, it is likely that much of the blood will be "peripheral" and therefore relatively uncontaminated by blood from the major organs. However, this is rarely the case. Femoral blood is typically drawn by a "stick" to the unligated femoral vein in the groin area, such that blood will be drawn from above and below the site of sampling. If the volume drawn is relatively small (e.g., 2 to 5 mL), it is unlikely that much blood will be drawn down from the central body cavity. However, with some skill, it is often possible to draw 50 mL or more of blood from a "femoral stick." Even with a limited knowledge of anatomy, it does not require much thought to realize that at least some of this blood will have been drawn down from the inferior vena cava, and hence from the liver. An alternative sampling technique is to cut the iliac vein at the side of the pelvis during autopsy, and only sample blood that is massaged out from the femoral vein directly into a test tube. Even if such a procedure ensures that the collected blood is from the femoral vein, some post-mortem changes may just as well have happened in this blood, too, e.g., diffusion from vessel walls and skeletal muscle. Since blood concentrations of some drugs have the potential for marked post-mortem change, it is good practice to analyze blood obtained from more than one site, plus tissue or other specimens where this may be useful.

Vitreous Humor

Vitreous humor, although limited in volume (e.g., 3 to 6 mL), is an extremely useful specimen. It has been used for years to verify post-mortem blood concentrations of ethanol, since post-mortem fermentation does not occur to any significant extent in the eye. However, vitreous humor has also been useful for a number of drugs. For example, it is well known that digoxin concentrations will rise after death in cardiac blood, due to post-mortem redistribution from myocardial tissue, and possibly other organs. Consequently, vitreous digoxin concentrations are more likely to reflect those in ante-mortem plasma.[5] Vitreous humor has been used to analyze a large number of other drugs, including barbiturates, cocaine, morphine, tricyclic antidepressants, and benzodiazepines.[6–10] However, interpretation of vitreous drug concentrations is difficult, in part because very few studies have been published that relate blood concentrations to those in vitreous humor, and in part because the large *ad hoc* data on vitreous drug concentrations is fragmented in innumerable case reports.

In general, however, those drugs that tend to be somewhat hydrophilic at physiological pH (e.g., digoxin, benzoylecgonine, acetaminophen, salicylate) are more likely to have concentrations approaching those in blood or plasma, than those drugs that are either highly protein bound (e.g., tricyclic antidepressants) or highly lipophilic (e.g., benzodiazepines). In fact, a significant negative correlation between the vitreous:blood concentration ratio and the degree of protein binding of different drugs has been reported.[11]

Because the eye is remote from the central body cavity and the abdominal organs, it has been suggested that vitreous may be a useful fluid for the determination of drugs that are subject to post-mortem redistribution. That may hold true for many drugs such as digoxin. However, others have shown that some drugs, notably cocaine, may increase in concentration in the vitreous humor after death.[9] Post-mortem diffusion of drugs to the vitreous from the brain, particularly in bodies lying in a prone position for an extended time, may be a possible source of error, and warrants systematic studies.

Liver

Many toxicologists rank the liver second only after blood in importance as a specimen of interpretive value in post-mortem toxicology. It is particularly valuable for the tricyclic antidepressants and many other drugs that are very highly protein bound. It is useful for the phenothiazine neuroleptics which have a very large dosage range, and hence range in "therapeutic" blood concentrations. Liver tissue is also of value for interpreting post-mortem concentrations of many other drugs where a sufficiently large database has been established, and particularly where blood is not available due to severe decomposition, fire, or exsanguination.

One other aspect of liver drug concentrations should be considered. It is known that post-mortem diffusion from the stomach may artifactually elevate concentrations of the drug proximal to the stomach — for example, after an overdose, where both the concentration and absolute amount of drug in the stomach are high.[12,13] However, little appears to have been done to assess the kinetics of drugs in the liver after therapeutic doses. For example, common sense would suggest that drug concentrations in the liver, and particularly those that are strongly protein bound, would increase dramatically in the period after a dose was taken, compared with that at steady state. This might be particularly important for drugs with a relatively long half-life and that are often taken in single nighttime doses, or divided with a large portion of the dose at night. As for other specimens, liver concentrations are extremely valuable for assessing the role of many drugs in a death, but only in conjunction with other analytical findings and history.

Gastric Contents

Interpretation of the analytical findings of drugs in the gastric contents is largely dictated by common sense. It is the *amount* of drug or poison remaining in the gastric contents that is important; the concentration of the drug is generally of far less importance. The tricyclic antidepressants offer a good example. Most forensic toxicologists regard total tricyclic concentrations greater than 2 to 3 mg/L, even in post-mortem "cardiac" blood, as at least potentially toxic or fatal. So what does a gastric tricyclic concentration of 1500 mg/L mean? The answer is, on its own, not much, except that the person may have consumed his or her medication a relatively short period prior to death. For example, 200 mg amitriptyline at night is a fairly common dosage. If the gastric volume was, say, 120 mL, then 1500 mg/L would be completely consistent with the person taking the normal dosage just prior to death — probably from unrelated causes. However, if in our example the gastric volume at autopsy was 900 mL, then a concentration of 1500 mg/L would calculate out to 1350 mg/900 mL in the stomach, and therefore almost certainly consistent with an overdose.

Conversely, a relatively low absolute amount of drug in the gastric contents, with or without a high concentration, does not rule out the possibility of an overdose. Numerous case histories have shown that it may take several hours for an individual to die from an intentional overdose, depending on the exact drugs or poisons ingested, the amounts, co-ingestion of alcohol, general state of health and age. It is not unusual for people to die from an oral overdose with less than a single therapeutic dose remaining in the stomach, notwithstanding the fact that an overdose of drugs can be irritant to the stomach lining and therefore delay gastric emptying. Extensive vomiting before death can also reduce the amount of drug remaining in the stomach at the time death occurs.

Two other aspects of "gastric toxicology" should be mentioned. The simple presence of a drug in the gastric contents does not necessarily mean that the drug was recently consumed, or even prove that the drug was taken orally. Most drugs will be re-excreted into the gastric contents through the gastric juice, maintaining an equilibrium between the gastric fluid and the blood. This is especially so for drugs that are basic (alkaline) in nature. This can readily be demonstrated where it is known that a drug has only been administered intravenously under controlled conditions, and yet can be found later in small concentrations in the gastric contents. The same phenomenon can be seen with drug metabolites where, invariably, concentrations can be found in the gastric fluid. While it could be argued that microbial metabolism could have occurred in the stomach, it is more likely that the majority of the metabolites found were secreted into the stomach via the gastric juice. Conversely, the presence of "ghost" tablets in gastric contents has been reported for at least one type of slow-release analgesic, where overdose or abuse was not suspected. Apparently, the wax-resin matrix of these sustained release tablets may remain in the gastric contents long after the active ingredient has diffused out.[14]

More commonly, significant amounts of conglomerated, unabsorbed tablet or capsule residue can be found in the stomach many hours, or even a day or two after a large overdose was consumed. These masses can occur after overdoses where large amounts of capsules or tablets may form a gelatinous mass, which is not readily dissolved or broken up, and which may lie slowly dissolving; they are called bezoars.[15] While the term can apply to unabsorbed masses of almost anything (e.g., hair balls), it is also applied to unabsorbed drug formulations. They occur, at least in part, because gastric emptying time is delayed significantly by irritants, including large amounts of undissolved drug residue. However, the phenomenon is also occasionally seen in patients where overdosage is extremely unlikely (e.g., controlled setting such as a hospital or nursing home), but where several unabsorbed tablets may be recovered from the stomach. This is more likely to occur where enteric-coated tablets are involved, which do not dissolve in the stomach, but may stick together to form a small mass of tablets. It is also more likely to happen in elderly individuals, or in other patients where gastric motility is abnormally slow.

Urine

It is almost universally accepted that, with few exceptions, there is very little correlation between urine and blood drug concentrations, and even less correlation between urine drug concentrations and pharmacological effect. So many factors affect urine concentration, such as fluid intake, rate of metabolism, glomerular clearance, urine pH, and the times of voiding relative to the dose, that any attempt to predict or even estimate a blood concentration from a urine concentration is pure folly. As always there are some exceptions. Urine alcohol concentrations can be used to estimate the approximate blood alcohol concentration, but only if the bladder is completely voided and the measurement made on the second void. Estimates of the body burden of some heavy metals are still made on 24-h urine collections.

Brain

The brain is the primary site of action of many forensically important drugs, such as the antidepressants, benzodiazepines, and narcotics. It is potentially a very useful specimen for the measurement and interpretation of drugs because it is remote from the stomach and other major organs in the body and would not be expected to be affected by post-mortem diffusion and redistribution. However, although drug concentration data in brain tissue are not hard to find in the literature, it is largely fragmented into innumerable case reports which seldom specify what anatomic region of brain tissue was analyzed. The brain is an anatomically diverse organ such that concentrations of many drugs vary significantly from one region to another — up to about twofold.[2,4]

Other Soft Tissues

Most of the major organs such as the kidneys, lungs, spleen, and myocardial tissue have at some time been analyzed to estimate the degree of drug or poison exposure. However, for most drugs, adequate reference databases are not available in the literature, so the interpretive value of these measurements may be limited. Skeletal muscle has the potential to be one of the most useful specimens for drug or poison determination, particularly where the body is severely decomposed, or where post-mortem redistribution or diffusion might affect measurement in blood or other organs. The problem is one of obtaining sufficient reference values for that drug in skeletal muscle in order to make a confident interpretation. Some studies have been published, but data are scattered and incomplete.[2,4,16]

The potential usefulness of bone marrow for the determination of both drugs and alcohol has been explored.[17–19] For drugs and other poisons at least, this could be very useful in cases where severe decomposition, fire, or the action of wild animals has made the major organs unavailable, but where bone marrow can still be harvested and analyzed. As for many other specimens, the problem is again one of establishing an adequate and reliable database of reference values.

Other Fluids

Bile has been used for decades as one of the primary specimens analyzed in the forensic toxicology laboratory, but mainly for the detection and measurement of morphine. However, the usefulness of bile has decreased in the past few years as sensitive immunoassays and mass spectrometry based assays have been developed for whole blood. For most drugs, including morphine, the interpretive value of bile is limited. Biliary drug concentrations may also be influenced by post-mortem diffusion from the liver and the stomach.

Cerebrospinal fluid (CSF) is also a potentially useful specimen for the measurement and interpretation of drugs, since it is the fluid that "bathes" the central nervous system, the brain, and spinal cord. Its limitation lies mainly in the fact that it is often more difficult to collect than blood post-mortem, and as for many other specimens, there is a very limited database of reference values. As for the vitreous, drugs that are highly protein bound or those that are lipophilic will tend to have significantly lower concentrations than in the blood.

Injection Sites, Nasal Swabs

Suspect injection sites are periodically excised and submitted for analysis, to support evidence of that route of administration. Certainly, it is not difficult to perform such analyses. However, the simple qualitative detection or even quantitative measurement of a drug in a piece of skin is evidence only that the drug was taken or used, not that it was necessarily injected, let alone at that site. Sometimes it is forgotten that most drugs are distributed throughout the body from any route of administration, such that any piece of skin will contain some amount of the drug. For such measurements to be useful, a similar piece of skin from another part of the body, not suspected to be an injection site, must be analyzed for comparison. Only if the concentration in the suspect site is substantially higher than that in the reference site can meaningful conclusions be drawn. Even then, a perfect injection may not cause persistent elevated drug concentrations at the intravenous injection site, in contrast to an intramuscular or subcutaneous site. Similarly, the simple detection of a drug such as cocaine in a nasal swab does not prove that the drug was "snorted." Any fluid secreted by the body, including sweat, vaginal fluid, and nasal secretions, will contain some concentration of the drug. In this instance, quantitative determination is difficult and interpretation even more so unless the concentration of drug in the nasal secretions is extremely high relative to the blood.

Hair

Most drugs and poisons will be absorbed by bone, nails, and hair. Hair has long been used for the determination of arsenic and heavy metals, and by cutting the hair into sequential sections, for estimating the duration of exposure to the poison.[20] More recently, hair has been used for the determination of drugs of abuse in workplace and probation testing. Further, hair analysis can also be applied to estimate compliance in drug substitution programs and may also prove useful in therapeutic drug monitoring. In drug-facilitated crimes, the detection of a particular poison, such as GHB,[21] zopiclone,[22] and thiopental[23] in hair has been used to document the exposure in several drug-facilitated crimes, but a negative finding can usually not exclude an exposure.[24] Finally, hair analysis has the potential to be useful in post-mortem situations, for example, to estimate the duration of exposure to a drug or toxin, and hence provide information about the subject's previous drug use.[25–29]

The incorporation of drugs into hair is to a large extent due to melanin binding.[30] Hence, comparisons of levels between individuals is very risky. Even if the melanin content in the hair is measured, there are different types of melanin, and besides, a correction for total melanin content can only be applied to drugs where the drug-melanin binding characteristics have been firmly established. For most drugs, such information is lacking, and hence, the exact hair drug concentration per se is rarely informative.

Nails, Bone

One advantage of analysis of keratinized materials that should be emphasized is the stability of drugs in hair and nails, which means that such samples can be stored in room temperature for very long periods without major degradation of incorporated drugs. Drugs are incorporated into nails via both the root of the growing nail and via the nail bed.[31] This implies that during the growth of the nail, drugs follow the movement of the keratinized matrix both upward and forward. In addition, the growth of nails is variable and generally slow. Hence, a temporal mapping of previous drug intake using analysis of nails is hardly possible. On the other hand, nails are almost always available for analysis, whereas hair is not; some subjects may present with alopecia totalis, or have shaved the hair on many body parts. Despite the limitations as to the growth rate of nails, this matrix has the potential to be a useful source for information about the drug use history of the decedent.

Most drugs and poisons will be taken up in bone and therefore, unless volatile, will be detectable in skeletonized remains. The interpretation of concentrations of certain drugs or poisons is relatively easy since either the normal or reference values are well established (e.g., arsenic; heavy metals), or the substance should not be present in any concentration (e.g., strychnine). However, interpretation of specific concentrations of pharmaceutical drugs or drugs of abuse is problematic because of limited reference levels. In addition, it should be recognized that bone is continuously remodeled; hence, drugs incorporated in bone tissue over time will be liberated and re-delivered to the blood. This means that a negative detection in bone does not rule out an exposure and a positive detection will not give very much information as to the time for exposure.

Paraphernalia: Syringes, Spoons, Glasses

Most forensic toxicologists are willing to analyze potentially drug-related exhibits found at the scene of death. Syringes or spoons can provide a valuable confirmation of drugs that may have been used prior to death. For example, heroin is so rapidly broken down to morphine that little or no heroin, or even monoacetylmorphine, may be detectable in post-mortem blood. The finding of morphine in, for example, blood, could indicate either use of heroin or a morphine salt (or codeine, if it was also found). However, it should be borne in mind that most addicts reuse syringes and therefore the presence of a drug in a syringe found in the same room as a body does not necessarily mean that drugs contained therein were involved in the death, although it may provide circumstantial evidence. The use or abuse of insulin in a person without diabetes is exceptionally difficult to prove, since blood insulin concentrations are so variable, are difficult to determine accurately in post-mortem blood, and even during life correlate poorly with blood glucose. Insulin abuse is uncommon,[32,33] but in those cases where it happens may be difficult to prove post-mortem without a good clinical history. However, detection of insulin in a used syringe near someone who was not prescribed the drug can provide useful circumstantial evidence of abuse. The presence of drug residues in drinking glasses or cups can provide evidence of at least the route of ingestion and in most cases assist with the determination of manner of death, especially if the drug residue is large and obvious. Care would obviously have to be taken to distinguish, say, a multiple drug overdose mixed in a glass of water, from two or three hypnotic tablets introduced into an alcoholic beverage for the purposes of administering a "Mickey Finn."

12.6.3 Pharmacokinetics

Although other parts of this book deal with the topic of pharmacokinetics in some detail, it is worth reviewing the basics as it relates to post-mortem interpretation. The kinetics of all drugs and poisons in the body are characterized by absorption, distribution, metabolism, and excretion. All these parameters affect the concentrations that will be found in the body after death, and therefore interpretation of analytical toxicology results.

12.6.3.1 Absorption and Distribution

Absorption may be via the oral route, parenteral (e.g., intravenous, intramuscular, subcutaneous), pulmonary, dermal, and rarely, rectal. The route of absorption can be very important to the interpretation. For example, many drugs are extremely toxic via the intravenous route, especially if given rapidly. For example, heroin, barbiturates, and many other drugs can cause severe hypotension, and may be fatal, if given rapidly, even though the total dose given is within the range normally considered "therapeutic." The resulting post-mortem blood concentrations may be below those normally considered fatal. At the other extreme, dermal absorption of medication is probably the slowest, such that even therapeutic concentrations in blood may take several hours to reach. Moreover, absorption of the drug may continue for several hours after the source of the drug, for example, a transdermal patch, is removed, due to the depot of medication which accumulates in the upper layers of the skin. In these circumstances the dose is difficult to control, and if toxicity occurs, it is important that the patient be monitored for several hours after the patch is removed, in case of continued toxicity.[34]

Morphine provides a good and common example of why interpretation of blood concentrations alone in isolation from case history is difficult. First, opiate tolerance can vary tremendously between individuals and even within the same individual over a relatively short time span (days or weeks). Tolerance is an important consideration both clinically, where opiates may be chronically administered for pain, and in abuse situations where they are used for their euphoric effect. In clinical situations the issue of tolerance is complicated by the fact that patients in severe pain can tolerate higher doses of opioids than those in whom the pain is mild. It is also accepted that less opioid is required to prevent the recurrence of pain than to relieve it.[35] The form of the opioids will affect how rapidly the drug crosses the blood–brain barrier and, therefore, how potent it is. For example, heroin (diacetylmorphine) is at least twice as potent as morphine, probably because it is more lipid soluble and reaches the central nervous system faster than the more hydrophilic drug, morphine. It has been suggested that heroin may simply be a pro-drug for morphine, but one that reaches the site of action more efficiently. As a result, blood concentrations of morphine seen in heroin abuse deaths are frequently lower than concentrations resulting from the therapeutic administration of oral or parenteral morphine in clinical situations. The situation is complicated further because morphine is extensively metabolized by conjugation with glucuronic acid.

Originally it was assumed that this resulted in exclusively water-soluble metabolites, which were pharmacologically inactive. However, while morphine-3-glucuronide is devoid of narcotic activity, morphine-6-glucuronide, which is typically present in blood at higher concentrations than unconjugated morphine, is more potent than morphine itself.[36–38] Furthermore, much of the case data published in the clinical and forensic toxicology literature does not even distinguish between unconjugated and "total" morphine, let alone the 3- and 6-glucuronides, which are seldom measured routinely. With all these variables, it is no wonder unconjugated morphine blood concentrations correlate poorly with analgesic effect and central nervous system depression. A good example of this has been described where prolonged respiratory depression was observed in three patients in renal failure where morphine concentrations were extremely low, but where morphine-6-glucuronide had accumulated to toxic levels.[39]

12.6.3.2 *Metabolism and Pharmacogenetics*

A detailed treatise on the mechanisms of drug metabolism and the accumulation of drugs or metabolites due to impaired metabolism is beyond the scope of this chapter. However, it is worth pointing out at least three different scenarios where impaired metabolism can have a significant impact on the interpretation of results. Metabolism can be impaired by liver disease, such as advanced cirrhosis. However, not all metabolic pathways will be impaired equally by liver disease, and indeed some pathways may be affected little, if at all. Oxidative pathways, which are easily saturable, are likely to be affected more than others, such as glucuronidation. A person's metabolism may be genetically deficient, for example, in cytochrome P4502D6 (CYP2D6), This pathway is responsible for many oxidative transformations such as ring hydroxylation of the tricyclic antidepressants, and genetically poor metabolizers can be identified post-mortem.[40] Third, co-ingested drugs can inhibit one or more drug metabolism pathways. For example, most or all of the selective serotonin-reuptake inhibitors (SSRIs) inhibit CYP2D6 and some are extremely potent in this regard. The degree of elevation of the drugs or metabolites affected depends very much on the respective dosages of the drugs involved and, not least, on the "metabolic reserve" of the individual patient. Some drug–drug interactions or genetic polymorphism may only result in slightly elevated drug or metabolite concentrations, perhaps necessitating lowering of dosage. However, in some circumstances the increases may be so dramatic as to cause life-threatening toxicity or death, particularly where the side effects were not sufficiently severe to alert the physician or patient that cardiotoxicity might be a problem. At least two cases involving probable impaired metabolism of imipramine have been described in the forensic literature.[41]

12.6.3.3 *Calculation of Total Body Burden*

Calculation of the total amount of drug ingested in self- or homicidal poisonings have been attempted many times over the years. This was attempted by the toxicologist who analyzed the remains found in the basement of Dr. Harvey Crippen, the renowned London poisoner who used hyoscine.[42] Calculations typically involve measurement of the drug or poison in the major organs including, where possible, skeletal muscle, and then taking into account the organ weights to arrive at a total estimate of the amount in the body. In some cases, the amounts have correlated very well with the available physical evidence (e.g., amount of drug in an empty injection vial or amount prescribed).[43,44] Doubtless, in some other examples attempted by toxicologists, correlation with the physical evidence was less convincing, or not possible. In order for such calculations to be meaningful, a number of factors must be assumed.

Perhaps most important, the particular part of the tissue or blood sample analyzed must be representative of the remainder of the organ or tissue. Since most organs are not homogeneous and because uneven post-mortem diffusion (as discussed later) can lead to non-homogeneity of concentration, being sure of the average concentration of drug within any one organ may be difficult without analyzing that entire organ. While it is easy to know the weight of individual organs such as the heart, lungs, liver, kidneys, and brain, it is very difficult to reliably estimate the total amount of tissue into which most drugs readily distribute including the skeletal muscle. While the mass of skeletal muscle can be estimated from medical tables, given a person's height and weight, there is no assurance that the concentration of drug measured in one or two portions of skeletal muscle is representative of that in muscle from all other parts of the body.

Similar arguments apply to adipose tissue, where it is more difficult to obtain representative samples and accurately assay. It should also be borne in mind that for a person chronically taking a drug with a very large volume of distribution and long half-life, the equivalent of many times the total daily dose will be *normally* present in the body, even after therapeutic doses. Estimation of the total body burden of a drug may not be without value in all cases; it must be done with caution and the variables well understood and acknowledged. It is the rare cases of homicidal poisoning where significant weight may be erroneously placed on such calculations and where the stakes are the highest.

12.6.3.4 *Estimation of Amount Ingested from Blood Levels*

Given the foregoing discussion, it should go without saying that using pharmacokinetic calculations to try to estimate dosage, given a post-mortem blood concentration, is of virtually no value and can be extremely misleading. Several factors make such calculations invalid. The blood drug concentration measured post-mortem must be representative of that present at the time of death. As discussed elsewhere in this chapter, that is often not the case, and it is very difficult to predict whether any given post-mortem drug concentration represents the concentration at the time of death, even for drugs for which post-mortem redistribution is thought to be minimal. Any toxicologist who has routinely analyzed drugs in multiple blood samples from the same case knows how often those concentrations unexpectedly vary from sample to sample. Also, the drug must be at steady state at the time the person dies. By the very nature of drug-related deaths, that is rarely the case. Even if the gastric contents contain relatively little drug, much of the drug could still be present in the ileum, or at least not have attained equilibrium with muscle, adipose tissue, and the major organs. Finally, the rate of absorption, bioavailability, volume of distribution, half-life, rate of metabolism, and clearance are seldom known for any specific individual and can vary tremendously between subjects. The estimation of dose from post-mortem blood concentrations is a practice of the foolhardy.

12.6.4 Post-Mortem Redistribution and Other Changes

One question should be asked before attempting to interpret post-mortem drug concentrations: Is the concentration found likely to represent, at least approximately, that present at the time of death? Unfortunately, the answer is often a flat no, or at least not necessarily. A number of factors need to be considered.

12.6.4.1 *Incomplete Distribution*

It is often the case that sudden deaths involving drugs are caused by abuse or suicidal drug overdose. Death will therefore usually occur before steady state has been reached. If a person is actively absorbing an overdose, it is likely that the concentration of the drug in blood leaving the liver (i.e., the inferior vena cava and right atrium) will have a somewhat higher concentration than, for example, venous blood returning from the peripheral vessels (e.g., femoral vein), for no other reason than a substantial amount of the drug will be absorbed during the course of circulation through the body. This has been demonstrated in living patients with concentration differences up to about twofold recorded between arterial and venous blood.[45,46] It is an open question if this is a practical issue in post-mortem toxicology. In two cases of almost instantaneous death following heroin injection, the concentrations of morphine and codeine in blood collected from heart, brachial veins, and femoral veins were uniform, indicating a very rapid equilibrium.[47]

12.6.4.2 Post-Mortem Redistribution and Post-Mortem Diffusion

Post-mortem redistribution and post-mortem diffusion involve the movement of drug after death along a concentration gradient. Although the differentiation of these terms is not always clear in the literature, post-mortem redistribution generally refers to the release of drugs from areas of higher concentration in organ tissues and subsequent diffusion into and through the capillaries and larger blood vessels of those organs. Post-mortem diffusion generally refers to the diffusion of drug along a concentration gradient, from an area of high concentration to an area of low concentration. The usual scenario is where a high concentration of drug in the stomach contents (e.g., after an overdose) causes elevated concentrations of the drug in nearby tissue (e.g., proximal lobe of the liver) or blood.

Much is still unknown about the extent to which post-mortem changes in drug concentration occur and the drugs affected; however, some generalizations can be made. Post-mortem redistribution is likely to be most marked for drugs that are highly protein bound, but particularly those sequestered in the major organs such as the lungs and liver (e.g., tricyclic antidepressants, propoxyphene, chloroquine). Post-mortem redistribution starts to occur within an hour after death and continues as the post-mortem interval increases. The most important quantitative changes in blood drug concentration occur within the first 24 h and are highly site dependent. In general, increases will be greater in blood from "central" sites, such as the vessels near the major organs, than in more peripheral sites, such as the femoral veins. However, blood drug concentrations can vary fivefold or more between cardiac, hepatic, and pulmonary sites.[2,4] Given the very close proximity of these major vessels to one another and the organs they serve, it is impossible to even estimate peri-mortem drug concentrations based on the post-mortem interval and site from which a blood sample was drawn. Even aside from the unpredictable nature of post-mortem redistribution per se, blood from the "heart," if labeled as such, could have come from either of the cardiac atria or ventricles, the pulmonary vein or artery, the aorta or the inferior vena cava.

Since it is known that many drug concentrations change after death, due to redistribution from the major organs, it is recommended, that post-mortem blood for drug and alcohol analysis be taken from a peripheral site such as the femoral vein. However, it should be emphasized that even if a "good" femoral blood sample is obtained, it is no guarantee that the drug concentrations subsequently measured will represent those present at the moment of death. In fact it is well established that femoral blood concentrations of many drugs can increase twofold or more after death. While it is possible that some of this increase is due to diffusion of released drug down the major vessels to the groin, it should be borne in mind that drug concentrations in skeletal muscle are often twofold or more higher than in the peri-mortem blood.[2,4] Given the mass of muscle surrounding these relatively small peripheral vessels, diffusion of drug directly into the blood across the vessel wall is very likely to occur. While in many of the published studies on post-mortem redistribution the vessels have been carefully ligated prior to taking blood samples, this is rarely done during routine medicolegal autopsies. Consequently, blood labeled as "femoral" may contain blood drawn down from the inferior vena cava. This is particularly likely to be the case where large volumes (e.g., 30 to 50 mL) have been obtained from a supposedly femoral site. It should also be obvious that it does not matter whether the syringe needle is pointing down toward the leg!

The mechanisms for post-mortem redistribution probably involve release of drug from protein-bound sites after death occurs, with subsequent diffusion into interstitial fluid, through the capillaries and into the larger blood vessels. Since this process appears to start within an hour or so of death, decomposition or putrefaction per se is not likely to play a role, at least in the early stages. It is more likely that cessation of active cellular processes and the rapid fall in blood and tissue pH that occurs after death would lead to changes in the conformation of proteins and therefore release of some proportion of drugs present from the protein-bound state. It is important to bear in mind that these changes start well before putrefaction and microbiological action are likely to play a role.

Other types of post-mortem diffusion can occur. For example, it has been demonstrated that over a period of a day or more, significant changes in drug concentrations in the major organs can occur. This has been shown for the tricyclic antidepressants, where concentrations in the lungs tended to decrease, commensurate with an increase in concentration in the liver.[48] This study was done in such a manner as to show that these changes can occur due to direct diffusion from one organ to the other, independent of the residue of drug in the stomach. However, the magnitude of these changes is not likely to affect interpretation of tissue drug concentrations to a significant extent. It has also been demonstrated that post-mortem diffusion of drug from the stomach can markedly increase drug concentrations in proximal lobes of the liver and lungs, as well as post-mortem blood in some of the central vessels.[12,13] Ironically, when organ tissue was analyzed in previous decades, post-mortem diffusion into the liver or lungs might have been less important since it was not uncommon to homogenize large amounts of organ tissue (e.g., 500 g), such that any local increases in concentration would be averaged out. However, today the tendency in many laboratories is to homogenize small amounts of tissue (e.g., 2 to 10 g), which could lead to a gross overestimation of the amount of drug in the organ if the sampled tissue was taken close to the stomach. The potential for post-mortem diffusion of drugs in this manner has been known for decades, but recent work has brought the issue the attention it deserves and better quantified the potential changes.

Aspiration of gastric contents can provide one more important mechanism whereby post-mortem blood concentrations can be artificially elevated.[49] This can occur agonally, as death is occurring, or after death, during transportation of the body. It is a factor that may more commonly occur after overdosage where the stomach contains a very concentrated cocktail of one or more drugs, with or without alcohol. However, it could also be very important to consider in deaths where therapeutic doses have been consumed and death occurs as a result of unrelated natural causes. It is not uncommon, for example, for tricyclic antidepressants to be taken as a single nightly dose, and in fact large doses of many antipsychotic drugs are taken at night. This can result in drug concentrations in the stomach of the order of grams per liter, which if aspirated could result in significant increases in some local post-mortem blood concentrations. Not surprisingly, the pulmonary vein and artery blood concentrations are elevated to the greatest extent following simulated aspiration. This is more significant than it might seem because much of the so-called "heart blood," which is often sampled at autopsy, is in fact blood of pulmonary origin drawn from the major pulmonary vessels or the left atrium. A comprehensive discussion of the possible mechanisms for post-mortem redistribution has been published.[50]

12.6.5 Other Considerations

12.6.5.1 Trauma

Severe trauma can affect the interpretation of both alcohol and drug concentrations. For example, it is not uncommon for severe motor vehicle accidents to result in rupture of the stomach and diaphragm. This can easily result in the release of gastric fluid into the body cavity. Because blood may be difficult to obtain from discrete vessels, pooled blood from the pleural cavity may be sampled. If an autopsy is performed, the origin and nature of the fluid so drawn should be obvious, and hopefully noted. However, if an autopsy is not performed and "blood" is sampled through the chest wall in an attempt to obtain cardiac blood, the coroner or medical examiner may be unaware that the sample is contaminated with gastric fluid. If even small, therapeutic amounts of drug remain unabsorbed in the gastric contents in these circumstances, it can result in what appears to be a grossly elevated "blood" drug (or alcohol) concentration. The release of microorganisms from the gastrointestinal tract and subsequent potential for fermentation is a well-recognized problem.

Trauma causing extended blood loss may also affect blood drug levels, since the physiological reactions include, in addition to increased heart rate and peripheral vasoconstriction, plasma volume refill. Hence, blood levels may increase or drop, depending on their concentrations in the restoration fluid. Experimentally, codeine and morphine blood levels were found to increase significantly after controlled exsanguination in rats[51] and a similar study showed that the analgesic effect of morphine was elevated when given to rats with hemorrhagic shock.[52] Although further studies are needed to determine the impact of and conditions for such antemortem redistribution for several drugs with different pharmacokinetic properties, the phenomenon should be considered in trauma cases with longer duration of blood loss.

12.6.5.2 Artifacts of Medication Delivery

Artifacts of absorption and distribution must be recognized when interpreting post-mortem blood concentrations. For example, it is quite common to find grossly elevated concentrations of lidocaine in cases where resuscitation has been unsuccessfully attempted. Concentrations may be two to five times those normally considered therapeutic when lidocaine is given by intravenous infusion for the treatment of cardiac arrhythmias. If lidocaine is administered as a bolus intracardiac injection and normal cardiac rhythm never established, very high local concentrations will result in the cardiac blood. These could be interpreted as "fatal" unless all the circumstances are considered.

Devices that automatically deliver medication by the parenteral route can lead to artificially high blood concentrations post-mortem. Most of these devices will continue to periodically dispense medication, usually narcotics, into the vein after a person dies, unless they are switched off and disconnected quickly. This can result in extremely high local concentrations of drug, which may be misinterpreted as an overdose.

Transdermal patches left on a body after death will give rise to locally high concentrations of the drug (e.g., fentanyl). Since these patches rely primarily on passive diffusion across a rate-limiting membrane for drug delivery, the concentration of the medication in the local area will continue to rise after death, albeit at a slower rate. Since blood circulation through the skin obviously stops after death, the drug will no longer be transported away except by diffusion, allowing a local build-up of drug. However, such a high concentration gradient exists between the gel containing the medication in the patch and the skin, that even modest post-mortem diffusion might be expected to raise the post-mortem blood and tissue concentrations up to several inches away.

12.6.5.3 Additive and Synergistic Toxicity

When interpreting drug concentrations it is important to take into account the sum of the effects of all of the drugs detected. This is often an issue in drug abuse deaths, particularly those involving prescription drugs. Such deaths often involve multiple drugs of the same type (e.g., benzodiazepines or narcotics), individually present in "therapeutic" amounts, and often in combination with alcohol. Interpretation of blood drug concentrations in these cases has to take into account disease that may be present, and the total amounts of drugs and alcohol. In many cases, these effects may simply be additive, i.e., simply the sum of the individual effects of the drugs involved. In other cases, the effect may be truly synergistic, where the toxicity is greater than would be expected based on the pharmacology and concentrations of the individual drugs. Cases where multiple drugs are present, with or without alcohol, are probably the most difficult to interpret and rely heavily on the experience of the interpreter and a reliable and complete case history.

12.6.5.4 Adverse Reactions

A death attributed to neuroleptic malignant syndrome (NMS) resulting from therapy with phenothiazine or some other neuroleptics is a good example of a fatal adverse drug reaction.[53] Combinations of drugs can result in similar syndromes, such as combination of a tricyclic antidepressant and a monoamine oxidase inhibitor (MAOI) causing serotonin syndrome.[54] Although not always fatal, a serotonin reaction can result in death and might be considered where there is no other reasonable cause of death and especially where there are elevated concentrations of MAOIs and either tricyclic antidepressants or SSRIs. It should be borne in mind that by the very nature of drug–drug or other adverse reactions, blood concentrations of the drug(s) involved are seldom predictive of the outcome and are often well within the range normally expected from therapeutic doses. In the absence of clinical observations, such fatalities can be very difficult to diagnose accurately.

12.6.5.5 Drug Instability

It should not be overlooked that many drugs are unstable in any biological fluid. Cocaine is probably the most notable example. It is broken down in aqueous solution and enzymatically in blood or plasma to benzoylecgonine and methylecgonine, neither of which has much pharmacological activity. While cocaine may be stabilized to some extent by the addition of fluoride after the blood is collected, the extent of breakdown between death and autopsy must be considered. Unfortunately, there are many variables to consider. First, the toxicity of cocaine itself correlates only poorly with blood concentration, even in the living. There is good evidence that cocaine concentrations in post-mortem blood can increase or decrease, depending on the exact site of collection.[55,56] There are probably competing effects due to variable breakdown in different areas of the body and true post-mortem redistribution. The collection and measurement of cocaine in vitreous humor has been attempted to overcome these problems. However, it has been shown that cocaine will often, if irreproducibility, increase in concentration with time in the vitreous humor. The mechanism for this has not been proved, but it likely involves post-mortem redistribution from the brain, where cocaine is known to concentrate relative to the blood, into the eye via the optic nerve and other soft tissue. It is possible that time-dependent post-mortem increases in vitreous concentrations may occur for other drugs where those drugs attain higher concentrations in the brain.

12.6.5.6 Interpretation Using Tables of Values

There probably is not a forensic toxicologist or pathologist alive who has not used published tables as a reference when trying to interpret post-mortem blood concentrations. Tables of such values became a necessary evil due to the sheer volume of medical and forensic literature. However, they unfortunately perpetuate the myth that post-mortem toxicology results can be interpreted solely using, or heavily relying on so-called "therapeutic," "toxic," and "fatal" ranges. Although tables of drug concentrations can serve as a useful reference point, it should be borne in mind that many of the values in these tables are derived from serum or plasma data from living patients, that the ranges are seldom referenced to published cases, and that they may not take into account or state other variables such as post-mortem redistribution, time of survival after intoxication, or the presence of other drugs, natural disease, or injury. Having stated that, one compilation has attempted to address some of these issues and indeed bases the post-mortem values it lists exclusively on carefully collected femoral blood samples.[57] In that compilation, values are also provided for "controls," consisting of deceased subjects, who with certainty died of causes other than intoxication, and who were not incapacitated at the time for the demise. Such data are equally important as levels in fatal cases and additional compilations using this approach are encouraged.

12.6.6 Conclusion

In the final analysis, post-mortem toxicology results must be interpreted with regard to all of the available information, including medical history, information from the scene, autopsy findings, nature and exact location of the post-mortem samples collected, and the circumstances of the death. Only after weighing all of these variables can post-mortem results be reliably interpreted. Even then, it must be admitted that *reliable* interpretation of some results is simply not possible based on the available information. In many respects, the desirable underlying approach to the interpretation of post-mortem drug concentrations is not much different from that used a century ago: a good scene investigation, medical investigation, laboratory investigation, and the application of common sense. We hope we are also wiser now.

REFERENCES

1. Logan, B.K. and Lindholm, G., Gastric contamination of postmortem blood samples during blind-stick sample collection, *Am. J. Forensic Med. Pathol.*, 17, 109, 1996.
2. Jones, G.R. and Pounder, D.J., Site dependence of drug concentrations in postmortem blood — a case study, *J. Anal. Toxicol.*, 11, 186, 1987.
3. Prouty, R.W. and Anderson, W.H., The forensic implications of site and temporal differences on predicting blood-drug concentrations, *J. Forensic Sci.*, 35, 243, 1990.
4. Pounder, D.J. and Jones, G.R., Post-mortem drug redistribution — a toxicological nightmare, *Forensic Sci. Int.*, 45, 253, 1990.
5. Vorpahl, T.E. and Coe, J.I., Correlation of antemortem and postmortem digoxin levels, *J. Forensic Sci.*, 23, 329, 1978.
6. Ziminski, K.R., Wemyss, C.T., Bidanset, J.H., Manning, T.J., and Lukash, L., Comparative study of postmortem barbiturates, methadone, and morphine in vitreous humor, blood, and tissue, *J. Forensic Sci.*, 29, 903, 1984.
7. Worm, K. and Steentoft, A., A comparison of post-mortem concentrations of basic drugs in femoral whole blood and vitreous humor, in *Proceedings of the International Congress of Clinical Toxicology, Poison Control and Analytical Toxicology, Lux Tox '90, Societe des Sciences Medicales du Grund-Duche de Luxembourg*, Wennig, R., Ed., Luxembourg, 1990, 438.
8. Bermejo, A.M., Ramos, I., Fernandzez, P., Lopez-Rivadulla, M., Cruz, A., Chiarotti, M., Fucci, N., and Marsilli, R., Morphine determination by gas chromatography/mass spectrometry in human vitreous humor and comparison with radioimmunoassay, *J. Anal. Toxicol.*, 16, 372, 1992.
9. McKinney, P.E., Phillips, S., Gomez, H.F., Brent, J., MacIntyre, M.W., and Watson, W.A., Vitreous humor cocaine and metabolite concentrations: do postmortem specimens reflect blood levels at the time of death? *J. Forensic Sci.*, 40, 102, 1995.
10. Robertson, M.D. and Drummer, O.H., Benzodiazepine concentrations in vitreous humor, *Bull. Int. Assoc. Forensic Toxicol.*, 25, 28, 1995.
11. Holmgren, P., Druid, H., Holmgren, A., and Ahlner, J., Stability of drugs in stored femoral blood and vitreous humor, *J. Forensic Sci.*, 49, 820, 2004.
12. Pounder, D.J., Fuke, C., Cox, D.E., Smith, D., and Kuroda, N., Postmortem diffusion of drugs from gastric residue: an experimental study, *Am. J. Forensic Med. Pathol.*, 17, 1, 1996.
13. Pounder, D.J., Adams, E., Fuke, C., and Langford, A.M., Site to site variability of postmortem drug concentrations in liver and lung, *J. Forensic Sci.*, 41, 927, 1996.
14. Anderson, D.T., Fritz, K.L., and Muto, J.J., Oxycontin: the concept of a "ghost pill" and the post-mortem tissue distribution of oxycodone in 36 cases, *J. Anal. Toxicol.*, 26, 448, 2002.
15. Ku, M.T., Bezoars, *Clin. Toxicol. Rev.*, 18, June 1996.
16. Christensen, H., Steentoft, A., and Worm, K., Muscle as an autopsy material for evaluation of fatal cases of drug overdose, *J. Forensic Sci. Soc.*, 25, 191, 1985.

17. Winek, C.L. and Esposito, F.M., Comparative study of ethanol levels in blood versus bone marrow, vitreous humor, bile and urine, *Forensic Sci. Int.*, 20, 1727, 1980.

18. Winek, C.L., Westwood, S.E., and Wahba, W.W., Plasma versus bone marrow desipramine: a comparative study, *Forensic Sci. Int.*, 48, 49–57, 1990.

19. Winek, C.L., Morris, E.M., and Wahba, W.W., The use of bone marrow in the study of postmortem redistribution of nortriptyline, *J. Anal. Toxicol.*, 17, 93–98, 1993.

20. Poklis, A. and Saady, J.J., Arsenic poisoning: acute or chronic? Suicide or murder? *Am. J. Forensic Med. Pathol.*, 11, 226, 1990.

21. Kintz, P., Cirimele, V., Jamey, C., and Ludes, B., Testing for GHB in hair by GC/MS/MS after a single exposure. Application to document sexual assault, *J. Forensic Sci.*, 48(1), 195–200, 2003.

22. Villain, M., Cheze, M., Tracqui, A., Ludes, B., and Kintz, P., Testing for zopiclone in hair application to drug-facilitated crimes, *Forensic Sci. Int.*, 145(2–3), 117–121, 2004.

23. Frison, G., Favretto, D., Tedeschi, L., and Ferrara, S.D., Detection of thiopental and pentobarbital in head and pubic hair in a case of drug-facilitated sexual assault, *Forensic Sci. Int.*, 133(1–2), 171–174, 2003.

24. Cheze, M., Duffort, G., Deveaux, M., and Pepin, G., Hair analysis by liquid chromatography-tandem mass spectrometry in toxicological investigation of drug-facilitated crimes: report of 128 cases over the period June 2003–May 2004 in metropolitan Paris, *Forensic Sci. Int.*, 153(1), 3–10, 2005.

25. Tagliaro, F., De Battisti, Z., Smith, F.P., and Marigo, M., Death from heroin overdose: findings from hair analysis, *Lancet,* 351(9120), 1923–1925, 1998.

26. Kronstrand, R., Grundin, R., and Jonsson, J., Incidence of opiates, amphetamines, and cocaine in hair and blood in fatal cases of heroin overdose, *Forensic Sci. Int.* 92(1), 29–38, 1998.

27. Darke, S., Hall, W., Kaye, S., Ross, J., and Duflou, J., Hair morphine concentrations of fatal heroin overdose cases and living heroin users, *Addiction,* 97(8), 977–984, 2002.

28. Musshoff, F., Lachenmeier, K., Wollersen, H., Lichtermann, D., and Madea, B., Opiate concentrations in hair from subjects in a controlled heroin-maintenance program and from opiate-associated fatalities, *J. Anal. Toxicol.*, 29(5), 345–352, 2005.

29. Kronstrand, R., Nystrom, I., Strandberg, J., and Druid, H., Screening for drugs of abuse in hair with ion spray LC-MS-MS, *Forensic Sci. Int.*, 145(2–3), 183–190, 2004.

30. Cone, E.J., Mechanisms of drug incorporation into hair, *Ther. Drug Monit.*, 18(4), 438–443, 1996.

31. Palmeri, A., Pichini, S., Pacifici, R., Zuccaro, P., and Lopez, A., Drugs in nails: physiology, pharmacokinetics and forensic toxicology, *Clin. Pharmacokinet.*, 38(2), 95–110, 2000.

32. Odei, E.L.A., Insulin habituation and psychopathy, *Br. Med. J.,* 2, 346, 1968.

33. Retsas, S., Insulin abuse by a drug addict, *Br. Med. J.,* 2, 792, 1972.

34. Duragesic Monograph, Janssen Pharmaceutica, Titusville, NJ, April 1992.

35. Jaffe, J.H. and Martin, W.R., Opioid analgesics and antagonists, in *Goodman and Gilman's The Pharmacological Basis of Therapeutics*, Gilman, A.G., Rall, T.W., Nies, A.S., and Taylor, P., Eds., Pergamon Press, New York, 1990, chap. 21.

36. Shimomura, K., Kamata, O., Ueki., S. et al., Analgesic affects of morphine glucuronides, *Tohoku J. Exp. Med.*, 105, 45, 1971.

37. Yoshimura, H., Ida, S., Oguri, K., and Tsukamoto, H., Biochemical basis for analgesic activity of morphine-6-glucuronide. I. Penetration of morphine-6-glucuronide in the brain of rats, *Biochem. Pharmacol.*, 22, 1423, 1973.

38. Westerling, D., Persson, C., and Hoglund, P., Plasma concentrations of morphine, morphine-3-glucuronide, and morphine-6-glucuronide after intravenous and oral administration to healthy volunteers: relationship to nonanalgesic actions, *Ther. Drug Monit.*, 17, 287, 1995.

39. Osborne, R.J., Joel, S.P. and Slevin, M.L., Morphine intoxication in renal failure: the role of morphine-6-glucuronide, *Br. Med. J.*, 292, 1548, 1986.

40. Druid, H., Holmgren, P., Carlsson, B., and Ahlner, J., Cytochrome P450 2D6 (CYP2D6) genotyping on postmortem blood as a supplementary tool for interpretation of forensic toxicological results, *Forensic Sci. Int.*, 99(1), 25–34, 1999.

41. Swanson, J.R., Jones, G.R., Krasselt, W., Denmark, L.N., and Ratti, F., Death of two subjects due to chronic imipramine and desipramine metabolite accumulation during chronic therapy: a review of the literature and possible mechanisms, *J. Forensic Sci.*, 42, 335, 1997.

42. Anonymous, The Crippen trial: special report of the medical evidence, *Br. Med. J.,* 2, 1372, 1910.

43. Saady, J.J., Blanke, R.V., and Poklis, A., Estimation of the body burden of arsenic in a child fatally poisoned by arsenite weedkiller, *J. Anal. Toxicol.*, 13, 310, 1989.

44. Pounder, D.J. and Davies, J.I., Zopiclone poisoning: tissue distribution and potential for postmortem diffusion, *Forensic Sci. Int.*, 65, 177, 1994.

45. Baud, F.J., Buisine, A., Bismuth, C., Galliot, M., Vicaut, E., Bourdon, R., and Fournier, P.E., Arterio-venous plasma concentration differences in amitriptyline overdose, *J. Toxicol. Clin. Toxicol.*, 23, 391, 1985.

46. Sato, S., Baud, F.J., Bismuth, C., Galliot, M., Vicaut, E., and Buisine, A., Arterial-venous plasma concentration differences of meprobamate in acute human poisonings, *Hum. Toxicol.*, 5, 243, 1986.

47. Druid, H. and Holmgren, P., Fatal injections of heroin. Interpretation of toxicological findings in multiple specimens, *Int. J. Legal Med.*, 112(1), 62–66, 1999.

48. Hilberg, T., Morland, J., and Bjorneboe, A., Postmortem release of amitriptyline from the lungs; a mechanism of postmortem drug redistribution, *Forensic Sci. Int.*, 64, 47–55, 1994.

49. Pounder, D.J. and Yonemitsu, K., Postmortem absorption of drugs and ethanol from aspirated vomitus — an experimental model, *Forensic Sci. Int.*, 51, 189, 1991.

50. Pelissier-Alicot, A.L., Gaulier, J.M., Champsaur, P., and Marquet, P., Mechanisms underlying post-mortem redistribution of drugs: a review, *J. Anal. Toxicol.*, 27, 53, 2003.

51. Kugelberg, F.C., Holmgren, P., and Druid, H., Codeine and morphine blood concentrations increase during blood loss, *J. Forensic Sci.*, 48, 664, 2003.

52. De Paepe, P., Belpaire, F.M., Rosseel, M.T., and Buylaert, W.A., The influence of hemorrhagic shock on the pharmacokinetics and the analgesic effect of morphine in the rat, *Fundam. Clin. Pharmacol.*, 12, 624, 1998.

53. Laposata, E.A., Hale, P., Jr., and Poklis, A., Evaluation of sudden death in psychiatric patients with special reference to phenothiazine therapy: forensic pathology, *J. Forensic Sci.*, 33, 432, 1988.

54. Sternbach, H., The serotonin syndrome, *Am. J. Psychiatry*, 148, 705, 1991.

55. Hearn, W.L., Keran, E.E., Wei, H., and Hime, G., Site-dependent postmortem changes in blood cocaine concentrations, *J. Forensic Sci.*, 36, 673, 1991.

56. Logan, B.K., Smirnow, D., and Gullberg, R.G., Lack of predictable site-dependent differences and time-dependent changes in postmortem concentrations of cocaine, benzoylecgonine, and cocaethylene in humans, *J. Anal. Toxicol.*, 20, 23, 1997.

57. Druid, H. and Holmgren, P., A compilation of fatal and control concentration of drugs in postmortem femoral blood, *J. Forensic Sci.*, 42, 79, 1997.

CHAPTER 13

Toxicogenetics

Edited by Steven B. Karch, M.D., FFFLM
Consultant Pathologist and Toxicologist, Berkeley, California

CONTENTS

Editor's Note: This chapter covers exciting new methods and materials that were largely experimental or unheard of at the time the first edition of this book was published. Sudden death goes unexplained at least 5% of the time, and perhaps even more often than that. The percentage is higher in children and young adults. Advances in molecular biology and DNA technology now make it possible to explain many of those deaths.

This development is not without irony. At the same time that many in clinical medicine are expressing frustration about the lack of tangible gains provided by the Human Genome Project 1, and pathologists are wondering about the viability of their field, DNA technology is about to reshape the field of forensic pathology, and most especially the field of drug death investigation. Emerging evidence suggests that the underlying cause of death in many is genetic, and that heart and liver abnormalities may play a role. The problem is that death from a wide variety of genetic defects leaves no histological markers. The ability to identify these "invisible diseases" with postmortem genetic testing has become a reality far more quickly than anyone had ever imagined. It may not yet be "standard of care" to test for cardiac channelopathies, or P450 polymorphisms, but it will be in the not-too-distant future. The introduction of these methods will have an enormous effect on the practice of forensic pathology, and so an introduction has been included in this edition. Some of the more important developments in the postmortem diagnosis of liver and heart disease are discussed in this chapter.

13.1 PHARMACOGENOMICS FOR TOXICOLOGY*

Robert M. White, Sr., Ph.D.[1] **and Steven H.Y. Wong, Ph.D.**[2]

[1] Technical Director, DSI Laboratories, Fort Myers, Florida

[2] Professor of Pathology, Director, Clinical Chemistry/Toxicology, TDM, Pharmacogenomics, and Proteomics, Medical College of Wisconsin, and Scientific Director, Toxicology Department, Milwaukee County Medical Examiner's Office, Milwaukee, Wisconsin

The Great Paracelsus (Phillipus Aureolus Theophrastus Bombastus von Hohenheim-Paracelsus, 1493–1541) is remembered by toxicologists for his famous quote: "All substances are poisons; there is none which is not a poison. The right dose differentiates a poison from a remedy."[2] Indeed, the basic principle from the quote still applies today. The right dose of morphine that will produce a blood level of approximately 0.07 to 0.083 mg/L is essential for the relief of pain. An overdose that results in a markedly increased blood level (0.2 to 2.3 mg/L) can cause death due to central nervous system depression.[3] In general, the same applies to all chemical substances. However, as an important exception to Paracelsus's statement, there are instances in which a drug should be avoided completely. An example is found in the administration of succinylcholine as a skeletal muscle relaxant in surgery patients. Most patients can convert succinylcholine into inert metabolites through an enzyme called pseudocholinesterase because most patients possess two alleles for the common gene that can produce active enzyme. However, a certain small percentage of patients carries the genes that are aberrant or silent and, thus, either produce protein (enzyme) that is defective in its function or cannot produce the protein that is capable of inactivating administered succinylcholine at all; these patients expire or suffer severe sequelae from administration of the drug.[4] Along the same line of thinking, the dose of a given drug for certain individuals may differ from that used for the majority of the population due to genetic differences between the individual and the general population (e.g., a reduced dose of 6-merecaptopurine in the presence of reduced thiopurine methyl transferase or TPMT activity due to a genetic deficiency in synthesis of the active enzyme).[5] Therefore, in the third millennium, an expansion of Paracelsus's statement might be that the "right dose" for one individual may not be the "right dose" or even the right drug for another due to differences in each individual's genetic makeup. The determination of what is the "right

* This chapter was partially rewritten with modifications and updates from Reference 1, with permission from the publisher, Medical Laboratory Observer.

Figure 13.1.1 Central dogma.

dose" and, in some cases, what is even the right drug for a given individual constitutes the reason for the development of the sciences of pharmacogenetics and pharmacogenomics.

Although often used interchangeably, there are subtle differences between pharmacogenetics and pharmacogenomics. Pharmacogenomics is concerned with the systematic assessment of how chemical compounds (e.g., drugs) modify the overall expression pattern in certain tissues. Pharmacogenomics is not focused on the differences between individuals. Rather, pharmacogenomics focuses on differences among several drugs or compounds with regard to a generic set of expressed or non-expressed genes. The focus in pharmacogenomics is on compound variability. In contrast, pharmacogenetics focuses on individual traits with respect to one compound or drug. Thus, pharmacogenetics, which historically actually preceded pharmacogenomics, looks at the responses of different individuals to one drug while pharmacogenomics studies the differences among several compounds with regard to a single genome.[6–11] For the purposes of this brief introduction, the two terms will be used interchangeably unless stated otherwise.

Before embarking upon a cursory journey through pharmacogenomics, a very brief discussion of DNA (deoxyribonucleic acid) and its products is in order. DNA is the genetic code that determines all of an individual's characteristics including the synthesis of the proper proteins essential for life. The so-called "central dogma" of molecular biology is outlined in Figure 13.1.1.[10] DNA is a long chain of chemically linked (phosphate bond), single nucleotides. Although there is a great deal more detail to the system due to phenomena such as splice variants,[8] etc., basically DNA is transcribed in the cell nucleus by an enzyme called RNA polymerase to yield messenger RNA or mRNA. DNA sequences called promoters and enhancers also are required to initiate RNA synthesis. Silencers balance the effects of promoters and enhancers when synthesis is not required. A stop codon (a series of the nucleotides that tells the polymerase to stop transcription) also is required so that only the required RNA and not an almost infinitely long RNA is produced. Regions of the mRNA from DNA that do not code for amino acids are called introns. The introns are spliced out before the completed mRNA is capped (*vide infra*) and exported from the nucleus for translation. The regions of the mRNA that do code for protein are called exons. RNA that has had the introns removed is capped on the 5′ end with a special nucleotide called 7-methylguanosine and has a poly-A (poly-adenosine) "tail" added to the 3′ end. The capped mRNA with its poly-A "tail" is then translated into protein in a cellular apparatus called a ribosome.[6]

Also required before pharmacogenomics can be discussed is a basic knowledge of proteins that are the end product of the transcription of DNA and the translation of RNA. Essentially, a protein is a long chain of chemically linked (amide or peptide bond) amino acids. The sequence in the chain of amino acids is called the primary structure. The chain may form loops and/or helices (secondary structure) and the loops and helices may fold to form the tertiary structure. Further, the protein may exist by itself, associate with other protein chains like itself (e.g., dimerize to form an aggregate of two like chains), or associate with dissimilar protein chains to form the final, active structure, which is known as the quaternary structure. Further, a protein may be chemically and functionally changed ("post-translational modification") by the addition of phosphate groups (phosphorylation), glucuronic acid groups (glucuronidation), or other groups or by the addition or removal of amino acids or short stretches of amino acids called polypeptides. The study of proteins, which is closely related, but separate from molecular biology, is called proteomics.[12]

Proteins can act as hormones (e.g., insulin, glucagons, chorionic gonadotrophin, etc.), enzymes, which are biological catalysts (e.g., lactate dehydrogenase, alkaline phosphatase, creatine kinase, etc.), structural components (e.g., troponin, collagens, etc.), receptors (e.g., opiate receptors, cholesterol receptors, etc.), and a plethora of other functions essential for life itself. When a protein is formed from DNA that was in the correct sequence, the DNA is correctly transcribed, and the RNA is correctly translated; a fully functional protein usually results. However, if the DNA code is incorrect (although exceptions exist here, also) or there is a defect in the machinery that creates the protein from the original DNA code, a partially functional protein, a non-functional protein, or even a protein that is deleterious to cell function may be produced. Gene duplication, where the gene is functional and codes for the correct protein, can result in the overproduction of protein.[13]

Also before pharmacogenomics can be discussed, it is helpful to review a few pharmacologic fundamentals. First, although it sounds obvious, before a drug can have any effect on an individual, the drug must somehow enter the individual's body. Entry can be accomplished through inhalation (e.g., a bronchodilator used for the treatment of asthma), absorption through the skin (e.g., a topical anesthetic such as cocaine or lidocaine) or mucous membranes (e.g., pilocarpine eye drops), parenterally (any number of drugs that may be delivered intravenously, intramuscularly, or subcutaneously), or, most commonly, orally (a large number of drugs including such common substances as aspirin and acetaminophen) where the drug is absorbed from the gastrointestinal tract. Once inside an individual, a drug needs to be transported to the site where it will have its effect. A drug may have no action whatsoever (e.g., inulin), may act directly on a receptor to produce the desired effect (e.g., morphine for analgesia), or may require activation (e.g., the production of morphine from codeine for analgesia). Both before and after the desired effect has been produced, drugs may be excreted (multiple routes such as urine and bile) unchanged (e.g., free morphine) or excreted as metabolites (e.g., the excretion of morphine glucuronide, which is an inactive metabolite of morphine) or a combination.[14] Proteins are essential to carry out all of the afore-mentioned steps in drug metabolism.

Proteins play an active role in the disposition of drugs and their metabolites (*vide infra*). Proteins in the intestinal enterocytes such as BCRP (breast cancer resistance protein), MRP2 (multidrug resistance-associated protein), and MDR1 (multidrug resistance protein) are involved in the transport of xenobiotics into the intestinal lumen. A member of the peptide transporter family such as PepT1 facilitates absorption from the gut lumen and tubular reabsorption in the kidney. Drugs such as valaciclovir, valganciclovir, and captopril are known to be transported by PepT1. OCTN2, which is part of the organic cation transporter family, is involved in both the efflux and influx of drugs such as quinidine and verapamil. Although numerous polymorphisms exist among the transporter proteins, their influence on pharmacogenomics is unclear and still in its infancy.[15] However, a clear example of how a protein and a mutation of that protein can affect a drug's absorption is found with the cardiac glycoside digoxin. *P*-Glycoprotein, which is a membrane protein that functions as an exporter of xenobiotics from cells, is a product of the MDR1 (<u>m</u>ulti<u>d</u>rug <u>r</u>esistance) gene. Although several models have been proposed for *P*-glycoprotein's action, basically *P*-glycoprotein acts to move xenobiotics from epithelial cells into the adjacent lumen. *P*-Glycoprotein is found in numerous cells associated with excretory function. In the case of digoxin (and certain other drugs), reduced intestinal absorption of the drug can be associated with induction (increased amounts) of the enzyme or the C3435T (cytosine replaces thymidine at position 3435 in the DNA sequence that codes *P*-glycoprotein) mutation of *P*-glycoprotein. Thus, the mutant form of the protein causes a lowered overall intestinal absorption of digoxin by excreting more back into the intestinal lumen than the wild-type protein.[16]

Once a drug has entered the bloodstream it is transported to various parts of the body where the drug may be activated or inactivated by certain enzymes (*vide infra*) by a process commonly

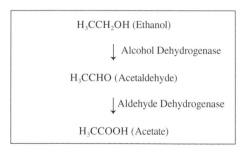

Figure 13.1.2 Metabolic pathway for oxidation of ethanol.

referred to as biotransformation or metabolism, be excreted unchanged, interact with a receptor or other location where the desired (and, sometimes, undesired or side effect) action(s) may take place, or be stored (e.g., the retention of [9]-tetrahydrocannabinol or THC in body fat or lead in bone) for future uses such as those previously described. Many drugs and other xenobiotics express their pharmacodynamic action by interacting with a specific protein receptor. As an example, morphine acts at what are called μ receptors. Indeed, polymorphism is exhibited by the various opiate receptors.[17]

Perhaps the best-characterized and most extensively studied area in pharmacogenomics is biotransformation, which is commonly referred to as metabolism. Fundamentally, biotransformation or metabolism can be divided into two areas – Phase I and Phase II. Both Phase I and Phase II are designed to make xenobiotics more polar and, thus, more water soluble. By being more polar and more water soluble, metabolites are more easily excreted into excretory fluids such as urine. Phase I reactions include hydrolysis, reduction, and oxidation. Phase I metabolism may activate a drug (known in this case as a prodrug) into a biologically active form, or Phase I may inactivate an active drug. An example of activation is seen with the conversion of Tegafur into the active anticancer agent 5-fluorouracil (5-FU). An example of deactivation is seen with the oxidation of ethanol into acetaldehyde by alcohol dehydrogenase and the further oxidation of acetaldehyde into acetate by aldehyde dehydrogenase. Phase II biotransformation may or may not be preceded by Phase I biotransformation. Phase II biotransformation reactions involve glucuronidation, sulfation, acetylation, methylation, conjugation with glutathione, and conjugation with amino acids such as glycine, taurine, and glutamic acid.[18]

Hydolysis as a Phase I chemical breakdown pathway has been mentioned above in the case of pseudocholinesterase and its variants. Reduction of the drug 5-fluorouracil, which was discussed above under activation of Tegafur, shows polymorphism in the 5-FU reduction when 5-FU is metabolized (deactivated) to its reduction product, 5-fluorodihydrouracil, in rare individuals who are deficient in the enzyme dihydropyrimidine dehydrogenase (DPD). Individuals who are deficient in DPD show toxicity, which may be fatal, to bone marrow and intestines due to increased levels of 5-FU.[15]

Since a more polar (and, thus, more water soluble) product usually results, oxidation is one of the commonest metabolic pathways in mammals. Due to genetic polymorphism, the metabolism of the most routinely observed analyte in toxicology, ethanol or ethyl alcohol, actually is more complex than usually visualized by the simple pathway depicted in Figure 13.1.2.

The first enzyme in the oxidation of ethanol, alcohol dehydrogenase, is a zinc-containing dimer, which means that the functional enzyme consists of two protein chains and the element zinc. The subunits are encoded on chromosome 4 by six different genetic loci (ADH1A, ADH1B*1, ADH1C*1, and ADH4 to ADH7; formerly ADH1 through ADH7, respectively). The subunits are designated α, β, γ, π, χ, or σ. ADH1A (formerly ADH1) codes the protein for α subunits. ADH1B (formerly ADH2) codes for β subunits. ADH1C (formerly ADH3) codes for γ subunits. To further add to the complexity of the system, there are three allelic variants of the beta subunit designated β_1, β_2, and β_3 and two allelic variants of the gamma chain designated γ_1 and γ_2 arising from, respectively,

ADH1B*1, ADH1B*2, ADH1B*3, ADH1C*1, and ADH1C*2. The nine subunits of ADH can combine to form homodimers (i.e., both chains are identical) and the α, β, and γ chains and their allelic variants heterodimers (i.e., the two chains are different) with each other, but not with the other types of chains. The different molecular forms of ADH are divided into four classes. Class I contains ADH1A, ADH1B*1, and ADH1C*1, which can be considered isozymes. ADH1B enzymes that differ in the type of β subunit are known as allelozymes as are ADH1C enzymes that differ in the type of γ subunit. Accordingly, the protein product of ADH1B*1 is an allelozyme composed of β_1 subunits, the protein product of ADH1B*2 is an allelozyme composed of β_2 subunits, and the protein product of ADH1B*3 is an allelozyme composed of β_3 subunits. Class II contains ADH4, which is made up of two π subunits. Class III contains ADH5, which is made up of two χ subunits. Class IV contains ADH7, which is made up of two σ subunits. It is the Class I and Class II ADH isozymes that are of the most interest to the practicing toxicologist as it is these isozymes that are involved in the oxidation of ethanol and methanol. The protein product of ADH1B*2 is an atypical isozyme that is responsible for an unusually rapid conversion of ethanol into acetaldehyde in 85% of Asians, but is expressed to a lesser degree in Caucasians, Native Americans, and Asian Indians. Conversely, in about 25% of African Americans there is an abundance of the $\beta_3\beta_3$ form. European Caucasians have a predominance of the homodimer from the ADH1B*1 gene.[20] Aldehyde dehydrogenase (ALDH) oxidizes aldehydes (like acetaldehyde) to the corresponding carboxylic acid. In all, 12 ALDH genes (ALDH1 through ALDH10, SSDH, and MMSDH) have been identified in humans. ALDH2 is primarily responsible for oxidizing simple aldehydes like acetaldehyde. A genetic polymorphism for ALDH2 has been identified in humans. A high percentage of Japanese, Chinese, Koreans, Taiwanese, and Vietnamese populations are deficient in ALDH2 due to a point mutation ($Glu_{487} \rightarrow Lys_{487}$). This inactive allelic variant of ALDH2 known as ALDH2*2 is found in the same population that has a high incidence of the atypical form of ADH, ADH2*2, which means that these individuals rapidly convert ethanol to acetaldehyde, but only slowly convert acetaldehyde to acetic acid. As a result, many Asians experience a flushing syndrome after consuming alcohol. Thus, what is considered to be very simple by most toxicologists; especially those who deal with driving under the influence (DUI) forensic cases, actually can be quite rich in detail for certain individuals within a diverse array of ethnic groups.[19–22]

In addition to the example of the oxidation of ethanol given above, numerous other oxidative pathways for xenobiotics exist in humans and other animals. Many of the oxidations of drugs are the result of a group of enzymes known as CYPs (from *CY*tochrome *P*450, the 450 being derived from the cytochrome's maximal absorbance of light at 450 nm). The cytochrome P450s or CYPs are categorized according to amino acid sequence homology. CYPs that have less than 40% homology are placed in the same family (e.g., 1, 2, 3, etc.). CYPs that are 40 to 55% identical are assigned to different subfamilies (e.g., 1A, 1B, 1C, etc.). P450 enzymes that are more than 55% identical are classified as members of the same subfamily (e.g., 2B1, 2B2, 2B3, etc.). The P450 enzymes are expressed in numerous tissues, but are especially prevalent in liver. CYPs so numerous that their complete description is beyond the scope of this basic introduction exist in mammalian physiology.[18] However, the CYPs that are important to human drug metabolism are within its scope.[23]

The final step in drug metabolism is elimination. As stated above elimination can occur with the unchanged drug, a drug that has been subjected to Phase I metabolism, a drug that has been subjected to Phase II metabolism, or a combination. Also as briefly discussed above, the proteins involved in elimination can be subject to polymorphism and, thus, are involved in pharmacogenomics.

A few brief examples of the applications of pharmacogenomics are given in the sections below.

13.1.1 Clinical Applications

Three applications of pharmacogenomics are demonstrated in depression, opiate toxicity and forensic toxicology.

13.1.1.1 Depression

To provide therapeutic efficacy, the tricyclic antidepressant nortriptyline must achieve serum levels of 5 to 150 ng/ml.[24] Usually, a therapeutic level is achieved by adjustment of a standard dose. Nortriptyline is metabolized to its hydroxy metabolite, 10-hydroxynortriptyline, by CYP2D6. Individuals with different genotypes and multiple copies of CYP2D6 metabolize nortriptyline at markedly different rates. When poor metabolizers of debrisoquin (a drug used to determine an individual's CYP2D6 status) with no functional CYP2D6 gene, extensive metabolizers with one functional CYP2D6 gene, extensive metabolizers with two functional CYP2D6 genes, ultra-rapid metabolizers with duplicated CYP2D6*2 genes, and one ultra-rapid metabolizer with 13 copies of the CYP2D6*2 gene are compared, the results are quite striking. On one end of the spectrum, the individuals with no functional copy of CYP2D6 have maximal levels of serum nortriptyline of 51 to 71 ng/ml. On the other end of the spectrum, an individual with 13 copies of the CYP2D6*2 gene had a maximal serum level of only 13 ng/ml. Needless to say, this represents an outstanding example where a "standard dose" will not necessarily achieve the required serum level of the active drug and, thus, the desired results.[13]

Selective serotonin-reuptake inhibitors such as fluvoxetine, paroxetine, and fluoxetine exert their action probably through the serotonin transporter protein. The serotonin transporter gene (5-HTT) shows several polymorphisms. One polymorphism is in the transcriptional control region upstream of the 5-HTT coding sequence. It is either a 44-base-pair insertion (long variant) or deletion (short sequence). One group has reported that individuals homozygous for the long variant and heterozygous individuals respond better to fluvoxamine than do individuals who are homozygous for the short variant.[25] Interestingly, another group reported just the opposite.[26] The disparity between the studies is a reminder that other factors that may never be separated out affect genomic expression and phenotypic response.

13.1.1.2 Opiate Toxicity

A 62-year-old male, who had previously received chemotherapy but currently was prescribed only valproate for post-traumatic generalized seizure, is admitted for bilateral pneumonia limited to the lower lobes.[27] Although there is no evidence of *Pneumocystis carinii*, yeast is found in the bronchoalveolar lavage. The patient is treated with ceftriaxone, clarithromycin, and voriconazole for yeast and codeine for cough. The patient's level of consciousness deteriorates. Serum BUN and creatinine levels that increase are normalized with hydration. Administration of naloxone results in a dramatic improvement in the patient's level of consciousness.

The patient's blood levels of codeine, morphine, and their metabolites were determined by liquid chromatography/mass spectrometry. The patient's level of codeine was above therapeutic as were the levels of morphine, morphine-3-glucuronide (active metabolite), and morphine-6-glucuronide (inactive metabolite). Duplication or multiduplication of the CYP2D6 gene was determined using restriction-fragment-length polymorphism analysis of the patient's genomic DNA. The CYP2D6 and CYP3A4 phenotypes also were determined.

Dextromethorphan was administered to the patient as a probe after he was stabilized. Because dextromethorphan is metabolized by CYP2D6 into dextrorphan and 3-hydroxymorphinan by CYP3A4, the ratio of dextromethorphan to dextrorphan was less than 0.0005, which was compatible with an ultra-rapid CYP2D6 metabolizer.

Normally, about 80% of codeine is converted into norcodeine by CYP3A4 or converted into codeine glucuronide. The conversion of codeine into morphine by CYP2D6 represents only about 10% of normal clearance of codeine. In the patient described, there was ultra-rapid conversion of codeine into morphine by his three or more CYP2D6 alleles. To exacerbate the situation, the patient's CYP3A4 was inhibited by administration of clarithromycin and voriconazole and the accumulation of glucuronides (acute renal failure).

Thus, in contrast to the clinical scenario in which 7 to 10% of the white population receive no analgesic benefit from codeine due to homozygosity for nonfunctional CYP2D6 alleles, that patient described above had a toxic amount of morphine and one of its active metabolites due to ultra-rapid metabolism. The patient's ultra-rapid metabolism due to multiple copies of the CYP2D6 gene was intensified by inhibition of CYP3A4 that normally metabolizes the majority of the codeine to norcodeine.

13.1.1.3 Forensic Toxicology

This section outlines the application of pharmacogenomics as molecular autopsy, as proposed by Figure 13.1.3.[28] Several upcoming chapters by Holmgren and Ahlner,[29] Sajantila et al.,[30] and Wong et al.[31] summarize the current practice of using pharmacogenomics as molecular autopsy — an adjunct for forensic pathology/toxicology, by considering long QT syndrome, and effect on driving. Several cases are included to illustrate the applications.

A 9-year-old born with probable fetal alcohol syndrome is treated with a combination of methylphenidate, clonidine, and fluoxetine for multiple behavioral problems. Over a period of time, the individual is hospitalized in status epilepticus followed by cardiac arrest and expires. Based on the levels of fluoxetine and its metabolite, norfluoxetine, in the deceased's post-mortem blood, the adoptive parents are suspected of homicide, and the remainder of the adopted children are removed from the household. Due to the vociferous claims of the adoptive parents that there was no foul play involved, the deceased individual is tested for genetic polymorphism. Indeed, a polymorphism in the CYP2D6, which resulted in the poor metabolism of fluoxetine, was discovered. Based on the results of the post-mortem genetic testing, the adoptive parents of the deceased were exonerated and reunited with the remainder of the children.[32]

One of the cases of a recently published study of assessing pharmacogenomic methadone death certification involved a 41-year-old woman who was 6 months pregnant and recently diagnosed with heart murmur and rheumatoid arthritis.[33] She was treated with methadone and tricyclic antidepressants for her depression. After celebrating New Year's Eve with her husband, she was found unresponsive in her living room the following morning. Toxicology analysis showed methadone, 0.7 mg/L, amitriptyline, 1.5 mg/L, and nortriptyline, 2.2 mg/L. Pharmaco-genomics tests showed CYP2D6*4 homozygous, corresponding to a poor metabolizer as a result of deficient CYP 2D6 enzyme. The lack of enzyme predisposed her to the inability to hydroxylate methadone, amitriptyline, and nortriptyline, resulting in an overall accumulation and drug tox-icity. Death certification showed the cause of death to be mixed drug overdose, and manner of death, accident.

In the study of 25 fentanyl cases, one decedent, a 44-year-old white woman, had a history of drug abuse including cocaine, marijuana, and pain medications and psychiatric problems.[34] Com-plaining to her boyfriend about her knee pain during a rummage sale, she obtained some narcotic patches and put them on. Later in the evening, her boyfriend noticed she seemed disoriented, and after about 24 h, she was found not breathing. One Duragesic fentanyl patch was found on her left upper arm, and another adhered to a blanket. Toxicology analysis showed: fentanyl 19 µg/L and norfentanyl 7.6 µg/L with a metabolic ratio of 2.5, cyclobenzaprine 0.16 mg/L, tramadol 0.06 mg/L, diphenhydramine 0.08 mg/L, and citalopram, 0.22 mg/L. Pharmacogenomics testing showed that she was compound heterozygous for CYP 3A4*1B and CYP 3A5*3, resulting in decreased enzyme activities. Death was certified to be mixed drug overdose for cause of death, and accident for manner of death. Together with findings from the other cases, the higher fentanyl concentration and high metabolic ratios in the individuals with CYP 3A5*3 homozygous variant suggested that CYP 3A5 mediates fentanyl metabolism. Thus, homozygous CYP 3A5*3 variant would result in decreased CYP3A5 enzyme activity.

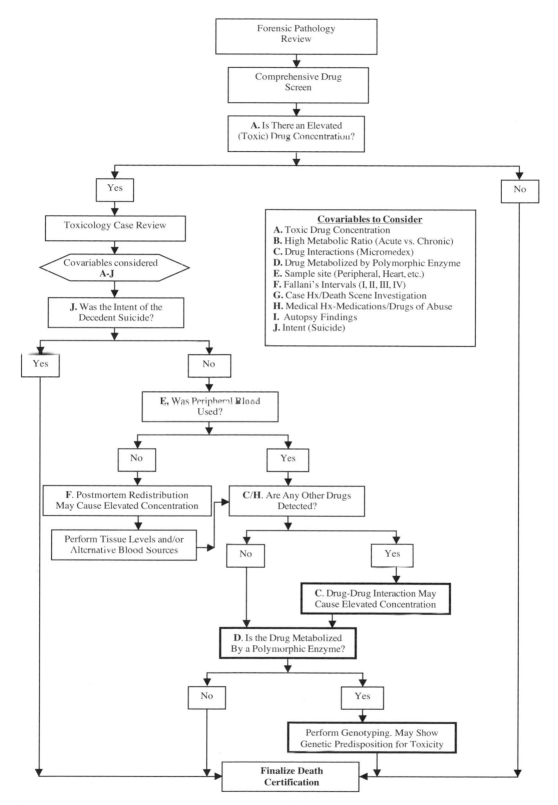

Figure 13.1.3 Application of pharmacogenomics as molecular autopsy.

13.1.2 Conclusions

Pharmacogenomics as molecular autopsy may serve as a useful adjunct for drug death certification for forensic pathology/toxicology. Since most drug deaths involved multiple drugs ingestion, drug–drug interactions will likely contribute to the toxicity and will complicate the interpretation. However, the knowledge derived from post-mortem pharmacogenomics studies would enhance the understanding of pharmacogenomics in "ante-mortem" drug metabolism/therapy, and hence, the emergence of personalized medicine.

GLOSSARY[35]

Allele: One or several forms of a gene of a single individual compared with other individuals. An allele is present on a specific site (genetic locus) of a chromosome controlling a particular characteristic and giving rise to noticeable hereditary difference. A single allele is inherited separately from maternal and paternal origin. Thus, with the exception of unmatched sex chromosomes, every individual has two alleles for each gene.

Genotype: The precise genetic constitution (i.e., genomes, genes, or alleles at one locus or place) that determines the phenotype (observable characteristics) of an organism.

Heterozygote: An individual who carries a pair of different alleles of a particular gene (inherited from two parents) on each member of a pair of chromosomes.

Homozygote: An individual whose genotype has two identical alleles (each derived one parent) at a given locus or place on a pair of homologous chromosomes.

Phenotype: The observable characteristics or physical appearance of an organism resulting from and determined by its expressed genes.

Polymorphism: "Many faces." The difference in genetic sequences among individuals, groups, or populations.

Wild-type: The allele, genotype, or phenotype that naturally occurs in the normal population or, in the case of microbes, the standard laboratory strain of a given organism.

Xenobiotic: A foreign chemical including drugs, industrial chemicals, pollutants, pyrolysis products in food, and toxins produced by plants and animals.

REFERENCES

1. White, R.M. and Wong, S.H.Y., Pharmacogenomics and its applications, *MLO*, 20–27, 2005.
2. Gallo, M.A., History and scope of toxicology, in *Casarett & Doull's Toxicology. The Basic Science of Poisons,* 6th ed., McGraw-Hill Medical, New York, 2001.
3. Baselt, R.C., Ed., *Disposition of Toxic Drugs and Chemicals in Man,* 7th ed., R C Baselt, ed., Biomedical Publications, Foster City, CA, 2004.
4. Moss, D.W. and Henderson, A.R., Clinical enzymology, in *Tietz Textbook of Clinical Chemistry,* 3rd ed., E.A. Ashwood and C.A. Burtis, Eds., W.B. Saunders, Philadelphia, 1999.
5. Innocenti, F., Iyer, L., and Ratain, M.J., Pharmacogenomics of chemotherapeutic agents in cancer treatment, in *Pharmacogenomics. The Search for Individualized Therapies*, J. Licinio and M.-L. Wong, Eds., Wiley-VCH, Weinheim, Germany, 2002.
6. Lindpainter, K., The role of pharmacogenomics in drug discovery and therapeutics, in *Pharmacogenomics. The Search for Individualized Therapies*, J. Licinio and M.-L. Wong, Eds., Wiley-VCH, Weinheim, Germany, 2002.
7. Ito, R.K. and Demers, L.M., Pharmacogenomics and pharmacogenetics: future role of molecular diagnostics in the clinical diagnostic laboratory, *Clin. Chem.,* 50(9), 1526–1527, 2004.
8. Wong, S.H.Y., Linder, M., and Valdes, R., Jr., *Principles of Pharmacogenomics and Introduction to PharmacoProteomics*, AACC Press, Washington, D.C., in press.
9. Moridani, M., Pharmacogenomics, *CAP Today*, 2004.

10. Strachan, T. and Read, A.P., DNA structure and gene expression, in *Human Molecular Genetics 3*, Garland Science/Taylor & Francis, London, 2004.

11. Strachan, T. and Read, A.P., Human gene expression, in *Human Molecular Genetics 3*, Garland Science/Taylor & Francis, London, 2004.

12. Proteins, in *Molecular Biology of the Cell*, B. Alberts, A. Johnson, J. Lewis, M. Raff, K. Roberts, and P. Walker, Eds., Garland Science/Taylor & Francis, London, 2002.

13. Dahlél, P., Dahl, M.-L., Ruiz, M.L.B., and Bertilsson, L., 10-Hydroxylation of nortriptyline in white persons with 0, 1, 2, 3, and 13 functional CYP2D6 genes, *Clin. Pharmacol. Ther.*, 63(4), 444–452, 1998.

14. Rozman, K.K. and Klaassen, C.D., Absorption, distribution, and excretion of toxicants, in *Casarett & Doull's Toxicology. The Basic Science of Poisons*, 6th ed., McGraw-Hill Medical, New York, 2001.

15. Tirona, R.G. and Kim, R.B., Pharmacogenomics of drug transporters, in *Pharmacogenomics. The Search for Individualized Therapies*, J. Licinio and M.-L. Wong, Eds., Wiley-VCH, Weinheim, Germany, 2002.

16. Fromm, M.F. and Eichelbaum, M., The pharmacogenomics of human P-glycoprotein, *Pharmacogenomics. The Search for Individualized Therapies*, J. Licinio and M.-L. Wong, Eds., Wiley-VCH, Weinheim, Germany, 2002.

17. Resine, T., Pharmacogenomics of opioid systems, *Pharmacogenomics. The Search for Individualized Therapies*, J. Licinio and M.-L. Wong, Eds., Wiley-VCH, Weinheim, Germany, 2002.

18. Parkinson, A., Biotransformation of xenobiotics, absorption, distribution, and excretion of toxicants, in *Casarett & Doull's Toxicology. The Basic Science of Poisons*, 6th ed., McGraw-Hill Medical, New York, 2001.

19. Jones, A.W., Disposition and fate of ethanol in the body, in *Medical-Legal Aspects of Alcohol*, 4th ed., J.C. Garriott, Ed., Lawyers & Judges, Tucson, 2003.

20. Jones, A.W., The biochemistry and physiology of alcohol: applications to forensic science and toxicology, in *Medical-Legal Aspects of Alcohol*, 4th ed., J.C. Garriott, Ed., Lawyers & Judges, Tucson, 2003.

21. Hurley, T.D., Edenberg, H.J., and Li, T.-K., Pharmacogenomics of alcoholism, in *Pharmacogenomics. The Search for Individualized Therapies*, J. Licinio and M.-L. Wong, Eds., Wiley-VCH, Weinheim, Germany, 2002.

22. Whitfield, J.B., Alcohol and gene interactions, *Clin. Chem. Lab. Med.*, 43(5), 480–487, 2005.

23. Wong, S.H.Y., Society of Forensic Toxicologists' Meeting, Washington, D.C., September, 2004.

24. Ashwood, E.A. and Burtis, C.A., Eds., *Tietz Textbook of Clinical Chemistry*, 3rd ed., W.B. Saunders, Philadelphia, 1999.

25. Smeraldi, E., Zanardi, R., Benedetti, F., Di Bella, D., Perez, J., and Catalona, M., Polymorphism with the promoter of the serotonin transporter gene and antidepressant efficacy of fluvoxamine, *Mol. Psychiatry*, 3, 508–511, 1998.

26. Kim, D.K., Lim, S.-W., Lee, S., Sohn, S.E., Kim, S., Hahn, C.G., and Carroll, B.J., Serotonin transporter gene polymorphism and antidepressant response, *NeuroReport*, 11(1), 215–219, 2000.

27. Gasche, Y., Daali, Y., Fathi, M., Chiappe, A., Cottini, S., Dayer, P., and Desmules, J., Codeine intoxication associated with ultrarapid CYP2D6 metabolism, *N. Engl. J. Med.*, 351, 2827–2831, 2004.

28. Jannetto, P.J., Wong, S.H.Y., Gock, S., Sahin, E., and Jentzen, J.M., Pharmacogenomics as an adjunct to forensic toxicology: genotyping oxycodone cases for cytochrome P450 (CYP) 2D6, *J. Anal. Toxicol.*, 26, 438–477, 2002.

29. Holmgren, P. and Ahlner, J., Pharmacogenomics for forensic toxicology — Swedish experience, in Wong, S.H.Y., Linder, M., and Valdes, R., Jr., Eds., *Principles of Pharmacogenomics and Introduction to PharmacoProteomics*. AACC Press, Washington, D.C., in press.

30. Sajantila, A., Lunetta, P., and Ojanper, I., Postmortem pharmacogenetics — towards molecular autopsies, in Wong, S.H.Y., Linder, M., and Valdes, R., Jr., Eds., *Principles of Pharmacogenomics and Introduction to PharmacoProteomics*. AACC Press, Washington, D.C., in press.

31. Wong, S.H., Gock, S.B., Shi, R., Jin, M., Wagner, M.A., Schur, C., Jannetto, P.J., Sahin, E., Bjerke, J., Nuwayhid, N., and Jentzen, J.M., Pharmacogenomics as molecular autopsy for forensic pathology and toxicology, in Wong, S.H.Y., Linder, M., and Valdes, R., Jr., Eds., *Principles of Pharmacogenomics and Introduction to PharmacoProteomics*. AACC Press, Washington, D.C., in press.

32. Wong, S.H.Y., Wagner, M.A., Jentzen, J.M., Schur, C., Bjerke, J., Gock, S.B., and Chang, C.J., Pharmacogenomics as an adjunct of molecular autopsy for forensic pathology/toxicology: does genotyping CYP 2D6 serve as an adjunct for certifying methadone toxicology, *J. Forensic Sci.*, 48, 1406–1415, 2003.

33. Salee, F.R., DeVane, C.L., and Ferrell, R.E., Fluoxetine-related death in a child with cytochrome P450 2D6 genetic deficiency, *J. Child Adolesc. Psychopharmacol.*, 27, 27–34, 2000.
34. Jin, M., Gock, S.B., Jannetto, P.J., Jentzen, J.M., and Wong, S.H.Y., Pharmacogenomics as molecular autopsy for forensic toxicology: genotyping cytochrome P450 *3A4*1B* and *3A5*3* for 25 fentanyl cases, *J. Anal. Toxicol.*, in press.
35. Zhang, Y.-H. and Zhang, M., *A Dictionary of Gene Technology Terms*, Parthenon, New York, 2001.

13.2 HERITABLE CHANNELOPATHIES AND MYOPATHIES

Kathryn A. Glatter, M.D., Jonica Calkins, M.D., and Sanjay J. Ayirookuzhi, M.D.
Department of Cardiology and Internal Medicine, University of California, Davis, California

Sudden cardiac arrest remains the major cause of death in the U.S. and the developed Western world.[1–3] Most cases are a consequence of cardiac ischemia, coronary artery disease, and acute myocardial infarction–induced ventricular fibrillation (arrhythmias). Autopsy findings generally reveal atherosclerosis and occluded cardiac vessels in these patients, leading to a clear diagnosis.

However, genetic causes of cardiac arrhythmias are not rare, and the first indication of their presence is often as unexplained sudden death. Some of these disorders may demonstrate gross morphologic alterations at autopsy; hypertrophic cardiomyopathy is the most obvious, but other disorders represent a diagnostic challenge for the forensic pathologists, because at autopsy the heart is structurally normal.

It is important to be familiar with these genetic causes of sudden cardiac death, and the diagnostic difficulties they present, so that they can at least be considered as possible causes of death when the autopsy is otherwise normal. Sudden death in cases of drug overdose may also be due to an ion channel disease and not a simple function of direct drug toxicity. Pathologists need to consider these disorders and other etiologies of cardiac death, as described below.

This chapter contains a brief discussion of the clinical presentation of genetic, molecular, and cellular abnormalities and the appropriate diagnostic measures for the evaluation of channelopathies, cardiomyopathies, and chemical causes of sudden cardiac death (see list below). Finally, we provide an overview for forensic pathologists on the appropriate methods for the collection of tissue samples used for molecular testing of these entities.

Disorders of the Ion Channel

1. Long QT syndromes (LQTS)
2. Brugada syndrome (BS)
3. Catecholaminergic polymorphic ventricular tachycardia (Ryanodine receptor defect) (CPMVT)

Disorders of the Heart Muscle

1. Arrhythmogenic right ventricular dysplasia (ARVD)
2. Hypertrophic cardiomyopathy (HCM)

Chemical Causes of Sudden Cardiac Death

1. Ephedra ("ma huang")
2. Methamphetamine
3. Cocaine

13.2.1 Disorders of the Ion Channel

13.2.1.1 Long QT Syndromes

LQTS is one of the more common and best known of the ion channelopathies.[4,5] It can be inherited as a dominant gene or can be seen in cases of acquired LQTS after taking common drugs including antipsychotics, anti-arrhythmic drugs, or allergy medications.[6,7]

Epidemiology

Currently it is estimated that 1 in 5000 people carry a LQTS genetic mutation.[4,5] With the inclusion of drug-induced or acquired LQTS cases, many of which have the same genetic ion channel defects as seen with congenital LQTS, some experts believe that the true incidence of LQTS is actually 1 in 1000.[8,9] Certainly it is one of the more common genetic causes of sudden death, and it is being diagnosed with increasing frequency as more pathologists become aware of its existence.

Clinical Features

Most patients with an LQTS mutation will never experience any symptoms. LQTS families are usually discovered when a young person tragically dies suddenly, has no findings at autopsy, and other family members are found to have a prolonged QT interval on electrocardiogram (ECG). At least 10% of affected patients may present with sudden death as their first (and last) symptom.[10–13]

Each genetic subtype (described below) has its own trigger for events (Table 13.2.1).[10–14] LQT1 patients usually experience symptoms (syncope, cardiac arrest, or sudden death) during catecholamine-driven types of activities such as running, exercise, or with strong emotion (e.g., during an argument). An unexplained drowning in a person able to swim could be due to an LQT1 mutation.[10,13,15,16] LQT2 (*HERG*) mutations may cause sudden death due to auditory triggers, as with an alarm clock or the telephone ringing.[15–17] Episodes in the rare LQT3 (sodium channel) subtype may occur during sleep or during periods of slow heart rates.[10,13]

Although LQTS is an autosomal disease, females are far more likely to experience symptoms than males.[10–14] In some cases LQTS can be diagnosed by noting a prolonged QT_C interval (>450 ms) on the ECG. However, up to 30% of gene-positive patients may have a normal or only borderline prolonged QT_C interval, making diagnosis impossible in some cases.[10–14,18] Exercise testing may reveal an otherwise concealed form of LQTS.[19,20]

There is a weak association in the literature between SIDS (sudden infant death syndrome) and LQTS, although probably fewer than 5% of all SIDS cases are due to ion channel mutations.[21,22] Other, more common causes of SIDS include placing the infant prone, co-sleeping with overlaying by adults, and inborn errors of metabolism.

As with many ion channelopathies causing unexplained sudden death, autopsy findings are unremarkable. Venous blood saved in an EDTA-tube (or perhaps snap-frozen myocardial tissue) can be tested at a research laboratory for the presence of LQTS ion channel mutations.

Table 13.2.1 Long QT Syndrome Genes

Disease	Chromosome Locus	Gene	Gene Product
LQT1	11p15.5	KVLQT1	I_{Ks}, subunit
LQT2	7q35-36	HERG	I_{Kr}, subunit
LQT3	3p21-23	SCN5A	Na channel
LQT4	4q25-27	ankyrin 2	ankyrin-B
LQT5	21p22.1	*minK* (*KCNE1*)	I_{Ks}, subunit
LQT6	21p22.1	*MiRP1* (*KCNE2*)	I_{Kr}, subunit
LQT7	17q23	KCNJ2	I_{Kr}, subunit

Pathophysiology

The fundamental defect in LQTS is prolonged ventricular repolarization and a tendency toward the occurrence of torsades de pointes (polymorphic ventricular tachycardia) and ventricular fibrillation.[4,5] The LQTS ion channel mutation leads to this abnormality in repolarization, and evidence of it can be seen on the ECG as a prolonged QT interval. Beta-blocker medications (described below) do not shorten the QT interval; they are believed to act, in part, by blocking EADs (early after-depolarizations), which initiate the ventricular arrhythmias.

Genetics

To date, a total of seven genes have been identified as causing long QT syndrome.[23–26] The mutant ion channel that causes clinical LQTS is inherited in an autosomal dominant fashion with incomplete penetrance and was originally known as the "Romano-Ward Syndrome." With the advent of genetic testing, it has become clear that each LQTS genetic subtype represents a unique disease, with different triggers to arrhythmias. The genes that encode the potassium channels *KVLQT1* (on chromosome 11) and *minK* (on chromosome 21) interact to form the cardiac I_{Ks} (inward slow potassium) current; mutations in each cause LQT1 and LQT5, respectively.[5,23,24] The potassium channels *HERG* (on chromosome 7) and *MiRP1* (on chromosome 21) interact to form the I_{Kr} (inward rapid potassium) current, and defects in each cause LQT2 and LQT6, respectively.[25] Mutations in the sodium cardiac channel SCN5A cause LQT3 (on chromosome 3).[26] The gene responsible for LQT4 was recently identified as a mutation in the ankyrin-B protein.[27] The potassium channel mutations cause a "loss of function" in the channel (or a "dominant-negative effect," in the case of the *HERG* mutation), whereas defects in the sodium channel cause a "gain of function."[4,5] LQT7 is due to a defect in the α-subunit of the I_{Kr} channel (gene product *KCNJ2*).

In the unlikely event that a mutant copy of the I_{Ks} channel is inherited from each parent (mutations in the *KVLQT1* and *minK* genes), the child will suffer from a clinically severe form of autosomal dominant LQTS, and from autosomal recessive congenital deafness. This condition is known as the "Jervell and Lange-Nielsen syndrome" (JLNS).[28,29] JLNS was first described in 1957 in a Norwegian family in which three congenitally deaf children died suddenly before the age of 10.[30] It is actually quite rare, with an estimated incidence of 1.6 to 6 cases per million.[29]

In a somewhat more likely event, it is possible that an individual carrying a *KCNH2* mutation on a mutant allele might also carry a different *KCNH2* polymorphism on the nonmutant allele. Relatives who inherit the one without the other would be asymptomatic, but when both mutations are simultaneously present, reduction of Ik would be substantial and result in a clinically significant form of LQTS. This situation has actually been demonstrated to occur in humans, raising the possibility that compound mutations may be more common than had previously been suspected.[31]

Treatment

There is no consensus on how to treat patients with LQTS.[4,13,32] Most physicians would advocate an implantable defibrillator (ICD) for those patients who have survived a cardiac arrest, or possibly even in those with syncopal events.[33] Dual chamber pacemakers, even with beta-blocker therapy, have been shown to be ineffective in symptomatic patients.[34]

It is generally recommended that beta-blocker therapy should be initiated in asymptomatic LQTS patients.[11–14] The exact dose or type of beta-blocker medication to be used is unclear. In patients unable (or unwilling) to take medications, an ICD may then be recommended. Restriction from heavy physical activity is also suggested in affected patients. Data from the International LQTS Registry have shown that symptomatic LQT1 patients have a low recurrence rate after starting beta-blocker medication (19% recurrence), LQT2 patients have an intermediate rate (41% recurrence), and LQT3 patients a higher rate (50%).[10] Sympathectomy to modify the effect of adrenaline upon the heart has been shown to be ineffective at preventing events.[34]

13.2.1.2 Brugada Syndrome

The Brugada syndrome (BS) is another inherited ion channelopathy that causes unexplained sudden death, particularly in middle-aged males.[35–37] It is relatively common in southeast Asia and should particularly be considered in the autopsy of subjects with this ethnicity.[38]

Epidemiology

A Brugada syndrome consensus report published in 2002 estimated the incidence of the disease worldwide at up to 66 cases per 10,000 people.[39] Although it is an autosomal dominant disease, it affects males more commonly than females, in an 8:1 male:female ratio. The reason for this gender difference is unknown. The gene is much more prevalent in Southeast Asia than in the U.S., and Brugada syndrome is thought to cause the entity known as *Lai Tai* ("death during sleep") in Thailand, a relatively common cause of sudden unexplained death among young healthy men.[38]

Clinical Features

The Brugada brothers reported eight cases of cardiac arrest in 1992, in young healthy patients with right bundle branch block patterns on ECG.[40] Since then, more has been learned about BS, although much about the disease remains a mystery.[41,42] It is not known why some patients with Brugada become symptomatic and others remain clinically silent. However, once BS subjects experience a symptom (syncope or aborted cardiac arrest), it becomes a very lethal disease with a high clinical penetrance.[43–45] Several studies have found that the 5-year recurrence rate following a resuscitated cardiac arrest was 62%.[39,41,43–45] Most arrhythmic events occur for the first time when patients are in their early 40s, but episodes have been described over a wide age range (2 to 77 years). Symptomatic patients with Brugada experience polymorphic ventricular tachycardia degenerating into ventricular fibrillation, leading to syncope or even death. The episodes occur most commonly during sleep but may also happen with exercise or at rest.

The ECG in a patient with Brugada is frequently abnormal and provides the best way to diagnose BS. A right bundle branch block-type pattern is often noted in right precordial leads V1–V3 with concomitant ST segment elevation.[35–37,46] In many patients with BS, the ECG abnormalities can normalize or be unmasked by pharmacologic challenge with a sodium channel blocking drug such as procainamide, flecainide, or ajmaline.[47,48]

Many patients with Brugada will have abnormal test results during invasive electrophysiology (EP) studies.[49,50] Inducibility of malignant ventricular arrhythmias in this group of patients is not rare, and it may portend a worse clinical prognosis than for those patients who have normal EP studies.[35–37,49,50] The usual cardiac tests in BS are normal including echocardiogram, cardiac magnetic resonance imaging (MRI), and biopsy. Autopsy findings of the heart in patients with BS are also unremarkable.

Pathophysiology

The mutation in the *SCN5A* gene results in either a reduced sodium channel current or failure of the sodium channel to express. The disease is caused by a defect in the α-subunit of the cardiac sodium channel gene (*SCN5A*).[37,41,51,52] Numerous *SCN5A* mutations have been described that produce BS, but most lead to a "loss of function" in the cardiac sodium channel. Interestingly, LQT3 (a completely different disease) is also due to mutations in the *SCN5A* gene but leads to a "gain of function" in the sodium channel.[51–55]

The mutant sodium channel demonstrates more abnormal function at higher temperatures. There are numerous reports in the literature of patients with BS experiencing symptoms during febrile illnesses.[35–37]

Recently it has been shown that the Y1102 polymorphism of the *SCN5A* gene is present in 13% of African Americans, and that its presence has been linked to the occurrence of lethal arrhythmias in African American families with ventricular tachycardia. The prevalence of the Y1102 polymorphism in a series of sudden deaths in this population has been established; it is present in 28% of African Americans who die of unexplained arrhythmias. Adjusted for age and sex, the relative risk of an unexplained arrhythmic death in individuals with this polymorphism was 8.4 (95% CI 2.1 to 28.6, $P = 0.001$) when compared with noncardiac deaths in this subgroup. The presence of the Y1102 allele appears to be a risk factor in African Americans for sudden cardiac death even in the absence of obvious morphological findings.[56]

Genetics

BS is an ion channelopathy inherited in an autosomal dominant fashion. To date, only 20% of Brugada cases have been linked to the *SCN5A* gene; the precise ion channel mutations causing the remaining 80% of cases are unknown.[40–42] The *SCN5A* gene is one of the largest ion channel genes known, with at least 28 exons identified thus far.[51,52]

Treatment

Medications are largely ineffective at treating BS.[39] Amiodarone, beta-blocker, and calcium channel blocking agents have all been tried and do not prevent sudden death in high-risk patients, although sotalol may be useful.[57] The recommended treatment for symptomatic patients with BS is ICD implantation, particularly as the recurrence rate for such subjects is high. Patients who have not yet experienced an arrhythmic event but spontaneously exhibit the abnormal ECG findings are at intermediate risk for an episode and may benefit from prophylactic implantation of a defibrillator.[49,50,58]

13.2.1.3 Catecholaminergic Polymorphic Ventricular Tachycardia

CPMVT is a newly described inherited disorder of cardiac calcium channels. It is another arrhythmogenic disorder characterized by sudden unexplained death associated with exercise.

Epidemiology

The disease has thus far been described in several Finnish and Italian families.[59–62] The epidemiology of this disorder has not yet been fully characterized and is so far limited to small case series. Its true incidence is likely much higher than is currently appreciated since most cases are undiagnosed.

Clinical Features

CPMVT was first described by Leenhardt et al. in 1995 in 21 children.[63] This disorder is characterized by syncopal spells in childhood and adolescence, which are often triggered by exercise or stress (catecholamines). Cardiac arrest and sudden death also occur. The disease has a mortality of 30 to 50% by the age of 30 in affected individuals.[62] Due to its autosomal dominant nature, there is often a family history of unexplained sudden death.

The resting ECG of a patient with this disorder is usually unremarkable, as are cardiac imaging studies (echocardiogram, angiogram, cardiac MRI, etc.).[62–65] Patients with CPMVT may experience bi-directional or polymorphic ventricular tachycardia with exercise stress testing, with emotional stress, or during infusion of adrenaline (isoproterenol).[64,65] Up to 30% of such patients have been initially misdiagnosed as having LQTS in one study.[61] Autopsy findings in subjects with CPMVT are generally normal.

Pathophysiology

Defective calcium channels formed as a result of the mutations in the ryanodine receptor gene *RyR2* lead to abnormal conduction, which predispose the heart to ventricular tachycardia and sudden death.[59–62,66] *RyR2*, the gene encoding the cardiac calcium channel, is responsible for mediating the coupling of the cell's electrical excitation and mechanical contraction. Cellular depolarization leads to release of Ca^{2+} from the sarcoplasmic reticulum via RyR2 and mechanical contraction. Sudden death is hypothesized to occur as the result of torsades de pointes or ventricular fibrillation due to the abnormal calcium channel handling.

Genetics

CPMVT is due to a defect in the cardiac ryanodine receptor (RyR2) gene, which is inherited in an autosomal dominant fashion.[59–62,66] Ryanodine receptors are intracellular calcium channels that regulate the release of calcium from different cell sites. Three different isoforms of the ryanodine receptor are known, and a different gene encodes each. They are the largest ion channels yet described. RyR2 (encoded by 105 exons) is characteristically found in the heart while RyR1 is found in skeletal muscle.

Because this entity is newly described and the genes encoding the mutant calcium channel are so large, no commercial genetic screening is currently available for CPMVT.

Treatment

Beta-blockers form the mainstay of therapy in this condition. In patients who have survived cardiac arrest or are felt to be at particularly high risk for sudden death, an ICD is offered.[61,65]

13.2.2 Disorders of the Heart Muscle

13.2.2.1 Arrhythmogenic Right Ventricular Dysplasia

ARVD is a newly recognized disorder that is a cause of unexplained sudden death in otherwise healthy young adults, particularly young athletic men.[67–69] Particularly in the early stages, affected patients may have grossly normal heart function.

Epidemiology

The true incidence of ARVD is unknown. In a prospective, detailed autopsy-based study in the Veneto region of northern Italy, 20% of unexplained sudden deaths in subjects under age 35 were found to have ARVD, including 22% of young athletic men who died suddenly in the region.[70] It is unclear if northern Italy simply has an abnormally high incidence of the disease, or if this reflects the true incidence of the disease. However, it is likely a much more common entity than initially appreciated as most cases go undetected.

Clinical Features

Unfortunately, the initial presentation of ARVD clinically is often the unexplained sudden death in a healthy, athletic male. Patients experience ventricular arrhythmias from the diseased right ventricle. These range from benign premature ventricular complexes (PVCs) to ventricular tachy-

Table 13.2.2   ARVD Diagnostic Criteria

ECG Findings
Epsilon wave of QRS in leads V1–V3
Late potentials on signal-averaged ECG
Arrhythmias
Right ventricular tachycardia or premature beats
Family history
Confirmed at autopsy
Structural findings
RV global hypokinesis with preserved LV function

cardia or even ventricular fibrillation and cardiac arrest.[71–74] ARVD was first described briefly in 1961, and in greater detail in 1977.[75,76] The Study Group on ARVD/C has defined specific criteria to aid in the diagnosis of ARVD (Table 13.2.2).[77]

ECG findings include a complete or incomplete right bundle branch block during normal sinus rhythm with T wave inversion in leads V_1 to V_3. An epsilon wave, a terminal notch in the QRS, may also be present.[67–69,71–73] A signal-averaged ECG (SAECG) is also characteristically abnormal.[77]

Echocardiographic findings may be normal or reveal a variety of abnormalities in the right ventricle including RV wall thinning, dilatation, or dysfunction.[67–69,71–73,78] Cardiac MRI can sometimes be useful as it may reveal the fibrofatty infiltration of the RV free wall.[79,80] Biopsy of the RV septum (done in the septum and not in the free wall, due to free wall thinning) is often not helpful because involvement of the septum in ARVD is sporadic.

ARVD represents one of the few genetically based causes of sudden death that can be identified at autopsy, at least in grossly abnormal cases. The pathologist may find diffuse or segmental loss of myocardium in the right ventricular free wall, with concomitant replacement with fibrofatty tissue.[67–69] Two thirds of such patients have patchy, acute myocarditis-type of findings with lymphocytic infiltration and cell death.[71–73] Up to 50% of patients with ARVD have right ventricular aneurysms at autopsy.[71–73,77]

Patients can have progressive dilatation and failure of the right ventricle over time, which can also occasionally involve the left ventricle, leading to a diffuse cardiomyopathy. One study found that 76% of ARVD subjects had histologic involvement of the left ventricle.[77]

Pathophysiology

The pathophysiology of ARVD is unclear. It likely represents a complex interplay among genetic predisposition, cellular mechanisms, and unknown environmental factors.[67–69,77] Several consistent features of ARVD can be noted: apoptosis (programmed cell death), a component of inflammatory heart disease (e.g., acute myocarditis), and myocardial dystrophy. The disease is progressive over decades in some patients, whereas it is relatively quiescent, for unknown reasons, in others.

Genetics

At least seven distinct chromosomal loci for ARVD have so far been located.[81–85] These loci include two on chromosome 10, two on chromosome 14, and one each on chromosomes 1, 2, and 3. One autosomal recessive form of ARVD is associated with palmoplantar keratoderma and woolly hair.[86] It is due to a mutation in the gene for plakoglobin. Another syndrome found in Ecuador involves a recessive mutation in the gene for desmoplakin.[87] Both are components of desmosomes, which form the major cell adhesion junctions. Currently, there is no commercial genetic testing available to diagnose ARVD.

For most cases of ARVD, the genetic linkage is unclear. Up to 30 to 50% of the cases will have an associated family history consistent with ARVD (including sudden death).[71–73,77]

Treatment

There is no consensus for how to treat ARVD.[77] In those patients who have survived cardiac arrest, implantation of an ICD is generally recommended to avoid sudden death.[88] Pharmacologic therapy with beta-blocker or antiarrhythmic medications has also been suggested.[77] Radiofrequency ablation during electrophysiology study of ventricular arrhythmias has also been attempted.[89]

13.2.2.2 *Hypertrophic Cardiomyopathy*

HCM is one of the oldest known non-atherosclerotic causes of sudden death. It was first described in 1958.[90] It has been called HOCM (hypertrophic obstructive cardiomyopathy) and also IHSS (idiopathic hypertrophic subaortic stenosis) despite that 75% of affected patients do not have a sizable resting outflow gradient.[91,92] It is a polygenic, relatively common, genetic cause of sudden death, particularly in young athletes.

Epidemiology

HCM is actually the most common genetically associated form of sudden cardiac death. It is estimated that 1 in 500 people (0.2% of the general population) carry an HCM genetic mutation.[93,94] However, the phenotypic presentation or clinical penetrance of the disease is much lower. Most patients with an HCM mutation will not demonstrate clinical manifestations of the disease during life.

Clinical Features

The hallmark feature of HCM, when present, is myocyte disarray.[92,95,96] The clinical diagnosis of HCM during life is made most reliably by echocardiography. Severe ventricular wall thickening can be noted. A normal left ventricular wall thickness is generally <12 mm, but thicknesses >30 mm are not unusual in severe cases of HCM.[97–101] Marked septal hypertrophy is often an age-dependent effect and may not be seen initially in young patients. In most cases, the left ventricle is affected diffusely, or it may demonstrate ASH (asymmetric septal hypertrophy).[95–101] In contrast, in the Japanese variant of HCM, the apical left ventricle is primarily affected and shows abnormal thickening.[92,95–101]

At autopsy using detailed pathologic examination, one can frequently see hypertrophied myocytes with bizarre shapes, chaotic cellular alignment, and gross cellular disarray in the left ventricle.[102–106] The disarray is most evident in the mid-portion of the septum. Patchy areas of myocardial scarring and fibrosis can be seen, a lesion that is thought to be due to the presence of abnormal intramural coronary arteries.[107,108]

Pathophysiology

Syncope in these subjects may occur due to arrhythmias, or it may be the result of outlet obstruction due to ventricular hypertrophy and cavitary obliteration.[90,97,98] Dehydration can trigger syncopal events in such patients. Sudden death in HCM is primarily due to electrical abnormalities generating ventricular arrhythmias.[92,97,109–112] In support of this view, one large study of patients with HCM, in whom defibrillators were implanted, demonstrated that nearly 25% of the patients had documented ventricular arrhythmias over a 3-year follow-up period.[113]

The disease may be progressive in certain individuals. Cardiomyocytes continue to hypertrophy over years, but in a clinically silent manner that may lead ultimately to an end-stage, dilated cardiomyopathic picture.[92,97,98] Depending on the timeframe during which the patient is evaluated, the HCM-affected heart could appear grossly normal, markedly hypertrophied, or dilated, which makes the diagnosis difficult.

Genetics

The polygenic and multicellular nature of HCM makes it a frustratingly difficult disease to diagnose unless gross histopathologic abnormalities are found on ECG or at autopsy. At least ten different genes encoding the cardiac sarcomere have been implicated in HCM.[92,97,98,114] More than 150 unique mutations have been reported since the first genetic cause for HCM was identified in 1990.[115] Most such mutations are missense mutations found in the proteins of the cardiac sarcomere and are located in the β-myosin heavy chain, cardiac troponin T, or myosin binding protein-C.[111–119] Although the disease is autosomal dominant, a family history of syncope or sudden death may be lacking, and the disease has variable clinical penetrance.

Within the β-myosin heavy chain gene (*MYH7*), numerous mutations have been described as malignant mutations associated with a poor clinical prognosis.[118–121] These particular mutations seemed to be associated with a severe clinical phenotype including progression to end-stage heart failure or sudden death, a relatively high penetrance of the disease, and extreme left ventricular wall thickness.[92,97,98,112,117,118]

Treatment

There are no formal guidelines for treating asymptomatic patients with HCM.[92,97,98] In symptomatic patients with shortness of breath, treatment with medications that reduce the outflow gradient remains the mainstay of therapy.[92,97,98,122,123] Such medications include beta-blockers or calcium channel blockers. In very symptomatic patients with a large (>50 mm) gradient, the outflow gradient can be reduced by surgical myomectomy or by catheter-based alcohol ablation.[92,97,98,124,125] The latter is a relatively new technique, which causes a controlled myocardial infarction and thus reduces the obstruction to outflow.

In those patients deemed at high risk for an arrhythmic event, an ICD may be implanted to avert sudden death.

13.2.3 Drug Causes of Sudden Death

Clearly, many medications and drugs of abuse can lead to cardiac arrhythmias and sudden death. A detailed description of these topics is beyond the scope of this chapter. However, we consider three major causes of sudden death that should be considered by the pathologist at autopsy: ephedra (or ma huang), methamphetamine, and cocaine.

13.2.3.1 Ephedra

Ma huang is a popular herb derived from the genus *Ephedra* used for over 5000 years in Chinese folk remedies.[126] It is a natural source of ephedrine taken in various vitamin or other supplements to promote weight loss and boost energy. Ephedrine and its derivatives function in the body by increasing the availability of naturally released catecholamines.[127] Its physiologic effects on the body include increasing the heart rate, raising the cardiac output, and elevating the vascular resistance.[128] It is excreted in the urine and has a serum half-life of 2.7 to 3.6 h.[129]

Before the supplements were withdrawn from the market, it was one of the most widely used herbal supplements in the world. Even though ephedra-containing supplements are no longer for sale, millions of consumers still use ephedrine on a daily basis in the form of over-the-counter asthma preparations. It is puzzling that these asthma preparations, which have been available for more than 50 years, were never associated with any of the complications attributed to the supplements. An estimated 12 million consumers in the U.S. alone purchased over-the-counter ephedra-containing preparations in 1999.[130–132] Caffeine is also a common ingredient in ephedra preparations;

the combination of the two drugs, when taken in excess, clearly can cause ventricular arrhythmias, hypertension, or cardiovascular collapse.

Numerous case reports have linked ma huang to cases of cardiovascular disorders, sudden death, and hemorrhagic stroke.[133] One analysis of adverse event reports evaluated 926 possible cases of ephedra toxicity reported to the FDA from 1995 through 1997.[130] The authors identified 37 major cardiovascular events they thought likely to be ma huang related, including 16 strokes, 11 cardiac arrests, and 10 myocardial infarctions. The average age of the 37 patients was only 43 ± 13 years and included 23 women.

Pathologists should consider testing for ephedra/ma huang particularly in young, otherwise healthy subjects who die suddenly with a normal autopsy, or if autopsy reveals early-onset vascular disease such as strokes or myocardial infarction.[134–137] Particular attention should be paid to a history of vitamin supplement ingestion in such patients.

13.2.3.2 Methamphetamine

Methamphetamine is a central nervous stimulant that was first synthesized by a German chemist in 1887.[138] It is an odorless, crystalline powder that is soluble in alcohol or water. Its precursors are ephedrine and pseudoephedrine.

Its sympathomimetic actions produce hypertension, elevated heart rate, ischemia, vasoconstriction, and other adrenergic-type of stimuli upon the heart. Acute aortic dissection has been described at autopsy in methamphetamine users.[139] Myocardial infarction, chest pain syndromes, and coronary artery disease have been found in such patients, and a direct toxic effect on myocytes has been implicated for methamphetamine.[140–142] Methamphetamine may promote ventricular arrhythmias and sudden death with its use.[143] Chronic use may lead to a dilated cardiomyopathy.[144–147]

Methamphetamine use is increasingly popular and should be considered in the autopsy evaluation when present, but usually there are other stigmata present suggesting the diagnosis, and sudden cardiac death with a negative autopsy is rare in a methamphetamine abuser.

13.2.3.3 Cocaine

Cocaine (benzoylmethylecgonine) is an alkaloid originally extracted from the leaves of the *Erythroxylon coca* plant.[147] It is estimated that at least 30 million people in the U.S. have used cocaine at some point. Cocaine acts at both the central and peripheral adrenergic nervous system by blocking the reuptake of norephinephrine and dopamine from presynaptic terminals. These effects lead to a net stimulatory effect upon the cardiovascular system.[148,149]

Cocaine causes a variety of cardiac complications. Its basic pathophysiologic effect is to induce an adrenergic overload leading to acceleration of the heart rate, proarrhythmic effects, and even cardiac collapse.[147,148,150,151] Cocaine increases myocardial oxygen demand acutely while concomitantly reducing myocardial oxygen supply with its direct vasoconstrictive effects on the coronary arteries. It promotes intracoronary thrombosis and platelet aggregation in the absence of coronary atherosclerosis, leading to vascular injury.[147,148,150–152] Finally, long-term cocaine use has been associated with premature and accelerated atherosclerosis.[155]

The pathologist should consider cocaine toxicity as an adjunctive diagnosis in the unexplained sudden death of seemingly healthy subjects. However, as is true for methamphetamine abusers, sudden death with a negative autopsy is an uncommon finding in a cocaine abuser.

In addition to its direct cardiac effects (e.g., myocardial infarction, stroke, aortic dissection, cardiac arrhythmias), cocaine has been found to directly block the *HERG* potassium channel.[157] This finding represents yet another way cocaine may cause sudden cardiac death, and is particularly important, since *HERG* blockade would not be associated with any identifiable anatomic markers.

13.2.4 Molecular Diagnosis of Cardiovascular Disease

With the explosion of molecular techniques, DNA testing on peripheral blood and tissue has revolutionized the diagnosis of genetic causes of sudden death. We describe the basic methods of tissue preparation and DNA analysis as a useful overview for the clinical pathologist and coroner.

13.2.4.1 Collection of DNA from Blood Samples

It is easiest to amplify DNA that will be used for genetic testing when it is taken from blood samples.[158,159] Ideally, the medical examiner or pathologist would collect the samples at the time of autopsy. At least 15 ml of blood should be collected in EDTA-containing tubes, in order to prevent coagulation and degradation of the DNA. The tubes are then stored at 4°C until the DNA can be extracted for analysis, which should be within 1 week, although sometimes DNA can be extracted up to 4 months after collection. If the blood samples are collected in tubes that do not contain an anticoagulant, the DNA should be extracted promptly (within days of the initial collection).

13.2.4.2 Collection of DNA from Tissue Samples

Extraction of high-quality DNA from tissue that can be used for PCR (polymerase chain reaction) amplification is much more problematic than using blood samples. It is often difficult to amplify long fragments of DNA from formalin-fixed and paraffin-embedded tissue because formalin fixation may damage the DNA, as may long storage in the tissue blocks prior to analysis. Formic acid may also form in the sample making PCR difficult, if not impossible[160,161] Formic acid hydrolyzes the DNA and creates single-strand nicks in the DNA. In post-mortem tissues fixed in nonbuffered formalin (usually in tissue preserved more than 20 years ago), DNA fragments longer than 90 base pairs cannot be amplified.

There are a variety of published methods to extract DNA from preserved tissue.[162,163] Many involve a phenol-chloroform digestion and washing step. Commercial kits are also available that may simplify the methodology. One recent paper described a "pre-PCR restoration process" in which the single-stranded DNA nicks are repaired with Taq polymerase prior to PCR amplification, greatly enhancing the length of DNA pieces that could be amplified.[164]

An alternative method for obtaining usable DNA from tissue collected at autopsy is to snap-freeze fresh myocardial tissue in liquid nitrogen, and store it at −80°C until DNA extraction is performed. Using this method allows the extraction process to be deferred for many months. Clearly, collection and preservation of tissue or blood samples for future DNA analysis is cumbersome, time-intensive, and costly. However, it may be of great assistance in determining the cause of death if tissue is carefully preserved for future DNA testing, especially in those cases where a genetic cause of sudden death is suspected.

Acknowledgments

This work was funded in part by an American Heart Association Beginning-Grant-in-Aid, Western States Affiliates, to Dr. Glatter.

REFERENCES

1. Escobedo LG, Zack MM. Comparisons of sudden and nonsudden coronary deaths in the United States. *Circulation* 1996;93:2033–6.

2. Goraya TY, Jacobsen SJ, Kottke TE, et al. Coronary heart disease death and sudden cardiac death. *Am J Epidemiol* 2003;157:763–70.

3. Zheng ZJ, Croft BJ, Giles WH, et al. Sudden cardiac death in the United States, 1989 to 1998. *Circulation* 2001;104:2158–63.

4. Wehrens XH, Vos MA, Doevendans PA, et al. Novel insights in the congenital long QT syndrome. *Ann Intern Med* 2002;137:981–92.

5. Vincent GM. The molecular genetics of the long QT syndrome: genes causing fainting and sudden death. *Annu Rev Med* 1998;49:263–74.

6. Zeltser D, Justo D, Halkin A, et al. Torsade de pointes due to noncardiac drugs: most patients have easily identifiable risk factors. *Medicine* 2003;82:282–90.

7. Al-Khatib SM, LaPointe NM, Kramer JM, et al. What clinicians should know about the QT interval. *JAMA* 2003;289:2120–7.

8. Yang P, Kanki H, Drolet B, et al. Allelic variants in long-QT disease genes in patients with drug-associated torsades de pointes. *Circulation* 2002;105:1943–8.

9. Roden DM. Pharmacogenetics and drug-induced arrhythmias. *Cardiovasc Res* 2001;50;224–31.

10. Schwartz PJ, Priori SG, Spazzolini C, et al. Genotype-phenotype correlation in the long-QT syndrome: gene-specific triggers for life-threatening arrhythmias. *Circulation* 2001;103:89–95.

11. Moss AJ, Schwartz PJ, Crampton RS, et al. The long QT syndrome: a prospective international study. *Circulation* 1985; 71:17–21.

12. Moss AJ, Schwartz PJ, Crampton RS, et al. The long QT syndrome. Prospective longitudinal study of 328 families. *Circulation* 1991;84:1136–44.

13. Zareba W, Moss AJ, Schwartz PJ, et al. Influence of genotype on the clinical course of the long-QT syndrome. International Long QT Syndrome Registry Research Group. *N Engl J Med* 1998;339:960–5.

14. Locati EH, Zareba W, Moss AJ, et al. Age- and sex-related differences in clinical manifestations in patients with congenital long-QT syndrome. *Circulation* 1998;97:2237–44.

15. Moss AJ, Robinson JL, Gessman L, et al. Comparison of clinical and genetic variables of cardiac events associated with loud noise versus swimming among subjects with the long QT syndrome. *Am J Cardiol* 1999;84:876–9.

16. Ali RH, Zareba W, Moss AJ, et al. Clinical and genetic variables associated with acute arousal and nonarousal-related cardiac events among subjects with long QT syndrome. *Am J Cardiol* 2000;85:457–61.

17. Wilde AA, Jongbloed RJ, Doevendans PA, et al. Auditory stimuli as a trigger for arrhythmic events differentiate *HERG*-related (LQTS2) patients from *KVLQT1*-related patients (LQTS1). *J Am Coll Cardiol* 1999;33:327–32.

18. Priori SG, Napolitano C, Schwartz PJ. Low penetrance in the long-QT syndrome: clinical impact. *Circulation* 1999;99:529–33.

19. Swan H, Viitasalo M, Piippo K, et al. Sinus node function and ventricular repolarization during exercise stress test in long QT syndrome patients with *KvLQT1* and *HERG* potassium channel defects. *J Am Coll Cardiol* 1999;34:823–9.

20. Swan H, Toivonen L, Viitasalo M. Rate adaptation of QT intervals during and after exercise in children with congenital long QT syndrome. *Eur Heart J* 1998;19:508–13.

21. Schwartz PJ, Priori SG, Dumaine R, et al. A molecular link between the sudden infant death syndrome and the long-QT syndrome. *N Engl J Med* 2000;343:262–7.

22. Ackerman MJ, Siu BL, Sturner WQ, et al. Postmortem molecular analysis of *SCN5A* defects in sudden infant death syndrome. *JAMA* 2001;286:2264–9.

23. Keating M, Atkinson D, Dunn C, et al. Linkage of a cardiac arrhythmia, the long QT syndrome, and the Harvey ras-1 gene. *Science* 1991;252:704–6.

24. Jiang C, Atkinson D, Towbin JA, et al. Two long QT syndrome loci map to chromosomes 3 and 7 with evidence for further heterogeneity. *Nat Genet* 1994;8:141–7.

25. Abbott GW, Sesti F, Splawski I, et al. *MiRP1* forms I_{Kr} potassium channels with *HERG* and is associated with cardiac arrhythmia. *Cell* 1999;97:175–87.

26. Wang Q, Li Z, Shen J, et al. Genomic organization of the human *SCN5A* gene encoding the cardiac sodium channel. *Genomics* 1996;34:9–16.

27. Mohler PJ, Schott JJ, Gramolini AO, et al. Ankyrin-B mutation causes type 4 long-QT cardiac arrhythmia sudden cardiac death. *Nature* 2003;421:634–9.

28. Chen Q, Zhang D, Gingell RL, et al. Homozygous deletion in KVLQT1 associated with Jervell and Lange-Nielsen syndrome. *Circulation* 1999;99:1344–7.

29. Splawski I, Timothy KW, Vincent GM, et al. Molecular basis of the long-QT syndrome associated with deafness. *N Engl J Med* 1997;336:1562–7.

30. Jervell A, Lange-Nielsen F. Congenital deaf-mutism, functional heart disease with prolongation of the Q-T interval, and sudden death. *Am Heart J* 1957;54:59–68.

31. Crotti L, Lundquist AL, Insolia R, et al. KNCH2-K897T is a genetic modifier of latent congenital long-QT syndrome. *Circulation* 2005;222:1251–8.

32. Chiang CE and Roden DM. The long QT syndromes: genetic basis and clinical implications. *J Am Coll Cardiol* 2000;36:1–12.

33. Groh WJ, Silka MJ, Oliver RP, et al. Use of implantable cardioverter-defibrillators in the congenital long QT syndrome. *Am J Cardiol* 1996;78:703–6.

34. Dorostkar PC, Eldar M, Belhassen B, et al. Long-term follow-up of patients with long-QT syndrome treated with beta-blockers and continuous pacing. *Circulation* 1999;100:2431–6.

35. Antzelevitch C, Brugada P, Brugada J, et al. Brugada syndrome: a decade of progress. *Circ Res* 2002;91:1114–8.

36. Gussak I, Antzelevitch C, Bjerregaard P, et al. The Brugada syndrome: clinical, electrophysiologic, and genetic aspects. *J Am Coll Cardiol* 1999;33:5–15.

37. Antzelevitch C. The Brugada syndrome: ionic basis and arrhythmia mechanisms. *J Cardiovasc Electrophysiol* 2001;12:268–72.

38. Nademanee K, Veerakul G, Nimmannit S, et al. Arrhythmogenic marker for the sudden unexplained death syndrome in Thai men. *Circulation* 1997;96:2595–2600.

39. Wilde AAM, Antzelevitch C, Borggrefe M, et al. The Study Group on the Molecular Basis of Arrhythmias of the European Society of Cardiology. Proposed diagnostic criteria for the Brugada syndrome: consensus report. *Circulation* 2002;106:2514–9.

40. Priori SG, Napolitano C, Gasparini M, et al. Natural history of Brugada syndrome: insights for risk stratification and management. *Circulation* 2002;105:1342–7.

41. Alings M and Wilde A. "Brugada" syndrome: clinical data and suggested pathophysiological mechanism. *Circulation* 1999;99:666–73.

42. Brugada P, Brugada J. Right bundle branch block, persistent ST segment elevation and sudden cardiac death: a distinct clinical and electrocardiographic syndrome. *J Am Coll Cardiol* 1992;20:1391–6.

43. Brugada J, Brugada R, Antzelevitch C, et al. Long-term follow-up of individuals with the electrocardiographic pattern of right bundle-branch block and ST-segment elevation in precordial leads V1 to V3. *Circulation* 2002;105:73–8.

44. Brugada J, Brugada R, and Brugada P. Right bundle-branch block and ST-segment elevation in leads V1 through V3. *Circulation* 1998;97:457–60.

45. Priori SG, Napolitano C, Gasparini M, et al. Clinical and genetic heterogeneity of right bundle branch block and ST-segment elevation syndrome. *Circulation* 2000;102:2509–15.

46. Smits JP, Eckardt L, Probst V, et al. Genotype-phenotype relationship in Brugada syndrome: electrocardiographic features differentiate *SCN5A*-related patients from non-*SCN5A*-related patients. *J Am Coll Cardiol* 2002;40:350–6.

47. Brugada R, Brugada J, Antzelevitch C, et al. Sodium channel blockers identify risk for sudden death in patients with ST-segment elevation and right bundle branch block but structurally normal hearts. *Circulation* 2000;101:510–5.

48. Priori SG, Napolitano C, Schwartz PJ, et al. The elusive link between LQT3 and Brugada syndrome: the role of flecainide challenge. *Circulation* 2000;102:945–7.

49. Brugada P, Brugada R, Mont L, et al. Natural history of Brugada syndrome: the prognostic value of programmed electrical stimulation of the heart. *J Cardiovasc Electrophysiol* 2003;14:455–7.

50. Kanda M, Shimizu W, Matsuo K, et al. Electrophysiologic characteristics and implications of induced ventricular fibrillation in symptomatic patients with Brugada syndrome. *J Am Coll Cardiol* 2002;39:1799–805.

51. Chen Q, Kirsch GE, Zhang D, et al. Genetic basis and molecular mechanism for idiopathic ventricular fibrillation. *Nature* 1998;392:293–6.

52. Balser JR, The cardiac sodium channel: gating function and molecular pharmacology. *J Mol Cell Cardiol* 2001;33:599–613.

53. Kurita T, Shimizu W, Inagaki M, et al. The electrophysiologic mechanism of ST-segment elevation in Brugada syndrome. *J Am Coll Cardiol* 2002;40:330–4.

54. Yan GX and Antzelevitch C. Cellular basis for the Brugada syndrome and other mechanisms of arrhythmogenesis associated with ST-segment elevation. *Circulation* 1999;100:1660–6.

55. Clancy CE and Rudy Y. Na+ channel mutation that causes both Brugada and long-QT syndrome phenotypes: a simulation study of mechanism. *Circulation* 2002;105:1208–13.

56. Burke A, Creighton W, Mont E, et al. Role of SCN5A Y1102 polymorphism in sudden cardiac death in blacks. *Circulation* 2005;112:798–802.

57. Glatter KA, Wang Q, Keating M, et al. Effectiveness of sotalol treatment in symptomatic Brugada syndrome. *Am J Cardiol* 2004;93:1320–2.

58. Kakishita M, Kurita T, Matsuo K, et al. Mode of onset of ventricular fibrillation in patients with Brugada syndrome detected by implantable cardioverter defibrillator therapy. *J Am Coll Cardiol* 2000;36:1646–53.

59. Laitinen PJ, Brown KM, Piippo K, et al. Mutations of the cardiac ryanodine receptor (RyR2) gene in familial polymorphic ventricular tachycardia. *Circulation* 2001;103:485–90.

60. Swan H, Piippo K, Viitasalo M, et al. Arrhythmic disorder mapped to chromosome 1q42-q43 causes malignant polymorphic ventricular tachycardia in structurally normal hearts. *J Am Coll Cardiol* 1999;34:2035–42.

61. Priori SG, Napolitano C, Memmi M, et al. Clinical and molecular characterization of patients with catecholaminergic polymorphic ventricular tachycardia. *Circulation* 2002;106:69–74.

62. Priori SG, Napolitano C, Tiso N, et al. Mutations in the cardiac ryanodine receptor gene (hRyR2) underlie catecholaminergic polymorphic ventricular tachycardia. *Circulation* 2001;103:196–200.

63. Leenhardt A, Lucet V, Denjoy I, et al. Catecholaminergic polymorphic ventricular tachycardia in children. A 7-year follow-up of 21 patients. *Circulation* 1995;91:1512–9.

64. Lahat H, Eldar M, Levy-Nissenbaum E, et al. Autosomal recessive catecholamine- or exercise-induced polymorphic ventricular tachycardia. *Circulation* 2001;103:2822–7.

65. Fisher JD, Krikler D, Hallidie-Smith KA. Familial polymorphic ventricular arrhythmias: a quarter century of successful medical treatment based on serial exercise-pharmacologic testing. *J Am Coll Cardiol* 1999;34:2015–22.

66. Tunwell RE, Wickenden C, Bertrand BM, et al. The human cardiac muscle ryanodine receptor-calcium release channel: identification, primary structure and topological analysis. *Biochem J* 1996;318:477–87.

67. Corrado D, Basso C, Thiene G. Arrhythmogenic right ventricular cardiomyopathy: diagnosis, prognosis, and treatment. *Heart* 2000;83:588–95.

68. Fontaine G, Fontaliran F, Hebert JL, et al. Arrhythmogenic right ventricular dysplasia. *Annu Rev Med* 1999;50:17–35.

69. Thiene G, Basso C. Arrhythmogenic right ventricular cardiomyopathy: an update. *Cardiovasc Pathol* 2001;May–Jun;10:109–17.

70. Thiene G, Nava A, Corrado D, et al. Right ventricular cardiomyopathy and sudden death in young people. *N Engl J Med* 1988;318:129–33.

71. Nava A, Bauce B, Basso C, et al. Clinical profile and long-term follow-up of 37 families with arrhythmogenic right ventricular cardiomyopathy. *J Am Coll Cardiol* 2000;36:2226–33.

72. Corrado D, Basso C, Thiene G, et al. Spectrum of clinicopathologic manifestations of arrhythmogenic right ventricular cardiomyopathy/dysplasia: a multicenter study. *J Am Coll Cardiol* 1997;30:1512–20.

73. McKenna WJ, Thiene G, Nava A, et al. Diagnosis of arrhythmogenic right ventricular dysplasia/cardiomyopathy. *Br Heart J* 1994;71:215–8.

74. Obata H, Mitsuoka T, Kikuchi Y, et al. Twenty-seven-year follow-up of arrhythmogenic right ventricular dysplasia. *Pacing Clin Electrophysiol* 2001;24:510–1.

75. Dalla Volta S, Battaglia G, Zerbini E. "Auricularization" of right ventricular pressure curve. *Am Heart J* 1961;61:25–33.

76. Fontaine G, Guiraudon G, Frank R, et al. Stimulation studies and epicardial mapping in ventricular tachycardia: study of mechanisms and selection for surgery. In: Kulbertus HE, ed. *Reentrant Arrhythmias: Mechanisms and Treatment.* Lancaster: MTP Press;1977:334–50.

77. Corrado D, Fontaine G, Marcus FI, et al. Arrhythmogenic right ventricular dysplasia/cardiomyopathy: need for an international registry. *Circulation* 2000;101:E101–6.

78. Basso C, Thiene G, Corrado D, et al. Arrhythmogenic right ventricular cardiomyopathy. Dysplasia, dystrophy, or myocarditis? *Circulation* 1996;94:983–91.

79. Midiri M, Finazzo M, Brancato M, et al. Arrhythmogenic right ventricular dysplasia: MR features. *Eur Radiol* 1997;7:307–12.

80. Tandri H, Calkins H, Nasir K, et al. Magnetic resonance imaging findings in patients meeting task force criteria for arrhythmogenic right ventricular dysplasia. *J Cardiovasc Electrophysiol* 2003;14: 476–82.

81. Danieli GA and Rampazzo A. Genetics of arrhythmogenic right ventricular cardiomyopathy. *Curr Opin Cardiol* 2002;17:218–21.

82. Rampazzo A, Nava A, Danieli GA, et al. The gene for arrhythmogenic right ventricular cardiomyopathy maps to chromosome 14q23-q24. *Hum Mol Genet* 1994;3:959–62.

83. Ahmad F, Li D, Karibe A, et al. Localization of a gene responsible for arrhythmogenic right ventricular dysplasia to chromosome 3p23. *Circulation* 1998;98:2791–5.

84. Li D, Ahmad F, Gardner MJ, et al. The locus of a novel gene responsible for arrhythmogenic right-ventricular dysplasia characterized by early onset and high penetrance maps to chromosome 10p12-p14. *Am J Hum Genet* 2000;66:148–56.

85. Melberg A, Oldfors A, Blomstrom-Lundqvist C, et al. Autosomal dominant myofibrillar myopathy with arrhythmogenic right ventricular cardiomyopathy linked to chromosome 10q. *Ann Neurol* 1999;46:684–92.

86. Protonotarios N, Tsatsopoulou A, Patsourakos P, et al. Cardiac abnormalities in familial palmoplantar keratosis. *Br Heart J* 1986;56:321–6.

87. Norgett EE, Hatsell SJ, Carvajal-Huerta L, et al. Recessive mutation in desmoplakin disrupts desmoplakin-intermediate filament interactions and causes dilated cardiomyopathy, woolly hair and keratoderma. *Hum Mol Genet* 2000;9:2761–6.

88. Link MS, Wang PJ, Haugh CJ, et al. Arrhythmogenic right ventricular dysplasia: clinical results with implantable cardioverter defibrillators. *J Interv Card Electrophysiol* 1997;1:41–8.

89. Fontaine G, Tonet J, Gallais Y, et al. Ventricular tachycardia catheter ablation in arrhythmogenic right ventricular dysplasia: a 16-year experience. *Curr Cardiol Rep* 2000;2:498–506.

90. Teare D. Asymmetrical hypertrophy of the heart in young adults. *Br Heart J* 1958;20:1–18.

91. Braunwald E, Lambrew CT, Rockoff D, et al. Idiopathic hypertrophic subaortic stenosis. *Circulation* 1964;30 (suppl IV):3–217.

92. Maron BJ. Hypertrophic cardiomyopathy: A systematic review. *JAMA* 2002;287:1308–20.

93. Maron BJ, Bonow RO, Cannon RO, et al. Hypertrophic cardiomyopathy. Interrelations of clinical manifestations, pathophysiology, and therapy. *N Engl J Med* 1987;316:780–9.

94. Maron BJ, Gardin JM, Flack JM, et al. Prevalence of hypertrophic cardiomyopathy in a general population of young adults. *Circulation* 1995;92:785–9.

95. Maron BJ, Epstein SE. Hypertrophic cardiomyopathy: a discussion of nomenclature. *Am J Cardiol* 1979;43:1242–4.

96. Klues HG, Schiffers A, Maron BJ. Phenotypic spectrum and patterns of left ventricular hypertrophy in hypertrophic cardiomyopathy. *J Am Coll Cardiol* 1995;26:1699–1708.

97. Spirito P, Seidman CE, McKenna WJ, et al. The management of hypertrophic cardiomyopathy. *N Engl J Med* 1997;336:775–85.

98. Maron BJ. Hypertrophic cardiomyopathy. *Lancet* 1997;350:127–33.

99. Spirito P, Bellone P, Harris KM, et al. Magnitude of left ventricular hypertrophy predicts the risk of sudden death in hypertrophic cardiomyopathy. *N Engl J Med* 2000;342:1778–85.

100. Louie EK, Maron BJ. Hypertrophic cardiomyopathy with extreme increase in left ventricular wall thickness. *J Am Coll Cardiol* 1986;8:57–65.

101. Elliott PM, Gimeno Blanes JR, Mahon NG, et al. Relation between severity of left-ventricular hypertrophy and prognosis in patients with hypertrophic cardiomyopathy. *Lancet* 2001;357:420–4.

102. Maron BJ, Roberts WC. Quantitative analysis of cardiac muscle cell disorganization in the ventricular septum of patients with hypertrophic cardiomyopathy. *Circulation* 1979;59:689–706.

103. Ferrans VJ, Morrow AG, Roberts WC. Myocardial ultrastructure in idiopathic hypertrophic subaortic stenosis. *Circulation* 1972;45:769–92.

104. St. John Sutton MG, Lie JT, Anderson KR, et al. Histopathological specificity of hypertrophic obstructive cardiomyopathy. *Br Heart J* 1980;44:433–43.

105. Varnava AM, Elliott PM, Mahon N, et al. Relation between myocyte disarray and outcome in hypertrophic cardiomyopathy. *Am J Cardiol* 2001;88:275–9.

106. Maron BJ, Anan TJ, Roberts WC. Quantitative analysis of the distribution of cardiac muscle cell disorganization in the left ventricular wall of patients with hypertrophic cardiomyopathy. *Circulation* 1981;63:882–94.

107. Maron BJ, Epstein SE, Roberts WC. Hypertrophic cardiomyopathy and transmural myocardial infarction without significant atherosclerosis of the extramural coronary arteries. *Am J Cardiol* 1979;43:1086–1102.

108. Basso C, Thiene G, Corrado D, et al. Hypertrophic cardiomyopathy and sudden death in the young: pathologic evidence of myocardial ischemia. *Hum Pathol* 2000;31:988–98.

109. Elliott PM, Poloniecki J, Dickie S, et al. Sudden death in hypertrophic cardiomyopathy: identification of high risk patients. *J Am Coll Cardiol* 2000;36:2212–8.

110. Maron BJ, Olivotto I, Spirito P, et al. Epidemiology of hypertrophic cardiomyopathy-related death: revisited in a large non-referral-based patient population. *Circulation* 2000;102:858–64.

111. McKenna WJ, England D, Doi YL, et al. Arrhythmia in hypertrophic cardiomyopathy. *Br Heart J* 1981;46:168–72.

112. Watkins H. Sudden death in hypertrophic cardiomyopathy. *N Engl J Med* 2000;342:422–4.

113. Maron BJ, Shen WK, Link MS, et al. Efficacy of implantable cardioverter-defibrillators for the prevention of sudden death in patients with hypertrophic cardiomyopathy. *N Engl J Med* 2000;342:365–73.

114. Seidman JG, Seidman C. The genetic basis for cardiomyopathy: from mutation identification to mechanistic paradigms. *Cell* 2001;104:557–67.

115. Geisterfer-Lowrance AA, Kass S, Tanigawa G, et al. A molecular basis for familial hypertrophic cardiomyopathy: a beta-cardiac myosin heavy chain gene missense mutation. *Cell* 1990;62:999–1006.

116. Watkins H, McKenna WJ, Thierfelder L, et al. Mutations in the genes for cardiac troponin T and alpha-tropomyosin in hypertrophic cardiomyopathy. *N Engl J Med* 1995;332:1058–64.

117. Watkins H, Rosenzweig A, Hwang DS, et al. Characteristics and prognostic implications of myosin missense mutations in familial hypertrophic cardiomyopathy. *N Engl J Med* 1992;326:1108–14.

118. Marian AJ. Pathogenesis of diverse clinical and pathological phenotypes in hypertrophic cardiomyopathy. *Lancet* 2000;355:58–60.

119. Moolman JC, Corfield VA, Posen B, et al. Sudden death due to troponin T mutations. *J Am Coll Cardiol* 1997;29:549–55.

120. Enjuto M, Francino A, Navarro-Lopez F, et al. Malignant hypertrophic cardiomyopathy caused by Arg723Gly mutation in beta-myosin heavy chain gene. *J Mol Cell Cardiol* 2000;32:2307–13.

121. Tesson F, Richard P, Charron P, et al. Genotype-phenotype analysis in four families with mutations in the beta-myosin heavy chain gene responsible for familial hypertrophic cardiomyopathy. *Hum Mutat* 1998;12:385–92.

122. Spicer RL, Rocchini AP, Crowley DC, et al. Chronic verapamil therapy in pediatric and young adult patients with hypertrophic cardiomyopathy. *Am J Cardiol* 1984;53:1614–9.

123. Gilligan DM, Chan WL, Joshi J, et al. A double-blind, placebo-controlled crossover trial of nadolol and verapamil in mild and moderately symptomatic hypertrophic cardiomyopathy. *J Am Coll Cardiol* 1993;21:1672–9.

124. Lakkis NM, Nagueh SF, Dunn JK, et al. Nonsurgical septal reduction therapy for hypertrophic obstructive cardiomyopathy: one-year follow-up. *J Am Coll Cardiol* 2000;36:852–5.

125. Qin JX, Shiota T, Lever HM, et al. Outcome of patients with hypertrophic obstructive cardiomyopathy after percutaneous transluminal septal myocardial ablation and septal myectomy surgery. *J Am Coll Cardiol* 2001;38:1994–2000.

126. Tyler VE. *The Honest Herbal: A Sensible Guide to the Use of Herbs and Related Remedies*. 3rd ed. New York: Pharmaceutical Products Press;1993:119–20.

127. Sapru HN, Theoharides TC. Autonomic nervous system. In: Theoharides TC, ed. *Essentials of Pharmacology*. 2nd ed. Boston: Little, Brown; 1996:58.

128. Hoffman BB, Lefkowitz RJ. Catecholamines, sympathomimetic drugs, and adrenergic receptor antagonists. In: Hardman JG, Limbird LE, Molinoff PB, Ruddon RW, Gilman AG, eds. *Goodman and Gilman's The Pharmacological Basis of Therapeutics*. 9th ed. New York: McGraw-Hill;1996:221.

129. Pentel P. Toxicity of over-the-counter stimulants. *JAMA* 1984;252:1898–1903.

130. Samenuk D, Link MS, Homoud MK, et al. Adverse cardiovascular events temporally associated with ma huang, an herbal source of ephedrine. *Mayo Clin Proc* 2002;77:12–6.

131. Haller CA, Benowitz NL. Adverse cardiovascular and central nervous system events associated with dietary supplements containing ephedra alkaloids. *N Engl J Med* 2000;343:1833–8.

132. Gurley BJ, Gardner SF, Hubbard MA. Content versus label claims in ephedra-containing dietary supplements. *Am J Health Syst Pharm* 2000;57:963–9.

133. Karch SB. Use of ephedra-containing products and risk for hemorrhagic stroke. *Neurology* 2003;61:724–5.

134. Shekelle PG, Hardy ML, Morton SC, et al. Efficacy and safety of ephedra and ephedrine for weight loss and athletic performance. *JAMA* 2003;289:1537–45.

135. Foxford RJ, Sahlas D, Wingfeld KA. Vasospasm-induced stroke in a varsity athlete secondary to ephedrine ingestion. *Clin J Sport Med* 2003;13:183–5.

136. Wooltorton E, Sibbald B. Ephedra/ephedrine: cardiovascular and CNS effects. *CMAJ* 2002;166:633.

137. Blechman KM, Karch SB, Stephens BG. Demographic, pathologic, and toxicological profiles of 127 decedents testing positive for ephedrine alkaloids. *Forensic Sci Int* 2004;139:61–9.

138. Yu Q, Larson DF, Watson RR. Heart disease, methamphetamine, and AIDS. *Life Sci* 2003;73:129–40.

139. Swalwell CI, Davis GG. Methamphetamine as a risk factor for acute aortic dissection. *J Forensic Sci* 1999;44:23–6.

140. Turnipseed SD, Richards JR, Kirk JD, et al. Frequency of acute coronary syndrome in patients presenting to the emergency department with chest pain after methamphetamine use. *J Emerg Med* 2003;24:369–73.

141. Carson P, Oldroyd K, Phadke K. Myocardial infarction due to amphetamine. *Br Med J* 1987;294:1524–6.

142. Furst SR, Fallon SP, Reznik GN, et al. Myocardial infarction after inhalation of methamphetamine. *N Engl J Med* 1990;323:1147–8.

143. Bashour TT. Acute myocardial infarction resulting from amphetamine abuse: a spasm-thrombus interplay? *Am Heart J* 1994;128:1237–9.

144. Hong R, Matsuyama E, Nur K. Cardiomyopathy associated with the smoking of crystal methamphetamine. *JAMA* 1991;265:1152–4.

145. Call TD, Hartneck J, Dickinson WA, et al. Acute cardiomyopathy secondary to intravenous amphetamine abuse. *Ann Internal Med* 1982;97:559–60.

146. Karch SB, Stephens BG, Ho CH. Methamphetamine-related deaths in San Francisco: demographic, pathologic, and toxicologic profiles. *J Forensic Sci* 1999;44:359–68.

147. Benzaquen BS, Cohen V, Eisenberg MJ. Effects of cocaine on the coronary arteries. *Am Heart J* 2001;142:402–10.

148. Kloner RA, Hale S, Alker K, et al. The effects of acute and chronic cocaine use on the heart. *Circulation* 1992;85:407–19.

149. O'Brien CP. Drug addiction and drug abuse. In: JG Hardman and LE Limbird, Eds. *Goodman and Gilman's The Pharmacological Basis of Therapeutics.* 10th ed. New York: McGraw-Hill: 2001, 621–42.

150. Minor RL, Scott BD, Brown DD, et al. Cocaine-induced myocardial infarction in patients with normal coronary arteries. *Ann Intern Med* 1991;115:797–806.

151. Mittleman RE, Wetli CV. Cocaine and sudden "natural" death. *J Forensic Sci* 1987;32:11–9.

152. Rod JL, Zucker RP. Acute myocardial infarction shortly after cocaine inhalation. *Am J Cardiol* 1987;59:161.

153. Simpson RW, Edwards WD. Pathogenesis of cocaine-induced ischemic heart disease. *Arch Pathol Lab Med* 1986;110:479–84.

154. Cooke CT, Dowling GP. Cocaine-associated coronary thrombosis and myocardial ischemia. *Pathology* 1988;20:242, 305–6.

155. Kolodgie FD, Virmani R, Cornhill JF, et al. Increase in atherosclerosis and adventitial mast cells in cocaine abusers: an alternative mechanism of cocaine-associated coronary vasospasm and thrombosis. *J Am Coll Cardiol* 1991;17:1553–60.

156. Kogan MJ, Verebey KG, DePace AC, et al. Quantitative determination of benzoylecgonine and cocaine in human biofluids by gas-liquid chromatography. *Anal Chem* 1977;49:1965–9.

157. Zhang S, Rajamani S, Chen Y, et al. Cocaine blocks HERG, but not KvLQT1 + minK, potassium channels. *Mol Pharmacol* 2001;59;1069–76.
158. Higuchi R. Simple and rapid preparation of samples for PCR. In HA Ehrlich, Ed. *PCR Technology: Principles and Applications for DNA Amplification.* New York: Stockton Press: 1989, 31–38.
159. Bajanowski T, Rossi L, Biondo B, et al. Prolonged QT interval and sudden infant death — report of two cases. *Forensic Sci Int* 2001;115:147–53.
160. Sato Y, Sugie R, Tsuchiya B, et al. Comparison of the DNA extraction methods for polymerase chain reaction amplification from formalin-fixed and paraffin-embedded tissues. *Diagn Mol Pathol* 2001;10:265–71.
161. Cao W, Hashibe M, Rao JY, et al. Comparison of methods for DNA extraction from paraffin-embedded tissues and buccal cells. *Cancer Detect Prev* 2003;27;397–404.
162. Mygind T, Ostergaard L, Birkelund S, et al. Evaluation of five DNA extraction methods for purification of DNA from atherosclerotic tissue and estimation of prevalence of *Chlamydia pneumoniae* in tissue from a Danish population undergoing vascular repair. *BMC Microbiol* 2003;3:19.
163. Konomi N, Lebwohl E, Zhang D. Comparison of DNA and RNA extraction methods for mummified tissues. *Mol Cell Probes* 2002;16:445–51.
164. Bonin S, Petrera F, Niccolini B, et al. PCR analysis in archival postmortem tissues. *Mol Pathol* 2003;56:184–6.

CONTENTS

14.1 DUI DEFENSES

Alan Wayne Jones, D.Sc.[1] and Barry K. Logan, Ph.D.[2]
[1] Department of Forensic Toxicology, University Hospital, Linköping, Sweden
[2] Director, Washington State Toxicology Laboratory, Department of Laboratory Medicine, University of Washington, Seattle, Washington

After prohibition was abolished in the United States in 1933, consumption of alcohol escalated as did many of the negative consequences associated with too much drinking. Among other things, the number of alcohol-related accidents within the home, at work, and on the roads increased alarmingly.[1,2] Alcohol and transportation made a poor mix, and in efforts to curb this new wave of road-traffic accidents and deaths on the highways, more effective legislative measures were urgently needed.[3,4]

The first laws prohibiting driving under the influence of alcohol (DUI) appeared in the 1920s, but the criteria used to demonstrate impairment and unfitness to drive were not very sophisticated. These included the smell of alcohol on the breath, the ability of a person to walk a chalk line, and various behavioral signs and symptoms of inebriation.[5] Gaining a conviction for drunk driving was by no means certain, unless the suspect showed obvious signs and symptoms of gross intoxication.[6] It was strikingly obvious that more sensitive and more objective methods were needed to decide whether a person was under the influence of alcohol. Following the lead of some European countries, efforts in the U.S. were directed toward measuring the concentration of alcohol in blood and other body fluids as evidence of intoxication.[7] However, quantitative studies of the relationship between blood-alcohol and impairment were virtually nonexistent at this time.

These efforts led to the first statutory limits of blood alcohol concentration (BAC) for driving being set at 150 mg/dL (0.15 g/dL), a conservatively high level.[8,9] Subsequently, this threshold BAC for driving has progressively been lowered, first to 100 mg/dL (0.10 g/dL) and in all U.S. states the limit is now set at 80 mg/dL (0.08 g/dL).[10] For young (< 21 y) drivers an even lower BAC, so-called zero tolerance limits, has been sanctioned (0.00 to 0.02 g/dL).[11] Legal limits of blood alcohol concentration differ from country to country and also within regions of the same country, e.g. the various states in Australia.[12] Lowering the legal alcohol limits for driving even further is supported by many national and international medical societies including the American Medical Association.[13] Judging by recent trends in Europe, it seems that most countries are aiming for a threshold BAC limit of 50 mg/dL (0.05 g/dL); France approved a 0.05 g/dL limit in 1995, whereas Sweden adopted 0.02 g/dL in 1990.[12]

Punishment and sanctions for those found guilty of drunk driving have become increasingly severe and include suspension of the driver's license, heavy fines, and sometimes a mandatory term of imprisonment.[14–16] The first DUI statutes stipulated that the concentration of alcohol present in body fluids (blood, breath, or urine) was admissible as presumptive evidence of unfitness to drive, but that this was a rebuttable presumption.[4,6] In contrast, most of the DUI statutes in operation today are the so-called per se laws, under which the person's BAC or breath alcohol concentration (BrAC) is the sole deciding factor necessary as proof of unfitness to drive.[15,16] In short, a person can be found guilty of drunk driving without exhibiting visible signs of intoxication when alcohol concentration per se statutes are in operation.[16] This legal framework, whereby the concentration of alcohol in a specimen of blood or breath determines guilt or innocence, places high demands on the analytical methods used for forensic purposes. Moreover, pre-analytical factors such as sampling, transportation, storage and handling of specimens needs to be carefully regulated and controlled. The combined influences of per se legislation, the compelling objective standard of proof provided to juries in the numerical value of the BAC or BrAC result, and the increasingly harsh penalties imposed on those found guilty of DUI explain, at least in part, the vigorous defense attacks against prosecution evidence based on results of BAC or BrAC determinations.

Soon after chemical tests for intoxication were introduced and used on a large scale, the reliability of the approved methods and the results obtained were increasingly being questioned.[4] The practice of running duplicate determinations on the same specimen or obtaining two or more specimens of the same or different body fluids (e.g., blood and urine) and testing these by different analytical methods has much to recommend it.[14,15] Defending drinking drivers has become a popular business and many lawyers specialize in this area of jurisprudence. A plethora of textbooks and newsletters are available that provide detailed information about the science and law of DUI litigation.[17-21] These typically present recent examples of DUI case law, reviews and opinion of articles published in scientific peer-review journals, and hints and tips for developing more effective strategies for defending and also for prosecuting drunk drivers.[22]

This review article discusses the strengths and weaknesses of common DUI defense challenges. The work is subdivided into four main sections. The first deals with general attacks on potentially incriminating evidence, the second focuses on challenging results of urine alcohol analysis, the third deals with scrutiny of blood sampling and analysis, and the fourth section is concerned with the use of evidential breath-alcohol instruments. Procedural aspects of the DUI offense, such as whether the arresting police officer followed the correct protocol when the driver was apprehended, had reasonable suspicion or probable cause for making the arrest, conducted the field sobriety tests properly, or gave the appropriate warnings demanded by the local rules and regulations prior to administering the chemical test, are not considered. The chemistry and physiology of forensic alcohol testing are the main focus of this review and much of the perpetual nit-picking about procedural issues often raised in DUI litigation are omitted.

An extensive list of references is provided, and most citations refer to articles published in peer-review U.S. and European English language journals. However, a bimonthly journal from Germany called *Blutalkohol* (blood-alcohol), is worthy of note. *Blutalkohol* is published by Steintor-Verlag, Lübeck and the first volume appeared in 1962/63. This periodical contains a wealth of information about forensic aspects of alcohol with direct relevance to the defense and prosecution of DUI suspects. Although most of the articles are written in German, English summaries are provided.

14.1.1 General Challenges

14.1.1.1 *Drinking after the Offense*

A frequent defense tactic is one in which the suspect claims to have consumed alcohol after driving or being involved in an accident such as a single-vehicle crash; this approach is sometimes called the hip-flask ploy.[23,24] Prosecution for DUI must necessarily relate driving with the consumption of alcohol at a time before or during the driving. In these cases however it is alleged that the drinking took place after the driving, but prior to obtaining a specimen of blood or breath for forensic analysis. For example, hit-and-run drivers often manage to drive home. When eventually apprehended by the police, they might claim to have been sober during the driving but needed alcohol to "calm their nerves" or alleviate the condition of shock caused by "hitting a bird or cat," and the resulting damage to the car. Subjects will often insist they drank alcohol after driving, even when they cannot produce any empty or opened bottle of liquor or any other credible evidence such as eye witnesses to support their story. Some of the more experienced DUI offenders, especially repeat offenders, may carry a bottle of alcohol in their coat pocket or glove compartment, for the express purpose of being able to drink after driving; hence the origin of the term hip-flask defense. In some jurisdictions the prosecutor must prove beyond a reasonable doubt that the allegation of drinking after the offense was untrue, or that in spite of the alcohol consumed after driving the suspect's BAC or BrAC at the time of driving still exceeded the legal limit. This is often a difficult task.

To deal with alleged drinking after the offense, the prosecutor has several options available and should seek help from qualified forensic experts when preparing the case. First, it is important to consider the testimony of the police or other witnesses who might have observed the actual driving, or the behavior and general appearance of the suspect when arrested. Such observations as the smell of alcohol on the breath, slurred speech, or unsteady gait are important to document before the driver has had the opportunity to drink any more alcohol. In cases where the subject has allegedly consumed a large quantity of alcohol immediately before being apprehended by the police, one would also expect to see a dramatic and progressive onset of symptoms of intoxication. Second, information regarding the quantity of alcohol allegedly consumed after driving, the time of intake and the sex, age, height, and body weight of the suspect can be used to calculate the expected BAC.[22] If this approach is used, the suspect should be given the "benefit of any doubt" by assuming that at the time of sampling blood and breath, absorption and distribution from the post-incident ethanol consumption was complete.

The Widmark equation (see Chapter 5.2) is commonly used to calculate the expected BAC on the basis of the person's body weight and drinking pattern.[25,26] Making an adjustment for elimination of alcohol through metabolism between the time of starting to drink and the time of sampling blood is usually warranted, especially when several hours have elapsed between the time of the driving and the time of obtaining a blood-sample. In this way, a theoretical mean BAC and its 95% confidence interval can be compared with the analytical report from the forensic laboratory. The resulting difference in BAC, if any, should reflect the BAC that existed prior to the post-incident drinking, and therefore the BAC before or during driving. The use of a 95% confidence interval is a safeguard to allow for inter-individual variations in absorption, distribution, and elimination patterns of alcohol (see Chapter 5.2 for details). Grossly exaggerated claims of the amount of alcohol consumed after the offense, such as drinking a whole bottle of liquor in a relatively short time span, are clearly unrealistic and should be given little credibility.

The limitations of urine alcohol concentration (UAC) are dealt with in the next section; however, if the police manage to obtain samples of urine and blood shortly after driving, the magnitude of the UAC/BAC ratio can help resolve whether alcohol was ingested within approximately 1 h of taking the samples. This approach was tested empirically by Iffland et al.[27] who found that UAC/BAC ratios between 1.0 to 1.15 indicated fairly recent drinking whereas ratios larger than 1.2:1 indicate that the drinking began much earlier. This fits with the observation that during the absorption phase of alcohol kinetics, before equilibration has been reached, UAC is generally less than or equal to BAC. In the post-absorptive phase of alcohol metabolism, UAC is usually 1.3 to 1.5 times higher than BAC.[28,29] The concentration of alcohol in pooled bladder urine mirrors the average concentration prevailing in the blood during the formation of urine in the kidneys and storage in the bladder.[28] Because urine has about 20% more water than an equal volume of whole blood, the concentration of alcohol in newly secreted urine is about 20% higher than BAC and a urine/blood ratio of 1.2:1 should be expected. Dividing the measured UAC by 1.2 gives an estimate of the lowest BAC at the time of voiding or since the bladder was last emptied. Moreover, a UAC/BAC ratio exceeding 1.3 suggests that the bulk of the alcohol was already absorbed into the blood and distributed throughout total body water. Whenever the police suspect that a person will assert consumption of alcohol after driving, efforts should be made to obtain two specimens of urine about 30 to 60 min apart. If the UAC of the second void is higher than the first void then it seems reasonable to assume that absorption of alcohol from the stomach is not complete at the time of sampling. Such a finding would support the claim of recent consumption of alcohol. If the UAC decreases between the first and second void 30 to 60 min later, this suggests that the post-absorptive phase has become well established and the main part of the alcohol was imbibed at least 1 to 2 h earlier. [28,29]

If the ratio of UAC/BAC is less than or close to unity, this supports the contention of recent consumption of alcohol and the BAC curve was probably still rising, or near the peak. If an alcohol-free pool of urine existed in the bladder before drinking started, this would tend to dilute the concentration of alcohol in primary urine secreted into the bladder and might suggest a rising UAC between the two successive voids, even though in reality the BAC curve was in the post-peak phase. Alternatively, evaluating the change in BAC between the times of taking two blood samples 30 to 60 min apart gives a good indication of whether a rising or falling BAC existed at the time of sampling.[30]

Forensic toxicologists in Germany have developed another way to deal with allegations of drinking after the offense and this method has become known as congener analysis.[31–34] In brief, this method entails analyzing the alcoholic beverage the suspect claims to have consumed after driving with the aim of identifying other volatile constituents besides ethanol. Pure ethanol does have a distinctive odor, although these other congeners (non-ethanol volatiles) produced during the fermentation process help impart the distinctive smell and flavor to the drink.[31] The results of the congener analysis are then compared with the volatiles present in a sample of blood or urine taken from the suspect in an attempt to match the components. Methanol, 1-propanol, 2-butanol, and 2-methyl-1-propanol are typical examples of congener alcohols that can be identified in body fluids depending on the particular kind of beverage consumed.[32] The results of congener analysis, together with other information, has been accepted by the courts in Germany when dealing with hit-and-run drivers who frequently claim drinking after the offense.[31–34] The usefulness of analyzing methanol as a congener in forensic casework is limited by the fact that this alcohol is produced naturally in the body and its concentration in body fluids increases after ingestion of ethanol because of competition for the metabolizing enzyme alcohol dehydrogenase.[35–37] Furthermore, if the beverage consumed before the incident is the same as that allegedly consumed afterwards, the congeners will be the same and this approach would not work.

Claims of drinking after the offense can be counteracted by appropriate legislation. For example, in Norway it is a separate offense for a motorist to consume alcohol within 6 hours of driving if there is good reason to believe that the police will want to investigate some event related to the driving. Thus, drinking within 6 h of an accident to reach a BAC in excess of the legal limit carries the same penalty as being found guilty of drunk driving (Norwegian traffic law, paragraph 22). Without this kind of legislation, the magnitude of the UAC/BAC ratio and the change in BAC between successive samples, or UAC between two successive voids, provides useful information to evaluate whether or not a person has consumed alcohol within an hour or so before taking the samples. Knowledge of the stage of alcohol kinetics is important not only in cases of alleged drinking after the offense but also when asked to engage in retrograde extrapolation of BAC to an earlier time. Accurate back-tracking of BAC to the time of driving is fraught with difficulties, and only an approximate result, and likely range of values is possible, based on known population averages for rate of alcohol elimination. Again, the need to back extrapolate can be avoided by statutory definition of the relevant BAC for prosecution as that existing at the time of sampling or within 2 to 3 h of the driving.

14.1.1.2 Laced Drinks

The "laced drinks" defense is another challenge that arises during prosecution of drunk drivers in their attempts to avoid punishment for DUI.[17,19–21] The usual story is that a friend or associate has added liquor (usually vodka) to a non-alcoholic drink or to beer when the person concerned was otherwise engaged or distracted. Another spin on this scenario is where the suspect has been invited to consume some kind of homemade beverage which was not recognized as containing a high alcohol content because the taste was masked by strong fruit flavoring. Unintentional intoxication through the over-consumption of alcohol-containing chocolates or alcohol-soaked fruit have also been documented. Only later, after being apprehended for DUI, was it apparent to the people in these cases that the drink must have contained an unusually high concentration of alcohol, which was not obvious from the taste. The subjective intoxication effects of alcohol differ widely among different individuals and this allows the defendant to argue that he or she was driving with a BAC above the limit but without intent, which although not a complete defense, may have some mitigating value.

Widmark calculations (see Chapter 5.2) are commonly used to estimate the BAC expected from the amount of alcohol inadvertently consumed in the laced drink.[24,25] However, relating a given BAC to a precise degree of intoxication is difficult because of the wide variations in consumption and concentration tolerance between different individuals. Dram-shop laws in the U.S. place responsibility on the host at the party, or the owner of the bar for damages caused by a drunk driver if that person was served alcohol while he or she was visibly intoxicated.[17-22] In a well-documented laced drinks case, a woman was acquitted after driving with a BAC of 0.17 g/dL. She admitted drinking from a "punch bowl" when visiting the home of some friends, although she denied knowledge of the fact that the drink was laced with 96% v/v ethanol, and claimed not to feel any definite impairment effects of alcohol despite the high BAC. The medicolegal experts called by the court refused to state with certainty that the woman must have felt under the influence of alcohol at a BAC of 0.17 g/dL. On appeal to the high court, the woman was acquitted of willfully driving under the influence. The prosecutor approached the supreme court but permission to review the case was refused.[38] The trend toward introducing lower legal limits and zero tolerance laws for young people should make the laced drinks defense, and thus driving over the limit without intent, a much more common defense tactic. This follows because of the great difficulty in recognizing symptoms of intoxication at very low BAC levels such as 0.02 g/dL where impairment may be minimal. The same applies to driving in the morning following an evening of heavy drinking, when low per se illegal concentrations of alcohol are enforced.

14.1.1.3 *Rising Blood-Alcohol Concentration*

Some DUI suspects argue that their BAC or BrAC was below the legal limit at the time of driving, but that the concentration of alcohol had risen to exceed the legal alcohol limit at the time of obtaining the samples for analysis. In short, if the prosecution BAC was 0.12 g/dL at the time of the test, it might be suggested that it was below 0.08 g/dL at the time of driving some time earlier.[39,40] The key question here is by how much can the BAC or BrAC rise after the last drink? To answer this question, details of the subject's drinking pattern before or during the driving, as well as the various time elements and intake of food, should be carefully investigated. The pharmacokinetics of alcohol show large inter-individual variations especially when small doses are taken after a meal.[41,42] This challenge is known as the rising BAC defense and the usual scenario according to the defendant is that he or she was engaged in moderate social drinking for several hours after work, perhaps with a meal or eating bar snacks. For some unexplained, and physiologically improbable reason, the alcohol ingested during the evening remained unabsorbed in the stomach until the person decided to leave for home or drive to the next bar. Shortly after driving the person is either involved in a collision or pulled over by the police because of a moving traffic offense, and in this connection is arrested for DUI. The defendant then claims that between the time of being apprehended and the time of providing the blood or breath-alcohol test, the alcohol in the stomach became absorbed into the blood, bringing the person over the legal limit.

Obviously, this scenario is unreasonable because alcohol, unlike many other drugs, starts to become absorbed from the stomach immediately following ingestion. Gastric emptying accelerates this process and leads to a rapid onset of the effects of alcohol on the brain. Indeed, people indulge in drinking primarily to experience alcohol's enjoyable pharmacological effects such as euphoria, relaxation, and diminished social inhibitions. In order for this to happen, the alcohol must become absorbed into the bloodstream and transported to the brain. The intoxicating effects of alcohol are more pronounced during the rising limb of the BAC profile, and people would surely be surprised if they had been consuming drinks for several hours without experiencing any effect! Unfortunately, only a handful of studies have looked at the pharmacokinetics of alcohol under real-world drinking conditions to establish, for a large number of subjects, the degree of rise in BAC and the time needed to reach the peak after the last drink.

Gullberg[43] reported a study in which 39 subjects drank various quantities of alcohol under real-world drinking conditions. The mean time required to reach the peak BAC after end of drinking was 19 min (span 0 to 80 min) and 81% of subjects reached a peak within 30 min. A study reported by Shajani and Dinn[44] also gives a clue to the time needed to reach peak BAC under social drinking conditions. In 8 men and 8 women who consumed known amounts of alcohol according to choice, the maximum BAC was reached 35 min (span 17 to 68 min) after end of intake. Taken together these studies and a few others suggest the low probability that the result of a blood or breath-alcohol test made some time after driving will be higher than at the time of driving which is often 1 to 2 h earlier. Zink and Reinhardt[45] made an important contribution when they allowed heavy drinkers to consume very large amounts of alcohol over periods of 6 to 10 h, resulting in peak BAC's in the range 0.10 to 0.38 g/dL. Venous blood was taken for analysis of alcohol at 15 min intervals during and after the drinking spree. In this way accurate information was obtained about the shape of the concentration-time profile and the time of reaching the peak as well as rise in BAC after the last drink. Importantly, they found that half the individuals had reached their peak BAC even before the last drink was taken (i.e., the rate of elimination exceeds the rate of consumption). The longest time necessary to reach a peak was 50 min after end of drinking (mean ± SD, 7.7 ± 22.9 minutes), and when a rise in BAC occurred between the end of drinking and the peak BAC it was invariably less than 0.02 g/dL. This study has important ramifications because many DUI suspects have blood-alcohol concentrations in this high range when they are apprehended.

Drinking alcohol together with a large meal was studied by Jones and Neri[42] who found that under these conditions, although the peak BAC was attained soon after the end of drinking for most subjects, a BAC plateau developed, and for some the BAC remained fairly constant for 2 to 3 h. Interestingly, in 10 of these subjects, 70% of the peak BAC had been attained within 15 min after the end of drinking. More studies are needed delineating the absorption kinetics of alcohol for different drinking conditions, with different beverages and formulations and with fast and slow ingestion of alcohol, on an empty stomach and after a meal.

Although a person's BAC or BrAC at the time of driving or when a road-traffic accident occurred might be considered the most relevant result for prosecution, it is fairly obvious that estimating this value can involve much uncertainty. This follows because the blood or breath-test is often made 1 to 2 h after the driving and there is a wide variation in absorption, distribution, and elimination patterns of alcohol in individual DUI suspects. Much can be gained by statutory definition of the relevant BAC or BrAC as that prevailing at the time of the chemical test and not at the time of driving. Unfortunately, many jurisdictions persist with using the BAC or BrAC at the time of driving as the relevant figure needed for prosecution of DUI suspects. Other jurisdictions accept the chemical test result, provided it was obtained within 2 h of the driving, as being equivalent to the BAC at the time of driving. Samples of blood or breath taken outside this time frame require the prosecution to estimate the BAC or BrAC prevailing at the time of driving. This entails making a back extrapolation of BAC from time of sampling to the time of driving and this calculation is always subject to much uncertainty. In cases where the statutory period of 2 or 3 h between the driving and the time of the test is exceeded, error in back extrapolation can be minimized (in the defendant's favor), by only extrapolating back to the end of the 2- or 3-h period.

Provided the subject was in the post-peak phase of alcohol absorption-distribution at the time of driving and at the time of sampling blood, extrapolating back with a conservative alcohol burn-off rate, such as 0.008 to 0.010 g/dL per hour, can be defended. Other safeguards against overestimation include an adjustment for absorption of alcohol contained in the last drink, and allowing for the possibility of a BAC concentration plateau existing, during which time the BAC remains more or less constant for several hours, as sometimes happens if alcohol is ingested together with a large meal. Other reasonable approaches include the use of population mean elimination rates, with 95% confidence intervals to establish the most likely upper and lower limits of BAC.

A recent study of double blood samples from 1090 DUI suspects arrived at a mean alcohol burn-off rate of 0.019 g/dL per hour with 95% limits of agreement, spanning from 0.009 to 0.029 g/dL/h.[46] These results suggest that making a back estimation of a person's BAC over long periods of time and assuming a relatively low and constant burn-off rate such as 0.008 to 0.01 g/dL/h will lead to a large underestimate of the BAC at the time in question, but always in the defendant's favor. While this approach gives a definite advantage to the suspect, the practice of making a back estimation of a person's BAC is inevitably a controversial issue in DUI litigation and should be avoided whenever possible.[47–50]

14.1.1.4 *Pathological States and Ethanol Pharmacokinetics*

The pharmacokinetics of many prescription drugs have been carefully investigated in patients suffering from various diseases.[51–53] Much less work has been done concerning the influence of disease states on absorption, distribution, and metabolism of the social drug ethanol. DUI suspects sometimes claim however that they suffer from certain medical conditions or pathological states, which they hope might explain their BAC being above the legal limit for driving. Various claims of this kind have been documented such as liver cirrhosis, kidney failure, or absence of a kidney or one lobe of the lung. Because only 2 to 5% of the total quantity of alcohol consumed is excreted in urine and breath, reduced efficiency of the lungs or kidney has marginal effect on the total amount of alcohol eliminated from the body. The rate of alcohol elimination from blood in patients with kidney failure scheduled for hemodialysis was no different from the burn-off rate in healthy control subjects.[54]

Major surgery to the gastro-intestinal tract, such as gastrectomy, is known to cause a more rapid absorption of alcohol leading to an overshoot peak, which tends to be somewhat higher than the maximum BAC expected.[55–57] A similar phenomenon is often observed when drinking neat liquor on an empty stomach.[41] However, 1 to 2 h after drinking ends, the BAC should approach the value expected for the dose of alcohol ingested and the person's gender and body weight because alcohol has now had sufficient time to equilibrate in the total body water. The rate of absorption of alcohol shows wide inter-individual variations even in apparently healthy individuals, and estimating the peak BAC from amount consumed is subject to considerable uncertainty.[41] Jokipii[58] devoted his thesis work to comparing blood-alcohol profiles under controlled conditions in healthy subjects and in those with various diseases (liver cirrhosis, acute hepatitis, hyperthyreosis, diabetes mellitus, and neurocirculatory asthenia or dystonia). This publication is unfortunately not widely available, although its salient features were reviewed with the conclusion that these particular pathological states did not cause distorted alcohol burn-off rates or abnormal distribution volumes of ethanol compared with healthy control subjects.[59]

Drunk drivers with de facto diseased liver, such as alcohol hepatitis or cirrhosis, insist that this renders them slow metabolizers of ethanol compared with individuals having normal liver function. Controlled studies of the effect of various liver diseases on the rate of disappearance of alcohol from blood are rather sparse. Ethical issues preclude embarking on detailed investigations of this topic. Those few studies available do not support the notion of a slower rate of metabolism outside the limits of 0.009 to 0.025 g/dL/h seen in healthy individuals.[60–63] Moreover, results of alcohol drinking experiments in patients with cirrhosis are often confounded by the problem of malnutrition in these binge drinkers. This also leads to a slower elimination rate of alcohol from blood.[52,63] In patients with cirrhosis and severe portal hypertension, where part of the blood is forced to bypass the liver, there is some evidence to suggest a slower rate of ethanol disappearance (0.007 g/dL/h). The reason for this finding is probably diminished flow of blood to the alcohol metabolizing enzymes, and not so much necrosis of the liver tissue.[64]

People suffering from chronic liver disease often accumulate a fluid in the peritoneal cavity called ascites.[65,66] Indeed, ascites is one consequence of long-term abuse of alcohol and alcohol-induced cirrhosis. Because the ascites fluid is mainly water, this furnishes a body fluid reservoir for ethanol, thus increasing the person's volume of distribution. The volume of ascites fluid can vary widely between different individuals, and up to 5 liters is not uncommon. An increased total body water in patients with ascites raises the volume of distribution for other hydrophilic drugs besides ethanol. The concentration of alcohol in ascites will be closer to the concentration in plasma and serum than in whole blood. When alcohol has been cleared from the blood circulation the pool of alcohol in the ascites fluid can redistribute back into the bloodstream. However, alcohol cannot concentrate in this fluid space and ascites fluid should therefore contain approximately 10 to 20% more alcohol than an equal volume of whole blood. Like the situation with urine (see Chapter 5.2), there should also be a time-lag in the clearance of the alcohol from ascites fluid compared with blood.

Most of the scientific evidence indicates that alcoholics generally tend to metabolize alcohol faster than moderate drinkers owing to induction of the microsomal enzyme denoted P4502E1, sd one of the consequences of long-term heavy drinking.[67] In a recent study in alcoholics undergoing detoxification with initial BACs of 0.20 to 0.45 g/dL, the burn-off rate (β-slopes) ranged from 0.013 to 0.036 g/dL/h with an average of 0.022 g/dL/h.[68] A similar mean value was reported when the work of several research groups based in Germany were compiled together; average elimination rate 0.022 ± 0.005 g/dL/h (mean ± SD).[69] Many DUI suspects are clearly alcoholics, and in a study of 1090 apprehended drunk drivers from whom two blood samples were taken 60 min apart, the mean β-slope was 0.019 g/dL/h with 95% limits of agreement of 0.009 to 0.029 g/dL/h, being in close agreement with values for alcoholics during detoxification.[46]

Individuals suffering from diabetes mellitus with impaired glucose metabolism might have elevated concentrations of ketone bodies, including acetone, circulating in their blood. Note that the acetone produced can also become reduced to isopropanol in the liver through the alcohol dehydrogenase pathway.[70] However, when modern gas chromatographic (GC) methods are used for blood alcohol analysis, acetone and isopropanol are easily distinguished, so defense challenges directed at the lack of specificity of GC methods are therefore pointless if two or more different stationary phases are used for the chromatography.[71] There is no evidence to suggest that the rate of ethanol metabolism should be any different in people suffering from diabetes compared with healthy control subjects.[72,73] The metabolic disturbances associated with insulin-dependent diabetes are not related to the enzymes involved in the disposal of ethanol.[74] Total body water and activity of alcohol dehydrogenase enzymes decreases in states of malnutrition and protein deficiency, and this is reflected in slower burn-off rates of alcohol.[75,76] However, moderate losses of body water after prolonged sauna bathing did not result in any marked differences in the shape of blood-alcohol profiles.[77] A low relative TBW/kg body weight is associated with a smaller volume of distribution for ethanol and this explains the well known male-female difference in peak BAC and area under the curve for the same dose of alcohol administered per kg body weight.[78] The distribution volume of ethanol was shown to decrease in male subjects between the ages of 20 to 60 years along with a decrease in total body water in the elderly.[79]

People involved in traffic accidents might be badly injured and suffer from shock and hemorrhage owing to massive losses of blood. This raises the question about the influence of trauma and shock on the hepatic metabolism of alcohol and the resulting blood-alcohol profiles.[80–82] In a recent study with 10 subjects involved in accidents when under the influence of alcohol, and suffering from poly-traumatic shock, a series of venous and arterial blood samples were obtained for determination of ethanol.[83] The rate of alcohol disappearance from blood ranged from 0.017 to 0.021 g/dL/h (mean 0.018 g/dL/h) and these values were the same regardless of whether arterial or venous blood sampling sites were used. The results of this study confirm many other anecdotes and case reports regarding alcohol pharmacokinetics in people injured when drunk.[80–82] Hypovolemic shock following massive loss of blood will result in a redistribution of body fluids and higher proportions of plasma enter the intravascular space to maintain an effective circulation and tissue perfusion.[84] This might alter the relative distribution of some protein-bound drugs and endogenous substances between body compartments, but the concentration of alcohol in the blood is not markedly influenced.[85,86] Nevertheless, some people continue to speculate about the impact of trauma on blood-alcohol concentrations and alcohol burn-off rates, even though a careful review of the literature shows that there is no substance to these opinions.[87]

14.1.1.5 Drug-Alcohol Interactions

The intake of various tonics (elixirs), cough syrups, over-the-counter medications, or even foodstuffs that might contain alcohol, will obviously result in alcohol appearing in the blood.[88] Some cough medicines, vitamin mixtures, pick-me-ups, and other health-store products may contain considerable quantities of alcohol (>10% v/v), and overdosing with these products will obviously elevate a person's BAC. By how much the BAC rises will depend on the quantities consumed and the time frame in relation to driving. Medication taken in tablet form or drugs applied externally can hardly be expected to lead to alcohol appearing in the blood. Psycho-pharmacological agents such as benzodiazepine derivatives may cause increased impairment when taken together with alcohol because of interaction at the GABA receptor complex in the brain.[89] However, there is no evidence to suggest that the resulting BAC will be any different from that expected if the same dose of alcohol had been taken without the drug.[90]

Intake of alcohol can modify the pharmacokinetics and behavioral effects of drugs that are metabolized by P4502E1 enzymes or that interact with the GABA receptor to elicit their effects on the central nervous system.[91] However, these changes do not result in an altered alcohol pharmacokinetics or a raised BAC above that obtained in control experiments when the same dose of alcohol was consumed on an empty stomach. One drug that does block the metabolism of alcohol is 4-methyl pyrazole (4-MP), which competes with ethanol for binding sites on the primary metabolizing enzyme ADH.[92] However 4-MP is not prescribed by physicians even though it may have legitimate therapeutic uses in the treatment of patients poisoned with methanol or ethylene glycol.[93,94]

14.1.1.6 Gastric Alcohol Dehydrogenase

The enzyme mainly responsible for the metabolism of alcohol is called alcohol dehydrogenase (ADH) and this is located primarily in the liver and to a minor extent also in other organs and tissue such as the kidney and the mucosa of the stomach.[95] Recent studies have shown that gastric ADH is seemingly less active in women compared with men and also in alcoholics compared with moderate drinkers, and the overall activity decreases with advancing age.[96] About 20 years ago the suspicion arose that part of the dose of alcohol consumed was metabolized in the stomach by gastric ADH. This process was known as pre-systemic metabolism or first-pass effect. This meant that the effective dose of alcohol reaching the systemic circulation depended on the efficacy of gastric ADH enzymes. Sex-related differences in gastric ADH offered another mechanism to explain why women reach a higher peak BAC than men for the same dose of alcohol.[97] If a part of the dose of ethanol is metabolized by gastric ADH, this would also explain the observation of a smaller area under the BAC-time profile after oral intake compared with intravenous administration of the same dose. Prolonged retention of alcohol in the stomach, such as after drinking together with or after a meal, allows more opportunity for pre-systemic oxidation by gastric ADH to occur.[98,99]

Interest in the role played by gastric ADH in the overall metabolism of ethanol received a boost when *in vitro* studies showed that the enzyme extracted from gastric biopsies was inhibited by certain commonly prescribed drugs. Among others, aspirin and the H_2-receptor antagonists, ranitidine and cimetidine, used in the treatment of gastric ulcers and inhibition of secretion of excess stomach acid, were capable of blocking the action of gastric ADH.[100,101] This led to the suggestion that people taking this medication, which is widely used in society, and now available without prescription, run the risk of obtaining higher than expected BAC's and, therefore, a potentially more pronounced impairment from the alcohol they consume.[102,103] The drugs seemingly promote the bioavailability of ethanol by removing the potential for oxidation of some of the alcohol already in the stomach.[102–104] Media coverage of this much publicized research triggered a large number of defense challenges from individuals who claimed to combine their H_2-receptor blocking drugs with intake of alcohol.[105] Studies purporting to show an enhanced bioavailability of ethanol, and a higher peak BAC from this drug–alcohol interaction were not very convincing. The number of volunteer subjects was often limited (N = 6) and very low doses of alcohol (0.15 to 0.3 g/kg) were ingested 1 h after a fat-rich meal. Moreover, the methods of alcohol analysis were not appropriate considering that the maximum BACs reached were only 0.015 to 0.025 g/dL, being far removed from the statutory limits for driving in most countries, namely, 0.05 to 0.08 g/dL.[106] Many subsequent studies involving larger numbers of subjects and a better experimental design failed to confirm the enhanced bioavailability of alcohol when H_2-receptor antagonist drugs were taken together with a moderate doses of ethanol 0.15, 0.30, or 0.60 g/kg.[106–111] Accordingly, this defense challenge holds little merit to explain a person's BAC being above the legal limit for driving without intent. Many factors influence the rate of absorption of alcohol from the gut and the bioavailability, particularly the amount of food in the stomach before drinking.[98,99] It is always good advice not to drink alcohol on an empty stomach.

14.1.1.7 *Endogenous Ethanol and the Autobrewery Syndrome*

With the help of sensitive and specific methods of analysis, very low concentrations of ethanol (0.5 to 1.5 mg/L) can be determined in body fluids from people who have not consumed any alcoholic beverages.[112–114] It seems that endogenous ethanol (EE) is produced in the gut by microbes, bacteria and/or yeasts acting on dietary carbohydrates, but other biochemical pathways also exist according to a comprehensive review of this subject.[115] Indeed, the existence of other metabolic precursors of EE was confirmed when ethanol was identified in blood and tissue samples from germ-free rats, because in these animals fermentation of carbohydrates by microflora inhabiting the gut cannot be invoked as an explanation.[116] Because the portal blood draining the stomach and intestine must pass through the liver before reaching the heart, lungs, and systemic circulation, any EE formed in the gut is probably eliminated through the action of alcohol metabolizing enzymes located in the liver.[117]

Abnormally high (0.05 g/dL) concentrations of EE were measured in blood and cerebrospinal fluid from hospitalized patients who had allegedly abstained from drinking alcohol.[118,119] The reports of this work were published in peer-reviewed journals, so these unusual findings give some cause for concern and warrant a carefully scrutiny. It seems that the methodology used for measuring ethanol in biological specimens was rather primitive involving wet-chemistry and oxidation, which is not a specific means of identifying ethanol. Whether dietary factors or even the medication prescribed to the patients were oxidized by the chemical reagents used in the assay, producing falsely elevated concentrations of EE needs to be explored.[120]

If for some reason large quantities of ethanol are synthesized in the gastro-intestinal tract and overwhelm the capacity of the alcohol-metabolizing enzymes in the liver, then much higher concentrations of EE could appear in the peripheral venous blood. This is exactly what was described in a group of Japanese subjects who were suffering from various disorders of the gut. Some had previously complained of experiencing feelings of drunkenness even without consumption of alcohol.[121–122] This condition seemed to appear after the subjects had eaten a carbohydrate-rich meal, such as rice. This study from Japan was difficult to fault because ethanol was identified in blood, urine, and breath with the aid of a reliable gas chromatographic method used for quantitative analysis.[121] The term used to describe this abnormal production of EE was "autobrewery syndrome" and to our knowledge this has been observed only in Japanese subjects.[123] It is widely known that the activity of alcohol metabolizing enzymes, especially aldehyde dehydrogenase, is diminished in Oriental populations compared with Caucasians, which might render Japanese and other Asians less able to clear ethanol from the portal blood.[59] Other requirements before "autobrewery syndrome" that should be seriously considered as contributing to a person's BAC include genetic predisposition (Oriental origin), a past history of gastrointestinal ailments, documented medical treatment for the problem, low tolerance to alcohol, and reports of fatigue and drunkenness after eating meals.

The occurrence of EE has also attracted interest in clinical and diagnostic medicine as an indirect way to furnish evidence of yeast infections in the gut.[123] After obtaining a control pre-treatment blood sample, the fasted patient receives a 5 g glucose load orally and a second blood sample is taken again after 1 h. If the concentration of EE in the second blood sample is significantly higher than in the first, this indicates the possibility of a bacteria or yeast overgrowth in the stomach or small intestine causing a gut-fermentation reaction. Many studies from various countries have confirmed the existence of EE in blood and other biological media from healthy human subjects, but the concentrations rarely exceed 1.0 mg/L, which is over 1000 times less than the statutory BAC for unfitness to drive in most countries (0.08 g/dL = 0.8 g/L = 800 mg/L). These vanishingly small concentrations lack any forensic significance except in exceptional circumstances such as that described for Japanese subjects suffering from gastrointestinal disorders (autobrewery syndrome).[121] Concentrations of EE in blood samples from people with diabetes mellitus, as well as other metabolic disorders, were not much different from the values in healthy control subjects.[113]

14.1.2 Urine Samples

It has been known for more than a century that only a small fraction (about 1 to 2%) of the quantity of alcohol a person consumes is excreted unchanged in the urine.[124,125] Indeed, collection and analysis of urine was recommended by Widmark as a chemical test to prove that a person had been drinking and as an aid in the clinical diagnosis of drunkenness.[125] When urine is used as a body fluid for analysis of alcohol in traffic law enforcement, great care is needed with the sampling protocol to ensure correct interpretation of results.[28,29,126,127] This follows because the concentration of alcohol in urine does not relate to the concentration in the blood at the time of emptying the bladder.[29] Instead, the UAC reflects the average BAC during the time period in which the urine is being produced and stored in the bladder after the previous void.[128] During this storage time, the BAC might have changed appreciably and even reached a zero concentration. In the morning after an evening of drinking it is not uncommon to find that the first urinary void contains a relatively high concentration of alcohol, whereas blood or breath-alcohol content are below the limits of detection with conventional analytical methods.[129] The morning UAC reflects the person's average BAC during the night after the last void before bedtime.

In the U.K. urine specimens were approved for evidential purposes after the Road Traffic Act of 1967, when an alcohol concentration of 80 mg/dl blood or 107 mg/dL urine was accepted as per se evidence of unfitness to drive safely.[14] However, the rules and regulations required the collection of two samples of urine about 30–60 min apart.[14] The first void empties the bladder of old urine, and the concentration of alcohol measured in the second void reflects the person's blood-alcohol concentration at the mid-point of the collection period. Because urine contains about 20% more water than an equal volume of whole blood, the concentration of alcohol in the urine entering the ureter will always be higher than the concentration in blood flowing to the kidney.[28,29] The urine/blood ratio in the post-peak phase of alcohol metabolism is about 1.33:1 on the average,

Table 14.1.1 **Evidential Breath-Alcohol Instruments Currently Used for Forensic Purposes in Europe and North America; the Statutory Limits of Blood-Alcohol (BAC) and Breath-Alcohol (BrAC) Concentration Are Also Reported**

Country	Breath analyzer	BrAC limit	BAC Limit
Sweden[a]	Evidenzer	0.10 mg/L and 0.50 mg/L	0.20 and 1.0 mg/g
Finland[a]	Alcotest 7110	0.22 mg/L and 0.53 mg/L	0.50 and 1.2 mg/g
Norway	Intoxilyzer 5000N	0.10 mg/L	0.20 mg/g
Great Britain	Intoxylizer 6000 Intoximeter EC/IR	35 µg/100 mL	80 mg/100 mL
Ireland	Intoxilyzer 6000	35 µg/100 mL	80 mg/100 mL
Holland	DataMaster	220 µg/L	0.50 mg/mL
Austria	Alcotest 7110	0.25 mg/L	0.50 mg/mL
France	Ethylométer 679T	0.25 mg/L	0.50 mg/mL
U.S.A.[b]	Alcotest 7110 Intoxilyzer 5000 & 8000 Intoximeter EC/IR DataMaster	0.08 g/210 L	0.08 g/100 mL
Canada	Intoxilyzer 5000C DataMaster C	0.08 g/210 L	80 mg/100 mL
Germany	Alcotest 7110	0.25 mg/L	0.50 mg/g
Denmark	None at present	0.25 mg/L	0.50 mg/g

[a] Sweden and Finland have a two-tier legal limit with more severe penalties for a DUI suspect with a high BAC.

[b] In some U.S. states several different breath-alcohol instruments are approved for forensic purposes.

although large inter- and intra-individual variations exist.[128] Studies have shown that the urine/blood ratio of alcohol as well as its variability increases as the blood-alcohol concentration decreases.[28,29] The mean ratio of 1.33:1 is higher than expected on the basis of water content differences (1.2:1), in part because of the time-lag between formation of urine in the ureter and storage in the bladder before voiding (see Chapter 5.2). With relatively short storage times the UAC/BAC ratio might be close to the value expected theoretically of 1.2:1. Note that in UK traffic-law enforcement, the DUI suspect's BAC is not estimated indirectly from the measured UAC. Instead, the legislature has adopted an alcohol concentration of 107 mg/dL in urine as being equivalent to 80 mg/dL in blood (107/80 = 1.33). This approach is similar to the way that the threshold limits of BrAC have been derived from the existing BAC, by dividing by the blood/breath conversion factor adopted by the legislature in the respective countries (see Table 14.1.1). Indeed, because of individual variations in the urine/blood and breath/blood ratios of alcohol, it is strongly recommended that UAC or BrAC not be converted into a presumed BAC as a measure of guilt in DUI prosecution. Instead, the threshold concentration of alcohol should be defined in terms of the substance analyzed whether this is breath or urine.[15,16]

Not many jurisdictions allow the concentrations of alcohol determined in urine specimens as binding evidence for prosecution in DUI, especially when per se statutes operate. This caution is well founded if the measured UAC has to be translated into the presumed BAC because the urine/blood ratio is highly variable between and within individuals and also changes as a function of the BAC. However, unlike most other drugs, the UAC/BAC ratio is not influenced by diuresis because alcohol is handled by the kidneys exactly like water in a passive diffusion process.[126] Increasing the volume of urine excreted by drinking large volumes of water may dilute the urine as reflected by its osmolality and creatinine content but the concentration of alcohol in the specimen will remain unchanged.[130] One objection often raised against the use of urine-alcohol evidence in prosecution of DUI suspects is that some people cannot completely empty their bladders on demand. The retention of old urine with a higher content of alcohol than expected for the prevailing BAC at the time of voiding introduces uncertainty.[131] The prevalence of urine retention in the population at large is hard to estimate although this problem is seemingly more common in elder men, and some studies have detected as much as 25 mL of residual urine.[131] However, the impact of urine retention on the concentration of alcohol determined in successive voids and the magnitude of error incurred if the UAC is converted into presumed BAC has not been demonstrated experimentally.

Because some people might have glucose in their urine,[132] especially those suffering from diabetes mellitus,[133] there is always a risk that ethanol can be produced *in vitro* through the fermentation of sugar by micro-organisms or yeasts infecting the bladder or urinary tract.[134,135] Some reports claim that ethanol can be produced in the bladder itself, so-called bladder beer.[136] This makes it important to include chemical preservatives such as sodium or potassium fluoride at a concentration of at least 1% w/v or sodium azide in the collecting tubes to inhibit microbial synthesis of ethanol.[136,137] Storage of urine specimens in a refrigerator immediately after collection will also help to hinder the synthesis of ethanol through the action of *candida albicans* acting on glucose as substrate.[137]

Some new research findings have demonstrated that production of alcohol directly in the bladder or in the collecting tubes in vitro after sampling can be detected by measuring in the urine the concentration of 5-hydroxytryptophol (5HTOL), a minor metabolite of serotonin.[138] The concentration of 5HTOL increases in blood and urine during hepatic oxidation of ethanol, so a normal concentration of 5HTOL in urine and an elevated concentration of ethanol suggest that the alcohol was synthesized after voiding from the action of bacteria or yeasts on carbohydrate or other substrates.[139]

14.1.3 Blood Samples

14.1.3.1 *Use of Alcohol Swabs for Skin Disinfection*

Blood specimens collected for alcohol analysis in traffic law enforcement are generally taken from an antecubital vein with the aid of sterile equipment such as evacuated tubes (Vacutainer) or a disposable plastic syringe and needle. Preparation of the skin at the site of blood sampling with disinfectants such as ethanol (70% v/v) or isopropanol (70% v/v) should obviously be avoided if specimens are intended for clinical or forensic alcohol testing. Because sterile equipment is used, disinfection of the skin at the site of sampling is not really necessary and, instead, cleaning the skin with saline or soap and water is sufficient. Nevertheless, alleged contamination by ethanol or isopropanol in the swabs used to disinfect the skin is sometimes raised as a defense challenge in attempts to invalidate results of blood-alcohol analysis.[140,141] Note, however, that the methods used for forensic alcohol analysis should be able to distinguish between ethanol and isopropanol.

Many studies have been done to evaluate the risk of carry-over of alcohol from the antiseptic used to swab the skin before the specimen of venous blood was taken for analysis.[142,143]

A classic example of giving the benefit of the doubt was demonstrated when several hundred convictions for DUI in the U.K. were deemed invalid and the sentences overturned. This was felt necessary because the swabs normally issued with kits used for blood-sampling from DUI suspects had been inadvertently switched to another brand, which contained isopropanol.[144] The legal alcohol limit in the U.K. is 35 µg/100 mL breath and if the result is between 40 and 50 µg/100 mL the suspect can opt to provide a blood sample instead and the BAC is then used as evidence for prosecution (threshold BAC = 80 mg/100 mL). Because of reported large discrepancies between BAC and BrAC in this kind of paired test, the swabs used to clean the skin before drawing blood became suspect. This suspicion was strengthened when the swabs were shown to contain alcohol (isopropanol). This led to an official investigation. The convictions of several hundred individuals who had pleaded guilty to DUI and had received their sentences were considered unsound and quashed. It appears that this decision was reached by the court of appeals because the integrity of the blood specimen was cast in doubt, and the defendants were not aware of this when they were asked to plead guilt or not guilty to DUI. This led to several controlled studies into the risk of carry-over of alcohol from the swabs used to disinfect the skin. The results, however, showed that contamination of the blood sample with various alcohols during venipuncture was highly unlikely and in most studies, only traces or no alcohol at all could be detected in the specimens.[145–149]

If evacuated tubes are used for sampling blood, then two tubes should be filled with blood in rapid succession and gently inverted several times to mix with the chemical preservatives. If some coagulation does occur, the sample should be homogenized prior to sampling to prevent inadvertent aliquoting of the serum fraction which would contain more alcohol than a specimen of whole blood. The chemical preservatives are typically sodium fluoride (NaF), which prevents glycolysis and inhibits certain enzymes and micro-organisms that might be present in the blood, and potassium oxalate which serves as an anticoagulant. These substances are already in the tubes as supplied by the manufacturer, although the necessity of having sodium fluoride in sterile Vacutainer tubes is open to discussion because contamination with bacteria can, in reality, only arise from the skin at the point of inserting the needle. Nevertheless, NaF should be included if only to prevent this defense challenge from being raised; the amount of NaF recommended for blood specimens taken from living subjects is 100 mg/10 mL blood (1% w/v). If the amount actually present is challenged then methods are available to assay blood samples for fluoride ions such as by using ion-sensitive electrodes or by other means.[150] In the event that alcohol-containing swabs are used, the practice of always taking two tubes of blood for analysis has the advantage that any unusually large discrepancies in the results of BAC between the two tubes can be detected. If present, this might suggest carryover or some other problem. However, the studies from the UK cited above confirm several earlier reports, which demonstrated that the risk of carryover of alcohol, even when 70% ethanol was used as an antiseptic, is virtually non-existent.[149,151] Another safeguard when filling evacuated tubes with blood is to remove each tube from the collecting needle and holder before withdrawing the needle from the puncture site.[151]

The concentration of alcohol in stored blood samples decreases on storage at 4°C despite the inclusion of 1% w/v NaF as preservative.[152] The rate of loss of alcohol is only about 0.003 g/dL per month, and evidently occurs by a non-enzymatic oxidation reaction that involves oxyhemoglobin.[152,153] If blood specimens are contaminated with microorganisms when the Vacutainer tubes are opened to remove aliquots for analysis, this can lead to a much more rapid disappearance of alcohol during storage compared with unopened tubes. It seems that various species of microorganism utilize alcohol as a food.[140] Other considerations regarding specimen collection include filling the tube with as much blood as possible, to avoid having a large airspace. Volatiles, including ethanol, will accumulate in the headspace and will be lost when the tube is opened. In the event that a tube is opened and closed repeatedly, this could result in appreciable losses of alcohol.

The question of uptake of alcohol through the skin as a mode of entry into the body to produce elevated BAC has been raised as a defense challenge by people working with large volumes of solvents. In fact, the absorption of ethanol through the skin was investigated many years ago by Bowers et al.[154] in controlled experiments with several children and one adult. The legs of the test subjects were wrapped in cotton soaked in 200 mL of 95% ethanol and secured with rubber sheeting and sealed with adhesive tapes. Blood samples were taken before and at various times after this treatment but neither clinical signs of inebriation nor raised BAC were noted. It seems safe to conclude that ethanol cannot accumulate in the body, and BAC is not increased by absorption through intact skin.

14.1.3.2 Trauma and Intravenous Fluids

Drunk drivers are often involved in serious road-traffic crashes causing injury and sometimes death. Trauma resulting in massive losses of blood precipitate a hypovolemic shock and this requires swift emergency treatment. This might involve administering medication at the site of the accident such as pain killers and intravenous fluids to counteract shock and replace depleted body fluids. More intensive treatment can be given on arrival at a surgical emergency unit and it is usually at this point that a blood sample is taken for clinical and/or medicolegal purposes. The sampling of blood for analysis of alcohol in a critically injured patient requires considerable deliberation to safeguard the integrity of the patient and the specimen. Errors incurred in sampling blood from trauma patients are not uncommon, and they are beyond the control of the forensic laboratory.[155] Care is needed if intravenous fluids are administered as a first aid for treatment of shock, and it is important that the blood sample for alcohol analysis is not taken downstream from the same vein used for infusion. Otherwise, this can result in a marked dilution of the specimen and a decrease in the concentration of alcohol. If dilution of the specimen is suspected, this can sometimes be verified by determination of hemoglobin.[155]

Routinely analyzing aliquots of blood from two Vacutainer tubes that are filled in rapid succession furnishes a useful way to reveal discrepant results and problems associated with blood sampling. If the tube-to-tube difference in BAC exceeds that expected from knowledge of random analytical errors and past experiences, this points to other influences such as pre-analytical factors. Abnormally large differences in BAC between the two tubes can often be traced to dilution or coagulation of one or both of the samples because of inadequate mixing after collection. Note that the concentration of alcohol measured in plasma or serum will be higher than in whole blood by about 10 to 15% as discussed in detail elsewhere.[156]

14.1.3.3 Blood-Water Content and Hematocrit

The water content of whole blood is easily determined by weighing an aliquot and heating overnight at 105 to 110°C to reach a constant weight.[156] The change in weight after desiccation can be used to calculate the water content of the blood specimen. According to the scientific literature whole blood contains 85 g water per 100 mL (95% range 83.0 to 86.5 g/100 mL).[157] The specific gravity of blood is 1.055 so the water content is 5.5% less when expressed in mass/mass units; 85.0% w/v corresponds to 80.6 % w/w.[157] Women tend to have approximately 1 to 2% more water than men for the same volume of whole blood owing to loss of red cells during periods of menstruation.[158]

Whole blood is composed of a plasma fraction, red blood cells (erythrocytes), white blood cells (leukocytes), and platelets. Blood hematocrit is defined as the volume of packed cells per 100 mL of whole blood when expressed as a percentage. Normal values for hematocrit in men are 42 to 50% compared with 37 to 47% in women.[159] The red cells (erythrocytes) carry the hemoglobin and contain about 73 mL of water/100 mL cells whereas plasma contains 93 mL of water/100 mL plasma. Assuming a hematocrit of 40%, the water content of whole blood should be $(0.40 \times 73) + (0.60 \times 93)$ or 85 mL water/100 mL of whole blood. This value agrees well with gravimetric determinations of blood-water by desiccation and a mean value of 85.6% w/v was reported.[156] Because the red cells contain so much water and because alcohol distributes in blood according to the water content of the various components, it must be obvious that even fairly wide variations in hematocrit will not make much difference to the concentration of alcohol per unit volume of whole blood.

This was confirmed empirically when blood was prepared in-vitro with hematocrit values of 18, 31, 39, and 60.[160] The specimens were spiked with the same amount of ethanol to give a BAC of 0.212 g/dL and the actual concentration in each blood sample was determined by gas chromatography to be 0.211, 0.211, 0.207, and 0.208 g/dL respectively. Thus, no influence of varying hematocrit from 18 to 60 on the alcohol concentration in the whole blood was observed.[160] However, if equilibrated headspace vapor above the same blood specimens had been analyzed, the specimen with lowest hematocrit (large plasma portion and more water per unit volume) would have had a lower headspace concentration of ethanol compared with the specimens with higher hematocrit (low plasma portion and therefore less water content per unit volume).[158] This follows because the concentration of alcohol in the vapor phase will be higher for the blood specimen with least water and therefore will contain a higher concentration of alcohol per mL blood-water.[158]

A blood sample with abnormally low hematocrit means a low number of blood cells and also a low hemoglobin content, which might be associated with a patient suffering from anemia. The other extreme is polycythemia, which is an overabundance of red cells per unit volume of blood and therefore an abnormally high hematocrit in this condition. The question of whether variations in hematocrit influence the maximum BAC reached from intake of a known amount of alcohol is difficult to answer because large changes in hematocrit are often associated with changes in the distribution of body water in general and therefore with an altered volume of distribution for ethanol.[161]

14.1.4 Breath-Alcohol Analysis

Historical developments in testing for alcohol intoxication by use of chemical analysis of blood or breath were recently reviewed.[162] Breath-tests for alcohol are currently used in forensic science practice and traffic law enforcement for two main purposes. The first and least controversial application involves roadside pre-arrest screening to furnish an objective indication of alcohol involvement and whether or not the driver might be above the critical legal limit for driving. In many situations, the police require probable cause before a chemical test for alcohol can be administered. This necessitates observations about the way the person was driving, and evidence of impairment from use of field-sobriety tests, which are important concerns before making an arrest and administering the chemical test for alcohol. Various hand-held devices are currently available for measuring breath-alcohol concentration at the roadside (Table 14.1.2). The most popular method of roadside breath testing involves the principle of electrochemical oxidation of alcohol with a fuel cell sensor and this technology is fairly selective because endogenous volatiles such as acetone and methane do not react with this kind of detector. However, if acetone is reduced in the body to isopropanol, this secondary alcohol is oxidized with the fuel cell sensor and can give a response that cannot be distinguished from ethanol.[163]

The results of roadside breath-testing might be displayed as colored lights such as pass (green), warn (yellow), or fail (red), or as a digital display of breath-alcohol concentration in units such as mg/L or g/210L depending on the particular jurisdiction (Table 14.1.1). If the screening test gives a positive response this indicates the driver has been drinking and may be over the legal limit, which is sufficient probable cause to demand a specimen of blood or breath for evidential forensic analysis. The suspect is then taken to a police station where an evidential breath-alcohol test is conducted; examples of instruments used in various countries are given in Table 14.1.1. When properly calibrated and operated, the hand-held screening devices can be as accurate as any other breath test instrument. Some of the limitations of screening devices when used for quantitative

Table 14.1.2 Examples of the Most Commonly Used Hand-Held Breath-Alcohol Devices for Roadside Breath-Alcohol Screening Purposes and for Estimating the Coexisting Blood-Alcohol Concentration[a]

Breath-test instrument	Method of alcohol analysis	Manufacturer and country
Alcolmeter SD-2	Electrochemical oxidation	Lion Laboratories, U.K.
Alcolmeter SD-400	Electrochemical oxidation	Lion Laboratories, U.K.
Alcotest 7410	Electrochemical oxidation	Dräger, Germany
Alcotest 6510	Electrochemical oxidation	Dräger, Germany
Alcosensor III and IV	Electrochemical oxidation	Intoximeters Inc., U.S.A.
Alcodoose II	Infrared Absorption (9.5 μm)	Seres, France
Lifeloc FC10	Electrochemical oxidation	Lifeloc Inc., U.S.A.

[a] To estimate BAC from BrAC, the breath analyzers must be pre-calibrated with a blood:breath conversion factor such as 2100:1 or 2300:1.

evidential purposes include: the lack of protection they provide against interference from mouth alcohol, the lack of blank tests or calibration control tests, the fact that they can generate low results at low temperatures, and also that for some older devices (Alcosensor III, Alcolmeter SD-2) the results are operator dependent; releasing the button before the reading has stabilized will generate a low result. Breath-alcohol instruments used for quantitative evidential purposes are generally more sophisticated than the hand-held screening devices and provide a printed record of results with date, time, location of the test as well as computer-storage of results for generating statistical reports. Moreover, these devices ensure that end-expired breath is being sampled and that residual alcohol in the mouth from recent drinking or regurgitation has not biased the result.

A critical element in performing an evidential breath-alcohol test is always to observe the suspect for at least 15 min before making the breath test. During this time he or she should not be allowed to drink, eat, smoke, or place anything in the mouth prior to completing the test. Moreover, a duplicate test should be made not less than 3 min and not more than 15 min after completion of the first test. The instrument calibration must be controlled in conjunction with testing the subject and this is accomplished with a breath-alcohol simulator device or alcohol contained in compressed gas tanks. Analysis of the room-air provides a blank test result before and between making the duplicate tests with the subject. All these requirements have been described in detail elsewhere and are important for ensuring a successful evidential breath testing program that will withstand scrutiny.[164] Regardless of these many new developments and improvements in the technology of breath-alcohol testing, challenges against the reliability of the results are far more common than against the results of blood-alcohol analysis. This probably stems from the fact that breath-testing is performed by police officers whereas blood-alcohol analysis is done at government laboratories by chemists, some of whom have research experience or a Ph.D. degree. Furthermore, the blood sample is usually retained and can be re-tested if there is any doubt about the results, whereas breath samples are generally not preserved and therefore cannot be re-tested.

14.1.4.1 *Mouth Alcohol and Use of Mouthwash Preparations*

Even during the first studies of breath-alcohol analysis as a test for intoxication, it was emphasized that testing should not be conducted too soon after the last drink.[165] Thus, Emil Bogen in his landmark article, which was published in 1927, made the following statement;

> "As soon as the disturbing factor of alcoholic liquor still in the mouth is removed, which occurs usually within fifteen minutes after imbibition, in the absence of hiccuping or belching, the alcoholic content of 2 liters of expired air was a little greater than 1 cc of urine."

A multitude of studies have been done since the 1930s to confirm the importance of a 15-min deprivation period after the last drink even though this problem is sometimes rediscovered from time to time.[166] Most experiments on the influence of residual mouth alcohol on breath-test results have generally involved human subjects initially alcohol-free who are required to hold solutions of alcohol (40% v/v) in their mouths for 1 to 2 min without swallowing.[167,168] Immediately after expelling the alcohol, the test subject undergoes a series of breath tests at 1- to 2-min intervals for 20 to 30 min. The results show that within 15 to 20 min after ejecting a strong solution of alcohol from the mouth, the response of the breath-alcohol analyzer is always less than 0.01 g/210 L, which is generally considered the threshold for baseline readings. Other study designs have involved measuring breath-alcohol in subjects after they drink alcohol to reach a certain BAC level.[169] After rinsing the mouth with more alcohol, breath tests are made repeatedly until the results recover to the pre-drinking BrAC. Under these test conditions, the time needed to clear the residual alcohol from the mouth was even less than 10 min.[169]

Accordingly, on the basis of experiments such as these, rules and regulations for evidential breath-alcohol testing stipulate a 15- to 20-min observation period before conducting an evidential breath-alcohol test. During this time the suspect should not be allowed to smoke or drink or place any material in the mouth, and if he or she regurgitates or vomits, the observation period must be started again. Although a 15-min observation period is not mandated prior to conducting roadside breath-alcohol screening tests, in practice, a considerably longer time will usually have elapsed since the last drink was taken, unless the drinking took place while the person was driving. The time involved in stopping the vehicle, and contacting the driver, as well as any necessary field sobriety testing will usually take longer than 15 min. For reliable quantitative determinations, however, the 15-min deprivation period should be observed and documented.

Many mouth-wash preparations contain alcohol as well as other organic solvents, and the concentrations sometimes are as high as 50 to 60% v/v. Obviously the use of these materials prior to conducting a breath-alcohol test would produce similar disturbances on breath-test results as having alcoholic beverages in the mouth. Provided that the 15 to 20 min observation time is maintained, use of breath fresheners containing alcohol will not have any negative impact on the reliability of the test result.[170] However, if these preparations are intentionally or unintentionally consumed, this will be a source of alcohol just like drinking an alcoholic beverage. In a recent study with commercial mouthwash products, Listerine (29.6% alcohol), Scope (18.9% alcohol), and Lavoris (6.0% alcohol), tests were made on a breath-alcohol analyzer after rinsing the mouth with these preparations. Within 2 min of rinsing the mouth, breath-test results were as high as 240 mg/dL (expressed as BAC equivalent) but within 10 min this had dropped dramatically and was well below the threshold limits for driving (0.08 to 0.10 g/dL). By 15 min post-rinsing, the readings were below 0.01 g/dL. Similar results, namely no significant response with an infrared breath-alcohol analyzer, were obtained 15 to 20 min or more after various mouthwashes, aftershave lotions, and perfumes in common use in Germany were tested.[171]

14.1.4.2 *Regurgitation and Gastro Esophageal Reflux Disease (GERD)*

The pioneer work by Bogen[165] indicated that hiccuping, burping, and belching might present a problem in connection with breath-alcohol analysis. Only very limited investigations of this problem have been made, and these indicate that the risk of elevating breath-alcohol readings is greatest shortly after the end of drinking as might be expected because the concentration of alcohol in the stomach is then at its highest.[172,173] A closely related problem is gastro-esophageal reflux disease (GERD).[174–177] Many people suffer from acid-reflux disorders, known as reflux esophagitis, whereby gastric secretions as well as other liquid contents erupt from the stomach into the esophagus and sometimes reach the mouth.[178–180] Indeed, this condition might be aggravated after drinking certain alcoholic beverages.[181,182] The impact of GERD on results of evidential breath-alcohol testing has not yet been investigated in any controlled studies. Nevertheless, this medical condition has been raised as a defense challenge from DUI suspects who maintain they experienced a reflux from the stomach into the mouth immediately prior to providing a breath-alcohol sample.[183] The higher the concentration of alcohol prevailing in the stomach during a reflux, the greater the risk of contaminating the breath-sample in a similar mechanism to the mouth-alcohol effect. From this follows the contention that GERD is the cause of a person's BrAC being above the legal limit for driving, and medical experts have testified to this effect, which has led to the acquittal of a DUI suspect.[184] However, the validity of this defense argument was strongly questioned by another expert as being one of the least convincing, and he also noted that the doctors appearing for the defense "ignored one of the basic maxims in the business," namely "what the subject says he has drunk is not evidence."[185]

Although most evidential breath test instruments feature "slope detection" to disclose the presence of mouth alcohol, in some cases these may not detect small contributions resulting from belching or burping. A far better approach to counter the GERD defense challenge is always to observe the subject carefully, and to perform duplicate breath-alcohol analyses, that is two separate exhalations 3 to 5 min apart.[185] Obtaining close agreement between the two independent results speaks against the influence of regurgitation of stomach contents having a high concentration of alcohol just prior to making the first breath-test or between the first and the second test. Also the risk of GERD elevating the breath test result decreases as the time after ingestion of alcohol increases because of the ongoing absorption of alcohol from the stomach and the emptying of the stomach contents into the duodenum. Evidential breath-alcohol programs that require only a single breath-alcohol test are out of date and should be abandoned especially if GERD is a recurring defense argument. The single chemical test for alcohol has no place in jurisdictions where per se statutes operate, regardless of whether blood or breath analysis is used for forensic purposes.

14.1.4.3 Dentures and Denture Adhesives

The question of people with dentures or individuals who might be fitted with special bridge-work where alcohol can be trapped has arisen as a possible cause of obtaining a falsely elevated breath-alcohol reading.[186,187] This challenge is therefore akin to having residual alcohol in the mouth from recent drinking. The empirical evidence supporting the notion that sufficient alcohol becomes trapped under denture plates or in other structures or cavities in the mouth for long periods of time is not very convincing, although a few isolated case reports support this defense argument.[188] A person suspected for DUI in the U.K. was acquitted when expert testimony raised a reasonable doubt about the validity of the evidential breath test performed using an Intoximeter 3000 breath alcohol analyzer. Alcohol allegedly was trapped in cavities in the mouth as a result of dental treatment.[186] However, the experiments and reasoning presented to support this defense argument were speculative, not very convincing, and were easy to fault.[187] An acquittal in a DUI case in the U.S. was obtained when expert evidence suggested that the breath-test results were suspect because of alcohol being absorbed by the particular kind of denture adhesive used by the defendant.[188]

The most convincing study appearing in a peer-reviewed journal dealing with breath-alcohol testing and the use of dentures involved the participation of 24 subjects.[189] They were tested under various conditions; with dentures intact, with dentures removed, and with dentures held loosely in place both with and without adhesives. The volunteers held 30 mL of 80 proof brandy in their mouths for 2 min without swallowing. After ejecting the alcohol, breath-alcohol tests were made with an Intoxilyzer 5000 instrument at regular intervals. After an elapsed time of 20 min, no results were above 0.01 g/210 L.[189] This argues convincingly against the idea of people who wear dentures obtaining falsely elevated breath-alcohol concentrations. The widely practiced deprivation period and observation time of 15 to 20 min seems adequate to eliminate the risk of mouth-alcohol invalidating results even in people with dentures.[190]

A recent report described experiments in a person with dentures who was suspected of DUI. The defendant alleged that the brand of denture adhesive used was responsible for the breath alcohol reading being above the legal limit of 0.10 g/210 L breath.[188] In one set of tests with a Breathalyzer model 900, which is not equipped with a slope detector, prolonged retention of alcohol was observed remarkably for several hours after 86 proof whisky was held in the mouth and when a certain brand of dental adhesive was used. These results suggest that some kinds of denture adhesives might retain alcohol for longer and lead to false high breath-alcohol readings. However, no corroborative reports of this have been published, and more controlled studies are necessary making use of duplicate measurements of blood and breath-alcohol concentration, weaker solutions of ethanol, and monitoring the shape of the BrAC exhalation profile in order to substantiate these surprising observations and conclusions.

Many of the latest generation of breath-alcohol analyzers used for evidential purposes are equipped with a slope-detector mechanism, which is designed to monitor the time-course of BrAC during a prolonged exhalation.[191,192] If the BrAC is higher at the start of an exhalation compared with at the end of the exhalation, this causes a negative slope and suggests a possible mouth alcohol effect or perhaps regurgitation of stomach contents or GERD. More work is necessary to evaluate the effectiveness of the slope detectors fitted to evidential breath-alcohol analyzers over a wide range of concentrations of alcohol in the mouth, and at various times after the end of drinking.

14.1.4.4   Alleged Interfering Substances in Breath

The alleged response of breath-alcohol instruments to interfering substances is a common DUI defense argument in many countries.[193] The interferents in question are either claimed to have been produced naturally in the body, so called endogenous breath volatiles, or volatile organic compounds (VOC) inhaled with the ambient air during occupational exposure. The question of whether substances other than ethanol give a response on evidential breath-alcohol instruments escalated dramatically in the early 1970s after infra-red absorptiometry started to become the technology of choice for evidential purposes.[194] Hitherto, the Breathalyzer model 900 dominated the field of breath-alcohol testing in the U.S. and this device incorporates wet-chemistry oxidation with photometric endpoint for determination of BrAC.[195] Although this represents a non-specific chemical oxidation reaction for the analysis of alcohol, provided the galvanometer on the Breathalyzer was read after exactly 90 seconds as per the instructions, the presence of acetone, toluene and other substances in the breath do not present a serious interference problem.[196,197] Most infrared evidential breath alcohol devices provide some control for the presence of interfering substances with the use of either multiple filters, or dual technology, such as electrochemical oxidation in conjunction with infrared.

Endogenous Breath Volatiles

Human expired air consists of a mixture of gases including oxygen, nitrogen, carbon dioxide, water, vapor, and in extremely small amounts a multitude of volatile organic compounds (VOCs).[198–200] The major endogenous breath volatiles are acetone, methane, and the unsaturated hydrocarbon isoprene (2-methyl-1,3-butadiene).[201–204] The concentration of acetone expelled in breath is usually between 0.5 and 5 µg/L but this can increase appreciably if a person is deprived of food or engages in a prolonged fast.[205] Moreover, during ketoacidosis, a condition often associated with hyperglycemia, diabetes mellitus, or alcohol withdrawal, the concentration of ketone bodies (acetone, acetoacetate and beta-hydroxybutyrate) circulating in the blood increases appreciably along with the concentration of acetone expelled in the breath.[205–208]

The question of whether VOCs other than ethanol might interfere with the results of evidential breath-alcohol testing started to become an issue of debate and concern shortly after the first Intoxilyzer instrument, a single wavelength (3.39 µm) analyzer, appeared for use in law enforcement.[194] The Intoxilyzer measures the C-H bond stretching and vibrational frequencies in ethanol molecules, which means that abnormally high concentrations of acetone (blood/air distribution ratio approximately 300:1) in breath becomes a major candidate as an interfering substance. However, this problem was quickly solved by monitoring the absorption of infrared radiation at two wavelengths such as 3.39 and 3.48 µm as currently used with the Intoxilyzer 5000.[193] Another approach to enhance selectivity is to incorporate two independent methods of analysis such as IR and electrochemical oxidation in the same unit as is used with the Alcotest 7110.[209]

When properly adjusted, the Intoxilyzer 5000 instrument corrects the ethanol signal for the presence of acetone in the breath. Moreover, if the concentration of breath-acetone exceeds 300 to 600 µg/L, corresponding to a blood concentration of 0.009 to 0.018 g/dL, the imbalance between the two filter signals exceeds a pre-set threshold value and the evidential test is aborted.[193] The instrument reports an interferant detected and the "apparent ethanol" concentration is stored in an internal memory of the software. If very high concentrations of acetone are present in the blood, this ketone can be reduced by alcohol dehydrogenase in the liver to produce isopropanol, which also absorbs infrared radiation at the wavelengths used and can masquerade as ethanol.[163] Methanol, which has highly toxic metabolites, presents a special problem if high concentrations are present in blood and breath because infrared breath-alcohol analyzers cannot easily distinguish this one-carbon alcohol from ethanol if only two infrared wavelengths are used. The potential for methanol to interfere with a breath test can best be addressed by a consideration of its toxicological properties.[94]

Isoprene is another endogenous VOC expelled in the breath. In experiments with 16 healthy subjects, the breath isoprene concentration ranged from 0.11 to 0.70 μg/L as determined by thermal desorption gas chromatography and UV detection.[201] These concentrations are much too low to interfere with the measurement of breath-alcohol with the infrared technology currently used for evidential purposes. Methane is produced in the gut by the action of colonic bacteria on disaccharides and this VOC can be detected in human expired air. It seems that some individuals are more prone than others to generate methane in the large intestine and the concentration of this hydrocarbon expelled in breath under different conditions requires more documentation.[204] Methane should perhaps be considered as a potential interfering substance in connection with forensic breath-alcohol testing by infrared methods, but more research is necessary on this topic before raising an alarm.[203]

Acetaldehyde is a VOC produced during the metabolism of ethanol by all known enzymatic pathways and is also a major constituent of cigarette smoke. The high volatility and low blood/air partition coefficient of acetaldehyde (190:1) means that this substance crosses the alveolar-capillary membrane of the lungs and enters the breath.[210] Because acetaldehyde absorbs IR radiation in the same region as ethanol (3.4 to 3.5 μm) this VOC might be considered a potential interfering substance in connection with evidential breath-alcohol testing. This problem was investigated empirically in tests with a single wavelength (3.39 μm) infrared analyzer under conditions when abnormally high concentrations of breath-acetaldehyde (50 μg/L) existed.[211] This was accomplished by inhibiting the metabolism of acetaldehyde by pretreatment of subjects with Antabuse-like drugs before they drank alcohol. Even under these extreme conditions, no false-high apparent ethanol readings were obtained. In recent reviews of the biomedical alcohol research literature, it seems that the concentrations of acetaldehyde in blood are very low during oxidation of ethanol (< 88 μg/L corresponding to 0.46 μg/L in breath) that this metabolite of ethanol cannot be seriously considered an interfering VOC when testing drunk drivers with the aid of infrared analyzers.[210,212]

Occupational Exposure to Organic Solvents

A few studies have dealt with the response of infrared breath-alcohol instruments after occupational exposure to solvent vapors, although no convincing evidence of an interference problem has emerged, provided that at least 20 min elapses after leaving the work environment.[213] In an effort to investigate the claims from two convicted drunk drivers that inhalation of solvents caused false high readings on an infrared breath-alcohol instrument, the men volunteered to spray cars with toluene/xylene/methanol-based paint thinner under extreme working conditions and without the use of protective clothing or face masks.[214] They worked for several hours in a small poorly ventilated room making use of 5 to 7 liters of paint during this time. It was noted that their eyes were watering and they were suffering from severe irritation, coughing regularly and complaining of sore throats. Tests with one of the subjects gave measurable apparent ethanol responses during the exposure. Results with an infrared breath analyzer (Intoximeter 3000) were consistently higher than those obtained with an electrochemical instrument (Alcolmeter S-D2). At times of 0 min, 15 min, and 30 min after leaving the small working environment, one subject gave BrAC results of 0.019, 0.010, and 0.002 g/210 L on the IR analyzer. The lack of any instrument responses for the other subject was explained by a considerably lower environmental temperature on the day of the testing, and this presumably led to a less efficient vaporization of the solvents.

Inhalation of gasoline fumes as might occur if a person sniffs this liquid or engages in siphoning gasoline between cars can cause falsely elevated readings on the Intoxilyzer 5000.[215,216] In an actual DUI case scenario, the Intoxilyzer reacted by aborting the test because an interfering substance or substances were detected.[193] Gasoline contains, among other things, a complex mixture of aliphatic and aromatic hydrocarbons and these were also qualitatively identified in a blood sample taken from the suspect whose blood-alcohol concentration was zero. Abuse of organic solvents such as thinner or glue is another source of interfering substances in connection with evidential breath-alcohol testing.[217] People who abuse these materials often tend to smell of the solvents they inhale, and may display characteristic symptoms of intoxication. If there is evidence to suggest solvent abuse, or extended exposure to solvent fumes, arrangements should be made for obtaining blood samples instead.

Diethyl ether is another solvent capable of interfering with the response of dual wavelength infrared breath-alcohol instruments and being mistakenly reported as ethanol.[218] This solvent is no longer widely used in industry or hospitals, so the risk of being exposed to ether in everyday life is not very high, although it is present in carburetor or starting fluid. Several other case reports have appeared suggesting that work-related inhalation of toluene and lacquer fumes in conjunction with normal occupational exposure gives readings on IR analyzers exceeding 0.10 g/210L.[219,220] However, the test subject who had been apprehended for DUI sometimes showed behavioral manifestations of solvent inhalation or abuse and was chronically exposed to these agents over a period of many years, so accumulation of toluene in body fat depots cannot be excluded. Some drunk drivers use technical spirits for intoxication purposes and these solvents contain ethanol, methanol, methyl ethyl ketone, ethyl acetate, and isopropanol as well as other VOCs. These substances absorb IR radiation and can be mistakenly identified as ethanol with some IR breath-alcohol analyzers.[221] By comparing the results from a pre-arrest roadside test utilizing an electro-chemical sensor for ethanol determination, with the results from infrared evidential analyzers, useful information can be gleaned about the presence of an interfering substance. The two detector systems (IR and Fuel cell) respond differently to different VOCs in the breath; electrochemical sensors don't respond to acetone or hydrocarbons.[222,223]

A comprehensive series of experiments on the subject of evidential breath-alcohol testing and the response to organic solvents was made in the U.K., where two infrared analyzers have been used for legal purposes since 1983.[224–226] Human volunteers were exposed on different occasions to toluene, 1,1,1-trichlorethane, butane, white spirit, and nonane under controlled conditions, and blood and breath were sampled at regular intervals after ending the exposure. The volunteers assumed a resting position talking and playing cards during a 4-h period of exposure to the solvents at concentrations close to the upper limits prescribed for the workplaces in the U.K. After inhalation of butane vapor a response was seen on the infrared breath analyzers lasting for 1 to 5 min after exposure, before rapidly declining to zero.[224] Exposure to toluene and 1,1,1-trichloroethane did not give any response on the IR analyzers although these substances were identified in blood samples for up to 8 h after exposure ended.[224] The concentration of the solvents in blood and breath decreased rapidly on ending the exposure, which supports the conclusion that normal occupational use of solvents would be unlikely to contribute to false high results on IR breath-alcohol analyzers. Similar negative findings on evidential breath-test results were reported after inhalation of nonane and white spirit.[225]

Elevation of blood and breath-alcohol concentrations as a result of inhalation of ethanol vapors by brewery or distillery workers or industrial workers required to handle ethanol-based solvents has been a recurring argument in DUI trials.[227] One of the first controlled studies was done in 1951 with subjects being exposed to varying concentrations of ethanol vapor for up to 6 h.[227] The results showed that alcohol could be absorbed into the blood by inhalation through the lungs, and that the BAC attained was proportional to the concentration of ethanol in the inhaled air and the rate of ventilation. However, extreme conditions were necessary to build-up a BAC exceeding 0.01 g/dL, and the methods of blood and breath-alcohol analysis were fairly primitive.[227] Note that between 6 to 8 g of ethanol can be metabolized per hour so uptake by inhalation and absorption through the lungs must exceed this amount before the BAC will increase above base-line levels. Moreover, it was noted that inhalation of air-alcohol concentrations of 10 to 20 mg/L caused coughing and smarting of the eyes and nose. Untoward effects were more pronounced at concentrations of 30 mg/L, and at 40 mg/L the situation was barely tolerable, making it impossible to remain in this atmosphere for any length of time.

Several more recent studies have looked in theory and practice at the reality of generating an elevated BAC from inhalation of ethanol vapor.[228–230] From these experiments we conclude that obtaining a BAC exceeding 0.003-0.005 g/dL is highly unlikely as a result of normal occupational exposure owing to the metabolism of ethanol that occurs during and immediately after ending the exposure.[231] However, if a person already has an elevated BAC before entering an atmosphere with a very high alcohol vapor concentration (simply sitting in a bar is not sufficient!), then the metabolism of alcohol and clearance of BAC might be delayed during the inhalation period. This would lead to a shallower β-slope than expected if the intake of alcohol by inhalation is sufficient to balance the amount eliminated by metabolism.[232] In short, caution should be exercised in interpreting breath test results from subjects with extensive solvent exposure immediately prior to the breath test. Most solvents are rapidly distributed and eliminated following environmental exposure. There is no evidence that casual exposure to solvents or solvent-containing products will exert an effect on an evidential breath test administered an hour or more later.

14.1.4.5 *Variability in the Blood/Breath Alcohol Ratio*

Historically, the first breath-alcohol instruments were developed and used as an indirect way of measuring a person's blood alcohol concentration. Breath-testing was considered more practical than blood-testing for traffic-law enforcement purposes,[162] because of the noninvasive sampling technique and the fact that an immediate indication of the person's blood-alcohol concentration and state of inebriation were obtained.[233] Conversion of a measured BrAC into the expected BAC was accomplished by calibrating the breath-analyzers with a constant factor (2100:1), which was known as the blood/breath ratio of alcohol. The figure of 2100:1 had been determined empirically by equilibration of blood and air at constant temperatures *in vitro* and also *in vivo* by taking samples of breath and venous blood at nearly the same time from a large number of volunteer subjects.[234,235] In the post-absorptive phase of alcohol metabolism, studies showed that the blood/breath ratio of alcohol was approximately 2100:1, and this figure was subsequently endorsed by several meetings of experts with international representation.[162] However, the blood/breath ratio is not a constant for all individuals and varies within the same individual from time to time and during different phases of alcohol metabolism.[236] This variability needs to be considered when the results of breath-alcohol testing are used in criminal litigation to estimate a person's blood-alcohol concentration.

All analytical results have inherent uncertainty, resulting from a combination of human error, systematic errors in calibration, random instrument error, etc. In a forensic context, the extent of any error should be known by analysis of appropriate standards and controls, and the contribution of error or uncertainty in the measurement should be considered when the result is interpreted. When measurements are being made of dynamic systems, such as exhaled human breath samples, further biological variation outside of the control of the analyst is introduced. The inherent variability in the blood/breath alcohol ratio among different individuals is an excellent example of this, and has emerged as a hot topic of discussion and debate in the scientific literature and in the courts.[17–22]

For many years, the results of breath-alcohol analysis in law enforcement were overshadowed by inherent variations in blood/breath ratio and allegations that BAC had been overestimated by use of breath-test instruments. Obtaining an estimated BAC that was too high was more likely during the absorption phase, when BAC was still rising, because of the existence of arterial-venous (A-V) differences in alcohol concentration. The time course of breath-alcohol concentration follows more closely the arterial BAC than the venous BAC, with the arterial BAC exceeding the venous during the absorptive phase, and vice versa during the elimination phase. Moreover, the 2100:1 ratio was originally determined by comparing venous BAC and BrAC in samples taken during the post-absorptive phase of alcohol metabolism when A-V differences are small or negligible.[234] The actual blood/breath conversion factor is clearly a moving target, and its value depends on many factors that are impossible to know or control in any individual subject at the time of testing. Several more recent studies comparing blood and breath-alcohol in DUI suspects show that in the field, the blood/breath ratio is closer to 2400:1 with a 95% range from 1900 to 2900, indicating a strong bias in favor of the suspect being breath-tested in comparison with the same person providing a specimen of blood for analysis at a forensic laboratory.[237–240]

In an attempt to quell much of the troublesome debate that was erupting over the continued use of a constant blood/breath ratio, experts in the field of chemical tests for intoxication met to discuss the scientific and legal issues involved. The fruits of this meeting came in the form of a signed statement endorsing the continued use of the 2100:1 ratio for clinical and forensic purposes. Several new studies verified that the 2100:1 ratio gives a generous margin of safety in favor of the subject by about 10% compared with venous BAC analyzed directly.[241,242] In controlled laboratory studies, with blood and breath samples taken during the post-absorptive phase of alcohol metabolism, a blood/breath ratio of 2300:1 was more appropriate to give unbiased estimates of venous BAC.[241] To eliminate the entire problem of variability in the blood/breath ratio and the need to convert BrAC to BAC, Mason and Dubowski suggested that the threshold alcohol limit for driving should be defined in terms of the person's BrAC at the time of the test.[242] This approach was clearly similar to the use of UACs in Great Britain, where the statutory limits for motorists are 80 mg/dL in blood or 107 mg/dL in urine, which implies a UAC/BAC of 1.33:1.[14] Because a blood-alcohol concentration limit of 0.10 g/dL was already widely accepted in the U.S., the corresponding threshold BrAC limit was set at 0.10 g/210 liters of breath. By including the 210 liters in the wording of the statute, the weight of alcohol (0.10 g) remained the same regardless of whether blood or breath-alcohol testing were used for analysis. Much is often made over these units given the fact that 210 L is a larger volume than any human could exhale. This is clearly a spurious issue, however, since only a portion of the breath (typically around 50 mL) is being tested, and the units used are g/210L. The results could equally well be expressed in μg/L, mg/mL, micromoles per liter, or any other concentration units. Any units can be used, provided that the instrument is calibrated with the appropriate standards, having concentrations of alcohol similar to the unknown breath samples.

Accordingly, a person's BAC or BrAC are now considered equivalent for the purpose of generating evidence of impairment at the wheel. Eliminating the need to convert BrAC into BAC in every single case led to a dramatic reduction in spurious litigation concerning blood/breath ratios of alcohol and inherent variability. Furthermore, the effects of alcohol on psychomotor performance, as well as roadside surveys of the risk of involvement in traffic accidents, have been conducted with breath-test instruments (e.g., the Grand Rapids survey) and not by the analysis of BAC directly. However, several U.S. states, among others New Jersey, still persist in translating the breath-alcohol readings into a presumed BAC. Indeed, the use of breath-alcohol testing was the subject of a vigorous defense challenge in 1989 in the State of New Jersey, where the Breathalyzer was well established for testing drinking drivers. The DUI statute in New Jersey stipulated that a person's blood-alcohol concentration should be estimated indirectly by analysis of the breath. The gist of the defense argument was that the 2100:1 blood/breath ratio was biased against the person being tested. Considerable expert testimony was called to answer questions about variation in the blood/breath conversion factor used. This "Downie case" was eventually settled by the Supreme Court of New Jersey ruling in favor of the continued use of the Breathalyzer 900 in law enforcement and also keeping the 2100:1 conversion factor unchanged. The bulk of the expert testimony and the most credible witnesses took the stance that breath-tests involving a 2100:1 ratio tended to underestimate the venous blood-alcohol concentration for samples taken in the post-absorptive phase of alcohol metabolism and when results are truncated to two decimal places.

When the countries in Europe introduced evidential breath-alcohol testing in the early 1980s, the threshold BrAC limits were derived from the pre-existing BAC limits on the basis of a presumed blood/breath ratio, either 2000:1, 2100:1, or 2300:1 depending on the country. Thus, 0.50 mg/mL, which is the statutory BAC limit in the Netherlands, became 220 μg/L in breath, being derived from 0.50/2300 = 0.000217 and rounding to 0.00022, before moving the decimal point to obtain appropriate units of μg and liters. The threshold BrAC limits corresponding to already established BAC limits in different countries are shown in Table 14.1.1.

14.1.4.6   Pulmonary Function (Chronic Obstructive Pulmonary Disease)

The basic premise of breath-alcohol testing is that the concentration of alcohol in pulmonary capillary blood equilibrates with alveolar air at normal body temperature.[243] However, the air in the upper airways and dead-space regions of the lungs also contains alcohol by a diffusion process from the mucous membranes receiving alcohol from blood supplying the tissue in the upper respiratory tract. Furthermore, alcohol from the upper respiratory tract may be picked up in the inspired air and deposited further down the tract during inspiration, only to be redistributed again during expiration, with some of the alveolar alcohol being deposited back into the depleted tissues of the upper airways.[244] The net effect is that the alcohol which appears on the expired breath does so as a result of a complex dynamic process, which varies in degree from individual to individual. As indicated in the previous section, however, where the law specifies a BrAC per se offense, the actual mechanism is not relevant, and the per se BrAC offense is readily justified in terms of impairment associated with BrAC.

Modern breath-alcohol instruments are equipped with automated procedures for sampling breath and these monitor the volume exhaled and the concentration of alcohol during a prolonged exhalation. If a person manages to exhale a certain minimum volume of breath for a given length of time to satisfy the sampling requirements, a portion of the end-expired air is captured for analysis of alcohol. Some individuals, particularly those with impaired lung function, will genuinely be unable to satisfy the sampling parameters of some evidential breath-alcohol analyzers currently being used.[245,246] Indeed, even subjects with healthy lungs, especially women of small stature and those who habitually smoke cigarettes, might have insufficient lung capacity to exhale for the minimum required time. Moreover, at high blood-alcohol concentration, the ability of a person to provide an approved sample of breath might be reduced compared with the sober state.[247]

The rules and regulations pertaining to evidential breath-alcohol testing should therefore contain an option for the suspect to provide a blood sample if he or she fails to satisfy the sampling requirements because of pulmonary limitations. In Great Britain, the policeman operating the instrument has to decide whether the suspect is not cooperating properly in providing the required sample. If this happens, the person can be charged with "failing to provide" as a separate offense that carries the same punishment as if the BrAC had been above the legal limit for driving.[14,245] Many people charged and prosecuted for "failing to provide" in the U.K. have later been vindicated by seeking medical advice and undergoing pulmonary function tests.[248,249] This prompted the British Home Office scientists to embark on a series of studies into the ability of people with small stature and impaired lung function to satisfy the sampling requirements of various breath-alcohol testing instruments.[245,250] Those individuals with forced expiratory volume in one second ($FEV_{1.0}$) of less than 2.0 L and forced vital capacity (FVC) of less than 2.6 L were unable to use some of the breath-testing equipment evaluated. In another study with healthy subjects less than 5 ft 5 in. (165 cm) tall, some were unable to provide the required breath sample.[250] This report, however, fails to specify the ages of the subjects, whether they were tested under the influence of alcohol, and whether they smoked cigarettes. These variables are important when the ability of a person to provide an approved breath sample has to be judged.

Asthma is an inflammatory disease of the airways causing obstruction to breathing and a reduction in air flow. Respiratory inhalers used by asthmatics contain salbutamol (β_2-adrenergic bronchodilator) as the active ingredient. It is the mainstay treatment for acute attacks of asthma. The use of this inhaled medication just prior to being breath-tested with Intoximeter 3000 (infrared) and Alcolmeter S-D2 (electrochemistry) failed to produce a response of apparent alcohol.[251] A similar lack of response was reported for a number of nasal sprays used by people with impaired lung function.[252] Some asthma inhalers contain ethanol as an ingredient and this means that a response is more likely to occur immediately after their use. However, within 2 to 9 min after using a wide range of inhalers and sprays, the small positive response on the breath analyzers was eliminated.[253]

To test the influence of chronic obstructive pulmonary disease (COPD) on breath-alcohol analysis, patients suffering from COPD received 60 to 70 g ethanol and their blood-alcohol concentration was compared with results using the Breathalyzer model 900 at various times after drinking. The resulting blood/breath ratios were consistently higher than the 2100:1 calibration factor used with the Breathalyzer 900 instrument, so breath-tests for alcohol are not detrimental to those individuals who suffer from COPD.[254] In a more recent study with 12 COPD patients as well as an age matched control group of subjects, alcohol (0.60 g/kg) was given by intravenous infusion and blood and breath-alcohol concentrations were determined for up to 4 h.[255] The blood/breath ratios of alcohol in the control group and patients with COPD varied with time after infusion of alcohol and in the post-peak phase of metabolism of alcohol, the values were mostly in excess of 2400:1.[255]

Summing up these experiments in patients with pulmonary disease, there is no solid evidence to suggest that impaired lung function (asthma, COPD, emphysema) puts them at risk of being unfairly prosecuted for drunk driving when per se alcohol limits operate.[256,257] If people with these pulmonary limitations manage to provide an approved breath sample, there is no reason to believe that the test result will be greater than for people with healthy lungs having the same blood-alcohol concentration. On the contrary, because of the higher blood/breath ratios in people suffering from COPD compared with age-matched control subjects, those with COPD who might be breath-tested have an advantage.[255]

14.1.4.7 *Breathing Pattern and Hypo- and Hyperthermia*

For a given individual, the concentration of alcohol expelled in the breath depends on the concentration existing in the pulmonary blood, which depends on the amount of alcohol consumed and the time after drinking when breath-tests are made.[243] However, the concentration of alcohol measured in the breath at a given blood-alcohol concentration depends on numerous factors, especially the person's pattern of breathing prior to exhalation and body temperature. Also, various design features of the breath-alcohol analyzer, such as the resistance to exhalation and the geometry of the breath-inlet tube, and also the kind of mouthpiece and spit-trap fitted to the instrument, are important to consider when variations in test results have to be explained.[258–260]

The influence of a person's breathing pattern prior to exhalation has been evaluated in several studies and variables such as breath-holding, hyper- and hypoventilation, as well as shallow breathing were investigated.[258] Most changes in the pre-exhalation maneuver decrease the BrAC in the final exhalation compared with a control sample comprising a moderately deep inhalation and forced end-exhalation. However, breath-holding or hypoventilation before providing breath for analysis increases the concentration of alcohol in the breath-sample by about 10 to 20%.[261,262] This higher BrAC is caused in part by a higher breath temperature and the longer time available for equilibration of alcohol with the mucous surfaces in the upper airways.[263] Body temperature has an important influence on BrAC because the temperature coefficient of alcohol solubility is ± 6.5% per degree centigrade.[264] Local cooling of the mouth and upper-airway by breathing cold air will decrease breath-temperature and breath-alcohol concentration.[265] Keeping ice in the mouth before and during exhalation leads to a marked lowering in the person's BrAC, in part because of the high solubility of alcohol in water condensing from the ice, and condensation of ethanol vapor in the mouth.[266] Isothermal re-breathing devices have been described for use with breath alcohol equipment.[267] The net effect of this device is to allow better equilibration of alcohol with all the tissues in the respiratory tract, thus raising the breath test result by about 10%, and showing a closer agreement to the blood alcohol result when a blood/breath ratio of 2100:1 is assumed.[267]

Controlled studies of the influence of hypo- and hyperthermia on breath-alcohol test results with Breathalyzer model 900 were reported by Fox and Hayward.[268,269] The deep-core body temperature was raised by keeping volunteer subjects immersed up to their necks in water at 42°C for 45 min. This caused a 2.5°C rise in body temperature and a 23% distortion (increase) in the breath-alcohol concentration. Immersion of the subjects up to the neck in cold water at 10°C for 45 min caused mild hypothermia and the breath-alcohol concentration decay curve was distorted downwards by 22%. When subjects were returned to normothermic conditions, the BrAC readings recovered to reach the values expected from past experience with the Breathalyzer 900, that is, results were about 10% less than the corresponding blood-alcohol concentration directly determined.

14.1.5 Concluding Remarks

The widespread use of statutory alcohol concentration limits for motorists simplifies the prosecution of drunken drivers and makes this process more effective. Accordingly, a person's blood or breath-alcohol concentration has become the single most important evidence for successfully prosecuting DUI suspects. It should, however, always be considered in the context of other evidence, such as observations about the subject's driving ability, outward behavior, and response to questions and performance in field sobriety tests. This has meant that defense arguments focus heavily on trying to discredit and cast doubt on the reliability of the result of analyzing alcohol in blood and/or breath. Of the two, it seems that results of measuring blood-alcohol are much less frequently questioned than those obtained by analyzing the breath. This probably stems from the earlier tradition of translating a measured BrAC into a presumed BAC for forensic purposes. The magnitude of variation in the conversion factor (blood/breath ratio) from person to person and in the same person over time triggered many defense challenges, which still persist today. The uncertainty in the sampling and analysis of breath and the conversion factors used have attracted much debate in the scientific literature and in the courts. The entire problem with blood/breath ratios should have been eliminated after defining the statutory alcohol limits for driving as the BrAC per se and thus sidestepping the need to convert BrAC into BAC.

Furthermore, mostly under the control of a built-in microprocessor, evidential breath-alcohol instruments are typically operated by police officers and not by chemists. This apparent vested interest in the outcome of the test result tends to make breath-alcohol testing more suspect according to some critics, and vulnerable to defense attacks compared with blood alcohol measurements performed at a forensic laboratory. Much could be done to improve forensic alcohol analysis by paying more attention to pre-analytical factors, in particular the methods and procedures used to obtain samples of body fluids (blood, breath, or urine). The responsibility for sampling, transport, and initial storage of specimens is usually in the hands of the police and other personnel who lack training in clinical laboratory methods.[270] The use of a checklist to document certain key aspects of the sampling protocol and the various precautions taken is highly recommended.[271] Any mishaps or unusual incidents that occur during sampling, as well as the behavior and appearance of the suspect, should be carefully noted. These might become important later when the results of alcohol analysis are interpreted by the court.

The trend toward accreditation of clinical and forensic laboratories will help to standardize and document analytical procedures and establish acceptable standards of performance that minimize the risk of laboratory blunders. Forensic tests for alcohol, however, should always be held to a high standard, and where there is error, mistakes, or uncertainty, this should be honestly recognized and accrue to the defendant's favor. As long as there is a lot of money to be made in defending drunk drivers, or testifying on their behalf, there will always be lawyers and expert witnesses prepared to embark on crusades to discredit the police, the laboratory, or both. To focus an attack on the scientific background of forensic alcohol testing, a defense lawyer requires the services of an expert witness.[272] There are plenty of these individuals available, many of whom can be located through professional directory listings of their names, addresses, academic qualifications, experience, and often their fee. Most of these experts are willing to testify for the defense, the prosecution, or both and will generally testify in either criminal or civil litigation.

During the highly publicized *Daubert* decision from the U.S. Supreme Court, much was written about the use of scientific evidence and how best to judge the testimony of expert witnesses.[273] At about this time, an editorial in the scientific journal *Nature* made the following statement about expert witnesses:[274]

> The so-called expert witness in court may be a hired-gun, willing to testify to anything for a fee, or a crackpot whose insupportable ideas are masked by an advanced degree (Ph.D.) often from a respectable university.

William S. Lovell (chemist and district attorney) made the following observation about the use and abuse of expert testimony in DUI litigation as long ago as 1972:[275]

> Courts are indeed plagued by the instant expert, who whether out of a misguided eagerness to earn his fee or an overreaction to his own self-described credentials, may expound far reaching opinions.

The courtroom can be a cruel place and skillful use of expert testimony plays a much bigger role in deciding the outcome of DUI trials held in the U.S. and Britain than in continental Europe. In Britain and the U.S., the adversarial system of justice operates, which aims to establish the truth by probing the strengths and weaknesses of defense and prosecution cases.[276] This opens the door for selecting expert witnesses known for their strong opinions and outspoken views about key elements of the scientific evidence crucial for the case. This is somewhat different from the situation in continental Europe and Scandinavia where the inquisitorial system operates and an investigating judge or judges appoint the necessary forensic experts who conduct tests and make investigations independent of the prosecution.[277,278] This gives the impression that forensic experts evaluate the scientific evidence in a more impartial way and arrive at an opinion based on their findings. This takes the form of a written report to the court, similar to a deposition, but occasionally the expert is also expected to appear in person to present his conclusions and receive questioning from the defense and prosecution attorney.

As far as possible, expert witnesses should base their testimony on personal experience and studies they have conducted themselves and the results of which have been published in the peer-reviewed literature. But even peer-reviewers make mistakes and publication per se does not make the results gospel. Scientists are not infallible and unsubstantiated opinion is no substitute for personal experience and well designed experiments. If scientific evidence is important in criminal or civil litigation, it might be better for the judge to appoint suitably qualified experts instead of relying on witnesses chosen by the opposing sides.[279] This was one of the recommendations of the *Daubert* decision of the U.S. Supreme Court, and has already been put into practice in Oregon, in a case concerning the health hazards of silicone breast implants.[280] Unfortunately, the demeanor and manner of the witness often determines whether or not the evidence they present is accepted by the jury, rather than the validity of the science on which the opinion is based.[281] Complex scientific issues can usually not be satisfactorily discussed and debated in the courtroom by lawyers posing set-piece questions to expert witnesses, many of whom have poor or inappropriate qualifications and questionable motives.[281,282] Other complicating factors are that the attorneys are often prepared to use any available means, including confusing the jury, obfuscating the issues, and impugning the expert testimony, in order to gain an acquittal, rather than pursuing an objective search for the truth.

REFERENCES

1. Heise, H.A., Alcohol and automobile accidents. *JAMA* 103, 739, 1934.
2. Heise, H.A., Halporn, B., Medicolegal aspects of drunkenness. *Penn Med J* 36, 190, 1932.
3. Holcomb, R.L., Alcohol in relation to traffic accidents. *JAMA* 111, 1076, 1938.
4. Borkenstein, R.F., Historical perspective: North American traditional and experimental response. *J Stud Alc Supp.* 10, 3, 1985.

5. Andréasson, R., Jones, A.W., Historical anecdote related to chemical tests for intoxication. *J Anal Toxicol* 20, 207, 1996.

6. Ladd, M., Gibson, R.B., The medicolegal aspects of the blood test to determine intoxication. *The Iowa State Law Review* 24, 1, 1939.

7. Bavis, D.F., Arnholt, M.F., Tests of blood and urine of drunken drivers. *Nebraska State Med J* 24, 220, 1939.

8. Newman, H.W., Fletcher, E., The effect of alcohol on driving skill. *JAMA* 115, 1600, 1940.

9. Newman, H.W., *Acute Alcoholic Intoxication; A Critical Review.* Stanford University Press, Stanford, CA, 1941.

10. Hingson, R., Heeren, T., Winter, M., Lowering state legal blood alcohol limits to 0.08%: The effect on fatal motor vehicle crashes. *Am J Pub Health* 86, 1297, 1996.

11. Wagenaar, A.C., O'Malley, P.M., LaFond, C. Lowered legal blood alcohol limits for young drivers: effects on drinking, driving, and driving after drinking behaviors in 30 states. *Am J Pub Health* 91, 801, 2001.

12. Jones, A.W., Blood and breath-alcohol concentrations. *Br Med J* 305, 955, 1992.

13. Council on Scientific Affairs, American Medical Association Council Report. Alcohol and the driver. *JAMA* 255, 522, 1986.

14. Walls, H.J., Brownlie, A.R., *Drink, Drugs and Driving.* Sweet & Maxwell, London, 1985.

15. Jones, A.W., Enforcement of drink-driving laws by use of per se legal alcohol limits: Blood and/or breath concentration as evidence of impairment. *Alc Drugs and Driving* 4, 99, 1988.

16. Ziporyn, T., Definition of impairment essential for prosecuting drunken drivers. *JAMA* 253, 3509, 1985.

17. Tarantino, J., *Defending Drinking Drivers.* James Publishing Inc., Santa Ana, CA, 1986.

18. Head, W.C., Joye, Jr. R.I., *101 ways to avoid a drunk driving conviction.* Maximar Publishing Company, Atlanta, 1991.

19. Fitzgerald, E.F., Hume, D.N., *Intoxication test evidence: Criminal and Civil.* The Lawyers Co-operative Publishing Company, 1987.

20. Nichols, D.H., *Drinking/Driving litigation: Criminal and Civil.* Callaghan, Deerfield, Il., 1985.

21. Erwin, R., *Defense of Drunk Driving Cases, Criminal/Civil.* Matthew Bender, New York, 1996.

22. Cohen, H.M., Green, J.B., *Apprehending and prosecuting the drunk driver.* Matthew Bender, New York, 1995.

23. Denney, R.C., The use of breath and blood alcohol values in evaluating hip flask defences. *New Law Journal*, Sept. 26, 923, 1986.

24. Lewis, M.J., The individual and the estimation of his blood alcohol concentration from intake with particular reference to the hip-flask drink. *J Forens Sci Soc* 26, 19, 1985.

25. Jones, A.W., Widmark's equation; Determining amounts of alcohol consumed from blood alcohol concentration. *DWI Journal; Law and Science* 3, 8, 1989.

26. Forrest, A.R.W., The estimation of Widmark's factor. *J Forens Sci Soc* 26, 249, 1986.

27. Iffland, R., Staak, M., Rieger, S., Experimentelle Untersuchungen zur Überprüfung von Nachtrunkbehauptungen. *Blutalkohol* 19, 235, 1982.

28. Biasotti, A.A., Valentine, T.E., Blood alcohol concentration determined from urine samples as a practical cquivalent or alternative to blood and breath alcohol tests. *J Forens Sci* 30, 194, 1985.

29. Jones, A.W., Ethanol distribution ratios between urine and capillary blood in controlled experiments and in apprehended drinking drivers. *J Forens Sci* 37, 21, 1992.

30. Grüner, O., Ludwig, O., Rockenfeller, K., Die Bedeutung der Doppelblutentnahmen für die Beurteilung von Nachtrunkbehauptungen. *Blutalkohol* 17, 26, 1980.

31. Bonte, W., *Begleitstoffe alkoholischer Getränke.* Verlag Max Schmidt-Röshild, Lübeck, FRG, 1988.

32. Iffland, R., Congener analysis of blood in legal proceedings: Possibilities and problems. In: W. Bonte, editor, Proc. In: Workshop on Congener Alcohols and Their Medicolegal Significance. University of Düsseldorf, 1987, p 236.

33. Bilzer, N., Grüner, O., Methodenkritische Betrachtungen zum Nachweis aliphatischer Alkohole im Blut mit Hilfe der Headspace-Analyze. *Blutalkohol* 20, 411, 1983.

34. Bonte, W., Contributions to congener analysis. *J Traffic Med* 18, 5, 1990.

35. Roine, R.P., Eriksson, C.J.P., Ylikahri, R., Penttilä, A.M., Salaspuro, M., Methanol as a marker of alcohol abuse. *Alcoholism Clin Exp Res* 13, 172, 1989.

36. Buchholtz, U., Blutmethanol als Alkoholismusmarker. *Blutalkohol* 30, 43, 1993.

37. Haffner, H.Th., Graw, M., Besserer, K., Blickle, U., Henssge, C., Endogenous methanol: variability in concentration and rate of production. Evidence of a deep compartment. *Forens Sci Intern* 79, 145, 1996.

38. Jones, A.W., Top-ten defence challenges among drinking drivers in Sweden. *Med Sci Law* 31, 429, 1991.

39. Jones, A.W., Status of alcohol absorption in drinking drivers. *J Anal Toxicol* 14, 198, 1990.

40. Jones, A.W., Jönsson, K.Å., Neri, A., Peak blood-alcohol concentration and the time of its occurrence after rapid drinking on an empty stomach. *J Forensic Sci* 36, 376, 1991.

41. Jones, A.W., Interindividual variations in the disposition and metabolism of ethanol in healthy men. *Alcohol* 1, 385, 1984.

42. Jones, A.W., Neri, A., Evaluation of blood-ethanol profiles after consumption of alcohol together with a large meal. *Can Soc Forens Sci J* 24, 165, 1991.

43. Gullberg, R.G., Variations in blood alcohol concentration following the last drink. *J Police Sci Admin* 10, 289, 1982.

44. Shajani, N.K., Dinn, H.N., Blood alcohol concentrations reached in human subjects after consumption of alcohol in a social setting. *Can J Forens Sci Soc* 18, 38, 1985.

45. Zink, P., Reinhardt, G., Der Verlauf der Blutalkoholkurve bei großen Trinkmengen. *Blutalkohol* 21, 422, 1984.

46. Jones, A.W., Andersson, L., Influence of age, gender, and blood-alcohol concentration on the disappearance rate of alcohol from blood in drinking drivers. *J Forens Sci* 41, 922, 1996.

47. Allanowai, Y., Moreland, T.A., McEwen, J., Halliday, F., Durnin, C.J., Stevenson, I.H., Ethanol kinetics — extent of error in back extrapolation procedures. *Br J Clin Pharmacol* 34, 316, 1992.

48. Lewis, K.O., Back calculation of blood alcohol concentration. *Br Med J* 295, 800, 1987.

49. Montgomery, M.R., Reasor, M.J., Retrograde extrapolation of blood alcohol data; An applied approach. *J Toxicol Environ Health* 36, 281, 1992.

50. Dossett, J.A., Breath tests, blood tests and back calculations. *The Law Society's Gassett,* 15 October, 2925, 1987.

51. McLean, A.J., Morgan, D.J., Clinical pharmacokinetics in patients with liver disease. *Clin Pharmacokinet* 21, 42, 1991.

52. Hoyumpa, A.M., Schenker, S., Major drug interactions: Effect of liver disease, alcohol, and malnutrition. *Ann Rev Med* 33, 113, 1982.

53. Koltz, U., Pathophysiological and disease-induced changes in drug distribution volume: Pharmacokinetic implications. *Clin Pharmacokinet* 1, 204, 1976.

54. Grüner, O., Bilzer, N., Walle, A.J., Blutalkoholkurve und Widmark-Werte bei dialyseabhängigen Patienten. *Blutalkohol* 17, 371, 1980.

55. Cotton, P.B., Walker, G., Ethanol absorption after gastric operations and in the coeliac syndrome. *Postgrad Med J* 49, 27, 1973.

56. Griffiths, G.H., Owen, G.M., Camphell, H., Shields, R., Gastric emptying in health and in gastroduodenal disease. *Gastroenterology* 54, 1, 1968.

57. Elmslie, R.G., Davis, R.A., Magee, D.F., White, T.T., Absorption of alcohol after gastrectomy. *Surg Gynacol Obstet* 119, 1256, 1964.

58. Jokipii, S.G., Experimental studies on blood alcohol in healthy subjects and in some diseases. Thesis for MD degree, University of Helsinki, 1951.

59. Jones, A.W., Biochemistry and physiology of alcohol: Applications to foresnic science and toxicology. In: *Medicolegal aspects of alcohol,* edited by J.C. Garriott, Lawyers & Judges Publishing Company, Inc., Tuson, 1996, p 85.

60. Lieberman, F.L., The effect of liver disease on the rate of ethanol metabolism in man. *Gastroenterology* 44, 261, 1968.

61. Ugarte, G., Insunza, I., Altschiller, H., Iturriage, H., Clinical and metabolic disorders in alcoholic hepatic damage. Chapter 29, In: *Alcohol and Alcoholism,* edited by R.E. Popham, Addiction Research Foundation, Toronto, 1969; p 230.

62. Mezey, E., Tobon, F., Rates of ethanol clearance and activities of the ethanol-oxidizing enzymes in chronic alcoholic patients. *Gastroenterology* 61, 707, 1971.

63. Bode, J.Ch., The metabolism of alcohol: Physiological and pathophysiological aspects. *J Roy Coll Phycns* 12, 122, 1978.

64. Mallach, H.J., von Oldershausen, H.F., Springer, E., Der Einfluß oraler Alkoholzufuhr auf den Blutalkoholspiegel von Gewohnheitstrinkern und Leberkranken unter verschiedenen alimentären Bedingungen. *Klin Wschr* 50, 732, 1972

65. Runyon, B.A., Care of patients with ascites. *N Eng J Med* 330, 337, 1994.

66. Aiza, I., Perez, G.O., Schiff, E.R., Management of ascites in patients with chronic liver disease. *Am J Gastroenterol* 89, 1949, 1994.

67. Teschke, R., Gellert, J., Hepatic microsomal ethanol-oxidizing system (MEOS): metabolic aspects and clinical implications. *Alcoholism; Clin Exp Res* 10, 20S, 1986.

68. Jones, A.W., Sternebring, B., Kinetics of ethanol and methanol in alcoholics during detoxification. *Alc Alcohol* 27, 641, 1992.

69. Haffner, H.T., Batra, A., Bilzer, N., Dietz, K., Gilg, T., Graw, M., et al., Statistische Annäherung an forensische Rückrechnungswerte für Alkoholiker. *Blutalkohol* 29, 53, 1992.

70. Monaghan, M.S., Olsen, K.M., Ackerman, B.H., Fuller, G.L., Porter, W.H., Pappas, A.A., Measurement of serum isopropanol and the acetone metabolite by proton nuclear magnetic resonance; Application to pharmacokinetic evaluation in a simulated overdose model. *Clin Toxicol* 33, 141. 1995.

71. Jones, A.W., Schuberth, J., Computer-aided headspace gas chromatography applied to blood-alcohol analysis: Importance of online process control. *J Forensic Sci* 34, 1116, 1989.

72. Coldwell, B.B., Grant, G.L., The disappearance of alcohol from the blood of diabetics. *J Forensic Sci* 8, 220, 1963.

73. Coldwell, B.B., A note on the estimation and disappearance of alcohol in blood, breath and urine from obese and diabetic patients. *J Forensic Sci* 10, 480, 1965.

74. Taylor, R., Agius, L., The biochemistry of diabetes. *Biochem J* 250, 625, 1988.

75. Bode, Ch., Buchwald, B., Goebell, H., Hemmung des Äthanolabbaues durch Proteinmangel beim Menschen. *Dtsch Med Wschr* 96, 1576, 1971.

76. Bode, Ch., Thiel, D., Hemmung des Äthanolabbaus beim Menschen durch Fasten: Reversibilität durch Fructose-Infusion. *Dtsch Med Wschr* 100, 1849, 1975.

77. Willner, K., Kretschmar, R., Die Veränderung des Verteilyngsfaktors nach akuten Körperwasserverlusten. *Blutalkohol* 2, 99, 1963.

78. Marshall, A.W., Kingstone, D., Boss, A.M., Morgan, M.Y., Ethanol elimination in males and females; relationship to menstrual cycle and body composition. *Hepatology* 3, 701, 1983.

79. Jones, A.W., Neri, A., Age-related changes in blood-alcohol parameters and subjective feelings of intoxication. *Alc Alcohol* 20, 45, 1985.

80. Brettel, H.F., Maske, B., Zur Alkoholbestimmung bei Blutnahme in Schockzustand. *Blutalkohol* 8, 360, 1971.

81. Brettel, H.F., Die Alkoholbegutachtung bei Traumatisierten und Narkotisierten. *Blutalkohol* 11, 1, 1974.

82. Brettel, H.F. and Henrich, M., Die Rückrechnung auf die sog, Tatzeitalkoholkonzentration bei Schockfällen. *Blutalkohol* 16, 145, 1979.

83. Kleemann, W.J., Seibert, M., Tempka, A., Wolf, M., Weller, J-P., Tröger, H-D., Arterielle und venöse Alkoholelimination bei 10 polytraumatisierten Patienten. *Blutalkohol* 33, 162, 1995.

84. Baskett, P.J.F., Management of hypovolemic shock. *Br Med J* 300, 1453, 1990.

85. Flordal, P.A., The plasma dilution factor: Predicting how concentrations in plasma and serum are affected by blood volume variations and blood loss. *J Lab Clin Med* 126, 353, 1995.

86. Ditt, J., and Schulze, G., Blutverlust und Blutalkoholkonzentration. *Blutalkohol* 1, 183, 1962.

87. Wigmore, J.G., Mammoliti, D.N., Comments on Medicolegal alcohol determination: Implications and consequences of irregularities in blood alcohol concentration vs time curves. *J Anal Toxicol* 17, 317, 1993.

88. Goldberger, B.A., Cone, E.J., Kadehjian, L., Unexpected ethanol ingestion through soft drinks and flavored beverages. *J Anal Toxicol* 20, 332, 1996.

89. Linnoila, M., Mattila, M.J., Kitchell, B.S., Drug interactions with alcohol. *Drugs* 18, 299, 1979.

90. Lane, E.A., Guthrie, S., Linnoila, M., Effects of ethanol on drug and metabolite pharmacokinetics. *Clin Pharmacokinet* 10, 228, 1985.

91. Lieber, C.S., Interaction of alcohol with other drugs and nutrients: Implications for the therapy of alcoholic liver disease. *Drugs*, 40 (suppl 3) 23, 1990.

92. Blomstrand, R., Theorell, H., Inhibitory effect on ethanol oxidation in man after administration of 4-methyl pyrazole. *Life Sci* 9, 631, 1970.

93. Blomstrand, R., Östling-Wintzell, H., Löf, A., McMartin, K., Tolf, B.R., Hedström, K.G., Pyrazoles as inhibitors of alcohol oxidation and as important tools in alcohol research: An approach to therapy against methanol poisoning. *Proc Natl Acad Sci* 76, 3499, 1979.

94. Jacobsen, D., McMartin, K.E., Methanol and ethylene glycol poisonings — mechanism of toxicity, clinical course, diagnosis and treatment. *Med Toxicol* 1, 309, 1986.

95. Estonius, M., Svensson, S., Höög, J.O., Alcohol dehydrogenase in human tissues: localisation of transcripts coding for five classes of the enzyme. *FEBS Letters* 397, 338, 1996.

96. Seitz, H.K., Egerer, G., Simanowski, U.A., Waldherr, R., Eckey, R., Agarwal, D.P., Goedde, H.W., Von Wartburg, J.P., Human gastric alcohol dehydrogenase activity; effect of age, sex, and alcoholism. *Gut* 34, 1433, 1993.

97. Frezza, M., DePadova, C., Pozzato, G., Terpin, M., Baraona, E., Lieber, C.S., High blood alcohol levels in women: the role of decreased gastric alcohol dehydrogenase activity and first-pass metabolism. *N Engl J Med* 322, 95, 1990.

98. Welling, P.G., Pharmacokinetics of alcohol following single low doses to fasted and non-fasted subjects. *J. Clin. Pharmacol.* 17, 199–206, 1977.

99. Wilkinson, P.K., Sedman, A.J., Sakmar, E., Lin, Y.J., Wagner, J.G., Fasting and non-fasting blood ethanol concentration following repeated oral administration of ethanol to one adult male subject. *J. Pharmacokinet. Biopharm.* 5, 41, 1977.

100. Roine, R., Gentry, T., Hernandez-Munoz, R., Baraona, E., Lieber, C.S., Aspirin increases blood alcohol concentration in humans after ingestion of ethanol. *JAMA* 264, 2406, 1990.

101 Julkunen, R.J.K., Tannenbaum, L., Baraona, E., Lieber, C.S., First-pass metabolism of ethanol: an important determinant of blood levels after alcohol consumption. *Alcohol* 2, 437, 1985.

102. Seitz, H.K., Bösche, J., Czygan, P., Veith, S., Simon, B., Kommerell, B., Increased blood ethanol levels following cimetidine but not ranitidine. *Lancet* 2 700, 1982.

103. Feely, J., Wood, A.J., Effects of cimetidine on the elimination and actions of ethanol. *JAMA* 247, 2819, 1982.

104. Caballeria, J., Baraona, E., Rodamilans, M., Lieber, C.S., Effects of cimetidine on gastric alcohol dehydrogenase activity and blood ethanol levels. *Gastroenterology* 96, 388, 1989.

105. Westenbrink, W., Cimetidine and the blood alcohol curve: A case study and review. *Can Soc Forens Sci J* 28, 165, 1995.

106. Bye, A., Lacey, L.F., Gupta, S., Powell, J.R., Effect of ranitidine hydrochloride (150 mg twice daily) on the pharmacokinetics of increasing doses of ethanol (0.15, 0.3, 0.6 g/kg). *Br. J. Clin. Pharmacol.* 41, 129, 1996.

107. Dauncey, H., Chesher, G.B., Palmer, R.H., Cimetidine and ranitidine; Lack of effect on the pharmacokinetics of an acute ethanol dose. *J Clin Gastroenterol.* 17, 189, 1993.

108. Fraser, A.G., Hudson, M., Sawyerr, A.M., Smith, M., Rosalki, S.B., Pounder, R.E., Ranitidine, cimetidine, famotidine have no effect on post-prandial absorption of ethanol 0.8 g/kg taken after an evening meal. *Aliment. Pharmacol. Therapeut.* 6, 693, 1992.

109. Raufman, J.P., Notar-Francesco, V., Raffaniello, R.D., Straus, E.W., Histamine-2 receptor antagonists do not alter serum ethanol levels in fed, nonalcoholic men. *Ann Int Med.* 118, 488, 1993.

110. Pedrosa, M.C., Russell, R.M., Saltzman, J.R., Golner, B.B., Dallal, G.E., Sepe, T.E., Oates, E., Egerier, G., Seitz, H.K., Gastric emptying and first-pass metabolism of ethanol in elderly subjects with and without atrophic gastritis. *Scand J Gastroenterol.* 31, 671, 1996.

111. Toon, S., Khan, A.Z., Holt, B.J., Mullins, F.G.P., Langley, S.J., and Rowland, M.M., Absence of effect of ranitidine on blood alcohol concentrations when taken morning, midday, or evening with or without food. *Clin Pharmacol Therap* 55, 385, 1994.

112. Lester, D., The concentration of apparent endogenous ethanol. *J. Stud. Alcohol* 23, 17, 1962.

113. Sprung, R., Bonte, W., Rüdell, E., Domke, M., Frauenrath, C., Zum Problem des endogenen Alkohols. *Blutalkohol* 18, 65, 1981.

114. Jones, A.W., Mårdh, G., Änggård, E., Determination of endogenous ethanol in blood and breath by gas chromatography-mass spectrometry. *Pharmacol. Biochem. Behav.* 18 Suppl. 1, 267, 1983.

115. Ostrovsky, Y. M., Endogenous ethanol — Its metabolic, behavioral and biomedical significance. *Alcohol* 3, 239, 1986.

116. Jones, A.W., Ostrovsky, Y.M., Wallin, A., Midtvedt, T., Lack of differences in blood and tissue concentrations of endogenous ethanol in conventional and germfree rats. *Alcohol* 1, 393, 1984.

117. Blomstrand, R., Observations on the formation of ethanol in the intestinal tract in man. *Life Sci.* 10, 575, 1971.

118. Agapejev, S., Vassilieff, I., Curi, P.R., Alcohol levels in cerebrospinal fluid and blood samples from patients under pathological conditions. *Acta Neurol Scand* 86, 496, 1992.

119. Agapejev, S., Vassilieff, I., Curi, P.R., Alcohol in cerebrospinal fluid (CSF) and alcoholism. *Hum Exper Toxicol* 11, 237, 1992.

120. Jones, A. W., Concentration of endogenous ethanol in blood and CSF. *Acta Neurol. Scand.* 89, 149, 1994.

121. Kaji, H., Asanuma, Y., Yahara, O., Shibue, H., Hisamura, M., Saito, N., Kawakami, Y., Murao, M., Intragastrointestinal alcohol fermentation syndrome; report of two cases and review of the literature. *J Forens Sci Soc* 24, 461, 1984.

122. Kaji, H., Asanumo, Y., Saito, N., Hisamura, M., Murao, M., Yoshida, T., Takahashi, K., The auto-brewery syndrome — the repeated attacks of alcoholic intoxication due to the overgrowth of Candida (albicans) in the gastrointestinal tract, *Materia Medica Polona,* 8, 429, 1976.

123. Hunnisett, A., Howard, J., Davies, S., Gut fermentation (or the 'Auto-brewery') syndrome: A new clinical test with initial observations and discussion of clinical and biochemical implications. *J Nutr Med* 1, 33, 1990.

124. Jones, A.W., Excretion of alcohol in urine and diuresis in healthy men in relation to their age, the dose administered, and the time after drinking. *Forens Sci Intern* 45, 217, 1990.

125. Widmark, E.M.P., Uber die Konzentration des genossenen Alkohols in Blut und Harn unter verschiedenen Umständen. *Skand Arch Physiol* 33, 85, 1915.

126. Blackmore, D.J., Mason, J.K., Renal clearance of urea, creatinine and alcohol. *Med Sci Law* 8, 51, 1968.

127. Miles, W.R., The comparative concentrations of alcohol in human blood and urine at intervals after ingestion. *J Pharmacol Exp Therap* 20, 265, 1922.

128. Lundquist, F., The urinary excretion of ethanol in man. *Acta Pharmacol Toxicol* 18, 231, 161.

129. Jones, A.W., Helander, A., Disclosing recent drinking after alcohol has been cleared from the body. *J Anal Toxicol* 20, 141, 1996.

130. Widmark, E.M.P., *Principles and application of medicolegal alcohol analysis.* Biomedical Publications, Davis, 1981, pp 1–163.

131. Mulrow, P.J., Huvos, A., Buchanan, D.L., Measurement of residual urine with I123 labeled diodrast. *J Lab Clin Med* 57, 109, 1961.

132. Fine, J., Glucose content of normal urine. *Br Med J* 1, 1209, 1965.

133. Alexander, W.D., Wills, P.D., Eldred, N., Urinary ethanol and diabetes mellitus. *Diab. Med.* 5, 463, 1988.

134. Sulkowski, H.A., Wu, A.H.B., McCarter, Y.S., In-vitro production of ethanol in urine by fermentation. *J Forens Sci* 40, 990, 1995.

135. Saady, J.J., Poklis, A., Dalton, H.P., Production of urinary ethanol after sample collection. *J Forens Sci* 38, 1467, 1993.

136. Muholland, J.H., Townsend, F.J., Bladder Beer: a new clinical observation. *Trans Am Clin Climatol Ass* 95, 34, 1983.

137. Chang, J., Kollman, S.E., The effect of temperature on the formation of ethanol by candida albicans. *J Forensic Sci* 34, 105, 1989.

138. Beck, O., Helander, A., Jones, A.W., Serotonin metabolism marks alcohol intake. *Forensic Urine Drug Testing,* September 1996, p 1–4.

139. Helander, A., Beck, O., Jones, A.W., 5HTOL/5HIAA as biochemical marker of post-mortem ethanol synthesis. *Lancet* 340, 1159, 1992.

140. Dick, G.L., Stone, H.M., Alcohol loss arising from microbial contamination of drivers' blood specimens. *Forens Sci Intern* 34, 17, 1987.

141. Heise, H.A., How extraneous alcohol affects the blood test for alcohol. *Am J Clin Pathol* 32, 169, 1959.

142. Goldfinger, T.M., Schaber, D., A comparison of blood alcohol concentration using non-alcohol and alcohol-containing skin antiseptics. *Ann Emerg Med* 36, 665, 1982.

143. Times Law Report. Power to quash convictions after guilty pleas., *The Times,* October 4, 1990.

144. Taberner, P.V., A source of error in blood alcohol analysis. *Alc Alcohol* 24, 489, 1989.

145. Peek, G.J., March, A., Keating, J., Ward, R.J., Peters, T.J., The effects of swabbing the skin on apparent blood alcohol concentration. *Alc Alcohol* 25, 639, 1990.

146. McIvor, R.A., Cosbey, S.H., Effect of using alcoholic and non-alcoholic skin cleansing swabs when sampling blood for alcohol estimation using gas chromatography. *Brit J Clin Prac* 44, 235, 1990.

147. Ogden, E.J.D., Gerstner-Stevens, J., Burke J., Young, S.J., Venous blood alcohol sampling and the alcohol swab. *The Police Surgeon*, October, 4, 1992.

148. Carter. P.G., McConnell, A.A., Venous blood sampling in drink driving offences and English law. *Alc Drugs and Driving* 6, 27, 1990.

149. Ryder, K.W,, Glick, M.R., The effect of skin cleansing agents on ethanol results measured with the Du Pont automatic clinical analyzer. *J Forensic Sci* 31, 574, 1986.

150. Kissa, E., Determination of inorganic fluoride in blood with a fluoride ion-sensitive electrode. *Clin Chem* 33, 253, 1987.

151. Dubowski, K.M., Essary, N.A., Contamination of blood specimens for alcohol analysis during collection. *Abs & Rev in Alcohol and Driving* 4, 3, 1983.

152. Brown, G.A., Neylan, D., Reynolds, W.J., and Smalldon, K.W., The stability of ethanol in stored blood. Part 1: Important variables and interpretation of results. *Anal Chim Acta* 66, 271, 1973.

153. Smalldon, K.W. and Brown, G.A., The stability of ethanol in stored blood. Part II: The mechanism of ethanol oxidation. *Anal Chim Acta* 66, 285, 1973.

154. Bowers, R.V., Burleson, W.D., Blades, J.F., Alcohol absorption from the skin in man. *Quart J Stud Alc* 3, 31, 1942.

155. Riley, D., Wigmore J.G., Yen, B., Dilution of blood collected for medicolegal alcohol analysis by intravenous fluids. *J Anal Toxicol* 20, 330, 1996.

156. Jones, A.W., Hahn, R., Stalberg, H., Distribution of ethanol and water between plasma and whole blood; Inter- and intra-individual variations after administration of ethanol by intravenous infusion. *Scand J Clin Lab Invest* 50, 775, 1990.

157. Lenter, C., Geigy Scientific Tables, Geigy Pharmaceuticals, Basel, 1992.

158. Jones, A.W., Determination of liquid/air partition coefficients for dilute solutions of ethanol in water, whole blood, and plasma. *J Anal Toxicol* 7, 193, 1983.

159. Ganong, W.F., *Review of Medical Physiology.* Lange Medical Publications, Los Altos, 1979.

160. Wilkinson, D.R., Haines, P., Morgner, R., Sockrider, D., Wilkinson, C.L., Spartz, M., The 2100/1 ratio used in alcohol programs is once again under attack. In: *Alcohol, Drugs and Traffic Safety,* Eds P.C. Noordzij and R. Roszbach, Elsevier Science Publishers, Amstedam, 1987, p 391.

161. Wright, B.M., Distribution of ethanol between plasma and erythrocytes in whole blood. *Nature* 218, 1263, 1968.

162. Jones, A.W., Measuring alcohol in blood and breath for forensic purposes — A historical review. *Forens Sci Rev* 8, 13, 1996.

163. Jones, A.W., Andersson, L., Biotransformation of acetone to isopropanol observed in a motorist involved in a sobriety control. *J Forensic Sci* 40, 686, 1995.

164. Dubowski, K.M., Essary, N., Quality assurance in breath alcohol analysis. *J Analyt Toxicol* 18, 306, 1994.

165. Bogen, E., Drunkenness; A quantitative study of acute alcohol intoxication. *JAMA* 89, 1508, 1927.

166. Spector, N.H., Alcohol breath tests: Gross errors in current methods of measuring alveolar gas concentrations. *Science* 172, 57, 1971.

167. Dubowski, K.M., Studies in breath-alcohol analysis: Biological factors. *Z Rechtsmed* 76, 93, 1975.

168. Caddy, G.R., Sobell, M.B. and Sobell, L.C., Alcohol breath tests: Criterion times for avoiding contamination by mouth alcohol. *Behav Res Meth Instr* 10, 814, 1978.

169. Gullberg, R.G., The elimination rate of mouth alcohol: mathematical modeling and implications in breath alcohol analysis. *J Forensic Sci* 37, 1363, 1992.

170. Modell, J.G., Taylor, J.P. and Lee, J.Y., Breath alcohol values following mouthwash use. *JAMA* 270, 2955, 1993.

171. Grüner, O., Bilzer, N., Untersuchungen zur Beeinflu barkeit der Alkomat — Atemalkoholmessungen durch verschiedene Stoffe des täglichen Gebrauchs (Mundwässer, parfüms, Rasierwässer, etc.). *Blutalkohol* 27, 119, 1990.

172. Denney, R.C. and Williams, P.M., Mouth alcohol: Some theoretical and practical considerations. In: *Proceedings, 10th International Conference on Alcohol, Drugs and Traffic Safety,* edited by Noordzij, P.C. and Roszbach, R. Amsterdam: Elsevier, 1987, p. 355-358.

173. Penners, B.M. and Bilzer, N., Aufsto en (Eruktation) und Atemalkoholkonzentration. *Blutalkohol* 24, 172, 1987.

174. Kahrilas, P.J., Gastroesophageal reflux disorders. *JAMA* 276, 983, 1996.

175. Fraser, A.G., Gastro-oesophageal reflux and laryngeal symptoms. *Aliment Pharmacol Therapeut* 8, 265, 1994.

176. Schoeman, M.N., Tippett, M., Akkermans, L.M.A., Dent, J., Holloway, R.H., Mechanisms of gastroesophageal reflux in ambulant healthy human subjects. *Gastroenterology* 108, 83, 1995.

177. Klauser, A.G., Schindlbeck, N.E., Müller-Lissner, S.A., Symptoms in gastro-oesophageal reflux disease. *Lancet* 335, 205, 1990.

178. Cohen, S., The pathogenesis of gastroesophageal reflux disease; A challenge in clinical physiology. *Ann Int Med* 117, 1051, 1992.

179. Pope, C.E., Acid-reflux disorders. *N Eng J Med* 331, 656, 1994.

180. Weinberg, D.S. and Kadish, S.L., The diagnosis and management of gastroesophageal reflux disease. *Med Clin North Am.* 80:411 1996.

181. Kaufman, S.E., Kaye, M.D., Induction of gastro-oesophageal reflux by alcohol. *Gut* 19, 336, 1978.

182. Pehl, C., Wendl, B., Pfeiffer, A., Schmidt, T., Kaess, H., Low-proof alcoholic beverages and gastroesophageal reflux. *Dig Dis Sci* 38, 93, 1993.

183. Wells, D., Farrar, J., Breath-alcohol analysis of a subject with gastric regurgitation. In *Abstracts of the 11th International Conference on Alcohol, Drugs, and Traffic Safety,* Chicago, 1989.

185. Wright, B.M., Medical problems with breath testing of drunk drivers. *Br Med J* 289, 1071, 1984.

184. Duffus, P., Dunbar J.A., Medical problems with breath testing of drunk drivers. *Br Med J* 289, 831,

186. Trafford, D.J.H., and Makin, H.L.J., Breath-alcohol concentration may not always reflect the concentration of alcohol in blood. *J Anal Toxicol.* 18;225-228, 1994.

187. Cowan, J.M., Apparent flaws in a breath-alcohol case report. *J Anal Toxicol* 19;128, 1995.

188. Cohen, H.M., Saferstein, R., Mouth alcohol, denture adhesives and breath-alcohol testing. *Drunk Driving Liquor Liability Reporter,* 6, 24, 1992.

189. Harding, P.M., McMurray, M.C., Laessig, R.H., Simley, D.O., Correll, P.J., Tsunehiro, J.K., The effect of dentures and denture adhesives on mouth alcohol retention. *J Forens Sci* 37, 999, 1992.

190. Katzgraber, F., Rabl, W., Stainer, M., Wehinger, G., Die Zahnprothese — ein Alkoholdepot? *Blutalkohol* 32, 274, 1995.

191. Dubowski, K.M., The technology of breath-alcohol analysis. *US Department of Transportation Report No. (ADM) 92-1728,* U.S. Goverment Printing Office, Wahington, DC, 1992.

192. Kramer, M., Haffner, H.T., Cramer, Y. and Ulrich, L., Untersuchungen zur Funktion der Restalkoholanzeige beim Atemalkoholtestgerät — Alcomat. *Blutalkohol* 24, 49, 1987.

193. Jones, A.W., Andersson, L., Berglund, K., Interfering substances identified in the breath of drinking drivers with Intoxilyzer 5000S. *J Anal Toxicol* 20, 522, 1996.

194. Harte, R.A., An instrument for the determination of ethanol in breath in law enforcement practice. *J Forensic Sci* 16, 167, 1971.

195. Borkenstein, R.B., Smith, H.W., The Breathalyzer and its applications. *Med Sci Law* 2, 13, 1961.

196. Oliver, R.D., Garriott, J.C., The effects of acetone and toluene on Breathalyzer results. *J Anal Toxicol* 3, 99, 1979.

197. Brick, J., Diabetes, breath acetone and Breathalyzer accuracy: A case study. *Alc Drugs Driving* 9, 27, 1993.

198. Manolis, A., The diagnostic potential of breath analysis. *Clin Chem* 29, 5, 1985.

199. Jones, A.W., Excretion of low molecular weight volatile substances in human breath: Focus on endogenous ethanol. *J Anal Toxicol* 9, 246, 1985.

200. Krotoszynski, B.K., Bruneau, G.M., O Neill, H.J., Measurement of chemical inhalation exposure in urban populations in the presence of endogenous effluents. *J Anal Toxicol* 3, 225, 1979.

201. Jones, A.W., Lagersson, W., Tagesson, C., Determination of isoprene in human breath by gas chromatography with ultraviolet detection. *J Chromatog* 672, 1, 1995.

202. Flores, A., Franks, J.F., The likelihood of acetone interference in breath alcohol measurement. *Alc Drugs and Driving* 3, 1, 1987.

203. Marks, V., Methane and the infrared breath-alcohol analyzer. *Lancet* ii, 50, 1984.

204. Peled, Y., Weinberg, D., Hallak, A., Gilat, T., Factors affecting methane production in humans. *Dig Dis Sci* 32, 267, 1987.

205. Dubowski, K.M., and Essary, N.A., Response of breath-alcohol analyzers to acetone. *J Anal Toxicol* 7, 231, 1983.

206. Mebs, D., Gerchow, J., Schmidt, K., Interference of acetone with breath-alcohol testing. *Blutalkohol* 21, 193, 1984.

207. Levey, S., Balchum, O.J., Medrando, V., Jung, R., Studies of metabolic products in expired air. 11 Acetone. *J Lab Clin Med* 63, 574, 1964.

208. Tassopoulos, C.N., Barnett, D., Fraser, T.R., Breath-acetone and blood-sugar measurements in diabetes. *Lancet* i, 1282, 1969.

209. Schoknecht, G., Hahlbrauck, B., Erkennung von Fremdgasen bei der Atemalkoholanalyse. *Blutalkohol* 29, 193, 1992.

210. Jones, A.W., Measuring and reporting the concentration of acetaldehyde in human breath. *Alc Alcohol* 30, 271, 1995.

211. Jones, A.W., Drug alcohol flush reaction and breath acetaldehyde concentration: No interference with an infrared breath alcohol analyzer. *J Anal Toxicol* 10, 98, 1986.

212. Eriksson, C.J.P., Fukunaga, T., Human blood acetaldehyde (Update 1992). In *Advances in Biomedical Alcohol Research,* eds P.V. Taberner and A.A. Badaway, Pergamon Press, Oxford, 1995, p 9.

213. Imobersteg, A.D., King, A., Cardema, M. and Mulrine, E., The effects of occupational exposure to paint solvents on the Intoxilyzer-5000 — a field study. *J Anal Toxicol* 17, 254, 1993.

214. Denney, R.C., Solvent inhalation and 'apparent' alcohol studies on the Lion Intoximeter 3000. *J Forens Sci Soc* 30, 357, 1990.

215. Cooper, S., Infrared breath-alcohol analysis following inhalation of gasoline fumes. *J Anal Toxicol* 5, 198, 1981.

216. Hümpener, R., Hein, P.M., Untersuchungen zur Beeinflußbarkeit der Alcomat-Atemalkoholmessung durch Benzin. *Blutalkohol* 29, 365, 1992.

217. Aderian R., Schmitt, G., Wu, M., Klebstoff-Lösemittel als Ursache eines Atemalkohol-Wertes von 1.96 promille. *Blutalkohol* 29, 360, 1992.

218. Bell, C.M., Gutowski, S.J., Young, S. and Wells, D., Technical Note — Diethyl Ether Interference with Infrared Breath Analysis. *J Anal Toxicol* 16, 166, 1992.

219. Edwards, M.A., Giguiere, W., Lewis, D., Baselt, R., Intoxilyzer interference by solvents. *J Anal Toxicol* 10, 125, 1986.

220. Giguiere, W., Lewis, D., Baselt, R., Chang, R., Lacquer fumes and the Intoxilyzer. *J Anal Toxicol* 12, 168, 1988.

221. Jones, A.W., Observations on the specificity of breath-alcohol analyzers used for clinical and medicolegal purposes. *J Forensic Sci* 34, 842, 1989.

222. Logan, B.K., Gullberg, R.G., Elenbaas, J.K., Isopropanol interference with breath alcohol analysis: A case report. *J Forensic Sci* 39, 1107, 1994.

223. Pennington, J.C., The effect of non-ethanolic substancs on the alcolmeter S-L2. *Can Soc Forens Sci J* 28, 131, 1995.

224. Gill, R., Hatchett, S.E., Broster, C.G., Osselton, M.D., Ramsey, J.D., Wilson, H.K., Wilcox, A.H., The response of evidential breath alcohol testing instruments with subjects exposed to organic solvents and gases. 1. Toluene, 1,1,1-trichlorocthane and butane. *Med Sci Law* 31, 187, 1991a.

225. Gill, R., Warner, H.E., Broster, C.G., Osselton, M.D., Ramsey, J.D., Wilson, H.K., Wilcox, A.H., The response of evidential breath alcohol testing instruments with subjects exposed to organic solvents and gases. 11 White spirit and nonane. *Med Sci Law* 31, 201, 1991b.

226. Gill, R., Osselton, M.D., Broad, J.E., Ramsey, J.D., The response of evidential breath alcohol testing instruments with subjects exposed to organic solvents and gases. 111. White spirit exposure during domestic painting. *Med Sci Law* 31, 214, 1991c.

227. Lester, D., Greenberg, L.A., The inhalation of ethyl alcohol by man. *J Stud Alcohol* 12, 167, 1951.

228. Mason, J.K., Blackmore, D.J., Experimental inhalation of ethanol vapor. *Med Sci Law* 12, 205, 1972.

229. Lewis, M.J., Inhalation of ethanol vapor; A case report and experimental test involving the spraying of shellac lacquer. *J Forens Sci Soc* 25, 5, 1985.

230. Lewis, M.J., A theoretical treatment for the estimation of blood alcohol concentration arising from inhalation of ethanol vapor. *J Forens Sci Soc* 25, 11, 1985.

231. Campbell, I., Wilson, H.K., Blood alcohol concentration following the inhalation of ethanol vapor under controlled conditions. *J Forens Sci Soc* 26, 129, 1986.

232. Kruhoffer, P.W., Handling of inspired vaporized ethanol in the airways and lungs with comments on forensic aspects. *Forens Sci Intern* 21, 1, 1983.

233. Harger, R.N., Lamb, E.B., Hulpieu, H.R., A rapid chemical test for intoxication employing breath. *JAMA* 110, 779, 1938.
234. Harger, R.N., Forney, R.B., Barker, H.B., Estimation of the level of blood alcohol from analysis of breath. *J Lab Clin Med* 36, 318, 1950.
235. Harger, R.N., Raney, B.B., Bridwell, E.G., Kitchel, M.F., The partition ratio of alcohol between air and water, urine and blood; estimation and identification of alcohol in these liquids from analysis of air equilibrated with them. *J Biol Chem* 183, 197, 1950.
236. Jones, A.W., Variability of the blood/breath alcohol ratio in vivo. *J Stud Alc* 39, 1931, 1978.
237. Harding, P.M., Field, P.H., Breathalyzer accuracy in actual law enforcement practice; A comparison of blood- and breath-alcohol results in Wisconsin drivers. *J Forensic Sci* 32, 1235, 1987.
238. Harding, P.M., Laessig, R.H., Field, P.H., Field performance of the Intoxilyzer 5000: A comparison of blood- and breath-alcohol results in Wisconsin drivers. *J Forensic Sci* 35,1022, 1990.
239. Taylor, M.D., Hodgson, B.T., Blood/breath correlations: Intoxilyzer 5000C, Alcotest 7110, and Breathalyzer 900A breath alcohol analyzers. *Can Soc Forens Sci J* 28, 153, 1995.
240. Jones, A.W., Andersson, L., Variability of the blood/breath alcohol ratio in drinking drivers. *J Forensic Sci* 41, 922, 1996.
241. Dubowski, K.M., O Neill, B., The blood/breath ratio of ethanol. *Clin Chem* 25, 1144, 1979.
242. Mason, M.F., Dubowski, K.M., Breath-alcohol analysis: Uses, methods, and some forensic problems — Review and opinion. *J Forensic Sci* 21, 9, 1976.
243. Jones, A.W. Physiological aspects of breath-alcohol measurement. *Alc Drugs and Driving* 6, 1, 1990.
244. George S.C., Babb, A.L., Hlastala, M.P., Dynamics of soluble gas exchange in the airways III. Single exhalation breathing maneuver. *J Appl Physiol* 75, 2439, 1993.
245. Gomm, P.J., Broster, C.G., Johnson, N.M., Hammond, K., Study into the ability of healthy people of small stature to satisfy the sampling requirements of breath alcohol testing instruments. *Med Sci Law* 33, 311, 1993.
246. Morris, M.J., Alcohol breath testing in patients with respiratory disease. *Thorax* 45, 717, 1990.
247. Neukirch, F., Liard, R., Korobaeff, M., Pariente, R., Pulmonary function and alcohol consumption. *Chest* 98, 1546, 1990.
248. Prabhu, M.B., Hurst, T.S., Cockcroft, D.W., Baule, C., Semenoff, J., Airflow obstruction and roadside breath alcohol testing. *Chest* 100, 585, 1991.
249. Morris, M.J., Taylor, A.G., Failure to provide a sample for breath alcohol analysis. *Lancet* i, 37, 1987.
250. Gomm, P.J., Osselton, M.D., Broster, C.G., Johnson, N.M., Upton, K. Study into the ability of patients with impaired lung function to use breath alcohol testing devices. *Med Sci Law* 31, 221, 1991a.
251. Gomm, P.J., Osselton, M.D., Broster, C.G., Johnson, N.M., Upton, K., The effect of salbutamol on breath alcohol testing in asthmatics. *Med Sci Law* 31, 226, 1991b.
252. Gomm, P.J., Weston, S.I., Osselton, M.D., The effect of respiratory aerosol inhalers and nasal sprays on breath alcohol testing devices used in Great Britain. *Med Sci Law* 30, 203, 1990.
253. Westenbrink, W., Sauve, L.T., The effect of asthma inhalers on the ALERT J3A, Breathalyzer 900A, and mark IV GC Intoximeter. *Can J Forens Sci Soc* 24, 23, 1991.
254. Haas, H., Morris, J.F., Breath-alcohol analysis and chronic bronchopulmonary disease. *Arch Environ Health* 25, 114, 1972.
255. Hahn, R.G., Jones, A.W., Billing, B., Stalberg, H.P., Expired-breath ethanol measurement in chronic obstructive pulmonary disease: implications for transurethral surgery. *Acta Anaesthesiol Scand* 35, 393, 1991.
256. Briggs, J.E., Patel, H., Butterfield, K., Noneybourne, D., The effects of chronic obstructive airway disease on the ability to drive and to use a roadside Alcolmeter. *Respir Med* 84, 43, 1990.
257. Crockett, A.J., Schembri, D.A., Smith, D.J., Laslett, R., Alpers, J.H., Minimum respiratory function for breath alcohol testing in South Australia. *J Forens Sci Soc* 32, 349, 1992.
258. Jones, A.W., How breathing technique can influence the results of breath alcohol analysis. *Med Sci Law* 22, 275, 1982.
259. Bell, C.M., Flack, H.J., Examining variables associated with sampling for breath alcohol analysis. In: *Proc 13th Intern Conf Alcohol, Drugs, and Traffic Safety,* Eds C.N. Kloeden and A.J. McLean, NHMRC Road Accident Research Unit, University of Adelaide, Australia, 1995, p 111.

260. Bell, C.M., What about the humble mouthpiece? Breath sample modification and implications for breath-alcohol analysis. *Proceedings 13th Intern Conf Alcohol, Drugs, and Traffic Safety,* Eds C.N. Kloeden and A.J. McLean, NHMRC Road Accident Research Unit, University of Adelaide, Australia, 1995, p 945.

261. Mulder, J.A.G., Neuteboom, W., The effects of hypo- and hyperventilation on breath alcohol measurements. *Blutalkohol* 24, 341, 1987.

262. Schmutte, P., Stromeyer, H., Naeve, W., Vergleichende Untersuchungen von Atem- und Blutalkoholkonzentration nach körperlicher Belastung und besonderer Atemtechnik (Hyperventilation). *Blutalkohol* 10, 34, 1973.

263. Jones, A.W., Quantitative relationships of the alcohol concentration and the temperature of breath during a prolonged exhalation. *Acta Physiol Scand* 114, 407, 1992.

264. Gatt, J.A., The effect of temperature and blood:breath ratio on the interpretation of breath alcohol results. *New Law Journal March* 16, 249, 1984.

265. Jones, A.W., Effects of temperature and humidity of inhaled air on the concentration of ethanol in a man's exhaled breath. *Clin Sci* 63, 441, 1982.

266. Gaylarde, P.M., Stambuk, D., Morgan, M.Y., Reduction in breath ethanol readings in normal male volunteers following mouth rinsing with water at differing temperatures. *Alc Alcohol* 22, 113, 1987.

267. Ohlson, J., Ralph, D.D., Mandelkorn M.A., Babb, A.L., Hlastala, M.P., Accurate measurement of blood alcohol concentration with isothermal rebreathing. *J. Stud. Alc.* 51, 6, 1990

268. Fox, G.R., Hayward, J.S., Effect of hypothermia on breath-alcohol analysis. *J Forens Sci* 32, 320, 1987.

269. Fox, G.R., Hayward, J.S., Effect of hyperthermia on breath-alcohol analysis. *J Forens Sci* 34. 836, 1989.

270. Chamberlain, R.T., Chain of custody: Its importance and requirements for clinical laboratory specimens. *Lab Med,* June: 477, 1989.

271. Dubowski, K.M., The role of the scientist in litigation involving drug-use testing. *Clin Chem* 34, 788, 1988.

272. Ayala F.J., Black, B., Science and the courts. *Am Sci* 81, 230, 1993.

273. Gold, J.A., Zaremski, M.J., Rappaport, E., Shefrin, D.H., Daubert v. Merrel Dow; The Supreme Court tackles scientific evidence in the courtroom. *JAMA* 270, 2964, 1993.

274. Editorial, Criteria for science in the courts. *Nature* 362, 481, 1993.

275. Lovell, W.S., Breath tests for determining alcohol in the blood. *Science* 178, 264, 1972.

276. Iwwinkelried, E.J., The evolution of the American test for admissibility of scientific evidence. *Med Sci Law* 30, 60, 1990.

277. Neufeld, P.J. and Colman, N., When science takes the witness stand. *Sci Am* 262, 46, 1990.

278. Havard, J.D.J, Expert scientific evidence under the adversarial system. A travesty of justice. *J For Sci Soc* 32, 225, 1992.

279. Annas, G.J., Scientific evidence in the courtroom; the death of the Frye rule. *N Eng J Med* 330, 1018, 1994.

280. Culliton, B.J., Scientific "experts" and the law. *Nature Med.* 3, 123, 1997

281. Eaton, D.L., Kalman, D., Scientists in the courtroom: basic pointers for the expert scientific witness. *Environ Health Perspect* 102, 668, 1994.

282. Kuffner Jr., C.A., Marchi, E., Morgado, J.M., Rubio, C.R., Capillary electrophoresis and Daubert; Time for admission, *Anal Chem,* April 1, 241A, 1996.

14.2 TESTING CLAIMS OF ADVERSE DRUG EFFECTS IN THE COURTROOM

Joe G. Hollingsworth, J.D. and Eric G. Lasker, J.D.*
Spriggs & Hollingsworth, Washington, D.C.

> There is something fascinating about science. One gets such wholesale returns of conjecture out of such a trifling investment of fact.

> — **Mark Twain,** *Life on the Mississippi* **(1874)**

Editor's note: This section on testing claims is a new, much-needed addition to this second edition. It can be almost guaranteed that anyone who has attended a forensic conference at any time in the last 10 years has been forced to sit through a lecture on the implications of the *Daubert* decision. It can also be guaranteed with equal certainty that most of those attending the lecture neither understood nor cared a great deal about what was being said. That is unfortunate, because this is a very important ruling, and it should have an enormous effect on the way we work and testify. Readers are very fortunate to have access to this section. By illustrating the problem with a real case and real plaintiff's arguments, the authors have made the magnitude of our problem frighteningly clear.

In today's litigious society, no textbook on the potential adverse health effects of drugs would be complete without a discussion of how claims of alleged adverse drug reactions are evaluated in the courtroom. While there are many examples of licit and illicit drugs that have scientifically established adverse effects, there are also many examples of medically indicated drugs that have been pulled from the market, in whole or in part, based on perceived risks that are not borne out by the objective scientific data. Over the past 20 years, the courts have been inundated with scientifically unfounded claims that pharmaceuticals or medical devices caused adverse health effects, starting with the allegations in the 1980s that the morning sickness drug Bendectin caused birth defects and continuing in the 1990s and 2000s with claims of autoimmune disease from silicone breast implants, and claims of strokes and cardiovascular diseases from the postpartum lactation drug Parlodel. These cases have led the courts to develop important evidentiary rules that — when properly applied — prevent such unfounded claims from reaching the jury.

Ever since the U.S. Supreme Court's landmark ruling in the Bendectin case *Daubert v. Merrell Dow Pharmaceuticals, Inc.,*[1] judges have been tasked with the obligation to serve as gatekeepers to keep scientifically unreliable and irrelevant expert testimony out of the courtroom. The standards set forth in *Daubert*, which the Supreme Court has described as "exacting,"[2] have had a significant impact on numerous areas of legal dispute, but perhaps no area has been more affected than toxic tort and pharmaceutical product liability litigation. Under *Daubert* and its progeny, *General Electric v. Joiner*[3] and *Kumho Tire Co., Ltd. v. Carmichael*,[4] a plaintiff can no longer get a product liability claim before a jury based solely on an expert's subjective opinion that the plaintiff's injury was caused by a particular drug. Rather, the plaintiff must demonstrate that the expert's opinion is scientifically valid, both on the general causation question of whether the drug could potentially cause the injury in any patient and the specific causation question of whether the drug in fact did cause the particular plaintiff's injury.[5]

---

* Messrs. Hollingsworth and Lasker are partners in the Washington, D.C. law firm Spriggs & Hollingsworth, where they specialize in pharmaceutical and toxic tort litigation.

[1] 509 U.S. 579 (1993).
[2] *Weisgram v. Marley Co.*, 528 U.S. 440, 455 (2000).
[3] 522 U.S. 136 (1997).
[4] 526 U.S. 137 (1999).
[5] *See, e.g., Raynor v. Merrell Pharms. Inc.*, 104 F. 3d 1371, 1376 (D.C. Cir. 1997).

Daubert has imposed a significant new obligation on trial courts, and many judges have struggled to understand the scientific principles that they must follow in their new role.[6] Plaintiffs' counsel and like-minded legal observers have sought to take advantage of this uncertainty by arguing that the Supreme Court provided ambiguous guidance regarding the admissibility of medical causation testimony and that courts should defer to the judgment of medical experts so long as they follow the same "differential diagnosis" reasoning in their expert testimony as they do in their clinical practice.[7] These arguments are wrong. The guidance provided by the Supreme Court is clear: expert testimony that a drug caused an adverse event is admissible only if it is based on the scientific method, i.e., evidence properly derived through the generating and testing of hypotheses. This guidance provides a simple framework for courts considering the variety of evidence generally put forth by causation experts in drug product liability litigation, whether it be epidemiology, animal research, chemical analogies, anecdotal information, or differential diagnosis.

In this chapter, we review the Supreme Court's adoption of the scientific method as the standard for admissibility of expert testimony and analyze how a court's proper understanding of the scientific method can guide it in evaluating the different types of causation evidence presented in pharmaceutical product liability litigation, both with respect to general and specific causation. Throughout this discussion and in the concluding section, we draw on our firm's experience as national defense counsel in a series of product liability cases involving the prescription drug Parlodel, in which these evidentiary issues have been analyzed in-depth in judicial opinions across the country. The Parlodel litigation has been described in another recent textbook as "the first significant products liability causation debate of the 21st century" and one that "will serve as a guide to understanding the significant causation issues that will continue to be involved, at increased rates of complexity, in the 21st century products cases."[8]

14.2.1 The Supreme Court's Directive: Expert Testimony Must Be Derived by the Scientific Method

In *Daubert*, the Supreme Court held that scientific testimony is not admissible unless it satisfies the dual requirements of scientific reliability and relevance. Scholarly debate regarding *Daubert* has often focused on the four factors suggested by the Court in determining scientific reliability: (1) testing, (2) peer review, (3) error rate and standards, and (4) general acceptance. However, a rote discussion of these factors misses the point. These factors are relevant only insofar as they assist the trial court in applying the overarching directive of *Daubert* that expert testimony must be based on the scientific method. The Supreme Court explained that "in order to qualify as 'scientific knowledge' an inference must be derived by the scientific method."[9] The Court defined the scientific method as follows: "Scientific methodology today is based on generating hypotheses and testing them to see if they can be falsified; indeed, this methodology is what distinguishes science from other fields of human inquiry."[10] Moreover, "[s]cientific validity for one purpose is

---

[6] A recent survey of 400 state trial judges found that while a large majority of judges agreed that the role of "gatekeeper" was an appropriate one for a judge, most judges did not have a proper understanding of the scientific principles set forth in *Daubert*. *See* Sophia I. Gatowski, et al., Asking the gatekeepers: a national survey of judges on judging expert evidence in a post-*Daubert* world, 25(5) *Law and Human Behavior* 433 (2001).

[7] *See, e.g.,* J. Kassirer and J. Cecil, Inconsistency in evidentiary standards for medical testimony: disorder in the courts, 288(11) *JAMA* 1382–87 (Sept. 2002); M. Berger, Upsetting the balance between adverse interests: the impact of the Supreme Court's trilogy on expert testimony in toxic tort litigation, 64 SUM *Law & Contemp. Probs.* 289 (Spring/Summer 2001).

[8] Terence F. Kiely, *Science and Litigation: Products Liability in Theory and Practice* 177 (CRC Press, Boca Raton, FL, 2002).

[9] 509 U.S. at 590.

[10] *Id.* at 593. The Supreme Court cited to two philosophical texts on the nature of scientific evidence. *See id.* (citing C. Hempel, *The Philosophy of Natural Science* 49 (1966) ("[T]he statements constituting a scientific explanation must be capable of an empirical test"); K. Popper, *Conjectures and Refutations: The Growth of Scientific Knowledge* 37 (5th ed. 1989) ("[T]he criterion of the scientific status of a theory is its falsifiability, or refutability, or testability")).

not necessarily scientific validity for other, unrelated purposes."[11] In other words, expert testimony is admissible only if empirical testing validates the specific theory to which the expert opines.[12]

Daubert also explains that while admissible expert testimony must be based on the scientific method, "there are important differences between the quest for truth in a courtroom and the quest for truth in the laboratory."[13] "[S]cientific conclusions are subject to perpetual revision. Law on the other hand, must resolve disputes finally and quickly."[14] Accordingly, expert testimony must be judged based on the current state of scientific knowledge, not on the possibility that additional knowledge may emerge in the future. The Court recognized that the requirement of existing empirical evidence "on occasion will prevent the jury from learning of authentic insights and innovation" but held that this "is the balance struck by Rules of Evidence designed not for the exhaustive search for cosmic understanding but for particularized resolution of legal disputes."[15]

Four years after *Daubert*, the Supreme Court provided further guidance on how judges should use the scientific method in evaluating expert testimony. In *Joiner*, the plaintiffs' experts contended that their opinion (that PCBs can cause lung cancer) should be admitted because they relied on epidemiology and animal studies, which are standard tools used by scientists in testing causal hypotheses. The Court rejected this contention, explaining that a faithful application of the scientific method requires more: "whether animal studies can ever be the proper foundation for an expert's testimony was not the issue. The issue was whether these experts' opinions were sufficiently supported by the animal studies on which they purport to rely."[16] In other words, expert testimony must be based on empirical testing that *validates* the conclusions reached.[17]

The *Joiner* Court held that the research cited by plaintiffs' experts did not validate their conclusions because the epidemiological studies did not report a statistically significant causal link between PCBs and lung cancer, lacked proper controls, and examined substances other than PCBs, and because the animal studies involved massive doses of PCBs and a different type of cancer and could not be properly extrapolated to humans. Plaintiffs' experts could not support their opinions under the scientific method because their conclusions ultimately rested on subjective leaps from the scientific evidence. "[N]othing in either *Daubert* or the Federal Rules of Evidence requires a district court to admit evidence that is connected to existing data only by the *ipse dixit* of the expert. A court may conclude that there is simply too great an analytical gap between the data and opinion proffered."[18]

Two years later, in *Kumho Tire*, the Supreme Court held that the *Daubert* requirements of reliability and relevance apply to all expert testimony, including experience-based testimony. Even in areas where the four factors proposed in *Daubert* are inapplicable, the Court explained that the overarching question remains the same: Is the expert's testimony supported by a methodology that has been objectively validated and supports the conclusions offered?[19] In evaluating this question,

---

[11] *Id.* at 591.

[12] The four factors discussed in *Daubert* provide different methods by which an expert's opinion can be analyzed for adherence to the scientific method. Two of the factors, testing and error rates, are integral parts of the scientific method itself. The other two factors, peer review and general acceptance, can provide independent support that the opinion was properly derived by the scientific method. Peer review, however, should not be mindlessly equated with publication. As the Supreme Court noted, publication "is but one element of peer review." *Daubert*, 509 U.S. at 593. Peer review, like general acceptance, refers more broadly to the concept that the theory at issue has been subjected to and found valid through empirical testing by the broader scientific community. *See generally* W. Anderson, et al., *Daubert's* backwash: litigation-generated science, 34 *U. Mich. J.L. Reform* 619 (2001); E. Chan, The "Brave New World" of *Daubert*: true peer review, editorial peer review, and scientific validity, 70 *N.Y.U. L. Rev.* 100 (1995).

[13] *Id.* at 596–97.

[14] *Id.* at 597.

[15] *Id.*

[16] 522 U.S. at 145.

[17] *See id.* at 146 ("conclusions and methodology are not entirely distinct from one another").

[18] *Id.*

[19] *See* 526 U.S. at 157 (noting with respect to challenged tire expert's testimony that "despite the prevalence of tire testing," plaintiffs did not "refer to any articles or papers that validate [the expert's] approach").

the Court instructed that courts should consider whether the expert "employs in the courtroom the same level of intellectual rigor that characterizes the practice of the expert in the relevant field."[20]

14.2.2 Evaluating General Causation Evidence under the Scientific Method

General causation opinions in drug product liability litigation may be based on a wide variety of evidence of differing scientific value, including, *inter alia*, epidemiology, animal studies, chemical analogies, case reports, and regulatory findings and other secondary sources. Some legal observers have argued that a medical expert's evaluation of this evidence involves a "complex inferential process" and that the expert accordingly should be allowed to simply lump this evidence together and reach "a subjective judgment about the strength of the evidence."[21] However, *Daubert* clearly requires more. Under *Daubert*, a trial court must consider each of these categories of evidence in light of the scientific method, and the expert's testimony may only be admitted if the expert can establish through scientific evidence that her causal hypothesis has been reliably tested and validated.

Further, causation experts cannot satisfy their *Daubert* burden by arguing that the scientific research necessary to test their hypothesis has not been or cannot be performed. *Daubert* requires trial judges to evaluate expert testimony based on the science that exists at the time, not the possibility of new scientific discoveries in the future or guesswork as to what those discoveries might show.[22] As Judge Posner of the U.S. Court of Appeal for the Seventh Circuit explained, "the courtroom is not the place for scientific guesswork, even of the inspired sort. Law lags science, it does not lead it."[23]

14.2.2.1 Epidemiology

Controlled epidemiological studies are generally considered the most reliable evidence for testing a hypothesis that a particular substance causes a particular injury in humans.[24] Epidemiological studies can be especially important in cases where the drug or substance at issue is widely used or where there is a measurable background rate of the alleged injury regardless of exposure. In these situations, epidemiology may be the only way to test the hypothesis that observed injuries in exposed individuals are reflective of an increased risk and a causal connection rather than pure statistical chance.[25] While the absence of epidemiology may not be fatal to a plaintiff's case,

---

[20] *Id.* at 152.

[21] Kassirer and Cecil, *supra* note 7, at 1384, 1386; *see also* Berger, *supra* note 7.

[22] 509 U.S. at 597.

[23] *Rosen v. Ciba-Geigy Corp.*, 78 F.3d 316, 319 (7th Cir. 1996).

[24] *See, e.g., Soldo v. Sandoz Pharms. Corp.*, 244 F. Supp. 2d 434, 532 (W.D. Pa. 2003) (epidemiology is "the primary generally accepted methodology for demonstrating a causal relation between a chemical compound and a set of symptoms or a disease") (quoting *Conde v. Velsicol Chem. Corp.*, 804 F. Supp. 972, 1025–26 (S.D. Ohio 1992), *aff'd*, 24 F.3d 809 (6th Cir. 1994)); *Hollander v. Sandoz Pharms. Corp.*, 95 F. Supp. 2d 1230, 1235, n.14 (W.D. Okla. 2000) ("In the absence of an understanding of the biological and pathological mechanisms by which disease develops, epidemiological evidence is the most valid type of scientific evidence of toxic causation"), *aff'd*, 289 F.3d 1193 (10th Cir. 2002); *Breast Implant Litig.*, 11 F. Supp. 2d 1217, 1224–25 (D. Colo. 1998) (same, citing cases).

[25] There has been recent controversy regarding whether certain types of epidemiological studies should be considered inherently more reliable than others in establishing causation. Historically, courts have understood that randomized controlled clinical trials are less likely to report erroneous associations than observational epidemiological studies, like cohort or case control studies. *See In re Rezulin Prod. Liab. Litig.*, 369 F. Supp. 2d 398, 406 (S.D.N.Y. 2005); *see also* David H. Kaye and David A. Freeman, *Reference Guide on Statistics*, Reference Manual on Scientific Evidence (2d ed. 2000) at 94–95. However, recent research suggests that this understanding may be mistaken, *see* John Concato, et al., Randomized, controlled trials, observational studies, and the hierarchy of research design, 342(25) *N. Engl. J. Med.* 1887 (2000); John Concato, Observational versus experimental studies: what's the evidence for a hierarchy? 1 *J. Am. Soc. Exp. NeuroTherapeutics* 341 (2004). In a recent review of the most highly cited clinical research (defined as studies cited more than 1000 times in the literature), a scientist concluded that 16% of the top-cited clinical research studies relating to medical interventions had been contradicted within the following 15 years and another 16% were followed by subsequent research suggesting that the initial findings may have been overstated. John P.A. Ioannidis, Contradicted and initially stronger effects in highly cited clinical research, 294(2) *JAMA* 218 (2005). While epidemiological evidence can provide the best evidence of causation, as explained below, even the best study cannot establish that causation in fact exists.

numerous courts have held that a plaintiff seeking to establish causation without such evidence will face a high evidentiary hurdle.[26]

When causation experts rely on epidemiological studies to support their opinions, a trial court must analyze those studies to determine whether they provide a proper foundation for the expert's testimony under the scientific method. The finding in an epidemiological study of an *association* between a substance and an injury is not equivalent to *causation*.[27] There are three reasons that a positive association may be observed in an epidemiological study: (1) chance, (2) bias, and (3) real effect.[28] As the Supreme Court recognized in *Joiner*, epidemiological research cannot provide a scientifically reliable basis for an affirmative causation opinion if it is statistically insignificant or inadequately controlled for bias.[29]

Epidemiologists attempt to account for the possibility of chance by calculating "confidence intervals" around point estimates of potential increased risk derived from epidemiological studies. An epidemiological study is considered to show a statistically significant association with an increased risk if the confidence interval of upper- and lower-bound estimates of risk does not include the possibility of no increased risk in the exposed population. The possibility of no increased risk is referred to as the "null" hypothesis, which is generally indicated by a relative risk or odds ratio of 1.0.[30] The generally accepted confidence interval in epidemiological studies is 95%, meaning that a study is not statistically significant unless the "null" hypothesis of no increased (or decreased) risk can be excluded with 95% confidence.[31] If an epidemiological study is not statistically significant, it cannot provide scientifically reliable evidence of an association, let alone causation.[32] Further, numerous courts have held that epidemiological evidence can only support a conclusion that a substance is more likely than not the cause of disease if it establishes a doubling of the risk of the disease.[33] The reasoning behind this requirement is that if exposure does not at least double the risk of injury, then more than half of the exposed population suffering from injuries allegedly caused by the substance would have been injured anyway through pure chance (based on the background risk of injury) thereby disproving "more likely than not" legal causation. Courts have also cautioned against reliance on statistically significant subgroup analyses, given the likelihood that numerous subgroup analyses will result in spurious statistical associations in some end points through chance alone.[34]

Bias in epidemiology is any systematic error that makes the two groups being compared different in more ways than just the variable being studied.[35] Common sources of bias include confounding factors (other factors associated with the studied factor that might account for a perceived increased risk), selection bias (uncontrolled differences between the studied populations), and information

---

[26] *See, e.g., Siharath v. Sandoz Pharms. Corp.*, 131 F. Supp. 2d 1347, 1358 ((N.D. Ga. 2001), *aff'd sub., nom Rider v. Sandoz Pharms. Corp.*, 295 F.3d 1194 (11th Cir. 2002).

[27] *See* Michael D. Green, *Reference Guide on Epidemiology*, Reference Manual on Scientific Evidence (2d ed. 2000) at 336.

[28] *See Magistrini v. One Hour Martinizing Dry Cleaning*, 180 F. Supp. 2d 584, 591 (D.N.J. 2002), *aff'd*, 68 Fed. Appx. 356 (3d Cir. 2003)); *Caraker v. Sandoz Pharms. Corp.*, 188 F. Supp. 2d 1026, 1032 (S.D. Ill 2001); *see also* Eddy A. Bresnitz, Principles of research design, in *Goldfrank's Toxicologic Emergencies* 1827–28 (Goldfrank, et al. eds. 6th ed. 1998).

[29] *See Joiner*, 522 U.S. at 145–46.

[30] *See Turpin v. Merrell Dow Pharms., Inc.*, 959 F.2d 1349, 1353 n.1 (6th Cir. 1992).

[31] *Id.*, at 723 (citing *DeLuca v. Merrell Dow Pharms., Inc.*, 791 F. Supp. 1042, 1046 (D.N.J. 1992), *aff'd*, 6 F.3d 778 (3d Cir. 1993)).

[32] *See Joiner*, 522 U.S. at 145; *see also Dunn v. Sandoz Pharms. Corp.*, 275 F. Supp. 2d 672, 681 (M.D.N.C. 2003) ("statistically insignificant results do not constitute proof" of causation); *Soldo*, 244 F. Supp. 2d at 533 ("Courts have emphasized that epidemiologic proof must be statistically significant,") (citing cases); *Caraker*, 188 F. Supp. 2d at 1034 (rejecting experts' causation opinions "inasmuch as they rely on selective use of statistically insignificant data from epidemiological studies").

[33] *See Magistrini*, 180 F. Supp. 2d at 591; *Siharath*, 131 F. Supp. 2d at 1356; *In re Breast Implant Litig.*, 11 F. Supp. 2d at 1225-26; *Hall v. Baxter Healthcare Corp.*, 947 F. Supp. 1387, 1403-04 (D. Or. 1996); *see also Daubert v. Merrell Dow Pharms., Inc*, 43 F.3d 1311, 1321 (9th Cir. 1995) ("*Daubert II*") ("A relative risk of less than two may suggest teratogenicity, but it actually tends to *dis*prove legal causation as it shows that Bendectin does not double the likelihood of birth defects"). *But cf. In re Hanford Nuclear Reservation Litig.*, 292 F.3d 1124, 1137 (9th Cir. 2002) (plaintiffs did not need to present epidemiological evidence showing a doubling of risk of cancer from ionizing radiation at specific exposure levels because capability of ionizing radiation to cause cancer generally has been recognized by scientific and legal authority).

[34] *See Newman v. Motorola, Inc.*, 218 F. Supp. 2d 769, 779 (D. Md. 2002), *aff'd* 62 Fed. R. Evid. Serv. 1289 (4th Cir. 2003).

[35] *See Magistrini*, 180 F. Supp. 2d at 592.

bias (systematic error in measuring data that results in differential accuracy of information).[36] A court must consider each of these sources of bias in interpreting an epidemiological study because bias can produce an erroneous association.[37] Thus, for example, courts have excluded expert causation testimony based on purported statistically significant epidemiologic evidence where the study failed to account for other confounding exposures that could have accounted for the apparent association.[38] Courts have rejected expert opinions that relied on epidemiological studies where the subjects were not blinded to the study hypothesis.[39] Courts have rejected expert testimony based on epidemiological studies that failed to adequately address the possibility that injured subjects would be more likely to recall a preceding exposure than healthy controls ("recall bias").[40] Courts have also rejected expert testimony that relied upon epidemiological studies that failed to articulate selection criteria for participants in the study and thus could not account for selection biases "that could lead to erroneous inferences regarding causation."[41]

The existence of a well-controlled epidemiological study that reports a statistically significant increased association with a specific injury does not, by itself, provide scientifically reliable evidence establishing causation.[42] "The strong consensus among epidemiologists is that conclusions about causation should not be drawn, if at all, until a number of criteria have been considered."[43] In analyzing the scientific reliability of epidemiological evidence under *Daubert*, a number of courts have been guided by a set of criteria published by the noted epidemiologist, Sir Austin Bradford Hill in 1965 ("the Bradford Hill criteria").[44] The Bradford Hill criteria can be summarized as follows: (1) strength of association, (2) consistency and replication of findings, (3) specificity with respect to both the substance and injury at issue; (4) evidence of a dose-response relationship, (5) temporal relationship, (6) biological plausibility, and (7) consideration of alternative explanations.[45]

In light of these criteria, courts have rejected statistically significant epidemiological research under *Daubert* where the reported relative risk is only slightly elevated[46] and have suggested that epidemiological research reporting a relative increased risk of less than three times indicates only a weak association (strength of association).[47] Courts have also rejected isolated, statistically

---

[36] *See Merrell Dow Pharms. v. Havner*, 953 S.W.2d 706, 719 (Tex. 1997); *see also* Bresnitz, *supra* note 28, at 1831–32; Michael D. Green, *et al.*, *Reference Guide on Epidemiology*, Reference Manual on Scientific Evidence at 389, 392, & 395 (2d ed. 2000) (discussing sources of bias); David A. Grimes and Kenneth F. Schuls, Bias and causal associations in observational research, 359 *Lancet* 248 (Jan. 19, 2002) (same, including real-world examples of confounding errors).

[37] *Magistrini*, 180 F. Supp. 2d at 591; *Caraker*, 188 F. Supp. at 1032; *see also Havner*, 953 S.W.2d at 719 ("Bias can dramatically affect the scientific reliability of an epidemiological study.").

[38] *Nelson v. Tennessee Gas Pipeline Co.*, 243 F.3d 244, 252–54 (6th Cir. 2001) (expert's failure to account for confounding factors in cohort study or alleged PCB exposures rendered his opinion unreliable).

[39] *See Allison v McGhan Med. Corp.*, 184 F.3d 1300, 1315 (11th Cir. 1999) (noting that the women participating in the study at issue "were aware of the hypothesis, a factor which could have created bias, skewing the results and ultimately making the conclusions suspect").

[40] *See Newman*, 218 F. Supp. 2d at 778; *see also Maras v. Avis Rent A Car Sys., Inc.*, No. Civ. 03-6191, 2005 WL 83828, * 5 (D. Minn. Jan. 14, 2005) (rejecting expert testimony based on epidemiological study that, among other failures, may have been influenced by recall bias).

[41] *In re TMI Litig.*, 193 F.3d 613, 707–08 (3d Cir. 1999); *see also Bouchard v. Am. Home Prods. Corp.*, 213 F. Supp. 2d 802, 809–10 (N.D. Ohio 2002) (excluding expert causation testimony to the extent based on epidemiological study tainted with selection bias).

[42] *See, e.g., Amorgianos v. Nat'l R.R. Passenger Corp.*, 137 F. Supp. 2d 147, 168 (E.D.N.Y. 2001), *aff'd*, 303 F.3d 256 (2d Cir. 2002).

[43] *Havner*, 953 S.W.2d at 718.

[44] *See Dunn*, 275 F. Supp. 2d at 677–78; *Magistrini*, 180 F. Supp. 2d at 592–93; *Amorgianos*, 137 F. Supp. 2d at 168; *Castellow v. Chevron USA*, 97 F. Supp. 2d 780, 786–87 & n.2 (S.D. Tex. 2000); *In re Breast Implants*, 11 F. Supp. 2d at 1233 n.5; *Havner*, 953 S.W.2d at 718 & n.2.

[45] *Id.*; *see also* Bresnitz, *supra* note 28 at 1827–28 (describing Bradford Hill criteria in detail); Grimes and Schulz, *supra* note 36 (same); Douglas L. Weed, Underdetermination and incommensurability in contemporary epidemiology, 7(2) *Kennedy Inst. Ethics J.* 107, 113–15 (1997) (same).

[46] *See Allison*, 184 F.3d at 1315 (noting that statistically significant epidemiological study reporting an increased risk of marker of disease of 1.24 times in patients with breast implants was so close to 1.0 that it "was not worth serious consideration for proving causation."); *In re Breast Implants Litig.*, 11 F. Supp. 2d at 1227 (same).

[47] *See Havner*, 953 S.W.2d at 719.

significant epidemiological findings that are not replicated in other epidemiological research (consistency).[48] Courts have rejected epidemiological studies reporting statistically significant associations with allegedly similar substances or allegedly similar injuries (specificity).[49] And courts have rejected alleged associations in epidemiological studies that did not demonstrate a dose–response relationship (dose response).[50] Moreover, courts have not accepted the mere incantation of the name of Bradford Hill as establishing the reliability of a causation hypothesis.[51] These criteria must be applied faithfully or they can also generate unreliable conclusions,[52] as demonstrated by two review papers published in 1989–1990 that both purported to use the Bradford Hill criteria to assess the epidemiological evidence regarding an association between alcohol consumption and breast cancer, but reached dramatically different conclusions.[53]

Causation experts sometimes attempt to bolster individually weak epidemiological studies by relying on "meta-analyses" in which otherwise insignificant or inconsistent findings are pooled to generate a single purportedly significant finding. This approach was rejected by courts in the Bendectin litigation,[54] and rightfully so. While meta-analyses can provide useful information if conducted pursuant to proper scientific methodology, they have frequently reported causal relationships that do not survive scientific scrutiny.[55] By pooling data from different studies, meta-analyses can paper over biases and other weaknesses in the underlying studies, disregard inconsistent findings, and improperly combine divergent population groups. As one commentator has explained, "[m]eta-analyses begin with scientific studies, usually performed by academics or government agencies, and sometimes incomplete or disputed. The data from these studies are then run through computer models of bewildering complexity, which produces results of implausible precision."[56] After finding that meta-analyses were frequently contradicted by subsequent large, randomized controlled trials, another investigator cautioned: "The popularity of meta-analysis may at least partly come from the fact that it makes life simpler and easier for reviewers as well as readers. However, simplification may lead to inappropriate conclusions."[57] Pursuant to *Daubert*, a court

---

[48] *See, e.g., Miller v. Pfizer, Inc.*, 196 F. Supp. 2d 1062, (D. Kan. 2002) (expert failed to address "fact that other research is contrary to his conclusion), *aff'd*, 356 F.3d 1326 (10th Cir.), *cert denied*, 125 S. Ct. 40 (2004); *Havner*, 953 S.W.2d at 727 ("if scientific methodology is followed, a single study would not be viewed as indicating that it is 'more probable than not' that an association exists").

[49] *See Joiner*, 522 U.S. at 145–46 (studies proffered as evidence of PCB-lung cancer link involved exposures to mineral oils or other potential carcinogens); *Burleson v. Tex. Dep't. of Criminal Justice*, 393 F.3d 577, 585–86 (5th Cir. 2004) (rejecting expert testimony where expert could not point to epidemiological studies demonstrating statistically significant link between thorium dioxide exposure and plaintiff's type of lung or throat cancer); *Allison*, 184 F.3d at 1315 (studies reported link to injuries not suffered by plaintiff); *Schudel v. Gen. Elec. Co.*, 120 F.3d 991, 997 (9th Cir. 1997) (studies involved exposures to organic solvents other than those at issue); *Magistrini*, 180 F. Supp. 2d at 603–04 (to same effect).

[50] *See Newman*, 218 F. Supp. 2d at 778 (no dose–response relationship found in study involving cell phone use and cancer); *Kelley v. Am. Heyer-Schulte Corp.*, 957 F. Supp. 873, 879 (W.D. Tex. 1997).

[51] *See Hollander*, 289 F.3d at 1204 (rejecting expert's causation testimony despite his claimed adherence to the Bradford Hill methodology): *Dunn*, 275 F. Supp. 2d at 677–78 (same).

[52] *See Lust v. Merrell Dow Pharms. Inc.*, 89 F.3d 594, 598 (9th Cir 1996) ("the district court should be wary that the [expert's] method has not been faithfully applied"); *O'Conner v. Commonwealth Edison Co.*, 13 F.3d 1090, 1106–07 (7th Cir. 1994) (excluding opinion where expert did not follow his own expressed methodology for establishing causation); *Knight v. Kirby Inland Marine, Inc.*, 363 F. Supp. 2d 859, 864 (N.D. Miss. 2005) (expert's "Bradford-Hill analysis is only as reliable as the underlying data upon which it is based"); *Hall*, 947 F. Supp. at 1400 (quoting *Lust*).

[53] *See Weed (1997) supra note 45 at 115, 116–18 (discussing Robert A. Hiatt, Alcohol consumption and breast cancer, 7 *Med. Oncol. Tumor Pharmacother.* 143 (1990) (concluding that women with risk factors for breast cancer should limit alcohol use) and Ernst L. Wynder and Randall E. Harris, Does alcohol consumption influence the risk of developing breast cancer? in *Important Advances in Oncology* 283 (V.T. Devita, S. Hellman, and S.A. Rosenberg eds. 1989) (concluding that there was no evidence of a causal link)).

[54] *See, e.g., DeLuca v. Merrell Dow Pharms., Inc.*, 791 F. Supp. 1042, 1046-59 (D.N.J. 1992), *aff'd without op.*, 6 F.3d 778 (3d Cir. 1993); *see also Knight*, 363 F. Supp. 2d at 866 (rejecting causation opinion based on meta-analyses of cancer risks to chemical industry employees).

[55] For examples, see Douglas L. Weed, Interpreting epidemiological evidence; how meta-analysis and causal inference methods are related, 29 *Int. J. Epidemiol.* 387 (2000); Jacques LeLorier, et al., Discrepancies between meta-analyses and subsequent large randomized, controlled trials, 337(8) *N. Engl. J. Med.* 336 (1997); Samuel Shapiro, Is meta-analysis a valid approach to the evaluation of small effects in observational studies? 50(3) *J. Clin. Epidemiol.* 223 (1997); Samuel Shapiro, Meta-analysis/Shmeta-analysis, 140(9) *Am. J. Epidiol.* 771 (Nov. 1994).

[56] Shapiro (1994), at 771, *supra* note 55.

[57] LeLorier (1997), at 541, *supra* note 55.

must look behind the "bewildering complexity" of meta-analysis and protect against "inappropriate conclusions" by requiring the expert to establish the reliability and relevance both of the different pieces of information going into the meta-analysis and the calculations used to combine the information into a single result.

14.2.2.2 Animal Research

Animal research may be a useful tool for raising suspicions that can then be tested in humans, but there are significant differences in humans and laboratory animals that limit the degree to which animal research can validate a causation hypothesis in humans.[58] There are numerous examples of apparent positive findings in animal studies that have subsequently been found inapplicable to humans. The most commonly cited example, perhaps, is saccharine, which was linked to bladder cancer in rats over 20 years ago but was recently removed from the National Toxicology Program list of potential human carcinogens after years of subsequent research failed to find any health risk in humans. Similarly, scientists have determined that a common insecticide, carbaryl, causes fetal abnormalities in dogs because dogs lack a specific enzyme involved in metabolizing carbaryl. Humans have the enzyme at issue and are accordingly not believed to be at risk.[59] Because of numerous such problems of extrapolation, courts repeatedly have held that animal studies alone cannot prove causation in humans.[60]

At a minimum, extrapolations from animal studies to humans are not considered reliable in the absence of a credible scientific explanation why such extrapolation is warranted.[61] In evaluating whether animal studies can form a reliable foundation for a causation opinion, trial courts should consider such factors as (1) whether the results followed a dose–response curve; (2) whether the animal studies involved massive doses, (3) whether the studies involved different routes of administration, (4) whether the studies are conducted in intact animals (as opposed, e.g., to isolated animal parts), (5) whether the results have been replicated in different animal species, and (6) whether the animal models have been shown to be reliable predictors of human experience.[62]

Animal toxicology studies are not designed to establish whether a substance is safe in humans but rather to allow scientists to study the types of effects a substance can produce under specified conditions.[63] Accordingly, animal studies are often conducted with the goal of inducing the greatest number of adverse effects. This is accomplished in a number of ways, including the use of extremely high doses and exposures through special routes designed to deliver the substance directly to a particular organ without allowing for normal absorption and metabolization.[64] While these models are useful and appropriate in the laboratory as a means to generate hypotheses for further testing, they create additional problems for extrapolating study findings to humans.

---

[58] See, e.g., Irva Hertz-Picciotto, Epidemiology and quantitative risk assessment: a bridge from science to policy, 85(4) Am. J. Public Health 484, 485 (1995) ("The uncertainty stemming from interspecies extrapolation is far larger than the uncertainty resulting from uncontrolled bias or errors in exposure information in epidemiological studies").

[59] See Bernard D. Goldstein and Mary Sue Henifen, Reference Guide on Toxicology, Reference Manual on Scientific Evidence 420 n.48 (2d ed. 2000). For additional examples of the often dramatic differences in responses among animal species and between animals and humans, see David L. Eaton and Curtis D. Klaassen, Principles of toxicology, in Casarett & Doull's Toxicology: The Basic Science of Poisons 25–26 (Curtis D. Klaassen ed., 6th ed. 2001); Elaine M. Faustman and Gilbert S. Omenn, Risk assessment, in Casarett & Doull's Toxicology: The Basic Science of Poisons, supra, at 88–90; Lorenz Rhomberg, Risk assessment and the use of information on underlying biological mechanisms: A perspective, 365 Mutat. Res. 175, 179–80 (1996); Jan M. M. Meijers, et al., The predictive value of animal data in human cancer risk assessment, 25 Regul. Toxicol. Pharmacol. 94 (1997).

[60] See Siharath, 131 F. Supp. 2d at 1367 (quoting Bell v. Swift Adhesives, Inc., 804 F. Supp. 1577, 1579–80 (S.D. Ga. 1992)); Wade-Greaux v. Whitehall Labs., Inc., 874 F. Supp. 1441, 1483–84 (D.V.I. 1994), aff'd without op., 46 F.3d 1120 (3d Cir. 1994).

[61] See Soldo, 244 F. Supp. 2d at 565; Siharath, 131 F. Supp. 2d at 1366–67 (citing cases).

[62] See, e.g., Joiner, 522 U.S. at 144; Hollander, 289 F.3d at 1209; Turpin, 959 F.2d at 1358–61; In re Rezulin Prod. Liab. Litig., 369 F. Supp. 2d at 406–07; Caraker, 188 F. Supp. 2d at 1037; Wade-Greaux, 874 F. Supp. at 1477.

[63] See Eaton and Klaassen, at 27, supra note 59.

[64] See Eaton and Klaassen, at 27, supra note 59; Karl K. Rozman and Curtis D. Klaassen, Absorption, distribution, and excretion of toxicants, in Casarett & Doull's Toxicology: The Basic Science of Poisons, at 111.

The existence of a dose–response relationship has been described as the most fundamental and pervasive concept in toxicology.[65] All substances, even water, become toxic at a high enough dose. Conversely, however, "it has long been recognized that acute toxicological responses are associated with thresholds; that is, there is some dose below which the probability of an individual responding is zero."[66] As stated by the oft-described father of chemical pharmacology, Paracelsus (1493–1541), "What is there that is not poison? All things are poison and nothing [is] without poison. Solely a dose determines that a thing is not a poison."[67] Accordingly, even leaving to one side the issue of inter-species variations, the fact that a high-dose study results in adverse effects in animals cannot be extrapolated into a scientifically reliable conclusion that the substance can cause such effects at normal exposure levels in humans.[68] To the contrary, because toxic effects in humans are generally expected to appear in the same range on the basis of dose per unit of body surface as in experimental animals, a finding of adverse events in animals at only very high doses may be more indicative of the safety of the substance in normal use.[69]

The route by which a substance enters the body can also have a significant effect on its toxicity. Animal researchers frequently administer chemical agents through special routes, including, *inter alia,* (1) intraperitoneal, (2) subcutaneous, (3) intramuscular, and (4) intravenous.[70] These routes of administration may bypass the normal mechanisms through which potential toxins are removed before reaching the general circulation. For example, many substances are biotransformed and detoxified by the liver; while these substances may demonstrate toxic effects when injected intravenously, intramuscularly, or subcutaneously, they are perfectly safe if ingested orally.[71] Likewise, animal researchers also use genetically designed or physically altered animals in which normal protective body mechanisms are removed.[72] These types of animal studies can be useful in studying how an animal's normal body mechanisms interact and how substances can affect isolated physiological systems, but they do not reflect real-world risks, even in the species being studied.

In conducting its *Daubert* inquiry, a trial court also must determine whether the findings in the animal studies "fit" the opinions being offered in the case. Thus, an expert cannot rely on animal research that relates to a different injury than the one at issue. For example, animal carcinogenicity studies indicate that animals "react differently and in much more diverse ways than man" and that "compared to humans much more variation occurs in the cancer sites in animals."[73] However, in cases in which a chemical has been associated with cancers in both animal studies and epidemiological studies, "the target organ is usually identical."[74] In *Joiner*, the Supreme Court thus rejected animal research in part because the animals had developed a different type of cancer than the cancer at issue in the plaintiff.[75]

---

[65] *See* Eaton and Klaassen, at 17–18, *supra* note 59.

[66] *Id.*, at 21.

[67] *Id.*, at 13.

[68] *See, e.g.,* Meijers, *supra* note 59, at 100 (concluding based on a comparison of animal and epidemiological studies for specific chemicals that "chemicals with little or no cancer potential in humans have been tested at too high concentrations in rodents... which resulted in the observed carcinogenic effect").

[69] *Id.*, at 27. Federal regulatory agencies such as the Environmental Protection Agency thus use high-dose animal research as a basis for establishing conservative regulatory safe exposure levels for humans (albeit at levels several multiples below that found to have no effect in animals). *See, e.g.,* Faustman and Omenn, *supra* note 59, at 92–94.

[70] *See* Rozman and Klaassen, *supra* note 64, at 111; *see also* Meijers, *supra* note 59 at 95–98; Irva Hertz-Picciotto, *supra* note 58, at 485.

[71] *See* Eaton and Klaassen, *supra* note 59, at 14; Rozman & Klaassen, *supra* note 64, at 111–14.

[72] *See, e.g.,* Rhomberg, *supra* note 59, at 181–83 (discussing carcinogenicity testing in animals engineered to be more susceptible to tumors).

[73] Meijers, *supra* note 59, at 98.

[74] *Id.*

[75] *See Joiner*, 522 U.S. at 145; *see also Glastetter v. Novartis Pharms. Corp.*, 252 F.3d 986, 991 (8th Cir. 2001).

14.2.2.3 Chemical Analogies

Causation opinions derived from chemical analogies rely on the hypothesis that a substance's effects can be predicted based on the established effects of similarly structured compounds. Trial courts should be very wary of such "guilt-by-association" evidence,[76] particularly where there is scientific research involving the actual substance at issue that demonstrates differences between it and its purported chemical cousins. Because even small changes in molecular structure can radically change a particular substance's properties and propensities, research in analogous substances does not reliably test the causal hypothesis at issue.[77]

The difficulty in relying on chemical analogies has been demonstrated by attempts to create computerized programs to assess the toxicity of chemical agents based on structure–activity relationships (SARs). These computerized models are far more sophisticated than the simplistic chemical analogies often relied on by causation experts in toxic tort litigation, and often rely on additional information regarding a substance beyond its chemical structure. Even so, while these models ultimately may prove helpful in setting research priorities or generating hypotheses, they have failed to provide reliable predictions as to a chemical's toxic effect.[78] As reported in a recent survey article, two prediction toxicity exercises conducted in recent years under the aegis of the National Toxicology Program have found that models that attempt to predict carcinogenicity "based solely on information derived from chemical structure" have been particularly unreliable, with the first exercise reporting that "overall accuracy in terms of positive or negative predictions was in the range 50–65%" and the ongoing second exercise reporting even higher error rates in preliminary results.[79] Moreover, "[a] clear limitation of almost all the prediction systems … was their excessive sensitivity, i.e., incorrectly predicting many non-carcinogens as positive."[80] Efforts to predict toxicity based on structure activity relationships have resulted in similar problems.[81]

14.2.2.4 Case Reports/Case Series

Case reports and case series are anecdotal observations of adverse effects occurring in coincidence with exposure to a given substance. If a sufficient body of similar case reports appear in the literature, they can spur epidemiological or other controlled research to test the hypothesis that a causal link exists.[82] However, as most courts have properly recognized, case reports themselves do

---

[76] *Caraker*, 188 F. Supp. 2d at 1038; *see also Soldo*, 244 F. Supp. 2d at 549 ("Other federal courts facing proffered expert testimony based on the effects of allegedly similar compounds have reached the same conclusion and rejected such contentions: these courts have found that consideration of the effects of *other* drugs can only lead away from the truth.") (citing cases).

[77] *See McClain v. Metabolife Int'l, Inc.*, 401 F.3d 1233, 1246 (11th Cir. 2005); *Rider*, 295 F.3d at 1200–01; *Glastetter*, 252 F.3d at 990; *Schudel*, 120 F.3d at 996–97.

[78] *See, e.g.*, Faustman and Omenn, *supra* note 59, at 86–87; A.M. Richard and R. Benigni, AI and SAR Approaches for Predicting Chemical Carcinogenicity: Survey and Status Report, 13(1) SAR and QSAR in Environmental Research 1 (2002); J. Ashby and R.W. Tenant, Prediction of rodent carcinogenicity for 44 chemicals: results, 9(1) *Mutagenesis* 7 (1994).

[79] *See* Richard and Benigni, *supra* note 78, at 8, 10.

[80] Richard and Benigni, *supra* note 78, at 8; *see also* Ashby and Tenant, *supra* note 78, at abstract ("carcinogenicity tends to be overpredicted by this integrated technique" of basing predictions on chemical structure, genotoxicity and rodent toxicity).

[81] *See* James D. McKinney, et al., Forum: the practice of structure activity relationships (SAR) in toxicology, 56 *Toxicol. Sci.* 8, 15 (2000) ("Given the huge range and variability of possible interactions of chemicals in biological systems, it is highly unlikely that SAR models will ever achieve absolute certainty in predicting a toxicity outcome, particularly in a whole-animal system.").

[82] *See* Howard Hu and Frank E. Speizer, Influence of environmental and occupational hazards on disease, in *Harrison's Principles of Internal Medicine* 19 (Braunwald, et al. eds. 15th ed. 2001) ("Case reports either sent to local authorities or published in the literature often prompt follow-up studies that can lead to the identification of new hazards"); David A. Grimes and Kenneth F. Schulz, Descriptive studies: what they can and cannot do, 359 *Lancet* 145 (Jan. 12, 2002) ("epidemiologists and clinicians generally use descriptive reports to search for clues of cause of disease — i.e., generation of hypotheses"); J.A. Arnaiz, et al., The use of evidence in pharmacovigilance: case reports as the reference source for drug withdrawals, 57 *Eur. J. Clin. Pharmacol.* 89–91 (2001).

not test the causal hypothesis and accordingly cannot support a causation opinion under *Daubert*.[83] Case reports are merely anecdotal accounts of observations in particular individuals; they are not controlled tests, frequently lack analyses, and frequently make little attempt to screen out alternative causes for a patient's condition.[84] As discussed above, when the substance at issue is widely used, it is statistically certain given general background rates of injury that there will be case reports in which an exposure and an injury coincidentally coincide. Accordingly, the existence of such case reports is of little scientific value.[85]

In drug product liability cases, causation experts may rely on so-called "causality assessments" of individual case reports. Causality assessments are algorithms used in some European pharmacovigilance regulatory schemes that seek to impose some structure on evaluation of individual case reports by creating standardized questions to be used in the review of such reports, such as:

- Was the adverse event a known consequence of the drug?
- Did the event occur in temporal proximity to the use of the drug?
- Did the symptoms disappear upon withdrawal of the drug ("dechallenge")?
- Did the symptoms reappear following reintroduction of the drug (rechallenge)?
- Are there alternative causes for the adverse event?

Reviewers then grade individual case reports using such terms as "not possible," "unlikely," "possible," and "probable."[86] Causality assessments are used by some regulatory agencies as a signaling tool, but "they have no objective reliability which would render them useful in a wider environment."[87] "None of the available causality assessment systems has been validated.... In other words the uncertainty [inherent in case reports] is not reduced, but categorized (at best in a semiquantitative way)."[88] Studies of standardized causality assessments have repeatedly found significant disagreements between graders using the same assessment methodology.[89] Accordingly, causality assessments carry no greater scientific weight than other case reports and likewise cannot provide the type of evidence required under *Daubert*.[90]

Some case reports include information regarding purported dechallenges or rechallenges, *i.e.*, reports that a patient's condition improved when the substance was removed or worsened when the substance was reintroduced. Where the dechallenge/rechallenge report is merely an after-the-fact account of an anecdotal observation, it suffers from similar reliability problems as other case reports. Many medical conditions result in fluctuations in symptomology in the ordinary course, and apparent temporal associations with exposure may be due to pure chance. Even if the dechallenge or rechallenge is conducted prospectively with the intent of testing a causal hypothesis, a

---

[83] *See McClain*, 401 F.3d at 1253–54; *Norris v. Baxter Healthcare Corp.*, 397 F.3d 878, 885 (10th Cir. 2005); *Rider*, 295 F.3d at 1199; *Hollander*, 289 F.3d at 1211; *Glastetter*, 252 F.3d at 989–90; *Soldo*, 244 F. Supp. 2d at 541; *Caraker*, 188 F. Supp. 2d at 1034–35; *Brumbaugh v. Sundoz Pharm. Corp.*, 77 F. Supp. 2d 1153, 1156 (D. Mont. 1999), *see also Siharath*, 131 F. Supp. 2d at 1361–62 (citing cases).

[84] *See Rider*, 295 F.3d at 1199; *Glastetter*, 252 F.3d at 989–90; *Soldo*, 244 F. Supp. 2d at 539–40; *see also* Ellenhorn's *Medical Toxicology: Diagnosis and Treatment of Human Poisoning* 1 (Ellenhorn ed. 2d ed. 1997) ("Case reports demonstrate a temporal but not necessarily causative relationship between exposure and health effects. This information is often confounded by the inability to exclude other causes of illness.").

[85] *See* Grimes & Schulz, *supra* note 82, at 148 (case reports, case series, and other descriptive studies "do not allow conclusions about cause of disease").

[86] *See* M.N.G. Dukes, et al., *Responsibility for Drug-Induced Injury: A Reference Book for Lawyers, the Health Professionals and manufacturers* 45–46 (2d ed. 1998); Ronald H.B. Meyboom, et al., Causal or casual? The role of causality assessments in pharmacovigilance, 17(6) *Drug Saf.* 374, 375–81 (1997).

[87] M.N.G. Dukes, *supra* note 86 at 46.

[88] Mayboom, *supra* note 86, at 382.

[89] *See Mayboom*, *supra* note 86 at 381; G. Miremont, et al., Adverse drug reactions: physicians' opinions versus a causality assessment method, 46 *Eur. J. Clin. Pharmacol.* 285, 288 (1994).

[90] *See Glastetter v. Novartis Pharms. Corp.*, 107 F. Supp. 2d 1015, 1037 n. 21 (E.D. Mo. 2000) ("like case reports ... a causality assessment involves only one individual, and, in any event, is not sufficient to establish causation") *aff'd*, 252 F.3d 986 (8th Cir. 2001); *Soldo*, 244 F. Supp. 2d at 545 (plaintiff has failed to show that the causality assessment "methodology — adopted for foreign regulatory purposes — meets any of the *Daubert* criteria, nor has plaintiff shown any other indicia of reliability.").

perceived effect in one person has limited scientific value at best.[91] Because the data are limited to a single observation, a trial court must be particularly diligent in determining whether the dechallenge/rechallenge was conducted under strict controls to account for potential confounding influences. Prospective dechallenge/rechallenge experiments — sometimes referred to as "single subject" or "n of 1" experiments — have numerous limitations that preclude general causation conclusions.[92] "[W]ithout strong assumptions regarding how an intervention on one individual relates to its effects on others, the results from a single-subject design provide little useful information … [and e]xamination of a single subject cannot verify those assumptions."[93] As courts have explained, a prospective dechallenge/rechallenge report "constitutes but one single, uncontrolled experiment."[94]

14.2.2.5 Secondary Source Materials

In addition to actual scientific or anecdotal data, causation experts will sometimes rely on secondary source materials that cite to the primary evidence, such as regulatory materials, textbooks, and internal company documents. These secondary materials do not add any additional scientific knowledge and are no more reliable than the evidence they cite.[95] They do not test a causal hypothesis; they merely report the findings of others.

In particular, regulatory findings do not provide relevant "peer review" for a causation opinion, because they are based on a risk–utility analysis that involves a much lower standard of proof than that which is demanded by a court of law.[96] For example, a recent article reported that the vast majority of regulatory withdrawals of approvals for drugs in Spain during the 1990s were based solely on case reports.[97] As one commentary observed, "law, societal considerations, costs, politics, and the likelihood of litigation challenging a given regulation all influence the level of scientific proof required by the regulator decision-maker in setting regulatory standards and make such standards problematic as reference points in litigation."[98]

14.2.3 Causation Opinions Based on Clinical Reasoning

The question whether clinical reasoning can reliably support a causation opinion must be considered separately with respect to general causation and specific causation. Doctors do not in their ordinary clinical practice reach scientifically reliable determinations regarding general causation; they make individualized treatment decisions based on the exigencies of the moment. Accordingly, clinical reasoning cannot reliably support a general causation opinion. On the other hand, clinical reasoning through a differential diagnosis may provide reliable support for a specific causation opinion, so long as the diagnosis is reached in a manner that it is faithful to the scientific

---

[91] See Dunn, 275 F. Supp 2d at 683; Soldo, 244 F. Supp. 2d at 541–42; Caraker, 188 F. Supp. 2d at 1035–36; see also Revels v. Novartis Pharms. Corp., No. 03-98-00231-CV, 1999 WL 644732, *5 (Tex. App. Aug. 26, 1999).

[92] See David M. Reboussin and Timothy M. Morgan, Statistical considerations in the use and analysis of single-subject designs, Med. Sci. Sports Exerc. 639, 640–642 (1996) (discussing limitations).

[93] Reboussin and Morgan, supra note 92, abstract.

[94] Soldo, 244 F. Supp. 2d at 541 (quoting Revels, 1999 WL 644732, at *5); see also McClain, 401 F.3d at 1254–55 ("dechallenge/re-challenge tests are still case reports and do not purport to offer definitive conclusions as to causation") (quoting Rider, 295 F.3d at 1200).

[95] See Soldo, 244 F. Supp. 2d at 513, 542; Caraker, 188 F. Supp. 2d at 1039; Siharath, 131 F. Supp. 2d at 1370; Glastetter, 107 F. Supp. 2d at 1034 n.18.

[96] See McLain, 401 F.3d at 1248–50; Rider, 295 F.3d at 1201; Glastetter, 252 F.3d at 991; Hollander, 289 F.3d at 1215; Conde, 24 F.3d at 814; Dunn, 2003 WL 21856420, at * 10; Soldo, 244 F. Supp. 2d at 513; see also Richard A. Merrill, Regulatory toxicology, in Casarett & Doull's Toxicology: The Basic Science of Poisons 1041–43 (discussing federal regulator's conservative risk-utility analysis); Joseph V. Rodricks and Susan H. Rieth, Toxicological risk assessment in the courtroom: are available methodologies suitable for evaluating toxic tort and product liability claims?, 27 Regul. Toxicol. Pharmacol. 21, 27 ("The public health-oriented resolution of scientific uncertainty [used by regulators] is not especially helpful to the problem faced by a court.").

[97] See Arnaiz, supra note 82.

[98] Rodricks and Rieth, supra note 96, at 30.

method. Differential diagnoses conducted for tort litigation purposes raise unique issues of reliability, however, because they generally are conducted *post hoc* and not in the context of medical treatment.

14.2.3.1 Clinical Reasoning and General Causation

Doctors in their day-to-day practice are required to make treatment decisions for individual patients based on the clinical information before them. These clinical judgments do not provide a reliable basis for a general causation opinion.[99] Doctors do not conduct scientific testing in their daily practice to determine whether particular substances can cause particular injuries. Indeed, few doctors have more than a rudimentary training in the scientific methods used to determine causation.[100] Instead, they reach working diagnoses and make conservative medical judgments based on their Hippocratic oath to "first, do no harm."[101] Thus, for example, if a patient reports a recent exposure to a new medication or chemical substance, the doctor may order the patient to avoid further exposures based not on a scientific determination of causality but simply as a no-risk prophylactic measure.[102]

While doctors may reach tentative opinions regarding causation in the course of providing treatment, their opinions are not reached pursuant to the scientific method, but are instead based on inferential leaps that allow them to provide immediate therapeutic care. Clinical causation opinions based on differential diagnosis are "a mixture of science and art, far too complicated for its accuracy to be assessed quantitatively or for a meaningful error rate to be calculated."[103] Moreover, differential diagnosis only "follow[s] the causal stream up to a point where intervention is possible" because, typically, physicians "do not care about a disease's etiology ... unless understanding causation would assist in diagnosis and treatment."[104] As one court recently explained,

> Doctors in their day-to-day practices stumble upon coincidental occurrences and random events and often follow human nature, which is to confuse association and causation. They are programmed by human nature and the rigors and necessities of clinical practices to conclude that temporal association equals causation, or at least that it provides an adequate proxy in the chaotic and sometimes inconclusive world of medicine. This shortcut aids doctors in their clinical practices because the most important objective day-to-day is to help their patients and "first do no harm," as their Hippocratic oath requires. Consequently, they make leaps of faith.... [This type of] clinical impression is not the sort of scientific methodology that *Daubert* demands.[105]

Plaintiffs' counsel seeking to rely on clinical reasoning to support a general causation opinion will often cite to the language in *Kumho Tire* that an expert must "employ in the courtroom the same level of intellectual rigor that characterizes the practice of the expert in the relevant field."[106] This argument is misplaced, because, as explained above, "the relevant field[s]" for a general causation opinion are epidemiology and toxicology, not clinical medicine.[107] Plaintiffs' counsel will also argue that differential diagnosis is a well-recognized, scientifically reliable technique. But differential

---

[99] *See Soldo*, 244 F. Supp. 2d at 508; *Siharath*, 131 F. Supp. 2d at 1362; *In re Breast Implant Litig.*, 11 F. Supp. 2d at 1230; *Hall*, 947 F. Supp. at 1413.

[100] *See* Hu and Speizer, *supra* note 82.

[101] *See Siharath*, 131 F. Supp. 2d at 1371; *see also* Miremont, *supra* note 89 at 288 (explaining finding that physicians are more likely to attribute causation to a drug as being due to their "necessarily more pragmatic approach to patients and diseases").

[102] *See* Kassirer and Cecil, at 1384.

[103] John M. Conley and John B. Garver, III, William C. Keady and the law of scientific evidence, 68 *Miss. L.J.* 39, 51 (1998).

[104] Herbert A. Simon, Artificial-intelligence approaches to problem solving and clinical diagnosis, in *Logic of Discovery and Diagnosis in Medicine* 72, 87 (Kenneth F. Schaffner ed. 1985).

[105] *Siharath*, 131 F. Supp. 2d at 1372.

[106] 526 U.S. at 152.

[107] *See Siharath*, 131 F. Supp. 2d at 1362; Michael B. Kent, Jr., *Daubert*, doctors and differential diagnosis: treating medical causation testimony as evidence, 66 *Def. Couns. J.* 525, 532–33 (1999).

diagnosis is a reliable methodology only for "ruling out" alternative causes of injury from a list of possible causes; it does not "rule in" a substance as a potential cause in the first instance.[108]

14.2.3.2 Clinical Reasoning and Specific Causation

Although insufficient for purposes of general causation, a differential diagnosis may provide a scientifically reliable basis for a specific causation opinion — *i.e.*, that an established toxin in fact caused a plaintiff's injury. However, an expert's bare assertion that the expert applied a differential diagnosis is not sufficient to satisfy *Daubert*. A trial court must determine whether the differential diagnosis is based on a reliable methodology. Accordingly, the expert must demonstrate that the differential diagnosis was based on a sufficient and valid clinical investigation.[109] The expert also must have a scientifically reliable basis for excluding alternative causes of the plaintiff's injury, including the possibility that the injury was idiopathic.[110]

In analyzing the reliability of a specific causation opinion based on differential diagnosis, trial courts must ensure that the expert employs "the same level of intellectual rigor" in the courtroom as a treating physician would employ in the ordinary care of patients.[111] An expert cannot simply look for all possible causes of a person's illness from the universe of potential causes and declare that each of them — including the exposure at issue — should be considered actual but for causes for purposes of tort liability.[112] Even if an expert can show reliable scientific evidence supporting some level of increased risk from a drug, the expert cannot reliably point to the drug as the cause of an individual plaintiff's injury if that plaintiff has other independent risk factors that are more strongly associated with the injury in question. For example, assume that there is scientifically reliable epidemiological evidence showing a three times statistically significant increased risk of stroke in patients who used a given drug X. That evidence may be sufficient to support an expert's specific causation opinion with regard to a plaintiff who has no other risk factor for stroke. However, it would not be sufficient to support a specific causation opinion with regard to a patient who also suffers from uncontrolled hypertension and has smoked a pack of cigarettes a day for the past 20 years, given the greater risks posed by those comorbid conditions. Where a plaintiff has other established risk factors that could have caused the plaintiff's injury, the expert must explain how he ruled out these other potential causes to reliably support an opinion that the injury was due instead to a drug exposure.[113]

A trial court also needs to evaluate an expert's differential diagnosis in light of the artificial circumstances in which it is reached. Unlike differential diagnoses conducted by doctors in their day-to-day practice, a differential diagnosis in a litigation context is often conducted in support of an already asserted legal claim of causation. This raises myriad possibilities of bias, both intentional and unintentional.

Consider a hypothetical example of typical large-scale drug product liability litigation. Based on anecdotal reports of adverse events and possibly pressure from special interest organizations like Public Citizen, the FDA recommends labeling changes or withdraws approval of a drug.[114] The same day, if not before, plaintiffs' firms will begin advertising for potential plaintiffs through

---

[108] *See Norris*, 397 F.3d at 885; *Soldo*, 244 F. Supp. 2d at 524; *Siharath*, 131 F. Supp. 2d at 1362–63; *Glastetter*, 107 F. Supp. 2d at 1027.

[109] *See Soldo*, 244 F. Supp. 2d at 551; *Pick v. Am. Med. Sys. Inc.*, 958 F. Supp. 1151, 1168–69 (E.D. La. 1997).

[110] *See Daubert*, 43 F.3d at 1319; *Soldo*, 244 F. Supp. 2d at 551–52; *Magistrini,*180 F. Supp. 2d at 608–10 (D.N.J. 2002); *Nelson v. Am. Home Prods. Corp.*, 92 F. Supp. 2d 954, 971 (W.D. Mo. 2000).

[111] *Kumho Tire*, 536 U.S. at 152.

[112] *See Cano v. Everest Minerals Corp.*, 362 F. Supp. 2d 814, 846 (W.D. Tex. 2005).

[113] *See Wills v. Amerada Hess Corp.*, 379 F.3d 32, 50 (2d Cir. 2004) (excluding expert's specific causation opinion that plaintiff's squamous cell carcinoma had been caused by polycyclic aromatic hydrocarbons where plaintiff was a smoker and heavy consumer of alcohol); *Easter v. Aventis Pasteur, Inc.*, 358 F. Supp. 2d 574, 577 (E.D. Tex. 2005) (expert could not reliably point to thimerosal in vaccine as a cause of plaintiff's neurological injuries where plaintiff had autism that could not be linked to vaccine and was independently associated with such injuries).

[114] As discussed *supra* at 1160, such regulatory action is not the equivalent of a finding of causation.

various forms of media, including the Internet, television, radio, and print media. Provided that the drug has been used by a relatively large number of patients, there will be a ready population of patients who had adverse events while taking the drug based solely on statistical chance due to the background rates of such events regardless of drug use. Accordingly, plaintiffs' counsel can quickly gather a large pool of potential plaintiffs.

Plaintiffs' counsel will then start weeding through that pool to exclude individuals with obvious alternative causes for their injuries and patients whose injury did not emerge in temporal proximity to their ingestion of the drug. At first blush, this might appear to be a reliable method for determining those individuals whose injuries were more likely due to the drug. That interpretation, however, is based on the false premise that medicine can always find a cause for an injury. In fact, there are many conditions for which medicine frequently cannot find a cause.[115] In other words, there is often a measurable background rate of *idiopathic* injuries, i.e., injuries with unknown causes. Plaintiffs' counsel's weeding out process, accordingly, often merely identifies the statistically expected population of patients who coincidentally had adverse events of unknown cause while taking the drug.

At the same time plaintiffs' counsel are reviewing their potential plaintiff population, they will also be looking for an expert witness to provide a specific causation opinion. Generally, plaintiffs' counsel will select an expert who is already prepared to offer a favorable general causation opinion. Plaintiffs' counsel will also select an expert witness who is predisposed toward providing a favorable specific causation opinion. This does not mean that the expert is intentionally biased or insincere in his or her opinion, but it does mean that the expert will enter the process with a preconceived assumption of causality.

By the time the expert and plaintiff are brought together for purposes of a differential diagnosis, the result is effectively preordained. The expert will start the examination from the premise that the substance at issue is dangerous and a likely cause of injury regardless of potential alternative causes. The plaintiff will not present with obvious alternative causes of injury sufficient to shake the expert from the initial presumption. Moreover, in cases where the expert is not the patient's treating physician, the expert will not test the initial diagnosis through ongoing observation and medical treatment.

This "differential diagnosis" bears little resemblance to a differential diagnosis conducted by treating physicians in their regular practice, and cannot provide the type of objective validation that *Daubert* requires for admissibility of an expert specific causation opinion. Trial courts must recognize that there is an inherent "selection bias" at work in mass drug product liability litigation and carefully evaluate the expert's specific causation opinion with this artificial background in mind.

14.2.4 The Parlodel Litigation

Over the past decade, a number of product liability cases involving the prescription drug Parlodel have been working their way through the courts. The Parlodel litigation has resulted in a body of *Daubert* case law that squarely addresses the issues of medical causation expert testimony discussed above and provides a detailed analysis of "all of the components of the 'causation' argument that are available to experts in the most contentious of products liability case[s]."[116]

There is now an emerging judicial consensus that plaintiffs' experts' causation opinions in the Parlodel litigation do not satisfy the requirements of *Daubert*. Three federal appellate courts, the Eighth, Tenth, and Eleventh Circuits, have unanimously affirmed district court opinions excluding the causation opinions of plaintiffs' experts, and four other published district court opinions

---

[115] *See*, e.g., Steven A. Kittner, et al, Cerebral infarction in young adults, 50 *Neurology* 890–94 (1998) (despite neurologists' careful review, in 50.5% of cases, no probable cause of stroke in young adults could be identified).

[116] Kiely, *supra* note 8. In addition to being used as a case study for legal scholars, the Parlodel litigation was discussed in an article published in the *Journal of the American Medical Association* by an unsuccessful *amicus* for plaintiffs appealing a Parlodel *Daubert* exclusionary ruling to the Eleventh Circuit Court of Appeals in *Rider*. *See* J. Kassirer and J. Cecil, *supra* note 7.

excluding this testimony were not appealed.[117] A few earlier district court opinions, two of which were drafted by the same magistrate judge, have gone the other way.[118] The Parlodel opinions thus provide a useful *Daubert* case study of courts that properly evaluated medical causation testimony based on the scientific method and those that do not.

14.2.4.1 Plaintiffs' Allegations Regarding Parlodel

Parlodel (bromocriptine mesylate) is an FDA-approved drug used for a variety of indications, including Parkinson's disease, amenorrhea/galactorrhea (lack of menses), infertility, and acromegaly (a growth disorder). From 1980 to 1994, Parlodel was also approved for the prevention of postpartum lactation ("PPL") in women who elected not to breast-feed. The manufacturer of Parlodel withdrew the drug from the market for this PPL indication following receipt of a number of case reports of strokes, seizures, and myocardial infarctions and an FDA advisory committee determination that there was limited need for pharmaceutical treatment for PPL. The FDA withdrew its approval of Parlodel for the PPL indication in 1995, based on its conclusion that the limited utility of the drug for PPL did not outweigh the possible risks.[119]

Plaintiffs' experts allege that Parlodel causes vasoconstriction (a narrowing of blood vessels), which they allege can cause stroke, seizures, and myocardial infarction. Plaintiffs' experts concede that the epidemiological studies conducted on the drug have not established a causal link with these injuries and that there is a body of controlled clinical research in humans that has found that Parlodel has the exact opposite effect of causing vasodilation (a widening of blood vessels). Plaintiffs' experts also concede that controlled intact animal research has not shown a causal link between Parlodel and strokes, seizures, or myocardial infarctions in animals. Plaintiffs' experts base their causation opinion on anecdotal case reports (including alleged dechallenge/rechallenge reports), animal research involving limited end points, chemical analogies, a variety of secondary source materials, and differential diagnoses.[120]

14.2.4.2 Opinions Admitting Plaintiffs' Experts' Causation Opinions

The district courts that have admitted plaintiffs' experts' causation opinions have relied primarily on differential diagnoses and the determination that lesser scientific evidence of general causation should be accepted because it allegedly would not be possible to conduct an epidemiological study of sufficient strength to adequately test plaintiffs' experts' causation hypothesis. Thus, one magistrate judge dismissed the lack of any direct scientific evidence supporting plaintiffs' experts' causation opinion, reasoning that "[s]cience, like many other human endeavors, draws conclusions from circumstantial evidence, when other, better forms of evidence [are] not available."[121] In a subsequent opinion, the same magistrate judge sounded a similar theme: "In science, as in life, where there is smoke, fire can be inferred, subject to debate and further testing."[122] The court was similarly deferential in its review of plaintiffs' experts' specific causation opinions. While noting that there were a number of alternative causes for the injuries at issue, the court found that the "debate creates a question about the weight to be accorded the plaintiffs' experts' opinions, but it does not affect the admissibility."[123]

---

[117] *Rider*, 295 F.3d 1194; *Hollander*, 289 F.3d 1193; *Glastetter*, 252 F.3d 986; *Dunn*, 275 F. Supp 2d 672; *Soldo*, 244 F. Supp. 2d 434; *Caraker*, 188 F. Supp. 2d 1026; *Brumbaugh*, 77 F. Supp. 2d 1153; *see also Revels*, 1999 WL 644732 (excluding Parlodel causation opinions on Texas analog of *Daubert*).

[118] *Brasher v. Sandoz Pharms. Corp.*, 160 F. Supp. 2d 1291 (N.D. Ala. 2001) (Putnam, M.J.); *Globetti v. Sandoz Pharms. Corp.*, 111 F. Supp. 2d 1174 (N.D. Ala. 2000) (Putnam, M.J.); *Eve v. Sandoz Pharms. Corp.*, 2001 U.S. Dist. LEXIS 4531 (S.D. Ind. Mar. 7, 2001).

[119] *See Caraker*, 188 F. Supp. 2d at 1028, 1040.

[120] *See generally Rider*, 295 F.3d 1194; *Glastetter*, 252 F.3d 986; *Caraker*, 188 F. Supp. 2d 1026.

[121] *Globetti*, 111 F. Supp. 2d at 1180; *see also Eve*, 2001 U.S. Dist. LEXIS 4531, at *75 (quoting *Globetti*).

[122] *Brasher*, 160 F. Supp. 2d at 1296; *see also id.* at 1297 ("Given the practical unavailability of other forms of scientific evidence, reliance on those that are available is all the more reasonable.").

[123] *Id.* at 1299.

Missing in these opinions is any recognition of the requirement in *Daubert* that the experts' causation opinions be based on the scientific method of testing and validating hypotheses. *Daubert* does not permit expert testimony to be admitted based on the smoke of anecdotal reports and inferences, nor does it allow courts to lower the bar of scientific reliability based on a perceived lack of relevant scientific evidence. In accepting plaintiffs' experts' lower showing of evidence, these courts abdicated their gatekeeping responsibility.

14.2.4.3 Opinions Excluding Plaintiffs' Experts' Causation Opinions

By contrast, in the Parlodel cases in which courts have evaluated plaintiffs' experts' opinions based on the scientific method, the experts' testimony has been excluded. These courts have conducted detailed analyses of each of the different categories of evidence discussed above, and their reasoning and conclusions are incorporated in that discussion. The overarching theme in these opinions is the courts' recognition that medical causation opinions are not admissible unless they are based on scientifically tested and validated hypotheses.

As these courts have explained, *Daubert* does not establish a "best efforts" test.[124] An expert cannot satisfy *Daubert* by arguing that the expert has "used the best methodology available under the circumstance,"[125] or that the expert has "done the best [the expert] could with the available data and the scientific literature."[126] Rather, the expert must answer the "key question," whether the "theory being advanced by the expert is testable or has been tested, the methodology of which is what distinguishes science from other fields of human inquiry."[127] "The hallmark of [*Daubert*'s] reliability prong is the scientific method, i.e., the generation of testable hypotheses that are then subjected to the real world crucible of experimentation, falsification/validation, and replication."[128] The "testing of hypotheses" is "a critical aspect of the application of the scientific method."[129] Expert opinions "reposed in the realm of 'may cause' or 'possibly could cause'" must be excluded.[130] "While hypothesis is essential in the scientific community because it leads to advances in science, speculation in the courtroom cannot aid the fact finder in making a determination of whether liability exists."[131]

These Parlodel cases forcefully answer critics of *Daubert* who argue for a lower standard based on deferential review of medical causation testimony:

> The *Daubert* trilogy, in shifting the focus to the kind of empirically supported, rationally explained reasoning required in science, has greatly improved the quality of the evidence upon which juries base their verdicts. Although making determinations of reliability may present the court with the difficult task of ruling on matters that are outside its field of expertise, this is less objectionable than dumping a barrage of scientific evidence on a jury, who would likely be less equipped than a judge to make reliability and relevancy determinations.[132]

The scientific method serves as a bulwark against subjective judgments and inspired guesswork masquerading as scientific knowledge. Courts that ignore the scientific method in their review of medical causation opinions do a disservice to the legal system and disregard the Supreme Court's mandate.

---

[124] *Siharath*, 131 F. Supp. 2d at 1373.
[125] *Id.* at 1371.
[126] *Hollander*, 289 F.3d at 1213.
[127] *Brumbaugh*, 77 F. Supp. 2d at 1156.
[128] *Caraker*, 188 F. Supp. 2d at 1030.
[129] *Soldo*, 244 F. Supp. 2d at 529.
[130] *Glastetter*, 107 F. Supp. 2d at 1025.
[131] *Dunn*, 275 F. Supp. 2d at 684.
[132] *Rider*, 295 F.3d at 1197.

14.2.5 Conclusion

Faced with the exacting standards of *Daubert*, plaintiffs' causation experts will often respond with a spaghetti-on-the-wall strategy in the hope that something will stick. The Supreme Court's adoption of the scientific method as the central guide to admissibility provides district courts with the solution they need to untangle the mess. For each strand in plaintiffs' expert's analysis, the questions are the same: Is the expert relying on evidence that has been tested and validated, and does the evidence fit the question at issue? Unless experts can answer both of these questions in the affirmative, they should not be allowed to serve up their opinions to a jury.

As Supreme Court Justice Breyer explained in his concurring opinion in *Joiner*, the evidentiary safeguards imposed by the courts against unreliable science provides an important bulwark against unfounded litigation that can threaten access to needed health care:

> [M]odern life, including good health as well as economic well-being, depends upon the use of artificial or manufactured substances.... [I]t may, therefore, prove particularly important to see that judges fulfill their *Daubert* gatekeeping function, so that they help assure that the powerful engine of tort liability, which can generate strong financial incentives to reduce, or to eliminate, production, points toward the right substances and does not destroy the wrong ones.[133]

While this book has focused primarily on the dangers of *drug abuse*, the potential dangers of *litigation abuse* on the availability of medically indicated pharmaceutical products also poses a threat to patient health that must not be ignored.

---

[133] *Joiner,* 522 U.S. at 148–49 (Breyer, J., concurring).

Appendices

CONTENTS

APPENDIX IA: GLOSSARY OF TERMS IN FORENSIC TOXICOLOGY

Compiled by H. Chip Walls, B.S.
Department of Pathology, Forensic Toxicology Laboratory, University of Miami, Miami, Florida

Absolute Method A method in which characterization is based on physically defined (absolute) standards.

Accreditation (1) A formal process by which a laboratory is evaluated, with respect to established criteria, for its competence to perform a specified kind(s) of measurement(s); (2) the decision based upon such a process; (3) formal recognition that a testing laboratory is competent to carry out specific tests or specific types of tests.

Accuracy Closeness of the agreement between the result of a measurement and a true value of the measured quantity.

Acetaldehyde The first product of ethanol metabolism.

Acute Severe, usually crucial, often dangerous in which relatively rapid changes are occurring. An acute exposure runs a comparatively short course.

Acute tolerance The development of tolerance within the course of a single exposure to a drug.

Alcohol dehydrogenase (ADH) The main enzyme that catalyzes the conversion of ethanol to acetaldehyde.

Aldehyde dehydrogenase (ALDH) The enzyme that converts acetaldehyde to acetate.

Aliquot (1) A divisor that does not divide a sample into a number of equal parts without leaving a remainder; (2) a sample resulting from such a divisor.

Analyte The specific component measured in a chemical analysis.

Analytical run (series) A set of measurements carried out successively by one analyst using the same measuring system, at the same location, under the same conditions, and during the same short period of time.

Analytical sensitivity The ability of a method or instrument to discriminate between samples having different concentrations or containing different amounts of the analyte. Slope of the analytical calibration function.

Analytical specificity   Ability of a measurement procedure to determine solely the measurable quantity (desired substance) it purports to measure and not others.

Analytical wavelength   Any wavelength at which an absorbance measurement is made for the purpose of the determination of a constituent of a sample.

Antemortem   Before death, occurring before death.

Ascites   An abnormal accumulation of fluid in the peritoneal cavity of the abdomen.

Assignable cause   A cause believed to be responsible for an identifiable change in precision or accuracy of a measurement process.

Beer's law   The absorbance of a homogeneous sample containing an absorbing substance is directly proportional to the concentration of the absorbing substance.

Bias   A systematic error inherent in a method or caused by some artifact or idiosyncrasy of the measurement system. Temperature effects and extraction inefficiencies are examples of errors inherent in the method. Blanks, contamination, mechanical losses, and calibration errors are examples of artifact errors. Bias can be either positive or negative, and several kinds of error can exist concurrently. Therefore, net bias is all that can be evaluated.

Blank   (1) The measured value obtained when a specified component of a sample is not present during the measurement. In such a case, the measured value (or signal) for the component is believed to be due to artifacts and should be deducted from a measured value to give a net value due solely to the component contained in the sample. The blank measurement must be made so that the correction process is valid.   (2) Biological specimen with no detectable drugs added, routinely analyzed to ensure that no false-positive results are obtained.

Blind sample   A control sample submitted for analysis as a routine specimen whose composition is known to the submitter but unknown to the analyst. A blind sample is one way to test the proficiency of a measurement process.

Calibrant   Substance used to calibrate, or to establish the analytical response of, a measurement system.

Calibration   Comparison of a measurement standard or instrument with another standard or instrument to report or eliminate, by adjustment, any variation or deviation in the accuracy of the item being compared.

Central line   The long-term expected value of a variable displayed on a control chart.

Certification   A written declaration that a particular product or service complies with stated criteria.

Certified value   The value that appears in a certificate as the best estimate of the value for a property of a certified reference material.

Certified reference material (CRM)   A reference material one or more of whose property values are certified by a technically valid procedure, accompanied by or traceable to a certificate or other documentation that is issued by a certifying body. [ISO Guide 30: 1981 (E)]

Chain of custody (COC)   Handling samples in a way that supports legal testimony to prove that the sample integrity and identification of the sample have not been violated as well as the documentation describing these procedures.

Chance cause   A cause for variability of a measurement process that occurs unpredictably, for unknown reasons, and is believed to happen by chance alone.

Check standard (in physical calibration)   An artifact measured periodically, the results of which typically are plotted on a control chart to evaluate the measurement process.

Chronic   Persistent, prolonged, repeated.

Chronic tolerance   The gradual decrease in degree of effect produced at the same blood concentration in the course of repeated exposures to that drug.

Coefficient of variation   The standard deviation divided by the value of the parameter measured.

Comparative method   A method that is based on the intercomparison of the sample with a chemical standard.

Composite sample   A sample composed of two or more components selected to represent a population of interest.

Concentration   Amount of a drug in a unit volume of biological fluid, expressed as weight/volume. Urine concentrations are usually expressed either as nanograms per milliliter (ng/ml), micrograms per milliliter (μg/ml), or milligrams per liter (mg/l).   (There are 28,000,000 micrograms in an ounce, and 1,000 nanograms in a microgram.)

Confidence interval   That range of values, calculated from an estimate of the mean and the standard deviation, which is expected to include the population mean with a stated level of confidence. In the same manner, confidence intervals can also be calculated for standard deviations, lines, slopes, and points.

Confirmation   A second test by an alternate chemical method to positively identify a drug or metabolite. Confirmations are carried out on presumptive positives from initial screens.

Control chart   A graphical plot of test results with respect to time or sequence of measurement together with limits in which they are expected to lie when the system is in a state of statistical control.

Control limits   The limits shown on a control chart beyond which it is highly improbable that a point could lie while the system remains in a state of statistical control.

Control sample   A material of known composition that is analyzed concurrently with test samples to evaluate a measurement process. (See also Check standard.)

Correlation coefficient   Measures the strength of the relation between two sets of numbers, such as instrument response and standard concentration.

Cross sensitivity   A quantitative measure of the response for an undesired constituent or interferent as compared to that for a constituent of interest.

Cross-reacting substances   In immunoassays, refers to substances that react with antiserum produced specifically for other substances.

Cutoff level (threshold)   Value serving as an administrative breakpoint (or cutoff point) for labeling a screening test result positive or negative.

Cytochrome P450   A detoxifying enzyme found in liver cells.

Detection limit or limit of detection (LOD)   The lowest concentration of a drug that can reliably be detected. Smallest result of a measurement by a given measurement procedure that can be accepted with a stated confidence level as being different from the value of the measurable quantity obtained on blank material.

Double blind   A sample, known by the submitter but supplied to an analyst in such a way that neither its composition nor its identification as a check sample or standard is known to the analyst.

Duplicate measurement   A second measurement made on the same or identical sample of material to assist in the evaluation of measurement variance.

Endogenous   Produced or originating within the body by natural processes such as intermediary metabolism.

Enzymes   Proteins whose function is to drive the chemical reactions of the body — a catalyst of biochemical reactions.

False negative   An erroneous result in an assay that indicates the absence of a drug that is actually present.

False negative rate   The proportion of true positive samples that give a negative result.

False positive   An erroneous result in an assay that indicates the presence of a drug that is actually not present.

False positive rate   The proportion of true negative samples that give a positive test result.

Fume   Gas-like emanation containing minute solid particles arising from the heating of a solid body such as lead, in distinctions to a gas or vapor. This physical change is often accompanied by a chemical reaction such as oxidation. Fumes flocculate and sometimes coalesce. Odorous gases and vapors are not fumes.

Hepatocyte   Name given to cells within the liver.

Hyperglycemia   An excessive amount of glucose in the blood.

Hypoglycemia   An abnormally low concentration of glucose in the circulating blood.

Impairment   Decreased ability to perform safely a given task.

Infrared   Pertaining to the region of the electromagnetic spectrum from approximately 0.78 to 300 microns (780 to 300,000 nanometers).

Insulin   A hormone produced in the islets of Langerhans in the pancreas as a response to elevated blood sugar levels. The hormone permits the metabolism and utilization of glucose.

Interferant   A chemical compound or substance other than the substance of interest (e.g., ethanol) to which the measuring instrument responds to give a falsely elevated result.

Interfering substances   Substances other than the analyte that give a similar analytical response or alter the analytical result.

Interindividual variation Distribution of the values of a type of quantity in individuals of a given set.

Intraindividual variation Distribution of the values of a type of quantity in a given individual.

Limit of quantification (LOQ) The lower limit of concentration or amount of substance that must be present before a method is considered to provide quantitative results. By convention, LOQ = 10 x so, where so = the estimate of the standard deviation at the lowest level of measurement.

Matrix The composition of the biological sample being analyzed, consisting of proteins, lipids and other biomolecules that can affect analyte recovery.

Matrix effects Influence of a component in the analytical sample other than the component being investigated on the measurement being made.

MEOS The microsomal ethanol oxidizing system, an enzyme system in liver that converts ethanol to acetaldehyde.

Metabolite A compound produced from chemical changes of a drug in the body.

Microsomal enzymes Detoxifying enzymes associated with certain membranes (smooth endoplasmic reticulum) within cells.

Ordinal scale Ordered set of measurements consisting of words and/or numbers indicating the magnitude of the possible values that a type of quantity can take.

Outlier A value in a sample of values so far separated from the remainder as to suggest that it may be from a different population.

Perimortem At or near the time of death.

Pharmacodynamics The study of the relationship of drug concentration to drug effects.

Pharmacokinetics The study of the time course of the processes (absorption, distribution, metabolism, and excretion) a drug undergoes in the body.

Physical dependence A state that develops in parallel with chronic tolerance and is revealed by the occurrence of serious disturbances (abstinence syndrome) when drug intake is terminated.

Postmortem After death, occurring after death, of or pertaining to a postmortem examination, an autopsy.

Precision Closeness of agreement between independent results of measurements obtained by a measurement procedure under prescribed conditions (standard deviation).

Presumptive positive Sample that has been flagged as positive by screening but that has not been confirmed by an equally sensitive alternative chemical method.

Proficiency-testing specimen A specimen whose expected results are unknown to anyone in the laboratory, known only by an external agency, and later revealed to the laboratory as an aid to laboratory improvement and/or a condition of licensure.

Psycho Pertaining to the mind and mental processes.

Psychoactive Affecting the mind or mental processes.

Psychochemical A substance affecting the mind or mental processes.

Psychology The science of mental processes and behavior.

Psychomotor Of or pertaining to muscular activity associated with the mental process.

Psychomotor functions Matters of mental and motor function.

Psychosis Severe mental disorder, with or without organic damage, characterized by deterioration of normal intellectual and social functioning and by partial or complete withdrawal from reality.

Psychotomimetic Pertaining to or inducing symptoms of a psychotic state.

Psychotropic Having a mind-altering effect.

Qualitative test Chemical analysis to identify one or more components of a mixture.

Quality assurance (QA) Practices that assure accurate laboratory results.

Quality control (QC) Those techniques used to monitor errors that can cause a deterioration in the quality of laboratory results. Control material most often refers to a specimen, the expected results of which are known to the analyst, that is routinely analyzed to ensure that the expected results are obtained.

Quantitative test Chemical analysis to determine the amounts or concentrations of one or more components of a mixture.

Repeatability Closeness of agreement between the results of successive measurements during a short time (within run standard deviation).

Reproducibility Closeness of agreement between the results of measurements of the same measurable quantity on different occasions, made by different observers, using different calibrations, at different times (between run standard deviation).

Screen A series of initial tests designed to separate samples containing drugs at or above a particular minimum concentration from those below that minimum concentration (positive vs. negative).

Sensitivity The detection limit, expressed as a concentration of the analyte in the specimen.

Specificity Quality of an analytical technique that tends to exclude all substances but the analyte from affecting the result.

Split specimen Laboratory specimen that is divided and submitted to the analyst, unknown to him or her, as two different specimens with different identifications.

Standard Authentic sample of the analyte of known purity, or a solution of the analyte of a known concentration.

Substrate The substance (molecule) acted upon by an enzyme; its conversion to a particular product is catalyzed by a specific enzyme.

Tolerance A state that develops after long-term exposure to a drug. Metabolic tolerance infers a faster removal, oxidation by the liver. Functional tolerance infers a change in sensitivity of the organ to the effects of the drug.

Tolerance interval That range of values within which a specified percentage of individual values of a population, measurements, or sample are expected to lie with a stated level of confidence.

Ultraviolet Pertaining to the region of the electromagnetic spectrum from approximately 10 to 380 nm.

Visible Pertaining to radiant energy in the electromagnetic spectral range visible to the human eye, approximately 380 to 780 nm.

Wavelength A property of radiant energy, such as IR, visible, or UV. The distance measured along the line of propagation, between two points that are in phase on adjacent waves.

APPENDIX IB: COMMON ABBREVIATIONS

Compiled by H. Chip Walls, B.S.

Department of Pathology, Forensic Toxicology Laboratory, University of Miami, Miami, Florida

ABS	Absorbance error (EMIT)
AM	Morning, antemortem
AMPH	Amphetamines
AP	Attending physician
APAP	Acetaminophen
ASA	Salicylates
ASCVD	Arteriosclerotic cardiovascular disease
ASHD	Arteriosclerotic heart disease
BAC	Blood alcohol concentration
BDS	Basic drug screen
BE	Benzoylecgonine
BENZO	Benzodiazepine(s)
Bld	Blood
BP	Blood pressure
BSV	Blue-stoppered vacutainer
CAP	College of American Pathologists
CBC	Complete blood count
CI	Chemical ionization (in mass spectrometry)
CID	Criminal investigation department
CN	Cyanide
CO	Carbon monoxide
Co	County
c/o	Complain(-ing), (-ed), (-t) of

COPD	Chronic obstructive pulmonary disease
DC	Death certificate
Decd	Decedent/deceased
DM	Diabetes melitus
DNR	Do not resuscitate
DOH	Department of Health
D/T	Due to
DUI	Driving under the influence
DUID	DUI for drugs
DWI	Driving while intoxicated
dx	Diagnosed
EB	Eastbound
ECD	Electron capture detector (GC)
EI	Electron impact ionization (in mass spectrometry)
EMIT	Enzyme-multiplied immunoassay testing
ER	Emergency room
ET	Evidence technician
EtOH	Ethanol/alcohol
Ext	Extract
Extn	Extraction
FH	Funeral home
FID	Flame ionization detector (GC)
FS	Fingerstick
FTD	Failed to detect
Fx	Fracture
g	Gram
g%	Gram percent
GC	Gastric contents, gas chromatography
GC/MS	Gas chromatography/mass spectrometry
gm	Gram
GSV	Gray-stoppered vacutainer
GSW	Gunshot wound
H2O	Water
HCT	Hematocrit
Hgb	Hemoglobin
HIV	Human immunodeficiency virus
HPLC	High performance liquid chromatograph(y)
HTN	Hypertension
Hx	History
ICU	Intensive care unit
L, l	Liter
LLQ	Left lower quadrant
LUQ	Left upper quadrant
MC	Mixed volatiles
MCT	Micro color test
MCV	Mean cell volume
Meds	Medications
MEO	Medical Examiner's Office
MeOH	Methanol
mg	Milligram
ml, mL	Milliliter
MSDS	Material safety data sheet
MVA	Motor vehicle accident
n	Number
NB	Northbound
ND	None detected
NDD	No drugs detected
Neg	Negative
ng	Nanogram
NOK	Next of kin
NP	Nurse practitioner

NPD	Nitrogen phosphorus detector
NR	Not requested
O2	Oxygen
OF	Ocular fluid (vitreous)
Opi	Opiates
p	After
P	Probation
Pb	Lead
PCC	Poison Control Center
PCP	Phencyclidine
pg	Picogram
PM	Postmortem, in the evening
PMH	Previous medical history
PO	Police officer, probation officer
Pos	Positive
PSV	Purple-stoppered vacutainer
p/u	Pick(ed) up
QA	Quality assurance
QC	Quality control
QNS	Quantity not sufficient
QS	Quantity sufficient
QS to _	Dilute to volume
R	Referral
RB	Reagent blank
RBC	Red blood cells
RIA	Radio immunoassay
RLQ	Right lower quadrant
R/O	Rule out
RSV	Red-stoppered vacutainer
RUQ	Right upper quadrant
Rx	Prescription
s	Without
S/A	Same address
SB	Southbound
SD	Standard deviation
Ser	Serum
SMA	Sympathomimetic amines
S/O	Sign-out
SOB	Shortness of breath
SOP	Standard operating procedure
Sp Gr	Specific gravity
SST	Serum separator tube
STD	Sexually transmitted disease
TAT	turn-around time
THC	Tetrahydrocannabinol
TLC	Thin-layer chromatography
Tx	Taken
U	Urine
VD	Venereal disease
VP	Venipuncture
w/	With
WAN	Weak acid/neutral
WB	Westbound
WBC	White blood cells
w/o	Without
x	Average
y/o	Year old
µL	Microliter (also uL)
µg	Microgram (also ug, ugm, µgm)
4-Br	Tetrabromophenolphthalein ethyl ester (a color test)
% sat	Percent saturation

APPENDIX IC: REFERENCES FOR METHODS OF
DRUG QUANTITATIVE ANALYSIS

Drug Name	Class	Fraction	UV	GC	LC	GC/MS	General
11-Hydroxy delta-9-THC	3	B		[1]	[2]	[3–9]	[10–12]
DELTA-9-THC	3	B					[10–12]
Acebutolol	2	B			[13]	[14]	[15–17]
Acetaminophen	1	WAN	[18–20]		[21–24]		[25–29]
Acetazolamide	5	B		[30]			
Acetylcarbromal	3	WAN					
Acetylsalicyclic acid	1	A		[31–33]	[34,35]		[36–38]
Albuterol	2	B			[39]		[40]
Alfentanil	1	B		[41]		[42]	[43,44]
Allobarbital	3	WAN	[45]	[46–55]	[46,56–60]		
Allopurinol	5	WAN					
Alphaprodine	1	B					[61]
Alprazolam	3	B/N		[62 63]	[64,65]	[66]	
Amantadine	1	B					
Amiodarone	2	B		[67,68]			
Amitriptyline	3	B		[69,70]	[71–76]	[77–80]	
Amlodipine	3	B			[81]		
Amobarbital	3	WAN			[82–85]	[86,87]	
Amoxapine	3	B		[88–90]			
Amphetamine	3	B			[91–93]	[94–101]	
Amyl nitrite	3	G					[102–106]
Aprobarbital	3	WAN		[50]		[107]	
Astemizole	4	B					[108]
Atenolol	2	B			[109]		
Atracurium	3	Q					[110]
Atropine (Hyoscyamine-D,L)	3	B				[111,112]	[113]
Azatadine	3	B					
Baclofen	1	B			[114, 115]		
Barbital	3	WAN			[116]	[117]	
Barbiturates	3	WAN			[118–123]		[51,120, 124–129]
Benzephetamine	3	B					[130–134]
Benzocaine	3	B					[135]
Benzoylecgonine	3	AMPHO			[136–139]		[140–145]
Benzphetamine	3	B				[146]	
Benztropine	3	B				[147]	
Bepridil	2	B					[67]
Betaxolol	2	B					
Biperiden	3	B					
Bisoprolol	3	B					
Bretylium	2	O					
Bromazepam	3	B			[148]	[149]	
Bromocriptine	3	B				[150]	
Bromdiphen-hydramine	4	B		[151,152]		[153,154]	
Bupivacaine	3	B		[155–157]	[158]		[159–161]
Buprenorphine	1	B			[162,163]	[164–166]	[167–169]
Bupropion	3	B		[170]		[171,172]	[173,174]
Buspirone	3	B		[62]	[175]	[175]	
Butabarbital	3	WAN			[176]		
Butalbital	3	WAN				[86,107,120,126]	
Butorphanol	1	B				[177]	[178]
Caffeine	3	WAN			[179–181]		[182–184]
Camazepam	3	B					
Carbamazepine	3	B		[185–187]	[188–190]		[191,192]
Carbinoxamine	3	B					

Drug Name	Class	Fraction	UV	GC	LC	GC/MS	General
Carfentanil	1	B				[124,193]	[194]
Carisoprodol	3	WAN		[195]		[196]	
Chlopropamide	5	WAN	[197]		[198]		
Chloral Hydrate	3	O		[199–202]		[203]	
Chlordiazepoxide	3	B		[202,204–206]	[201,202]		
Chloropromazine	3	B		[207]	[208]	[209]	
Chloroquine	5	B			[210,211]		
Chlorpheniramine	3	B	[212]	[213]			
Chlorphentermine	3	B					
Chlorpromazine	3	B		[214,215]	[208,216]		
Chlorpropamide	5	WAN					[197]
Chlorprothixene	3	B					
Chlorzoxazone	3	WAN, B					
Cimetidine	5	B			[217]		
Clemastine	3	B					
Clobazam	3	B			[218,219]	[220]	
Clomipramine	3	B			[221–224]		
Clonazepam	3	B		[225–228]	[229–231]	[227]	
Clonidine	2	B				[232,233]	
Clorazepate	3	B		[234,235]		[236]	
Clotiazepam	3	B					
Clozapine	3	B		[237–239]	[240–243]		[244]
Cocaethylene	3	B			[245]	[140,245–248]	[138,249]
Cocaine	3	B		[248]	[250–253]	[140,145, 254–257]	
Codeine	1	B		[258]	[259]	[260–264]	[265]
Colchicine	5	B			[266,267]		
Cotinine	5	B		[268]		[269–271]	
Cyclizine	3	B				[272]	
Cyclobenzaprine	3	B			[72]	[73,273]	[274]
Cyclopane	5	WAN					
Cyproheptadine	3	B					[275]
delta-9-THC- Carboxylic acid	3	A		[276]		[3,7,10, 277–279]	
Demoxepam	3	B			[201,280, 281]	[202,282]	
Desalkylflurazepam	3	B			[283]	[284,285]	[286]
Desflurane	5	G				[287]	
Desipramine	3	B					
Dextromethorphan	4	B			[288,289]		
Dextrorphan	4	B			[288,289]		
Diazepam	3	B		[234,235, 290]]	[283,291, 292]	[236]	
Diclofenac	1	A			[293,294]		
Dicyclomine	5	B				[295]	
Diethylpropion	3	B					[296]
Diflunisal	1	WAN					[297]
Dihydrocodeine	1	B				[298,299]	
Diltiazem	2	B				[300]	
Diphenhydramine	4	B		[152]		[153]	
Diphenoxin	1	B			[301]		
Diphenoxylate	1	B			[301]		
Disopyramide	2	B			[302,303]	[304,305]	[300]
Doxepin	3	B			[306]		[307]
Doxylamine	4	B				[308]	
Ecgonine methyl ester	3	B			[250, 251, 309–311]	[254,312–315]	

Drug Name	Class	Fraction	UV	GC	LC	GC/MS	General
Encainide	2	B					[316,317]
Enflurane	5	G				[318]	[319]
Ephedrin	4	B			[320]	[183]	
Esmolol	2	B					
Estazolam	3	B			[321]	[149]	
Ethanol	5	G		[322–329]			
Ethchlorvynol	3	O		[330–334]			[335,336]
Ethinamate	3	WAN					
Ethosuximide	3	WAN			[337–339]		[340,341]
Ethylene	5	G					
Ethylflurazepam	3	B					
Etodolac	1	A					
Etomidate	3	WAN		[342]			
Famotidine	3	B				[343]	
Felbamate	3	WAN, B		[344]	[189,345, 346]		[347]
Felodipine	2	B		[348]			
Fenfluramine	3	B			[349]		
Fenoprofen	1	A			[350]		
Fentanyl	1	B		[351]		[124,193, 352–355]	[356]
Flecainide	2	B			[357–359]	[300]	
Flunitrazepam	3	B		[62, 63]	[360–363]		
Fluoxetine	3	B		[364–367]	[368]	[369]	
Fluphenazine	3	B				[370]	
Flurazepam	3	B					
Flurbiprofen	1	A					
Freon	5	G					
Gasoline	5	G					
Glipizide	5	WAN			[371]		
Glutethimide	3	WAN		[372,373]			[374,375]
Glyburide	5	WAN			[371]		
Halazepam	3	B					
Haloperidol	3	B			[376–379]	[380–382]	
Hexobarbital	3	WAN		[129,383, 384]		[120,125, 126]	[385]
Hydrocodone	1	B					[386]
Hydromorphone	1	AMPHO			[387–389]	[264,390]	
Hydroxychloroquine	5	B			[211,391]		
Hydroxyzine	3	B		[392]			
Ibuprofen	1	WAN			[294,393]	[394–397]	
Imipramine	3	B		[398]	[398–401]	[402]	
Indomethacin	1	WAN		[403,404]	[350,405–407]		
Insulin	5	O					[408–412]
Iso-metheptene	5	B					
Isoflurane	3	G				[318]	
Isopropanol	5	G					[413–419]
Isoxsuprine	2	B					
Isradipine	2	B					[420]
Ketamin	3	B		[421]	[422]	[423,424]	
Ketazolam	3	B					
Ketoprofen	1	WAN			[425–427]		
Ketorolac	1	B			[428–431]	[432]	
l-methamphetamine	3	B				[433–435]	
Lamotrigine	3	B					[436–438]
Levallorphan	1	B				[439]	
Levodopa	5	O					
Levorphanol	1	AMPHO					[440]

Drug Name	Class	Fraction	UV	GC	LC	GC/MS	General
Lidocaine	5,2	B			[155,156, 441]		
Lithium	3	O					
Loperamide	1	B					
Lorantadine	3	B					
Lorazepam	3	B			[281]	[442–444]	
Loxapine	3	B					
LSD	3	B			[445–447]	[448,449]	
Maprotiline	3	B				[450,451]	
Mazindol	3	B					
MDEA	3	B				[132]	
Meclizine	3	B					
Medazepam	3	B				[361]	
Mefenamic Acid	1	A					
Meperidine (Pethidine)	1	B				[157]	
Mephentermine	3	B					
Mephenytoin	3	B					
Mephobarbital	3	B					
Mepivacaine	3	B					
Meprobamate	3	WAN		[195,452]		[453]	[375,454, 455]
Mescaline (Peyote)	3	B					[456]
Mesoridazine	3	B			[457]		[458]
Methadone and metabolite	1	B		[459]		[460–462]	
Methamphetamine	3	B		[463]		[133,464, 465]	
Methanol	5	G		[418,466– 468]			
Methapyrilene	3	B					
Methaqualone	3	WAN,B		[235,469]		[470]	
Methocarbamol	3	WAN					
Methohexital	3	WAN					
Methsuximide	3	WAN			[471]		[340]
Methylenedioxy amphetamine (MDA)	3	B				[132,472]	
Methylenedioxymethamphetamine (MDMA; Ecstasy)	3	B				[132,472]	
Methylphenidate	3	B					
Methyprylon	3	WAN					
Methysergide	3	B					
Metoclopramide	5	B					
Metoprolol	2	B		[473]	[474]	[474]	
Mexiletine	2	B		[475]		[300,476]	
Midazolam	3	B			[422,477, 478]	[479]	
Molindone	1	B					
Monoacetylmorphine	1	B		[480]	[481]	299,482– 484]	
Moricizine	2	B					
Morphine	3	AMPHO			[485–487]	[488–490]	
Morphine-3-glucuronide	3	AMPHO			[491–494]		
Nadolol	2	B					
Nalbuphine	1	B					[178,495]
Naproxen	1	WAN			[294]		
Nicotine	5	B			[496]	[269,497, 498]	
Nifedipine	2	B		[499]	[500,501]	[502]	
Nitrazepam	3	B			[149,321, 360,363]		

Drug Name	Class	Fraction	UV	GC	LC	GC/MS	General
Nitrous oxide	3	G					
Nomifensine	3	B					
Nylidrin		B					
Orphenadrine	3	B					
Oxazepam	3	B			[292]	[503]	
Oxycodone	1	B				[504,505]	[506]
Oxymorphone	1	B				[505]	
Pancuraonium	3	Q					[507,508]
Papaverine	2	B				[509]	
Paradehyde	3	O					
Paroxetine	3	B					[510]
PCP	3	B		[511–513]		[514,515]	
Pemoline	3	B					[516]
Pentazocine	1	B		[517–519]			
Pentobarbital	3	WAN		[49,54]		[520]	[521–524]
Pergolide	3	B					[525]
Perphenazine	3	B					
Phendimetrazine	3	B					[526]
Phenelazine	3	B					
Phenobarbital	3	WAN			[189,339, 527–529]		
Phensuximide	3	WAN					
Phentermine	3	B			[530]	[134,531]	
Phenylpropanolamine	3	B		[532]			
Phenyltoloxamine	4	B					
Phenytoin (Diphenyl-hydantoin)	3	WAN			[528,533, 534,338]		
Piroxicam	1	A					
Prazepam	3	B			[62,321, 360,535]		
Primidone	3	WAN			[189,527, 529]	[536,537]	
Procainamide	2	B			[303]		[538,539]
Procaine	5	B					
Promazine	3	B					
Promethazine	3	B			[540]		
Propafenone	3	B			[541]		
Propanolol	2	B		[473]	[542–544]	[545,546]	
Propofol	3	B			[547]	[548]	
Propoxyphene	1	B		[469,549–552]		[553–556]	[557–559]
Protriptyline	3	B			[74,222, 376,560]		[385,561–564]
Pseudoephedrine	4	B					[94,565]
Psycylobin	3	O					
Pyrilamine	4	B				[308,566]	
Quazepam	3	B		[567]	[568]		[569]
Quinidine	2	B			[570]		[538]
Quinine	5	B				[571]	
Ranitidine	5	B			[572,573]		
Risperidone	3	B			[574,575]		[576,577]
Scopolamine	3	B				[578,579]	
Secobarbital	3	WAN			[580]		[581]
Selegiline	3	B		[582]	[583]	[584,585]	[586]
Sertraline	3	B				[587]	[510]
Sotalol	2	B					
Strychnine	5	B					[588]

Drug Name	Class	Fraction	UV	GC	LC	GC/MS	General
Succinylcholine	3	Q					[589,590]
Sufentanil	1	B					[193,591]
Sumatriptan	1	B					[592]
Talbutal	3	WAN				[86,593, 594]	
Temazepam	3	B			[595]		[596,597]
Terbutaline	4	B			[598]	[599,600]	
Terfenadine	4	B					
Tetracaine	5	B					[601]
Tetrazepam	3	B					
Theophylline	4	WAN			[83,338, 602, 603]		[603–607]
Thiamylal	3	WAN			[608,609]		
Thiopental	3	WAN		[610]	[405]		
Thioridazine	3	B			[399,457]		
Thiothixene	3	B					
Tocainide	2	B					[300]
Tolazamide	3	WAN					
Tolmetin	1	WAN					[126]
Toluene	5	G		[611]		[612–614]	[615–617]
Tolutamide	3	WAN					
Tramadol	1	B					[618]
Tranylcypromine	3	B					
Trazodone	3	B		[619–621]			
Triazolam	3	B			[321]	[66,622– 624]	
Trichloroethylene	5	G		[625]			
Trifluoperazine	3	B					[67]
Triflupromazine	3	B					
Trihexyphenidyl	3	B		[626]			
Trimethadione	3	WAN					[627]
Trimethobenzamide	3	B					[628,629]
Trimipramine	3	B		[398]	[630]	[402]	[631]
Tripelennamine	4	N		[517,518, 632]			
Triprolidine	4	N					
Tubocurarine	5	Q					
Valproic acid	3	WAN		[633–635]	[636,637]	[638]	[639]
Venlafaxine	3	B					[640,641]
Verapamil	2	N		[642–644]			[645,646]
Xylene	5	G					[102,647– 650]
Zolpidem	3	B			[651–655]		

KEY: Fraction (extraction): A = acid, B = Base, WAN = weak acid neutral, Ampho = amphoteric, Q = quantanary, O = Other

Pharmacological Classification

1 **Analgesics and Antiinflamatory**
Nonsteroidal antiinflammatories
Opioids
Central analgesics
2 **Cardiovascular/DiureticDrugs**
Antiarrhythmics
Antihypertensives
Beta blockers
Calcium channel blockers
Inotropic
Nitrates
3 **Central Nervous System Drugs**
Anticonvulsants
Antiemetics/ antivertigo
Depressants
Hallucinogens
Psychotherapeutic agents
Antianxiety
Antidepressants
Antipsychotics
Sedatives and hypnotics
General anesthetics
Barbiturates
Nonbarbiturates
Gases
Volatile liquids
Muscle relaxants
Parkinsonism drugs
Stimulants
Analeptics
Amphetamines
Anorexiants
4 **Respiratory Drugs**
Antihistamines and antiallergics
Bronchodilators
Cough and cold
5 **Other**

REFERENCES

1. Ritchie, L.K., Caplan, Y.H., and Park, J., delta-9-Tetrahydrocannabinol analysis in forensic blood specimens using capillary column gas chromatography with nitrogen sensitive detection, *Journal of Analytical Toxicology*, 11, 205–209, 1987.
2. Moffat, A.C., Williams, P.L., and King, L.J., Combined high-performance liquid chromatography and radioimmunoassay method for the analysis of delta 9-tetrahydrocannabinol and its metabolites in plasma and urine, NIDA Research Monograph, 42, 56–68, 1982.
3. Hattori, H., Detection of cannabinoids by GC/MS. Part I. Quantitation of delta-9-THC in human urine and blood plasma., *Nippon Hoigaku Zasshi,* 35, 67–72, 1981.
4. Huestis, M.A., Mitchell, J.M., and Cone, E.J., Detection times of marijuana metabolites in urine by immunoassay and GC-MS, *Journal of Analytical Toxicology*, 19, 443–449, 1995.
5. McCurdy, H.H., Lewellen, L.J., Callahan, L.S., and Childs, P.S., Evaluation of the Ion Trap Detector for the detection of 11-nor-delta 9-THC-9-carboxylic acid in urine after extraction by bonded-phase adsorption, *Journal of Analytical Toxicology*, 10, 175–177, 1986.
6. Clatworthy, A.J., Oon, M.C., Smith, R.N., and Whitehouse, M.J., Gas chromatographic-mass spectrometric confirmation of radioimmunoassay results for cannabinoids in blood and urine, *Forensic Science International*, 46, 219–230, 1990.

7. Wilkins, D., Haughey, H., Cone, E., Huestis, M., Foltz, R., and Rollins, D., Quantitative analysis of THC, 11-OH-THC, and THCCOOH in human hair by negative ion chemical ionization mass spectrometry, *Journal of Analytical Toxicology*, 19, 483–491, 1995.

8. Kudo, K., Nagata, T., Kimura, K., Imamura, T., and Jitsufuchi, N., Sensitive determination of delta-9-tetrahydrocannabinol in human tissue by GC/MS, *Journal of Analytical Toxicology*, 19, 87–90, 1995.

9. Moeller, M.R., Doerr, G., and Warth, S., Simultaneous quantitation of delta-9-tetrahydrocannabinol (THC) and 11-nor-9-carboxy-delta-9-tetrahydrocannabinol (THC-COOH) in serum by GC/MS using deuterated internal standards and its application to a smoking study and forensic cases, *Journal of Forensic Sciences*, 37, 969–983, 1992.

10. Huestis, M.A., Henningfield, J.E., and Cone, E.J., Blood cannabinoids. I. Absorption of THC and formation of 11-OH-THC and THCCOOH during and after smoking marijuana [see comments], *Journal of Analytical Toxicology*, 16, 276–282, 1992.

11. Huestis, M.A., Henningfield, J.E., and Cone, E.J., Blood cannabinoids. II. Models for the prediction of time of marijuana exposure from plasma concentrations of delta 9-tetrahydrocannabinol (THC) and 11-nor-9-carboxy-delta 9-tetrahydrocannabinol (THCCOOH) [see comments], *Journal of Analytical Toxicology*, 16, 283–290, 1992.

12. Kemp, P.M., Abukhalaf, I.K., Manno, J.E., Manno, B.R., Alford, D.D., and Abusada, G.A., Cannabinoids in humans, *Journal of Analytical Toxicology*, 19, 285–291, 1995.

13. Meffin, P.J., Harapat, S.R., Yee, Y.G., and Harrison, D.C., High-pressure liquid chromatographic analysis of drugs in biological fluids. V. Analysis of acebutolol and its major metabolite, *Journal of Chromatography*, 138, 183–191, 1977.

14. Siren, H., Saarinen, M., Hainari, S., Lukkari, P., and Riekkola, M., Screening of beta-blockers in human serum by ion-pair chromatography and their identification as methyl or acetyl derivatives by gas chromatography-mass spectrometry, *Journal of Chromatography*, 632, 215–227, 1993.

15. Leloux, M., Niessen, W., and van der Hoeven, R., Thermospray liquid chromatography/mass spectrometry of polar beta-blocking drugs: preliminary results, *Biological Mass Spectrometry*, 20, 647–649, 1991.

16. Ghanem, R., Bello, M.A., Callejon, M., and Guiraum, A., Determination of beta-blocker drugs in pharmaceutical preparations by non-suppressed ion chromatography, *Journal of Pharmaceutical & Biomedical Analysis*, 15, 383–388, 1996.

17. Segura, J., Pascual, J.A., Ventura, R., Ustaran, J.I., Cuevas, A., and Gonzalez, R., International cooperation in analytical chemistry: experience of antidoping control at the XI Pan American Games, *Clinical Chemistry*, 39, 836–845, 1993.

18. Davey, L. and Naidoo, D, Urinary screen for acetaminophen (paracetamol) in the presence of N-acetylcysteine, *Clinical Chemistry*, 39, 2348–2349, 1993.

19. Novotny, P.E. and Elser, R.C, Indophenol method for acetaminophen in serum examined, *Clinical Chemistry*, 30, 884–886, 1984.

20. Bailey, D.N., Colorimetry of serum acetaminophen (paracetamol) in uremia, *Clinical Chemistry*, 28, 187–190, 1982.

21. Wong, A.S., An evaluation of HPLC for the screening and quantitation of benzodiazepines and acetaminophen in post mortem blood, *Journal of Analytical Toxicology*, 7, 33–36, 1983.

22. West, J.C., Rapid HPLC analysis of paracetamol (acetaminophen) in blood and postmortem viscera, *Journal of Analytical Toxicology*, 5, 118–121, 1981.

23. Manno, B.R., Manno, J.E., Dempsey, C.A., and Wood, M. A., A high-pressure liquid chromatographic method for the determination of N-acetyl-p-aminophenol (acetaminophen) in serum or plasma using a direct injection technique, *Journal of Analytical Toxicology*, 5, 24–28, 1981.

24. Colin, P., Sirois, G., and Chakrabarti, S., Rapid high-performance liquid chromatographic assay of acetaminophen in serum and tissue homogenates, *Journal of Chromatography*, 413, 151–160, 1987.

25. Ashbourne, J.F., Olson, K.R., and Khayam-Bashi, H., Value of rapid screening for acetaminophen in all patients with intentional drug overdose, *Annals of Emergency Medicine*, 18, 1035–1038, 1989.

26. Campbell, R.S. and Price, C.P., Experience with an homogeneous immunoassay for paracetamol (acetaminophen), *Journal of Clinical Chemistry & Clinical Biochemistry*, 24, 155–159, 1986.

27. Dasgupta, A. and Kinnaman, G, Microwave-induced rapid hydrolysis of acetaminophen and its conjugates in urine for emergency toxicological screen, *Clinical Chemistry*, 39, 2349–2350, 1993.

28. Price, L.M., Poklis, A., and Johnson, D.E., Fatal acetaminophen poisoning with evidence of subendocardial necrosis of the heart, *Journal of Forensic Sciences*, 36, 930–935, 1991.

29. Slattery, J.T., Nelson, S.D., and Thummel, K.E., The complex interaction between ethanol and acetaminophen. [Review], *Clinical Pharmacology & Therapeutics*, 60, 241–246, 1996.

30. Wallace, S.M., Shah, V.P., and Riegelman, S., GLC analysis of acetazolamide in blood, plasma, and saliva following oral administration to normal subjects, *Journal of Pharmaceutical Sciences*, 66, 527–530, 1977.

31. Asselin, W.M. and Caughlin, J.D., A rapid and simple color test for detection of salicylate in whole hemolyzed blood, *Journal of Analytical Toxicology*, 14, 254–255, 1990.

32. Morris, H.C., Overton, P.D., Ramsay, J.R., Campbell, R.S., Hammond, P.M., Atkinson, T., et al., Development and validation of an automated, enzyme-mediated colorimetric assay of salicylate in serum, *Clinical Chemistry*, 36, 131–135, 1990.

33. Trinder, P., Rapid determination of salicylates in biological materials, Biochemical Journal, 57, 1954

34. Levine, B. and Caplan, Y.H., Liquid chromatographic determination of salicylate and methyl salicylate in blood and application to a postmortem case, *Journal of Analytical Toxicology*, 8, 239–241, 1984.

35. Dipietra, A.M., Gatti, R., Andrisano, V., and Cavrini, V., Application of high-performance liquid chromatography with diode-array detection and on-line post-column photochemical derivatization to the determination of analgesics, *Journal of Chromatography*, 729, 355–361, 1996.

36. Chan, T.Y., Chan, A.Y., Ho, C.S., and Critchley, J.A., The clinical value of screening for salicylates in acute poisoning, *Veterinary & Human Toxicology*, 37, 37–38, 1995.

37. Asselin, W.M. and Caughlin, J.D., A rapid and simple color test for detection of salicylate in whole hemolyzed blood, *Journal of Analytical Toxicology*, 14, 254–255, 1990.

38. Jammehdiabadi, M. and Tierney, M., Impact of toxicology screens in the diagnosis of a suspected overdose: salicylates, tricyclic antidepressants, and benzodiazepines, *Veterinary & Human Toxicology*, 33, 40–43, 1991.

39. Bland, R.E., Tanner, R.J., Chern, W.H., Lang, J.R., and Powell, J.R., Determination of albuterol concentrations in human plasma using solid-phase extraction and high-performance liquid chromatography with fluorescence detection, *Journal of Pharmaceutical & Biomedical Analysis*, 8, 591–596, 1990.

40. King, W.D., Holloway, M., and Palmisano, P.A., Albuterol overdose: a case report and differential diagnosis. [Review], *Pediatric Emergency Care*, 8, 268–271, 1992.

41. Bjorkman, S. and Stanski, D.R., Simultaneous determination of fentanyl and alfentanil in rat tissues by capillary column gas chromatography, *Journal of Chromatography*, 433, 95–104, 1988.

42. Mautz, D., Labroo, R., and Kharasch, E., Determination of alfentanil and noralfentanil in human plasma by gas chromatography-mass spectrometry, *Journal of Chromatography B: Biomedical Applications*, 658, 149–153, 1994.

43. Van, B.H., Van, P.A., Gasparini, R., Woestenborghs, R., Heykants, J., Noorduin, H., et al., Pharmacokinetics of alfentanil during and after a fixed rate infusion, *British Journal of Anaesthesia*, 62, 610–615, 1989.

44. Meistelman, C., Saint-Maurice, C., Lepaul, M., Levron, J., Loose, J., and Mac, G.K., A comparison of alfentanil pharmacokinetics in children and adults, *Anesthesiology*, 66, 13–16, 1987.

45. Schumann, G.B., Lauenstein, K., LeFever, D., and Henry, J.B., Ultraviolet spectrophotometric analysis of barbiturates, *American Journal of Clinical Pathology*, 66, 823–830, 1976.

46. Gill, R., Stead, A.H., and Moffat, A.C., Analytical aspects of barbiturate abuse: identification of drugs by the effective combination of gas-liquid, high-performance liquid and thin-layer chromatographic techniques, *Journal of Chromatography*, 204, 275–284, 1981.

47. Lillsunde, P., Michelson, L., Forsstrom, T., Korte, T., Schultz, E., Ariniemi, K., et al., Comprehensive drug screening in blood for detecting abused drugs or drugs potentially hazardous for traffic safety, *Forensic Science International*, 77, 191–210, 1996.

48. Mule, S. and Casella, G., Confirmation and quantitation of barbiturates in human urine by gas chromatography/mass spectrometry, *Journal of Analytical Toxicology*, 13, 13–16, 1989.

49. Wallace, J.E., Hall, L.R., and Harris, S.C., Determination of pentobarbital and certain other barbiturates by capillary gas-liquid chromatography, *Journal of Analytical Toxicology*, 7, 178–180, 1983.

50. Budd, R.D., Gas chromatographic properties of 1,3-dialkyl barbiturate derivatives, *Clinical Toxicology*, 17, 375–382, 1980.

51. Barbour, A. D., GC/MS analysis of propylated barbiturates, *Journal of Analytical Toxicology*, 15, 214–215, 1991.

52. Christophersen, A. S. and Rasmussen, K. E., Glass capillary column gas chromatography of barbiturates after flash-heater derivatization with dimethylformamide dimethylacetal, *Journal of Chromatography*, 192, 363–374, 1980.

53. Budd, R. D. and Mathis, D. F., GLC screening and confirmation of barbiturates in post mortem blood specimens, *Journal of Analytical Toxicology*, 6, 317–320, 1982.

54. Sun, S. R. and Hoffman, D. J., Rapid, sensitive GLC determination of pentobarbital and other barbiturates in serum using nitrogen-specific detector, *Journal of Pharmaceutical Sciences*, 68, 386–388, 1979.

55. Marigo, M., Ferrara, S. D., and Tedeschi, L., A sensitive method for gas-chromatographic assay of barbiturates in body fluids, *Archives of Toxicology*, 37, 107–112, 1977.

56. Gill, R., Lopes, A. A., and Moffat, A. C., Analysis of barbiturates in blood by high-performance liquid chromatography, *Journal of Chromatography*, 226, 117–123, 1981.

57. Drummer, O. H., Kotsos, A., and McIntyre, I. M., A class-independent drug screen in forensic toxicology using a photodiode array detector, *Journal of Analytical Toxicology*, 17, 225–229, 1993.

58. Chan, E. M. and Chan, S. C., Screening for acidic and neutral drugs by high performance liquid chromatography in post-mortem blood, *Journal of Analytical Toxicology*, 8, 173–176, 1984.

59. Ferrara, S. D., Tedeschi, L., Frison, G., and Castagna, F., Solid-phase extraction and HPLC-UV confirmation of drugs of abuse in urine, *Journal of Analytical Toxicology*, 16, 217–222, 1992.

60. Lehane, D. P., Menyharth, P., Lum, G., and Levy, A. L., Therapeutic drug monitoring: measurements of antiepileptic and barbiturate drug levels in blood by gas chromatography with nitrogen - selective detector, *Annals of Clinical & Laboratory Science*, 6, 404–410, 1976.

61. Van Vunakis, H., Freeman, D. S., and Gjika, H. B., Radioimmunoassay for anileridine, meperidine and other N-substituted phenylpiperidine carboxylic acid esters, *Research Communications in Chemical Pathology & Pharmacology*, 12, 379–387, 1975.

62. Gaillard, Y., Gay-Montchamp, J. P., and Ollagnier, M., Simultaneous screening and quantitation of alpidem, zolpidem, buspirone and benzodiazepines by dual-channel gas chromatography using electron-capture and nitrogen-phosphorus detection after solid-phase extraction, *Journal of Chromatography*, 622, 197–208, 1993.

63. Lillsunde, P. and Seppala, T., Simultaneous screening and quantitative analysis of benzodiazepines by dual-channel gas chromatography using electron-capture and nitrogen-phosphorus detection, *Journal of Chromatography*, 533, 97–110, 1990.

64. Akerman, K. K., Jolkkonen, J., Parviainen, M., and Penttila, I., Analysis of low-dose benzodiazepines by HPLC with automated solid-phase extraction, *Clinical Chemistry*, 42, 1412–1416, 1996.

65. Shimamine, M., Masunari, T., and Nakahara, Y., [Studies on identification of drugs of abuse by diode array detection. I. Screening-test and identification of benzodiazepines by HPLC-DAD with ICOS software system], *Eisei Shikenjo Hokoku—Bulletin of National Institute of Hygienic Sciences*, 47 56, 1993.

66. Cairns, E. R., Dent, B. R., Ouwerkerk, J. C., and Porter, L. J., Quantitative analysis of alprazolam and triazolam in hemolysed whole blood and liver digest by GC/MS/NICI with deuterated internal standards, *Journal of Analytical Toxicology*, 18, 1–6, 1994.

67. Pollak, P. T., A systematic review and critical comparison of internal standards for the routine liquid chromatographic assay of amiodarone and desethylamiodarone, *Therapeutic Drug Monitoring*, 18, 168–178, 1996.

68. Flanagan, R. J., Storey, G. C., and Holt, D. W., Rapid high-performance liquid chromatographic method for the measurement of amiodarone in blood plasma or serum at the concentrations attained during therapy, *Journal of Chromatography*, 187, 391–398, 1980.

69. Fernandez, G. S., Witherington, T. L., and Stafford, D. T., Effective column extraction from decomposed tissue in a suspected overdose case involving maprotiline and amitriptyline, *Journal of Analytical Toxicology*, 9, 230–231, 1985.

70. Bailey, D. N. and Jatlow, P. I., Gas-chromatographic analysis for therapeutic concentrations of amitriptyline and nortriptyline in plasma, with use of a nitrogen detector, *Clinical Chemistry*, 22, 777–781, 1976.

71. Vandel, S., Vincent, F., Prudhon, F., Nezelof, S., Bonin, B., and Bertschy, G., [Comparative study of two techniques for the determination of amitriptyline and nortriptyline: EMIT and gas chromatography]. [French], *Therapie*, 47, 41–45, 1992.

72. Poklis, A. and Edinboro, L. E., REMEDi drug profiling system readily distinguishes between cyclobenzaprine and amitriptyline in emergency toxicology urine specimens [letter], *Clinical Chemistry*, 38, 2349–2350, 1992.

73. Wong, E. C., Koenig, J., and Turk, J., Potential interference of cyclobenzaprine and norcyclobenzaprine with HPLC measurement of amitriptyline and nortriptyline: resolution by GC-MS analysis, *Journal of Analytical Toxicology*, 19, 218–224, 1995.

74. Attapolitou, J., Tsarpalis, K., and Koutselinis, A., A modified simple and rapid reversed phase high performance liquid chromatographic method for quantification of amitriptyline and nortriptyline in plasma, *Journal of Liquid Chromatography*, 17, 3969–3982, 1994.

75. Rop, P. P., Viala, A., Durand, A., and Conquy, T., Determination of citalopram, amitriptyline and clomipramine in plasma by reversed-phase high-performance liquid chromatography, *Journal of Chromatography*, 338, 171–178, 1985.

76. Hartter, S. and Hiemke, C., Column switching and high-performance liquid chromatography in the analysis of amitriptyline, nortriptyline and hydroxylated metabolites in human plasma or serum, *Journal of Chromatography*, 578, 273–282, 1992.

77. Oliver, J. S. and Smith, H., Amitriptyline and metabolites in biological fluids, *Forensic Science,* 3, 181–187, 1974.

78. Spiehler, V., Spiehler, E., and Osselton, M. D., Application of expert systems analysis to interpretation of fatal cases involving amitriptyline, *Journal of Analytical Toxicology*, 12, 216–224, 1988.

79. Bolster, M., Curran, J., and Busuttil, A., A five year review of fatal self-ingested overdoses involving amitriptyline in Edinburgh 1983–'87, *Human & Experimental Toxicology*, 13, 29–31, 1994.

80. Bailey, D. N. and Shaw, R. F., Interpretation of blood and tissue concentrations in fatal self-ingested overdose involving amitriptyline: an update (1978–1979), *Journal of Analytical Toxicology*, 4, 232–236, 1980.

81. Pandya, K. K., satia, M., Gandhi, T. P., Modi, I. A., Modi, R. I., and Chakravarthy, B. K., Detection and determination of total amlodipine by high-performance thin-layer chromatography: a useful technique for pharmacokinetic studies, *Journal of Chromatography B: Biomedical Applications*, 667, 315–320, 1995.

82. Svinarov, D. A. and Dotchev, D. C., Simultaneous liquid-chromatographic determination of some bronchodilators, anticonvulsants, chloramphenicol, and hypnotic agents, with Chromosorb P columns used for sample preparation, *Clinical Chemistry*, 35, 1615–1618, 1989.

83. Meatherall, R. and Ford, D., Isocratic liquid chromatographic determination of theophylline, acetaminophen, chloramphenicol, caffeine, anticonvulsants, and barbiturates in serum, *Therapeutic Drug Monitoring*, 10, 101–115, 1988.

84. Kabra, P. M., Stafford, B. E., and Marton, L. J., Rapid method for screening toxic drugs in serum with liquid chromatography, *Journal of Analytical Toxicology*, 5, 177–182, 1981.

85. Kabra, P. M., Koo, H. Y., and Marton, L. J., Simultaneous liquid-chromatographic determination of 12 common sedatives and hypnotics in serum, *Clinical Chemistry*, 24, 657–662, 1978.

86. Liu, R. H., McKeehan, A. M., Edwards, C., Foster, G., Bensley, W. D., Langner, J. G., et al., Improved gas chromatography/mass spectrometry analysis of barbiturates in urine using centrifuge- based solid-phase extraction, methylation, with d5-pentobarbital as internal standard, *Journal of Forensic Sciences*, 39, 1504–1514, 1994.

87. Pocci, R., Dixit, V., and Dixit, V., Solid-phase extraction and GC/MS confirmation of barbiturates from human urine, *Journal of Analytical Toxicology*, 16, 45–47, 1992.

88. Osiewicz, R. J. and Middleberg, R., Detection of a novel compound after overdoses of aspirin and amoxapine, *Journal of Analytical Toxicology*, 13, 97–99, 1989.

89. Taylor, R. L., Crooks, C. R., and Caplan, Y. H., The determination of amoxapine in human fatal overdoses, *Journal of Analytical Toxicology*, 6, 309–311, 1982.

90. Wu Chen, N. B., Schaffer, M. I., Lin, R. L., Hadac, J. P., and Stein, R. J., Analysis of blood and tissue for amoxapine and trimipramine, *Journal of Forensic Sciences*, 28, 116–121, 1983.

91. Bourque, A. J., Krull, I. S., and Feibush, B., Automated HPLC analyses of drugs of abuse via direct injection of biological fluids followed by simultaneous solid-phase extraction and derivatization with fluorescence detection, *Biomedical Chromatography*, 8, 53–62, 1994.

92. Achilli, G., Cellerino, G. P., Deril, G. V. M., and Tagliaro, F., Determination of illicit drugs and related substances by high-performance liquid chromatography with an electrochemical coulometric-array detector, *Journal of Chromatography*, 729, 273–277, 1996.

93. Michel, R. E., Rege, A. B., and George, W. J., High-pressure liquid chromatography/electrochemical detection method for monitoring MDA and MDMA in whole blood and other biological tissues, *Journal of Neuroscience Methods*, 50, 61–66, 1993.

94. Paul, B. D., Past, M. R., McKinley, R. M., Foreman, J. D., McWhorter, L. K., and Snyder, J. J., Amphetamine as an artifact of methamphetamine during periodate degradation of interfering ephedrine, pseudoephedrine, and phenylpropanolamine: an improved procedure for accurate quantitation of amphetamines in urine, *Journal of Analytical Toxicology*, 18, 331–336, 1994.

95. Suzuki, S., Inoue, T., Hori, H., and Inayama, S., Analysis of methamphetamine in hair, nail, sweat, and saliva by mass fragmentography, *Journal of Analytical Toxicology*, 13, 176–178, 1989.

96. Hornbeck, C. L., Carrig, J. E., and Czarny, R. J., Detection of a GC/MS artifact peak as methamphetamine, *Journal of Analytical Toxicology*, 17, 257–263, 1993.

97. Nakahara, Y., Detection and diagnostic interpretation of amphetamines in hair. [Review], *Forensic Science International*, 70, 135–153, 1995.

98. Kalasinsky, K. S., Levine, B., Smith, M. L., Magluilo, J., Jr., and Schaefer, T., Detection of amphetamine and methamphetamine in urine by gas chromatography/Fourier transform infrared (GC/FTIR) spectroscopy, *Journal of Analytical Toxicology*, 17, 359–364, 1993.

99. Lillsunde, P. and Korte, T., Determination of ring- and N-substituted amphetamines as heptafluorobutyryl derivatives, *Forensic Science International*, 49, 205–213, 1991.

100. Logan, B. K., Methamphetamine and driving impairment. [Review], *Journal of Forensic Sciences*, 41, 457–464, 1996.

101. Rasmussen, S., Cole, R., and Spiehler, V., Methamphetamine in antemortem blood and urine by RIA and GC/MS, *Journal of Analytical Toxicology*, 13, 263–267, 1989.

102. Premel-Cabic, A., Cailleux, A., and Allain, P., [A gas chromatographic assay of fifteen volatile organic solvents in blood (author's transl)]. [French], *Clinica Chimica Acta*, 56, 5–11, 1974.

103. Astier, A., Chromatographic determination of volatile solvents and their metabolites in urine for monitoring occupational exposure, *Journal of Chromatography*, 643, 389–398, 1993.

104. Oliver, J. S. and Watson, J. M., Abuse of solvents "for kicks," *Lancet*, 1, 84–86, 1977.

105. Ghittori, S., Fiorentino, M. L., and Imbriani, M., [Use of gas chromatography with flame ionization (GC-FID) in the measurement of solvents in the urine], *Giornale Italiano di Medicina del Lavoro*, 9, 21–24, 1987.

106. Houghton, E., Teale, P., and Dumasia, M. C., Improved capillary GC/MS method for the determination of anabolic steroid and corticosteroid metabolites in horse urine using on-column injection with high-boiling solvents, *Analyst* (London), 109, 273–275, 1984.

107. Maurer, H. H., Identification and differentiation of barbiturates, other sedative-hypnotics and their metabolites in urine integrated in a general screening procedure using computerized gas chromatography-mass spectrometry, *Journal of Chromatography*, 530, 307–326, 1990.

108. Kingswood, J. C., Routledge, P. A., and Lazarus, J. H., A report of overdose with astemizole, *Human Toxicology*, 5, 43–44, 1986.

109. Law, B. and Weir, S., Fundamental studies in reversed-phase liquid-solid extraction of basic drugs; II: Hydrogen bonding effects, *Journal of Pharmaceutical & Biomedical Analysis*, 10, 181–186, 1992.

110. Logan, B. K. and Case, G. A., Identification of laudanosine, an atracurium metabolite, following a fatal drug-related shooting, *Journal of Analytical Toxicology*, 17, 117–119, 1993.

111. Xu, A., Havel, J., Linderholm, K., and Hulse, J., Development and validation of an LC/MS/MS method for the determination of L-hyoscyamine in human plasma, *Journal of Pharmaceutical & Biomedical Analysis*, 14, 33–42, 1995.

112. Saady, J. J. and Poklis, A., Determination of atropine in blood by gas chromatography/mass spectrometry, *Journal of Analytical Toxicology*, 13, 296–299, 1989.

113. Cugell, D. W., Clinical pharmacology and toxicology of ipratropium bromide. [Review], *American Journal of Medicine*, 81, 18–22, 1986.

114. Fraser, A. D., MacNeil, W., and Isner, A. F., Toxicological analysis of a fatal baclofen (Lioresal) ingestion, *Journal of Forensic Sciences*, 36, 1596–1602, 1991.

115. Millerioux, L., Brault, M., Gualano, V., and Mignot, A., High-performance liquid chromatographic determination of baclofen in human plasma, *Journal of Chromatography* 729, 309–314, 1996.

116. Bailey, D. N. and Jatlow, P. I., Barbital overdose and abuse, *American Journal of Clinical Pathology*, 64, 291–296, 1975.

117. Varin, F., Marchand, C., Larochelle, P., and Midha, K. K., GLC-mass spectrometric procedure with selected-ion monitoring for determination of plasma concentrations of unlabeled and labeled barbital following simultaneous oral and intravenous administration, *Journal of Pharmaceutical Sciences*, 69, 640–643, 1980.

118. Moriya, F. and Hashimoto, Y., Application of the Triage panel for drugs of abuse to forensic blood samples, *Nippon Hoigaku Zasshi—Japanese Journal of Legal Medicine*, 50, 50–56, 1996.

119. Chankvetadze, B., Chankvetadze, L., Sidamonidze, S., Yashima, E., and Okamoto, Y., High performance liquid chromatography enantioseparation of chiral pharmaceuticals using tris(chloro- methylphenylcar-bamate)s of cellulose, *Journal of Pharmaceutical & Biomedical Analysis*, 14, 1295–1303, 1996.

120. Qiu, F. H., Liu, L., Guo, L., Luo, Y., and Lu, Y. Q., [Rapid identification and quantitation of barbiturates in plasma using solid-phase extraction combined with GC-FID and GC-MS method], *Yao Hsueh Hsueh Pao—Acta Pharmaceutica Sinica*, 30, 372–377, 1995.

121. Thormann, W., Meier, P., Marcolli, C., and Binder, F., Analysis of barbiturates in human serum and urine by high-performance capillary electrophoresis-micellar electrokinetic capillary chromatography with on-column multi-wavelength detection, *Journal of Chromatography*, 545, 445–460, 1991.

122. Minder, E. I., Schaubhut, R., and Vonderschmitt, D. J., Screening for drugs in clinical toxicology by high-performance liquid chromatography: identification of barbiturates by post-column ionization and detection by a multiplace photodiode array spectrophotometer, *Journal of Chromatography*, 428, 369–376, 1988.

123. Mangin, P., Lugnier, A. A., and Chaumont, A. J., A polyvalent method using HPLC for screening and quantification of 12 common barbiturates in various biological materials, *Journal of Analytical Toxicology*, 11, 27–30, 1987.

124. Cody, J. T. and Foltz, R. L., GC/MS analysis of body fluids for drugs of abuse, in *Forensic Applications of Mass Spectrometry*, Yinon, J., CRC Press, Boca Raton, FL, 1995, pp. 1–59.

125. Kojima, T., Taniguchi, T., Yashiki, M., Miyazaki, T., Iwasaki, Y., Mikami, T., et al., A rapid method for detecting barbiturates in serum using EI-SIM, *International Journal of Legal Medicine*, 107, 21–24, 1994.

126. Abadi, M. and Solomon, H. M., Detection of tolmetin and oxaprozin by a GC/MS method for barbiturates [letter], *Journal of Analytical Toxicology*, 18, 62, 1994.

127. Gibb, R. P., Cockerham, H., Goldfogel, G. A., Lawson, G. M., and Raisys, V. A., Substance abuse testing of urine by GC/MS in scanning mode evaluated by proficiency studies, TLC/GC, and EMIT, *Journal of Forensic Sciences*, 38, 124–133, 1993.

128. Pocci, R., Dixit, V., and Dixit, V. M., Solid-phase extraction and GC/MS confirmation of barbiturates from human urine, *Journal of Analytical Toxicology*, 16, 45–47, 1992.

129. Chen, X. H., Wijsbeek, J., van Veen, J., Franke, J. P., and de Zeeuw, R. A., Solid-phase extraction for the screening of acidic, neutral and basic drugs in plasma using a single-column procedure on Bond Elut Certify, *Journal of Chromatography*, 529, 161–166, 1990.

130. Logan, B. K., Methamphetamine and driving impairment. [Review] [37 refs], *Journal of Forensic Sciences*, 41, 457–464, 1996.

131. Long, C. and Crifasi, J., Methamphetamine identification in four forensic cases, *Journal of Forensic Sciences*, 41, 713–714, 1996.

132. Ensslin, H. K., Kovar, K. A., and Maurer, H. H., Toxicological detection of the designer drug 3,4-methylenedioxyethylamphetamine (Mde, Eve) and its metabolites in urine by gas chromatography mass spectrometry and fluorescence polarization immunoassay, *Journal of Chromatography B: Biomedical Applications*, 683, 189–197, 1996.

133. Valentine, J. L., Kearns, G. L., Sparks, C., Letzig, L. G., Valentine, C. R., Shappell, S. A., et al., GC-MS determination of amphetamine and methamphetamine in human urine for 12 hours following oral administration of dextro-methamphetamine: lack of evidence supporting the established forensic guidelines for methamphetamine confirmation, *Journal of Analytical Toxicology*, 19, 581–590, 1995.

134. Meatherall, R., Rapid GC-MS confirmation of urinary amphetamine and methamphetamine as their propylchloroformate derivatives, *Journal of Analytical Toxicology*, 19, 316–322, 1995.

135. Arufe-Martinez, M. I. and Romero-Palanco, J. L., Identification of cocaine in cocaine-lidocaine mixtures ("rock cocaine") and other illicit cocaine preparations using derivative absorption spectroscopy, *Journal of Analytical Toxicology*, 12, 192–196, 1988.

136. Clauwaert, K. M., Vanbocxlaer, J. F., Lambert, W. E., and Deleenheer, A. P., Analysis of cocaine, benzoylecgonine, and cocaethylene in urine by HPLC with diode array detection, *Analytical Chemistry*, 68, 3021–3028, 1996.

137. Fernandez, P., Lafuente, N., Bermejo, A. M., Lopezrivadulla, M., and Cruz, A., HPLC determination of cocaine and benzoylecgonine in plasma and urine from drug abusers, *Journal of Analytical Toxicology*, 20, 224–228, 1996.

138. Logan, B. K., Smirnow, D., and Gullberg, R. G., Lack of predictable site-dependent differences and time-dependent changes in postmortem concentrations of cocaine, benzoylecgonine, and cocaethylene in humans, *Journal of Analytical Toxicology*, 21, 23–31, 1997.

139. Sosnoff, C. S., Ann, Q., Bernert, J. T., Jr., Powell, M. K., Miller, B. B., Henderson, L. O., et al., Analysis of benzoylecgonine in dried blood spots by liquid chromatography—atmospheric pressure chemical ionization tandem mass spectrometry, *Journal of Analytical Toxicology*, 20, 179–184, 1996.

140. Thompson, W. C. and Dasgupta, A., Confirmation and quantitation of cocaine, benzoylecgonine, ecgonine methyl ester, and cocaethylene by gas chromatography/mass spectrometry, *American Journal of Clinical Pathology*, 104, 187–192, 1995.

141. Corburt, M. R. and Koves, E. M., Gas chromatography/mass spectrometry for the determination of cocaine and benzoylecgonine over a wide concentration range, *Journal of Forensic Sciences*, 39, 136–149, 1994.

142. Okeke, C. C., Wynn, J. E., and Patrick, K. S., Simultaneous analysis of cocaine, benzoylecgonine, methylecgonine, and ecgonine in plasma using an exchange resin and GC/MS, *Chromatographia*, 38, 52–56, 1994.

143. Gerlits, J., GC/MS quantitation of benzoylecgonine following liquid–liquid extraction of urine, *Journal of Forensic Sciences*, 38, 1210–1214, 1993.

144. Aderjan, R. E., Schmitt, G., Wu, M., and Meyer, C., Determination of cocaine and benzoylecgonine by derivatization with iodomethane-D3 or PFPA/HFIP in human blood and urine using GC/MS (EI or PCI mode), *Journal of Analytical Toxicology*, 17, 51–55, 1993.

145. Abusada, G. M., Abukhalaf, I. K., Alford, D. D., Vinzon-Bautista, I., Pramanik, A. K., Ansari, N. A., et al., Solid-phase extraction and GC/MS quantitation of cocaine, ecgonine methyl ester, benzoylecgonine, and cocaethylene from meconium, whole blood, and plasma, *Journal of Analytical Toxicology*, 17, 353–358, 1993.

146. Kikura, R. and Nakahara, Y., Hair analysis for drugs of abuse. XI. Disposition of benzphetamine and its metabolites into hair and comparison of benzphetamine use and methamphetamine use by hair analysis, *Biological & Pharmaceutical Bulletin*, 18, 1694–1699, 1995.

147. Rosano, T. G., Meola, J. M., Wolf, B. C., Guisti, L. W., and Jindal, S. P., Benztropine identification and quantitation in a suicidal overdose, *Journal of Analytical Toxicology*, 18, 348–353, 1994.

148. Le Solleu, H., Demotes-Mainard, F., Vincon, G., and Bannwarth, B., The determination of bromazepam in plasma by reversed-phase high-performance liquid chromatography, *Journal of Pharmaceutical & Biomedical Analysis*, 11, 771–775, 1993.

149. Yoshida, M., Watabiki, T., Tokiyasu, T., Saito, I., and Ishida, N., [Determination of benzodiazepines by thermospray liquid chromatograph-mass spectrometer. Part 1. Nitrazepam, estazolam, bromazepam, flunitrazepam]. [Japanese], *Nippon Hoigaku Zasshi Japanese Journal of Legal Medicine*, 47, 220–226, 1993.

150. Haring, N., Salama, Z., and Jaeger, H., Triple stage quadrupole mass spectrometric determination of bromocriptine in human plasma with negative ion chemical ionization, *Arzneimittel Forschung*, 38, 1529–1532, 1988.

151. Hindmarsh, K. W., Hamon, N. W., and LeGatt, D. F., Simultaneous identification and quantitation of diphenhydramine and methaqualone, *Clinical Toxicology*, 11, 245–255, 1977.

152. Meatherall, R. C. and Guay, D. R., Isothermal gas chromatographic analysis of diphenhydramine after direct injection onto a fused-silica capillary column, *Journal of Chromatography*, 307, 295–304, 1984.

153. Tonn, G. R., Mutlib, A., Abbott, F. S., Rurak, D. W., and Axelson, J. E., Simultaneous analysis of diphenhydramine and a stable isotope analog (2H10)diphenhydramine using capillary gas chromatography with mass selective detection in biological fluids from chronically instrumented pregnant ewes, *Biological Mass Spectrometry*, 22, 633–642, 1993.

154. Vycudilik, W. and Pollak, S., [Detection of diphenhydramine in autolytic brain tissue in poison-induced brain death syndrome], *Zeitschrift für Rechtsmedizin—Journal of Legal Medicine*, 95, 129–135, 1985.

155. Lorec, A. M., Bruguerolle, B., Attolini, L., and Roucoules, X., Rapid simultaneous determination of lidocaine, bupivacaine, and their two main metabolites using capillary gas-liquid chromatography with nitrogen phosphorus detector, *Therapeutic Drug Monitoring*, 16, 592–595, 1994.

156. Demedts, P., Wauters, A., Franck, F., and Neels, H., Simultaneous determination of lidocaine, bupivacaine, and their two main metabolites using gas chromatography and a nitrogen–phosphorus detector —selection of stationary phase and chromatographic conditions, *Therapeutic Drug Monitoring*, 18, 208–209, 1996.

157. Coyle, D. E. and Denson, D. D., Simultaneous measurement of bupivacaine, etidocaine, lidocaine, meperidine, mepivacaine, and methadone, *Therapeutic Drug Monitoring*, 8, 98–101, 1986.

158. Clark, B. J., Hamdi, A., Berrisford, R. G., Sabanathan, S., and Mearns, A. J., Reversed-phase and chiral high-performance liquid chromatographic assay of bupivacaine and its enantiomers in clinical samples after continuous extraplural infusion, *Journal of Chromatography*, 553, 383–390, 1991.

159. Zakowski, M. I., Ramanathan, S., Sharnick, S., and Turndorf, H., Uptake and distribution of bupivacaine and morphine after intrathecal administration in parturients: effects of epinephrine, *Anesthesia & Analgesia*, 74, 664–669, 1992.

160. Bailey, C. R., Ruggier, R., and Findley, I. L., Diamorphine-bupivacaine mixture compared with plain bupivacaine for analgesia, *British Journal of Anaesthesia*, 72, 58–61, 1994.

161. Martin, J. and Neill, R. S., Venous plasma (total) bupivacaine concentrations following lower abdominal field block, *British Journal of Anaesthesia*, 59, 1425–1430, 1987.

162. Kintz, P., Cirimele, V., Edel, Y., Jamey, C., and Mangin, P., Hair analysis for buprenorphine and its dealkylated metabolite by RIA and confirmation by LC/ECD, *Journal of Forensic Sciences*, 39, 1497–1503, 1994.

163. Debrabandere, L., Van Boven, M., and Daenens, P., Analysis of buprenorphine in urine specimens, *Journal of Forensic Sciences*, 37, 82–89, 1992.

164. Kuhlman, J. J., Magluilo, J., Cone, E., and Levine, B., Simultaneous assay of buprenorphine and norbuprenorphine by negative chemical ionization tandem mass spectrometry, *Journal of Analytical Toxicology*, 20, 229–235, 1996.

165. Shiraishi, Y., Sakai, S., Yokoyama, J., Hayatsu, K., Mochizuki, T., Moriwaki, G., et al., [The plasma concentration of buprenorphine during its continuous epidural infusion after catheterization at different vertebral levels], *Masui—Japanese Journal of Anesthesiology*, 42, 371–375, 1993.

166. Battah, A.-K. and Anderson, R. A., Comparison of silyl derivatives for GC/MS analysis of morphine and buprenorphine in blood. in 26th International Meeting of the International Association of Forensic Toxicologists. 1989. Glasgow, Scotland.

167. Kuhlman, J. J., Lalani, S., Magluilo, J., Levine, B., Darwin, W. D., Johnson, R. E., et al., Human pharmacokinetics of intravenous, sublingual, and buccal buprenorphine, *Journal of Analytical Toxicology*, 20, 369–378, 1996.

168. Ohtani, M., Kotaki, H., Uchino, K., Sawada, Y., and Iga, T., Pharmacokinetic analysis of enterohepatic circulation of buprenorphine and its active metabolite, norbuprenorphine, in rats, *Drug Metabolism & Disposition*, 22, 2–7, 1994.

169. San, L., Torrens, M., Castillo, C., Porta, M., and de la Torre, R., Consumption of buprenorphine and other drugs among heroin addicts under ambulatory treatment: results from cross-sectional studies in 1988 and 1990, *Addiction*, 88, 1341–1349, 1993.

170. Rohrig, T. P. and Ray, N. G., Tissue distribution of bupropion in a fatal overdose, *Journal of Analytical Toxicology*, 16, 343–345, 1992.

171. Fogel, P., Mamer, O. A., Chouinard, G., and Farrell, P. G., Determination of plasma bupropion and its relationship to therapeutic effect, *Biomedical Mass Spectrometry*, 11, 629–632, 1984.

172. Friel, P. N., Logan, B. K., and Fligner, C. L., Three fatal drug overdoses involving bupropion, *Journal of Analytical Toxicology*, 17, 436–438, 1993.

173. Spiller, H. A., Ramoska, E. A., Krenzelok, E. P., Sheen, S. R., Borys, D. J., Villalobos, D., et al., Bupropion overdose: a 3-year multi-center retrospective analysis, *American Journal of Emergency Medicine*, 12, 43–45, 1994.

174. Butz, R. F., Welch, R. M., and Findlay, J. W., Relationship between bupropion disposition and dopamine uptake inhibition in rats and mice, *Journal of Pharmacology & Experimental Therapeutics*, 221, 676–685, 1982.

175. Jajoo, H. K., Mayol, R. F., LaBudde, J. A., and Blair, I. A., Metabolism of the antianxiety drug buspirone in human subjects, *Drug Metabolism & Disposition*, 17, 634–640, 1989.

176. Scott, E. P., Application of postcolumn ionization in the high-performance liquid chromatographic analysis of butabarbital sodium elixir, *Journal of Pharmaceutical Sciences*, 72, 1089–1091, 1983.

177. Mulvana, D. E., Duncan, G. F., Shyu, W. C., Tay, L. K., and Barbhaiya, R. H., Quantitative determination of butorphanol and its metabolites in human plasma by gas chromatography electron capture negative-ion chemical ionization mass spectrometry, *Journal of Chromatography B: Biomedical Applications*, 682, 289–300, 1996.

178. Combie, J., Blake, J. W., Nugent, T. E., and Tobin, T., Furosemide, Patella vulgata beta-glucuronidase and drug analysis: conditions for enhancement of the TLC detection of apomorphine, butorphanol, hydromorphone, nalbuphine, oxymorphone and pentazocine in equine urine, *Research Communications in Chemical Pathology & Pharmacology*, 35, 27–41, 1982.

179. Rodopoulos, N. and Norman, A., Determination of caffeine and its metabolites in urine by high-performance liquid chromatography and capillary electrophoresis, *Scandinavian Journal of Clinical & Laboratory Investigation*, 54, 305–315, 1994.

180. Jin, X., Zhou, Z. H., He, X. F., Zhang, Z. H., and Wang, M. Z., [Solid-phase extraction and RP-HPLC screening procedure for diuretics, probenecid, caffeine and pemoline in urine], *Yao Hsueh Hsueh Pao —Acta Pharmaceutica Sinica*, 27, 875–880, 1992.

181. Leakey, T. E., Simultaneous analysis of theophylline, caffeine and eight of their metabolic products in human plasma by gradient high-performance liquid chromatography, *Journal of Chromatography*, 507, 199–220, 1990.

182. Fligner, C. L. and Opheim, K. E., Caffeine and its dimethylxanthine metabolites in two cases of caffeine overdose: a cause of falsely elevated theophylline concentrations in serum, *Journal of Analytical Toxicology*, 12, 339–343, 1988.

183. Garriott, J. C., Simmons, L. M., Poklis, A., and Mackell, M. A., Five cases of fatal overdose from caffeine-containing "look-alike" drugs, *Journal of Analytical Toxicology*, 9, 141–143, 1985.

184. Miceli, J. N., Aravind, M. K., and Ferrell, W. J., Analysis of caffeine: comparison of the manual enzyme multiplied immunoassay (EMIT), automated EMIT, and high-performance liquid chromatography procedures, *Therapeutic Drug Monitoring*, 6, 344–347, 1984.

185. Lensmeyer, G. L., Isothermal gas chromatographic method for the rapid determination of carbamazepine ("tegretol") as its TMS derivative, *Clinical Toxicology*, 11, 443–454, 1977.

186. Schwertner, H. A., Hamilton, H. E., and Wallace, J. E., Analysis for carbamazepine in serum by electron-capture gas chromatography, *Clinical Chemistry*, 24, 895–899, 1978.

187. Toseland, P. A., Grove, J., and Berry, D. J., An isothermal GLC determination of the plasma levels of carbamazepine, diphenylhydantoin, phenobarbitone and primidone, *Clinica Chimica Acta*, 38, 321–328, 1972.

188. Martens, J. and Banditt, P., Validation of the analysis of carbamazepine and its 10,11-epoxide metabolite by high-performance liquid chromatography from plasma: comparison with gas chromatography and the enzyme-multiplied immunoassay technique, *Journal of Chromatography*, 620, 169–173, 1993.

189. Romanyshyn, L. A., Wichmann, J. K., Kucharczyk, N., Shumaker, R. C., Ward, D., and Sofia, R. D., Simultaneous determination of felbamate, primidone, phenobarbital, carbamazepine, two carbamazepine metabolites, phenytoin, and one phenytoin metabolite in human plasma by high-performance liquid chromatography, *Therapeutic Drug Monitoring*, 16, 90–99, 1994.

190. Rainbow, S. J., Dawson, C. M., and Tickner, T. R., Direct serum injection high-performance liquid chromatographic method for the simultaneous determination of phenobarbital, carbamazepine and phenytoin, *Journal of Chromatography*, 527, 389–396, 1990.

191. Schmidt, S. and Schmitz-Buhl, M., Signs and symptoms of carbamazepine overdose, *Journal of Neurology*, 242, 169–173, 1995.

192. Chai, C. and Killeen, A. A., Carbamazepine measurement in samples from the emergency room, *Therapeutic Drug Monitoring*, 16, 407–412, 1994.

193. Schwartz, J. G., Garriott, J. C., Somerset, J. S., Igler, E. J., Rodriguez, R., and Orr, M. D., Measurements of fentanyl and sufentanil in blood and urine after surgical application. Implication in detection of abuse, *American Journal of Forensic Medicine & Pathology*, 15, 236–241, 1994.

194. Tobin, T., Kwiatkowski, S., Watt, D., Tai, H., Tai, C., Woods, W., et al., Immunoassay detection of drugs in racing horses. XI. ELISA and RIA detection of fentanyl, alfentanil, sufentanil and carfentanil in equine blood and urine, *Research Communications in Chemical Pathology & Pharmacology*, 63, 129–152, 1989.

195. Kintz, P., Mangin, P., Lugnier, A. A., and Chaumont, A. J., A rapid and sensitive gas chromatographic analysis of meprobamate or carisoprodol in urine and plasma, *Journal of Analytical Toxicology*, 12, 73–74, 1988.

196. Backer, R. C., Zumwalt, R., McFeeley, P., Veasey, S., and Wohlenberg, N., Carisoprodol concentrations from different anatomical sites: three overdose cases, *Journal of Analytical Toxicology*, 14, 332–334, 1990.

197. Kaistha, K. K., Selective assay procedure for chlorpropamide in the presence of its decomposition products, *Journal of Pharmaceutical Sciences*, 58, 235–237, 1969.

198. Meatherall, R. C., Green, P. T., Kenick, S., and Donen, N., Diazoxide in the management of chlorpropamide overdose, *Journal of Analytical Toxicology*, 5, 287–291, 1981.

199. Levine, B., Park, J., Smith, T. D., and Caplan, Y. H., Chloral hydrate: unusually high concentrations in a fatal overdose, *Journal of Analytical Toxicology*, 9, 232–233, 1985.

200. Meyer, E., Van Bocxlaer, J. F., Lambert, W. E., Piette, M., and De Leenheer, A. P., Determination of chloral hydrate and metabolites in a fatal intoxication, *Journal of Analytical Toxicology*, 19, 124–126, 1995.

201. Lister, R. G., Abernethy, D. R., Greenblatt, D. J., and File, S. E., Methods for the determination of lorazepam and chlordiazepoxide and metabolites in brain tissue, *Journal of Chromatography*, 277, 201–208, 1983.

202. Song, D., Zhang, S., and Kohlhof, K., Determination of chlordiazepoxide in mouse plasma by gas chromatography-negative-ion chemical ionization mass spectrometry, *Journal of Chromatography B: Biomedical Applications*, 660, 95–101, 1994.

203. Heller, P. F., Goldberger, B. A., and Caplan, Y. H., Chloral hydrate overdose: trichloroethanol detection by gas chromatography/mass spectrometry, *Forensic Science International*, 52, 231–234, 1992.

204. Bailey, D. N., Blood concentrations and clinical findings following overdose of chlordiazepoxide alone and chlordiazepoxide plus ethanol, *Journal of Toxicology—Clinical Toxicology*, 22, 433–446, 1984.

205. Dixon, R., Brooks, M. A., Postma, E., Hackman, M. R., Spector, S., Moore, J. D., et al., N-desmethyldiazepam: a new metabolite of chlordiazepoxide in man, *Clinical Pharmacology & Therapeutics*, 20, 450–457, 1976.

206. Stronjny, N., Bratin, K., Brooks, M. A., and de Silva, J. A., Determination of chlordiazepoxide, diazepam, and their major metabolites in blood or plasma by spectrophotodensitometry, *Journal of Chromatography*, 143, 363–374, 1977.

207. Bailey, D. N. and Guba, J. J., Gas-chromatographic analysis for chlorpromazine and some of its metabolites in human serum, with use of a nitrogen detector, *Clinical Chemistry*, 25, 1211–1215, 1979.

208. Ohkubo, T., Shimoyama, R., and Sugawara, K., Determination of chlorpromazine in human breast milk and serum by high-performance liquid chromatography, *Journal of Chromatography*, 614, 328–332, 1993.

209. Nishigami, J., Takayasu, T., and Ohshima, T., Toxicological analysis of the psychotropic drugs chlorpromazine and diazepam using chemically fixed organ tissues, *International Journal of Legal Medicine*, 107, 165–170, 1995.

210. Walker, O. and Ademowo, O. G., A Rapid, Cost-effective liquid chromatographic method for the determination of chloroquine and desethylchloroquine in biological fluids, *Therapeutic Drug Monitoring*, 18, 92–96, 1996.

211. Volin, P., Simple and specific reversed-phase liquid chromatographic method with diode-array detection for simultaneous determination of serum hydroxychloroquine, chloroquine and some corticosteroids, *Journal of Chromatography B: Biomedical Applications*, 666, 347–353, 1995.

212. Murtha, J. L., Julian, T. N., and Radebaugh, G. W., Simultaneous determination of pseudoephedrine hydrochloride, chlorpheniramine maleate, and dextromethorphan hydrobromide by second-derivative photodiode array spectroscopy, *Journal of Pharmaceutical Sciences*, 77, 715–718, 1988.

213. Masumoto, K., Tashiro, Y., Matsumoto, K., Yoshida, A., Hirayama, M., and Hayashi, S., Simultaneous determination of codeine and chlorpheniramine in human plasma by capillary column gas chromatography, *Journal of Chromatography*, 381, 323–329, 1986.

214. Bailey, D. N. and Guba, J. J., Gas-chromatographic analysis for chlorpromazine and some of its metabolites in human serum, with use of a nitrogen detector, *Clinical Chemistry*, 25, 1211–1215, 1979.

215. Garriott, J. C. and Stolman, A., Detection of some psychotherapeutic drugs and their metabolites in urine, *Clinical Toxicology*, 4, 225–243, 1971.

216. Fenimore, D. C., Meyer, C. J., Davis, C. M., Hsu, F., and Zlatkis, A., High-performance thin-layer chromatographic determination of psychopharmacologic agents in blood serum, *Journal of Chromatography*, 142, 399–409, 1977.

217. Lin, Q., Lensmeyer, G. L., and Larson, F. C., Quantitation of cimetidine and cimetidine sulfoxide in serum by solid-phase extraction and solvent-recycled liquid chromatography, *Journal of Analytical Toxicology*, 9, 161–166, 1985.

218. Borel, A. G. and Abbott, F. S., Metabolic profiling of clobazam, a 1,5-benzodiazepine, in rats, *Drug Metabolism & Disposition*, 21, 415–427, 1993.

219. Streete, J. M., Berry, D. J., and Newbery, J. E., The analysis of clobazam and its metabolite desmethylclobazam by high-performance liquid chromatography, *Therapeutic Drug Monitoring*, 13, 339–344, 1991.

220. Schutz, H., [A screening test for Nor-clobazam, a principal metabolite of the new 1,5 benzodiazepine clobazam (Frisium)], *Archiv für Kriminologie*, 163, 91–94, 1979.

221. Coudore, F., Hourcade, F., Moliniermanoukian, C., Eschalier, A., and Lavarenne, E., Application of HPLC with silica-phase and reversed-phase eluents for the determination of clomipramine and demethylated and 8-hydroxylated metabolites, *Journal of Analytical Toxicology*, 20, 101–105, 1996.

222. Altieri, I., Pichini, S., Pacifici, R., and Zuccaro, P., Improved clean-up procedure for the high-performance liquid chromatographic assay of clomipramine and its demethylated metabolite in human plasma, *Journal of Chromatography B: Biomedical Applications*, 669, 416–417, 1995.

223. McIntyre, I. M., King, C. V., Cordner, S. M., and Drummer, O. H., Postmortem clomipramine: therapeutic or toxic concentrations? *Journal of Forensic Sciences*, 39, 486–493, 1994.

224. Nielsen, K. K. and Brosen, K., High-performance liquid chromatography of clomipramine and metabolites in human plasma and urine, *Therapeutic Drug Monitoring*, 15, 122–128, 1993.

225. Marliac, Y. and Barazi, S., [Determination of unchanged clonazepam in plasma by gas-liquid chromatography]. [French], *Annales de Biologie Clinique*, 47, 503–506, 1989.

226. Miller, L. G., Friedman, H., and Greenblatt, D. J., Measurement of clonazepam by electron-capture gas-liquid chromatography with application to single-dose pharmacokinetics, *Journal of Analytical Toxicology*, 11, 55–57, 1987.

227. Wilson, J. M., Friel, P. N., Wilensky, A. J., and Raisys, V. A., A methods comparison: clonazepam by GC-electron capture and GC/MS, *Therapeutic Drug Monitoring*, 1, 387–397, 1979.

228. Petters, I., Peng, D. R., and Rane, A., Quantitation of clonazepam and its 7-amino and 7-acetamido metabolites in plasma by high-performance liquid chromatography, *Journal of Chromatography*, 306, 241–248, 1984.

229. Shaw, W., Long, G., and McHan, J., An HPLC method for analysis of clonazepam in serum, *Journal of Analytical Toxicology*, 7, 119–122, 1983.

230. Haver, V. M., Porter, W. H., Dorie, L. D., and Lea, J. R., Simplified high performance liquid chromatographic method for the determination of clonazepam and other benzodiazepines in serum, *Therapeutic Drug Monitoring*, 8, 352–357, 1986.

231. Doran, T. C., Liquid chromatographic assay for serum clonazepam, *Therapeutic Drug Monitoring*, 10, 474–479, 1988.

232. Haering, N., Salama, Z., Reif, G., and Jaeger, H., GC/MS determination of clonidine in body fluids. Application to pharmacokinetics, *Arzneimittel-Forschung*, 38, 404–407, 1988.

233. Arrendale, R. F., Stewart, J. T., and Tackett, R. L., Determination of clonidine in human plasma by cold on-column injection capillary GC/MS, *Journal of Chromatography*, 432, 165–175, 1988.

234. Linnoila, M. and Dorrity, F., Jr., Rapid gas chromatographic assay of serum diazepam, N-desmethyldiazepam, and N-desalkylflurazepam, *Acta Pharmacologica et Toxicologica*, 41, 458–464, 1977.

235. McCurdy, H. H., Lewellen, L. J., Cagle, J. C., and Solomons, E. T., A rapid procedure for the screening and quantitation of barbiturates, diazepam, desmethyldiazepam and methaqualone, *Journal of Analytical Toxicology*, 5, 253–257, 1981.

236. Kudo, K., Nagata, T., Kimura, K., Imamura, T., and Noda, M., Sensitive determination of diazepam and N-desmethyldiazepam in human material using capillary GC/MS, *Journal of Chromatography*, 431, 353–359, 1988.

237. Lovdahl, M. J., Perry, P. J., and Miller, D. D., The assay of clozapine and N-desmethylclozapine in human plasma by high-performance liquid chromatography, *Therapeutic Drug Monitoring*, 13, 69–72, 1991.

238. Jennison, T. A., Brown, P., Crossett, J., Kushnir, M., and Urry, F. M., A rapid gas chromatographic method quantitating clozapine in human plasma or serum for the purpose of therapeutic monitoring, *Journal of Analytical Toxicology*, 19, 537–541, 1995.

239. Lin, G., McKay, G., Hubbard, J. W., and Midha, K. K., Decomposition of clozapine N-oxide in the qualitative and quantitative analysis of clozapine and its metabolites, *Journal of Pharmaceutical Sciences*, 83, 1412–1417, 1994.

240. McCarthy, P. T., Hughes, S., and Paton, C., Measurement of clozapine and norclozapine in plasma/serum by high performance liquid chromatography with ultraviolet detection, *Biomedical Chromatography*, 9, 36–41, 1995.

241. Gupta, R. N., Column liquid chromatographic determination of clozapine and N-desmethylclozapine in human serum using solid-phase extraction, *Journal of Chromatography B: Biomedical Applications*, 673, 311–315, 1995.

242. Olesen, O. V. and Poulsen, B., On-line fully automated determination of clozapine and desmethylclozapine in human serum by solid-phase extraction on exchangeable cartridges and liquid chromatography using a methanol buffer mobile phase on unmodified silica, *Journal of Chromatography*, 622, 39–46, 1993.

243. Chung, M. C., Lin, S. K., Chang, W. H., and Jann, M. W., Determination of clozapine and desmethylclozapine in human plasma by high-performance liquid chromatography with ultraviolet detection, *Journal of Chromatography*, 613, 168–173, 1993.

244. Liu, H. C., Chang, W. H., Wei, F. C., Lin, S. K., Lin, S. K., and Jann, M. W., Monitoring of plasma clozapine levels and its metabolites in refractory schizophrenic patients, *Therapeutic Drug Monitoring*, 18, 200–207, 1996.

245. Clauwaert, K. M., Van Bocxlaer, J. F., Lambert, W. E., and De Leenheer, A. P., Analysis of cocaine, benzoylecgonine, and cocaethylene in urine by HPLC with diode array detection, *Analytical Chemistry*, 68, 3021–3028, 1996.

246. Bailey, D. N., Cocaethylene (ethylcocaine) detection during toxicological screening of a university medical center patient population, *Journal of Analytical Toxicology*, 19, 247–250, 1995.

247. Cone, E. J., Hillsgrove, M., and Darwin, W. D., Simultaneous measurement of cocaine, cocaethylene, their metabolites, and "crack" pyrolysis products by gas chromatography-mass spectrometry, *Clinical Chemistry*, 40, 1299–1305, 1994.

248. Hime, G. W., Hearn, W. L., Rose, S., and Cofino, J., Analysis of cocaine and cocaethylene in blood and tissues by GC-NPD and GC-ion trap mass spectrometry, *Journal of Analytical Toxicology*, 15, 241–245, 1991.

249. Bailey, D. N., Comprehensive review of cocaethylene and cocaine concentrations in patients, *American Journal of Clinical Pathology*, 106, 701–704, 1996.

250. Nishikawa, M., Nakajima, K., Tatsuno, M., Kasuya, F., Igarashi, K., Fukui, M., et al., The analysis of cocaine and its metabolites by liquid chromatography/atmospheric pressure chemical ionization-mass spectrometry (LC/APCI-MS), *Forensic Science International*, 66, 149–158, 1994.

251. Peterson, K. L., Logan, B. K., Christian, G. D., and Ruzicka, J. Analysis of polar cocaine metabolites in urine and spinal fluid, in 46th Annual Meeting of the American Academy of Forensic Sciences, San Antonio, TX, 1994.

252. Logan, B. K. and Stafford, D. T., High-performance liquid chromatography with column switching for the determination of cocaine and benzoylecgonine concentrations in vitreous humor, *Journal of Forensic Sciences*, 35, 1303–1309, 1990.

253. Masoud, A. N. and Krupski, D. M., High-performance liquid chromatographic analysis of cocaine in human plasma, *Journal of Analytical Toxicology*, 4, 305–310, 1980.

254. Thompson, W. C. and Dasgupta, A., Confirmation and quantitation of cocaine, benzoylecgonine, ecgonine methyl ester, and cocaethylene by gas chromatography/mass spectrometry. Use of microwave irradiation for rapid preparation of trimethylsilyl and T-butyldimethylsilyl derivatives [see comments], *American Journal of Clinical Pathology*, 104, 187–192, 1995.

255. Cardenas, S., Gallego, M., and Valcarcel, M., An automated preconcentration-derivatization system for the determination of cocaine and its metabolites in urine and illicit cocaine samples by gas chromatography/mass spectrometry, *Rapid Communications in Mass Spectrometry*, 10, 631–636, 1996.

256. Kintz, P. and Mangin, P., Simultaneous determination of opiates, cocaine and major metabolites of cocaine in human hair by gas chromotography/mass spectrometry (GC/MS), *Forensic Science International*, 73, 93–100, 1995.

257. Hearn, W. L., Keran, E. E., Wei, H. A., and Hime, G., Site-dependent postmortem changes in blood cocaine concentrations, *Journal of Forensic Sciences*, 36, 673–684, 1991.

258. Delbeke, F. T. and Debackere, M., Influence of hydrolysis procedures on the urinary concentrations of codeine and morphine in relation to doping analysis, *Journal of Pharmaceutical & Biomedical Analysis*, 11, 339–343, 1993.

259. Posey, B. L. and Kimble, S. N., High-performance liquid chromatographic study of codeine, norcodeine, and morphine as indicators of codeine ingestion, *Journal of Analytical Toxicology*, 8, 68–74, 1984.

260. Vu-Duc, T. and Vernay, A., Simultaneous detection and quantitation of O6-monoacetylmorphine, morphine and codeine in urine by gas chromatography with nitrogen specific and/or flame ionization detection, *Biomedical Chromatography*, 4, 65–69, 1990.

261. Bowie, L. J. and Kirkpatrick, P. B., Simultaneous determination of monoacetylmorphine, morphine, codeine, and other opiates by GC/MS, *Journal of Analytical Toxicology*, 13, 326–329, 1989.

262. elSohly, H. N., Stanford, D. F., Jones, A. B., elSohly, M. A., Snyder, H., and Pedersen, C., Gas chromatographic/mass spectrometric analysis of morphine and codeine in human urine of poppy seed eaters, *Journal of Forensic Sciences*, 33, 347–356, 1988.

263. Wu Chen, N. B., Schaffer, M. I., Lin, R. L., and Stein, R. J., Simultaneous quantitation of morphine and codeine in biological samples by electron impact mass fragmentography, *Journal of Analytical Toxicology*, 6, 231–234, 1982.

264. Saady, J. J., Narasimhachari, N., and Blanke, R. V., Rapid, simultaneous quantification of morphine, codeine, and hydromorphone by GC/MS, *Journal of Analytical Toxicology*, 6, 235–237, 1982.

265. Gygi, S. P., Colon, F., Raftogianis, R. B., Galinsky, R. E., Wilkins, D. G., and Rollins, D. E., Dose-related distribution of codeine and its metabolites into rat hair, *Drug Metabolism & Disposition*, 24, 282–287, 1996.

266. Tracqui, A., Kintz, P., Ludes, B., Rouge, C., Douibi, H., and Mangin, P., High performance liquid chromatography coupled to ion spray mass spectrometry for the determination of colchicine at ppb levels in human biofluids, *Journal of Chromatography B: Biomedical Applications*, 675, 235–242, 1996.

267. Clevenger, C. V., August, T. F., and Shaw, L. M., Colchicine poisoning: report of a fatal case with body fluid analysis by GC/MS and histopathologic examination of postmortem tissues, *Journal of Analytical Toxicology*, 15, 151–154, 1991.

268. Thompson, J. A., Ho, M. S., and Petersen, D. R., Analysis of nicotine and cotinine in tissues by capillary GC and GC/MS, *Journal of Chromatography*, 231, 53–63, 1982.

269. Urakawa, N., Nagata, T., Kudo, K., Kimura, K., and Imamura, T., Simultaneous determination of nicotine and cotinine in various human tissues using capillary gas chromatography/mass spectrometry, *International Journal of Legal Medicine*, 106, 232–236, 1994.

270. Deutsch, J., Hegedus, L., Greig, N. H., Rapoport, S. I., and Soncrant, T. T., Electron-impact and chemical ionization detection of nicotine and cotinine by gas chromatography-mass spectrometry in rat plasma and brain, *Journal of Chromatography*, 579, 93–98, 1992.

271. Jacob, P. d., Yu, L., Wilson, M., and Benowitz, N. L., Selected ion monitoring method for determination of nicotine, cotinine and deuterium-labeled analogs: absence of an isotope effect in the clearance of (S)-nicotine-3′,3′-d2 in humans, *Biological Mass Spectrometry*, 20, 247–252, 1991.

272. Backer, R. C., McFeeley, P., and Wohlenberg, N., Fatality resulting from cyclizine overdose, *Journal of Analytical Toxicology*, 13, 308–309, 1989.

273. Tasset, J. J., Schroeder, T. J., and Pesce, A. J., Cyclobenzaprine overdose: the importance of a clinical history in analytical toxicology [letter], *Journal of Analytical Toxicology*, 10, 258, 1986.

274. Levine, B., Jones, R., Smith, M. L., Gudewicz, T. M., and Peterson, B., A multiple drug intoxication involving cyclobenzaprine and ibuprofen, *American Journal of Forensic Medicine & Pathology*, 14, 246–248, 1993.

275. Baehr, G. R., Romano, M., and Young, J. M., An unusual case of cyproheptadine (Periactin) overdose in an adolescent female, *Pediatric Emergency Care*, 2, 183–185, 1986.

276. Law, B., Mason, P. A., Moffat, A. C., Gleadle, R. I., and King, L. J., Forensic aspects of the metabolism and excretion of cannabinoids following oral ingestion of cannabis resin, *Journal of Pharmacy and Pharmacology*, 36, 289–294, 1983.

277. elSohly, M. A., Little, T. L., Jr., and Stanford, D. F., Hexadeutero-11-nor-delta 9-tetrahydrocannabinol-9-carboxylic acid: a superior internal standard for the GC/MS analysis of delta 9-THC acid metabolite in biological specimens, *Journal of Analytical Toxicology*, 16, 188–191, 1992.

278. Moeller, M., Doerr, G., and Warth, S., Simultaneous quantitation of delta-9-tetrahydrocannabinol (THC) and 11-nor-9-carboxy-delta-9-tetrahydrocannabinol (THC-COOH) in serum by GC/MS using deuterated internal standards and its application to a smoking study and forensic cases, *Journal of Forensic Sciences*, 37, 969–983, 1992.

279. Kemp, P. M., Abukhalaf, I. K., Manno, J. E., Manno, B. R., Alford, D. D., McWilliams, M. E., et al., Cannabinoids in humans. II. The influence of three methods of hydrolysis on the concentration of THC and two metabolites in urine, *Journal of Analytical Toxicology*, 19, 292–298, 1995.

280. Wolff, K., Garretty, D., and Hay, A. W. M., Micro-extraction of commonly abused benzodiazepines for urinary screening by liquid chromatography, *Annals of Clinical Biochemistry*, 34, 61–67, 1997.

281. Tanaka, E., Terada, M., Misawa, S., and Wakasugi, C., Simultaneous determination of twelve benzodiazepines in human serum using a new reversed-phase chromatographic column on a 2-mu-m porous microspherical silica gel, *Journal of Chromatography B: Biomedical Applications*, 682, 173–178, 1996.

282. Needleman, S. B. and Porvaznik, M., Identification of parent benzodiazepines by gas chromotography/mass spectroscopy (GC/MS) from urinary extracts treated with B-glucuronidase, *Forensic Science International*, 73, 49–60, 1995.

283. Peat, M. A. and Kopjak, L., The screening and quantitation of diazepam, flurazepam, chloridazepoxide, and their metabolites in blood and plasma by electron-capture gas chromatography and high pressure liquid chromatography, *Journal of Forensic Sciences*, 24, 46–54, 1979.

284. Song, D., Zhang, S., and Kohlhof, K., Gas chromatographic-mass spectrometric method for the determination of flurazepam and its major metabolites in mouse and rat plasma, *Journal of Chromatography B: Biomedical Applications*, 658, 142–148, 1994.

285. Clatworthy, A. J., Jones, L. V., and Whitehouse, M. J., The GC/MS of the major metabolites of flurazepam., *Biomedical Mass Spectronomy*, 4, 248–254, 1977.

286. Aderjan, R. and Mattern, R., [A fatal monointoxication by flurazepam (Dalmadorm). Problems of the toxicological interpretation (author's transl.)]. [German], *Archives of Toxicology*, 43, 69–75, 1979.

287. Abel, M. and Eiscnkraft, J. B., Erroneous mass spectrometer readings caused by desflurane and sevoflurane, *Journal of Clinical Monitoring*, 11, 152–158, 1995.

288. Hartter, S., Baier, D., Dingemanse, J., Ziegler, G., and Hiemke, C., Automated determination of dextromethorphan and its main metabolites in human plasma by high-performance liquid chromatography and column switching, *Therapeutic Drug Monitoring*, 18, 297–303, 1996.

289. Lam, Y. W. and Rodriguez, S. Y., High-performance liquid chromatography determination of dextromethorphan and dextrorphan for oxidation phenotyping by fluorescence and ultraviolet detection, *Therapeutic Drug Monitoring*, 15, 300–304, 1993.

290. Wallace, J. E., Schwertner, H. A., and Shimek, E. L. j., Analysis for diazepam and nordiazepam by electron-capture gas chromatography and by liquid chromatography, *Clinical Chemistry*, 25, 1296–1300, 1979.

291. St-Pierre, M. V. and Pang, K. S., Determination of diazepam and its metabolites by high-performance liquid chromatography and thin-layer chromatography, *Journal of Chromatography*, 421, 291–307, 1987.

292. MacKichan, J. J., Jusko, W. J., Duffner, P. K., and Cohen, M. E., Liquid-chromatographic assay of diazepam and its major metabolites in plasma, *Clinical Chemistry*, 25, 856–859, 1979.

293. Plavsic, F. and Culig, J., Determination of serum diclofenac by high-performance liquid chromatography by electromechanical detection, *Human Toxicology*, 4, 317–322, 1985.

294. Blagbrough, I. S., Daykin, M. M., Doherty, M., Pattrick, M., and Shaw, P. N., High-performance liquid chromatographic determination of naproxen, ibuprofen and diclofenac in plasma and synovial fluid in man, *Journal of Chromatography*, 578, 251–257, 1992.

295. Garriott, J. C., Rodriquez, R., and Norton, L. E., Two cases of death involving dicyclomine in infants, *Journal of Toxicology—Clinical Toxicology*, 22, 455–462, 1984.

296. Shimamine, M., Takahashi, K., and Nakahara, Y., [Studies on the identification of psychotropic substances, *Eisei Shikenjo Hokoku—Bulletin of National Institute of Hygienic Sciences*, 67–73, 1992.

297. Levine, B., Smyth, D., and Caplan, Y., A diflunisal related fatality: a case report, *Forensic Science International*, 35, 45–50, 1987.

298. Hofmann, U., Fromm, M. F., Johnson, S., and Mikus, G., Simultaneous determination of dihydrocodeine and dihydromorphine in serum by gas chromatography-tandem mass spectrometry, *Journal of Chromatography B: Biomedical Applications*, 663, 59–65, 1995.

299. Musshoff, F. and Daldrup, T., Evaluation of a method for simultaneous quantification of codeine, dihydrocodeine, morphine, and 6-monoacetylmorphine in serum, blood, and postmortem blood, *International Journal of Legal Medicine*, 106, 107–109, 1993.

300. Maurer, H. H., Identification of antiarrhythmic drugs and their metabolites in urine, *Archives of Toxicology*, 64, 218–230, 1990.

301. Pierce, T. L., Murray, A. G., and Hope, W., Determination of methadone and its metabolites by high performance liquid chromatography following solid-phase extraction in rat plasma, *Journal of Chromatographic Science*, 30, 443–447, 1992.

302. Angelo, H. R., Bonde, J., Kampmann, J. P., and Kastrup, J., A HPLC method for the simultaneous determination of disopyramide, lidocaine and their monodealkylated metabolites, *Scandinavian Journal of Clinical & Laboratory Investigation*, 46, 623–627, 1986.

303. Proelss, H. F. and Townsend, T. B., Simultaneous liquid-chromatographic determination of five antiarrhythmic drugs and their major active metabolites in serum, *Clinical Chemistry*, 32, 1311–1317, 1986.

304. Anderson, W. H., Stafford, D. T., and Bell, J. S., Disopyramide (Norpace) distribution at autopsy of an overdose case, *Journal of Forensic Sciences*, 25, 33–39, 1980.

305. Kapil, R. P., Abbott, F. S., Kerr, C. R., Edwards, D. J., Lalka, D., and Axelson, J. E., Simultaneous quantitation of disopyramide and its mono-dealkylated metabolite in human plasma by fused-silica capillary gas chromatography using nitrogen-phosphorus specific detection, *Journal of Chromatography*, 307, 305–321, 1984.

306. McIntyre, I. M., King, C. V., Skafidis, S., and Drummer, O. H., Dual ultraviolet wavelength high-performance liquid chromatographic method for the forensic or clinical analysis of seventeen antidepressants and some selected metabolites, *Journal of Chromatography*, 621, 215–223, 1993.

307. Pounder, D. J. and Jones, G. R., Post-mortem drug redistribution—a toxicological nightmare, *Forensic Science International*, 45, 253–263, 1990.

308. Wu Chen, N. B., Schaffer, M. I., Lin, R. L., Kurland, M. L., Donoghue, E. R., Jr., and Stein, R. J., The general toxicology unknown. II. A case report: doxylamine and pyrilamine intoxication, *Journal of Forensic Sciences*, 28, 398–403, 1983.

309. Virag, L., Mets, B., and Jamdar, S., Determination of cocaine, norcocaine, benzoylecgonine and ecgonine methyl ester in rat plasma by high-performance liquid chromatography with ultraviolet detection, *Journal of Chromatography B: Biomedical Applications*, 681, 263–269, 1996.

310. Peterson, K. L., Logan, B. K., and Christian, G. D., Detection of cocaine and its polar transformation products and metabolites in human urine, *Forensic Science International*, 73, 183–196, 1995.

311. Balikova, M. and Vecerkova, J., High-performance liquid chromatographic confirmation of cocaine and benzoylecgonine in biological samples using photodiode-array detection after toxicological screening, *Journal of Chromatography B: Biomedical Applications*, 656, 267–273, 1994.

312. Crouch, D. J., Alburges, M. E., Spanbauer, A. C., Rollins, D. E., and Moody, D. E., Analysis of cocaine and its metabolites from biological specimens using solid-phase extraction and positive ion chemical ionization mass spectrometry, *Journal of Analytical Toxicology*, 19, 352–358, 1995.

313. Wang, W. L., Darwin, W. D., and Cone, E. J., Simultaneous assay of cocaine, heroin and metabolites in hair, plasma, saliva and urine by gas chromatography-mass spectrometry, *Journal of Chromatography B: Biomedical Applications*, 660, 279–290, 1994.

314. Mule, S. J. and Casella, G. A., Confirmation and quantitation of cocaine, benzoylecgonine, ecgonine methyl ester in human urine by GC/MS, *Journal of Analytical Toxicology*, 12, 153–155, 1988.

315. Matsubara, K., Maseda, C., and Fukui, Y., Quantitation of cocaine, benzoylecgonine and ecgonine methyl ester by GC-CI-SIM after Extrelut extraction, *Forensic Science International*, 26, 181–192, 1984.

316. Ahnoff, M., Ervik, M., Lagerstrom, P. O., Persson, B. A., and Vessman, J., Drug level monitoring: cardiovascular drugs. [Review], *Journal of Chromatography*, 340, 73–138, 1985.

317. Braggio, S., Sartori, S., Angeri, F., and Pellegatti, M., Automation and validation of the high-performance liquid chromatographic-radioimmunoassay method for the determination of lacidipine in plasma, *Journal of Chromatography B: Biomedical Applications*, 669, 383–389, 1995.

318. Saito, K., Takayasu, T., Nishigami, J., Kondo, T., Ohtsuji, M., Lin, Z., et al., Determination of the volatile anesthetics halothane, enflurane, isoflurane, and sevoflurane in biological specimens by pulse-heating GC-MS, *Journal of Analytical Toxicology*, 19, 115–119, 1995.

319. Heusler, H., Quantitative analysis of common anaesthetic agents, *Journal of Chromatography*, 340, 273–319, 1985.

320. Ohtsuji, M., Lai, J. S., Binder, S. R., Kondo, T., Takayasu, T., and Ohshima, T., Use of REMEDi HS in emergency toxicology for a rapid estimate of drug concentrations in urine, serum, and gastric samples, *Journal of Forensic Sciences*, 41, 881–886, 1996.

321. Boukhabza, A., Lugnier, A. A., Kintz, P., and Mangin, P., Simultaneous HPLC analysis of the hypnotic benzodiazepines nitrazepam, estazolam, flunitrazepam, and triazolam in plasma, *Journal of Analytical Toxicology*, 15, 319–322, 1991.

322. Charlebois, R. C., Corbett, M. R., and Wigmore, J. G., Comparison of ethanol concentrations in blood, serum, and blood cells for forensic application, *Journal of Analytical Toxicology*, 20, 171–178, 1996.

323. O' Neal, C., Wolf, C. E., 2nd, Levine, B., Kunsman, G., and Poklis, A., Gas chromatographic procedures for determination of ethanol in postmortem blood using t-butanol and methyl ethyl ketone as internal standards, *Forensic Science International*, 83, 31–38, 1996.

324. Macchia, T., Mancinelli, R., Gentili, S., Lugaresi, E. C., Raponi, A., and Taggi, F., Ethanol in biological fluids: headspace GC measurement, *Journal of Analytical Toxicology*, 19, 241–246, 1995.

325. Skrupskii, V. A., [Gas chromatographic analysis of ethanol and acetone in the air exhaled by patients]. [RUSSIAN], *Klinicheskaia Laboratornaia Diagnostika*, 4, 35–38, 1995.

326. Jones, A. W., Edman-Falkensson, M., and Nilsson, L., Reliability of blood alcohol determinations at clinical chemistry laboratories in Sweden, *Scandinavian Journal of Clinical & Laboratory Investigation*, 55, 463–468, 1995.

327. Clerc, Y., Huart, B., Charotte, J. M., and Pailler, F. M., [Validation of blood ethanol determination method by gas chromatography (letter)]. [French], *Annales de Biologie Clinique*, 53, 233–238, 1995.

328. Cox, R. A. and Crifasi, J. A., A comparison of a commercial microdiffusion method and gas chromatography for ethanol analysis, *Journal of Analytical Toxicology*, 14, 211–212, 1990.

329. Jones, A. W. and Schuberth, J., Computer-aided headspace gas chromatography applied to blood-alcohol analysis: importance of online process control, *Journal of Forensic Sciences*, 34, 1116–1127, 1989.

330. Bridges, R. R. and Jennison, T. A., Analysis of ethchlorvynol (Placidyl): evaluation of a comparison performed in a clinical laboratory, *Journal of Analytical Toxicology*, 8, 263–268, 1984.

331. Winek, C. L., Wahba, W. W., Rozin, L., and Winek, C. L., Jr., Determination of ethchlorvynol in body tissues and fluids after embalmment, *Forensic Science International*, 37, 161–166, 1988.

332. Winek, C. L., Wahba, W. W., and Winek, C. L., Jr., Body distribution of ethchlorvynol, *Journal of Forensic Sciences*, 34, 687–690, 1989.

333. Flanagan, R. J., Lee, T. D., and Rutherford, D. M., Analysis of chlormethiazole, ethchlorvynol and trichloroethanol in biological fluids by gas-liquid chromatography as an aid to the diagnosis of acute poisoning, *Journal of Chromatography*, 153, 473–479, 1978.

334. Flanagan, R. J. and Lee, T. D., Rapid micro-method for the measurement of ethchlorvynol in blood plasma and in urine by gas-liquid chromatography, *Journal of Chromatography*, 137, 119–126, 1977.

335. Bailey, D. N. and Shaw, R. F., Ethchlorvynol ingestion in San Diego County: a 14-year review of cases with blood concentrations and findings. [Review], *Journal of Analytical Toxicology*, 14, 348–352, 1990.

336. Kelner, M. J. and Bailey, D. N., Ethchlorvynol ingestion: interpretation of blood concentrations and clinical findings, *Journal of Toxicology—Clinical Toxicology*, 21, 399–408, 1983.

337. Berry, D. J. and Clarke, L. A., Gas chromatographic analysis of ethosuximide (2-ethyl-2-methyl succinimide) in plasma at therapeutic concentrations, *Journal of Chromatography*, 150, 537–541, 1978.

338. Richard, L., Leducq, B., Baty, C., and Jambou, J., [Plasma determination of 7 common drugs by high performance liquid chromatography], *Annales de Biologie Clinique*, 47, 79–84, 1989.

339. Schmutz, A. and Thormann, W., Determination of phenobarbital, ethosuximide, and primidone in human serum by micellar electrokinetic capillary chromatography with direct sample injection, *Therapeutic Drug Monitoring*, 15, 310–316, 1993.

340. Miles, M. V., Howlett, C. M., Tennison, M. B., Greenwood, R. S., and Cross, R. E., Determination of N-desmethylmethsuximide serum concentrations using enzyme-multiplied and fluorescence polarization immunoassays, *Therapeutic Drug Monitoring*, 11, 337–342, 1989.

341. Stewart, C. F. and Bottorff, M. B., Fluorescence polarization immunoassay for ethosuximide evaluated and compared with two other immunoassay techniques, *Clinical Chemistry*, 32, 1781–1783, 1986.

342. Haring, C. M., Dijkhuis, I. C., and van Dijk, B., A rapid method of determining serum levels of etomidate by gas chromatography with the aid of a nitrogen detector, *Acta Anaesthesiologica Belgica*, 31, 107–112, 1980.

343. Qin, X. Z., Ip, D. P., Chang, K. H., Dradransky, P. M., Brooks, M. A., and Sakuma, T., Pharmaceutical application of LC-MS. 1—Characterization of a famotidine degradate in a package screening study by LC-APCI MS, *Journal of Pharmaceutical & Biomedical Analysis*, 12, 221–233, 1994.

344. Poquette, M. A., Isothermal gas chromatographic method for the rapid determination of felbamate concentration in human serum, *Therapeutic Drug Monitoring*, 17, 168–173, 1995.

345. Wong, S. H. Y., Sasse, E. A., Schroeder, J. M., Rodgers, J. K., Pearson, M. L., Neicheril, J. C., et al., Totally automated analysis by robotized prepstation and liquid chromatography—direct-sample analysis of felbamate, *Therapeutic Drug Monitoring*, 18, 573–580, 1996.

346. Annesley, T. M. and Clayton, L. T., Determination of felbamate in human serum by high-performance liquid chromatography, *Therapeutic Drug Monitoring*, 16, 419–424, 1994.

347. Friel, P. N., Formoso, E. J., and Logan, B. K. GC/MS analysis of felbamate, a new antiepileptic drug, in postmortem specimens, in American Academy of Forensic Science, Seattle, WA, 1995.

348. Nishioka, R., Umeda, I., Oi, N., Tabata, S., and Uno, K., Determination of felodipine and its metabolites in plasma using capillary gas chromatography with electron-capture detection and their identification by gas chromatography-mass spectrometry, *Journal of Chromatography*, 565, 237–246, 1991.

349. Ferretti, R., Gallinella, B., Latorre, F., and Lusi, A., Direct high-performance liquid chromatography resolution on a chiral column of dexfenfluramine and its impurities, in bulk raw drug and pharmaceutical formulations, *Journal of Chromatography*, 731(1–2): 340–345, 1996.

350. Moore, C. M. and Tebbett, I. R., Rapid extraction of anti-inflammatory drugs in whole blood for HPLC analysis, *Forensic Science International*, 34, 155–158, 1987.

351. Watts, V. and Caplan, Y., Determination of fentanyl in whole blood at subnanogram concentrations by dual capillary column gas chromatography with nitrogen sensitive detectors and gas chromatography/mass spectrometry, *Journal of Analytical Toxicology*, 12, 246–254, 1988.

352. Mautz, D. S., Labroo, R., and Kharasch, E. D., Determination of alfentanil and noralfentanil in human plasma by gas chromatography-mass spectrometry, *Journal of Chromatography B: Biomedical Applications*, 658, 149–153, 1994.

353. Smialek, J. E., Levine, B., Chin, L., Wu, S. C., and Jenkins, A. J., A fentanyl epidemic in Maryland 1992, *Journal of Forensic Sciences*, 39, 159–164, 1994.

354. Levine, B., Goodin, J. C., and Caplan, Y. H., A fentanyl fatality involving midazolam, *Forensic Science International*, 45, 247–251, 1990.

355. Ferslew, K., Hagardorn, A., and McCormick, W., Postmortem determination of the biological distribution of sufentanil and midazolam after an acute intoxication, *Journal of Forensic Sciences*, 34, 249–257, 1989.

356. Poklis, A., Fentanyl: A review for clinical and analytical toxicologists [Review], *Journal of Toxicology Clinical Toxicology*, 33, 439–447, 1995.

357. Hoppe, U., Krudewagen, B., Stein, H., Hertrampf, R., and Gundert-Remy, U., Comparison of fluorescence polarisation immunoassay (FPIA) and high performance liquid chromatography (HPLC) methods for the measurement of flecainide in human plasma, *International Journal of Clinical Pharmacology, Therapy, & Toxicology*, 31, 142–147, 1993.

358. Stas, C. M., Jacqmin, P. A., and Pellegrin, P. L., Comparison of gas-liquid chromatography and fluorescence polarization immunoassay for therapeutic drug monitoring of flecainide acetate, *Journal of Pharmaceutical & Biomedical Analysis*, 7, 1651–1656, 1989.

359. Straka, R. J., Hoon, T. J., Lalonde, R. L., Pieper, J. A., and Bottorff, M. B., Liquid chromatography and fluorescence polarization immunoassay methods compared for measuring flecainide acetate in serum, *Clinical Chemistry*, 33, 1898–1900, 1987.

360. Berthault, F., Kintz, P., and Mangin, P., Simultaneous high-performance liquid chromatographic analysis of flunitrazepam and four metabolites in serum, *Journal of Chromatography B: Biomedical Applications*, 685, 383–387, 1996.

361. Kleinschnitz, M., Herderich, M., and Schreier, P., Determination of 1,4-benzodiazepines by high-performance liquid chromatography electrospray tandem mass spectrometry, *Journal of Chromatography B: Biomedical Applications*, 676, 61–67, 1996.

362. Robertson, M. D. and Drummer, O. H., High-performance liquid chromatographic procedure for the measurement of nitrobenzodiazepines and their 7-amino metabolites in blood, *Journal of Chromatography B: Biomedical Applications*, 667, 179–184, 1995.

363. Benhamou-Batut, F., Demotes-Mainard, F., Labat, L., Vincon, G., and Bannwarth, B., Determination of flunitrazepam in plasma by liquid chromatography, *Journal of Pharmaceutical & Biomedical Analysis*, 12, 931–936, 1994.

364. Lantz, R. J., Farid, K. Z., Koons, J., Tenbarge, J. B., and Bopp, R. J., Determination of fluoxetine and norfluoxetine in human plasma by capillary gas chromatography with electron-capture detection, *Journal of Chromatography*, 614, 175–179, 1993.

365. Rohrig, T. P. and Prouty, R. W., Fluoxetine overdose: a case report [published erratum appears in *Journal of Analytical Toxicology* 14, 63, 1990], *Journal of Analytical Toxicology*, 13, 305–307, 1989.

366. Orsulak, P. J., Kenney, J. T., Debus, J. R., Crowley, G., and Wittman, P. D., Determination of the antidepressant fluoxetine and its metabolite norfluoxetine in serum by reversed-phase HPLC with ultraviolet detection, *Clinical Chemistry*, 34, 1875–1878, 1988.

367. Nash, J. F., Bopp, R. J., Carmichael, R. H., Farid, K. Z., and Lemberger, L., Determination of fluoxetine and norfluoxetine in plasma by gas chromatography with electron-capture detection, *Clinical Chemistry*, 28, 2100–2102, 1982.

368. Nichols, J. H., Charlson, J. R., and Lawson, G. M., Automated HPLC assay of fluoxetine and norfluoxetine in serum, *Clinical Chemistry*, 40, 1312–1316, 1994.

369. Eap, C. B., Gaillard, N., Powell, K., and Baumann, P., Simultaneous determination of plasma levels of fluvoxamine and of the enantiomers of fluoxetine and norfluoxetine by gas chromatography mass spectrometry, *Journal of Chromatography B: Biomedical Applications*, 682, 265–272, 1996.

370. Miller, R. S., Peterson, G. M., McLean, S., Westhead, T. T., and Gillies, P., Monitoring plasma levels of fluphenazine during chronic therapy with fluphenazine decanoate, *Journal of Clinical Pharmacy & Therapeutics*, 20, 55–62, 1995.

371. Sener, A., Akkan, A. G., and Malaisse, W. J., Standardized procedure for the assay and identification of hypoglycemic sulfonylureas in human plasma, *Acta Diabetologica*, 32, 64–68, 1995.

372. Flanagan, R. J. and Withers, G., A rapid micro-method for the screening and measurement of barbiturates and related compounds in plasma by gas-liquid chromatography, *Journal of Clinical Pathology*, 25, 899–904, 1972.

373. Shipe, J. R. and Savory, J., A comprehensive gas chromatography procedure for measurement of drugs in biological materials, *Annals of Clinical & Laboratory Science*, 5, 57–64, 1975.

374. Bailey, D. N. and Shaw, R. F., Blood concentrations and clinical findings in nonfatal and fatal intoxications involving glutethimide and codeine, *Journal of Toxicology Clinical Toxicology*, 23, 557–570, 1985.

375. Bailey, D. N. and Shaw, R. F., Interpretation of blood glutethimide, meprobamate, and methyprylon concentrations in nonfatal and fatal intoxications involving a single drug, *Journal of Toxicology Clinical Toxicology*, 20, 133–145, 1983.

376. Hoffman, D. W. and Edkins, R. D., Solid-phase extraction and high-performance liquid chromatography for therapeutic monitoring of haloperidol levels, *Therapeutic Drug Monitoring*, 16, 504–508, 1994.

377. Aravagiri, M., Marder, S. R., Van Putten, T., and Marshall, B. D., Simultaneous determination of plasma haloperidol and its metabolite reduced haloperidol by liquid chromatography with electrochemical detection. Plasma levels in schizophrenic patients treated with oral or intramuscular depot haloperidol, *Journal of Chromatography B: Biomedical Applications*, 656, 373–381, 1994.

378. Jann, M. W., Chang, W. H., Lam, Y. W., Hwu, H. G., Lin, H. N., Chen, H., et al., Comparison of haloperidol and reduced haloperidol plasma levels in four different ethnic populations, *Progress in Neuro Psychopharmacology & Biological Psychiatry*, 16, 193–202, 1992.

379. Park, K. H., Lee, M. H., and Lee, M. G., Simultaneous determination of haloperidol and its metabolite, reduced haloperidol, in plasma, blood, urine and tissue homogenates by high-performance liquid chromatography, *Journal of Chromatography*, 572, 259–267, 1991.

380. Haering, N., Salama, Z., Todesko, L., and Jaeger, H., GC/MS determination of haloperidol in plasma. Application to pharmacokinetics, *Arzneimittel-Forschung*, 37, 1402–1404, 1987.

381. van Leeuwen, P. A., Improved GC/MS assay for haloperidol utilizing ammonia CI and SIM, *Journal of Chromatography and Biomedical Applications*, 40, 321–330, 1985.

382. Hornbeck, C. L., Griffiths, J. C., Neborsky, R. J., and Faulkner, M. A., GC/MS chemical ionization assay for haloperidol with SIM, *Biomedical Mass Spectrometry*, 6, 427–430, 1979.

383. Coudore, F., Alazard, J. M., Paire, M., Andraud, G., and Lavarenne, J., Rapid toxicological screening of barbiturates in plasma by wide-bore capillary gas chromatography and nitrogen-phosphorus detection, *Journal of Analytical Toxicology*, 17, 109–113, 1993.

384. Soo, V. A., Bergert, R. J., and Deutsch, D. G., Screening and quantification of hypnotic sedatives in serum by capillary gas chromatography with a nitrogen-phosphorus detector, and confirmation by capillary gas chromatography-mass spectrometry, *Clinical Chemistry*, 32, 325–328, 1986.

385. Mahoney, J. D., Gross, P. L., Stern, T. A., Browne, B. J., Pollack, M. H., Reder, V., et al., Quantitative serum toxic screening in the management of suspected drug overdose, *American Journal of Emergency Medicine*, 8, 16–22, 1990.

386. Meeker, J. E., Som, C. W., Macapagal, E. C., and Benson, P. A., Zolpidem tissue concentrations in a multiple drug related death involving Ambien, *Journal of Analytical Toxicology*, 19, 531–534, 1995.

387. Bouquillon, A. I., Freeman, D., and Moulin, D. E., Simultaneous solid-phase extraction and chromatographic analysis of morphine and hydromorphone in plasma by high-performance liquid chromatography with electrochemical detection, *Journal of Chromatography*, 577, 354–357, 1992.

388. Sawyer, W. R., Waterhouse, G. A., Doedens, D. J., and Forney, R. B., Heroin, morphine, and hydromorphone determination in postmortem material by high performance liquid chromatography [see comments], *Journal of Forensic Sciences*, 33, 1146–1155, 1988.

389. O' Connor, E. F., Cheng, S. W., and North, W. G., Simultaneous extraction and chromatographic analysis of morphine, dilaudid, naltrexone and naloxone in biological fluids by high-performance liquid chromatography with electrochemical detection, *Journal of Chromatography*, 491, 240–247, 1989.

390. Cone, E. J. and Darwin, W. D., Simultaneous determination of hydromorphone, hydrocodone and their 6alpha- and 6beta-hydroxy metabolites in urine using selected ion recording with methane chemical ionization, *Biomedical Mass Spectrometry*, 5, 291, 1978.

391. Croes, K., McCarthy, P. T., and Flanagan, R. J., Simple and rapid HPLC of quinine, hydroxychloroquine, chloroquine, and desethylchloroquine in serum, whole blood, and filter paper- adsorbed dry blood, *Journal of Analytical Toxicology*, 18, 255–260, 1994.

392. Kintz, P., Godelar, B., and Mangin, P., Gas chromatographic identification and quantification of hydroxyzine: application in a fatal self-poisoning, *Forensic Science International*, 48, 139–143, 1990.

393. Naidong, W. and Lee, J. W., Development and validation of a liquid chromatographic method for the quantitation of ibuprofen enantiomers in human plasma, *Journal of Pharmaceutical & Biomedical Analysis*, 12, 551–556, 1994.

394. Maurer, H. H., Kraemer, T., and Weber, A., Toxicological detection of ibuprofen and its metabolites in urine using gas chromatography-mass spectrometry (GC-MS), *Pharmazie*, 49, 148–155, 1994.

395. Zhao, M. J., Peter, C., Holtz, M. C., Hugenell, N., Koffel, J. C., and Jung, L., GC/MS determination of ibuprofen enantiomers in human plasma using r(-)-2,2,2-trifluoro-1-(9-anthryl)ethanol as derivatizing reagent, *Journal of Chromatography B: Biomedical Applications*, 656, 441–446, 1994.

396. Seideman, P., Lohrer, F., Graham, G. G., Duncan, M. W., Williams, K. M., and Day, R. O., The stereoselective disposition of the enantiomers of ibuprofen in blood, blister and synovial fluid, British *Journal of Clinical Pharmacology*, 38, 221–227, 1994.

397. Theis, D. L., Halstead, G. W., and Halm, K. A., Development of capillary GC/MS methodology for the simultaneous determination of ibuprofen and deuterated ibuprofen in serum, *Journal of Chromatography*, 380, 77–87, 1986.

398. Jourdil, N., Pinteur, B., Vincent, F., Marka, C., and Bessard, G., Simultaneous determination of trimipramine and desmethyl- and hydroxytrimipramine in plasma and red blood cells by capillary gas chromatography with nitrogen-selective detection, *Journal of Chromatography*, 613, 59–65, 1993.

399. Maynard, G. L. and Soni, P., Thioridazine interferences with imipramine metabolism and measurement, *Therapeutic Drug Monitoring*, 18, 729–731, 1996.

400. Nielsen, K. K. and Brosen, K., High-performance liquid chromatography of imipramine and six metabolites in human plasma and urine, *Journal of Chromatography*, 612, 87–94, 1993.

401. Koyama, E., Kikuchi, Y., Echizen, H., Chiba, K., and Ishizaki, T., Simultaneous high-performance liquid chromatography-electrochemical detection determination of imipramine, desipramine, their 2-hydroxylated metabolites, and imipramine N-oxide in human plasma and urine: preliminary application to oxidation pharmacogenetics, *Therapeutic Drug Monitoring*, 15, 224–235, 1993.

402. Eap, C. B., Koeb, L., and Baumann, P., Determination of trimipramine and its demethylated and hydroxylated metabolites in plasma by gas chromatography-mass spectrometry, *Journal of Chromatography*, 652, 97–103, 1994.

403. Hunt, J. P., Haywood, P. E., and Moss, M. S., A gas chromatographic screening procedure for the detection of non-steroidal anti-inflammatory drugs in horse urine, *Equine Veterinary Journal*, 11, 259–263, 1979.

404. Sibeon, R. G., Baty, J. D., Baber, N., Chan, K., and Orme, M. L., Quantitative gas-liquid chromatographic method for the determination of indomethacin in biological fluids, *Journal of Chromatography*, 153, 189–194, 1978.

405. Hannak, D., Scharbert, F., and Kattermann, R., Stepwise binary gradient high-performance liquid chromatographic system for routine drug monitoring, *Journal of Chromatography A*, 728, 307–310, 1996.

406. Caturla, M. C. and Cusido, E., Solid-phase extraction for the high-performance liquid chromatographic determination of indomethacin, suxibuzone, phenylbutazone and oxyphenbutazone in plasma, avoiding degradation of compounds, *Journal of Chromatography*, 581, 101–107, 1992.

407. Cosolo, W., Drummer, O. H., and Christophidis, N., Comparison of high-performance liquid chromatography and the Abbott fluorescent polarization radioimmunoassay in the measurement of methotrexate, *Journal of Chromatography*, 494, 201–208, 1989.

408. Bauernfeind, M. and Wood, W. G., Evaluation of a fully mechanised immunoassay—Enzymun-Test System ES 300—and comparison with in-house methods for 8 analytes, *European Journal of Clinical Chemistry & Clinical Biochemistry*, 31, 165–172, 1993.

409. Patel, F., Fatal self-induced hyperinsulinaemia: a delayed post-mortem analytical detection, *Medicine, Science & the Law*, 32, 151–159, 1992.

410. Fletcher, S. M., Insulin. A forensic primer. [Review], *Journal Forensic Science Society*, 23, 5–17, 1983.

411. Heyndrickx, A., Van Peteghem, C., Majelyne, W., and Timperman, J., Detection of insulin in cadavers, *Acta Pharmaceutica Hungarica*, 50, 201–206, 1980.

412. Dickson, S. J., Cairns, E. R., and Blazey, N. D., The isolation and quantitation of insulin in post-mortem specimens—a case report, *Forensic Science*, 9, 37–42, 1977.

413. Jones, A. W., Severe isopropanolemia without acetonemia: contamination of specimens during venipuncture? [letter; comment], *Clinical Chemistry*, 41, 123–124, 1995.

414. Chan, K. M., Wong, E. T., and Matthews, W. S., Severe isopropanolemia without acetonemia or clinical manifestations of isopropanol intoxication [see comments], *Clinical Chemistry*, 39, 1922–1925, 1993.

415. Jerrard, D., Verdile, V., Yealy, D., Krenzelok, E., and Menegazzi, J., Serum determinations in toxic isopropanol ingestion, *American Journal of Emergency Medicine*, 10, 200–202, 1992.

416. Davis, P. L., Dal Cortivo, L. A., and Maturo, J., Endogenous isopropanol: forensic and biochemical implications, *Journal of Analytical Toxicology*, 8, 209–212, 1984.

417. Kelner, M. and Bailey, D. N., Isopropanol ingestion: interpretation of blood concentrations and clinical findings, *Journal of Toxicology Clinical Toxicology*, 20, 497–507, 1983.

418. Baker, R. N., Alenty, A. L., and Zack, J. F., Jr., Toxic volatiles in alcoholic coma. A report of simultaneous determination of blood methanol, ethanol, isopropanol, acetaldehyde and acetone by gas chromatography, *Bulletin of the Los Angeles Neurological Societies*, 33, 140–144, 1968.

419. Alexander, C. B., McBay, A. J., and Hudson, R. P., Isopropanol and isopropanol deaths-ten years' experience, *Journal of Forensic Sciences*, 27, 541–548, 1982.

420. Brogden, R. N. and Sorkin, E. M., Isradipine. An update of its pharmacodynamic and pharmacokinetic properties and therapeutic efficacy in the treatment of mild to moderate hypertension. [Review], *Drugs*, 49, 618–649, 1995.

421. Kochhar, M. M., Bavda, L. T., and Bhushan, R. S., Thin-layer and gas chromatographic determination of ketamine and its biotransformed products in biological fluids, *Research Communications in Chemical Pathology & Pharmacology*, 14, 367–376, 1976.

422. Adams, H. A., Weber, B., Bachmann, M. B., Guerin, M., and Hempelmann, G., [The simultaneous determination of ketamine and midazolam using high pressure liquid chromatography and UV detection (HPLC/UV)], *Anaesthesist*, 41, 619–624, 1992.

423. Feng, N., Vollenweider, F. X., Minder, E. I., Rentsch, K., Grampp, T., and Vonderschmitt, D. J., Development of a gas chromatography-mass spectrometry method for determination of ketamine in plasma and its application to human samples, *Therapeutic Drug Monitoring*, 17, 95–100, 1995.

424. Lau, S. S. and Domino, E. F., Gas chromatography mass spectrometry assay for ketamine and its metabolites in plasma, *Biomedical Mass Spectrometry*, 4, 317–321, 1977.

425. Carr, R. A., Caille, G., Ngoc, A. H., and Foster, R. T., Stereospecific high-performance liquid chromatographic assay of ketoprofen in human plasma and urine, *Journal of Chromatography B: Biomedical Applications*, 668, 175–181, 1995.

426. Lovlin, R., Vakily, M., and Jamali, F., Rapid, sensitive and direct chiral high-performance liquid chromatographic method for ketoprofen enantiomers, *Journal of Chromatography B: Biomedical Applications*, 679, 196–198, 1996.

427. Palylyk, E. L. and Jamali, F., Simultaneous determination of ketoprofen enantiomers and probenecid in plasma and urine by high-performance liquid chromatography, *Journal of Chromatography*, 568, 187–196, 1991.

428. Chun, I. K., Kang, H. H., and Gwak, H. S., Determination of ketorolac in human serum by high-performance liquid chromatography, *Archives of Pharmacal Research*, 19, 529–534, 1996,

429. Tsina, I., Tam, Y. L., Boyd, A., Rocha, C., Massey, I., and Tarnowski, T., An indirect (derivatization) and a direct hplc method for the determination of the enantiomers of ketorolac in plasma, *Journal of Pharmaceutical & Biomedical Analysis*, 15, 403–417, 1996.

430. Tsina, I., Chu, F., Kaloostian, M., Pettibone, M., and Wu, A., Hplc method for the determination of ketorolac in human plasma, *Journal of Liquid Chromatography & Related Technologies*, 19, 957–967, 1996.

431. Sola, J., Prunonosa, J., Colom, H., Pcraire, C., and Obach, R., Determination of ketorolac in human plasma by high performance liquid chromatography after automated online solid phase extraction, *Journal of Liquid Chromatography & Related Technologies*, 19, 89–99, 1996.

432. Logan, B. K., Friel, P. N., Peterson, K. I., and Predmore, D. B., Analysis of ketorolac in postmortem blood, *Journal of Analytical Toxicology*, 19, 61–64, 1995.

433. Sievert, H. J. P., Determination of amphetamine and methamphetamine enantiomers by chiral derivatization and GC/MS as a test case for an automated sample preparation system, *Chirality*, 6, 295–301, 1994.

434. Cooke, B. J., Chirality of methamphetamine and amphetamine from workplace urine samples, *Journal of Analytical Toxicology*, 18, 49–51, 1994.

435. Nagai, T., Kamiyama, S., Kurosu, A., and Iwamoto, F., [Identification of optical isomers of methamphetamine and its application to forensic medicine]. [Japanese], *Nippon Hoigaku Zasshi Japanese Journal of Legal Medicine*, 46, 244–253, 1992.

436. Wallace, S. J., Lamotrigine—a clinical overview, *Seizure*, 3, 47–51, 1994.

437. Rambeck, B. and Wolf, P., Lamotrigine clinical pharmacokinetics. [Review], *Clinical Pharmacokinetics*, 25, 433–443, 1993.

438. May, T. W., Rambeck, B., and Jurgens, U., Serum concentrations of lamotrigine in epileptic patients —the influence of dose and comedication, *Therapeutic Drug Monitoring*, 18, 523–531, 1996.

439. Kintz, P., Flesch, F., Jaeger, A., and Mangin, P., GC-MS procedure for the analysis of zipeprol, *Journal of Pharmaceutical & Biomedical Analysis*, 11, 335–338, 1993.

440. Xu, Y. Q., Fang, H. J., Xu, Y. X., Duan, H. J., and Wu, Y., [Studies on the analysis of anileridine, levorphanol, nalbuphine and ethamivan in urine], *Yao Hsueh Hsueh Pao—Acta Pharmaceutica Sinica*, 26, 606–610, 1991.

441. Benko, A. and Kimura, K., Toxicological analysis of lidocaine in biological materials by using HPLC, *Forensic Science International*, 49, 65–73, 1991.

442. Cirimele, V., Kintz, P., and Mangin, P., Detection and quantification of lorazepam in human hair by GC-MS/NCI in a case of traffic accident, *International Journal of Legal Medicine*, 108, 265–267, 1996.

443. Higuchi, S., Urabe, H., and Shiobara, Y., Simplified determination of lorazepam and oxazepam in biological fluids by gas chromatography-mass spectrometry, *Journal of Chromatography*, 164, 55–61, 1979.

444. Koves, E. M. and Yen, B., The use of gas chromatography/negative ion chemical ionization mass spectrometry for the determination of lorazepam in whole blood, *Journal of Analytical Toxicology*, 13, 69–72, 1989.

445. Twitchett, P. J., Fletcher, S. M., Sullivan, A. T., and Moffat, A. C., Analysis of LSD in human body fluids by high-performance liquid chromatography, fluorescence spectroscopy and radioimmunoassay, *Journal of Chromatography*, 150, 73–84, 1978.

446. Veress, T., Study of the extraction of LSD from illicit blotters for HPLC determination, *Journal of Forensic Sciences*, 38, 1105–1110, 1993.

447. Cai, J. and Henion, J., On-line immunoaffinity extraction-coupled column capillary liquid chromatography/tandem mass spectrometry: trace analysis of LSD analogs and metabolites in human urine, *Analytical Chemistry*, 68, 72–78, 1996.

448. Nelson, C. C. and Foltz, R. L., Determination of lysergic acid diethylamide (LSD), iso-LSD, and N-demethyl-LSD in body fluids by gas chromatography/tandem mass spectrometry, *Analytical Chemistry*, 64, 1578–1585, 1992.

449. Bukowski, N. and Eaton, A. N., The confirmation and quantitation of LSD in urine using GC/MS, *Rapid Communication Mass Spectrometry*, 7, 106–108, 1993.

450. Ackermann, R., Kaiser, G., Schueller, F., and Dieterle, W., Determination of the antidepressant levoprotiline and its N-desmethyl metabolite in biological fluids by gas chromatography/mass spectrometry, *Biological Mass Spectrometry*, 20, 709–716, 1991.

451. Alkalay, D., Carlsen, S., Khemani, L., and Bartlett, M. F., Selected ion monitoring assay for the antidepressant maprotiline, *Biomedical Mass Spectrometry*, 6, 435–438, 1979.

452. Stidman, J., Taylor, E. H., Simmons, H. F., Gandy, J., and Pappas, A. A., Determination of meprobamate in serum by alkaline hydrolysis, trimethylsilyl derivatization and detection by GC/MS, *Journal of Chromatography*, 494, 318–323, 1989.

453. Kintz, P. and Mangin, P., Determination of meprobamate in human plasma, urine, and hair by gas chromatography and electron impact mass spectrometry, *Journal of Analytical Toxicology*, 17, 408–410, 1993.

454. Bailey, D. N., The present status of meprobamate ingestion. A five-year review of cases with serum concentrations and clinical findings, *American Journal of Clinical Pathology*, 75, 102–106, 1981.

455. Hamman, B., Meprobamate, in *Methodology for Analytical Toxicology: Volume I*, Sunshine, I., Ed., CRC Press, Boca Raton, FL, 1984, 219–221.

456. Foltz, R. L., Fentiman, A. F., Jr., and Foltz, R. B., GC/MS assays for abused drugs in body fluids. [Review], *NIDA Research Monograph*, 32, 1–198, 1980.

457. Poklis, A., Wells, C. E., and Juenge, E. C., Thioridazine and its metabolites in post mortem blood, including two stereoisomeric ring sulfoxides, *Journal of Analytical Toxicology*, 6, 250–252, 1982.

458. Schurch, F., Meier, P. J., and Wyss, P. A., Acute poisoning with thioridazine [German], *Deutsche Medizinische Wochenschrift*, 121, 1003–1008, 1996.

459. Kintz, P., Mangin, P., Lugnier, A. A., and Chaumont, A. J., A rapid and sensitive gas chromatographic analysis of methadone and its primary metabolite, *Journal de Toxicologie Clinique et Experimentale*, 10, 15–20, 1990.

460. Alburges, M. E., Huang, W., Foltz, R. L., and Moody, D. E., Determination of methadone and its N-demethylation metabolites in biological specimens by GC-PICI-MS, *Journal of Analytical Toxicology*, 20, 362–368, 1996.

461. Wilkins, D. G., Nagasawa, P. R., Gygi, S. P., Foltz, R. L., and Rollins, D. E., Quantitative analysis of methadone and two major metabolites in hair by positive chemical ionization ion trap mass spectrometry, *Journal of Analytical Toxicology*, 20, 355–361, 1996.

462. Baugh, L. D., Liu, R. H., and Walia, A. S., Simultaneous gas chromatography/mass spectrometry assay of methadone and 2-ethyl-1,5-dimethyl-3,3-diphenylpyrrolidine (EDDP) in urine, *Journal of Forensic Sciences*, 36, 548–555, 1991.

463. Jacob, P., 3rd, Tisdale, E. C., Panganiban, K., Cannon, D., Zabel, K., Mendelson, J. E., et al., Gas chromatographic determination of methamphetamine and its metabolite amphetamine in human plasma and urine following conversion to N-propyl derivatives, *Journal of Chromatography B: Biomedical Applications*, 664, 449–457, 1995.

464. Dallakian, P., Budzikiewicz, H., and Brzezinka, H., Detection and quantitation of amphetamine and methamphetamine—electron impact and chemical ionization with ammonia-comparative investigation on Shimadzu Qp 5000 GC-MS System, *Journal of Analytical Toxicology*, 20, 255–261, 1996.

465. Valtier, S. and Cody, J. T., Evaluation of internal standards for the analysis of amphetamine and methamphetamine, *Journal of Analytical Toxicology*, 19, 375–380, 1995.

466. Wu, A. H., Kelly, T., McKay, C., Ostheimer, D., Forte, E., and Hill, D., Definitive identification of an exceptionally high methanol concentration in an intoxication of a surviving infant: methanol metabolism by first-order elimination kinetics, *Journal of Forensic Sciences*, 40, 315–320, 1995.

467. Pla, A., Hernandez, A. F., Gil, F., Garcia-Alonso, M., and Villanueva, E., A fatal case of oral ingestion of methanol. Distribution in postmortem tissues and fluids including pericardial fluid and vitreous humor, *Forensic Science International*, 49, 193–196, 1991.

468. Winkel, D. R. and Hendrick, S. A., Detection limits for a GC determination of methanol and methylene chloride residues on film-coated tablets, *Journal of Pharmaceutical Sciences*, 73, 115–117, 1984.

469. Kintz, P., Tracqui, A., Mangin, P., Lugnier, A. A., and Chaumont, A. A., Simultaneous determination of dextropropoxyphene, norpropoxyphene and methaqualone in plasma by gas chromatography with selective nitrogen detection, *Journal de Toxicologie Clinique et Experimentale*, 10, 89–94, 1990.

470. Liu, F., Liu, Y. T., Feng, C. L., and Luo, Y., Determination of methaqualone and its metabolites in urine and blood by UV, GC/FID and GC/MS, *Yao Hsueh Hsueh Pao Acta Pharmaceutica Sinica*, 29, 610–616, 1994.

471. Streete, J. M., Berry, D. J., Clarke, L. A., and Newbery, J. E., Analysis of desmethylmethsuximide using high-performance liquid chromatography, *Therapeutic Drug Monitoring*, 17, 280–286, 1995.

472. Poklis, A., Mackell, M. A., and Drake, W. K., Fatal intoxication from 3,4-methylenedioxyamphetamine, *Journal of Forensic Science*, 24, 70–75, 1979.

473. Quaglio, M. P., Bellini, A. M., and Minozzi, L., Simultaneous determination of propranolol or metoprolol in the presence of benzodiazepines in the plasma by gas chromatography, *Farmaco*, 47, 799–809, 1992.

474. Li, F., Cooper, S. F., and Cote, M., Determination of the enantiomers of metoprolol and its major acidic metabolite in human urine by high-performance liquid chromatography with fluorescence detection, *Journal of Chromatography B: Biomedical Applications*, 668, 67–75, 1995.

475. Holt, D. W., Flanagan, R. J., Hayler, A. M., and Loizou, M., Simple gas-liquid chromatographic method for the measurement of mexiletine and lignocaine in blood-plasma or serum, *Journal of Chromatography*, 169, 295–301, 1979.

476. Minnigh, M. B., Alvin, J. D., and Zemaitis, M. A., Determination of plasma mexiletine levels with gas chromatography-mass spectrometry and selected-ion monitoring, *Journal of Chromatography B: Biomedical Applications*, 662, 118–22, 1994.

477. Bourget, P., Bouton, V., Lesnehulin, A., Amstutz, P., Benayed, M., Benhamou, D., et al., Comparison of high-performance liquid chromatography and polyclonal fluorescence polarization immunoassay for the monitoring of midazolam in the plasma of intensive care unit patients, *Therapeutic Drug Monitoring*, 18, 610–619, 1996.

478. Mastey, V., Panneton, A. C., Donati, F., and Varin, F., Determination of midazolam and two of its metabolites in human plasma by high-performance liquid chromatography, *Journal of Chromatography B: Biomedical Applications*, 655, 305–310, 1994.

479. de Vries, J. X., Rudi, J., Walter-Sack, I., and Conradi, R., The determination of total and unbound midazolam in human plasma, *Biomedical Chromatography*, 4, 28–33, 1990.

480. Vu-Duc, T. and Vernay, A., Simultaneous detection and quantitation of O6-monoacetylmorphine, morphine and codeine in urine by gas chromatography with nitrogen specific and/or flame ionization detection, *Biomedical Chromatography*, 4, 65–69, 1990.

481. Hanisch, W. and Meyer, L. V., Determination of the heroin metabolite 6-monoacetyl-morphine in urine by high-performance liquid chromatography with electrochemical detection, *Journal of Analytical Toxicology*, 17, 48–50, 1993.

482. Kintz, P., Mangin, P., Lugnier, A. A., and Chaumont, A. J., Identification by GC/MS of 6-monoacetyl-morphine as an indicator of heroin abuse, *European Journal of Clinical Pharmacology*, 37, 531–532, 1989.

483. Schuberth, J. and Schuberth, J., GC/MS determination of morphine, codeine and 6-monoacetylmorphine in blood extracted by solid phase, *Journal of Chromatography*, 490, 444–449, 1989.

484. Wasels, R. and Belleville, F., Gas chromatographic-mass spectrometric procedures used for the identification and determination of morphine, codeine and 6-monoacetylmorphine, *Journal of Chromatography A*, 674, 225–234, 1994.

485. Rotshteyn, Y. and Weingarten, B., A highly sensitive assay for the simultaneous determination of morphine, morphine-3-glucuronide, and morphine-6-glucuronide in human plasma by high-performance liquid chromatography with electrochemical and fluorescence detection, *Therapeutic Drug Monitoring*, 18, 179–188, 1996.

486. Pacifici, R., Pichini, S., Altieri, I., Caronna, A., Passa, A. R., and Zuccaro, P., HPLC electrospray mass spectrometric determination of morphine and its 3- and 6-glucuronides: application to pharmacokinetic studies, *Journal of Chromatography B: Biomedical Applications*, 664, 329–334, 1995.

487. Pacifici, R., Pichini, S., Altieri, I., Caronna, A., Passa, A. R., and Zuccaro, P., High-performance liquid chromatographic-electrospray mass spectrometric determination of morphine and its 3- and 6-glucuronides: application to pharmacokinetic studies, *Journal of Chromatography B: Biomedical Applications*, 664, 329–334, 1995.

488. Tyrefors, N., Hyllbrant, B., Ekman, L., Johansson, M., and Langstrom, B., Determination of morphine, morphine-3-glucuronide and morphine-6-glucuronide in human serum by solid-phase extraction and liquid chromatography mass spectrometry with electrospray ionisation, *Journal of Chromatography*, 729, 279–285, 1996.

489. Moeller, M. R. and Mueller, C., The detection of 6-monoacetylmorphine in urine, serum and hair by GC/MS and RIA, *Forensic Science International*, 70, 125–133, 1995.

490. Levine, B., Wu, S., Dixon, A., and Smialek, J., An unusual morphine fatality, *Forensic Science International*, 65, 7–11, 1994.

491. Romberg, R. W. and Lee, L., Comparison of the hydrolysis rates of morphine-3-glucuronide and morphine-6-glucuronide with acid and beta-glucuronidase, *Journal of Analytical Toxicology*, 19, 157–162, 1995.

492. Aderjan, R., Hofmann, S., Schmitt, G., and Skopp, G., Morphine and morphine glucuronides in serum of heroin consumers and in heroin-related deaths determined by HPLC with native fluorescence detection, *Journal of Analytical Toxicology*, 19, 163–168, 1995.

493. Wright, A. W., Watt, J. A., Kennedy, M., Cramond, T., and Smith, M. T., Quantitation of morphine, morphine-3-glucuronide, and morphine-6-glucuronide in plasma and cerebrospinal fluid using solid-phase extraction and high-performance liquid chromatography with electrochemical detection, *Therapeutic Drug Monitoring*, 16, 200–208, 1994.

494. Rop, P. P., Grimaldi, F., Burle, J., De Saint Leger, M. N., and Viala, A., Determination of 6-monoacetylmorphine and morphine in plasma, whole blood and urine using high-performance liquid chromatography with electrochemical detection, *Journal of Chromatography B: Biomedical Applications*, 661, 245–253, 1994.

495. Yoo, Y. C., Chung, H. S., Kim, I. S., Jin, W. T., and Kim, M. K., Determination of nalbuphine in drug abusers' urine, *Journal of Analytical Toxicology*, 19, 120–123, 1995.

496. McManus, K. T., deBethizy, J. D., Garteiz, D. A., Kyerematen, G. A., and Vesell, E. S., A new quantitative thermospray LC-MS method for nicotine and its metabolites in biological fluids, *Journal of Chromatographic Science*, 28, 510–516, 1990.

497. Cooper, D. A. and Moore, J. M., Femtogram on-column detection of nicotine by isotope dilution gas chromatography/negative ion detection mass spectrometry, *Biological Mass Spectrometry*, 22, 590–594, 1993.

498. Deutsch, J., Hegedus, L., Greig, N. H., Rapoport, S. I., and Soncrant, T. T., Electron-impact and chemical ionization detection of nicotine and cotinine by gas chromatography-mass spectrometry in rat plasma and brain, *Journal of Chromatography*, 579, 93–98, 1992.

499. Lesko, L. and Miller, A., Rapid GC method for quantitation of nifedipine in serum using electron-capture detection, *Journal of Chromatographic Science*, 21, 415–419, 1983.

500. Ohkubo, T., Noro, H., and Sugawara, K., High-performance liquid chromatographic determination of nifedipine and a trace photodegradation product in hospital prescriptions, *Journal of Pharmaceutical & Biomedical Analysis*, 10, 67–70, 1992.

501. Nitsche, V., Schuetz, H., and Eichinger, A., Rapid high-performance liquid chromatographic determination of nifedipine in plasma with on-line precolumn solid-phase extraction, *Journal of Chromatography*, 420, 207–211, 1987.

502. Martens, J., Banditt, P., and Meyer, F. P., Determination of nifedipine in human serum by gas chromatography-mass spectrometry: validation of the method and its use in bioavailability studies, *Journal of Chromatography B: Biomedical Applications*, 660, 297–302, 1994.

503. Kintz, P., Cirimele, V., Vayssette, F., and Mangin, P., Hair analysis for nordiazepam and oxazepam by gas chromatography—negative-ion chemical ionization mass spectrometry, *Journal of Chromatography B: Biomedical Applications*, 677, 241–244, 1996.

504. Dickson, P. H., Lind, A., Studts, P., Nipper, H. C., Makoid, M., and Therkildsen, D., The routine analysis of breast milk for drugs of abuse in a clinical toxicology laboratory, *Journal of Forensic Sciences*, 39, 207–214, 1994.

505. Smith, M. L., Hughes, R. O., Levine, B., Dickerson, S., Darwin, W. D., and Cone, E. J., Forensic drug testing for opiates. VI. Urine testing for hydromorphone, hydrocodone, oxymorphone, and oxycodone with commercial opiate immunoassays and gas chromatography-mass spectrometry, *Journal of Analytical Toxicology*, 19, 18–26, 1995.

506. Drummer, O. H., Syrjanen, M. L., Phelan, M., and Cordner, S. M., A study of deaths involving oxycodone, *Journal of Forensic Sciences*, 39, 1069–1075, 1994.

507. Poklis, A. and Melanson, E. G., A suicide by pancuronium bromide injection: evaluation of the fluorometric determination of pancuronium in postmortem blood, serum and urine, *Journal of Analytical Toxicology*, 4, 275–280, 1980.

508. Briglia, E. J., Davis, P. L., Katz, M., and Dal Cortivo, L. A., Attempted murder with pancuronium, *Journal of Forensic Sciences*, 35, 1468–1476, 1990.

509. Paul, B. D., Dreka, C., Knight, E. S., and Smith, M. L., Gas chromatographic mass spectrometric detection of narcotine, papaverine, and thebaine in seeds of *Papaver somniferum*, *Planta Medica*, 62, 544–547, 1996.

510. Eap, C. B. and Baumann, P., Analytical methods for the quantitative determination of selective serotonin reuptake inhibitors for therapeutic drug monitoring purposes in patients [Review], *Journal of Chromatography B: Biomedical Applications*, 686, 51–63, 1996.

511. Miceli, J. N., Bowman, D. B., and Aravind, M. K., An improved method for the quantitation of phencyclidine (PCP) in biological samples utilizing nitrogen-detection gas chromatography, *Journal of Analytical Toxicology*, 5, 29–32, 1981.

512. Kintz, P., Tracqui, A., Lugnier, A. J., Mangin, P., and Chaumont, A. A., Simultaneous screening and quantification of several nonopiate narcotic analgesics and phencyclidine in human plasma using capillary gas chromatography, *Methods & Findings in Experimental & Clinical Pharmacology*, 12, 193–196, 1990.

513. Holsztynska, E. J. and Domino, E. F., Quantitation of phencyclidine, its metabolites, and derivatives by gas chromatography with nitrogen-phosphorus detection: application for in vivo and in vitro biotransformation studies, *Journal of Analytical Toxicology*, 10, 107–115, 1986.

514. Slawson, M. H., Wilkins, D. G., Foltz, R. L., and Rollins, D. E., Quantitative determination of phencyclidine in pigmented and nonpigmented hair by ion-trap mass spectrometry, *Journal of Analytical Toxicology*, 20, 350–354, 1996.

515. Kidwell, D. A., Analysis of phencyclidine and cocaine in human hair by tandem mass spectrometry, *Journal of Forensic Sciences*, 38, 272–284, 1993.

516. Jin, X., Zhou, Z. H., He, X. F., Zhang, Z. H., and Wang, M. Z., [Solid-phase extraction and RP-HPLC screening procedure for diuretics, probenecid, caffeine and pemoline in urine]. [Chinese], *Yao Hsueh Hsueh Pao—Acta Pharmaceutica Sinica*, 27, 875–880, 1992.

517. Mackell, M. A. and Poklis, A., Determination of pentazocine and tripelennamine in blood of T's and Blue addicts by gas-liquid chromatography with a nitrogen detector, *Journal of Chromatography*, 235, 445–452, 1982.

518. Poklis, A. and Mackell, M. A., Pentazocine and tripelennamine (T's and Blues) abuse: toxicological findings in 39 cases, *Journal of Analytical Toxicology*, 6, 109–114, 1982.

519. Poklis, A. and Mackell, M. A., Toxicological findings in deaths due to ingestion of pentazocine: a report of two cases, *Forensic Science International*, 20, 89–95, 1982.

520. Liu, R. H., McKeehan, A. M., Edwards, C., Foster, G., Bensley, W. D., Langner, J. G., et al., Improved GC/MS analysis of barbiturates in urine using centrifuge-based solid-phase extraction, methylation, with d5-pentobarbital as internal standard, *Journal of Forensic Science*, 39, 1504–1514, 1994.

521. Turley, C. P., Pentobarbital quantitation using immunoassays in Reye's syndrome patient serum, *Therapeutic Drug Monitoring*, 11, 343–346, 1989.

522. Earl, R., Sobeski, L., Timko, D., and Markin, R., Pentobarbital quantification in the presence of phenobarbital by fluorescence polarization immunoassay, *Clinical Chemistry*, 37, 1774–1777, 1991.

523. Li, P. K., Lee, J. T., and Schreiber, R. M., Rapid quantification of pentobarbital in serum by fluorescence polarization immunoassay, *Clinical Chemistry*, 30, 307–308, 1984.

524. Sarandis, S., Pichon, R., Miyada, D., and Pirkle, H., Quantitation of pentobarbital in serum by enzyme immunoassay, *Journal of Analytical Toxicology*, 8, 59–60, 1984.

525. Bowsher, R. R., Apathy, J. M., Compton, J. A., Wolen, R. L., Carlson, K. H., and DeSante, K. A., Sensitive, specific radioimmunoassay for quantifying pergolide in plasma, *Clinical Chemistry*, 38, 1975–1980, 1992

526. Shimamine, M., Takahashi, K., and Nakahara, Y., [Studies on the identification of psychotropic substances. IX. Preparation and various analytical data of reference standard of new psychotropic substances, N-ethyl methylenedioxyamphetamine, N-hydroxy methylenedioxyamphetamine, mecloqualone, 4-methylaminorex, phendimetrazine and phenmetrazine], *Eisei Shikenjo Hokoku—Bulletin of National Institute of Hygienic Sciences*, 66–74, 1993.

527. Moriyama, M., Furuno, K., Oishi, R., and Gomita, Y., Simultaneous determination of primidone and its active metabolites in rat plasma by high-performance liquid chromatography using a solid-phase extraction technique, *Journal of Pharmaceutical Sciences*, 83, 1751–1753, 1994.

528. Kouno, Y., Ishikura, C., Homma, M., and Oka, K., Simple and accurate high-performance liquid chromatographic method for the measurement of three antiepileptics in therapeutic drug monitoring, *Journal of Chromatography*, 622, 47–52, 1993.

529. Liu, H., Delgado, M., Forman, L. J., Eggers, C. M., and Montoya, J. L., Simultaneous determination of carbamazepine, phenytoin, phenobarbital, primidone and their principal metabolites by high-performance liquid chromatography with photodiode-array detection, *Journal of Chromatography*, 616, 105–115, 1993.

530. Binder, S. R., Adams, A. K., Regalia, M., Essien, H., and Rosenblum, R., Standardization of a multi-wavelength UV detector for liquid chromatography-based toxicological analysis, *Journal of Chromatography*, 550, 449–459, 1991.

531. Wu, A. H., Onigbinde, T. A., Wong, S. S., and Johnson, K. G., Identification of methamphetamines and over-the-counter sympathometic amines by full-scan GC-ion trap MS with electron impact and chemical ionization, *Journal of Analytical Toxicology*, 16, 137–141, 1992.

532. Cui, J. F., Zhou, Y., Cui, K. R., Li, L., and Zhou, T. H., [Study on metabolism of phenmetrazine-like drugs and their metabolites], *Yao Hsueh Hsueh Pao—Acta Pharmaceutica Sinica*, 25, 632–636, 1990.

533. Rambeck, B., May, T. W., Jurgens, M. U., Blankenhorn, V., Jurges, U., Korn-Merker, E., et al., Comparison of phenytoin and carbamazepine serum concentrations measured by high-performance liquid chromatography, the standard TDx assay, the enzyme multiplied immunoassay technique, and a new patient-side immunoassay cartridge system, *Therapeutic Drug Monitoring*, 16, 608–612, 1994.

534. Logan, B. K. and Stafford, D. T., Direct analysis of anticonvulsant drugs in vitreous humour by HPLC using a column switching technique, *Forensic Science International*, 41, 125–134, 1989.

535. Lensmeyer, G. L., Rajani, C., and Evenson, M. A., Liquid-chromatographic procedure for simultaneous analysis for eight benzodiazepines in serum, *Clinical Chemistry*, 28, 2274–2278, 1982.

536. Eadie, M. J., Formation of active metabolites of anticonvulsant drugs. A review of their pharmacokinetic and therapeutic significance. [Review] [86 refs.], *Clinical Pharmacokinetics*, 21, 27–41, 1991.

537. Streete, J. M. and Berry, D. J., Gas chromatographic analysis of phenylethylmalonamide in human plasma, *Journal of Chromatography*, 416, 281–291, 1987.

538. Kim, S. Y. and Benowitz, N. L., Poisoning due to class IA antiarrhythmic drugs. Quinidine, procainamide and disopyramide. [Review], *Drug Safety*, 5, 393–420, 1990.

539. Sonsalla, P. K., Bridges, R. R., Jennison, T. A., and Smith, C. M., An evaluation of the TDX fluorescence polarization immunoassays for procainamide and n-acetylprocainamide, *Journal of Analytical Toxicology*, 9, 152–155, 1985.

540. Bagli, M., Rao, M. L., and Hoflich, G., Quantification of chlorprothixene, levomepromazine and promethazine in human serum using high-performance liquid chromatography with coulometric electrochemical detection, *Journal of Chromatography B: Biomedical Applications*, 657, 141–148, 1994.

541. Bohm, R., Ellrich, R., and Koytchev, R., Quantitation of R- and S-propafenone and of the main metabolite in plasma, *Pharmazie*, 50, 542–545, 1995.

542. Botterblom, M. H., Feenstra, M. G., and Erdtsieck-Ernste, E. B., Determination of propranolol, labetalol and clenbuterol in rat brain by high-performance liquid chromatography, *Journal of Chromatography*, 613, 121–126, 1993.

543. Kwong, E. C. and Shen, D. D., Versatile isocratic high-performance liquid chromatographic assay for propranolol and its basic, neutral and acidic metabolites in biological fluids, *Journal of Chromatography*, 414, 365–379, 1987.

544. Lindner, W., Rath, M., Stoschitzky, K., and Uray, G., Enantioselective drug monitoring of (R)- and (S)- propranolol in human plasma via derivatization with optically active (R,R)-O,O-diacetyl tartaric acid anhydride, *Journal of Chromatography*, 487, 375–383, 1989.

545. Ehrsson, H., Identification of diastereomeric propranolol-o-glucuronides by GC/MS., *Journal of Pharmacy and Pharmacology*, 27, 971–973, 1975.

546. Ehrsson, H., Simultaneous determination of (–)- and (+)- propranolol by GC/MS using a deuterium labeling technique, *Journal of Pharmacy and Pharmacology*, 28, 662, 1976.

547. Altmayer, P., Buch, U., Buch, H. P., and Larsen, R., Rapid and sensitive pre-column extraction high-performance liquid chromatographic assay for propofol in biological fluids, *Journal of Chromatography*, 612, 326–330, 1993.

548. Guitton, J., Desage, M., Lepape, A., Degoute, C. S., Manchon, M., and Brazier, J. L., Quantitation of propofol in whole blood by gas chromatography-mass spectrometry, *Journal of Chromatography B: Biomedical Applications*, 669, 358–365, 1995.

549. Amalfitano, G., Bessard, J., Vincent, F., Eysseric, H., and Bessard, G., Gas chromatographic quantitation of dextropropoxyphene and norpropoxyphene in urine after solid-phase extraction, *Journal of Analytical Toxicology*, 20, 547–554, 1996.

550. Margot, P. A., Crouch, D. J., Finkle, B. S., Johnson, J. R., and Deyman, M. E., Capillary and packed column GC determination of propoxyphene and norpropoxyphene in biological specimens: analytical problems and improvements, *Journal of Chromatographic Science*, 21, 201–204, 1983.

551. Wolen, R. L., Gruber, C. M., Jr., Baptisti, A., Jr., and Scholz, N. E., The concentration of propoxyphene in the plasma and analgesia scores in postpartum patients, *Toxicology & Applied Pharmacology*, 19, 498–503, 1971.

552. Wolen, R. L. and Gruber, C. M., Jr., Determination of propoxyphene in human plasma by gas chromatography, *Analytical Chemistry*, 40, 1243–1246, 1968.

553. Wolen, R. L., Obermeyer, B. D., Ziege, E. A., Black, H. R., and Gruber, C. M., Jr., Drug metabolism and pharmacokinetic studies in man utilising nitrogen-15- and deuterium-labelled drugs: the metabolic fate of cinoxacin and the metabolism and pharmacokinetics of propoxyphene, In: Baillie, T. A., Ed., *Stable Isotopes*, Baltimore, University Park Press, QV, 20, 1978.

554. Wolen, R. L., Ziege, E. A., and Gruber, C., Jr., Determination of propoxyphene and norpropoxyphene by chemical ionization mass fragmentography, *Clinical Pharmacology & Therapeutics*, 17, 15–20, 1975.

555. Nash, J. F., Bennett, I. F., Bopp, R. J., Brunson, M. K., and Sullivan, H. R., Quantitation of propoxyphene and its major metabolites in heroin addict plasma after large dose administration of propoxyphene napsylate, *Journal of Pharmaceutical Sciences*, 64, 429–433, 1975.

556. Wolen, R. L., Ziege, E. A., and Gruber, C. M., Determination of propoxyphene and norpropoxyphene by chemical ionization mass fragmentography., *Clinical Pharmacological Therapy*, 17, 15–20, 1974.

557. Flanagan, R. J., Johnston, A., White, A. S., and Crome, P., Pharmacokinetics of dextropropoxyphene and nordextropropoxyphene in young and elderly volunteers after single and multiple dextropropoxyphene dosage, *British Journal of Clinical Pharmacology*, 28, 463–469, 1989.

558. Kaa, E. and Dalgaard, J. B., Fatal dextropropoxyphene poisonings in Jutland, Denmark, *Zeitschrift für Rechtsmedizin—Journal of Legal Medicine*, 102, 107–115, 1989.

559. Kintz, P. and Mangin, P., Abbott propoxyphene assay: evaluation and comparison of TDx FPIA and GC/MS methods, *Journal of Analytical Toxicology*, 17, 222–224, 1993.

560. Preskorn, S. H. and Fast, G. A., Therapeutic drug monitoring for antidepressants: efficacy, safety, and cost effectiveness [published erratum appears in *Journal of Clinical Psychiatry*, 52, 353, 1992]. [Review], *Journal of Clinical Psychiatry*, 52, 23–33, 1991.

561. Power, B. M., Hackett, L. P., Dusci, L. J., and Ilett, K. F., Antidepressant toxicity and the need for identification and concentration monitoring in overdose. [Review], *Clinical Pharmacokinetics*, 29, 154–171, 1995.

562. Henry, J. A., Alexander, C. A., and Sener, E. K., Relative mortality from overdose of antidepressants [see comments] [published erratum appears in *British Medical Journal*, 8, 310(6984):911, 1995], *British Medical Journal*, 310, 221–224, 1995.

563. Rao, M. L., Staberock, U., Baumann, P., Hiemke, C., Deister, A., Cuendet, C., et al., Monitoring tricyclic antidepressant concentrations in serum by fluorescence polarization immunoassay compared with gas chromatography and HPLC, *Clinical Chemistry*, 40, 929–933, 1994.

564. Poklis, A., Soghoian, D., Crooks, C. R., and Saady, J. J., Evaluation of the Abbott ADx total serum tricyclic immunoassay, *Journal of Toxicology Clinical Toxicology*, 28, 235–248, 1990.

565. Brooks, K. E. and Smith, N. S., Lack of formation of methamphetamine-like artifacts by the monoacetates of pseudoephedrine and related compounds in the GC/MS analysis of urine extracts [letter], *Journal of Analytical Toxicology*, 17, 441–442, 1993.

566. Yeh, S. Y., N-depyridination and N-dedimethylaminoethylation of tripelennamine and pyrilamine in the rat, *Drug Metabolism & Disposition*, 18, 453–461, 1990.

567. Bun, H., Coassolo, P., Ba, B., Aubert, C., and Cano, J. P., Plasma quantification of quazepam and its 2-oxo and N-desmethyl metabolites by capillary gas chromatography, *Journal of Chromatography*, 378, 137–145, 1986.

568. Gupta, S. K. and Ellinwood, E. H., Jr., Liquid chromatographic assay and pharmacokinetics of quazepam and its metabolites following sublingual administration of quazepam, *Pharmaceutical Research*, 5, 365–368, 1988.

569. Kales, A., Quazepam: hypnotic efficacy and side effects. [Review] [137 refs.], *Pharmacotherapy*, 10, 1–10, 1990.

570. Brandsteterova, E., Romanova, D., Kralikova, D., Bozekova, L., and Kriska, M., Automatic solid-phase extraction and high-performance liquid chromatographic determination of quinidine in plasma, *Journal of Chromatography A*, 665, 101–104, 1994.

571. Cosbey, S. H., Craig, I., and Gill, R., Novel solid-phase extraction strategy for the isolation of basic drugs from whole blood, *Journal of Chromatography B: Biomedical Applications*, 669, 229–235, 1995.

572. Lloyd, T. L., Perschy, T. B., Gooding, A. E., and Tomlinson, J. J., Robotic solid phase extraction and high performance liquid chromatographic analysis of ranitidine in serum or plasma, *Biomedical Chromatography*, 6, 311–316, 1992.

573. Karnes, H. T., Opong-Mensah, K., Farthing, D., and Beightol, L. A., Automated solid-phase extraction and high-performance liquid chromatographic determination of ranitidine from urine, plasma and peritoneal dialysate, *Journal of Chromatography*, 422, 165–173, 1987.

574. Aravagiri, M., Marder, S. R., Van Putten, T., and Midha, K. K., Determination of risperidone in plasma by high-performance liquid chromatography with electrochemical detection: application to therapeutic drug monitoring in schizophrenic patients, *Journal of Pharmaceutical Sciences*, 82, 447–449, 1993.

575. Le Moing, J. P., Edouard, S., and Levron, J. C., Determination of risperidone and 9-hydroxyrisperidone in human plasma by high-performance liquid chromatography with electrochemical detection, *Journal of Chromatography*, 614, 333–339, 1993.

576. Borison, R. L., Diamond, B., Pathiraja, A., and Meibach, R. C., Pharmacokinetics of risperidone in chronic schizophrenic patients, *Psychopharmacology Bulletin*, 30, 193–197, 1994.

577. Springfield, A. C. and Bodiford, E., An overdose of risperidone, *Journal of Analytical Toxicology*, 20, 202–203, 1996.

578. Deutsch, J., Soncrant, T. T., Greig, N. H., and Rapoport, S. I., Electron-impact ionization detection of scopolamine by gas chromatography-mass spectrometry in rat plasma and brain, *Journal of Chromatography*, 528, 325–331, 1990.

579. Oertel, R., Richter, K., Ebert, U., and Kirch, W., Determination of scopolamine in human serum by gas chromatography ion trap tandem mass spectrometry, *Journal of Chromatography B: Biomedical Applications*, 682, 259–264, 1996.

580. Quatrehomme, G., Bourret, F., Zhioua, M., Lapalus, P., and Ollier, A., Post mortem kinetics of secobarbital, *Forensic Science International*, 44, 117–123, 1990.

581. Sharp, M. E., Wallace, S. M., Hindmarsh, K. W., and Peel, H. W., Monitoring saliva concentrations of methaqualone, codeine, secobarbital, diphenhydramine and diazepam after single oral doses, *Journal of Analytical Toxicology*, 7, 11–14, 1983.

582. Paetsch, P. R., Baker, G. B., Caffaro, L. E., Greenshaw, A. J., Rauw, G. A., and Coutts, R. T., Electron-capture gas chromatographic procedure for simultaneous determination of amphetamine and N-methylamphetamine, *Journal of Chromatography*, 573, 313–317, 1992.

583. La Croix, R., Pianezzola, E., and Strolin Benedetti, M., Sensitive high-performance liquid chromatographic method for the determination of the three main metabolites of selegiline (L-deprenyl) in human plasma, *Journal of Chromatography B: Biomedical Applications*, 656, 251–258, 1994.

584. Maurer, H. H. and Kraemer, T., Toxicological detection of selegiline and its metabolites in urine using fluorescence polarization immunoassay (FPIA) and gas chromatography-mass spectrometry (GC-MS) and differentiation by enantioselective GC-MS of the intake of selegiline from abuse of methamphetamine or amphetamine, *Archives of Toxicology*, 66, 675–678, 1992.

585. Reimer, M. L., Mamer, O. A., Zavitsanos, A. P., Siddiqui, A. W., and Dadgar, D., Determination of amphetamine, methamphetamine and desmethyldeprenyl in human plasma by gas chromatography/negative ion chemical ionization mass spectrometry, *Biological Mass Spectrometry*, 22, 235–242, 1993,

586. Meeker, J. E. and Reynolds, P. C., Postmortem tissue methamphetamine concentrations following selegiline administration, *Journal of Analytical Toxicology*, 14, 330–331, 1990.

587. Rogowsky, D., Marr, M., Long, G., and Moore, C., Determination of sertraline and desmethylsertraline in human serum using copolymeric bonded-phase extraction, liquid chromatography and GC/MS, *Journal of Chromatography B: Biomedical Applications*, 655, 138–141, 1994.

588. De Saqui-Sannes, P., Nups, P., Le Bars, P., and Burgat, V., Evaluation of an HPTLC method for the determination of strychnine and crimidine in biological samples, *Journal of Analytical Toxicology*, 20, 185–188, 1996.

589. Stevens, H. M. and Moffat, A. C., A rapid screening procedure for quaternary ammonium compounds in fluids and tissues with special reference to suxamethonium (succinylcholine), *Journal of the Forensic Science Society*, 14, 141–148, 1974.

590. Forney, R. B., Jr., Carroll, F. T., Nordgren, I. K., Pettersson, B. M., and Holmstedt, B., Extraction, identification and quantitation of succinylcholine in embalmed tissue, *Journal of Analytical Toxicology*, 6, 115–119, 1982.

591. Woestenborghs, R. J., Timmerman, P. M., Cornelissen, M. L., Van Rompaey, F. A., Gepts, E., Camu, F., et al., Assay methods for sufentanil in plasma. Radioimmunoassay versus gas chromatography-mass spectrometry, *Anesthesiology*, 80, 666–670, 1994.

592. Rochholz, G., Ahrens, B., Konig, F., Schutz, H. W., Schutz, H., and Seno, H., Screening and identification of sumatriptan and its main metabolite by means of thin-layer chromatography, ultraviolet spectroscopy and gas chromatography/mass spectrometry, *Arzneimittel-Forschung*, 45, 941–946, 1995.

593. Qiu, F. H., Liu, L., Guo, L., Luo, Y., and Lu, Y. Q., [Rapid identification and quantitation of barbiturates in plasma using solid-phase extraction combined with GC-FID and GC-MS method]. [Chinese], *Yao Hsueh Hsueh Pao—Acta Pharmaceutica Sinica*, 30, 372–377, 1995.

594. Laakkonen, U. M., Leinonen, A., and Savonen, L., Screening of non-steroidal anti-inflammatory drugs, barbiturates and methyl xanthines in equine urine by gas chromatography-mass spectrometry, *Analyst*, 119, 2695–2696, 1994.

595. Tjaden, U. R., Meeles, M. T., Thys, C. P., and van der Kaay, M., Determination of some benzodiazepines and metabolites in serum, urine and saliva by high-performance liquid chromatography, *Journal of Chromatography*, 181, 227–241, 1980.

596. Pounder, D. J., Adams, E., Fuke, C., and Langford, A. M., Site to site variability of postmortem drug concentrations in liver and lung, *Journal of Forensic Sciences*, 41, 927–932, 1996.

597. Walash, M. I., Belal, F., Metwally, M. E., and Hefnawy, M. M., A selective fluorimetric method for the determination of some 1,4-benzodiazepine drugs containing a hydroxyl group at C-3, *Journal of Pharmaceutical & Biomedical Analysis*, 12, 1417–1423, 1994.

598. McCarthy, P., Atwal, S., Sykes, A., and Ayres, J., Measurement of terbutaline and salbutamol in plasma by high performance liquid chromatography with fluorescence detection, *Biomedical Chromatography*, 7, 25–28, 1993.

599. Van Vyncht, G., Preece, S., Gaspar, P., Maghuin-Rogister, G., and DePauw, E., Gas and liquid chromatography coupled to tandem mass spectrometry for the multiresidue analysis of beta-agonists in biological matrices, *Journal of Chromatography A*, 750, 43–49, 1996.

600. Lindberg, C., Paulson, J., and Blomqvist, A., Evaluation of an automated thermospray liquid chromatography-mass spectrometry system for quantitative use in bioanalytical chemistry, *Journal of Chromatography*, 554, 215–226, 1991.

601. Altieri, M., Bogema, S., and Schwartz, R. H., TAC topical anesthesia produces positive urine tests for cocaine, *Annals of Emergency Medicine*, 19, 577–579, 1990.

602. Hannak, D., Haux, P., Scharbert, F., and Kattermann, R., Liquid chromatographic analysis of phenobarbital, phenytoin, and theophylline, *Wiener Klinische Wochenschrift. Supplementum*, 191, 27–31, 1992.

603. Mounie, J., Richard, L., Ribon, B., Hersant, J., Sarmini, H., Houin, G., et al., Methods of theophylline assay and therapeutic monitoring of this drug [published erratum appears in *Annales de Biologie Clinique* (Paris) 48, 447, 1990]. [Review], *Annales de Biologie Clinique*, 48, 287–293, 1990.

604. Zaninotto, M., Secchiero, S., Paleari, C. D., and Burlina, A., Performance of a fluorescence polarization immunoassay system evaluated by therapeutic monitoring of four drugs, *Therapeutic Drug Monitoring*, 14, 301–305, 1992.

605. Jones, L. A., Gonzalez, E. R., Venitz, J., Edinboro, L. E., and Poklis, A., Evaluation of the Vision Theophylline assays in the emergency department setting, *Annals of Emergency Medicine*, 21, 777–781, 1992.

606. Sessler, C. N., Theophylline toxicity: clinical features of 116 consecutive cases. [Review], *American Journal of Medicine*, 88, 567–576, 1990.

607. el-Sayed, Y. M. and Islam, S. I., Comparison of fluorescence polarization immunoassay and HPLC for the determination of theophylline in serum, *Journal of Clinical Pharmacy & Therapeutics*, 14, 127–134, 1989.

608. Costantino, A. G., Caplan, Y. H., Levine, B. S., Dixon, A. M., and Smialek, J. E., Thiamylal: review of the literature and report of a suicide, *Journal of Forensic Sciences*, 35, 89–96, 1990.

609. Stockham, T. L., McGee, M. P., and Stajic, M., Report of a fatal thiamylal intoxication, *Journal of Analytical Toxicology*, 15, 155–156, 1991.

610. Yashiki, M., Kojima, T., and Okamoto, I., Toxicological study on intravenous thiopental anesthesia—interrelation between rate of injection and distribution of thiopental, *Forensic Science International*, 33, 169–175, 1987.

611. Garriott, J. C., Foerster, E., Juarez, L., de la Garza, F., Mendiola, I., and Curoe, J., Measurement of toluene in blood and breath in cases of solvent abuse, *Clinical Toxicology*, 18, 471–479, 1981.

612. Inoue, H., Iwasa, M., Maeno, Y., Koyama, H., Sato, Y., and Matoba, R., Detection of toluene in an adipoceratous body, *Forensic Science International*, 78, 119–124, 1996.

613. Kawai, T., Mizunuma, K., Yasugi, T., Horiguchi, S., and Ikeda, M., Toluene in blood as a marker of choice for low-level exposure to toluene, *International Archives of Occupational & Environmental Health*, 66, 309–315, 1994.

614. Jones, A. D., Dunlap, M. R., and Gospe, S. M., Jr., Stable-isotope dilution GC-MS for determination of toluene in submilliliter volumes of whole blood, *Journal of Analytical Toxicology*, 18, 251–254, 1994.

615. Von Burg, R., Toluene. [Review] [85 refs.], *Journal of Applied Toxicology*, 13, 441–446, 1993.

616. Lof, A., Wigaeus Hjelm, E., Colmsjo, A., Lundmark, B. O., Norstrom, A., and Sato, A., Toxicokinetics of toluene and urinary excretion of hippuric acid after human exposure to 2H8-toluene, *British Journal of Industrial Medicine*, 50, 55–59, 1993.

617. Saker, E. G., Eskew, A. E., and Panter, J. W., Stability of toluene in blood: its forensic relevance, *Journal of Analytical Toxicology*, 15, 246–249, 1991.

618. Xu, Y. X., Xu, Y. Q., Zhang, C. J., and Shen, L., [Analysis of tramadol and its metabolites in human urine]. [Chinese], *Yao Hsueh Hsueh Pao—Acta Pharmaceutica Sinica*, 28, 379–383, 1993.

619. Anderson, W. H. and Archuleta, M. M., The capillary gas chromatographic determination of trazodone in biological specimens, *Journal of Analytical Toxicology*, 8, 217–219, 1984.

620. Caccia, S., Ballabio, M., Fanelli, R., Guiso, G., and Zanini, M. G., Determination of plasma and brain concentrations of trazodone and its metabolite, 1-m-chlorophenylpiperazine, by gas-liquid chromatography, *Journal of Chromatography*, 210, 311–318, 1981.

621. Lambert, W., Van Bocxlaer, J., Piette, M., and De Leenheer, A., A fatal case of trazodone and dothiepin poisoning: toxicological findings, *Journal of Analytical Toxicology*, 18, 176–179, 1994.

622. Senda, N., Kohta, K., Takahashi, T., Shizukuishi, K., Mimura, T., Fujita, T., et al., A highly sensitive method to quantify triazolam and its metabolites with liquid chromatography—mass spectrometry, *Biomedical Chromatography*, 9, 48–51, 1995.

623. Joynt, B. P., Triazolam blood concentrations in forensic cases in Canada, *Journal of Analytical Toxicology*, 17, 171–177, 1993.

624. Koves, G. and Wells, J., The quantitation of triazolam in postmortem blood by gas chromatography/negative ion chemical ionization mass spectrometry, *Journal of Analytical Toxicology*, 10, 241–244, 1986.

625. Kostrzewski, P., Jakubowski, M., and Kolacinski, Z., Kinetics of trichloroethylene elimination from venous blood after acute inhalation poisoning, *Journal of Toxicology—Clinical Toxicology*, 31, 353–363, 1993.

626. Kintz, P., Godelar, B., Mangin, P., Chaumont, A. J., and Lugnier, A. A., Identification and quantification of trihexyphenidyl and its hydroxylated metabolite by gas chromatography with nitrogen-phosphorus detection, *Journal of Analytical Toxicology*, 13, 47–49, 1989.

627. Maurer, H. H., Detection of anticonvulsants and their metabolites in urine within a "general unknown" analytical procedure using computerized GC/MS, *Archives of Toxicology*, 64, 554–561, 1990.

628. Jones, R., Klette, K., Kuhlman, J. J., Levine, B., Smith, M. L., Watson, C. V., et al., Trimethobenzamide cross-reacts in immunoassays of amphetamine/methamphetamine [letter; see comments], *Clinical Chemistry*, 39, 699–700, 1993.

629. Colbert, D. L., Possible explanation for trimethobenzamide cross-reaction in immunoassays of amphetamine/methamphetamine [letter; comment], *Clinical Chemistry*, 40, 948–949, 1994.

630. Pok Phak, R., Conquy, T., Gouezo, F., Viala, A., and Grimaldi, F., Determination of metapramine, imipramine, trimipramine and their major metabolites in plasma by reversed-phase column liquid chromatography, *Journal of Chromatography*, 375, 339–347, 1986.

631. Fraser, A. D., Isner, A. F., and Perry, R. A., Distribution of trimipramine and its major metabolites in a fatal overdose case, *Journal of Analytical Toxicology*, 11, 168–170, 1987.

632. Poklis, A., Case, M. E., and Ridenour, G. C., Abuse of pentazocine/tripelennamine combination. Ts and Blues in the city of St. Louis, *Missouri Medicine*, 80, 21–23, 1983.

633. Pokrajac, M., Miljkovic, B., Spiridonovic, D., and Varagic, V. M., An improved gas chromatographic determination of valproic acid and valpromide in plasma, *Pharmaceutica Acta Helvetiae*, 67, 237–240, 1992.

634. Vajda, F. J., Drummer, O. H., Morris, P. M., McNeil, J. J., and Bladin, P. F., Gas chromatographic measurement of plasma levels of sodium valproate: tentative therapeutic range of a new anticonvulsant in the treatment of refractory epileptics, *Clinical & Experimental Pharmacology & Physiology*, 5, 67–73, 1978.

635. Berry, D. J. and Clarke, L. A., Determination of valproic acid (dipropylacetic acid) in plasma by gas-liquid chromatography, *Journal of Chromatography*, 156, 301–307, 1978.

636. Liu, H., Montoya, J. L., Forman, L. J., Eggers, C. M., Barham, C. F., and Delgado, M., Determination of free valproic acid: evaluation of the Centrifree system and comparison between high-performance liquid chromatography and enzyme immunoassay, *Therapeutic Drug Monitoring*, 14, 513–521, 1992.

637. Liu, H., Forman, L. J., Montoya, J., Eggers, C., Barham, C., and Delgado, M., Determination of valproic acid by high-performance liquid chromatography with photodiode-array and fluorescence detection, *Journal of Chromatography*, 576, 163–169, 1992.

638. Yu, D., Gordon, J. D., Zheng, J., Panesar, S. K., Riggs, K. W., Rurak, D. W., et al., Determination of valproic acid and its metabolites using gas chromatography with mass-selective detection: application to serum and urine samples from sheep, *Journal of Chromatography B: Biomedical Applications*, 666, 269–281, 1995.

639. Dupuis, R. E., Lichtman, S. N., and Pollack, G. M., Acute valproic acid overdose, *Drug Safety*, 5, 65–71, 1990.

640. Levine, B., Jenkins, A. J., Queen, M., Jufer, R., and Smialek, J. E., Distribution of venlafaxine in three postmortem cases, *Journal of Analytical Toxicology*, 20, 502–505, 1996.

641. Parsons, A. T., Anthony, R. M., and Meeker, J. E., Two fatal cases of venlafaxine poisoning, *Journal of Analytical Toxicology*, 20, 266–268, 1996.

642. Shin, H. S., Ohshin, Y. S., Kim, H. J., and Kang, Y. K., Sensitive assay for verapamil in plasma using gas-liquid chromatography with nitrogen-phosphorus detection, *Journal of Chromatography B: Biomedical Applications*, 677, 369–373, 1996.

643. Levine, B., Jones, R., Klette, K., Smith, M. L., and Kilbane, E., An intoxication involving BRON and verapamil, *Journal of Analytical Toxicology*, 17, 381–383, 1993.

644. Crouch, D. J., Crompton, C., Rollins, D. E., Peat, M. A., and Francom, P., Toxicological findings in a fatal overdose of verapamil, *Journal of Forensic Sciences*, 31, 1505–1508, 1986.

645. Ashraf, M., Chaudhary, K., Nelson, J., and Thompson, W., Massive overdose of sustained-release verapamil—a case report and review of literature, *American Journal of the Medical Sciences*, 310, 258–263, 1995.

646. Brogden, R. N. and Benfield, P., Verapamil—a review of its pharmacological properties and therapeutic use in coronary artery disease [review], *Drugs*, 51, 792–819, 1996.

647. Akisu, M., Mir, S., Genc, B., and Cura, A., Severe acute thinner intoxication, *Turkish Journal of Pediatrics*, 38, 223–225, 1996.

648. Etzel, R. A. and Ashley, D. L., Volatile organic compounds in the blood of persons in Kuwait during the oil fires, *International Archives of Occupational & Environmental Health*, 66, 125–129, 1994.

649. Mannino, D. M., Schreiber, J., Aldous, K., Ashley, D., Moolenaar, R., and Almaguer, D., Human exposure to volatile organic compounds: a comparison of organic vapor monitoring badge levels with blood levels, *International Archives of Occupational & Environmental Health*, 67, 59–64, 1995.

650. Ramsey, J., Anderson, H. R., Bloor, K., and Flanagan, R. J., An introduction to the practice, prevalence and chemical toxicology of volatile substance abuse, *Human Toxicology*, 8, 261–269, 1989.

651. Stanke, F., Jourdil, N., Lauby, V., and Bessard, G., Zopiclone and zolpidem quantification in human plasma by high performance liquid chromatography with photodiode-array detection, *Journal of Liquid Chromatography & Related Technologies*, 19, 2623–2633, 1996.

652. Meeker, J. E., Som, C. W., Macapagal, E. C., and Benson, P. A., Zolpidem tissue concentrations in a multiple drug related death involving Ambien, *Journal of Analytical Toxicology*, 19, 531–534, 1995.

653. Ahrens, B., Schutz, H., Seno, H., and Weiler, G., Screening, identification and determination of the two new hypnotics zolpidem and zopiclone, *Arzneimittel-Forschung*, 44, 799–802, 1994.

654. Tracqui, A., Kintz, P., and Mangin, P., High-performance liquid chromatographic assay with diode-array detection for toxicological screening of zopiclone, zolpidem, suriclone and alpidem in human plasma, *Journal of Chromatography*, 616, 95–103, 1993.

655. Debailleul, G., Khalil, F. A., and Lheureux, P., HPLC quantification of zolpidem and prothipendyl in a voluntary intoxication, *Journal of Analytical Toxicology*, 15, 35–37, 1991.

APPENDIX II: SAMPLE CALCULATIONS

Barry K. Logan, Ph.D.
Director, Washington State Toxicology Laboratory, Department of Laboratory Medicine, University of Washington, Seattle, Washington

Alan Wayne Jones, D.Sc.
Department of Forensic Toxicology, University Hospital, Linköping, Sweden

This section presents some typical scenarios based on authentic DUI cases, and the application of some of the issues discussed in Chapter 13. Bear in mind that statutory "per se" alcohol limits are somewhat arbitrary, and that a person's driving might be influenced below the so-called "legal limit." For this reason, the quantitative measurement of blood or breath alcohol, and related calculations, should be one element of any DUI case, and not the entire case.

Example 1. The defendant (male, 175 lb) had been drinking for 3 h, but gulps down a "double vodka," (assumed to be 2 oz of 40% v/v) immediately before leaving the bar, and is arrested for DUI 15 min later. His BrAC 30 min after arrest is 0.10 g/210 L. Could his BrAC have been below 0.08 at the time of driving?

This question relates to the significance of the last drink as a factor in raising the BrAC. Since this pattern of drinking represents a small bolus on top of a pre-existing BrAC, it is likely that the last drink was substantially absorbed within 15 min, i.c., at the time of the arrest. The small amount of alcohol unabsorbed would not be enough to account for the difference between 0.08 and 0.10 g/210 L. Note that no allowance was made for alcohol metabolism (often called burn-off) in this example. Assuming some alcohol elimination occurred between the time of the arrest and the breath test, this would make it even less likely that the BrAC at the time of the arrest was below 0.08 g/210 L.

It is possible to construct a scenario whereby the defendant's version could be supported, and might involve some kind of delayed gastric emptying, an unusually low volume of distribution for the alcohol, and a low alcohol elimination rate. This latter scenario, however, is much less likely than the former, and needs to be evaluated in the context of other available information in the case. For example, what was the reason for the driver being stopped in the first place? These situations require the application of some scientific common sense, and the principle of Occam's razor, namely that the fewer assumptions one has to invoke to explain a set of facts, the more likely that explanation is. Note also that intra-individual variations in absorption and elimination of alcohol make any kind of reconstruction or repeat of the circumstances in question of dubious value.

Example 2. The defendant (male, 230 lb) claims he consumed ten 12-oz beers of 4.2% v/v alcohol content in 1 h, then drove immediately afterward, and was arrested 10 min after his last drink. The BrAC was 0.17 g/210 L, 1 h later. Could the suspect's BrAC have been below 0.10 g/210 L at the time of driving?

In this scenario, one has to make fewer assumptions in order for the defendant's BrAC to be below 0.10 g/210 L at the time of driving. Absorption of alcohol after drinking so much beer could result in a delayed peak. The drinking pattern is unusual, however, based on Widmark's formula it could account for the measured BrAC. Credible corroboration of the defendant's story would be important in presenting this case to the jury, and would have to be considered in the context of other evidence of his behavior, his driving, his statements at the time of arrest, etc. It has to be said that even if true, this pattern of drinking followed by driving is not likely to engender much sympathy from the jury.

Example 3. The defendant (male, 150 lb) admits to having a few drinks before an accident, but alleges he drank 4 oz of 40% v/v whisky to steady his nerves after the accident. His BAC at the time of blood sampling about 1 h later was 0.15 g/dL. Could his BAC at the time of the accident have been below 0.08 g/dL?

This scenario relates to whether the contribution from post-accident drinking can account for the difference between the measured BAC and an administrative legal limit. According to Widmark's formula, the contribution to BAC from the post-accident drinking would be approximately 0.08 g/dL. Given the uncertainty in this estimate (~0.06 to 0.09 g/dL), there is a significant possibility that he could have been below 0.08 g/dL at the time of the accident. Important factors to consider would be the accuracy of the estimate of how much post-accident drinking actually took place (if indeed it did), the actual times of the accident and blood sampling, and some corroboration of the pre-accident drinking pattern. A large amount of drinking immediately before the accident could further raise the likelihood of the BAC being below 0.08 at the time of the accident. In some countries, drinking within a certain time period after an accident is itself considered a punishable offense, and certainly displays poor judgment on the part of the defendant.

Example 4. Defendant (male, 230 lb) is arrested and an evidential breath test shows 0.21 g/210 L. He claims he only consumed two 16-oz beers over a 3-h period. Application of Widmark's formula shows that the volume of beer required to produce this BrAC is about 230 oz of 3.5% v/v beer. How can this discrepancy be resolved?

The defendant maintains that the discrepancy suggests a malfunction in the breath test instrument. This comes down to an evaluation of the credibility of the defendant's story against the accuracy and reliability of the breath test. Safeguards followed when conducting the breath test, such as duplicate testing, room air blank tests, and simulator control tests with each subject test, will help to validate the accuracy of the result. Again, other factors such as the defendant's driving pattern, performance in field sobriety tests, and behavior at the time of the arrest will either help or hurt his story. It is the experience of most people working in this field that defendants will invariably underestimate their actual consumption, and may not recall the brand of beer or liquor they were drinking.

Example 5. The defendant (female 120 lb) leaves the scene of an accident, but is eventually arrested and a blood sample is collected 4 h later. Her BAC at the time of sampling is 0.05 g/dL. What was her BAC at the time of the accident ?

This is a clear-cut case regarding the validity of retrograde extrapolation, or estimating back. If one assumes that the defendant was fully post-absorptive at the time of the accident, estimating back 4 h and allowing a mean burn-off rate of 0.019 g/dL/h (with a range from 0.009 g/dL/h to 0.030 g/dL/h) would produce a most likely BAC of 0.126 g/dL (range 0.086 to 0.170 g/dL). However, since a BAC plateau might have occurred, especially with food in the stomach, the validity of this assumption of a decreasing blood alcohol curve for 4 h is perhaps open to question.

Another approach, which is more defensible, can be applied if there is a statutory time limit that applies to the measured BAC. For example, there may be a presumption in the law that a BAC within 2 h of driving is representative of the BAC at the time of driving. In this case, estimating back only 2 h, to place the defendant within the 2-h statutory window, is more reliable and produces a most likely BAC of 0.088 g/dL within a range of 0.068 to 0.110 g/dL.

The larger question in this case would be whether the woman was under the influence of alcohol at the time of the accident, and the estimated BAC is only one element of that determination.

Example 6. The defendant has a breath alcohol concentration of 0.16 g/210L. An expert called by the defense claims that the suspect's elevated body temperature (102.9°F) resulting from a fever, raised his breath level over his blood level by 20%. He claims that the defendant held his breath before exhaling into the instrument, raising his BrAC by 10%. He claims that the defendant may have had some acetone on his breath, but not enough to trigger the interference detector on the instrument, resulting in up to 0.009 g/dL apparent ethanol response from acetone. He notes the "margin of error" on the instrument is 0.01 g/210 L. He also claims that alcohol from the defendant's upper airways was picked up by his breath during the expiration, suggesting that the alcohol entering the instrument did not come from alveoli, or deep lung regions of the airway. The net effect is that the defendant's "actual" BrAC could have been as low as 0.08 g/210 L.

This shotgun approach, perhaps tied to one of the other rising BAC scenarios discussed above, is very common in DUI litigation, as it seeks to present a barrage of details attacking the validity of breath testing in general, and this defendant's test in particular. The various assertions need to be evaluated individually. First, if the jurisdiction has separate blood and breath statutes, the blood/breath ratio resulting from elevated temperature is not relevant. Breath holding will elevate breath alcohol concentrations compared with rapid, repeated inspiration and expiration. However, breath holding is not part of the breath test protocol, and a well-documented 15-min observation period can challenge this assertion. The acetone issue is discussed in detail in Chapter 13; however, the amount of acetone required to produce an apparent BrAC of 0.009 g/210 L, would result only from extreme fasting (including abstinence from alcoholic beverages) or diabetes, which is not a transient condition. The defendant's medical records can determine whether he or she is diabetic. The "margin of error" issue is frequently raised when the result is close to the legal limit. What "margin of error" means is not clear; it is certainly not a scientific term. Most instrument protocols that include a control with each breath test will require that the control is within ±0.01 g/210 L of a reference value; however, these same instruments will also include optical controls which typically must meet much more stringent parameters. The kinetics of alcohol deposition and evaporation from the airways during inspiration and expiration have been alluded to in Chapter 13; however, the bottom line is that breath testing is recognized as a valid measurement of impairment, and breath alcohol concentration, regardless of the complexity of the respiration physiology, is a valid indicator of intoxication. The best approach in these cases is again to contrast the contrived circumstances that are required for the defendant's version to be valid, with the generally more straightforward explanation that the defendant had consumed too much alcohol, was arrested because of impaired driving, failed field sobriety tests, and gave a breath test that reflects his true breath alcohol concentration and is consistent with his impairment.

Example 7. The defendant has a BrAC of 0.05 g/210 L, and performs field sobriety tests well. To what extent was the subject's driving affected?

One can say with some confidence that certain elements of the driving task are influenced at fairly low BrAC levels even in experienced drinkers. However, certain kinds of driving tasks are more likely to be affected than others. Driving down a straight, country road with no other traffic, in good weather, during daylight hours requires less skill than driving on a busy city street at night, in the rain, with pedestrians around, and distractions in the car such as intoxicated companions or loud music. In a case such as this, one must look at the driver's actual driving performance and determine first if it was impaired, then second if other explanations exist for that impairment besides drinking, including possibly fatigue, drug use, or inattention. This BrAC on its own says relatively little about the extent of driving impairment.

APPENDIX III: PREDICTED NORMAL HEART WEIGHT (G) AS A FUNCTION OF BODY HEIGHT IN 392 WOMEN AND 373 MEN[a]

Body height (cm)	Women				Men		
	(in.)	L95	P	U95	L95	P	U95
130	51	133	204	314	164	232	327
132	52	135	207	319	167	236	333
134	53	137	210	324	170	240	338
136	54	139	214	329	173	243	344
138	54	141	217	334	175	247	349
140	55	143	220	338	178	251	355
142	56	145	223	343	181	255	361
144	57	147	226	348	184	259	366
146	57	149	229	353	187	263	372
148	58	151	232	358	189	267	378
150	59	153	236	363	192	271	383
152	60	155	239	368	195	275	389
154	61	157	242	372	198	280	395
156	61	159	245	377	201	284	400
158	62	161	248	382	204	288	406
160	63	163	251	387	207	292	412
162	64	165	254	392	209	296	417
164	65	167	258	397	212	300	423
166	65	169	261	401	215	304	429
168	66	171	264	406	218	308	435
170	67	173	267	411	221	312	440
172	68	176	270	416	224	316	446
174	69	178	273	421	227	320	452
176	69	180	277	426	230	324	458
178	70	182	280	431	233	328	463
180	71	184	283	435	235	332	469
182	72	186	286	440	238	336	475

Body height	Women				Men		
(cm)	(in.)	L95	P	U95	L95	P	U95
184	72	188	289	445	241	341	481
186	73	190	292	450	244	345	487
188	74	192	295	455	247	349	492
190	75	194	299	460	250	353	498
192	76	196	302	465	253	357	504
194	76	198	305	469	256	361	510
196	77	200	308	474	259	365	516
198	78	202	311	479	262	369	522
200	79	204	314	484	265	374	527
202	80	206	318	489	268	378	533
204	80	208	321	494	271	382	539
206	81	210	324	499	274	386	545
208	82	212	327	508	276	394	557
210	83	214	330	508	279	394	557

[a] P = predicted normal heart weight; L95 = lower 95% confidence limit; U95 = upper 95% confidence limit.

From Kitzman, D. et al., Age related changes in normal human hearts during the first 10 decades of life. Part II (Maturity): A quantitive anatomic study of 765 specimens from subjects 20 to 99 years old, *Mayo Clinic Proc.*, 63:137–146, 1988. With permission.

Index

B

C

I

O

R

T

83. Barrett, C., Good, C., and Moore, C., Comparison of point-of-collection screening of drugs of abuse in oral fluid with a laboratory-based urine screen, *Forensic Sci. Int.* 122, 163, 2001.

84. Yacoubian, G.S., Jr., Wish, E.D., and Perez, D.M., A comparison of saliva testing to urinalysis in an arrestee population, *J. Psychoactive Drugs* 33, 289, 2001.

85. De Giovanni, N., Fucci, N., Chiarotti, M., and Scarlata, S., Cozart Rapiscan system: our experience with saliva tests, *J. Chromatogr. B Anal. Technol. Biomed. Life Sci.* 773, 1, 2002.

86. Samyn, N. and van Haeren, C., On-site testing of saliva and sweat with Drugwipe and determination of concentrations of drugs of abuse in saliva, plasma and urine of suspected users, *Int. J. Legal Med.* 113, 150, 2000.

87. Jehanli, A., Brannan, S., Moore, L., and Spiehler, V.R., Blind trials of an onsite saliva drug test for marijuana and opiates, *J. Forensic Sci.* 46, 1214, 2001.

88. Kolbrich, E.A., Kim, I., Barnes, A.J., Moolchan, E.T., Wilson, L., Cooper, G.A., Reid, C., Baldwin, D., Hand, C.W., and Huestis, M.A., Cozart RapiScan Oral Fluid Drug Testing System: an evaluation of sensitivity, specificity, and efficiency for cocaine detection compared with ELISA and GC-MS following controlled cocaine administration, *J. Anal. Toxicol.* 27, 407, 2003.

89. Walsh, J.M., Flegel, R., Crouch, D.J., Cangianelli, L., and Baudys, J., An evaluation of rapid point-of-collection oral fluid drug-testing devices, *J. Anal. Toxicol.* 27, 429, 2003.

90. Niedbala, R.S., Feindt, H., Kardos, K., Vail, T., Burton, J., Bielska, B., Li, S., Milunic, D., Bourdelle, P., and Vallejo, R., Detection of analytes by immunoassay using up-converting phosphor technology, *Anal. Biochem.* 293, 22, 2001.

91. Nath, N., Eldefrawi, M., Wright, J., Darwin, D., and Huestis, M., A rapid reusable fiber optic biosensor for detecting cocaine metabolites in urine, *J. Anal. Toxicol.* 23, 460, 1999.

92. Tsai, J.S.C., Deng, D., Diebold, E., Smith, A., Wentzel, C., and Franzke, S., The latest development in biosensor immunoassay technology for drug assays, *LABOLife*, 4/02, 17, 2002.

93. Weiss, A., Concurrent Engineering for Lateral-Flow Diagnostics, *IVD Technol.* 5, 48, 1999.

94. Klimov, A.D., Tsai, S.-C.J., Towt, J., and Salamone, S.J., Improved immuno-chromatographic format for competitive-type assays. *Clin. Chem.* 41, 1360, 1995.

95. Yang, J.M. and Lewandrowski, K.B., Urine drugs of abuse testing at the point-of-care: clinical interpretation and programmatic considerations with specific reference to the Syva Rapid Test (SRT), *Clin. Chim. Acta* 307, 27, 2001.

96. Phillips, J.E., Bogema, S., Fu, P., Furmaga, W., Wu, A.H., Zic, V., and Hammett-Stabler, C., Signify ER Drug Screen Test evaluation: comparison to Triage Drug of Abuse Panel plus tricyclic antidepressants, *Clin. Chim. Acta* 328, 31, 2003.

97. Ferrara, S.D., Tedeschi, L., Frison, G., Brusini, G., Castagna, F., Bernardelli, B., and Soregaroli, D., Drugs-of-abuse testing in urine: statistical approach and experimental comparison of immunochemical and chromatographic techniques, *J. Anal. Toxicol.* 18, 278, 1994.

98. George, S. and Braithwaite, R.A., A preliminary evaluation of five rapid detection kits for on site drugs of abuse screening, *Addiction* 90, 227, 1995.

99. Peace, M.R., Tarnai, L.D., and Poklis, A., Performance evaluation of four on-site drug-testing devices for detection of drugs of abuse in urine, *J. Anal. Toxicol.* 24, 589, 2000.

100. Gronholm, M. and Lillsunde, P., A comparison between on-site immunoassay drug-testing devices and laboratory results, *Forensic Sci. Int.* 121, 37, 2001.

101. Leino, A., Saarimies, J., Gronholm, M., and Lillsunde, P., Comparison of eight commercial on-site screening devices for drugs-of-abuse testing, *Scand. J. Clin. Lab. Invest.* 61, 325, 2001.

102. ROSITA Deliverable D4, Evaluation of different roadside drug tests, 2000. (www.rosita.org)

103. Taylor, E.H., Oertli, E.H., Wolfgang, J.W., and Mueller, E., Accuracy of five on-site immunoassay drugs-of-abuse testing devices, *J. Anal. Toxicol.* 23, 119, 1999.

104. Kadehjian, L.J. Performance of five non-instrumented urine drug-testing devices with challenging near-cutoff specimens, *J. Anal. Toxicol.* 25, 670, 2001.

105. Schwartz, R.H., Clark, H.W., and Meek, P.S., Laboratory tests for rapid screening of drugs of abuse in the workplace: a review, *J. Addict. Dis.* 12, 43, 1993.

106. George, S. and Braithwaite, R.A., Use of on-site testing for drugs of abuse, *Clin. Chem.* 48, 1639, 2002.

107. Hammett-Stabler, C.A., Pesce, A.J., and Cannon, D.J., Urine drug screening in the medical setting, *Clin. Chim. Acta* 315, 125, 2002.